VARIETY
Film Reviews

Garland Publishing, Inc.
New York and London
1986

Contents

Variety

Film Reviews
1983–1984

VOLUME EIGHTEEN

Includes an Index to Titles
for 1981–1984

Garland Publishing, Inc.
New York and London
1986

Library of Congress Cataloging-in-Publication Data
(Revised for vol. 18)

Variety film reviews.

    Vols. 1–16 have title: Variety film reviews,
1907–1980.
    Contents: v. 1. 1907–1920—v. 2. 1921–1925—
[etc.]—v. 18. 1983–1984.
    1. Moving-pictures—Reviews.   I. Daily variety.
II. Title: Variety film reviews, 1907–1980.
PN1995.V34   1983   791.43′75   82-15691
ISBN 0-8240-5200-5 (v. 1 : alk. paper)
ISBN 0-8240-5218-8 (v. 18)

Manufactured in the United States of America

Printed on acid-free,
250-year-life paper

Preface

The reviews contained in this volume are complete and comprehensive reproductions of the original reviews printed in *Variety*. Only full-length feature films are included. Short subjects and made for television films are not included.

User's Guide

The reviews in this collection are published in chronological order, by the date on which the review appeared. The date of each issue appears at the top of the column where the reviews for that issue begin. The reviews continue through that column and all following columns until a new date appears at the top of the page. Where blank spaces occur at the end of a column, this indicates the end of that particular week's reviews. An index to film titles for the years 1981–1984 is published in this volume.

1983

America: From Hitler To M-X
(COLOR & B&W-DOCU-16m)

A Parallel Films release of a Parallel and Fourth Wall Repertory production. Created and directed by Joan Harvey. Camera (color), John Hazard and Jeff Wayman; producers, Albee Gordon; Ralph Klein, Saul Newton; sound, Gordon; editors, Harvey, Ken Eluto, Trudy Bagdon; additional photography, Mark Benjamin, Michael Camerini, Andy Ferullo, John Krauss, Stuart Math, Peter Schnall, Jeffrey Victor. Reviewed at Parallel Films screening room, N.Y.C., Dec. 29, 1982. (No MPAA Rating.) Running time: **90 MINS**.
With: Daniel Ellsberg, Rep. Ronald V. Dellums, Sen. David Pryor, Herbert Scoville Jr., Paul Warnke, Sidney Lens, Sen. Max Baucus.

Pulling no punches and hitting the United States' defense policy from a decidedly left of center point of view, "America: From Hitler To M-X" is a revealing, provocative documentary that sees cynicism and danger in the Reagan Administration's drive to upgrade its nuclear arsenal.

Given the dire concerns worldwide over The Bomb, one-time actress Joan Harvey's pic is a natural for continued film festival exposure (it's already unspooled at recent London and Leipzig fests). Pic is also suited for European tv broadcast, but theatrical release here or abroad may be tricky because of its unrelenting pessimism. "Atomic Cafe" this film is not.

Gloom and doom saturate the docu. Gruesome footage of nuke damages to life and property alternates with interviews with more than 60 former Defense Department officials, ex-CIA operatives, labor union leaders, politicians, scientists and antiwar activists.

These present some shocking scenarios, arguing that civil defense in the face of nuclear destruction is like "rearranging deck chairs on the Titanic," for example, or that the explosion of one nuclear weapon could cause widespread communication breakdown between friends and foes, and the computers controlling defense systems would fail, thus increasing chances for successive nuclear launches.

Theorizing that the proposed M-X missile system would not be built in the Midwest and wait to be hit by the Russians, the docu charges U.S. foreign policy is aggressive rather than defensive. Harvey, who grew up in Hollywood, as the daughter of a producer who worked with Cecil B. DeMille, charges in her film that the U.S. is preparing for a first-strike alternative in the event of, say, more Persian Gulf conflicts.

In an even graver indictment that could use more substantiation than it gets, the film says that big business is behind the nuclear arms buildup, thus echoing major corporations' alleged collusion with the Third Reich. For example, German reconnaissance planes were made by Pratt-Whitney, DuPont maintained contracts with a German company that manufactured poison gas, and Harry Truman himself is quoted attacking Standard Oil for selling patents to the Nazis.

The film makes these charges supported only by newspaper article excerpts.

While worthwhile truisms emerge in "America..." (most notably, the insanity of embellishing nuclear arms when the existing bombs can already evaporate continents, and the inanity of "limited" nuclear war), the Administration's viewpoint should have been directly represented at some point. A dialog, rather than a diatribe which this film often becomes, would have put the government's allegedly faulty policies into clearer focus.

Still, this important docu benefits from testimony from a wide range of experts including former government officials, such as chief SALT II negotiator Paul Warnke and ex-deputy director of the CIA Herbert Scoville Jr., who by their own job experience make them Harvey's most credible witnesses.
—*Binn.*

Gedaechtnis
(Remembrance)
(WEST GERMAN-B&W-DOCU-16m)

Berlin, Dec. 22.
A Common Film Production, Berlin, in coproduction with Westdeutscher Rundfunk (WDR), Cologne. Stars Curt Bois, Bernhard Minetti. A documentary film by Bruno Ganz and Otto Sander. Camera (black and white), Wolfgang Knigge, Michael Steinke, Uwe Schrader, Karl Koshnick, Rene Perraudin; sound, Theo Kondring, Slavco Hitrov; editors, Susann Lahaye, Bruno Ganz; production manager, Helmut Wietz; tv-producer, Martin Wiebel. Reviewed at Berliner Screening Room, Berlin, Dec. 22, '82. Running time: **90 MINS**.

This unusual document deals with two aged and respected actors on the Berlin stage: Curt Bois, 80 and Bernhard Minetti, 77. They are interviewed by two corresponding younger acting colleagues: Otto Sander and Bruno Ganz, both well known as Berlin actors through their Schaubuehne am Halleschen Ufer productions (as well as film careers). The idea was to have the acting trade discussed by equals among equals, and it has its merits — indeed, Ganz and Sander's "Remembrance" has many fine moments to set it apart from others of its sort.

Bois was at the top of the ladder when he emigrated from Germany in 1933 just after the Nazis rose to power. Thereafter, he had a tough time of it as a bit player of small stature in Hollywood prods, and he thus felt the pangs of exile more than most of his Berlin colleagues. He speaks of oldtime variety acts (his demonstrated routine of "putting-on-his-suitcoat" is priceless!), recalls the pleasure of watching Gypsy Rose Lee at Minsky's upon arriving in New York, and remembers meetings with Bertolt Brecht, Buster Keaton (they played together in Richard Oswald's "The Lovable Cheat"), and Charles Laughton (on the set of "The Hunchback of Notre Dame"). Bois summarizes his life as a kind of eternal pursuit of women and horses, the passions leading Sander and Ganz to Michelle (a Berlin nite spot for lonely gentlemen) and the local racetrack at Marienfelde.

The same fascination stems from recollections of Minetti, whose love for the stage and soccer-games consumes most of his waking hours up to the present. He is shown rehearsing Goethe's "Faust" in a Berlin legit prod, and a visit is paid to an empty Olympic Stadium with friends to muse over a couple of memorable soccer matches. Minetti obviously likes to talk about his craft, all the richer in view of his ever growing reputation as the favorite actor of dramatist Thomas Bernhard. He is also well liked by the younger generation of play directors — a current walk-on is in Shakespeare's "Hamlet" staged by the Berliner Schaubuehne.

Docu's one fault is that a double-appearance of Bois and Minetti doesn't take place. But that's a minor aspect. For those who know and like German legit, the interviews could easily have been twice as long. —*Holl.*

Enigma
(BRITISH-FRENCH-COLOR)

Okay spy thriller in for lukewarm returns.

Hollywood, Jan. 3.
An Embassy release of a Filmcrest International Corp. presentation of a Peter Shaw production. An Archerwest Ltd.-S.F.P.C. coproduction in association with I.F.I., G.F.I., Peroquet Productions. Produced by Peter Shaw, Ben Arbeid. Producer (France), Andre Pergament. Directed by Jeannot Szwarc. Stars Martin Sheen, Brigitte Fossey, Sam Neill. Screenplay, John Briley, based on the novel by Michael Barak; camera (uncredited color), Jean-Louis Picavet; editor, Peter Weatherley; art direction, Francois Comtat; sound, Jean-Louis Ducarme; assistant director, Michel Cheyko. Reviewed at CFI Labs, Hollywood, Jan. 3, 1983. (MPAA Rating: PG.) Running time: **101 MINS**.

Alex Holbeck	Martin Sheen
Karen	Brigitte Fossey
Dimitri Vasilkov	Sam Neill
Kurt Limmer	Derek Jacobi
Bodley	Michael Lonsdale
Canarsky	Frank Finlay
Molton	David Baxt
Bruno	Kevin McNally
Hirsch	Michael Williams
Konstantin	Warren Clarke

As in the last couple of years, Embassy Pictures is out of the gate with the first release of the new year. An English-French coproduction, "Enigma" is a well-made but insufficiently exciting spy thriller which rather pleasingly emphasizes the emotional vulnerabilities of the pawns caught up in East-West intrigue. Film should do passable b.o. as an early season replacement for Christmas fatalities.

Martin Sheen ably portrays an East German refugee who, after working as a Radio Free Europe-type broadcaster out of Paris, is recruited by the CIA to return to East Berlin. Assignment: steal a coded micro-processor, or scrambler, from the Russians before the KGB proceeds with the assassination of five Soviet dissidents living in the West.

After neatly making his way to his destination, Sheen locates old flame Brigitte Fossey who, while resisting the idea of resuming their romance, sympathizes with his unexplained cause.

On the other side, the KGB and the East German authorities are hot on Sheen's trail, but one of the more amusing aspects of the tale is the competition and divisiveness to be found between those supposed allies. The Germans, naturally, are anxious to handle the case themselves, and are none too fond of the high-handed tactics of the KGB, personified here by up-and-coming agent Sam Neill.

Although not a spy herself, Fossey willingly follows Sheen's request that she begin a relationship with Neill for the sake of the mission. Situation is similar to that in "Notorious," in which Ingrid Bergman gave herself to Nazi agent Claude Rains to help Cary Grant, and although the result is hardly as brilliant here, contrivance remains interesting and emotionally potent.

Enlisting the aid of some subversive students and donning several disguises at various points, Sheen eventually creates severe havoc for his adversaries as diversions from his theft of the scrambler. As befits any thriller, there are still a couple of twists to come once the deed is accomplished, and it would be unfair to disclose them. Suffice it to say the emotional payoff, while low-keyed, is gratifying, and enriches what could easily have been stock hero-and-villain characterizations.

Although it never becomes boring, pic does bog down in the middle stretch when it becomes unclear just what Sheen is up to. He sort of muddles about in assorted pursuits, none of which, at the time, seem pressingly related to the achievement of his mission.

John Briley's screenplay keeps everything coherent, not always easy with this sort of fare, and Jeannot Szwarc's direction is very handsome indeed, even if he does go in for too many red herring shock setups, which are invariably followed by cheap payoffs that are the equivalent of surprise handshake buzzers.

To someone who's not been there, at least, depressing East Berlin setting is convincingly presented, with heavy emphasis being paid to police state trappings. Jean-Louis Picavet's lensing is excellent, as is the score by a composer who goes nameless in the press materials provided by Embassy.

Some of the actors, notably Michael Lonsdale as a CIA agent, appear to have been dubbed. Also, full nudity by Fossey in an interrogation scene is somewhat surprising given the PG rating.—*Cart.*

Graesaenklingar
(Grass Widowers)
(SWEDISH-COLOR)

Copenhagen, Dec. 28.

A Drakfilm/Europa Film Production, AB Europa Film (Stockholm) release. Directed by Hans Iveberg. Features entire cast. Executive producer, Peter Hald. Production management, Rune Hjelm, Brita Werkmaester. Screenplay, Ake Cato, Jan Richter; camera (Eastmancolor), Petter Davidson, Gunnar Nilsson; production design, Mona Theresia Forsen; costumes, Karin Sundwall; editors, Roger Sellberg, Sten Valegren; music, Bjoern Jason Lindh. Reviewed at the ABCinema, Copenhagen, Dec. 28, 1982. Running time: 95 MINS.

Gary	Goesta Ekman
Lasse	Janne Carlsson
Viveka	Marika Lindstroem
Maggan	Lena Nyman
Inga Lil	Mona Seilitz
Lillian	Lis Nilheim
Mia	Aase Bjerkeroth
Nina	Lena Olin
Hypnotized lady	Kim Anderzon

"Grass Widowers" is the second feature helmed by Hans Iveberg, who scored mightily at the boxoffice in Sweden with last year's "Who Pulled The Plug?" a rather heavy-handed compilation of sightgags. This time he has turned to subtler material with Ake Cato and Jan Richter's mild-mannered satire about two youngish husbands who expect the exact opposite of what they actually get when presented with a sudden opportunity to be alone and independent in town when their wives go abroad for a week.

Goesta Ekman plays the befuddled architect who has hoped for quiet days of work and philosophical repose. Beefy Janne Carlsson is the mechanic who has pals and broads lined up for fun & games as soon as his wife has left. But the two, very different men, somehow get involved with each other in a friendship from which both will benefit. The architect is thrown into a week of all-embracing fun that wears his body down but refreshes his spirit. The mechanic does step out but not nearly to the extent he had planned. He has kids that the architect gets him to feel more responsible for.

Especially the architect gets into ridiculous situations, including an affair where he cannot get his pants off because he has forgotten to remove his shoes first, and a bank robbery where the hold-up man's submachine gun gets its muzzle stuck in the architect's coat-pocket. Meanwhile, the mechanic takes over as a lecturer about urban planning for a better way of life. All of it is pretty unlikely nonsense that is somehow made to make sense anyway because Iveberg rarely overworks his given lines and situations and because Ekman and Carlsson are both accomplished players of comedy with a truly human touch.

Already sold to all Scandinavian territories, "Grass Widowers" might have appeal in other foreign theatrical situations but will more likely be received as a heaven-sent by tv programmers of feature film slots around about midnight.

—*Kell.*

Flucht Aus Pommern
(Flight From Pomerania)
(WEST GERMAN-B&W)

Berlin, Dec. 23.

An Elan-Film Gierke & Comp. Production, Munich, in coproduction with Zweites Deutsches Fernsehen (ZDF), Mainz. Features entire cast. Written and directed by Eberhard Schubert. Camera (color), Wedigo von Schultzendorff; sets, Herwig Libowitzky; tv-producer, Klaus Riemer. Reviewed at ZDF Screening Room, Berlin, Dec. 23, '82. Running time: 100 MINS.

Cast: Armin Mueller-Stahl (Lyssek), Marie-Charlotte Schueler (Marlene), Edith Behleit (Guste), Klaus Hoehne (Jakob), Andre Wilms (Armand), Rudolf Schuendler (Mutschke), Siegmar Schneider (Hermann), Stephan Schwartz (Heinrich), Stefan Makk (Lew), Alexander Radszum (Lieutenant).

For those with a yen for historical tracts on the last war, Eberhard Schubert's docu-fiction "Flight from Pomerania" is highly recommended: it's the story of a group of German refugees fleeing from their homes just a few steps before the Red Army in the winter of 1944-45.

"Flight from Pomerania" is the story of this eastern-province of Prussia in its death-throes. The war has long been lost, but the civilian population is kept in line with a fast-fading hope of a "wonder-bomb" by Hitler's minions. Now as the mortar-batteries and feared tanks rumble in the distance, even the long-suffering believers know that it's time to evacuate before it's too late. And so the flight from Pomerania begins on Christmas Eve at the manorhouse of a Pomeranian landowner, the estate managed by a caretaker with a conscience.

The principal figures are the caretaker Lyssek (Armin Mueller-Stahl), a young woman from Hannover assigned by government officials to work in Prussia (her own

home had been bombed out and her husband is serving in the army), and an assortment of women, children, and elderly — all loaded into wagons to be pulled over frozen roads by horses. The adventures they experience along the way could serve as a catalog of fear, deprivation, and misery heaped upon any civilian population caught on the front between two lines of battle, the main difference being that this account is taken from stories by eyewitnesses who actually went through the ordeals as described.

In the beginning, German officials assure the population that all will be well — in other words, the innocent can serve as a buffer zone should things go from bad to worse and a retreat is necessary. A film of Russian atrocities on the eastern front is shown two soldiers who deserted the Wehrmacht are quickly tried and executed by a provisonal military tribunal; and prisoners-of-war (French) find it more humane and commendable to help the German civilians than wreak a revenge of their own on the enemy or simply surrender to the approaching Soviets.

The air of tragedy hangs almost everywhere once the flight is attempted (it's made against orders from authorities but encouraged by the common soldier, one of whom is Marlene's own husband). A farm is visited at which the entire household has committed suicide while cows in the stalls let out a bellow to be miled. A mother witnesses the death of her own child in her arms, from cold and hunger. A corps of teenage recruits combat a tank, and succeed in putting one out of action. And confusion reigns as backroads are sought to find a way out of No Man's Land.

It's the French POWs that come to the rescue in the moment of direst need. When the wornout escapees take refuge in a building, the Soviet soldiers happen almost immediately upon the scene. The French send the Germans to the cellar for their own protection, then convince the Russians that they are truly POWs. But a search leads to the discovery of the hidden-away women and children under Lyssek's protection, and a rape of the women is about to take place — when a Russian officer speaking German arrives in time to spare the humiliation. The humanistic officer recalls the rape and death of members of his own family before Leningrad, but a short time before. Later, the French POWs lead the decimated group to the banks of the Elbe River to cross over into safety.

This pacifist-minded film is one of the best produced in West Germany on the Second World War. It's sensitively directed and acted. The tragic elements apply to all such

victims of war at any time and place: a universal message. —*Holl.*

Midnight
(COLOR)

Okay low-budget horror opus from Pittsburgh.

An Independent-International Pictures release of a Congregation Co. production. Executive producers, Samuel Sherman, Daniel Kennis. Produced by Donald Redinger. Directed by John A. Russo. Features entire cast. Screenplay, Russo, from his novel; camera (Eastman color), Paul McCollough; editor, McCollough; music, The Sound Castle; songs, One Man's Family; sound, Eric Baca; special makeup effects, Tom Savini; assistant camera, John Rice. Reviewed at Liberty theatre, N.Y., Jan. 1, 1983. (MPAA Rating: R). Running time: 91 MINS.

Bert Johnson	Lawrence Tierney
Nancy Johnson	Melanie Verliin
Tom	John Hall
Hank	Charles Jackson
Harriet Johnson	Doris Hackney
Abraham	John Amplas
Cynthia	Robin Walsh
Cyrus	David Marchick
Luke	Greg Besnak

"Midnight" is a 1980 Pittsburgh-made horror thriller which, while lacking the scares of its many competitors, at least varies from the rigid format of recent shockers. Horror novelist John Russo, who scripted the Pittsburgh classic, "Night Of The Living Dead," develops enough twists on traditional Satanism and road movie formulae to keep the fans interested.

Heroine Nancy Johnson (Melanie Verliin) runs away from home when her cop stepdad (Lawrence Tierney) tries to rape her. Diverted from her goal of joining a sister in California by two young men who pick her up hitchhiking, she becomes a captive of a local family of devil worshipers who slate her for human sacrifice on midnight, Easter Sunday.

Familiar elements here include the devil cultists retaining their clan matriarch in mummified form (a la "Psycho") and the usual gimmick of a backwoods family preying on unsuspecting travelers. One switch is the emphasis upon the story's racial angles, with several black victims and local prejudice surfacing against the racially mixed trio on the road.

Special makeup effects by a top artist in the field Tom Savini are effective (particularly a realistic decapitation simulation), but the picture's low budget shows in its unatmospheric, routine visuals, amateurish performances in small roles and a 1960s-style music track. Though the premise has heroine and her road buddies headed south, autumn locations (belying Easter Sunday premise) all look similar, evidently filmed within shouting distance of the Pittsburgh home base.

Forties star Lawrence Tierney has fun as the heroine's stepdad, veering from initial comical villainy to a stalwart protector in the final reel. Other leads, many of whom are familiar faces from George A. Romero films, perform functionally. —*Lor.*

Hot Touch
(CANADIAN-COLOR)

Winnipeg, Dec. 11.

An Astral film production in cooperation with Trans-Atlantic Enterprises. Produced by Harold Greenberg. Directed by Roger Vadim. Features entire cast. Screenplay, Peter Dion, based on story by Dion, Jean-Yves Pitoun; camera (color); Francois Protat; production design, Ted Watkins; editor, Stan Cole and Yurij Luhovy; music, Andre Gagnon; sound, Joseph Champagne and Jack Burman. Reviewed at Towne Cinema 8, Winnipeg, Dec. 11, 1982. Running time: 92 MINS.

Danny Fairchild	Wayne Rogers
Dr. Emilienne Simpson	Marie-France Pisier
Severo	Lloyd Bochner
Samantha O'Brien	Samantha Eggar
Vincent Reblack	Patrick Macnee
Max Reich	Melvyn Douglas
Kelly	Gloria Carlin
Lincoln Simpson	Allan Kolman
Ivan Strauss	Norwich Duff
Judge Jackson	James Douglas
Martha	Jan Lapp
Sir Arthur Bloomfield	Victor Knight

"Hot Touch" presents a tepid romantic thriller set in the world of art forgery. It's a film without heroes where sympathies lie with the brighter elements among con men, murderers, thieves and innocent bystanders.

While an intriguing backdrop for a film, the world of classic painting pales considerably at the hands of director Roger Vadim. The script by Peter Dion is an inferior reworking of such jewel thief capers as "To Catch a Thief" and provides a much less accomplished swindle than either "The Sting" or "Paper Moon." Set against the earlier films "Hot Touch" can be promptly dismissed.

The story centers around Wayne Rogers, an accomplished duplicator of Picasso and other sought-after artists. Rogers and Patrick Macnee are partners in a company which authenticates valuable paintings on their way to the auction block.

Their scam has been undetected for years. However, this ends with the arrival of Lloyd Bochner, the mysterious strong arm of an unscrupulous art speculator. Bochner threatens both public exposure and physical harm unless Rogers agrees to forge masterpieces by Van Gogh and El Greco which disappeared during World War II.

He accepts reluctantly, but plots to turn the tables on Bochner and his unknown accomplice with a little help from girlfriend Marie-France Pisier. The story sounds much more ominous than played. Even so, director Vadim struggles unsuccessfully to blend both the light romance and the implicit violence of the situation.

Matters are not helped by a script overflowing with sub-plots serving only to confuse the main action. The story jumps frantically from the art auction houses of New York City to Roger's Montreal base with reason stranded somewhere between in mid-air.

Pisier struggles with an unsuccessful marriage, Rogers frets over the safety of his mentor, played by the late Melvyn Douglas looking ashen, and Macnee battles to keep a straight face. Only Bochner emerges with a balanced performance suitably revelling in his character's villainy.

The film's major problem is the clumsy manner in which the scam evolves. Vadim is too coy and mysterious about its working, so there's no way for an audience to fully appreciate the cunning of the forgers (who said there's honor among thieves?). The chicanery is presented pretty much as a fait acompli.

Technical credits are good overall. The film's settings and forgeries are quite acceptable and presented with some skill.

However, "Hot Touch" will leave audiences cold and in the dark. The charm and personality of the cast just can't overcome discrepancies in the story, characters and situations. There's a sketch for a strong idea but the image remains obscure. —*Klad.*

In Viaggio Con Papa
(My Trip With Dad)
(ITALIAN-COLOR)

Rome, Dec. 28.

A Titanus release, produced by Augusto Caminito for Scena Films. Stars Alberto Sordi, Carlo Verdone. Directed by Alberto Sordi. Screenplay, Rodolfo Sonego, A. Sordi, Carlo Verdone; camera (color), Sergio D'Offizi; sets, Emilio Baldelli; editing, Tatiana Casini Morigi; music, Piero Piccioni. Reviewed at Barberini Cinema, Rome, Dec. 28, 1982. Running time: 115 MINS.

Armando	Alberto Sordi
Cristiano	Carlo Verdone

This is a big comedy hit put together with two top b.o. stars, veteran Alberto Sordi and relative newcomer Carlo Verdone. Sordi, who also helmed "My Trip With Dad," has been directing his own films for some time now in association with scripter Rodolfo Sonego and producer Augusto Caminito. "Trip" is a much more successful effort than the mannered "I Know That You Know That I Know" released by Scena Films this summer.

Sordi and Verdone, cast together for the first time, click perfectly as pater and fils. Though the Romanness of the humor and importance of dialog (much of it improvised) will make pic primarily exportable to other Latin and Mediterranean markets, "Trip" is a fair choice for fests interested in sampling some of

the better contemporary Italo comedy.

Storyline is thin, just enough to hold together a loose series of comic sketches featuring one or both of the stars.

Well-to-do businessman Armando (Sordi) is about to take off to join his beautiful young lover for summer vacation when his idiot son Cristiano (Verdone) unexpectedly turns up. Having missed a rendezvous with a group of meditating neohippies, Cristiano tags along with Papa to mother's house.

Far more of a puritan than his parents, Cristiano is shocked by mama's cohabiting with a tv screenwriter, an arrangement that suits his father just fine. The duo hits the trail again, passing through a luxurious resort, a tent camp in Corsica and finally Armando's girlfriend's seaside villa. There Armando's constant urging finally bears fruit and Cristiano is initiated into adult life — as luck and script would have it, by his father's mistress.

Verdone is an excellent creator of characters and spares no punches with the childishly goody-goody Cristiano. Sordi seems restrained in contrast as the aging Latin Lover shackled with an overgrown son more interested in bandaging seagulls' wings than learning the facts of life first-hand.

There is a strange resemblance between the two stars — overfed, thin of hair and baby-faced — who represent two generations of Italian comedy. Pic's jokes may not be the freshest and script shamelessly exploits local audiences' titillation with racy slang. But Verdone's demented son routines that foil Sordi's most earnest lessons at Don Juanism are often irresistible. As a helmer Sordi is simple and direct, his years of experience in the business paying off with no-nonsense steady technique.

Pic knows how to exploit its gorgeous exteriors (it was shot entirely on summer seacoast locations) and maintains a fittingly relaxed pace for nearly two hours.

For an unpretentious picture meant only to clean up at the Christmas boxoffice, "Trip" gives an affectionately critical portrait of the Italian middle-class that harks back to some of Sordi's best efforts of past decades. Could be a good introduction to those unfamiliar with this important comic. —*Yung.*

Hard Feelings
(CANADIAN-COLOR)

Winnipeg, Dec. 12.

An Astral film production and release. Produced by Harold Greenberg. Directed by Daryl Duke. Features entire cast. Screenplay, W.D. Richter, John Herzfeld, based on novel by Don Bredes; camera (color), Harry Makin; production design, Douglas Higgins; editor, Tony Lower; music, Mickey Erbe, Maribeth Solomon;

sound, Richard Lightstone, David Appleby, Dino Pigat. Reviewed at Towne Cinema 8, Winnipeg, Dec. 12, 1982. Running time: 106 MINS.

Bernie Hergruter	Carl Marotte
Winona Lockhart	Charlaine Woodward
Russell Linwood	Vincent Bufano
Lathom Lockhart	Grand Bush
Barbara Hollard	Lisa Langlois
Fred Hergruter	Michael Donaghue
Jean Hergruter	Sylvia Llewellyn
Lee Bridgeman	Allan Katz
Leslie Wolstein	Stephanie Miller
Mr. Holland	Vlasta Vrana

"Hard Feelings" is an admirable, if flawed, look at the perils of growing up. In some respects it mirrors such recent films as "Breaking Away" and "My Bodyguard." However, the story is not as neatly told and while it may be more accurate in substance, its convoluted plot will hinder potential commercial playoff.

Directed by Daryl Duke, the script, based on a novel by Don Bredes, is certainly not lacking ambition. Set on Long Island in 1963, it concerns an aimless high school senior played by Carl Marotte.

Superficially, he's much like his classmates with scholastic, athletic (tennis) and social interests. Also typical is his middle-class home where his parents bicker about money and worry about fidelity.

The major difference in Marotte's life is he's been singled out by school bully Vincent Bufano as an object of persecution. Bufano accosts him verbally with a stream of physical threats. And it's obvious from their physical differences, Marotte's no match for his adversary.

Despite obvious parallels, the film bears only a slight resemblance to "My Bodyguard." Bufano is but one of the perplexing aspects in the young man's life. He's also confused about sex and in this area the intensity of his family situation reflects poorly on his attitude toward his girlfriend (Lisa Langlois).

The story takes an abrupt turn when the combination of anxieties lead Marotte to run away. His worldly riches add up to a ticket to Atlanta where he encounters an environment as alien to him as a trip to the moon.

In Georgia he encounters Winona (Charlaine Woodward), a young black woman, and her brother Grand Bush. They offer him an alternative lifestyle which though unfamiliar, Marotte relates to strongly. It also provides him with the courage to return home and confront his problems directly.

Duke's film is really more concerned with questions than in providing neat answers. It's a highly perplexing tale which overcomes many of the plot vagaries as a result of the director's ability to focus on highly recognizable situations and to elicit sympathetic performances from his actors, particularly Marotte and newcomer Woodward.

Technical credits are also strong with Harry Makin's camerawork employing a subtle use of soft focus to enhance the period setting. The film, however, is far from a slick-looking production.

Despite its period setting, "Hard Feelings" is very much a contemporary subject. It will nonetheless require special marketing geared toward a sophisticated audience in international territories. —Klad.

Heat And Dust
(BRITISH-COLOR)

Classy, engrossing Merchant-Ivory revisit to timeless India.

London, Jan. 12.

Curzon Film Distributors release of a Merchant-Ivory production, produced by Ismail Merchant. Directed by James Ivory. Features entire cast. Screenplay by Ruth Prawer Jhabvala (based on her novel); camera (color), Walter Lassally; production design, Wilfred Shingleton; art direction, Maurice Fowler, Ram Yadekar; music, Richard Robbins; editor, Humphrey Dixon; sound, Ray Beckett; assistant directors, Kevan Barker, David Nichols. Reviewed at Curzon Cinema, London Jan. 11, 1982. (BBFC rating: 15 (AA).) Running time: 133 MINS.

Anne	Julie Christie
Douglas Rivers	Christopher Cazenove
Olivia	Greta Scacchi
Mr. Crawford	Julian Glover
Mrs. Crawford	Susan Fleetwood
The Nawab	Shashi Kapoor
The Begum	Madhur Jaffrey
Harry	Nickolas Grace
Inder Lal	Zakir Hussain
Maj. Minnies	Barry Foster
Lady Mackleworth	Amanda Walker
Dr. Saunders	Patrick Godfrey
Mrs. Saunders	Jennifer Kendal
Chief princess	Sudha Chopra
Rita	Ratna Pathak
Mother	Tarla Mehta
Child	Charles McCaughan
Dr. Gopal	Jayut Kripilani
Dacoit chief	Sajid Khan
Leelavati	Leelabhai

If "Gandhi" is about a man and his mission to free India from British bondage, "Heat and Dust" is far more about India itself, its timelessness and the quicksand of the spell it seems to cast. The Indian subcontinent has been the subject of previous entries ("Shakespeare Wallah," etc.) by the dogged 21-year partnership of producer Ismail Merchant and director James Ivory, but possibly never with as much sense of historical continuity and variety of detail. Film's more a pinpoint tapestry than a vast mosaic with teeming incident. Commercial playoff prospects are obviously limited but potentially satisfying.

Scripted from her own novel by Merchant-Ivory repeater Ruth Prawer Jhabvala, "Heat and Dust" intercuts the stories of two women and of India past and present. The device is sometimes irritating in its jumps but ultimately successful in conveying the essential immutability of India's mystic character and ambivalent appeal — evidently a state of mind as much as one of place.

Julie Christie, as a distinctly modern Englishwoman researching and to some extent reliving the Indian past of a late great aunt, is the top name in a fine and well-matched Anglo-Indian cast. But the principal impact, partly by virtue of role, is supplied by British newcomer Greta Scacchi. Portraying the great aunt as a young bride of scandalous behavior in colonial India, she creates an impressive study of classic underplayed well-bred English turmoil as her affections oscillate between loyal husband and an Indian potentate. Only her second film and first of consequence, she handily qualifies as something of a "find" with a future.

As was great aunt before her, Christie too becomes seduced, not only by the Indian mystique but by a native stud as well. Both femmes become pregnant as a result, but unlike Scacchi who aborts in confusion and disgrace, the unmarried Christie elects to go to term. As to any symbolism in her choice, it's best left to the mind of the beholder.

Inevitably, the film's also about the English too, specifically the upperclass colonial mentality. Throughout the unfolding dual narrative of two women of two times there is also an engrossing interplay of mutually suspicious, snobbish and contemptuous cultures — not in the style of "Gunga Din" but with understated and acute perception. As an ironic lesson in the ultimate futility of "civilizing" conquest by means of imperial arrogance, "Heat and Dust" serves nicely.

Ivory has handled all this, the interpersonal and cultural conflicts, with accomplished fluency of consistent interest. The intercutting by him and editor Humphrey Dixon achieves a sense of pace and dramatic movement that belies the film's 133-minute length. "Heat and Dust," with solid lensing by Walter Lassally, is anything but static storytelling.

Christie's own performance is confident and appealing within the limitations of a basically reactive role as a young woman more or less open to experience all that India has to offer, including carnal knowledge.

Besides newcomer Scacchi, the film's other sharp impression is created by Shashi Kapoor as an impecunious prince with all the trappings of dishonest wealth, a portrayal in which he radiates a compulsive magnetism and power.

Christopher Cazenove, with the stalwart looks of a matinee idol, is good as Scacchi's noble, bemused husband, and there are fine efforts by Nickolas Grace as a bachelor Englishman with something of an identity crisis, and Charles McCaughan as a young American dropout who's found a guru and karma and disillusion in that order.

The visual stimulation of "Heat and Dust" also owes considerably to production designer Wilfred Shingleton and Barbara Lans's costumes. Other topnotch credits include music by Richard Robbins.
—Pit.

Independence Day
(COLOR)

Diffuse drama of small-town America and the "need to get out." Despite fine acting, pic self-destructs.

A Warner Brothers release and production. Produced by Daniel H. Blatt, Robert Singer. Directed by Robert Mandel. Features entire cast. Screenplay, Alice Hoffman; camera (color), Chuck Rosher, prints by Technicolor; editor, Dennis Virkler, Tina Hirsch; music, Charles Bernstein; songs, Bernstein, Jim Messina; sound, Willie Burton; assistant director, Jerry Sobul; production manager, Ann Kindberg; production design, Stewart Campbell; set decoration, George R. Nelson; stunt coordinator, Gary Jensen. Reviewed at Warner Brothers screening room, N.Y., Jan. 12, 1983. (MPAA Rating: R). Running time: 110 MINS.

Mary Ann Taylor	Kathleen Quinlan
Jack Parker	David Keith
Carla Taylor	Frances Sternhagen
Les Morgan	Cliff DeYoung
Nancy Morgan	Dianne Wiest
Sam Taylor	Josef Sommer
Red Malone	Bert Remsen
Evan	Richard Farnsworth
Shelly	Brooke Alderson
Andy Parker	Noble Willingham
Rose Parker	Anne Haney

"Independence Day" is an unpleasant dramatic study of young people in a small southwestern town facing family problems and the perennial career decision: to stay home or trek to the big city. Despite some yeoman acting by a talented cast of character actors, the predictable and contrived storyline of the Daniel Blatt-Robert Singer production proves intractable, spelling a most difficult task for Warner Bros. to find an audience for this pic.

Alice Hoffman's unfocused screenplay centers upon two people in their 20's: Mary Ann Taylor (Kathleen Quinlan), a waitress in her dad's diner in the tiny southwestern town of Mercury and Jack Parker (David Keith), a gas station mechanic just returned home after an unsuccessful stay at engineering school.

While the duo's romance blossoms, Parker is coping with his suicidal sister Nancy (Dianne Wiest), her philandering, wife-beating husband Les (Cliff DeYoung) and his own brutish father (Noble Willingham). He is also prepping his high-performance Camaro for the annual Fourth of July race in nearby Bearsville, while Mary Ann tends to her cancer-stricken mom (Frances Sternhagen) and holds out hopes of being accepted at a California art school to pursue a career in photography.

The film's accelerating revelations of "all is not well" below the placid surface of middle America echo modern gothic horror films, but the realistic depiction of mental illness and domestic violence here is jarring with the pastoral overall romance of the story. While the material probably wouldn't have worked as an expose, it is manifestly unpleasant in the matter of fact, non-fantastic mode adopted. Latter half of the picture is packed with incredible contrivances and even a silly deus ex machina in the form of Bert Remsen popping in as the heroine's photography idol, visiting town to announce that she's won a full scholarship to study with him.

Director Robert Mandel, making the big jump from his fine 1980 AFI short "Nights At O'Rears" to a major feature, again demonstrates winning ways with actors and small-town atmospherics, but cannot make the disparate personal problems presented here either compelling or entirely credible.

Film's commercial chances rest upon critics (and public) responding to some solid performances. Keith reinforces his image as a likable and forceful young performer while Quinlan demonstrates the ambivalence of love vs. a career quite skillfully. She is upstaged (the script's fault) by Dianne Wiest in an extraordinary rendering of the submissive, battered wife who can find no solution to her domestic hell. Supporting cast is uniformly effective within the strained situations of this story.

Technical credits are fine, with the country music score highlighted by a pleasant wraparound themesong "Follow Your Dreams" by Jim Messina. —*Lor.*

Alexander Der Kleine
(Alexander The Little)
(EAST GERMAN-RUSSIAN-COLOR)

East Berlin, Jan. 17.
A coproduction between DEFA Studios, Group Berlin, East Berlin, and the Maxim Gorki Studio for Youth Films, Moscow. Features entire cast. Directed by Vladimir Fokin. Screenplay, Ingeborg Kretzschmar, Valentin and Vladimir Yeshov, Vladimir Fokin; camera (color), Sergei Filippov; sets, Erich Kruellke; music, Eduard Artemyev; editor, Tamara Belyeyeva; co-director, Helge Trimpert; dramaturg, Gudrum Deubner, Andrei Ivanov; production manager, Dietmar Richter, Arkadi Kushlyansky. Reviewed at DEFA Screening Room, East Berlin, Jan. 7, '83. Running time: 98 MINS.
Cast: Boris Tokaryev (Captain Zvetov), Yuri Nasarov (Starshina), Mikhail Kokshenov (Privat Kurykin), Ute Lubosch (Tessa), Walfriede Schmitt (Frau Flechsig), Hans Uwe Bauer (Walter).

Aimed for the youth audience, this lopsided glance at the postwar scene leaves much to be desired in painting a rather heroic picture of Soviet soldiers coming to the rescue of an entire village off the beaten path on the way to Berlin. Tale has a new mayor just out of prison caring for a load of orphaned kids in a barn in the summer of 1945, the area threatened by hoodlums and diehard Nazi youth who are not above raids and the killing of innocent people for the losing Fatherland.

The title refers to a name given to a newborn baby by the Russians-"he's too small to be Alexander the Great, so Alexander the Little" — and there's a bloody shootout in the end as the fascists attack the town for revenge or something. —*Holl.*

The Sting II
(COLOR)

Weak followup.

Hollywood, Jan. 14.
A Universal Pictures release of a Jennings Lang production. Produced by Jennings Lang. Directed by Jeremy Paul Kagan. Stars Jackie Gleason, Mac Davis, Teri Garr, Oliver Reed. Screenplay, David S. Ward; camera (Technicolor), Bill Butler; editor, David Garfield; production design, Edward C. Carfagno; costumes, Burton Miller; music, Lalo Schifrin; sound, Ronald G. Cogswell; assistant director, L. Andrew Stone. Reviewed at the Cinerama Dome, Hollywood, Jan. 14, 1983. (MPAA Rating: PG.) Running time: 102 MINS.
Gondorff .... Jackie Gleason
Hooker .... Mac Davis
Veronica .... Teri Garr
Macalinski .... Karl Malden
Lonnegan .... Oliver Reed
Kid Colors .... Bert Remsen

Universal's "The Sting II" is a sequel to a very successful picture and as such should do a healthy amount of initial business. But even had it been the first one out of the gate, it's likely this story of conflicting con games would have difficulty catching on. Although Teri Garr brightens things up in a nice supporting performance, stars Jackie Gleason and Mac Davis come nowhere close to evoking the charming onscreen qualities of Paul Newman and Robert Redford. Combined with the slow pace and overdone exposition, part two is mostly just a chore to watch.

Though screenwriter David S. Ward concocts as viable a story as he did in the original, the trouble is there is still an original. Had there not been it might not be as difficult to watch many of the similar types of plot twists and character devices. Had there even been a change of theme or dynamics it might not have mattered as much. But with the spirit here being so close to part one, the overriding feeling is how much better it was all done before.

In this story, Gleason plays the master con man out to make a big score with the help of fellow huckster Davis. The chief patsy is tacky nightclub owner Karl Malden while Oliver Reed does a less than distinctive turn as a mysterious gangster watching it all happen.

So much of the intricate plot is explained in dialog that the first half of the film often seems like someone reading an instruction book. Exception is Garr, who provides what little life there is as a slick, seasoned trickster who becomes involved in the scam.

The second half picks up a bit as the plan goes into effect and this is

where the performances come into play. Because Gleason and Davis fail to charm or even stir up much interest in their characters, it's hard to care what will happen in the end. There is a surprise in the last few frames that concludes things on a nice note, but by that time it's too late in coming.

Technical elements all work quite well. Bill Butler has photographed the action smartly while production design by Edward C. Carfagno and music (original and adapted) by Lalo Schifrin capture the period. But director Jeremy Paul Kagan lets the action lapse much too often while failing to spur the actors on to creating much more than what's on paper. With that lacking all the technical backing in the world can't really help.

Certainly Universal can't be faulted for going ahead with making a sequel to one of its most successful pictures, particularly in this age of sequelmania. But with what they've offered in "Sting II" audiences certainly can't be faulted if they don't respond. —*Berg.*

Lianna
(COLOR)

A woman's twilight transformation. Intelligent but talky. Urban art site potential.

United Artists Classics release of a Winwood Company production. Written, directed and edited by John Sayles. Produced by Jeffrey Nelson, Maggie Renzi. Features entire cast. Camera (Du-Art Color), Austin de Besche; camera operator, Frank Coleman; music, Mason Daring; art direction, Jeanne McDonnell; assistant director, Carol Dysinger; sound, Wayne Wadhams, Thomas Brandau, Fred Burnham. Reviewed at Cinema II, N.Y., Jan. 19, 1983. (MPAA Rating: R). Running time: 110 MINS.
Lianna .... Linda Griffiths
Ruth .... Jane Hallaren
Dick .... Jon DeVries
Sandy .... Jo Henderson
Theda .... Jessica Wight MacDonald
Spencer .... Jesse Solomon
Jerry .... John Sayles
Bob .... Stephen Mendillo
Cindy .... Betsy Julia Robinson
Kim .... Nancy Mette
Sheila .... Maggie Renzi

John Sayles, the prolific screenwriter who scored a resounding critical success with his first directorial effort, "The Return Of The Secaucus Seven," again uses a keen intelligence and finely tuned ear to tackle the nature of friendship and loving in "Lianna." For all its virtues, however, this story of a married woman coming to grips with her late-blooming lesbianism emerges as an even more specialized entry that probably can't count on media consensus to duplicate the rags-to-modest riches success of "Secaucus." Careful handling in urban art enclaves is in order.

That's not to belittle the considerable accomplishments of this frequently involving story of a 33-year old woman (Linda Griffiths), saddled with an arrogant and unsupportive professor-husband (John DeVries) who downplays her efforts to return to school for her degree and constricts her life until she finds herself falling in love, for the first time, with a woman teacher (Jane Hallaren).

Following her husband's casual cruelties and infidelities, however, the sudden rush of love blinds Griffiths to the painful practical realities of her choice. Kicked out of her home by DeVries (who finds it a convenient excuse to alienate himself and their two kids from her in good conscience), she is forced to start a new life that proves as complicated, and frequently as painful, as what preceded it.

Fadeout finds her at a certain level of healthy self-awareness and self-sufficiency (along with some reconciliation with children and friends), but far from a happily-ever-after. Crux of Sayles' message, it seems, is that friendship is a more durable and necessary commodity than romantic bliss.

With significant success, "Li-anna" takes a story that could have easily indulged the tragic-roman-tic parameters of a true confession mag (or, alternatively, could have slipped into an exploitation mold) and concentrates instead on the realistic personal dynamics of its situation, without ever resorting to special pleading or proselytising.

Key means of conveying those dynamics is through Sayles's forte — finely honed dialog — emerging largely as a progression of ear-per-fect conversations that unfold with a naturalism that makes the hero-ine's conflicts intensely credible. As telling as it is about her immersion into an alternate lifestyle, it's just as insightful in detailing the effects of that choice on others.

Particularly well-drawn are her husband's doubly-hurt sense of sex-ual betrayal, the half-formed understandings of her children, who've only just become aware of conventional sexual realities, and the ambivalence of once-close women friends suddenly fearful and embarrassed for the affection and touches they indulged in be-fore her transition.

Unfortunately, the same low-keyed, casually structured, stead-fastly realistic tone that makes the interplay so credible also works against a steady dramatic thrust and the film fails to build to a truly satisfying peak. As immediate as it all seems while unfolding, the net effect is curiously neutral once the film leaves the screen.

Paced by Griffiths' excellent pivotal performance, the film is marked by fine acting overall, par-ticularly Hallaren as the catalytic lover scared off by the intensity of Griffiths' feelings; DeVries as the acerbic, insecure academic mate; Jo Henderson as the retroactively frightened best girlfriend, and Jes-se Solomon as the wise-beyond-years pubescent son. Sayles himself appears to good effect as a sup-portive friend. Though its low-bud-get origins are evident in some visual rough-edges, technical as-pects are all good, with an es-pecially good use of pop music counterpoints. —*Step.*

Meurtres A Domicile
(Home Murders)
(BELGIAN-FRENCH-COLOR)

Brussels, Jan. 8.

An Elan Films release of a coproduction ODEC (Brussels)-Babylone Films (Paris). Produced by Violette and Jacques Vercruyssen. Screenplay, Jean Van Ham-me, based on the novel "Hotel Meuble" by Thomas Owen; camera, Ken Legargeant; editor, Marc Lobet, France Duez; as-sociate producer, Romaine Hacquard. Di-rected by Marc Lobet; art direction, Luc Monheim; sound, Ricardo Castro; cus-tumes, Anne Verhoeven; assistant direc-tor, Chris Vanden Broeke. Reviewed at Cinema Empire, Brussels, Nov. 28, 1982. Running time: **87 MINS.**

Inspector Aurelia Maudru . Anny Duperey
Max Queyrat .... Bernard Giraudeau
Oswald Stricker .... Andre Bernier
Madame Vianna .... M.A. Dutheil
Julius Zepernick .... Daniel Emilfork
Ange Auber .... Alain Flick
Raoul Queyrat .... Idwig Stephane

"Home Murders" is, so far, one of the few Belgian films aimed at entertaining a large audience. But the mixture of classic whodunit, bizarre and fantastic elements and broad caricature doesn't work out. Pic is based on the novel "Hotel Meuble" by Belgian writer Thomas Owen who was an advocate of com-bining thriller with black humor.

French actress Anny Duperey plays a part that is traditionally re-served for men: a police inspector who is assigned to a murder case. The fact that the job is done by a woman gives the film a chance to invert the genre's stereotypes and makes her investigation somewhat original.

The murder was committed in the old building where she has an apartment. All her neighbors are suspected and all seem to have a motive for the crime. They all have their strange obsessions and cur-ious behavior. Among them: a nec-rophilic undertaker, a fortune teller who practices exorcism, an old photographer, a sculptor who lives with his young model and an ego-maniacal theatre actor. This part is played by Bernard Giraudeau, who is miscast as a thespian who could play Othello.

Acting, except by the two leads, is way over the top. Most of the action is lensed in a glowering Brussels house where each apartment seems to hold a dark secret. Suspense is well sustained till the end, and the solution of the murder mystery comes as a big surprise. It's a pity that the director didn't find a right balance.

Thanks mostly to the billing of two popular French actors, pic has been moderately successful in Belgium. —*Pat.*

Murder By Phone
(CANADIAN-COLOR)

A New World Pictures release of a Co-Co Film Prod./Famous Players/Canadian Film Development Corp. production. Executive producer, Stanley Colbert. Pro-duced by Robert Cooper. Directed by Michael Anderson. Features entire cast. Screenplay, Michael Butler & Dennis Shy-rack, John Kent Harrison; camera (De Luxe color), Reginald Morris; editor, Mar-tin Pepler; music, John Barry; music orchestrated and performed by John Petersen, Jonathan Elias; sound, Peter Shewchuk; production manager, Phil McPedran; assistant director, Steve Wright; production design, Seamus Flan-nery; co-producer, Brian Walker; assoc. producer, Michael Hadley; stunt coordi-nator, Bob Hannah; special effects, Bill Myatt, Henry Piersig, Kenneth Estes. Re-viewed at National 1 theatre, N.Y., Jan. 7, 1982. (MPAA Rating: R). Running time: **79 MINS.**

Nat Bridger ...... Richard Chamberlain
Dr. Stanley Markowitz .. John Houseman
Ridley Taylor .... Sara Botsford
Noah Clayton .... Robin Gammell
Det. Meara .... Gary Reineke
Fred Waits .... Barry Morse

Filmed in Toronto in 1980 as "Bells," "Murder By Phone" is a sorry excuse for a horror/sci-fi pro-grammer. Picked up for distribu-ion by New World (and briefly flirting with an alternate monicker "The Calling"), it's due for a quick playoff.

The picture's gimmick is a crazed killer baffling the local po-lice by killing at a distance using a sophisticated apparatus which transmits through the telephone system, zapping victims through their phone receivers. New World's release title for the film unwit-tingly tips off the age of this hoary plot device, used as the basis for a stilted 1935 "Murder By Television."

Richard Chamberlain, sporting a handsome beard and an unsteady country-boy accent, toplines as Nat Bridger, a science teacher investi-gating the mysterious death of one of his students. Tracking her death to a Toronto subway phone which was found melted, Bridger seeks aid in vain from his former pro-fessor Stanley Markowitz (John Houseman), now an environ-mental consultant for Inter-World Telephone Co.

In one of many preposterous script cogs, Bridger befriends art-ist Ridley Taylor (Sara Botsford), painting a huge technology mural in the phone company's lobby, who conveniently has access to all the labs and files in the supposedly high security installation. Aided by local police detective Meara (Gary Reineke) they trace and trap the killer.

British director (now a Can-adian resident) Michael Anderson fails to pump any excitement or suspense into the picture, prefer-ring to immerse the viewer in tele-phone lore and load every scene with a different type of phone re-ceiver. Cumulative effect is campy rather than scary, not surprising given the impersonal, definitely un-horrific reliance on "murder at a distance." Each killing consists of a victim shaking, bleeding profusely and then, with hokey special effects, flying across the room in slow mo-tion.

With silly, cliched dialog (and time out for pompous militant speeches by Chamberlain con-cerning controlling our destiny and protecting the environment), cast plays by the numbers. Redhead Sara Botsford is introduced here as an attractive heroine, subse-quently having made two more hor-ror films "Still Of The Night" and "Night Eyes," while Barry Morse is quite predictably up to no good as the president of IWT. Tech credits are subpar, particularly the murky photography. For an effective and intentionally funny paranoia film about the phone company, one still has to turn to "The President's Analyst." —*Lor.*

Timerider
(COLOR)

Enjoyable sci-fi escapism.

Hollywood, Jan. 25.

A Jensen-Farley Pictures release, pro-duced by Harry Gittes. Directed by Wil-liam Dear. Exec producer, Michael Nes-mith. Screenplay, William Dear and Mich-ael Nesmith; camera (Color), Larry Pi-zer; editors, Suzanne Pettit, Kim Secrist, R.J. Kizer; art direction, Linda Pearl; music, Michael Nesmith. Reviewed at the Pacific Theatre, Hollywood, Jan. 21, 1983. MPAA rating: PG. Running time: **93 MIN.**

Lyle Swann .... Fred Ward
Clair .... Belinda Bauer
Reese .... Peter Coyote
Padre .... Ed Lauter
Claude .... Richard Masur
Carl ....Tracey Walter
Potter.................... L.Q. Jones
Daniels .... Chris Mulkey
Dr. Sam .... Macon McCalman
Jesse .... Jonathan Banks

"Timerider" is the kind of pic-ture small distributors like Jensen-Farley dream of: too cheap and amateurish to attract the majors' interest, but just right for a certain segment of the paying audience. Should do terrific in action houses.

Conceding the picture is pap that any concentrated attention will make shambles of, it's nonetheless a pleasant, enjoyable 93 minutes that noodles with what might hap-pen if a fellow rode a motorcycle through a time warp and wound up in the middle of a bunch of bandits in the Wild West.

Fred Ward is just fine as the cyc-list, terrific on wheels, but a bit too dense to ever figure out quite what's happened to him. And Peter Coy-ote is a good match as the outlaw chief who covets Ward's wheels.

Rounding out a generally good cast are pretty Belinda Bauer, sexy with a pistol, Richard Masur and Carl Dorsett as Coyote's rather hapless henchman and Ed Lauter, solid in a somewhat confusing part (he might have been preferable in Coyote's role.)

Director William Dear cranks his story up and roars along with little concern for the ecology of logic, but he has fun and reaches a neat end-ing. If this be escapism, make the most of it. —*Har.*

Treasure Of The Four Crowns
(COLOR-3-D)

Fatiguing adventure fantasy fails to advance the cause of 3-D.

A Cannon Films release of an M.T.G. (Lupo-Anthony-Quintano) and Lotus Films S.A. (Spain) coproduction. Execu-tive producer, Menahem Golan, Yoram Globus. Produced by Tony Anthony, Gene Quintano; associate producer, Marshall Lupo. Directed by Ferdinando Baldi. Stars Tony Anthony. Screenplay, Lloyd Battista, Jim Bryce, Jerry Lazarus, from a story by Tony Petito, Gene Quintano; camera (Metrocolor, 3-D), Marcello Masciocchi, Giuseppe Ruzzolini; editor, Franco Fraticelli; music, Ennio Morricone; 3-D technical advisor, Stan Loth; art direction, Luciano Spadoni; special effects, Fredy Unger, Germano Natali, Carlo de Marchis; stunt director, Neno Zamperla; sound effects, Roberto Arcangeli; filmed with Marks 3-Depix Converter & Arriflex cameras. Reviewed at Gemini 1 theatre, N.Y., Jan. 21, 1982. (MPAA Rating: PG). Running time: **99 MINS.**

J.T. Striker	Tony Anthony
Liz	Ana Obregon
Edmund	Gene Quintano
Socrates	Francisco Rabal
Rick	Jerry Lazarus
Brother Jonas	Emiliano Redondo
Prof. Montgomery	Francisco Villena
Possessed woman	Kate Levan
Popo	Lewis Gordon

"Treasure Of The Four Crowns" is topliner-producer Tony Anthony's failed attempt to emulate the adventure and fantasy of "Raiders Of The Lost Ark" in 3-D format. Public interest in depth pictures (spurred by Anthony's previous "Comin' At Ya" film) should assure good openings, but eye-taxing visuals and weak story values spell trouble in building a wider audience.

Sharing "Comin' At Ya's" problem in over-emphasizing gimmickry, "Treasure" often resembles a silent-era trick film, stringing together 3-D gags at the expense of continuity and narrative. After the obligatory "Star Wars"/serial-styled intro crawl, credits sequence presents the wording on a different plane from the action, creating focusing problems for the viewer. First 20 minutes of the picture are sans dialog, as adventure Striker (Tony Anthony) undergoes an incoherent series of perils in a Spanish castle in order to fetch a magic key.

Delayed exposition establishes a quest initiated by Prof. Montgomery (Francisco Villena) to recover two ancient crowns containing golden balls that hold the powers of good and evil, fashioned by the Visigoths. Striker organizes a "Mission: Impossible" crew to retrieve them from European religious cult leader (hailing from Brooklyn) Brother Jonas (Emiliano Redondo): the prof's assistant Edmund (Gene Quintano), a drunken mountain climber Rick (Jerry Lazarus), circus strongman (now clown) Socrates (Francisco Rabal) and his trapeze artist daughter Liz (Ana Obregon).

Final 40 minutes of the picture detail the team's assault on Jonas's fortress, executed with fine physical action scenes, pryotechnics and stuntwork.

Problem is that the filmmakers include too frequent an array of negative parallax shots, that is, objects photographed to appear rapidly moving off the screen into theatre space. Combination of fast-cutting and rapid movement of objects does not allow one's eyes to easily adjust to the changes in stereo convergence. Result is strain, fatigue and another setback in the effort to make 3-D a viable, standard filmmaking tool.

On the plus side, "Treasure" has effective sets and many pleasing depth shots amidst the flashy ones. Aerialists performing in a circus look good in 3-D, as do exploding miniatures and other fireworks. Hampered by inadequate dubbing, the cast performs well physically, with no discernible doubles during the exciting hanging-from-the-ceiling caper to steal the crowns.

Special effects are hokey, with Anthony's spinning head and subsequent good/evil makeup when he gets the crowns' power proving to be laughable. Action is carried by solid sound effects and an alternately driving or romantic Ennio Morricone musical score.

Numerous raids on "Raiders" include Obregon's sassy intro to Anthony, which echoes Karen Allen's greeting to Harrison Ford; large flaming balls rolling after Anthony; a mist-filled trunk instead of ark holding the key and a silly finale with flame-throwers emanating from Anthony's hands at the baddies. Instead of getting mad at this imitation, hopefully George Lucas and/or Steven Spielberg will make their own 3-D adventures, and thereby validate the process. —*Lor.*

Vigilante
(COLOR)

Violent and topical message picture. Too grim for general audiences.

An Artists Releasing Corp. release through Film Ventures International of a Magnum motion picture. Produced by Andrew Garroni and William Lustig. Stars Robert Forster, Fred Williamson. Directed by Lustig. Screenplay, Richard Vetere; camera (TVC color), James Momel; editor, Lorenzo Marinelli; music, Jay Chattaway; sound, Gary Rich, Arthur Sokalner; assistant director, Randy Jurgensen; production manager, Randee Lois Smith; special makeup effects, Cecelia Verardi; production design, Mischa Petrow; special effects coordinator, Gary Zeller; additional photography, Michael Spera; exec producers, John Packard, Jerry Masucci, Kenneth Pavia. Reviewed at RKO 86th St. 2 theatre, N.Y., July 23, 1982. (MPAA Rating: R). Running time: **90 MINS.**

Eddie	Robert Forster
Nick	Fred Williamson
Burke	Richard Bright
Vickie	Rutanya Alda
Prago	Don Blakely
Ramon	Joseph Carberry
Rico	Willie Colon
Eisenberg	Joe Spinell
D.A. Fletcher	Carol Lynley
Rake	Woody Strode
Judge Sinclair	Vincent Beck
Horace	Bo Rucker
Mr. "T"	Peter Savage

"Vigilante" is an extremely violent, hard-edged action picture in the familiar genre popularized by "Death Wish." Literally a case of "overkill," film's plotting and violent effects are quite unpleasant, meaning that while it stands to clean up in action houses "Vigilante" will likely prove a turnoff to wider audiences.

Bound to provoke controversy, picture portrays contemporary New York City as a battleground, with neighborhood spokesman Nick (Fred Williamson) uniting with fellow factory workers to beat up or even blow away the punks, drug pushers and pimps that make their life hell.

Coworker Eddie Merino (Robert Forster) resists Nick's simplistic vigilante solution to the problem, but is put on the spot when the punks, mainly Puerto Ricans, terrorize his family, killing his child and viciously knifing his wife (Rutanya Alda). As events progress in a downward spiral, even he joins the vigilantes in an orgy of exploding blood-pack killings.

With pictures such as "The Exterminator" and others blurring once and for all the moral issues involved, it is not surprising to have today's John Garfield-esque hero Forster rooted on as a "motivated" but cold-blooded good guy killer. However, helmer William Lustig and writer Richard Vetere resort to an increasingly far-fetched route to get him (and the vicariously identifying audience) there.

After his son's murder, police round up the suspects and Eddie has D.A. Mary Fletcher (Carol Lynley) prosecute the gang leader Rico (salsa singing star Willie Colon). At the trial, the idiotic judge sides with corrupt defense lawyer Eisenberg (Joe Spinell) and, over Fletcher's objections, lets Rico off with a two-year suspended sentence. Physically attacking the judge in court, Eddie is thrown in prison for contempt. While Nick and his pals are rounding up and killing drug dealers and their higher-ups, Eddie emerges from prison ready to kill the whole gang and even the judge.

This negative, wish-fulfillment fantasy is enacted with considerable technical skill. Production team, encoring from their Joe Spinell terror vehicle "Maniac," portrays the violent scenes as in a horror picture, with noisy Dolby stereo effects enhancing the impact. Even without the ultra-violence, "Vigilante" is simply too grim and nihilistic to justify its existence as entertainment.

Under the circumstances, Forster and especially Williamson are powerful forces as the anti-heroes. Alda is very impressive as Forster's victimized wife, even putting across an impossible scene where she walks out on him just as he's released from prison. Film's best moments are provided by Woody Strode, who projects a quiet authority as a fellow prisoner who creates a show-stopping scene when he beats up two monstrous young thugs terrorizing Forster in prison. —*Lor.*

(Film recently opened in Paris. U.S. release is slated for March.— Ed.)

Stark Raving Mad
(U.S.-COLOR)

Thrill killer a soft entry.

Winnipeg, Jan. 18.
John J. Burzichelli in association with Bernard Block presents an Independent Artists release of a Round Picture production. Produced by Tiger Warren and Don Gronquist; executive producers, Robert and Swigert Warren; directed by George F. Hood; screenplay, uncredited; camera (color), J. Wilder; editor, Hood; art direction, W.S. Warren. Reviewed at Towne Cinema 8, Winnipeg, Jan. 18, 1983. Running time: **88 MINS.**

Richard Stark	Russell Fast
Laura Ferguson	Marcie Severson
Francis Porter	B. Joe Medley
David Jenkins	Mike Walter
Barbara Farmington	Janet Galen
Norman Stark	Don Beekman
Dorothy Freeman	Mildred Card
Maid	Marjorie Hall
Lucius Davis	Don Finley

"Stark Raving Mad" recounts Charlie Starkweather's killing spree of 1958. The incident already served as the basis for the exceptional "Badlands" made in 1973 and while the new film cannot match Terrence Malick's in substance or craft, it is nonetheless a compelling, if modest, work.

Produced on an extremely low budget and shot in 16m with primarily non-pro performers and technicians, "Stark Raving Mad" benefits from the grittiness of its images. It is a relatively faithful account of the Starkweather affair which involved his 14-year-old girlfriend Caril Ann Fugate though there are echoes of such couple-on-the-run films as "You Only Live Once" and "They Live by Night."

Russell Fast plays Starkweather, called Richard Stark (hence the title) in the film. In the opening moments he's seen being shaved on his way to the electric chair and a voice-over narration labels him "the most remorseless killer of our time."

Action then moves backwards to Fast's first meeting Marcie Severson, the Fugate character renamed Laura Ferguson. She asks him to buy her and her giggly girlfriends cigarettes. They're soon holding hands at the malt shop in their Nebraska town.

Fast, a garbageman with a James Dean fixation, isn't deemed a suitable date by Severson's stepfather. After Fast gets fired for fighting on the job, he picks up Severson and tells her they'll face her step-father. However, his plan to leave with the young girl is met by anger and in the ensuing fight, Fast kills the man with a poker.

On the run, Fast kills six more people in the process of changing cars and eluding the authorities. Severson remains a knowing by- stander witnessing the murders, and in one case, a rape. However, when they're finally cornered by police she decides to feign inno- cence after a brief flirtation with turning gun moll.

Considering the severe working limitations, director George Hood gets highly competent perform- ances from his two leads. Fast has a brooding presence and is genuine- ly chilling when reflecting on his sudden notoriety. Severson has an unaffected air suited to the role and natural screen charm.

The supporting characteriza- tions are all unexceptional and technical work is no more than competent apart from some well- paced editing. Hood has made as- tute artistic decisions with the only real embarrassment being some dreadful reportorial voiceovers which open and close the film.

The film falls into the difficult bind of being neither high-brow nor exploitation. Its modest trappings would suggest the latter but the sub- dued violence and one fleeting bit of nudity are hardly selling points on the grind circuit. It's unlikely "Stark Raving Mad" will find an audience that's truly receptive to the film. Nonetheless, it's quite playable and should recoup its modest investment. —Klad.

Kill And Go Hide
(COLOR)

Interesting horror cheapie.

A New American Films release of a Pan- orama Films production. Exec producer, Harry Novak. Produced by Robert Dada- shian. Directed by Robert Voskanian. Fea- tures entire cast. Screenplay, Ralph Lu- cas; camera (Eastmancolor), Mori Ala- vi; editor, Voskanian, Dadashian; music, Rob Wallace; sound, John McDonald; spe- cial makeup effects, Jay Owens, assistant director-production manager, Smith John- son. Reviewed at Magno Preview 9 screen- ing room, N.Y., Jan. 6, 1983. (MPAA Rating: R). Running time: 83 MINS.
Alicianne .... Laurel Barnett
Rosalie .... Rosalie Cole
Mr. Nordon .... Frank Janson
Len Nordon .... Richard Hanners
Mrs. Whitfield .... Ruth Ballan

"Kill And Go Hide" is an inter- esting gothic horror film, rising above the obvious limitations of its low budget and derivative origins. Released in 1977 as "The Child" by Boxoffice International, picture's reissue should be of interest to hor- ror buffs.

Familiar gothic story set in the 1930s has the heroine Alicianne (Laurel Barnett) arriving as an outsider figure to be governess for the child Rosalie (Rosalie Cole), whose family has a history of men- tal illness.

The child crystallizes her morbid imagination by making line draw- ings of what she wants to happen. This voodoo-style premise is mani- fested in ghouls carrying out the child's wishes.

Hampered by some flat acting and overuse of low and wide angle camerawork, the picture even- tually generates a powerful night- marish quality as Alicianne and Rosalie's brother are trapped by the ghouls in a climactic sequence that explicitly acts out the "return of the repressed" theme later pop- ularized by critic Robin Wood in his analyses of major horror films. The film's nihilistic conclusion is less ef- fective, however.

Director Robert Voskanian milks certain thriller set-pieces over- much (e.g., the car engine that won't start) but generally delivers the chills. Sound and other techni- cal credits are below par, and the ghouls unfortunately look too much like extras in Halloween skeleton costumes. —Lor.

Himala
(Miracle)
(FILIPINO-COLOR)

Manila, Jan. 24.
An Experimental Cinema of the Philip- pines production and release. Executive producer, Charo Santos Concio. Directed by Ishmael Bernal. Stars Nora Aunor, Veronica Palileo, Spanky Manikan, Gigi Duenas, Laura Centeno. Screenplay, Ricardo Lee; camera (color), Sergio Lobo. Reviewed at the opening of the 1983 Manila International Film Festival, Manila Film Centre, Philippines, Jan. 24, 1983. Running time: 120 MINS.
Elsa .... Nora Aunor
Nimia .... Gigi Duenas
Orly .... Spanky Manikan
Mrs. Alba .... Veronica Palileo
Chayong .... Laura Centeno
(In Tagalog with English subtitles.)

French-trained Filipino director Ishmael Bernal has finally reached his creative peak and total accep- tance in the Philippine film industry when "Himala" swept the major awards at the recent Metro Manila Film Fest and then was invited to prestigiously open the 1983 Manila International Film Festival. Ber- nal has long been neglected and he is the most-nominated Manila film- maker for the local critics' derby. His "Manila After Dark," how- ever, won best picture last year.

"Himala" has also been touted as the first Tagalog picture to have been produced by the Experi- mental Cinema of the Philippines, an arm of the annual MIFF for 3,- 000,000 pesos. It will circulate to five leading international filmfests, in- cluding the forthcoming Berlin Film Festival, then to Cannes' Di- rectors' Fortnight.

The film bitingly, hypnotically and realistically captures the mixed-up and often confused rural Philippine traditions that are full of

contradictions quite similar to what was shown in Francesco Rosi's "Christ Stopped At Eboli." It is a situation where religion, fanatic- ism, superstition and cliched soap opera characters intermix. The film opens in the dappled and moody darkness of an eclipse which sets the tone of the supernatural theme that's been blended with the harsh realities experienced by a young girl who gets victimized by circumstances beyond her control. It is rich in details of backward village life that should fascinate foreign viewers intrigued with ex- otic Third World poverty, hunger, oriental funeral services, physical ugliness and handicapped human bodies cinematically framed by the magic of faith healing as its main theme.

The provincial setting is the sleepy town of Cupang (shot on location in lovely Ilocos Norte) which has supposedly been cursed after driving away a leper. The small, dissipated and forgotten dusty town without rainfall awak- ens to exploitation and com- mercialism when an innocent girl called Elsa (Nora Aunor) claims to have seen an apparition of the Bles- sed Virgin. She later acquires heal- ing powers. Along the lines of Lourdes, the whole village be- comes a bustling commercial venue for mass-produced statue saints and bottled holy or tonic water. In later excursions into sub- plots, a close friend of Elsa who becomes a woman of easy virtue returns to Cupang, a virginal sister who is totally devoted to the re- ligious mission, some enterprising matrons, then a kaleidoscopic look at hundreds of sick people with dis- eased bodies. A pivotal character is a cynical and young film director (Spanky Manikan) with a con- science. The latter becomes obses- sed in capturing Elsa's healing ses- sions on celluloid which leads to his candidly catching on film (by acci- dent) a dark secret of Elsa, a secret which prompted the suicide of her sister.

Here is an eloquent, powerful film that is full of grandeur and sim- ple segments. It shows an at- mospheric environment where il- literate but adulating, praying crowds desperate for a cure can be a hostile mob when the miracle they crave for doesn't materialize.

Nora Aunor as Elsa gives a sen- sitive, polished and highly passive and consistently low-key per- formance. She is letter-perfect for the role. Meanwhile, Gigi Duenas (a stage actress) as a girl on the wrong side of the tracks who op- erates a "cabaret-whorehouse" is singularly brilliant and provides a striking contrast to the spiritual life of Elsa.

If there is anything wrong with the production, it is just the length and repetitious sequences.

Towards the middle, a weird and startling denouement is shared with the viewers to sustain their high level of fascination. The Tagalog screenplay is suitably hard boiled and not affected as in common local features. There is excellent eerie soundtrack music.

"Himala" is the kind of quality festival film that brightens the Philippines' tarnished name in the field of films geared for inter- national consumption and release. The picture brings out the fact that there are more Filipino directors to discover. —Mel.

Comeback
(U.S.-COLOR)

Romantic meller looking for theatrical life beyond tele- vision.

Winnipeg, Jan. 25.
A 20th-Century Fox release of a Hall Bartlett production. Produced and direct- ed by Hall Bartlett; Associate producers, Cathy Bartlett, David Leonard, William Kushner. Stars Michael Landon. Screen- play by Bartlett; camera (Deluxe color), Andrew Laszlo; art direction, Dan Lom- ino; underwater special effects by Ira and Barbara Anderson, Al Broussard and Mike Edmonson; editor, Jay Lash Cassidy; music, Klaus Doldinger; sound, Don MacDougall, David Dockendorf, Richard Tyler; reviewed at the Capitol 2, Winni- peg, Jan. 17, 1983. Running time: 127 MINS.
John Everingham .... Michael Landon
Keo Sirisomphone .... Moira Chen
General Siegfried Kapler Jurgen Prochnow
Derek McBracken ... Edward Woodward
Sandy Redford .... Priscilla Presley
Steve Hammond .... David Leonard
Cathy Hammond .... Cathy Bartlett
Georges .... Gabriele Tinti
Clive .... William Kushner
Frank Moseley .... Eric Miller
Madeleine .... Dee Barouch
General Khams .... Kuhn Ram Vortan

Producer-director Hall Bartlett, best known for his production of "Jonathan Livingston Seagull," re- turns to the screen with "Come- back," a heavily melodramatic ro- mantic adventure based on the true exploits of Australian photo-jour- nalist John Everingham.

Michael Landon plays Evering- ham, a long-time resident in Laos who was exiled for spying in 1977. However, he returned the follow- ing year to rescue his Laotian fi- ancee in a daring underwater operation.

The photo-journalist's attempts to make a successful crossing of the Mekong River between Thailand and Laos in scuba gear account for the film's most exciting moments. The remainder of the film, a Far Eastern romance, is fascinating if familiar fare. And Bartlett, who also wrote the screenplay, offers lit- tle more than cliche to explain the enduring love between Evering- ham and his Laotian girl friend.

The film opens with Evering- ham's first attempt at a rescue mis- sion. The stunning underwater pho- tography and rapid cutting make for a hard act to follow. At more than two hours, "Comeback" plods through a dense jungle of exposition for most of its running length.

After the first failure, the story flashes back a year earlier to Landon's first meeting with Moira Chen. Unbeknowst to him, Chen is working for Jurgen Prochnow, the German-Russian head of Pathet Lao espionage. Prochnow suspects embarassing stories and photos leaking to the west originate from the photo-journalist.

So, he commissions Landon to photograph for a travel brochure and Chen is assigned as his model. However, things don't work out as Prochnow planned. Landon's sincerity and concern for the Laotian people convinces Chen the Communist regime is not beyond reproach.

Prochnow suspects a wavering in her loyalty and as insurance has his own men track Landon. While Chen insists his activities are not subversive, Prochnow collects enough damaging evidence to put Landon on trial and soon has him expelled as an undesirable.

Prochnow's true intentions toward Chen then become quite evident. He begins to groom her as his mistress and begins a campaign to discredit her ex-lover. Meanwhile, working from Thailand, Landon concocts his kamikaze rescue plan with the aid of Edward Woodward, an ex-British naval frogman.

Bartlett has spliced the various elements of the true story together quite awkwardly. He bookends the film's most visually impressive moments — the two underwater rescue attempts — and offers little real action in between. An exception is a grudge match between Landon and Prochnow where they use western and eastern boxing techniques respectively.

The story grows from an exotic romance laden with poetic dialog into an aquatic "Rocky" as Woodward pushes Landon to increase his lung capacity and strength as if preparing for a sporting event. There is simply no sustaining momentum in the narrative.

Shot in Thailand, the film at least has a sense of authenticity. And this aspect sustains viewer interest when the story turns sugary. The film is marginally better than other recent romantic yarns thanks to its basis in fact.

Landon, in his first large screen role in two decades, is a touch too subdued for this obsessive role. His coolness contrasted with Prochnow's fierce villainy results in an old fashioned melodramatic effect not intended for the tale. Incidently, though the real Everingham is Australian, there's no attempt to identify his nationality.

Chen, an Indonesian actress, however, offers the right note to the proceedings. She has just the right degree of awkwardness required

for this east meets west affair. And Edward Woodward registers well in his supporting role.

Technical credits are strong in the large screen venture. "Comeback" was to go to U.S. television over Bartlett's strong objections but may yet see theatrical dates in the States thanks to its strong opening in Canada. However, picture is best suited to a quick playoff rather than a sustained run. —Klad.

Amici, Miei, Atto 2
(All My Friends 2)
(ITALIAN-COLOR)

Rome, Jan. 20.

A Gaumont release, produced by Luigi and Aurelio De Laurentiis for Filmauro. Stars Philippe Noiret, Ugo Tognazzi, Gastone Moschin, Adolfo Celi and Renzo Montagnani. Directed by Mario Monicelli. Screenplay, Leo Benvenuti, Piero De Bernardi, Tullio Pinelli and Monicelli; camera (Eastmancolor), Sergio D'Offizi; editor, Ruggero Mastroianni; art director, Lorenzo Baraldi; music, Carlo Rustichelli. Reviewed at Garden Cinema, Rome, Jan. 20, 1983. Running time: 120 MINS.
Giorgio Perozzi . . . . Philippe Noiret
Count Lello Mascetti . . . . Ugo Tognazzi
Prof. Sassaroli . . . . Adolfo Celi
Giambaldo Melandri . . . Gastone Moschin
Necchi . . . . Renzo Montagnani
Alice Mascetti . . . . Milena Vukotic

Seven years after helming "Amici Miei," a well-crafted comedy based on an idea by Pietro Germi just before his death, Mario Monicelli brings a second "act" to the screen with virtually the same cast, writers, and technicians. All attempts to duplicate the phenomenal success of the original, which topped Italo b.o. charts in the '75-76 season, are annulled by a dullish script and the general re-run quality of the follow-up. Pic is big box-office and now leading all but one of this year's comedy hits. Export potential is mainly in Italo comedy markets.

Like the first version, pic counts heavily on its five principals to carry the anecdotal story along to its arbitrary cut-off point. The five, all appealing middle-aged actors with solid careers behind them, play close buddies living in Florence who have a bent for practical jokes. Ugo Tognazzi is a penniless count living in squalor with his wife and unattractive daughter, who gets pregnant out of wedlock. Philippe Noiret, the newspaper man who was killed off at the end of Act I, is resuscitated here for the sake of script necessities and the French market; most episodes take place in the past to keep him in scene.

As the surgeon, Adolfo Celi plays some nasty tricks on a doddering moneylender who is convinced he needs a double kidney transplant. Gastone Moschin falls for a religious freak and ends up interpreting Jesus in a highly profane passion play. Renzo Montagnani, only new face in the film, plays a cuckolded bar owner.

Though the situations are yawningly old, firstrate thesping from all hands makes pranks come alive briefly, like match flames. But the bitter-sweet aftertaste and malicious barbs that occasionally distinguished its predecessor (and all the better comedies of Pietro Germi and Monicelli) come off looking forced and unconvincing (Tognazzi winding up in a wheelchair at pic's end).

To its credit, pic sidesteps the current fad for spicing dialog with words teenagers snigger at and easy laughs from dialect jokes. Its nothing-sacred stance takes aim at everything from religion to children, contortionists to medicine, often skirting vulgarity but aspiring to a more mature form of humor. More's the pity it was made with so little invention. —Yuna.

Sapiches
(Private Popsicle)
(ISRAELI-COLOR)

Tel Aviv, Jan. 10.

A Golan-Globus production, distributed by Noah Films. Produced by Menahem Golan and Yoram Globus. Written and directed by Boaz Davidson. Features entire cast. Script adviser: Eli Tavor; editor, Bruria Davidson; camera (color), Adam Greenberg; costumes, Tami Mor; art director, Ariel Roshko. Reviewed at the Shahaf Cinema, Tel Aviv, Jan. 10, 1983. Running time: 100 MINS.
Cast: Yiphtakh Katzur, Tzahi Noi, Jonathan Segal, Dvora Kedar, Menashe Warshawsky, Joseph Shiloah, Sonia Martin, Moshe Ish-Kassit.

Boaz Davidson is back at his old "Lemon Popsicle" formula, which, at least as far as the domestic audience is concerned, simply can't go wrong. In only a few weeks it has already beaten all competition for the top moneymaker of the year, in spite of bad reviews.

This is the fourth time the formula is used, and obviously running out of inspiration; ideas from previous sequels are inserted again, with slight changes. What is more qualified to please the crowd than something that has already pleased them in the past?

The three teenage musketeers, who have walked through adolescent crises of all sorts, are finally drafted into the army — which doesn't quench their insatiable thirst for the opposite sex and their incapability to think about anything else.

What does seem to be apparent, is that Davidson and his crew are going through the motions without trying too much. The plot consists of mediocre vaudeville sketches, notable for their vulgarity, such as falling into a latrine, and substantial gay innuendos. Thus, the musketeers have ample chance to display their talents in drag and there are double entendre jokes to please everybody.

Tzahi Noi has his obligatory bare behind scene, an Austrian

actress is brought in to play the older woman with the craving for tender flesh, and the soundtrack is adequately adorned with sighs and grunts. In any case, the film's English title gives a pretty accurate idea of the type of humor

In what is a pretty slack and lackadaisical piece of work, one point has been taken care of. Except for a bus bearing a Hebrew inscription, there is nothing in this film to identify it as Israeli, in any manner, and whoever has gone through his military service here, will have difficulty recognizing the events on the screen as anything familiar.

This will certainly serve the distributors in those territories where Israel may not be very popular nowadays, and judging by results of the earlier "Popsicles," the trick has worked. —Edna.

S.A.S. a San Salvador
(S.A.S.-Terminate With Extreme Prejudice)
(FRENCH-W. GERMAN-COLOR)

Paris, Jan. 5.

UGC release of an Elephant productions/UGC-Top 1/Malko Films/CCC Filmkunst coproduction. Produced by Raymond Danon. Stars Miles O'Keeffe. Directed by Raoul Coutard. Screenplay, Gerard de Villiers, from his novel, "Terreur a San Salvador;" camera (color), Georges Liron; art directors, Pierre Louis Thevenet, Gotz Heyman, Jurgen Rieger; editor, Helene Plemianikov; music, Michel Magne; sound, Jean-Philippe Leroux; reviewed at the UGC Normandie theatre, Paris, Dec. 29, 1982. Running time: 95 MINS.
S.A.S. Malko Linge . . . . Miles O'Keeffe
Chacon . . . . Raimund Harmstorf
Reynolds . . . . Anton Diffring
Maria Luisa . . . . Dagmar Lassander
Rosa . . . . Catherine Jarret

Raoul Coutard, the brilliant French cinematographer, is back for another stab at directing, and it's a pretty feeble lunge. Coutard showed some ambition in his earlier pictures, but is apparently now content to handle hack assignments, for which he's unsuited.

"S.A.S. a San Salvador" is the first thriller based on Gerard de Villiers' books featuring His Serene Highness Malko Linge, an Austrian prince who moonlights for the CIA in order to pay for the upkeep of the family castle. De Villiers wrote the screenplay, and all one can say is it's a poor advertisement for the book.

For this first screen adventure, Linge is ordered to civil war-torn San Salvador to do away with a vicious right wing terrorist. He does so. In between there's a little sex, a little violence (generally directed against women), and lots of boredom.

Miles O'Keeffe, who was Tarzan to Bo Derek's Jane, plays the supercool hero, poorly dubbed into French. It's not much of a performance, but then it's not much of a part. The other principals, most of them German — it's a Franco/West German coproduction — don't shine either, and tech credits are dull. The mediocrity of Georges Liron's color photography suggests Coutard's indifference to the material. —*Len.*

Il Conte Tacchia
(Count Tacchia)
(ITALIAN-COLOR)

Rome, Dec. 23.

A Gaumont release, produced by Carlo Valerio and Luciano De Feo for D.A.C. Productions in association with RAI-TV 2 and Adige Film 76 Productions. Stars Enrico Montesano, Vittorio Gassman, Paolo Panelli. Directed by Sergio Corbucci. Screenplay, Corbucci, Luciano Vincenzoni, Sergio Donati, Massimo Franciosa; camera (color), Luigi Kuveiller; editor, Ruggero Mastroianni; art director Maco Dentici; music, Armando Trovaioli. Reviewed at Imprecom Studio, Rome, Dec. 22, 1982. Running time: 111 MINS.

County Tacchia .... Enrico Montesano
Prince .... Vittorio Gassman
Checco's father .... Paolo Panelli

Popular helmer Sergio Corbucci and star Enrico Montesano strive to recapture a forgotten bit of turn-of-the-century Roman history and duplicate the boxoffice feats of "The Marquis of Grillo."

Story of a carpenter's son who is made a count has an undeniable charm that finally outdistances some easy gags and an occasionally halting script. Indications are for brisk boxoffice onshore with good export potential for other Latin and Mediterranean markets.

Checco (Montesano) is a lively little carpenter who likes to dress well and take his pretty girlfriend out in style. His friendship with a noble, impoverished and perennially drunk Prince (Vittorio Gassman) is partly based on his delusion he is the Prince's illegitimate son. Mockingly called Count Tacchia after the wedge of wood he is wont to slip under wobbly furniture legs, Checco carries the masquerade too far to court a foolish young Duchess and becomes the laughingstock of decadent Roman aristocracy.

But Checco is such a plucky fellow he is actually made a count by King Humbert in order to fight a duel with a French swordsman whom the real aristocrats are too cowardly to face. Through stratagems, luck and the Prince's aid, Count Tacchia wins both the duel and his girl back by the end of an epic length film lasting almost two hours.

Montesano, a comic actor known for playing humble Roman characters with sympathetic realism, does well in "Tacchia" to tone down some of his broader humor and aim at a more three-dimensional character. Entire pic gives the impression of a middle range product upgraded with a sincere effort from

a quality crew and determined performers. Besides the star, two strong supporting thesps help out: Gassman as the aged Prince still roaring with life, the sole nostalgic representative left of a truly "noble" class; and Paolo Panelli, a perfect counterpoint as Checco's carpenter father, unsentimental and utterly realistic.

Count Tacchia was a real historical person, ennobled by the Pope to fight the duel pic records. Script shows a commendable effort to rework this historical material into an entertaining but not trivialized film. Some of the gags are blatantly aimed at contemporary audiences' limp sense of humor. Others are more situational and tinged with plot-related feeling, like Count Tacchia's revenge on the aristocrats who snub his tragicomic attempt to throw a high-class party.

The ably recreated atmosphere of 1910 Rome accounts for a large part of pic's fascination, thanks to Marco Dentici's sets, Clelia Gonzalez's costumes, and Luigi Kuveiler's lensing. —*Yung.*

Blue Thunder
(COLOR)

Slam-bang aerial action picture looks to be a b.o. smash.

Hollywood, Jan. 28.

A Columbia release of a Rastar-Gordon Carroll production. Produced by Carroll. Executive producers, Phil Feldman, Andrew Fogelson. Directed by John Badham. Stars Roy Scheider. Screenplay, Dan O'Bannon, Don Jakoby. Camera (Deluxe color, Panavision), John A. Alonzo; editors, Frank Morriss, Edward Abroms; music, Arthur B. Rubinstein; art direction, Sydney Z. Litwack; set design, Catie Bangs; set decoration, Mickey S. Michaels; costume design, Marianna Elliot; sound, John Glascock, Tim Cooney; visual consultant, Phillip Harrison; special effects supervisor, Chuck Gaspar; special effects, Jeff Jarvis; special effects electronics, Peter Albiez; associate producer, Gregg Champion; assistant directors, Jerry Ziesmer, Danny McCauley; second unit director, aerial, James Gavin; second unit director, stunt, Terry Leonard. Reviewed at the Avco, West L.A., Jan. 28, 1983. (MPAA Rating: R.) Running time: 108 MINS.

Murphy .... Roy Scheider
Cochrane .... Malcolm McDowell
Braddock .... Warren Oates
Kate .... Candy Clark
Lymangood .... Daniel Stern
Icelan .... Paul Roebling
Fletcher .... David S. Sheiner
Montoya .... Joe Santos
Sgt. Short .... Ed Bernard
Mayor .... Jason Bernard
Himself .... Mario Machado

"Blue Thunder" is a ripsnorting live-action cartoon which will give action audiences everywhere their money's worth. Utterly implausible but no less enjoyable for that, pic has been shrewdly structured and crafted for maximum commercial impact. Columbia isn't opening this Rastar-Gordon Carroll production until May 13, but held heavily advertised previews last Friday night to spread word that it has another winner on its hands. Audience response was rousing to say the least.

Except for "The Road Warrior," no film in recent memory has been so jam-packed with visceral, unusual action. Opening 15 minutes take vet L.A. police helicopter pilot Roy Scheider and rookie Daniel Stern on nocturnal rounds, which encompass apprehension of some liquor store hold-up men, a little voyeurism outside the window of a sexy babe doing nude exercises and, more seriously, trying to help stem an assault on a female city councilwoman at her home, which ends in her death.

Reprimanded by boss Warren Oates for the sex-show detour, Scheider is nevertheless invited to a demonstration of the Feds' latest creation, Blue Thunder, a top-secret anti-terrorist chopper loaded with artillery and all manner of privacy invasion technology, such as shotgun microphones that can penetrate bedroom and building walls, long-distance zoom lenses, heat detectors and computer file data on citizens and organizations.

Craft has been brought to L.A. for possible use against subversives during the 1984 Olympic Games, and among those in charge of the program is cardboard villain Malcolm McDowell, with whom Scheider served in Vietnam. For sketchy reasons, they hated each other then and they hate each other now, so much so that the snotty Englishman sabotages Scheider's and Stern's ship in an attempt to put them out of the picture.

Taking Blue Thunder out for a ride, the hot-shot cops manage to eavesdrop on, and record, a conversation linking McDowell, some heavyweight politicos and thug types to the killing of the councilwoman as well as to an insidious military conspiracy aimed at U.S. citizens.

Suspected of possessing the tape, Stern is brutally murdered, whereupon Scheider embarks upon a desperate plan to expose the conspiracy, and, incidentally, save his own neck. His spunky g.f., Candy Clark, helps in getting the tape from its hiding place to a tv station for broadcast, while Scheider, having commandeered Blue Thunder, simultaneously tries to protect Clark, ward off two F-16 Air Force planes dispatched to down him, and fight a final duel with McDowell, all while darting in and out around skyscrapers in downtown Los Angeles.

The aerial stuff, providing countless provocative and distinctively new views of L.A., is exciting enough as it is, but what will really make the picture work for the public is its extremely clever play on audience sympathies and attitudes.

On the one hand, viewers can revel in the high technology and militaristic trappings, which are everywhere in evidence. On the other, they will root strongly for the loner, vaguely anti-establishment personality of Scheider, a macho combat veteran with enough knowledge of the military to know how dangerous it can be.

Further, opening sequences serve to illustrate what a good job the cops and choppers can do in tracking down criminals, promulgating a solid law and order p.o.v. System's excesses, however, are shown up by a daring, enterprising individual, and pic's ending represents a vindication of moral decency and a repudiation of the callousness of the Military Industrial Complex. Ideologically, film is all over the map, but very cleverly manages to have it both ways when it comes to audience's love-hate relationship with things military.

Climactic sequence, which lasts a full half-hour, is truly impressive. Flight of F-16s (filmed via miniatures) zooming into downtown L.A. and blowing up one of the Arco Towers with a missile is astonishing, and the cat-and-mouse game played by Scheider and McDowell behind towering monoliths is inspired both in conception and execution.

Although brief Vietnam flashbacks punctuate the film to "explain" animosity between Scheider and McDowell, streamlined script by Dan O'Bannon and Don Jakoby has been shorn of almost all psychology and complexity, and it hardly matters.

As a Vietnam vet who, for once, is portrayed as a hero, Scheider fills the bill perfectly, and the enthusiastic, slightly goofy Stern proves an ideal foil for him. Candy Clark amusingly sets the cause of woman drivers back 50 years in the final reels, and the late Warren Oates, to whom film is dedicated, is good and gruff as he is constantly obliged to chew out his underlings for their boisterous irreverence.

Enormous technical and logistical challenge posed by the project has been admirably surmounted by director John Badham, aerial second unit director James Gavin, stunt second unit director Terry Leonard, lenser John A. Alonzo, editors Frank Morriss and Edward Abroms, the special effects team, large sound unit and all other hands. — Cart.

Videodrome
(CANADIAN-COLOR)

Effects-laden sci-fi thriller delivers.

Winnipeg, Jan. 24.

A Universal Pictures release of a Filmplan International production. Produced by Claude Heroux; executive producers, Pierre David and Victor Solnicki; associate producer, Laurence Nessis. Direction and screenplay, David Cronenberg. Features entire cast. Camera (color), Mark Irwin; production design, Carol Spier; special makeup effects, Rick Baker; editor, Ronald Sanders; music, Howard Shore. Reviewed at the Odeon, Winnipeg, Jan. 23 1983. (MPAA Rating: R). Running time: 88 MINS.

Max Renn .... James Woods
Bianca O'Blivion .... Sonja Smits
Nicki Brand .... Deborah Harry
Harlan .... Peter Dvorsky
Barry Convex .... Les Carlson
Prof. Brian O'Blivion .... Jack Creley
Masha .... Lynne Gorman
Briley .... Julie Khaner
Moses .... Reiner Schwarz
Rafe .... David Bolt
Rena King .... Lally Cadeau
Bum .... Sam Malkin

Horror specialist David Cronenberg has come up with his most densely plotted and talky film in "Videodrome." However, neither factor gets in the way of the picture's visceral charms, which are considerable. It should easily score another commercial success for Cronenberg and his producers.

Story concerns a small-time cable tv outlet in Toronto. The quasi-clandestine operation is run by Max Renn (James Woods) who's ever on the lookout for offbeat and erotic material.

He becomes fascinated with a program called Videodrome, picked up from a satellite by a sta-

tion technician. The show appears to be little more than a series of torture sequences, primarily involving women. Initially thought to originate in the Far East, the scrambled transmission is eventually tracked to Pittsburgh.

Renn pursues the program but is blocked at every turn. One of his suppliers warns him that the activities on the show are not staged. However, he perseveres, making contact with a McLuhanesque media guru named Brian O'Blivion (Jack Creley). O'Blivion is actually a victim of Videodrome, which has the power to create hallucinations through its emissions. Although dead, his daughter Bianca (Sonja Smits) has maintained this secret by running his old videotapes.

Film is dotted with video jargon and ideology which proves more fascinating than distancing. And Cronenberg amplifies the freaky situation with a series of stunning visual effects including a breathing television set and a chest cavity which opens and closes to serve as a gun holster or a video playback unit.

The dark nature of the tale and most of Cronenberg's earlier films — no heroes, black comedy, and a message of fatalism rather than hope — should continue to enthrall audiences. Despite the bizarre nature of the story, there's an underlying credibility to the proceedings which is frightening.

Renn's path eventually takes him to Videodrome's mastermind. And he goes on a wild journey thanks to a helmet created to conceptualize the wearer's thoughts.

Casting, sometimes a Cronenberg weakness in the past, is first-rate in "Videodrome." Woods aptly conveys Renn's obsession and eventual bondage to the television nightmare. Smits is an alluring and mysterious femme fatale and Deborah Harry seems just right as Renn's girlfriend who thrives on and is undone by Videodrome's games of cruelty.

Supporting cast members are all strong with memorable turns from Creley, Lynne Gorman and Les Carlson as Videodrome's mastermind, an optician aptly named Barry Convex.

Technical credits have a clean polish thanks to Mark Irwin's crisp camera work, Carol Spier's inventive production design and the ingenious makeup effects by Rick Baker. Overall, it's Cronenberg's most accomplished film in all areas of production.

Picture is a real find for horror buffs looking for new thrills and may attract a videophile audience with its high-tech prophesizing. "Videodrome" should attract strong initial business thanks to its ability to elicit shock. There are a number of truly gruesome effects but its boxoffice staying power will

hinge on turning on more than tuning out the audience. — Klad.

Bingo Bongo
(ITALIAN-COLOR)

Rome, Jan. 28.

A Columbia Pictures release, produced by Mario and Vittorio Cecchi Gori for Intercapital Films. Stars Adriano Celentano and Carole Bouquet. Directed by Pasquale Festa Campanile. Screenplay by Enrico Oldoini, Franco Ferrini, Laura Toscano, Franco Marotta. Camera (Technicolor), Alfio Contini; editor, Amedeo Salfa; music, Pinuccio Pirazzoli. Reviewed at Europa Cinema, Rome, Jan. 27, 1983. Running time: 100 MINS.
Bingo Bongo .... Adriano Celentano
Laura .... Carole Bouquet

A comedy made with a little extra care and a few more ideas than usual, "Bingo Bongo" perhaps for that very reason has come in below expectations at the local Christmas boxoffice, despite a cast headlined by popular actor-singer Adriano Celentano and French star Carole Bouquet. However, the absence of specifically national references, dialect jokes and dirty words that may have hurt "Bingo" onshore, could prove pluses for Columbia in exporting to sister markets. Might even go farther marketed as a children's film. ("Bingo" is a smash hit outside the big cities. —Ed).

Picture has a theme of sorts, the relations between human and animal kingdoms, which is developed with a light touch. Bingo Bongo (Celentano), who grew up in the jungle with the monkeys, is captured as an adult and brought back to civilization. A pretty scientist Laura (Carole Bouquet) trains him to speak and eat spaghetti properly. Bingo falls in love. When Laura balks at marriage, the apeman turns his energies to upholding animal rights around the world, eventually winning her over.

Pic's unsophisticated humor plays on Bingo's ability to talk to the animals and cute scenes with Bouquet's pet chimp, who is as talented an actor as his costars. Athletic, rough and at odds with urban living, Celentano makes a perfect missing link. Story was obviously written for his physical talents, with a discotheque production number and several mimed skits reminiscent of old silent comedy.

Bouquet, the icy beauty who tames the beast, is a classic in the old fashioned part in which she switches from severe ethnologist to sensual woman by simply taking off her glasses and slipping into a transparent nightgown. Her apartment full of pets wins her automatic sympathy.

A particular plus is the pulsating rock score by Pinuccio Pirazzoli. Helmer Pasquale Festa Campanile has tried a little harder on this pic, which moves along at a fast clip. —Yung.

Without A Trace
(COLOR)

Low suds meller. Spotty b.o.

Hollywood, Jan. 18.

A 20th Century-Fox release of a Stanley Jaffe production. Produced, directed by Stanley R. Jaffe. Screenplay, Beth Gutcheon, based on her novel, "Still Missing." Stars Kate Nelligan, Judd Hirsch. Camera (Deluxe color), John Bailey; editor, Cynthia Scheider; music, Jack Nitzsche; production design, Paul Sylbert; art direction, Gregory Bolton; set decoration, Alun Hicks; costume design, Gloria Gresham; sound, Jack C. Jacobson; associate producer, Alice Shure; assistant director, Terry Donnelly. Reviewed at the 20th Century-Fox Studios, West L.A., Jan. 18, 1983. (MPAA Rating: PG). Running time: 120 MINS.

Susan Selky .... Kate Nelligan
Al Menetti .... Judd Hirsch
Graham Selky .... David Dukes
Jocelyn Norris .... Stockard Channing
Margaret Mayo ...... Jacqueline Brookes
Philippe .... Keith McDermott
Ms. Hauser .... Kathleen Widdoes
Alex Selky .... Daniel Bryan Corkill
Pat Menetti .... Cheryl Giannini
Eugene Menetti .... David Simon
Polygraph Operator .... William Duell
Vivienne Grant .... Joan McMonagle
Malvina Robbins .... Louise Stubbs

A muted melodrama about a woman whose young son simply disappears one day, "Without A Trace" seems to be of two minds about its own emotional content. On the one hand, film bends over backwards to be restrained and civilized, to avoid cliched treatment of a rather conventional dramatic situation. On the other, pic privately wants to devastate the audience, a secret let out of the bag in the last 10 minutes with a delirious conclusion of "Rocky"-esque proportions. Fox should be able to generate some biz despite lack of b.o. names, although a more than moderate final tally could hardly be expected.

Kate Nelligan, currently the toast of Broadway due to her acclaimed performance in "Plenty," for the first time plays an American on the screen, an English teacher at Columbia whose six-year-old son vanishes from the Brooklyn streets while on his two-block walk to school.

His mother, of course, is deeply disturbed by the turn of events, and her emotional state is not helped by the fact that her husband, David Dukes, has left three months earlier to shack up with a girl in Greenwich Village. But she retains her composure to an admirable degree, even when the cops and the media invade and virtually take over her home to work on the case.

In fact, the police marshalls its forces impressively, spending hundreds of man hours on this single story among millions in the naked city. Leading the investigation team is Judd Hirsch, almost too perfectly cast as an overworked detective.

The domestic tragedy is bannered in the sensationalist dailies, Nelligan appears on tv, her friends post placards throughout the neighborhood, and everyone is supportive as all get-out, but still no kid. Finally, the police arrest Nelligan's former maintenance man, a young, seemingly sympathetic gay who in fact is a kinky S&M freak in whose possession are · found the missing boy's underpants. The case is thus closed, but Nelligan, believing her employe's protestations of innocence, continues to hope her son will somehow turn up.

Stanley R. Jaffe, directing for the first time, could have bathed Beth Gutcheon's tale in undiluted sentimentality from beginning to end, but has instead shied away from some of the most obvious potential dramatic developments. Some storytellers would have had Nelligan· and the cop fall in love, but there's nary a hint of that. Set-up also provides easy excuse for her and her estranged husband to get back together, but no dice there either. And had a warm, cute actress like Sally Field played the lead, audience response would have been much different than is the case with Nelligan, who seems set on preserving her dignity. Actress' fundamental humorlessness keeps viewer at arm's length, and while one can admire her strength and determination, one doesn't come to feel terribly close to her despite her dire predicament.

Without giving away the ending, it must nevertheless be said that Jaffe pulls out all the stops, and creates an almost mind-boggling advertisement for the police in the process. In another context it might have proved as rousing as he intended it, but what has come before is so underplayed that ending seems to be part of some other picture.

Performances are solid down the line. After "Bent" and "The First Deadly Sin," it's nice to see David Dukes with a full head of hair again, and Kathleen Widdoes has a· nice scene as a psychic called in for assistance. Outstanding among the supporting players is Cheryl Giannini, who works wonders with the ultra-conventional role of Hirsch's neglected wife, and William Duell, riveting as a polygraph operator who interviews Nelligan.

Although the gay character is let off the hook, some will undoubtedly object to the stereotyped portrait of him as an unstable sociopath with a penchant for little boys.

Production credits are all modest but pro, and Brooklyn locales make for a nice change of pace from usual mid-town Manhattan settings. Film is overlong at two hours, considering that in an overtly dramatic sense, little happens during the long middle stretch when there are no leads in the case.

Final credits have the phrase, "This film has been rated PG," imprinted directly upon them as part of the film itself, a change from the usual informational slug normally tacked on at the end of a picture.

—Cart.

Party, Party
(BRITISH-COLOR)

London, Jan. 21.

Twentieth Century-Fox (U.K.) release of a Film and General Production for A&M Films, produced by Clive Parsons and Davina Belling. Directed by Terry Winsor. Features entire cast. Screenplay by Daniel Peacock and Winsor. Executive producer, Derek Greene; camera (color), Syd MacCartney; editor, Eddie Joseph; art direction, Deborah Gillingham; music consultant, Richard Hartley. Reviewed at the British Academy of Film and Television Arts, Jan. 13, 1983. (BBFC rating: 15 (AA) Running time: 98 MINS.

Toby	Daniel Peacock
Johnny	Karl Howman
Larry	Perry Fenwick
Sam Diggins	Sean Chapman
Rebecca	Phoebe Nicholls
Terry	Gary Olsen
Bobby	Clive Mantle
Shirley	Caroline Quentin
Brenda	Kim Thomson

It may have been conceived as a compassionate look at the pains of growing up, but "Party, Party" looks now like a calculated commercial sortie on the youth market, combining tasteless English humor with a pounding music track that reviews much of the contemporary rock scene.

The film's concept was originally realized by helmer Terry Winsor as his graduation piece for the National Film School. The winning moments are in the feature, but single idea that postpubescence is a rarely satisfied quest for sexual satisfaction is insufficient to sustain the longer format.

The film opens on a car chase without thrills, then puts its youth characters in costume as police and choirboys in a manner that cracks psychological credibility. By the time the fun starts, interest in the leading players is bound to be slight.

It's just possible that young audiences will feel there is some veracity in the interchanges over the party floor, but older viewers will not be enlightened as to the attitudes and mores of the younger generation.

Comic moments are well timed, and all the young players carry their caricatured roles with finesse. The chief actor Daniel Peacock is clearly a comic find, but in this case he pushes his role over the top.

Despite the fact that many of the crew are also first timers, other departments are fine, and there is no lack of energy to enthuse a sympathetic audience. —Japa.

One Dark Night
(COLOR)

Some good scares.

Hollywood, Jan. 10.

ComWorld Pictures Inc. release. Produced by Michael Schroeder. Exec producer, Thomas P. Johnson. Directed by Tom McLoughlin. Features entire cast. Screenplay, McLoughlin, Michael Hawes; camera (Movielab), Hal Trussel; editor, Charles Tetoni, Michael Spence; production design, Craig Stearns; sound, Trevor Black; music, Bob Summers; assistant director, Dennis White. Reviewed at the Paramount Theatre, Hollywood, Jan. 10, 1983. (MPAA Rating: PG). Running time: 89 MINS.

Cast: Meg Tilly, Robin Evans, Leslie Speights, Elizabeth Daily; Adam West, Melissa Newman, David Mason Daniels.

ComWorld Pictures' "One Dark Night" is a good low-budget suspenser that should do nicely in the appropriate markets. Though it would hardly win any awards for originality, the film serves up the necessary scares while at the same time keeping excessive gore in check. That alone is an achievement these days.

The plot has "nice girl" Meg Tilly (in a far cry from her supporting role in "Tex") desperate to get accepted into a "tough" club of some of her femme high school classmates. Nasty group leader Robin Evans, who also happens to be the jilted "ex" of Tilly's boyfriend, has devised all kinds of nasty initiations that Tilly has passed with flying colors. But then she comes up with the ultimate test.

Tilly is to spend the night in a mausoleum where Evans and the gang plan to scare her into defeat. Just so happens that, "coincidentally," the building houses the crypt of a dead man with telekinetic powers. Seems these powers allowed him to murder some innocent teens some days ago by draining the energy out of their bodies, a pattern one of his former associates fears he could repeat from beyond. So guess what happens?

Director and coscripter Tom McLoughlin creates an adequate amount of tension even if the story is a pencil-by-number example of the genre. Tech credits are respectable considering the budget limitations and the actors perform what's expected of them.

Of course, the lingering question is how many more of these teenager-in-peril films can there possibly be before the market is saturated. That's something they'll probably be asking 20 years from now. —Berg.

Le Prix du Danger
(The Prize of Peril)
(FRENCH-COLOR)

Paris, Jan. 17.

UGC release of a Swanie Productions/TF 1 Film Production/UGC-Top 1/Avala Films (Belgrade) coproduction. Produced by Norbert Saada. Stars Gerard Lanvin, Michel Piccoli, Marie-France Pisier, Bruno Cremer, Andrea Ferreol. Directed by Yves Boisset. Written by Boisset and Jean Curtelin, based on the story by Robert Sheckley; camera (color), Pierre-William Glenn, music, Vladimir Cosma; art director, Serge Douy; editor, Michelle David; sound, Raymond Adam. Reviewed at Club 13, Paris, Jan. 17, 1983. Running time: 99 MINS.

Francois Jacquemard	Gerard Lanvin
Frederic Lemaire	Michel Piccoli
Laurence Ballard	Marie-France Pisier
Antoine Chirex	Bruno Cremer
Elizabeth Worms	Andrea Ferreol

"The Prize of Peril" is a trite update of "The Most· Dangerous Game" theme, with television cast in the role of the villain, a sort of corporate Count Zaroff.

Inspired by a Robert Sheckley tale, Yves Boisset's speculative thriller tells of a phenomenally popular televised manhunt in a future society eroded by massive unemployment and manipulated by morally bankrupt tv and advertising minds. Two years ago, Bertrand Tavernier offered "Deathwatch," a more thoughtful variation on a similar sci-fi theme. (The late Elio Petri's 1965 "The Tenth Victim" has a similar premise, also taken from a Sheckley novel.— Ed.).

The show, called :"The Prize of Peril," is a home screen bread-and-ciruses event concocted by unscrupulous tv execs (Marie-France Pisier and Bruno Cremer). It offers $1,000,000 to a desperate candidate — recruited from the swelling ranks of the unemployed — who can stay alive as five amateur killers, each angling for a $100,000 bounty, hunt him down in the city. The macabre fun is monitored live from a dirigible and filmed by a battery of motorized cameramen, while the show's host emcées from the studios, where the sponsors outlandishly peddle their wares to millions of rapt viewers.

Gerard Lanvin is the hero of the piece, a young, sullen protagonist of drive and daring. He is resourceful enough to get rid of his pursuers and even expose the trumped-up mechanics of the game, but not cunning enough to outwit the producers, who have him finally carted off the air to an insane asylum, thus protecting their jackpot and program.

Boisset is a clever commercial filmmaker, brought up on classic American action films at the Cinematheque, who has made a name for himself treating serious political and social topics in glossy, popular modes.

But here he largely botches both the medium and the message. One would not mind the obvious, elephantine ironies of the script's anti-media broadsides, if the pure suspense elements were handled with more ingenuity and directorial flair. Though the premise is catchy and the pacing brisk, there are few dramatic moments that have the viewer leaning forward expectantly in his seat.

Despite the prestigious billing, the principal roles are undistinguished, and many of the supporting players are downright awful.

Most of the exteriors were shot on location in Belgrade, which is supposed to represent the nondescript cosmopolitan city of the near future. Pierre William Glenn, who extracted the brooding menace of Glasgow for Tavernier's "Deathwatch," has lensed with his usual competence, but with less dramatic inspiration. —*Len.*

Xtro
(BRITISH-COLOR)

A New Line Cinema release of an Amalgamated Film Enterprises Ltd. production. Executive producer, Robert Shaye. Produced by Mark Forstater; associate producer, James M. Crawford. Directed by Harry Bromley Davenport. Features entire cast. Screenplay, Robert Smith, Iain Cussie, based upon original script by Michel Parry, Davenport; additional dialog, Jo Ann Kaplan; camera (Kay color), John Metcalfe; editor, Nick Gaster; music, Davenport with synthesizer effects by Shelton Leigh Palmer; assistant director, Jake Wright; production manager, Vivien Pottersman; art direction, Andrew Mollo; sound, John Midgley; special makeup effects, Robin Grantham, John Webber; creature effects, Francis Coates; special effects, Tom Harris; camera operator/add'l photography, John Simmons. Reviewed at RKO Century National 2 theatre, N.Y., Jan. 28, 1983. (MPAA Rating: R). Running time: **80 MINS.**

Sam Phillips	Philip Sayer
Rachel Phillips	Bernice Stegers
Joe Daniels	Danny Brainin
Tony Phillips	Simon Nash
Analise	Maryam D'Abo
Michael	David Cardy
Miss Goodman	Anna Wing
Clown	Peter Mahdell

"Xtro" (known in pre-production under the more descriptive but less commercial title "Judas Goat") is an imitative, chintzy British monster picture. Well-timed for release and obviously exploitable for horror film audiences, film is too silly and underdeveloped in story values to expand beyond the diehard fans.

Despite ad copy and title reminiscent of "E.T.," project actually predates public awareness of that Steven Spielberg classic, instead choosing to copy his earlier "Close Encounters Of The Third Kind" and its never-filmed but widely publicized sequel "Night Skies."

Absurd plot has Britisher Sam Phillips (Philip Sayer, with a saturnine visage) snatched by aliens while playing with his son Tony (Simon Nash), the event represented poorly by a sudden eclipse, windstorm and bright light/lens flare in the sky.

Three years later, he is deposited back on Earth in the altered form of what resembles a humanoid grasshopper (and looks very fake and rubbery) that attacks a pretty blonde woman and infects her with makeup effects copying that influential hit "Alien." Next day she gives birth to a full grown Sam Phillips, in perhaps the film's only inventive moment for horror film scholars to analyze.

Back in action, practically the first thing Phillips does is to phone home, setting in motion an undeveloped and asinine subplot of "deserted" wife Rachel (Bernice Stegers) saddled with both hubby and live-in lover Joe (Danny Brainin) in the house. Besides this triangle, film also explores ever-popular father/son relationships, except that early on in a quite irritating scene, Phillips bites his son on the shoulder, infecting him with alien spores.

Horror fans will recognize an aping of David Cronenberg's famed "They Came From Within" picture, as son Tony proceeds to bite the family's foxy au pair girl Analise (Maryam D'Abo) on the tummy, and she becomes encased in a large cocoon. Pointlessly ripping off another hit, "Time Bandits," "Xtro" segues into the odd subplot of Tony using supernatural mental powers to bring his G.I. Joe and clown dolls to full-scale life, with the dwarf clown left at film's finish tending Analise's larvae-like offspring. Pic has no ending, just Tony in monster makeup exiting in a cheap spaceship as mom looks on.

Filmmaker Harry B. Davenport builds little suspense, and no thrills in a film devoid of stuntwork or action scenes. It's just another "check out that makeup" exercise, consisting of brief scenes and poor continuity. Acting is flat, with Stegers (fine as femme lead in Fellini's "City Of Women") inexpressive and unattractively styled. It took five writers to devise the weak story and functional "Don't go in there!" dialog, while Bromley takes the rap himself for the boring electronic keyboards musical score.

Absence of credible spaceship effects and no ending spell poor word-of-mouth for this opus. —*Lor.*

Manila Fest

Onimasa
(JAPANESE-COLOR)

Manila, Jan. 27.

A Toei Company release of a Shigeiu Okada production. Directed by Hideo Gosha. Script by Koje Takata and Gosha, based on Tomiko Miyao's novel. Camera (Fujicolor), Fujio Morita; music, Mitsukai Karno; editor, Isamu Ichida; production design, Yoshindon Nishioka. Reviewed in the competition section of the 1983 Manila Film Festival, Manila Film Center, Jan. 27, 1983. Running time: **146 MINS.**

Onimasa	Tatsuya Nakadai
Matsue	Masako Natsume
Uta	Shima Iwashita
The Big Boss	Tetsuro Tamba
Hanako	Kaori Tagasugi
Hanako's Mother	Akiko Kana
Second Mistress	Emi Shindo
Third Mistress	Akika Nakamura
Opponent's Mistress	Mari Natsuki

For sheer cinematic splendor in drama, cinematography, production design and acting, Hideo Gosha's "Onimasa" will be hard to beat as a contender for this year's Golden Eagle best picture award. Whether the jury will find film's subject matter sufficiently uplifting (a quality much looked for at this event) is another thing. (Film is Japan's official submission for 1982 foreign language Academy Award consideration. —Ed).

Working from a script based on a highly praised novel, Gosha has created a work of purest cinema. Each frame has composition, flash and style without in any way interfering with the story's dramatic flow. Actually, the pictures form a truly natural part of the narrative's endless energy.

Although much human abuse is shown in "Onimasa," it does end on an uplifting note, scoring a triumph of a kind for the obdurate spirit, particularly the female one. The title figure, though, is a man, a handsome Mafia chieftain in the town of Shikoku in the years between 1921 and 1941. His energy in all matters borders on madness. He has a wife, two mistresses, but no children, and so he adopts Matsue, a girl nearing her teens. Matsue notes the displays of power, political as well as sexual, personified in Onimasa, with some trembling. But, early on, she forms an attachment to her new father, which is reciprocated. This feeling is not diminished when Onimasa later on succeeds in fathering a daughter of his own with one of the mistresses.

Scenes of life in the Onimasa house with all its male brutality being shrewdly curbed by various female devices and designs, interchange with scenes of gang warfare. The latter has political aspects and later on, Matsue goes away with Tanabe, a young socialist. She does not give up her attachment to Onimasa, however, nor to her kid sister, Hanako. And as Onimasa's wife is dying with typhoid, Matsu insists on sharing her room until she dies.

Since all characters are drawn with multi-layered characteristics, some good, some very bad, all this comes out less sentimental than a brief resume might indicate. Audiences, as a matter of fact, are kept in constant suspense about what direction the story might take. But whatever happens, the outcome appears logical enough.

Tatooed bodies in sexual action figure strongly in a film that nevertheless has nine of the "Empire Of Passion" single-mindedness about it. Violence of several kinds explodes as the natural results of carefully built-up suspense. At one point, Onimasa tries to rape Matsue. She fights him off successfully by trying to kill herself, not him, with a piece of broken glass. The way this sequence runs makes it quite reasonable that Onimasa and his adopted daughter love each other even more afterwards.

The film is full of such surprises, so it does not appear too fanciful, either, the Matsue survives to the end of the picture as the only member of the family who can walk away — with a swirl of her parasol — into a new sunrise.

Masako Natsume is the actress who adds sweetness and light to the film in the Matsue role. While creditable performances are given also by Shima Iwashita as Onimasa's wife, it is Tatsuya Nakadai in the title role who will be remembered the longest. His bursts of softness and sad resignation come as truly human touches amidst his parading of macho attitudes. Nakadai, used by Akira Kurosawa in "Kagemusha, The Shadow Warrior," seems destined to become as internationally known and respected as Toshiro Mifune.
— *Kell.*

Byala Magia
(White Magic)
(BULGARIAN-COLOR)

Manila, Jan. 31.

A Bulgariafilm production and release. Story and script, Konstantin Pavlov. Directed by Ivan Andonov. Camera (color), Victor Chichov; production design, Peter Goranov; music, Georgi Genkov. Reviewed at the Manila Film Center, Manila Intl. Film Festival (in competition), Jan. 31, 1983. Running time: **96 MINS.**

Cast: Plamena Getova, Peter Slabakov, Georgi Kaloyanchev, Kounka Baeva, Ilka Zafirova, Velvo Kunev, Ivan Grigorov.

Konstantin Pavlov writes film scripts like descriptive poems with very little dialog. Ivan Andonov as director turns Pavlov's "White Magic" script into a feature film with perfect empathy. Their joint work has some of the "madness" of Latin American fantastic reality literature, but is maybe more closely linked to painter Marc Chagall's famous scenes of Slavic village life with their topsy-turvy imagery and cleverly naive love of all God's — and the Devil's — creations.

It will be understood from this that "White Magic" is not any ordinary feature film, but it is in no way murky or too remote for appeal to ordinary audiences. Careful handling could bring "White Magic" beyond the festival circuit and into specialized situations almost anywhere.

With sly humor, poetic distance and slices of robust realism, Pavlov and Andonov serve up episodes and characters during a market day in a mountain village early in this century. A little boy gets drunk on wine and goes through the village shouting "death to the tyrant." A young widow is raped and kills her sated rapist with a pitchfork. Later in the day her marriage to somebody is celebrated while the market fair's bearded lady "shaves" for the night. A barber with pretentions to be a surgeon uses — in vain — a gramophone to attract a young woman. Indirectly, one is presented with the forces of good and evil fighting towards some commonsensical compromise.

A lot of other things happen. Some characters do inexplicable things, but that is all right, too. The muted cinematography, the quietly convincing playing by all actors, the general mood all serve to make "White Magic" as entertaining as any fairy-tale. Lots of philosophic insights can be read into it and they are probably there, but the play remains the thing. —*Kell.*

Moral
(FILIPINO-COLOR)

Manila, Jan. 29.

A Jesse Ejercity production. Directed by Marilou Diaz Abaya. Screenplay, Ricardo Lee; camera (color), Manolo Abaya; art direction, Fiel Zabat; editing, Abaya; music, George Canseco; sound, Rollie Ruta. Reviewed at the Manila Film Festival (in competition). Jan. 29, 1983. Running time: 135 MINS.
Loreta . . . . Lorna Tolentino
Maritess . . . . Anna Marin
Sylvia . . . . Gina Alajar
Kathy . . . . Sandy Andolong

One of the entries to the competition section of MIFF, "Moral" had won an earlier award as second best picture of the local Metro Manila Film Fest last December. The story of four young campus girls trying to live it up as the new breed of liberated females is an interesting concoction of different unconventional lifestyles.

Fancy-free Loreta is a junkie who sleeps with half the male population of the school although she is quite in love with a classmate who is actively involved in socialistic propaganda, but unfortunately married. Maritess marries into a big family which believes that a wife's role in this world is to beget children and lives with her in-laws and a large brood of nephews and nieces.

Sylvia is a singer, but a bad one, who had to go to bed with a recording company sales agent so she could make it to the top. And Kathy, the most sober of the quartet, has her own marital problem. She has separated from her husband who is living with a homosexual.

In the end, however, compassion develops and brings the three into a harmonious though strange relationship. There is a tender scene in which Kathy, her husband and the boyfriend dance in tandem while mood music plays in the background. The subplots are neatly trussed at the end and everything ends with a happy note.

"Moral" got praise from local critics and was endorsed by an association of top women writers in the country. It is, however, cut out for the local audience and will stand a lot of editing and rehashing if it is to be exhibited outside domestic domain. —*Gron.*

Oro, Plata, Mata
(Gold, Silver, Bad Luck)
(FILIPINO-COLOR)

Manila, Jan. 29.

An Experimental Cinema of The Philippines production and release. Original story and screenplay, Jose Xavier Reyes. Directed by Peque Callaga. Camera (Color) Rody Lacapp; editor, Jesus Navarro; music, Jose Gentica; executive producer, Charo S. Concio; production design, Don Escudero, Rodell Cruz; costume design, Salvador Bernal. Reviewed as an official competition entry in the Manila International Film Festival, Jan. 29, '83 at Manila Film Center's main theatre. Running time, 195 MINS.
Trining . . . . Cherie Gil
Miguel . . . . Joel Torre
Maggi . . . . Sandy Andolong
Nena . . . . Liza Lorena
Viring . . . . Lorli Villanueva
Hermes . . . . Ronnie Lazaro
Melchor . . . . Abbo De La Cruz
Don Claudio . . . . Manny Ojeda
Jo Russell . . . . Maya Valdes
Inday Lorenzo . . . . Fides Cuyugan Asensio

"Oro, Plata, Mata" means steps one, two and three on a staircase, and you keep counting the same three till you have reached the top. Then you must take an invisible step if you have ended up on "Mata," which means death or bad luck. Most Filipinos do not even know the expression. It belonged to the old Spanish aristocracy, a family of which here is followed during its four years of first mountain, then jungle exile during the Japanese occupation.

Film, which is too long and burdened with many other faults as well, is an ambitious project. It may benefit from considerable shortening, but will more likely reach some foreign sales in the South East Asia area divided up into a miniseries for tv. It has handsome production values, some teenage love scenes and nudity and many sudden spurts of carnage, blood and gore in between its arid stretches of mood establishing and infinite slowness in character presentation and development.

Of the wealthy Ojeda family, the grandfather, the women and two young boys plus all the servants go to their consecutive hideouts, first a mountain estate, then a jungle cottage, when all the grown men have taken up arms elsewhere. It takes close to two hours to establish that the youngsters are fumbling at love, while one of the mothers is a snob and greedy about her wealth as well. One woman has style, another has guts, one of the teenage girls will one day turn into a snob, too, while the other will prove to have guts and eventually marry the shy astronomy-happy boy. The latter thinks for a long time that he is a coward, but in a long sequence that would make Sam Peckinpah feel queasy he proves his manhood by killing off not only a servant who was a thief and a deserter but also about 50 jungle bandits.

Unfortunately, both script person and continuity person on the film must have been sleeping badly on their respective jobs. Events are forever muddled. All characters constantly sport freshly laundered suits and dresses. And in most true action scenes, they are filmed with their faces hidden in darkness. Still, when a few of the characters finally move out of their cardboard shadows, we see some fine acting, and in the strictly atmospheric scenes (aristocracy hard at work at doing nothing) film is pretty (and often pretty funny) to look at. —*Kell.*

Saarbruecken Festival

Das Glueck Beim Haendewaschen
(The Pleasure of Washing One's Hands)
(WEST GERMAN-AUSTRIAN-SWISS-ITALIAN-B&W)

Saarbruecken, Feb. 1.

A Tura Film Production, Munich, in coproduction with Zweites Deutsches Fernsehen (ZDF), Mainz, ORF (Austrian Television), SRG (Swiss Television), and RAI (Italian Television). German producer, Michael Wiedemann; ZDF-TV producer, Hans Kutnewsky. Directed by Werner Masten. Screenplay, Joseph Zoderer, Masten, based on Zoderer's novel with the same title; camera (b&w), Klaus Eichhammer. Reviewed at Saarbruecken Film Fest (Max Ophuls Prize), Jan. 20, '83. Running time: 125 MINS.
Cast: Mario Baumgartner (Andreas Hittaler), Peter Gamer, Martin Abram, Brigitte Karner, Guido von Salis.

The fact that Werner Masten's "The Pleasure of Washing One's Hands" has lensed in Austria (mostly in Bregenz) but set in Switzerland (much of the spoken text is Swiss German), makes the debut feature by a graduate of the Munich Film Academy with an Italian passport all the more intriguing. Indeed, it was one of the genuine surprises at Saarbruecken, (even though pic had already been aired on Second Television in "Das kleine Fernsehspiel" series).

Drawing on a novel with the same title by Joseph Zoderer, the story is autobiographical, dealing with a German-speaking region in South Tirol, just over the Austrian border in northern Italy. Before the First World War, this was a part of Austria-Hungary — after the war, it was ceded to Italy. As the Second World War broke out, the population largely tended to Germany, choosing the Third Reich over Austria. But since Hitler wished to maintain good relations with his ally Mussolini, the question of South Tirol was shoved under the table for the time being. Today, the wounds are still open.

Andreas Hittaler, the protagonist, comes from a poor peasant family in this disputed section belonging to the Italian fascists in 1941, when he enters school. His father

(who like his German-speaking neighbors refused to learn Italian) feels that union with Germany is the only chance, and we next find the family in Graz at the end of the war under the control of British occupation forces.

The lad's native dialect here sets him apart from other boys in town, and the family fortune is now worse than ever. Thus, when a kindly religious order offers to give the lad a strict Catholic upbringing in a not-too-distant Swiss-German cloister, the family accepts.

Andreas, again an outsider with an Austrian accent, must now learn to speak Swiss German in the classroom. And when he returns home on one occasion for a visit with his new Italian passport, he can't say a word in Italian at the border. In short, he has lived in four different worlds before even finishing his primary school education; he finds himself still in search of a "homeland" in language.

Andreas has meanwhile picked up other bits of knowledge along the way. He makes the acquaintance of a "dance-partner" in the officers' club in Graz, steals bread for himself and his friends in times of postwar starvation (befriending a German soldier in hiding in the process), and is so pleased to be able to wash his hands with soap in the Swiss Catholic seminary that he announces this newly found happiness to schoolmates at the very moment when silence is normally required.

The boy's days in the school are happy and profitable ones for the most part: he's intelligent and learns quickly. But upon returning home for a visit, he is introduced to the literary merits of an important Swiss author through a book that is forbidden in the cloister-school. The school's attempt to block this new avenue to learning by taking away the book leads to protest and, finally, his decision to leave the school. On the outside, now a young man of 15, Andreas goes to work in a nearby slaughterhouse, where he ultimately begins to discover his own identity, and the meaning of language and fatherland to boot.

Strikingly lensed in black-and-white against wintery landscapes, "The Pleasure of Washing One's Hands" makes for a moving experience from start to finish. Afterwards, one tends to agree with filmmaker Werner Masten that this Saarbruecken entry is best described as "an authentic Suedtirol film production." —*Holl.*

Wilde Clique
(Wild Bunch)
(WEST GERMAN-COLOR-16m)

Saarbruecken, Feb. 1.

A Hannelore Conradsen Film Production, Berlin. Features entire cast. Directed by Dieter Koester. Screenplay, Hannelore Conradsen and Dieter Koester;

camera (color), Koester; music, Extrabreit, Marianne Rosenberg. Reviewed at Saarbruecken Film Fest (Max Ophuls Prize '83), Jan. 19, '83. Running time: 85 MINS.

Cast: Annette Berndt (Madine), Marni Held (Vivienne), Dorothea Moritz (Waltrand), Martin Kukula (Pellworm), Oliver Wilckens (Beule), Rainer Dellmuth ("42").

Hannelore Conradsen and Dieter Koester's "Wild Bunch" ("Wild Clique" is the direct translation) scores as a fine low budget pic on the West Berlin scene. Indeed, it should put a lot of the favored "subsidy films" to shame, for Conradsen-Koester made this delightful comedy entirely on their own, together with friends, without a single pfennig of state aid.

The husband-wife team shared scripter-helmer-lenser duties, while the thesps (mostly nonprofessional) are Berliners in the fullest sense of the term. Result: a realism that recalls the authenticity of Robert Siodmak and Billy Wilder's "People On Sunday" (1929).

"Wilde Clique" might just as well be called "People on a Weekend." The story is pretty much the same as "People On Sunday," save that the action extends a day longer. The protagonists are two young couples, both about to leave their youth behind for the uncertain world of adulthood, who meet by chance (one couple via a magazine contact ad) to experience the varied urban attractions of West Berlin as they are today. It's this light touch, the coming-and-going, that makes it a hit.

The script is constructed around a bit of make believe. Neither the ad contact couple, Vivienne and Pellworm, nor the tag alongs, Madine and Beule, let the others know who they really are or what they do for a living during the working days (these surprises are saved for the ending). It's a question here only of a bit of adventure, a touch of romance, a slice of life for what it is. But therein lies the pic's depth. Ordinary people do have fantasies and dreams, a thirst for personal fulfillment, and a certain pleasure in playing roles that don't necessarily fit but allow for momentary escape and amusement.

Helmer Dieter Koester has made a number of highly professional tv productions for youth aired on Sender Freies Berlin (SFB): "Pretty Dull Vacation" (1980), "Drippel Droppel" (1981), "Berlin Wall Gang" (1981), and one critically acclaimed tv documentary on a camping-site in northern Germany on the North Sea coast, "A Bit of Freedom" (1982). "Wild Bunch" is his first feature, made in collaboration with his wife, Hannelore Conradsen. He's a coming talent in the socalled "Berlin Film School" — an unusual talent at that, for he has an eye for the visual narrative, a handful for comedy and comic situations, and a refined feel for the human condition as it's found in everyday life. He (and his wife, as scripter) are born storytellers.

Thesp performances in "Wild Bunch" are casual and disarmingly at ease before the camera. The six principals (another couple on the edge of the thin plot line) carry each of the scenes as constructed (the film is a collection of "episodes") while the city offers a charm of its own that hints the pic might just as well be titled "Berliners" or "What Happens When Weekly Boredom Gives Way to the Unknown Delights of a Weekend Lark!" This is one of those pics that points a new direction in the Berlin film scene: a low-budget production free of tv cliches and uninspired stereotyped acting. Pic could be effectively programmed abroad. —Holl.

The Heartbreakers
(WEST GERMAN-COLOR)

Saarbruecken, Feb. 1.

A Tura-Film Production, Munich, in coproduction with Project Film in Filmverlag der Autoren, Munich, and Westdeutscher Rundfunk (WDR), Cologne. Produced by Michael Wiedemann; tv-producer, Alexander Wesemann. Features entire cast. Directed by Peter F. Bringmann. Screenplay, Matthias Seelig; camera (color), Helge Weindler; sets, Toni Luedi; music, Lothar Meid; editor, Annette Dorn; assistant director, Werner Masten; production manager, Herbert Rimbach. In Dolby stereo. Reviewed at Saarbruecken Film Fest (Max Ophuls Prize), Jan. 21, '83. Running time: 110 MINS.

Freytag .... Sasha Disselkamp
Lisa .... Mary Ketikidou
Schmittchen .... Uwe Enkelmann
Horn .... Mark Eichenseher
Guido .... Harmut Isselhorst
Pico .... Michael Klein
Sieglinde .... Ester Christinat
Lisa's Father .... Rolf Zacher

Far and away the most professional film to unspool at Saarbruecken in the Max Ophuls Competition, and the best German pic to appear on the scene in the new season, Peter F. Bringmann's "The Heartbreakers" (ditto for German title) should make its mark on the local scene despite the absence of name thesps. Further, given an international festival push, both the film and the director should now command a position of respect and promise in the vanguard known as "New Generation" German directors — in addition to scripter Matthias Seelig and producer Michael Wiedemann of Tura-Film in Munich.

The story is as old as they come in the musical film genre. A pop band from a remote industrial town is trying to make a breakthrough in the 1960s just like the Beatles and other rock bands have done before them. These are mostly kids just about to age into their knowing teens, but each has a distant personality and all have the drive to make it on their own, cost what it may. Moreover, the script is so tightly penned that gags, humor, and laughs augment and support the musical numbers early in the game.

It's Recklinghausen in 1966, a time of innumerable rock groups and beat-bands playing the circuit those days; it was The Rolling Stones — and if they could make it, why not The Heartbreakers? In fact, it's after being picked up by the police during a wild time at a Stones concert that the group gradually begins to form during the precinct interrogation.

The next step is to get some musical instruments with loudspeaker vibes, and after that the all male group has to decide on letting a femme thrush, Lisa, into the act (doing mostly imitation hits, to begin with). The loudmouth of the group, Freytag, wants to oust Lisa at the outset, and doesn't perceive any quality in her singing voice even after he falls in love with her. Meanwhile, Lisa has a serious problem at home with a drunken father and a brother in a teenage gang.

Paralleling this dramatic conflict is another along the same lines: Schmittchen likes to romance the girls on and off the job, but he can't make any headway with an attractive blond despite trying every trick in the book. Then there's Horn, whose chubby fingers exercise an accomplished touch on every musical instrument in sight (even the organ at a high mass); Guido, the deadpan bass-guitarist; and Pico the band's pintsized, cigaret-puffing manager. The gags are neatly constructed on visual motifs and verbal puns, and there are subtle twists in the story line — but the charm lies entirely in the hands of the six teenage thesps and this evocation of the 1960s as lived and experienced by the entire production unit.

Technical credits are top quality. This, too, is the result of a longstanding collaboration among helmer Bringmann, scripter Seelig, producer Wiedemann, and lenser Weindler going back to the mid-1970s. The Seelig-Bringmann tandem began with the first "Theo" film, "Invitation to Dance" (1976), and matured to perfection with the making of "Paul Is Back" (1977); "Theo against the Rest of the World" (1979), and now "The Heartbreakers" (1982). —Holl.

Aufdermauer
(WEST GERMAN-B&W)

Saarbruecken, Feb. 1.

A Munich Film & Television Academy Production, in coproduction with Second German Television (ZDF), Mainz; Eckhart Stein, tv-producer. Features entire cast. Written and directed by Lutz Konermann. Camera (b&w), Toni Sulzbeck; editing, Konermann. Reviewed at Saarbruecken Film Fest (Max Ophuls Prize), Jan. 19, '83. running time: 100 MINS.

Cast: Klaus Abramowsky (Albert Aufdermauer), Klaus Gruenberg, Susann B. Winter, Lutz Konermann, Barbara Bertram, Thiemo Bauch.

Lutz Konermann's "Aufdermauer" refers in the title to a prison case; Albert Aufdermauer, who spent 30 years behind bars for manslaughter and experiences a week of freedom on his own by breaking parole on his first one-day pass. It's a very fine diploma film at the Munich Film Academy that flowered into a fortunate coproduction in 35m with Second German TV due to the interest taken in the project by tv producer Eckhart Stein of "Das kleine Fernsehspiel." Pic turned out to be a sleeper at the Max Ophuls competition in Saarbruecken.

Lensed in black and white, this frank and probing portrait of a lifer draws heavily upon an actual happening two years ago, an unusual occurrence that attracted the attention of the press and was reported upon in "Stern" (the German-style "Life" magazine). Konermann, in turn, did his own research into the details of the case, and came up with a human-interest portrait of a man who sees the world anew with inquisitive, questioning eyes in and around the city of Bielefeld in the Westphalian section of Northrhine-Westphalia. One might say this is docu-ficton in the best sense of the term.

Albert Aufdermauer, a sensitive and intelligent man, apparently made one fatal mistake in life — he took part in a robbery, injured his victim who later died of the injuries, and was convicted of manslaughter. The case normally calls for eventual parole, but other circumstances led to the longer duration of the sentence. It's this factor that makes the story interesting, for the prisoner is badly treated by fellow inmates behind bars — thus winning the sympathy of the viewing public. On the other hand, the inquiring reporter (symbolic of the mass media) takes an interest in the case more or less to further his own career. This leads to a release of the prisoner for a one-day outing in the hands of the reporter. He thereupon runs away.

Now begins the drama, one of minute observation both of the outsider on the loose and the people he meets. Aufdermauer sleeps in haymows, in abandoned factories, wherever he can. He tramps along country roads, his elation at experiencing freedom underscored by pop hits of bygone days on the soundtrack. He observes a group of young people on motorcycles, for he was at this age when he was arrested and convicted of a crime he has since long regretted. A young girl, in particular, catches his attention. With a pocketful of change given to him for work in prison, he manages to hold out for a week's time while on the run in the immediate neighborhood.

Meanwhile, the reporter is so messed up that he goes on a drunken spree, nearly loses his job, and comes slowly around to recognizing the error of his ways in the Aufdermauer case. But when the runaway runs out of money and is ready to return peacefully to prison, he phones the reporter to request his help and apologize at the same time for the inconvenience he has caused. They arrange a meeting to turn the lifer in at a nearby prison; but because it's after working hours, he is picked up by the police as an escaped fugitive instead. Thus the chance of ever returning to society is possibly denied forever.

A remarkable diploma film, "Aufdermauer" well deserves a fest slot and marks Lutz Konermann (23 years old) as a director to watch in the future. —Holl.

Ziemlich Weit Weg
(Quite Far Away)
(WEST GERMAN-COLOR-16m)

Saarbruecken, Feb. 1.
A Dietrich Schubert Film Production, Cologne. Written and directed by Dietrich Schubert. Camera (color), Henning Zick; music, Bernhard Schmitz; assistant director, Katharina Schubert. Reviewed at Saarbruecken Film Fest (Max Ophuls Prize), Jan. 20, '83. Running time: 90 MINS.
Cast: Burkhart Klaussner, Christine Lemm, Wolfgang Krassnitzer, Christine Kaufman, Barbara Grupe.

Following a long string of successful documentary films, Dietrich Schubert has made his first feature film, "Quite Far," with some noticeable docu touches. Considering that this 16m pic was made with modest coin funding from the Northrhine-Westphalian Film Fund, it does the trick in covering all the bases intended — but a concrete story is missing to carry the whole over the patchy parts.

Similar in theme to Alain Tanner's "Jonas, Who Will Be 25 in the Year 2000" and John Sayles's "Return of the Secaucus Seven," this is the story of a group of aging revolutionaries from the student reform and peace movement days who gather one day to look at old newsreels on those times, then go their separate ways without much to say to each other about how they realized the dreams proposed back in 1968.

Three of the group — a woman with a child, her husband, and a friend — live in an abandoned railway station not far from Cologne, but "quite far away" so far as contact with the real world is concerned. These outsiders — the men are, natch, in the creative professions of filmmaker and graphic artist — also maintained an apartment in the city, at least for a while.

Pic's main figure is the filmmaker, whose latest project, a docu on an unknown worker-writer, goes down the drain upon the subject's unexpected death. Nevertheless, a chat with an acquaintance of the deceased miner makes for one of the best scenes in the film: the writer's verses are spoken and sung in the manner of a naively composed ballad, and deal with an old fighter facing a firing-squad and bidding farewell to his comrades (it's a convincing parallel to the protagonist's own lost cause). The fire of intellectual protest has obviously gone out.

Then comes a key scene in which the filmmaker, by chance, meets a laboratory scientist working at a gigantic radio-telescope lab, and they discuss infinity and the beginning of the universe — all of which adds up to the world and life itself as a mass of insoluble riddles. The filmmaker now decides to become a permanent dropout: he will never leave the railway-station homestead again. His new theme is a study of people in the area, whatever that means, while making a complete break with his past and his current friends.

Despite a ripe theme that has yet to be treated sufficiently well in West Germany, there's not much to cheer about in the long run. The film, unfortunately, never cuts itself off from its documentary roots. —Holl.

...Schwierig Sich Zu Verloben
(...Difficult To Become Engaged)
(EAST GERMAN-COLOR)

Saarbruecken, Feb. 1.
A DEFA Film Production, "Roter Kreis" Group, East Berlin; world rights, DEFA Aussenhandel, East Berlin. Features entire cast. Written and directed by Karl-Heinz Heymann. Camera (color), Guenter Haubold; music, Reinhard Lakonny. Reviewed at Saarbruecken Film Fest (Max Ophuls Prize), Jan. 19, '83. Running time: 85 MINS.
Cast: Ulrike Krumbiegel (Brigitte), Werner Tritzschler (Wolfgang), Monika Lennartz, Petra Hinze, Gerd Steiger.

A debut pic by newcomer Karl-Heinz Heymann, "May I Say Petruschka to You?" (1980), on a ballet-dance theme, introduced a writer-director talent who came up through the ranks in the German Democratic Republic. Upon graduating from the East German Academy for Film and Television in 1972, Heyman worked first as a cameraman and assistant director, and then for television before receiving his initial directorial assignment; he was also a trained mechanic on steel-construction before entering the film school. His "...Difficult to Become Engaged," preem-ing at the Saarbruecken fest, was the single entry from East Germany and the opening night.

This is a film for and about youth and specifically about the first bitter fruits of romance in life. It's also about the working class, offering a fair share of revealing moments on construction work as such and comeraderie among members of a "batallion" on the job at an outdoors site. But it's mostly about the problems young people (who might be anywhere) have making up their minds on love, marriage, and the rest.

Wolfgang and Brigitte live in a small town. He's on his way to becoming a skilled worker in a factory or in construction, but dreams of finding a job that will allow him to travel abroad ("perhaps building a bridge in Ethiopia"). She's employed in a furniture-sales position, but does her job well enough to get a promotion to continue studying for a more qualified job. They meet at a youth gathering and take a liking for each other, after which he tries to make an impression on her parents, and they find ways to have an affair on the side. Meeting at his place whenever it's convenient, she becomes pregnant, and develops qualms about revealing her mistake in not using the pill.

The relationship goes on the rocks for a time: both have affairs with others, which doesn't really solve anything — they realize that they're pretty much meant for each other. Meanwhile, Wolfgang has found his way to an outdoor construction site through a friendly contact, but this doesn't lead to the desired chance for an overseas assignment. He eventually opts to voluntarily serve with the military. As for Brigitte, should she accept the offer to continue her training, it will mean leaving town and thereby losing Wolfgang for a time.

The situation leads to an abortion, separation, reunion, and finally to a willingness to look towards the future and sort their problems out, remarkably without outside advice from parents, an agency, or a friendly Dutch Uncle. Further, the future doesn't seem very rosy — save for the security of having a job — and the types the young couple meet are not necessarily on the positive side, nor are they very exemplary. Life is shown to be a grab-bag in cut-and-dried realistic terms: what's missing is a strong plausible ending leaving everything open-ended and questioning. —Holl.

Betrayal
(BRITISH-COLOR)

Kingsley and Irons names will boost interest in decent Pinter adaptation. Viable for art circuit.

Hollywood, Jan. 13.
A 20th Century-Fox International Classics release of a Horizon film. Produced by Sam Spiegel. Directed by David Jones. Features entire cast. Screenplay, Harold Pinter, based on his play; camera (uncredited color), Mike Fash; editor, John Bloom; music, Dominic Muldowney; production design, Eileen Diss; costume design, Jane Robinson; Patricia Hodge's costumes, Jean Muir; sound, Brian Simmons; associate producer, Eric Rattray; assistant director, Ted Morley. Reviewed at the 20th Century-Fox Studios, West L.A., Jan. 13, 1983. (MPAA Rating: R.) Running time: 95 MINS.
Jerry ....Jeremy Irons
Robert ....Ben Kingsley
Emma ....Patricia Hodge

As it was onstage, "Betrayal" is an absorbing, quietly amusing chamber drama for those attuned to Harold Pinter's way with words. Capably made by British hands under the auspices of Sam Spiegel, in a production unusually modest for him, film's release will benefit from the rising stars of male leads Jeremy Irons and, particularly, Ben Kingsley, whose deft performance proves his versatility on the heels of his "Gandhi" triumph. Nevertheless, intellectual bent on the material necessarily limits pic to more art-oriented venues, where it should generate decent biz.

In laying out his study of a rather conventional menage-a-trois among two male best friends and the wife of one of them, Pinter's gambit was to present it in reverse chronological order. Tale thus starts in the present and gradually steps backwards over the course of nine years. Play divided nine scenes over two acts, and film announces each time change with titles reading "Two years earlier," etc.

Opening section, which lasts nearly a half-hour, has literary agent Irons and Patricia Hodge meeting in a quiet London pub two years after their affair has ended. At first, the clipped, pause-laden delivery of the dialog seems almost unreally pronounced, but before long the fine edge of comic stylization becomes apparent. Conversations throughout largely consist of domestic and professional banalities, but Pinter here is in close to top form in transforming seeming small talk into incisive commentaries on the foibles of the head and heart.

First time jump delivers characters back two years to the fizzling of the romance. Action a year before that is set in Venice, Italy, where Hodge reveals the existence of the affair to her husband, Kingsley, a diffident but extremely clever book publisher. Dramatic and thespian highlight comes immediately thereafter, during a London luncheon between Irons and Kingsley, when latter tries to drown in drink the nervousness he feels in confronting his friend for the first time armed with the knowledge of what's been pulled off behind his back.

Remaining scenes are relatively short, as they sketch in the lovers taking a flat for their daytime sessions and, climactically, beginning their affair during a party.

Despite some reservations that the flip-flopped narrative smacked too much of a stunt or a purely intellectual exercise, "Betrayal" was one of Pinter's more commercially successful plays, and is in no way confusing.

As usual with the playwright, effectiveness of the pic depends to a great extent on the precision and expressiveness of the players in fleshing out the subtext beneath the spare surface of the dialog. On this score, Kingsley comes across best, as the film only springs fully to life when he's onscreen. His is an immaculate performance, brimming with subtle shadings, suspicions and accusations unspoken but hinted at in his eyes and vocal inflections.

Having performed Pinter in the theatre, Irons also seems very much at home with the required style and believably etches an essentially good and civilized man who is nevertheless capable of betraying his best friend on a long-term basis.

As the fulcrum of the tale, Hodge knows her way around dialog but pales somewhat in the presence of the two men and lacks the allure to them, as well as to the audience, that the character should possess. Blythe Danner was incandescent in this role on Broadway and Hodge, unfortunately, suffers by comparison.

In his film debut, theatre and television director David Jones moves the talk along at a good clip and has been responsive to most of Pinter's nuances, although overall result is somewhat less effective than what is arguably the best Pinter play on film, Peter Hall's version of "The Homecoming." For his part, the playwright has naturally remained extremely faithful to his own work, but has also managed to open it up nicely to include numerous varied locations. Behind-the-scenes contributions are all solid.

For the record, Michael Gambon, Penelope Wilton and Daniel Massey played the leading roles when play was first staged in London in 1978, while Raul Julia, Danner and Roy Scheider starred in the 1980 Broadway production.
— Cart.

The Courtesans Of Bombay
(BRITISH-COLOR-16m)

London, Feb. 1.

A Merchant Ivory Production for Channel Four Television. Produced, directed and written by Ismail Merchant, James Ivory, Ruth Prawer Jhabvala. Camera (color), Vushny Mathar; editor, Amit Bose. Reviewed at the National Film Theatre, London, Jan. 31, 1983. Running time: 73 MINS.
Features Saeed Jaffrey, Sohra Segal, Kareem Samar and the people of Pavan Pool.

This semi-documentary pic is an intimate look at an Indian community of singing and dancing girls fallen on hard times. Approach to the subject is characteristic of much work by this creative trio, particularly their Manhattan dancehall feature, "Roseland."

What the film attempts is not a phychological exploration of various characters who offer their performing services to visiting menfolk, but an explanation of the social and cultural context in which they operate.

Acted scenes objectify the insight of the film's creators about the community and its visitor. Saeed Jaffrey plays a film actor besotted with a particular girl. Kareem Samara is the bribeable rent collector and Sohra Segal a retired courtesan. All play their parts with an amateurish feel that blends with the general tone.

But pic is most affecting when it peers at the indolent and useless males in the community or gazes at the courtesans.

Contrasting styles ultimately help to illumine this dark corner of India where the traditional value system is maintained in inverted form. Sense of authenticity reflects knowledge and interest on the part of its makers. —Japa.

Table For Five
(COLOR)

Good tear-jerker should find solid acceptance.

Hollywood, Feb. 2.

A Warner Bros. release of a CBS Theatrical Films presentation of a Voight-Schaffel production. Produced by Robert Schaffel. Stars Jon Voight. Directed by Robert Lieberman. Screenplay, David Seltzer; camera (Deluxe color), Vilmos Zsigmond; editor, Michael Kahn; music, Miles Goodman, John Morris; production design, Robert F. Boyle; art direction, Norman Newberry; set decoration, Arthur Jeph Parker; costume design, Vicki Sanchez; sound, Jeff Wexler; second unit camera, Victor Goss; assistant director, Newton Arnold. Reviewed at The Burbank Studios, Burbank, Feb. 2, 1983. (MPAA Rating: PG.) Running time: 122 MINS.
J.P. Tannen .... Jon Voight
Mitchell .... Richard Crenna
Marie .... Marie Christine Barrault
Kathleen .... Millie Perkins
Tilde .... Roxana Zal
Truman-Paul .... Robby Kiger
Trung .... Son Hoang Bui
Mandy .... Maria O'Brien
Old Man .... Nelson Welch

A slick but emotionally effective tear-jerker, "Table For Five" marks a solid re-entry into feature film production by CBS Theatrical Films after a period of managerial regrouping. Well-written drama concerns an errant father who takes his three children on an ocean voyage in an effort to close the gap that's grown between them, pic earns most of its emotional points honestly and will touch most anyone who's ever taken the responsibilities of parenting seriously, either in fact or theoretically. If Warners' marketing can open it solidly, good biz with legs should loom.

At the opening, Voight's kids have lived with their mother, Millie Perkins, and her new man, attorney Richard Crenna, for several years. Voight them swoops into New York to take the moppets off on a luxurious sea cruise aboard a Scandinavian liner with the promise of a new-found sense of responsibility.

But Voight quickly realizes that he really doesn't know how to communicate with his kids who, for their part, resent the fact he's more interested in chasing blondes in the bar than hanging out with them. A mid-Atlantic stand-off sees Voight asking them to try to consider him as a friend rather than a father, an approach which has a depth-charge negative reaction with his adopted Vietnamese son, who has already been abandoned by two fathers in his young life.

Despite the attempted interference of his sharp daughter, Voight manages to initiate a shipboard romance with a sympathetic French woman, Marie Christine Barrault, and after about an hour, group arrives at its first port-of-call, Rome. First-time director Robert Lieberman indulges in just a moderate amount of typical travelog footage of famous sights (the Colosseum, the Parthenon in Athens, Pyramids and Sphinx in Egypt) and for the most part eschews foreign ethnic characterizations among the natives, keeping the focus on the principals.

Out at sea again, Voight receives tragic news over a bad wireless phone connection — Perkins has been killed in an automobile accident. Crenna, who loves the kids and has cared for them as if they were his own, is there to meet them at the next stop, Athens, but Voight asks for a little time to break the news to the kids.

In great pain and filled with remorse over never having truly resolved his relationship with his ex-wife, Voight manages to contain himself until group reaches Egypt, where, in front of the ancient monuments, he finally drops the bombshell on the children. It's a beautifully written and performed speech, one which fully expresses the notion that, no matter how gently and loving such news is delivered, there's no way to cushion the initial blow.

Given Crenna's legal expertise, there at first seems to be no way Voight is going to manage to keep his kids but, with encouragement from Barrault, he resolves to try to do so. Seed for his climactic effort has been too obviously planted earlier, when he tells his youngest son, who seems unable to learn to read, never to say "can't." But having come to love his kids, there's no way he's going to give up now without a fight, and matter is resolved reasonably at fade-out.

Voight's irresponsible father occasionally reminds of his boorish loser characterization in the recent "Lookin' To Get Out," but fortunately the positive side of his character prevails. A lot of the child remains in this grown-up, which sometimes makes it terribly difficult for him to maintain constant authority, and his abrupt impatience initially causes kids to think he hates them. It's a winning performance.

Crenna is solid as a bastion of fairness and civility, Barrault is engagingly warm and emotionally direct as Voight's confidante and occasional bedmate, while Perkins, in a return to the screen after a long absence, looks gorgeous and is excellent in her brief early scenes.

During his career as a commercials director, Lieberman earned a strong reputation for his handling of youngsters, which he has lived up to here in his work with the three kids. A cutie on the verge of adolescence, Roxana Zal exudes a maturity still held in check by her years and is highly appealing. Robby Kiger will break many hearts as the youngest of the bunch, while Son Hoang Bui, with his pent-up resentment over his outsider status, prompts substantial feeling for his special dilemma.

Although it holds the attention throughout, film is still about 10 minutes too long at 122 minutes, as many individual scenes are pushed just a bit further than needed.

Tech contributions are all fine, and film overall should prove satisfying to the mass audience. —Cart.

The Lords Of Discipline
(COLOR)

Absorbing but brutal.

Hollywood, Jan. 27.

A Paramount release of a Herb Jaffe/Gabriel Katzka production. Produced by Jaffe, Katzka. Directed by Franc Roddam. Features entire cast. Screenplay, Thomas Pope, Lloyd Fonvielle, based on the novel by Pat Conroy; camera (Eastmancolor), Brian Tufano; editor, Michael Ellis; music, Howard Blake; production design, John Graysmark; art direction, Alan Cassie; set decoration, Peter Howitt (U.K.), George DeTitta (U.S.); costume design, John Mollo; sound, Bruce White (U.K.), Alan Bernard (U.S.); associate producer, Basil Rayburn; assistant directors, Michael Murray, Roger H. Lyons. Reviewed at the Paramount Studios, L.A., Jun. 27, 1983. (MPAA Rating: R.). Running time: **102 MINS.**

Will	David Keith
Bear	Robert Prosky
General Durrell	G.D. Spradlin
Abigail	Barbara Babcock
Alexander	Michael Biehn
Pig	Rick Rossovich
Mark	John Lavachielli
Trudd	Mitchell Lichtenstein
Pearce	Mark Breland
Poteete	Malcolm Danàre
Macabbee	Judge Reinhold
Teresa	Katharine Levy

"The Lords Of Discipline" laces a military school Watergate saga with heavy doses of sadism, racism and macho bullying. Designed as an expose of the corruption to be found within the hallowed walls of a venerable American institution, pic wants to have it both ways in "entertaining" the audience with verbal and physical brutality, then condemning it all as an obscene way of life. Unusual nature of the story and expert craftsmanship make for an absorbing film, but appeal of the main unsavory details to a mass public is questionable and women will probably find little to like.

Set around 1964 but stripped of any topical references save for LBJ fright masks and numerous pop tunes, drama follows cadet David Keith through his senior year at the Carolina Military Institute, a strict academy so proud of its reputation that extreme lengths are taken to ensure that no unworthy young men are bestowed with its ring, the supreme token of graduation.

Year in question is a notable one for the school because the first black cadet in its history has been enrolled. All entrants are treated in a manner that makes the basic training of "An Officer And A Gentleman" look like summer camp, but one can be sure that special treatment will be accorded the black youth by the uniformly bigoted school population. If Southern gents were really all like this, the Ku Klux Klan would have a waiting list of applicants miles long.

As far as the new recruits, or "knobs," are concerned, the poop hits the fan on "hell night," which is just as bad as it sounds. With the full sanction of the faculty, upper classmen are permitted, even encouraged, to turn strong young men into oatmeal, running them through an evening of physical horrors under the guise of building character. One boy dies as a result, which leads outsider-type Keith onto the existence of The Ten, a secret society to ferret out undesirables.

Keith has also quietly been assigned to watch over the black cadet (Mark Breland) to make sure nothing too nasty happens to him. After an ever-worsening series of assaults, however, things do get out

of hand, and Keith barely manages to save Breland from being castrated and probably killed by The Ten.

Incensed, Keith recruits his reluctant roommates (Rick Rossovich, John Lavachielli and Mitchell Lichtenstein) in an effort to uncover the identities of The Ten. Ultimately, this endeavor leads to the highest levels of the school, giving it strong Watergate overtones.

Because of the layer-by-layer unveiling of successive outrages, tale undeniably has its compelling side, and Thomas Pope and Lloyd Fonvielle have done a good job condensing Pat Conroy's 500-page novel, sacrificing little save a romantic subplot (women appear in the film in only the most incidental of ways.) Dialog is loaded with barracks and locker room-type grossness, which carries scenes along, and situation is so incendiary as to rivet the attention. Like it or not, cesspools are often worth looking into, but there's considerable doubt as to the relevance of this one in terms of everyday life or even social conditions.

Having attracted considerable notice with his debut feature, "Quadrophenia," Franc Roddam nevertheless had to wait over three years to make his American directorial debut and, ironically, ended up doing most of this film in Britain when no domestic (U.S.) school would allow lensing on its grounds (some locationing was done in South Carolina and film seems utterly American in all aspects).

Pic leaves no doubt about Roddam's talent — his instinct for muscular camera set-ups, choice of lenses and dynamic cutting is much in evidence, and his work with the mostly young cast is exemplary.

Keith and his buddies are all excellent, as are Robert Prosky as the school's genially scheming second-in-command and G.D. Spradlin as the academy's crusty leader. One might have wished some expansion of Breland's beleaguered black recruit role from that of a mere victim, although he is given one good scene in which he explains why he's determined to survive at all costs.

Technical work, notably Brian Tufano's lensing, Michael Ellis' editing and John Graysmark's production design, with support from art director Alan Cassie and set decorators Peter Howitt and George Detitta, is superior. —*Cart.*

Testa O Croce
(Heads or Tails)
(ITALIAN-COLOR)

Rome, Jan. 6.
A C.I.D.I.F. release, produced by Luigi and Aurelio De Laurentiis for Filmauro in association with Intercontinental Film.

Stars Nino Manfredi, Renato Pozzetto. Directed by Nanni Loy. Screenplay, Franco Ferrini, Nanni Loy, Enrico Oldoini, Nino Manfredi and Renato Pozzetto; camera (Eastmancolor), Claudio Cirillo; editor, Franco Fraticelli; art director, Elena Ricci Poccetto, Umberto Turco; music, Carlo and Paolo Rustichelli. Reviewed at Adriano Cinema, Rome, Jan. 6, 1983. Running time: **100 MINS.**

Don Emidio	Renato Pozzetto
Teresa	Mara Venier
The Bedouin	Nino Manfredi
Stefania	Ida Di Benedetto
Grandfather	Paolo Stoppa

Respectable comic helmer Nanni Loy tries his hand at a dual-episode film featuring popular comedians Nino Manfredi and Renato Pozzetto. The Luigi and Aurelio De Laurentiis production, aimed at mass audiences with a short attention span, manages to put a little meat on the structural bones and upgrade the genre through a script dealing with realistic characters and problems.

Result is an intelligent national product that has done well at local boxoffices and with a future in Latin and Mediterranean markets.

The two episodes are distinctly different in flavor and each is custom-made for its star. First 50 minutes is a scathingly anti-clerical, anti-provincial attack disguised as a mini-sex comedy. Pozzetto, a straight-laced roly-poly priest from a little Northern town, has amnesia on a train and ends up having a wild ten-day fling with a pretty Milanese girl (Mara Venier). The party ends when his superiors locate him and drag him back to Varese, but Father Emidio never quite becomes the same tyrannical pastor his flock once revered.

Unfortunately story ends before the episode's time slot does, and a lot of repetitive padding blunts the punch. Venier is highly believable as the sophisticated girlfriend, but Pozzetto's unexercised physique stretches plausibility as a romantic partner.

If first episode is a grotesque fable lampooning repressed ids, second segment assumes a more realistic tone. Manfredi plays a raucous-voiced Roman construction worker whose pride-and-joy son, a junior soccer star, turns out to be gay. Plot is trite, message predictably progressive. The detailed reconstruction of the characters' humble home and working lives gives the story some breadth. Manfredi's portrait of the confused father, a widower who sneaks home at night after visiting his girlfriend to keep from scandalizing his teenage son, is the tale's strong point. Good supporting thesps are Paolo Stoppa as a busybody grandfather and Neapolitan actress Ida Di Benedetto as the girlfriend.

—*Yung.*

Ascendancy
(BRITISH-COLOR)

London, Feb. 3.
A British Film Institute production, in association with Channel Four Television. Exec producer, Peter Sainsbury. Produced by Penny Clark and Ian Elsey. Directed by Edward Bennett. Features entire cast. Screenplay, Bennett and Nigel Gearing; camera (color), Clive Tickner; editors, Charles Rees, George Akers; art direction, Jamie Leonard; music, Ronnie Leahy. Reviewed at Preview One, London, Feb. 1, 1983. Running time: **85 MINS.**

Connie	Julie Covington
Ryder	Ian Charleson
Wintour	John Phillips
Nurse	Susan Engel
Dr. Strickland	Phillip Locke
Dr. Kelso	Kieran Montague

"Ascendancy" is the most successful attempt so far by any British filmmaker to formulate a creative response to Britain's long-standing "Irish problem." The resulting film is necessarily downbeat, but through avoidance of simplifying rhetoric poses the issues in a manner bound to provoke discussion on festival and arthouse circuits.

It's an okay feature debut for helmer Edward Bennett, who has three documentaries to his credit, but sophisticated visual understanding is not matched by real mastery of actors and narrative techniques.

Pic's central concept is an intriguing one, a girl of prosperous family who protests with her body against the horrors of Belfast shortly after World War I. First, her right arm loses its power when her brother, who went unwillingly to war, dies in the trenches. Her response to the growing antagonism between Protestant and Catholic that led to the partition of Ireland is a mute fast.

Psychological exploration is clearly difficult with a character whose sense of horror will not be vocalized, but audiences generally will share with the British soldier, played by Ian Charleson, some uncertainty as to what is happening in the mind of the girl for whom he forms an affection. And without that information it's impossible to evaluate her response.

There's a partial explanation, of course, in the scenes of conflict on the streets and in the factory where the girl's father is complicit in solidifying a conflict. The model by which he weakly justifies his efforts to protect his own, leading the two sides to bloody war, is clearly just what her sullen passivity avoids.

The film's impact is dependent on its imagery; the house from which Connie, the girl, views the world, the shrine to her brother represented in the books, clothes and pictures that crowd his room, and scenes of street violence which are effectively done.

The potent musical score combines allusions to the music of composers who lived through the era and traditional Irish airs, linking Connie's response to the mood of post-war intellectuals. Quality photographic and art departments should ensure the pic wide cable and tv playoff after a limited theatrical release. —Japa.

The Evil Dead
(COLOR)

Suspenseful gorefest shapes up as a strong performer in horror market.

A New Line Cinema release of a Renaissance Pictures Ltd. production. Produced by Robert Tapert. Exec producers, Tapert, Bruce Campbell, Sam M. Raimi. Stars Bruce Campbell. Directed by Sam M. Raimi. Screenplay, Raimi; camera (Du Art color), Tim Philo; prints by Technicolor; editor, Edna Ruth Paul; music, Joe LoDuca; sound, John Mason; photographic special effects supervisor, Bart Pierce; special makeup effects, Tom Sullivan; second unit camera, Joshua M. Becker. Reviewed at RKO Century National 2 theatre, N.Y., Feb. 4, 1963. (No MPAA Rating). Running time: 85 MINS.
Ash .... Bruce Campbell
Cheryl .... Ellen Sandweiss
Linda .... Betsy Baker
Scott .... Hal Delrich
Shelly .... Sarah York

Filmed in 1980 on Tennessee and Michigan locations as "Book Of The Dead," "The Evil Dead" emerges late in the horror film cycle as the *ne plus ultra* of low-budget gore and shock effects. Neophyte Detroit-based filmmakers Bob Tapert, Sam Raimi and Bruce Campbell have built a better horror picture, which despite the crudities of its blowup from 16m and low (under $400,000) budget, should clean up in the fright marketplace. Currently poised for domestic release in unrated (and uncensored) form, question is whether "The Evil Dead" can attract a wider audience.

Story premise has five youngsters (in their 20s) holed up in a remote cabin where they discover a Book Of The Dead. Archaeologist's tape recording reveals it having been found among the Khandarian ruins of a Sumerian civilization. Playing the taped incantations unwittingly summons up dormant demons living in the nearby forest, which possess the youngsters in succession until only Ash (Bruce Campbell) is left intact to fight for survival.

While injecting considerable black humor, writer-director Sam Raimi maintains suspense and a nightmarish mood in between the showy outbursts of special effects gore and graphic violence which are staples of modern horror pictures. Powerful camerawork (simulating crane and Panaglide shots) suggests the lurking presence of the huge-scale demons in the forest, reminiscent of the scary first-person camera of Daniel Haller's "The Dunwich Horror."

The possessed youngsters are presented in makeup (replete with green pea soup effusions) derived from "The Exorcist," while the level of explicit eye-gouging, dismemberment and other mayhem exceeds that of the higher-priced competition. Very effective in the final reel is Bart Pierce's stop-motion animation, integrated with the ongoing makeup effects to present the victims' disintegration with the Book is thrown into the fireplace.

Although the 35m blowup is grainy and color mismatched in spots, film boasts atmospheric lighting, pro crosscutting and excellent pacing. Cast is functional, frequently called upon to venture into a spooky cellar or threatening forest in order to evoke a superior feeling audience's warnings. Dynamic sound is overbearing.

—Lor.

Wacko
(U.S.-COLOR)

Lameduck horror spoof.

Winnipeg, Jan. 26.
A Jensen Farley release of A Greydon Clark production. Produced and directed by Greydon Clark. Executive producer, Michael R. Starita; screenplay, Dana Olsen, Michael Spound, M. James Kauf Jr. and David Greenwalt; camera (color), Nicholas von Sternberg; editors, Earl Watson, Curtis Burch; music, Arthur Kempel. Reviewed at Towne Cinema 8, Winnipeg, Jan. 25, 1983. (MPAA Rating: PG). Running Time: 84 MINS.
Dick Harbinger .... Joe Don Baker
Marg Graves .... Stella Stevens
Doctor Graves .... George Kennedy
Mary Graves .... Julia Duffy
Norman Bates .... Scott McGinnis
Tony Schtonginini .... Andrew Clay
Bambi .... Elizabeth Daily
Rosie .... Michele Tobin
Zeke .... Anthony James
Looney .... David Drucker
Weirdo .... Sonny Davis
Dr. Moreau. .... Victor Brandt
Harry Palms .... Jeff Altman
Patrick O'Hara .... Charles Napier
Dr. Denton .... Wil Albert
Damien Graves .... Michael Lee Gogin

"Wacko" is a spoof aimed at the recent spate of teenage horror movies. Its story is most noticeably culled from "Halloween" and "Prom Night" with a barrage of non-sequitur gags in the "Airplane" tradition.

While many of the situations are genuinely humorous, director Greydon Clark may have overplayed his comedy by sticking so closely to the stories of the horror hits. The uninitiated may well find "Wacko" too far out to comprehend.

Story centers on the notorious Lawnmower Killer who murdered a girl 13 years earlier. Joe Don Baker, looking like the Michelin tire boy, plays a cop named Harbinger who insists the killer is about to strike again. However, the experts he calls in do little to help his case.

Meanwhile, the kids at Hitchcock High are preparing to put on their annual Halloween Pumpkin dance. Among the seniors is Mary Graves (Julia Duffy), the younger sister of the murdered girl. She's haunted by Lawnmower dreams and the terrible images everyone says "will screw her up for the rest of her life."

The rest of the class is filled with the usual assortment of nymphets, studs and shy, serious types. The teaching staff is a veritable looney bin, from a vice-principal with a masochistic strain to a science teacher named Dr. Moreau who's experimenting with a new serum.

Clark and his screenwriters miss few opportunities to send up the genre but in the process of identifying the origin of the spoof, a lot of the comedy is lost. The best material in the fast-paced film is visual and unrelated to horror pics.

Large cast is dotted with new faces saddled with playing stereotypes. The presence of Baker, George Kennedy and Stella Stevens does nothing for the story or commercial prospects of the film.

Technical credits are modest, suggesting the same slap-dash quality apparent in the script. "Wacko," like last year's "Student Bodies" has a limited audience which would much rather scream than laugh at its horror. Likely to be a fast and quickly forgotten release. —Klad.

Lovesick
(COLOR)

And probably fatal.

Hollywood, Feb. 3.
A Ladd Co. release through Warner Bros. Produced by Charles Okun. Stars Dudley Moore. Directed, written by Marshall Brickman. Camera (Technicolor), Gerry Fisher; editor, Nina Feinberg; music, Philippe Sarde; production design, Philip Rosenberg; set decoration, Gary Brink; costume design, Kristi Zea; sound, Stephen Scanlon; assistant director, Thomas Reilly. Reviewed at Warner Hollywood Studios, Feb. 3, 1983. (MPAA Rating: PG.) Running time: 95 MINS.
Saul Benjamin .... Dudley Moore
Chloe Allen .... Elizabeth McGovern
Sigmund Freud .... Alec Guinness
Larry Geller, M.D. .... John Huston
Otto Jaffe .... William Shawn
Lionel Gross, M.D. .... Alan King
Mrs. Mondragon .... Renee Taylor
Ted Caruso .... Ron Silver
Frantic patient .... Gene Saks

Prospects are dark for "Lovesick." An engaging idea — Dudley Moore as a successful, married shrink who becomes obsessed with a beautiful patient (Elizabeth McGovern) — is rendered inoperable by Marshall Brickman's witless script and uninspired direction. This Ladd Co. release, through Warner Bros., is a particular disappointment because it wastes so many fetching talents: McGovern, Alec Guinness, John Huston, among them.

From the heights of "10" and "Arthur" through the flop of "Six Weeks" to the nadir of "Lovesick," Moore's pictures have done a loop that leaves one numb. Adding to the troubles here are a grandiose but hokey music score out of sync with the intended romantic-comedic tone and murky cinematography that adds to the gloom of the whole endeavor.

What has long been a cliche target of satire, psychoanalysis, becomes a long, tiresome joke. Moore is okay, ranging from a cool, controlled psychiatrist to a shambles of a lovesick doctor, but no amount of individual artfulness can shore up slight rigging. McGovern (also caught in a tailspin here, following "Ordinary People" and "Ragtime") plays a New York playwright with the power to enthrall. With those intense, glowing eyes, she literally dispatches her first shrink, played by William Shawn, when he expires in anguished ectasy. The dapper, rich, professional Moore "inherits" McGovern and he's soon gone to the world, at one point stealing her key and sneaking into McGovern's apartment, where she discovers him behind the shower curtain. Love blossoms but the rest, including scenes at the Juilliard School where McGovern is rehearsing a play, is a hapless series of scenic diversions.

Perhaps most descriptive of the script's desperation is the gimmicky inclusion of Sigmund Freud, who mystically materializes in the person of Alec Guinness whenever Moore seeks professional help. Guinness properly plays it straight and slightly aloof, telling Moore that his obsession with McGovern "reminds us what we really are — animals — take it or leave it." Pure Freud.

Cinematically, the film is unimaginative, marred by an edgy, uncertain rhythm, and Gotham never looked more drab. Pic is devoid of style.

Ron Silver is fine as an arrogant actor but Gene Saks (the director) as a suicidal patient, Huston and Alan King as stuffy doctors, and Renee Taylor as a patient are all embarrassing. —Loyn.

Utu
(NEW ZEALAND-COLOR)

Napier, N.Z., Jan. 31.
A Kerridge Odeon release of a Geoff Murphy production. Produced and directed by Geoff Murphy. Features entire cast. Screenplay, Murphy, Keith Aberdein; camera (color), Graeme Cowley; editor, Michael Horton; production design, Ron Highfield; costumes, Michael Kane; music, John Charles; sound, Graham Morris; assistant director, Lee Tamahori; 2nd unit director, Rory O'Shea; production manager, Pat Murphy; executive producers, Don Blakeney, Kerry Robins and David Carson-Parker. Reviewed at the Odeon Theatre, Napier, N.Z., Jan. 29, '83. Running time: 120 MINS. (GA rating).

Te Wheke	Anzac Wallace
Williamson	Bruno Lawrence
Scott	Kelly Johnson
Wirimu	Wi Kuki Kaa
Colonel Elliot	Tim Eliott
Emily	Ilona Rodgers
Kura	Tania Bristowe
Vicar	Martyn Sanderson
Henare	Faenza Reuben
Matu	Merata Mita

The rumbling, underground buzz presaging Geoff Murphy's "Utu," the first N.Z. feature in the blockbuster category, is just about right.

Set during 19th century times of savage encounter between European and Polynesian (Maori), the behind-celluloid word was the pic would be a breakthrough for the home film industry in successfully meshing theme and story of epic scale. It would also demonstrate the breadth and expertise of proven tech talent now involved in an industry that after only five short years is rapidly achieving maturity.

"Utu," the buzz asserted, could be the first N.Z. pic to attract big grosses overseas; set the seal on international recognition of N.Z. movie making prowess.

On the local front, it will surprise if "Utu" is not as big a success with New Zealanders as "The Man From Snowy River" is with Australians.

Murphy, the film's initiator, director and cowriter, knows his at-hand audience. His earlier "Goodbye Pork Pie" still sits securely at the head of top-grossing N.Z.-made features on the home market.

With "Utu" (the Maori word for revenge), however, Murphy has been far more ambitious. In a N.Z. western of the North American Indian-white settler school, he has fashioned a fast-moving visual tale of archetypal passion and action that should appeal well beyond these shores.

Central figure is rebel leader Te Wheke (Anzac Wallace) during the wars between European settlers and the native Maoris in New Zealand of the late 19th centuy.

At first sympathetic to the European (pakeha) cause, Te Wheke turns guerrilla when his village is wiped out by British soldiers protecting the settlers. He retaliates in kind while recruiting supporters. As his actions become increasingly despotic and cruel, he is tracked down, captured and finally shot.

With a main theme of "those who live by the sword, die by the sword" — no matter what race, no matter what circumstance — Murphy has produced powerful images and strong performances, particularly from Wallace, Wi Kuki Kaa (as Wirimu) and a big cast of Maori actors. Action sequences, special effects, and visual exploitation of a rugged, high country location in central New Zealand are superb.

European characters fare less well. In the cases of settler William-son (Bruno Lawrence) and Lieutenant Scott (Kelly Johnson) it seems character development and clarity have been sacrificed for action.

There is a strong, original music score from John Charles, although themes might have been more strongly pointed. But these are minor blemishes in what must rate as the most powerful, expert and audience-appealing film yet to be wholly conceived and executed in this country.

What is more (and despite the absence of overseas stars) it should travel well. —*Nic.*

La Baraka
(Stroke of Luck)
(FRENCH-COLOR)

Paris, Jan. 3.
Parafrance release of an Elephant Production/S.F.P.C./FR 3 coproduction. Produced by Raymond Danon. Stars Roger Hanin. Directed by Jean Valere. Screenplay, Valere, Henri Graziani, Daniel Saint Hamont; camera (color), Christian Bachmann; sound, Georges Vaglio; editor, Kenout Peltier; art director, Jean-Francois Corneille; music, Jacques Arel. Reviewed at the Monte Carlo Theatre, Paris, Dec. 26, 1982. Running time: 105 MINS.
Aime Prado	Roger Hanin
Julien	Gerard Darmon
Catherine Prado	Magali Renoir
Mother Prado	Marthe Villalonga
Fisherman	Henri Tisot

Algerian-born French actor Roger Hanin has hit a popular vein with colorful portrayals of "Pied Noir" (French Algerian) types, notably in the top grossing films of his compatriot, Alexandre Arcady. "La Baraka," a drama directed by Jean Valere, is in the same mold and offers Hanin a moderately interesting vehicle for his talents.

Here Hanin is a top Pied Noir (black foot) chef who runs a highly rated bouillabaisse restaurant in Marseilles. Essentially goodhearted but overbearing and bigoted towards Arabs, Hanin submits to a severe test of his self-professed generosity and beliefs when he brings into his household a solitary young poacher who has saved his life on one of his regular fishing trips.

At Hanin's insistance, the sullen young man (Gerard Darmon) allows his stand-offish reserve to be chipped away and even begins to bed the chef's pretty, footloose daughter. This doesn't disturb Hanin unduly until Darmon finally admits that not only is he half-Arab, but he's an escaped convict who'd been sentenced for having (accidentally, he claims) killed a man. Hanin manages to overcome his prejudices and make an ultimate gesture toward saving Darmon, but unforeseen complications lead to tragedy.

Script is little more than serviceable pretext for Hanin to show what he can do, and he does it pretty well, incarnating the exuberant Pied Noir more convincingly than he's done in Arcady's pics. Darmon is a quietly eloquent foil in an underwritten part, and Marthe Villalonga provides some comic relish as Hanin's stubbornly tradition-bound mother.

Valere, who made his first film in 1957, with Hanin billed, has directed adequately and tech credits are good. —*Len.*

As Aventuras da Turma de Monica
(The Adventures of Monica's Friends)
(BRAZILIAN-COLOR/B&W-ANIMATED)

Rio de Janeiro, Dec. 30.
An Embrafilme release and production. Directed by Mauricio de Sousa. Screenplay, Reinaldo Waisman, De Sousa; storyboard, Waisman; art direction, Roberto Barbist, Fumiomi Yabuki, Alice Keiko Takeda; editing, Mauro Alice, Jair Correa; musical direction, Remo Usai; songs, Mauricio de Souza, Gao Gurgel, Remo Usai, Marcio de Sousa, Eduardo Leao Waisman; lyrics, Vilma Camargo, Yara Maura Silva; special effects, Pedro C.O. Azevedo, Ives Ribeiro; animation, Jose Eliseo Villa, Nova Conceicao; production director, Eduardo Leao Waisman; executive producer, Marcos Urbani Saraiva; sound, Rancho Studios. Reviewed at Embrafilme screening room, Rio de Janeiro, Dec. 30, 1982. Running time: 80 MINS.

Feature cartoons are an odd product in Brazilian cinema, although four of them have officially been produced since 1952. In fact, except for the "Troublemakers" series, children's pics are practically nonexistent among Brazil's 80 native releases a year; less than 5% of them are actually created for moppet audiences.

"Monica," therefore, is an exception. Author Mauricio de Sousa has managed to turn his characters into the most popular of local comic strips, reportedly sold to 21 countries. "Monica And Her Friends" has also achieved a good marketing position, the names selling everything from tomato concentrates to soap and shampoos all over the country.

Strip's success encouraged De Sousa to jump with his drawings into films and Embrafilme to coproduce it (picture had a $550,000 budget, high by local standards). Early boxoffice figures (item has just open in Sao Paulo) have shown that pic may return its investment, even if it is not a smash.

Technically, experience has proven to be satisfactory. If not rich, animation is fluent and characters — Monica, Cebolinha, Cascao, Magali, Franjinha — remain at least as attractive as in the comic strips. Author seems to have dealt with the lack of a good story satisfactorily. He's put four small vignettes together, filling them with his own presence, which is questionable as a brilliant solution from the audience's stand. Characters con-sequently move well, but they do not know exactly where to go or what to say, which could certainly be frustrating for the Monica fans.

Such problems, however, do not hamper the crew's efforts. Evaluation of the problems involved in this cartoon narrative will be most helpful in making the sequels planned by the producers. As a unique experience of its kind in Brazil, "Monica," besides the solid animation, has voices that are pertinent and well placed; sets are okay as is the music. More carefully written and narrated, it would certainly amuse the children even more than the comics have already done. —*Hoin.*

Sabine Kleist, 7 Jahre
(Sabine Kleist, 7 Years Old)
(EAST GERMAN-COLOR)

East Berlin, Jan. 7.
A DEFA Film Production, Berlin Group, East Berlin; world rights, DEFA Aussenhandel, East Berlin. Features entire cast. Written and directed by Helmut Dziuba. Camera (color), Helmut Bergmann; sets, Heinz Roeske; music, Christian Steyer; editor, Barbara Simpn; dramaturg, Anne Pfeuffer; production manager, Guenter Schwaack. Reviewed at DEFA Screening Room, East Berlin, Jan. 7, '83. Running time: 80 MINS.
Cast: Petra Laemmel (Sabine Kleist), Simone von Zglinicki (Edith), Martin Trettau (Karl Schindler), Heide Kipp (Frau Marloch), Gerd Guetschow, Gudrun Ritter, Carl Heinz Choynski, Johanna Clas, Juergen Huth.

One of the finest children's films to emerge from a Socialist country in recent memory, Helmut Dziuba's "Sabine Kleist, 7 Years Old" is a standout because it appeals equally to adults and credits are tops in every category. Dziuba has dealt almost exclusively in kidpics, since his "Moor And The Ravens Of London" (1969), but this time he has outdone himself by raising the difficult genre to a philosophical parable on human foibles.

This is the story of an orphan, seven-year-old Sabine Kleist, who runs away one day from the orphanage because she feels that her favorite schoolmistress is deserting her by getting pregnant and going on leave to have the baby. Sabine herself lost both her parents in a tragic auto accident some years before. She then spends two days and nights on her own, while her beloved schoolmistress (with her husband) and the authorities are out looking for her. Much as in the vein of Morris Engel's "The Little Fugitive" (1953), this is a perspective on the human condition from the eyes and feelings of a very sensitive young lady marvelously played by child thesp Petra Laemmel.

Her first contact with the outside world is with a circus troupe on its way to downtown Alexanderplatz in East Berlin. Then she attends the funeral of a dignitary and joins the brass band to pull off a couple of monkeyshines with a friendly hornblower. She helps a lost Polish lad on the street who can't speak German, and whom she dumps at the local police station without getting caught herself in the act. Then she's at a hospital for newborn children, and on a group picnic with other kids on a boat who have but one parent to look after them.

She ends up at a beach to play with a family group, and she spends the first evening with an elderly pensioned worker who has celebrated a bit too much on the day of his retirement. In all these cases she's the one who turns out to be the most helpful and attentive, while the grownups are hardly the mature and understanding types — indeed, she even helps the police in a roving squad car to "find" and identify her, and then bring her back to the orphanage, free and willing.

Packed with humor and several fine touches, pic is a winner due to helming and lensing plus finely etched character roles. "Sabine Kleist" is reportedly on its way to the competition at Manila. —Holl.

The House On Sorority Row
(COLOR)

Fair horror item acceptable for appropriate venues.

Hollywood, Jan. 26.

An Artists Releasing Corp. thru Film Ventures International release of a VAE Productions presentation. Produced by Mark Rosman, John G. Clark. Coproducer, Ed Buyer. Executive producers, John Ponchock, W. Thomas McMahon. Directed, screenplay by Rosman. Additional dialog, Bobby Fine. Camera (TVC color), Timothy Suhrstedt; editors, Jean-Marc Vasseur, Paul Trejo; music, Richard H. Band; art direction, Vincent Perranio; sound, Steve Rogers; associate producer, Alec Rabinowitz; assistant director, Paul Schiff; second unit director, production associate, Rene Eram. Reviewed at the Paramount, Hollywood, Jan. 26, 1963. (MPAA Rating: R). Running time: 91 MINS.
Katherine .... Kathryn McNeil
Vicki .... Eileen Davidson
Liz.......................Janis Zido
Jeanie .... Robin Meloy
Diane .... Harley Kozak
Morgan ....Jodi Draigie
Stevie .... Ellen Dorsher
Mrs. Slater .... Lois Kelso Hunt
Dr. Beck ... . Christopher Lawrence

"The House On Sorority Row" is a fair to middling girls-in-jeopardy horror entry. Indie-financed item was shot outside Baltimore in the summer of 1981 under the title "Seven Sisters," was picked up last year by Edward L. Montoro and was test marketed in Las Vegas and Albuquerque in November. Initial b.o. results in its L.A. break were okay, and pic will prove an acceptable, if unexciting, exploitationer for its intended market.

Ladies in question all seem nice enough upon meeting them, but when their house mother freaks out upon learning that they intend to throw a party on June 19, some of the young collegiates turn murderous and end up drowning the old bag in the swimming pool. One thinks they could have reached some sort of compromise concerning the party.

As it turns out, on June 19 some 20 years before, poor Mrs. Slater had given birth to a son via an experimental process for barren women, and she was never the same after that. Thus, on the kid's birthday, someone's running amok around the house, knocking off the sorority sisters one by one.

Not unexpectedly, the girls are mostly types — the sultry blonde bombshell who instigates the crime, the plain Jane, the tough, practical one and the clear-eyed intellectual who perseveres — but the acting isn't bad for this sort of fare. In fact, first-time director Mark Rosman, formerly an assistant to Brian De Palma, displays more talent and sympathy dealing with the actresses than with the mechanics of horror manipulation.

Pic bogs down when Rosman boxes himself into the corner of having to come up with diverse ways of killing off his heroines, and impatience for the climax builds long before it finally arrives. Gore level is moderate.

Nevertheless, film is competently made for a low-budget entry, and care has been invested in such matters as casting, lensing and, particularly, the music. Richard H. Band's full-bodied romantic suspense score summons up memories of Bernard Herrmann's work and aids immeasurably in smoothing over various rough edges and bland stretches.

In the nominal lead, Kathryn McNeil projects intelligence along with a gravity which seems a bit heavy in context. Eileen Davidson is a looker with a lot of spunk who does well with the bad girl role, and Harley Kozak reveals an appealingly offbeat personality as another of the sisters. —Cart.

Twilight Time
(U.S.-YUGOSLAV-COLOR)

Mild family film aimed at ethnic and overseas markets.

An MGM-UA Entertainment release of a Dan Tana and Centaur production for United Artists. Executive producer, Milan Zmukic. Produced by Dan Tana. Stars Karl Malden. Directed by Goran Paskaljevic. Screenplay, Paskaljevic, Filip David, Tana, Rowland Barber; camera (Rank color), Tomislav Pinter; editor, Olga Skrigin; music, Walter Scharf; title song, Buck Ram, Morty Nevins, Al Nevins; sound, Claude Hitchcock; assistant director, Zoran Andric; production manager, Alexsandar Radulovic; art direction, Niko Matul; associate producer, Andrew Wood. Reviewed at MGM screening room, N.Y., Feb. 3, 1963. (MPAA Rating: PG). Running time: 102 MINS.
Marko ....Karl Malden
Lena ....Jodi Thelen
Ivan ....Damien Nash
Ana ....Mia Roth
Pashko ....Pavle Vujisic
Tony ....Dragan Maksimovic

"Twilight Time" is an old-fashioned family picture lensed in Yugoslavia. Topliner Karl Malden gives an engaging performance as the grandpa caring for two cute kids, but thin writing and a combination of slow pacing and sentimentality make this entry an unlikely candidate to score in the domestic marketplace.

Slight story, burdened with flat, strictly functional English-language dialog, concerns Marko (Karl Malden), a septuagenarian farmer known locally as Americano for his 20-year stay in the U.S. before returning home to a tiny Yugoslav village. He is looking after his grandchildren Ivan (Damien Nash) and Ana (Mia Roth), whose parents are in Germany as immigrant workers. Marko befriends an attractive new schoolteacher Lena (Jodi Thelen), whose main problem is getting Ivan to come to class, as the pre-teenage boy is increasingly taking over the duties of running Marko's farm and household.

With Marko predictably dying, uneventful picture ends with the two children working the farm and evidently standing up for traditional values in defiance of their parents' "modern" materialistic abandonment of family and homeland. Theme will appeal to nostalgic audiences, but lacks the dramatics and story development required for more demanding venues.

Malden earns his star billing with an earthy, at times moving portrayal of an old man living with his memories (signified by frequent playing of his favorite old standard, the 1944 "Twilight Time" hit), but weak material and an inadequate supporting cast let him down. Thelen, very attractively photographed by top-ranked European lenser Tomislav Pinter, reprises her perpetual smile from her pic debut in "Four Friends," and her sincere but goody-goody performance is irritating.

The kids are merely okay, and the Yugoslav minor actors have been dubbed disconcertingly into English, spoiling the otherwise adequate use of direct-sound dialog recording of the principal players. An unrealized romantic interlude between Thelen and Dragon Maksimovic is particularly pointless.

Credit producer Dan Tana and his team of filmmakers with attempting to bring back the family entertainment (with which MGM was synonymous in the Golden Age) of yore, but failing to develop adequate story material. Helmer Goran Paskaljevic, for his first English-language entry, directs as if walking on eggshells. The technical side is okay, especially Pinter's laudable still-life landscape shots, but "Twilight Time" is a lifeless film. —Lor.

The King Of Comedy

De Niro & Scorsese team with Jerry Lewis for in-joke laden picture. Limited outlook.

Hollywood, Feb. 1.

A 20th Century-Fox release, produced by Arnon Milchan. Directed by Martin Scorsese. Exec producer, Robert Greenhut. Stars Robert DeNiro, Jerry Lewis. Screenplay, Paul D. Zimmerman; camera (Technicolor), Fred Schuler; editor, Thelma Schoonmaker; sound, Les Lazarowitz; production design, Boris Leven; assistant director, Scott Maitland; associate producer, Robert F. Colesberry; music, Robbie Robertson. Reviewed at 20th Century-Fox, L.A., Feb. 1, 1983. (MPAA rating: PG.) Running time: 101 MINS.
Rupert Pupkin...........Robert De Niro
Jerry Langford ....Jerry Lewis
Rita ....Diahnne Abbott
Masha ....Sandra Bernhard
Cathy .... Shelley Hack
Himself ....Tony Randall
Himself ....Ed Herlihy
Band leader ....Lou Brown
Receptionist .... Margo Winkler

"The King Of Comedy" is a royal disappointment, although another off-center teaming of director Martin Scorsese and star Robert De Niro will work up enthusiasm in certain limited quarters. But it's an enthusiasm that's not likely to be shared by the majority.

To be sure, De Niro turns in another virtuoso performance for Scorsese, just as he's done in their four previous efforts. But once again — and even more so — they've come up with a character that it's hard to spend time with. Even worse, the characters — in fact, all the characters — stand for nothing.

"King" is too shallow for drama; too somber for comedy. It can't be satire and it can't be farce. There's a real feeling, in fact, that there must have been a lot that went before the cameras that hasn't made it into the final cut.

De Niro plays a would-be standup comic, determined to start at the top by getting a gig on Jerry Lewis' popular talk show. He's also a nut nearly totally removed from reality. Finally, he's brash, boring, pushy and beyond any sympathy whatsoever, not deserving much less earning anything others really work for.

Worse still, he has a sidekick, Sandra Bernhard, who's even nuttier than he is, only slightly more likable because she's slightly more pathetic in her desperate fantasy love for Lewis.

When all else fails, the pair kidnap Lewis to get what they want: He a spot on the show, she a night of amour. With any clear intent, it would still be tough to bring that absurdity off. But Scorsese doesn't seem to know where to go at any given point, persistently setting up audience expectations he doesn't fulfill.

Bernhard is winsome, but her character is totally confusing and ill-drawn, especially when she turns suddenly wealthy in the middle of the picture and finally disappears into the night with no further reference.

Taking a totally dramatic turn, Lewis is solid, but his part is largely reactive and sketchy. There's a feeling here, especially, that he surely must have been drawn to a more solid role than is on the screen. Diahnne Abbott is excellent as a girl embarrassingly drawn into De Niro's fantasy world.

After all this, unfortunately, comes an empty ending, which shan't be given away. Suffice to say it's totally unsatisfying and bleakly cynical. Hardly worth waiting for is too much praise. —*Har.*

The Mediterranean
(COLOR)

Vidbound festpic has craft, minimal b.o. potential.

Berkeley, Jan. 11.

No distrib. A Camera Verde Films production. Executive producer, Sophia Pigozzi. Produced by John V. Fante and Yan Nascimbene. Directed and written by Nascimbene. Camera (color), Fante; editor, Susan M. Slanhoff; music, Martin Bresnick; sound, Dan Gleich; assistant director, Penelope Dunham; assistant camera, Martin Rosenberg. Reviewed at Pacific Film Archive, Berkeley, Calif., Jan. 11, 1963. (No MPAA Rating.) Running time: 87 MINS.
Paul .... Conrad Selvig
Joan .... Joan Parazette
Sophie .... Noemie Nascimbene
Greg .... Stuart Schwarz
Mailcarrier .... Julia Freiberg
Phoneman .... Ernie Fossellus

This semi-autobiographical, well-crafted study of an artist cracking up has been booked at seven fests, including upcoming New Delhi and San Remo, but has yet to attract distrib bids other than for vidsale. Pic appears a tough sell as a theatrical feature, with title somewhat of a turn-off going in, but it does serve to tip the potential of writer-director-coproducer Yan Nascimbene, 37, who lived in Paris and Rome before coming to the Frisco area to study art and photography in 1969.

In a sense, this is a home movie. Nascimbene's wife and daughter play two of the three leads, as the wife and daughter of newcomer Conrad Selvig, who limns the character of an artist unable to create anything except his own emotional deterioration. Selvig's inability to deliver lines dissipates the believability of his crack-up, yet the woman and the child, latter a four-year-old when pic was lensed in

Hollister, Calif., ranchlands, deliver effective jobs in their first thesping.

Pic is tantamount to a series of stills within stills. Scenes are quite brief, and often affecting. Selvig busies himself shooting stills of his family and surroundings, taping the sounds of the house, preserving labels from canned goods — attempting, says Nascimbene, to freeze time.

Tale of this routine-numbed couple is marred by b&w comments by each, described by writer-director as "diary entries." They don't work; neither do flashbacks to earlier life in Antibes.

But there is a distinct lushness (shot in 16m with a 35m blow-up via Du Art labs) to the Hollister footage, a style and symmetry reflecting Nascimbene's artistic background. John V. Fante's lensing is a class act.

With a fleshed-out, more cohesive screenplay and a more compelling leading man, this pic could click. It's evident Nascimbene has a feature future. —*Herb.*

Te Engle Og Fem Loever
(Three Angels And Five Lions)
(DANISH-COLOR)

Copenhagen, Jan. 1.

An A/S Panorama (Just Betzer) pjoduction (with the Danish Film Institute) and release. Directed by Sven Methling. Features entire cast. Screenplay, Bjarne Reuter, Sven Methling, based on Reuter novel; camera (Eastmancolor), Claus Loof; production deisgn, Henning Bahs; music, Fuzzy; costumes, Annelise Hauberg; editor, Leif Axel Kjeldsen; executive producer, Christian Clausen. Reviewed at the Palads, Copenhagen, Dec. 29, 982. Running time: 68 MINS.
Uncel Georg .... Otto Brandenburg
Father .... Jesper Langberg
Mother .... Lisbeth Dahl
Aunt Gyda .... Elin Reimer
Bertram .... Michael Nezer
Winnie .... Henriette Holm
Oscar .... Jesper Lund
Anders .... Tobias Fog

Sven Methling's second kiddie & family entertainment based on one of novelist Bjarne Reuter's successful and baroquely funny books about a down-at-heels family with four kids and an irresponsible, but charming uncle who plunges everybody headly into various semicriminal ventures has a funny title, "Three Angels And Five Lions," has neither the angelic charm nor the animal roar and gusto of "Kidnapped," its predecessor. While it seems sure to make its money back at home, "Three Angels," would appear to be of limited appeal even on kiddie tv abroad.

Although "Three Angels" was shot simultaneously with "Kidnapped," it does not seem directed, played and otherwise handled by the same professional people. The acting is tired, the director must have been absent-minded, the scriptwriting, totally uninspired and lacking in dramatic logic, and if

there had been any material for the editor to salvage, he did not manage to do so.

It is a pity since the plot is made to order for a good farcical comedy (art thieves get their precious Three Angels canvas swapped with Little Oscar's innocent oil painting of lions and the hunt is on with Uncle Georg outsmarting himself as usual).

"Kidnapped" climaxed in a wonderful and swiftly managed chase sequence. When "Three Angels" gets to its grand finale chase through the Copenhagen Tivoli Gardens, every opportunity for fun and suspense is fumbled. Danish children have nevertheless laughed lustily at showings here since Otto Brandenburg as Uncle Georg and Michael Nezer as Little Oscar are popular figures already and they do their expected amount of slipping and geneal tumbling about. —*Kell.*

Midnite Spares
(AUSTRALIAN-COLOR)

Sydney, Jan. 25.

A Roadshow Australia release of a Filmco presentation. Exec producer, John Fitzpatrick. Produced by Tom Burstall. Directed by Quentin Masters. Features entire cast. Screenplay, Terry Larsen; camera (Eastmancolor), Geoff Burton; production manager, Jenny Day; sound, Lloyd Carrick; location manager, John Warran; editor, Andrew Prowse; music, Cameron Allan. Reviewed at the Roadshow theatrette, Jan. 14, 1983. (Commonwealth Film Censor rating: M). Running time: 96 MINS.
Steve .... James Laurie
Ruth .... Gia Carides
Tomas .... Max Cullen
Wimpy .... Bruce Spence
Rabbit .... David Argue
Howard .... Tony Barry
Vincent .... John Clayton
Sidebottom .... Graeme Blundell
Uncle Harry .... Terry Camilleri
Chris the Rat .... John Godden
Wayne .... Jonathan Coleman
Janelle .... Amanda Dole
Panton .... Ray Marshall

An action-adventure which makes few pretenses, "Midnite Spares" is a cinematic demolition derby of screeching tires, mangled metal and pyrotechnics, orchestrated by suitably raucous rock music. While chunks of dialog are lost in the din, the teenagers and young adults to whom pic is dedicated are not likely to have much trouble following the plot.

It opens Down Under in February, distrib figuring to do good business in capital city hardtops initially before widening to suburban drive-ins. Film has already been sold to Germany (for a reported $200,000, a handsome stipend for an Oz offering), where fast play-off strategy will probably pay the best dividends.

Title refers to a gang of criminals who specialize in stealing autos, stripping them, and selling the parts. The baddies come into collision — quite literally — with an honest bunch of tow-truck op-

erators and Steve, a young sprint-car driver whose father mysteriously disappeared after refusing to join the cartel.

When Steve isn't whizzing around the speedway and endeavoring to find out what happened to his dad, he carries on a pretty tepid romance with Ruth, who works at the hot-dog stand. His allies are Tomas, his dad's partner, and two oddball mechanics, Wimpy and Rabbit.

In the end, rough justice is meted out to the villains, who are variously crushed, shot, and incinerated. Director Quentin Masters keeps the accent throughout on the action, interspersed with bursts of crude humor (breaking wind "jokes" predominate). The one or two serious themes in Terry Larsen's script (e.g. the relationship between free-spirited Ruth and her over-possessive mother and relatives) are either poorly developed or glossed over.

While the stuntwork is impressive, it should be noted that a camera assistant was killed during filming when a sprintcar ran off the track, sparking calls for a new safety code to protect Australian technicians and actors.

As Steve and Ruth, James Laurie and Gia Carides are a fairly insipid leading duo; Bruce Spence and Davis Argue put a bit more bite and flair into their sidekick roles; Max Cullen as Tomas wrestles none too well with his curiously drawn character; and the bad-guys are straight out of stock.

Geoff Burton's high-standard camerawork gives the pic more class than its other elements probably deserve. —*Dogo.*

Manila Fest

My Memories of Old Beijing
(CHINESE-COLOR)

Manila, Jan. 30.

A China Film Export & Import release of a Shanghai Film Studio production. Features entire cast. Directed by Wu Yigong. Screenplay, Yi Ming from a novel by Lin Haiyn; camera (color, wide screen), Cao Weiye. Reviewed at Main Theatre, Manila Film Center, January 30, 1983. Running time: 92 MINS.
Cast: Shen Jie, Zheng Zhenyao, Zhang Min, Zhang Fenjyi, Yan Xiang, Yuan Jiayi.

Set 50 years ago in the charming streets of the old Chinese capital, this story is meant to carry the evocations of a Taiwan-born woman, then just a 10-year-old girl. She is seen in the process of discovering life and the surrounding social reality, asking her mummy where do babies come from and claiming not to know the meaning of the world "future." She also finds out that, in her day's China, parents used to sell their children, thieves robbed for surviving, and students were shot to death by the police.

Politics, however, is by no means the main subject in this old-fashioned romantic story. Ovverwhelmingly ingenuous, it wil perhaps be able to bring some tears out of raw Oriental audiences, but is almost unable to get an emotional involvement from cinematically more sophisticated western viewers. In fact, director Yigong does not seem to care for any stronger involvement, pushing it away by turning his narrative as slowly as possible. He chooses no more than two or three different shots for each location, so the field is immediately read by the viewer, who tends to seek for any further visual information. No way, though. The camera barely moves, leaving the audiences along with characters portraying quite childish roles by the contemporary standards.

There are some outstanding sequences, as when the girl meets her thief friend during the school's graduation ceremony. But seldom getting any emotion from the plot — smart little girls are not exactly the ultimate discovery of the film industry —'item fails to offer a local narrative accent, for the Chinese filmmaking still seems to be highly influenced by the American pics of the '50s. Trapped in small sets (despite the wide screen) with nice but uninteresting people, audience has therefore the sensation of, say, spending two hours at the Beijing airport, without having a chance either to visit the city or to chat with their locals. —*Hoin.*

(Pic won top prize at the festival. —Ed.)

El-aar
(The Shame)
(EGYPTIAN-COLOR)

Manila, Feb. 1.

An Adwaa el Cinema production, Falcon Company (Cairo) foreign release. Directed by Ali Abd el Khalek. Features entire cast. Original story and script, Mahmoud Abu Zeid; camera (Eastmancolor), Said el Shimy; editor, Hassen Afifi; music, Hassan Abu el Soud. Reviewed as an official competition entry in the Manila International Film Festival at the Manila Film Center's Main Theatre on Jan. 31, 1983. Running time: 120 MINS.

Kamal . . . . Nur el Sharif
Adil . . . . Mahmoud Ab'd el Asis
Roka . . . . Noura
Ahmed . . . . Hossein Famy

"The Shame" befalls a Cairo family when the old father, a much respected spice merchant and all around do-gooder, dies. It is then disclosed, but only to the family, that the heritage is not the business, the home, the assets in the bank since all that has been set riding on a huge shipment of cocaine yet to be retrieved from its cache in the open sea.

The old gentleman was a crook, but his sons want to reap their inheritance without turning criminal themselves. Film then goes to great length to depict their moral quandary (one of the sons is the Public Prosecutor, another a doctor, the third is more than ready to follow into his father's business footsteps and to other lengths to tell about the decision to retrieve the dope and to sell it). There is a bit of death involved, a drowning and a suicide, and the moral of the story is that crime does not pay, but mostly Ali Abd el Khalek's overlong and fuzzily lensed feature plays it for laughs.

Some laughs are to be had, but Western audiences will find it hard to sit still through the long stretches between them. Severe editing might help film to get across some borders, but a story otherwise rich in tragi-comic possibilities is not helped either by rather sleep walking acting in all major parts. —*Kell.*

Wild Horses
(NEW ZEALAND-COLOR)

Manila, Jan. 30.

An Endeavour Production in association with the New Zealand Film Commission. Exec producer Gary Hannam, produced by John Barnett. Features entire cast. Directed by Derek Morton. Screenplay, Kevin O'Sullivan. Camera (Eastmancolor) Doug Milsome; music, Dave Fraser; editor, Simon Reece; sound recordist, Mike Westgate; sound mixers, Don Reynolds, Brian Shenna; production design, Joe Bleakley. Reviewed Jan. 30, 1983 at Manila Int'l Film Festival (competing), Manila Film Center. Running time: 88 MINS.

Mitch . . . . Keith Aberdein
Jack . . . . .John Bach
Harry . . . . Kevin J. Wilson
Sara . . . . Robyn Gibbes
Tyson . . . . Bruno Lawrence
Mary . . . . Kathy Rawlings
Sam . . . . Tom Poata
Andy . . . . Marshall Napier
Jones . . . . Martyn Sanderson
Benson . . . . Michael Haigh

The horses and stunning scenery are the real stars of this richly lensed but disjointed film about horse exploiters vs. horse haters. Strong performances by Keith Aberdein, Kevin Wilson and especially John Bach add to audience involvement, but fail to overcome a script marred by narrative holes and a tendency to only hint at motivations rather than reveal what truly drives the main participants.

Derek Morton's direction helps tell the story, but scenes seem to start mid-stride and much of the narrative must be gleaned between the lines. Script itself, originally penned by costar Wilson under a pseudonym, apparently suffers from too many collaborators, including other thesps in the picture. As a result, pic lacks a clear focus story-wise, and fails to build real tension. Limited word of mouth calls for careful handling. Equine

theme, rural characters and setting look to garner best results in non-urban markets.

Story entails three laid-off loggers, Mitch and the two Sullivan brothers, Jack and Harry, who turn to capturing and selling horses running wild in New Zealand's Tongariro National Park as a source of income. Initially they are ill-qualified and meet with no success. At the same time, other jobless loggers have hired on with a venison export biz to hunt deer in the park. However, with the trio chasing horses about, it spooks the deer and the deer hunters' boss comes up with a simple solution — shoot the horses.

The hunters are as hapless at shooting horses as the trio is at capturing them. But the horse chasers join forces with the nature-wise Sam and his horse-loving and comely sidekick Sara, who teach them how to capture horses and a respect for leaving the best in the herd to breed even better horses.

But the deer company hires Tyson, a sinister, black-garbed exterminator dressed in black, who efficiently begins to eliminate the horses. To him it's just a job, but to Sara it's murder and the inevitable confrontations with Tyson and the deer hunters escalate into ugliness. Along the way (it's never clear to the audience just why) Mitch develops an obsession to capture a striking stallion and strikes a pragmatic bargain with Tyson to leave the stallion unscathed — the other horses are fair game. The two brothers soon tire of Mitch's obsessive and fruitless pursuit and break up the tacit partnership.

Climax has Mitch going on a rampage after Sara is apparently molested when trapped along with the last of the horses in a night hunt by the bad guys. Venison exec Benson and the hunters get their nonfatal comeuppance, and Tyson perishes in an ironic twist when he attempts to renege on his bargain with Mitch.

Pic has its well-timed funny moments, especially a barroom brawl scene that's romping good fun (though the punches are pathetically phony). Dialog also has high points, especially the brotherly banter between Jack and Harry, but heavy Kiwi accents pose problems in some scenes.

John Bach gets high marks as Jack, the hot-headed loudmouth brother, and his hapless horsemanship contributes to the overall effect. Kevin Wilson as Harry, the loyal, easygoing brother, gets kudos for sensitive interpretation and understated thesping. Keith Aberdein was infinitely better in last year's critical Kiwi success "Smash Palace," but fleshes out Mitch's character beyond limitations of the script.

Marshall Napier as a boorish, thick-headed hunter and Martyn Sanderson as a hunter sympathetic to the horse chasers are bright spots in the supporting cast. Newcomer Robyn Gibbes fails to impress as Sara, and Bruno Lawrence as Tyson plays the heavy too stiffly.

Doug Milsome's camerawork is impressive, though setting gave him lots to work with. Sound quality is okay but Dave Fraser's music is less so, and it often seems at odds with the mood onscreen. Simon Reece's editing leaves the pic choppy and disjointed. Other tech values are fine. —*Mich.*

Alsino Y El Condor
(Alsino And The Condor)
(NICARAGUAN-CUBAN-MEXICAN-COSTA RICAN-COLOR)

Manila, Feb. 2.

An ICAIC release of a Nicaraguan Film Institute/The Cuban Film Institute/Latinamerican Film Producers of Mexico/The Costarican Film Cooperative production. Features entire cast. Executive producer, Hernan Littin. Directed by Miguel Littin. Screenplay, Miguel Littin, Isidora Aguirre, Thomas Perez Turrent; camera (color), Jorge Herrera, Pablo Martinez; sound Germinal Hernandez; music, Leo Brower; art direction, Ely Menza; editing, Miriam Talavera; assistant director, Rafael Vargas, Francisco Fasano, Elias Nahmias. Reviewed at Main Theatre, Manila Film Center, Manila, Feb. 2, 1983. Running time: 89 MINS.

Cast: Dean Stockwell, Alan Esquivel, Carmen Burnster, Alejandro Parodi, Delia Casanova, Marta Lorenza Perez, Reinaldo Miravalles, Marcelo Gaete, Jam Kees de Roy, Rogelio Blain, Raul Eguren, Marcelo Gaete.

Miguel Littin has generally been acknowledged as one of the most skillful directors among Latin American revolutionary filmmakers. Chilean-born, he used to work as head of his country's Educational Television, as well as the top man at government-owned Chile Films. He moved to Mexico following Chile's military coup and in exile he has accomplished some of his most important works, including "Actas de Marusia," nominated in 1975 for an Oscar.

This new production is supported by three Latin American revolutionary groups, besides the Cuban government itself. It is a reasonable guess, therefore, that some political propaganda would be involved, as in the previous work of the same artist. In fact, the action is set in an imaginary Latin American country, where U.S. military troups are taking the task of organizing a repression system against guerrillas. Military chief is Frank (Dean Stockwell), who meets a 10-year-old peasant, Alsino (Alan Esquivel), whose dream is to be able to fly "like a bird." Frank takes him in his helicopter, but Alsino is not happy. Dreams and realities cannot be blended to fulfill one's aims.

The repression strategy gets stronger after a U.S. official is killed. Oddly enough, guerrillas are never seen except when victimized by a slaughter. Nevertheless, Littin keeps the movement and the interest of his story. Alsino holds the dream of also meeting Manuel (Rogelio Blain), the guerrilla leader who lives with the mother of Alsino's little friend Lucia (Marta Lorenza Perez). In his search for freedom and strength, Alsino falls from a tree and is disabled, but is never discouraged. Professionally acted (especially by Stockwell and Esquivel), picture often transcends its immediate goals. It gives us an idealized view of guerrilla movements in Latin America, though with a cinematic approach as sophisticated as the Cuban cinema has recently been able to achieve.

Locations at Ticuantepe, a small village near Managua, Nicaragua, were conveniently set so to give some credibility to the action. One wonders how far can the Cuban cinema go when filmmakers would be able to diversify their subjects.
— *Hoin.*

I'm Going To Be Famous
(U.S.-COLOR)

Manila, Jan. 30.

An L.T. Productions Ltd. production, International Film Sales Division release (Los Angeles). Original story, script, edited and directed by Paul Leder. Produced by Leder and Joe Terry. Associate producers, Bruce Cook and Mimi Leder. Camera (Eastmancolor), Joel King; production design, Anne Welch; sound, Bill Fiege. Features entire cast. Music and lyrics by Jay Asher, title song lyrics by Dennis Spiegel. Reviewed in market section of the Manila International Film Festival at Screening Room 1 on Jan. 29, 1983. Running time: 96 MINS.

The Director	Dick Sargent
Susan Barker	Meredith MacRae
Ron Michaels	Paul Coufos
Harold Green	Greg Mullavey
Kitty March	Roslyn Kind
Kevin McGraw	Joe Terry
Laura Lowell	Vivian Blaine

"I'm Going To Be Famous," shown in an answer print, was well received by a large and youthful audience of mainly Filipinos at a midnight showing here. And the youth market at home in the U.S. is surely where this indie production of largely unpretentious proportions could win back its modest costs. Later foreign and tv sales would be icing on the cake. Some critical kudos are to be expected, too, since producer-writer-director-editor Paul Leder has done smooth and efficient work in all departments, aided nicely by a crew and cast of professionals and non-professionals.

The set-up of crew and cast fits in just fine with the story itself which is, of course, variant number 117 of every showbiz ambition story from "A Star Is Born" to "A Chorus Line." This time, a famous New York playwright-director (Dick Sargent) auditions young hopefuls for his new work which is to open in L.A. prior to its Gotham presentation.

Among the hopefuls are a young part-time gigolo with a pregnant girlfriend and a dependency on the rich, elderly lady who backs the show; an idealistic parole officer torn between the dramatic demands of his work with young criminals and his stage ambitions; an alcoholic young singer tormented by her mother's fame, and boyish Kevin McGraw (Joe Terry) who acts as if he already had the part, but inside he's insecure and suicidal.

It turns out that there will be roles to play for everybody but one. The director is a fair-minded man, but will he be influenced unfairly by his own actress-wife (Meredith MacRae)? Will the parole officer ever reach the rehearsals at all when he has to take guns away from young wards who kidnap his secretary? Will the rich woman want the gigolo out of the way when he no longer comes to her bed? Will the singer throw away pills and bottles in time?

Everything is both very trite and true, but Leder makes the trueness of these showbiz-driven people carry the day. They are all believable, even the rich woman (a nice performance by veteran Vivian Blaine) and the singer, although the latter's motivations for her plight are not very convincingly given. She is played rather mutedly by Roslyn Kind, who perhaps consciously did not want to emulate too much of her older sister's, Barbra Streisand's, more abrasive personality. Kind also sings two songs by Jay Asher nicely enough, this time more in her sister's highly dramatic manner. An especially credible performance is given by Greg Mullavey as the parole officer.

Film has an explosive and bloody ending to underscore how the pressure these people live under can be a dangerous one. For most of them, however, healthy egotism will win out. While one is led away by police for murder, the others immediately get into an argument about who plays what role in some other upcoming production. Some of the plot twists are a bit contrived, but the generally honest feel of a slice of showbiz recaptured remains. —*Kell.*

Desire
(FILIPINO-COLOR)

Manila, Jan. 2.

A Hemisphere Pictures (Philippines) production and release. Produced, written and directed by Eddie Romero. Camera (color) Manolo Abaya; production design, Claire Guthrie; music, Ryan Cayabyab; editor, Manolo Abaya. Reviewed in the films in exhibition section of the Manila International Film Festival, screening room 1, Jan. 27, 1983. Running Time: 117 MINS.

Joe Hale	John Saxon
Bessie	Tetchie Agbayani
Bessie's Mother	Charito Solis
Phil Seaver	Ken Metcalfe
Julie Seaver	Judith Chapman
Bong	Mark Gil
Cris Arias	Maria Richwine

"Desire" is a Filippino feature melodrama with aspects of romantic comedy, skillfully handled by veteran writer-director Eddie Romero who says he will edit the film further for foreign sales. On the strength of the John Saxon name and the introduction of young Tetchie Agbayani, these sales may well go beyond tv and into minor theatrical situations in some markets.

Film has an incest theme and some sex scenes and nudity, but all done with too much discretion to make "Desire" a "hot" item on those scores. Plot has Joe Hale (Saxon) coming to Manila to straighten things out in an American ad agency that seems to be mismanaged by his old friend Phil. Hale soon has Phil's wife (Judith Chapman) in his bed, but only because she wants to get there. He also gets involved briefly with a rich local girl (Maria Richwine). Joe is a twice-divorced man of easygoing attitudes, but no real skirt-chaser.

With John Saxon and his Sean Connery looks and a role written very inoffensively, this Joe is almost too good to be true, but he does have to stop and reconsider his life and its direction, when young Bessie (Tetchie Agbayani) thinks that she has found out that she is his daughter through a G.I. relation between Joe and her Mother (Charito Solis). When they find out that they are not dad and daughter after all, Bessie wants Joe and Joe is clearly tempted, but they decide to go out to a fish restaurant instead.

What explosives this story contains are carefully defused most of the way by quite arid stretches of talk. Agbayani has appeared as a centerfold in Playboy magazine's non-U.S. editions, but here she is very much the typical Filippino teenager, all sweetness and mild rebellion against manners and mores. Her mother is played with customary wounded-but-proud looks by Solis, an established character actress. Casting in all roles appear to be just right for the purposes. Some of cinematographer Manolo Abaya's frames are a bit underlit, but the general look and production dress of "Desire" is quite handsome. —*Kell.*

Return To Eden
(BRITISH-DOCU-COLOR-16m)

Manila, Jan. 25.

A Newlords Ltd. (London) production and release. Directed by Geoff Hogg. Camera (Eastmancolor, 16m), Mike Coles, Av. Rix and (underwater) Werner Schulz. Starring and narrated by Omar Sharif. Written by Marc Alexander. Produced by Omer Ahmed. Music, David Scholastique, Patrick Victor, Ton Pa. Reviewed at VCR Room 2, Phillippine Convention Center as a Film Market presentation during the Manila International Film Festival, Jan. 25, 1983. Running time, 58 MINS.

Natan Scheinwald of Australia has acquired "Return To Eden" for the South East Asia area mainly with a view to tv sales. The neat and shinily produced documentary about the Seychelles Islands has been picked up by the BBC and other tv sales into less demanding programming situation should not be hard to negotiate. Less demanding, since docu carefully avoids any reference to political realities of the island republic in the Indian Ocean. Not even the likely presence of flies or mosquitoes is mentioned.

If the presence of Omar Sharif in almost every frame as guide and narrator of words he speaks in a natural enough way although he did not write them himself can be considered a true attraction (the star is in good trim, his voice is pleasant and his moustache has grown slightly larger), then alright, but any invisible narrator might have done the actual information job as well.

We hear random facts of Seychelles history and of the Seychellois population and are introduced to exotic flora and fauna (including male and female coconuts of phallic and vaginal likeness, scorpion fish, giant turtles and fruit bats, etc.). We meet a few of the islanders who all appear to be happy and at ease and we attend a sumptuous wedding.

If there is any degree of poverty on the many Islands, we hear neither about that nor about anything else disagreeable. On the Island of Praslin, Britain's General Gordon is said to have placed the original Garden of Eden in a hidden valley.
—*Kell.*

Faleze De Nisip
(Sand Cliffs)
(RUMANIAN-COLOR)

Manila, Jan. 27.

Film Company 1 production. Directed by Dan Pita. Screenplay, Bujor Nedelcovici, Dan Pita; camera (color), no credit. Features entire cast. No other credits available. Reviewed at Film Centre Guilding, Manila, Jan. 27, '83. Running time: 97 MINS.

Cast: Victor Rebengiuc, Marin Moraru, Gheorghe Visa, Carmen Galin, Valentin Uritescu, Vasile Cosma, Ion Vilcu.

What starts out as a simple case of mistaken identity, as a thief steals a radio and some personal effects on a beach, careens off tangentially into an analysis of the psyches of accusor and accused.

After capture of the seeming culprit, a simple, introverted carpenter who from the start is seen to be patently innocent, pic changes tack and starts to delve into the compulsive yearning of a surgeon, who was witness to the theft, to put the accused behind bars.

Following some rather far-fetched police questionings and a mockery of a trial, the young man is convicted and sentenced to jail. But upon release, after doing his time, he is still hounded by the doctor who, for his own satisfaction and peace of mind continues to try to wring a confession of guilt from the carpenter, while his own marriage goes on the rocks.

Some audiences might read all kinds of symbolisms into the simple plot, but barring such approaches pic doesn't have much going for it to generate interest. All the characters are presented in an annoying vein, the fuss made over a minor theft in modern Rumania seems exaggerated and the story is rather too slight to be spun out into a full-length feature. Thesping and direction of the middling sort, with poor color quality. —Besa.

Siege
(CANADIAN-COLOR)

Manila, Jan. 28.

A Summa Vista (domestic) and Manson International (overseas) release of a Salter production, exec produced by Philip M. Robinson. Produced by Michael Donovan, John Walsch, Maura O'Connell, Paul Donovan. Directed by Paul Donovan, O'Connell. Features entire cast. Screenplay by Paul Donovan, based on an idea by Marc Vautour; camera (Eastmancolor), Les Krizsan; editor, Ian McBride; sound, Pierre Dostie; music, Peter Jermyn, Drew King; production design, Malachi Salter. Reviewed at Manila Film Center, Jan 28, 1983. Running time: 83 MINS.

Horatio .... Tom Nardini
Barbara .... Brenda Bazinet
Cabe .... Doug Lennox
Chester .... Darel Haney
Daniel .... Terry Despres
Goose .... Jeff Pustil
Patrick .... Jack Blum
Steve .... Keith Knight
Ian .... Brad Wadden
Lloyd .... Gary Dempster

This violent exploitationer marks the directorial debut of Paul Donovan and Maura O'Connell, who merit kudos for fast pacing, solid framing and continual tension in the storytelling. Pic delivers the goods on most levels without being overdone, and fact that dialog, bloodshed and characterizations are realistic should add to appeal beyond the bigger urban markets.

Broad premise of pic is civilian anarchy resulting from a police strike in Halifax, Nova Scotia, but actually concerns two related incidents over one night — and oh, what a night. Opening is slow, with local rowdies harassing the shuttered police station. From there, aud sees a carload of goons with clubs entering a homosexual nitery, The Crypt (aptly named), to "correct" the supposed perversion inside. Entry scene looks too phony, however,

with these right-wingers, members of an org called the "New Order," smacking clubs (to a man) into their palms. When the bartender is fatally impaled on a broken bottle in a scuffle, the thugs call leader Cabe (Doug Lennox) about what to do.

The icy-cool Cabe arrives and methodically executes the bound and gagged witnesses in a gripping and powerful scene that shows the victims' faces as they realize death is near and inevitable. Daniel (Terry Despres) manages to escape, however, and the baddies follow him to the apartment of Horatio (Tom Nardini) where he seeks refuge. Horatio refuses to surrender Daniel while girlfriend Barbara (Brenda Bazinet) doesn't want to get involved and opines they should turn Daniel over to the thugs. Horatio wins out and the siege begins.

The New Order can't seem to do anything without Cabe, who arrives with a high-tech arsenal, infra-red rifle scopes and walkie-talkies. The good guys meanwhile, gird for the assault with a rifle (with two bullets) and a hunting bow (with one arrow) supplied by staid handyman neighbor Chester (Darel Haney) who also assembles a homemade rocket and a flamethrower made with a candle and spray deodorant, as well as electrifying the doors and windows in the apartment building, located in a deserted industrial area.

Countless bullets fly as the New Order attacks, inflicting their first casualty when the blind Steve (Keith Knight) exits the apartment against his pals' wishes and ends up providing target practice for the New Order. Homemade ingenuity ultimately wins out over heavy weaponry, but not without the defenders paying a heavy price. But just when Horatio and the survivors think it's all over, Cabe, who's been directing the assault from a safe distance, takes matters into his own hands. After stalking the apartments and garroting Chester, Cabe gets what's coming to him. Surprise ending details the police strike ended after 42 days, but it turns out the sole New Order survivor is a cop.

Nardini and Bazinet turn in okay perfs, and though their characters seem fairly humdrum, they bring out nuances of ordinary folk under pressure. Jeff Pustil as Goose, the loud-mouthed and sadistic goon, makes his character the most memorable of the right-wingers, and his high-pitched voice adds to his impish nature. Lennox plays the heavy to the hilt, but as Cabe there's little characterization beyond the strong, silent stereotype. Brad Wadden as a wimpy right-winger, Ian, is also worth noting.

Camerawork by Les Krizsan is murky throughout, but this adds to

pic's realism and is helped by moody lighting. Pierre Dostie's sound could stand improvement, especially in some dialog sequences, and synthesized music track by Drew King and Peter Jermyn fails to build tension as well as it should. Ian McBride's editing is crisp and adds to overall pace. Carolyn van Gurp's special effects makeup displays the carnage without overdoing it, but it's still not for the meek. —Mich.

Saarbruecken Festival

Nach Wien
(To Vienna)
(WEST GERMAN-COLOR)

Saarbrucken, Jan. 24.

A Ludolf Weyer Film Production, Munich, in coproduction with Norddeutscher Rundfunk, Hamburg. Features entire cast. Written and directed by Friedemann Beyer. Camera (color), Ludolf Weyer. Reviewed at Saarbruecken Film Fest, Jan. 23, '84. Running time: 87 MINS.

Cast: Friedrich Steinhauer, Axel Witte.

A debut pic that rose out of the low-budget ranks due to tv-subsidy support, Friedemann Beyer's "To Vienna" scored at Saarbruecken as an audience fave. Thesp Friedrich Steinhauer is also known as "The Nightingale of Ramersdorf" for his beer-saloon, singing-waiter melodies in and around Munich. Pic is constructed entirely around Steinhauer's naive and oft primitive acting performance.

"To Vienna" comes across like Bavarian Volkstheater comedy. Two friends down on their luck decided to take what cash they have on hand and drive from Munich to Vienna for a weekend. Friedrich has just lost his job as a singing waiter in a small Gasthaus (the place is closing), and can't handle the oversize beer-mugs at the Oktoberfest drinking sprees. Axel had to give up his taxi job, and is now driving a delivery truck. The two set off on the trip to Vienna like two Laurel-and-Hardy innocents in a broken-down Volkswagen: after many adventures, they reach their goal but experience only the underbelly of the city of their dreams. That's enough to add up to a goodly bundle of local gags and puns, but Bavarian humor alone doesn't guarantee b.o. legs, even in Germany.

All the same, Friedemann Beyer has a refined touch for comedy and has a number of delightful twists in his pic, each episode building upon the mistakes or miscalculations in the scene before. Steinhauer will delight German film buffs who are familiar with Werner Herzog or Herbert Achternbusch pics, and there were many at Saarbruecken who went wild over his high-

soprano warbling, both in the film (two occasions) and in town itself. —Holl.

Catch Your Dreams...
(WEST GERMAN-COLOR)

Saarbruecken, Jan. 23.

A Tantra Film Production, Munich. Features entire cast. Written and directed by Moritz Boerner. Camera (color), Andreas Schulz; music, Kitaro. Reviewed at Saarbruecken Film Fest (Max Ophuls Prize) Jan. 22, '83. Running time: 90 MINS.

Cast: A. Jacobsen, A. Lilleystone, P. Panther, C. Piel, B. Panzer, N. Mueller, A. Schaerer, N. Oehlrich, P. Lunghard, P. Schmidt.

Unspooled in a latenight slot at Saarbruecken, Moritz Boerner's "Catch Your Dreams..." is exactly what its title hints at: wet-dream blue movie passing at a fest for a purification of mind and body via total release of any inhibitions, and syruped with Wagner and other classical music. The bed partners on a weekend joy-spin in a remote castle with antique furniture and silk sheets are all wishful Venus and Adonis types engaging in various acts of exhibitionism, each more or less "directed" by the women themselves.

Since none of the principals is from the ranks of porn-stars, pic has an "art" tab slapped on the film cans in an attempt to escape the "club-kino" circuit, but the ruse is not liable to work: this is not peekaboo porn, like "Bilitis" or "Egon Schiele," and it has none of the critical flair of "Obscene" (a riotous spoof of the porn trade and leftist politics). It's drawing-room Victorianism in the buff, for what that's worth. —Holl.

Tscherwonez
(WEST GERMAN-COLOR/B&W)

Saarbruecken, Jan. 24.

A Werner Grassmann Film Production, Hamburg, in coproduction with Zweites Deutsches Fernsehen (ZDF), Mainz. Features entire cast. Directed by Gabor Altorjay, Janos Marton, and Randi Marie Hoffmann. Screenplay, Altorjay; camera (color/b&w), Joerg Jeshel; music, The Wirtschaftswunder; sets, Michael Tonke, Uschi Cyriax, Bolek Gruzinsky; production manager, Klaus Dzuck. Reviewed at Saarbruecken Film Fest (Max Ophuls Prize), Jan. 23, '83. Running time: 96 MINS.

Cast: Peter Halas (Captain of Russian wheat-freighter "Sovjetskij Sojus"), Stephen Balint (Party Secretary of ship), Eva Buchmueller (woman sailor), Peter Berg (drunken sailor), Tom Dokoupil (Dimitri), Sheryle Sutton (Olivia), Gabor Altorjay, Thamas Staub, Karo Heinecke, Otmar Hitzelberger, Sid Gautama, Rene Durand, Angelo Galizia, Joram Bejerano, Oskar O. Hancke, Ahmadschah Ahmadi, Uli Dietzel, Knud Knabe.

Gabor Altorjay's "Tscherwonez" refers in its title to the gold piece used as monetary exchange in Russia since the 15th century, the coin still commonly in use in the Soviet Union today. In German banks the 10-ruble gold piece is worth approximately 200 marks, or circa $85. In the film it's the one sure way for an escaped sailor on a Russian freighter in the port city of Hamburg to get around the city on his own — he simply has to cash in the coin for marks at the local bank.

The comedy satirizes two well known film classics' "Potemkin" and "Ninotchka," both apparent in opening shots and delightfully integrated into the plot from the start. A sailor named Dimitri Bogomas is in search of his long-lost brother, Boris, who settled in Hamburg many years ago due to his father's German nationality. Dimitri is worried because he hasn't heard from Boris in four years. So with a handful of gold-rubles, he decides to "abandon ship" for an illegal day's leave to comb the waterfront dives for his kin. He does so by ducking his companions in an American-style Burger King, whereupon the chase for the fugitive Dimitri is on.

A subplot involves the murder in an elevator of the lift's operator: it later turns out that the victim was a former Nazi criminal now returned from abroad to deal in illegal trade. Further, due to the fact that the Soviet Secret Police has left the freighter in search of their runaway sailor, the German Secret Police sets out on the tracks of both Dimitri and the KGB.

The gags are often fresh and original. The thesps (the leads played by members of the Hungarian-based SQUAT theatre, now active in Gotham) are a riot in deadpan roles that require little, if any, verbal text to put the point across. And the in-jokes are more than amusing: one involved the quirky, bouncy soundtrack throughout the chase, and another is the eye-catching mixture of sepia-tones in a mixed b&w and color print. All in all, "Tscherwonez" is a film buff's film — a sure bet in a repertory house with either "Potemkin" or "Ninotchka" on a double-bill. Winner of the UNIFILM (Saarbruecken University Students) Prize at Saarbruecken. —*Holl.*

Nuclearvision
(WEST GERMAN-COLOR)

Saarbruecken, Jan. 24.

A Robot Film Production. Features entire cast. Written and directed by James Jacobs and Guenther Seltmann. Camera (color). Jacobs. Reviewed at Saarbruecken Film Fest (Max Ophuls Prize), Jan. 23, '83. Running time: 82 MINS.

Cast: Peter Ambach (Tom Broken), Jutta Ilzhoefer, Roland Eisenmenger, Werner Eichhorn.

James Jacobs and Guenther Seltmann's "Nuclearvision" was made for the Peace Movement and Disarmament Protest Groups in West Germany and Europe, its message aimed at the White House and the Kremlin, however. The idea is to show how an ordinary journalist can be awakened to the catastrophe threatening all of humanity by a contract to make a film on something like "What To Do in Case of Atomic War" (the title of the proposed tv-production is never given).

The journalist, shown to be a rather shallow individual in the beginning, travels to Houston to visit an American military base and learns there at first hand that a computer in a sterilized control-center practically governs the fate of humanity without much interference from a debilitating presidency in the White House. He also feels that the West German Ministry of Defense in Bonn has the blinders on as well, so he tries to eject himself from the project in mid-flight.

This leads to some consternation on his employers' part, and our journalist becomes a security risk. There's also a dream sequence in the film dealing with Hiroshima victims, whose images are superimposed on healthy nude skin surfaces for the purpose of dialectical argument. Pic is stuffed with stop-the-bomb hypo. —*Holl.*

Klassengefluester
(Class Whispers)
(SWISS-B&W)

Saarbruecken, Feb. 1.

An Odyssee Film Production, Zurich. Features entire cast. Directed by Nino Jacusso and Franz Rickenbach. Screenplay, students and apprentices from Wasseramt/Solothurn; camera (b&w), Pio Corradi; music, Ben Jeger. Reviewed at Saarbruecken Film Fest (Max Ophuls Prize), Jan. 21, '83. Running time: 90 MINS.

Cast: students and apprentices from Wasseramt (Solothurn, Guido von Salis, Danielle Giuliani; Gian Toendury, Hans Heinrich Ruegg.

Nino Jacusso and Franz Rickenbach's "Class Whispers" scores as a top quality challenger among the Swiss German entries at Saarbruecken in the prestigious Max Ophuls Competition. Half fiction, half documentary, it's a portrait of an entire secondary school class in the year before graduation (at circa 12-years-old, a year lived through with aching impatience). The filmmakers recruited a dozen or more high school kids, and others of the same age bracket already apprenticed in trade professions, to work with them intimately on the project from the start to finish. In effect, the screenplay became a collective exercise for the schoolclass without any outside interference.

It's a fascinating idea, one that has been tried with success before in German cinema (Dietrich Schubert's fiction-documentary on a boy graduating from high school into a tool and dye apprenticeship, "Just Let It Pass For Now") and even on the German stage (British director Pip Simmons's production on the Baader-Meinhof/Group, "The First Baader-Meinhof Play"). The idea is that once a spontaneous notion or improvised scene has been nailed down via rehearsals to portray reality, the acting before the camera takes on an unaffected and totally natural mode of expression. Further, this is how the school class sees its own milieu in frank and uncompromising terms.

Naturally, certain motifs rise to the surface in the process of preparing such a fiction-documentary treatment. The first is the arrival of a new student in the school: she's not readily accepted by the others and experiences a time of loneliness, until one of the boys takes a liking for her and appreciates her self-assurance despite the obstacle she faces. Later, when that relationship is betrayed (one love affair burns out, another apparently begins for the lad), she feels deeply hurt and loses, for a moment, that very self-assurance that previously supported her.

The second is that age-old problem of an uncaring teacher who tyrannizes his class instead of awakening a love for knowledge. A student, another girl, is forced one day to stay after school to write out a task as punishment, whereupon she steals his "black book" of notes and comments on the class members. The teacher threatens to expel the culprit and demands that the class suffer as a whole until justice is done, so the girl lets her schoolmates know that she is guilty. The finale has the entire class turning the tables on the sadistic teacher, and winning the day.

A final scene shows life after graduation. A different class passes through a bottling-factory, and the camera in conclusion pans to two girls (our former protagonists) standing wearily on an assembly line. This recalls the closing shot in that Italian classic made by Ermanno Olmi: "Il Posto" showing youth snuffed out almost overnight by the dire necessity of simply working to earn a living. —*Holl.*

Das Zweite Gesicht
(The Second Face)
(WEST GERMAN-COLOR)

Saarbruecken, Jan. 23.

A Tura Film Production, Michael Wiedemann, producer, in coproduction with Bayerischer Rundfunk (BR), Munich. Features entire cast. Written and directed by Dominik Graf. Camera (color), Helge Weindler; music, Bela Bartok. Reviewed at Saarbruecken Film Fest (Max Ophuls Prize), Jan. 22, '83. Running time: 101 MINS.

Cast: Thomas Schuecke, Greta Scacchi, Franz Buchrieser, Brigitte Karner.

Upon winning a German Film Prize last year for his episode "Running Blue" in the omnibus feature "Noon City," Dominik Graf made his first debut feature, "The Second Face," along much the same lines: a combination horror and suspense thriller with nods to Alfred Hitchcock and Roman Polanski.

A young man returns after a prolonged vacation abroad to Munich and a routine job in an optical firm, although he knows that he's not about to fit in anywhere in today's society. He meets a girl who works in a bookstore: this young lady is tormented mentally by deja-vu images of having been in an apartment building before and a nightmare of possibly having committed suicide here a hundred years ago. In the end, it all comes true: boy murders girl in a bloodsquirting affair.

For the first half-hour, tight editing and a visual finesse (lensing by the very competent Helge Weindler) offer some promise, but it all leads to naught mid-way through tale and falls flat in its own ketchup in the end. One of pic's puzzling aspects is the music and sound effect-laden soundtrack, much of which disrupts the continuity of the horror theme. —*Holl.*

Milo Barus - Der Staerkste Mann Der Welt
(Milo Barus - The Strongest Man in the World)
(WEST GERMAN-COLOR)

Saarbruecken, Jan. 23.

A Tura Film, Hamburg, coproduction with Film Kompanie, Pro-Ject Film in Filmverlag der Autoren, Munich, and Westdeutscher Rundfunk (WDR), Cologne. Features entire cast. Directed by Henning Stegmueller. Screenplay, Stegmueller, Detten Schleiermacher; camera (color), Paco Joan; music, Jim Sust. Reviewed at Saarbruecken Film Fest (Max Ophuls Prize), Jan. 22, '83. Running time: 110 MINS.

Cast: Guenther Lamprecht (Emil Bahr, alias Milo Barus), Maria-Agnes Reintgen, Horst Raspe, the Mai Family.

Debut pic by a grad of the Munich Film Academy, Henning Stegmueller, "Milo Barus - The Strongest Man in the World" is one of those projects buried under the weight of its ambitions — in the end, it comes across as a stereotyped German tv-production. Lensed partially in Czechoslovakia, it's the story of a real-life "Strongest Man in the World" from the Sudetenland section across the border in present-day Czechoslovakia — one Emil Bahr (his German name), or Milo Barus (his artistic monicker), who claimed the title in a 1935 world competition.

The rub in the story is that this circus-type strongman and one-time wrestler (he killed a man in the ring by accident) is despised by the Nazis in his village because he apparently likes everyone and disowns his Aryan heritage. During the war, he was active in the Czech resistance, was jailed for a time, and then forever after plagued by ex-Nazis when he attempted to perform in his traveling-circus act. Later, he drifts to Sweden to escape his tormentors, then back to West Germany again — and finally to East Germany, where his independent stance and outspoken ways get him into trouble again. Pretty mild moviemaking. —*Holl.*

Herzlichen Glueckwunsch
(Warm Congratulations)
(WEST GERMAN-COLOR)

Saarbruecken, Jan. 23.

A Quest-Voigt Film, Berlin. Features entire cast. Written and directed by Wolfgang Quest and Axel Voight. Camera (color), Guenther Fehrer. Reviewed at Saarbruecken Film Fest (Max Ophuls Prize), Jan. 22, '83. Running time: 88 MINS.

Cast: Harald Maack, Jochen Kolenda, Frank Schuster, Rudi Knauss.

One doesn't have to have the entire series of recent and current German "worker films" before your eyes to appreciate Wolfgang Quest and Axel Voight's "Warm Congratulations," but it helps. This is an hilarious spoof of would-be leftist filmers attempting to make a documentary on a typical laborer. Quest and Voight recently graduated from the Berlin Film Academy, and their previous effort as colloaborating scripters was on Manfred Stelzer's comedy "Pearl of the Caribbean" (1980), a howl of a diploma film for all concerned.

Picture three committed filmers from a film school in search of a young worker to make a leftist docu classic imitative of the 1970s. This projected "Portrait of a Worker" takes on flesh-and-blood when "Dieter — One of Us" is found tinkering on his jalopy one sunny afternoon. Dieter is naive enough to bed the students down in his apartment (naturally, three on one mat), whereupon these German Film Academy students construct a myth around their captive subject. After a visit to Dieter's family, interviews with the boss, and angling to get Dieter's small print-shop to join a union, they move to get the three new union-members to call a strike, and so on.

The "worker" features of the 1970s had their rightful place in New German Cinema history, and so do several serious documentaries made by Klaus Wildenhahn, Dietrich Schubert, and others. But some German production companies have recently moved in with working-class families with camera and microphone in search of a questionable on-the-spot authenticity. These heavy-handed filmers grind out films like newborn Joris Ivens types: docus without humor and laden with endless self-deprecating gab — plus the Marxist magic of a strike-threat to cure the ills of Capitalist society.

"Warm Congratulations" is an accurate observation of this ongoing syndrome in contemporary German cinema. It's also a riotous satire, one that should not be missed by scribes and historians who are also out to write the authentic history of the New German Cinema movement. —*Holl.*

Ente Oder Trente
(Put Up or Shut Up)
(WEST GERMAN-COLOR)

Saarbruecken, Jan. 24.

A C&H Film Production, Berlin, in co-production with Westdeutscher Rundfunk (WDR), Cologne. Features entire cast. Directed by Rigo Manikofski. Screenplay, Guenter Schulz; camera (color), Gunther Damm. Reviewed at Saarbruecken Film Fest (Max Ophuls Prize), Jan. 23, '83. Running time: 92 MINS.

Cast: Gottfried John (Glentz), Ute Cremer (Katharina), Leslie Malton, Ricci Mainz, Tobias Hoesl, Barbara Stanek, Albert Heins.

Rigo Manikofski's "Put Up or Shut Up" (a rough translation of the prison-jargon German title) is his first independent feature. He previously codirected with Karsten Wichniarz a low-budget diploma feature film, "No Land" (1980), at the Berlin Film Academy, another portrait of an outsider surviving on the edge of the underworld.

This time, a former Foreign Legion recruit is trying to go straight with a new job as a store detective. But he takes his work too seriously and beats the petty criminals he catches to a pulp. Glentz (played convincingly by Gottfried John) just doesn't know his own strength, and has to be reluctantly let go by the department store owner. The chances for further employment turn out to be nil, for he has to show his papers first, and his past alone makes him suspect. He soon turns to his old ways, and ends up in prison for drunkenly clubbing a woman with whom he has had a brief affair.

Here comes the twist: the former lady friend, a social worker, was caught by Glentz in the act of shop-lifting some time before, and now she feels guilty for getting her legionaire into trouble for something that is equally her fault. So she refuses to press charges for the attack, personally picks him up at the jailhouse, and invites him to join her commune, the WG Front. This makes for a problem of readjustment, but it soon become clear that the commune is as antisocial as they come — shoplifting and break-ins are okay so far as the greedy establishment is concerned.

At the urging of the fiery members of the WG Front, he organizes a break-in at the place he formerly guarded as a house detective. It turns out to be a bit of an embarrassment when one of the kids goes off on his own, and gets caught. Glentz pulls up stakes again, and leaves town — on the run once more.

Tale has more than enough potential to score, but too much was packed into the film to offer anything more than modest b.o. success. Gottfried John, a former character-actor in Rainer Werner Fassbinder films, carries the film on his performance alone. Manikofski, who obviously has a feeling for the cops-and-robbers milieu, is a name to watch in the German "New Generation" movement.

— *Holl.*

Local Hero
(COLOR)

Delightful comedy will need patient push to allow for word-of-mouth.

Hollywood, Feb. 8.

A Warner Bros. release of an Enigma production for Goldcrest. Produced by David Puttnam. Stars Burt Lancaster. Written and directed by Bill Forsyth. Camera (color), Chris Menges; editor, Michael Bradsell; music, Mark Knopfler; production design, Roger Murray-Leach; art direction, Richard James, Adrienne Atkinson. Frank Walsh, Ian Watson; sound, Louis Kramer; special effects, Wally Veevers; associate producer, Iain Smith; assistant director, Jonathan Benson. Reviewed at The Burbank Studios, Burbank, Feb. 8, 1983. (MPAA Rating: PG). Running time: 111 MINS.

Felix Happer	Burt Lancaster
Mac MacIntyre	Peter Riegert
Ben	Fulton MacKay
Gordon Urquhart	Denis Lawson
Moritz	Norman Chancer
Danny Oldsen	Peter Capaldi
Geddes	Rikki Fulton
Watt	Alex Norton
Marina	Jenny Seagrove
Stella	Jennifer Black
Victor	Christopher Rozycki
Rev. Macpherson	Christopher Asante

After making the grade internationally with the sleeper hit, "Gregory's Girl," Scottish writer-director Bill Forsyth has broken the sophomore jinx the only way he could, by making an even better film. While modest in intent and gentle in feel, "Local Hero" is loaded with wry, offbeat humor and is the sort of satisfying, personal picture that is becoming an increasingly rare commodity these days. David Puttnam's first production since "Chariots Of Fire" has little in the way of obvious commercial hooks, and Warners will have to give it a chance to breathe if it's to make its way in the world, but good reviews followed by word of mouth could build it into a steady b.o. performer.

Essentially a comedy about a serious situation, pic is dominated by a constantly surprising sense of whimsicality which never becomes predictable and therefore catches the viewer off guard throughout. Basic story has Peter Riegert, rising young executive in an enormous Houston oil firm, sent to Scotland to cinch a deal to buy up an entire village, where the company intends to construct a new oil refinery.

Given the ecological consciousness that's spread in recent years, first switch on normal expectations is that, far from being resistant to the idea of having their surroundings ruined by rapacious, profit-minded Yankees, local Scots can hardly wait to sign away their town, so strong is the smell of money in the air.

Naturally, negotiations take somewhat longer than expected, which means that Riegert can't help but become involved in the affairs of the natives. But there is no predictable romance, no con-vulsive occurrence to push the film into false melodrama. Basically, whole story is comprised of delight-ful human moments, with just enough narrative push to keep it moving.

Back in Houston, oil magnate Burt Lancaster keeps up to date on the deal's progress with occasional phone calls to Riegert, but is more concerned with his prodding, sadis-tic psychiatrist and his obsessive hobby of astronomy, which seems to dictate everything he does. Char-acter is a looney conception, and Lancaster gives it a marvelously bonkers reading, although ending of the film falls somewhat flat due to the illogical nature of the man's cli-mactic decisions.

Almost in the manner of classic American comedies of the 1930s, pic is overflowing with memorable supporting characters. There's Riegert's Scottish oil company counterpart, whose accent is so thick one thinks they might not be able to communicate well in Eng-lish, but who turns out to speak over a half-dozen languages; the local parson, a man named Mac-pherson, who happens to be a black African; the manager and cook of the village's only inn, who wears another hat as the chief negotiator of the deal; a beautiful young woman with a special interest in the sea, who physically seems to have begun a transformation into a mer-maid, and a visiting Russian sailor with an active interest in Western investment markets and a very un-usual style as a country-western singer.

Just when it appears that Riegert has finally struck a deal with the locals, a major snag crops up and Lancaster himself turns up on the beach to iron things out. Although it's been well prepared for, ending nevertheless comes off as uncon-vincing, given the economic imperatives of the oil business.

Riegert's underplaying initially seems a bit inexpressive, but ulti-mately pays off in what emerges as a droll performance with a soup-con of moral and emotional awak-ening. As his Scottish buddy, the gangling Peter Capaldi is vastly amusing, and Denis Lawson is very good as the community's chief spokesman.

Two main women present, Jenny Seagrove as the aptly named Marina and Jennifer Black as Law-son's warm wife, are terrifically at-tractive and provide ample fan-tasy material for Capaldi and Rie-gert, respectively.

Pic not only benefits from the beautiful Scottish setting, but from the remarkable contrast between it and Houston. In look and tempera-ment, two locales could hardly be more dissimilar, an aspect which quietly underlines one of film's im-portant themes.

Given a larger canvas, director Forsyth has in no way attempted to overreach himself or the material, keeping things modest and inti-mate throughout, but displaying a very acute sense of comic insight. Tech work is fine, and a lot of imagi-nation has gone into the fabulous design of Lancaster's penthouse abode. —*Cart.*

Le Battant
(The Cache)
(FRENCH-COLOR)

Paris, Feb. 7.

AMLF release of an Adel Productions film. Produced and directed by and star-ring Alain Delon. Screenplay, Delon and Christopher Frank, from a novel by Andre Caroff. Camera, Jean Tournier; art di-rector, Theo Meurisse; editor, Michel Lewin; music, Christian Dorisse; sound, Michel Desrois; production manager, Henri Jacquillard. Reviewed at Gaumont Ambassade theatre, Feb. 6, 1983. Running time: 122 MINS.
Jacques Darnay .... Alain Delon
Ruggeri .... Francois Perier
Rouxel .... Pierre Mondy
Clarisse ..... Marie-Christine Descouard
Mignot .... Michel Beaune

No surprises, alas, from Alain Delon His new film proudly bears his name as producer, director, co-screenwriter and, of course, star, leaving no doubt about who's to blame for the numbing mediocrity of this thriller without thrills, drama or anything else usually associated with good commercial entertain-ment. Delon continues to be faith-ful to the image he thinks the public wants to see. But to judge from ear-ly boxoffice returns, the public may be tiring of his refrigerated mag-netism and scrappy suspense ve-hicles.

Script casts Delon as a lone-wolf hood who's just served a prison term for a jewelry job in which the dealer was killed. Intent on re-covering the gems he'd stashed away before his arrest, he finds himself up against other gangsters and police also interested in the loot. Killing his antagonists and hood-winking the cops he manages to get away with the goods (and the girl).

Surround himself as he may with good actors (Francois Perier, Pierre Mondy, Michel Beaune) and competent technicians, Delon can-not hide the dismaying vacuity of script and unfeeling predictability of his direction and performance.

Delon, by the way, dedicated this film to director Rene Clement, "my master," who helped pave the ac-tor's way to stardom in the early '60s. A dubious compliment, given the results. —*Len.*

Doctor Faustus
(DUTCH-COLOR-16m)

Amsterdam, Jan. 25.

An Eerste Amsterdamse Filmassociatie production. Features entire cast. Directed by Rene Seegers. Screenplay. Seegers, Leon de Winter. Jean van de Velde, Peter de Baan; producer, van de Velde. Camera (color), Sjoerd Jansen. No other credits provided. Reviewed at Filmmuseum, Am-sterdam, Dec. 23, 1982. Running time: 80 MINS.
Johan Vuist .... Krijn ter Braak
Margriet Vuist .... Jara Lucieer
Mephisto .... Bruce Gray
Kees .... Peter de Baan
Aga .... Anita Menist

Three young men who met at the Netherlands Film Academy in 1974 left in 1977 loudly protesting that the courses were not worthwhile. Rene Seegers, Jean van de Velde and Leon de Winter have since then (from '80 onwards under the name Eerste Amsterdamse Filmasso-ciatie) made three documentaries, three feature films, and a number of television programs.

They write regularly, as a three-some or individually, for news-papers and magazines, and De Winter ranks with his short stories and novels among the top Dutch authors of his generation. Their work is original, offbeat without be-ing precious, and shows a fresh, striking approach to meaningful image-making. They are intelli-gent and very painstaking.

Their third feature, "Doctor Faustus," is neither documentary nor fiction, but a combination. Its main theme is the sense of doom which permeates the thoughts and feelings of many in this atomic age. A subsidiary theme is the disap-pearance of belief in Progress of which Goethe's Faust is seen as a kind of representative.

In the fictional part, a film-maker, Johan Vuist ("vuist" is the Dutch translation of the German noun "Faust") undergoes many kinds of tribulation. His wife leaves him; he can't communicate with other people except, somewhat, with his young daughter Margriet.

Vuist (brilliantly played by Krijn ter Braak) loses faith in his current work, a documentary about man-kind's progress to Doomsday. The documentary seg contains a num-ber of interviews with well-known economists, psychologists, politi-cians and sociologists

Some of them furnish explana-tions for the sudden or gradual stop-ping of the automatic growth which has been labelled progress. None of them has a panacea. They seem re-signed, or perplexed, that progress can be withering.

The feature part of the film does not offer any solution either. It ends gloomily or does it? The fear of doom seems to become less im-portant than the dread of empti-ness. Seegers admits that he gives "no answer to the existential ques-tion, the meaning of death," and adds "there is nothing for it but to go on searching." And Mephisto (yes, he does appear in the film) is jeal-ous of all human beings, because they always have a choice "and I, poor devil, haven't."

Notwithstanding the thematic complexity and the philosophical undertones the film manages to re-main quite simple and clear. This is due to the strong structure and the subtle mixture of fiction and docu-mentary.

"Doctor Faustus," though incon-clusive, remains intriguing. —*Wall.*

Le Japon De Francois Reichenbach
(Francois Reichenbach's Japan)
(FRENCH-DOCU-COLOR)

Paris, Feb. 8.

GEF/CCFC release of a Films des Deux Mondes/France Opera Films/FR3 copro-duction. Produced by Jean-Loup Puzenat. Exec producer, Jean-Jacques Four-geaud. Directed by Francois Reichen-bach. Commentary, Tada Takemoto; camera (color), Reichenbach, Gerard de Battista; sound, Bernard Ortion; Akira Kurosu, Akira Ishizaki; music, Jean-Claude Eloi; editor, Yves Deschamps; production manager, Alain Coiffier; asso-ciate producer, Film Company Stuttgart. Reviewed at the Cine Beaubourg Theatre, Paris, Feb. 6, 1983. Running time: 90 MINS.

The Japan of docu filmmaker Francois Reichenbach is certainly exotic enough, but curiously cheer-less and unenticing. Reichen-bach's 90-minute promenade through a complex and contradic-tory culture is full of images that should hold the viewer, yet one feels indifferent, when not slightly re-pelled. It's an anti-tourism trave-log.

Reichenbach films what one would expect a Westerner to film: traditional rites and customs, mar-tial arts exercises, urban Japan in the grips of dehumanizing technol-ogy and the incursions of Western culture, etc. There are no inter-views, and the faces the filmmaker has chosen for closeups are some-times terrifying in their inexpres-siveness. Is contemporary Japan-ese life as soulless as this film would have us believe?

The director assembles his foot-age without much rhyme or reason and provides little indication or analysis for what we see. Only com-mentary are rather abstract thoughts spoken on the soundtrack by Japanese writer Tada Take-moto, offering such tantalizing ob-servations as: "The Japanese are the only people who think about nothing ..." What such pronounce-ments might mean doesn't seem to rpeoccupy Reichenbach unduly, who is content to record and let the viewer make what he can of it.
—*Len.*

Le Ruffian
(The Ruffian)
(FRENCH-CANADIAN-COLOR)

Paris, Jan. 19.

AMLF release of a Films Christian Fechner/Parma Films/Corporation Image (Montreal) coproduction. Pro-duced by Christian Fechner. Stars Lino Ventura, Bernard Giraudeau. Written and directed by Jose Giovanni. Camera (color), Jean-Paul Schwartz; music, En-

nio Morricone; art director, Willy Holt; editor, Jacqueline Thiedot; sound, Patrick Rousseau. Reviewed at the Gaumont Ambassade theatre, Paris, Jan. 15, 1983. Running time: 107 MINS.
Aldo .... Lino Ventura
Gerard .... Bernard Giraudeau
The Baroness .... Claudia Cardinale
Eleonore .... Beatrix Van Til
John .... Pierre Frag

Novelist-filmmaker Jose Giovanni has earned his best screen credits as adaptor of his own novels for other filmmakers, notably Jacques Becker ("Le Trou"), Jean-Pierre Melville ("Le Deuxieme Souffle"), and Claude Sautet ("Classe tout Risque"). As his own director, his tales of male bonding and exhilarating adventure have rarely reached beyond the cliche and a sort of lumpish romanticism.

His new film "Le Ruffian" is hardly different, though the more pleasantly watchable of his recent efforts due to an appealing cast and good, eye-filling locations. The first and last parts are best, as Giovanni concentrates on action in the Canadian wilds. It's the soggy midsection — devoted to the extolling of male camaraderie, with the women coaching amorously from the sidelines — that slows the film down. Fortunately, there are Lino Ventura, Bernard Giraudeau and Claudia Cardinale to keep it from getting too sticky.

Ventura is a footloose adventurer who's working in a north Canadian goldmine when bandits attack the camp and slaughter all but him and two Indian laborers. The three kill their assailants and decide to split the gold themselves, but Ventura dumps his companions and makes off with the booty when he realizes that they have no intention of sharing with him.

Ventura loses the cases of gold when his canoe goes over a waterfall. He returns to Montreal broke, and links up with his old buddy (Giraudeau), a racing car nut who was paralyzed in the legs in an accident, but is succored by an adoring wife (Beatrix Van Til). Together they decide to mount an expedition to retrieve the gold. With the support (especially financial) of Ventura's now and again mistress (Cardinale) and another buddy, (Pierre Frag) they manage to salvage the treasure, overcoming new interventions from the two Indians and a third potential claimant.

The plotting is hoary and the characters stereotyped. But, at least there are the camera-worthy performers (Cardinale is as lovely as ever, even though she has little to do); they manage to fend for themselves, despite the foolishness of the situations and dialog.

No less important an asset is the on-location shooting in Canada, with the Rockies splendidly photographed by Jean-Paul

Schwartz, and a catchy theme by Ennio Morricone. —Len.

Sorceress
(COLOR)

Sword and skin film. Regional playoff item.

A New World Pictures release. Produced by Jack Hill. Directed by Brian Stuart. Stars Leigh Harris, Lynette Harris, Bob Nelson. Screenplay, Jim Wynorski; camera (color), Alex Phillips Jr.; editor, Larry Bock, Barry Zetlin; music, uncredited; sound, Manny Tompkins; assistant director, Mark Conway; production manager, Michael Lima; art direction, Joe Greenman; special effects, New World Effects; creature design & fabrication, John Buechler; stunt coordinator, Robin Martin; animation design, Deborah Gaydos; post-production supervisor, Clark Henderson. Reviewed at Rivoli 1 theatre, N.Y., Feb. 11, 1983. (MPAA Rating: R). Running time: 75 MINS.
Mira .... Leigh Harris
Mara .... Lynette Harris
Erlik .... Bob Nelson
Pando .... David Millbern
Baldar .... Bruno Rey
Dellisia .... Ana De Sade
Traigon .... Robert Ballesteros

New World's lensed-in-Mexico "Sorceress" demonstrates that a "Conan"-type heroic fantasy film can be made on a modest scale, a point soon to be underscored by the dozens of Italian-made imitations poised to hit the market. The Jack Hill production directed by Brian Stuart emphasizes nudity and vulgar humor, with the resulting package likely to appeal to cable-tv viewers after completing its current theatrical run.

Okay storyline by Jim Wynorski is set in an ancient time, deals with twin girls (Leigh and Lynette Harris) brought up as boys and hidden from their evil wizard father Traigon (Robert Ballesteros), who plans to sacrifice the first-born to the forces of darkness in return for increased supernatural powers. Traigon is allied with the beautiful princess Dellisia (Ana De Sade), while the twins are aided in their quest for revenge against their father (who killed their mother) by warrior Erlik (Bob Nelson) and Baldar (Bruno Rey) and friendly satyr Pando (David Millbern).

Punctuated by frequent (and unexciting) sword battles and even some martial arts fights this abbreviated adventure film is largely an excuse for the shapely Harris twins (previously featured in the "I, The Jury" remake) to bare their charms. Hero Bob Nelson provides equal time with nude beefcake scenes but his good ole boy accent (typical of the film's poor dubbing) is just one among many indicators that the filmmakers are spoofing the fantasy genre. In fact, the phony beards, tacky sets and silly jokes make "Sorceress" resemble the quaint softcore porn pageants (e.g., "The Lustful Turk") of the 1960s.

Title is a misnomer, as the well-executed optical effects done at

New World's Venice facility are generally extraneous to the story. Fantasy content includes a meaningless and static finale battle between two opposing gods in the heavens, a silly fight with horny zombies in the catacombs · (as Baldar says, they've been buried for a thousand years) and various cheap makeup creatures such as the red-brown haired monkey men (also horny).

The gimmick of the twins sharing their feelings and experiences at a distance provides a cute sex comedy scene of Mira reacting orgiastically when captured Mara miles away is deflowered by Erlik. Ultimately, the oft-repeated "The two who are one" epithet for the twins is just an excuse for a sex joke at fadeout. They are briefly upstaged by the stunning-looking dark villainess, played by Latin actress Ana De Sade. —Lor.

Schwarzfahrer
(Joy Ride)
(WEST GERMAN-COLOR)

Berlin, Dec. 23.
A Tura Film Production, Munich, in co-production with WDR Cologne and SFB Berlin; producers, Mike Wiedemann and Alexander Wesemann (WDR). Features entire cast. Directed by Manfred Stelzer in collaboration with Gerd Moebius. Screenplay, Stelzer, Gerd Weiss; camera (color), David Slama; editing, Peter Przygodda; sound, Detlev Vichiner; sets, Erwin Wengoborski; music, Kevin Coyne; production manager, Michael Mueller. Reviewed at Kant Kino, Berlin, December 23, '82. Running time: 106 MINS.
Cast: Rolf Zacher (Chris), George Meyer-Goll (Alois), Harald Henschel-Franzmann (Harry), Iris Berben (Lisa), Alisa L. Saltzman (Alisa), Jendrich Mann (court baliff), Diethardt Wendland (Gun Handler), Johanna Karl-Lory (Frau Feuerbach), Nora Bendig (Frau Buske), Bernhard Daessner (Chicken Thrower), Klaus Muenster (Truck Driver), Heinz G. Diesing (Gardener), Martha Kusitzky (Pensioned Woman), Marcus Kiessling (Tommy).

Manfred Stelzer's "Joy Ride" — the German title "Schwarzfahrer" refers to stealing a car for a joy ride — is his second independent feature, following his graduation film from the Berlin Film & TV Academy, "Pearl of the Caribbean" (1981). Before that, he made a number of eye-catching documentaries in collaboration with Johannes Fluetsch.

"Joy Ride" is also about conmen in the Berlin Underworld. Chris (Rolf Zacher) does little else save keep his head just above water, but now he's down on his luck as the court-bailiff is after him to pay the rent on the apartment and other outstanding bills. So he steals a car, and is off for a joy ride — no place in particular, and of course with a newly-found buddy: Alois, who punctures car tires for the quirky fun of it.

The duo becomes a trio when the pair help out another brash type,

Harry, who has a riverboat on a canal and earns a living as a wheeler-dealer. It's when the three happen upon a possible heist — a payroll robbery with a twist: the money is being transferred, quite legally but all too carelessly from West to East Berlin in a pokey little East German "shoebox" vehicle — that the film comes to life and shifts into a thriller gear.

The rest is in the fumbling tradition · of Alec Guinness's mob in "Ladykillers" and Humphrey Bogart's in "Beat the Devil" — no one takes them very seriously, until the job is there on the screen and all the buffoonery adds up to a killing! It's what leads up to that that catches the most attention, however. Stelzer has an easy hand with nonprofessionals and vet thesps (Zacher) in improvised scenes, and he lets his actors carve out their own screen personalities along the way. "Joy Ride" thus is more like a "talking-blues" happening than a filmic narrative line (an element badly needed to become a b.o. winner).

Credits are all a good cut above the average, particularly lensing and directorial flair. Pic has comic touches galore, and Berlin has seldom looked more engaging as a seamy backdrop for smalltime gangsters. Further, there's the political rub: the snatch highlights the incongruity of two Germanys with but a thin wall between them so far as money transactions are concerned. Among the robust gags is one that tends to bring the house down: the installation of peep-holes ("guckies") in apartment doors, a ruse that works to perfection on the unwary bourgeois citizen in modern housing developments.

Catch this one at German Film Weeks or on the fest circuit. Manfred Stelzer is a coming name on the German film scene. —Holl.

Solothurn Fest

Max Haufler, Der Stumme
(Max Haufler, "The Mute")
(SWISS-COLOR-DOCU-16m)

Solothurn, Feb. 15.
A Richard Dindo Film Production, Zurich. Written and directed by Richard Dindo. Camera (color), Rainer Trinkler, Juerg Hassler; sound, Alain Klarer; editing, Dindo, Rainier Trinkler. With Janet Haufler in an acting role. Reviewed at Solothurn Film Days, Jan. 29, '83. Running time: 90 MINS.

Richard Dindo is considered in many quarters to be Switzerland's leading documentary filmmaker, enjoying a reputation for creative thematic treatment equalled in German-language cinema only by Klaus Wildenhahn of West Germany and Wilfried Junge of East Germany. He is particularly a specialist at interpretative sketches of prominent or forgotten Swiss personalities, people whose lives offer keys to comprehending complex chapters in Swiss history this century.

Dindo's latest — "Max Haufler, 'The Mute'" — is about a popular Swiss character actor, Max Haufler, whose greatest ambition was to be a film director. Haufler's pet project was to film Swiss writer Otto F. Walter's novel, "The Mute," but disappointment at not finding backers for the production led to his death by suicide in 1965.

Dindo's interest in the project extends to a short reconstruction of passages in the novel with Janet Haufler, Max's daughter, interpreting the role of the mute as the commentary is read by Walter himself from his bestseller. In general, the ploy works — only the viewer tends to lose sight of Haufler when attention is shifted throughout most of the second half of the film to the aborted production (later produced for German television and directed by an inferior talent than Haufler).

Haufler's biography is the story of frustration facing Swiss cinema as a whole throughout the 1930s, 1940s, and 1950s. Only Haufler's "Farinet" (a Ramuz adaptation) and "People Passing By" (based on a Carl Zuckmayer play) have gone down in film history books, both made during the turbulent 1940s; thereafter, the promising director had to earn his bread as a popular film actor in primarily commercial dramas. His international reputation was also secured in Orson Welles's adaptation of Franz Kafka's "The Trial" (1962), and he was next in Hollywood as supporting actor to Marlon Brando in Bernhard Wicki's "Morituri" (1964).

West German tv-viewers saw him in Peter Lilienthal's "A School of Skills" (1962) and "Striptease" (1963) (scripted by Slawomir Mrozek). There is little doubt that Haufler could earn his bread at home and abroad as an able stage and screen actor — but he was obsessed with the idea of directing "The Mute."

Dindo's version of the Walter book has a quiet; effective approach to a difficult theme: a mute a young man in story, seeks his long-lost father, at a working site, takes a job next to him, and hopes that one day the fateful recognition will take place between father and offspring. One wonders in the course of the film exercise whether such a human tragedy could have been rendered palatable for the commercial audience in the first place. Perhaps Haufler's wary potential backers were right in dropping the lid on the project back then. —Holl.

Giro
(SWISS-B&W-16m)

Solothurn, Feb. 15.

A Hugo Sigrist. Ombra-Film Production. Bern. Features entire cast. Directed by Hugo Sigrist. Screenplay. Max Rueflinger; camera, Clemens Klopfenstein; sets. Serena Kiefers; sound, Pavol Jasovsky; editor, Sigrist. Reviewed at Solothurn Film Days. Jan. 26. Running time: 75 MINS.

Cast: Christine Lauterburg (Chrige), Marianne Derendinger (Lisa), Francesco Micieli (Carlo). Max Ruedlinger (Andy).

A film without a real beginning or an end, Hugo Sigrist's debut pic, "Giro," is about restlessness and boredom among young people. As in many contemporary French, German and Swiss features, nothing is really supposed to happen to disrupt the mood fashioned at some pains by the shooting team. As a matter of fact, both the theme and the direction lean heavily — much too heavily — in the direction of Michelangelo Antonioni, particularly "L'Avventura" of a full generation ago.

Chrige lives with Andy in a Bern commune, whose preoccupations are presently with archaeological diggings. They have a spat over the community dinner-table, then she's off with a girlfriend, Lisa, on a trip to Umbria in Italy. There Lisa is kept busy with a job, but Chrige lolls around with nothing to do but maintain a loose contact with Andy by telephone and letters. Next comes Carlo, Lisa's cousin, who owns the apartment they're living in and a relationship develops. However, they're from two different worlds, and that too, along with the film, comes to naught. —Holl.

Trans Atlantique
(SWISS-COLOR)

Solothurn, Jan. 29.

An Ariane Film and Limbo Film Coproduction, Zurich. Features entire cast. Written and directed by Hans-Ulrich Schlumpf. Camera (color), Pio Corradi; art direction, Beatrice Pfenninger, Thema Selection Zurich; sound, Hans Kuenzi; music, Baden Powell; editor, Fee Liechti. Reviewed at Solothurn Film Days, Jan. 29, '83. Running time: 108 MINS.

Cast: Zaira Zambelli (Zaira Gelbert), Roger Jendly (Roger Wiedmer), Renate Schroeter, Balz Raz, the crew and passengers of the "Eugenio C."

"Trans Atlantique" is helmer Hans-Ulrich Schlumpf's first feature after making a number of docus and shorts. It also scores as the one outstanding feature at the 1983 Solothurn Film Days, where the year's productions are unspooled over a six-day stint. Pic has enough in the way of polished credits and comic acting to guarantee it a slot at an international fest or two, although offshore chances are limited to the arthouse circuit.

The joke is on right from the beginning: a Zurich enthnologist is determined to retrace the steps of his favorite author and book, Claude Levy-Strauss's "Tristes Tropiques," across the Atlantic on a ship from Genoa to Rio de Janeiro. Although married and cushioned with an academic job, he feels hemmed-in by life and professional restrictions — besides, his wife would like to crown a decade of marriage with a child, which would mean the end of our protagonist's long-desired Levy-Strauss adventure. But picture an ethnologist who can't speak a word of Portuguese, with visions of ethnographic research dancing in his head like sugarplums, and you have the general drift of this shipboard comedy — the straight-laced Swiss nerd is going to rocket into space at the drop of the first lady passenger's handkerchief.

The lady happens to be a born-and-bred Brazilian who is returning home to mother and family after bumming around Europe for two years as a would-be student and go-go dancer. The two communicate in French, but the principal line of chatter is about the difference between two continents and two civilizations. When the anthropologist says he hopes to study the Brazilian Indians first-hand, the girl simply leads him down to the engine-room to watch one at work. And when he gabs on about his job, she cues him into doing taperecorded interviews with the passengers — it provides the film with some of its most spontaneous and detailed footage: tourists, emigrants, crew, missionaries, and one mad-hatter of a stowaway who keeps getting into our researcher's hair.

In the end, as the boat nears Rio, the ethnologist is more interested in a roll in the hay than his hearth at home or the rigors of his proposed venture into the jungles of Brazil, so the girl proposes he stay in Rio and let Daddy help find him a job there — for it's definite that she won't tag along with him as his interpreter and companion. They part at Rio, and our hero is left alone on board as the boat cruises further down coast in the direction of "Tristes Tropiques" country.

Lensing is topnotch (Pio Corradi is one of Switzerland's best cameramen), which more than makes up for lapses in story line. —Holl.

Melzer
(SWISS-W. GERMAN-COLOR)

Solothurn, Jan. 27.

A Heinz Buetler Film production, in coproduction with Zweites Deutsches Fernsehen (ZDF), Mainz, tv-producer, Christoph Holch. Features entire cast. Written and directed by Heinz Buetler. Camera (color), Hansueli Schenkel; sets, Kurt Hiltebrand; music, Jan Garbarek, Charlie Haden, Egberto Gismonti; sound, Florian Eidenbenz, Hanspeter Fischer; editor, Markus Fischer, Heinz Buetler, Peter Schneider. Reviewed at Solothurn Film Days, Jan. 27, '83. Running time: 90 MINS.

Cast: Ruediger Vogler (Mauro Melzer), Ingo Lampe, Nicolas Lansky, Adelheid Arndt, Christel Foertsch, Ingeborg Arnoldi, Susanne Peter, Erwin Parker, Heinrich Trimbur.

Upon making an impressive docu on schizophrenia, "For the Improvement of the Individual" (1981), helmer Heinz Buetler tried his hand at much the same theme in his first feature, "Melzer," the tale of a successful painter who voluntarily commits himself to a psychiatric clinic. Mauro Melzer (Ruediger Vogler) is in a crisis, a situation he looks upon as related to the creative retreat of Robert Walser, a Swiss scribe venerated in these parts as another Franz Kafka and Melzer's favorite writer. Naturally, when an artist of some repute wants to be looked upon as mad, objections arise in all quarters — the clinic's psychiatrist, in particular, agrees with a gallery proprietress in her idea to present a full retro of the painter's work. In fact, the clinic purchases a Melzer original for hanging — our painter practically has a fit at this affront.

During the exhibit, Melzer is free to leave the clinic to attend the affair. But instead of going to the gallery, he wanders the streets and has an affair in a darkened alley with an accommodating whore at the very moment when a cocktail party in the gallery allows for a similar form of intellectual masturbation. Thereafter, he visits his former apartment to meet the new tenant — a lovely young lady with an understanding glimmer in her eye for his peculiar idiosyncrasies — our painter ventures up on the roof in the course of the evening, and the comic absurdity of it all seems, in the end, to be leading him out of the crisis.

Despite credits being on the plus side, the story doesn't have a point-of-view to carry it along — save that a lot of normal people occupy nuthouses, while the real nuts pass as normal individuals at cocktail parties. —Holl.

Xunan
(The Lady)
(SWISS-COLOR-DOCU-16m)

Solothurn, Jan. 30.

A Margrit Keller Film Production, Zurich, in coproduction with Cinov Film, Bern. Directed by Margrit Keller, Peter von Gunten. Screenplay, Margrit Keller; camera (color), Peter von Gunten; editor, Fredi M. Murer; sound, Thomas Pfister, Pavol Jasovsky. Reviewed at Solothurn Film Days, Jan. 29, '83. Running time: 107 MINS.

Margrit Keller and Peter von Gunten's "Xunan" (The Lady) was two years in the making, filmed in Mexico in 1980 and 1982 with a year's pause in between when Keller could not finish the docu (then titled "Point of No Return"), with lenser Peter M.

Schneider and Gunten called in to finish the project. In the original version, the focus was entirely on a former Bern resident, Gertrude Dueby-Blom, who left Switzerland 40 years ago to work with refugees in Mexico due to her commitment tô the anti-fascist Resistance Movement. She stayed in the country upon marrying an oil businessman-turned-archeologist, and settled in a large mansion in the Chiapas jungles after the war to befriend the Lacandonae Indians (descendants of the Mayans now in some danger of extinction).

"Xunan" (The Lady) is the name the Indians themselves have given to Dueby-Blom, while tourists and adventure-minded students from North American campuses simply settle for "Trudi" in referring to the well-liked octogenarian (born in 1901). For Keller's film, she led the shooting crew on a trip into the jungle to visit tribes of this declining civilization, a trip on horseback and by canoe over rather rough terrain. The emphasis changed, however, upon the arrival of von Gunten: he decided to focus on the clearing of the forests, particularly the mass stripping of mahogany trees. It is indeed painful to watch these magnificent trees that took some 500 years to reach their noble stature cut down in a matter of minutes and hauled off to a sawing mill in the area. Interviews with workers on the job and various business people indicate that the entire mahogany forests are to be cleared for an enormous profit — thereafter, roads through the jungle are to be constructed to reach the rich oilfields near the Guatemala border.

One of the film's moving scenes is an interview with an Indian named Chan K'in, an elderly Lacandona, who recalls the past before the missionaries came, followed by the exploiters of the forests. It's clear from his account that the Mayan race will now move swiftly in the direction of extinction due to the recent oil discovery on the border. —Holl.

Unsere Eltern Haben Den Ausweis C
(Our Parents Have the Foreigners' Work Permit C)
(SWISS-COLOR-DOCU-16m)

Solothurn, Jan. 28.

A Film & Video Collectif Film Production, Ecublens. Written, directed, and photographed by Eduard Winiger, assisted by Mia Froelicher. Sound, Luc Yersin. Winiger; editing. Hannelore Kuenzi, Franziska Wirz. Reviewed at Solothurn Film Days, Jan. 27, '83. Running time: 150 MINS.

Eduard Winiger's docu, "Our Parents Have the Foreigners' Work Permit C" deals with foreign workers from the Mediterranean

countries, from Spain to Turkey, working in Switzerland. A two-part tv production, the first film is titled "Change of Shifts" and the second "Way to School — Between Two Worlds." As these titles hint, the first has to do with the families and their reasons for coming to Switzerland in the first place, while the second tackles the problem of the kids beginning Swiss schools and thus learning a new culture and way-of-life different from the one at home.

Winiger has analyzed the problem so completely that to see the film to comprehend the lot of foreign-workers in a technically advanced country. One conclusion is obvious: most of these workers find it easier after a while to stay in their newly adopted country rather than return to the uncertainties of their own homelands with shaky economic standards. A most informative docu on a quite complex problem. —Holl.

Die Verborgenen Taenze
(Hidden Dances)
(SWISS-COLOR-16m)

Solothurn, Jan. 26.

A Filmkollektiv Zurich Production, in collaboration the Society for Research and Preservation of Folk Music in Oberwallis. Features entire cast. Written and directed by Peter Schweiger. Camera (color), Rob Gnant; editor, Georg Janett; music, Oberwalliser Spillit; sound, Roger Bonnot; lighting. Werner Santschi; sets, Hans Gloor. Reviewed at Solothurn Film Days, Jan. 26, '83. Running time: 55 MINS.

Cast: Inhabitants of Binntal, Oberwalliser Spillit, Walpen Brothers.

Peter Schweiger's "Hidden Dances" is a docu-fiction account of music and musicians in an Oberwalliser (Upper Valais) village, a kind of folkloric heritage pic.

A pair of young musicians travel from the city to visit the Walpen Brothers in their mountain cabin to hear them play their latest composition for homemade zither-like instruments. The playing attracts neighboring villagers, and soon the whole community is dancing to "spillit" tunes on an improvised wooden platform. Between each number a village tells a tall tale about "hidden dances" experienced in the hills — way back when it was forbidden to dance to music in this remote, puritanically minded area, and the offenders were thereafter condemned to dance on the glacier until the Last Judgment.

Each tale is thereby acted out by nonprofessionals with warming charm as the music is heard and integrated into the story-line. The twist in each story is that the live musician is regularly invited to join these "damned souls" in their all-night merriment, the end effect being that no one really believes the

tall tale in the long run or simply joins in a "try and beat this one" competition. And these inhabitants of Binn Valley — a mountain folk speaking an almost incomprehensible Swiss-German dialect — obviously enjoy having guests drop by to hear their peculiar brand of dance-music.

The final shot is a gem: in the night as darkness gives way to sunrise, the villagers (who also played the exiled souls) make their way up the side of a mountain in a silhouetted "dance of death" fashion common to medieval paintings — to the edge of the glacier. —Holl.

Windplaetze: Aufgerissen
(Windy Places: Torn Apart)
(SWISS-COLOR-16m)

Solothurn, Jan. 29.

An Achziger Film Production, Zurich. Features entire cast. Written and directed by Pius Morgen. Camera (color), Hans X. Hagen; art direction, Su Meili; music, West Block; sound, Andres Bosshard; editor, Morgen. Reviewed at Solothurn Film Days, Jan. 28, '83. Running time: 96 MINS.

Pius Morgen's "Windy Places: Torn Apart" deals with Switzerland, and Zurich in particular, in a metaphor-packed mixture of documentary and improvised fiction scenes with some striking visual impact. It's a good example of the kind of film portraits cited by Solothurn fest coordinator Stephan Portmann in his opening speech: dark films, often couched in allegorical or concealed film language in making statements on everyday Swiss life and realty.

The very title — torn-apart windy-places imagery — implies what the viewer can expect throughout: docu footage on parliamentary meetings, the passive countenances of a consumer society, then a kidnapping scene and a switch to a trial in a courtroom, followed by shots of garbage-disposal to the music of Mozart's "Don Giovanni" as the protagonist is swallowed up by a gaping hell.

It's the absurdities in the Swiss portrait that catch the eye, while the political statements can best be interpreted by observant Swiss critics. Less fiction than documentary, it can best be described as a collage compilation film. —Holl.

Pi-Errotische Beziehungen
(Pi-errotic Relationships)
(SWISS-COLOR-16m)

Solothurn, Jan. 28.

A Gruppe Ansia Film Production, Zurich. Features entire cast. Written and directed by Beat Kuert. Camera (color), Hansueli Schenkel, Bernhard Lehner; sound, Kuert; editor, Kuert. Reviewed at Solothurn Film Days, Jan. 27, '83. Running time: 80 MINS.

Cast: Barbara Melzl, Michael Maassen, Hansueli Schenkel.

As the title indicates, helmer Beat Kuert is out to analyze the "Pierrot" side of humanity via our "erotic relationships" — thus "Pi-errotic Relationships," with a clear reference to the comic figure in Commedia dell'Arte farces. For those familiar with Kuert's previous critical portraits of contemporary society — "Mulungu" (1974), "Schilten" (1979), "Nestbruch" (1980), and "Evil Times" (1982) — this is another of his studies of relationships at their most intimate level. It makes for fascinating cinema — provided the viewer is into Freudian psychology and/or behaviorism in order to make the necessary "bridges" between dream and reality, love and fear, role-playing and purging-of-the-self.

Three individuals face the camera to speak about their erotic fantasies, these "confessions" paired with fiction scenes to illustrate the depth of their relationships to others. One of these, an actor, talks of his first homosexual contacts — a revelation commanding attention and personal respect, which may be what the film is all about. The rest is slow and plodding. And heavy going, as a whole. —Holl.

Die Leidenschaftlichen
(Passionate People)
(W. GERMAN-SWISS-AUSTRIAN-COLOR-16m)

Solothurn, Jan. 29.

A Polyphon Film & Television Production, Hamburg, in coproduction with Zweites Deutsches Fernsehen (ZDF), Mainz, Austrian Television (ORF), and Swiss Television (SRG). Features entire cast. Directed by Thomas Koerfer. Screenplay, Hans Christoph Buch, Koerfer; camera (color), Thomas Mauch; art direction, Goetz Heymann; music, Ernst Koelz; sound, Luc Yersin; editor, Fee Liechtl. Reviewed at Solothurn Film Days, Jan. 29, '83. Running time: 110 MINS.

Cast: Lutz Weidlich (Goethe/Werther), Sunnyi Melles (Charlotte Buff), Hanns Zischler (Georg Christian Kestner), Wolf Kaiser, Sigfrit Steiner, Paul Burian (Karl Wilhelm Jerusalem), Norbert Schwientek, Karl-Heinz Martell.

Thomas Koerfer's "Passionate People" was produced primarily by West Germany's Second Channel (ZDF) for airing during the "Goethe Year" of 1982, commemorating the 150th anniversary of the German poet's death. It was co-produced by both Austrian and Swiss television, the director himself a German Swiss writer-filmmaker with auteur credentials — Koerfer previously made the impressive literary adaptation of Robert Walser's "The Assistant" (1976). The film on Goethe is presently making the rounds of the world's Goethe Institutes under a West German Inter Nationes banner.

"Passionate People" is about Goethe writing that classic of German Romanticism, "The Sorrows of Young Werther" (1774), based on true-life experiences while assigned duties as an advocate at the Imperial Appellate Court in Wetzlar. The novel parallels his own love affair with Charlotte Buff, who was engaged at 20 to marry the notary Georg Christian Kestner. Charlotte chose Kestner and young Goethe departed from the scene, still burning with the flames of passion for "Lotte" as the story formulated in his head. The impulse was given when another Wetzlar acquaintance, the poet-mystic Karl Wilhelm Jerusalem, committed suicide for love of the wife of another friend, borrowing the fatal weapon from Kestner. Goethe immediately transferred Jerusalem's fate to Young Werther's in his autobiographical book, killed Werther in the novel to give himself peace; and thus fashioned the work that became at publication the rage of Europe.

Koerfer weaves his story of "Passionate People" on three levels: (1) the arrival of Goethe in this provincial town to begin a career in law and meet the "Lotte" who was to change his destiny; (2) the integration, ever so gradually, of the "Sorrows of Young Werther" into Goethe's true-life experiences; and (3) the perspective on both gaining in focus by transferring the setting to the arrival of Napoleon in Germany at the head of a victorious army, the emperor taking time out to discuss "Werther" with Goethe, now in an advanced age. Any introductory college course on Goethe and the German classic would appreciate such an intelligently constructed and narrated tale, but there's more to the tv-production than that.

"Passionate People" is wrapped in a superlative set of credits. Not only are all the personages correctly cast and directed, but the courtly and rustic sets are right as well as the sundry elements that make up a respectable costume feature. Lensing is in soft browns and golds with a care for lighting in and out of doors (Thomas Mauch), and there are twists of humor and other light touches (a magic lantern show) to catch the eye as the tale unfolds. Indeed, the story has such an immediacy that the academic game of analyzing the Goethe/Werther double-role need not even be applied to appreciate the whole.

Koerfer's "Passionate People" might find its way into selected art houses with proper handling of a 35m blow-up. All the same, it should be presented at German Film Weeks or Goethe salutes. It's a gem of a literati pic along the lines of the best of Shakespeare films. —Holl.

The Pirates Of Penzance
(COLOR)

Delightful adaptation of musical stage hit. Simultaneous theatrical-pay tv debut creates b.o. question mark.

Hollywood, Feb. 17.
A Universal release of an Edward R. Pressman presentation of a Joseph Papp production. Produced by Joseph Papp. Coproducer, Timothy Burrill. Executive producer, Edward R. Pressman. Directed, screenplay by Wilford Leach. Stars Kevin Kline, Angela Lansbury, Linda Ronstadt, George Rose, Rex Smith, Tony Azito. Camera (Technicolor, Panavision), Douglas Slocombe; editor, Anne V. Coates; words, Sir William Schwenck Gilbert; music, Sir Arthur Seymour Sullivan; music adapted, orchestrated, conducted by William Elliott; choreography, Graciela Daniele; production design, Elliot Scott; art direction, Ernest Archer, Alan Cassie; set decorator, Peter Howitt; costume design, Tom Rand; sound (Dolby), David Hildyard; assistant director, Barry Langley. Reviewed at the Universal Studios, Universal City, Feb. 16, 1983. (MPAA Rating: G.) Running time: 112 MIN.
The Pirate King	Kevin Kline
Ruth	Angela Lansbury
Mabel	Linda Ronstadt
Major-General	George Rose
Frederic	Rex Smith
Sergeant	Tony Azito

Gilbert & Sullivan's durable "The Pirates Of Penzance" has been turned into an elaborate screen musical by basically the same hands responsible for Joseph Papp's smash New York Shakespeare Festival and Broadway stage production, and result is a delight. Although the impact of full-blown stage theatricality is necessarily reduced somewhat onscreen, everything about this rendition has been done with a hip professionalism that is refreshing.

Probably because of the decision to premiere the film on pay tv last Thursday (17), the same day it went into theatrical release, a cloud of sorts has hung over the picture, with exhibs proclaiming they wouldn't play it. Results of the experiment will be known soon enough, but there can be little doubt that this effort looks and sounds better on a big screen than it would on the tube.

That a few G & S purists might object to the somewhat irreverent tone of this staging was rendered quite irrelevant by the fact that director Wilford Leach introduced thousands of new spectators to the pleasures of comic light opera. The decades-old starch was taken out of the material, and rock stars Linda Ronstadt and Rex Smith fit in quite nicely with the other outstanding legit cast members.

For the film, shot at Shepperton Studios' in England, a charming artificiality of style was arrived at, which is most immediately apparent in Elliot Scott's beautifully witty production design. While by no means simply a photographed stage play, piece reflects its origins in the pastel painted backdrops,

forced perspective sets, paper trees and even a dyed cow. Settings therefore provide the perfect context for the exaggerated thesping required to put G&S over.

Simple tale has orphan Rex Smith leaving, upon turning 21, the band of pirates with whom he's been raised. Upon hitting land, he encounters eight sisters and becomes smitten with one of them, Linda Ronstadt. Pirate King Kevin Kline is not about to let Smith go straight so easily, however, and informs him that, having been born on Feb. 29, he's actually only had five birthdays, and will therefore be obliged to remain with the gang until 1940 or so.

Smith has a hard time tearing himself away from Ronstadt, but finally joins Kline and company in an assault on the home of the girls' father, Major-General George Rose. Madcap chase ends up onstage during a production of "H.M.S. Pinafore," with pirates finally prostrating themselves beneath a statue of Queen Victoria before pairing off with assorted daughters.

With the exception of Angela Lansbury, entertaining as the pirates' nursemaid and aide-de-combat, all principal cast members have repeated their Broadway performances here, and in exemplary fashion. Kline adds a touch of the fop to his dashing, flamboyant pirate leader and is winning all the way, seemingly ever-ready for a sword fight and never walking when running, jumping or swinging on a rope will do.

Smith is a delightful surprise in the romantic lead, and fact that Kline and Smith are two of the best looking young actors on the screen these days won't hurt femme appreciation of the film.

Similarly easy on the eyes is Ronstadt, who's terribly fetching in her amorous skirmishes with Smith and sings beautifully. Her performance here actually reminds of silent screen star Clara Bow, a resemblance emphasized by her red button mouth and big brown eyes.

George Rose makes his entrance with the show-stopping "Major-General" number, and Tony Azito, as the head cop with the responsibility of apprehending the pirates, amazes with his elastic dancing.

Production is classy all the way. Douglas Slocombe's expertly lit lensing is marred only occasionally by some close-up graininess, and Anne V. Coates' editing is sharp. Of particular quality is William Elliott's adaptation and orchestration of the Sullivan score. To the musically inclined, subtle instrumentation achieves a sly humor all its own. Graciela Daniele's choreography is also humorous and resists temptation toward undue athleticism.

Pic does run down a bit in the attack and chase sequences prior to

climax, and those who loved the stage production may feel that the sense of exuberance achieved live doesn't quite transfer on the screen, but that's the nature of the beast.

Not only will the full scope of the production not be felt on television, but a major problem for home viewers is that it was shot in widescreen Panavision. In certain instances, people sing at each other from opposite ends of the screen, a framing dilemma impossible to solve adequately on the tube. In this and other ways, film was probably not the ideal guinea pig for the simultaneous theatrical/pay-tv experiment, and filmmakers can only hope that their work will have a life in film houses beyond this weekend. —Cart.

Zu
(Warriors From The Magic Mountain)
(HONG KONG-COLOR)

Hong Kong, Feb. 11.
A Golden Harvest presentation. Produced by Raymond Chow. Directed by Tsui Hark. Stars Cheng Siu Tsou (Adam Cheng), Lau Chung Yan, Yuen Biao, Meng Hai, Lin Chin Hsia, Tsui Siu Keung, Judy Ong, Fung Hark On, Samo Hung. Screenplay, Sze To Chung Hong; camera (color), Bill Wong; music, Tang Siu-Lam; theme song, Joseph Koo; art director, Chung Suk-Ping; special effects, Robert Blalack, Peter Kuran, Arnie Wong, John Scheele. Reviewed at State Theatre, Hong Kong, Feb. 10, 1983. Running time: 100 MINS.
(Cantonese soundtrack with English subtitles)

Publicized as the most expensive movie ever made in Hong Kong (HK $30-Mil) with the most innovative local director around, Tsui Hark of "Butterfly Murders" fame "Zu" has top tv, movie and recording stars, well-known martial artists (Samo Hung, Meng Hai, Yuen Biao) and special effects provided by professionals especially imported from Japan, America and Taiwan. With such irresistable come-ons, one would also expect it to be the best picture of the year.

Unfortunately, "Zu" is merely a zoo of bizarre Chinese characters of the mythological variety ... a cavalcade of non-stop special effect images. It may be a boxoffice success but an artistic failure. Everything was done to excess. "Zu" is no exception, as the often grotesque personages clothed in Chinese high fashion of some unspecified time and space spend most of their time flying around fighting each other in mysterious castles. And despite an expensive budget, one still sees the wires that make the mortals and gods fly high. The concept has been executed before, but on a shoestring budget. The action is nonstop so viewers may find it difficult to nourish some of the creative imagery.

The flat storyline is merely encounters between mortals and the gods in the land of Zu, which has been made complicated with the forces of evil battling with the good ones. "Zu" is a magic mountain where peace abounds and goodness prevails.

Tsui Hark, who is truly imaginative and talented, has never been a good storyteller as his brilliant, big ideas tend to dissipate into kaleidoscopic chips on screen that mean little. His talent can be compared to' raw energy that must be harnessed and disciplined to accomplish a total picture of merit that excels in the different aspects of film-making. —Mel.

Duel To The Death
(HONG KONG-COLOR)

Hong Kong, Jan. 17.
A Golden Harvest Production for Paragon Films. Ltd. Produced by Raymond Chow. Directed by Ching Siu Tung. Stars Lau Chung Yan, Tsui Sui Keung, Flora Cheong Lee, Kao Hsiung, Yeung Chak Lam, Chang Chung and Ka Sa Fa. (No other credits provided by producers). Reviewed at Queen's Theater, Jan. 12, 1982. Running time: 100 MINS.
(Cantonese soundtrack with English subtitles)

"Duel To The Death" is a pretentiously boring and self-conscious work of new director Ching Siu Tung (an ex-martial arts choreographer). It comes from Golden Harvest Productions, following a number of tepid variations or comedy-horror-kung fu elements. This one is no exception, despite the fact that the ingredients of exotic Chinese sword fighting and mysterious Japanese Ninjas have been added.

The basic storyline (if one may call it that) centers on a contest between supposedly famous swordfighters from China and Japan. The duel tournaments happen once in a while on a regular basis, something like the Olympic Games. The main protaganists are Chinese Po Ching-Wan (Lau Chung-Yan who is best known for his "Roving Swordsman" TV series) and Japanese Hashimota (Tsui Sui-Keung). For dramatic counterpoint, an influential warlord type who is willing to compromise with the Japanese steps in just to allow her daughter (also a martial arts expert) Shing Lan (Flora Chong-Lee) to participate in hte marathon battle to ensure the man's lost prestige. And it must be a duel to the death as the one who wins has the totality of dominance, plus the spiritual advantage of a victory that transcends human expression.

And so viewers are treated to nasty eyeball-to-eyeball glances between the major characters and movements of grave seriousness. After a series of fleeting atmospheric visual elegance that are sandwiched between programmed meetings in scenic places, the film dissolves into another routine Hong Kong kung-fu, chop-suey muddle.

Flora Cheong Lee, who also provides the romantic link is no actress. but is an elegant screen personality who can fashion-show her period costumes well and look extremely serious without depth. Impeccably dressed for duels and sword encounters, she moves gracefully in battletic scenes where she emerges goddess-like amidst clouds of fog, possibly the leftover mist that once carpeted the scenic mountain visuals of three King Hu movies.

"Duel To The Death" like the others in the genre is another sham picture made by yet another moviemaker who needs more proper direction to organize his abilities on the right track. There is nothing new here, merely another production that relies heavily on the visuals and image wizardry. It may satisfy the eyes but it insults the mind and is generally a stale martial arts film attuned to local and foreign Chinatown tastes. --Mel.

Das Ganze Leben
(The Whole Of Life)
(SWISS-B&W/COLOR-DOCU-16m)

Solothurn, Jan. 29.
A Bruno Moll Film Production, Aarburg. Written and directed by Bruno Moll. Camera (b&w/color), Edwin Horak; art direction, Greta Roderer, Edith Peter; music, Ben Jeger, Philip Roland; sound, Florian Eidenbenz, Hans-Peter Fischer; editor, Franziska Wirz. Reviewed at Solothurn Film Days, Jan. 28. Running time: 112 MINS.
With Serena Wey in acted portions.

Bruno Moll's "The Whole of Life" is about a 50-year old woman whose lifespan has taken her through correction homes, prisons, prostitution, and a generally miserable existence as one of society's incorrigible outsiders. Barbara, a real-life woman, is of interest to the director because she wrote him suggesting a film to be made on her life, so Moll decided to do so by engaging an actress, Serena Wey, to interpret episodes in Barbara's past in semi-documentary fashion. In addition, Barbara herself appears on the scene as a consultant on the project. A lesbian with a wealth of life-experiences behind her, she steals the show each time she's on camera.

The Barbara sequences are filmed in black-and-white, while Wey's acted segs are in color to provide a possible contrast with young people today in the same boat as that of the protagonist in the past. Since the story is mostly of youthful rebellion and the miserable conditions in a prison for criminals (undeserved for the most part, for the girl is more of a runaway than a convicted criminal, it appears), it has some value for discussion purposes. A pure docu sans fiction seems to be a rarity among Swiss-German and German directors these days, and now in "The Whole of Life" the mixed fiction-documentary technique loses its credibility in the long run. The interpretative performance is particularly weak. —Holl.

Yogoreta Eiyu
(Dirty Hero)
(JAPANESE-COLOR)

Tokyo, Feb. 14.
A Toei release of a Kadokawa Production. Produced and directed by Haruki Kadokawa. Features entire cast. Production assistants, Shinichi Hashimoto, Kosaku Wada; screenplay, Shoichi Maruyama, based on the novel by Haruhiko Oyabu; camera, (color), Sezo Sengen; music, Yuichiro Oda; music production, Tadao Takakuwa; art, Chikara Imamura; lighting, Mitsuo Watanabe; sound, Tetsuo Segawa; editing, Kioaki Saito, assistant director, Yoshikun Matsunaga. Reviewed at Toei Central, Tokyo, Feb. 9, 1983. Running time: 102 MINS.
Akio Kitano . . . . Masao Kusakari
Azusa Ogata . . . . Atsuko Asano
Keiji Oki . . . . Hiroshi Katsuno
Ken Kashima . . . . Satoshi Sadanaga
Takashi Mamiya . . . . Yutaka Hayashi
Muneyuki Ogata . . . . Eiji Okada
Christine Adams . . . . Rebecca Holden

This story of a professional road racer and the successful fashion designer and wealthy businesswoman who loves him is yet another addition to that cinematic genre, "People With Good Looks and Lots of Money Have Problems, Too."

Road racer Akio Kitano (Masao Kusakari), for example: even though he's able to maintain his independent racing status, not to mention an enviable life style, thanks to financial contributions from the women he makes love to, he is constantly troubled by the prospect of sudden, fiery death every time he mounts his 500cc motorcycle. Or Monacan tycooness: even though she's young, attractive, wealthy and has countless minions at her beck and call, she's not always lucky in love, which fact is conveyed to us by a scene in which she moodily dines alone at an approximately 30-foot long, candle-lit banquet table.

Producer Haruki Kadokawa, making his directorial debut, has liberally topped his concoction with International Flavor. Kitano lives in a two-story apartment, personal swimming pool and body-building alcove on the lower level, state-of-the-art audio system and walk-in closet filled with Giorgio Armani suits on the upper level. No floors of straw and sliding doors of paper for this boy.

Indeed, there is very little that is Japanese about the Japanese on view: their houses, their apartments, their clothes, their favorite coffee shops are Western and they shake hands when they meet. (The only person bowing in this film is the tycoonness' right hand man, who kowtows upon receiving orders from his boss.) Other Occidentalia include thematic elements from both the "Rocky" trilogy (with triumphal music accompanying the conclusion of a race borrowing liberally from Bill Conti's score) and "Shane," with the son of Kitano's pit crew chief taking an enormous liking to the gigolo-racer.

Kitano, unsurprisingly, is played by Western-looking nonactor, Masao Kusakari, who is required to pitch woo in English. Although half-American, he obviously had to learn his lines phonetically, resulting in diction at least as smooth as that of Charlie Chan.

Racing sequences, especially those intended to represent the "Japan Road Racing Championship" are excitingly well done. The musical soundtrack, like those of past Kadokawa productions contains much that is eminently hummable, particularly the theme song, composed by Yuichiro Oda and sung by Rosemary Butler.

What, finally, is most remarkable about "Yogoreta Eiyu" is that it took Kadokawa so long to get around to making it. After all, there is hardly a subject more suitable for treatment for this master of the commercial tie-in. —Bail.

Aces Go Places II
(HONG KONG-COLOR)

Hong Kong, Feb. 10.
A Cinema City Company Ltd. production. Produced by Carl Mak, Dean Shek. Directed by Eric Tsang. Stars Sâm Hui, Carl Mak, Sylvia Chang, Sue Wang, Yasuki Kurata, Joe Dimmick, Hector Britt. Co-produced by Raymond Wong; production supervisor, Paul Lal; art director, Oliver Wong; editor, Tony Chow. Reviewed at President Theater, Hong Kong, Feb. 9, 1983. Running time: 100 MINS.
(Cantonese soundtrack with English subtitles).

Cinema City repeats their boxoffice formula of 1982 and will likely retain their kingly status as the most successful and financially stable independent film company in Hong Kong.

That flamboyant formula consists of providing 100 minutes of non-stop visual slapstick type comedy combined with James Bond carbon copy shenanigans and Cantonese humour. It's never a 'dull moment fun film for kids and adults with young minds attuned to things that are basic and elementary. There is nothing intellectual here and it's meant to be nothing more, simply a well-calculated commercial movie.

The cast of "Aces I" and "II" are basically the same. Fancy-free jewel thief and footloose King Kong (Sam Hui), last seen assisting the law, headed by Kodojak (Carl

Mak) and Superintendent Ho (Sylvia Chang), is now a responsible citizen. However, his tranquility is broken because revengeful members of the Italian Mafia are still upset about the capture of their chief thief. They send a robot to liquidate King Kong. The robot fails and assorted baddies, foreigners, Orientals and a lovely girl decoy, Juju (Sue Wang), are summoned.

Predictable young love takes over. King Kong and Juju start making eyes and music together. The final confrontation takes place when another robot, Black Knight II (more powerful than the first) endanger King Kong and Kodojak. Hui is beginning to be an adept comedian with good timing though he still mugs a lot.

"Aces II" is better seen than described.

In many ways, the frenetic pace reflects the fast Hong Kong lifestyle of its residents. It may lack detailed plot construction and polished wit but the film sells. Directed rigorously by Eric Tsang for the second time, in his usual Keystone Kops style. —Mel.

Na De Liefde
(After Love)
(BELGIAN-COLOR)

Brussels, Feb. 5.
An Elan Films release of an F3 O.D.E.C. production (Brussels). Produced by Godfried Courtmans. Written and directed by Jaak Boon. Camera (color), Yves Vandermeeren; editor, Monique Rysselinck; art direction, Luc Monheim; music, Jean Blaute; production managers, Tom Coene and Guy De Lombaert. Reviewed at the Albert I theatre, Palais des Congres, Brussels, Jan. 19, 1983. Running time: 90 MINS.
Gerard ... Raymond van het Groenewoud
Pierre .... Frank Aendenboom
Ingrid .... Nicole Colchat
Denise .... Guusje van Tilborgh
Mother ....: ... Alice Toen
Father ....:... Oswald Maes
Van Schaemel .... Max Schnur
Pol .... Leo Rozenstraeten
Elvira .... Mia Vaerman

"After Love" marks the acting debut of Raymond van het Groenewoud, a well-known Flemish rock-singer. But despite his reputation and popularity among young people, his first film venture proved a disaster at the boxoffice. This may have less to do with the downbeat subject than with the poor quality of the script and banality of the subject.

Film draws the portrait of a freewheeling man in his early thirties who hasn't settled down yet and who behaves like an outcast. He runs an antique shop and dreams of becoming a great novelist, though he makes no effort to start writing. He blames his upper-class parents for his failure, has great fun in provoking his entourage (unfortunately for the audience he's the only one) and seems to enjoy his situation as a born loser.

Weak story-line concentrates on his relationship with his beloved sister and with an ex-mistress, who reappears in his disorganized life and tempts him with her dreams of a middle-class marriage.

First-time director-screenwriter Jaak Boon throws in a lot of social-minded ideas along the way (from unemployment to the difficult choice of having children) but he hasn't bothered to construct a viable dramatic framework for his catalogue of "problems" all treated so superficially that they remain platitudes.

Scenes alternating sarcastic humor, pathos and melodrama are seldom effective. But the main factor in the failure of the film is the incapacity of the leading actor to arouse any sumpathy. Directing on the whole is dull. —Pat.

Der Kleine Bruder
(The Little Brother)
(WEST GERMAN-COLOR)

Berlin, Dec. 23.
An Ufa-Fernsehproduktion, Berlin, in coproduction with Zweites Deutsches Fernsehen (ZDF), Mainz. Features entire cast. Directed by Rainer Soehnlein. Screenplay, Klaus Poche; camera (Color), Guenter Marczinkowsky; music, Juergen Knieper; tv-producer, Wolfgang Baecker. Reviewed at ZDF Screening Room, Berlin, Dec. 23, '83. Running time: 90 MINS.
Cast: Herbert Stass (Paul), Ilsemarie Schnering (Hilde), Hannes Messemer (Reini), Claudia Blutenuth (Vera), Friedhelm Ptok (Harry), Brigitte Stockmann (Iene), Ruediger Wandel (Robert).

Rainer Soehnlein's "The Little Brother" is one of those modest Berlin productions that stands out for its contemporary relevance: it deals with a retired railwayman from East Germany who comes to live permanently in West Germany. He's 65, now a widower, and has worked for 30 years on the same job. He has a sister in the West, a widow (she has grown children, and is now living along). Since the older sister and "little brother" were close in childhood, both feel that things will work out in the long run.

Scripter Klaus Poche, however, has a few cards up his sleeve in penning this delightful comedy. The former East German writer knows the incongruities between the two Germanys only too well. The old man smuggles his saved-up retirement pay (10,000 East marks) across the border in a flower-pot it's worth little on this side, he discovers. Then, after a year in the West, he also discovers that the Federal Republic will offer him a retirement sum of the same amount — this time in hard-currency "West marks"! But he can't forget his old buddies back home: to while away the time, he is always on the telephone to a former crony — but when the friend shows up for a visit, the experience leaves a bad taste because one can't live a life

---

with feet planted on both sides of the "fence."

The most revealing scene of all is a vacation in a winter wonderland shared by brother and sister. It's at this moment that the ex-GDR citizen realizes that he has wasted so much of his life "on the other side," and it's now too late to make up for lost time — so he turns grumpy again and takes it out on the defenseless but understanding sister. In the end, they come as close together as they did in the past, even though the "little brother" feels that he should be buried (when the time comes) next to his wife in the GDR.

Credits are tops in this tv-prod with an optional chance for art-house spinoff, particularly the three senior citizens: Herbert Stass, Ilsemarie Schnering, Hannes Messemer. What makes it work is the accuracy of the lines and situation-factors, for Poche has only recently left East Germany himself to settle in the West — as has lenser Guenter Marczinkowsky. This is a sociopolitical comedy worth a classroom seminar due to its detailed richness, for many lines are packed with appropriate metaphors or revealing symbols. It is not a coincidence that Big Sister lives in the West and Little Brother in the East, for instance. Nor that both sides constantly demonstrate that they do, in fact, know very little about each other's living standards, everyday cares, and contrasting ideologies.

Poche is a masterful social critic and delightful satirist. His skills as a screenplay writer are extensive and a boon to the new generation of contemporary German cinema.
— Holl.

Tu Mi Turbi
(You Disturb Me)
(ITALIAN-COLOR)

Rome, Feb. 9.
A Titanus release, produced by Ettore Rosboch for Best International Films. Starring and directed by Roberto Benigni. Screenplay, Roberto Benigni, Giuseppe Bertolucci, camera (Eastmancolor), Luigi Verga; editor, Gabriella Cristiani; art director, Giorgio Luppi and Maurizia Narducci; music, Paolo Conte. Reviewed at the Bertoloni screening room, Rome, Feb. 9, 1983. Running time: 100 MINS.
Benigni .... Roberto Benigni
Bank director .... Giacomo Piperno
Angela .... Olimpia Carlisi
Soldier .... Claudio Bigagli

A festival film that will have trouble being understood outside its native land, an alternately brilliant and boring monolog of sarcastic wit disguised as the babbling of a fool, "You Disturb Me" is indeed a disturbing film, one of the most original and difficult to be made by the "new comics." Roberto Benigni, a young actor from Tuscany who became big a few years ago on television and brightened up several

---

humdrum films, makes his helming debut in a four-part episode picture centered around himself. The humor is trenchant, repetitive and abstract, based on the verbal and nonverbal nuances of Italian. Although Benigni has a loyal following, pic looks like a hard sell onshore as well as off.

"Disturb" was written by the helmer with the help of Giuseppe Bertolucci, who directed him in "I Love You Berlinguer," an even more demented sample of the comic's taste and talent. Pic began as a series of skits for tv before producer Ettore Rosboch decided to release it theatrically. It remains a one-man show featuring the long-haired, weak-chinned, thick-lipped Benigni, targets for whose bizarre sense of humor range from baby-sitting for the Baby Jesus to doing guard duty at the Tomb of the Unknown Soldier. Most have a metaphysical ring.

In the first episode Benigni is a poor shepherd in the year "5 A.D." who's lost his flock out of pure distraction. His old girlfriend Mary and her husband Joseph get him to look after Jesus while they go out. The child, perfectly silent, listens to Benigni's ruminations on God, stands on top of the bath water, and leaves an impression of his face on the towel.

Second story has Benigni searching for his runaway guardian angel, a very corporeal spirit (Olimpia Carlisi) who says he's bored with their relationship and has fallen in love with God.

Funniest and most coherent is the tale of Benigni going into a bank to get a loan to buy a house. Refusing to be intimidated by the contemptuous bank director (Giacomo Piperno), he gives a tour de force performance that ends with his being locked in a jail cell — his new home.

Last skit shows him as a bersagliere guarding the eternal flame before the Tomb of the Unknown Soldier and tormenting his straight-laced companion (Claudio Bigagli) to tears with nerve-wracking jokes like "telephone calls" on his sword. In the cold of the night they snipe at each other and discuss the existence of a mysterious "Buch" who knows for sure whether God exists.

As a helmer Benigni opts for extreme simplicity, to the point of shooting the entire Unknown Soldier skit in five austere camera angles that are continually alternated. Result is a stagey look that heightens the abstraction of the dialog. Props and actors are also reduced to a minimum, furthering concentrating attention on the main character. A performer of unquestionable talent, Benigni is side-splitting when he clicks with the situation; deadly when the ideas run out. Unfortunately the gems are

buried in long stretches of un-directed filler whose lack of compactness is soporific. "You Disturb Me" is blessed with a melodious score by Paolo Conte that gives the film a sense of magic and grace.
—*Yung.*

Die Dicke Tilla
(Fat Tilla)
(EAST GERMAN-COLOR)

East Berlin, Jan. 7.

A DEFA Film Production, Johannisthal Group, East Berlin; world rights, DEFA Aussenhandel, East Berlin. Features Entire cast. Directed by Werner Bergmann. Screenplay, Rosel Klein, based on her children's book with the same title; camera (color), Bergmann, Ingo Baar; sets, Hans-Jorg Mirr; music, Kirill Cibulka; editor, Karin Kusche; dramaturg, Andreas Scheinert; production manager, Dorothea Hildebrandt. Reviewed at DEFA Screening Room, East Berlin, Jan. 7, '83. Running time: 90 MINS.

Cast: Carmen Sarge (Tilla), Jana Mattukat (Anna), Matthias Manz (Knut), Maurice Woynowski (Felix), Peter Bause (Teacher Eckart), Carl Heinz Choynski (Tilla's Father), Guenter Junghans (Anne's Father), Carmen-Maja Antoni (Anne's Mother).

It's not often that the director and photographer are one and the same, yet in this case Werner Bergmann is nationally known as one of the best lensers at the DEFA Studios (he worked on all of Konrad Wolf's prizewinning features) and apparently enjoyed tackling the double-chores on this children's film based on a bestselling book.

"Fat Tilla" has much of the flavor of Hal Roach's "Our Gang" in that this class of fifth graders go through all the paces of grownups, particularly when it comes to bossing others around and constantly ploying the subtleties of one-upmanship whenever possible.

"Die dicke Tilla" is the terror of her class, but she can't get the newcomer, Anna, to bend to her will, come what may. Anna is just the opposite of her antagonist: thin, shy, and sensitive. Yet both opponents have one thing in common: a strong streak of stubbornness — neither will give in to the other in the long run, and thus they slowly become the best of friends without even being fully aware of it.

By and by, it becomes clear why the fatty in the class plays the role of a dictator — she is without a mother and is now pretty much on her own despite two older twin brothers and a busy father (he's a policeman). As for Anna, she often drifts into a fantasy world of her own, a magic kingdom where she can carry on conversations with talking fish and being taken on transports in her dreams. The showdown comes when Tilla wrecks Anna's bike, and then is forced to replace the intentionally damaged wheel to avoid punishment at home (the teacher has found out about the tiff between the two by chance).

It's when Tilla has the upper hand that Anna feels too humiliated to go home after school, so she hides out under a bridge over a creek. And who finds her to scold her about worrying her mother — Tilla, who's without a mother she clearly misses. After another personality clash, which leads to the two being trapped in a barn hayloft, all is well when the brothers and another friend help them down to Mother Earth. They're still at each other's throats in the end, but the differences of opinion are now only minor.

Credits are on the plus side, and the leads are a riot when together.
—*Holl.*

Dusty
(AUSTRALIAN-COLOR)

Melbourne, Feb. 22.

Kestrel Films Production with Film Victoria release. Produced by Gil Brealey. Directed by John Richardson. Stars Bill Kerr, Noel Trevarthen, Carol Burns. Screenplay, Sonia Borg, based on the novel by Frank Dalby Davison; camera (Eastmancolor), Alex McPhell; music, Frank Strangio; editor, David Greig; assistant director, Colin Fletcher; production manager, Mark Ruse; art director, Ivana Perkins; sound, John Phillips. (Commonwealth Film Censor rating: G). Running time: 88 MINS.

Tom .... Bill Kerr
Harry .... Noel Trevarthen
Clara .... Carol Burns
Railey Jordan .... John Stanton
Jack .... Nick Holland

In the seemingly unlimited category of "a boy and his dog" tales, this pic enters the class in a refreshing and expansive way. Based on the Australian children's classic by Frank Dalby Davison, "Dusty" is the story of the ill-fated bond between an old man and his canine companion, helmed by John Richardson in an unsentimental yet touching style. Yet Richardson takes this nearly naive yarn a step further, and enriches the pic with philosophical overtones about the right to be different and about the experience of freedom.

Aged hired hand Tom Lincoln (Bill Kerr) unsuspectingly buys Dusty for $5 to assist him on the Morrison family's sheep farm, unaware that the dog is part dingo (wild Australian breed who are inherent sheep killers) and part kelpie (champion sheepdog). The growing bond between Tom and Dusty is delicately portrayed, as Tom raises the dog to clearly become a champ, filled with loyalty and trustworthiness — the definitive kelpie traits. When the Morrison family starts losing sheep at the same time that Dusty happens to simultaneously be missing, it becomes evident that Dusty is yielding to his part-savage heredity and stalking out in the bush at night. Meanwhile, a tight emotional attachment has evolved between Tom and Dusty, so Tom decides to leave the farm when the decision has been made that Dusty must be destroyed.

Jordan, the cunning dingo hunter, is urged by the Morrisons to get Dusty, but he feels, "Shooting an old man's pet — there's no challenge in it." Dusty, who has rejoined Tom in the bush, ultimately returns to the Morrison ranch, signalling some distress in Tom's life, and the final drama is culminated in Tom's death and Dusty's ultimate release into the wild bush.

In a far from heavy-handed manner, Richardson unravels another layer in the pic via the symbol of Dusty: all men have noble and savage aspects to their natures and reveal each side under appropriate circumstances. High marks go to Alex McPhee's beautiful lensing of the bush in Northern Victoria and for creative camera angles from the dog's p.o.v. The dialog is economical yet full characters emerge. The farm family, especially Harry (Noel Trevarthen) and Clara (Carol Burns) are appropriately unpretentious and earthbound. The understated dramatizations embellish the man-dog relationship without getting overly unctuous or gushy, although it's tough not to get out your hankies for the final moments.

Appeal should range from tots to adults for this pic is done with maturity and style, with the bonus of a lush travelog view of the Aussie countryside. —*Dogo.*

Bad Boys
(COLOR)

Youths in prison film packs a wallop.

Hollywood, March 1.

Universal Pictures and Associated Film Distribution release from EMI Films of a Robert Solo production. Produced by Solo. Directed by Richard Rosenthal. Features entire cast. Screenplay, Richard Dilello; camera (Technicolor), Bruce Surtees, Donald Thorin; editor, Antony Gibbs; production design, J. Michael Riva; music, Bill Conti; assistant directors, Tom Mack, Pat Kehoe. Reviewed at Plitt's Century Plaza Theatre, Feb. 25, 1983. (MPAA Rating: R). Running time: 123 MINS.

Mick O'Brien .... Sean Penn
Pramon Herrera .... Reni Santoni
Paco Moreno .... Esai Morales
Horowitz .... Eric Gurry
Gene Daniels .... Jim Moody
J.C. Walenski .... Ally Sheedy
Viking Lofgren .... Clancy Brown
Tweety .... Robert Lee Rush
Wagner .... John Zenda

EMI's "Bad Boys" is a troubling and often riveting drama about juvenile delinquency that will leave an indelible impression on audiences. Director Richard Rosenthal has done a topnotch job of bringing to life the seedy, hopeless environment of a jail for juvenile offenders and has gotten some terribly convincing performances from his young cast, notably topliner Sean Penn. But the Universal-AFD release will have to be carefully sold as the portrait presented is a disturbing one that might prove unappealing to a large portion of filmgoers, particularly without top name stars. However, there should be a market for a film as gripping as this one.

If it goes on a bit too long for its own good and often finds the pieces of its story fitting together a bit too perfectly, the explosive emotions contained within the picture more than make up for the lapses. Richard Dilello's original screenplay sets up a viable structure into which Rosenthal and the actors pour all of the overheated angers and frustrations felt by the delinquents and those around them. It's a world where everyone lives very close to the edge. The film manages to be just restrained enough to have nearly all of the incidents ring true.

From the first scene where 16-year-old tough guy Penn breaks the window of a car and steals a woman's purse, it's clear this is not going to be the picture of youth most people are used to. The raging, embittered look on Penn's face leads through a dark neighborhood where teengers think nothing of running drugs, carrying guns and assaulting anyone who gets in their way.

Penn's only safety is in the love of girlfriend Ally Sheedy, the one person who has ever seemingly seen the softer side of his nature. Though she urges him to be careful, he is too sure of himself and disdainful of everyone else to ever feel he is in danger.

That confidence is put to a stop when in a robbery attempt by a high school gang he finds himself shooting at people in the street and accidentally running over the little brother of a gang leader. With an arrest record a mile long, Penn is thrown into a juvenile correctional facility where his cohorts are other young murderers, rapists, arsonists and the like.

It is in this area that the film really takes off, pitting Penn against the abuses of his fellow inmates and the inherent hopelessness of his situation. Though he rises to top man (boy) in jail, his world begins to crack again when the gang leader on the outside rapes Penn's girlfriend to avenge his brother's death and gets sentenced to the same correctional facility.

Penn is nothing short of terrific in the key role, which, given a minimal amount of dialog, calls for him to rely primarily on his emotional and physical abilities. It's a subtle, studied performance that others might likely have played much more broadly to much less effect. Eric Gurry, Clancy Brown, Robert Lee Rush and a host of other actors (some real delinquents) provide solid support as other teenagers while Reni Santoni and Jim Moody give ample balance as the adults assigned to keep them in line.

There are some problems in believability (Sheedy's character just happens to be wandering alone in a dangerous area the night she is raped) and in character (the intellectual inmate played by Gurry is a little bit too convenient). There is also the feeling that at just over two hours, Rosenthal lost some of the ongoing intensity of the situation, especially in the middle section.

But overall the filmmakers have managed to effectively dramatize a major social problem without ever sounding preachy. That combination of entertainment and intelligence is something all too rare in most films these days. —Berg.

Ghosts Galore
(HONG KONG-COLOR)

Hong Kong, Feb. 10.

A Shaw Brothers production. Presented by Sir Run Run Shaw. Executive producer, Mona Fong. Directed by Hsu Hsia. Stars Chen Hsiao Hou, Yang Tsing Tsing, Chiang Chin, Lo Lieh, Lung Tien Chiang, Pei Ju Hua. Screenplay, Yeh Chia; camera (color), Kuan Mu; editors, Chiang Hsing Lung, Fang Peo Hua; art directors, Cheng Ching Shen, Ho Chien Sheng; martial arts directors, Hsu Hsia, Yuan Hui. Reviewed at Jade Cinema, Hong Kong. Feb. 1, 1933. Running Time: 100 MINS.
(Cantonese soundtrack with English sub-titles).

"Ghosts Galore" tells the story of two run-of-the-mill con exorcists-fortune tellers (Chiang Chin, Chien Hsiao Hou) who're trying to trick illiterate country folks for a living.

When they bump into their elder master (Lo Lieh), without realizing that he is their master's brother, the two have a good time teasing him. Later, when they are being pursued by a ghost-nymph after failing to exorcise her, the elder master comes to their rescue.

Meanwhile, a gang of Japanese ninjas headed by their master is after renegade ninjas who'd fled to China. When these characters collide, a vicious fight takes place and ends with Chiang Chin and a renegade killed. Chien Hsiao Hou manages to save a female ninja (played by Yang Tsing Tsing). When the master ninja decides to take on the two himself, they turn to the elder master for help. After a series of black magic duels, the master ninja is blown to bits. And the elder master, who has fullfilled his Dao Hun (mission), ascends to heaven.

With sci-fi films laden with lavish special effects and stunts being so popular abroad, Hong Kong filmmakers are following the same trail, producing their own versions. "Ghosts Galore" is one of those films that should have been shelved. This one is strictly for grind houses of Chinatowns abroad.

In "Ghosts Galore," the period takes place in ancient China, and it has to prolong the fighting scenes to fill up the time. The dialog has corny jokes, smart street talks in contemporary style. The special visual effects are amateurish.

"Ghosts Galore" is supposed to be a kung-fu-comedy, so the audience well familiar with this format, know that all starts well ends well, thus depriving the audience of possible suspense. —Mel.

Twinkle, Twinkle, Little Star
(HONG KONG - COLOR)

Hong Kong, Feb. 14.

A Shaw Brothers production. Presented by Sir Run Run Shaw. Executive producer, Mona Fong. Director, Alex Cheung (Chang Kuo Ming). Stars Yi Lei, Cherry Chung (Chung Chun Hung), Tan Tien Nan, Liang Tien, Paul Che, Liu Yi Fan, Feng Feng, Hsi Kao Pao. Screenplay, C. Wen, L.C. Shao, C.C. Yuan, K.M. Chang; camera (color), Chang Kuo Ming; editors, Chiang Hsing Lung, Fang Pao Hua; art director, Hohnson Tsao; special effects, Chua Lan; music directors, Stephen Shing, So Chun Hou; martial arts director, Cheng Hsiao Tung; action director, Teng Te Chiang. Reviewed at Jade Cinema, Hong Kong, Feb. 13, 1983. Running time: 100 MINS.

(Cantonese soundtrack with English sub-titles).

Yi Tien (Yi Lei) and Ah Chen (Cherry Chung) have one thing in common, they are both born losers. He, as a private eye who yearns to become another Sherlock Holmes, but his undignified assignments leave him confused that he plans suicide. She, in spite of a pretty face and body, is just a dumb broad who is incapable of doing anything right. When she's about to become a rich man's wife, she claims that she has been molested by a space alien from a UFO, thus losing her so-called virginity. Her disbelieving fiance drops her.

Yi and Ah meet while trying to jump under a train, but narrowly escape death. Yi Tien vows he will prove her story as true to make them famous.

Ah Chen is still unable to convince anyone of what she has seen, until one day, a certain Dr. Lu (Liang Tien) confirms her encounter of the fourth kind, and she catapults to fame as a sex-object. The mountain where Ah Chen has her encounter is suddenly filled with girls who want to experience likewise.

Yi Tien and sidekick Kung Lun Pu (Tan Tien Nan), dress in drag and mingle with the girls at the scene of encounter. They discover a flying saucer and Yi gets inside. There's a duel to death with the hostile monster, then he unravels the identity of the alien.

Among the three local films during the Chinese lunar new year, Alex Cheung's "Twinkle, Twinkle, Little Star" is the definite loser, for it fails on many counts. If it's meant to make the audience laugh, it hardly raises a giggle. If it's meant to impress with its cheap-looking but expensive special effects, the outcome looks like a cross between a B-movie and some low-budget Taiwanese love story-musical.

Chung, a gorgeous thing to behold, is sadly no actress, or anywhere near. Yi Lei, one of Hong Kong's more popular comedians, is simply wasted here. —Mel.

Spring Fever
(CANADIAN-COLOR)

A Comworld Pictures release of an Amulet Pictures presentation. A Tournament Prods. Ltd. production, made with the participation of Canadian Film Development Corp. and Famous Players. Produced by John F. Bassett. Directed by Joseph L. Scanlan. Features entire cast. Screenplay, Stuart Gillard, Fred Stefan; camera (Film House color), Donald Wilder; editor, Kirk Jones; music, Fred Mollin; sound, Don Cohen; assistant director, Tony Lucibello; art director, Bruno Rubeo. Reviewed at RKO Cinerama 2 theatre, N.Y., Jan. 16, 1983. (MPAA Rating: PG). Running time: 100 MINS.

Stevie Castle	Susan Anton
Louis Corman	Frank Converse
Celia Berryman	Jessica Walter
Neil Berryman	Stephen Young
Karen Castle	Carling Bassett
Melissa Berryman	Shawn Foltz

A Canadian production filmed in Sarasota, Florida in 1981 under the title "Sneakers," "Spring Fever" is a mild and dull picture about preteen girls trying to be the next Chris Evert of the tennis world. The film is being sold as another of the popular teen hi-jinks comedies, but except for the inclusion (a la "Bad News Bears") of precocious kids spouting foul language for cheap laughs, "Fever" has little to offer fans of softcore sex-tease.

Padded with endless montages of tennis matches, the picture unfolds as a corny tale of poor little K.C. (Carling Bassett), an underdog, unseeded 13-year-old entrant in the Junior National tennis tournament. She is ostracized because of her beautiful and too-flashy Las Vegas showgirl mom Stevie Castle (Susan Anton).

While mom becomes involved romantically with a reporter (Frank Converse) covering the tournament, K.C. befriends Missy Berryman (Shawn Foltz), top-seeded daughter of a rich socialite (Jessica Walter). Before the big final match against Missy, K.C. finds time to hustle money games against unwary male adult opponents (take that, Bobby Riggs!).

With five writers credited with "additional material" beyond the main screenplay, "Spring Fever" is unfortunately uneventful. Outside of a drug bust at a disco which nearly halts Missy's career, the pic divides equally between limning the activities of the pre-teens and their adult parents, with no teenagers (presumably the target audience) on view. Lame script even resorts to having Missy's dad (Stephen Young) suffer a heart attack during the final match in a dubious effort to create viewer interest in the outcome.

Casting (including obvious nepotism) has the young girls impressive on the court but evidencing little acting skill. Lead Carling Bassett is laughable in dramatic scenes and her duly-recorded grunting every time she hits a ball is irritating enough to keep one awake during the matches.

The adult cast has little to do, except for Jessica Walter, most impressively hard and nasty, reminding one of her underutilized big-screen potential since her extraordinary "Play Misty For Me" performance. —Lor.

Verszerzodes
(Blood Brothers)
(HUNGARIAN-COLOR)

Budapest, Feb. 15.

Hungarofilm release of a Dialog Studio, Mafilm, production. Features entire cast. Directed by Gyorgy Dobray. Screenplay, Peter Horvath, Dobray; camera (Eastmancolor), Gabor Szabo; music, Gyula Babos. Reviewed at Hungarian Film Week, Feb. 13, '83. Running Time: 78 MINS.

Pici (Tiny)	Istvan Bubik
Tulak	Attila Epres
Eva	Agi Bihari
Kriszta	Judit Toth

Straight-forward action film, doubtless influenced by American cinema. Pici and Tulak are buddies doing military service. Pici is an extrovert, confident, a womanizer; Tulak is shy, muddle-headed, indecisive. Pici takes his friend to meet his girlfriend, only to discover she's getting married to another man, though pregnant by Pici. There's a brawl, and it's the unfortunate Tulak who ends up wounding one of the wedding guests with a broken bottle. The pair are jailed, but after a while make a run for it, with Tulak killing a probation officer. They pick up a couple of girls, but needless to say any possibilities of happiness are short-lived.

Film is well-made, fast-moving and technically tops. Attila Epres as the born loser, Tulak, is very good, and there is good support down the line. This is a more commercial offering from Magyar film production, and though it lacks depth is OK of its kind. —*Strat.*

Talpra, Gyozo!
(Be Tough, Victor!)
(HUNGARIAN-COLOR)

Budapest, Feb. 15.

Hungarofilm release of an Objektiv Studio, Mafilm, production. Features entire cast. Directed by Rezso Szoreny. Screenplay, Mihaly Sukosd; camera (Eastmancolor), Peter Jankura; music, Zdenko Tamassy. Reviewed at Hungarian Film Week, Feb. 15, '83. Running Time: 98 MINS.
Victor .... Laszlo Helyey
Gabor .... Laszlo Vajda
Gabor's first wife .... Eva Almasi
Gabor's second wife .... Erika Bodnar
Mother-in-law .... Hedi Temessy
Alcoholic .... Istvan Iglodi
Friend .... Andras Balint

Somewhat obscure, precious treatment of recent Hungarian history, presented in a highly artificial and theatrical style. The tumultuous events of the early fifties, the tragic days of 1956, and the period of mild student revolt of the late sixties are all encapsulated in a strange tale of a childish 35-year-old insurance agent, Victor, who is 'adopted' by a plump opera singer, Gabor.

Acting as a kind of chorus to the stylized glimpses of history are Gabor's two wives and his sentimental mother-in-law. This could be an item for local audiences, though customers at the public screening caught sat through it all in stony silence. This kind of brittle pageant has to be done very well before it can begin to work, and director Rezso Szoreny mixes it with a very heavy hand. More was expected from the director of the very promising "Happy New Year" (1978). Safe to say that this current item will have almost no chances internationally. —*Strat.*

Hungarian Film Week

Szerencses Daniel
(Daniel Takes a Train)
(HUNGARIAN-COLOR)

Budapest, Feb. 15.

Hungarofilm release of a Hunnia Studio, Mafilm, Production. Features entire cast. Directed by Pal Sandor. Screenplay, Zsuzsa Toth, Zsuzsa Biro, from a short story by Andras Mezel; camera (Eastmancolor), Elemer Ragalyi; music, Gy-

orgy Selmeczi. Reviewed at Hungarian Film Week, Feb. 14, '83. Running time: 90 MINS.
Daniel Szerencses .... Peter Rudolf
Gyuri Angeli .... Sandor Zsoter
Marianne Erdelyi ....Kati Szerb
Mrs. Erdelyi .... Mari Torocsik
Mr. Erdelyi ....Dezso Garas
Mr. Angeli .... Gyula Bodrogi
Kapas .... Andras Kern

In recent years, Hungarian films have explored the recent past with increasing directness, looking back at the early days of Communism ("Angi Vera") or the early Sixties ("Time Stands Still"). Now Pal Sandor confronts one of the most sensitive of periods, 1956 itself, when Hungarians fought Soviet troops in the streets of Budapest.

"Daniel Takes a Train" is set in December of that year. The central character, Daniel, is not directly involved in the tumultuous events; he's hopelessly in love with Marianne, the girl next door. But now thousands of Hungarians are fleeing the country, including Marianne's parents. Daniel's best friend, Gyuri, has a more pressing reason to leave; he was a soldier whose entire platoon joined the insurgents, and now he's on the run. Daniel decides to join Gyuri on a train headed for the Austrian border. This is the start of a most exciting thriller, a tense and gripping tale of people caught up in a national catastrophe.

The train journey itself belongs in the same class as other memorable screen train journeys of the past, with the crowded carriages filled with refugees as well as police and security men. When the train stops at a village close to the border and the characters find themselves staying at a little hotel waiting for their chance to cross into Austria, the tension never lets up. At the same time, Daniel and Marianne have the opportunity, amid the turmoil, to consummate their relationship.

The film is forthright in capturing the complexities and passions of this terrible time, with longstanding hatreds coming to the surface as former comrades viciously turn on each other. A confrontation with young Russian soldiers is at the same time a tense and grimly funny sequence. Sandor, best known for "A Strange Role" (1975, known as "Improperly Dressed" in Britain) and the underrated "Deliver Us from Evil" (1976) has come up with his best film here, immeasurably aided by the pristine camerawork of Elemer Ragalyi. Performances are tops down the line. This one has commercial possibilities in situations where other top quality Hungarian films have succeeded, and should certainly represent its country at a major Festival in the near future.

It won the prize of Best Film of the Year from local jury. —*Strat.*

A Kutya eji Dala
(The Dog's Night Song)
(HUNGARIAN-COLOR)

Budapest, Feb. 15.

A Hungarofilm release of a Tarsulas Studios, Mafilm production. Features entire cast. Directed by Gabor Body. Screenplay, Sandor Erdelyi, Body, based on Vilmos Csaplar story; camera (Eastmancolor), Johanna Heer; music, Bizottsag Group. Reviewed at Hungarian Film Week, Feb. 10, '83. Running Time, 146 MINS.
The priest .... Gabor Body
The astronomer ......Attila Grandpierre
The invalid .... Andras Fekete
The army officer .... Janos Dersi
His wife .... Marietta Mehes
The consumptive woman . Gabriella Seres

Gabor Body is an unusual figure on the Hungarian film scene, an experimental filmmaker who makes an occasional narrative feature, his last being the four-hour romantic epic, "Narcissus and Psyche" (1980). His new film, adapted from a short story by Vilmos Csaplar, has moments of brilliance but overall emerges as an overlong and frequently obscure opus.

The story, when one can be deciphered, concerns a priest (played by Body himself) who arrives in a small village. He befriends a former local Communist Party Chief, now confined to a wheelchair after being hit by a sniper's bullet during the tumultuous events of 1956. He also tries to help a consumptive woman who comes to confession. Also in the village is an astronomer who sings with a punk group, The Running Coroners. The astronomer is friendly with a small boy, son of an erratic army officer and his wife; the latter quarrels with her husband and decamps for the city to become a cloakroom attendant in a nightclub. The husband and a friend track her down there. Meanwhile, the invalid man has attempted suicide and the consumptive woman dies when apparently accidentally impaled by a pin given her by the priest. Furthermore, the priest is revealed to be a phoney.

The film has a whiff of phoniness about it, too. Though Johanna Heer's camerawork is sometimes dazzling, it's often infuriatingly pretentious as it wanders around all over the place, frequently deliberately decapitating the characters on-screen. The punk scenes seem endless, and comparisons between Christianity and Communism (with Stalin being compared to Christ at one point) are naive. No doubting that Body has talent, but it's undisciplined and chaotic. Hard to see an audience for this lengthy and needlessly obscure film, even on home ground. However, it's visually OK, with some striking moments and complex video effects. Dolby sound, too, so no effort has been spared on what could only have been, in the West, a low-budget 16m production. Body's

own performance, as the phony priest, is suitably manic.

Film has been picked for the Forum in the upcoming Berlin Film Fest. —*Strat.*

Visszaesok
(Forbidden Relations)
(HUNGARIAN-COLOR)

Budapest, Feb. 15.

Hungarofilm release of an Objektiv Studio, Mafilm, Production. Features entire cast. Written & directed by Zsolt Kezdi Kovacs. Camera (Eastmancolor), Janos Kende. Reviewed at Hungarian Film Week, Feb. 12, '83. Running Time: 89 MINS.
Juli .... Lili Monori
Fodor .... Miklos B. Szekely
Mother .... Mari Torocsik
Father .... Jozsef Horvath
Brother ....Jozsef Toth
Pista ....Tibor Molnar
Doctor .... Gyorgy Banffy
Policeman .... Laszlo Horvath

Film about incest, based on a true story, which is simply told but exceptionally effective. Director Zsolt Kezdi Kovacs heard about the real-life couple from a newspaper story, met them, and wrote a script based on their experiences. The story takes place in a small village. Juli's husband hangs himself for no apparent reason one night; she's pregnant, but decides to have an abortion, and goes to live with her parents. One day, on a local bus, she meets Fodor, who lived in the village as a child and now, after two failed marriages and trouble with the police, is returning home.

The two are instantly attracted to each other and start a passionate affair before Juli discovers to her horror that Fodor is her stepbrother, son of her mother by a former marriage. But by now the lovers are obsessively involved with each other and there seems to be no turning back. Juli gets pregnant. When her mother discovers the truth, she reports the pair to the authorities and they're arrested. Fodor is sent to prison, Juli gets a suspended sentence. Her baby is born and is normal. But after a year, Fodor is released, and the affair starts up again, with Juli quickly becoming pregnant again.

Incest is a taboo not often explored in films, though there have been some notable examples. In "Forbidden Relations," Kezdi Kovacs confronts the situation head-on, and the audience soon finds itself siding with the passionate lovers. In actuality, it seems, the couple now have five normal children. Lead performances by Lili Monori, first used to advantage in an earlier Kezdi Kovacs film, "When Joseph Returns" (1975) and later seen in several Marta Meszaros pics, and newcomer Miklos B. Szekeley are splendid. Their intimate scenes are frank, desperate and suitably passionate. Also standout is veteran actress Mari Torocsik as Juli's mother who feels partly responsible for what she sees as an unholy alliance; the guilt drives her mad. Janos Kende's beautiful images are beyond praise; the village and its environs are hauntingly photographed, and one sequence of a sudden rainstorm on the plain is of surpassing beauty.

The theme and the way it's handled may shock some, but the film deserves to find its way into the market and should certainly represent Hungary at a major Festival later this year. —*Strat.*

Dogkeselyu
(The Vulture)
(HUNGARIAN-COLOR)

Budapest, Feb. 15.

Hungarofilm release of a Dialog Studio, Mafilm, production. Features entire cast. Directed by Ferenc Andras. Screenplay, Miklos Munkacsi, Andras, from a novel by Munkacski; camera (Eastmancolor), Elmer Ragalyi; music, Gyorgy Kovacs. Reviewed at Hungarian Film Week, Feb. 12, '83. Running time: 108 MINS.
Jozsef Simon .... Gyorgy Cserhalmi
Mrs. Halmos .... Hedi Temessy
Mrs. Szanto .... Zita Perczel
Cecilia Halmos ...... Maria Gladkowska

A fatalistic thriller about a loser who finally decides to strike back. Simon is a qualified engineer reduced to driving a taxi. He's divorced and unhappy in his private life. To top it all, he has a bad cold. Two chatty old ladies take his cab after attending a funeral, and when they leave he discovers they've stolen his life savings from his wallet. The authorities are skeptical about his story, his father won't help, nor will his ex-wife.

But Simon has picked up a clue from the conversation the two thieves had in the cab, and manages to track one of them down. Instead of reporting his success, he decides to take private revenge, especially as the old lady seems to him almost indecently well off. He makes elaborate plans to kidnap her daughter and hold her for ransom.

Director Ferenc Andras, who previously made the appealing "It's Rain and Shine Together" (1977) makes the best of what is basically rather a routine enterprise. He moves the film along at a good pace, filling it in with interesting characters and details. Performances are quite adequate, though little attempt is made to make the protagonist a very sympathetic character. It picks up towards the end as the details of Simon's plan to collect the ransom are gradually revealed, though in the early stages Andras tends to err on the side of obscurity, puzzling his audience a bit unnecessarily.

All in all a perfectly competent but quite unremarkable film. It's set to represent Hungary in the upcoming Berlin Film Festival.
— *Strat.*

Hatasvadaszok
(Midnight Rehearsal)
(HUNGARIAN-COLOR)

Budapest, Feb. 15.

Hungarofilm release of a Dialog Studio, Mafilm, production. Features entire cast. Directed by Miklos Szurdi. Screenplay, Peter Endre Varkonyi, Istvan Verebes, Szurdi; camera (Eastmancolor), Andras Szalai; music, Zsolt Dome. Reviewed at Hungarian Film Week, Feb. 11, '83. Running Time: 100 MINS.
Adam Horkai .... Sandor Szakacsi
Andrea ...'........... Dorottya Udvaros
The playwright .... Gyorgy Linka
The theatre manager ..... Tamas Vegvari
Kati .... Eniko Eszenyi
Andrea's husband .... Peter Trokan

A provocative, witty and stylish first feature which marks an auspicious debut as director for former actor Miklos Szurdi.

The setting is a provincial theatre where the director, Adam Horkai, is rehearsing his lacklustre cast in a tired production of a Schubert musical. Horkai is having an affair with Andrea, his leading actress, who is married to a doctor. The doctor has been treating a famous, award-winning writer who has only two weeks left to live. Back in 1951 he'd written a provocative play, "The Jacobins," set during the French Revolution, which had been banned by the Hungarian authorities. His great ambition is to see the play produced, finally, before he dies.

Horkai decides to stage an elaborate charade in respect of the admired author; the company will rehearse the play, knowing it can never be staged, and the writer can come to watch the rehearsals. However, the delighted author decides to stick around, despite his illness, for the play's opening; he doesn't know that everything is faked. Little by little, Horkai and his cast even fool themselves into thinking the play will actually go on. In one superb scene, Horkai (a rather dissolute character in reality) bullies an extraordinary performance out of one of his actresses, having lost sight of the fact that no audience will ever see it.

Judging by the reactions of the local audience at the screening caught, the dialog is funny and clever. Yet the film obviously has a serious theme which is pushed to the limit by director Szurdi. He himself worked in a provincial theatre, so doubless much of the film's intricate detail comes from first-hand knowledge. Acting is flawless down the line, starting with Sandor Szakacsi as the opportunistic director, though Dorottya Udvaros as his mistress is also worth noting. There are also some fine cameos among smaller roles, including one of the local Party member who comes to see a rehearsal.

Visually handsome, with fine production qualities and sharp photography by Andras Szalai, this

is a very promising first feature which should show up at a key Festival later in the year. It could also find specialized commercial success in major cities where the best Hungarian films have caught on. —*Strat.*

Viadukt
(Matushka)
(HUNGARIAN-U.S.-
W. GERMAN-COLOR.)

Budapest, Feb. 15.

Peer J. Oppenheimer presentation of a Hunnia Studio, Mafilm-Peer J. Oppenheimer-Andre Liblik production, in association with Wescom Productions Inc. Stars Michael Sarrazin. Directed by Sandor Simo. Screenplay, Peer J. Oppenheimer, Egon Eis; camera (Eastmancolor), Tamas Andor; music, Zdenko Tamassy; sets, Alexander Trauner; associate producer, Don Stern. Reviewed at Hungarian Film Week, Feb. 12, '83. Running Time: 95 MINS.
Sylvester Matushka .... Michael Sarrazin
Dr. Epstein .... Towje Kleiner
Ilona Almasi .... Constanze Engelbrecht
Kovacs .... Ferenc Bacs
Magda Matushka .... Herlinde Latzko
Tetzlaff .... Armin Mueller-Stahl
Inspector Balogh .... Geza Tordy

The English language version of this Hungarian-U.S.-W. German co-production is a misguided affair in which a disastrous soundtrack mixes uneasily with superb visuals and a fascinating story. To take the positive view first, the film deals with a real character, Sylvester Matushka, who was in the Austro-Hungarian army during the First World War and became obsessed with sabotaging trains.

Cause of his obsession is obscure, but even after he was apparently happily married and a father he kept sneaking off to damage the railway tracks. This obsession climaxes with the spectacular demolition, in Hungary in 1931, of the Orient Express, a piece of terrorism blamed on the Communists. The film suggests that the unstable Matushka was an unknowing pawn in the hands of sinister Hungarian Fascist elements, led by the mysterious Kovacs.

The story is quite fascinating, and visually the film is superb. With topnotch set design by veteran Alexander Trauner and sumptuous photography by Tamas Andor, "Matushka" delights the eyes.

But not the ears. The dialog, credited in this version to Peer J. Oppenheimer alone, though the Hungarian credits list only Egon Eis, is terrible. Anachronisms abound; people in the early thirties did not use expressions such as "No sweat!" or "Get lost!", but the film uses them in abundance. The leaden dialog jars with the visuals at every turn, and had the Budapest audience laughing in some of the more serious moments. This is certainly a career low for Michael Sarrazin, who has to deliver the worst of the dialog, and is frequently visibly ill-at-ease.

Film could be saved by releasing a well-produced Hungarian/German version, with subtitles in English territories; all the film's problems are in the crude English dialog.

Director Sandor Simo (remembered for "Happy Years of My Father" (1977), one of the best Magyar films of recent years), does what he can with the material. He is surely responsible for the film's handsome gloss, and it's a pity he couldn't have done something with the dialog. All in all, "Matushka" is an exceptionally frustrating experience. —*Strat.*

Adj Kiraly Katonat!
(The Princess)
(HUNGARIAN-B&W)

Budapest, Feb. 15.

Hungarofilm release of a Tarsulas Studio, Mafilm, Production. Features entire cast. Directed by Pal Erdoss. Screenplay, Istvan Kardos; camera, (black and white) Lajos Koltai, Ferenc Pap, Gabor Szabo. Reviewed at Hungarian Film Week, Feb. 10, '83. Running time: 115 MINS.
Jutka .... Erika Ozsda
Zsuzsa .... Andrea Szendrei
Peter .... Denes Diczhazy
Andras .... Arpad Toth
Jutka's sister .... Juli Nyako
Truck Driver .... Lajos Soltis

A first feature made in the now familiar style of Hungarian docudrama, "The Princess" rises above the limitations and technical deficiencies of the genre thanks to a perceptive script, knowing direction, and above all the heart-tugging performance of Erika Ozsda in the leading role.

She's a 15-year-old country girl, Jutka, who comes to the city with her best friend, Zsuzsa, to get work in a textile factory. Zsuzsa quickly becomes pregnant, but daren't tell her strait-laced parents, and when she visits home the baby girl is passed off as Jutka's. Meanwhile Jutka herself has lost her virginity to a smooth-talking circus acrobat (much more unromantically than it sounds, in fact) and has met Peter, a pleasant fellow who, she thinks, will marry her. She, too, becomes pregnant, but when she's brutally raped by one of Peter's drunken friends, she decides to have an abortion. Then she agrees to care for her friend's baby, and for a short while finds a new meaning to life.

After a slow start, the film quickly develops into a captivating character study of this country girl trying to get by in unfamiliar and often hostile surroundings. There are plenty of implicit criticisms of society here, from the cops who suddenly turn up in a bar checking customers' I.D.'s, to the factory foreman who indulges in unthinking sexual harassment, or to the four stone-faced women who represent the Abortion Board. In one of the film's happier sequences, Jutka and Peter go to the cinema and laugh their way through Milos Forman's "Loves of a Blonde," and indeed Jutka is in many ways a similar character to the heroine of Forman's Czech-produced movie, being similarly naive and optimistic. In her film debut, freckle-faced, wide-eyed Erika Ozsda proves to be quite a find.

A pity that the film's potential is undermined by the unnecessarily grainy black and while photography, or the frequent and irritating noise of the camera itself, proof that Hungarian filmmakers have yet to master the recording of direct sound. Despite its technical inadequacies, the film could be well received on its universal theme and the depth of Ozsda's performance.

Pic's original title literally means "King, Give Us a Soldier!", and is a reference to a children's game.

—*Strat.*

Nyom Nelkul
(No Clues)
(HUNGARIAN-COLOR)

Budapest, Feb. 15.

Hungarofilm release of a Budapest Studio, Mafilm, production. Features entire cast. Directed by Peter Fabry. Screenplay, Istvan Nemes; camera (Eastmancolor), Andras Peterffy; music, Laszlo Des, Dimenzio Group. Reviewed at Hungarian Film Week, Feb. 11, '83. Running Time: 85 MINS.

Peter	Tamas Cseh
Buksi	Miklos B. Szekely
Karesz	Karoly Dunai
Kis	Zoltan Bezeredy
Letra	Istvan Hunyadkurty
Szkall	Karloy Eperjes

Thriller about a shop-window dresser who is the secret mastermind of a series of ingenious robberies. This completely unbelievable film at least comes up with three ingenious robbery ideas. In one, thieves steal an icon from a church and sell it to West German dealers for a vast sum; then they cause the returning Germans to crash their car, and retrieve the icon, replacing it in the church and leaving the cops completely out of it. Next, a safe is stolen from under the very eyes of nightwatchmen via a judicious use of modern video techniques — this is a very well-conceived notion. Finally, an antique store is robbed of valuable diamonds, with the thief concealing the jewels in a hollowed table he'd already sold the store; later the table is resolt, and the jewels smuggled out.

Any one of these well-constructed scams might have made the basis for a thriller, but writer Istvan Nemes does nothing with them, and the film has minimal structure. None of the characters are developed in the slightest, and in the end the film just abruptly stops, in one of the most anti-climactic finishes in memory.

Visually the film is fine with occasionally some unusual effects as the frustrated cops use computers to try to locate the mysterious mastermind. But with a little more serious plotting, "No Clues" could have been a superior thriller; as it stands, it will be quickly forgotten.

— *Strat.*

Elveszett Illuziok
(Lost Illusions)
(HUNGARIAN-COLOR)

Budapest, Feb. 16.

Hungarofilm release of Objektiv Studio, Mafilm, production. Features entire cast. Directed by Gyula Gazdag. Screenplay, Miklos Gyorffy, Gyorgy Spiro, Gazdag, from a novel by Honore Balzac; camera (Eastmancolor), Miklos Jancso Jr; music, Istvan Martha. Reviewed at Hungarian Film Week, Feb. 16, '83. Running Time: 103 MINS.

Laszlo Sardi	Gabor Mate
Kriszta	Dorottya Udvaros
Luszto	Robert East
Daniel	Boguslaw Linda
Mrs. Barsony	Agi Margittai
Mrs. Deszkas	Ilona Beres
Flora Koves	Juli Basti
Finta	Laszlo Sinko
Dori	Ferenc Bessenyei

Transposing a Balzac novel to Budapest in 1968 is an interesting idea which remains somewhat unfulfilled in this diffuse tale of a young man's overweening ambition. Laszlo Sardi arrives from the provinces hoping to make his mark in the literary circles of Budapest, aided by his mistress, an older woman. But she soon drops him on the advice of a friend, and he has to make his own way. Through a variety of contacts he soon gets a job as critic for an influential magazine, and starts a passionate love affair with an ambitious young actress. But this cocky young man is making enemies along the way, and before long he finds himself disgraced and ousted from his position.

Film is a bit unmotivated, and the central performance of Gabor Mate as the ambitious Sardi lacks the ruthlessness required. On the other hand, Dorottya Udvaros makes an impression as the young actress who throws over her middle-aged lover to take up with the apparently up-and-coming protagonist. The bitchiness and back-biting of the literary world of the late Sixties is well etched, though one glaring anachronism has characters studying Polaroid photos of a type not in use until many years later. Production dress is handsome, with fine photography by Miklos Jancso Jr. —*Strat.*

A Sertes
(The Insult)
(HUNGARIAN-COLOR)

Budapest, Feb. 15.

Hungarofilm release of a Dialog Studio, Mafilm, and Hungarian Television production. Features entire cast. Directed by Peter Bacso. Screenplay, Basco (based on short stories by Vassili Shukshin); camera (Eastmancolor), Tamas Andor; music, Szabolcs Fenyes. Reviewed at Hungarian Film Week, Feb. 13, '83. Running Time: 93 MINS.

The Insult

Man	Geza Tordy
Wife	Piroska Molnar

Son ... Kalman Solyom

Conversation in a Restaurant

Old man	Sandor Suka
Young man	Laszlo Vajda

The Unexpected Guest

The artist	Miklos Gabor
The wife	Judit Meszleri
The husband	Laszlo Huszar
The daughter	Klara Leviczky

Three short stories by the late Soviet writer-director Vassili Shukshin have been adapted by director Peter Bacso for this uneven omnibus film, originally made for television. The first story, "The Insult," runs 22 minutes and is both the shortest and the best of the three. A man and his small son are shopping when a shop assistant, mistaking the man for someone else, accuses him of drunkenness. The father is outraged, the more so when another customer insults him too. It leads to a brawl, which resolves nothing. Despite its rather abrupt ending, this is an amusing anecdote set, like all three stories, in the U.S.S.R., which seems to reflect quite accurately the problems faced by shoppers in that country.

Second story, "Conversation in a Restaurant" (33 minutes), has an old, lonely man meet a young worker from Siberia in a night-club. Both are fascinated by the singer and get drunk. The young man promises to take the old man back to Siberia with him, but next day leaves without him.

Lastly, "The Unexpected Guest" (30 minutes) is a rather depressing tale of an alcoholic artist who travels to a small village in search of his long-lost daughter.

The stories themselves are rather charming, but Bacso's handling is disappointingly pedestrian. Only in the first tale is any real wit and tension generated, making the subsequent too anti-climactic. The last story is especially turgid and self-pitying. Bacso has made interesting films in the past, including the long-delayed "The Witness," made in 1968 but released only a couple of years ago; but on the whole he seems better suited to meaty drama than to subjects requiring a light touch. Technically, film is adequate, having been blown up to 35m from a 16m original. —*Strat.*

Voros Fold
(Red Earth)
(HUNGARIAN-COLOR)

Budapest, Feb. 15.

Hungarofilm release of a Tarsulas Studio, Mafilm, production. Features entire cast. Directed by Laszlo Vitezy. Screenplay, Istvan Darday; camera (Eastmancolor), Ferenc Pap, Mate Darvas. Reviewed at Hungarian Film Week, Feb. 13, '83. Running Time: 100 MINS.

Laszlo Szanto	Imre Nemeth
Kovacs	Sandor Kocsis
Torok	Kalman Toronyi
Kelemen	Ferenc Toth
Jozsef Kraft	Vilmos Gadori

Totally gripping, gritty film which angrily exposes flaws in the relations between workers and management in today's Hungary. It may sound dull, and probably has limited commercial possibilities, but it's an eye-opener all the same. In style, the film seems to owe something to the critical Polish films of Kieslowski and others, or possibly to British helmer Kenneth Loach.

Laszlo Szanto is an honest, hard-working middle-aged man who works in a bauxite mine in western Hungary. He also has a small farm, and one day his pigs turn up bauxite deposits right on the surface of his property. Excited, he reports his find to the management, but is ignored; it seems the authorities find this new discovery simply too much trouble to deal with, and they'd rather keep working the established mine. Matters change, however, when it's discovered the existing mine is affecting a local thermal spring which has been bringing in tourists for health cures. Now the bosses find Szanto's discovery suddenly more attractive.

In short order, the area is transformed as the mining equipment is moved in. Szanto's neighbors are outraged, and he's ostracized. Worse, he can't get the compensation he feels he deserves for his land, or even an adequate reward for his original discovery. In a sequence of tremendous irony, he's summoned to an award-giving ceremony in a chauffeur-driven car, and gets a token award, less than those given to the management who ignored him earlier. And to add insult to injury, nobody bothers to drive him home again and he's force to hitch-hike. Eventually he's evicted from his home.

Full credit to the Hungarian film industry for making such a film in which the system itself comes under intense criticism. A scene in which a V.I.P. from Moscow is shown around the mine speaks volumes in itself. The film is a bit talky, but constantly involving in its human drama and wider implications. As the little man up against the system, Imre Nemeth is quite splendid.

Director Laszlo Vitezy, making his second film, also injects plenty of visual humor, as in the opening scene where Mass is being said and at the conclusion of the service a curtain is pulled back to reveal portraits of Lenin, Marx and Engels behind the 'altar' in this all-purpose village hall. Script by Istvan Darday also deserves commendation. "Red Earth," unfortunately, won't be an easy film to sell, but it deserves to be widely seen.

—*Strat.*

Cha Cha Cha
(HUNGARIAN-COLOR)

Budapest, Feb. 15.

Hungarofilm release of an Objektiv Studio, Mafilm, production, in association with Hungarian Television. Features entire cast. Directed & screenplay by Janos Kovacsi. Camera (Eastmancolor), Miklos Jancso Jr.; Music; Hungaria. Reviewed at Hungarian Film Week, Feb. 10, '83. Running Time: 83 MINS.

Gruber	Peter Rudolf
Virag Fekete	Rita Tallos
Sztasni	Matyas Usztics
The Dancing Master	Frigyes Hollosi
The Dancing Mistress	Dorottya Geczy
Gruber's father	Tibor Kristof
Gruber's mother	Terez Varhegyi

A familiar tale of the coming-of-age of a shy teenager in 1962, "Cha Cha Cha" is a slight comedy which seems overlong at 83 minutes. However, in his handling of actors and some of his ideas, first-timer Janos Kovacsi could bear watching in the future.

Gruber is about 16, and naturally interested in sex. While dozens of people who inhabit the Budapest apartment house where he lives crowd round a neighbor's antique black and white tv set to watch the stirring tales of "William Tell," Gruber eyes a lucky fellow kissing a girl in the back of the room. However, the main focus of Gruber's life, and indeed about 90% of the film, is taken up with the Sunday afternoon dancing class where an avuncular dancing master and his vapidly grinning assistant endeavour to teach a roomful of "young gentlemen and ladies" how to dance the fox-trot, the waltz, and even the cha-cha-cha. For the teenagers, this is the closest they've come to physical contact with the opposite sex.

There are a few laughs here in the antics of the kids and the attitudes of the little orchestra (the drummer getting plastered, the pianist surreptitiously reading the sports pages), but not enough to carry a feature length film. Nor is the overtly explicit and rather brutal climax too successful. However, there are plenty of pleasant performances, and Peter Rudolf as the central character gives an incisive study in teenage eagerness and, finally, pain. Interesting to note that in Budapest in 1962, talk between boys and girls seems to revolve entirely around a new Lollobrigida film currently playing in a city theatre, again underlining the point that people are much the same everywhere when you get down to the basics. —*Strat.*

Egyutteles
(Coexistence)
(HUNGARIAN-W. GERMAN-COLOR)

Budapest, Feb. 15.

Hungarofilm release of an Objektiv Studio, Mafilm/Infafilm (Munich) production. Features entire cast. Directed by Livia Gyarmathy. Screenplay, Geza Boszormenyi; camera (Eastmancolor), Ferenc Pap. Reviewed at Hungarian Film Week, Feb. 13, '83. Running Time: 83 MINS.

Centering around a wedding, this documentary explores the on-going frictions between people of different ethnic backgrounds in south-

eastern Hungary. Film traces the background, showing that waves of German migrants settled in this area in the 18th century after the local population had been thinned out by 150 years of Turkish occupation. But the Germans retained their own customs and ways, and hardly mixed with the locals. After World War 2, many Germans were evicted from homes where their families had lived for 200 years and sent back to Germany; their places were taken by Hungarians from the south-east, a province that became part of Rumania.

Over the years, the differences between the various displaced peoples always remained. Now, a girl of German stock is to marry a boy of Hungaro-Rumanian stock. Both families oppose the match, but the young people are determined. Film culminates in the wedding celebrations, held partly in one village, partly in another to mollify both families.

There are a lot of talking heads in the early stages, but the material is interesting and newsreel archive footage is well used. The final wedding sequences are charming, with everyone, including the bridegroom, having a good cry. Hard to see commercial prospects for this, but it could be interesting for tv, maybe with a little condensation. —*Strat.*

Csak semmi Panik ...
(Don't Panic, Please!)
(HUNGARIAN-COLOR)

Budapest, Feb. 15.

Hungarofilm release of a Budapest Studio, Mafilm, production. Features entire cast. Directed by Sandor G. Szonyi. Screenplay, Istvan Bujtor; camera (Eastman color), Gyula Bornyi; music, Karoly Frenreisz. Reviewed at Hungarian Film Week, Feb. 11, '83. Running Time: 88 MINS.

Lt. Otvos	Istvan Bujtor
Dr. Kardos	Andras Kern
Lt. Boros	Gyula Bodrogi
Sibille Gudrat	Petra Hinze
Matsuka	Laszlo Banhidy
Granddaughter	Monika Kossovits
Tar	Gabor Koncz
Henrik Rombeld	Dioko Rosic

This mundane comedy-thriller is the third in a series scripted by actor Istvan Bujtor and centering on himself as a tough cop in the Lake Balaton district of Hungary.

Bujtor (brother of late actor Zoltan Latinovits) seems to model himself on Italian Bud Spencer; he's a big, bearded fellow with fists of iron. However, this lacklustre vehicle, involving buried treasure, a kidnapped German woman tourist, and an unscrupulous gang of crooks, is only for the most undemanding local audiences. The fights and chases are poorly staged, the humor is obvious and childish, and even a classic scene of suspense, involving a bomb planted in the hero's car, is botched. Strictly for home consumption. —*Strat.*

Berlin Film

Heller Wahn
(A Labor of Love)
(W. GERMAN-FRENCH-COLOR)

Berlin, March 1.

A Bioskop-Film Production, Munich, in coproduction with Les Films du Losange, Paris, and Westdeutscher Rundfunk (WDR), Mainz. Producers, Eberhard Junkersdorf (Germany), Margaret Menegoz (France). Features entire cast. Written and directed by Margarethe von Trotta. Camera (color), Michael Ballhaus; sets, Juergen Henze; music, Nicolas Economou, Carole King, Robert Schumann; editing, Dagmar Hirtz. Reviewed at Berlin Film Fest (competition), Feb. 24, '83. Running time: 105 MINS.

Cast: Hanna Schygulla (Olga), Angela Winkler (Ruth), Peter Striebeck (Franz), Christine Fersen (Erika), Franz Buchrieser (Dieter), Wladimir Yordanoff (Alexej), Agnes Fink (Mother), Felis Moeller (Christof), Jochen Striebeck (Bruno), Therese Affolter (Renate), Werner Eichhorn (Schlesinger), Helga Ballhaus (Gallery Owner), Peter Aust (Hansen), Carla Egerer (Frau Hansen).

"A Labor of Love" is a miscarriage, speaking from a feminist point-of-view. This is the fourth feature by cine-feminist filmer Margarethe von Trotta on the same theme with only slight variation.

"A Labor of Love" stars Hanna Schygulla (Maria Braun, alias Olga) and Angela Winkler (Katharina Blum, alias Ruth) as the two new sisters dependent on each other's love and affection. Schygulla is the outgoing type, a literature professor at the university teaching a seminar course. She's separated from her stage-director husband, and has a teenaged son at home, as well as a Russian pianist for a lover. Winkler is shy and withdrawn, married to a "peace expert" who needs her to maintain his own self-confidence. She is a ripe candidate for suicide, save that she can save herself by painting on the side. There are scenes in the Provence and in Cairo, as well as at the university and stage-rehearsals (the leading male, Peter Striebeck, is a theatre manager in Hamburg in fact — he's the pic's peacemaker).

Lensing (Michael Ballhaus) and Trotta's knack for pacing are the pluses. The logic of some scenes is mind-boggling, while the emotional component is disturbing. Perhaps Trotta could offer a female's point-of-view on masculinity, and then the rest on women's rights could be sorted out from there. The problem with Trotta's films is that it's difficult to figure out what she getting at.

There's talent buried under all those non-sequiturs. She's a better director than writer. "A Labor of Love" is the apogee of the German "Autor" film. —*Holl.*

Neupline Zatmeni
(Incomplete Eclipse)
(CZECH-COLOR)

Berlin, March 1.

A Barrandov Film Studios Production, Prague. Features entire cast: Directed by Jaromil Jires. Screenplay, Jires, Daniela Fischerova; camera (color), Emil Sirotek; editing, Josef Valuslak; sound, Antonin Kravda; music, Zdeněk Pololanik. Reviewed at Berlin Film Festival, Feb. 19, 1983. Running time: 48 MINS.

Czech director Jaromil Jires specializes in films concerning problems of young. "Incomplete Eclipse" recounts the struggle of a 14-year-old girl, Marta, growing up facing the loss of her sight as a result of an accident caused by her spoiled, younger sister.

Most of the action takes place in a school for the blind where Marta, convincing played by Lucie Patikova, clings to her illusion she will regain her sight in time as she has been led to believe by her mother. When she realizes her blindness will be permanent, she resents her mother bitterly, retreats into an inner world and contemplates suicide. But a psychologist, Dr. Mos, excellently portrayed by Oldrich Navratil, eventually succeeds in imparting enough confidence in the girl so that she can cope with her fate.

Despite competent credits and direction, film is a downer without the redeeming inspiration of "The Miracle Worker." The transition from despair and withdrawal to a stand up to fate resolution lacks conviction. Little Continental commercial prospects, no offshore possibilities. —*Kind.*

Krieg Und Frieden
(War and Peace)
(W. GERMAN-COLOR-DOCU)

Berlin, March 1.

A coproduction of Pro-ject Filmproduktion im Filmverlag der Autoren, Bioskop-Film, and Kairos-Film, Munich; world rights, Filmverlag der Autoren, Munich. A documentary and fiction film by Heinrich Boell, Volker Schloendorff, Alexander Kluge, Stefan Aust, and Axel Engstfeld (fiction sequences scripted by Boell). Camera (color), (for Kluge), Werner Luering, Thomas Mauch, (for Schloendorff), Franz Rath, Igor Luther, (for Aust), Franz Rath, (for Engstfeld), Bernd Mosblech; editing, Beate Mainka-Jellinghaus, Carola Mai, Dagmar Hirtz, Barbara von Weitershausen; production managers, Gerd von Halem (Bioskop-Film) and Daniel Zuta (Kairos-Film). Reviewed at Berlin Film Fest (out-of-competition), Feb. 19, '83. Running time: 120 MINS.

With Juergen Prochnow, Guenter Kaufmann, Manfred Zapatka, Karl-Heinz Merz, Heinz Bennent, Edgar Selge, Angela Winkler, Michael Gahr, Hans-Michael Rehberg, Dieter Traier.

The omnibus film, "War and Peace," directed by Alexander Kluge, Volker Schloendorff, and Stefan Aust, with an extra episode directed by Axel Engstfeld and three fiction segments scripted by Heinrich Boell, follows in line with earlier German history lessons made by Kluge, Schloendorff &

Company: "Germany in Autumn" (1978) and "The Candidate" (1980). The first two were up-to-date portraits of West Germany and its political climate, whereas "War and Peace" is the case of a chronicle-film losing its raison d'etre due to a shift in government midway through the project.

"War and Peace," as the title indicates, has to do with the Peace Movement. Back on Oct. 10, 1981, there was an enormous crowd gathering in Bonn for a peace march, the message being aimed then at Helmut Schmidt's Social Democrat Party and the government's stand on the NATO agreements. A few months later, the Schmidt government fell from power (due to the swing in the coalition government by the partner Free Democrat Party). This brought about a rise to power of Helmut Kohl and the Christian Democrat Union/Christian Socialist Union parties, again in coalition with the Free Democrats. In addition, a new election has been set for March 6, just five days after the close of the Berlin fest and and only week after the nation-wide release of "War and Peace." This means that the directors would logically have to decide on whether to support the policy of the Social Democrats or condemn it, at least insofar as the Armament Issue is concerned.

The outcome is that "War and Peace" doesn't have a clear point-of-view at all. The first half of the film drifts in the general direction of the Peace Movement, with refined ironical statements by Kluge on the threatening situation of two superpowers stationing nuclear warheads smack on the West German border to the Socialist Bloc countries within target range of the Soviet Union. The filmmakers as a whole also deploy the ideology of a nuclear war in today's age of the super-kill. Then, shifting gears, the film has a whack at Chancellor Helmut Kohl, offering a parody of the political figure at home and abroad — particularly at the White House with President Reagan.

As for the Heinrich Boell episodes — titled "Space Talk," "Atom Bunker," and "Kill Your Sister" — these are definitely in the vein of the Peace Movement and threat of nuclear war, but they are embarrassingly staged and acted against cheap sets, and thereby lost their effectiveness. Previously announced tracts on former Chancellor Helmut Schmidt in talks with East Germany's Erich Honnecker have also been dropped.

. In short, the film has been too long in coming. Indeed, the German tv-reportage on the American bishops and church leaders in Europe could be seen on the same evening as the film's preem — with the result that the religious spokesmen are stronger voices than those of the filmmakers on the question of

"War and Peace" today. One has the feeling that Kluge & Co. wanted very much to turn their cameras on Bonn entirely. Even the comment on the Summit Conference in France — comprised mostly of protocol jokes (helicopter landings, a canceled boat-trip, Reagan's face when Francois Mitterand unexpectedly condemned Israeli aggression in Lebanon) — is without sting and only amusing as a witty afterthought.

Lastly, the film is dull in far too many episodes. The juxtaposition and editing of key scenes and episodes are without logic, or the rationale is known only to the filmmakers with little chance of the audience unraveling the clues and metaphors. —Holl.

La Belle Captive
(The Beautiful Prisoner)
(FRENCH-COLOR)

Berlin, March 1.
An Argos Films Production. Executive Producer, Bernard Bouix. Directed by Alain Robbe-Grillet. Features entire cast. Screenplay, Robbe-Grillet, Frank Verpillat; camera (color), Henri Alekan; editing, Bob Wade; sound, Gerard Barra; production design, Aime Deude; costumes, Piet Bolscher. Reviewed at Berlin Film Festival, Feb. 25, 1983. Running time: 88 MINS.
Walter .... Daniel Mesguich
Marie-Ange .... Gabrielle Lazure
Sara .... Cyrielle
Inspector Francis ...... Daniel Emilfork
Van de Reeves .... Roland Dubillard
Dr. Morgentodt ..... Francois Chaumette

Alain Robbe-Grillet, writer-filmmaker, and a leading novelist and theorist of France's "nouveau roman," has turned out a classy, literary-based opus with elements of E.A. Poe, Gothic castles, Greek legend, symbols, vampirism and bizarre doctors, all within a nightmarish dream sequence.

Film represents an intellectual exercise, with images and eroticism in part based on painter Rene Magritte's "La Belle Captive" painting, the source of the film's title. Walter, with wife Sara, has just moved into a new apartment, where he experiences a terrifying nightmare during which the legend of "The Fiancee of Corinth" unfolds. Walter becomes infatuated with a beautiful young woman at a discotheque, who disappears and is found again under mysterious circumstances. In searching for her, he learns that the girl had died in an accident seven years before from her father, a medic who indulges in parapsychic experiments in an effort to contact the dead.

In line with the legend, the deceased girl's father offers Walter shelter for the night. Film, whose music score was adapted from Franz Schubert's D-minor string quartet and Duke Ellington's "The Mooch," skillfully matches a Kafka-esque element of fatal inability to carry out an urgent task because of unexpected events. The disjointed dream-sequence plot re-

plete with the usual symbolic dream logic, seems to say the dreams reflect the false reality of another world, or the other way round, the real world is false. Like Alain Resnais' "Last Year at Marienbad," scripted by Robbe-Grillet, film mixes the unconscious mind, memory and reality with erotic fantasy. European playoff best bet with art theatres and specialty houses most likely outlets. Little popular appeal, despite excellent credits. Television prospects faint. —Kind.

Yaju-Deka
(The Dropout)
(JAPANESE-COLOR)

Berlin, March 1.
A Toei Company Production. Directed by Eiichi Kudo. Stars Ken Ogata, Ayumi Ishida; Screenplay, Kumio Kanami; camera (color), Seizo Sengen; editing, Isamu Ichida; sound, Hideaki Kuriyama; music, Katsuo Ono; production design, Akira Takahashi. Reviewed Feb. 21, 1983 at the Berlin Film Festival. Running Time: 122 MINS.
Seiji Otaki .... Ken Ogata
Keiko Yamane .... Ayumi Ishida
Toshiaka Sakagami ..... Shigeru Izumiya
Kuroki .... Mikio Narita
Miura .... Kaoru Kobayashi

Director Eiichi Kudo, whose credits include Samurai films made in the 1950s and a number of gangster films in the 1960s, has a reputation for skillful handling of violence including brutal fight scenes. He carries on in "The Dropout," a routine melodrama depicting the usual police headquarters scenes, barroom brawls, sex, drugs and murder climaxed by a multi-squad car chase of a driver in Osaka in a stolen car in the final frames.

Plot revolves around the fatal stabbing of a young girl, allegedly a student, but in reality a call girl in high circles. Detective Otaki (Ken Ogata), known as "Wild Beast" for his hard, unconventional methods on the homicide squad, investigates. After being suspended from duty for beating up a suspect, he refuses to give up and concocts a plan to trap the psychopathic killer using his girlfriend as a decoy.

Plot is complicated by the return from prison of the husband of Otaki's mistress, who dies when the plan backfires. Action takes place in a realistic backdrop of Osaka. Film score is western pop style and ends with a song in English, extolling "freedom" and choice of lifestyles. An outmoded genre, prospects for any media are questionable. —Kind.

Echtzeit
(Realtime)
(W. GERMAN-COLOR-DOCU/FICTION)

Berlin, March 1.
A coproduction of B-Pictures, Hamburg, with von Vietinghoff Film Production, Berlin, in collaboration with Westdeutscher Rundfunk (WDR), Cologne.

Features entire cast. Directed by Hellmuth Costard and Juergen Ebert. No screenplay. Camera (color), Costard, Thomas Schwan, Martin Manz, Carolyn Swartz; editing, Costard, Ebert, Sigrid Halvensleben-Gaul; sound, Freudigmann, Ebert, Joerg Priesner, Egon Bunne; animation, Raimund Krumme, Sibylle Hofter, Costard, Ebert; electronics, Winfried Wolf. Reviewed at Berlin Film Fest (out-of-competition), Feb. 19, '83. Running time: 111 MINS.
With Adolf Hornung, Reiner Weber, Erwin Quednau, Manfred Huebschmann, Ernst Weihreter, Ernesto Adam, Hans Rainer Kraft, Leo M. DeMayer, Freiherr von Adelsheim, Konrad Zuse, Klaus Schubert, Winfried, Schrempp, Gottfried Muehlhaupt, Presidents Francois Mitterand-Karl Carstens-Ronald Reagan, News commentator Friedrich Nowottny, Georg Kraemer, Ruth Bierich, Christian Brueckner, Susanna Bonasewicz.

Hellmuth Costard and Juergen Ebert's "Realtime" refers in the title to computer terminology, and it's billed by the directors as "a film without a screenplay" (apparently as an answer to those German subsidy commissions that demand a screenplay to begin with for consideration). Of course, a script of some kind is visible in the end — at least for the fiction scenes — but the weight of the film is in the direction of documentary and animation-experimental genres, rather than a narrative story in the feature-film tradition. Pic was unspooled in the fest's Zoo Palast in an out-of-comp slot.

"Realtime" refers to the technology concept of a computer keeping up with an actual event it is supposed to control — that is (as the filmmakers note themselves), "when the analysis, calculation, and control of a process coincide without a time-lag." This said, Costard and Ebert present the case of military satellites measuring the earth's surface-landscapes whereby an image on a camera-like "thinking" computer-screen of any desired spot on the face of the earth can be "played with" by the computer-lords as in the example of video computer games.

"Realtime" contrasts a scientist who now feels he is redundant with his alive young girlfriend who works with porpoises in an entertainment water-tank attraction, the end result being that the scientist loses control of his senses, imagines he too is cruising over the face of the earth, and falls (as in the Icarus legend) to his death during the fatal imagined flight. The girl finds him dead in an empty field. Other intellectual statements on man's conceptual prowess includes a tour of architect Balthasar Neumann's grand staircase design in the castle of Wuerzburg and, naturally enough, the Reagan-Carstens meeting of recent tv-coverage wintage at Bruehl Palace near Cologne (another Neumann creation) for extra commentary on the follies of the technically oriented egghead of modern civilization — these Neumann-designed staircases far exceed in beauty and perfection the images on a computerized date-screen.

Oddly enough, Costard himself is obsessed with technology and the wizardry of computerized cartoons and "thinking cameras" coughing up landscape images from relaying satellites. One has the feeling that he aches to get his hands on the equipment and play with it in an impishly sarcastic manner. If anything, "Realtime" is a docu on computerized filmmaking, and a rather enchanting one, when the focus is entirely on the possibilities of the medium. Only for special auds. —Holl.

Via Degli Specchi
(Street of Mirrors)
(ITALIAN-COLOR)

Berlin, March 1.

A Tangram Film, Rome, production in collaboration with RAI. Produced by Roberto Levi, Claudio Bioni. Stars Nicole Garcia. Directed by Giovanna Gagliardo. Screenplay, Gagliardo, Jean Grault; camera (color), Camillo Bazzoni; music, Pino Donaggio; costumes, Danda Or; production design, Francesco Bronzi. Reviewed at Berlin Film Festival, Feb. 23, 1983. Running time: 90 MINS.

Francesca	Nicole Garcia
Gianfranco	Heinz Bennent
Veronica	Milva
Consigliere Bianchi	Massimo Serrato
Giuseppe	Claudio Bigagli

Female director Giovanna Gagliardo's second feature film, "Street of Mirrors," fails to come off. A woman magistrate in a municipal justice department investigates the apparent suicide of a young girl, which at first appears to be a routine case.

During the course of her investigations, she discovers that the girl had a lover, who turns out to be her own husband. The slowly unravelling plot takes a gimmicky turn near the end but cannot rescue the film, whose style is more suited for television than theatre. A nervous, intruding music score, stilted acting, and slow pace for a mystery, preclude any offshore possibilities with even tv playoff unlikely. —Kind.

Hakkari'de Bir Mevsim
(A Season in Hakkari)
(TURKEY-W. GERMAN-COLOR)

Berlin, March 1.

A Kentel Film (Munich) and Data A.S. Istanbul co-production. Directed by Erdin Kiral. Stars Genco Ercal. Screenplay, Onat Kutlar (based on novel by Ferit Edgue); camera (color), Kenan Ormanlar; editing, Yilmaz Atadeniz; sound, Cemil Kivanc; music, Timur Selcuk. Reviewed at Berlin Film Festival, Feb. 23, 1983. Running time: 109 MINS.

An elementary school teacher is transferred to a remote village in a rugged mountainous area in the north-eastern corner of Anatolia in southwest Turkey. The teacher, an idealist played movingly by Genco Ercal, finds the village in primitive conditions, with no electricity, roads, post, doctor or medicines. His pupils have no textbooks, notebooks or pencils.

In his loneliness amidst the stones, snow and indifference, the teacher reveals personal conflicts through interior monologs. But these begin to pale compared with the harsh life of the villagers, who live according to their own rules untouched by the passing of time. Their total isolation is indicated by lack of medical attention from outside after a mysterious epidemic takes the lives of many babies in the province.

The teacher becomes involved with the villagers' problems but feels, in the final analysis, unable to help, coming from a different world. When winter is finally over, the teacher sadly takes leave of his pupils and returns to civilization. A slow-paced, visually beautiful film in quasi-documentary style, there is little action and more mood. Credits are excellent.

Director Erdin Kiral's third feature film could find outlets in art theatres, education television channels and the fest circuit. Commercial possibilities limited to domestic market and Turkish cinemas in West Germany, which has a large Turkish worker population.

—Kind.

Dies Rigorose Leben
(Nothing Left to Lose)
(WEST GERMAN-COLOR)

Berlin, March 1.

An Atossa Film Production, Munich, in coproduction with Roxy Film, Munich, and in collaboration with Zweites Deutsches Fernsehen (ZDF), Mainz; world rights, Weltvertrieb im Filmverlag der Autoren, Munich. Features entire cast. Written and directed by Vadim Glowna. Screenplay assistance (English language), Christopher Doherty; camera (color), Martin Schaefer; music, Peer Raben; sets, Dieter Flimm, Ute Truthmann, Kathryn Long, Nellie Ben; production manager, Mark Shelly (USA), Udo Heiland (West Germany); assistant on location, Gabriele Rohrer. Reviewed at Berlin Film Fest (Competition), Feb. 22, '83. Running time: 99 MINS.

Angela Molina (Rosa), Jerzy Radiwilowicz (Joseph), Vera Tschechowa (Salka), Viveca Lindfors (Ada), Elfriede Kuzmany (Martha), Jose Sierra (George Lone Tree), Federico Rodigues (Johnny), Dolores Davis (Lorraine), Beth Gottlieb (Juicy Lucy), Helen Pesante (Ruby).

A noted German actor, Vadim Glowna turned to directing and scored on his debut with "Desperado City." Now he's back with "Nothing Left to Lose" (literal translation of title is "This Rigorous Life"), one of the three West German entries at Berlin.

Glowna has a bit more left to lose than he figured: the film is pretty much of a disaster so far as the mainstream of the arthouse mart is concerned. There just isn't much to say about a slick attempt to shoot a film in English at a roadstop in a Texas desert with a German and international cast (no Yanks or Brits in any of the leads) and then dubbed back into German for the Berlinale audience — save to add that it might just as well have been left in the same desert from which it originated.

Glowna went off the deep end by attempting the impossible in the first place: American cinema German-style, with the option to dub it all back into German for the home audience. The English-lingo version was not unspooled at Berlin, but the direction the film takes indicates that too much was improvised and patched together along the line to cloud even the general drift of the story.

The setting is the Southwest where two highways cross in the desert — there's a gas station, a bordello-trailor with "Lorraine's" in neon, a garage, a snack-bar, the remains of a drive-in amid a scrapheap. The story is about a group of stranded German emigrants huddled together in mobile-homes.

Joe loves Rosa who shacks up with truckers, one of whom he kills as he's sure this is a rape. Joe gets five years in prison; meanwhile, his mother dies and he's back just in time for a burial on boot-hill. His sister chucked a wedding with an honest sodbuster of the Mennonite school, for she really loves Joey and is about to go off her nut at the death of the mother — or head across the street to the roadhouse.

The action picks up when Rosa gets involved with another trucker, and decides to run off with him. The trucker takes his vengeance on the innocent rival by attempting to kill Joey by knocking over the derrick where Joseph is puttering around with his projector at the drive-in in broad daylight. Our hero decides to set everything on fire: the gas-station and the snack-bar, the inferno reaching its height when the enraged trucker, losing his girlfriend to Joey, drives smack into the mountain of flames for a climactic explosion.

Sole saving grace is Martin Schaefer's light-splashed lensing. —Holl.

Empfaenger Unbekannt
(Addressee Unknown)
(WEST GERMAN-COLOR-16m)

Berlin, March 1.

A Creative Age Film Production, Wiesbaden, in coproduction with Zweites Deutsches Fernsehen (ZDF), Mainz. Features entire cast. Written and directed by Sohrab Shahid Saless. Camera (color) Ramin Reza Molai; editing, Cornelia Palme; sets, Claus-Juergen Pfeiffer; music, Wolfgang Heinze; costumes, Monika Grube; collaborator, Imke Bellfuss; tv-producer, Eckhart Stein. Reviewed at Berlin Film Fest (Forum of Young Cinema), Feb. 19, 1983. Running time: 86 MINS.

Cast: Iris von Reppert-Bismarck (the wife), Manfred Zapatka (the husband), Umran Ertok (the foreigner).

Sohrab Shahid Saless's "Addressee Unknown" is a low-budget 16m project about the alienation foreigners feel in Germany — in this case, a Turkish architect without a job. Unspooled in the Forum of Young Cinema, it's one of two films by the director in the Berlinale — the other being "Utopia" in the competition.

It's along the lines of his usually perceptive view of contemporary German society as presented in "Far from Home" (1975), "Coming of Age" (1976), "Diary of a Lover" (1977), and "Order" (1980). But this time the drama is missing, while the tale of a broken marriage is coated in tones of black-and-white simplicity. The Turkish architect has taken up with the wife of a separated couple, whose husband has chucked his 1968 Student Reform ideals for the soft life of a successful businessman. The question is whether the husband's efforts via letters to mend the fences of a broken relationship will work in the end or not: the wife, however, can't make a decision, and the matter is left open.

Saless focuses more on the estranged husband, with his villa and children and regular ticket for the theatre, than he does on the wife's dilemma. It amounts to throwing away a trump-card in the long run. Further, much time is wasted on chatting about the state-of-things in a Germany dependent, for better or for worse, on the foreign-worker for the duration (the same is true of all the highly industrial countries of Europe). The theme of the sensitive foreign-worker in an alienated situation was the theme of Saless's earlier "Far from Home."

Saless's aim was apparently to take the pulse of a Germany facing an economic crisis, thereby deepening the gulf between the native-in-a-pinch and the foreigner-looking-for-a-job. Once the viewer sizes up the story during the first exchange of letters, there's not much else to do but settle back and soak in the stylistic traits the director is noted for: slow camera pans, a soundtrack loaded with muted noises and light musical score, and a sparse deadpan dialog. "Addressee Unknown" is a tiring summation of Saless's style, without adding anything new or thematically convincing. —Holl.

La Laguna De Dos Tiempos
(The Lagoon of the Two Ages)
(MEXICAN-COLOR-DOCU)

Berlin, March 1.

An Instituto Nacional Indiginista-FONAPAS Production. Produced by Coca Gaxiola, Saul Serrano. Directed by Eduardo Maldonado. Camera (color), Francisco Bojorquez; editor, Maldonado; sound: Jesus Sanchez Padilla; research, Maldonado, Manuel Uribe, Diana Roldan, Victoria Novelo. Reviewed at the Forum of the

Young Cinema, Berlin, Feb. 20, 1983. Running time: 105 MINS.

This documentary, largely shot under the previous Portillo regime and released after the last elections in Mexico, is defined by the director himself as a film intended for home consumption first of all. The main concern is to give deprived people who usually have no access to the media, a chance to express themselves on the plights of a country which has been brutally brought back to grim realities, after drifting for years in illusions of richness and plenty.

For a non-Mexican audience, the main interest here is to see the effects that the mixed blessing of oil has had on a Third World country. Furthermore, it ties in the industrialization of rural environments with the destruction of popular traditional culture as such, with ecological disasters and a general pauperization of the population, which has to switch from agrarian work to factory labor, and suffer a considerable decrease in their standard of living.

Dividing his treatise in three different chapters, dealing with the past, the present and an appraisal of the future in view of the facts submitted, Maldonado follows in the tracks of Paul Leduc, who tried similar approaches to the ethnic destruction and radical changes Mexican society is going through.

It is obvious, from this film, that oil is not necessarily the miracle solution for a poor nation, for it will only make the rich richer and the poor poorer, there is no doubt that the damage done to the environment by the explosion of industries springing up around the oil production is irreparable, and that labor conditions in this industry, for the unskilled peasants whose land has been poisoned by pollution, are demeaning. On the other hand, as the last part of the film seems to realize, progress is here to stay and the struggle should be not to abolish it but to use it in order to create a better order of things to come.

While Maldonado makes his points succinctly, he could have certainly benefitted from a more objective editor (instead of doing the job himself) for the final result is lax and repetitive. Camera work is not always on the same level, indicating probably the conditions under which the footage was shot, yet, it manages to find as much eerie beauty in the steel constructions of the New World as it is normal to find in the midst of unspoiled nature. It is only a pity that, while clearly accusing a state agency, Pemex (the Mexican Oil Industries) of not assuming its responsibilities towards the ecological problems arising from its activities, it does nothing to clarify why such an attitude is possible. Maldonado does hint that any further research in this direction might have endangered the existence of the entire film, but without it, the result is incomplete. —Edna.

Utopia
(WEST GERMAN-COLOR)

Berlin, March 1.
A Multimedia Film Production, Hamburg, Eberhard Hauff, producer, in coproduction with Ullstein Tele Video and Zweites Deutsches Fernsehen, Mainz. Features entire cast. Directed by Sohrab Shahid Saless. Screenplay, Saless, Manfred Grunert; camera (color), Ramin R. Molai; music, Rolf Bauer; sets, Claus Juergen Pfeiffer; editing, Christel Orthmann; tv-producer, Willy Segier. Reviewed at Berlin Film Fest (Competition), Feb. 20. Running time: 198 MINS.
Cast: Manfred Zapatka (Heinz), Imke Barnstedt (Renate), Gundula Petrovska (Rosi), Gabriele Fischer (Susi), Johanna Sophia (Helga), Birgit Anders (Monika).

Sohrab Shahid Saless, the Iranian-born director living and working in Germany, is well known to the Berlin fest: his Iranian-produced films, "Still Life" (1974) and "A Simple Event" (1973), appeared respectively in the Berlinale competition and the Forum of Young Cinema in 1974, and he was back a year later with "Far From Home" (1975) in comp and, at later intervals in the Forum and other sidebars, with "Coming of Age" (1976) and "Diary of a Lover" (1977). His "Order" (1980) appeared at Cannes recently in the Directors' Fortnight. Now he's back in Berlin with "Utopia" in Competition and "Addressee Unknown" in the Forum.

"Utopia" is a disappointment to Saless admirers. Over 3 hours in length, it appears, in fact, to be a parody of his own slow-moving style: the usual rhythm is gone, the words fall flat, realism is substituted for metaphor (always a unique aspect in his other film), and he has lost control of his actors in group formations.

This is a film about a pimp and his prostitutes in a Berlin apartment-bordello. Heinz works the streets at first with Renate, then decides to better his position by opening a "Club Arena" for walk-in customers with five ladies on his leash. He is a no-nonsense type, bitter and cruel, a man who can brutally humiliate women in bending them to his will. In appearances he comes across as a well-dressed gentleman, but his links are apparently with other brutal types of the Berlin Underworld — in any case, he suffers periodically from migraines or other undetermined head-pains, and he receives a threatening visit from old cronies on one occasion.

As for the girls, they come from all walks of life: a divorcee, a young university student, types who don't know exactly what else to do and enjoy each other's company. Renate, the lady-in-charge when Heinz is away, is aging and losing her charm, which leads to a black-and-blue beating for not drawing the customers as readily any more. It's she at the end who does Heinz in with a scissors-stab in the gut when matters have gone too far, the others joining in on the kill. Then she takes the establishment over to run it as before.

Credits suffer from underlighting in lensing of bordello interior, but otherwise a plus — particularly the integration of noises and music on the soundtrack.
—Holl.

High Road To China
(COLOR)

High road company version of 'Raiders.'

Hollywood, March 8.
A Warner Bros. release of a Golden Harvest and Jadran Film presentation, produced by Fred Weintraub. Directed by Brian G. Hutton. Exec producer, Raymond Chow. Stars Tom Selleck, Bess Armstrong. Screenplay, Sandra Weintraub Roland, S. Lee Pogostin, based on book by Jon Cleary; camera (Technicolor), Ronnie Taylor; editor, John Jympson, sound, George Stephenson; production design, Robert Laing; associate producer, Frederick Muller; aerial camera, Peter Allwork; assistant director, Bert Batt; costumes, Betsy Heimann, Franco Antonelli; music, John Barry. Reviewed at The Burbank Studios, Burbank, Calif., Feb. 22, 1983. (MPAA rating: PG.) Running time: 120 MINS.
O'Malley .... Tom Selleck
Eve .... Bess Armstrong
Struts ....Jack Weston
Tozer .... Wilford Brimley
Bentik ....Robert Morley
Suleiman Khan .... Brian Blessed
Alessa ....Cassandra Gava

"High Road To China" is a lot of old-fashioned fun and, with Tom Selleck in the lead, should attract solid business, though hardly on a level with "Raiders Of The Lost Ark."

Comparisons to "Raiders" are inevitable because "China," though an older project, was revived for Selleck after his tv schedule kept him from taking the Harrison Ford role in "Raiders." Ford clearly got the better deal because "China" just isn't as tense and exciting.

But "China" has the same Saturday-matinee spirit, with director Brian G. Hutton nicely mixing a lot of action with a storyline that never seems as absurd as it is, allowing the two hours to move by very quickly.

Selleck is perfect as a grizzled, boozing biplane pilot whom 1920s flapper Bess Armstrong is forced to hire to help her find her father before he's declared dead and her inheritance is stolen. Selleck and Armstrong make a cute couple, even though their bantering, slowly developing romance is deliberately predictable throughout.

Jack Weston is also a delight as the inevitable sidekick and Brian Blessed gets a good turn as a tribal chieftain. Wilford Brimley is also on the mark as the missing father. Only Robert Morley, unfortunately, is more or less wasted in an ill-defined role as the villain plotting the couple's downfall.

Shot in Yugoslavia, "China" has transferred a lot of production value to the screen and Hutton handles the big scenes well. As might be expected, some of the scenery is spectacular. Though the saga proceeds to a thoroughly dopey conclusion, it's nonetheless an enjoyable journey. —Har.

My Tutor
(COLOR)

Gets a C plus.

Chicago, March 4.

Crown International Pictures release of a Marimark Production. Produced by Marilyn J. Tenser. Directed by George Bowers. Screenplay by Joe Roberts; camera (Deluxe). Mac Ahlberg; editor, Sidney Wolinsky; art director, Linda Pearl; music, Webster Lewis; assistant director, Steven Esthelman. Reviewed at the State-Lake Theatre, Chicago, March 4, 1983. (MPAA rating: R). Running time: 97 MINS.

Terry	Caren Kaye
Bobby	Matt Lattanzi
Mr. Chrystal	Kevin McCarthy
Billy	Clark Brandon
Don	Bruce Bauer
Mrs. Chrystal	Arlene Golonka
Jack	Crispin Glover

For years now, Crown International has been churning out benignly lightheaded fare, long on sex and laughs and short on brainpower. With "My Tutor," the Crown tradition continues in especially good style. Moderate-to-good b.o. looms.

This pic is yet another in the older-woman-introduces-young-man-to-the-lessons-of-love vein milked in recent months by Jensen Farley's "Homework" and "Private Lessons." What distinguishes "My Tutor" to some degree is its strong comic underpinning revolving about some horny highschoolers' perpetual quest for sex.

The plot of this one is elementary: a rich Southern California couple hires an attractive, 30-ish tutor (Caren Kaye) to take up residence one summer in their palatial, neo-Spanish-styled home and teach French to their post-pubescent son (Matt Lattanzi).

He, of course, winds up getting French and a lot more, much to the consternation of his tippling father (Kevin McCarthy) who leches after the tutor. The developing romance-liaison is alternated with comic bits involving confrontations between the boy's high school chums and, in no particular order, a motorcycle gang and inhabitants of a local brothel.

What renders "My Tutor" slightly non-formulaic is the way which director George Bowers, scripter Joe Roberts and producer Marilyn Jacobs Tenser (whose father founded Crown and whose husband, Mark, is its president) worked out the romantic interlude of the boy and the tutor.

Instead of milking the situation strictly for sniggers and low-ball humor, the creators have presented a plausible situation with at least a stab at genuine romantic sentiment. The laughs and bedroom scenes — a sine qua non of this type of enterprise — are here in abundance. But so is a tidy little story of a pleasant young man coming of age.

Kaye looks attractive and turns in a creditable job in the title role. Lattanzi, seen briefly in "Rich and Famous" but best-known as Olivia Newton-John's boyfriend, is nicely cast as the male lead. He wears an expression of astonished ingenuousness throughout that makes his character sympathetic.

Production values, especially Mac Ahlberg's sharp photography, are surprisingly good.
— *Sege.*

Trenchcoat
(COLOR)

A mystery as to why they made it.

Hollywood, March 3.

Buena Vista release of a Jerry Leider production. Produced by Leider. Directed by Michael Tuchner. Features entire cast. Screenplay, Jeffrey Price, Peter Seaman; camera (Technicolor), Tonino Delli Colli; editor, Frank J. Urioste; production design, Rodger Maus; music, Charles Fox; set decoration, Harry Cordwell; assistant director, Carlo Cotti. Reviewed at the Writer's Guild Theatre, March 3, 1983. (MPAA Rating: PG.) Running time: 91 MINS.

Mickey Raymond	Margot Kidder
Terry Leonard	Robert Hays
Inspector Stagnos	David Suchet
Eva Werner	Gila Von Weitershausen
Nino Tenucci	Daniel Faraldo
Princess Aida	Ronald Lacey
Marquis De Pena	John Justin
Lizzy O'Reilly	Pauline Delany
Sean O'Reilly	P.G. Stephens

All the makers of Buena Vista's "Trenchcoat" have done is paste together a series of random events in the most obvious of ways in the hopes of a film turning up. Almost nothing in it works, and audiences will probably leave it off their plans for the evening.

It's a shame that Disney Studios should fall back into the trap of making such a cliche, behind-the-times film. Assuming there was ever a commitment to make a witty mystery, the studio needs to at least have the courage to give it some sense of contemporary reality. Disney, more than anyone else, should know that cartoon-like characters and situations usually work best in cartoons, not live action.

Margot Kidder is given the unfortunate task of starring as a court stenographer taking a two-week vacation in Malta to write a mystery novel (even Agatha Christie probably didn't work that fast). Through a series of ridiculous, contrived and thoroughly unbelievable mishaps she slowly finds herself involved in her own set of murder mysteries which, in turn, translate into her book.

Though Kidder gets to deliver one or two amusing lines, the concept of the script by firsttimers Jeffrey Price and Peter Seaman is annoyingly cute and relentlessly oversold. Judging from the way the story unfolds one would conclude they were either under severe constraints by Disney or suffer from a true sense of unreality.

British director Michael Tuchner, who has done some top notch work in television, makes his U.S. film debut here and succumbs to similar pitfalls. But why he, Kidder, costar Robert Hays and a host of others ever consented to be associated with the project is the real mystery of "Trenchcoat."— *Berg.*

Baby, It's You
(COLOR)

Fine new actress can't save romantic mismatch. Limited b.o.

Hollywood, March 1.

A Paramount release of a Double Play production. Produced by Griffin Dunne, Amy Robinson. Features entire cast. Directed, written by John Sayles, based on a story by Robinson. Camera (Movielab color), Michael Ballhaus; editor, Sonya Polonsky; production design, Jeffrey Townsend; set decoration, Carol Nast; costume design, Franne Lee; sound, Scott Smith; associate producer, Robert F. Colesberry; assistant director, Raymond L. Greenfield. Reviewed at Paramount Studios, Hollywood, March 1, 1983. (MPAA Rating: R.) Running time: 105 MINS.

Jill	Rosanna Arquette
Sheik	Vincent Spano
Mrs. Rosen	Joanna Merlin
Dr. Rosen	Jack Davidson
Mr. Capadilupo	Nick Ferrari
Mrs. Capadilupo	Dolores Messina
Miss Vernon	Leora Dana
Mr. Ripeppi	William Joseph Raymond
Mr. McManus	Sam McMurray
Jody	Liane Curtis
Beth	Claudia Sherman
Debra	Marta Kober
Leslie	Tracy Pollan
Shelly	Rachel Dretzin
Chris	Susan Derendorf

Despite some strong thematic material and a vibrant central performance, "Baby, It's You" remains an essentially unfulfilled romantic drama. John Sayles' third directorial outing improves as it moves along from 1966 to a slightly later time frame, but can't recoup from the ultimately unbelievable pairing of leading characters. Paramount opened this negative pickup Friday (4) in Seattle, where a receptive audience should be found if it exists anywhere, and will play it at Filmex next month. But pic falls into the unfortunate honorable failure category and is a dubious bet for more than specialized, college-area venues.

Admittedly, opposites can attract and many unlikely couples can be found in real life, but this doesn't mean that just any match-up will hold water dramatically. In a nutshell, that's the fatal problem with this film, which has an elegantly dressed Italian street kid with the mysterious name of Sheik pursue, win, lose and, at length, haunt the emotional life of a bright, ambitious and terribly attractive high school drama student.

Sheik goes through many of the predictable macho motions with the inexperienced Jill — hot rodding in a fast car, taking her drinking in a seedy bar with some tough friends and trying to make her feel guilty for not going all the way. For her part, Jill is simply trying to get through high school on her way to entering Sarah Lawrence, and to figure out if she's got what it takes to become an actress.

When the pair split at the time of her prom, after an affectionate but still chaste courtship, the two travel radically different roads from Trenton, N.J., she to school and encroaching hippiedom, and he to Miami to follow his dream of being Frank Sinatra.

Latter turn of events reveals latent comedy in Sayles' screenplay, penned from a story by coproducer Amy Robinson, in that the only gig the self-styled lounge lizard can get is lip-synching tunes by Sinatra and others in a seedy boite patronized by oldsters who may well have seen Sinatra when he first appeared back in bobby-soxer days.

Writer-director Sayles seems even more at home gently satirizing the dope-smoking, psychedelic scene into which Jill somewhat uncomfortably falls. He displayed sharp insight into the foibles of counterculture adherents in "Return Of The Secaucus Seven" and similarly scores his best points here when confronted with material obviously close to his heart.

Nevertheless, film has been set up as an oddball romance and feels obliged to follow through with the duo's mutual story, when an exploration of their separate tales (for separate they are clearly destined to be) would appear considerably more interesting. On a break from school, Jill feels compelled to hie to Miami to visit Sheik, where she finally yields to his imposing physicality, with evidently disappointing results. Faced with his own lack of prospects, he then chases her back to Sarah Lawrence, where a suitable resolution ensues.

In spite of a character which could have used more fleshing out in the writing, it's Rosanna Arquette who makes "Baby, It's You" persistently watchable. Startling as Gary Gilmore's wild lover in "The Executioner's Song," she here plays a nice girl who latches on to the wrong guy by default and gradually loses her bearings when turned loose from home. Resembling something of a more voluptuous cross between Nastassia Kinski and Audrey Hepburn, to whom her character is compared in the film, Arquette is clearly one of the sexiest young actresses on the screen today and her exceedingly alive performance shows great potential.

As the Sinatra idolator, Vincent Spano, with his hair greased back and clothes beautifully pressed, looks just like the poor man's idea of elegance he's supposed to embody. He does a good turn, but unavoidably suffers from miscasting of his character opposite Arquette's. In fact, it's almost as unbelievable as if someone like Sylvester Stallone were cast opposite the young Audrey Hepburn. It just doesn't wash.

Other, more minor, irritants include an uncertainty as to Sheik's status in school. He looks somewhat older than the rest of the kids and is always wandering the halls, seemingly at will. It's only when he's expelled that one knows for certain he's been a student all along. Although the period is set by nearly two dozen 1960s pop tunes, anachronistic use of four modern numbers by Bruce Springsteen is mystifying in context, even if they do express elements of teenaged angst and rebellion implicit in the tale.

Because the humor surfaces so infrequently, and the characters have been explored in less depth than possible, feeling persists that Sayles, the director, has not fully served Sayles, the writer. Tech contributions are modest, and it should be noted that the late Rainer Werner Fassbinder's frequent cinematographer, Michael Ballhaus, makes his American debut on this picture. —Cart.

Pauline a la Plage
(Pauline at the Seaside)
(FRENCH-COLOR)

Paris, March 2.
A.A.A. release of a Films du Losange/-Films Ariane coproduction. Produced by Margaret Menegoz. Features entire cast. Written and directed by Eric Rohmer. Camera (color), Nestor Almendros; editor, Cecile Decugis; sound, Georges Prat; music, Jean-Louis Valero; reviewed at the Ponthieu screening room, March 1, 1983. Running time: 94 MINS.
Pauline .... Amanda Langlet
Marion .... Arielle Dombasle
Pierre .... Pascal Greggory
Henry .... Feodor Atkine
Sylvain .... Simon de la Brosse
Louisette .... Rosette

Eric Rohmer is slumming again. "Pauline a la Plage" is the third in his "Comedies and Proverbs" cycle, and like the preceding entries, revolves around young people. One senses the pleasure Rohmer takes in writing for the working class with the hub of youthful talent that has formed around him since his 1978 feature, "Perceval." One senses too that, even in the relatively minor dramatic range in which the filmmaker has previously worked quiet wonders, these new pictures are kids' stuff — as if Rohmer were on a working holiday, waiting for a theme or subject that would implicate his special talents fully.

That said, Rohmer's newest is still a breezy, intelligent entertainment, an urbane comedy of morals and manners among a group of young Parisians vacationing on the

Normandy coast. Rohmer has directed with his usual limpidness, and Nestor Almendros has lensed pleasingly. One could ask for more, but one could do much worse.

A recently divorced young woman (Arielle Dombasle) arrives at her family's coastal villa in company of her young cousin, Pauline (Amanda Langlet). There she meets an old friend (Pascal Greggory), who has always nursed an idealistic love for her. He tries to woo her at a party, but Dombasle prefers to throw herself into the arms of a cynical writer (Feodor Atkine), who plays up to her romantic illusions about their budding relationship but is in fact fooling around with an empty-headed candy peddler (Rosette). As for Langlet, she flirts with an engaging boy her own age, (Simon de la Brosse), whom she meets on the beach.

The pivotal incident of the story, through which all the characters' pronouncements about love, passion and personal rapports are put to the test, comes when Dombasle who has gone off for the day returns to see Atkine, who is in the upstairs bedroom with Rosette. To cover his deceit, Atkine shoves Brosse into the room with Rosette, making it look like the two are having a fling. Dombasle falls for the coverup and the ensuing scenes involve further complications as Greggory and Atkine try, each in their own manner, to straighten out the tangle.

In "Le Beau Mariage," Rohmer constructed his film around a tedious nuisance. Here he does a neat juggling act with several characters who (with the exception of the two teenagers) are either vain, pretentious or odious. It's a measure of his talent and control that he can make us sit in their dubious company for an hour and a half and pay attention, even if they fail to touch us.

Pic won the directing award at the recent Berlin Film Festival. It should do nicely in art house situations where Rohmer has a following. —Len.

Berlin Film Reviews

Cap Canaille
(FRENCH-BELGIAN-COLOR)

Berlin, Feb. 28.
A Babylone Films, UGC, Top 1 (Paris), ODEC, F3, (Brussels) production. Produced by Ken Legargeant and Romaine Legargeant. Directed by Jean-Henri Roger, Juliet Berto. Features entire cast. Written by Jean-Henri Roger, Claude Vesperini, Juliet Berto, with dialogs by Boris Bergman and Jean-Henri Roger; camera (color), William Lubtchansky; editor, Nicole Lubtschansky; sound, Ricardo Castro, Miguel Rejas; sets, Max Berto; costumes, Ingrid Schumann; music composed and performed by Elisabeth Wiener. Reviewed at the Berlin Film Fest (In Competition), Feb. 28, 1983. Running time: 103 MINS.

Paula Barretto .... Juliet Berto
Verges .... Richard Bohringer
Kebadjan .... Jean-Claude Brialy
Wim .... Patrick Chesnais
Nino .... Gerard Damon
Mayolles .... Richard Anconina
Dugrand .... Nini Crepon

The Berto-Roger tandem attracted attention a couple of years ago, in Cannes, with their first joint effort, "Neige" (the French slang term for heroin), which displayed great sensitivity in dealing with the hapless drop-outs destroying themselves around Place Pigalle. Now they are back again, together, to tackle a subject which has been often discussed on French front pages in the last years, the scandals of forest fires initiated by underworld organisms who need the space for real estate development.

The French Riviera has been constantly plagued by these man-made disasters, with the culprits quite often known to the police; but going scotfree, nevertheless.

Berto and Roger, start from the political aspect of the problem and work their way into a thriller concerning Berto's burned property, a newsman's investigation and police corruption. The point they wish to make is clear from the very beginning: financial interests rule the Southern coast of France and control every aspect of government there. Legitimate investors who believe they can get assistance from the organized crime and keep their hands clean find out otherwise soon enough, and whoever makes the slightest attempt to throw a wrench into the works is pitilessly eliminated, notwithstanding family relations or obligations.

As a thriller, this is pretty much predictable stuff, not expertly enough handled to make it truly exciting. But Berto and Roger obviously intended their film to be more than that, to bear some of the pain and despair of their previous effort and to make a valid statement about the situation in France.

Berto, playing the lead as a sort of drifter who lives with an individualistic armed robber who doesn't trust partners, is supposed to reflect the disgust and rejection felt by a scion of an underworld family (her father, it is hinted, died while distilling drugs, her brother is involved head over heels in the real estate plot), for her surroundings. The back streets of Marseilles, its sleazy bars and the violence rampant there are part of the general picture, and the impossibility of making any changes is reflected, among other things, in the attitude of a reporter who covers the beat, lets himself serve as a tool for the sort of misinformation which will serve organized crime, but can't help asking, once in a while, embarrassing questions that make the police inspector squirm. Such as: why would a suicide use a silencer on his gun?

As worthy followers of Jean-Luc Godard (both started with him, Berto as a thesp, Roger collaborating on some of the scripts), the two co-directors make abundant use of cinematic quotes.

Editing is loose, dialog tries for a combination of tough street talk and poetical expressions that sound forced, acting is mostly on the apathetic side and characters lack the urgency which was the main appeal of "Neige." Camera work includes a lot of hand-held material and what appear to be documentary footage of authentic forest fires and the soundtrack features songs written and interpreted by Elisabeth Wiener. In both cases, too much use is made of what should be means to an end and not an end in itself. Reception in Berlin was mixed and commercial prospects will depend on the amount of interest raised by politico-economical scandals behind this story. —Edna.

Mo Sheng De Peng You
(Strange Friends)
(CHINESE-COLOR)

Berlin, March 1.
A Peking Film Studio Production, Peking (Chinese spelling: Beijing); producers Liang Kemin, Liu Yunchang. Features entire cast. Directed by Xu Lei. Screenplay, Li Baoyuan, Xu Lei, Xu Tianxia; camera (color), Huang Xinyi; music, Zhang Piji; conductor, Yan Fang; sets, Duan Zhengzhong, Hu Hongyuan. Reviewed at Berlin Film Fest (Competition), Feb. 25, '83. Running time: 80 MINS.
Cast: Li Ling, Zhang Chao, Zhan Jingo, Wang Yunxia, Zhao Wande, Huang Zhong, Jin Feng, Liu Xiaohua, Liu Antai, Han Tingqi, Cheng Mu, Zhang Yuede, Xue Jianshe, Shen Guanchu, Zhang Tongsheng, Wang Chong, Xu Yanyan, Cai Ming.

Xu Lei's "Strange Friends" comes across as an official state entry by the formidable Peking Film Studio at a major international film festival. The film follows a simple narrative line, has unmistakable message value for the general moviegoing public, and leaves no doubt that good will conquer over evil in the long run.

These observations aside, the unveiling of such honest truths as the presence of hoodlums on trains and in the streets of large cities is remarkable for a country like China making significant strides in the direction of a common living standard for the masses. It may not have been an inside bet in the Berlinale sweepstakes, but nonetheless this is only a step or two away from solid festival contention in the future.

"Strange Friends" is set on a train from Peking to Shanghai, a trip requiring a couple of days traveling time. Three passengers sharing a compartment strike up an acquaintance to pass the time away — rather, two young men do, and wonder why the girl sitting beside them won't say a single word. One of the lads is an outgoing, comical type; the other is reserved and serious, but with a kind heart for others.

It turns out, via flashbacks, that the girl is fleeing her employers, who feel she's a good-for-nothing on the job, and her past as well. She apparently fell into bad company in Peking, and is now trying to "go straight" in the face of adversity. One of her aims is to see the seashore of her youth again, even if it means that she will be shortly arrested for running away from her job and other responsibilities.

The girl gets off in Nanking, and she's immediately spotted by hoodlums as a likely victim for shady dealings. But just as two thugs are preparing to make off with her, our hero from the train appears on the scene in the nick of time — he has followed her on a hunch. After the rescue, they continue on to Shanghai — where the third friend is waiting for them, also on a hunch. It turns out that the rescuer was also once a criminal type, but has seen the light to become a committed member in a youth group. It's also revealed that the girl's father had been injustly imprisoned under the old regime run by the Gang of Four.

A bit preachy, but an indication of things to come from China. —Holl.

Dans La Ville Blanche
(In The White City)
(SWISS-PORTUGUESE-COLOR)

Berlin, March 1.
A Metro Filme, (Lisbon), and Filmographe (Geneva). Coproduction; producers, Paulo Branco, Alain Tanner, Antonio Vaz de Silva. Stars Bruno Ganz. Written and directed by Alain Tanner. Camera (color), Acacio de Almeida; sets, Maria Jose Branco; music, Jean-Luc Barbier; editing, Laurent Uhler. Reviewed at Berlin Film Fest (Competition), Feb. 26, 1983. Running time: 108 MINS.
Paul .... Bruno Ganz
Rosa .... Teresa Madruga
Elisa .... Julia Vonderlinn
Patron .... Jose Carvalho
Thief with knife .... Francisco Baiao
Second thief .... Jose Wallenstein
Barkeeper .... Victor Costa
Barmaid .... Lidia Franco
Friend in the tavern .... Pedro Efe
Lady on the train .... Joana Vicente

Among Alain Tanner's quite impressive string of tightly woven stories of ousiders and would-be outsiders his latest film, "In The White City," comes across as an improvised short story. Nevertheless, the film is a direct extension of everything else he's done and will be an immediate success to Tanner fans on the arthouse circuit, particularly if the Berlin Fest and other fest showcases give the pic the push it needs.

Tanner won a director's kudo at Cannes in 1981 for "Light Years Away," an odd tale of a youth leaving a barkeeping job in an Irish city to converse with a Russian-born, self-styled mystic holed up in a garage-shed far off the beaten path. There was a girl the young man had

an affair with — now she's back as a barmaid in the port city of Lisbon having an affair with a ship's mechanic. The mechanic, played by Bruno Ganz, is another of Tanner's patented dropouts from society: for him, time has stood still — just like the clock running backwards in the bar-hotel he visits, and never quite leaves, for the duration of the film.

Pic is without a plot to speak of. The mechanic takes Super-8 shots of "the white city" and the girl he has shacked up with from the hotel bar; he sends the reels home to his wife in German-Switzerland, together with letters that don't seem much sense at all. The loner is apparently about to go off his rocker. Meanwhile, he runs into a couple of thugs in a poolroom, who steal his money. Ganz pawns his gold Swiss watch, and keeps wandering around.

The barmaid loves him, but knows this all has to end somewhere. It just about ends on a slab in a morgue, for Ganz has a run-in again with one of the thieves, is seriously stabbed, but then recovers. He trades his camera for room-payment, buys a train ticket, and may be on his way home (or some unknown destination) at the end. Meanwhile, his girl has left him to seek employment in France.

"In The White City" has its imperfections. Somehow, in a Tanner film, they seem to be intentionally there to tititlate the viewer. All the same, proper handling is a must for offshore spinoff. —Holl.

Klassenfeind
(Class Enemy)
(WEST GERMAN-COLOR)

Berlin, March 4.
A Regina Ziegler Filmproduktion, Berlin, in coproduction with Project Filmproduktion im Filmverlag der Autoren, Munich, and Sender Freies Berlin (SFB); producer, Regina Ziegler, tv-producer, Christa Vogel; world rights, Weltvertrieb der Filmverlag der Autoren, Munich. Features entire cast. Directed by Peter Stein. Screenplay, Stein, Juergen Klose, based on Nigel Williams's play "Class Enemy" camera (color), Robby Mueller; sets, Karl-Ernst Herrmann; costumes, Dorothea Katzer; editing, Inge Behrens; costumes, Dorothea Katzer; assistant director and script, Karin Viesel; production manager, Carlo Rola. Reviewed at Berlin Film Fest (out-of-competition), Feb. 26, 1983. Running time: 123 MINS.
Bernd Engel,
  "Angel" .... Greger Hansen
Norbert Pichler,
  "Pickel" .... Stefan Reck
Erwin Klose,
  "Koloss" .... Jean-Paul Raths
Wolfgang Volkmann,
  "Vollmond" .... Udo Samel
Ernst Fitzlaff,
  "Fetzer" .... Ernst Stoetzner
Ahmed Kitapci,
  "Kebab" .... Tayfun Bademsoy
Teacher .... Michael Maassen

The curiosity about Peter Stein's "Class Enemy" is that this is a film version of his own adapted stage

production of British playwright Nigel Williams's 1978 award-winning play with the same title. When Williams's drama on the miserable conditions in a South London Comprehensive School appeared five years ago at the Royal Court theatre in London, the author was voted the season's "Most Promising New Playwright" by British critics. And as such plays of documentary realism often go, it was thematically transposed to the run-down Kreuzberg section of West Berlin where Peter Stein's Schaubuehne am Halleschen Ufer was located in 1981 (the Schaubuehne Ensemble has now moved to comfortable new quarters at Lehninerplatz on Berlin's Kudamm boulevard).

This means that "Class Enemy" is no longer a play about South London, but instead Berlin Kreuzberg. In fact, the names of the leading figures were changed to strike a note of immediacy: Williams's "Iron" is Stein's "Fetzer," "Skylight" is "Vollmond," "Snatch" is "Kebab," "Nipper" is "Koloss," "Racks" is "Pickel," and "Sweetheart" is "Angel." Further, the problems of these social losers are oriented towards the Berlin-German scene of unemployed youth, foreign-worker ghetto (the Turks in Berlin), and the prevalence of growing violence in a dehumanizing slum-district. When the stage production was reviewed by observant German critics in 1981, hardly anyone missed the implication that the "class enemy" was on West Germany's doorstep rather than abroad in violence-ridden London.

Personally viewed, the tip of the hat goes to Nigel Williams so far as the dramatic success of Peter Stein's "Class Enemy" is concerned, while the film adaptation owes much to Stein's creative ingenuity and Robby Mueller's exemplary camera work. All the thesps in the film played their roles countless times on the Schaubuehne stage, the play itself confined to a claustraphobic school-room setting that is gradually torn apart as fevers rise to pitched violence. The action moves at a swift pace when each of the protagonists is spotlighted to reveal the strengths and weaknesses of his personality within the peer group. And the camera (Robby Mueller was Wim Wenders's ace lenser on his early pics) suitably captures the intensity of the key conflict scenes. Filmed theatre, to be sure, but of a very special nature, for Stein always stages plays cinematically.

"Class Enemy" is a breakthrough for German cinema. Not only does the helming and lensing of Williams's play make this a "film" rather than "theatre" (it is skedded for release shortly in German theatres), but this was the finest

West German pic at the Berlinale in the main program. There's little doubt that pic will surface at a prominent North American fest and thereafter find its way to Yank arthouses.

Why "Class Enemy" didn't surface in the Berlin fest competition is a bit of a puzzle, considering how the three official entries fell flat on their faces. But through the vision and encouragement of Theo Hinz of the Filmverlag der Autoren it scored a brilliant audience success at the 33rd Berlinale, which will assure its run at home and abroad. One hopes that Stein and Mueller will work together again on another project similarly aimed at the general public, and away from the Schaubuehne all-too-prevalent esthetic belly-button gazing. —Holl.

Exposed
(COLOR)

Unusual meller with more politics than sex. Careful push needed.

Hollywood, Feb. 24.

An MGM/UA release. Produced, directed, written by James Toback. Executive producer, Serge Silberman. Stars Nastassia Kinski, Rudolf Nureyev. Camera (Metrocolor), Henri Decae; editor, Robert Lawrence, Annie Charvein (France); music, Georges Delerue; production design, Brian Eatwell; art direction (France), Robert Luchaire; set decoration, John Godfrey (U.S.), Carlos Conti (France); costume design (France), Aude Bronson-Howard; sound, James Sabat (U.S.), Daniel Brisseau (France); associate producer, Brian Hamill; assistant directors, William Hassell (U.S.), Michel Cheyko, Alain Tasma (France). Reviewed at the MGM Studios, Culver City, Feb. 23, 1983. (MPAA Rating: R). Running time: 100 MINS.

Elizabeth Carlson	Nastassia Kinski
Daniel Jelline	Rudolf Nureyev
Rivas	Harvey Keitel
Greg Miller	Ian McShane
Margaret	Bibi Andersson
Curt	Ron Randell
Vic	Pierre Clementi
Marcel	Dov Gottesfeld
Nick	James Russo
Bridgit Gormann	Marion Varella
Hotel Manager	Murray Moston
Leo Voscovitch	James Toback

Intelligent and illogical, beautiful and erratic, "Exposed" is a provocative, jet-setter's visit to the worlds of high fashion and international terrorism. Neither a full-blown political thriller nor an out-and-out romance, pic mixes the exoticism of various chic milieu in pursuit of its fundamentally serious thematic concerns. Although all the elements don't entirely coalesce, it's an intriguing brew that's promotable to the intelligentsia via the attractive topliners and stands a commercial chance as an offbeat entry.

This is the third directorial outing by James Toback, a fact remarkable in itself since his first two pics, "Fingers" and "Love And Money," received the barest theatrical releases imaginable (he also wrote the superior but low-grossing "The Gambler.")

Also credited here as writer and producer, Toback has again served up an unusual cast in which highbrow literary and artistic concerns are overlaid on low-down criminality and thuggery.

For the first time in his work, however, a woman occupies center stage. After a prolog in which a foxy blonde is observed blowing up a Paris cafe, Toback himself, as a college English teacher, breaks up romantically with one of his students, Nastassia Kinski.

Kinski returns to her home in Wisconsin to tell her parents that she's quitting school to pursue her destiny in New York City, where she's beset by a Bronx Zoo-full of cretins and is frustrated in her desire to be appreciated as a serious pianist. So, plausibly enough considering her looks, she becomes this year's model instead, the hottest item on the international fashion scene.

In one of the film's most striking, and convincing, sequences, Kinski is attending an exhibition of photos featuring her when her eye is caught by Rudolf Nureyev. A bit embarrassed, she quickly glances away, then can't help but look at him again, fascinated. From the beginning, casting of these two together seems preordained and almost magical, for in her second look she registers unmistakably her knowledge that she's found her perfect male twin.

After a bizarre, cat-and-mouse courtship, the inevitable big love scene arrives. It's quite unusual, and perhaps the most that should be said is that Nureyev, playing a professional violinist, makes decidedly novel use of his bow. Scene is also discreet, however, and it would be a mistake for ad promo to push any lurid expections based on film's title.

As it happens, Nureyev is also a dedicated terrorist fighter with intensely personal motives, and when Kinski follows him to Paris, she naively becomes involved with the very forces Nureyev is intent upon wiping out. Through the blonde glimpsed earlier, Kinski is delivered into the lair of Carlos-type terrorist Harvey Keitel, a provocateur dedicated to random violence. Amazingly, Keitel eventually allows her to go free, which helps set up the climactic confrontation between himself and Nureyev.

In the uncertain first half-hour, Toback raises doubts about his natural abilities as a director — rhythms seems off, and the camera is rarely in the right place. However, he appears to grow more confident just as the story becomes more shaded and intriguing, and by the conclusion, comes close to investing his grave tale with the tragic dimensions it was clearly designed to possess. The most significant death at the end is as inevitable as that of a Shakespearean hero, yet a truly poignant sadness accompanies the bleaching of the screen from color to black and white as the characters' vision eclipses.

Film boasts numerous other fresh, startling scenes — Kinski's discovery as a model while working as a waitress, a wild ambiguous dance she performs alone in a room, her meeting which the blonde terrorist in a bookshop and subsequent lunch at a Paris McDonald's, Keitel's brutal killing of a disloyal associate while sitting with Kinski in the back seat of a car, and a car chase through the French capital which is compellingly scored with severe classical music.

As usual with Toback, he has populated the film with an implausibly high percentage of beautiful femmes (even for a pic partially set in the fashion world), and, with the exception of Nureyev, nearly all the men are macho bullies with a propensity for stupid violence. Political angles are not developed with much specificity, which is acceptable given the oblique treatment given the films other concerns.

Performers seem to have been chosen mostly for their physical attributes, and Kinski and Nureyev lead the way in ably fleshing out characters who are meant to remain mysterious. Vet French producer Serge Silberman served as exec producer here, and tech contributions, notably Henri Decae's beautifully muted lensing and George Delerue's somber score, are aces. —Cart.

Now And Forever
(AUSTRALIAN-COLOR)

Sydney, March 7.

A Roadshow Distributors (Australia) release. Produced by Treisha Ghent and Carnegie Fieldhouse. Director, supervising editor, Adrian Carr. Stars Cheryl Ladd, Robert Coleby. Screenplay, additional material directed by Richard Cassidy, based on the novel by Danielle Steel; camera (color), Don McAlpine; art direction, wardrobe design, Rene and Rochford; associate producer, Rea Francis; music composed by Bruce Rowland; production manager, Carol Williams. Previewed at Colorfilm theatrette, Sydney, March 4, 1983. (Commonwealth Film Censor rating: M). Running time: 90 MINS.

Jessie Clarke	Cheryl Ladd
Ian Clarke	Robert Coleby
Astrid Bonner	Carmen Duncan
Margaret Burton	Christine Amor
Bethanie	Aileen Britton
Andrew Wyndham	Alex Scott
Matilda Spencer	Kris McQuade
Martin Harrington	John Allen
Geoffrey Bates	Rod Mullinar
Jock Martin	Kevin Healy
William Horton	Michael Long
Kent Adams	Tim Burns
Barry York	Henri Szeps
Judge	
(Supreme Court)	Redmond Phillips

Based on the best-selling book by American author Danielle Steel, "Now And Forever" is a syrupy melodrama, a cinematic equivalent of the Mills and Boon novel, well typified in the title song written and performed by Air Supply, highly successful purveyors of schmaltz.

Considering the problems which plagued the production — original director Richard Cassidy exited abruptly early in the shoot, and Adrian Carr, the film's editor, stepped up to help his first feature — tech and artistic standards are more than passable.

Pic is due to bow theatrically in the U.S. this month via Interplanetary Pictures. North American pay-tv and vidcassette rights have been acquired by Universal/MCA, and Roadshow will release it here midyear.

Prospects will probably rely largely on the popularity of the novel, and the heretofore untested b.o. appeal of topliner Cheryl Ladd. The de-winged "Charlie's Angel" limns as a successful boutique proprietor in Sydney, whose husband, a not so successful novelist played by local thesp Robert Coleby, is accused of rape. We know he's innocent — Coleby puts up a little token resistance while he's being seduced by a woman he met in a restaurant — but, and here's the twist, he's found guilty and carted off for 12 months in an island jail. This enforced separation understandably puts strains on their marriage, Ladd resorts to pills and booze, Coleby immerses himself in his second novel and divorce seems inevitable until the conventional happy ending.

Story moves at a fast clip and maintains interest fairly well, despite a few holes in the plot (why doesn't Ladd press Coleby for an explanation of what happened until after he's committed for trial, a long way into the narrative?) and abundant cliches (there's even a tall dark handsome stranger on horseback who nearly, but not quite, gallops off with Ladd's divided heart).

While Ladd looks a million dollars, she is not so richly endowed in the talent department, at least on the evidence of this perf, inhibited by a limited range of emotions and expressions. She has her best moments when her character is falling apart.

Coleby is stilted and unconvincing early in the piece, but grows surer and stronger as the pic progresses, while Christine Amor nearly steals the show as the alleged victim, urgent and erotic in the seduction scene, quivering and defiant in the witness box.

Photography by Don McAlpine, a longtime associate of Bruce Beresford, gives the pic a high-gloss finish, with lots of shots of the Opera House, Harbour Bridge and lush Aussie countryside to please American audiences.

Composer Bruce Rowland, who did a fine job adding atmosphere and feeling to "The Man From Snowy River" has gone for the overkill here; those trilling violins are a rather heavy-handed accompaniment to what is a fairly simple, modestly-mounted yarn.

—Dogo.

Savage Weekend
(COLOR)

Lame gore thriller for the lower-half of double bills.

A Cannon Films release of an Upstate Murder Co. production. Executive producer, John Mason Kirby. Produced by Kirby, David Paulsen. Features entire cast. Written and directed by David Paulsen. Camera (Technicolor, Berkey Pathe Humphreys color), Zoli Vidor; editor, Zion Avrahamian, Jonathan Day; music, Dov Seltzer; assistant director, Peter Kean; sound, Rick Waddell. Reviewed at Lyric Theatre, N.Y., March 12, 1983. (MPAA Rating: R). Running time: 83 MINS.

Nicky	Christopher Allport
Robert	James Doerr
Marie	Marilyn Hamlin
Shirley	Kathleen Heaney
Mac	David Gale

Jay .... Devin Goldenberg
Greg .... Jeffrey David Pomerantz
Otis .... William Sanderson

"Savage Weekend" is a poorly-made terror film, lensed in 1976 as "The Killer Behind The Mask" and released domestically by Cannon in 1981. Picture is also known under the title, "The Upstate Murders," and is reviewed here for the record.

Story has several couples (adults; this film precedes the successful "teens in jeopardy" horror format of late) visiting a remote upstate N.Y. country house for the weekend. Undeveloped (and oddly distracting) subplot has a vast wooden ship half-built in the barn, with the men discussing its completion schedule.

Apart from nominal story values, "Weekend," is structured as a softcore pornography film, with frequent extraneous sex and/or nude scenes, and even the genre's utilitarian fantasy flashbacks. With soft photography by Zoli Vidor, no horror atmosphere is created during this lazy idyll, and the closeup gore shots when a killer-in-a-mask starts picking off the cast seem tacked on.

Lethargic dialog readings and poor scene construction (Paulsen emphasizes one-shot closeups that don't cut together well) make for rough going until some minimal suspense in the final reel. Paulsen demonstrated a more professional approach in his subsequent Cannon assignment, the 1980 "Schizoid" (aka "Murder By Mail"). —*Lor.*

The Funny Farm.
(CANADIAN-COLOR)

Vancouver, March 15.

A New World-Mutual Pictures release of a Filmplan International Inc. Production. Produced by Claude Heroux. Written and directed by Ron Clark. Stars Miles Chapin, Eileen Brennan, Jack Carter, Tracy Bregman. Camera, (color) Rene Verzier; editor, Marcus Manton; music supervision, Pierre Brousseau; sound, Joseph Champagne; art direction, Carol Spier; production manager, Roger Heroux. Reviewed at the Odeon Granville theatre, Vancouver, March 5, 1983. Running time: 96 MINS.
Mark Champlin .... Miles Chapin
Amy Lowell .... Tracy Bregman
Gail Corbin .... Eileen Brennan
Philly Beekman .... Jack Carter
Stephen Croft .... Peter Aykroyd
Bruce Nutter .... Mike MacDonald
Larry Pound .... Howie Mandel
Peter Bowman .... Jack Blum

U.S.-based writer Ron Clark, Canadian-born, has made his rep as both dramatist ("Norman, Is That You?") and as gag-man for both Mel Brooks ("High Anxiety"), and for Blake Edwards ("The Revenge Of The Pink Panther"). Now he debuts as director of his own script in this mildly involving comedy-drama about the agonies and the ecstasies of being a young, scorned stand-up comic.

Miles Chapin, a performer with a Jack Lemmon delivery, plays a young man from Cleveland who goes to L.A. to make his name. Settling into the friction-fraught "Funny Farm" club, run by a tough harridan, neatly limned by Eileen Brennan, Chapin befriends other young hopefuls and finds out about failure.

His exposure to the downs of the game, via harsh, corrupt old-timer Jack Carter, and the reclusive Mike MacDonald, adds a dramatic element to the fable that comes off as just plain portentous.

A nimble showcase for a handful of Canadian spritzers, including Dan Aykroyd's brother, Peter, "The Funny Farm" is handled in a very unassuming fashion by Clark. Tech credits are passable, apart from some grainy daytime exteriors, and a rudimentary music track. —*Gran.*

Joysticks
(COLOR)

Vulgar video games comedy for fast playoff.

A Jensen Farley Pictures release of a Greydon Clark production. Produced and directed by Greydon Clark. Stars Joe Don Baker. Screenplay, Al Gomez, Mickey Epps, Curtis Burch; camera (Movielab color), Nicholas von Sternberg; editor, Larry Bock; music supervision, John Caper Jr.; songs, Ray Khennetsky, Bill Scott; sound, Al Ramirez; production manager, Daryl Kass; art direction, Donn Greer. Reviewed at RKO Cinerama I theatre, N.Y., March 11, 1983. (MPAA Rating: R). Running time: 88 MINS.
Mr. Rutter .... Joe Don Baker
Eugene Groebe .... Leif Green
J.A. McDorfus .... Jim Greenleaf
Jefferson Bailey .... Scott McGinnis
King Vidiot .... Jonathan Gries
Patsy Rutter .... Corinne Bohrer
With: John Diehl, John Voldstad, Logan Ramsey, Reid Cruckshanks, Morgan Lofting, Kym Malin, Kim G. Michel, Jacqulin Cole, Hugo Stanger.

Originally titled "Video Madness," Greydon Clark's "Joysticks" is a teenage sexploitation picture in which the video arcade replaces yesteryear's diner or drive-in as the hangout where episodic action takes place. Not funny enough to justify its plotless existence, film is due for a short life in its theatrical runs.

Corny premise has the young people of River City attempting to keep their beloved video arcade open against the opposition of irate parent Mr. Rutter (Joe Don Baker). Remainder of the film is the usual youthful hijinks, desultory execution of which make for a tedious picture.

With Joe Don Baker playing straight opposite an undistinctive, overacting young cast, filmmaker Clark has to rely on flatulence gags as "savers," with Jim Greenleaf as the gross-out character, a former high school class president now gone to seed under the influence of video games. Leif Green as the

stock nerd is an imitation of Charlie Martin Smith ("American Graffiti"), while the film's de rigeur set of punk-styled troupers is led by King Vidiot (Jonathan Gries) who despite the multi-colored hairdo and already-dated hip mannerisms is just a recycling of the Harvey Lembeck as Eric Von Zipper routines in the "Beach Party" films. Most disturbing "new" element is Corinne Bohrer's nearly unintelligible portrayal of Baker's daughter as a Valley Girl. If the upcoming group of trend films devoted to that lamentable phenomenon are as irritating as her eye-popping and voice-cracking work here, exploitation film fans are in for a long summer.

Though there is plenty of music, "Joysticks" lacks the dynamic score and rhythmic editing which makes other films of this type work. Clark also errs by including an excess of attempted phallic humor plus some softcore sex material which clashes with the light-hearted tone and are likely to limit the film's potential audience. One distressing sign of the times is that Clark, who began directing with blaxploitation films such as "Tom" and "Black Shampoo," employs only whites in speaking roles here. —*Lor.*

The Territory
(PORTUGUESE-U.S.-COLOR)

Paris, March 1.

Hors Champs (Paris) release of a V.O. Films coproduction, in association with Roger Corman (New World Pictures). Produced by Pierre Cottrell and Paulo Branco. Directed by Raul Ruiz. Features entire cast. Screenplay, Ruiz and Gilbert Adair; camera (color), Henri Alekan; sound, Joaquin Pinto, Vaso Pimentel; editor, Valeria Sarmiento; music, Jorge Arriagada. Reviewed at Republic Cinema, Paris, Feb. 25, 1983. Running time: 100 MINS.
With: Isabelle Weingarten, Rebecca Pauly, Jeffrey Carey, Jeffrey Kime, Paul Getty Jr., Ethan Stone, Camila Mora, Jose Nascimento.

(English soundtrack)

"The Territory" is noteworthy for Henri Alekan's evocative color photography and the fact that German helmer Wim Wenders "borrowed" the cast and techniques to make "The State of Things," also shot in Portugal.

Otherwise, there's little that distinguishes this vacuous tale about a group of young Americans who get lost during a hike in a large natural park and are reduced to cannibalism to survive.

Writer-director Raul Ruiz, a talented Chilian filmmaker who has been essentially working in France since self-imposed exile from his homeland in 1974, attempts to weave a parable from familiar dramatic elements. Macabre humor, surrealism and metaphysics are part of the non-realistic narrative, but the whole suffers irremediably from its transparent symbolic effects and the outrageously goofy performances.

"The Territory" is obviously destined for the festival trail and specialized art house playoff. It will probably delight semiologists, and amateurs of Borgesian intrigues. Lovers of lurid sensationalism should abstain.

(Pic was shot in English, with British critic Gilbert Adair sharing credit on the dialog). —*Len.*

J'Ai Epouse une Ombre
(I Married a Dead Man)
(FRENCH-COLOR)

Paris, March 1.

AMLF release of a Sara Films/TF-1 Film Productions coproduction. Produced by Alain Sarde. Stars Nathalie Baye and Francis Huster. Directed by Robin Davis. Screenplay, Davis and Patrick Laurent, based on William Irish's novel; camera (Kodacolor), Bernard Zitzermann; art director, Ivan Maussion; music, Philippe Sarde; editor, Marie-Castro Vasquez; sound, Michel Laurent; production manager, Jacques Ristori de la Riventosa. Reviewed at the Gaumont Colisee theatre, Paris, March 1, 1983. Running time: 110 MINS.
Helene .... Nathalie Baye
Pierre .... Francis Huster
Frank .... Richard Bohringer
Lena .... Madeleine Robinson
Mr. Meyraud .... Guy Trejan
Fifo .... Victoria Abril

"J'Ai Epouse un Ombre" is an oddly chaste Gallic transposition of the William Irish (Cornell Woolrich) tale, "I Married A Dead Man," about a pregnant young drifter who assumes the identity of another woman killed in a train crash. Hollywood director Mitchell Leisen filmed it in 1950 as "No Man Of Her Own," with Barbara Stanwyck in the main role.

Many of Irish's local admirers have come down hard on this new version, charging writer-director Robin Davis and coscripter Patrick Laurent of having emasculated what was powerfully harsh and ambiguous in the book. Maybe so, but the pic's problems have less to do with infidelity to the source, than with weaknesses of its alternate dramatic line.

Nathalie Baye is a rootless young woman, left pregnant and alone by a ne'er-do-well boyfriend (Richard Bohringer). On a train, she befriends a young newlywed, pregnant like herself, who lends her some personal items and allows her to rest in the couple's compartment. The train is derailed, with the couple among the many dead. Baye awakes in a hospital and learns that not only has she given birth in the wreck, but is mistaken for the dead girl by the latter's in-laws, who had never met her.

Baye and her baby are taken into the bosom of the family (which runs a lucrative viticultural business) and she finds it increasingly difficult to destroy their illusions — the ailing mother (Madeleine Robinson) dotes on her, and the remaining son (Francis Huster) falls in love with her. Slowly overcoming her guilt, she begins to adapt, but Bohringer suddenly reappears and tries to blackmail her and the family. Baye kills him. Robinson, in a deathbed gesture of love, signs a letter claiming responsibility for the crime. Baye and Huster can now marry and look forward to a cozy, unclouded future.

The story, as transposed to France, doesn't come across very credibly, and Davis and Laurent deal with the problem by simply ignoring it. How is it, for instance, that nobody bothers to check the identity papers of the dead girl, which Baye recovers and consults in one scene in order to familiarize herself with her new role? Since much of the drama depends on Baye not being found out, it's a persistently nagging problem, one not helped by the realistic tone of the direction.

. The role has apparently been tailored to Baye's popular image. Her previous role as a Paris hooker in Bob Swaim's "La Balance" (for which she's won the Cesar award for best actress) hopefully indicated a new direction for her towards personages of a darker psychological cloth. Not so here. She's back as the Nice French Girl, stuck in a "film noir" plot, but remaining morally aloof of its conventions.

Still, Baye is good here and, if one can forget its abiding faults, "J'Ai Epouse un Ombre" is fairly involving and occasionally touching. Davis, who directs ably, banks heavily on the relationship between Baye and Robinson, (whose screen appearances have become all too rare), and their scenes create a cogent emotional texture. Less interesting is the romantic angle, with Huster dull in a rather conventional role. Bohringer is aptly detestable as the ex-lover.

Tech credits are excellent. Film is cleaning up locally and stands fair pickup chances abroad. —Len.

Als Je Begrijpt Wat Ik Bedoel
(If You Know What I Mean)
(DUTCH-COLOR-ANIMATED)

Amsterdam, Feb. 11.

Verenigde Nederlandse Filmcompagnie release of a Rob Hower's Filmcompagnie production. Producer and story-editor, Rob Hower. Animation, Bjorn Frank Jensen, Bob Maxfield; backgrounds, Ben van Voorn; music, Herman Schoonderwalt; songs (text and music), Harrie Geelen. Scenario, storyboard, direction, Bert Kroon, Harrie Geelen, Bjorn Frank Jensen, based on Marten Toonder story and comic strip; artistic supervision, Houwer and Toonder. Reviewed at City Theatre, Amsterdam, Feb. 19, 19, 83. Running time: 80 MINS.

Noted Dutch producer Rob Houwer has come up with Holland's first full-length animated film which took three years and $2,000,000 to make. It has already opened

well locally and if now-producing foreign translations match up to the quality of the original text and voicecasting is handled as adroitly, it will travel.

The film is reminiscent in some ways of older Disney pictures and there is an "E.T." type appeal attached to one of the main characters, Swellbelly. But this is no case of mere emulation or plagiarism. The cartoon characters, from the pen of Marten Toonder, Holland's famed strip creator, have a long heritage of popularity and the differences between this film and Disney's are greater than the similarities (here the human beings look like animals rather than animals acting like humans).

The text of the film is at least as important as its visual images. Toonder not only created distinctive figures, he developed personal styles of speech for some of them. The characters are so familiar locally that a number of their words and expressions have slipped into the language.

Main characters are Tom the cat and Ollie B. Bommel, a rich, pompous, socially snobbish, kind and none-too-bright bear. He has an even more pompous valet. They all live in Rommeldam, which also has a mayor, police chief, newspaperman plus good burghers and their wives who have been known nationally (since 1939) through the daily blatts and other publications.

For the film, this world is invaded by an egg, blown into town by a storm, from which emerges a Zwelgbast (Swellbelly), an unknowing offspring of a monster from the other side of the Black Mountains. Swellbelly, who figures the bear is his ma, has some devastating little ways — he can swell up to the size of King Kong and can only be mollified in such moods by his adopted mum.

But life becomes complicated in town, notably when Bommel is accused of robbing a bank. The cat, who is the ingenious one of the bunch, sorts it all out and gets the monsterfils back to his real mother.

The animation is well done, the characters appealingly drawn. But the visuals have not been allowed to dominate the dialog. That's one of its great strengths. —Wall.

Stadt der Verlorenen Seelen
(City of Lost Souls)
(W. GERMAN-COLOR)

Rotterdam, Feb. 16.

Produced, written, directed and edited by Rosa von Praunheim. Camera (color), Stephan Koster; music, Alexander Kraut, Jayne County, Angie Stardust. Reviewed at Film Festival Rotterdam, Feb. 5, 1983. Running time: 90 MINS.

Stars: Jayne County, Angie Stardust, Judith Flex, Gary Miller, Joaquin La Habana.

Cult director Rosa von Praunheim (aka Holger Mischwitzki)

makes pics about sex and people in all their diversity — controversial and provocative stuff which has made him something of a licensed film-jester of West German television and international film festivals.

His films are in color but his statements are in black and white. Characters are either idiots or geniuses. But he seems to love them all.

Such certainty is the case in "City Of Lost Souls," a warm, fast (but never frantic) film crowded with temperamental, eccentric and egocentric characters. Lacking any real plot line, the film is a framework on which sequences are hung.

The city of lost souls, natch, is Berlin and the souls are those of American singers, dancers and actors stranded there or just around because they like that wide open town. The sexual mix is an exotic one — hetero's, gays, transvestites and transsexuals (one of the latter, now a woman, develops lesbian tendencies) — exuding brittleness, vulnerability, warmth and kindness.

Essentially a form of cabaret, the film phases through the sentimental and witty to the plain funny and explicit. But it's never hardnosed or pornographic.

The players know their job: the camerawork is inventive. And the music is good. —Wall.

Ator
(COLOR)

Laughable sword and sorcery.

Hollywood, March 9.

Comworld Pictures release. Directed and written by David Hills. Produced by Alex Susmann. Features entire cast. Camera (color), Frederick Slonisco; editor, David Framer; art direction, John Gregory; music, Maria Cordio; assistant director, Sam Stone. Reviewed at the Paramount Theatre, Hollywood, March 9, 1983. (MPAA Rating: PG) Running time: 100 MINS.

Cast: Miles O'Keeffe, Sabrina Siani, Ritza Brown, Edmund Purdom, Laura Gemser.

There are so many unintentional laughs in Comworld Pictures,' "Ator" that one almost couldn't blame the company for releasing it as a comedy. Unfortunately, it's being billed as a new sword and sorcery film starring Miles O'Keeffe (last seen as Bo Derek's "Tarzan"). The sheer incompetence of the effort defies much analysis. B.o. performance should reflect that.

O'Keeffe didn't know how lucky he was to be without dialog in the Derek film. In this one, writer-director David Hills uses him as a beefy mythical hero trying to defeat the evil "black knights" in so many countlessly absurd situations that even a Newman or Redford would find it difficult to charm themselves into respectability. Needless to say, O'Keeffe doesn't either.

Though much of the picture bears more than a resemblance to Uni-

versal's Arnold Schwarzenegger starrer, "Conan, The Barbarian," Hills has put in some of his own touches. The evil hero worships spiders and the cast alternates between medieval talk and contemporary southern California-type lingo. O'Keeffe utters such diverse pearls of wisdom as "altruism doesn't fit you any more than the maternity route" (to a woman taken with him) and "Well, if we gotta go ..." (when faced with proceeding with a dangerous journey.

The entire picture appears to have been photographed at different times of the day, the soundtrack mostly sounds like it's been piped in through a megaphone and the overall production values raise the schlock sci-fi pics of the fifties to new levels of excellence. —Berg.

10 To Midnight
(COLOR)

Solid b.o. for action fans.

Hollywood, March 12.

A Cannon Group release of a Golan-Globus Production. Produced by Pancho Kohner and Lance Hool. Stars Charles Bronson. Directed by J. Lee Thompson. Written by William Roberts. Camera (color), Adam Greenberg; editor, Peter Lee Thompson; music, Robert O. Ragland; art direction, Jim Freiburger; set director, Cecilia Rodarte; sound mixer, Craig Felburg; assistant director, Barbara Michaels. Reviewed at SRO Paramount Theatre, March 11, 1983. (MPAA Rating: R.) Running time: 100 MINS.
Leo Kessler .... Charles Bronson
Laurie Kessler .... Lisa Eilbacher
Warren Stacey .... Gene Davis
Paul McAnn .... Andrew Stevens
Dave Dante .... Geoffrey Lewis
Captain Malone .... Wilford Brimley
Nathan Zager .... Robert Lyons
Bunny .... Iva Lane

A sexually deranged killer slices up five young women like melons, two in the early going of "10 to Midnight" and three in the final minutes in a scene curdlingly reminiscent of the shocking Richard Speck murders of eight student nurses in Chicago in 1966. The killer (well enough played by Gene Davis) is literally getting away with murder because of bureaucratic red tape and a pending insanity plea. As cop Charles Bronson puts it: "I remember when legal meant lawful. Now it means loophole." So Bronson takes matters into his own hands as this Cannon Group release of a Golan-Globus production adds the latest variation to Bronson's earlier "Death Wish" pair. Boxoffice outlook for the action crowd appears solid.

The public crowd in the opening screening in Hollywood whooped when Bronson dispatched the psycho, and chortled when Bronson told his by-the-book sidekick (Andrew Stevens) "Forget what's legal and do what's right." Cries of "I love it" — not sarcastic — filled the theatre when the movie ended.

Bronson is a gnarled veteran on the force. When he can't nail his man legally, he plants evidence on him. He's found out and disgraced but no matter. He's a hero all the way. William Roberts' screenplay, while it sags in the middle, is damnably clever at dropping in its vicious vigilante theme without being didactic, and J. Lee Thompson's direction, borrowing from Hitchcock's editing in "Psycho," creates the full horror of blades thrusting into naked bellies without the viewer ever actually seeing it happen.

The title means nothing in the context of the film. "10- to Midnight" is supposed to suggest a kind of "High Noon" tension, but during the slaughter of the student nurses, with the cops already alerted, the slayings meander along for what seems like eternity. Lisa Eilbacher plays Bronson's daughter and the beautiful, major target of the killer. Geoffrey Lewis is very good as a self-serving defense attorney who tells his warped client to be cool because "you'll walk out of a crazy house alive."

Production catches the grimy, tacky side of L.A. but the sound quality of the print reviewed was poor, with dialogue definition frequently blurred and echoey.

—Loyn.

Second Thoughts
(COLOR)

They should have had second thoughts about this one.

Hollywood, Feb. 10.

A Universal release from EMI Films of a Turman-Foster Company production. Produced by Lawrence Turman, David Foster. Directed by Turman. Features entire cast. Screenplay, Steve Brown, from story by Brown and Terry Louise Fisher; camera (Technicolor), King Baggot; editor, Neil Travis; music, Henry Mancini; production design, Paul Peters; set design, Robert Goldstein; set decoration, Linda DeScenna; costume design, Julie Weiss; sound, Darin Knight; assistant director, Jerry Grandey. Reviewed at Universal Studios, Universal City, Feb. 10, 1983. (MPAA Rating: PG.) Running time: 98 MINS.

Amy	Lucie Arnaz
Will	Craig Wasson
John Michael	Ken Howard
Janis	Anne Schedeen
Dr. Eastman	Arthur Rosenberg
Dr. Martha Carpenter	Peggy McCay
Sharon	Tammy Taylor
Hondo	Alan Stock
Chief Staab	James O'Connell
Sgt. Cabrillo	Louis Giambalvo
Officer Behncke	Alex Kubik
Judge Richards	Charles Lampkin

The folks at EMI and, down the line, at Universal, should have had second thoughts when they decided to go ahead with this screenplay. Indeed, so dismal is it that one can only wonder what possibly made them think a film made from it could emerge as either commercial or entertaining. Look for this one in short order on tv, where the potential audience will be quite large, since few viewers will have seen it in theatres.

Almost everything about the premise, as well as the execution, is preposterous. For some reason, Santa Fe attorney Lucie Arnaz has taken leftover hippie and street musician Craig Wasson as a lover after divorcing high-powered banker Ken Howard. Although the psychology of her choice is never explored, Arnaz must have a mighty strong masochistic streak, for rarely have two such emotional Fascists as these men are popped up in a single film before.

Understandably, Arnaz finally decides to break up with Wasson, a dippy idealist who is still amazed when the police haul him in even though the same thing has undoubtedly been happening to him for years. Problem is Arnaz discovers she's 10 weeks pregnant. After due deliberation, she decides maybe Wasson isn't the best potential father for her child and checks into the hospital for an abortion.

Getting wind of this, Wasson kidnaps her, takes her out to a shack in a desert ghost town and chains her to a bed where he evidently intends to keep her until it's too late to go through with the abortion. In the meantime, because Howard has refused him a loan (a reasonable decision considering Wasson's prospects), Wasson terrorizes the financial institution by stuffing a pizza into the night deposit slot and placing stinking dead fish in a safety deposit box.

Much of the dialog consists of debate over Arnaz's right to end her pregnancy, with Wasson ranting and raving about how he won't let her do it. Even right to lifers would probably disown Wasson as a spokesman for their cause.

Labored efforts at farce drag pic down even further, and supporting characters, such as Howard's bimbo of a second wife and a thoroughly creepy abortion specialist at the hospital, are outright embarrassments.

After all the arguing and issue-taking film even chickens out of taking a stand, solving the dilemma via a dopey case of mistaken identity back at the hospital. —*Cart.*

Berlin Film Reviews

Der Aufenthalt
(Held For Questioning)
(EAST GERMAN-COLOR)

East Berlin, Feb. 18.

A DEFA Film Production, East Berlin, "Babelsberg" Film Group; world rights, DEFA Aussenhandel, East Berlin. Features entire cast. Directed by Frank Beyer. Screenplay, Wolfgang Kohlhaase, based on Hermann Kant's novel; camera (color), Eberhard Geick; sets, Alfred Hirschmeier; editing, Rita Hiller; music, Guenther Fischer; dramaturg, Dieter Wolf; production manager, Herbert Ehler. Reviewed at DEFA Screening Room, East Berlin, Feb. 18, '83. Running time: 101 MINS.

Cast: Sylvester Groth (Mark Niebuhr), Fred Dueren (General Eisensteck), Klaus Piontek (Major Lundenbroich), Matthias Guenther (Hauptsturmfuehrer), Horst Hiemer (Gasmann), Guenter Junghans (Gestapo Commissioner Rudloff), Hans-Uwe Bauer (Coporal Fensko), Alexander von Heteren (Jan Beveren), Gustaw Lutkiewicz (Pan Szybko), Zygmunt Maciejewski (Pan Eugoniusz), Andrzej Pieczynski (Lieutenant), Krzysztof Chamiec (Chief), Roman Wilhelmi (Ohnehals), Andrzej Krasicki (Doctor).

Originally slated for competition in the Berlin Film Festival, Frank Beyer's "Held for Questioning" was then withdrawn by the East Germans themselves at the last minute. It appears, according to a reliable source, that the objection to showing the film in the Berlinale came from Poland, and the German Democratic Republic reluctantly complied with its neighbor's wishes. As a result, there wasn't a competing East German film in the festival — an embarrassment primarily for the Socialist countries, but a ticklish matter for the Berlinale as well.

In the long run, however, the matter will be resolved at one or other of the international festivals on the season's circuit, for "Held for Questioning" (the original German title means a "stop" or "sojourn") doesn't step on any country's toes — and hardly Poland's — just because the setting happens to be a Polish prison in the immediate aftermath of World War II.

"Held for Questioning" is a true-to-life story, based on writer Hermann Kant's own experiences as a young 19-year-old German soldier drafted into the Wehrmacht just after the fateful seige of Stalingrad. Taken prisoner, the young man is mistakingly identified by a distraught mother who is convinced that he was the same SS-man responsible for the death of her daughter in Lublin some time before. The soldier is immediately imprisoned and held for interrogation.

The drama begins in the prison. Young Mark Niebuhr (Sylvester Groth) doesn't know, first of all, why he is being held. Further, when he is isolated, the methods used to wring the truth out of him tax all his energies. In fact, the apparent hope is that he will die by accident while on dangerous prison-yard work assignments. This doesn't happen, and the questioning goes on. Then he's shifted to a cell reserved for several German officers and soldiers together — and here the pressure is worse than ever, for the Germans hold by military protocol and are mostly convicted Nazi criminals waiting for trial and execution. It's here that Niebuhr learns the bitter truth of the horrors of Lublin and Auschwitz and other extermination camps, and methods perpetrated by the Nazis.

As a member of the Wehrmacht (with only a few weeks of military service), Niebuhr protests his innocence. And as a youth of 19, he offers a credible argument that he is completely ignorant of any of the Nazi atrocities. This puts him as much in disfavor with the other German prisoners as it angers his Polish captors. To add to this dilemma, one of the lad's own company companions, who was with him from the beginning of military service, refuses to open his mouth in defense of the accused (apparently for fear of implicating himself in some way).

The outcome is an investigation leading to a declaration of innocence, but without much of an apology from the Polish officers for the mistaken-identity treatment. But in the meantime the lad had narrowly escaped a self-righteous execution on the part of the imprisoned Germans with their damning code of conduct.

Beyer's direction is fluid and suspenseful, while Wolfgang Kohlhaase's dialog is appropriately sparse. Both German and Polish actors appear in the film, many of the characters roles being standout performances. Pic would have been in easy contention for laurels in direction or acting departments at the Berlin fest, and it's a shame that a filmmaker of Frank Beyer's integrity and standing — he made the impressive "Jacob the Liar" (1974), a Berlinale Silver Bear winner set in the Warsaw Ghetto during the Holocaust — should fall amiss of an oversensitive national film commission. The real "heavies" in this prison expose are the Germans in prison, not the Poles running it.

—Holl.

Die Puppe
(The Doll)
(WEST GERMAN-COLOR-16m)

Berlin, March 2.

A Detlev Fechtmann Film Production. Features entire cast. Directed by Detlev Fechtmann. Screenplay, Fechtmann, Ronald Wedekind; camera (color), Wedekind; editing, Ingrid Hause; music, Hainer Dutjer; sets, Werner Burhop, Rudolf Skupin. Reviewed at Berlin Film Fest (Forum), Feb. 21, '82. Running time: 93 MINS.

Cast: Sabine von Maydell (Anne), Elke Rensing (Anne as Child), Ingrid Slowak (Mother), Christian Haisch (Father), Sara Fruchtmann, Heinz Gerling.

Unspooled in the Information Program on New German Cinema at the International Forum of Young Cinema, Detlev Fechtmann's "The Doll" marks the helmer as a name to watch among New Generation talent. It's the story of a young girl whose contact with her grandfather was more important than that with her own working parents who were seldom at home when it counted. The death of the grandfather leaves her entirely on her own, and the 12-year-old sinks into a fantasy world due to her shyness and inability to make close friends at school. Her partner now is a doll, with whom she begins to communicate as a substitute for the departed grandfather.

Later, the girl now grown to adulthood, we are presented with a case history of a schizophrenic. Anne is recuperating from a mental and physical breakdown in a clinic. After a time, she is released and returns home to a normal existence again — but also has to confront an alter ego in the form of a grown doll. Chances are even that she will find her way out of the deadend situation at the end.

"The Doll" is a modest low-budget film made without subsidy coin on the director's own shoestring. The quality of the credits and self-assurance in handling the theme should guarantee more visibility for Detlev Fechtmann in the future. —Holl.

Eine Liebe Wie Andere Auch
(A Love Like Any Other)
(WEST GERMAN-COLOR)

Berlin, March 8.
A Janus Film Production, Frankfurt. Features entire cast. Written and directed by Hans Stempel, Martin Ripkens. Camera (color), Michael Teutsch; music, Chet Baker, Frederick the Great, Friedrich Georg Handel, Tantra, Giuseppe Verdi, Boris Vian; editing, Alexander Rupp; production managers, Rosy Gockel, Helo Gutschwager. Reviewed at Berlin Film Fest (Forum), Feb. 23, '83. Running time: 104 MINS.
Cast: Klaus Adler (Wieland), Stuart Wolfe (Wolf), Christa Maerker (Christa), Paul Lotter (Paul), Dieter Bachnick, Thomas Bloecker, Michael Foester, Herta von Klewitz, Johannés Kuester, Bernd Langschied, Friehelm Lehmann, Klaus D. Lucas, Heinz Rathsack, Susanne Schlaepfer, Hendrik de Wit.

After the appearance of Frank Ripploh's "Taxi zum Klo" (1980) on the hang-ups of being gay, followed by Alexandra von Grote's "Depart to Arrive" (1982) on the existential anxieties within a lesbian relationship, it's only natural that a light social comedy like Hans Stempel and Martin Ripkens's "A Love Like Any Other" should come along. Pic preemed at the Berlin Forum of Young Cinema, and may find its way abroad to more international oasis and certainly to Gay Fests in Gotham, Frisco, and elsewhere.

Pic reduces homosexuality to an innocent parlor game, somewhat like turning an Ernst Lubitsch comedy inside out. It has to be seen to be believed and experienced to be taken at its word.

The story is about a pair of young gays in their late twenties living in Berlin: one is a high-school teacher, the other a bookseller dreaming of a shop of his own one day. This is a city made for alternative life-styles, so the pair come across as rather normal and quite bourgeois throughout the film. They are, however, quite independent individuals: the teacher leans towards a defense of "house-squatters" in his courses, and discovers that one of his pupils is gay; the bookseller is an admirer of Klaus Mann (author of "Mephisto"), threatening to put an end to the relationship by finding temporarily a new boyfriend and then going through a bit of a trauma at the death of his father.

The humor is found in the human comedy that is life itself. Their neighbor, Christa, has one affair after another without finding a married boyfriend to last. An inheritance leads to renting a more expensive apartment rather than giving up security for the risks of starting a bookshop of one's own. There's also a recipe for making chocolate mousse, a rug delivery to a Berlin Gay house, and several moments of table-talk that are precious to say the least. —Holl.

Hadisat An Nusf Meter
(The Incident of the Half-Meter)
(SYRIAN-COLOR)

Berlin, March 4.
A National Film Organization Production, Damascus. Features entire cast. Written and directed by Samir Zikra. Camera (color), Abdul Kadar al Shurbagy; music, Marcel Kalipheh; sets, A. Farhoud; sound, E. Sa'adeh; editing, Antonette Azarieh, Hanna Ward; production manager, George Bishara. Reviewed at Berlin Film Fest (Forum), Feb. 23, '83 Running time: 110 MINS.
Cast: Abdul Fatah al Mozaeen, Gyana Ide, Ali Assed, Hassan Yoness, Nizar Charaby, Vilda Samoor, Najah Hafcez, Fahed Kaikati; Ahmad Mahayni.

Unspooled previously at fests in Carthage, Nantes, and Venice, debut helmer Samir Zikra's "The Incident of the Half-Meter" introduces a new talent in Arabic cinema. Pic is a social comedy, one that blends irony with criticism in deciphering the weaknesses in a patriarchal society in Syria as well as being a commentary on the human side of an inoffensive bureaucracy for what it is. Zikra, like several other Third World directors of note, graduated from the Moscow Film School (VGIK) in 1973 and made several shorts and newsreels before this feature film.

The scene is Damascus, 1967. A civil servant in the government tax office travels daily on the bus to work, and falls in love with a young student riding the same bus but a half-meter away from him. His daily existence in the office supplies more than enough material for a satire, for the red-tape is matched with hierarchical rules and dubious reports of Syrian successes at the war front.

The war ends in defeat for the Syrians. Then the second defeat has to be met: the girl decides to break off her relationship with the indecisive government clerk. Love and war are just not his strong points so far as a self-assertive character is concerned. His main concern in life revolves around how to keep his suit clean and neat on and off the job in a city that dumps its garbage regularly into the middle of the street.

Credits are a major plus in this social comedy with a light satirical touch. Zikra is not only a promising new name in Arabic cinema, but he has also thrust Syrian cinema to the forefront this past season. "The Incident of the Half-Meter" deserves more fest invitations and exposure abroad. One of its strong aspects is the view of everyday life today in one of the world's oldest living cities. —Holl.

Clementine Tango
(FRENCH-COLOR)

Berlin, Feb. 26.
A Creation production with Vladimir Forgency, London. Written and directed by Caroline Roboh. Features entire cast. Camera (color), Mario Barroso; editor, Dany; sound, Gerard Lecas; production design, Pierre Simonini, Arturo Brachetti; make-up; Josephine Larsen, Arturo Brachetti; choreography, Michel Renault, Caroline Roboh. Reviewed at the Filmkunst 66 Cinema, Berlin, Feb. 26, 1983. Running time: 100 MINS.
Cast: Claire Pascal, Francois Helvey, Arturo Brachetti, Josephine Larsen, Caroline Roboh, Ronald Fuhrer, Michel Renault, Margarethe Russel, Fabio Ceresa.

This is impertinent and unconventional enough to become a cult movie, if pushed and promoted the right way. It certainly offers enough transvestism, incest, decadence and outrageous scenes to please camp followers. It could have done with a more substantial plot and with less confinement in closed sets, obviously caused by budget limitations, but the midnight crowds in Berlin didn't seem to mind.

It is all about the snobbish scion of a noble family who investigates one of his father's past love affairs and discovers its traces in a freakish Pigalle nightclub. There he finds an English-speaking singer and her daughter, Clementine, mad about tango and fascinating. He also encounters a bisexual crowd which throws him into a state of emotional confusion. He also has to cope with the younger sister who shares his flat, a shy, ugly duckling, always complaining that she is not sufficiently taken care of, and incidentally being played by helmer Caroline Roboh herself.

The plot is an excuse to tie together a number of nightclub acts, well performed by Arturo Brachetti and Josephine Larsen, who are particularly talented at breaking down accepted sexual barriers. That they have also been involved in the art direction and make-up comes as no surprise, this film having the looks of a communal effort in which each participant contributed in more than one way to create the final effect. Thus, Michel Renault, credited as choreographer, plays this part, with a lusty gay touch, in the film with Roboh herself contributing her own share of dance suggestions.

The effect is that of a wild party, small in dimensions but enjoyed by everybody present. The camera work may not be that secure and carefully planned, but this shouldn't worry an audience in the general improvisational mood prevalent here. Spoofing moral righteousness and bourgeois prissiness, this item is amusing most of the time, if accepted on its own level — that of a grotesque caricature. Francois Helvey is just right as the insufferable blueblood with a streak of decadence in his veins. Claire Pascal plays Clementine with an air of innocence that belies the surroundings in which she has grown up, but the film's main assets, are without any doubt, Brachetti and Larsen who handle with amazing ease all the different, and equally stratagem disguises they go through. —Edna.

Kaj Ti Je Deklica
(Red Boogie)
(YUGOSLAV-COLOR)

Berlin, March 9.
A Viba Film Production, Ljubljana; world rights, Yugoslavija Film, Belgrade. Features entire cast. Directed by Karpo Godina. Screenplay, Branko Somer; camera (color), Vilko Filac; music, sets, Belica Skerlak; music, Janez Gregorc; editing, Godina; production manager, Ivan Mazgon. Reviewed at Berlin Film Fest (Market), Feb. 26, '83. Running time: 90 MINS.
Cast: Ivo Ban, Boris Cavazza, Jozef Roposa, Peter· Mlakar, Marko Derganc, Zvonko Coh, Zo: an Predin, Edi Stefancic, Ursula Rebek.

Following the success of Karpo Godina's debut film, "The Raft of Medusa" (1980), his latest, "Red Boogie," was looked forward to with expectation. The cameraman-turned-director from Slovenia contributed his talents also to lensing and editing this portrait of the troubled postwar years, when Yugoslavia cut herself off from Stalinist influence in the Soviet Union and went it alone without even support from the capitalist West. Pic has some strong aspects, but the sting of Branko Vucicevic's script (the screenplay writer for "The Raft of Medusa") is missing to guarantee success.

During a Five-Year-Plan, a radio station sends its band of musicians around the countryside to raise morale at working sites and collective farms. But the musicians are captivated by the idea of playing jazz, boogie-woogie, and blues melodies instead of the conventional stilted folkloric tunes that are required. Each time they try to slip in the forbidden "red boogie," however, they are reprimanded by party secretaries, secret policemen, and yes-men of every type.

The comedy lies in the tricks the group resort to in order to pull the wool over the eyes of watching naysayers. Further, they have their wreck of a pick-up truck to drive quickly from village to factory to working collective, so when things get too hot — they simply move on to the next stop. The musicians are talented, full of humor, and with a measure of idealism. In the finale, one of them makes a dash for the border, and is shot.

The first half of "Red Boogie" holds real promise, but then the wind goes out of the sails, and the ending is too abrupt to score anywhere else than on the festival circuit. Nonetheless, Godina is one of Yugoslavia's masterful cinematic talents, one to keep a close eye on the future. —Holl.

Der Stille Ozean
(The Silent Ocean)
(AUSTRIAN-W. GERMAN-B&W)

Berlin, March 1.

A Teamfilm Production, (Vienna) Oesterreichischer Rundfunk (ORF), Vienna, and in coproduction with Zweites Deutsches Fernsehen (ZDF), (Mainz). Features entire cast. Directed by Xaver Schwarzenberger. Screenplay, Gerhard Roth, Walter Kappacher, camera (black and white) Schwarzenberger; sets, Frank Geuer; music, Bert Breit; editing, Uli Schwarzenberger. Reviewed at Berlin Film Fest (competition), Feb. 27, '83. Running time: 95 MINS.

Ascher .... Hanno Poeschl
Zeiner .... Bert Breit
Widow Egger ..,........... Maria Emo
Florence .... Marie-France Pisier
Hofmeister ....,...... Bruno Dallansky
Rogy ....,....Johannes Thanheiser
Luescher .... Marius Cella
First Sister .... Paola Loew
Second Sister .... Maria Martina
Regina ...?....,.,....... Gerlinde Ully
Frau Melzer ..,........ Liliane Nelska
Policeman .... Emanuel Schmied
Doctor ..,............ Herbert Steinmetz

"The Silent Ocean" is the debut film by Xaver Schwarzenberger, cameraman of Rainer Werner Fassbinder for the latter's later films, and it's a beauty to watch. As director-cameraman for this Austrian-W. German entry at the Berlinale, Schwarzenberger turns the trick without a hitch.

This is the story of a young doctor who accidentally caused another's death. To find himself, he travels alone to an isolated Austrian village. It's autumn as it changes to winter, a misty landscape much appreciated by hunters during the season on fat pheasants and rabbits. The villagers treat strangers coldly, but when he passes himself off for a biologist during a rabies epidemic, the peasants take to his presence as a kind of savior who happened upon the scene at just the right time. When one of the villagers is bitten by a diseased animal, however, it soon becomes known who he is.

Meanwhile, he contemplates suicide. His wife, who writes him letters, comes for an occasional visit. The epidemic begins to worry everyone, thus setting the stage for a philosophical reflection on fear and death, violence and suicide. Most of all, the distraught doctor watches village life with its cus-

toms and traditions pass before him. One villager loses a court case, takes justice into his own hands, and kills his neighbors — now he's hunted like game. The doctor, during this final episode, awakens to life by looking into the face of death. In the end, he leaves the village as he came.

"The Silent Ocean" matches breathtaking images with poetic verbal metaphors and philosophical truths, all without being pretentious or overbearing. If there's a minus at all, it's the drawback of being a concise piece of Austrian literature. Scripter Gerhard Roth belongs to the Graz school of writers, whose novel "The Silent Ocean" appeared in 1980. Schwarzenberger has made a film that in literati circles would go down as a quality tv production, save that it needs the breadth of a movie screen to be fully appreciated and comprehensible. --Holl.

Kto Stuchitsya V Dverj Ko Mne?
(Who's Knocking On My Door?)
(SOVIET-COLOR)

Berlin, March 9.

A Mosfilm Production, Moscow; world rights, Goskino, Moscow. Features entire cast. Directed by Nikolai Skubjin. Screenplay, Tatyana Chlopnikova; camera (color), Genri Abramyam; music, Yefim Podgaiz; sound, L. Terechovskaya. Reviewed at Berlin Film Fest (Forum), Feb. 21, '83. Running time: 85 MINS.

Cast: Tamara Akulova, Sergei Shakurov, Svetlana Toma, Shanna Bolotova, Vadim Spiridonov.

A debut film on the everyday in Moscow, Nikolai Skubjin's "Who's Knocking on My Door?" marks a concern with new aspects of Soviet life. A contrast is presented between pessimistic youth and the complacent middle-class, but offered in such a context that the self-assurance of professional people (a cross-section of Soviet uppercrust living) is shaken to the roots.

"Who's Knocking" is a young girl seeking refuge on a wintry evening at an apartment filled with company. Once the hosts get involved with the girl's fate, a string of events occur that lead to a stabbing and run-in with a street gang. For the most part, the director is on the side of a skeptical, questioning youth in this "mirror of the times," but the main thrust of the opening scenes loses in the course of the complex plot maneuvers that ends in a police station with arrests of the girl and youths.

Try to catch "Knocking" at a Soviet Film Week or on the fest circuit. In any case, helmer Skubjin is a coming name in Soviet cinema to keep an eye on in the future. —Holl.

Maerkische Forschungen
(Research In Mark Brandenburg)
(EAST GERMAN-COLOR)

Berlin, March 8.

A DEFA Film Production, Roter Kreis Group, East Berlin; world rights, DEFA Aussenhandel, East Berlin. Features entire cast. Written and directed by Roland Graf, based on Guenter de Bruyn story with the same title. Camera (color), Peter Brand; sets, Dieter Adam; music, Guenther Fischer; costumes, Barbara Braumann; editing, Monika Schindler; production manager, Volkmar Venzke. Reviewed at Berlin Film Fest (Info Show), March 1, '83. Running time: 95 MINS.

Cast: Hermann Beyer (Poetsch), Kurt Boewe (Prof. Menzel), Jutta Wachowiak (Frau Poetsch), Eberhard Esche (Bradke), Dieter Franke (Fritz), Trude Bechmann (Grandma Alwine), Marylu Poolman (Erau Eggenfels), Michael Gwisdek (Dr. Albin), Simone von Zglinicki (Frau Unverloren), Horst Schulze (Alfons Lepetit), Barbara Dittus (Frau Menzel).

Roland Graf's comedy is based on Guenter de Bruyn's satire with the same title, "Research in Mark Brandenburg," which deals with a hoax in academic circles — all the more provocative, because the egg is on the face of a committed East Berlin professor. The literary professor has spent 10 years researching the life and fragmented writings of an early 19th-century revolutionary poet, Max von Schwedenow, who turns out in the end to be none other (in his later years) than one Maximilian von Massow, a reactionary writer who went far out of his way to condemn the Jacobins of the time. And the man who stumbles on the truth is a village-teacher in Mark Brandenburg (the area of woods and marches surrounding Berlin).

Thus we have the rib-tickling situation of a professor having to shuck his pet theories in the face of new evidence, all of which might just put an end to his career. The plump egoist decides to play his trump card and prevent the manuscript of his village colleague from being printed. So the stubborn village research struggles on by himself at the end in his lone quest for the truth.

The comedy lies in the fanaticism of two researchers in the first place. Jokes are pinned to the legend of the visionary Schwedenow, enough to make the viewer wonder how many revolutionaries and peasant leaders have been extolled to the skies in remote corners of Socialist lands in East Europe. Hopefully, there'll be more satires along these lines produced in the German Democratic Republic and elsewhere.

The richness of "Research in Mark Brandenburg" is in the adapted story rather than in the film version. Guenter de Bruyn, once a village-teacher who knows what he's talking about in this tale of thumped-up revolutionary forerunners, has hit every nail on the head. For that matter, Hermann Beyer in his alter ego role, that of

the village schoolteacher, sweeps all before him when he appears on the scene at his pompous professor's birthday party. It's the scene that makes the whole film. —Holl.

Konopielka
(POLISH-B&W)

Berlin, March 10.

A Film Polski Production, Perspektywa Unit, Warsaw; world rights, Film Polski, Warsaw. Features entire cast. Written and directed by Witold Leszczynski, based on Edward Redlinski's novel with the same title. Camera (black and white), Zbigniew Napiorkowski; music, Wojciech Karolak; art direction, Maciej Putowski; editing, Lucja Osko. Reviewed at Berlin Film Fest (Market), Feb. 21, '83. Running time: 92 MINS.

Cast: Krzysztof Majchrzak (Kaziuk), Anna Seniuk, Jerzy Block, Marek Sludym, Tomek Jarosinski, Joanna Sienkiewicz (teacher), Franciszek Pieczka, Anna Milewska.

Lensed in the summer months in a backwoods village, Witold Leszczynski's "Konopielka" (a woman's name referring to cloth made from flax) is a fitting sequel to his earlier "Days of Matthew" (1968). It breathes village life, folklorica, country humor, religious superstition, and tradition for the blind sake of tradition.

The film has a clear moral, religious, mystical, and philosophical bent, one best understood by Poles themselves but readily grasped by any who has lived "down on the farm" for a good part of his life.

Kaziuk is a stubborn peasant with a child-bearing wife and an ill temper when his authority is challenged on his own homestead. He and the villagers are visited on day by a couple who might just pass for "the Lord" and "the Virgin Mother" — in any case, strange things begin to happen: an enchanted horse, a tree of knowledge, the fruit of good and evil, the very temptation of the devil in the person of a lovely new schoolteacher sent to the area. The teacher, in fact, stirs erotic fantasies in the imagination of Kaziuk: she pursues him naked in the fields, she makes love with another in her room at the peasant's farmhouse (where she has rented a room), and she does indeed make love with Kaziuk himself. Whether all of this is imagined, or perhaps a real slice of life, is left open for the viewer to muse over.

Then there's the question of time-honored traditions. In a fit of frustration, Kaziuk decides to cut down the family tree next to the ancient farmhouse; this amounts to a sacrilege in the eyes of his family. But when he goes a step further and begins to cut wheat with a grass-scythe, instead of the usual reaping-blade, the entire village is aroused to protest. Just at this moment, a crash of lightning sets his farmhouse afire. Added to this are the twists in the dialog that tickle to the bone: the film comes across like a medieval morality play in the long run.

"Konopielka" deserves some fest exposure, but its real audience will be found at Polish Film Weeks abroad. Credits are far on the plus side, particularly thesps and lensing. —Holl.

Was Tun Pina Bausch Ihre Taenzer In Wuppertal?

(What Are Pina Bausch and Her Dancers Doing In Wuppertal?)
(W. GERMAN-COLOR-DOCU-16m)

Berlin, March 15.

A Coproduction of Norddeutscher Rundfunk (NDR), Hamburg, and Westdeutscher Rundfunk (WDR), Cologne; tv-producers, Rainer Hagen, Horst Koenigstein, Christhart Burgmann. Written and directed by Klaus Wildenhahn. Camera (color), Wolfgang Jost; editing, Petra Arciszowski; sound, Wildenhahn. Reviewed at Berlin Film Fest (Forum), Feb. 26, '83. Running time: 115 MINS.

The tv-documentary by Klaus Wildenhahn, "What Are Pina Bausch and Her Dancers Doing in Wuppertal?" (1982), is the third in a trilogy on art, life, and culture in Northrhine-Westphalia of western Germany that includes "A Message for Posterity" (1980) and "Bandonion" (1981). The connection emerges from an examination of thematic content. "Pina Bausch" opens with a segment from her Wuppertal stage production of the original dance-ballet, "Bandonion," a few years back.

For the neophyte, Pina Bausch is a hot name in dance theatre. Her Wuppertal company is watched by admirers and critics as closely in Gotham as in European cultural circles.

Wildenhahn was invited to share the company's daily life and tough round of rehearsals (in addition to performing schedules in Wuppertal), which meant that he was on hand for a couple of months and assembled some 20 hours of shot footage that had to be whittled down to two hours on television. One senses that the slow pace of putting a new ballet together demanded much more time than allowed for a finished film, but what is there is well worth watching. Further, Wildenhahn is a socially engaged documentarist, not a cultural chronicler of esthetic trends — so he appears to be lost in relating the dance troupe to social and political questions.

Pic begins with a dance critic offering sagacious comments on ballet dancers finishing their careers in the mid and late thirties — just when the interpretation of such existential aspects as "misery," "suffering," and "fear of death" should be a part of the dancer's spiritual and psychological make-up, and thus draw

the best from the performer. Rehearsals for "Bandonion" and "Walzer" are shown, with Bausch (her newly born child in arms) taking her international dancing troupe through the motions (language at rehearsals is German, French and English, by the way). The whole is then related to a working-class woman and texts by two of Wuppertal's literary lights, Friedrich Engels and Else Lasker-Schueler (the German-Jewess poet-dramatist).

Ballet enthusiasts might be disconcerted that this form of avant-garde dancing on the whole foot, rather than the tip of the toes, is not traditionally esthetic enough, but Wildenhahn's camera catches the whole body in motion and highlights the beauty of a gesture, "What is Pina Bausch" deserves a round of fest and German Film Week exposure, yet docu is best comprehended in connection with its preceding portraits of poet Westerhoff and the origin of the bandonion. —Holl.

Der Steinerne Fluss
(The Stone River)
(WEST GERMAN-COLOR)

Berlin, March 15.

A Regina Ziegler Filmproduktion, Berlin, in coproduction with Sender Freies Berlin (SFB). Features entire cast. Written and directed by Thorsten Naeter. Camera (Color), Jacques Steyn; sets, Holger Scholz, Frank Tauchmann; music, Guenther Fischer; editing, Naeter. Reviewed at Berlin Film Fest (Info Show), Feb. 26, '83. Running time: 96 MINS.
Cast: Cora Naeter (Anna), Mark Naeter (Mario), Peter Roggisch (Rudi), Gunter Berger (Anna's Father), Monika Ogorek (Anna's Mother), Sabine Lorenz (Mario's Mother), Peter Schlesinger (Baker), Horst Pinnow (Stranger), Alexander Troll (Dirk), Stephan Kuno (Olli), Volker Lehnert (Jens), Guido Meyn (Clown), Wolfgang Bruhns (Woodcutter), Hannelore Carstens (Teacher), Mathias Josten (Trumpeter).

Unspooled in both the Info Show and the kidpic sidebar, Thorsten Naeter's "The Stone River" attempts to weave all the social problems that plague Berlin (and most German cities) into a meaningful youth film. But the message is so heavy-handed and the images so stagnant that pic is best scored as a nod in the right direction with little to back it up. Only Jacques Steyn's lensing shines on the plus side in this tale about the construction of a new expressway through a wooded area — and smack through the hideaway of a sad-faced retired magician. The kids, natch, save the day. —Holl.

Das Gespenst
(The Ghost)
(WEST GERMAN-B&W)

Berlin, March 15.

A Herbert Achternbusch Filmproduktion, Buchendorf. Features entire cast. Written and directed by Herbert Achtern-

busch. Camera (black and white), Joerg Schmidt-Reitwein; sets, Gunter Freyse; costumes, Ann Poppel; editing, Ulrike Joanni; sound, Sylvia Tewes. Reviewed at Berlin Film Fest (Info Show), Feb. 27, '83. Running time: 88 MINS.
Cast: Herbert Achternbusch (Superior), Annamirl Bierbichler (Sister Superior), Kurt Raab (Poli), Dietmar Schneider (Zisti), Judit Achternbusch (Sister I), Rut Achternbusch (Sister II), Ann Poppel (Woman), Sepp Bierbichler (First Soldier, Second Soldier), Alois Hitzenbichler (Deputy, Third Soldier), Franz Baumgartner (Priest), Werner Schroeter (Bishop), Gabbi Geist (wife), 30 Fools (bit players).

"The Ghost" is Herbert Achternbusch's 10th film in eight years, each pretty much like the other. This one finds him on a note of blasphemy: he's J.C. who's come down from the cross to romance the Mother Superior and feed on bread-and-wine when not working the miracle of transubstantiation. His crown-of-thorns gets in the way at times, there's a visiting bishop investigating the affair, and the local cops come across Roman legionaires of today without a hint of what's going on before them at the inn.

Great for Achternbusch fans (the Bavarian writer-director has many), but not much exciting in the way of screen fare for the masses. — Holl.

Heinrich Penthesilea Von Kleist
(WEST GERMAN-COLOR)

Berlin, March 15.

A Regina Ziegler Filmproduktion, Berlin, Features entire cast. Written and directed by Hans Neuenfels, based on Heinrich von Kleist's play "Penthesilea." Camera (color), Thomas Mauch; music, Heiner Goebbels; editing, Dorete Voelz; sets, Neuenfels, Anna Viebrock; sound, Detlef Fichtner, Uwe Griem. Reviewed at Berlin Film Fest (Forum), Feb. 26, '83. Running time: 144 MINS.
Cast: Elisabeth Trissenaar (Penthesilea), Hermann Treusch (Achilles), Verena Peter (Meroe), Liselotte Rau (High Priestess of Diana), Nicole Hessters (Asteria), Ulrich Hass, Joerg Holm, Edith Robbers, Berta Drews, Hans Neuenfels.

Hans Neuenfels's "Heinrich Penthesilea von Kleist" is based on his own production of Heinrich von Kleist's "Penthesilea" at the Schiller-Theater in West Berlin, in 1981 during the Prussian Art Exhibit. The idea of transposing a play to film in a modern setting (Berlin today) with a mixture of stage costumes (Prussian military uniforms, Amazonian loin-cloths) is not new, but the question is why do it in the first place?

Neuenfels, a top legit director, is shown pursued by blithe spirits of his stage production until the smoke-screen clears and a shortened form of "Penthesilea" finally hits the screen. Thereafter, it's filmed theatre with a few visual twists to help it along for the two-hours-plus stretch.

For the record, Neuenfels's stage production appropriately and professionally manipulated the audience's sensibilities back then with film interludes of thesps romping across Berlin meadows as Penthesilea, the Amazonian Queen, battles Achilles and his Greeks. —Holl.

Concurs
(Orientation Course)
(RUMANIAN-COLOR)

Berlin, March 6.

A Romaniafilm Production, Bucharest, Group Three; world rights, Romaniafilm, Bucharest. Features entire cast. Written and directed by Dan Pita. Camera (color), Vlad Paunescu; sets, Calin Papura; costumes, Irina Katz; sound, Sotir Caragata; music, Adrian Enescu; editing, Cristina Ionescu. Reviewed at Berlin Film Fest (Market), Feb. 25, '83. Running time: 101 MINS.
Cast: Marin Moraru, Gheorghe Dinica, Catalina Murgea, Adriana Schiopu, Claudiu Bleont, Vladimir Juravle, Vladimir Uritescu, Stefan Iordache, Teodor Danetti.

Dan Pita's "Orientation Course" scores as one of the best Rumanian pics to surface to recent years.

"Orientation Course" follows much the same formula, as his "Philip the Good" but in an allegorical context. People from various walks of life enter a contest that will take them over an obstacle course in a wilderness: the trick is to orientate one's self to the difficulties and tests of strength, mind, and spirit the course provides. A young lad enters the contest on the side of one group at the last minute, and it is he who pulls the others through as each fails in the test of character.

Meanwhile, screams are heard in the distance. Unknown to the group, a girl has been raped and murdered. While the group of weaklings head for home in their bus, the lad is left alone to ponder the tragedy. The trick is to figure out what it all means, and that's not at all easy despite credits on the plus side in nearly every category. Pic deserves a fest slot. —Holl.

Vlublen Po Sobstvennomu Zelanij
(Love By Request)
(SOVIET-COLOR)

Berlin, March 4.

A Lenfilm Production, Leningrad; world rights, Goskino, Moscow. Features entire cast. Directed by Sergei Mikaelyan. Screenplay, Mikaelyan, Alexander Vassinsky; camera (color), Sergei Astachov; sound, Natalya Levitina; music, Igor Tsvetkov; sets, Alexei Rudyakov. Reviewed at Berlin Film Fest (Competion), Feb. 28, '83. Running time: 86 MINS.
Cast: Oleg Yankovsky (Oleg), Yevgenia Glushenko (Vera), Vsevold Shilovsky (Nikolai), Irina Resnikova (Natasha), Gladimir Beloussov (Gena), Yuri Dubrovin (Petrushin), Yuri Kopych (Michail Petrovich).

Sergei Mikaelyan's "Love By Request" stirred little critical enthusiasm at the Berlin fest, although helmer is fairly well known for his 1974 sociopolitical pic, "The Premium," which treated corruption in a labor union.

This one is about a drunken good-for-nothing who is favored by a plain-looking girl librarian out of humanistic, sympathetic reasons, the encounter leading to a mutual "love" agreement whereby will power and enlightened thinking can solve just about everything — or so the books say.

The twist in this comedy and social melodrama is that both individuals are losers in society: Oleg was always second in sports, and gradually gave into alcohol as the only solution to constant disappointment; Vera is such a wallflower that someone to care for is almost a matter of life and death, while a real love affair means that she's now fulfilled her life and "is ready to die" if need be.

Pic offers a genuine portrait of "little people" in Socialist society. Direction is straightforward and unimaginative, but thesp performances are solid in this game of mental therapy to cure the drinking habits and loneliness of lead characters. (Yevgenia Glushenko won best actress prize at Berlinale for her role in the pic.) —Holl.

Born In Flames
(U.S.-COLOR)

Berlin, March 1.
Produced by Lizzie Borden and the Jerome Foundation. Written and directed by Lizzie Borden. Features entire cast. Camera (color), Ed Bowes, Al Santana, Phil O'Reilly; editor, Lizzie Borden; music: The Bloods, the Red Crayolas, Ibis. Reviewed at the Berlin Forum for the Young Cinema, Feb. 20, 1983. Running time: 90 MINS.
Cast: Honey, Jeanne Satterfield, Adele Bertei, Becky Johnston, Pat Murphy, Kathy Bigelow, Flo Kennedy.

Lizzie Borden's independent production, which took some two years to complete, appears to have all the advantages and the disadvantages of a home movie. It is impertinent, audacious, abounding in fresh ideas, considerably untraditional ideas. On the other hand, it is disjointed, with no real characters, preachy, the script unsufficiently developed and the acting often amateurish. What's more, not only was it shot in 16m, but the print at Berlin was the wrong one, the color oversaturated, the sound distorted and out of sync, so no valid technical evaluation was possible.

Situated in the near future, during the next 10 years, after America has gone through a socialist revolution which has turned it into a sort of one-party progressive democracy, the story deals with the condition of women in that new society, conditions that, in Borden's opinion, changed very little from those prevalent today, in spite of the other major transitions in the American way of life.

Starting with portrayal of women movements as small, separate and ununified little groups, each set in its own opinions and ways, from the Establishment-affiliated ladies who believe that change will come gradually inside the system, to the activists who believe that only outright revolution, including the use of violence, has any chance of truly improving the woman's lot. Borden shows how the extremists are proven right, and how such a revolution should be prepared in future.

Some of the ideas she spreads around are present with a definite ironical slant, such as the bicycle riding vigilante squad saving ladies in distress. Other suggestions, like mobilizing the media to serve the cause of the revolution, have been kicked around often, and the common cause of women from different parts of the world, hinting at the possible cooperation between them, is a thesis still to be proved.

The film's main grace is its sense of humor, a rare quality indeed in a militant film. Nervously edited, with an almost documentary touch in the use of the camera on real New York locations, and a powerful beat soundtrack, effectively used, since two radio stations are taking an active part in the proceedings and their sound accompanies most of the plot, the movie is bound to find favor in the eyes of the women's movement. Borden, when questioned about possible distribution, doubted whether she will manage to find an audience in the U.S., suspecting the film's looks are too uncommercial. But judging by the enthusiastic reaction of the Berlinese crowd, admittedly consisting mostly of women already identified with Borden's cause, may point out to a possible market on a larger scale.
—Edna.

Monty Python's The Meaning Of Life
(BRITISH-COLOR)

As tasteless and as funny as usual.

Hollywood, March 17.
Universal Pictures release. Produced by John Goldstone. Directed by Terry Jones. Written by and featuring Graham Chapman, John Cleese, Terry Gilliam, Eric Idle, Terry Jones, Michael Palin; camera (Technicolor), Peter Hannan; editor, Julian Doyle; production design, Harry Lange; sound, Garth Majshall; costumes, Jim Acheson; animation, Gilliam; music, Idle, Jones, Palin, Chapman, Cleese, John du Prez, Dave Howman and Andre Jacquemin; assistant director, Ray Corbett. Reviewed at Universal Studios, Room 1, Hollywood, March 17, 1983. (MPAA Rating: R.) Running time: 103 MINS.
Cast: Chapman, Cleese, Gilliam, Idle, Jones, Palin, Carol Cleveland, Simon Jones, Patricia Quinn, Judy Loe, Andrew MacLachlan, Mark Holmes, Valerie Whittington, Jennifer Franks, Imogen Bickford-Smith, Angela Mann, Peter Lovstrom, Victoria Plum, Anne Rosenfeld, George Silver.

Gross, silly, caustic, tasteless and obnoxious are all adjectives that alternately apply to Universal's "Monty Python's The Meaning Of Life" though probably the most appropriate description would simply be funny. Typically disregarding any semblance of traditional moral standards, the seasoned British comedy troupe has this time come up with an expertly biting, off-the-wall satire of life's various passages that will undoubtedly offend as many as it will entertain. Any controversy the picture creates will certainly only help its financial cause as it looks to be Monty Python's most potent domestic boxoffice performer.

There is something to be said for the skillful way the troupe utilizes its sheer lack of restraint in the context of this picture. While many filmmakers employ that approach and come up only with a series of gratuitous bits, there is often an underlying thread of serious social commentary in many scenes here. To be sure there is a lot of unabashed juvenile humor (one vignette where a very fat man orders food in a fancy restaurant is up there with the bean scene in "Blazing Saddles" as one of filmdom's most grossly hysterical moments) but it is all put in framework that ultimately makes a lot of sense.

Pic opens with an amusing short film of its own where elderly workers unite against their younger bosses and then segues to the real task—finding the meaning of life. Tracing the human existence from birth through death, the group touches on such areas as religion, education, marriage, sex and war in a way it was no doubt ever taught in school or in the home. Though there are some rough spots along the way (some of the passages on war don't register) most of the sections get

their maximum comedic punch by not being allowed to linger for too long.

Among the most imaginative and scathing of the sequences is an all-out musical number (a la "Oliver") condemning the way religion deals with birth control. Don't expect the clergy to embrace any of the goings-on here nor the medical profession once it gets a glimpse of Python's reenactment of medical procedure during a typical hospital birth. Though the group's past pics have had their protestors it only seems to encourage Python to continue working the way it always has — a strategy that definitely pays off this time out.

If any film were a collaborative effort this one is and is rightly billed so. Python members Graham Chapman, John Cleese, Terry Gilliam, Eric Idle, Terry Jones and Michael Palin share equal credit as cast and screenwriters (they also cowrote the songs) while Jones served as director and Gilliam supervised some superior animated sequences.

As actors each of the men shine as they play both male and female roles with equal aplomb. The writing truly offers bits of comedic brilliance though, like any film of this nature, has a few duds mixed in. Jones seems to have been allowed a great deal of freedom to do what he wanted as director and has managed to keep everything moving quite nicely within the structure of story. Rest of the cast and tech work also help things along.

Some have reasoned that several of the past Python films suffered with segments of the American audience for being "too British" in their stylized delivery or a little "too esoteric" in the subjects they tried to address. But with "The Meaning Of Life" Monty Python has touched on universal areas that look like they will pay off creatively and financially as well. —Berg.

Tough Enough
(COLOR)

Especially on the audience.

Hollywood, March 15.
A 20th Century-Fox release of an American Cinema production, produced by William S. Gilmore. Directed by Richard O. Fleischer. Features entire cast. Exec producers, Michael Leone, Andrew D.T. Pfeffer. Screenplay, John Leone; camera (Technicolor), James A. Contner; editor, Dann Cahn; sound, Jack C. Jacobsen; production design, Bill Kenney; assistant director, Peter Bogart; associate producer, Mark Fleischer; music, Michael Lloyd, Steve Wax. Reviewed at 20th Century-Fox Studios, L.A., March 15, 1983. (MPAA rating: PG.) Running time: 107 MINS.
Art Long .... Dennis Quaid
Caroline Long .... Carlene Watkins
P.T. Coolidge .... Stan Shaw
Myra .... Pam Grier
James Neese .... Warren Oates
Tony Fallon .... Bruce McGill

Bill Long . . . . Wilford Brimley
Gert Long . . . . Fran Ryan

"Tough Enough" is a pretty flabby picture, totally void of dramatic focus and padded throughout with uninteresting brawling that can please only hard-core action crowds.

Film's first problem is its concern with a fadette that received a flurry of press attention some time back but never really swept the country: So-called "tough man" contests that pitted various brutes against each other until the last survivor won.

A a failing young country singer trying to support a wife and child, Dennis Quaid is drawn to the contests as a financial alternative to his tree-trimming job which he hates.

Good with his fists, Quaid wins the first $5,000 after a series of totally boring elimination bouts. Never once is there any doubt that Quaid will triumph over all these lunks who are flailing away.

As a grizzled fight promoter, Warren Oates comes off as a pretty good guy who makes no bones about wanting to exploit Quaid as he moves on to the national finals, where there's never much doubt who's going to win there either.

One of the problems with this film, in fact, is there aren't any real villains, except some of Quaid's meaner opponents, all cardboard and scowls. Quaid is nice, his wife Carlene Watkins is nice, father Wilford Brimley is nice and so are their friends, Stan Shaw and Pam Grier.

Everybody shows moments of doubt and discomfort, but the moments are brief, indeed, and never very compelling. Meanwhile, the fighting goes on and on. —Har.

Eddie Macon's Run
(COLOR)

John Schneider's smooth debut.

Hollywood, March 21.

A Universal Pictures release of a Martin Bregman production. Produced by Louis A. Stroller. Written, directed and edited by Jeff Kanen, based on novel by James McLendon. Features entire cast. Exec producer, Peter Saphier. Camera (Technicolor), James A. Contner; sound, Maury Harris; production design, Bill Kenney; assistant director, Michael R. Haley; music, Norton Buffalo. Reviewed at Universal Studios, L.A., March 21, 1983. (MPAA Rating: PG.) Running time: 95 MINS.
Marzack . . . . Kirk Douglas
Eddie Macon . . . . John Schneider
Jilly Buck . . . . Lee Purcell
Chris . . . . Leah Ayres
Kay Potts . . . . Lisa Dunsheath
Daryl Potts . . . . Tom Noonan
Shorter . . . . J.C. Quinn
Logan . . . . Gil Rogers
Rudy Potts . . . . Jay O. Sanders

It may come as a surprise to car-crash "Dukes Of Hazzard" fans that in this first film starring role in "Eddie Macon's Run" John

Schneider isn't involved in an auto chase until 10 minutes before the end — and he isn't even driving. It may come as even a bigger surprise to "Dukes" detractors that "Macon" is actually an involving, enjoyable picture.

Most of the credit for that, however, goes to Kirk Douglas who brings interesting nuances to his part as the policeman in pursuit, and Lee Purcell as a bored but influential rich girl who gets more involved than she wants to in helping Schneider elude Douglas.

Schneider himself is okay and certainly brings more to his role than anything required of him on television. Without reaching towering dramatic heights, he nonetheless ably portrays the anguish of a young husband/father wrongly sent to prison and determined to escape to rejoin his family in Mexico.

With Schneider fleeing on foot for most of the picture, "Macon" has a tendency to drag in spots, especially in the beginning, but writer-director Jeff Kanen wisely keeps cutting back to Douglas in plotting his chase and figuring out the angles. He's an engaging character, even if womewhat forced into a stereotype.

Meanwhile, out in the backwoods, the action picks up when Schneider encounters a family of half wits determined to hang him in their living room as a cattle rustler. This trio — Lisa Dunsheath, Tom Noonan and Jay O. Sanders — are quite good in maintaining a chilling menace to a situation that could have been nothing more than caricature.

"Macon" really starts moving, though, when Schneider encounters Purcell and her luxury car, slumming in redneck country. As she notes, "it's a slow Wednesday," so she decides to help him make it across the border.

Naturally, she's attracted to Schneider's sexy body, but equally impressed that he's determined to stay faithful to his devoted wife, Leah Ayres. Purcell, too, adds depth to a part that could easily have been shallow.

It's quite possible, of course, that Schneider's tv fans won't like any of this, especially because Norton Buffalo's score only resorts to fiddles for the briefest of passages. Language and sexual suggestion may also be a problem for parents to the age group associated with "Hazzard."

Otherwise, "Macon" runs smoothly. —Har.

Scusate Il Ritardo
(Sorry I'm Late)
(ITALIAN-COLOR)

Rome, March 8.

A Cineriz release, produced by Mauro Berardi for Yarno Cinematografica. Stars and directed by Massimo Troisi. Screenplay, Troisi, Anna Pavignano; camera (Technicolor), Romano Albani; editor, Antonio Siciliano; art director, Bruno Carafalo; music, Antonio Sinagra. Reviewed at American Cinema, Rome, March 7, 1983. Running time: 110 MINS.
Vincenzo . . . . Massimo Troisi
Anna . . . . Giuliana De Sio
Tonino . . . . Lello Arena

Massimo Troisi, boy wonder whose first low budget comedy, "Starting From Three," came out of nowhere and took country by storm a couple years ago, topping the year's b.o. charts, has crafted a second, more austere but not less interesting picture. A good film with limited appeal.

In comparison to its predecessor, "Sorry I'm Late" is conceived in a more restricted physical and psychological environment — a handful of scenes set in middle class Naples. The simple story, excessive, nervous dialog and laughter tinged with a bittersweet aftertaste make duplication of helmer's debut hit unlikely.

Festival life as well as foreign markets will be hampered by the language problem, since pic is based on non-stop conversation in heavy Neapolitan that is not even universally comprehensible throughout national territory.

Vincenzo (Massimo Troisi), a do-nothing living at home with his mother and sister's family, meets a pretty girl at a party and has a brief affair with her. Anna (Giuliana De Sio) is a bright young woman torn between living in Naples and Perugia, where she had a job. Her final choice is left hanging, but clearly depends on Vincenzo growing into a more responsive and caring partner.

Divided into a chain of long, talky scenes like a theatre piece, pic requires a good grasp of the dialect to follow fully, as characters work out their relationships through words and gestures that seem to multiply to fill a menacing void. "Sorry" is the kind of comedy that has to be enjoyed line by line, as at the level of pure story it is too thin to work, and the marathon sequences trend to drag.

Pic's strong point is Troisi, a talented comic with a charismatic screen presence that accounts for much of his pictures' success. Perhaps knowing this he features himself prominently in every scene. Blending the right amounts of warmth and egotism, modernity and neurosis, Vincenzo represents a character young audiences can believe in and identify with, Neapolitan or not.

De Sio as the girlfriend remains a serious, naturalistic theatre actress on celluloid who makes Anna believable but not sparkling. Third important character is Lello Arena as Tonino, Vincenzo's despairing friend whose girlfriend walked out on him for a Swede, "because I'm so ugly." Arena injects touching

humor into the character, who benefits greatly from thesp's new restraint.

As a helmer Troisi opts for the simplest pictorial solutions to scenes, with few camera angles or movements, frequent close-ups. Technical credits are standard, notable for colorful interior sets overflowing with local knick-knacks, courtesy of art director Bruno Carafalo. —Yung.

Nana
(ITALIAN-COLOR)

London, March 10.

A Cannon Group production. Produced by Menahem Golan and Yoram Globus. Executive producer, Alexander Hacohen. Features entire cast. Directed by Dan Wolman. Screenplay, Marc Behm; camera (color), Armando Nannuzzi; music, Ennio Morricone. Reviewed at the Cannon Classic cinema, Shaftesbury Avenue, London, March 8, '83 BBFC rating 18 (X). Running time: 92 MINS.
Nana . . . . Katya Berger
Muffat . . . . Jean-Pierre Aumont
Sabine . . . . Mandy Rice-Davies
Satin . . . . Debra Berger
Zoe . . . . Shirin Taylor
Steiner . . . . Yehuda Efroni

Not only is "Nana" almost totally lacking in quality, it fails even to provide sufficient erotic content to draw its apparently intended market.

Producers claim the film is "loosely based" on Emile Zola's classic novel, but it's difficult to believe that anyone involved read the book, judging from a story totally lacking in dramatic coherence.

Among many problems is a lead actress without a trace of the feminine mystique necessary to explain her power over men (and women), or her infinite capacity for evil. Given the weak center and inept scripting, it's no surprise that everyone else ends up as cardboard. Result is that there's nothing credible in this tale of a 19th-century courtesan who first persuades a banker to set her up in the best part of Paris, then expels him to take up with an even more stupidly generous government minister, whose son she seduces from his wedding party before leaving for India in a balloon.

Incompetent direction and editing reach rock bottom in the pic's two set pieces: the hunt of four naked ladies through the woods, and the fight to the death between a white man and a Black on whom Nana's lover has staked his family house. Both scenes offer no thrills, and that just about sums up the picture. —Japa.

Auftrage
(The Missioner)
(U.S.-W. GERMAN)

Berlin, March 1.

A co-production of the New York Film Group and Aria-Film (Munich) productions. Produced, directed, written and edited by Parviz Sayyad. Features entire cast. Camera (Eastmancolor), Reza Aria; art direction, Seyed Safavi; sound, Jousef Shahab. Reviewed at the Zoo Palast, Berlin, March 1, 1983. Running Time: 106 MINS.

Daoud Moslemi . . . . Parviz Sayyad
Malieheh . . . . Mary Apick
Colonel Ghafar . . . . Houshang Touzie

Iranian exile Parviz Sayyad has concocted an interesting thriller in "The Missioner," shown in competition at Berlin. While modest in its technical aspects, the film displays enormous imagination in its story and could well go on to some pleasing commercial results.

Nonetheless, Sayyad appears slightly overwhelmed by the task of directing, writing and editing, in addition to starring in this intriguing tale. The rough-hewn quality of the production works against the elements of international intrigue found in the story.

Sayyad plays an assassin sent to the United States to eliminate a former Iranian political boss. However, shortly after his arrival, he sees a news report indicating his target has already been eliminated. He's quickly given another assignment. This time he's to get rid of a former army official.

Matters rapidly complicate the task. Tracking his victim, he's forced to aid him when the army officer is mugged in a subway station. The thankful man insists the presumed ally accept an invitation to dinner and is elated to discover a fellow countryman.

The assassin accepts, assuming this will make his job easier. However, he had not counted on the man having two children. His attachment to the family is further intensified when he meets the army officer's sister-in-law. They are physically attracted to one another but find themselves arguing over political ideologies.

Sayyad winds up arguing with his American contacts about the sanction. He finds excuses not to kill the former official as his political beliefs are eroded away by his newfound Iranian friends. He attempts to flee his obligation but winds up a victim himself.

Shot on a low-budget, "The Missioner" is a familiar tale of a political assassin undone by his assignment. The novel twist is the currency of its politics and setting. Both aspects help to minimize the embarrassing political exchanges and simplistic outlook of the script.

Sayyad enhances his modest production with crisp editing and elicits natural performances from his small cast. Unlike more polished spy yarns, the film comes across on a human level which is readily understandable and accessible to an audience.

Marketing the film will be problematic. It just falls short in its technical polish to enter mainstream distribution and lacks the philo-

sophical bite to attract an art house crowd. Nonetheless, the picture deserves a better fate than limited festival screenings and alternative cinema bookings. —*Klad.*

Ana
(PORTUGUESE-COLOR)

Berlin, Feb. 21.

A Portuguese Institute of Cinema presentation. Produced by Antonio Reis, Margarida Cordeiro, Paulo Branco. Direction and screenplay by Reis and Cordeiro, text, Rainer Maria Wilke. Features entire cast. Camera (color), Acacio de Almeida, Elso Roque; art direction, sound, Antoinr Bonfanti; editors, Reis and Cordeiro. Reviewed at the Delphi, Berlin, Feb. 21, 1983. Running Time: 115 MINS.

With: Ana Maria Martins Guerra, Octavio Lixa Figueiras, Manuel Ramalho Eanes, Aurora Afonso, Mariana Margarido.

Husband and wife filmmaking team of Antonio Reis and Margarida Cordeiro have produced an interesting curiousity from Portugal entitled "Ana." While recent Portuguese films have attracted attention at film festivals, this film is unlikely to open doors for international distribution.

Set in a remote mountain area of Portugal, the film centers on a primitive family and a group of ethnographers. The film relies on incident rather than establishing a narrative flow to the event. The effect is disjointed and irritating for audiences.

Film' strongest point is Acacio de Almeida's camerawork which captures both the darkness and sombre quality of the primitive mountain folk and the sunnier coastal hues. However, "Ana" displays more style than substance and eventually one is uncertain whether these people actually exist or are the creation of the filmmakers.

Action around the family unfolds at a tortoise's pace and their inability or reluctance to communicate verbally does little to convey a sense of the characters. If the incidents are meant to be symbolic, then this is lost in translation. Conversely, the scientists speak volumes about a possible Mesopotamian link to the area which fails to pay off dramatically.

"Ana" appears confined to festival slottings where audiences will find the film more curious than revealing. —*Klad.*

L'Africain
(The African)
(FRENCH-COLOR)

Paris, March 7.

AMLF release of a Renn Productions picture. Produced by Claude Berri. Stars Catherine Deneuve and Philippe Noiret. Directed by Philippe de Broca. Screenplay, de Broca and Gerard Brach. Camera, Jean Penzer; art director, Francois de Lamothe; sound, Jean Labussiere; makeup, Jackie Reynal; costumes, Sylvie Gautrelet; editor, Henri Lanoe; music, Georges Delerue; stunt director, Daniel

Verite; Reviewed at the AMLF screening room, Paris, Feb. 28, 1983. Running time: 101 MINS.

Charlotte . . . . Catherine Deneuve
Victor . . . . Philippe Noiret
Planchet . . . . Jean-Francois Balmer
Bako . . . . Joseph Momo
Josephine . . . . Vivian Reed
Patterson . . . . Jacques Francois
Poulakis . . . . Jean Benguigui

Philippe de Broca's new film is unexceptional but likeable enough. To its credit are eye-catching African backgrounds, fine production credits, reasonably airy direction and relaxed performances from an appealing cast, headed by Catherine Deneuve and Philippe Noiret. Where the film stumbles is in a script that beats a predictable path through the cliches of romantic comedy adventure.

Deneuve and Noiret play an ill-assorted and estranged couple who meet up again in central Africa. She is a no-nonsense Club Mediterannee exec who comes to the Dark Continent scouting for a future resort site. But she runs into resistance from Noiret, who, since their separation, has settled there as village grocer and pilot. Naturally he is opposed to the encroachments of European society, particularly when it's represented by his former mate. But their mutual animosity is deflected by a band of ivory traffickers who are massacring elephants in the region. Deneuve winds up their hostage and Noiret goes after them into the heart of pygmy country. Together they foil the traffickers' plans and pave the way to a future reconciliation.

De Broca and his co-screenwriter Gerard Brach don't ring any new variations on the theme of a bumpy relationship tidied over by physical danger, and the last part of the film slides regrettably into rather conventional jungle pursuit melodramatics, complete with friendly pygmies, and villains cutting a rope bridge suspending the hero over an awesome abyss. Rather than kid these scenes (as he used to do in some of his earlier successes), De Broca serves them fairly straight.

There is welcome comedy, though mostly bunched into the first half of the story: facile but amusing jokes based on incongruity (a rudimentary jungle airport serviced by sophisticated public announcement system) as well as hoary gags (like the bumbling policeman trying to unholster his gun only to shoot himself in the foot). But the film owes much of its genuine good humor to the gruff warmth of Noiret, who gives freshness to his familiar verbal matches with Deneuve. Deneuve is a competent foil, and Jean-Francois Balmer adds to the proceedings as her reluctant lackey-associate and sometimes suitor.

Yank singer Vivian Reed is on hand as Noiret's current girl-friend,

a role that seems more an afterthought to accommodate her participation. Apart from some bits of warbling, she is called upon to throw some fits of jealousy when Deneuve shows up.

Other supporting players are good with Jacques Francois sporting an English accent as the region's conservation officer, and Jean Benguigui offering a Greek accent as the chief villain.

Pic was shot on location in Kenya, and De Broca has not failed to get a maximum of picturesque detail through Jean Penzer's excellent camerawork.

"The African" is doing fairly well locally, and should find offshore possibilities on its director-cast combination. —*Len.*

Hollywood Out-Takes & Rare Footage
(COMPILATION-B&W/ COLOR-16m)

A Manhattan Movietime release. Produced by Ronald Blackman. Compilation directed by Blackman and Bruce Goldstein; editor, Doug Rossini. Reviewed at Magno Preview 4, N.Y., Feb. 16, 1983. (No MPAA Rating). Running time: 81 MINS.

After several years of testing odd reels (mainly obtained from collectors) on audiences at a local repertory theatre, "Hollywood Out-Takes & Rare Footage" emerges as a pleasant compilation feature aimed primarily at film buffs. There is enough humor, nostalgia and camp value in the package to attract wider audiences, however, as demonstrated in its strong recent opening at a Greenwich Village firstrun theatre.

Presented without narration (and with a minimum of identifying cards or titles), package consists of several types of footage: out-takes of familiar stars blowing their lines and then swearing; various public service pitches by stars, usually related to the World War II effort; and films of movie premieres and awards ceremonies boasting dozens of familiar faces.

Though prominent in the film's title, the out-takes here are its weakest element. Brief but repetitive, they feature mainly Warner Bros. talent of the 1930s and 1940s and offer the trivia of seeing usually composed stars losing their temper, among them James Cagney, Humphrey Bogart, Pat O'Brien, Kay Francis, John Garfield, Edward G. Robinson, Errol Flynn and Barton MacLane.

Far better is the series of pitchmen short films. Shirley Temple's legendary screen presence is amply demonstrated in a spot for the Red Cross, Bette Davis impressively hawks war bonds and with the late Ruth Donnelly selling a 1935 GE dishwasher, Frank Sinatra sings and preaches a pro-tolerance message in an RKO short. Best of all is the priceless "At Home With Joan Crawford," as the much-maligned star puts her children to bed (an offscreen "Good night, mommy dear" is voiced over) and asks us to help kids in need by contributing to the Red Sox-Variety Clubs' anti-cancer "Jimmy Fund" campaign.

Camp value of the Crawford spot is topped only by a 1937 "Daily Beauty Rituals" short starring Constance Bennett. In yellow and blue-dominated Cinecolor, she intimately demonstrates her skin care secrets in a show-stopping segment.

Special segments give much attention to Bette Davis, Judy Garland & Mickey Rooney and Marilyn Monroe. Garland contributes a moving rendition of "Over The Rainbow" in a filmed radio show with Bob Hope, while Monroe is featured in an intriguing screen test opposite Richard Conte plus home movies shot at a party given by Ray Anthony.

Including some low-quality tv kinescope material, the awards and premiere segs are nostalgia trips including the 1954 "A Star Is Born" launch and 1939 Oscars ceremony. Best bit is the 1960 Golden Globe winners, with an impressively jiggly Jayne Mansfield interacting with host Ronald Reagan and Mickey Rooney.

Though generally upbeat, film climaxes with a ghoulish segment: Gig Young interviewing James Dean off the set of "Giant," in which Dean (providing almost a textbook of his physical and vocal mannerisms) warns of the dangers of fast driving on the highways. In common with the Crawford material, the black humor provided by the audience's hindsight is strictly a matter of taste. —Lor.

Blind Rage
(FILIPINO-COLOR)

A Trans World Films release of a Metropolitan Film Prods. production. Directed by Efren C. Pinon. Features entire cast. Screenplay, Jerry Tirazona, Leo Fong; camera (color), Den Lobo; editor, Edgardo Vinarao; assistant director, Jose Torres. Reviewed at Selwyn Theatre, N.Y., March 16, 1983. (MPAA Rating:R). Running time: **80 MINS.**
With: D'Urville Martin, Leo Fong, Tony Ferrer, Fred Williamson, Dick Adair, Darnell Garcia, Charlie Davao, Leila Hermosa, Carlos Padilla Jr., B.T. Anderson, Jose Garcia, Chuck Doherty, Max Alvarado, Nick Miranda.

Filmed with the more appropriate title "Steal 'Em Blind" in 1977, "Blind Rage" is a funny, inept action film as yet undiscovered by connoisseurs of camp.

Filipino production (with American guest actors) was filmed in globe-hopping locations, amounting to an unwitting cheapie parody of the international (superim-

posed card: "Paris 5:30 p.m.") thriller genre.

"Foolproof alibi" gimmick has five blind men, led by familiar blaxploitation actor D'Urville Martin, rounded up to execute a bank robbery in the Philippines. A pretty, poorly-dubbed Filipino heroine (Leila Hermosa) trains them, with funny dialog, such as the caper run-through beginning with her saying: "Let's begin by synchronizing your Braille watches."

Adequate tension is maintained during the robbery, though the blind quintet's movements often resemble sighted people merely disguised in dark glasses. Poor continuity has a bright, daylit robbery, yet the police cars arrive at the bank in the dead of night.

After an hour's running time devoted to standard recruitment, training and caper execution (plus periodic martial arts outbursts), story premise is suddenly unraveled as the Filipino police immediately (through the aid of an informer) hunt down blind suspects. The heroes escape, hidden in the vast tank of a gasoline truck (a la "White Heat"), which suddenly crashes explosively into a jet plane to end the main narrative.

For the tacked-on final reel, the local crime mastermind flees to Los Angeles, where CIA agent Jesse Crowder (Fred Williamson reprising the tough-talking, stogie-smoking screen character from his own films such as "No Way Back") has a showdown with him at the International House Of Pancakes. Zipping breezily in and out of the film, Williamson (only his stogie is mussed during some hectic chasing and fighting) gets a tagline which sums up the film's philosophy: "Next time you want some of Uncle Sam's money, ask for it." —Lor.

A Taste Of Sin
(COLOR)

Enjoyable Hitchcockian horror cheapie.

An Ambassador Pictures release of a New West Films production. Executive producers, Gary Gillingham, Tim Nielsen, James Honore. Produced and directed by Ulli Lommel. Features entire cast. Screenplay, Lommel, John P. Marsh, Ron Norman; camera (Getty color), Lommel, Jochen Breitenstein, Jon Kranhouse, Dave Sperling. Jorg Walther; editor/coproducer/2d unit director, Terrell Tannen; music, Joel Goldsmith; production manager, Ron Nehemiah; London location supervisor, Zelda Baron. Reviewed at RKO Fordham 4, Bronx, N.Y., March 19, 1983. (MPAA Rating: R). Running time: **84 MINS.**
Olivia .... Suzanna Love
Michael Grant .... Robert Walker
Richard .... Jeff Winchester
Mother .... Bibbe Hansen
Olivia, age 6 .... Amy Robinson
G.I. .... Nicholas Love
Detective .... Ulli Lommel

Filmed half in London and half in Arizona in 1981 with the shooting ti-

tle "Faces Of Fear," "A Taste Of Sin" is an effective psychological horror thriller from prolific Germany-to-U.S. filmmaker Ulli Lommel. Biggest treat here for film buffs and horror fans is Lommel's equal-time raiding of not merely the works of Alfred Hitchcock, but also the Hitchcock-derived thrillers of Brian De Palma.

Prior to its present (tacked-on to suit a sex-themed ad campaign) monicker, picture bore a series of better titles: "Beyond The Bridge," "Double Jeopardy" and "Olivia."

Opening (culled from Hitchcock's "Marnie") has 6-year-old Olivia (Amy Robinson) watching (through a keyhole) her British prostitute mother servicing a G.I. who's into bondage. She helplessly sees mom killed by the G.I. Fifteen years later, Olivia (played as an adult by Suzanna Love, star of all seven of Lommel's U.S.-made pics) has a brutish husband Richard (Jeff Winchester), and dresses up at night to relive her mom's experience as a street-walker near London Bridge. Controlled by her (imagined) mom's voice from beyond the grave, she starts killing her customers while being racked with guilt for not coming to mom's aid vs. the G.I.

Olivia falls in love with Michael Grant (Robert Walker), an American working on a project to restore the bridge. In a fight with Richard over her that takes place on the bridge, Grant is victorious, and Richard ends up hurtling into the water below.

With the film half over, scene shifts to Arizona four years later where London Bridge has been transplanted (along with its fatalistic associations for the lead characters). Grant finds Olivia working as a condominium saleslady using a new name (Jenny) and with a new mousy appearance and American accent. Suspenseful plot twists (and red herrings) involve lifts from "Vertigo," "Obsession," "Sisters," "Psycho," — you name it.

Though this type of derivative filmmaking is hotly criticized these days (with De Palma perhaps the number one whipping boy), Lommel plays it straight and comes up with an entertaining B-picture. He obviously enjoys the Hitchcock association, even casting Vera Miles from "Psycho" in his next film "Brainwaves" (opposite Tony Curtis instead of Janet Leigh) and recalling Walker (son of "Strangers On A Train" namesake and near-lookalike) for the lead in "Devonsville Terror."

Suzanna Love is quite impressive in the chameleon lead role, calling for at least three distinct personalities. Walker, still looking boyish at age 40, is an empathetic hero, though one keeps expecting him to become sinister, given Hitchcock's switcheroo casting of

his dad 30 years earlier. Joel Goldsmith's synthesizer music score is effective, but the film is hampered by drab would-be film noir visuals, for which five cinematographers are credited. —Lor.

King Blank
(U.S.-BLACK & WHITE-16m)

Berlin, Feb. 20.
A King Blank production in association with Metafilms Inc. Produced and directed by Michael Oblowitz. Features entire cast. Screenplay, Oblowitz, Rosemary Hochschild; camera (black and white), Oblowitz; editor, Susanne Rostack; music, Anton Fig; sound, Bob Kragen. Reviewed at the Atelier, Berlin, Feb. 20, 1983. Running time: **71 MINS.**
Queenie Blank ..... Rosemary Hochschild
King Blank .... Ron Vawter
Bar Customer .... Will Patton
Bouncer .... Pete Richardson

"King Blank," first feature by American-based, South African-born Michael Oblowitz, suggests promise for the filmmaker but will have a difficult time entering commercial distribution. In addition to the obvious problems marketing a 16m black and white production, the film poses problems in both its explicit language and crude subject.

Story centers on King Blank, an Army veteran, and nis wife, Queenie, who've shut themselves up at a motel near a New York City airport. Action unfolds in both their hotel room and a nearby bar and involves the couple with drunks, perverts and prostitutes.

The battling couple carry on at an hysterical pitch as their relationship dissolves. And they can find no respite on the outside from the frustrated lounge lizards and sexual deviants. From the outset it's clear there's no happy ending in store.

Despite its crude technique — spotty sound, unsteady camera — Oblowitz and actress Rosemary Hochschild invest tremendous vitality into the film. While the material is repugnant, there's an energy to the proceedings which is difficult to ignore. Overall effect is like watching a time capsule of a long-forgotten New York experimental director.

Commercial prospects are limited to specialized screenings where the film may find a devoted audience. However, the film will be competing with much slicker and accessible product currently being produced by independents. —Klad.

Canale Grande
(W. GERMAN-AUSTRIAN-COLOR)

Berlin, March 8.
A Primadonna Film Production, Munich. Written and directed by Friedrike Pezold. Features entire cast. Camera (color), Elfi Mikesch, Wolfgang Pilgrim, Fritz Oelberg; sound, Margit Eschenbach, Anke-Rixa Hansen, Ebba Jahn; editing, Henriette Fischer. Reviewed at

Berlin Film Fest (Forum), Feb. 23, '83.
Running time: 95 MINS.
  With Friedrike Pezold.

More documentary than fiction, Friedrike Pezold's homemade "Canale Grande" features the Austrian filmmaker-author-artist — videofreak-superstar in a utopian search for a reality that corresponds to her fantasies, dreams, and wishes.

Her thesis is that the world is a brace of pre-programmed systems, thereby allowing little room for self-expression and emancipation. For most of the film, she is an inquiring reporter with a closed-circuit tv-set on her back wandering around Berlin. The effect is somewhat like a news-camera-person filming a video-artist in action. Her previous film, or video-film, was "Toilette" (1979), and this one took three years to make.

—Holl.

Au Clair De
La Lune
(Moonshine Bowling)
(CANADIAN-COLOR)

Berlin, Feb. 26.

A National Film Board of Canada production and release. Produced by Bernard Lalonde, Louis Laverdiere. Directed by Andre Forcier. Features entire cast. Screenplay, Forcier, Jacques Marcotte, Michel Pratt, Guy L'Ecuyer, Michel Cote, Bernard Lalonde; camera (color), Francois Gill, Andre Gagnon; editor, Francois Gill; art direction, Gilles Aird; music, Joel Bienvenue; sound, Alain Corneau, Marcel Fraser. Reviewed at the Berlin Film Festival, Feb. 26, 1983. Running Time: 88 MINS.
Albert (Bert) Bolduc ...... Guy L'Ecuyer
Francois (Frank) .... Michel Cote
Maurice Dieumegarde .... Robert Gravel
Leopoldine Dieumegarde ... Lucie Miville
T-Kid Radio .... Gaston Lepage
Philosopher .... Michel Gagnon
Alfred .... J. Leo Gagnon
Emil .... Andre Forcier

Andre Forcier's long-delayed "Au Clair de la Lune" (Moonshine Bowling) proves to be a whimsical, absurdist comedy which will have a difficult time penetrating outside the borders of Quebec. Shot four years ago, the picture has had a rocky post-production history which has not been overcome despite the long period of tinkering.

Central characters are Frank, a white-thatched drifter who claims to come from distant Albinoland and Bert, a former bowling star now confined to carry a sandwich board for Moonshine Bowling. Although Forcier's past films have all had fantastical elements, this is certainly his most bizarre work.

The relationship between the two men flip-flops as Frank coerces his way into Bert's good graces as the ex-bowler exploits his naivete in exchange for allowing the albino to set up camp in his vintage model Chevy. The film's many vignettes, introducing a strange variety of characters, lead up to Bert's comeback tournament and Frank's

crafty manner at securing the trophy for his friend.

Tale is too offbeat and rooted in local jokes to find an international release but should hit an emotional chord in Quebec. Forcier gets strong performances for both Michel Cote as Frank and Guy L'Ecuyer as Bert which stress the characters' humanity when all around threatens to go wildly absurd.

Technical credits are excellent with Farncois Gill and Andre Gagnon's camerawork a standout for creating a surreal environment for the out of the ordinary tale. However, story is too facile to sustain interest in the minor victories of the principals and sub-plots further dissipate the film's dramatic impact.

"Au Clair de la Lune" fails to hit a responsive note but may attract some festival interest on Forcier's past credits and his unique observations in this escapist film. —Klad.

Track Two
(CANADIAN-COLOR-DOCU)

Berlin, Feb. 25.

A DEC film release of a KLS Production. Produced by Gordon Keith, Jack Lemmon, Harry Sutherland. Directed by Sutherland. Features entire cast. Script and research, Jack Lemmon; camera (color), Leo Zourdoumis; sound, Karin Michael; music, Carol Pope, Kevin Staples. Reviewed at the Atelier, Berlin, Feb. 25, 1983. Running Time: 87 MINS.
With: Ken Popert, John Sewell, Brent Hawkes, Christine Bearchell, Arnold Bruner, John Bart, Gerald Hannon, George Hislop, Allan Sparrow, June Callwood, Alan Bovoroy, Laurier LaPierre, Margaret Atwood.

Harry Sutherland's documentary on Toronto's "Gay Bath Raids" of 1981, "Track Two" is a relatively straightforward reconstruction of a politically hot issue. As such, it is slightly more ambitious and consuming than a television news documentary and could find theatrical release in selected situations.

Title derives from a Toronto police term for the area where the raids occurred. The actual event resulted in 286 arrests, the second highest number in Canada after 1970's War Measure Act which put troops into the streets after a political assassination.

Film primarily focuses on the community hostility toward gays as exemplified by various events prior to 1981. Catalyst was the murder of a young shoeshine boy in 1977, attributed to a gay gang. The issue eventually worked its way into civic politics and the defeat of Toronto mayor John Sewell, lauded in the film for his courage in defending Toronto's homosexual community.

The production also delineates the ironic aftermath which resulted, according to the filmmakers, in solidifying a desperate group. This strength and a chang-

ing public attitude meant the suspension of 139 of 167 cases which went to trial.

"Track Two" lacks the invention or scope to register as a wide theatrical release despite its technical skill. Best results will be found in television distribution and in nontheatrical situations. —Klad.

Abuse
(U.S.-BLACK & WHITE-16m)

Berlin, Feb. 24.

A Promovisional International release of an Arthur J. Bressan Jr. production. Produced by Steven McMillin. Executive producer, Frederick Schminke. Direction and screenplay, Arthur Bressan Jr. Features entire cast. Camera (black and white), Douglas Dickinson, Carl Teitelbaum; editor, Arthur Bressan; music, Shawn Phillips, additional music, Jeffrey Olmsted. Reviewed at the Berlin Film Festival, Feb. 24, 1983. Running Time: 93 MINS.
Larry Porter .... Richard Ryder
Thomas Carroll .... Raphael Sbarge
Dr. Bennett ....Steve James
Kathy Logan .... Kathy Gerber
Professor Rappaport .... Jack Halton
Laura ....Mickey Clark
Mr. Carroll .... Maurice Massaro
Mrs. Carroll .... Susan Schneider
Dean Kinkaid .... Jean Garrett
Samantha .... Pam Poitier

Arthur Bressan's heavily autobiographical drama, "Abuse," works as both solid entertainment and factual documentary. It's a consuming tale which adeptly juggles social issues with insight, humor and compassion. It should escape its modest origins and prove a modest commercial success.

Story centers on Larry Porter (Richard Ryder), a film student working on a child-abuse documentary for his degree. Porter finds Thomas Carroll (Raphael Sbarge) at a hospital and strikes up a friendship with the teenager who's been beaten and burned by his parents.

Breaking through to the boy proves difficult for several reasons. Above all he loves his parents and it's only after he realizes the filmmaker is gay, like himself, that he truly opens up.

Bressan weaves both the child abuse and homosexual elements of the tale together without turning into crusader. The facts — 200,000 beatings, 65,000 sexual assaults reported annually — speak for themselves and the documentary footage is far more eloquent than possible diatribes.

This allows greater attention to be paid to the relationship between filmmaker and subject. As such, it raises fascinating questions about a different kind of exploitation and allows subtle distinctions to be made between abuse, concern and protectiveness.

Shot in 16m and black and white, the film still manages to have a technical polish suitable for commercial distribution. Bressan isn't always successful with the primarily non-pro cast members who

tend to be stiff when called upon to register horror. However, both Ryder and Sbarge register admirably.

Strong asset of "Abuse" is its use of ironic humor to lighten the weighty subject matter. Ryder's character particularly gets needled for misunderstanding his material even after completion of the presumed in-depth documentary.

Nature of the film and low-budget trappings will limit commercial playoff but film should do well in large urban centers. It has obvious non-theatrical spin-off potential and educational usage which will serve it well in the long haul. —Klad.

Un Chien dans un Jeu
de Quilles
(A Dog in a Game
of Nine-Pins)
(FRENCH-COLOR)

Paris, March 15.

A.A.A. release of a Fideline Films production. Produced by and starring Pierre Richard. Co-stars Jean Carmet. Directed by Bernard Guillou. Screenplay, Guillou and Claude Gallot. Camera (Eastmancolor), Claude Agostini; music, Patrice Caratini; sound, Alain Lachassagne; editor, Marie-Sophie Dubus; makeup, Jacky Bouban; costumes, Michele Marmande; art director, Gerard Daoudal; production manager, Jean-Claude Bourlat. Reviewed at the Gaumont Ambassade Theatre, Paris, March 13, 1983. Running time: 90 MINS.
Pierre Cohen .... Pierre Richard
Joseph Cohen .... Jean Carmet
Alexandre ....Julien Guiomar
Marjolaine ....Sylvie Jolie
Francoise .... Beatrice Camurat
Rose .... Helene Surgere

Comedian Pierre Richard tries something different from his usual grind of scatter-brained farces with this rural comedy set in Britanny, but local audiences, perhaps unappreciative of such efforts, have chosen to snub the film at the wickets. Too bad: it's a sympathetic try, with Richard abandoning his frenzied peabrains for a role somewhat more nuanced and human.

He plays a worldly Paris psychologist who returns to his Breton birthplace to aid his farmer brothers (Jean Carmet) in his battle against a local squire's attempts to dispossess him of his land. Richard is an advocate of psychological warfare, but his methods don't always have the required effect, particularly when his jealous girlfriend (Beatrice Camurat) turns up to survey his activities. All ends well, and Richard winds up a local hero, in spite of himself.

Much less vulgar than most Parisian-minded rustic comedies, this one is handsomely produced, but doesn't get enough fresh comic observation into its situations to raise it above competent routine.

Bernard Guillou, who has helmed one feature previously, wrote the original story and directs ade-

quately. The performances are bright, with a lovely little surprise from the classy Helene Surgere, touching here as Carmet's mute but attentive wife. It's too bad the script gives her little to do, because she makes one of the stronger unconventional impressions in the film.
—Len.

Le Demon dans l'Isle
(The Demon of the Isle)
(FRENCH-COLOR)

Paris, March 1.

AMLF release of a Films 7 production. Produced by Patrick Delauneux. Stars Anny Duperey and Jean-Claude Brialy. Directed by Francis Leroi. Screenplay, Leroi and Owen T. Rozmann; camera (Fujicolor), Jacques Assuerus; editor, Caroline Grombergh; sound editor, Corinne Yvonnet; storyboard designs, Giorgio Fenu; art director, Bruno Bruneau; special effects, Marc Marmier; costumes, Cidalia Branger; music, Christian Gaubert; sound, Paul Berthaud; reviewed at the Avoriaz film festival, Jan. 16, 1983. Running time: 102 MINS.
Doctor Gabrielle Martin ...Anny Duperey
Doctor Paul Marshall Jean-Claude Brialy
The mayor .... Pierre Santini
Marie Talbot .... Cerise
The Pharmacist .... Gabriel Cattand

With its Pavlovian plot mechanics, Francis Leroi's "Demon In The Isle" is a reasonably effective if uninspired entry into the glutted international horror pic market. Skillful production and above average acting (by genre standards) give it okay chances in non-French playoffs.

Story is set on an island community off the French coast, where inhabitants are literally being attacked by household appliances they've all bought in the same department store.

Embroiled in this epidemic of macabre incidents is Anny Duperey, a young doctor recently arrived from the mainland, who is trying to erase the personal tragedy that claimed the lives of husband and child.

Called upon to treat the victims, she picks up a trail of clues that leads back to another island physician (Jean-Claude Brialy), whose strange, aloof manner has alienated him from his clientele. Brialy tries to draw her in as accomplice, but she resists and soon exposes his activities, which revolve around an overgifted child with unusual mental powers.

Leroi, who has previously worked in the local porno industry, wrote the script (with Owen T. Rozmann) and has directed with a sure sense of audience manipulation, though, like too many directors, he gets carried away with graphic special effects. (In one grisly scene, a housewife's arm gets caught in a kitchen oven and is literally roasted to a crisp; Leroi, like the oven, just won't let go. But the special effects, like the housewife's arm, are well done.)

Considering the rather stock roles, Duperey and Brialy give surprisingly subtle performances, which do much to enlist audience involvement. —Len.

Sapore Di Mare
(A Taste of Sea)
(ITALIAN-COLOR)

Rome, March 5.

A Medusa release, produced by Pio Angeletti and Adriano De Micheli for International Dean Film. Stars Jerry Cala, Marina Suma. Directed by Carlo Vanzina. Screenplay, Carlo and Enrico Vanzina; camera (Technicolor), Beppe Maccari; music, Edoardo Vianello, Mariano Perrella; editor, Raimondo Crociani. Reviewed at Reale Cinema, Rome, March 3, 1983. Running time: 96 MINS.
Marina .... Marina Suma
Luca .... Jerry Cala
Susan .... Karina Huff
Gianni .... Gianni Ansaldi
Adriana .... Virna Lisi

Young helmer Carlo Vanzina concocts a frothy, rewarmed but bankable pastiche of memories about middle-class teens in the Sixties. Pic touches enough comic and nostalgic keys to please onshore audiences, who either remember their youth or, more likely, are underage but familiar with the decade's stereotypes. With a big cast of young actors aping "Grease" and "American Graffiti" to the tune of vintage Italian hit songs. "Taste of Sea" lacks the on-target inventiveness of first-rate parody, though in a sea of interchangeable light comedies it paradoxically passes for something original. "Sea" is well shot and pleasant enough to watch, however, and should do well in the usual Latin and Mediterranean markets.

Story is set in a seaside resort during the summer, where vacationing kids pass carefree days going to parties, riding motorboats and motorbikes, and scrambling after the opposite sex. Luca (Jerry Cala) is the plump rich boy from Milan who flirts with pretty Marina (Marina Suma), from a social-climbing Neapolitan family. Susan (Karina Huff) is the "fast" English girl who breaks hearts and wins personality contests. Gianni (Gianni Ansaldi) is the little intellectual of the group who temporarily dumps his girlfriend for a frustrated but very sexy older woman (Virna Lisi).

Twenty years later in the Eighties, the characters meet again briefly, married and unmarried, happy and unhappy, to take a last heart-twanging look at each other and the ravages of time.

Scripters Carlo and Enrico Vanzina (sons of vet helmer Steno) struggle mightily to keep the situations light and devoid of even momentary drama or tension that would break the idyllic atmosphere. Result is that the petty jealousies, betrayals and fights that

animate the story lack dramatic and emotional power to involve audience.

Vanzina and crew do a good job technically and give the comedy a graceful, natural look. Old songs help establish an atmosphere better than occasional references to Italian television and political figures of the time, obscure to younger audiences.

Outstanding troupers are Virna Lisi, so vital and magnetic she injects believability into a cliched role, and Marina Suma, whose screen presence is on another level from the rest of the competent cast. —Yung.

De Witte Paraplu
(The White Umbrella)
(DUTCH-COLOR-16m)

Rotterdam, Feb. 16.

Produced by Rolf Orthel. Written, directed and edited by Heddy Honigmann, Noshka van der Lely. Stars Josje Janse, Irene Ypenburg. Camera (color), Angela Linders. Reviewed at Film Festival Rotterdam, Feb. 5, 1983. Running time, 65 MINS.

This is a first feature by Heddy Honigmann and Noshka van der Lely who have previously collaborated on short subjects. It's a part autobiographical tale about two women, active nuclear disarmers, who make a film together.

The intoxicating experience of filming the 1981 no-nukes demo in Amsterdam, when an estimated 450,000 people were on the streets, affects the fictionalized filmers and leaves them with a moralistic hangover. Self doubt creeps in. After all, what's been changed?

The women handle the depression in different ways, each ultimately coming to terms with reality, and come back together to make further films.

It's a small, gentle story without overblown pretentions and it is filmed carefully, if modestly. Money on screen matters less when filmmakers have style and are in harmony with the subject. Lack of stridency notwithstanding, parts of it linger in the memory. It may surprise and do well on the festival beat, though commercially its prospects are limited. —Wall.

L'Enfant Secret
(The Secret Child)
(FRENCH-B&W)

Paris, March 1.

Gerick distribution release of a Philippe Garrel production. Produced, written, directed and edited by Philippe Garrel. Script collaborator, Annette Wademant; camera (b&w), Pascal Laperrousaz; sound, Allan Villeval; music, Faton Cahen; reviewed at the Olympic Luxembourg theatre, Paris, Feb. 20, 1983. Running time: 95 MINS.
With: Anne Wiazemsky, Henri de Maublanc.

"L'Enfant Secret" is your average French intimate drama about the difficulties of forming a couple, revised by an avant-garde filmmaker, Philippe Garrel, who is 35 and has been directing since 1964 (with 13 pictures to his credit).

Garrel's style is austere: black & white lensing, one shot sequences, minimal dialog, non-linear, fragmented narrative, non-emotive acting. One thinks of Jean-Luc, Godard, Jean Eustache, Robert Bresson. Particularly the last-named, since Garrel has cast two Bresson graduates, Anna Wiazemsky and Henri de Maublanc ("The Devil, Probably").

Maublanc plays a filmmaker, Wiazemsky an actress, living alone with her child. They meet, fall in love, come together, separate, etc. He has a nervous depression, she a fit of immobilizing despair.

It's boring and unmoving. Garrel strains to transcend the banality, but his direction is itself banal in its sterile, self-conscious mannerisms. The actors and photography are no less glum and inexpressive.

Still, Garrel has a local following that considers him a genius, and this film picked up the 1982 Jean Vigo prize. —Len.

The Headless Eyes
(COLOR)

Obscure gore film for horror completists.

A J.E.R. Pictures release of a Lavinia-que Films production. Executive producers, Chandler Warren, David Bowman. Produced by Ronald Sullivan. Features entire cast. Written and directed by Kent Bateman. Camera (color), uncredited; associate producer, Bayard Stevens. No other credits on print. Reviewed at 8th St. Playhouse, N.Y., March 17, 1983. (MPAA Rating: X). Running time: 79 MINS.
With: Bo Brundin, Gordon Ramon, Kelley Swartz, Mary Jane Early.

"The Headless Eyes" is a 1971 gore thriller so obscure that no credits or details about it are listed in comprehensive horror encyclopedias. It is reviewed here, finally, for the record.

Set in New York, picture opens with lead Bo Brundin robbing a woman in her apartment to raise his rent money (he's a struggling artist). Defending herself with a teaspoon, the victim pokes his eye out, setting off Brundin's grisly mania of killing women and gouging out their eyes with a spoon of his own.

Generically related to the familiar mad sculptor/wax museum films, story has Brundin creating plastic artwork incorporating the eyes. Plentiful blood and adequately simulated gore account for the picture's X-rating, awarded by the MPAA in 1973.

Technical quality is extremely poor, with a grainy blowup from 16m lensing.

Director Kent Bateman did an about-face by helming the G-rated 1977 wilderness adventure "Land Of No Return" starring Mel Torme. "Eyes" is interesting for the earnest overacting of Brundin, who later moved up to a leading role opposite Robert Redford in "The Great Waldo Pepper." —*Lor.*

The Outsiders
(COLOR)

Well-crafted but unexciting restless youth drama.

Hollywood, March 19.

A Warner Bros. release. Produced by Fred Roos, Gray Frederickson. Directed by Francis Coppola. Features entire cast. Screenplay, Kathleen Knutsen Rowell, based on novel by S.E. Hinton; camera (Technicolor, Panavision), Stephen H. Burum; editor, Anne Goursaud; music, Carmine Coppola; production design, Dean Tavoularis; set decoration, Gary Fettis; special visual effects, Robert Swarthe; costumes, Marge Bowers; sound design, Richard Beggs; sound (Dolby), Jim Webb; associate producer, Gian-Carlo Coppola; assistant director, David Valdes. Reviewed at the Pacific 4, Sherman Oaks, Calif., March 19, 1983. (MPAA Rating: PG). Running time: **91 MINS.**

Ponyboy Curtis	C. Thomas Howell
Dallas Winston	Matt Dillon
Johnny Cade	Ralph Macchio
Darrel Curtis	Patrick Swayze
Sodapop Curtis	Rob Lowe
Cherry Valance	Diane Lane
Two-Bit Matthews	Emilio Estevez
Steve Randle	Tom Cruise
Bob Sheldon	Leif Garrett
Tim Shephard	Glenn Withrow
Randy Anderson	Darren Dalton
Marcia	Michelle Meyrink
Jerry	Gailard Sartain
Buck Merrill	Tom Waits
Store Clerk	William Smith

Francis Coppola has made a well acted and crafted but highly conventional film out of S.E. Hinton's popular youth novel, "The Outsiders." Although set in the mid-1960s, pic feels very much like a 1950s drama about problem kids, such as those directed by Nicholas Ray and Elia Kazan, but is nowhere as penetrating or electric as the best work of those directors.

Warners is opening the film at 800 theatres nationwide and initial returns should be solid based on young people's attraction to the material and good-looking thesps, as well as enduring interest in Coppola. But overall b.o. may only be modest, in line with pic's achievement.

Hinton wrote "The Outsiders," her first novel, while still in high school and since 1967 it has reportedly sold several million copies on the young adult circuit. Simple and direct in its humanization of small town "greasers" who are limited in education and feel like outcasts no matter what they do, tome takes a personal "us against the world" attitude which makes for easy teen identification.

Screenplay by Kathleen Knutsen Rowell is extremely faithful to the source material, even down to having the film open with the leading character and narrator, C. Thomas Howell, reciting the first lines of his literary effort while we see him writing them.

But as with such writers as Hemingway and Fitzgerald, dialog which reads naturally and evocatively on the page doesn't play as well on screen, and there's a decided difficulty of tone during the early sequences, as Howell and his buddies, Matt Dillon and Ralph Macchio horse around town, sneak into a drive-in and have an unpleasant confrontation with the Socs, rival gang from the well-heeled part of town.

When the Socs attack Howell and Macchio in the middle of the night, latter ends up killing a boy to save his friend, and the two flee to a hideaway in an abandoned rural church. Whole passage of their isolation reminds forcibly of the Sal Mineo-James Dean relationship in "Rebel Without A Cause," and it is here that one of the most familiar themes of serious 1950s teen pics, that of "sensitive" youths trapped in a tough environment, comes to the fore.

It is also during this mid-section that the film starts coming to life, largely due to the integrity of the performances by Howell and Macchio. Younger, at about 16, and smaller than most of his cohorts, Howell is clearly a product of his deprived environment and upbringing (his parents died in an accident, leaving him and his two older brothers to fend for themselves), but also enjoys something of the budding intellectual's remove. He recites poetry, moons over the Socs' prettiest girl, Diane Lane, and makes it through the days on the lam by reading "Gone With The Wind" (some of the visual effects of red-drenched sunsets backdropping the characters strongly evoke similiar shots in "GWTW").

When the duo rescues some little kids from a fire in the church, they become the town's unlikely heroes. Macchio, however, is mortally injured in the blaze, and it just so happens that the Greasers and Socs have scheduled an all-out rumble, in which Howell and Dillon participate with a "win one for Johnny" attitude.

Upon Macchio's death, Dillon, not his best friend Howell, freaks out, robs a store and is gunned down by the cops, while Howell is seen back at work on his tome.

It's all done with the utmost sincerity and, one might even say, reverence for the material, a feeling emphasized by Carmine Coppola's highly dramatic score, one which intensely evokes Leonard Rosenman's work on the James Dean pics "Rebel Without A Cause" and "East Of Eden."

Although the kids in "Rebel" basically wanted to be understood and to feel part of society, a major difference with "The Outsiders" is that there is very little sense of rebellion. Nor are there any authority figures providing resistance to them. They're totally on their own, with marginal pasts and no definable futures, and the lack of concrete context for their behavior lessens the urgency of the tale as well as the fun often provided in such pics by cultural reference points.

Most satisfying elements remain the performances. Howell is truly impressive, a bulwark of relative stability in a sea of posturing and pretense. Macchio is also outstanding as his doomed friend, and Patrick Swayze is fine as the oldest brother forced into the role of parent. Only Dillon, star of the first Hinton film adaptation, "Tex," and the only b.o. name present, tends to overdo it, dragging on his cigarets with self conscious intensity and behaving in hyperkinetic fashion.

All craft work, notably Dean Tavoularis' production design and Stephen H. Burum's lensing, maintains the high standards expected in a Coppola film, but overall this seems at first viewing like the director's least personal and least ambitious pic in over a decade. Visually, film is characterized by heavy emphasis on the elements — fire, wind and water. Final impression is one of a respectable, but relatively unexciting, picture.

—*Cart.*

Max Dugan Returns
(COLOR)

Uplifting Neil Simon tale.

Hollywood, March 19.

A 20th Century-Fox release, produced by Herbert Ross and Neil Simon. Directed by Herbert Ross. Exec producer, Roger M. Rothstein. Features entire cast. Screenplay, Neil Simon; camera (DeLuxe color), David M. Walsh; editor, Richard Marks; sound, Al Overton, Jr.; production design, Albert Brenner; assistant director, Jack Roe; art direction, David Haber; music, David Shire. Reviewed at the Sherman Oaks Cinema, L.A., March 19, 1983. (MPAA rating: PG.) Running time: **98 MINS.**

Nora McPhee	Marsha Mason
Max Dugan	Jason Robards
Brian Costello	Donald Sutherland
Michael McPhee	Matthew Broderick
Mrs. Litke	Dody Goodman
Coach Roy	Sal Viscuso
Luis	Panchito Gomez

"Max Dugan Returns" is a consistently happy comedic fable which should please romanticists drawn again to another teaming of Neil Simon, Marsha Mason and Herbert Ross.

Once more, Simon's pen turns to the problems of parental relationships — especially reunion after long estrangement — but largely leaves aside any heavy emotional involvement or rapid fire comedy.

To be sure, there's a heart tug here and there and a fair share of Simonized one-liners. Mainly, though, "Dugan" is there to be enjoyed for the uplift.

Struggling to raise a 15-year-old son, Matthew Broderick, on a meagre teacher's salary, widow Mason maintains a wonderful attitude as her refrigerator breaks, her old car barely runs but gets stolen to boot, and life generally never quite works. Even on the playing field, every baseball game comes down to Broderick's ninth inning batting ability — and he always strikes out.

But Mason takes the bad hands without despair. And there are some bright spots. Broderick is a good kid who accepts her poor-but-honest morality very well. In addition, there's a budding romance with Donald Sutherland, an exceptionally intelligent detective who's investigating the theft of her car.

Out of a dark night, however, returns Max Dugan (Jason Robards), the father who abandoned Mason when she was nine years old. Dying of a heart ailment, Robards is carrying a satchel full of remorse and a suitcase crammed with cash left over from a checkered career in Las Vegas.

Robards wants to swap the money for a last chance to get to know his grandson and Mason, too, if she will let him. But father and daughter have slightly different views on the honesty of where the money came from, a source of interest also to both the police and the mob.

Too good to turn him out, Mason finds out she's also too confused to turn Robards off in his determination to fill their lives with sudden wealth, including every appliance buyable, a luxury car, and complete renovation of her house. He even buys famed Chicago White Sox batting coach Charlie Lau to give lessons to Broderick.

The new wealth naturally raises the suspicions of straight-laced Sutherland, aided by the nosiness of neighbor Dody Goodman. Will Mason and Sutherland break up? Will Mason and Robards take root? Will Broderick be corrupted and/or finally hit a homer in the last of the ninth? These are hardly gritty questions within totally unbelievable circumstances. But they are fun, nonetheless.

As usual, Ross directs this first rate cast with great assurance and each one of them is a delight, although the whole project hardly challenges the abilities of anybody involved. —*Har.*

The Black Stallion Returns
(COLOR)

Fifth in a four horse race.

Hollywood, March 21.

MGM-UA release from Zoetrope Studios. Produced by Tom Sternberg, Fred Roos, Doug Claybourne. Directed by Robert Dalva. Features entire cast. Exec producer, Francis Coppola. Screenplay, Richard Kletter and Jerome Kass based on the novel by Walter Farley; camera (Technicolor), Carlo DiPalma; editor, Paul Hirsch; art director, Aurelio Crugnola; costumes; Danda Ortona, music, Georges Delerue; assistant directors, Doug Claybourne, Giovanni Arduini. Reviewed at MGM Studios, Hollywood, March 21, 1983. (MPAA Rating: PG). Running time: 93 MINS.

Alec Ramsay	Kelly Reno
Raj	Vincent Spano
Kurr	Allen Goorwitz
Meslar	Woody Strode
Abu Ben Ishak	Ferdinand Mayne
Tabari	Jodi Thelen
Alec's Mother	Teri Garr
Tiny Man	Doghmi Larbi

Well-intentioned though it may be, MGM-UA's "The Black Stallion Returns" is little more than a contrived, cornball story that most audiences will find to be an interminable bore. Much of the charm and innocence of the original are absent here as now young teen hero Kelly Reno follows the unlikeliest of searches through the Sahara desert for his devoted horse. There should be a minimum amount of boxoffice action from youngsters and those looking for a sequel to the successful 1979 pic. But overall this one doesn't look like a winner.

This time out Reno is not a cute little boy finding an almost magical horse, but rather a wide-eyed teenager taking care of a pet he dearly loves. The stallion itself seems reasonably happy, ensconced in Reno's barn in N.Y. and allowing its owner to ride him in an occasional race.

But all this is to change. A band of supposed "good guy" Moroccans steal the horse in order to bring him back to his real home in the deserts of northern Africa (where he will run in a once-every-five-years horse race) much to the chagrin of the "bad guy" Moroccans who represent a supposedly evil tribe. It's all highly ridiculous in the context presented, especially as Reno's hysterical mom Teri Garr (in a cameo) runs around in hair curlers wondering who burned down the barn.

Still, the film forges ahead. Reno follows the horsenappers and finds they are going to take his animal to a remote village near Casablanca (this should only be as good as the Bogart film). After phoning Mom to say he won't be home to dinner, he then easily stows aboard a jet that takes him to his destination. Then he just as easily makes contact with some children who show him around.

His luck doesn't run out there. In fact, it never runs out. From almost the moment he lands in Casa-blanca, Reno meets various people who point him in the right direction of his horse and is eventually able to trek across the desert with the help of his own personal local tour guide. You'd almost think he had consulted a travel agent before taking the trip.

Naturally, Reno is reunited with the animal, who is being primed for the all-important race that each of the tribes is determined to win. As in the original, the film builds to the inevitable competition conclusion but adds the unlikeliest of plot twists at the end that renders most of the previous action meaningless.

Robert Dalva, who edited the "Black Stallion," served as director here but doesn't manage to convincingly merge the feelings of fantasy and reality that made the first film so charming. Screenwriters Richard Kletter and Jerome Kass, writing from Walter Farley's novel, don't help matters with a silly story that is not imaginative enough to emerge as engaging fantasy or pointed enough to ever be threatening in real terms. Carlo Di-Palma's photography captures some nice shots along the way but doesn't come close to the extraordinary work done by Caleb Deschanel (who is credited with some additional photography here) in the original.

The middle-Eastern type accents affected by several of the actors, notably Allen Goorwitz and Jodi Thelen, are ludicrous, though Vincent Spano somehow manages to pull it off and be convincing as Reno's friend and guide. For his part, Reno had a great deal more charm when he was younger.

— Berg.

Spring Break
(COLOR)

A little education is a dangerous thing.

Hollywood, March 25.

A Columbia Pictures release. Produced and directed by Sean S. Cunningham. Features entire cast. Executive producers, Mitch Leigh, Milton Hersong. Screenplay, David Smilow; camera (color), Stephen Poster; editor, Susan Cunningham; music, Harry Manfredini; production design, Virginia Field; art director, Nicholas Romanac; costume design, Susan Denison. Sara Denning; sound, Kim Ornitz; asst. director, Brian Frankish. Reviewed at Columbia Pictures, Hollywood, March 25, 1983. (MPAA Rating: R.) Running time: 101 MINS.

Nelson	David Knell
O.T.	Steve Bassett
Adam	Perry Lang
Stu	Paul Land
Eddie	Richard B. Shull
Joan	Corinne Alphen
Susie	Jayne Modean
Ernest Dalby	Donald Symington

B 'n' B — bosoms and bottoms — ripen the title opticals and most of the rest of this otherwise conventional teen spree celebrating the rites of spring at Ft. Lauderdale.

"Spring Break," released over the weekend by Columbia Pictures, is hitting its target audience at prime time with $and, $urf, and $ex.

Producer-director Sean S. Cunningham, whose recent milieu has been horror movies ("Friday the 13" and "A Stranger Is Watching"), generates a pair of distinctive and appealing characterizations from David Knell and Steve Bassett, but David Smilow's script suggests a '60s beach blanket narrative line. More to the point, the pic recalls MGM's old Ft. Lauderdale saga, "Where the Boys Are" (1960). There's more skin this time out, and no inhibitions about sex. But, graphically, the film is pretty tame and celebrates youthful innocence more than orgiastic consumption.

Susan Cunningham's editing and Harry Manfredini's score keep most scenes jumping and noisy. But it takes 30 minutes for the outlines of a plot to even unfold. That deals with the misadventures of four young men sharing a room and the efforts of one of them (Knell) to escape the clutches of a nasty, rich stepfather.

The thin narrative is punctuated by hordes of attractive teens jumping up and down at assorted contests (the Wet T-Shirt, the Wet He-Shirt, the Teenie-Weenie Bikini, the Belly Flop, etc). Kids are always pouring beer over each other.

Much of the film looks like a Chamber of Commerce pitch. Richard B. Shull adds some fun as a sweaty hustler, and 1982 Penthouse Pet of the Year Corinne Alphen gleams in the rather frozen manner of a centerfold.

Only once are kids in bed together and that's played for laughs. Language is mild. For all its fever, it's unlikely a PG ("Spring Break" is an R) would have raised an eyebrow. —Loyn.

Man, Woman And Child
(COLOR)

Good, but not to the last drop.

Hollywood, March 9.

A Paramount Pictures release. Produced by Elmo Williams and Elliott Kastner. Features entire cast. Directed by Dick Richards. Exec producer, Stanley Beck. Screenplay, Erich Segal, David Z. Goodman, based on Segal's novel; camera (De-Luxe Color), Richard H. Kline; editor, David Bretherton; sound, David Ronne; production design, Dean Edward Mitzner; associate producer, Stacy Williams; assistant director, Tommy Thompson; music, Georges Delerue. Reviewed at Nosseck's Screening Room, L.A., March 9, 1983. (MPAA rating: PG.) Running time: 99 MINS.

Bob Beckwith	Martin Sheen
Sheila Beckwith	Blythe Danner
Jean-Claude	Sebastian Dungan
Jessica Beckwith	Arlene McIntyre
Paula Beckwith	Missy Francis
Bernie	Craig T. Nelson
Gavin	David Hemmings
Nicole	Nathalie Nell
Margo	Maureen Anderman
Louis	Jacques Francois

"Man, Woman and Child" is a sweetly dramatic picture which, unfortunately, reaches so hard for sobs at the end that all logic is suspended. This will probably hurt word-of-mouth and, in any case, the film probably arrives too late in the "family crisis" cycle of the past three years.

Despite the problems in the screenplay adaptation of Erich's Segal's novel by Segal and David Z. Goodman, there are still some fine performances here, tautly directed (until the ill-considered conclusion) by Dick Richards. •

Martin Sheen is superb as a happily married husband of Blythe Danner and father of Arlene McIntyre and Missy Francis. But trouble arrives with news that a brief fling of the past in France (seen in flashback with Nathalie Nell) has caused a problem for the present.

Nell has been killed in an accident, leaving a son by Sheen that he never knew about. For Sheen, the only decent thing to do is confess all to Danner and invite the boy to the U.S. for a get-acquainted visit.

Danner is also excellent in her hurt reaction, torn between love for her husband and resentment of the young intruder, who really isn't to blame for anything. And young Sebastian Dungan is a real discovery as the visitor who doesn't know Sheen is his father.

There's a good feeling throughout that this is an unfortunate situation that actually could have happened to fundamentally decent and innocent people. And with that feeling comes hope that, once the hurts are suffered and put aside, they will all live happily ever after.

And perhaps they do, as set up by the script and Richards, they easily could have with little trouble. But "Man, Woman," concludes with one of those annoying film situations where the characters have several choices of what to do— and select the one that makes the least sense.

It's the kind of ending, in fact, that makes people mad that they wasted emotion on what led up to it. —Har.

La Traversee de la Pacific
(Odyssey Of The Pacific)
(CANADIAN-FRENCH)

Vancouver, Jan. 10.

A Cine-Pacific (Montreal) — Babylone (Paris) films production. Produced by Claude Leger, executive producer, Bruce Mallen. Directed by Fernando Arrabal. Features entire cast. Screenplay, Arrabal, Roger Lemelin; production design, Rene, Petit; music, Edith Butler. Reviewed at the National Film Board, Vancouver, Jan. 10, 1983. Running Time: 78 MINS.

Emperor of Peru	Mickey Rooney
Toby	Jonathan Starr
Liz	Anick
Han	Ky Huot Uk
Uncle Alex	Jean-Louis Roux
Aunt Elsa	Monique Mercure
Flora	Vera Dalton

Fernando Arrabal, author and sometime filmmaker, takes a radical departure from his past works with "Odyssey Of The Pacific." However, the usually surprising and bizarre nature of Arrabal's work is nowhere to be found in this inane children's yarn. The picture will have a most difficult time finding theatrical outlets.

Story centres on a young boy and his sister living with their aunt and uncle in an idyllic rural setting. They are both too cute and cuddly to be embraced by audiences and the boy, Toby (Jonathan Starr), is downright irritating as he fantasizes great adventures for himself.

Into their midst comes a Cambodian orphan whom their aunt and uncle have taken into their home. He is initially disoriented but soon joins in the children's activities.

It is during one of their forays that they discover a crippled eccentric who identifies himself as the Emperor of Peru (Mickey Rooney). He beguiles the children with tall tales and the former locomotive engineer reveals his most prized possession — a hidden engine called The Pacific.

The Cambodian child sees the engine as his ticket home and enlists his friends to help him. The Emperor teaches them how to operate the machine but rather than join their escapade stays behind to face probable internment in an old folk's home.

Arrabal listlessly directs the lightweight fantasy. There are touches of surrealism, broad acting from Rooney and little narrative momentum. It's not surprising the film lacks poignancy and fails to compel us with the orphan's tragic story.

Commercial prospects are poor. While the film has made a pay-tv sale in Canada, it has yet to lock up a theatrical run. Technical credits are uneven and the print viewed suffered from a particularly bad English dub. —*Klad.*

Order Of Death
(ITALIAN-COLOR)

Berlin, Feb. 22.

A Jean Vigo production in association with Radiotelevision Italia. Produced by Elda Ferri. Directed by Robert Faenza. Features entire cast. Screenplay, Faenza. Ennio de Concini, Hugh Fleetwood, based on novel by Fleetwood; camera (color). Giuseppe Pinora; editor. Nino Baragli; art direction. Luigi Barchieliano; music. Ennio Morricone. Reviewed at the Berlin Film Festival. Feb. 22. 1983. Running time: 113 MINS.
Lt. Fred O'Connor .... Harvey Keitel
Lenore Carvo .... Nicole Garcia
Bob Carvo ....Leonard Mann
Leo Smith .... John Lydon
Margaret Smith .... Sylvia Sidney

"Order of Death" proves an interesting psychological thriller behind cops and robbers trappings.

The Italian production, shot in English in New York City, leads the audience down several dead ends before settling into its story of a corrupt cop and a young man who terrorizes him despite being his hostage.

Initially, the film appears to be about tracking down a cop killer. Harvey Keitel and Leonard Mann play two of the city's finest who after hours are not above a little skimming. It's never made clear what their illegal racket is but it affords them a shared second apartment.

The secrecy of their abode is shattered by a mysterious young man who knocks on the door and identifies himself as the cop killer to Keitel. However, the cop's not buying the confession and locks the stranger up, later beating him up in hopes of getting to the truth.

Mann is horrified by Keitel's brutal actions and in a scuffle he's killed by his partner. Keitel then has the young man slit Mann's throat in the style of the cop killer and dumps the body. However, when he attempts to shoot his captive and tie up the case, he discovers he's out of bullets and the young man escapes.

Up to this point "Order of Death" is pretty standard fare. The young man, identified as Leo Smith (John Lydon) after posing under several false names, quickly changes from victim to embarrassment for Keitel.

However, stranger things are to occur. Leo returns to the apartment and begins to take over Keitel's life. He orders him how to act and raises hell when he's disobeyed. Their roles completely reversed, Leo strikes up a bargain with his collaborator that he'll leave if Mann's wife, a reporter (Nicole Garcia), is murdered.

Running throughout the film is the constant suggestion of aberrant behavior. There's the suggestion Keitel and Mann's relationship is for more than business purposes. Keitel's manhood is put into question by both his encounters with Lydon and Garcia and this ties in nicely with the way in which Lydon dominates him by ruthlessly preying on his sense of Catholic guilt.

The plot is too complex for its own good but the final surprise twist is well worth the wait.

Keitel makes a marvelously ambiguous character with a hopelessly obsessive streak and a nagging conscience. However, the film's big asset is Lydon, better known as former punk singer Johnny Rotten. In his dramatic film debut he creates a truly frightening manipulator.

Technical credits are solid, particularly Giuseppe Pinora's camerawork and a restrained but effective Ennio Morricone score. The film lacks the name value and

action to become a major release but should do well in specialized situations where it has a chance to build an audience. —*Klad.*

Doll's Eye
(BRITISH-COLOR)

Berlin, Feb. 25.

A British Film Institute Production. Direction and screenplay, Jan Worth. Features entire cast. Camera (color), Anne Cottringer; editors, Christine Booth, Alan Mackay; art direction, Gemma Jackson; sound, Moya Burns. Reviewed at the Atelier, Berlin; Feb. 25, 1983. Running time: 80 MINS.
Jane ....Sandy Ratcliffe
Jackie ....Bernice Stegers
Maggie .... Lynne Worth
Also .... Richard Tolan, Paul Copley, Nick Ellsworth

The latest from the British Film Institute, "Doll's Eye" focuses on three women trying to make the best of things in an unsympathetic London. It is a social-sexual polemic of specialized interest unlikely to repeat the mainstream acceptance of the BFI's "The Draughtsman's Contract."

Trio is comprised of a journalist with a young child, another single mother working as a prostitute and a third struggling along as a switchboard operator and babysitter. They are neighbors with overlapping lives but not necessarily homogeneous backgrounds and views. Director-writer Jan Worth seems determined to set up barriers between her characters in the film's structure.

Incidents don't quite connect from scene to scene and the natural flow of action is repeatedly interrupted by speeches deploring Britain's prostitution laws and the inequity of male-female relationships in the business world. The film suffers from its sense of indignation and lack of subtlety and humor. Nonetheless, actresses Sandy Ratcliffe, Bernice Stegers and Lynne Worth do their best to bring depth and humanity to their roles.

Technical work is a bit ragged with a garbled soundtrack making it difficult to discern many conversations. "Doll's Eye" is likely only to reach the already converted and even they will have a difficult time slogging through its message. —*Klad.*

Scissere
(CANADIAN-COLOR/B&W-16m)

Vancouver, March 15.

A Collaborative Effort Production, Toronto. Features entire cast. Directed and written by Peter Mettler. Produced by Mettler, Ron Repke; camera, (color/black & white), Mettler; editor, Mettler; sound, Henry Jesionka, Bruce McDonald. Reviewed at the Ridge Theatre, Vancouver, March 5, 1983. Running time: 85 MINS.
Ex-patient .... Greg Kranze
Drug addict ....Sandy MacFadyen
Young mother ....Natalie Olanick
Entomologist ....Anthony Downes

Avant-garde, underground pics follow no fewer rules than your average Hollywood genre pic, and are no less hidebound. Peter Mettler's strenuously abstract and self reflective feature debut is no exception.

Presented at the 1982 Toronto Festival of Festivals, and shortly thereafter a winner of three awards at the Canadian National Film Festival, "Scissere" is at worst a compendium of countless out-takes from National Film Board of Canada docus: snow galore; machinery pumping and growling madly; broken window-panes overlooking deserted terrain; shabby scenes on public transport.

The highly disjointed narrative commences with some actuely disturbing imagery of a young man on the threshold of a psychiatric home. His role is rapidly superseded by the saga of a drug-addict guitarist prowling the city. Embroiled in his itinerary are a young mother and an elderly scientist, who had discovered a species of moth newly come to Canada.

Mettler cleverly interweaves the actions of this trio with some arresting imagery. His command of the medium is versatile-stop-motion, slow-motion, shuddering editing- but this mastery is purely at the service of established precepts of the avant-garde. Mettler's skills are shown in a 15-minute prelude of clouds, lakes and woods. For many "Scissere" will be a taxing experience. For others it will confirm that the avant-garde cinema changes whilst remaining the same. Okay prospects on campus, and at midnite shows. —*Gran.*

Zappa
(DANISH-COLOR)

Copenhagen, Feb. 25.

A Per Holst Film production with The Danish Film Institute, Kaerne ApS release. Directed by Bille August. Features entire cast: Script, Reuther and Bille August, based on Bjarne Reuther novel; camera (Eastmancolor), Jan Weincke; production management, Ib Tardine, Janne Find; production design, Kirsten Koch; costumes, Gitte Kolvig; editor, Janus Billeskov Jansen; music, Bo Holten. Reviewed at the Danish Film Studio, Kgs. Lyngby, Denmark. Feb. 25, 1983. Running time, 100 MINS.
Sten ....Peter Reichhardt
Bjoern .... Adam Toensberg
Mulle ....Morten Hoff
Sten's mother .... Solbjoerg Hoejfeldt
Sten's father ....Bent Raahauge
Bjoern's brother ....Thomas Nielsen
Bjoern's father ....Arne Hansen
Bjoern's mother ....Lone Lindorff
Mulle's father ....Jens Okking

"Zappa" serves up strong dramatic meat along with the casting of a lovingly ironic glance at teenage life in an outlying, middle-class district of Copenhagen, circa 1961. Three young teenage classmates join in a seemingly innocent gang. The leader of the gang is Sten, son of wealthy parents who either ignore him or urge him on to winning positions in all fields.

Bjoern is the nice guy who goes along with the gang even when he would rather be elsewhere, nursing various small amours. Mulle, the fatso of the class, is flattered when asked to join even if he promptly finds himself abused as the target of Sten's many cruel bits of wit.

Eventually, Sten leads the gang into a series of criminal activities, including knocking down shop-owners. The violence is never planned by Sten, but he obviously shares many of the characteristics of the small predatory fish called Zappa kept in a tank in his home. When Bjoern and Mulle at various times want out of the gang, Sten punishes them by molesting their property. Towards the end, Sten goes to even greater and more vicious length to bolster his weakened position as gang leader. Mulle, the born workingclass hero of the story, revolts first, Bjoern only reluctantly.

While director Bille August sometimes lets his film's dramatic build go astray in sweet and precise portraiture of family life, he stays on the track most of the time. He has a sure hand with well-chosen amateur child players as well as with the few adult professionals. His film's gang life is like a microcosm of big city youth gang life versus society seen in many U.S. features, and apart from its occasional bursts of overt violence, "Zappa" works best at showing the pressures building from within.

The period atmosphere is richly but still discreetly given, the playing throughout is excellent, even the caricatures of the rich have a certain zainy charm and credibility. Sten is fortunately drawn as a character not quite beyond redemption. Pic has obvious value as youth fare of high gloss as well as of depth. It is reported as a hopeful for competition entry in this year's Cannes event and would not be ill placed there. —Kell.

I Dismember Mama
(COLOR)

Horror oldie can't live up to that title.

A Valiant International release of a Romal Films production. Produced by Leon Roth; associate producer, Jack Marshall. Directed by Paul Leder. Features entire cast. Screenplay, William Norton; camera (Pacific Film Industries color), William Swenning; editor, uncredited; music, Herschel Burke Gilbert; sound, Kirk Francis; song, Gilbert, w/lyrics by Rocket Roden. Reviewed at 8th St. Playhouse, N.Y., March 24, 1983. (MPAA Rating: R). Running time: 78 MINS.
Albert .... Zooey Hall
Annie .... Geri Reischl
Mrs. Robertson .... Joanne Moore Jordan
Detective .... Greg Mullavey
Alice .... Marlene Tracy
Dr. Burton .... Frank Whiteman

With: Elaine Partnow, Rosella Olson, Robert Christopher.

———

A modest B-film lensed as "Poor Albert And Little Annie" in 1972, this ineffectual psycho-on-the-loose picture enjoys an enduring notoriety by virtue of its title change to "I Dismember Mama." Though the material is suitably distasteful and morbid, meek presentation will disappoint gorehounds lured by that title.

Quite impressive as the outwardly cool but deranged killer, Zooey Hall escapes from a sanitorium after the authorities prohibit him from watching stag movies in his room. Beginning a string of killings with a bald orderly, he's out to punish his rich mother (Joanne Moore Jordan) whom he blames for having him sent there and cut off from the family's $30,000,000 nest egg.

Arriving at the family mansion, Hall terrorizes and kills the busty redhead housekeeper (Marlene Tracy). When her pre-teen daughter Annie (Geri Reischl) returns home from school, the film segues into a U.S. version of the French classic "Sundays and Cybele," as romantic music, lyrical montages and a generally pleasant mood accompany Hall and Reischl's idyll together. At night, his warped sexual urges surface, but resisting the impulse, Hall sublimates by going out and picking up an adult blonde woman at an L.A. pool hall.

Besides the absence of gore, film relies upon unbelievable police procedure to keep its narrative going, and script is fatally flawed by the absence of a confrontation between Hall and his mom. (In fact, they have no footage together). Among the more familiar cast members, Greg Mullavey (of tv's "Mary Hartman") is miscast as the incompetent detective on the case.

Low-budget filming is poorly lit (multiple shadows abound) and lacking in action until the derivative chase through a warehouse of mannikins finale. Punchy big-band score by Herschel Burke Gilbert is a plus.

Director Paul Leder went on to film the 3-D "Ape," and more recently "I'm Going To Be Famous" with Mullavey in the latter. Scriptwriter William Norton would appear to be the same one who worked on half a dozen Levy-Gardner-Laven productions such as "Sam Whiskey" and "Gator," distinct from the B.W.L. Norton (of "Cisco Pike," "More American Graffiti"), but confusing credits over the past decade still need to be sorted out (e.g., Bill Norton Senior of "Night Of The Juggler" and William Norton Senior of "Dirty Tricks"). —Lor.

Day Of The Woman
(COLOR)

Attenuated revenge picture lacks credibility.

A Cinemagic Pictures release. Produced by Joseph Zbeda. Written and directed by Meir Zarchi. Stars Camille Keaton. Camera (Eastmancolor), Yuri Haviv; editor, Zarchi; sound, Steven Sklar; production manager, Bill Tasgar; assistant director, Michael Penland. Reviewed at 8th St. Playhouse, N.Y., March 12, 1983. (MPAA Rating: R). Running time: 101 MINS.
Jennifer .... Camille Keaton
Johnny .... Eron Tabor
Matthew .... Richard Pace
With: Anthony Nichols.

———

"Day Of The Woman" is a 1978 vengeance picture which owes its notoriety to its alternate release title of "I Spit On Your Grave" (courtesy of distributor Jerry Gross), as well as the reactionary diatribes written by several critics attacking its violence and audience-baiting. In a typical boomerang effect, film's current press kit turns Chicago's Roger Ebert and Gene Siskel's soapbox attacks on the film into selling points.

Beyond the hype, "Woman" bears the familiar vengeance structure of Yanick Bellon's 1977 French film "L'Amour Viole" (Rape Of Love), in which the heroine is gang-raped, leading her to a painstaking "balancing the accounts" revenge on her male attackers. Unlike that prototype picture, or the late Bob Kelljan's effective 1974 "Rape Squad," "Woman" is reduced to mere camp value as filmmaker Meir Zarchi exaggerates the violence, generating laughter instead of audience involvement.

Part of the problem here is one shared by most 1970s revenge pictures: an excess of motivation. After shaggy-dog opening reels of fair-skinned, attractive heroine Jennifer (Camille Keaton) tempting both the audience and local men in voyeuristic shots as she enjoys her summer novel-writing vacation by a lake in upstate New York, she is predictably attacked and raped by a foursome in the woods. Following the "last straw" premise of this genre, Zarchi has the same group rape her again in another part of the woods after she recovers and wanders off, followed fatalistically by them waiting at her home to beat her and molest her a third time. Instead of nightmarish, this format (with Keaton becoming progressively muddier and more bedraggled) becomes silly.

Though the peaceful, green-saturated locale is well-shot as a natural contrasting backdrop to mayhem, Zarchi's conception of sex and violence is unrealistic, derived from the "groan louder" school of softcore porn. Emphasis upon a black humor nerd-character (Richard Pace) goaded on by the others to prove his manhood insures that the viewer will be laughing at the violence.

Illogical final reels detail an over-directed Keaton sadistically wreaking her gory vengeance on the quartet. After the three rape encounters, she improbably decides to seduce the villains, who unbelievably succumb to her come-on.

By substituting sadism and cheap thrills for the efficient catharsis of successful revenge films (ranging all the way from William S. Hart silents to Charles Bronson starrers), Zarchi ends up with a padded, unconvincing exploitation film. —Lor.

Banzai
(FRENCH-COLOR)

Paris, March 17.
AMLF release of a Renn Production film. Produced by Claude Berri. Stars Michel Coluche. Directed by Claude Zidi. Screenplay, Zidi, Didier Kaminka, Michel Fabre; camera (color), Jean-Jacques Tarbes; music, Vladimir Cosma; sound, Michel Laurent; editor, Nicole Saulnier; art director, Payling Wang (Hong Kong), Claude Guilhem (Tunisia); special effects director and cameraman, Derek Meddings, Paul Wilson; production managers, Pierre Gauchet, Michel Choquet (Tunisia), Michael Nosik (New York), Philip Lee (Hong Kong); exec producer, Pierre Grunstein. Reviewed at the AMLF screening room, Paris, March 17, 1983. Running time: 100 MINS.
Michel Bernardin .... Michel Coluche
Isabelle Morizet .... Valerie Mairesse
Cousin Paul .... Didier Kaminka
Boss .... Francois Perrot
Businessman .... Jean-Marie Proslier
Mrs. Bernardin .... Marthe Villalonga
Carole .... Eva Darlan

———

Michel Coluche, the caustically anti-Establishment stand-up comic who traded in his barbs for screen fame as France's cuddly comedy favorite, is the brow-beaten star of this hugely expensive, misshappen laugh machine that wheezes its way around the globe, with on-location scenes in Tunisia, New York and Hong Kong.

Though producer Claude Berri sank more than $3,000,000 into the film, it seems evident that the cash wasn't spent on the script. Director Claude Zidi, who can boast a long, unbroken string of commercial hits, has never been strong on ambition, but he has on occasion showed a flair for low comedy invention. Backed by Didier Kaminka and Michel Fabre, Zidi here miscalculates on a wide scale, fashioning a story without momentum or genuine imagination. It will probably cash in locally and in markets where Zidi and Coluche are familiar names, but it doesn't seem likely to break new commercial ground in other situations.

Coluche is an employee in a Paris-based international organization that provides advice and aid to tourists in distress. This provides the source of various misadventures when he is assigned to hop on planes to repatriate French travellers who've been hospitalized abroad. Part of his problems is that he's afraid of flying. An when he gets to his destination, all the wrong things happen.

Sent to a desert hospital in a civil-war torn African nation, Coluche accidentally springs a rebel leader and inadvertently contributes to a coup d'etat. Dispatched to New York to bring back a black musician from a Harlem hospital, he is set upon by three blacks who mistake him for a drug carrier. Flown to Hong Kong, he becomes an ignorant pawn in the hands of underworld masterminds.

One is left numb by the desperately unfunny, and often tasteless, nature of small-minded gags and the discrepant means for their execution. In this regard, the climactic Hong Kong sequence is particularly appalling, with elaborate firstrate special effects — a jet crashlanding on an aircraft carrier and keeling over into the sea — wasted on throwback frace of the lowest order.

As for Coluche, his one-time cocky disrespect has given way to sentimentality and squealing.

The abrasive comic who once ran for the French presidency to show his scorn for the political system has now become a Gallic Lou Costello. —Len.

Bella Donna
(WEST GERMAN-COLOR)

Berlin, March 29.
A Joachim von Vietinghoff Film Production, Berlin, in coproduction with Westdeutscher Rundfunk (WDR) and Sender Freies Berlin (SFB); tv-producers, Joachim von Mengershausen (WDR) and Hans Kwiet (SFB). Features entire cast. Written and directed by Peter Keglevic. Camera (color), Edward Klosinski; editing, Sigrum Jaeger; music, Astor Piazolla; artistic advisor, Arno Ziebell; production manager, Klaus Keil. Reviewed at Cinema Paris, Berlin, March 18, '83. Running time: 105 MINS.
Cast: Fritz Praetorius (Fritz), Krystyna Janda (Lena), Erland Josephson (Max), Brigitte Horney, Angela Gockel, Kurt Raab.

Peter Keglevic came to his first feature, "Bella Donna," from television. The Austrian-born helmer's best known work there was the two part tv documentary, "Years Pass By," and the detective pic, "Admitted for Evidence," in the "Tatort" whodunit series. Despite an international cast, in the end he has little to show for it.

"Bella Donna" is about a down and out saxophonist in love with a singer with an entertainment band on a showboat cruising a Berlin lake. The singer has a husband who adores her but suffers as she takes lover after lover to quiet her nerves. Meanwhile, the sax player can't get his love life straightened out either, so he roams about with his instru-

mental case under his arm in search of an identity.

A girlfriend of the singer is dying of cancer, which adds another odd twist to a plot which ambles aimlessly.

"Bella Donna" (as the title hints) appears to be in the genre spawned by Rainer Werner Fassbinder's "Lili Marleen" and "Lola" — the glittering tinsel world of nightclub singers: respectively in the aforementioned films and this one. Although it's a pity her talents are wasted on fluff, Krystyna Janda manages to save more than a few scenes with a pleasing flair for torch numbers. Another plus is lenser Edward Klosinski, Andrzej Wajda's cameraman for "Man of Marble" and "Man of Iron." —Holl.

Syndicate Sadists
(Rambo Sfida La Citta)
(ITALIAN-COLOR)

A Summit Associates Ltd. presentation of a Dania Film-Medusa Produzione production. Produced by Luciano Martino. Directed by Umberto Lenzi. Stars Tomas Milian. Screenplay, Vincenzo Mannino; camera (Eastman color), Federico Zanni; editor, Daniele Alabiso; music, Franco Micalizzi; assistant director, Alessandro Metz; sets, Giacomo Cardocci. Reviewed at Lyric Theatre, N.Y., March 26, 1983. (MPAA Rating: R). Running time: 92 MINS.
With: Tomas Milian (Rambo), Joseph Cotten (Paterno), Maria Fiore, Mario Piave, Luciano Catenacci, Femi Benussi, Guido Alberti, Shirley Corrigan, Evelyn Stewart.

Underneath its misleading U.S. release title, "Syndicate Sadists" is a 1975 Italian crime picture originally named (in translation) "Rambo Takes On The City." Film is typical of the scores of routine Italo actioners ground out in the 1970s, many of which grind away at domestic action houses and drive-ins with little fanfare, subbing for the nearly extinct U.S.-made B-level action film.

Tomas Milian toplines as an unkempt (clad throughout in black leather jacket and red and black outfit) sort of local hero named Rambo who returns to Milan to visit a buddy who works for the local Mondialpol (a private police force). When the pal is killed, Rambo goes seeking vengeance, foiling kidnappers and cleaning up two rival gangs which are operating while (as they seem to say in every Italian crime pic) the police stand by "powerless."

With his motorcycle goggles adding to his comic strip figure appearance, Milian is presented as a subject of hero worship for the kids in the film, though his amoral, undefined personality and appeal is likely to mystify U.S. audiences. As a blind gang leader specializing in gambling, Joseph Cotten has little to do here, though his self-dubbing in English is far superior to the low-

quality voicing afforded the rest of the cast.

Prolific director Umberto Lenzi demonstrates his ability to stage a chase and keep things moving, but the picture's minor-league story climaxes at about the halfway point when Rambo seemingly outwits the kidnappers, and in the barest of switches has to retreat in order for 40 minutes more padding to occur. —Lor.

La Petite Bande
(Thé Little Bunch)
(FRENCH-COLOR)

Paris, March 16.
Gaumont release of a Hamster Films /Gaumont/Stand'Art/FR3/Elefilm coproduction. Produced by Denis Mermet. Features entire cast. Directed by Michel Deville. Screenplay, Deville, Gilles Perrault; music, Edgar Cosma; camera (Eastmancolor), Claude Lecomte; editor, Raymonde Guyot; art direction, Michel Guyot, Regis des Plas; sound, Andre Herve, Joel Beldent; animation, Cartoon Farm — Jose Xavier; production managers, Franz Damamme and Roger Fleytoux; exec producer (England), Bob Kellet. Reviewed at the Gaumont Colisee theatre, Paris, March 16, 1983. Running time: 91 MINS.
The children: Andrew Chandler, Helene Dassule, Nicole Palmer, Catherine Scrimgeour, Hammisch Scrimgeour, Nicolas Sireau, Remy Husquin. The adults: Francois Marthouret, Francoise Lugagne, Roger Desmare, Alain Janey, Henri Viscogliosi, Robin Remucci, Pierre Forget, Nathalie Becue, Alain Maratrat, Roland Amstutz, Jean-Pierre Bagot.

After a Patricia Highsmith adaptation ("Deep Water"), the eclectic Michel Deville now tackles a children's fantasy with a tale of some London schoolchildren who leave home one day for some marvelous and terrifying adventures abroad.

This modern fairy tale, told without dialog, but with a pervasive musical score by Edgar Cosma (uncle of French film composer Vladimir Cosma) is based on an actual escapade in 1979 by some British kids who made their way unimpeded across the English Channel and had a lark in France before authorities could catch up with them.

Deville asked writer Gilles Perrault (author of "Dossier 51," which Deville filmed in 1978) to imagine a scenario using this situation. Perrault came up with a fanciful tale that draws heavily on the conventions and cliches of fairy tales and children's literature.

It's a sympathetic effort, though it doesn't really come off. Perrault's script tries to make something new from old, but a certain banality prevails. Deville shows a felicitous light touch in the earlier, more realistic part of the film, but his imaginative eye and control weaken as the story shifts gradually into a purely fantastic universe of childish awe and terror. The flights of fancy have clipped wings.

Action begins relatively down to earth with an exposition of home and school life for seven youngsters — four boys, three girls — in a humdrum London suburb. One day they suddenly decide to skedaddle and stow away in a car transporter headed for Dover. There they slip aboard a Channel ferry.

Once in France, they wander carefree, wreak mischievous havoc in a village, succour a dying old woman, hoodwink an entire clinic of psychiatrists. But malevolent forces are at work, and the little band find themselves menaced by strange figures: a priest in a Rolls-Royce, a tattooed nun, a family of canal pirates, etc.

In fact, these mysterious characters are part of a cult with evil designs on childhood. They kidnap children and submit them to the aging rays of a diabolical machine in a secret grotto. But the runaways, aided by a providential cat, and a sort of guardian angel in the form of an omniscient young man, foil their plans and make their escape on a boat. Finally, they are shipwrecked on a desert isle where their innocence can no longer be threatened.

The seven English children were all recruited from bi-lingual schools near Paris and are charming. However, the several dozen adult actors who pass through the film do not always find the spirit Perrault and Deville look for.

Tech credits are fine, and pic should please young audiences in various situations, particularly as there are no sub-titling or dubbing problems. Adults may be somewhat more demanding with the film's affected naivete. —Len.

Le Lit
(The Bed)
(BELGIAN-COLOR)

Brussels, Feb. 15.
A Cinelibre/Progres Films release of a Man's Films production (Brussels). Produced by Marion Hansel. Associated producer, Jean-Marc Anchor, Eos Films (Chene-Bourg Suisse). Written and directed by Marion Hansel, based on the novel by Dominique Rolin. Camera (color), Walter Vanden Ende; editor, Susana Rossberg; art direction, Maris-Francoise Manuel; music, Serge Kochyne; sound, Henri Morelle; production manager, Jacques De Pauw; production director, Michele Troncon. Reviewed at the Albert I theatre, Palais des Congres, Brussels, Jan. 24, 1983. Running time: 80 MINS.
Martin Y.................Heinz Bennent
Eva..................... Natasha Parry
Martin's first wife....... Francine Blistin
Doctor .... Johan Leysen

"Le Lit" is a courageous but nevertheless uninvolving drama about the suffering of a sculptor who dies after a long illness. Two women are at his bedside: his second wife and the first wife who tries to comfort her. Film depicts the gradual disintegration of the sick man, but also shows the strong moments of hope when the pain disappears for a while and death seems suddenly further away.

In spite of the downbeat subject, it's also a film about the strength of life in situations when people confront death. The painful observation of the last 24 hours in the life of the man are intercut with flashbacks of happier moments in the life of the couple. Thanks to the memories of their passionate love, the woman finds the courage to prepare for an existence without the other.

The agony of the man takes place mostly on a barge, lost in a misty, grey landscape. The restriction of the decor give pic a claustrophobic feeling; near the end we feel trapped like the characters in the fatal cycle of life and death.

Theatre actress Marion Hansel directs her first feature film with a great sensitivity, carefully avoiding all melodramatic pitfalls. Sound is also used effectively to suggest the unbearable situation of the two women listening to the screaming and suffering of the dying man.

Unfortunately, the distant approach of the director eventually works against the film. Considering the intensity of the drama, pic is cold and uninvolving. Film is furthermore weakened by so-so acting and the artificial wisdom of the dialogue.

Considering the unpleasantness of the subject, pic needs careful handling but seems a natural for fest circuits and art house playoff.
—*Pit.*

Axe
(COLOR)

Unusual, minimalist horror exercise.

A New American Films release of a Boxoffice Pictures International presentation; a Frederick Prods. production. Executive producer, Irwin Friedlander. Produced by J.G. Patterson Jr. Written and directed by Frederick R. Friedel. Features entire cast. Camera (color), Austin McKinney; editor, Friedel, Patterson Jr.; music, George Newman Shaw, John Willhelm; sound, Shaw; production manager, Philip Smoot; makeup, Worth Keeter. Reviewed at 8 th St. Playhouse, N.Y., March 12, 1983. (MPAA Rating: R). Running time: 67 MINS.

Lisa .... Leslie Lee
Steele .... Jack Canon
Lomax .... Ray Green
Billy .... Frederick R. Friedel
Grandfather .... Douglas Powers
Aubrey .... Frank Jones

Filmed in Charlotte, North Carolina about a decade ago (picture was rated by the MPAA in 1974, its alternate title: "Lisa, Lisa"), "Axe" is a fascinating but totally uncommercial film noir exercise in the horror genre, recently reissued to take advantage of public's appetite for gore-shockers. Recalling the B-films of old in its one-hour (plus elongated credits) running time, picture will be of more interest to film students than exploitation film fans.

Filmmaker Frederick R. Friedel, working on apparently a student film budget, emphasizes detail closeshots and inserts, with punchy, accelerating editing to maintain tension in the absence of a strong narrative. Picture opens with abstract tracking shots and moody closeups as a trio of gangsters terrorize an underling in a seedy hotel room. Typical of a nobudgeter, his falling out the 12thstory window takes place entirely off-screen, with a scream and sound effect.

Rest of the film has the gangsters hiding out down south, invading the remote house inhabited by a shy young girl Lisa (Leslie Lee) and her paralyzed, catatonic grandpa. As the gangsters singly try to attack her, Lisa dispatches two of them with a straight razor and the title axe, while the third (played by director Friedel in an evident economy move) is accidentally offed by the police at film's end.

Abstracting his minimal material, Friedel evidences a good camera eye here. A piano, ondioline-style electronic keyboard and percussion score help to sustain the hypnotic mood, but for general audiences, lack of solid story values combined with amateur acting are bound to be disappointing. One example of the latter is that both Friedel and attractive heroine Lee fall back upon the device of gazing floorward to appear shy and vulnerable.

Little has been heard of Friedel since this promising effort, but cameraman Austin McKinney has made many low-budgeters and makeup man Worth Keeter is still in North Carolina, directing Earl Owensby's 3-D extravaganzas.
—*Lor.*

A Private Life
(W. GERMAN-COLOR)
Berlin, March 15.

A Peter Almond Film Production, in co-production with Film for Thought. Stars Lotte Palfi, Paul Andor. Directed by Mikhail Bogin. Screenplay, Nancy Musser, Peter Almond; camera (color), Alicia Weber; music, Evelyne Crochet; sets, Jody Moore; editing, Charles Musser; sound, Morning Pastorok; costumes, Jody Moore. Reviewed at Berlin Screening Rooms, March 15, '83. Running time: 50 MINS.

Cast: Lotte Palfi (Margot Lerner), Paul Andor (Karl), Joe Parsons Perdito.

Unspooled in the nine-film retro in honor of German exiled thesp Paul Andor (Wolfgang Zilzer, his real name, is found in German screen credits), Mikhail Bogin's "A Private Life" (1979) scores as a gem of a short feature set in Uptown Manhattan today. Pic's director, Mikhail Bogin, is a Soviet filmmaker-in-exile, whose home now is also Gotham. This is not to be confused with Raizman's "Private Life," currently playing in N.Y.

This is a story of elderly German-Jewish emigrants living in an upper West Side section of New York. Lotte Palfi plays a warmhearted, now unattached, somewhat lonely but quite active individual, Margot, whose closest friend is Karl, played by Paul Andor, a widower with a shy nature and an evident need to recall at regular intervals his youth in Berlin of the Golden 1920s. Together, they take walks in Central Park, talk of "old times" in Germany, and recall the Expressionist period, New Objectivity, the Bauhaus, and all the other movements in art, on the stage, and in film studios of the day.

Gradually, as the deep relationship extends even to a review of family albums and poetry readings (Karl reciting, Margot listening), the two plan a vacation together abroad; and in preparation for the journey, Margot begins to learn Portuguese. Then comes the news: Karl's son in a distant city wants his father to pull up stakes in New York, transfer his belongings to a nearby Old Peoples Apartment Building, and thus be separated from Margot save for letters and an intermittent visit. Karl, the dreamer, will make this decision, while the goodhearted Margot can only wish him well in despair that they have never declared their love for each other, nor taken the last step necessary to share their last years together.

The magic of "A Private Life" is in the common connection to a bygone past. Both Palfi and Andor (Wolfgang Zilzer) had budding careers in German theatre and film studios, she in Friedrich Hollaender's cabaret revues, and he in lead film roles. Their touching recollections sanctify the destinies of several German emigrants who withered on the vine in Hollywood or New York, their talents reduced to bit roles and walk-ons. One hopes that "A Private Life" will lead to a sequel of some sort for all concerned on the modest project.
—*Holl.*

Fearless Hyena II
(HONG KONG-COLOR)

Hong Kong, March 5.

A Lo Wei Motion Picture Co. Ltd. Production. Executive Producer, Lo Wei. Directed by Chan Chun. Stars Jackie Chan (Sing Lung), Dean Saki. (No other credits provided by the producer). Reviewed at President Theater, Hong Kong, March 5, 1983. Running Time: 100 MINS.
(Cantonese soundtrack with English subtitles)

The enterprising filmmakers of the world have done it to Bruce Lee ("The Game of Death") and Peter Sellers was not spared ("Trail of the Pink Panther"), so why shouldn't it be done to Jackie Chan, still a popular kung-fu figure. He's very alive and well and working for himself and Golden Harvest in Hong Kong. "Fearless Hyena" was a Lo Wei martial arts cheapie made during the kung-fu craze which starred Chan at the beginning of his golden career.

A lot of footage was shot and now that the boy wonder with the sympathetic unwashed and underdog look is a clean-cut man marking the foreign boxoffice scene, it's inevitable on the part of Lo Wei to revive, rehash and rehabilitate several outtakes and unused bits and pieces to create a surgical editing job.

The outcome of this exploitative exercise is "Fearless Hyena II" which has many unrelated Chan comedy sequences forced into a feature. A look-alike who does not look like Chan has been hired to connect the scenes which don't connect. Any local idiot can detect the changing color quality of the film, the lack of continuity, the nonsense plot and the hairdo of Chan which changes in every episode.

There is nothing good that can be said about this surgery production, except that there are some unseen Jackie Chan reels showing his youthful kung fu and charisma which centers on his looking helplessly funny, yet victorious, in the end. As added interest, Chan wanted to sue the producers before the release date but later changed his mind as Godfather Lo Wei claims to have every right to do what he wants with old footage from several vintage films. Chan was once under contract with Lo Wei Productions before his sojourn to Seasonal Films and then to Golden Harvest's super ladder to international fame. —*Mel.*

Zwarte Ruiter
(Black Rider)
(DUTCH-COLOR)

Amsterdam, Feb. 11.

A Joop van den Ende production. Exec producer, Gijsbert Versluys. Directed by Wim Verstappen. Features entire cast. Screenplay, Gerard Cox; camera (color), Eduard van der Enden; sound, Rene van den Berg; music, Clous van Mechelen. Reviewed at City Theatre, Amsterdam, Feb. 11, '83. Running time: 95 MINS.

Fons Ruiter .... Hugo Metsers
Rinus Ijzerman .... Rijk de Gooyer
His daughter .... Cristel Braak
Milou .... Pleuni Touw

This is a flatfooted and predictable yarn about post-war butter smuggling at the Dutch Belgian border. Outside the Netherlands, it's unlikely to rate more than second-feature playoff.

The story mix of old friends on opposite sides of the law, Resistance workers turned criminal, Mafia gun-running, love and jealousy should have been enough to get some excitement going.

But direction and editing are pedestrian and though the intention to style lead Hugo Metsers as a Dutch Jean-Paul Belmondo was obvious, it didn't come off. Other good seasoned actors, such as Pleuni Touw and Rijk de Gooyer, go through the motions without much conviction. —*Wall.*

New Directors/New Films

Joe's Bed-Stuy
Barbershop:
We Cut Heads
(COLOR-16m)

Okay student film.

A First Run Features release of an N.Y.U. Graduate Film School production. Produced by Zimmie Shelton, Spike Lee. Written and directed by Spike Lee. Features entire cast. Camera (Du Art Color, 16m), Ernest Dickerson; editor, Lee; music, Bill Lee; sound, Mark Quinlan; production manager, Sonia Alvarez; art direction, Felix DeRooy. Reviewed at New Directors-New Films series, 57th St. Playhouse, N.Y., March 27, 1983. (No MPAA Rating). Running time: 60 MINS.

Zachariah Homer .... Monty Ross
Ruth Homer .... Donna Bailey
Teapot .... Stuart Smith
Nicholas Lovejoy ....Tommie Hicks
Joe Ballard .... Horace Long

Titled after the neon sign above the community gathering spot, "Joe's Bed-Stuy Barbershop: We Cut Heads" is a diverting fictional student film by 25-year-old Spike Lee. Filmed as a master's thesis project using student crew and pro thesps, hour-long opus is well-lensed as a slice of life of black people coping with neighborhood problems and the influence of the numbers racket.

After his partner Joe (Horace Long) is murdered for skimming off the barbershop's numbers trade, Zachariah (Monty Ross) takes over the haircut business, but finds no customers when he tries to steer clear of the rackets. His social worker wife Ruth (Donna Bailey) places one of her charges, a youngster nicknamed Teapot (Stuart Smith), as a helper in the shop, and everyone prospers as Zachariah agrees to let numbers kingpin Nicholas Lovejoy (Tommie Hicks) re-establish the site as a local betting parlor.

With filmmaker Spike Lee glossing over the moral crises, Zack eventually takes a stand against the rackets and pic's open ending offers no solution to everyman's dilemma in trying to survive (or escape) a harsh, limiting environment. Eschewing the sex and violence cliches of blaxploitation gangster films, Lee delivers a friendly portrait of black folkways that, except for the convincing street language and wit, is probably too mild to capture a sizeable audience.

With the married lead characters a trifle unconvincing, film's best role (in an all-black cast except for one bit part) is numbers magnate Nicholas Lovejoy (said to be patterned after the early career of Cleveland's fight promoter Don King), well-enacted as a cool, smooth philosopher by Tommie Hicks.

Ernest Dickerson's camerawork and other tech credits are pro quality, and film is aided by a jazz score by the director's father, bassist Bill Lee. —*Lor.*

Sekka Tomurai Zashi
(Irezumi — Spirit
Of Tattoo)
(JAPANESE-COLOR)

A Daiei Films (Kyoto Studio) production and release. Produced by Yasuyoshi Tokuma, Masumi Kanamaru. Directed by Yoichi Takabayashi. Features entire cast. Screenplay, Chiho Katsura, from a novel by Baku Akae; camera (color), Hideo Fujii; music, Masaru Sato; art direction, Seiten Shimoishizaka; planning, Yo Yamamoto; lighting, Reijiro Yamashita; sound, Tashiyuki Shozu. Reviewed at New Directors/New Films series, 57th St. Playhouse, N.Y., March 20, 1963. (No MPAA Rating). Running time: 109 MINS.

Kyogoro ....Tomisaburo Wakayama
Akane ....Masayo Utsunomiya
Fujieda .... Yuhsuke Takita
Harutsune .... Masaki Kyomoto
Katsuko .... Harue Kyo
Haruna .... Naomi Shiraishi

"Irezumi — Spirit·Of Tattoo" is an unconvincing and tedious Japanese film using the tattooing ritual as a springboard for tortured passion and corny plot twists. Obvious film fest fodder (where seriousness of tone is often confused with art), picture's U.S. import chances are nil.

Initial story premise, adapted by scripter Chiho Katsura from a Baku Akae novel, harks back to silent-era melodrama (e.g., Tod Browning's 1927 "The Unknown," wherein Lon Chaney Sr. had his arms amputated to please his neurotic lover Joan Crawford). Librarian heroine Akane (Masayo Utsunomiya) agrees to have her back elaborately and painfully tattooed over a two-year period to satisfy her boss and lover Fujieda (Yuhsuke Takita), who has a tattoo fetish in addition to his "beauty of a woman's skin" fetish.

Akane is presented as a willful character, but what she sees in the nondescript and bossy Fujieda is never explained or demonstrated. Picture segues instead to its main emphasis upon the tattooist Kyogoro (Tomisaburo Wakayama), who has evolved a peculiar method of his art requiring the woman to be made love to while being tattooed. Amidst much portentious mumbo-jumbo about "living tattoos" and the implication of the art, the viewer is treated to bloody close-ups of simulated tattooing and standard softporn genre closeups of Akane groaning with a mixture of pain and pleasure.

Heavy-handed direction by Yoichi Takabayashi demonstrates almost no narrative skill: every plot detail and twist is first introduced with an emphatic camera movement or racking of focus before its revelatory repetition later, and story periodically halts for a reel or two of lameduck, illustrated flashbacks. Overall effect is akin to a silent film where the dramatic content is developed in the inter-titles rather than through the shots and montage.

By the time the last plot shoe drops, story structure resembles a timid incest film, in which each of the six main characters is multiply intertwined with one another via blood or sexual relations: foster father, stepfather, second husband, etc. Though the characters are driven (even to suicide) by these contrived linkages, there is no emotional impact provided for the viewer.

In the unplayable lead role, Masayo Utsunomiya has a beautiful face which is about all one can carry away from the picture's trite visual imagery. Her acting is hard to assess, as Takabayashi inconsistently has her strike poses to fit contradictory scenes. As the tattooist, Tomisaburo Wakayama (familiar stocky hero from the Baby Cart series seen here as "Shogun Assassin") presents a dull workman, far removed from the mythical, mystical character in the script. Despite the lurid material, "Irezumi's" sexual and nude content is minimal. —*Lor.*

Oridathu Oru Phayalvaan
(There Lived A Wrestler)
(INDIAN-COLOR)

Thundathil Films (Trivandrum) production. Producer, R. Suresh Features entire cast. Written, edited and directed by P. Padmarajan. Camera (color), Vipindas; sound, Devadas; music, Johnson; make-up, K.G. Ramu. Reviewed at the 57th St. Theatre, New York, as part of the New Directors/New Films series, March 23, 1983. Running time: 120 MINS.

Cast: Rasheed, Nedumudi Venu, Jayanthy, K.G. Devaki Amma, Ashok, Jayadevan, Karliachen, Krishnankutty Nair.

(Malayalam soundtrack; English subtitles).

Chronologically, India has one of the longest film histories and for much of that time it has been one of the most prolific filmmaking nations. Yet its output is so little known to the West that it's now included in the Third World countries. One of these reasons is that the national style is so non-conforming when it comes to international tastes (and a great reluctance to change) that most of its efforts are self-defeating.

Unfortunately, although P. Padmarajan's "There Lived A Wrestler" does omit the lengthy, dull musical passages which weigh down the average Indian film (at least in the print shown), his style of writing, directing and acting is as old-fashioned as they come.

There's virtually little story — the adventures of a wrestler who's adopted by a village which hopes to benefit by their wagers on him and the accompanying publicity but finds only unhappiness in his stay. Much of the story deals with the actions of the wife provided by the villagers, who's neglected, rather than the athlete himself. Rasheed, as the wrestler, is physically excellent (like the contrast of a sumo wrestler with the average Japanese) but his idea of acting is mostly sighs and sidelong glances.

Technically, the film is average, with bad lighting but rather good color definition. In two years Padmarajan has made only three films. What he really needs are a few lessons from Satyajit Ray. —*Robe.*

Serangan Fajar
(The Dawn)
(INDONESIAN-COLOR)

PPFN (Pusat Produksi Film Negara) production. Features entire cast. Written and directed by Arifin C. Noer. Camera (Kodacolor), M. Soleh Ruslani; editor, Supandi; music, Embie C. Noer; art directors, Fred Wetik, F. Effendhy, Nahali. Reviewed at the 57th Street Theatre, New York, as part of the New Directors/New Films series, March 23, 1963. Running time: 170 MINS.

Cast: Dani Marsuni (Temon), Suparmi, Amorso Katamsi, Suwastinah, Anthonius Yacobus, Nunuk Khaerul Umum, Susanto Anthonius, Rini Satiti, Charlie Sahetapy, Jajang C. Noer dan Faqih Syahrir.

(Bahasa Indonesian soundtrack: English subtitles).

Indonesian filmmaker Arifin C. Noer might have better made three films, rather than one, about the early days of his country's independence as the three-part "The Dawn" makes for 170 minutes of propaganda and mawkish drama.

Interestingly, national patriots depicted in the film do not include Sukarno (nor is there any intimation of his later dictatorship). The period of the film is mostly 1945 which could be subtitled "the year of really living dangerously." A third of the film is almost in documentary form, spotted with historical highlights; another third deals with the social split among the various Indonesian classes; the rest of the film turns on the adventures of a small boy who spends his time awaiting the return of his father from the war

The real central figure is Ragil, the uncle of the boy, who is a servant in the Romo family household (and in love with one of their daughters) and a revolutionary soldier. Dani Marsuni as Temon, the small lad, plays most of his role with wide eyes and a continual sniff.

For the patriotic Indonesian audience only. —*Robe.*

Heart Like A Wheel
(COLOR)

Strong biopic of first femme racing driver. Appeal's there, but smart sell needed.

Hollywood, March 29.

A 20th Century-Fox release of an Aurora Production in association with Michael Nolin. Produced by Charles Roven. Executive producers, Rich Irvine, James L. Stewart. Directed by Jonathan Kaplan. Features entire cast. Screenplay, Ken Friedman; camera (Deluxe color), Tak Fujimoto; editor, O. Nicholas Brown; music, Laurence Rosenthal; production design, James William Newport; set design, Tom Duffield; set decoration, Peg Cummings; costume design, William Ware Theiss; sound, Robert Gravenor; associate producer, Arne Schmidt; assistant director, Steve Lim; second unit director, Conrad E. Palmisano. Reviewed at the 20th Century-Fox Studios, West L.A., March 29, 1982. (MPAA Rating: PG.) Running time: 113 MINS.

Shirley Muldowney	Bonnie Bedelia
Connie Kalitta	Beau Bridges
Jack Muldowney	Leo Rossi
Tex Roque	Hoyt Axton
Don 'Big Daddy' Garlits	Bill McKinney
John Muldowney (age 15-23)	Anthony Edwards
Sonny Rigotti	Dean Paul Martin
Chef Paul	Paul Bartel
Mickey White	Dick Miller
Angela	Missy Basile
NHRA Boss	Michael Cavanaugh
Mrs. Marianne Kalitta	Ellen Geer
Nurse North	Nora Heflin
John (age 10-13)	Byron Thames
Tiny	Tiny Wells
John (age 5-8)	Brandon Brent Williams

"Heart Like A Wheel" is a surprisingly fine biopic of Shirley Muldowney, the first professional female race car driver and three-time winner of the National Hot Rod Assn. world championship. What could have been a routine good ol' gal success story has been heightened into an emotionally involving, superbly made drama which nicely balances the woman's achievement and sacrifice, kicks and suffering, in what is probably the best effort of its type since "Coal Miner's Daughter."

Fox will have to sell the film with the utmost precision, as it is hardly just a racing picture and will have enormous appeal to women if they can be lured in spite of the redneck milieu expectations. Film opened in initial markets Friday (1).

In fact, first of many surprises is that story isn't set in the South at all, but in Schenectady, N.Y., and, later, California. Winning prolog has pa Hoyt Axton letting his little daughter take the wheel of his speeding sedan, an indelible experience which prefigures Shirley, by the mid-1950s, winning drag races against the hottest rods in town.

Happily married to her mechanic husband Jack and with a young son, Shirley finds her innate ability compelling her, by 1966, to enter her first pro race. Roadblocked at first by astonished, and predictably sexist, officials, Shirley proceeds to set the track record in her qualifying run, and her career is underway.

But her husband ultimately can't take her career-mindedness, and she's forced to set out on her own, with the support of w.k. driver Connie Kalitta. When Kalitta is barred from competing indefinitely, he throws himself entirely behind her efforts, and also becomes the lover of the driver known, in 1972, as "Cha-Cha" Muldowney.

Despite a serious injury and the deterioration of her relationship with Kalitta, Muldowney, by the mid-1970s, becomes a champ, a position she still maintains in real life.

Director Jonathan Kaplan has served a long apprenticeship on such road action exploitationers as "Truck Turner" and "White Line Fever," but nothing he has done before, including the provocative, little-seen "Over The Edge," prepares one for his mature, accomplished work here. The textures and compositons he'd worked out with lenser Tak Fujimoto make the film endlessly interesting visually, and the scenes of emotional connection and separation are handled with particular intelligence.

Best of all, however, is the leading performance by Bonnie Bedelia. Always an intriguing actress, Bedelia here makes clear that she's never before been seen to maximum advantage. In a role spanning some 25 years, Bedelia moves beautifully from winsome bride to very married lady, toughened divorcee and proud winner. Throughout, she displays a continuing suspicious, askance attitude toward good fortune that seems realistic and lends pic a welcome hard edge. It's a terrific performance.

As the helpful but unreliable Kalitta, Beau Bridges allows himself to appear more grimy and lowdown than usual and emerges with his best performances in some time. Leo Rossi registers forceful emotional integrity as the abandoned husband, Axton is ingratiating as Muldowney's father, Anthony Edwards impresses as her son, and Paul Bartel, of "Eating Raoul," has an amusing scene of comic relief as a tv chef on whose show the driver incongruously appears.

Ken Friedman's dialog is superior, but script does suffer from a few structural problems, notably in the jump from the 1960s to the 1970s and in clarification of the apparently amorous, but emotionally ill-defined, relationship between Muldowney and Kalitta.

Tech contributions are expert, and Laurence Rosenthal's music blends nicely with pop tunes from the eras involved. Muldowney herself is billed as creative consultant, and she has been rewarded with a relative rarity, a fine contempo biopic. —Cart.

Het Veld Van Eer
(The Field Of Honor)
(DUTCH-COLOR-16m)

Rotterdam, Feb. 17.

Film International release, produced by Neon Film/Kees Kasander. Directed by Bob Visser. Features entire cast. Screenplay, Rien Vroegindeweij, J.A. Deelder, Bob Visser; camera (color), Dick Verdult; sound, Mark Glynne; music, Tuxidemoon/ Au Pairs. Reviewed at Film Festival Rotterdam, Feb. 3, '83. Running time: 90 MINS.

Ada	Leos Luca
Louis	Ralph Wingens
Hotelmanager	Guido Louwaert

Debutante feature director Bob Visser, who cut his teeth in television, based this downbeat tale on an unpleasant episode that befell his sister. Maybe he should have kept it in the family.

Yarn is part thriller, part war film, part underground and part comedy, an ill-assorted mix not enhanced by different styles of acting and uneven photography.

Inexperience behind the camera shows despite the good intentions and enthusiasm of the filmmakers.

Plot details how a newlywed husband turns out to be a war freak and expects his bride to share his interest in arms, fortresses and war graves. They honeymoon in Verdun, one of the grimmest battlegrounds of WWI.

If that's no fun for the bride, neither is her spouse's attempt to murder her after a fight. His subsequent death is no turn-on either.

Leos Luca as the bride does her best to get credibility into the character but it's uphill stuff. And the mix of allegory and dreams, madness and sanity, passion and pusillanimity never jell.

Commercially blah. —Wall.

A Marriage
(COLOR)

Nicely executed marital breakup.

A Cinecom Intl. release of a Filmco Production. Produced by David Greene. Written and directed by Sandy Tung. Features entire cast. Camera (Technicolor), Benjamin Davis; editor, Michael R. Miller; music, Jack Waldman; art direction and associate producer, Farrel Levy Duffy. Reviewed at the 57th St. Playhouse, N.Y. (New Directors/New Films) March 30, 1983. (No MPAA rating). Running time: 90 MINS.

Ted	Ric Gitlin
Nancy	Isabel Glasser
Jane	Jane Darby
Mark	Jack Rose

A creditable debut feature from film editor and tv director Sandy Tung, "A Marriage" is a well-executed contemporary drama with comedic hues focusing on the growth and collapse of an all-American couple's relationship, a universal theme which, if carefully exploited, could produce a sleeper success.

Highlighted by naturalistic performances from newcomers Isabel Glasser and Ric Gitlin, the film was made in Staten Island, Manhattan and New Jersey on the thinnest of shoestring budgets (somewhere in excess of $100,000). The indie pic's technical achievements are good given the fiscal constraints.

Tung, 32, scripted "A Marriage" admittedly basing it on his own experiences and Stanley Donen's "Two For The Road." He traces the ups and downs of Ted and Nancy's long love affair beginning with their nervous adolescent crushes and first, humorously brief, sexual encounter. They marry and clash head-on with vocational adversity and financial pressures that ultimately wreck the marriage.

The couple's love-and-love-lost story is told in flashbacks sprinkled throughout a 24-hour period leading up to the signing of their final divorce decree. Tung handles the rather complicated structure with authority and also excels at light comedic turns (although a slapstick film within the film that Ted makes to get into film school is a bit lame).

Since the flashbacks cut in and out singly from Ted's point of view, a case could be made for the critical lack of attention to Nancy's outlook. And some may find it implausible that the pair stayed together for 12 years, since he's so arrogant, she so materialistic and both are pretty selfish. Yet the paradox rings true.

Pic's overall strengths and appeal overcome these minor false notes for a successfully realized autobiographical effort. "A Marriage" also exemplifies the sustained potential of U.S. indie filmmaking as well as its value as an industry alternative. (Noteworthy are the risky references to Ric's sexual dysfunction brought on by his marital woes, a plot turn rarely treated in major pictures with major stars).

Concurrent with its world premiere at the recent New Directors/New Films, the pic was acquired by Cinecom Intl. —Binn.

Insel Im See
(The Island on the Lake)
(EAST GERMAN-COLOR)

Berlin, March 22.

A Production of the Academy for Film and Television in the GDR, Potsdam-Babelsberg; world rights, DEFA Aussenhandel, East Berlin. Stars Hertha Thiele. Directed by Wolfgang Muenstermann. Screenplay, Wolfgang Voigt; camera (color), Ali Bayram; music, Voigt editing, Gerda von Dorszevski. Reviewed at Berlin Screening Room, March 15, '83. Running Time: 52 MINS.

Cast: Herta Thiele (Grandmother), Hans-Christian Klein, Guenter Junghans, Renate Reinicke, Eberhard Mellies.

Wolfgang Muenstermann's "Island on the Lake" (1980) was unspooled for the Hertha Thiele retro during the recent Berlin Film Fest. It's a production of the East German Film & TV Academy in Potsdam-Babelsberg, a diploma film that attracted quite a bit of attention via its airing on DDR II in October 1981.

Thiele is a grandmother living with her son's family in a house on a lake near Berlin. The grandson, a student, has to defend her honor one day before the other kids who're making fun of her. It appears she always rows out to an island in the lake with provisions at regular intervals for collecting water-reeds that could be found anywhere else on the lake, and is thereby taken to be a bit looney. The grandson asks his father in bits and pieces of contemporary reality surrounding Thiele herself.

The boy learns that his grandmother hid a POW on the island under the noses of the Nazis during the war years. She would go at regular intervals to the island by rowboat to bring him something to eat. One day, she was called in for questioning: the POW had been caught, and she was held as an accomplice. Her defense was simply that she was collecting water-reeds to make baskets.

With scarcely more than a few lines of dialog, Thiele lends to "Island on the Lake" a quiet dignity of purpose. The tragic character of the tale is not rooted to ideological principles, but a person's own fate as an engaged individual acting in the cause of humanity. Her figure of a grandmother, keeping herself useful by weaving baskets at a lakeside villa, becomes an enigmatic symbol of lonely vigilance as the story of her past begins to surface in the narrative. Who was this POW on the island: a lover, a German or a Russian soldier, a Jew perhaps — we never know.

Thiele emigrated to Switzerland in 1937, lived, after the war, in, Switzerland (as a Swiss citizen) and East Berlin. Beginning in 1966, she was seen again in East German films and on the stage in East Berlin. —Holl.

The Kid Who Couldn't Miss
(CANADA-COLOR-DOCU)

Winnipeg, March 15.
A National Film Board of Canada production and release. Produced by Paul Cowan, executive producer, Adam Symansky. Features entire cast. Direction and screenplay, Paul Cowan. Camera (color). Cowan; editors, Sidonie Kerr, Cowan; music, Ben Low ;narrated by William Hutt. Reviewed at the National Film Board,

Winnipeg, March 15, 1983. Running Time: 79 MINS.
With: Eric Peterson as Billy Bishop and Walter Bourne and Cecil Knight, Lord Balfour, Arthur Bishop, Louis Loumez, Alexander McKee.

Canadian World War I flying ace William (Billy) Avery Bishop was credited with 72 kills — the highest total for any British pilot. However, the authenticity of his record and deflating the myths which have grown up around him consume most of "The Kid Who Couldn't Miss."

Bishop is easily Canada's best-known war hero. Most recently he was the subject of the musical, "Billy Bishop Goes To War," which played extensively in Canada as well as London and New York. Originally, director Paul Cowan simply planned to translate the play to the screen but doing research for the project prompted him to expand his horizon.

The resulting film consists of interviews with those who knew Bishop during the war, a rendering of the events of his life and excerpts from the play plus actor Eric Peterson in the role of Bishop's mechanic Walter Bourne offering his views on the man and the myth. It's like a crazy quilt with a disquieting design. Cowan can only pose questions and raise suspicion rather than concretely letting the air out of the Bishop legend.

The only thing raised which appears credible is the assertion Bishop was a poor pilot but an excellent marksman. Otherwise, he appeared to suffer the same battle exhaustion experienced and chronicled by other pilots in the film. Cowan's portrait of the experience is quite fascinating but provides no added understanding of Bishop.

Film holds obvious interest in Canada and will most assuredly attract an audience in specialized screenings and on television. However, foreign sales appear minimal for this story of a home-grown hero. —Klad.

Ferestedah
(The Mission)
(U.S.-W. GERMAN-COLOR)

A New Film Group (N.Y.) and Aria Film Prod. (Munich) co-production. Produced and directed by Parviz Sayyad. Stars Sayyad, Mary Apick, Hooshang Touzie. Screenplay, Sayyad, from a story by Hesam Kowsar, Sayyad; camera (Du Art color)/co-producer, Reza Aria; editor, Sayyad; sound, Yousef Shaham. Reviewed at New Directors/New Films series, 57th St. Playhouse, N.Y., March 31, 1983. (No MPAA Rating). Running time: 108 MINS.
Agent from Teheran ... Hooshang Touzie
The Colonel .... Parviz Sayyad
Maliheh .... Mary Apick
His Eminence ... Mohammad B. Ghaffari
Maziar .... Hatam Anvar
Farzaneh .... Hedyeh Anvar
Gaffar .... Kamran Nozad
(In Farsi; subtitled in English.)

Filmed in New York City last year by expatriate Iranian filmmaker Parviz Sayyad, "The Mission" is a sugar-coated political tract in the form of a comedy-thriller about a hit man who ends up befriending his likable target. With a bloated running time about twice as long as the material demands, Farsi-language entry is destined for a limited audience.

Sayyad's threadbare plot peg is to cast himself as the hale and hearty ex-army colonel now working as a nightshift janitor in Gotham, who quickly wins over the friendship of Teheran agent (Hooshang Touzie) sent to kill him by local contact known as His Eminence (Mohammad B. Ghaffari). The hit is actually a substitute for Touzie's original mission, which was nullified when a tv news report indicates his previous target has been assassinated in Washington, D.C.

With the colonel's cute kids who speak English (his wife is stuck back in Teheran due to emigration restrictions) plus their feisty young aunt (Mary Apick) as romantic sparring interest, the sullen agent played by Touzie becomes part of the family group and eventually uses the rationalization that Eminence has possibly chosen the colonel as a target for personal reasons rather than a Teheran-ordered cause as his excuse for not completing the mission. Film's trick ending relies upon equal parts of off-screen "surprise" twists and trite sentimental effects.

Between tedious dialectic discussions in which Sayyad and Apick are the filmmaker's mouthpieces for tolerance and a variety of platitudes, film alternates between dull "thriller" footage and cornball situation comedy. Sayyad gives the only interesting performance, as lead Touzie presents a taciturn facade that doesn't jibe with his supposed crisis of conscience. Apick is an initially appealing young actress, but soon becomes a political cartoon berating "religious zealot" Touzie for the faults of the Khomeini regime.

Film's 35m blowup from 16m lensing is okay (only night footage is grainy), but picture lacks style. Color is drab and the absence of a musical score adds to film's ponderous effect. —Lor.

Here Are Ladies
(IRISH-DOCU-COLOR-16m)

An Arthur Cantor presentation of a Sedgemoor Prods. production. Executive producer, Martin C. Schute. Produced by Marvin Liebman, Davis Fasken. Directed by John Quested. Stars Siobhan McKenna. Camera (color), Dudley Lovell; editor, Mamoun Hassan; music, David Fanshawe; assistant director, Redmond Morris. Reviewed at Thalia theatre, N.Y., March 28, 1983. (No MPAA Rating). Running time: 60 MINS.

With: Siobhan McKenna, Niall Buggy, May Clusky, Paul Farrell, Sarah Gallagher, Maireni Ghrainne, Pat Layde, Patsy Madden, Bernadette McKenna, Owen McMahon, Brian Murray.

Siobhan McKenna's "Here Are Ladies" is an informative and very entertaining documentary filmed in 1971 in Ireland which represents several female characterizations created by Irish writers ranging from George Bernard Shaw to James Joyce. Instead of transcribing her one-woman legit show of the same title (presented in London in 1970 by Laurence Harvey and Wolf Mankowitz, followed by a 1971 Joseph Papp New York presentation and 1973 Broadway revival, all staged by Sean Kenny), McKenna has filmed the picture on actual locations where the writers lived and wrote about, and has added fine supporting performances by Abbey Theatre players. Result is an engrossing and educational hour's entertainment, aided immeasurably by the star's anecdotes and concise delivery of historical background material.

Exposing McKenna's versatility, picture presents her in a moving closeup performance as Mrs. Tancred from Sean O'Casey's "Juno And The Paycock," a sad, wistful essaying of a graveside scene from John Millington Synge's "Riders To The Sea" as Moira laments the passing of the last of her six sons, and a sparkling reading of, Winnie (buried in sand on a beach) excerpted from Samuel Beckett's "Happy Days." The context of these on-location perfs is often significant, as in McKenna's portrayal of George Bernard Shaw's "St. Joan," filmed in a moodily-lit Irish jail.

The film's major highlight is a scene taken from Abbey Theatre writer Lennox Robinson's play "Drama At Inish." On stage, McKenna essayed all four roles herself, but here she is surrounded by three top Abbey players in an hilarious rendering of grand over-acting, as a scene from a mock Russian drama is enacted for two uncomprehending Irish folk. McKenna's handling of varied Irish and British accents and widely divergent acting styles is on view.

Picture ends with a lengthy two-handed scene of women washing clothes at a stream taken from James Joyce's "Finnegan's Wake." Displaying the musicality and hypnotic rhythms of Joyce, scene carries over a problem from McKenna's legit version, in that the thick accents employed resist intelligibility. Film suffers from the omission of the live show's highlight, the Molly Bloom soliloquoy from Joyce's "Ulysses," but still it preserves, for posterity, a fine sampling of McKenna's thesping art, significantly since she has only appeared in a dozen feature films in her career.

Direction by John Quested (who also helmed "Philadelphia Here I Come" with McKenna) is simple and effective, and picture deserves wider distribution, having fallen into obscurity since winning a prize at the 1971 Venice Film Festival. Cable or broadcast tv usage would be a natural.

Documentary has no writing credit, but given the personal nature of some anecdotal material it is likely that McKenna wrote the commentary. Other works excerpted in addition to those noted above are O'Casey's "The Plough And The Stars," four Crazy Jane Poems by W.B. Yeats, and James Stephens' "The Crock Of Gold."—*Lor.*

The One-Armed Executioner
(FILIPINO-COLOR)

A Super-Pix Prods. release of a B.A.S. production. Executive producers, Gene S. Suarez, Rey Q. Santos. Produced and directed by Bobby A. Suarez. Stars Franco Guerrero. Screenplay, Wray Hamilton; camera (color), Juan Pereira; editor, Joe Zucchero; music director, Gene Kavel; associate director, Pepito Diaz; assistant director, Butch Santos; special effects, Benny Macabale. Reviewed at Lyric Theatre, N.Y., March 26, 1983. (MPAA Rating: R). Running time: **88 MINS.**

With: Franco Guerrero, Jody Kay, Pete Cooper, Nigel Hogge, Mike Cohen, James Gaines, Brian Smith, Leopoldo Salcedo, Joe Zucchero, Joe Sison, Odeth Khan, Danny Rojo, Joe Cunanan, Nestie Mercado, Celso Lindaya.

"The One-Armed Executioner" is a 1980 Filipino picture attempting, with meager achievement, to provide an action alternative to the still-dominant chop-socky films. Though the actors in a mixed cast (orientals, whites and blacks) articulate in English, the dubbing job is poor, marking the picture for undiscriminating audiences only.

Title derives from predicament of hero Ortega (Franco Guerrero) an Interpol agent in the Philippines whose arm is cut off by drug smugglers after they kill his bride Ann (Jody Kay), a blonde from San Francisco. Before Orteg sets out on his inevitable quest for revenge, picture bogs down in several interminable reels of Ortega's self-pity and padding as an ex-agent (now restaurateur) undertakes to train him in martial arts and compensatory reliance upon his other physical talents and senses.

Though filmmaker Bobby A. Suarez delivers okay fight sequences and shootouts (with mucho explosions and other special effects), the emphasis here is on weaponry and fist fights rather than kungfu displays. Guerrero is a bland hero, and instead of the expected "Bad Day At Black Rock" excitement of a one-armed man taking on all comers, payoff is routine.—*Lor.*

Megilah '83
(ISRAELI-COLOR)

Tel Aviv, March 13.

A Berkey-Pathe-Humphries & Telefilm Production. Produced by Tommy Lang. Directed by Ilan Eldad. Features entire cast. Haim Heffer; Screenplay, adapted by Ilan Eldad, Tommy Lang; camera (color), Ilan Rosenberg; editor, Naomi Peres-Aviram; art direction, Arnon Adar; music composed, arranged and conducted by Dov Seltzer; lyrics, Itzik Manger; translated by Jerry Hyman, Mitch Hiller; choreography; Sharon Pinsley. Reviewed at the Lev Cinema, Tel Aviv, March 12, 1983. Running time: **000MINS.**

Cast: Jonathan Segal, Nitza Shaul, Michael Schneider (with the singing voice of Albert Cohen), Shlomo Bar-Abba, Aviva Paz, Jerry Hyman.

Based on a musical based on a story by Yiddish poet Itzik Manger, Ilan Eldad's film deals with the Book of Esther in the Old Testament.

Keeping close to the basic construction of the show, a play within a play (travelling actors presenting the story of Esther), Eldad and Lang try to add new twists, including a sequence to give the show the additional dimension of dealing not only with Jewish Diaspora in the Persian Empire and Eastern Europe, but also with the Holocaust, which is a bit too much. The plot is unsufficiently clear, the performances would fit much better the stage parody than the realistic style imposed by the camera, the sets look theatrical and the recordings do not take into consideration they are intended for a soundtrack.

The songs themselves are already very popular, for the show has been presented for Jewish audiences everywhere (there is an ensemble producing it on the Israeli stage now). Most of the film is sung, with the original Yiddish lyrics being combined with English (or German, for the version to be released in West Germany) dialog, but these lyrics may supply the selling point to market this production, particularly in spots with heavy Jewish audiences. —*Edna.*

Quan Shui Ding Dong
(Our Aunt Tao)
(CHINESE-COLOR)

Berlin, March 15.

A Shanghai Studio Film Production; world rights, China Film Export and Import Corporation, Peking. Features entire cast. Directed by Shi Xiao-hua. Screenplay, Wu Yian-xin; camera (color), Yu Shi-shan; music, Liu Yan-xi; sets, Xue Yian-na. Reviewed at Berlin Screening Rooms, March 15, '83. Running time: 97 MINS.

Cast: Zhang Rui-fang (Aunt Tao), Zhang Ling-fei (Xue-li), Niu Ben (Big Liu), Shi Shu-gui (Yue'e), Chen Xu-de (Old Hou).

This children's film, unspooled at the Berlin Film Fest. Shi Xiao-hua's "Our Aunt Tao," is the work of a talented woman director at the Shanghai Film Studio. It's about a retired schoolteacher whose health is ailing, the reason being that she has dedicated her life to her profession without ever leaving the city in 40 years. And she still can't leave in good conscience to take a much needed cure — for she notices unattended children in city playgrounds, left on their own because both parents have to work and there's no such thing as a state-kindergarten, or day-nursery.

Aunt Tao invites the children to her modest apartment during the day, settles a few family squabbles in the course of her goodheartedness, and breaks with her own niece due to the latter's need for quiet to continue her music lessons. It all works out in the end, however, including the good lady's cure at a sanitorium to restore her health and return to her "mission in life."

"Our Aunt Tao" deserves more exposure at kidpic fests. Its plus is in the credits and the natural screen personalities of the child thesps. It's a film that stays close to the story line and sugar-coating its heartwarming side. One of the best of the entries in the Berlinale's children's fest. —*Holl.*

Virgin People
(FILIPINO-COLOR)

Manila, Feb. 6.

A Topaz Film Productions. Executive producer, Juan T. Dominguez. Written and directed by Celso Ad Castillo. Stars Janet Bordon, Myrna Castillo, Pepsi Paloma, Joonee Gamboa, William Zafran, Ernie Garcia. Camera (color), Gani Sioson; music, Rey Rames; editing, Do Hulleza. Reviewed at the Manila International Film Festival at PICC, Manila, Feb. 4, 1983. Running Time: Approximately 120 MINS.
(Version previewed is for international release).

The controversial and censor-prone film of erratic Filipino director Celso Ad Castillo was the sensation of the recent Manila International Film Festival though not legitimately part of the filmfest. Shown uncut in 29 Metro Manila theatres in its original version, the erotic softcore pic was presold and pre-packaged as pornographic (by Philippine standards) which helped tremendously at the boxoffice. It grossed over 10,000,000 pesos in two weeks.

Sad to say but true is the fact that "Virgin People" is neither authentic porno nor a masterpiece in the field of erotic cinema. It is nothing but a crude, technically inept teaser created by Castillo in an unsophisticated pseudo-arty style that can be best described as an example of exploitative film for third world folks. To those familiar with "cinema erotique" (Continental or French style), this movie is more of a delirious camp that's been directed by a man trying to titillate his audience with a cheap "peep" Philippine strip show.

The lovemaking sequences look forced, with the man wearing his jeans most of the time. It shows a great deal of perverse or uncomfortable ways of making love.

The film's popularity can also be attributed to the Philippines' strict censorship on female and male nudity and simulated sex acts. The temporary lifting of censorship during the MIFF week gave a lot of sex-starved Filipinos a chance to see their favorite "bomba" stars in different stages of undress as they take a bath, sleep, or make love.

The plot is minimal, three young supposedly virginal girls (Janet Bordon, Myrna Castillo, Pepsi Paloma) live in a remote and rural village. Their innocence is shattered when two men arrive. The first is a lecherous uncle (Joonee Gamboa) and Isaac (Ernie Garcia), a stuttering stud.

Isaac becomes the object of excitement, competition, envy and deceit as the three enlivened and suddenly worldly girls now turned into wanton women bordering on nymphomania. They fight for the hero's attention, time and sexual favours. The superficial dramatic performances of the three shapely stars were somewhat covered-up by their constant physical exposure and fake orgasms. The overlong film definitely needs drastic editing if and when released abroad.

The best parts, which are also the funniest, are the lovemaking sessions which come only after a series of long conversations, repetitive shots of flora and fauna. They can be likened to a pause that refreshes, as the viewer has to wait long for something heated to develop seriously. However, to some, part of the fun is to see the feminine resistance which easily turns to total submission.

The incorporation of pretentious symbolisms about God, Christ and Satan in the vestal paradise of the virginal residents (which flounders into murder, revenge and retribution) make this film even more ridiculous and at times incomprehensible.

To those raised on other directors, Castillo's "Virgin People" would be nothing but a small sex joke from the Philippines without finesse nor redeeming artistic values. But to locals or domestics who have been taught to look the other way when dealing with human bodies, pysches, and sex acts, the movie is a shocking and important one for undemanding voyeurs and sensation seekers, for lovers of low-budget celluloid thrills with a tropical setting and for those easily pleased by surface lures.
— *Mel.*

Uiin Monogatari — Jemin Y To S
(Vienna Story — Gemini Y and S)
(JAPANESE-COLOR)

Tokyo, Feb. 18.

A Toho release. Produced by Sai Ogura and Johnny Kitagawa. Directed by Yoshihiro Kawasaki. Features entire cast. Screenplay, Genyo Takahashi, Konosuke Fuji, Yoshihiro Kawasaki; camera (color), Masahiro Ueda; art, Yukio Higuchi; sound, Nobuyuki Tanaka; lighting, Shinji Kojima; music, Kazuo Oya. Reviewed at Toho Central, Tokyo, Feb. 7, 1983. Running time: 96 MINS.

Koichi Wakakusa	Toshihiko Tahara
Yutaka Irie	Yoshio Nomura
Hayato Shibata	Masahiko Kondoh
Bunsaemon	Sou Yamamura
Masako	Emiko Tsushima
Yuka Irie	Tomoko Ikuta
Katarina	Hiroko Grace
Kyoko Shibata	Naomi Nagaya

The narrative inventiveness which characterized the Tanokin Trio's four previous cinematic outings is again in evidence in the latest release from this wildly popular threesome (Toshihiko Tahara, Masahiko Kondoh and Yoshio Nomura). Tahara, who portrayed a student of dance in New York in the third Tanokin adventure, "Good Luck Love," is here a student of music in Vienna. And whereas he discovered his long-lost father in the aforementioned film, in this he discovers his long-lost twin.

He is aided and abetted by Yoshio Nomura, an employee in a N.Y. Japanese restaurant in "Good Luck Love," but is now an apprentice cook in a Viennese bakery. Masahiko Kondoh, who rode a motorbike through "High Teen Boogie" (the trio's previous release), enters Vienna on a motorbike.

It could, of course, be argued that the Marx Brothers — to name another trio that made audiences laugh, albeit intentionally — never changed their screen personae from film to film; but then, they not only had the talent to get away with it, they had the able assistance of such brilliant screenwriters as George Kaufman and S. J. Perelman. The Tanokin Trio has neither, although it must be admitted that Nomura, a progressively more vestigial presence with each successive film, is rapidly turning into another Zeppo (the least talented Marx).

Just as "Good Luck Love" presented such slices of Americana as a blonde, blue-eyed whore, Big Apple punks preying on a single Japanese woman and a black wino capable of blowing a mean trumpet, so "Uiin Monogatari" leaves no Viennese cliche unturned. Tahara and his girl friend, Hiroko Grace, are serenaded by the Vienna Boys Choir; Tahara, Kondoh and Grace quaff a few at a beer garden; Tahara skis down pristine slopes; Tahara and Kondoh elude villains by ducking into the Austrian capital's famed sewers. And in the background can be heard the "Third Man Theme," performed, of course, on the zither.

Although Tahara, Nomura and Kondoh are ensnared in Vienna's well-known web of intrigue, they manage to escape by employing the James Bondian method succintly summarized by one writer as: "and with a single bound, he was free." At one juncture, Kondoh and Nomura, who have heretofore demonstrated a remarkable ability to pummel into insensibility hulking Westerners twice their size, are pinioned by villainous Occidentals; the camera then cuts to an organ-playing Tahara, who is immediately joined — without explanation — by his two little pals, looking remarkably unrestrained.

The film belongs to Tahara, who is required to speak German, convince the audience that he is half-foreign and sing. Which task he performs least well is a matter for each individual member of the audience to decide. —*Bail.*

Jidaiya No Nyobo
(The Antique Dealer's Wife)
(JAPANESE-COLOR)

Tokyo, March 13.

A Shochiku release, produced by Shigemi Sugisaki and Kanji Nakagawa. Directed by Azuma Morisaki. Features entire cast. Screenplay, Haruhiko Arai, Keiji Nagao, based on novel by Tomomi Muramatsu; music, Toshiyuki Komori; camera (color), Hiroshi Takemura; sound, Shinichi Harada; mixing, Koji Matsumoto; lighting, Hiroshi Ijima; editing, Yoshi Sugihara. Reviewed at Shochiku Central, Tokyo, March 9, 1983. Running time: 97 MINS.

Yasu	Tsunehiko Watase
Mayumi & Misato	Masako Natsume
Owner of Sunrise	Masahiko Tsugawa
Yuki	Tomiko Nakayama
Youth	Hiroyuki Okita
Drycleaner	Shiro Osaka

Most understandable is the decision of Shochiku to release "Jidaiya No Nyobo" on a double bill at its chain theatres with "Kamata Koshinkyoku" (Kamata March), named best picture of 1982 at the sixth annual Japan Academy Awards, the 25th annual Blue Ribbon Awards and the 37th annual Mainichi Film Concours. Without the pulling power of the latter film, it's doubtful many viewers here will be drawn to see the former.

Not that the film is a bad one. It has its virtues, almost all of which can be stated negatively: it is not overly long, not hammily acted, not too uninterestingly directed and its inconsequential plot is not quite light enough to allow the pic to float right off the screen.

To the old downtown curiosity shop run by Yasu (Tsunehiko Watase) come two stray cats, one literal, the other — Mayumi (Masako Natsume) — figurative. Natsume moves in with Watase, becomes his common-law wife, sometimes goes wandering off for days at a time.

On one such occasion, Natsume vanishes long enough for several unrelated subplots to come stumbling onto center stage. When the watering hole run by Masahiko Tsugawa goes under, his old girl friend (Tomiko Nakayama) and her new boy friend take over; an old railway ticket found in a beat-up valise sets Mr. Imai, the dry cleaner (Shiro Osaka), to reminiscing; Misato, a Brillo-haired 24-year-old with a surprising resemblance to the the missing Mayumi (not unusual as she is also played by Natsume) has a one-night stand with Yasu before heading off to get married. Mayumi eventually returns before the final credits roll and life in and around Yasu's establishment presumably goes on in as unengaging a manner as the 97-minute slice of it just presented the viewer.

Whether the fault lies with Tomomi Muramatsu's novel, the screenplay by Haruhiko Arai and Keiji Nagao or the direction by Azuma Morisaki, the film is characterized by a jarring, jangling tone. Bittersweetness segues into slapstick with all the grace of a log jam in a dry creek bed.

Watase's is a genuinely affecting, understated performance, his longing for the temporarily absent Natsume achingly palpable. So good is he that one almost fails to notice the cameo appearance of Mitsuru Hirata, winner of the Japan Academy Award best actor nod for his performance in "Kamata Koshinkyoku." It's unfortunate that the vehicle given Watase is as creaky as most of the items in his little shop. —*Bail.*

Chichi To Ko
(Father and Child)
(JAPANESE-COLOR)

Tokyo, Feb. 21.

A Toho release of a Sanrio Film production. Executive producer, Shintaro Tsuji. Produced by Teruyuki Ogisu, Ryuzo Kikushima, Komei Fuji. Features entire cast. Directed by Nobuhiko Hosaka. Screenplay, Ryuzo Kikushima; camera (color), Hiroshi Murai; lighting, Yoshimasa Tanaka; sound, Fumio Yanoguchi; art, Nobuo Kurihara; editor, Sachiko Yamachi; assistant director, Akio Kondoh; music, Shinji Tanimura. Reviewed at Toho Central, Tokyo, Feb. 10, 1983. Running time: 107 MINS.

Takeichi Kudo	Keiju Kobayashi
Takashi Kudo	Keichi Nakai
Tomoko Minegishi	Junko Mihara
Young wife	Mieko Harada
Toyoko	Junko Miyashita
Marie	Toshi Kusonoki
Yuri	Mieko Takamine

This is an astonishingly multi-layered film, its concerns ranging from the difficulty of maintaining completely honest relationships to the immutable nature of prejudices.

Father is Keiju Kobayashi, proprietor of a mobile bookstore, and his only child is high school senior Keichi Nakai, but they seem related hardly at all. There is an almost palpable gap between the two that develops into a veritable chasm when Nakai, a straitlaced lad for whom honesty is the only policy, learns from his natural mother that she divorced his father because he deliberately concealed from her the facts about his family background. The truth is that Kobayashi is the eldest son of the operator of a rural crematorium.

Furious at what he regards as his father's duplicity, Nakai takes out his anger on his teacher, stabbing him — nonfatally — with a knife. Called to the school to pick up his son, Kobayashi decides to take the boy to his, Kobayashi's, home town. There Nakai learns why Kobayashi felt compelled to run away, leaving his younger brother to continue performing a necessary service.

With a most winning subtlety and sensitivity, director Masahiko Hosaka demonstrates the deleterious effect on relationships of societal pressure to conceal rather than reveal, the preserve superficial harmony at the expense of being, at times, painfully honest. Further, it would not be stretching matters to say that this film is a gentle, understated plea for us to examine how our prejudices can force others to lead lives of fearful dissemblance.

Veteran character actor Kobayashi is predictably reliable, while relative newcomer Nakai shows much promise. A pleasant surprise is pop star Junko Mihara, who give a winning performance as a young woman concealing certain unpleasant portions of her past.

This, the first Toho release of 1983, is a profoundly heartening film. If subsequent releases from this and other studios maintain its standards, this will be a banner year for the Japanese cinema.
— *Bail.*

The Drummer
(HONG KONG-COLOR)

Hong Kong, March 13.

A Sincere Film Production Co. release. Executive producer, Sin Kam Wing (Chow Chung). Directed by Yueng Kuen. Stars Leslie Chung, David Lo, Ng Wui, Paul Chung, Daisy Cheung, Fred Carpio Jr.; Elaine Chow, Dolly Carpio. Production Manager, Wan Siu Kuen; music composed and arranged by Joseph Koo; drumming adviser, Tony Hui. Reviewed at State Theatre, Hong Kong. No other credits provided. March 12, 1983. Running Time: 96 MINS.

(Cantonese soundtrack with English subtitles)

Leslie Cheung, Hong Kong actor-singer, 27, is the perennial teenager in Cantonese movies. He continues his post-adolescent screen character in yet another youth-oriented drama about showbiz aspirations. Along the lines of Neil Diamond's "Jazz Singer," there is nothing jazzy nor classy to brag about, as it ends up looking like a B-grade beach blanket movie.

Produced by Sincere Film Company, another independent, it is headed by ex-actor Chow Chung.

His ambition is to produce an exemplary and inspiring film that school masters would recommend, but he failed with dismal results as director (Yueng Kuen) did not and was not able to capture the "feel" of today's generation.

Cheung is Chan Chi Yeung, a secondary student who dreams of being a professional drummer despite the discouragement of his screenwriter father (David Lo), but understanding grandfather. Chan later meets a professional but has-been Filipino drummer (Fred Carpio Jr.) and convinces him to be his teacher.

The photography is passable, while the acting is embarrassing with the exception of Carpio, who gives some mature depth to all the ridiculous situations presented. Heroines Daisy Cheung and Elaine Chow are useless decorations. Singer Dolly Carpio makes a cameo performance as a female drummer and main competitor of Chan. There is no evidence of any flair and creativity. —Mel.

Das Letzte Jahr
(The Last Year)
(W. GERMAN-COLOR-DOCU)

Berlin, March 11.

A Regina Ziegler Film Production, Berlin, in coproduction with Zweites Deutsches Fernsehen (ZDF), Mainz. Directed by Wolf Gremm. Camera (color), Hartmut Lange; editing, Doerte Voelz. Reviewed at Filmbuehne am Steinplatz, Berlin, March 11, '83. Running time: 60 MINS.

Wolf Gremm's "The Last Year" could be caught in the German Series section of the Berlin Film Fest about the same time as Dieter Schidor's "The Wizard of Babylon" in the Info Show, and perhaps both docus should be seen back-to-back. They both deal with the last working days of Rainer Werner Fassbinder, who died at 37 (not 36, as most biographies state) in circumstances that inspire legends, biographies, and personal documentaries.

Gremm's own "Kamikaze 1989" stars RWF in his last acting role. Both this film and Fassbinder's last, "Querelle," were lensed in Berlin. During the work on these pics, RWF stayed on as guest of Gremm and his producer-wife, Regina Ziegler.

We see Gremm directing Fassbinder in "Kamikaze" and clips from this pic. There are also several intimate close-ups of RWF shooting "Querelle," but without clips of the film introduced for contrast. What's revealing is the wear-and-tear on the director's countenance, his heavy dependence on bourbon-and-ginger ale during working hours, and a passion for every detail of film production in its stylistic perfection (particularly the framing of a shot and an intuitive

knowledge of how one shot relates to another).

"The Last Year" was unspooled on Second Television shortly after RWF's death. It should find its way to international fests featuring retros or selected features from Fassbinder's film legacy. —Holl.

Ostanovilsya Poyesd
(The Train Stops Here)
(RUSSIAN-COLOR)

Berlin, March 14.

A Mosfilm Production, Moscow; world rights, Goskino, Moscow. Features entire cast. Directed by Vadim Adbrashitov. Only credits available. Reviewed at Sovexport Screening Room, Berlin, March 14, '83. Running time: 90 MINS.
Cast: Anatoli Solonitsin.

Vadim Adbrashitov's "The Train Stops Here" (1982) follows in line with his other Mosfilm productions on moral problems, court cases, and questions of guilt. In each, investigators and other principal characters in the "search for truth" make moral decision in their own lives as a consequence of what they learned.

In "The Train Stops Here" Adbrashitov wraps his investigation in a tight narrative formula a la the American thriller. There's an investigator on the scene of an accident that might add up to a crime with several individuals guilty. A train locomotive crashed, and the death of the locomotive-driver is hailed by all as a "deed of bravery," for many lives were saved through his apparent self-sacrifice. It's the investigator's job to find out what really happened. In the meanwhile, a reporter has been assigned to write a popular story on the heroic engineer. The two bunk together in the same room at a crowded hotel in the provinces.

It turns out, ever so gradually, that many people were guilty of the crash and the engineer's death; in fact, the cause of everything happening for the worst was negligence all the way down the line. But the reporter is set on his story of heroism, and the common people appear to prefer this version of the accident to a mass implication of guilt. The investigator, by and bye, is urged to simply leave town. In the end, the story is written pretty much as prescribed, the population has the expected hero's burial, and a handful of guilty officials and workers at the station are left to face a collective guilty conscience.

Well-paced and acted in all principal roles, "The Train Stops Here" should find its way abroad for the broad critical recognition it deserves. About the time of the pic's tour through West German cinematheques in a Soviet Film Week, news emerged from Moscow related to just this theme: Party Secretary Yuri Andropov assailed in the Soviet press the waste due to

negligence and even corruption on the country's railway transportation lines. This was thesp Anatoli Solonitsin's last screen appearance before a premature death due to cancer. The gifted son (prominent in Tarkovsky and Shepitko films) plays the news reporter.
— Holl.

Larose, Pierrot Et La Luce
(CANADIAN-COLOR)

Berlin, Feb. 25.

Produced and distributed by Yoshimura Gagnon Inc. Produced by Yuri Yoshimura Gagnon, Claude Gagnon. Directed, written and edited by Claude Gagnon. Features entire cast. Camera (color), Andre Pelletier; art direction, Jacques Tardif; music, June Wallack; sound, Louis Dupire. Reviewed at the Berlin Film Festival, Feb. 25, 1983. Running time: 101 MINS.
Jacques Larose .... Richard Niquette
Pierrot Joyal .... Luc Matte
La Luce .... Louise Portal
Secretary .... Celine Jacques
Notary .... Daniel St-Pierre
Marilou .... Noemie Gelinas
Suzanne .... Camille Pelletier
Ti-Georges Tanguay .... Alain Gelinas
Johanne .... Madeleine Dubreuil

"Larose, Pierrot et la Luce" marks the second dramatic feature for Quebec-born, Japanese-trained filmmaker Claude Gagnon. The odd, comic tale of an unlikely trio is unlike to attract a large audience in Quebec or abroad. There's just too much whimsey and not enough substance.

Action turns on Jacques Larose's (Richard Niquette) inheritance of an old house in a small Quebec town. He decides to quit his civil service job to renovate the structure. However, he's ill-equipped to take on the task. So, he attempts to enlist his childhood friend Pierrot Joyal (Luc Matte) in the endeavour.

The job allows both men to escape other things which have consumed and frustrated their lives. Neither has ever been a success professionally or romantically. The house is to be their act of redemption, so Pierrot signs on, quits the bars and brings along current girlfriend, la Luce (Louise Portal).

It's difficult to understand why la Luce tolerates the men's childish behavior. They argue relentlessly and Pierrot winds up in the bars after one of these differences.

Gagnon paints a disparaging portrait of his principals which he attempts to shore up with humor quite unsuccessfully. Pierrot, in particular, seems a hopeless case and Larose is extremely pathetic. Yet, Gagnon insists on pulling out some eleventh hour optimism.

He concocts a Mexican holiday for the trio which allows Larose to look for a woman for whom he's been carrying a flame for years. The device is wholly artificial and capped off with the trio's return to

open a Mexican restaurant in the renovated house.

"Larose, Pierrot et la Luce" is consistent in forcing both its drama and humor on an audience. However, rather than effecting charm, one resents the characters' actions and attitudes and remains confused at what keeps them together.

Performances and technical work is good but hardly up to the task of overcoming the script. Commercial prospects outside Quebec appear limited to festivals and the picture is unlikely to stir much interest or recognition at home.
—Klad.

Eisenhans
(Strange Fruits)
(WEST GERMAN-B&W)

Berlin, March 8.

A Bavaria Film Studios Production, Munich, in coproduction with Westdeutscher Rundfunk (WDR), Cologne; world rights, Bavaria Atelier, Munich. Producer, Helmut Krapp. Directed by Tankred Dorst. Features entire cast. Screenplay, Dorst, Ursula Ehler; camera (black & white), Juergen Juerges; music, Bert Grund; editing, Stefan Arnsten; sets and costumes, Peter Pabst; sound, Guenther Stadelmann; production manager, Lutz Hengst. Reviewed at Berlin Film Fest (Forum), Feb. 25, '83. Running time: 100 MINS.
Schroth .... Gerhard Olschewski
Marga .... Susanne Lothar
Frau Schroth .... Hannelore Hoger
Habek .... Michael Habeck
Feininger .... Hans Michael Rehberg
Ingrid .... Angelika Milster
Innkeeper .... Helmut Pigge
Hilde .... Angelika Bartsch
Ida .... Sofie Keeser
Social Worker .... Irm Hermann
Edi .... Dieter Gackstetter
Furniture Salesman ...... Dieter Augustin
Fiancee .... Udo Suchan
Andi .... Martin May
Dream Figure .... Gisela Koenig
Guests .... Werner Wettermann
                     Hans Joachim Wettermann

A member of Germany's literati, Tankred Dorst made his first independently directed film, "Mosch," in 1980 and has now followed with this Forum of Young Cinema entry, "Strange Fruits" (the literal translation of German title "Eisenhans" is on the order of "Iron Jack"). He has often been associated in the past with theatre, film and television director Peter Zadek on various collaborative efforts. Dorst ranks with the top echelon of German dramatists and writers for two decades now.

"Strange Fruits" is about incest. It concerns a beer-truck driver who has had a long standing relationship with his employer: as "Iron Jack" he protected his weakling schoolmate in their youth. But the strongman has a retarded daughter, whom he also wants to protect above all and prefers her company over that of his wife and older daughter. However, the more time Eisenhans spends in his free time with the simple-minded Marga, the more the neighbors are up in arms over the scandalous affair. Finally, a social worker manages to have the girl sent to a pastor's family in another town before a family tragedy takes place.

Lensed in black-and-white by ace cameraman Juergen Juerges, "Strange Fruits" works its screen magic for the first half, then begins to burst at the seams for lack of a fitting denouement to a promising narrative line. Thesp performances and production credits are top-grade as befits the current quality work emerging from the Bavaria Studios in Munich. Pic deserves a fest slot, but offshore chances are possible only with special handling. —Holl.

Hakhoref Ha'Acharon
(The Last Winter)
(ISRAELI-COLOR)

Tel Aviv, Feb. 14.

A Lerko Films Productions. Produced by Ya'akov Kotzky, Avi Lerner and Mota Garfung. Stars Kathleen Quinlan, Yona Elian. Directed by Riki Shelach. Screenplay, Riki Shelach, Yona Elian, Nava Semel, Dror Schwartz, based on an original idea by Dan Wolman; camera (color), Amnon Salomon; editor, Kevin Connor; music, Nahum Heyman. Reviewed in Tel Aviv, Feb. 14, 1983. Running time: 90 MINS.
Cast: Kathleen Quinlan, Yona Elian, Steven Macht, Zippora ,Peled, Michael Schneider, Brian Aron, Yehuda Fuchs.

This is a first attempt to develop Israeli production in a new direction. Shot in English with two actors, Kathleen Quinlan and Macht, who have some appeal in the international market, it is already sold for tv in several territories. This Lerko production has cost at least three times as much as an average local film but, supposedly, has the chance to recover most of it.

To director Riki Shelach's credit, he handles his first feature smoothly and concedes nothing to the normal standard of American tv features, with which he will probably have to compete. The story, based on an idea by an Israeli filmmaker, Dan Wolman, exploits one of the painful topics this area has to face, touching only the human interest side of it, and adroitly avoiding any sort of political involvement.

Quinlan plays an American who comes to Israel, immediately after the first truce during the Yom Kippur War, for her husband has volunteered to go to the front, and no news has reached her since his mobilization. Pestering the officers in charge of disappeared persons, she meets an Israeli journalist in a similar predicament. While watching films of war prisoners in an Egyptian camp, both believe they have identified their husbands in the same person. First, each reacts spitefully towards the other, but as time goes by and no additional proof is made available and no more information seeps through from Egypt, a friendship blossoms

between the two women, which leads them to identify with the other's plight.

Flashbacks indicate that the American couple were going through a period of crisis before the war, while the Israeli journalist bears a heavy burden of guilt for preferring her career to her baby, in spite of her husband's wish.

While everything is kept on a very emotional and melodramatic level, no attempt is made to go deeper into the psychological and political factors behind the people concerned, which could have complicated its merchandising by adding controversial material. The result is a painful but pretty accurate reminder of late 1973 in Israel and the mood prevailing at the time, something that has been too often ignored by the rush of events since that time.

Amnon Salomon and Nahum Heyman have been both awarded, for the camera work and the music, and if Quinlan and Yoan Elian hit a false note, here and there, the reason might be Shelach's lack of experience. Macht, in a guest performance, lends a convincing present to the character of the released POW. —Edna.

Das Beil Von Wandsbek
(The Axe of Wandsbek)
(EAST GERMAN-B&W)

Berlin, March 7.

A DEFA Film Production, East Berlin; world rights, DEFA Aussenhandel, East Berlin. Features entire cast. Directed by Falk Harnack. Screenplay, Wolfgang Staudte, Werner Joerg Lueddecke, based on Arnold Zweig's novel; camera (black and white), Robert Baberske; sets, Erich Zander, Karl Schneider; music, Ernst Roters. Reviewed at Arsenal-Kino, Berlin, March 3, '83. Running time: 90 MINS.
Cast: Erwin Geschonneck (Albert Teetjen), Kaethe Braun (Stine Teejen), Geflon Helmke (Physician), Willy A. Klainau (Footh), Arthur Schroeder, Ursula Meissner, Hellmuth Hinzelmann, Blandine Ebinger, Hilde Sessak, Claus Holm, Erika Dannhoff, Fritz Wisten, Albert Garbe, Hermann Stoevesand. Gert Schaefer, Maly Delschaft, Claus-Peter Luettgen, Raimund Schelcher, Gisela May.

The late preem of Falk Harnack's 1951 DEFA production, "The Axe of Wandsbek," so far as West Berlin and West Germany are concerned, was greeted with a full house at the Arsenal Kino on the occasion of the writer-producer-director's 70th birthday, the event capped by moving speeches by dignitaries from East and West Berlin. The print was made available by the East German archive for the eight-film Harnack retro, and due to the fact that this is the uncut version of the long-forbidden film, "The Axe of Wandsbek" scores as an authentic premiere some 30 years after its production.

Harnack's life career is of special interest to historians of every ilk. He was a member of the Munich resistance group, the Scholls'

"White Rose" movement, and stood before Peoples Court Judge Roland Freisler in 1943, winning acquittal only for lack of evidence. Thereafter, while on the front lines as a soldier, he deserted and joined the Greek Resistance. After the war, he was engaged at various theatres in Germany as a director and artistic advisor, then took a position at DEFA in East Berlin at the end of the 1940s, for which he served as artistic director.

His first film production, "The Axe of Wandsbek," was based on the Arnold Zweig novel published in 1947. Shortly after the film's problems with the East German censors, Harnack left East for West Berlin to become a noted film, stage, and television director there and in West Germany.

"The Axe of Wandsbek" — recently filmed again by Horst Koenigstein and Heinrich Breloer, in a Norddeutscher Rundfunk (NDR) tv-production — originated in book form in exile; in fact, it was first published in Hebrew in Haifa in 1943. The tale was derived from fact: in 1938 in the Hamburg suburb of Wandsbek, a butcher was hired to execute four Communist demonstrators during a harbor strike with a meat-axe. Zweig penned his story at intervals between 1938 and 1942, finishing it while on the move in London. He tried to analyze the Nazi mentality as a whole, and fairly succeeded in doing so from the distance of his forced exile.

Erwin Geschonneck_ plays the butcher, whose fate follows him like Macbeth's bloody deeds until he has lost all his customers; experiences the despairing suicide of his wife, and is driven in the end to his own self-destruction. Credits are all top grade, and pic could still find an echo abroad at fests and retros.
—Holl.

Avant La Bataille
(Before The Battle)
(BELGIAN-COLOR-DOCU)

Berlin, March 16.

A Politifilm Production, Brussels, in collaboration with Polish Cinematography. Features entire cast. Written and directed by Janusz Kijowski. Camera (color), Patrice Payen; music, Fabien Audooren; editing, Dominique Van Goolen. Reviewed at ZDF Screening Room, Berlin, March 16, '83. Running time: 90 MINS.
Cast: Simon Zaleski, Seweryn Blumsztajn, Marek Edelmann, Tadeusz Konwicki, Jacek Kuron, Adam Michnik, Lech Walesa.

Janusz Kijowski made a series of important features — "Index" (1977), "Kung Fu" (1979), and "Voices" (1981) — during the recent Polish Film Revival, and then departed for Belgium to make this documentary coproduction with Polish Solidarity filmmakers and a Belgian camera team. Lensed in October-November 1981, before the curtain fell in December, it was air-

ed last January on West Germany's Second Channel (ADF) and is, without a doubt, an authentic statement on the artistic aspirations of the Solidarity movement. Further, in light of the current "sit-down strike" within the Polish film industry (little work is being done nowadays in film and tv studios), "Before the Battle" stands as an informative, uncompromising statement on the status quo of Polish Cinematography.

"Before the Battle" is a political documentary. The discussion in both features on the unrest in March, 1968 forms a point-of-departure. "Before the Battle": A Polish-Jewish actor, Simon Zaleski, left the country in 1968 on the grounds that a recognizable form of antiSemitism was rearing its head once more, and thereafter took up residence in Belgium. Now, 12 years later, he and his friends in Belgium decide to look into the question of free democratic unions and artistic freedom in the performing arts.

"Before the Battle" follows Zaleski on his search for the truth. With Kijowski looking over his shoulder, he visits his former wife; spends time with a Solidarity union, and interviews Lech Walesa. He talks to workers and farmers, attends religious services in churches and synagogues, and chats with the man-on-the-street. The optimistic side is clearly visible, but some advise him to return.

The document features key individuals; Lech Walesa, Jacek Kuron (founder of "Core"), Adam Michnik, Marek Edelmann, Tadeusz Mazowiecki, Karol Modzelewski, Jan Rulewski, Tadeusz Konwicki, and many others. Zaleski and Kijowski visit Konwicki during the location shooting of the latter's adaptation of Czeslaw Milosz's "Issa's Valley," and footage from the production is presented in the docu. He also includes a synagog clip out of Jerzy Kawalerowicz's "Austeria." Both films have been recently completed, and can be currently seen at selected film festivals.

"Before the Battle" accomplishes its purpose without extra commentary or an analysis of the situation. It's simply an atmospheric portrait of the times. Pic should be seen in a fest slot, although the material is now somewhat dated. In the future, it will certainly interest film historians and docu enthusiasts, to say nothing of solidarity fans. —Holl.

Lone Wolf McQuade
(COLOR)

Chuck Norris and the baddies mix it up near the border. Good b.o. in action situations.

Hollywood, April 4.

An Orion release of an 1818 Production in association with Top Kick Prods. Produced by Yoram Ben-Ami, Steve Carver. Directed by Carver. Features entire cast. Screenplay, B.J. Nelson, from story by H. Kaye Dyal. Nelson; camera (Deluxe color), Roger Shearman; editor, Anthony Redman; music, Francesco De Masi; production design, Norm Baron; set decoration, Robert Zilliox; sound, Robert Wald, associate producers, Kathryn Petty, Aaron Norris; assistant director, Jerram Swartz. Reviewed at the Orion Screening Room, West L.A., April 4, 1983. (MPAA Rating: PG). Running time: 107 MINS.

J.J. McQuade	Chuck Norris
Rawley Wilkes	David Carradine
Lola Richardson	Barbara Carrera
Jackson	Leon Isaac Kennedy
Kayo	Robert Beltran
Dakota	L.Q. Jones
Sally	Dana Kimmell
T. Tyler	R.G. Armstrong
Jefe	Jorge Cervera Jr.
Molly	Sharon Farrell
Falcon	Daniel Frishman
Snow	William Sanderson
Burnside	John Anderson

Fans of Soldier of Fortune magazine will think they've been ambushed and blown away to heaven by "Lone Wolf McQuade." Every conceivable type of portable weapon on the world market today is tried out by the macho warriors on both sides of the law in this modern western, which pits Texas Ranger Chuck Norris and his cohorts against multifarious baddies who like to play rough. B.o. for Norris' pics has slipped on his last couple of outings, but there's enough hard action here to amply satisfy intended audience, so results on Orion's first inhouse production since taking over Filmways should be satisfactory.

Opening sequence, showing the grizzled Norris busting up a gang of Mexican horse rustlers, makes it clear that film's primary source of inspiration is Sergio Leone. Brooding closeups, broad acting and gunpoint confrontations all ape the Italian master, and Francesco De Masi's music throughout sounds like a recycling of Ennio Morricone, particularly his score for "The Good, The Bad And The Ugly."

Needless to say, the imitation pales in the shadow of the original, and B.J. Nelson's screenplay fails to hew to a sufficiently straight and clean narrative line, but the tensions of the characters are such that it seems that whenever someone new walks into the frame, someone else feels the need to cock his gun, and frequently to use it.

Being a Norris picture, and one with David Carradine, no less, there are also a couple of occasions when only karate will do to settle the score, but it's clear that the star is now trying to carve a slightly different, less specialized screen persona for himself, more along the lines of Clint Eastwood (as if in homage, he at one point visits Eastwood Hospital in the film).

Norris' sagebrush Dirty Harry likes to operate alone and tries to shed the Hispanic greenhorn imposed upon him by his boss. Young partner is played by Robert Beltran, an immensely likeable actor who had title role in "Eating Raoul," and he's saddled with some of the most embarrassing "Ay Chihuahua"-type dialog heard since the heyday of Cisco and Pancho. That Beltran manages to ultimately emerge with his dignity intact reps a sizable tribute to the thesp.

Vile Carradine is in the business of hijacking U.S. Army weapons shipments and selling them to Central American terrorist groups. Uneasily allied with Carradine is the Mexican Mafia, and this may be the first mainline American pic to make a connection between latter group and contempo insurgents.

Norris and FBI agent Leon Isaac Kennedy finally locate Carradine's secret airstrip, and after a setback there, track him down at a compound loaded with all manner of armaments. Macho men in fatigues fight it out with bazookas, grenades, machine guns and tanks and, after an obligatory karate fight between Norris and Carradine, a high-octane finale sends most of the lowlifes to their rewards.

Some domestic scenes featuring Norris with his daughter and estranged or divorced wife are inserted in rudimentary fashion, but it's impossible to figure out what beauteous Barbara Carrera is up to; at one moment she's hanging out with Carradine, who killed her husband, and at the next she's bedding down and mud wrestling with Norris.

Director Steve Carver lifts motifs from all sorts of earlier pics and doesn't manage to maintain the Leone-esque intensity of the opening scene, but achieves the bottom line of getting lots of rough stuff up there on the screen. Tech credits, including a wide variety of stunts and explosions, are all serviceable.
—*Cart.*

Street Kids
AUSTRALIAN-DOCU-COLOR-16m)

Melbourne, April 5.

A York Street Film Production in association with Film Victoria. Directed by Leigh Tilson and Rob Scott. Camera, (color), Leigh Tilson; sound, Rob Scott. No other credits provided. Screened at York St. Film Productions, Melbourne, March 24, 1983. Running time: 72 MINS.

A hauntingly honest examination of the plight of homeless teenagers is the gripping subject of this docu. Leigh Tilson and Rob Scott actually lived in a sleazy boarding house in an area of Melbourne that attracted these wayward youths, and consequently got to know the kids, establish trust and friendship, and thus pursue their filmmaking. Out of this relationship the kids in the pic were able to honestly verbalize their feelings of isolation, hopelessness, and powerlessness.

Docu combines close-up confessions by the kids, interviews with cops on the beat, revelations by a Jesuit street worker, and occasional peeps into kiddie prostitution solicitations and drug taking. What emerges is the surprising articulation of these teens, their emotional pleas for establishment of family relationships, their frustrations about their inability to change their situations, and their assessment of a bleak lifespan. Only snag for overseas is the occasional Down Under down-home accents, but the spirit of the speech is still communicated.

Tech qualities are admittedly shaky. While one filmmaker shot, the other sound recorded. They used available light at all times and at night filming they pushed the film stock way beyond its recommended limits.

But this unobtrusive process (on 16m) results in the docu's dignity and authenticity. The pic was shot in Melbourne, but the pervasiveness of this social dilemma in western society transcends its Aussie locale. —*Devo.*

Losin' It
(COLOR)

Not worth a search, but okay if stumbled upon.

Hollywood, March 31.

An Embassy Pictures release, produced by Bryan Gindoff and Hannah Hempstead. Directed by Curtis Hanson. Features entire cast. Exec producers, Joel B. Michaels, Garth H. Drabinsky. Screenplay, B.W.L. Norton; camera (color), Gil Taylor; editor, Richard Halsey; sound, Kirk Francis; production design, Robb Wilson King; assistant director, Patrick Crowley; art direction, Vance Lorenzini; music, Ken Wannberg. Reviewed at MGM Studios, March 31, 1983. (MPAA rating: R.) Running time: 104 MINS.

Woody	Tom Cruise
Dave	Jackie Earle Haley
Spider	John Stockwell
Kathy	Shelley Long
Wendell	John P. Navin Jr.
El Jefe	Henry Darrow
Chuey	Hector Elias
Taxi Driver	Daniel Faraldo

"Losin' It" is a virtuous entry in the current cycle of deflower-power pics, aided by a talented young cast working hard at a light-weight project that should play off without great excitement, yet deserving no derision.

As often noted, the problem with porno is that there are only so many ways to show people having sex; the problem with films like "Losin'" is that there are only so many ways to show teenagers not having sex.

But director Curtis Hanson makes a commendable effort with a rather obvious story about three teenage boys who head for a wild weekend in Tijuana, hoping to trade hard cash for manly experience.

Though none is really very experienced, each is sophisticated to a stereotyped degree: There's the high-school hunk, John Stockwell, who's actually had a girl; the blustering faker, Jackie Earle Haley, whose experience is limited to his own imagination; and the sensitive innocent, Tom Cruise, who isn't sure he wants it, but is destined for the best time to be had by all.

Naturally, they are acompanied by wimpy John P. Navin Jr., brought along only because he has the necessary cash to make the trip possible. And along the way they pick up crazy — but nice — Shelley Long, on the lam from her husband and heading for a Mexican divorce she really doesn't want.

South of the border, the group encounters the friendly-like car upholsterer Hector Elias, the unfriendly-like policeman Henry Darrow and the funny-like taxi driver Daniel Faraldo, winding up in various social disasters, solved naturally enough by a car chase.

This doesn't sound like much and it isn't. But each of the leading characters tries hard to get as much out of the part as possible and the picture is a solid credit for all involved. Especially good are Haley, Navin and Darrow.

"Losin' it," to be sure, is not a find. But it's far from a lost cause.
—*Har.*

Io, Chiara E Lo Scuro
Me, Light and Darkness)
(ITALIAN-COLOR)

Rome, April 4.

A Titanus release, produced by Gianfranco Piccioli and Marco Valsaria for Hera Productions. Stars Francesco Nuti. Directed by Maurizio Ponzi. Screenplay, Francesco Nuti, Maurizio Ponzi, Franco Ferrini, Enrico Oldoini; camera (color), Carlo Cerchio; editing, Sergio Montanari; sets, Giudi Iossia; music, Barluna. Reviewed at Ariston Cinema, Rome, April 4, 1983. Running time: 103 MINS.

Francesco	Francesco Nuti
Chiara	Giuliana De Sio
"Scuro"	Marcello Lotti

A small but savory all-Italo comedy centered around champion pool playing. Helmer Maurizio Ponzi and cabaret comic Francesco Nuti team up a second time in a young-spirited, pulled together pic bound to cop some of this year's prizes. The very fact this unpretentious film doesn't try to dodge its local Roman setting and aim at being "international" boosts its prospects for a broader off-shore quality market (including fests). It is doing brisk business at home.

Star of the show is thesp and co-writer Nuti, a personable, good-looking young comedian who leans heavily on his Tuscan background to flesh out his character. A lonely hotel porter, Nuti turns into a tiger at night in the neighborhood pool hall, where his prowess nets him a surprise win over the swarthy, undisputed champ known as "Scuro" (Marcello Lotti). Nuti's decline begins when Lotti coaxes him into playing for money. At the same time the forces of good appear in the guise of a pretty neighbor, Chiara (or "light"), played by Giuliana De Sio as anything but an angelic character, who astutely pulls him out of his woeful debts.

Using only a handful of sets and a lot of skillful shooting (thanks also to the moody nighttime lensing of cameraman Carlo Cerchio), helmer Maurizio Ponzi takes a giant step beyond the first Nuti vehicle ("Oh What A Quiet Night"). Result is an absorbing narrative film lensed with confidence and rhythm. A large share of pic's fascination is watching Lotti as Scuro (thrice Italian pool champ in real life) make impossible billiard shots.

But even more amazing is star Nuti's phenomenal stunt playing. The actor trained for months to be up to the part; almost all his dazzling shots are done in unedited single takes, where it is obvious no double was used. This adds enormously to pic's credibility.

Nuti projects a feeling of warmth and humanity into his role, in stark contrast to costar De Sio's cold defensiveness slowly turning into trust. De Sio, a newcomer who is on the crest of popularity right now with three films out simultaneously, is a mannered actress but also a trouper (she studied saxophone playing for her part as Chiara, and brings it off convincingly).

Well done technical credits.
—Yung.

Mortelle Randonee
(Deadly Circuit)
(FRENCH-COLOR)

Paris, April 3.

GEF/CCFC release of a Telema/TF 1 Film production. Produced by Charles Gassot. Stars Isabelle Adjani, Michel Serrault. Directed by Claude Miller. Screenplay, Michel and Jacques Audiard, from novel "Eye of the Beholder" by Marc Behm; camera (color), Pierre Lhomme; editor, Albert Jurgenson; art director, Jean-Pierre Kohut-Svelko; costumes, Emilie Poirot & Renee Renard; makeup, Catherine Desmaemacker; sound, Paul Laine; music, Carla Bley; production manager, Bernard Grenet. Reviewed at the Publicis Theatre, Paris, April 1, 1983. Running time: 120 MINS.
The Eye .... Michel Serrault
Catherine .... Isabelle Adjani
Schmith Boulanger ..... Genevieve Page
The Pale Man .... Guy Marchand
Woman in Grey .... Stephane Audran
Ralph .... Sami Frey
Madeleine .... Macha Meril

After their tour-de-force collaboration with the theatrical limitations of the 1981 drama, "Garde a Vue," screenwriter Michel Audiard and director Claude Miller let out all stops for "Mortelle Randonnee," an extravagant, generally gripping thriller whose obsessive protagonists carom around Europe like uncontrolled pinballs.

Isabelle Adjani and Michel Serrault are in top form as a gold-digging pathological murderess who sweeps around the continent seducing and slaughtering rich young socialites, and a desperately neurotic private detective who follows her bloody trail and soon becomes her protector and father-figure.

Like "Garde a Vue," pic is based on a Yank detective novel: "Eye of the Beholder" by Marc Behm, set in the U.S. and spread over a period of two decades. Audiard, who was taken with the book to the point of buying the film rights, went to work with his son, Jacques, adroitly transposing the action to Europe and compressing the time span to a neat, but credible year and a half. The result is tainted by some arty pretense — the Oedipal intrigue is so overladen with notations and symbols as to put Freudians in a cold sweat — but it's dramatically trenchant and Audiard's special gift for tart dialog, spiced with sardonic humor, is in full evidence. The writer who can sometimes appear extremely lazy, has obviously invested himself completely in the project.

Adjani is beautiful and disturbingly mysterious as the chameleon-like criminal who, to erase the memories of a miserable childhood and a pathetically impotent father, embarks on a career as a female Landru, executing husbands and lovers with blood-curdling abandon, and moving immediately on to her next prey.

On her trail is Serrault, as the morbid professional investigator who remains traumatized by the death of a daughter he never really knew and whom he cannot identify in a classroom photo he has touted around for years.

In his tortured mind, he begins to view Adjani as his lost offspring and soon becomes a detached accomplice-by disposing of the bodies to prevent her arrest. But when Adjani seriously falls in love with a blind architect (Sami Frey), Serrault is seized by jealousy and causes the latter's death. The despairing Adjani resumes her deadly itinerary and at last seeks sanctuary in her home town, where Serrault makes a final, ineffectual attempt to save her from a narrowing police dragnet. Rather than surrender, the girl commits suicide; the detective subsequently realizes his own long-standing death wish.

Miller who has a penchant for dark, obsessional personages and intrigues (as witness his Patricia Highsmith adaptation, "This Strange Sickness"), directs with feverish intensity, sustaining an atmosphere of protracted, glossy nightmare. Though there's a lot less here than meets the eye, one is enthralled by film's breathless virtuosity. Lenser Pierre Lhomme, designer Jean-Pierre Kohut-Svelko, editor Albert Jurgenson and composer Carla Bley can all lay claim to part of the pic's dazzle, and holding power.

Supporting players are all excellent, especially Genevieve Page as Serrault's affected agency boss, Sami Frey as Adjani's soft-spoken lover, and Guy Marchand and Stephane Audran as a pair of sleazy blackmailers.

Producer Charles Gassot has spared no expense in providing the action with on-location filming in Belgium, Italy, Germany and France. Pic has done only moderately good business here, but has strong prospects for offshore festival and commercial playoffs.
—Len.

Valley Girl
(COLOR)

It's a tubular girl movie, fer shurr.

Hollywood, April 7.

An Atlantic Releasing Corp. release, written and produced by Wayne Crawford and Andrew Lane. Directed by Martha Coolidge. Features entire cast. Exec producers, Thomas Coleman, Michael Rosenblatt; camera (Color Lab Color), Frederick Elmes; editor, Eva Gordos; sound, David Brownlow; production design, Mary Delia Javier; assistant directors, Nancy Israel, Michael Hacker; music, various artists. Reviewed at the Writers Guild Theatre, Beverly Hills, April 7, 1983. (MPAA rating: R.) Running time: 95 MINS.
Randy .... Nicolas Cage
Julie .... Deborah Foreman
Loryn .... Elizabeth Daily
Tommy .... Michael Bowen
Fred .... Cameron Dye
Stacey .... Heidi Holicker
Suzie .... Michelle Meyrink
Samantha .... Tina Theberge
Beth Brent .... Lee Purcell
Sarah Richman .... Colleen Camp
Steve Richman .... Frederic Forrest

It may be sexist to say that "Valley Girl" shows the clear imprint of its female director. If so, it's nonetheless positive because the end result is far superior to the usual teen sexploitation picture cranked out by a lot of leering males. If the young audience relates, it could do snappy summer business.

"Valley" is very good simply because director Martha Coolidge obviously cares about her two lead characters and is privileged to have a couple of fine young performers, Nicolas Cage and Deborah Foreman, to make the audience care.

To be sure, the script by producers Wayne Crawford and Andrew Lane does not offer anything profoundly original in another variation of the problems of a cross-cultural love affair. But the dialog is crisp, the thoughts are heart-felt and there are a number of chuckles along the way.

Though surrounded by a surprising number of able young performers for a low-budget feature like this, Cage and Foreman elevate what could have been typical teen silliness to an involving level.

As the title suggests, she's a definitive valley girl, mouthing all the nonsensical catch phrases recently popularized in song and book. He's a Hollywood punker who normally wouldn't venture over the hills into the square valley, except to crash a party where they meet.

Their blazing romance, which shocks her high-school friends, ultimately becomes too socially threatening for Foreman and she cuts it off. Cage's pain and frustration over the rejection is quite affecting, as is Foreman's confusion and guilt.

For a change, there aren't any cartoon problem adults on hand as there often are in these pictures. True, the parents may be a little oversexed or absurdly tolerant, but never clearly beyond belief. Interesting in that regard, is the presence as Foreman's ex-hippie parents of Frederic Forrest and Colleen Camp, a pair with far bigger feature credits which leads to suspicion they are probably appearing here as a favor. Clearly, their parts do not measure up to their talents.

Of course, Coolidge does not eschew nudity and rough language — this after all is a picture for young people. But it's all relatively restrained and reasonably in context, helping "Valley" to reach its peak. —Har.

Un Dimanche de Flics
(A Cops' Sunday)
(FRENCH-COLOR)

Paris, March 23.

Prodis release of a Filmax/SFPC coproduction. Produced by Gabriel Boustani. Stars Victor Lanoux, Jean Rochefort, Barbara Sukowa. Written and directed by Michel Vianey, based on the novel, "Off Duty" by Andrew Coburn. Camera (color), Robbie Muller; music, Jean-Pierre Mas; sound, Bernard Ortion; art director, Jean-Pierre Bazerolles; editor, Pierre Gillette; associate producers, Nader Atassi and Bashar Nasri; production manager, Anne-Marie Otte. Reviewed at the Publicis screening room, Paris, March 15, 1983. Running time: 99 MINS.
Franck .... Victor Lanoux
Rupert .... Jean Rochefort
Patricia .... Barbara Sukowa
Fred .... Maurice Biraud
Dansevitch .... Jean-Roger Milo
The Lawyer .... Armin Mueller Stahl

Writer-director Michel Vianey, who ladled a lot of soupy psychoanalytical notions over a routine thriller plot in his last film, "Un Assassin Qui Passe," is back with another psychological crime drama. "Un Dimanche de Flics" is less murky than its predecessor, but no less predictable and dramatically lame, despite its sturdy male leads.

Based on a Yank mystery novel (again!), pic deals with two middle-aged plainclothes cops (Victor Lanoux and Jean Rochefort) who intercept a heroin pickup and decide to chuck the dope and keep the loot for themselves. This doesn't sit well with the underworld kingpin who arranged the affair; he wants his money back and is ready to kill as many cops as it takes to get it. He puts a psychopathic hood on their trail, who viciously murders a retired detective buddy (Maurice Biraud, in his last screen appearance) who took part in their unethical action. Lanoux decides to surrender his part of the appropriated money, but Rochefort won't let go and is finally shot down.

That's not all. There's a secondary dramatic line concerning Rochefort's male menopause crisis. He meets a beautiful young girl and decides to leave his wife to shack up with her. Lanoux, who's always been in love with his buddy's spouse, decides to move in with her. Not surprisingly, Rochefort's new companion proves fickle and the cop wants his wife back.

Vianey weaves these two strands together to no real thematic or dramatic effect and the while film suffers from obvious character development and equally foreseeable narrative turns.

Lanoux is acceptable in his role, more so than Rochefort, who cannot give much depth to a transparent part. Rochefort's wife is played, for no apparent reason, by Polish actress Barbara Sukowa, who has virtually nothing to do except look concerned. A German, Armin Mueller Stahl, plays the gangster, complete with a neck brace a la Stroheim.

Tech credits are routine, including the lensing by Robby Muller. —Len.

Sans Soleil
(Sunless)
(FRENCH-COLOR)

Paris, April 7.

An Argos Films production and release. Produced by Anatole Dauman. Written, directed, photographed & edited by Chris Marker. Additional footage, Sana Na N'hada, Jean-Michel Humeau, Mario Marret, Eugenio Bentivoglio, Daniele Tessier, Haroun Tazieff; assistant director, Pierre Camus; assistant editors, Anne-Marie L'Hote, Catherine Adda; mixing, Antoine Bonfanti, Paul Bertault; special effects, Hayao Yamaneko. Reviewed at the Studio Action Christine. Paris, April 1, 1983. Running time: 100 MINS.
Narrators: Florence Delay (French soundtrack). Alexandra Stewart (English soundtrack).

The singular French non-fiction filmmaker Chris Marker pursues his solitary path away from beaten docu tracks with this intriguing feature-length film essay, shot over a period of several years, in Japan and Africa essentially.

Much in the line of "documented point of view" formula (coined by Jean Vigo), "Sans Soleil" would appear to be a reflection of the themes of time and memory, though one viewing doesn't seem sufficient to determine if the film has a discernible center. Rather, Marker has "composed" his work, in a musical sense (The title "Sunless" refers to a song cycle by Modest Mussorgsky). Though one may not see the point of it, the audiovisual melody casts its spell.

Marker invents a fictitious veteran cameraman who has travelled extensively and who corresponds regularly with the female commentator (Florence Delay in the French version, Alexandra Stewart on the English track), to whom he confides his impressions. The poles of his wanderings are Japan, a civilization bloated by technological advances, and some of the most wretched corners of Black Africa; but there are also digressions to Iceland, France and San Francisco, where the protagonist conducts an obsessive pilgrimage to the sites used by Alfred Hitchcock in "Vertigo."

Full of anecdotes and acute observations, both in image and text, "Sans Soleil" will undoubtedly be a much discussed item for festival circuits and specialized art house situations.

Producer-distrib Anatole Dauman has quietly booked it into a single Paris art cinema, where it is discreetly holding its own. Pic is slated for Filmex this month in the English version. —Len.

De Vlaschaard
(The Flax Field)
(BELGIAN-DUTCH-COLOR)

Brussels, Feb. 7.

A Belga Films release of a coproduction Kunst En Kino (Brussels) — Cine-Vista (Hilversum). Written and directed by Jan Gruyaert, based on the novel "De Vlaschaard" by Stijn Streuvels. Produced by Jan Van Raemdonck. Associate producer, Gerrit Visscher; camera (color), Ben Tenniglo; editor, Susana Rossberg; art direction, Philippe Graff; sound, Peter Flamman; music, Rogier van Otterloo; costumes, Yan Tax; assistant director, Hans Kemna; production manager Gerard Vercruysse; unit manager; Jef Van de Water. Reviewed at the Albert I theatre, Palais des Congres, Brussels, Jan. 29, 1983. Running time: 90 MINS.
Vermeulen . . . . Vic Moeremans
Barbele . . . . Dora Van der Groen
Louis . . . . Rene van Sambeek
Schellebelle . . . . Gusta Gerritsen
Bert . . . . Dirk Celis
Jan . . . . Daan Hugaert
Ivo . . . . Mark Peeters
Martha . . . . Mieke De Groote

"The Flax Field" is a new screen version of the best known novel, written in 1907, flemish author Stijn Streuvels, of whom it has been said that he is to Flanders what Knut Hamsun is to Norway. His realistic tale of simple countryside life was previously filmed by the Germans — under the title "Wenn die Sonne wieder scheint" ("when the sun shines again") — during the Nazi occupation of Belgium in the Second World War.

At the centre of the rural drama, where an often hostile nature entirely dominates the peasants, is the enmity between a stubborn, disgruntled farmer and his son in a little village in the West of Flanders. The tyrannical father thinks unjustly that his son threatens his authority. Tensions flare up over the choice where the flax should be sown. The old man, who doesn't want to admit that his strength is ebbing, is also upset because his son falls in love with the new milkmaid, whom he believes an unfitting match for his heir. Events move to a tragic climax during which the son is nearly killed. The incident provokes the breakdown of the intolerant patriarch.

The story is dated, and the young helmer, himself, (this is his first commercial venture after his art film debut, "Incluis") doesn't seem to believe in the material. Power should come from within the strong central conflict, but the director constantly diverts attention with inserts of insects, plants, crops and idyllic images. The heavy-handed approach is particularly irritating in the ponderous photographic style and the artificial camera set-ups. Pic jumps from one undeveloped scene to another without any overall dramatic impact or concern.

In spite of all the insistent details (and over-worked close-ups), "The Flax Field" doesn't express any sincere feeling or understanding for the harsh reality of peasant life at the beginning of the century. Pic is further hampered by a poorly judged music score, stilted, unnatural dialogue and the flat acting of the younger thesps. Film's best moments are provided in the emotional confrontations between the old farmer and his submissive, suffering wife, mostly thanks to the sensitive acting of Dora Van der Groen. Another isolated, powerful moment, and one of great pictorial beauty, is the violent rainstorm across the fields.

On the whole, pic is uninvolving and may only attract an audience that detects a certain exotic quality in Flemish countrylife. —Pat.

Rumours Of Glory
(CANADIAN-COLOR-16 m)

Toronto, April 4.

An Extra Modern Production. Produced by Bill House and Peter Walsh. Associate producer, Bernie Finkelstein. With participation of the Canadian Film Development Corp. Directed by Martin Lavut. Features entire cast. Camera (color), Vic Sarin, Henri Fiks, Robert Fresco. Rene Ohashi, Barry Stone; editor, Les Brown; production design, Peter Kanter; stage designer, Jim Plaxton; assistant director, David Pamplin; sound, John Thomson; lighting, Frank Merino; soundtrack producer, Eugene Martynec; soundtrack engineer, Gary Gray. Reviewed at Simcom, Toronto, April 4, 1983. Running time: 80 MINS.
With Bruce Cockburn, Bob Disalle, Jonathon Goldsmith, Hugh Marsh, Kathryn Moses, Dennis Pendrith.

Concert films have tough sledding in theatrical release and "Rumours Of Glory" might be no exception. But it's such a careful and successful exercise in faithfully filming a concert by Canadian singer-composer Bruce Cockburn that it could be a hot tip for audiences who care to listen and not be jabbed by electric camera tricks to hype the music.

This effort is bang on. It's straightforward and succeeds in being no more than what it obviously planned to achieve.

Director Martin Lavut, ably aided by a five-camera team, keeps at a proper distance yet stays close enough, lenses virtually always on the stage and not jumpily intercut by shots of adoring fans.

Cockburn, who plays acoustic and electric guitar, sings and is backed by an excellent, crisp-sounding five-person band, delivers 15 strong songs he's written. They range from social commentary to mood pieces about loners, a sexy "Mama Just wants To Barrelhouse All Night Long" and the title piece, a gospel-peppered "Rumours Of Glory."

Refreshingly free of apparent mannerisms, Cockburn changes mood easily and gives no introduction to any number and no afterramble. Lyrics that are always compelling and music matter most here and the lack of chat makes the pic flow with a well-plotted energy.

A planned 35m print will have Dolby sound. As it is, the film is dandy for tv and runs this month on Canada's First Choice paycabler and debuts theatrically at Los Angeles Filmex. —Adil.

Rock & Rule
(CANADIAN-ANIMATED-COLOR)

Toronto, April 6.

MGM/UA release of a Nelvana Films production. Produced by Patrick Loubert, Michael Hirsh with participation of the Canadian Film Development Corp. Directed by Clive A Smith. Screenplay, Peter Sauder, John Halfpenny from story by Patrick Loubert and Peter Sauder; art direction, Clive A. Smith, Louis Krawgna; score composer, performer, Patricia Cullen; designer; design of principal characters, Frank Nissen; set design, Louis Krawagna, Don Marshall, Paul Rivoche; storyboard, Raymond Jafelice, Patrick Loubert, Michael Hirsh, Clive A. Smith. Camera (color), Leonora Hume; animators, Anne Marie Bardwell, Dave Brewster, Charles Boniface, Robin Budd,

Chuck Gammage, Frank Nissen, Bill Speers, Tom Sito, Gian-Franco Celestri; producer special animated effects, Norman Stangel; director animated special effects, Keith Ingham; editor, G. Scott Labarge; sound editor, Tom Jobin. Reviewed at Famous Players screening room, Toronto, April 5, 1983. (MPAA Rating: PG). Running time: 83 MINS.

Voices of Don Francks, Paul LeMat, Susan Roman, Sam Langevin, Dan Hennessy, Catherine O'Hara, Greg Duffell, Chris Wiggins, Brent Titcomb, Donny Burns, Martin Lavut, Catherine Gallant, Keith Hampshire, Melleny Brown, Anna Bourque, Nick Nichols, John Halfpenny, Maurice LaMarche.

Songs: "Angel's Song," "Invocation Song," Send Love Through," by Chris Stein and Deborah Harry, vocals Deborah Harry; "Pain & Suffering" by Iggy Pop and Ivan Kraal, vocals Iggy Pop; "My Name Is Mok," "Triumph" by Lou Reed, vocal, Lou Reed; "Born To Raise Hell," "I'm The Man," "Ohm Sweet Ohm" by Rick Nielsen, vocals Cheap Trick; "Dance, Dance, Dance" by Beloyd Taylor, vocal Earth Wind and Fire; "Hot Dogs & Sushi" by Patricia Cullen and Melleny Brown, vocals Melleny Brown.

———

"Rock & Rule," produced by Nelvana, Canadian animation house, is one of the first — but probably not the last — feature-length rock music cartoons.

It's the Saturday morning cartoon funnies come of age, with an appealing, appalling cartoon villain who has Mick Jagger's lips, acts like Peter O'Toole and sounds like Darth Vader, as well as a score featuring Deborah Harry, Cheap Trick, Lou Reed and Iggy Pop, although the best piece comes from Earth, Wind & Fire.

Its heart is in the '70s. Indeed, with Mok, the aging superstar (voice by Canadian actor-singer Don Francks), whose quest for power is the hinge on which the story swings, one can detect elements of Paul Williams' evil record mogul in "Phantom Of The Paradise."

Its target audience is in the '80s, that generation of rock fans, 14-24, who grew up after the Beatles parted and had at least a passing interest in the gutter glitter of Alice Cooper and Kiss.

Visually, the fantasy comes halfway between Disney and Heavy Metal magazine, full of effect and mood. Movement is minimal, although director Clive Smith has managed to disguise this kinetic inertia well.

The story is Victorian in its love of grime, squalor and suppressed, unexplained sexuality. Mok kidnaps Angel, the young singer with a young rock group. He needs her voice to summon up the demon who'll bring him even greater power.

With the exception of Beloyd Taylor's "Dance, Dance Dance" and EW&F's patently slick production of it, this is a decidedly second-rate collection of pieces. Only Lou Reed and Iggy Pop touch on the spirit of the project, not because of what they're singing but how they're singing it. They know future decadence when they've lived it. —Goda.

Flashdance
(COLOR)

———

Gals really get physical in femme "Saturday Night Fever." Some b.o. assured, but extent of fantasy appeal tough to gauge.

———

Hollywood, April 13.

A Paramount release of a Polygram Pictures production. Produced by Don Simpson. Jerry Bruckheimer. Executive producers, Peter Guber, Jon Peters. Directed by Adrian Lyne. Features entire cast. Screenplay, Tom Hedley, Joe Eszterhas, story by Hedley; camera (Movielab color), Don Peterman; editors, Bud Smith, Walt Mulconery; music supervision, Phil Ramone; original music, Giorgio Moroder; production design, Charles Rosen; set decoration, Marvin March; choreography, Jeffrey Hornaday; costume design, Michael Kaplan; sound (Dolby), Jim Webb; associate producers, Tom Jacobson, Lynda Rosen Obst; assistant director, Albert Shapiro. Reviewed at the Village Theatre, West L.A., April 13, 1983. (MPAA Rating: R.) Running time: 96 MINS.

Alex Owens	Jennifer Beals
Nick Hurley	Michael Nouri
Hanna Long	Lilia Skala
Jeanie Szabo	Sunny Johnson
Richie	Kyle T. Heffner
Johnny C.	Lee Ving
Jake Mawby	Ron Karabatsos
Kate Hurley	Belinda Bauer
Cecil	Malcolm Danare
Frank Szabo	Phil Bruns
Rosemary Szabo	Micole Mercurio

———

Watching "Flashdance" is pretty much like looking at MTV for 96 minutes. Virtually plotless, exceedingly thin on characterization and sociologically laughable, pic at least lives up to its title by offering an anthology of extraordinarily flashy dance numbers to the accompaniment of over a dozen high-powered tunes. Attempt at a femme "Saturday Night Fever" forfeits any claim to credibility by totally eschewing realism, so b.o. will depend entirely upon film's voyeuristic appeal to young men and fantasy allure for teenage gals. Some biz is foreseen, but upper ceiling is hard to call.

Appealing newcomer Jennifer Beals plays an 18-year-old come to Pittsburgh to toil in a steel mill by day and work off steam at night by performing wild, improvised dances in a local bar (much of Beals' dancing was reportedly done by an uncredited double).

Basic situation is fraught with implausibilities: Beals has no family that's mentioned; she claims to have already saved enough money to support herself through ballet school should she be accepted, and could the sort of avant-garde, new-wavish dancing possibly go down at a blue-collar bar largely populated by middle-age, beer-guzzling Steelers fans? Not likely.

What story there is sees Beals trying to get up the courage to audition for formal dance study and dealing with the advances of her daytime boss Michael Nouri who, to her fury, secretly intervenes to get her admitted to the school.

Sociologically, film is oddly fascinating as a Beverly Hills fantasy of working class life. Nouri drives a Porsche and lives in a film producer-type mansion, while Beals lives in a converted warehouse which would be the envy of any New York loft artist. Wardrobes are all startling, no one is unemployed and grimy Pittsburgh is made to look like an industrial, high tech paradise.

Female performances all come off as if the sole directorial command was, "All right, girls, let's get physical!" Pic features better bodies and more crotch shots than "Personal Best," and every effect is of the most vulgar and obvious variety. Subtlety has been banished from the artistic vocabulary.

But, for all that, "Flashdance" can hardly be called boring. This may be the first mainline commercial film to incorporate trendy "break" dancing into its proceedings, and aspects of disco. Aerobicize and even Kabuki new wave are provocatively on view in the closest feature film equivalent yet to music promo videos.

Much of the dancing is spectacular, and that may be enough for intended audiences, along with the compendium of pop tunes, four of which were composed by Giorgio Moroder. Title song, performed by Irene Cara, seems destined for popularity.

Tech credits are as slick as they come. —Cart.

The Ploughman's Lunch
(BRITISH-COLOR)

———

London, April 13.

A Goldcrest and Michael White presentation of a Greenpoint Film. Produced by Simon Relph and Ann Scott. Directed by Richard Eyre. Features entire cast. Written by Ian McEwan; camera (color), Clive Tickner; production designer, Luciana Arrighi; editor, David Martin; music, Dominic Muldowney; sound, David Stephenson. Reviewed at 20th Century-Fox preview theatre, London, April 12, 1983. Running time, 100 MINS.

James Penfield	Jonathan Pryce
Jeremy Hancock	Tim Curry
Ann Barrington	Rosemary Harris
Matthew Fox	Frank Finlay
Susan Barrington	Charlie Dore
Gold	David De Keyser
Mr. Penfield	Nat Jackley
Lecturer	Bill Paterson

———

"The Ploughman's Lunch" marks the theatrical debut for Richard Eyre, otherwise a legit and tv helmer. It's such a searing account of current British politics and morality that it'll wow the U.K. intelligentsia and anyone scornful of the English.

Pic is set in the heartland of bourgeois England among its media creators and academic pontificators, and runs the period from the first spark of last year's Falklands warlet to the victory speech of Prime Minister Margaret Thatcher at her party's gungho autumn shindig.

But those events are only a backdrop to the multi-layered story of a group of people who are either off the rails or suffering an acute lack of human commitment. It's a plot that could have turned out over-schematic, but Eyre's strong directorial hand shows in delicately ambivalent performances from all players. There's no one in this canvas of cynicism with whom the audience can easily identify, but the spectacle of moral bankruptcy and social gaucheness is not without interest.

The film evidently springs from its author's heart in characterizing the radio journalist played by Jonathan Pryce as lacking in virtue and understanding. His sins include political convictions that blow with the wind; neglect of a dying mother, leading on an older woman, and a fruitless infatuation with the tv researcher played by Charlie Dore.

Dore, who's a singer in life, pulls off the trick of combining moderate bitchiness with a worldliness that makes her cruelly sensible in her dealings with the pursuer. Film reaches an astonishing climax during the Conservative party conference, where crew and cast filmed undercover. Pryce finally realizes he's on a losing wicket and reproaches his friend Jeremy for foul play, just as Thatcher's jingoistic rhetoric reaches its peak.

Frank Finlay and Rosemary Harris counterpoint these goings on, representing former idealists who have largely put away their hopes to hide behind creature comforts.

Pic is always visually interesting, thanks to Eyre's direction and photography by Clive Tickner who does marvels with rustic locations. —*Japa.*

Return Engagement
(U.S. COLOR-DOCU)

Hollywood, March 31.
An Island Pictures presentation of an Alive Enterprises production. Produced by Carolyn Pfeiffer. Directed by Alan Rudolph. Features entire cast. Camera (Foto-Kem Industries Color). Jan Kiesser; editor, Tom Walls; music. Adrien Belew; sound, Douglas Vaughn; associate producer, Barbara Leary; assistant director, Bruce Chevillat. Reviewed at the Warner Hollywood Studios, L.A., March 31, 1983. No MPAA Rating. Running time: 89 MINS.
Features: G. Gordon Liddy, Timothy Leary, Carole Hemingway.

Near the end of "Return Engagement," a documentary on the vaudeville team of G. Gordon Liddy and Timothy Leary, a journalist says to the men, "You two sound like an old married couple." Comment is apt in that, no matter how much the two bicker, score points and attempt to maintain the facade of animosity for the sake of the box-office of their "debate" tour, a basic compatibility underlies their relationship which gives the impression that they were, in some way, meant for each other.

World preemed last Thursday (14) at Filmex, Alan Rudolph's first docu feature will be of interest to pop historians and has a solid future at fests, specialized commercial venues and, in a limited way, on television.

Liddy, famed for his role in the Watergate break-in, and Leary, self-styled hippie guru and drug advocate, are billed as the highest paid team on the lecture circuit, and pic covers eight days surrounding a recent appearance at the Wilshire Ebell Theatre in Los Angeles. Centerpiece of the film is this public performance, at which both men, along with moderator Carole Hemingway, spout off in front of a giant American flag, a la "Patton." More amusing and revealing, however, is the off-stage time spent both together and separately, when each gets the chance to expound more coherently, and less defensively, on his beliefs, and when they can be caught in less guarded moments.

Although Rudolph keeps his film moving along so as not to bore, viewer reaction will naturally be predicated to a great extent upon personal feelings about Liddy and Leary. Immaculately groomed, very proper and tremendously fit, Liddy confounds most preconceived notions about him through his easy command of history and articulate manner in which he sometimes twists logic to rationalize his criminal actions.

Leary, too, is able to talk a good game, but anyone who ever thought he was a flake is unlikely to change one's mind on the evidence presented here. Admitting that he's still a "cheerleader" for the postwar generation, whom he encourages to seize power quickly, Leary is glimpsed playing video games and spouting such nonsense as, "You're going to see Shakespeare in the future in video arcades," as well as lecturing to aging hippies at Esalen.

One of the most amusing revelations to non-experts on these gentlemen is that, 16 years earlier, it was assistant d.a. Liddy who busted Leary for drugs in rural New York. Urging his friend on film to get high, Leary maintains that Liddy is a lost soul because he's concerned with the past, and history, instead of the future, while Leary exposes himself as a utopian idealist who, in Liddy's opinion, might have lost quite a few brain cells to his countless drug trips.

And so it goes, back and forth, like Alphonse and Gaston, at a Hollywood party thrown in their honor, at a wine-enhanced dinner and at a Chateau Marmont breakfast shared with their very amiable wives. In spare time, Leary works on a book on a word processor, while Liddy exhibits fine marksmanship at a firing range and rides choppers with Hell's Angels, one of whom served time

with him at Terminal Island and respects Liddy because he wasn't a snitch. In a way, whole film goes to show that you never know where you might find new friends.

Pic was blown up impressively from 16m to 35m, and tech aspects are all solid. —*Cart.*

The Trail
(HONG KONG - COLOR)

Hong Kong, April 2.
A Golden Harvest production, presented by Raymond Chow. Produced by Michael Hui. Directed by Ronny Yu. Production Supervisor, Louis Sit. Stars Ricky Hui, Cheng Jut Si, Tin Lian, Hsu Siu Ning, Miao Tin, Chung Fat. Screenplay, Michael Hui, Ronny Yu; production designer, David T.W. Chan; camera (color), James Chan; associate producers, Oliviu Mok, Barbie Tung; editor, Cheung Yiu Chung; theme song sung by Agnes Chung; music, Bobby Chan. Reviewed at State Theater, Hong Kong, April 1, 1983. Tunning time: 100 MINS.
(Cantonese soundtrack with English sub-titles).

The gathering of reliable talents in a picture does not assure quality nor boxoffice success. Another shining example in this category is "The Trail," coproduced and written by "comedy king" Michael Hui ("Private Eyes"), directed by often competent, American-trained Ronny Yu ("The Saviour") and starring third brother of the Hui Brothers ensemble, Ricky Hui.

Together, they have created a film that deserves a five star yawn award. Golden Harvest, which has now mastered the technique of making mass produced horror-comedy-kung fu oddities, even shot this film on location in Taiwan to showcase a different locale, yet it is no different from any ordinary Samo Hung starrer in hometown Hong Kong dealing with corpses and exorcists in ancient times.

This time, it is set in China in the early 1920s where people supposedly would do any odd jobs to earn upkeep to survive. Smuggling of opium is rampant in such a situation and the occult is a powerful force. The superstitious provincials and residents contend with the unknown with grave seriousness. The central character is simpleminded, average-man Ricky Hui, who belongs to a group or sect whose trade is to "Walk The Stiffs Home." This service is provided to those people who die somewhere else and would like to return home to their families. Magic is somehow called upon to "walk" the corpses to their destination for a decent burial. This particular job can only be done at night.

With such an interesting and exotic framework, one would expect entertaining possibilities of having something to laugh at and then occasionally be scared with the presence of baddies who roam the scenic territory. Except for the cinematography, "The Trail" leaves nothing behind for the viewers to re-

member, for a collection of nonsensical, stilted characters and dull direction. The time-worn revenge scenario is laden with blatant copies from popular foreign movies, with special focus on Brian De Palma ideas, done without shame. There is little refreshing in this production, though there are some bits and pieces of high comedy that are easily forgotten. —*Mel.*

La Vie Est Un Roman
(Life is a Novel)
(FRENCH - COLOR)

Paris, April 12.
AAA release of a Philippe Dussart / Films A2 / Fideline Films / Films Ariane / Filmedis co-production. Produced by Philippe Dussart. Stars Vittorio Gassman, Ruggero Raimondi, Geraldine Chaplin, Fanny Ardant. Directed by Alain Resnais. Written by Jean Gruault; camera (Fujicolor and Eastmancolor), Bruno Nuytten; art directors, Jacques Saulnier and Enki Bilal; music, Philippe-Gerard; editor, Albert Jurgenson; sound, Pierre Lenoir; costumes, Catherine Leterrier; production manager, Jean Lara. Reviewed at Club 13, Paris, April 6, 1983. Running time: 110 MINS.
Walter Guarini .... Vittorio Gassman
Michel Forbek .... Ruggero Raimondi
Nora Winkle .... Geraldine Chaplin
Livia Cerasquier .... Fanny Ardant
Elizabeth Rousseau .... Sabine Azima
Robert Dufresne .... Pierre Arditi
Claudine Obertin .... Martine Kelly
Zoltan Forbek ....Samson Fainsilber
Nathalie Holberg ...... Veronique Silver
Raoul Vandamme ...... Andre Dussolier

Much talent and money has been mobilized for one of the most joyless and vacuous film spectacles to come out of France in a long while.

"La Vie Est Un Roman" was written by Jean Gruault, directed by Alain Resnais, and produced at an astronomical cost of more than $3,500,000, an especially mind boggling sum when you consider that this is not a film that will automatically knock 'em dead in Toulouse or Pittsburgh. Though its makers refer to it without a trace of irony as an "entertainment," it can be considered diverting only by a long stretch of the imagination. And imagination is essentially what's missing in this compleat snob trap, whose intellectual conceits have left perplexed even those who fell into a swoon over the previous Gruault-Resnais collaboration, "Mon Oncle D'Amerique."

In fact, "La Vie Est Un Roman" is something of a sequel to that film, which won honors at Cannes and earned Resnais his greatest commercial success. Without recourse to any preconceived scientific notions on behavior or philosophy, Gruault has come up with a tripartite script that presumably treat themes like the quest for happiness, intellectual and emotional fulfillment, and other hot boxoffice topics.

In the first of three contrapuntally interwoven episodes, set just before and after the First World War, a battily mystic Lithuanian count (opera star Ruggero Raimondi, in his first straight dramatic film role) gathers a group of selected friends in loonily baroque castle he has built in the Ardennes woods to house a cult of happiness, complete with memory-erasing potions, Chinese attendants and pseudo-poetic group gropes. But the rightful skepticism of one participant (Fanny Ardant), loved by Raimondi, brings the entire enterprise to collapse.

The second narrative is set in the same castle in the present, now become the site of a fashionable private school. A group of pedagogues are gathered there for a gaseously high-minded seminar (on the "teaching of imagination"). There enter on the scene three new guests: an American anthropologist (Geraldine Chaplin), a celebrated Italian architect (Vittorio Gassmann) and a young schoolteacher (Sabine Azima) whose idealized theories on life, love and education are put to a rude test by the shabby morality, hypocrisy and cynicism of her peers.

The third strand, set in a purely imaginary universe with fanciful decors and fairy tale personages, recounts a young prince's pursuit and execution of the murderous tyrant who usurped his throne.

It's hard to believe that dedicated, intelligent artists got together to commit this cinematic foolishness which defies good sense and commercial logic with its studied naivetes, windy platitudes, and an assortment of nudniks whom you'd flee like the plague at a cocktail party.

And what did Gruault and Resnais think they were doing in having their personages suddenly break out into song every once in a while, as if they'd just strayed in from a Jacques Demy set? Sad to note that the excellent composer Philippe-Gerard, who has done all too little film work, has lent his talent to this saddening nonsense.

As for Resnais, it must be said that his directing has never been more flavourless; any competent director of lesser abilities, but a stronger sense of humour, could have breathed a bit more life and humanity into the vain goings-on. Even Resnais' fussy editing mannerisms are absent here.

There is little to retain of the acting. A nice slice of the budget probably went into Raimondi's and Gassman's pockets, but neither is interesting. Only Sabine Azima, a little known tv and stage actress, is memorable as the vulnerable, naive schoolteacher; her performance is a welcome pocket of warmth, humanity and spontaneity, holding out against the hot air blowing around it.

Art house circuits and festival exposure will probably offer pic its best chances. —*Len.*

Bar Esperanca-O Ultimo Que Fecha
(Bar Esperanca: Last To Close)
(BRAZILIAN-COLOR)

Gramado, Feb. 21.

An Embrafilme release of a CPC/Embrafilme production. Features entire cast. Directed by Hugo Carvana. Screenplay, Carvana, Armando Costa, Denise Bandeira, Euclydes Marinho, Martha Alencar; camera (Eastmancolor), Edgar Moura; art direction, Mario Monteiro; editing, Lael Rodrigues; music, Thomas Improta; makeup, Antonio Pacheco; costumes, Rita Murtinho; executive production, Luiz Carlos Lacerda; continuity, Rita Erthal; assistant director, Lael Rodrigues; sound, Juarez Dagoberto. Reviewed at Cine Embaixador, Gramado Film Festival, Gramadao, Brazil, Feb. 21, 1983. Running time: 105 MINS.

Cast: Marilia Pera, Hugo Carvana, Anselmo Vasconcellos, Nelson Dantas, Louise Cardoso, Luiz Fernando Guimaraes, Julio Braga, Antonio Pedro, Paulo Cesar Pereio, Sylvia Bandeira, Sandro Solviatt, Thelma Reston, Wilson Grey, Maria Gladys, Eliana Araujo, Tessy Calado, Carlos Gregorio, Oswaldo Loureiro, Tiao Ribas D'Avila, Alvaro Freire, Rui Polanah, Thereza Mascarenhas, Daniel Filho and the children Luiza Marcier and Jonas Torres.

Hugo Carvana, an actor who six years ago directed his first feature, "Vai Trabalhar Vagabundo," so far the most accurate portrait of the "Carioca" (Rio de Janeiro-born) way of life, is a character of the world he is concerned with in his films. Traditional bohemian of the Carioca nights, his third feature is a kind of report on himself and his closest friends. Subject is a fictional Rio de Janeiro bar, meeting point for drunkers and intellectuals, where frustrated novelists, desperate journalists, junkies and the friendly waiter of every night get together to drink, to be mutually complacent, hostile sometimes but especially to forget the exterior signs of life.

It is not a comedy, as were two previous Carvana's pics, although there are some funny moments, particularly in the sequence where Carvana, a fired tv writer recently separated from his wife (Marilia Pera), finds a haven in the place of a journalist friend (Nelson Dantas) and both discuss whether they have the delirium tremens or not.

As usually in Carvana's works, characters are real and intelligently directed. At this time, they are especially well photographed by Edgar Moura ("Gaijin") and the set is an harmonious combination of many Carioca bars of this kind. In addition, the big cast is in fact a selection of many of Carvana's friends. Some of them give outstanding performances, especially Marilia Pera, Nelson dantas, Paulo Cesar Pereio and Carvana himself.

Director's main sin is not allowing his film to develop naturally. The main plot, the struggle for reconciliation among couples, is often reiterated and even some bar characters are forced to be constantly insisting in their definitions.

So what Carvana gets in technical achievement, he may be losing in emotional involvement.

Perhaps that will make his film easily understandable for foreign audiences. There is certainly an appeal in this sense. And "Bar Esperanca" does not lose the Carioca spirit that makes its author one of the most integrated in the complexity of the Rio de Janeiro culture. —*Hoin.*

Otto er et naesehorn
(Otto Is A Rhino)
(DANISH-COLOR)

Copenhagen, April 4.

A Metronome (Bent Fabricius-Bjerre) production with The Danish Film Institute. Warner-Metronome release. Features entire cast. Screenplay, Rumle Hammerich, Mogens Kloevedal, based on Ole Lund Kierkegaard novel. Directed by Rumle Hammerich. Camera (Eastmancolor), Dan Lausten; production design, Henning Bahs, Sven Wickman; music, Jacob Groth; production management, Lise Lense-Moeller, Sanne Arnt; editor, Niels Pagh Andersen, Vinca Wiedemann; animation, Joergen Klubien, Jacob Kock; main titles, Jacob Stegelmann, Jeff Varba; optical effects, Bent Barfoed. Reviewed at the Palads, Copenhagen, April 4, 1983. Running time: 85 MINS.

Topper	Kristjan Markersen
Viggo	Erik Petersen
Mr. Lion	Axel Stroebye
Mrs. Flora	Kirsten Rolffes
Mr. Holm	Egon Stoldt
Erling	Ole Meyer
Topper's Auntie	Judy Gringer
Police Lt.	Joergen Kiil
Topper's Daddy	Leif Sylvester Petersen
Sille	Henriette Damsgaard
The Baker	Jan Zangenberg
Baker's wife	Margrethe Koytu
Fire Chief	Peter Steen
Fisherman	Anthony Michael
Teacher	Jannie Fauerschou

Producer Bent Fabricius-Bjerre had a minor international hit with his kiddie and adults entertainment, "Rubber Tarzan," voted best children's feature by UNESCO two years ago. Now he is likely to go one better with "Otto Is A Rhino," another burlesque story based on a novel by the late Ole Lund Kierkegaard, a creator of very close-to-life fantasy worlds in which children overcome the frustrations imposed upon them by dour or downright malignant adults through various merry flights of fancy.

First-time director Rumle Hammerich has been put in charge of "Otto Is A Rhino" in which a magic pencil enables a lonely boy (his father seems to be forever away on the high seas) to draw anything on any wall and then to see it come to life. When he draws a rhino, a beautiful yellow rhinoceros is suddenly at large on the second floor of an apartment house in a small town by the sea.

The rhino (a beautiful piece of technical, very lifelike work) has to be fed enormous quantities of dark bread and bales of hay. He is a friendly even humorous animal, siding quite naturally with such inhabitants of the house who will feed and accept him while taking no guff at all from the downstairs inn-

keeper who wants to steal the magic pencil to start a brewery of his own.

The innkeeper (a tour de force of The Eternal Tyrant by Axel Stroebye) has long been bullying the pencil-wielding boy Topper and his own son Viggo (both boys played with muted melancholy and far from any cutesy manners by amateurs). Now he gets, of course, his come-uppance. But even without their revenge, they have been seeking and finding much consolation in rather poetic wanderings around town with an old pram which they take turns at either pushing or reclining in.

The little world of Topper is drawn in a particular kind of poetic baroque that will have children everywhere enjoying the innocent suspense of the plot while adults will laugh out loud at old-fashioned punch-lines and comical characters and new-fangled visual fun, everything being handled swiftly and with much cinematographic imagination and inexpensive, but sweetly convincing imagery by director Hammerich. Production and special effects credits are also of a high order, and all major as well as minor characters are drawn with the nicest touches of human compassion, including the villain who is, towards the happy ending, threatened with drowning in his own beer.

With Fabricius-Bjerre's already well-established international sales connections, "Otto Is A Rhino" should be a shoo-in as a theatrical kiddie entertainment everywhere, especially if post-synched foreign language versions are made. Both the fun and the sweetness of the poetry recalls the best of Disney entertainments with most of the technical credits matched as well.

—*Kell.*

Misterio
(Mystery)
(MEXICAN-COLOR)

Hollywood, March 28.

An Azteca Films release of a Conacine, S.A. de C.V. production. Produced by Pablo Buelna. Directed by Marcela Fernandez Violante. Features entire cast. Screenplay, Vincente Lenero (adapted from his novel, "Studio Q"); camera (color), Daniel Lopez; editor, Jorge Bustos; music, Leonardo Velazquez. Reviewed at the MGM Studios, Culver City, March 28, 1983. No MPAA Rating. Running time: 97 MINS.

Alex	Juan Ferrara
TV director	Victor Junco
Silvia	Helena Rojo
Gladys	Beatriz Sheridan
TV producer	Jorge Fegan

(In Spanish; English subtitles)

Let the record read that Mexico's "Misterio" (Mystery), directed by Mexico's major woman filmmaker, Marcela Violante, last year took eight Ariels (the Mexican equivalent of the Oscar). Eight is a very large number for a film as tiresome and belabored as this one. Mystery indeed.

The concept deals with the confusion between illusion and reality. A weary soap opera star in Mexico City (Juan Ferrara) finds life before the cameras and life at home with his wife increasingly indistinguishable. Everything he does privately becomes an action on the television screen. Life is just like tape. His wife and leading lady, his home and the soap opera set, become telescoped into the same maddening vortex.

This is all played with a certain crazy charm; moments on the soap set, under the vise-like grip of a marionette of a director (Victor Junco), occasionally suggest some of the sound stage stuff in "Tootsie." The critical point, however, is that there's an intellectual arrogance, an archness, to "Mystery" that decimates the film once the gimmick has worn off — say about 15 minutes into the film.

The acting is fine — in the case of the hero it verges on fastidious exhaustion — but the double mirrors on view here too quickly begin to reflect the same, single joke. Credit the film for its claustrophobia, but the price exacted is repetition. --*Loyn.*

Turkey Shoot
(AUSTRALIAN-COLOR)

Sydney, April 12.

A Filmco-Hemdale-FGH Production. Executive producers, John Daly, David Hemmings; producers, Anthony I. Ginnane, William Fayman. Features entire cast. Directed by Brian Trenchard-Smith; screenplay, Jon George, Neill Hicks, based on a story by George Schenck, Robert Williams. David Lawrence; camera (color, Panavision), John McLean; music, Brian May; editor, Alan Lake; production design, Bernard Hides; special effects, John Stears. Reviewed at Barclay Cinema, Sydney, April 9, 1983. (Australian Censorship Rating: M). Running time: 92 MINS.
Paul Anders .... Steve Railsback
Chris Walters .... Olivia Hussey
Charles Thatcher .... Michael Craig
Jennifer .... Carmen Duncan
Mallory ....Noel Ferrier
Rita Daniels ....Lynda Stoner
Ritter .... Roger Ward
Tito .... Michael Petrovitch
Red .... Gus Mercurio
Dodge ....John Ley
Griffin .... Bill Young
Alph ....Steve Rackman

During the 92 minutes of "Turkey Shoot," a sadistic, futuristic bloodbath belatedly released on its home territory though bearing a 1981 dateline, the following acts of ultra-violence occur. A young woman is savagely beaten, punched and kicked to death by a prison guard. Another prisoner is taunted and then incinerated. A mutant breaks the back of a screaming victim. Later, the same mutant is sliced in half by a bulldozer. A man is filled with arrows, then deliberately run over and crushed by a car. A man's hands are chopped off by the leading lady. A man is shot in the groin. A woman's naked body, covered with lac-

erations, is found with an arrow thrust down her throat and emerging from her neck. A man is killed by a massive wooden booby-trap which hits him between the legs. A man's skull is split open. A man is literally shot to pieces. A woman is stabbed in the face with an exploding arrow.

The excuse for all this savagery and blood-letting is an inept updating of the old "Hounds of Zaroff" formula in which authorities of the future amuse themselves by hunting down unarmed "deviates" given a head start and let loose in the jungle. Nobody connected with this travesty can take any credit. One or two members of the cast or production team have, in the past, done better things in other countries; one can only hope they were well paid.

This is exactly the kind of mid-Pacific monstrosity worrying local craft unions and others concerned for the future of the Australian film industry. Presumably "Turkey Shoot" wasn't made with an Australian audience in mind (it has been released locally for a limited one-week season in a couple of hardtops and some drive-ins; Saturday evening downtop hardtop business, at the session caught, appeared to be calamitous), but it's hard to see just what audience would respond to this inane and singularly unpleasant material. A few attempts at comedy fall very flat.

Special effects and make-up are quite convincing, adding to the stomach-churning horrors. —*Strat.*

Zaman
(BELGIUM-COLOR)

Antwerp, March 30.

A Visie Filmproduction, Brussels. Produced by Roland Verhavert. Directed by Patrick Le Bon. Screenplay, Paul Koeck, Patrick Le Bon; camera, (Kodak-Eastmancolor) Walther vanden Ende; editor, Ludo Troch; music, Francois Glorieux; production manager, Nadine Borreman; costumes, Chris Willems; sound, Jules Goris; make-up, Therese Glbert; assistant director, Styn Coninx. Reviewed at Rex Theatre, Antwerp, March 29, 1983. Running time: 90 MINS.
Zaman .... Marc Janssen
Frank .... Herbert Flack
Magda .... Gerda Lindekens
Katie .... Mieke Bouve
Kaplan ....Herman Gilis
Commissioner .... Paul's Jongers
Valerie .... Sylvia Sabbe
Zaman's son .... Patrick Brabants
Red Door .... Dirk Luyten
Frank's wife .... Ann Nelissen

From the original screenplay by popular Belgian writer Paul Koeck and Flemish director Patrick Le Bon, "Zaman" has become the first Flemish police-film that really works. Le Bon has made a film about ordinary people who have their ups and downs, doubts and fears, friends and colleagues and a family life. Pic takes a look at the real people behind the uniforms.

This cop, who goes by the name of Zaman, is past his forties and has been a cop all his life. He's fascinated by his work, although this has led to the destruction of his private life. His first marriage ended in divorce and his daughter left home and works in a topless bar. Zaman's second marriage is not much of a success either. He spends all his time working, and at home his wife treats him as a stranger. His relationship with his young son is somewhat better. The boy looks up to his father and often asks him about his job. He understands Zaman better than his wife.

One day Zaman gets a new partner, Frank. He is young and has different opinions about the job. The two disagree constantly. Frank can't understand that a policeman's job consists of paperwork. Their relationship is cold in the beginning, and Zaman often shows off his experience to Frank. The latter often accuses him of playing it safe, nailing only the little guys, while the big fry go free.

Still, after a while they become friends. When Zaman wants to arrest some big underworld figures, his search leads him into the municipality of the city. A policeman's investigation cannot be tolerated in these circles, and Zaman gets suspended.

His wife now realizes she has always misunderstood her husband's devotion. She tells him she always admired him for the way he wanted to do his job honestly. This gives him the strength to carry on. Only this time, he loses his job because of his determination.

The human aspect and the results that a job like this can have on someone's family life are excently presented in this pic. No spectacular car chases and big shoot-outs, but an everyday reality that policemen all over the world will find much easier to relate to.

Director Le Bon looks at things the way they are. He's objective and his characters are no heroes.

Entire cast consists of actors and actresses well-known in Belgian theatre, and it is fascinating to see all these familiar faces in one film. Marc Janssen as Zaman, turns his role into a man who could be your next door neighbor. In all his simplicity, he is extremely convincing as a man torn between his job and his life. Same thing goes for Herbert Flack, as Frank. This versatile actor shows us someone tender and strong at the same time; Gerda Lindekens is impressive as Zaman's wife. Her part could lead into hysterics, but she plays it cool.

Technical credits are excellent with Walter van den Enden's camerawork a standout for creating the atmosphere of a sleazy Antwerp port town. Business in Belgium is very good and with a bit of pruning,

could find appeal with regular as well as selective audiences abroad.
—*Dave.*

Curtains
(CANADIAN-COLOR)

A Jensen Farley Pictures release of a Simcom production. Executive producer, Richard Simpson. Produced by Peter R. Simpson. Directed by "Jonathan Stryker" (pseudonym; see review). Stars John Vernon, Samantha Eggar, Linda Thorson. Screenplay, Robert Guza Jr.; camera (Film House color), Robert Paynter; additional photography-camera operator, Fred Guthe; editor, Michael MacLaverty; music, Paul Zaza; assistant director, Tony Thatcher, Stephen Wright; production manager, Gerry Arbeid, Ilana Frank; sound, Bryan Day; production design, Roy Forge Smith; special effects, Colin Chilvers; stunt coordinator, Bob Hannah. Reviewed at RKO Cinerama I theatre, N.Y., April 8, 1983. (MPAA Rating: R). Running time: 89 MINS. .
Jonathan Stryker ....John Vernon
Samantha Sherwood ... Samantha Eggar
Brooke Parsons ....Linda Thorson
Laurian Summers ...... Anne Ditchburn
Patti O'Connor .; ....Lynne Griffin
Tara Demillo .... Sandra Warren
Christie Burns .... Lesleh Donaldson
Amanda Reuther ...... Deborah Burgess
Matthew .... Michael Wincott

"Curtains" is an insulting horror picture that started shooting in November, 1980 and emerges finally (after considerable reshooting) with questionable credits and meager results. Fright genre fans deserve better than this, which unfortunately even fails to make the "so bad it's good" category.

In a rather dubious film history first, "Curtains" director is credited as Jonathan Stryker, which happens to be the fictional character name of lead actor John Vernon, who portrays a film director. Principal photography was actually directed by Richard Ciupka, a cinematographer who numbers the lauded "Atlantic City" among his credits. Actress Sandee Currie (of "Terror Train" and "Gas") is billed as Sandra Warren. Film's end credits account for the re-shooting by listing two separate 60-person crews, jokingly attributed with filming "Act I" and "Act II" of this one-part film.

Not surprisingly, picture is a mishmash, lacking simple transition scenes and the usual continuity. A simple "Ten Little Indians" story of six actresses invited to audition (and be killed) at film director Stryker's remote mansion, picture's main fault is not technical problems but its repeated cheating and misleading the audience. Most fright scenes (and even simple narrative scenes such as a rape and a lesbian sequence) turn out to be false: either a nightmare-plus-wakeup or rehearsal exercise. Cumulative effect of being jerked around in this fashion is viewer frustration. Even the explicit gore and on-screen violence usually doled out to energize the fans is absent here.

Vernon is far too serious in the leading role, not jibing with the picture's attempted tongue-in-cheek approach. Samantha Eggar, latterly involved in far too many terrible films, tries very hard but to no avail in essaying a contradictory mad woman role. The other actresses, including tv's "Avengers" star Linda Thorson and ballerina Anne Ditchburn, are merely decorative, though Lynne Griffin has the closest thing to a characterization, portraying a standup comic. Very obvious clues telegraph who is the killer amongst them.

Format of insulting the viewer culminates explicitly with a final scene played to an on-screen audience of insane asylum inmates. Film's title refers to the hoary, repetitive device of beginning each new sequence with an optical effect of black curtains parting on screen to represent a play. Horror fans used to be frightened by the prospect of monsters and maniacs.
—*Lor.*

Sargento Getulio
(Sergeant Getulio)
(BRAZILIAN-COLOR)

Gramado, March 24.

An Embrafilme release of an Hermano Penna/Embrafilme production. Features entire cast. Directed by Hermano Penna. Screenplay, Penna, Flavio Porto from novel by Joao Ubaldo Ribeiro; dialog, Joao Ubaldo Ribeiro; camera (Ektachrome 16m blown up to 35m), Walter Carvalho; executive producer, Alvaro Pedreira; editing, Laercio Silva; sound, Mario Masetti; art direction, costumes, makeup, Percival Rorato; musical direction, Jose Luiz Penna; original songs, Jose Luiz Penna, Tiago Araripe, Paulinho Costa; continuity, Lia Pereira Camargo; assistant direction, Flavio Porto. Reviewed at Embaixador Theatre, Gramado Film Festival, Brazil, March 24, 1983. Running time: **90 MINS.**

Cast: Lima Duarte, Orlando Vieira, Inez Maciel, Fernando Bezerra, Flavio Porto, Antonio Leite, Amaral Cavalcante, Marieta Fontes, Marcia de Lima, Otavio Sales, Luiz A. Barreto, Etel de Souza, Carlos Rocha.

Originally made as a pilot for a tv series, "Sargento Getulio" easily transcends its purpose. Inspiration is a famous Brazilian novel by Joao Ubaldo Ribeiro which has become a must among local intellectuals. It deals with the Brazilian northeastern story on the late 1940s, set in the state of Sergipe, where two political parties, PSD and UDN, struggle for power. Getulio is a sergeant at the service of PDS who takes an UDN prisoner from the village of Poco Verde to the capital Aracaju.

Through an atmosphere of violence and no respect for the most elementary human rights, travel is punctuated by all sort of arbitration, especially when Getulio finds out that the political situation has changed in Sergipe: even his boss does not want the prisoner any more, but the Sergeant is now obsessed to finish his mission.

Movie features extraordinary acting by Lima Duarte, one exponent of Brazilian TV, and the camerawork (blown up from 16 to 35m in the U.S.) could hardly be more

impressive. Director Hermano Penna works with very few actors, often in locations as small as the interior as a car, sometimes in the biggest spaces of the Northeastern "caatinga," and manages to be equally involving and technically correct.

Ubaldo's text has been consciously adapted, allowing Penna to create intelligent and emotional material. For obscure reasons, he waited five years to publicly release his film. Shown for the first time in Gramado, it got the warmest reactions from the audience. There is no question that "Sargento Getulio" will be one of the leading items of Brazilian production for this year. —*Hoin.*

La Voie Lumiere
(The Lumiere Approach)
(FRENCH-COMPILATION-
B&W/COLOR)

A Service des Archives du Film, Centre National de la Cinematographie (Bois d'Arcy) compilation, organized by Franz Schmitt. Reviewed at Museum of Modern Art, N.Y., April 2, 1983. Running time: **100 MINS.**

"La Voie Lumiere" is a valuable compilation film of 96 short French pictures, including some of the oldest motion pictures extant. Emphasizing the documentary work of Auguste and Louis Lumiere, program in 35m is presented in silent format without commentary with well-preserved, amazingly sharp technical quality to most of the entries.

Besides some 59 films by the Lumiere brothers, compilation includes representative work by several of their contemporaries. Eleven early films (running only 3-5 seconds in length each) by Jules-Etienne Marey present the people and animals in motion studies in the manner of Edward Muybridge. More interesting are seven films by Georges Demeny, a former collaborator of Marey. These street scenes filmed in 1895-6 (including an early example of tinted, hand-colored footage) benefit from having been shot in the 60m format, presented here in high-definition 35m reduction prints. Also quite sharp is a Place de la Madeleine shot by Grimoin-Sanson, which evidences, as do many of these early documentaries, people ogling the camera.

The Lumiere films, which stress movement in the static, one-shot per film frame, are grouped to present people working, leisure time activities, family life, travel films, military subjects and several staged comedy skits.

Over 2,000 Lumiere films were catalogued in 1905 (made from 1898-1905), and those shown here give a cross-section of the several hundred which have survived. The most impressive is a shot of washerwomen on the river bank

which is a vertical composition depicting three levels of movement at different elevations with everything in sharp focus. The only fantasy film included is Gaston Velle's 1903 "La Marmite Diabolique," using trick-photography to show a devil emerging from a cooking-pot after the chef has stuffed his dwarf assistant into the concoction. One of the most striking Lumiere shorts is a panorama at Belle-Vue, shot by a camera mounted on a cablecar descending down the mountains.

While the Lumieres display one of the earliest examples of an exploitation film (four women fighting until interrupted by a dog), a Dr. Doyen shot a lengthy segment recording the 1902 separation of Siamese twins Dokika and Radika, which some 80-plus years after is still hard to watch. High-speed photography (up to 20,000 frames per second) from the Marey Institute catches slow-motion athletes and animal studies, plus some time-lapse photography of flowers blooming.

Compilation ends with some rather boring, attenuated films. The work (dating from 1910-27) of banker-turned-filmmaker Albert Kahn's cameramen differs from earlier films in the reliance upon a panning camera and the editing sequentially of shots taken from different camera setups. Kahn material on view is dull, ranging from an early example of sleaze film (shots outside a Parisian public urinal observing men emerging, hand on crotch) to a nearly five-minute-long sequence (it seems interminable) depicting huge throngs demonstrating in 1927 to support Sacco & Vanzetti.

The French archive has several other compilation films completed in 1982, covering the work of Georges Melies and his peers, plus a survey of early color, sound and animated works. All are musts for students of film history. —*Lor.*

Vida E Sangue De Polaco
(Life And Blood Of The Polish)
(BRAZILIAN-COLOR-DOCU 16m)

Gramado, March 21.

An Embrafilme release of an Embrafilme/Secretary of Culture and Sports of the State of Parana/Silvio Back production. Directed by Silvio Back. Screenplay and research, Back, Maraidit Flores; camera (16m, Kodacolor), Adrian Cooper; sound, Romeu Quinto; music, Henrique de Curitiba, Polish Folk Songs; editing, Mario Queiros Jr.; executive production, Maraidit Rne. Flores. Reviewed at Cine Embaixador, Gramado Film Festival, Brazil, March 21, 1983. Running time: **56 MINS.**

Silvio Back is a filmmaker from Parana (Brazilian south) lately quite concerned with the forgotten culture of southern Brazil. He directed a feature on the war of Pelados ("A Guerra dos Pelados"), "Aleluia Gretchen," on the German colonization in the south, "Revolution of 30," when the south

politicians took over the federal power, "Republica Guarani," on south Indians, and many shorts.

"Vida e Sangue de Polaco" is a docu on the Polish colonization of some villages in the Brazilian south. It follows a structure divided in five parts: the Polish today, the Polish origins, the Polish religiosity, the Polish within the society, and the integrated Polish. Back accomplishes his research using especially from sensitive and rich images of the Polish life in Brazil today. His film is not a report but a set of well-photographed images, encouraging reflection and virtually forcing a strong emotional involvement with the subject.

Back is right when he states that the Brazilian south culture has been forgotten, perhaps in favor of much stronger ties between the Northeast and Africa, for example. Thus his work has the cultural importance of partially repairing such omission. More than this, "Vida e Sangue de Polaco" is an essay about human beings and an ethnic and social miscegenation barely known, even a few miles away from the Polish villages in Brazil. —*Hoin.*

G'Ole
(BRITISH-COLOR-DOCU)

London, April 12.

A Drummond Challis-Michael Samuelson film presented by IVECO in association with Ladbroke Entertainments. Produced by Drummond Challis and Michael Samuelson. Directed by Tom Clegg. Written by Stan Hey; camera (color), Harvey Harrison; editor, Chris Blunden; music, Rick Wakeman; sound, Alan Paley; narrator, Sean Connery. Reviewed at the Classic, Shaftesbury Avenue, London, April 11, 1983. (BBFC rating, PG (A)). Running time, **100 MINS.**

"G'Ole' proudly declares itself the "official" record of last year's World Cup Soccer tournament, in which 24 teams played at 15 locations across the Iberian peninsula. But boxoffice prospects would be more promising if film's makers were not looking over their shoulders to ensure approval by the international football association FIFA.

What could have been a general interest look at both the spectacle and politics of football is in fact a bland collection of sporting cameos which functions best as an "aide memoire" for pigskin enthusiasts.

But technical departments for the widescreen presentation cannot be faulted, and there are many thrilling moments in the chronological account of goals and very frequent fouls.

There's also charm in the characterization of various teams, particularly the nervous amateurs from New Zealand and the bluff optimists of Cameroon. The carnival atmosphere created by Brazil's supporters provides a colorful backdrop.

But there's no sustaining theme, either in the tapestry of personalities and groups, or in off-field looks at fans and less-interested Spaniards. Film culminates in top-heavy accounts of the final matches involving Poland, Italy, Germany and France.

A commentary packed with superlatives is rendered in resonant tones by Sean Connery. Rick Wakeman's score is more than a trifle heavy-handed. —*Japa.*

O Rei Da Vela
(King of Candle)
(BRAZILIAN-COLOR)

Gramado, March 22.

An Embrafilme release of a 5° Tempo Produces Artisticas e Culturais/Secretary of Culture of the State of Sao Paulo/-Embrafilme production. Directed by Jose Celso Martinez Correia. Noilton Nunes. Screenplay, Correia. Nunes; camera (Eastmancolor/b&w), Carlos Alberto Egbert, Rogerio Noel, Pedro Farkas, Adilson Ruiz, Jorge Bouquet, Anselmo Serrat, Noilton Nunes, Edson Elito, Werner Penzel; art direction and costumes. Helio Eichbauer; direct sound, Riva, Silvio Da-Rin, Carlao, Romeu Quinto, Augusto Seva, Jom Tob Azulay, David Pennington, Valtinho; editing, Noilton Nunes; sound editing, Dominique Paris, Martha Luz, Goulart; mixing, Roberto, Jacare, Maranhao; music, Rogerio Duprat, Caetano Veloso, Damiano Cozella, Luis Fernando Guimaraes, Joel Cardoso, Edgar Ferreira, Sandy Celeste, Feliciano Paixao. Reviewed at Cine Embaixador, Gramado Film Festival, March 22, 1983. Running time: 106 MINS.

Cast: Jose Wilker, Ester Goes, Renato Borghi, Maria Alice Vergueiro, Renato Dobal, Silvia Werneck, Flavio Santiago.

Originally a play written in 1933 by Oswald de Andrade, one of the major exponents of Brazilian modernism (a movement born in the early '20s), "O Rei da Vela" got its most famous staging in 1967 by avant-garde group "Oficina," under the direction of Jose Celso Martinez Correia. Correia himself started filming the play in 1971 but had to discontinue it due to several reasons, ranging from lack of funds to political pressures.

A political activist, Correia was arrested, then exiled in Europe for a few years, living also in Africa for some time. He resumed its project in 1979, working for almost three more years, the last of them in close collaboration with filmmaker Noilton Nunes, who became responsible for the editing and the shooting of many additional sequences. When the film was finished, in May 1982, the final result was an almost three-hour long pic, shot in both 16 and 35m, video, in color and black and white, and considerably distant from the 1971 idea, not to mention the 1967 staging. In many ways a commercially and culturally anarchistic product, as is the director's temperament.

From Oswald de Andrade's hands came out the story of Abelardo, a funerary candles seller who gets involved with Brazilian rural aristocracy as well as with

Americans, drawing an allegoric profile of the political-economical relations within his country. In Correia's view, "O Rei da Vela" turns out to be also the story of his own group and his struggle for the achievement of a "popular art". (At the early '70s, Correia went deep in the Brazilian north, trying to stage "O Rei" and other plays at public squares and even in the jungle for mostly illiterate audiences, despite the narrative complexity of his work — a partial record of this period being edited in the film).

Such contradiction is an enlightening sign of the romantic vein of Correia as an artist. He juxtaposes the 1971 staging in Sao Paulo with portions of the same staging in the Northern squares. Often just an explosion of images and personal statements — always with a very carefully conceived sound track — "O Rei da Vela" exhibits the deepest conflicts and anxieties of its director.

Like in Glauber Rocha's "A Idade da Terra," there can hardly be found any commercial commitment and the screen is constantly filled with encoded if not completely arbitrary images. It is nevertheless the testimony of the difficult process of disenchantment and perplexity experienced by one of the top contemporary Brazilian stage directors. —*Hoin.*

The Hunger
(COLOR)

Sexy, bloody modern vampire tale may fall in a b.o. limbo.

An MGM/UA release of a Richard Shepherd Co. production. Produced by Shepherd. Directed by Tony Scott. Screenplay, Ivan Davis, Michael Thomas, based on the novel by Whitney Strieber. Stars Catherine Deneuve, David Bowie, Susan Sarandon. Camera (Metrocolor), Stephen Goldblatt; editor, Pamela Power; music Michel Rubini, Denny Jaeger; music supervision, arrangement, Howard Blake; production design, Brian Morris; art direction, Clinton Cavers, Vicky Paul (N.Y.); set decoration, Ann Mollo, Janet Rosenbloom (N.Y.); makeup illusions, Dick Smith, Carl Fullerton; special makeup, Anthony Clavet; costume design, Milena Canonero; sound, Clive Winter, John Bolz (N.Y.); assistant director, David Tringham, William Hassell (N.Y.). Reviewed at the MGM Studios, Culver City, April 22, 1983. (MPAA rating: R). Running time: 97 MINS.

Miriam	Catherine Deneuve
John	David Bowie
Sarah Roberts	Susan Sarandon
Tom Haver	Cliff De Young
Alice Cavender	Beth Ehlers
Lt. Allegrezza	Dan Hedaya
Charlie Humphries	Rufus Collins
Phyllis	Suzanne Bertish
Ron	James Aubrey

"The Hunger" is the latest in chic trash. Like so many other films from British commercials directors, pic is all visual and aural flash, although this modern vampire story looks so great, as do its three principal performers, and is so bizarre that it possesses a certain perverse appeal. Boxoffice prospects seem quite limited, as the art house crowd attracted to the cast will be turned off by the monumental amount of gore, and mainstream horror fans will find the proceedings entirely too outre.

Opening sequence provides viewers with a pretty good idea of what's in store.

To the accompaniment of a throbbing musical track, extraordinary-looking pair of Catherine Deneuve and David Bowie pick up a couple of punky rock 'n rollers who imagine they've just hit the sexual jackpot.

But the kids end up paying the ultimate price for their pleasure, as Deneuve and Bowie commit a double murder in their elegantly appointed New York apartment, and the prevailing motif of sex mixed with bloody death is established.

Although Deneuve and Bowie privately vow to stay with one another forever, Bowie soon notices himself growing rapidly older and visits author-doctor Susan Sarandon, who is preoccupied with the problem of accelerated aging. Shunned by her, Bowie deteriorates quickly and assumes the equivalent of the Janet Leigh role in "Psycho" by disappearing early on, as Deneuve buries him in a box in her attic next to her previous lovers.

Distraught over her mistreatment of Bowie, Sarandon begins visiting Deneuve, and a provocative highlight is their seduction and lovemaking scene, done in very classy fashion but with considerable kissing and nudity. Thus does Deneuve, without doubt the most beautiful vampire ever to grace the screen, infect Sarandon with "The Hunger," which requires one to feed on human blood once a week.

Situation and pervasive mood of decadent sexual sickness reminds of the "Cat People" remake, although this film is even more sophisticated and accomplished visually.

In his feature debut, director Tony Scott, brother of Ridley, exhibits the same penchant for eleborate art direction, minimal, humorless dialog and shooting in smoky rooms (indeed, characters smoke so much in the early going that it comes to seem like a gag).

On a purely technical level, there is a great deal to admire. Stephen Goldblatt's cinematography is extraordinary, creating a visual feast of light, color and shadow, and much of the cutting seems to have been preplanned for startling effect. Brian Morris' design of Deneuve's apartment exquisitely reflects her personal history as accumulated over 2,000 years on earth, and score by Michel Rubini and Denny Jaeger imaginatively calls upon an impressively wide range of music and sounds. Bowie's aging process reps a tour de force for makeup artists Dick Smith, Carl Fullerton and Antony Clavet.

Fortuitous casting of Deneuve marks an astute evaluation of her appeal. About 40 now, actress is as gorgeous as ever but has also taken on an aspect of elusive agelessness that calls to mind Marlene Dietrich and is ideal for this diabolical creature who is impervious to the passage of time. Slightly mannish, confidently bisexual and alluringly discreet, she is a supreme seductress, a master/mistress of love and death.

Sarandon acquits herself well, and is a good partner visually for Deneuve, as is Bowie, although latter doesn't get much to do besides lament his growing old.

Story is dismissable as folderol, and Scott's grim seriousness in telling it could understandably move many to regard the whole thing as silly when an occasionally lighter hand might have helped viewers warm up to the patently unbelievable tale. But most spectators will surely object to the unrestrained bloodletting, which makes one dread each successive killing and creates a sour mood for what, at times, becomes an insidiously intriguing vampire tale. —*Cart.*

All The Wrong Spies
(HONG KONG-COLOR)
Hong Kong, April 12.

A Cinema City Company Ltd. production and release. Executive producers, Wellington W. Fung, Carl Mak, Deak Shek. Co-producer & screenplay, Raymond Wong. Directed by Teddy Robin. Production design, Tsui Hark & Nansun Shi. Production supervisor, Paul Lai, art director, Kenneth Yee; music, Chris Babida; camera (color), Johnny Koo. Reviewed at President Theater, Hong Kong, April 9, 1983. Running Time: 102 MINS.

Cast: Lam, Teddy Robin, Lin Ching Hsia, Paul Chin Pei and Tsui Hark.

(Cantonese with English subtitles).

———

"All The Wrong Spies" is set in 1939. War is raging in Europe. The key to its outcome lies in the secret formula to the atomic bomb held by a Jewish scientist (Ray Cordiero).

Private Eye Yoyo (Lam) has been assigned to assist the scientist in passing the secret to the Americans. The place of exchange is Hong Kong. The secret formula falls into the hands of the head of the Hong Kong Police who intends to sell it to the Japanese. Yoyo enlists the help of Inspector Robin (Teddy Robin). And so it oes.

"Spies," which has already grossed HK$12 million, is supposedly a sequel to Hark Tsui's highly successful "All The Wrong Clues," but is actually a variation of the latter movie with two main characters carried over. The new story line is not connected in anyway but the nostalgic 30s ambiance is retained.

Singer/songwriter/producer/actor Teddy Robin makes his debut as director, together with his Cinema City teammates. They manage to present a pleasant slapstick copycat comedy for the masses.

This film has all the right spices, cooked-up to the audience's mentality. It is yet another item that one forgets as soon as the last frame runs out and has no legs abroad.
—Mel.

Angelo, My Love
(COLOR)

Duvall-helmed gypsy overview has marvy moppet, minimal form. Tough sell looms.

———

San Francisco, April 17.

A Cinecom release of a production written and directed by Robert Duvall. Features Angelo Evans and Steve "Patalay" Tsigonoff. Associate producer, Gail Youngs; camera (color), Joseph Friedman; editor, Stephen Mack; music director, Michael Kamen; lighting, John Drake; sound editor, Dennis Fierman; assistant directors, Carl Clifford, Jeffrey Silver, Christopher Stoia, Youngs. Reviewed at the Castro Theatre, San Francisco International Film Festival, April 17, '83. (No MPAA rating reported). Running time: 120 MINS.

Angelo Evans .... Himself
Michael Evans .... Himself
Ruthie Evans .... Herself
Tony Evans .... Himself
Debbie Evans .... Herself
Steve "Patalay" Tsigonoff ...... Himself
Millie Tsigonoff .... Herself
Frankie Williams .... Himself
George Nicholas .... Himself
Patricia .... Katerina Ribraka
School Teacher .... Timothy Phillips
Student Reporter .... Lachlan Youngs
Student Reader .... Jennifer Youngs
Hispanic Student .... Louis Garcia
Old Woman .... Margaret Millan Gonzalez
Country Singer .... Cathy Kitchen
Mother .... Jan Kitchen
Peaches .... Debbie Ristick
Opera Singers William Duvall, John Duvall
The Wedding
God parents .... Nick Costello, Diana Costello
Bride's Parents .... Johnny Ristick, Yelka Ristick
Greek Dancer .... John Williams
Wedding Guests .... The Ufie Family, The Ristick Family, The Costello Family, The Lucky Brothers
Also features: Toma Lakataca, Jimmy "Italiano" Mitchell, George "Apples" Thompson, "Fat Harry," "Potatoes," "Big Bob" Stevenson, "Baby Nicky," Jay "Boya" Stevenson, Miller Nicholas, Sam Uvanowich, Tony Vlado, and Gypsy Musicians, Johnny Mitchell, Steve Mitchell, and Marko Cristo.

———

This is the first dramatic feature helmed by thesp-Robert Duvall, who financed himself ("just over $1,000,000") and says he spent nearly five years on the project. (Duvall did direct a 1975 feature-length docu, "We're Not the Jet Set," a tale of plains life which won a London Film Festival award.)

The Angelo of the title is a gypsy kid from Duvall's Manhattan neighborhood of whom actor was so enamored he built this entire yarn around him, with mixed success.

Because the bulk of the cast plays themselves (gypsies) and several of them do not read English, including Angelo, scripting is pocked with improvisation, and occasional sub-titling. Remarkably — or perhaps expectedly because of gypsy facility with the put-on — the performances are firstrate; Duvall gets more out of his gypsies than his story line, and the audiences who do find this pic (it already has a late April booking in New York and mid-May date in L.A.) will be amused and touched by the work and the persona of devilish Angelo Evans.

"Angelo" has much more of a docu feel and style than the earlier "King of the Gypsies" feature but, just as "King," moves episodically without helping you understand the motivational history of this ethnic strain.

The con is hinted at but never fully developed, and several scenes are overlong, particularly a boisterous "trial" involving the theft of Angelo's birthright ring by charming heavy Steve "Patalay" Tsigonoff, whom Duvall says he discovered washing cars on Sunset Boulevard.

Much of the plot involves the boy's attempt, with the help of older brother Michael Evans, to nail Tsigonoff — in Manhattan and on a trip to Quebec.

At the heart of Angelo's character is cultural ambivalence — wanting to be both an American and a gypsy. And he fits both ways. An early scene in which he disrupts a classroom while faking reading is the pic's best moment.

Three warblers have interesting bits in the pic: Duvall's brothers William and John, in a restaurant scene, and C-W moppet Cathy Kitchen, with whom Angelo comes on strong in an amusing seg.

Angelo the kid never stops being interesting. "Angelo" the pic needed the same sort of consistency. --Herb.

Bearn
(La Sala de las Munecas)
(SPANISH-COLOR)

Madrid, April 14.

Jet Films S.A., Kaktus Producciones Cinematograficas S.A. production. Presented by Alfredo Matas. Director, Jaime Chavarri. Features entire cast. Screenplay, Salvador Maldonado, based on novel by Llorenc Villalonga; camera (Eastman color) Hank Burmann; music, Francisco Guerrero; art direction, Gil Parrondo; costumes, Yvonne Blake; editor, Jose L. Matesanz; exec producer, Helena Matas. Reviewed at Cine Capitol (Madrid), April 14, 1983. Running time: 122 MINS.

Don Antonio .... Fernando Rey
Xima .... Angela Molina
Maria Antonia .... Amparo Soler Leal
Juan .... Imanol Arias
Mado Francina .... Concha Bardem
Vicario .... Alfredo Mayo
Barbara Titana .... Juana Ginzo
Dr. Wassman .... William Layton
Also: Eduardo Mc Gregor, Elena Ceva, Mateu Grau, et al

Director Jaime Chavarri, best known so far for his prize-winning "To An Unknown God," here turns his talents to a period drama set in Mallorca in 1865 based on a novel which enjoys something of the popularity of Lampedusa's "The Leopard," and to which it bears some resemblance.

Alfredo Matas, the producer, has spared no expenses to provide pic with handsome sets, costumes, and production values as a backdrop of yarn relating the final demise of an aristocratic Mallorcan family.

But despite its over two-hour running time, many of the seemingly inconclusive points in the story are not clarified until the final scenes, when we learn of the masonic connections of the philosophical patriarch (Fernando Rey) and his relationships with a pretty cousin, mysterious strangers, the Pope and other personages; even so much is unfortunately left unexplained.

The dolls' room, to which the sub-title refers, is at the very end of the film, and is where the masonic secret files have been kept. There are also some sketchy allusions to local politics which leave even local audiences in doubt.

Fernando Rey plays his usual mellow, paternal role with dignity and expertise; Angela Molina, who appears only fleetingly at the beginning and end of the film, is the main buoyant element of the story, though she looks even more haggard than in "Demons in the Garden;" Amparo Soler Leal is perfect as the simple-minded, distracted wife of Don Antonio; and Imanol Arias, as the young, confused bastard son/cum priest who spins the whole yarn in one long flashback, is cautiously competent but rather lifeless.

Pic jumps about in its locations from the Mallorcan villa, where the profligate Don Antonio has been reunited with his estranged wife (his supposed brink of financial ruin is not reflected in the sets), to a trip to Paris where Don Antonio pilots a balloon, and to Rome for an audience with the Pope, to whom he mysteriously presents a document. The abrupt demise of story comes when wife Maria Antonia inadvertently poisons herself. Don Antonio voluntarily follows her cue, and Xima (Angela Molina) is seen floating Ophelia-like in a stream. Presumably her death and that of a neighbor are the result of masonic intrigue, though this is never clearly explained. —Besa.

The Deadly Spawn
(COLOR)

Strictly amateur night for these eels from space.

———

A 21st Century Distribution release of a Filmline Communications production. Produced by Ted Bohus. Directed by Douglas McKeown. Features entire cast. Screenplay, McKeown, from story by Bohus, John Dods, McKeown; add'l dialog, Tim Sullivan; camera (Technicolor), Harvey Birnbaum; processing, Studio 16; editor, Marc Harwood; music, Michael Perilstein; add'l music, Ken Walker, Paul Cornell; sound-lighting director, Frank Balsamo; special makeup effects, Arnold Gargiulo; special effects-assoc. producer, John Dods; add'l photography, Carl Santoro. Reviewed at RKO National 1 theatre, N.Y., April 23, 1983. (MPAA Rating: R). Running time: 78 MINS.

Charles ..... Charles George Hildebrandt
Tom .... Tom De Franco
Frankie .... Richard Lee Porter
Ellen .... Jean Tafler
Kathy .... Karen Tighe
Aunt Millie .... Ethel Michelson
Uncle Herb .... John Schmerling
Sam .... James Brewster
Barbara .... Elissa Neil

"The Deadly Spawn" is a non-pro horror film lensed in New Jersey in 1981, with yet another set of monsters inspired by that influential hit "Alien." Resolutely low-budget, picture is a minor entry in the Yowl-and-Growl genre.

Pre-credits teaser establishes the monsters as having arrived on Earth via a meteorite shower. Sightless (no eyes) but sensitive to sound, the fast-multiplying beasties resemble the "chest-burster" critter that felled John Hurt in "Alien," and when full-grown their toothy mouths are constantly dripping in the manner of the adult

"Alien." Bulk of the picture has them in the basement preying on a family and friends.

The tyro filmmakers are, obviously fans of B-monster movies, judging by knowing verbal references, attractive posters, a thank-you credit to fan supremo Forrest J. Ackerman and even a discussion of the psychology of terror. Pic's hero has a bedroom filled with monster masks, and given the okay gore effects and cute puppet monster footage here, he represents the target audience. He also ingeniously saves the day with a homemade monster zapper and a trusty extension cord, while his older brother (an unimaginative science student) folds under pressure.

A cheap slide-shot of a miniature is used for film's exterior atmosphere and finale, and editing is haphazard (including mismatched reverse shots crossing the center line). Blowup from 16m is quite grainy. The paradox with cheapies such as this one is that its fans-turned-filmmakers would undoubtedly avoid sitting through such a picture, opting instead for pro B's such as "The Monster That Challenged The World" ("Spawn's" obvious forebear) or a film cited explicitly, "It! The Terror From Beyond Space" (which inspired "Alien"). —*Lor.*

Rio Babilonia
(Rio Babylon)
(BRAZILIAN-COLOR)

Gramado, March 24.

An Embrafilme release of a Cineville Producoes Cinematograficas CPC Helio Paulo Ferraz Embrafilme production. Features entire cast. Directed by Neville D'Almeida. Screenplay, Neville D'Almeida, Ezequiel Neves, Joao Carlos Rodrigues; art direction, Yurika Yamazaki; costumes, Liege Monteiro; camera (Eastmancolor), Edson Santos; assistant directors, Liege Monteiro, Jirges Ristum, Marco Antonio Cury; make-up, Jaque Monteiro; executive production, Carlos Alberto Diniz; music, Jorge Ben, Lincoln Olivetti, Robson Jorge; songs, "Rio Babilonia" (Ben), "Babilonia Rock" (Olivetti, Jorge). Reviewed at Embaixador theatre, Gramado Film Festival, March 24, 1983. Running time: 110 MINS.

Marciano	Joel Barcelos
Vera Moreira	Christiane Torloni
Liberato	Jardel Filho
Claudia	Denise Dummont
Dante	Paulo Villaca
Eduardo	Pedro Aguinaga
Regina	Tania Boscoli
Bira	Antonio Pitanga
Linda Lamar	Pat Cleveland
Madame Solange	Norma Benguell

Also: Paulo Cesar Pereio, Sergio Mamberti, Nildo Parente, Mauricio do Valle, Renato Pedrosa, Maria Gladya, Wilson Grey, Guara Rodrigues, Sandro Solviatt, Lygia Durand, Claudia O'Reilly, Marcus Vinicius, Julio Braga, Carlinhos Pandeiro de Ouro, Helio Braga, Romeu Evaristo, Paulo Bacellar, and the transvestite cast of Jorge Mourao, Mariza Unica, Paulo Angel, Vanessa, Valeria and Munique Lamarque.

This Neville D'Almeida pic was the most ambitious of his career (his previous features include "A Dama do Lotacao" and "Os Sete Gatinhos") and one of the most promising Brazilian productions for this year. Filmmaker worked with almost no restrictions to his budget and absolute creative freedom. As usual, he managed to work with a very rich screenplay. At this time, he had in hands a bright panel of the "carioca" social life, its conflicts, its craziness and especially its mundanity. D'Almeida himself is a part of this world: a socialite in Rio, his project was ultimately a comment on the gloomy social life surrounding himself.

Unfortunately his aim did not completely succeed. In part due to what seems to be Neville's misunderstanding of the screenplay in which he collaborated (though mostly written by Neves and Rodrigues). Partly for deep problems with art direction and the casting, in respect to figuration (protagonists were consciously hired). Partly due to D'Almeida's problems in directing the cast. Reasonably enough, "Rio Babilonia" was accused in Gramado of being just another "pornochanchada" with no further background. This can be true in respect to the final product, although false if one examines the original project.

Such potential does not completely disappear, though. The anarchistic view of Rio de Janeiro social life survives, and very good moments arise. The strong eroticism persists in part, although one cannot say that it really succeeds. (Brazilian censorship banned almost ten minutes, what turns some sequences, especially the strong finale, almost incomprehensible). A the level of intentions, Neville's work could be outstanding, an anarchistic approach to a world of corruption, drugs, sex and hypocrisy. Such level, however, does not count. Neville has made a film with great commercial potentiality, perhaps even for the foreign market. But he has failed to materialize an extraordinary project, which is, to say the least, twice as regrettable. —*Hoin.*

1990: The Bronx Warriors
(ITALIAN-COLOR)

The Bronx, all 'Italiana.

A United Film Distribution Corp. release of a Deaf International Films production. Produced by Fabrizio de Angelis. Directed by Enzo G. Castellari. Stars Vic Morrow, Christopher Connelly, Fred Williamson, Mark Gregory. Screenplay, Dardano Sacchetti, Elisa Livia Briganti, Castellari from story by Sacchetti; camera (Telecolor), Sergio Salvati; editor, Gianfranco Amicucci; music, Walter Rizzati; production manager, Pasquale Vannini; production design-costumes, Massimo Lentini. Reviewed at Rivoli I theatre, N.Y., April 22, 1983. (MPAA Rating: R). Running time: 84 MINS.

Hammer	Vic Morrow
Hot Dog	Christopher Connelly
The Ogre	Fred Williamson
Trash	Mark Gregory
Anne	Stefania Girolami
Ice	John Sinclair

Also with: Ennio Girolami, George Eastman, Betty Dessy, Rocco Lerro, Massimo Vanni, Angelo Ragusa, Enzo Girolami (Castellari).

"1990: The Bronx Warriors" is an exceedingly silly Italian action picture, masquerading as part of the futuristic sci-fi genre of "The Road Warrior" and "Escape From New York." It is likely to be laughed off the screen at all but the most marginal grindhouses.

Very poorly scripted (with risible tough-guy dialog in English), picture pits a ruthless agent of the Manhattan Corp. named Hammer (no it's not star Fred Williamson who used to use this nickname, but rather the late Vic Morrow) against various gang leaders in the Bronx, a no man's land beyond the scope of 1990's police or military. The prize is Anne (Stefania Girolami), heiress to control of Manhattan Corp. and kidnappee of various gangs. Skimpy plot twists involving petty treachery and periodic rumbles are eventually nullified by Hammer adopting a scorched earth policy involving horsemen bearing flamethrowers.

The film sadly lacks atmosphere, with its filmed on Bronx locations exteriors (interiors lensed in Rome) looking peaceful and ordinary. Action scenes are dull, with director Enzo G. Castellari emphasizing rituals and posed setpieces at the expense of dynamic thrills. Dubbing is subpar (though leads articulate in English).

In his penultimate film role pre-"Twilight Zone" tragedy, Vic Morrow has been dubbed by another's voice, and is disappointing as a stock exterminator character. Fred Williamson, filling the Isaac Hayes role (from "Escape From New York" model) as the self-appointed king of the Bronx, comes off best in the cast, handling himself smoothly in fight scenes which owe more to Italian sword 'n sandal programmers than recent violent epics.

Campiest moments are provided by the nominal hero, a dark-complexioned young Italian actor named Mark Gregory, who as "Trash" struts around with toolight on his feet posturings that are guaranteed to generate catcalls and jeers from the fans. Hopefully the scores of futuristic Italian action films upcoming will incorporate fantasy elements, sorely lacking in this junker. —*Lor.*

A Idolatrada
(The Loved One)
(BRAZILIAN-COLOR)

Gramado, March 23.

An Embrafilme release of a Government of State of Minas Gerais/Embrafilme production. Features entire cast. Directed by Paulo Augusto Gomes. Screenplay, Paulo Augusto Gomes, Mario Alves Coutinho, based on story by Gomes; camera (Eastmancolor), Dileny Campos; editing, Jose Tavares de Barros; art direction, Carlos Prieto; music, Tavinho Moura; sound, Evandro Lemos da Cunha; produced by Tarcisio Teixeira Vidigal. Reviewed at Embaixador Theatre, Gramado Film Festival, March 23, 1983. Running time: 90 MINS.

Cast: Denise Bandeira, Eduardo Machado, Mario Lago, Carmen Silva, Jose Mayer, Maria Lucia Dahl, Jota D'Angelo.

Very few among the 90 films yearly produced in Brazil are made outside the Rio-Sao Paulo area. Minas Gerais, despite being one of the wealthiest states of the Federation, an agricultural and banking center, seldom contributes with a feature for the national film industry.

"A Idolatrada" is one of the few exceptions. Directed by a young newcomer, Paulo Augusto Gomes, who also wrote the screenplay and the original story, pic has no purpose of raising social and political issues. Instead, it brings the private problem of an elderly couple on the evening of their 50th wedding anniversary. Following the usual party, the husband tells his wife about an old love affair: 46 years before, he fell in love with a young woman but was afraid of breaking his marriage, a fact that he regretted for the rest of his life. The magic of the golden wedding anniversary turns out to be a moment of sorrow, pain and disillusion.

Gomes' narrative is as conventional as his story, which is ultimately a sign of coherence. So old fashioned are both of them that sometimes it is hard to believe that the author is a young man in his early thirties. Nevertheless, acting is good, especially by Mario Lago, Carmen Silva (the couple), Denise Bandeira, Eduardo Machado (the lovers 50 years before). Cinematography, and music by Tavinho Moura ("Cabaret Mineiro") is creative and rich as usual.

Ingenuous and raw especially in respect to the dialog, "A Idolatrada" could be at the most a sign that the author may come out with crafty works at the future, if only his forthcoming films would be more committed to his times. —*Hoin.*

De Vierde Man
(The Fourth Man)
(DUTCH-COLOR)

Amsterdam, March 23.

Verenigde Nederlandse Filmcompagnie release of a Rob Houwer production. Produced by Rob Houwer. Directed by Paul Verhoeven. Screenplay, Gerard Soeteman, based on novel by Gerard Reve; camera (color), Jan de Bong; music, Loek Dikker; editing, Ine Schenkkan; art direction, Roland de Groot. Stars Jeroen Krabbe, Renee Soutendijk. Reviewed at City Theatre, Amsterdam, 23 March '83. Running time: 92 MINS.

Gerard	Jeroen Krabbe
Christine	Renee Soutendijk

Gerard Reve — one of the three or four best and bestselling Dutch novelists, blatant homosexual, vociferous convert to Catholicism (his personal version), stridently right wing in politics, expert in clamorous publicity and calculated scandal — two years ago wrote a slight, spirited, ironical novella.

The protagonist, a gay writer, also called Gerard Reve (although the story as such is not autobiographical), gives a lecture in a coastal town, spends the night, to his own astonishment, in the bed of a local belle, stays on for a few days. While she is in Germany to fetch her fiance whom the writer hopes to seduce, the novelist discovers that the woman has had three husbands each of whom died accidental deaths. Afraid of being the fourth, he flees back to Amsterdam.

The successful Dutch film-trio (i.a. "Turkish Delight," "Katje Tippel," "Soldier of Orange"), producer Rob Houwer, director Paul Verhoeven, and scenario writer Gerard Soeteman, fleshed out the story. Where the living Reve makes fun of the paper Reve — his greed for sex and money, his need to fantasize, to make up stories about any object, person or situation he encounters — the film introduces an atmosphere of magic realism. All the fantasies might be "real," the mysterious might be mystical.

The woman who, in the book, is an attractive, sexy but rather insipid owner of a beauty parlor, becomes in the film a "femme fatale" who might be a genuine honest-to-badness witch.

The scenario is very effective, the direction skillful. Jeroen Krabbe is excellent as the inveterate weaver of tales who believes in his own make-believe and, like a child, frightens himself with his own stories.

Renee Soutendijk gets little chance for acting. The story doesn't decide if her character is that of an emancipated business woman, a wanton or a witch. She just has to look beautiful and enigmatic, which she does.

But the real stars, which provide the magic and the tension, are the fabulous photography of Jan de Bont, the subtle editing of Ine Schenkkamp and the insinuating music of Loek Dikker.

Their manipulation of the audience is most competent, but never obvious. And they make the film look more expensive than its $1,-000,000 budget. Abroad, with good marketing, pic should be attractive to the slightly higher brows. —Wall.

Modern Day Houdini
(COLOR)

Indianapolis, April 14.

A Mid America Promotions Inc. presentation. Produced by Ron Hostetler, Eddie Beverly Jr. Executive Producer, Bill Shirk. Directed by Eddie Beverly Jr. Features entire cast. Screenplay, Steven Meyers; camera (color), Steve Posey; editor, Ron Hostetler; music, Jeffry Boze. Reviewed at Eastwood Theatre, Indianapolis, April 14, 1983. (MPAA Rating: PG). Running time: 90 MINS.
Shirk .... Bill Shirk
Weiss .... Milbourne Christopher
Sharky .... Peter Lupus
The Bruiser .... Dick the Bruiser
Doug Meyers .... Gary Todd
Polly .... Terry Mann
Stormy .... Cynthia Johns
Sylvia .... Elizabeth Bechtel
Mike Winden .... Sam Graves
Hardin .... Robert James Poorman Jr.
Butch .... Dave Dugan
Bubba .... Larry Battson

"Modern Day Houdini" is the product of what seems to be Bill Shirk's obsessions: death, escapology and young (but not quite classy) broads. These are things most would keep private, but not Shirk. He has chosen to reveal his inner sanctum to anyone who might care to look, and in the process has handed Indiana its first locally-produced feature film, although one without a U.S. distributor as yet has been turned down for U.S. distribution.

Shirk, in real life the owner of an Indianapolis AM radio station, probably does know a thing or two about escapology. In the past he has pulled genuine, Houdini-like stunts to promote WXLW. Once he allowed himself to be buried alive with a boa constrictor and other creatures, like rats and spiders. Another time he escaped in a mere 9.8 seconds from a straight jacket 1,-600 feet above ground, hanging by his feet from a helicopter. The gimmicks must have worked at the time: he still owns the station.

But now in real life the station is at risk again. The station has been hocked to make this film — the one about using publicity stunts to save the station from a takeover bid by a conglomerate of mostly black business tycoons. But don't confuse this with art imitating life. There is hardly any life here, and definitely no art.

So back to stunts it is. As this issue goes to press, Shirk is 6 ft. under, with six rats, waiting for the first performance of "Modern Day Houdini" to sell out at Indianapolis' Eastwood Theatre. Only then will he allow himself to be dug up.

Out of the local cast, including a few names from the ranks of central Indiana media figures, no one displays much talent. Direction by Eddie Beverly Jr. is undetectable. More obvious is the editing, which accounts for rambling jerks. Only Indianapolis succeeds in this film.

proving herself to be a suitable backdrop for a wide variety of urban shots. —Tuch.

The Wicked Lady
(BRITISH-COLOR)

And fairly funny, too, as intended.

London, April 18.

A Columbia release (U.K.) MGM/UA release (U.S.) of a Cannon Group presentation. Produced by Menahem Golan and Yoram Globus. Directed by Michael Winner. Stars Faye Dunaway, Alan Bates, John Gielgud. Screenplay, Winner, Leslie Arliss (based on "The Life and Death of the Wicked Lady Skelton" by Magdalen Kinghall); additional dialog, Gordon Glennon. Aimee Stuart; camera (color), Jack Cardiff; art direction, John Blezard; music, Tony Banks; editor, Arnold Crust; sound, John Pyner, Terry Poulton, James Roddan; assistant director, Ron Purdie. Reviewed at Leicester Sq. Theatre, London, April 18, '83. (BBFC rating: 18). Running time: 98 MINS.
Lady Skelton .... Faye Dunaway
Jerry Jackson .... Alan Bates
Hogarth .... John Gielgud
Sir Ralph Skelton ...... Denholm Elliott
Lasy Kingsclere .... Prunella Scales
Kit Locksby .... Oliver Tobias
Caroline .... Glynis Barber
Aunt Agatha .... Joan Hickson
Moll Skelton .... Helena McCarthy
Doll Skelton .... Mollie Maureen
Jackson's girl .... Marina Sirtis
Ned Cotterell .... Nicholas Gecks
Uncle .... Hugh Millais
Landlady .... Guinevere John

Sex, humor and even a facsimile of style, or all the things the indifferent 1945 original with Margaret Lockwood lacked, distinguish Michael Winner's entertaining remake of "The Wicked Lady" as a comedy-drama of rogue-ridden 17th-century England with Faye Dunaway an effective title star. Okay b.o. looms.

Winner, who coauthored the piece with Leslie Arliss, has pumped some amusing life and typically brisk pace into a basically tired old (and even campy) story about an alluring high society dame for whom seduction, highway robbery and even murder are all in a day's work. After marrying Denholm Elliott for his money, Dunaway turns to a life of nocturnal crime, solo at first, but later in cahoots with legendary stagecoach robber Alan Bates. Death by ironic twist awaits both. However permissive the update may be with its nudity and passionate love scenes, it's also very moral in an old-fashioned way.

Film has a number of good jokes, with much of the routine dialog itself constituting a spoof of the genre. Besides abundant displays of female form, for kinkier fans there's also a pretty good duel of whips between Dunaway and Bates' doxy. But as screen violence goes, the sequence qualifies as no more than mere titillating digression. Like the nudity and sex, gratuitous, yes, but excessive, hardly.

Dunaway performs her dominating role with satisfying conviction, straight face and all. Ditto Elliott as her scorned and cuckolded husband. Bates makes for a charming but all-too-brief rogue, while John Gielgud as a Godfearing retainer has a marvelous deadpan time of it kidding himself.

Film was shot last year, largely in rural England, where Jack Cardiff's lensing shows to best effect. Glynis Barber, Oliver Tobias and, especially, Prunella Scales all perform efficiently in key secondary parts.

John Blezard's art direction, Tony Banks' score and other tech credits are all up to snuff. —Pit.

L.A. Filmex

Wild Style
(COLOR)

Hollywood, April 16.

A Wild Style production. Produced, directed, written by Charlie Ahearn. Features entire cast. Camera (uncredited color), Clive Davidson, John Foster; editor, Steve Brown; music, Fred Brathwaite, Chris Stein; sound, Bernie Nobel, Larry Sharf; associate producers, Frederick Brathwaite, Jane Dickson; assistant directors, Colen Fitzgibbon, Rex Piano. Reviewed at the El Rey, L.A., April 16, 1983. (No MPAA Rating.) Running time: 82 MINS.
Raymond (Zoro) ... Lee George Quinones
Phade .... Frederick Brathwaite
Virginia .... Patti Astor
Zroc .... Andrew (Zephyr) Witten
Raymond's brother ...... Carlos Morales
Boy with broom .... Alfredo Valez
Art patroness .... Niva Kislac
TV producer .... Bill Rice
Museum curator .... Glenn O'Brien
Features: Grand Master Flash, Chief Rocker Busy Bee, Fantastic Five, Cold Crush Four, Double Trouble.

"Wild Style" succeeds admirably in its limited ambition of directly expressing the vitality and energy of its subjects, who are the graffiti artists, rappers and dancers of one of the nation's most blighted ghettos, the South Bronx. Pic received a spirited reaction at its public screening at Filmex and is the sort of indie effort with which a small, hustling distributor might be able to score some modest returns in major urban markets.

Producer-director-writer Charlie Ahearn began by making experimental documentaries, and a strong docu flavor permeates this fictional feature, which is cast with actual street kids as well as an impressive lineup of rap performers and break-dancers.

Many New Yorkers consider their graffiti-adorned subway cars as major eyesores, but "Wild Style" makes them into things of imagination, if not beauty. The outlaw art entails the risk of sneaking into subway yards at night, and the fruits of one's labor can only be briefly glimpsed by chance as the trains clack by during the day, unless one earns neighborhood employment by decorating otherwise drab buildings.

Raymond, the self-styled maverick of the area who calls himself "Zoro," refuses to enter the mainstream and persists in painting trains until a newspaper reporter drags him to a chic downtown party replete with condescending poseurs and a new character to the screen, a graffiti artist groupie.

When Zoro finally accepts a commission, it's to paint a large bandshell where his promoter buddy Phade has arranged to stage a giant rap concert. Put on the spot like this, Zoro suffers from creative block until his sort-of girlfriend gets him out of his rut.

That's about it for plot, and Ahearn adds little in terms of psychological or sociological examination. But pic gains plenty from characters' frequent listenings to local rap performers such as the celebrated Grand Master Flash, Busy Bee and others, from a unique display of poetry in motion on the basketball court by the Cold Crush Four, and from some dance units and soloists who show the latest moves in the break-dancing phenomenon.

As played by Lee George Quinones, Zoro is a shy kid whose insistence on artistic independence is unexplained but appealing, and Frederick Brathwaite as the promoter is brashly entertaining. Patti Astor as the white, bleached-blonde reporter comes to co-op the scene for the hip intelligentsia but ends up just digging the action, and pic overall reveals a very optimistic, upbeat attitude toward the self-expressive, achievement-oriented and entrepreneurial activities of society's outcast youths.

Ahearn clearly admires his subjects, and film is of, rather than about, the scene it depicts. Technical aspects are quite acceptable under the low-budget circumstances.
—Cart.

Comedienne
(COLOR-DOCU-16m)

Hollywood, April 11.

A Straightface Films presentation. Produced, directed by Katherine Matheson. Features entire cast. Camera (uncredited color), Robert Chappell, John Hazard, Robert Levi, Thomas Hudson Reeve, Gerald Saldo; editor, Donna Marino; sound, Leo Orloff, Edward Novick; associate producer, Paula Mazur. Reviewed at the American Film Institute Screening Room, L.A., April 11, 1983. (No MPAA Rating.) Running time: 82 MINS.

Features: Cheryl Klein, Zora Rasmussen, Red Lightening, Jerry King, Pat Joyce, Vinnie Platania, Nancy Sigworth, Sterling Swan, Ula Hedwig, Lenny DelDuca, Wayne Matteson.

A study of two aspiring female stand-up comics, "Comedienne" represents a sobering object lesson in the difficulty of a showbiz career. Lensed over a four-year period, absorbing docu follows two women as they make the New York rounds of improv spots, clubs and other venues willing to give unknowns a few minutes to try out their material onstage. This has wide appeal as documentaries go and should have a good future at fests, specialized commercial houses, in non-theatrical markets and on pay and public tv.

Producer-director Katherine Matheson covered the budding careers of comics Cheryl Klein and Zora Rasmussen from 1978-1982. Although there was no way to know it at the beginning, choices proved fortuitous from a dramatic point of view, as Rasmussen rose from improv dates to mini-cult status on national television shows, while Klein basically went nowhere fast.

Because of the long gestation period, feature provides a rare look at how comic schtick is developed and refined, then frozen once it clicks with audiences. At the outset, both Klein and Rasmussen offer routines full of largely undigested real life experiences. Speaking for many comedians over the years, Klein aptly comments at one point that, "Everything that ever made me cry now makes people laugh."

A zany blonde with slightly crossed eyes, Rasmussen holds up an enlargement of her exceedingly straight high school yearbook portrait and makes light of the years she spent as the student to be avoided because she had "cooties." As a refugee from Brooklyn who minored in Spanish men in college, Klein dwells relentlessly on her Jewish heritage and in the process illustrates the limitations of strictly ethnic humor.

Initially, the pic offers a sharp glimpse at the compulson towards aggressiveness, hyperness and always being "on" felt by such performers, but becomes much more trenchant, and painfully touching, when it becomes clear that Klein isn't making it. In an enormously poignant moment, camera catches Klein, after bombing at a club called The Comic Strip, walking off alone into the night carrying her umbrella. One wonders how she can pick herself up after such an experience.

Gradually, Rasmussen begins appearing in increasingly posh settings, leading up to slots on major tv. Klein, on the other hand, can find nowhere to perform but at old folks' bars and for a group of firemen, and eventually, and commendably, shifts gears a bit by writing scripts and making no-budget videos for cable tv.

While Rasmussen becomes somewhat more remote as a person after she starts spinning in the upward spiral success syndrome, Klein has the insight and honesty to admit that comedy serves as a salvation for her, an escape from, and revenge upon, her mother for the limited upbringing afforded her.

Matheson has intercut the two women's stories expertly, and is to be lauded for undertaking such an ambitious project and pulling it off with such aplomb. —Cart.

Leuchtturm Des Chaos
(Lighthouse of Chaos)
(W. GERMAN-COLOR)

Hollywood, April 17.

Produced by Wolf-Eckert Buhler. Directed by Buhler, Manfred Blank. Features entire cast. Camera (color), Bernd Fiedler; editor, Manfred Blank. Reviewed at the El Rey Theater, L.A., April 17, 1983. (No MPAA Rating.) Running time: 119 MINS.

Principal cast: Sterling Hayden.
(In English)

Whatever predisposition you may have to the life and ruminations of actor-rebel-latter day-Dutch bargeman Sterling Hayden, this German-made, autobiographical film is the stuff of human, often painful candor.

A few years ago a young German documentary crew climbed aboard Hayden's colorful barge on a leafy river in Holland, pointed a camera in his direction, and, to use Hayden's favorite phrase in the film, "let her rip." The result is a fascinating confessional, intercut with stills, clips, and garish Commie-hit man headlines from Hayden's largely B-movie Hollywood career of the 1950s.

Why it remained for Europeans, rather than Americans, to record Hayden's flamboyant odyssey is hard to tell. But Hayden, filmed on his boat in sackcloth and beard and alternately swiggling from a fifth of Ballantine's, talks to his filmmakers with almost a paternal urgency. This translates to a remarkably honest self-portrait. Indeed, Hayden occasionally plays the great guru, a self-parodying Ernest Hemingway.

But "Lighthouse of Chaos" (his barge is named Pharos of Chaos) is so full of the cutting edge of self-revelation that there's a universality in the human spill.

Those who have read his autobiographical "The Wanderer," named for the yacht on which he absconded with his four kids to sail to Tahiti in the late 1950s, will find more update here. During one dramatic moment in the film, the filmmakers intercede in the proceedings to recount off-screen how Hayden, the evening before, had come aboard his barge so drunk that he fell into the water and had to be rescued by his son (one of his four who still lives with him). We see Hayden deal with this when he regroups the next morning, and his thoughts on alcohol, like his haunted feelings about betraying friends before the House UnAmeri-can Activities Committee during the Red hearings in 1951, are voiced with calm but tense laconic struggle.

There's humor, too, in the sudden burst of an outrageous thought or story, but when things matter there's no bravado. For those who recall how Hayden despised his Hollywood movies — he literally made six a year between 1951 and '58, when he fled from it all — Hayden also signals out two that he's proud of John Huston's "The Asphalt Jungle" (1949) and Stanley Kubrick's "Dr. Strangelove" (1962). Clips of his Army general's breakdown in "Strangelove" are intercut with Hayden recalling his near-breakdown shooting that movie. "I was creatively impotent," he says, near to the point of "crying" during one scene with Peter Sellers that took 48 takes. Whatever, the performance on film comes across as one of his best, and the filmmakers let it speak for itself. Hayden also pays a brief, off-hand tribute to Robert Altman (with whom he made "The Long Goodbye").

German producer, codirector Wolf-Eckert Buhler never takes the camera off Hayden except for black-and-white Hollywood flashbacks. To see Hayden walking like Moses along a Flemish riverbank and then to cut to an old Los Angeles Examiner headline — "Four Stars for Hayden! He Names Commies" — is a job that keeps the contradictions overwhelming.

This American premiere, a solo screening last weekend at Filmex, stacks up as a good bet for a U.S. distributor (print source is Red Harvest Films, based in Munich). To pair this with one of Hayden's better films on the art house circuit, or for PBS or specialized distribution seems eminently negotiable. —Loyn.

The Spirit Moves
(DOCU-B&W)

Hollywood, April 11.

Produced and directed by Mura Dehn. Camera (black and white), John Cohan; editors, Herbert Matter, Mura Dehn. Reviewed at the American Film Institute, L.A., April 10, 1983. (No MPAA rating). Running time: 140 MINS.

"The Spirit Moves" is definitely strictly for devotees to the art of dance, not the art of cinema. The spirit may move in this 30-year chronicle of Black dance in the U.S., but the film doesn't.

Produced and directed by dance historian Mura Dehn, "Spirit" has been praised as the only existing record of the influence and style of jazz dancing and how it affected modern dance. So be it for those who really care.

For others, the quality of the black-and-white film is technically poor and the camera work so static the mind goes numb. Much of the work is no more than dancers doing their steps in a poorly lit bare studio while the camera never moves.

Narration is exceedingly pedantic and academic, usually over dull and crude exposition titles, with black leaders tossed in sometimes for connections.

Finally, except for experts, a lot of those old dances look a lot alike and it's near impossible for the novice to appreciate what's been shown, especially when required to recall unclear narration of moments before. And there's a strong suspicion some of the music was laid in later because movement and rhythm don't always seem to match. —Har.

Black Wax
(U.K./U.S.-COLOR-DOCU-16m)

Hollywood, March 11.

A Mugg-Shot production for Channel 4. Produced, directed, edited, set design by Robert Mugge. Written by Mugge, Gil Scott-Heron. Camera (uncredited color), Lawrence McConkey; music, Scott-Heron; sound, Lee Dichter. Reviewed at the Universal Studios, Universal City, March 11, 1983. No MPAA Rating. Running time: 79 MINS.
Features: Gil Scott-Heron, Ed Brady, Robert Gordon, Glen (Astro) Turner, Kenny Powell, Carl Cornwall.

Gil Scott-Heron calls himself a "bluesologist," but "Black Wax" reveals him as considerably more than that. Framed around an engaging nightclub performance with the Midnight Band, feature docu presents Scott-Heron the hipster, history teacher, poet and political commentator as he gives a counter-culture alternative to a Cook's tour of his native Washington, D.C. Made for Channel 4 in London, film should be embraced Stateside in appropriate music-oriented venues, and where entertainer's irreverent social analysis will be appreciated.

Foremost impression Scott-Heron makes is as a skilled monologuist, whether or not his spiels are accompanied by music. Smooth talking in a rhyming, sing-song manner reminiscent of the best of Muhammad Ali, the young jazz-man addresses such subjects as the civil rights movement, apartheid, illegal aliens and former Philadelphia Mayor Frank Rizzo in highly successful social protest tunes, and contrasts the official monuments of the nation's capital with the poverty-stricken side of the city that few tourists ever see.

One of his most devastating numbers is "B-Movie," in which President Ronald Ray-gun, as he's called, is cast in the leading role of a low-budget film in which the rest of the population plays supporting, or non-supporting parts, as the case may be.

Scott-Heron also pays a visit to a local Wax Museum, where he confronts and tweaks the noses of prominent American historical figures with playfully trenchant commentary.

Robert Mugge, whose "Sun Ra: A Joyful Noise" played at Filmex two years ago, is clearly fully responsive to Scott-Heron's music and message, and has come up with one of the more entertaining and edifying music docus of recent times, one which strongly communicates the personality of the subject. It's all Scott-Heron's show, as no one else is allowed to share the spotlight with him and one doesn't at all get to know the neighborhood he claims as his own, but film still represents a fine introduction to a vibrant, nervy talent.
—Cart.

Doctora
(Doctor)
(COLOR-DOCU)

Hollywood, April 21.

A Cultural Research and Communication, Inc. production. Produced, directed by Linda Post, Eugene Rosow. Camera (color), Antonio Equino; editor, Eugene Rosow; sound, Alberto Villanpando. Reviewed at The Redd Foxx Screening Room, L.A., April 21, 1983. (No MPAA rating). Running time: 56 MINS.
Principal cast: Dr. Ruth Tichauer.
(In English and Bolivian Indian dialects)

Documentary directors-producers Linda Post and Eugene Rosow last spring and summer, on a budget of $120,000, plunged into the jungles and barrios of Bolivia to film the story of Dr. Ruth Tichauer, a 74-year old exile from Nazi Germany who ministers to the ancient Aymara Indian community in South America's poorest country.

Known as "Dr. Schweitzer of the Andes," Tichauer is a remarkable woman and this docu, shot by Bolivia's single, best-known film-maker, Antonio Equino, amply demonstrates the power of a beacon in the midst of darkness. Traversing mountains and valleys in a mobile medical van, taking vegetables and fruit as pay from her Indian patients, Tichauer is an elite European bringing sophisticated medical techniques to people ignored by Bolivia's own elite and who have never seen a doctor in their lives.

Tichauer, according to the filmmakers, didn't want to do the film but relented when she thought the production might inspire outside funding for her operation (she receives no help from the Bolivian government). The "doctora," as everyone calls her, strikes an uncanny trust with the superstitious Indians, who are seen in unintended comic poses, huddled on outdoor clinics under their bowler hats and ponchos with thermometers sticking out of their mouths.

The directness and simplicity of Tichauer are enormously impressive and so, too, are the occasional vistas of the land, which ultimately blend into the story and become as one with its humanity. —Loyn.

Itineraire Bis
(Sideroads)
(FRENCH-COLOR)

Hollywood, April 9.

Produced by Rene Feret. A Films Arquebuse production. Directed by Christian Drillaud. Features entire cast. Screenplay, Christian Drillaud, J.C. Carriere; camera (color), Eduardo Serra; editor, Christiane Lack; music, Jean Musy. Reviewed at The Burbank Studios, Burbank, April 9, 1983. (No MPAA rating). Running time: 90 MINS.
Charles .... Georges Wilson
Cyprien .... Rufus
Marthe .... Claire Maurier
Robert .... Andre Marcon
Jeanne .... Martine Kalayan
Pelletti .... Marc Fayolle
(In French, English subtitles)

Aptly entitled, "Sideroads" (Itineraire Bis) is a meandering odyssey loosely anchored by a young man who careens around the suburbs of France in search of commercial enterprise. Apparently, director Christian Drillaud's intention was to create an artful and playful patchwork of youthful dreams overlaid with a soupcon of eccentric characters and absurd twists.

The result, however, is unappetizing. There are several reasons for this: although the movie is not an anti-narrative experiment, the deliberate abandonment of any ordinary structure muddies up the film. Focus continually shifts between the youth and his dream of buying a pizza truck to a pair of strange middle-aged brothers who share this great old house which in a curious fairytale way becomes the star of the film. The boy himself (Andre Marcon) is callow and unappealing, and the brothers (the wheelchair-bound Georges Wilson and the puzzling Rufus (give eccentricity a bad name. Stylistically, the film shifts from the lyrical to the mundane to the bizarre, and thematically it's uncertain. Life may be quirky, full of disorder and even occasional charm but at a minimum we expect a film to give it shape. This film is shapeless and too impatient with itself.

The handicapped brother gives the boy money for his truck. The boy's girl (Martine Kalayan, in a nice performance) joins the melange. There's a comic-tragic accidental killing of the brother in the wheelchair. And a sensual performance by Claire Maurier who lives with an ascetic young man — down the road, so to speak. What hurts is that the idiosyncrasies are not even particularly French.
—Loyn.

Les Yeux Des Oiseaux
(Eyes of the Birds)
(BRITISH-FRENCH-COLOR)

Hollywood, March 23.

A Channel 4 (London) production. Produced by Daniel Vaissaire. Directed by Gabriel Auer. Features entire cast. Screenplay, Carlos Andreau, Gabriel Auer; camera (color), Jean-Yves Escoffier; editor, Joelle Nache; music, Francois Tusques, Carlos Andreau. Reviewed at Universal Studios, Universal City, March 23, 1983. Running time: 83 MINS.
Cast: Roland Amstutz, Philippe Clevot, Jean-Claude Leguay, Bernard Waver.
(In French, English subtitles)

Based on events which reportedly happened in the "model" prison of Libertad in Uruguay, this French film is a chilling indictment of both political repression in Uruguay and the callowness of a Red Cross prison inspection team that's too weak-willed to fight for the human rights of prisoners.

Although ostensibly a fiction/narrative, the Uruguayan prison setting and the starchness of the telling create a haunting, documentary tone. Unlike the genre jail-house movie, even those based on factual conditions, "Eyes of the Birds" is quiet, not riotous. Human deterioration is psychological, not physical. And because the violence is implicit — trucks driving prisoners away into the night — the atmosphere of abuse is more terrifying.

Heightening the tension, and irony, is a prison so antiseptic in its spotlessness that the film is almost odorous with disinfectant; and director, co-writer Gabriel Auer finds the exact cinematic form — a burnished clarity — to tell the story.

Cast with professional actors and non-pros, the narrative centers on supposedly private interviews between inmates and a three-man delegation from the International Committee of the American Red Cross. But prison authorities are secretly recording the 'private' conversations. Even when presented with reports of that betrayal, the head of the delegation, citing political expediency, compels his Red Cross teammates to keep their mouths shut. And prisoner reprisals follow.

The film is crisply edited and one of the first theatricals produced by the new Channel 4 in London.
—Loyn.

Xi Ying Men
(The In-Laws)
(CHINESE-COLOR)

Hollywood, March 12.

A Shanghai Film Studio production. Directed by Zhao Huanzhang. Screenplay, Xin Xianling; camera (color), Peng Enli, Cheng Shiyu. Reviewed at The Burbank Studios, Burbank, March 12, 1983. (No MPAA rating.) Running time: 103 MINS.
Features: Wang Shuqin, Wen Yujuan, Yu Shaokang, Wang Yumei, Zhang Liang, Ma Xiaowei, Hong Xuemin.

Watching "The In-Laws," one might never suspect that a communist revolution once took place in China. True, there are a few references to the commune, the brigade leader, work points and party meetings, but this cheerful domestic drama set in a rural community posits above all the value and virtue of family life as the backbone of society. Made in 1981, film satisfies an ongoing curiosity about what is happening culturally in China these days, but also raises the question of whether this is representative of current fare, or merely an aberration. Fests and other one-shot bookings comprise the domestic market for this determinedly apolitical picture.

In theme and even style, film could almost have been made at MGM in the 1930s. In a tranquil, fertile area which could pass for the Napa Valley, the Chen family lives in a common housing unit until the temperemental wife of the eldest son hordes some meat dumplings. Most upset, Grandpa decides to move out and tremendous friction is generated among diverse family members until reason prevails and everyone sits down to supper over a tableful of dumplings.

Not much of a plot, to be sure, and based on what dialog is translated by subtitles, it's frequently difficult to figure out what all the characters are getting so worked up about. Accusations and recriminations fly like fur in a cat fight, but issues invariably seem like minor ones. Even by fade-out the precise relationships of many of the characters remain rather confusing, blame for which is hard to attribute.

In any event, approach is conventional in the extreme, with broad acting, bright, clean lighting and a straightfaced acceptance of the soap opera plot being the order of the day. Plenty of old-fashioned homilies are delivered, the elderly are treated with great deference, and traditional methods of problem-solving are endorsed.

On a technical level, pic appears to have been post-synched, and the sound overall has a studio quality in which the dialog and background noises have not been integrated in the naturalistic manner expected by Western audiences. There is also a considerable amount of zooming employed to reframe scenes when characters move around.

Film won the best film award from the Ministry of Culture in China and was selected for export from among three pics produced in 1981 by the Shanghai Film Studio.
— Cart.

I Apenati
(The Woman Across The Way)
(GREEK-COLOR)

Hollywood, March 15.
A Giorgos Panoussopoulos Ltd., Greek Film Center/Greka Film M. Lefakis S.A.

production. Produced, directed, edited by Giorgos Panoussopoulos. Screenplay, Panoussopoulos, Philippos Drakontaidis, Petros Tatsopoulos; camera (color), Aris Stavrou; music, Stavrous Logaridis. Reviewed at the Warner Hollywood Studios, L.A., March 15, 1983. (No MPAA rating.) Running time: 110 MINS.
Stella .... Bette Livanou
Haris .... Aris Retsos
Features: Georges Siskos, Dimitris Poulikakos, Dora Volanaki.
(In Greek: English subtitles)

"The Woman Across The Way" is not an unskillful but overly monotonous study of a young man's obsession with a neighboring lady. Second feature of former cinematographer Giorgos Panoussopoulos is actually most interesting as a glimpse of the American cultural colonialization of Greek teenagers, but is not sufficiently dramatic to have commercial potential domestically.

Young Haris lives with his widowed mother in a bland apartment building in suburban Athens and spends most of his time gazing through his telescope while listening to rock tunes on American Forces Radio.

Although ostensibly interested in astronomy, he more often trains his lens, not on the stars, but on a handsome woman who lives across the street. By the hour he observes her going through her boring daily routines, arguing with her husband and tending to her child. Eventually he starts phoning her, but hangs up after saying little or nothing to her.

Uncommunicative and downright rude to his mother, Haris wanders the streets from time to time but is sullen with his friends and turns down job opportunities, as work would undoubtedly interfere with his voyeuristic pursuits.

But these nocturnal promenades do provide a look at the America-obsessed Greek youths, who dance to English-language tunes, wear U.S. university t-shirts, pose as though they've just sat through a James Dean retrospective and race motorcycles on public thoroughfares.

All along, it's difficult to know what Haris' intentions are. Finally, he crashes a party at her place and establishes some initial contact, a move reciprocated when the woman, rather surprisingly, visits and makes love to him. Climactic scene is abruptly, almost unnaturally, truncated, leaving in doubt both parties' emotional and physical reactions. But indications are that, goal accomplished, Haris can now proceed with other aspects of his life.

By refusing to enter psychological territory, Panoussopoulos limits the scope of his picture, making it a rather cold, detatched work of only marginal interest for its sociological nuances and observations. Camerawork and other technical

aspects are fine, although English subtitles are sloppy in the extreme.
— Cart.

A Deusa Negra
(Black Goddess)
(NIGERIAN-BRAZILIAN-COLOR)

Hollywood, March 29.
A Magnus Filmes/Afrocult Foundation production. Produced by Jece Valadao. Directed, screenplay by Ola Balogun. Camera (color), Philippe Gosselet, Edison Baptista; music, Reni Kababa. Reviewed at the Warner Hollywood Studios, L.A., March 29, 1983. (No MPAA rating.) Running time: 90 MINS.
Features: Jorge Coutinho, Sonia Santos, Zozimo Bulbul, Lea Garcia.
(In Wolof: English subtitles)

"Black Goddess" belongs in cultural, not artistic, film festivals. Paucity of storytelling or technical skills makes viewing this a painful experience, and goodwill brought to one of the few Nigerian films to be seen on these shores quickly dissipates under the weight of awkward direction and dialog, and artistic aspirations which are obvious in the first five minutes. Commercial opportunities for this four-year-old film are zilch.

To state that this represents an attempt at a "Roots" set in South America pretty much says it all. A young African promises his dying grandfather that he'll return to Brazil and bring what remains of their family there back home. Armed only with the carving of a goddess, Babatunde tracks down the appropriate religious group in Rio and meets a ceremonial dancer through whom the goddess speaks to him.

To get to the source of their origins, duo travels toward Bahia along with a jealous admirer of the dancer. In a fight scene so poorly staged that it makes fisticuffs in old Republic serials look convincing, the jealous b.f. tumbles off a little hill to his death, whereupon the remaining couple blithely proceeds toward their destination.

Shortly thereafter, one is treated to a half-hour flashback detailing slave life in the region some 200 years earlier, which at least relieves some of the tedium by offering a modicum of dramatic confrontation. But all that emerges from the tale is that Babatunde and the dancer were destined to meet in modern Brazil. And that the boyfriend can just be left lying in the ditch, with no burial, investigation or further mention.

Director Ola Balogun is said to have made eight features in the last decade, including three since completing this one. Surely they could not have been of less interest than "Black Goddess." — Cart.

Maria Chapdelaine
(CANADIAN-FRENCH-COLOR)

Montreal, May 3.
An Astral Film Production, in collaboration with Radio Canada (Canadian Broadcasting Corp.) and La Societe nationale de programmes T.F. 1 (France). Executive producer, Harold Greenberg. Producers Murray Shostak, Robert Baylis. Directed by Gilles Carle. Features entire cast. Screenplay, Carle, Guy Fournier, based on novel by Louis Hemon; art direction, Jocelyn Joly; camera (color), Pierre Mignot; costumes, Michele Hamel; film editing, Avde Chiriaeff, Michel Arcand; music, Lewis Furey; special effects, Bill Orr, John Thomas. Reviewed at Cinema Le Dauphin, Montreal, April 27, 1983. Running time: 108 MINS.
Marie Chapdelaine .... Carole Laure
Francois Paradis .... Nick Mancuso
Father Cordelier .... Claude Rich
Laura Chapdelaine .... Amulette Garneau
Samuel Chapdelaine .... Yoland Guerard
Eutrope Gagnon .... Pierre Curzi
Lorenzo Surprenant ...... Donald Lautrec
Marie-Ange .... Marie Tifo
Also: Gilbert Sicotte, Guy Thauvette, Stephan Query, Josee-Anne Fortin, Louis-Philippe Milot, Gilbert Comtois, Patrick Messe, Claude Evrard, Paul Berval, Guy Godin, Dominique Briand, Claude Pregent, Angele Arsenault, Jean Ricard, Guy L'Ecuyer, Roland Bedard, Raoul Duguay, Michel Rivard, Gilles Valiquette, Michel Langevin, Cedric Noel, Jose Ledoux, Renee Girard, Roch Demers, Yvon Sarrazin, Claude Trudeal, Jean-Pierre Rheaume, Georges Levchtouk, Gilbert Moore.

Harold Greenberg, executive producer of the highest-grossing picture in the history of the Canadian film industry, "Porky's," can now lay claim to making "The Great Canadian Film."

"Maria Chapdelaine," after a world premiere here on April 28, opened in its original French-track version in 24 theatres across Quebec. The English version and television mini-series are both projected for the fall.

The long-awaited pic, based on the 1913 international bestseller by Louis Hemon, is the effort of one of Canada's most accomplished director, Gilles Carle.

Carle co-scripted "Maria" with Guy Fournier, principal author of the Fournier Report, the Quebec film and video policy review which included many recommendations now in Bill 109, the draft of a proposed law now before Quebec's parliament.

Faithfully translated to the screen, "Maria" is beautiful to look at, lyrical, and haunting.

The story of a French-Canadian farmer's daughter (Laure), promised in marriage to the timid farmer next door (Curzi), pursued by a rich city slicker (Lautrec), but tragically in love with a handsome woodsman (Mancuso), the film describes the harsh conditions and hardships of turn-of-the-century rural life in Quebec's north.

This was not an easy film to make. The prop master personally logged 7,200 miles on his truck during the first few weeks of shooting. Location was 300 kilometers (200 miles) north of Montreal. The area, with an average annual snowfall of

110 inches, barely got 10 inches in the unusual winter of 1982-83.

The set, a village including a church, general store, post office, homes, barns, and a logging camp, was completely constructed by the film crew. The results were worth it.

The photography and art direction are flawless. The music, composed by Lewis Furey, is sumptuous but sometimes too loud and too present. The performances are polished. The luscious Laure and the macho Mancuso are even prettier than the scenery. But they're both too old for the parts.

Carle should have risked going with teen-agers. Only then would many of the ill-considered and rash actions of the principals make sense.

This is the third version of the film. First made in 1934 by Julien Duvivier, the original featured Madeleine Renaud and Jean Gabin. The 1949 Marc Allegret remake starred Michele Morgan and Phillippe Lemaire. The English versions of both were titled "The Naked Heart."

Boxoffice is a question mark. Depending on the marketing, this could be a hit or could slip by unnoticed. Reception in the French-speaking world should be excellent.

Pic was produced with the participation of the Canadian Film Development Corporation, the Quebec Film Institute, and the Aluminum Company of Canada. —*Zerb*.

Doctor Detroit
(COLOR)

A double, but dull, life.

Hollywood, April 28.

A Black Rhino/Brillstein Co. production of a Michael Pressman Film for Universal. Produced by Robert K. Weiss. Directed by Michael Pressman. Stars Dan Aykroyd. Screenplay, Carl Gottlieb, Robert Boris, and Bruce Jay Friedman; story by Bruce Jay Friedman (based on his novel, "Detroit Abe"); camera (Technicolor), King Baggot; editor, Christopher Greenbury; music, Lalo Schifrin; production design, Lawrence G. Paull; set decorator, Hal G. Gausman; costume design, Betsy Cox; sound, William Kaplan; associate producer, Peter V. Herald; assistant director, Gary Daigler. Reviewed at Universal Studios, April 28, 1983. (MPAA Rating: R). Running time: **89 MINS.**

Clifford Skridlow	Dan Aykroyd
Smooth Walker	Howard Hesseman
Diavolo Washington	T.K. Carter
Monica McNeil	Donna Dixon
Thelma Cleland	Lynn Whitfield
Jasmine Wu	Lydia Lei
Karen Blittstein	Fran Drescher
Mom	Kate Murtagh
Arthur Skridlow	George Furth
Margaret Skridlow	Nan Martin
Harmon Rousehorn	Andrew Duggan
Bandleader	James Brown
Judge	Parley Baer

Dan Aykroyd's first solo-starring picture, "Doctor Detroit," centered on a meek college professor who leads a double life as a Windy City mobster, is a frantic, glossy, sputtering comedy too inchoate to promise much boxoffice fun for Universal.

Concept is promising enough: a naive professor of Chivalry in Literature is hurtled into protecting a band of penthouse prostitutes as a fictitious Doctor Detroit. He wears crimson velour jackets, lavender trousers, and a great bush of a wig in his rush from academia to a rhinestone underworld. But there's a curious old-fashioned quality, both about the story and the style, that suggests a glitzy, Runyonesque-inspired comedy that could have been made in the 1950s. Pic, however, is devoid of charm or ballast.

Director Michael Pressman and Aykroyd indeed generate some laughs but there are long periods when there are no laughs. Start of the film is okay, when pimp Howard Hesseman flees from tangle with rival mobster Mom (played by rotund Kate Murtagh) and hands his working girls over to Aykroyd, following some wild bar-hopping on Rush Street.

The sleek foursome of girls, who look pretty good cuddled around the dauntless hero in the leather folds of limousines, certainly qualify as a fantasy quartet but not once do they ever suggest that they are hookers, which is a petty annoyance. Visually leading the pack is vaulting blonde Donna Dixon, whose giggly and ethnic support team comprises black Lynn Whitfield, Oriental Hawaiian Lydia Lei and a Brooklyn Jewish princess type, Fran Drescher.

Hesseman is wasted, out of the pic in minutes, big Mom is tiresome in the uninspired hands of Murtagh; and George Furth, as Aykroyd's dad and college head, is overcome by his role's single-note anxiety. Aykroyd shines much better as the staid professor; his antics as Doctor Detroit never fly and the result is silly rather than humorous.

Actor who does register strongly is comic T.K. Carter, as Aykroyd/Hesseman's jivey chauffeur. Andrew Duggan and Nan Martin are along for the ride.

The sense of desperation on screen suggests too many hands on the script; the credited writers are Bruce Jay Friedman (whose novel, "Detroit Abe," is basis for script), Carl Gottlieb; and Robert Boris.

Production values, particularly a Translite penthouse illusion of the Chicago skyline, are fine. —*Loyn.*

The Terry Fox Story
(CANADIAN-COLOR)

Winnipeg, April 27.

A 20th Century-Fox (Canada) release of an Astral Film production in co-operation with CTV and the Bank of Montreal (HBO for U.S.). Produced by Robert Cooper. Executive producers, Gursten Rosenfeld; Michael Levine; associate producer, John Eckert. Directed by Ralph L. Thomas. Stars Robert Duvall, Eric Fryer. Screenplay, Edward Hume, story, John and Rose Kastner; camera (color) Richard Ciupka; art direction, Gavin Mitchell; editor, Ron Wisman; music, Bill Conti. Reviewed at the Odeon screening room, Winnipeg. April 26, 1983. Running time: **96 MINS.**

Bill Vigars	Robert Duvall
Terry Fox	Eric Fryer
Doug Alward	Michael Zelniker
Darrell Fox	Chris Makepeace
Rika Noda	Rosalind Chao
Betty Fox	Elva Mai Hoover
Rolly Fox	Frank Adamson
Judith Fox	Marie McCann
Dr. Simon	R.H. Thomson
Dan Grey	Saul Rubinek
Gregg	Gary Darycott
Bob Cady	Matt Craven
Wilson	Chuck Shamata
Peg Leg	Patrick Watson

"The Terry Fox Story" chronicles the heroic life of the young Canadian man whose 1980 Marathon Of Hope resulted in raising more than $20,000,000 for cancer research. It's an uplifting, emotional tale guaranteed to become a major boxoffice champion in Canada with strong theatrical prospects in international markets. The film, while specific, has an obvious universal theme and plays on a visceral level audiences need few subtitles to understand. It will be released in the U.S. via Home Box Office.

Newcomer Eric Fryer plays the title role with tremendous conviction. The story opens in Vancouver in 1977, prior to the time Fox lost his right leg to cancer. In short order, the film dispenses with the diagnosed malignancy, Fox's convalescence, the fitting of a prosthetic leg and his decision to run across Canada to raise money for cancer research.

The opening section suffers slightly as a result of brevity and awkward dramatics. However, once the film moves into the actual run, it never loses its emotional grip or falters in pacing and involvement.

Despite initial parental and medical opposition, Fox's dream begins in April 1980. He enlists the aid of his friend, Doug Alwood (Michael Zelniker) to drive a camper and watch his progress but cannot convince his girlfriend, Rika (Rosalind Chao), to leave her job and join the marathon. Simply, he maps out a schedule to run 5,150 miles by doing a daily marathon.

With official support from the Cancer Society pending, he begins by dipping his foot in the Atlantic off the coast of Newfoundland. At the outset, there are only a handful of supporters but as he continues, interest and monetary involvement grow.

The film maintains a refreshing honesty about its subject. Fox remains a sympathetic character despite his obvious human failings. The 21-year-old is viewed as egocentric and abusive to friends with a hint of a suicidal streak as he pushes himself to the limits of his physical endurance.

The tension and rapport between Fox and Alward are particularly well-defined as the initial stages of the marathon take a severe mental toll on the one-legged runner. In Quebec, the people and the media virtually ignore him but he's greeted royally when he crosses into Ontario.

At this stage in his progress, Ontario Cancer Society rep Bill Vigars (Robert Duvall) enters the picture. Vigars approaches the event with a salesman's zeal, staging media events, speeches and receptions to capitalize on potential donations. There appear to be no limits to where Vigars will seek sponsorship, yet he attempts to maintain a dignity to Fox's activities. It's a difficult balancing act for all concerned.

Fox was forced to end his marathon shortly after he passed the half-way point. The film takes us up to his collapse and hospitalization in Thunder Bay, Ont. where it was diagnosed he'd developed cancer in his lungs. A voice-over by Duvall, as Vigars, tells of his death the following year and the lasting contributions Fox initiated.

A genuinely moving tale, "The Terry Fox Story" would be difficult to accept were it not true. The film captures the rallying emotional effect the event had in Canada and how Fox's marathon elevated him to the status of modern-day hero. His courage is not easily won which makes the story all the more credible.

Directed adroitly by Ralph L. Thomas, the film supports strong technical contributions including Richard Ciupka's handsome lensing and a restrained, effective musical score from Bill Conti. Edward Hume's script, based on research by John and Rose Kastner, combines humor and pathos to underplay the fierce emotional elements surrounding Fox's tale.

Fryer, an acting newcomer and himself an amputee, shows no rough edges in his performance. He's appropriately awkward in his relationship with his girlfriend and quite moving as he finds the strength to address crowds as spokesman for a cause. Rarely has a film concerning emotional growth been told so directly and honestly.

Duvall as Vigars has another accomplished, gutsy role. He playfully suggests a lack of integrity in his character but pulls through as an essentially well-meaning, honest type. He has a rare facility for duplicitous roles.

Once again Thomas draws fine performances from a large supporting cast. Particularly good are Zelniker as Fox's close friend who accepts a thankless position and Chao as Fox's hardpressed girlfriend.

The film, opening in late May, has already lined up the largest simultaneous opening of any Canadian picture in Canada to date. It will have no problem attracting a sizable audience thanks to its subject and craft. Meanwhile, U.S. audiences will see the film a week earlier when it premieres on HBO pay service, a major financier in the picture.

"The Terry Fox Story" is the first movie (dubbed HBO Premiere Films) HBO has funded expressly for its service. It's difficult to pre-guess the picture's U.S. impact in this pilot situation but one guesses HBO might have gotten better mileage from the film by going theatrically first. However, this would defeat the intent of the experiment. —*Klad.*

Something Wicked This Way Comes
(COLOR)

So-so film version of Ray Bradbury favorite—an iffy b.o. proposition.

Hollywood, April 27.

A Buena Vista release of a Walt Disney/Bryna Co. production. Produced by Peter Vincent Douglas. Directed by Jack Clayton. Features entire cast. Screenplay, Ray Bradbury, based on his novel; camera (Technicolor), Stephen H. Burum; editor, Argyle Nelson; music, James Horner; production design, Richard MacDonald; art direction, John B. Mansbridge, Richard James Lawrence; set decoration, Rick Simpson; special visual effects, Lee Dyer; costume design, Ruth Myers; sound (Dolby), Bruce Bisenz; associate producer-assistant director, Dan Kolsrud. Reviewed at the Walt Disney Studios, Burbank, April 27, 1983. (MPAA Rating: PG.) Running time: 94 MINS.
Charles Halloway . . . . Jason Robards
Mr. Dark . . . . Jonathan Pryce
Mrs. Nightshade . . . . Diane Ladd
Dust Witch . . . . Pam Grier
Tom Fury . . . . Royal Dano
Will Halloway . . . . Vidal Peterson
Jim Nightshade . . . . Shawn Carson
Miss Foley . . . . Mary Grace Canfield
Mr. Crosetti . . . . Richard Davalos

Long-anticipated film version of Ray Bradbury's popular novel "Something Wicked This Way Comes" must be chalked up as something of a disappointment. Possibilities for a dark, child's view fantasy set in rural America of yore are visible throughout, but various elements have not entirely congealed into a unified achievement. Visually imposing production has been mounted with taste and care, but estimated cost of $20,000,000 means an unlikely shot at profits for Walt Disney Prods.

Location scenes shot in an astonishingly beautiful Vermont autumn stand in for early 20th century Illinois, where two young boys are intrigued by the untimely arrival of a mysterious carnival troupe. By day, fairgrounds seem innocent enough, but by night they possess a strange allure which leads local inhabitants to fall victim to their deepest desires.

Like all humans, citizens of Green Town have frailties to which they are particularly vulnerable. Town librarian Jason Robards,

father of one of the two lads, feels old, suffers from a weak heart and perhaps suspects he has wasted his life buried in books; barber Richard Davalos yearns for the attentions of beautiful women; schoolmarm Mary Grace Canfield would love to be a beautiful young thing, and one-armed, one-legged bartender James Stacy would give anything to be returned to his full-bodied, football-star form.

Thanks to the diabolical talents of carnival leader Mr. Dark, played by the suitably sinister Jonathan Pryce, these wishes can be granted, but at the price of becoming a member of the traveling freak show. Mr. Dark decides that little Will and Jim would make excellent recruits and pursues them vigilantly until the apocalyptic finale.

Small-town setting has been sumptuously created by ace production designer Richard MacDonald, and textures caught by lenser Stephen H. Burum could hardly have been more beautiful. But there still is slightly threadbare, artificial feeling to the evocation of typical Americana, something that Hollywood studio pics, from "It's A Wonderful Life" to "Margie," used to be able to capture so well.

Beyond that, the fantasy elements have not been integrated with seamless ease into the more straightforward narrative structure. A sense of absolute, Mephistophelian evil which threatens the townspeople seems somewhat diluted, and the manner in which they are threatened or seduced into capitulating to it comes across as less than startling.

Pic literally catches fire with special effects in the final reel, as Mr. Dark flings years of Robards' life to the ground and suffers a horrible fate when his efforts to kidnap the boys go awry. Storm which sends the carnival to oblivion recalls both "The Wizard Of Oz" and "The Ten Commandments" in look.

Despite a couple of mild attempts, film is never really scary, although a scene of a tarantula attack on the kids will inspire some squeamishness, and proceedings remain safely within PG boundaries.

In terms of the memorable work director Jack Clayton has done with children before, in "The Innocents" and "Our Mother's House," lightning has not hit a third time here. In his first film since "The Great Gatsby" nine years ago, Clayton has done a fine job visualizing the screenplay by Bradbury himself, but has missed really connecting with the heart of the material and bringing it satisfyingly alive.

Major themes of aging, missed opportunities and reflective vs. active life are embodied in the Robards character, and actor is gently responsive to them. Most other adult performances are appropriate but on single notes, and Vidal

Peterson and Shawn Carson neatly play kids respectively afraid of adventure and actively looking for it.

As indicated, physical aspects of the film are genuinely impressive, and James Horner's full-bodied score is a strong asset. —*Cart.*

Same As It Ever Was
(AUSTRALIAN-COLOR)

Sydney, April 15.

Alpha Communications Pty. Ltd. Production. Produced, directed and photographed (color), by Albert Falzon. Music, Brian Eno, Talking Heads; editors, Rhonda McGregor, Calli Cerami. Reviewed at Valhalla Cinema, Glebe, Australia, April 15, 1983. Running time: 90 MINS.

"Same As It Ever Was" is aimed at a specific audience, conditioned to accept its purely visual and musical presentation of India's Kumbha Mela Festival. Opening titles tell us the Festival, an important holy event, is held every three years and attracts millions of pilgrims from all over the country.

The film, however, is not a straightforward documentary of the event. Rather, it's a "head" film for young people (and aging hippies) who get off on its psychedelic sights and sounds. For the converted, the film could be an exciting experience; for the uninitiated, it will be a crashing bore.

The first 40 minutes consist solely of images of waterways, shot with distorted lens and equally distorted color, while Brian Eno's sonorous music drones on the soundtrack; the intention is to give the viewer "an impression of weightlessness and flight" per the handout. Later, music by Talking Heads livens up the soundtrack, but the images remain on the same spaced-out level, with scenes of river bathing, crowds gathering, holy men, and the final procession to the river.

Filmmaker Albert Falzon scored a success in the mid-1970s with his original surf film, "Crystal Voyager" and also with "Morning Of The Earth." "Same As It Ever Was" will need to tap the same tuned-in youth audience to make its mark, and in territories where such an audience exists it could become a cult item. Crossover to more general audiences, however, seems most unlikely. —*Strat.*

Een Zaak Van Leven En Dood
(A Matter of Life and Death)
(DUTCH-COLOR)

Amsterdam, April 13.

A Digma Films production. Producer, Matthijs Van Heijningen. Written and directed by George Schouten, based on a Hans Vermoot novel. Stars Peter Faber, Carla Hardy. Camera (color), Marc Felperlaan; editor, Edgar Burchsen; sound, George Bosseors. Reviewed at City Thea-

tre, Amsterdam, April 12, 1983. Running time: 95 MINS.
Hans . . . . Peter Faber
Eva . . . . Carla Hardy
Jack . . . . Derek de Lint
Cecil . . . . Judy Doorman
Lucas . . . . Gerard Cox

Limited foreign prospects seem in store for this, the third of George Schouten's three pictures to date. Prized and accoladed for his earlier efforts, the young director here bases his film on a successful Dutch novel by Hans Vermoot about phobias, psychological deviation and troubled minds. The boxoffice looms to be the most troubled of all.

Plot outlines a young woman, happily in love, who develops attacks of mortal fear, hyperventilation and deep depressions. She leaves her husband for another victim of similar misfortune and a master-slave relationship develops. Anyhow, the woman goes over a 10-story balcony and what the husband tries to find out is: was she pushed?

Unfortunately, by the end of the pic few will care. Schouten couldn't make up his mind whether he wanted to make a psycho-thriller, an allegory on the no man is an island theme, or maybe a new twist: it's normal to be abnormal.

To the director's credit he does create his own style.

The actors did their best to put life into these puppets-in-crisis but, despite some very good work, they succumbed. —*Wall.*

The Lost Tribe
(NEW ZEALAND-COLOR)

Wellington, N.Z., April 2.

A Meridian Films and Film Investment Corp of NZ presentation. Produced by Gary Hannam and John Laing. Written and directed by John Laing. Features entire cast. Camera (color) Thom Burstyn; editor, Philip McDonald; art director, Gerry Luhman; music, David Fraser; sound, Ken Saville; first assistant director Jim Mitchell; production manager, Lynnette Gordon. Reviewed at special preview Kings Two, Wellington, N.Z. April 2, '83. Running time: 114 MINS.
Edward Scarry . . . . John Bach
Ruth Scarry . . . . Darien Takle
Katy . . . . Emma Takle
Inspector Ford . . . . Terry Connolly
Sergeant Swain . . . . Don Selwyn
Bill Thorne . . . . Martyn Sanderson
Mears . . . . Ian Watkin
Eileen . . . . Adele Chapman

One of the four new titles to be unspooled by the New Zealand film industry at this year's Cannes festival is John Laing's psycho-thriller "The Lost Tribe."

While it is unlikely to receive the hype of Geoff Murphy's "Utu," officially selected for screening in the fest's main program, it could prove a sleeper.

At a special before-Cannes preview ("Tribe" is not being released on the home market until later this year), the film proved a fascinating adjunct to the preponderance of strong on adventure and action pics being made here. Director Laing pre-warned "Tribe" could have something of the flavor of '40s Carol Reed mystery thrillers. And it has.

It is there in the look of the movie (even if color, not black and white), and in the methodical pacing of the plot and unravelling of its intricate tracings.

There is also the feel of Hitchcock about, and a whiff of that 1970s Nicolas Roeg sleeper "Don't Look Now" starring Donald Sutherland and Julie Christie.

Yet these echoes of other works and styles are just that. Laing's hand is sure and his own in this his second feature. As writer, director and co-producer he is his own master.

Search for a mysterious lost tribe is the apparent reason for the disappearances of anthropologist Maxwell Scarry in a remote southern fiordland. At first neither his twin brother Edward (John Bach) nor his wife Ruth (Darien Takle) are greatly concerned.

Only his young daughter Katy (Emma Takle), who has inherited her father's seemingly prescient powers, is aware that something extremely out of the ordinary is taking place.

When Edward is interrogated by the police on suspicion of murdering a hooker, he is finally compelled not only to delve into the enigma surrounding the crime, but also to concern himself with Max's disappearance and his long-sublimated desire for sister-in-law Ruth.

Final denouements are played out when Edward, Ruth and Katy travel to the fiordland and find themselves entangled in an explosive and deadly series of events, involving Max and the "lost tribe," from which there is no escape.

While Laing has tended to overload the plot and its mysteries with infinite embellishment, thus making for a longish and at times tooslow a film, "Tribe" nevertheless succeeds on its own merits in most departments.

Technically (camera is Torontobased Thom Burstyn), it looks and sounds first class with excellent acting from John Bach in his first starring role. The film's integrity hinges on the Bach performance and he gives it full throttle ensuring a strong center to the piece.

Darien Takle provides most of what is necessary for the rather enigmatic Ruth, while her in-reallife young daughter, Emma, ably assumes Katy.

A stand-out in the supporting cast is Adele Chapman as the hooker Eileen caught up in the murder investigation.

Chapman's performance in a cameo has the subtle finesse of a big Antipodean star in the making. —*Nic.*

Strata
(NEW ZEALAND-COLOR)

Auckland, April 15.

A Phase Three Films production and release. Produced by John Maynard. Directed by Geoff Steven. Stars Nigel Davenport, Judy Morris. Screenplay, Ester Krumbachova, Michael Havas, Steven; camera (Eastmancolor), Leon Narbey; music, Mike Nock; editor, David Coulson; art director, Dean Cato; wardrobe, Elizabeth Mitchell; makeup, Bryony Hurden; assistant director, Bill Harman. Reviewed at Amalgamated Theatres theatrette, Auckland, April 15, 1983. Running time: 118 MINS.
Victor .... Nigel Davenport
Steve .... John Banas
Margaret .... Judy Morris
Eric .... Tom Brennan
Keith .... Roy Billing
Tony .... Peter Nicoll
Gaylene ....: ..... Mary Regan
Thomas .... Ctibor Turba
Quarantine director .... Patrick Smyth

"Strata" pays its audience the compliment of assuming that it does not have to use tricks or beguilement to claim total attention. Though essential plot details only emerge along the way, and all the usual production values are accounted for, direction and narrative style are straightforward. The scenery is spectacular enough by any standards, but it is used organically.

The drama is worked out against the backdrop of a high, aridly beautiful volcanic plateau, including the rim of a still active crater, with the title linking the geological evidence of recent eruptions with the layers of motive and character revealed in the film's participants.

Five passengers on an international flight, suspected of contact with a cholera outbreak, are being held in an isolated New Zealand medical research center. They escape from quarantine and head for what they think is a nearby town, but become lost in mountainous country. The group comprises Tom Brennan, an American businessman, Roy Billing, a New Zealander and a sorehead, young newly-weds Mary Regan and Peter Nicoll and Ctibor Turba, a remote, Central European figure. After several days on the mountain they are rescued by a vulcanologist, played by Nigel Davenport, and a writer and photographer, Judy Morris and John Banas. They are putting together a book on Davenport, who is making a scientific study of the area.

Brennan, it turns out, is involved in an arms deal and Turba, a political assassin, is trailing him. In the intimacy of their flight and struggle for survival Regan indulges in a consummated, if brief, passion for Billing. Turbas is cheated of his intended victim, but his bottled-up aggression has its eruption near the film's end when the photographer, who has been ignoring Turba's requests not to be photographed, asks him what he does for a living. With a chilling lack of emotion, and in the flattest of

tones, the assassin answers, "I show you."

As he did in "Skin Deep," director Geoff Steven shows he can draw particularly sensitive, natural performances from women. Australian actress Judy Morris is icily poised yet encouraging enough toward the aging vulcanologist to explain the gentle pass that he makes at her, and the title of her book on him, seen at the publisher's party that closes the film, is "Surface Readings," which makes its quiet point. Mary Regan, in her first film role, gives body to what might have been rather a slight character on paper, making Gaylene (the name will have a heavy 'suburban' ring for local audiences) a contradictory amalgam of vulnerability and strength.

Turba, a mime artist in his native Czechoslovakia, constructs a believable killer disguised as a bearlike oddball with an English-language problem.

Davenport's portrayal is exceptional. It goes against the extrovert grain of his usual work, as in the "Chariots of Fire" Lord Birkenhead; there is an air of gentle resignation about him, and there is no doubt that, of all the people in the film (and this is impressively demonstrated in his relaxed handling of the dangerously overwrought Turba) the vulcanologist is most at peace with himself.

A fine score by jazz composer-pianist Mike Nock provides a sensual and dramatic assist, and like the rapt camerawork of Leon Narbey, does not obtrude.

Among all the films of the New Zealand renaissance "Strata" is the least regional, and this is not wholly because of the script involvement of Czech Ester Krumbachova. The picture has a probing, European style, which should be an added plus for offshore audiences. —*Dub.*

Orechi No Vedingu
(Our Wedding)
(JAPANESE-COLOR)

Tokyo, April 22.

A Shochiku release of an NTV-Central Arts co-production. Produced by Mitsuru Kurosawa and Tatsuhiko Goto; Production assistants, Tsuyoshi Yamaguchi and Tatsuro Shibagaki. Directed by Kichitaro Negishi. Features entire cast. Screenplay, Shoichi Maruyama; camera (color), Yonezo Maeda; lighting, Mitsuo Watanabe; art direction, Yoshie Kikukawa. Reviewed at Shochiki screening room, April 13, 1983. Running time: 104 MINS.
Hitomu Omura .... Saburo Tokito
Makiko Ogura ......:.._ Yoshiko Miyazaki
Hiroshi Okamura .. .:..:.... Masato Ibu
Tokiko Ota .... Jun Miho
Kohei Tajima .... Shiro Itoh

This film would be improved immeasurably if, through some intercutting process, a more talented actor's performance could be substituted for that of Saburo Tokito.

Unfortunately for the fabric of this absurdist, dark-hued comedy, that is not possible. Tokito plays a

young man whose bride is stabbed (nonfatally) on their wedding day by — or so it appears — a distraught woman who then blows herself up. The rest of the film is spent trying to unravel the mystery of the assault.

It is a tribute to Tokito's co-stars that the film itself is not completely unravelled. Yoshiko Miyazaki, playing Tokito's wife, shows herself to be a winningly perky comedienne. Even more of a pleasure to watch is Jun Miho, a former softcore porn actress who has managed a very effective mainstream crossover.

Another refugee from bump-and-grind cinema is Kichitaro Negishi, who directed, though certainly not with as much ability as in his critically acclaimed "Enrai."

To give credit where it's due, Tokito is tall, tanned and blessed with a winning smile. —*Bail.*

Educating Rita
(BRITISH-COLOR)

Required viewing.

Hollywood, April 27.

Columbia Pictures release. Produced and directed by Lewis Gilbert. Exec producer, Herbert L. Oakes. Coproducer William P. Cartlidge. Stars Michael Caine, Julie Walters. Screenplay, Willy Russell; camera (Technicolor), Frank Watts; editor, Garth Craven; art director, Maurice Fowler; music, David Hentschel; sound Daniel Brisseau; Michel Cheyko. Reviewed at Columbia Pictures Screening Room 24, Burbank, April 27, 1983. (MPAA Rating: PG.) Running time: 110 MINS.
Dr. Frank Bryant .... Michael Caine
Rita .... Julie Walters
Brian .... Michael William
Trish .... Maureen Lipman
Julia .... Jeananne Crowley
Denny .... Malcolm Douglas
Rita's Father .... Godfrey Quigley
Elaine .... Dearbhla Malloy

Producer-director Lewis Gilbert has done a marvelous job of bringing the charming British play "Educating Rita," to the big screen. Aided greatly by an expert film adaption by its playwright, Willy Russell, Gilbert has come up with an irresistible story about a lively lower-class British woman hungering for an education and the rather staid, degenerating English professor who reluctantly provides her with one. Columbia Pictures has acquired worldwide rights (except in the U.K.) and appropriately plans a slow platform release in the fall for the British pic. That seems the way to go since American audiences will have to slowly become educated to the joys the film offers.

It would be a shame if the British flavor doesn't translate to the American market, for the character of "Rita" is one of those memorable screen personas that seem to be lacking nowadays. Witty, down-to-earth, kind and loaded with common sense, she's the antithesis of the humorless, stuffy and stagnated academic world she so longs to infiltrate. Julie Walters injects her with just the right mix of comedy and pathos, in what certainly ranks as one of the top femme performances so far this year.

The irony of Rita's plight provides the cutting edge for the serious side of the picture. Though Walters is given more than her share of outrageous, off-handed comments, Russell never forgets to remind the audience that she is in danger of leaving behind that very charming manner as she becomes more and more the academic. In one of his better screen appearances of late, Michael Caine embodies the foibles of that world as the sadly smart, alcoholic teacher who knows the fundamentals of English literature, but long ago lost the ability to enjoy life the way his uneducated pupil does.

The contradictions of the two characters are at the core of the picture, as Walters goes from dependent housewife to intelligent student and Caine begins to learn what it's like to feel again. Various details of their respective personal lives are employed as subplots (not always to the best advantage) but Gilbert wisely never lets the story slip too far away from Walters and Caine.

Particularly impressive here, in light of the many recent legit to screen adaptions, is the fact that this piece comes off as a real motion picture rather than just a filmed theatre presentation. Any of the "staginess" of the original work has been removed, a quite admirable feat since it might have been tempting (and easy) to keep many of the scenes as classroom exchanges between the two main characters.

If there are weaknesses, it might be in the somewhat convenient way some of the subplots are resolved. Late in the picture Walters happens to run into her husband on the steet while Caine and his girlfriend's relationship is not ever fleshed out to have much meaning as it disintegrates. There is also a pivotal event near the conclusion involving Walters' friend, a woman the audience never really is given a chance to know and thus care about.

But ultimately those become minor points in light of how many basic human conflicts the film touches upon. While it might be compared to the classic "Pygmalion" tale, Russell manages to lace in many contemporary problems within the classic teacher-student dynamic.

Pic works nicely in all technical departments, giving the intimacy of a low-budget venture without sacrificing any of the quality. Gilbert, who had a solid performer in 1966 as producer-director of another British import, "Alfie" (which also starred Caine), seems to have worked similar magic here.

Though the market has changed quite a bit since then, "Educating Rita" certainly has the chance to follow a similar path. —Berg.

Janete
(Janete)
(BRAZILIAN-COLOR)

Gramado, March 26.
An Embrafilme release of a Tatu Filmes/Embrafilme production. Directed by Chico Botelho. Features entire cast. Screenplay, Botelho, Andre Klotzel, Ines Castilho; camera (Eastmancolor), Jose Roberto Eliezer; direct sound, Walter Rogerio; executive producer, Claudio Kahns; production manager, Wagner Carvalho; art direction and costumes, Teresinha de Jesus; editing, Alain Fresnot; musical direction, Arrigo Barnabe; theme song sung by Caetano Veloso; assistant direction, Andre Klotzel and Mario Masetti; continuity, Dulcines Gil; still, Adrian Cooper; mixing, Jose Luis Sasso. Reviewed at Gramado Film Festival, March 26, 1983. Running time: 90 MINS.
Cast: Nice Marinelli, Flavio Guarnieri, Lilian Lemmertz, Luiz Armando Queiroz, Ruthinea de Moraes, Lelia Abramo, Claudio Mamberti, Turibio Ruiz, Maria Silvia, Silvia Leblon, Jayme del Cueto, Ursula Marcondes, D'Artagnan Junior, Denoy de Oliveira, Dalton Tangara, Cleo Busatto, Alberto Baruque, Regina Rheda, Tereza Dione, Hilda Zerlotti, Maria Angelica Chaves, Dalva de Souza, Margot Ribas, Clarita Steinberg, Maria Rita Costa.

In some way, "Janete" is a female version of "Pixote": a 19 year old girl, abandoned by her family, eventually becomes a prostitute in Sao Paulo and is taken to a "reformatory" where she is forced to make love with other female prisoners and with the house director, an older woman who falls in love with her. Janete manages to escape, trying to follow a circus, from which she had known one of the performers weeks before. The circus has gone very far and in order to get there Janete is forced to take truck driver lifts in exchange for her favours.

Finally she finds the circus and manages to work there, falling in love with her circus friend. After a performance, however, a man tries to rape her: he is the local chief of police, who later will arrest her again for lack of documents, as a pretext to have her. Janete sleeps with him and early in the morning leaves her circus boy friend, again getting on the road.

Botelho is able to create some good images, but is defeated by the weakness of the screenplay and the conventionalism of his own direction. Himself a newcomer, as is Nice Marinelli in the role of Janete, he is worried about not making a big mistake, rather than trying to accomplish something new or daring. As a result, "Janete" is often a crafty work though lacking any stronger emotional involvement, despite the potential strength of its theme. Cinematography and editing make it a fine, although academic, work. —Hoin.

The Settlement
(AUSTRALIAN-COLOR)

Sydney, April 12.
A Queensland Film Corp. presentation of a Robert Bruning Production. Produced by Robert Bruning. Directed by Howard Rubie. Stars Bill Kerr, John Jarratt, Lorna Lesley. Screenplay, Ted Roberts; camera (Eastmancolor), Ernest Clark; composer, Sven Libaek; film editor, Henry Dangar; art director, John Watson; production supervisor, Irene Korol; assoc. producer, Anne Bruning. Previewed at the Film Australia theatre, Sydney, April 8, '83. (Commonwealth Film Censorship rating: M). Running time: 96 MINS.
Kearney .... Bill Kerr
Martin .... John Jarratt
Joycie .... Lorna Lesley
Crowe .... Tony Barry
Mrs. Crowe .... Katy Wild
Lohan .... Alan Cassell
Mrs. Lohan .... Elaine Cusick
Fr. Kieran .... David Downer
Mrs. Gansman .. .. Babette Stephens
Girl .... Vanessa Wilkinson

One of the handful of new Aussie feature films being unveiled at Cannes this year, "The Settlement" is a charming, old-fashioned love story about three characters, society outcasts, who are drawn together into a remarkably innocent menage-a-trois.

A contradicition in terms? Not so. Ted Roberts' script and Howard Rubie's direction treat the subject in a wholesome, smut-free fashion, and while there is a little activity between the various sheets, the accent is on the participants' affection for each other, and their mutual dependence, threatened by an increasingly hostile township which does not like or understand them.

Theatrical prospects Down Under are okay, primarily for the over-25 market, while absence of star-names, and the pic's gentle, understated mood, will probably incline it more towards paycable in the U.S. and tv in Europe.

Bill Kerr and John Jarratt, both seasoned Aussie thesps, topline as two drifters, "swagmen" in the local vernacular, who drift into a small outback town in the 1950s. They find a kindred spirit in Lorna Lesley, a girl with a colorful past, also newly arrived in the district, and after she is evicted from the local hotel, where she was working, the trio set up house in a ramshackle hut on the outskirts of town. It's a happy, if unconventional home, punctuated by the occasional tiff, but the outside world is closing in. The town's resentment against the fringe-dwellers grows, and in a highly effective, climactic scene, a posse of women attack Lesley and set fire to the shack. It goes up in smoke but the threesome survives, and hits the road again, presumably to live happily ever after.

Underlying the light, lilting narrative, pic makes a few telling observations about small town prejudices and hypocrisy, eloquently personified in the frigid wife of the police sergeant, who listens to the preacher's sermons with lust in her heart for the reverend gentleman, while her husband satisfies his lust with Lesley.

Kerr plays the wily old fox role to perfection, while Jarratt as the young pup is perhaps a touch too wide-eyed and ingenuous. Lesley as the harlot with a heart of gold lacks the necessary earthiness, but gets the other facets of her character just right.

Essaying his first theatrical feature, Howard Rubie, an experienced tv director, has a fine feeling for the relative simplicity and naiviety of the 1950s era, and keeps the story percolating, without fully realizing the possibilities of the big screen. —Dogo.

L.A. Filmex

My Love Letters
(U.S.-COLOR)

Winning romantic drama.

Hollywood, April 25.
A New World Pictures release. Produced by Roger Corman. Executive producers, Mel Pearl, Don Levin. Directed, screenplay by Amy Jones. Features entire cast. Camera (Deluxe color), Alec Hirschfeld; editor, Wendy Greene; music, Ralph Jones; art direction, Jeannine Oppewall; set decoration, Lisa Fischer; sound, Jan Brodin; associate producer, Charles Skouras III; assistant director, Peter Manoogian. Reviewed at Filmex (Joe Shore Screening Room, L.A.), Apr. 25, 1983. (M-PAA Rating: R.) Running time: 98 MINS.
Anna .... Jamie Lee Curtis
Oliver .... James Keach
Wendy .... Amy Madigan
Danny .... Bud Cort
Mr. Winter .... Matt Clark
Mrs. Winter .... Bonnie Bartlett
Ralph .... Phil Coccioletti
Edith .... Shelby Leverington
Chesley .... Rance Howard
Marcia .... Betsy Toll
Sally .... Sally Kirkland

"My Love Letters" is a fine intimate drama from writer-director Amy Jones. Although overly schematic and lacking a certain humor that might have been welcome, film is much closer to the tradition of personal European filmmaking than anything ever produced before at New World Pictures, and thus constitutes a most welcome surprise from producer Roger Corman. While star name of Jamie Lee Curtis means something to mainstream customers, pic should be nurtured slowly from exclusive openings, where supportive reviews could make it a modest performer with college-age and upscale urban audiences.

Formerly an editor, Jones bowed as a director last year with the exploitationer "Slumber Party Massacre." By contrast, new effort reps a largely successful attempt at a work to be judged on the most serious level, as well as a film which rewardingly bears the mark of having been directed by a woman.

Under other circumstances, material might well have served as the basis for a poignant short story.

Although in no way intended to seem typical, Curtis is seen living a life that is certainly shared by many young contempo women. Self-possessed socially and reasonably successful (as a public radio d.j.) at an early age, she hasn't yet found the key relationship for which she's vaguely looking.

Suddenly, barely past age 40, Curtis'·mother dies, and the daughter discovers a collection of old letters which reveal the secret love of her mother's life, a love which can stand as a pure ideal to Curtis. Despite their exalted emotions, the two married lovers never ran off together, and only their correspondence remains as a source of both tragedy and inspiration to Curtis.

While pouring over the missives, Curtis meets prosperous photographer James Keach, a 40-ish married man with two kids. As if compelled to fashion a romance as monumental as her mother's, Curtis allows herself to fall deeply, then desperately, in love with Keach. Latter is hardly a cad and takes reasonable risks to maintain the relationship without destroying his marriage, but there's never much doubt that his family comes first.

Tale is tied up in very near literary fashion, but predictability of Curtis' compulsively parallel behavior is far overshadowed by the rich observations of a single woman's life. Curtis lives on the canals in Venice, and view of L.A. is a uniquely naturalistic and quiet one, and for once the city is seen not as a zoo full of weirdos but as a place where relationships, careers and lives can be pursued as seriously as they are onscreen in New York, Paris or anywhere else.

Also believable are the intense and sweaty sex scenes, into which Curtis throws herself with increasing abandon, and the exchanges with her best friend, Amy Madigan, who delivers conventional put-downs of modern men by way of rationalizing a vow of celibacy.

Less successful are Curtis' tense encounters with her drunken, wasted father, with whom she's forced into awkward intimacy by her mother's death. He's too much the total loser for many nuances or meanings to spring from obvious distance between them.

In a decided change of pace from her horror roles, Curtis is onscreen constantly and holds her own impressively, never flinching from the bare emotional and physical demands of the part. Keach expresses the called-for seriousness and sensitivity and fortunately never seems as though he's merely exploiting her. Bud Cort is in briefly as another d.j. at the radio station.

Doubtlessly working on a very low budget, craft and technical staff have contributed fine efforts, and film is frequently very imaginative visually. —Cart.

Montgomery Clift
(ITALIAN-COLOR-DOCU)

Hollywood, April 26.
Produced by Donatella Baglivo for Ciak Studio. Directed, written by Claudio Masenza. Camera (color), Giancarlo Formichi; editor, Baglivo; sound, Kyle Kibbe. Reviewed at the El Rey, L.A., April 26, 1983. (No MPAA rating.) Running time: 122 MINS.
Features: Brooks Clift, Kevin McCarthy, Augusta Dabney, Robert Lewis, Jane Fonda, Jean Levy, William Massena, Patricia Bosworth, Robert La Guardia, Flip McCarthy, William Gunn, Blaine Waller, Judy Balaban, Jack Larson, Maureen Stapleton, Lee Remick, Susannah York.

(English soundtrack)

The sad life of Montgomery Clift has been well evoked in two different recent written biographies, and this Italian documentary represents a third fine telling of the late actor's rapid rise to stardom and gradual descent into what Robert Lewis herein calls "the longest suicide in the American theatre." Film ideally fulfills its purpose and is an excellent bet for appropriate theatrical situations and television. Despite Italian origins, this is entirely in English and needs no adaptation whatsoever for domestic market.

Born in 1920 and raised largely in Europe by a domineering mother with aristocratic aspirations, Clift was caught at various times in his youth in home movies which have been fortuitously located and secured by the docu team of Donatella Baglivo and Claudio Masenza.

More than in any written account, therefore, one is impressed here by what an extraordinary-looking, happy-go-lucky young man he was when he began appearing on Broadway in the 1930s, a period when he seemed "the personification of the young prince."

Clearly, the world was his for the taking, and by the late 1940s he had become the first of a new breed of film star, the "sensivite" leading man whom women adored and wanted to mother, and into whom men could funnel emotions not usually associated with the tough guys who dominated the screen.

But Clift began to change. Friends increasingly sensed that he was tormented by a double life forged by his bisexuality, and after his disfiguring automobile accident during the filming of "Raintree County," he became a slave to drink and drugs. By the end of his life in 1966, he was virtually washed up as an actor.

Due to the incessant parade of visual documentation, including not only clips from Clift's key motion pictures but from a rich variety of home movies and occasional film premiere newsreels, one is nearly overwhelmed by the tragic decline of this complex man. The testimony of many of those interviewed proves that he certainly didn't lack for friends who loved and would help him, but he held most of his women friends at a certain distance and seemed to systematically alienate many through silly behavior and irrational demands.

Early home movie footage and eloquent descriptions by such friends as Kevin McCarthy, his then-wife Augusta Dabney and Jean Levy particularly brings to life Clift's mercurial, zany side, and one can truly believe Dabney's comment that, "everything was heightened" in his presence.

McCarthy, who was driving directly in front of his friend when the car accident occurred, vividly narrates his account of the tragedy, and fact that none of the interviewees can pin down precise reason for Clift's torment thereafter merely reaffirms the mystery that has always surrounded his private demons.

Brooks Clift, whose halting speech patterns startlingly recall those of his brother, personally blames "Freud" director John Huston for Clift's final plunge, although he wrongly claims that it was Huston who brought suit against the actor in the aftermath of the picture when it was really Universal. He then says, "I have to think that maybe his premature death was for the best, because it was painful to live."

Made with intelligence, and a tactful but probing attitude, film is a richly satisfying example of the documentary form. —Cart.

Take It Or Leave It
(BRITISH-COLOR)

Hollywood, March 12.
A Nutty Stiff production. Produced, directed by Dave Robinson. Screenplay, Robinson, Phil MacDonald. Stars Madness. Camera (uncredited color), Nic Knowland; editor, Michael Ellis; music, Madness; art direction, Bert Davey; sound (Dolby), Wally Plummer; associate producer, Adrian Rawle. Reviewed at The Burbank Studios, Burbank, March 12, 1983. (No MPAA rating.) Running time: 85 MINS.
Features: Suggs McPherson, Mark 'Bedders' Bedford, Lee 'Kix' Thompson, Carl 'Chas' Smash, Woody Woodgate, Chris Foreman, Mike 'Barso' Barson (aka Madness).

"Take It Or Leave It" is a likeable, fitfully amusing dramatic re-creation of the career of the British ska band Madness. Starring the band members themselves, modes pic demonstrates how lower-class kids with guitars can become cult sensations in a very short time and somewhat demystifies the London club scene where it all began. Not really exciting enough to create substantial want-see among non-musical specialists, film's appeal is sufficient for slotting in appropriate youth-oriented venues.

Still playing together, unlike many original New Wave bands, Madness is one of the most popular of the various, largely interracial groups to have been inspired both by traditional rock 'n' roll and reggae. For and of English working class youth, ska sound found an avid but distinctly limited following in the U.S.

Staged with the actual performers and presumably on the locations where it all happened, film begins in Camden Town in 1976, where two buddies begin learning to play in very rudimentary fashion by copying Fats Domino and Chuck Berry records.

A year later, their group, then called The Invaders, makes a truly awful debut playing "Jailhouse Rock" in a rockabilly vein. One might have been tempted at that time to tell them to give up, but they shortly thereafter incorporate some reggae into their repertoire, and by 1978 they are able to celebrate rambunctiously after a successful gig at Acklam Hall.

At times, pic seems to be emulating "A Hard Day's Night," notably in a funny sequence which finds the band speeding across London trying to squeeze two engagements into one night. Audience at the second club on the evening's agenda is kept waiting almost until closing time, but group finally appears and saves the establishment from spontaneous demolition.

Film doesn't get too close to the musicians individually and doesn't bring much of their personal lives to bear on the chronicle of career success, which leaves the spectator a bit remote. But, to those familiar with Madness' first recordings, it's almost astonishing to witness the group cutting its first tracks in the most dingy studio imaginable and to reflect on how far these little sessions took the band.

Neither penetrating nor an outright kick, amiable film is worth a look for those interested in the contempo music scene. Tech contributions are all fine. —Cart.

The Deception Of Benjamin Steiner
(U.S.-B&W-16m)

Hollywood, March 11.
A Hanooka-Wolotzky production. Produced by Izhak Hanooka, Ron Wolotzky. Directed, screenplay by Hanooka. Features entire cast. Camera (black and white), Ronny Dana, Chris H. Lapus; editor, Wolotzky; music, Rick Hamouris, Todd Gould; art direction, Salomon Illouz; associate producer, David Langer. Reviewed at Universal Studios, Universal City, March 11, 1983. (No MPAA rating.) Running time: 81 MINS.
Benjamin Steiner .... Bob Gould
Bob .... Fred Thorp
Jean Steiner .... Elizabeth Dietrich
Dana .... Alison Belle
Bill Bradley .... Rick Bartlett
Marsha Bradley .... Edie Berry
Hustler .... Clim Jackson
Drug Addict .... Jan Johnson
Security Guard .... Johnny Dee

"The Deception Of Benjamin Steiner" was allegedly made for under $18,000, and looks it. Technically abysmal and dramatically void, pic is a skeleton which should best be kept in the director's closet. Commercial prospects don't exist.

On a superficial level, this embodies all the worst cliches of indie filmmaking — wobbly camerawork, jazzy cutting to camouflage lack of coherence, grizzled "realism" which supposedly equates with "truth" and unsynched sound all recall an underground movement that was supposed to be over 20 years ago.

But beyond that, the insipid tale ill-serves what 'could have been a pertinent subject, that of urban violence and paranoia. For reasons not worth elaborating, title character roams the streets of L.A. trying to decide who to kill, Walking time-bomb idea could create extensive anxiety stemming from fear of random crime, but Steiner is just a poor simpleton who can never screw up the courage or energy to do anything at all.

Perhaps one reason character is so tired is that he traverses the city constantly, and L.A. audiences will chortle at supposedly continuous scenes which mix locations in Westwood, Hollywood, Santa Monica and West Hollywood.

Wind-up is cheap and unsatisfying, and next time out, director should not only scrounge up more money but locate some more inspiration as well. —Cart.

Citizen: The Political Life Of Allard K. Lowenstein
(U.S.-COLOR-DOCU-16m)

Hollywood, April 21.

An MJ & E production. Produced by Julie Thompson, Brogan de Paor. Directed by Thompson. Executive producers, Mike Farrell, Michael Jaffe. Camera (color), Frederick Elmes; editor, de Paor; music, Stephen Thompson; sound, Algis Kalpis; associate producers, Lynda Gilman, Ann Dollard. Reviewed at the El Rey, L.A., April 21, 1983. (No MPAA rating.) Running time: 72 MINS.
Features: Midge Costanza, David Halberstam, Emory Bundy, Dr. Sherman Bull, Greg Craig, Barney Frank, Ivanhoe Donaldson, Aaron Henry, Jenny Lowenstein Littlefield, Frank Lowenstein, Clinton De Veaux, Rick Weidman, Sam Brown, Curtis Gans, Edward M. Kennedy, Harriet Eisman, Sondra Shapiro, Betty Schlein, Jackie Richman, Hannah Kommanoff, Ellie Chandler, Mimi Purr, Tommy Lowenstein, Pete McCloskey, Dorothy Di Cintio, William F. Buckley Jr., Gary Bellow, Harvey Lippman, Mildred Johnson, Mildred Tudy, Peter Yarrow.

This feature docu represents an unabashed tribute to the late political activist Allard K. Lowenstein. Long an organizer behind the scenes and briefly a Congressman himself, Lowenstein meant a lot to a great many people and was crucially involved with both the civil rights movement and anti-war effort of the 1960s. Some limited commercial dates could materialize in urban situations, but principal markets for film lie in non-theatrical and public tv areas.

As described here, Lowenstein was a political animal virtually from birth. He gained headlines for the first time in 1959, when he testified before the United Nations on lamentable conditions in South West Africa after a visit there.

A few years later, he was one of the organizers of the Mississippi voter registration drive on behalf of blacks, and in 1967 he was cofounder of the "Dump Johnson" campaign and key man behind the presidential candidacy of Eugene McCarthy.

The following year, Lowenstein himself was elected a Congressman in Long Island, but in 1972 he sued for a new election after losing to machine politician John Rooney in Brooklyn, only to lose in the second primary. In 1980 he was shot to death by former protege Dennis Sweeney, who was subsequently declared insane.

Producer-director Julie Thompson has rounded up over 30 people who knew the subject well, including his family, and ranging from such diverse politicos as Sen. Edward Kennedy and William F. Buckley Jr. to Brooklyn housewives who worked on his behalf. They're all clearly speaking about the same man, one of unalterable dedication to human rights, incredible energy and an admirable ability to instill hope and positive direction in others.

Given the unanimity of opinion about him (even his ideological opponent Buckley endorsed his Congressional bid), film emerges as rather straightforward and simple, and one wishes to hear a bit less from his champions and more from Lowenstein himself. A few clips of his speechmaking and campaigning are presented, but there's a lack of direct, human talk from him. One would think that, in a life that was so public, more footage would have been available of the man.

Film may prove particularly informative to those too young to have been aware what it took to secure black voting rights in the South and to oust LBJ. There's plenty of coverage of the racial tensions in Mississippi, as well as of the exciting period during the first half of 1968 which saw the entrance of McCarthy and Robert Kennedy into the Democratic primaries and the decision by LBJ not to run.

But for the basically one-note, entirely laudatory information about Lowenstein provided, film seems a bit overlong even at 72 minutes, and impression is left that more depth would have been possible. —Cart.

The Yin & The Yankee
(U.S.-COLOR-DOCU-16m)

Hollywood, April 26.

An Armand Hammer production. Produced by Kenneth Locker, Mishka Harnden. Directed by Locker. Features entire cast. Camera (color), Kevin O'Brien; editor, Bill Haugse; sound, John Glascock. Reviewed at the El Rey, L.A., April 26, 1983. (No MPAA rating.) Running time: 86 MINS.
Features: Malcolm Forbes, Tim Forbes, Cook Nielson, Clifford May, Dennis Fleck, Kip Clelland, Tsui Shu Yi, Zuo Zhiyang 'George,' Chen Hanz Hang, Sun Jaowa, Yang Xuming, Zhao Ziyang, Dr. Armand Hammer.

In October, 1982, Malcolm Forbes and several companions were given permission to embark upon what was called a hot air balloon/Harley Davidson caravan across the People's Republic of China. Also present was a film crew, and result is this curious documentary.

Several strains run through Kenneth Locker's films, none of them fully realized, but all with a certain interest. It is, unavoidably, a privileged look at backwater, rural area of China that haven't been glimpsed by westerners in several decades. As a mere document, pic has its value.

Also on view are numerous first hand examples of live action diplomacy. Although ostensibly allowed to fly his balloon, Forbes encountered excuses and roadblocks all along the way and very rarely got to go aloft. Much of the footage is devoted to always polite but undeniably tense encounters between Forbes and various Chinese officials, with latter telling the American that presence of nearby military installations forbids flight except when balloon is connected to the ground by an umbilical cord rope.

Most of all, there is the surreal sight of a bunch of macho capitalists plowing through impoverished Chinese villages on their monster choppers. At one point, it's wonderful how poor American Southerners would react if a group of Maoist bikers came charging through their territory, and one can only speculate as to whether they would be treated with the same cordiality with which these Yankees are received.

But this extreme contrast of cultures stirs up some rather unpleasant undercurrents. For one thing, Forbes, chairman and editor-in-chief of Forbes magazine, is not a particularly open or charming camera subject, and his younger companions exude a barely concealed sense of superiority to their hosts which doesn't sit well. Forbes' evident irritation and petulance upon repeatedly being denied permission to fly makes one think he hasn't put his position in China into proper perspective, and that the Chinese officials must have better things to do than deal with a rich American selfishly pursuing his recreational interests.

After biking nearly 2,000 miles, Forbes and company were allowed to fly the balloon around Beijing and created a momentary international incident when they landed accidently on a military base. This is not seen, although the agitation of the Chinese increases noticeably.

Although unique, film ultimately seems rather trivial in that a strong point of view is taken neither by the participants in the trip nor the filmmakers. At the end of the voyage, both Forbes and the Chinese had to be awfully glad it was over.

Pic was backed by Occidental Petroleum topper and diplomat extraordinaire Armand Hammer, who managed to secure permission for Forbes' project after even Henry Kissinger was unable to do so. —Cart.

WarGames
(COLOR)

Solid b.o. looms for exciting
pic with middling plot.

Hollywood, May 7.

An MGM UA Entertainment release of a
United Artists production, produced by Harold Schneider. Directed by
John Badham. Exec producer, Leonard
Goldberg. (in association with Sherwood
Prods.) Features entire cast. Screenplay,
Lawrence Lasker, Walter F. Parkes; camera (Metrocolor), William A. Fraker;
editor, Tom Rolf; sound, Willie D. Burton;
production design, Angelo P. Graham; art
direction, James J. Murakami; assistant
director, Newton D. Arnold; music, Arthur B. Rubinstein. Reviewed at the Bruin
Theatre, L.A., May 7, 1983. (MPAA rating:
PG). Running time: 110 MINS.

David	Matthew Broderick
McKittrick	Dabney Coleman
Falken	John Wood
Jennifer	Ally Sheedy
Gen. Beringer	Barry Corbin
Pat Healy	Juanin Clay
Cabot	Kent Williams
Watson	Dennis Lipscomb
Conley	Joe Dorsey
Richter	Irving Metzman

Competing against "War-
Games," arcades can kiss at least
20 quarters goodbye for every kid
who's hooked on electronic fantasy, which should guarantee the
picture a mountain of summer silver at the boxoffice.

Although the script by Lawrence
Lasker and Walter F. Parkes has
more than its share of short circuits, director John Badham nonetheless solders the pieces into a
terrifically exciting story charged
by an irresistible idea for today's
young audience: an extra-smart
kid can get the world into a whole lot
of trouble that it also takes the same
extra-smart kid to rescue it from.

Matthew Broderick is on the
mark as the bright teenager, bored
by traditional high school subjects
like biology, but brilliant with computers. Knowing the latter so well,
of course he doesn't have to worry
about the former since he can crack
the school's computer code and
change his grades at will.

When determined, in fact, he can
break into just about any computer
system anywhere. Unfortunately,
thinking he's sneaking an advance
look at a new line of video games, he
taps into the country's Norad mis-
sile-defense system to challenge its
computer to a game of global
thermonuclear warfare.

To say the least, this is an excellent premise, just true enough and
possible enough to be thoroughly
chilling. (A recent Wall Street Journal story, in fact, recounted how
much woe young whizzes are causing breaking into supposedly secure corporate computer systems.)

"WarGames'" weakness, sad to
say, is that the adult side of the yarn
is not peopled with very realistic
characters, although the performances are fine. Once wise to what
Broderick has done, the elders re-

fuse to accept that he just stumbled
upon a flaw, but remain convinced
he's part of a Communist conspiracy and arrest him, forcing him to
escape and save the world under
even more difficult circumstances.

Likewise, despite an abundance
of contrary evidence, the U.S. missile command remains convinced
of an impending Russian attack, refusing to lose faith in the computer
Broderick so easily tampered with.
And, from a structural standpoint,
the film hurdles the heroes from
Oregon to Colorado at the last minute with a real lurch — and in a Jeep
when a helicopter would have been
much more logical.

But these are — in the jargon of
the film itself — acceptable losses
on the way to the film's ultimate
victory. And the final moral — the
futility and insanity of contemplating nuclear war — may not be
fresh, but it is certainly timely.

Among the other players, Ally
Sheedy is perfectly perky as Broderick's girlfriend (she also gets the
best line in the film). Dabney Coleman brings his usual dissonance to
the role of the computer-reliant defense specialist but John Wood's
large talents aren't fully used in a
somewhat confusing part as the
misanthropic eccentric who designed the computer. Best turn of
all comes from Barry Corbin, who
makes the commanding general
something different than the usual
war-mongering stereotype.

All of this, however, seems less
important as the final seconds tick
away and Broderick frantically
tries to outwit the runaway computer and avert World War III.
Clearly, Badham is pushing but-
tons to manipulate his audience.
But he's pushing the right ones.
—Har.

Still Smokin'
(COLOR)

Burnt out.

Hollywood, May 6.

Paramount Pictures release. Produced
by Peter MacGregor-Scott. Directed by
Thomas Chong. Stars Cheech Marin,
Thomas Chong. Exec producer, Joseph
Mannis. Screenplay, Chong, Cheech
Marin; camera (Cineco/Movielab color),
Harvey Harrison; editors, David Ra-
mirez, James Coblenz; art director, Ruud
Van Dijk; music, George S. Clinton; as-
sistant director, Peter Carpenter. Re-
viewed at the Fox Theatre, Hollywood,
May 6, 1983. (MPAA Rating: R.) Running
time: 91 MINS.

Cheech	Cheech Marin
Chong	Thomas Chong
Promoter	Hans Van In't Veld
Hotel Manager	Carol Van Herwijen
Assistant Manager	Shireen Strooker
Hotel Maid	Susan Hahn
Bellboys	Arjan Ederveen, Kees Prins

Whatever Cheech & Chong are
'Still Smokin',' they'd be well-ad-
vised to provide it to those stepping
into the theatre to attend their new
Paramount picture. For that would
appear to be the only way anyone

could "appreciate" what the duo
were going for with this amateurish, incompetent excuse for filmmaking. Since Cheech & Chong had
some proven audience there should
be some boxoffice returns. But their
marquee power has shrunk with
each film they've put out and should
reach an all-time low here.

The biggest offense of the whole
affair (which contains lots of offensive material), is that they've been
given access to the money needed to
roll cameras when so many talented unknowns struggle to even
put together the semblances of a
small 16m film. But ability has
never been the sole prerequisite for
a green light, as this picture so aptly
demonstrates.

For the record, the plot (?) involves Cheech & Chong arriving in
Amsterdam (they are at first somehow mistaken for Burt Reynolds
and Dolly Parton) for the country's
first film festival. No other stars
ever show up and, after wandering
around the streets caught up in elaborate fantasies, the guys eventually perform a live act to save the
event (this includes footage from a
C&C Amsterdam concert).

The routines manage to insult
various minorities to little payoff,
variously center around leering
sex, excrement and tired drug references (not necessarily in that
order) and, most importantly,
aren't funny.

Maybe the whole affair would be
better if one were hopelessly under
the influence of some natural or unnatural substance. But it's doubtful. At the very least, it would be less
painful. —Berg.

Gabriela
(BRAZILIAN-COLOR)

Rio de Janeiro, March 30.

A UA Classics release of a Sultana production. Produced by Harold Nebenzal and
Ibrahim Moussa. Features entire cast. Directed by Bruno Barreto. Screenplay, Leopoldo Serran, Bruno Barreto, from the novel "Gabriela, Cravo e Canela," by Jorge
Amado; camera (Technicolor, Technovision), Carlo di Palma; music, Antonio Carlos Jobim; theme song sung by Jobim and
Gal Costa; editing, Emanuelle Castro; art
direction, Helio Eichbauer; costumes,
Diana Eichbauer; sound, Jean Claude
Laureux. Reviewed at Roxy Theatre, Rio
de Janeiro, March 30, 1983. Running time:
102 MINS.

Gabriela	Sonia Braga
Nacib	Marcello Mastroianni
Tonico Bastos	Antonio Cantafora
Coronel	Paulo Goulart
Capitão	Nelson Xavier
Engeneer	Nuno Leal Maia
Tuisca	Fernando Ramos
Malvina	Nicole Puzzi
Gloria	Tania Boscoli
Ramiro	Jofre Soares
Prince	Paulo Pilla
Dona Olga	Claudia Gimenez
Professor Josue	Ricardo Petraglia
Doctor	Antonio Pedro
Colonel Melk	Ivan Mesquita
Dona Arminda	Zeni Pereira
Mundinho	Flavio Galvao

"Gabriela, Cravo e Canela," perhaps the most famous work by nov-

elist Jorge Amado, became, as a
soap opera, a smash in Brazilian
television, and quickly spread to
many other countries, especially
Portugal and Latin America. This
$3,000,000 film version was di-
rected by Bruno Barreto, who
turned another Amado novel,
"Dona Flor And Her Two Husbands," into an international hit for
the Brazilian cinema.

Now working for foreign producers and with an international
crew, Barreto was forced to cope
with several authorship problems.
Screenwriter Leopoldo Serran rejected the film following its preview, with heavy public complaints against the director and producers. A few days later, the critics
showed their disappointment with
the work.

Such reaction can mainly be credited to the pic's approach to the novel, originally (and even in the tv
version) a rich description of the
political conflicts and social tension in the state of Bahia over the
second decade of this century. On
the screen, however, everything is
reduced to a love affair between a
wealthy bar owner of Turkish origin (Mastroianni) and his young
and attractive employee (Sonia
Braga).

Both are finely directed, and Braga (who starred in both "Dona
Flor" and the tv version of "Gabriela") is always a strong support to
Amado's characters. Yet they
seem to be living anywhere but in
the complexity of the social environment of the agricultural center of
Ilheus 60 years ago. (Pic was actually shot in Parati, a colonial
coast city 120 miles south of Rio,
now a tourist resort). Reconstitution is poor, but most regrettable is
that all the transcendence of the
situation in which Nacib falls for
Gabriela seems to be irreversibly
lost, to the point where much of the
character's behavior cannot be understood.

So many times has the screenplay been rewritten that perhaps
this dilution is just a result of a mistaken production system. As for
Barreto's work, it seems to be obviously shy, seldom recalling the inventiveness of "Dona Flor," but
with some good mements in the
Mastroianni/Braga scenes.

Parati is nicely photographed by
Carlo di Palma, and music by Antonio Carlos Jobim, although not
nearly as inspired as the best moments of this outstanding Brazilian
composer, is doubtless amazing.

In short, "Gabriela" seems to be
the result of a production in which
the extension of everyone's authorship freedom was never properly
defined. From a novel even better
than "Dona Flor," with the same
screenwriter, the same director,
the same actress and the enriching
presence of Mastroianni, di Palma
and very attractive means of pro-

duction. this adaptation results in something much smaller, suggesting that in a creative process nothing can ever be taken for granted. —*Hoin.*

Le Dernier Combat
(The Last Combat)
(FRENCH-BLACK & WHITE)

Paris, April 27.

Gaumont release of a Films Loup production. Produced and written by Luc Besson and Pierre Jolivet. Features entire cast. Directed by Luc Besson. Camera (CinemaScope, b&w), Carlo Varini; art directors, Christian Grosrichard, Thierry Flamand, Patrick Lebere; costumes, Marine Rapin, Marie Beau; editor, Sophie Schmit; sound effects, Andre Naudin; sound, Patrick Alessandrin; makeup, Maude Baron; music, Eric Serra. Reviewed at the Gaumont Colisee theatre, Paris, April 26, 1983. Running time: **90 MINS.**
With: Pierre Jolivet, Jean Bouise, Fritz Wepper, Jean Reno, Maurice Lamy, Michel Doset, Pierre Carrive, Bernard Have, Jean-Michel Castanie, Petra Muller, Christiane Kruger.

"The Last Combat" is one of those end of the world, survival of the fittest adventure fantasies, but despite its predictable dramatic lines, is a modest triumph of ingenuity and energy over limited means.

It follows the adventures of one young survivor of cataclysm (Pierre Jolivet) in a devastated world especially lacking in women. Anxious to find a mate, he manufactures a small aircraft and makes his way to what's left of a metropolis where he falls in with a sympathetic doctor (Jean Bouise) holed up in a medical clinic, which is fortified against the persistent aggressions of a brutish would-be interloper (Jean Reno).

Jolivet soon learns that Bouise has a woman, apparently a mental patient, sequestered in the building. But before he can follow through on a courtship, Bouise is killed and the brute manages to get into the clinic and savagely slaughters the girl. Jolivet has a showdown with the aggressor and kills him.

Shot in black and white and CinemaScope, and containing not a single line of dialog — the unnamed cataclysm appears to have affected the vocal chords of the survivors — pic won double honors from jury and press at the last Avoriaz film festival. It marks, with Francis Leroi's concurrent "Demon In The Island," France's move into the international sci-fi and horror market.

Its director, Luc Besson, is only 24 and has clearly spent countless hours in front of the sci-fi genre classics, not to mention samurai epics and the recent Mad Max pics, all of which come to mind in the action scenes, handled briskly, but without innovation. Rather, much of pic's charm comes in its quieter moments, particularly in the small details dreamed up to suggest a planet reduced to desert wastes and isolated urban structures, and in the touching rapport between Bouise and Jolivet, spiced with a humor that deflates the occasional pretentiousness.

"The Last Combat" doesn't especially herald a startling new sensibility on the local scene or a future Gallic Lucas or Spielberg. But it's a generally clever and engaging little entertainment that makes the most of its modest budget and natural settings (mostly abandoned urban buildings). Handled right, it has reasonable commercial chances abroad.
—*Len.*

The City's Edge
(AUSTRALIAN-COLOR)

Sydney, April 28.

New South Wales Film Corp. presentation of a C.B. Films Production. Produced by Pom Oliver and Errol Sullivan. Directed by Ken Quinnell. Stars Katrina Foster, Mark Lee, Tommy Lewis, Hugo Weaving. Screenplay, Robert Merritt, Quinnell, based on the novel by W.A. Harbinson; camera (color), Louis Irving; sound recordist, Noel Quinn; editor, Greg Ropert; art director, Robert Dein; assoc. producer, Barbara Gibbs. Reviewed at Supreme Studios, Sydney, April 13, 1983. Running time: **90 MINS.**
Jack Collins . . . . Tommy Lewis
Jim Wentworth . . . . Mark Lee
Laura Wentworth . . . . Katrina Foster
Cripple . . . . Ralph Cotterill
Andy White . . . . Hugo Weaving

Claimed to be the first Australian feature which explores the dilemma of the urban Aboriginal, "The City's Edge" is a dark, brooding, low-budget drama set in the decaying Sydney oceanfront suburb of Bondi.

While the producers figure the black element will appeal to international audiences, particularly Europeans, pic's bleak, claustrophobic atmosphere will probably nix theatrical prospects in many markets, and tv appears the more realistic route.

Boxoffice outlook Down Under is not bright, unless watching a bunch of misfits, drop-outs and ne'er-do-wells popping pills, shooting up, swigging whisky, haranguing each other and sinking further into a pit of depression is your idea of an enjoyable night out.

Tommy Lewis, so impressive in the title role of "The Chant of Jimmie Blacksmith," Fred Schepisi's powerful historical saga of an Aboriginal wreaking revenge on the white society who ostracized him, is less effective here as the owner of a dingy, roach-infested boardinghouse and manipulator of its low-life residents.

There's Mark Lee (co-lead of "Gallipoli") as a drug addict, who blames himself for his father's death, Katrina Foster as his sister, who is burdened by the guilt of having had an abortion at age 16 after an incestuous interlude with her brother, Ralph Cotterill as a ranting cripple, and Hugo Weaving as a naive country boy who stumbles into this chamber of horrors.

Foster bed-hops from Lewis to Weaving, Lee throws himself in front of a train, Lewis and Weaving get involved in a fight on the beach with several white rednecks, one of whom is killed, and in the climax police lay siege to Lewis, who's holed up in his boardinghouse. He takes a swift, violent exit.

Although he musters a fair amount of dramatic momentum and energy towards the finale, Lewis lacks the strength and authority to be credible as a black overlord, dominating and directing the whites, early in the piece. Also, he is stymied by some leaden lines in the script by helmer Ken Quinnell and Aboriginal playwright Robert Merritt. Homilies like "When you stop hating, you're dead," and "There are things that hurt worse than bullets," would defeat more experienced and artful actors than Lewis.

Foster gives an uneven and confused perf, Weaving does not project much, and it is Lee who registers the strongest.

Working to a tight budget, first-time feature director Quinnell keeps the production values at an acceptable level, but often allows the pace to lag and does not invite much understanding or sympathy for his characters, and there are few inspired, or inspiring, moments to enliven a remorselessly grim tale. —*Dogo.*

Edith Et Marcel
(Edith and Marcel)
(FRENCH - COLOR)

Paris, April 14.

Parafrance release of a Films 13 - Parafrance production. Produced, written and directed by Claude Lelouch. Stars Evelyne Bouix, Marcel Cerdan Jr., Jacques Villeret, Francis Huster, Jean-Claude Brialy, Jean Bouise, Charlotte de Turckheim, Charles Gerard. Script collaborators, Gilles Durieux and Pierre Uytterhoeven. Camera (Eastmancolor), Jean Boffety; editor, Hughes Darmois; original music, Francis Lai; original lyrics, Charles Aznavour; art director, Jacques Bufnoir; sound, Harald Maury; costumes, Catherine Leterrier; makeup, Reiko Kruk; production manager, Eugene Bellin; producer, Tania Zazulinsky. Reviewed at the Publicis theatre, Paris. Running time: **162 MINS.**
Edith Piaf/Margot
de Villedieu . . . . Evelyne Bouix
Marcel Cerdan . . . . Marcel Cerdan Jr.
Jacques Barbier . . . . Jacques Villeret
Loulou Barrier . . . . . . Jean-Claude Brialy
Francis Roman . . . . Francis Huster
Lucien Roupp . . . . Jean Bouise

Claude Lelouch bluffs his way through his new film, "Edith and Marcel," a purported dramatization of the famous love affair between singer Edith Piaf and middleweight boxing champ Marcel Cerdan in the late 1940's. Unfortunately, Lelouch lacks only two things to make this flashy $4,000,000 production a success: Piaf and Cerdan, precisely.

The passionate couple is portrayed by Evelyne Bouix, who had a major role in the director's previous extravaganza, "Les Uns Et Les Autres" and played the seduced and abandoned Fantine in Robert Hossein's "Les Miserables," and Marcel Cerdan Jr., son of the famous prizefighter, who was working on the film as technical advisor for the fight scenes. When actor Patrick Dewaere, who was to star, committed suicide just days before start of production, Lelouch desperately shunted him into the role of his father, since not only is he himself a former boxer, but he bears a striking resemblance to his dad.

But Cerdan Jr. can't act, and Lelouch hasn't asked him to — he merely cut or rewrote all of the heady emotional scenes with Piaf, so that their relationship limps across the screen with all the fury and emotion of a casual flirt. Junior has an affable grin and a charmingly awkward manner that works well in some scenes, but as a character he's nonexistent.

Still, he has a surface authenticity utterly lacking in Bouix's Piaf, whom Lelouch attempts to apotheosize with his typically giddy camerawork and a thick overlay of Dolby-ized Piaf song playbacks. But Bouix is unable to convey the strength of character, gut-deep hunger for affection and overbearing professional exigencies that made the great singer a national myth in her own lifetime. Bouix is all careful makeup and studied physical mimicry — she resembles Piaf like a pebble resembles a boulder.

Around this yawning dramatic vacuum, Lelouch erects another one of his glossy period reconstitutions. The script spans the entire decade of the '40s, beginning with the eve of the war, when Piaf and Cerdan won their first respective laurels and were still ignorant of each other's existence, and concluding with the boxer's death in a plane crash in 1949.

Not one to do things simply, Lelouch drags in the war, the Occupation, the Liberation, and even a parallel romance between two ordinary people (Jacques Villeret and Bouix, again, as if she didn't have enough to do), which takes up no less than a third of this artificially overextended waxworks. At times one has the impression of looking at a scaled-down remake of "Les Uns Et Les Autres," with the Ravel "Bolero" replaced by Piaf tunes.

There are small compensations here and there, particularly in some of the supporting roles — like Jean-Claude Brialy as Piaf's agent Loulou Barrier, and Jean Bouise's unobtrusively solid portrayal of Cerdan's manager. And there is the sympathetic sight of singer Charles Aznavour playing himself — 30 years younger!

Aznavour and Francis Lai, by the way, have written some new songs "in the Piaf manner" for the film, which are performed (as are some of the true classics, for which existing recordings are of poor quality) by a Piaf sound-alike named Mama Bea. They only aid in pointing up the synthetic nature of the whole enterprise. —*Len.*

Breathless
(COLOR)

Sharp Hollywood remake of Godard classic. Richard Gere in sexy role spells strong initial b.o.

Hollywood, May 6.

An Orion release of a Martin Erlichman/Miko production. Produced by Erlichman. Executive producer, Keith Addis. Directed by Jim McBride. Stars Richard Gere, Valerie Kaprisky. Screenplay, L.M. Kit Carson, McBride, based on the screenplay by Jean-Luc Godard of the story by Francois Truffaut, camera (Deluxe color), Richard H. Kline; editor, Robert Estrin; original music, Jack Nitzsche; production design, Richard Sylbert; set decoration, George Gaines; costume design, J. Allen Highfill; sound, Bruce Bisenz; assistant director, Jack Baran. Reviewed at the Orion Screening Room, L.A., May 6, 1983. (MPAA Rating: R.) Running time: **100 MINS.**

Jesse Lujack	Richard Gere
Monica Poiccard	Valerie Kaprisky
Birnbaum	Art Metrano
Lt. Parmental	John P. Ryan
Paul Silverstein	William Tepper
Sgt. Enright	Robert Dunn
Berrutti	Gary Goodrow
Salesgirl	Lisa Persky
Grocer	James Hong
Tolmatchoff	Waldemar Kalinowski
Hwy. Patrolman	Jack Leustig
Dr. Boudreaux	Eugene Lourie

More than a little guts was required to remake such a certified film classic as Jean-Luc Godard's "Breathless," and the generation of film critics that had their lives changed by the 1959 film will easily be able to argue on behalf of the artistic superiority of the original. But the comparison remains virtually irrelevant to youthful audiences, who should find this update a suitably jazzy, sexy entertainment. Richard Gere's first release since "An Officer And A Gentleman" opens in 1,100 theatres Friday (13) and seems a good bet for strong b.o., at least initially.

Godard's film, based on a story by Francois Truffaut, starred then-little-known Jean-Paul Belmondo as a smalltime hood who idolized Bogart and whose love for American-in-Paris Jean Seberg turned out to be a fatal mistake. Freewheeling street shooting, rule-breaking jump-cut technique and total freshness seemed revolutionary at the time, and remake's director, Jim McBride, and co-writer, L.M. Kit Carson, were among those whose eyes were opened by the film.

New version follows the original structurally, moves the action to contempo L.A. and transposes the nationalities of the two leads, but has quite a different feeling and aesthetic. Although lensed mainly on location, pic has a pop culture, almost artificial ambiance which arrests the eye and is surprisingly appealing, an asset bolstered by a barrage of over a dozen imaginatively-chosen rock tunes.

In his manic behavior and naive destructiveness, Gere's lowlife hustler could be a brother to Robert De Niro's character in either "Mean Streets" or "The King Of Comedy." On his way back from Las Vegas in a stolen car, Gere accidentally mortally wounds a cop, then heads for the L.A. apartment of French UCLA student Valerie Kaprisky, with whom he's had just a brief fling but whom he is also convinced he loves.

She seems a relatively serious sort and initially discourages his further advances, accurately calling him "crazy, disgusting person, jerk," but all the other men in the picture come off as such scumbags or twerps that the irresponsible Gere, before long, seems rather winning. While clearly a candidate for quick burn-out, Gere is a live wire, and one has little trouble believing her decision to go along for the ride, up to a point.

A real romantic who dreams of escaping down to Mexico with his inamorata, Gere behaves as if he's oblivious to the heat closing in on him after the cop dies, continuing to steal cars right and left and freely wandering around town. Inevitably, he's hunted down, and film's one severe disappointment is the ending. Original had Seberg turning Belmondo in, with latter then being gunned down in the streets. Not wishing to give it away, one can only say that the finale of the remake is a cop-out.

It's a simple and, now, seemingly classical story which has been fleshed out nicely, both literally and figuratively. Gere's status as a sex star is certainly reaffirmed here, and not only does he appear with his shirt off through much of the pic, but he does some full-frontal scenes highly unusual for a major actor. This is also his most kinetic, spirited performance to date.

Fresh and attractive, Kaprisky also does numerous scenes semi-clad or less, although one suspects full potential for her role was not reached. The two sides of the character's personality — the academic and the devil-may-care — are indicated but not entirely felt, so that her betrayal of her lover doesn't possess the devastating impact it should.

One important sex scene, performed in relief against a film theatre screen on which the B gangster classic "Gun Crazy" is unspooling, represents at once a good example of the pic's unreal, exaggerated visual style, as well as a homage to the sort of Hollywood melodrama which inspired Godard in the making of his film.

Heightened atmosphere is constantly provided by fabulous locations, which include an enormous auto graveyard, a procession of vivid Venice murals, various seedy dives, the Bonaventure Hotel and assorted architectural pop icons, as well as by occasional process work. Flashy, loud color, particularly reds, predominate, and production designer Richard Sylbert and lenser Richard H. Kline, among other hands, have made superior contributions here.

Musical selections are also tops. Jerry Lee Lewis' original "Breathless" is also covered by the New Wave group "X," and Jack Nitzsche has provided some fine additional scoring.

Impotent ending is indeed unfortunate, but most of what comes before marks a lively, long-overdue Hollywood directorial debut for Jim McBride, heretofore best known for his memorable New York underground feature, "David Holzman's Diary." —*Cart.*

Screwballs
(COLOR)

Or "Porky's 1½."

Hollywood, May 4.

A New World Pictures release of a Maurice Smith production. Produced by Smith. Directed by Rafal Zielinski. Features entire cast. Executive producers, screenplay, Jim Wynorski, Linda Shayne; camera (uncredited color), Miklos Lente; editor, Brian Ravok; music, Tim McCauley; additional songs, Johnny Dee Fury; art direction, Sandra Kybartas; costume design, Nancy Kaye; associate producers, Peter McQuillan, Nicky Flan. Reviewed at the Beverly Hills Screening Room, L.A., May 4, 1983. (MPAA Rating: R). Running time: **80 MINS.**

Rick McKay	Peter Keleghan
Purity Busch	Lynda Speciale
Howie Bates	Alan Daveau
Brent Van Dusen III	Kent Deuters
Melvin Jerkovski	Jason Warren
Bootsie Goodhead	Linda Shayne
Tim Stevenson	Jim Coburn
Miss Anna Tommical	Raven De La Croix
Principal Stuckoff	Donnie Bowes
Chesty Colgate	Terrea Foster

"Screwballs" is a poor man's "Porky's." Undeniably, this compendium of horny high school jokes is full of youthful exuberance and proves utterly painless to watch, but is so close in premise and tone to its model that negative comparisons can't help but be drawn. Using simple ads which also startlingly resembled those of "Porky's," New World release did only likewarm biz in its Los Angeles release, so domestic prospects seem iffy, especially as major competition grows in the coming weeks and months.

Press materials state that this tale of shenanigans at T & A High is set in 1965, but there's no way of knowing that based on the film itself. Five lads receive detentions for such infractions as posing as a doctor during girls' breast examinations and straying into the gals' locker room.

Responsible for the boys' plight is snooty homecoming queen Purity Busch, evidently the only female virgin left at the school. Five guys dedicate themselves to de-purifying her, and remainder of the film describes their goonlike attempts on her innocence.

Just as "Porky's" had its shower scene, so "Screwballs" had to come up with one particularly gross sequence which would send kids out to tell their friends, "You gotta see that!" Here it's a zany contest of strip bowling in which the nerdy loser remarkably manages to get a bowling ball attached to his privates and then somehow scores a strike.

That it's all a cartoon is emphasized by frequent speeded-up action interludes. Original title of "Hide The Salami" is invoked in a drive-in scene in which Linda Shayne, who also cowrote and was co-exec producer, plays the game with her date.

Film was lensed in Toronto, which can only make one wonder why all these studies of randy young Americans come from north of the border. —*Cart.*

Vroeger Kon Je Lachen
(One Could Laugh In Former Days)
(DUTCH-COLOR)

Amsterdam, April 27.

A Bert Haanstra Films production, produced and directed by Bert Haanstra. Features entire cast. Screenplay, Simon Carmiggelt; camera (color), Anton van Munster; music, Jurre Haanstra; editor, Rob Hakhoff. Reviewed at Tuschinski Theatre, Amsterdam, April 26, 1983. Running Time: **98 MINS.**

This film represents a successful marriage of two of Holland's most noted talents — author Simon Carmiggelt and filmmaker Bert Haanstra.

Locally, Carmiggelt has become everyone's friend via a series of press columns. "Kronkels," which he ground out six times a week for 30 years. Latterly, he's down to one a week but compilations of his column still sell in book form and garner good ratings when read on tv, which happens several times a month.

Carmiggelt likes people and projects them as endearing and funny. Ditto Haanstra, who ranks among the most internationally known and accoladed of Dutch filmmakers (his docu "Glass" won an Oscar in 1958).

Thus it seems natural for the pair who are friends and sometime collaborators, to come up with a theatrical version of the "Kronkels" — dialog-intensive cameos on rdinary folks' thoughts. habits. feelings.

With a bunch of domestically recognizable talent featured (even in walkon:), the combo has succeeded in patching together all types of acting from traditional histrionic to modern cabaretesque, via three generations of thesps, to come up with a film that sometimes moves, sometimes amuses but never bores.

Carmiggelt is an offscreen observer in some sequences but appears in footage linking the vignettes. Haanstra gracefully included one of the several "Kronkels" previously filmed by young Helmer Otto Jongerius for tv, and which majored on visuals. Haanstra's approach has been to let the dialog carry the story and to shape the mood by clever editing which underlines the role of the camera as an ironic (but never satirical) observer.

While the author makes this film a presold entity locally, its prospects offshore seem limited since Carmiggelt's following is largely domestic. —Wall.

Diablito de Barrio
(Little Devil From the Quarter)
(ARGENTINE-COLOR)

Buenos Aires, May 10.

A Cinematografica Victoria release and production. Produced by Hector Bailez. Directed by Tito Cunill. Stars Juan Carlos Calabro, Lorena Paola. Story and screenplay. Elio Eramy; camera (Eastmancolor), Leonardo Rodriguez Solis; art director, Miguel Angel Lumaldo; costumes, Horace Lannes; music, Mike Rivas; special effects, Trentuno. Reviewed at the Normandi theatre, B.A., April 1, 1983. Running time: 90 MINS.

Cast: Juan Carlos Calabro, Lorena Paola, Cristina Del Valle, Marcos Zucker, Dalma Milevos, Tristan, Eloisa Canizares.

The appeal of top comedian Juan Carlos Calabro and moppet star Lorena Paola are diluted by a weak script about a chemist who is trying to find a magic formula for happiness, helped by a frolicsome young niece, and routine direction.

Commercial fiasco has been the predictable outcome of such lack of effort. Technical credits are okay. —Nubi.

Grijpstra & De Gier
(Outsider In Amsterdam)
(NETHERLANDS-COLOR)

Hollywood, March 15.

A Verenigade Nederland Filmcompagnie production. Produced by Rob Houwer. Directed by Wim Verstappen. Screenplay, Verstappen, Kees Holierhoek. Stars Rutger Hauer, Rijk de Gooyer. Camera (color), Marc Velperlaan; editor, Jutta Brandstadter; music, Rogier van Otterloo; art direction, Roland de Groot. Reviewed at the Warner Hollywood Studios, L.A., March 15, 1983. (No MPAA Rating). Running time: 85 MINS.

Brigadier Rinus
de Gier .... Rutger Hauer
Adjutant H.F.
Grijpstra .... Rijk de Gooyer
Constanze ...... Willeke Van Ammelrooy
Habberdoedas
van Meteren .... Donald Jones
Rechercheur Cardozo . Frederik de Groot
Helen .... Marina de Graaf
(In Dutch; English subtitles)

"Outsider In Amsterdam" is an R-rated "Starsky And Hutch" in Dutch with English subtitles. With its light-hearted, smart-alecky attitude toward grisly crime and glaringly obvious direction which rubs the viewer's nose in a smorgasbord of vulgarities, pic is commercial fodder all the way, but possesses some appeal to U.S. distribs thanks to toplined Rutger Hauer.

Policier follows two Amsterdam plainclothesmen — charismatic Hauer and his older, more mundane associate, played with wry humor by Rijk de Gooyer — on their rounds. Story is packed with such exploitative elements as weird sex, oily drug dealers, pathetic addicts and religious cults, to the extent that director and cowriter Wim Verstappen seems largely to be playing ringmaster to a freak show populated by the most exhibitionistic members of his city's fringe

It's all directed to the most obvious possible effect, with commercial instead of artistic ends in sight. Dutch programmer would have no interest for Yank audiences whatsoever except for the presence of Hauer, who's begun carving a substantial American career for himself and who could possibly attract audiences to this before word gets out as to how crass it really is.

Music, in particular, seems to ape the worst in U.S. tv scores. Among pic's most prominent features is a parade of beauteous Dutch damsels, hardly the least of which is the commanding Willeke Van Ammelrooy, who hooks up with Hauer when he's not otherwise occupied. —Cart.

Fruehlingssinfonie
(Symphony Of Love)
(W. GERMAN-E. GERMAN-COLOR)

Berlin, April 15.

An Allianz Film, Berlin, and Peter Schamoni Film, Munich, in coproduction with Second German Television (ZDF), Mainz, and DEFA Filmproduktion, East Berlin; released by Warner-Columbia. Stars Nastassia Kinski, Rolf Hoppe, Herbert Groenemeyer. Written and directed by Peter Schamoni. Screenplay assistance, Hans A. Neunzig; camera (Fujicolor), Gerard Vandenberg; editing, Elfi Tillack; sound, Gerard Rueff; sets and art direction. Alfred Hirschmeier; costumes. Christiane Dorst; assistant director; Harald Fischer Guenter Kraeae; production manager. Horst Hartwig, Lilo Pleimes. Music by Robert Schumann, performed by Babette Hierholzer, Dietrich Fischer-Dieskau, Wilhelm Kempf, Gidon Kremer, Ivo Pogorelich, Manfred Rosenberg, Wolfgang Sawallisch, Berliner Hymnentafel. Reviewed at Cinema Paris, Berlin, April 15, '83. Running time: 103 MINS.

Clara Wieck .... Nastassia Kinski
Friedrich Wieck .... Rolf Hoppe
Robert Schumann . Herbert Groenemeyer
Clara as Child .. Anja-Christine Preussler
Mutter Schumann .... Edda Seippel
Felix Mendelssohn-
Bartholdy .... Andre Heller
Nicolo Paganini .... Gidon Kremer
Baron von Fricken ...... Bernhard Wicki
Baronin von Fricken ..... Gisela Rimpler
Ernestine von Fricken . Sonja Tuchmann
Christel .... Margit Geissler
Becker .... Uwe Mueller
Karl Banck .... Gunter Kraeae
Clemenza Wieck .... Inge Marschall
Alwein Wieck .... Helmut Oskamp

The remarkable element in Peter Schamoni's musical spectacle, "Symphony of Love" (German title translates "Spring Symphony"), is that this biography of composer Robert Schumann was filmed on original locations in and around Leipzig, presently in the German Democratic Republic, where Schumann fought for, and won, the love of pianist Clara Wieck. "Spring Symphony," his first, was composed in 1841, a year after marrying Clara Wieck — and at the end of a turbulent five-year love affair with the gifted 16-year-old piano virtuoso, who was the daughter of his teacher. Via a special arrangement with DEFA in East Germany, this Second German Television (ZDF) funded film, in coproduction too with Alliance Film (Berlin) and Peter Schamoni's own production company (Munich), is arguably the first authentic East-West German coproduction on a grand scale. Further, if the super-spectacle had been filmed entirely in West Germany, the cost on sets and art direction alone would hage been too prohibitive to begin the project at all. Pic cost around $3,000,000, DEFA in East Germany receiving the rights for the Socialist lands.

"Symphony of Love" begins in 1928: Schumann is 18, Clara Wieck 9. He's about to give up the study of law forever, she's well on her way to becoming a child prodigy at the piano under the direction of her father and teacher, Friedrich Wieck. Both, in fact, are music students under the dictatorial father; and, beginning in 1835 (he 25, she 16), Robert and Clara enter upon a relationship that the father opposes until Schumann brings the matter to the courts, and wins his love in a bitterly fought court case.

Schamoni's biography stays close to the facts without attempting a romantic or melodramatic embellishment of the story. Schumann's music is also kept mostly in the background on the soundtrack.

For those familiar with the historical figures of the time, the personalities of Clara and Robert Schumann, Friedrich Wieck, composer Felix Mendelssohn, violinist Paganini, and others will offer an attraction. As a film, however, the script is stiff and uninspired to the point of embarrassment in certain dialog passages. Nastassia Kinski as Clara Wieck and Herbert Groenemann as Robert Schumann make an interesting, historical, true-life-looking pair of screen lov-

ers, while the central figure of Rolf Hoppe steals the show in the fashion of the devil-having-all-the-best-lines.

The pic's glaring weakness has to do with compressing historical time into a rush of spliced images that carry the audience on Clara's piano tours of Europe — in Germany around Leipzig, then Paris, Vienna and Venice. "Symphony of Love" also threw away its trump-card by limiting musical numbers to a couple of bars at regular intervals. Offshore chances require proper handling, and are limited to the musical biography circuit.

(Katharine Hepburn played Clara Schumann in Metro's 1947 "Song of Love" -Ed.) —Holl.

Wajda's Danton
(BRITISH-COLOR-DOCU-16m)

Oberhausen, April 23.

A Documentary produced by Tomasz Pobog-Malinowski and Witold Stok, in coproduction with Channel Four, London. World Sales, Cori & Orient, London, Los Angeles, Tokyo. Directed by Tomasz Pobog-Malinowski. Camera (color, 16m), Witold Stok. Reviewed at Oberhausen Short Film Festival (market), April 22, '83. Running time: 50 MINS.

Features Andrzej Wajda, Igor Luther, Gerard Depardieu, Angela Winkler, Wojciech Pszoniak.

This revealing documentary on Andrzej Wajda's filming of his French-Polish coproduction, "Danton," is a must for any film buff and Polish historian. Tomasz Pobog-Malinowski's "Wajda's Danton" was produced for British television as one of those accompanying docus timed for airing when the feature film goes into general release. It was made in Paris and environs just six months after the imposition of martial law in Poland, lensed by Witold Stok — the same cameraman who collaborated with Pobog-Malinowski on his equally impressive documentary on the erection of the Gdansk memorial, "100 Days" (1981).

"Wajda's Danton" shows the Polish director and his Slovakian-born cameraman, Igor Luther, working on the guillotine scenes in "Danton" after finishing the Danton-Robespierre showdown in the National Assembly. Interviews are with thesps Gerard Depardieu (Danton), Wojciech Pszoniak (Robespierre), and Angela Winkler (whose observations offer more insight into the actress herself than the project she's currently working on). But the main emphasis is on Wajda: how he occupies himself with infinite details in preparing each scene, his respect for actors and the shooting team, the moments off the set taking a snooze in a car or sketching camera placements with a cigar-butt in his mouth, the director's restless preoccupation with his craft.

Just as informative is the comparison, ever so subtle at times (but constantly visible to the insider), between the two "revolutions" (French and Polish) highlighted in both the feature film and the analyzing documentary.

Pobog-Malinowski goes right to the heart of the matter: why the Poles are playing the Robespierrists, and the French the Dantonists. One of the side-comments on the visual side has to do with members of the Polish team watching the world soccer match on television last summer between Poland and the Soviet Union.

A documentarist with a refined sense for placing his subject-matter within a visually thematic context, Tomasz Pobog-Malinowski makes docus in the manner of Richard Leacock in America and Klaus Wildenhahn in Germany. —Holl.

Fanny Hill
(BRITISH-COLOR)

London, April 27.

Brent Walker release of a F.H. Productions film, produced by Harry Alan Towers. Directed by Gerry O'Hara. Screenplay, Stephen Chesley. Features entire cast. Camera (color), Tony Spratling; art direction, Geoffrey Tozer; editor, Peter Boyle; sound, Laurie Clarkson; assistant director, Tony Hopkins. Reviewed at the Prince Charles Theatre, London, April 26, 1983. (BBFC rating, 18 (X). Running time: 92 MINS.
Fanny Hill .... Lisa Raines
Mr. Barville .... Wilfrid Hyde White
Mrs. Cole .... Shelley Winters
Mr. Widdlecombe .... Oliver Reed
Mrs. Brown .... Paddy O'Neil

You have to enjoy nubile ladies to appreciate "Fanny Hill," but that aside the film is a thoroughly tasteful piece of erotica. Stylistic finesse and cracking pace will not guarantee b.o. potential but may provide for satisfactory playoff on cable outlets. Pic has been picked up for U.S. release by Playboy Enterprises.

The theme comes from the novel that sent the British establishment apoplectic back in the 18th century. It follows the adventurous antics of Fanny Hill from destitute girl newly arrived in the city to savvy million-airess with a live-in lover. And, at least in the film version, Fanny falters in her progress only for an occasional weep.

One cannot say that Lisa Raines exactly acts the part of Fanny, but she goes about her erotic tasks with a sense of "joie de vivre" that is entrancing and affects the entire cast. Oliver Reed and Wilfrid Hyde White in particular ham up their roles outrageously.

There's a lot of simple good fun as Fanny first observes the joys of carnal knowledge, is initiated by members of both sexes, then learns the joys of heterosexual abandon before passing on to the pleasures of

equestrian sex and lewder pastimes.

There's no attempt to force a message, and although a bit of psychological exploration might have helped the film to a wider audience, the pic stands as a jolly romp through 18th century lowlife. Period flavor is conveyed through carriages and costumes. —Japa.

With Prejudice
(AUSTRALIAN-COLOR-16m)

Sydney, May 3.

Australian Film Institute release of a Sirocco Visual Production. Produced by Don Catchlove. Directed by Esben Storm. Features entire cast. Screenplay, Leon Saunders; camera (color), Peter Levy; executive producer, Jim George. No other credits available. Reviewed at Chauvel Theatre, Paddington, Sydney, May 2, 1983. Running time: 73 MINS.
Ross Dunn ....:.....:...... Scott Burgess
Tim Anderson .... John Ley
Paul Alister .....:.:.:...... Terry Serio
Richard Seary ....:. David Slingsby
Detective Rogerson .... Chris Haywood
Detective Krawczyk .... Max Cullen
Detective Middleton .... Richard Moir
Detective Hamilton .... P.J. Jones
Detective Burke .... John Clayton
Judge Nagle .... Redmond Phillips
Adams .... Tony Barry
Einfeld .:,.....:........ David Downer
Tueno ....,...... Tim McKenzie
Gregory .... Phillip Hinton
Bodor .... Peter Whitford

"With Prejudice" is an engrossing, low-budget 16m feature whose script mainly follows the transcript of a controversial criminal case still fresh in the public memory in Australia. However, since the case is of rather local interest, and since the filmmakers have made little effort to dramatize the story outside the confines of the courtroom, overseas chances will be very limited. This is a pity, because there's some fine acting to be found here.

During a Conference of Commonwealth leaders held in Sydney in February, 1978, there was a bomb outrage at the Hilton hotel, where most of the foreign guests were housed; there were some fatalities, including a policeman, but none of the Commonwealth leaders was injured. At the time it was suggested by the authorities that those responsible were members of the Ananda Marga, a religious sect. A year later, in February, 1979, three members of the Ananda Marga, Ross Dunn, Tim Anderson and Paul Alister, were brought to trial on quite another matter; police alleged they were arrested with a bomb in their possession, a bomb they intended to plant at the home of a right-wing politician.

The three accused denied the charges, which were brought about as a result of information given to the police by a paid informer, Richard Seary, who had infiltrated the organization. During the trial, police evidence was conflicting, and the result was a hung jury. End titles inform us that at a second trial,

held six months later, the three accused were found guilty and sentenced to long prison terms.

Director Esben Storm, whose last film was "In Search of Anna" (1977), has done a competent job on the restricted budget available; film is done in television style, and is only just passable as a cinema presentation. Of interest, however, is the thesping: several prominent actors — among them Chris Haywood, Richard Moir, Tony Barry, David Downer and Max Cullen — appear as either detectives or members of the legal profession. Storm and producer Don Catchlove were certainly fortunate to attract so many top performers to the project, an indication, perhaps, of widespread interest in a case generally considered to be a grave miscarriage of justice. —Strat.

The MGM Three Stooges Festival
(COMPILATION-COLOR/B&W)

Weak archive entry will disappoint Stooges fans.

A United Artists Classics release of a compilation of MGM productions. Directed by Jack Cummings, others. Stars Ted Healy; features Howard, Fine & Howard & Bonny; music, Al Goodhart, Dmitri Tiomkin, others. No other credits provided. Reviewed at St. Marks Cinema, N.Y., April 30, 1983. (No MPAA Rating). Running time: 95 MINS.
With: Ted Healy, Moe Howard, Larry Fine, Curly Howard, Bonny Bonnell, others.

"The MGM Three Stooges Festival" is a welcome compilation of 50-year-old short films for buffs but a letdown for contemporary young fans of the Three Stooges, as they play supporting roles to manager/teammate Ted Healy here. UA Classics has minted four 35m prints for repertory theatre use.

Before embarking on their still-extremely popular (and worth exploiting as midnight movie fare) series of Columbia short subjects, the Stooges appeared in several MGM feature films such as "Dancing Lady" and "Meet The Baron." The MGM festival compilation covers nearly all their short films for the studio, "Nertsery Rhymes." "Beer and Pretzels" and "Plane Nuts" from 1933 and "The Big Idea" from 1934, as well as a Curly Howard solo venture "Roast-Beef and Movies." Missing is "Hello Pop" from 1933, for which no negative was available to create a new print.

Best work on display is "Beer and Pretzels" which plays well as slapstick comedy in the vein of later Stooges shorts, only with Healy as the leader of the group working as waiters. Healy dishes out punishment in what eventually became Moe's slot. Also on hand is a fifth member of the group, Bonny Bon-

nell, whose monotone singing and eccentric dancing have dated badly.

Two of the five shorts, namely "Nertsery Rhymes" and "Roast-Beef" are in two-strip Technicolor, with reddish-brown and green tones predominating.

In common with the other two weak items, there is not much Three Stooges material on view, with lengthy musical production numbers (photographed and staged in the familiar Busby Berkeley-Dave Gould fashion) involving chorus lines. MGM producer Jack Cummings is credited with helming "Plane Nuts" and "Nertsery Rhymes." This musical content (including impressive kaleidoscopic numbers), plus other nostalgia material such as a radio comedy trio doing impressions of Arthur Tracy and Bing Crosby, suggest that the film could be marketed to buffs in the manner of the Busby Berkeley reissue "The Gang's All Here." Pitching it to Stooges fans is bound to create false hopes. —Lor.

A Fist Full Of Talons
(HONG KONG-COLOR)

Hong Kong, April 22.

An Eternal Film (H.K.) Co. Ltd. production and release. Produced by Pal Ming. Directed by Sun Chung. Stars Billy Chong, Hwang In Shik, Pai Ying, Liu Hao I, Chang Shan, Cheng Kay Ying, Chiang Tao. Screenplay, Wong Ping Yiu; Cannes (color) Woo Ying; editor, Poon Hung Yiu; music, Stephen Shing, So Chun Hou; set designer, Ting Yuen Ta; martial art instructor, Leung Siu Hung. Reviewed at State Theatre, Hong Kong, April 20, 1983. Running time: 98 MINS. (Hong Kong Version) International Version is approximately 89 MINS.
(Two versions available, Cantonese with English sub-titles or English soundtrack)

During the first troubled years of the Chinese Republic, a group of ex-Imperialists were meeting with six generals headed by Nai Sin (Hwang In-shik), a former Ching official. They had heard that Ding Wei Chung (Pai Ying), a northern territories general turned Republican agent, was on his way to deliver secret documents to the Republican government Nai order Ding's death.

Ching I Ming (Billy Chong) meets Ding at his father's post station and feels sympathetic. Later, Ching realizes that Ding is involved in a desparetely important mission and resolves to look for him and offer his help. On the way, Ching meets Eagle Girl Ma (Liu Hao I), daughter of a local sheriff. She develops a liking for the handsome young man. Meanwhile, Ding is waylaid by two of Nai's men and injured. His horse, stolen by Little Bandit (Lao K-shun) who tries to sell it in the market, is spotted by Ching.

"A Fist Full Of Talons," a.k.a. "Wind, Forest, Fire and Mountain" is director Sun Chung's first film for Eternal Film Prod., and he brings with him the grandiose studio style he mastered in his Shaw Brothers' heydays. Reportedly produced with a HK$5 million budget, it is a bold move, considering that straightforward kung-fu genre is in its lowest ebb in Hong Kong and overseas. English version will be at Cannes this May. —Mel.

Hostage - The Christine Maresch Story
(AUSTRALIAN - COLOR)

Sydney, May 2.
Roadshow Release of a Frontier Films presentation of a Klejazz Production. Produced by Basil Appleby, Frank Shields. Directed and written by Frank Shields. Features entire cast. Co-writer, John Lind; camera, (color), Vincent Monton; art director, Phil McLaren; sound, Bob Allen; editor, Don Saunders; music, Davood Tabrizi. Reviewed at Roadshow Theatrette, Sydney, April 29, '83. (Commonwealth Film Censorship rating: M). Running time: 90 MINS.
Christine Maresch .... Kerry Mack
Walter Maresch .... Ralph Schicha
Mrs. Lewis .... Judy Nunn
Mrs. Hoffman .... Doris Goddard
John Hoffman .... Michael Harrs
Freda Hoffman .... Claire Binney
Wolfgang .... Henk Johannes
Helmut .... Bert Cooper
Gary .... Ian Mortimer
Zoltar .... Moshe Kedem

Twice during the opening credits of "Hostage — The Christine Maresch Story" the viewer is assured "This is a true story;" one can readily, understand the insistence of the claim, because if this were not a true story it would be dismissed as utterly implausible.

Christine Lewis, a 16-year-old girl from an Australian country town, leaves an unhappy home and joins a travelling carnival. There she meets the handsome Walter Maresch, an itinerant German, and starts an affair with him (discarding a previous lover). It quickly becomes evident that Walter is unstable and dangerously so; he threatens to kill himself if Christine refuses to marry him, and does indeed shoot himself, but not fatally. They marry and have a daughter, and before long she's desperately unhappy but pregnant again. In 1977, he takes her and their daughter to Munich, promising an abortion at the other end. Instead, he keeps her a virtual prisoner, and when she manages to get an abortion in Holland, he blackmails her into joining him in a bank robbery.

It's now revealed he's a member of a neo-Nazi organization, members of which force him to leave the country for fear that police searching for the bank robbers will be led to them via him. The couple, their daughter, and a friend head off in a Volkswagen, apparently intending to drive to Asia. In a Turkish village, they're attacked by members of a family who want to 'buy' Christine, and Walter, though wounded, manages to

kill one of their assailants. Eventually they make it back to Australia, where Walter forces Christine to commit another bank robbery and wounds her more than once before his inevitable capture. The film's final titles contain photography of the real Christine and Walter, the latter now serving a long prison sentence.

It's certainly an incredible story, which piles disaster after disaster onto its long-suffering heroine. First-time feature director Frank Shields (who some years ago made an excellent documentary, "The Breaker," about Breaker Morant, the real-life character, not the successful Bruce Beresford movie), has tried to pack too much narrative into too short a running time. For once, one can safely say a film should have been longer.

The early scenes have a staccato rhythm that is needlessly unsettling, and characters become caricatures as a result. This cinematic shorthand also gives rise to some appallingly cliched dialog along the lines of "Let me take you away from all this" and "If you leave with him, don't ever come back." However, once the action shifts to Europe, the tension starts to build, and the bulk of the film is quite gripping, even if this true story still seems almost incredible.

Kerry Mack gives a spirited performance as the beleagured Christine, while Ralph Schicha has something of the charisma of Rutger Hauer as the pathological Walter. Some of the supporting players are less convincing, and the sequence with the Turks resorts to the same kind of national stereotyping for which "Midnight Express" was criticized.

Technically tops, the film was shot on locations in Australia and Germany, with the Turkish scenes shot Down Under. Vincent Monton's photography is fine, though Don Saunders' editing seems too severe. Pic should do good to very good business locally, though it doesn't mark a return to the best quality Australian films of a year or so ago. Consequently, overseas results could be iffy. —Strat.

Mausoleum
(COLOR)

Entertaining, old-fashioned supernatural horror cheapie.

A Motion Picture Marketing (MPM) release of a Western International Pictures production; a Robert Barich film. Produced by Robert Barich, Robert Madero. Executive producers, Jerry Zimmerman, Michael Franzese. Directed by Michael Dugan. Features entire cast. Screenplay, Madero, Barich, from an original screenplay and story by Katherine Rosenwink. camera (Getty color), Barich; editor, Richard C. Bock; music, Jaime Mendoza-Nava; supervising sound editor, Michael Sloan; assistant director-production man-

ager, Charles Norton; special effects makeup, John Buechler, Maurice Stein; art direction, Robert Burns; stunt coordinator, Joel Kramer; special effects, Roger George. Reviewed at Rivoli 1 theatre, N.Y., May 6, 1983. (MPAA Rating: R). Running time: 96 MINS.
Oliver Farrell .... Marjoe Gortner
Susan Farrell .... Bobbie Bresee
Dr. Simon Andrews ...... Norman Burton
Ben, the gardener .... Maurice Sherbanee
Elsie .... La Wanda Page
Aunt Cora .... Laura Hippe
Dr. Roni Logan .... Sheri Mann
Susan, age 10 .... Julie Christy Murray

Filmed in 1981, "Mausoleum" is an engaging minor film concerning demonic possession, presenting variations on "The Exorcist" format. Not the stab 'n slab genre picture one might infer from its title, film should please afficianados of old-fashioned B-horror films, but lacks the scares to yield more than modest returns in the current fright market.

A beautiful blond actress Bobbie Bresee (vaguely resembling Susannah York) toplines as Susan Farrell, a 30-year-old woman who has been possessed by a demon at age 10 after strolling into the family mausoleum, carrying on a centuries-old family curse affecting the first-born. Twenty years after, the demon has finally taken over, going on a killing spree that arouses the suspicions of her husband Oliver (Marjoe Gortner). Friend and psychiatrist Dr. Andrews (Norman Burton) is enlisted to help Susan and ultimately bests the demon.

The filmmakers (it's not entirely clear who did what, since the press kit information does not agree with credits on screen) have adhered to traditional horror film motifs, updated with tantalizing displays of Bresee's physical charms plus modern makeup effects and gore. Too slowly paced and decorative rather than suspenseful, "Mausoleum" is nonetheless a well-told tale.

Bresee is extremely seductive here in the femme fatale role, complete with stock victims such as the shady gardener, unwary delivery boy, etc. Star Gortner's role is written for a bland Kent Smith type, never tapping the actor's evangelical background despite the opportunities in "Exorcist" country. La Wanda Page is hilarious as their maid, exclaiming "There's some strange s--t going on here" and evoking fond memories of the fun generated decades ago by Willie Best in similar situations.

Lensing in a handsome mansion and on California locations is attractive, replete with Steadicam work and unusual overhead tracking shots in the mausoleum. Make-up effects, especially the varied monster masks for Bresee, are solid for a low-budgeter and her glowing green eyes' effect during telekinesis scenes is quite realistic. A nice little picture. —Lor.

Heartbreaker
(COLOR)

Just another automobile rally.

Hollywood, May 4.
A Monorex presentation of an Emerson Film Enterprises release. Produced by Chris D. Nebe and Chris Anders. Directed by Frank Zuniga. Features entire cast. Screenplay, Vicente Gutierrez; camera (Eastmancolor), Michael Lonzo; editor, Larry Bock; music, Rob Walsh; art direction, Pamela Warner, Mario Torero; sound, Sanford S. Berman; associate producer, Lionel Heredia; assistant director, Ron Martinez. Reviewed at the Commerce Theatre, East Los Angeles, May 4, 1983. (MPAA Rating: R.) Running time: 90 MINS.
Beto .... Fernando Allende
Kim .... Dawn Dunlap
Hector .... Peter Gonzales Falcon
Angel .... Miguel Ferrer
Hopper .... Michael D. Roberts
Wings .... Robert Dryer
Loco .... Pepe Serna
Alfonso .... Rafael Campos
Minnie .... Carmen Martinez
Gato .... Carlo Allen

Indie production keyed to cross-cultural romance between a Chicano and the new blonde in town, against background of customized lowriders in multiethnic mix of East Los Angeles, lifts "Heartbreaker" above a Latino gang movie with potential for fast playoffs on broad neighborhood fronts.

Although cinematically unsteady and carrying the burden of a story that is notable for its lack of violence and sex, the film features a top Latin name, Fernando Allende, and a dazzling array of garishly-painted lowriders that should alert car club enthusiasts, particularly in California and the Southwest where the material has its cultural identity.

First-time distributor Monorex, which produced the film two summers ago for $1,000,000 with non-union, below-line talent, could recoup on a select regional distrib plan.

Pic unfurled in East L.A. to Hispanic drumbeating but irony is that the movie carefully works at avoiding Latino tag, with characters representing spectrum of Latins, blacks, and whites. Chief among latter is fetching Dawn Dunlap as the love interest and Robert Dryer as a rival car club bully. Most talented member of the young cast is dude Michael D. Roberts. Able support is delivered by Peter Gonzales Falcon's callow cad, Miguel Ferrer's misguided lowrider, Pepe Serna's self-described Loco, and Jesse Aragon's self-possessed, yellow-jacketed groupie.

Film, which all the majors passed up for distribution, per coproducer Chris Nebe, would be an easy PG except for smattering of four-letter words. Sex is innocent, even distractingly gooey in Allende-Dunlap trysts.

Conflict, in script by Vicente Gutierrez, develops much too slowly and fails, given the chance, to really render any social insights to life in a Latin-dominated community beyond belonging to a car club.

Sum of results is undeniably bland (ditto the handsome Allende, doing his first film in English), but there's a decency here, too, that's appealing. Director was Frank Zuniga. —*Loyn.*

Los Fierecillos Se Divierten
(The Shrews Have Fun)
(ARGENTINE-COLOR)

Buenos Aires, May 10.
An Aries release and production. Directed by Enrique Carreras. Stars Jorge Porcel, Alberto Olmedo. Story and screenplay, Carreras, Jose Dominianni; camera (Eastmancolor), Leonardo Rodriguez Solis; art director, Alvaro Duranona y Vedia; music, Oscar Cardozo Ocampo; costumes, Horace Lannes; assistant director, Orlando Zumpano. Reviewed at the Sarmiento Theatre, B.A., Feb. 24, 1983. 90 MINS.
Cast: Jorge Porcel, Alberto Olmedo, Luisa Albinoni, Susana Traverso, Mario Sapag, Javier Portales, Nelly Beltran, Mario Sanchez, Elizabeth Killian, Pimpinela and the groups I Medici Concert and Luna de Cristal.

Second Porcel-Olmedo vehicle aimed at the moppet audience, it seems to have been hastily concocted after the tremendous b.o. success attained last year with "Los Fierecillos Indomables" (The Untamable Shrews). This one depends entirely on the magnetism of fat Porcel and thin Olmedo, two ace comics of almost irresistible appeal for large audiences in Argentina and some foreign lingo spots, since there is a minimum of funny material in the script.

A parody of Ravel's "Bolero," as it was danced by Jorge Donn in "Les Uns Et Les Autres," and another of a basketball game, excite laughs in undiscriminating patrons. No other effective moments come to mind. Technical credits acceptable. —*Nubi.*

Buenos Aires Rock
(ARGENTINE-COLOR)

Buenos Aires, Feb. 10.
An Aries release and production. Directed by Hector Olivera, Carlos Orgambide and Renata Schussheim. Features entire cast. Script, Olivera and Daniel Ripoll; camera (Eastmancolor), Victor Hugo Caula. Reviewed at the Callao theatre, B.A., Jan. 20, 1983. 91 MINS.
Cast: Litto Nebbia, Raul Porchetto, Leon Gieco, Spinetta-Jade, Piero, Riff, Pedro and Pablo, Starc-Lebon, Ruben Rada, Alejandro Lerner, Los Abuelos de la Nada, Orions and La Torre.

This documentary puts on screen the peak moments of the BARock IV, a festival held during four days at the Obras stadium in B.A. Most of the top names in Argentine contemporary pop music are seen and heard not only on stage but also in brief interviews.

Hector Olivera and his aides, Renata Schussheim and Carlos Orgambide, have also caught the reactions of the young audiences, having given a generally updated look to his technical work. Topical lyrics, some of strong critical content, and not a few poetic accomplishments, have won enthusiastic support for native rock among youths and young adults.

"B.A. Rock" is aimed at this clientele. —*Nubi.*

El Poder de la Censura
(The Power of Censorship)
(ARGENTINE-COLOR)

Buenos Aires, April 26.
A Negocios Cinematograficos release of a Total Cinematografica production. Directed by Emilio Vieyra. Features entire cast. Screeenplay, Hebert Posse Amorin; camera (Eastmancolor), Rinaldo Pica; editor, Oscar Esparza; music, Luis Maria Serra; executive producer, Juan Carlos Fisner; assistant director, Felipe Lopez. Reviewed at the Monumental theatre, B.A., March 31, 1983. Running time: 90 MINS.
Jorge .... Victor Laplace
Cristina .... Fernanda Mistral
Pepe .... Hector Bidonde
Roberto .... Carlos Moreno
Alicia .... Constanza Maral
Actress .... Reina Reech
Dr. Achaval .... Norman Ehrlich
Marcela .... Monica Vehil
Press Secretary .... Carlos Ferreira

How could a film titled "The Power of Censorship" be made in the country with the tightest film censorship in the Western world? Certainly the step taken by producer-director Emilio Vieyra puzzled everyone in and out the film industry, specially after the National Film Institute helped finance the project. Afterwards, the Film Classification Board blocked the pic's first unspooling, but finally gave it the greenlight, apparently without cuts.

Vieyra and his scripter, critic Hebert Posse Amorin, might have been encouraged by some liberties that censorship tolerated last year to Aristarain's "Last Days of the Victim," Ayala's "Easy Money" and Maria Luisa Bemberg's "Nobody's Wife." Also they presumably bet on the backing they would get from the presently outspoken print media if the pic was eventually banned. In any case what they took was a very carefully calculated risk.

Story centers on an actor, a friend, a director and a toymaker who decide to produce an adult film, financed by the latter. Once the lensing is underway the actor fears they are being too daring and convinces the others to either soften or suppress scenes that might be objected to by censorship. Although this self-pruning weakens the pic, censorship bans it. They hire an influential character who manages to obtain, at ministerial level, the lifting of the ban.

Meanwhile the toymaker's wife divorces him and his mistress is diagnosed as terminally ill, the actor starts an affair with a journalist (daughter of the influential man) and the actor's friend is felled by a heart attack. In short, the fear of censorship ruins either the ideals, the health or the pocket of the people committed to the film, and the film itself.

Vieyra's film's main merit is its denunciation of censorship, but an epidermic treatment, more journalistic than dramatic, deprives it of both depth and emotion. One cannot but sympathize with it, but that's all. Maybe its lack of impact explains why the censorship didn't bother to forbid it. It is basically truthful but intrinsically innocuous.

Acting can't go beyond the shallowness of the characters. There are a few sex scenes, until recently unusual in Argentine pics. Technical credits generally okay. —*Nubi.*

Sekando Rabu
(Second Love)
(JAPANESE-COLOR)

Tokyo, April 23.
A Toei release. Produced by Tatsuo Yoshido and Katsuhiro Maeda. Directed by Hoichi Higashi. Features entire cast. Screenplay, Yoichi Higashi and Masako Tanaka; assistant director, Taseshi Kurihara; camera (color), Koichi Kawakami; lighting, Hidenori Isozaki; art direction, Ikuro Ayabe; sound, Sachio Kubota; music, Michi Tanaka; editing, Keiko Ichihara. Reviewed at Toei screening room, April 18, 1983. Running time: 103 MINS.
Kazumi .... Reiko Ohara
Hideo .... Kaoru Kobayashi
Machiko .... Reiko Nakamura
Tomoharu .... Ai Jooji
Yamano .... Hatsunori Hasegawa
Isomura .... Tokuma Nishioka

"Sekando Rabu" represents a long overdue return to the screen, after a four-year absence, by Reiko Ohara and confirms Yoichi Higashi's preeminent position as Japan's best "women's director," which is to say not only a skillful director of women, but a director who genuinely cares about women.

Most of Higashi's films since 1973 constitute a thematically related body of work which, at this stage, looks like the first half of what might be labelled "The Seven Stages of Woman:" in "Mo Hozue Wa Tsukanai," college student Kaori Momoi gains her independence after caroming between two dead-end affairs; in "Zo Reipu," Yuko Tanaka, a career woman in her mid-twenties, elects to put her private life on public display in order to secure the conviction of a criminal; and in "Sekando Rabu," over-thirty Reiko Ohara survives in the inevitable emotional buffetings of remarriage in a country where few men want to be second in line.

Because Ohara is both older and more "experienced" than husband Kaoru Kobayashi (it's his first marriage, her second), he is forever discovering "evidence" of her unfaithfulness in everything from annoying phone calls to a dead prowler in their kitchen. She, nonetheless, responds with displays of enormous strength of character that do not lead to a "happily-ever-after" resolution.

When a pregnant Ohara is injured and hospitalized near the end of the film, it is virtually impossible to avoid mentally jump-cutting ahead to what appears to be the film's ultimate, predictable destination: a tearful reconciliation brought about by Ohara's brush with near-tragedy. But just before the expected happens, Higashi makes brilliant use of that overworked visual device, the freeze frame, to suggest the ambiguous course of the couple's future.

Typically Higashion flourishes here include dry, almost Western humor (the husband sulks in a locked room and the wife breaks down the door) and love scenes characterized by a playful tenderness rather than sweat-stained eroticism.

Higashi is virtually the only filmmaker in Japan whose heroines are strong, intelligent and, above all adult. His films deserve to be seen by anyone interested in the what it means to be a woman in Japan. —*Bail.*

Stelle Emigranti
(Wandering Stars)
(ITALIAN-COLOR-DOCU)

Hollywood, May 1.
A CIAK Studio producton for RAI-TV Channel 1. Directed by Francesco Bortolini, Claudio Masenza. Camera (Color), Eugenic Bentivoglio, Giuseppe Lanci, Robert Levi; editor, Donatella Baglivo. Reviewed at the El Rey, Los Angeles, April 30, 1983. (No MPAA Rating). Running time: 58 MINS.
Features: Gina Lollobrigida, Sylva Koscina, Virna Lisi, Claudia Cardinale, Giorgia Moll, Rossella Falk, Marisa Pavan, Stefania Casini, Claudio G. Fava, Stewart Stern, Pauline Kael.
(In Italian; English subtitles)

"Wandering Stars" features an agreeably unusual premise, the casual study of the careers of eight Italian actresses who, at various times over the past 30 years, worked on Hollywood pictures. Such a group is a natural, but this valid approach hasn't been taken much by scholars except to study the German and other European emigres of the 1930s. Results here are interesting, if not profound, and display women with more intelligence, humor and personality than they were permitted to exhibit in their American pics. Italian subtitles limit possibilities for domestic exposure, but this could have a slight market in special, art house situations as well as non-theatrically.

Of the actresses under consideration, Gina Lollobrigida was imported in the early 1950s by Howard Hughes but broke away from him to enjoy a respectable international career; Marisa Pavan, sister of the late Pier Angeli, acted in English-language pics from 1952 on; Rossella Falk is a stage actress who journeyed to Hollywood in the late 1960s for Robert Aldrich's "The Legend Of Lylah Clare;" Stefania Casini went to New York in the 1970s for "Andy Warhol's Bad," while Sylva Koscina, Virna Lisi; Claudia Cardinale and Giorgia Moll were put under exclusive contracts and groomed as sexpots by various studios during the 1960s.

Those closely connected to studios mildly complain of having been "remade" to resemble certain Americans stars — Marilyn Monroe in the case of Lisi, Doris Day, astonishingly for Cardinale. Lisi reveals that, when she turned down "Barbarella," she was forced to repay money on her seven-year contract, and Moll hilariously describes how her figure was hugely padded to conform with the studio's standard notion of sexuality.

Clever editing brings out the impression, repeated by several of the women, that they were bowled over by Hollywood to begin with, were immoderately impressed with the organization and efficiency of Yank filmmaking, and that performers in general are better treated here than in Italy, where Lollobrigida remarks that they are treated "worse than dogs."

General shared feeling was that Hollywood represented an interesting adventure, actresses seem intelligently philosophical about their careers there. Lisi, however, goes a little deeper, opining that she ultimately found the U.S. "the loneliest place in the world," a place where "you don't feel like a human being."

Writer Stewart Stern describes how he discovered Pier Angeli in Italy, while critic Pauline Kael offers some good common sense evaluations of the limited possibilities for foreign-accented actresses in Hollywood.

Film is made with thorough professionalism, although subtitles are not as complete as they should have been. —Cart.

Chytilova Vs. Forman
(BELGIAN-COLOR-DOCU-16m)

Hollywood, April 30.
An Iblis Film production for Belgische Radio en Televisie. Produced by Pierre Drovot, Daniel Van Avermaet. Directed by Vera Chytilova. Camera (color). Michel Baudour; Colin Mounier; editor, Jiri Brozek; associate producer, Joz. Van Liempt. Reviewed at the El Rey, Los Angeles, April 30, 1983. (No MPAA Rating). Running time: 84 MINS.

Features: Milos Forman, Vera Chytilova, Michael Weller, Howard E. Rollins, E.L. Doctorow.

Milos Forman and Vera Chytilova were students together and represented two of the leading lights of the brief Czech New Wave of the mid-1950s. Since then, Forman has gone on to fame and fortune in the U.S., while Chytilova remained behind to combat the vagaries of communist-state-controlled filmmaking. Made largely against the opulent sets for Forman's extravagantly expensive "Ragtime," this feature documentary seems to promise, by its title, an artistic and ideological showdown between two former comrades who have radically parted ways. Disappointingly, nothing of the sort occurs, and pic, at bottom line, stands as simply a mildly interesting portrait of Forman and his working methods.

Commercial prospects are limited to film buff congregations.

Notion of a confrontation between the two Czechs is intriguing, not for the possibilities of verbal bloodshed, but for the opportunity to shed light on the distinctions between commercially and politically-rooted filmmaking.

Although life was far from easy for Forman until his triumph with "One Flew Over The Cuckoo's Nest" in 1975, Chytilova has clearly had the rougher time of it over the last 13 years, and parallel accounts of their respective careers might well have proved illuminating on any number of levels.

Instead, Chytilova, who directed the docu for Belgian television, is self-effacing to the point of perversity, bending over backwards to cut herself out of the frame when she is sitting talking to Forman, and speaking Czech and fractured French while her subject responds in English, further obliterating any impression she might make on the viewer.

Forman is seen working with Brad Dourif, Elizabeth McGovern and a group of black actors on "Ragtime." Howard E. Rollins testifies to his pleasure in working with the director, and Forman is seen lolling around his farm and, amusingly, lying in bed at New York's Chelsea Hotel, where he spent most of his penniless days.

For the most part, Forman resists any attempt at self-analysis, but describes his process of selecting projects, his love of cinema and his obsession with precise casting of actors. Rather like his friend Roman Polanski, Forman seems to have an iron will, an absolute determination to prevail which surely accounts for some of his success in the commercial film industry.

Chytilova pads her film with strangely amateurish travelog stuff of the key cities in Forman's life, Prague and New York, as well as

with nutty footage of the man jogging and strolling the streets. But most frustrating is Chytilova's incomprehensible refusal to touch on politics, their time together in school, Forman's flight to the West and his observation on filmmaking Here and There. Pic ultimately emerges as one of the most bizarre and idiosyncratic studies of a director ever made. —Cart.

Cannes Festival

L'Argent
(Money)
(FRENCH-COLOR)

Paris, May 3.
AMLF release of a Marion's Films/-FR3/Eos Films coproduction. Produced by Jean-Marc Henchoz. Features entire cast. Written and directed by Robert Bresson, inspired by "The Counterfeit Note" by Leo Tolstoy. Camera (color). Pasqualino de Santis, Emmanuel Machuel; editor, Jean-Francois Naudon; art director, Pierre Guffroy; sound, Jean-Louis Ughetto and Luc Yersin; executive producer, Antoine Gannage; associate producers, Jean-Pierre Baste, Patricia Moraz. Reviewed at the Publicis screening room, Paris, April 28, 1983. In Cannes Film Fest (competitive). Running time: 84 MINS.
With: Christian Patey, Sylvie Van Den Elsen, Michel Briguet, Caroline Lang, Vincent Risterucci, Beatrice Tabourin, Didier Baussy, Marc Ernest Fourneau, Bruno Lapeyre.

Although no film by Robert Bresson is fully assessable upon a single viewing, "L'Argent," his first picture in six years, would seem to be one of his least compelling. It runs a typically concise 84 minutes and deals, as did "The Devil Probably," with spiritually dessicated contemporary youth, in the filmmaker's usually ascetic manner.

That austerity of style here too often borders on aridity and inexpressiveness. As the title indicates, the film's theme is the corrupting power of money — epitomized by a counterfeit bill — but that banal theme, submitted to Bresson's rigorously selective sensibility, acquires no new force or revelation.

Inspired by a short story by Tolstoy, Bresson traces the tragic course of a young Parisian workman, who is the victim of a petty counterfeiting swindle initiated by a couple of bourgeois youths. The latter pass off a fake 500 franc note on some shopkeepers, who themselves dump the bill on the protagonist (Christian Patey), who is making a delivery of fuel oil. To save their skin the shop owners file a false testimony in court.

The young man loses his job and subsequently agrees to take part in a bank robbery. He is arrested and sentenced to prison, during which time his daughter dies and his wife leaves him. When he is released, he finds refuge in a suburban home of a working woman. Despite her generosity however, his long pent-up rage explodes, and he takes an axe to his benefactor and her family,

murdering the entire household. He gives himself up to the police.

The film's abiding problem is not a new one for Bresson: in the director's gallery of dead-pan protagonists, Patey is possibly the blankest, the least readable, even as a cipher in Bresson's bone spare cinematic design. The viewer understands virtually nothing of his drift into crime and murder, and if his final surrender is a sign of redemption — Bresson apparently refers to Dostoyevsky's "Crime and Punishment" — it is not evident in the character or Bresson's presentation.

One is left to coldly admire, or be bored by, the filmmaker's minimalist narrative, though the color photography reminds us nostalgically that Bresson has worked better in black and white, which is more suited to his conception.

Still, local critical response to "L'Argent" is generally enthusiastic. Pic will obviously generate much buff criticism and commentary and should follow the usual fest and art house circuits. — Len.

Caracteres Chinois
(Chinese Characters)
(FRENCH-COLOR-DOCU-16m)

Paris, May 3.
A Tricontinental Production. Produced by Antoine Fournier and Francois Leclerc. Directed by Antoine Fournier. Editor, Olivier Froux. Camille Cotte, Francoise Beloux. Reviewed at the Centre National du Cinema, Paris, April 26, 1983. Part of Cannes Fest's Perspectives in French Cinema. Running time: 65 MINS.

Producers Francois Leclerc and Antoine Fournier, who went into the Soviet Union a few years ago to make the clandestine docu, "Behind the Curtain," have repeated their exploit in Red China. "Chinese Characters" is a modest but winning record of a handful of ordinary folk living and working in Canton, in southern China.

Director Fournier and a reduced crew made three trips to the Communist nation in 1981 and 1982, where they filmed the family and friends of a young exile whom Leclerc had met in New York, and who accompanied the team as interpreter. The successive journeys give the reportage a certain progression as we watch the camera subjects — in particular a young brother and sister, both touching and funny in their wistful simplicity — move from a certain reserve to more frank observations about themselves.

Well shot in 16m, this intimate multiple portrait may say more about contemporary Chinese life than projects of more ambitious sweep and means. Though it may not have the mettle for the theatrical playoffs its makers desire, it has certain potential for tv and non-theatrical careers on the international marketplace. —Len.

Return Of The Jedi
(COLOR)

Great creatures and effects equals smash b.o. for trilogy's finale, but weak on the human side.

Hollywood, May 9.

A 20th Century-Fox release of a Lucasfilm Ltd. production, produced by Howard Kazanjian. Exec producer, George Lucas. Directed by Richard Marquand. Features entire cast. Screenplay, Lawrence Kasdan, George Lucas; camera (Rank Color; prints by Deluxe), Alan Hume; editors, Sean Barton, Marcia Lucas, Duwayne Dunham; sound (Dolby Stereo), Tony Dawe, Randy Thom; sound design, Ben Burtt; production design, Norman Reynolds; visual effects supervisors at Industrial Light & Magic, Richard Edlund, Dennis Muren, Ken Ralston; costumes, Aggie Guerard Rodgers, Nilo Rodis-Jamero; assistant director, David Tomblin; makeup and creature design, Phil Tippett, Stuart Freeborn; music, John Williams. Reviewed at the Academy of Motion Picture Arts & Sciences, Beverly Hills, May 9, 1983. (MPAA Rating: PG). Running time: 133 MINS.

Luke Skywalker .... Mark Hamill
Han Solo .... Harrison Ford
Princess Leia .... Carrie Fisher
Lando Calrissian ...... Billy Dee Williams
C-3PO .... Anthony Daniels
Chewbacca .... Peter Mayhew
Emperor .... Ian McDiarmid
Darth Vader .... David Prowse
Vader voice .... James Earl Jones
Ben Kenobi .... Alec Guinness
Yoda .... Frank Oz
Anakin Skywalker .... Sebastian Shaw
R2-D2 .... Kenny Baker
Other cast: Michael Pennington, Kenneth Colley, Michael Carter, Denis Lawson, Tim Rose, Dermot Crowley, Caroline Blakiston.

Additional Production Credits
Production supervisor, Douglas Twiddy; location camera, Jim Glennon, assistant directors, Roy Button, Michael Steele; art direction, Fred Hole, James Schoppe; special effects supervisors, Roy Arbogast, Kit West; stunts, Glenn Randall, Peter Diamond; choreography, Gillian Gregory; conceptual artist, Ralph McQuarrie; co-producers, Robert Watts, Jim Bloom.

Miniature & Optical Effects Unit Credits
Visual effects art direction, Joe Johnston, optical photography supervisor, Bruce Nicholson; matte-painting supervisor, Michael Pangrazio; modelshop supervisors, Lorne Peterson, Steve Gawley; visual effects editor, Arthur Repola; animation supervisor, James Keefer; stop motion animation, Tom St. Amand.

There is good news, bad news and no news about "Return Of The Jedi." The good news is that George Lucas & Co. have perfected the technical magic to a point where almost anything and everything — no matter how bizarre — is believable. The bad news is the human dramatic dimensions have been sorely sacrificed. The no news is the picture will take in millions regardless of the pluses and minuses.

As heralded, "Jedi" is the conclusion of the middle trilogy of Lucas' planned nine-parter and suffers a lot in comparison to the initial "Star Wars," when all was fresh. One of the apparent problems is neither the writers nor the principal performers are putting in the same effort.

Telegraphed in the preceding "Empire Strikes Back," the basic dramatic hook this time is Mark Hamill's quest to discover — and do something about — the true identity of menacing Darth Vader, while resisting the evil intents of the Emperor (Ian McDiarmid). Unfortunately, this sets up a number of dramatic confrontations that fall flat.

Though perfectly fine until now as daringly decent Luke Skywalker, Hamill is not enough of a dramatic actor to carry the plot load here, especially when his partner in so many scenes is really little more than an oversized gas pump, even if splendidly voiced by James Earl Jones.

Even worse, Harrison Ford, who was such an essential element of the first two outings, is present more in body than in spirit this time, given little to do but react to special effects. And it can't be said that either Carrie Fisher or Billy Dee Williams rise to previous efforts.

But Lucas and director Richard Marquand have overwhelmed these performer flaws with a truly amazing array of creatures, old and new, plus the familiar space hardware. The first half-hour, in fact, has enough menacing monsters to populate a dozen other horror pics on their own.

The good guys this time are allied with a new group, the Ewoks, a tribe of fuzzy, sweet little creatures that continually cause ahhs among the audience (and will doubtlessly sell thousands of dolls). Carrying their spears and practicing primitive rites, they also allow Lucas to carry on the "Star Wars" tradition of borrowing heavily from familiar serial scenes.

Though slow to pick up the pace and saddled with an anticlimatic sequence at the finish, "Jedi" is nonetheless reasonably fast paced for its 133-minute length, a visual treat throughout. But let's hope for some new and more involving characters in the next chapters or more effort and work for the old. —Har.

Blue Skies Again
(COLOR)

More bunt than homerun.

Hollywood, May 4.

A Warner Bros. release. Produced by Alex Winitsky and Arlene Sellers. Directed by Richard Michaels. Features entire cast. Screenplay, Kevin Sellers; camera (Technicolor), Don McAlpine; editor, Danford B. Greene; sound (Dolby Stereo), Howard Warren; art direction, Don Ivey; assistant director, Michael Daves; music, John Kander. Reviewed at the Directors Guild of America, L.A., May 4, 1983 (MPAA rating: PG.) Running time: 96 MINS.

Sandy .... Harry Hamlin
Liz .... Mimi Rogers
Dirk .... Kenneth McMillan
Lou .... Dana Elcar
Paula .... Robyn Barto
"Brushback" .... Marcos Gonzales
"Wallstreet" .... Cilk Cozart
Calvin .... Joey Gian
Carroll .... Doug Moeller
Ken .... Andy Garcia
Roy .... Tommy Lane

A sunny little baseball picture, "Blue Skies Again" steals home on a bunt and should provide pleasant family filler until the big summer pictures arrive.

Like other professional sports, baseball remains one of the land's last outposts of sexual segregation — a natural target for producers Alex Winitsky and Arlene Sellers who, along with director Richard Michaels, have gotten the most out of writer Kevin Sellers' question: What would happen if a girl dared try out for a major league team?

The answer, of course, is a lot of foot-shuffling, bluster and protest from the males, all of whom are essentially likable beneath their short-sighted chauvanism. Best of all is Harry Hamlin as the wealthy bachelor team owner who won't even consider a female player until he starts to fall for her manager, Mimi Rogers.

As the freckle-faced second baseman anxious for a fair chance for the fair sex, Robyn Barto proves quite winsome in her film debut. And Kenneth McMillan seems to be on a relaxing lark as the sympathetic but cowed manager.

If after five minutes, anybody doubts Barto is going to ultimately make the big play and earn a spot on the team, then they're the kind of person who makes sure there's a Weiner in the hot dog before passing the money back down the line.

Even if expected, though, the big crack of Barto's bat is a good capper for a light-hearted inspiration to the little girls in the audience, even if the boys are tempted to groan.
—Har.

Spacehunter: Adventures In The Forbidden Zone
(COLOR-3-D)

Poorly-scripted sci-fi actioner looks to big openings via 3-D gimmick, but is a weak entry in summer b.o. competition.

A Columbia Pictures release of a Columbia-Delphi production. Executive producer, Ivan Reitman. Produced by Don Carmody, John Dunning, Andre Link. Directed by Lamont Johnson. Features entire cast. Screenplay, Edith Rey & David Preston, Dan Goldberg & Len Blum, from a story by Stewart Harding. Jean LaFleur; camera (Twin Panavision, Metrocolor), Frank Tidy; editor, Scott Conrad; music, Elmer Bernstein; 3-D consultant, Ernest McNabb; sound, Richard Lightstone; production design, Jackson DeGovia; special makeup effects, Thomas R. Burman; assistant director, Tony Lucibello; production manager, William Zborowsky; stunt coordinator, Walter Scott; special effects coordinator, Dale Martin. Reviewed at Loews State 2 theatre, N.Y., May 5, 1983. (MPAA Rating: PG). Running time: 90 MINS.

Wolff .... Peter Strauss
Niki .... Molly Ringwald
Washington .... Ernie Hudson
Chalmers .... Andrea Marcovicci
Overdog McNabb ...... Michael Ironside
Grandma Patterson ...... Beeson Carroll
Chemist .... Hrant Alianak
Meagan .... Deborah Pratt
Reena .... Aleisa Shirley
Nova .... Cali Timmins
Jarrett .... Paul Boretski
Duster .... Patrick Rowe
Barracuda Leader .... Reggie Bennett

Visual Effects Credits
Special visual effects produced by Fantasy II Film Effects: art direction, Michael Minor; special effects supervisors, Gene Warren Jr., Peter Kleinow; production supervisor, Leslie Huntley; model shop supervisor, Dennis Schultz; pyrotechnics, Joseph Viskocil; camera operator, John Huneck; matte paintings, Matte Effects; effects animation, Ernest D. Farino. Special optical effects, Image 3; optical photography, Phil Huff, Mike Warren.

Columbia's big-budget ($12-13,-000,000) entry in the current 3-D revival, "Spacehunter: Adventures In The Forbidden Zone" is a muddled action film, lacking the story values which could attract a wide audience. By virtue of its release timing ahead of other summer product, it should generate very strong openings, but shapes up as easy prey for the big guns to come.

Science fiction tale is set in the mid-21st Century on planet Terra Eleven of a double-star system, an Earth colony reduced to "Road Warrior"-style rubble by wars and a plague. Weak story premise, lacking urgency or any sense of importance, has salvage ship pilot Wolff (Peter Strauss) and other "Earthers" including orphaned waif Niki (Molly Ringwald) and Wolff's former training school colleague, now sector chief Washington (Ernie Hudson), searching the planet for three shipwrecked, later kidnapped girls.

Episodic treatment pits them against many local dangers including a well-executed set of puffy monsters, en route to a showdown at the lair of local tyrant McNabb, known as Overdog (Michael Ironside, in skull-like makeup reminiscent of actor Reggie Nalder).

The film's single theme, of man fighting machine, is repeated over and over in comic relief, gladiatorial contests and even the slotting of villain Overdog as a cyborg.

Aside from fine stuntwork in an early battle with misfits aboard a vast sail-rigged galleon running on railroad tracks and the impressive depth effects in the final reel battles at Overdog's iron sculpture-plus-neon fortress, "Spacehunter" is a dull trek picture. Strauss and Ringwald's verbal bickering as they move from one sudden peril to the next is unengrossing and lacks the wit or clash-of-wills entertainment of models ranging from "The African Queen" to Strauss's earlier (opposite Candice Bergen) "Soldier Blue." Strauss, Hudson and Ironside are effective in one-note performances, but Ringwald's abrasive brat portrayal becomes obnoxious. In common with most of the supporting players, she is stuck with truly awful pidgin-English dialog, supposed to represent futuristic lingo but yielding unintentional howlers instead. Andrea Marcovicci, belying her billing, appears briefly in a gimmick role.

Technical highlights in "Spacehunter" are the vast metal sculpture sets, plus impressive and well-matched miniatures and explosions. The outer space mattework and vehicles footage is brief and seemingly tacked-on to suggest a space picture in what is strictly a Terra Firma adventure. Director Lamont Johnson, who entered the picture midstream after original helmer Jean LaFleur was bounced, handles the action scenes well but editing opposes viewer involvement, taking one out of each hectic action scene before its impact can be assimilated and enjoyed.

The film's 3-D process, utilizing a bulky twin-camera system developed by Ernest McNabb, has yielded mixed results. At best, the film's vast, barren vistas recall the depth effects of other depth-enhancement processes such as Cinerama, particularly the "Dawn Of Man" introduction to "2001: A Space Odyssey." At other times, light levels are variable and the near-absence of negative parallax shots (objects projecting beyond the screen into theatre space) is an unduly timid overreaction to the recent excesses of "eye-poking" shots in 3-D pictures.

Vigorous sound effects and Elmer Bernstein's rousing though sparse musical score are assets. Ultimate commercial prospects may be brighter overseas, where heavy action scenes can mitigate the very weak story. Film's abbreviated running time is slightly over 80 minutes, plus nearly 10 minutes' worth of credits sequences. —Lor.

Claretta And Ben
(Permette Signora Che Ami Vostra Figlia)
(ITALIAN-FRENCH-COLOR)

An Aquarius Film release presented by Terry Levene, of a Champion (Rome)/-Madeleine Films (Neully) production. Produced by Carlo Ponti. Directed by Gian Luigi Polidoro. Stars Ugo Tognazzi, Bernadette Lafont. Screenplay, Rafael Azcona, Leo Benvenuti, Piero de Bernardi, Polidoro from a story by Polidoro; camera (Technospes color), Mario Vulpiani; music, Carlo Rustichelli. Reviewed at Beekman Theatre, N.Y., May 6, 1983. (No MPAA Rating). Running time: 102 MINS.
Gino Pistone ....Ugo Tognazzi
Sandra ....Bernadette Lafont
With: Franco Fabrizi, Lia Tanzi, Gigi Ballista, Quinto Parmeggiani, Ernesto Colli, Felice Andreasi, Rossana di Lorenzo.

"Claretta And Ben" is an effective black comedy vehicle for Ugo Tognazzi. Filmed and released in Italy in 1974 with an original title

that roughly translates as "Madam, Permit Me to Love Your Daugher," picture arrives Stateside at this late date on the latter-day popularity of Tognazzi from "La Cage Aux Folles."

American release title refers to a play-within-the-film, penned by touring actor-playwright Gino Pistone (Tognazzi) as a starring vehicle for himself and his lover-leading lady Sandra (Bernadette Lafont) to portray the romantic story of Benito Mussolini and his mistress Claretta Petracci.

Picture limns the travails of a modest theatre group touring the provinces, with director Gian Luigi Polidoro getting in swipes against the dreaded competitor television, the financial necessities which can force actors into porno jobs and the inevitable (for an Italian film) political confrontations. When the troupe puts on its play in Mussolini's home region, the local communists throw rotten tomatoes at the actors and disrupt the performance until Gino finally wins them over by emphasizing the romantic side of his opus.

Still timely with its examination of the tendency to apologize for and romanticize the past (as witness the recent Hitler diaries hoax), "Claretta" benefits from varied use of real locations and an unfamiliar supporting cast of talented, convincing types. Both Tognazzi and French thesp Lafont excel in their star turns. Tognazzi, who worked previously with Polidoro in such films as their never released domestically 1968 "Satyricon" (superceded by Fellini's version), is wonderful as the haughty, selfish ham actor, who gradually begins to live his role as Il Duce, actually shaving his head and becoming a petty tyrant. Well-dubbed in Italian, Lafont is a solid comic foil, especially effective in the on-stage scenes. —Lor.

On The Wrong Track
(HONG KONG-COLOR)

Hong Kong, April 23.

A Shaw Brothers production and release, presented by Sir Run Run Shaw. Executive producer, Mona Fong. Directed by Huo Yao Ling. Stars Yueh Hua, Lau Tak Wash, Yim Chiu Wah, Chien Hui Yi, Liu Kuo-cheng, Liu Me-chun. Screenplay, Shaw's Creation Department; camera (color), Shao Yuan Chih; art director, Li Yao Kuang; editors, Chiang Hsing Lung, Liu Shao Kuang; music director, Li Hsiao Tien. Reviewed at Jade Theatre, Hong Kong, April 22, 1983. Running time: 98 MINS.
(Cantonese soundtrack, English subtitles).

Chen Shou-cheng (Yueh Hua), a divorced police warden, is a tyrant to teenage sons Paul (Lau Tak Wah) and Billy (Yim Chiu Wah). He especially arouses their dissatisfaction with his relationship with Winnie (Chien Hui Yi), a new

girlfriend after being estranged from his wife, now residing in Taiwan.

His two sons mix with young hooligans, and are often involved in daredevil games. Paul, always blamed for not controlling his younger brother, meets Hsiao Szu, a Vietnamese refugee (Liu Mei-chun) and falls in love, even though he knows she has an illegitimate child. The two brothers, and a group of youngsters, are caught trying to get diapers for Szu's baby at a supermarket. They are thrown out by the proprietress, the mother of Winnie. When their father learns this, he punishes his sons badly. To vent his indignation, Billy leads a group of youngsters to storm the supermarket at night. He is accidentally killed by Chen's friend, Sgt. King Kong (Liu Kuo-cheng). Paul is arrested and sent to prison.

After his discharge, Paul, who has lost all his friends, comes to the refugee camp to see Hsiao. When he is stopped from getting close, he creates trouble, which ends up in her being taken to a closed camp. To prevent her from being emigrated from Hong Kong, Paul begs his father's permission to marry her, but his request is rejected. Paul rescues Hsiao from the closed camp, but King arrives to take her away. He challenges King to a death duel, which ends in another tragedy.

This is director Huo Yao Ling's second outing. "On The Wrong Track" shows some filmic improvements. But he still sacrifices content for image and indulges in visual flamboyance. It is another movie about disturbed youth in the juvenile delinquent mould, but lacks spontaneity. The film is fast moving and well acted. —Mel.

Cannes Fest Competing

La lune dans le caniveau
(The Moon In The Gutter)
(FRENCH-ITALIAN-COLOR)

Cannes, May 12.
A Gaumont/TF1 Productions/SFPC (Paris)/Opera Film Produzione (Rome) production, Gaumont (Paris) release. Based on novel by David Goodis. Stars Gerard Depardieu, Nastassia Kinski. Screenplay and directed by Jean-Jacques Beineix. Executive producer Lise Fayolle. Camera (Eastmancolor, Anamorphic Panavision), Philippe Rousselot with Dominique Brenguier; editors, Monique Prim, Yves Deschamps; music, Gabriel Yared; production management, Hubert Niogret, Luicano Balducci; production design, Hilton McConnico, Sandro dell'Orco, Angelo Santucci, Bernhard Vezat; costumes, Claire Fraisse. Reviewed at Cannes Film Festival, (competitive) May 12, 1983. Running time, 137 MINS.
Gerard ....Gerard Depardieu
Loretta ....Nastassia Kinski
Bella ....Victoria Abril
Newton Channing ...Vittorio Mezzogiorno
Frank ....Dominique Pinon
Lola ....Bertice Reading
Tom ....Gabriel Monnet
Frieda ....Milena Vukotic
Jesus ....Bernard Farcy
Dora ....Anne-Marie Coffinet

Some of the near-unanimous hissing that met Jean-Jacques Beineix' "The Moon In The Gutter" after its Cannes competition showings may be due to the frustrations caused by overblown expectations. After all, Beineix had blessed the world of films artistically and commercially with his first feature "Diva" and now for his second effort he had been working neck to neck with Federico Fellini in Rome's Cinecitta for three months, using big stars and a big budget (25,000,000 francs against "Diva's" mere seven).

Alas, even the firmest Beineix enthusiasts this time around must make do with a big, beautiful bag, empty of anything but high technical gloss and cinematic trickery. "The Moon," is a love-cum-whodunit comedy featuring frames to hang worthily in any museum of photography, some good acting, some stagey acting, plus a plot and a dialog that together constitute a catalog of all the favorite corny twists and mouthings of yesterday's popular films and novels. None of this works even as tongue-in-cheek satire. Superficial value is all this film has and no amount of scholarly analysis of hidden intents will alter that fact.

Beineix, a confessed conoisseur of trashy novels (he likes to empty spaces in them, ready to be filled with his imagery), has based his script on a murder novel by David Goodis. It would be interesting to read the book since Beineix leaves us with no solutions, only more riddles. He has a big, solid longshoreman Gerard (played with muted strength by Gerard Depardieu) continuing a restless search for the rapist who caused his adult kid sister to borrow his razor and commit suicide with it, leaving blood for the moon of the title to be reflected in.

In its in extremis picturesque natural and artificial decor, film is clearly a case of nostalgie de la boue, almost literally nostalgia for the gutter. Gerard lives with his kid brother and father, both layabouts and alcoholics, in a derelict house near the city port. The houses also serves as a cheap bar and a brothel, where his regular girl-friend Bella works (a vivacious performance by Victoria Abril). A modicum of rough order is maintained by the father's black wife (Bertice Reading, screaming her dialog in an amusing way). To this place comes one night a rich young man, Newton Channing (Vittorio Mezzogiorno), who stays on with the obvious intent of drinking himself to death. His sister turns up to bring him home. She is Loretta, and she is played with sly, warm smiles by Nastassia Kinski, appearing ready to burst into sexual maturity any minute now. (Actually, Beineix spotted her from exactly that newly gained quality in Francis Coppola's "One From The Heart," a film "Moon" in many ways is a close parallel to, anyway).

Bernard and Loretta are drawn towards each other. She takes the initiative, he is reluctant (and Bella is madly jealous). Bernhard pursues his training of the murderer. The drunks drink, the inamorated couple play with fire and with dreams of marriage, and Bernard gets involved in fist-fights with other workers, and there is an attempt by design on his own life. Romantic music swells and is then toned down into the near-silence of suspense-building. A vertical laser beam lies down horizontally to become the stripe of light coming out from under a door. Loretta is found with her throat cut. Later she marries Gerard at midnight in a deserted catehdral. Then he wakes up in the black woman's bed, is thrown out, climbs to rest with an enthused Bella who shows him that his wedding band is breakable, it was made of plastic.

Film goes on to have a couple of endings or new beginnings maybe. But most audiences will by then have ceased to care long ago. "The Moon" is sure to get some sales and exposure because of the success enjoyed by "Diva," but there really is no big coin — or any other reward — shining back at the moon from this gutter of stylish dreams. —Kell.

Vokzal dla dvoish
(Station For Two)
(USSR-COLOR)

Cannes, May 8.
A Mosfilm production, Sovexport release. Features entire cast. Directed by Eldar Riaznov. Original story and script by Emil Braguinski and Eldar Riazanov; camera (color) Vadim Alissov; production design, Alexander Borissov; music, Andrei Petrov. Reviewed at the Cannes Film Festival (competing) May 7, 1963. Running time: 127 MINS.
Platon ....Oleg Bassilashvili
Vera .... Lyudmila Gurchenko
Vera's boyfriend .... Nikita Mikhalkov
The other
   waitress............ Nonna Mordukova

It appears amazing that the Russians care to be represented in international competition with such a minor effort as "Station For Two" — and even more amazing that the Cannes selection committee did not reject the offering. Film is an excessively long romantic comedy with dashes of social satire, some pratfalls and a few attempts at the lightest imaginable eroticism, all of it presented by writer-director Eldar Riazanov in an insecure mix of cinematic styles and artistic intents.

Story has pianist Platon, more or less on the run from a traffic accident for which he has taken the blame properly belonging to his frivolous wife, getting involved romantically with a waitress at a rather large and very lively railroad station where he is stuck for a couple of days and nights and where all kinds of mishaps come upon him: he loses his ticket, his passport, has his money stolen, etc. Meanwhile, he finds solace with the waitress, herself approaching middle age and with much disillusion in her heart.

While the two sympathetic characters (played stolidly by Oleg Bassilashvili and more vivaciously by Lyudmila Gurchenko, currently Russia's most popular comedienne) grope with infinite slowness towards the new comforts of the decisive embrace (in a side-tracked sleeping car), nice sketches of satire are devoted to rather innocent black-market activity and bureaucratic nonsense, etc. flourishing in and around the train station and particularly in its restaurant, the latter offer looking more like a field canteen than a nightclub.

"Station For Two" falls in two parts of equal length and might amuse an international audience as a tv offering, mainly because the aforementioned eroticism, innocent as it is, and the spice of satire of the "System" are quite unexpected. Otherwise, all that is made clear is that waiting around railroad stations in Russia is as much of a drag as anywhere else in the world. Except that the Russians have live music around the clock and waitresses humming "Raindrops Keep Falling On My Head." —Kell.

Camminacammina
(ITALIAN-COLOR)

Rome, May 3.
A Gaumont release, produced by RAI-TV and Scenario Film. Features entire cast. Written, directed, photographed, edited, set and costume designs by Ermanno Olmi. Music, Bruno Nicolai. Reviewed at C.D.S. Rome, April 3, 1983. Running time: 165 MINS.
Mel, the Priest .... Alberto Fumagalli
Rupo, the boy .... Antonio Cucciarre

Ruled off-limits to under-14's by the bizarre Italian censors for "gratuitous obscenities" (ban has since been lifted under pressure), Ermanno Olmi's mini-epic "Camminacammina" is, on the contrary, a beautiful children's film, a personal vision also capable of holding adults — and not particularly pious ones — for its lengthy duration. This story of the Magi lovingly retold from a mixture of unconventional sources would make an ideal Christmas picture anywhere in the world, while its four-hour version for tv (perhaps

pic's most congenial outlet) awaits airing.

A bright star whooshes across the night sky and Mel, the astronomer-priest, aided by his boy assistant, organizes a party of believers into a caravan to pay their respects to the "King of Kings," as the Scriptures direct. A motley crew dressed in rags and sent off by the King's guards represents not so much an official delegation (though local authorities entrust them with a chest of precious objects to honor the new potentate) as the people's spontaneous desire to see the magnificent new ruler with their own eyes.

The journey is long and hard. To the director's credit, it is rarely tedious to watch. An excellent sense of pacing (Olmi edited, as well as photographed, scripted, and designed costumes and sets) keeps the pilgrimage moving forward, facing the usual woes of wagon train westerns.

Then the caravan wakes up one morning and finds thevselves face to face with an elephant and a camel, it takes them a while to realize they've stumbled across the other two "Magi" — common men like them, following the star. The actual encounter with a tiny pink fist sticking out of the manger is hardly how they expected their tiring march to end. These wise men consult and decide they have no choice but to be "certain" this is the Saviour. They hurriedly depart on the long trek home, leaving the slaughter of the innocents behind them.

A devout Catholic and a thoughtful artist, Olmi has made an effort not simply to recreate the classic Biblical stories in their most familiar version, a la Zeffirelli, but to find a key in more realistic popular legends, which lend pic an air of authenticity and personal religious experience, simplicity, humility and faith.

A film into which the director has evidently poured a great deal of himself (three years of work), "Camminacammina" is also enjoyable on a non-religious level as a well-told adventure tale with a sober ending. Bruno Nicolai's score is dominated by one very listenable tune, which now and then gives the caravan a needed pick-up. The non-professional cast selected from among the director's friends and locals from Volterra, where pic was lensed, is led by Alberto Fumagalli's human, noble, mystical priest Mel, a complex figure of intellectual and sage. Special mention goes to the self-willed little boy Rupo (child actor Antonio Cucciarre) from whose mouth come those few naughty words the censors came down on. —Yung.

Nostalghia
(Nostalgia)
(USSR-ITALIAN-COLOR/B&W)

Cannes, May 16.
A RAI Rete 2, Opera Film (Italy) production in collaboration with Sovin Film (Moscow), Gaumont Distribution. Directed by Andrei Tarkovsky. Features entirecast. Screenplay by Tarkovsky, Tonino Guerra; camera (Technicolor alternating with black and white), Giuseppe Lanci; production design, Andrea Grisanti; costumes, Lina Nerli Taviani; editors, Amedeo Salfa, Erminia Marani; music consultant, Gino Peguri; executive producer, Francesco Casati. Reviewed (in competition) at the Cannes Film Festival, May 16, 1963. Running time: 130 MINS.
Gorciakov .... Oleg Jankovski
Eugenia .... Domiziana Giordano
Domenico .... Erland Josephson
Gorciakov's wife .... Patricia Terreno

"Nostalghia" is the first feature film by Russia's Andrei Tarkovsky to be shot outside his homeland. Only five percent of the film was shot in Russia, the rest in and around the Vignoni thermal baths in a small 14th-century village in the Tuscan hills.

To this place comes Gorciakov (Oleg Jankovski) as a Russian professor of architecture to study the sites and buildings he has taught his students about. he is accompanied by a strongwilled, temperamental woman (Domiziana Giordano) who serves as his interpreter.

An impossible love affair between the two is indicated, but she revolts early on when Gorciakov submerges himself both in the ever-present still and moving waters that are the filmmaker's obsession as well and in what he sees as his own mirror image — the elderly, slightly mad Italian professor of mathematics Domenico (Erland Josephson).

The Italian long ago forbade his family to leave the confines of their house, being obsessed with the conviction that the end of the world would come any day now. Towards the end of the film, Domenico appears in a larger town on top an equestrian statue in the role of Doomsday prophet. He tells people that they have destroyed the purity of the world's waters, but Tarkovsky's and co-scripter-poet Tonino Guerra's message is hardly an ecological one alone.

Domenico sets fire to himself, but first he has told the Russian that he may save the world by keeping a candle burning while walking the length of the bottom of the thermal bath.

Learned treatises and books are sure to be written about "Nostalghia," and Tarkovsky himself has offered clues about the impossibility of two cultures to ever really understand each other's art until all borders are torn down. His nostalgia also has to do with longing for his homeland, physically and within man's soul.

Only very devout people will be able to both enjoy the exquisite imagery and frames of Tarkovsky's film and truly understand the rather murky incantations of the dialog. "Nostalghia" is simply not a film to be understood at one sitting and certainly not a work that will ever be appreciated by general audiences (it will be shown on Italian tv one year from its theatrical release).

Tarkovsky's reputation along with his obvious mastery of the medium as visual art will assure "Nostalghia" of worldwide sales and interest in specialized situations.

As a filmmaker, Tarkovsky could be said to be a poet of the most beautifully lit darkness. His landscapes' curves are caressed by mists. His interiors are dripping, watery halls of muted dreams. On the soundtrack, music is very rarely heard (Beethoven's "Ode To Joy" bursts forth briefly), while the whizzing of some industrial saw or the falling of water drops are heard almost continuously.

Tarkovsky uses color mostly for interiors, black and white for exteriors, but you cannot count on any regularity. The shifts come quite naturally, though.

Awaiting the above-mentioned learned treatises, discerning audiences will sink themselves in the waters of Tarkovsky's moody imagery and accept the dialog as pure sound, music in a way, to be absorbed by the senses rather than by the brain. Oleg Jankovski's lean, dark face reflects the urge to explore endlessly, to search stubbornly for light.

Erland Josephson appears like a fallen patriarch of an unrequited faith, and Domiziana Giordano, looking like a more voluptuous and certainly more savage Botticelli's Venus, has beauty as well as the most luminous star quality. —*Kell.*

La Mort de Mario Ricci
(The Death of Mario Ricci)
(FRENCH-SWISS-COLOR)

Cannes, May 8.

A Pegase Films-Television Suisse Romande/Swanie Productions-F.R. 3/-Tele Muenchen production. Produced by Yves Peyrot and Norbert Saada. Written and directed by Claude Goretta. Features entire cast. Camera (Eastmancolor), Hans Liechti; production design, Yanko Hodjis; editor, Joele van Effenterre; music, Arie Dzierlatke, The Orchestre Osmose, plus excerpts of Vivaldi and Monteverdi pieces. Reviewed at Cannes Film Festival (competing) May 8, 1983. Running time: 97 MINS.

Bernard Fontana ....Gian-Maria Volonte
Didier Meylan ...... Jean-Michel Dupuis
Henri Kremer ....Heinz Bennent
Cathy Burns ....Mimsy Farmer
Solange .... Magali Noel
Stephane Coutaz .... Lucas Belveaux

Claude Goretta of "The Lacemaker" fame has shaped his new feature "The Death of Mario Ric-

ci" in his usual chamber music tones and frames and is once again looking at universal matters through the microcosmos of people and events in the narrowest of communities, this time the imaginary Swiss village of Etiolaz, where the Italian worker of the title has just been killed in what appears to be a traffic accident.

A much respected, elderly·TV interviewer, Bernard Fontana, and his young assistant Didier Meylan have just arrived at the local inn. They are preparing to do a program with Henry Kremer, a scientist and an expert on solutions of world famine, who is now living here as a disillusioned recluse with his younger lover-companion Cathy Burns. The latter would like to help Fontana in nudging Kremer back into an active life. While pursuing their main objective, Fontana and everybody else gets sidetracked in various ways. Fontana has a brief affair with the inn's waitress Solange, his assistant similarly attaches himself to Cathy Burns when Cathy is saddened by the scientist's renewed reneging on the world after a brief opening up towards Fontana.

And when the diseased Mario Ricci proves to have been the victim of an attack by young hoodlums, Fontana, though partly crippled, makes a pitch to bring out the truth, thus proving himself a man not to be persuaded by bad events to refrain from involving himself in matters of others' life and death.

Gian-Maria Volonte's great Mount Rushmore face, now framed by a curly white mane, is as expressive as ever of a man's sensitivity intelligent reactions to the wayward behavior of everybody, including himself. He plays the tv humanist with quiet compassion against the nervous pulse-beat of Heinz Bennent's performance as the scientist. But Goretta is great at having everybody (including Magali Noel as the waitress and Mimsy Farmer as Cathy Burns) playing their roles to the hilt without every straining for effort. Film is full of significant little observations, and if it at times appears dull in its avoidance of the story's build-in dramatic possibilities, it retains the particular life of the perfect miniature closely observed.

Both the Goretta name and the subject matter of "The Death of Mario Ricci" should carry this film beyond the festival circuit into specialized theatrical situations in many countries before being lost in the netherworld of cultural tv film programming. —*Kell.*

L'Ete Meurtrier
(One Deadly Summer)
(FRENCH-COLOR)

Cannes, May 10.

SNC production and release, in co-production with CAPAC and TF 1 Films Production. Produced by Gerard Beytout. Stars Isabelle Adjani and Alain Souchon. Directed by Jean Becker. Screenplay, Sebastien Japrisot, from his novel; camera (Eastmancolor), Etienne Becker; editor, Jacques Witta; art director, Jean-Claude Gallouin; music, Georges Delerue; sound, Guillaume Sciama; production manager, Alain Darbon. Reviewed at the Cannes film festival (competitive) May 10, 1983. Running time: 130 MIN.
"She" .... Isabelle Adjani
Pin Pon .... Alain Souchon
Cognata .... Suzanne Flon
Pin Pon's mother ....Jenny Cleve
Mickey ....Francois Cluzet
Boubou .... Manuel Gelin
Gabriel ....·.... Michel Galabru
She's Mother .... Maria Machado

Sebastien Japrisot's best-selling suspense novel, "One Deadly Summer," has finally made it to the screen in an adaptation by the author, and Jean Becker (son of the late Jacques Becker) has directed this psychological drama about a dangerously neurotic girl's obsession with a family shame. Often questionable in matters of credibility and wobbly in its dramatic conception, pic is nonetheless fairly engrossing, thanks to Isabelle Adjani, astonishing in the central role.

Story is set in a small southern French town where Adjani, recently arrived with her timid German mother and invalid father (Maria Machado and Michel Galabru), quickly earns the reputation of a local tinsel sexpot, empty-headed, volatile and unattainable.

In fact, she has much on her tortured mind. Traumatized by the knowledge that her mother was raped by three Italian immigrants before she was born, Adjani thinks she's on the trail of vengeance when she is courted by a young garage mechanic (Alain Souchon), whose father, now dead, was an Italian immigrant who owned a mechanical piano, the only clue to the identity of her mother's aggressors. Adjani plans to use Souchon and his family to avenge her mother and exorcize her own emotional wounds, but she literally goes mad when she learns that the two Italians whom she believes to be the aggressors are innocent and that her father had long ago secretly exacted vengeance on the real rapists. She is committed to an asylum, and Souchon, who thinks she had been raped by the two men she had been plotting against, shoots them down in cold blood.

Japrisot retains in his screenplay the multiple narrative idea that supposedly gave his novel its particular ironic force: the action is related alternately from the viewpoints of several characters, including Adjani, Souchon and Su-

zanne Flon, as the humane, partly deaf aunt.

But in the film this shifting is translated by alternating voiceover commentaries. If an asset in the novel, it becomes something of an obstacle in the film, because Becker fails to differentiate the narratives visually. The action owes its movement more to the performances and Japrisot's tangy dialog than to the director's handling of camera.

Adjani's performance of a disturbed young woman moving implacably towards madness is so electrifying it manages to forestall any questions one might have about the unlikely plot turns. The rest of the cast offers solid support.

Tech credits are all fine and pic should have good commercial chances at home and abroad.
—*Len.*

Carmen
(SPANISH-COLOR)

Cannes, May 13.

An Emiliano Piedra production. Directed by Carlos Saura; screenplay and choreography by Carlos Saura and Antonio Gades; camera (Eastmancolor), Teo Escamilla; music, Paco de Lucia (excerpts of Georges Bizet's "Carmen" performed by Joan Sutherland and Mario del Monaco); sets, Felix Murcia; costumes, Teresa Nieto; editor, Pedro del Rey; sound, Carlos Faruolo. Reviewed at Palais du Festival (Cannes) (Competing) May 13, '83. Running time: 102 MINS.
Antonio ....Antonio Gades
Carmen .... Laura del Sol
Paco .... Paco de Lucia
Cristina ....Cristina Hoyos
Juan/husband .....Juan Antonio Jimenez
Escamillo .....Sebastian Moreno
Pepe Giron .... Jose Yepes
Pepa Flores .... Pepa Flores

The new Carlos Saura-Antonio Gades version of "Carmen" is a visual delight which promises to have art audiences lining up at the theatres as the team that earlier scored with "Blood Wedding" again spin filmic and dance magic on the screen. (Item was picked up by Orion at Cannes).

Producer Emiliano Piedra has beat other "Carmen" producers to the punch, and this version of the famous tale of Prosper Merimee, done by the Spaniards themselves, will constitute a yardstick against which forthcoming versions will be measured. Despite some adagio dips in the pacing, item moves along briskly on the whole, with highpoints the dance numbers at the Tobacco Factory and Carmen's love scene.

Rather than filming a full-dress version of the Bizet opera, Saura and Gades have opted for a flamenco-ballet presentation, using at times excerpts from the opera, at other times resorting to flamenco rhythms adapted to the Carmen yarn.

But the rehearsals of "Carmen" are intermingled, often with typically Sauralike touches, with a contemporary love story between Gades and Laura del Sol, who has been chosen to play the "Carmen" part.

At other times, such as the "toreador" scene, Saura and Gades parody the French opera; throughout they are aware of the cliches in foreigners' concepts of Spain, but gleefully mimic them. Strongpoint of pic is not its story, but some of the stunning musical numbers performed without props or sets on an empty stage. It is the stark artistry of pure dance and a mesmerizing mixture of classic music and modern flamenco that held many in the audience here spellbound, and which make for a memorable film, certainly one of Carlos Saura's best to date. —Besa.

Cannes
Non-Competing

Gib Gas — Ich Will Spass
(Step on the Gas!)
(WEST GERMAN-COLOR)

Cannes, May 15.
A Solaris Film Production, Munich produced by Peter Zeuk; world rights, Atlas International, Munich. Features entire cast. Directed by Wolfgang Bueld. Screenplay, Bueld, Georg Seitz; camera (color), Heinz Hoelscher; sound, Winfried Heubner, Klaus Eckelt; editing, Peter Fratscher; sets, Erhard Engel; music, Nena, Markus, Morgenrot, and Extrabreit. Reviewed at Cannes Film Festival (Market) May 9, '83. Running time: 91 MINS.
Cast: Nena (Tina), Markus (Robby), Enny Gerber, (Asias), Morgenrot (Tino), Karl Dall.

Wolfgang Bueld's rep was a Teutonic helmer of punk-and-rock music — his docus include "Punk in London" (1977), "Reggae in Babylon" (1978), and "British Rock" (1979) — until he ventured into the feature film with an episode titled "Disco Satanica" in the omnibus film "Neon City" (1981). Now he's scored a b.o. hit with "Step on the Gas!" (a rough translation of the German pop-hit title "Gib Gas — ich will Spass"), starring "New Wave" songs by Nena, Markus, Morgenrot, and Extrabreit. Nena, in particular, is currently second only to David Bowie on the European song hit parade. Pic does little more than supply ample opportunities for the pop stars to sing their numbers in playback against open-air film backdrops.

The story is slim pickings: Tina falls in love with a bump-car attendant named Tina at the fairgrounds, where she works after school. A highschool chum, Robby, in turn has a crush on her — so when Tina follows Tino to the next fairgrounds to run away with him, Robby tags along in pursuit and to help out if need be. Pic is packed with a solid line of visual gags, the best featuring Karl Dall in a series of walk-ons. Indeed, cabaretist Dall should be given a feature of his own.
— Holl.

Sliozy Kapali
(Tears Are Flowing)
(USSR-COLOR)

Cannes, May 11.
A Mosfilm production, Moscow; world rights, Goskino, Moscow. Features cast. Directed by Georgi Danelia. Screenplay, Danelia, Kir Bulychev, Alexander Volodin; camera (color), Yuri Klimenko; sets, Alexander Boim, Alexander Makarov; music, Guy Kancheli. Reviewed at Cannes Film Fest (Market), May 11, '83. Running time: 90 MINS.
Cast: Yevgeni Leonov/Iya Savvina, (Pavel Ivanovich Vasin), Nina Grebeshkova, Olga Mashnaya, Boris Andreyev.

Georgi Danelia's comedies on the common people living in and around Moscow are known to fest followers: "Afonya" (1975), "Mimino" (1977), and "Autumn Marathon" (1979). His latest feature, "The Tears Are Flowing," is slated for entry in the upcoming Moscow festival, where he has become a house director of sorts.

"Tears Are Flowing" refers in its title to a popular expression and song hit. It's the story of a minor official in a provincial town who suddenly breaks out of his working routine to the amazement and consternation of his family, friends, and office colleagues. Geared as a fantasy from start to finish, there's a reference to Hans Christian Andersen's fairy tale of the wicked troll who uses a mirror to reflect everything as ugly and disturbing in the eye of the beholder — in this case, one Pavel Ivanovich Vasin on his way home from work after a rather trying day at the office. For the next 24 hours, a tragicomedy unfolds as a good man goes berserk to the point of attempted self-destruction at whatever cost to the people about him who know and love him in an entirely different light.

The first people our little-man antihero gets even with are his wife and family. The lady of the house is forever on the telephone, while the daughter and her student-husband don't even pay much attention to the granddaughter, whose babysitter is the tv set. Pavel Ivanovich lets everybody know that he's irritated by the noncommunicative noise of jabbering voices in every room of the small apartment: he hangs up the phone on his wife, and suggests that his son-in-law go out and earn a living. Then he packs a toothbrush, and leaves the house himself.

Throughout the night, he finds himself unwanted in the local hotel without proper identification, and can't even find a bed at the home of a friend. The next day at the office, he tells off everybody in sight who are guilty of some form of corruption by greasing the palms of town officials for one personal favor or another. Since his job has to do with the distribution of housing and garage space in the community, the phone fairly rings itself off the hook from morn to eve. One thing leads to another — until Pavel Ivanovich does such crazy things like telling his driver to run the official car into a convenient mud-hole on a construction site. Next, he tries suicide — without much success, as the fixture on the ceiling of an apartment is too weak to hold his weight, and the end result in a gaping hole in the floor of the apartment above.

So our little man tries walking out into the town lake, breaking the ice in his stubborn path to end it all. A girl passing by stops that attempt by wading out after him. In the end, he calms down enough to talk with his granddaughter on the phone, who magically offers the remedy for his illness: simply blow your top to get it all out, and then let the tears flow ... It works, and everything is back to normal again.

Yevgeni Leonov, a vet Danelia thesp, is a charmer in this modern fairy tale. Although the story is slighter than usual for the Georgian director who ranks as Mosfilm's leading comic helmer, "The Tears Are Flowing" is a compact work of subtle visual fantasy.
—Holl.

Runners
(BRITISH-COLOR)

Cannes, May 14.
A Hanstoll Production for Goldcrest Films and Television Ltd. Produced by Barry Hanson. Directed by Charles Sturridge. Features entire cast. Screenplay, Stephen Poliakoff; camera (color), Howard Atherton; editor, Peter Coulson; music, George Fenton; production design, Arnold Chapkis; art direction, Mark Nerini; costume design, David Perry. Reviewed at Cannes Festival (noncompeting) May 9, 1983. Running time: 110 MINS.
Tom . . . . James Fox
Helen . . . . Jane Asher
Rachel . . . . Kate Hardie
Wilkins . . . . Robert Lang
Gillian . . . . Eileen O'Brien
Lucy . . . . Ruti Simon

There are a lot of interesting ideas in "Runners," but they're never really shaped into a coherent film. It's evident that directing "Brideshead Revisited," the rambling tv series with which helmer Charles Sturridge secured international acclaim, was not the best education in cinematic structure.

The meandering plot follows a father, played by James Fox, who searches for his daughter long after everyone else, including his wife, have given up. Tracking her down to a car hire firm, rather than some perverse religious sect as he had expected, he is horrified at her reluctance to return.

Along the way, the father strikes up with a woman from a different social class who is hunting for her son. There are some interesting nuances in this relationship, but eventually it is the trival details of the hunt that dominate the screen.

One is two thirds of the way through the film before the question is even raised of why this girl fled. And it's doubtful whether the sullen sadness in the girl's face or cheap accounts of a world without hope really serve the bill, except for naturally sympathetic youth.

It's a view of the world that writer Poliakoff has played with before in tv plays like "Bloody Kids" and "Caught On A Train." He just doesn't seem to have the guts to tackle the theme of alienated youth head on, and consequently he's easily diverted down byways.

Technical credits are all fine, although the music score is a trifle on the heavy side. Fox and Asher give as much to the roles as they can.
—Japa.

Austeria
(POLISH-COLOR)

Cannes, May 15.
A Film Polski Production, "Kadr" Film Unit, Warsaw; world rights, Film Polski, Warsaw. Features entire cast. Directed by Jerzy Kawalerowicz. Screenplay, Tadeusz Konwicki, Kawalerowicz, Julian Stryjkowski, based on Stryjkowski's novel with the same title; camera (color), Zygmunt Samosiuk; music, Leopold Kozlowski; sets, Jerzy Skrzepinski; sound, Jerzy Blaszynski; editor, Wieslawa Otocka; production manager, Urszula Orczykowka, Zygmunt Wojcik. Reviewed at Cannes Film Fest (Market), May 10, '83. Running time: 109 MINS.
Cast: Franciszek Pieczka (Tag), Wojciech Pszoniak (Shamiz), Jan Szurmiej (Cantor), Ewa Domanska (Kasia, or Kathy), Liliana Glabczynska (Yevdokha), Golda Tencer (Blanca), Marek Wilk (Bum), Wojciech Standello (Tzaddiq), Szymon Szurmiej (Wilf).

Jerzy Kawalerowicz's "Austeria" preemed abroad last November at the London Film Festival, and was in the running until the last minute for entry at Cannes. It's his first film since "Death of the President" (1978), and stands as a kind of testament — or summary of a career stretching over three decades. Kawalerowicz's preoccupation with Christian and Jewish cultures blending to form a rather unique Polish national tradition was visible previously in his "The Real End of the Great War" (1957), "Mother Joan of the Angels" (1960), "Pharaoh" (1965), and "Magdalena" (1969), the last named an Italian production. Now it gushes to the surface in "Austeria," based on Julian Stryjkowski's novel and scripted in collaboration with the writer and the equally prominent poet-writer-director Tadeusz Konwicki.

It's set in Polish Galicia in 1914, on the eve of WWI. This border area was peopled by three nationalities and cultures: Polish, Ukrainian, Jewish, thus absorbing Eastern and Western influences. That unique composite of religious traditions was wiped out by two world wars, but preserved by Stryjkowski's novel published in 1966, an autobiographical work. Kawalerowicz, too, goes far out of his way to preserve on film the magic of a vanished culture.

The scenery is a country inn. The neighboring village is being abandoned by the Jewish community, who are only a few steps ahead of the advancing Cossacks. The inn, an "Austeria" in Galician, is maintained by a worldwise old Jew, Tag, who sees no sense in running away from the pursuing fates. Soon, his inn houses the desperate Jews, an Austrian baroness also on the run from the town, and an Hungarian hussar cut off from his battalion — in addition to the local priest who sympathizes with the lot of the losers.

A pair of young lovers cue the tragedy: they have strayed off, and she is killed by a Cossack bullet in the meadow. The innkeeper's maid tempts Tag with her sensuality; the Hungarian has an affair with a married woman in the group; and the town is set ablaze by the invading Cossacks. The Hasidic custom of singing and dancing occupies the attention of the Jews as their fate points to doom, but the more practical Tag and the village priest make every effort to bury the dead girl in hallowed ground of the community. In the end, fire torches and gunfire raze everything to the ground, the Hassidic community staining the river with their blood as sacrificial victims.

An impressive film, but one that will have its troubles even on the arthouse circuit due to the special nature of the theme. Credits are a plus, and pic deserves more fest exposure. —Holl.

Equateur
(Equator)
(FRENCH-COLOR)

Cannes, May 13.

Gaumont release of a Corso Productions / TF 1 / Gaumont co-production. Produced y Charles Mensah. Stars Francis Huster, Barbara Sukowa. Written and directed by Serge Gainsbourg, based on the novel, "Le Coup de Lune," by Georges Simenon. Camera (color) Willy Kurant; sound, Michel Brethez; editor, Babeth Si Ramdane; music, Serge Gainsbourg; art director, Jean Ladislaw; production manager, Louis Wipf. Reviewed at the Cannes film festival (non-competitive) May 11, 1983. Running time: 85 MINS.
Adele .... Barbara Sukowa
Timar .... Francis Huster
Eugene .... Rene Kolldehoff
Commissioner ; .... Francois Dyrek
Magistrate .... Jean Bouise
Bouilloux .... Julien Guiomar

"Equateur" is the second feature film written and directed by Serge Gainsbourg, the gifted

French songwriter with a special talent for creating scandals. Pic, based on a Georges Simenon novel set in French equatorial Africa in the 1930's, finally has less to do with Simenon than with Gainsbourg's often morbid carnal obsessions. As self-portrait, this picture is about as complete as could be: grungy, feverish, self-centered, disconcerting, maddening.

Gainsbourg retains the shell of Simenon's story about an idealistic young man (Francis Huster) embarking in Africa with hopes about making his fortune there. But he falls in with a woman of shady background (Barbara Sukowa), who turns out to be a murderess as well; as a result of her deceit and amorality, he returns to Europe empty and broken.

Ridding the plot of all of Simenon's nuanced psychological observations, Gainsbourg creates a series of scenes without conventional dramatic development, but which perfectly reflect his own vision of passion in all its torrid sometimes brutish physicality. For Gainsbourg, the African setting is less a geographical reality, than a projection of his characters' state.

Gainsbourg is not the first to shoot a steamy love scene through a mosquito net and neither the overhead camera angles nor explicitness make the sexual strophes any more original.

Ironically, the film is most remarkable when it doesn't deal with sex, but simply with elemental ambiance. Gainsbourg shows his true cinematic abilities when he combines a sure camera sense with his proven gifts as composer. Sequences like those depicting Huster's arrival on a freighter (no music, but forcefully composed natural sounds) or his descent down river in a native canoe are memorable in their translation of oppressive experience. Of course, Willy Kurant's lensing must claim its share of what's best in the film.

Huster and Sukowa have no trouble enacting their roles since the film was shot on location in Gabon where the climate put them quickly in the necessary mood. The others are no less sweatily adequate.

Pic will no doubt infuriate many. But if Gainsbourg can put together a screenplay worthy of the name and get some more distance on his material, he could easily come up with a first-rate piece of artful provocation. —Len.

Polioty Vo Sne Naiavou
(Dream Flights)
(SOVIET-COLOR)

Cannes, May 10.

A Studio Alexander Dovzhenko Film Production, Kiev; world rights, Goskino, Moscow. Features entire cast. Directed by Roman Balayan. Screenplay, Victor Mere-jko; camera (color), Vilain Kaluta; sets,

Vitali Volynski; music, Vadim Khrapachev. Reviewed at Cannes Film Fest (Market), May 10, '83. Running time: 90 MINS.
Cast: Oleg Yankovski (Sergei Makarov), Lyndmila, Gurchenko, Nikita Mikalkov, Oleg Tabakov, Lyudmila Zorina, Elena Kostina.

Roman Balayan made a name for himself with his debut film, "The Lone Wolf" (1978), an adaptation of a Turgenev story that preemed at the Berlin fest. Now the Ukrainian director has made a feature in a Chekhovian vein: "Dream Flights," unspooled in the Cannes mart but a likely entry in the future on the fest circuit.

"Dream Flights" deals with a man of 40 in the midlife crisis. He lives in a provincial town, is bored by his job as an architect, doesn't have a going relationship with either his wife or his mistress, and resorts to innocent pranks whenever and wherever the chance avails itself. His friends suspect that something is wrong, but no one really understands his moods and wouldn't know what to do with a dropout in any case. Since the guy is a likeable comic too, it's best to humor him.

In the course of a day or so, our hero Sergei Makarov has a number of adventures. His speedy driving costs him a ticket after giving the police car a bit of a chase. He happens upon a film crew shooting a film, and finds himself in a dialog with the director (played by Nikita Mikalkov, the noted actor-director). He fakes drowning in a lake on a company outing, but this joke wears a bit thin: it's a cool autumn day, and to rescue him would be in vain in any case — for he's hiding out, soaking wet, just out of eyesight to see what everybody will do.

Pic's strength is lead thesp's virtuoso performance: Oleg Yankovsky (also Andrei Tarkovsky's lead in "Nostalghia") incarnates a dropout much like those in Western films and letters. —Holl.

Story of the Dolls
(HONG KONG-GERMAN-COLOR)

Cannes, May 9.

A First Distributors (HK) Ltd. production and release. Executive producers, Hoi Wong, Wolfgang von Schiber. Stars Tetchie Agbayanai, Max Thayer, Carina Schally, Josephine Manuel, Brigitta Cimarolli, Vanessa Vaylord, Sabine Mucha, Leo Hermosa, Mario Layco, Hubert Frank and Richard Cable. Directed by Hubert Frank. from an original screenplay by Frank. Production manager, Luis Mayr; camera (color), Franz X. Lederle, Michael Gast. Reviewed at Cannes Film Festival (Market), May 8, 1983. Running Time: 98 MINS.
(English version for international release).

Shot on location in the tropical Philippines, which looks like a lost paradise in the South Seas, this is the first major coproduction ex-

cursion of Hong Kong-based First Films with a German company since their "Shocking Asia" documentary series. The lead attraction is Tetchie Agbayani, a controversial Filipina model-actress whose springboard to international fame were her poses for a German Playboy layout issue, which brought her to court by ired Catholics in her native country.

The charge was obscenity, as she apparently damaged the whiter than white image of Filipina women, now considered outmoded in contemporary and Americanized Manila.

The story is really immaterial and unnecessary for this type of feature. It is the age-old tale about a handsome foreign photographer (Max Thayer) washed ashore after a severe typhoon and the provincial lass who finds through him skyrockets to fame, glory and wealth. He incidentally also saves her (Tetchie Agbayani) from being raped by a crazed beau in the old-fashioned B-movie in the tropics tradition. He takes her to the big city. But the road to success as we know is rocky, and the innocent girl is corrupted to an eastern Dolce Vita through high fashion, beauty contest, bitchy models, photographic sequences. The poor lass pays the price in the end and finds solace amongst her folks where she truly belongs.

There is no denying that the plot is sappy, mawkish and childish. It's a predictable Cinderella story welded on the kind of film that has the visual impact of an animated girlie cartoon striptease that is quite unremarkable but would obviously entertain the soft core market that it so clearly aims at. The "Story of the Dolls" targets at soft erotica and it hits the mark with the mandatory nudity, simulated sex, lesbian acts, orgasmic moans spiced with heterosexual escapades in the eye-filling touristy sights in and out of Manila environs. The latter should bring some armchair travelers to life while the "dolls" stimulate the other senses.

"Dolls" is well suited for potent exploitation and exotic escapism. Some would know that Tetchie's reel role is not too far removed from the real life drama of the 21-year-old actress.

The producers and screenwriter have concocted ideas inspired from past Oriental favorites in the genre. The cinematography transforms some of the landscapes into looming, threatening presences while the different "ladies" are lovingly exposed in different stages of undress.

Director Hubert Frank who doubles as the local pastor spitting sermons about the glory of God to the villagers directs like a cut-rate porno moviemaker turned semi-respectable. He could have spared the viewers some of the heartaches from this sex-tainted workhorse had he concentrated more on the luscious tanned body, delectable charms and histrionic talents of Agbayani.

The problem with the picture is that it tries too hard to please and this shows in the general tone created. It lacks naturalness and spontaneity despite the soft-focus images and vaselined lens to glamourize each feminine bump and grind for all the voyeurs of the world.

The English dubbing is better than average. As expected, the intellectual content is nil in this type of movie. —*Mel.*

The Sign Of Four
(BRITISH-COLOR)

Cannes, May 14.

A Mapleton Films Production. Produced by Otto Plaschkes. Directed by Desmond Davis. Features entire cast. Executive producer, Sy Weintraub; screenplay Charles Pogue; camera (color), Denis Lewiston; editor, Timothy Gee; art director, Eileen Diss; sound, Tony Dawe; costume designer, Julie Harris. Reviewed at Cannes Film Festival (Market) May 13, 1983. Running time: 100 MINS.
Sherlock Holmes . . . . Ian Richardson
Dr. Watson . . . . David Healy
Major John Sholto . . . . Thorley Walters
Inspector Layton . . . . Terence Rigby
Jonathan Small . . . . Joe Melia
Mary Morstan . . . . Cherie Lunghi
Mordecai Smith . . . . Michael O'Hagan

Planned as the first of 13 adaptations of the Conan Doyle detective stories, "The Sign Of Four" fails to capture the atmosphere of the originals. It makes do as a tepid adventure story.

"The Sign Of Four" is the tale of an ex-convict getting revenge on an army major who many years back left him in a penal colony and ran off with a stolen treasure hoard. But the con's an easy catch for Holmes, with his wooden and dwarf companion whose favorite food is human.

The excitement of the original stories lies in the process by which a mystery is unravelled. But "The Sign Of Four" puts all that aside by revealing the crime prior to Holmes's arrival on the scene.

There's no compensation in any attempt to round out the character of the U.K.'s most notorious fictional detective, or inject psychological credibility into the other characters. Holmes's sidekick Doctor Watson is unutterably stupid, and makes the flesh creep as he embarks on the amorous pursuit of a wronged maiden played by Cherie Lunghi. Some of the performances would embarrass even a college thespian.

It's a shame really since period details are loving recreated and settings such as fairground, riverside and chambers decorated in Indian style provide plenty of scope for atmosphere. —*Japa.*

En flicka paa halsen
(Saddled With A Girl)
(SWEDISH-COLOR)

Cannes, May 8.

A Golden Films/Mats Arehn/Europa Film production, released by Europa Film. Original story, script and directed by Tomas Loefdahl. Camera (Eastmancolor) Lasse Bjoerne, Bertil Rosengren; editor, Lasse Hagstroem; music, Ragnar Grippe; production design, Goesta Engstroem. Reviewed at Cannes Film Festival (Market Section) May 8, 1982. Running time: 90 MINS.
Johan . . . . Bjoern Skifs
Pia . . . . Liv Alsterlund
Gangster boss . . . . Goesta Ekman
His bodyguard . . . . Roland Jansson
The Professor . . . . . . Stig Ossian Ericsson
Marie-Louise . . . . Anki Liden

Tomas Loefdahl's near little farcical comedy, "Saddled With A Girl," is an innocent item of kiddie and family entertainment which is neither moralizing nor very consistent in its handling of comedy techniques, but has vigor and lots of charm in its telling of a rather mad—

The latter has to do with a young chemical researcher who is not only saddled with a lot of homework for a nutty professor, but also with the tiny tot of the title. She is left behind in the old apartment house by her father, who is on the run from a couple of cartoon gangsters. When he cannot pay a debt, they want to catch him to punish him. Later, they try to kidnap the little girl.

Film is murkily lit, but the comedy talents especially of Goesta Ekman and Roland Jansson as the two crooks, shine brightly. Bjoern Skifs, otherwise a much respected young man of music, plays the worried researcher with a nice flair for the befuddled mien. Minor characters are sketched in with quite bold strokes. —*Kell.*

Limpan
(Loafie)
(SWEDISH-COLOR)

Cannes, May 11.

An SF Svensk Filmdustri production and release. Directed by Staffan Roos. Features entire cast. Screenplay, Allan Edwall, based on his own novel; camera (Eastmancolor) Petter Davidsson and Dan Myhrman; production design, Lars Westfelt; costumes, Inger Pehrsson; editor, Thomas Holewa; music Bjoern Isfaelt. Reviewed at the Cannes Film Festival (non-competing), May 11, 1983. Running time: 85 MINS.
Loafie Lindberg . . . . Allan Edwall
Institution manager . . . . . . Boerje Ahlsted
Manager's wife . . . . Anna Godenius
Danish fishmonger . . . . Ove Sprogoe
Asa . . . . Jonna Arb

"Loafie" is a satirical comedy about an inmate in a home for alcoholics who runs away and then cannot get back in because of the staff's stubborn sticking to bureaucratic rules and regulations about when and under what circumstances a patient can be admitted. Allan Edwall, one of Sweden's best actors of stage and screen, plays the lead role in Staffan Roos' slight

feature that is based on Edwall's own novel.

While the original novel has sly humor along with vicious satire and some grotesque shadings of the Kafkaesque, film staggers along limply as a piece of indecisive old-fashioned cinematic realism, a style clashing embarrassingly with the rather unlikely turns of the plot. Edwall's own acting is best when he finally gets to play the relapsed alcoholic, worst when he wears the beatific smile of a reformed sinner. What little spark and bubble "Loafie" has will hardly allow film to travel far beyond Swedish borders. —*Kell.*

Die Flambierte Frau
(A Woman Flambee)
(WEST GERMAN-COLOR)

Cannes, May 12.

A Robert van Ackeren Film Production, Berlin, in coproduction with Dieter Geissler Film Production, Munich; world rights, Weltvertrieb im Filmverlag der Autoren, Munich. Features entire cast. Directed by Robert van Ackeren. Screenplay, van Ackeren, Catharina Zwerenz; camera (color), Juergen Juerges; music, Peer Raben; lighting and sets, Achim Lorenz, Dieter Baer; editing, Tanja Schmidbauer. Reviewed at Cannes Film Fest (Directors' Fortnight), May 11, '83. Running time: 106 MINS.
Cast: Gudrun Landgrebe (Eva), Mathieu Carriere (Chris), Hanns Zischler (Kurt), Gabriele La Fari (Yvonne).

Robert van Ackeren has been a figure on the sidelines of New German Cinema for the past two decades, whose best films, "Harlis" (1972) and "Das andere Laecheln" (Another Smile) (1979), were remarkable for their dry humor and bittersweet irony in an erotic-neurotic atmosphere. His latest, "A Woman Flambee," unspooled at the Directors' Fortnight and is his best film to date.

As the title hints, "the woman in flame" is a prostitute in Berlin who is introduced to her trade under somewhat unusual circumstances. At the outset, she's a married woman who plans to finish her doctorate at the university in due time, but she can't seem to fit into an orderly household for her husband's fashionable friends. So she simply walks out on him during a dinner party at their apartment, and finds herself now without a penny and few prospects for a career — save as a high-priced prostitute for visiting businessmen, tourists, and other clientele in this "German Las Vegas" (as Berlin is sometimes referred to). But first she has to break into the ranks.

A friend arranges for the first customers on a commission basis, pointing out the needs and idiosyncrasies of the rich and pampered male. These scenes set the tone of the film. Shortly, Eva makes the acquaintance of Chris at a party,

and the two become lovers. Chris, being a highly paid male prostitute, suggests that they set up housekeeping together: he services the ladies, she the men, and sometimes vice versa — for Chris has a longstanding male relationship with Kurt, a patron of the arts, so to speak. It's these interrelationships that tickle the funny bone.

Since Chris is getting a bit old for the profession, he can't perform as readily as expected. Meanwhile, Eva has learned something new about herself in the trade: she prefers to play the dominant role in sex, and thus begins to come out of her shell to become a self-assured woman. And so the happy couple fall victim to jealousy on the part of the male prostitute for his female counterpart — indeed, Chris wants to invest their money in a fashionable restaurant, settle down with Eva, and raise a family. Eva rebels, and during a fight one day the "flambee" scene is neatly constructed before the camera: the woman whose trade is passion is set aflame quite literally like a waiter showing his stuff at a deluxe restaurant. The final twist at the end — Eva and Yvonne, her trade-sister, reminiscing on the past and present — marks helmer van Ackeren as an "Autor" to keep an eye on.

Credits are all on the plus side. A witty script, sharp lensing (Juergen Juerges), and fine thesping by Gudrun Landgrebe and Mathieu Carriere made "A Woman Flambee" one of the highlites of the Quinzaine des Realisateurs. —*Holl.*

Horatio I.P.I.
(HONG KONG-BRITISH-COLOR)

Cannes, May 13.

A Kent International Films Ltd. and Capital Enterprises Corporation production. Produced by K.L. Lim & Roy McAree. Stars Lawrence Tan, Laurens Cornelis, Mike Kelly, Rowena Cortes, Jenny Tarren, Michael James, Stella Poon, Michael Lovatt, Kong To. Directed by Lau Shing-Hon. Screenplay, Patrick M. Dunlop. Executive Producer, Leonard L. Bianchi; camera (color) Johnny Koo; music, Anders Nelson; title theme sung by Rowena Cortes. Reviewed at Cannes Festival (Market) May 13, 1983. Running time: 90 MINS.
(English dialogue version)

Horatio is Horatio Lim, a tall, charming Chinese detective with an American accent who's athletically alive and living quite well in Hong Kong. He's portrayed by new find Lawrence Tan, a martial arts specialist and enthusiast born of Chinese parents in Connecticut, U.S. Discovered by a Hong Kong-based movie company, Kent International Film Ltd., this overseas Chinese has an appealing screen charisma that should skyrocket him to better things after the advance showings of his first starring role as Horatio at the Cannes International Film Festival market section.

Tan's magic is that he is not menacing like Oriental superman Bruce Lee nor an oversized muscleman who happens to be funny like Jackie Chan. Tan is more like a confident Mr. Average with a very pleasant personality, a person we'd likely meet. This makes him believable and likeable.

Better than the standard martial arts Hong Kong concoction, the film excels in its high production quality, cinematography and general presentation. It is action packed and frenetic in pace so it should please the action markets around the world. "Horatio I.P.I." may have been·produced cheaply but is definitely not cheap looking and Hong Kong does not look like a bargain basement Asian tourist trap. The glossy photography of the many fascinating unseen and unused Hong Kong sights should more than please the city's tourist association. But the richness of the visuals does not apply to the stereotype characters. In other words, Horatio is a neat surprise but the deficiency in the plot·department is blatant.

The story goes like this: Lawrence Cornelis, a white naval officer and his black buddy Mike Kelly are attacked by Hong Kong thugs upon arrival. They are on shore leave for a good time. Horatio saves them. Later, Kelly disappears and the hero Lawrence join forces to locate the missing friend. In the process, they unravel some big time connections with the local drug traders. Some gangster uglies appear led by an odd character known as Gold Tooth Wang.

Everything else is predictable, yet the movie has several excellent scenes, especially the fight and chase sequence at the Cantonese opera open theatre. Smaller roles have been cast with a desire for performers who can provide talent for character detail. Unfortunately, the only one who shines in this department is professional Hong Kong-resident stage actress Jenny Tarren who tries to give some emotional content to her wronged and bitter wife role. Meanwhile, singer Rowena Cortes as Horatio's younger sister persists in her irritating imitation of a Sandra Dee character without her Troy Donahue. She looks good but a dreadful actress who's even been asked to sing the awful theme song that sounds like an imitation 007 incidental theme for the closing credits.

On the technical side, the music often overpowers the dialogue.

The main selling point here are Lawrence Tan and exotic Hong Kong. He's "simpatico" and the picture looks good.

Director Lau Shing Hon, an American trained local director

first made his name via the arty route ("House of the Lute") and movies. He shows flair in "Horatio" and should be encouraged to do a more polished one as follow-up to this action packed 90-minute entertainment that's been advertised as —"Horatio" — some guys use fists like others use guns. More content and creativity in the scenario should help besides guns and modern kung fu fists in the next Kent-Capital coproduction effort. —Mel.

We Will Rock You
(CANADIAN-COLOR-DOCU)

Cannes, May 14.

A Mobilevision/Yellowbill presentation of a Woodlarks Production. Produced by Saul Swimmer and Jim Beach. Executive producer, Adrian Scrope. Directed by Swimmer. Camera (color) Richard E. Brooks; editor, Robert M. Brady; musical production, Mack; music mix, Power Station. Reviewed Cannes Film Festival (Market) May 13, 1983. Running time: 100 MINS.
Features Freddie Mercury, Roger Taylor, Brian May and John Deacon.

"We Will Rock You" is a "straight" concert film recorded at two shows given by the Queen group at the Montreal Forum, Canada. As such, it should draw large parts of the group's substantial following. There will be extra interest for presentations in the largescale Dynavision format.

But through intelligent direction and editing, the film is also an intriguing record of how a band works together and builds rapport with an audience. There are no gratuitous shots of the audience or offstage gallivantings which are so much part of this genre. Instead, every shot has something to say.

The opening shots capture the event's scale but then the attention is all on the band. Each player receives due attention and the pic's restrained style, combined with the effects from smoke and banks of roving lights, effectively captures the primeval qualities of the rock music.

The film's 21 numbers reflect a range of moods. Included are "Crazy Little Thing Called Love," "We Are The Champions," "Under Pressure" and "Another One Bites The Dust."

What's stupid about the film is that it has one climax over half way through, with passionate calls for 'encore." Then everyone changes costume and starts again, guaranteeing that only the truly converted will stay with it. —Japa.

Caballo Salvaje
(Wild Horse)
(VENEZUELAN-COLOR)

Cannes, May 12.

A Cimarron Producciones S.R.L. production, produced and directed by Joaquin Cortes. Features entire cast. Screenplay,

Cortes; camera (color) Pablo E. Courtalon; Editor Cortes; sound, Simon Fleszler. Reviewed at Cannes Film Festival, (Un Certain Regard). May 10, 1983. Running time: 99 MINS.
Cast: Asdrubal Melendez, Alberto Carrillo, Martha Pavon, Sammy Akinin, Josefina Camarata, Pepe de Negri, Isoris Tovar, Evelio Leal, Irene Le Maitre and Felix Lugo.

The taste of the French in matters of Latin-American cinema is often unfathomable and the selection of "Wild Horse" in an official section (Un Certain Regard) at Cannes is, at best, surprising.

Joaquin Cortes, who produced, directed, wrote and edited the film, has a background in documentaries and does not yet seem at ease in a fiction format. The story is poorly developed and it is also quite clear that Cortes is inexperienced in handling actors or, for that matter, in casting adequately.

The film deals with feudalism in the Venezuelan "llanos" (plains). Alberto, a cowboy who had emigrated to Caracas, returns to the countryside after living for a time in the capital's slums. There is an attempt to establish a parallel between him and a powerful and rebellious horse, while Don Marcos, the landowner, is a feudal prototype. Then there are also the latter's son and his friends from the city, who have even less respect for the peasants.

The social comment implied by events and this set of characters, although theoretically valid, is displayed in a manner that turns it into a caricature of Third World cliches.

Even some scenes of a more documentary nature are unimpressive and the same can be said for the technical credits. —Amig.

Peppermint Frieden
(Peppermint Peace)
(WEST GERMAN-COLOR)

Cannes, May 14.

A Nourfilm Production, Munich; producer, Gerard Samaan; executive producer, Monica Aubele. Features entire cast. Written and directed by Marianne Rosenbaum. Camera (color), Alfred Tichawsky, Thilo Pongratz; sets, Franz Tyroller, Eva Moschler, Sw. Deva Mani; music, Konstantin Wecker. Reviewed at Cannes Film Festival (Market), May 13, '83. Running time: 118 MINS.
Cast: Peter Fonda (Mister Frieden), Saskia Tyroller (Marianne), Gesine Strempel (Marianne's mother), Hans Peter Korff (Marianne's father), Elisabeth Neumann-Viertel (Marianne's grandmother), Cleo Kretschmer (Nilla Gruenapfel), Sigl Zimmerschied (Mr. Aria), Hans Brenner (village priest).

Marianne Rosenbaum's debut film, "Peppermint Peace," toplines Peter Fonda in a portrait of postwar Germany, when Yank soldiers were something like saviours to children of Lower Bavaria with their handfuls of chewing gum and peppermints. But since the entire film is viewed through the eyes of a 6-year-old, Marianne, the

whole comes across as a kind of children's film lensed in an experimental vein.

Pic captures the milieu and has several stylistic traits to recommend it: grey-tinted photography, pop music of the late '40s on the soundtrack, costumes and sets, and a light hand with children. Saskia Tyroller in the lead role also has a dreaming look in her eyes; so when the village priest predicts doom for all those who sin, naturally she imagines all kinds of bad things happening to "Mister Peace," the Yank soldier (Peter Fonda) romancing the village trollop on the side.

Marianne Rosenbaum is a femme filmer to watch on the future, judging from her gift for style. Pic deserves fest slot on the season's circuit. —Holl.

Kassensturz
(Banks and Robbers)
(WEST GERMAN-COLOR)

Cannes, May 14.

A Frankfurter Filmwerkstatt coproduction with Roxy-Film, Munich, Luggi Waldleitner. Features entire cast. Written and directed by Rolf Silber. Camera (color), Marian Czura; sound, Kurt Eggmann; editor, Raimund Barthelmes; sets, Thomas Deutschmann; music, Peter Schmitt; producer, Michael Smeaton; executive producer, Daniel Zuta. Reviewed at Cannes Film Festival (Market), May 13, '83. Running time: 84 MINS.
Cast: Christoph Marius Ohrt (Erich Bauermann), Britta Pohland (Franzi), Kai Fischer, Tilo Prueckner.

Rolf Silber's debut pic, "Banks and Robbers," proposes to be a comedy on a frustrated young bank clerk, who falls for a young thesp in a communal road company. When a bank robbery takes place, the accommodating robber·leaves a pile of bills behind by accident, which the clerk pockets to help out his friends with a loan. Later, he leaves the bank to join the troupe and thus break out on his own. There's also his father, who's an aging Elvis Presley freak, and a line-up of oddball bank·employees, geared to illustrate the idiocy of working for a living.

Pic is a good example of the inanities of German screenplays at present — there's not one of this sort, but several, on the scene today as new generation writer-directors angle for subsidy paydirt. —Holl.

De Lift
(The Elevator)
(DUTCH-COLOR)

Amsterdam, May 3.

Tuschinski release of a Sigma Films Production, produced by Matthijs van Heijningen. Directed by Dick Maas. Features entire cast. Screenplay, Maas; camera (color), Marc Fleperlaan; art direction, Harry Ammerlaan; editor, Hans van Dongen. Stars Huub Stapel, Willeke van Ammelrooy, Josine van Dalsum. Reviewed at Tuschinski Theatre, Amsterdam, May 3, '83. Running time: 95 MINS.
Felix Adelaar . . . . Huub Stapel
Mieke de Beer . . . Willeke van Ammelrooy
Saskia Adelaar . . . . Josine van Dalsum

Humor from charcoal gray to pitch black, fine suspense, murders and thrills, and all of it without gratuitous gore combine for a jaunty entertainment in "De Lift" (The Elevator), director Dick Maas' first theatrical test, which he passes handsomely. Pic has opened across Holland to jumbo biz, with worldwide rights (except for Benelux countries) just obtained by Warner Bros.

Background on young (32) Maas is that up to his feature bow his screen medium was the short, which he often crammed with considerable imagination and, typically, black humor. He also has numerous tv drama credits. In short, he's one to watch.

Hero of "De Lift" is an elevator maintenance man. The anti-hero is the elevator itself — an eccentric, malign, office-building conveyance whose passengers either suffocate, are decapitated by the doors or dumped down the shaft.

With the aid of a femme journalist sniffing for a story, the vexed maintenance man (whose life is complicated by a jealous wife) finally gets to the bottom of the mystery. Before he does, thanks to adroit performances and special effects, there are plenty of laughs and thrills.

Maas has a well-developed sense of irony as well as a knack for the unusual sight gag. Film has echoes of Stanley Kubrick and Brian de Palma, but at bottom it's no imitation but an original Maas.

In its home market pic shapes as one of the biggest smashes ever. Warners should do very well with it in at least some other territories.
—Briel.

L'Indic
(The Informer)
(FRENCH-COLOR)

Paris, May 15.

GEF/CCFC release of a Consortium Financier de Production de Films/Compagnie Francaise Cinematographique/TF 1 by Jean Kerchner production. Produced by Jean Kerchner. Directed by Serge Leroy. Stars Daniel Auteil, Thierry Lhermitte, Pascale Roeard. Screenplay, Didier Decoin; Serge Leroy, Jean Kerchner, based on the novel by Roger Borniche; camera (Eastmancolor), Andre Domage; editor, Francois

Ceppi; sound, Bernard Aubouy; music, Michel Magne; production manager, Gille Schneider. Reviewed at the UGC Biarritz theatre, Paris, May 7, 1983. Running time: 95 MINS.
Bertrand . . . . Daniel Auteuil
Dominique . . . . Thierry Lhermitte
Sylvie . . . . Pascale Rocard
Malaggione . . Bernard Pierre Donnadieu
Legoff . . . . Michel Beaune
Michelesi . . . . Christian Bouillette

Director Serge Leroy quickly followed up his last thriller, "Legitime Violence" with yet another crime drama, "L'Indic." Though based on a novel by Roger Borniche, a former policeman turned novelist, pic is utterly conventional in characterization, plotting and direction, though it moves fast enough to forestall boredom.

Thierry Lhermitte, cast as a hood in "Legitime Violence," is in the new one as well — as another hood. Here he's the righthand man to a brutal underworld kingpin (Bernard-Pierre Donnadieu, who physically resembles Gerard Depardieu and played the real Martin Guerre in Daniel Vigne's "The Return Of Martin Guerre"). But Lhermitte falls in love with an innocent young provincial girl (Pascale Rocard), who is unaware of his gangland affiliations but doesn't much mind when she finds out.

Lhermitte promises her that after one more "affair" he'll pull out. But a hot-shot young detective (Daniel Auteuil), bent on nabbing Donnadieu, coerces Rocard into informing on her lover's associates. The plans go awry: Donnadieu escapes the police dragnet, confronts Lhermitte and shoots him down when latter assumes responsibility for Rocard's treachery. Auteuil subsequently gets his man but loses the girl (on whom he'd developed a crush, naturally).

In short, a routine cops and robbers drama like any other, bearable when its a question of guns, sticky when there are girls around. —Len.

Bill Cosby-'Himself'
(COLOR)

No-frills comedy concert.

A 20th Century-Fox Intl. Classics release of a Jemmin Inc. production. Exec producer, Dr. William H. Cosby Jr. Directed and written by Cosby. Starring Bill Cosby. Camera (color), Joseph M. Wilcotts; editors, Ken Johnson and Steve Livingston; production manager, Mary Waller; assistant director, David Shepherd. Reviewed at Gotham Cinema, N.Y.C., May 22, 1983 (MPAA rating: PG). Running time: 105 MINS.

"Bill Cosby-'Himself'" is a no-frills concert film documenting the likeable comic intensity of Bill Cosby in a milieu he has treaded less frequently in recent years in favor of commercials, tube series and variety shows, and films. Theatrical outlook seems fair to middling.

The 45-year-old comedian displays a winning ease and expertise on the stage (in this case the Hamilton Place in Hamilton, Ontario), but his material harbors no surprises. That will limit the audience to Cosby partisans who can't wait for the pic to reach cable tv, where "Himself" will likely be headed very soon.

The standup comic (who in fact is sitting on a chair for most of the show) begins his routine with drug-oriented humor. That's the last material that will appeal to younger audiences. Subject matter for the rest of the picture is focused on Cosby's manic embellishments of the woes of child-rearing and life in the Cosby clan.

As such, pic may have been better titled "Bill Cosby And His Family." Indeed the film opens with a still photo montage of Cosby offspring with the sometime singer warbling his self-penned "Just The Slew Of Us." Despite Cosby's generally brilliant delivery and timing, the jokes will consistently amuse parents only.

Cosby has somehow incorporated the concept of home movies into a one-man comedy act, and the result is sometimes painfully akin to the boredom and confinement a guest feels when his host screens family flicks.

Culled from four performances Cosby gave in Hamilton, Ont., May 5 and 6, 1981, the film benefits from fine camera work and editing. The subtle changing of colored lights illuminating the screen behind is effective. Crew is predominantly Canadian.

Still, a better Cosby concert film has yet to be made, perhaps one blending updated material from his classic comedy albums along with new material with wider appeal.
—Binn.

The Salamander
(U.S.-BRITISH-ITALIAN-COLOR)

A Lew Grade and William R. Forman presentation of an ITC Films production. (Copyright: Orbi S.A.) Executive producer, Forman. Produced by Paul Maslansky. Directed by Peter Zinner. Features entire cast. Screenplay, Robert Katz, from a novel by Morris West; camera (color), Marcello Gatti; editor, Claudio Cutry; music, Jerry Goldsmith; sound, Tonino Testa; art direction, Giantito Burchiellaro; production manager, Giuseppe Pollini; assistant director, Antonio Brandt; costume design, Fabrizio Caracciolo. Reviewed at Magno Preview 4 screening room, N.Y., May 18, 1983. (No MPAA Rating). Running time: 101 MINS.
Dante Matucci . . . . Franco Nero
Bruno Manzini . . . . : Anthony Quinn
Stefanelli . . . . Martin Balsam
Lili Anders . . . . Sybil Danning
Director Baldassare . . . . Christopher Lee
Major Malinowsky . . . . Cleavon Little
Leporello . . . . Eli Wallach
Elena . . . . Claudia Cardinale
The Surgeon . . . . Paul Smith
Roditi . . . . John Steiner
Girgione . . . . Renzo Palmer
Princess . . . . Anita Strindberg
Also with: Marino Mase, Jacques Herlin, Gita Lee.

Filmed in 1980, "The Salamander" is a dull suspense film about Italian political intrigues, made by Lew Grade and the late Pacific Theatres president William R. Forman for Associated Film Distribution (but not acquired for U.S. distribution by Universal or any other outlet). With an impressive name cast, film has already played overseas, but is backing into its first U.S. date at a Gotham Cinema 5 house (owned by Pacific Theatres) after having already appeared on Home Box Office cable tv.

The handsomely-mounted Paul Maslansky production suffers terminally from storytelling handled verbally rather than enacted through action scenes and dramatics. Robert Katz's adaptation of Morris West's novel is far too chatty and static despite its globe-hopping locations (West's own adaptation of his novel, "The Devil's Advocate," last time out in 1976 for Geria Productions in West Germany also failed to obtain U.S. distribution, however). Debuting director Peter Zinner (an Oscar-winning film editor) directs his high-priced cast as waxworks delivering exposition. It's a far cry from the exciting political thrillers of the late Elio Petri or Francesco Rosi's engrossing "Illustrious Corpses."

Franco Nero toplines as a counter-intelligence officer investigating the death of an Italian army general, uncovering a plot for a fascist coup de'etat planned by another General (Eli Wallach). Salamander of the title (referring to creature's status as a survivor and representing justice) is personified by Anthony Quinn, portraying a wealthy industrialist and W.W. II Partisan who has been tracking down war criminals.

Most of the interesting action takes place off-screen, with Nero the narrator telling us about it or listening to another player's verbal report. What action segments we get are awkwardly-staged and unconvincing bursts of gunplay or automobile zooming.

With the central Quinn character reduced to an extended cameo, Nero has to carry the picture on his back and plays it too heavily, especially considering the wry, cynical dialog he has. His romance with a spy played by lovely but ice-cold Sybil Danning doesn't ignite and is oddly directed at a G-rating level, despite Danning's memorable skin displays in previous films.

Of the supporting cast, only Christopher Lee as Nero's duplicitous superior makes a strong impression by virtue of his regal bearing and imposing dialog delivery. Villain Paul Smith ("Midnight Express") portrays a sadistic torturer as a laughable cartoon character, disrupting the genteel tone of the film.

Tech credits are good, but not supportive of the material, as Marcello Gatti's brightly-lit visuals convert dangerous situations into pleasant travelog scenes. Cornball climax has Quinn and Nero rounding everybody up for a party, locking them in and doing a William Powell summation number.
—Lor.

The Gates Of Hell
(Paura Nella Citta Dei Morti Viventi)
(ITALIAN-COLOR)

A Motion Picture Marketing (MPM) release of a Dania Film-Medusa-National Cinematografia production. Executive producer, Robert Warner. Directed by Lucio Fulci. Features entire cast. Screenplay, Fulci, Dardano Sacchetti; camera (Luciano Vittori color; prints by MGM), Sergio Salvati; editor, Vincenso Tomassi; music, Fabio Frizzi; special effects, Gino de Rossi; assistant director, Roberto Giandalia; stunt coordinator, Nazzareno Cardinali. Reviewed at Rivoli 2 theatre, N.Y., May 20, 1983. (No MPAA Rating; self-applied equivalent X rating). Running time: 93 MINS.
Peter Bell .... Christopher George
Mary .... Katriona MacColl
Sandra .... Janet Agren
Jerry .... Carlo de Mejo
With: Antonella Interlenghi, Venantino Venantini, Robert Sampson.

Filmed in 1980, "The Gates Of Hell" is a supernatural horror film by specialist Lucio Fulci (currently grinding out "Road Warrior" imitations) with enough gore and scares to satisfy the fringe market for shockers. Film is being released stateside with an adults only (17 and over) warning, as was Fulci's previous "Zombi 2" ("Zombie" in U.S.) and current domestic rival "The Evil Dead."

Set (story uncredited) mainly in macabre author H.P. Lovecraft's mythical Massachusetts town of Dunwich, film vaguely resembles John L. Moxey's 1960 classic in the genre "City Of The Dead" (aka "Horror Hotel"). Newspaper reporter Peter Bell (Christopher George) and the premature burial victim whom he saved, Mary (Katriona MacColl) travel from New York to Dunwich to investigate mysterious murders. Wave of terror, fulfilling portents written in the eldritch Book of Enoch, has been set off by the suicide of a local priest, releasing Dunwich's dead from their graves.

Story, which unfortunately bears no resemblance to Lovecraft's tales of ancient evil attacking Earth from other dimensions, and characters are prosaic, with film's real star as usual being its grisly makeup effects. An extremely realistic drill-

through-the-head routine is Fulci's major setpiece, amidst the usual outpouring of butcher shop bright-red animal parts that have been diverting a sizable fringe audience since Herschell Gordon Lewis's "Blood Feast" twenty years ago.

Acting is unimpressive, with Fulci maintaining a brisk pace and effective control of atmosphere and tension. Color is drab in the extreme, with cheaple production values below par for the genre. Film has gone through numerous title changes, including "The Fear," "Fear In The City Of The Living Dead," "City Of The Living Dead" and "Twilight Of The Dead." —Lor.

Sao Daet Deeo
(Teenaged Girl)
(THAI-COLOR)

Bangkok, May 15.

A Kanyaman Film release. Produced by Banchong Kanyaman. Written and directed by Dokdin Kanyaman. Features entire cast. Camera (color), Manat Tohpayat; music, Virat Yuthaworn; sound recording, Cinelab Siam; art director, Anuphap Kanyaman; assistant director, Bandhit Kanyaman. Reviewed at Chalerm Thai, Bangkok, May 15, 1983. Running time: 120 MINS.
Cast: Sorapong Chatri, Suriwan Suriyong, Dokdin Kanyaman, Orasa Issarangkura Na Ayudhya, Metta Rungrath, Sor Asanachinda, Marasri Issangkura Na Ayudhya.

Dokdin Kanyaman's new comedy marks his first effort using Suriwan Suriyong, better known as an action star rather than a comedienne. What he has in mind is to let her combine action skills with her first try at comedy. At the same time, this also allows comedy teammates, Dokdin and Orasa, to join Suriwan in several action-comedy scenes.

It cannot be helped, however, that Suriwan must also play opposite Sorapong Chatri, the lead actor in Dokdin's comedies for several years now, primarily on the strength of the director's rule of using the most popular Thai actor.

Sorapong plays all kinds of roles, but he is an awkward comedian — suave and debonair-looking but also uptight and stiff when he's supposed to make people laugh.

Served once a year, people still flock to see a Dokdin pic, with predictable comic stuff and patented jokes. But then, even his unchanging comic style is still funnier than most other local comedies, and that in itself has always been his main advantage. —Cano.

Reaching Out
(COLOR)

Stillborn indie soul-searching picture.

A PAR Films production and release. Written, produced and directed by Pat

Russell. Features entire cast. Camera (TVC color), David Sperling; editors, Russell, Sperling, Jim McCreading; music, Elizabeth Mazel; assistant director, Ellen Rabinawich; sound, Bob Geraldini, Ed Gray. Reviewed at Embassy 72d St. 1 theatre, N.Y., May 19, 1983. (MPAA Rating: R). Running time: 87 MINS.
Pat Stuart .... Pat Russell
John Stevens .... Tony Craig
Frank Mesina .... Frank McCarthy
Mrs. Stuart .... Betty Andrews
Mr. Stuart .... Douglas Stark

Filmed in 1973, one-woman filmmaker Pat Russell's "Reaching Out" is an earnest but amateurish self-analysis, covering the travails of an Ohio girl trying to find her way and break into the acting profession in the Big Apple.

Russell toplines as a depressed young girl, on her own after her parents' deaths and rebounding from a failed marriage to an egocentric young businessman (Tony Craig). Ultimately she finds encouragement and companionship from an outgoing actor-sculptor (Frank McCarthy).

Crippled by a poor central performance by Russell, whose technique of scrunching up her face and shouting turns key scenes such as crying at Mom's graveside or bawling out her husband for being unfaithful into unintentionally funny, campy outbursts. As a filmmaker, she shows more promise in sidebar vignettes where Greenwich Village types quite naturalistically are observed playing backgammon, panhandling or accosting her. Film's final reel manifesto, delivered by her acting teacher (Marketa Kimbrel) stresses unfettered self-expression in thesping, but film itself is at its best in low-key moments.

Tech credits, including variable direct-sound recording, are below par, with a grainy 35m blowup from 16m featuring saturated, bright colors at odds with the "I'm depressed" intended mood. —Lor.

Effraction
(Break-In)
(FRENCH-COLOR)

Paris, May 10.

Parafrance release of an ATC 3000 production. Produced by Benjamin Simon. Stars Jacques Villeret, Bruno Cremer, Marlene Jobert. Directed by Daniel Duval. Screenplay, Duval and Francis Rcyk, based on the latter's novel; camera, (color), Michel Cénet; music, Maurice Vander; art director, Antoine Roman; editor, Eva Zóra; sound, Georges Vaglio. Previewed at the Paramount City-Triomphe theatre, Paris, May 5, 1983. Running time: 90 MINS.
Val .... Jacques Villeret
Kristine .... Marlene Jobert
Pierre .... Bruno Cremer
Commissioner .... Jean-Pierre Dravel

Daniel Duval, a young filmmaker who once showed promise with a couple of personal feature films, "Le Voyage d'Amelie" (1974) and "L'Ombre des Chateaux" (1976), before finding anonymous mainstream success in 1979 with

"La Derobade," checks in with another dispiriting commercial drama, "Effraction," based on a novel by suspense writer Francis Ryck, who collaborated on the script but later disowned pic as having little to do with what he wrote.

Tale is a banal thriller about a disturbed, sexually-impotent crook who panics during a bank job and guns down both employes and his own accomplices. He makes off with the loot and finally holes up in a Riviera hotel where he takes a couple hostage, and escapes with them into the back country, where police finally gun him down.

Jacques Villeret, the rotund stand-up comic who has made a number of screen appearances, plays the killer: an unusual bit of casting, though not a successful one. Bruno Cremer and Marlene Jobert are the couple, who have met only hours earlier but who are very much involved by the time Villeret bursts into their hotel room to turn their idyll into a nightmare.

Duval directs adequately, and he's certainly more accomplished than the hordes of other commercial directors churning out thrillers these days. But the script is a bummer, and nothing the helmer does can make us forget its utter predictability.

Tech credits are okay. —Len.

Circulez Y'A Rien a Voir
(Move Along, There's Nothing To See)
(FRENCH-COLOR)

Paris, May 17.

AMLF release of a Christian Fechner/-Films A2 production. Produced by Christian Fechner. Stars Michel Banc, Jane Birkin, Jacques Villeret. Directed by Patrice Leconte. Screenplay, Patrice Leconte, Martin Veyron; camera (color), Robert Fraisse; music, Ramon Pipin and Jean-Philippe Goude; sound, Alain Lachassage & Bernard Ortion; art director, Eric Moulard; editor, Joelle Hache; production manager Daniel Riche. Reviewed at the Gaumont Ambassade Theatre, Paris, May 15, 1983. Running time: 90 MINS.
Helene Duvernet .... Jane Birkin
Leroux .... Michel Blanc
Pelissier .... Jacques Villeret
Marc .... Michel Robbe
Martine .... Gaelle Legrand
Reska .... Louis Rego

The title just about sums up this mirthless romantic farce about a runty police investigator (Michel Blanc) who gets a crush on an elegant young widow (Jane Birkin) he meets in the course of a routine investigation. Inventing the slightest professional pretexts he begins to follow her day and night, remaining unaware that Birkin is involved in a traffic of stolen art works. Blanc's dogged pursuit of his unattainable lady leads both through a series of incidents from which they emerge finally a couple, but on the lam from the law.

Director Patrice Leconte was responsible for "Viens Chez Moi,

J.'Habite Chez une Copine," probably the best of the featherweight comedies produced by Parisian cafe-theatre talent, and one has come to expect a certain guarantee of diversion from him and his habitual star, Michel Blanc. But the script for "Circulez ...," co-authored with Martin Veyron, is poor in concept, characterization, development, and gags, and unbelievable even on its own farce terms. Blanc and Birkin try hard to pump some charm into the proceedings, but pic remains dull and humourless. Comic Jacques Villeret is on hand in a thankless foil role as Blanc's associate.

Comedy has been enjoying a brisk success locally. —*Len.*

Undated Wedding
(TAIWAN-COLOR)

Bangkok, May 15.
A Wu Tian Film release. Executive producers, Wu Tian and Tu Yu Lin. Written and directed by Wang Shih-Hsen. Features entire cast. No other credits available. Reviewed at Krung Kasem, Bangkok, May 15, 1983. Running time: 95 MINS.
Cast: Kenny Bee, Sum Ngan, Fong Chien, Li To-Hung, Lu I-Chang.

Kenny Bee and Sum Ngan have become a very popular romantic comedy love team, following the success of "The Girl From The South" last year. Their new pic opens with events immediately preceding a wedding, held in a chapel located in a factory compound. It is an economical, factory-sponsored wedding, and most of the guests are workers, who take their lunch before going to the wedding.

A drunkard accidentally spills bathroom cleanser in the wedding soup, causing most of the wedding party, including the bridegroom, to be indisposed.

Afterward, recurrent wedding cancellations supply the running joke up to the finish. Subsequent failures to start or complete the ceremony are always blamed on Kenny Bee, who plays an easygoing character, who claims that from childhood he has always been unlucky every time he encounters a dog. It so happens that on his wedding day, a poodle urinates on his wedding trousers.

In such a movie, the more things go wrong, the more the audience has fun watching it, and things are expertly manipulated under Wang Shih-Hsen's direction. Bee sticks to his usual style as the naive butt of jokes. Co-star Sum Ngan has much less to do compared to her previous teaming up with Kenny. —*Cano.*

Daijoobu, Mai Furendo
(All Right, My Friend)
(JAPANESE-COLOR)

Tokyo, April 22.
A Toho release of a Kitty Film. Producer, Hidenori Taga. Written and di-
rected by Ryu Murakami and based on his original story. Features entire cast. Camera (color), Kozo Okazaki; assistant to director, Loichi Nakajima; art director, Osamu Yamaguchi; sound, Hideo Nizhizaki; lighting, Kazuo Shimomura; editing, Sachiko Yamaji; music director, Kazuhiko Katoh. Reviewed at Toho screening room, Tokyo, April 15, 1983. Running time: 119 MINS.
Gonzy Traumerai . . . . Peter Fonda
Doctor . . . . Jinpachi Nezu
Mimimi . . . . Reona Hirota
Hachi . . . . Hiroyuki Watanabe
Monika . . . . Yoshiyuki Noo
Reiko . . . . Kumi Aoichi

In "Daijoobu, Mai Furendo," Peter Fonda plays a superstrong man from outer space who falls to earth, where he is chased by evildoers called the Doors, who want to clone him and build a master race. Sheltering him from harm are three Japanese who, even though they speak only Japanese, have no trouble understanding this English-speaking alien. At any rate, Fonda the extra-terrestrial, by film's end, is able to say, "Flown home."

You get the feeling that this film came about when Mickey Rooney and Judy Garland turned to a group of their peers and said, "Hey, kids, let's put on an allegory." The Doors, with their somber suits and ties and short haircuts, are, it seems, meant to represent conservative, male-dominated Japanese society: upon capturing Reona Hirota, they dress her in a kimono and set her to arranging flowers. They apparently lobotomize Hiroyuki Watanabe so that he performs his assigned job with uncomplaining, robotic efficiency.

The main failing of this supposedly trenchant social criticism is that the libertarian alternative to the Doors is symbolized by three unattractive simps with the studiedly "cute" nicknames Mimimi, Monika (who is male) and Hachi. They are played by, respectively, Reona Hirota, Yoshiyuki Noo and Hiroyuki Watanabe. Hirota is reasonably pleasant and has a rather nice figure; Noo isn't and doesn't. Watanabe is on his way to becoming another Victor Mature.

The scenarist and director is Ryu Murakami, a winner of Japan's most prestigious literary prize whose well-known love of films is evidenced by several cinematic references: Jinpachi Nezu's Doctor, with his Mandarin manners and Mao-style grey tunic, is a virtual copy of "Dr. No;" Hirota and Noo, and in a throwaway scene recalling "Blow-Up," play tennis without rackets or balls; and, of course, the film's central premise — alien comes to earth — is composed of parts of "E.T.," "The Man Who Fell to Earth" and "Superman." That Fonda's strength is sapped by ordinary, garden variety tomatoes suggests that Murakami is even
familiar with the cornball SFer, "Attack of the Killer Tomatoes." Good for him. —*Bail.*

Geek Maggot Bingo
(COLOR-16m)

Amateur monster film for undiscriminating midnight shows.

A Weirdo Films production and release. Executive producer, Donna Death. Produced and directed by Nick Zedd. Features entire cast. Screenplay, Zedd, from story idea by Robert Kirkpatrick, Zedd; camera (color, 16m), Zedd; editor, Zedd; sound, Ella Troyano; production design, Zedd; sets, Donna Death, Zedd; special effects, Tyler Smith, Ed French; monster design & creation, illustrations, Smith. Reviewed at St. Marks Cinema, N.Y., April 5, 1983. (No MPAA Rating). Running time: 73 MINS.
Dr. Frankenberry . . . . . . Robert Andrews
Buffy . . . . Brenda Bergman
The Rawhide Kid . . . . Richard Hell
Scumbalina . . . . Donna Death
Host . . . . Zacherle
Geeko . . . . Bruno Zeus
Flavian . . . . Gumby Sangler
Dean Quagmire . . . . Jim Giacama
Street hawker . . . . Robert Martin
Victim . . . . Bob Elkin

"Geek Maggot Bingo" (subtitled: "or the Freak from Suckweasel Mountain") is a poorly-made monster movie spoof shot in Brooklyn last year. Filmmaker Nick Zedd, who has previously made a Super 8m feature and a 16m short, needs to do considerable woodshedding before putting his work before the general public, but on curiosity value this one can play as a minor midnight offering.

Using the Frankenstein and vampire traditions as his starting point, Zedd tries too hard for camp value, with laughs provided by poor reaction shots, tacky sets and silly dialog. Robert Andrews is suitably pompous as Dr. Frankenberry, launching into endless monologs concerning his experiments in "chemosynthetic regeneration." Seeking to reanimate dead tissue, he succeeds in creating a Formaldehyde Man (played by the film's special effects expert Tyler Smith), a two-headed multiple-limbed concoction which works better on screen than the awkward, two-actor "two-headed transplants" of a decade ago.

Parallel plot has a vampiress Scumbalina (Donna Death) biting people with cheapo effects but bat-to-human transformation footage. The monster ends up battling the vampires, with cheap but gory disintegration makeup effects a la Rob Bottin's "The Thing" work.

Supporting cast works in contradictory styles, with Bruno Zeus no threat to the memory of Dwight Frye in his role as hunchback assistant Geeko, who cross-dresses as a femme prostitute to acquire bodies for the monster creation. With a nasal delivery and sleazy, see-through outfits, Brenda Bergman aims for grotesque humor without
much success. Singer Richard Hell (of the Voidoids) has a nothing role as a cowboy.

Poor sound and lighting, library music and crude hand-drawn backgrounds (as a dumb gag, even the telephones are two-dimensional cardboard here) exemplify this low-budget effort. Tv monster movie host Zacherle hosts the film, demonstrating an unimpressive tie-in gimmick, a giveaway Drool Cup imprinted with the film's logo. Zedd's in-joke approach reaches rock-bottom with the screen appearance of the editor of Fangoria magazine, credited with doing an impression of the editor of the Sleazoid Express newsletter. Strictly infra dig. —*Lor.*

Blues Country
(COLOR/B&W-DOCU-16m)

Seattle, May 7.
Written and produced by Joe Vihikow. Associate producer, Julie Sakahara; sound, Glenn (Chip) Hughes; narrated by Taj Mahal. No other credits provided. Reviewed in Seattle, May 7, 1983. Running time: 84 MINS.

This tribute to old time blues singers, banjo and guitar players includes film clips recorded in the 1960s and 1970s by the Seattle Folklore Society, and from other performers filmed and recorded by Joe Vinikow, Julie Sakahara and Glenn Hughes in a quick trip through the southeast. Among the around 25 artists featured are such legendary picker-singers as Sonny Terry, Furry Lewis, Johnny Shines, Lightnin' Hopkins, John Cephas, Elizabeth Cotten and Leadbelly, among others. Mamie Smith is represented in a 1939 film short, singing "Harlem Blues."

Vinikow, who got an Academy Award nomination in 1977 for a short, "Banjo Man," featuring Uncle Homer Walker, made while a student at Yale, discovered a treasure trove of short films, nearly 20-hours all told, in vaults of KCTS-TV and in the U. of Washington's Ethnomusicology archives. He got a $20,000 grant from the National Endowment for the Humanities, years with hopes that showings of the doc might help the performers still alive and working, and, in addition, get on record these performers who today are nearly forgotten.

Vinikow, a guitarist himself, appears to be too much enamored of closeups of fingering and picking by the performers featured, but even so, the down-to-earth, vibrant melancholy of the songs comes through vigorously.

The docu is in three distinct sections, each 28 minutes, so any can be used separately for a 30-minute program on tv, or as a theatrical short. First part is "Roots," tracing the beginnings of the blues to black African roots, with stills of slave ships and other elements of slavery; part two is "Recording" (the best of the three) featuring the heyday of recordings of black artists in the period between the two World Wars, and the third is "Revival," tracing some memorable figures of the blues revival in the 1940s.

Film quality is uneven, naturally, but doesn't detract; narration by Taj Mahal is a plus, but what is remembered is the many talented oldsters singing (from the heart) the real, lowdown blues.

First showing of the docu was the week of May 5-8 in the Broadway Performance Hall. —Reed.

Cannes Non-Competing

Another Time, Another Place
(BRITISH-COLOR)

Cannes, May 17.
Umbrella Films Production for Redifusion Films, Channel Four Television and the Scottish Arts Council. Produced by Simon Perry. Directed by Michael Redford. Features entire cast. Screenplay, Radford, based on the novel by Jessie Kesson; executive producer, Timothy Burrill; camera (color), Roger Deakins; editor, Tom Priestley; music, John McLeod; art direction, Hayden Pearce. Reviewed at the Palais Croisette, May 16, 1983. Running time: 101 MINS.

Janie	Phyllis Logan
Luigi	Giovanni Mauriello
Umberto	Gian Luca Favilla
Paolo	Claudio Rosini
Dougal	Paul Young
Beel	Gregor Fisher
Finlay	Tom Watson
Kirsty	Jennifer Piercey
Meg	Denise Coffey
Jess	Yvonne Gilan

It's not often that a British film is realized with as much creative integrity as "Another Time, Another Place." The pic's slow pace will limit its general appeal, but lyrical tone and emotional content guarantee a healthy art house career.

The plot springs from the cultural difference between the inhabitants of a bleak Scottish agricultural village and a trio of Italians confined to the community during WWII One Italian in particular, the passionate Neopolitan Luigi (Giovanni Mauriello); mesmerizes Janie (Phyllis Logan) by seeming to offer an alternative to an emotionally cold marriage and a laborious penny-pinching life. The rest of the Scottish community remain suspicious of the strangers in their midst.

The developing relationship is narrated with a light and humorous touch, even though both parties are drawn to each other out of desperation. Absence of subtitles for Italian speech is an effective device to convey the girl's growing fascination.

Central to the film's effectiveness is the performance of Phyllis

Logan as the girl entranced. Eyes and gestures capture the initial longing followed by the remorse that follows surrender. Giovanni Mauriello as the Neapolitan has the necessary charisma.

The film's impact derives also from representations of daily life and a landscape that changes with the seasons. It is the misery of a northern autumn and winter that most fosters in the Italians a deeper sense of exile.

Pic was shot in super 16m but 35m blowup looks great thanks to photography and camera work by Roger Deakins, who also has an eye for the telling composition. Emotional impact is largely a credit to editing by Tom Priestley who previously did John Boorman-helmed movies "Deliverance," "The Heretic" and "Excalibur." Only downer on the creative side is a score that remains monotonous despite diverse orchestrations of the central theme. —Japa.

Can She Bake A Cherry Pie
(U.S.-COLOR)

Cannes, May 12.
An International Rainbow Pictures Presentation of a Jagfilm Production. Produced by M.H. Simonson. Features entire cast. Written and directed by Henry Jaglom. Camera (color), Bob Fiore; music, Karen Black. Reviewed at the Andre Bazin Auditorium. (Un Certain Rigard). Canes, May 12, 1983. Running time: 90 MINS.
Cast: Karen Black, Michael Emil, Michael Margotta, Frances Fisher, Martin Frydberg.

Henry Jaglom follows his Cannes hit of two years ago, "Sitting Ducks," with a similar opus. This is once again a talky comedy, in which the scripter-director puts his characters in a number of sitcom situations, feeds them the opening lines of their scenes and lets them embroider the rest on their own, cutting off superfluities in the editing.

The result is the kind of fare that may not be to everyone's taste, but has some felicitous moments that are not to be ignored. Starting from the basic premise that human beings suffer from their inability to communicate with their fellow men, and will go to any length to establish valid relationships, Jaglom builds up a romance of sorts between a fresh divorcee who is still not emotionally rid of her husband, and a man who has been living on his own for some years, therefore is better settled in his ways of bachelorhood.

Moving his actors from one location to another, from a streetside cafe to an apartment, then to another apartment, to an office, and so on, and letting the actors improvise their dialog much of the time, he gets a feeling of authenticity that

is sometimes uncanny, for instance when Karen Black tries to make up her mind what to order in a restaurant, but, as it will often happen when this method is used, scenes tend to drag on longer than necessary, points often take too long to be made and the audience is required to accept the deliberate hesitancy of the plot as part of the general picture.

Characters are built very much around the personality of the two main actors, Black giving a beautiful performance, humorous, edgy, nervous and implying deep fears and pains hidden barely under the surface, and Michael Emil (incidentally the director's brother and who had much to do on the production side as well) brings back many of the peculiarities of his part in "Sitting Ducks," such as his galloping hypochondria, his original theories on sex and his total self-centered interest, doing this with all the commitment of someone playing himself. His attempt to measure his pulse while having intercourse, in order to assess the extent of his sexual excitement, is just one of his part's many quirks.

Very much a New York film, with the feeling of the city, and the special breed of intellectuals living on its fringes, the film also uses some nice poetic touches, such as Michael Margotta's trained pigeon, which always returns to its master, an allegory to what some humans would like their relationship to be.

Probably less compact than "Sitting Ducks," which had a frame narrative to keep all its components together, this will basically appeal to the same sort of audience, and may do quite well in specialized positions. —Edna.

Rodnia
(Family Relations)
(SOVIET-COLOR)

Cannes, May 14.
A Mosfilm Production, Moscow; world rights, Goskino, Moscow. Features entire cast. Directed by Nikita Mikhalkov. Screenplay, Victor Merezhko; camera (color), Pavel Lebenshev; music, Eduard Artemiev, sets, Alexander Adabachian, Alexander Samuelekin. Reviewed at Cannes Film Fest (Market), May 14, '83. Running time: 90 MINS.
Cast: Nonna Mordyukova (Maria Konovalova), Svetlana Kryuchkova, Andrei Petrov, Ivan Bortnikov, Yuri Bogatyrev.

Nikita Mikhalkov has become one of the hottest directors on the Moscow film scene, besides being a popular actor in heavy demand by the major Soviet studios. His "Slave of Love" (1976) had a good run in Yank arthouses, and this success was followed by a string of "discoveries" in the Cannes mart: "Unfinished Piece for a Player Piano" (1977), "Five Evenings" (1978), and

"A Few Days in the Life of I.I. Oblomov" (1979).

Mikalkov's "Family Relations" (or "Kin") was tipped at fest as one of Cannes topper Gilles Jacob's preferential Soviet choices. It received, instead, a slot in the mart, and is thus available for other international fests on the season's circuit.

Pic stars Nonna Mordyukova, a vet thesp of 30 years on Soviet screens, and this film appearance might score as a tip-of-the-hat to an acting tradition. In any case, this is minor Mikhalkov—a comedy on Moscow mores based on an original screenplay with none of his usual directorial subtleties.

Maria Konovalova (played by Mordyakova), is a busybody. She lives in a provincial village not far from the Big City, and has raised a family by herself after divorcing her husband. But after a daughter grew up and married and provided her with a granddaughter, her closest kin moved away to the city and left her behind, lonely and frustrated. So off she goes to find out why life in the provinces is not good enough for the family relations, including her ex-husband.

From the moment she arrives on the scene, Maria Konovalova takes issue with everything. She pokes her nose in her daughter and son-in-law's affairs, scolds her granddaughter for being too modern and impolite, and talks back to neighbors and people-on-the-street. She even meddles in her ex-husband's affairs. It's quite clear, that her closest relatives have fled from the grasp of this mother spider. In the end, however, she senses the errors of her way, and tearfully takes leave of her kin — until a happy reunion at the railway station promises a reconciled future.

Not much to get excited about, even as an arthouse prospect, "Family Relations" has some witty original moments — the restaurant scene, for instance, when Nikita the actor does a cameo for Mikhalkov the director as an eccentric waiter. —Holl.

Job Lazadasa
(Revolt Of Job)
(HUNGARIAN-W. GERMAN-COLOR)

Cannes, May 18.
A Mafilm production release by Libra Films. Directed by Imre Gyongyossy, Barna Kabay. Features entire cast. Screenplay, Gyongyossy, Kabay, Katalin Petenyi; camera (Eastmancolor), Gabor Szabo; editor, Katalin Petenyi; music, Zoltan Jeny. Reviewed at Cannes (Market), May 18, 1983. Running Time: 97 MINS.

Job	Ferenc Zenthe
Roza	Hedi Temessy
Lacko	Gabor Feher
Jari	Peter Rudolf
Ilka	Leticia Caro

"The Revolt Of Job" is an outstanding, human account of a Holo-

'caust story set in Hungary in 1943. Expertly and originally told, the film should have few problems finding an arty audience in North America and Europe.

Story concerns an elderly Jewish couple — Job and Roza — who adopt a non-Jewish child in an effort to pass on their wealth and knowledge to him before Nazi oppression consumes Hungary. Job selects the unruly Lacko and authorities agree to backdate papers to facilitate the couple.

The warm tale incorporates both humor and social observation seamlessly into the plot. However, its main thrust is the taming of the wild child through understanding and patience by the couple he grows to regard as his parents.

The persecution of Jews in Hungary occurred late in the war, though rapidly. It hangs over the proceedings like a grey cloud with stray incidents suggesting the creeping horror. A Passover meal that is both joyful and sad eloquently conveys how little time the couple has to enjoy freedom.

The rapport between Ferenc Zenthe as Job and the young Gabor Feher makes the film a truly emotionally consuming experience. Job's dignity in the face of an impossible situation and his canniness are beautifully illustrated. The ultimate persecution is dramatically powerful material.

A handsomely-crafted production, "The Revolt Of Job" was coproduced by Hungarian and Western German TV. It's a highly accessible story on an emotional level. American release version will have a brief forword to clarify the story's historical context.

Picture should register well in specialty houses and in large urban centers. Its strong emphasis on humanity elevate the tale above the specific context of the Holocaust and its facility to show character and demonstrate humor are highly laudable. —*Klad.*

La Bete Lumineuse
(Shimmering Beast)
(CANADIAN-COLOR-DOCU)

Cannes, May 9.

A National Film Board of Canada production and release. Produced by Jacques Bobet. Directed by Pierre Perrault. Features entire cast. Research by Yvan Dubuc. Camera (color). Martin Leclerc; editor, Suzanne Allard; sound, Yves Gendron. Reviewed at Cannes (Certain Regard), May 9, 1983. Running time: 128 MINS.

With: Louis-Philippe Lecuyer, Philippe Cross, Stephane-Albert Boulais, Maurice Chaillot, Bernard L'Heureux, Michel Guyot, Barney Descontie, Maurice Aumont, Claude Lauriault, Laurier Prevost.

Filmmaker Pierre Perrault has specialized in ethnographic studies for more than two decades. His latest, "La Bete Lumineuse," examines at great length the popular mania for urban dwellers to fly into remote Northern regions of Quebec and hunt for moose. The film's title is a Quebec idiom for the beast.

In minute detail Perrault follows a group of hunters from home to a lodge near Maniwaki, Quebec. It's evident in this case that most of the men participate primarily to escape family pressures. Tracking the animal is less important than drinking, pranks and demoralizing games.

The picture is much too long to sustain audience interest. Perrault repeatedly covers the same ground in the course of the film's two hours. And his participants often appear to be playing for the camera rather than dropping inhibitions.

The same material was covered in dramatic form a decade ago in Francis Mankiewicz' "Le Temps d'une Chasse," and little would appear to have changed. Major difference is Perrault's hunters fail even to sight their objective but the irony is hollow in context.

Theatrical prospects are as remote as the picture's title character and even television potential is limited by the film's current form. Perhaps edited into an hour program for tv the film could make its points more precise and concise. —*Klard.*

Faits Divers
(News Items)
(FRENCH-COLOR-DOCU)

Paris, May 17.

Pari Films release of an Antenne 2/-Unite de Programmes Pascale Breugnot/Copyright Films. Produced by Pascale Dauman, Raymond Depardon. Directed and photographed (color) by Raymond Depardon. Editor. Francoise Prenant. Reviewed at the Cannes Film Festival ("Un Certain Regard" section), May 9, 1983. Running time: 108 MINS.

With: the staff of the police commissariat of the 5th arrondissement, Paris.

Raymond Depardon, who wears two hats as a leading photo journalist (he is cofounder of the Gamma photo news agency) and a documentary filmmaker, took his camera into a police station in the fifth arrondissement in Paris and came out with this extraordinary feature-length docu, "Fait Divers."

As the title indicates, Depardon was only interested in the more routine assignments of the 60-man commissariat, the kind of incidents that at best get a paragraph or two in local papers. Working alone, skillfully lensing and sound recording with compact material, Depardon managed, in the space of three months, to become a near imperceptible, objective cog in the operations of the station, winning the confidence of the policemen and thus getting maximum impact from the events he witnessed.

Depardon records a variety of incidents: the investigation of a rape charge, attempts to revive a suicide, the transportation of an hysterically senile old woman to the hospital, the pickup of a badly-hurt drug addict, an inquiry into a strange couple living by candlelight in the windowless storage room of an apartment building, etc.

Depardon combines the best qualities of photographer, filmmaker and humane observer to capture all that is essential in a scene without giving the impression of voyeurism or facile sensationalism (though at certain moments the viewer inevitably feels special discomfort with what he is seeing). Most important the filmmaker offers us an unconventional portrait of police officers at work that goes far in deflating some widespread cliches.

Often deeply moving, and at times unexpectedly hilarious, "Faits Divers" confirms Depardon as a top-ranking docu artist of skill and sensibility. Pic may not be as popular here as his hugely successful "Reporters" a couple of years ago, but it should have a larger outlook on the international scene, with fest and art house playoffs likely. —*Len.*

Cross Country
(CANADIAN-COLOR)

Cannes, May 19.

A New World Pictures (MGM-UA in U.S.) release of a Filmline/Ronald Cohen production in association with Yellowbill Productions. Produced by Pieter Kroonenburg, David J. Patterson. Executive producers, Ronald Cohen, Jim Beach. Directed by Paul Lynch. Features entire cast. Screenplay, John Hunter, William Gray, based on novel by Herbert Kastle; camera (color), Rene Verzier; editor, Nick Rotundo; art direction, Michel Proulx; music, Chris Rea; sound, Patrick Rousseau. Reviewed at the Olympia, Cannes (market), May 9, 1983. Running time: 100 MINS.

Evan Bley .... Richard Beymer
Lois Hayes .... Nina Axelrod
Ed Roersch .... Michael Ironside
John Forrest .... Brent Carver
Harry Burns .... Michael Kane
Glen Cosgrove ...... August Schellenberg
Nick Overland .... Paul Bradley
Elma Jean .... Roberta Weiss
Lt. Roberts .... George Sperdakos

"Cross Country" is a convoluted thriller dotted with grisly violence and graphic sex. The ingredients are hardly the recipe for success in this Canadian-made film. The picture, though sporting classy production values, is squarely aimed at an audience used to crude exploitation fare.

Action revolves around the brutal murder of a call girl with initial suspicion falling on Evan Bley (Richard Beymer), a tv advertising director involved with the woman. Bley, however, is on vacation and the evidence against him is too slim for an arrest.

Story twists and turns from Bley's cross-country car trip to the investigating detective (Michael Ironside), convinced of his guilt. Bley has acquired two passengers — a model and her guitar-playing male friend — and promptly establishes a reign of psychological terror in the automobile for unknown reasons.

Major problem of the film rests with the monotonous cross-cutting which oddly diminishes the tension of the tale. Ideally, the two narrative lines should be converging and the anticipation heightening from incident to incident.

However, the script provides direction for neither stream resulting in an aimlessness to the proceedings. The character of Bley particularly lacks clear rationale. His paranoid tendencies are not properly established.

Faring slightly better is the character of the detective who is withholding evidence for private reasons. It provides the film's most fascinating twist but is introduced far too late in the plot. Conversely, the tip-off to the real murderer's identity comes too soon and the structure of circumstances pushing and pulling the thriller collapses on its own lack of cleverness.

Actor Richard Beymer, rarely seen on screen in the past 20 years (his last appearance was in "Innerview" in 1974 which he also directed), is much too mannered and obvious as the thriller's prime suspect. His performance throws off the work of both Nina Axelrod and Brent Carver playing virtual prisoners.

Far more interesting is Ironside as the detective with questionable ethics. Ironside, usually cast as a heavy, proves equally adept at playing an offbeat sympatic role.

Print viewed credits John Hunter with co-scripting the film while ads list Logan N. Danforth, the writer's nom de plume. Erratic quality suggests Hunter and credited William Gray were responsible for separate aspects of narrative rather than collaborators.

Sturdy Canadian cameraman Rene Verzier has done outstandingly slick work in the picture which is somewhat muted by sloppy editing. Story really requires nuance but director Paul Lynch can't seem to resist going for shock value.

"Cross Country" should have no difficulty playing as an exploitationer and would benefit from saturation bookings. Audience would appear to be limited to a hardcore group and is unlikely to build on a word-of-mouth campaign. —*Klad.*

Kiez
(Hell's Kitchen)
(WEST GERMAN-COLOR)

Cannes, May 9.

An Entenproduktion, Rolf Buehrmann, producer; world rights. Transocean International. Features entire cast. Directed by Walter Bockmayer and Rolf Buehrmann. Screenplay, Hans Eppendorfer; camera (color), Thomas Mauch; editor, Alexander Rupp; sets, Thomas Schappert; music, Gunther Erfurt; costumes, Tabea Blumenschein; production manager, Felix Hock. Reviewed at Cannes Film Festival (Market), May 9, '83. Running time: 105 MINS.

Cast: Wolf-Dietrich Sprenger (Knut), Katja Rupe (Heinke), Brigitte Janner (Ditte), Rainer Philippi (Nil), Kral-Heinz von Hassel.

Walter Bockmayer and Rolf Buehrmann's previous lowbudget comedies on Super-8 and 16m — "Pretzels I & II" (1975), "Jane Is Jane Forever" (1976); and "Flaming Hearts" (1977) — made the directors' names as offbeat commentators on the pop cult in Germany. Then they shifted into high gear and attempted straight melodrama in "Looping" (1980) and now "Hell's Kitchen" (the German title "Kiez" means "turf" in the sense of a tightly knit urban neighborhood), both disappointments — although "Kiez" did find its way to the competition at Manila.

"Hell's Kitchen" (also a stage production by Bockmayer/-Buehrmann in Cologne, invited to the 1982 Berlin Theatre Festival) deals with the waterfront underworld in Hamburg, and follows the moves of an ex-seaman pimp, his goodhearted whore, and a smalltime crook through the joints on St. Pauli's Reeperbahn. Outside of bundles of flesh and rather helpless orgies for the sake of sin-and-sex, dope-and-grog, "Hell's Kitchen" is mostly crude pulp-magazine fare. —Holl.

Das Luftschiff
(The Airship)
(EAST GERMAN-COLOR)

Cannes,, May 15.

A DEFA Film Production, Johannisthal Film Group, East Berlin; world rights, DEFA Aussenhandel, East Berlin. Features entire cast. Directed by Rainer Simon. Screenplay, Fritz Rudolf Fries, Simon, based on Fries's novel with same title; camera (color), Roland Dressel; sets, Hans Poppe; music, Friedrich Goldmann; production manager, Horst Hartwig. Reviewed at Cannes Film Fest (Market), May 15, '83. Running time: 105 MINS.

Cast: Joerg Gundzuhn (Stannebein), Elisa Montes (Dona Mathilde), Gudrun Ritter (Polonia), Katrin Knappe (Flora), Victor Garvajal (Sorigueta), Hermann Beyer (Kiessling), Johanna Schall (Johanna), Daniel Roth (Chico).

Rainer Simon, best known for his kidpics, seems out of his genre in this complex tale of an aeronautic engineer whose wild plans to construct an airship that's a cross between a Zeppelin and a helicopter go awry.

Based on a true story, Franz Xaver Stannebein was obsessed in his youth at the turn-of-the-century by the desire to fly. He plays Leonardo and Icarus by jumping off a hill with homemade wings, and nearly kills himself. He doesn't give up his dream during his orphanage years, and is supported by a kindly prostitute to go on with his engineering plans.

Later, as a successful merchant in Spain, he invests all his savings in pipedreams to construct his own patented airship for buyers in Latin America; the gamble busts him. Then the German government under the newly-elected Nazis hire him to build an airfield in Spain, which is used in time by the Condor Legion in the Spanish Civil War.

Stannebein returns to Germany to protest — and lands in a madhouse for the rest of his days. His grandson, in postwar 1945, searches into his papers for an answer to the man's enigma.

Pretty dull film storywise, "The Airship" catches a bit of the turn-of-the-century atmosphere to recommend it for DEFA Film Weeks.
—Holl.

Hysterical
(U.S.-COLOR)

Cannes, May 8.

An Embassy Pictures release of a Cinema Works presentation of a H&W presentation. Produced by Gene Levy. Executive producer, William Immerman. Directed by Chris Bearde. Features entire cast. Screenplay, William, Mark and Brett Hudson, Trace Johnston; camera (DeLuxe color), Donald Morgan; editor, Stanley Frazen. Reviewed at the Olympia, Cannes (market), May 8, 1983 (MPAA Rating: PG). Running Time: 87 MINS.
Frederick Lansing ...... William Hudson
Paul Batten .... Mark Hudson
Fritz .... Brett Hudson
Kate .... Cindy Pickett
Capt. James Howdy .... Richard Kiel
Venetia .... Julie Newmar
Dr. John .... Bud Cort
Ralph .... Robert Donner
The Mayor .... Murray Hamilton
The Sheriff .... Clint Walker
Leroy .... Franklin Ajaye
Count Dracula .... Charlie Callas
Old Fisherman .... Keenan Wynn
TV Announcer .... Gary Owens

"Hysterical" is rock-bottom comedy which desparately clutches at straws to turn The Hudson Brothers into the '80s Marx Brothers. The former television headliners pale in comparison to the Marx, Ritz or even the Smith Brothers. Commercial outlook is slim.

Essentially a horror spoof culling from such offerings as "The Amityville Horror," "The Exorcist" and "Night Of The Living Dead," the picture is hysterically childish rather than funny. William Hudson plays a pulp novelist who buys a haunted Oregon lighthouse in fictional Hellview. He adopts a new identity and begins to write a serious novel.

His pursuit is interrupted by the spirit of the lighthouse lamp, a vengeful spurned mistress of a former sea captain. She recalls her former lover who kills the townsfolk who promptly become zombies

saying, "what difference does it make?"

Brothers Mark and Brett are adventurers specializing in occult phenomena. Gag is they're closet cowards. It's a very thin premise to maintain a feature comedy.

Director Chris Bearde, who also engineered the Hudsons' tv show, directs as if it were an extended comedy-variety show. The humor is vignettish and relies on tired situations and characters, displaying a paucity of imagination.

Jeffrey Ganz is credited as film's "comedy consultant" but obviously the filmmakers required divine intervention. The frantic style produces an extremely amateurish effort with scant marketability. —Klad.

Bolero
(WEST GERMAN-COLOR)

Cannes, May 15.

A Monika Nuechtern Filmproduktion, in coproduction with Artus Film, Trio Film, Jurg Marquard, and Radio Bremen. Features entire case. Directed by Ruediger Nuechtern. Screenplay, Monika and Ruediger Nuechtern; camera, (color) Jacques Steyn; sound, Stani Litero; editor, Helga Beyer; music, Joerg Evers. Reviewed at Cannes Film Festival (Market), May 10, '83. Running time: 103 MINS.

Cast: Katja Rupe (Lena), Michael Koenig (Pete), Maxi Nuechtern (Benny), Daniel Nagel, Kurt Raab, Hans Brenner, Paul Hubschmid.

Ruediger Nuechtern, a grad of the Munich Film Academy, has proven to be a competent craftsman in the director's seat, but the thematic content of all his features leave much to be desired. His last outing, "Night of the Wolves" (1982), was a cornball transplant of "West Side Story" gang warfare to the ice-cream parlors of Munich. And now he's tackled the hip world of art shows and pop records in "Bolero."

This is the heart-crunching story of Pete, who has left his rock group to go it alone as a solo songwriter, and his wife Lena, who believes in the future of her art gallery as much as her marriage ensconced in chic decorative displays — if the cliches in the script are to be taken seriously. And, natch, there's the preschool son Benny to add a bit more sugar to the story. Pete's self-pity and Lena's gallery-come-true chatter go on and on without relief, until one wonders why two gifted thesps just didn't chuck the chestnuts in the script and make at least an improvised effort to save their own careers. "Bolero" is the best evidence of the season for the absolute need of a dialog & script specialist on future German tv subsidized film productions. —Holl.

(Title is not to be confused with upcoming Cannon film release by same name to star Bo Derek. — Ed.)

Mission Thunderbolt
(HONG KONG-COLOR)

Cannes, May 15.

An IFD Films and Arts Limited Production. Executive producers, Joseph Lai, Betty Chan. Directed and written by Godfrey Ho. Stars Jonathan Stierwald, Chan Wai-Man, Steve Daw, Chan Kun Tai, Tina Matchett, Summer Dora, Phillip Ko, John Ladalski, Melisa Taylor, Phoenix Chu, Shih Chung Tin, Johnny Shen. Camera (color), Tony Fan; martial arts director, Allan Wong; music, Johnny Tsang. Reviewed at New Palais Theatre, Cannes Film Festival (Market Section), May 12, 1983; Running time: 96 MINS.
(Available in English and Chinese version with English subtitles)

There must be a market for this type of Hong Kong-made chop suey kung-fu or there wouldn't be so many made, especially during these hard times. IFD Films, producer and distributor of domestic and foreign-made celluloid oddities, has made this action drama that should serve the grind houses 'round the world.

The film begins with a series of murders in London, New York and Sydney. One practically expects a travelog to follow but three vicious professional white assassins enter the picture headed by a man called White Tycoon. The killers dispose of their unsuspecting victims in the most ingenious Chinese-inspired torture method imaginable which includes lethal finger claws meant for the skull. The motive of the White Tycoon is to create confusion, conflict and complete dissent between the two prominent rival gangs, the Scorpions and the Serpents, so that he can take over their profitable gangster business.

The situation brings about ample opportunities to present chase sequences and countless fights to the death. This is what the film is all about. It is the best photographed film made by IFD but producer Joseph Lai definitely needs a professional screenwriter and dialog instructor if he wishes to upgrade his future Thunderbolt flicks. Classy and better-looking actresses are also required to back-up the action stars who need not look extra-special. One cannot really be extra critical about "Mission Thunderbolt" as it knows exactly the specific audience which enjoys mass murder capers in Hong Kong low-life style. —Mel.

Grenzenlos
(Open Ends)
(WEST GERMAN-COLOR)

Cannes, May 17.

A Ruebezahl-Film, Josef Roedl Film, and Project im Filmverlag der Autoren, Munich; world rights, Weltvertrieb im Filmverlag der Autoren, Munich. Features entire cast. Written and directed by Josef Roedl. Camera (color), Frank Bruehne; music, Peer Raben; editing and sound, Fritz Baumann; sets, Winfried Henning; executive producer, Peter Voiss. Reviewed at Cannes Film Fest (Directors'

Fortnight), May 14, '83. Running time: 109 MINS.

Cast: Therese Affolter (Agnes), Sieg-fried Zimmerschied (Adi), Antonia Roedl (Mother); Richard Witll (Neighbor), Ur-sula Staetz (Rosa), Georg Berner (Young Boy), Andrea Wolf (Hanna), Franz Kuch-ler (Old Pastor), Josef Schiessl (Mayor), Herbert Jung (Franz), Richard Kattan (Max), Georg Schlessl (Politician), Jo-hanna Karl-Lory (Mourner).

Josef Roedl scored an immed-iate critical hit with his diploma film at the Munich Film Academy, "Albert — Why?" (1978), a tale of a country dolt who is plagued by neighbors and alcohol until he com-mits suicide. Now he's at Cannes in the Directors' Fortnight with his second film, "Open Ends," a simi-lar story of a confined individual who can't quite cope with her ex-istence due to being raped as a young girl, during which the of-fender died. Both films are semi-documentary in style and subject, for some are real people from Roedl's own Bavarian village and its surroundings.

Agnes and Adi are farmers in a small community; and since they are neighbors, their families hope that they will marry, and thus join the two farms. Adi loves Agnes, but the feeling as yet is not mutual. Further, the people in the com-munity, including the village priest, tend to look upon Agnes as a bad-luck omen — perhaps even posses-sed by the devil.

Events take a turn for the worst when the barn on Agnes's farm burns down, and a young mute boy with a crush on the girl dies in the fire by accident. The dead boy's mother swears revenge. Agnes de-cides one day to leave the com-munity and journeys to a larger town to visit a girlfriend — there she discovers that her friend works in a nite-bar-cum-bordello, instead of as the salesgirl she claimed to be. Agnes is tempted to spend the night with one of the town lotharios, but backs out at the last minute when Adi happens upon the scene. They return home, and spend the night together — perhaps now she is washed clean of her nightmarish fantasies, although the ending too is "open-ended."

A slow-moving film featuring ac-tors and nonactors, "Open Ends" is too stylistic to score as potentially commercial. Roedl, quite clearly, is a bona fide member of the Bavar-ian school of storytelling — in the vein of some of Rainer Werner Fassbinder films and Franz Xaver Kroetz's plays. Indeed, the "Autor" references to RWF (Fassbinder's "Fear Eats the Soul" is unspooling in the village cinema) extend even to Peer Raben's music, one ele-ment that works to the film's detri-ment. On the plus side are Frank Bruehne's lensing and his quiet handling of actors moving at times almost in slow-motion.

Look for "Open Ends" at other fests on the season's circuit, or Ger-man Film Weeks. Roedl is de-veloping gradually into a talented helmer of offbeat rural chronicles.
—Holl.

Danni
(WEST GERMAN-COLOR)

Cannes, May 15.

An Astral Film Production, Munich; produced by Wolfgang Odenthal; world rights, Weltvertrieb im Filmverlag der Autoren, Munich. Features entire cast. Written and directed by Martin Gies. Camera (color), Axel Block; sound, Peter Kaiser; editor, Jean-Claude Piroue; sets, Erhard Engel; music, Lothar Meid. Reviewed at Cannes Film Festival (Mar-ket), May 13, '83. Running time: 106 MINS.

Cast: Brigitte Karner (Danni), Robert Hunger-Buehler (Stefan), Dominik Graf, Barbara Freier, Walter Weber.

Martin Gies's debut film "Danni" shows some moments of directorial talent, but in general it's an em-barrassment script-wise — a film that might have scored as a com-pact short feature, as many of this variety have in the past.

It's a psychological tale. Stefan, who's a proficient but shy sound-man at a recording studio, meets Danni in a Munich bar one nite. Since she doesn't have a place to stay, and he's sharing a room apartment with a friend presently on a New York trip for a long period of time, the two settle down for some serious housekeeping. But Danni is not all there, and becomes so possessive that she threatens to kill herself if left alone in the apart-ment. By and bye, Stefan is caught in her web. The upshot is that her suicide leads to accidental murder — whereupon the last love act is performed on a corpse.

Apparently meant to be a study of paranoia, the game is much too voyeuristic to be taken seriously in the long run. Thesping is the sort that grates rather than entices in the sort of film that particularly de-mands accomplished dual acting.
—Holl.

Utilities
(CANADIAN-COLOR)

Cannes, May 9.

A New World Pictures release of a Rob-ert Cooper presentation. Produced By Rob-ert Cooper. Executive producers, Gurston Rosenfeld, Mike MacFarland. Directed by Harvey Hart. Features entire cast. Screen-play, David Greenwalt, M. James Kouf Jr., based on a story by Greenwalt, Kouf and Carl Manning; camera (color), Richard Leiterman; editor, John Kelly; pro-duction design, Bill Boeton; music, John Erbe and Mickey Solomon. Reviewed at the Olympia (market), Cannes, May 9, 1983. Running Time: 91 MINS.

Bob Hunt .... Robert Hays
Marion Edwards .... Brooke Adams
Roy Blue .... John Marley
Kenneth Knight .... James Blendick
Eddie .... Ben Gordon
Dr. Martha Rogers .... Jane Mallet
Gilda Hoffman .... Toby Tarnow
Ruby Blue .... Helen Burns
Jack Reynolds .... Lee Broker
Leland Thompson .... J.P. Linton
The Hook .... George Touliatos

Mort .... Jan Rubes
Wendell .... Tony Rosato

It's easy to see why the light, anti-establishment comedy, "Utilities," has been sitting on the shelf for two years. Despite a reasonably ap-pealing premise, the film has neither the wit nor the romance to capture a large audience.

Robert Hays plays a big-hearted social worker in Chicago (actually Toronto) who goes up against "the system" and wins. The material is of a type best rendered by Frank Capra in the '30s but today, under the direction of Harvey Hart, dead-ly "Capracorn."

Action hinges on Hays' des-perate attempt to stop an electric company from disconnecting ser-vice to elderly Jane Mallet. His ef-forts to physically block entry are thwarted by plainclothes officer Brooke Adams in a clever ploy.

Initially, the verve and original-ity and chemistry of Hays and Adams overcome pedestrian plot-ting. However, their courtship soon bogs down into cliches. It blends poorly with the more serious under-pinnings in the tale.

Mallet's elderly neighbors man-age to raise enough money to re-connect her utilities but a tech-nicality prevents the resumption of her service. After a cold snap, she's rushed to hospital and dies.

Adopting Peter Finch's credo from "Network," Hays proceeds, with inventor friend Ben Gordon, to bilk major utilities by reprogram-ming their computers. At the same time, power magnate James-Blendick is politically manipulating a rate increase and city invest-ment in his company. He capital-izes on Hays' activities by hiring an arsonist and blaming his man's ac-tions on Hays.

Final confrontation has the two men appealing to city hearing board and citizens to determine the outcome. Clearly, there's no con-test.

Film's primary stumbling block is incorporating romance, comedy and social satire. All three wind up diluted in a picture which already appears to have been trimmed to the bone. Performers with major billing have been left with cameo roles.

Hays and Adams simply can't register enough charisma to over-come the banalities in the script. Both performers rely on cuteness and charm to wade through the story's implausibilities.

Technical credits are smooth, particularly Richard Leiterman's crisp images. However, the pic-ture has been edited into a crazy quilt and continuity problems in-clude alternating scenes where snow magically appears and dis-appears.

"Utilities" should function as a quick programmer, eventually winding up as fodder for pay tv.
—Klad.

Miss Lonelyhearts
(U.S.-B&W)

Cannes, May 14.

A H. Jay Holman Production, in asso-ciation with the American Film Institute Center for Advanced Film Studies. Execu-tive producer; H. Jay Holman. Directed by Michael Dinner. Features entire cast. Screenplay, Dinner, Robert Bailey, based on a novel by Nathaniel West; camera (black and white), Juan Ruiz-Anchia; edi-tor, J.A. Stewart; production designer; Thomas A. Walsh; music, Leonard Rosen-man. Reviewed at the Palais Croisette, Cannes, May 14, 1983. Running time: 37 MINS.

Miss Lonelyhearts .... Eric Roberts
Shrike .... Arthur Hill
Faye Doyle .... Conchata Farrell
Doyle .... John Ryan
Mary Shrike .... Sally Kemp
Goldsmith .... Greg Itzin
Farkis .... Rita Taggart
Betty .... Martina Deignan

A slight incident, concerning the running time of this film, originally announced as over 60 minutes and then proving to be slightly under it, prevented its inclusion in the Cam-era d'Or competition of the Cannes Festival, dedicated to first films of feature length.

Which may be a pity for the film, if it is to be accepted on any terms, it is as a first film which indicates that helmer Michael Dinner knows his way around professionally. How much insight he can bring to this skill of his, remains to be proven.

Once again this is a not very suc-cessful attempt to handle a Nath-aniel West subject for the cinema, specifically one which had already served Vincent Sherman for his Montgomery Clift vehicle of the 1950s. West, who made his living and nurtured his frustrations for a long time in Hollywood, seems to be striking posthumously back at his profession with every effort to bring him to the screen failing in some respect.

In this case, Dinner does okay by the narrative, a story about a young journalist pigeonholed into hand-ling the "Miss Lonelyhearts" col-umn in provincial newspaper. Get-ting too involved with the troubles he encounters every day in his readers" letters, feeling too much compassion for them and unable to disassociate himself from his job, he disintegrates emotionally and falls prey to his own phantasms and those of his readers.

West, a disillusioned man who had a running battle with the media all his life, intended this as a harsh pitiless portrayal of hardboiled, in-sensitive journalism, using his own vitriolic style, in which he brought sarcasm to such a degree it almost implied pity. But, as has been the case before, the literary qualities of the original get lost on the way, Dinner, keeping close to the plot but tending to go for easy solutions, as far as characterization is concerned. Acting is satisfactory, no wonder when such veterans as Arthur Hill and Conchata Farrell participate, and the technical credits are remarkable, taking into consideration the limitations of a first film. Dinner was invited to go on Public TV only after the final result was reviewed by both the television people and by United Artists, who are still holding the film rights to the novel.

As an introduction, Dinner should be pleased with himself and his film, but the inclusion of the film in this year's Cannes Directors' Fortnight, featuring the most popular, and unadventurous selection ever (which may explain its tremendous public appeal), was a bit too ambitious for its own good. —*Edna.*

Cannes Fest Competing

Narayama-Bushi Ko
(The Ballad of Narayama)
(JAPANESE-COLOR)

Cannes, May 15.

A Toei release. Produced by Jiro Tomoda. Directed by Shohei Imamura. Features entire cast. Screenplay, Shohei Imamura based on novel by Shichiro Fukazawa; camera (color), Masao Toshizawa; editor, Hajime Okaiasu; music, Shin'ichiro Ikebe. Reviewed at the Grande Salle, New Palais, Cannes Film Festival (Official Competition), May 15, 1983. Running time: 130 MINS.

Cast: Sumiko Sakamoto, Ken Ogata, Aki Takejo, Mitsuko Baisho, Nijiko Kiyokawa.

While broad marketing points are lacking, Shohei Imamura's "The Ballad Of Narayama" is excellently crafted, strongly acted and directed, and well shot.

Focus is on the now-past Japanese custom of taking their elderly to the mountains to die; in this case, a determined 69-year-old woman, portrayed convincingly by actress Sumiko Sakamoto, 47, who puts her own family in order and, though healthy, demands to be left on the mountain well before she becomes infirm. Her eldest son protests, but leaves her to the elements.

Imamura shows village life with all its gossip, friendship and abrupt violence and adds a few raw sex scenes that add rather than detract and avoid exploitation.

Pic is a shade long for its telegraphed plot, but for those who take the time there are rewards.

Sakamoto is only one of a top cast which does work like a family united with admirable result. And the characters are a mixed bag; a shy elder son who must marry first, a second son who loses his lover when her family proves to be criminals

and is buried alive by the village folk, and a third roisterous son who in a counterpoint subplot has sex with another of the village's old ladies.

Camerawork by Hajime Okaiasu is always first rate as is the music and other technical values. An art pic that rates an audience and another accomplishment for Imamura. Playing fests would be its best introduction for art house possibilities. —*Adil.*

(Film won the Golden Palm top prize at Cannes this year. -*Ed.*)

Merry Christmas, Mr. Lawrence
(NEW ZEALAND-JAPANESE-BRITISH-COLOR)

Cannes, May 11.

A Recorded Picture Company Production (Universal Classics release in U.S.). Produced by Jeremy Thomas. Executive producers: Masato Hara, Eiko Oshima, Geoffrey Nethercott, Terry Glinwood. Directed by Nagisa Oshima. Features entire cast. Screenplay, Oshima, Paul Mayersberg, based on novel, "The Seed and the Sower," by Laurens van der Post; camera (Eastmancolor), Toichiro Narushima; production designer, Shigemasa Toda; art director, Andrew Sanders; editor, Tomoyo Oshima; sound, Tetsuya Okashi, Mike Westgate; music, Ryuichi Sakamoto. Reviewed at the Cannes Festival (competing), May 11, 1983. Running time: 122 MINS.
Celliers .... David Bowie
Lawrence .... Tom Conti
Yonoi .... Ryuichi Sakamoto
Hara .... Takeshi
Hicksley .... Jack Thompson
With: Johnny Okura, Alistair Browinig, James Malcolm, Chris Broun, Yuya Uchida, Ryunosuke Kaneda, Takashi Naito, Tamio Ishikura.

By no means an easy picture to deal with, this thinking man's version of "The Bridge On The River Kwai" makes no concessions to the more obvious commercial requirements, unless it is the selection of David Bowie, the pop star, for the leading dramatic role, which has no singing whatsoever in it (it even includes a joke, when the Bowie character, Celliers, reflects that he would like to be able to sing but he can't).

The strongest points of the script, penned by Oshima and Paul Mayersberg from a novel by South African author Laurens van der Post, are the philosophical and emotional implications, brought up in a careful and intricate comparison between Orient and Occident on every possible level.

The weakest point is its construction, sturdy and compact up to the point when it has to use flashbacks in order to explain the British side of the allegory. Once this is done, the tense, sharply-focused atmosphere of a Japanese prisoner camp in Java, during World War II, tends to disintegrate, the pic slipping from a powerful, many-sided, realistic story, to a fable, cleverly contrived and certainly

very meaningful intellectually, but losing some of its emotional weight because of it.

The plot has a Japanese captain, Yonoi (Ryuichi Sakamoto), trying to impose his own ideas of discipline, honor, order and obedience, in a clash with a British major, Celliers (David Bowie), represents the diametrically opposed train of thought. Yet there are many similarities between these two, not the least being that they both feel confined, Celliers since he is a prisoner, Yonoi because he had been denied the right to face his enemy on equal terms at the front.

There is also a strong homosexual fascination working between them, which helps build up the film's climax, and both carry over, from the past guilty feelings they try to expiate, each in his own way.

The conflict between the two leading figures is better verbalized by Colonel Lawrence (Tom Conti), who lends his name to the film's title, and Hara (Takeshi), the Japanese sergeant whose popular origins allow him much more freedom of emotions and of expressions than anything his commander could afford.

Lawrence, an intellectual who speaks Japanese and is in some ways the bridge between the two poles, believes that he understands his enemy and knows how he should be handled, which of course he doesn't, while Hara can display extreme violence and cruelty, but is also capable of kindness and bursts of humor that no self-respecting Japanese officer would allow himself.

The film's conclusion, in an epilog taking place in 1946 (another one of those leaps and bounds which mark the script construction in the second part of the film) is quite explicit: Orient and Occident may indeed be vastly different in every respect, but they are both victims of leaders who believe they are always right, while the truth is no one can always be right.

Oshima handles his directorial chores with a sure hand, he knows exactly what he wants to achieve and there seems to be perfect understanding between him and his crew. There is remarkable consistency in the rhythm, shape and atmosphere of the prisoner camp scenes, which accentuates all the more the incongruity of flashbacks to England that are out of tune with the rest of the picture.

Out of tune, but on purpose, is also Bowie when he attempts to open his mouth and sing. Bowie plays his part straight, no make-up displays and no eccentric behavior and does a remarkably credible job. Conti shows much intelligence, feeling and pain in the part of Colonel Lawrence, while Jack Thompson brings to the part of Colonel Hicksley something of Alec Guinness'

performance in "The Bridge On The River Kwai."

On the Japanese side, Ryuichi Sakamoto gives a perfectly stylized performance as the code-bound commander of the prisoner camp, and also contributes highly original soundtrack music, which confirms the talent that has made him one of the top Japanese musicians today. Takeshi, a comic of wide following in Japan, manages to imply both sadism and good humor in the part of Hara.

Excellent photography add to the impressive credits of this, which needs careful handling but could attract mainstream audiences outside the art house boundaries, which were Oshima's until now.
—*Edna.*

Cross Creek
(U.S.-COLOR)

Cannes, May 16.

A Universal Pictures-Associated Film Distribution release of a Thorn-EMI production. Produced by Robert B. Radnitz. Directed by Martin Ritt. Features entire cast. Screenplay, Dalene Young, based on the memoirs of Marjorie Kinnan Rawlings; camera (Technicolor), John Alonzo; editor, Sidney Levin; production design, Walter Scott Herndon; music, Leonard Rosenman. Reviewed at Cannes (Competition), May 16, 1983. Running time: 122 MINS.
Marjorie Kinnan
 Rawlings .... Mary Steenburgen
Marsh Turner .... Rip Torn
Norton Baskin .... Peter Coyote
Ellie Turner .... Dana Hill
Geechee .... Alfre Woodard
Mrs. Turner .... Joanna Miles
Paul .... Ike Eisenmann
Floyd Turner .... Cary Guffey
Tim's Wife .... Toni Hudson
Leroy .... Bo Rucker
Charles Rawlings .... Jay O. Sanders
Tim .... John Hammond
Maxwell Perkins ..... Malcolm McDowell
Man in Rocking Chair ..... Norton Baskin

Author Marjorie Kinnan Rawlings' novel, "The Yearling," is among the most widely taught works in the U.S. However, relatively little is known of the author. The release of "Cross Creek," based on her memoirs, will do little to change that situation.

The film, produced by Robert Radnitz and directed by Martin Ritt, offers a sanitized vision of her early struggle to publish a novel and the Florida backwoods which inspired her prose. It's an uncompelling, yet warm, tale which lightly skips over the woman's travails by illustrating a series of vignettes of rural humanity. The overall effect trivializes a life and provides little insight into the artistic process.

Story opens in 1928 with Rawlings (Mary Steenburgen), deciding to leave the security of a marriage to a wealthy New Yorker for the uncertainty of life in a remote region of Florida. She has bought, sight unseen, an orange grove and plans to maintain herself from her crop while devoting her remaining time to writing Gothic romances.

However, the land is hardly fertile. Nonetheless, thanks to the generosity of neighbors, the grove is reactivated and she' able to spend almost all her time at the type-writer.

The drama, what little exists in the film, centers on Rawlings' inability to sell her work until she begins writing about the events of the Florida swamp folk. Her friends Marsh Turner (Rip Torn) and his daughter Ellie (Dana Hill) will become the inspiration for "The Yearling" and "Jacob's Ladder" evolves from the lives of a handyman and his wife.

Remainder of the film focuses on Rawlings' relationship with local hotelier Norton Baskin (Peter Coyote), the recovery of her land and the warm relationship between the author and her young black housekeeper. It's all very pleasant fare told with warmth and humor but lacks tension and currency.

The method of demonstrating the creative process is less than satisfyingly portrayed. And the credibility of the situation is further muted by turning the supposed squalor into a picturesque locale worthy of The Waltons.

Dalene Young's script relies heavily on voice-over passages from Steenburgen which sound less like poetry and more like real estate huckstering. One has to make an enormous leap of faith to accept the situation as being difficult and strenuous.

"Cross Creek" serves Steenburgen poorly. Her shrill demeanor suggests she is incapable of portraying a sympathetic heroine and her off-beat qualities would be better suited to comedy. Only a couple of scenes demonstrate her depth.

Torn once again provides a thoroughly watchable and entertaining performance in an otherwise slow-moving film. Also registering strongly is Alfre Woodard as Geechee, Rawlings' spunky and clever housekeeper. However, Peter Coyote as the film's romantic interest offers few sparks and Hill is rather undimensional as Torn's daughter.

Technical credits are excellent, perhaps to a degree detrimental to the picture. John Alonzo's photography might have seemed more appropriate had it been murkier and had the art direction and settings suggested a "dirt poor" area. Leonard Rosenman's score simply complements the unreal images with lush, romantic arrangements.

The old-fashioned biographical style of "Cross Creek" is clearly out-of-step with contemporary tastes. Commercial prospects are slim for the class production which is aimed as a family entertainment by producer Radnitz. It may fare slightly better outside theatrical exhibition but hardly indicates a film of enormous appeal. —*Klad.*

Kharij
(The Case is Closed)
(INDIAN-COLOR)

Cannes, May 16.

A Neelkanth Films (Calcutta) production. Features entire cast. Written and directed by Mrinal Sen, from a story by Ramapada Chowdhury. Camera (Eastmancolor), K. K. Mahajan; art director, Mitish Roy; editor, Gangadhar Naskar; music, B. V. Karanth. Reviewed at the Cannes film festival (official competition), May 11, 1983. Running time: **95 MINS.**
Mamata . . . . Mamata Shankar
Andan Sen . . . . Anjan Dutt
Sreela . . . . Sreela Majumder
Pupai . . . . Indranil Moitra
Hari . . . . Debapratim Das Gupta
Inspector . . . . Nilotpal Dey

Mrinal Sen, one of India's noted filmmakers, represented his country in the official competition at Cannes for the second time with "The Case Is Closed." Similar in setting and style to his 1979 "Ekdin Pratidin," it is a naturalistic study of a lower middle-class family in a crisis situation.

In "Ekdin Pratidin," Sen analyzed a family unit thrown into a self-centered panic when the eldest daughter, who virtually supports the household, fails to come home from work one evening. In this new film, set in a similar Calcutta tenement, a young couple, sympathetic but overly concerned with their bourgeois strivings, are stricken with guilt and terror when their servant boy is found dead one morning in their locked kitchen.

It turns out that the boy, hired out by his peasant father for some desperately needed income, did not share the comforts the couple reserved for their own child, and during a cold wave, left his sleeping space under a damp staircase to curl up in the warmth of a coal oven, where he was overcome by carbon monoxide poisoning.

Sen dramatizes the deepening disarray of the couple as the police pursue their investigation and the threat of legal sanctions looms. Their dread increases with the arrival of the grief-stricken father with other members of the family and friends and the couple fear violent reprisals. But no court action is made and the peasants meekly return home.

Sen directs with the same dry concision that marked "Ekdin Pratikin" and the dramatic intensity is skillfully maintained. Yet "Kharij" remains a bit disappointing because it doesn't probe deeply enough into the mental states of its protagonists. Too, the performances of its leads, Anjan Dutt and the lovely Mamama Shankar, who has appeared in several of Sen's recent films, are a bit pale. —*Len.*

Le Mur
(The Wall)
(FRENCH-COLOR)

Cannes, May 17.

MK2 production and release, in co-production with Guney Productions-TF1 Films Productions-the French Ministry of Culture. Produced by Marin Karmitz. Features entire cast. Written and directed by Yilmaz Guney. Camera (Fujicolor), Izzet Akay; sound, Serge Guillemein; makeup, Francois Chapuis; editor, Sabine Mamou; music, Ozan Garip Sahin and Stetrak Bakirel; production manager, Catherine Lapoujade. Reviewed at the Cannes Film Festival (Official Competition), May 17, 1983. Running time: 117 MINS.
Cast: Tuncel Kurtiz, Ayse Emel Mesci, Malik Berrichi, Nicolas Hossein, Isabelle Tissandier, Ahmet Ziyrek, Ahmet Ziyrek, Ali Berktay, Selahattin Kuzuoglu, Jean-Pierre Colin, Jacques Dimanche, Ali Dede Altuntas, Necdet Nakiboglu, Sema Kuray, Zeynep Kuray, Habes Bounabi, Bernard Certeaux, Jeremie Nassif, Christina Castillo, Aicha Arouali, Betty Nocella, Joelle Guigui, Sylvie Flepp, Schahla Aaalam.

Yilmaz Guney's first film since his escape from Turkey in October, 1981, is something of an event but less than 'first-rate as a film. Only months after sharing the Gold Palm at last year's Cannes Film Festival, the one time matinee idol-turned-socially conscious filmmaker wrote and directed "The Wall," made on French soil, under the combined auspices of indie producer Marin Karmitz, the state television web TF-1, and culture minister Jack Lang, who put his government's relationship with Turkey on the line by aiding financing from state coffers.

Set entirely in a Turkish prison, "The Wall" was shot a mere 40 miles north of Paris, in a former abbey transformed by the production crew into a grim, claustrophobic institution. The actors, most of them children, are predominantly non-professional and an extraordinary melting pot of French, South Americans, North Africans and expatriate Turks. Among the few professional actors is Tuncel Kurtiz, who was in Guney's 1979 feature, "Suru," cast here as a humane, paternalistic guard.

Thus it's a genuine feat and a tribute to the dedication and professionalism of Guney, Karmitz and company that their film comes across with a credible veristic surface, despite all the heterogeneous elements that went into its making. (Pic was post-synched into Turkish, its original version.)

But the picture itself is a disappointment. A denunciation of the repressive methods of the military regime in Turkey (as well as a probable exorcism of his own 12 years in Turkish penal institutions on and off between 1961 and 1981), Guney's drama is an unrelenting depiction of an actual prison revolt that took place in an Ankara prison in 1976, which was brutally suppressed.

What was different about this uprising was the rebels were children. Their dormitory was one of the most sordid in a complex in which men, women and adolescents were carefully kept apart (but in which common law criminals and political prisoners were locked up together).

Obviously such subject matter cannot fail to have a minimal dramatic impact and the squeamish will find enough violence, dramatized or implied, from which to cringe, as the script has its share of beatings, shootings and humiliations.

But apart from its exotic setting and the youth of its victims, the film is too often commonplace in scripting and predictable in direction (this is the first film Guney has helmed himself since his last sentencing in 1975). It's not Guney's fault if the atrocities of prison life have been banalized in countless motion pictures, but he must be faulted for not being able to transcend certain dramatic conventions and cliches.

Despite its abiding weaknesses, "Le Mur" will undoubtedly be the subject of discussion and controversy, which will fortify its commercial outlook internationally. Karmitz, who is also distrib, has released the film in 30 Parisian cinemas, a considerable spread for a dramatic film of this kind. —*Len.*

Erendira
(Erendira)
(MEXICAN-FRENCH-
W. GERMAN-COLOR)

Cannes, May 16.

A Cine Qua Non, S.A. (Mexico), Les Films du Triangle (Paris) and Saskia Film production. Produced by Alain Queffelean. Directed by Ruy Guerra. Features entire cast. Screenplay, Gabriel Garcia Marquez, based on his novel "The Sad And Unbelievable Story Of Candid Erendira And Her Diabolic Grandmother;" camera (color), Denys Clerval; editing, Kenout Peltier; music, Maurice Lecoeur; costumes, Alberto Negron; decors, Pierre Cadiou, Rainer Chaper; sound, Claude Villand, Roberto Martinez. Reviewed at Cannes Film Festival (in competition), May 14, 1983. Running time: 105 MINS.
The grandmother . . . . Irene Papas
Erendira . . . . Claudia Ohana
The Senator . . . . Michael Lonsdale
Ulysses . . . . Oliver Wehe
The photographer . . . . Rufus
Ulysses' mother . . . . Blanca Guerra
Ulysses' father . . . . Pierre Vaneck

Gabriel Garcia Marquez's stories and novels, whose style is often described as "magic realism," would seem a natural for cinema on account of their rich imagery. However, despite several attempts, he has not yet found a filmmaker ideally suited to bringing his very special world to life on the screen. Ruy Guerra's film may be one of the better attempts to date, but this doesn't prevent it from having serious shortcomings.

"Erendira" was first written as a screenplay and only later as a novel; if taken literally, this tale of a young girl forced into prostitution by her grandmother could appear rather sordid, but she never loses her innocence and the world created around her is simultaneously real and surreal, with larger than life characters, endless spaces, oranges that grow with a diamond inside, etc. The story of candide Erendira can be taken at its face value or interpreted as a symbol of confining structures, family and otherwise, in Latin-American life.

It is above all a visual world and in this respect Guerra tends to be uneven and neither powerful nor imaginative enough to sustain the film's metaphor. Realism too frequently gets the upper hand over the exuberant images of the Garcia Marquez novel. It is a case of roller coaster-like ups and downs, in which the spectator is drawn into the film, only to be ejected moments later. The elements of humor, also found in the story, tend to get lost.

The acting of the multinational cast is uneven and Irene Papas becomes too much of a caricature of the grandmother. It is not so much a matter of individual interpretations being good or bad, but of their not blending. Each actor does his own thing but the problems of style implicit in a film like this are not solved. Technical credits are good.

The film's fate on the international market will basically depend on the drawing power of the Garcia Marquez name in different territories. —*Amig.*

Psycho II
(COLOR)

Ingenious sequel looms as a b.o. smash.

A Universal Pictures release of a Universal-Oak Industries production. Executive producer, Bernard Schwartz. Produced by Hilton A. Green. Directed by Richard Franklin. Stars Anthony Perkins. Screenplay, Tom Holland, based on characters created by Robert Bloch; camera (Technicolor), Dean Cundey; editor, Andrew London; music, Jerry Goldsmith; assistant director, Don Zepfel; production manager, Bill Gray; sound, Jim Alexander, Mark Server; sound design, Andrew London; production design, John W. Corso; special visual effects, Albert Whitlock; makeup, Michael McCracken, Chuck Crafts; matte artist, Syd Dutton. Reviewed at Rivoli 2 theatre, N.Y., May 31, 1983. (MPAA Rating: R).Running time: 113 MINS.

Norman Bates	Anthony Perkins
Lila Loomis	Vera Miles
Mary	Meg Tilly
Dr. Raymond	Robert Loggia
Toomey	Dennis Franz
Sheriff Hunt	Hugh Gillin
Ms. Spool	Claudia Bryar
Statler	Robert Alan Browne
Judge	Ben Hartigan
Myrna	Lee Garlington
Josh	Tim Maier
Kim	Jill Carroll
Deputy Pool	Chris Hendrie
Deputy Norris	Tom Holland

"Psycho II" is an impressive, 23-years-after followup to the late Alfred Hitchcock's 1960 Paramount suspense classic, which was the second-best grossing film that year after the costly epic "Ben-Hur." Sequel, which was produced by Hilton A. Green economically last summer as a $4,000,000-budgeter targeted by backer Oak Industries for the pay-cable market following its theatrical exposure via co-financer Universal, has backed into U's prime summer of 1983 release slot. Its mixture of suspense, shocks and plot twists should yield massive returns in today's market.

Using novelist Robert Bloch's characters and boasting numerous visual homages to Hitchcock's original film, as well as a shadow profile "cameo appearance" conjuring up the master, "Psycho II" is actually indebted equally to the French masters of suspense, novelists Thomas Marcejac and Pierre Boileau, whose specialty of convoluted, twist-filled shock stories is best represented on screen by Henri-Georges Clouzot's 1954 film "Les Diaboliques," a picture much-admired by Hitchcock. Writer Tom Holland has piled on similar twists here, with Aussie director Richard Franklin smoothly executing them in a refreshing riposte to the nearly plotless horror thrillers of late.

Picture opens in black & white with a reprise of the notorious Janet Leigh shower murder from the original (a sequence reputedly directed not by Hitchcock but by his title designer Saul Bass) complete with the late Bernard Herrmann's music. New story, set 22 years later,

has Norman Bates (Anthony Perkins) released from a mental institution on the petition of his psychiatrist, Dr. Raymond (Robert Loggia), over the objections of Lila Loomis (Vera Miles) whose sister he murdered (Leigh in the first film). Familiar gothic melodrama structure has Bates returning to his ancestral home, stirring up memories and, per Raymond's plan, forcing him to face up to the repressed conflicts (particularly his having poisoned his mother many years before) that originally drove him crazy.

Securing a job as cook's assistant at a local diner, Bates is befriended by a young waitress Mary (Meg Tilly) who moves into his house as an empathetic companion. A series of mysterious murders ensue, beginning with the killing of the obnoxious manager Toomey (Dennis Franz), who has turned the Bates family business into a hot-sheets motel. It quickly becomes clear that someone is trying to convince Bates that his mother is still alive and responsible for the mayhem.

Ultimately (until eliminated one by one via knife wounds) all the leading characters are suspect, with "Psycho II" earning but not displaying a "please do not reveal the story" tagline which was appended to "Les Diaboliques" when it was released. Holland, who also appears on-screen as a deputy, has enough twists to keep anyone guessing, though the final one is extremely farfetched despite well-laid hints along the way.

Director Franklin deftly keeps the suspense and tension on high while doling out dozens of shock-of-recognitions shots drawn from the audience's familiarity with "Psycho." Tech credits for this modestly-lensed opus are quite effective, including tight editing and scary sound designed by Andrew London as well as Jerry Goldsmith's supportive musical score.

Reprising his famous role, Perkins is very entertaining, whether stammering over the pronunciation of "cutlery" or misleading the audience in both directions as to his relative sanity. For a sequel that comes so long after the original, he also uncannily looks virtually unchanged. Tilly, the cute heroine of "Tex" and veteran of an earlier spooker, "One Dark Night," is a valuable asset here as that rare lady in jeopardy who can appear sympathetically vulnerable and yet credibly able to defend herself in any situation.

For the first half of "Psycho II," Franklin admirably proves that shocks and thrills are still possible without gore, but he switches to explicit mayhem for the final reels. Purists may balk at approving this decision, but it will probably add to the ultimate b.o. tally. —*Lor.*

The Man With Two Brains
(COLOR)

Pic displays split personality: funny and unfunny. Prospects good if not great.

Hollywood, May 31.

A Warner Bros. release of an Aspen Film Society/William E. McEuen/David V. Picker production. Producer by Picker, McEuen. Directed by Carl Reiner. Stars Steve Martin. Screenplay, Reiner, Martin, George Gipe; camera (Technicolor), Michael Chapman; editor, Bud Molin; music, Joel Goldsmith; production design, Polly Platt; art direction, Mark Mansbridge; set design, Robert Sessa; set decoration, Bruce Gibeson; sound, Bud Alper; assistant director, Michael Grillo. Reviewed at the Burbank Studios, Burbank, May 18, 1983. (MPAA Rating: R). Running time: 93 MINS.

Dr. Michael Hfuhruhurr	Steve Martin
Dolores Benedict	Kathleen Turner
Dr. Alfred Necessiter	David Warner
Butler	Paul Benedict
Dr. Pasteur	Richard Brestoff
Realtor	James Cromwell
Timon	George Furth
Dr. Brandon	Peter Hobbs

"The Man With Two Brains" is a fitfully amusing return by Steve Martin to the broad brand of lunacy that made his first feature, "The Jerk," so successful. Erratic at best, pic offers enough aural and visual non-sequiturs to please the comedian's most ardent fans, but general audiences will also notice that the comic shotgun blasts miss more often than they hit. B.o. should land agreeably, if not overwhelmingly, somewhere between that of "The Jerk" and his last effort, "Dead Men Don't Wear Plaid."

Plot is a frayed crazy quilt barely held together as if by clothespins. Ace neurosurgeon Martin almost kills beauteous Kathleen Turner in an auto accident, only to save her via his patented screwtop brain surgery technique. As manipulative and devious as she was in "Body Heat," Turner proves to be a master at withholding her sexual favors from her frustrated husband, who decides to take her on a honeymoon to Vienna in an attempt to thaw her out.

While there, Martin visits the lab of colleague David Warner and meets the love of his life, a charming woman and marvelous conversationalist who also happens to be a disembodied brain suspended in a jar, her body having been the victim of a crazed elevator killer. As Martin puts it, "For the first time, I'm aroused by a mind." What he needs to find, of course, is a wonderful new body to contain the lovely brain, and with Turner acting nastier and nastier all the time, there's little doubt where Martin's thoughts will lead him.

Presence of a medical background hardly accounts for the preponderance of anatomical humor offered up, and Martin seems to be developing a real fetish for the running gag of a gorgeous woman lewdly, and amusingly, sucking on an object (Rachel Ward on bullets in "Dead Men," Turner on his finger here). Much humor, of course, stems from the befuddled Martin groveling at the feet of the knockout gal he comes to call a "scum queen," but too much of the film seems devoted to frantic overkill to compensate for general lack of bellylaughs and topnotch inspiration.

Although less so than Mel Brooks before him, Martin nevertheless seems drawn to film parody as an essential mode of comedy, what with the mad scientist-type laboratory, "Bride Of Frankenstein"-like climax and Jack the Ripper subplot. Buff aspect is probably what limited b.o. on "Dead Men," and while there's no reason to avoid this altogether, it is to be hoped that Martin essentially pushes toward original ideas in future instead of recycling cliches for easy laughs.

Martin delivers all that's expected of him as a performer, and Turner is a sizzling foil for his comic and pent-up sexual energy. Revelation of the identity of the elevator killer reps a genuinely hilarious surprise, one which is well guarded by the pic's credits.

Tech contributions are adequate, and production design contributes at least one inspired sight gag in the form of Warner's gothic lab lying behind the blandest possible condominium hallway.

—Cart.

I Do
(HONG KONG-COLOR)

Hong Kong, April 15.
A Wing-Scope Co. production, presented by Alan Tang. Executive producer, Maria Chung. Directed by Hilda Chan ("New Year's Eve"); Annette Sham ("Please, Please Me"); Angela Mak ("I Do"). Stars Jenny, Alan Tang, Kenny Bee. Screenplay, Eunice Lam; camera (color), Yeung Ping Tong, Paul Chan, Wong Nga Tai; music, Lam Man Eiee. Reviewed at Hong Kong Lab, Prince Edward Road, Hong Kong, April 14, 1983. Running time: 96 MINS.
(Cantonese soundtrack with English subtitles)

Here's a photoplay featuring three short, unrelated stories about people who made promises in the past and break them later. Glossily presented in gossipy feminine fashion, the setting spotlights Hong Kong's contemporary bourgeois society and nouveau riche. These are composed of well-off Cantonese, who've been infected by western ways. There's opulence in the presentation, which shows generally good taste in the overall production.

The three stories were written by local novelist, Eunice Lam, who specialize in escapist romance-type stories. The total effect is charming, entertaining and captivating as well as exposing some showy beha-

vioral patterns in modern Hong Kong where millionaires abound and Rolls Royces are common.

Story I is "New Year's Eve," directed by Holda Chan. It is the best of the lot. Ching Yi (Jenny) and Wai Lap make a very handsome married couple. Although Wai is a womanizer, Ching remains faithful. The husband has changed a lot, judging from the flashbacks. She discovers that he is in fact having an affair with an old classmate and this leaves her heartbroken and insecure.

On New Year's Eve, Wai leaves Ching alone at home while he goes out with friends. She then decides to dress-up and go out on her own. The outing is not fruitful, as she is not the single-mingle type. She returns home alone only to find her house is about to be robbed. Why not seduce the burglar? What better sweet revenge on an unfaithful husband? A frozen smile is seen on her lips as the episode ends.

Story II, "Please, Please Me" is directed by Annette Sham. Gei Ming and Tung-tung are a young couple living together. Gei Ming (Kenny Bee) has a rule to their relationship: they can talk about love, but never about the responsibility of marriage, for lovers are happier than husband and wife.

One day, Tung-tung finds Lindy, a colleague, in the house with Gei, and she moves out in anger. Lindy moves in. But Gei discovers as the days go by that it is Tung-tung that he really loves. He pursues her to the airport. The ending is happy for Tung-tung, they marry and their relationship is for life.

Story III "I Do!" is directed by Angela Mak. Love between a man and a woman joined by a vow which even death cannot break, is the theme of this story. Sung (Alan Tang) and Keet Ming met abroad and, on their engagement, return to Hong Kong. They go to Sung's huge old mansion on the hill which is being looked after by Sung's old friend Ah Wai (a painter) and his paraplegic but glamorous look-alike dead sister.

Upon arrival, Keet Ming becomes aware immediately that something strange is going on. She becomes the near-miss targets of several near-accidents. She discovers that Sung used to live in this same house with his ex-fiancee, Heung Yue.

It is apparent that the wandering ghost of Heung Yee is still in the house, and seeks to get rid of her new rival. The only way Sung can protect Keet is to keep his vow to Heung in an expected finale. The ghost story provides variety and excels in creating atmospheric images meant to pleasurably scare viewers with calculated precision that works well most of the time.

—Mel.

Trading Places
(COLOR)

Dan and Eddie get acting lessons.

Hollywood, May 25.
A Paramount Pictures release, produced by Aaron Russo. Directed by John Landis. Exec producer, George Folsey Jr. Features entire cast. Screenplay, Timothy Harris, Herschel Weingrod; camera (Metrocolor), Robert Paynter; editor, Malcolm Campbell; sound, James J. Sabat; production design, Gene Rudolf; assistant director, David Sosna; associate producers, Sam Williams, Irwin Russo; music, Elmer Bernstein. Reviewed at the Village Theatre, L.A., May 25, 1983. (MPAA rating: R.) Running time: 106 MINS.
Louis Winthorpe 3d .... Dan Aykroyd
Billy Ray Valentine .... Eddie Murphy
Randolph Duke .... Ralph Bellamy
Mortimer Duke .... Don Ameche
Coleman .... Denholm Elliott
Ophelia .... Jamie Lee Curtis
Beeks .... Paul Gleason
Penelope .... Kristin Holby
Todd .... Robert Curtis-Brown

"Trading Places" is a light romp geared up by the schtick shifted by Dan Aykroyd and Eddie Murphy, whose billing should guarantee success for a venture that might have failed in lesser hands.

Happily, it's a pleasure to report also that even those two popular young comics couldn't have brought this one off without the contributions of three veterans — Ralph Bellamy, Don Ameche (in his first feature since "The Boatniks" 13 years ago) and the droll Englishman, Denholm Elliott.

As written by Timothy Harris and Herschel Weingrod, "Places" is neither a crackling comedy nor a penetrating social satire. But director John Landis knows well the strength of his performers and unleashes them for delightful individual moments and wacky interaction.

Aykroyd plays a stuffy young financial wizard who runs a Philadelphia commodities house for two continually scheming brothers, Bellamy and Ameche. Unaware of their dark side, Aykroyd enjoys the upper-class preppy rewards of his efforts, including butler-chauffeur Elliott and equally stuffy fiancee, nicely played by Kristin Holby.

Conversely, Murphy has grown up in the streets and lives on the con, including posing as a blind, legless veteran begging outside Aykroyd's private club. (His hilarious "cure" when confronted by cops is one of the film's highpoints.)

On a whim motivated by disagreement over the importance of environment vs. breeding, Bellamy bets Ameche that Murphy could run the complex commodities business just as well as Aykroyd, given the chance. Conversely, according to the bet, Akyroyd would resort to crime and violence if suddenly all friends and finances were stripped away from him.

So their scheme proceeds and both Aykroyd and Murphy are in

top form reacting to their new situations. At this point, an odd effect takes temporary hold on the film.

Up until the point where's he's done in by the brothers' uncaring manipulation, Aykroyd has been thoroughly dislikable. But his downfall is so complete — and no fault of his own — that his plight becomes too sympathetic for laughs. He is, after all, a decent enough honest guy beneath the bumptiousness.

The only cost, however, is a midsection stretch without laughs, still made enjoyable by the presence of Jamie Lee Curtis as a good-hearted hooker who befriends Aykroyd.

Ultimately, Murphy, Aykroyd, Curtis and Denholm get wise to the brothers and team up to ruin them by upsetting a commodities swindle they're plotting with the help of a menacing investigator, well-acted throughout by Paul Gleason.

The conclusion is fast-paced and a lot of fun, culminating no doubt in a four-letter word Ameche never thought he'd ever be saying on film when he started four decades ago. But it makes a great capper. —Har.

Coup de Foudre
(FRENCH-COLOR)

Paris, May 18.
Gaumont release of a Partner's Productions/Alexandre Films Hachette Premiere/Films A2/SFPC coproduction. Produced by Ariel Zeitoun. Directed by Diane Kurys. Stars Miou-Miou, Isabelle Huppert. Screenplay, Diane Kurys and Alain Le Henry; camera (color), Bernard Lutic; music, Luis Bacalov; art director, Jacques Bufnoir; sound, Harald Maury and Alix Conte; costumes, Mic Cheminal; production manager, Michel Frichet. Reviewed at the Marignan theatre, Paris, May 15, 1983. Running time: 108 MINS.
Madeleine ....,...... Miou-Miou
Lena ....Isabelle Huppert
Costa .... Jean-Pierre Bacri
Michel .... Guy Marchand
Raymond .... Robin Renucci
Carlier .... Patrick Bauchau

Diane Kurys' third film (after "Peppermint Soda" and "Cocktail Molotov") is her skillful best. A well-observed drama about the friendship between two young women in the early 1950s and the resultant breakup of their marriages, it is apparently inspired by Kurys' own family history, with the couple played by Isabelle Huppert and Guy Marchand modelled on her parents.

Kurys begins her film during the war, tracing the separate destinies of her two heroines. Huppert is a Jewish girl of Russian origin in a French internment camp who agrees to marry a Frenchman (Marchand) to avoid deportation. Unfortunately, he too, is Jewish and they must flee across the Alps.

Miou-Miou is a young art student in Lyon whose fiancee is shot down before her eyes during a skirmish between resistance fighters and police. Later she drifts into a marriage with a young actor, and has a child.

Marchand and Huppert settle in Lyon after the war, where he opens a garage, with his wife and two daughters. When the two women meet at a school fete, they take to each other immediately and become inseparable friends.

But their liaison brings home to each the boredom and banality of the lives they have passively accepted. Burning with artistic ambitions, Miou-Miou leaves her husband, and urges her friend to do the same. Huppert is more hesitant and her mate, aware of Miou-Miou's negative influence, tries to keep them apart. Finally, Huppert decides to leave Marchand.

Kurys has neatly avoided the pitfalls of decorative nostalgia in her evocation of '50s provincial France, and, with the invaluable aid of art director Jacques Bufnoir and costume designer Mic Cheminal (and Bernard Lutic's lensing) has rendered the period quintessentially.

Miou-Miou and Huppert are both adequate, though their scenes together haven't that tacit, deep-felt urgency needed to give their rapport true poignancy. Rather, acting palms go to the men: Jean-Pierre Bacri, fine as Miou-Miou's sympathetic ne'er-do-well mate, always up on the latest losing affair; and Guy Marchand, whose portrayal of a mediocre, hard-working man very much devoted to his family and broken by his wife's departure, should put him up for a French academy award next year.
—*Len.*

Chained Heat
(U.S.-W. GERMAN-COLOR)

Disappointing but commercial women's prison pic.

A Jensen Farley Pictures release of a Heat GBR/TAT-Film/Intercontinental Films production. Executive producers, Ernst R. von Theumer, Louis Paciocco. Produced by Billy Fine. Directed by Paul Nicolas. Stars Linda Blair, John Vernon, Sybil Danning, Tamara Dobson, Stella Stevens. Screenplay, Vincent Mongol, Nicolas; camera (color), Mac Ahlberg, editor, Nino di Marco; music, Joseph Conlon; assistant director, Nancy King; production manager, Mark Tarnawskv. sound, Anna De Lanzo; art direction, Bob Ziembicki. Reviewed at Rialto 1 theatre. N.Y., May 27. 1983. (MPAA Rating: R) Running time: 95 MINS.
Carol .... Linda Blair
Warden Backman .... John Vernon
Ericka .... Sybil Danning
Duchess .... Tamara Dobson
Captain Taylor .... Stella Stevens
Val .... Sharon Hughes
Lester .... Henry Silva
Kaufman................... Nita Talbot
Bubbles .... Louisa Moritz
Martin .... Michael Callan
Also with: Susan Meschner, Greta Blackburn, Robert Miano, Edy Williams, Jennifer Ashley, Kendall Kaldwell, Dee Biederbeck, Leila Chrystie.

"Chained Heat" is a silly, almost campy followup to producer Billy Fine's women's prison hit, "The Concrete Jungle," that manages to pack in enough sex tease and violent action to satisfy undiscriminating action fans. Boasting an impressive cast list for a B-pic, film is a step down from the modest but fun genre films of a decade ago and is unlikely to gain the loyal following of similarly-titled Jonathan Demme's 1974 "Caged Heat" once it finishes its saturation playoff.

Linda Blair toplines as Carol, an innocent young girl serving an 18-month stretch in a California prison run by Warden Backman (John Vernon) and Captain Taylor (Stella Stevens), as corrupt a pair as the scripters can imagine. Real power in stir is shared by statuesque Ericka (Sybil Danning) and Duchess (Tamara Dobson), lording it over the white and black prison populations, respectively.

Though working for Backman, Taylor has a private drugs and prostitution scam run by her lover Lester (Henry Silva) who is also two-timing and plotting against her with Ericka. The in-fighting and doublecrossing ultimately climaxes in a prison break in which arch-enemies Ericka and Duchess improbably stop beating up each other and unite with Carol against the authorities.

German director Paul Nicolas displays little feel for the prison genre, emphasizing archaic sex-for-voyeurs scenes, reaching a nadir in the warden's tacky office which features a hot tub next to his desk for frequent quickies with the prisoners. Hard action scenes are in scarce supply, with only Tamara Dobson (erstwhile "Cleopatra Jones" of a decade ago) convincing in battle.

Blair displays her new uninhibited image here, but remains an unconvincing performer in dramatic scenes. Vernon has fun in several lowdown softcore sex scenes. Miscasting has the beautiful mannequin Danning supposed to be a tough-as-nails match for Dobson. If Stevens and Danning had exchanged roles, film would have played more convincingly with Danning as an Ilsa, Shewolf of the S.S.-type assistant warden and Stevens the rugged inmate.

Sharon Hughes is spotlighted as Blair's best pal with the rest of the cast, including dyed-redhead perennial starlet Edy Williams, getting lost in the shuffle. Tech credits are okay. —*Lor.*

Cannes Fest Competing

Storia Di Piera
(Story of Piera)
(ITALIAN-COLOR)

Rome, May 26.
A CIDIF release, produced by Achille Manzotti for Faso Films. Stars Hanna Schygulla. Isabelle Huppert. Marcello Mastroianni. Directed by Marco Ferreri. Screenplay, Pierra Degli Esposti, Dacia Maraini. Ferreri; camera (color), Ennio Guarnieri; editor, Ruggero Mastroianni; art director, Luciana Levi; music, Renato Angiulini. Reviewed at Flamma Cinema, Rome, May 25. 1983. Running time: 110 MINS.
Eugenia .... Hanna Schygulla
Piera, child .... Bettina Gruhn
Piera, adult ....Isabelle Huppert
Lorenzo .... Marcello Mastroianni

After filming Bukowski's "Tales of Ordinary Madness," Marco Ferreri tackles the controversial autobiography of esteemed theatre actress Piera Degli Esposti, based on the book she coauthored with feminist writer Dacia Maraini.

Despite the title, this "story" is mainly about Piera's free-spirited mother Eugenia, and obsessively focuses on the mother and daughter's incestuous relations as the core of their rapport. High on shock potential, "Piera" is liberally dosed with frontal nudity and suggestiveness, but avoids explicit sex scenes.

Onshore, "Piera" has been doing well but not brilliantly. With a bankable name like helmer Ferreri, pic is a natural for the international erotic art film market. A fine Italo-German-French cast should help it over the barrier of a difficult script lacking structure and a clear point of view.

Eugenia (Hanna Schygulla), the eccentric wife of a mild-mannered but equally spacy professor (Marcello Mastroianni), leads a life of total, all-consuming, guiltless sexual freedom in a provincial Italian town in the early '50s. Unselfconscious and provocative, Eugenia aggressively pedals around town on her bicycle, sits at the train station talking to men, and distractedly exudes affection on her husband and 12-year-old daughter Piera. She is quite an extreme for her day and place, and either for that reason or because she is really unbalanced, she's in and out of mental hospitals throughout the film.

Eventually she involves Piera, who has been morbidly following her love affairs at a distance, in relations with her lovers. Going out on "dates" at night with her mother in high heels and tight dresses, Piera is a child without a childhood, drawn into an intense sexual vortex that totally distorts her familial relations and affects her health.

As a young woman (played by Isabelle Huppert), Piera is forced to watch both her mother and father deteriorate mentally. Now a successful actress, Piera goes to see her gentle father in a barren madhouse and at long last acquiesces to a sexual act (suggested, not seen) with him. Eugenia also has to be visited in her clinic, and film ends with the aged but still sensual mother and grown-up, neurotic daughter embracing naked on a windy beach.

Ferreri is torn between open admiration for Eugenia's unrepressed, unconditioned sexuality and ambiguous, morbid curiosity about how precocious incest affects Piera. Rejecting a smooth, fluid narrative style, filmmaker opts for brief flashes showing events that take place over a period of years, only connected by the two women. Result is often confusing for audiences, who have trouble following the characters popping into hospitals, beds and emotional situations without preparation or segue. To the film's credit, it rivets attention.

What's lacking is a definite incident or emotional moment that would crystalize the meaning of Piera's and Eugenia's experience. Ferreri, who has been at pains to state "Piera" is neither a feminist nor anti-feminist film, leaves the balance sheet open on the bizarre relations between the two women, and given the inconclusive nature of the material, most viewers will have to do the same.

Hanna Schygulla, as focus performer, was unanimously awarded best performance prize at Cannes. She is at her peak of animal-like sensuality. Child actress Bettina Gruhn (as young Piera) is remarkably intense and mature.

On the plus side is Ennio Guarnieri's clean, precise lensing and Luciana Sevi's sets, inspired by Fascist architecture. Pic is one of Ferreri's best visual efforts.
—*Yung.*

El Sur
(The South)
(SPANISH-FRENCH-COLOR)

Cannes, May 19.
An Elias Querejeta (Madrid) — Chloe (Paris) coproduction, with participation of Spanish Radio-television. Directed by Victor Erice. Features entire cast. Screenplay by Jose Luis Lopez Linares based on story by Adelaida Garcia Morales; assistant director, John Healey; production director, Primitivo Alvaro; camera (Eastmancolor), Jose Luis Alcaine; editor. Pablo G. del Amo; sets. Antonio Belizon; costumes, Maiki Marin. Reviewed at Palais des Festivals. Cannes Film Fest (in competition). May 18. '83. Running time: 94 MINS.
Agustin ....Omero Antonutti
Estrella (Age 8) .....Sonsoles Aranguren
Estrella (Age 15) ....Iciar Bollan
Julia ....Lola Cardona
Milagros .... Rafaela Aparicio
Casilda ....Maria Caro
With: Francisco Merino. Jose Vivo. Jose Garcia Murilla. Aurore Clement and Germaine Montero.

Victor Erice's long-awaited "El Sur" is a landmark in the history of Spanish cinema and, for many, one of the highpoints of the Cannes Film Festival. Nine years after astounding critics with his "Spirit Of The Bee-Hive," and having made no other film in the interim, Erice returns with this exquisitely-limned opus which is sure to run the gamut of the fest circuits this year, culling awards as it goes along. After the recent success of "La Colmena" in Berlin and "To Begin Again" in Hollywood, this is Spain's crowning achievement.

The behind-the-scenes controversies concerning the film are bound to haunt it for the remainder of its existence. Near the end of pic's lensing, helmer Erice and producer Elias Querejeta quarrelled and the production was stopped. Rather than leave it in eternal limbo, Querejeta took the parts that had been shot and edited them into the present film. It will never be known whether the result would have been better still with Erice working on the film to the end. What is certain is that pic, as it stands, is a masterpiece.

Story is set in a small farmhouse and a nearby village in northern Spain in 1957. Tale is narrated by a young girl, Estrella, and is a long flashback in which she remembers some of the key events of her childhood, especially her relationship with her father, a visit from her grandmother and an aunt from the South, and to a lesser degree her mother.

The dominating personage of the film is Estrella's father, a doctor in the village. As film proceeds, we glean, first through the child's and then through the adolescent's eyes, snippets of the father's past: he was on the "wrong" side in the Spanish Civil War, he is not religious, he once had a romance with a minor film star and he had to leave "the south" after violent arguments with his father.

Erice manages to spin a spellbinding mood which is not broken until the last frame of the film, when Estrella, after a lifetime in the cold, rainy inhospitable North, finally decides to see for herself the fabled "South."

Thesping all around is superb, with an especially memorable performance by Omero Antonutti ("Padre Padrone") as the father. Estrella at both ages is wonderfully acted, as are supporting roles by Rafaela Aparicio ("Mom Turns 100") and Lola Cardona. As always, Jose Luis Alcaine's lensing is superb. In view of the film's difficulties, perhaps the final kudos go to editor Pablo G. del Amo, who was able to select and put together this film.

Commercially, pic is bound to be picked up internationally by classics divisions and/or major distribs in virtually every sophisticated market in the world.
—Besa.

Cannes Non-Competing

Rien Qu'un Jeu
(Just A Game)
(CANADIAN-COLOR)

Cannes, May 13.
A Cine-Groupe production. Produced by Monique Messier, Yvon Michon and Jacques Pettigrew. Directed by Brigitte Sauriol. Features entire cast. Screenplay, Sauriol, Monique Messier; camera (color), Paul Van der Linden; editor, Marcel Pothier; art direction, Gaudeline Sauriol; music, Yves Laferriere. Reviewed at Cannes Film Festival (Directors Fortnight), May 13, 1983. Running Time: 101 MINS.
Mychele .... Marie Tifo
Andre .... Raymond Cloutier
Catherine .... Jennifer Grenier
Julie .... Julie Mongeau

"Rien Qu'un Jeu" concerns the problem of incest in a middle class Quebec family. The film provides no particularly novel insight or reflection on its subject, preferring to play the story quite dead-pan. Rather than humanizing the material, director Brigitte Sauriol creates an arid textbook atmosphere.

Action occurs during a young couple's summer vacation at a Quebec resort area. Initially, one suspects the tension between the father, Andre (Raymond Cloutier), and his young teenage daughter Catherine (Jennifer Grenier) has to do with his protective nature. However, he shows his real intentions when he drives to a secluded location and demands she provide him with sexual release.

Script implies the situation has gone on for several years, and Catherine has only just begun to understand and reject her father's demands. She runs away briefly, attempting to tell a friend of her plight unsuccessfully. When she finally returns, her mother Mychele (Marie Tifo) adds to her frustration with accusations of loose conduct.

Further complications arise when Catherine recognizes her father is asking for sexual favors from her younger sister Julie (Julie Mongeau). The entire situation finally blows up when Mychele catches Andre and Julie in the act one afternoon.

At first she is shocked and angry, but later she simply wants to ignore the issue. Andre promises tearfully he will stop his compulsion and Mychele takes his side over her daughters.

The story is straightforward, frank and very dull. Production values are good and the performances can't be faulted generally. However, one feels very much like the older daughter — frustrated by the stasis of the situation. And rather perplexed by the lack of drama and confrontation.

"Rien Qu'un Jeu" may gain some distribution outside Quebec on subject matter alone. However, theatrical prospects are quite limited. —Klad.

Uliisees
(WEST GERMAN-COLOR)

Cannes, May 16.
A Werner Nekes Film Production, Muelheim. Features entire cast. Written and directed by Werner Nekes, based loosely on Homer, James Joyce, and Neil Oram. Camera (color), Bernd Upnmoor; music, Anthony Moore, Helga Schneider; collaborators, Bernd Upnmoor, Dore O., Birger Bustorff, Herbert Jeschke, Volker Bertzky. Reviewed at Cannes Film Fest (Market), May 14, '83. Running time: 94 MINS.
Cast: Armin Woelfl, Tabea Blumenschein, Russel Derson, Shezad Abbas.

Werner Nekes, primarily an experimental filmmaker with 60 titles to his credit, marks a progression to the avant garde full-length feature "Uliisses" (1982), financed in part by the Northrhine-Westphalian film fund. As the title hints, pic is based loosely on the James Joyce classic, "Ulysses," but has additional references to Homer and Neil Oram (according to the author's own notes). The first screening of "Uliisses" took place in Dublin at a James Joyce Symposium.

Without doubt, this is Nekes's own personal reflection on one of the most controversial books in modern history. And just as Leopold Bloom in the original was depicted in a state of complete physical and mental nakedness, so, too, a full measure of bare flesh orchestrates the theatrically staged happenings in "Uliisses." What the rest is about is anybody's guess; visually striking images amid an assortment of poetic metaphors.
—Holl.

Les Trois Couronnes du Matelot
(The Three Crowns of the Sailor)
(FRENCH-COLOR-16m)

Cannes, May 20.
An I.N.A./Antenne 2 production. Directed by Raul Ruiz. Features entire cast. Screenplay, Ruiz, Emilio de Solar, Francois Ede; camera (color), Sacha Vierny; sound, Jean-Claude Brisson; editor, Janine Verneau and Valeria Sarmiento; music, Jorge Arriagada. Reviewed at the Cannes Film Fest (Perspectives on French Cinema), May 11, 1983. Running time: 117 MINS.
With: Jean-Bernard Guillard, Philippe Deplanche, Jean Baudin, Nadege Clair, Lisa Lyon.

Raul Ruiz is a prolific, 42-year-old Chilean-born filmmaker who left his homeland in 1974 and settled in France where he has worked with various fringe producers and directed for experimental television production units. His best pictures are baroque, intellectual puzzles of rich visual invention and offbeat humor, though his last-released film, "The Territory," an English-language production shot in Portugal, was far beneath his imaginative best.

"The Sailor's Three Crowns" shows Ruiz back in full sail, however. Made for television — it was produced by the Antenne 2 web and the enterprising Institut National de l'Audiovisuel — it unspooled last month in the Perspectives on French Cinema program at Cannes, where it was voted best of the crop.

Veteran producer Pierre Braunberger saw the pic, fell in love with it and has committed himself to launching the pic theatrically, in a 35m blowup version, this fall. Though very much a specialized product, it well deserves international exposure, and could help win Ruiz the following that has consistently eluded him.

Film opens in a fog-bound port where a student, who has just committed a murder, is buttonholed by a mysterious sailor, who offers to tell his story in exchange for three Danish crowns. They repair to an ornate dance hall where the seaman (Jean-Bernard Guillard) recounts his macabre odyssey: how he shipped out of his native Valparaiso aboard a vessel that turned out to be a damned ship manned by phantoms, on which he was the only living crewman, condemned to sail until he found someone to replace him.

The world-weary mariner had been all over the world encountering a bizarre assortment of prostitutes, gangsters, dockside sages and other ghosts, none of whom could offer relief from his nautical calvary. At dawn, after hearing him out, the student beats him to death on the docks and takes his place.

Ruiz has drawn richly on various cinematic and literary sources (the Flying Dutchman legend, the tales of Robert Louis Stevenson, the "poetic realism" of the Thirties French Cinema) to concoct this breathlessly flamboyant fable, full of savoury anecdote and incident. Sacha Vierny, working with color filters, has lensed with inspiration (the film was shot in Paris and Portugal, but the numerous geographic contrasts are cleverly suggested) and Jorge Arriagada's tangy Latin score is a distinct delight. Guillard heads a generally solid cast. —Len.

Das Gold er Liebe
(The Gold of Love)
(WEST GERMAN-COLOR)

Cannes, May 18.
A Martin Moszkowicz Star Film Production, Munich, Eric Moss, executive producer. Features entire cast. Written and directed by Eckhart Schmidt. Camera (color), Bernd Heinl; art direction, Michael Domant; music, D.A.F., Blumchen Blau, Wanderlust; editing, Patricia Rommel. Reviewed at Cannes Film Fest (Market), May 16, '83. Running time: 89 MINS.

Cast: Alexandra Curtis (Patricia), Marie Colbin, Hermann Strobl, Regina van Tom, Andre Heller, Andrea Wurstbauer, Allegra Curtis.

Eckhart Schmidt's debut feature, "Trance" (1982), featured pop entertainer Desiree Nosbusch killing and then eating her pop idol, when her fantasies declared that no one but this fan will possess him forever.

His latest feature moves in the same weird direction: "The Gold of Love" has another 16-year-old pop fan (played by Alexandra Curtis, daughter of Tony Curtis and Christine Kaufmann) traveling to Vienna to visit a concert given by pop-group D.A.F., whereupon she witnesses a ritual murder and "flees into the night" on a trip-fantasy.

The rest is blood-and-guts horror against the background on nonstop pop music. The film was apparently conceived for the sprouting video bars, hip urban locales where the video-film serves as mutual word killer off in the background. As a film-film, it's an empty-seater. —Holl.

Un Bruit Qui Court
(A Rumour)
(FRENCH-COLOR)

Cannes, May 20.
A Feravec/FR3 coproduction. Executive producer, Michele Dimitri. Written and directed by and starring Jean-Pierre Sentier and Daniel Laloux. Camera (color), Jean-Noel Ferragut; sound, Antoine Bonfanti; music, Pierre Alrand; editor, Joelle Barjolin; art directors, Jackson Stricanne and Gilles Laboulandine; costumes, Charlie Moro; makeup, Dominque Germain. Reviewed at the Cannes Film Festival (Perspectives on French Cinema), May 12, 1983. Running time: 88 MINS.
With: Jean-Pierre Sentier, Daniel Laloux, Pierre Ballot, Alain Frerot, Josiane Stoleru, Pierre Bolo, Jacques Grand-Jouan, Jacques Boudet, Pierre Fabre, Claude Duneton, Armand Babel.

Actor-director Jean-Pierre Sentier has an original sense of humor and has been trying to communicate it through film. His first directorial effort, "L'Arret au Milieu," in 1978, was a medium length comedy, quirky and refreshing. Two years ago he tackled his first feature length project, "The Gardener," which had several precious moments of invention, but showed strain in filling out its allotted length.

Now Sentier is back with a new feature, seconded in script, direction and performance — this is Sentier's first role in his own film — by fellow zany Daniel Laloux. Together they have cooked up an engaging little absurdist parable about two forgotten bureaucrats on a desert island, a sort of "Not Waiting for Godot."

Sentier and Laloux are two civil servants who, once upon a time, were posted on an island by the Ministry of Toil to manufacture boxes for Camembert cheese. But due to a administerial slip-up, (their identity cards fell behind the filing cabinet) their employers forgot about their existence. So the two merely carried on their jobs faithfully, all the while creating new identities and lifestyles for themselves.

The ministry finally comes across its error and immediately dispatches sophisticated up to date material (a goat) to the island, followed by a small reindoctrination task force. But the two administrative castaways will have nothing to do with this invasion and effectively repel the intruders.

Sentier and Laloux make for an amusingly deadpan duo who have forgotten almost all their basic human instincts but remain ever-curious about life.

Sentier is still far from filling the void left by Jacques Tati, but his films are welcome wafts of daft charm.

Film's subtitle, by the way, is "Some people mislay their citizens like others their umbrellas." —Len.

Nesto Izmedju
(Something in Between)
(YUGOSLAV-COLOR)

Cannes, May 31.
A Centar Film Production, Belgrade. Features entire cast. Directed by Srdjan Karanovic. Screenplay, Karanovic, Miroslav Marinovic, Andrew Horton; camera (color), Zivko Zalar; sets, Miljen Kljakovic; music, Zoran Simjanovic; editing, Branka Ceperac. Reviewed at Cannes Film Fest (Certain Regard), May 16, '83. Running time: 107 MINS.
Cast: Caris Corfman (American journalist), Predrag Manojlovic (surgeon), Dragan Nikolic (playboy), Zorka Doknic-Janojlovic, Renata Ulmanski, Gorica Popovic, Sonja Savic, Nina Kirsanova, Petar Ilic-Hajne.

(English soundtrack)

Srdjan Karanovic has made four features. "Something in Between" is slated in the "Certain Look" section at Cannes. He is far and away the leading intellectual filmmaker in Yugoslavia, a Serb associated with Centar Film in Belgrade who studied at the Prague Film School (FAMU).

"Something in Between" deals with an American journalist, Caris Corfman, in her first film role, and her relationship with two Yugoslavs, both friends and intent on winning her attention, if not her heart. Pic is shot in English, but in view of the nature of the theme, the jumbled English and half-baked Serbo-Croatian works as a meeting of two cultures in the land where East meets West. The story follows the girl as she travels from New York to Belgrade to Istanbul, with a stopover in Dubrovnik.

The fun is in the dialog itself. The American journalist notes the contradictions in the life style of Belgrade Yugoslavs: flying to Dubrovnik for a fish dinner, eight rotating presidents of the country, strict family codes with the mother at the center, and the odd tie between a responsible surgeon and a likable ne'er-do-well. The rogue romances her even though she's attached to his friend; she, in turn, takes a liking for the wrong guy, on the grounds that the rogue has more pluck and charm than the straight-laced physician. It's a constant game of humorous one-upmanship from beginning to end, some of the twists (like receiving a love-note in flight via a radiogram) quite original.

Karanovic labels his film as "social commentary" — it's that, and a comedy of manners as well. One of the in-jokes has to do with stringing together American movie titles to get across punch lines; Karanovic knows film history backwards!

"Something in Between" should find its way to other fests on the upcoming circuit, and could enjoy as well a modest spinoff at arthouses with proper handling. —Holl.

La Rosa de los Vientos
(The Rose of the Winds)
(CUBAN-VENEZUELAN-SPANISH-COLOR)

Cannes, May 18.
An I.C.A.I.C. (Cuba), Universidad de los Andes (Venezuela) and Paraiso Films (Spain) production. Directed by Patricio Guzman. Features entire cast. Screenplay, Guzman, Gloria Laso, Jorge Diaz; camera (color), Pablo Martinez; music, Leo Brouwer, editing, Nelson Rodriguez. Reviewed at Cannes Film Festival (Directors' Fortnight) on May 17, 1963. Running time: 96 MINS.
Cast: Patri Andion, Jose A Rodriguez, Nelson Villagra, Asdrubal Melendez, Fernando Birri, Gloria Laso, Coca Rudolfi, Hector Noguera, Henry Zacca, Eliana Vidal.

Patricio Guzman has been making films since 1965 but except for a couple of student shorts, his work had up to now been in the field of documentaries, the best known of which is "The Battle of Chile."

Now, at age 41, this exiled director from Chile enters a quite different phase of his career and "The Rose of the Winds," which could loosely be described as a fiction film, is liable to lead to extreme reactions. Although there will probably be a consensus that it is beautiful to behold, some will consider it as rather pretentious and repetitive symbolic twaddle, both confusing and not properly thought out.

Others will have a diametrically opposed viewpoint and these divergences may well turn Guzman's film into a cult item, particularly among those interested in Latin American cinema.

Over the next year, "The Rose" should have plenty of further exposure on the festival circuit and it will no doubt find its way into art houses, both in Europe and in the U.S.

The film's main theme is the survival of Latin American culture and identity from the arrival of Columbus and the Spanish conquerors up to the present, in spite of unceasing attacks from foreign elements and also from alienated local power structures. This subject is not developed as straight narrative, but in what could be described as successive concentric circles, each covering a different period, with Jorge Agricola — a mythical character — as a timeless link. .

The film was mostly shot in the Venezuelan Andes of the state of Merida, at an altitude of over 5,000 meters and also in Cuba's Jaruco jungle. These locations are powerfully used throughout, creating a pantheistic atmosphere of man's communion with nature.

There are moments when the dialog tends to become too rhetorical, but although strongly symbolic, the storyline also has a clear inner logic and — although this will not be a unanimous verdict — "The Rose of the Winds" is a powerful and highly personal film. —Amig.

Octopussy
(BRITISH-COLOR)

Lucky No. 13 in James Bond series boasts exceptional stuntwork, conventional storyline. Should be a solid b.o. performer worldwide.

An MGM-UA Entertainment release of a United Artists presentation of an Eon Prods. Ltd. production. Produced by Albert R. Broccoli. Executive producer, Michael G. Wilson. Directed by John Glen. Stars Roger Moore. Screenplay and screen story, George MacDonald Fraser, Richard Maibaum & Michael G. Wilson, based on stories, "Octopussy" and "The Property of a Lady," by Ian Fleming; camera (Technicolor, Panavision; prints by Metrocolor), Alan Hume; supervising editor, John Grover; editors, Peter Davies, Henry Richardson; music, John Barry; theme song "All Time High," music, Barry, lyrics, Tim Rice, sung by Rita Coolidge; production design, Peter Lamont; art direction, John Fenner; set decoration, Jack Stephens; sound (Dolby stereo), Derek Ball; special effects supervision, John Richardson; second unit direction & camera, Arthur Wooster; costume design, Emma Porteous; assistant director, Anthony Waye; production supervisor, Hugh Harlow; action sequences arranger, Bob Simmons; driving stunts arranger, Remy Julienne; stunt supervisors, Martin Grace, Paul Weston, Bill Burton; aerial team director, Philip Wrestler; associate producer, Tom Pevsner. Reviewed at RKO National 2 theatre, N.Y., June 2, 1983. (MPAA Rating: PG). Running time: **130 MINS.**

James Bond	Roger Moore
Octopussy	Maud Adams
Kamal	Louis Jourdan
Magda	Kristina Wayborn
Gobinda	Kabir Bedi
Orlov	Steven Berkoff
Twins	David & Tony Meyer
Vijay	Vijay Amritraj
"Q"	Desmond Llewelyn
"M"	Robert Brown
Gogol	Walter Gotell
Minister of Defense	Geoffrey Keen
Gwendoline	Suzanne Jerome
Midge	Cherry Gillespie
Sadruddin	Albert Moses
Fanning	Douglas Wilmer
009	Andy Bradford
Miss Moneypenny	Lois Maxwell
Penelope Smallbone	Michaela Clavell

Even before its release, "Octopussy" has emerged triumphant by beating a rival James Bond film starring series original Sean Connery to market by several months. This Roger Moore-starrer, his sixth entry and the fourth produced solo by Albert R. Broccoli since buying out partner Harry Saltzman, is a lavishly-mounted but utterly conventional action entertainment film. Thrilling stuntwork largely covers the singular absence of a worthy villain for Britain's finest agent to go up against, giving "Octopussy" very strong b.o. potential in all markets.

Topical storyline concerns a scheme by hawkish Russian General Orlov (Steven Berkoff) to launch a first-strike attack with conventional forces against the NATO countries in Europe, relying upon no nuclear retaliation by the West due to weakness brought about by the current Peace Movement in Europe.

Orlov is aided in his plan by a beautiful smuggler Octopussy (Maud Adams), her trader-in-art-forgeries underling Kamal (Louis Jourdan) and exquisite assistant Magda (Kristina Wayborn). James Bond (Roger Moore) is set on their trail when fellow agent .009 (Andy Bradford) is killed at a circus in East Berlin, but delivers a fake Faberge egg art object to the British Ambassador's residence before dying. The British deduce that the Russians have fabricated the fake to raise western currency for some scheme, and Bond is off and running when Kamal outbids him for the real egg at a Sotheby's auction.

Trail takes Bond to India (lensed in sumptuous travelog shots) where he is assisted by local contact Vijay (tennis star Vijay Amritraj in a pleasant acting debut). Surviving an impromptu "Hounds of Zaroff" tiger hunt turned manhunt and other perils, including a thug wielding a yoyo device bearing a circular saw blade, Bond pursues Kamal to Germany for the hair-raising race against time conclusion.

Encoring from the last picture, "For Your Eyes Only," John Glen directs smoothly and with less gimmickry than is usual for the series. Film's high points are the spectacular aerial stuntwork marking both the pre-credits teaser and extremely dangerous-looking climax. The rest of the action scenes are well-executed but suffer from a sense of deja vu, as in a lengthy stunt sequence atop a speeding train that recalls Sean Connery's derring-do in "The Great Train Robbery" (wherein Connery did similar stunts himself while Moore here is obviously replaced by a stuntman).

Roger Moore is eminently effective in the Bond role and presumably will be cajoled to return a seventh time in the next entry, "From A View To A Kill," announced in the end credits. Maud Adams defies tradition by becoming the first leading lady to repeat a romantic heroine role in a Bond picture when she predictably switches from adversary to ally midstream. Newcomer from Sweden Kristina Wayborn (who has portrayed Greta Garbo on tv) is the most beautiful Bond heroine in many years but comes off as cool and remote as her recent predecessors. Bond could use an earthy, more emotional companion in future.

Since Adams' initial slotting as a heavy doesn't pay off, villainy in "Octopussy" falls to Louis Jourdan, his chief henchman portrayed by Middle Eastern star (of Italy's "Sandokan" series) Kabir Bedi and Berkoff's mad Russian. They are merely okay, with Jourdan mellow and resolutely not larger-than-life, while Bedi is just ominous rather than delivering the requisite danger opposite Bond. As for Berkoff, his hammy performance is designed mainly to ensure that the viewer differentiates between hopefully level-headed, peacenik Russian leaders and one bad apple. Though the Bond formula still works, apparently Ian Fleming's Cold War-era concept of SMERSH making the USSR the official villain is gone forever.

Tech credits are, per usual, tops, with special kudos going to lighting cameraman Alan Hume for the handsome visuals and to the stunt crew for their yeoman efforts.

—*Lor.*

Superman III
(COLOR)

Unspecial followup to second gem, though Pryor should lure lotsa funny business.

A Warner Brothers release of an Alexander Salkind presentation of an Alexander and Ilya Salkind production, made by Dovemead Ltd. Executive producer, Ilya Salkind. Produced by Pierre Spengler. Directed by Richard Lester. Stars Christopher Reeve, Richard Pryor. Screenplay, David and Leslie Newman, based on characters created by Jerry Siegel and Joe Shuster; camera (Rank color, Panavision), Robert Paynter; editor, John Victor Smith; music, Ken Thorne, with original Superman themes by John Williams; songs, Giorgio Moroder; production design, Peter Murton; art directors Terry & Brian Ackland-Snow, Bert Davey; set decoration, Peter Young; sound mixer (Dolby), Roy Charman; director of special effects & miniatures, Colin Chilvers; flying and second unit director, David Lane; costumes, Evangeline Harrison; assistant director, Dusty Symonds; production manager, Vincent Winter; stunt coordinator, Paul Weston; makeup, Paul Engelen, Stuart Freeborn; associate producer, Robert Simmonds; film services in association with UAA Ltd. Reviewed at Criterion 2 theatre, N.Y., June 6, 1983. (MPAA Rating: PG). Running time: **123 MINS.**

Superman/	
Clark Kent	Christopher Reeve
Gus Gorman	Richard Pryor
Perry White	Jackie Cooper
Jimmy Olsen	Marc McClure
Lana Lang	Annette O'Toole
Vera Webster	Annie Ross
Lorelei Ambrosia	Pamela Stephenson
Ross Webster	Robert Vaughn
Lois Lane	Margot Kidder
Brad	Gavan O'Herlihy

Additional Special Visual Effects Unit Credits

Supervisor of optical and visual effects, Roy Field; front projection by the Zoptic System, consultant, Zoran Perisic. Model unit: director of photography, Harry Oakes; camera, Ginger Gemmell; art director, Charles Bishop. Process unit: director of photography, John Harris; camera, John Palmer; Zoptic front projection supervisor, David Wynn Jones; traveling matte supervisor, Dennis Bartlett; lighting effects, Lightflex System. Process Backgrounds: Aerial Wesscam photography, Ronald Goodman; background photography, Bob Bailin. Optical unit: optical printers, Dick Dimbleby, David Docwra; matte artists, Peter Melrose, Charles Stoneham; optical & matte cameras, Peter Harman, Martin Body; optical effects by Optical Film Effects Ltd.

Particularly since it follows in the wake of the original "Superman's" superior and extremely successful sequel, "Superman III" emerges as a surprisingly soft-cored disappointment. Putting its emphasis on broad comedy at the expense of ingenious plotting and technical wizardry, the film does have distinct commercial promise which will be largely hinged on Richard Pryor's comic lure and the built-in "Superman" audience. But there's virtually none of the mythic or cosmic sensibility that marked its predecessors and while initial biz should be strong indeed, the film's legs may be far from indestructable within the summer competition.

Off to a promising start, the film begins with an hilarious pre-credits sequence in which Pryor, an unemployed "kitchen technician," is kicked off the unemployment roster and, courtesy of a borrowed matchbook, decides to embark on a career as a computer programmer. As the credits begin to roll, an ingenious and equally hilarious chain-reaction of disasters on a Metropolis street, indulging director Richard Lester's longtime knack for slapstick and sight-gaggery, sets the tone of broad silliness which will mark the remainder of the film.

Set-up then cross-cuts between Clark Kent (Christopher Reeve) returning to his midwestern childhood town of Smallville for a soft feature story on a high school reunion, and Pryor's employment as an instant computer whiz at a conglomerate headed by Robert Vaughn, where he quickly learns how to program an embezzlement scheme.

As comic-book fate would have it, Vaughn, a crooked megalomaniac intent on taking over the world economy, recognizes devious talent when he sees it, and dispatches Pryor to a small company subsid in Smallville, where he programs a weather satellite to destroy Colombia's coffee crop (and make a market-cornering killing for Vaughn).

Foiled by Superman (who's saved a chemical plant from destruction and rescued the young son of Clark's onetime crush Lana Lang (Annette O'Toole) in the meantime), Pryor uses the computer to concoct an imperfect form of Kryptonite — using cigaret tar to round out the formula.

With Vaughn as a weak and unspectacular nemesis (he seems no more villainous than any power-crazed conglomerate owner), David and Leslie Newman's screenplay opts for the novelty of using the Kryptonite to split the Clark Kent/Superman persona into two bodies, respectively good and evil. Despite the quirky novelty of a mean, macho, 5 o'clock-shadowed Superman, indulging in arrogant sexual posturings, bar-room brawls and generally unsavory behavior (like straightening the Tower of Pisa out of spite), the confrontation between the two personalities, culminating in a mean-spirited, jarringly violent physical battle, still fails to set the screen soaring.

In fact, virtually none of the film's set action and spectacle pieces — the conflagration at the chemical plant, the shifting of Colombia's weather, the abduction of mid-Atlantic oil tankers and a final confrontation with a destructive computer with a mind of its own — has the scope or the technical imagination of either of the previous pics.

In one of the few exceptions, the missile launch pursuit of Superman through the Grand Canyon (cross-cut with a video game version that seems destined for home use) does manage to perfectly meld action and sly humor. But most of the action relies on explosive pyrotechnics and careening stuntpersons.

At the romantic level, the film does paint a nice relationship between Reeve (as Kent) and O'Toole, and the good guy actually gets the girl, though she's hardly a charismatic screen presence (spunky Margot Kidder has a too-brief bookending appearance as Lois Lane). Pryor is excellent, as usual, when the writing allows him to be, but is probably too broad overall. Apart from Vaughn (constrained by a weak cartoon-like persona), Pamela Stephenson as his deceptively dumb bimbo sidekick, and Annie Ross as his tough-as-nails villainous sister, there's little more at hand than cameo turns from the old Daily Planet crowd.

Technical credits, as usual, are firstrate, with flying sequences (now taken for granted), miniatures and matte-work all A-calibre. This entry does lack the stylish lensing that characterized the first two "Superman" pics, and apart from recalled strains of John Williams' original theme, the music is notably unspecial, including a new love theme and a couple of tunes from Giorgio Moroder. —Step.

Smorgasbord
(U.S.-COLOR)

Paris, May 22.

A Warner Bros. (domestic), Orion (overseas) release. Produced by Peter Nelson and Arnold Orgolini. Directed by Jerry Lewis. Stars Jerry Lewis. Screenplay by Lewis and Bill Richmond; camera (color), Gerald Perry Finnerman; art direction, Terry Bousman; editor; Gene Fowler Jr.; music, Morton Stevens. Reviewed at the Colisee, Paris, May 21, 1983. (MPAA Rating: PG) Running Time: 83 MINS.
Warren Nefron/Dr. Perks ... Jerry Lewis
Dr. Jonas Pletchick ...... Herb Edelman
Waitress .... Zane Busby
Pilot .... Foster Brooks
Passenger .... Buddy Lester
Female Patient .... Milton Berle

Also with Dick Butkus, Francine York, Bill Richmond, Robin Bach, Paul Davidson.

Jerry Lewis is back in "Smorgasbord" which is currently enjoying a critical-commercial run in Paris where the actor-filmmaker is adored. It's unlikely to repeat this success in either area when released on the other side of the Atlantic. North Americans appear less inclined to flock to a rehashing of already familiar Lewis material which dominates the film.

Story concerns a hapless bungler named Warren Nefron played by Lewis. Warren's repeated suicide flubs have sent him scurrying to shrink Herb Edelman who dubs him "the worst case I've ever seen" on his first visit.

The patient-doctor set-up allows Lewis to recall past failures, so the film is simply a series of vignettes. It also winds up being a retrospective of past Lewis gags, often without new twists. The little story which exists attempts to put him back on his feet.

As with "Hardly Working," Lewis again plays a guy who can't hold a job. It serves as a one-gag running joke for the film. This might not have been so unpalatable if Lewis were not so insistent at milking the material so dry. Situations go on far beyond their comic potential.

There are nonetheless, as with all Lewis films, a couple of novel jibes. Lewis' satire on cut-rate air fares begins promisingly but runs out of gas about mid-way through the vignette. More successful is his exchange with Zane Busby as an obnoxiously helpful waitress.

Production credits are average and, surprisingly, Lewis attempts few interesting camera set-ups or visual experiments. Most scenes simply shoot Lewis in mid-shot as if he were performing on stage.

Apart from Lewis there's little for anyone else to do. Edelman has the only other role which runs the course of the film. And his task is to play straight man rather unconvincingly. Busby is the only supporting role that really registers.

It would be a genuine surprise if "Smorgasbord" repeated the North American boxoffice of "Hardly Working." There is a genuine Lewis audience still, but it is certain to tire of this rehash. He even gets out a closing dig at current pic fare which predicts "Smorgasbord's" failure and audience's preference toward fantasy and horror films. It appears he's been looking into an accurate crystal ball. —Klad.

Balles Perdues
(Stray Bullets)
(FRENCH-COLOR)

Paris, May 30.

Films Galatee release of a La Cecilia/-Ombre et Lumiere/Transcontinental Films/Cinevog/Gaumont coproduction. Produced by Martine Marignac. Features entire cast. Directed by Jean-Louis Comolli. Screenplay, Comolli and Clarence Weff, based on Weff's novel, "Mince de Pince;" camera (color), William Lubtchansky; art director, Emmanuel de Chauvigny; costumes, Marianne Di Vettimo; editors, Catherine Roitevin, Elisabeth Moulinier; sound, Alix Comte; music, Michel Portal; additional music, Louis Dandrel. Reviewed at the Gaumont Ambassade theatre, Paris, May 3, 1983. Running time: 91 MINS.
Maryvonne .... Andrea Ferreol
Vera .... Maria Schneider
Sam Witchner .... Serge Valletti
Madam Teufminn .... Capucine
Mr. Teufminn .... Charles Millot
Eric .... Andre Dupon
Natacha .... Micky Sebastien
Ludovic .... Alexandre Arbatt
Johnny .... Stephan Meldegg

"Balles Perdues" is yet one more detective spoof, directed by an unlikely helmer, Jean-Louis Comolli, a former editor of the Cahiers du Cinema revue who turned to filmmaking in 1974. His previous theatrical features were a pair of solemn political dramas, "La Cecilia" and "The Red Shadow," the latter about some French Communist agents caught up in the Stalinist purges of the late 1930s.

"Balles Perdues" is based on a lampoon mystery novel by Clarence Weff, who collaborated on the screenplay, and has no other ambition but to amuse. But this tale of an amateur private eye reluctantly thrown into a murder investigation and pursued by the usual clutch of hit men, femmes fatales and mysterious Chinamen has nothing new to offer and is executed with uninspired technical competence. The cast, which includes Andrea Ferreol, Maria Schneider, Serge Valletti and Capucine, manages to inject some moments of brightness, but not enough to lift the material above deja vu parody.

Pic looks good and sounds good: best thing about it is the marvelous jazz score by Michel Portal, who won a Cesar award for his music for Daniel Vigne's "The Return of Martin Guerre." Hopefully Portal will be heard more regularly in cinemas from now on. —Len.

Eureka
(BRITISH-COLOR)

So much gold, so little payoff.

London, May 27.

UIP (UA) Classics in U.S. release, produced by Jeremy Thomas. Directed by Nicolas Roeg. Stars Gene Hackman, Theresa Russell, Rutger Hauer. Screenplay, Paul Mayersberg (based on a novel by Marshall Houts); camera (color), Alex Thomson; music, Stanley Myers; production designer, Michael Seymour; art director, Les Dilley; sound, Paul LeMare, editor, Tony Lawson. Reviewed at Screen on the Hill theatre, London, May 27, '83. BBFC rating: 18 (X) Running time: 129 MINS.
Jack McCann .... Gene Hackman
Tracy .... Theresa Russell
Maillot van Horn .... Rutger Hauer
Helen McCann .... Jane Lapotaire

Perkins .... Ed Lauter
Aurelio .... Mickey Rourke
Mayakofsky .... Joe Pesci
Frieda .... Helen Kallianiotis
Worsley .... Corin Redgrave
Roger .... James Faulkner
Webb .... Tim Scott

Even by his own standards, Nicolas Roeg's "Eureka" is an indulgent melodrama about the anticlimactic life of a greedy gold prospector after he has struck it rich. Pic reeks of pretentious Art, not just visually but also in a strained, confusing and overstretched plot on the theme of (what else?) obsession. MGM-UA won't have an easy time selling it, and neither will UIP in the foreign markets.

Gene Hackman performs with predictable credit as the man whose jackpot fortune only leaves him bored, surly and suspicious of being ripped off by one and all, family included.

Since Paul Mayersberg's script offers precious few clues as to why so rich a man should live out his remaining years in splendid misery, including his very own tropical island, one can only assume it was genetic destiny, or some such Anyway, with striking lack of self-confidence, the film concludes with a gratuitous piece of voice-overed philosophy to the effect that the excitement comes from the quest rather than the achievement. If an audience has to be so told, what's the point of the preceding two hours-plus of tortured, convoluted narrative?

Intended or not as an Orson Welles homage, "Eureka" is rife with "Citizen Kane" echoes — obsessed characters, moody mansion, air of gloom and doom, even a "rosebud" equivalent in the form of a strange white stone. Not to mention some Welles-angled camera shots.

To all of which Roeg has added his own touches — a fetish for the Canadian moon, camera zooms, cycloramic landscape shots, ejaculating gold fields (a phantasmic effect that has to be seen), steamy Caribbean orgy, etc. Every thought, every scene is resonant with Significance in this Roeg elephant film.

It's when the narrative, with its literary airs, gets down to people and all that anguish that the film really moves into numbing stride. Theresa Russell, who had a rough emotional time of it in Roeg's "Bad Timing," isn't much happier as the girl-woman daughter of a rich man who rebelliously marries a putative gigolo, Rutger Hauer, whom paranoid Papa psychs as a fortune hunter. Mother Jane Lapotaire, meanwhile, driven to the sauce by an uncaring husband, drifts through life in the tropics with sulky sarcasm.

Violent menace permeates pic, radiated by Joe Pesci as a Yiddish-speaking "entrepreneur" who, foiled in his bid to buy a piece of Hackman's island in order to establish a casino, finally sends the hoods after Hackman, leading up to a gruesome pre-finale.

Most of the film's characters are basically familiar to the point of corny, and with most it's just hard to give a damn. It isn't easy, either, to admire such lines as "gold smells stronger than a woman" and similar affectations. That line notwithstanding, the one thing "Eureka" doesn't do is really explore the obsession with which it's obsessed.

Despite the odds, the performances are all very good, even that of Helen Kallianiotis in the ridiculous part of a gold rush landlady-cum-soothsayer.

Alex Thomson's lensing and the mixture of orchestral and solo piano music by Stanley Myers are both suitably Roeg-ish. —Pit.

Fuori Dal Giorno
(Outside the Day)
(ITALIAN-COLOR-16m)

Ischia, May 28.
Produced by Paolo Bologna for Mebo Produzione. Stars Leonardo Treviglio. Written, directed and edited by Paolo Bologna. Camera (Color-16m), Roberto Meddi; music, Maurizio Giammarco. Reviewed at Cinema delle Vittorie, Forio, May 28, 1983. Running time: 81 MINS.
Cast: Leonardo Treviglio, Ennio Fantastichini, Angelica Ippolito, Andrea Franchetti, Vinicio Diamanti, Francesco Comegna.

The most hard-won debut at Ischia's recent young cinema competition was "Outside the Day," scripted, shot, edited and financed by Paolo Bologna, 27, over a two-year period. Result is a quality, post-modern film noir reminiscent of the New York school of New Wave indie filmmaking. The picture would be a respectable addition to any independent cinema festival, and heralds an upcoming talent with the courage to be experimental in a market like the Italian one, geared to the numbingly familiar.

A disconnected day in the life of homeless, alienated young filmmaker Leo (Leonardo Treviglio) is the thread of the film, shot in 16m largely at night with a fine sensibility for natural lighting and the photogenic quality of the modern, run-down quarters of the city (an unrecognizable Rome, without a single monument or familiar building). Leo finances his cinema habit with drug dealing and, by the end of the day, is on the lam

"Day's" disciplined dialog is kept to an absolute minimum. Treviglio, tall, gaunt, with a mocking expression on his face, breathes life into the central character, quite an achievement in a difficult part. Though Leo is not a sympathetic

character (he is shown pushing cocaine, having a tantrum with his film cutter, sardonically mocking a harmless bookseller), he has a true anti-hero's perverse fascination that holds the attention.

Bologna creates a recurrent juxtaposition between the film Leo is editing on the moviola — a chase sequence in which a character played by Leo is being pursued by a gunman — and the larger film in which Treviglio is playing the part of a character on the run. By privileging transition shots — characters travelling in taxis and subway cars, walking down the street, through empty halls, taking elevators — the director creates a disjointed contemporary environment of seemingly aimless perpetual movement, showing the city at its most everyday level, peopled with strange figures we never get more than a fleeting glimpse at.

Besides Roberto Meddi's fine lensing, Maurizio Giammarco's soundtrack shows rare attention to counterposing music and image, and boasts some notable jazz cuts.
—Yung.

L'Homme Blesse
(The Wounded Man)
(FRENCH-COLOR)

Paris, May 26.
Gaumont release of a Partner's Production/Renn Productions/Ollane Productions/Azor Films/FR3 coproduction. Produced by Ariel Zeitoun, Marie-Laure Reyre and Claude Berri. Features entire cast. Directed by Patrice Chereau. Screenplay, Chereau and Herve Guibert; camera (Eastmancolor), Renato Berta; art director, Richard Peduzzi; sound, Michel Vionnet; costumes, Caroline de Vivaise; makeup, Joel Lavau; production manager, Armand Barbault. Reviewed at the Gaumont Ambassade theatre, Paris, May 25, 1983. Running time: 109 MINS.
Henri .... Jean-Hughes Anglade
Jean .... Vittorio Mezzogiorno
Bosmans .... Roland Bertin
Elizabeth .... Lisa Kreuzer
Father .... Armin Mueller Stahl
Mother .... Annik Alane
Client .... Claude Berri
Crying Man .... Gerarde Desarthe

Patrice Chereau, the dynamic young stage and opera director who's now running one of the country's most important drama centres at Nanterre, has another go at filmmaking with "L'Homme Blesse" which repped France officially at Cannes last month. After "The Flesh of the Orchid" (1974), an adaptation of a James Hadley Chase thriller, and "Judith Therpauve" (1978), a drama about the death of a once prestigious newspaper, starring Simone Signoret, Chereau has turned to more urgently personal material in this lurid tale of a homosexual passion that ends in murder.

Chereau's script, written with journalist Herve Guibert, is about an idle young man of modest background (Jean-Hughes Anglade) who's sucked into the netherworld

of a large provincial train station where he becomes romantically obsessed with a brutishly mysterious older man (the Italian actor Vittorio Mezzogiorno, here dubbed by Gerard Depardieu). Himself pursued by another station habitue, a voyeuristic homosexual doctor (Roland Bertin), the young man awkwardly tries to win the attentions of his strange idol, who remains aloof, yet tantalizing, and even submits to sexual hustling (his first and only client is played by producer-director Claude Berri, who coproduced the film). Anglade at last consummates his passion when he makes love to a drugged and helpless Mezzogiorno, and then climaxes the moment by strangling him to death.

One cannot help but think of Jean Genet, though Chereau's desperate romanticism is far from the great writer's homophile mysticism. Yet there is an attempt to create a poetic universe, stressed by the ellipses of the script, the ambiguity of the characters, and encapsuled in Renata Berta's darkly beautiful color photography.

But the film too often remains anchored to a certain gutter naturalism and accepted cliches of homosexual loneliness and despair (as epitomized in Bertin's personage). Chereau's characters are irritating puppets enacting a morbid roundelay of frustrated courtships and violent encounters. Chereau confirms that he has a sense of cinematic style, but he continues to direct with an icy hand that makes empathy difficult (coldness of manner is an abiding affliction of Chereau's stage work as well, as is a complete lack of humor).

Anglade, a 28-year-old legit player, makes a sensitive screen debut as the emotionally rootless teenager (he had a bit part in Pierre Lary's "L'Indiscretion" last year), Mezzogiorno provides the right tone of brutal ambiguity as his virile hero, and Bertin skillfully salvages his role from banality. German actress Lisa Kreuzer is wasted in a pointless and poorly written part as Mezzogiorno's passive girl friend.

Film will obviously demand special handling, though it has been doing fairly well in its local commercial bow. Some will certainly be shocked by the subject matter, though the action's several sexual encounters, despite flashes of frontal nudity, have nothing hardcore about them. —Len.

La Casa Del Tappetto Giallo
(House of the Yellow Carpet)
(ITALIAN-COLOR)

Ischia, May 28.
A Gaumont release, produced by Filiberto Bandini for R.P.A. Productions with RAI-TV Channel 2. Stars Beatrice Romand, Erland Josephson. Directed by

Carlo Lizzani. Screenplay, Lucio Battistrada, Filiberto Bandini; camera (Eastmancolor), Giuliano Giustini; editor, Angela Cipriani; art director, Elena Ricci Poccetto; music, Stelvio Cipriani. Reviewed at Cinema delle Vittorie, Rome, May 27, 1983. Running time: 134 MINS.
Franca .... Beatrice Romand
The stranger .... Erland Josephson
Antonio .... Vittorio Mezzogiorno
The woman .... Milena Vukotic

Returning behind the camera after his four-year stint as director of the Venice Film Festival, Carlo Lizzani steps off with a thriller stuffed with all the classic elements and twists of the genre. Capable lensing and a sterling if eclectic cast of international thesps should boost b.o. appeal. Another offshore plus is pic's determined adherence to the mystery genre, which makes it so unspecific it hardly seems like an Italian film. Though lacking cleverness, depth and believability, pic should have good prospects if marketed for general audiences.

Golden rug of the title is the starting point for a young housewife's tale of horror. A mysterious stranger (Erland Josephson) gets into the house on the pretext of buying the carpet, but soon reveals his real intention is to terrorize and murder the spunky heroine. Beatrice Romand, the newcomer who copped the Best Actress award at Venice last year for "Le Beau Mariage," turns out a high-pitched performance as Franca (dubbed into Italian with distracting disattention to lip-synch) that tends to veer above the lines. There is a fascination, however, in her long girl-and-murderer duet with Josephson, a restrained and inventive actor, however oft-seen the various psychological tortures

Franca finally turns the tables and kills her jailer with his own knife. Soon a mysterious woman (Milena Vukotic) rings the bell, claiming to be the wife of the deceased, who was merely a wacky out-of-work actor into "house theatre." Next we find (little to our surprise) that the actor-murderer isn't really dead at all and is in cahoots with Franca's mysteriously missing husband Antonio (Vittorio Mezzogiorno). The explanation is a little more original than one might suppose, but no more plausible. Pic concludes with an odd piece of black humor.

Entire story takes place in the claustrophobic environs of the couple's modern apartment, whose location "could be any modern metropolis." Far from a limitation, Lizzani's and cameraman Giuliano Giustini's talent at framing and lensing in subdued light makes the closeness of the film a visual pleasure.

Though Vukotic and Mezzogiorno are fine actors, the small ensemble's acting lacks a unified direction that would allow the audience to build up some identification and sympathy with the characters. The two strangers are a humorous pair of oddballs, Romand plays her part as realistically as possible, Mezzogiorno has a role so banal he never comes off as anything but a plot necessity with an embarrasingly intense face. Struggling with an overloaded story that recalls a mesh of many other chillers, pic never finds a tone of its own or gets a handle on its multiple plot reversals and story strands.

Perhaps the best way to view "Yellow Carpet" is as a collection of entertaining chills that make for a nice evening out. —*Yung.*

Twilight Zone The Movie
(COLOR)

Mixed blessings, but packs a wallop.

Hollywood, June 14.

A Warner Bros. release. Produced by Steven Spielberg, John Landis. Executive producer, Frank Marshall. "The Twilight Zone" created by Rod Serling. Music, Jerry Goldsmith; production design, James D. Bissell. Prologue: directed, written by Landis; camera (Technicolor), Steve Larner; editor, Malcolm Campbell; associate producer, George Folsey Jr. Segment 1: directed, written by Landis; camera, Larner; editor, Campbell; associate producer, Folsey; art direction, Richard Sawyer; set decoration, Barbara Paul Krieger; costume design, Deborah Nadoolman; special effects, Paul Stewart; sound, Bill Kaplan; assistant director, Elie Cohn. Segment 2: directed by Spielberg, written by George Clayton Johnson, Richard Matheson, Josh Rogan, from a story by Johnson; camera, Allen Daviau; editor, Michael Kahn; associate producer, Kathleen Kennedy; set design, William J. Teegarden; set decoration, Jackie Carr; sound, Tommy Causey; special effects supervision, Mike Wood; assistant director, Pat Kehoe. Segment 3: directed by Joe Dante, written by Matheson, from a story by Jerome Bixby; camera, John Hora; editor, Tina Hirsch; associate producer, Michael Finnell; set design, Teegarden; set decoration, Carr; sound, Causey; special makeup effects design and creation, Rob Bottin; special effects supervision, Wood; cartoon supervision, Sally Cruikshank; assistant director, Kehoe; Segment 4: directed by George Miller, written by Matheson from his story; camera, Daviau; editor, Howard Smith; associate producer, Jon Davison; art direction, James H. Spencer; set design, Teegarden; set decoration, Carr; sound, Causey; special makeup effects creation, Craig Reardon, Michael McCracken; special effects supervision, Wood; monster conceptual design, Ed Verreaux; visual effects, Peter Kuran, Industrial Light & Magic, David Allen; assistant director, Kehoe. Reviewed at the Samuel Goldwyn Theatre, Beverly Hills, May 25, 1983. (MPAA Rating: PG). Running time: 102 MINS.

Prologue

Passenger	Dan Aykroyd
Driver	Albert Brooks

Segment 1

Bill	Vic Morrow
Larry	Doug McGrath
Ray	Charles Hallahan
German Officers	Remus Peets, Kai Wulff

Segment 2

Mr. Bloom	Scatman Crothers
Mr. Conroy	Bill Quinn
Mr. Weinstein	Martin Garner
Mrs. Weinstein	Selma Diamond
Mrs. Dempsey	Helen Shaw
Mr. Agee	Murray Matheson
Mr. Mute	Peter Brocco
Miss Cox	Priscilla Pointer
Young Mrs. Weinstein	Tanya Fenmore
Young Mr. Agee	Evan Richards
Young Mrs. Dempsey	Laura Mooney
Young Mr. Mute	Christopher Eisenmann
Mr. Grey Panther	Richard Swingler
Mr. Conroy's Son	Alan Haufrect
Daughter-In-Law	Cheryl Secher
Nurse No 2	Elsa Raven

Segment 3

Helen Foley	Kathleen Quinlan
Anthony	Jeremy Licht
Uncle Walt	Kevin McCarthy
Mother	Patricia Barry
Father	William Schallert
Ethel	Nancy Cartwright
Walter Paisley	Dick Hiller
Sara	Cherie Currie
Tim	Bill Mumy
Charlie	Jeffrey Bannister

Segment 4

Valentine	John Lithgow
Sr. Stewardess	Abbe Lane
Jr. Stewardess	Donna Dixon
Co-Pilot	John Dennis Johnston
Creature	Larry Cedar
Sky Marshal	Charles Knapp
Little Girl	Christina Nigra
Mother	Lonna Schwab
Old Woman	Margaret Wheeler
Old Man	Eduard Franz
Young Girl	Margaret Fitzgerald
Young Man	Jeffrey Wiesman
Mechanic No. 1	Jeffrey Lambert
Mechanic No. 2	Frank Toth

"Twilight Zone — The Movie" plays much like a traditional vaudeville card, what with its tantalizing teaser opening followed by three sketches of increasing quality, all building up to a socko headline act. Feature film spinoff from the late Rod Serling's perennially-popular tv series of 20 years ago possesses plenty of built-in want-to-see via title and filming talents involved, but will still have to prove that the segmented, omnibus style encompassing separate stories and casts is not a boxoffice limitation for American audiences, as it normally has been in the past. Biz will assuredly be hefty, although format will probably impose ceiling on this funhouse.

This is also the film, of course, which received, and continues to receive much unwanted publicity in connection with the deaths of actor Vic Morrow and two Vietnamese child thesps. Some trade talk in the intervening months has centered on whether or not the fatal helicopter accident would cast a pall over the entire project and, indeed, there was considerable internal discussion over the possibility of jettisoning the entire John Landis episode because of it. As has been reported, sequence involving the chopper and kids is nowhere to be seen, and trade awareness of the tragedy and its aftermath may foster a distorted impression of its looming importance to the public at large.

Pic consists of prolog by Landis as well as vignettes, none running any longer than original tv episodes, by Landis, Steven Spielberg, Joe Dante and George Miller, all of whom have previously evinced an affinity for the fantasy, sci-fi and/or horror genres. Ironically, the lesser known of the quartet, Dante and Miller, manage to shine the brightest in this context, a fact which will considerably raise their stock in the industry.

Landis gets things off to a wonderful start with a comic prolog starring Dan Aykroyd and Albert Brooks. Driving down a deserted highway, they engagingly shoot the breeze, sing some tunes and discuss, with no self-consciousness whatever, favorite "Twilight Zone" episodes before Aykroyd shows Brooks something "really scary." Placing entire "Twilight Zone" phenomenon in cultural context, sequence ideally sets up the feature as a whole.

Landis' principal episode, however, is a downbeat, one-dimensional fable about racial and religious intolerance. An embittered, middleaged man who has just been passed over for a job promotion, Morrow sports a torrent of racial epithets aimed at Jews, Blacks and Orientals while drinking with buddies at a bar. Upon exiting, he finds himself in Nazi-occupied Paris as a suspected Jew on the run from the Gestapo. After a prolonged chase and brush with death, he is then transported to the American South, where the Ku Klux Klan is about to lynch him. In short order, he is plopped down in Vietnam, where both the Yanks and the Viet Cong threaten his existence. Back in Paris, he is rounded up with a crowd of Jews for shipment to a concentration camp.

Intent is noble and dramatic situations faced by Morrow are intense, but having made its only point early on, sequence misses the sort of catharsis which was reportedly part of the story to begin with, wherein the bigoted man would experience a change of heart. Desperately sweaty throughout, Morrow strongly conveys the insecurity lying shallow beneath the character's aggressive hatefulness, but dramatic payoff is thin.

This is the only sequence in the film not derived from an actual tv episode, although it does bear a thematic resemblance to a 1961 installment titled "A Quality Of Mercy," in which Dean Stockwell portrayed a marauding American lieutenant in the Philippines during World War II who is changed into a besieged Japanese soldier on Corregidor.

Based on the episode originally called "Kick The Can" (none of the segments are given titles in the feature), Spielberg's entry is sweetly sentimental and quite the most down-to-earth of all the stories.

In a retirement home filled with oldsters living in the past, spry Scatman Crothers encourages various residents to think young and, in organizing a game of kick the can, actually transforms them into their childhood selves again.

Filmette is filled with delightful characterizations by both the old and young performers, and is entirely recognizable as a Spielberg work via the sense of awe and wonder expressed by the characters as they recapture a childhood p.o.v. of the world. But despite fact that no theme could be closer to the director's heart, sequence has the air of pencil sketch rather than a fully-painted picture, and impact is no more than lightly charming. Jerry Goldsmith, who provides strong and varied music for the entire film, has come up with scoring for Spielberg which sounds for all the world like that of John Williams, and emotionally it peaks far too soon in the tale.

Most bizarre contribution comes from Joe Dante, who wrings considerable changes on a story first called "It's A Good Life." Outsider Kathleen Quinlan enters the Twilight Zone courtesy of little Jeremy Licht, who lords it over a Looney-Tune household by virtue of his power to will anything into existence except happiness.

Afraid of what the young progeny might unleash upon them, Licht's family grovels before him in exaggerrated 1950s tv style, and house itself is a masterpiece of expressionistic art direction in the manner of "The Cabinet Of Dr. Caligari."

Classic cartoons are forever playing on tv in the background, and payoff comes when he brings some of the more monstrous cartoon characters to life in the living room. It's a unique and startling sequence, one which also contains the most sustained explosion of special effects in the entire film.

For the record, Billy Mumy, who played the boy on tv, can be seen in a preliminary roadside diner scene, as can Dick Miller in a reprise of his Walter Paisley characterization.

But, wisely, the best has been saved for last. George Miller's reworking of "Nightmare At 20,000 Feet," about a man who sees a gremlin tearing up an engine wing of an airplane, is electrifying from beginning to end. This Australian and former medic proved with "Mad Max" and "The Road Warrior" that he is the most talented action director to have come down the pike in years, and now he has created another amazing work in his first shot in Hollywood.

Dropping the character of the man's wife, Miller zeroes right in on the fully justifiable paranoia of John Lithgow, who grows increasingly crazed as he, and only he among the passengers and crew, catches glimpses of the monster wreaking havoc on the aircraft as it flies through a storm.

Rarely has the sense of movement in flight been so strongly evoked, and lensing and editing superbly contribute to rapidly building tension throughout the sequence, which passes like the wind. Furthermore, Lithgow brilliantly delineates the deteriorating mental state of a man into whom all can project their own fear of flying.

Only flaw lies in the realm of nitpicking — exterior of the plane is an old Boeing 707, while interior is of the widebody variety.

Burgess Meredith, who acted in more than one "Twilight Zone" episode, has provided some introductory remarks, while the familiar recording of Serling is laid in at conclusion.

Overall, pic is a mixed bag of mostly moderate pleasures which has been expertly, and not too lavishly, produced.

For the record, original "Kick The Can" episode was written by George Clayton Thomas and directed by Lamont Johnson. "It's A Good Life" was penned by Serling from a Jerome Bixby short story, and was directed by James Shelton. "Nightmare at 20,000 feet," adapted from his own story by Richard Matheson, who has contributed heavily to the feature, was directed by Richard Donner.

—Cart.

The First Time
(COLOR)

Pleasant rites-of-passage comedy.

A New Line Cinema release and production of a Goldmine Co. film. Produced by Sam Irvin. Executive producers, Robert Shaye, Lawrence Loventhal. Directed by Charlie Loventhal. Stars Tim Choate, Krista Errickson. Screenplay, Charlie Loventhal, Susan Weiser-Finley, William Franklin Finley; camera (TVC color), Steve Fierberg; editor, Stanley Vogel; music, Lanny Meyers; sound, Anna de Lanzo; art direction, Tom Surgal; creative consultant, Brian De Palma; associate producer, Sara Risher. Reviewed at Magno Preview 9 screening room, N.Y., June 8, 1983. (MPAA Rating: R). Running time: 95 MINS.
Charlie .... Tim Choate
Dana .... Krista Errickson
Prof. Rand .... Marshall Efron
Wendy .... Wendy Fulton
Ron .... Raymond Patterson
Prof. Goldfarb .... Wallace Shawn
Eileen .... Wendie Jo Sperber
Glorida .... Cathryn Damon
Also with: Jane Badler, Bradley Bliss, Eva Charney, Bill Randolph, Rex Robbins, Robert Trebor, Larry (Bud) Melman.

"The First Time," lensed in 1980 as "Goldmine," is a mild but entertaining first feature by writer-director Charlie Loventhal and producer Sam Irvin, former assistants to Brian De Palma on his 1979 indie picture, "Home Movies." Dealing fictionally with Loventhal's growing-up adventures while a student at formerly all-girls school Sarah Lawrence, the comedy owes much to De Palma's freewheeling satires made in the 1960s. Pic has already played in the sticks and (following a recent trend) had cable-tv exposure prior to its Gotham theatrical debut.

Charlie (Tim Choate) is an odd-man-out at college: unable to score with the pretty (but believably so) girls there while his black roommate Ronald (Raymond Patterson) shows off and gives him tips. In his film class, presided over by eccentric, pretentious Prof. Goldfarb (Wallace Shawn), he wants to make comedies while his classmates are strictly into experimental, avant-garde exercises.

While pursing an unattainable dream girl Dana (Krista Errickson), Charlie links up with another lonely soul Wendy (Wendy Ful-

ton), and ultimately loses his virginity with the inevitable older woman Karen (Jane Badler) in an unsuccessful subplot of rather sinister implications.

Filmmaker Loventhal achieves a nice balance of character humor and painful "outsider" undertones in the picture, which is somewhat out of step with the raunchy youth hi-jinks films currently in vogue. Film-within-a-film motif of the hero's making a James Bond spoof is an effective device.

Top-notch cast delivers solidly. Choate is very sympathetic in the lead role, matched by the sex appeal of Errickson, naturalism of Fulton and comedy sex-bomb Wendie Jo Sperber. Shawn's pretentious film prof and Marshall Efron's know-it-all psych prof are delightful revuestyle turns. Tech Credits are good, with Steve Fierberg's cheery, colorful 16m lensing blowing up well to 35m. —Lor.

La Palombiere
(The Bird Watch)
(FRENCH-COLOR)

Paris, May 30.
Gaumont release of a Partner's Production/FR3 coproduction. Produced by Ariel Zeitoun and Claude Gildas. Features Jean-Claude Bourbault and Christiane Millet. Directed by Jean-Pierre Denis. Screenplay, Jean-Pierre Denis and Denis Gheerbrant; camera (Eastmancolor), Denis Gheerbrant; editor, Anne Baudry; sound, Daniel Ollivier; art director, Pierre Saiet; music, Jean Musy; lyrics, Laurence Matalon; reviewed at the Club 13 screening room, Paris, May 30. Running time: 90 MINS.
Paul .... Jean-Claude Bourbault
Claire .... Christiane Millet
The rival .... Daniel Jegou
Sylvette .... Nadine Raynaud
The father .... Georges Vaur

Jean-Pierre Denis, 37, made a noted debut in 1980 with his first feature, "Histoire d'Adrien," a regional drama which had the particularity of having been made in a dialect (Occitan). It was shown in the International Critics Week at the Cannes fest that year and won the Camera d'Or.

Denis returned to Cannes last month with his new film, "La Palombiere," which was in the Perspectives on French Cinema program. Though set in the same region of France (the Dordogne, in the southwest) as "Histoire d'Adrien," this one was cast with two Parisian legit actors and was made in French. It doesn't fulfill the promise of Denis' debut.

Denis' script (written in collaboration with Denis Gheerbrant, who lensed as well) is an obvious tale about a brief but passionate fling between a municipal workman in a rural township (Jean-Claude Bourbault) and an attractive substitute teacher assigned there for a three-month stint.

He is immediately taken with [her] but is too timid and put off by [her] politely distant manner. When [he] finally confesses his passion she first rejects him, but later su[r]renders to him. But they b[oth] realize their relationship is a pas[s]ing one.

Denis is good at portrayi[ng] provincial life and the beauties [of] the countryside, but his handling [of] the central human rapport is d[ull] and unconvincing. He especia[lly] fails in the film's most importa[nt] scene when the laborer and t[he] teacher finally make love in t[he] tree-top cabin (the "palombiere" [of] the title) where the former lur[es] passing flocks of migratory pi[g]eons and bags them with his rif[le.] Neither the direction, the ph[o]tography nor the actors succeed [in] lifting the sequence out of the co[m]monplace.

Millet is okay as the teacher, su[b]tly drawn into an affair she does[n't] want by the sensuousness of h[er] surroundings. Bourbault is bland [as] the diffident yokel, right physically, but without a regional a[c]cent, which jars the film's na[t]uralistic texture. —Len.

Camera d'Afrique:
20 Years of African Cinema
(FRENCH-TUNISIAN-DOCU-B&W/COLOR-16m)

Cannes, May 18.
A Ferid Boughedir production, with [the] collaboration of the French Ministry [of] Cooperation, the French Ministry of Ext[er]ior Relations and the SATPEC (Tunisi[a]). Written, produced and directed by Fe[rid] Boughedir. Camera (Eastmancolor[)], Sekou Ouedraogo, Charly Meunier; sou[nd], Abdelkader Alouani, Alain Garnier; edit[or,] Andree Davanture, assisted by Julia[?] Sanchez; music, folk music of Niger, Ma[li,] Burundi and Upper Volta. Reviewed at [the] Cannes Film Festival ("A Certain R[e]gard" section), May 13, 1983. Runni[ng] time: 95 MINS.
With: Med Hondo, Ousmane Sember[e,] Dikongue Pipa, Safi Faye, Oumar [?] Ganda, Ola Balogun, Souleymane Ciss[e,] Gaston Kabore.

Documentaries about the cinem[a] should both inform and give [the] average viewer the desire to see t[he] films evoked. "Camera d'Af[ri]que," which traces the growth [of] film expression in several Bla[ck] African nations, gets low marks [in] both categories.

The disappointment is all t[he] greater because the director, Fer[id] Boughedir, seemed the man for t[he] job. A former assistant director [to] helmers like Alain Robbe-Grill[et] and Fernando Arrabal, he is a Tun[i]sian critic and filmmaker with [a] doctorate from the Sorbonn[e] where he did a dissertation on Bla[ck] African and Arab cinemas. He h[as] also directed several festivals, no[t]ably the Panafrican fest of Carth[ag]age, a leading showcase for Thi[rd] World cinema.

But his film leaves one dissatisfied. The commentary is copious but unenlightening, and the scattered interview segments add little. The essence of the film is of course the film clips — from 18 titles which are supposed to epitomize the growth of African cinematic expression — but all one can say is that these films, whatever their overall quality and power may be, do not lend themselves to effective anthologizing.

Pic is available in French and English versions. Its best chances seem fest, tv and non-theatrical presentations. —Len.

L'Homme au Chapeau de Soie
(The Man in the Top Hat)
(FRENCH-COMPILATION-B&W/COLOR)

Cannes, May 14.
A Films Max Linder production. Produced, written and directed by Maud Londer. Editors, Suzanne Baron, Pierre Gillette. Music, Jean-Marie Senia; orchestral direction, Carlo Savina; musical arrangements, Theirry Durbet. Reviewed at the Cannes Film Fest (homage screening), May 13, 1983. Running time: 96 MINS.
With: Max Linder.

Maud Linder carries on the essential task of rehabilitating her father, the great pioneer film comic Max Linder. "The Man In the Top Hat" comes 20 years after her first compilation work, "In Company of Max Linder," a superb montage of the comic's three American features of the 1920's, notably "The Three-Must-Get-Theres," a hilarious parody of Alexandre Dumas' "The Three Musketeers" and the Douglas Fairbanks screen version.

This new film is less conventional in conception and is a fine addition to the regrettably small number of films about the cinema's formative years. What Maud Linder has done is use clips from her father's films — 42 of the more than 80 titles recovered that do contributed to the montage — to present not only a biography of the comedian, but also a picture of the epoch that bred him and feted him as the first international motion picture star.

This is possible because in the more than 500 films that Linder wrote, directed and starred in between 1905 and 1925, the comedian proposed a dandyish comic personage close to his own elegant private image and often used personal experiences for the subjects of his comedies. Linder's early stage career, for example, later inspired a particularly funny short in which he tries to dignify a stage tragedy but is defeated by a recalcitrant wig.

In addition to recreating past personal moments in a humorous vein, Linder also mixed fiction and documentary realism in an extra-ordinary series of films made during an international tour, during which he debuted as a toreador in a Madrid arena with a real bull — and recorded it all on film.

Maud Linder has assembled these astonishing documents with skill and sensitivity, herself providing the commentary with touching discretion. Though these images date back over 70 years, they still look splendid, thanks not only to Linder's real cinematic talents, but also to the care and expertise with which his daughter has restored them, beautifully tinted and toned and presented with an excellent musical score by Jean-Marie Senia.

This makes a perfect companion piece to the first Linder compilation and should help stir interest in discovering Linder's comedies in their full versions. Maud Linder is currently hunting funds to continue her work and put Linder's comedies back into circulation, notably through television. Her recently completed biography of her dad is scheduled to be published here later this year, commemorating the centenary of the comedian's birth.
—Len.

Careful, He Might Hear You
(AUSTRALIAN-COLOR)

Sydney, June 5.
A Syme International Production, in association with the New South Wales Film Corporation. Produced by Jill Robb. Directed by Carl Schultz. Features entire cast. Screenplay, Michael Jenkins (from novel by Summer Locke Elliott); camera (Eastmancolor, Panavision), John Seale; production design, John Stoddart; music, Ray Cook; sound recording, Syd Butterworth; editor, Richard Francis Bruce. Reviewed at Film Australia Theatrette, Lindfield, Sydney, May 27, 1983. Running time: 116 MINS.
Vanessa Scott .... Wendy Hughes
Lila Baines .... Robyn Nevin
P.S. (William
Scott Marriott) ...... Nicholas Gledhill
Logan .... John Hargreaves
Vere .... Geraldine Turner
Agnes ....,........ Isabelle Anderson
George Baines .... Peter Whitford
Ettie .... Colleen Clifford
Diana .... Julie Nihill

A top quality production about the struggle between two sisters for custody of an eight-year-old boy, their nephew, "Careful, He Might Hear You" is a completely involving emotional experience. Although the theme may sound similar to that of "Kramer vs. Kramer," the approach of the film is entirely different.

Indeed, the Summer Locke Elliott novel on which Michael Jenkins' excellent screenplay is based was, for many years, a project for Joshua Logan with, at one point, Elizabeth Taylor announced for the role of Vanessa Scott, the lonely, frigid spinster who causes all the trouble, and who is played, commandingly, here by Wendy Hughes.

Story is set in the Depression in Sydney. The boy, nicknamed "P.S." by everyone, is homeless after the death of his mother and the departure of his feckless father, Logan, for the goldfields. He's taken in by a loving but impoverished aunt and uncle (Robyn Nevin and Peter Whitford), working-class people struggling to make ends meet, but genuinely caring for the boy.

Their lives are disrupted, however, by the arrival of Vanessa, another sister, but from the moneyed side of the family, who has just returned from a long visit to England. It is learned that Vanessa was jealous of her dead sister and had loved Logan, the boy's father, herself; now she wants custody of the child. Climax of the film comes with a court case to decide the boy's future, followed by an unexpected tragedy.

This is the third feature film directed by Carl Schultz, and his best. He had already indicated last year in the underrated "Goodbye Paradise" that he was a skillful and imaginative filmmaker, and this new film amply confirms that promise. Visually, the film is a treat with John Seale's camerawork outstanding and the production design of John Stoddart (contrasting the fabulously wealthy waterside house of Vanessa with the shabby but warm and cozy home of Lila and George) is also worthy of kudos. Ray Cook provides a lush music score in the grand tradition, if a bit rich by today's standards.

As for the performances, they're impeccable. Hughes, one of Australia's best actresses, looks fabulous and gives a well-rounded, bitchy-but-insecure, interpretation of Vanessa. Robyn Nevin and Peter Whitford are perfectly contrasted as the boy's original foster parents. John Hargreaves, as Logan, the boy's weak father, has a tiny role but makes an enormous impression in it; this is his most memorable film role to date. All this talent might have gone to naught without the perfect casting of the boy playing "P.S.;" young Nicholas Gledhill (son of actor Arthur Dignam) is a real find and gives a relaxed and natural performance.

This is the film the Australian film industry needed right now, a reaffirmation that a wholly indigenous production can be made without compromises towards international distribution. Because it is a fine film, "Careful, He Might Hear You" should do smash business locally and find profitable overseas sales into the bargain. It should also be heard from at festivals. —Strat.

Chicken Ranch
(BRITISH-U.S.-DOCU-COLOR-16m)

A First Run Features release of a Central Independent Television (G.B.) production, made in association with Churchill Films; partial funding by the National Endowment for the Arts. Produced by Nick Broomfield. Directed by Broomfield and Sandi Sissel. Camera (color, 16m), Sissel; editor, Julian Ware; assistant editor, Ezra Nathan; assistant camera, Christine Burrill; sound, Broomfield; dubbing mixer, Colin Martin. Reviewed at Film Forum 1 theatre, N.Y., June 3, 1983. (No MPAA Rating). Running time: 78 MINS.

Filmed last year at a Nevada brothel, "Chicken Ranch" is a tedious, ill-conceived cinema verite exercise made to fill time on British tv and, as is increasingly the case with G.B. tube product of late, acquired for theatrical distribution in the U.S. This schlock-doc consists mainly of talking-heads footage of inarticulate prostitutes aimed at curiosity-seekers interested in taking a peek inside a legalized whorehouse and snickering at the lowlife people on display.

Novelty value of directors Nick Broomfield (who did a nice job last time out with Joan Churchill on doc "Soldier Girls") and Sandi Sissel's project is nil, since the exact same territory was assayed in the mid-1970s in Robert Guralnick's "Mustang: The House That Joe Built," filmed at a more famous Nevada brothel which is briefly alluded to by one of the prosties here. Major difference between the two docs is that Guralnick included nudity, while Broomfield and Sissel's chaste approach makes the goings-on behind closed doors as cryptic as can be.

Slackly edited, "Ranch" makes the pretense of an "invisible camera," observing the prostitutes coming out for the repetitive ritual of selection by geek-esque customers, their chatty personal anecdotes, views of a tough-as-nails manageress barking orders, and comical footage of the pompous owner, whose sentimental Thanksgiving Dinner speech sounds as if it were written by Prof. Irwin Corey.

Since the directors make the basic mistake of assuming the camera's presence will not affect the subjects being observed, it is not surprising that much of the doc seems like an inept home movie, with the women engaging in childish horseplay on their off-hours, and pouring out bitter, man-hating banalities during group discussion sessions. Even the "johns" (customers) come off as false, obviously aware they are being photographed except for a group of Japanese tourists who are here callously treated as figures of fun.

Self-congratulatory finale to this ephemeral opus has the owner ordering the filmmakers to surrender

their film and stop shooting when he catches them lensing footage of one of the prostitutes angrily packing to leave after she has quit/been fired due to a disagreement with the boss over payment for services. He threatens to sue, the film ends, but Broomfield and Sissel have their film for exhibition including the disputed sequence. Big deal.
—Lor.

Nelly's Version
(BRITISH-COLOR)

London, June 3.
Mithras Films production for Channel Four Television, produced by Penny Clark. Directed by Maurice Hatton. Screenplay, Hatton; camera (color), Curtis Clark; editor, Thomas Schwalm; production design, Grant Hicks; art direction, Pete Nutton; music, Michael Nyman. Reviewed at the Channel Four Cinema, June 1, 1983. Running time, 98 MINS.

Nelly	Eileen Atkins
George	Anthony Bate
Miss Wyckham	Barbara Jefford
Inspector Leach	Nicholas Ball
David	Brian Deacon
Susan	Marsha Fitzalan
Carmelita	Stella Maris
Brush Salesman	Hugh Fraser
Vagrant	Hilton McRae
Narrator	Susannah York

Maurice Hatton's second feature since "Praise Marx And Pass The Ammunition" in 1967 is a mystery thriller with many twists. But it's also portentious art that droops with symbolism and lacks the narrative thrust to assure broad appeal, even in art house locations.

Plot concerns an amnesiac woman who seems to recognize none of those who claim her as friend, wife or mother. Nor is she much interested in the detective who suggests that she's linked with various crimes and disasters.

The woman, played by Eileen Atkins for stubborn ordinariness, passes the first half of the film in a hotel retreat, then goes back to her husband and rediscovers the tedium of life as a bourgeois housewife. However, by the time the film reaches its enigmatic finale the audience still hasn't learned much about the problems of living that were the source of the amnesia.

The camerawork emphasizes the woman's sense of alienation, but a heavyhanded musical score only drives home the film's failure to create dramatic interest. What could have been an intriguing feminine portrait ends up as a game for film buffs. —Japa.

The Hound Of The Baskervilles
(BRITISH-COLOR)

Cannes, May 15.
A Mapleton Films production. Produced by Otto Plaschkes. Directed by Douglas Hickox. Executive producer, Sy Weintraub. Features entire cast. Screenplay, Charles Pogue; camera (color), Ronnie Taylor; editor, Malcolm Cooke; production designer, Michael Stringer; cos-

tumes, Julie Harris. Reviewed at the Cannes Film Festival (non-competing), May 15, 1983. Running time, 100 MINS.

Sherlock Holmes	Ian Richardson
Dr. Watson	Donald Churchill
Sir Henry Baskerville	Martin Shaw
Jack Stapleton	Nicholas Clay
Dr. Mortimer	Denholm Elliott
Geoffrey Lyons	Brian Blessed
Inspector Lestrade	Ronald Lacey

There's nothing especially innovative about Douglas Hickox's remake of "The Hound of the Baskervilles," but narrative pace and a skillfully evoked air of mystery ensure good entertainment values. It's altogether a better augury for any future episodes in the "Sherlock Holmes" series planned by Mapleton Films than the previously-reviewed "Sign of the Four."

"Baskervilles" is, of course, one of the more famous of the Conan Doyle tales. It's got social commentary of sorts, a hint of the supernatural, all set in the bogs and mists of rural England.

The master sleuth is seemingly absent throughout, but in fact works undercover in the disguise of a local gypsy. That leaves the often misled Doctor Watson to learn what he can of the local community and put the murderer off his guard in preparation for the final denouement.

Numerous clues and false trails, set against an atmospheric backdrop, will keep audiences not already in the know guessing throughout. The hound itself is intriguingly evoked and there's romantic interest as usual provided by Doctor Watson.

There's a raft of experienced names among the acting credits. All act out the incident-packed story in the spirit of plain good fun. Technical credits are fine. —Japa.

The Herdsman
(CHINESE-COLOR)

Cannes, May 17.
A Shanghai Studios production. Directed by Xie Jin. Screenplay by Li Zhun. Camera (color), Xu Qi. No other credits available. Reviewed at Cannes (Certain Regard), May 17, 1983. Running Time: 90 MINS.
With: Zhu Shimao, Chong Shan, Liu Qiong, Niu Ben.

"The Herdsman" from the People's Republic of China, screening out of competition at Cannes, is a simple tale of father-son tension. While the film shares common problems with recent Chinese productions, its evocation of western society should prove of interest to European and particularly American audiences.

Film opens with the reunion of father and son who have been separated for 30 years. The father abandoned the family and moved to the U.S. where he established a successful business career. The son eventually suffered from guilt by

association and was forced into a reeducation program.

Rather than a clash of wills between men, there is merely a confrontation of alien sensibilities. The son, who has spent much of his life herding horses in a remote northern area, embraces simple virtues. He's highly uncomfortable in Beijing where the reunion occurs, looking like a duck out of water in the modern hotel complete with disco.

Through flashback, one sees the rigors of the son's life and the development of a warm, family situation with a timid, country girl. Also, the son's tremendous devotion to her and their young son.

Typical of Chinese productions, dialog is naive and the tale is both direct and chaste. One constantly senses points are being made for the home audience as a part of the narrative flow, thus creating a dramatic awkwardness for westerners.

The film is unlikely to secure commercial distribution but due to theme and references to America will likely earn festival and specialty screening in the U.S. Technical work is competent but the acting in "The Herdsman" lacks the natural, unpretentious quality seen in better recent Chinese productions. —Klad.

Handgun
(COLOR)

Just misses its target.

London, June 2.
Thorn EMI Film release (WB in U.S.) of a Kestrel production. Produced and directed by Tony Garnett. Features entire cast. Screenplay, Garnett; camera (color), Charles Stewart; editor, William Shapter; music, Mike Post; production design, Lilly Kilvert; costumes, Janet Lawler. Reviewed at the ABC Cinema, Shaftesbury Avenue, London, June 1, 1983. BBFC rating, 18 (X). Running time: 101 MINS.

Kathleen Sullivan	Karen Young
Larry Keller	Clayton Day
Nancy	Suzie Humphreys
Miss Davis	Helena Humann
Chuck	Ben Jones

Like Tony Garnett's only previous helming venture, "Prostitute," "Handgun" takes a subject which is the stuff of exploitation and steers it towards social commentary. The result is an intelligent analysis of the political and sexual values of male society in Texas that may annoy both those in search of slick action and facile social analysis. Consequently, pic won't have an easy time in the marketplace.

Pic is cast in three chapters that follow the maturing of a pretty young girl who goes to the midwest to teach history after a protected Catholic upbringing in Boston. She's just too soft to counter the approaches of a macho attorney who's obsessed with guns and hunting. It's

only when he decides to have his own way with her that she realizes what she's up against.

First section of the film is a relatively straightforward account of the process by which the girl becomes fascinated by the values of the community in which she's placed herself. The stylistics of the British realist school, combining long observational shots with improvised dialog, work well here in conveying the atmosphere of the male-oriented society of Texas.

Karen Young is harp in her depiction of a nervy girl whose eyes are slowly opened. And Clayton Day plays all the subtleties of a decent chap who, nevertheless, has swallowed whole a value system that debases women and seeks to protect its integrity through violent confrontation.

But if some audiences feel let down by the elliptic depiction of the girl's rape at gunpoint, they'll also be mystified by the somewhat fetishistic account of the girl's acquisition of mastery in the art of shooting. There are not many clues as to what is happening in her head, and that makes somewhat flat the scenes in which she hunts down her man.

Behind the mystery, what is happening is the development of a different value system that passes on both the ideals of hippy peace and love, as well as the Catholic idea of forgiveness, and adapts the Wild West principles, to which the gun club adhere, to its own end.

Stylistically, these sections seem unhappily caught between classic documentary values and the gut punch approach of much U.S. filmmaking. That maybe because camera and editing credits were taken by Britishers who also worked on "Prostitute." —Japa.

El Arreglo
(The Deal)
(ARGENTINE-COLOR)

Buenos Aires, June 7.
An Aries release and production. Produced by Hector Olivera and Luis Osvaldo Repetto. Directed by Fernando Ayala. Stars Federico Luppi, Julio De Grazia. Screenplay, Roberto Cossa, Carlos Somigliana; camera (Eastmancolor), Victor Hugo Caula; editor, Eduardo Lopez; music, Jorge Valcarcel; art director, Oscar Piruzanto; costumes, Marta Albertinazzi. Reviewed at the Normandie theatre, B.A., May 18, 1983. Running time: 90 MINS.

Luis Bellomo	Federico Luppi
Best Friend	Julio De Grazia
Foreman	Rodolfo Ranni
Mrs. Bellomo	Haydee Padilla
Daughter	Susu Pecoraro
Son	Fernando Alvarez
Young daughter	Andrea Tenuta

Director Fernando Ayala and producers Hector Olivera and Luis Osvaldo Repetto, who attained the greatest hit of 1982 in Argentina with "Plata Dulce" (Easy Money), have scored again with another look at depressing realities of contemporary Argentina life, this time those related with widespread bribery at all levels of the social spectrum although the story mirrors what happens in one street of a humble neighborhood. But any viewer with a standard I.Q. can easily detect in it a parable of the so-called "ilicitos" (illicit deeds), mainly attributed to public officials, that have mushroomed in recent years.

Federico Luppi is a house painter who works hard to support wife Haydee Padilla and teenage-daughter Andrea Tenuta with the help of young son Fernando Alvarez, a repairer of tv aerials. He also lends a hand to elder daughter Susu Pecoraro and her husband in their effort to build a small house before their first child is born.

Main problem for this family and their neighbors is the lack of running water but one day a crew appears and starts digging along the middle of the street. The foreman explains the ditch they are excavating is the dividing line between two counties, so they will provide running water to just one side of the street.

After the initial outburst of protests and anger, the people from the other side starts talking with the foreman about a "deal" aimed at getting illegal extensions of the water pipe line to their homes. Terms of the bribe are agreed on but the foreman insists that all the neighbors have to contribute, as a guarantee that if everybody is guilty nobody will talk.

Luppi refuses to be drawn into the scheme, even when pressed by relatives, friends and neighbors to forget his principles and accept the fact that there is no other way to get the water. Luppi puts decency above need. A loving father and a true friend, he endures the painful rejection of his children and his cronies when they fail to understand the ethical motivation of his stand. He becomes isolated among his own people and eventually realizes that in an amoral environment a honest person is deemed a lunatic. Then his will weakens. Luppi goes to see the foreman to yield to his demand but when the foreman scorns him he can no longer control his rage and shame, a fistfight ensues, he knocks down his hated rival and ends in jail. For being faithful to his self-respect he loses everything else that counts in life, even his freedom. Decency doesn't pay.

Penners Cossa and Somigliana have given a straightforward treatment to the story, with rather few comedy touches once the central conflict starts to change the relationships between the main characters. Director Ayala keeps a lively pace without losing either emotion or social comment, proving once more his fine craftmanship.

Acting is first rate. Luppi, besides injecting both strength and warmth to the protagonist, makes one feel his disenchantment with a society subdued by corruption that destroys all the hopes he had for himself and his loved ones. Julio De Grazia, Rodolfo Ranni, Haydee Padilla, Susu Pecoraro and young Fernando Alvarez attain convincing portrayals of all other main characters, while shrewdly-chosen supporting actors lend credibility to the minor parts.

Victor Hugo Caula's good camerawork, Eduardo Lopez's tight editing and Jorge Valcarcel's effective score contribute to the overall satisfying result of this topical comedy. —Nubi.

Luggage Of The Gods
(COLOR-16m)

Minor caveman comedy.

A General Pictures production. Produced by Jeff Folmsbee. Directed by David Kendall. Features entire cast. Screenplay, Kendall; camera (color, 16m). Steven Ross; editor, Jack Haigis; music, Cengiz Yaltkaya; sound, Stuart Deutsch; assistant director, Folmsbee; production manager, Annie Allman; art direction. Joshua Harrison; makeup, Arnold Gargiulo; costumes, Dawn Johnson; special effects, Glenn Van Fleet. Reviewed at Bombay Cinema, N.Y., June 1, 1983. (No MPAA Rating). Running time: 74 MINS.

Yuk .... Mark Stolzenberg
Tull .... Gabriel Barre
Hubba .... Gwen Ellison
Zoot, the chief .... Martin Haber
Kono, Zoot's mate .... Rochelle Robins
Flon, lead hunter .... Lou Leccese
Gurn, Flon's sidekick ...... Dog Thomas
Whittaker ...:............ John Tarrant
Lionel .... Conrad Bergschneider

"Luggage Of The Gods" is a mild indie comedy filmed in New York last year by tyro filmmakers that recalls Carl Gottlieb's 1980 "Caveman." Producer Jeff Folmsbee and helmer David Kendall have gotten technical value from a tiny budget, but the wryly-titled opus lacks the punch or invention needed to escape the "specialized U.S. indie" ghetto and find more commercial markets.

Story premise recalls Ismail Merchant-James Ivory's 1972 "Savages" and Jamie Uys's recent international hit "The Gods Must Be Crazy," in limning the impact of modern civilization and its products upon an untouched tribe of primitives. Yuk (Mark Stolzenberg) is a cave painting artist exiled from his tribe (living unchanged from prehistoric times somewhere in North America) for violating a taboo by looking up at the jet planes that periodically fly overhead.

With his sidekick Tull (Gabriel Bare), Yuk rummages through and puts to use a treasure trove of luggage jettisoned from a plane. A lame subplot has two crooks looking for a crate of rare paintings (dropped from the plane) and fighting

with the tribe until defeated by Yuk and Tull.

Slowly-paced picture lags between gags, most of which are repetitive variations of the basic feeling-superior reaction of watching a savage misuse or ingeniously invent a new use for a familiar modern object. Writer-director Kendall fails to develop his material beyond the level of an elongated blackout sketch. One missed opportunity occurs when Yuk finds a one-hand miniature 8m film projector. Instead of developing the cultural shock (commonly observed among primitives who have never seen a movie before) of the incident, Kendall has Yuk immediately assimilate the artificial image of a silent G-rated (not stag) film and introduce "the kiss" to his tribe.

Funniest motif, when the tribe takes the 1960s pop song, "Build Me Up, Buttercup" (heard on a radio found in the luggage) as its chant, is little more than a variation on the discovery of polyrhythms around the campfire that was the highpoint of "Caveman." Without the money to compete with major productions, tyro filmmakers should concentrate on creating a novel alternative to mainstream fare, rather than a small-scale version of it.

Leads Stolzenberg, Barre and heroine Gwen Ellison are physically expressive in roles utilizing a made-up, simple language; some extraneous English narration is voiced-over to bookend the film. Cengiz Yaltkaya's marimba playing and his background musical score are the dominant contrast during much of the heroes' uneventful trek through New York parks. —Lor.

The Survivors
(COLOR)

Won't survive summer competition.

Hollywood, June 21.
A Columbia release of a Delphi-Rastar-William Sackheim production. Produced by Sackheim. Executive producer, Howard Pine. Directed by Michael Ritchie. Stars Walter Matthau, Robin Williams, Jerry Reed. Screenplay, Michael Leeson; camera (Metrocolor), Billy Williams; editor, Richard A. Harris; music, Paul Chibara; production design, Gene Callahan, art direction. Jay Moore; set decoration, Herb Mulligan; costume design, Ann roth; sound, Dennis Maitland; second unit director, Peter Norman; assistant director, Tom Mack. Reviewed at the Writers Guild Theatre, Beverly Hills, June 18, 1983. (MPAA RAting: R). Running time: 102 MINS.

Sonny Paluso .... Walter Matthau
Donald Quinelle .... Robin Williams
Jack Locce .... Jerry Reed
Wes Huntley .... James Wainwright
Candice Paluso .... Kristen Vigard
Doreen ....:...Annie McEnroe
Betty .... Anne 'Pitonisf
Tv station manager ..... Bernard Barrow
Jack's wife .... Marian Hailey

An aimless, unfocused social comedy, "The Survivors" misfires on just about every level. Finding what laughs it has to offer solely in the personal performing talents of Walter Matthau and Robin Williams, pic is perhaps no sillier than many other comedies which have found favor with the public of late, but is also offputting in a manner that will undoubtedly make it one of the early summer boxoffice casualties.

Given basic storyline, film could have been angled in one of at least two different ways, but indecisive mish-mash will leave audiences gasping in wonder at what the point of the whole thing was supposed to be.

Exec Williams and gas station owner Matthau both become unemployed at the outset, and through a bizarre coincidence are thrown together as intended victims of professional hitman Jerry Reed. A la something like "The In-Laws," pic might have concentrated upon the comic possibilities of the characters' nutty misalliance, but they are so thinly drawn in the writing that the two stars must work overtime to breathe any life or interplay into their scenes together.

On the other hand, tale also offers the potential for satiric treatment of American social conditions and organizations, something director Michael Ritchie has been drawn to time and again. Confronted with the threat of another attack by Reed, Williams becomes a maniacal gun enthusiast and joins a survival training unit run in the snowy mountains by James Wainwright, who greets his recruits by saying, "Welcome to the new Middle Ages," and encourages his disciples to look forward to their day of takeover after Western Civilization goes entirely to pot.

It feels as though the script, such as it was, was tossed out the window once action moves to the New Hampshire compound (scenes were actually shot in Vermont and, when snow didn't materialize, in the Tahoe area). All of Williams' dialog from this point on sounds like lifts from crazed comic monologs he might deliver onstage, and at least one scene, in which he challenges Reed by phone to come up from New York to try to knock him off, is hilarious. But good social satire should be founded on some kind of realistic premise, and by this time any sense of dramatic and comic coherence has long since been jettisoned.

Matthau, who replaced Joseph Bologna after a couple of weeks lensing, at least makes things watchable thanks to his masterful comic timing and resourceful reactions to the lunacy surrounding him; it's frightening to think what the film would have been like without him.

Williams seems as if he was left basically to his own devices, resulting in a performance of erratic comic effectiveness and no believability. Reed firmly plays a nasty good ole boy with a curious soft spot and Wainwright, as the mercenary military fanatic seems to have been cast mainly for his strong resemblance to Gen. Alexander Haig.

Tech contributions are okay.
—*Cart.*

Touched
(U.S.-COLOR)

Cannes, May 14.

A Lorimar production is association with Wildwoods Partners. Produced by Dirk Petersmann and Barclay Lottimer. Directed by John Flynn. Features entire cast. Screenplay by Lyle Kessler; camera (Technicolor), Fred Murphy; editor, Harry Keramidas; production design, Patricia Von Brandenstein; music, Shirley Walker. Reviewed at the Olympia (market), Cannes Film Fest, May 13, 1983. No MPAA Rating). Running Time: 93 MINS.
Daniel .... Robert Hays
Jennifer .... Kathleen Beller
Herbie .... Ned Beatty
Ernie .... Gilbert Lewis
Timothy .... Lyle Kessler
Thomas .... Farnham Scott

"Touched" offers an offbeat romance between two young people who escape from a mental institution and attempt to make a life for themselves on the outside. There's a faint trace of "David and Lisa" in the story without the early film's rawness or acute observation. This film is glossier, more fanciful and less emotionally involving.

Robert Hays plays Daniel, a patient who bolts the institution when he learns the counselors want him to be trained as a messenger boy. He winds up at a nearby boardwalk where he lands a job in a dunk tank. For him, the step is a major accomplishment and prompts him to return to the institution to spirit

out his girlfriend Jennifer (Kathleen Beller).

The two set up house and experience a kind of normalcy which proves beneficial to both. It's nonetheless a rocky transition, plagued by doubts and temporary failures.

Essentially a two-character study, the script by Lyle Kessler fails to flesh out supporting roles. Kessler plays his dunk tank partner who dreams of buying a pony, moving to Arizona and setting up a photography business. It provides a momentary contrast to Daniel's situation but is abruptly dropped.

Also curiously underdeveloped is Gilbert Lewis' role as an institution warden who wants to sabotage Daniel and Jennifer's love nest. The threat from Lewis runs through the movie without providing a real dramatic effect.

Filmed under the title "On the Boardwalk Some Sunny Day," one can see how the new title is a slight improvement. Still, it will do little to attract audiences to this hard-sell picture.

Production credits are strong but John Flynn's direction gives the film a claustrophobic quality better suited to the small screen. Intention may have been to make the story more intimate but instead the technique diminishes the drama.

Both Hays and Beller are excellent in difficult roles, bringing lots of charisma to the film. However, much of this strength is undone by the unadventurous, poorly-developed script. Kessler falls back on movie cliches too often to portray the couple's doll-house existence.

Commercial prospects would appear to be very modest. Neither performers nor subject have guaranteed appeal. Careful marketing and possible favorable reviews could build a small following for picture. —*Klad.*

Surprise Party
(FRENCH-COLOR)

Paris, June 10.

Prodis release of a Uranium Films production. Produced by Georges Glass. Stars Caroline Cellier, Mylene Demongeot, Michel Duchaussoy. Special guest stars, Robert Hossein, Maurice Ronet. Written and directed by Roger Vadim. Camera, (color), Georges Barsky; music, Michel Magne, Sergio Renucci; art director, Jean-Francois Corneille; editor, Raymond Lewin; costumes, Sylvianne Combes; production manager, Gerard Adeline. Reviewed at the Marignan-Concorde theatre, Paris, May 24, 1983. Running time: 100 MINS.
Lisa Bourget .... Caroline Cellier
Francois Lambert ..... Michel Duchaussoy
Andre Auerbach .... Robert Hossein
Georges Levesque .... Maurice Ronet
Genevieve Lambert .... Mylene Demongeot
Anne Lambert ·..Philippine Leroy-Beaulieu
Christian Bourget .... Christian Vadim
Marie-Jo Le Kellec .... Charlotte Walior
Madam Gisele .... Pascale Roberts
Marco .... Michel Godin
David Auerbach .... Charly Chemouni

Roger Vadim has come a long way since his splashy beginnings

in 1956 with his "And God Created Woman" and for many the direction has been downward. He now returns to France with a youth comedy-drama, "Surprise Party;" once a creator of trends, Vadim is now content to exploit those already in the air.

"Surprise Party" is a predictable cross between "American Graffiti" and the French hit "La Boum," and other films in the same vein. Set in a provincial French city in the 1950's, it follows several freshfaced youths on the social scene, as they date and mate, with the usual joys and heartaches, misunderstandings, flirts and unrequited loves.

Technically, it's neatly packaged, and the youngsters (among them, Christian Vadim, the helmer's son) are bubbly or melancholic enough, but there's virtually nothing here to distinguish it scriptwise (Vadim is solely credited for the screenplay). There's a shadow of the old Vadim in a scene in which two nubile girls (Charlotte Walior and Philippine Leroy-Beaulieu) awaken to each other's sexual charms during a night-long escapade in a museum castle, but it's a pale one; not daring, just tritely naughty.

Among the adults, Maurice Ronet makes his last screen appearance, a cameo, as Christian Vadim's outlaw father, on the lam for his collaborationist activities during the German Occupation. His scene provides the only unusual note to an otherwise conventional product, which could have been turned out by any competent director. —*Len.*

Zig Zag Story
(FRENCH-COLOR)

Paris, June 14.

AAA release of a Chloe Production. Produced by Jean-Pierre Fougea. Features entire cast. Written and directed by Patrick Schulmann. Camera, (Fujicolor) Gilberto Azevedo; art director, Pierre Voisin; editor, Aline Asseo; sound, Claude Bertrand; music Patrick Schulmann; production manager, Edith Colnel; associate producer, Francoise Fougea. Reviewed at the Marignan-Concorde theatre, Paris, June 10, 1983. Running time: 100 MINS.
Cat .... Diane Bellego
Gil .... Christian Francois
Bob .... Fabrice Luchini
Romo .... Ronny Coutteure
Inspector .... Philippe Khorsand

Writer-director Patrick Schulmann scored big in 1978 with his comedy feature debut, "Et la Tendresse? Bordel," and struck out big two years later with a follow-up, "Rendez Moi Ma Peau." Now he's back with a third comedy of love and sex, which is a slight improvement over his previous film, but still shows the strain of a filmmaker trying to prove he's both sensitive and clever.

Somewhat in the manner of his hit first film, Schulmann juxtaposes sex-obsessed eccentricity and healthy romantic love, with narrative emphasis on the developing relationship between a patient, good-natured and cool young (color-blind) artist and a temporarily handicapped attractive radio producer, whom the young man nurses during a long convalescence period. The sex nut is the artist's photographer roommate, played by Fabrice Luchini, who was Eric Rohmer's "Perceval."

After a spectacular opening gag sequence of Rube Goldberg-like complexity, script quickly switches gears into a humdrum sentimental comedy of surprisingly little charm or warmth. Unlike the neatly balanced parallel tales in "Tendresse," this pic "zig-zags" through some secondary characters and subsidiary incidents (a kidnapping investigation), but without any apparent dramatic purpose or design. The leads, Diane Bellego and Christian Francois, are newcomers to film, but are unable to give the drab script any personal flavor. Overall, despite its pretences, "Zig Zag Story" lacks genuine feeling and invention. —*Len.*

Purumeria No Densetsu Tengoku No Kissu
(The Legend of Plumeria — Heaven's Kiss)
(JAPANESE-COLOR)

Tokyo, June 12.

A Toho release of a Toho-Sun Music co-production. Produced by Masauki Takubo. Directed by Yoshihiro Kawasaki. Features entire cast. Screenplay, Yoshihiro Kawasaki, Kyohei Nakaoka, Ayuko Anzai, Haruo Tanami, from story by Kyohei Nakaoka; camera, (color), Tadashi Furuyama; art, Yukio Higuchi; sound, Nobuyuki Tanaka; lighting, Takeshi Awakihara; music, Ryo Fukui. Reviewed at Toho screening room, Tokyo, June 9, 1983. Running time: 90 MINS.
Emiko Hayasaka .... Seiko Matsuda
Shinji Terao .... Kiichi Nakai
Yuko Hirose .... Miyuki Ono
Akira Kuniyoshi .... Shinji Yamashita
Mayumi Kishimoto .... Miki Jimbo
Tatsuro Hayasaka ..... Akira Takarada
Mrs. Hayasaka .... Akiko Koyama

The Hawaiian locale of "Purumeria No Densetsu — Tengoku No Kissu" is immediately established in opening shots featuring a potpourri of lithe, long-limbed bodies, in the midst of which is rudely plopped top-lined Seiko Matsuda, resulting in a jarring juxtaposition not unlike that occurring later in the film when a scene suddenly shifts from the emerald-green waters lapping the shores of Oahu to the sludge-colored waves washing over Chigasaki in Japan.

Matsuda, in contrast to the usual on-location Toho release, is not a native of Japan who has some marvelous adventure in Hawaii while on a group tour, but rather a native of Hawaii who, shortly before graduating from college, makes her first ever trip to Mom and Pop's homeland, there to find true love in the person of windsurfing enthusiast Kiichi Nakai.

Unlike Matsuda, who comes from a well-to-do family, Nakai is a man of modest means. Nonetheless, even though Matsuda's parents hope she'll agree to an arranged marriage with wealthy Shinji Yamashita, they cheerfully accept their daughter's choice of a future mate.

Alas, Yamashita — who, it develops, is a selfish, two-faced blackguard — tries to eliminate his rival and succeeds only in hurting the one he loves: Matsuda is struck on the head in a boating accident and expires just as her sweetheart wins a windsurfing championship. Her father, in a display of that inscrutable stoicism with which screen Orientals 40 years back always met misfortune, says that his daughter's death was brought about not by any one person, but by "fate."

By no means is this the only instance of cringe-inducing dialog. A kindly bartender, referring to a windsurfer who died in an accident not long ago, says to two of the late lad's friends: "He isn't really dead. He lives in your heart and my heart, too."

Given that Matsuda is a pop vocalist whose stage persona is one of unsullied purity, it is somewhat surprising that unpleasant reality is occasionally allowed to intrude on her screen vehicle. The ex-girlfriend of Yamashita informs him that she has had an abortion. Even more surprising, given the general absence of kissing in youth films, not to mention the fact that Ken Takakura and Chieko Baisho, this country's leading adult romantic team, have never kissed on screen, are Matsuda's long kiss scenes with her co-star. In the local context, it's pretty hot stuff.

Unfortunately, with this initimation of sex comes a threat of violence: in an exploitative attempt to recall an actual assault on Matsuda earlier this year by a former mental patient, she is here threatened by a knife-wielding juvenile.
—Bail.

House of The Long Shadows
(BRITISH-COLOR)

Gothic fun for nostalgia freaks.

London, June 24.

A Cannon release of a Menahem Golan-Yoram Globus production. Directed by Pete Walker. Stars Vincent Price. Christopher Lee. Peter Cushing. Screenplay. Michael Armstrong; camera (color). Norman Langley; music. Richard Harvey; art direction. Mike Pickwoad; editor. Robert Dearberg; ass't directors. Brian Lawrence. Glynn Purcell. Paul Carnie. Nick Goodden. Reviewed at Classic Haymarket Theatre. London. June 23. 1983. (B-BFC rating: 15). Running time: 96 MINS.

Lionel	Vincent Price
Corrigan	Christopher Lee
Sebastian	Peter Cushing
Kenneth Magee	Desi Arnaz Jr.
Lord Grisbane	John Carradine
Victoria	Sheila Keith
Mary Norton	Julie Peasgood
Sam Allison	Richard Todd
Diana	Louise English
Andrew	Richard Hunter
Stationmaster	Norman Rossington

With Vincent Price, Christopher Lee, Peter Cushing and John Carradine reviving their old scaremongering number, Cannon's "House Of The Long Shadows" is a kind of kidding-on-the-square homage to the bygone gothic chiller. It could have been both scarier, wittier and more mocking, but clever promotion of its nostalgia value could spell okay returns once the summer crop of biggies has passed its peak.

Michael Armstrong's screenplay is an affectionate, elaborate red herring with not one but two trick endings, the second by far the bigger surprise. Suffice that the plot involves a bizarre family reunion at a dilapidated Welsh manor house where a young American author (Desi Arnaz Jr.) holes up on a bet to race the clock and crank out one of those over-the-top suspense novels.

Indubitably, the durable senior set steals the show, as the fans would expect, with Cushing, Price and Lee afforded the best opportunities to flamboyantly register. Sheila Keith also scores in a spooky style reminiscent of Judith Anderson as Mrs. Danvers in "Rebecca."

Pete Walker's direction is competent, and the pic is very good on atmosphere as it reproduces just about every cliche in the book — remote setting, rain and lightning, clattering shutters, squeaky doors, unexpected black cats, etc. Mike Pickwoad's art direction speaks well for itself, ditto Norman Langley's lensing and Richard Harvey's music.

Young Arnaz isn't stretched any but performs satisfactorily and with some appeal as the bemused author. Louise English and Richard Hunter as a young couple on the rocks are particularly plausible, with okay efforts by Richard Todd

and Julie Peasgood as Arnaz' publisher and romantic interest respectively. —Pit.

The Final Solution
(SWISS-B&W-DOCU)

Sydney, June 22.

An Arthur Cohn production. Producer. Arthur Cohn; dramatization, Dieter Hilderbrandt, based on the book by Gerhard Schoenberner; editors, Erno Sethy, Helga Kruska; technical advisor and introduction, Simon Wiesenthal; camera (black and white), no credit; narrator, Alexander Scourby. Reviewed at the Sydney Film Festival, June 16, 1983. Running time: 82 MINS.

Swiss-based producer Arthur Cohn's docu on the Holocaust inevitably traverses a lot of familiar territory in examining what Nazi hunter Simon Wiesenthal terms in his brief but poignant intro as "the greatest crime in history."

Unlike other films on the subject, however, "The Final Solution" pinpoints the burning of books by Nazi stormtroopers and students at Berlin University in 1933 as the beginning of the persecution and harassment which culminated in the genocide of 6,000,000 Jews.

The full nightmarish horror of the Jews' suffering is retold in film drawn from 42 archives in 14 countries. While film quality is patchy in parts, scenes etch themselves on the memory: the Warsaw ghetto, the cattle trucks, the ovens and gas chambers, bodies being bulldozed into open graves. No narration is furnished with some stills, and none is needed.

Excerpts from German propaganda films are intercut with the archival material, to telling effect, and speeches by Hitler and his henchmen are translated verbatim, monsters damned by their own words.

It is important to explain what happened and why, to prevent it happening again, says Wiesenthal, adding, "It serves as a remembrance, a lesson and a warning." Impeccably researched, produced and presented, "The Final Solution" will earn its place at any fest.
—Dogo.

Yellowbeard
(BRITISH-COLOR)

The meaning of no-life.

Hollywood, June 20.

An Orion release of a Seagoat Production. Produced by Carter De Haven. Executive producer, John Daly. Directed by Mel Damski. Features entire cast. Screenplay. Graham Chapman, Peter Cook, Bernard McKenna; camera (De Luxe), Gerry Fisher; editor, William Reynolds; music, John Morris; production design, Joseph R. Jennings; art decorator, Jack Shampan; set decoration, Tim Hutchinson, Peter James, Teresa Pecanins; costume design, T. Stephen Miles; sound, Brian Simmons, Manuel Topete;

first assistant directors, Clive Reed, Ted Morley, Mario Cisneros. Reviewed at the Directors Guild Theatre, Hollywood, June 20, 1983. (MPAA Rating: PG.) Running Time: 101 MINS.

Yellowbeard	Graham Chapman
Moon	Peter Boyle
El Segundo	Richard (Cheech) Marin
El Nebuloso	Tommy Chong
Lord Lambourn	Peter Cook
Gilbert	Marty Feldman
Dan	Martin Hewitt
Dr. Gilpin	Michael Hordern
Commander Clement	Eric Idle
Betty	Madeline Kahn
Captain Hughes	James Mason
Blind Pew	John Cleese
Lady Churchill	Susannah York

One can second-guess what went wrong with this aptly entitled Seagoat Production until the grog runs dry. Suffice that the picture is a disaster. It's that bad. Suffice also that Orion Pictures' press kit and publicity stunts are infinitely more entertaining than the film. If ever a picture needed inventive showmanship, "Yellowbeard" is it. There's no other way the film is going to draw money.

Debuting theatrical director Mel Damski, with several impressive tv credits behind him, helms a treasure chest of players, not to mention Mexican, English, and American crews, as if he were pouring ingredients into a blender. But Damski's trouble is an incoherent script, which titular star and co-writer Graham Chapman reports was an effort to tell "the true story of Treasure Island" — more precisely, to turn Robert Louis Stevenson "inside out." That it does.

The picture is the first of producer Carter De Haven's multi-pic deal with Orion. John Daly was exec producer. Perhaps most revealing, the idea for the pic was inspired by late rocker Keith Moon, who was going to play the evil bosun played by Peter Boyle (called Moon in the film). Another melancholy note is that the picture is the last work of Marty Feldman, who died near the end of the production in Mexico City. He portrays a sniveling spy.

Those cutups identified with Monty Python and Beyond the Fringe — Chapman, Peter Cook, John Cleese, Eric Idle — give the film its bewigged, besotted British identity. Cheech and Chong, Madeline Kahn, James Mason, Susannah York, even Martin Hewitt (the boyfriend in "Endless Love"), and many, many more, are thrown into the porridge. One fast shot is of David Bowie.

Every scene is frenetic. The pirate plot is an arabesque of maddening contortion that is incomprehensible. Watching snippets of this movie in TV trailers can be amusing but when the pieces are strung together, with no pacing or rhythm or structure, the end result is a migraine. —Loyn.

Porky's II: The Next Day
(COLOR)

More of same.

Hollywood, June 24.

A 20th Century-Fox release of a Simon/Reeves/Landsburg Prods. & Astral Bellevue Pathe presentation. Produced by Don Carmody, Bob Clark. Executive producers, Melvin Simon, Harold Greenberg, Alan Landsburg. Features entire cast. Directed by Clark. Screenplay, Roger E. Swaybill, Alan Ormsby, Clark. Camera (Deluxe color), Reginald H. Morris; editor, Stan Cole; music, Carl Zittrer; art direction, Fred Price; set decoration, Richard Helfritz; costume design, Mary E. McLeod; sound, Alan Bernard; associate producers, Gary Goch, Ken Heeley-Ray; assistant director, Ken Goch. Reviewed at the Hollywood Pacific, L.A., June 24, 1983. (MPAA Rating R.) Running time: **96 MINS.**

Pee Wee	Dan Monahan
Tommy	Wyatt Knight
Billy	Mark Herrier
Mickey	Roger Wilson
Tim	Cyril O'Reilly
Meat	Tony Ganios
Wendy	Kaki Hunter
Brian	Scott Colomby
Balbricker	Nancy Parsons
John Henry	Joseph Running Fox
Carter	Eric Christmas
Reverend Bubba Flavel	Bill Wiley
Gebhardt	Edward Winter
Sandy Le Toi	Cisse Cameron
Mrs. Morris	Else Earl

If the general rule holds that, the more similar a sequel to the original, the better the b.o., "Porky's II: The Next Day" should do very well indeed. Pic opens with a recapitulation of the first film, which was a surprise smash to the tune of over $53,000,-000 in domestic rentals, and the remaining hour-and-a-half offers ample evidence that the youthful characters haven't matured a single bit in the interim.

Plot follows in the grand tradition of many early rock 'n' roll quickies, in which self-righteous upholders of comic morality attempted to stomp out the threat posed by the new primitive music. Replacing Chuck Mitchell's Porky as the heavy here is Bill Wiley's bigoted Rev. Bubba Flavel, who makes a crusade out of shutting down the school's Shakespeare festival due to the lewdness he finds strewn throughout the Bard's work.

Enlisted in his cause is the ample girls' gym teacher Miss Balbricker and the local contingent of the Ku Klux Klan, who are each the victims of two of the film's three "big scenes." Everyone who saw it remembers "that scene" from the original. Here, some of the boys get back at Balbricker by sending a snake up into her toilet, and the KKK guys get theirs when their heads are shaved in a most undignified manner and they are forced to run nude through the streets.

Clearly, then, director Bob Clark has not allowed success lead him astray into the dreaded

realm of good taste. Furthermore, he has wisely retained basically the same cast and made a picture which looks just as cheap as the first one.

However, it should not go unnoticed that the commercial victory of "Porky's" has emboldened its makers to express a social conscience this time out, that the new film bravely takes a stand against right-wing bigots, religious fanatics, duplicitous politicians and hypocrites of all persuasions. It's good to see that Hollywood hasn't lost the guts to tackle such controversial issues head on.
—*Cart.*

Play Catch
(HONG KONG-COLOR)

Hong Kong, June 13.

A Cinema City Company Ltd. production. Produced by Karl Maka, Dean Shek; coproducers, Raymond Wong. Features entire cast. Directed by Lau Kar Wing. Screenplay, Raymond Wong, Clifton Ko; camera (color), Peter Ngor Chi-kwan; production designer, Nansun Shi; production supervisor, Paul Lai; executive producer, Wellington W. Fung; art direction; Sita Yeung; editor, Tony Chow; music, Teddy Robin, Tang Shiu-lam. Reviewed at State Theatre, Hong Kong, June 12, 1983. Running time: **96 MINS.**
Cast: Alan Tam, Olivia Cheng, Eric Tsang, Wong Ching.

(Cantonese soundtrack, English subtitles)

"Play Catch" is Cinema City's summer offering to Hong Kong residents as they try to escape the sweltering summer heat in air conditioned theatres. The film is an exhilarating diversion with the usual, predictable and cliched elements concocted to perfection in the patented comedy-drama.

"Play Catch," obviously was inspired by the Goldie Hawn-Chevy Chase "Foul Play," adapted to Cantonese slapstick terms, sequences.

Corrupt and public figure billionaire Law and his gang are conspiring to murder an influential judge. The plan is overheard by a detective who records the meeting on a cassette. When Law discovers this, he orders that the tape be found. The spy is killed but before he dies, he hides the alleged tape in a reporter's (Olivia Cheng) handbag.

In comes the young hero, Law Kim Long (Alan Tam), a refugee from China, on the lookout for his father now living in Hong Kong. Law Kim Long is mistaken for the son of billionaire Law and meets up with lady reporter.

Cheng and Tam make a handsome couple, but the material doesn't ask much from them except to look good and energetic. Everybody searches, runs, hide jumps and runs some more in hide and seek fashion. The search finally ends at the climactic colorful circus segment.

"Play Catch" is proving popular at the boxoffice, but there's really nothing super-special, but locals trust Cinema City's ability to produce wholesome commercial family pics at a price that practically all can afford and judging from the public response they are apparently getting their money's worth from their tickets.
—*Mel.*

Waltz Across Texas
(COLOR)

Limping all the way.

Hollywood, June 16.

An Atlantic Releasing Corp. release, produced by Martin Jurow. Directed by Ernest Day. Features entire cast. Screenplay, Bill Svanoe; camera (Metrocolor), Robert Elswit; editor, Jay Lash Cassidy; sound, Jan Brodin; coproducer, Scott Rosenfelt; associate producer, Mark Levinson; production design, Michael Erler; assistant director, Jan Wieringa; music, Steve Dorff. Reviewed at Atlantic Releasing, L.A., June 16, 1983. (MPAA rating: PG). Running time: **99 MINS.**

Gail	Anne Archer
John	Terry Jastrow
Joe	Noah Beery
Kit	Mary Kay Place
Luke	Josh Taylor
Frank	Richard Farnsworth
Bill	Ben Piazza

"Waltz Across Texas" limps across the screen, not as a bad film but oddly out of its time and clearly unnecessary, a dim commercial prospect.

A self-proclaimed throwback to the romantic comedies of Spencer Tracy and Katharine Hepburn, "Waltz" clearly shows its ambitions, but Anne Archer and Terry Jastrow don't come up to the standard, though both are certianly good.

Husband and wife in real life, Jastrow and Archer are clearly carrying out a family-project, providing the story for the script by Bill Svanoe. Somebody should have advised them to redo the living room instead.

Archer plays a beautiful, admirable and strong-willed geologist and Jastrow a handsome, likable wildcatter. She's scientific; he plays hunches. She's from the East; he's a proud Texan. She's cosmopolitan; he's down-to-earth. With all these conflicts, they're sure to despise each other at first, fall in love, spat and separate until they live happily ever after.

You can't get 10 minutes into all of this without thinking, "This picture is going to end up with them dancing and hugging beneath an oil gusher." And sure enough, fate takes them into partnership on a do-or-die wildcat well and there's never a moment's real doubt what lies below that drill bit.

Incidentally, another problem with "Waltz" is a whole lot of shots of oil-well digging equipment at work, which adds little cinematic excitement unless you're heavy into petroleum.

On the plus side, Archer and Jastrow do work well together and all their scenes come off nicely. But they and director Ernest Day just don't have any place to go.
:—*Har.*

Funny Money
(BRITISH-COLOR)

London, June 22.

Cannon Film Distributors release (in U.K.) of a Greg Smith production. Directed by James Kenelm Clarke. Features entire cast. Screenplay, Clarke; camera (color), John Wyatt; production designer, Harry Pottle; editor, Bill Lenny. Reviewed June 21, '83, at the Classic Haymarket, London. (BBFC rating: 18). Running time: **92 MINS.**

Ben	Gregg Henry
Cass	Elizabeth Daily
Banks	Gareth Hunt
Diana	Annie Ross
Sanderson	Derren Nesbitt
Limping man	Joe Praml

"Funny Money" is a lowercase programmer about the megabuck traffic in stolen credit cards. Lacking names, style or dramatic punch, the prospect is for soft b.o. and limited playoff as and when it gets a U.S. distrib. A fast segue to the late-late show slots is likely.

The yarn, scripted by director James Kenelm Clarke (he also scored pic, uncredited), tracks two Yanks in London, Gregg Henry as a hotel lounge pianist and Elizabeth Daily as a basically good chick on the make, who collab to collect as much plastic as they can from the hotel's guests. Suffice that insipid plotting fumbles both its action and kinky sex opportunities.

Most arresting scene has Henry demonstrating how a pro can alter credit plastic so as to defy the computers. Amex, Diners' Club, et al, may well wince. Otherwise all is corny and predictable including foregone redemption of the lead duo.

None of the actors are overtaxed. Henry and Daily are oke, ditto Annie Ross, Gareth Hunt, Derren Nesbitt and Joe Praml in principal support.

John Wyatt's lensing, including a brief opening sequence in the Las Vegas environs, is standard. Other tech credits are routine.—*Pit.*

L'Amour Fugitif
(Bad Hats)
(FRENCH-BRITISH-COLOR)

Paris, June 20.

A Productions Audiovisuelles (LPA)/TF1 Films Production/Channel Four (London) coproduction. Produced by Pierre Heros. Stars Marcel Bozzuffi, Mick Ford. Directed by Pascal Ortega. Screenplay, Mick Ford, Robert Hickson; camera (color), Gerard Sterin; sound, Laurent Quaglio; editor, Christopher Kelly; art director, Claude Chevant; music, Jeff Cohen; executive producer, Bernard Lorain. Reviewed at the Cinematheque Francaise, Paris, June 18, 1983. Running time: **85 MINS.**

Rochon	Marcel Bozzuffi
Chapin	Mick Ford
Catherine	Catherine Lachens

"L'Amour Fugitif" is an undistinguished drama about two deserting soldiers during the first World War. Financed in part by England's new Channel Four, it has already aired on British home screens last winter under the title "Bad Hats," and unspooled at the Cannes film fest as a Perspectives of French Cinema selection.

Scripted by Robert Hickson and actor Mick Ford, who plays the British lead, story follows the adventures of two infantrymen in 1917 France, one English, the other French (Marcel Bozzuffi), who decide to leave the war to others and split for Ireland. Making their way from the front to the coast, they steal a skiff (with Ford killing a fisherman in the process) and head out to sea. But Bozzuffi's self-professed navigating talents prove weak, and they find themselves back on French soil, once again near the butchery they both will have nothing more to do with.

Rather than try flight by sea again, and seeing a firing squad imminent, they decide to live for the moment and run into a young war widow (Catherine Lachens), who's of the same mind. She decides she wants a child from the both of them, and they willingly oblige. After some time at this curiously utopic, bucolic life, Ford is mistaken as the enemy by a French soldier and shot. Bozzuffi, who prefers to withdraw into total silence, ends up in front of a French firing squad.

A parable is evidently intended, but lacks the suggestive richness of character and incident needed. The scripters water down the contrast between the two soldiers by giving Bozzuffi a perfect command of English (and Lachens, too, proves to be equally fluent), which makes the choice of nationalities seem arbitrary. Ford is all mad-dog vulgarity, and Bozzuffi phlegmatic pretence. Beyond that there's little else to set them apart. The director, Pascal Ortega, a former stage and film assistant making his helming debut, doesn't give any of this any novel accent or flavor.

Intended for theatrical release in France, pic might have better chances on television, where its dramatic sketchiness may come across to better effect. Tech credits are passable. —Len.

Pink Motel
(COLOR)

The pits.

A New Image release of a Mike MacFarland-Don McCormack film, produced in association with Wescom Prods. Executive producer, McCormack. Produced by M. James Kouf Jr. and Ed Elbert. Directed by MacFarland. Features entire cast. Screenplay, Kouf; camera (Getty

color; prints by Movielab); Nicholas von Sternberg; editor, Earl Watson; music, Larry K. Smith; sound, Al R. Ramirez; assistant director, George W. Perkins; production manager, Daryl Kass; associate producer, Bren Plaistowe. Reviewed at Criterion 1 theatre, N.Y., June 4, 1983. (M-PAA Rating: R). Running time: 88 MINS.
With: Terri Berland, Brad Cowgill, Cathryn Hartt, Andrea Howard, Tony Longo, Squire Fridel, Heidi Holicher, John Maccia, Christopher Nelson, Phyllis Diller, Slim Pickens.

"Pink Motel" is an interminably dull attempt at sexploitation situation comedy. Filmed last year under the title "Motel," film's opening credits actually read only "Motel," but in pink lettering, indicating the distributor didn't bother to make the title change on the prints.

Cheap about sums up this annoying, unfunny picture. Slim Pickens and Phyllis Diller portray the owner-managers of a small California motel. The film recounts the brief stays one night of five couples, using sluggish cross-cutting between them in a vain attempt to hold the viewer's interest. Format and content resemble the 1970 tv series "Love — American Style," but production values are inferior to most hardcore porn films.

The attractive cast of familiar thesps is okay, but burdened with unplayable cliched roles: a massive fullback who is still a virgin, bedding down a hooker; adulterous lovers quibbling over the chintziness of the motel; a conceited young stud who could give even porn star Jack Wrangler lessons in smug, ham acting.

Writer M. James Kouf Jr. has delivered a nonstop stream of banalities in his talky script, directed by Mike MacFarland in static, extended shots or catatonic series of reverse-shot choker closeups. Though there is a modicum of nudity, "Motel"'s few sight gags don't come off and it lacks the raunchiness which has allowed many schlock comedies recently to ride the b.o. coattails of "Porky's."

Tech credits are unimpressive, with murky color. —Lor.

Le Prefere (Rock and Torah)
(The Favorite (Rock And Torah)) (FRENCH-COLOR)

Paris, June 17.
Coline Distribution release of a Harvert Productions/Films de la Rose production, with participation of the Culture Ministry. Produced, written and directed by Marc-Andre Grynbaum. Features entire cast. Co-producers, Louis Albert Serrut and Olivier Zameczkowski. Camera (Eastmancolor), Thierry Arbogast; art director, Patrice Renault; editor, Georges Klotz; costumes, Christiane Saussier; sound, Harrik Maury; music, Jean-Philippe Goude, Ramon Pipin; lyrics, Pierre Grosz, Marc-Andre Grynbaum. Reviewed at the Gaumont Colisee theatre, Paris, June 7, 1983. Running Time: 97 MINS.
Isaac .... Christian Clavier
Joseph .... Charles Denner

Esther .... Rosy Varte
Christine .... Patricia Fauron
Norbert .... Michel Boujenah
Angel Gabriel .... Jean-Luc Bideau
El Sublimo .... Thierry Lhermitte
Simone .... Rebecca Potok

Jewish humor in French film is a rarity, and Marc-Andre Grynbaum, a former talent agent-turned producer, tries to fill the gap in this comedy, which he wrote and directed, and which bears the subtitle "Rock and Torah."

Grynbaum sets his comic parable in the Sentier district of Paris, one of the city's Jewish quarters and, not surprisingly, the center of France's garment industry. An enterprising young man (Christian Clavier) abandons his parents' business to launch himself into show business with a best-selling disc and the creation of a Jewish rock group ("Rock and Torah" — with five swinging Hassids). He has success in all his undertakings, since he's one of God's favorites, being in fact a reincarnation of a Biblical patriarch, who preferred to make music rather than work in his dad's idol shop. The Lord rewarded him by giving him a people and a subway map of the Promised Land (Paris).

Grynbaum squanders some amusing collegiate humor ideas and a talented cast (including Charles Denner, Rosy Varte and Jean-Luc Bideau) on a screenplay that's a flavourless mishmash of parody, satire and sentimental comedy. The direction lacks chutzpah. —Len.

Sarah
(FRENCH-COLOR)

Paris, June 20.
UGC release of a Cineastes Associes/Films A2/UGC-Top 1 co-production. Produced by Rene Feret. Stars Jacques Dutronc, Lea Massari, Heinz Bennent, Jean-Claude Brialy, Gabrielle Lazure. Written and directed by Maurice Dugowson. Camera (color), Jean-Francois Robin; sound, Michel Brethez; editor, Jean-Bernard Bonis; art director, Carlos Conti; music, Gabriel Yared. Reviewed at the UGC Normandie theatre, Paris, June 10, 1983. Running time: 106 MINS.
Arnold Samson .... Jacques Dutronc
Carla Angelli .... Lea Massari
Pierre Baranne .... Heinz Bennent
Gabriel Larcange ...... Jean-Claude Brialy
Marie/Sarah .... Gabrielle Lazure
Paul Jarry .... Gabriel Yared
Maggy .... Evelyne Dress

"Sarah" is one of those films about filmmaking that attempts to blur the borderlines of reality and fantasy. Shot on location in Spain, it recounts the difficulties of a production unit mired in inactivity when its principal set is one night destroyed in a mysterious blaze. One thinks immediately of Wim Wenders' previous "The State of Things," shot in Portugal, and which deals with a film brought to a halt by lack of funds. In fact, writer-director Maurice Dugowson says his screenplay

antedates Wenders' pic by several years, and that he was in part inspired by the shooting of novelist Romain Gary's motion picture, "Les Oiseaux Vont Mourir au Perou," which was temporarily paralyzed during its Spanish location shooting by a prolonged storm.

All of this is incidental to the fact that "Sarah" is a beautiful-looking but fairly-empty drama, for which Dugowson seems to have overreached his real talents. It is certain that he has drawn his characterizations from real life and personal cinematic experience, but his straining to elevate the material to a more poetic plane lead to attitudinizing and sterile emotional content. Shot for shot it is well-composed and fascinating, but the accumulative effect is lacking in resonance and real feeling.

The principal character is outside the movie business: Jacques Dutronc is an insurance investigator who is assigned to assess the damage to the production. On his way down, he has met a lovely, mysterious young woman (Gabrielle Lazure) in a hotel. Arriving in the town where the film unit is holed up in idle disarray, he learns that the girl was a neophyte actress whom the director (Heinz Bennent) had discovered to play a lead role in his picture. But during the filming of a key scene, she suddenly disappeared and has not returned since. Dutronc's fascination with the missing girl turns to obsession, and as he comes into contact with each of the self-centred film company, from conceited director and his temperamental companion/star (Lea Massari), to philosophical actor (Jean-Claude Brialy) and emotional makeup girl (Evelyne Dress), his own perceptions of reality become distorted. In a final feverish denouement, he finds himself as part of the film in the making, reunited with the ephemeral Lazure.

The acting is far from excellent, with fine players like Brialy, Bennent and Massari proving unable to give their irritating personages any human resonance. Only Dutronc and Lazure suggest the tone Dugowson aims for, and achieves occasionally through Jean-Francois Robin's admirable lensing.

—Len.

Klakier
(The Applause-Getter) (POLISH-COLOR)

Cannes, May 31.
A Film Polski Production, Warsaw, Film Unit Silesia; world rights, Film Polski, Warsaw. Features entire cast. Directed by Janusz Kondratiuk. Screenplay, Kondratiuk, Wlodzimierz Preyss; camera (color), Zygmunt Samosiuk; sets, Andrzej Przedworski, Czeslaw Siekiera; music, Krzy-

sztof Mayer; editing, Jaroslaw Ostanowko; sound, Leszek Wronko; production manager, Henryk Parnowski. Reviewed at Cannes Film Fest (Market), May 17, '83. Running time: 90 MINS.

Cast: Zuzanna Lozinska (Gertrude), Michael Bajor (Fred), Wlodzimierz Borunski (Gusty), Wlodzimierz Musial (Bobojajne), Wlodzimierz Preyss (the Monkey's Owner), Joanna Szezepkowska (Pola), Leszek Teleszynski (Georgie).

Janusz Kondratiuk made a name for himself two decades ago by contributing the script for Roman Polanski's short film, "Mammals" (1962). He also wrote and directed "Shave, Please" (1966), an Oberhausen prizewinner and a short feature with black humor connotations.

His "The Applause-Getter" (or "The Claqueur") (1982) unspooled in the Cannes film mart, is packed with enough absurd wit to bear the writer-director's stamp. A troupe of would-be actors on a tour of the provinces feature a once great actress in the top billing, the woman now deaf, dumb, and senile. In order to keep the production alive, the young impresario doubles as local "claqueur" or "applause-getter" to assure the elderly actress that she's not playing before empty or disapproving houses. This leads to a gimmick to bring in the crowds: he spreads the rumor that the elderly actress just may die at one of the next performances — right on the stage before the audience! Of course, it's S.R.O. crowds thereafter.

Kondratiuk throws in a pinch of bare flesh to beef the plot up a bit, and there is the usual run of backstage jokes as the amateur entrepreneur battles his critics and competitors. The comedy ends with the expected twist on the very gimmick that has kept the show alive.

Worth a fest slot on the season's circuit, "The Applause-Getter" scores as the best Poland has to offer these days of shuttered studios and drama in the streets — an amusing, tongue-in-cheek comedy. —Holl.

Young Heroes
(HONG KONG-COLOR)

Hong Kong, June 14.
A Bluebird Movie Enterprises Ltd. presentation. Produced by Miranda Yang (Xia Meng). Directed by Tun Fei Mou S. Features entire cast.

Cast: Zhang Xiao Yan, Hao Yong, Hu Yi Lin, Lu Li, Zhang Yong, Li Dian Fang, Zu Mei Ling. (No other credits provided by producers). Reviewed at Nanyang Theater, Hong Kong, Feb. 13, 1983. Running time: 98 MINS.
(Cantonese soundtrack with English subtitles).

Following the footsteps of "Shaolin Temple," a tremendous hit, BlueBird's "Young Heroes" is a bit of a letdown. Watching the promising first 15 minutes in King Hu's "Dragon Inn" style, one would think we

are really on to something big and with substance. After all, Bluebird produced "Boat People." But it soon bogs down to one long tiresome chase with five villains trying to track down five innocent kids. There's practically no sub-plot, no detailed development of characters and no time for the audience to breathe.

The producer of "Young Heroes" has a keen sense, though, of knowing what the average audience wants and when they'll swoon with delight. No doubt about it, the production values are high.

The composition of the choreographed fights and crowd scenes is spectacular. Unfortunately, more sophisticated viewers won't rely only on visual values. They need dramatic counterpoints and solid performances which, in this case, is provided by one performer, a whiz-kid called Kho Yun. He plays "Big Man," a 10-year-old, who's been married to a 20-year-old woman fighter.

The storyline is set in Shih-Tsing in the late Ching (Manchu) years. It shows how some of the young heroes (mostly children) of the legendary Tien-ti Hui (Society of Heaven and Earth) cleverly and bravely get rid of their pursuers during their escape.

"Young Heroes," despite its deficiencies, may find some market abroad solely on its exotic China appeal, touristy sights of a frozen waterfall, pastoral views and authentic oriental martial arts for the action market.—Mel.

Last Plane Out
(U.S.-COLOR)

Cannes, May 15.
A Jack Cox production. No distributor. Produced by Jack Cox and David Nelson. Directed by David Nelson. Screenplay by Ernest Tidyman; camera (color), Jacques Haltkin. Features entire cast. No other credits available. Reviewed at the Olympia (market), Cannes Film Festival, May 15, 1983. Running time: 92 MINS.
Jack Cox .... Jan-Michael Vincent
Maria Cardena .... Julie Carmen
Liz Rush .... Mary Crosby
Jim Corley .... David Huffman
James Caldwell .... William Windom
Anastasio Samosa .... Lloyd Battista
Harry Clarke .... Yeg Wilson
Ramon .... Anthony Feijo
Luis .... Ronnie Gonzalez

The last days of Nicaragua's Samosa regime, as seen by an American journalist who was there, serves as the plot of "Last Plane Out." Attempted as a docu-drama, the film comes out more like a propaganda-piece for the USIA. Characters and situations are cut and dried in this unconvincing historic reconstruction.

Journalist Jack Cox (Jan-Michael Vincent, who also served as the picture's coproducer), arrives in Nicaragua toward the end of the

Samosa regime. Latin America has been his beat for several years and despite the internal turmoil Cox swims through the maelstrom to talk to both Samosa and the rebels. The latter group is convinced he's working for the CIA and suggests he leave and not return.

However, Cox does return during the last minutes of Samosa's rule. The Nicaraguan leader escapes but Cox and his crew find themselves trapped. Worse, the guerrillas know of his presence and plan to kill him before he can get an airplane out of the country.

Script by Ernest Tidyman is decidedly pedestrian. He loads the story with stereotypes ranging from cute kids running a taxi to a female love interest for Cox who happens to be a rebel leader. The final clutch has her choosing between a cause and her love for the journalist.

Social and political observations are planted like flashing neon signs. The picture's likable Samosa, actor Lloyd Battista, tells Cox "the real story" now that Washington has turned its back on the freedom-loving government. The scene demands an enormous suspension of disbelief.

Quickie, low-budget item suffers from cardboard performances and lacklustre production values. Quality rates below better television feature offerings, so North American theatrical prospects are poor. Picture may fare slightly better in foreign markets and could find some life as a pay-tv offering in the U.S.
—Klad.

Des 'Terroristes' a la Retraite
('Terrorists' in Retirement)
(FRENCH-COLOR-DOCU-16M)

Paris, June 20.
An Antenne 2/Centre National du Cinema/Top n. 1/La Cecilia co-production. Produced by Evelyne July. Directed by Mosco. Camera (color), Jean Orjollet, Daniel Desbois, with collaboration of Francois Catonnet, Guy Chanel, Philippe Rousselot, Edouardo Serra, Carlo Varini, Guy Auguste Boleat; lighting, Jean-Claude Panzera; music, Jean Schwarz and Benoit Charvet; editors, Christiane Leherissey and Beatrice de Chavagnac, with collaboration of Chantal Remy and Martine Gousse; sound, Michel Kharat, with the collaboration of Gerard Barrat, Patrice Nola and Bernard Rochut; reviewed at the Cinematheque Francaise, Paris, June 19, 1983. Running time: 83 MINS.
Narrators: Simone Signoret, Gerard Desarthe.

"Des 'Terroristes' a la Retraite" is a moving, pertinent documentary feature about the French Resistance during World War II. No, not just one more evocation of a much covered subject, but a singular spotlight on a lesser known aspect of the underground struggle: the major role played by immigrant resistance units, mobilized in the early part of the German Oc-

cupation by the French Communist Party.

Mosco, a young IDHEC film school graduate who has made some shorts, hunted up a handful of these veterans and asked them not only to recall their experiences, but in part to relive them as well. The subjects, all of Eastern European origins (Poland, Hungary, Rumania, etc.), most Jewish and one-time militant Communists, all fled persecution in their homeland and settled in France, in the years before the second World War. After the nation's fall in 1940, they proved to be among the most devoted and motivated of freedom fighters.

Today living in modest anonymity (and almost all working in Paris' garment industry), the survivors tell their fascinating story and even return to the scenes of clandestine activities to reenact several of their exploits (sometimes with the aid of actors dressed in military uniform, a rather unnecessary touch that tends to trivialize these "reconstructions"). In one scene, a veteran shows how he used to manufacture bombs in his kitchen, while another subject takes the camera crew to a Paris metro station where in 1942, he participated in the execution of a German officer.

Inevitably the souvenirs come around to the infamous "Affiche rouge" affair, in which the Gestapo rounded up several hundred Paris-based resistants in 1943 and tried 23 of them, all immigrants led by the Armenian poet Manouchian, in a brief show trial that ended in their execution by firing squad. Days later the Germans plastered Paris with red posters bearing photos of the Manouchian group and denouncing all Resistance activity as the work of foreign communists.

Mosco also interviewed other resistance figures, a couple of historians, and the widow of Manouchian. The film tends to support a controversial theory that the French Communist Party "sacrificed" the Manouchian group in order to play down the foreign, Jewish elements in the underground, and eventually emerge on the post-war political scene with a homogenous, "made in France" image in its bid for power.

Made for television, film could stir interest in situations here and abroad in both theatrical, non-theatrical and tv. —Len.

Sydney Film Festival

Lucien Brouillard
(CANADIAN-COLOR)

Sydney, June 23.
An ACPAV production. Produced by Rene Gueissaz. Directed by Bruno Carriere. Features entire cast. Assoc. producer, Marc Daigle; screenplay, Jacques

Jacob, Jacques Paris, Carriere; camera (color), Pierre Mignot; editor, Michel Arcand; art director, Gilles Aird; sound, Serge Beachemin. Reviewed at the Sydney Film Festival, June 23, 1983. Running time: 88 MINS.

Lucien Brouillard .... Pierre Curzi
Jacques Martineau .... Roger Blay
Alice .... Marie Tifo
Andre Morin .... Paul Savoie
Premier Provencher ...... Jean Duceppe

Another of the world preem events at the Sydney Film Festival, "Lucien Brouillard" is an absorbing, consistently entertaining drama played out against the turbulent backdrop of Montreal politics.

First feature from Montreal helmer Bruno Carriere, its plusses are an intelligent, thought-provoking script, first-class acting and imaginative direction.

French dialog will be a minus holding the pic back from wide release, but it should find a niche in art-houses known for programming quality foreign films and, with subtitles or dubbing, serve as agreeable tv fare in many markets. Theatrical and tv distribution has been lined up in Canada and a German tv sale has been firmed, said Carriere in Sydney for the fest.

Pacy narrative centres on two men who formed a strong bond of friendship in their youth — both were in an orphanage — and which continues despite the widely different courses each pursues in life.

Title character is a political radical, headstrong and fiery, who champions the poor and oppressed and rails against the rich and powerful. Martineau is a well-heeled, urbane lawyer whose ambitious drive carries him into Parliament and the ministry as a lieutenant to the Premier.

Brouillard languishes in jail for two years, a trumped-up police charge adding to the catalog of offenses he committed as an activist. The friends see little of each other until after Martineau's wife and child are killed in an accident, and he falls from the Premier's favour. Suddenly drawn together again, they plot their revenge, for different reasons, agaisnt the Premier. In a tense, cleverly-contrived climax Brouillard realizes that he has been betrayed by Martineau and their friendship counted for nought, and they destroy each other.

Pierre Curzi as Brouillard and Roger Blay as Martineau turn in marvelous performances, ably supported by Marie Tifo as Brouillard's wife who supports him until even she can endure no more. Tech credits are fine. —*Dogo.*

SL-1
(U.S.-DOCU-COLOR)

Sydney, June 21.

Beecher Films production. Producer-directors, Diane Orr, C. Larry Roberts. Screenplay, Orr; camera (color) Roberts; editors, Orr and Roberts; music, Brian Eno, Popol Vuh. No further credits supplied. Reviewed at the Sydney Film Festival, June 21, 1983. Running time: 60 MINS.

Given its world preem at the Sydney Film Festival, "SL-1" is a chilling re-enactment of the first fatal nuclear accident in the United States. Title refers to a reactor at a testing station in Idaho which blew up Jan. 3, 1961, killing three operators. Cause of the explosion was well established — an 80-pound central control rod was lifted by hand from the reactor cone — but the motive for what investigators termed "an abnormal act" will never be known for sure.

Docu by Diane Orr and C. Larry Roberts, indie filmmakers from Salt Lake City, fictionalises the final 72 hours in the life of one of the nuclear plant operators and painstakingly examines the aftermath of the disaster, drawing on government documents and interviews with various personnel involved, including Atomic Energy Commission investigators, scientists, physician and pathologist (curiously, none is named).

Archival film and new footage are skilfully integrated to achieve a frightening degree of realism, the sense of urgency and drama of the event heightened by slow-motion techniques.

Weight of opinions voiced supports the view that one of the operators, beset with marital problems, lifted the rod in a bizarre suicide act. Which is probably cold comfort to three of the 790 people exposed to significant radiation at that time, who in 1981 were reported to be suffering from lung, throat and colon cancer

While the human element remains, the docu warns, such accidents could happen again. A powerful and poignant blend of journalism and drama, "SL-1" is compelling viewing, and seems assured of a long life on the fest circuit. —*Dogo.*

The Disappearance of Harry
(BRITISH-COLOR)

Sydney, June 20.

Labrahurst Ltd. production for Channel 4. Producer-director, Joseph Despins. Stars Annette Crosbie. Screenplay, Despins, Howard Wakeling; assoc. producer, Chris Griffin; camera (color), Phil Meheux; editor, Tony Lawson; production designer, Herbert Westbrook; music, Nick Bicat. Reviewed at the Sydney Film Festival, June 15, 1983. Running time: 97 MINS.

Liz Webster .... Annette Crosbie
Freddie Mason .... Cornelius Garrett
Geoff Graddon .... Leonard Preston
Pat Graddon .... Cora Kinnaird
Felix Guthfrithson .... Philipe Locke
Stan Harris .... Dudley Sutton
Dr. Glynis Abbeydale ... Rosalind Knight
Harry Webster .... David Lyons

Screened in the "New British Cinema" section of the Sydney Film Festival, "The Disappearance of Harry" is a stylish, well-crafted suspenser, the third feature from Canadian-born, British-based helmer Joseph Despins.

Commissioned by indie English web Channel 4, pic is agreeable small-screen fare but does not register strongly enough to warrant theatrical exposure.

Eponymous Harry is a seemingly conventional suburban type — middle-aged, happily married with a married daughter, steady job, neat home in Nottingham — who leaves home the morning after his birthday party, never to return. A farewell note, discovered several days later, indicates he could not continue leading a "double life." A confession of bigamy? A closet homosexual?

Nothing so simple. Various clues, unsubtly dropped by director and co-writer Despins, point to Harry' involvement with a bunch of latter-date Luddites, reincarnations of an 18th century group of machine-wreckers, who are systematically bombing factories in the Midlands. Harry's wife Liz searches high and low, aided by that hoary old plot device, the sympathetic young newspaper reporter, but the trail — and the film — fizzle out at a fairground, and the viewer can but guess what happened to Harry.

The leave-them-up-in-the-air technique employed here, recalling such films as Peter Weir's "Picnic at Hanging Rock" is fine if you enjoy puzzling for hours over cryptic crosswords and conundrums; frustrating and annoying if you don't.

Pic is enhanced by a spirited perf by Annette Crosbie as Liz; and Cornelius Garrett is serviceable as Freddie, the reporter, although the scene in which Liz forgets her anxiety and tumbles between the sheets with friendly Freddie is as implausible as it is incongruous.

Tech credits are excellent, and the grey sombreness of Nottingham, adroitly captured by Phil Meheux's camerawork, is an atmospheric backdrop for a whodunit which furnishes no answers. —*Dogo.*

My Country, My Hat
(SOUTH AFRICAN-COLOR)

Sydney, June 21.

Bensusan Film production. Producer-director, David Bensusan. Stars Allette Bezuidenhout, Regardt van den Berg, Peter Se-Puma. Screenplay, Bensusan; camera (color), Michael Buckley; editor, Dereck Ward; sound, Robin Harris; music, Colin Shapiro, Barry Bekker. Reviewed at the Sydney Film Festival, June 20, 1983. Running time: 84 MINS.

Sarah .... Alletta Bezuidenhout
Piet .... Regardt van den Berg
James .... Peter Se-Puma

Touted by Sydney Film Festival organizers as the first anti-apartheid feature made entirely by South Africans, at least in modern times, "My Country, My Hat" is an angry denunciation of the nation's Pass system for registering non-whites.

For a black man, no Pass means no job, no food, no hope and no identity, as depicted in this first feature from David Bensusan, Johannesburg-based writer, producer and director. While many will sympathize with the filmmaker's sentiments, pic serves as a fairly heavy-handed exercise in didacticism, downplaying its entertainment value and probably restricting it to festivals and limited arthouse runs.

In Bensusan's Johannesburg, the whites are openly racist, regarding the blacks with either fear, suspicion or outright contempt. The blacks, on the other hand, are uniformly cheerful, decent folk trying to improve their lot but continually being frustrated and persecuted by the system.

Piet, a white garbage truck driver, kills a black man whom he suspects of burgling his house and attacking his wife, Sarah. Enter James, a young black struggling to support his wife and child, who is hired by Piet to do menial tasks around the house. James has no Pass and is working illegally, which Piet discovers. James then learns of Piet's crime, there is a stalemate, and at film's end, Piet goes free and James walks away with the dead man's Pass.

Peter Se-Puma brings a lot of verve and style to the role of James, while eliciting the high degree of sympathy intended by the director. Regardt van den Berg, an imposing screen presence with his bald pate and aggressive posture, is as detestable as no doubt intended as Piet, and Alletta Bezuidenhout is unremittingly sour and morose as the neurotic Sarah.

Shooting mostly with natural light, Bensusan has achieved an almost docu-like realism but his good work is belaboured by static camerawork and conscience-on-its-sleeve proselytizing. —*Dogo.*

Autour du Mur
(About "The Wall")
(FRENCH-COLOR-DOCU-16m)

Paris, June 22.

Mk2 production and release. Produced by Marin Karmitz. Directed and photographed (color) by Patrick Blossier. Editor, Luc Barnier; assistant director, Dominique Toussaint; production manager, Catherine Lapoujade. Reviewed at the Cinematheque Francaise, Paris, June 22, 1983. Running time: 75 MINS.
With: Yilmaz Guney, cast and crew of "Le Mur."

This is a 75-minute reportage about the shooting of "The Wall," the French-produced theatrical feature by exiled Turkish helmer Yilmaz Guney, which competed at the Cannes festival this year. Docu unspooled at the fest in the Perspectives on French Cinema program, just the day before official screening of subject film.

"The Wall" began shooting in France exactly one year after Guney's escape from a Turkish prison. Marin Karmitz, an indie distrib and exhibitor, produced it, and commissioned Patrick Blossier, a young former assistant director and cameraman, to follow the making of the pic at Pont-St. Maxence, where a former monastery, now a school, was transformed into a composite Turkish prison. Here Guney recreated a children's revolt in an Ankara prison back in 1976.

Chiefly this is a good portrait of the filmmaker as a director of actors. Aficionados of technique will be disappointed by the little footage devoted to production logistics and there is nothing about Guney's general views of film aesthetics (as he says early in the film during an indoctrination session for the actors; "The Wall" was conceived as a propaganda piece against the current Turkish military regime.)

The interest here is Guney's handling of his main actors, most of them youngsters recruited from Turkish immigrant communities in Germany, and all alien to cinema and performance.

Pic has stirred some mild controversy over some scenes in which Guney is shown slapping a young player in order to get him to cry. Apparently, what has shocked some is the discordant method of a crusading filmmaker whose pictures are compassionate denunciations of social injustice.

But it's clear that Guney is not a brute, though Blossier's camera records his authoritative, sometimes pompous manner, fits of anger and impatience, and lack of spontaneous warmth. One of the values of this film is in its demystification of the filmmaking process, reminding us that directors don't always extract good performances through mystical communion or kind, patient wheedling.

Guney's browbeating tactics and mild manhandling are certainly less shocking than the psychological terrorism of other filmmakers. —Len.

Stroker Ace
(COLOR)

One ace misdealed.

Hollywood, June 28.

A Universal Pictures release, produced by Hank Moonjean. Directed by Hal Needham. Stars Burt Reynolds. Screenplay, Hugh Wilson, Hal Needham, based on novel, "Stand On It," by William Neely and Robert K. Ottum; camera (Technicolor), Nick McLean; editors, Carl Kress, William Gordean; sound, Jack Solomon; art direction, Paul Peters; assistant director, Tom Connors; associate producer, Kathy Shea; music, Al Capps. Reviewed at Universal Studios, Universal City, June 28, 1983. (MPAA rating: PG.) Running time: 96 MINS.
Stroker Ace .... Burt Reynolds
Clyde .... Ned Beatty
Lugs .... Jim Nabors
Pembrook .... Loni Anderson
Aubrey .... Parker Stevenson
Arnold .... Bubba Smith
Doc .... John Byner
Dad .... Frank O. Hill

Burt Reynolds and director Hal Needham may not have achieved high art with their "Smokey" and "Cannonball," pics, but they at best elevated them with some charm, humor and exciting stunts. Teamed again on "Stroker Ace," however, they're just coasting in circles, trying to pick up whatever prize money might be attracted by their track record.

A top stuntman in his time, Needham as director proved he could also staged some top-notch action, especially with cars. But the most spectacular crashes in "Stroker" are contained in old stock racing footage, suggesting where the creative standards went once the deal came in the window.

In one sequence, Reynolds blazes across town in a car with a missing front wheel and when it turns corners, you can see the rigging of the gag beneath the axle, suggesting where care went, also.

Otherwise, story is no more than a cartoon, with ace driver Reynolds lured into an onerous contract with fried-chicken king Ned Beatty. Don't be surprised if Reynolds has to wear a chicken suit before he gets out of the deal.

Loni Anderson is a virginal public relations exec for the chicken shacks whose innocence is irresistable for the womanizing Reynolds. Don't be surprised if she gets drunk and decides to go to bed with him, but falls asleep before the action starts.

Jim Nabors is a good-hearted hick of a mechanic. Don't be surprised if he says "Goh-ah-ah--lly" before the picture is half over.

Continuing the "Smokey," trademark, the end titles run along with outtakes from the film just seen. Don't be surprised if they're better than picture that preceded. —Har.

Hong Kong Playboys
(HONG KONG-COLOR)

Hong Kong, June 16.

A Sir Run Run Shaw Production, Shaw Brothers. Produced by Mona Fong, Wong Ka Hee. Directed and written by Wang Tsing. Stars Alexander Fu Sheng, Shih Hsien, Chen Pai Chiang, Chung Chu Hung, Liu Hsuen Hua, Li Tien Lang, Shi Chi, Chiang Chin, Chien Hui Yi. Camera (color), Li Hsin Yeh; editors, Chiang Hsing Lung, Liu Shao Kuang; art director, Chen Ching Shen; music, Stephen Ching, So Chun Hou. Reviewed at Jade Theatre, Hong Kong, June 15, 1983. Running time: 100 MINS.
(Cantonese soundtrack, English subtitles)

Popular Hong Kong kung-fu actor Alexander Fu Sheng gets a rare opportunity to display his comedic talents in this Shaw Brothers modern comedy about romance in local high society. He portrays a rich playboy leading a carefree life until his mother, who lives overseas, returns to convince him to look for a suitable wife. She is accompanied by a private nurse (Cherry Chung) who shows disinterest in the handsome bachelor.

Fu Sheng courts a tv actress (Liu Hsueh-Hua) and a rich heiress (Chien Hui-yi) but without problems and competition from a lothario, Valentine (Shih Hsien) and a fumbling tv actor, Lolanto (Chen Pai-chiang). The competitiveness to woo and win the young ladies serve as the heart of this fast-paced comedy laced with colloquial jokes and humor that will be best appreciated by those living in the colony.

This is one of the better-produced current films from Shaw Brothers who seemed to have learned from the style of Cinema City. The result is pleasantly positive as the studied and predictable wholesale elements work well at the boxoffice.

As local comedies go, there is lack of subtlety and most movements are either exaggerated or overacted as if director Wang Tsing is afraid that his scenario won't be understood by the audience.

There are some very frolicsome moments that involve the ma jong, disco dancing and references to local celebrities, nostalgic trivia and Cantonese movie stars. The overall production is average but one thing is sure, the moviegoers are laughing on the way out of the theatre. —Mel.

The Winds Of Jarrah
(AUSTRALIAN-COLOR)

Sydney, June 28.

A Film Corporation of Western Australia Production. Produced by Mark Egerton, Marj Pearson. Directed by Mark Egerton. Features entire cast. Screenplay, Egerton, based on a screenplay by Bob Ellis and Anne Brooksbank from the Harlequin/Mills & Boon novel "The House in the Timberwoods," by Joyce Dingwall; camera (Eastmancolor, Panavision), Geoff Burton; production design, Graham Walker; costumes, David Rowe; editor, Sara Bennett; music, Bruce Smeaton; sound recording, Gary Wilkins. Reviewed at Pitt Center Cinema, Sydney, June 15, 1983. Running Time: 104 MINS.
Marlow .... Terence Donovan
Diana Venness .... Susan Lyons
Jock Farrell .... Harold Hopkins
Clem Matheson .... Steve Bisley
Ben .... Martin Vaughan
Mrs. Sullivan .... Dorothy Alison
Helen Marlow .... Isabelle Anderson
Andy .... Emil Minty

If readers of Mills and Boon books also go out to the cinema, "The Winds of Jarrah" could be a commercial success. This rather predictable romance, about a young Englishwoman who takes a job as tutor to three children who live in wooded bush country with their embittered uncle, is not for sophisticates; but neither was "The Man from Snowy River," and that became Australia's highest-grosser.

There are no prizes for guessing that, eventually, the Englishwoman, recovering from an unhappy love affair, will wind up with her truculent boss; but there may be an audience for a film which is so very attractive to look at, utilizing to the full the magnificent scenery around Dorrigo in northern New South Wales.

Susan Lyons, a statuesque actress who towers over the men in the film, is quite effective as the unhappy heroine. Terence Donovan makes a rather dour hero, while Harold Hopkins is lively as an earnest young man in love with Lyons and Steve Bisley reaffirms that he is of potential star material (if only he could find the right role) as a local rough diamond.

Mark Egerton, formerly assistant director to some of Australia's top filmmaker's including Peter Weir, Gillian Armstrong and Bruce Beresford, has handled his first full directorial assignment in a craftsmanlike way (he previously took over direction of "Crosstalk" during production); he could have injected a bit more passion into the story, which is told rather flatly, and the dialog he provides is frequently trite. However, Egerton and cinematographer Geoff Burton, give the film a magnificent visual gloss, which should be a help.

It's a pity more wasn't made of the plight of unemployed ex-soldiers (the film is set in 1946), which for a while promises to become a sub-plot more interesting than the main story — but this direction winds up in a dead end.

This is not a film for critics, and will need a hard sell to find its potential audience; however, it could pay off on its exotic locations and all-Australian theme. Emil Minty, remembered as The Feral Kid in "The Road Warrior" ("Mad Max

2") is good as the youngest of the three children who eventually succumbs to a fatal disease. —*Strat.*

Iso Valee
(Big Blonde)
(FINNISH-COLOR)

Copenhagen, June 22.

A Sateenkaarifilmi Oy/Rainbow Film Ltd. (Helsinki) production and release. Directed by Veikko Kerttula. Features entire cast. Based on Veijo Meri's novel "Summer Of The Ice-Hockey Player," screenplay, Meri and Kerttula; camera (Eastmancolor) Pekka Aine, Kari Sohlberg; editor, Tapio Suominen; music, Heiki Valpola. Reviewed at The Danish Film Institute screening room, Copenhagen, June 22, 1983. Running time: **90 MINS.**
Salme....................Kirsti Otsamo
Illu ....Kimmo Tuppurainen

As played by Kirsti Otsamo, the title character (Salme) of Veikko Kerttula's feature film, "Big Blonde," is easily believable as the harsh-edged beauty of fading youth who intrigues men of all ages in the small Finnish community around a military barracks.

The time is the early 1950s, and it seems that war-time wounds are not quite healed. Especially Salme suffers from memories of a time when she fell prey to the advances of German soldiers on Finnish soil. She now lives alone as a semi-whore, but is wary of sleeping alone, too, and she drinks too much.

When Illu, a young ice-hockey player spending the summer as a woodsman, turns up, Salme opts for a sudden marriage. She has instant relapses, though, but his rather innocent stubbornness may save the day and a future for them both.

Film has a lot of steamy sex dialog and some rough-and-tumble sex scenes, but otherwise alternately crawls and jumps along as a rather freeform slice of realistic cinematic poetry. People and landscapes around the main protagonists are given in a fresh variety of tableaux. "Big Blonde" was generally overlooked when given two special screenings at the Cannes Fest in May, but should do better on the minor festival rounds with at least some tv sales and maybe even a few theatrical openings abroad possible — as a piece of esoteric erotica, in broodingly Finnish style. —*Kell.*

Jukai No Mosukiito
(Mosquito On The Tenth Floor)
(JAPANESE-COLOR)

Tokyo, June 25.

An ATG release of a New Century Producers production. Produced by Yoshihiro Yuki. Directed by Yoichi Sai. Features entire cast. Screenplay, Yoichi Sai, Yuya Uchida; camera, (color) Masaru Mori; lighting, Isao Koyama; sound, Fujio Satoh; art, Terumi Hosoichi; editing, Shinji Yamada; music, Katsuo Ono; assistant director, Ichiro Isomura. Reviewed at

Toho screening room, Tokyo, June 17, 1983. Running time: **108 MINS.**
Man ....Yuya Uchida
Woman Thief ....Ann Lewis
Rie ....Kyoko Koizumi
Keiko ....Reiko Nakamura
Bar Proprietress ... .Junko Miyashita

A rock and roller whose long career is attributable less to talent than tenacity, Yuya Uchida is a compelling screen presence, uncharismatic in the extreme, yet practically daring you not to watch him. He is a character actor and the character he specializes in is the disaffected wage earner, burnt-out on the surface, a short fuse burning inside.

"Jukai No Mosukiito," which Uchida co-scripted with Yoichi Sai, whose interesting directorial debut this is, reprises much of Uchida's '82 starrer, "Mizu No Nai Puuru:" he is once again a man with no name in a job with no future; his relations with his family are strained; his various sexual couplings are dichotomous acts of rage and pitiful attempts to connect; he is arrested for his transgressions.

In a world where money is everything, and its acquisition by virtually whatever means possible perfectly acceptable, then a man who lives a poor but honest life will be scorned. Money is the connective tissue in most of policeman Uchida's relationships: his ex-wife, though currently living quite well, badgers him about keeping up his alimony payments; his daughter, who hangs out with leather-jacketed hoods, comes around only when she wants to put the touch on him for more allowance money; the proprietress of the bar he frequents sends him home with a cheerful reminder to clear up his accumulated bills.

Living alone in a government dwelling, he purchases a companion — a personal computer, which affords him the illusion of human interaction. This technological wonder having put a dent in his budget, he takes out a loan, gambles the money away at speedboat races, takes out another loan, gambles that money away, repeats the cycle until the authorities make him stop.

Although Uchida's lowly position on the police force is due to his having repeatedly failed departmental examinations, his wife and daughter do not hold him in contempt so much for any lack of brains, as far as his failure to emulate their instructive example and do something — anything — to "get his."

The parallel with society at large is not too difficult to discern: differences in ability — academic or otherwise — are accepted with relative equanimity; however, more and more people, misunder-

standing the meaning of democracy, are unable to accept that all slices of the economic pie cannot be the same.

Uchida is ably supported by a cast including Biito Takeshi, good in what amounts to a cameo appearance; Reiko Nakamura, making this third appearance as Uchida's main squeeze (the other two: "Mizu No Nai Puuru" and "Waika"); and Kyoko Koizumi as Uchida's daughter. —*Bail.*

Ben Lokeach Bath
(Young Loves)
(ISRAELI-COLOR)

Tel Aviv, June 20.

A Guy Films Production. Produced by Avi Kleinberger and Gideon Amir. Written and directed by Michal Bat Adam. Features entire cast. Camera (color); Nurith Aviv; editor, Hagith Anin; sound, Eli Yarkoni; production designer, Laddie Wilhelm; costumes, Esther Zevko; music, Nurith Hirsch. Reviewed in Tel Aviv, June 20, 1983. Running time: **82 MINS.**
Cast: Einath Helpman, Assaf Zur, Amalia Dayan and children and adults from the kibbutzim Ma'ayan Baruch and Kfar Glickson including Hillel Ne'eman, Gaby Eldor, Tammy Spivak, Ilan Dar, Esther Zevko, Dina Limon, Shai Golan.

Michal Bat Adam's third feature is a natural outgrowth of her previous one, in which she had the protagonist, a little girl, sent by her parents to spend time in a kibbutz. This is the starting point for the plot here, out of which she spins a tale that attempts to be an Israeli equivalent of Francois Truffaut's "Pocket Money."

It is about the little things, first friendships and pangs of jealousy, as experienced by the little girl in an alien surrounding, one which ends up so dear to her that she finds it difficult to go back to her own parents.

There is no real plot, to speak of, but more a combination of children confronting each other, the kibbutz life going on in its normal routine, with Bat Adam inserting some clear anti-militaristic messages that are rather disturbing in what is generally kiddie fare.

Children performances are not always sufficiently polished and natural, some stilted declamatory poses mar the natural charm they obviously possess when caught unawares by Nurith Aviv's sensitive camera, and the grown-ups are kept mostly in the background. For an audience interested in the kibbutz atmosphere, this is a faithful rendition, but a stronger story line would have certainly helped to keep audience attentive.

Released for the summer crowd, in hope of drawing very young audiences, this will have to do battle with some pretty aggressive competition for which it may prove too soft. —*Edna.*

Kazoku Geemu
(The Family Game)
(JAPANESE-COLOR)

Tokyo, May 27.

A Toho release of an Art Theatre Guild production. Produced by Shiro Sasaki, Yu Okada and Shiro Sasaki. Features entire cast. Written and directed by Yoshimitsu Morita, based on a book by Yohei Honma. Camera (color), Yoneo Maeda; lighting, Kazuo Yabe; sound, Hitoshi Onodera; art, Tatsumi Nakazawa; editing, Akimasa Kawashima; assistant director, Shusuke Kaneko. Reviewed at Toho screening room, Tokyo, May 27, 1983. Running time: **106 MINS.**
Yoshimoto ....Yusaku Matsuda
Mr. Numada ....Juzo Itami
Mrs. Itami ....Saori Yuki
Shigeyuki ....Ichirota Miyagawa
Shinichi ....Junichi Tsujita

To judge by only two examples from his admittedly limited body of work thus far, scenarist-director Yoshimitsu Morita, 33, is already in a class by himself. Visually, his pics have usually been uncluttered, though it would be stretching matters to say that this is his main claim to distinction. Rather, it is his slightly askew sense of humor that makes him an original.

After attracting attention with an 8m film, "Live in Chigasaki," Morita made his feature directorial debut in '81 with "No Yonamono," a breezy comedy. Then followed three relatively undistinguished pics — a Toei vehicle for a popular singing trio and a brace of Nikkatsu soft-core numbers. And now, renewing hope, is "Kazoku Geemu."

Describing just what Morita does is a problem not satisfactorily dealt with even by the publicity departments of the companies which distribute his films. Simply put, it is a cockeyed, wicked look at the Way We (which is to say, the Japanese) Live.

Juzo Itami and Saori Yuki are a prototypical, apartment-dwelling suburban couple. This petit bourgeois twosome has one bright and one not-so-bright son: Junichi Tsujita has recently been admitted to a good high school, while younger brother, Ichirota Miyagawa, struggles through his third year in high school. For their less gifted offspring, mom and pop engage a tutor, Yusaku Matsuda.

The enigmatic Matsuda descends on the household like a crusader against middle class stultification. His presence is due not only to the parents' attitude towards education — an attitude Morita submits to some very judicious tweaking — but to their own abrogation of parental roles. Morita makes deft incisions here and there, each serving to help us see anew the smotherly mother-feckless father-directionless kiddies composition of the Japanese family.

The acting is uniformly crisp. Eerily, funnily effective is Yusaku Matsuda, whose career offers proof that redemption can come at any time in an actor's life: in less than a decade, he has moved from the machismo of "Ningen no Shomei" and "Yomigaeru Kinro" to subtle, masterly performances in "Kagerouza" and now this.

As for Morita, hope has given way to expectation. As long as he continues to work for the independents, we can reasonably expect him to continue edifying and amusing. —*Bail.*

Pocukido Bame Un-Nka
(Shall the Cuckoo Sing at Night?)
(SOUTH KOREAN-COLOR)

Pesaro, June 18.
Produced by Woo Jin Film Co., Ltd. Stars Lee Dae Gun, Ghung Yoon Hee. Directed by Chung Jin Woo. Screenplay, Kim Kang Yoon; camera (color), Chung Woon Kyo. Reviewed at Pesaro Film Festival, June 18, 1983. Running time: 110 MINS.
Suni ....Lee Dae Gun
Hyunbo ....Chung Yoon Hee

A finely made, moving film with the power of a fable, "Shall the Cuckoo Sing at Night?" won the best film prize at the Grand Bell Awards in 1980, and was screened at Pesaro's Asian festival as an appetizer for next year's Korean cinema showcase. Veteran helmer Chung Jin Woo combines believable characters and a setting of great natural beauty in a tragic love story of mountain people. A classic festival item that could be marketed more widely with special handling.

On a remote mountaintop Hyungo, a stalwart, simple-minded young coal maker, lives with his aged mother. One day they find a little girl, Suni, who has been abandoned by her mother, and take her to live with them. Suni grows into a beautiful young woman, marries the coal maker, and lives with him in idyllic happiness until their lives are shattered by a lustful forest guard, who gets Hyunbo sent to prison for 10 years. Loyal to her husband, Suni revenges him by dragging the evil forester into the coal fire with her, where both perish.

Thesps deserve much credit for keeping this bittersweet fairy tale poignant but not mawkish. Lee Dae Gun is delicate-looking but inwardly strong as the heroine Suni, a simple girl whose spontaneity and naturalness of feeling protect and guide her. When Hyunbo is arrested she bravely carries on the heavy tasks of coal-making by herself; when a well-meaning friend tries to take her to the city, she has the wisdom to refuse. In the role of Suni's bearish hillbilly husband, Chung Yoon Hee wins sympathy for his pure and unflagging love for his wife. The villains, in the guise of the

forces of senseless social law, are depicted as totally evil creatures out of a nightmare.
Film is beautifully lensed.
—*Yung.*

Pesaro Film Festival

Puen-Paeng
(Puen and Paeng)
(THAILAND-COLOR)

Pesaro, June 12.
Produced by Chantana Songsri for Cherdchai Productions. Stars Chanuteporn Visitsophon, Sorapong Chatri. Directed by Cherd Songsri. Screenplay, Thom Thatree, from short story from Jacob; camera (color), Kawee Kiattina; art direction, Narong Puernprapai; editing, Kacha Rajapratarn; music, Samra Karnchanapalin and Kadee Attakorn. Reviewed at Pesaro Film Festival June 12, 1983. Running time: 129 MINS.
Paeng ....Chanuteporn Visitsophon
Lorr ....Sorapong Chatri
Puen ....Kanungnit Reksasarn

A lavishly lensed, finely acted drama about star-crossed lovers, noble hearts and evil deeds, set in a picturesque village in 1930's Thailand. A winning heroine, played by newcomer Chanuteporn Visitsophon, gives the familiar story freshness and charm. "Puen and Paeng" is an easy to digest film for foreigners and could well have a commercial life apart from the fest circuit.
Pic opens with a series of lyrical scenes of Paeng's life as an unloved little girl, cruelly mistreated by her father and mocked by the villagers who favor her beautiful older sister Puen. Paeng's defender is Lorr, a handsome and hard-working youth who is the pride of the village.
Story gets underway when Lorr and Puen are engaged to be married. Paeng, mischievous, comical and unrepressed, does everything to win Lorr away from her sister. But when Lorr comes down with malaria the girls' true character comes out: Paeng keeps a faithful vigil at his bedside, while Puen accepts the attentions of a Don Juan cousin.
As in the best fairy tales, Paeng nobly hides the truth from her beloved, intent on sacrificing herself to his love for Puen. Lorr discovers the truth and he and Paeng spend a fateful night together that ends in tragedy.
Helmer Cherd Songsri's lensing of the old village life, untouched by the modern civilization that has already reached Bangkok, is movingly beautiful, with nostalgic scenes of riding water buffaloes, chanting in the rice paddies, going to the shadow play. Music, lensing and thesping work together in an absorbing narration with some magical moments. —*Yung.*

Dibalik Kelambu
(Under the Mosquito Net)
(INDONESIAN-COLOR)

Pesaro, June 13.
Produced by P.T. Sukma Putra Film. Stars Christine Hakim, Slamet Rahardjo. Directed by Teguh Karya. Screenplay, Teguh Karya, Slamet Rahardjo; camera (color), Tantra Suryadi; art director, Satari S.K5 and Benny Benhardi; editing, George Kamarullan; music, Eros Djarot. Reviewed at Pesaro Film Festival, June 13, 1983. Running time: 100 MINS.
Hasan .... Slamet Rahardjo
Nurlela ....Christine Hakim

A predictable drama from Indonesia about the vicissitudes of a young married couple. A middle-range product with a soap-opera style story, "Under the Mosquito Net" will have limited commercial appeal for most off-shore audiences, who can watch similar local items on tv.

Hasan, a poor man who has married into a higher social caste, his beautiful wife Nurlela and their two kids have a hard time cohabiting with the rich in-laws. They don't have the money to rent an apartment of their own. Hasan's father-in-law picks on him day and night. Nurlela gets sick, Hasan loses his job and starts driving a cab in secret. Hasan, who is not a very sympathetic character in spite of his problems, reacts by lying compulsively, beating his wife and leaving her for another woman who doesn't know he's married. Against all odds pics opts for a happy ending with husband giving up girlfriend, and wife joyfully forgiving all.

Only thing that indicates "Mosquito Net" comes from Indonesia is the glossed over question of whether Hasan's womenfolk are going to put up with him taking a second wife or not — a complication not foreseen by most daytime drama, but rich in possibilities. "Net" doesn't play up the idea, but the picture that emerges of the modern Indonesian woman trying to support herself while saddled with crushing family obligations is oppressive enough. To pic's credit is thesp Christine Hakim, a sympathetic heroine we don't blame for being almost driven to suicide. Slamet Rahardjo (credited as co-scripter) fails to bring across the charm, warmth or dignity that would make Hasan worth fighting over. —*Yung.*

Feilai De Xianhe
(The Magic Crane Flew By)
(CHINESE-COLOR)

Pesaro, June 14.
Produced by Changchun Film Studios. Features entire cast. Directed by Chen Jialin. Screenplay Wang Xingdong, Wang Zhebin, Liu Zicheng; camera (color), Chen Chan-an, Zhang Baoxi. Reviewed at Pesaro Film Festival, June 14, 1983. Running time: 112 MINS.
Cast: Yang Tong, Wang Shangxin, Sun Caihua, Zhang Weixin and Li Tiyun.

Little boy has to choose between his beloved adoptive parents and real father and mother. Main virtue of this unabashed tearjerker — other than its interest value in hailing from Mainland China — is extremely fine lensing and poetic imagery. Western audiences are likely to find it slow-moving and predictable.

Bai Lu, a pretty ballet dancer in Peking, one day remembers her 10-year-old son, Xiang, whom she was forced to give up at birth when she and her husband were exiled to the steppes by the Gang of Four. Now comfortably rehabilitated, Bai Lu journeys incognito to the crane preserve where the boy is living with a pair of kindly peasants.

When Xiang's foster folks accidentally learn who Bai Lu is, they nobly sacrifice their beloved son to allow him to be "educated" in the city. This seems to chiefly consist in learning to play the piano, which Xiang can't stand, and after many heart-wrenching tears he runs away to the farm, just as the cranes are migrating north again.

Though simplistic, helmer Chen Jialin's first feature is graced with some breathtaking nature photography of cranes on the moody, storm-ridden marsh and picturesque lensing of peasant life (two DPs are credited, Chen Chan-an and Zhang Baoxi). Arty freeze-frames and teary close-ups of suffering faces banalize the beauty of the images, which would have done much better with low-key treatment. With no villainous characters or selfish sentiments (everyone wants to do what's best for the child), pic's conflict is simply left to when Xiang will come back to his heart-broken foster parents. The heavy symbolism put on the birds Xiang loves should tip off the sleepiest viewer.
All hands turn in fine thesping performances, including the child actor. —*Yung.*

Lingju
(Neighbors)
(CHINESE-COLOR)

Pesaro, June 13.
Produced by Young People's Film Studios of the Superior Film Institute of Peking. Stars Feng Hanyuan. Directed by Zheng Dongtian, Xu Guming. Screenplay, Ma Lin, Znu Mei, Da Jiangfu; camera (color), Zhou Kun, Gu Wenkai; art direction, Liu Guang'en, Wang Honhai; editing, Zhang Lanfang, Zhao Qihua. Reviewed at Pesaro Film Festival, June 13, 1983. Running time: 118 MINS.
Liu Lixing ....Feng Hanyuan
Yuan Chifang ....Wang Pei
Xi Fengnian ....Xu Zhongquan
Li Zhanwen ....Feng Weidong

A long, drawn-out story of fighting bureaucracy for decent housing in Mainland China, "Neighbors" may have more sociological fascination than conventional entertainment value for

Western viewers. Through a rambling and not always evenly-paced chain of anecdotes around a cast of characters — hard to keep track of — pic offered one of the broadest overviews of life in contemporary China on view at the Asian film festival, of particular interest to those concerned with contemporary Chinese culture and society.

Six families are crowded into temporary quarters where they share a communal kitchen in the hallway. While they wait to be assigned to new apartments, they see building funds being diverted to construct a hotel for foreigners and secret luxury apartments for government officials. The protest of the boarders is led by old Liu, a retired ex-cadre who still has friends in high places.

Sweeping a look at many different social classes, from the well-to-do head of the architectural project to rehabilitated officials, teachers, students and housewives, the gap between young and old, and jealousies between different generations of functionaries, "Neighbors" achieves its aim of describing contemporary life realistically. The story is carefully lightened with humorous elements and many characters have their charm. Some political references are obscure to the unprepared viewer, and the film is permeated by a post-Gang of Four optimism and eagerness to work together for the welfare of the country and one's neighbors that strikes the Westerner as a committee-made sentiment. Pic was, in fact, codirected by Zheng Dongtian and Xu Guming. Though not a personalized film, "Neighbors" has the fascination of a firsthand report on a little-known country. Acting is professional, technical credits adequate. — *Yung.*

Man Chu
(Late Autumn)
(SOUTH KOREAN-COLOR)

Pesaro, June 17.

Produced by Dong-A Exports Co. Stars Jong Dong Hwan, Kim Hae Ja. Directed by Kim Soo Yong. Screenplay, Kim Ji Hun; camera (color), Chung Il Sung. Reviewed at Pesaro Film Festival, June 17, 1983. Running time: 95 MINS.
The woman . . . . Jong Dong Hwan
The man . . . . Kim Hae Ja

Made in 1981, "Late Autumn" is a graceless festival film that fails to absorb the viewer into its implausibly tragic story or convince of its sincerity. Veteran Korean helmer Kim Soo Yong is a master of photogenic lensing, but sensitive photography is powerless against pic's dragging pace, that of a tired workhorse staggering under its load. With practically only two cha-

racters on the screen for its entirety and a single sad tune played over and over maddeningly, pic has a definite marketability problem abroad.

The characters are nameless. A depressed-looking woman gets on a train with a stern-faced matron who eventually leaves her. The man opposite her tries to strike up a conversation but she won't say a word. He persists, and follows her to her mother's grave in a small town. Finally he takes her to a hotel, but immediately dashes off to murder a shady underworld figure. When he returns she is gone. They meet just in time to say goodbye before she is escorted back to prison by the matron (having killed her husband years before in a flashbacked fit of jealous) while he is arrested for his crime.

Despite the reminiscent title, Kim Soo Yong is no Ozu and "Autumn" doggedly refuses any type of social setting or significance. The two characters (of whom the man is the more interesting, if only because he talks) seem designed as stick figures, representatives of some vague human condition that is characterized by solitary suffering and paired salvation. Like the rocky landscape of the little town, the empty vastness of the hotel and the monotonous familiarity of the train, pic is stripped down and barren-looking, proudly self-conscious of its own nudity as though it was the height of art.

The finale is more depressing than poignant, and anyway comes as no surprise since it opens the picture. — *Yung.*

Staying Alive
(COLOR)

Travolta's hot, but Rocky's not.

Hollywood, July 8.

A Paramount release of a Robert Stigwood production. Produced by Stigwood, Sylvester Stallone. Executive producer, Bill Oakes. Directed by Stallone. Stars John Travolta. Screenplay, Stallone, Norman Wexler, based upon characters created by Nik Cohn; camera (Metrocolor), Nick McLean; editors, Don Zimmerman, Mark Warner; songs by The Bee Gees; music coordination, Robin Garb; production design, Robert F. Boyle; art direction, Norman Newberry; set decoration, Arthur J. Parker; costume design, Thomas M. Bronson; finale costume design, Bob Mackie; sound (Dolby), Jeff Wexler; choreography, Demnon Rawles, Sayuber Rawles; associate producer, Linda Horner; second unit director, Thomas J. Wright; assistant director, William Beasley. Reviewed at the Paramount Studios, L.A., July 8, 1983. (MPAA Rating: PG.) Running time: 96 MINS.
Tony Manero . . . . John Travolta
Jackie . . . . Cynthia Rhodes
Laura . . . . Finola Hughes
Jesse . . . . Steve Inwood
Mrs. Manero . . . . Julie Bovasso

The bottom line is that "Staying Alive" is nowhere as good as its six-year-old predecessor, "Saturday Night Fever." More to the point for this summer's young audiences, however, is that, despite lots of visible sweat expended in the cause, the dance and music-dominated feature doesn't generate the heat and sense of style that have made Paramont's own "Flashdance" such an unexpected sensation. Double-barrelled threat posed by its sequel status and trendy genre will mean plenty of immediate b.o., abetted here by John Travolta, who is in amazing shape and looks great.

When last heard from, Travolta's Tony Manero had left Brooklyn for an uncertain future in Manhattan. Now, he's on the rounds of casting calls and auditions for Broadway dance shows and pulling in a little change as a modern dance instructor.

He's also got a comfortable but uncommitted relationship going with fellow struggling dancer and sometime saloon singer Cynthia Rhodes, who loves him a lot. Nevertheless, Travolta doesn't think twice about her feelings when he spots alluring British dancer Finola Hughes and hooks up with her while winning a background role in a show in which she will be starring.

Hughes is a pragmatic, ruthless woman who espouses a use-unto-other approach to life which Travolta finds confusing, but he repeatedly stands up Rhodes while deluding himself that he may be able to land promiscuous Hughes just for himself.

By close to showtime, Travolta and Hughes loathe each other, and she's none too pleased when this unknown upstart manages to replace her faltering costar in the

male lead of the production. Even though it looks like a Ken Russell reimagining of a sub-Bob Fosse extravaganza, the show, entitled "Satan's Alley," emerges as an opening night smash, and Tony Manero is a success at last. But asked by his loyal girlfriend if he might like to step out to celebrate, he utters the following classic line: "You know what I wanna do? You know what I wanna do? Strut," upon which he hits the pavement again to the strains of the Bee Gees' "Staying Alive," reprised from the earlier pic.

Centerstage throughout, of course, is Travolta, who, having been put through an intense physical training program by director Sylvester Stallone, is an astonishing physical specimen. He is also as winning as before in this characterization, and it's a pleasure to watch the actor work.

Unfortunately, the musical aspect of the film is a distinct disappointment. The five new tunes turned out by the Bee Gees would seem to have none of the chart-busting potential of their "Saturday Night Fever" collection, and the other numbers, many of which were cowritten and performed by Frank Stallone, are none too catchy.

Like a contempo "Footlight Parade," film concludes with three elaborate "Satan's Alley" production numbers, which feature Travolta in a loin cloth and are pretentiously populated by writhing dancers, a high-tech cage of a set and all manner of stage gimmicks. Here, as elsewhere, bright lights, overly-kinetic cutting and a predominance of close-ups prevent good prolonged looks at the dancing itself.

Rhodes is sweet and sympathetic as the proper lady in Travolta's life, while Hughes comes on strong as his temptress. For his part, Stallone, who also coproduced with Robert Stigwood and cowrote with Norman Wexler, puts in a Hitchcockian cameo in the early going.

Pic has the hard-edged but slick look which is virtually becoming a Paramount house style. — *Cart.*

Red Monarch
(BRITISH-COLOR)

London, June 30.

An Engima production for Goldcrest Films & TV Ltd. Produced by Graham Benson. Executive producer, David Puttnam. Directed by Jack Gold. Stars Colin Blakely, David Suchet. Screenplay, Charles Wood; camera (color), Mike Fash; production design, Norman Garwood; editor, Laurence Mery-Clark; asst. director, Gary White. Reviewed at the Channel Four Cinema, London, June 6, 1983. Running time: 101 MINS.
Stalin . . . . Colin Blakely
Beria . . . . David Suchet
Brown . . . . : . . . Carroll Baker
Shaposhnikov . . . . Ian Hogg
Molotov . . . . Nigel Stock
Lee . . . . Lee Montague

Vlasek . . . . Glynn Edwards
Sergo . . . . David Kelly

In its attempt to portray the lighter side of life at the Kremlin under Russian despot Josef Stalin, "Red Monarch" clearly figures as an oddball entry in the market. Although the theme of the pic, to be distributed in the U.S. by the Sam Goldwyn Co., may stir some audience interest, generally the film falls flat both as comedy and an expose of a dictator's mind.

What is lacking from the episodic story is any narrative thrust. It's a package of incidents. The Politburo meet to discuss Russia's defeat in a basketball contest. Stalin plays snooker while riposting approaches from this drunken sot of a son. A meeting with China's Mao Tse-tung ends up as an arm-wrestling contest. And director Jack Gold pulls out all the stops for Stalin's interview with an American journalist played by Carroll Baker.

The scenes portrayed feel authentic enough, not surprisingly since Charles Wood's script derived from a set of short stories written by Yuri Krotkov from his own experiences of Stalin. Additionally, both production designer Norman Garwood and lenser Mike Fash did a fine job of "Russianizing" the U.K. locations.

Colin Blakely as Stalin and David Suchet as his sidekick, Beria, create comic performances that fall well short of clowning. The red monarch himself is portrayed as an eccentric buffoon burdened by the responsibilities of power. And his accomplice comprises an interesting mix of lechery, sycophancy and hatred of his master.

Ultimately, however, the film's makers failed to find a style that would make a peculiarly Russian form of satire of interest to a wide international audience. —Japd.

Zelig
(BLACK & WHITE/COLOR)

Woody back in grace with inspired pseudo-docu. Class prospects great.

An Orion Pictures/Warner Brothers release, distributed by WB, of a Jack Rollins and Charles H. Joffe production. Executive producer, Joffe. Produced by Robert Greenhut. Directed by Woody Allen. Stars Allen, Mia Farrow. Screenplay, Allen; camera (b&w/color), Gordon Willis; editor, Susan E. Morse; music, Dick Hyman; sound, James Sabat, Frank Graziadel; supervising sound editor, Dan Sable; sound editor, Marjorie Deutsch; production manager-associate producer, Michael Peyser; assistant director, Fredric B. Blankfein; production design, Mel Bourne; art direction, Speed Hopkins; costume design, Santo Loquasto; makeup design, Fern Buchner; special makeup effects, John Caglione; choreography, Danny Daniels; still photography, Kerry Hayes; photo retouchers, Karen Dean, Judith Lumb; optical effects; Joe Hynick, Stuart Robinson. R/Greenburg Associates; stills

animation, Steven Plastrik; newsreel artcards, Karen Siegel Engel; narrator, Patrick Horgan. Reviewed at Beekman Theatre, N.Y., July 6, 1983. (MPAA Rating: PG). Running time: **84 MINS.**

Leonard Zelig . . . . Woody Allen
Dr. Eudora Fletcher . . . . Mia Farrow
Actor Zelig . . . . Garrett Brown
Sister Meryl . . . . Stephanie Farrow
Rally chancellor . . . . Will Holt
Martin Geist . . . . Sol Lomita
Paul Deghuee . . . . John Rothman
Lita Fox . . . . Deborah Rush
Actress Fletcher . . . . Marianne Tatum
Sister Ruth . . . . Mary Louis Wilson
Also appearing in comporary interviews: Susan Sontag, Irving Howe, Saul Bellow, Bricktop, Dr. Bruno Bettelheim, Prof. John Morton Blum.

With a film as uniquely conceived and subtly entertaining as "Zelig," Woody Allen, never a talent to be tied by convention or taken for granted, has likely regained a good portion of the smiled-upon paradise he largely lost since 1979's "Manhattan."

Lampooning documentary tradition by structuring the entire film as a meticulously crafted bogus docu, Allen tackles some serious stuff en route (namely the two-edged sword of public and media celebrityhood) but manages to avoid the recent self-oriented seriousness that's alienated many of his onetime loyalists. More positively, "Zelig" is consistently funny, though more academic than boulevardier. Critical response should be strong and business in urban climes promises to be brisk.indeed. Typically less assured are prospects closer to the grass roots.

Allen himself plays the eponymous Leonard Zelig, subject of the "documentary" that traces this onetime legend of the 1920s-30s whose weak personality and neurotic need to be liked caused him to become the ultimate conformist. Changing not only his personality, but even his facial features and body and shape to suit his company, Zelig is traced, via "vintage" newsreels, recordings and interviews (including real-life contempo intellectuals) through his progress from medical marvel to a celebrity in his own right.

Through the use of doctored photos and staged black and white footage cannily — and usually undetectably — matched with authentic newsreels and stock footage of the period, Allen is seen intermingling with everyone from the Hearst crowd at San Simeon, Eugene O'Neill and Fanny Brice to the likes of Pope Pius XI and even Adolf Hitler. To describe his adventures in any detail would spoil too much fun.

The narrative that does emerge (the entire film is narrated between docu and interview segments) limns the efforts of a committed psychiatrist (played with tact and loveliness by Mia Farrow) to give Zelig a single self, a relationship that blossoms, predictably, to love by fadeout.

Trashing psychoanalytic convention and jargon along the way, the film follows his path from "Elephant Man"-type freak (his half-sister makes a fortune off him) to high society, casting a scathing look at public appetites (and fickleness) as Zelig is first merchandised (toys, games, watches, a "Chameleon Dance" craze and even clips from a bogus 1935 WB biopic, which distorts and glamorizes his tale in typical Hollywood fashion) and later turned upon.

Basically parodic, "Zelig" is like one of Allen's New Yorker pieces come to staggering life and, as such, is often on the academic level, a sense buffeted (and self-mocked) through present-day interviews (a nice swipe at "Reds") with contempo intellectual types, including Saul Bellow, Bruno Bettelheim, Susan Sontag and Irving Howe, all acting as if they knew Zelig when.

There are a number of truly inspired sight gags and a constant flow of epigrams along with some expected one-liners, but the core of the film's humor comes from its absurdist juxtaposition of the eternal nebbish in the great tide of history. The concept eventually wears a bit thin, but the curtailed running-time stops it all just when it should.

Technically, "Zelig" is a masterwork. With Allen deftly staging his own and the large cast's performances, conforming to but not exaggerating the conventions of the docu mold, major plaudits go to Gordon Willis's largely black and white cinematography, which blends its own style, texture and essence with the stock footage; Susan E. Morse's prodigious editing job; Dick Hyman's period-parody "Zelig" songs, and Santo Loquasto's era-perfect costumes.
—Step.

Class
(COLOR)

Crudely written & executed 'older woman' saga. Quick exploitation in order.

Hollywood, July 6.

An Orion release of a Martin Ransohoff production. Produced by Ransohoff. Executive producer, Cathleen Summers. Directed by Lewis John Carlino. Features entire cast. Screenplay, Jim Kouf, David Greenwalt; camera (Deluxe color), Ric Waite; supervising editor, Stuart Pappe; editor, Dennis Dolan; music, Elmer Bernstein; art direction, Jack Poplin; set decoration, Bill Fosser; Bisset's costume design, Donfeld; sound, Ray Cymoszinski; associate producers, Kouf, Greenwalt, Jill Chadwick; assistant directors, L. Andrew Stone, Scott Maitland. Reviewed at the Samuel Goldwyn Theatre, Beverly Hills, July 6, 1983. (MPAA Rating: R.) Running time: **98 MINS.**

Skip . . . . Rob Lowe
Ellen . . . . Jacqueline Bisset
Jonathan . . . . Andrew McCarthy
Balaban . . . . Stuart Margolin
Mr. Burroughs . . . . Cliff Robertson
Roscoe . . . . John Cusack

Roger . . . . Alan Ruck
Allen . . . . Rodney Pearson
Kennedy . . . . Remak Ramsey
Lisa . . . . Virginia Madsen
Susan . . . . Deborah Thalberg

"Class" is anything but classy. Abysmally written, crudely made and visibly schizophrenic in its intentions. Martin Ransohoff production does offer some overtly commercial "elements" which will put it over with certain segments of the public, notably teenaged boys, so hard sell behind wide national release will produce some decent b.o. But pic's legs can't compare with those of its star.

About a brainy but virginal prep school student who unwittingly begins an affair with his upper-class roommate's sexy mother, film seems something like an unofficial remake of one of Jacqueline Bisset's first Hollywood efforts, the 1969 "The First Time," in which she initiated the nerdy Wes Stern in the pleasures of the flesh. Throw in aspects of "The Graduate," with the young fellow's best friend, instead of girlfriend, getting mad at the betrayal, and you get the idea.

Whether it was the case or not, script by Jim Kouf and David Greenwalt seems like it was written once for the dramatic impact of the situation, then rewritten to pack in some inane boy's school hijinx. Or vice versa. In any event, opening stretch crassly announces "outrageous" aspirations, what with the two guys running around in lingerie and one of them barfing on a double date and disrupting a sedate meeting at a girls' school, while final half-hour lurches into more serious territory as the pals try to mend their relationship after the discovery of the transgression.

But worse than that is the utter implausibility of the affair between Bisset and self-described "turd" Andrew McCarthy (by now, a whole category of Bisset's films has her hooking up with younger men). She picks him up in a Chicago singles' bar, where, unbelievably, he is not carded even though he looks many years younger than anyone else there, then practically rapes him in, of all places, an exposed, see-through elevator.

All of a sudden a new-born study, McCarthy continues to rendezvous with his lusty lady until, on a trip to New York, she ditches him upon discovering that he's just a preppy instead of the Northwestern Ph.D. candidate he had claimed. It all hits the fan when Bisset's self-possessed son (Rob Lowe) brings McCarthy home for Christmas.

Amazingly, Bisset sneaks into McCarthy's room at night, and keeps calling him in the following weeks, even though he wants nothing more to do with her. Brief mention is made of Bisset's "neurosis," but no attempt at all is made to explain her character's bizarre behavior. Is she a nympho? Does she just need some attention, something she doesn't get from stuffy, wealthy hubby Cliff Robertson? Aren't there any other men in Chicago? Is she genuinely into young boys? There's really no figuring her out, and it's not the actress' fault.

McCarthy and Lowe carry most of the picture, and both acquit themselves reasonably well under the circumstances. Lewis John Carlino's direction is frequently awkward, notably in the nudity-less sex scenes; R rating has been won strictly on the basis of mucho vulgar dialog.

Ric Waite's lensing is surprisingly murky, given quality of most of his recent work, and one imagines a rock song score would have been more suitable for intended audience than the more traditional Elmer Bernstein effort offered up. Other tech contributions are equally lackluster. —Cart.

The Return of Captain Invincible
(AUSTRALIAN-COLOR)

Sydney, July 6.

Seven Keys Film Distributors release of a Philippe Mora film. Produced by Andrew Gaty. Directed by Philippe Mora. Stars Alan Arkin, Christopher Lee, Kate Fitzpatrick, Bill Hunter. Screenplay, Steve de Souza, Gaty; director of photography (color), Mike Molloy; art director, Owen Patterson; sound, Ken Hammond; editor, John Scott; production designer, David Copping; original score, William Motzing; assoc. producer, Brian Burgess. Reviewed at Hoyts Theatre, Sydney, July 5, 1983. (Commonwealth Film Censor rating: NRC). Running time: **90 MINS.**

Captain Invincible	Alan Arkin
Mr. Midnight	Christopher Lee
Patty Patria	Kate Fitzpatrick
Tupper/Coach	Bill Hunter
Australian Prime Minister	Graham Kennedy
U.S. President	Michael Pate
Kirby	Hayes Gordon
Admiral	Max Phipps
General	Noel Ferrier

The eponymous Captain, a.k.a. the Man of Magnet and the Legend in Leotards, is a superhero who, after being hounded out of the U.S. by the McCarthyites (his red cape was a dead giveaway), seeks refuge in the bottle and the Australian outback, until he is dragged back into service by the American President to save the world from the incarnation of evil, Mr. Midnight.

A terrific premise for escapist fantasy, which is muddled in its execution. Result is an uneven, inconsistent film which is inspired, nearly brilliant in parts, but which fails to jell as a whole. As a musical comedy it is light on laughs; as an adventure it has moments of edge-of-the-seat excitement, but loses momentum when it most needs it: in the final 15 minutes.

Boxoffice prospects in Australia, where it's being released by Seven Keys, and in the U.S., where it's slated to play in 800 cinemas via Jensen Farley Pictures, are moderate at best.

Pic has had a troubled passage to the screen. Director Philippe Mora and producer Andrew Gaty had creative disagreements, and Gaty recut the film in New York. The Australian Home Affairs Minister expressed doubts about the project's origins (screenplay is credited to Gaty and American writer Steve de Souza) and creative control, and refused to grant a final certificate, a pre-requisite for the 150% tax deduction for investors, which Gaty is appealing in court. None of which could or should matter to cinema patrons, but it may help explain the odd juxtaposition of some scenes, and the intervals when narrative sags.

Mora sets the scene beautifully in the opener: a series of rapid-fire mock newsreel segs, recapping the superhero's exploits and his eventual fall from grace. Switch to Australia, where the not-so-invincible Captain had become a drunken bum. Then, a world crisis: the top-secret hypno-ray is stolen, and the U.S. President's SOS to the man who was his boyhood hero.

Rehabilitated with a little assistance from Aussie policewoman Kate Fitzpatrick, and gradually regaining his awesome powers, our hero sets out to thwart Mr. Midnight, who has a fiendish plan to purify New York: persuade the ethnic minorities to buy homes on the coastline, then have them float out to sea with the aid of some well-directed torpedoes.

Alan Arkin brings a lot of energy, style and guile to his role as the comic strip hero, while Christopher Lee as Mr. Midnight seems to enjoy himself hugely, without developing the menacing edge which would have made his character more effective.

Fitzpatrick, an erstwhile actress who has earned a solid reputation in many stage plays and tv appearances, makes an awkward transition to the big screen, a cold and sterile presence. Michael Pate hams it up to the point of overkill as the U.S. President, and Graham Kennedy is a bumbling buffoon as Australian Prime Minister.

The flying sequences — Invincible zooming over Sydney and Manhattan, Fitzpatrick perched awkwardly on his back — are unremarkable, despite the deployment of the same front projection technique used on the "Superman" films, while some of the other special effects, such as the attack-of-the-Kill-er-vacuum cleaners sequence — works like a charm. Mr. Midnight's offsider, a dwarf who looks like he was cross-bred from the "Star Wars" and "Dark Crystal" factories, is a shriek.

Production numbers, including contributions from the "Rocky Horror Show's" Richard Hartley and Richard O'Brien, are outstanding in every aspect. If only the other elements of this patchwork picture were as classy, "Captain Invincible" might fly a lot higher. — Dogo.

Phar Lap
(AUSTRALIAN-COLOR)

Sydney, July 5.

A Hoyts Distribution release of a John Sexton presentation in association with Michael Edgley International. Produced by John Sexton. Directed by Simon Wincer. Stars Tom Burlinson, Martin Vaughan, Judy Morris and Ron Leibman. Screenplay, David Williamson; camera (Panavision, color), Russell Boyd; music, Bruce Rowland; production design, Larry Eastwood; sound: Gary Wilkin; costume design, Anna Senior; editor, Tony Paterson. Reviewed at Film Australia Theatrette, Lindfield, July 4, 1983. Running Time: 118 MINS.

Tommy Woodcock	Tom Burlinson
Harry Telford	Martin Vaughan
Bea Davis	Judy Morris
Dave Davis	Ron Leibman
Vi Telford	Celia de Burgh
Lachlan McKinnon	Vincent Ball
Emma	Georgia Carr
Jim Pike	James Steele
Eric Connolly	John Stanton
Bert Wolfe	Peter Whitford

Phar Lap was a champion racehorse, a legend in his own lifetime, who met a mysterious death in California in 1932. "Phar Lap" is the second feature film production backed by multi-media entrepreneur Michael Edgley; his first, "The Man from Snowy River," met with critical brickbats but went on to become not only the most successful Australian film to date, but for a while was the No. 1 boxoffice title in the history of Down Under distribution.

Against all odds, "Phar Lap" is a much better film than "Snowy River." Director Simon Wincer, whose previous theatrical outings were the inane thrillers "Snapshot" (1979) and "Harlequin" (1980), has delivered the goods; the film may not win critical awards, but should be a huge success on the home market and do very respectably overseas into the bargain.

It's a big, handsome, entertaining story about a scrawny horse that becomes a champion, a poor man who becomes rich, and a shy stable-boy who helps train one of the greatest race-horses ever. There's also the amiably rascally American who has a part-interest in the horse, plus some sinister racetrack types who at one stage threaten the life of the champion horse and his trainer and who, ultimately, may be responsible for his sudden death.

Film's one flaw is its opening: it begins with Phar Lap's illness and death, and while every schoolboy in Australia knows this is how the story ended, a little suspense might have been retained for overseas viewers. Problem is compounded by the ill-advised printing of the opening titles over this sequence, which further robs it of impact. However, once the flashbacks begin and Phar Lap's story is told, the film takes off. It may not be particularly original, but David Williamson's screenplay is a model of its kind, and Wincer gives it pacing and narrative clarity all too rare in Australian cinema. Added to this is the very superior cinematography of Russell Boyd, a bouncy musical score by Bruce Rowland, and glorious costumes (Anna Senior) and sets (Larry Eastwood). Racing scenes are superbly handled, though the slow-motion gimmick is a bit overworked.

Performances are all fine. Tom Burlinson, the young lead from "Snowy River," is very effective as the shy stable-boy who becomes devoted to the courageous horse. Martin Vaughan is impressive as the grimly determined trainer who leases the horse in the first place, as is Celia de Burgh, luminous as his loyal but neglected wife. Ron Leibman practically walks away with the picture as Davis, the smooth American horseowner, and Judy Morris is quietly effective as his naive, talkative wife. Also worthy of mention is Vincent Ball, very smooth as an ultra-conservative member of Australia's horse-racing elite, equally opposed to what he sees as an inferior horse, and to its Jewish-American owner.

Incidentally, the character played by Burlinson, Tommy Woodcock, is still alive; now a sprightly 78, he acted as adviser on the production. Mention must also be made of Towering Inferno, the magnificent horse who plays Phar Lap with absolute conviction.

"Phar Lap" looks set to be another huge success, probably equalling or even besting "Snowy River," locally. Overseas, too, it stands an excellent chance for success as, basically, it's a good story well told. Another shot in the arm for the troubled Aussie film industry. —Strat.

Don't Go In The Woods
(COLOR)

A grammatical and film-making error.

A Seymour Borde & Associates release of a JBF presentation. Produced by Roberto and Suzette Gomez. Directed by James Bryan. Features entire cast. Screenplay, Garth Eliassen; camera (color), Henry Zinman; editor, uncredited; music, H. Kingsley Thurber; sound, Gerry Klein; production manager, Jonathan Bliss. Reviewed at Movieland theatre, N.Y., July 1, 1983. (MPAA Rating: R). Running time: **81 MINS.**

Peter	Nick McClelland
Craig	James P. Hayden
Ingrid	Mary Gail Artz
Joanie	Angie Brown
Monster	Tom Drury

Also with: David Barth, Larry Roupe, Ken Carter.

Filmed during the horror production boom of 1980, "Don't Go In The Woods" finally arrives in New York as one of the poorest amateur efforts in the genre, reviewed here for the record.

Plotless wonder was lensed in photogenic Brighton, Utah and environs, though the grainy blowup from 16m and "can't afford a tripod" blurry camerawork belie that potential value. Premise has a "monster" (revealed in the third reel to be a hairy, club & spearwielding man) preying on hikers venturing into the hillside forests. Requisite gore is provided in the form of bloody killings, but without the adventurous makeup effects audiences have come to expect in horror flicks.

Acting is terrible, with the unphotogenic lead quartet of youngsters given no characterizations: they're just potential meat for the yowling baddie. When two of the foursome escape to civilization and a hospital, script logic falls apart completely, with the male lead returning to the forest on a one-man rescue mission and the girl actually brought back there by the local posse on the flimsiest of pretexts. In line with the film's lame attempts at black humor (e.g., a guy in a wheelchair trying to ascend the steep grade), open-ending poses a cute orphaned kid as the monster's successor.

Poor, artificial sound and a repetitive, abrasive electronic music track also contribute to this test of endurance for even the hardiest of horror film completists. After a deputy sums up the proceedings with a line typical of pic's writing: "Makes you kind of wonder," out-theme is a garbled version of "Teddy Bears' Picnic," which at least gets the title warning fixed: "Don't go out in the woods tonight..."—*Lor.*

Deadly Force
(COLOR)

Disposable actioner.

An Embassy Pictures release of a Sandy Howard/Hemdale production. Executive producer, John Daly. Produced by Sandy Howard. Directed by Paul Aaron. Stars Wings Hauser. Screenplay, Ken Barnett, Barry Schneider, Robert Vincent O'Neil; camera (CFI color), Norman Leigh, David Myers; editor, Roy Watts; music, Gary Scott; sound, Ronald Judkins; assistant director, Ronald Colby; production manager, Roger La Page; production design, Alan Roderick-Jones; special makeup effects, Mark Shostrom. Reviewed at Loews State 1 theatre, N.Y., July 9, 1983. (MPAA Rating: R). Running time: 95 MINS.
Stoney Cooper .... Wings Hauser
Eddie Cooper .... Joyce Ingalls
Joshua Adams .... Paul Shenar
Sam Goodwin .... Al Ruscio
Ashley Maynard .... Arlen Dean Snyder
Otto Hoxley .... Lincoln Kilpatrick

Filmed late last year (with an alternate title of "Fierce Encounter"), "Deadly Force" is a nondescript imitation of "Dirty Harry" made by the team responsible for "Vice Squad." Unappealing lead players and a ho-hum script make for a desultory action picture, due for a short life in hit-and-run saturation release.

Episodic format introduces devil-may-care, gun-for-hire Stoney Cooper (Wings Hauser, the maniac from "Vice Squad"), juggling New York and Los Angeles assignments. In latter locale, his trackdown of a mass murderer is obstructed by his ex-associate on the police force, Otto Hoxley (Lincoln Kilpatrick), while Cooper fortuitously makes up with his estranged wife Eddie (Joyce Ingalls), a tv newshen who is also covering the murder case.

Fitting by default in the B-picture category, "Force" lacks the unusual plotting or colorful gallery of characters which once distinguished this form of filmmaking. Key plot twists, particularly the identify of the power behind the killer, are telegraphed so that the audience is at least two reels ahead of the slow-witted leads. Aimed at the action audience, picture features many minority players but casts them in stereotyped roles, except for Lincoln Kilpatrick as the *de rigeur* tough policeman, making a strong impression in an otherwise undistinguished frontline.

As the oversize, toothy lead, Hauser likewise made an impression as the nut terrorizing Season Hubley in "Vice Squad," but the attempt to convert him into a recurring Eastwood-like (or rather, a B-level Robert Ginty-like) hero fails. Manhandling lowlifes throughout the film's poorly-knitted episodes, Hauser plays his new role as if he were still essaying a violent maniac, eliciting no sympathy in the process. While in Don Siegel's "Dirty Harry," the hunt and confrontations with killer Andy Robinson were carefully dominant over the episodes of routine Eastwood business, here the mad killer plot has no impact or urgency and differs from the subplots and filler along the way only in terms of body count.

Supporting Hauser in a stock role originally announced for Cindy Pickett, Joyce Ingalls delivers bored, monotone readings. Laying in a noisy musical score fails to hide the unexciting, "let's wrap this one up" nature of Paul Aaron's direction, which loses all credibility in the final reel when Hauser battles the main villain in comic strip "unkillable" scenes. Tech credits are okay. — *Lor.*

Munich Film Festival

The Ballad Of Gregorio Cortez
(U.S.-COLOR)

Munich, June 23.

A Moctesuma Esparza Production. Produced by Michael Hausman, associate producer, Richard Soto; world rights, Embassy Pictures, Los Angeles, London. Stars Edward James Olmos. Directed by Robert M. Young. Screenplay, Victor Villasenor, based on Americo Paredes's book, "With His Pistol in His Hands"; camera (color), Ray Villalobos, Young; art direction, Stuart Wurtzel; music, W. Michael Lewis, Edward James Olmos; editor, Richard Soto. Reviewed at Munich Film Fest, June 23, '83. Running time: 104 MINS.
Gregorio Cortez ....Edward James Olmos
Boone Choate .... Tom Bower
Sheriff Frank Fly ...... James Gammon
Captain Rogers .... Brion James
Bill Blakely .... Bruce McGill
Romaldo Cortez .... Pepe Serna
Sheriff Mike Trimmell .... Alan Vint
Abernethy .... Barry Corbin
Sheriff Morris .... Tim Scott
Carolot Munoz .... Rosana DeSoto

Now considered to be a "father figure" in the rapid development of the American Independents movement, Robert M. Young has won mounting praise at several European fests for "The Ballad of Gregorio Cortez," an offbeat Western on the plight of native-born Mex-Americans in Texas at the turn-of-the-century.

Set for a commercial release this September, "Ballad" should prove that Yank indies are a commercial entity to deal with both at home and abroad, for this is an outstanding piece of low-key writing-directing-acting technique as presently practiced by leading American independents today in seeking an alternative audience to Hollywood production formulas.

Young developed his film during the 1981 summer workshops at Robert Redford's Sundance Institute in Utah, together with thesps Edward James Olmos and Tom Bower (pic's main protagonists).

"The Ballad of Gregorio Cortez' is based on a popular "corrido" (or ballad) sung today along the Mexican border in Texas, where the events of June 1901 actually took place. Cortez, a cowhand working the ranges around San Antonio, kills a sheriff in self-defense when he's about to be arrested in a case of mistaken identity and due to an inept translation of the charges by an accompanying Mexican-speaking deputy. Then begins an 11-day manhunt led by Texas Rangers as Cortez flees on horseback from Gonzales (near San Antonio) for the Mexican border; some 600 pursuers were not able to catch him although surrounded and trapped on several occasions. The reports on the manhunt in local newspapers made Cortez a legend, particularly when he apparently gave himself up upon realizing that his family

was arrested and held as hostages. The trial in Gonzales, Texas, forms the epilog.

Sharply lensed (in Super-16, then blown up to 35m), ably acted (Olmos is tops) down to bit parts, and competently directed, "Cortez" made such an impact at the Munich fest that buyers from Socialist lands lined up to secure rights and other European fests (Belgrade in Yugoslavia, where Young appeared a few years ago with "Alambrista!") have put in bids to show the film. The attraction here is the tale of an authentic American ethnic folkhero.

Little doubt, film will find its way to art houses peopled by film buffs and Yank indie supporters, but it also has a better than even chance to hit it commercially stateside. The first half of the film follows a "Rashomon" flashback technique, whereby contrasting stories on the shootout between the sheriff and Cortez are explored in a "who's really telling the truth" manner. The second half brings the viewer into the jury seat as Cortez is tried and narrowly escapes a lynching mob in the process. The original jail and courthouse at Gonzales, plus an oldtimer train used in the pursuit of Cortez, add to the authenticity of the setting and the narrative. —*Holl.*

Posledni Zhelania
(Last Wishes)
(BULGARIAN-COLOR)

Munich, June 21.

A Bulgarian Film Production, Sofia; world rights, Bulgarofilm, Sofia. Features entire cast. Directed by Rangel Vulchanov. Screenplay, Miryana Basheva, Vulchanov; camera (color), Radoslav Spassov; sets, Borislav Neshev; music, Kiril Donchev. Reviewed at Munich Film Fest, June 21, '83. Running time: 95 MINS.
Cast: Stefan Mavrodiev, Antonia Zhekova, Diana Sofronieva, Georgi Mamalev, Aleko Minchev.

Rangel Vulchanov's "Last Wishes" marks a new twist in the career of the distinguished Bulgarian director — it's a satire on the First World War. "Last Wishes" has good intentions, but doesn't quite get off the ground to rank with similar Western satires on the Great War and family squabbles among Europe's royalty.

Pic opens with a truce being called on the central European battle-lines. This requires a photographer to take the visiting royalty's pictures, whose job up to then has been taking snapshots of the dead. A rural farm setting is selected as the site for the one-day truce, and appropriate entertainment is ordered. One leader of the royalty is dumber than the other, so that the company of czars, kings, emperors, and respective princes can't even figure out why they're fighting each other in the first place. It's the pomp and circumstance, the uniforms and the fanfare that make this family gathering at an inopportune time necessary, it seems.

As for the princelings, they go off to play a few cruel games of their own. A particularly tyrannical grandson of the Habsburg Emperor decides to put one of his young cousins on trail for treason and execution, and the rest of the kids go senselessly along with him. Meanwhile, a plot has been hatched among the entertainment ladies to plant a bomb in the midst of the eminent group, and thus be done with the war and its instigators at one and the same time. The bomb, however, is discovered, and the wrong lady is blamed for the plot. Thereupon, the photographer valiently offers himself as a willing substitute for his newly found love, is given his "last wishes" (he busies himself with camera snapshots of the event), and is shot before the portable toilet facilities. The truce is over, and the war begins again.

Some of the visual jokes are a delight — for instance, two double-winged planes crashing midair, and the complications of getting the airship up, but the rest has the look and polish of a cabaret revue enacted before a camera. Undoubtably, too, the humor has a Bulgarian ring. The Westerner, on the other hand, may have a bit of trouble telling the royal families part. —Holl.

Punkty Za Pochodzenie
(Points for Parentage)
(POLISH-COLOR)

Munich, July 2.

A Film Polski production, Aneks Film Unit, Warsaw; world rights, Film Polski, Warsaw. Features entire cast. Written and directed by Franciszek Trzeciak. Camera (color), Wlodzimierz Precht; sets, Andrzej Skoczylas, Maciej Dybowski; editor, Walentyna Wojciechowska, Barbara Krasnicka; production manager, Halina Kawecka. Reviewed at Munich Film Fest, June 23, '83. Running time: 87 MINS.

Cast: Michal Juszczakiewicz (Wladek), Barbara Rachwalska (Wjadek's mother), Wladyslaw Dewoyno (Wladek's father), Jozef Pieracki (the Old Professor), Teresa Mikolajczuk (Professor's Wife), Jolanta Wollejko (the Elocution Professor), Erwin Nowiaszek (the Stage Director).

Polish debut helmer Franciszek Trzeciak came from acting, and is known to home auds through his tv-roles. "Points for Parentage" is his first feature after a string of shorts and docus, and it's more or less an autobiographical tale of how he, as a peasant lad from the villages, became an actor.

Title has to do with the "points" a peasant lad can make from his humble background in a Socialist state to win entrance to the acting school in Warsaw, or another large city. Even when the young aspirant to the arts has his foot in the door, however, he still becomes the butt of jokes and pranks among his peers because he's condemned to act like a country bumpkin.

Further, he falls prey to seductive floozies and homosexuals in the higher echelons of the acting school and theatre companies. And, of course, he's embarrassed by his past when his mother appears upon the scene just as he's starting to get ahead.

Put all of this together, and you have a quietly entertaining satire on career-climbing in the Polish arts scene. —Holl.

Josephs Tochter
(Joseph's Daughter)
(WEST GERMAN-SPANISH-COLOR

Munich, June 19.

A Gustav Emck Film in coproduction with Maran-Film, Munich, and Jezabel Film, Madrid; world rights, Transocean International, Munich. Stars Linda Manz. Written and directed by Gustav Emck. Camera (color), Gerard Vandenberg; editing, Timothy Gee, Karl Fugunt; music, Roland Baumgartner; sets, Benjamin Fernandez; costumes, Maria Eugenia Escriva. Reviewed at Munich Film Fest. June 19, '83. Running time: 90 MINS.

Cast: Linda Manz (Linda), Walt Davis (Joseph), Marie-Christine Barrault (Jane), Ana Torrent (Barbara), May Heatherly (Cilly), Luis Bar-Boo (Erik), Jose Moreno (Dursun), Andreas Nutzhorn (Marty), Ofelia Angelica (Erik's Wife), Andres Mejuto (Zapata), Marisa Porcel (Beppy).

Gustav Emck has made his reputation in New German Cinema circles as a specialist in entertainment pics, often dipping into the kidpic genre. Two of his best films were "Trace of a Girl" (1967) and "Fire at Midnight" (1977). Now he's entered the arena of English-language productions with an international cast: "Joseph's Daughter," with Linda Manz, Walt Davis, Marie-Christine Barrault, and Ana Torrent in the lead roles.

"Joseph's Daughter" was shot in Spain, but the ambiguity of the setting could put the tale in focus on the Californian-Mexican border, or anywhere in the American Southwest, for that matter. It's about a truckdriver, Joseph, who manhandles his wife, Jane, and mistreats his teenaged daughter, on occasion. It's not that he doesn't appreciate them; it's just that this is the way a tough guy shows affection around the house, particularly if the wife is a submissive type. Linda (played by Linda Manz, last seen in Dennis Hopper's "Out of the Blue") is a tomboy teenager with a mind of her own; she feels it's time to fight back, so she eventually talks her mother into running away when things at home start getting worse. The last scene has the good-looking mother of 35 with her matured teenaged daughter hitching a ride on the highway to nowhere in particular.

Pic's rambling story has its moments of authenticity, and Manz is a standout as a bundle of raw energy. But character motivation is miss-

ing, while the dubbed German version unspooled at the Munich fest gives every indication that such hybrid multi-lingo productions are neither fish nor fowl in the long run. Emck is a professional talent to watch in future. —Holl.

Dolina Issy
(Issa's Valley)
(POLISH-COLOR)

Munich, June 22.

A Film Polski production, Perspektywa Film Unit, Warsaw; world rights, Film Polski, Warsaw. Features entire cast. Written and directed by Tadeusz Konwicki, based on Czeslaw Milosz's novel with same title. Camera (color), Jerzy Lukaszewicz; music, Zygmunt Konieczny; sets, Andrzej Borecki; sound, Nikodem Wold-Laniewski; editor, Krystyna Rutkowska; production manager, Ryszard Chutkowski. Reviewed at Munich Film Fest, June 21, '83. Running time: 110 MINS.

Cast: Anna Dymna (Magdalena), Maria Pakulnis (Barbarka), Danuta Szalarska (Grandmother Mary), Ewa Wisniewska (Helena), Krzysztof Gosztyla (Balthazar), Jerzy Kamas (Romuald), Jerzy Kryszak (Devil), Edward Dziewonski (Grandfather Surkont), Maciej Mazurkiewicz (Tomaszek/Tommy), Marta Lipinska (Tommy's Mother), Jozef Duriasz (Jozef Czarny), Marek Walczewski (Masiulnis).

Based loosely on Czeslaw Milosz's novel (published in 1955), Tadeusz Konwicki's "Issa's Valley" evokes a childhood in rural Lithuania between the wars shared by both the Nobel Prize-winning poet and the writer-director but a generation apart — Milosz was born there in 1911, Konwicki in 1926. The novel centers on the period between 1910 and 1920, while the film moves beyond this period to mirror the climate in independent Lithuania shortly after the First World War.

Packed with metaphors and symbols — the most prominent of which is a naked girl leading a white horse through an enchanted forest — this is both an idyllic portrait of rural, unblemished Lithuania as well as a sketch of the revolutionary forces in the air. Most of all, it's Konwicki's vision of his birthplace as "a land of poets and natural beauty." As "a cradle of poets," this land bequeathed creative inspiration to Adam Mickiewicz and Czeslaw Milosz, and painters Marc Chagall and Mikalojus Konstantinas Ciurlionis.

"Issa's Valley" doesn't follow a narrative line so much as focusing (Jerzy Lukaszewicz's lensing is outstanding) on magic glades and mysterious lakes in the midst of primeval forests. The chief protagonist, a country lad named Tommy, realizes that the Issa Valley he lives in during the fateful 1920s is about to be torn apart by internal political conflicts and social unrest among the mixed population of Lithuanians, Poles, Russians, and Jews. But he is in his preteens, and is captivated by the hunting and

wandering paradise surrounding him, as well as open to the life experiences he witnesses firsthand. His fantasies transport him, on one occasion, to a confrontation with the Devil himself — he witnesses evil and death, and the tragedy of an ill-fated love affair.

Tommy lives on a rich estate, the land situated on the Polish border. It's during this aftermath of the World War 1 that tempers rise, and hate and distrust break out even between Poles and Lithuanians. A metaphor for the mounting tragedy in the area is supplied by a forbidden love between a priest and his housemaid, the consequences being death and a haunting spectre of evil in the world.

A film based purely on nostalgia and childhood remembrances, "Issa's Valley" impresses as an esthetic treatise. Pic deserves its present fest slot, and could even find critical recognition at selected arthouses and Polish Film Weeks. —Holl.

Summerspell
(U.S.-COLOR)

Munich, June 26.

A Lina Shanklin Film Production, produced by Shanklin and Joanne D'Antonio. Features entire cast. Written and directed by Lina Shaklin. Camera (color), Robert Elswit; editing, Gloria Whittemore; music, Toni Marcus. Reviewed at Munich Film Fest, June 26, '83. Running time: 90 MINS.

Cast: Dorothy Holland (Bernice Wisdom), Jennifer Mayo (her daughter), Frank Whiteman (Lowell Wisdom), Michael Holmes, Joan Crosby, Kay Freeman, Gay Hagen, Coleman Creel, Bert Transwell, Ed Wright.

Lina Shanklin's low-budget autobiographical feature, "Summerspell," preemed at the USA Film Festival in Dallas last May, has surfaced in the tribute to American Independents at the Munich Film Fest. Costing a miniscule $80,000 but lensed patiently over a three-year stretch in the Los Angeles area, "Summerspell" outshone all the other Yank indies on the slate (including Susan Seidelman's "Smithereens," another $80,000 arthouse and fest fave) by scoring a half-page critical report-and-interview in the prestigious Sueddeutsche Zeitung (one of Germany's leading dailies).

Shanklin has etched a family saga in the literary tradition of Eugene O'Neill, Tennessee Williams and early William Faulkner. "Summerspell" takes place on July 4, 1948 on a patriarchal homestead in Texas, this particular family reunion leading to a confrontation between the couple managing the farm, Bernice and Lowell Wisdom, and visting relatives. The tale follows the classical dramatic unities of time and place in and around the homestead over a two-day stretch.

The couple are seen at the beginning arranging for the family reunion, and since the patriarch of the family is nearing death and suffering from senility, the reunion may be the last as well as a crucial one for all concerned. The Wisdoms have a teenaged daughter, who is beginning to question family matters — she wants to know why her mother and father stay permanently on the farm in the first place. Lastly, Bernice Wisdom as a city-bred girl has given her life to be with her husband out on the hot Texas plains, apparently because he was needed to save the estate from bankruptcy and ruin during the Depression Years.

It turns out in the course of the story that the patriarch had tricked his son Lowell into giving up a promising law career to return to the farm. The family was in no danger ever of losing the homestead, but Lowell was the only son competent enough to run the place among a brood of inept kin — so the sacrifice was made at the cost of one's own happiness. It's the daughter who notes particularly the sacrifice of her own mother, a woman never fully accepted by the jealous relatives.

Strikingly lensed and directed with a firm hand at a slow pace, "Summerspell" marks the debut of a talented Yank femme director with an unusually refined eye for pictorial composition and natural rural beauty. The minor faults — too much theatrical chatter, too many characters to keep track of — stem understandably from a drama company Shanklin developed her story with. Musical score, too, is a bit heavy and overdone. Otherwise, credits are tops, and Shanklin is a name to watch among Yank indies. —*Holl.*

Man Of Flowers
(AUSTRALIAN-COLOR)

Melbourne, July 12.

Flowers International Pty. Ltd. Production. Produced by Jane Ballantyne, Paul Cox. Directed by Paul Cox. Stars Norman Kaye, Alyson Best, Chris Haywood, Sarah Walker. Associate producer, Tony Llewellyn-Jones. Screenplay, Paul Cox; dialogue, Bob Ellis; camera (color), Yuri Sokol; art director, Asher Bilu; sound recordist, Lloyd Carrick; editor, Tim Lewis. Reviewed at the Melbourne Film Festival July 2, '83. Running time: 94 MINS.

Charles Bremer	Norman Kaye
Lisa	Alyson Best
David	Chris Haywood
Jane	Sarah Walker
Art teacher	Julia Blake
Psychiatrist	Bob Ellis
Postman	Barry Dickins
Coopershop man	Patrick Cook
Angela	Victoria Eagger
Father	Werner Herzog
Mother	Hilary Kelly
Young Charles	James Stratford
Aunts	Eileen Joyce and Marianne Baillieu
Florists	Lirit Bilu and Juliet Bacskai
Cleaning lady	Dawn Klingberg
Church warden	Tony Llewellyn-Jones

At the world preem of "Man Of Flowers" in the Melbourne Film Festival, producer-director Paul Cox called for "a bit more dedication and less greed" from filmmakers and a switch of focus from "the money brokers and lenders."

His visually compelling picture was shot in Melbourne in three weeks, completed in eight, for a remarkable $A250,000. It is an elegantly crafted feature that looks as though it might have been produced with a far more generous budget and a far more luxurious deadline.

"Man Of Flowers," which contains a cameo, silent-role appearance by the German filmmaker Werner Herzog, the Dutch-born helmer's close friend, appears to be targeted mainly at the European cinema and tv market where "Kostas," an earlier Cox picture, received some attention. It promises bright arthouse b.o. if given U.S. distrib.

Cox's film, flickering between realism and fantasy, follows the progress of Bremer, a rich naive eccentric (Norman Kaye), whose inherited wealth both protects him from the coldness of the outside world and isolates him from its warmth. He is cocooned in a childlike innocence, dwelling on the sexual exploration of his boyhood.

"Man Of Flowers" opens with an astonishingly erotic strip by Lisa, the model. She strips, nothing more, nothing less. Is her stated affection for him genuine, or is she attracted by his money? Cox keeps the bond teasingly ambiguous.

Bremer believes there are many kind people around him. The man who sold him the swimming pool is kind, because he gave the water away free, and the psychiatrist who said he should stay in hospital apparently changed his mind after receiving a check.

At times "Man Of Flowers" creates Hitchcock-like tension, but when the suspense becomes uncomfortable Cox lets his audience off the hook with a little wry humor. The expected black climax is never quite allowed to occur.

Norman Kaye delivers a wonderful, understated performance as Bremer and Best is a delightfully enigmatic Lisa. They get fine back-up from thesps in minor roles, with Julia Blake, Barry Dickins and Sarah Walker outstanding.

Musically, too, "Man Of Flowers" is rich. There are generous excerpts of Donizetti's "Lucia di Lammermoor," sung by Montserrat Caballe and Jose Carreras with the New Philharmonia conducted by Jesus Lopez Cobos.

"Man Of Flowers" is a photographer's vision of loneliness, rather than a writer's assessment. The flaws are those seeds planted somewhere between Cox's imagination and writer Bob Ellis's interpretation.

Ellis is strong on the humorous relief (e.g. a scene on the psychiatrist's couch in which Ellis himself appears), but he appears uncertain as to the overall intention. It would be fascinating to see what Cox could do with a really powerful script. —*Bec.*

Le Jeune Marie
(The Young Bridegroom)
(FRENCH-COLOR)

Paris, July 12.

AMLF release of a T. Films/Adel Productions coproduction. Produced by Alain Terzian. Stars Richard Berry, Brigitte Fossey. Directed by Bernard Stora. Screenplay, Stora, Luc Beraud; camera (color), Ricardo Aronovich; art director, Serge Douy; sound, Harrik Maury; editor, Jacques Comets; music, Luis Bacalov; production manager, Pierre Pardon. Reviewed at the Studio 28, Paris, July 7, 1983. Running time: 97 MINS.

Billy	Richard Berry
Viviane	Brigitte Fossey
Nina	Zoe Chauveau
Baptiste	Richard Anconina
Durbec	Daniel Russo
Billy's mother	Francoise Seigner

"Le Jeune Marie" is about a young man who marries one girl, falls for another just hours after the ceremony, and spends the rest of the film pursuing her. The original screenplay by Bernard Stora, who directed, and Luc Beraud (himself a writer-director) bears obvious resemblance to Elaine May's satiric comedy, "The Heartbreak Kid;" but where the Yank film dwelt on cruel caricatures, Stora intends an ironic comedy-drama with feeling and well-observed characters.

The young bridegroom of the title is Richard Berry, a young highway construction laborer, who slips rather too casually into marriage with a young girl (Zoe Chauveau) he's only known for six

months. They move into a still-uncompleted housing project, whre, on the very eve of the wedding, Berry mistakes his floor and walks into the wrong apartment. There he finds Brigitte Fossey, a bourgeois spouse whose husband has just walked out on her. Without telling her that he's married and lives just floors above, Berry, immediately smitten, plays up to her. Fossey at first succumbs, but quickly realizes that their affair is folly and flees to her parents' Paris home.

Berry chucks his job and tender-loving wife and follows, but the hide-and-seek ends in a truce when Fossey finds tentative reconciliation with her husband, and Berry begins to take some clear-eyed stock of himself. But Chauveau's outraged father turns up, and after an accident caused by their dispute, Berry is brought back to the fold and assumes his role as a model husband.

Film is small-scale but fine, funny and touching. Director Stora has served a long apprenticeship as assistant director and displays a firm command of narrative, camera and the direction of actors — there's a subtle rightness of tone and touch that announces a promising film maker of sensibility.

As the young workman who swaps one misconception of love for another, Berry confirms his status as one of the best new young French actors of the moment, and Fossey is at her radiant best as his unattainable object of desire. Among supporting players of note is Richard Anconina, as Berry's bosom pal, who seems destined to molre important screen roles.

Technical credits are excellent. And a tip of the hat to Alain Delon, who coproduced this promising debut. — *Len.*

Mr. Mom
(COLOR)

Misses ... Bomb.

Hollywood, July 13.

Twentieth Century-Fox release of Sherwood Production. Produced by Lynn Loring, Lauren Shuler. Features entire case. Directed by Stan Dragoti. Exec producer, Aaron Spelling. Screenplay, John Hughes; coproducer, Harry Colomby; camera (Metrocolor), Victor J. Kemper; editor, Pattrick Kennedy; production design, Alfred Sweeney; music, Lee Holdridge; assistant director, Jim Dyer. Reviewed at Darryl F. Zanuck Theatre, Hollywood, July 12, 1983. (MPAA Rating: PG). Running time: 91 MINS.

Jack	Michael Keaton
Caroline	Teri Garr
Alex	Frederick Koehler
Kenny	Taliesin Jaffe
Megan	Courtney & Brittany White
Ron	Martin Mull
Joan	Ann Jillian
Jinx	Jeffrey Tambor
Larry	Christopher Lloyd
Stan	Tom Leopold
Humphries	Graham Jarvis

The comic talents of Michael Keaton and Teri Garr are largely wasted in Sherwood Productions' "Mr. Mom," an unoriginal romantic comedy that amounts to little more than a mediocre episode of a tv sitcom. Idea of using two stars as the perennial breadwinner-husband and homemaker wife who switch roles has been done so many times before that one marvels it can still serve as the centerpiece for a contemporary feature film — much less the first picture from production companies headed by industry vets like David Begelman (prez of Sherwood) and Aaron Spelling (exec producer and topper of Aaron Spelling Prods.). Distributor 20th Century-Fox is in trouble with this one since it's difficult to imagine audiences paying to see a poorly executed idea they have no doubt viewed for free on the tube.

Though Keaton and Garr occassionally manage to evoke some pathos and laughs, it's an uphill battle that is won solely on the strength of their individual personalities. Screenwriter John Hughes, from "National Lampoon" fame, provides no new insights and many tired sight gags. Cinematographer Victor J. Kemper has for some unknown reason shot a light comedy in a darkened, often subdued atmosphere (is a supermarket ever dimly lit?). And director Stan Dragoti, injecting no sense of style, focus or imagination, seems to have done nothing more than aim the camera.

This would all signal total disaster were it not for Keaton and Garr. Keaton, close to perfection as the husband and father depressed by unemployment but always a sport with his family, is already a known bundle of comic energy. But he especially shines here in some more dramatic moments with his children, suggestions a future in more serious-comedic turns.

Garr, as always, is a delight to watch though it would be nice to see her in a role where she wasn't someone's wife or mother. Still, her inspired double takes continue to say more than pages of dialog while her keen timing helps somewhat in the more beleaguered scenes.

But neither one can save the picture. When Keaton loses his job as a car designer and Garr then immediately gets employment as an ad exec, one hopes for some variations on the familiar working wife, hubby at home scenes. What is offered are things like Keaton screwing up in the housework (he puts too much soap in the washer) while pondering romantic advances from horny divorcee Ann Jillian (in a thankless part). Garr is forced to fight off the predictable advances from strange, lecherous employer Martin Mull while using her expertise as a housewife to save a multimillion dollar tuna fish account.

The writers of "I Love Lucy" did far better with the premise 30 years ago. —Berg.

Le Batard
(The Bastard)
(FRENCH-COLOR)

Paris, July 7.
Cyrile Distribution release of a Mallia Films/FR 3 coproduction. Produced and directed by Bertrand Van Effenterre. Features entire cast. Screenplay, Bertrand Van Effenterre and Pierre-Alain Maubert, based on the novel "The Bastard," by Erskine Caldwell; camera (Fuji), Francois Catonne; art director, Geoffroy Larcher; editor, Joelle Van Effenterre; sound, Pierre Gamet; music, Norbert Aboudarham; title song lyrics, Pierre Gross. Reviewed at the Saint-Andre-des-Arts cinema, Paris, July 7, 1983. Running time: 110 MINS.
Patrice ....Gerard Klein
Marie ....Julie Jezequel
Jean ....Didier Flamand
Foreman's wife ....Brigitte Fossey
Brigitte ....Mylene Demongeot
Betty.......................Victoria Abril
Foreman............Jean-Jacques Biraud
Dan ....Patrick Bruel

Bertrand Van Effenterre's new film is a misfire, and all the more disappointing because this talent young writer-director's pictures are few and far between — three in 10 years, beginning with "Erica Major" in 1973, and "Mais Ou Et Donc Ornicar" in 1978. For "Le Batard" Van Effenterre has adapted an Erskine Caldwell novel, "The Bastard," but the pitfalls of transposition and an inadequate lead actor sink this ambitious venture.

Film concerns the wanderings of a Paris garage mechanic who is summoned to Marseille to identify the body of his murdered mother, an aging bar floozie who abandoned him years ago as a child. Fired by some long-buried filial feeling, the protagonist kills his mother's cynical boss and sets off on an aimless journey through southern France, during which he has numerous encounters, mostly sexual. Finally weary of the road, he decides to set up house with a young teenage musician, and embarks her, pregnant, to Paris. But the humdrum cloistered family life drives her into melancholic inertia, and the mechanic finds the only solution in deserting her and their child and hitting the road again.

In transposing Caldwell's drama to France, Van Effenterre and co-adaptor Pierre-Alain Maubert come up with some neat geographical and sociological equivalents, but the south of France is not the American South, and the cultural and moral tensions between film and model remain naggingly unreconcilable. The direction accordingly flounders as Van Effenterre tries unsuccessfully to exploit the tragicomic and grotesque elements that one finds in much American southern literature, and

which only render the characters more alien and unsympathetic.

The title role is played by Gerard Klein, a popular French radio announcer-turned-film actor with a substantial supporting part in the last Romy Schneider vehicle, "La Passante du Sans Souci" (1981). Klein has real screen presence but severely limited acting abilities. Van Effenterre has helped him get rid of some of his amateurish stiffness, but has failed to draw any fire or feeling, so that he virtually walks through the film more or less impassively. — Len.

Hells Angels Forever
(DOCU-COLOR)

Hollywood, July 11.
An RKR Releasing release of a Baytide Films production in association with Wescom Prods. Produced by Richard Chase, Sandy Alexander, Leno Gast. Executive producers, Jerry Garcia, Clare Frost. Directed by Chase, Kevin Keating, Gast. Screenplay, Peterson Tooke, Chase; camera (uncredited color), Keating; associate producer, Tooke; narration, Morgan Paull. Reviewed at the Hollywood Pacific, L.A., July 11, 1983. (MPAA Rating: R). Running time: 90 MINS.
Features: The Hells Angels, Willie Nelson, Jerry Garcia, Johnny Paycheck, Bo Diddley.

"Hells Angels Forever" is an academic, unexciting apologia for the world's most notorious bikers. Some 10 years in production, docu features random footage said to have been shot by the Angels themselves, as well as a plethora of self-justifying interviews and coverage of the government's questionable efforts to break up the organization via legal and other means. Opening week b.o. in Los Angeles was modest, and pic is simply too uneventful to generate much enthusiasm even from those who would normally patronize fictional chopper sagas.

Few American figures can compete with the Angels when it comes to iconographic weight; their uncompromising defiance of society's norms brands them as outcasts and outlaws, and, in film terms, many a biker cheapie has remained watchable by virtue of the gang members' extreme attitudinizing, as well as by some visual attraction of their cycles and tough get-up.

A documentary, particularly one which is at least partly an outside job, provides the chance to get beneath these surfaces, but this piece is bent upon displaying the Angels as basically o.k. guys who are unfairly persecuted by a threatened society. Predictably, it's just the naughty behavior of a small handful which has given the entire group a bad name, with the Angels supposedly getting rough only with those who step on their toes.

Unfortunately, all the allegedly trumped-up charges against the Angels are refuted in only the

vaguest of terms, even though two trials involving Angels president Sonny Barger ended with juries unable to agree on a verdict. But if profitable racketeering and drug operations were not being run by the Angels, as the state charged, then how do these people make a living? Pic never bothers to address the point.

With so many swastikas and SS insignias on view, subjects of Naziism, racism and anti-Semitism can't be avoided altogether, but responses are typically inarticulate. On the subject of women, however, the Angels are clear: they're here to obey their men, polish their bikes and take a left to the jaw if they get out of line.

Pic opens with a photo recap of the California small town biker melee which inspired the 1954 "The Wild One" with Marlon Brando, which in turn popularized the whole biker mystique and which is briefly excerpted, as is "Hell's Angels '69." Offered at greater length are some concert performances by such Angel-approved singers as Jerry Garcia, Johnny Paycheck, Bo Diddley and Willie Nelson.

Given the sometimes washed-out quality of the home movie material, film has been quite professionally produced. Originally the brainchild of New York Angel Sandy Alexander, pic boasts some of the most unusual credits ever seen, with various producers and directors identified along with the dates they were involved with the project. —Cart.

Femmes
(Women)
(FRENCH-COLOR)

Paris, July 12.
Planfilm release of an Accord Productions/Orphee Arts/Transcontinental/Balcazar coproduction. Produced by Lucien Duval. Stars Alexandra Stewart, Helmut Berger. Written and directed by Tana Kaleya. Camera (color), Edmond Sechan; editor, Nicole Berckmans; art director, Yves Brover; music, Yves Dessca and Marc Hillman; sound, Juan Quiles. Reviewed at the Publicis Theatre, Paris, July 10, 1983. Running time: 92 MINS.
With: Alexandra Stewart, Helmut Berger, Tina Sportoralo, Eva Cobo, Dirke Altevogt.

"Femmes" is just another installment in the glossy erotica vein established by "Emmanuelle," "Madame Claude" and the like and nothing to take a cold shower about. Tana Kaleya, a professional commercial photographer, wrote and directed, and it's about as insipid and dull a women's effort as "Conte Pervers," the 1980 film made by Regine Desforge, a local specialist in erotic literature.

Kaleya's feeble story concerns a handsome, globetrotting hedonist (Helmut Berger, who apparently had nothing better to do) who drops off on a lush Mediterranean isle to see an old flame (Alexandra Stewart, in another demeaningly nonexistent role). In the course of his stay, he rekindles Stewart's fires, deflowers her all-too-willing teenage daughter, and puts away a lesbian couple, who are happily AC/DC when Berger gets through with them. What a man! And this is supposed to reflect female sex fantasies.

Needless to say that "Femmes" doesn't herald a new filmmaking talent. — *Len.*

The White Lions
(COLOR)

Tame wildlife picture.

An Alan Landsburg Prods. (a Reeves Communications Co.) production. Executive producer, Alan Landsburg. Produced by Paul Freeman and Howard Lipstone. Directed by Mel Stuart. Stars Michael York. Screenplay, Corey Blechman, Peter Dixon from Chris McBride's book; camera (CFI color), Robert Jessup; African locations photography, Michael Dodds; editor, Art Stafford; music, William Goldstein; song lyrics, Judith Barron; sound, Robert Wald; assistant director, Bob Bender; production manager-associate producer, F.A. Miller; art direction, Roger Pancake; set decoration, Mike Parsons. Reviewed on Home Box Office, N.Y., July 12, 1983. (MPAA Rating: PG). Running time: **96 MINS.**

Chris McBride	Michael York
Jeanie McBride	Glynnis O'Connor
Vreeland	Donald Moffat
Aniel	J.A. Preston
John Kani	Roger E. Mosley
Laura McBride	Lauri Lynn Meyers

Lensed in the spring of 1979 and MPAA-rated two years later, "The White Lions" is a mild family picture which failed to get domestic theatrical distribution and is currently providing pleasant tv diversion.

With educational value for the younger set, picture toplines Michael York as real-life naturalist Chris McBride, who with wife and daughter in tow returns to an African wildlife preserve where he was born, to study animal behavior. Easy-going narrative (with York voicing over lots of background material about lions and their habits) is short on conflict, the main issue being wife Jeanie (Glynnis O'Connor) wishing to go back to the U.S. and resume a normal, academic family life.

Ultimately she comes around and serves as still photographer, accepting McBride's dictum: "We gave up the creature comforts and gained the creatures." When they discover a cute pair of white-colored (but not albino) lion cubs, argument is between the femmes' desire to help them survive vs. McBride's hard stance of non-interference. Dad finally compromises (while maintaining a firm opposition to zoos) but the cubs' fate is hinted at by a theme song nicely sung by Maureen McGovern: "Enough To Let Me Go."

Lead thesps give earnest performances, with York balancing the preachy demands of his role adroitly and O'Connor a sympathetic helpmate/adversary. A corny subplot has Donald Moffat as a poacher aiming to exploit the cubs.

Wildlife photography is attractive but unexciting, with not enough integration of the actors and animal subjects (reflecting the dichotomy between second unit African lensing and principal filming at a Texas wildlife park).

Commercially, though wilderness adventure pictures have had a big family audience, traditional British entries in the "Born Free" tradition such as "Living Free" and "The Belstone Fox" have not made a b.o. dent Stateside, marking "White Lions" as mainly of ancillary interest. —*Lor.*

The Instructor
(COLOR)

Chop-socky, Buckeye style.

Akron, O., July 2.

An American Eagle Film International Release. Executive producer, Richard F. Lombardi. Stars Bob Chaney, Bob Saal, Lynda Scharnott. Written, produced, and directed by Don Bendell. Camera (Eastmancolor), Ron Hughes; supervising editor, Shirley Bendell; art director, Joyce Edwards, Music, Marti Lunn. Reviewed at the Civic Theatre, Akron, O., July 1, 1983. (No MPAA Rating). Running time: **91 MINS.**

The Instructor	Bob Chaney
Bud Hart	Bob Saal
Dee Walton	Lynda Scharnott
Mr. Fender	Bruce Bendell
Ben Sloan	Tony Blanchard
Thumper Rhodes	Don Bendell
Shank Ballinger	Jack Holderbaum
Grasshopper Gordon	Hank Gordon
Choo Choo Casey	Denise Blankenship
Alex Reason	Bob Huey
Roach Cramer	Bradley Norfolk
Karen Rhodes	Denise Phillips
Rick Runninghorse	Bob Dorman
Al Butcher	Steve Boergadine

For advocates of karate, "The Instructor" provides an action-packed 91 minutes, plus the philosophy of a dedicated holder of a black belt. Don Bendell, who wrote, directed and produced the film, is a firm believer that the true philosophy of karate has been distorted in many chop-socky films of recent vintage.

Returning to the scene of his youth in the Akron, Ohio area, he filmed his picture to demonstrate karate is not a means of vengeance and cruelty, but is a discipline; a way of life based on controlled behavior whereby the "good guy" can utilize his physical powers to become a worthy citizen to cope with today's harsh challenges.

Then there are the bad guys. They use their knowledge as a cruel, selfish and vicious design for greed and power. They pay the price, of course, at the end. Never mind that the plot is simplistic; dialog bordering on the banal and

acting amateurish. The scenes where the black belts perform are worth the price. Add to this a vehicle chase through the Greater Akron area, and the totality more than offsets the negatives in this $3,000,000 production.

Bob Chaney, a black belt who runs his own school in private life, is "The Instructor" who catches Bob Saal (Bud Hart) the bad guy. Saal, off-screen, is coach of the U.S. AAU karate team. Lynda Scharnott, (Dee Walton) the love interest, not only shows flashes of film potential, but holds a black belt and demonstrates her capability by upending a group of would-be thugs.

Following showing in the Akron area, "The Instructor" takes off for a limited run in several western states. Bendell returns to his Colorado home for shooting of his next film. —*Mark.*

Night Of The Zombies
(COLOR)

Offbeat, tongue-in-cheek horror cheapie.

An NMD Film Distributing release, presented by Nicholas Demetroules. Produced by Lorin E. Price, in association with Evelyn Waxman. Directed by Joel M. Reed. Stars Jamie Gillis. Screenplay, Reed; camera (TVC color), Ron Dorfman; supervising editor, Victor Kanefsky; editor, Samuel Pollard; music, Onomatopoeia Inc., Matt Kaplowitz, Maggie Nolin; sound, Chat Gunter, Alvar Stugard; production manager, Kenneth Bowser; makeup, David E. Smith; special effects, Peter Kunz. Reviewed on videocassette in N.Y., June 8, 1983. (No MPAA Rating). Running time: **88 MINS.**

Nick Monroe	Jamie Gillis
Dr. Proud	Ryan Hilliard
Susan	Samantha Grey
Capt. Fleck	Ron Armstrong
Sgt. Freedman	Richard de Faut
Officer Schuller	Juni Kulis
C.I.A. agent	Alphonse de Noble
Neo-Nazi	Joel M. Reed
Prostitute	Shoshana Ascher
Priest	Lorin E. Price
C.I.A. chief	Ron Dorfman

Filmed in 1979 as "Gamma 693," "Night Of The Zombies" is a failed horror film that has an unusual premise but not enough budget to carry it out. Writer-director Joel M. Reed (whose earlier gore opus "Bloodsucking Freaks" continues in release) has included oddball humor but doesn't deliver the scares. Picture displays an "R" rating, but has never been rated, according to the MPAA.

C.I.A. agent Nick Monroe (Jamie Gillis) is sent to West Germany to investigate the murder of two NATO officers and to find missing canisters of Gamma 693, a U.S. experimental gas developed in 1944. Teaming up with scientist Dr. Proud (Ryan Hilliard) and his niece Susan (Samantha Grey), he ventures to a remote, snow-scaped Bavarian village where local legend claims zombies now inhabit the site of a W.W. II battlefield.

Far-fetched science fiction premise maintains that the missing Gamma 693 was invented to put wounded soldiers in a state of suspended animation, attempting to prolong their lives. In practice, it has been used to extend the lives of unaging U.S. and German W.W. II soldiers, who prey on human flesh in order to counteract the decaying side-effect of the gas. The opposing troops are supposedly still fighting the war, a corny gimmick that reflects "Zombies" having originally been set in the Far East about an isolated Japanese regiment before a budget-induced rewrite switched locale and lessened story credibility.

Disarmingly silly dialog and spoofing of the international intrigue genre makes this slow-paced picture watchable. Cheap makeup on the soldier zombies plus too-bright lighting renders fright scenes ineffective. Reed's conception of light-hearted zombies, who lack the expected catatonic stare and like to joke around, bears little connection to earlier screen versions, though an expert notes authoritatively: "Zombies don't devour human flesh — ghouls do."

Location lensing in Germany is attractive, but lengthy, static exposition scenes and lack of convincing action footage betray the film's low budget, financed by legit theatre producer ("George M.," etc.) Lorin Price. Familiar porn star Jamie Gillis is physically right as the tough-guy hero, but too laid-back for the role. Supporting cast is unimpressive and features many of the behind-the-camera personnel doubling as performers.
—*Lor.*

Bekhinath Bagruth
(Finals)
(ISRAELI-COLOR)

Tel Aviv, June 1.

A Itzhak Shani - Josef Dimant production for Berkey-Pathe-Humphries. Produced by Naftali Alter. Features entire cast. Written and directed by Assi Dayan; based on a novel by Galila Ron-Feder. Camera (color); Ilan Rosenberg; editor, Yossi Rabinovitz; music, Naftali Alter. Reviewed in Tel Aviv, June, 1983. Running time: **90 MINS.**

Cast:

Ronnie	Dan Toren
Orna	Irith Frank
Ruthie	Ariela Rabinovitz
Omri	Ronnie Pinkovitz
Dalia	Maya Kadishman
Yoav	David Beth-On
Orna's father	Itzhak Hizkiah
Orna's mother	Irith Alter

The material used here is identical to the stuff which made "Lemon Popsicle" and its sequels the most successful films in the history of the Israeli cinema. It is all about high school loves, first sexual encounters, jealousy, perfidy, making up, and so on. The treatment, however, is diametrically opposed to everything "Lemon Popsicle" stands for, as characters here are treated in a subdued manner, never made fun of, and there is no attempt to go for the easy, vulgar and obviously crowd-pleasing humor, typical not only of the aforementioned hits, but also of many previous Assi Dayan-Naftali Alter ventures.

The approach may have been determined by the fact that this tandem, who have put together up to now eight features, has used as the basis for this one an extremely successful novel which attempts furnish young readers with a didactic instruction in sex life, at an age when asking parents is awkward.

The pivotal point here, in the relationship between two 17-year-olds, Ronnie and Orna, is first the fear that she might be pregnant, which leads to a pedagogical visit to a gynecologist who preaches against abortion, and later a second crisis erupts around the same topic, when a better educated girl who already knows what the pill is, forgets to use it the right way.

Throughout this double crisis, the plot tries to give a general image of the way high-school kids live, nowadays in Israel, the worries they have, and unlike the pure, undiluted entertainment supplied by the competition, it even mentions the fact that Israel is at war, and war is no fun. As a matter of fact, one of the more endearing characters is a high school dropout who joins the army and is sent to the front. It may not be all that integrated into the plot, but at least it is there.

The script seems to be made out of model situations, put together without too much concern for dramatic construction, for the purpose of teaching the young audience how to extricate itself, once they fall into similar predicaments, and, as such, it requires unusually naive characters, for through them, the test case is best proven. This doesn't help the actors, and they are often in an uncomfortable position, acting unnaturally. Still, Dan Toren and Ronnie Pinkovitz give creditable performances and they will be certainly be heard from again, in future.

Technical credits are okay and film is already doing brisk business in its initial release in Israel.

— *Edna.*

Krull
(COLOR)

Derivative fantasy bodes less than legendary b.o.

Hollywood, July 22.

A Columbia release of a Ted Mann-Ron Silverman production. Produced by Silverman. Executive producer, Mann. Directed by Peter Yates. Features entire cast. Screenplay, Stanford Sherman; camera (Metrocolor, Panavision), Peter Suschitzky; editor, Ray Lovejoy; music, James Horner; production design, Stephen Grimes; art direction, Tony Reading, Colin Grimes, Norman Dorme, Tony Curtis; set decoration, Herbert Westbrook; visual effects supervision, Derek Meddings; special makeup design, Nick Maley; visual effects photography, Paul Wilson; optical effects photography, Robin Browne; costume design, Anthony Mendleson; sound (Dolby), Ivan Sharrock; associate producer, Geoffrey Helman; assistant director, second unit director, Derek Cracknell. Reviewed at the Directors Guild of America Theatre, L.A., July 22, 1983. (MPAA Rating: PG.) Running time: 112 MINS.

Colwyn	Ken Marshall
Lyssa	Lysette Anthony
Ynyr	Freddie Jones
Widow of the Web	Francesca Annis
Torquil	Alun Armstrong
Ergo	David Battley
Cyclops	Bernard Bresslaw
Kegan	Liam Neeson
Seer	John Welsh
Titch	Graham McGrath
Turold	Tony Church
Eirig	Bernard Archard
Vella	Belinda Mayne
Bardolph	Dicken Ashworth
Oswyn	Todd Carty
Rhun	Robbie Coltrane

Although inoffensively designed only to please the senses and appeal to one's whimsical sense of adventure, "Krull" nevertheless comes off as a blatantly derivative hodgepodge, the recipe for which includes ingredients from nearly every successful film in the fantasy genre. This "Excalibur" meets "Star Wars" has been lavishly mounted at a reported cost of $27,000,000, but the collection of action set pieces never jells into an absorbing narrative which takes on a life of its own. Columbia's jumbo ad promo campaign will try to cash in on continuing interest in this sort of film, but b.o. results will undoubtedly come closer to those of "Dragonslayer" than to the much higher levels originally hoped for.

Plot is as old as the art of storytelling itself. Young Prince Colwyn (whose name, as pronounced by some of the other characters, often sounds like "Goldwyn") falls heir to a besieged kingdom, but must survive a Ulysses-scaled series of tests on the way to rescuing his beautiful bride from the clutches of the Beast, whose army of slayers imperils his journey every step of the way.

Format opens up a field of infinitive possibilities for incident, particularly since the tale has been placed in an unhistorical setting which is neither past nor future. Characters live in medieval style castles and ride horses to get about, but their weaponry lights up a la "Star Wars" when put to use.

Crucial to Colwyn's quest is his recovery of the glaive, a razor-tipped, spinning boomerang which will enable him to combat the Beast. This fancy piece of magical jewelry holds the same importance as the Excalibur sword did for Arthur, or the Force did for Luke Skywalker, and he is led to it by wise old Freddie Jones who, it cannot be avoided, bears an uncanny plot resemblance to Alec Guinness' Ben Kenobi in "Star Wars."

Citing inspirations for the characters and incidents in "Krull" is not an exercise in film buff obscuritanism because, in this case, borrowings have been so obviously made from many of the most popular films of all time, just about any film fan over the age of 12 will have seen most of the antecedents.

Colwyn picks up a ragtag band of accomplices, a la Robin Hood and "The Wizard Of Oz." One of his destinations is "The Emerald Temple;" the Beast is able to take on many forms, as in "The Thing;" one of the characters is Cyclops, out of "The Odyssey." At one point, in a rush, the band's horses take to the skies just as the bicycles did in "E.T.," and several of the action escape sequences bar distinct overtones of "Raiders Of The Lost Ark."

Even though the specifics are different, almost everything about the film seems terribly familiar, and it lacks the freshness and zip which would have been required to make one forget the past in favor of current pleasures.

Stanford Sherman's script, filled with incident as it is, holds the attention on a moment to moment basis, but lacks an inner drive or a compelling raison d'etre. Professionalism of director Peter Yates, the large array of production and technical talents and, particularly, the mainly British actors keep things from becoming genuinely dull or laughable. But there's no denying that the enterprise fell far short of the intended mark.

Stephen Grimes' production design is a riot of influences, from the space-aged to the ancient to the surreal, and the sheer number of different settings is astounding. For some reason, however, pic has a rather murky, bluefish look which, in sharpness and luster, isn't on a par with most grand scale features of late. James Horner's score, lushly conceived, also becomes somewhat overbearing at times.

As Colwyn, Ken Marshall has the right spirit but is a bit bland, and Lysette Anthony's beauty takes care of the only demands made on her as his kidnapped bride. David Battley manages some decent comic relief, and

Alun Armstrong delivers well as the outlaw leader who brings his men over to Colwyn's side.

—*Cart.*

El Grito de Celina
(Celina's Cry)
(ARGENTINE-COLOR)

Buenos Aires, June 12.

A Cono Sur release. Directed by Mario David. Features entire cast. Screenplay, David, based on Bernardo Kordon's short story, "Celina's Eyes;" camera (Eastmancolor), Adelqui Camusso; music, Victor Proncet; art director, Renee David. Reviewed at the Opera theatre, B.A., May 26, 1983. Running time: 96 MINS.

Cast: Maria Rosa Gallo, Selva Aleman, Pablo Alarcon, Miguel Angel Sola, Maria Vaner, Aldo Barbero, Alba Mujica.

"Celina's Cry" was lensed in 1975 but its release was long delayed, firstly due to commercial reasons and then to the blacklisting of some members of its cast. Both obstacles removed, it was finally shown with poor b.o. results, although most of its players have more drawing power nowadays, at least on stage and tv, than when the pic was made.

Besides the fact that time has taken its toll — the film looks unsophisticated for present standards — another handicap is a misplacement of the story about a fiery mother who plots the murder of a daughter-in-law unwilling to accept her tyrannical handling of the family, eventually forcing her two sons (one of them the husband of the victim) to kill the girl by exposing her to a snake's bite.

This story was inspired by a real incident that involved primitive people in a remote area of the Chaco jungle but was transplanted to a civilized rural area of Buenos Aires province, where such a barbarian thing is unbelievable (and not only because there are poisonous snakes there!). --*Nubi.*

Risky Business
(COLOR)

How to succeed in shady business.

Hollywood, July 13.

A Geffen Company release through Warner Bros. of a Steve Tisch/Jon Avnet production. Produced by Avnet, Tisch. Directed, screenplay by Paul Brickman. Features entire cast. Camera (Technicolor), Reynaldo Villalobos, Bruce Surtees; editor, Richard Chew; music, Tangerine Dream; production design, William J. Cassidy; set decoration, Ralph Hall; costume design, Robert de Mora; sound (Dolby), Scott Smith; associate producer, James O'Fallon; assistant director, Jerry Grandey. Reviewed at the Burbank Studios, Burbank, July 13, 1983. (MPAA Rating: R.) Running time: 96 MINS.

Joel Goodson	Tom Cruise
Lana	Rebecca DeMornay
Barry	Curtis Armstrong
Barry	Bronson Pinchot
Glenn	Raphael Sbarge
Guido	Joe Pantoliano
Joel's father	Nicholas Pryor
Joel's mother	Janet Carroll
Vicki	Shera Danese

Rutherford.................Richard Masur
Jackie ....Bruce A. Young
Chuck.................Kevin C. Anderson

"Risky Business" is like a promising first novel, with all the pros and cons that come with that territory. Appealingly personal and humorously observant much of the time, directorial bow by screenwriter Paul Brickman also capitulates on occasion to the crass commerciality it depicts, thereby creating a muddled grab-bag of tones. But, "Class" notwithstanding, this is as close to a contempo "The Graduate" as has come along in awhile, and that, coupled with some exotic story angles, gives pic potential sleeper status, with possibility to build as word gets around.

High schooler Tom Cruise could literally be a next-door neighbor to Timothy Hutton in "Ordinary People" on Chicago's affluent suburban North Shore. Serious, well-reared and admirably principled, lad seems well positioned for acceptance at a good college and for success in adult life, although his relatively cloistered environment has cut him off from experimentation with life's, and his own, wilder side.

That changes virtually overnight, however, when he meets sharp-looking hooker Rebecca De Mornay, who begins by divesting Cruise of his virginity, then proceeds in short order to relieve him of his innocence.

On the lam from her slimy pimp, she shacks up in Cruise's splendid home while his parents are out of town and, since he's anxious to prove himself as a Future Enterpriser in one of his school's more blatantly greed-oriented programs, convinces him to make the house into a bordello for one night.

To this end, De Mornay invites dozens of her slinky girlfriends over to the pad to service the neighborhood's young men, guys with plenty of dough in their pockets but without sufficient nerve to search out these same gals in downtown Chicago.

Premise is provocative, and storytelling is approached in a manner that often proves fresh and unpredictable. Particularly in the early-going, Brickman spikes the narrative with some very effective dream and fantasy vignettes, and dark, roving camera style creates a restless, anxious mood which nicely underlines Cruise's uncertainty as to what he's going to do, not only with his weekend, but with his life.

Further tension stems from such surface plot points as whether or not Cruise is going to get in trouble for landing his father's Porsche in the lake and allowing the pimp to steal all of his parents' furniture, as well as from the overtly predatory nature of De Mornay. Cruise

begins to covet her as a potential real girlfriend, not just a business associate, and normally one would expect her to soften up a bit and show her vulnerable side. But character remains quite remote and self-possessed throughout, and so manipulative of her prey that one somewhat resents her influence on him.

But most unsettling aspect of the film is that it's impossible to really know what it's about. Script is more sensitive than most to the value of various moral attitudes, and is appreciative of such notions as the fear of growing up and the restrictions that a "good" upbringing can impose on the full development of one's personality.

But ultimately, pic seems to endorse the bottom line, going for the big buck, above all other considerations. In fact, not only is Cruise rewarded financially for setting up the best little whorehouse in Glencoe, but it gets him into Princeton to boot.

Brickman can therefore be accused of trying to have it both ways, but there's no denying the stylishness and talent of his direction. While not always successful, Brickman is not afraid to try to mix moods, to inject high comedy into an anxiety-filled situation. Furthermore, as lensed by Reynaldo Villalobos and Bruce Surtees, film is marvelous to look at.

Their characters hardly seem made for each other, but both Cruise and De Mornay acquit themselves in fine fashion. Of supporting cast, Curtis Armstrong has the best role, that of a gadfly who pushes Cruise to forget his inhibitions and take risks, whether they are well considered or not.

Pic is ultra-slick in all departments. — *Cart.*

Jaws 3-D
(COLOR-3D)

Bruce has had a sex change and teeth extracted.

Hollywood, July 22.
Universal Pictures release of an Alan Landsburg production. Produced by Robert Hitzig. Directed by Joe Alves. Exec producers, Alan Landsburg, Howard Lipstone. Features entire cast. Screenplay, Richard Matheson, Carl Gottlieb; story, Guerdon Trueblood; suggested by the novel, "Jaws," by Peter Benchley; camera (Technicolor), James A. Contner; underwater operator, Jeff Simon; editor, Randy Roberts; music, Alan Parker, shark theme, John Williams; production design, Woods Mackintosh; visual creative consultant, Roy Arbogast; visual design consultant, Philip Abramson; art rction, Chris Horner, Paul Eads; sound, Jack C. Jacobsen; costume supervisor, Dresden Urquhart; assistant directors, Scott Maitland, J. Alan Hopkins, David Sosna; second unit director, Rupert Hitzig. Reviewed at Universal Studios, Universal City, July 22, 1983. (MPAA Rating: PG.) Running time: 97 MINS.
Mike Brody...................Dennis Quaid
Kathryn Morgan...........Ness Armstrong
Philip FitzRoyce....Simon MacCorkindale
Calvin ....Louis Gossett Jr.

Sean Brody.................John Putch
Kelly Ann Bukowski........Lea Thompson
Jack Tate...................P.H. Moriarty
Dan..........................Dan Blasko

The "Jaws" cycle, eight summers after the first bite that was felt around the boxoffice world, has reached its end and nadir with this surprisingly tepid 3-D version. Curiosity alone should spell a hot opening weekend (just concluded), but the film has no fins and should drown quickly.

There's nothing wrong with bringing back a story that gives people a terrific time. The trick is not to stray too far from the original and not to stick too close to it either. But "Jaws 3-D" strays much too far; it isn't particularly scary; and, as the bellwether 3-D movie of the year, it doesn't point to much of a future for three dimensional film. If 3-D can't enhance a pic about a devouring shark, what's left except lame novelty?

Since the first "Jaws" was such a phenomenon, some financial perspective is in order. The seminal entry grossed approximately $550,000,000 worldwide, reaping some $270,000,000 in rentals, with $133,000,000 of that domestic. "Jaws II," released in the summer of 1978, did $220,000,000 worldwide gross, about $110,000,000 in rentals, with some $60,000,000 of that domestic. "Jaws 3-D," although imaginatively enough conceived from a story by Guerdon Trueblood with a scenario by Richard Matheson and veteran "Jaws" hand Carl Gottlieb, reportedly reached $15,000,000 in production costs. A Universal pickup of an Alan Landsburg Production, its filmmakers face a stiff road if they're to break even.

Gone are Roy Scheider, the summer resort of Amity, and even the ocean. They have been replaced by Florida's Sea World, a lagoon and an Undersea Kingdom that entraps a 35-foot Great White, and a group of young people who run the tourist sea park.

The picture includes two carryover characters from the first two "Jaws," Scheider's now-grown sons (Mike and Sean Brody), who are played by nominal star Dennis Quaid as the older brother turned machine engineer and kid brother John Putch (the son of Jean Stapleton). Park supervisor is routinely essayed by Louis Gossett Jr., in a role that's certainly a letdown following his mark with "An Officer and a Gentleman."

Femme cast is headed by Bess Armstrong as an intrepid marine biologist who lives with Quaid. Simon MacCorkindale is an egotistical underwater photographer who wins the distinction of winding up inside the shark, with POV from MacCorkindale as he frantically

struggles to swim through the shark's jaws to safety.

A word about the 3-D glasses. The effect is much greater if you sit far back and in the center. But director Joe Alves, who was instrumental in the design of the first "Jaws" shark and was the unsung production hero in both the first two pictures, fails to linger long enough on the Great White. The action sequences become blurred in a rush of water. And the horror is missing. Most symbolic of uneventful things to come are the opening moments. Instead of human beings getting chomped — the now famous night bather in #1 and the underwater cameraman in #2 — this time the first gore you see is only the chopped-off head of a fish.

As in "Jaws II," the body count is limited to some five or six unfortunates. With the desire for PG rating, the blood count is low. And, with a more mechanically sophisticated shark, not to mention 3-D, there is yet nothing in the film that even manages to suggest that wonderful second with Robert Shaw got it in the '75 picture.

Film, out of the lagoon, is a series of dull interludes around Sea World that look like a promo for the park. Further, the by-now familiar cuts from underwater suspense to serene chat topside, become predictable and boring. Characterization is sorely missing, proving once again that character is action, and that without it, even with things coming at you in 3-D, that particular moviegoing experience is only a brief novelty. —*Loyn.*

Kurt og Valde
(Kurt and Valde)
(DANISH-COLOR)

Copenhagen, July 20.
A Nordisk Film (with Danish Film Institute aid) production and release. Features entire cast. Original story and manuscript by Peter and Stig Thorsboe; script, Erik Balling, Erik Bahs; directed by Hans Kristensen; camera (Eastmancolor) Claus Loof; editors, Lars Brydesen, Leif Axel Kjeldsen; music, Svend Skipper, Jesper Klein; production design, Henning Bahs; executive producer, Bo Christensen; production management, Karsten Groenborg, Lene Christiansen. Reviewed at the Palads, Copenhagen, July 19, 1983. Running time: 97 MINS.

Kurt...................Lars Knutson
Valde..................Arne Hansen
The Professor..............Olaf Ussing
Knudsen....................Ove Sprogoe
Bank Manager......Bjoern Watt Booelsen
Innkeeper 1..............Ole Thestrup
Innkeeper 2..............Buster Larsen
2's wife..................Lisbet Dahl
Kasper....................Thomas Eje
Mette.....................Eva Jensen

With all of the venerable Nordisk Film production knowhow behind it, "Kurt and Valde" emerges as a surprisingly heavy item where the lighter farcical comedy fun had been expected. Hans Kristensen has directed from a script by Erik Balling and Henning Bahs (of "Olsen Gang" fame and fortune) and has done so with maybe too much care: every plot device, gag, pratfall is delivered with so much advance preparation and warning that the shots fail to surprise and thus to amuse.

Hans Kristensen, who has earlier done both brilliant thrillers and comedy, likes his characters to come out truly believable as human beings. He works here in the opposite interests of a script that cries out for straight-out farce and fast fun. The title characters are a couple of small-time touring actors, down on their luck and reduced to skipping their hotel bills with the aid of primitive trickery.

One day, dressed up in disguises, they are taken to be friends and confidantes of an inventor who exploded himself to death without disclosing to the local business community the formula for the perfect ersatz gasoline he had just proven totally effective. Without really wanting to, but starved and otherwise at wits' end, Kurt and Valde are forced to play out their new roles as the only possessors of the magical chemical letters and ciphers.

While Kurt and Valde are played amiably by Lars Knutzon and Arne Hansen as a couple of really nice guys doing their best against all odds, everyone else involved just goes through the motions of a predictable sitcom. A certain amount of social satirical intent is in evidence in the script, but the satire never bites deeper than cliche level.

As Valde, Arne Hansen delivers a performance with mock hammy gusto worthy of grand theatre, but there is nothing in the interplay between him and Lars Knutzon to indicate that a new comedy team has been established here, let alone a new comedy series to replace Nordisk's "Olsen-Gang" that ran to 13 successful installments before it was finally laid to rest three years ago. —*Kell.*

Ah Ying
(HONG KONG-COLOR)

Hong Kong, July 17.

A Feng Huang Motion Picture Co. Production. Released by Sil-Metropole Organization Ltd. Directed by Allen Fong Yuk-Ping. Features entire cast. Screenplay, Sze Yeung-Ping, Peter Wang; camera (color), Chang Lok-Yee; music, Violet Lam; sound recording, Wong Kwok-Hung. Reviewed at Sil-Metropole Organization preview room, Sunbeam Commercial Bld., Kowloon, Hong Kong, July 16, 1983. Running Time: 100 MINS.

Cast: Hui So-Ying, Peter Wang, Hui Piu, Yao Lin-shum, Cheng Chi Hung, Shu Kei, Rachel Zen, Wong Kee-Chee, Charles Ng, Wong Chi.

(Cantonese, Mandarin, English soundtracks).

In a money-motivated city like Hong Kong, where films are con-

ceived merely for commerce and are geared to either viewers with young minds or just plain, non-thinking and visually oriented patrons, director Allen Fong is a rarity ... a sort of a gem in a sea of dollar coins. It is even more surprising that his projects manage to get reasonable financing.

Fong Yuk-ping (also known as Allen) is the American-trained filmmaker from Shaukiwan who surprised Hong Kongites in 1981 with "Father and Son;" an exquisite domestic drama about an ordinary Chinese family in a resettlement estate. He is unique in the sense that he has the distinction of being the only local filmmaker who's been exposed to western culture yet has managed to retain his "Chineseness" in cinematic expression of feelings, subtlety and sensitivity, attitudes and presentation of things Oriental.

"Ah Ying," the name of a young girl, is the title of Fong's new film. It was supposedly inspired by actress Hui So Ying whose real life became the basis for the pic, then incorporated with the brief Hong Kong sojourn of American-Chinese artist Koh Wu who died in Hong Kong in 1982, a close friend of the director.

Hui and Koh worked together and their platonic relationship serves as the core of this impressive and intimate film that is definitely not in the common mainstream of Cantonese filming.

The lead actress is a non-professional and is a fish vendor in real life. Her entire family appears as her "reel family" and the only professional actor is Peter Wang who portrays the drama coach Cheung. He contributed most of his dialog. For authenticity, Fong used direct sound and for realism, the dialog is a mixture of Cantonese, Mandarin, and English, the three most-used languages in Hong Kong.

Ah Ying earns $HK500 a month, so she has to suffer the overcrowding at home. Her relationship with the family members is not especially harmonious and her interest in modern music and the arts is not shared by her sisters. Her determination to improve herself emotionally, culturally and artistically leads her to a film society, then to an acting school where she meets her mentor, Cheung Chung Pak, an American-Chinese brought to Hong Kong to make a film. In many ways, Cheung serves as the alter ego of the director.

The film has already been invited to represent Hong Kong in the Manila International Film Festival in 1984. "Ah Ying" is convincing because of its unpreten-

tious naturalness. It has warmth and a lot of humanity. Fong's pic is without gimmick and will survive time because it is basic yet necessary Chinese. —*Mel.*

Moscow Film Festival

Amok
(MOROCCO-COLOR)

Moscow, July 14.

A Casablanca release of a Moussa Diakite, Cheikomar Barry, Vera Kaiss production. Features entire cast. Directed by Souheil Ben Barka. Screenplay, Ben Barka, Michel Constantin, Francois Rabati; music, Miriam Makeba. No other credits provided. Reviewed at Central Festival Hall, 13th Moscow Film Festival, July 13, 1983. Running time: 118 MINS.

Cast: Robert Liensol, Miriam Makeba, Douta Seek, Richard Harrison.

Except for Senegal, we seldom see good films coming from Africa. Technical achievements are still in the first development stage, and the political situation in most countries encourages state-subsidized items that serve as more than subtle propaganda of the regime and national values of the moment.

"Amok" is not an exception, although it manages to go much further. Subject is apartheid in South Africa, where a substantial part of this footage was shot. A Zulu living in the north is forced to go to Johannesburg, and there all possible misfortunes happen to himself and his black fellows. The plot is by no means as ingenuous as it seems in the beginning: Souheil Ben Barka, a usual collaborator with French filmmakers (especially Claude Lelouch), can extract from his script a cinematically fascinating story. The dramatic action is coherent, well developed and technically good. But the tone of the film is often questionable, turning into an inflated and demagogic discourse.

Such an approach conflicts with the whole structure of the film, which does not avoid using a great deal of humor to criticize the civilizations it is dealing with. In short, a very big advance over the average African feature, "Amok" still suffers from the cinematographic content problems within its continent. But it seems to be as clear as water that from Ben Barka's crafty hands very good films are to come in the nearest future.
— *Hoin.*

Jon-Kertomus Maailman Lopusta
(Jon - A Story About The End of the World)
(FINNISH-COLOR)

Moscow, July 9.

A Tambur Oy release and production. Produced by Tambur Oy. Features entire cast. Directed by Jaakke Pyhala. Screenplay, Py-

hala, Heikki Vuente, based on an original story by Pyhala; camera (color), Pertti Mutanen; sound, Paul Jyrala, Matti Kuortti; editing, Pyhala; music, Antti Hytti. Reviewed at the Central Festival Hall, Moscow Film Festival, July 8, 1983. Running time: 125 MINS.

Cast: Kari Vaananen, Vesa-Matti Loiri, Pia-Beate Tellefsen, Nils Utsi.

There is a strong scent of Scandinavia in this finely photographed item. Perhaps it comes from the ocean, for the film is mainly set in a small fishing village in northern Norway.

A young Finnish man, Jon, escapes to the small burg when he becomes tired of the capital city of Helsinki. He's on the run from the police, after beating up his metropolitan lover, and has no better alternative but to work in a fish-processing plant in the remote village, said to be the Norwegian equivalent of Siberia.

As he arrives in his new home, he becomes the theme for a Swedish tv crew which is shooting a documentary about migrant workers in Scandinavia.

The story of "Jon" turns out to be the story of the documentary. He doesn't have much to say, neither does the film. But his life is rich and colorful, as is the docu. Narrative and acting may look strange, for they are mostly fragmented and artificial. This characteristic by no means implies that the work itself suffers; it has its inner consistency and is technically correct.

Jaakke Pyhala, 27, seems to be a young director not much commited to the staging, but very much sensitive to the environment, which ultimately is the main character of this, his second feature film. —*Hoin.*

Pastorale Heroica
(Pastorale Heroica)
(POLISH-USSR-COLOR)

Moscow, July 8.

A Film Polski release of a Polish Corporation for Film Production Zespoly Filmowe, Iluzjon unit production, in cooperation with Mosfilm. Features entire cast. Directed by Henryk Bielski. Screenplay and dialog, Jerzy Janicki; music, Jerzy Maksymiuk; camera (color), Maciej Kijewski; production designer, Roman Wolniek; sound, Ryszard Krupa; editing, Ursula Sliwinska. Reviewed at Central Festival Hall, Moscow Film Festival, July 8, 1983. Running time: 82 MINS.

Cast: Wirgiliusz Gryn, Krystyna Krolowna, Zygmunt Malanowicz, Marek Kendrat, Leon Niemczyk.

The action is set at the end of World War II, when the Polish and Soviet armies are already approaching Berlin. As a GI barber, Josef Lopuch does not have much to do, except to claim that bullets can never touch him, since he was born in a graveyard. He is granted a license to visit his home, where he he hasn't been for five years, nor has his wife answered any of the 24 letters he has sent her. On his way home, he is surprised by two bits of news: his wife has married Wikter, and Wikter is responsible for the land reform which takes place in the village.

The new conjugal status is, of course, difficult to solve (Lopuch's wife claims she never got any letter and was told that the husband had died at the beginning of the war); now Lopuch must also cope with land problems.

Eventually ambiguity sets in. An armed band breaks into Sabina's house to take Wikter away. Wikter sacrifices himself for Lopuch whose wife's cause turns out to be more important than anything else. Land and faith are the causes for which he doesn't hesitate to test his immortality. Bielski's thesis, though muddled, could well be that land reform and faith in the holy spirit are not conflicting ideas, but homogeneous parts of such a complex culture as the Polish. —*Hoin.*

Dhil Al-Ardh
(Shadow of the Earth)
(TUNISIAN-FRENCH-COLOR)

Moscow, July 8.
A Satpec. (Tunis), and Films Moliere, (Paris), coproduction. Features entire cast. Directed by Taieb Louhichi. Screenplay, Taieb Louhichi. Only credits available. Reviewed at Moscow Film Fest (Competition), July 8, '83. Running time: 89 MINS.
Cast: Despina Tomazani, Helene Catzaras, Mouna Noureddine.

Taieb Louhichi's "Shadow of the Earth" scored at other international fests (Cannes Critics Week, 1982) before finding an appreciative audience at Moscow. It's far and away one of the finest films to emerge from an African Arab nation, and may be in the running for deserved kudos.

This is the story of nomads in the Tunisian deserts. It chronicles the family life of a tribe, loosely connected to other nomads in the area, one of whom is the acknowledged leader due to age or heredity. The modestly living group has sheep and goats, plus a few camels, and they live according to ancient laws and customs for the most part. The first half of the film covers these rites and rituals from a humanistic viewpoint, for a child is born while the elder in the family is becoming weak with age.

The son responsible for the group's care and livelihood decides one day to leave his family to work for a period in a nearby city, for the grazing is presently bad and a few sheep have caught a strange disease — should the entire herd become infected, the nomads would indeed be in dire straits. Some time later, the son returns with money and presents, and a happy reunion takes place. One of

the presents is a tv set, operated by a generator, which causes a stir when a kiss is seen on the screen by shocked women in the family.

A turn-of-events then disrupts the family. First, a census is taken by visiting military and government officials. Then the son is drafted into the army, and soldiers arrive to take him away. He resists, but it is hopeless. Again, time passes, and news comes that the son (husband and father to other in the family) has died. The wife decides to go alone to Tunis to claim the body.

It is this trip from the desert into the distant city that is worth all the documentary-like footage before it. The woman travels by bus into the more populous areas, then arrives in the teeming-with-life Tunis to look for the port authorities. On this particular day, all the offices are closed. She must wait until the weekend is over, but meanwhile a coffin is lifted from the hold of a ship to hang suspended in air as the shot freezes to make its silent commentary.

Tightly directed and lensed, "Shadow of the Earth" deserves more fest exposure plus skedding in Arab (or Tunisian) Film Weeks.
— *Holl.*

The Star Chamber
(COLOR)

Judges as vigilantes.

Hollywood, July 19.
A 20th Century-Fox release, produced by Frank Yablans. Directed by Peter Hyams. Features entire cast. Screenplay, Roderick Taylor, Peter Hyams; camera (Deluxe Color), Richard Hannah; editor, Jim Mitchell, sound, Gerry Jost; production design, Bill Malley; assistant director, Bill Beasley; associate producers, Kurt Neumann, Jonathan A. Zimbert; art direction, Robert Welch; music, Michael Small. Reviewed at 20th Century-Fox studios, L.A., July 19, 1983. (MPAA rating: R.) Running time: 149 MINS.
Hardin ....Michael Douglas
Caulfield..................... Hal Holbrook
Lowes.....................Yaphet Kotto
Emily ....Sharon Gless
Lewin...............James B. Sikking
Cooms.....................Joe Regalbuto
Monk.......................Don Calfa
Wickman.....................John DiSanti
Flowers..................DeWayne Jessie
Hingle......................Jack Kehoe
Wiggen.....................Larry Hankin
MacKay...........Dick Anthony Williams

Though "The Star Chamber" admirably tackles a national threat just as destructive as nuclear holocaust, the film fails to hold onto its focus and collapses about halfway through. That, combined with a sci-fi title that doesn't fit, spells probable boxoffice doom.

Producer Frank Yablans and director Peter Hyams exhibit an excess of faith in today's educational system if they think the bulk of today's filmgoing audience will know the title's 15th-Century derivation as an extra-judicial body.

In any case, "Chamber" does start out on an important note: The U.S. criminal justice system is not only collapsing but what's left has been perverted until the victims of crime have no hope of satisfaction nor protection.

As a decent, conscientious judge, Michael Douglas deals with the problem daily, forced by straining legal precedent to free the obviously "guilty."But he sincerely believes the rule of law must prevail until faced with the anguish of a father, perfectly played by James B. Sikking, whose young son was one of several kids drugged and murdered by a child-porno ring.

Circumstantial evidence clearly points to the pair in Douglas' court, but he feels compelled to let them go on the grounds of a legal hairsplit in their favor by a questionable stop-and-search. But when Sikking pulls a pistol in court in a futile attempt at revenge and wounds a cop instead, there's no question who's going to serve hard time while his accused tormentors roam free.

Severely stricken by these events, Douglas turns to his friend and mentor, Hal Holbrook, who is secretly part of a group of judges who mete out their own fatal sentences on criminals who've been through their real courts and gone free.

Getting to this point in the film, there's a pleasure in rediscovering intelligent dialog, ably provided by Hyams and Roderick Taylor. But the talk is haunted by concern that this intellectual morass cannot be solved within the confines of cinema.

Sure enough, Hyams and the script let go eventually when it turns out that the pair originally accused of killing the kid are innocent — but have already been marked for execution by the judges meeting in secret.

From that point on, the story goes from able to addled as Douglas, the mild-mannered judge, puts himself in all sorts of peril to find the accused and try to persuade them to leave town. Failing that, he's willing to sacrifice himself, his family and all the other judges for the wrong they've done, even if convinced that the two thugs in question probably have escaped punishment for other killings, though falsely accused of this one.

In the midst of all this, also, dialog surrenders to action until all involvement in the original moral-legal problem fades away. But it's good to come across a sincere attempt, anyway. —*Har.*

Toki Wo Kakeru Shojo
(The Little Girl Who
Conquered Time)
(JAPANESE-COLOR)

Tokyo, July 25.
A Toei release of a Kodokawa Production. Exec producer, Haruki Kadokawa. Produced by Norihiko Yamada, Kyoko Obayashi. Directed by Nobuhiko Obayashi. Features entire cast. Screenplay, Wataru Kenmotsu; camera (color), Zenshi Sakamoto; art director, Kazuko Satsuya; sound, Shohei Hayashi; music, Masataka Matsutoya; lighting, Akio Watanabe; editing, Nabuhiko Obayashi; assistant director, Shuji Natio. Reviewed at Toei screening room, Tokyo, July 15, 1983. Running time: 104 MINS.
Yoshiyama ....Tomoyo Harada
Fukamachi ....Ryoichi Takayanagi
Horikawa...................Toshinori Oki
Mariko ....Yukari Tsuda
Fukushima ....Ittoku Kishibe

To give credit where it's due, this Kadokawa Production, for a bit over half its 104 minutes, is more affecting than affected, informed less by cloying sentimentality and relatively honest sentiment. The titular young girl is Tomoya Harada, a hopelessly romantic 16-year-old caught up in the beauty of stars and the fragrances of flowers, and falling in love for the first time.

Although she sounds like the sort of person guaranteed to send diabetics into insulin shock, the heroine is no cutesy-baby doll, but rather a soft-spoken, winningly gentle-spirited soul. Making her screen debut, Tomoyo Harada proves herself a natural. Although she is convincing at what she does, the evidence here suggests she might not have the range to do much of anything else.

Not unusual for a teenager with a dreamy outlook on life, Harada begins having clearly focused dreams resembling precognitive experiences resembling clearly-focused dreams), "participating" in various events some 24 hours before they actually transpire. Alas, with the unravelling of the mystery comes the unravelling of the film.

Prior to presenting the solution to the conundrum troubling Harada, Nabuhiko Obayashi, perhaps Japan's most technique-obsessed director, hold his well-known addiction to visual gimmickry in check, one of his few indulgences being a self-referential opening lifted intact from his "Tenkosei." His use of a b&w-to-color transition, while serving a dramatic purpose in the earlier film, does not do so here. But this is a misdemeanor to the felony of Obayashi's pulling out the stops, which consists of relying on special effects that look exceptionally cheap.

The cause of Harada's time-trekking tribulations turns out to be the object of her affections, Ryoichi Takayanagi, a classmate and de facto visitor from another world whose highly romantic outlook on life is the result of mysterioso input from Harada's personality and whose delivery of lines is undoubtedly the result of his brain-waves being controlled by a galaxy inhabited by monotonous no-talents. The epilog to this inter-galacto-cosmic argle-bargle not unexpectedly suggests the punch line of a shaggy dog story, with Harada made up as a confirmed spinster of 27, a melancholy lab technician still carrying a torch for her spaceman. So this is what it's like to get old. —*Bail.*

Twice Upon A Time
(ANIMATED-COLOR)

Limited by identity problem.

Hollywood, July 29.
A Ladd Co. release through Warner Bros. Produced by Bill Couturie. Directed by John Korty and Charles Swenson. Features entire cast. Exec producer, George Lucas. Screenplay, John Korty, Swenson, Suella Kennedy and Couturie based on a story by Korty, Couturie and Kennedy; technical director, John Baker; supervising animator, Brian Narelle, editor, Jennifer Gallagher; art director, Harley Jessup; sound, Walt Kraemer. Reviewed at Burbank Studios, Room 5, July 29, 1983. (MPAA Rating: PG). Running time: **75 MINS.**

Ralph .... Lorenzo Music
Fairy Godmother Judith Kaham Kampmann
Synonamess Botch .... Marshall Efron
Rod Rescueman/
  Scuzzbopper .... James Cranna
Flora Fauna .... Julie Payne
Greensleeves .... Hamilton Camp
Narrator, Chief of Stage,
  Judges And Bailiff .... Paul Frees

As the success of various recent Walt Disney Prods. reissues proves, there is room in the marketplace for animated films. But the Ladd Co.'s "Twice Upon A Time" hardly seems capable of finding its niche. An unfocused, often confusing good vs. evil tale from director-writer John Korty done in cooperation with Lucasfilm, the pic ultimately emerges as too sophisticated for the kids and just too dull for adults. Boxoffice prospects for distrib Warner Bros. are limited.

Although the animation and overall look of the film are fine (a new Lumage animation process was employed), "Twice" falters on the crucial element — story. It appears the filmmakers are trying to bring across a world where animated creatures are responsible for both the dreams and nightmares of the outside world. There's a fight for control (that rests with obtaining the spring of the "cosmic clock") and an ultimate showdown between the bad guys and the good guys. It would be difficult to figure out more than that without a press kit.

In addition, character names like Synonamess Botch, Greensleeves and Scuzzbopper don't aid in clarity for the kiddies nor does the fairly undistinctive look of many of the figures used onscreen. There are a few humorous moments with a Jewish-mother type "fairy godmother" but nothing that hasn't been seen before.

High point comes when one of the creatures asks about a particularly strange onscreen character. The creature is told not to worry, "it's just the writer." Indeed.
—*Berg.*

Stella
(FRENCH-COLOR)

Paris, July 25.
Fox-Hachette release of a Sara Films/Hachette-Fox coproduction. Produced by Alain Sarde. Stars Nicole Garcia, Thierry Lhermitte, Jean-Claude Brialy, Charles Denner, Victor Lanoux. Directed by Laurent Heynemann. Screenplay, Heynemann, Pierre Fabre; camera (color), Jean-Francois Gondre; music, Philippe Sarde; art director, Jean-Baptiste Poirot; editor, Armand Psenny; makeup, Jackie Reynal; sound, Paul Laine; costumes, Catherine Leterrier, Marie Helene Daumal; production manager, Christine Gozlan. Reviewed at the Gaumont Colisee Theatre, Paris, July 15, 1983. Running time: **98 MINS.**
Stella .... Nicole Garcia
Yvon .... Thierry Lhermitte
The Swiss .... Victor Lanoux
Caron .... Jean-Claude Brialy
Paulet .... Gerard Desarthe
Richard .... Charles Denner

"Stella" is a war-time drama about a young Frenchman during the German Occupation who joins the Gestapo in order to free his Jewish lover, who has been denounced and sent to an internment camp for eventual deportation.

Though he succeeds in liberating her, their idyll is cut short by news of the disembarking Allied forces and the menace of retaliation by Resistance forces attempting to round up collaborators.

Laurent Heynemann, who last made the adroit romantic thriller, "Il Faut Tuer Birgit Haas," has here set his sights much higher in his dramatization of a true story, but the conventional scripting, with its typed secondary characters representing different viewpoints and providing a moral sounding board for the main personages, fails to do justice to the ambiguity of the theme.

Most problematic is the casting: the illicit lovers are played by Nicole Garcia and Thierry Lhermitte. Garcia is often praised for her intelligence and subtlety, but here one wishes she'd been less cerebral and more visceral — she hardly convinces as a woman blinded by her passions. As for Lhermitte, he has the most extraordinary pair of blue eyes, but they don't compensate for a lack of dramatic force; powerful emotions just seem to slide off his bland good looks.

What's left are some fairly interesting descriptive passages of French underground and collaborationist circles in the panic and chaos of August 1944, and a few savory performances: notably Jean-Claude Brialy as Lhermitte's hardbitten Gestapo chief, and Victor Lanoux as a totally corrupt and cynical Swiss profiteer. Technically, film is fine, with a poignantly expressive score by Philippe Sarde.

But this drama about passion and moral prostitution fails to arouse enough urgent concern for its colorless protagonists. —*Len.*

Private School
(COLOR)

Lewd, and long, exploitationer.

Hollywood, July 29.
A Universal release of an R. Ben Efraim production from Unity Pictures Corp. Produced by Efraim, Don Enright. Directed by Noel Black. Features entire cast. Screenplay, Dan Greenburg, Suzanne O'Malley; camera (Metrocolor), Walter Lasally; editor, Fred Chulack; production design, Ivo Cristante; set decoration, K.C. Scheibel; sound, Susumu Tokunow; sound unit director, Ric Rondell; assistant director, Stephen Lofaro. Reviewed at Universal Studios, Universal City, July 29, 1983. (MPAA Rating: R.) Running time: **97 MINS.**
Christine .... Phoebe Cates
Jordan .... Betsy Russell
Jim .... Matthew Modine
Bubba .... Michael Zorek
Miss Dutchbok .... Fran Ryan
Betsy .... Kathleen Wilhoite
Chauncey .... Ray Walston
Ms. Copuletta .... Sylvia Kristel
Roy .... Jonathan Prince
Rita .... Kari Lizer
Mr. Flugel .... Richard Stahl
Coach Whelan .... Julie Payne
Mr. Leigh-Jensen .... Frank Aletter
Birdie Fallmouth .... Frances Bay

"Private School" gets an "A" in Phys Ed, but merits a "D-minus" in all other courses. A determinedly lewd teen sexploitationer with a strong dirty old man voyeuristic streak, pic is the third Universal release in a month's time not to be advance press screened for fear that bad notices would harm biz on the all important opening weekend. It can't be said that the studio was wrong in this case.

R. Ben Efraim production falls squarely in the "Animal House"-"Porky's" genre, and at least half the film seems dedicated to efforts of a group of pea-brained guys to try to ogle the young ladies of the Cherryvale Academy for girls in various states of undress.

This, of course, sets up endless opportunities for the viewer to gaze upon nubile lasses in the locker room, in their dorms, and even riding bare breasted on horseback. Quotient of nudity is quite high compared with other recent genre efforts, which will please the boys, but perhaps somewhat put off the dating crowd.

Unfortunately, pacing is dreadfully slow, both within individual scenes and overall, and pic should have been cut by about 10 minutes from its 97 minutes, which seems like two hours. Director Noel Black flubs the payoffs of numerous comic gags, which accounts for preponderance of dead air, and characterizations are limited to one note posing.

But the girls, notably Phoebe Cates and Betsy Russell, are cute, the soundtrack is packed with lively tunes, and no one's mind will be forever warped by the proceedings, so things could be worse. Sylvia Kristel, star of Efraim's previous moneymaker, "Private Lessons," has a desultory bit as a sex education teacher, and is about the only femme in the show who keeps her clothes on all the time.
—*Cart.*

Deserters
(CANADIAN-COLOR-16m)

Vancouver, July 25.
An Exile Productions Ltd. (Vancouver) presentation. Produced by Tom Braidwood, Jack Darcus. Directed by Darcus. Features entire cast. Screenplay, Darcus; camera (color), Tony Westman; art director, Darcus; editor, Darcus; sound, Larry Sutton, Barry P. Jones; music score, Michael Conway Baker. Reviewed at Ridge Theatre, Vancouver, July 25, 1983. Running time: **98 MINS.**
Sgt. Ulysses Hawley .... Alan Scarfe
Peter .... Jon Bryden
Val .... Barbara March
Noel .... Dermot Hennelly
Army Captain .... Ty Haller
  Also with: Bob Metcalfe, Robin Mossley.

Jack Darcus' fourth feature is an offbeat bout of largely undiluted theatrics that harks back to an era (1969) when U.S. draft-dodgers fled to Canada to evade the Vietnamese war.

Aided by the New Play Centre of Vancouver, and especially by veteran thespian Henry Woolf, Darcus reworked his original one-hour tv drama as a vehicle suited to the talents of actor Alan Scarfe. He takes the role, tailored for him specifically, of Sarge, a hardnosed drill-instructor hot on the heels of two fugitive trainees who have made a fool of him in front of an officer.

Sarge finds a haven of sorts in the home of Noel and Val, an unhappy young couple, who prey upon the refugees from the draft. Noel is a sappy idealist, possibly with a gay urge, who has sheltered wimp escapee Peter and has glamorized him into a daring activist. Val enjoys the occasional sexual favors of Noel's protegees. Sarge has a charisma that obliges other men to take a cue from his intransigence and to play the macho game to shore up their shrunken masculinity.

In its claustrophobia and dingy, trapped look "Deserters" is reminiscent of William Fruet's 1972 debut feature "Wedding in White." Darcus has clearly sharpened his scripting knowhow and, although he continues to function as a one man band filmmaker, has chosen wisely to let protagonist Scarfe run with a set of riveting soliloquies.

The other three actors are quite subsidiary, though Jon Bryden as draft-dodger Peter is immaculately callow, and Barbara March as Val has a mystery and a pathos all too real.

Technical credits are okay, for a low-budget pic shot on a tight schedule. Tony Westman's lensing is flexible and adroit. The score of Michael Baker is muted and effective. "Deserters" is likely to prove the final film to be shot on location at the notorious British Columbia Penitentiary, scheduled for demolition within a year. It was also the first B.C. production to benefit from salary deferments with the IATSE local, to a figure of almost 50% of the total budget, which was under $250,000. —*Gran.*

Winners & Sinners
(HONG KONG · COLOR)

Hong Kong, July 9.
A Golden Harvest Group production. Distributed through Golden Communications. Executive producer, Raymond Chow. Directed by Samo Hung. Stars Jackie Chan, Samo Hung, Richard Ng, Charlie Ching Shung Lin, John Sham, Fung Shiu Fam. (No other credits provided by producers). Reviewed at State Theatre, Hong Kong, July 8, 1983. Running time: **100 MINS.**
(Cantonese soundtrack with English subtitles.)

Teapot (Samo Hung), Exhaust Pipe (Richard Ng), Vaseline (Charlie Ching Shung Lin), Curly Jerk (John Sham) and Ranks (Fung Shiu Fam), all petty thieves, become friends while in prison. Fresh out, they swear they will reform. They even form a cleaning company to prove it. Meanwhile, Boss Chau of the underworld, also released from prison, decides to do otherwise. He reactivates his counterfeit money operation.

Exhaust Pipe and Vaseline vie for the attention of Curly Jerk's kid sister (Chung Chor Hung), but she likes self-effacing Teapot better. Moments of minor crises and continuous hilarity occur.

Crack CID detective Jackie Chan is after the counterfeit ring. He is on the point of busting it when the printing plates disappear and end up by accident in the cleaning van. Poor Jackie is chewed out by his superior.

The five, unaware of all this, gatecrash Chau's party. The five escape from the party only to learn Boss Man (Gheung Chung) of a rival gang is holding kid sister in exchange for the plates. And in the finale, there's a dog fight in the warehouse. The five manage to put Chau and Man in their proper place — behind bars. But surely not for long before a sequel.

"Winners and Sinners" is a summer winner for Golden Harvest which needs a local solid hit to retain its showbiz leadership. There is obvious evidence of positive merger and chemistry to combine the various talents of the five major local stars.

There are cameo roles of popular Hong Kong faces and despite the exploitation of Jackie Chan's presence, his role is really a minor one (but still, he and Samo Hung shoulder most of the action sequences). Samo Hung (who also directed) and fellow sinners dominate the scenario. Ng is super-hilarious as he bares all in an amusing "invisible" sequence. But the more dangerous stunts seem to have been done by a double, said to have been imported from Japan.

Budgeted at $HK10,000,000, "Winners and Sinners" should prove to be a Golden Harvest bonanza in Hong Kong and other standard marketplaces. — *Mel.*

Buddies
(AUSTRALIAN-COLOR)

Sydney, July 21.
A J.D. Productions Pty. Ltd. Production, in association with the Queensland Film Corporation. Produced by John Dingwall. Directed by Arch Nicholson. Features entire cast. Screenplay, Dingwall; camera (color), Panavision), David Eggby; editor, Martyn Down; music, Chris Neal; production design, Philip Warner. Reviewed at Film Australia, Lindfield, N.S.W., July 1, 1983. Running time: **99 MINS.**

Mike	Colin Friels
Johnny	Harold Hopkins
Stella	Kris McQuade
Ted	Bruce Spence
Andy	Dennis Miller
Alfred	Simon Chilvers
George Spencer	Norman Kaye
Jennifer Spencer	Lisa Peers
Peter	Andrew Sharp
Merle	Dinah Shearing

There's nothing particularly original about "Buddies," but it achieves everything it sets out to do; it's an enjoyable, old-fashioned entertainment. Set in and around the evocatively-named diamond mining townships of Emerald and Rubyvale in Central Queensland, which form a spectacularly dusty, fly-blown setting for the action, it's about two pals, Mike (Colin Friels) and Johnny (Harold Hopkins) who scratch for sapphires and live in fairly primitive conditions with their friend Ted (Bruce Spence) in "The Road Warrior") and a woman miner, Stella (Kris McQuade). Conflict arises when the unscrupulous Andy (Dennis Miller) tries to take over the friends'; mining claim by force, but there's never much doubt that the villain will be defeated in the end.

John Dingwall, who scripted and produced, is best known for his screenplay for Ken Hannam's 1974 "Sunday too Far Away," also about male camaraderie. He's provided an expansive, amusing story this time out, and provided plenty of interesting characters. These include a middle-aged doctor and his wife, plus their pretty daughter and her stodgy boyfriend. They turn up as tourists towing a caravan, but stay on to become involved with the diamond miners, and there are no prizes for guessing the daughter will wind up with one of the miners at fadeout.

Another endearing character is Alfred (Simon Chilvers), who arrives in this remote outback spot wearing a suit and tie in order to sell the buddies a light aircraft; a highlight of the film is a sequence where he drunkenly tries to give them a flying lesson, a sequence combining excellent stunt flying (by Barry Hemple) and broad comedy. Alfred, too, stays on and winds up with Stella.

Not only has Dingwall filled his script with unusual amusing characters, he's also got a knack of building up to what appears to be a climax — a love scene, a fist fight — and then defusing the moment, giving the film plenty of unexpected twists. There is a climax, however: when Mike and Andy fight a duel involving a giant bulldozer and a front-end loader.

This is the theatrical debut for Arch Nicholson, who's made his name over the years with excellent documentaries and tv features; he does a good job, keeping the action and the laughs moving along at a cracking pace. Only major flaw in a disarming film is the rather heavy-handed opening sequence in which Mike and Stella make violent love — it's out of key with what follows.

Engaging performances down the line, starting with the two leads, though maybe Chilvers as the dignified Alfred is stand-out. Technical credits are pro, with handsome location photography by David Eggby, and a catchy music score by Chris Neal.

Buddy films have been a bit out of vogue lately, but there should be an audience for this sprightly effort, with its neat blend of comedy and suspense and its numerous happy endings. The exotic locale won't hurt either. —*Strat.*

National Lampoon's Vacation
(COLOR)

A trip to remember.

Hollywood, July 26.
A Warner Bros. release, produced by Matty Simmons. Directed by Harold Ramis. Features entire cast. Screenplay, John Hughes; camera (Technicolor), Victor J. Kemper; editor, Pem Herring; sound, Marty Bolger; production design, Jack Collis; assistant director, Robert P. Cohen; associate producer, Robert Grand; music, Ralph Burns. Reviewed at the Academy of Motion Picture Arts & Sciences, Beverly Hills, July 26, 1983. (MPAA rating: R.) Running time: **94 MINS.**

Clark Griswold	Chevy Chase
Ellen Griswold	Beverly D'Angelo
Rusty Griswold	Anthony Michael Hall
Aunt Edna	Imogene Coca
Cousin Eddie	Randy Quaid
Audrey Griswold	Dana Barron
Lasky	John Candy
Walley	Eddie Bracken
Girl	Christie Brinkley

"National Lampoon's Vacation" is an enjoyable trip through familiar comedy landscapes which stays just far enough from Sillyville to keep from getting lost. With little left to compete with for laughs this summer, the film should turn out to be one of Chevy Chase's better grossers.

Fortunately, Chase is perfectly mated with Beverly D'Angelo as an average Chicago suburban couple setting out to spend their annual two-week furlough. Determined to drive, Chase wants to take the two kids to "Walley World" in California.

She would rather fly.

Despite home-computer planning, this trip is naturally going to be a disaster from the moment Chase goes to pick up the new car from the agency and gets stuck with an ugly station wagon nobody likes.

No matter how bad this journey gets — and it gets pretty disastrous —Chases perseveres in treating each day as a delight, with D'Angelo's patient cooperation. His son, beautifully played by Anthony Michael Hall, is a help, too.

"Vacation" peaks early with the family's visit to Cousin Eddie's rundown farm, rundown by the relatives residing there. As the uncouth cousin, Randy Quaid almost steals the picture. He's funny.

Enjoyment of the whole film, in fact, is heightened by the wealth of characters the family encounters along the way in small roles. Credit director Harold Ramis for populating the film with a host of well-known comedic performers in passing parts.

Speaking of small roles, however, model Christie Brinkley's film debut hardly lives up to the advance hoopla. Essentially, she's just another beautiful blonde, an extended version of Suzanne Somers' silent part driving by in "American Graffiti." As Chase's fantasy temptress, Brinkley finally gets a few lines, but nothing to remember.

After all that's gone wrong before, it's no surprise Walley World turns out to be temporarily closed, finally driving Chase to bizarre steps. Even though John Candy adds much to this sequence it's somewhat anticlimatical.

For many, "Vacation" may come off as just too obvious. Still, there's plenty of fun here for anybody who can relate from the front or back seat. —Har.

Moscow Film Festival

Proshchanie
(Farewell)
(SOVIET-COLOR)

Moscow, July 14.
A Mosfilm Production, Moscow; world rights, Goskino, Moscow. Features entire cast. Directed by Elem Klimov. Screenplay, Larissa Shepitko, R. Turin, Klimov, based on Valentin Rasputin's novel, "Farewell to Matyora;" camera (color), A. Rodionov, Y. Skhirtladze, S. Taraskin; art direction, V. Petrov; music, V. Atemyev, A. Shnitke; editing, V. Belova. Reviewed at Enthusiast Cinema, Moscow, July 14, '83. Running time: 140 MINS.
Cast: S. Staniuta, L. Durov, A. Petrenko, L. Kryuk, V. Yokovenko, Yu. Katin-Yortsev, Denis Luppov, Maya Bulgakova.

The opening scene in Elem Klimov's "Farewell" shows a boat crossing a river, the five occupants (four men and a woman) clothed in white plastic coverings of a mysterious spiritual nature. The haze blanketing the river, the soundless movement of the boat, and the gentle following sway of the camera give every hint that this is a solemn moment. Surely it is: Klimov is bidding farewell to his wife, film director Larissa Shepitko, who died tragically in a car accident with four members of her crew during the first days of location work on the filming of Valentin Rasputin's novel, "Farewell To Matyora." Klimov took over the project "in her name" after his wife's death.

As for Rasputin's novel, "Farewell to Matyora" (published in 1976) is considered to be a high point in contemporary Soviet literature. The Siberian author is a passionate observer of peasant life and mourns in general the passing of old, revered traditions.

Theme of the book is the fate of a 300-year-old island village, named Matyora (Mother Earth), soon to sink below water after a dam is built that will soon turn the river into a man-made lake.

Pic's principal figure, Daria (Maya Bulgakova) refuses to leave the island-village during its final summer; other old women decide to follow suit, even though others are leaving and homes are being burnt to the ground upon departure. It's a question of ethics and tradition, of a past connected to the village cemetery.

Their stubbornness is reflected in a futile attempt by demolition workers to destroy an ancient tree in the community—neither a buzz-saw, nor a backhoe, and not even fire can kill it in a metaphysical, spiritual sense (although the tree is consumed by flames in the end). It's depicted at the end in all its natural glory — as is the "resurrected" village itself.

Meanwhile, the officials are generally shown as misguided bureaucrats, the age of the machine directing their motivation. In contrast, when it comes time to bid farewell to her house, Daria washes its walls and floors to pay the last respects as in the case of a dead person being prepared for burial. Then, as the waters rise, the elderly women disappear into a morning fog just as the last boat arrives to make the transfer to the mainland. Daria's son, Pavel, representative of the new order, also gets lost in the rising mist: the last shot has him shouting the name of the disappeared "Matyora," and he does so quite frantically.

Although it is hardly proper to speculate on the same literary adaptation in the hands of Shepitko, one can lament nevertheless the absence of humanistic feeling for rural, peasant life. Klimov approaches his subject in a romantically intellectual vein: the images are overwhelmingly striking and beautiful, yet author Rasputin's feel for peasant life is missing. All the same, the central motifs in the novel are respected to the spiritual letter.

As in the case of Andrei Tarkovsky's "Andrei Rublev" (completed 1966, released 1971) and Klimov's own "Agonia" (completed 1976, released 1981), the Klimov-Shepitko-Rasputin "Farewell to Matyora" may take a half-decade to reach the sanctuary of an international "A" festival (both Cannes and Venice are reportedly seeking this film). When it does, several

critics will rightly hail it as one of the most important Soviet films of the present decade. Direction, lensing, and acting — particularly Maya Bulgakova as Daria — make this a must on any film buff's list, despite dim commercial chances for an arthouse epic of this rare breed.

"Farewell" is a film elegy, one of the few in world cinema. —Holl.

Five Fingers Of A Hand
(MONGOLIA-COLOR)

Moscow, July 11.
A Mongolkino Film Production. Features entire cast. Directed by I. Niamgavaa and B. Baljinniam. Screenplay, I. Niamgavaa. Only credits available. Reviewed at Moscow Film Festival (Competition), July 11, '83. Running Time: 105 MINS.
Cast: O. Oyuntsetseg, N. Batamgalan, M. Bathishig.

The Mongolian entry at Moscow, I. Niamgavaa and B. Baljinniam's "Five Fingers of a Hand," ranks as one of the best to be made in this socialist republic neighboring the Soviet Union. More of a film for youth than one for the general audience, the theme is that of a father who leaves his wife and family of five children to live with another woman.

The twist is that the wife and mother supported her husband with a menial job in a brick-factory until he could study and get a degree in engineering. Once his position is secured, the man falls in love with a young widow and begins to have an affair. Eventually, a decision has to be made — so he opts to leave his whole family for a love he has always dreamed of. Not long thereafter, the broken-hearted wife dies of a broken spirit (her health was not strong to begin with).

This leaves the oldest among the children, the only girl with four brothers, to carry on by herself: she takes her mother's factory job, and sacrifices herself to raise the children and keep them all in school.

When the father returns one day to offer help — he suggests an adopted foster-family for some of the children — the girl reacts vehemently by saying that the five fingers belong to one hand, and so none of the children will be separated from each other. Later, she meets a young man who is studying journalism, and he writes a story about her courage. In the end, they marry.

Warmly acted and directed, "Five Fingers of a Hand" deserves a fest slot at a kidpic rendezvous.
—Holl.

The Outcasts
(IRISH-COLOR)

Moscow, July 9.
An Irish Film Production, Dublin. Features entire cast. Produced, written and directed by Robert Wynne-Simmonds. Camera (color), Semus Corcoran. No other credits available. Reviewed at Moscow Film Festival (Information Section), July 9, '83. Running Time: 114 MINS.
Cast: Mary Ryan, Mick Lally, Cyril Cusack.

"The Outcasts" is set in the 19th century, and features a name actor (Cyril Cusack) in a tale of village life that is hardly the romantic Eire portrayed in the usual American production. Yet the picturesque beauty of the countryside, together with the mythical structure of the plot, are more than enough to mesmerize the viewer nurtured on folklore.

A young girl is the "outsider" in her village. She is made fun of by her peers, but is befriended one evening by a mysterious stranger with devilish powers. He bears her to a high branch of a tree to observe the foibles of friends and acquaintances. There they watch a couple in a love embrace — the forbidden act is then turned into a game-of-horror by the stranger's magical powers of changing guises to frighten the couple.

This is the period of the Irish emigration to the United States and elsewhere. The fatalism of the film is felt at the outset, the motif of the outcast picked up in folk songs and dances. One moment is particularly striking: when a young couple marry, a band of strolling minstrels with straw baskets covering their heads play for the wedding. The mingling of rocky seashore, green rolling hills, and sad nostalgic music make this modest production a memorable one. —Holl.

Bes Svideteley
(Without Witnesses)
(SOVIET-COLOR)

Moscow, July 10.
A Mosfilm Production, Moscow; world rights, Goskino, Moscow. Stars Irina Kupchenko, Michael Ulyanov. Directed by Nikita Mikalkov. Screenplay, Mikalkov, Sofia Prokofyeva. Ramiz Fataliyev, based on Prokofyeva's drama "A Talk Without Witnesses;" camera (color), Pavel Lebeshev; art direction, Alexander Adabadashyan, Igor Makarov, Alexander Samulekin; music, Eduard Artemyev. Reviewed at Moscow Film Fest (Information Section), July 9, '83. Running time: 92 MINS.
Cast: Irina Kupchenko, Michael Ulyanov.

Nikita Mikalkov's adaptation of Sofia Prokofyeva's "Without Witnesses" (a.k.a. "In Private" at the Moscow fest) was originally conceived as both a stage and film production — that is, the seven-week rehearsal period for the play served the needs of making a film at the same time. However, the legit preem never took place in the end, so only the film version is left. Pic was unspooled in the Info Show and the Film Mart at Moscow, and it deservedly shared the FIPRESCI Critics' Prize (with Manuel Gutierrez Aragon's "Demons in the Garden," the Spanish entry in the competition).

"Without Witnesses" scores as the best pic on display at the Moscow fest. It features but two actors in a drama of constant one-upmanship. The performances by Irina Kupchenko and Michael Ulyanov are simply outstanding.

The action takes place entirely in a two-room flat. "He" (Ulyanov) decides one evening to visit his wife; "she" (Kupchenko) is watching a classical concert on television, when she is disturbed by the unexpected visit. The couple were once married, and have a son (presently living with the mother, but away from home on this occasion). They are now divorced, but family albums and wall photographs indicate that they were once happily married. What happened to sour the relationship becomes soon the occasion of the conversation; meanwhile, the ex-husband tries at repeated opportunities to seduce her again, failing each time.

It comes to light that Kupchenko is about to marry her ex-husband's colleague, upon whom Ulyanov is now dependent in an office-oriented position. Further, Ulyanov has resorted to various devious devices to promote his own career above both family and friends, all of which have now sealed his fate as a failure. His wife's future marriage is therefore unbearable, which he will now, of course, resort to anything to hinder. His tactic is an anonymous letter, which he feels he can now use to force a showdown with Kupchenko and thus win a moral and complete victory in the end.

The filmed drama is tense from the start: first, he wins a round; then, she is able to turn the tables. The last round, however, is won by Ulyanov: he forces a telephone call to his rival, the end result of which is a tearful "farewell." But the final scene offers a surprise ending, which does not necessarily have to be considered a comforting epilog. This is a psychological war-of-words in the best tradition of Chekhov and Gorky. It's also Nikita Mikalkov's best film in a fast-rising career that places him now at the forefront of contemporary Soviet cinema. —Holl.

Patsani
(Kids)
(SOVIET-COLOR)

Moscow, July 15.
A Lenfilm Production, Leningrad; world rights, Goskino, Moscow. Features entire cast. Directed by Dinara Asanova. Screenplay, Yuri Kleptikov. Only credits available.

Reviewed at Moscow Film Fest (Information Section), July 13, '83. Running time: 90 MINS.
Cast: V. Priemykhov, M. Levtova.

Reportedly taken off the shelves for selected showings at the Soviet national fest in Leningrad earlier this year and then the Information Section of the Moscow fest, Dinara Asanova's "Kids" ("Hoodlums" might be a better translation) found an appreciative audience among Moscovites during its screening. Chances are the film would score abroad on the fest circuit, for this is undoubtedly the best film on juvenile delinquency in the Soviet Union since Nikolai Ekk's "Road To Life" (1931), to which it bears a remarkable resemblance.

Femme helmer Dinara Asanova, of the Leningrad school of realism, won recognition earlier with "The Key Not To Be Passed On" (1976), a film on the problems of high school teachers. For "Kids," she collaborated with one of the key screenplay writers in the Soviet Union, Yuri Kleptikov.

Pic opens with interviews of a documentary nature. Teenagers are asked why they have turned to stealing, assault, and other misdemeanors; the responses are in the expected areas of broken homes, bad environments, drunken or uncaring parents, and the like. Then a counselor of a youth sports-labor camp enters the picture: he is willing to take the kids truly asking for help out of a correction home for rehabilitation. The camp is situated in a wilderness area next to a lake with an island on it, and the time is, of course, summer. One of his assistants, however, is a strict authoritarian of the nonloving school, so conflicts arise at the start.

The rest is along the lines of a semidocumentary. The kids give everyone trouble, even themselves. When two loners prefer to live by themselves on the island, the counselor brings them food and leaves them be; it's when they attack a young couple, however, on an excursion to the island that things turn from bad to worse. One of the pair later fakes an appendicitis attack to enable him to run away from the camp entirely.

Other seg features a young boy who fears that his drunkard-father has taking to beating his sister at home, so he steals the camp's flare gun and thus get his revenge. Then there's the moment when the camp is left unfortunately in the sole care of the disciplinarian — upon which the kids revolt, and tear the place apart. The counselor is now ready to throw in the towel, when one of the lads, serving as the leader, saves the day. Gradually, all the juvenile delinquents stand behind the man they have learned to respect. This, in contrast to parents shown in such a light that many of them should obviously be sent to a correction school, instead of the juveniles.

A strong film, packed with universal truth. Despite apparent cuts, "Kids" stands at the forefront of a new realistic trend in Soviet cinema. — Holl.

Izbrannye
(The Elect)
(SOVIET-COLOMBIAN-COLOR)

Moscow, July 7.
A Mosfilm Coproduction with Dinavillon LTDA, Productiones Casablanca LTDA, Colombia, with the participation of Sovinfilm (USSR) & Focine (Colombia). Features entire cast. Directed by Sergei Soloviev. Screenplay, Soloviev, Alfonso Lopes Michelson, based on the novel by Lopes Michelson; camera (color), Pavel Lebeshev; art direction, Alesander Adabashyan, Alexander Samulekin; music, Mozart, Beethoven, Maler, Shostakovich, Sviridov, Shavartz, Tishenko, Castro. Reviewed at Moscow Film Fest (out-of-competition), July 7, '83. Running time: 140 MINS.
Cast: Leonid Filatov (B.K.), Tatyana Drubich (Olga), Amparo Grisales, Raul Cervantes, Santiago Garcia, Carl West.

The opening nite presentation at the Moscow fest, Sergei Soloviev's "The Elect" was highlighted more as a Soviet-Colombian coproduction than as a prime example of cinematic art. It's an average literary adaptation of a penned 30 years ago novel dealing with ex-Nazis and German emigrants living in Latin America at the end of World War II. The theme, however, is fascinating from start to finish, and pic only narrowly missed being a winner in all respects. Novelist Alfonso Lopes Michelson collaborated on the script.

A rich industrialist, a Baron B.K., was never a friend of National Socialist leaders; in fact, he was repulsed by Hitler's excess, although he was too weak in character to do anything in conscience about it. It's when he manages to leave Germany for a Latin American country in 1944, where his capital is invested, that he finally awakens to the truth, partially by watching newsreels on the fall of Germany in local cinemas. He also awakens to love, having an affair with a girl from the lower classes.

They have an affair, and she then makes an attempt to save his life from a tyrannical American consul officer. It appears that Baron B.K. is about to be arrested in view of his German passport, but the Yank consul is also in love with the elusive Olga. Olga sacrifices herself in the offices of the American consulate, hoping to save the man she loves.

Meanwhile, a Nazi secret agent confronts B.K. with forged documents pointing to his guilt as a Nazi collaborator in his industrial dealings. B.K. kills the man, and then hopes to destroy the evidence. He meets his fate, however, at the hands of an orphan-lad he and Olga befriend: the boy is tormented by his playmates into believing that Olga has become a whore, so he kills B.K. with a gun he stole from the German's hiding-place. Ironically, the German baron dies in May 1945.

Thesp performances in lead roles and lensing by cameraman Pavel Lebeshev (one of the best in the Soviet Union) are the plus factor. Pic was shot entirely on locations in Colombia, with native actors in supporting roles. —Holl.

Ezhavathu Manithan
(The Seventh Man)
(INDIAN-COLOR)

Moscow, July 8.
A Palai N. Shanmughan Film Production, Madras. Features entire cast. Written and directed by K. Hariharan. Camera (color), Dharma; editing, K.N. Raju; music, Vaithilaxman; dialog, Somasundareswar, Arunmozhi. Reviewed at Moscow Film Fest (competition), July 8, '83. Running time: 124 MINS.
Cast: Raghuvaran, Ratna, Satyajit, Deepak, Anitha Mathews, Satyendra, Ranga.

The Indian entry at Moscow, K. Hariharan's "The Seventh Man," deals with a workers' strike at a cement-mixing factory in the Tirunelvelli district of Tamil Nadu, home of the Indian poet Bharathi — whose poetry dealing with India's modernization is employed frequently in the film.

Anand, a university engineering graduate, decides to seek employment in a rural area rather than city factories. While working in the area's only source of employment, a cement factory, he takes note of the misery of the workers and fights against their exploitation by company gangs. The death of two friends forces a showdown between Anand and the factory owner's son.

In the end, a union organizer and Communist trade lawyer saves the day by traveling to the rural community to help the strikers. When the owners decide to blow up the factory with TNT to collect the insurance, the workers discover the plot and take over production under a cooperative arrangement.

"The Seventh Man" doesn't measure up to the recent high standards reached in Indian cinema. At times, it is naively exaggerated sociopolitical cinema. Tamil cinema has a way to go to catch up with Calcutta and Bombay as major "art cinema" production centers. —Holl.

Zille und Ich
(Zille and Me)
(EAST GERMAN-COLOR)

Moscow, July 14.
A DEFA production and release. Features entire cast. Directed by Werner Wallroth. Screenplay, Dieter Wardetsky. No other credits provided. Reviewed at Central Festi-

val Hall, Moscow Film Festival, July 13, 1983. Running time: **119 MINS.**
Cast: Kurt Nolse, Daniella Hoffmann, Thomas Zieler.

A fine item from the German Democratic Republic, this is a musical about the life of Heinrich Zille, a well known painter who once decided to dedicate his work to politics. Set in Berlin during the Kaiser period, film is filled with good sense of humor and a severe attention to details. Songs, which cover some 50% of the narrative, bring Kurt Weill to mind, and are reinforced by a modern and attractive choreography.

Wallroth's obstination to impregnate a Hollywood musical style of the 1950s has to cope with the difficulties of a lack of such tradition in the cinema of East Germany, but the final result is surprisingly satisfactory. Cinematography (unfortunately not disclosed in the press information in Moscow) helps a lot, but the best achievement is perhaps that of the art direction, which brings to the screen a diversified and rich atmosphere of Berlin at the beginning of the century.

From the commercial viewpoint, item is no less attractive, both for children and for adults sensible to a good Berliner beer. —*Hoin.*

Vassa
(SOVIET-COLOR)

Moscow, July 19.

A Mosfilm Production, Moscow; world rights, Goskino, Moscow. Stars Inna Churikova. Written and directed by Gleb Panfilov, based on Maxim Gorky's play, "Vassa Zheleznova." Camera (color), Leonid Kalashnikov; music, Vadim Bibergan. Reviewed at Moscow Film Fest (Competition), July 18, '83. Running time: **140 MINS.**
Cast: Inna Churikova (Vassa Zheleznova), Nikolai Skorobogatov, Valentina Telichkina (Rachel), Valentina Yakunina, Yana Poplavskaya.

A Gold Medal (First Prize) winner at the Moscow fest, Gleb Panfilov's "Vassa" is based on Maxim Gorky's play, "Vassa Zheleznova," and has all the pluses and minuses of a theatrical film production. The performances are outstanding, but the camera serves only as a static observer of plot's action. All the same, pic should find its way to theatrical release abroad and will enhance helmer Gleb Panfilov's career as one of the Soviet Union's foremost art-cinema directors.

This is the tragic story of a rich merchant family in 1913, the Zheleznovs owning a steamship line on the Volga and residing in a plush family villa in Nizhny Novogorod. Vassa is the backbone of the enterprise, her wastrel husband facing a court trial for a moral misdemeanor that could ruin the family in the long run. She convinces him to take his life to save his family from scandal, particularly the two

daughters now teenagers and soon to marry. He does, and thereafter Vassa hardens against all about her to protect her and the family's interests, come what may.

An elaborate spying system in the house keeps a close eye on a high-living brother, the dissatisfied servants, and the flighty daughters. The land is in revolt, and even on a ship-cruise, the passengers become aware of the dawn of the new order when a revolutionary among the crew is killed by a secret agent of the government.

The tables are turned in Vassa's plans when her daughter-in-law arrives from Switzerland with the news that her son is nearing death from an incurable illness. Rachel, a Jew with revolutionary ideas of her own, wishes to take her young son, now in Vassa's care, back with her to Switzerland and eventually to schooling in Paris. She has traveled to Russia under false papers. Vassa refuses to give up her grandson, and there is a moral showdown between Vassa and Rachel.

Vassa wins, but in the night she dies of a heart attack at her desk. When the body is discovered in the morning by the servants and family, everyone tries to steal what he can from the family fortunes. With war on the doorstep, it's clear that the day of revolution has arrived.

Much can be said for the dual performances of Inna Churikova (Vassa) and Valentina Telichkina (Rachel), and lensing, too, is a major plus. But filmed theatre doesn't make an equally esthetic film production. Churikova has been in practically all of Panfilov's films, and usually in the key role. And although she might be considered a bit too young for the role of Vassa, her performance is one of high quality thesping in contemporary Soviet cinema. Indeed, she carries the film easily on the expression in her eyes and the mastery of controlled gestures.

Next skedded out-of-comp at Venice, pic should make the rounds of international fests thereafter. It's a must-see. —*Holl.*

Get Crazy
(COLOR)

Enjoyable and high-spirited but iffy in depth.

Hollywood, Aug. 5.

An Embassy release of a Herbert Solow/D & P production. Produced by Hunt Lowry. Executive producer, Solow. Directed by Allan Arkush. Features entire cast. Screenplay, Danny Opatoshu, Henry Rosenbaum, David Taylor; camera (Metrocolor), Thomas Del Ruth; supervising editor, Mark Goldblatt; editors, Kent Beyda, Michael Jablow; art direction, Elayne Ceder; set decoration, Thomas Roysden; costume design, Roseanna Norton; sound (Dolby), Thomas Causey; original music, Michael Boddicker; special visual effects, Robert Blalack, Praxis Filmsworks, Inc.; visual effect supervision, Nancy Roshlow; assistant director, Clifford Coleman. Reviewed at CFI Labs, L.A. Aug. 5, 1983 (MPAA Rating: R.) Running time: **92 MINS.**

Reggie Wanker	Malcolm McDowell
Max Wolfe	Allen Goorwitz
Neil Allan	Daniel Stern
Willy Loman	Gail Edwards
Sammy Fox	Miles Chapin
Colin Beverly	Ed Begley Jr.
Susie	Stacey Nelkin
King Blues	Bill Henderson
Auden	Lou Reed
Captain Cloud	Howard Kaylan
Nada	Lori Eastside
Piggy	Lee Ving
Toad	John Densmore
Chantamina	Anna Bjorn
O'Connell	Robert Picardo
Mark	Bobby Sherman
Marv	Fabian Forte
Cool	Franklyn Ajaye
Nurse Gwen	Denise Galik
Arthur	Tim Jones
Joey	Dan Frischman
Violetta	Mary Woronov
Stagehand	Barry Diamond
Dr. Carver	Paul Bartel
Susie's Mom	Jackie Joseph
Susie's Dad	Dick Miller
Taxi Driver	Charlie Stavola
Debby	Charity James
Minister	Sam Laws

Genuinely enjoyable pictures set in the rock 'n' roll milieu have been few and far between, and now "Get Crazy" can be added to the list. Set at a contempo New Year's Eve concert featuring a diverse collection of acts, high-spirited comedy takes light-hearted jabs at all the participants, and is hip without being too inside for young viewers, who will find plenty to recognize. Nevertheless, rock pics of any stripe, particularly those with backstage or concert aspects ("American Hot Wax," "Sparkle," "Roadie," etc.), have generally had tough sledding at the b.o., and this, combined with less than wholehearted promo for the film (it was not press screened in advance) augurs for iffy sustained biz.

Story is a bouillabaisse of gentle send-ups of the music scene. Promoter Allen Goorwitz puts out a "deathbed" request for reclusive poet-rocker "Auden" to put in an appearance; a band of hippies shows up for the concert, 15 years late; punks dive-bomb out of the balcony; someone puts acid in the water cooler; the villainous proprietor of the auditorium wants to tear it down and build an 88-story

office building; Rastamen show up with foot-long reefers, and naked gals get it on with rockers backstage.

Not all the gags work, of course, but director Allan Arkush's rambunctious pacing and amusing cartoon-like style, which often reminds of Frank Tashlin, puts the whole thing over engagingly.

Pic's center of gravity, if there is one, is Daniel Stern as the concert stage manager. From his office bed, Goorwitz tries to pull all the loose ends of the event together, smarmy landlord Ed Begley Jr. tries to sabotage the proceedings, Stern's teenage sister, Stacey Nelkin, sneaks away from home to attend, and, one by one, the performers arrive to do their specialties at the type of mixed-bag concert that has long since disappeared as an expected attraction.

As a rock veteran who has certain traits in common with Mick Jagger, Rod Stewart and Roger Daltrey, Malcolm McDowell arrives on his private, coke-laden 747 and has a field day as the narcissistic superstar. Lou Reed is similarly amusing as the Dylanesque Auden, Fear lead singer Lee Ving is a riot as, basically, himself, a hardcore punker, and Lori Eastside has all the steps down as the foremost member of an all-girl group.

Other cast members whose presence will amuse music fans are Howard Kaylan as a leftover hippie spokesman, Doors' drummer John Densmore, Bobby Sherman and Fabian Forte as Begley's obnoxious henchmen, and Bill Henderson and Franklyn Ajaye as r&b performers.

Music's sound is appropriate, but one somewhat misses inclusion of some real hit songs, which would have really souped up the track. Notion of having assorted artists doing wildly varied renditions of "Hoochie Coochie Man" is funny enough, but less than exciting in the execution.

Appropriately, pic does not look too classy, having the appearance of having been shot quickly and almost off-the-cuff. Nevertheless, art director Elayne Geder has made excellent use of L.A.'s abandoned Wiltern Theatre as the principal setting, and frequent special and animation effects are zippy.
—*Cart.*

Kuni Lemel In Cairo
(ISRAELI-COLOR)

Tel Aviv, July 7.

A Roll Films Presentation. Produced by Israel Ringel and Yair Pradelsky. Written and directed by Yoel Zilberg. Features entire cast. Camera (color), Nissim (Nitcho) Leon; editor, Atara Horenstein; music, Kobi Oshrath; lyrics, Avi Koren; costumes, Maya Meroskek; set designer, Qeer Lickter. Reviewed at the Pe'er Cinema, Tel Aviv, July 7,

1983. Running time: **90 MINS.**
Cast: Mike Burstein, Hana Laszlo, Avraham Mor, Moshe Ibgi, Uri Gavriel, Igor Borisov.

This is the third sequel in the adventures of Kuni and Muni Lemel, the twins born in Central European Yiddish operetta, who have become a standard staple of the Israeli kid-oriented cinema.

This time around, the orthodox, God-fearing Kuni, and the good for nothing nightclub entertainer Muni, are involved in an improbable plot concerning the transfer of a Torah (Holy Scroll) from Israel to the Jewish community of Cairo, for which the community will reciprocate with a gift of priceless antique coins.

The scoop here is that, for the first time, an Israeli production has shot scenes in Egypt. The Egyptians allegedly gave in after arguments, but judging by what has been left in the film, they shouldn't have worried, for besides stock shots showing Cairo crowds, traffic and skyscape, the only real action comes in several tourist sequences, in which Mike Burstein rides a camel in front of the pyramids, drives by the Sphinx, etc.

The thin story is peppered, as usual in the Kuni Lemel series, with songs which lack originality, particularly one aping "Do Re Mi" in "The Sound of Music." There are many jokes in Yiddish, intended for Jewish-American audiences, who have shown sympathy, in the past, the main character.

Burstein, who, has shown stamina on Broadway, in "Barnum," doesn't over-exert himself here, and neither does anybody else. Response at home has been lukewarm, but the small faithful audience across the ocean, may still give it a chance. —*Edna*.

Daffy Duck's Movie: Fantastic Island
(COLOR-ANIMATED)

Summer fun from Daffy & pals.

Hollywood, July 29.
A Warner Bros. release, produced and directed by Friz Freleng. Exec producer, Jean H. MacGurdy. Screenplay, John Dunn, David Detiege, Friz Freleng; editor, Jim Champin; sequence directors, David Detiege, Friz Freleng, Phil Monroe; associate producer, Hal Geer; production design and layout, Bob Givens, Michael Mitchell; backgrounds, Richard H. Thomas; animators, Brenda Banks, Warren Batchelder, Bob Bransford, Brad Case, Terrence Lennon, Bob Matz, Norm McCabe, Sam Nicholson, Jerry Ray, Richard Thompson; music, Screenmusic West. (Others also credited for previously released cartoon segments). Reviewed at the Goldwyn Theatre, July 29, 1983. (MPAA Rating: G). Running time: **78 MINS.**
Voices: Mel Blanc. Additional voice characterizations, June R. Foray, Les Tremayne.

Fourth in a series of full-length cartoons dispatched by Warner Bros. Cartoons since 1979, Daffy Duck gets his first starring theatrical, in a "Fantasy Island"-inspired takeoff conceived by late, vet animation writer John Dunn, to whom the movie is dedicated. All three recent Warner's cartoon movies ("Bugs Bunny/Road Runner," "The Looney Looney Looney Bugs Bunny Movie," and "Bugs Bunny's Third Movie: 1001 Rabbit Tales") have made money and there's no reason to doubt the financial forecast will be any different this season.

Formula remains consistent: a third of the material, the Daffy Duck island stuff, is new animation and the rest is segments from other Warner's cartoons, primarily from the early 1950s. Under the helm of producer-director Friz Freleng, the feature has done a marvelous job of matching the look of the old cartoons to the new animation.

The '50s segments were shot on black and white film through separation color filters and converted to Eastman Kodak stock to match the new material. The result defies any layman's ability to distinguish the old material from the new.

With the incomparable Mel Blanc supplying the voices, both in the classic shorts and the Fantastic Island sequences, film is a cornucopia of enduring characters disembarking on Daffy Duck's isle: Bugs Bunny, Foghorn Leghorn, Porky Pig, Miss Prissy, Sylvester, Pepe Le Pew, among others. Yosemite Sam and his mate Tasmanian Devil negotiate their own island invasion.

There's a nostalgic pull to the material if you grew up with these figures and probably a certain fascination for the current Saturday a.m. generation to see their favorites ballooned to blown-up movie house size.

On the down side, the flat animation style grows repetitive and the interlocking of one-two minute sequences from other cartoons fails to generate the seamless superchase you'd like. The brevity of the gags is fine but too much of the '50s material too obviously belongs anywhere but a tropical island. Will the kids care? No way. Here's another cartoon movie for the summer that's the real thing.
— *Loyn.*

Space Raiders
(COLOR)

Recycled sci-fi from the bottom of the barrel.

W. Palm Beach, July 23.
A New World Pictures release of a Millennium presentation. Produced by Roger Corman. Directed by Howard R. Cohen. Features entire cast. Screenplay, Cohen; camera (Deluxe color), Alec Hirschfeld; editor, Anthony Randel, R.J. Kizer; music, James Horner; songs, Murphy Dunne; assistant director, Gordon Boos; sound, Mark Ulano; special effects supervisor, Tom Campbell; special effects makeup, Mike Jones; second unit director, Mary Ann Fisher. Reviewed at AMC Cross Country Mall 6 theatre, West Palm Beach, Fla., July 22, 1983. (MPAA Rating: PG). Running time: **82 MINS.**
Hawk....................Vince Edwards
Peter...................David Mendenhall
Amanda.....................Patsy Pease
Flightplan............Thom Christopher
Ace.....................Luca Bercovici
Aldebarian..................Drew Snyder
Also with: Ray Stewart, George Dickerson, Dick Miller.

With "Space Raiders," producer Roger Corman hits the lowest ebb of his career, fashioning a nonsensical, uninteresting Outer Space picture out of leftovers from an earlier film. Aimed to sop up the crumbs left behind by George Lucas's latest sci-fit hit, "Raiders" is likely to anger even stalwart fans addicted to Corman cheapies.

Trouble with the film is telegraphed immediately, as the musical score turns out to be James Horner's work for Corman's 1980 "Battle Beyond The Stars," already repeated without credit in such New World releases as "Sorceress" and excerpted in "Screwballs." Enough already.

Space footage and models here look suspiciously like those from "Battle Beyond The Stars," too, representing Corman's substantial initial investment in special effects. Reusing old material is not intrinsically bad, as witness Corman's fun 1976 spoof "Hollywood Boulevard," in which clips from his Filipino-lensed chaingang-women films were cleverly intercut with new footage. With "Raiders," however, the space battles are incoherent and not integrated with the dull shots of the heroes at their control panels, and worse yet, the same footage is repeated endlessly, as with a distinctive explosion seen at least half a dozen times.

Nominal plotline pits a motley crew led by Col. Hawkins, known as Hawk (Vince Edwards) against the undefined "Company," another symbol of soulless technocracy as used in the films "Alien" and "Outland." "Raiders" begins a la "Star Wars" in the middle of an action scene, as Hawk and cohorts steal a spaceship in which a cute kid named Peter (David Mendenhall) has stowed away together with his pet insect (a nice but very brief dollop of stop-motion animation). Heroes are hired to steal four spaceships from the Company, must battle a massive robot ship (reminiscent of you-know-who's Death Star) and try to take the kid home to his planet Proscian 3.

Writer-director Howard Cohen tries for humor, scoring only in a few gags such as a bit by a "Space hooker," an alluringly sleazy-dressed femme at a "Star Wars"-style cantina who turns around to reveal her hideous alien makeup mask. Spoofing futurism, he has star Edwards in his spaceship imbibing beer from archaic ringpull cans, and features a hologram of a used-spaceship salesman.

Acting is poor, with wide-eyed little Mendenhall becoming annoying early on. Florida audience cheered only when the heroes were killed off one by one, amidst gross continuity errors such as a lead's chest wound switching to the opposite side between shots. In the spirit of ripoff, "Raiders'" poster features a character drawn in the likeness of Chewbacca the Wookiee from "Star Wars" but no such creature pops up in the film.
—*Lor.*

Off The Wall
(COLOR)

Prison comedy misfires.

W. Palm Beach, July 23.
A Jensen Farley Pictures release of a Hot Dogs Inc. presentation. Executive producer, Lisa Barsamian. Produced by Frank Mancuso Jr. Directed by Rick Friedberg. Features entire cast. Screenplay, Ron Kurz, Dick Chudnow, Friedberg; camera (Movielab color), Donald R. Morgan; editor, George Hively; music, Dennis McCarthy; assistant director, Steve Perry; production design, Richard Sawyer; stunt coordinator, Everett Creach. Reviewed at AMC Cross Country Mall 1 theatre, W. Palm Beach, Fla., July 22, 1983. (MPAA Rating: R). Running time: **85 MINS.**
Warden Castle...............Paul Sorvino
Governor's daughter....Rosanna Arquette
Randy...................Patrick Cassidy
Rico Santiago................Billy Hufsey
Johnny Hammer............Ralph Wilcox
Miskewicz...................Dick Chudnow
Governor................Monte Markham
Jennifer....................Brianne Leary
Also with: Mickey Gilley, Gary Goodrow, Biff Manard, Stu Gilliam, Jenny Neumann, Lewis Arquette, Jeana Tomasino, Roselyn Royce.

"Off The Wall" is a freewheeling comedy picture set in a Tennessee prison that only occasionally lives up to the humor implicit in its title. With several "film surgeons" cited in the end credits, it is difficult to parcel out blame or credit for the finished film, but in any event "Wall" is not funny enough or in step with popular tastes to make much of a dent at the theatrical b.o., with its future clearly as a sleeper to be sampled via cable telecast.

Randy (Patrick Cassidy) and Rico (Billy Hufsey) are Yankee boys hitchhiking in the South, picked up by the beautiful daughter (Rosanna Arquette) of the governor of Tennessee. She leaves them holding the bag for a car accident, and after a poor defense by their black lawyer (Stu Gilliam), they end up with six months' time at Snake Canyon Prison.

In stir, Randy falls in love with Jennifer (Brianne Leary), the daughter of Warden Castle (Paul

Sorvino), while Rico becomes the romantic object of the prison's leading wrestler, ultimately becoming his tag-team partner. Amidst various running gags, duo learn the ropes from their roommate, a black escape artist Johnny Hammer (Ralph Wilcox).

Director Rick Friedberg and his co-scripters Ron Kurz and Dick Chudnow (latter doubling as the warden's sidekick) have engineered some amusing situations, but the film over-relies on rather dated Southern stereotypes to launch its gags. Best of these is Stu Gilliam's bit as a lawyer right out of "Amos 'n Andy." Star Paul Sorvino has a ball as the redneck, paranoid warden, but his overplaying, in common with that of most of the cast, is of the desperate sort. An on-target satire could have been played straight with stronger material.

Biggest disappointment here is that second-billed Rosanna Arquette, who since filming "Off The Wall" has become an important young star in "The Executioner's Song" and "Baby, It's You," has a relatively small role. Physical production is impressive, with an atmospheric prison locale and excellent stuntwork by the great vehicle specialist Everett Creach.

Following "Wall," producer Frank Mancuso Jr. hit paydirt with 3-D in "Friday The 13th Part 3" and the current "The Man Who Wasn't There," but what this comedy lacks is not another dimension but simply better writing.
— *Lor.*

Cabaret Tears (Send In The Clowns)
(HONG KONG-COLOR)

Hong Kong, July 22.

A Cinema City Company Ltd. production and release. Produced by Karl Maka, Deak Shek, Raymond Wong and Wong Yen-Shong. Directed by Lin Ching Cheih. Stars Chang Shio-Yen, Sylvia Chang, Li Muh-Chern, Guu Feng. Production designer, Sylvia Chang; screenplay, Wu Nien-Gen; executive producer, Chu Fung Kang; art director, Li Fu Shung; music, Lo Ta Yu, Tang Lin; camera (color), Liaw Ching-Song; editor, Hwang Chiou-Guey. Reviewed at the Cinema City Preview Room, Hong Kong, July 21, 1983. Running time: 100 MINS.
(Cantonese, Mandarin versions available with English subtitles)

"Cabaret Tears" is Cinema City's serious contribution to its long list of formula boxoffice comedies. Conceived and produced in Hong Kong, but shot on location in Taiwan, it is a soap opera about ordinary people's survival. It is shopworn but interesting when presented in the Asian context and locale.

The original title of this film was "Send In The Clowns" but was changed recently to "Cabaret Tears" which is more appropriate. It is a re-telling of the old saying

that life for many is a bed of thorny roses. The film sensitively describes the tightrope existence between the realities of failure intermingled with dreams for success or the harrowing experiences of small time, provincial notoriety that will not blossom into big city fame.

It is a rich film, emotionally that is, and though laden with typical Asian sentimentality, emanates great optimism, inspiring humanity and projects the dignity of hard work. These are human values not often offered in Hong Kong-financed films meant for the masses, except possibly when they're geared for the Taiwanese market.

"Cabaret Tears" centers on a troupe of travelling entertainers who struggle to make a hand-to-mouth existence by staging cheap shows in sleazy theatres and dilapidated music halls. Boxoffice takings are on the decline and so is the quality of the audience. The scenario zooms into the lives of two sisters who are part of the troupe.

The elder one, Chang Mei-yu (Chang Shio-yen) keeps trying to push her younger sister, Chang Mei-hui (Sylvia Chang) into the solo act for better pay and the chance of being discovered. However, Mei-hui sees no real future in her job as a chorus girl. A young journalist is fascinated by the gypsy-life existence of the group as they compete and later falls in love with Mei-hui.

The aggressiveness of Chang Mei-yu pays off and they are off to the City of Taipei billed as mud wrestlers from Korea. But her younger sister decides that the dehumanizing world of entertainment is not really her calling. Mei-hui believes that married life offers more security, marries the journalist and the elder sister's dream for the big time is shattered.

The role of big sister in less skillful hands could have deteriorated into a caricature performance, but the dramatic eloquence of Chang Shio-yen is one of the best performances this year. She is perky, loud, jaded, sly but at the same time vulnerable and very much a woman. Sylvia Chang, without hesitation, deglamorizes herself and shows her potential as a maturing dramatic actress in a role that defies her early screen image.

The cinematography is impressive, not so much for the arty angles and the stylish camera movements but for the realistic recreation of the squalid atmosphere that the Taiwanese ghettos exude. "Cabaret Tears" did reasonably well in Taiwan but has still to make it in Hong Kong and should do more as Cinema City's official rep in film festivals.
—*Mel.*

Lovely But Deadly
(COLOR)

Unusual low-budget actioner is worth a peek.

Ft. Lauderdale, July 26.

A Juniper Releasing Co. presentation of an Elmtree Prods. Ltd., Picturemedia Ltd. production. Executive producer, V. Paul Hreljanovic. Produced by Doro Vlado Hreljanovic and David Sheldon. Directed by Sheldon. Features entire cast. Screenplay, Sheldon, Patricia Joyce from story by Lawrence D. Foldes; camera (color), Robert Roth; editor, Richard Brummer; music, Robert O. Ragland; assistant director, John Cummins; sound, Art Names. Reviewed at Thunderbird Drive-In 6, Ft. Lauderdale, Fla., July 25, 1983. (MPAA Rating: R). Running time: 93 MINS.
Lovely .... Lucinda Dooling
Franklin Van Dyke .... John Randolph
Honest Charlie .... Richard Herd
Martial arts teacher ...... Susan Mechsner
Also with: Mel Novak, Marie Windsor, Mark Holden, Rick Moser, Mary McDonough, Pamela Bryant, Irwin Keyes, Judd Omen, Linda Shayne, Vincent Roberts, Wendell Wright, Jeana Tomasina.

In an era when the B-grade action film market is dominated by lookalike martial arts pictures and vengeance mellers, "Lovely But Deadly" is an entertaining novelty, combining elements of both genres into a teenage wish-fulfillment format. It represents a tough sell commercially, but pic will provide pleasant diversion for both action fans and students of current trends.

Filmmaker David Sheldon has adapted the current vigilante trend in films to teen pics, with pert young brunette Lucinda Dooling toplining as a California high school student, Mary Ann Lovett (nicknamed "Lovely"), mounting a one girl campaign to wipe out the drug dealers and higherups in her community, in order to avenge her kid brother's drug-induced death.

Sheldon styles Dooling as an underage, female version of James Bond (with topgrade martial arts skills to boot), a gimmick which proves to be fun since she is a normal-looking young girl rather than such macho femmes as Pam Grier, Cheri Caffaro, Monica Vitti, Cornelia Sharpe and Marilyn Chambers who have previously essayed similar roles. Also to the film's advantage is the staging of Bond-like action scenes in prosaic settings such as the school locker room. If you can't compete with $30,000,000 budgeters, you can at least have fun with the format.

Cast mixes old pros (Marie Windsor as heroine's aunt, Richard Herd and John Randolph as behind the scenes heavies) with young talent with generally effective results. Dooling, in particular, overcomes the occasionally preachy anti-drugs script with her forceful, physically convincing performance. Teen genre conventions such as cheerleaders' action and several rock songs belted on-camera by the anti-hero slow up

the narrative, but the final action payoff on the docks when karate teacher Susan Mechsner and her class of diminutive high school girls come to Dooling's rescue from assorted thugs is priceless.

Lensing is cheap, using available light for many scenes. The musical score by Robert Ragland is in the same rousing bag as his recent "10 To Midnight" offering and features a scene-setting title song which has the tone of a Shirley Bassey-Bond theme. — *Lor.*

Un Ragazzo Come Tanti
(A Boy Like Many Others)
(ITALIAN-COLOR)

Taormina, July 27.

Produced by TV CINE 2000. Features entire cast. Written and directed by Gianni Minello. Camera (color), Silvio Fraschetti; art director, Franco Ceraolo; editor, Emanuele Foglietti; music, Enrico Pieranunzi. Reviewed at the Taormina Film Festival, July 27, 1983. Running time: 96 MINS.
Pino .... Stefano Mioni

Veteran co-op head Gianni Minello goes a long way on a shoestring budget in his second feature, which explores the problems of a country boy who comes to the big city and survives on the fringes of society. Production circumstances, notably a 14-day shoot with non-pro actors, leave their mark on the film, whose rough edges as well as serious subject matter and frank treatment of homosexuality and male prostitution will give it a rocky time finding an onshore distribber. Possible fest play abroad.

Pino, played by former stuntman Stefano Mioni, is an introverted boy "like many others" with no ambitions or expectations from life except getting out of the country. He meets a young hustler at the station who encourages him to make some money off his pretty face with casual prostitution, which he does with a sense of repugnance and shame.

Film details Pino's succession of depressing, exploitative encounters: with a mild-mannered professor who wants a live-in lover, a young hippy girl who has a relationship with a lesbian, a frustrated older woman who runs an art gallery, dope pushers, and so on. After brief forays into drug dealing and petty crime, Pino ends up as a lonely kid listlessly slumped on the steps of public monuments. In an odd-up ending, Pino finds affection and understanding from a gay commercial artist

Structured like an amalgam of case histories by some social worker in the slums, "Boy Like Many Others" has a strange fascination that hooks the filmgoer on Pino's sad tale; perhaps because in spite of generally wooden acting pic comes across with unmistakable sincerity and realism. Refusing to give Pino a past, a future, or a distinct personality, helmer Minello is less concerned with bringing the character to life than honestly portraying a sordid social reality.

— *Yung.*

Moscow Film Festival

Ravnovessie
(Balance)
(BULGARIAN-COLOR)

Moscow, July 23.

A Bulgarofilm Production, Sofia; world rights, Bulgarofilm, Sofia. Features entire cast. Directed by Lyudmil Kirkov. Screenplay, Stanislav Stratiev, based on his novella "Carpenter Bees;" camera (color), Dimko Minov; art direction, Georgi Todorov; music, Boris Karadimchev. Reviewed at Moscow Film Fest (Competition), July 16, '83. Running time: **119 MINS.**

Cast: Pavel Poppandov (Milko), Plamena Getova (Elena), Katerina Evro (Maria), Georgi Georgiev-Getz (the Scriptwriter), Konstantin Kotsev (the Director), Stefan Danailov (the Actor), Vanya Tsvetkova (the Actress), Luchezar Stoyanov (the Cameraman).

Winner of a Silver Medal at the Moscow Film Fest, Lyudmil Kirkov's "Balance" well deserved the prize: this is his third collaboration with gifted writer-dramatist Stanislav Stratiev, and by far the latter's best screenplay. Their other films together were "Short Sun" (1979) and "A Nameless Band" (1981).

This is a story of three losers, their lives told in flashbacks, and of a screenplay writer on a film project who awakens to the truth about him by indirectly participating in the tragedy of a lost life through suicide. Using a clipped narrative style, Kirkov traces the background of a taxi driver who is having an affair with an assistant director on a film location, then shifts to the stories of two women in his life: his wife, who is the cashier on the film project, and the aforementioned assistant director (or scriptgirl), with whom he's presently having an affair. It becomes evident that each of these individuals has had much bad luck in her life, while the crisis of middle-aged failure keep mounting. In the end, the wife, the most vulnerable of the three, drowns herself.

Via flashbacks, one notes that the taxi-driver is a goodhearted sort, but left school for sports, then failed as a coming boxer by suffering a severe arm injury in a streetfight with rowdies. His chance for marital happiness is ruined when his wife has a miscarriage while he's on his army service tour; after that, their relationship sours, and he has affairs with other women — first while on a factory job, then as a taxi-driver.

As for his wife, who has had the miscarriage, she cared for a ailing mother until her death, thus robbing her of an education at the university and forcing her to take a menial job at a factory to keep things at home going. The miscarriage happened at the same time as the death of the mother.

The third party, a girl who can't control her sex life and drifts from male to male, is shown as a victim of an early seduction. Her good looks have proven to be a cross more often than not in the flashbacks, and the last affair with the taxi-driver develops out of loneliness and a desire to be loved by someone.

This complex human web of relationships is then matched with the pretense of the film crew on location. The scriptwriter thinks only of scoring a hit, for he is a successful writer. As for the rest: the director is a comic, the cameraman a macho, the actors spoilt stars — in short, the film is going to be a dud in every respect.

One evening, on the day of the shooting, the taxi-driver quarrels with his wife, and the break is final. Next door to their hotel-apartment, the scriptwriter hears everything, and witnesses the departure of the wife. She later commits suicide and the writer is pained afterwards by a guilty conscience, for he might have saved her life. He quits the film project altogether.

"Balance" is a fine psychological study so far as examining the social structure and mores of a society. The performance by Plamena Getova in the role of the suicide is outstanding. Credits too are top grade, particularly the collaboration of scripter Stratiev and helmer Kirkov. Pic deserves more festival exposure. — *Holl.*

El Escarabajo
(The Bicycle Racer)
(COLOMBIAN-COLOR)

Moscow, July 23.

A Marcos Jara Film Production, Colombia. Features entire cast. Written and directed by Lisandro Duque Naranjo. Only credits available. Reviewed at Moscow Film Festival (Competition), July 19, '83. Running time: **83 MINS.**

Cast: Eduardo Bazcon, Argeiro Castiblanco, Carlos Parada, Cina Morett.

Lisandro Duque Naranjo's "The Bicycle Racer" scored at Moscow fest as a delightfully entertaining pic on youth in Colombia. The subject is bicycle racing, a popular sport in and around the city of Bogota. Three young friends work together to make one of them a racing champion, and indeed sucess in an important race is attained at the outset. Then a pretty girl enters the picture, and training goes out the window — until the big race approaches at the climax.

Pic's easy-going narrative style is the major plus, along with the comic antics of the three lead figures. Feature's semidocumentary flavor is another plus, particularly crowd shots during the bicycle racing. — *Holl.*

Pasla Kone Na Betone
(Concrete Pastures)
(CZECHOSLOVAK-COLOR)

Moscow, July 23.

A Czechoslovak Film Production, Koliba Film Studio, Bratislava; world rights, Ceskoslovensky Filmexport, Prague. Features entire cast. Directed by Stefan Uher. Screenplay, Milka Zimkova, Uher; camera (color), Stanislav Szomolanyi; art direction, Anton Krejcovic; music, Svetozar Stur; sound, Milan Nemethy; editing, Maximilian Remen. Reviewed at Moscow Film Fest (competition), July 17, '83. Running time: **82 MINS.**

Cast: Milka Zimkova (Jolana), Veronika Jenikova (Pavlinka), Peter Vons (Studniar), Peter Stanik (Berty), Marie Logojdova (Jozefka), Mikulas Las (Michal), Ferdinand Macurak (Ondo).

One of Czechoslovaki's best known directors, Stefan Uher recently has not enjoyed the same success he did in the 1960s. Now he's made a light bittersweet comedy, "Concrete Pastures," and the pic won him a Silver Medal at Moscow.

Film is based on a collection of stories penned by Milka Zimkova, who also plays the central role of Jolana, an unmarried mother in an East Slovak village whose daughter is now about to experience the same fate. The woman once had a brief affair with a well-digger on their village homestead, became pregnant and bore a child; in the meanwhile, she has given her best years for the good of a collective farm.

Her daughter, now at the tender age of 20, has a similar affair with a passing soldier. This leads, of course, to another unfortunate pregnancy. So what does the mother do? She advertises in a newspaper for a potential husband for her daughter.

The ad works its own magic: a young man does respond, and he turns out to be a bargain at that. The wedding day is set, and in the bloom of life the girl puts on her wedding dress. The whole village celebrates — but the husband doesn't show up, so the crowd of relatives and friends keep right on with the festivities on this warm summer day. In the midst of it all, as mother and daughter shrug their shoulders in face of a common fate, the birth pains start. So it's a mad rush to the hospital — just as the belated bridegroom arrives (his car has had a breakdown along the way). In the end, the community is still celebrating just for the joy of life.

This merry satire on village life starts slow, but the last sequences are fresh and warmly amusing. "Concrete Pastures" well deserves a slot or two on the fest circuit after its success at Moscow. It's one of the best films to emerge from Czechoslovakia in a long time. — *Holl.*

Nelesita
(ANGOLA-COLOR)

Moscow, July 23.

A Laboratorio Nacional de Cinema production, Angola. Features entire cast. Written and directed by Ruy Duarte. Only credits available. Reviewed at Moscow Film Fest (Competition), July 18, '83. Running time: **90 MINS.**

Cast: Antonio Tyitenda, Francisco Munyele, Tyiapinga Primeira.

Ruy Duarte's "Nelisita" leans heavily on national folklore in making this first truly native feature produced in Angola. The folk tale is about a young man who resourcefully conquers evil spirits about him, thus liberating the good embodied in a mother-figure. The legend has it that Nelisita thus saved all of humanity and other life on earth via his brave deeds.

Although the story is a quaint one, there's little to chew on otherwise in the film. Apparently, such a film has an appeal to the natives of Angola, and certainly it is propagandistic in concept and distribution aims. As a fest entry, it stands as an oddity. — *Holl.*

Sunset Street
(CHINESE-COLOR)

Moscow, July 9.

A Beijing Film Studio Production, Beijing. Features entire cast. Directed by Wang Haowei. Screenplay, Su Shu-yang; Camera (color), Li Chenseng; art design, Liu Yi, Lin Chaoxiang. Reviewed at Moscow Film Festival (Competition), July 9, '83. Running Time: **104 MINS.**

Back at the Moscow fest with an official entry after a long absence, Wang Hao-wei's "Sunset Street" proved to be an entertaining film on a social level. It's the tale of a street in Beijing (Peking) on which a row of low-level housing allows for community sharing of every sort, from a common waterpipe to courtyard gatherings. All the families know each other intimately, the daily encounters supplying the thread of a social drama: some of the kids are lazy, others honest and industrious; some of the adults are asocial and greedy, others generous and neighborly.

The main thread of this human comedy concerns a father who is bartering his daughter to gain a dowry. It turns out that the prospective marriage partner is, in fact, a swindler, and the girl is saved from her fate in the nick of time. Another drama concerns the love of a young man for an older woman, both of whom find each other after some painful moments of deliberation. Not everything turns out for the better in the end, however, for life has too many twists and turns to guarantee a happy ending for all. One of the film's poignant moments is the closing scene: the quaint community housing on Sunset Street is abandoned for a high-rise apartment (due to a widening of the street to construct a boulevard). The old, maybe more humane style of living has passed.

Credits and performances are even throughout. Pic could tour in Chinese Film Week in view of its "slice of everyday life" human factor. —*Holl.*

Ve Noi Gio Cat
(Back to the Sand Village)
(VIETNAMESE-COLOR)

Moscow, July 11.
A Central Film Studios Production, Vietnam. Features entire cast. Written and directed by Huy Thanh. Only credits available. Reviewed at Moscow Film Fest (Competition), July 11, '83. Running time: 114 MINS.
Cast: Tran Vinh, Huoung Xuan, Vi Cuong.

Huy Thanh's "Back to the Sand Village" deals with the period of post-war Vietnam, a time of crisis and doubt for many living in a locale known as Sand Village in central Vietnam.

It takes a while for the Communist chairman in the region to win the confidence of the people living in three neighboring villages on the sea coast, particularly as some adherents of the old order plan to block any change in their usual habits or social status. A plot to kill the new leader is uncovered in the nick of time.

Credits are poor in this humdrum tale of revolutionary zeal.
—*Holl.*

Guerrillera Del Norte
(Guerrilla from the North)
(MEXICAN-COLOR)

Moscow, July 23.
A Productora Mazateca dn Estudios America coproduction, Mexico. Produced by Gustavo Bravo Ahuja. Features entire cast. Directed by Francisco Guerrero. Screenplay, Xavier Robles; camera (color), Manuel Tejada; music, Rafael Carrion; editing Francisco Chiu. Reviewed at Moscow Film Festival (Competition), July 19, '83. Running time: 94 MINS.
Cast: Juan Valentin, Macaria, Ernesto Gomez Cruz, Jose Carlos Ruiz, Jorge Humberto Robles, Silvia Manriquez.

Francisco Guerrero's "Guerrilla From The North" amounts to an uninspired actioner on the Mexican Revolution. The guerrilla fighter, Melesio Cabanas, fights against the cruel Captain Ortiz, but he also manages to take time out for a moment of tender love with "La Calandria." One shootout follows another, often involving rather large mob scenes and guerrilla warfare on horseback on a grand scale. Our hero dies for the cause of the Revolution in the end,

but "La Calandria" bears him a daughter. The dawn of a new democratic order is breaking at the finale.

Lotsa blood-and-guts but little else in the way of plot or dialog.
— *Holl.*

Bonheur D'Occasion
(The Tin Flute)
(CANADIAN-COLOR)

Moscow, July 13.
A Marie-Josee Raymond Film Production, Canada. Features entire cast. Directed by Claude Fournier. Screenplay, Marie-Josee Raymond, Claude Fournier, based on Gabrielle Roy's novel "Bonheur d'Occasion" (roughly: "Second-Hand Happiness"), translated into English as "The Tin Flute." Camera, Claude Fournier. Only credits available. Reviewed at Moscow Film Fest (Competition), July 13, '83. Running time: 123 MINS.
Cast: Mireille Deyglun, Marilyn Lightstone, Michel Forget, Pierre Chagnon.

Based on a well known Canadian novel by Gabrielle Roy titled in French "Bonheur d'Occasion" (Second-Hand Happiness) and in English "The Tin Flute" (published in 1945), this two-hour literary adaptation directed and lensed by Claude Fournier is skedded to open in French and English versions at the upcoming Montreal and Toronto fests. The Moscow entry was the English one, which appears to be dubbed in a rather word-thudding manner. Since the book by the French Canadian authorities was published originally in French, the version in that language would be naturally preferable at an international fest.

Roy was one of the first Canadian writers to depict the problems of urban life in French Canada, and "Bonheur d'Occasion" won her the rather prestigious Prix Femina in 1947, a French award. Her theme in the novel was the erosion of human values in the face of increased industrialization and urbanization. Turned into film terms, the narrative appears today to be too charged with melodramatic motifs — indeed, the film comes across as a good old-fashioned weeper. On the other hand, the times of which she was writing were hard: it was the end of the Depression and the advent of the Second World War, the uncertain late 1930s.

Pic's central figure is a young working girl, the oldest in a large family whose father is a dreamer and whose mother is a struggling saint trying desperately to make ends meet as best she can. The working daughter, a waitress in a diner, keeps only the tips for herself, while turning her pay over to her mother to help pay the bills. One day, in the diner, she meets a slick talker who invites her to go to the movies, then stands her up. During a second meeting, the fast-talker woos her with more smooth words, and the girl falls for him.

They have a brief one-night affair, and the girl becomes pregnant.

Meanwhile, the father loses his job by using the company truck to take the kids on an outing; the use of private property for family luxury is not permitted, so he's fired from his job. This causes the family to move out of their modest quarters to a ramshackle, dehumanizing place near a railroad track. It's here that the youngest in the family catches a lung infection, and has to be hospitalized. That misery is coupled with the mother's pregnancy once again. When the sick boy's other older sister comes to visit him in the hospital ward, she brings along a tin flute — it is his last play-toy before dying of tuberculosis. The boy is buried just as the mother gives birth to a new son.

Meanwhile, our heroine faces the shame of being an unmarried mother. So she resourcefully manages to become engaged to another shy young man, and takes her chances on a "second-hand happiness." The war has already come along, her husband has been drafted, and she now sees him off at the station with the words that "they may be three" upon his return. The father, too, has put on a uniform in order to send his pay back to the needy wife and family at home. However, the daughter now has the opportunity to move into a large house — and bring her mother and the kids into the household with her.

Filmed in and around Montreal, pic neatly captures the atmosphere of the times: the diner, the movie house, the streets and buildings and cars of the late Depression years. Pic's only fault is the literary heaviness of the whole, despite commendable performances in the main roles. —*Holl.*

Furusato
(Home Village)
(JAPANESE-COLOR)

Moscow, July 19.
A Seijiro Koyama, Yutaka Osawa, and Toshio Goto Film Production. Features entire cast. Written and directed by Seijiro Koyama, based on a novella by Kosuke Hirakata. Only credits available. Reviewed at Moscow Film Fest (Competition), July 18, '83. Running time: 107 MINS.
Cast: Yoshi Kato, Hiroyuki Nagato, Fumie Kashiyama.

Helmer Seijiro Koyama learned his trade working under Kaneto Shindo, whose "The Island" made film history a few decades back. Koyama shares Shindo's concern for people in remote corners of Japan, and his "Home Village" treats the fate of a mountain community that is suddenly awakened to the industrial world due to the construction of a dam. Once the dam is completed, the villagers will have to leave their homes — for the

entire area will be submerged under water. The question of relocation forms the thematic content.

The Maruyama family covers all generations from grandfather to grandson, the key figure being the grandfather now approaching the age of senility. The grandmother has just died, and he imagines she is still in the household to converse with on the problems of the day. The daughter-in-law cares for him with a warm compassion — and understanding that a tradition is passing.

Pic is straightforward in narrative style without the poetic or imaginative touches one might expect in a theme of this sort. Credits are professionally adequate.
—*Holl.*

Al Mas A La Al Kubra
(Clash of Loyalties)
(IRAQI-COLOR)

Moscow, July 12.
A Diaa Al Bayati Film Production, Baghdad. Features entire cast. Directed by Mohammed Shukri Jameel. Screenplay, Latif Jorephani, Mohamed Jameel, Ramadan Gatea, Roger Smith. Only credits available. Review at Moscow Film Fest Competition), July 12, '83. Running time: 127 MINS.
Cast: Oliver Reed, Ghazi Tikrity, James Bolam.

Mohamed Shukri Jameel's "Clash Of Loyalties" deals with a fascinating chapter in modern Iraqi history: it's a tale of the Liberation Movement in the 1920s, when Iraqi revolutionaries struggled to throw off the British yoke. Further, the central figure, Dari Mahmud, was one of the leaders of the uprising who gave his life for the cause. This is mostly his story.

As an historical chronicle, "Clash of Loyalties" will find an appreciative audience, for there is little in the way of feature films made on this period in the Middle East and Iraq in particular. The presence of Oliver Reed in the film lends an authenticity to the proceedings. Lastly, the action scenes are well handled. What's missing is a tighter dramatic unity and sharply penned dialog scenes. Still, Iraqi cinema is maturing year by year, and this film offers a strong prognosis of things to come at the well-geared Baghdad studios. British thesps in Iraqi pics assure a universal appeal for historical themes: just as much care should be given to all-around top-quality production credits. —*Holl.*

Mi Socio
(My Friend)
(BOLIVIAN-COLOR)

Moscow, July 12.
An UKAMAU Film Production. Features entire cast. Directed by Paolo Agazzi. Screenplay, Oscar Soria, Raquel Romero,

Agazzi. Only credits available. Reviewed at Moscow Film Fest (Competition), July 12, '83. Running time: **82 MINS.**

Cast David Santalla, Gerardo Suarez.

Paolo Agazzi's "My Friend" is a delightly rendered "youth film" that should make the rounds of kid-pic fests on the seasonal circuit. The leads, a truckdriver and his young helper, travel across Bolivia on a delivery route, encountering various types along the way and experiencing a number of adventures. As an ethnographic catalog on life in Bolivia, the pic is particularly recommended. On the film going side, it has the appeal of a family film for grownup kids.

The truckdriver needs a helper on his route, and is reluctant to take an orphaned kid still wet behind the ears. But the boy proves persistent by being a stowaway, and is accepted. Thereafter, the driver stops along the way: losing his money in a game of craps, fighting with his wife (left at home with a number of kids), romancing girls as he pleases at every stopover, helping an Indian woman to bring her produce to market, assisting at the delivery of a child, and so on. Gradually, the two become friends.

Then comes the twist of fate. Upon making the delivery, they share the payment money and start back on the return trip. The boy has bought a dog, however, and that brings about his unfortunate death: he chases the pup across a busy road — and is hit by a passing truck. — *Holl.*

Vivement Dimanche
(Let It Be Sunday)
(FRENCH-B&W)

Locarno, Aug. 15.

A Roissy Films Presentation of a Films du Carrosse/Films A2/Soprofilms Production. Features entire cast. Directed by Francois Truffaut. Screenplay, Francois Truffaut, Suzanne Schiffman, Jean Aurel. Based on "The Long Saturday Night" by Charles Williams; camera (black and white), Nestor Almendros; editor, Martine Barraque, Marie-Aimee Debril; production designer, Clinton McConnico; music, Georges Delerue. Reviewed at Piazza Grande, Locarno, Aug. 5, 1983. Running time: **106 MINS.**

Cast: Fanny Ardant, Jean-Louis Trintignant, Philippe Laudenbach, Caroline Sihol, Philippe Maurier-Genoud.

Francois Truffaut must have enjoyed himself immensely doing this picture. It is obviously a labor of love dedicated to actress Fanny Ardant, for whom this film is a real showcase, putting forward not only her considerable physical charms but also a remarkable talent for elegant comedy. This more than confirms the promise of Truffaut's earlier "La Femme a Cote" in which she was featured in a darker and more passionate part.

Also Truffaut has a second chance here to pay tribute to his favorite director, Alfred Hitchcock. In the past, he had already bowed to the master of suspense in "The Bride Wore Black," but now he argues that film was too luminous and precise for his taste. Hence the use of black and white here and the explicit choice of night sequences are in the spirit of the classical American thriller.

Truffaut also uses extensively his predilection for quotations. In one instance, a cinema cashier gives a cockeyed summary of Kubrick's "Paths of Glory," a browsing eye catches the title of Andrzej Zulawski's French film, "L'Important c'est d'Aimer," an amateur theatrical group repeats a Victor Hugo play (Truffaut had dedicated an earlier film to the playwright's daughter) and there are at least two occasions to recall Truffaut's own "L'Homme qui Aimait Les Femmes," once when the protagonist peeks at women's legs from a basement window, and again, when the villain confesses that he loves all women passionately and would like to possess them all.

These embellishments are all important, sometimes more so than the plot itself, which was inspired by a Charles Williams thriller. In it, a real estate dealer is accused of having murdered his wife's lover, but it is his lovely secretary, secretly in love with him, who unravels the whole mystery. To do so, she practically jails her boss in his own office, while she is taking charge of the enquiry. Illicit love affairs, crooked private detectives, clumsy policemen and a profitable prostitution ring, are some of the

milestones she covers before turning out the real culprit.

The ploy is typical Hitchcock with a couple of twists. Mr. Everyman is charged with a crime he doesn't know anything about, but here he solves it by proxy, the entire initiative being that of the secretary, indicating possibly the changes that have taken place in the relationship between the sexes in the last few years. Also, Truffaut not only picks a brunette for the lead, he actually goes as far as to poke fun at the cool blondes Hitch used to favor.

But the extensive attention paid these details detracts from the treatment of the narrative as such. It is easy to admire the expert handling of the camera by Nestor Almendros, and the humorous points Truffaut makes with it; the editing is brisk and impressive, the kind that was the trademark of the American B-pictures in the thirties and forties. But Truffaut carries too far the theory that accidents are a legitimate part of the story, and he stresses the light touch so exclusively, that no one will bite his nails waiting for the ending, for it is inconceivable that it could be anything but happy.

Even the characters aren't really built up, except for the secretary, Barbara, the rest being limited to supporting background, altogether, and that includes the accused man himself, played by Jean-Louis Trintignant. It is no real surprise to discover that most of the acting is also slightly overdone, as if the cast was conscious of doing an affectionate tribute rather than constructing something independent.

As an opener for the Locarno Fest this proved to be a judicious choice, light, accessible and fully appreciated. For Truffaut, this may be a minor, but fully enjoyable opus, if accepted on its own terms. — *Edna.*

A 20th-Century Chocolate Cake
(CANADIAN-COLOR)

Winnipeg, July 12.

A Chocolate Cake Film Corp. presentation. Produced and directed by Lois Siegel. Coproduced and written by Gregory Van Riel. Features entire cast. Camera (color), uncredited; editor, Lois Siegel; music, Andre Vincelli. Reviewed at the National Film Board, Winnipeg, July 12, 1983. Running time: **72 MINS.**

Charles.................Gregory Van Riel
Greg...................Charles Fisch Jr.
Jeannine...............Jeannine Lasker
Mechanic.................Peter Brawley
Customer.................Stephen Lack
Himself.............The Great Antonio
and Thomas Schnumacher

"A 20th-Century Chocolate Cake" is a rag-tag low budget concoction of half-baked ideas. Filmmaker Lois Siegel's first feature effort was shot over an extended

period of time and suffers from the stop-start filming. No clear storyline emerges from this series of disjointed vignettes.

Ostensibly, the film is about Greg, a straight-arrow type and Charles, who says he lives to paint and dance. Both characters lead an aimless existence. Their experiments with a variety of jobs forms the basis of what little plot exists in the film.

For instance, they go out into the streets to record the thoughts of children. Although sometimes amusing, this material only contributes to furthering an already disjointed tale. Another vignette involving a chance encounter with a mysterious woman in a cafe ultimately has an unconvincing conclusion.

An exchange between a man with car trouble and a mechanic is genuinely amusing but completely unrelated to anything else in the film. It's difficult to comprehend whether Siegel and Van Riel, credited with the script, were attempting a docu-drama or a fictional slice-of-life tale on English Montreal.

Technical work is as erratic as the plot. Apparently more than 10 cameramen contributed to the final film in addition to a long list of technicians. Siegel was unable to bring the right proportions for her film recipe together in the cutting room.

"A 20th-Century Chocolate Cake" is reminiscent of feature-length student works of more than a decade ago. One would have expected a new wave of these type of films to be more sophisticated in content and technique. Commercial prospects will have to be directed to specialty houses with a penchant for failed experiments. —*Klad.*

Smokey and the Bandit — Part 3
(COLOR)

Smokey now only dying embers.

Hollywood, Aug. 12.

Universal release of a Mort Engelberg production. Stars Jackie Gleason. Produced by Mort Engelberg. Directed by Dick Lowry. Screenplay, Stuart Birnbaum, David Dashev; camera (Technicolor), James Pergola; art director, Ron Hobbs; editors, Byron (Buzz) Brandt, David Blewitt, Christopher Greenbury; music, Larry Cansler; Howard Warren; sound, costumes, Andre Lavery, Linda Benedict; set decorator, Don K. Ivey; assistant director, Ron Bozman; stunt coordinator, David Cass; 2nd unit camera, John Winner. Reviewed at Universal Studios, Universal City, Aug. 12, 1983. (MPAA Rating: PG). Running time: **88 MINS.**

Buford T. Justice.........Jackie Gleason
Cletus/The Bandit...........Jerry Reed
Junior......................Mike Henry
Dusty Trails.............Colleen Camp
Big Enos................Pat McCormick
Little Enos..............Paul Williams
Tina.......................Faith Minton

The Real Bandit ....Burt Reynolds
Police woman ....Sharon Anderson

"Smokey and the Bandit" veterans Burt Reynolds and director Hal Needham have stepped aside but producer Mort Engelberg has kept enough old signposts, chiefly Jackie Gleason to clone another copy of this backroads moneymaker for Universal.

First picture, in 1977, rang up $61,055,000 in domestic rentals; second version, three years later, tallied rentals in U.S. and Canada of $40,002,000. Now, with the formula thinning and Reynolds materializing in the Bandit's Trans Am for only a brief fantasy sequence, commercial outlook appears entirely dependent on quick bucks in opening, and staggered; rounds.

Filmmakers, including first-time theatrical director Dick Lowry, have wisely returned to the non-stop car-chasing destruction derby of the first movie. But the sense of fun in that original is missing and the countless smashups and near-misses are orchestrated randomly. Result is a patchwork of arbitrary mayhem as Gleason's sheriff Buford T. Justice, who tires of retirement in Florida, pursues Jerry Reed and sidekick Colleen Camp through the South. Except for the closing and opening moments, film is so devoid of structure that reels could be shown in reverse order without any loss of coherence.

Gleason, in a testament to endurance, remains funny, and his dimwit son is still humorously parlayed by Mike Henry. All Reed has to do is grin a lot and he's fast becoming a parody of former film roles. Pat McCormick and Paul Williams, reprising their rich and nasty father-son combo, are tiresome caricatures.

Writers Stuart Birnbaum and David Dashev have delivered a very slight variation on the theme. For students of the genre, the cargo in the first movie was illegal beer; in the second film, Reynolds was hauling an elephant to a Republican convention. This time, with Gleason mistaking Reed for the real bandit Reynolds, the featured cargo is a replica of a "Jaws" shark advertising McCormick's new sea-food chain. As always, the drivers have a deadline to meet.

Replacing Sally Field as the girl in the passenger seat is Colleen Camp, whose cool blondeness and campus demeanor are too urbane to convey the Dogpatch look.

However brief, Sharon Anderson has a sharp moment as a police woman ticketing the flustered Gleason. Also in for a brief moment, in very brief clothes, is Playboy magazine's upcoming Miss November, Veronica Gamba. Music by Larry Cansler is a plus. — *Loyn.*

Cujo
(COLOR)

A very rabid film.

Hollywood, Aug. 12.

A Warner Bros. release of a Taft Entertainment Co. presentation of a Daniel H. Blatt & Robert Singer production. Produced by Blatt, Singer. Directed by Lewis Teague. Stars Dee Wallace. Screenplay; Don Carlos Dunaway, Lauren Currier, based on the novel by Stephen King; camera (CFI color), Jan De Bont; editor, Neil Travis; music, Charles Bernstein; production design, Guy Comtois; set design, Joseph Garrity; set decoration, John Bergman; costume design, Jack Buehler; sound, Mark Ulano; animal action, Karl Lewis Miller; special visual effects makeup, Peter Knowlton; associate producer, Neil A. Machlis; assistant director, Jerry Grandey. Reviewed at the Burbank Studios, Burbank, Aug. 12, 1983 (MPAA Rating: R.) Running time: **91 MINS.**
Donna Trenton................Dee Wallace
Tad Trenton.............. Danny Pintauro
Vic Trenton............Daniel Hugh-Kelly
Steve Kemp ....Christopher Stone
Joe Camber.....................Ed Lauter
Charity Camber ....Kaiulani Lee
Brett Camber................Billy Jacoby
Gary Pervier................Mills Watson

Although well-made, this screen adaptation of Stephen King's "Cujo" emerges as a dull, uneventful entry in the horror genre, a film virtually devoid of surprises or any original suspense. Novel about a mad dog on the rampage occupies a low place in the King canon, which is understandable if the film's stupefying predictability is an accurate reflection of the book. Yet another summer release not screened in advance for critics, pic is exploitable for an opening week or two of biz, but little more.

Opening sequence has a lovable looking St. Bernard bitten on the nose by a bat, whereupon audience is introduced to the Trentons, a family of young parents and a son which is disintegrating, mostly thanks to Dee Wallace's sideline affair with a local worker.

In a red herring that doesn't go anywhere, little Tad is dreadfully scared of the dark and of the monsters he's afraid reside in his bedroom closet, but story basically marks time until, at least halfway through, the dog begins attacking Maine seacoast locals (pic was shot in Northern California).

The poor, victimized doggie progressively appears with more and more bloody goop on his face until, inevitably, the big setpiece in which the isolated Dee Wallace and her son are trapped in a car with the pooch lurking in wait outside. There's the expected battle between (wo)man and beast, as well as the modern cliche of the presumably eliminated villain rising from the dead for one more assault on the besieged mortals.

That's really about all there is to it, unless one cares to explore the recurrent King theme of the endangered nuclear family unit. But, except for the appealing kid played by Danny Pintauro, the charac-ters are of little interest, and the tragedies that befall them are entirely too predictable.

Lewis Teague, who replaced Peter Medak as director early in the shoot, has done a pro job of putting this marginal material on the screen, and Jan De Bont's lensing is very attractive, although a bit too much attention has been put on wide-angle perspectives. Acting is okay in a low-key way, and Charles Bernstein's score is nicely modulated.

Warners release bears a Sunn Classics Pictures copyright.
— *Cart.*

Curse Of The Pink Panther
(BRITISH-COLOR)

Great gags, but the format doesn't work without Peter Sellers.

An MGM-UA Entertainment release of a United Artists presentation of a Titan Prods. feature from Blake Edwards Entertainment. Executive producer, Jonathan D. Krane. Produced by Blake Edwards, Tony Adams. Directed by Edwards. Features entire cast. Screenplay, Blake Edwards, Geoffrey Edwards; camera (Technicolor), Dick Bush; editor, Ralph E. Winters, Bob Hathaway, Alan Jones; music, Henry Mancini; assistant director, Ray Corbett; production supervisor, Denis Johnson Jr.; production design, Peter Mullins; supervising art director, Tim Hutchinson; art direction, Alan Tomkins, John Siddall; set decoration, Jack Stephens; costume design, Patricia Edwards; stunt arranger, Joe Dunne; sound, Roy Charman; second unit director Terry Marcel; second unit camera, Derek Browne. Reviewed at Embassy 3 Theatre, N.Y., Aug. 12, '83. (MPAA Rating: PG). Running time: **109 MINS.**
Clifton Sleigh .... Ted Wass
Sir Charles Litton............David Niven
George Litton..............Robert Wagner
Dreyfus.....................Herbert Lom
Chandra...................Joanna Lumley
Lady Litton.....................Capucine
Bruno.....................Robert Loggia
Professor Balls...........Harvey Korman
Cato........................Burt Kwouk
Clouseau...................Roger Moore
Juleta Shane...................Leslie Ash
Also: Graham Stark, Andre Maranne, Peter Arne, Patricia Davis, William Hootkins.

The eighth entry in United Artists' hit comedy series, "Curse Of The Pink Panther" resembles a set of gems mounted in a tarnished setting. Abetted by screen newcomer Ted Wass's flair for physical comedy, filmmaker Blake Edwards has created genuinely funny sight gags but the film's rickety, old-hat story values waste them.

Lensed simultaneously last year with the outtakes- plus-Peter Sellers highlights compilation film, "Trail Of The Pink Panther," "Curse" boasts all-new footage but virtually repeats the prior release's storyline. Instead of a newshen tracking down the missing Inspector Clouseau, this time Interpol's Huxley 600 computer (an uppity machine named Al-dous) is secretly programmed by Clouseau's boss (Herbert Lom) to select the world's worst detective to search for his unwanted employe.

N.Y. cop Clifton Sleigh (Ted Wass) is the bumbling man for the job, simultaneously trying to discover who has stolen (again) the Pink Panther diamond. As with "Trail," format has him encountering and interviewing characters from earlier films in the series, with the sketchy plotline merely there to set up the gags.

In the animated opening credits placing the Pink Panther character in videogame land, Wass's character is drawn as an invisible man and unfortunately for the film he remains as such. He is introduced in the live action in a lengthy sequence dressed in drag, and when finally given a normal persona he lacks distinctive characteristics beyond his spectacles and odd hats. This Detective Sleigh is just a pinch-hitter, creating the same comic mayhem Clouseau did. As with Alan Arkin's "Inspector Clouseau" feature of 1968 (helmed by Bud Yorkin rather than Edwards), Wass is not able to fill Sellers' shoes.

He does provide moments of hilarity, fighting a windstorm at an airport, dealing with pesky inflatable dolls and engaging in strenuous stunts. Guest stars David Niven (in his final film appearance, though his work in Bryan Forbes' "Better Late Than Never," filmed a year earlier, is due out last), Robert Wagner and Capucine have little to do, while a pert British blonde Leslie Ash is briefly impressive as a lethally-kicking martial arts partner for Wass when Edwards segues his film into James Bond territory.

Enjoying himself is a slapstick comedy turn, James Bond's Roger Moore pops up as Clouseau after plastic surgery. He is credited as one Turk Thrust II, an in-joke reprising the nom de film used by Forbes in a cameo role in Edwards' "A Shot In The Dark."

Technical credits for "Curse" are excellent and Henry Mancini has provided an ingratiating clarinet theme for Wass's character as well as re-orchestrating the Pink Panther theme. —*Lor.*

The Man Who Wasn't There
(COLOR-3-D)

He should disappear.

Hollywood, Aug. 11.

Paramount Pictures release of a Frank Mancuso Jr. production. Produced by Mancuso Jr. Directed by Bruce Malmuth. Features entire cast. Screenplay, Stanford Sherman. Camera (Movielab), Frederick Moore; editor, Harry Keller; art director, Charles Hughes; music, Miles Goodman; visual consultant, Robb Wilson King; costumes, Sandi

Love; assistant director, Robert P. Cohen. Reviewed at the Directors Guild Of America, Hollywood, Aug. 11, 1983. (MPAA Rating: R.) Running time: 111 MINS.

Cast: Steve Guttenberg, Jeffrey Tambor, Lisa Langlois, Art Hindle, Morgan Hart, Bill Forsythe, Bruce Malmuth, Ivan Naranjo, Clement St. George, Vincent Baggetta, Charlie Brill, Michael Ensign, Richard Paul.

If only "The Man Who Wasn't There" could vanish via some unknown chemical substance in the way its star Steve Guttenberg does within the confines of its story. Then its makers would not have to undergo the inevitable roasting from film critics, distributor Paramount would not have to shell out millions of dollars in an assuredly thankless marketing attempt and, most importantly, audiences would not have to be interminably bored. But since this is real life the film will have to disappear the traditional way — through disinterest.

Seriously lacking in structure, continuity and pacing, the picture seems to have been made only to cash in on the possible commercial interest in a summer 3-D comedy. That would be fine if it even appeared there was some attempt to turn out something coherent. Unfortunately, there are so many plot holes, lapses in continuity, and carelessness in the final product that one wonders what those behind the film were aiming or.

After too many unexplained characters and situations in the first 20 minutes, it finally comes to light that Guttenberg (a kind of government aide on international relations though he's described in the welcome press kit as an assistant protocol clerk) has innocently gotten a hot formula that makes people disappear. All kinds of good and bad guys are after the recipe, which was given to Guttenberg by a dying invisible man, and it's up to our hero to get it to some unknown source.

Guttenberg almost immediately begins rubbing the obviously dangerous substance on his body and immediately disappears himself. As they say in the promos, "that's where the fun starts" as Guttenberg gets in a myriad of mundane adventures.

Aside from drifting from one unreal situation to another, the picture is populated with an endless array of unexplained characters and other truly baffling moments that have no payoff.

There are also many sloppy spots in particular when Guttenberg's invisible girlfriend reappears with a purse containing the formula that she didn't have in an earlier scene.

The 3-D Optimax III process works adequately though there are only a handful of effects in the 111 minutes. Why the 3-D gimmick was not utilized to some greater end is just one more mystery here not worth figuring out. — *Berg.*

Joy
(FRENCH-CANADIAN-COLOR)

Paris, Aug. 9.
UGC release of an ATC 3000 (Paris)/RSL Films (Montreal) coproduction. Produced by Benjamin Simon. Stars Claudia Udy. Directed by Serge Bergon. Screenplay, Marie-Francoise Hans, Christian Charriere, Serge Bergon, based on the book by Joy Laurey; camera (Fujicolor), Rene Verzier, Richard Ciupke (Canada); art director, Eric Moulard; editor, Michel Lewin; costumes, Claire Fraisse; makeup, Aida Thivat-Carange; sound, Henri Roux; music, Francois Valery (theme song) and Alain Wisniak; "Joy" sung by Debbie Davis. Reviewed at the UGC Normadie theatre, Paris, Aug. 7, 1983. Running time: 100 MINS.
Joy..........................Claudia Udy
Marc................Gerard Antoine Huart
Margo.....................Agnes Torrent
Joelle...............Elisabeth Mortensen
Alain......................Manuel Gelin
Bruce................Keneth Le Gallois
(French Track)

The screen version of Joy Laurey's bestselling erotic memoir is just another timid piece of emmanuelized softcore slush, resembling less a film than a bunch of glossy publicity spots for la dolce vita, strung out on a feeble Freudian plotline. One of the (many) things wrong with this kind of product is that its makers continue to associate eroticism and luxury, an idea utterly banalized by the advertising world. Like most of its fashion-conscious predecessors, "Joy" is ornamental and sanitized, where even the heavy breathing and orgasms maintain decorum. Boring.

Joy is a classy, freewheeling photographic model, who would seem to have everything, but doesn't. She doesn't have love, for her heart belongs to daddy. And daddy left one day when she was a child, never to return, presumably because little Joy surprised him one night making love in front of the fireplace.

All of which, of course, has made of Joy a problematic and unattainable adult. But she does find herself in love with a man, handsome and (naturally) middle-aged, who doesn't mind sharing his love between two women, and dragging the docile Joy through kinky Paris pleasure haunts to spike his own sex fantasies. The relationship, not surprisingly, finally goes to pieces, but Joy does find her father in the end. In last shot we see her boarding a plane for New York (leaving us in doubt as to whether it's merely her heart that lucky old dad gets.)

Claudia Udy, a 23-year-old U.S.-born, Canada-raised model with some previous legit and tv experience, plays the title role, but if she's easy on the eyes, her acting is no pleasure.

Serge Bergon, who coscripted and directed, has made alot of commercials before and, as far as "Joy" is concerned, is still in the same field.

The Franco-Canadian coproduction has reportedly already been sold in many international markets. "Joy" to the world, but no joy to the world. —*Len.*

Come Dire
(How Would You Say....)
(ITALIAN-COLOR)

Locarno, Aug. 6.
A Lab 80 presentation of an A&B Films Production. Directed by Gianluca Fumagalli. Features entire cast. Screenplay, Fabio Carlini, Gianluca Fumagalli, from subject by Fumagalli; camera (color), Fabio Cianchetti; sound, Dino Pasquadibisceglie; editor, Osvaldo Bargero; music, Gaetano Liguori. Reviewed at the Morettina Center, Locarno, Aug. 6, 1983. Running time: 82 MINS.
Carlina.............Alessandra Comerio
Nanni...............Francesco Guzzetti
Adriana..............Mariella Valentini
Alberto...............Silvano Cavatorta
Skirtchaser..............Claudio Disio

A first film by a director who prefers to call this a "jazz movie" but acts like sorcerer's apprentice, in more ways than one. Completely smitten with the latest technical developments of the media, he crams them all into his story and his extensive use of handheld camera hints at a beginner's enthusiasm with the tools of his profession.

The jazz reference may be justified, insofar as the entire construction here is based on free improvisation by the character of a young singer-composer desperately searching for the right subject of the first song she is about to record, a plight similar to that of the filmmaker on his own first outing. While riding the Milanese subway, she imagines a sort of hide 'n' seek game involving a girl from out of town and her own boyfriend. Most of the action is shot in the streets of Milan, but its free radio stations, tv studios, video arcades, cafes equipped with closed circuit tv and different media personalities pop up every inch of the way.

The film's main charm is in a sort of freewheeling approach to acting and atmosphere in Milan, but the plot is so loosely built and the narrative devices to prolong it so contrived, that a general audience may tire well before the happy ending of this game within a game.

Technical credits are above average, considering the modest size of the production, and their importance here is obvious, since it is clear that how to say things, in this instance, is more important than the things said. —*Edna.*

Opera in the Vineyard
(Opera Ve Vinci)
(CZECH-COLOR)

Mill Valley, Calif., Aug. 1.
No U.S. distrib. Barrandov Film Studios production. Director, Jaromil Jires. Screenplay, Vladimir Merta, Jires; camera (color), Emil Sirotek; set design, Jindrich Goetz; editing, Josef Valusiak; music Famos Hrebacka-Mikulecky, Zdenek Pololanik, Vladimir Misik; sound, Antonin Kravka. Features entire cast. Reviewed at Sequoia Theater, Mill Valley Film Festival, Aug. 11, '83. (No MPAA rating). Running time: 90 MINS.

Pic has never had U.S. release and doesn't figure to because of what would strike even artsy audiences here as convoluted simplicity. "Opera in the Vineyard" is a musical with subtleties about socialism's infringement on simpler, rural times. The grapelands are pretty, the lensing often affecting, the performances all right.

But yarn about adventurous young rock singer and dying old folk song writer, played, respectively, by Jan Hartle and Josef Kemr, evolves into elder's production of pastoral opera that is neither interesting nor musically enticing.

Continuity is lacking, sub-titles sometimes moves too quickly, pace is supra-laconic. Impression is a more compelling pic could have evolved with concentration on relationship between rocker and folker. But that never happens. —*Herb.*

War Years
(NEW ZEALAND-DOCU-B&W)

Wellington, N.Z., July 17.
A New Zealand National Film Unit presentation. Produced by Hugh MacDonald. Devised and directed by Pat McGuire. Editor, Chris Lancaster; sound, Kit Rollings; film restoration, Clive Sowry, Ron Cameron, Les Bloomfield; executive producer, Frederick Cockram. Reviewed at world premiere Embassy Theater, Wellington, N.Z., July 13, '83. Running time: 90 MINS.

New Zealand's state-financed National Film Unit has done country and people a service in compiling "War Years."

Gleaned from newsreel stock from the time the NFU made newsreels for regular cinema screening here, this full-length documentary is an entertaining and informative social history of the years 1939-45. While its emphasis is on Kiwi involvement in the last great European and Pacific wars, there is enough included of events at home to provide a reasonably rounded picture of what it takes to be a New Zealander down under.

Gallipoli was part of a war fought almost three generations previously by New Zealanders, as well as Australians, and it is something of a shock to recall, from the vantage point of 1983, just how irresistible war jingoism can be. Laundered, clean-cut, get out there and fight for king and country attitudes seemed just as strong in 1939 as 1914.

It was only in the latter stages of World War II (and there are startling clips of New Zealanders fighting in the Italian and Greek campaigns, and in the Pacific), that this image toughened into a more questioning realism.

Of special interest in "War Years" is the almost equal attention given Maori and pakeha (European) New Zealanders. The return from overseas of the decimated famous Maori battalion to mourning maraes (Maori meeting places) provides the most moving sequences.

The visit here of Eleanor Roosevelt and the varied impact of U.S. Marines upon the population during the early 1940s are among other highlights.

But most of all, inside and outside the war effort, "War Years" celebrates an active, inventive, ingenious (if sometimes ingenuous) people in close touch with their land, in a country which is the last stop before Antarctica.

All those involved in assembling this film are to be congratulated, and particularly the trio involved in restoring film from old stock — Clive Sowry, Ron Cameron and Les Bloomfield. —*Nic.*

Wavelength
(COLOR)

Bumbling sci-fi fantasy. Modest returns loom.

Chicago, Aug. 10.
A New World Pictures release. Produced by James Rosenfield. Features entire cast. Written and directed by Mike Gray. Executive producer, Maurice Rosenfield; camera (uncredited color), Paul Goldsmith; editors, Mark Goldblatt, Robert Leighton; sound, Ron Judkins; asst. director, Nick Marck; art direction, Linda Pearl; music, Tangerine Dream. Reviewed at Film Media Center, Chicago, Aug. 4, 1983. (MPAA rating: PG). Running time: **87 MINS.**
Bobby .... Robert Carradine
Iris .... Cherie Currie
Dan .... Keenan Wynn
Gen. Ward............. Cal Bowman
Col. MacGruder .... James Hess
Capt. Hinsdale .... Terry Burns
Dr. Cottrell.......... Eric Morris
Dr. Stern .... Bob McLean
Dr. Sidey .... Eric Heath
Dr. Wolf .... Robert Glaudini

"Wavelength" is a thoroughly nonsensical outing from writer-director Mike Gray, best known as the original scripter of "The China Syndrome." Tossed out during the late-summer booking hiatus, this low-budgeter looks in for minimal to modest returns.

For better or worse, mostly worse, the film has a Chicago origination. Gray once ran an indie film org. here that came up with such docus as "American Revolution II," about 1960's politico-social turmoil, and "The Murder of Fred Hampton," about the death of the Black Panther leader in Chi.

Gray departs his usual socially-conscious tack in "Wavelength" to ludicrous result. Pic was fi-

nanced for less than $2,000,000 by exec producer Maurice Rosenfield ("Bang the Drum Slowly"), the brother of Martin Rosenfield, a founder and officer of M&R Amusement Corp. in Skokie, Il., which runs the Chi area's most profitable theatre circuit. Producer of this pic is Maurice's son, James M. Rosenfield. (The Rosenfields and Gray were put in touch by Chi political consultant Don Rose.)

Plot involves detention of three bald and unclothed creatures from outer space by the U.S. Air Force in a underground cavern located — in of all places — the Hollywood Hills. A Chi hand quips that given the usual populace of the area, it's a wonder anyone would notice the newcomers.

Seems the creatures, unlike those in Steve Spielberg's "Close Encounters of the Third Kind," aren't completely benevolent. Military worries about their powers to zap humans on contact and the possibility of a general, all-purpose plague getting underway.

So, creatures are detained for medical experimentation in what appears to be an abandoned military facility. Living nearby is a pop singer (Robert Carradine) of no discernible talent. His terminally cute girlfriend (played with distracting smugness by Cherie Currie) finds she receives powerful vibrations from the apparently abandoned site. The two investigate.

Several dull plot turns later, the adventurous couple find themselves captives of the military brass, and manage an escape in concert with the three creatures aided by a grizzled prospector (Keenan Wynn).

Enough said that the performances are undistinguished, the dialog is straight-out cartoon captions, the direction (by Gray, it's his first pic as a helmer) is shaky, and the production values and special effects are generally inadequate. New World Pictures has domestic rights; Manson International is handling overseas sales.

Although "Wavelength's" plot strongly suggests "Close Encounters" and "E.T.," Gray says he wrote the pic in 1977 before both pics were released. — *Sege.*

Bus II
(DOCU-COLOR)

Mill Valley, Calif., Aug. 6.
No distrib. Producer, Haskell Wexler. Filmmakers, Bonnie Bass Parker, Tom Tyson, Wexler; editor, Michael Ornstein. Reviewed at Sequoia Theatre, Mill Valley, Calif., Aug. 6, 1983. (No MPAA rating.) Running time: **82 MINS.**

Prospects are dim for this docu on cross-country, two-week bus trip of 30 anti-nukers from L.A. to the UN. Financed by vet protest

observer Haskell Wexler and his mother Lottie, pic becomes interesting, and meaningful, only in final moments, with footage of thousands of marchers in Manhattan at June 12, 1982, Disarmament Rally. Wexler says he's had "no luck" in finding a distrib and that potential of a PBS playoff is hampered by lack of underwriting sponsor.

Major handicap of the bus bit is its passenger list. The people simply aren't interesting and spend endless time on petty, indecisive squabbling, including one seg in which several knock one woman for "trying to be a movie star."

Manhattan march footage — faces without dialogue — bespeaks the cause with far more atriculation than the busload of self-awareness mavens. It's amazing that Wexler and colleagues didn't ask for a transfer early on. —*Herb.*

Un Loco en Accion
(A Nut In Action)
(ARGENTINE-COLOR)

Buenos Aires, May 29.
An Argentina Sono Film release of a Todo Show production. Written and directed by Enrique Dawi. Stars Carlos Bala. Camera (Eastmancolor), Hector Collodoro; music, Horacio Malvicino. Reviewed at the Sarmiento theatre, B.A., May 5, 1983. Running time: **93 MINS.**
Cast: Carlos Bala, Santiago Bal, Marcos Zucker, Cristina Del Valle, Rolo Puente, Alberto Anchart Jr., Vicky Shocron, Julio Lopez.

Intended to make some fast money exploiting the popularity of tv comic Carlos Bala among the moppet audience, the pic fails because its story of a secret agent and his dumb double lacks wit while the action promised by the title never materializes properly.

Only now and then Bala manages to make his fans laugh. And that's all. —*Nubi.*

Occhei, Occhei
(Okay, Okay)
(ITALIAN-COLOR)

Taormina, July 24.
A CIC release, produced by Piero La Mantia for PLM Film Produzione. Stars Paula Molina. Directed by Claudia Florio. Screenplay, Claudia Florio, Gianni Galassi; camera (color), Armando Nannuzzi; editor, Nine Baragli; art director, Franco Velchi; music, Gaetano Liguori. Reviewed at the Taormina Film Festival, July 24, 1983. Running time: **92 MINS.**
Bianca..................... Paula Molina
Rosy .... Giulia Salvatori
Egidio .... Walter Ricciardi
L.P...................... Luigi Laezza
Priest .... Ninetto Davoli
Grandmother.............. Anna Maestri

Fast-paced and uninhibited, this dressed-up tale of teenage love, sex and friendship shamelessly caters to the domestic youth market and should get it, if Italo censors say okay, okay to a pruned

version. The day of pic's fest premiere in Taormina, producer Piero La Mantia received word of the official thumbs-down on the grounds the film is "obscene" and "pervasively erotic." "Occhei" is neither, but it has enough frankness about youthful behavior and titillation through costumes and situations to bank on an occasional shock effect. These elements could draw audiences onshore and in related Mediterranean markets.

Firsttime helmer Claudia Florio, who worked her way up through the ranks, has a professional touch that lightens a ponderously predictable story.

Bianca (Paula Molina) is a pretty laundress; Rosy (Giulia Salvatori), her comical friend, works in a beauty parlor. Like all girls of 16, implies pic, their heads are filled with nothing but boys, clothes, sex and disco. Though supposedly mad about all things made in the U.S. (ergo title) and a fantasized American lifestyle, characters are 100% Italian.

Bianca's boyfriend (Walter Ricciardi) woos her tenderly at first, but seduced is immediately followed by abandoned for a far less pretty girl. To spite him Bianca performs an exhibitionistic solo at the disco, goes off with three toughs and gets gang raped. Boyfriend's response is to dissociate himself because now she has a bad reputation.

The girls go to live in the country with Bianca's fortune-telling grandmother. In a tame climax, they get some mild revenge on the rapists and male chauvinists in general, then hit the road, leaving parents, jobs and reality behind. Plot is defused in a fairy-tale ending.

Though the two heroines are painted with a nice sense of female camaraderie, pic's treatment of the hard facts of life, like rape and family conflicts, is disturbingly cursory and superficial, as though Florio was afraid to spoil the fun.

Unusual in an Italian film is the fast and snappy dialog. Nino Baragli's cutting gives pic a quick clip, in synch with the disco beat of featured punk singer, Luna.

The youthful cast of newcomers headlines Angela Molina's little sister Paula, more soap and water than Spanish fire, and likable Giulia Salvatori, daughter of actors Renato and Annie Girardot. Thrown in for good measure are vets Anna Maestri as the girls' fairy godmother and Ninetto Davoli as a hippie priest who tells Bianca God forgives a girl who goes all the way faster than he pardons a tease (another source of scandal for the censors.) — *Yung.*

Pula Fest

Zadah
(Body Scent)
(YUGOSLAV-COLOR)

Pula, July 24.

A Film Danas (Belgrade) and Viba Film (Ljubljana) corproduction. Features entire cast. Directed by Zivojin Pavlovic. Screenplay, Pavlovic, Slobodan Golubovic Leman; camera (color), Aleksandar Petkovic; art direction, Miodrag Miric; music, Izbor. Reviewed at Pula Film Fest, July 24, '83. Running time: 98 MINS.
Cast: Dusan Janicijevic, Rade Serbedzia, Metka Franko Ferrari, Lijiljana Medjesi.

Winner of the Golden Arena at Pula, Zivojin Pavlovic's "Body Scent" is vintage thematic cinema by a director long considered to be "national in expression" by home and foreign critics. Pic summarizes Pavlovic's other films to some extent, but it should be added that this Serbian director — who often had to work in Slovenia on projects considered too controversial in Belgrade film circles — was once tagged as a maker of unwanted "black films" on social mores in Yugoslavia.

In this regard, his Slovenian pics deserve mention. "The Enemy" (1965) (based loosely on Dostoevsky's "The Double"), "Red Wheat" (1970), "Flight of the Dead Bird" (1973), and "See You in the Next War" (1980) are striking forerunners to the Pula Grand Prix winner.

Once again, writer-director Pavlovic draws on his own literary source for "Body Scent," the main character being a dropout, or outsider, in the usual social context. Bora Markovic, a railwayman, decides that his life and job are the essence of boredom, so he leaves his family and changes his habits immediately for no evident reason at all.

He goes to another town, falls in with a merrymaker named Amigo, and meets another woman who attracts him in his lonely bitterness. The shift from one safe way of life to a more challenging but dangerous one leads in the end to an existential act of killing.

Pic's strong aspects are the restless camera tracking, sketches of life's seamy sides in bars and cafes seldom seen by tourists to Yugoslavia, and strong thesp performances (Rade Serbedzia and Ljiljana Medjesi are top legit performers). But story in itself lacks the tough sociopolitical backbone common to the best of Pavlovic's films: "The Rats Wake Up" (1967) and "When I Am Dead and White" (1968) (both scripted by Gordan Mihic and Ljubisa Kozomara), and his self-scripted "Ambush" (1969). One has the feeling that, due to the "black-film" stigma formerly attached to these latter films, a score

has been finally settled in awarding "Body Scent" at this year's Pula. —Holl.

Balkan Ekspres
(Balkan Express)
(YUGOSLAV-COLOR)

Pula, July 23.

An Art Film 80, Belgrade, and Inex Film, Belgrade, coproduction. Features entire cast. Directed by Branko Baletic. Screenplay, Gordan Mihic; camera (color), Zivko Zalar; art direction, Vladislav Lasic; music, Zoran Aimjanovic. Reviewed at the Pula Film Fest, July 23, '83. Running time: 102 MINS.
Cast: Dragan Nikolic, Bora Todorovic, Bata Zivojinovic, Tanja Boskovic, Olivera Markovic.

"Balkan Express" is Branko Baletic's second feature; the adept director of satirical comedies debuted at Pula last year with "Plum Juice." Scripted by Gordan Mihic, one of the best scribes in East European Socialist cinema, "Balkan Express" is a madcap tale of thieves, conmen, and roving musicians plying their trade in Serbia at the outbreak of the Second World War. Pic was the Pula arena and fave at fest.

Title refers to the "Balkan Express Band" — the guise under which the thieves move around the country. Nothing much really happens during the first half of the film, save to show how each member of the groups specializes in his trade. Often enough, they spend more time trying to outfox each other than working together on a common hijacking caper. Since it's the beginning of the war, and plenty of people are on the move, it's easy to pick and choose among potential customers: train pickpocket robbery, house-breaking, stolen vehicles, impersonations, etc.

The humor of the situation increases when the Nazis happen upon the scene. Their presence at a niteclub leaves little doubt that things are getting hot in the Big City, so when a German officer takes a fancy to the chanteuse in the Balkan Express Band, the mob decides to make the most of it. The main thing is to get their hands on proper ID papers, which only the smitten German officer can provide. In the meanwhile, the first deportation of Jews and aliens takes place — and the group of soft-hearted crooks are suddenly left with a refugee Jewish lass of 10 on their hands. They hide the girl in a potbellied stove for the duration.

Then the Underground Resistance gets in on the act. A plan is devised to blow up the riverboat niteclub with the German officers on board for an evening of entertainment, then escape with the Jewish girl on waiting getaway boats. The finale of this misguided ruse makes heroes of entire lot in a

manner only Mihic could dream up.

Credits are tops across the board. With proper handling, "Balkan Express" might make its mark at offshore arthouses — in any case, try to catch it at a hip Yugo Film Week or an enterprising film fest. —Holl.

Medeni Mjesec
(Honeymoon)
(YUGOSLAV-COLOR)

Pula, July 27.

An Adriafilm (Zagreb) Croatia Film (Zagreb) and Radna Zajednica Film coproduction. Features entire cast. Written and directed by Nikola Babic. Camera (color), Andrija Pivcevic; art direction, Zeljko Senecic; music, Alfi Kabiljo. Reviewed at Pula Film Fest, July 27, '83. Running time: 113 MINS.
Cast: Slobodan Milovanovic, Biserka Ipsa, Nada Abrus, Ljubisa Samardzic, Toso Jelic, Zvonko Lepetic, Pavle Vujisic, Fabijan Sovagovic.

One of the most titillating, show-it-all films every shown in the Pula arena, Nikola Babic's "Honeymoon" is a mixture of police capers with roll-in-the-hay antics for the commercial audience.

A country bumpkin leaves his store-country in the provinces to pursue a conman who has taken his girlfriend away from him. Our wet-behind-the-ears hero then falls into the arms of the waiting Vanda in the Big City, whose pad is a front for crime and corruption. And so it goes — through the longest sex scene in Yugo film history — to a finale that has the lad awaken to the purity of the good and honest life. —Holl.

Treci Kljuc
(The Third Key)
(YUGOSLAV-COLOR)

Pula, July 25.

A Centar Film, Belgrade, and TV Zagreb Coproduction. Features entire cast. Directed by Zoran Tadic. Screenplay, Pavao Pavlicic; camera (color), Goran Trbuljak; art direction, Ante Nola; music, Aleksandar Bubanovic. Reviewed at Pula Film Fest, July 25, '83. Running time: 81 MINS.
Cast: Bozidar Alic, Vedrana Medjimorec.

Zoran Tadic's debut film, "The Rhythm of Crime" (1981), won him deserved critical attention; now he's back with a blown-up tv-film, "The Third Key," which certifies his credentials as an intellectual helmer with a yen for psychological thrillers.

"The Third Key" has a lot in common with Carol Reed and Roman Polanski films: it's difficult to figure how the film really ends, due to the complicated pattern of building tension and suspense throughout. A young married couple move into a long-awaited new apartment, only to find that strange people are watching them and funny things happen when

they're away — as though someone else has a "third key" to the apartment, besides the two they themselves use. Yet nothing is ever stolen — instead, strange letters with cash enclosed in the envelopes keep arriving. Since the couple have little extra money of their own to meet expenses at this time, the money is welcomed — but what's the set of mysterious deliveries all about. The rising tension leads to nervous explosions, and the couple are all the more concerned due to the wife's expectancy.

The drama for two comes across like topnotch kammerspiel drama, skillfully penned and directed. Tadic is a Yugo helmer to watch.
— Holl.

Druga Generacija
(The Second Generation)
(YUGOSLAV-COLOR)

Pula, July 23.

An Art Film 80, Belgrade, and TV Novi Sad Coproduction. Features entire cast. Directed by Zelimir Zilnik. Screenplay, Zelnik, Miroslav Mandic; camera (color), Ljub. mir Becejski; art direction, Kolektivna; music, Disciplina Kicme i Azra. Reviewed at Pula Film Fest, July 23, '83. Running time: 87 MINS.
Cast: Vladimir Sinko, Petar Bosancic, Sanja Zlatkovic.

Zelimir Zilnik, one of Yugoslavia's most talented directors, hasn't had a film in the Pula arena or the Army Center (where the annual competition for Yugo features is held) since 1969 — when he won the Golden Bear for "Early Works" at the Berlin fest and won strong critical praise by home and visiting journalists at Pula. "Early Works" went on the shelf shortly thereafter. Thus, when his "Second Generation" was unspooled at Pula this year (on opening nite in the arena), the resulting press conference meant a packed house for an hour-long discussion of both the film and the director's "excommunication" for a decade.

"The Second Generation" was originally produced for tv, then blown up for the arena presentation. It deals with Yugoslav children of second-generation foreign workers abroad, one youth having spent 11 years with his parents in Stuttgart and another about the same in Melbourne, Australia. The boy's German rearing and background now conflicts with his high-school education in Yugoslavia while living with his grandmother. It seems that several youths are, more or less, forced to return home for their last years of education (not to mention military duty), and the cultural gap leaves them pretty much as outsiders in their own country.

The 15-year-old Pavel feels that he doesn't fit in anywhere, so he runs away from his grandmother's home and returns to Stuttgart. There he discovers that his parents are not allowed to take him in anymore, nor can he attend school in Germany. So it's back to Novi Sad and a well-established boarding-school with other lads in somewhat the same boat as he. This new environment works for a while, an Pavel makes the acquaintance of a gypsy girl he likes enough to become intimate with. But a schoolboy prank gets him into trouble again, and he grows into a man by sorting himself out in the end.

A semi-documentary feature, "The Second Generation" is one of several tv-films made along the lines of cinema-verite or direct cinema in Yugoslavia of late. Zilnik draws natural performances from his leading protagonists, who are "second generation" teenagers of parents living and working abroad. —*Holl.*

Kako Sam Sistematski Unisten Od Idiota
(How I Was Systematically Destroyed By An Idiot)
(YUGOSLAV-FRENCH-COLOR)

Pula, July 28.

An Avala Film (Belgrade) Branko Vukajlovic. (Paris) and Union Film (Belgrade) coproduction. Features entire cast. Directed by Slobodan Sijan. Screenplay, Moma Dimic, Sijan; camera (color), Milorad Glusica; art direction, Miljen Kljakovic; music, Archive Music. Reviewed at Pula Film Fest, July 28, '83. Running time: 97 MINS.
Cast: Danilo Stojkovic, Jelisaveta Sablic, Rade Markovic, Stevo Zigon, Desa Muck, Svetozar Cvetkovic, Zika Milenkovic, Dorbrica Jovanovic, Svetislav Goncic.

After the international success of "Who's That Singing Over There?" (1980) and "The Marathon Family" (1982), Slobodan Sijan became almost overnight the most interesting and provocative filmmaker in Yugoslavia. His metier is the black comedy, comparable to the best that has emerged from Poland and Yugoslavia. Sijan's latest, "How I Was Systematically Destroyed by an Idiot," may not appeal to the same broad audience as his earlier films, but it is a gem for anyone who has lived, and suffered, through student politics and university reform movements.

The time is 1968. Our hero, Babi Popusko, a self-made Marxist poet-lecturer-agitator, belives that he has picked up the torch dropped by his fallen hero, Che Guevara. A self-effacing revolutionary, his higly orthodox ideals don't permit him to do much else save fear he's dying of cancer and keep on spreading the gospel among deaf-eared materialists. All the same, Babi has to eat, and he's not opposed to a pinch of bare behind when the opportunity presents itself. And he has his coterie of de-

voted followers, even though they don't seem to grasp half of what he's trying to say in a land already dedicated to the ideals of Marxist-Leninism.

Wearing his Spanish beret at an angle, Babi wanders into a student sitdown at the University of Belgrade. There, as history actually recorded it in the heady revolutionary days of 1968, a distinguished actor from the National Theatre spoke his lines from Georg Buechner's classic tragedy, "Danton's Death" — those in the play of Robespierre. That speech, delivered in the costume of the French Revolution, sparks Babi to give his own fiery speech, thus unsettling the students and confusing everyone. The old revolutionary suddenly realizes that deeds around him speakk louder than words, even tose of Guevara.

The end is tragic: Babi falls out of a window, and breaks his bones on the pavement below. As he breathes his last for the cause, and his body is carried off to an awaiting ambulance, another elderly revolutionary dressed as ancient Karl Marx himself picks up the fallen hero's papers, and walks off with Che's speeches under his arm. One guesses right off that this is the very character about whom the entire film has been made in the first place. There's one in every city, usually on the doorsteps of the university.

The pity that probably only the "in" crowd will full appreciate this one-man-show by Danilo Stojkovic, a remarkable actor in a role that challenges every bit of his professional skill for the full length of a feature film. Catch this one at an enlightened film fest or Yugo Film Week. —*Holl.*

Mahovina Na Asfaltu
(Moss-Covered Asphalt)
(YUGOSLAV-COLOR)

Pula, July 22.

An Avala Film (Belgrade) and Croatia Film (Zagreb) coproduction. Features entire cast. Directed by Jovan Rancic. Screenplay, Veroslav and Jovan Rancic; camera (color), Milivoje Milivojevic; art direction, Miodrag Miric; music, Arsen Dedic. Reviewed at Pula Film Fest, July 22, '83. Running time: 93 MINS.
Cast: Dragomir Felba, Dusko Janicijevic, Alenka Rancic, Vladan Zivkovic, Rados Bajic, Nadezda Vukicevic, Drasko Roganovic, Jelena Munjic, Mirko Lazic.

An aud fave at Pula, Jovan Rancic's "Moss-Covered Asphalt" is a kidpic with a feel for the rural countryside, in contrast to the disrupting rhythms of city life.
Pic opens with a young lad in a mountain village, whose companions are a dog and a rabbit and whose playground features a woods and a old water-mill. Then the family moves to the city, and the pastoral life is left behind. The boy has to adjust to new surround-

ings, while the parents learn something about the joys of childhood at the same time.
Recommended for kidpic fests. —*Holl.*

Halo Taksi
(Hello, Taxi)
(YUGOSLAV-COLOR)

Pula, July 28.

An Avala Pro-Film Production, Belgrade. Features entire cast. Written and directed by Vlastimir Radovanovic. Camera (color), Bozidar Nikolic; art direction, Milenko Jeremic; music, Kornelije Kovac. Reviewed at Pula Film Fest, July 28, '83. Running time: 97 MINS.
Cast: Velimir (Bata) Zivojinovic, Svetlana Bojkovic, Gorica Popovic, Pavle Vujisic, Mladen Andrejevic, Dragomir Bojanovic, Voja Brajovic, Irfan Mensur, Nada Bojnovic, Lepomir Ivkovic.

Entertainment pic with the indestructable Velimir Zivojinovic in the lead role of an ex-boxer, now driving taxis for a living, Vlastimir Radovanovic's "Hello, Taxi" proved to be prime Pula arena entertainment for rabid Yugo action fans.
The driver stumbles on a drug-ring by accident, when he realizes to his dismay that his wife is a drug-addict. This gets him into trouble as he sets out to take revenge as a one-man Private Eye, but the entire taxi-fleet of Belgrade comes to his rescue at the end. —*Holl.*

Maskarada
(Masquerade)
(YUGOSLAV-COLOR)

Pula, July 22.

A Viba Film (Ljubljana) and Kinematografi (Zagreb) coproduction. Features entire cast. Directed by Bostjan Hladnik. Screenplay, Vitomil Zupan; camera (color), Jure Pervanje; art direction, Milan Pogacnik; music, Bojan Adamic. Reviewed at Pula Film Fest, July 22, '83. Running time: 97 MINS.
Cast: Miha Baloh, Vida Jerman, Igor Galo, Blanka Jenko, Bojan Setina.

Produced in 1971, and then shelved for the duration due to its questionable moral viewpoint, Bostjan Hladnik's "Masquerade" surfaced at this year's Pula fest to put the record straight. Little doubt, the contemporary Yugo entertainment pic offers sex scenes much more explicit than those shown in "Masquerade" — so the original charge has lost its sting in the meantime. All the same, pic is hardly worth defending as a lost work of art.
A young athlete attracts the attention of the fun-loving wife of a sports director. The affair between the young man and the older woman leads to jealousy compromising situations, but in the end the young man cannot forget his forbidden love. Pic has all the earmarks of being made for the then liberated

Yugo mart in the style of the East German innocent sexpic. —*Holl.*

Tesna Koza
(A Tight Spot)
(YUGOSLAV-COLOR)

Pula, July 29.

A Film Danas Production, Belgrade. Features entire cast. Dircted by Mica Milosevic. Screenplay, Sinisa Pavic; camera (color), Aleksandar Petkovic; art direction, Dragoljub Ivkov; music, Vojislav Kostic. Reviewed at Pula Film Fest, July 29, '83. Running time: 91 MINS.
Cast: Nikola Simic, Milan Gutovic, Ruzica Sokic, Rahela Ferrari.

Light comedy, about a clerk who can't meet all his family's demands on his small salary. The long-suffering father has a daughter with a law degree who can't find work, another offspring who is a lifetime student of astronomy without any intention ever of working, and a young son who badly wants a second-hand Honda to run around on. Financial worries go from bad to worse — until the only hope is a strike-it-rich win at the football-pool.
Pretty fair sitcom. —*Holl.*

Kakav Deda Takav Unuk
(Like Grandfather, Like Grandson)
(YUGOSLAV-COLOR)

Pula, July 24.

A Film Danas production, Belgrade. Features entire cast. Directed by Zoran Calic. Screenplay, Calic, Jovan Markovic; camera (color), Bozidar Nikolic; art direction, Predrag Nikolic; music, Dimitrije-Mikan Obradovic. Reviewed at Pula Film Fest, July 24, '83. Running time: 91 MINS.
Cast: Dragomir Gidra Bojanovic, Jelena Zigon, Marko Todorovic, Rialda Kadric, Vladimir Petrovic, Mihajlo Jeftic.

Family comedy, about a lad with two grandfathers — one likes to monkey-around, the other the cultural things of life.
Zoran Calic's "Like Grandfather, Like Grandson" follows the antics of the favorite, Opa, who finds ways to take his grandson off to the playground at the slightest excuse. Family conflicts almost separate the two chums, but warm hearts win out in the end. —*Holl.*

Covek Sa Cetiri Noge
(The Four-Legged Man)
(YUGOSLAV-COLOR)

Pula, July 25.

An Inex Film Production, Belgrade. Features entire cast. Written and directed by Radiovje-Lola Djukic. Camera (color), Milorad Markovic; art direction, Aleksandar Milovic; music, Ildi Ivanji Pro Musica. Jacques Offenbach. Reviewed at Pula Film Fest, July 25, '83. Running time: 96 MINS.
Cast: Mija Aleksic, Milena Dravic, Tanja Boskovic, Djokoca Milakovic, Dragan Zaric, Danilo Stojkovic, Mica Tomic.

Light comedy, Radivoje-Lola Djukic's "The Four-Legged Man"

open with a rib-tickling scene right out of the legit tradition of Ben Travers and the French farces of Feydeau and Labiche. A respected business-man finds himself in an embarrassing position on New Year's Eve; due to a power shortage, his lovely young neighbor is locked out of her apartment — and stands before his door wrapped only in a bath-towel. Of course, in the course of the evening, one visitor after anothr happens by — including a photo-reporter. When the news hits the papers, the morality of the distinguished citizen is questioned.

Played by some of Yugoslavia's best comic talents, the show is nonetheless stolen by the shy posing of comedienne Tanja Boskovic in her wrap-around. —*Holl.*

DIH
(A Breath of Air)
(YUGOSLAV-COLOR)

Pula, July 26.

A Viba Film Production, Ljubljana. Features entire cast. Directed by Bozo Sprajc. Screenplay, Zeljko Kozinc; camera (color), Valentin Perko; art direction, Jani Kovic; music, Jani Golob. Reviewed at Pula Film Fest, July 26, '83. Running time: 113 MINS.

Cast: Draga Potocnjak, Ivo Ban, Milena Zupancic, Faruk Begoli, Zvone Hribar, Vojko Zidar, Polde Bibic.

After making a remarkable debut film, "Spasm" (1979), helmer Bozo Sprajc has pursued his social orientation in a feature on hospitals and doctors in the futuristic 1990s: "A Breath of Air."

It's a tale of medical ethics, about newly born children dying of a mysterious lung infection. A young femme doctor is sure that, unless something is done, an apocalyptic catastrophe will threaten the entire world. A run-of-the-mill scifier done at a clip narrative pace, "A Breath of Air" should make its mark on the commercial home mart. — *Holl.*

Igmanski Mars
(The Igman March)
(YUGOSLAV-COLOR)

Pula, July 26.

A Centar Film Production, Belgrade. Features entire cast. Directed by Zdravko Sotra. Screenplay, Slobodan Stojanovic; camera (color), Bozidar Nikolic; art direction, Milenko Jeremic; music, Kornelije Kovac. Reviewed at Pula Film Fest, July 26, '83. Running time: 95 MINS.

Cast: Tihomir Arsic, Lazar Ristovski, Zelka Cvjetan, Branislav Lecic, Bata Zivofinovic, Slavko Stimac, Aleksandar Bercek.

The only partisan "eastern" unspooled at Pula this year, Zdravko Sotra's "The Igman March" takes place in the ice-cold winter of 1941-42 in Bosnia. The Proletarian Brigade, surrounded by the German Army, made the famous Igman March past Sarajevo over the mountains on the night of January 27-28, some of the partisans hit by gangrene later when their feet froze.

The second half of the film dips into the horror genre as medical operations are made on camera to remove infected toes from the spreading gangrene. An actioner for patriots, but not for the squeamish. —*Holl.*

Eva
(YUGOSLAV-COLOR)

Pula, July 22.

A Viba Film Production, Ljubljana. Features entire cast. Directed by Franci Slak. Screenplay, Ana Rajh; camera (color), Zoran Hochstaetter; art direction, Sreco Papic. Zdravko Papic; music, Begnagrad. Reviewed at Pula Film Fest, July 22, '83. Running time: 87 MINS.

Cast: Miranda Caharija.

One of the best Yugo films of the season, Franci Slak's "Eva" received high critical praise at its Pula debut — particularly for thesp Miranda Caharija of the Slovenia theatre across the border in Trieste. She plays the title role, a bored widow with two teenaged children, a comfortable house of some luxury, and a career position in an architectural firm. She even has a lover on the side.

As in similar Antonioni films of restless boredom, Slak lets his Eva drift aimlessly from scene to scene, rather than motivating the action in any way. She settles into the background at home like another object in a still-life painting. Her every gesture and movement are guarded poses for the public eye, hardly the result of motivated impulse.

Slowly, she appears to be falling apart inside — for on occasion an image disturbs her, as the appearance of a stranger in her that she didn't expect. At the outset, her state-of-mind is shown via a lonely drive on the expressway; indeed, her only outlet for relief appears to be a drive somewhere in the car. Not even the daily affairs of her teenaged children capture her interest, while the affair with the younger lover is beginning to wear thin.

A change of pace is offered when she is assigned a new project: she is to redesign prison cells in the construction of a new penal institution. So she drives to the rural area and pays a visit to the director of the prison, a slow-speaking half-baked intellectual who shows her a cell used for solitary confinement. Next comes a fruitless visit to her father, a retired academic type living alone on a lovely old-fashioned estate.

Then comes the first break with her frustrations. Earlier in the film, Eva goes to a film theatre and sees Jean-Luc Godard's "Breathless" — Jean-Paul Belmondo's act of liberating violence offers a way out of her dilemma. She steals money from an unguarded cashbox at a postoffice, then a gun — with which she apparently shoots her lover after a night of love-making. Always composed in outer behavior, Eva leaves the apartment for her car — and an uncertain future.

Slak punctuates his film with cinematic footnotes. Just before the film, she sees a young man standing before a fish-tank, a reference to his first feature, "Year of Crisis" (1981). The encounter at the postway with Eva Ras at the switchboard is out of Dusan Makavejev's "Tragedy of the Switchboard Operator" (1967). And one of the prisoners walking in the courtyard of the penal institution just happens to be Zelimir Zilnik, who had great difficulty finding work after making "Early Works" (1969).

Trained at the Polish Film School in Lodz, Slak brings a visual perfection to his work. He is already a mature talent, and more psychological thrillers of merit are expected of him in the future.

— *Holl.*

Daniel
(COLOR)

Curiously uninvolving Rosenberg-era conscience piece.

A Paramount release of a John Heyman production. Produced by Burtt Harris. Directed by Sidney Lumet. Screenplay, E.L. Doctorow, from his novel "The Book Of Daniel." Features entire cast. Exec producers. Doctorow, Lumet; camera (Technicolor; prints, Metrocolor); Andrzej Bartkowiak; editor, Peter C. Frank; production design, Philip Rosenberg; costumes, Anna Hill Johnstone; traditional songs sung by Paul Robeson; associate producer, John Van Eyssen. Reviewed at Paramount Pictures screening room, N.Y., Aug. 10, '83. (MPAA Rating: R). Running time: 129 MINS.

Daniel	Timothy Hutton
Paul	Mandy Patinkin
Rochelle	Lindsay Crouse
Jacob Ascher	Edward Asner
Phyllis Isaacson	Ellen Barkin
Frieda Stein	Julie Bovasso
Linda Mindish	Tovah Feldshuh
Selig Mindish	Joseph Leon
Fanny Ascher	Carmen Matthews
Mr. Gulgliemi	Norman Parker
Susan Isaacson	Amanda Plummer
Jack Fein	Lee Richardson
Robert Lewin	John Rubinstein
Lise Lewin	Maria Tucci

Faithfully adapted by E.L. Doctorow from his own acclaimed novel, "The Book Of Daniel" and directed by Sidney Lumet with his customary intensity and subjective commitment, "Daniel" is nonetheless a curiously detached filmization of the highly charged book.

Though it's generally well acted and occasionally evokes the sense of tragedy surrounding the effect of Julius and Ethel Rosenberg's trial and eventual execution as Russian atom spies (fictionalized in the novel and film), viewers who bring no background knowledge of the era's polarized social and political forces may be left stranded.

Though the film will probably benefit from resurgence of media interest in the Rosenberg puzzle following recent publication of a major investigative tome, commercial fight will be uphill, though urban art site openings may be deceptively brisk.

Taking its form from the novel, the film flashes back and forth in time between 1967 — as Daniel Isaacson (Timothy Hutton) an aloof, uncommitted grad student is prodded by the near-suicide of his activist sister (Amanda Plummer) into probing the events behind his parent's execution — and the period of his parents' last years from the 1930s to 1953. Entire chain of events is seen through the son's eyes and a child's sensibilities.

Lumet, somewhat tritely alternating between golden visual hues for the past, and a cold blue tint for the present, unfolds the events like a puzzle or detective story (Daniel is determined to know once and for all whether his parents were truly guilty or the framed victims of anti-Red hysteria). But the constant time shifts and resultant fragmentation make any overall mounting emotional involvement near impossible.

Though Lumet has effectively staged a number of political rallies, confrontations, mini-cell meetings, socialist picnics etc., the climate of the times is never fully realized. Most effective portions of the film are those chronicling the parents (Lindsay Crouse in a staggeringly subtle performance as Daniel's mother, Mandy Patinkin superb as his father). Even here, though, miscasting of the younger Daniel and his sister (cipher-like portrayals by Ian M. Mitchell-Smith and Jena Greco) makes the filial tragedy less harsh.

With much of the dialog having a Yiddish intonation to it, the unevenness of the performances is particularly evident. With Crouse, Patinkin and, most of the time Hutton, on the plus side, inappropriate turns by Daniel's adoptive parents John Rubinstein and Maria Tucci (and the ethnically appropriate but overacted performance by Tovah Feldshuh as the defensive daughter of the family friend who betrayed the Isaacsons) are strong negatives. Edward Asner is understated and quite effective as the Isaacsons' friend and defense attorney, in stark contrast to Plummer's actorly exaggerations as the mentally ill sister.

The film, which makes no final judgment on the parents' innocence or guilt, has a happy ending of sorts (Daniel becomes politicized and his parents' socially committed spirits will live on through him), but no catharsis.

Physically, "Daniel" is harsh and unattractive as lensed by Andrzej Bartkowiak, most likely an intentional tone, but nonetheless grating. —Step.

Upir z Feratu
(Ferat Vampire)
(CZECH-COLOR)

Petaluma, Calif., Aug. 13.
No U.S. distrib. Barrandov Film Studios production. Features entire cast. Directed by, Juraj Herz; screenplay, Jan Fleischer and Herz, from story by Josef Nesvadba; camera, (color), Richard Valenta; set design, Vladimir Labsky; editor, Jaromir Janacek; music, Petr Hapka. Reviewed at Mill Valley Film Festival, Plaza Theatre, Petaluma, Calif., Aug. 13, '83. (No MPAA rating.) Running time: 90 MINS.
Dr. Marek ....Jiri Menzel
Mima ....Dagmar Veskrnova
Kriz ....Petr Cepek
Luisa-Klara ....Jana Brezkova
Dr. Kaplan ....Jan Schmid
Madam Ferat ......Zdena Prochazkova
Grandma ....Blanka Waleska
Secretary...............Zdenek Ornest
Autopsy Prof ....Ilja Racek
Autopsy Dr. ....Vit Olmer

This thinly disguised, and thin, traffic safety metaphor poses as a vampire send-up before, no pun intended because there's a unique

kind of fuel involved here, running out of gas. Jean-Luc Godard covered much the same highway, and more effectively, in "Weekend" in 1967.

"Ferat Vampire" is an often (but not often enough) amusing lecture on the automobile's potentiality for being a deadly weapon. At one point, in not-too-subtle throwaway dialog, actual traffic accident statistics are quoted.

Premise of the stretched yarn is that Madame Ferat's new sports model, called the Vampire and looking like something designed by the Spielberg-Iacocca Motor Works, is powered by blood. The "fuel-injection" method is a sharp-pronged accelerator pedal taking transfusions from the right foot of whoever's driving, in this case two lovelies. That the drivers eventually turn into zombies, needing quick hits of blood themselves, should come as no surprise to advanced students of the Count.

Jiri Menzel, nominally a director, portrays the earnest physician who starts investigating this odd vehicle after his girl friend, the ambulance driver, begins racing the Vampire.

All the elements of basic, skewed horror are here: coffins, a nocturnal visit to a cemetery, identity confusion, a Strangleovian mechanic, reappearing passersby, neck hickeys. Director Juraj Herz even inserts the Paul Henreid schtick of lighting two cigarets at once, except here the lighter is the gay Madam Ferat and the lightee her curvy secretary.

Technicals are fine, especially in the racing scenes. But the stretching of the scenario serves to drive a spike into the heart of "Ferat Vampire." — Herb.

Strange Brew
(COLOR)

This beer is flat.

Hollywood, Aug. 12.
An MGM-UA Entertainment Co. release of an MGM production. Executive producer, Jack Grossberg. Produced by Louis M. Silverstein. Stars Dave Thomas, Rick Moranis. Directed by Dave Thomas, Rick Moranis. Screenplay, Thomas, Moranis, Steven de Jarnatt; camera (Metrocolor), Steven Poster; editor, Patrick McMahon; music, Charles Fox; sound, David Lee; assistant director-associates producer, Brian Frankish; production manager, Marc Dassas; production design, David L. Snyder; art direction, Suzanna Smith, Debra Gjendem; set decoration, Gustave Meunier, Elena Kenney; second unit director, Larry Pall; animator, John Wash; matte artist, Matthew Yuricich. Reviewed at the MGM Studios, Culver City, Aug. 12, 1983. (MPAA Rating: PG). Running time: 90 MINS.
Doug McKenzie ....Dave Thomas
Bob McKenzie ....Rick Moranis
Brewmeister Smith ....Max von Sydow
Claude Elsinore ....Paul Dooley
Pam Elsinore...............Lynne Griffin
Jean LaRose ....Angus MacInnes

Also with: Tom Harvey, Douglas Campbell, Brian McConnachie, Len Doncheff, Jill Frappier, David Beard, Thick Wilson and Mel Blanc (voice of Mr. McKenzie).

"Strange Brew" is such an innocuous concoction that it manages to make a virtue of inoffensiveness. Item reps initial screen adventures of those "hosers" from north of the border, Bob and Doug McKenzie, characters introduced by Dave Thomas and Rick Moranis on "SCTV" a few seasons back. Effect is something like drinking near beer for an entire evening — you might get a slight buzz on, but it doesn't really get you high. B.o. prospects are meagre.

As with many star vehicle comedies, plot and construction are virtually irrelevant. Instead, pic resembles one giant Canadian joke, in that socio-cultural idiosyncrasies of the characters are gently satirized ad infinitum. "Hosers" can be identified by, among other things, their predilection for plaid shirts, furlined parkas, ski hats, earmuffs, an infinite capacity for beer and a tendency to end every sentence with the query, "eh"?

Given that the film's humor is pretty much limited to these matters, it's amazing that 90 minutes could be filled out. Actually, only about 20 minutes are filled out — the rest are vaguely occupied in one way or another.

The McKenzies are interested in nothing more than their (admittedly large) daily quotient of beer, but end up becoming involved in a plot by evil brewmaster Max von Sydow to kidnap the Elsinore Brewery heiress and subsequently take over the world by addicting drinkers to his newly spiked beverage.

Action prompts the anticipated escapes, chases, close calls and rescues, all done in a perfunctory, but entirely good natured style which only a grouch could call meretricious, but which only a mindless fan could call genuinely amusing.

As directed by Thomas and Moranis themselves, pic attempts to include the audience in the fact that it's all just a home movie that's been thrown together, and the guys provide seemingly impromptu opening and closing dialogs designed to disarm the critics. Indeed, how many pics have ever ended with the leading players delivering a ready-made film review?

Team's limited brand of comedy certainly works better in short format of sketches or even disks (they had one hit record), but then again, Cheech and Chong managed to parlay one basic joke into a hugely successful career. Thomas and Moranis are much less wild and

raunchy, just as beer is less potent than dope, but they have a certain mangy appeal nonetheless.

This is an oddity on all counts.
— Cart.

Easy Money
(COLOR)

When a good credit card is needed.

Hollywood, Aug. 11.
An Orion Pictures release, produced by John Nicolella. Directed by James Signorelli. Stars Rodney Dangerfield. Exec producer, Estelle Endler. Screenplay, Rodney Dangerfield, Michael Endler, P.J. O'Rourke. Dennis Blair; camera (Technicolor), Fred Schuler; editor, Ronald Roose; sound, Les Lazarowitz; production design, Eugene Lee; assistant director, Robert Girolami; music, Laurence Rosenthal. Reviewed at the Academy of Motion Picture Arts & Sciences, Beverly Hills, Aug. 11, 1983. (MPAA rating: R.) Running time: 95 MINS.
Monty.................Rodney Dangerfield
Nicky.......................Joe Pesci
Mrs. Monahan........Geraldine Fitzgerald
Rose....................Candy Azzara
Julio........................Taylor Negron
Louie.......................Val Avery
Paddy.....................Tom Noonan
Belinda....................Lili Haydn
Clive......................Jeffrey Jones
Scrappleton...............Tom Ewell
Allison ....Jennifer Jason Leigh
Bill.......................Jeffrey Altman
Hector.....................David Vasquez

"Easy Money" will have to labor for whatever it gets in the marketplace, but the film is an acceptable comedy effort whose worst fault is that its star didn't sacrifice his own mediocre role to highlight an inspired supporting effort. But that's a lot to ask of a star.

Although his nervous stage mannerisms are absolutely maddening when stretched over the length of a feature film, Rodney Dangerfield is nonetheless close to the mark as a likable slob given to an excess of eating, drinking, smoking and gambling, qualities that endear him to wife Candy Azzara, but not mother-in-law Geraldine Fitzgerald.

Dangerfield wrote the picture with three others and for a full half hour at least it seems none of the quartet gave any thought to how individual gags might be melded into a plot. It's at least that long — and maybe longer — before a story finally develops that has Dangerfiled standing to inherit $10,000,000 from Fitzgerald if he gives up all his worldly pleasures for a year.

Considering the wait, it's not much of a story, fraught with predictable scenes of Dangerfield in the woes of withdrawal. At his best, though, the veteran comic makes some of it work quite well.

Adding to Dangerfield's vexations is the pending marriage of his daughter, Jennifer Jason Leigh, to a Puerto Rican gang member, Julio. Suffice to say, portrayed by Taylor Negron, Julio is wonderful — an overly greased reminder of all those Valentino look-alikes from "Mondo Cane."

On his wedding night, Julio brings along an oversized radio, quarters for the vibrating bed and a copy of 'El Joy de Sexo." But nothing works out right and Leigh flees home to her parents. Trying to woo her back, Negron uplifts the picture.

Though it could have made a picture in itself, this subplot is unfortunately underdeveloped and dangling in inconsistencies as the focus stays on Dangerfield's eventual triumph over temptations.

The payoff for that, too, is weak and hardly worth the buildup. But despite the problems, director James Signorelli shows an eye for interesting shots in his feature debut, though he also hasn't learned to cover all his mistakes. All said, however, this is Dangerfield's picture, plus and minus. —*Har.*

Metalstorm: The Destruction of Jared-Syn

(COLOR-3-D)

Needs Magnets

Hollywood, Aug. 19.
Universal release of a Charles Band Film. Produced by Charles Band, Alan J. Adler. Directed by Charles Band. Features entire cast. Exec producer, Albert Band, Arthur H. Maslansky. Screenplay, Alan J. Adler; camera (color), Mac Ahlberg; editor, Brad Arensman; sound, James Thornton; music, Richard Band; art director, Pamela B. Warner; conceptual designer, Douglas J. White; costumes, Kathie Clark; makeup effects, Douglas J. White, Allan A. Apone, Francis X. Carrisosa; stereovision 3-D lenses, Chris J. Condon; sculptor, Kenny Myers; live action stunts, Speed Stearns, Larry Howe; associate producer, Gordon W. Gregory; assistant director, Matia Karrell. Reviewed at Universal Studios, Universal City, Aug. 19, 1983. (MPAA rating: PG.) Running time: **84 MINS.**

Dogen................:.........Jeffrey Byron
Rhodes.....................Tim Thomerson
Dhyana ....Kelly Preston
Jared-Syn ....Mike Preston
Hurok.......................Richard Moll
Baal.........................David Smith
Poker Annie..................Mickey Fox

A poor man's "Mad Max 2," this Universal pickup of an Albert Band International Prod. has narrow mileage with the 6-12-year-old audience. Coming on the tail end of a woolly effects-picture summer, pic was held from the press till its shotgun opening Friday (19). Slight lure is centered on the okay Stereovision 3-D, bizarre makeup and costumes, and a clutch of funky, four-wheel desert vehicles.

Elements that could spark broader appeal, such as a coherent narrative, sustained imaginative stunts, and charismatic performances (with exception of Tim Thomerson as a funny-cynical sidekick) are absent.

"Metalstorm" is also belabored with a garrulous subtitle, "The Destruction of Jared-Syn," which

any exhibitor would do well to leave off the marquee even given the room. Director Charles Band (who helmed the 3-D "Parasite") and his coproducer and writer Alan J. Adler rather brashly dip into material that's derivative of the "Star Wars" films, particularly a saloon scene that's emblematic of the movie's frequent, skimpy look. Darth Vadar-type visages also abound.

Star Jeffrey Byron, steely-eyed, plays a Peacekeeping Ranger dispatched to the barren, desert of another planet to strike down an evil in the universe, which is personified by Aussie actor Mike Preston with a comically out of place English accent. Most of the story, entangled with a plot about a potent crystal whose powers are muddied in the telling, remains land-bound.

Picture has dry, California sagebrush look (it was shot last February-March in Simi Valley and Box Canyon near Palm Springs) and requires belief suspension to call it a space-age western. Formula is old Hollywood Western with grotesquely hooded characters and cars.

Byron, the intense man behind the good wheel, has a pretty blonde passenger, in this case actress Kelly Preston. Thomerson is welcome, ragged relief, in a cliche role that he turns to his advantage.

There's a terrific shot of a car diving and exploding at the bottom of a huge cliff. But best moment is a ghastly reptilian creature that bursts from underneath the sand. Sound work and music are pro and give the film some feeble pulse.
— *Loyn.*

Yor, The Hunter From The Future

(TURKISH-ITALIAN-COLOR)

None of the budget went for wigs.

Hollywood, Aug. 19.
A Columbia release of a Diamant Film production through Kodiak Films. Produced by Michele Marsala. Directed by Anthony M. Dawson (Antonio Margheriti). Features entire cast. Screenplay, Robert Bailey, Dawson, based on the novel by Juan Zanotto, Ray Collins. Camera (Luciano Vittori color) Marcello Masciocchi; editor, Alberto Moriani; music, John Scott; additional music, Guido, Maurizio De Angelis; art direction, Walter Patriarca; costumes, Enrico Luzzi; special effects, Edward, Tony Margheriti; sound, Cinzia Rossi; associate producers, Sedat Akdemir, Ugur Terzioglu; assistant director, Ignazio Dolce. Reviewed at The Burbank Studios, Burbank, Aug. 19, 1983. (MPAA Rating: PG.) Running time: **88 MINS.**
Yor.........................Reb Brown
Ka-Laa.....................Corinne Clery
Overlord.....................John Steiner
Ena.........................Carole Andre
Pag.........................Alan Collins
Roa.........................Ayshe Gul
Ukan.......................Aytekin Akkaya
Tarita....................Marina Rocchi
Kay........................Sergio Nicolai

This is the first picture in a long time to have both dinosaurs and a space ship in it. For the first hour or so, the loinclothed title character runs about beating on all his adversaries with an ax. But then, lo and behold, he finds a plastic radio receiver in the sand, and it turns out we're in a post-holocaust future, so Yor must quickly learn how to handle laser guns and dynamite. Call it "Conan Meets Darth Vader." Columbia pickup is one of the cheesiest pics to bear a major studio imprimatur recently, and will have to grab the under-12 crowd on opening weekend or two to pay off. Nobody older than that will buy it.

Mostly dubbed dialog has some howlers in the opening reel, and femme Corinne Clery, having been saved from the jaws of a giant reptile by the eponymous muscle man, utters the immortal line, "Why is Yor so different from other men?" Answer seems to be that he wears a blond heavy metal-style wig instead of black mops, or maybe it's that he's able to annihilate entire tribes singlehandedly.

Lensed in Turkey and Italy, film can at least be said to have brought unfamiliar faces to the screen, although promise of a sequel in the wrap-up narration probably won't make too many people hold their breath in anticipation. —*Cart.*

Boogeyman II

(COLOR)

Recycled horror, overloaded with introspection.

A New West Films production, presented by Ulli Lommel. Executive producers, Jochen Breitenstein, David DuBay. Produced by Lommel, Bruce Starr. Directed by Starr. Features entire cast. Screenplay, uncredited; camera (Pacific color), Philippe Carr-Forster, David Sperling; editor, Terrell Tanen; music, Tim Krog; additional music, Craig Hundley, Wayne Love; associate director, Paul Willson; special effects, CMI Ltd., Craig Harris; makeup, Shirley Howard; assistant director, Bruce Perlstein; associate producers, Mark Balsam, James Dudelson. Reviewed on VC II videocassette, N.Y., Aug. 11, 1983. (No MPAA Rating). Running time: **79 MINS.**
Lacey.....................Suzanna Love
Bonnie.....................Shannah Hall
Mickey Lombard ....Ulli Lommel
Joseph..................Sholto von Douglas
Bernie.....................Bob Rosenfarb
Also with: Ahley DuBay, Rhonda Aldrich, Sarah Jean Watkins, Rock MacKenzie, Rafael Nazario, Leslie Smith, Mina Kolb, Ann Wilkinson, David D'Arnel.
Appearing in flashbacks only: John Carradine, Ron James, Nicholas Love, Felicite Morgan, Bill Rayburn, Llewelyn Thomas.

Made in 1982, "Boogeyman II" is an unsuccessful followup to Ulli Lommel's 1980 horror hit. Carrying sequelitis to a distressing extreme, about half the current picture's running time consists of flashback highlights from the earlier film, amounting to virtually a condensed version. Small wonder that, in common with many other

marginal films of late, the pic has had no theatrical release but has gone instead directly into the homevideo market.

Uncredited screenplay is built around the first film's heroine Lacey (Suzanna Love) moving from Maryland to L.A. six months after the supernatural murders recounted in part 1. Much of the pic's early reels consists of flashback material as she tells her story to friends and film director Mickey Lombard (Ulli Lommel).

Beyond recapitulation of already-released footage, "Boogeyman II" is a vehicle for expatriate German filmmaker Ulli Lommel to express his misgivings about the Hollywood scene. Recalling (no doubt unintentionally) the theme of an unsung little film-about-films "The Other Woman" by the Czech actor-director Hugo Haas, the picture has Lommel (under protest) shooting some skin shots to spice up his current art film entitled "Nathalie And The Age Of Diminishing Expectations." His producer has already retitled the epic "Kiss And Tell."

As Haas did 30 years ago, Lommel (in character) sounds off about the commercial vicissitudes of filmmaking. Thumbing through a copy of Kenneth Anger's "Hollywood Babylon," he spots a photo of Erich von Stroheim and comments cynically about the "good old days when Hollywood destroyed real people instead of toys." Regarding spiraling costs and waste, once again the target is a familiar one, as Lommel's agent expresses the low-budget filmer's refrain: "Brian De Palma spent $18,000,000 on that bomb of his 'Blow Out;' you could make 50 movies for that."

Amidst this griping, the lethal mirror shard brought along from "Boogeyman" by Lacey goes on the rampage again, possessing the butler Joseph (Sholto von Douglas). With extremely cheap blood and gore effects, various household objects are supernaturally levitated and used to kill off the creepy guests at a Hollywood party. Besides a garden hose, hedge-clipper, corkscrew and barbecue tongs, the appliances employed in this weak spoof of the "power tools of death" horror genre extend to an electric toothbrush and even a girl smothered by shaving cream. It's a feeble exercise in black humor, right up through the inevitable graveside ending (ripped off from De Palma's "Carrie").
—*Lor.*

C.O.D.

(W. GERMAN-U.S.-COLOR)

Minor sex tease comedy suitable for drive-ins.

A Lone Star Pictures International release of a Geiselgasteig Film Prod. GmbH, Metro Film GmbH production. Executive producer,

Wolfgang von Schiber. Produced and directed by Chuck Vincent. Features entire cast. Screenplay, Vincent, Rick Marx, Johnathan Hannah from story by von Schiber; camera (color), Larry Revene; editor, James Macreading; music, Hannah; assistant director, Bill Slobodian; production manager, Mark Silverman; sound, Dale Whitman; production design-costumes, Robert Pusilo. Reviewed on vidcassette. N.Y., Aug. 10, 1983. (MPAA Rating: PG). Running time: **94 MINS.**

Albert	Chris Lemmon
Holly Fox	Olivia Pascal
Lydia	Jennifer Richards
Lisa Foster	Teresa Ganzel
Cheryl	Corinne Alphen
Debbie	Marilyn Joi
Countess Bazzini	Carol Davis
Christina Werner	Dolly Dollar

Made over two years ago with the title "Snap!," "C.O.D." is a fitfully amusing German-backed but American-made sex comedy which is too soft (PG-rating instead of today's near-obligatory R) for much usage beyond the drive-in circuit and subsequent tv exposure.

West Germany has been exporting scores of light sex comedies (notably the endless "Schoolgirls" series) over the past decade which unspool at U.S. drive-ins in R-rated or soft X-rated dubbed versions with little public notice. "C.O.D." is similar in format to these (especially a mid-1970s title "Penthouse Playgirls"), dealing with the efforts of peripatetic young adman Albert (Chris Lemmon) to sign five beautiful and famous international women to contracts endorsing Dumore Industries' line of brassieres.

Along the way, there are some effective slapstick and gags, but the main thrust of the picture is to display an impressive assemblage of actresses known for their top-heavy superstructures. Former Penthouse mag pinup Corinne Alphen appears as a Hollywood star seen filming a satirical horror flick "The Zombies' Revenge," Teresa Ganzel (of "The Toy") is cast as the president's dizzy blonde daughter, black actress-stripper Marilyn Joi is alluring as a disco singer, Carol Davis is a fiery Italian countess and German starlet Dolly Dollar appears as a top-heavy wrestler. In context, the lovely German actress Olivia Pascal (memorable in "Vanessa") is cast as Albert's plain-Jane secretary. Even the running gags involving Albert's opposition are handled by the divertingly busty Jennifer Richards.

With all this pulchritude on the bill, "C.O.D." opts for an old-fashioned risque approach in its teasing avoidance of nudity or sex scenes, which have become a staple of comedies of late. A big plus is the work of Jack's son Chris Lemmon, carrying his hectic role with enthusiasm and solid comic timing. Also of value is the original English soundtrack recording which separates this from the throwaway dubbed project.

Chuck Vincent's direction is fast-paced, boosted by location-hopping production values that are way above average for the genre. Robert Pusilo's costume and production designwork is suitably garish. —Lor.

Le Cercle des Passions
(Circle Of Passions)
(FRENCH-SPANISH-COLOR)

Paris, Aug. 12.

Ginis Films release of a Dedalus Films/Intercontinental Productions/Figaro Film (Barcelona) coproduction. Produced by Henry Lange. Directed by Claude D'Anna. Features entire cast. Written by D'Anna and Laure Bonin; camera (Fujicolor), Acacio d'Almedia, Manuel Mateos; music, Egisto Macchi, Giuseppe Verdi, Giacomo Puccini; art directors, Vianet Brinte, Pierre Cadiou, Tony Roman, Didier Sainderichin; editors; Claude d'Anna, Patric de Coninck; production managers, Bernard Guiremand, Carmo Moser; executive producer, Jean-Marie Bertrand; associate producers, Alfred Gutman, Franck Hoggart. Reviewed at the Gaumont-Amassade theatre, July 19 1983. Running time: **110 MINS.**

Anthony Tursi	Giuliano Gemma
Carlo di Vilalfratti	Max Von Sydow
Elisa di Villafratti	Assumpta Serna
Turiddu Zangara	Marcel Bozzuffi
Renata Strauss	Francoise Fabian
Rosaria Croce	Ofelia Angelica
Silvio Croce	Federico Pacifi
Lucia	Dora Calindri
D'Amico	Raul Freire

"The Circle Of Passions" offers a dosage of murder, incest, madness and lust against the backdrop of turbulent Sicilian society in the 1950s, when the Mafia is beginning to encroach on the privileges of landed aristocracy. Claude D'Anna's Franco-Spanish coproduction, released in Italian and French versions, strives for a certain operatic intensity reminiscent of Visconti, though falls short of its intended grandeur.

Original script by D'Anna and Laure Bonin deals with a young Sicilian-American who finds himself mixed up with a decadent aristocratic family when he returns to Sicily to bury his father on native soil. Invited to the count's home, he is immediately set upon by latter's luscious half-idiot daughter, who's already incestuously wrapped up with her father (he'd unwittingly jumped her one night, thinking she was his wife, who later committed suicide on discovering the act).

Domestic tensions are reflected in the family's public life, where striking plantation workers, and bloody confrontations between Communist agitators and Mafia gunmen precipitate the tragedy that leaves the Count broken and alone.

The excessive rapports and incidents are the stuff of grand opera, and D'Anna has dutifully set some major sequences at the opera house, helping himself to large servings of Verdi and Puccini. But he is unable to provide his driven decadents with the larger-than-life theatricality that would help transcend the hackneyed and the ridiculous.

Still, a generally good cast keeps the ludicrous at bay. Max Von Sydow brings his authoritative presence to the perverse but pathetic aristocrat, though, alas, he is not an actor to be dubbed with impunity. The lovely Spanish actress Assumpta Serna is well in control of a delicate role of the nymphomaniac daughter; Francoise Fabian has a classy cameo in a flashback as the count's opera star spouse, who learns of what Von Sydow has done before going on stage to sing; and Marcel Bozzuffi is reliably caddish as Von Sydow's conniving right arm. Only Giuliano Gemma looks dispensable as the strayed Sicilian-American, the kind of catalyst-observer personage often glossed over by screenwriters.

D'Anna is a fringe figure in the French industry, who has managed to earn a certain prestige in buff circles. But this film doesn't seem likely to draw him into a larger spotlight. —Len.

Flics de Choc
(Shock Cops)
(FRENCH-COLOR)

Paris, Aug. 16.

Planfilm release of a Films de la Tour/TF1 Films Production coproduction. Produced by Adolphe Viezzi. Features entire cast. Directed by Jean-Pierre Desagnat. Screenplay, Jean Ardy, Guy Perol, Patrick Laurent, from the novel by Serge Jacquemard; camera (color), Maurice Fellous; sound, Paul Laine; music, Emilenco; executive producer, Guy Perol. Reviewed at the Marignan-Concorde theatre, Paris, Aug. 10, 1983. Running time: **92 MINS.**

Cast: Pierre Massimi, Chantal Nobel, Jean-Luc Moreau, Pierre Banderet, Marc Chapiteau, Mylene Demongeot, Laetitia Gabrielli, Anne Tihomiroff, Yannick Groell, Nathalie Hayat, Nadine Alari, Jacques Balutin, Michel Barbey, Christophe Bourseiller, Henri Virlogeux, Catherine Lachens.

"Flics de Choc" is conventional cops and robbers fare, with a collective hero of five super-snoopers (four guys and a gal who packs a pistol better than her colleagues) on the trail of a prostitution ring that preys on attractive young runaways for a classy clientele. Some of the girls manage to escape their velvet prison, but are relentlessly stalked by the pic's deputized villain, a black leather-clad motorcyclist, whom the cops finally get in the end, but not before he's provided a quota of corpses.

Helmer Jean-Pierre Desagnat matches an obvious and sloppy script with insensitive direction; when he's not busy dwelling on the breezy, wisecracking manner of his heros, he's lingering rather distastefully on the terror of the nubile victims, as if to emphasize some underlying seriousness in the story. But this is oafish comic book stuff, which its principal players try much too hard to pep up. —Len.

La Crime
(Coverup)
(FRENCH-COLOR)

Paris, Aug. 17.

UGC release of a T. Films/Films A2 production. Produced by Alain Terzian. Stars Claude Brasseur, Jean-Claude Brialy, Jean-Louis Trintignant, Gabrielle Lazure, Dayle Haddon. Directed by Philippe Labro. Screenplay, Jacques Labib, Jean-Patrick Manchette; camera (Fujicolor), Pierre—William Glenn; sound, Michel Desrois; art director, Serge Douy; costumes, Catherine Leterrier; editor, Thierry Derocles; music, Reinhardt Wagner; production manager, Armand Barbault; reviewed at Club 13, Paris, Aug. 17, 1983. Running time: **102 MINS.**

Commissioner Martin Griffin	Claude Brasseur
Rambert	Jean-Claude Brialy
Sybille Berger	Gabrielle Lazure
Suzy Thompson	Dayle Haddon
Christian Lacassagne	Jean-Louis Trintignant
Avram Kazavian	Robert Hirsch
Antoine Gomez	Luc-Antoine Dicquero
Philippe d'Alins	Daniel Jegou

Philippe Labro is a prominent French journalist and author who's moonlighted as filmmaker, turning out a handful of commercial thrillers in the early '70s, notably two Jean-Paul Belmondo vehicles. Now, after an eight-year absence, he's back behind the camera with "La Crime," which is a proficiently produced and acted crime melodrama.

Jean-Patrick Manchette, a popular French detective novelist (whose books are regularly snapped up by producers here) is responsible for the screenplay and dialog (working on an original story by Jacques Labib), but that doesn't prevent the film from suffering from a few unlikely setpieces and obvious peripeties.

Picture begins with the first (post-credit) sequence, in which two "cops" march imperiously into the Palace of Justice in Paris, and ceremoniously execute a respected attorney in his study, mysteriously sparing the young legal trainee who witnesses the murder. As the plot develops, and one comes across loads of characters trying to cover up for influential folks in high places, it's a wonder why the catalyzing crime hadn't been engineered with more discretion and ambiguity. Labib and Manchette hunger for flamboyant set-ups, without seeming to consider if they fit logically into the train of events and the corrupt psyches.

The conventional alternates with the incredible as an embittered but fundamentally decent police commissioner pushes stubbornly on with his investigation, despite the moral rot encroaching on him, bolstered by the affections of an attractive young femme journalist.

There are generally brisk performances, including Claude Brasseur as the seedy hero, Jean-Claude Brialy as the double-dealing colleague assigned to survey his moves in order that he should not stumble on to the truth, Jean-Louis Trintignant as an implicated French government minister who commits ritualistic suicide with a kitchen knife, and Dayle Haddon as the murdered advocate's distraught mistress, who is terrorized and finally killed in the film's most florid scene, as she is doused with gasoline and set afire in an elevator.

Labro directs much of this with bland efficiency, tending to dote excessively on individual scenes and characterizations. At times — as in the confrontation between Brasseur and one prime suspect (played by legit actor Robert Hirsch) — one has the feeling of a parody of classic thrillers, in which memorable supporting actors vied for attention with the lead players in brilliantly idiosyncratic performances.

"La Crime" sums up as another melodrama in which the world-weary but uncorruptible hero triumphs over evil and is rewarded with the love of an equally upright woman. —*Len.*

Befrielsesbilleder
(Liberation Pictures)
(DANISH-COLOR/B&W)

Copenhagen, Aug. 11.
A Danish Film Studio For The Danish Film School production and release. Directed by Lars von Trier. Features entire cast. Screenplay, Trier, Tim Elling, based on original story by Trier; camera (color, b&w) Tom Elling; editor, Thomas Gislasoln; sound, Morten Degnbol, Iben Haahr; executive producer, Per Arman; music, Ars Nova, Bo Holten. Reviewed at Danish Film Institute Little Theatre, Aug. 11, 1983. Running time: **60 MINS.**

"Liberation Pictures" (also, tentatively, called "Image Of A Relief") is the film school graduate work of Lars von Trier, who is currently at work on his first feature, "The Elements Of The Crime — Or The Last Tourist in Europe" for Per Holst Productions. Film won a second prize at last year's European Film School Competition in Munich and was immediately snapped up for the U.K. by Channel Four.

While very much on the experimental side of filmmaking, von Trier's work bears the obvious marks of a creative artist in full dramatic and technical control of his medium. He uses color sparingly, mostly to grade softly from the glaring into long passages of black & white, the latter being lab-processed to the point of becoming pitch black shapes and outlines in which the light areas take on a certain luminous quality.

Sound (choral music, a ballad or two) is worked into the pictorial texture of the film as a natural adjunct. Dialog is used sparingly. All acting and action is highly stylized and the story developed rather through hints and off-beat accents and obvious symbolic gambits than through ordinary moving picture narrative, yet the suspense is held from the first frame to the last.

Film is just as open for interpretation as any of Andrei Tarkovsky's work. Trier must obviously be inspired by the great Russian. The latter's use of dripping water, shimmering lights and vague poetic verbal statements are often in evidence in "Liberation Pictures." Film tells of lovers being tested by the moods and sentiments and flaring tempers of that day in May 1945 when Denmark was liberated from the German occupiers.

A German officer (played with mute strength) by Danish feature film director Edward Fleming) fails to kill himself in the subterranean prison where Resistance men keep guard while burned bodies pass by, hanging from moving wire in front of cremation ovens. He escapes to look up a Danish woman (Kirsten Olsen, looking like a sweetly tragic twin sister of a young Ingrid Bergman). She tells him that he cannot pass all responsibility for the blinding of a teenage boy on to the SS. She then appears to help him find an escape route through a forest, but instead has him trapped by the Resistance. She blinds him with a wooden dagger and leaves him to crawl among the trees where he once, as a child and also later, made attempts to make conversation with the birds.

Docu clippings of real Resistance fighters making street arrests indicate that random violence and lack of respect for human values were not a German prerogative and "Liberation Pictures" has been blamed for taking a pro-German stand on occupation and liberation facts & fiction. This is, of course, far from von Trier's interest although he does seem to like to poke fun gently — and by the way — at a few popular faiths and taboos. Full of moods and gaunt pictorial beauty, film is an obvious item for further festival exposure plus careful tv programming. —*Kell.*

Noc Poslije Smrti
(Night After Death)
(YUGOSLAV-COLOR)

Pula, July 23.
An Adria Film (Zagreb) and Televisija Zagreb coproduction. Features entire cast. Directed by Branko Ivanda. Screenplay, Zora Dirnbach, based on a short story by K.S. Djalski; camera (color), Drago Novak; art direction, Zelko Senecic; music, Alfi Kabiljo.

Reviewed at Pula Film Fest, July 23, '83. Running time: **84 MINS.**
Cast: Milena Dravic, Rade Serbedzia, Sven Lasta.

Branko Ivanda, a grad of the Zagreb Academy for Film, Theatre and Television, came to film direction from criticism, and went to work mostly in tv after a successful debut pic in 1968, "Gravitation." "Night After Death" aired first as a tv-film under the title "Nocturno" over two years ago, then was blown up for film distribution under its present tag.

Pic is based on a short story by Ksaver Sandor Djalski (penname of Ljubo Bratic), in the imagination tradition of Edgar Allan Poe. Djalski (1854-1935), as a novelist, was concerned with the decay of the Croatian nobility at the turn-of-the-century, chronicling Croatian society of the 1880s and 1890s. His works are singular for their melancholy, pessimism, and tinge of mysticism, appropriate to his aristocratic nature and upbringing.

"Night After Death" portrays a distraught nobleman in northern Croatia, whose wife died and left him heartbroken. When he has a vision of his wife appearing to him, he resorts to spiritualism to get her back — until he is convinced that she has returned from beyond. Straight tv-drama, but fascinating in thematic content. —*Holl.*

The Perfect Wife
(HONG KONG-COLOR)

Hong Kong, Aug. 12.
A Cinema City Company Ltd. presentation. Produced by Karl Maka. Co-producer and screenplay, Raymond Wong. Directed by Dean Shek. Stars Dean Shek, Eric Tsang, Liu Juel Chi, Paul Chin Pei, Brenda Lo. Production designers, Tsui Hark, Nanshun Shi; executive producer, James Lau; camera (color) Johnny Koo; editor, Tony Chow; art director, Raymond Li; music, Teddy Robin. Reviewed at President Theater, Hong Kong, Aug. 11, 1983. Running Time: **100 MINS.** (Cantonese soundtrack with English subtitles)

The mere fact that the lead of the film is also responsible for the direction and production will make one wonder if professionalism and creativity are now drying up at Cinema City, once the most innovative of Hong Kong's independent companies.

Dean Shek's high-blown acting is the ultimate ham to end all ham. Loud, excessive overacting, unglamorous women, unexplained motivations, and a naive plot are some of the major reasons why this film is the absolute pits.

"The Perfect Wife' tries to capture the spirit of Benny Hill's madcap comedy and Rock Hudson's handsome bachelor days, but it turns out to be a most imperfect film as it strains desperately for laughs that just aren't there.

Cinema City seems to have forgotten the rule of keeing audiences awake and that is "If the film don't measure up, put 'em back in the can or do it again." —*Mel.*

Possessed
(HONG KONG-COLOR)

Hong Kong, July 29.
A Johnny Mak Productions Ltd. production and release. Executive Producer, Johnny Mak, assistant producers, Hon Yee Sang, George Ma. Director, David Lai. Stars Lau Siu Ming, Siu Yuk Lung, Sue Chan, Irene Wan. Screenplay, John Au; camera (color), Bob Thompson. (No other credits provided by producer). Reviewed at State Theater, Hong Hong, July 28, 1983. Running time: **100 MINS.** (Cantonese soundtrack with English subtitles).

There is usually something good, laughable, entertaining, appetizing and intriguing to be derived from contemporary Cantonese ghoulash that's been patterned after foreign screen creepies and screamies. One good example is "Possessed," the latest, relatively low-budget feature from Johnny Mak Productions, directed by David Lai, a young talent who shot to fame with his "Lonely Fifteen" debut.

Lai has the flair for rehashing western styles for Oriental appreciation.

The production succeeds in paying tribute to everyone's favorite horror-thriller sequences, and tailoring them for Hong Kong-inspired special effects.

Oldtime policeman Lau Siu Ming and handsome bachelor cop Siu Yuk Lung are close friends. One evening, they are nearly knocked down by a car. They follow but it disappears near a dilapidated country house. From the dark, they hear a woman screaming for help. Ming and Siu enter the house and finds a man chasing the woman with a chopper. In fright, Ming shoots the man to protect himself from being attacked.

Since the incident, Ming and Siu experience a series of eerie events. Some unknown force enhabits Siu's house, kills his sister, and rapes his Korean girlfriend, and unable to get any clue, Ming and Siu go to a fortuneteller and with the help of the supernatural, the mystery finally unfolds.

The ending leaves sufficient opportunities for a sequel. But locals were unsatisfied as they like a definite end. A "hanging", or vague finale with some of the mysteries remaining unsolved irritate Cantonese viewers.

"Possessed" has plenty of splash and feminine skin exposure to satisfy both local and foreign (horror being visual and universal) filmgoers. After all, scaring people is still good business especially the "Possessed" variety which will "eeeeekk" out sufficient blood in the form of Hong Kong currency at the boxoffice without fear of failure. Ex-stuntman Siu Yuk Lung makes an excellent debut as male lead. This film should lead him to other parts. —*Mel.*

Jeanne Dielman, 23 Quai Du Commerce, 1080 Bruxelles
(BELGIAN-FRENCH-COLOR)

Mill Valley, Aug. 4.

New Yorker release of a Paradise Films (Brussels) and Unite Trois (Paris) production. Directed and written by Chantal Akerman. Camera (color), Babette Mangolte. Stars Delphine Seyrig, Jan Decorte. Reviewed at Sequoia Theatre, Mill Valley, Calif., Aug. 4, 1983. (No MPAA Rating.) Running time: **198 MINS.**

Billed, at least at Mill Valley film fest, as a "feminist" pic, "Jeanne Dielman" has already had a commercial run earlier this year in Manhattan and is slotted for split-week runs this summer in two other Bay area venues, Frisco and Berkeley.

Pic was first released in 1975 and made by all-woman aggregation. At time of lensing, director-writer Chantal Akerman was 25 years old. In terms of helming, writing and techs, pic is first-rate, and experimental, meticulously realistic, inside-out look at a 40ish Brussels widow who's a compulsive cleaner-upper and an at-home prostitute.

Yarn is so very real that it quite often is numbing, thus manifesting commercial problems: a patient, understanding, intelligent audience is required, and such an audience obviously is limited. Nearly full house here treated pic rudely — laughing, hollering at central character's orderliness and, in significant numbers, walking out.

As honest a work as this is, one must question its playability.

Dialog is sparse. Scenes, many void of any action or business, stretch endlessly. Settings are narrow, claustrophobic. The cumulative effect is discomfort, yet that's what "Jeanne Dielman" is all about. Akerman makes the audience eyewitnesses to an empty, cold, narrow life. But she makes no judgments, no statements. This is a film of pure observation.

But what you must observe along the way are such mundane, and brutalizing, chores as cooking, cleaning, dusting, bedmaking, shoe-shining, the tasks which, sadly, encumber so many lives, particularly that of the title figure, who covers all emotion by being obsessed with the routine.

Chores take as long on the screen as they do in life: the preparation of a meatloaf, making of coffee, cleaning of a bathtub, turning on lights, turning off lights, opening and closing doors, riding up and down an elevator, eating, spoonful by spoonful, soup.

It is as if the cutaway had not been discovered, and of course there are no cutaways in the real world.

The control of Delphine Seyrig in these long, long takes is impeccable. Her etching of the character's composure slippage in the final day of this three-day observation is particularly skilled. Her restlessness, her struggle to maintain control, becomes your restlessness. The work of Seyrig is complemented by the disciplined performance of Jan Decorte as her teen-aged son.

One really has to stand in awe of Akerman's work here. But the true test with "Jeanne Dielman" is sitting, until the surprising, homicidal ending, in awe. For most, the length will tarnish the breadth.
—*Herb.*

Moj Tata Na Odredjone Vreme
(My Temporary Father)
(YUGOSLAV-COLOR)

Pula, July 22.

An Avala Film (Belgrade) and Croatia Film (Zagreb) coproduction. Features entire cast. Directed by Milan Jelic. Screenplay, Predrag Perisic, Jelic; camera (color), Djordje Nikolic; art direction, Slobodan Mijacevic; music, Vojislav Kostic. Reviewed at Pula Film Festival, July 22, '83. Running time: **90 MINS.**
Cast: Ljubisa Samardzic, Milena Daravic, Boris Dvornik, Baa Zivojinovic, Nikola Kojo, Jeslisaveta Sablic, Olivera Markovic.

All the popular vet stars of Yugo cinema are to be found in Milan Jelic's family comedy, "My Temporary Father" — Ljubisa Smardzic, Milena Dravic, Bata Zivojinovic, Boris Dvornik, Olivera Markovic. The formula is such that just about everyone in the fest audience could go away satisfied.

A divorced mother with a 12-year-old son has a passing relationship with a boyfriend, who has a temporary job while looking for something permanent. The ex-husband returns into the picture, and he hopes to win his wife back by hinting that the boyfriend is having another affair on the side with the lady at the employment office.

One misunderstanding deserves another, but helmer Jelic handles everything deftly. He's become one of Yugoslavia's most popular directors of situation comedies.
—*Holl.*

Dreamland
(COLOR-DOCU)

Mill Valley, Calif., Aug. 6.

First-Run Features release of Inter-American/MG production. Executive producer. Richard Lourie; producer, Jonathan Stathakis; directors, Oz Scott, Nancy Baker, Joel Schulman. Features entire cast. Written by Baker and Lourie; camera (color), Joe Mangine and Don Lenzer; music, Butler, editing, Baker and Jay Freund; sound, Nigle Noble. Reviewed at Sequoia Theater, Mill Valley, Calif., Aug. 6, 1983. (No MPAA rating.) Running time: **83 MINS.**
Cast: Joanne Crayton, Henry Butler, Charles Elloie.

This thoroughly entertaining, musically upbeat pic has been sitting around for three years waiting for (1) a distrib, which it now has in firstrun, and (2) commercial bookings. Appears salable to jazz-oriented audiences and in black situations but might, with savvy marketing, perhaps even involving soundtrack exploitation, work in selected artsy houses. Although yarn does look at gospel, it crosses over mostly into jazz, so should have better b.o. possibilities than "Gospel," performance pic unspooled at the '82 Mill Valley fest, or "Say Amen, Somebody," an overview of gospel history.

The drama element of this docudrama is quite fetching and believable, centering on the ambitions of gospel-spawned warbler Joanne Crayton, who works as Lady B.J., to ankle New Orleans and hit it big as a club singer in "The Apple." Director Oz Scott says he was summoned to fashion this story line and then integrate it into mucho previously lensed footage on New Orleans music, heavy on Mardi Gras shooting.

The integration is deft, and for once cinema verite gabbing is terse, articulate, relevant to story line. Crayton and blind tunesmith-pianist Henry Butler, latter now hotsy in L.A. club circles, are both engaging in musical and "thesping terms." There even is a slick element of conflict in the person of Crayton's "manager," Charles Elloie, who struggles with Butler over guiding Crayton's career.

In a small sense, this is a "Flashsong," the hope of a young performer to escape the confines of a time and place, "to stretch myself out a little bit as an artist ... because God wants me to sing."

There is spirit and stamina throughout this pic; it'll take at least those two qualities to sell it.
—*Herb.*

Shaolin Drunkard
(HONG KONG-COLOR)

Hong Kong, Aug. 12.

A First Distributors (H.K.) Ltd. presentation. Executive producer, Hoi Wong. Directed by Yuen Wo Ping. Martial arts director, The Yuens Clan. Stars Simon Yuen Jr., Yuen Cheung Yan, Yuen Shun Yi, Yuen Chun Yong, Chan Tien Loong and Young Hoi Yee. Camera (color), Michael K.W. Ma; music, Tang Siu Lam. Reviewed at President Theater. Hong Kong, Aug. 11, 1983. Running time: **100 MINS.**
(Cantonese soundtrack with English subtitles).

The plot, acting and plausibility are all secondary to this kind of gimmicky kung fu fare. Yuens Clan's latest effort "Shaolin Drunkard," should please even insatiable kung-fu fans. One look at all the (by now familiar) Yuens family parade of bizarre characters, dressed-up in what looks like the same costumes, could be mistaken as a sequel to their previous Halloween outings with the Shaws, Golden Harvest and other independent productions.

With all the cartoon characterizations, impeccably choreographed fighting sequences and childlike black magic voodoo duels, "Shaolin Drunkard" is comparably inoffensive and almost like an adult animated kungfu in which everyone suffers from heavy karate blows and still stays alive.

But, no one is complaining as the visually alert local audiences leave the theatre wondering what's in the Yuens clan's sleeves the next time around. The Yuens have mastered their craft well so they don't waste a single minute. Each sequence is overcrowded with gimmicks galore.

Produced by Hoi Wong of First Films, "Shaolin Drunkard" has sufficient non stop visuals to fill in the wafer-thin storyline dealing with the encounters of a martial arts expert with black magic practitioners. Foreign audiences may find some of the strange names either ridiculously exotic or just plain silly.

This film oddity should do well in the region and Chinatown markets abroad — because the low intellectual level and content are maintained in this Kung Fu with Asian-made special effects. — *Mel.*

Il Pianeta Azzurro
(The Blue Planet)
(ITALIAN-DOCU-COLOR)

Petaluma, Calif., Aug. 13.

No U.S. distrib. Production of 11 Marzo Cinematografica s.r.l., Rome. Producer. Silvano Agosti. Directed, photographed and edited by Franco Piavoli. Assistant director, Neria Poli; sound, Giuliana Zamariola, Fausto Ancillai; music, Maderna, Josquin des Pres. Reviewed at Mill Valley Film Festival, Plaza Theatre, Petaluma, Calif., Aug. 12, '83. (No MPAA rating.) Running time: **83 MINS.**

This lovely to look at, and aurally fascinating, docu inspection of the rhythms of the seasons of life played at the '82 Venice fest and won top honors from the Italian Film Critics Assn, plus a UNESCO award. Pic is the first full-length effort of Franco Piavoli, 50, who essayed four docu shorts in 1961-64, then no other film work until "The Blue Planet," a spinoff of his '61 shortie "Stagioni" (Seasons).

(In a magazine interview, he described the lengthy period between pics as "years of constrained inactivity, but as well as period of preparation for this film.")

His intention, the director-shooter-cutter says, was "four narrative veins: the geology of primordial life, the poetic story of the seasons, the simple story of daily life, and through these three fabrics appears clearly the story of life."

Yes, and no. The human condition takes a back seat to rain, shadows, clouds, fields of grain, rivers, lakes, ponds, trees, algae, fish, worms, moths, frogs, snails, dawn, dusk, fireflies, a reaper, crickets and the victory of a spider.

Yet "Blue Planet" is a toughie for commercial audiences. At the first screening of pic at this year's Mill Valley fest, at the Sequoia twinner in Mill Valley, there were reports of laughter and walkouts. It's likely that art houses would, even with a brief booking, come up short at the b.o.; further, the pic is too "big" for television. College circuits, and specialized situations, may be the only outlets for this effort. —*Herb.*

Hong Kong, Hong Kong
(HONG KONG-COLOR)

Hong Kong, July 25.

A Shaw Brothers Production and release. Executive Producer, Mona Fong. Directed by Clifford Choi. Stars Cherrie Chung (Chung Chor-Chung), Alex Man (Man Che-Leung), Kwan Hoi-San. Camera (color), Bob Huke. Music, Lam Man-Yee. (No other credits provided by producers). Reviewed at Jade Cinema, Causeway Bay. Hong Kong. July 24, 1983. Running time: **100 MINS.**
(*Cantonese soundtrack with English subtitles*).

There are more than 5,000,000 official citizens in the tiny colony of Hong Kong, a city living on borrowed time. But some sources claim that there's another hidden quarter of 1,000,000 unlisted residents, composed mainly of unknown aliens, refugees, practicing con-men and overstaying tourists. Most come to Hong Kong either to turn their money dreams into realities or to bury a bleak shady past for a fresh new one. All congregate in the popular transient resort of the Orient.

Each resident has a story to tell and Sir Run Run Shaw's latest film centers on two ordinary characters, a street-wise man who is an overseas Chinese from Thailand and an innocent, childlike woman, a "boat people" escapee from mainland China. Both are ambitious and want a new life, with all the trappings of a nouveau riche.

Strangely enough, the original Chinese title, which is "A Man And A Woman" is more apropos than, the gimmicky concept of repeating the name of the city twice, as in New York, New York.

Hong Kong is shown as a vital, progressive and fast moving city. It is both exotic and modern,

highly competitive and demanding, seductive as well as sinister, habit forming like heroin. It provides energy but at the same time saps life's energies from its people.

In "Hong Kong, Hong Kong," Cherrie Chung is a well-intentioned woman from China who craves for bourgeoisie and a materialistic life, while her lover, Alex Man, is a man's man who wants both fame as a boxer and the money that comes with the prestigious champion title. Chung, for survival and to obtain the much revered Hong Kong identity card, consents to give a child to an aging carpenter, a homely bachelor known as Uncle Kwai. In exchange, she gets free board, lodging and a small fee for her services after the delivery of the baby.

Unlike the pessimistic, long-winded films from the third world countries, the characters here face their problems with solutions. They solve them with head on practicality and realism, instead of the typical holier-than-thou attitude and excessive melodrama. The principle here is not to question how it's done to survive but the positive end result that satisfies. And through a love story, the social problems currently facing Hong Kong are dramatized in fiction form.

The streamlined pacing is in keeping with the frenetic life in Hong Kong. This mood is expressed in an intimate lovemaking sequence in a park above a highway active with non-stop traffic.

Lead feminine star Chung, an actress with limited emotional projection, finally graduates from her ingenue roles into a "bold" actress of stature. She gets a chance to project a series of emotions but sadly bereft of facial expressions with depth.

Clifford Choi is a filmmaker who shows great promise as a director, if given a strong screenplay that can seriously go all the way. He can be intellectually and emotionally competent if provided the chance to get to the core of the subject, without the compromises of commercial cinema as can be seen in this ambitious project.

This modest Shaw Brothers modern social drama maintains a high level of conviction and aspiration. It clearly shows the upgrading quality process currently undergoing in that once staid film factory. Responsible for the right changes and new course is Mona Fong, the right-hand lady of Run Run Shaw. —*Mel.*

Mohana
(Confluence)
(BANGLADESH-COLOR)

Moscow, July 14.

An Alamgir Kabir and Joyasree Kabir Film Production. Features entire cast. Written and directed by Alamgir Kabir. Only credits available. Reviewed at Moscow Film Fest (Information Show), July 14, '83. Running time: **108 MINS.**
Cast: Joyasree Kabir, Bulbul Ahmed, Ahmed Sharif.

Alamgir Kabir's "Confluence" is about the social problems confronting Bangladesh today. Set in the rural districts, it's a tale of young doctors trying to educate and assist the poorer classes by establishing a village medical center.

The opposition of a rich landowner brings about a dramatic conflict, the doctors succeeding to some degree in the end by winning the confidence of the villagers. Production credits leave a lot to be desired. —*Holl.*

Ett Berg Pa Manen's Baksida
(A Hill On The Dark Side Of The Moon)
(SWEDISH-COLOR)

Copenhagen, Aug. 14.

A MovieMakers production with The Swedish Film Institute, Swedish TV-SVT 1, Sandrews, Film Institute release. Directed by Lennart Hjulstroem. Director, Agneta Pleijel; camera (Eastmancolor) Sten Holmberg, Rolf Lindstroem; production design, Stig Boquist; editor, Lasse Lundberg; music, Lars-Erik Brossner; executive producer, Bert Sundberg; production manager, Gustav Wiklund. Reviewed at the Delta Bio, Copenhagen, Aug. 14, 1983. Running time: **94 MINS.**
Sonya Kovalevsky . . . . Gunilla Nyroos
Maxim Kovalevsky . . . . . Thommy Berggren
Foufa . . . . Lina Pleijel
Ann-Charlotte Leffler . . . . . . Bibi Andersson

Attaining the highest of intellectual achievements along with total happiness in love would surely rate anybody to have "A Hill On The Dark Side Of The Moon" named for her or him.

Sonya Kovalevsky was a woman who would settle for nothing less. It seems that she was born in the wrong century. She lived as a Russian university professor of mathematics in Sweden from 1883 until her death in 1891, and had a young daughter through an unhappy Russian marriage and an intense love affair, a battle of wills, with Maxim Kovalsky, also a Russian but no relation.

Writer Agneta Pleijel has lifted her from history and helped director Lennart Hjulstroem put her into a feature film that displays much muted drama amidst its self-imposed limits of a conversation piece. Film also has handsome production values (mostly interiors, but there is never any sense of stage suffocation) and beautifully honed performances by gaunt-faced Gunilla Nyroos and softer-looking Thommy Berggren.

Sonya's love for Maxim is hardly unrequited, but he is the intellectual who shies away from the heated words and declarations of love. She alternates between fits of jealousy and despondency, and the

gauntness of her visage is only illuminated into beauty in moments where her love is so fulfilled that she actually does not know where to go from there. Maxim sees to it — by stubbornly insisting on their either co-existing as separate individuals or splitting up — that she ultimately has no other choice: no moon hill will be named for her since "love as entry into a cathedral" is beyond her.

Fortunately, feminist topicality is rarely allowed to attain the shrill ring of polemics in Pleijel and Hjulstroem's slow but fluent movements of their set-pieces. It could be argued that extravagant demands such as Sonya's could hardly be met even in a more enlightened century that the nineteenth. Film has an incidental plot of Sonya's best friend, a novelist (Bibi Andersson) basking in physical beauty and a freedom attained through the spurning of an unloved husband, while Sonya's child Foufa remains a rather sad but brave shadow in the background of a mother who is, after all, self-centered to the point of cruelty, even to herself.

Although the director is a man, "A Hill On The Dark Side Of The Moon" would serve well in feminist film slots on the festival circuit or even in more specialized theatrical situations. Tv-programming, again specialized, should be obtainable everywhere.—*Kell.*

Locarno Festival

L'Allegement
(SWISS-B&W)

Locarno, Aug. 13.

A Cactus Films Presentation of A Film & Video Collectif/Film & Video Productions/SSR Production. Produced by Gerard Reuy and Miguel Stucky. Features entire cast. Directed by Marcel Schuepbach. Screenplay, Marcel Schuepbach and Yves Yersin based on a story by Jean-Pierre Monnier; camera (black and white), Hughes Ryffel; edited by Elisabeth Waelchli; music by Michel Hostettler; sound: Laurent Barbey. Reviewed at the Morettina Center, Locarno, Aug. 12, 1983. Running time: **80 MINS.**
Rose-Helene . . . . Anne Caudry
Grandmother . . . . Anne-Marie Blanc
Valentin . . . . Serge Avedikian
Diego . . . . Hanns Zischler

The black and white photography in this Swiss entry at the Locarno competition is probably the best thing about it, for almost every frame could be lifted out and exhibited on its own, for its esthetic values.

Sadly, this is all this film has going for it. The surrealist treatment, the subject matter and the overused symbolic language have all been put to better use in the past, and quite often, too.

An old woman tries to understand the reasons that drove her granddaughter, a nurse, away from her country home. While doing so she perceives the similarities between the young woman and her own mother, who went mad and died on her lover's grave.

The young girl is restless from the first moment because she experiences an urge for terrible passion that she cannot find in her home surroundings, and it is this urge, a romantic notion that is particularly meaningful in a country known for its staid nature, that finally draws her away into the white, snowy wilderness.

Schuepbach, who uses a novel as his starting point but avoids the plot and prefers to create a climate rather than a definite story, displays a whole set of cinematic images that have grown tired from so much use: tree trunks as phallic symbols, groomed stallions for eroticism, mirrors to move from one world to another, and for anyone who still has not grasped the message, the girl writes in her diary: "There is a fire in me that I can't grasp."

To make sure there is no trace of realism in his film, Schuepbach has concocted his entire soundtrack in the studio. The music does its best to alert the audience to the important significance of the images through its intricate complexities, and the set avoids establishing any definite period for the story, to infuse a kind of eternal value to its contents.

While there is no doubt that everything was carefully planned and executed, the film overstates its case and will have a hard time finding a receptive audience outside the strict circuit of the cineclubs on the lookout for new names. — *Edna.*

Killer Aus Florida
(Killer From Florida)
(SWISS-COLOR-16m)

Locarno, Aug. 14.

A Xanadu Film AG Production. Produced by George Reinhart. Stars Bruno Ganz. Written and directed by Klaus Schaffhauser; camera (color, 16m), Lukas Strebel; edited by Fredi M. Murer; sound, Felix Singer; music, Rossini. Reviewed at the Morettina Center, Locarno, Aug. 13, 1983. Running time: **50 MINS.**

Cast: Bruno Ganz, Renate Schroeter.

This offbeat item should have found its way into the fest's tv movies section, which it fits eminently, both in its conception and its running time.

Inspired by an interview given to the French daily Le Monde by a professional killer, the script narrowly follows a gunman who flies into Zurich to fulfill a contract. While the plot is fictitious, the style is rigorously documentary, and the action is divided into days.

The camera sticks to the protagonist, as he changes identities, switches rented cars, moves from one hotel to another, shadows his

victim, zeroes in carefully and acts only when the right moment comes along. All with the cool, detached approach of a professional, enhanced by his sober clothes, remote attitude and controlled behavior. Except for the gun he totes, he looks just like any respectable bank executive.

Slow, deliberate and sometimes agonizingly dwelling on details to stress the drab and unspectacular side of this job, the film is better enjoyed in retrospect, once its message has been transmitted, for the story itself avoids on purpose any excitement which might give the film a flashy look.

The camera settings are unobtrusive, inviting the audience to consider the activity in a detached way, and the soundtrack consists of everyday street noises, two voices reading the interview as if there was nothing more normal than a killer imparting his professional secrets to a journalist, and here and there, mocking Rossini music, to counterpoint the sinister endeavour of the killer.

This is Schaffhauser's first attempt at a tv-length movie, and while both length and downbeat approach may not help theatrical distribution, this could find its slot in special tv programming, and indicates an author of promise.
— *Edna.*

La Java Des Ombres
(Shadow Dance)
(FRENCH-COLOR)

Locarno, Aug. 13.

A Marin Karmitz MK2 Production. Written and directed by Romain Goupil. Features entire cast, Camera (color): Renan Poles, Richard Andry, Olivier Petitjean; editor, Helene Viard, I. Devinck; music by Gabriel Yared. Reviewed at the Morettina Center, Locarno, August 11, 1983. Running time: **90 MINS.**

Cast: Tcheky Karyo, Franci Camus, Anne Alvaro, Jean-Pierre Aumont.

Romain Goupil showed great promise with his first feature film, "Mourir A 30 Ans" (To Die at 30), a combination of fiction and documentary about the lost generation of the 1968 student uprising in Paris. Now with his fully fictionalized sequel, about the same generation 15 years later, Goupil slips into the easy mold of a militant director whose films may be in color, but who sees reality strictly in black and white.

Presented as a political thriller, his new venture attempts to show what happens to one of the old-time dissidents who is released now from prison (by the security authorities) knowing that he will immediately set on a track of revenge to kill one of the right-wing extremists who has hit him and his friends in the past and put the law on his tracks.

As plot unfolds it turns out that even the security is too weak to measure up to the fascists, who have infiltrated the police as well, and the downbeat end is intended to prove there is no hope of democracy in France, and all dissidents are exterminated before they get a chance to do anything.

His mind set on proving this premeditated political thesis, Goupil succumbs to all the pitfalls of militant films. All good leftists who refuse to conform are slightly disheveled, their eyes tired, but their minds determined. All the fascists look like androids escaped from "Blade Runner," expressionless faces of teleguided killers. The security forces (not to be mistaken for the police, who in this case are villains) are made up of weak-minded masterminds, who haven't seen sufficient thrillers to know what is in store for them. And the plot is manipulated to such an extent that it becomes simply ludicrous.

On top of it all, there are obvious pretenses here at poetry, the characters moving suddenly from naturalistic dialog and acting, to strange-sounding declamatory phrases and camerawork here and there trying to recapture the journalistic touch of Goupil's previous opus. And whenever the dramatic emphasis seems to dwindle a little, in comes the music to add some impact.

Goupil pledged in Locarno to go on with a third and final sequel to this trilogy about the '68 generation, which is his own. After those who were destroyed on the spot (the first part), those who drifted into terrorism (the second part), he says the third will be about the dropouts, those who escaped into suicide and drugs. One can only hope that the image he will elicit in the future will be more balanced, and consequently, more interesting than his present offering.
— *Edna.*

Paesaggio Con Figure
(Landscape With Figures)
(ITALIAN-B&W)

Locarno, Aug. 13.

A Bilicofilm/Iceberg Film Production. Directed by Silvio Soldini. Features entire cast Screenplay, Soldini, Luca Bigazzi, Anni Amati, Carlo Bella with dialogs by Soldini; camera (black and white), Luca Bigazzi; edited by Michele Bonelli; music by Matteo di Guida. Reviewed at the Morettina Center, Locarno, Aug. 13, 1983. Running time: **80 MINS.**

Cast: Anni Amati, Carla Chiarelli, Vanni Corbellini, Mario Sala.

A shoestring production made by a group of Milanese enthusiasts, headed by a 25-year-old director fresh out of NYU, htis is a pretentious hodgepodge of avant-garde ideas that have been used many

times before, but are presented here with all the earnestness of a discovery.

Most of the film consists of a car driving at night through fog and smog, a (sort of tribute to Wim Wenders' "road movies") or men walking, preferably showing only their feet. There are references which should remind audiences of Luis Bunuel and his eye impediment in the last years of his life; a character bears the name of Zazie, possibly in honor of Louis Malle, and Milano by night should hopefully recall Jean-Luc Godard's "Alphaville" atmosphere.

The dialog fools around with the significance of language, hints that people talk always to themselves, never to other people. There are lateral travelings, black frames and more such stylistical preciosities, all probably intended as tributes. But all this does not lead anywhere, and the only explanation is that young filmmakers often take the means to an end to be the end itself.

Even if there is a certain logic in choosing black and white or exaggerating the grain in the blowup from 16m to 35m, and the directsound is intended to give an authentic aural image, after the first few minutes, one doesn't care what it all means. — *Edna.*

Rodnik
(The Spring)
(SOVIET-COLOR)

Locarno, Aug. 14.

A Mosfilm Production, Moscow; world rights, Goskino, Moscow. Features entire cast. Directed by Arkadi Sirenko. Screenplay Vladimir Lobanov, based on a story by E. Nossov; camera (color), Elishar Karavaev; only credits available. Reviewed at Locarno Film Festival (Competition), August 11, '83 Running time: **90 MINS.**

Cast: Vladimir Gostyukin, Valentina Fedotova, Ivan Lapikov, Eduard Bocharov.

Arkadi Sirenko's debut feature, "The Spring," followed on the heels of his prizewinning short "Veterans" at the Cracow fest in 1979. Pic was lensed in 1981, and is based on a story by E. Nossov set at the dawn of World War II. Helmer Sirenko described "The Spring" at Locarno as being an antiwar film, although a more proper designation would by idyllic patriotism.

Scene is a typical Russian village at harvest time in 1941. The idyllic countryside, lensed in lovely late-autumn hues of browns-and-yellows, speaks of peace and tranquility, of a life undisturbed by outside forces or the presence of evil in the world. A family is singled out for observation: a father with a modest farm and family — pregnant wife, a tableful of kids, and an elderly mother. During the harvesting, which involves the entire village, a man on horseback arrives with news of the German invasion. Later, a "greetings" letter from the government arrives each able-bodied man in the village is to be drafted. In the end, the rollcall is taken by a recruiter sent to the district, and the elders, wives, and children of the village watch as the men march off to war.

"The Spring" scores as a still-life portrait of a Russian village at harvesting time, the action anchored to the earth by a stationary camera groomed only for the questionable esthetic of wide-angle zoom-shots. — *Holl.*

Der Rechte Weg
(The Right Way)
(SWISS-COLOR-16m)

Locarno, Aug. 14.
A T&C Film Production, Zurich. Features entire cast. Written and directed by Peter Fischli and David Weiss. Camera (color), Pio Corradi; music, Stephan Wittwer; editing, Rainer Trinkler. Reviewed at Locarno Film Festival (Critics' Section), Aug. 12, 1983. Running time: **55 MINS.**
Cast: Peter Fischli, David Weiss (voices of Alfred Pfeifer, Ingold Wildenauer).

The sequel to Peter Fischli and David Weiss's debut pic, "The Slightest Resistance" (1981), also written-directed-produced-interpreted by the duo, "The Right Way" finds them again in their oversized "bear" and "rat" costumes wandering through the Swiss countryside on another observation-and-conversation lark. The filmmakers' tic of relying entirely on verbal puns and in-jokes on Swiss life and the wonders of nature leaves little room for a festival audience to cue in on their sense of humor and point-of-view.

Both the "rat" and the "bear" (our directors in costume) approach nature as a phenomenon new to their experience — good for a few laughs when ecology cares are underscored, but tiring and repetitive in the long run. — *Holl.*

System Ohne Schatten
(System Without Shadow)
(WEST GERMAN-COLOR)

Locarno, Aug. 14.
A Moana Film, Berlin, and Anthea Film, Munich, coproduction; producers, Rudolf Thome, Hans Brockmann; world rights, Munic Films, Munich Features entire cast. Directed by Rudolf Thome. Screenplay, Jochen Brunow; camera (color), Martin Schaefer; art direction, Michael Wetterling; music, Laurie Anderson (singing "Closed Circuit"), Dollar Brand, Die Wikinger (Zurich); editing, Ursula West; sound, Detlev Fichtner, Uwe Griem; costumes, Barbara Baum. Reviewed at Locarno Film Fest (Competition), August 13, '83. Runing time: **119 MINS.**
Cast: Bruno Ganz (Faber), Dominique Laffin (Juliet), Hanns Zischler (Melo), Sylvie Kekule (Renate), Joachim Grigo (Agostini), Halbe Jelinek (Cordano), Konstantin Papanastasiou (Nino), Mikro Rilling (First Musician).

Rudolf Thome's "System Without Shadow" marks nearly 20

years in the helmer's career since he began making shorts in 1964; over that stretch, he has made a dozen features while dipping from time to time into documentaries and experimental personal statements. Among his early features were German-style thrillers — "Detective" (1968), "Red Sun" (1969) — and a critical breakthrough on home ground was recently achieved with "Berlin Chamissoplatz" (1980), a film on house squatters in the Kreuzberg section of the city.

"System Without Shadow" is another Berlin portrait. It's the story of a computer-expert who figures out a way to cheat a bank by the simple process of tinkering with its computerized accounts-system. The idea is supported by a new girlfriend, a French stage actress now weary of her profession, and a chance acquaintance at a reception for an art exhibit, a drug dealer and all around "fixer" with a yen for big money.

Like breaking-the-bank at a casino, the trio decide to open an account in Switzerland and attempt a computerized switchover of funds via a foolproof ruse: the trick is to find a way to manipulate, unnoticed, the computer system at the Berliner Discount Bank.

Now comes the twist right out of "Rififi" and "The Lavendar Hill Mob": gangsters have to be brought into the picture. A break-in has to be engineered at the bank, whereby the computer-expert, Victor Faber, can tamper with the system, and thereby effect a minor breakdown. Thus, it is hoped, the computer firm will be telephoned for the necessary repairs, and Faber can program, quite neatly, the transfer of millions to his own account in a Zurich bank (registered under a false passport).

The trio have only to get to Zurich within a few days, remove the money from the account in a cash on the barrelhead transfer, and then hightail it to a distant retreat somewhere in the world to enjoy the booty.

The "system without shadow" has its hitch, however. During the bank break-in with professional gangsters, a guard is killed by a quirk of fate: he happens by when he's not supposed to. Faber is now involved in an unwanted killing, and the killers decide to blackmail him for a larger payoff than originally agreed upon. However, the repairs on the bank's computer are required as predicted — and the transfer to the Zurich account works like magic. Off the trio goes to pick up the bundle. The rest is a surprise twist at the end of the tale.

Pic needs tightening to score as an art house thriller. Indeed, the idea is better than the thematic realization: leisurely direction and lame dialog mark the whole, par-

ticularly when the plot finally gets moving in the right direction.

Lensing is a strong plus: that and the subtle one-upmanship among the three thesps (Bruno Ganz, Dominique Laffin, Hanns Zischler) at improvised intervals. In one scene, for instance, Ganz and Laffin go to a movie in Zurich at the Nord-Sued arthouse — to see Laffin herself in Jacques Doillon's "La Femme Qui Pleure" (1978). It's a pretty good movie, says Ganz later to Zischler. To say the same about "System Without Shadow" is, unfortunately, not possible in its present state of uncut festival largesse.
— *Holl.*

Alexandre
(SWISS-COLOR)

Locarno, Aug. 7.
A Hatari Film Distribution of a Jean-Francois Amiguet/Film & Video Collectif/ Television Suisse Romande Production. Features entire cast. Directed by Jean-Francois Amiguet, Anne Gonthier. Screenplay, Jean-Francois Amiguet, Anne Gonthier, Gerard Ruey; camera (color), Rainer Klausmann; editor, Daniela Roderer; sound, Luc Yersin; music, Gaspard Glaus. Reviewed at the Morettina Center, Locarno, Aug. 7, 1983. Running time: **82 MINS.**
Cast: Didier Sauvegrain, Michel Voita, James Mason.

This is a typical Swiss film, doting on all the themes that have preoccupied this national cinema in the last 10 years, without bringing any really new dimension to them. There is solitude and lack of purpose in life, non-communication and fear of making decisions, a certain lyricism evolving from the scenery itself (the surroundings of Vevey) but also a certain kind of stilted inner monologs, or pretentious games and poses leading to another image futility, insufficiently sustained by the plot.

A substitute teacher, jilted three years before by a girl, decides to look for her again, but all he finds is another man who had been subjected to the same treatment. The two strike up an uneasy sort of relationship which grows closer, through their common search after the missing girl, but which comes to an end once she turns up.

Featured in a brief guest part, James Mason plays the father, probably a symbol of the financial security of the older generation which doesn't have much of a meaning for the new one.

Out of it all emerges once again the picture of emotional immobility accompanied by physical restlessness and a capitulation before the mysteries of human nature, which shouldn't be analyzed or gone into any depth. Needless to say, it is a legitimate opinion, but it has been said before and

better, for even incommunicability has to be communicated to the audience, in order to make real sense.— *Edna.*

Moscow Film Festival

Al-Infigar
(Explosion)
(LEBANESE-COLOR)

Moscow, July 11.
An Aifif Mudallal Film Production, Beirut. Features entire cast. Written and directed by Rafic Hajjar. Only credits available. Reviewed at Moscow Film Fest (Information Section), July 11, '83. Running time: **113 MINS.**
Cast: Abdul Majid Magzub, Madeleine Tabbar Churi, Ahmed Zein.

Rafic Hajjar is a young Lebanese director with a number of politically-oriented docus on the Middle East question to his credit. He had also treated the problems of the country's illiterates, as well as the emancipation of women in Arab lands. His first feature, "The Fugitive," was unspooled at the 1981 Moscow fest; that film dealt with the Civil War in Lebanon of 1975-76. Now he's back with his second feature, "Explosion."

"Explosion" is again set in 1975, on the eve of the Civil War. It concerns a couple from separate religious backgrounds, the girl a Christian and the boy a Muslim, whose love relationship is ill-fated from the outset. Because their family, relatives, and friends belong to opposing warring groups, pro and anti Palestinian, there is little they themselves can do to resolve the issue in their own lives. The "explosion" is imminent, and the boy is killed.

Pic has a human dimension not often seen in Arab cinema dealing with the PLO Question. The Romeo and Juliet context hints that much of the animosity surrounding the couple is alien to life, living, and peaceful coexistence. Credits are a cut above the average in contemporary Arab cinema. — *Holl.*

Hiver '60
(Winter, 1960)
(BELGIAN-COLOR)

Moscow, July 23.
A Les Films d'Hiver Film Production, Bruxelles, Thierry Coene, in coproduction with RTBF, Liege. Features entire cast. Directed by Thierry Michel. Screenplay, Jean-Louis Comolli, Jean Louvet, Thierry Michel, Christine Pireaux; camera (color), Walther Vanden Eede; sets, Francoise Hardy; music, Marc Herouet; sound, Ricardo Castro, Miguel Rejas; editing, Fernando Cabrita. Reviewed at Moscow Film Fest (Competition), July 16, '83. Running time: **90 MINS.**
Cast: Philippe Leotard, Christian Barbier, Francoise Bette, Ronny Coutteure, Paul Louka, Marcel Dossogne, Alain Soreil, Jenny Cleve, Jean Louvet.

Thierry Michel's "Winter, 1960" leans heavily on previously shot docu footage, supplied for this feature by Frans Buyens (released in 1960-61 under the title "Fighting for Our Rights"). That was the winter of a general strike that paralyzed the country for five weeks: it began in December 1960 and continued until the end of the following January. The occasion for the strike was the proposal of the Loi Unique, an emergency law provoked not only by clashes between the Flemish and Walloon factions in the country, but also labor unrest in the Belgian coal mines and the riots in the Belgium Congo of the preceding years. Economic and social reforms were necessary, and it wasn't until 1965 that the country made provisions for a dual-language constitutional amendment.

The semi-documentary "Winter, 1960" offers some remarkable scenes of the bloody general strike from the available archival footage. This is blended into a story of key people involved in the strike movement, two of them a young couple who find each other during the melee, have a brief affair, and then suffer the tragic consequences.

Pic should appear to special auds with a yen for historical chronicles and portraits of labor movements. Credits are topnotch.
—*Holl.*

Paweogo
(The Emigrant)
(UPPER VOLTA-COLOR)

Moscow, July 16.
A CINAFRIG Film Production, Upper Volta. Features entire cast. Written and directed by Sanou Kollo. Only credits available. Reviewed at Moscow Film Fest (Information Section), July 16, '83. Running time: **80 MINS.**
Cast: Bila Ouedraogo, Marie-Claire Coeffe, Jules Tassembedo.

Sanou Kollo's "The Emigrant" deals with the eternal problem of a rural community adjusting to industrial change. The "emigration" is from a village to a city, the problem is unemployment, and the main role features a young man breaking with obsolete traditions to seek a new life. The twist in this case is that "civilization" does not offer much more, if anything, than the emigrant has already left behind.

The second conflict in the film has to do with caste prejudice: a situation develops in which the young man cannot marry due to ancient customs and tribal laws. Neither this problem, nor that of employment, is fully resolved in the film, much to the director's credit.

Upper Volta, whose capital is Ouagadougou, recently hosted the African Film Festival. This part of Africa maintains ties to France; thus Upper Volta tends to compare well with Senegal and Mali as a leading film production land. "The Emigrant" proved to be the Moscow fest's representative Black African film this year, and not a bad one at that. —*Holl.*

Kirik Bir Ask Hikayesi
(A Broken-Hearted Love Story)
(TURKISH-COLOR)

Moscow, July 23.
An Alfa Film Production. Omer Kavur and Necip Saricioglu, producers. Features entire cast. Directed by Ömer Kavur. Screenplay, Selim Ileri, Kavur; camera (color), Salih Dikisci; music, Cahit Berkay. Reviewed at Moscow Film Fest (Information Section), July 18, '83. Running time: **98 MINS.**
Cast: Kadir Inanir, Humeyra, Halil Ergun, Mamuran Usluer, Guler Okten, Neriman Koksal, Ozlem Onursal.

A newcomer of the Turkish film scene, helmer Omer Kavur scored a critical success with his first film, "Emine." Thereafter, he made a prizewinning children's film, "Yusuf and Kenan," followed by a human drama pic about a truckdriver in love with a prostitute, "O, Lovely Istanbul." Kavur's latest, "A Broken-Hearted Love Story," deals with mores in the provinces, and it doesn't fail to impress within the framework of a melodrama.

A literature teacher is assigned to replace a retired colleague in a provincial town on the seacoast. Her presence, however, stirs a community molded by traditional ways, enough to set people against her. The woman from Istanbul is a bit too progressive, both for the school and the community as a whole. Pic describes her ordeal as the quiet, dignified woman fends off the constant disfavor her presence causes.

Credits are a cut above average for Turkish cinema. —*Holl.*

A Hot Summer In Kabul
(SOVIET-AFGHANISTAN-COLOR)

Moscow, July 23.
A Mosfilm (Moscow) and Afghanfilm (Afghanistan) coproduction. Features entire cast. Directed by Ali Khamrayev. Screenplay, Vadim Trunin, Asadulla Habib; camera (color), Yuri Klimenko; art direction, Chavkat Abdussalamov; music, Eduard Artemiev. Reviewed at Moscow Film Fest (Information Section), July 19, '83. Running time: 90 MINS.
Cast: Oleg Yakov, Nikolai Olialin, Gulboston Tachbaeva, Djamal Moniava, Matlyuba Alimova.

Any way you look at it, the presence of Ali Khamrayev's "A Hot Summer in Kabul," an Afghan-Soviet coproduction, in the official program of the Moscow fest treads on the goodwill of many international guests, even though it's only categorized under the Information Section. The tenor of the film is more Soviet than Afghan (theme, direction, production staff), and there is no certified proof that the film was entirely lensed in Afghanistan (particularly the war sequences).

Helmer Ali Khamrayev works generally out of the Uzbekistan studios in Tashkent. His string of actioners often treated the revolution in Central Asia, one of quite remarkable in demonstrating guerrilla warfare in the 1920s. "The Bodyguard" was lensed in Tadzhikistan, just over the border from Afghanistan.

This is the story of a surgeon from Moscow coming to Kabul to work in a hospital for a long, hot, conflict-ridden summer. The war continues in the streets as well as in the mountains, and on one occasion the rebels attack a military transport and down the helicopter carrying the physician. He is rescued in the nick of time.

A deft mix of humanism and propaganda, the striking aspect is Yuri Klimenko's lensing. —*Holl.*

Intoarcerea Din Iad
(Return from Hell)
(RUMANIAN-COLOR)

Moscow, July 23.
A Rumanian Film Production, "Three" Film Unit, Bucharest; world rights, Rumania Film, Bucharest. Features entire cast. Written and directed by Nicolae Margineanu, based on Ion Agirbiceanu's short story "The Policeman." Camera (color), Vlad Paunescu; art direction, Radu Corciova; costumes, Desdemona Lozinschi; music, Cornel Taranu; editing, Cristina Ionescu. Reviewed at Moscow Film Fest (Competition), July 15, '83. Running time: **93 MINS.**
Cast: Constantin Branzea, Remus Margineanu, Maria Ploae, Ana Ciontea, Ion Sasaran, Lucia Mara.

Nicolae Margineanu progressed from cameraman to director, one of his best jobs as lenser being Dan Pita's "A Summer Tale" (1976). He then collaborated with Pita as codirector on "This Above All" (1978), followed by his solo debut on "The Painter" (unspooled at the 1982 Karlovy Vary fest). Now he's in Moscow with "Return from Hell," based on a short story by Ion Agirbiceanu.

This passionate tale of forbidden love and loyal comradeship during the First World War has its heavy melodramatic moments, but in general it holds together as a human portrait of wartime misery. A former country constable inherits the family fortune and comes back to the village of his youth — only to find that the girlfriend of his youth has meanwhile married an honest peasant. The protagonist marries another, but can't forget his first love, and they enter upon a forbidden love affair.

Then comes the war, and the two rivals for the same girl go to the front. There the peasant saves the life of the rival, eventually sacrificing his life for the man who has stolen the heart of his wife. When the lone survivor returns home from the war, he cannot forget his friend's sacrifice, nor his own moral turpitude of the past and he goes mad.

Lensing is pic's top credit, particularly war sequences. —*Holl.*

Das Haus Im Park
(The House in the Park)
(WEST GERMAN-COLOR)

Moscow, July 23.
An Ottokar Runze Film Production, Berlin. Features entire cast. Directed by Aribert Weis. Screenplay, Regine Heuser, Jochen Brunow; Weis; set, Goetz Heymann; editing Regine Heuser; sound, Detlef Fichtner; music, Wilhelm Dieter Siebert; production manager, Michael Beier. Reviewed at Moscow Film Fest (Information Section), July 14, '83. Running time: **103 MINS.**
Cast: Wilfried Labmeier, Ulrich Pleitgen, Renate Heuser, Christine Pascal.

Listed in the Moscow fest catalogue under West Berlin, Aribert Weis's "The House in the Park" scores in non-Socialist lands as a West German production. This is Weis's first feature film, and working as a cameraman for Rosa von Praunheim and other Teutonic helmers over the past decade.

"The House in the Park" is conventional thriller pap. A young bankrobber stumbles on another source of quick money by stealing a Mercedes that turns out to have a corpse in the trunk. By tracing the car to the owner, a rich industrialist, our hero Andi figures to move into the culprit's luxurious villa as the blackmailing know-it-all. The rest is in the vein of a politthriller with a psychological twist, too much for a story line that is thin to begin with. —*Holl.*

Kieselsteine
(Little Stones)
(AUSTRIAN-COLOR)

Moscow, July 9.
A Satel Film, Vienna, Production. Features entire cast. Directed by Lukas Stepanik. Screenplay, Nadja Seelich; camera (color), Bernd Neuburger; sets, Ernst Wurzer; production manager, Walter Maitz. Reviewed at Moscow Film Fest (Competition), July 9, '83. Running Time: **102 MINS.**

Lukas Stepanik's "Little Stones" is one of those films that covers all its bets in a padded script, so that all the viewer has to do is sit back and either nod or shake his head as one cliche after another is heavily handled on the Jewish Question. Regrettably a bloodless film, it might have been a convincing one nonetheless in an entirely different stylistic context.

Hanna, a young Austrian Jew, cannot forget the Holocaust, even though she is not socially or politically engaged and doesn't share strong religious convictions on the matter. She lives with a non-Jew and has a satisfying editorial job on a magazine. Friedrich, whose father was a Nazi doctor, pursues Hanna from afar, believing that his German origin destines him to have an affair with the Jewish girl.

Throughout the film, they meet each other regularly in circumstances that always bring up the past. Even though Friedrich's proud stuffiness is unbearable for Hanna and her friends, she is interested to know what makes him tick. Her curiosity leads to rape in the end, all readily predictable in the course of the naively constructed dialog sequences.

"Little Stones" as a statement on a still potent issue in Middle Europe, particularly German-language countries, is a step backward rather than forward. Even Jewish Film Festivals will be troubled by the mired arguments of self pity and soul searching, although the filmmaker's heart is in the right place. —*Holl.*

Yunost Geniya
(The Youth of a Genius)
(SOVIET-COLOR)

Moscow, July 23.

An Uzbekfilm and Tadzhikfilm coproduction; world rights. Goskino, Moscow. Features entire cast. Directed by Elier Ishmukhamedov. Screenplay, Odelsha Agishev, Ishmukhamedov; camera (color), Tatyana Loginova; art direction, Emmanuel Kalantarov; music, Eduard Artemiev. Reviewed at Moscow Film Fest (Information Section), July 18, '83. Running time: **90 MINS.**

Cast: Bakhtier Zakirov, Ato Mukhamedzhanov, Rano Kubaev, Furkat Faiziev.

An Uzbek director, Elier Ishmukhamedov scored a number of critical successes early in his career — the short "Rendezvous" (1963), "Tenderness" (1966) and "In Love" (1969) — establishing himself together with scripter Odelsha Agishev and lenser Dilshat Fatkhullin (his colleagues at VGIK, the Moscow Film School). Next he made "Meetings And Partings" (1974) and "The Birds Of Our Hopes" (1977), and now "The Youth Of A Genius."

"The Youth Of A Genius" (scripted again by Agishev) covers the childhood of Avicenna (980-1037 A.D.), the great medieval philosopher and physician who lived in Persian Bukhara (near Tashkent in today's Uzbekistan Republic of the Soviet Union). Avicenna, or Abu Ali Ibn-Sina, lived in a Bukhara governed by the enlightened Samanid dynasty, which came to an abrupt end in the philosopher's youth. Ishmukhamedov's historical epic covers the glories of the ancient city in unfolding a conventional story of a young genius in touch with a flow of cultures, traditions, religions, and the like on one of the busiest trade routes of the time.

The outlay of costumes alone is impressive in this spectacle. There is an attention to detail that is rare in today's epics, for months were spent researching museums and libraries, as well as conferring with scholars of Oriental history, in preparation for the film. — *Holl.*

Yahalu Yeheli
(The Friends)
(SRI LANKA-COLOR)

Moscow, July 12.

A Mark Jayawardena and Roy Jayawardena Film Production. Features entire cast. Directed by Sumitra Peries. Screenplay, Karunasena Jayalath. Only credits available. Reviewed at Moscow Film Fest (Information Section), July 12, '83. Running time: **82 MINS.**

Cast: Tony Ranasingghe, Sanath Guantileka, Nadika Gunasekera.

Cinema in Sri Lanka has received a major boost by the recent recognition given to Lester James Peries, considered by several critics to be the equal of India's Satyajit Ray in hiw own right as a chronicler of life and society in Sri Lanka. Now his wife, Sumitra Peries, has tried her hand at directing: pic was selected for a slot in the Info Show at the Moscow fest.

"The Friends" deals with a relationship between a landowner and his neighboring poor tenants. The landowner is so greedy that he employs his henchmen to berate and exploit the poorer classes, particularly when he notes that his daughter has made friends with the undesirable neighbors. One night, the father of the boy is killed by the landowner, the crime leaving little doubt among the villagers as to the guilty party. Yet justice cannot be done in a social structure that gives all the rights to the rich. It's the girl who stands up to the truth in the end: she defies her father and family.

A rather conventional story unfolded in a slow monotonous rhythm. — *Holl.*

Fire And Ice
(ANIMATED-COLOR)

Frazetta's art says it all.

Hollywood, Aug. 17.

Twentieth Century-Fox release of a Producer Sales Organization presentation. Directed by Ralph Bakshi. Produced by Bakshi and Frank Frazetta. Screenplay, Roy Thomas, Gerry Conway. Characters created by Bakshi and Frazetta. Executive producers, John W. Hyde, Richard R. St. Johns. Animation camera, R&B EFX; music, William Kraft; editor, A. Davis Marshall; production supervisor, Scott Ira Thaler; animation supervisor, Michael Svayko; sound, Bill Varney, Steve Maslow, Gregg Landaker; layout, John Sparey, Michael Svayko; background pictures, James Gurney, Thomas Kincade. Reviewed at 20th Century-Fox, Aug. 17, 1983. (MPAA Rating: PG). Running time: **81 MINS.**

Voices:
Juliana	Susan Tyrrell
Teegra	Maggie Roswell
Larn	William Ostrander
Nekron	Stephen Mendel
Tutor	Clare Nono
Envoy	Alan Koss
Defender captain	Hans Howes
Subhumans	Ray Oliver, Nathan Purdee, Le Tari

Ralph Bakshi's newest animation feature is interesting for two special reasons: (1) the production represents a clear design on Bakshi's part to capture a wider and younger audience than any of his previous films, and (2) the animation marks the film debut of America's leading exponent of heroic fantasy art, Frank Frazetta, who coproduced with director Bakshi.

A 20th Century-Fox pickup from Producer Sales Organization, the feature moves cautiously into the marketplace this weekend, with selected openings. Both kids and a groundswell of older Frazetta and/or Bakshi cult followers could turn a profitable dollar for this latest wrinkle on the sword and scorcery genre. Abetting the film is William Kraft's symphonic score (in Dolby stereo), which enriches the primeval struggle in a world divided between good and evil characters inhabiting volcanic lands and advancing glaciers (i.e., "Fire and Ice.").

The film, Bakshi's seventh since his X-rated "Fritz the Cat" in 1972, is the first time Bakshi has sublimated his own control in a feature to accommodate another artist in his own right. Known for his classic comic book and poster art, Frazetta's works some of his famous illustrations into the film, such as his "Death Dealer" painting portraying an axe-wielding figure on horseback. Populating an Armageddon embellished with subhumans and flying dragonhawks are a blond hero, Larn, a sensuous-vulnerable dream girl in distress, Teegra, and an icy sorcerer and his willful mother, Lord Nekron and Juliana (Stephen Mendel and Susan Tyrrell).

Bakshi, as in his last two, and more ambitious films ("American Pop" and "Lord of the Rings"), shot live actors first, to lay the foundation for the animation, in a process called Rotoscope. Action sweeps among ice caverns, steep volcanic cliffs, and moody swamps. Fights are not balletic swordplay but of the hacking, tearing variety.

Bakshi and Frazetta create some nice illusions of depth, never to be taken for granted in animation. But curiously, in a technique that distracts, scenes frequently dissolve and cut through flashy optical wipes that have no place in such a picture.

Story, based on characters created by Bakshi and Frazetta, was written by pair of former Marvel Comics hands, Roy Thomas and Gerry Conway. In an effort to backoff former narrow band demographics, narrative is almost fairy-tale simplistic in its war between good and evil. Result represents quite a switch for Bakshi whose previous pics dealt with social criticism ("Heavy Traffic"), polemics ("Wizards" coincidentally also a Fox PG release), and racial controversy ("Coonskin"). —*Loyn.*

Getting It On
(COLOR)

Warm and winning teen comedy.

A Comworld Pictures release of a William Olsen Production. Executive producer, Michael Rothschild. Produced by Jan Thompson, William Olsen. Written and directed by Olsen. Features entire cast. Camera (TVC color), Austin McKinney; editor, Olsen; additional dialog, Timothy L. Bost, Barbara Dixon, Deborah Wakefield; music, Ricky Keller; sound, Bill Shaver, Michael Carton; production manager, Jan Thompson; art direction, James Eric. Reviewed at RKO National 1 theatre, N.Y., Aug. 21, 1983. (MPAA Rating: R). Running time: **96 MINS.**

Alex Carson	Martin Yost
Sally Clark	Heather Kennedy
Nicholas Byers	Jeff Edmond
Marilyn White	Kathy Brickmeier
Richard Byers	Mark Alan Ferri
Principal White	Charles King Bibby
Mrs. White	Sue Satoris
Mr. Carson	Terry Loughlin
Mrs. Carson	Caroline McDonald
Jenny	Kim Saunders
Chuck Sugar	Dan Thompson
Taxi driver	Bryan Elsom

Originally titled "American Voyeur" but released as "Getting it On," this North Carolina-lensed teenage comedy nimbly pumps new life into the overdone high school hijinks genre. Though marketed as another raunchy "Porky's" followup, the William Olsen production is a well-acted, sweet and funny picture.

Filmmaker Olsen targets our consumerist and video-obsessed culture for some ribbing in this story of high school freshman Alex Carson (Martin Yost), with a crush on the girl next door, Sally (Heather Kennedy). Devising a video software business to earn money, Alex borrows his startup capital (at 15% interest) from his very businesslike dad, and with the help of his cutup classmate Nicholas (Jeff Edmond) uses the video equipment to record hidden camera footage of Heather and other pretty girls. When Nicholas is kicked out of school by mean principal White (Charles King Bibby), the heroes enlist the services of a friendly prostitute (Kim Saunders) to record footage of White in flagrante delicto.

What makes this material work is a fresh, enthusiastic cast, witty writing and direction by Olsen that bears no hint of malice. Though Alex's parents are caricatures, more interested in getting the latest satellite dish installed in the backyard than in their son's future, they are drawn as ingratiating characters, and even the practical joke directed against the principal turns out to benefit everyone, with no hard feelings. The script even includes a subplot reminiscent of "Tex," concerning Nicholas and his older brother living without parental supervision.

Young, attractive cast members match the teenage role requirements, though the pleasant lead player Martin Yost, an empathetic Timothy Hutton type, is of course older than the virginal 14-year-old in the script. Of special note is Bryan Elsom, very funny in a small role as a loquacious young Southern cab driver.

Tech credits for this modestly-budgeted effort are fine.
— *Lor.*

The Golden Seal
(COLOR)

Boy loves seal. Boy loses seal. Adults foiled.

A Samuel Goldwyn Company production and release. Produced by Samuel Goldwyn. Directed by Frank Zuniga. Features entire cast. Screenplay, John Groves, based on James Vance Marshall novel, "A River Ran Out Of Eden;" camera (Metrocolor), Eric Saarinen; editor, Robert Q. Lovett; music, John Barry, Dana Kaproff; production design, Douglas Higgings; second unit director, Joe Canutt; sound, Larry Sutton; assistant director, Gordon Mark. Review in New York screening room, Aug. 22, 1983. (MPAA Rating: PG) Running time: **94 MINS.**

Jim Lee	Steve Railsback
Tania Lee	Penelope Milford
Crawford	Michael Beck
Eric	Torquil Campbell
Gladys	Sandra Seacat
Semeyon	Seth Sakai
Alexei	Richard Narita

For his first personal production since "Cotton Comes To Harlem" and "Come Back Charleston Blue," Samuel Goldwyn Jr. has turned to the "Wilderness family genre" with mixed results. Having a small boy befriend and defend a rare golden seal, ostensibly in the Aleutian Islands but actually made in British Columbia (plus a little second unit work), the slim story is only kept alive by the antics of the title character and the evil handiwork of almost all the grown-ups in the film.

Legend has a golden (actually it's a regular seal with a Clairol-type rinse) seal appear after several years and spends the rest of the film evading assorted hunters, all aiming for a bounty posted years before and, by now, amounting to quite a sum considering the accrued interest — sort of an unclaimed Money Market Account. The small son of one of the hunters finds the seal first, hides it and when the hunt gets hot, fights off the grown-ups, including his own father. Good will prevail and all the nasty adults finally agree that they'd best let such an endangered species go untouched.

Actually, the best performance is given by Michael Beck as a nasty type who only sees the seal as a valuable hide, followed closely by Canadian boy actor Torquin Campbell as the valorous lad (valorous because he has to jump into the icy waters for a romp with the seal that causes ice crystals to form in the audience). Most of the rest of the cast, including Steve Railsback and Penelope Milford as the parents and Seth Sakai and Richard Narita as a pair of Japanese-looking natives, tend to over-react.

Eric Saarinen's camerawork is first-rate with the seal scenes especially beautiful, but John Groves' script avoids plotlines too much to give the story much meaning. You never know why people in the film choose to live where they do or what causes the obvious tensions in their domestic lives.

Market for the film, based on its early release, has been in the same area as the "Wilderness Family" product which is, at best, limited.
— *Robe.*

El Desquite
(The Revenge)
(ARGENTINE-COLOR)

Buenos Aires, Aug. 23.

A Yasi release of an Arte 10 production. Produced and directed by Juan Carlos Desanzo. Stars Rodolfo Ranni. Screenplay, Ruben Tizziani, based upon his own novel; music, Baby Lopez Furst; executive producer, Maria Teresa Nieto. Reviewed at the Callao theatre, B.A., Aug. 4, 1983. Running time: **95 MINS.**

Cast: Rodolfo Ranni, Julio De Grazia, Silvia Montanari, Hector Bidonde, Ricardo Darin, Gerardo Sofovich, Gabriela Giardino, Lucrecia Capello, Jorge Sassi, Pablo Drichta.

Cinematographer turned director Juan Carlos Desanzo hit the jackpot with his opera prima thanks to a sudden liberalization of the hitherto tight Argentine film censorship, which seemingly looked the other way when the sequences of softcore sex and violence in this gory tale were unspooled for examination in its screening room (just a few days before the censors had banned a scene from Juan Jose Jusid's "Esperame Mucho" which seems rather innocent when compared with the heavier stuff of "El Desquite").

Desanzo's opus sold nearly 150,000 tickets in its first week at 32 theatres of metropolitan and suburban areas, favored by a strong word of mouth generated mainly by the amazement of viewers that could hardly believe what they had seen for the first time in a native pic since the heyday of actress Isabel Sarli in the early '60s. For the Argentine-cinema aficionados in the under-35 age group it was a complete novelty, since this kind of hot material had been allowed only in some offshore attractions during the recent months.

Yarn centers on the experiences of story editor and frustrated novelist Rodolfo Ranni after he meets childhood pal Gerardo Sofovich, now owner of a sophisticated discotheque and lover of sultry Gabriela Giardino. Sofovich is killed by some gangsters but before dying decides Ranni will be the heir of 51% of his estate, the remainder going to Giardino and his cronies Julio De Grazia and Ricardo Darin.

As soon as Ranni decides to keep Sofovich's business going the discotheque is attacked and smashed by the gangsters. One of them is identified, captured and savagely beaten on a dunghill by former boxer De Grazia. Under such pressure he reveals his boss is Hector Bidonde, apparently a rival of Sofovich in another field, drug peddling. Ranni & Co. attack and destroy a warehouse owned by Bidonde, who retaliates with an attempt to kidnap Ranni's family, which leads to accidental death of one of latter's daughters. Afterwards Ranni corners and shoots to death Bidonde and his henchmen. Another goon has been murdered earlier by De Grazia when he found him in bed with a gay partner.

Along these developments Ranni and Giardino have become lovers, first in a low-motion, dimly-lit nude scene in bed, then in a brightly lit encounter in a bathtub.

Story lacks motivations, convincing characters and other essentials of sound narrative, but it provides a thread for the shocking sequences shrewdly schemed to excite a strong response in the domestic market and foreign-lingo spots abroad. Thesps lend a professional coating to cardboard parts. Sexy, husky-voiced newcomer Gabriela Giardino could have a successful career. A very popular tv personality, producer-director-penner-emcee Gerardo Sofovich, does his big-screen debut in an ably played cameo.

Desanzo's craftmanship shines in the action sequences, which are neatly above local standards. Good camerawork, tight editing, contemporary music and well chosen locations are other pluses helping to give an updated look to this erratic but effective entertainment that seemingly opens the way for film permissiveness in gaucho-ville. — *Nubi.*

Planeta Krawiec
(The Planet "Tailor")
(POLISH-COLOR)

Locarno, Aug. 9.

A Film Polski Production, X Film Unit, Warsaw; world rights, Film Polski, Warsaw. Features entire cast. Directed by Jerzy Domaradzki. Screenplay, Wieslaw Saniewski, Andrzej Bianusz, Domaradzki; camera (color), Stanislaw Szymanski; music, Marek Wilczynski; sets, Teresa Smus; editor, Elzbieta Kurkowska; production manager, Tadeusz Drewno. Reviewed at Locarno Film Fest, Aug. 9, '83. Running time: **88 MINS.**

Cast: Kazimierz Koczor (Romanek), Slawomira Lozinska, Liliana Glabczynska, Wladyslaw Kowalski.

Helmer Jerzy Domaradzki, once an assistant director to Andrzej Wajda (on "Land of Promise") and one of the three debut helmers in the omnibus film "Test Shots" (1977), has made a career mostly in television. As a writer-director, his string of prods is impressive: "The Long Wedding Night" (1977), "White Harvest" (1978), "Laureat" (1980), "The Great Race" (1981), and now "The Planet 'Tailor'."

"The Planet Tailor" is based on a true story: Romanek in Domaradzki's film is, in actuality, one Adam Giedrys, a tailor who turned to sky-gazing as a hobby and avocation after being hospitalized for a serious illness. For the sake of a good script, the tale takes on metaphorical dimensions: instead of just being a comedy on an amateur astronomer causing a stir in his smalltown with the provincial authorities, one can read into it a record of recent sociopolitical mishaps in Poland.

Naturally enough, only a Pole could decipher all the nuances referring to the contemporary scene, so foreign auds are left with mostly assumptions of an amusing nature. In other words, what if the "tailor" Romanek stood for the electrician Walesa, then the "planet" might have something to do with an ethereal dream of newly-discovered independent unions!

In any case; in the 1950s, a village tailor drinking with his friends has an attack that puts him into a hospital emergency room — it's his damaged kidneys that nearly spell curtains. Given a reprieve on life, Romanek decides that he has somehow communicated with the distant stars while in a brief coma. He decides to give up tailoring altogether to commit his life to research — perhaps he could even discover a distant, unknown planet on the edge of the universe. A small telescope is not enough for his grand schemes, so he engages friends in the village to help him construct an observatory. Meanwhile, the children of the neighborhood flock around the new born scientist for lessons and instructions. Even the country authorities back him for a while.

Then comes the bitter awakening. Although our tailor makes the newspapers as an amateur scientist, his wife can't live with his obsessions anymore — so she packs up and leaves. And just about this time, the first Soviet sputnik goes up in the heavens — so Poland's chief ally is not too happy to find there's an unauthorized planet-gazer taking telescopic photographs of passing space phenomena. The town council calls on Romanek to abandon his plans.

Meanwhile, there's a astronomical convention being held in nearby Varna — and Romanek has been invited to attend. Off he goes with his lunch-basket and briefcase under his arm. He becomes the sensation of the conference — not however by talking on his planet Tailor, but by guessing the clothing measurements of delegates to the convention! Once back in Poland, the tailor realizes that his pipe-dream may be over — yet he still can't help staring out into space in quest of his vaunted planetarian discovery. Not bad — for an allegory. As an entertainment pic for arthouses, only so-so.

— *Holl.*

Pismo-Glava
(Heads Or Tails)
(YUGOSLAV-COLOR)

Pula, July 25.

A Sutjeska Film (Sarajevo) and Croatia Film (Zagreb) coproduction. Features entire cast. Directed by Bata Cengic. Screenplay, Miroslav Jancic, Nebojsa Pajkic, Cengic; camera (color), Karpo Godina Adamic, Zivko Zalar; art direction, Dragan S. Stefanovic; music, Bojan Adamic. Reviewed at Pula Film Fest, July 25, '83. Running time: **105 MINS.**
Cast: Mladen Nelevic, Mira Furlan, Zijah Sokolovic, Vladica Milosavljevic.

Bata Cengic's "Little Soldiers" (1968) unspooled at that disrupted Cannes fest as the official Yugoslav entry, thus introducing a prominent new talent from Sarajevo. The Bosnian director followed with two of the strongest films of the early 1970s: "My Family in the World Revolution" (1971) and "Scenes from the Life of a Shock Worker" (1972), both scripted by the able Branko Vucicevic and lensed by the talented Karpo Godina-Acimovic. As poli-

tical treatises, these two features were considered too hot for general release, so they were ultimately shelved — and Cengic along with them for more than a decade.

"Head or Tails" is Cengic's welcome-back film. It's mild stuff in comparison with his past record, but competent filmmaking within the limits of the genre; a youth film about unemployment, first love, moral character versus corruption and neglect, and the coming-of-age of a lad who is momentarily seduced by temptation about him. The scene is Sarajevo; a peasant recruit leaving military service decides to stay in the city and work on a construction job, where he falls in with both good and bad companions. By selling his deceased father's farm, he invests in a niteclub, only to see the errors of his ways in the end. Nicely etched character roles and a strong new thesp (Mladen Nelevic in the lead). Pic should surface abroad in Yugo Film Weeks.—*Holl.*

El Crack Dos
(The Crack, Part 2)
(SPANISH-COLOR)

Madrid, Aug. 18.

A Lola Films S.A. - Lima, S.A. - Nickelodeon S.A. production. Directed by Jose Luis Garci. Features entire cast. Exec producers, Francisco Hueva, Carlos Duran. Screenplay, J.L. Garci, Horacio Valcarcel; camera (Eastmancolor), Manuel Rojas; sets, Julio Esteban; editor, Miguel G. Sinde; music, Jesus Gluck. Reviewed at Cine Coliseum, Madrid, Aug. 18, '83. Running time: **116 MINS.**
German Areta . . . . Alfredo Landa
Carmen . . . . Naria Casanova
Cardenas . . . . Miguel Rellan
Don Ricardo . . . . Jose Bodalo
Don Miguel . . . . Rafael de Penagos
Don Gregorio . . . . Arturo Fernandez
Also: Manuel Lorenzo, Luis Maria Delgado, Agustin Gonzalez, Jose Luis Merino, Jose Manuel Cervino, Maite Marchante et al.

Jose Luis Garci, this year's Oscar winner for "To Begin Again," continues the adventures of his Madrid-based private eye, Areta, in the second part of "El Crack" which drew kudos from most critics and audiences here and abroad. Again the erstwhile funnyman Alfredo Landa becomes the steely-eyed, hard-as-nails dick whose quips and slang try to approximate that used in Raymond Chandler's stories (to whom film is dedicated).

But after a quick-paced start, reminiscent of that used in the first "El Crack," story slows down ponderously as Areta and Don Ricardo have innumerable tete a tetes and Garci indulges in magnificent but ultimately pointless mood shots of Madrid streets and skylines during the wee hours. Just as the yarn seems to build up into a bit of action, Garci pulls the plug and his hero flies off to a vacation in Italy.

Sitting in his shabby office in the old part of the Gran Via, Areta receives a client, supposedly for a fast job: it's to find the client's lover, who, after 20 years of domestic bliss, has flown the coop. The "lover" is another gay. Areta tracks him down fast enough, but just as he thinks he's wrapped the case, police pick up the private eye and tell him both his client and the lover are dead.

Cold-shouldering his wife, who's ready to leave him if they cancel their proposed vacation to Capri, Areta nonetheless decides to get to bottom of the killings. These ultimately involve a multi-national business dealing in selling doctored medicines and hospital equipment. But it is "too big to buck," and Areta rather disappointingly leaves it at that.

All technical credits are top-notch, and thesping by Landa, Bodalo, Rellan and Casanova are excellent; Manuel Rojas's lensing is superb. The story is interlaced with humor and touches of irony, but at the end Landa's deadpan stare becomes a little tiresome. Commercial outlook is rather less than that of its predecessor.

— *Besa.*

Microwave Massacre
(COLOR)

Overdone cannibalism comedy.

A Reel Life Prods. presentation. Produced by Thomas Singer, Craig Muckler. Directed by Wayne Berwick. Stars Jackie Vernon. Screenplay, Singer from story by Muckler; camera (color), Karen Grossman; editor, Steve Nielson; music, Leif Horvath; sound, Susumo Takumo; assistant director-production manager, Donald P.H. Eaton; art direction, Robert Burns. Reviewed on Midnight Video videcassette, N.Y., Aug. 20, 1983. (No MPAA Rating). Running time: **76 MINS.**
Donald . . . . Jackie Vernon
Roosevelt . . . . Loren Schein
Philip . . . . Al Troupe
May . . . . Claire Ginsberg
Dee Dee Dee . . . . Lou Ann Webber
Chick . . . . Anna Marlowe
Evelyn . . . . Sarah Alt
Susie . . . . Cindy Gant
Neighbor . . . . Karen Marshall
Knothole girl . . . . Marla Simon
Sam . . . . Phil de Carlo

Filmed about five to six years ago and finally emerging as a homevideo release, "Microwave Massacre" is an amateurish comedy dwelling on cannibalism in its lampooning of gory horror films. Vaguely resembling the spoof-of-a-spoof "Please Don't Eat My Mother" (a takeoff on "Little Shop Of Horrors" made a decade ago), this film is suited for fanciers of grotesque black humor only.

Standup comic Jackie Vernon toplines as a mild construction worker Donald, engaged in Bickersons-style arguments with his stout wife May (Claire Ginsberg), especially over her penchant for inedi-

ble gourmet repasts prepared in her large microwave oven. In a rage, he kills her, and cuts the body into pieces (including a very cheap plaster head) and stores them neatly wrapped in aluminum foil with the frozen meat.

When Donald accidentally nibbles on one of his wife's hands for a midnight snack, he discovers he likes the taste and begins cooking the human flesh in the microwave, sharing the results at lunch with his friendly co-workers. Now a bachelor again, he starts picking up pretty girls, but ends up killing them while having sex and eating the corpses.

Filmmakers Wayne Berwick, Thomas Singer and Craig Muckler overplay this material for cheap laughs, with mugging actors including the usually deadpan Vernon. Gore is very fake-looking, aiming at viewers laughing at the production rather than being outraged by realism. Emphasizing vulgar gags and slowing down the dialog delivery results in an embarrassing, generally unfunny exercise, punctuated by the usual quota of female nude shots.

Budget is microscopic, with passable technical credits. In explaining Donald's final comeuppance (yes, even in amoral farragoes such as this there lurks some form of retribution), picture briefly intimates a supernatural element, but this is not enough to attract the interest of traditional horror film fans. — *Lor.*

Angel Of H.E.A.T.
(COLOR)

She's all tease.

A Studios Pan Imago presentation of a Schreibman/Kant film. Executive producer, Hal Kant. Produced and directed by Myrl A. Schreibman. Features entire cast. Screenplay. Helen Sanford; camera (Deluxe color), Jacques Haitkin; editor, Barry Zetlin; music, Guy Sobell; song written & performed by Denise McCann; assistant director, Mary Lou MacLaury; production manager, Fred Slark; android prosthetics created by William Munns, executed by Gordon Greio. Reviewed on Cinemax, N.Y., July 8, 1983. (MPAA Rating: R). Running time: **93 MINS.**
Angel Harmony . . . . Marilyn Chambers
Mark Wisdom . . . . Stephen Johnson
Samantha Vitesse . . . . Mary Woronov
Harry Covert . . . . Milt Kogan
Andrea Shockley . . . . Remy O'Neill
Albert Shockley . . . . Dan Jesse
Peter Shockley . . . . Harry Townes
Hans Zeisel . . . . Gerald Okamura
Mean Wong . . . . Andy Abrams
Randy Small . . . . Jerry Riley

Filmed in 1981 (and retaining its original shooting title as a subtitle "The Protectors, Book #1"), "Angel Of H.E.A.T." is a softcore sex-science fiction comedy failing to establish porn star Marilyn Chambers, in her second R-rated opus after "Rabid," as a female James Bond. Same territory was covered a decade ago in the successful "Ginger" series starring Cheri Caffaro, but the theatrical market has changed, leaving "H.E.A.T." unreleased and currently being telecast as cable-tv filler, as well as a homevideo title.

Stuck with an unfunny, sniggering screenplay, filmmaker Myrl A. Schreibman goes for a silly tongue-in-cheek approach reminiscent of the spy spoofs of the 1960s, but the cast's arch readings become tiresome. His previous sci-fier (made with director Robert Fiveson) "Parts: The Clonus Horror," was also silly, but at least played straight.

Hokey plotting, which features numerous pauses in the action for verbal plot exposition, recaps and even a final wrapup, provides a surplus of good guys and a paucity of villains. Angel Harmony (Marilyn Chambers) leads a special unit of The Protectors, ex-intelligence agents turned international vigilantes, called H.E.A.T. (acronym undefined), while Mark Wisdom (Stephen Johnson) and Samantha Vitesse (Mary Woronov) are government agents working parallel to her on the same mission.

Everyone's goal is to stop megalomaniacal scientist Albert Shockley (Dan Jesse), who is out to control the world with the aid of his android henchmen and high-frequency communications. Preposterous gimmick has his dwarf aide Randy Small (Jerry Riley) fronting a casino in Lake Tahoe where lab employees are bilked, forcing them to steal micro-circuits to pay their gambling debts and thus facilitate Shockley's Earth takeover bid.

Unfortunately, film wanders for the first few reels, with lots of dumb puns, bare breasts and failed gags, such as subtitles (with Yiddish words) for an all-American guy who talks with a Chinese accent and German accent for an oriental martial arts expert. There's also mud wrestling as a diversion and sex-crazed androids but precious little attention to the story.

Martial arts action scenes are poorly-executed, with the picture lacking the budget to compete with James Bond in stunts and special effects gimmickry. Chambers is convincingly sexy but the R-rated format restricts her and the film to teasing only. Interesting casting has the star of "Eating Raoul," Mary Woronov, who vaguely resembles Chambers physically (but is much taller) cast opposite her as a rival agent and later teammate. A surprisingly amoral touch has Woronov's lesbian role treated quite matter-of-factly.

Tech credits are good, with attractive lensing by Jacques Haitkin in the Lake Tahoe region. As lightweight, low-involvement entertainment, feature could work on the drive-in circuit or overseas where Bond imitations have an audience. — *Lor.*

Hercules
(ITALIAN-COLOR)

More pecs than sex.

Hollywood, Aug. 26.
An MGM/UA and Cannon Group release of a Golan-Globus production. Produced by Menahem Golan, Yoram Globus. Executive producer, John Thompson. Directed, screenplay by Lewis Coates (Luigi Cozzi). Stars Lou Ferrigno, Sybil Danning, Brad Harris. Camera (Technicolor), Alberto Spagnoli; editor, Sergio Montanari; music, Pino Donaggio; costume design, Adriana Spadaro; sound, (Dolby) Gerry Humphries, Robin O'Donoghue; director of optical effects, Armando Valcauda; special effects, Fabio Traversari; assistant director, Giancarlo Santi. Reviewed at the Hollywood Pacific, L.A., Aug. 26, 1983. (MPAA Rating: PG). Running time: **98 MINS.**
Hercules . . . . Lou Ferrigno
Circe . . . . Mirella D'Angelo
Arianna . . . . Sybil Danning
Cassiopea . . . . Ingrid Anderson
King Minos . . . . William Berger
King Augias . . . . Brad Harris
Zeus . . . . Claudio Cassinelli
Hera . . . . Rossana Podesta
Athena . . . . Delia Boccardo

Almost 20 years ago, there was a picture called "Hercules Against The Moon Men." Now, the ubiquitous Golan and Globus have corralled "The Incredible Lou Ferrigno" to topline in a cheesy epic that could just about be titled "Hercules In Outer Space." Since a lumpy space suit would cover Ferrigno's mighty physique from view, the all-powerful one travels through the universe wearing nothing but his gladiatorial briefs, which is a good thing since b.o. will depend upon those anxious to watch the star flex his pecs at all times.·

When imagining a Hercules pic, such as the global b.o. hit of 1959 which starred Steve Reeves, one thinks of swords, sun and sandals, as well as backlot ancient temples and hordes of extras. By contrast, this "Hercules" seems to have no more than two dozen people in it, including extras (the one battle assuredly consists of footage hijacked from an earlier pic), and almost all of it is set in murky, blue and black-drenched studio sets.

A lot of it also takes place on the moon, as Zeus and wife and daughter Hera and Athena toy from above with the fate of mortals. It is Hercules' tasks to try to rescue the Princess Cassiopea from the clutches of her evil kidnappers, and given the changing times, the muscleman doesn't have to battle cardboard monsters, but hi-tech mechanical beasts made of metal and which emit deadly laser blasts from their jaws.

Hercules also possesses a wonderful talent for flinging objects into orbit in outer space. Opening day matinee audience in Hollywood went into seizures of laughter when, finding his father killed by a giant bear, Hercules proceeded to beat up the animal and then, with a mighty heave, to toss it into the stratosphere, where it formed the Ursa Major constellation.

Director of optical effects Armando Valcauda clearly worked overtime filling almost every shot in the picture with visual effects of one kind or another. As in last week's barbarian-of-the-future pic, "Yor," simple clanging swords aren't good enough anymore; due to the "Star Wars" influence, all combat must now be accentuated by electronic zaps and video game-type wipe-outs.

Although dubbed by another, Lou Ferrigno is perfectly affable, and physically (if not physiognomally) he more than lives up to his billing. Sybil Danning, Mirella D'Angelo and Ingrid Anderson comprise a fetching trio of femmes.

But, somehow, this isn't the "Hercules" children of the 1950s and 1960s knew and loved. —*Cart.*

Hannah K.
(FRENCH-COLOR)

Paris, Aug. 30.
Gaumont release Universal-U.S. of a K.G. Prods./Gaumont/Films A2. Produced by Michele Ray-Gavras. Stars Jill Clayburgh. Directed by Constantine Costa-Gavras. Screenplay, Costa-Gavras, Franco Solinas; camera (Fujicolor), Ricardo Aronovich; editor, Francoise Bonnot; music, Gabriel Yared; Yiddish songs performed by Talila and the Kol Aviv ensemble; art director, Pierre Guffroy; sound, Pierre Gamet; costumes, Edith Vesperini; production manager, Gerard Crosnier. Reviewed at the Gaumont Ambassade theatre, Paris, Aug. 19, 1983. Running time: **108 MINS.**
Hannah Kaufman . . . . Jill Clayburgh
Victor Bonnet . . . . Jean Yanne
Josue Herzog . . . . Gabriel Byrne
Selim Bakri . . . . .·. . . . . Mohamed Bakri
Amnon . . . . David Clennon
Professor Leventhal . . . . Shimon Finkel
The stranger . . . . Oded Kotler

Constantine Costa-Gavras' customary dramatic punch is missing in his new film "Hannah K.," an unpersuasive French-produced, English-language drama about a young American Jewish woman's sentimental and ideological conflicts in modern-day Israel. Apart from the problem of Jill Clayburgh's bland central performance, film suffers from a script by the director and the late Franco Solinas (his last), too mild-mannered and diffuse to make any potent dramatic points.

Though it touches on issues even more explosive than those tackled in "Missing," "Hannah K." is low in controversy value, yet there could be outraged commentary about the portraits of the representative "sabra" (native Israeli), an arrogant young district attorney of hawkish inclination, and the inversely sympathetic young Palestinian trying to reclaim his ancestral home on the occupied Left Bank. (Latter is played by a real Arab, Mohamed Bakri, while an Irish actor, Gabriel Byrne, is the Israeli.)

Unfortunately, their political differences are distorted through a private optic, since both are intimately involved with Clayburgh. This paves the way for the story's climactic crisis and its ironic coda, but they don't work convincingly because the preparatory character development remains unsatisfactory.

Male characters are subordinate to Clayburgh, however, whose interreacting emotional and political confusions are the focus of the film. She's an idealistic, first-generation American Jew, of European Holocaust heritage. Separated from a French husband who still loves her, she has come to Israel, struggled for a law degree and landed a job in a law firm.

Her most recent lover is the Israeli district attorney; she is bearing his child but she has refused to join him in conventional marriage. An "Adam's Rib" situation develops when she is assigned to defend the young Arab, whom the d.a. sees as a terrorist in disguise. When, in the course of the story, Clayburgh and the Palestinian become lovers, the Israeli resorts to an odious subterfuge to separate them.

Costa-Gavras' apparent intent here is to evoke the contradictions of Israeli life through the dilemma of an impressionable Jewish foreigner, but neither script nor Clayburgh composes a personage of palpable experience or personality. At its weakest, film looks a bit like "An Unmarried Woman Goes to Jerusalem."

Byrne is passable as the haughty Israeli, and Bakri appealing as the Palestinian, too appealing, in fact, as if Costa-Gavras wanted to back away as far as possible from the racist cliches about Arabs.

Best performance comes from Jean Yanne, in an episodic part of Clayburgh's wryly wistful French hubby, who comes running when she calls for help. Yanne reminds us that he can be a fine actor.

Costa-Gavras' direction is at its assured best in the more expansive, public scenes, such as the film's opening in which Israeli soldiers are seen rounding up suspected terrorists (Bakri among them) in an Arab settlement, and then dynamiting the dwelling in which they were found. (Though most of the film was shot on location in and around Jerusalem, this sequence was filmed in Italy, not surprisingly.)

English-language production was apparently a commercial concession, and it tears the realistic texture of the film. Here the Arabs speak Arabic, but the Israelis all speak fluent English (though they all drop "Shalom" on each other.) In Costa-Gavras' earlier political melodramas, language was not a problem because the settings were vaguely mythic. But the Israel of "Hannah K." is unmistakably genuine, and at least in the scenes without Clayburgh, there's no reason why the characters should not speak Hebrew. —Len.

Lucie Sur Seine
(Interdit Aux Moins de 13 Ans)
(FRENCH-COLOR)

A Nicole Jouve Interama (U.S.) release of a Uccelli Prod. in association with Janus Film. Produced and directed by Jean-Louis Bertuccelli. Features entire cast. Screenplay, S. Majerowitcz, adapted by Bertuccelli; camera (GTC color), Jean-Francois Robin; editor, Andre Gaultier; music, Gabriel Yared; sound Laurent Caglio; assistant director, Olivier Peray. Reviewed at Museum of Modern Art, N.Y., Feb. 19, 1983. (No MPAA Rating). Running time: 90 MINS.
Louis .... Patrick Depeyrat
Lucie .... Sandra Montaigu
Nonoeil .... Akim Oumaouche
Chantal .... Maryline Even

Jean-Louis Bertuccelli, best known in the U.S. for his 1970

"Ramparts Of Clay" and more recently the Annie Girardot-starrer "No Time For Breakfast" (originally, "Dr. Francoise Gailland") is back with an offbeat realistic drama "Lucie Sur Seine." Though lacking European star names, picture could find a niche on the arty circuit via its unusual look at a side of Paris (its suburban slum areas) omitted from most Gallic filmers' itineraries.

Styled as a film noir in the vein of Marcel Carne's classics, "Lucie" concerns a young towel deliveryman Louis (Patrick Depeyrat), unhappily married to Chantal (Maryline Even). To escape his routine, he robs the store where Chantal works, killing two people in the process.

A pretty girl working there, Lucie (Sandra Montaigu) sees the crime but instead of turning Louis in teams up with him as the film segues into the U.S. type of "They Live By Night" and "You Only Live Once" genre. A key subplot deals with Lucie's precocious half-brother Nonoeil (of Arabic extraction), who with the other local street urchins arranges for strip shows and other porno acts for underage youngsters' viewing. (Film's 1982 French release title "Interdit Aux Moins de 13 Ans" refers to this, translating as "Forbidden to Those Under 13 Years Old.)

Strong on atmosphere (particularly the night visuals of Paris), "Lucie" is burdened with an unconvincing climax in which the inevitable police confrontation with the anti-hero doesn't play well.

Depeyrat is inexpressive in the lead role, but Sandra Montaigu (who also collaborated in the script-writing) is an attractive heroine. Gabriel Yared (who also scored "Invitation Au Voyage") has provided hypnotic musical background. —Lor.

The Big Chill
(COLOR)

Just misses despite all the right elements.

Hollywood, Aug. 25.

A Columbia release of a Carson Prods. Group, Ltd./Columbia Delphi production. produced by Michael Shamberg. Executive producers, Marcia Nasatir, Lawrence Kasdan. Directed by Kasdan. Features entire cast. Screenplay, Kasdan, Barbara Benedek; camera (Metrocolor), John Bailey; editor, Carol Littleton; production design, Ida Random; set decoration, George Gaines; sound, Gene S. Cantamessa; associate producer, Barrie M. Osborne; assistant director, Michael Grillo. Reviewd at the Gomillion Studios, L.A., Aug. 25, 1983. (MPAA Rating: R.) Running time: 103 MINS.
Sam .... Tom Berenger
Sarah .... Glenn Close
Michael .... Jeff Goldblum
Nick .... William Hurt
Harold .... Kevin Kline
Meg .... Mary Kay Place
Chloe .... Meg Tilly
Karen .... JoBeth Williams

Richard .... Don Galloway
Minister .... James Gillis
Peter The Cop .... Ken Place

"The Big Chill," which has its world premiere at the Toronto Film Festival Fri. (9) night and will shortly kick off the New York Film Festival, is an amusing, splendidly-acted but rather shallow look at what's happened to the generation formed by the 1960s. Like a high-gloss version of John Sayles' "Return Of The Secaucus Seven" with a classy cast, Lawrence Kasdan's misleadingly-titled second feature as a director should be very well received by upscale viewers in their 30s, as contemporaries of the characters will find plenty to "relate to." But commercial breakout to a significantly wider public is doubtful.

Framework set up by scenarists Kasdan and Barbara Benedek has seven old college friends gathering on the Southeastern seaboard for the funeral of another old pal, who has committed suicide in the home of happily-married Glenn Close and Kevin Kline.

Others in attendance are: sharp-looking Tom Berenger, who has gained nationwide fame as a Tom Selleck-type private eye on tv but is forlorn in the wake of his recent divorce; Jeff Goldblum, horny wiseacre who writes for People magazine; William Hurt, the Jake Barnes of the piece by virtue of having been strategically injured in Vietnam; Mary Kay Place, a successful career woman who just hasn't met the right man, and Jo-Beth Williams, whose older husband returns home to the two kids before the weekend has barely begun, leaving Williams to explore the possibilities of a fresh start.

Also provocatively on hand is Meg Tilly, much younger girl-friend of the deceased who doesn't react with sufficient depth to the tragedy in the eyes of the older folk.

Ensconced in Kline and Close's lovely oceanside home, group gets the official grieving over with early on, and spends the remainder of the weekend sorting through their lives and, in some cases, trying to strike new sparks. Williams, who in college went with Hurt, and Berenger had a longstanding but unconsummated thing for each other, and she sees to it that the latter condition is remedied, despite his hesitations.

Most engaging, however, is Place's dilemma. In her mid-30s, like the others, Place ruminates over the pros and cons of her lifestyle and declares herself absolutely ready to have a baby at this point, even if the father wants to take no responsibility.

What's more, she proclaims herself physically right that weekend to conceive, and gets the word out to Berenger that she'd like Mr.

TV Stud to be the father of her child. When that doesn't work out, pic reaches its comic highlight when Close performs the ultimate act of wifely selflessness in giving her blessing to a night of love between her close friend and her husband (and in her own bed, yet!).

Unlike its obvious predecessor, "Secaucus Seven," film devotes little time to characters dwelling on their pasts, to the point where some long-ago personal relations and political activities are decidedly vague. Indeed, in a film so crammed with talk, evasion of much direct discussion about the ideals of youth vs. the realities of adult life is rather surprising, given a structure that invites thematic exploration of the subject.

Except perhaps for Hurt, who still takes drugs heavily and is closest in personality to the dead man, characters are generally middle-of-the-roaders, and pic lacks a tough-minded spokesman who might bring them all up short for a moment. Film will therefore seem rather mild and lightweight to those who aren't enjoying seeing so many aspects of themselves up on the screen.

On the positive side, one can believe that these people were once tight friends, which is a tribute to the ensemble acting by the marvelous group of actors assembled by Kasdan. All of them are given opportunities to shine, and all rise to the occasion with seeming effortlessness.

After scoring in his directorial debut with "Body Heat" two years ago, Kasdan has appropriately played down the stylistic flashiness here in a solid piece of work. It's just too bad he was willing to be satisfied with a film of hundreds of behavioral niceties when more depth was possible.

All credits are strongly pro, and soundtrack is strewn with well over a dozen familiar pop tunes — mainly of the late 1960s — which will bring pleasant smiles of recognition to the faces of the intended audience. —Cart.

Eddie And The Cruisers
(COLOR)

Poorly-scripted rock music nostalgia drama. Strong soundtrack and new talent will create some interest.

An Embassy Pictures release of an Aurora presentation of a Martin Davidson film. Executive producers, Rich Irvine, James L. Stewart. Produced by Joseph Brooks, Robert K. Lifton. Directed by Martin Davidson. Features entire cast. Screenplay, Martin Davidson, Arlene Davidson, from a novel by P.F. Kluge; camera (Technicolor; prints by CFI), Fred Murphy; editor, Priscilla Nedd; music and songs, John Cafferty; musical supervision-production, Kenny Vance; musical advisor, Joseph Brooks; sound, Maryte Kavaliauskas; art direction, Gary Weist; set decoration, Chris Kelly; production manager, Robert Girolami; assistant director, Henry Bronchtein; technical advisor, Southside Johnny Lyon. Reviewed at Loews 34th St. Showplace 2 theatre, N.Y., Sept. 4, 1983. (MPAA Rating: PG). Running time: **92 MINS.**

Frank Ridgeway	Tom Berenger
Eddie Wilson	Michael Pare
Doc Robbins	Joe Pantoliano
Sal Amato	Matthew Laurance
Joann Carlino	Helen Schneider
Kenny Hopkins	David Wilson
Wendell Newton	Michael "Tunes" Antunes
Maggie Foley	Ellen Barkin
Lew Eisen	Kenny Vance
Keith Livingston	John Stockwell

"Eddie And The Cruisers" is a mish-mash of a film, combining elements of the ongoing nostalgia for rock music of previous decades with an unworkable and laughable mystery plotline. Two very impressive new actors in featured roles plus an arresting songs score will give Embassy Pictures some marketing angles, but too many scenes self-destruct due to pompous, catch phrases dialog.

Lensed in New Jersey and New York in the spring of 1982 as an indie Aurora production (investment outfit that also backed Don Bluth's "The Secret Of NIMH"), "Eddie" opens, in strict "Citizen Kane" fashion as tv news mag reporter Maggie Foley (Ellen Barkin) is using old clips to pitch her investigative story on the early 1960s rock group Eddie And The Cruisers. Unit disbanded in 1964 with the suicide of its leader Eddie Wilson (Michael Pare).

She needs a news hook, and settles on the unlikely gimmick that Eddie (whose body was never found) is still alive and that a search for the missing tapes of his final, unreleased recording session of nearly 20 years ago will solve the mystery of his disappearance. Foley interviews other surviving group members, including the lyricist-keyboard man Frank Ridgeway (Tom Berenger), who is prompted to remember (in frequent flashbacks) those glory days of 1962-63.

Film takes a disastrous turn when Frank is reunited with the group's beautiful femme singer Joann (Helen Schneider). Amidst howler lines that belabor the obvious ("What's going on?," "Where are the tapes?"), picture segues into the structure (but minus the thrills) of a "he's returned x years after" horror film leading to a stupid anti-climax.

Under Martin Davidson's tedious direction (he also coscripted with his sister Arlene), "Eddie" only comes alive during the flashbacks when John Cafferty's songs provide a showcase for the magnetic screen presences of Pare and Schneider. In his film debut, Pare, who shares the arresting screen qualities of other young talent such as Matt Dillon and Eric Roberts, lip-synchs vocals sung by Cafferty

very well and is dynamic in his sketchy (flashbacks only) role. Real-life rock singer Schneider is very sexy on screen, but her contemporary scenes are ruined by unplayable dialog plus makeup and styling that do not age her one day in supposedly 20 years.

In the lead role Berenger is too bland, probably baffled a bit by the plot incongruities, as well as the "Great Gatsby" structure that continually has Pare upstaging him.

Tech credits are very fine throughout, especially in capturing the period look. Though the young target audience may not notice or care, Cafferty's new songs (following authentic 1961 hits here by Del Shannon and Dion) are somewhat anachronistic, spotlighting the 1970s work of his own Beaver Brown Band as well as the distinctive Bruce Springsteen sound. —*Lor.*

Nightmares
(COLOR)

Weak 4-part horror film diverted from tv to theatres.

A Universal Pictures production and release. Executive producers, Andrew Mirisch, Alex Beaton. Produced by Christopher Crowe. Directed by Joseph Sargent. Features entire cast. Screenplay, Crowe (Chapters 1-3), Jeffrey Bloom (Chapter 4); camera (Technicolor), Gerald Perry Finnerman (Chap. 1-2), Mario DiLeo (Chap. 3-4); editor, Rod Stephens, Michael Brown; music, Craig Safan; additional music, Black Flag, Rik L. Rik, Fear; sound, Jim Alexander; production design, Dean Edward Mitzner; art direction, Jack Taylor; set decoration, Lee Poll; assistant director, Kevin Cremin; production manager, Zane Radney; stunt coordinator, Gary Jensen; videogame special effects, Bo Gehring Associates; associate producer, Alan Barnette. Reviewed at Loews 83d St. Quad 3 theatre, N.Y., Sept. 2, 1983. (MPAA Rating: R). Running time: **99 MINS.**

1. Terror In Topanga

Wife	Cristina Raines
Husband	Joe Lambie
Store clerk	Anthony James
Gaspump man	William Sanderson

2. Bishop Of Battle

J.J. Cooney	Emilio Estevez
Mrs. Cooney	Mariclare Costello
Mr. Cooney	Louis Giambalvo
Pamela	Moon Zappa
Zock	Billy Jacoby

3. The Benediction

MacLoed	Lance Henriksen
Del Amo	Tony Plana
Sheriff	Timothy Scott
Bishop	Robin Gammell

4. Night Of The Rat

Steven Houston	Richard Masur
Claire Houston	Veronica Cartwright
Brooke Houston	Bridgette Andersen
Mel Keefer	Albert Hague

"Nightmares" is an adequately scary but overly-predictable four-part horror omnibus, aimed at the "Twilight Zone — The Movie" audience but actually closer in spirit to the successful British Amicus productions of a decade ago. Originally paid for by NBC as a two-hour pilot telefilm, picture has been released to theatres first by Universal, where it should easily cover

its modest $2,000,000 or so production nut.

Writer-producer Christopher Crowe (and cowriter Jeffrey Bloom) have failed to provide enough plot twists to make nightmares fully satisfying, but director Joseph Sargent expertly eliminates flab with solidly realistic direction. The four segs split between psychological and supernatural horror, with the film at its best in exploring credible, everyday fears.

Top material is upfront, leading off with Cristina Raines in "Terror In Topanga," portraying a young woman in jeopardy. Foolishly driving out one night to get a pack to satisfy her cigaret habit, she's at the mercy of a well-publicized, knife-wielding Canyon killer. Segment boasts the film's best twist, and is aided by solid casting of two sinister actors Anthony James and William Sanderson (latter unfortunately omitted from the credits.)

Emilio Estevez toplines in "Bishop Of Battle," an animated-effects laden episode about a videogames arcade champ who meets his match in a supernatural game. Good effects and direction are limited here by a telegraphed conclusion.

Lance Henriksen limns the role of a priest who's lost his faith in "The Benediction." Giving up his vocation and driving off down the highway, he is absurdly brought back in line by a demonic black minivan in a story lifted from Universal's earlier features "The Car" and "Duel." Nice 180-degree car stunts and a car bursting out of the ground (a la Chuck Norris in "Lone Wolf McQuade") are the best moments in a silly segment.

Finale written by Jeffrey Bloom puts Veronica Cartwright back in familiar territory (remember "Alien") hunting for her kitty-cat and expressing wide-eyed terror when a man sized rat attacks her house. As her hubbie, Richard Masur is stuck with the unplayable role of a macho guy so sure of himself that even a monster in the woodwork is just another minor daily problem. This silly finale betrays the film's absence of a sizable budget; instead of the usual Universal display of scary monsters by a Rob Bottin or Rick Baker master, there are fake-looking composite shots using a real rat.

Tech credits throughout are modest. The R-rating for "Nightmares" is probably due to a gory scene that precedes the initial segment. —*Lor.*

Jos Ovaj Put
(Just Once More)
(YUGOSLAV-COLOR)

Pula, July 24.

An Avala Film, (Belgrade) and Croatia Film, (Zagreb) coproduction. Features entire

cast. Directed by Dragan Kresoja. Screenplay, Milan Jelic; camera (color), Predrag Popovic; art direction, Vladislav Lasic; music, Mladen and Predrag Vranesevic. Reviewed at Pula Film Fest, July 24, '83. Running time: **94 MINS.**

Cast: Aleksandar Bercek, Bata Zivojinovic, Rada Zivkovic-Bambic, Vladica Milosavljevic, Branko Vidakovic, Dusan Janicijevic, Josuf Tatic, Mica Tomic, Dragoljub Milosavljevic, Milan Gutovic.

A warmhearted tale of two convicts whose friendship enables them to wrestle with fate once more and break even, "Just Once More" scores as a fine debut pic by vet docu filmer and tv-film director, Dragan Kresoja. The script is by another able writer-director-actor talent, Milan Jelic (whose own "My Temporary Father" unspooled at Pula).

Somewhat like a Butch Cassidy and Sundance Kid pair, Aleksandar Bercek is a convicted drug-pusher from the social side of the tracks, while Bata Zivojinovic has been in and out of prison for a number of raps. Bercek has left behind a wife and newly born son when caught peddling dope "just once more," and he now wants to discover what's happened to his wife after a number of years in the can. He gets a weekend pass, just as his prison buddy, Zivojinovic, is conditionally discharged due to failing health. They go off in search of a lost past, during which Zivojinovic dies — this changes Bercek's view of the world altogether, as he looks for a way to make his life meaningful for the first time.

Melodrama, of the tough he-man variety, in which sentiment is hard won. — *Holl.*

La Femme de Mon Pote
(My Buddy's Girl)
(FRENCH-COLOR)

Paris, Aug. 31.

AMLF release of a Sara Films Productions coproduction. Produced by Alain Sarde. Stars Isabelle Huppert, Coluche, Thierry Lhermitte. Directed by Bertrand Blier. Screenplay, Blier, Gerard Brach; camera (Eastmancolor), Jean Penzer; art director, Theo Meurisse; sound, Bernard Bats, editor, Claudine Merlin, costumes, Michele Cerf, music, J.J. Cale, production manager, Alain Depardieu, executive producer, Pierre Grunstein. Reviewed at the Marignan-Concorde theatre, Paris, Aug. 31, 1983. Running time: **99 MINS.**

Cast: Coluche, Isabelle Huppert, Thierry Lhermitte, Daniel Colas, Francois Perrot, Farid Chopel.

Director Bertrand Blier has taken the classic romantic triangle on some truculent joyrides in the past, but his new film, "La Femme de Mon Pote," is thoroughgoing sentimental fare, obviously carpentered as a vehicle for the endearing talents of Coluche, the roly-poly stage comic-turned-film star. Though he shares top billing with Isabelle Huppert and Thierry Lhermitte, Coluche looms over the predominantly single-set proceedings like a Raimu silhouette.

Script, by Blier and Gerard Brach, has Huppert as a bargain basement Paris vamp, who embarks on an Alpine ski vacation and worms her way quickly into the heart and home of Lhermitte, a local sportswear vendor with a cozy little chalet on the ski slopes. Coluche, a disk jockey and Lhermitte's long-standing best friend, is initially wary of his buddy's new flame, until he finds himself falling for her in the first big passion of his life.

Blier's erstwhile sexual anarchy has been tamed, giving way to conventional lump-in-the-throat sex comedy, and he's not very good at it here, either as writer or director. "La Femme de Mon Pote" is virtually undistinguishable from the spate of other desperately casual romantic romps cranked out each year in France. —*Len.*

Autumn Born
(CANADIAN-COLOR)

A Monterey Home Video release of a Lloyd A. Simandl presentation of a North-American Pictures production. Executive producers, Simandl, Sharon Christensen. Directed by Simandl. Associate directors, Christensen, Sharon Elder. Features Dorothy Stratten. Screenplay, Christensen, Shannon Lee, Ihor Procak; camera (color), Simandl; lighting, Vic Ondricek; editor, Ed Smith, Christensen, Simandl; music, Don Bouchai; sound, Ed Smith. Reviewed on vidcassette, N.Y., July 9, 1983. (No MPAA Rating). Running time: **75 MINS.**.

With: Dorothy Stratten (Tara Dawson), Ihor Procak, Dory Jackson, Gisselle Fredette, Nate MacIntosh, Jocelyne Fournier, Roberta Weiss, Roman Buchok, Sharon Elder, Ludmila Kanevski, Benjamin Esteban, Anita Durand, Kim Elder, Lorraine Pelletier, Robert Light, Jerry Towle, Paul Sweatman, Anne Wallace.

Made in Winnipeg, Manitoba in 1979, "Autumn Born" is an unreleased softcore pornography feature which would undoubtedly have remained in the vault except that it toplines the late Dorothy Stratten, former Playboy playmate and victim of a sensational murder. Of obvious curiosity value, this amateurish film is currently circulating on the homevideo market.

Already the subject of a tv biopic starring Jamie Lee Curtis and an upcoming Bob Fosse-helmed biopic starring Mariel Hemingway, Stratten is featured here in the film's lead role, that of heiress Tara Dawson, who is kidnapped on her uncle's orders and taken to Morgan Estates, an "obedience" school for girls.

Tedious picture lamely attempts to present Victorian-era porno in modern guise, with poor Stratten subjected to frequent birchings and sensory deprivation in four months of isolation, in order to break her spirit and have her sign over her inheritance to the uncle.

Bondage motifs and a stock lesbian head mistress of the school are the primary diversions of the repetitive, uneventful footage.

Though there are some nude scenes, the sexual content of "Autumn Born" is quite tame by contemporary standards. Stratten is literally on display in her undergarments for voyeuristic purposes, but the device ultimately becomes fetishistic. Amidst generally awful, one-take acting by the cast, her transition from sexy 17-year-old to submissive little girl is earnestly portrayed and projects some of the appeal shown in her smaller role in Peter Bogdanovich's "They All Laughed" and far more interesting than her walkthrough as a robot in her other film "Galaxina."

Ragged editing, sloppy sound mix and a dull keyboards musical score create a dull film, which is heavily padded by opening and end credits to reach a 75-minute feature length. —*Lor.*

Le Destin de Juliette
(Juliette's Fate)
(FRENCH-COLOR)

Paris, Aug. 25.
Gaumont release of a Laura Productions/Films A2 coproduction, with the participation of the French Culture Ministry. Features entire cast. Directed by Aline Isserman. Screenplay, Aline Isserman and Michel Dufresne; camera (color), Dominique Le Rigoleur; art director, Danka Semenovicz; costumes, Maritza Gligo; editor, Dominique Auvray; sound, Francois de Morant; music, Bernard Lubat. Reviewed at Gaumont screening room, Neuilly, Aug. 24, 1983. Running time: **115 MINS.**

Juliette...................Laure Duthilleul
Marcel.................Richard Bohringer
Renee.....................Veronique Silver
Ferdinand.................Pierre Forger
Etienne....................Didier Agostini
Pierre.................Hippolyte Girardot

A low-keyed drama about small, bogged lives, "Le Destin de Juliette" follows the long, arid detour in a young woman's life. Aline Isserman, 35, a former journalist and cartoonist, hasn't taken an easy way out in centering her first feature around unassuming ordinary folk, but genuine filmic skill and perceptiveness make this one of the more promising, if commercially difficult, local debuts in some time.

Pic's fatalistic protagonist is Juliette (Laure Duthilleul) a simple farm girl who seems contentedly earmarked for sedate rural existence as a shepherd's mate, but passively finds herself shunted into marriage with a sullen, mediocre railway employee (Richard Bohringer) in order to save her disintegrating family from poverty and homelessness.

Tragically, her sacrifice is ultimately in vain, but she is now locked into a lonely and sorrowful wedlock, which the birth of a child and

sympathetic social pressures have cemented.

Transferred from one outpost to another, Bohringer sinks slowly into alcoholism and inertia, and eventually dies. Finally free, Duthilleul can now look to remaking her life.

Subtle performances from Duthilleul and Bohringer and a keen sense of narrative ellipse and choice of detail keeps film emotionally pertinent and generally free of the melodramatic or case study dullness.

Unspooled at Cannes in the Critics week sidebar, pic is getting normal commercial release via Gaumont here, though cheerless subject matter and subdued treatment will make this an essentially art house and fest item. —*Len.*

Kalibaliken i Bender
(The Big Bang In Bender)
(SWEDISH-COLOR)

Malmoe, Aug. 23.
A Viking Film (Bo Jonsson)/Europa Film production, Europa Film release. Story idea and executive producer, Bo Jonsson. Script, Rolf Bjoerlind. Features entire cast. Directed by Mats Arehn. camera (Eastmancolor), Joergen Persson; production design, Erik Lisin Johnson; editor, Sylvia Ingemarsson. Costumes, Inger Pehrsson. Music, Stefan Nilsson; production management, Christer Abrahamsen. Reviewed during Malmoe Film Days at the Camera, Malmoe, Sweden, Aug. 23, 1983. Running time: **97 MINS.**
Charles XII..............Goesta Ekman
Lt. Lagercrona..............Lasse Aberg
Orderly Kruus........Brasse Brannstroem
Princess Serina...Ayse Emel Mesci Kuray
Colonel Grothusen........Sten Ljunggren
Army chaplain................Lars Amble
General Lagercrona......Sture Hovstadius
Hultman............Carl-Gustav Lindstedt
Paniatowski..............Donald Arthur
Grand Vizir...............Walter Gotell
Sultan's Mother............Ayten Kuyululu

"The Big Bang in Bender" is based on a historical incident, a curious footnote to world history, and it tells what really happened when Sweden's early 18th century Hero King, Charles XII, had got himself stuck for an embarrassing while in the Turkish town of Bender. He had been given sanctuary there by the Grand Vizir after defeat by Czar Peter, whose empire the Swede had thought himself able to conquer. Now the Turks began conniving with the Russians to put Charles either into Russian hands or just back to Sweden, while the King still thought he had a chance to get armies together for further battle in Russia.

Producer Bo Jonsson has been toying with an idea to build a large-scale comedy-drama around these events for years, and he finally allied himself with scripter Rolf Bjoerlind and director Mats Arehn, the latter a filmmaker of bright achievement in several genres, and muscular Europa Film about making "The Big Bang" with a lavish budget and seven weeks of location

shooting in Hungary. Jonsson wanted his film to come out as primarily an adventure story for young-adult audiences.

By wanting it too many ways — comedy-drama, adventure story, farcical fun plus history re-telling with social hindsight and slightly satirical intent (debunking the King's hero myth in particular) — Jonsson has now delivered a big, gorgeous-looking piece of moviemaking that never gathers momentum in one single direction by looking frantically all the time for the right chair to sit on.

The historical episode is presented to us mainly through the trials and tribulations of a gangly, clumsy, good-natured Swedish lieutenant (Lasse Aberg, a superb comedy actor in the farcical comedies he himself writes and directs such as "The Charter Trip") and his rather brighter orderly (Brasse Brannstroem). The two men are entrusted with bringing a Sultan's gift — a beautiful princess — to Charles XII in Bender. Not a very attractive task since it seems widely known that Charles never in his life came near a woman and did not want to, either.

A gift of Charles' weight in gold and diamonds is simultaneously meant to pay the Swede to get out of Turkey. The two gifts are interchanged. And after much plotting and intrigue in various courts — and some half-heartedly cavalry charges) plus considerable clowning, the scene is prepared for the Big Bang. This we only get to hear in the distance, though, as the Lieutenant and the orderly are rejoined by the rejected Princess on their way home to Sweden.

There are nice cameo roles well played by Swedish, English and Turkish actors, but the expected erotic ambiance between Brannstrom's orderly and Ayse Emel Mesci Kuray is never made to appear likely, she being hidden behind a veil and he behind too much greasepaint, or else the script has just simply failed them on his point. Lasse Aberg as the lieutenant seem to be a lone wanderer in the wrong comedy, while Goesta Ekman's Charles XII is a shining example of high comedy held firmly in the control of the best of realistic acting. The King, woman-shy and burdened by a too big belly on a frail frame, seduced by his own isolation in a threatened power, is made a laughing stock, but one that remains curiously and appealingly human.

With production credits of the most shining order, superior cinematography by Joergen Persson, elegantly convincing designs by Erik Lisin Johnson and costumes by Inger Pehrsson, as usual combining the down-to-earth with the appealingly fanciful, "The Big Bang" has all the looks of great filmmaking, but the full-toned, happy noise to make it heard and seen far beyond Sweden's own borders remains absent in most departments. —*Kell.*

Terror On Tour
(COLOR)

Slasher sludge.

An Intercontinental World Distributing production in association with Four Features Partners Ltd. of a Tour Features picture. Executive producers, Rick Whitfield, Alex Rebar. Produced by Sandy Cobe. Directed by Don Edmonds. Features entire cast. Screenplay, Dell Lekus; camera (United color), James Roberson; editor, Bob Ernst; music, The Names; sound, Greg McCulloch; production manager, Buck Flower; assistant director, Evzen Kolar; art direction-set decoration, Verkina Flower; special effects make-up, Jack Petty; special effects, Charlie Spurgeon; second unit camera, James Tynes; stunt coordinator, Don Edmonds. Reviewed on Media Home Entertainment vidcassette, N.Y., Sept. 5, 1983. (No MPAA Rating). Running time: **88 MINS.**
The Band:
Fred .... Rick Styles
Ralph .... Chip Greenman
Henry .... Rich Pemberton
Cherry .... Dave Galluzzo
Tim .... Larry Thomasof
Herb .... Jeff Morgan
Jeff .... Dave Thompson
Jane .... Lisa Rodriquez
Lt. Lambert .... John Green
Carol .... Sylvia Wright
Nancy .... Lindy Leah

Made in 1980, "Terror On Tour" is a theatrically unreleased stab and slash feature film currently available to homevideo users. Uninvolving programmer has little to offer horror addicts.

Premise has a hard-rock group the Clowns (wearing makeup reminiscent of Kiss) doing a Grand Guignol-style live act (similar to such trend-setters as Alice Cooper), caught up in a murder investigation when someone wearing their makeup starts stabbing girls for real. The victims are prostitutes, and script rather tediously keeps hammering away at the relationship between drugs, rock music and violence. Filmmakers even have the temerity to end on a note imploring the audience to stop displaying its enthusiasm for violent, "sick" entertainment.

Belying its title, low-budget feature has no tour, with barely any exterior scenes and the group rooted in one spot. Only a handful of extras appear in the concert footage. Performing is dull, though lovely Lisa Rodriquez has a nice little role as a prostie working undercover for the police. Identity of the killer is obvious early on by the process of elimination.

Biggest surprise is absence of extreme gore, since "Tour" was directed by Don Edmonds, whose two "Ilsa" gore spectaculars of a decade ago have become cult favorites. He may have cleaned up his act, but the result is a failure to

meet the minimum requirements of the exploitation genre. —*Lor.*

Soesken pa Gud's jord
(Children Of God's Earth)
(NORWEGIAN-COLOR)

Oslo, Aug. 20.
An A/S Elan Film, Norsk Film A/S release. Based on Arvid Hanssen's novel. Script and directed by Laila Mikkelsen. Features entire cast. Advisors on script, Arvid Hanssen, David Wingate; camera (Fuji color), Rolv Haan; executive producer, Kirsten Bryhni; production management, Fred Sassebo, Merete Lindstad; editor, Fred Sassebo; music, Pete Knudsen; production design and costumes, Torunn Mueller. Reviewed at Norsk Film A/S screening room, Jar, Oslo, Aug. 19, 1983. Running time: **78 MINS.**
Margit .... Anneli Marian Drecker
Baela .... Torgils Moe
Kristian .... Odd Furoy
Simon .... Frode Rasmussen
Johanna .... Randi Koch
Arild .... Ernst Rune Huemer
Vavva .... Merete Moen

"Children's Of God's Earth" is an austere, sparse story laid out in a slow-moving feature of the kind that would seem a shoe-in for an Ecumenical prize at any international film festival. Laila Mikkelsen's first film after the strong and instantly moving "Little Ida" (about the wartime child of a Norwegian woman and a German soldier) should also be assured audiences at least a little wider through its clean-cut visuals and skilled handling of the set-pieces of the poor-folks, rural melodrama.

On some remote Norwegian island (so remote that public authorities seem forever nonexistent), subteenager Margit is the ward of a peasant and his wife, a couple soured on life and on each other. Their other wards include another girl, a mute, who is clad in an old sack and kept in a dark sheep's bin, and Baela, the classical mild-mannered giant of half-wit. Nearby lives the peasant's fisherman brother who one day promises Baela a huge sum of money to tear the other man's head off.

Margit of the clean-scrubbed, wide-eyed face looks at all this impending violence and tries to counteract its outcome, but to not much avail. There is also another teenager on the island, a consumptive boy who expires when trying to run after Margit when he has failed to embrace her beyond a shyly allotted kiss. All this is the classical stuff of simple melodrama, often bordering on the unvoluntarily farcial and acceptable only because of Laila Mikkelsen's use of frames, landscapes, dialogue and characters in a way to tempt audiences to explore hidden depths and/or symbolism.

While left to ponder whether these island folks are driven by inner forces or outward isolation or by sheer fear of a God they refrain from mentioning, audiences are

sure to feel both trapped and elated by the clean, almost angelic stare and visage of Anneli Marian Drecker playing Margit. ("Children Of God's Earth" would still appear to have dim commercial prospects beyond very specialized situations such as fests of "arty" programming by ambitious state-run stations. — *Kell.*

The Last Fight
(COLOR)

Minor boxing picture showcases new talent from the Salsa music biz.

A Best Film & Video release of a Movie and Pictures International production. Produced by Jerry Masucci. Directed by Fred Williamson. Features entire cast. Screenplay, Williamson from a story by Masucci; camera (color), James Lemmo; editor, Daniel Loewenthal; music, Jay Chattaway; songs, Cary King, Ruben Blades. Reviewed at RKO National 2 theatre, N.Y., Aug. 31, 1983. (MPAA Rating: R). Running time: **88 MINS.**
Joaquin Vargas .... Willie Colon
Andy "Kid" Clave .... Ruben Blades
Jesse Crowder .... Fred Williamson
Boss .... Joe Spinell
Sally .... Darlanne Fluegel
Nancy .... Nereida Mercado
Frankie .... Anthony Sirico
Vinny Argiro .... Det. Pantane
Ex-champ .... Jose "Chegui" Torres
Also with: Don King, Salvador Sanchez, Bert Sugarman.

"The Last Fight" is a low-budget boxing picture that showcases Panamanian-born Salsa recording star Ruben Blades as a singer-turned-fighter. After working with several of the same crew members and cast as exec producer of "Vigilante," Fania Records owner Jerry Masucci has conceived and produced an unexciting little film, which will have its greatest appeal to music fans rather than the action-pic trade.

Blades, who projects a handsome and empathetic screen presence resembling a Latino Bobby Darin, portrays Andy "Kid" Clave, a successful recording star aiming at the junior lightweight boxing title. Prone to running up big gambling debts, he is strong-armed into boxing for New York City nightclub owner Joaquin Vargas (Willie Colon), who provides Clave with the services of his beautiful girl friend Sally (Darlanne Fluegel) as part of the deal.

Taking a nod from the films noirs of the 1940s, writer-director Fred Williamson has created a doomed atmosphere for the lead players, including Clave's pretty g.f. Nancy (Nereida Mercado), leading up to Clave risking his life (blood clot on his brain from a bar accident) in a title bout. Williamson, however, portrays his familiar "Dirty Harry"-like screen persona, ex-cop Jesse Crowder (seen in several earlier films such as "No Way Back"), so there's no question of him surviving to return another day. As an actor, his

smooth manner, tongue-in-cheek dialog and action ability brighten up the film.

Picture is dedicated to the late featherweight champion Salvador Sanchez (killed in an auto accident shortly after lensing wrapped in early 1982), who knocks the daylights out of Clave in the title bout. Promoter Don King is fun in a cameo role, but most of the cast (particularly the femme leads) is under-directed by Williamson in his seventh outing as a feature helmer. Boxing footage is lensed from cameras outside the ring and overall the film remains too static (and with too many closeups) to energize action fans.

Biggest diasappointment of "The Last Fight" is the absence of a positive role model for the Hispanic audience. In films of late, Puerto Ricans and Chicanos have become the stock baddies, with Willie Colon again a hissable villain as in "Vigilante." The musical talent, as evidenced here by Blades' pleasant vocals, needs to be harnessed with an upbeat story, not the flawed, doomed fighter saga conveyed in this picture. —*Lor.*

BrainWaves
(COLOR)

Engrossing medical science fiction thriller.

A Motion Picture Marketing (MPM) release of a CinAmerica Pictures Corp. production. Executive producers, Charles Aperia, Gary Gillingham, Tim Nielsen; line producer, Jochen Breitenstein. Produced and directed by Ulli Lommel. Stars Keir Dullea, Suzanna Love. Screenplay, Lommel; additional dialog, Buz Alexander, Suzanna Love; camera (Getty color), Jon Kranhouse, Lommel; editor, Richard Brummer; music, Robert O. Ragland; sound, Ed Christiano, John Huck; assistant director, Bruce Starr; production manager, Ron Norman; art direction, Stephen E. Graff; special effects, N.H.P. Inc.; associate producer, David DuBay. Reviewed on Embassy Home Entertainment vidcassette, N.Y., Aug. 30, 1983. (MPAA Rating: PG). Running time: **81 MINS.**
Julian Bedford................. Keir Dullea
Kaylie Bedford............. Suzanna Love
Marian.................. Vera Miles
Dr. Robinson............. Percy Rodrigues
Dr. Clavius .... Tony Curtis
Dr. Schroder................. Paul Wilison
Danny Bedford............... Ryan Seitz
Willy Meiser............... Nicholas Love
Lelia Adams............. Corinne Alphen
Miss Simpson.............. Eve Brent Ashe

"BrainWaves" is a briskly-told, engaging 1982 psychological thriller dealing with the sci-fi concept of transferring thought processes and memories electronically between different people (similar territory to Douglas Trumbull's upcoming big-budget "Brainstorm"). Representing German emigre filmmaker Ulli Lommel's best U.S. work to date, picture lacks the shock effects and hardware prevalent in today's sci-fi and horror market, probably accounting for its release in home-video form (via Embassy) prior to theatrical launch by distrib MPM.

Suzanna Love (Mrs. Lommel off-screen) toplines as Kaylie Bedford, a young San Francisco housewife who suffers a severe brain trauma (leaving her in a coma-like trance) in an auto accident. Her husband, Julian (Keir Dullea), and mother (Vera Miles) agree to an experimental medical procedure for her masterminded by Dr. Clavius (Tony Curtis), unaware that it has not yet been tested on humans.

Designed to transfer corrective patterns by computer from a donor brain to the victim's damaged brain areas, process goes awry when the donor turns out be a murdered girl (Corinne Alphen). Kaylie is physically and mentally rehabilitated, but plagued with traumatic first-person memories of the murder. Worse yet, the murderer is now after her, to forestall exposure regarding a death previously classified by the police as an accident.

Well-edited by Richard Brummer, picture zips along with admirable verisimilitude. Dullea as the husband and father of a young boy (Ryan Seitz) is very sympathetic, with solid suspense generated as he pieces together clues to the killer's identity. Suzanna Love handles the lead character's shifts adroitly, and the trick-casting of her real brother, (who resembles her) Nicholas Love, as the killer pays off. Name players in the supporting cast (particularly a glum-looking Tony Curtis) have little to do.

Director Lommel has kept his usual homages to Alfred Hitchcock to a minimum here ("Vertigo," etc.) with good results. Tech credits are pro. —Lor.

El Harrif
(Street Player)
(EGYPTIAN-COLOR)

Moscow, July 23.

A Sohba Film production, Cairo. Features entire cast. Directed by Mohammed Khan. Screenplay, Beshir El Deck. Only credits available. Reviewed at Moscow Film Fest (Competition), July 19, '83. Running time: 114 MINS.

Cast: Adel Imam, Fardous Abdel Hamid.

Mohammed Khan's "Street Player" has to do with a common phenomenon in Cairo — street-soccer played by semi-professionals for gamblers and by-standers rooting for local heroes. Seldom has this ever been treated in Egyptian films, and the thematic material alone made it worth a critical once-over at Moscow.

The protagonist lives on the edge of society, and is the victim of middlemen who organize the gambling games on empty lots and back streets. His own booking agent cheats him regularly out of his share of the booty. Further, he is growing old, has a young son,

and is divorced. His other menial job in a shoe factory does not meet all his financial needs, so the street games and other forms of hustling are all he has to keep him going. An aging and sick father living in destitution adds to the situation.

In the end, the street player makes his final appearance on a back lot and leads his team from behind to victory — he thereby gets even with his betting exploiters. This slice of Egyptian realism recalls the Italian neorealism movement, and is a welcome contrast to star-oriented national production. Overall credits, however, are subpar for offshore handling.
— Holl.

Raskenstam
(Raskenstam)
(SWEDISH-COLOR)

Malmoe, Aug. 18.

An Artistsfilm, Swedish Film Institute, Swedish TV-2, Centrum Radio, Sandrews production. Sandrews release (domestic) Swedish Film Institute (foreign sales). Story and script, Brigitta Stenberg, Gunnar Hellstrom. Produced and directed by Gunnar Hellstrom. Features entire cast. Camera (Eastmancolor), Lars Bjoerne; executive producer, Brian Wikstroem; production management, Ann Collenberg, Anita Tessler, Susanne Ruben; editor, Lars Hagstroem; music, Lasse Samuelsson; costumes, Mago; production design, Anders Barreus. Reviewed at Sandrews 1-2-3, Malmoe, Aug. 18, 1983. Running time: 109 MINS.

Raskenstam .... Gunnar Hellstrom
Lisa Matsson .... Agneta Faeltskog
Malla av Tidaholm .... Lena Nyman
Cecilia Andersson ...... Harriet Andersson
Katarina Andersson .... Gunvor Ponten
Almquist .... Thomas Hellberg
Anna-Greta Kjellgren ..... Inga Gill
Marta Ohlin .... Yvonne Lombard
Agnes Bengtsson .... Lis Nilheim
Erik Branner ...... Carl Gustav Lindstedt
Defense Attorney ...... Kim Anderzon

Gunnar Hellstrom, director of 36 "Gunsmoke" episodes and several rounds of "Dallas," returned last year to his native Sweden to produce, co-write, direct and star in "Raskenstam," a sentimental period piece and comedy feature based on the 1942-45 real-life trials and tribulations of a con-man specializing in swindling money out of love-hungry women.

The real Raskenstam had an earlier conviction and a jail stretch behind him when he, at 42, picked up his peculiar career to become rather successful at it — at least he had gotten 120 women to fork over their savings to him, while being sexually active with most of them and officially engaged to at least two of their number when they all, three years later, refused to sue him but rather followed him tearfully and throwing kisses when he entered a prison-cell filled to overflowing with red roses. Actually, Raskenstam fell as the victim of an over greedy male blackmailer.

As Hellstrom tells about him — and plays him — Raskenstam comes around as a rotund, but

rather elegant and mild-mannered gentleman of both refinement and persuasive erotic charm. He is also seen as a brave man who just cannot let down any of his many women (we get to know only a handful of them). He struggles valiantly to lay his hands on more money to satisfy the relentless blackmailer while keeping up both ardor in his erotic commitments and a convincing front as a straight-laced businessman — first as president of a gravestone enterprise, later as a banker. Since some of his women are up to various tricks of their own, Raskenstam is really in a fix around the clock.

With actresses Harriet Andersson, Inga Gill, Yvonne Lombard and Lena Nyman putting in vigorous, romping performances and the ABBA pop group's blonde Agneta Faeltskog debuting handsomely as the fisherman's daughter who remains sweet and faithful even into her second pregnancy as Raskenstam's fiancee, plus Thomas Hellberg giving one of his expert "slimy" acts as the blackmailer, the burden of acting still lies with Hellstrom himself, and he shoulders it with humor and conviction and much showing of quiet desperation throughout.

As a director-producer he allows his film to run on too long, but it never loses its old-fashioned charm nor the equally old-fashioned way it makes its storytelling points. "Raskenstam" will have obvious appeal to all Scandinavian markets, while its theatrical future elsewhere would appear dimmer than its tube and video prospects. All production credits are first rate. —Kell.

Montreal Fest

Stranger's Kiss
(U.S. — COLOR/B&W)

Montreal, Aug. 24.

An Orion Classics release of a Michael White presentation. Produced by Doug Dilge. Executive producer, Michael White. Associate producer, Sean Ferrer. Directed by Matthew Chapman. Features entire cast. Screenplay, Chapman, Blaine Novak, based on a story by Novak; camera (color), Mikail Suslor; visual consultant, Michael Riva; editor, William Carruth; music, Gato Barbieri. Reviewed at the World Film Festival (non-competing), Montreal, Aug. 24, 1983. Running Time: 94 MINS.

Stanley .... Peter Coyote
Carole Redding .... Victoria Tennant
Stevie Blake .... Blaine Novak
Sidney Ferris .... Dan Shor
Frank Silva .... Richard Romanus
Shirley .... Linda Kerridge
Estoban .... Carlos Palomino

"Stranger's Kiss" is a glowing homage to '50s melodrama set in the film world. Though shot on a modest budget, picture has a lush look aided by strong artistic and technical contributions and should

find a ready market in art house situations with potential mainstream playoff in sophisticated markets.

The love triangle tale is mirrored in both the real life and film-within-a-film structure of the production. However, inventive director and cowriter Matthew Chapman emphasizes the differences in the two situations developing a humor and irony which raises the tale beyond its modest origins.

Principals are Carole Redding (Victoria Tennant), a young woman kept by a gangster (Richard Romanus) who agrees to finance the film's film and costar, Stevie Blake (Blaine Novak, who also cowrote the script), a hustler who soon becomes consumed by Carole's mysterious background. Aware of potential problems in the circumstance, Stanley (Peter Coyote), the director, keeps Stevie in the dark to capitalize on his emotions. The charades promote an uneasiness among all parties which effectively maintains the material when it threatens to become too glib and facile.

Both stories concern a boxer and a dancehall girl who fall in love but her past debt to a hoodlum threatens to destroy the relationship. Plot is reminiscent of Stanley Kubrick's "Killer's Kiss" and several other low budget items circa 1955, the setting of the picture.

The real-life story develops a genuine threatening edge thanks to Coyote's megalemaniacal performance and Romanus' sudden flashes of temperament. The make-believe tale is rather more concerned with style and happy endings. Shot in black-and-white with an accent for chiaroscuro lighting, the film-within-a-film plays wonderfully on that era's movie cliches.

The production meanwhile manages to avoid most of the conventions with showing how films are made. And there's a marvellously comic screening-room sequence watching takes of a kiss between the principals complicated by Novak's rather large nose.

Chapman, whose previous credit was "Hussy," provides both a sense of fun and mystery to "Stranger's Kiss." Handsomely produced with excellent credits from cameraman Mikail Suslor and a moody score from Gato Barbieri, the film has an intimate quality which complements the less expansive elements of what is essentially a hoary yarn.

Victoria Tennant is radiant as Carole with a genuine screen presence suited to her role. In sharp contrast, Novak has a forceful presence which demands our attention and eventually wins our affection.

"Stranger's Kiss" should capture strong critical response and play well with the cogniscenti.

Wider audience appeal will depend on initial reaction with probable further market strength to be found in foreign markets. —*Klad.*

The Wild Duck
(AUSTRALIAN-COLOR)

Montreal, Aug. 19.

An Orion (overseas) Pictures release of a Tinzu Pty. Ltd. production. Produced by Phillip Emanuel, co-producer Basil Appleby. Directed by Henri Safran. Features entire cast. Screenplay, Safran, Peter Smalley, John Lind based on play by Henrik Ibsen; camera (color), Peter James; production design, Darrell Lass; editor, Don Saunders; music, Simon Walker. Reviewed at the World Film Festival (Competition), Montreal, Aug. 19, 1983. Running Time: **96 MINS.**

Gina Ackland ....Liv Ullmann
Harold Ackland ....Jeremy Irons
Henrietta Ackland ....Lucinda Jones
Major Ackland ....John Meillon
Gregory Wardle ....Arthur Dignam
George Wardle ....Michael Pate
Mollison.......................Colin Croft
Dr. Roland ....Rhys McConnochie
Bertha Summers ....Marion Edward
Peters ....Peter De Salis
Johnson ....Jeff Truman

Henrik Ibsen's stage chestnut, "The Wild Duck," receives an interesting, if not wholly satisfactory, translation set in turn of the century Australia. While the change of locale from Norway has no perceptible effort on the material, there's a disquieting quality in both performance and interpretation which unbalances the material. Direction and tone leave little room for interpretation and the result is overtly melodramatic.

Jeremy Irons plays the central role of Harold Ackland, a failed scientist plying his trade as a photographer. The Ackland household is filled out by Harold's wife, the hard put upon Gina (Liv Ullmann), daughter Henrietta (Lucinda Jones) and his father, the Major (John Meillon), another failure who lives in past glories and the bottle.

The relative quiet of their existence is interrupted by the arrival of Gregory Wardle (Arthur Dignam), a former classmate of Harold and the son of the town's leading merchant, the Major's former partner. Gregory is unhinged by Harold's situation and his contempt for his father. Gina is a former Wardle housekeeper that he believes carried on an affair with his father. Henrietta is actually the spawn of that liaison and Gregory sets up to reveal this fact to Harold.

Director Henri Safran, who adapted Ibsen with a handful of others, attempts a very complicated interpretation of the title character. In the opening frames, George Wardle shoots down but does not kill the duck. However, rather than do in the bird, he agrees to give it to one of his employes who in turn offers it to

the Major as part of his attic menagerie. It figures into the plot later when Henrietta, believing her father despises her, offers up the animal as a love sacrifice.

The symbolic use of the wild duck is quite heavy handed. Safran and his collaborators err toward the obvious in this rendering, allowing for several overblown performances and a pervasive, emotionally-telegraphed musical score. An earlier adaptation, by West German Hans W. Geissendorfer, ranks considerably better beside the Australian effort.

Irons, the man undone by the truth, plays his role on the edge of hysteria. There's no denying the effectiveness, at times, of the performance but it is ultimately too many hand gestures and tantrums. Conversely, Ullman remains overly subdued and rational for the union to remain credible.

Also somewhat unidimensional is Arthur Dignam as the self-righteous Gregory. He appears hell-bent to save his friend with no sense of the compassion of his action, albeit misguided, emerging. Only John Meillon, as the pathetic Major, manages a suitable balance and humanity in his characterization.

Technical work is lush, and too lush in the case of the music. The sense of claustrophobia and sobriety in Ibsen withers in the presence of Peter James' bright images and the filmmakers' physical expansion of the play.

"The Wild Duck" offers an intriguing, flawed interpretation. Cast name value should spark some art house interest in North America but the ultimate audience is severely limited in size and likely will remain unmoved by this production. — *Klad.*

My Iz Djaza
(The Jazz Man)
(SOVIET-COLOR)

Montreal, Aug. 20.

A Mosfilm production released by International Film Exchange. Directed by Karen Chakhnazarov. Features entire cast. Screenplay Chakhnazarov, Alexandre Borodianski; camera (color), Vladimir Chevtzik; art direction, Constin Forostenko; editor, Karen Chakhnazarov; music, Anatoli Kroll. Reviewed at the World Film Festival (Competition), Montreal, Aug. 20, 1983. Running Time: **88 MINS.**

Kostia.........................Igor Skoliar
Stepan .....Alexandre Pankratov-Tchiorny
Jora ....Nikolai Averiunchkine
Ivan Bavourine ....Piotr Schterbakov
Katia ....Elena Tzyplakova
Cuban Singer ....Larisa Dolana
Papa ....Jaruslav Yevestignev

"The Jazz Man," unspooling in competition at Montreal's World Film Festival, certainly ranks among the most accessible and commercially potent Soviet films of recent years. The tale of a '30s era jazz quartet overcoming official censure and suspicion is a win-

ning combination of history, humor and compassion. It's a disarming, charming venture filled with mirth and music.

Title character is a conservatory student from Odessa who shocks teachers and students with his advocacy for so-called "American decadent" music. Nonetheless, he persists maintaining jazz comes from the oppressed and is therefore revolutionary. Thankfully, this exchange transpires with good humor and tongue-in-cheek pokes at the party line.

Kostia (Igor Skoliar), the jazz man, first enlists two street musicians with the lure of steady work. Instead, they are removed forcibly from their first audition. He maintains things will improve once they acquire a saxophonist.

In the interim they get the odd job playing for closet jazz aficionados and after a row at a nightclub reach their low point in jail. There, they meet their saxophonist and head for Moscow and hopefully more sophisticated audiences. However, first they must learn the art of musical improvisation which sounds easier than it appears on screen.

Director and cowriter Karen Chakhnazarov in his second feature documents the ups and downs of the group with skill and humor. The film has the charm of a vintage musical with fantasy mixing freely with more realistic situations as the quartet proceeds to win respect and official sanction.

Based on the experiences of actual jazz exponents, the film relates a fanciful memory of the early years of Soviet jazz. Music offers variations of swing, ragtime and dixieland themes contrasted sharply with progressive movement in the epilogue.

The novelty of subject and genuine good humor is strong draw in this well-crafted outing. Technical and artistic elements are strong and "The Jazz Man's" ability to surprise in a frank, but uncritical, fashion will prove almost revelatory to foreign audiences.

"The Jazz Man" should register strong response on art house circuit and emerge as one of the more popular Soviet films of the past decade.—*Klad.*

Right Of Way
(U.S.-COLOR)

Montreal, Aug. 23.

A Schaefer/Karpf production in association with Post-Newsweek Video for HBO. Executive producer, Merrill Karpf. Produced and directed by George Schaefer. Co-producer, Philip Parslow. Features entire cast. Screenplay, Richard Lees, based on his play; camera (color), Howard Schwartz; editor, Sid Katz; production design, Jack Chilberg; music, Brad Fiedel. Reviewed at the Montreal Film Festival (Competition), Aug. 23, 1983. Running time: **106 MINS.**

Mini Dwyer..................Bette Davis
Teddy Dwyer..............James Stewart

Ruda Dwyer................Melinda Dillon
Mrs. Finter...............Priscilla Morrill
G. Clayburn................John Harkins
Mrs. Belkin...........Jacque Lynn Colton
Kahn......................Louis Schaeffer

Unspooling in Montreal's main competiton, "Right of Way" is HBO's first U.S. production intended for pay-tv first release in America. The story of an old couple who plan a joint suicide, rather than face death separately, lacks both commercial appeal or novelty necessary to ensure possible foreign theatrical sales. However, the sheer experience of seeing James Stewart and Bette Davis together will be a strong lure for television outings. .

Coupling of the two veteran actors will draw immediate comparisons with screen version of "On Golden Pond." Also, both stories are derived from stage plays, although "Right of Way" has been limited to regional productions. Here, comparison ends and the differences pay off in "On Golden Pond's" favor.

Stewart and Davis play Teddy and Mini Dwyer, a retiring couple who live in a rundown house in Santa Monica with a platoon of cats named after contemporary male screen performers. The son of a wealthy family, Teddy is consumed with his books and Mini makes specialty dolls, an art learned from her mother.

The normality of their life masks a bizarre plan they've been brewing. They explain to their daughter, Ruda (Melinda Dillon), that Mini has a terminal blood disease and they've chosen to kill themselves. Ruda, after much discussion, realizes their seriousness and attempts to dissuade her parents.

However, her good intentions backfire. She sends a social worker to see them who, upon hearing their plan, reacts in horror. Soon, city officials, lawyers and the press are taking up the story and Ruda finds herself regretting her earlier action.

Prime weakness of the material is finding the levity in the grim conviction of the couple. There is a marvelous rapport between Teddy and Mini which emerges in their daily existence but this dissipates whenever the subject of their suicide arises. And forcing the humor only diminishes the facile nature of the writing and situation.

Nonetheless, both Stewart and Davis fight valiantly to rise above their material with Stewart demonstrating a conviction and sensitivity in his role. Davis fares slightly worse, appearing too cute and doll-like as if she were one of her own creations. The latter actually occurs and serves as a rather unconvincing bond between mother and daughter.

Director George Schaefer fails to establish the irony of this lively couple contemplating their own end. The film has a fairy tale quality which is further heightened by the prettiness of the Southern California locations. It's just too bright and cheerful to convey the earnest underpinnings.

The supporting work by Dillon is fine in an underdeveloped role. Her character must bridge a rift with her mother and realize the unwitting damage of her action without benefit of supporting scenes in the script. Too much is left to discretion of the viewer.

"Right of Way" remains a production of noble intentions which squanders the skills of two accomplished actors. Less cleverness and more attention to detail should have been applied to this material.
—*Klad.*

Red Bells: I've Seen The Birth Of The New World
(SOVIET-MEXICAN-ITALIAN-COLOR-70M)

Montreal, Aug. 25.

A co-production of Mosfilm Studios (USSR), Conacite-2 (Mex) and Vides International (Italy). Directed by Sergei Bondarchuk. Features entire cast. Screenplay, Bondarchuk, Antonio Saguera; camera (color), Vadim Yousov; art direction, Levan Shengeliya; music, Georgy Sviridov. Reviewed at the World Film Fetival (non-competing), Montreal, Aug. 25, 1983. Running Time: 137 MINS.
Lenin................Anatoly Ustiuzhaninov
John Reed.......:..........Franco Nero
Louise Bryant................Sydne Rome

"John, you just slept through the revolution," a fellow journalist informs a sleeping John Reed near the end of Sergei Bondarchuk's second installment of "Red Bells," subtitled "I've Seen the Birth of the New World." The line receives an unintentional laugh and those dozing at the epic will likely be awakened for the film's spectacular finale storming of the Winter Palace.

The second and final episode in what was originally conceived as a three-part film, is a wholesale "redwash" of John Reed's (Franco Nero) coverage of the events leading up to 1917. Bondarchuk presents an earnest, humorless portrait of the 10 days that shook the world according to Reed's book. In comparison to "Reds," Warren Beatty's film of the same subject, "Red Bells" has the sensibility of a Classics Illustrated comic book and can only boast of filming on the actual locations as an advantage over the Beatty production.

Film opens in Moscow with Reed and Louise Bryant (Sydne Rome) contemplating how to cover the tumultuous events of early 1917. The first part of "Red Bells" closed with Reed's coverage of the Mexican revolution, so one assumes the establishing material with Bryant was scrapped with the decision to make only two parts to the epic.

With the monarchy overthrown in Russia, a fierce power struggle begins between the new government and the Bolsheviks led by V.I. Lenin (Anatoly Ustiuzhaninov). Lenin denounces the government as landowners with little regard for the peasantry and demonstrations fuel the crowd against the country's involvement in the First World War.

Like Reed, Bondarchuk views the incidents at arm's length developing no more than cardboard emotions. Although Lenin is given top billing in part 2, he's viewed at a distance with no indication of the man underneath the revolutionary. Conversely Reed and Bryant remain well-meaning, naive foreigners distressed about their true commitment to the cause.

As mentioned, the climactic storming of the Winter Palace provides the film's most stunning moments. The director's ability with crowds and action cannot be denied and one assumes no courtesy was withheld in the making of the closing scenes.

However, where Bondarchuk ranks as a professional technically, he is a rank amateur dramatically. The players of the revolution, with few exceptions, are thumb-nail, monolithic portraits. Rome offers a flyweight interpretation of Bryant and Nero is too old and thick-headed to convince as Reed. None of this is aided by dialog, spoken in Russian, English and French.

As with the earlier "Red Bells: Mexico in Flames," the Soviet-Mexican-Italian coproduction "Red Bells: I've Seen The Birth Of The New World" offers no more than a curiosity look. Commercial prospects are decidedly dim and initial plans in many areas are to attempt exploitation through television rather than theatrical playoff. Ironically, the film's technical strength will be diminished on the small screen and its lack of intimacy further accentuated. —*Klad.*

Home Free All
(U.S.-COLOR)

Montreal, Aug. 27.

A P.O.P. Company production. Produced by Stewart Bird, Peter Belsito. Directed and written by Stewart Bird. Features entire cast. Camera (color), Robert Levi; editor, Daniel Loewenthal; music, Jay Chattaway; sound, Ed Novick. Reviewed at the World Film Festival (non-competing), Montreal, Aug. 27, 1983. Running Time: 92 MINS.
Barry Simon................Allan Nicholls
Al........................Roland Caccavo
Marvin.....................Lorry Goldman
Cathy.......................Muary Ellyn
Custodian............Jose Ramon Rosario

Impotent, left-over leftists have become the target of much recent comedy. Director Stewart Bird's first feature creates a jaundiced but sympathetic portrait of hero Barry Simon, a former radical and

future writer, who is constantly being told to grow up.

Barry lives on East 10th St. in New York, and in the first two sequences, he suffers the worst that can befall a Jewish intellectual New Yorker. He loses both his shrink and his girl, who moves out, leaving him time to renew an old friendship from his adolescence with Al, a successful suburban husband and father dissatisfied with his lot.

Al shows Barry how grown-ups live, and Barry shows Al how little fun all the free and easy village life really is. They play tennis and handball and lust after the same or similar women. Al moves in with Barry and behaves like a man used to having things done for him which irritates Barry. The dialog is psychologically acute and their respective situations ring true without ever resorting to cliches.

About midway into the film, they meet another old classmate, Marvin, who wields power in the Jewish mafia. A glimpse at a Jewish "Mean Streets" ensues, as Barry picks up some work from his mafioso buddy and then tries to back out. But nobody gets hurt.

Only violence in the film is felt in the threat from the landlord wanting to get rid of his low-rent tenants by torching their apartments. Barry's neighbor, the custodian, gets killed by some thugs, while Barry is out wandering the city trying to negotiate a reconciliation with his girlfriend. Her pregnancy gives them reason to believe they can settle down, and the final sequence is a celebration with both families reunited over turkey and football at Al's suburban home.

Stewart Bird has benefitted from his years of winning awards as the docu helmer of socially conscious pics like "The Wobblies," and "Coming Home," a docu about Vietnam vets that preceded the Hollywood production. He knows and develops his characters with tolerance and a great deal of humor, and displays a gift for straightforward story-telling about psychological complexity. Central to each of the principal's life is his experience in Vietnam, confessed to a montage of black-and-white flashbacks. The device does not interfere and slowly develops Barry's worst fears about confirmity.

New York locations and very good ethnic casting gives the pic a feeling of being a new angle on some tried and true situations. The poignant moments are handled without sentimentality, ironies never overstated. New Yorkers and frustrated people everywhere are bound to love laughing at themselves and their loss of innocence mirrored in the characters. The peppy pacing never loses the au-

dience and makes it seem bigger than it actually is.

As a modest production, it seems geared for the art house circuit but ought to find bigger boxoffice, as word-of-mouth generates interest in a public looking for human comedy. Although it is a natural for tv, Bird has opened it up and the lensing looks like hard-edged realism on the big screen. —*Kaja.*

Benvenuta
(BELGIAN-FRENCH-COLOR)

Montreal, Aug. 20.

An UGC release of a Nouvelle Imagerie-Opera films production. Produced by Jean-Claude Batz. Directed by Andre Delvaux. Features entire cast. Screenplay, Delvaux, based on novel, "La Confession Anonyme," by Suzanne Lilar; camera (Eastmancolor), Charles Van Damme; set design, Claude Pignot; editor, Albert Jurgenson; music, Frederic Devreese. Reviewed at the World Film Festival (Competition), Montreal, August 20, 1983. Running Time: 103 MINS.
Benvenuta..............Fanny Ardant
Livio................Vittorio Gassman
Jeanne.............Francoise Fabian
Francois...........Mathieu Carriere
Inge................Claire Wauthion
Father.............Philippe Geluck
Mother..............Anne Chappuis

Flemish filmmaker Andre Delvaux is an infrequent producer of highly idiosyncratic tales for the cinema. "Benvenuta," (note: winner of Montreal's Special Jury Prize) is his first feature in five years and relates the story of a woman's passionate, impossible love for a married man.

Definitely aimed at a specialty audience, the film should garner some interest in several European markets and a limited art house release in North America. However, despite the presence of such name talent as Vittorio Gassman and Fanny Ardant, commercial prospects will be limited and wider audiences elusive.

The story begins with scriptwriter Mathieu Carriere tracking down the author of a once-scandalous novel. His aim is to adapt the work for screen but several elements of the novel he finds difficult to comprehend. The author, Jeanne (Francoise Fabian), is initially cautious of relaying information, insisting the presumably autobiographical book in no way relates to her personal life.

However, eventually she takes the man into her confidence to tell the background of Benvenuta (Fanny Ardant). She paints the picture of a musical virtuouso who against her better judgment becomes involved with an Italian magistrate played by Vittorio Gassman. It's a no-holds-barred passion of hot temperaments doomed to a miserable conclusion.

In addition to detailing a liaison described by the protoganist where "the sweetest thing in love is violence," Delvaux appears consumed with the boundaries between fact and fiction. As Francois develops his script, he informs the author that it will have to be updated. In an instant, the flashbacks switch from period to modern settings.

Later, he has the scriptwriter almost bump into the supposedly fictional Benvenuta in the street. And when Jeanne dies, it is Benvenuta who burns her personal records.

It's a fascinating premise but Delvaux lacks the imagination to elevate the incidents above a stilted, arch rendering. The entire production becomes trivialized in games of reason better suited to "The Twilight Zone."

Still, both Gassman and the dazzling Ardant develop a strong screen chemistry providing the film's best moments. The framing story is considerably more reserved and constrained and artifically artistic. Apart from lush production values, one might assume they'd stumbled across a lost product from the French new wave.

Careful marketing may provide some added life to "Benvenuta." However, Delvaux's split loyalty between the two parallel threads of his story weakens both and finally, the entire picture: —*Klad.*

Venice Festival

Streamers
(U.S.-COLOR)

Venice, Sept. 4.

A Nick J. Mileti production, United Artists Classics release. Produced by Nick J. Mileti, Robert Altman. Screenplay, based on his own stage play, David Rabe. Directed by Robert Altman. Features entire cast. Camera (Eastmancolor) Pierre Mignot; editor, Norman Smith; production design, Wolf Kroeger; art director, Steve Altman; costumes, Scott Bushnell; music, the song Stephen Foster's "Beautiful Dreamer" with new words added, executive producers, Robert Michael Geisler, John Roberdeau. Reviewed as an official competition entry in the Venice Film Festival, Casino La Perla, Venice, Sept. 4, 1983 Running time, 118 MINS.

Billy .... Matthew Modine
Carlyle .... Michael Wright
Richie .... Mitchell Lichtenstein
Roger .... David Allen Grier
Martin .... Albert Macklin
Sgt. Rooney .... Guy Boyd
Sgt. Cokes .... George Dzundza

Recently enamored with working for the legit stage, Robert Altman now follows up on his dual theatre and film effort, "Come Back To The Five & Dime," with "Streamers," a feature film based on David Rabe's stage play (originally a Joseph Papp production directed by Mike Nichols). From an all-female cast, Altman now has an all-male one, but from a technique of the quickly shot, almost improvised film he, this time, offers a carefully crafted work.

It remains, however, a much more stage-bound affair, while it also — and very un-Altmanish — allows each actor to finish whatever string of words he has more or less mumblingly launched before the other guy takes over. This makes for a certain clarity of meaning, but hardly for a realism that is never more than token. "Streamers" is a highly stylized set of theatricals describing an existentialist hell among a small group of men in a military barracks.

Apart from allowing the camera to occasionally peek through a curtain, Rabe and Altman have their 1965 soldiers await orders to go to Vietnam and spending the waiting time either lying around on their bunks or returning drunk from saloon or whorehouse outings. They mostly taunt each other with tales of their own past history, but the taunts are socially, racially and sexually loaded, two of the soldiers being black, a third being an Ivy League homosexual and the fourth an intellectual "from the sticks." Two sergeants are seen as cardboard brutes.

Playing on the themes of their various hang-ups or passions, the soldiers all play a game to the death. The sergeants, in a musically mounted sequence, emulate paratroopers (the men are all of the Screaming Eagle Regiment) descending in slow rhythms through the air. They sing "Beautiful Dreamer" all the while, but with new words to make us know that the film's title refers to paratrooper lingo for a soldier whose chute has not opened. To otherwise entertain audiences that will probably be restricted to diehard Altman fans, the camera is lingering lovingly and possibly meaningfully in various symbolic ways on faces, feet, beer bottles and light bulbs, etc.

Things do, of course, explode in blood-gushing violence and general sadness when the possibilities of the thematic monotony have been exhausted in this overlong, over-emphatic film. The actors all, with the exception of the men playing the sergeants, attempt to look and sound like everyday men, but the

Under Fire
(U.S.-COLOR)

Venice, Sept. 2.

An Orion Pictures release of a Lion's Gate Film. Produced by Jonathan Taplin; executive producer, Edward Teets. Directed by Roger Spottiswoode. Stars Nick Nolte, Gene Hackman. Screenplay, Ronald Shelton, Clayton Frohman; story, Frohman; camera (color), John Alcott; art direction, Agustin Ytarte; music, Jerry Goldsmith; editing, Mark Conte. Reviewed at Venice Film Festival (Venice by Night Information Section), Sept. 2, '83. Running time: 100 MINS.

Russell Price .... Nick Nolte
Alex Grazier .... Gene Hackman
Claire Stryder .... Joanna Cassidy
Marcel Jazy .... Jean-Louis Trintignant
Oates .... Ed Harris
Hub Kittle .... Richard Masur
Somoza .... Rene Enriques
Regis Seydor .... Hamilton Camp
Isela .... Alma Martinez
Miss Panama .... Jenny Gago
Pedro .... Eloy Casados
Rafael .... Jorge Zepeda

Films dealing with revolutionary moments in modern history are quite plentiful these days, and some directors — Constantine Costa-Gavras and Peter Weir, to name the most prominent — seem of late to be making a career out of the historical drama. Now comes Roger Spottiswoode's highly commended "Under Fire," the best feature film made to date on Nicaragua; others in the past have been Peter Lilienthal's "The Uprising" (West Germany) and Miguel Littin's "Alsino and the Condor" (Nicaragua-Mexico). And in light of the recent political developments in Latin America, particularly Nicaragua, pic should get a better critical response and playoff than otherwise.

The American media are strongly taken to task in "Under Fire." This is the story of two correspondents (one working for Time, the other Public Radio) and an on-the-scenes war photographer. The action begins in the African bush of Chad, then moves on to Nicaragua — and a feature-film rehearsal of that tragic televised killing of the ABC correspondent by a Somoza government soldier in the late 1970s as he was covering the fighting with the winning Sandinista rebels. In view of the fact that the public media have a way of stumbling over their own wire services in covering hot political news, these newshounds are fair game for a critical motion picture like this. Another attempt in the same direction was made by Volker Schloendorff in covering the Lebanese Crisis through the eyewitness accounts of writer-journalist Nicholas Born, but his "Circle of Deceit" (1981) failed miserably in taking a serious point-of-view. Not so "Under Fire."

Three individuals cover the Chad conflict in the late 1960s: the 30-year-old photog Russell Price (Nick Nolte), the 50-year-old senior correspondent for Time mag Alex Grazier (Gene Hackman), and the circa 40-year-old radio newslady Claire Stryder (Joanna Cassidy). All are tough professionals, yet clearly in the tradition of the vulnerable, somewhat romantic protagonists of the Hollywood genre action film: for them, good old-fashioned loyalty is more important than sympathy with the downtrodden or the underdog. But Grazier has become tired of it all, and Price will end up with the same feeling in Nicaragua. It's the same with Stryder, whose affections

gradually grow for the photo-journalist after the Time newsman (her

erstwhile lover as well as close colleague) returns briefly home to the States to take a new job as an anchor man on tv for $10,000 a month and a home on Long Island. It's living on the periphery of danger that attracts them all, just as it did Ernest Hemingway and countless name journalists of the recent past.

There's a fourth individual who surfaces now and then: he's a hired mercenary, a killer by trade, whom lenser Nolte meets from time to time, first in Chad and later in Nicaragua. It's the mercenary's cold-blooded killing habit that eventually forces the photographer to take "sides" as well as "pictures" — particularly when he sees the wanton killing in the streets and villages by Somoza's troops, while the dictator himself receives the comforting support of the CIA and other Washington officials. General publicized accounts of underhanded Yankee involvement in Latin America are known via released papers by American government agencies (a feather, by the way, in the cap of democracy) but this is probably the first time that both the American media and p.r. agencies on the side of the Somoza regime (read the character named Oates in this case) are openly taken to task in an American feature film production aimed for stateside commercial release. Hats off.

In the course of covering the events Nolte and Cassidy opt to search for a certain rebel leader named Rafael among the revolutionary Sandinistas, for Rafael has never been photographed nor interviewed by the American press. When they do reach an enclave of the rebels, they discover that Rafael has been killed in an ambush. But the rebels want Nolte to photograph him in such a position that he appears to be alive — the photo thereupon to be released to the world press for certification. In this way the Sandinistas can expect support from Western supporters (including Americans) to carry on the revolution. Nolte gives in — but here's the twist: the photo becomes the sensation of New York and causes Hackman to return to the scene in order to convince Nolte to lead him to Rafael for an interview. This move results in the death of Hackman at the hands of the Somoza militia, the fatal encounter photographed by Nolte.

Further, Nolte's photos of the rebels play into the hands of a double-agent, the Frenchman (Jean-Louis Trintignant), who uses them to hunt down and kill the key Sandinista leaders. So now Nolte is guilty indirectly of their deaths. Moral factors like these are the core of the action — to the end, when Somoza abandons ship for sunny Florida. All the same, the motivational elements are never clarified by Spottiswoode — a broadcast, for instance, on Nicaraguan TV of the Somoza killing of Hackman stretches credulity in the plot to the breaking point.

Lensing is top grade, the chores handled by John Alcott. Thesping is also on the plus side, particularly Nolte in a role cut to his proportions, and the script has several succinct dialog exchanges penned by Clayton Frohman and Ronald Shelton. Roger Spottiswoode, after a couple of earlier actioners, has great potential, if the signs are right in this warm-up venture.

"Under Fire" should do well on home front, although it tends to split the European critics down the middle on its ambivalent handling of the external political issues.
—*Holl.*

Never Cry Wolf
(U.S.-COLOR)

Venice, Sept. 1.

A Buena Vista release of a Walt Disney Pictures production of a Carroll Ballard film. Executive producer, Ron Miller. Produced by Lewis Allen, Jack Couffer, Joseph Strick; associate producer, Walker Stuart. Directed by Carroll Ballard. Screenplay, Curtis Hanson, Sam Hamm, and Richard Kletter, based on a book by Farley Mowat; narration, C.M. Smith, Eugene Corr, Christina Luescher; camera (Technicolor, Panavision, Dolby Stereo), Hiro Narita; art direction, Graeme Murray; music, Mark Isham; editing, Peter Parasheles, Michael Chandler; sound, Alan R. Splet. reviewed at Venice Film Fest (Young Venice competition), Sept. 1, '83. Running time: 105 MINS.
Tyler . . . . Charles Martin Smith
Rosie . . . . Brian Dennehy
Ootek . . . . Zachary Ittimangnaq
Mike . . . . Samson Jorah
Drunk . . . . Hugh Webster
Woman . . . . Martha Ittimangnaq
Hunter No. 1 . . . . Tom Dahlgren
Hunter No. 2 . . . . Walker Stuart

For the masses out there who love nature films, and even those who don't, Carroll Ballard's "Never Cry Wolf" more than fits the commercial bill and should score well too with critical auds on several counts. Pic ws two years in production in the wilds of the Yukon and Alaska, and it measures up to the promise Ballard amply provided in his first feature, "The Black Stallion."

It's already a leading contender for the kudos in the Young Venice competition (open for first two pics of a new director), taking a lot of top crits by surprise who went into the screening with expectations of seeing a run of the mill outdoor life elegy, one bearing the Walt Disney stamp of family approval. It's all of that, of course — and something refreshingly more.

Basically, this is a story about the life-and-times of white wolves in the Arctic. It's based on a best-seller, Farley Mowat's "Never Cry Wolf" (an autobiographical account of the popular writer's experiences as a government biologist in the Canadian Northwest).

The stretch of location shooting in and around Dawson City, Yukon, and Nome, Alaska, tried the talents of the entire crew, from the documentarist Ballard to actor Charles Martin Smith in the role of the young biologist Tyler — it was seasonal work requiring proper lighting, patient animal training and performance, and simply two years of hard work. The results of this sweat-and-labor are all to be found in the film's powerful images and comprehending feel for the wonders and mysteries of Mother Nature.

The story is simple: idiotically simple. Biologist Tyler is sent to survive in the Arctic while investigating whether the predatory wolf is responsible for the gradual disappearance of the caribou herds. Tyler, a naive lad, could hardly survive a winter alone in any case, so a friendly but reticent Eskimo, Ootek, fortunately happens by the helpless biologist's stake-out in the dead of winter to rescue him — both the greenhorn and his supplies are then transported to an isolated hut, whereupon Tyler is left on his own again.

When the weather begins to change, Tyler falls through the ice on a lake during an expedition, but finally the idiot-biologist hardens into a practical scientist by learning everything the hard way — including eating mice to survive when his supplies run out.

Then begins the study of the white wolf. It turns out to be just like numerous recent articles and Mowat's own book: the wolf is, after all, an intelligent creature and deft provider with warm family ways, hardly the villain he's so often made out to be and certainly not the reason for the ongoing decrease in the caribou herds. Indeed, it's the wolf that's being wantonly hunted for the bounty on his pelt. Biologist Tyler, in some of the wittiest, funniest, and most human scenes in the film, comes to know his research-quarry quite intimately as George and Angeline living with their family of three pups in a nearby den. When Eskimos Ootek and Mike later join him for company, the wisdom of this production surfaces in their light conversation on man and nature.

In the end, when the caribou arrive on a trek of their own, the final proof is garnered on the innocence of the wolf — even though the kill of one weak caribou is registered (it's evidence instead of Nature's way of removing the weak to strengthen the strong). Man also appears on the scene in a most undignified manner: the wilderness is gradually being exploited for commercial gain without bothering in the lest for relevant ecological needs.

All this said, the most praise goes to the imagery of this poetic fiction-documentary as fashioned by Ballard, together with his able cameraman Hiro Narita and soundman Alan R. Splet. The style of the film, indeed, questions the efficacy of labeling "Never Cry Wolf" under the usual genres. One guess is that film historians will probably classify Carroll Ballard's "Black Stallion" and "Never Cry Wolf" as fable-documentaries or poetic nature-epics; and if there is any weakness to note at all, it lies in the rather extreme poetic and romantic polish of the director's vision. No biologist is that dumb, to begin with, on an expedition into the wilds of the Northwest. And if he was, he should have taken Jack London's "Call of the Wild" along with him to read in his spare time.

Yet the magic of the film is in that quaint comic performance rendered by thesp Charles Martin Smith. He's the Goofy of the Walt Disney nature series. — *Holl.*

1919
(SPANISH-COLOR)

Madrid, Aug. 29.

A T.V.E., S.A. (Spanish Television) presentation, produced by Ofelia Films, S.A. - Carlos Escobedo. Associate producer, Kaktus P.C. Features entire cast. Directed by Antonio Jose Betancor; Screenplay, Lautaro Murua, Antonio Jose Betancor, Carlos Escobedo, Javier Moro, based on novel "Cronica del Alba" by Ramon J. Sender; camera, (Eastmancolor), Juan A. Ruiz Anchia; sets, Felix Murcia; costumes, Javier Artinano; editor, Eduardo Biurrum; sound, Jim Willis; music, Riz Ortolani. Reviewed at Cine Avenida, Madrid Aug. 29, 1983. Running time: 85 MINS.
Pepe . . . . Miguel Molina
Isabelita . . . . Cristina Marsillach
Checa . . . . : . . . . Walter Vidarte
Lucas . . . . Jose Antonio Correa
Valentina . . . . Emma Suarez
    Also, Saturno Ferra, Conchita Leza, Marisa de Leza, Alfredo Luchetti, Fernando Sancho, Juan Jose Otegui, Claudio Rodriguez et al.

Antonio Jose Betancor's continuation of the "Dawn Chronicle," based on the Ramon J. Sender story, is very much in the line of the foregoing "Valentina," but the lack of Anthony Quinn in the cast as a drawing card will probably lessen commercial interest in it.

Like "Valentina," it is sensitively directed and atmospheric, but the action is too sporadic to enable interest to build. It is series of vignettes in provincial Spain of 1919; there are overtones of the Communist and Anarchist troubles that were to sunder the country in 1936, but all this is left inconclusively to impress the adolescent Pepe, now a decade older.

The meagre storyline sees Pepe's family moving to another province while he, aged 15, stays on in Zaragoza as a pharmacy apprentice. He's still carrying a torch for Valentina, who has been sent off to a nun's school, but meanwhile meets a new girl, Isabelita,

in a cinema, therewith providing him (and her) with his first sexual experience.

He visits Valentina once at her school, but the encounter remains inconclusive; her family is dead set against Pepe. Returning to Zaragoza, he watches with fascination as his anarchist acquaintances have a shoot-out with the police and are killed or captured; finally, after graduating from school, he joins up again with Isabelita.

Thesping is fine throughout. Miguel Molina (brother of Angela Molina) is a bit stiff and self-conscious, but this goes well with the part he plays; Cristina Marsillach (daughter of Spain's well-known legit director and actor Adolfo Marsillach) steals the scenes whenever she comes on; and Walter Vidarte plays to perfection the hounded, idealistic revolutionary whose fate is a foregone conclusion. — *Besa.*

(Pic is official competing entry at the Venice Film Festival).

Ja, vi elsker ...
(Last Gleaming)
(NORWEGIAN-COLOR)

Oslo, Aug. 20.

A Filmgruppe 1 A/S production, foreign sales: Norsk Film A/S. Based on an idea by Soelve Skagen, Malte Wadman. Script for fiction part, Oeystein Loenn. Features entire cast. General structuring, narration (English) and editor, Andrew Szepesy. Directed by Soelve Skagen, Malte Wadman. Camera (Eastmancolor), Bahram Manocheri; production management, Laila Mikkelsen, Gaute Kristiansen. Trond documentary footage, NRK, Norsk Ukerevy, Visnews, BBC; poetry quotations, Jan Erik Vold, Rudolf Nilsen, Arnulf Oeverland, Georg Johannesen, Henrik Wergeland, Bjoernstjerne Bjoernson; music, Richard Nordraak, Fartein Valen, Arne Nordheim, Torgrim Sollid, Jan Garbarek, Voemmoel Spellmannslag, etc. Reviewed at Norsk Film screening room, Jar, Oslo, Aug. 20, 1983. Running time: 115 MINS.
    Cast: Roy A. Hansen, Hildegunn Eggen, Ib Kjoelsen, Asle Bjelland, Sverre Anker Ousdal, Georg Arntzen, Kristin Hauge, Joerund Flaa.

"Ja, vi elsker" (Meaning "Yes, we do love ...," these being the first words of Norway's national anthem) will be marketed abroad as "Last Gleaming" with a reference to Soelve Skagen and Malte Wadman's use of a drowning man's reliving of his past to frame their summing up in partly-straight, partly-mock documentary form, with interviews interspersed, of life after 1968 for the then active young radical and intellectuals. The framing later is revealed as being strictly phony, but it adds about the only dash of humor to the somber, pessimistic proceedings: it seems that actually 70 Norwegians, most of them drunk, fall out of small boats and drown every year.

The drowning man is a high school teacher, who has come to

lack conviction when he tells his pupils about the world according to Marx & Co. He is divorced, father of a son, and he remembers his own father. He remembers how his only real relationship to the working classes had to do with making a poor girl pregnant. He sees scenes of life with father and sex with the girl, he hears friends of his youth talking shrilly to each other without ever listening to other opinions than their own about women's lib, the New Man, etc.

Poets are quoted with urgent lines about accepting responsibility for the various evils of the modern world. Docu shots of concentration camp corpses and Hitler yelling and being applauded are thrown in along with similar — and to Norwegians always embarrassing — thousands of Oslovites giving the Hitler salute to the Gestapo head of their German occupiers in 1941. The mushroom cloud is in there, too, of course. But in the filmmakers' pessimistic view, everything has been for nothing.

While pessimism may be legitimate enough, it is definitely detrimental to its message when it is expressed sullenly, heavily and with endless repetition in an overlong film that is also almost totally devoid of any filmic rhythm or cinematic suspense. It just keeps plodding on like a weary, beaten infantryman blaming all the world's trouble on his feet, while viewing the world from the same feet's perspective.

It is hard to see any future either in theatres at home or via tv or festivals abroad for "Last Gleaming" even if English narration has been supplied from the outside by Andrew Szepesy, a Norwegian-based former London Film School teacher and BBC-2 producer.

—*Kell.*

Strange Invaders
(COLOR)

Solid special effects in sci-fi/horror winner.

Hollywood, Sept. 9.

An Orion Pictures release of a Michael Laughlin production for Orion Pictures in Association with EMI. Produced by Walter Coblanz. Features entire cast. Directed by Michael Laughlin. Screenplay. William Condon, Michael Laughlin; camera (Deluxecolor, Louis Horvath; editor, John W. Wheeler; production and costume design, Susanna Moore; art director, Emad Helmy; music, John Addison; set decoration, Gus Meunier; sound, Peter Shewchuk; assistant director, David Shepherd; associate producers, Richard Moore, Joel Cohan; special visual effects, Private Stock Effects Inc., Chuck Comisky, Ken Jones, Larry Benson; visual effects design, John Muto, Robert Skotak. Reviewed at Orion Pictures, Century City, Calif., Sept. 8, 1983. MPAA rating: PG. Running time: 94 MINS.

Charles Bigelow	Paul LeMat
Betty Walker	Nancy Allen
Margaret	Diana Scarwid
Willie Collins	Michael Lerner
Mrs. Benjamin	Louise Fletcher
Earl	Wallace Shawn
Waitress/Avon lady	Fiona Lewis
Arthur Newman	Kenneth Tobey
Mrs. Bigelow	June Lockhart
Professor Hollister	Charles Lane
Elizabeth	Lulu Sylbert

Striking special effects keyed to the shriveling of the human form into the membrane and bug-like features of outer-space aliens position this Orion release for a respectable early autumn payoff. More intriguing, to filmgoers satiated with sci-fi and horror/suspense, is a script (by director Michael Laughlin and William Condon) which has some fun flapping together the decades of the 1950s and '80s.

Paul LeMat, a professor caught in the time warp, and Nancy Allen, a tabloid journalist, make an engaging, offbeat team. Prospects could be surprisingly rosy, given the timing of the release, the film's craftsmanship, and the sly sense of affection for source material zeroing back to "The Day the Earth Stood Still" and ranging forward to "E.T."

Dominant genre theme, again, is that distant planets are inhabited by beings of superintelligence. In this case, they materialize in a small, midwestern hamlet in the no-nonsense year 1958 and assume the bodies of the town's small populace. The real people disappear via glowing, white-speckled blue spheres.

The nice technical achievement here, notwithstanding the horrific human transformations, is the light humor the filmmakers distill into the 1950s. Susanna Moore's production decor and cinematographer Louis Horvath's soft-focus and bucolic-tinged vision effectively counterpoint contemporary New York and the beginning of LeMat's pursuit for his little daughter (Lulu Sylbert, whose father is Oscar-winning production designer Richard

Sylbert). LeMat, refreshing, off-hand and low-key, hooks up with Allen, a cynical but sunny exploitation reporter for The National Informer.

Nub of plot centers on fact that LeMat's ex-wife, played with appropriate stone-face by Diana Scarwid, is one of the aliens who has opted for life on earth. Now the aliens, in the form of those 1958 midwestern farmers, have come to Gotham to retrieve the wife and daughter.

Scary bait in these scenes involve villainess Fiona Lewis, apartment maintenance man Wallace Shawn, and a shocker in a hotel room when one of the aliens rips off his skin and skull to resume his bug shape. After encounters with U.S. government scientist Louise Fletcher and alien victim Michael Lerner, principals converge on the midwestern hamlet to solve the mystery.

The problem with the picture is its perceptible shift in tone, from light satire to straight-away horror. This unevenness is rather joltingly resolved when those blue spheres reappear and bring everyone back to life. Pic's end, in fact, strongly suggests the very end of "The Wizard of Oz." Filmmakers try to have it too many ways, but that unsteadiness does not, finally, seriously detract from aforementioned virtues. — *Loyn.*

Revenge Of The Ninja
(COLOR)

Strong on action, weak on acting.

An MGM-UA and Cannon Group release of a Golan-Globus production. Produced by Menahem Golan, Yoram Globus. Directed by Sam Firstenberg. Stars Sho Kosugi. Screenplay, James R. Silke; camera (TVC color), David Gurfinkel; supervising editor, Michael J. Duthie; editor, Mark Helfrich; music, Rob Walsh; add'l music, W. Michael Lewis, Laurin Rinder; sound, Les Udy; assistant directors, Michael Schroeder, Dennis White; art direction, Paul Staheli; set decoration, Diane Perryman; fight choreography, Sho Kosugi; stunt coordinator, Steven Lambert; special effects, Joe Quinlivan; second unit camera, Reed Smoot; additional photography, Hanania Baer; optical effects, Cineffects Visuals; associate producer, David Womark. Reviewed at RKO Warner 2 theatre, N Y., Sept. 11, 1983. (MPAA Rating: R). Running time: 88 MINS.

Cho Osaki	Sho Kosugi
Dave Hatcher	Keith Vitali
Lt. Dime	Virgil Frye
Braden	Arthur Roberts
Caifano	Mario Gallo
Grandmother	Grace Oshita
Cathy	Ashley Ferrare
Kane Osaki	Kane Kosugi

Also with: John La Motta, Melvin C. Hampton, Oscar Rowland, Prof. Toru Tanaka, Dan Shanks.

Cannon's "Revenge Of The Ninja" is an entertaining martial arts actioner, following up company's "Enter The Ninja" but lacking that film's name players and Far East locale. Designed as a bread-and-butter (or more precisely mat-

zoh-and-butter) picture, film is weak in the story and acting areas, but makes up for these failings in solid action sequences spotlighting Japanese topliner Sho Kosugi. There is a third film in the series already in preparation, but distrib MGM-UA is unlikely to add another hit series to its James Bond, Pink Panther and Rocky Balboa legacy from United Artists.

After a brief intro set in Japan, where Cho Osaki (Sho Kosugi) witnesses most of his family wiped out by black-clad ninjas, action shifts to an unidentified U.S. locale (filmed in Salt Lake City) six years later. Osaki, with his surviving child and its grandma, runs a gallery featuring imported Japanese dolls, which unbeknownst to him is a front for heroin smuggling (inside the dolls) run by his pal Braden (Arthur Roberts). Braden is involved with an unscrupulous U.S. mobster Caifano (Mario Gallo), and having trained as a ninja for many years in Japan, dons the black garb and a mask to go on a rampage of bloodletting against Caifano's men to convince their boss to play ball with him.

Revenge occurs when Braden kills grannie, kidnaps the child Kane (Kane Kosugi) and later kills Osaki's best friend, martial arts expert Dave Hatcher (Keith Vitali). After numerous battles, pic climaxes in a photogenic, rooftop ninja vs. ninja free-for-all.

Fine fight choreography by Kosugi, including fast and often funny moves by him, keeps the film cooking. When Israeli-born director Sam Firstenberg stops for a dramatic scene however, he delivers truly awful acting by all the leads. Gallo and Frye overact while Vitali and Roberts are stiff and give monotone readings. Ferrare adds pulchritude but is unconvincing in an ambiguous role. Kosugi is best in action, with his precocious son Kane a physically agile, scene-stealing little performer.

Tech credits are okay, with an overbearing synthesizer-plus-percussion score. —*Lor.*

Stryker
(FILIPINO-COLOR)

A New World Pictures release of an HCI International Pictures production. Produced and directed by Cirio H. Santiago. Features entire cast. Screenplay, Howard R. Cohen; camera (Technicolor), Ricardo Remias; editor, B. Samos; music, Ed Gatchalian; production manager, Aurelio Navarro; special effects, J. Sto. Domingo. Reviewed at UA Rivoli II theatre, N.Y., Sept. 2, 1983. (MPAA Rating: R). Running time: 84 MINS.

Cast: Steve Sandor (Stryker), Andria Savio, William Ostrander, Michael Lane, Julie Gray, Monique St. Pierre, Jon Harris 3d, Ken Metcalfe.

A Grade-D imitation of "The Road Warrior," "Stryker" offers little for today's action audience.

Nearly-plotless assemblage of stray footage is a step down for veteran action director Cirio H. Santiago, and will certainly die quickly at the boxoffice once the word gets out on its contents.

Inane script credited to Howard R. Cohen (who also perpetrated another recent New World schlocker "Space Raiders") is set in a post-Nuclear War future where locals are fighting for water, the key to survival and power. Plot catalyst is a young woman Diala, who wants to share her colony's hoard of a fresh spring of water with neighboring colonies, thus setting everyone against her except a stalwart protector Stryker (ugly Steve Sandor, introed as a combination imitation of Indiana Jones and Mad Max).

With a bald villain named Cardiz to oppose and his brother Trune as ally, Stryker hops into an old Mustang for many very-slowly driven car chases to pad out the running time. Santiago's shots rarely match, making for sloppy editing and enervating tedium.

Sci-fi element here is dispensed of in an opening stock footage shot of a U.S. A-bomb blast. The remainder of the film is populated by pretty girls (including former Playboy Playmate Monique St. Pierre in a nothing role) in leather short-shorts, a tribe of nice-guy dwarfs modeled after George Lucas's Shell Dwellers (in "THX 1138") and Jawas (in "Star Wars") and cheap battle scenes. Poorly-dubbed dialog provides a few howlers, but is mainly of the "Come on, let's go," variety aimed at illiterate audiences.

Cast is not identified with their roles in end-credits. —Lor.

El Pico
(The Needle)
(SPANISH-COLOR)

Madrid, Sept. 3.

An Opalo Films S.A. production, with the collaboration in Euzkadi of Guarko Filmeak S.A. directed by Eloy de la Iglesia; exec producer, Jose Antonio Perez Giner; screenplay, Eloy de la Iglesia and Gonzalo Goicoechea; camera (Gevacolor), Hans Hurmann; sets, Josep Rosell; editor, Jose Salcedo; music Luis Iriondo. Reviewed at Carreno (Madrid), Sept. 2, '83. Running time: 107 MINS.

Comandante Evaristo
Torrecuadrada .....Jose Manuel Cervino
Paco ....Jose Luis Manzano
Urko ....Javier Garcia
Aramendia...................Luis Iriondo
Mikel...............Enrique Sanfrancisco
Also: Lali Espinet, Queta Ariel, Marta Molins, Pedro Nieva Parola, Alfred Luchetti, Ovidi Montllor et al.

This is the sort of film most critics will hate, but audiences in Spain may be drawn to in droves. The title, "El Pico," has a double meaning in its context (it also has a scatological meaning in such countries as Chile and Panama), first, the needle whereby narcotics are injected into the veins of addicts, and also the three-cornered hat of Spain's Civil Guards.

The double-meaning partly sums up the background of the film. As in most of his previous pics, Eloy de la Iglesia opts for the most controversial and sensationalist topics at hand, with a clear eye to the maximum commercialization of his product. In this case he mixed the teen-age drug addict scene in Spain, the plight of Civil Guards living in the Basque area, prostitution, homosexuality, murders, the generation gap and a sprinkling of local politics. All of it seasoned with the street slang used by today's Spanish youth.

Surprisingly, for the most part it works. Though the fastidious may wince at the close-ups of needles entering veins, and the aesthetically discerning balk at what occasionally totters on the edge of melodrama, and just about everyone may shrink from the ghastly musical score that has been thrown helter-skelter into the background and which positively detracts from the story, De la Iglesia keeps you riveted to your seat. The pacing is fast and the outcome uncertain as the writers alternately take pokes at the Civil Guards, at the Basque nationalists (who come off best in the film), and at the drug scene in Spain.

Filmed in Bilbao, story concerns sons of a Civil Guard commandant and of a Basque political leader who have got hooked on cocaine and are forced to push it in order to pay for their doses. One of the boys, Paco, is also carrying on an off-and-on homosexual affair, and both hang out in the house of an Argentine prostitute. After finally kicking the habit by going cold turkey, they are again drawn into it by the prostitute. Action heightens near end, as the boys gun down their pusher with the Civil Guard's service pistol.

Item is bound to raise controversy here, especially in the way the Civil Guard is handled. In several scenes we see the Guards beating up suspects during questioning; also bound to offend some advocates of law and order is final scene in which the Civil Guard father throws his gun, a package of cocaine and his three-cornered hat into the sea, symbolically turning his back on drugs and police intransigence, but also tacitly condoning his son's crime and destroying all evidence of it.

Pic should do brisk biz in Spain, and probably will do well among less sophisticated youth audiences in other parts of the world. Significantly, pic has been chosen for the official section in the fourthcoming San Sebastian Film Festival, and will screen in the prestigious Saturday night slot. —Besa.

Debout les Crabes, la Mer Monte!
(On your feet, Crabs, the Tide's Up)
(FRENCH-COLOR)

Paris, Aug. 19.

Parafrance release of a Trinacra production. Produced by Yves Rousset-Rouard. Features entire cast. Directed by Jacques Grandjouan. Screenplay, Grandjouan and Philippe Dumarcay, based on an original idea by Dumarcay and Bertrand Blier; script collaborators, Pascal Aubier and Pierre Fabre; camera (color), Eduard Serra; art director, Jean-Pierre Braun; editor, Annick Rousset-Rouard; sound, Alix Conte; music, Eric Demarsan; production manager, Patrick Desmaretz; executive producer, Denis Mermet. Reviewed at the Paramount Mercury theatre, Paris, Aug. 18, 1983. Running time: 90 MINS.

Cast: Martin Lamotte, Veronique Genest, Virginie Thevenet, Richard Bohringer, Valerie Mairesse, Dominique Lavanant, Roland Dubillard, Luis Rego, Jean-Pierre Sentier, Laszlo Szabo, Jacques Chailleux.

"Debout les Crabes ..." is a tediously prolix farce that has a tart premise, but develops it poorly through a series of mostly static mono-and duologs that succeed each other without rhythm or dynamics. Writer-director Jacques Grandjouan is a young proponent of the French dialog tradition (in the vein of Jacques Prevert, Henri Jeanson, and the like) and has obvious gifts for slangy gab and cockamamie characterizations, but his lack of overall story movement and leadbooted direction (as evidenced in his previous film, "Rue du Pied-de-Grue" in 1979) are a deadweight on his caustically winged ambitions.

Story deals with a fast-talking young hooker (Veronique Genest), fresh out of prison and sex-starved, who throws herself at a young bourgeois liberal (Martin Lamotte) in a train compartment and gets herself invited to his home (one is not surprised to note that Bertrand Blier, who made "Going Places," is credited on original story idea).

While she merrily goes about corrupting all the members of the family, Genest is plotting vengeance against the blind pimp (Jean-Pierre Sentier) who framed her on a murder charge, and similarly uses Lamotte to take the rap for her when she bumps off Sentier.

The talk is fast and furious, but only intermittently on target, and the eager young players (of whom Sentier comes out best) don't modulate the flow of verbiage to less monotonous effect.

Grandjouan, who shot the film on an ultra-rapid schedule, invariably filmed his action, or lack of it, from pointless low-angle setups, which heightens the oppressive sense of dramatic stasis. —Len.

Udenrigskorrespondenten
(Haiti Express)
(DANISH-COLOR)

Copenhagen, Aug. 31.

An HTM (Tivi Magnusson) production with The Danish Film Institute, HTM Film release. Features entire cast. Based on idea by Joergen Melgaard and outline by Klaus Rifbjerg and Joergen Leth; written and directed by Joergen Leth. Dialog, Joergen Leth and Hanne Uldal; camera (Fujicolor) Alexander Gruszynski; executive producer, Tivi Magnusson; editor, Kristian Levring; music, Fuzzy; additional music, D.P. Express; production management, Vibeke Windeloev; assistant director, Ake Sandgren. (Filmed entirely on Haiti and El Salvador locations). Reviewed at the Dagmar, Copenhagen, Aug. 30, 1983. Running time: 90 MINS.

Alex Hansen...............Henning Jensen
The Woman...................Hanne Uldal
UIP man, El Salvador.....John Newhagen
General Assembly President,
El Salvador Roberto
D'Aubuisson .... Himself
Haiti hotelowner...................Al Seitz
Haiti contact..............Francois Latour
Haiti art dealer..........Aubelin Jolicoeur
Voodoo priest.............Max Bauvoir
Santo Domingo hooker...Jocasta Maspuda

"Udenrigskorrespondenten," actually "The Foreign Correspondent," but to be marketed outside Denmark as "Haiti Express" is neither an homage to Michelangelo Antonioni nor indebted to Constantine Costa-Gavras' political thriller style, but is Danish poet and prolific poetic documentary filmmaker (French bicycle racing, American ballet, Chinese railroads) Joergen Leth's willfully anti-dramatic and existentialist and lyrical-romantic first feature film.

Filmed entirely on Haitian and El Salvadorean locations and based on day to day scripting and dialog-writing, story focusses with an extreme of patience on the morose visage of Henning Jensen as the reporter who seems to be looking mostly into the embarrassing emptiness of whatever soul he is left with after undefined events in his personal past history.

The reporter tries to get an interview in Haiti with Baby Doc. In El Salvador, he surveys fields of skeletons of dead guerrillas. His heart is in neither task. He interrupts his open-mouthed soul-searching (a narrator who identifies more and more with the protagonist is given voice by American Joseph Benti and most of film's dialog is in English) mostly to sit in bars, dance in discos or look for sex, all of it very absent-mindedly. When he accidentally meets a pretty Danish woman (played by Hanne Uldal and looking rather like a Gauguin Polynesian), he has a both tender and strongly physical affair with her. She then disappears without a trace and he spends the rest of the film looking for her and neglecting his journalistic assignments. His final telex from Port-au-Prince is a quote from Nobel-winning Danish poet-novelist Johs. V.

Jensen: "Nothing is worthwhile, nothing is true."

Such words and such anti-dramatic filmmaking do not constitute much entertainment value, but while often bordering on self-parody and getting hopelessly muddled in his mistaken notions of being able to work best under the duress of having no regular script, Leth still manages (with the aid of cinematographer Alexander Gruszynski) to convey a moving panorama of exotic vignettes of people and places against a backdrop of events that remain evasive. (Real action has evidently taken place elsewhere as the journalist overhears accidentally on a radio newscast about the outbreak of the Falkland hostilities). The "Haiti Express" of the English title refers to a noisy, sugarcane-carrying train pushing its way through the streets of Port-au-Prince and even entering one of the journalist's nightmares.

Any symbolism here or elsewhere is admitted by Leth to be strictly accidental, however clearly savored by him. Film's best bid at home and abroad would be for a minor cult following. —*Kell.*

Home At Hong Kong
(HONG KONG – COLOR)

Hong Kong, Aug. 27.

A Golden Fountain Publishing Company Ltd. production. Executive Producer, Au Yeung Tin. Directed by King Hoi Lam. Stars Andy Lau Tak-Wah, Chu Hai-Ling, Ku Fang, Carol Gordon, Lai Hon-chee and Kau Hung-Ping. Screenplay, Chan Man Kwei; camera, Adbul Mohamed Rumjahn; music, Ng Tai Kong and songs by James Wong. Reviewed at the State theatre, August 26, 1983. Running time: **100 MINS.**

(Cantonese soundtrack with English subtitles).

"Home At Hong Kong" will suffer heavily when likened to the quite realistic, similar and quite satisfactory re-creation of modern Hong Kong in Shaw Brothers' current success "Hong Kong, Hong Kong." The latter was blatant in what it wanted to achieve when compared to the confused graffiti-scarred style of Golden Fountain's pic that presents the current social issues and problems of the city on a superficial level, then getting them waylaid on the nearby harbor from sheer heavy load. The company was on line with its debut feature "Cream Soda and Milk" but obviously out of line, this time around.

"Home At Hong Kong" is something like a tabloid newspaper jam-packed with sensationalistic bits of current social, political, business, racial, and cultural themes that are interestingly presented but never fully developed. Thus, the messy film merely teases, provokes but lacks the guts and power to get to the core of complexities of the issues presented.

The film merely cashes in on the emotional fears of local residents. It also adheres obediently to the commandments laid down by fashionably talking about today's conditions and tomorrow's insecurities which have obvious boxoffice lure.

The scenario sets up, a series of standard setpieces of lovers and fighters, winners and losers that partially mirrors Hong Kong as a city dedicated only to those who make the grade, a common big city ailment. This means that Hong Kong is heaven for the moneyed, purgatory for the average and hell for the failures. Sadly, "Home" fails to match its dizzying premises, images and hollow statements.

Director King Hoi Lam has clearly bitten more than he can chew and handle when portraying the Hong Kong "experience." The following subjects were brought up: illegal immigrants, decadent high society, corrupt business practices, anti-Japanese campaign, Eurasian racism, labor problems, retardation, mental illness etc. etc.

The film's cinematography, like its acting is uneven and erratic. Andy Lau Tak Wah, who was a revelation in Ann Hui's "Boat People," apparently got his role on the basis of his new "star" status. In the film, he is made into a matinee idol and though he photographs well, he is not mature enough to portray the confusion of an innocent who wanders off accidentally into the battle zone of big business, then falls in love with a simple illegal immigrant from Mainland China because she is "pure and innocent."

"Home At Hong Kong" is indeed rich in material, just like the city it portrays but all the exploration went to waste, akin to a boat that never reached its final destination. —*Mel.*

'Gator Bait
(COLOR)

Okay B-picture from the '70s.

A Sebastian Films Ltd. production and release. Produced and directed by Ferd and Beverly Sebastian. Features entire cast. Screenplay, Beverly Sebastian; camera (color), Ferd Sebastian; editor, Ron Johnson; music, Ferd Sebastian; music arranged by William A. Castleman, William Loose; vocal by Lee Darin. No other credits provided. Reviewed on Independent United Distributors vidcassette, N.Y., Aug. 27, 1983. (MPAA Rating: R). Running time: **88 MINS.**
With: Claudia Jennings (Desiree), Sam Gilman, Doug Dirkson, Clyde Ventura, Bill Thurman, Don Baldwin, Ben Sebastian, Janit Baldwin, Tracy Sebastian.

Reviewed here for the record, " 'Gator Bait," a low-budget effort with limited theatrical distribution a decade ago but now making the rounds on homevideo and on cable tv, is no lost "gem" but still a cut above the average exploitation film. Part of film's commercial problem may have been that it has neither the crassness of standard exploitation fare nor the production values necessary to make it a mainline feature.

Item stars the late Claudia Jennings, a cult favorite of the '70s for her numerous "B" films, as Desiree, a no-nonsense Cajun huntress who tends faithfully after her two younger siblings. At a time (1973-75) when women were being banished from leading roles in mainstream films Jenning's "swamp queen" anticipates the currently developing trend toward female action stars.

Scripted by Beverly Sebastian and codirected by her and husband Ferd Sebastian, the filmmakers know how to make their dramatic points quickly and economically. A montage of Jennings and her little brother early in the film establishes their bond that even with a hint of prepubescent knowingness fosters a tone of D.W. Griffith-like pastoral innocence.

Into this boggy paradise come five intruders: two father and son(s) teams and a patriarch who mistakenly believes Jennings has murdered his son. When Jenning's sister is victimized, the quest for revenge becomes mutual. With the help of her brother the Cajun woman launches a guerrilla war by drawing her enemies further into the swamp, a tactic also used by Cajuns in Walter Hill's more somber and high-minded "Southern Comfort" seven years later.

There are a number of violent deaths in " 'Gator Bait" (including what must be one of the most obviously Freudian murders ever done onscreen) but the stagings are neither prolonged nor graphic and because of the familial links between the characters the killings are not treated casually as in most actioners. The climax, while a good deal less than rousing, manages to be dramatically satisfying.

Tech credits are good for a film of this budget, but some of the post-production dubbing is all too apparent. The lensing by Ferd Sebastian is striking and sometimes achieves some painterly effects. As for the acting, Jennings has a minimum of dialog but can be clearly seen doing her own stunts. The rest of the cast acquit themselves at least competently.

" 'Gator Bait" could be seen on commercial TV with minor cuts and while it may be less than edifying would be far more palatable than most of the low-grade indie fare appearing on local stations. — *Lomb.*

Los Enemigos
(The Enemies)
(ARGENTINE-COLOR)

Buenos Aires, Sept. 6.

A Negocios release of an Eduardo Calcagno Cine production. Features entire cast. Directed by Calcagno. Screenplay, Alan Pauls; camera (Eastmancolor), Roberto Mateo; editor, Juan Carlos Macias; music, Luis Maria Serra. Reviewed at the Monumental theatre, B.A., Aug. 18, 1983. Running time: **90 MINS.**
Cast: Ulises Dumont, Nelly Prono, Mirtha Busnelli, Mario Luciani, Margara Alonso, Walter Soubrie, Vicky Olivares, Max Berliner.

Some 14 years after he made his opera prima, "You Were Mine One Summer," commercials helmer Eduardo Calcagno attempts in his second feature-length effort an elliptic approach to the ugliest facts of Argentine life in recent times: violence, repression, fear, deceit, unfulfillment, decadence.

Alan Pauls' screenplay evolves around Ulises Dumont, a shy, confused character who runs a funeral business inherited from his father and at the same time auditions for a small part in a film, which eventually he wins only to fail miserably at the real lensing. Dumont, who has a girlfriend in the film milieu and also beds a young servant at home, endures a constant pressure from his dominant mother, Nelly Prono, who despises what she deems his lack of guts. Prono starts to spy on a young couple who moves to an apartment across the street and make love in full view of the neighbors. She develops such a hate toward the lovers that she plots to kill them and forces Dumont to be the executioner. In the last second he changes his mind, aims the gun at his mother and pulls the trigger.

Seemingly more interested in the symbolism related with the parable on Argentine political and moral crisis, Calcagno and Pauls have forgotten here and there the requirements of credibility of the main story. Or maybe they have eschewed reality to avoid problems with censorship, which was still very tight at the time "Enemies" was produced. As a consequence the film is uneven, although with more ups than downs both in entertainment and meaning for the native audiences.

One main asset is the brilliant performance by Ulises Dumont, who shrewdly caught the viewers' attention with the tortuous psychology and unpredictable behavior of his irresolute character. Prono also shines as the voyeuristic, envious and merciless mother. Guest appearances by Sergio Renan, Pepe Soriano, Fernanda Mistral and Miguel Angel Sola are pluses for the domestic and satellite markets. Technical credits generally good. —*Nubi.*

Frightmare
(COLOR)

Misguided horror spoof.

A Saturn International Pictures release of a Screenwriters Prods. picture. Executive producer, Henry Gellis. Produced by Patrick and Tallie Wright. Directed by Norman Thaddeus Vane. Stars Ferdinand Mayne. Screenplay, Vane; camera (CFI color), Joel King; editor, Doug Jackson; music, Jerry Moseley; music arranged by Jack Manning; sound, Mary Jo Devenny; assistant director-second unit director, Sam Baldoni; art direction, Anne Welch; special effects makeup, Jill Rochow; special effects, Knott Ltd., Chuck Stewart; associate producers, Hedayat Javid, Harold D. Young. Reviewed on Vestron Video videocassette, N.Y., Sept. 3, 1983. (MPAA Rating: R). Running time: **86 MINS.**

Conrad	Ferdinand Mayne
Saint	Luca Bercovici
Mrs. Rohmer	Nita Talbot
Wolfgang	Leon Askin
Meg	Jennifer Starrett
Etta	Barbara Pilavin
Eve	Carlene Olson
Bobo	Scott Thomson
Donna	Donna McDaniel
Stu	Jeffrey Combs
Comm'l director	Peter Kastner
Detective	Chuck Mitchell
Professor	Jesse Ehrlich

Lensed in 1981 with the more appropriate title "The Horror Star," "Frightmare" is an off-putting combination of homage, satire and shocks. Pic is already available in the homevideo market ahead of its theatrical release, at which time its new monicker is bound to create confusion with Pete Walker's 1974 unrelated British feature "Frightmare."

A very well-cast Ferdinand Mayne (better known in his billing in earlier films as Ferdy Mayne, e.g., as Roman Polanski's nemesis in "Fearless Vampire Killers") toplines as Conrad, a classic horror film star modeled after Bela Lugosi, Christopher Lee and others. Idolized by the college film society led by students Saint (Luca Bercovici) and Meg (Jennifer Starrett), Conrad starts the picture off in a promising vein reminiscent of the Vincent Price black comedy "Theatre Of Blood," as he kills two of his directors, announcing "take 19 ... take 20," a riposte to their demands upon him as an actor.

Screenwriter Norman Thaddeus Vane (adding a director's cap on this one) quickly loses his way with an uncomfortable mixture of mockery and the standard gore-saturated "teens in jeopardy" horror format. Giving an explicit credit to the Errol Flynn-John Barrymore incident, the film society teens steal Conrad's corpse from his mausoleum after he has succumbed to a heart attack.

Conrad's widow Etta (Barbara Pilavin) brings him supernaturally back to life through the aid of a spiritual medium Mrs. Rohmer (Nita Talbot), and Conrad follows her wishes to destroy the body snatchers. Quite improbably, the surviving teens remain rooted in a spooky mansion with Conrad, even though they are aware that their peers are being brutally killed right and left.

Vane encourages eye-popping overacting, ensuring that his film will be taken as black humor rather than straight horror, but it is as unfunny as any of the numerous flop spoofs of the genre made in recent years. Though there are some marketable extreme gore effects on display (kids beheaded or having a tongue torn out by Conrad), tech credits are subpar, with smeared, whited-out window and sky shots and an annoying, almost non-stop use of thunderstorm sound effects.—*Lor.*

Esperame Mucho
(Wait For Me A Long Time)
(ARGENTINE-COLOR)

Buenos Aires, Aug. 30.
An Argentina Sono Film presentation of a Jusid Prods. production. Produced and directed by Juan Jose Jusid. Features entire cast. Screenplay, Jusid and Isidoro Blaisten, based upon latter's short story; camera (Eastmancolor), Felix Monti; editor, Cesar D'Angiolillo; music, Baby Lopez Furst; art director, Luis Diego Pedreira; executive producer, Isidro Miguel; assistant director, Norberto Cesca. Reviewed at the Sarmiento theatre, B.A., Aug. 11, 1983. Running time: **90 MINS.**
Cast: Alicia Bruzzo, Victor Laplace, Arturo Bonin, Alberto Segado, Villanueva Cosse, Catalina Speroni, Marzenka Nowak, Lucrecia Capello, Alicia Zanca, Roberto Catarineu, Mimi Pons, Federico Olivera, Ximena Diaz Alarcon.

After the overthrow of the first Peronist government in 1955 no pic was made depicting Argentine life at any time of the decade that regime lasted in power. Based on an Isidoro Blaisten's short story, Juan Jose Jusid visualizes in "Wait For Me A Long Time" the memories — voiced off screen — of a man who lived his pre-teen age between 1950, at the height of the Peron rule, and 1952, when Evita died. This means the pic might excite the curiosity of under-40 people who never had a chance to see what happened during those days in their country.

The story evolves around a family who owns a modest hardware shop in a working-class quarter. Its members, as well as their neighbors, are either Peronists or anti-Peronists, but no major conflicts — political or personal — develop between them, not even when an uncle of the child is temporarily jailed because of his outspoken criticism of the regime.

The reminiscences are tinged with nostalgia, having their best moments when the children talk about sex as if they knew about it and when clips of old newsreels are cut in, showing briefly personalities and picks of the period; longer footage is devoted to Evita's funeral.

Since both characters and situations are seen thru the child's eyes, the pic lacks both a political stand and an adult approach to the developments of the story. For same reason it is difficult to find convincing performances. Alicia Bruzzo, as the mother, is the only thesp who manages to inject some life to her part. Moppet Federico Olivera is okay in his acting debut.

Censorship scissored a scene showing several children in a bathroom with some of them trying to sodomize a companion. Technicolor credits professionally adequate.
—*Nubi.*

Koks i kulissen
(Awry In The Wings)
(DANISH-COLOR)

Copenhagen, Aug. 22.
A Danish Film Studio with The Danish Film Institute (Joergen Melgaard) production, Kommunefilm release. Original story and script, Helle Ryslinge, Anne Marie Helger, Christian Braad Thomsen. Features entire cast. Directed by Christian Braad Thomsen. Camera (Eastmancolor), Dirk Bruel; music, Helle Ryslinge and the Paravion rock group; editor, Grete Moeldrup; production management, Per Arman, Sanne Arnt; costumes, Tove Berg. Reviewed at the Dagmar, Copenhagen, Aug. 22, 1983. Running time: **100 MINS.**

Micha	Helle Ryslinge
Laura	Anne Marie Helger
Lennart	F1. Quist Moeller
Hans-Henrik	Hans Henrik Clemmensen
Ole	Arne Simsen

"Awry In The Wings" is a title to indicate comedy fun, and there is lots of fun, wordplay and provocative Dario Fo-ish stage counterpointing here, but Christian Braad Thomsen remains a man of rather solemn scepticism so his new feature has his usual implicit quota of dry-to-sour social commentary. To general audiences in Denmark and in selected off-shore situations including the festival circuit and easily obtainable tv slots, film will come over, however, first and foremost for its gamely provocative and generally slapdash-funny new way of handling old feminist themes.

Micha and Laura are on the road with a frankly feminist, but not any too intellectualized Two Women Show. Micha is hurting from being forever spurned by a musician-boyfriend who never promised her a rose garden, anyway. Laura is smug in her conviction that she can forever combine her touring stage life with life as wife of a lawyer and mother of their two small children. The lawyer seems happy, too, but becomes less so when he by chance drops in on one of the girls' performances, the latter featuring much rough language and physical sexual posturing.

Essentially, story is schematic from the outset, but it radiates vigorous charm and conviction until almost the very end when too many plot and polemic threads are woven roughly together. Fine playing in the leads (dialogue co-written by the two actresses) and satisfactory reporting about life on the road and in the wings of impromptu stages will help "Awry In The Wings" go over as general entertainment, while its most enthusiastic response will probably still be yielded when programmed at festivals in Women's Film slots.
— *Kell.*

Night Warning
(COLOR)

Effective horror opus, boasting an outstanding Susan Tyrrell perf.

A Comworld Pictures release of an S2D Associates picture, a Royal American Pictures production. Executive producers, Richard Carrothers, Dennis D. Hennessy. Produced by Stephen Breimer, Eugene Mazzola. Directed by William Asher. Features entire cast. Screenplay, Breimer, Alan Jay Glueckman & Boon Collins, from story by Glueckman & Collins; camera (CFI color), Robbie Greenberg; editor, Ted Nicolaou; music, Bruce Langhorne; song, Joyce Bulifant; sound, Art Names; production manager, Mazzola; assistant director, Don Yorishire; stunt coordinators, Paul Baxley, Tom Huff; special makeup effects, Al Apone. Reviewed on Thorn EMI Video vidcassette, N.Y., Sept. 4, 1983. (MPAA Rating: R). Running time: **94 MINS.**

Billy Lynch	Jimmy McNichol
Cheryl Roberts	Susan Tyrrell
Det. Carlson	Bo Svenson
Margie	Marcia Lewis
Julie Linden	Julia Duffy
Sgt. Cook	Britt Leach
Coach Landers	Steve Eastin
Phil Brody	Caskey Swaim
Frank	Cooper Neal
Eddie	William Paxton

Filmed in 1980 under the title "Thrilled To Death," and marginally released theatrically, "Night Warning" is a fine psychological horror film currently available in homevideo format. As the maniacally possessive aunt and guardian of a 17-year-old boy, Susan Tyrrell gives a tour-de-force performance which represents the genre's best acting since the "Baby Jane" mature femme roles of the 1960s.

Picture has gone through several other title changes, also known as "Butcher, Baker, Nightmare Maker" and the too dead-on "Momma's Boy." Despite production headaches, which saw William Asher replace Michael Miller in the director's chair, Robbie Greenberg replace lenser Jan De Bont and co-scripter Richard Natale missing from the final credits, film turned out well.

Story conforms to the over-familiar horror format relating to holidays, anniversaries and coming-of-age: Billy (Jimmy McNichol) is a 17-year-old basketball player at high school who has been brought up by his aunt Cheryl (Susan Tyrrell) after his parents died in a car crash (great stunt footage) 14 years ago. An old maid, Cheryl is over-protective, opposing Billy's desire to go to college in Denver on a hoped-for athletic scholarship to be with his girlfriend.

In a sublet reminiscent of Francois Truffaut's "The Green Room," Cheryl maintains a candle-lit memorial to an old boyfriend in the basement. The film's horror content begins (replete with slow-motion violence and plenty of blood) when she kills a young tv repairman after failing to seduce him. Cop on the case Detective Carlson (Bo Svenson, bulling his way through the film a la·his prior Buford Pusser role) is very closedminded, ignoring the facts and insisting on linking the crime to a homosexual basketball coach, making Billy the prime suspect instead of his aunt.

Becoming increasingly unbalanced, Cheryl takes to spiking Billy's milk to keep him ill and staying at home with her, as well as sabotaging his big game (for college scouts). Final reels greatly increase the film's body count and include a nice identity revelation.

Elevating "Night Warning" out of the routine is the pleasurable levity injected into the proceedings, which does not destroy the narrative (as is common with spoofs). In particular, Tyrrell brings that larger-than-life theatrical manner (recently shown in her legit perf in "Coupla White Chicks...") to her role, not decreasing its menace but adding a tongue-in-cheek layer. It's a one-of-a-kind portrayal, and makes this picture memorable. —*Lor.*

Alien Contamination
(ITALIAN-COLOR)

A Cannon Group release: production company unidentified. Produced by Charles (Claudio) Mancini. Written and directed by Lewis Coates (Luigi Cozzi). Features entire cast. Camera (color), Joseph (Giuseppe) Pinori; editor. Nino Baragli; music, Goblin: production design, Massimo Antonello Geleng; special-effects. John Corridori; alien cyclops design. Claudio Mazzoli; associate producer. Ugo Valenti. Reviewed on Paragon vidcassette. N.Y., July 14, 1983. (MPAA Rating: R). Running time: **85 MINS.**
Hubbard....................Ian McCulloch
Col. Holmes ....Louise Monroe
Lt. Tony Aris.................Martin Mase
Hamilton...............·.....Siegfried Rauch
Hamilton's ass't ....Lisa Hahn

"Alien Contamination" is a poorly-written horror cheapie shot in 1980 and released by Cannon in the U.S. in 1981 with no New York exposure to date. Currently circulating in the homevideo market, picture's anglicized credits (plus some N.Y. location shots) do not hide its Italian origins, with the usual poor dubbing of (articulated in English) silly English dialog another giveaway.

Using "Alien," "Invasion Of The Body Snatchers" and other sci-fi horror hits as his inspiration, filmmaker Luigi Cozzi (who has subsequently directed two "Hercules" films for Cannon) has concocted a routine tale. A monster from Mars (called a cyclops because of its single, light-radiating eye) has arrived on Earth, with astronaut Hamilton, who encountered it on a space mission to Mars two years back, acting as its stooge by running a coffee factory in South America that ships the monsters' eggs around the world.

When a deserted ship arrives in the port of New York harbor with its crew dead and the hold filled with eggs in coffee cartons, an unlikely team is assembled to track down and destroy their source: Col. Holmes (an Italian actress credited as "Louise Monroe"), a U.S. government security officer; astronaut Hubbart (British thesp Ian McCulloch), who was on the Mars mission with Hamilton; and Brooklyn cop Tony Aris (Martin Mase), who found the eggs in the ship's hold.

Science fiction elements are minor here, with the antiquated Martian threat running counter to space missions' data that has pegged the planet as lifeless. Cozzi's actors·are also lifeless, stuck with asinine dialog such as "She's married to a test tube and a whip," or an early nod to "Alien" 's spaceship named after a Joseph Conrad novel, when they board the deserted ship, one searcher says "It's right out of Conrad," and the response is "It's like something out of a movie." ·

Gore effects are of the butchershop variety and the cyclops, wisely photographed in semi-darkness, is an unimpressive latex mound. Other tech credits are okay, with a rhythmic keyboards score by the Italian rock group Goblin.—*Lor.*

Meu-Peun
(Gunman)
(THAI-COLOR)

Moscow, July 15.
A C.S.P. Film Production (Soraping Chatri), Bangkok. Features entire cast. Written and directed by Chatri C. Yukol. Camera (color), Yukol; music, Pisate Sangsuwan; art direction, Thaveesakdi Tusakorn. Reviewed at Moscow Film Fest (Information Section), July 15, '83. Running time: **144 MINS.**
Cast: Sorapong Chatri (Sommai), Rhone Rithichai (Dhanu), Chalita Patamapun (Nid), Saksiti Mingprayoon (Chalaem), Somsakdi Chaisongkarm (Chaem), Kamara Satethe (Kusuma).

Prince Chatri Yukol has made 24 feature films to date, the best known of which is "The Citizen" (unspooled in the film mart at the 1981 Berlinale, when the director served on the International Jury). "Gunman" is a conventional actioner about a gunman hired by higher-ups to rub out marked victims for a price. The twist is that tale unfolds in such a manner as to reveal the motivation for being a killer via flashbacks of war scenes in neighboring Laos, Cambodia, or possibly Vietnam. The gunman turns out to be a human being with a tragic wartime past.

Once the killings take place, a brutal, coldblooded police inspector sets out on the trail. It turns out that the policeman had been a coward in wartime, and now uses his authority to wantonly kill his victims.

In the end, the gunman is tracked down by surveying the hospital in which the son is being cared for.

But this resourceful Jesse James-type finds his way into the ward, rescues his son, and manages to send him to safety by using the police chief as a hostage. Then comes the final shootout. A tough terrific Thai thriller. —*Holl.*

Piratene
(The Pirates)
(NORWEGIAN-COLOR)

Oslo, Aug. 20.
A Norsk Film A/S and release. Original story and script, Bjoern Erik Hanssen. Features entire cast. Directed by Morten Kolstad. Camera (Eastmancolor) Halvor Naess; executive producer, Harald Ohrvik; production management, Hans Lindgren, Peter Boe; production design, Ingeborg Kvamme; costumes, Kiri Elfstedt; editor, Tore Tomter; music, Odd A. Eilersten. Reviewed at Norsk Film A/S screening room, Jar, Oslo, on Aug. 19, 1983. Running time: **92 MINS.**
Joergen..........Kristian Fr. Figenschow
Ronnie.................Trond Petter Much
May........................Guri Johnson
Hermansen....................Per Jansen
The Mayor..........Lars-Andreas Larssen

"The Pirates" is a swiftly and precisely told youth protest story with some refreshing difference. In his feature debut, Bjoern Erik Hanssen has a trio of unemployed youngsters, nice and cleancut, set up a mobile, hard-to-trace pirate radio station to broadcast a mix of rock music (the staid Norwegian network monopoly prefers staider fare) and sarcastic appeals to the burghers of their tiny Northern island community to get them work rather than welfare doles.

One of the youngsters is the son of a local merchant-bigwig who is just about to be initiated in the local Freemason chapter. Another boy's father is a fisherman-turned-truck driver for lack of work at sea. Both parents, for various reasons, hate to have their own offspring create any kind of trouble.

While never lifting his film out of its facile, tv-format story-telling and even burdening it with a fate-heavy ending of violent death, Hanssen still keeps a brisk pace and has his young actors play in a remarkably true-to-life way in roles that are nicely individualized.

The gutsiness of the story itself should, however, along with its general abstaining from facile preaching, carry the day for "The Pirates" as an easy program feature in foreign situations. —*Kell.*

Venice Film Festival

Prenom Carmen
(First Name Carmen)
(FRENCH-SWISS-COLOR)

Venice, Sept. 8.
A Sara Films (Paris), Jean-Luc Godard Productions (Switzerland) production, Alain Sarde (Paris) release. Original story, script and directed by Jean-Luc Godard. Features entire cast. Camera (Eastmancolor) Raoul Coutard; editor, Godard; music, Beethoven Quartets no. 9, 10, 14, 1?, 16 played by the Qua-

tor Prat, and Tom Waits singing "Ruby's Arms;" script and adaptation advisor, Anne-Marie Mieville. Reviewed as an official competition entry in the Venice Film Festival at the Grande Sala on Sept. 8, 1983. Running time: **85 MINS.**

Carmen X ....Maruschka Detmers
Joseph Bonaffe ....Jacques Bonaffe
Claire ....Myriel Roussel
The Boss ....Christophe Odent
Uncle Jean...............Jean-Luc Godard

As Jean-Luc Godard used contemplation of classical paintings to counterpoint calmly the fragmented cinematic prose-poetry style of his previous feature film "Passion," in "First Name Carmen" he interspersed the main action throughout with close looks at the Quator Prat ensemble rehearsing and playing a series of Beethoven quartets. He also has Raoul Coutard's expert camera divert to shots of the sea and of Paris traffic.

Film has no Bizet, but the title character is rather a gypsy, attached to a group of terrorists, working for an unnamed cause. Having held up a bank, Carmen starts what develops into a love affair with the young cop, Joseph, who tried to stop her from getting away. He is rather wishy-washy and also just as jealous as the lover of the original novel and opera. There all resemblance ends, but Godard has a good title plus a diving-board for his further playing-around with a plot outline that has himself as a stubble-bearded patient in a mental hospital taking on assignment as a filmmaker to serve as a cover for a kidnapping plotted by the terrorists. He is seen chomping away at a cigar and carrying huge tomes on Buster Keaton and copies of *Variety* and generally making obscurely witty remarks with many references to Cinema & Life.

Carmen and Joseph occasionally go to bed with each other, but most of the time they just undress, fight, and dress again. There is some mayhem in the film, but it is always treated mostly as a joke: the chairwoman in the bank taking trouble not to disturb the dead bodies while she sweeps the floor clean of blood, or innocent bystanders just keeping their noses in their newspapers while large-scale killing goes on right next to them, etc. A sure laugh-getter has Carmen and Joseph handcuffed to each other when she has to go to the washroom and Joseph insists on her using the men's room where there are only urinals to serve them.

There is, on the whole, more crude humor and less poetical-political philosophy in "First Name Carmen" than in most of Godard's earlier works of any period. He calls his new film a Western. He originally wrote the title role for Isabelle Adjani, but the old-fashioned sultry look of Adjani's Dutch replacement Maruschka Detmers serves Godard's purposes well. Since production coffers still seem to be open to his projects, venues will probably also appear for the showing of "First Name Carmen" even outside the festival circuit.

Pic won the top prize in the Venice festival. — Kell.

E La Nave Va
(And The Ship Sails On)
(ITALIAN-FRENCH-COLOR)

Venice, Sept. 10.

A Franco Cristaldi for RAI/VIDES (Rome), Gaumont (France) production, Aldo Nemmi for S.I.M. associated production. Gaumont release. Original story and script, Federico Fellini, Tonino Guerra. Directed by Federico Fellini. Features entire cast. Camera (Eastmancolor), Giuseppe Rotunno; production design, Dante Ferretti; costumes, Maurizio Millenotti; editor, Ruggero Mastroianni; song lyrics, Andrea Zanzotti; music, Gianfranco Plenixio; production management, Pietro Notarianni, Lucio Orlandini. Reviewed in the main program, out of competition in the Venice Film Festival at the Sala Volpi, Sept. 9, 1983. Running time: 132 MINS.
Orlando ....Freddie Jones
Ildebranda Cuffari ....Barbara Jefford
Fuciletto ....Victor Poletti
Sir Reginald................Peter Cellier
Teresa Valegnani ....Elisa Mainardi
Sir Reginald's wife............Norma West
Orchestra conductor ....Paolo Paolini
Dorothy ....Sarah Jane Varley
Grand Duke of Harzock ....Florenzo Serra
Princess Lheremia ....Pina Bausch
Count of Bassano ....Pasquale Zito
Ines Ione.....................Linda Polan
Prime Minister ....Philip Locke
Ricotin ....Jonathan Cecil
Ziloev ....Maurice Barrier
Lepori ....Fred Williams
Edmea Tetua ....Janet Suzman

Federico Fellini counts "And The Ship Sails On" as his 18th feature film, and he has launched a vessel that is chock-full of his best gags, visual fun and love of cinema as artful technique. Ship's journey, however, is a long one, and since there is not much in the direction of spiritual cargo, it also occasionally proves a tedious one and dangerously close to foundering in shallow waters.

The whole production is magnificently mounted. Everything is done inside the Cinecitta studios and jokes are made from the beginning of the sets not being the real thing. A setting sun is described by one character as looking as if it were painted on, which it very obviously is. Still, the ocean liner interiors have a solidity about them that occasionally makes one wonder if Fellini wanted the thriller aspects of his story about a ship of fools taken seriously after all. If so, he will hardly get away with it. Audiences not happy with all the fun may rather be angered and will certainly be missing the haunting poetry, this time only sketched in cautiously, of the Maestro's best work.

Story, in spite of all its comical story-telling appearance, could be deadly serious. After a sepia-toned

silent-pic tribute of great humorous impact, an ocean liner leaves Naples in the summer of 1914 in full color and full steam ahead towards a small island where the great soprano Edmea Tetua was born and where she now, dead at a young age, wants her ashes scattered by the passengers on the Gloria N.

These passengers are, so to speak, a motley crew. Showbiz businessmen, opera colleagues, musicians, comedians, hangers-on plus the party of the fat boy Arch Duke of Harzog, his blind sister, his prime minister, etc. All are given an emcee introduction by Orlando (Freddie Jones, a British actor of muted comical radiance), an elderly, slightly bewildered journalist, often in his cups, who is along to do a story on the voyage.

The Fellini gallery of grotesques is as lively drawn as ever, and the non-things they say to each other and little pieces of bitchery and intrigue they involve themselves in are also in the writer-director's grand old style.

Instead of following his usual ring around the rosy story telling technique, Fellini rather randomly picks up and drops his various subplots. Instead he stages great passages of grand opera that virtually are opera.

At the end and at the beginning of the film, magnificent opera chorus renditions are given of original lyrics by Andra Zanzotti and music by young Gianfranco Plenizio. The latter manages to create pieces that sound charmingly recognizable as classical opera. Elsewhere, he makes do with a tingling piano or — in a sequence of rare fun and beauty — the street organ rhythms and modulations of a suite for wine glasses, performed among the ship's chefs and pantry workers.

The elite of the first class very often descend into the belly of the ship, where they are greeted with enthusiasm. Holding their distance, they even condescend (mostly because of internal jealousies) to sing arias in the boiler-room.

There are other, non first classers aboard: a whole flock of Serbo-Croatian freedom fighters, now on the run from their fateful deed at Sarajevo. An Austro-Hungarian man-o'-war turns up to demand that these stowaways are delivered immediately or else there will be shooting. The shooting is only postponed long enough for the Serbo-Croats to perform a ballet and for one of their number to be joined by the ingenue of the passenger list. The scattering of ashes is also allowed to take place, and Fellini does this scene with tact and a finesse close to true sentiment: it is obvious that he loves all the world's crazies — in parti-

cular those of showbiz (the late soprano is seen in newsreel footage run by one of her most devoted admirers in his cabin all through the film. She is played by Janet Suzman).

Cannons then start booming. There is fire and belching smoke everywhere, all this more stagey than anything else in the film. We do not actually see the Gloria N. sink into the sea, but we are told by Orlando that most of the passengers were saved. He himself sits at the end in a life-boat along with a rhino that had been on its way to some zoo. Orlando happily says that the animal has proven good at giving milk. A rather feeble joke, maybe, to serve as the punchline gag of a film of such size.

Fellini, as usual, works wonders of fluid movement and finely shaded lighting with his cameraman (Giuseppe Rotunno).

All production designs are fully up to Fellini standards. He has been wise in using lesser-known talent for his huge gallery of characters, and along with Freddie Jones, Barbara Jefford as a Die Asta lookalike, Peter Cellier as the cuckolded but ever-enthusiastic Sir Reginald and Victor Poletti as the lustiest of opera singers will surely hear from Hollywood's casting directors after their performances here. Fellini's "Ship" does not really sink. It only barely keeps afloat as cinema art of the higher order. Its sailing into the international boxoffice sea should be assured, but it might not be the smoothest ride. —Kell.

Jogo De Mao
(Sleight of Hand)
(PORTUGUESE-COLOR)

Venice, Aug. 31.

A Paisa Film Production, cofinanced by the Portuguese Film Institute, Lisbon. Features entire cast. Directed by Monique Rutler. Screenplay, Edgar Gonsalves Preto, Eduardo Guerra Carneiro, Rutler; camera (color), Mario Barroso; music, Luis Cilia; editing, Rutler; sets, Fernando Filipe; sound, Carlos Alberto Lopes. Reviewed at Venice Film Fest (Competition), Aug. 31, '83. Running time: 115 MINS.
Cast: Joao Lagarto (Roberteiro), Julio Cesar (Alberto), Sao Jose Lapa (Isabel), Teresa Roby (Teresa), Carlos Wallenstein (Antonoi Cardeal), Isabel de Castro (Maria de Jesus).

A debut feature entered as well in the main competition at Venice, Monique Rutler's "Sleight of Hand" introduces a talented newcomer to Portuguese cinema. Her previous pics included: "Vera" (1970) (a Super-8 feature), "Such As Old Rags" (1979) (16m feature), and "Men on a Business Trip" (1983) (a tv production). The newest is a brace of four short stories introduced by a street entertainer, who uses his hand-puppets to sketch the characters and outline the moral of each individual tale. One story is particularly a delight,

and all deal with the tragedy of love — or lack of it.

"Sleight of Hand" begins with a shoeshine boy on the streets of Lisbon. The lad has two women he entertains on the side, neither of whom knows about the other as he finds ways with a glib tongue to deceive them. This goes on until one day both catch him off guard, so to speak — and his lies don't fit the situation anymore. A memorable scene is a Sunday at the beach: the shoeshine dutifully takes one of his girlfriends with her young daughter on the outing, but he's interested mostly in following a soccer game on his transistor radio.

The second tale is the best. A street-seller specializing in furs has an ugly temper, and the only satisfaction in his drab life is getting drunk and beating his wife. She takes everything stoically, although having to ride in the rear of their truck on cold days to guard the pelts borders on slavery in a marriage of convenience. One day, a jerk of the truck on an upgrade results in the woman falling from the vehicle, together with some of the furs. When the distraught husband returns on the highway upon noticing the mishap, he finds the woman carrying the pelts on her head as she trudges on the side of the road to catch up. That final shot says everything necessary on the exploitation of women in today's lower classes.

Next comes a pair of stories on the upper classes that complement each other. The first has to do with a young lady who decides to test the authority of a lady of the night against male macho types. But to reach her aims, she must learn the trade to begin with, and this leads not only to some humiliations of the opposing sex, but also a slug-it-out with another prostitute at a bar for raiding her territory.

The last focuses on the rich and well-to-do. After a dinner party, at which the host recounts a past conquest in his youth at the University of Coimbra (wearing a Dracula outfit), the offender (a judge) in the aforesaid rape incident invites his friends to a niteclub for an evening of carousing. It ends with the culprit having a fatal heart-attack in bed.

"Sleight of Hand" features a brace of solid thesp performances in the four episodes. —Holl.

Mitten Ins Herz
(Straight to the Heart)
(WEST GERMAN-COLOR)

Venice, Aug. 31.

Al Olga Film Production, Munich, in coproduction with Westdeutscher Rundfunk (WDR), Cologne; producer, Denyse Noever. World rights, Munic Film, Munich. Features entire cast. Directed by Doris Doerrie. Screenplay, Jelena Kristl; camera (color), Michael Goebel; sets, Klaus Emberger; editing, Thomas Wigand; costumes, Barbara

Grupp;.production manaager, Harald Kuegler. Reviewed at Venice Film Fest (Opera Prima Competition), August 31, '83. Running time: **90 MINS**.

Cast: Beate Jensen (Anna), Sepp Bierbichler (Armin), Gabriele Litty (Marlies), Nuran Filiz), Jens Mueller-Rastede (messenger), Joachim Hoepner (supermarket manager).

Doris Doerrie's career before her first feature, "Straight to the Heart," has been in documentaries and tv-productions since 1977. This explains, to some extent, the polish achieved in her debut pic — little doubt about it, she's easily one of the most talented German femme filmers on the scene today. A sharply sketched narrative tale of one-upmanship between two eccentric, quite narcissistic individuals intent only on satisfying their own selves without getting involved in any necessary social obligations "Straight to the Heart" scores as a comedy of manners turned inside out.

Anna Blume is a young independent lady working as a cashier in a supermarket. She spends her free time in her drab apartment writing letters to herself, and she doesn't particularly like being told what to do. So when the supermarket manager finds her helping out the mother of a foreign-worker family by not ringing up the cash charges properly, she just up and decides to leave the job on the spot. Then she dyes her hair an eye-catching blue to achieve a desired nonchalant "I Don't Care" presence on the streets.

Anna's independent nature, however, attracts the attention of a dentist during her search for a new apartment (she doesn't have any of the amenities of life in the old one, not even a refrigerator). He decides to invite her to live with him in his comfortable villa as a salaried "lady-of-the-house" with no strings attached. One might think that she's to be the rich man's geisha on the side, but in fact the dentist is lonely and only desires company of sorts since his recent divorce. The girl agrees to the odd relationship, then becomes quickly bored with nothing to do — save spend her $1,000 per month on whatever takes her fancy.

Not even an open warm-hearted invitation to a roll in the hay works at the outset: this only comes about after she gets desperately drunk and then soaked to the skin on a rainy night.

The girl finally hits upon the idea of feigning pregnancy to win her host's affection, for what it's worth. He's delighted — and now Anna is in deeper water than expected. So she leaves on a long-term trip to have the supposed child in a Frankfurt clinic — that is, she up and steals a new-born baby from the arms of a Turkish woman, and successfully makes off with it. Our dentist doesn't really know the dif-

ference, nor does he care even after reading the truth of the crime by accident in a discarded newspaper. In desperation once again, Anna impulsively kills the only man in her life she has ever really cared for. The last scene has her on-the-run to nowhere with the baby in her arms.

An eerie tale of a cold, self-centered relationship, "Straight to the Heart" benefits from a tight script, peppered with comical twists and amusing dialogue. Lensing and thesping are more pluses, particularly newcomer Beate Jensen and vet Sepp Bierbichler in the lead roles. All the same, it's difficult to sympathize with a kookie, kinky heroine who bluntly steals another woman's newly-born baby just to score a couple game-points back at the ranch — a narrative line between irony and decency has to be drawn somewhere. —*Holl.*

Una Gita Scolastica
(A School Outing)
(ITALIAN-COLOR)

Venice, Sept. 1.

An A.M.A. Film Production, in collaboration with RAI Televison (Channel 1), Citta di Porretta Terme, Provincia di Bologna, Credito Romagnolo and Roberto Colletti. Produced by Antonio Avati. Features entire cast. Directed by Pupi Avati. Screenplay, Pupi and Antonio Avati; camera (color), Pasquale Rachini; music, Riz Ortolani; sets, Basili-Scarpa, Annalisa Cecchini; editing, Amedeo Rachini. Reviewed at Venice Film Fest (Competition), Sept. 1, '83. Running time: **90 MINS**.

Cast: Carlo Delle Piane (Carlo Balla), Tiziana Pini (Serena Stanzani), Rossana Casale (Rossana), Cesare Barbetti (Head Master), Ferdinando Orlandi (Owner of Hotel Passo), Bob Tonelli (Cocchi Brother), Gianpaolo Cocchi (Second Cocchi Brother), Gianfaranco Mari (Singing Waiter).

Pupi Avati's "A School Outing" is one of those light comedies on the last years of youth and the first of adulthood. It's the spring of 1911, and a school outing is arranged for 30 kids (18 boys, 12 girls) at a Bologna high school just before matriculation — they're all around 18-20 years of age, with the usual crushes on the fairest in the class and a yen for all-out adventure on the three-day trip. Add to this a bombshell of an art teacher (named "Serena") and a puritanical but vulnerable Italian professor (aching to hit it off with Serena), and you have the ingredients of a farce on wrestling with the libido.

The outing lasts three days, as the group wanders through the lush countryside from Bologna to Florence. Along the way, they stop at the estate of the inventor Marconi, and communicate with the winds of the forest (a touch out of romantic paintings of the period) to allow them passage into an enchanted domain. Gradually, the defenses of morality are lifted: a purification bath is requested at the first lodg-

ing, a couple of the girls set their sights for the Romeo in the group, and the lads spar off to demonstrate their physical prowess. The upshot is that the art mistress educates a lad each evening to the bliss of a first affair, while teasing her bachelor colleague on his fumbling ways with the opposite gender. It appears that the pretty young art teacher has only recently married, and wishes to talk about the general theme of sexual freedom. Picture the lady as a full-bodied blithe spirit, and our puritan as a little squirt with illusions of manhood — then the rest develops pretty much as expected.

At the end of the trip and back at school once again, the scandal of the art teacher giving free courses outside of class provokes the wrath of the Head Master. And who comes to the rescue of the damsel in distress? Off our puritan goes with his desired Serena in the end — while the school kids applaud the finale of their last school outing.

Conventional gags and the cliches of the farce offer little room otherwise for a sophisticated twist or two to save this outing from an esthetic deadend. Nonetheless, there's an audience for this kind of nostalgic pap, and with proper handling "A School Outing" might enjoy a modest spinoff on the art circuit or at Italian Film Weeks. —*Holl.*

Eine Liebe In Deutschland
(A Love in Germany)
(W. GERMAN-FRENCH-COLOR)

Venice, Sept. 7.

A coproduction between CCC-Filmkunst, Berlin, and Gaumont-TF1 Films Production-Stand'art, Paris. Produced by Artur Brauner; executive producer, Peter Hahne; associate producer, Emmanuel Schlumberger. Features entire cast. Directed by Andrzej Wajda. Screenplay, Boleslaw Michalek, Agnieszka Holland, Wajda, based on Rolf Hochhuth's novel with same title; camera (color), Igor Luther; music, Michel Legrand; sets, Allan Starski, Goetz Heymann, Juergen Henze; editor, Halina Prugar-Ketling; costumes, Ingrid Zore, Krystyna Zachwatowicz-Wajda. Reviewed at Venice Film Fest (Competition), Sept. 6, '83. Running time: **132 MINS**.

Paulina Kropp .... Hanna Schygulla
Maria Wyler ..... Marie-Christine Barrault
Mayer .... Armin Muller-Stahl
Elsbeth Schnittgens .. Elisabeth Trissenaar
Wiktorczyk .... Daniel Olbrychski
Stanislaw Zasada .... Piotr Lysak
Karl Wyler .... Gerard Desarthe
Dr. Borg .... Bernhard Wicki
Schulze .... Ralf Wolter
The Narrator .... Otto Sander
Klaus .... Ben Becker
Melchior .... Sigfrit Steiner
Frau Melchior .... Erika Wackernagel
Martha .... Dorothea Moritz
Old Zinngruber .... Juergen von Alten

One of the inside favorites to win the Golden Lion at Venice, Andrzej Wajda's "A Love in Germany" is the Polish director's second film abroad since winning the Golden

Palm in Cannes in 1981 for "Man of Iron" in between, he made "Danton" (1982) (also unspooled at Venice in the "Venice by Night" section). In this regard, one should state at the outset that Wajda's two features abroad are clearly for and about Poland, employing an exiled team of Polish screenplay writers, actors, and technicians. In this case they are Boleslaw Michalek and Agnieszka Holland (scripters), Daniel Olbrychski and Piotr Lysak (actors), and Krystyna Zachwatowicz (costumes), plus Slovak-born cameraman Igor Luther (with whom Wajda communicates in Polish). There is even a short scene in the film featuring a dialogue between the two Polish actors in Polish, is undoubtably meant for his countrymen in reference to contemporary Poland.

That Wajda is able to make both a commercial film on one hand, while loading it with relevant symbols and meaningful nuances of every ilk and gender on the other, confirms his status as one of modern cinema's great directors. Consider the hidden messages in Jean Renoir's "The Rules of the Game" (France at end of the 1930s) and Carl Theodor Dreyer's "Day of Wrath" (Denmark in the wartime 1940s) — both directors had to leave the country shortly thereafter — and one can easily "read into" Wajda's two post-martial-law films, "Danton" and "A Love in Germany," without too much difficulty. The only prerequisite is perhaps the good fortune of having seen and appreciated the director's brilliant "Man of Marble" (1976) and "Man of Iron" (1981), a pair of political statements on (so to speak) the Passion, Death, and Resurrection of Poland as a nation. Danton was, indeed, a Lech Walesa before the guillotine, just as Stanislaw Zasada in "A Love in Germany" surely predicts a dim future for the rebellious Pole under a military dictatorship.

Nevertheless, "A Love in Germany" contains enough Rolf Hochhuth to bear the German writer's stamp-of-approval as well. It's a tale, too, of Germany's own agony under a regime that brooked no breaking of inhuman racist laws, particularly in the middle of the Second World War when victory was still a tangible dream for the population. The setting is a small town on the Swiss border, and the incident really happened as recorded in Hochhuth's documented nonfiction bestseller. A young Polish POW had an affair with a German fruit-and-vegetable shopkeeper, which was reported to the authorities and resulted in a mock-trial (an attempt to Aryanize the lad to save his life), followed by a fumbling execution in a stone-quarry. Indeed, as Hochhuth describes the case, the whole story is painfully and tragically characterized by one blunder and non sequitur after another — something like the hanging of Mary Surratt during the hysteria following the Lincoln assassination.

Hanna Schygulla plays the shopkeeper, too much a dumb-blonde type and too little a middle-aged and sex-starved victim of circumstances, but adequate for the role all the same. Piotr Lysak is the POW, too green-behind-the-ears and callow for the part, but naive and vulnerable enough to win sympathy. The ladies of the village who accelerate the tragic course of events are along the lines of Shakespeare's busybodies of Windsor, yet they too fill the bill pretty much as one might expect. Then the boy is arrested — and the story really gets off the ground with the introduction of the male characters: stormtrooper Armin Muller-Stahl, country doctor Bernhard Wicki, and military attache Ralf Wolter. While Schygulla ventures on her own Way of the Cross by becoming an object of ridicule in the village and is imprisoned for her crime of consorting with a Slav as a German of the super-class, the young POW is offered his life if he agrees to pass a rigged Aryan-test.

He refuses — and is led to his own crucifixion. To say more would perhaps rob the viewer of fully appreciating Wajda's masterful orchestration of the ending in word, image, and montage.

Muller-Stahl gives the performance of his career since leaving East for West Germany five years ago. The hanging-scene matches the guillotine-scene in "Danton" in dramatic impact, but surpasses it in depth of emotion. And the framing of the story by introducing into the Hochhuth original a narrator from today has its vindication in the closing scene: an aged Schygulla mourns the mistakes of her past before a tv-screen on which Lech Walesa proclaims the Gdansk agreement during a strike heard around the world. — *Holl.*

Biquefarre
(FRENCH-COLOR)

Venice, Aug. 31.

A Midas Sa/Millia Films Production. Producers, Marie-Francois Mascaro, Bertrand van Effenterre, William Gilcher. Directed by Georges Rouquier. Camera (color), Andre Villard; assistant cameraman, Pierre-Laurent Chenieus; editing, Genevieve Louveau; music, Yves Gilbert; sound, Alain Sempe, Pierre Lorrain. Reviewed at Venice Film Fest (Competition), August 31, '83. Running time: **90 MINS.**

Cast: Henri Rouquier (Henri), Maria Rouquier (Maria), Roget Malet (Raoul Padral), Marius Benaben (Lucien), Helene Benaben (Hortense), Andre Benaben (Marcel), Francine Benaben (Martine), Marie-Helene Benaben (Genevieve), Roch Rouquier (Roch), Raymond Rouquier (Raymond), Georgette Rouquier (Jeannette).

When Georges Rouquier's classic portrait of a French farm community, "Farrebique" (1947), was made 35 years ago, the film was labeled a documentary, and rightly so: it dealt with life and death in a community, the changing of the seasons, and the daily routine of farm life — all played by nonprofessionals. Today, film historians tend to classify the same genre as fiction-documentary, for the simple reason that reality was creatively manipulated by directors like Robert Flaherty ("Louisiana Story"), Lionel Rogosin ("On The Bowery"), and Rouquier. By the end of the 1940s and early 1950s, it was fairly common to find docu filmers packing 35m equipment into the great outdoors; and by the 1960s, the lightweight 16m shoulder-camera made cinema-verite fiction-documentaries the order of the day. Thus, at Venice 1983, the chance to see the classic "Farrebique" back-to-back with its sequel of today, "Biquefarre," amounted to a unique cinematic experience — indeed, one of the highlights of the fest's first week.

Returning to the scene of documentary action is not new these days. A West German documentary team recently visited Ireland and the island site of Flaherty's "Man of Aran" to search out old familiar faces, and a Bulgarian team did the same in revisiting the village chosen by Dutch docu filmer Joris Ivens in making the Bulgarian portion of "The First Years" — on both occasions, it was a glance back over the shoulder at more than a half-century of gradual progress amid a timeless stability in isolated communities. In Rouquier's case, however, he kind of takes up where he left off: we are introduced to the new generation on the same Farrebique farm, the tie between the two films accomplished by a film-within-a-film flashback technique.

Credits on pic and press release credit three Yank film professors at Ivy League universities for making the sequel possible via an application to the National Endowment for the Humanities to secure the initial funds to begin shooting again: the trio were William Gilcher and John Weiss of Cornell and Laurence Wylie of Harvard, Bill Gilcher's name appearing among the production credits. It was apparently during a Cornell film seminar on Rouquier's films (his career spans 50 years and 20 docu projects) that the idea was realistically hatched to make the sequel.

In the original the dramatic moment is the coming of electricity to the farm, while the solemn moment is the handing on of the farm by the dying patriarch to the oldest son — after a new grandson has already been born into the family to ensure the family tradition. In the sequel the dramatic moment is the selling of the neighbor's Biquefarre farm to the highest bidder upon that farmer's retirement, while the dramatic moment is the purchase of Biquefarre by the grandson of the first film even though he must incur debts to do so.

The rest is a seasonal observation of new farming methods, along with a near tragedy when a bag of insecticide falls upon the young heir and nearly endangers his life (due to lack of proper body covering in handling the poisonous powder). In the end, however, the road sign leading to both Farrebique and Biquefarre is replaced by a new one only to Farrebique. And the two elderly brothers, seen as youngsters in the original, stand before the grave of their parents to communicate the latest news.

The closing sequence is quite moving. Upon the gravestone of the departed is projected a moment from the 1947 "Farrebique" as the director's token of affection. Try to catch both classics together, if possible. — *Holl.*

Edith's Tagebuch
(Edith's Diary)
(WEST GERMAN-COLOR)

Venice, Aug. 31.

A coproduction of Hans W. Geissendoerfer Filmproduktion, Munich, Roxy-Film Luggi Waldleitner, Munich, Pro-ject Filmproduktion im Filmverlag der Autoren, Munich, and Zweites Deutsches Fernsehen (ZDF), Mainz. World rights, Filmverlag der Autoren, Munich. Stars Angela Winkler. Written and directed by Hans W. Geissendoerfer, based on Patricia Highsmith's novel with same title; camera (color), Michael Ballhaus; sets, Toni Leudi; music, Juergen Knieper; editing, Helga Borsche; costumes, Katharina von Martius; production manager, Rolf M. Degener; tv producer, Willi Segler. Reviewed at Venice Film Festival (Competition), Aug. 31, '83. Running time: **108 MINS.**

Edith Baumeister	Angela Winkler
Paul Baumeister	Vadim Glowna
Chris Baumeister	Leopold von Verschuer
Uncle George	Hans Madin
Katharina Ems	Sona MacDonald
Sabine Angerwolf	Irm Hermann
Bernd Angerwolf	Wolfgahg Condrus
Dr. Bleibig	Friedrich G. Beckhaus
Dr. Star	Werner Eichhorn

Selected as the opening night presentation at the Venice fest, Hans W. Geissendoerfer's "Edith's Diary" marks the second time the helmer has filmed a Patricia Highsmith psycho-thriller: he adapted "The Glass Cell" (pub. 1965) in 1977, then immediately negotiated with producer Luggi Waldleitner for her "Edith's Diary" (published 1977), hot off the press. With the author's permission (Highsmith appeared at the Venice press conference), he updated the time and place of the original from an American provincial town in the late 1960s to West Germany (specifically: Berlin) in more or less the present (a tv broadcast in the film shows the new West German Chancellor, Helmuth Kohl, being elected this spring). Geissendoerfer even changed the names of the principal characters, from Edith and Brett Howland to Edith and Paul Baumeister.

One might conclude that the whole is "loosely based on Highsmith," save that the main thread of the tale, the psycho-thriller element, has been honed to a fine edge. Just as Edith in the original mixes dream with reality to the point of creating an imaginary diary of fictional family events, so too does our German Edith withdraw from the burden of reality about her to retreat into a voluntary and salutary world of her own in order to survive at all.

In Highsmith's America, the conflict is clearly outlined in the schizophrenic handling of news by the media: the Yank intellectual has been shaken to the depths of his and her conscience by the daily death-counts and napalm fire-bombings in Vietnam (the news dished up on a silver platter just before the evening repast), followed by the Watergate crisis and the young "amoral generation."

Geissendoerfer has not been so lucky: he lets us assume that Edith Baumeister's emotional conflicts stem in part from her stance as dedicated editor in chief of a Left-oriented intellectual journal, Signal, — all well and good, but the viewer is not permitted even to glimpse the contents of the political editorials in this journal. Thus, a goodly portion of patented Highsmith motivation (so crucial in appreciating her work) is jettisoned for lack of a solid script.

Geissendoerfer's approach is to place all his chips on thesp Angela Winkler's talent for interpreting emotionally disturbed and psychologically pressured heroines — indeed, the Edith Baumeister appears to be a natural extension of her Katharina Blum in Margarethe von Trotta and Volker Schloendorff's adaptation of Heinrich Boell's "The Lost Honor of Katharina Blum" (1975). Supporting performances by Vadim Glowna as her jelly-fish husband and new-comer Leopold von Verschuer as her dropout, asocial son are also solid — when given something meaty in the way of dialog to chew upon.

middle-class and middle-aged couple moving into a new home in Berlin's plush villa section. Paul (apparently a publisher, but it's left undetermined) is having an affair with his secretary, and the marriage that Edith thought was quite secure has suddenly fallen apart for no reason at all. Yet it's well within Paul's wishy-washy character: his grown son is a painful family disappointment and complete psychological mess; while his neurotic, invalid uncle simply moves into the house to be under Edith's nursing care (instead of being properly committed to a humane old age home) — so the husband ducks every responsibility at home, knocks up the secretary, divorces and remarries to begin life anew. Edith has little other recourse than to turn to her politically conscious Signal and, finally and exclusively, to her diary.

This is where the film gets interesting. Geissendoerfer spans five years by this literary device, from 1978 to the present, a time in which the son flunks his matriculation exams to enter the university, becomes a paranoic parents-hater, and even attempts suicide to put an end to it all. Then he reads his mother's diary by accident — and realizes that, in her imagination, her own future world was built around her son's growth into a mature and responsible individual whose sole aim in life was to fulfill her mother's dreams. Gradually, the son replaces his father in the family hierarchy, then murders the invalid uncle, and fends off the psychiatrist sent by Paul to examine Edith's mental state. Just as the two prepare to depart the villa for good, Edith, in her hurry, falls down the staircase to crack her skull against the railing.

Deftly handled from the technical side, "Edith's Diary" confirms HWG as one of German cinema's major craftsmen. A two-story set, constructed in the Berlin Ufa-studios, is used to the maximum by lenser Michael Ballhaus, and the music, too, offers some clues to Edith's growing emotional state-of-mind (a romantic theme in the diary sequences). What's badly missing is a continuity line over the five year stretch and necessary motivational dialog to delineate the characters. Pic, HWG's best, could enjoy a modest spinoff on the arthouse circuit with proper handling. —Holl.

Maraa Le Ibni
(A Wife For My Son)
(ALGERIAN-COLOR)

Venice, Sept. 3.

An Oncic production and release. Written and directed by Ali Ghanem. Camera (Eastmancolor), Mahmoud Lekhal; editor, Youcef Tobni; music, Philippe Arthuys; production design, Mohammed Reda, Belghoul, Haoucine Menguellat; costume, Abedelhamid Ouaked. Reviewed in the Venezia Giovani program of the Venice Film Festival at the Excelsior screening room, Sept. 3, 1983. Running time: 90 MINS.
Fatiha .... Isma
Hocine .... La Him Laboul
    With Chafia Boudraa, Mustafa Kesdarli, Farida, Mustafa El Anka.

In the capital city of today's Algeria women rarely wear veils, but when they do, they make a great fuss about it. Fatiha, 18 years old, would rather do any work outside her home, but her parents have entered into a contract with 35-year-old Hocine's parents for the two to get married as soon as Hocine returns from Paris where he has been a guest worker.

"A Wife For My Son" by Ali Ghanem mixes the present-day ethnological with fine flashes of whimsical insights in manners and morals and the particular characteristics of his cast of people caught in all the expected turmoils of a cultural clash.

Hocine wants to go back to Paris, when he can get no work at home, but he does not feel up to taking his yong wife with him. She meanwhile, does not like Life With Mother-In-Law and, late in her pregnancy, returns to her own home even though she knows that she thereby brings shame upon it. Nor are the newlyweds alone in facing the consequences of mixing old and new ways of life.

Ali Ghanem treats his subject with warmth and humor and nuances even the less sympathetic of his story's characters. Everybody plays well in a story that may be structured too schematically, but still entertains nicely in a way that should gain film access to much TV programming outside Algeria.

All production credits are of a handsome order and cinematographer Mahmoud Lekhal lights his often quite inventively composed frames with a very special skill and finesse. —Kell.

Hotel Tsentral
(Hotel Central)
(BULGARIAN-COLOR)

Venice, Aug. 31.

A Bulgarian Film Production, Sofia; world rights, Bulgarofilm, Sofia. Features entire cast. Written and directed by Vesselin Branev. Camera (color), Yatsek Todorov; editing, Nedejda Tseneva; sets, Anastas Yanakiev; music, Bozhidar Petkov. Reviewed at Venice Film Festival (Opera Prima Competition), Aug. 31, '83. Running time: 100 MINS.
    Cast: Irena Krivochieva-(Tina), Jivko Garvanov (Yonchev), Renata Dralcheva (Nelli), Anton Radichev (Stavri), Boriana Puncheva (Lena), Velentine Gadjokov (Stefo), Tsoyan Stoev (Benio).

A tv director now making his first cinema feature, Vesselin Branev conceived "Hotel Central" pretty much in the style of theatre and television productions: conventional camera placements and unembellished acting. But the film by this writer-director has something in the daring of the theme to recommend it — the story is about a girl compelled to become a prostitute in a provincial town in 1934, due initially to a mistake on the part of the authorities (they believe that she is a member of a vice ring) and then to a brutal rape by a policeman taking her to live and work at the Hotel Central.

The girl soon hardens into a professional whore, taking orders from the hotel manager and fending for herself as best she can. This is the time of the fascist government under Tsar Boris, a time, too, of budding revolutionary movements.

Several types visit the hotel, but few offer her the same solace as a pile of romantic postcards in her belongings: by viewing the married couples of her dreams, she imagines a different world and a better future. Then comes a group of traveling actors to the town, one of them quoting the Russian poet Pushkin. And thereafter she gets the courage to break with her life of degradation by simply running away. A new life in a new society is on the horizon, one is led to hope.
—Holl

Montreal Fest

La Bete Noire
(FRENCH-COLOR)

Montreal, Aug. 21.

A Forum release of a Stardust and Cinetheque production. Produced by Catherine Bouguereau. Directed by Patrick Chaput. Feature entire cast. Screenplay, Chaput, Patrick Yalaoui, Jean-Pierre Bastid; camera (color), Richard Copans; art direction, Roland Fruytier; editor, Christiane Sauvage; music, Jean-Claude Vannier. Reviewed at the World Film Festival (non-competing), Montreal, Aug. 21, 1983. Running Time: 101 MINS.
Guy Boissieux .... Richard Bohringer
Daniel Ben-Yacine .... Philippe Sfez
Karen .... Sabine Haudepin
Guyot .... Georges Geret
Pepe .... Jean Bouise
Mme Guyot .... Isabelle Sadoyan
Antonia .... Bernadette Lafont
Bar Owner .... Eddie Constantine
Young Daniel .... Frederic Wizmane
Daniel's Mother ...... Catherine Gandois
Robert .... Nini Crepon

First-time director Patrick Chaput comes up with an effective thriller in "La Bete Noire." The modest tale of a juvenile delinquent who's befriended by scriptwriter has an invention and pace which should earn it foreign sales. Although less successful than "Diva," the production recalls some of the style and story-telling of the earlier successful thriller and again features Richard Bohringer in the role of the scriptwriter.

The title character is a 17-year-old named Daniel (Philippe Sfez) who tells his story to Guy (Bohringer), working on a film project on delinquency, for a fee. Daniel relates his early years as a foster child in a small village. He's obviously out of place in the setting and develops anti-social behavior which eventually lands him in, what he calls, "a school for gifted neurotics."

Paralleling Daniel's memories is his current situation of petty hustles in Paris. His desperate, precarious situation is seen by Guy who is preplexed by the dilemma of aiding the boy or simply listening in detached fashion to his predicament.

The downbeat conclusion, foreshadowed at the opening, fortunately doesn't diminish its impact. Chaput, who also cowrote the screenplay, provides a balance of humor, insight and observation to cushion the inevitable darkness of the material.

However, the complex time jumps at times prove distracting, artificially pushing the narrative along. Fortunately, the material avoids the obvious trap in turning into a sincere, sociological study. Chaput deals with this is a particular situation drawing a number of incongruous characters together and explores that particular dynamic rather cleverly.

Focus is clearly on Daniel rather than Guy, thus avoiding the narcissism of films about filmmaking. There's also an effective contractg painted of the sunny rural locales with the increasingly dark alleys of Paris. The versatile camerawork of Richard Copans becomes an important part of "La Bete Noire's" compelling nature.

Remaining technical credits are strong throughout and performances are all first-rate. There's a nice array of acting styles allowed for thanks to the diversity of settings and moods. The two central Daniels — Sfez as the teenager and Frederic Wizmane as the boy — exude a dark charm which remains the film's most intriguing aspect.

"La Bete Noire" should have no problem acquiring international distribution with obvious specialty and cross-over appeal in North America. Chaput reckons to be an important filmmaking name if his first effort is any clue to his skill with off-beat material and technical creativity. —Klad.

Les Annees 80
(Golden 80s)
(BELGIAN-COLOR)

Montreal, Aug. 28.

A Paradise films production. Produced by Marilyn Watelet. Directed by Chantal Akerman. Features entire cast. Screenplay, Akerman, Jean Gruault; camera (Fuji color), Michael Houssaiu; editors, Nadine Keseman, Francine Sandberg; art direction, Viviane Druez; music, Marc Herouet, lyrics, Akerman. Reviewed at the World Film Festival (Competition), Montreal, Aug. 28, 1983. Running Time: 82 MINS.
    With: Aischa Bentebouche, Francesca Best, Warre Borgmans, Amid Chakir, Aurore Clement, Harry Cleven, Patricia Frans, Herman Gillis, Martine Kivits, Marie-Line Lefevre, Xavier Lukornsky, Estelle Marion, Magali Noel, Yvette Poirier, Pascale Salkin, Nora Rilly, Nicole Valberg, Florence Vercheval, Michel Weinstadt, Bernard Yerles, Simon Zaleski.

Flemish filmmaker Chantal Akerman is best noted for offbeat productions catering to specialty audiences. While "Les Annees 80" is indeed out of the norm, it has an infectious charm which should win wider audiences for the female director.

In the simplest sense, Akerman divides her film into two parts. The first consists of a series of auditions on videotape for a proposed musical followed by filmed portions of the actual production. Although basically a sketch piece, the film is wholly satisfying in and of itself.

One of the film's great strengths is Akerman's insistence of ridiculing the process rather than the individuals involved. The opening section progresses from script readings to reaction shots, movement tests and scenes where she tests her participants with one another and as dancers and singers. Apparently, she culled from some 40 hours of tapes for her lively, versatile 50 minutes of film.

Akerman also steps in front of the camera to record a song. It's a wonderful sequence and one wonders whether the filmmaker is commenting on her own prowess or asking the audience to serve as casting agent.

The actual filmed musical sequences remind one of Demy's "Umbrellas of Cherbourg" or Renoir's musical section of the multi-part "Le Petit Theatre de Jean Renoir." In any event, the sections combine the energy of vintage musicals with modern surroundings such as a clothing store and a studio street.

Although just a taste of a possible feature, the vignettes register effectively and one craves to see Akerman given the go ahead for a full production. As with Orson Welles' "F for Fake," "Les Annees 80" is a kind of found film which owes no apologies, thanks to invention and style.

The film has an art house appeal and one might only wish Akerman had the budget to shoot more production and rely less heavily on the auditions. Her voice-over closing comment is "next year in Jerusalem," suggesting the hope for the budget and backing on a full fledged musical extravaganza. It's to be hoped her desire comes through based on her initial promising tests. Already "Les Annees 80" has received a warm reception in a non-competition category at Cannes, competition in Montreal and will be at the forthcoming New York film festival, where it gets a special midnight showing. —*Klad.*

The Wild Side
(U.S. - COLOR)

Montreal, Aug. 22.
A New World Pictures release of a Roger Corman-Bert Dragin presentation. Produced by Bert Dragin. Features entire cast. Written and directed by Penelope Spheeris.

Camera (color), Timothy Suhrstedt; editor, Ross Albert; art direction, Randy Moore; music, Alex Gibson. Reviewed at the World Film Festival (non-competing), Montreal, August 27, 1983. Running Time: 94 MINS.
Evan .... Bill Coyne
Jack .... Chris Pedersen
Skinner .... Tim O'Brien
Sheila .... Jennifer Clay
Joe .... Wade Walston
Razzle .... Mike B: the Flea
Ethan .... Andrew Pace
Keef .... Grant Miner
Bill Rennard .... Donald Allen
Skokes .... Jeff Prettymen
Jim Triplet .... Robert Peyton

One of producer Roger Corman's (and in association with Bert Dragin), early independent efforts, "The Wild Side" (shown at the fest under previous title "Suburbia") emerges as a tough, somewhat compassionate look at the punk generation. Writer-director Penelope Spheeris works wonders with a low budget, non pro cast in a film of commercial appeal with exploitable elements for both art and mainstream audiences.

Story centers on Evan (Bill Coyne), product of a suburban home of divorced parents. Household tension and a sense of worthlessness eventually sees his exit and a chance meeting at a punk rock concert lands him with a group of homesteading young people.

He quickly adopts their dress, hair style and lifestyle and receives a ritual tattoo stamp of T.R. (The Rejected). Not surprisingly the presence of the group near a residential area creates tension in the community. Neighborhood vigilantes blame the group for every local problem and although several accusations are deserved, several are totally unfounded.

Spheeris portrays the group quite favorably as a make-shift family without sentimentalizing their situation. There's no doubt it's a dead end proposition with potentially violent overtones. Several incidents convey the sudden, brutal nature of the existence and no attempt is made to soften this horror.

Action builds on the tension with several neighbors and the insistence of the community to blame the kids for local vices. There's no way they will get a fair shake and matters begin to crumble when one of the group commits suicide. A city cop, who happens to be the stepfather of one of the T.R.'s, suggests they move but ultimately they stay to confront the vigilantes.

The production maintains Corman's style of low budget, sensationalized subject fare. However, it's to Spheeris' credit that she conveys a sense of sophistication in the material and elicits strong portraits from her young, largely untrained, cast.

Adult performances are less sympathetic and accomplished in general and technical credits while ragged convey an honest sense of the environment. On balance, shortcomings in script and craft values are easily outweighed by energy and milieu.

Picture is natural extension of Spheeris' earlier "Decline of Western Civilization" which captured the American punk scene with conviction. The same authority permeates "The Wild Side" without any sense of an artificially induced dramatic structure.

Despite the strength of presentation, film will require careful handling. There's no cushioning of story with the prospect of known performers to convey a fictional distance. The commendable ferocious tone will have to be overcome with creative critical and word of mouth campaign. —*Klad.*

A Bell For Nirvana
(KOREAN-COLOR)

Montreal, Aug. 23.
A Se-Kyung Enterprises Production. Produced by Kim Hwa-Shik. Directed by Park Chul-soo. Features entire cast. Screenplay, Ahn Jin-woo; camera (color), Son Hyon-Chae; editor, Kim Hyon; music, Chung Min-sup. Reviewed at the World Film Festival (non-competing), Montreal, Aug. 23, 1983. Running time: 94 MINS.
Jongdu .... Chung Yoon-hee
Sukhawa .... Kim Dong-hyon
Ingu .... Hwang Hae

Korea's "A Bell For Nirvana" is a breathtaking, yet intimate, epic yarn centering on the creation of a sacred bell. The bell in question was removed by the Japanese during the Second World War for their war machine. According to legend, the only way for the dead to reach paradise is by hearing the sound of the bell.

So, the necessity of a new chime is paramount. The task falls to Jongdu whose father and grandmother were killed on the day the Japanese entered the village. Years later he scours villages for odd bits of brass to complete the task.

Complicating matters is his growing attachment for a young woman from the city. Sukhawa, an artist from Seoul, reciprocates his attention but both her father and a suitor do their utmost to quash the liaison.

The filmmakers quite successfully develop a Buddhist fairy tale incorporating elements of modern and traditional Korea. The strains from these elements producing a fascinating tale of a culture at the crossroads and a universally accessible love story.

Also striking is the visual elegance of the production. "A Bell For Nirvana" lacks the dramatic and textual impact of the bell-casting section of Andrei Tarkovsky's classic "Andrei Roublev" but its emphasis on the human dynamic compensates quite nicely.

Despite technical polish and accessibility, "A Bell For Nirvana" will be a hard sell in non-Oriental markets. It's unlikely even the current Korean attention will be of much use for this essentially delicate and warm tale. Festival attention appears assured with possible commercial potential in specialty situations and markets already disposed to Far Eastern production. —*Klad.*

Mat Maria
(Mother Maria)
(USSR-COLOR)

Montreal, Aug. 27.
A Mosfilm production. Features entire cast. Directed by Servei Kolosov. Screenplay, Kolosov, Yelena Mikulina; camera (color); Valentin Zhelezniakov; No other credits available. Reviewed at the World Film Festival (non-competing), Montreal, August 27, 1983. Running Time: 92 MINS.
Mother Maria .... Ludmilla Kasatkina
Ilya Isadoravich .... Leonid Markov
Daniel .... Igor Gorbachev
Sofia Borisnava ...... Yevgenia Khanaeva
Yuri .... Alexi Timoshin

Unspooling in Montreal festival's special Soviet cinema section and repping that country in Venice, "Mother Maria" is an earnest, sombre tale of a Russian exile's heroic efforts in France during World War II. The bleak tone of the effort will severely limit its distribution and the rather pat approach to the material further restricts its commercial outlook.

Title character is a privileged woman who left her homeland after the 1917 revolution and took up the veil. She eventually settled in Paris where a large emigre population existed and ran a building for displaced countrymen. Her selflessness earned her many patrons and enormous local respect.

With the outbreak of war in 1939 and Nazi rule the following year, Mother Maria began collaborating with the Resistance. However, eventually her complicity is revealed and she winds up in a concentration camp where she sacrifices her life for another woman.

Veteran Soviet director Sergei Kolosov steeps his story in party polemics, painting his heroine as a staunch supporter of her homeland during its darkest hour. In contrast, her fellow emigres side with Hitler in hopes of returning home.

While critical of the Nazis, film skirts such issues as French co-operation and presents not a single identifiable Jewish character in the course of the action. The exclusions are too obvious and strain at the credibility of the already angelic portrait of the title character.

The story suggests a truly unique real-life heroine but despite a dignified performance by Ludmilia Kasatkina, the portrait emerges as propaganda laden with sentiment. One can easily anticipate each new development and character response given the leaden direction and artificiality of many situations.

Kolosov puts his subject under the microscope and slowly dissects her without revealing the nature of her conviction or the strengths of her beliefs. The result is a hollow portrait more befitting a still life than a motion picture. —*Klad.*

Nagua
(Drifting)
(ISRAELI – COLOR)

Montreal, Aug. 22.

A Kislev Films Ltd. production. Produced by Amos Guttman, Jonathan Sagalle, Edna Mazia. Directed by Amos Guttman. Features entire cast. Screenplay, Guttman, Mazia; camera (color), Yosi Vine; editor, Anna Finkelstein; music, Arik Rudich; sound, Shabtai Sarig. Reviewed at the World Film Festival (non-competing), Montreal, Aug. 22, 1983. Running Time: **80 MINS.**

Robi	Jonathan Sagelle
Ilan	Ami Traub
Ezri	Ben Levine
Rachel	Dita Arel
Effi	Boaz Torjemann
Baba	Blanka Metsner
Robi's Father	Mark Hasmann

First-time feature director Amos Guttman offers up a semi-autobiographical story of repressed homosexuality in "Drifting." The low budget, even by Israeli standards, production relies heavily on earnestness and Angst. Prospects outside specialty screening would appear to be minimal.

Robi (Jonathan Sagelle) is a young filmmaker hoping to secure financing for his first feature. However, there appears to be little interest from government or private sources in his story of the local gay community. So, to eke by, he works in his grandmother's grocery store.

Guttman paints a rather hopeless existence for the young man. His mother is an actress working in Germany, his father is estranged from his son. He has a lover named Ilan (Ami Traub) who refuses to leave his wife and to cap matters, Rachel (Dita Arel), an ex-lover unaware of his current sexuality, arrives to renew their relationship.

The heavy plot-laden narratives also wander aimlessly through the local gay scene of bars and pickup spots. Here a sub-plot emerges of Robi's befriending of Ezri (Ben Levine). However, his advice to his acquaintance goes unheeded and later Ezri is seen plying a living as a male hustler.

The rather frank depiction of the milieu will no doubt be a problem is in its native land and will limit distribution of "Drifting" in many foreign markets. However, the film's major problem is in its lack of focus and inability to compel us with Robi's plight. Eventually, he abandons his "dream" project but emerges better equipped to deal with his homosexuality. Dramatically, the transition remains unconvincing.

The tale itself remains too self-conscious but Guttman demonstrates a flair for both handling performers and technicians. Despite modest resources the film smooths many rough edges through its direction. "Drifting" should be of interest on the festival circuit and may garner some art house exhibition. However, it remains too oblique for wide spread exploitation. —*Klad.*

Okinawa No Shonen
(Okinawan Boys)
(JAPANESE-COLOR)

Montreal, Aug. 23.

A Pal Entertainments production. Produced by Wataru Suzuki. Directed by Taku Shinjo. Features entire cast. Screenplay, Shinjo, Shinichiro Nakata, Zazuo Takagima; camera (color), Shinsaku Himeda; editor, Junbashima, music, Shinichiro Ikebe. Reviewed at the World Film Festival (non-competing), Montreal, Aug. 23, 1983. Running time: 117 MINS.

Tsuneo	Ippo Fujikawa
Young Tsuneo	Takeshi Naito
Mariko	Miyuki Ono
Young Mariko	Nana Okada
Ishigaki	Ken Ogata

Taku Shinjo's first film, "Okinawan Boys," is yet another new film at Montreal's World Film Festival dealing with a young man's determination to make a feature film. It also mirrors numerous entries in its structure of evolving its story through juxtaposition of modern and historic narrative lines. However, while flawed, the film retains a fascination for audiences which could earn it distribution outside Japan.

The central character, Tsuneo (Ippo Fujikawa), works as a laborer in Tokyo and moonlights in the ailing film industry. It's 1970 and Tsuneo's dream project is to film a story of life in his birthplace, the American-held, Japanese-populated Okinawa.

His thoughts wander to 1959 and growing up in the military-occupied island. His family runs a brothel for the G.I.s and young Tsuneo develops a passion for movies. What develops from portraits of these two eras and locations is his sense of displacement. He clearly remains an outsider through a quirk of fate.

Director-cowriter Shinjo is on firm ground in his observations of the young man. Less assured are the melodramatic elements of the plot. The story is filled with tragedy — death, suicide, lost hopes — and sentimentality. Still, the unique elements of location and era make much of this material more palatable for the viewer.

Technical credits are excellent with particularly impressive reaction of Okinawa in the late '50s and early '60s. And Shinjo assembles a fine young cast for the production. However, his seesawing between the two periods and locales becomes somewhat annoying and disorienting.

"Okinawan Boys" introduces a new Japanese talent in the raw. Shinjo should become an important filmmaker once he expels his personal demons. In the interim, his first film offers something novel for the festival circuit with a modest appeal on the art house scene. —*Klad.*

Mennyei Seregek
(Heavenly Hosts)
(HUNGARIAN-COLOR)

Montreal, Aug. 26.

A Hungarofilm release of a Mafilm production. Directed by Ferenc Kardos. Features entire cast. Screenplay, Istvan Kardos; camera (color), Lajos Koltai, music, Gyorgy Selmeczy. Reviewed at the World Film Festival (Competition), Montreal, Aug. 26, 1983. Running Time: 84 MINS.

Miklos Zrinyi	Viktor Fulop
Zsofia Lobl, his wife	Eva Ras
The Archbishop	Antal Pager
The Angel	Sandor Szoter
Lieutenant Guzics	Dioko Rosic
Captain Simonffy	Gyorgy Cserhalmi

"Heavenly Hosts" is not an historical epic, but rather a kind of historical sleight-of-hand. Just when the historical relevance begins to emerge, it disappears again behind the fogged up photography and heavy-handed symbolism. Based on a droll conceit of seventeenth century Hungarian history, it portrays what might have been the last day in the life of a Hungarian count, Miklos Zrinyi, who actually was an important military leader and poet in the Turk-beleaguered Hungary of November 18, 1664, when time stood still for a 24-hour miracle.

That miracle involves an angel falling into a tree while the Count is out hunting with his retinue. They have just wounded a boar, when the angel is discovered, rescued, and brought back to lie in a grotto. The angel, suitably wan and ethereal, inspires a variety of reactions from the Hungarian inhabitants ranging from the exploitative to the worshipful. The lords and ladies of the Hapsburg era first come to pay their respects, interpreting the presence of the angel in various ways. One sees it as a heavenly sign that they will fend off the Turks. Another thinks the angel can prevent her from aging. The Archbishop sees a shot at the papal throne, should he take the angel to Rome, where the church could benefit from the miracle. Count Zrinyi himself believes this must be God's way of appointing him commander of Hungarian national unity, an effort which shatters when the sundry nobility of the fiefdoms get lost in debate in the banquet hall before the grotto.

Another event is likewise seen as a miracle, when the Turks send a captive Captain Simonffy home to the Count. A religious fanatic, Captain Simonffy equips himself with wooden wings to appear in a mystery play staged to inform and illustrate the nature of this fallen angel. Soldiers in boots and sheets prance around in this piece of theatre, until one of them attempts to assassinate Count Zrinyi, but the bullet is stopped by a crucifix. Another sign from heaven.

The theatricality of the drama, the center-piece of the film, comes to an abrupt climax when the Captain abruptly decides to fly and leaps in his wooden wings from the parapets. He plunges to his death, and everybody agrees that it was no miracle. The angel has, meanwhile, disappeared and been found hiding in a hen house, detracting from his glory. The Count decides to release the angel again to the heavenly hosts, and he returns him to the open air. He tests his healed wings, ascends, and flies away. Running through the thicket watching the angel's flight, Count Zrinyi is attacked by the wounded wild boar from the opening sequence. It is fatal.

Besides indulging in tenuous and obscure allegory, the historical references in "Heavenly Hosts" are left unclear. Such intellectual conceptions of history and artistic ambitions have consistently kept director Ferenc Kardos from directing a film with international appeal.

Scripted by the director's brother, Istvan Kardos, the dialog often becomes monolog, and whatever political parallels it may have with modern Hungary are lost beyond the Hungarian border. The symbolism of the miracle exploited by man for his own purposes does not justify an entire pic. Viktor Fulop in the lead is a face known from many Hungarian films, as is Gyorgy Cserhalmi playing the Captain with soldiering vigor. As good as such thesps are, they seem bigger than the story.

Beyond its line-up in the Montreal competition, film is unlikely to find even festival outlets, despite its elegant period costumes and literary premise. For Hungarian film weeks, it is a good example of the influence of Miklos Jancso on his filmmaking compatriots. — *Kaja.*

Pura Sangre
(Pure Blood)
(COLOMBIAN-COLOR)

Montreal, Aug. 24.

A Luis Ospina production. Directed and produced by Ospina. Associate producer, Rodrigo Castano. Features entire cast. Screenplay, Ospina, Alberto Quiroga; camera (color), Ramon Suarez; art direction, Karen Lamassonne; music, Hermanos Ossa; editor, Ospina. Reviewed at the World Film Festival (non-competing), Montreal, Aug. 24, 1983. Running Time: **88 MINS**.

Florencia ....Florina Lemaitre
Perfecto ....Carlos Mayolo
Ramon ....Humberto Arango
Adolfo.................Luis Alberto Garcia
El Monstro ....Gilberto "Fly" Forero
Don Roberto ....Franky Linero

A hit in its native Colombia, "Pura Sangre" will have some difficulty registering outside Spanish-speaking markets. The macabre tale of modern, human vampires plays somewhere between bizarre comedy and low-budget slasher fare. The particular sociological implications don't travel well outside South America.

Action hinges on the precarious survival of a sugar baron. The victim of a rare blood disease, the man requires frequent transfusions of fresh blood. His son and heir manages this difficult requirement by enlisting the aid, through blackmail, of three employees. They wander the streets, luring children and teenagers into their blood bath.

The disappearance of the young people develops into local panic and the creation of a mythic "monster of the valley." The activity is also uncovered by business interests who threaten exposure before a series of ironic conclusions.

Debuting writer-director Luis Ospina's intent was the creation of something more ambitious than a "snuff" film. To a large extent he succeeds but the modesty of his technical resources provide a gritty look reminiscent of the very films he mocks. As a result many social-political observations are lost in the context.

Also somewhat difficult to sort out are the film's elements of black comedy. The Hughes-like tycoon serves as a wonderfully benign creation hooked up to life-support systems and watching vintage movies. One, "Citizen Kane," does not register well with the old man.

Performance level is erratic but several portraits truly capture the bizarre tone Ospina wished to convey. Florina Lemaitre as one of the trio of killers, whose real job is as a nurse, best contrasts the respectable life with the dark purposes of the characters. And there's a wonderful scene in which a demented character, not associated with the murders, confesses to the crimes.

"Pura Sangre" will need careful marketing to penetrate foreign markets. It's easy to misinterpret the intent of the filmmakers but attempting to sell the film as a shocker would be misplaced. The trick is to cue the audience into the film's layers of meaning without giving away too much.—*Klad.*

The Returning
(U.S.-COLOR)

Montreal, Aug. 25.

A Willow films production. Produced by Sally Faile. Directed by Joel Bender. Features entire cast. Screenplay, Patrick Nash; camera (color), Oliver Wood; art direction, Stebe Finkin; editor, Dan Loewenthal; music, Harry Manfredini. Reviewed at the World Film Festival (non-competing), Montreal, Aug. 25, 1983. Running Time: **90 MINS**.

John Ophir ....Gabriel Walsh
Sybil Ophir ....Susan Strasberg
Jason Ophir ....Brian Foleman
Al Lyons.....................Victor Arnold
Grace ....Ruth Warrick
Dr. Rizer ...................H.E.D. Redford
Medicine Man ....Mostea Oshley
Spikee ....Rick Barker

"The Returning" is a modest, well-crafted mystical tale rooted in Indian superstition. As such, it lacks the visceral thrills to qualify for the horror exploitation market and will have to earn its wings in more highbrow situations. However, livelihood commercially may be limited in its present form which falls short of establishing proper tension of its tale of possession.

Tale centers on a Utah family who acquire a rock with odd qualities during a family expedition to the Mojave desert. Initially it induces visions and odd noises. Later its power appears to cause the death of the son in a freak highway accident. His grieving father then begins to adopt childish behavior and assume the boy's traits.

It gradually evolves that the father and the driver of the truck which killed the son are linked through the spirits of long dead Indian warriors. The wife must seek out an old Indian shaman to quell the spirits before the men have a bloody confrontation.

This novel variation of the possession theme sustains much of the film's shortcomings in script and tension. Also commendable are strong central performances by Gabriel Walsh as the father, John Ophir, Susan Strasberg as Sybil Ophir and Victor Arnold as Al Lyons, the driver unwittingly involved in the curse.

Still, the production has an overall earnest tone unrelieved by humor which needs to be lightened. Director Joel Bender appears to want to create the impression of examining a case study rather than develop a fanciful, engrossing story of inexplicable, strange powers.

There's also an overemphasis of cutting between separate actions of the two men which begs for a juxtaposition of intents not necessarily warranted by the material. The effect is more irritating than anxiety-raising as a more linear movement would suffice.

Careful marketing will be important to relate the nature of the story which sounds more horrific than what's on view. Title also suggests ghoulish fare although real terror remains primarily cerebral.

Technical credits have a polish suggesting a considerably more expensive budget than that available to the filmmakers. Prospects, despite reservations should be above average for commercial release, foreign sales and eventual television exploitation.—*Klad.*

Liberty Belle
(FRENCH-COLOR)

Montreal, Aug. 20.

A Gaumont release of Films du Losange production. Produced by Nicole Flipo. Directed by Pascal Kane. Features entire cast. Screenplay, Kane, Pascal Bonitzer; camera (color), Robert Alazraki; editor, Martine Giordano; music, Georges Delerue; sound, P.L. Lemennel. Reviewed at the World Film Festival (non-competing), Montreal, Aug. 20, 1983. Running Time: 113 **MINS**.

Julien Berg ....Jerome Zucca
Elise ....Dominique Laffin
Vidal ....Andre Dussollier
Brinon ....Jean-Pierre Kalfon
Gilles ....Philippe Caroit

Set in 1959, at the height of France's Algerian crisis, "Liberty Belle" examines a young man's liberal advocacy and his personal dilemma between political concerns and sexual awakening. However, the issues often become confused muddying the drama and providing a less than satisfactory conclusion.

Julien Berg (Jerome Zucca) attends a private school in Paris where the chief topics of discussion are Algeria and girls. While interested in both, he lacks the conviction to pursue either passionately. However, his friendship with a new student, Gilles (Philippe Caroit) eventually draws him deeper.

Gilles runs with a fast set of monied older students which dazzles the young man. One of their hangouts is a club which turns out to be a center for right-wing activities. However, Julien's sympathies remain with the National Liberation Front and this serves to alienate the two men.

Caught attempting to destroy evidence which threatens to expel a classmate, Julien winds up on the outside. Eligible for the army, he enlists the aid of a liberal teacher (Andre Dussollier) to hide him and offers to become a courier for his activities with the NLF.

Further complications arise as a result of Julien's attraction to Elise (Dominique Laffin), the teacher's girlfriend and the discovery of his whereabouts and activities by Gilles' group. He eventually winds up transporting dangerous papers across the border but not before the teacher is killed and he consummates his affair with Elise.

The epic nature of Julien's progress is ill-suited to Pascal Kane's modest production. Too much information and not enough explanation leaves the audience more confused than enlightened in the course of the film. Relationships are often contrived and conclusions veer toward the melodramatic opting for cliches.

Julien alternates between motivator and cypher to the action and the full import of his relationship with Gilles goes underdeveloped. This proves fatal to later sections in the film. Also, the portrait of Vidal, the politicized teacher, proves sketchy and unsatisfying. Characters never quite connect in a way which would illuminate the particular period of political activity. Matters are too vague to accept the story as an allegory in foreign markets.

Despite a technically polished quality, "Liberty Belle" is mired in ill-conceived plotting. Commercial prospects are slim, so one is more likely to view this failed attempt in festival or specialty situations. —*Klad.*

Amagi Goe
(Amagi Pass)
(JAPANESE-COLOR)

Montreal, Aug. 25.

A Shochiku/Kiri production. Produced by Yoshitaro Nomura and Hideji Miyajima. Directed by Haruhiko Minura. Features entire cast. Screenplay, Mimura, and Tai Kato, based on novel by Seicho Matsumoto; camera (color), Yoshimasa Hanetkata; art direction, Yutaka Yokoyama; editor, Masuichi Tsuruta; music, Mitsuaki Kanno. Reviewed at the World Film Festival (Competition), Montreal, Aug. 25, 1983. Running Time: **99 MINS**.

Tajima ....Tsunehiko Watase
Hana ....Yuko Tanaka
Kenzo Onodera ....Mikijiro Hira
Kenzo as a boy ....Yoichi Ito
Kenzo's Mother ....Kazuko Yoshiyuki
Vagrant ....Kenzo Kaneko
Kenzo's Uncle ....Ichiro Ogura

Japanese entry at Montreal's World Film Festival, "Amagi Pass," provided an interesting, flawed debut for director Haruhiko Mimura. The thriller tells of an unsolved murder and the detective who doggedly pursues the real murderer for 40 years. Finally, though often compelling material, the climax is too facile and predictable to be truly satisfying.

Action opens in modern Japan. Detective Tajima places manuscripts of his famous cases with a local printer, who not uncoincidently, was a witness to a murder trial some 40 years earlier. Action then abruptly moves backward to printer Kenzo Onodera's youth in 1940.

The story evolves in flashback to the murder of a vagabond and the suspicion of homicide falling on a prostitute named Hana (Yujo Tanaka). Criss-crossing between confrontations between detective and printer and the 1940 sleuthing, the picture slowly emerges. Young Kenzo met both the victim and prostitute when he briefly ran away from home. In the latter meeting, he developed a warm friendship, so early appearances suggest his reluctance to divulge information stems from a sense of protectiveness for her.

It is perhaps the last time in the picture we are sent down a blind alley. Soon it becomes apparent Hana is innocent and the boy killed the man to defend the woman: Mimura, who also cowrote the film, hides the important questions of guilt and silence in fancy narrative jumps. It's like pulling punches on the drama, particularly considering the all-knowing coyness of the detective.

The murder stems from rage and frustration rather than premeditated plotting. Therefore, Kenzo's guilt over the years must be based on his silence. This is muted by the knowledge Hana was acquitted, despite a confession, due to lack of concrete evidence.

Apart from the initial intrigue, the plot offers few surprises. The measured pace allows the audience to remain ahead of the action, so characterization becomes paramount. In this department Tanaka as Hana offers a truly dazzling performance (note: she won the acting prize at Montreal) in a considerably better than a "hooker with a heart of gold" cliche.

Remaining cast is strong along with excellent technical credits and handsome recreation of the era. Sour note is a full-blown Ennio Morricone-inspired score by Mitsuaki Kanno.

Neither a gripping thriller (Japan has a 15-year statute of limitations on murder) or a psychological study, "Amagi Pass" ultimately lacks much needed emotional punch. The distant reflection will have difficulty tapping foreign markets although some specialty and festival screenings should be in the offing.—*Klad.*

Bullshot
(BRITISH-COLOR)

London, Sept. 7.

A Handmade Films presentation. Produced by Ian La Frenais. Directed by Dick Clement. Features entire cast. Executive producers, George Harrison, Denis O'Brien. Written by Ron House, Diz White and Alan Shearman. Camera (color), Alex Thomson; editor, Allan Jones; sound, Jim Roddan; production design, Norman Garwood; associate producer, David Wimbury; assistant director, Gary White; music, John Du Prez. Reviewed at the Bijou preview theatre, London, Sept. 5, 1983. (BBFC rating: PG). Running time: 85 MINS.
Captain Hugh "Builshot"

Crummond	Alan Shearman
Miss Rosemary Fenton	Diz White
Count Otto von Bruno	Ron House
Fraulein Lenya	
von Bruno	Frances Tomelty
Prof. Rupert Fenton	Michael Aldridge
Dobbs	Ron Pember
Lord "Binky" Brancaster	Christopher Good
"Crouch"	Mel Smith
"Hawkeye" McGillicuddy	Billy Connolly

"Bullshot" marks a new direction for producer Handmade Films in that it's a comic item that sports no contribution from the Monty Python team. And the comparative video inexperience of the Low Moan Spectacular troupe, who scripted and play the major parts, shows in the partial failure of this parody of things British to be funny.

The pic moves at a cracking pace through a lavish concoction of slapstick, displays of English eccentricity and carefully laid contempo jokes. But the '20s militaristic stereotype at the center of the story is not as automatically amusing as the film's makers seem to have supposed. And the pic neglects the dramatic potential available from the pitched battle between the forces of (British) civilization and the barbarous Hun.

The pic's quasi-hero is a military captain who practised his own form of barbarism during WWI (he was the only member of his regiment to emerge physically undamaged). Finding life somewhat tedious in peacetime, he's keen to go to the rescue of a damsel in distress and confront his former German rival.

The plot's development hinges on the evil German's search for a scientific secret uncovered by the lady's father, of whose significance the script gives no clue till the very end. Lacking that information, the audience is also deprived of any sense of suspense.

Pic reveals its theatrical origins in a series of shrill performances which nevertheless allow for some well-rounded characterization. Alan Shearman plays the captain whose heroism is largely the result of stupidity but who has an extraordinary physique and mathematical powers. Diz White is the silly but often courageous damsel. Ron House is restrained as the German force of evil who's partnered with sex-hungry Frances Tomelty.

Although the pic derives something from an awful seam of '30s British moviemaking, the Bulldog Drummond pics, the long-partnered filmmakers Ian la Frenais and Dick Clement resisted the temptation to give the film a tacky look. Camerawork and art direction make the most of country house locations and period forms of transport.

A series of action sequences bring the pic to its climax. Crummond, the captain, wins a battle with a giant octopus, leaps onto a flying plane and falls to safety via the damsel's parachute and the back seat of the car which he entered into the London to Brighton race.

What the pic lacks is that dose of imaginative flair which would inspire its local audience to laugh at what once they supposedly were. But it's just possible that in offshore markets where the English are considered funny per se, the film's humor will have appeal.
—*Japa.*

La Republica Perdida
(The Lost Republic)
(ARGENTINE-DOCU-B&W/COLOR)

Buenos Aires, Sept. 13.

A Noran release and production. Produced by Enrique Vandi. Directed by Miguel Perez. Written by Luis Gregorich; music, Luis Maria Serra; narrator, Juan Carlos Beltran; executive producer, Diana Frey. Reviewed at the Luxor theatre, B.A., Sept. 1, 1983. Running time: 135 MINS.

The documentary takes a look as fascinating as it is biased at Argentine political life between the first military coup (Sept. 6, 1930) and the last (March 24, 1976). Released just two months before the first elections to be held in the country in 10 years, amid an atmosphere of growing political tension, it excites both the interest and the emotions of the citizenry of all ideological shades since this kind of stuff has been long-banned for both the big and the small screens. For the younger audiences it is a complete novelty, almost a revelation, and for older people it reminds of key developments. Hence the strong appeal it has shown in its initial engagements is no surprise, with an almost certain chance to increase as a result of the rather heated arguments generated by what the film remembers and what it forgets about recent Argentine history.

In a prolog before main credits, "Republic" states the country was ruled by a ranchers' oligarchy until the advent of Hipolito Yrigoyen, who led blue- and white-collar workers in a movement that eventually attained political victory, making him president in 1916. He ruled until 1922 and was elected for a second term in 1928, but two

years later was overthrown by a coup which linked the cattle barons with the military, giving birth to governments spawned from electoral fraud until Peron, in the mid-'40s, retook the Yrigoyen nationalist line, championed social justice and became chief executive for a decade. In 1955 he was sacked by another coup, some weak semi-democratic regimes followed, in 1966 the military again took over, in 1973 Peron did his comeback, dying the following year to be succeeded by his widow Isabel as president until another coup installed the present self-called Process in 1976.

The pic's oligarchy-versus-people theme is an oversimplified way of focusing the complexities, contradictions, irrationalities and struggles that combined to send Argentina in half a century from sixth place among the richest nations of the world to the humiliatingly low level it precariously clings to today. Besides, its seemingly deliberate omissions of well-known historical facts will certainly mislead several million youths who ignore them and who need more accurate information before Oct. 30, when they will vote for the first time.

Although produced by Radical Party politician Enrique Vanoli, "Republic" is not a pro-Radical pic, at least not openly. Editor-director Miguel Perez and political writer Luis Gregorich have done a shrewd job of threading personalities and developments in a way aimed at getting viewers' response. Their opus, although highly debatable, is undoubtedly effective.

Fine lab processing of material from vintage newsreels as well as old photographs. —*Nubi.*

Trespasses
(NEW ZEALAND-COLOR)

Auckland, Sept. 1.

A Finlayson-Hill Production. Produced by Tom Finlayson and Dean Hill. Directed by Peter Sharp. Screenplay, Finlayson and Maurice Gee; camera, (Eastmancolor) Leon Narbey; music, Bernie Hill; designer, Lindsay Waugh; editor, David Coulson; costumes, Glenys Hitchens; makeup, Jill Mills. Reviewed at St. James Theaterette, Auckland, Aug. 31, 1983. (NZ Censor's rating: R13.) Running time: 113 MINS.

Fred Wells	Patrick McGoohan
Katie Wells	Emma Piper
Albie Stone	Andy Anderson
Doug Mortimer	Terence Cooper
Stan Gubbins	Frank Whitten
Dave Gilchrist	Sean Duffy
Bob Storey	Don Selwyn
Sandra Foster	Vivienne Laube
Billie MacIntyre	Paula Keenan
Mrs. Mac	Kate Harcourt
Andy MacIntyre	Peter Rowley

In other hands, given the melodramatic potential of the plot, the fate of "Trespasses" would not be nice to think about. In the central character of Fred Wells we have än Old Testament style religious fanatic still brooding over the death of his wife 25 years ago. He lives alone with his daughter (his wife died giving birth to her) in a deserted coastal region, communing with his fundamentalist God in his private chapel and working up a smouldering head of resentment at the signs he sees of his daughter's desire to break away. The girl has become a substitute for his dead wife and his talk of hellfire and sin conceals his unconscious incestuous desire.

Led by a well-meaning, love-smitten youth, daughter Katie makes the break in quite the wrong direction — first to the opposite extreme of a drunken beach party crowd and then to the permissive "family" of a nearby commune. When he tracks her down and tries to drag her away, Wells is thrown off the property, still raving of hellfire and sin. As it happens he is not far off the mark for the incident impels the commune's guru (played with leering arrogance by Frank Whitten) to deflower Katie in a kind of ritual initiation.

The guru's subsequent murder comes as no surprise, and there is a police investigation during which the love-smitten youth comes under suspicion. The climax comes when the facts emerge and the police arrive to take Wells away. It is then that father and daughter realize the true nature of his love, he with horror, she with womanly compassion. The scene is played without dialog and is a natural lead-in for the freeze frame, fade and end title treatment, but nonetheless moving.

In a role that must have invited over the top histrionics, Patrick McGoohan's Wells is a tightly-controlled performance which is perhaps the finest of his career. Imported from England for the part of Katie, Emma Piper is remarkable. A subtlety that might be lost on all but Down Under audiences is her unerring ear for the New Zealand accent, different from that of Australia and not easy to imitate. The nasal drawl helps the honest image of Katie's character, a young woman caught in an unhealthy relationship and rebelling against a life of repressive religion and spinsterhood.

Credit for the film's restraint must go also to Peter Sharp, directing his first feature, and to scripters Maurice Gee and Tom Finlayson. The feature developed from a successful Television New Zealand police-drama series called "Mortimer's Patch," but while the main production creative talent and supporting cast are carry-overs, "Trespassers" is a story of complex human relationships and self-revelation first and a murder mystery very much second.

Another factor that checks the Eugene O'Neill overtones that might have made this a really heavy night at the cinema are the serene coastal and farmland locations, all within an hour's drive from Auckland, which allowed cast and crew to commute daily.

— *Dub.*

George Kuchar: The Comedy Of The Underground

(COLOR-DOCU-16m)

Champaign, Ill., Sept. 7.

Cinemasque Productions release. Produced by David Hallinger. Directed by Hallinger and Gustavo Vasquez. Editor: Curt McDowell. With Curt McDowell, Stella Kuchar, Mike Kuchar, Marion Kuchar, Marion Eaton. No other credits available. Reviewed at Picture Start Screening Room, Champaign, Ill., Sept. 7, 1983. (No MPAA Rating). Running time: **66 MINS.**

Bronx twin brothers George and Mike Kuchar brought humor to the underground art film circuit in the mid '60s. George's cheap, yet lavish and loving, parodies of Hollywood crime and melodrama predated similar commercial efforts by John Waters and Paul Morrissey. "Hold Me While I'm Naked" (1966) and others continue in art house revival.

Since 1972, George has taught and affected filmmaking at the San Francisco Art Institute, so that an entire generation of young filmmakers has emerged imbued with his visual touch: hand-drawn sets, baroque costuming and posing, heavily stylized acting, and intentionally cheap sexual theatrics. Two of Kuchar's former students created this documentary homage, with Curt McDowell — George's most talented graduate — editing.

Interspersed are key scenes from Kuchar films, "Hold Me ...," "Eclipse of the Sun Virgin," "The Devil's Cleavage" and others. The body of the film, and the most compelling footage, is of Kuchar himself, lecturing deadpan about his life being enhanced by filmmaking. "I'm supposed to be washed up," he begins a lecture shyly. "People say 'whatever happened to him?' You can't help what you are doing, and you can't stop either because it feels so good."

Kuchar conducts a tour of his San Francisco apartment, filled with odd statuary and kitch relating to Santa Claus, Jesus and Aunt Jemimah. One room is filled entirely with religious trinkets to differentiate it from the street life outside. "Sex activities have to go elsewhere, though," he explains. He flips through his scrapbook of clippings and reviews, lamenting the fact that he has apparently been dropped from "Who's Who."

Other interviews come from Kuchar's old-fashioned mother from the Bronx and his former cowork-

ers. McDowell pegs Kuchar as an active filmmaker in the tradition of Edgar Ulmer and Edward Wood ... with sex. McDowell also notes that George really wanted to be a weatherman or an actor, and Kuchar still makes annual trips to study weather in Oklahoma.

Kuchar keeps track of his former actors, explaining how one now models in fish cake ads in Vancouver, another sells underwear in Texas. His method for making films is "to start from rock bottom and work with rock bottom people. Money would be the end of my career."

Hallinger and Vasquez clearly are paying appreciative respect to Kuchar with this film, and Kuchar does come off as a thoroughly likable and unpretentious filmmaker. Technical credits are fine, if pedestrian, with one complaint being unidentified film clips. Sound is also sometimes less than crisp.

What does the future hold for Kuchar? He foresees calmly, "More and more obscurity. Weight problems."

"George Kuchar: The Comedy of the Underground" has already done a partial tour of the festival circuit, but seems suitable for other venues as well, in particular certain cable outlets and as an accompaniment or introduction to revivals and collections of Kuchar's own films. — *Pege.*

An Bloem

(DUTCH-COLOR)

Amsterdam, Sept. 5.

A Frans Rasker Film production. Directed by Peter Oosthoek. Screenplay, Ton Vorstenbosch, based on his stage play Scheiden (Divorce). Camera (color), Frans Bromet; editor, Ton Ruys; music, Bob Zimmerman. Reviewed at City Cinema, Amsterdam, Sept. 2, 1983. Running Time: **96 MINS.**

An Bloem . . . . Kitty Courbois
Dik . . . . Rijk de Gooyer
Loedie . . . . Renee Soutendijk
Lucia . . . . Marina de Graaf
Frans . . . . Ben Hulsman
Landlady . . . . Diane Lensink

Peter Oosthoek, 48, has worked in the theatre for 24 years, directed more than 100 plays and has been much prized. He has some tv credits but "An Bloem" is his first feature. It does not come off.

Pic will have a difficult time at home and, despite its Grand Prix at the Knokke Festival, is unlikely to travel outside the Low Countries, even as femme fare.

The story is an adaptation by Ton Vorstenbosch of his play which Oosthoek staged some years ago. An Bloem is the middle-aged wife of a stolid dullard who keeps a drab tobacconist's shop. The elder of the two grownup daughters is looking after Number One, and seeking a shortcut to the good things in life; the younger, loud-mouthed and big-hearted, is a singer in a punk group.

An decides to break out but has no special plans. She gets a job and an apartment. She also gets involved with a new man, probably just as dull as her husband, but younger and richer.

Things look good, till the elder daughter steals the man, gets herself pregnant and safely wed. An accepts the situation and becomes a kind of housekeeper in her daughter's affluent home, until the newlyweds decide to send her back to her husband and his dingy shop.

Oosthoek had the benefit of good and experienced technicians, every one of them does his thing well. Unfortunately, the picture doesn't jell. Oosthoek believes that "in cinema every sequence (and he's got 154 of them) should be a little explosion."

The fireworks fizzled. Frantic cutting brings confusion here, not fast storytelling. What keeps the pic from disintegrating altogether is the superb acting of Kitty Courbois in the title role.

The part of the elder daughter provides little scope for Renee Soutendijk's undoubted acting abilities. Marina de Graaf is excellent as the extrovert punk girl.

— *Wall.*

Sorte Fuger

(Black Crows)

(NORWEGIAN-SWEDISH-COLOR)

Oslo, Aug. 19.

A Marcus Film (Oslo), Europa Film (Stockholm) production. A/S Norsk Film release. Based on short story by Espen Haavardsholm. Script by Haavardsholm and Lasse Glomm. Features entire cast. Directed by Lasse Glomm. Camera (Eastmancolor) Erling Thurmann Andersen; editor, Lars Hagstroem; music, Anne-Grete Preus; costumes, Anne-Siri Brynni; executive producer, Bente Erichsen; production management, Bente Erichsen (Oslo, Frankfurt), Jean-Luc Millorit, Helen Perzon (Paris). Reviewed at Norsk Film A/S screening room, Jar, Oslo, Aug. 19, 1983. Running time. **90 MINS.**

Simone Cambrai . . . . Bibi Andersson
Steiner Carlsen . . . . Bjoern Skagestad
Celeste . . . . Anouk Ferjac
Jean-Claude . . . . Henri Serre
Elisabeth . . . . Micki Sebastian
Asil . . . . Minken Fosheim
Lindtner . . . . Keve Hjelm
Secretary . . . . Laila Nilsen
Inger . . . . Janny Hoff Brekke

"Black Crows" explores the emotional wasteland into which a couple of intellectuals plunge themselves when indulging in a spontaneous sexual relationship. She is a handsome 40-ish French seller for France's Edition Stock, he is a considerably younger, but equally eyecatching cover designer for Norway's Aschehoug. They meet at Frankfurt's International Book Fair one year. The next year, she does not turn up. In between, they have made love in Frankfurt's Zoo and in her Paris apartment, but beyond sexual embrace they have never truly reached each other. The age difference is not mentioned in the script and is not supposed to have anything to do with developments, although the visuals of the film undeniably will make audiences think along those lines. What destroys the relationship would rather seem to be murky points in the woman's past (we guess that she has had a female lover long before we are being overtly told so) and the man's lack of strength to really ignore the life she led before, even if he valiantly struggles to do so.

Action moves back and forth between Oslo and various places in France. Much of the lovers' communication is via letters or tapes. Dialog and encounters remain generally mired in cliches. Much footage is wasted on illustrating location shifts through departure of trains or taking-off and landings of planes. Playing by young Bjoern Skagestad and veteran Ingmar Bergman beauty Bibi Andersson seems partly smothered by Lasse Glomm's routine direction of a story that lacks conviction in its own protest points and tired verities. As an item for tv programming, "Black Crows" may get some international exposure on Bibi Andersson's name value and film's unusual book fair framing.
— *Kell.*

Mi Tia Nora
(My Aunt Nora)
(ECUADOR-COLOR)

Montreal, Aug. 23.
Produced and directed by Jorge Preloran. Screenplay by Mabel Preloran. Camera (color), Jaime Cuesta; editor, Jorge Preloran; music, Claudio Jacome. Reviewed at the World Film Festival (non-competing), Montreal, Aug. 22, 1983. Running Time: 92 MINS.
Beatriz . . . . Isabel Casanova
Nora . . . . Guiomar Vega
Virginia . . . . Ana Miranda
Sebastian . . . . Alejandro Buenaventura
Donna Eleanora . . . . Blanca Hauser
Raul . . . . Alfonso Naranjo

The opening title card of "My Aunt Nora" states the events of the story "could happen in any Latin American city." The expectations created by this picture from Ecuador are for a tale of social and political implications. It's a false hope. "My Aunt Nora" is no more than an old-fashioned melodrama with a plot easily transferred to almost any urban center of the world.

Beatriz comes from a wealthy Ecuadorian family still ruled by the presiding wishes of her grandmother. As the story begins, it is Christmas and the family is together physically. The children of Donna Eleanora, the matriarch, are a wimpy businessman (Beatriz's father), a fast-talking hustler now living in Miami and the painfully repressed spinster Nora.

Only Beatriz's mother, Virginia, possesses the driving ambition which surely is responsible for the family's fortune. Not surprisingly,

on the old woman's death, Virginia ensures she gains the lion's share of money and leaves Nora shackled with payments on a house she cannot afford.

Nora's predicament mushrooms as she gives her American-based brother her meagre savings to invest and he promptly squanders the money. And neither her family nor the church will offer help. She attempts to earn money as a seamstress but is clearly unsuited to the work and is finally evicted from the house and put into an asylum.

The angst-ridden tale, seen from Beatriz's perspective, is unrelenting. The young woman certainly identifies with her aunt and wants to avoid becoming the helpless spinster Nora typifies. Beatriz too has a domineering mother opposed to her noises of liberation.

The Latin soap operatics lack the currency or emotion to escape into the world marketplace. The high-pitched theatrics of Jorge Preloran's picture verge on the comical, though one never questions his sincerity. Technical credits are modest and performances rather one-dimensional apart from Isabel Casanova's Beatriz.

Some Spanish-language markets may more readily accept the picture, but mainstream exploitation, or even additional festival screenings, in the U.S. appear doubtful.
—*Klad.*

Andra Dansen
(Second Dance)
(SWEDEN-B&W)

Montreal, Aug. 21.
A Swedish Film Institute-Sandrews production. Produced by Jonas Cornell and Per Berglund. Directed by Larus Oskarsson. Screenplay by Lars Lundholm. Camera (color), Goran Nisson, Jan Pehrsson; editor, Ann-Christine Lindstrom; music, Jan Bandell. Reviewed at the World Film Festival (non-competing), Montreal, Aug. 20, 1983. Running time: 93 MINS.
Jo . . . . Kim Anderzon
Anna . . . . Lisa Hugoson
Isak . . . . Hans Bredefeldt
Hitch-hiker . . . . Tommy Johnsson

Sweden's 'Second Dance" is a demanding tale of two women drifters who form a brief partnership in what might be termed a distaff road picture. While certainly a work of ambition, the film is too bleak and oblique to register outside festival and specialty screenings. The emphasis has been placed on the interior journey of the women and the more outward aspects of the tale have a tendency to be brutally alienating.

The women — Anna, a prostitute and Jo, an avant garde jazz musician — meet in a roadside cafe. Anna simply invites herself along when she learns Jo is driving north. Jo appears to be gathering inspiration for a composition and Anna wants to go back to her father's farm.

Along the route there are the usual pitfalls. They encounter an amorous salesman, a drunk hitchhiker, the eccentric owner of a remote mansion and a compassionate woodsman. The tone of the incidents is usually sombre and intensified by Anna's beligerance. There's little evidence of humor or rapport between the women until late in the proceedings. Particularly difficult is the attempted rape of Anna by a group of lumberjacks.

Shot in black and white, the picture is quite handsomely, if darkly, mounted. The two central performances are strong even if the actresses have to voice some tired cliches.

The difficult journey finally pays off dramatically at the end of the road. However, considering the miles covered, "Second Dance" is not artistically fuel efficient.
— *Klad.*

An Epitaph For Barbara Radziwill
(POLAND-COLOR)

Montreal, Aug. 28.
A Film Polski release of a Perspektywa unit production. Directed by Janusz Majewski. Screenplay by Halina Auderska and Stanislaw Kasprzystak. Camera (color), Zygmunt Samosiuk; editor, Janina Niedzwiecka; art direction, Andrzej Halinski; music, Zdzislaw Szostak and Bohdan Mazurek. Reviewed at the World Film Festival (non-competing), Montreal, Aug. 27, 1983. Running time: 94 MINS.
Barbara Radziwill . . . . Anna Dymna
Zygmunt August . . . . Jerzy Zelnik
Queen Bona . . . . Aleksandra Slaska
Annonimus . . . . Krzysztof Kolberger
Zygmunt Stary . . . . Zdzislaw Kozien
Ostoja . . . . Stanislaw Zatloka
Radziwill Czarny . . . . Jerzy Trela
Radziwill Rudy . . . . Boguslaw Sochnacki
Queen Elzbieta . . . . Bozena Adamek
Kmita . . . . Leonard Pietraszak

"An Epitaph for Barbara Radziwill" is a handsome period romance, expertly crafted but nonetheless of limited appeal outside its native Poland. The historical tale, directed by the acclaimed Janusz Majewski, is a visual and dramatic spellbinder clearly destined to win more critical than commercial kudos.

Set in the 16th century, the tale centres on the ill-fated liaison between a king and a woman from a wealthy but untitled family. Told in a series of flashbacks, the film opens with striking images of the woman, Barbara Radziwill, being prepared for burial. The king, Zygmunt August, has mounted an elaborate funeral cortege to take her from Cracow to her native Lithuania.

En route, the story evolves, Zygmunt August's arranged political marriage was a romantic nightmare. Elizabeth, his first wife, was frigid and epileptic and in the manner of kings, or future kings, he was encouraged by his mother to

travel the realm and take a mistress.

In Lithunia he falls for the charms of Barbara but commits the cardinal sin of indiscretion. This will later prove difficult when Elizabeth dies and he seeks his mother's consent to marry Barbara. She disapproves but Barbara's ambitious brothers maneuver a shotgun wedding.

Majewski expertly foretells the coming tragedy through oblique references during the final journey to Cracow. Barbara's coronation was refused by both the old Queen and the parliament but Zygmunt August defiantly overruled their decree. Unfortunately, Barbara's death provided him with a hollow victory.

Aided by lush production values and superb performances, "An Epitaph for Barbara Radziwill" should captivate viewers. The difficulty is, of course, that this type of production has fallen out of favor outside Eastern-bloc countries and, lacking obvious commercial hooks, the film ill-suits the rigors of the commercial marketplace. Nonetheless, a worthwhile choice on the festival circuit. — *Klad.*

Toronto Fest

My Brother's Wedding
(U.S.-COLOR)

Toronto, Sept. 14.
A Charles Burnett production. Produced by Charles Burnett and Gaye Shannon-Burnett. Written and directed by Charles Burnett. Features entire cast. Camera (color), Burnett; editor, Tom Pennick. Reviewed at the Festival of Festivals, Toronto, Sept. 13, 1983. Running time: 116 MINS.
Pierce Monday . . . . Everett Silas
Mrs. Monday . . . . Jessie Holmes
Sonia . . . . Gaye Shannon-Burnett
Soldier Richards . . . . Ronnie Bell
Wendell Monday . . . . : . . . . . . Dennis Kemper
Sonia's Father . . . . Sy Richardson
Sonia's Mother . . . . Frances Nealy

Independent black filmmaker Charles Burnett has come up with a well-observed, handsomely-crafted human drama in his second feature, "My Brother's Wedding." In terms of marketability, he's made dramatic strides from his worthy but difficult 1977 debut "Killer of Sheep." The new film has obvious appeal for black and art house crowds and with careful marketing should make significant inroads in mainstream bookings.

Pierce Monday (Everett Silas) works in his family's Watts (Calif.) cleaning and laundry store. Unmarried and 30, he carries on a love-hate relationship with the tightly-knit black community. Pierce feels a commitment to the people he grew up with but carries a sense of hostility about his underprivileged status. The latter, however, is largely of his choosing.

He's highly critical of his brother, a lawyer, and contemptuous of his future sister-in-law, raised in an affluent home. For him, they've sold out and part of his dilemma is effecting change without adopting the status and qualities of upwardly-mobile blacks. This attitude also brings him into constant conflict with his mother who feels Pierce could be doing more constructive things with his life.

Burnett has a strong feel for his subject without having to hammer his points home. The picture has a facility for incorporating secondary characters, comic observation and local color into the story and still maintaining the central focus.

The essential irony of Pierce's plight eventually boils down to a quirk of circumstances. He's confronted with attending his brother's wedding — a ritual demanded by family pressure — and his best friend's funeral. Both events are to take place on the same day and short of cloning himself, there's no way to fulfill both obligations. He simply can no longer waiver between personal and external commitments.

Using primarily novice and semi-pro performers, Burnett manages to create an authentic flavor to his film. Particular strong are Silas as Pierce and Jessie Holmes playing the family matriarch. The shooting, spanning almost a year, shows no strain from its modest financial resources. However, one still feels the picture could benefit from minor excisions to tighten the narrative.

An admirable effort, "My Brother's Wedding" should be snapped up by one of the specialty distribution companies. While hardly a blockbuster, both domestic and foreign prospects as a quality picture are evident and one looks forward to Burnett securing a budget equal to his talent and ambition.
— *Klad.*

East 103rd Street
(BRITISH-U.S.-DOCU-COLOR)

Toronto, Sept. 16.

A Central TV/Institute for the Study of Human Issues Production. Produced by Chris Menges and David A. Feingold. Directed by Chris Menges. Camera (color), Menges; editor, Kit Davies. Reviewed at Toronto Festival of Festivals, Toronto, Sept. 16, '83. Running time: **70 MINS.**

In the summer of 1980, cameraman/director Chris Menges parked his van outside a tenement apartment on Spanish Harlem's East 103d Street to chronicle an American family "with a drug history at the end of the opium trail." The result is a painfully honest and occasionally compassionate journey into a Puerto Rican family's heroin habit and, by extension,

into the social mores and street life in a New York City slum, which would appeal to an arty, socially concerned crowd.

Not for the emotionally fragile, very detailed footage reveals Toni and her common-law husband mainlining with their teenage son Danny, the latest family member to join the shooting gallery. Amid the drug ritual, Danny claims "I'm going to change my life," and reprimands his mother, "You gotta rise up on your feet and get a job."

Only his beautiful sister Candy, a roller-skating saleswoman of loose joints, provides a voice of hope as she desperately pleads with Danny to kick the habit and tries to convince her mother to become less self-defeatist.

Extreme close-ups during monologs and interactions among family members give this docu a hot, claustrophobic feeling that acutely communicates the suffocation of the family's plight. Soundtrack sharply records a cacophony of street sounds over the chaotic dialog.

But the message from the neighbors and friends on East 103d Street is simple: you're programmed to fail. "Everything is negative, negative," one friend says. "Heroin has become for many of us an underground economy. If you're unfortunate, you get hooked. The money goes up your arm."

Menges provides a gripping peek into this culture, but manages to inject an occasional element of hope through discussions between Candy and Danny, who voice the possibilities of regaining self-respect and solidarity as a family. —*Devo.*

Cold Feet
(U.S.-COLOR)

Toronto, Sept. 17.

A Cinecom International film release. Produced by Charles Wessler, executive producer, Theron van Dusen. Written and directed by Bruce van Dusen. Camera (color), Benjamin Blake; editor, Sally Jo Menke; production design, Tom Randol; music, Todd Rundgren. Reviewed at the Festival of Festivals, Toronto, Sept. 16, 1983. Running time: **91 MINS.**

Tom Christo .... Griffin Dunne
Marty Fenton .... Marissa Chibas
Leslie Christo .... Blanche Baker
Bill .... Mark Cronogue
Harold Fenton .... Joseph Leon
Psychiatrist .... Marcia Jean Kurtz
Louis .... Kurt Knudson
Dr. Birbrower .... Peter Boyden
Susan Josephson .... Mary Fogarty
TV Executives .... Dan Strickler
                              John Jellison

Debuting filmmaker Bruce van Dusen provides a tale of love in the big city (Manhattan) in "Cold Feet." The low-budget tale from this graduate of tv ads is a pleasant, undemanding story with modest market potential. However, there's still much to admire in the collective work of the young talents involved.

Griffin Dunne stars as a television writer-director married to the child-like, neurotic Blanche Baker. Opposite is Marissa Chibas as a research scientist also involved in a dead-end relationship. The initial problem is unburdening Dunne and Chibas of their current mates and effecting their meeting. The latter occurs at a party given by Dunne and Baker.

Van Dusen doesn't have any new wrinkles to the age-old dilemma. Baker and Mark Cronogue, as Chibas' boyfriend, are clearly unsuitable mates. The slight novelty involved is the uncharacteristic slow development of Dunne and Chibas' affair after each experiences a series of comic and disastrous blind dates.

However, the twist is never fully exploited. Although there are elements of social satire, "Cold Feet" is clearly intended as a traditional romantic comedy. The two principals are just more coy in realizing their passion.

The familiarity of the material verges on the banal but the central performances have a charm which involves rather than alienates audiences. Still, apart from Dunne and Chibas, the supporting cast leans toward pushy characterization which doesn't always complement the central plot.

Dan Strickler and John Jellison as obsequious, network toads provide some of the better comic moments. While played for humor, there's more than a grain of truth in the political maneuvering surrounding Dunne's child abuse movie-of-the-week. One can hardly wait for the new project on what's referred to as "cross-dressers."

Technical contributions contribute to a handsome looking production. The look provided by Benjamin Blake's camerawork and Tom Randol's design are up to large-budget studio standards.

"Cold Feet" should attract some interest in larger markets with an eye toward subsequent cable and pay-tv saturation. The intimacy of the story seems better suited for smaller screens and theatrical situations specializing in independent and foreign product. — *Klad.*

The Sky On Location
(W. GERMAN-U.S.-DOCU-COLOR)

Toronto, Sept. 16.

A Babette Mangolte/ZDF (FDR) Television production. Produced, directed, written, camera and editing by Babette Mangolte. Music, Ann Hankinson; narration, Mangolte, Honora Ferguson, Bruce Boston. Reviewed at the Festival of Festivals, Toronto Sept. 15, 1983. Running time: **79 MINS.**

Cinematographer Babette Mangolte turns director for "The Sky On Location," a record of a

foreigner's (French) observations of the American west. In intention this film is not dissimilar to Chris Marker's "Sans Soleil" but clearly the latter picture is superior in every way.

Mangolte criss-crosses the west to record such natural wonders as Zabriskie Point, Monument Valley and Old Faithful. She calls her many vistas "great movie locations" and the voice-over narration hints at this year-long diary being a film scouting expedition rather than a project in and of itself.

The film's three voices render the most weighty, pretentious sentiments. The text imagines the awe of the 19th-century pioneers and nature as the safety valve for contemporary U.S. urban tension. The result is a rather stunning looking travelog with an awful pop psyche narration.

American audiences will find the production baffling in its observation. However, European television may just snap up the film as gospel. In any case, theatrical possibilities are minimal. —*Klad.*

Variety
(U.S.-COLOR)

Toronto, Sept. 11.

Produced by Variety Motion Pictures in association with ZDF Television (FRG) and Channel 4 (London). Producer, Renee Shafransky. Directed by Bette Gordon. Screenplay by Gordon and Kathy Acker. Features entire cast. Camera (color), Tom Dicillo, John Foster; editor, Ela von Hasperg; music, John Lurie; props and costumes, Elyse Goldberg. Reviewed at the Bloor Cinema, Festival of Festivals, Toronto, Sept. 10, 1983. Running time: **90 MINS.**

Christine .... Sandy McLeod
Mark .... Will Patton
Louis .... Richard Davidson
Jose .... Luiz Guzman
Nan........................... Nan Goldin

New York avant-garde filmmakers Bette Gordon and Renee Shafransky assay their first fiction feature with "Variety." The snappy title refers to the place of employ of the central character — a porno theatre, Variety Photoplays.

The tale of a young woman whose job selling tickets leads her into a sexual fantasy world and a possible organized crime operation is both technically and artistically bargain-basement "L'Avventura" material. The filmmakers simply don't have the expertise to pull off an ambitious, ambiguous tale where interior motivation takes supremacy over plot.

Christine (Sandy McLeod) takes a job with the theatre after all other employment possibilities have been exhausted. The clientele of the Manhattan operation is what you'd expect with the odd exception. One, Louie (Richard Davidson), appears to be a well-dressed businessman of some sensitivity. Christine is attracted to him and one day follows him into an adult video and magazine store which lands her an invitation to join him at a Yankees baseball game.

However, during the game he's forced to excuse himself and Christine winds up following him to what appears to be a mysterious rendezvous. She continues to stalk his trail but there's no evidence to uncover the mystery of his activities. Meanwhile, the woman slips further into a fantasy world inspired by the banalities on the movie house's screen.

The disjointed narrative ambles along with the tease of a big payoff, which never happens and whose lack will immediately limit the film's audience appeal. And for the art house circuit there are just too many long passages of silent observation to justify allusions of profound meaning.

The film also misses capturing the milieu or establishing the characters in Christine's life. It would be too easy to say her empty environment mirrors an empty life.

Limited finances show in both the film's look and performances. Apart from the odd colorful vignette, the film is remembered for long silent tracking sequences and Christine's stillness. — *Klad.*

Chia-Ju Wo Shih Chen-Te
(If I Were For Real)
(TAIWANESE-COLOR)

Toronto, Sept. 11.

A Yung Sheng Production. Directed by Wang T'ung. Features entire cast. Screenplay, Sha Yeh-hsin, Li Sho-ch'eng, Yao Ming-te, adapted by Chang Yung-hsiung; camera (color), Lin Hung-chung; music, Ch'en Hsin-yi; editor, Hsieh Y-hsiung. Reviewed at Toronto Festival of Festivals, Toronto, Sept. 11, '83. Running time: 96 MINS.
Cast: T'an Yung-lin, Hu Kuan-chen, Hsiang Ling, Ko Hsiang-t'ing.

A post-Gang-of-Four China as a society of special privileges and favor according to rank is the prevailing theme of this Taiwanese gem, "Chia-Ju Wo Shih Chen-Te" (If I Were for Real). Based on an original screenplay by three writers from the People's Republic of China, this pic has been banned in China and Hong Kong.

A rural farmworker wants to get transferred back to Shanghai in order to marry his pregnant fiancee. Through a maze of planned events and serendipitous circumstances, he impersonates the son of a Peking official while on leave to Shanghai. He manages to convince all the bureaucrats he encounters of his position, deftly sprinkling his conversation with hilarious anecdotes about his father's political career. Shades of "The Inspector General" emerge as his effective portrayal affords him a glimpse into the world of special treatment that comes with the territory of government higher-ups.

When the gig is up and his "father" confronts him, the worker protests, "you people on top don't know our suffering. I had no hope on the farm." The boy is consequently arrested and kills himself in prison.

In his first directorial effort, Wang T'ung is not heavy-handed or melodramatic in his political message. He combines light satire with the occasional scabrous dig to revel the still-prevalent corruption and Party advantages. He extracts fully realized and endearing performances from T'an Yung-lin and Hu Kuan-chen as the star-crossed lovers. Tech credits are very fine. —*Devo.*

En Haut Des Marches
(At the Top of the Stairs)
(FRENCH-COLOR)

Toronto, Sept. 17.

A Diagonale film production. Directed and written by Paul Vecchiali. Camera (color), Georges Strouve; art direction. Benedict Bauge; editor, Vecchiali; music, Roland Vincent; sound, Jean-Francoise Chevalier. Reviewed at the Festival of Festivals, Toronto, Sept. 16, 1983. Running time: 92 MINS.
Francoise Canavaggia ..Danielle Darrieux
Suzanne ....Helene Surgere
Michele ....Francoise Lebrun
Police Commissioner ....Nicolas Silberg
Rose.........................Giselle Pascal
Catherine ....Sonia Saviange
Charles ....—.........Max Naldini
Christine ....Christine Laurent
Mathilde ....Micheline Presle

Paul Vecchiali's "En Haut des Marches" is a demanding, complex story of memory, affection and political fortunes. One certainly can't fault the filmmaker for ambition but there are clearly problems of grasp in this picture. The production will no doubt find its share of defenders and detractors but popular appeal will likely elude this think-piece.

Dedicated to his mother, the film concerns Francoise Canavaggia (Danielle Darrieux), a woman whose husband was mysteriously killed shortly after the Second World War presumably for supposed Petainist sympathies. Francoise arrives in Toulon in 1963 after more than a decade's absence. It's gradually revealed that her plan is to murder the people who live in the villa she was forced to sell. The act is more ritual than blood vendetta.

Her journey through the town on the way to her mission provides for a series of vignettes and philosophical ramblings. The soundtrack is punctuated by old speeches from Petain and De Gaulle and encounters with old acquaintances mingle with real and imagined memories.

The structure of the film is as eclectic as its concerns. It's a dense jungle of words and images without a core, strung together by a tenuous thread. For most, the overall result is elusive and unsatisfying.

The general somber tone is not without humor. When Francoise tells her sister, Suzanne, played memorably by Helene Surgere, about a chance meeting with an old servant, she's told the woman had died years earlier. Then, a moment later, Suzanne realizes she'd been thinking of someone else, relieving the intrusion of pretention. However, a musical interlude with Darrieux provides a fantasy quality less suitable to the film.

Darrieux is excellent as an anchor for this difficult and varied material. Also strong is Francoise Lebrun as Darrieux's niece, a lawyer who confronts Francoise with her most nagging self-doubts in a series of real and imagined encounters.

A technically polished film, "En Haut Des Marches" is nonetheless more confounding than explanatory. The whole nature of political revisionism never quite jells with the filmmaker's desire to develop a loving homage to his mother and tackle the inner workings of memory and fact.

Ideal for art house screenings, the film will need careful cultivation to acquire the sympathy of audiences. Definitely a difficult commercial proposition despite its noble intentions. —*Klad.*

Enormous Changes At The Last Minute
(U.S.-COLOR)

Toronto, Sept. 13.

An Ordinary Lives, Inc. production. Produced by Mirra Bank. Features entire cast. Directed by Mirra Bank, Ellen Hovde, and Muffie Meyer. Screenplay, John Sayles, Susan Rice, based on short stories by Grace Paley; camera (color), Tom McDonough; editor, Mirra Bank, Ellen Hovde, Muffie Meyer. Reviewed at Toronto Festival of Festivals, Toronto, Sept. 13, '83. Running time: 110 MINS.
Cast: Ellen Barkin, Kevin Bacon, Maria Tucci, Lynn Milgrim, Sudie Bond.

"Enormous Changes At The Last Minute" is an enormously uneven trilogy of modern urban woman's dilemma in the precarious area of relationships with men. Pic provides a complementary vehicle for Ellen Barkin ("Diner," "Tender Mercies") and Kevin Bacon ("Diner") to display their wares, but subject matter may banish the commercial future to women's studies circuit.

Pic is first fictional feature for the 3 producer/directors, Mirra Bank, Ellen Hovde, and Muffie Meyer, all film editors. First vignette pits Virginia (Ellen Barkin) as a housewife with 3 kids who is newly deserted by her husband, and thus has to resort to welfare. Barkin succumbs to the advances of a former boyfriend (now married with kids), who is also the

landlord's son, while she flashes to steamy scenes of seduction with her ex-husband. Barkin's abilities range from self-deprecating humor to touching self-analysis, and she brings tenderness and spark to her character.

In second entry, Faith (Lynn Milgrim) makes a trek to visit her artsy, literary parents in an old-age Jewish residence, to tell her father that she's separated from her husband Ricardo. Her father then informs her that he would like to be divorced from her mother, but reveals that they never got married — "they were idealists." This is the weakest and least successful section, failing to capture the potential intimacy and poignancy of the encounter.

Alexandra (Maria Tucci) is a middle-aged, divorced, social worker who has a ludicrous affair with frenetic cab driver/punk rocker Dennis (Kevin Bacon), who first seduces her by declaring, "Your eyebrows are outasight." Dennis, who drives a cab to help him "keep tabs on the bourgeoisie," is given enormous charm and energy by Bacon, who is a charismatic screen presence. When Alexandra becomes pregnant by Dennis and decides to have the baby, she vehemently decides to go it alone and raise it herself. But Dennis is not an old-school cad, and is hurt and confused by his forced exclusion from the event.

Screenplay by John Sayles ("Return of the Secaucus Seven") and Susan Rice has some bright spots, but is widely inconsistent. Sound track was out-of-sync with the pic during this screening, which detracted from concentration.

The lack of any successful relationship in this trio of tales adds to the overall sentiment of futility and sadness in trying to secure a tight bond. But some shining performances elevate it from a market solely appealing to feminists.

—*Devo.*

Pinkel
(DUTCH-DOCU-COLOR)

Toronto, Sept. 10.

A Rotterdam Films Production. Features entire cast. Written and directed by Dick Rijneke and Mildred Van Leeuwaarden. Camera (color), Dick Rijneke; music, Tandstickorshocks, Rondo. Reviewed at Toronto Festival of Festivals, Toronto, Sept. 10, '83. Running time: 70 MINS.

"I had a job and I became a punk overnight," reminisces Pinkel, the subject of the bleak Dutch docu about the transformation of a rebellious punk rocker to a right-wing conservative laborer and family man.

Filmmakers Dick Rijneke and Mildred Van Leeuwaarden shot pic in 1979 and again in 1982, thus documenting the changes with footage from both phases of Pinkel's life.

Pinkel joined the Dutch punk scene at 14 and played guitar in the group Tandstickorshocks, espousing the rhetoric of the day in such lyrics as "No god's gonna tell me what to do." Clips of him shopping for punk military fatigues, rinsing the dye out of his Indian-scalp coif, and spray-painting "To Hell with Shell" on brick factory walls support the grim negativism and political anarchy of the movement.

Cut to Pinkel 5 years later, now a paperhanger who lives in the Rotterdam slums with his girlfriend and baby, talking to life insurance agents about the most cost-effective policies and spewing his ultra right-wing stance on foreigners, housing, and the economy to the interviewers. "I was born in Rotterdam and I feel I deserve a house. Maybe it sounds fascist — but I'm a true Dutch. I have the right."

Pic effectively outlines Pinkel's isolation and alienation, but lack of enough background material on his evolution dilutes any effect of caring for the subject. The tech credits are fine, but there's limited commercial appeal with this downbeat docu. —Devo.

Casta Diva
(DUTCH-B&W)

Toronto, Sept. 14.

A Frans Raskers film production. Produced by Raskers. Directed by Eric de Kuyper. Screenplay by Kuyper, based on ideas by Emile Poppe and others. Camera (b&w), Michel Houssiau; editor, Ton de Graaf; music, Puccini, Offenbach, Bellini, Berlioz, et al. Reviewed at the Festival of Festivals, Toronto, Sept. 13, 1983. Running time: 110 MINS.

With Jack Post, Emile Poppe, Ben Kettenis, Paul Verstraten, Walter Nuyens, etc.

Dutch filmmaker Eric de Kuyper's "Casta Diva" is a highly experimental film aimed almost solely at specialty and festival audiences. Shot in black and white with virtually no dialog, the picture examines a series of men involved in such mundane activities as shaving, eating and preparing a bow tie.

The activities are generally accompanied by the strains of classical music pieces. However, one sequence includes off-camera directions presumably from the director and another a voice-over by a man cutting his hair. In the majority of situations the individuals are looking into mirrors, so one can assume the director wants to express an opinion on narcissism.

Although several sections display humor of observation, the overall effect is tedious and difficult to fathom. One feels he is viewing an in joke which simply does not translate.

Prospects are extremely limited outside the festival circuit.
— Klad.

Venice Festival (Competition)

Sasame Yuki
(The Makioka Sisters)
(JAPANESE-COLOR)

Venice, Sept. 3.

A Toho Film Production, Tokyo. Executive producer, Tomoyuki Tanaka. Features entire cast. Directed by Kon Ichikawa. Screenplay, Shinya Hidaka, Ichikawa, based on a novel by Junichiro Tanizaki; camera (color), Kiyoshi Hasegawa; editor, Chizuko Nagata; music, Shinnosuke Okawa; sets, Shinobu Muraki, sound, Tetsu Ohashi; costumes, Hiroshi Saito. Reviewed at Venice Film Fest (Competition), Sept. 2, '83. Running time: 140 MINS.

Cast: Keiko Kishi (Tsuruko, the oldest sister), Yoshiko Sakuma (Sachiko, the second oldest sister), Sayuri Yoshinaga (Yukiko, the third oldest sister), Yuko Kotegawa (Taeko, the youngest sister), Juzo Itami (Tatsuo, Tsuruko's husband), Koji Ishizaka (Teinosuke, Saschiko's husband).

Kon Ichikawa's "The Makioka Sisters" is based on one of the classics of Japanese literature by the celebrated writer Junichiro Tanizaki. This is a rambling family epic along the lines of Thomas Mann's "Buddenbrooks," Booth Tarkington's "The Magnificent Ambersons," and John Galsworthy's "The Forsyte Saga." Running at two hours-plus at Venice, it made for an elegant view of life in Japan a half-century ago.

A wealthy Osaka family, the Makiokas, owe their social standing to their recently deceased father, a onetime rich merchant who ended up in debt. He has four daughters, two of them now married. The oldest of the four sisters, Tsuruko, is the legal heir, but of nothing to speak of save the home. Tsuruko's husband works in a bank.

The second oldest sister, Sachiko, is married to a salesman in a department store. It's at their modest home that the two younger sisters, still unmarried, prefer to live. The reason for this goes back to a family scandal of minor proportions, one that involved the good names of both of the younger sisters, Yukiko and Taeko, when Taeko unfortunately became infatuated with a suitor and wanted to run away with him. The incident was reported in the papers, albeit with the wrong name of the innocent Yukiko (instead of Taeko). When the husband of the oldest sister meddled in the same affair, the matter got worse — so it's with the second oldest sister that the younger pair now intend to live with. This, in turn, hurts the feelings of the oldest, Tsuruko.

Then comes the second family problem. The husband of the second oldest sister falls in love with the gentle, retiring Yukiko — all of which disturbs Sachiko (the second oldest). Eventually, however, Yukiko finds a suitor she likes — and soon she will marry into wealth and position (the natural right of a Makioka sister, so to speak).

But that, too, is complicated by the youngest falling in love with a poor and lowly bartender, an honest man, but not up to snuff for the family's tastes. Further, the husband of the oldest wants to leave Osaka for Tokyo — he's been offered a better position in the bank. In the end, Tsuruko agrees to leave what has been her home since childhood to be with him.

With such a family epic of melodramatic proportions (often found in Japanese films on a lesser scale in the "shomen-geki" genre, melodramas excelled in particularly by Ozu and Naruse), there is rich opportunity for ensemble acting — and it's here to perfection in Ichikawa's hands. Another aspect is the show of costumes, the compositional images of interiors of homes, and the catalog of emotions associated with Japanese manners — in other words, a certain reflection of a particular time and place in a not too distant past.

For those film buffs fed on Ozu's family traditions and Naruse's tragic female figures, Kon Ichikawa's "The Makioka Sisters" should provide vintage cinema for a lengthy night's entertainment. The rest of the public will at least sense that this is an epic that deserves to be read as well as seen. — Holl.

Die Macht Der Gefuehle
(The Power of Emotion)
(WEST GERMAN-COLOR-B&W-DOCU/FICTION)

Venice, Sept. 7.

A Kairos Film Production, Munich; world rights, Futura Film, Munich. Features entire cast. Produced, directed, written and narrated by Alexander Kluge. Camera (color, b&w), Werner Luering, Adam Olech; sound, Olaf Reinke, Karl-Walter Tietze; assistant director and consultant, Carola Mai; production managers, Daniel Zuta, Karin Petraschke. Reviewed at Venice Film Fest (Competition), Sept. 6, '83. Running time: 115 MINS.

With: Hannelore Hoger, Alexandra Kluge, Edgar Boehlke, Klaus Wennemann, Erwin Scherschel, Beate Holle, Uwe-Karsten Koch, Suzanne V. Borsody, Paulus Manker, Barbara Auer, Daniel Lucoend.

Alexander Kluge's "The Power of Emotion" is neither fiction nor documentary: yet it's a little bit of both, but mostly a film treatise on the philosophical-psychological-legal (and what have you) definition of the human emotion. Kluge saves himself from splitting hairs on the subject by prefacing everything with the word "power" — just about anything can happen when the power of emotion takes over, opines our filmmaker.

Fortunately, too, Kluge has issued a booklet with his film for the viewer's later contemplation. And at his press conference in Venice, he emphasized the film's central theme: "all emotions believe in a happy ending." This said, here's the breakdown of his film's 12 separate sequences (reading like chapters of a book): Act Five, The Shot, The Confusion of Emotions, The Hour of Death, Her Last Show, The Objects, The Power Plant of Emotions, The Plot, The Change, The Burning of the Opera House, Bought for Her Own Sake, and The Undoing of a Crime by Means of Cooperation.

There's not much else to say save to recommend that the film buff see the treatise for himself. Several critics and other professionals were quite impressed with Kluge's argumentative logic. German observers could easily relate figures from the Bonn political world (FDP's Mischnick next to SPD's Wehner, for instance) to the treatise without much trouble, in view of the recent change in government in West Germany. This reviewer's guess is that the material for making his reflective opus has been laying around in Kluge's drawer over the past couple years, waiting for the writer to become a filmmaker once again.

In any case, just as it's pleasant to hear a Dylan Thomas read his poetry and poetic prose on occasion, one should order a videotape of AK's film-treatise for the home library. What he has to say makes a great deal of sense for reference — but not for moviegoing.

The film has already been called "a film on emotion made without any emotion at all." In fact, this is the coldest film Alexander Kluge ever made. — Holl.

Mat'r Marija
(Mother Maria)
(RUSSIAN-COLOR)

Venice, Sept. 10.

A Mosfilm production, Sovexport release. Story and script by Sergei Kolosov, E. Mikulina. Directed by Sergei Kolosov. Camera (color) Valentin Zeleznjakov; editor, S. Guralskaja. Music, Alexej Rybnikov; production design, Michail Kartasov; costumes, E. Priede. Reviewed in competition at Venice Film Festival, Sept. 9, 1983. Running time: 93 MINS.

Mother Maria .... Ljudmila Kasatkina
Jura .... A. Timoskin
Sofija Pilenko .... V. Polonskaja
Madame Lanje .... E. Chanaeva
Danila Skobtsov .... Leonid Markov

"Mother Maria" by veteran director Sergei Kolosov is an old-fashioned wartime melodrama, filmed mostly on Paris locations and telling the story of the real life pre-revolutionary poetess Elisaveta Jurevna Kuzmina Karavaeva whose soul was so disrupted by exile that she left her poet-husband Alexander Blok to become a nun. World War II turned her into an organizer in France of other Russian exiles then wanted by the Germans. She was later arrested by the SS along with her adult son. She went to her death voluntarily in a concentration camp, having taken on the identity of a mother of three whom she wanted to save.

Kolosov has used his Paris locations along with old uniforms and various other period items with care and skill, but he totally fails to develop his characters, including a fittingly pale and efficient-looking Ljudmila Kasatkina in the title role, into anything but props and pawns. His way of depicting Germans is even more cliche-ridden.

Story picks up some interest when the theme of Russians helping each other across the political issues that tore them apart in the first place is introduced, but that introduction is not followed up too sincerely. A final sequence in the concentration camp has the look of being filmed directly on a clumsy stage setting. After Venice, "Mother Maria" will probably cease her foreign traveling and go home to an early tv rest. —Kell.

Glut
(Embers)
(SWISS-W. GERMAN-COLOR)

Venice, Sept. 7.
A Cactus Film Production, Zurich, in coproduction with Prokino Film Production, Munich, Thomas Koerfer Film, Zurich, SRG (Swiss Television), and ZDF (Second German Television). Produced by Edi Hubschmid. Features entire cast. Directed by Thomas Koerfer. Screenplay, Koerfer, Dieter Feldhausen; camera (color), Frank Brühne; music, Peer Raben; sound, Rainer Wiehr; sets, Bernhard Sauter; editing, Georg Janett. Reviewed at Venice Film Fest (Competition), Sept. 6, '83. Running time: 115 MINS.
Cast: Armin Müller-Stahl (Francois Korb, Andres Korb), Katharina Thalbach (Claire Korb), Mathias Habich (Albert Korb), Sigfrit Steiner (Colonel Wettach), Thomas Luecking (Andres) Agnes Zielinski (Anna), Krystyna Janda (Hanna Drittel), Barbara Freier (Antonia), Gudrun Geier (Lina), Walther Ruch (Karl), Jan Groth (Polish Internee), Gert Heinz (German Ambassador), Michael Tittermann (British Ambassador), Robert Tessen (General).

Thomas Koerfer has established himself as one of German Switzerland's most promising Autor (author) filmmakers with but five features to his credit: "The Death of the Flea Circus Director" (1973), "The Assistant" (1975) (based on à Robert Walser novel), "Alzire, or The New Continent" (1978), "The Passionate" (1982) (Goethe writing his "Sorrows of Young Werther"), and "Embers" (1983). He is an intellectual with a yen for stylized acting always cutting against the grain of usual narrative storytelling, which in turn makes him accessible only to the initiated in German film circles.

"Glut" — a difficult title to translate, but given in English as "Embers" at Venice by the producer — treats for the first time the wealthy class during WW-II. It's 1944 and signs are that Germany will lose the war. The situation, however, doesn't bother the arms manufacturer Korb in the least, as he sells to both sides anyway.

Korb is considered to be an upright businessman and patriot by his peers, for the Swiss army also needs arms in times like these. But all is not well at home: his wife is having an affair with his brother, and his school-age son lives a desperately lonely life with a teddybear as his sole companion. So the Korbs decide to take in a refugee Polish girl as a temporary guest at the family villa. The two become fast friends.

There's also an elderly grandfather at the villa, a former military officer and a gentleman. When a Polish refugee soldier happens upon the scene, the children hide him with the help of the grandfather — then the grandfather exchanges uniforms with the Pole to help him escape. The industrialist Korb, however, mistakes the old man for the refugee — and kills him by firing a shot at the mysterious retreating figure on the roof of the villa. The point of involuntary homicide has been made, so far as the film is concerned.

But there's an aftermath, a flashback running throughout the film. The Polish girl returns to Switzerland 40 years later. There she meets her childhood friend, who has grown into the identical figure (thesp Armin Müller-Stahl in a double role) as his father of long ago.

Slow-moving and rather predictable, "Embers" is nonetheless a quite fascinating portrait of the well to do in the land of plenty. Lensing by Frank Brühne is particularly striking. This is one of those fest items that well deserves more exposure. —Holl.

Rue Cases Nègres
(Street Of The Black Shacks)
(FRENCH-MARTINIQUEN-COLOR)

Venice, Sept. 9.
A SU.MA.FA, ORCA, N.E.F. coproduction, N.E.F. Diffusion (Paris) release. Based on novel by Joseph Zobel. Written and directed by Euzhan Palcy. Camera (Fujicolor) Dominique Chapuis; editor, Marie-Joseph Yoyotte; music, Groupe Malavoi, Roland Louis, V. Vanderson, Brunoy Tocnay, Max Cilla, Slap-Cat; production design, Hoang Thanh At. Costumes, Isabelle Filleul; executive producer, Jean-Luc Ormieres; production management, Christine Renaud. Reviewed as a competition entry in the Venezia Giovani program of the Venice Film Festival at the Excelsior screening room Sept. 9, 1983. Running time: 100 MINS.
José......................Garry Cadenat
Grandmother Tine......Darling Legitimus
Old Medouze..................Douta Seck
Leopold..................Laurent Saint-Cyr
Monsieur Saint-Louis........Joby Bernabe
Leopold's mother.........Marie-Jo Descas
The teacher..................Henri Melon
Carmen......................Joel Palcy

Euzhan Palcy came from the Antilles to France in 1975. She made two recordings of children's songs, but soon established herself as a film professional, doing editing work for Serge Kollo, among others. "Street Of The Black Shacks" is her feature debut and an auspicious one. Film, a multi-prize winner at Venice, has already beaten "E.T.'s" records at the Martinique-Guadalupe box-office and is doing well in France, too. Basing her script on a memoir-cum-novel by Joseph Zobel, Palcy evokes an era (1931-33) in French colonial history in sepia-toned colors and handsomely composed frames without ever falling into the pitfalls of shrill propaganda. Her viewpoint in the film is that of a young teenager, José, who lives with his grandmother in the shantytown indicated in the title, but gets out of it by being both intelligent and stubborn.

Of course, the French "Whitey" is not seen in too sympathetic a light, but to José he is just there and there is nothing to do except get around him. At home, he is a boy like other boys, rather wild at times; he even gets drunk once and sets fire to a shack. He gets whipped by his grandmother, who is classically tough-but-tender, and is taught words of wisdom by an old, freed slave (Darling Legitimus and Senegal's Douta Seck play these adult roles and are the only professionals in the film). The boy is also unswervingly industrious and earns a scholarship to go to high school in the city of Fort-de-France. His grandmother goes with him, but soon decides to go back to the sugar plantation to die.

Considering the obvious melodramatic possibilities of her story, Palcy has opted for a style that has all dramatic counterpoints blunted too severely to make the film easily marketable outside home territories. Still, "Street of the Black Shacks" stands as an extremely subtle piece of filmmaking in which amateurs act naturally in surroundings and situations that often seem to belong more to a docu-drama than to an outright fiction feature. All production credits are deserving of high praise for accuracy and for never imposing themselves too much on the narrative flow. —Kell.

Lontano Da Dove
(Far From Where)
(ITALIAN-COLOR)

Venice, Sept. 8.
A Gaumont release, produced by Effe P.C., RAI-TV Channel 2 and Gaumont Opera Film. Features entire cast. Written and directed by Stefania Casini and Francesca Marciano. Camera (Kodacolor), Romano Albani; editor, Mauro Bonanni; costumes, Ornella Pisano; music, Lucio Dalla. Reviewed at the Venice Film festival, (Young Directors Competition), Sept. 8, 1983. Running time: 95 MINS.
Daniela....................Monica Scattini
Mario..............Claudio Amendola
Desideria.................Stefania Casini
Giacomini..............Victor Cavallo

A RAI-TV/Gaumont entry featured in the competitive young directors section of the Venice Film Festival, "Far From Where" marks the unusual debut of two femme helmers, Stefania Casini and Francesca Marciano, directing in tandem. Both are actresses (Casini was glimpsed in Bernardo Bertolucci's "1900," Marciano in Wertmuller's "Seven Beauties") and sendup of Italian kids starry-eyed over the pervasive myth of New York as glamorous Fun City, it soon becomes apparent pic isn't many steps ahead of its colorless, cliched characters and ends up taking them all seriously. The film's calculated "young" look is aimed at the Italo youth market, but it lacks the non-stop clowning and oomph that usually signal a local winner.

Story steps off with Mario (Claudio Amendola), an aimless young Roman, arriving in Gotham for the first time and instantly being deluged by sex, drugs and money. Mario is taken under the wing of a compatriot who has already established himself as a record importer. Everyone he meets is having the time of his life basking in the laid-back, easy-money atmosphere of what to them is the capital of the empire.

Point-of-view abruptly shifts to a slightly more realistic and sympathetic character, Daniela (Monica Scattini), who pays for acting lessons by working as a parttime waitress. Director Casini appears in a caricatured role as Desideria, a glamorous jet-setter prone to name-dropping the likes of Dustin Hoffman, Ringo Starr and Andy Warhol. But she's played so above the lines we're never sure whether she really knows any celebrities or not.

Completing the Italian cast is Giacomini (Victor Cavallo), a political journalist and aging leftie who mourns the passing of interest in Angela Davis and the Black Panthers. He opts for repatriation when a flighty newswoman usurps his place by sending home pieces on Italian youth in New York (pic's self-parody?).

Most of the American characters are unrecognizable in speech and act, with some naive racism and sexism casually tossed in for a laugh.

The neophyte-directors show considerable talent using a camera and manage to make some comic scenes work. Perhaps with a professional scripter and dialog writer they can develop their bent for irony and clean shooting technique. Music is by mellow folk singer Lucio Dalla. Among the cast, Monica Scattini and Claudio Amendola are most natural and convincing. — *Yung.*

Tisicrocna vcela
(The Millennial Bee)
(CZECH-W. GERMAN/ITALIAN-COLOR)

Venice, Sept. 6.

A Slovensky Film (Bratislava), Janus-Film, HR/ORF/RAI-TV-1/SACIS co-production, Slovensky Film release, Beta-Film (Munich) foreign. Based on novel by Peter Jaros. Script, Juraj Jakubisko, Peter Jaros. Directed by Juraj Jakubisko. Camera (Eastmancolor), Stanislav Dorsic; editor, Judita Fatulova; music, Petr Hapka; production design, Viliam Pausek, Milos Kalina; costumes, Mila n Corbu. Zdenka Bocankova. Reviewed as official competition entry in the Venice Film Festival, Sept. 6, 1983. Running time: **175 MINS. (Part 1: 98 MINS, Part 2: 77 MINS).**

Samo	Stefan Kvietik
Martin	Jozef Kroner
Maria	Ivana Valesova
Valent	Michal Docolomansky
Kristina	Eva Jakoubkova
Ruzena	Jana Janovska

Often returning to the metaphors of the life of the bees, Juraj Jakubisko, an accomplished Slovakian filmmaker in the great tradition of his country, tells in "The Millennial Bee" of the ups and downs during thirty years of a village family in a remote Czechoslavakian corner of the Austro-Hungarian empire. In Part 1, events are centered around an elderly beekeeper and bricklayer. Trials and tribulations, plenty of love affairs (very sensual and physical stuff here) and intrigue are mounted with beautiful cinematographic style, lively acting and a generally jolly way of telling almost too many stories at the same time.

Part 2 strikes more somber tones when Samo, the eldest son, in the days before World War I engages himself in social-democratic politics. During the war itself, his flour-mill is taken over by the military and he loses two sons in military action. However, all these people are seen to possess truly inventive spirits and sturdy hopes so there is a happy — politically fit ting, too — kind of ending.

However beautiful to look at and often very funny to boot, "The Millennial Bee" is told in too dramatically fragmented a manner to sustain audience excitement during its overlong run. All acting is brilliant, the production values are pure marvels and the director's little human insights are often touching, but still his film gets bogged down in excess. By wanting to present a whole world in microcosm, he enlarges every detail of that same microcosm to command an interest that is rarely followed through. Faces and fates flash by along with touches of magic that distract from, rather than enhance the elements of true drama. Film is sure to be applauded at festivals, but on foreign shores it will more likely find a tv market. Even tv programming will be difficult because of the fragmentary way Jakubisko has chosen to tell his story. Its two main parts are just not suited to be cut into still shorter episodes. — *Kell.*

Il Momento Dell'Avventura
(The Moment of Adventure)
(ITALIAN-COLOR)

Venice, Sept. 3.

A SACIS release, produced by Carlo Tuzii for RAI-TV Channel 1 and Pont Royal Film TV. Stars Peter Chatel and Laura Morante. Directed by Faliero Rosati. Screenplay by Giovanni Lombardo Radice, Marian Garroni and Faliero Rosati. Camera (Eastmancolor), Cristiano Pogany; editor, Anna Napoli; art director, Luciano Spadoni; music, Manuel De Sica. Reviewed at the Venice Film Festival, (Young Directors Competition), Sept. 3, 1983. Running time: **107 MINS.**

Andrea	Peter Chatel
Anna	Laura Morante
Doyle	William Berger
Voltera	Fausto Di Bella

One of Italy's more dignified entries in the competitive young directors section of the Venice Film Festival, "The Moment of Adventure" heralds the arrival of a talented new filmmaker to watch. Faliero Rosati, known for an acclaimed 1978 tv film called "Death of a Cameraman" here makes the leap into features with a sober, off-beat tale about an art forger's quest for buried treasure. Too slow and introspective to succeed as an adventure film, pic's interest lies in its breathtaking images and contemplation of the forger hero as artist-thief. Though a hardsell in domestic markets, pic should have a busy fest life and a crack at offshore playoff, perhaps, with specialized handling.

Adept international cast is led by Peter Chatel as Andrea, an art restorer who makes copies of the museum's sculpture collection in his spare time and switches his fakes for the originals. He sells them to a classy American art dealer, Doyle (William Berger), who is also doing a deal with an art forger named Volterra (Fausto Di Bella).

Andrea's big chance comes when the museum gets hold of an ancient Roman corpse with a strange cylinder embedded in its skull. Adding an impromptu surgical operation to his nocturnal pilfering, he extracts the cylinder and inside finds a map. Volterra does some fast library research and concludes it leads to an important undiscovered archaeological site — a sculptor's studio just off the Italian coast. Andrea and Volterra join forces to look for the treasure but are outmaneuvered by Doyle and his mysterious helpmate Anna (Laura Morante). Volterra dies of a heart attack; Andrea is forced to feel the country to avoid the police.

Rosati is a declared pupil of Michelangelo Antonioni's, and the master's influence is apparent in the carefully composed shots, measured pacing, interest in character rather than action, and spare (sometimes off the wall) dialog. In place of angst and boredom, Rosati's characters labor under the burden of cynicism, self-interest and mutual mistrust. Intelligent thesping from Chatel and Morante help cover some awkward moments, though nothing can explain the odd fact that Andrea habitually goes diving underwater with all his clothes on.

With its remarkable pictorial sensitivity for imagery and abstract natural forms (thanks also to cameraman Cristiano Pogany), it is a pity that "Adventure" is so maladroit as an actioner, unable to build sequences into emotionally resonant drama. Even the sensitive, restrained performances of the pro cast are in a certain contrast to the subject matter. Technical credits are high quality.
— *Yung.*

Hon vong phu
(Dust of Empire)
(FRENCH-VIETNAMESE-COLOR)

Venice, Sept. 6.

A Uranium-Film, FR-3 production, Prodis (Paris) release. Original story and script by Henry Colomer, Lam-Le. Directed by Lam-Le. Camera (Eastmancolor) Gerard de Battista; editor, Catherine Renault; music, Nguyen Thien Dao; production design, Lam-Le with Jacques d'Orido; executive producers, Yvon Guezel, Yves Gasser. Reviewed in the competition section of the Venezia Giovani section of the Venice Film Festival, Sept. 6, 1983. Running time: **103 MINS.**

The missionary	Dominique Sanda
The sergeant	Jean-Francois Stevenin
The carpenter	Thang Long
The Eurasian	Yann Roussel
The French Woman (both epochs)	Anne Canovas
The Vietnamese Woman (both epochs)	Hoang Lan
The singer	Myriam Mezieres
The boy messenger	Tra Huu Phuc

Lam-Le, born in 1948 in Vietnam and a French resident since 1966, worked with theatre groups as a production designer before he tried his hand at various film chores such as doing story-boards for, among others, Claude Miller. Actually, story-boarding of an exquisite order provides a solid foundation for the striking visuals of "Dust of Empire," Lam-Le's first feature film. Title refers to the several empires, including French colonial rule, that have crumbled on Vietnam soil. But the Vietnamese title can be translated as Waiting Stone. This stone is a meteoric formation in the mountains of Thanh-Hoa. It has a myth attached to it, marking both the departure and separation point of lovers and close friends and the point to which they must one day return, dead or alive.

In the 1950s, just after Dien-bien Phu, a missionary (Dominique Sanda) and a French sergeant live through days and nights of ghoulish hiding from an advancing "enemy." A small Vietnamese boy is entrusted with the passing on a written message which is a rather cryptic reference to the Waiting Stone. He is to give it to the wife of a resistance fighter. She is supposed to live in a certain Villa des Roses in Saigon, but the boy sees her boarding a ship bound for France. By now, the missionary and the sergeant have been seen to die rather wantonly from sniper bullets. The message, now folded into a flat fan, passes from hand to hand, it turns up in Paris at a Vietnamese reunion, and it strikes fear and longing in many hearts until one day, twenty years later, it is laid to rest in a hole in the Waiting Stone by the daughter of the woman from the Villa des Roses.

Lam-Le wants the poetic-mythical qualities of the legend to suffice as metaphor for Vietnamese faith and endurance, but plenty of room for interpretation is left open for audiences of analytical inclination. "Dust of Empire" is genuine poetry throughout even though it has a good deal of the gruesome, the grotesque and the wryly funny thrown in as realistic baits. Lam-Le composes and "colors" frames that currently cannot avoid comparison with those of "Diva's" Jean-Jacques Beineix — for better or for worse. Much seems too contrived, but nothing is less than striking.

Dominique Sanda's name and demurely beautiful presence may help sell "Dust of Empire" into worldwide theatrical situations of the more demanding order, but exactly in such situations Lam-Le's film should be able to thrive modestly on its own merits. —*Kell.*

Il Disertore
(The Deserter)
(ITALIAN-COLOR)

Venice, Sept. 3.

As Istituto Luce/SACIS release, produced by RAI-TV Channel 2. Stars Irene Papas and Omero Antonutti. Directed by Giuliana Berlinguer. Screenplay by Berlinguer and Massimo Felisatti, based on the novel by Giuseppe Dessi; camera (color), Sandro Messina; editor, Romano Trina; art director, Tommaso Passalacqua. Reviewed at the Venice Film Festival, (Young Directors Competition), Sept. 3, 1983. Running time: **106 MINS.**

Mariangela	Irene Papas
Father Coi	Omero Antonutti
Saverio	Mattia Sbragia

Giuliana Berlinguer's "The Deserter" was one of Italy's three entries in the Silver Lion young directors competition at Venice Film

Festival. As a simple, dignified story with many rich insights into how people come to terms with complex moral choices, pic would be an ideal tv fest entry. Produced by RAI-TV Channel 2 and shot by an acclaimed tv helmer, it retains a stubborn small screen aura that will weigh heavily against its chances at onshore theatrical release. An added problem is that pic was rigorously shot in a regional dialect not easily comprehensible to audiences — though this drawback dissolves with subtitles.

Top performances by Irene Papas and Omero Antonutti and a good, solid script based on the Giuseppe Dessi novel give pic quality points, but aren't enough to get it off the ground. Emotionally and politically, it remains correct, but uninvolving.

In a remote Sardinian village in 1922, town fathers are collecting funds for a war memorial, but the poor villagers show little interest and the richer ones keep a tight hold on their purse strings. Only Mariangela, who has lost her two sons in the war and feels the dead must have their names written down and remembered, sacrifices 15 years of savings for the cause. The organizers suspect they are being taunted by Father Coi (Antonutti), for whom Mariangela works as a maid, and give the money back. More determined than ever, Mariangela secretly donates it again.

Father Coi, who doesn't understand her gesture, is opposed to the rhetoric of the pompous monument committee, more interested in burying all memory of the war under fine words than remembering the sacrifices it entailed and its meaning for the people.

In a series of flashbacks we see the truth about the death of Mariangela's beloved younger son: Saverio (Mattia Sbragia), officially listed as missing, actually deserted after killing his captain and returned home critically ill with fever. Mariangela nursed him in a secret mountain hut with the complicity of Father Coi. There the boy died, asking not to be delivered to the authorities even after death.

Papas appears in the familiar role of the black-clad Mater Dolorosa, following her conscience with unshakable conviction. Antonutti paints a complex portrait, torn between his feelings toward the boy and his duty as priest and citizen to give him up to the authorities, first living, now dead. In the end, after the celebration for the inauguration of the monument ends in a bloody clash between fascists and local miners, Father Coi and Mariangela both silently conclude that Saverio's place is outside official rhetoric, and his grave remains a secret as a symbol of protest. —*Yung.*

Venice Fest (Non-Competing)

Unknown Chaplin
*(BRITISH-COLOR-DOCU-16m)

Venice, Sept. 3.
A Thames Television Production, produced by Kevin Brownlow and David Gill. Production assistants, Janice Brackenridge, Betty Kenworthy, Elizabeth Kemp. Screenplay, Gill, Brownlow; consultant, Raymond Rohauer; cinematographic research, Ian Lewis, Iwona Barycz; music, Charles Chaplin, Carl Davis; sound, Ron Thomas; editing, Trevor Waite; videotape editing, Tom Kavanaugh, Terry Badham, Grant Goodwin. Reviewed at Venice Film Fest (Venice by Day section), Sept. 2, '83. Running time: 154 MINS.
With: Virginia Cherrill, Georgia Hale, Sydney Chaplin, Alistair Cooke, Lita Grey Chaplin, Robert Parrish, Dean Riesner.

Enough can be found in the general press on the finding of lost footage (rather, unused stored footage) from Charles Chaplin films, but the heavy turnout at Venice to see these three assembled docus from a Thames Television production is worth a review for several reasons — one of which is that "finds" like this simply cannot be repeated enough in film journals and newspapers. It was indeed a pity that Kevin Brownlow and David Gill's "Unknown Chaplin" could not be presented in the Grand Salle of the festival palace, in the same manner as the restored Judy Garland classic, "A Star Is Born," was unspooled.

The series is rightly listed in the fest catalogue as "the coup of the century," for this is the first time in some 70 years that the public has had a chance to view discarded outtakes of Charlie's two-reelers and features. Part One is labeled "My Happiest Years, 1916/17," Part Two "Great Director, 1918/31," and Part Three "Hidden Treasures." So far as pure unadulterated Chaplin is concerned, "Hidden Treasures" deserves full scale release — perhaps with a few more overlooked treasures that could not be included within the proscribed time span of a tv-production.

"My Happiest Years" refers to his days with the Mutual Film Company. He made a dozen two-reelers at this time, 1916-1917. The gem of the lot is "The Cure," in which Chaplin went through several approaches to comedy at a spa. His rehearsals with Edna Purviance are also eye-catchers.

"Great Director" shows the planned but discarded ending to "The Gold Rush." There are also clips of distinguished guests at his new studio, and a home-movie on "How to Make Movies" there. The great vaudevillian, Sir Harry Lauder, can also be seen in one of his rare (if not the only) screen appearance: he and Charlie exchange costumes and then imitate each other. Other golden moments are interviewed with the ingenues in his feature films: Lita Grey (married to Chaplin), Georgia Hale, and Virginia Cherrill. The Cherrill interview on being hired, fired, and rehired for "City Lights" is particularly of note.

"Hidden Treasures" has the discarded sequences from "City Lights" and "Modern Times" that had the Venice aud in stitches. Rather than spoil the potential viewer's own amusement, let's just say that the sequence with the piece of wood stuck in the grating of a sidewalk vent before a department store window will surely go down in film history books. Were there any more like this that were discarded and seemingly lost forever? Keep looking out there!
— *Holl.*

Histoire D'Une Rencontre
(Story of an Encounter)
(ALGERIAN-COLOR)

Venice, Sept. 3.
An Oncic Film Production, Algeria. Features entire cast. Directed by Brahim Tzaki. Screenplay, Yamina Kesar; camera (color), Yahiaui Allel; sound, Bonafia Rachid; editor, Rachid Mazouza; music, Safy Bontella. Reviewed at Venice Film Fest (Special Program section), Sept. 2, '83. Running time: 80 MINS.
Cast: Belasri Boumedine (deaf-mute girl), Matthis Carine (deaf-mute boy), Gill Alan (father of the girl), Arbouz Mohamed, Bryan Lynn, Ben Bourak Arab, Bouch Ichi Ohra.

One of three Algerian pics unspooled at Venice, this one-shot presentation pulled the heartstrings as a sentimental human-interest story about two deaf-mutes who have only each other to meet the world — and eventually have to be separated due to the exigencies of their family backgrounds and the expected departure of one family due to the father's traveling job requirements.

The deaf-mute girl is an American visiting Algeria: her father works in the oil-fields. The deaf-mute boy is from the area near the Algerian oil-field, and his father raises chickens as both a hobby and a living. Once the two come to know each other and exchange experiences in their rather needy way, it seems a shame to separate them. The exchange also includes the playthings of two opposing cultures, whereby the initial communication is made. In the end, it's these two cultures that drive them unwillingly apart, although a strong and necessary friendship has been made on a strictly human level. —*Holl.*

Sogno Di Una Notte D'Estate
(A Midsummer Night's Dream)
(ITALIAN-COLOR)

Venice, Sept. 5.
A Giangi Film release, produced by Sergio Lentati for Politecne Cinematografica and RAI-TV Channel 2. Stars Flavio Bucci and Gianna Nannini. Written and directed by Gabriele Salvatores (from the Shakespeare play). Camera (color), Dante Spinotti; editor, Gabriella Cristiani; art director, Gianmaurizio Fercioni; music, Mauro Pagani. Reviewed at the Venice Film Festival, (noncompeting), Sept. 5, 1983. Running time: 95 MINS.

Oberon	Flavio Bucci
Titania	Gianna Nannini
Puck	Ferdinando Bruni
Hippolyta	Erika Blanc
Theseus	Alberto Lionello
Helena	Sabina Vannucchi
Hermia	Augusta Gori
Demetrius	Giuseppe Cederna
Lysander	Luca Barbareschi

Surprise hit of this year's heavy-handed Italian Showcase at the Venice Film Festival was a no-holds-barred rock musical based on Shakespeare's "A Midsummer Night's Dream." Young Milanese helmer Gabriele Salvatores comes from a theatrical background and pic began life as a hit rock musical on stage. Unabashedly mixing the Bard of Avon with punk, avant-garde and Hollywood citations, "Midsummer Night" could become Italy's first midnight cult movie.

Salvatores wisely chooses to use the Elizabethan text strictly as a framework, though he also gets some laughs out of bizarrely casting the famous characters. With prominent thesp Flavio Bucci and popular rock star Gianna Nannini playing Oberon and Titania, the King and Queen of the Night come ready-made with distinctive faces and personalities. Italo audiences may also be amused at the whimsical pairing of stage thesp Alberto Lionello and photoromanzo face Erika Blanc as Theseus and his consort Hippolyta.

The young couples are less inspired. Both girls are pretty but too similar, while handsome Luca Barbareschi as Lysander is unevenly pitted against Giuseppe Cederna's pony-tailed little Demetrius.

But it's the imaginative technical work that gives life to the film, with atmospheric nighttime sets in a crumbling tower designed by Gianmaurizio Fercioni; superbly suggestive lighting, often murky darkness illuminated by torches or the moon; the work of cameraman Dante Spinotti; and Mauro Pagani's rock score, which was rewritten for Nannini's searingly raucous voice and style. Choreography is basic leaping around and not all numbers are equally successful, but flaws don't put out the general fireworks. Pic's most serious problem is a structural one, with the best effects used up and the novelty worn off before the text's obligatory end. The final play by the country comedians and marriage round-up feels drawn out and anticlimactic, despite astute staging.

Salvatores plays for multimedia thrills (the fairies' erotic dance numbers) and camp twists (having Demetrius and Lysander fall in love with each other instead of the girls.) Inserting flash images of missiles and bullfights, having Theseus and Hippolyta dance a habanera and showing Oberon romping through a girls' shower room demonstrate the director's surprising ability to bring disparate, eclectic material together under one roof and make it work.
— *Yung.*

Voyage Au Pays De Rimbaud
(Voyage to Rimbaud Country)
(FRENCH-COLOR)

Venice, Sept. 5.
An Ina/FR3 production, Paris. Features entire cast. Written and directed by Dariush Mehrjui. Camera (color), Jacques Parmat. Eric Robert; editor, Dominique Bellfort. Veronique Parnet; sound, Jean Minondo. Andre Sierkierski. Reviewed at Venice Film Fest (Special Program section), Sept. 4, '83. Running time: **65 MINS.**
Cast: The Troupe del Theatre Ern: Cercle Pierre Bayle, Nicolas Joly (Rimbaud at 16), Mathieu Joly (Rimbaud at 8).

This French tv production of just over an hour was an intellectual teaser at Venice. The director is the best known and respected of Iranian film exiles: Dariush Mehrjui, educated at UCLA in both the film and philosophy departments, onetime editor of the Partisan Review, and the maker of several key Iranian films that always ran into trouble with the government, before the fall of the Shah.

Mehrjui is probably best known abroad for "The Postman" (1971) (an adaptation of George Büchner's "Woyzeck," transplanted to Iran), as well as the cut version of his "Mina Circle" (1974), the last film of importance to leave Iran in the trying days before the revolution.

Now Mehrjui has made a medium-length feature for French tv on the importance of Rimbaud, a revolutionary poet, for past and present, East and West. The twist: just as Rimbaud had gone to the East as a Westerner to seek a meaning to his life, so too an Eastern artist (Mehrjui) has ventured to the West to live and find himself. But just what is he looking for, since a man is the direct result of his own native culture? In this regard, Mehrjui spends a lot of time talking about the problem through both the past experiences of the French poet and the Iranian director's own life-in-exile today. One

man's thoughts correspond to the others, so it seems. Okay for a hip arthouse audience. —*Holl.*

Les Folles Annees Du Twist
(The Foolish Years of the Twist)
(ALGERIAN-COLOR)

Venice, Sept. 5.
An Oncic/Fennec Productions Film. Features entire cast. Produced and directed by Mohamed Tahar Harhoura. Screenplay Mahmoud Zemmouri; camera (color), Sma Lakhdar Hamina; editor, Youcef Tobni; music, Richard Anthony; sound, Vartan Kara keusian. Reviewed at Venice Film Fest (Venice by Day section), Sept. 4, '83. Running time: **90 MINS.**
Cast: Mustapha El Anka (Kadoer), Malik Lakhdar Hamina (Boualem), Fawzi B. Saichi (Salah), Jacques Villeret ("Hohn Wahne"), Keltoum (Boualem's Mother), Hassan El Hassani (Triti), Richard Bohringer (Signor Gomez).

Part of a three-film Algerian program at Venice, Mohamed Tahar Harhoura's "The Foolish Years of the Twist" appears to draw its inspiration from the filmmaker's own youth. It's set in the troubled years of 1960-62, just as Algeria was about to free herself from French jurisdiction. In fact, the background of the film has to do with the common population's agony over whom to side with: the French Occupational Forces or the rebel FLN.

The focus is on two lads of 20 who care for little else at the present than the dance craze known as the "twist." Like most young people, their first concern is money and how to get it without having to work as the average man does. Their petty thievery is heightened, in turn, by a worsening of the political situation — until it becomes clear that both of them will have to take sides in the ensuing political conflict. One of the pair leans towards being an opportunist, but the other has a conscience that tells him to side with his own people. For Boualem, the key figure, the leisure moments filled with twist dance numbers are over, and he is thrust into manhood by the revolution. —*Holl.*

Metropoli
(Metropolis)
(ITALIAN-COLOR)

Venice, Sept. 6.
Produced by Rosanna Benvenuto and Nando Di Lena for Maxima Film Coop. Directed by Mario Franco. Stars Ferdinando Di Lena and Rosanna Benvenuto. Camera (Eastmancolor), Renato Tafuri; editor, Anna Napoli; art director, Enrico Di Lauro; music, Luciano Berio. Reviewed at the Venice Film Festival (non-competing), Sept. 6, 1983. Running time: **96 MINS.**
Marco   Ferdinando Di Lena
Rosanna   Rosanna Benvenuto
Giulio   Leonardo Treviglio
Aldo   Tatti Sanguineti

Screened in the Venice by Day special program section instead of

the Italian Showcase, Mario Franco's "Metropolis" is a bizarrely confused and inconclusive story about a scriptwriter trying to rewrite the Fritz Lang silent film classic. The director is a founding father of the Naples film club movement and has been making shorts and documentaries since 1966. Considering he employs a prestige crew of technicians led by cameraman Renato Tafuri, pic's failure to tell a story, create an atmosphere or get a convincing line of dialog across is especially puzzling.

Story, such as it is, begins with Marco (Fernando Di Lena) returning to the wife he left two years earlier (Rosanna Benvenuto) to finish the screenplay of "Underground City." This is supposed to be shot by an American tv director on the wife's vacation resort. Brushing aside all objections to setting the film in a plain outdoor building complex, Marco continues to be so stubbornly unrealistic that we can see he is heading for disaster when the director arrives and gets a look at the script.

Meanwhile, a recurrent flashback of a girl getting run over in some kind of hit-and-run accident seems meant to suggest Marco and Rosanna have a dark secret in their past, but exactly what it is or whom is responsible is never clarified. Tension fails to build, in spite of introducing a sinister actor, Giulio (Leonardo Treviglio), who unwittingly jogs their memory with grave consequences.

Besides giving too little information about the characters, Franco has cast two unattractive leads (the film's real-life producers) not particularly gifted in the thespian art.

Sad to tell, most enjoyable sequence is a lyrical interlude without actors, when the camera is simply pointed out the window of a car driving through the night for the entire duration of a lovely English folk song that has nothing to do with the picture. —*Yung.*

Brainstorm
(COLOR-70M)

Spectacular visual effects dominate the storyline in Douglas Trumbull's mind odyssey. Natalie Wood's final perf intact; outstanding thesping by Louise Fletcher.

Hollywood, Sept. 7.
An MGM-UA Entertainment release of an MGM presentation of a J F Prod. of a Douglas Trumbull film. Executive producer, Joel L. Freedman. Produced and directed by Trumbull. Features entire cast. Screenplay, Robert Stitzel, Phlip Frank Messina, from story by Bruce Joel Rubin; camera (Metrocolor, Super Panavision), Richard Yuricich; editors, Edward Warschilka, Freeman Davies; music, James Horner; production design, John Vallone; art direction, David L. Snyder; set design, Marjorie Stone; set decoration, Tom Pedigo, Linda DeScenna; special visual effects created by Entertainment Effects Group (Trumbull-Yuricich); sound, Art Rochester; costume design, Donfeld; assistant directors, David McGiffert, Brian Frankish, Robert Jeffords, Eugene Mazzola; production managers, Jack Grossberg, John G. Wilson; stunt coordinator, Bill Couch; special effects, Robert Spurlock, Eric Allard, Martin Bresin; Experiential sequence consultants, Stanislav & Christina Grof; scientific consultants, Durk Pearson, Sandy Shaw; associate producer, Richard Yuricich; special purpose lenses by Omnivision. Reviewed at MGM Studios, Culver City, Calif., Sept. 6, 1983. (MPAA Rating: PG). Running time: **106 MINS.**
Michael Brace .... Christopher Walken
Karen Brace .... Natalie Wood
Lillian Reynolds .... Louise Fletcher
Alex Terson .... Cliff Robertson
Gordy Forbes .... Jordan Christopher
Hal Abramson .... Joe Dorsey
Landon Marks .... Donald Hotton
Robert Jenkins .... Alan Fudge
James Zimbach .... Bill Morey
Chris Brace .... Jason Lively
Wendy Abramson ...... Georgianne Walken

Special Visual Effects Unit Credits
Entertainment Effects Group personnel: director of photography, Dave Stewart; optical effects supervisor, Robert Hall; Compsy (computer-synthesized) effects supervisor, Don Baker; visual effects supervisor, Alison Yerxa; action props & miniatures supervisor, Mark Stetson; matte artist, Matthew Yuricich; post-prod. supervisor, Robert Hippard; ass't editor-visual effects, Jack Hinkle; optical lineup, Michael Backauskas; Compsy technical supervisor, Richard Hollander; animation & graphics, John C. Wash; additional photography, James R. Dickson; optical camera operator, Chuck Cowles; consulting engineer, Evans Wetmore; visual consultant, Virgil Mirano.

Long awaited, shaken and embattled during its completion phase, and carrying the still-vivid memory of Natalie Wood's death, MGM's "Brainstorm" is a high-tech movie essentially dependent on the visualization of a fascinating idea, not characterization or plot.

Producer-director Douglas Trumbull's effects wizardry — and the concept behind it — is the movie. The fetching idea, visually enhanced by periodically leaping from 35m non-anamorphic Panavision to 70m Super Panavision, is a brain-wave device that gives characters the power to record and experience the physical, emotional and intellectual sensations of another human being. Special effects, building finally to an awesome crossover from this world into the infinite, create interior travels that frequently conjure the uncanny sense of experiencing someone else's dream.

On the downside, majority of players, including stars Christopher Walken and Wood as a married couple in a research environment, seem merely along for the ride.

The film's acting surprise, because it is so unanticipated, is Louise Fletcher, whose flinty, career scientist is a strong flavorful, workaholic portrait, arguably her best role since Nurse Ratchet in "One Flew Over The Cuckoo's Nest" eight years ago.

A film in which speculation is more important than characters or story line is a risky shot, "2001" notwithstanding. Nearly two years and $18,000,000 later — $6,000,000 of that from insurance carrier Lloyds of London when Trumbull was fighting to complete the special effects — "Brainstorm" remains a timely but tricky release. MGM is readying one of the largest 70m openings on record (175 theatres, before the movie goes wide in November). Curiosity and the technical lure that helped pull crowds to the same company's "WarGames" should spell initial legs. Thereafter, off-beat, intriguing concept of a machine that snaps on your head and records your feelings like a psychic home movie will have to generate its own momentum. Straight 35m houses will have a tougher haul.

The film offers irrefutable evidence that Natalie Wood's drowning (Nov. 29, 1981) did not cause the filmmakers to drastically re-write or re-shoot scenes. Her work appears intact and, reportedly, only one scene had to be changed (with actor Joe Dorsey replacing Wood in a scene with Walken). Unfortunately, Robert Stitzel and Philip Messina's script, from a story by Bruce Joel Rubin, doesn't give Wood much to do. It's almost totally a reactive role as she plays an industrial designer at first estranged from Walken and then, with the help of that playback brain-wave machine, returning to him. Emotionally, she has only one solid moment in the film, a funny bit in a fancy restaurant when Walken and Wood start telling each other off, i.e., "Go to hell," "You go to hell," which grows into a chorus.

Cliff Robertson earnestly plays the compromising head of a vast research complex that employs colleagues Walken and Fletcher. Predictably, a government bogeyman is trying to gum up pure science for the sake of national security.

To the film's creit, humor raises its welcome head both in the zany self-destruction of the lab and when a scientist almost self-destructs when he uses the story's revolutionary invention to store up a sex-

ual orgasm with a lab technician for leisurely playback at home.

Walken turns in a serviceable performance. But the most chilling moment belongs to the chain-smoking Fletcher when she suffers a heart attack, flips on that multi-channel, sensory headset, goes off into the beyond, and gets it all on tape! It's Walken's experience with that same tape that closes the movie on its wondrous, space odyssey note. —*Loyn.*

Dot and the Bunny
(AUSTRALIAN-ANIMATED/LIVE-COLOR)

Sydney, Sept. 20.
A Yoram Gross Film Studio production. Produced, directed and original story by Yoram Gross. Features entire cast. Animation director, Athol Henry; scriptwriter, John Palmer; Camera (live action) John Shaw and Film Australia; animation camera, Jenny Ochse, Graham Sharpe; assoc. producer, Sandra Gross; original music, Bob Young; editor, Christopher Plowright. Reviewed at Yoram Gross Film Studio theatrette, Sydney, Sept. 13, 1983. (Commonwealth Film Censor rating: G). Running time: 80 MINS.
Character voices: Drew Forsythe, Barbara Frawley, Ron Haddrick, Anne Haddy, Ross Higgins, Robyn Moore.

Fifth Australian feature from Sydney-based producer-director Yoram Gross, and the third in the "Dot" series, this is another well-crafted offering to amuse and entertain the pre-teen set.

Targeted at the cable and videocassette markets in the U.S., pic has already notched healthy sales there distribbed by Satori, and rights to most other territories were firmed at the American Film Market.

Matching animation with live-action footage is Gross speciality, a technique which adds another dimension to what would otherwise be straightforward animation.

Eponymous Bunny has an identity problem: he's a rabbit, but he wants to be a kangaroo so he can take the place of Joey, a real roo for whom Dot is searching.

The hunt takes Dot and her floppy-eared sidekick through the Australian outback, where they meet and learn about flying foxes, koalas, snakes, turtles, crocodiles, emus and other residents of the bush.

Deft Gross artistry has animals, photographed in their natural habitat, dissolving into animated characters, each with a different personality.

And there's a moral slyly tucked in there, a gently delivered homily about accepting who you are and the folly of trying to be someone else.

Bob Young's music, including six original songs, is a lively and tuneful accompaniment, and lyrics and dialog are peppered with enough wit to make adults smile.
—*Dogo.*

Le Faucon
(The Falcon)
(FRENCH-COLOR)

Paris, Sept. 16.
Planfilm release of a Belstar Productions/Joseph Productions coproduction. Produced by Jacques Dorfmann. Stars Francis Huster. Directed by Paul Boujenah. Screenplay, Boujenah, Hubert and Alain Attal. Camera (color), Bernard Zitzermann; editor, Marie-Caro Vazquez; art directors, Frederico and Frederique Lapierre; music, Del Rabenja; sound, Harrick Maury; executive producer, Louis Duchesne. Reviewed at the Marignan-Concorde theatre, Paris, Sept. 17, 1983. Running time: 90 MINS.
With: Francis Huster, Guy Pannequin, Maruschka Detmers, Anastacia Menzel, Vincent Lindon, Audrey Dana.

"Le Faucon," part of the local season's new crop of thrillers, has some professional credentials, but is for the most part rankly amateurish in writing, direction and performance. Topbilled Francis Huster, a legit and screen star of disputed abilities, plays a tormented lone-wolf cop who spends most of the film literally running after a mad killer, and after an hour and a half of cross-town sprinting, finally gets his man.

Debutant director Paul Boujenah and his screenwriters would seem to be on their knees before their star and concoct some subsidiary situations — like a young daughter left in a coma after a road accident that killed his spouse (Maruschka Detmers, Jean-Luc Godard's Carmen) — to complete the showcase of his talents. But his acting is as ludicrous as the screenplay and pretentious direction.

Huster's name might draw some business locally, but commercial chances elsewhere seem about zero. — *Len.*

Mortuary
(COLOR)

Okay stab-and-slab offering.

An Artists Releasing Corp. release through Film Ventures International of a Hickmar Prods. picture. Produced by Marlene Schmidt, Howard Avedis. Directed by Avedis. Features entire cast. Screenplay, Schmidt, Avedis; camera (color), Gary Graver; editor, Stanford C. Allen; music, John Cavacas; special effects makeup, Tim Gillespie, Diane Seletos; assistant director-production manager, Herman Grigsby; art direction, Randy Ser. Reviewed at SRO's Hollywood theatre, Sept. 13, 1983. (MPAA Rating: R). Running time: 91 MINS.
Christie ....Mary McDonough
Greg Stevens ....David Wallace
Eve Parsons ....Lynda Day George
Dr. Hank Andrews .....Christopher George
Paul Andrews ....Bill Paxton

As splatter movies go, "Mortuary," filmed in 1981, is no worse and perhaps a bit better than the hundreds of lowbudget offspring that have proliferated since the surprise success of "Halloween" in 1978. Certainly there is nothing original about "Mortuary," but for those with a morbid curiosity about the mechanics of embalming, pic may prove enlightening.

All the traditional elements are present here: the young romance threatened by a jealous psychotic, the disbelieving parents, the red herring and some suitably bloody knife wielding.

David Wallace and his girlfriend Mary McDonough (of "Walton's" fame) get tangled up with Christopher George, the town's slick but suspicious mortician, when they observe him holding a black magic seance. Soon after that Mary, whose father was recently drowned in the family swimming pool under questionable circumstances, notices she is being followed by a strange black car.

Her mother, Lynda Day George, of course, doesn't believe her. When mom is discovered sneaking off to take part in the secret ceremonies, she and the undertaker become prime suspects.

But there's still time for the entrance of Bill Paxton, the mortician's unbalanced son whose claim to insanity is quite legitimate based on too many hours in the embalming lab. Furthermore he has a deadly crush on Mary.

Though not too different from your normal unbalanced youth in these kind of pics, director Howard Avedis gives an inkling of the boy's troubled psychology and constructs one or two interesting scenes around the lad's quirky personality and fondness for Mozart.

In the lab, Paxton does some rather deft work with a trocar, an embalming tool which extracts the body fluids and replaces them with the preserving juices. Needless to say the poor disturbed boy is also fairly accomplished at using the tool on people who are not yet ready to go. — *Jagr.*

Pieces
(ITALIAN-SPANISH-COLOR)

An Artists Releasing Corp. release through Film Ventures International of a Spectacular Film Prods. production. Produced by Dick Randall, Steve Minasian. Directed by Juan Piquer Simon. Features entire cast. Screenplay, Randall, John Shadow; camera (color), John Marine; music, CAM. No other credits on print. Reviewed at Rivoli 1 theatre, N.Y., Sept. 23, 1983. (No MPAA Rating; self-imposed equivalent X rating). Running time: 85 MINS.
Lt. Bracken ....Christopher George
Dean ....Edmund Purdom
Mary Riggs ....Lynda Day George
Willard ....Paul Smith
Sgt. Holden ....Frank Brana
Kendall...........................Ian Sera
Prof. Brown...................Jack Taylor
Dr. Jennings.................Gerard Tichy

Filmed in 1982 in Madrid and Boston by Italian-based producer Dick Randall, "Pieces" (originally titled "1000 Cries Has The Night") is an insulting, poorly-made gore film. Randall, who 15 years ago produced the tasteless "Wild, Wild World of Jayne Mansfield" (which mixed travelog footage of the late star with a simulation of her fatal car crash and decapitation), is still cranking out sleaze. Domestic distrib Film Ventures has adopted the cornball ploy of advertising "Absolutely no one under 17 admitted," but this drivel will quickly exhaust the fringe audience seeking cheap thrills.

Teaser opening has a young boy beheading his nasty mom in Boston, 1942, after she nastily bawls him out for putting together a nude jigsaw p⁻ ·. (Tacky production features closeups of a push button phone supposedly extant in 1942!)

Forty years later, the kid's a grownup maniac, stalking pretty girls on a college campus and using a chainsaw to gather body parts in a fullscale version of putting together a jigsaw puzzle. Christopher George (who's been in too many of these lowgrade horror films lately) portrays the dim-witted cop on the case, sending his real-life wife Lynda Day (portraying a former tennis star named Riggs) undercover on the case.

Identity of the killer is telegraphed midway through the film, leaving the audience to wait through tedious stalking footage and periodic outbursts of gouts of blood spurting amidst dismemberments. Spanish helmer Juan Piquer Simon (known previously for his low-budget Jules Verne adaptations and other sci-fi films) slavishly imitates Italian horror maestro Dario Argento, even including a keyboards and bass musical score by a group called CAM (named after the publishing company) that copies Argento's favorite group, Goblin.

The inane dialog is poorly dubbed, with slack editing leaving all of Chris George's post-synched stops-and-starts intact. Wife Lynda has one show-stopping howler of a scene when she starts screaming in anger, while Paul Smith (Bluto in "Popeye") wins the ham award here by making silly faces as the sinister gardener. Young student cast gives away the film's European origins — they look very continental.

After a busy finale, pic ends on a shock-element sight gag which exposes the filmmakers' utter contempt for their audience. —Lor.

Favoriti E Vincenti
(Favorites and Winners)
(ITALIAN-COLOR)

Venice, Sept. 7.

Produced by Salvatore Maira and Angelo Iacono for Fidelio Film. Stars Carlo Mammucari. Directed by Salvatore Maira. Screenplay by Maira and Massimo Franciosa; camera (color), Gianlorenzo Battaglia; editor, Alfredo Muschietti; art director, Joseph Teichner; music, Alfredo E. Muschietti. Reviewed at the Venice Film Festival, Sept. 7, 1983. Running time: 100 MINS.

Michele . . . . Carlo Mammucari
Loy . . . . Loris Bazzocchi
Mellina . . . . Lorella Morlotti

One of the more commercial entries in the Italian Showcase section of the Venice Film Festival, Salvatore Maira's "Favorites and Winners" spices up the sociologically-drawn saga of a handsome young dishwasher from the south with robbery, race tracks and murder. Result is wishy-washy, but this first feature generally holds attention and stands a fighting chance at onshore box-offices.

Michele (Carlo Mammucari) is a childish, dreamy southerner in Rome who flits from one job to another. When he doesn't have a bed for the night he crashes in a railway car at the train station with the rest of the local bums and lowlife. He throws his money away at the off-track betting window, where he meets Loy (Loris Bazzocchi), a suavely dressed gangster with a gorgeous moll (Lorella Morlotti).

Michele has a nice, dull policeman brother and a sweet African girlfriend named Fatima. Fortunately, he gets a great job as a houseboy (uniformed) to a kindly man he looks up to as the father he never had. Unfortunately, his bad companions want him to kill the man. Michele finds he can't pull the trigger and, in a bloody finale, gives the gangsters what they deserve, a nauseating dose of lead in each leg, thereby freeing himself forever from a life of crime.

This odd blend of B-movie scripting, unbelievable characters, stagey dialog and bad thesping is a close cousin to the current crop of *telefilm noir*. Only the studied attention given to the hero's origins and psychology suggest the pic has serious intentions. Message is simple and moralistic — it's all society's fault if nice kids go astray, but their instincts can lead them back to a decent life.

Music and lensing are pluses.
—Yung.

La Fiancee Qui Venait Du Froid
(The Fiancee Who Came In From the Cold)
(FRENCH-COLOR)

Paris, Sept. 21.

A Prodis release of a Uranium Films/Ginis Films co-production. Produced by Georges Glass and Daniel Cohen. Stars Thierry Lhermitte, Barbara Nielsen. Directed by Charles Nemes. Screenplay, Charles Nemes, Christian Watton and Jean-Jacques Tarbes; camera (Eastmancolor), Geroges Barsky; editor, Adeline Yoyotte-Husson; sound, Michel Vionnet; art-director, Raoul Albert; music, Robert Charlebois; production manager, Gerard Adeline. Reviewed at the U.G.C. Normandie theatre, Paris, Sept. 21, 1983. Running time: 95 MINS.

Paul . . . . Thierry Lhermitte
Zosia . . . . Barbara Nielsen
Maurice . . . . Gerard Jugnot
Anne . . . . Sophie Barjac
Ula . . . . Alexandre Szpulska
Marek . . . . Stephan Paryla
Alexandre . . . . Wlodek Press
Paul's mother . . . . Catherine Sauvage
Zosia's mother . . . . Ida Krottendorf

Behind the unappetizing (and misleading) title is a quietly touching romantic comedy with a pertinent story idea: what happens to a young Frenchman who agrees to a phony marriage with a Polish dissident in order to get her out of her homeland, where a long prison term is imminent.

Director Charles Nemes, who was touted as a promising newcomer with his 1979 comedy, "Les Heros N'Ont Pas Froid Aux Oreilles" (which nonetheless failed commercially) actually went through the ordeal himself in 1980, which gives a sharper edge to his seriocomic screen rendition. The autobiographical angle also helps strengthen credibility of the Polish scenes, which were shot in and around Vienna, in fact. Having to reduce the scope of these sections, Nemes has still been able to often suggest what he can't show.

New Gallic hearttrob Thierry Lhermitte comes across with his most winning screen performance to date as a casual, essentially good-hearted young Parisian (like Nemes, he directs tv commercials) who nonchalantly accepts the marriage, but finds more than he bargained for when he gets to Warsaw to "rejoin" his fiancee.

Lhermitte and the girl (who is lovely, needless to say) get hitched in a small civil ceremony and immediately go off on a honeymoon, joined by the real fiance, and some unmistakeable Polish police agents.

When Lhermitte has done his time, he returns to Paris, assured that the girl's passport will be forthcoming. But there are complications, and the young man, realizing that he cares more for the Pole than he thought, jumps in his car and drives all the way to Warsaw (since there's an air traffic controller's strike).

They leave the country and become lovers on their way back to France. Hooked on her, Lhermitte is frustrated by the demands made by the exile's fellow refugees. She finally decides to leave for the U.S., but the two meet up accidently in the airport a year later, where she is en route for Poland to take part in the Solidarity movement. Reaffirming their feelings, they promise to reunite soon, and she boards her plane.

But the film ends in a pained question mark, as a final title suggests she arrived home in time to be imprisoned in the harsh government crackdown.

Lhermitte's entirely credible characterization is matched beautifully by a young Polish actress, Barbara Nielsen, who has appeared in West Germany and Austria. If the film works its bittersweet charm, it is largely due to her looks and talent.

There is good support from Sophie Barjac, as Lhermitte's old girlfriend, and Gerard Jugnot, who was the lead in Nemes' first film, and here plays the protagonist's kookily parasitic roommate.

Pic's premise and cast appeal may give it an overseas reach, though a title change should be considered. —Len.

Better Late Than Never
(BRITISH-COLOR)

Sydney, Sept. 21.

A Warner Bros. release of a Golden Harvest Group production. Produced by Jack Haley Jr., David Niven Jr. Executive Producer, Raymond Chow. Director, Screenplay, Bryan Forbes. Camera (Technicolor), Claude Lecomte (additional camera, Gerry Fisher); music, Henry Mancini; production design, Peter Mullins; editor, Philip Shaw. Reviewed on Pan American flight 815 (L.A.-Sydney), Sept. 16, 1983. Running Time: 87 MINS.

Nick Cartland . . . . David Niven
Charley Dunbar . . . . Art Carney
Anderson . . . . Maggie Smith
Bridget . . . . Kimberley Partridge
Sable . . . . Catherine Hicks
Bertie Hargreaves . . . . Lionel Jeffries
Marlene . . . . Melissa Prophet

It's not surprising that Warners has not yet theatrically released this Golden Harvest Group production, which seems to have gone direct to the airline movie circuit. Tepid Bryan Forbes pic is lumbered with a familiar plot, limp script, routine direction and tired performances.

David Niven, looking visibly haggard in one of his last screen roles, portrays a tenth rate song and dance man eking a living in a Riviera nightclub when he receives a message from lawyer Lionel Jeffries. Seems that years ago Niven was the pre-war lover of a woman who subsequently married a rich Count. She had another lover at the time, an American who's now a struggline New York photographer (Art Carney) who is also summoned to the south of France.

The lady was pregnant before her marriage, but never knew whether the father was Niven or Carney; her daughter and son-in-law have died in an accident, leaving a precocious 10-year-old in the care of a nanny (Maggie Smith), and now the old lady herself is dead and in her will has left a fortune to whichever of her two old flames the little girl chooses as her grandfather.

Pic develops sans surprises from this point, as Niven and Carney both vie for the affections of one of the least endearing child actresses to come along in quite a while (Kimberley Partridge). Though Forbes' screenplay has a few mildly amusing one-liners, it's hackneyed material, lacking anything in the way of genuine comedy. Riviera locations are quite attractive, but also rather over-familiar.

It's sad to see Niven struggling to breathe life into such sub-standard material, though he tries manfully. A scene where he picks up a young American girl (Catherine

Hicks) on the beach appears to have landed on the editing floor; now, he simply appears with her, no explanation.

Carney brings some experienced comedy timing to his sketchy role, and Smith exudes her usually warmth in a less-than-nothing part. It's especially sad to see Forbes' name on such flaccid material.

The film contains several plugs for Pan American, so it seems only too appropriate that this screening was caught on a Pan-Am trans-Pacific flight. —*Strat.*

Brandende liefde
(Burning Love)
(DUTCH-COLOR)

Amsterdam, Sept. 12.

Verenigde Nederlandsche Filmcompagnie release of a Rob Houwer Filmcompagnie production, produced by Rob Houwer. Directed by Ate de Jong. Screenplay, De Jong and Houwer, based on a novel by Jan Wolkers; camera, Paul van den Bos; music, Laurens van Rooyen; sound, Wim Hardeman; editor, Edgar Burcksen. Reviewed at Tuschinski Theatre, Amsterdam, Sept. 12, 1983. Running time: 94 MINS.
Anna . . . . Monique van de Ven
Jan . . . . Peter Jan Rens
Mademoiselle Bonnema . . . . . Ellen Vogel
Father Bonnema . . . . Siem Vroom
Louis Laman . . . . Berend Boudewign

Rob Houwer, the only Dutch producer to get four pics on *Variety's* list of 50 top-grossing films, may get a fifth with "Burning Love."

The first one, "Business is Business" (followed in 1973 by "Turkish Delight") was based on a novel by Jan Wolkers, starred Monique van de Ven and Rutger Hauer. "Burning Love" is also a Wolkers story, again stars van de Ven, and might spark an international career for a new actor.

Topcast Peter Jan Rens looks good, oozes charm, comes over as intelligent and can act.

Houwer, who started as a director, puts his personal stamp on productions. They're well made, hold the interest and tend to shock. They are not sexploitation pics, but Houwer knows that sex (within limits) never hurt a film's gross. He has an uncanny instinct of knowing just how far to go, and in what way.

"Burning Love," for example has, nudity aplenty, frontal and in the round; wind-and-water gags in atrocious taste; the birth of a baby; a scene which might well be a ferociously militant feminist's answer to the notorious sequence in "Last Tango in Paris." All with very outspoken dialog.

But humor and good manners counterbalance the bad taste. And, adding to the tease, the protagonists never go to bed together.

Pic's aim is entertainment, no more. Love, life and death, more often than not, are seen here as just occasions for pranks. The characters are shallow, but quite nice company for 96 minutes.

There is very little story. Episodes follow each other as in a musical. The music, unfortunately, is no more than just adequate although the score has an important role in the film.

Set in the '50s, the film is about a young art student in Amsterdam who must learn French to win a scholarship in Paris.

He gets free lessons from a mean, soured, pixilated spinster in exchange for doing chores and looking after her crusty old father. In her house a violinist and his beautiful and quick-witted wife occupy an apartment. The student lusts after the wife. She plays with his feelings. He tries to play on hers. That's the theme — and there are plenty of variations.

Van de Ven, more beautiful than ever, and newcomer Rens, show great virtuosity on this very thin ice. Ellen Vogel manages to keep the vastly overwritten part of the teacher from sliding into pure caricature. Siem Vroom as the father is superb.

Ate de Jong, in his first collaboration with Houwer, does not manage to keep his directing as relatively free from the producer's influence as Paul Verhoeven did for instance in "Soldier Of Orange" or "The Fourth Man," but the individual sequences (except the "Tango-in-Paris" one) move neatly enough, and the underlying playfulness is well kept up through-out the whole pic.

De Jong did not restrain Paul ven den Bos from adding to his generally good camera work superfluous exercises in mobility and in arty lighting. What the camera can't help is that the featured oil paintings, which are supposed to have made the artist famous, look awful.

Edgar Burcksen's editing is skillful, fast and witty. "Burning Love" (which by the way is the name of a plant) will undoubtedly make boxoffices happy in the Netherlands and should also be able to produce some steam abroad. —*Wall.*

Amore Tossico
(Toxic Love)
(ITALIAN-COLOR)

Venice, Sept. 5.

A Gaumont release, produced by Giorgio Nocella for Iter International. Stars Cesare Ferretti and Michela Mioni. Directed by Claudio Caligari. Screenplay by Guido Blumir and Claudio Caligari; camera (Eastmancolor), Dario di Palma; editor, Enzo Meniconi; art directors, Lia Morandini and Maurizio Santarelli; music, Detto Mariano. Reviewed at the Venice Film Fest., Sept. 5, 1983. Running time: 90 MINS.
Cesare . . . . Cesare Ferretti
Michela . . . . Michela Mioni
Enzo . . . . Enzo Di Benedetto
Ciopper . . . . Roberto Stani

A serious anti-heroin picture shot in Rome's outer suburbs of Pasolini memory with non-pro actors, "Toxic Love" was one of the two films in the Venice Film Festival's De Sica section (Italian Showcase) to receive laurels. It is helmer Claudio Caligari's second feature, after much documentary video work.

Pic began life as a low-budget indie project, which shows in the grainy quality of 16m blown to 35m and the blurry sound (which is to be remedied with the prize money). At a certain point project got a leg up from Marco Ferreri, who took pic under his wing and got producer Giorgio Nocella involved. Gaumont picked up distribution. The subject's stark realism ends in a highly dramatic climax that should attract viewers who like a tough, laying it on the line style peppered with gunplay and sudden death.

But pic's heart is in the right place. Caligari and co-scripter Guido Blumir, a sociologist considered one of the country's leading drug experts, aims at a more factual representation of teenage junkies in the Roman seaport-slum of Ostia. The kids, led by Cesare Ferretti and Michela Mioni, aren't great actors but they come across as friendly and likeable, seemingly having turned to drugs out of sheer boredom with their prison-like environment, or for innocent thrills.

Now that they're hooked life revolves around the next fix and they're drawn against their will into prostitution and armed robbery. Climax, when Michela goes into convulsions from an from an adultered shot of cocaine, is played out under the ugly modern monument to Pasolini. While his girl is dying in the hospital, Cesare tries to commit suicide and fails, but is immediately shot to death, almost accidentally, by two cops.

Though characters are carefully limned, little feeling comes through for them (here wooden acting takes its toll). Most memorable and shocking images in the film are closeups of needles plunging into veins and battered, bruised arms — obviously the real thing. Cameraman Dario di Palma's clean lensing manages to shine through the grainy print, and Detto Mariano's music is a plus.
— *Yung.*

Hans Het Leven Voor de Dood
(Hans, Life Before Death)
(DUTCH-DOCU-COLOR & B/W)

Amsterdam, Sept. 8.

A Spectrum Film Production. Scenario, Louis van Gasteren. Directed and edited by Van Gasteren. Camera (color), Paul van den Bos, Fred van Kuyk, Jos van Schoor; music, Misha Mengalberg, Hans van Sweden, Brian Eno; sound, Rene van den Berg, Andre Patrouillie, Jan Wouter Stam. Reviewed at Leidseplein Theatre, Amsterdam, Sept. 6, 1983. Running time: 155 MINS.

This film deserves to be seen because of Louis Van Gasteren's consummate mastery of the medium and because of the subject: the first of the lost generations after World War II.

However, it's unlikely to be played outside the Low Countries because it mainly consists of interviews to which neither subtitles nor even dubbing could convey the significant nuances of style, intonation and accents. This generation was specifically Dutch and names and faces of the 53 interviewees, many of whom will mean little outside the Netherlands.

The "Hans" of the title is Hans van Sweeden, born 1939, a gifted composer, writer and occasional actor. He was part of the post-war subculture which experimented with poetry, music, theater; with sex and drugs and life. He killed himself in 1963.

Van Gasteren, born in 1922 into a family of actors and singers, is a colorful personality and stubborn perfectionist, who has made dozens of docus and tv programs. Some have had a distinct influence on Dutch public opinion (riots and police; treatment of concentration camp victims). He has lectured on film history in Holland and abroad (Harvard, Los Angeles) and Van Sweeden was a friend of his.

Van Gasteren has worked on pic since 1964, made 80 interviews, shot more than 100 hours of film and spent three and a half years cutting to the present length.

The result is less a biography of Van Sweeden than a requiem for a lost generation which had feverishly looked for a new meaning and a new way of life and has mostly settled for just going on living.

Van Sweeden, rarely seen, is the pivot on which the film hinges. The interviewees, the other people, are the film.

Personally involved though he is, Van Gasteren manages to keep his distance, but he involves the viewer and attention doesn't sag during the two and a half hours.

Van Gasteren achieves this partly through a quiet but intense use of the camera, but mainly through masterly editing, nearly imperceptible changes of rhythm, short pauses, the integration in one sequence of voices and sentences from different interviews, changing, as it were, dialogs into general discussions, and clean transitions from one scene to the next, never abrupt.

A must for serious film fests, pic should be study material at every film school. — *Wall.*

Molly
(AUSTRALIAN-COLOR)

Sydney, Aug. 25.

A New South Wales Film Corp., Greater Union Film Distributors and M & L Pty. Ltd. presentation. Exec producer, Richard

Brennan. Produced by Hilary Linstead. Directed by Ned Lander. Features entire cast. Screenplay, Phillip Roope; Mark Thomas, Linstead, Lander; camera (Eastmancolor), Vincent Monton; musical director, Graeme Isaac; art director, Robert Dein; costume designer, Laurel Frank; editor, Stewart Young, sound editor, Greg Bell; production supervisor, Barbara Gibbs. Reviewed at the Lyceum Theatre, Sydney, Aug. 25 '83 (Commonwealth Film Censor rating: G). Running time: 85 MINS.

Maxie Ireland . . . . Claudia Karvan
Jones . . . . Garry McDonald
Old Dan . . . . Reg Lye
Aunty Jenny . . . . Melissa Jaffer
Mrs. Reach . . . . Ruth Cracknell
Bill Ireland . . . . : . . . . Leslie Dayman
Stella . . . . Robin Laurie
Gina . . . . Tanya Lester
Molly . . . . Herself

Titled character is a dog who sings. Well, not so much warbles as whines off-key, but that should not strike too jarring a note with the moppets at whom this picture is squarely aimed.

Tots at the preview screening may not have laughed that often, nor been drawn to the edge of their seats, but pic held their attention throughout, which is no mean feat with the age 6-10 brigade.

The villain, Garry McDonald, was nasty enough to earn his quota of hisses, the pooch was cute enough to inspire a few affectionate "oohs" and "aahs," and as for the adults, it was, well, bearable.

Theatrical prospects Down Under seem okay, restricted to day sessions during holiday periods while cable and television playoff is probably the most that can be hoped for internationally.

Fairly thin plot concerns the efforts of McDonald, disguised variously as a clown and a nun, to steal Molly from her young custodian, Claudia Karvan. McDonald thinks he can make a fortune out of the not so musical mutt, but she will perform only for those who love her, and he is plainly not an aficionado.

Much of the latter half is set in a circus (Claudia is befriended and protected by a performing troupe) and it is here that the film gets most of its color and energy.

Chief flaw is pacing. Director Ned Lander, whose previous film "Wrong Side of the Road" was an interesting narrative about the on-the-road experiences of two Aboriginal rock bands, allows the plot to amble along, when more zip was needed.

Tyro Claudia Karvan is awkward and unconvincing at times, while McDonald, an old pro, does his utmost to bring some humor and pathos to a basically one-dimensional character. —Dogo.

L'Ami de Vincent
(A Friend of Vincent)
(FRENCH-COLOR)

Paris, Sept. 20.
An AMLF release of a Sara Films/T. Films/Films A2 co-production. Produced by Alain Sarde and Alain Terzian. Stars Philippe Noiret, Jean Rochefort. Directed by Pierre Granier-Deferre. Screenplay, Christopher Frank, Pierre Granier-Deferre, Jean-Marc Roberts, based on the latter's novel; camera (Eastmancolor), Etienne Becker; music, Philippe Sarde; art director, Willy Holt; editor, Jean Ravel; sound, Guillaume Sciama; costumes, Catherine Leterrier; makeup, Monique Granier; production manager, Gerard Gaultier. Reviewed at the Gaumont Champs-Elysees theatre, Paris, Sept. 19, 1983. Running time: 93 MINS.
With: Philippe Noiret, Jean Rochefort, Francoise Fabian, Fanny Cottencon, Marie Dubois, Marie-France Pisier, Anna Karina, Jane Birkin, Tanya Lopert, Sylvia Joly, Beatrice Agenin, Catherine Samie, Christiane Tissot, Chantal Deruez, Alexandre Rignault, Francois Perrot, Pierre Vernier.

"L'Ami de Vincent" is the third film adaptation of a novel by Jean-Marc Roberts, a prize-winning, 29-year old novelist, whose book, "Des Affaires Etrangeres," provided director Pierre Granier-Deferre with one of his best films in 1981: "Une Etrange Affaire." Last year the helmer's son, Denys, made his directorial debut with a second Roberts novel. Now Granier-Deferre senior, after a return to Georges Simenon country (which he knows well) with "L'Etoile du Nord," again adapts Roberts. As with "Une Etrange Affaire" his script collaborators are the author and fellow novelist Christopher Frank.

"Vincent's Friend" is about a man who has always taken a childhood friend for granted and is suddenly forced into taking a closer look at his buddy's life.

Philippe Noiret is the leader of a music hall orchestra, who leads a stable professional and private life (no wonder, he's married to Francoise Fabian). His friend, Jean Rochefort, is a bachelor trumpet-player in the same orchestra and a compulsive womanizer, never having cemented a solid relationship with the opposite sex.

Rochefort is badly shaken when a strange young woman enters their dressing room one night and takes some potshots at him with a pistol, claiming he has destroyed her sister. Rochefort holes up in his apartment and asks Noiret to track down his own romantic conquests to find out whom he could have wronged so tragically.

Out of friendship Noiret complies but his meeting with Rochefort's old flames turn up nothing, though provide a better understanding of his friend's true nature and emotional fickleness.

The story thus resembles something of a detective story, with the action mapped out by a series of voyages and confrontations, and eventually leading to "solution."

Unfortunately, if it resembles a mystery scheme, it's missing a basic ingredient — suspense. In this case, psychological suspense. Though Noiret is dismayed by some of the women he encounters, his fidelity to Rochefort is only mildly tried, and there are no real obligatory scenes putting their friendship to the test. As for Rochefort, his hollow personality becomes sufficiently clear too early in the action for us to care about whether or not he finds the woman he "destroyed" (though he does find her in a conclusion that strains credibility).

The screenplay unimaginatively distends the action in linear fashion, providing neat, but dramatically self-conscious cameos for the gallery of female talent playing women who've passed through Rochefort's arms in the past: Jane Birkin, Fanny Cottencon, Marie Dubois, Anna Karina, Tanya Lopert and Marie-France Pisier.

Granier-Deferre has directed dully, and, despite their professionalism and screen presence, Noiret and Rochefort do not make us greatly believe in their long-standing, if unquestioned, friendship. This is particularly surprising since the two have in the past created some wonderful dramatic duets, as in Bertrand Tavernier's "The Clockmaster" and Laurent Heynemann's "Il Faut Tuer Birgitt Haas."

Despite its lackluster theatrics, pic may get by commercially both at home and abroad on the basis of its cast list, though none of the performances is outstanding. Tech credits are passable. —Len.

Deadly Games
(COLOR)

Too many in-jokes, not enough thrills.

A Monterey Films presentation of a Raymond M. Dryden production for Great Plains Entertainment Corp. Executive producer, Robert H. Becker. Produced by Raymond M. Dryden. Written and directed by Scott Mansfield. Features entire cast. Camera (color), R. Michael Stringer; editor, Stuart Eisenberg; music, Hod David Schudson, Richard S. Thompson; assistant director, Eisenberg; production manager, Nicole Scott; art direction, Tana Cunningham-Curtis; set decoration, Laura Richarz; special effects-stunts, John Eggett; post-production supervisors, Dryden, Cunningham-Curtis; co-producers, Phillip J. Randall, Martin Wiviott; associate producers, Mac Greenberg, Mel Edelstein. Reviewed on Cinemax, N.Y., Sept. 12, 1983. (MPAA Rating: R). Running time: 96 MINS.
Roger Lane . . . . Sam Groom
Keegan . . . . Jo Ann Harris
Billy Owens . . . . Steve Railsback
Joe . . . . Dick Butkus
Linda . . . . Alexandra Morgan
Randy . . . . Colleen Camp
Chris . . . . Christine Tudor
Marge Lawrence . . . . June Lockhart
Mary . . . . Denise Galik
Carol . . . . Robin Hoff
Sooty . . . . Jere Lea Rae

Filmed with the title "Who Fell Asleep?" during the horror production boom at the end of 1979, "Deadly Games" is an unsuccessful thriller marginally released last year and currently getting pay tv exposure and available on vidcassette. Filmmaker Scott Mansfield has piloted a good cast to okay performances, but failed to provide the requisite thrills.

Routine story, frequently undercut by knowing horror buff references, has Keegan (Jo Ann Harris), a writer for a music magazine, returning to her sleepy home town where a rash of murders (detailed in usual stalk-and-slash, heavy breathing on the soundtrack fashion) has broken out. Though laid-back cop on the case Roger Lane (Sam Groom) doesn't acknowledge it, the chief suspect is his scarred, Vietnam War pal Billy Owens (Steve Railsback), whom the camera virtually indicts in the opening reels.

While Keegan is meeting her mom (June Lockhart in a very small role) and old chums, picture drifts into old-fashioned romantic idylls, touch football games and other diversions, dissipating the atmosphere of danger.

Harris gives a fun, personable performance as the independent heroine who can take care of herself, but the rest of the cast is relegated to stock roles. Film's release title refers to a horror movie board game Groom and Railsback play, parallel to the real-life killings. Railsback works as a projectionist in a horror movie theatre (star trio watch the 1932 "The Monster Walks" after-hours there one night), setting up many genre notations in the script.

Ultimately, the fairly-predictable killer turns out to be merely seeking some excitement in a too-dull community, leading to a wholly unsatisfying, convenient freeze-frame ending. Tech credits are okay. — Lor.

The Delta Fox
(COLOR)

Dim action pic.

A Sebastian International Pictures presentation of a Delta Fox Prods. Picture. Produced and directed by Ferd and Beverly Sebastian. Stars Stuart Whitman, John Ireland, Richard Jaeckel, Richard Lynch, Priscilla Barnes. Screenplay, the Sebastians; camera (color), uncredited; editor, Robert Angus; sound, James Allen Corbett; stunt coordinator, Craig Baxley. Reviewed on Independent United Distributors vidcassette, N.Y., Sept. 7, 1983. (No MPAA Rating). Running time: 93 MINS.
David Fox . . . . Richard Lynch
Karen . . . . : . . . . Priscilla Barnes
The Counselor . . , ... Stuart Whitman
Lucas Johnson . . . . John Ireland
Santana . . . . Richard Jaeckel
Tiny . . . . Julius W. Harris
With: Tracy Sebastian, Damon Reicher, Larry Gelman, Richard Lockmeister, Susan Holloway.

"The Delta Fox" is a theatrically unreleased 1977 production (currently on view via the homevideo market) that aspires to the mood of the 1940s film noir (in 1970s setting) but lacks the required narrative skill. Besides its familiar roster of name actors who pop up frequently in B-pictures, it features an early leading role for Priscilla Barnes (of tv's "Three's Company") and an unusual tortured hero performance by familiar screen heavy Richard Lynch.

Most of the exposition here is provided in lengthy, typed-out opening and end credits, with the film proper conforming to the streamlined structure of 1970s action films such as the classic "Vanishing Point." (Low-budgeter also relies heavily on Ma Bell dialog, with star-billed Stuart Whitman literally phoning in most of his performance).

Lynch portrays David Fox (with "Delta Fox" nickname), a con let out of prison (to exploit his stock car driving ability) to aid the government in catching a San Francisco-based tax shelter specialist (Stuart Whitman) wanted for tax evasion. Lynch hops into his Camaro which he proceeds to destroy in various chases around the Miami harbor.

Stealing Priscilla Barnes' landscaping truck, he also acquires her (in true road movie fashion) as a teammate and bedmate, traveling through Georgia (to pick up his exquisite Porsche) to an idyll in New Orleans. Justice Dept. agent Johnson (John Ireland) is on Fox' back seeking results, but the hero is torn between his mission and seeking revenge against whoever killed his brother years before.

With somewhat confusing continuity, pic climaxes back in Florida, with the expected Whitman-Lynch showdown and an unconvincing happy ending (disclosed mainly in the end titles).

Lynch is impressive here in a surprisingly sympathetic role for the man who terrorized Al Pacino memorably in "Scarecrow" over a decade ago. Another switch is the camera's unsparing display of his heavily-scarred neck and chest, used as a film noir plot point when Barnes comments on his disfigurement in an apres-sex scene, Lynch blaming it on "the war."

Barnes is lovely and feisty as his romantic sparring partner, though, as with her other 1977 starring role in the Telly Savalas-helmed 'Mati," stuck in a film vehicle which did nothing for her career, being left on the shelf. Rest of the cast, despite top billing, is along for the ride, with a certain amount of reflexive in-joking going on. Whitman, for example, tells a client to silence his investors, clamoring for a return, by saying their money was invested in a flop movie. In context, he's pretty convincing. —Lor.

Stations
(CANADIAN-COLOR)

Toronto, Sept. 17.
A MacGillivray Film production. Produced, directed and written by William MacGillivray Jr. Camera (color), Lionel Simmons; edited by MacGillivray and Simmons. Reviewed at the Festival of Festivals. Toron-
to, Sept. 16, 1983. Running time: **95 MINS.**
Tom Murphy.....William MacGillivray Jr.
Murphy's father .William MacGillivray Sr.
Harry.....................Richard Boland
Gordon......................Michael Jones
Train porter..............Bernard Cloutier

A promising beginning about a young seminarian, Murphy who, along with his friend Harry leaves the priesthood, becomes an unnecessarily complex narrative about a failed journalist looking for meaning on a trainride across Canada. An existential media journalist at a crisis in his life and career comes up with one abortive project after another. A show about his friend Harry ends with Harry's implied suicide. He is given leave by his station manager, starts to go on vacation with his wife and son, is called back to do a series of interviews with a motley assortment of Canadians in transit across the country, and then decides not to finish the job with his cameraman Gordon. Instead, he goes home to Halifax and finds his roots, making peace with his father for having left the ministry.

Flashforwards and flashbacks pose a chronological dilemma which, when coupled with the movement of the train posing geographical problems, is meant to show uprootedness but, in fact, leaves the pic in limbo. It is definitely Canada from a regional point of view, since the dialog seems to be an irreverent response to expectations of "Canadian content." Film-within-a-film devices abound, using both the protagonist's profession, which exploits only the cliches of such work, as well as the home movies of the director's family for flashbacks.

Ambitions were too inflated and the budget too low for an autobiographical film about having no calling as a priest, no calling as a journalist and, apparently, no calling as a Canadian. Best one-liner: "Being part of the Canadian Confederation is like being an extra in the movies ... they're always telling us to get out of the way." Yet, even the Canadian theatrical potential is very weak. — Kaja.

Au Rhythme De Mon Coeur
(To the Rhythm of My Heart)
(CANADIAN-B&W)

Toronto, Sept. 11.
A Cinak film production. Produced, directed and written by Jean-Pierre Lefebvre. English narration by Barbara Easto; camera and music by Lefebvre; unedited; animation, Yves Richard. Reviewed at the Festival of Festivals, Toronto, Sept. 10, 1983. Running time: **80 MINS.**

Basically a film diary, "To the Rhythm of My Heart," is far more interesting in concept than execution. Prolific Canadian filmmaker Jean-Pierre Lefebvre recorded images over two years on his 16m Bolex camera and presents them chronologically without editing. His only additions have been a voice-over narration and some music.

The period covered in his personal life includes the death of his wife, his remarriage, the birth of a child and periodic visits to film co-operatives across Canada. In some cases Lefebvre simply explains the context of a situation, at other times it's an opportunity to observe philosophically. Sections are punctuated with such titles as "From One Image to Another" and "As If on Another Planet."

In a way one marvels at his abililty to maintain an audience's attention. However, the mixture of reality and poetry is not always fluid. He admits at one point of tiring of the experiment and it's obvious there's only so far one can drive the pictures forward with words. After all, there were days where he preferred not to record, creating abrupt time and continuity gaps.

As an experiment "To the Rhythm of My Heart" has some merit but is hardly likely to spawn similar efforts. It's ideal for filmmaking classes and cine clubs and, to a degree, provides an insight into the director's psyche. However, after a point, Lefebvre begins to repeat himself and overstate what has already been gleaned. —Klad.

Se Acabo' El Curro
(The Sting Is Over)
(ARGENTINE-PERUVIAN-COLOR)

Buenos Aires, Sept. 20.
A Eurocine production and release, coproduced with undisclosed Peruvian partners. Directed by Carlos Galettini. Screenplay, Geno Diaz and Galettini; camera (Eastmancolor), Anibal Di Salvo; music, Luis Maria Serra; assistant director, Daniel Pires Mateus; executive producer, Juan Carlos Fisner. Reviewed at the Sarmiento theatre, B.A., Sept. 1, 1983. Running time, **90 MINS.**
Cast: Victor Laplace, Tulio Loza, Moria Casan, Javier Portales, Julio De Grazia, Dalma Milevos, Noemi Alan, Adriana Brodsky.

The sudden, although hitherto limited opening of Argentine film censorship has allowed local filmmakers their own chance to produce quickies aimed at getting fast bucks by hooking viewers with themes and stuff long forbidden here, with a total disregard for quality and integrity. This pic is an example.

One of its angles, apparently of prime concern for the offshore coproducer, follows Peruvian comic Tulio Loza as a sex maniac tourist in some of his experiences with fleshy B.A. prosties such as those played by Moria Casan and Adriana Brodsky. He has come from his country to take advantage of the exchange rate which now allows foreigners to afford most of what is unreachably dear for them outside Argentina. That's why Loza enjoys a shopping spree, for himself and his friends at home, when not enjoying other things in bed (censors have scissored, for local audiences, the hottest footage of the sex scenes, which almost certainly will be seen abroad.)

The other angle has Victor Laplace as an Argentine who befriends Loza but hopes to cheat him with some scheme to take away his greenbacks. Laplace alleges this will be a revenge since he was left without his business by the manipulations of the "financial fatherland," name given by many Argentines to the complex mixture of monetary laws, banking adventurism, boundless greed, savage repression and total impunity that corrupted their country's economy, leading thousands of industries and business to bankruptcy and skyrocketing the foreign debt to $40 billion without explanation.

That such a socially tragic subject had been irresponsibly exploited in a cheap, witless pic, offends almost everybody here. Besides, its seriousness doesn't mix with Loza's coarse antics, presumably aimed at his Peruvian followers. Some scenes were shot in Peru. Acting is generally poor, technical credits uneven. — Nubi.

Divergenze Parallele
(Parallel Divergences)
(ITALIAN-COLOR)

Venice, Sept. 1.
Produced by Viva Edizioni (Padua). Written, directed by and starring Renato Meneghetti. Camera (Kodacolor), Caludio Mainardi and Lorenzo Trento; art director, editor and music. Renato Meneghetti. Reviewed at the Venice Film Festival (Sept. 1.) Running Time: **102 MINS.**
The Artist..............Renato Meneghetti

Film is endless minutes of classic navel contemplation by "multimedia artist" Renato Meneghetti, or MR as he sometimes signs his works. The ideator-director-editor-composer-set and costume designer is almost the sole person appear in this indulgent minimalist feature from the Paduan avantgarde, screened in the Venice Film Festival's Italian Showcase. Director's previous credits are revealing — all shorts on related subjects: "MR Painting," "MR Sculpture," "MR Photography," "MR Music," "MR Performances" and "MR Theatre."

"Parallel Divergences" intrepidly charts a course through the artist's troubled psyche, apparently split between pure spiritual creation and a recurring yen for recognition, admiration and money. We are allowed a lengthy peek at an exhibition of land art in which hundreds of lighted candles are arranged on the lawn, while the artist froths at the mouth and writhes on the ground. Another recurring sequence shows the frivolity of museumgoers, more interested in each other than the paintings (pic's most watchable scenes, probably because devoid of The Artist).

Initial hopes that pic is a spoof on the myth of the self-consumed artist quickly turn to dust. As one drawn-out sequence succeeds another, with Meneghetti in a paint-splattered white robe conducting an orchestra of store dummies, climbing an infinite winding staircase and throwing his arms out to heaven as a blinding light engulfs him, hope for parody evaporate.

Meneghetti's one successful moment shows him at work painting over the blown up photo of a store mannequin, a kind of pleasant demonstration of technique. Modern saxophone track, presumably of his own composition, is quite listenable. But as an example of experimental filmmaking, pic really lacks new ideas. —*Yung.*

Sweet Sixteen
(COLOR)

Modest psycho-thriller, with fine cast.

A CI Films of California release of a Sweet 16 Prods. picture for Productions Two. Executive producers, Martin Perfit, June Perfit. Produced and directed by Jim Sotos. Features entire cast. Screenplay, Erwin Goldman; camera (color), James L. Carter; editor, Drake Silliman; music, Tommy Vig; sound, Tim Cooney; assistant director, Tony Loree; production manager, Betsy Pollock; makeup, Jim Gillespie; second unit camera, Gary Graver; associate producer, Sandy Charles; creative consultant, Billy Fine. Reviewed on Vestron Video vidcassette, N.Y., Sept. 3, 1983. (MPAA Rating: R). Running Time: 90 MINS.

Dan Burke	Bo Hopkins
Joanne Morgan	Susan Strasberg
Billy Franklin	Don Stroud
Marci Burke	Dana Kimmell
Melissa Morgan	Aleisa Shirley
Jason	Don Shanks
Hank Burke	Steve Antin
Jimmy	Logan Clarke
George Martin	Michael Pataki
John Morgan	Patrick Macnee
Earl	Larry Storch
Greyfeather	Henry Wilcoxon
Kathy	Sharon Farrell

Filmed in 1981, "Sweet Sixteen" is an okay psychological horror film, peopled with talented actors but too close to formula to attract much attention in the glutted market for scare pics. Film is currently in theatrical release (regionally) as well as being available in homevideo stores.

Familiar story structure is built around the sixteenth birthday party for Melissa Morgan (Aleisa Shirley), new girl in a small Texas town. Her mom (Susan Strasberg) has recently returned to her home town (the usual gothic horror setup) after many years away, accompanying her archaeologist husband (Patric Macnee) on a local dig excavating Indian burial grounds.

A rash of murders breaks out (with an odd wrinkle for horror pics: all the victims are male) and evidence plus local prejudices point the finger of guilt at Indians

Jason (Don Shanks) and Greyfeather (film veteran Henry Wilcoxon). They become the scapegoats for the crimes, with Greyfeather found hanged, probably the victim of a lynching.

Local sheriff Dan Burke (Bo Hopkins) is investigating the murders, aided by his inquisitive kids (Dana Kimmell and Steve Antin). Final revelation of the murderer's identity is no surprise.

Filmmaker Jim Sotos directs at a leisurely pace, with slow-motion emphasis during the violent scenes. Hopkins and attractive Kimmell (as his mystery buff daughter) are the cast standouts, capturing the bulk of the viewer's empathy. In the central role, Aleisa Shirley, who resembles a dark-eyed Meg Foster, is unremarkable and too old for the part. There is also a problem with inconsistent accents among family members (Patrick Macnee replaced Leslie Nielsen in the role of her father and doesn't match). Tech credits are fine. —*Lor.*

Falasha: Exile of the Black Jews
(CANADIAN-DOCU-COLOR)

Toronto, Sept. 12.

A Pan-Canadian release of a Matari Film production. Produced by Simcha Jacobovici and Jamie Boyd. Associate producer, Susan Price. Directed and written by Simcha Jacobovici. Camera (color), Martin Duckworth, Peter Raymont; editor, Roger Pyke; music, Sara Jacobovici. Reviewed at Toronto Festival of Festivals, Toronto, Sept. 12, '83. Running time: 72 MINS.

The systematic persecution and destruction of black Ethiopian Jews — Falashas — is the subject of this incisive docu.

The Falashas (translation: exiles) have lived for over 2,000 years in Ethiopia, practicing a literate, orthodox, pre-Talmudic Judaism. They were massacred after the Marxist military coup in 1974 by counter-revolutionaries who feared they would join the revolution, while revolutionaries persecute them for not relinquishing Judaism for Communism. These Jews have been denied land-holding rights, have suffered from famine, and as inhabitants of Gondar province, have been victim of the governor's policy of forced cultural assimilatio. Thousands of Jews flee to Sudan and wind up in refugee camps, where they pretend to be Christian for fear of being killed once identified as Jews.

Docu team of Simcha Jacobovici, Jamie Boyd, and Susan Price took great risks and traveled into the obscure Simien Mountains to remote Falasha villages, where they have come up with unique — and incriminating — footage about the plight of this vanishing tribe.

Interviews tell of harrowing tales of escape and torture from Eth-

iopia. Crew journeyed to the Sudan to film refugee camps, where Falashas were afraid to be photographed. Docu footage of famine in Ethiopia in late '70s is also included. Glimpses into a Falasha family living in Israel conducting a Sabbath dinner are particularly touching.

Interspersed throughout are clips with Jewish leaders including Yitzhak Rabin), who assure the public that "everything is being done" to save the Ethiopian Jews (whose numbers are estimated to be between 15-25,000 still in Ethiopia), cut with interviews with reps of North American Jewish relief agencies who claim the issue is given extremely low priority on Israel's agenda.

Docu drives home the point effestively that the issue is intentionally shrouded in mystery and especially zooms in on the quandary: Falashas are Jews among blacks in Ethiopia and blacks among Jews in Israel.

Pic should do well on the Jewish festival circuit, and with crafty marketing could also be extended to art houses for politically astute audiences. —*Devo.*

The Fire in the Stone
(AUSTRALIAN-COLOR)

Sydney, Sept. 21.

A South Australian Film Corp. production, in association with the Australian Children's Television Foundation. Exec producer, Jock Blair. Produced by Pamela Vanneck. Directed by Gary Conway. Features entire cast. Screenplay, Graeme Koestveld, based on the novel by Colin Thiele; camera (color), Ross Berryman; art director, Derek Mills; editor, Philip Reid; sound, Lloyd Carrick. Reviewed at the Coober Pedy Progress Assn. Hall, South Australia, Sept. 18, '83. Running time: 94 MINS.

Ernie	Paul Smith
Sophie	Linda Hartley
Nick	Theo Pertsinidis
Willie	Andrew Gaston
Robbie	Alan Cassell
Dosh	Ray Meagher

The South Australian Film Corp. and author Colin Thiele are a winning combination. Their collaboration on Thiele's novels "Storm Boy" and "Blue Fin" won admiring notices from critics and garnered healthy receipts around the world, and now comes "The Fire in the Stone" from the same stable.

Like the two forerunners, latest Thiele adaptation is aimed at the family audience, but differs in that it was made specifically for the tv market.

In an unusual distribution ploy, "The Fire in the Stone" will be circulated through 1,000 Australian schools by Young Australia Films of Sydney in 1984, before it's cleared for tv and homevid release here.

First international screenings will be at Mifed Indian Summer and then the American Market for Intl. Programs (A-MIP) in Miami.

Set in the marvelously scenic opal mining town of Coober Pedy in the South Australian desert, film concerns efforts by three teenagers to recover $A300,000 worth of the precious stone, stolen by one of the miners.

Elevating it above the Boys' Own adventure level is the subplot dealing with the sometimes turbulent relationship between one of the trio, Ernie, and his father, a perennial loser whose wife walked out on him, and who can't face responsibility.

Studding the narrative is some neat stunt work with a light aircraft; a budding romance between Ernie and Sophie which, contrary to the usual game plan, has girl chasing boy; and interesting chemistry between Willie, a young black, and his white friends. If Willie is the target of a lot of racist remarks, at least most are good-natured, and in response to those which aren't, he gives as good as he gets.

The opals are eventually retrieved, and the villain gets his come-uppance but there is no conventionally happy ending in the father-and-son saga, as Ernie quits the opal town for a new life in the capital city.

Performances by Paul Smith (who impressed as a rebellious teenager in Michael Caulfield's feature "Fighting Back") as Ernie, Linda Hartley as Sophie, and Andrew Gaston as Willie, are uniformly excellent. Alan Cassell invites sympathy as the well-meaning but weak-willed father, and Ray Meagher is suitably menacing as the villain.

Gary Conway, helming his first feature after a solid background in tv series and the miniseries "Sara Dane" displays a deft hand, and Ross Berryman's camerawork makes effective use of the outback landscapes.

Brought in on a budget of $A1,-700,000, "The Fire in the Stone" is a gem which figures to yield more paydirt for producer and author. —*Dogo.*

Never Say Never Again
(COLOR)

Connery's back with good adversary. Upbeat prospects for off-season.

Hollywood, Oct. 1.

A Warner Bros. release of a Taliafilm production. Produced by Jack Schwartzman. Executive producer, Kevin McClory. Stars Sean Connery. Directed by Irvin Kershner. Screenplay, Lorenzo Semple Jr., based on an original story by McClory, Jack Whittingham, Ian Fleming; camera (Technicolor, Panavision), Douglas Slocombe; supervising film editor, Robert Lawrence; editor, Ian Crafford; music, Michel Legrand; production design, Philip Harrison, Stephen Grimes; supervising art director, Leslie Dilley; art directors, Michael White, Roy Stannard; set decorator, Peter Howitt; costume design, Charles Knode; sound, Simon Kaye, David Allen; second unit director, Michael Moore; underwater sequence director, Ricou Browning; special visual effects supervisor, David Dryer; special effects supervisor, Ian Wingrove; associate producer, Michael Dryhurst; assistant director, David Tomblin. Reviewed at The Burbank Studios, Burbank, Sept. 30, 1983. (MPAA Rating: PG) Running time: 137 MINS.

James Bond	Sean Connery
Largo	Klaus Maria Brandauer
Blofeld	Max Von Sydow
Fatima Blush	Barbara Carrera
Domino	Kim Basinger
Felix Leiter	Bernie Casey
"Q" Algy	Alec McCowen
"M"	Edward Fox
Miss Moneypenny	Pamela Salem
Small-Fawcett	Rowan Atkinson
Lady in Bahamas	Valerie Leon
Kovacs	Milow Kirek
Lippe	Pat Roach
Lord Ambrose	Anthony Sharp
Patricia	Prunella Gee
Jack Petachi	Gavan O'Herlihy
Nicole	Saskia Cohen Tanugi

He said it would never happen, but after a 12-year hiatus, Sean Connery is back in action as James Bond in "Never Say Never Again." As opulently mounted as the mainline series entries produced by Albert Broccoli and, formerly, by him and Harry Saltzman, and now toplined by Roger Moore, new entry, produced by Jack Schwartzman, marks something of a retreat from the far-fetched technology of many of the later Bonds in favor of intrigue and romance.

As genial as the film is, however, a heavy sense of deja vu hangs over the proceedings, with few surprises now being possible within the standard format. Due to postproduction delays which prevented a summer opening, "Never" becomes the first Bond in nearly 20 years not to have been released either in summer or at Christmas. This fact, along with recent Bond exposure in "Octopussy," creates slight suspicion that reaching the customary domestic rentals level of $30,000,000 or so may be more difficult than usual.

Although it is not acknowledged as such, pic is roughly a remake of the 1965 "Thunderball." World-threatening organization SPECTRE manages to steal two U.S. cruise missiles and announces it will detonate their nuclear warheads in strategic areas unless their outrageous ransom demands are met.

Bond is summarily pulled out of retirement as a teacher in order to save the globe from destruction. Funny, but it seems like we've seen that one somewhere before.

Given the familiarity of the mission, pic's success depends entirely upon the moment-to-moment pleasure it can provide and results here are moderately good, but hardly enthralling. After a lacklustre war games opening, 007 is put on a health regimen to get him back in shape, with dry martinis out and herb tea in.

One of the nicest touches is Alec McCowen's "Q," the armaments specialist who complains of insufficient funding, would love an offer to transfer to the CIA and whose factory (so extravagant in the other films) looks like a second-rate autobody shop. As a parting remark to Bond, he says, "Now that you're on the case, I hope we're going to have some gratuitous sex and violence."

In short order, Bond hooks up with dangerous SPECTRE agent Fatima Blush (Barbara Carrera), who makes several interesting attempts to kill her prey, and later makes the acquaintance of Domino (Kim Basinger), g.f. of SPECTRE kingpin Largo, who enjoys the challenge presented by the secret agent as long as he thinks he holds the trump card.

Yarn mainly takes place in the lovely environs of the Bahamas and the French Riviera, as well as on Largo's spectacular technological yacht, and the principal action set piece is a rousing car-and-motorcycle chase through the narrow streets of Monaco. By contrast, climactic underwater battle for possession of the warhead is pointedly less spectacular and more personal than its parallel scene in "Thunderball."

What clicks best in the film is the casting. A recurring problem in some recent Bonds has been a confusion and softening of the villainy, as well as a reluctance to make the femmes real bad girls. In this line, Klaus Maria Brandauer, who came to world attention in "Mephisto," makes one of the best Bond opponents since very early in the series. Fabulously rich, noticeably charming, and much younger than the norm for such characters, Brandauer's Largo, although foreign, almost seems like a Ted Turner-type entrepreneur, who goes his own way and doesn't mind whose feathers he ruffles.

As for the ladies, Carrera lets out all the stops as an egocentric witch who relishes the idea of being the one who cuts down Bond once and for all, while Basinger is luscious as the pivotal romantic and dramatic figure.

Max von Sydow is in very briefly as the cat-caressing SPECTRE mastermind Blofeld, while Bernie Casey and Edward Fox efficiently carry out the remaining roles of importance, CIA agent Felix Leiter and Bond's boss "M," respectively.

And then, of course, there's Connery. In fine form and still very much looking the part, he gets knocked around more than Bond is accustomed to and has cut down a bit on both his vices and his quips, but the actor has brought Bond very gracefully, and pleasurably, into middle-age.

In his first film since "The Empire Strikes Back," Irvin Kershner has staged the action to good effect, although pace is extremely relaxed and running time of 137 minutes proves excessive given pic's lack of anything new to offer. Tone struck by him and scenarist Lorenzo Semple Jr. is less glib or smug than usual, although major differences stem mainly from lack of the accustomed accoutrements of the series, such as the Maurice Binder credits and familiar musical theme. Title song here is unimpressive, as is Michel Legrand's rather thin score.

Tech contributions are all strongly pro, from Douglas Slocombe's smooth lensing to Philip Harrison and Stephen Grimes' imaginative production design and the special effects, which include a B-1 bomber and the two missiles in extended flight.

Copyright for the film is credited to numerous banks and financial institutions. — Cart.

All The Right Moves
(COLOR)

Ace youth-themed pic. Big sleeper potential.

Hollywood, Sept. 26.

A 20th Century-Fox release. Executive producer, Gary Morton. Produced by Stephen Deutsch. Directed by Michael Chapman. Screenplay, Michael Kane; co-producer, Phillip Goldfarb; camera (color), Jan DeBont; art director, Mary Ann Biddle; editor, David Garfield; music, David Campbell; sound, Robert Gravenor; set decorator, Ernie Bishop; costumes, Deborah Hopper, Joseph Roveto; assistant director, Jerry Grandey. Reviewed at 20th Century-Fox, Sept. 26, 1983. (MPAA rating: R). Running time, 91 MINS.

Stef	Tom Cruise
Nickerson	Craig T. Nelson
Lisa	Lea Thompson
Pop	Charles Cioffi
Salvucci	Paul Carafotes
Brian	Christopher Penn
Suzie	Sandy Faison
Tracy	Paige Price
Bosko	James A. Baffico
Coach	Donald A. Yannessa
Rifleman	Walter Briggs
Shadow	Leon Robinson

A smash directorial debut by well-known cinematographer Michael Chapman and a gritty script by Michael Kane spiral this teen genre film to a height no other youth pic has achieved this year.

One of the surprises of the early fall, and another benchmark for top-lined Tom Cruise (coming on the heels of "Risky Business"), "All the Right Moves" crackles with authenticity. The story is centered on characters fighting to get out of a dying Pennsylvania mill town to make a better life for themselves. That is not unique, but the execution and texture deliver enough right moves to give this film a muscular boxoffice forecast.

Environment in the film (Johnstown, Pa.) has the reality of a gob of mud. High school football sequences, conveyed in the mud and rain of a turf so real you taste it, meld the visceral and human factors into the kind of jock footage seldom encountered on the screen. The filmmakers, which include Gary Morton in his debut as an exec producer and Stephen Deutsch in his second outing as producer, take the ingredients associated with the ritual of the prep school Friday night game and turn them into a metaphor that throbs with the sense of an American experience.

Source of the film was an article (in Geo magazine) by Pat Jordan. And Kane's screenplay, dramatizing father-son, boy-girl, and coach-player relationships, avoids cliches and sentimentality, ending on an affirmation that is wholly satisfying instead of sticky. Character addictions are not sex, drugs, and rock but the drive to impress well enough on the playing field to land a scholarship and escape the bleak, life-sapping options at home.

In a nice twist on expectations, the driven include Cruise's girlfriend, sharply played by newcomer Lea Thompson, whose own aspirations take the frill out of the coed image, and the hard-nosed high school coach, superbly portrayed by Craig T. Nelson, who wants the big time as much as Cruise, his star safety.

Another welcome surprise is the touching relationship between high school senior Cruise and his father. For once, here's a pop in a redneck town who treats his son like a human being, and Charles Cioffi, however brief his screentime, conveys a durable dignity. There are losers in this story, too, and they are etched with the slap of credulity: Christopher Penn as an SC-bound linebacker who woefully has to settle for a shotgun marriage and Paul Carafotes as the guy who makes the crucial end zone play and whose later desperation underscores the choices in a steel town of "dagos, Polacks, and blacks."

Cinematographer Jan DeBont captures the grime of smokey streets and the dampness of slushy autumnal afternoons on the practice field. Editor David Garfield (son of actor John Garfield) expertly punctuates the rhythms. And the soundtrack album features a strong selection of writers and performers.

The sex in the film, between Cruise and Thompson, is artfully low-key and dramatically responsible. But it is the charged conflict between Cruise and Nelson that illuminates the theme and arrests attention.

Only a couple of false moves qualify the achievement: an early locker room musical number rings untrue and a pair of classroom scenes involving actor Carafotes stretch believability. —*Loyn.*

The Osterman Weekend
(COLOR)

Good-looking, well-made Peckinpah 'comeback' film. Okay chances.

Hollywood, Sept. 28.

A 20th Century-Fox release of a Michael Timothy Murphy and Guy Collins presentation of a Davis-Panzer production. Produced by Peter S. Davis, William N. Panzer. Executive producers, Murphy, Larry Jones, Marc W. Zavat. Stars Rutger Hauer, John Hurt. Directed by Sam Peckinpah. Screenplay, Alan Sharp; adaptation, Ian Masters, based on the book by Robert Ludlum; camera (Deluxe color), John Coquillon; editors, Edward Abroms, David Rawlins; music, Lalo Schifrin; art direction, Robb Wilson King; set decoration, Keith Hein; sound, Richard Bryce Goodman, Bayard Carey; associate producers, Don Guest, E.C. Monell; assistant director, Win Phelps; second unit director, Rod Amateau; second unit camera, Jacques Haitkin. Reviewed at the 20th Century-Fox Studios, L.A., Sept. 27, 1983, (MPAA Rating: R.) Running time: 102 MINS.

John Tanner	Rutger Hauer
Lawrence Fassett	John Hurt
Bernard Osterman	Craig T. Nelson
Richard Tremayne	Dennis Hopper
Joseph Cardone	Chris Sarandon
Ali Tanner	Meg Foster
Virginia Tremayne	Helen Shaver
Betty Cardone	Cassie Yates
Stennings	Sandy McPeak
Steve Tanner	Christopher Starr
Maxwell Danforth	Burt Lancaster

Sam Peckinpah's first film in five years, "The Osterman Weekend" is a competent, professional but thoroughly impersonal meller which reps initial adaptation of a Robert Ludlum tome for the big screen. Tale of CIA manipulation of people's fates reeks of paranoia, betrayal and insidious invasions of privacy, and a good cast manages to make the hokum relatively palatable even though it's impossible to take it seriously for one second. Fox should be able to market this to okay effect during the fall season.

One of the 1970's most prolific directors, Peckinpah has suffered both career and personal difficulties since the release of his last pic, "Convoy," in 1978. It's no secret that he took the reins on "Osterman" as the first step in a comeback, to prove he could still do the job, and aficionados can hope that the film serves its purpose in that regard. By any conventional standards, it looks good and is well made.

Story, however, is pretty convoluted and more than stretches viewer credulity. CIA chief Burt Lancaster, who harbors presidential ambitions, recruits operative John Hurt to convince powerful tv journalist Rutger Hauer that several of his closest friends are actually Soviet agents. Hauer is about to host an annual weekend get-together with his buddies and their wives, and finally agrees to work with Hurt when presented with incriminating videotapes (as well as in the hope of getting the elusive Lancaster on his interview show).

After Hurt has equipped the California ranch house with a warehouse-full of sophisticated surveillance gear, Hauer warily bids welcome to his guests, who include: hot-tempered financier Chris Sarandon and his sexually unsatisfied wife, Cassie Yates; writer and martial arts expert Craig T. Nelson; doctor Dennis Hopper, and his wife, cocaine addict Helen Shaver. After an aborted attempt to send them away for the weekend, Hauer's wife Meg Foster and son Christopher Starr also remain for the festivities.

After a videotape foul-up, the pals get wind of Hauer's suspicions of them, and the domestic situation rapidly deteriorates. Then the twists commence, as Hurt and his men begin eliminating the visitors and force the survivors into life-and-death struggles.

Although a thoughtful postmortem enables one to pretty much figure out what was going on, essential preposterousness of the action discourages taking any of it very seriously, and it remains to be seen whether or not Ludlum's millions of readers will flock to theatres to see what's been done to their popular pulp.

Essentially, Peckinpah and writer Alan Sharp have played it straight, and have neither attempted to transform it nor send it up. Climactic section, in which Hauer must defend his home against maurauding intruders, bears some relation to Peckinpah's "Staw Dogs," but violence has been played way down and action is only moderately visceral in its impact.

With an accent that is now virtually 100% American Hauer is solid as the off-balance but determined protagonist. Hurt effectively plays most of his role isolated from the others in his video command post, and Lancaster socks over his bookend cameo as the scheming CIA kingpin.

Of the others, Craig T. Nelson stands out as the eponymous character. As for the women, each has her moments, but it may be noted by the director's longtime feminist adversaries that nary an opportunity is lost for them to disrobe and act vulgar.

Tech contributions are all excellent, notably John Coquillon's cool lensing. — *Cart.*

The Lonely Lady
(COLOR)

Zadora and Robbins names could spark some initial interest.

Hollywood, Oct. 1.

A Universal Pictures release, produced by Robert R. Weston. Stars Pia Zadora. Directed by Peter Sasdy. Screenplay, John Kershaw and Shawn Randall, based on novel by Harold Robbins; camera (Technicolor), Brian West; editor, Keith Palmer; sound, Claude Hitchcock; production design, Enzo Bulgarelli; associate producer, Tino Barzie; assistant director, Gerald Morin; music, Charles Calello. Reviewed at Universal Studios, Sept. 30, 1983. (MPAA rating: R). Running time: 92 MINS.

Jerilee	Pia Zadora
Walter	Lloyd Bochner
Veronica	Bibi Besch
Vincent	Joseph Cali
Guy	Anthony Holland
George	Jared Martin
Joe	Ray Liotta
Carla	Carla Romanelli
George	Olivier Pierre
Joanne	Kendal Kaldwell

Given its sure shot at redefining awful, "The Lonely Lady" is disappointingly ordinary, offering moments of the memorably mundane but no more. However, Pia Zadora's current media blitz and a Harold Robbins title should attract the initially curious.

As has been widely reported, this is the second Zadora film encouraged by her multimillionaire husband, raising again the question of whether she can really act. It is a difficult question, but largely irrelevant under the circumstances. Suffice to say she is there to do her job in nearly every frame of the film.

Accepting the probability that Zadora does as much with her part as could be done under the circumstances, if not uniquely nor certainly beyond imitation, the second burning question presents itself: Is "The Lonely Lady" sexy?

By some comparisons, say to a documentary on William Howard Taft's roads and harbors program, it is sexy, indeed. By the prevailing cinema standards expected of it, however, "Lady" is lukewarm.

There are brief glimpses of bare breasts and a lot of semi-nude wallowing, but none of this carries a hint of eroticism. Real passion is seldom apparent, even in the shower scene between Zadora and macho Jared Martin. When she sinks down out of camera view, for example, it's entirely believable that she may have had a sudden urge to clean the drain.

As a novelist, of course, Robbins has a knack for taking formula plots and fleshing them out into fairly decent yarns. Stripped of his excesses, however, the film version is left with nothing but the shopworn.

First met in pigtails, Zadora is an aspiring high-school writer who ultimately weds an older successful Hollywood writer, suavely played by Lloyd Bochner. Impotency, jealousy and other ills beset their marriage and she eventually sets out on her own.

Without going to bed with various men and women, she finds it difficult to sell her screenplay legitimately in Hollywood. So she goes to bed with men and women, winning an award for her efforts and shocking the town with her curtain speech before walking off alone.

If "Lady'" has a message, it's the difficulty of getting a good script onto the screen. For sure, for sure. —*Har.*

Beyond The Limit
(BRITISH-COLOR)

Tedious Graham Greene filmization. Poor prospects.

Hollywood, Sept. 27.

A Paramount release of a World Film Services Ltd. production in association with Parsons & Whittemore Lyddon Ltd. Produced by Norma Heyman. Directed by John Mackenzie. Stars Michael Caine, Richard Gere. Screenplay, Christopher Hampton, based on the novel "The Honorary Consul" by Graham Greene. Camera (Rank color; prints by Movielab), Phil Meheux; editor, Stuart Baird; music, Stanley Myers; theme composed by Paul McCartney; additional music, Richard Harvey; production design, Allan Cameron; art direction, Terry Pritchard, Xavier Rodriguez (Mexico); costume design, Barbara Lane; sound, David John; associate producer, Richard F. Dalton; assistant director, Simon Hinkly. Reviewed at Paramount Studios, L.A., Sept. 26, 1983. (MPAA Rating: R.) Running time: 103 MINS.

Charley Fortnum	Michael Caine
Dr. Eduardo Plarr	Richard Gere
Colonel Perez	Bob Hoskins
Clara	Elpidia Carrillo
Leon	Joaquim De Almeida
Aquino	A Martinez
Marta	Stephanie Cotsirilos
Diego	Domingo Ambriz
British Ambassador	Geoffrey Palmer

"Beyond The Limit" represents a weak attempt to adapt Graham Greene's 1973 novel, "The Honorary Consul," for the screen. Strong talents on both sides of the camera haven't managed to breathe life into this intricate tale of emotional and political betrayal and result is a steady dose of tedium. Paramount's last-minute switch to the ludicrous, exploitation-style title and lack of ballyhoo and even print ads within two days of opening indicate lack of distrib confidence, but paltry b.o. would undoubtedly eventuate no matter what.

Greene's central character was one Eduardo Plarr, a half-Paraguayan, half-British doctor in provincial Argentina who quietly assists some revolutionaries in their attempt to kidnap the American ambassador and equally casually impregnates the very young native wife of the besotted honorary consul from Britain, Charley Fortnum.

The rebels blunderingly capture Fortnum instead of the intended Yank, but detain and threaten to execute him anyway unless some of their comrades are released from prison. Plarr is hardly committed to their cause, but secretly acts as an intermediary out of sympathy for the ineffectual consul as well as in the hope that his father, a political prisoner, might be one of those released.

First handicap pic creates for itself is the casting of Richard Gere as the dispirited Englishman, and it's an obstacle that is never overcome. Actor's accent only manages to stay on course when his lines consist of five words or less and has the effect of straightjacketing his range of expressions even more than usual.

What's more, Gere performs another of his seemingly obligatory post-shower nude scenes here, as well as a couple of in-the-buff sex scenes with Elpidia Carrillo, who was first seen here in "The Border" and who acquits herself in decent fashion as a former prostie who opts for a life of leisure with the consul.

Acting honors easily fall to Michael Caine as the small-time, dipsomaniacal diplomat suddenly thrust into the center of a political tempest by virtue of a tragi-comic mistake. Character in the book was in his 60s, but Caine proves an ideal choice and makes Fortnum's self-acknowledged weakness and shortcomings as moving as they can possibly be under the muted circumstances of the rest of the film.

In an offbeat piece of casting, Bob Hoskins, who scored as the London gangland boss in director John Mackenzie's previous pic, "The Long Good Friday," registers strongly as a heartless but engaging South American police chief who violently puts an end to the sticky hostage situation.

Playwright Christopher Hampton's script faithfully follows the dramatic line of the Greene tale, but virtually eliminates the subtle religious, moral and political discussions which were really the substance of the work. Greene's self-described "entertainments" have often made for fine films, but his weightier novels continue to elude successful screen transfer.

Using Mexican locales, Mackenzie and lenser Phil Meheux have evoked a good sense of place, but end result is on the dull side. At least at screening caught, sound quality was subpar which, combined with mix of English and Latin accents, rendered a fair amount

of the dialog incomprehensible. Other tech credits are good.
— *Cart.*

Patu!
(NEW ZEALAND-COLOR)

Wellington, N.Z., Sept. 19.
Produced and directed by Merata Mita. Camera (color), Barry Harbert; editor, Annie Collins; sound, Gerd Pohlmann; original music, Diatribe; vocals, Tia Kingi; no other credits provided. Reviewed at Academy Cinema, Wellington, N.Z. September 14, '83. Running time: **110 MINS.**

"Patu!" which its publicity quite rightly describes as "a unique historical record," was given its world premiere at the recent Wellington Film Festival. It received a rapturous, standing ovation from a capacity audience most of whom would have had first-hand knowledge of, if not involvement in, the events the film portrays.

For an audience outside New Zealand in 1983, the Springbok rugby tour which so divided this country in the (southern) winter of 1981 might be of small and passing interest.

But here, reverberations continue with the probable effect of ensuring Mita's film runs strongly and for some time at the smaller, art house cinemas in the main centers.

"Patu!" was filmed over 12 months, documenting the growth of a movement deeply opposed to South African apartheid which resulted in an eruption by many thousands of New Zealanders, Maori and European, against the rugby sporting event.

The protests and violence that resulted mesmerized the country throughout the Springboks' stay as police and demonstrators did battle on the streets, along the perimeters and, sometimes, on the rugby fields of the nation.

Two games were cancelled and the tour was cut short as a result.

Whether "Patu!" meaning in Maori to kill or strike out, will have major appeal outside New Zealand is arguable. While Kiwis viewing the film know the background, including the almost religious fervor that rugby arouses among significant sections of the New Zealand and South African populations, other peoples could be mystified by a lack of information.

At the same time, this remarkable documentary of one side of the story, directed and produced by a Maori woman filmmaker, with the support of other filmmakers outraged by the events of the tour, has an excoriating power that will leave few people anywhere unaffected.

As a starter, it leaves this country for the London Festival in November. —*Nic.*

Running Brave
(CANADIAN-COLOR)

Minor Olympics-themed pic.

Hollywood, Sept. 24.
A Buena Vista release of an Englander Productions Inc. production. Produced by Ira Englander. Directed by "D.S. Everett." Written by Henry Bean and Shirl Hendryx; camera (Medallion color), Francois Protat; editor, Tony Lower, Earl Herdan; music, Mike Post; art director, Barbra Dunphy; set decorator, Rose Marie McSherry, Jim Erickson; sound, Rob Young; associate producer, Maurice Wolf; assistant director, Martin Walters. Reviewed at Mann's National Theatre, L.A., Sept. 23, 1983. (MPAA Rating: PG). Running time: **106 MINS.**
Billy Mills	Robby Benson
Coach Easton	Pat Hingle
Pat Mills	Claudia Cron
Dennis	Jeff McCraken
Billy's father	August Schellenberg
Frank	Denis Lacroix
Eddie	Graham Greene
Catherin	Margo Kane

Combining the appeal of "Chariots Of Fire" and the American fervor for the upcoming Olympics, "Running Brave," the story of Billy Mills, gold medalist in the 10,000-meter run in the 1964 Tokyo Olympics, should be an audience pleaser. Despite uplifting subject matter, pic, however, is riddled with cliches.

The Mills story is a natural for the screen. A Sioux Indian from South Dakota, Mills attended the U. of Kansas in the early '60s. He achieved some recognition there as a long-distance runner, but had difficulty adjusting to the white man's world.

Mills married and joined the Marines where he trained himself for the 1964 Olympics. His dramatic victory at Tokyo against a field of world class runners is regarded by some sports experts as the most sensational upset in Olympic history.

The real Billy Mills is obviously a formidable person and it is his strength of character which manages to come through the often hackneyed script, poor character development and unconvincing performances.

Robby Benson was reportedly chosen by Mills himself for the role, but it was not a wise choice.

The problem, however, is not all Benson's; he has lost his personality somewhere in the script. The difficult problems and trying relationships in Mills' life are all simplified and predictable. Pat Hingle is suitably gruff as Mills' demanding coach at Kansas.

An interesting area that goes pretty much unexplored is Mills' relationship with his classmates. Jeff McCracken rejects Mills as a fellow runner, but when thrown together as roommates, they have a reconciliation which could have been used to explore the whole area of white-Indian prejudices, but goes untapped.

Claudia Cron as Billy's girlfriend and eventual wife, Pat, is given even less to work with. The bulk of her role is sitting in the stands and smiling as Billy wins another race. The clash of cultures between them is touched on but Pat just doesn't hold her weight as a character.

Billy's Indian relatives come and go throughout the picture and behave pretty much as stereotypical Indians. One is bitter and hateful of white men, the other is a crushed alcoholic with unrealized talent.

The emotional payoff at the Olympics in Tokyo is more manipulated than earned, but oddly moving just the same. The real-life triumph of Mills still manages to shine through.

Filmed on location in Alberta, Canada and on the Edmonton and Drumheller reservations, technical credits are all first rate. Pic was financed by Ermineskin Band of Cree Indians, an oil-wealthy group in Canada. Everyone involved clearly had honorable intentions for "Running Brave," but sometimes that isn't enough.
—*Jayr.*
(Director Donald Shebib took his name off the film's credits.—*Ed.*)

The Sword Of The Barbarians
(ITALIAN-COLOR)

Novelty nil, special effects weak, chances slim.

A Cannon Releasing release of a Filman/Visione Cinematografica production. Executive producer, Ettore Spagnuollo. Produced by Pino Buricchi. Directed by Michael E. Lemick. Features entire cast. Screenplay, Pietro Regnoli; camera (Gevaert color), Giancarlo Ferrando; editor, Alessandro Lucidi; music, Franco Campanino; assistant director, Ettore Arena; set design, Franco Cuppini; master of arms-stunt sequences director, Robert Alexandri; production supervisor, Giulio Dini; special effects, (John) Corridori; dialog supervisor, Ted Rusoff. Reviewed at RKO Warner 1 theatre, N.Y., Sept. 30, 1983. (MPAA Rating: R). Running time: **88 MINS.**
With: Peter MacCoy (Sangral), Margareta Rance, Yvonne Fraschetti, Anthony Freeman, Sabrina Siani (Rani, the Golden Goddess), Xiomaria Rodriguez, Al Huang.

"The Sword Of The Barbarians" is a chintzy Italian imitation of "Conan The Barbarian," one of dozens of pasta fantasies ground out recently. Cannon pickup (released independently, not part of the MGM-UA distribution deal) is minus the novelty or fantastic special effects which could earn it much of a following theatrically.

Story has Sangral (Peter MacCoy), son of Ator, uniting his tribe of peaceful plains people in prehistoric times with Belem's tribe, after saving Belem's foxy daughter Aki from an attack by nasties belonging to evil Naluk's tribe. Naluk is protected by the Golden Goddess, Rani (Sabrina Siani), to whom he makes human sacrifices, officiated by his set of hunchbacked priests. Rani, who periodically appears via cheap special effects behind the altar fire, has declared war upon Sangral, and in one skirmish Naluk's men kill Sangral's beautiful, platinum blonde wife Leni.

Strictly copying the format of the "Conan" film, Sangral vows to bring his wife back to life, and accompanied by Aki and an oriental friend Lee Wa Twan, he treks to visit a black magician Rudak to obtain the secret of rebirth. Rudak can't help but sends him instead on a mission to the Ark of the Templars, from which Sangral extracts a laughably oversize crossbow which shoots three arrows at once. Dull climax has Sangral dutifully wiping out Naluk and even the goddess.

Director credited as Michael E. Lemick (only some of the Italian names are anglicized on this film) tries to stretch his minimal budget with over-use of low-angle and wide-angle shots but to no avail. Underpopulated picture features beasts that are actors in the cheapest makeup imaginable and virtually none of the promised sorcery. It's just hand-to-hand battle nonsense in the vein of the Hercules and Maciste films of over 20 years ago.

Peter MacCoy has the right muscleman build for the lead role and has appeared in several other local items including two "Gunan" features. Judging from the opening narration, his character here is apparently a descendant of the Miles O'Keeffe "Ator," though no family tree of prehistoric Italian schlock heroes has yet been charted. As the evil goddess, Sabrina Siani, also a vet of many of these pics, is an alluring personage, resembling the young Claudia Cardinale.

— *Lor.*

Stuck On You
(COLOR)

Also stuck on plot.

Hollywood, Sept. 30.

A Troma release, produced by Lloyd Kaufman and Michael Herz. Exec producers, William E. Kirksey, Spencer Tandy, Joseph L. Butt. Features entire cast. Directed by Michael Herz and Samuel Weil. Screenplay, Stuart Strutin, Warren Leight. Don Perman, Darren Kloomok, Melanie Mintz, Anthony Gittleson, Duffy Ceaser Magesis, Michael Herz, Lloyd Kaufman; camera (Guffanti Color), Lloyd Kaufman; editors, Darren Kloomok, Richard Haines; art direction, Barry Shapiro; costumes, Rosa Alfaro, Walter Steihl, Assistant directors, Kate Eisemann, Susan Demter; music, various artists. Reviewed at Aidikoff Screening Room, L.A., Sept. 29, 1983. (MPAA rating: R.) Running time: **88 MINS.**
Judge Gabriel.................Irwin Corey
Carol......................Virginia Penta
Bill......................Mark Mikulski
Artie.........................Albert Pia

"Stuck On You" claims to have been shot for the modest sum of $800,000, which could be an exaggeration on the high side judging by the way it looks. It also claims to have already grossed $9,500,000, which is hopefully a bit of an exaggeration as well. If not, teenage taste has declined even further than previously feared.

"Stuck" lists nine writers in its credits and could well name 9,000 more if every borrowed gag was fully acknowledged, up to and including, "Do you smoke after sex?"

Ripped on today's headlines, picture features pretty Virginia Penta and handsome Mark Mikulski locked in a "palimony" dispute before Judge Irwin Corey who is really an angel trying to win his wings by getting the couple back together. To do so, Corey belches a lot, smears his face with food and from time to time grabs himself in private places, which makes him one of the more unusual angels of recent film history.

There are various flashbacks on the couple's loving life together and their zany escapades, fleshed out with historical similarities that all ask the same madcap question: Just how much fun can be had with bodily functions?

In addition to the nine writers, the film lists two directors, Michael Herz and Samuel Weil. It is not clear whether each director supervised the work of four-and-a-half writers, whether they both worked together or whether one took the first three drafts while the other followed with the remaining six.

It is not clear, but it also does not make any difference. — *Har.*

Summertime
(ITALIAN-COLOR)

Rome, Sept. 21.

Produced and directed by Massimo Mazzucco. Stars Luca Barbareschi. Screenplay by Massimo Mazzucco and Michelle Reedy. Camera (color), Charles Rose; editor, Gianfranco Amicucci. Reviewed at the ANICA screening room, Rome, Sept. 21, 1983. Running time: **70 MINS.**
Marco................Luca Barbareschi
Valerie....................Susi Gilder
Friend..............Douglas Ferguson
Insurance agent.........Malcolm Botway

One of the two winners of the Venice Film Festival's Italian Showcase (De Sica section), "Summertime" is a quiet, intelligent little atmosphere film made on a shoestring budget with savvy and charm. Young fashion photographer Massimo Mazzucco's first feature, shot in super 16m and blown up to 35m, takes a whimsical look at a foreigner's three-day impressions of New York City. Merits fest play. Trouble lies ahead for Italo release mainly due to English-language soundtrack (with subtitles; dubbing would be pointless). Could possibly find playoff in specialized U.S. outlets.

With virtually no story, pic relies heavily on the sensitive performance of Luca Barbareschi — a tall, handsome stage actor and director in his own right. He projects a winsome sincerity that is highly attractive as the Italian tourist, Marco. Pic begins with Marco's arrival in New York and meeting a boy on the airport bus who offers him a place to stay.

A disappointing reunion with an old girlfriend (Susi Gilder superbly portrays the most obnoxious fashion model ever) puts a pall over the trip. So does the cold New York winter (pic's title is a subtle reminder of what Marco longs for). He has a one-night stand with a black girl with whom he can't communicate because she only speaks French. The next night the model stands him up and — possibly — he is drawn into a relationship with his host, a transvestite. Unfortunately Mazzucco cut some shots that made this explicit. Gentle and fragile as it is, pic could have done with a shot of stronger stuff.

"Summertime" is a charming picture in which almost nothing happens. It has a refreshing humility and lack of sentimentality or cuteness towards reality. Mazzucco shies away from story and action to concentrate on character sketches (often amusingly on-target) of various New York types, as seen from the outside. Helmer is skillful at turning necessity (like infrequent lip-synch) into a virtue (interesting use of off-screen sound).

Charles Rose's bravura lensing beautifully captures the city in all its tawdriness and wonder.

— *Yung.*

San Sebastian

La Chiave
(The Key)
(ITALIAN-COLOR)

San Sebastian, Sept. 23.

A San Francisco Film production. Directed by Giovanni Tinto Brass. Features entire cast. Screenplay, Tinto Brass, based on novel of same name by Junichiro Tanizaki; camera (color), Silvano Ippoliti; sets, Paolo Biagetti; costumes, Vera Cozzolino, Michela Gisotti; editor, Tinto Brass; music composed and conducted by Ennio Morricone; producer, Giovanni Bertolucci; associate producers, Selenia Cinematografica and International Video Service S.R.L.; choreography, Gabriella Borni; sound, Gaetano Carito. Reviewed at Cine Victoria Eugenia, San Sebastian, Sept. 23, 1983. Running time: **116 MINS.**
Nino Rolfe..................Frank Finlay
Teresa Rolfe..........Stefania Sandrelli
Lazlo Apony..........Franco Branciaroli
Lisa Rolfe...............Barbara Cupisti
Also: Armando Marra, Maria Grazia Bon, Gino Cavalieri, Piero Bortoluzzi, Pietro Lorenzoni, Irma Veithen, Emilia Corinaldi, Giovanni Michelagnoli.
(Film is being distributed by Gaumont)

The latest Giovanni Tinto Brass film, very loosely based on the Japanese novel of the same name, nixed for screening at the recent Venice fest but entered here in the official section, has all the looks of a big international moneymaker. Sophisticates and critics may cavil at its doubtful literary and filmic values, and frown upon its silly intellectual pretensions, but Tinto Brass has injected enough decadent sex scenes into the film to make it attractive to those audiences seeking quality titillation and urbane sexual excitement.

The physical charms of Stefania Sandrelli will certainly appeal to even the most blase male audiences; seeing her on screen is like leafing through a copy of Playboy or Penthouse. With the faded beauty of the most decadent of European cities, Venice, as a backdrop, and an excellent performance by Frank Finlay as the kinky, elegant husband, pic is tailored for success.

As in "Emmanuelle," no one need take the philosophizing seriously, nor will many note mistakes in the reconstruction of Venice of 1940; the mood of sex and Sandrelli's beauty will be what will hook the immense majority of audiences.

The "key" of the film's title is that fitting a private drawer used by both husband and wife to keep their secret diaries in. Each spouse in turn reads the other's entries, but also knows that his and hers is being read as well. Knowledge of what the wife or husband is doing, his or her erotic feelings, acts as a further incentive for sexual play and endless variations and interactions between them and the lovers they associate with.

Story is set in 1940, at the height of Mussolini's power in Italy, but the historical background is used only as a slate on which to tell the story and never becomes a factor in the story itself. Shots of Venice, reconstructions of the period in dresses and decor, good musical score by Ennio Morricone all add to cushion the lush goings-on as we wait for the next sex scenes, occasionally humorous for a change of pace.

Some frontal nudity is used, as well as scenes showing male members, which will cause pic to be nixed in countries with strict censorship. The almost two-hour running time is really not justified, but perhaps Tinto Brass felt that the non-sex padding was needed to prevent the sex scenes from succeeding each other too rapidly and thus starting to bore audiences. Some may be bored anyway.

Yarn ends when the husband, after repeated warnings from his doctor that he had better desist from coitus, has a stroke and shortly thereafter dies. But there is no sense of tragedy in the death, for we know he has lived his life the way he wanted. His coffin is conveyed across the Grand Canal in a gondola, crossing its path with another, brim full of boisterous fascists. Nino Rolfe has made his exit at the right moment. —*Besa.*

I Am The Cheese
(U.S.-COLOR)

San Sebastian, Sept. 19.

An Almi Films release, of A Jack Schwartzman, Albert Schwartz and Michael S. Landes presentation, produced by David Lange. Directed by Robert Jiras. Screenplay, David Lange and Robert Jiras based on novel "I Am the Cheese" by Robert Cormier; camera (TVC color), David Quaid; editor, Nicholas Smith; music, Jonathan Tunick; assistant director, Jeff Silver; sound, Nat Boxer; production manager-assoc. producer, C. Mac Brown; (MPAA Rating, PG). Reviewed at Cine Victoria Eugenia (San Sebastian), Sept. 18, 1983. Running time: 95 MINS.

Adam	Robert Macnaughton
Betty Farmer	Hope Lange
David Farmer	Don Murray
Dr. Brint	Robert Wagner
Amy	Cynthia Nixon
Mr. Grey	Lee Richardson
Arnold	John Fiedler
Edna	Sudie Bond
Young Adam	Frank McGurran

Decidedly slight but sometimes touching pic shot in Vermont about a lonely 15-year-old-boy who has always been the "cheese" (in song "Farmer in the Dell," he who is left over at the end). Three time levels are juxtaposed in the story, which may confuse some audiences since it is never made sufficiently clear what action is in the present and what is in the two different flashbacks.

After a slow start, pic accelerates nicely after plot thickens, giving us an upbeat ending. (Finale contradicts theme and finish of Robert Cormier's source novel.— *Ed.*)

An adolescent is undergoing psychiatric treatment in an institution; in daily sessions, a shrink tries to ascertain how much the boy remembers of his past. During his confinement within the guarded grounds, the boy daily cycles about the compound, imagining he is on the open road hastening back to his parents and a girl he knew at school. The persons he sees around him in the institution become the evil adversaries of his daydreams.
· Reason for the questionings is that the boy's father had once been a journalist who had testified in a famous court case; his life was so endangered that he simulated an accident and his own death, changed his name, and moved to rural Vermont, where he had holed up since, keeping a low profile and not telling his son of his past or even what his real name is. The father's true identity however is discovered by those after him, and he and his wife are killed in a car "accident," witnessed by the boy.

Between sessions with the doctor and imaginary rides, mixed with flashbacks, the boy gradually comes to understand that his captors are his father's adversaries and that he too is in danger. Okay thesping by Robert Macnaughton as the confused and reticent, but then assertive youth; Robert Wagner similarly all right as the psychiatrist, and all technical credits up to crack in what has the look of a very modest-budgeted film. Item could garner word-of-mouth audiences in select playoffs for domestic release, but seems more apt for the tv and cable market. — *Besa.*

Une Pierre Dans La Bouche
(A Stone in the Mouth)
(FRENCH-COLOR)

San Sebastian, Sept. 17.

An Helia Films and Salsaud International production. Produced and directed by Jean-Louis Leconte. Features entire cast. Screenplay, Gerard Brach and Laconte; camera (Fujicolor), Henri Alekan; editor, Genevieve Letellier; music, Egisto Macchi; sets, Jean-Pierre Bazerolle and Colombe Anouilh. Reviewed at Cine Miramar (San Sebastian), Sept. 16, '83. Running time: 106 MINS.

The Fugitive	Harvey Keitel
Victor	Michel Robin
Jacky	Catherine Frot
Marc	Richard Anconina

Also: Jeffrey Kime, Bruno Balp, Genevieve Mnich, Hughes Quester and Jacques Boudet.

A Yank gangster on the lam who holes up for three days in the villa of a blind ex-actor generates some wry Gallic humor that alternates with mock adventure in a tragicomic vein. Script lurches unevenly, sometimes scoring with witty dialog, then slowing to a ponderous pace.

Mainstay of pic is Michel Robin as the delightfully dithering blind man whose country mansion becomes the temporary refuge of the escaping, wounded gangster. A sort of symbiotic relationship springs up between the two; the owner of the house is amused at the novelty of such an encounter. Helmer Jean-Louis Leconte contrasts the histrionic polish of the old, blind, cultivated actor with the crude abrasiveness of the uncouth mobster.

Pacing changes with the arrival of the blind man's useless nephew, bringing in tow a pretty girlfriend of three days' vintage. Latter flirts with the hood while the boyfriend fumes and finally gives the mobster away to his cohorts, who're seeking him to settle an old score. At the end they catch up with the fugitive and gun him down, placing a stone in his mouth, the sign of a stool pigeon.

Technical credits are up to snuff and Robin's performance is superb; same can't be said for Harvey Keitel, who mopes about, frowns and occasionally switches from his accented French into gutteral English to let loose a barrage of curses. Pic will be a hard sell outside France, though some art houses might nibble at it. — *Besa.*

El Arreglo
(The Arrangement)
(SPANISH-COLOR)

San Sebastian, Sept. 19.

A Fuentealamo production, written and directed by Jose Antonio Zorrilla. Camera (Eastmancolor), Andres Berenguer; exec producer, Jose Maria Ramos; editor, Jose Salcedo; sets, W. Burman; direct sound, George Stephenson. Reviewed at Cine Miramar (San Sebastian), Sept. 18, '83. Running time: 110 MINS.

Cris	Eusebio Poncela
Mari Cruz	Isabel Mestres
Ana	Mamen del Valle
Leo	Pedro Diez del Corral

Also: Francisco Portes, Felicidad Blanc, Pilar Alcon, Carmen Rossi, Mery Leyva, Marta F. Muro, Jose L. Barcelo, Emilio Fornet, Avelino Canovas, Angel Roman, Elisenda Ribas et al.

(Not to be confused with Argentine film with same title, directed by F. Ayala and reviewed in the June 15, 1983 issue of Variety.)

There has recently been a rash of Spanish films about detectives, police inspectors and the Civil Guard, starting with Jose Luis Garci's "El Crack." "El Arreglo" is the latest effort in this vein, but remains a minor Spanish pastiche of the well-known genre.

The plight of the maverick police inspector hot on the trail of an international political plot, as his boss gives him 48 hours to solve a host of mysteries and murders, has become a filmic set piece. This Spanish version adds nothing new. Plot has so many twists and is so confusing that it would defy even a sleuth to make sense of the disjointed episodes and wordy explanations.

Eusebio Poncela as the inspector, who occasionally trembles and has fits that leave him unconscious, is unconvincing as the tough cop he's supposed to be; he has more the air of a student or intellectual than a tough flatfoot. On screen, he is never made to physically confront his adversaries. At most, he'll point a gun at them, as though he were play acting. Nor do we ever see him use the knife he straps to his leg at the beginning of the film. It's all bluff.

Plot concerns a political assassination engineered by a Latin American government which has even set up an elaborate torture chamber to extract confessions. A new girlfriend for the cop is thrown in to provide some romantic interest, but remains equally shadowy. There are also a few political asides, referring to police operations in the period before the Socialists came into power, but most of pic has the inspector tripping about Madrid, talking to suspects and occasionally ducking his would-be killers.

Item was nonetheless quite well received here and might do okay biz in the local market; it is unlikely to generate any interest abroad.
— *Besa.*

Brussels By Night
(BELGIAN-COLOR)

San Sebastian, Sept. 22.

A Real Reel Films production. Written and directed by Marc Didden. Camera (color) Willy Stassen; editor, Ludo Troch; exec producer, Erwin Provoost; music, Raymond van het Groenewoud. Features Francois Beukelaers, Ingrid De Vos, Amid Chakir, Michel Mentens, Senne Fouffaer, Alfred Van Kuryk, et al. Reviewed at Cine Miramar (San Sebastian), Sept. 21, '83. Running time: 90 MINS.
(Soundtrack mostly in Flemish, with some French as well)

Francois Beukelaers gives a tour-de-force performance in this well-scripted, taut tale of a man on the loose in Brussels after a personal tragedy at home. In the role of "Max," Beukelaers runs the gamut from savage anti-social behavior to cynical humor, as we drift with him for a night and a day in Brussels, his mood sometimes distraught, sometimes vicious. Occasionally, just when interest starts to lag, helmer Marc Didden comes up with some new twist, keeping audiences guessing till the final frames.

Opening scene of pic has Max, a tough truck driver, putting a gun into his mouth and pulling the trigger. But the bullet chamber is empty. He hops a train, the first that comes along, which takes him to Brussels where he strikes up a friendship with a barmaid and a North African who works as a streetcar driver. An old crony he happens to meet in the street joins the group, with Max' relationship to each changing mercurially in the course of the story, from tenderness to hate to condescension to ridicule.

The vein of savage humor and slashing gibes culminates with a wanton crime, as Max jettisons the African over a railing to his death. Throughout the film Max has been trying to reach a phone number which doesn't answer. Finally, when he is in police custody, we learn the phone number is that of his house where he has slain his wife and child.

Pic has enough going for it to interest audiences anywhere and should be a natural for tv and other marts. Flemish track may cut its potential in Francophone areas, which would be a pity. — *Besa.*

Truhanes
(Rogues)
(SPANISH-COLOR)

San Sebastian, Sept. 22.

A P.E. Films S.A. production, directed by Miguel Hermoso. Screenplay, Manolo Marinero, Mario Camus, Jose Luis G. Sanchez and Miguel Hermoso; camera (Eastmancolor), Fernando Arribas; editor, Blanca Guillem; sets, Antonio de Miguel; music, Jose Nieto; production director, Jose Jacoste. Reviewed at Cine Victoria Eugenia (San Sebastian), Sept. 21, '83. Running time: 100 MINS.

Gines	Francisco Rabal
Gonzalo	Arturo Fernandez
Marta	Isabel Mesatres
Nati	Lola Flores

Also: Vicky Lagos, Rafael Diaz, Elena Arnao, Angel Alcazar, Alberto Fernandez, Emilio Fornet, Fernando Bilbao, Elias Rodriguez, Silvia Gambino, Juan Cueto.

"Truhanes" is a well-paced, amusing comedy, sometimes bordering on the slapstick, bound to please local audiences more than it will critics who may cavil at its facile humor. As a commercial product it comes across very nicely and could rack up some sales in offshore markets, especially in Latin America and the U.S. Hispano circuit.

Yarn concerns a high class crook sentenced to his first term in prison. Intimidated and set upon by the prison rabble, he strikes up a friendship with a certain Gines (Paco Rabal). They make a simple deal. Gines will protect and take care of the playboy in the clink and latter will help the old jailbird when he's released a few months hence.

At this point, the yarn could have developed into an action-drama, but instead veers off amusingly into a comedy as the playboy is forced to take on the ex-con as a gardener; latter spends more time meddling in the former's business affairs than in pruning hedges, which makes for some chuckles.

Characters of the debonair playboy and the ex-con contrast amusingly, as Rabal puts in one of his best performances in a long time. Lola Flores has a cameo role as the tavern owner the rogues seek out in Barcelona after escaping from Madrid police. Arturo Fernandez is foppishly expressionless, which is what the part calls for, but is overshadowed by Rabal.

— Besa.

Tin Man
(U.S.-COLOR)

San Sebastian, Sept. 22.

A Goldfarb Distributors Inc. presentation of a John G. Thomas and Aaron Biston Film in association with Westcom Productions. Produced and directed by John G. Thomas. Features entire cast. Screenplay, Bishop Holiday; camera (color), Virgil Harper; editor, Drake Silliman; associate producer, Brian Avery; exec producer, Aaron Biston; music, Bishop Holiday. No other credits available. Reviewed at Cine Victoria Eugenia, San Sebastian Film Fest, Sept. 21, '83. Running time: 95 MINS.

With: Timothy Bottoms, Deana Jurgens, John Phillip Law, Troy Donahue.

"A computer is just a machine. What about people?" "I thought he loved me too. That hurts," "Gee, he's so wrong." These are some of the immortal lines uttered by Deana Jurgens in a film that makes most afternoon tv soap operas look like sophisticated fare by comparison. The pic has about as much depth as a crêpe on the pan and is topped by an irritating vein of self-righteousness as the expressionless Jurgens mouths every romantic cliche in the book.

Story concerns a good-natured deaf boy working in an auto repair shop, who on the side has fiddled around with computers and built a machine through which he can hear and talk by pressing the right keys. Enter a girl who works in a clinic for the deaf and who has contacts with a computer company. Not only does she get his hearing medically fixed, but also finds him a fat contract with the rascally company.

Boy genius then builds an electronic robot, which can answer virtually any question put to it and has a "personality" of its own. Sound familiar? Smooth romantic sailing between the boy genius and the save-the-world demoiselle is interrupted twice: once when it is learned he has "never had a girl," again when he starts to relose his hearing. But all ends well as he socks the mean computer company guy in the mouth and his girlfriend and he decide to go on a vacation.

Timothy Bottoms' performance is competent, but everyone else in the cast is pure pasteboard. Pic seems apt for tv, but is an unlikely contender for theatrical release.

— Besa.

The Right Stuff
(COLOR)

Smashing depiction of Mercury astronauts. Hit potential.

Hollywood, Oct. 7.

A Ladd Company release through Warner Bros. of a Robert Chartoff Irwin Winkler production. Produced by Winkler, Chartoff. Executive producer, James D. Brubaker. Directed, written by Philip Kaufman, based on the book by Tom Wolfe. Features entire cast. Camera (Technicolor), Caleb Deschanel; music, Bill Conti; editors, Glenn Farr, Lisa Fruchtman, Stephen A. Rotter, Tom Rolf, Douglas Stewart; production design, Geoffrey Kirkland; art direction, Richard J. Lawrence, W. Stewart Campbell, Peter Romero; set design, Craig Edgar, Joel David Lawrence, Nicanor Navarro; set decoration, Pat Pending, George R. Nelson; special visual creations, Jordan Belson; visual consultant, Gene Rudolf; special visual effects supervisor, Gary Gutierrez; costume supervision, Jim Tyson; sound (Dolby), David R.B. MacMillan; assistant director, Charles A. Myers. Reviewed at The Burbank Studios, Burbank, Oct. 7, 1983. (MPAA Rating: PG). Running time: 192 MINS.

Chuck Yeager	Sam Shepard
Alan Shepard	Scott Glenn
John Glenn	Ed Harris
Gordon Cooper	Dennis Quaid
Gus Grissom	Fred Ward
Glennis Yeager	Barbara Hershey
Pancho Barnes	Kim Stanley
Betty Grissom	Veronica Cartwright
Trudy Cooper	Pamela Reed
Deke Slayton	Scott Paulin
Scott Carpenter	Charles Frank
Wally Schirra	Lance Henriksen
Lyndon B. Johnson	Donald Moffat
Jack Ridley	Levon Helm
Annie Glenn	Mary Jo Deschanel
Scott Crossfield	Scott Wilson
Louise Shepard	Kathy Baker
Marge Slayton	Mickey Crocker
Rene Carpenter	Susan Kase
Jo Schirra	Mittie Smith
Minister	Royal Dano
Liaison Man	David Clennon
Air Force Major	Jim Haynie
Recruiters	Jeff Goldblum, Harry Shearer
Chief Scientist	Scott Beach
Nurse Murch	Jane Dornacker
Gonzales	Anthony Munoz
Head of Program	John P. Ryan
Life Reporter	Darryl Henriques
Eric Sevareid	Eric Sevareid
Slick Goodlin	William Russ

"The Right Stuff" is a humdinger. Full of beauty, intelligence and excitement, this big-scale look at the development of the U.S. space program and its pioneering aviators provides a fresh, entertaining look back at the recent past for those old enough to remember, and will serve as an eye-opening introduction to the subject for the large filmgoing audience that wasn't born when it all happened. Ladd Company release through Warner Bros. therefore has across-the-board appeal to all spectrums of the public and looks to do strong, sustained biz.

Film version of Tom Wolfe's best selling revisionist history has been some three years in the making, and this is one of those pics where all the elements, especially timing, have come together for maximum payoff. Initial media attention has focused on Sen. John Glenn's bid for the Democratic presidential nomination, but, a number of other factors will help foster acceptance of the film — renewal of interest in space travel thanks to the successful shuttle flights, a somewhat revived sense of patriotism and awareness of things military over the past three years and even the return of short haircuts and a "clean" look for men. Just a few years ago, getting gung-ho about "The Right Stuff" simply couldn't have been possible for young hipsters.

Tale spans 16 years, from ace test pilot Chuck Yeager's breaking of the sound barrier over the California desert to Vice President Johnson's welcoming of the astronauts to their new home in Houston with an enormous barbecue inside the Astrodome. Telling takes over three hours, but it goes by lickity-split under Philip Kaufman's direction and is probably the shortest-seeming film of its length ever made.

Emblematic figure here is Yeager, played by a taciturn Sam Shepard. As the ace of aces who was passed by for astronaut training due to his lack of college degree, Yeager, for Kaufman as for Wolfe, is the embodiment of "the right stuff," that ineffable quality which separates the men from the boys, so to speak. Throughout the film, Kaufman periodically cuts back to Yeager and his fellow test expert Scott Crossfield (played by Scott Wilson), who continue to push the limits of new aircraft while the young whippersnapper astronauts receive gobs of publicity even before they've gone aloft.

Once the Russians launch the first Sputnik, enormously amusing scenes have House Minority Leader Johnson, President Eisenhower and other officials reacting in near-panic and rushing to win the race for space. After rigorous, often humiliating tests, the final seven men are selected for the Mercury program amidst vividly recreated public fanfare.

As in the book, the wives' viewpoints are not neglected, but Kaufman has chosen to focus primarily upon four of the astronauts — Alan Shepard, John Glenn, Gordon Cooper and Virgil (Gus) Grissom. All want to be first in space, of course, and Glenn, due to his piousness, impossibly high moral tone and lack of a sense of humor about himself, rather sticks out from the bunch.

An incident over some flyboy groupies sets off a dynamic confrontation between Glenn and Shepard (certainly not the sort of thing reported in the press at the time), but the men all pull together for the good of the program and, despite early setbacks due to exploding rockets and the Russians getting there first, Project Mercury ultimately becomes a rousing success.

Assembling and structuring all this material could not have been easy, but Kaufman has proved equal to the task and has managed to ease many humanizing touches into the historical fabric. Especially with the addition of Bill Conti's high-profile music, tone tends toward the heroic rather than the irreverent, but latter element is still present, as in bits such as the men having to produce sperm samples on command during testing, Shepard having to relieve himself in his spacesuit while waiting out a delay on top of his rocket, and LBJ becoming foolishly furious when the shy, stuttering Mr. Glenn refuses to appear with him on television.

Even though upbeat end results are historically known, pic also manages two gripping episodes, wherein Grissom, America's second space voyager, has his capsule sink after splashdown and must endure suspicion and relative shame due to the mishap, and Glenn comes close to burning up upon re-entry when his heat shield comes loose.

Actors chosen to play the astronauts all bear resemblances to their real-life counterparts, and characterizations are ultra-realistic down the line. Dennis Quaid is particularly good at conveying the enthusiastic egoism of Cooper, Scott Glenn gets across Shepard's refusal to be pushed too far, Fred Ward appealingly projects Grissom's rough, regular-guy quality, and Ed Harris is absolutely right as Glenn, the best known of the group today.

Unfortunately, astronauts Slayton, Carpenter and Schirra never really register, appearing only on the periphery of the action, which would appear to be a disservice to men equally as deserving of attention as the others.

Of the wives, Veronica Cartwright's Betty Grissom, Pamela Reed's Trudy Cooper and Mary Jo Deschanel's Annie Glenn have the most screen time, and all are superb.

Casting is on the button down to the smallest roles. Donald Moffat does a physically uncanny impersonation of the ambitious, p.r.-minded LBJ, Barbara Hershey nicely etches Yeager's attractive wife, Kim Stanley is the salty-mouthed proprietress of the fliers' desert hangout, and Eric Sevareid even plays himself. Chuck Yeager, who served as technical consultant, plays a cameo as a barman.

Technically, the film is a wonder of verisimilitude and a triumph of mixed elements. Newly-lensed footage has been expertly combined with documentary and NASA footage to recreate space launches, public receptions and the like, and special effects play an important role in portraying the soaring flights of Yeager and the orbits executed by Glenn. Production hands contributing to these successes are too numerous to mention, but all deserve salutes.

Caleb Deschanel's cinematography is lustrous and impeccably clean, and experimental filmmaker Jordan Belson is credited with special visual creations.
—*Cart.*

No Habra Mas Penas Ni Olvido
(There Will Be No More Sorrows Nor Oblivion)
(ARGENTINE-COLOR)

Buenos Aires, Oct. 4.

An Aries release and production. Produced by Fernando Ayala and Luis Osvaldo Repetto. Directed by Hector Olivera. Stars Federico Luppi, Miguel Angel Sola, Ulises Dumont, Julio De Grazia, Rodolfo Ranni. Screenplay, Roberto Cossa and Olivera, based on Osvaldo Soriano's novel; camera (Eastmancolor), Leonardo Rodriguez Solis; editor, Eduardo Lopez; music, Oscar Cardozo Ocampo; art director, Emilio Basaldua; costumes, Maria Julia Bertotto; special effects, Ricardo Lanzoni, Jorge de la Reta and Mario Gabriel; makeup, Maria Laura Lopez; sound, Norberto Castronuovo; executive producer, Ricard Vacas; assistant director, Horacio Guisado. Reviewed at the Gran Rex theatre, B.A., Sept. 22, 1983. Running time: 80 MINS.

Fuentes.................Federico Luppi
Juan.................Miguel Angel Sola
Cerviño.................Ulises Dumont
Garcia.................Julio De Grazia
Sheriff Llanos.............Rodolfo Ranni
Major Guglielmini.........Lautaro Murua
Suprino..................Hector Bidonde
Toto.....................Arturo Maly
Rossi......................Raul Rizzo
Reinaldo.................Victor Laplace
Mrs. Fuentes.............Graciela Dufau
Mateo...................Jose Maria Lopez
Girl......................Maria Socas
Moyano.................Fernando Iglesias
Ricardito...............Fernando Olmedo

Nothing could be more unexpected in Argentine cinema nowadays than a film taking a critical look at Peronism just on the eve of national elections the Peronists hope to win. Director Hector Olivera, who supports the other top contender in the presidential race, Radical Party candidate Raul Alfonsin, has attained tremendous impact, besides stirring heated controversies, with this depiction of how rivalries between right- and left-wing factions within Peronism led to full-scale battles, merciless tortures and cold-blooded murder, with total disregard for both political and human values.

Yarn follows almost step by step a short novel by exiled writer Osvaldo Soriano, first printed in Europe (France, Italy, Poland) and only several years later in Argentina, where it has become a best-seller. Although apparently inspired by the shooting between ultrarightists and ultraleftists near the Ezeiza international airport the day Peron returned to the country in 1973, causing countless victims among the crowd, the story of "Oblivion" takes place in a small rural town, Colonia Vela, in 1974. In a wider context, what happens there symbolizes not only the plight of Peronism but of entire Argentina after it was caught in the crossfire between deadly extremist forces.

Hector Bidonde, local Peronist boss, plots with county mayor Lautaro Murua and union leader Victor Laplace scheme that might lead to the ousting of Colonia Vela's deputy mayor Federico Luppi, to whom he is indebted. Invoking orders from above they tell Luppi he has to fire his assistant Jose Maria Lopez because he is a Marxist. When Luppi refuses, arguing Lopez is a loyal Peronist, the others get tough, engaging the help of police chief Rodolfo Ranni.

Luppi, far from intimidated, decides to fight for what he deems just, convinced that Peron would see it that way, too. He turns his office into a fortress, assisted by Lopez, a police agent he promotes to corporal (Julio De Grazia), an old gardener (Fernando Iglesias) and a drunkard just escaped from jail (Miguel Angel Sola). After they resist the first police assault, Murua summons a death squadron, which attacks with heavy gunfire but is turned back by clouds of an insecticide sprayed from a plane piloted by Ulises Dumont, a pal of Sola's.

Meanwhile leftist youths have abducted sheriff Ranni, threatening to kill him if the attack on Luppi doesn't stop. But the confrontation is already unstoppable. Eventually almost all the main contenders, who have been either friends or good neighbors in the formerly peaceful Colonia Vela, are killed. Luppi dies after being tortured in a classroom where portraits of Argentina's founding fathers have been downed by the bullets. Dumont is shot on his plane.

Viewers follow these developments in fascination. It is an unprecedental experience for them because Argentine pics almost never have dealt with contemporary political subjects.

Entertainmentwise, a major asset of "Oblivion" lies in its many humor touches, specially the funny grotesque shades that brilliant comedians Miguel Angel Sola, Ulises Dumont and Julio De Grazia inject into their characters.

Moreover, the comic details and often witty dialogs strengthen, by contrast, the emotional impact of the second half. In fact, the tragicomedy treatment underlines the basic authenticity of the story, since many Argentines took as a sort of joke the early stages of clashes for power that rather ironically grew until becoming lethal for thousands and ruinous for the nation.

Olivera and his writers, Soriano and Cossa tell the story in terms of fastpaced action. Motivations and psychologies are hinted more by what the characters do than by what they say. Fine acting, tight editing and generally topnotch credits are other pluses. Title is a lyric taken from a tango classic, "My Beloved Buenos Aires."
—*Nubi.*

Scherzo Del Destino In Agguato Dietro L'Angolo Come Un Brigante Di Strada
(A Joke of Destiny Lying In Wait Around the Corner Like a Robber)
(ITALIAN-COLOR)

Rome, Sept. 30.

A Gaumont release, produced by Giuseppe Giovannini for Radiovideo Service. Stars Ugo Tognazzi, Piera Degli Espositi. Directed by Lina Wertmuller. Screenplay, Lina Wertmuller and Age; camera (color), Camillo Bazzoni; art director, Enrico Job; editor, Franco Fraticelli; music, Paolo Conte. Reviewed at Fiamma Cinema, Rome, Sept. 30, 1983. Running time: 105 MINS.

Vincenzo De Andreiis .... Ugo Tognazzi
Maria Teresa.........Piera Degli Espositi
Minister of the Interior...Gastone Moschin
Minister's assistant.. ..Roberto Herlitzka
Capt. of the Digos.......Renzo Montagnani
Terrorist...................Enzo Jannacci
Adalgisa...................Valeria Golino
Young Carabiniere ...Massimo Wertmuller

Lina Wertmuller bounces back to the screen after a five-year absence with a social allegory about the minister of the interior getting locked in his bulletproof, soundproof car. Cowritten with veteran comedy scripter Age, pic is obviously aimed at domestic markets and has enough flair and crazy antics to be a hit. However, it could also overleap national boundaries and recover some of the helmer's fans from her golden era, when her grotesque sense of humor won wide American art house audiences.

After the interval of the dramatic "Nightful of Rain" and Sicilian melodrama, "Blood Feud," Wertmuller wisely returns to a more popular blend of politics and irreverent laughs. True to form, pic craftily avoids taking sides and indiscriminately lampoons politicians, right-wingers, feminists, '68 militants, police and terrorists.

Gastone Moschin plays the menacing if helpless Minister trapped in a limo with a broken computer. The accident occurs in front of the art deco villa of a Christian Democrat deputy named De Andreiis (Ugo Tognazzi), who offers the minister hospitality in his garage while a fruitless rescue is attempted.

Meanwhile, De Andreiis' kooky wife Maria Teresa (Piera Degli Espositi) runs around the house hysterically while hiding her lover, an escaped terrorist, in the basement. As the head of the Secret Services (Renzo Montagnani) learns, her secret identity is "Rosa Luxemburg," a terrorist sympathizer and accomplice.

Memorable caricature is one of the strong points of "Scherzo." Tognazzi outdoes himself as the brittle career-bent politician whose human side emerges only when his wife threatens to leave him for another. De Andreiis' ingratiating bigwig gets laughs and viewer sympathy from the first minute he starts bowing obsequiously.

Degli Espositi, a stage performer, fits less comfortably into the role of the shrill militant (Wertmuller also makes her a rich aristocrat to complicate things). This flighty feminist in love with a wimpy terrorist nobody could like is likely to anger feminists and raise (deliberately) the same polemics "Swept Away" did about men's and women's roles.

Helmer again reverts to the trick of stacking the cards idologically in favor of the "right" character, Maria Teresa, while letting the "wrong" one, the conservative husband, get all the audience's sympathy. Whether this device can stimulate b.o. trade is a question.

Madcap cast is completed by a reefer-smoking grandmother, a fetching teenage daughter (Valeria Golino) in love with a young cop (the slowest subplot in the film is her flirtation with Massimo Wertmuller), and the minister's deadpan assistant, marvelously limned by Roberto Herlitzka.

Camillo Bazzoni's fine photography and Enrico Job's extravagant fantasy sets make pic technically very watchable, while Paolo Conte's music sometimes gives scenes an ironic touch.
— *Yung.*

Romantic Comedy
(COLOR)

The long and the short of it.

Hollywood, Oct. 3.
An MGM/UA release of a Walter M. Mirisch Prod. of an Arthur Hiller Film for UA/Taft Entertainment. Produced by Walter Mirisch, Morton Gottlieb. Executive producer, Marvin Mirisch. Directed by Arthur Hiller. Stars Dudley Moore, Mary Steenburgen. Screenplay, Bernard Slade, based on play by Slade; camera (Metrocolor), David M. Walsh; editor, John C. Howard; sound, Al Overton Jr.; production design, Alfred Sweeney; music, Marvin Hamlisch; costume. design, Joe I. Thompkins; associate producer, David Silver; assistant director, Joe Roe. Reviewed at MGM Studios, Oct. 3, 1983. (MPAA rating: PG.) Running time: **103 MINS.**
Jason . . . . Dudley Moore
Phoebe . . . . Mary Steenburgen
Leo . . . . Ron Leibman
Allison . . . . Janet Eilber
Kate . . . . Robyn Douglass
Blanche . . . . Frances Sternhagen

Dudley Moore and Mary Steenburgen, enacting an unlikely pair

of successful Broadway writing partners who endure and finally resolve nine years of "unsynchronized passion," are a winsome and resilient romantic team under Arthur Hiller's direction of adapter Bernard Slade's 1979 stage comedy.

The title, so casual it's almost a conceit, signals an old-fashioned time and place in the realm of popular movie romances, notwithstanding the film's contemporary wit and framework. "Romantic Comedy" is certainly the stuff of Broadway boxoffice but in today's movie market it's a curiosity whose appeal seems essentially limited to older crowds. For Moore, the result is a sure step forward following his last two misses ("Six Weeks," "Lovesick"), but commercial prospects look iffy.

Producers Walter Mirisch and Morton Gottlieb, who earlier teamed on the screen adaptation of Slade's "Same Time, Next Year," complement this updated Cinderella story with a class, Sutton Place townhouse-look from production designer Albert Sweeney. Cinematographer David Walsh captures equivalent Manhattan tones and costume designer Joe Tomkins deftly spans a near-decade in changing fashions. But technical sheen and engaging performances fail to overwhelm lack of narrative propulsion.

Supporting players in the six-character drama are competently limned by Ron Leibman, whom Steenburgen marries out of desperation; Robyn Douglass, svelte sexpot actress who loves her art well enough to go to bed with it; Janet Eilber, in a rather undimensional role as Moore's sophisticated wife; and Frances Sternhagen, as the helpful, seen-it-all literary agent. Trouble with thee crucial support roles is that Douglass and Sternhagen are saddled with characters close to cliches, Eilber is more bland than knowing, and Leibman's odd-man-out character, as written, is undeveloped and a tough challenge to crack.

The film thus depends totally on the Moore-Steenburgen fireworks, particularly Moore in terms of boxoffice. His character is subtly layered, and the stars hit the tuning fork right off when Steenburgen, a would-be dramatist from the New England woods, meets Moore on the day of his wedding and becomes his collaborator. Their first effort is a flop but fame follows. Their potential love always out of sync with the contingencies of their personal lives, Moore and Steenburgen bring to the screen a caustic insecure humor (his) and a vulnerability tinged with a Yankee sting (hers).

Slade nicely conveys the sense of playwrights who are actually writers, while most of their dialog is

personal. Fantasy element is the filmmakers' misguided use of booze. Moore is hardly ever without a drink in his hand, day or night, but, unlike "Arthur" or "10," Moore remains the image of control. It's that out-of-sync touch with whatever passes as sophistication that symbolizes the film's tired roots. — *Loyn.*

Un Foro Nel Parabrezza
(A Hole In The Windshield)
(ITALIAN-YUGOSLAVIAN-COLOR)

Venice, Sept. 3.
Produced by Corrado and Allesandro Canzio for RAI-TV, C.C.T., and Jadran Film (Zagreb). Stars Vittorio Mezzogiorno, Mimsy Farmer. Directed by Sauro Scavolini. Screenplay by Carlo Bernari and Sauro Scavolini, based on Carlo Bernari's novel; camera (color), Cristiano Pogany; editor, Alessandro Lucidi; art director, Ertha Schwartz. Reviewed at the Venice Film Festival, Sept. 3, 1983. Running time: **110 MINS.**
Eugenio . . . . Vittorio Mezzogiorno
Daniza . . . . Mimsy Farmer
Elsa . . . . Pamela Villoresi

A psychological thriller without much bite, Sauro Scavolini's first feature "A Hole in the Windshield" was screened in the Italian Showcase of the Venice Film Festival. The Italo-Yugoslav coproduction, taken from a novel by Carlo Bernari who co-scripted, will find its just outlet on tv in a slightly fuller version. On a market as glutted as the Italian one, product will have trouble distinguishing itself for theatrical release.

Story starts with a newspaper editor's obsession with a huge Citroen that keeps stealing his parking space. There is a sinister bullet hole through the windshield that further arouses his curiosity. When he finally meets the owner, Danzia (Mimsy Farmer), a lovely blonde foreigner with a shady past, his irritation turns to love. Eugenio (Vittorio Mezzogiorno) leaves his wife (Pamela Villoresi in a rare and uninteresting screen appearance) and children for the stranger, about whom he knows nothing. Not even why the Mob (and/or the police?) is trying to wreck their affair.

Though equipped with all the mysterious characters, stormy nights and unexplained disappearances desirable in a mystery, "Hole" is slow in involving the viewer in its political-editorial intrigues. By the time we get a glimpse of Daniza's husband, a former Mafia lawyer turned state witness and vegetablized by his ex-cronies, it's too late to care. Eugenio's stubborn persistence in chasing the woman he loves all over Italy and Yugoslavia ends in tragedy, yet finale is more frustrating than dramatic.

Shot entirely in Croatia, pic suffers from unrealistic setting

(Rome, for example, is depicted by a hospital, a newspaper office and a car). Thesps have a similar difficulty constructing believable characters with whom the audience could identify.

Lensing is good; a nice musical theme is worked to death. — *Yung.*

Attention, Une Femme Peut En Cacher une Autre
(Warning, One Woman May Be Hiding Another)
(FRENCH-COLOR)

Paris, Sept. 26.
Gaumont release of a Gaumont International/Marcel Dassault Productions coproduction. Produced by Alain Poiré. Stars Miou-Miou, Roger Hanin, Eddy Mitchell. Directed by Georges Lautner. Screenplay, Jean-Loup Dabadie; camera (color), Henri Decae; music, Philippe Sarde; art director, Alain Gaudry; editor, Michelle David; sound, Bernard Aubuoy, Philippe Lemenuel; production managers, Marc Golstaub, Bernard Marescot. Reviewed at the George V cinema, Paris, Sept. 25, 1983. Runing time: **110 MINS.**
Alice . . . . Miou-Miou
Philippe . . . . Roger Hanin
Vincent . . . . Eddy Mitchell
Cynthia . . . . Charlotte de Turckheim
Solange . . . . Dominique Lavanant
Simon . . . . Rachid Ferrache
Madam Le Boucau . . . . Renee Saint-Cyr

"Attention, une Femme Peut en Cacher une Autre" is mostly agreeable romantic corn cooked up by writer Jean-Loup Dabadie and served by helmer Georges Lautner. It's the kind of Gallic neo-fairy tale that occasionally strikes a responsive chord in foreign audiences with its nonchalance, good humor and affection for people in love. Dabadie is a past master in all of these, though he does tend to trade a bit much on facilities and cliches of a much exported brand of local bittersweet winsomeness.

His script asks us to believe Miou-Miou is a vivacious young French woman unneurotically leading a double love life. Three days a week she's a surgeon's assistant in Paris, happily married to a boisterous French Algerian pilot (Roger Hanin), with whom she has a young (precocious) son.

The rest of the week she's a therapist in a Normandy town where she's no less happily shacked up with a cuddly schoolteacher (Eddy Mitchell), and their two kids. Of course, the real feat here is that neither male is aware of the other's existence for a long while. And when the obligatory plot complications do come along, both men spend the rest of the screen time haggling over who has rights to Miou-Miou.

It's the old French ménage-a-trois situation, without any real insight or proximity to real life to give it any density, but the Dabadie confection has its fair share of deft comic and sentimental vignettes to make it a relaxing sit-through.

Miou-Miou, engaging when she's not trying to be the heavyweight dramatic actress, here rides nicely on her natural sweetness and warmth, skimming over the artificial makeup of her personage. Hanin overacts with his usual Mediterranean panache. Mitchell, one of France's biggest rock singers, confirms a genuine acting sensibility and phlegmatic comedic skill. In subsidiary parts as Miou-Miou's two girlfriends, both trying to make do with exasperating romantic situations, Charlotte de Turckheim and the wryly kooky Dominique Lavanant add positively .

Director Lautner, who's worked in a variety of genres in his recent pictures, has given script and actors attention and feeling to make this his best helming assignment in a long time. He has in turn been served well by composer Philippe Sarde and lenser Henri Decae.

—Len.

De Illusionist
(The Illusionist)
(DUTCH-COLOR)

Utrecht, Oct. 1.

A Jos Stelling Filmproducties production. Produced and directed by Stelling. Features entire cast. Executive producers, Bart De Groot, Stanley Hillebrandt. Screenplay, Freek De Jonge, Stelling, based on story by DeJonge; camera (color), Theo Van De Sande; editor, Rimko Haanstra; music, Willem Beruker; sound, Bert Flantua; art director, Gert Brinkers. Reviewed at Dutch Film Days, Utrecht, Sept. 30, 83. Running time: **90 MINS.**
The Illusionist ....Freek De Jonge
His brother ....Jim Van Der Woude
His mother ....Catrien Wolthuizen
His father ....Gerard Thoolen
His grandfather ....Carel Lapere
Magician.......:..........Craig Eubanks
His assistant ....Gerrie Van Der Klei

An international pic, inasmuch as it contains no dialog, an original story, intriguing storytelling, beautiful photography, ingenious editing, and a bravura performance by its lead, Freek De Jonge, should ensure boxoffice possibilities for this film in many countries, provided marketing is done with some imagination.

Director Jos Stelling's first feature ("Mariken Ban Nieumaghen") was in the Cannes competition in 1975 and his biopic of Rembrandt won some international prizes. Both features were distributed widely and owed their success mainly to the imagery.

De Jonge, very popular in the Netherlands through his work on stage and tv, is a mixture of stand-up comic and clown, keyed to verbal dexterity and incisive and satirical treatment of serious themes, in combination with pratfall humor.

"The Illusionist" is his first film. He and Stelling took the risk of excluding dialog, and succeeded. Due to a clever script and an imaginative score, the viewer hardly realizes there are no words. Phenomenal editing of Rimlo Haanstra makes it possible to follow without any difficulty the fantastical imaginings of a character who — right at the beginning of the film — is vaguely seen looking around the door.

Reality and illusion seemlessly fuse in the story of two brothers, one with narrow-minded, bigoted, penny-pinching and soul-cramping ideas and ambitions, and the younger one, mentally retarded, a child in a man's body.

Latter is sent to a mental hospital. The older son, the illusionist, tries to rescue him. Told this way, it's not much of a story. But the film is often very funny, sometimes melancholy, creepy at times and is always fascinating.

There are cunning running gags. There's clowning. There are references to the Bible (Cain and Abel). And there are, in addition to De Jonge, excellent performances, many (as always in Stelling's films) by amateurs.

Catrien Wolthuizen, a provincial amateur actress, scores as the illusionist's mother. The meeting of De Jonge (with a strict Puritanical background) and Stelling (impulsive, from a more lighthearted Catholic family) sparks off a brilliant interplay of thoughts and feelings.

The images of Stelling's former pics have been compared with medieval paintings, for instance Breughel. This time they occasionally remind of Fellini, but Stelling did not merely imitate.

The main virtue of the film is that it's never heavy-handed or preachy, due to Stelling's imaginative helming and De Jonge's writing and acting. *—Wall.*

The Dead Zone
(COLOR)

Solid thriller for the fright market.

A Paramount Pictures release of a Dino DeLaurentiis Corp. production. Produced by Debra Hill. Directed by David Cronenberg. Features entire cast. Screenplay, Jeffrey Boam, from Stephen King's novel; camera (Technicolor), Mark Irwin; editor, Ronald Sanders; music, Michael Kamen; sound, Bryan Day; assistant director, John Board; production manager, John M. Eckert; production design, Carol Spier; art direction, Barbara Dunphy; set decoration, Tom Coulter; special effects coordinator, Jon Belyeu; underwater camera, John Stoneman; stunt coordinators, Dick Warlock, Carey Loftin. Reviewed at Paramount screening room, N.Y., Sept. 30, 1983. (MPAA Rating: R). Running time: **102 MINS.**
Johnny Smith ....Christopher Walken
Sarah Bracknell ....Brooke Adams
Sheriff Bannerman ....Tom Skerritt
Dr. Sam Weizak ....Herbert Lom
Roger Stuart ....Anthony Zerbe
Henrietta Dodd ....Colleen Dewhurst
Greg Stillson................Martin Sheen
Frank Dodd ....Nicholas Campbell
Herb Smith ....Sean Sullivan
Vera Smith ....Jackie Burroughs
Sonny Elliman ....Geza Kovacs
Alma Frechette............Roberta Weiss
Chris Stuart ....Simon Craig

Joining the half-dozen shock-oriented directors who have filmed novelist Stephen King's horror and suspense yarns, David Cronenberg turns "The Dead Zone" into an accomplished psychological thriller sure to scare up a healthy share of Halloween-frame b.o.

Cronenberg seems to have been the logical choice to film "The Dead Zone," one of King's less gruesome but no less bone-chilling works. Shunning the explosive excesses in "Scanners" and "Videodrome," the Toronto filmmaker eases up on the violent visuals (but not the tension) and gets some appealing performances to depict the inner turmoil of his lead character.

In this case, his (and King's) focus is Johnny Smith, a shy schoolteacher who snaps out of a long coma with the questionable gift of second sight. Convincingly played by Christopher Walken, Johnny can see into anybody's past or future merely by grasping the person's hand. The "dead zone," not clearly defined in the pic, seems to refer to the brain damage that enables him to change the outcome of events he "sees" and knows will result in catastrophe.

Five years after his Volkswagen crashes into a milk truck (in one of the film's several dynamically staged scenes), Johnny awakens in a hospital under the care of Dr. Weizak (Herbert Lom). His first premonition enables a nurse to save her daughter from a domestic conflagration. The news of the patient's ESP spreads quickly and he experiences some pretty horrible incidents, inside and outside his head.

Although Cronenberg, scripter Jeffrey Boam, and producer Debra Hill (as an uncredited contributor) trim and condense King's manifold narrative in the right places, a lot happens in the 102-minute suspenser. There's the girlfriend (Brooke Adams) Johnny loses to his near-fatal accident and regains for awhile. There's also a sheriff (Tom Skerritt) who desperately needs a psychic solution to crack a murder case, and the wealthy businessman (Anthony Zerbe) who hires Johnny to tutor his problem son (Simon Craig).

As it turns out in the smoothly paced series of events, each of Johnny's clairvoyant spells makes him weaker and weaker. The prospect of a slow death amid the widely publicized pressures of the Power spurs him to a courageous but fatal deed to spoil the political fortunes of a secretly vile populist politician, Greg Stillson (Martin Sheen).

The scene establishing Stillson's cruelty and corruption is another example of the pic's finely crafted episodes. Walken's alternately eerie and eye-popping flashbacks and flashforwards also create enough intensity to earn the pic's R rating. Walken links each episode together quite well, accurately conveying the character's growing mental, physical and emotional anguish. He also makes it quite easy to suspend disbelief in such phenomena.

Quality of the remaining cast's work varies. Zerbe, Skerritt and Sheen all stand out in the crowded ensemble. Doctor Lom, g.f. Adams and parents Jackie Burroughs and Sean Sullivan add nothing to serviceable characters. Colleen Dewhurst gives her terse cameo a lot of impact as the protective mother of Skerritt's murderous deputy (Nicholas Campbell).

Cinematographer Mark Irwin films the story (which does include one grisly scene, that of Campbell's suicide by scissors) in grainy faded color. He and production designer Carol Spier strike the right mood with the cold rural settings. Michael Kamen's music works well, too.

Among Brian DePalma ("Carrie"), Tobe Hooper ("Salem's Lot," a tv MOW), Stanley Kubrick ("The Shining") and Lewis Teague ("Cujo"), Cronenberg's "The Dead Zone" stands as one of the better King adaptations. Those down the pike include the upcoming "Christine," by John Carpenter, "Firestarter" by Mark Lester, and, in the pre-production stage, George Romero's "The Stand." *—Binn.*

Karantin
(Quarantine)
(RUSSIAN-COLOR)

Vancouver, Oct. 11.

A Gorky Studio Production. Released by Sovexportfilm. Directed by Ilya Frez. Features entire cast. Screenplay, G. Sherbacova; camera (color), A. Kirillov; music, A. Rybnikov. No further credits available. Reviewed at Robson Square Cinema Vancouver (2d Annual Vancouver Kidfest), Oct. 2, 1983. Running time: **81 MINS.**
With Lila Kremer, E. Simonova, Y. Duvanov, S. Nemoliaeva, Y. Bogatriov.

Sprightly and gleeful, this fast-paced family comedy deals insouciantly with the grim stuff from which neorealist mellers used to be hewn. A workaholic young couple wrestle with the crisis in day care for their five-year-old Masha, once her kindergarten has been shut down, placed under quarantine. Without that lynchpin of their hectic urban grind the couple fights hammer and tongs.

Though her parents can impose upon the extended family that lives close by — 8 adults, spanning four generations — at times the intrepid tyke is left in the care of coworkers and even subordinates. Mom is a research scientist, dad a museum artisan. Invariably, irrepressible

Masha wanders off unmoored to mix with benevolent oldsters.

A genuine fairytale mood is sustained, though occasionally it has to be force-fed, thanks to a merry pop music score and a wealth of neatly-etched turns from a large cast.

The humor at times strays into that heavy-handed Russian terrain that Western audiences find grotesque. All technical credits are exceptional, when compared with standard Soviet kidpics. The camerawork is particularly confident and showy. An ingratiating look at contemporary Soviet lives that should fare okay in overseas sales.
—*Gran.*

Rumble Fish
(B&W/COLOR)

Visually interesting but overwrought Coppola teen film.

Hollywood, Oct. 5.

A Universal Picture release, produced by Fred Roos and Doug Claybourne. Directed by Francis Coppola. Features entire cast. Exec producer, Coppola. Screenplay, S.E. Hinton, Francis Coppola, based on Hinton's novel; camera (b&w), Stephen H. Burum; editor, Barry Malkin; sound, David Parker; production design, Dean Tavoularis; assistant director, David Valdes; music, Stewart Copeland. Reviewed at Universal Studios, L.A., Oct. 5, 1983. (MPAA Rating: R). Running time: **94 MINS.**
Rusty-James ....Matt Dillon
Motorcycle Boy ....Mickey Rourke
Patty ....Diane Lane
Father ....Dennis Hopper
Cassandra ....Diana Scarwid
Steve ....Vincent Spano
Smokey ....Nicolas Cage
B.J. ....Christopher Penn
Midget ....Larry Fishburne
Patterson ....William Smith

"Rumble Fish" is another Francis Coppola picture that's overwrought and overthought with camera and characters that never quite come together in anything beyond consistently interesting. Like his other adaptation of an S.E. Hinton novel, "The Outsiders," it's probably looking at limited success.

Coppola is certainly too clever to fail at a project as simple as "Fish," but not wise enough to avoid the traps of teenage intellectualism he's trying to appeal to or encourage. Beautifully photographed in black and white by Stephen H. Burum, the picture really doesn't need all the excessive symbolism Coppola tries to cram into it.

For those who want it, however, "Fish" is another able examination of teenage alienation, centered around two brothers who are misfits in the ill-defined urban society they inhabit.

One, Matt Dillon, is a young tough inspired to no good purposes by an older brother, Mickey Rourke, once the toughest but now a bit of an addled eccentric,

though remaining a hero to neighborhood thugs.

It's pretty clear from the start that Rourke has reached the end and it's only a question of how Dillon will turn out. But it's hard to care all that much, even if the issue were resolved, which it isn't.

Dillon and Rourke, though, turn in good performances as does Dennis Hopper as their drunken father and Diane Lane as Dillon's dumped-on girlfriend. Diana Scarwid is unfortunately underused as an addict hung up on Rourke. Nicolas Cage is a strong presence with a small part that's potentially more interesting than the brothers, but never pursued.

Title and a lot of the symbolism stem from Siamese fighting fish (photographed in color composite shots) which are unable to coexist with their fellows, or even an image of themselves. But as nature-film documentarians know, it's never a good idea to attribute human motives to wildlife behavior. And it can be equally dangerous to try the reverse. — *Har.*

Bush Christmas
(AUSTRALIAN-COLOR)

Sydney, Oct. 11.

A Hoyts Release of a Bush Christmas Production, in association with the Queensland Film Corporation. Produced by Gilda Baracchi, Paul Barron. Directed by Henri Safran. Features entire cast. Screenplay, Ted Roberts; camera (color), Malcolm Richards, Ross Berryman; editor, Ron Williams; music, Mike Perjanik; sound, Don Connolly; production design, Darrell Lass. Reviewed at Film Australia, Lindfield, July 1, 1983. Running Time: **91 MINS.**
Bill..........................John Ewart
Sly...........................John Howard
Helen.......................Nicole Kidman
Michael......................Mark Spain
Manalpuy.......................Manalpuy
Johnny...................James Wingrove
Father......................Peter Sumner
Mother...................Vineta O'Malley

"Bush Christmas" is one of the most enjoyable family films yet made in Australia and confirms that director Henri Safran, who also made "Storm Boy," has a talent for this kind of film. Set in the lush Koorabyn Valley in Queensland, the story's about a trio of plucky kids who, with a stoical Aboriginal stockman, track down the two thieves who stole their prize horse, Prince, without whom their father can't hope to win the New Year's Day horserace and save his farm.

For Northern Hemisphere audiences, the exoticism of a swelteringly hot Christmas down under will add plenty of novelty to the film; the film includes a visitor from England, Michael (played by a chubby Mark Spain) in order to wonder at the tradition of eating hot meals and having Christmas trees with cotton-wool snow despite the high temperatures, and also to pine for a white Christmas

back home. The local kids are played by Nicole Kidman, very good as the adolescent leader of the group who's just starting to become a bit conscious of her sex, and cheeky young James Wingrove, as resourceful a moppet as Disney ever introduced. Manalpuy is also effective as the Aboriginal boy who helps them, catching them lizards and even grubs to eat.

The thieves are played for laughs: Bill (John Ewart) is short and fat while Sly (John Howard) is tall and thin. Both players get plenty of laughs from their roles, and wind up being wholly sympathetic. Other adult roles are less persuasively drawn. In addition to its humor, film has plenty of suspense, including a scene where three of the children are trapped in a pit filling up with water, and the climactic horse-race. Needless to say, there's a happy ending.

Ted Roberts' screenplay is credited as being adapted from the original 1946 Rank Organization film; this is not strictly accurate, as the original version of "Bush Christmas" was produced by the Children's Film Foundation and released in Britain by Rank (Universal in the U.S.); nowhere in the remake is credit given to the original's writer-producer-director, Ralph Smart, who is believed to be living in Queensland. (Aussie actor Chips Rafferty was the original villain.) Director Safran gives the film plenty of polish and seems more at home here than with his more prestigious projects with imported actors. Location shooting by Malcolm Richards and Ross Berryman is an added plus, though Mike Perjanik's music is jarring at times.

Given the right promotion, pic should do very well locally in school holidays and could also find a very positive overseas response.
—*Strat.*

San Sebastian

Le Voyage D'Hiver
(Winter Journey)
(BELGIAN-COLOR)

San Sebastian, Sept. 18.

A Les Films d'Hiver production. Directed by Marian Handwerker. Features entire cast. Screenplay, Luc Jabon; editor, Dominique Van Goleti; camera (Fuji-color), Walter Van den Ende; sets, Chris Corniz; music, Marc Herouet. Reviewed at Cine Miramar (San Sebastian), Sept. 17, '83. Running time: **116 MINS.**
Adam ....Patrick Bauchau
Salomon ....Miescyslaw Voit
Corbin ....Christian Barbier
Rachel ....Simone Barry
Also: Jean Franval, Silvie Miuhaud, Francois Beukelaers.

The first half hour of this East-West spy yarn is reminiscent of the best filmic versions of John Le Carré's work, but pic gets bogged down in sub-plots, jejune philo-

sophizings on the fate of mankind and story intricacies which were often impossible to follow. Certainly, pruning 20 minutes of its excessive running time wouldn't have hurt.

Salomon is an aging Russian agent who worked in the Brussels Resistance movement during World War II and then went to live in Russia. Now, in his 60s, he is sent to West Berlin to liquidate a political target and obtain a secret notebook containing a list of names. But Salomon decides not to return to the East, and journeys to Belgium to look up a hospitalized former flame and her son, who may also be his.

Story takes on endless twists involving Russian agents trying to kill Salomon, Belgian agents getting in on the act, the son's break-up with his wife, a young daughter, etc. It adds up to a confused jumble performed under a constant air of mystery; explanations are few and far between and never satisfactory.

Best part is when Salomon, well acted by Miescyslaw Voit, is on screen as the weary, aging agent. About halfway through the film he is assassinated by the Russians, and the lead passes to his rather bland son; interest drops. Instead of the film ending there, it drags on for over a half hour. At the end we learn Salomon is miraculously alive, but by then curiosity in clearing up the murky muddle of motivations and past actions has evaporated. —*Besa.*

Los Enemigos
(The Enemies)
(ARGENTINE-COLOR)

San Sebastian, Sept. 18.

An E.C. Cine S.R.L. production. Produced and directed by Eduardo Calcagno. Screenplay, Alan Paulus from an original idea by Edardo Calcagno; camera (Eastmancolor), Roberto Mateo; editor, Juan Carlos Macias; sets, Abel Faccello; sound, Anibal Libenson; costumes, Nora Renan. Reviewed at Cine Miramar (San Sebstian), Sept. 17, '83. Running time: **94 MINS.**
Carlos Maria ....Ulises Dumont
The Mother ....Nelly Prono
Ana ....Mirtha Busnelli
Herminia....................Esther Goris
Young couple ....Patricia Etcheverry
                     and Mario Luciani
Also: Fernanda Mistral, Vicky Olivares, Sergio Renan, Miguel Angel Sola, Pepe Soriano and Ludovica Squirru.

Despite some nice touches of droll humor and good thesping by Ulises Dumont, Nelly Prono and Mirtha Busnelli, "Los Enemigos" has rather too slight a storyline to make it click; at times yarn is drawn out tediously, veering occasionally from lighthearted character studies and humor to brutal violence.

Story involves a meatball-faced nebish and his saturnine mother. The nonentity, who works in a funeral parlor, has got a job to do a bit part in a film, where he is to play a tough guy and shoot someone. A girlfriend eggs him on in preparing for the role, which he feels incapable of doing. Mother, meanwhile, is obsessed with a young couple that has moved into an apartment across the street and who spend a large part of the day making love with their blinds up.

Mother urges her son, Carlos Maria, to "do something" about the scandalous goings-on the other side of the block, but he is far too timid to comply. The mother, and the film, turn nasty when in her wrath mama enlists the help of an employee of the funeral parlor, who arranges for three thugs to smash up the lovers and their apartment, a deed witnessed with glee by the old crone.

Pic ends somewhat out of character with the son helping his mother to shoot the couple through the window, a far too contrived ending. Pic might have been better if helmer had concentrated on the son's would-be career as a bumbling actor. — *Besa.*

La Linea Del Cielo
(Skyline)
(SPANISH-COLOR)

San Sebastian, Sept. 22.

A La Salamandra P.C. production. Written and directed by Fernando Colomo. Camera (Eastmancolor), Angel Luis Fernandez; production director, Antonio Isasi; editor, Miguel Angel Santamaria; associate producer, Ana Huete. Features Antonio Resines, Beatriz Perez-Porro, Jaime Nos, Roy Hoffman, Irene and Whit Stillman, Patricia Cisarano. Reviewed at Cine Victoria Eugenia (San Sebastian), Sept. 21, '83. Running time: 83 MINS.

Helmer Fernando Colomo, best known for his 1980 film "La Mano Negra," has tackled a most promising subject, the difficulties foreign talent have breaking into the U.S. scene. But Colomo never comes to grips with it and his film is a deadpan, outsider's view of a world he doesn't even begin to understand.

As a comedy, the film is a complete dud, as Antonio Resines stumbles through repetitive scenes and wafer-thin comic situations which are embarrassingly bad. In addition, half the film is in English, meaning that in Spain it will either have to be re-dubbed or run with subtitles. In latter case it signifies its elimination from all but "art circuits."

Story, the little there is of it, concerns a Spanish photographer (not once in the film do we ever see him with a camera), who arrives in New York ingenuously trying to sell photos of Gotham buildings to Life or Newsweek. Film is shot almost entirely in a loft in Greenwich Village; the only exteriors are a few scenes in Village streets and on

the docks near the Battery. After a few minor misadventures, useless English classes, abortive efforts at making it with a Catalan girl, the photog wisely decides to return to Madrid.

Colomo, in fact, has got together a few of his friends and acquaintances in New york including sales rep Whit Stillman, and haphazardly shot the footage at their homes. The result, not surprisingly, is wholly amateurish. With the exception of deadpan Resines, none others in cast seem to have thesping experience. An occasional touch of wry humor is a mere grain of sand in the sea of inanity.
— *Besa.*

La Guerre Des Demoiselles
(The Young Ladies' War)
(FRENCH-COLOR)

San Sebastian, Sept. 21.

FR3 and Adriafilm (Jean-Yves Rondiere) coproduction. Directed by Jacques Nichet. Screenplay, Nichet, Christian Guillon and J.L. Benoit; camera (color), Guillon; editor, Catherine Quesemand; costumes, Alain Chambon; sets, Christine Rabot-Pinson; music, Georges and Pierre-Maria Baux; sound, Claude Bertrand. Features Jean-Paul Roussillon, Jean-Quentin Chatelain, Roger Souza, Gilbert Gilles, Albert Icart, Jean-Louis Benoit, Anne Clement. Reviewed at Cine Victoria Eugenia (San Sebastian), Sept. 20, '83. Running time: 90 MINS.

The "young ladies" of the title refer to French peasants who, in 1830, dress up as men to fight, kill and terrorize the inhabitants of the remote Ariege region of France. Their purpose is to prevent the industrialization of the area by new metal forges.

The subject as such has its possibilities and the first 10 minutes, as a new judge is sent to the village of Saint-Girons and closely escapes with his life as his cart driver is set upon by the "ladies," is promising enough. But after that nothing much else happens. We never see the "demoiselles" in action, their leader seems a dull country bumpkin who never utters a word when in captivity, and scenes seemingly leading up to some sort of activity suddenly fizzle out to dwell on further yakking or excruciatingly slow camera shots.

By the end of the film, when the judge has decided to throw in the towel and leave the district, we really know as little as we did at the beginning. Moreover, talk among the villagers is in a local dialect (Languedoc), which is incomprehensible to the judge and must be translated by his aides, which makes the pace even more plodding.

Above all, there is no story development and no dramatic sense in the film so the 90 minutes seem like three hours. — *Besa.*

Peri Erotos
(On Love)
(GREEK-B&W)

San Sebastian, Sept. 19.

A Maria Gavala, Thodoros Soumas and directed by Gavala and Soumas. Features entire cast. Camera (black & white), Philippos Koutsaftis; editor, Despina Danae Maroulakou, sound, Marinos Athanassopoulos and Pavlo Sidropoulos. Reviewed at Cine Miramar/San Sebastian), Sept. 18, '83. Running time; 83 MINS.

Chrysanthe .... Yota Festa
Jason .... Yannis Zavradinos
Anna .... Hara Angeloussi
Areti .... Sofia Kakarelidou
Also: Iphigenia Mela, Costis Koutsourelis.

Two neophyte directors have a fling at the subject of love and sex, outcome being uneven and, in the second yarn, overlong. Using a grainy 16m black and white stock and a shoestring budget, first portion of film directed by Maria Gavala limns a touching miniature portrait of a young girl who has run away from her village and in Athens has had her first unsuccessful fling at love and sex. Action is confined to one day in the girl's life, starting from the time she awakens in a girlfriend's bed through an encounter with her erstwhile lover, the writing of a letter to her parents and a chat with a male friend who describes to her the scene-by-scene action of a porno film he has seen out of boredom.

The mood of disappointment and forlorn futility is similarly conveyed in the second part of this film, directed by Theodoros Soumas, anent a would-be novelist who disdains the love of one girl, but vainly quests after that of another; he stakes out the latter's house, spends two hours in front of it each day, only to find that the charmer is already living with someone else. Long, lingering camera technique makes for mounting tedium. Final scene has lovestruck writer determining to convert his experience into the Great Greek Novel.

Both directors happily eschew explicit sex scenes and generally steer clear of undue intellectualizing. Pic is, if anything, non-erotic. Of the two directors, Gavala shows more promise in this, her first feature film. — *Besa.*

La Conquista De Albania
(The Conquest of Albania)
(SPANISH-COLOR)

San Sebastian, Sept. 23.

A Frontera Films Irun S.A. production. Directed by Alfonso Ungria. Features entire cast. Exec producers, Angel Amigo, Luis Calparsoro. Screenplay, Arantxa Urretavizcaya. Angel Amigo, Alfonso Ungria; camera (color), Alfredo Fernandez Mayo; editor, Julio Pena; sets, W. Burmann; special effects, Juan Ramon Molina; music, Alberto Iglesias; songs, Xabier Lasa. Reviewed at Cine Victoria Eugenia, San Sebastian, Sept. 23, '83. Running time: 122 MINS.

Cast: Xabier Elorriaga, Chema Munoz, Klara Badiola, Walter Vidarte, Miguel Arri-

bas, Alicia Sanchez, Enaut Urrestarazu, Patxi Bisquert, Ramon Balenciaga, Ramon Barea, Jesus Sastre, William Layton, Amaia Lasa, Jose Luis Aguirre, Imanol Gaztelumendi, Paco Sagarzazu, Jose Maria Tasso, Roberto Cruz, Paco Sanz.

This would-be historical epic is the biggest film ever financed by the Basques and presumably is intended as a flagship for other productions to follow. Scripters have fished out an obscure episode, an anecdotal footnote, to the history of Navarra (before the unification of Spain in 1492) in which King Carlos II decides to send his brother Luis at the head of a military expedition to conquer Albania, a territory rightfully his as a dowry of Jeanne of Anjou, whom Luis has wed.

Working with $500,000 budget, the producers have attempted to limn a medieval adventure film, but neither do they have the physical facilities to pull that off, nor a tight-enough script to prevent the two-hour-plus film from sinking into a sea of tedium.

Rather than movement, action and drama there are endless palavers and static camerawork as personages listlessly walk in and out of the frames, grandiloquently yak away, and sing songs about their homeland. When the battle scene finally comes, after an hour and a half of dull preliminaries, it falls pathetically short of expectations. The Basque "army" seems to number 30 men, and the enemy even less. The expedition's leader, Luis, has his hand lopped off and dies in the arms of his wife. Whereupon the Basques wisely decide to return home. Why the producers should have chosen such a downbeat story is a mystery.

Though Alfonso Ungria has helmed some good films in the past, and thesp Xabier Elorriaga has put in good performances in other Spanish films, both seems to be hopelessly adrift in this pointless film. Even as an exaltation of the Basques it falls short of its mark. About the only breath of life in the film is thesp Walter Vidarte, who plays a tough captain in the army.

Even in a shortened version, pic will be a tough sell, though some may be hoodwinked by pressbook and promo reel. —*Besa.*

Vestida En Azul
(Dressed In Blue)
(SPANISH-DOCU-COLOR)

San Sebastian, Sept. 19.

A Serva Films S.A. production. Written and directed by Antonio Gimenez-Rico. Camera (Eastmancolor), Teo Escamilla; editor, Jose Antonio Rojo; sound, Bernardo Menz and Carlos Faruolo. Features Lorenzo Arana Orellano, Rene Amor Fernandez, Jose Antonio Sanchez, Francisco Perez de los Cobos Avila, Juan Muñoz Santiago, Jose Ruiz Orejon Casado. Reviewed at Cine Victoria Eugenia (San Sebastian), Sept. 18, '83. Running time: 96 MINS.

Docu concerns transvestites in Madrid, their lives, passions, fears and aspirations via interviews, friends and even families. Subjects — about a half-dozen are interviewed — all work as male prostitutes and supplement their income working in night clubs and shows.

Helmer Gimenez Rico focuses mostly on the light side of the transvestites' lives, showing them in a jocular vein as they reminisce about the past and kid about the present. Most striking sequence is filming of chest surgery in which the patient has silicone breasts medically implanted.

Pic is not a docu in the classical sense, but a chatty, intimate portrait of the transvestites' lives and opinions on their own condition. Some of the interviews are touching, even comical and as such might be of some interest for tv and cable pickup. — Besa.

Kouzelne Dobrodruzstvi

(Romantic Story)
(CZECH-COLOR)

San Sebastian, Sept. 21.

Directed by Antonin Kachlik. Screenplay, Kachlik and J. Hanzlik based on the novel by Alain Fournier, "Les Grandes Meaulnes;" camera (color), Jaroslav Kucera; sets, Boris Moravec; music, Oldrich Flosman; editor, Jaromir Janacek; sound, R.M. Novotny. Features David Prachar, Ivan Gogal, Julie Juristova, Zdenek Rehor, Ondrej Pavelka, Valerie Zawadska, Frank Towen. Reviewed at Cine Victoria Eugenia (San Sebastian), Sept. 20, '83. Running time: 105 MINS.

Romantic meller is set in the 19th century anent dreams and loves of a student. Slow pacing and confusing flashbacks make for a muddled yarn, served to us piecemeal. Despite beautiful sets, scenery and lensing, story is far too thin to hold interest. Pic is dragged out with agonizing torpor.

Student has multiple escapades, meets lovely bucolic girls, all of them statuesque, while dream and reality are jumbled together.

He leaves one of the beauties pregnant, but a friend marries her, only to have the student return several years later to claim the offspring.

Technical credits are excellent, acting stiff and story deadly dull. (Novel was previously filmed in France in 1967 by Jean-Gabriel Albicocco, released in the U.S. as "The Wanderer," a critically-lauded picture starring Brigitte Fossey. —Besa.

Green
(ISRAELI-COLOR)

San Sebastian, Sept. 20.

Written and directed by Gideon Kolirin. Camera (color), Josef Wajn; editor, Zion Abrahyam; music, Arik Rudich; sets, Emanuel Amrami; sound, Itammar Ben Yaacov. Features Josef Shiloach, Aliva Paz, Peter Freistadt, Amos Lavi, Israel Gorion, Rolf Brin. Reviewed at Cine Miramar (San Sebastian), Sept. 19, '83. Running time: 90 MINS.

This is a sloppily made, amateurish and totally confusing film about a private eye trying to solve a mystery involving the closing down of a textile mill. Technically, scenes are handled so badly as to be unbelievable; the bad guys drive around in a broken-down Volkswagen, the detective is physically unattractive and the constant sex skits are an ordeal to watch.

The production values of this pathetic film are so poor that when a warehouse has to be blown up, the camera moves away from the building and all we hear is the sound. This is the sort of film where you can see the passerby turning around to look curiously at the scene being shot. Thesping is as bad as the script and direction are clumsy. —Besa.

N.Y. Film Festival

Last Night At The Alamo
(B&W-16m)

Earnest but claustrophobic regional slice-of-life.

An Alamo Films production. Executive producer, Ed Hugetz. Produced by Kim Henkel. Directed by Pennell. Features entire cast. Screenplay, Henkel; camera (b&w), Brian Huberman, Eric A. Edwards; editor, Henkel, Pennell; music, Chuck Pinnell, Wayne Bell; sound, Philip Davis; assistant director, John Hayes; production manager-associate producer, Tina Brawner; art direction, Fletcher Mackey. Reviewed at Alice Tully Hall, N.Y. Film Festival, Oct. 1, 1983. (No MPAA Rating). Running time: 80 MINS.

Cowboy Regan .... Sonny Carl Davis
Claude .... Louis Perryman
Ichabod .... Steve Matilla
Mary .... Tina-Bess Hubbard
Janice .... Doris Hargrave
Steve .... J. Michael Hammond
Lisa .... Amanda LaMar
Ginger .... Peggy Pinnell
Lionel .... Kim Henkel

Also with: David Schied, George Pheneger, Henry Wideman, John Heaner, Ernest Huerta, Pam Feight.

"Last Night At The Alamo" is a low-budget Texas film that boasts a lot of actors' energy but lacks the cinematic style to let it escape from the specialized category. With nearly all the action set in a small Houston bar, pic perilously recalls a Southern-fried "Iceman Cometh."

Filmmakers Eagle Pennell and Kim Henkel (latter a co-scripter of Tobe Hooper's "The Texas Chainsaw Massacre") are fans of "The Wild Bunch," but what they have taken from that film is not its style or themes but rather the folksy, vibrant dialog of Walon Green and Sam Peckinpah. This gives "Alamo" considerable verbal texture, as characters carry on in local argot or chat about clothing bought at the "Monkey Ward's" department store.

Opening reel is so densely packed with four-letter expletives that

the initially disarming device becomes tiresome. So, too, do the players, declaiming endlessly in the pipe dreams and complaints manner of barflies. Ichabod (Steve Matilla) is a scrawny young man, shooting pool, picking fights and trying to scoot his gal Mary (Tina-Bess Hubbard) off to the nearest hot-sheets motel. Claude (Louis Perryman) is a loud and foul-mouthed guy with wife trouble, constantly (and tediously) on the phone at the Alamo bar.

A late arrival is made by Cowboy Regan (Sonny Carl Davis), a smug, egocentric guy who believes he can "save" the Alamo, which has been sold by its owner and is due for immediate demolition to make way for high-rise buildings, appealing by phone to his old college roommate and now a state representative. Though he beats up an old high school rival Steve (J. Michael Hammond) who dares to doubt this claim, the effort to save the bar is, of course, just another pipe dream.

Director Pennell errs in shooting this film in a style reminiscent of live tv drama in the 1950s: low-key (for high contrast) lighting in black-and-white and claustrophobic framing (such as a foreground head, typically Claude's on the phone, dominating mid-ground action). Cumulative effect is oppressive. His actors are on too long a leash, with Louis Perryman's initially entertaining explosive swearing routine ending up sounding like a Steve Landesburg stand-up parody of a "good ole boy" dialect.

Lead player Davis, a balding young actor resembling Robert Stack and Robert Duvall, carries much of picture by underplaying compared to the rest of the cast. Steve Matilla as "don't call me Ichabod" is quite funny in small doses and scripter Henkel has written himself in a cute John Sayles-esque deadpan role as Lionel, so laconic a critter that everyone else has to tell his personal anecdotes for him. The women's roles are seriously underwritten.

Tech credits are acceptable, though the direct sound-recorded dialect gets a bit thick during some of the shouting matches. — Lor.

Seeing Red
(DOCU-COLOR/B&W-16m)

Good and affectionate, perhaps too affectionate, portrait of U.S. Communists.

A Heartland Productions film. No distributor. Produced and directed by James Klein and Julia Reichert. Camera (color), Stephen Lighthill, Sandi Sissel, Martin Duckworth; archival research, Martha Olson; associate producer, Aaron Ezekiel; sound, Klein; assistant camera, Judy Hoffman, Jocelyn Coblenz, Cathy Dorsey; sound editor, Joan Morris; consulting editors, Deborah Shaffer, Susan Martin, Jill Godmilow; additional camera, Nancy Schreiber, Gordon Quinn; production managers, Andrea Primdahl, Martha Olson, Ezekiel; additional archival research, Pierce Rafferty, Dolores Neuman, Tony Heriza, Anne Bohlen, Lorraine Gray; music consultant, David K. Dunaway; recording mixer, Tom Fleischman; voices, Fio Lorenz, Leon Hollster. Reviewed at Alice Tully Hall, N.Y., Sept. 28, 1982. Running time: 100 MINS.

With: Bill Bailey, Dorothy Healey, Howard "Stretch" Johnson, Pete Seeger, Stanley Postak, Rose Krysak; also, Ronald Reagan, Richard Nixon, Hubert Humphrey, J. Edgar Hoover, Herbert Philbrick.

Taking viewers on a tour of nearly 50 years of Communist Party activity on these shores, Ohio-based filmmakers Julia Reichert and James Klein come up with a generally absorbing and enlightening docu on American citizens who chose Karl Marx over capitalism. This N.Y. Film Fest entry will best find its audience on the international film fest circuit and Public Television.

Theatrical release in any market other than the largest urban areas with a liberal-minded populace will be chancey even though the filmmakers apparently succeeded in what they set out to do. Their interviews of some 400 present and former U.S. Communists (conducted over the past five years) have been distilled into an affectionate portrait of thinking men and women who merely wanted to close the cavernous gap between wealth and poverty.

The idea that all Communists were villainous radicals craving coups d'etat is quickly dispelled in the recently conducted interviews with selected party members. The directors make it easy to like, for example, Irish longshoreman Bill Bailey, black college prof Stretch Johnson, folk singer Pete Seeger, and petite union organizer Dorothy Healey. Articulate, and gifted with a sense of humor, they are as charismatic as (but a bit younger than) the witnesses in Warren Beatty's "Reds."

"Seeing Red," subtitled "Stories Of American Communists," also recalls "Atomic Cafe" with its discovery and use of dramatic and comedic archive footage and jaunty period music. ("Cafe" codirector Pierce Rafferty gets a research credit here.)

However, the docu falls victim to the cliche use of the post-World War II exploits of Richard Nixon, seen here cutting his political teeth during the Red Scare. Have any of the agit-prop docu makers ever tried to interview Nixon today rather than rely on outdated film? Even Nixon must have second thoughts on the era and his own public behavior.

Likewise, additional vault footage depicts the anti-Red postures of Ronald Reagan, Harry Truman, J. Edgar Hoover, et al., but for reasons of longevity and the directors' focus, only the American Communists have the opportunity to discuss their beliefs and behavior with the benefit of hindsight. Significantly, the pic establishes that some of the former Reds didn't want to be interviewed because they wished to keep their affiliation a secret, while many of the witnesses remain party members.

"Seeing Red" takes a dramatic turn toward the 100-minute pic's conclusion when it covers the destructive blows to the Communist Party USA. A lion's share of the party's 1,000,000 members who enlisted between 1930 and 1950 quit following Nikita Khruschev's revelations of Josef Stalin's murderous purges. The filmmakers capture the gamut of reactions from total alienation to apologistic resignation.

As revealed at a press conference following the pic's screening at the N.Y. Film Fest, "Seeing Red" is open to criticism for glossing over the U.S. Communist Party's faults, for example, the lack of democratic structure and the line of command stretching from Moscow. Still, the pic allowed at one point that the party harbored "its own seeds of destruction."

On the other hand, "Seeing Red" traces the party's legacy as the arguable sower of the seeds of Social Security, unemployment insurance, and civil rights. Yet, the pic's strength is not the pros and cons of Communism and capitalism, or U.S. Communism and Soviet Communism, but the ideological growth of the steel mill workers, printers, auto makers, secretaries, farmers and other workers who are profiled herein.—*Binn.*

Mélies Et Ses Contemporaires
(Mélies)
(FRENCH COMPILATION-B&W/COLOR)

A Service des Archives du Film, Centre National de la Cinématograhie (Bois d'Arcy) compilations, organized by Franz Schmitt. Reviewed at Museum of Modern Art, N.Y., Oct. 2, 1983. Running time: **124 MINS.**

"Mélies And His Contemporaries" is a valuable compilation film comprising 36 short motion pictures produced between 1896 and 1909. Prepared in 1981 under the supervision of Franz Schmitt at the French film archive in Bois d'Arcy, feature presents the films in their complete form and is of definite interest to students and buffs.

It is almost a truism in film history that fantasy films have a lasting impact while realistic pictures become dated. Certainly, supernatural, horror, science fiction and fantasy films produced in every era are continuously being revived and treasured by fans of these genres, while most contemporary-themed (and lacking fantasy elements) films, even those winning awards and great initial popularity, are considered passé by succeeding generations. One has only to look at the youth-oriented pictures of slightly over a decade ago (e.g. "Easy Rider"), which are rarely shown or requested today.

The trick films of pioneer Georges Melies and his peers that are complied here further bolster this notion, as their highly-accomplished special effects and editing gimmickry are still fascinating after 80 years. By contrast, more realistic shorts in the compilation are mainly of interest due to preserving the look of an earlier locale or era, rather than for content.

The 15 Melies pictures included here number among them his 1902 "A Trip To The Moon," probably the most widely-seen (today) of that era's product. It is fascinating to then compare, projected immediately afterwards, the 1903 imitation bearing the same title, directed by Ferdinand Zecca and Lucien Nonguet. Copying Melies' shots and ideas almost frame-for-frame, (including the man-in-the-moon live face), the followup film is even more effective, and sports beautiful color tinting. Director Nonguet also contributes an excellent (and lengthy) 1907 film of "The Dreyfus Affair" which dramatically outshines Melies' static and stilted 1899 pic of the same title.

Elsewhere, Melies' well-matched trick editing, which causes people and objects to appear and disappear at will, his composite photography and other innovations are preserved in funny shorts such as "The Man With The Man With The Rubber Head" (1902), "An Impossible Voyage" (1904) and "Extraordinary Dislocation" (1900) featuring clown André Deed. A very early example of the nudie-cutie is Melies' "After The Ball ... The Tub" (1897) featuring Jehanne D'Arcy stripping for a nude-derrière bath. As a useful historical device, the compilation follows this film with a similar pic by Zecca, "Through The Keyhole" (1902).

Preservation quality of the films on view varies considerably, though several are in beautiful 35m condition. Many tinted and hand-colored pictures (featuring multiple colors in every shot) are quite arresting, particularly Albert Capellani's 1907 pic for Pathé-Freres, "The Sheep's Hoof." This colorful fantasy combines pageantry, the frenzied movement in the frame one rather associates with Melies and numerous fantasy effects (including riding on a huge snail), set in motion when a forest goddess gives the hero a magical sheep's hoof.

Absence of a musical track makes this two-hour silent film more of interest to college campus exhibition rather than general audiences, as evidenced by the restive reaction when unspooled at the Museum of Modern Art to a mainly old folks crowd. —*Lor.*

Vancouver Kidfest

Planeta Na Sukrovishtata
(BULGARIAN-ANIMATED-COLOR)

Vancouver, Oct. 2.

A Bulgariafilm production, (Sofia Studio). Directed by Roumen Petkov. Screenplay, Boris Anghelov, Yossif Peretz. No further credits available. English-language narration. Reviewed at Robson Square Cinema, Vancouver (2d Annual Vancouver Kidfest), Oct. 2, 1983. Running time: **64 MINS.**

Long John Silver running amok in outer space is the best summary of this gaudy and simple-minded animated feature, which may cause Robert Louis Stevenson to turn over in his grave once again.

Felip is a space cadet who gains employment as a cabin boy in the year 2581 A.D. on the space craft Hispanola under Commander Smollett, en route to the fabulous and secret Treasure Planet of Cap'n Flint. Naturally a dog, a peg-leg and a couple of ornery sea-dog types join the cruise.

Animation is rudimentary, using endless lethargic tracking shots and moody zooms. In space, time is tedium, according to Commander Smollett. Ditto in theatres where "Treasure Planet" may unspool. It's truly a pedestrian voyage, populated by grotesque characters whose frantic antics are nicely commented upon in a breezy Yank-style narration. Puny chances of any overseas sales.
— *Gran.*

Was Kostet Der Sieg?
(What Price Victory?)
(AUSTRIAN-COLOR)

Vancouver, Oct. 11.

A Bannert-Film production & release. Directed by Walter Bannert. Features entire cast. Screenplay, Bannert, Klaus Kemetmuller; camera (color), Hans Polak; editor, Bannert; music, Hans Kann. No further credits available. Reviewed at National Film Board Theatre, Vancouver, (2d Annual Vancouver Kidfest), Sept. 29, 1983. Running time: **92 MINS.**

Coach Berger	Heinz Peter Puff
Andreas	Alexander Bauer
Michael	Andras Bauer
Walter	Rene Wrba
Peter	Nikolas Vogel
Heinz	Peter Wundsam
Anna	Eva Furst

This film's key dramatic premise — an overzealous soccer coach who rides roughshod over his wards — is developed with acumen by writer-director Walter Bannert. But though it's a polished and intense production, Bannert's pic suffers from its failure to go no farther than to state, restate and hammer home one more time its theme. It's an allegory about fascism, written small.

Coach Berger is a tyrant left to his own nefarious devices at Kolonitzplatz High School in Vienna. He likes foul play, so long as cheating is instrumental in making his team the champs. Berger sacrifices the physical and mental well-being of his wards, and is totally impervious to their feelings. The school principal colludes with Berger in the crusade.

But what makes Berger tick? Despite the plausibility of the script and the verisimilitude of the players, the film never reveals the roots of the coach's mania. None of his colleagues intervene. No parent protests. Surely all Austrians aren't that soccer crazy?

On the level of sheer filmmaking verve Bannert wins hands down. He handles the kids and the drama impeccably. But, and it's a big but, the storyline is utterly predictable and our villainous coach never has a second of self-doubt, or a thought that might distract him from the soccer field.

Unhappily, the filmmakers are no less single-minded, if not bloody-minded, than Coach Berger. The film wears blinkers akin to those of any sports fanatic who ignores the richness of life outside of athletics. Though "What Price Victory?" is undeniably a solid, thoughtful slice of life delivered with a high gloss, it suffers from too much undisclosed pathology, like a textbook rendition of enthusiasm gone totally off the rails.

Bannert's film will appeal to all ages and especially to sports enthusiasts, even though its intent is harshly critical. Could attract overseas sales for both paycable and vidtape. —*Gran.*

Sensei
(The Teacher)
(JAPANESE-COLOR)

Vancouver, Oct. 11.

An Eizo Kikaku Co. Production. A Daiei release. Directed by Yutaka Ohsawa. Features entire cast. Screenplay, Kou Seki; camera (color), Shun Yamamoto; music, Masaru Sato. No further credits available. Reviewed at National Film Board Theatre, Vancouver (2d Annual Vancouver Kidfest), Sept. 29, 1983. Running time: **100 MINS.**

Takeko Yamaguchi	Megumi Igarashi
Nobuhiko Komine	Yasumasa Miyazaki
Etsuko Komine	Aya Shikaya (Age 7)
	Tomoko Saito (Adult)
Dr. Takada	Kei Yamamoto

The setting of this highly effective tearjerker is the serene, sunlit coastal city of Nagasaki, 27 years after the A-bomb ruined it on Aug.

9, 1945. An epilog brings the viewer up to 1982, enriching the anti-nuclear message of a touching fable. With irony the pic describes itself as being "based upon a true story, but not entirely."

An openly sentimental case history of one of the many, many victims of radiation who continue 40 years later to drop like flies, the film centers upon vivacious schoolteacher Takeko Yamaguchi. A mischievous figure on her motorcycle, she promptly wins over her new pupils. The Komine kids, newcomers to the vicinity, their mother dead and father a workaholic, are particularly under Yamaguchi's sway.

Abruptly the teacher succumbs to aplastic anemia, has to be hospitalized, and dies the usual lingering death. Before her demise Yamaguchi shares with the Komines her experiences on the day the A-bomb was dropped.

Shot in vivid colors with moments of sheer poetry, the pic seemingly suffers from a heroine who is too good to be true. Yet director Yutaka Ohsawa quickly lures the viewer deep inside a naive fairytale with a sting in its denouement. His parable for our times carries a hefty punch.

Simple pans across today's Nagasaki, nestled amid sea and hills, are cleverly interwoven with shots of the setting sun that instantly create a strong sense of foreboding. Had Ohsawa dived headfirst into a morbid account of the tragedy, his film would have flunked the course.

Ingenious monochrome footage powerfully recreates the heroine's exposure to radiation. Her medical regimen is chillingly portrayed, and may be too harsh for some moppets. All technical credits are top notch. An unusually involving kidpic that should earn exposure overseas for its eloquent anti-nuke stance. —Gran.'

Phatikchand
(Phatik And The Juggler)
(INDIAN-COLOR)

Vancouver, Oct. 11.

A.D.K. Films Enterprise Production. Directed by Sandip Ray. Features entire cast. Screenplay, Satyajit Ray, from his own story; camera (color), Soumendu Roy; editor, Dulal Dutta; music, Satyajit Ray. No further credits available. Reviewed at National Film Board Theatre, Vancouver (2d Annual Vancouver Kidfest), Sept. 27, 1983. Running time: 104 MINS.
With Rajib Ganguly, Kamu Mukherji, Biplab Chatterji, Haradhan Bannerji.

Scripted and scored by world-renowned Bengali filmmaker Satyajit Ray, but directed by his cousin Sandip, this atmosphere-laden thriller for kids begins crisply with the abortive kidnaping of a wealthy 12-year-old, Bablu. Swift-

ly the tale degenerates into a leaden-footed pursuit melodrama with its stress upon character. Sandip Ray was his cousin's assistant director on the 1977 "The Chess Players."

After being hijacked by a gang of bumbling crooks, Bablu suffers a concussion during an auto crash which destroys his memory. Adopted by a kindly street entertainer, the boy works as a waiter in a teashop where he is recognized by the gang's leader. The chase is on, though it's more a matter of the tortoise than the hare.

Although lenser Soumendu Roy, a vet colleague of Satyajit Ray, has shot the pic with a classic simplicity, even his deft handiwork fails to salvage the venture from tedium. Director Ray has wisely kept dialog to a minimum during the initial reels, but great dollops of talk bog down the narrative after reel two.

A genuine flaw in the acting is the dimwittedness of the crooks. This pair has a crying need for the proverbial lamp bulbs over their heads as the penny excruciatingly drops whenever there's a decision to be made.

The senior Ray has composed a sprightly score that is melodious throughout. As writer he has fallen into an attitude of condescension towards the moppet audience: he has underestimated their sophistication, and their eager grasp of narrative. A real chore for Western viewers, despite attractive playing from the principals. Little chance of overseas sales. —Gran.

Sonata Pro Zrzku
(Sonata For A Redhead)
(CZECH-COLOR)

Vancouver, Oct. 11.

A Gottwaldov Film Studio Production. A Czechoslovak Filmexport release. Directed by Vit Olmer. Features entire cast. Written by Olmer, Vojtech Vacke; camera (color, Juraj Fandli; editor, Antonin Strojsa; music, Petr Ulrych. No further credits available. Reviewed at Robson Square Cinema, Vancouver (2nd Annual Vancouver kidfest), Oct. 5, 1983. Running time: 79 MINS.
Petra 'Ginger' ......Stanislava Coufalova
Mother ....Ladislava Kozderkova
Prof. Knitl ....Lubor Tokos
Petr.....................Michal Dvorak
Honza ....Matej Forman
Pavel ....Vladimir Vondra
Doriana...............Marketa Valentova

Torn between fame as a concert pianist, fun as a soccer goalkeeper, and a fancy for dashing, blond Pavel, a sophisticated teenager from Prague, heroine Ginger is a run-of-the-mill tomboy, coated with freckles and straight from the storybook cliche factory.

Director Vit Olmer did fashion a superlative kidpic after this one, his 1981 "House of Glass" (Skelneny Dum), a highlight of the 1st Vancouver kidfest. Here his work is routine and lacking in any gen-

uine spark of vitality. The narrative flow is damaged repeatedly by flamboyant dream sequences, and far too many brief scenes that lack pungency.

Clearly all redheads are not doomed to being temperamental and hard to handle. That myth should be put to rest. The torment of first love is not the exclusive domain of carrot tops.

The many soul-destroying piano lessons that Ginger has to take with demanding Prof. Knitl prove also to be an ordeal for the viewer. Olmer's pic has too much bouncy music, which he ill-judgedly attempts to accompany by bouncy visuals to no avail. Lack of real confidence in the kidpic genre would seem to be this writer-director's handicap.

The print suffered from faulty English subtitles. Frequent absurd misspellings and various other errors distract the reader/viewer. Tech credits, otherwise, were routine, although the colors were too strong in green and yellow, lending the print a faded look. Not much chance of any overseas sales, in any format. — Gran.

Richard Pryor Here And Now
(COLOR)

Usual bawdy laughs with some added bite. Good prospects.

Hollywood, Oct. 13.

A Columbia Pictures release. Produced by Bob Parkinson and Andy Friendly. Exec producer, Jim Brown. Written and directed by Richard Pryor. Camera (color), Vincent Singletary, Kenneth A. Patterson, Joe Epperson, Tom Geren, Johnny Simmon, Dave Landry; editor, Raymond Bush; sound, Doug Nelson; assistant director, Bernard Basley. Reviewed at the Academy of Motion Picture Arts & Sciences, Beverly Hills, Oct. 13, 1983. (MPAA rating: R.) Running time: 94 MINS.
Sole performer: Richard Pryor.

As a concert film, "Richard Pryor Here And Now" should attract and please those who appreciate him as a standup comic, meaning many, many. But beyond the ample laughs, there is a beautiful monolog that's so painfully acute it would entrance even those who never laugh at his other stuff.

His third concert film (let's not quibble that the first was actually two), "Here and Now" is a mixture of the ones done before and after the fire that almost killed him. Drug-free and still grateful for a second chance, Pryor remains much more mellow, but less self-examining and contemplative than last year's "Live On Sunset Strip."

But some of the hostility and bite have returned, though well under control. In most of his prepared material, in fact, it barely shows through more than any comedian looking at sex, marriage, racism, drinking, poverty, etc. But when he ad libs or exchanges with the audience, a lot of anger can still be seen lurking.

As usual, there's little of the 94 minutes that could be quoted in what used to be called polite company. But by now all the once-shocking language is so commonplace, it's either barely noticeable or merely repetitious. Sometimes, it seems he's even bored with it and only throwing out what the audience expects, remembering to add the words other comedians used to be fearful of letting slip out.

In any case, it's the concepts that count and Pryor always comes through with those, whatever the subject. Having been clean and dry now for several months, he's especially funny dealing with the foibles of those under the influence.

On top of the laughs, he also displays a deepening sympathy for those doomed by substances. Taking a heroin addict from idle amusing prattle awaiting injection, into the euphoric aftermath and muddled agonies over a life that is getting him close to overdose, Pryor is masterful.

Somewhere down the line is a complete dramatic picture, that could be the truly great film he's been waiting for. —Har.

Hapnimia
(Fun)
(ISRAELI-COLOR)

Tel Aviv, Oct. 18.
A Nachshon Films presentation of a Y.N.I.L. production. Produced by Doron Eran. Directed by Yaud Levanon. Features entire cast. Screenplay, Itzhak Ginsberg; camera (color), Gad Danzig; sound, Ya'akov Goldstein; editor, Irith Raz; production designer, Emmanuel Amrami; music, Ronny Brown, Yorik Ben David. Reviewed at the Limor Cinema, Tel Aviv, July 29, 1983. Running time: 85 MINS.
Cast: Ben Levin, Semadar Kaltchinsky, Alon Abutbul, Sarith Nahum, Uri Vardi, Einath Tzafrir, Zazi Kreiner, Tuvia Dobleru, Shmuel Vilozny, Alex Munte.

The English title of this production indicates the intention of its makers, rather than the result. One more side offspring of the enormously successful "Lemon Popsicle" syndrome, Yaud Levanon's second feature attempts to exploit the obvious penchant of local audiences for youthful romps with sexual, but never very explicit, innuendoes.

An uninspired script, awkward direction and clumsy performances leave little to be recommended, as the insecure plot follows a bunch of teenagers through one year in a boarding school (indeed, the original Hebrew title is "Boarding School"); Intersecting puppy loves, power plays between the boys and charm competitions between the girls lack the slightest inkling of originality with the inexperienced young actors looking sad and lost on the screen.

Still, the picture had a successful run at home, not the least reason being a clever tie-in with the biggest evening paper in Israel (Yaud Levanon is a member of its staff, incidentally) which added a considerable promotion clout to the initial release. —Edna.

Flipper
(Pinball)
(ITALIAN-COLOR)

Venice, Sept. 3.
Produced by Roberto Cicutto for RAI-TV Channel 2 and Aura Film. Stars Andrea Mingardi. Directed by Andrea Barzini. Screenplay by Tullio Pinelli and Andrea Barzini; camera (Eastmancolor), Luigi Verga; editing, Sandro Peticca. Reviewed at the Venice Film Festival, Sept. 2, 1983. Running time: 110 MINS.
Toni Zappa .... Andrea Mingardi
Arnalda .... Luciana Negrini
Aida .... Paola Pitagora
Pio .... Alessandro Haber

A two-hour tv film with a few minutes nipped off for possible theatrical release, "Pinball" was preemed in the Venice Film Festival Italian Showcase. Pic is a first feature by Andrea Barzini, son of writer Luigi. The young helmer's experience with tv documentaries shows through in pic's generally high technical level.

A desire to depict the lazy provincial feeling of the Emilia-Romagna coast has attracted many beginning helmers, going back to Fellini. "I Vitelloni" has been a hard act to follow and neither Luciano Manuzzo's black comedy "Out of Season" nor Barzini's realistic "Pinball" has managed to stir as much interest in the deadbeat natives and bleak winter beaches of these tourist towns.

Pic is a collection of stories about a bunch of friends in their 30s who are drifting apart. Central figure is a local folk singer, Toni Zappa, played by talented crooner Andrea Mingardi. While Zappa faces the trials and humiliations of setting up gigs in discotheques where the kids would rather hear imitation American punk than native talent, his wife Arnalda (Luciana Negrini) has a weird flirtation with the town looney (another sterling cameo for Alessandro Haber). Her rich friend Aida (Paola Pitagora) searches restlessly for some kind of identity, but is booed off the beach when she tries to give a poetry reading. Everybody gets together in their local bar to read letters from Aida's husband, who is running his father's hotel in Dallas.

In spite of its title, pic is not an energetic film; it seems to catch some of the slow pace of its subject. But it has a few inspired moments and a good jazz and rock track (uncredited). Thesping is quite even throughout (Mingardi is notable in his first film role).
— Yung.

Burroughs
(DOCU-COLOR/B&W-16m)

Interesting but overlong portrait of an author and all-around cutup.

A Citifilmworks Inc. production. Produced by Howard Brookner, Alan Yentob. Directed by Brookner. Camera (color, 16m), Richard L. Camp, Mike Southon, James Lebovitz, Tom Dicillo, Brookner, Cathy Dorsey, Larry Shiu; editor, Scott Vickrey, Ben Morris; sound, Jim Jarmusch, Peter Miller, G. Osborne, Edward Novik, Kevin Gordon, David E. Houle, Cathy Barnes, Peter Kuhn; special effects (makeup), Kevin Cloutier, Rob Allen; video camera, Kevin Dowd; b&w films by Antony Balch. Reviewed at Alice Tully Hall, N.Y. Film Festival, Oct. 8, 1983. (No MPAA Rating). Running time: 89 MINS.
With: William S. Burroughs, Allen Ginsberg, Herbert Huncke, William S. Burroughs Jr., James Grauerholz, Terry Southern, Brion Gysin, Lucien Carr, John Giorno, Mortimer Burroughs, Jackie Curtis, Francis Bacon, Otto Belue, Patti Smith, Lauren Hutton.

"Burroughs" is a feature-length examination of William S. Burroughs, the influential novelist who is now doubling as an entertaining reader of excerpts of his work at night club gigs for young audiences who weren't around during his trailblazing days in the 1950s and 1960s. Debuting director Howard Brookner, who expanded this work from a short student film begun five years ago, mixes documentary material with exhibitionist footage of Burroughs the mythmaker, with pruning of some scenes advisable. In its present form, picture deserves non-theatrical, college campus bookings and ultimately public tv usage.

With his verite cameras trailing Burroughs from his current N.Y. "Bunker" flat to his St. Louis, London and Moroccan former stomping grounds, Brookner fleshes out the man's life with recollections by many of his pals and colleagues. Their talking heads' testimony is suspect, however, as when poet Allen Ginsburg turns unconvincing apologist, blaming Burroughs' wife Joan for "egging him on" to a 1951 fatal William Tell-style shooting incident. Burroughs admits to killing his wife and seems honestly remorseful about it.

Interspersed throughout the film are evocative vintage b&w underground scenes of Burroughs, filmed by British helmer Antony Balch (who has the 1973 film "Horror Hospital" to his credit and tried to launch a film version of "Naked Lunch" in 1971). Also highlighting the docu are excerpts of Burroughs reading passages from his works such as "Naked Lunch" and "Nova Express," in a droll, highly amusing manner. Misguided efforts include a staged grand guignol performance for the camera of Burroughs, as Dr. Benway, aided by nurse Jackie Curtis in cutting up a patient with gory special effects one associates with recent horror films.

Low point of the picture consists of interviews with Burroughs' self-styled amanuensis James Grauerholz, a pompous young man who admits to having slept with Burroughs and feeling more like a son to the writer than was the late William S. Burroughs Jr. Brookner also includes morbid footage of Junior, called by one interviewee "the last beatnik" and bent on self-destruction through drugs, liquor, etc.

After a funny start, the film becomes rather dull in its second half with too much footage of Burroughs, obviously enjoying the spotlight. At feature length, this picture could have more efficiently covered his whole circle, including Jack Kerouac who is relegated to a couple of still photos and allusions. Brookner even indulges his subject with a lengthy scene showing the iconoclast demonstrating his gallery of weapons (ranging from a blowgun to a vicious-looking knife) ready for use against intruders. This silly scene is almost identical in content to one of Dennis Hopper showing off his guns (and willingness to use them) in a 1971 portrait docu, "The American Dreamer," and in both cases represents straying from the subject into audience-baiting. —Lor.

Digital Dreams
(BRITISH-COLOR-16m)

Hollywood, Oct. 3.
A Ripple Production. Produced by Bill Wyman, Astrid Wyman. Executive producer, Eric Gardner. Directed by Robert Dornhelm. Screenplay, Richard O'Brien; camera (uncredited color), Karl Kofler; editor, Tina Frese; art direction, John Beard; music, Bill Wyman, Mike Batt; animation sequences, Gerald Scarfe; sound, Willi Buchmuller; choreography, Arlene Phillips. Reviewed at the VIP Screening Room, West L.A., Oct. 3, 1983. (No MPAA Rating.) Running time: 72 MINS.
Features: Bill Wyman, Astrid Wyman, James Coburn, Richard O'Brien, Stanley Unwin, Patrick Moore, Stephen Wyman, Desmond Askey, Cecilia Sundin, Karin Lonnborg.

Self-funded and originally made for television, "Digital Dreams" represents a modest, self-effacing cinematic autobiography by Bill Wyman, one of The Rolling Stones. By turns amusing, naive and embarrassing, pic is neither long nor substantial enough for theatrical situations (it just concluded a one-week world preem run at the Monica in Santa Monica) and would assuredly be seen to better advantage in the medium for which it was first intended.

Bass player and least-known member of the rock 'n' roll band, Wyman has long been the Stones' self-appointed historian, and film begins with him picking out his life story on a home word processor.

His longtime ladyfriend Astrid unsuccessfully attempts to lure his interest away from his muse and ultimately complains that she is a "computer widow." Astrid has virtually nothing but criticism to offer of her mate throughout, and while the two are seen strolling into the sunset together at fadeout, it is not surprising, given the internal evidence, to learn the two have since separated.

Film delves at length into the material within Wyman's computer, recreating his deprived childhood (as well as Astrid's affluent one in Sweden), his departure from his job once the Stones get rolling, and a few snippets of early Stones concert footage. Group's drummer, Charlie Watts, appears briefly at Wyman's opulent country home, but the Stones are really incidental to the concerns of the film, and music fans attending due to interest in the band will be disappointed.

Essentially a lavish home movie, "Digital Dreams" has its share of incidental pleasures and moments of light humor, mainly stemming from Wyman's pleasant but hardly overpowering personality. Money has provided him with the opportunity to live exactly as he pleases, and he is clearly doing so, as a country gentleman with few pretentions.

James Coburn amusingly pops up in different guises from time to time, notably as a cowboy in a Wyman fantasy. Screenwriter Richard O'Brien overdoes the comic relief as a manic butler.

Deftly directed by Robert Dornhelm in the service of Wyman's purposes, pic also features some nice animated work by Gerald Scarfe and a mostly traditional score by Wyman and Mike Batt.

—Cart.

Testament
(COLOR)

Tremendously moving depiction of people coping with Nuclear Holocaust. Despite morbid subject matter, could build a serious-minded audience.

A Paramount Pictures release of an Entertainment Events production in association with American Playhouse. Produced by Jonathan Bernstein, Lynne Littman. Directed by Littman. Stars Jane Alexander. Screenplay, John Sacret Young, from story "The Last Testament" by Carol Amen; camera (CFI color), Steven Poster; editor, Suzanne Pettit; music, James Horner; sound, Lee Alexander; production design, David Nichols; art direction, Linda Pearl; production manager, Peter Cornberg; assistant directors, William Hassell, Peter Bogart; stunt coordinator, Jewse Wayne; special effects, Chuck Stewart; associate producer, Andrea Asimow. Reviewed at Paramount Pictures screening room, N.Y., Oct. 14, 1983. (MPAA Rating: PG). Running time: 89 MINS.

Carol Wetherly ....Jane Alexander
Tom Wetherly ....William Devane
Brad Wetherly ....Ross Harris
Mary Liz Wetherly............Roxana Zal
Scottie Wetherly.............Lukas Haas
Hollis ....Philip Anglim
Fania ....Lilia Skala
Henry Abhart ....Leon Ames
Rosemary Abhart ....Lurene Tuttle
Cathy Pitkin ....Rebecca DeMornay
Phil Pitkin ....Kevin Costner
Mike ....Mako
Larry ....Mico Olmos
Hiroshi.....................Gerry Murillo

"Testament" is an exceptionally powerful film dealing with the survivors of a nuclear war. Debuting director Lynne Littman, who has numerous honors for her tv work, brings an original approach to the grim material, presenting Paramount with the marketing challenge of attracting an audience to this serious, rewarding picture. Film was backed by public tv's American Playhouse series, where it will be broadcast after its theatrical exposure.

The segment of science fiction films devoted to W.W. III and its irradiated aftermath began in 1951 with Arch Oboler's "Five" in which William Phipps and Susan Douglas set out to start over after

the Holocaust. The genre peaked a decade later with such films as "The World, The Flesh And The Devil," "On The Beach" and Ray Milland's classic of survival "Panic In Year Zero." The next films dealt with the paranoia of nuclear war's approach, rather than its effects: "This Is Not A Tst," "Dr. Strangelove" and "Fail-Safe," with Peter Watkins in 1965 producing the ultimate in realism in his documentary-style "The War Game."

Based on Carol Amen's magazine story "The Last Testament," Littman's "Testament" avoids the sensationalism of earlier films to focus on the probable consequences of nuclear war on the average family. Set in the small California town of Hamlin, film's opening reel depicts a normal, complacent community. In the Wetherly family, dad Tom (William Devane) is preoccupied with concerns of the moment, such as his bike-riding, while mom Carol (Jane Alexander) takes a longer view, worrying over son Brad (Ross Harris) becoming eligible for the draft in five years.

The town's calm is shattered when a tv newscast announces that nuclear devices have exploded in New York and on the east coast, with the film proper suddenly going to yellow and whiteout, indicating blasts on the west coast as well. Ham radio operator Henry Abhart (Leon Ames) becomes Hamlin's communications link to the outside world, receiving conflicting reports as to who started W.W. III. He can't raise anything east of Keokuk, Iowa, on his radio, or any major city.

Isolated, Hamlin's residents attempt to survive on canned food and community activities, but within a month over 1,000 people have died from radiation sickness. A young couple (Rebecca DeMornay and Kevin Costner), whose baby has died, drive off in search of "a safe place," but the Wetherlys and orphaned kids they have taken in remain at home trying to cope with the inevitable.

Littman's skill and restraint with this increasingly morbid storyline are exemplary. There are no on-camera death scenes, only the increasing sense of loss in the faces of the survivors as each protagonist succumbs. Holding it all together as a tower of strength is actress Jane Alexander, coping with the deaths of her family and friends in truly heroic fashion via an understated performance that deserves Academy Award consideration.

The supporting cast is particularly strong, with a warm, affectionate turn by William Devane as the husband, deeply felt portrayals by Leon Ames and music teacher

Lilia Skala as elders passing on the baton to the youngsters, and a moving portrait of a young mother by Rebecca DeMornay (in a versatile stretch from her sexy lead role in "Risky Business"). Littman demonstrates a sure hand with kids, ranging from bit players acting in the pertinent allogorical school play-within-the-film ("The Pied Piper Of Hamelin") to the leading roles of the Wetherly children. Ross Harris as the eldest, Roxana Zal and particularly newcomer Lukas Haas create young people, the concern over whose fate will elicit a tremendous emotional response from any audience.

The musical score by James Horner is spare and to the point, with a sustained siren-like wail injected in the opening theme and use of ethereal choral effects to underscore Alexander's sensitive monolog to her daughter, Zal, explaining the closeness two people experience making love, something she'll never grow up to find out for herself. Other credits are adequate, reflecting the project's tv-movie budget constraints.

Renewed public awareness of nuclear peril is reflected on the screen with this summer's "Fail-Safe" update "WarGames," tv's "The Day After," which will be shown two weeks after "Testament" debuts, and a projected tv miniseries remake of "On The Beach." Still timely, producers might consider filming at long last the classic sci-fi novels in the genre: "Earth Abides," "Alas, Babylon" and "A Canticle For Leibowitz." — Lor.

El Hombre de Arena
(The Sandman)
(ARGENTINE-COLOR)

Buenos Aires, Aug. 4.
A Producciones El Churqui release and production. Produced, written and directed by Mario Cañazares. Features entire cast. Associate producer, Sabina Sigler. Camera (Eastmancolor), Poy Melendez; editor, Jorge Fridman; assistant director, Jorge Calvetti. Reviewed at the Lorca theatre, Buenos Aires, Aug. 4, 1983. 90 MINS.
Cast: Jorge Rodriguez, Teresa Terraf, Cristian Carrizo, Antonio Grimau, Ana Maria Picchio.

Very few regional films have been made in Argentina and most of them have had an amateurish look, not to talk about technical flaws. Mario Cañazares' "The Sandman" is the first made in Salta, 1,000 miles northwest of Buenos Aires, by a filmmaker born in that Andean province who shows professional prowess although neither he nor his staff had experience in the native film industry.

Unfortunately Cañazares, who studied his craft in the U.S. and Europe, seems to have lent too much attention to the technical side of filmmaking than to story devel-

opment and character buildup. His tale about a rugged man who earns a few pesos and asserts his independence by shoveling sand in a dry river bed gives a true picture of the life among poor, down-to-earth people in a distant frontier zone but is weakened by repetitions and speech-like monologs. A pity, since the authenticity of the background and the honesty of the central characters are plusses lost in the deficit of entertainment.

Jorge Rodriguez as the sandman and Teresa Terraf as his wife, who vainly struggles to make him accept some less independent but more reliable job near home, are convincing, as is moppet Cristian Carrizo as their son. Ironically, guest appearances by Antonio Grimau and Ana Maria Picchio, two popular tv stars, add nothing more than their names for promotion, but both have had to cope with cardboard characters.

Camerawork by newcomer Poy Melendez is good. Editor Jorge Fridman could have trimmed a lot of the footage. — Nubi.

Fräulein Berlin
(W. GERMAN-B&W-16m)

Berlin, Sept. 21.
A Lothar Lambert Film Production. Features Ulrike S. Produced, written, directed, edited, photographed and sound by Lothar Lambert. Reviewed at Unisono Tonstudio, Berlin, Sept. 18, '83. Running time: 90 MINS.
With: Ulrike S., Helke Sander, Norman Jewison, Hans-Dieter Frankenberg, Dorothea Moritz, Erika Rabau, Bette Gordon, Jim Jarmusch, Dagmar Beiersdorf, Carina Conti, Eric Mitchell, Hans Marquardt.

"Fräulein Berlin" is the latest in Lothar Lambert's extensive (more than a dozen) line of Berlin Underground films.

Much in the manner of Rosa von Praunheim's cruising of the Gotham and fest scene, "Fräulein Berlin" is the story of a Berlin Underground Star, Ulrike S., who wants to further her career by abandoning her past and severing her connections with a filmmaker who only wants her to undress in such personal epics as "Monster Woman" (a twist on L.L.'s own "Nightmare Lady" of a year ago). She goes to a film festival (Toronto) where her film should be shown as an "added attraction" oddity, speaks to a famous movie director (Norman Jewison) about a job or breaking into the big time, and then is off to Gotham to visit with a few other Underground wizards with 16m cameras (Bette Gordon, Jim Jarmusch).

Finally, quite frustrated with it all (apparently, Ulrike S.' own fate), she gives up being an Underground Star — and returns to her former job in a pharmacy (visited by helmer Helke Sander, who needs something to cure her sore throat). That's about it, so far as plot goes.

It's rather fun in the beginning to watch Lambert parody himself, and for insiders it's a pleasure to see so many familiar faces from Germany, Canada and the U.S. on screen at one time. But this parade of stars has all the earmarks of being a kind of cameo-pegged "Greatest Story Ever Told" on the Underground circuit. One is always wondering "who's on next" instead of receiving a pleasant jolt from a naive improvisation from one of the richest Underground playgrounds in contemporary cinema — Berlin — as was the case in former Lambert pics.

"Fräulein Berlin" was shot in English, so far as the sequences in Toronto and New York are concerned. The best moments are the tongue-in-cheek conversations between Ulrike S. and Jewison and critic David Overbey at the Toronto festival, where a full retro of Lambert's films were unspooled for posterity. —*Holl.*

The Burning Of The Imperial Palace
(CHINESE-COLOR)

Hong Kong, Sept. 20.
A New Kun Lun Film Co./China Film Co-Production Corporation co-production released by Southern Film. Directed by Li Hang Chiang. Stars Liu Xiaoqing, Liang Jiahui, Chen Ye, Zhang Shuyi, Siang Kun, Wang Pei, Lu Qian, Zhang Tielin. Screenplay, Yang Cunbin; assistant director, Xu Tongjun, Wang Shuyan; music, edited from Li Hang Chiang's early films. Reviewed at Southern Film Co., Hong Kong, Sept. 18, 1983. Running time: 100 MINS.
(Mandarin with English subtitles)

"The Burning of the Imperial Palace" & "Reign Behind Curtain" — Li Hang Chiang's two-part epic on the Empress Dowager & the late Ching Dynasty during the chaotic 1850s is as ambitious a work as the colorful real life of the Empress herself.

The two films, of which part one is actually the extension of part two, is co-produced by the newly-formed New Kun Lun Film Co. (Hong Kong-based company) and the China Film Corporation.

They had the unique permission to film on the subject's actual locations, namely the Ancient Palace, Chengde Resort and other assorted locations in mainland China. It's a dream come true for scholarly Li Hang Chiang, who spent many years with Shaw Brothers as a contract director doing low-budget skin flics.

Shaw's still own the biggest studio in Hong Kong and provided Li with the breeding ground for many of his large-scale costume dramas and historic epics. He's actually the first Chinese director to be exposed to the western world with more than 70 films to his credit.

It's almost logical for Li that after years of making period palace extravaganzas on studio sets to make one shot on authentic locations. The dream was finally realized with this two-part epic.

"The Burning of the Imperial Palace" is mild in intensity when compared to "Reign Behind a Curtain." The film begins with an overlong but lavish ceremony for the enthronement of the six-year-old emperor (the tenth emperor of the Ching Dynasty) and then flash backs to the 15-year old Cixi (then known as Yulan), mother to the emperor. The Empress Dowager Cixi (1835-1908) known before as Yehonala, was born of the Manchu family. She was selected as a low-ranking concubine of Emperor Hsieng-feng in 1851 and later promoted to Second Class Imperial Consort when she gave birth to the Emperor's only heir. And when the Emperor died in 1861, Cixi, then in her late 20s, used her position as mother of the child emperor to increase her position and craving for power. By now known as Empress Dowager of the West Palace, she became co-regent with the senior consort Empress Dowager Cian (a.k.a. Empress Dowager of the East Palace). Thus, begins the "Reign Behind a Curtain" of which Cixi, the ruthless, unscrupulous, shrewd and cunning woman of great ability, charm and wit, went on to rule China for 46 years, causing damage that weakened and deteriorated China as a nation.

The primary shortcoming of "The Burning of the Imperial Palace" is that instead of developing the characters first, it sacrifices the story-line and characterizations for breathtaking scenes and eye-filling sets. And the boring textbook style narration is no help either, thus leaving most viewers uninspired. Majestic and serious in style, grand and marvelous in scope, the film lacks impact due to a weak script and paper-thin storyline that's been overstretched. Foreign eyes will surely be dazzled by Chinese history, culture, cuisine, costumes, artifacts and thousands of extras, but they may find Part 1 lacking in western-style pacing as the director is basically a traditional and conservative filmmaker (though the director used the 1:1.85 ratio instead of CinemaScope for the first time, thus providing the pictures with more depth).

The end result is still rather empty and dull at times. Li's immaculate, well-researched and detailed visuals on things Chinese are impressive but fall short on sequences involving the British and the French, with Chinese extras costumed in what looks like their army uniforms with imitation red beards to look foreign. Understandable though, as there aren't

enough white-skinned players to fill the cast of a whole brigade.

And for those who have experienced the realism of "Waterloo," "War and Peace" or the dramatic intensity of "Kagemusha," the battle sequences in "The Burning of the Imperial Palace" are lacklustre by comparison. But in its own context and to millions of Chinese, it is quite an experience. Together with "Reign Behind a Curtain," if re-edited as one film, it would definitely be perfect international film festival material as it is very Chinese (unlike the local westernized productions) with a touch of patriotism or subject nationalism. — *Mel.*

Die Wilden Fuenfziger
(The Roarin' Fifties)
(WEST GERMAN-COLOR)

Berlin, Sept. 27.
A Bavaria Film Production, Munich, in coproduction with Second German Television (ZDF), Mainz. Executive producer, Guenter Rohrbach. World rights, Atlas International, Munich. Features entire cast. Directed by Peter Zadek. Screenplay, Wolfgang Bornheim, loosely based on motifs in Johannes Mario Simmel's novel, "Hurrah, We're Still Alive;" camera (color), Jost Vacano; sets, Rolf Zehetbauer; studio architect, Herbert Strabel; costumes, Charlotte Fleming; music, Klaus Doldinger; editing, Max Benedikt; production manager, Dieter Minx. Reviewed at Atelier am Zoo, Berlin, Sept. 27, '83. Running time: 120 MINS.
Cast: Juraj Kurkura (Jakob Formann), Boy Gobert, Peter Kern, Nora Barner, Christine Kaufmann, Sennyi Melles, Beatrice Richter, Eva Mattes, Dietrich Mattausch, Paul Esser, Hermann Lause, Klaus Hochn, Ilya Richter. Willy Millowitsch, Freddy Quinn, Sona McDonald, Christa Berndl, Ingrid Caven, Brigitte Mira, and (as guests) Burkhard Driest and Ivan Desny.

Known in German legit circles as a stage director with an eye for the bloated gesture and other titillating excesses, particularly when it comes to the classics, Peter Zadek has made on occasion a theatrically oriented film production: "I'm an Elephant, Madame" (1968) and "Ice Age" (1975). Now he's tackled a bestseller by Johannes Mario Simmel, "Hurrah, We're Alive," but the writer himself refused to allow, in the end, his name to be associated with the production at the Bavaria Studios, so pic was redubbed "The Roarin' Fifties" with the added note that everything in it is only loosely based on "motifs" in Simmel's original.

This is a film of and about excess, more or less Zadek's specialty. Pic is set during the so-called "Economic Miracle," when West Germany pulled itself up from the bootstraps to become Europe's leading financial power by virtue of the revived D-mark. Simmel's novel cruised over these years in popular bestseller fashion, contrasting the orgies of the rich with the fortunes of the common people in struggling simply to get ahead,

The 1978 novel was an immediate hit, selling 3,000,000 copies, thus whetting the appetite of Bavaria Atelier in Munich-Geiselgasteig to reshape the whole into an overblown comic strip on the times. Zadek, whose job was apparently to send some 70 actors and personalities through their paces, as at a circus performance in the big top, seemed to be the right man for the job.

But the whole of this circa $3,-000,000 production is stuck in the mud of theatricality from the very beginning. The rise of multi-millionaire Jakob Formann (Slovak thesp Juraj Kurkura) skips over years from 1946 to just about the present as though a plot narrative should hardly be necessary at all. The production appears, in Zadek's view, to be only a question of eating, drinking, partying, romping, and wheeling-and-dealing. That, plus a few documentary excerpts to indicate these were the years in which a Berlin Airlift and an Iron Curtain also happened to take place. As is often the case in features that turn to historical film archives for effect, the documentary sequences are the strongest moments in the film. In fact, they shouldn't have been used at all, for in this case the clips simply kick the spoofs of that same reality right off the screen.

Then there's the unfortunate decision of impersonating real-life figures from time to time. The American generals and senators get their whacks, along with the "nouveau riche" one finds today frequenting the casinos and music festivals in Bayreuth or Salzburg; even insider jabs at literary and show-biz figures are plentiful. But each thesp does his number before the camera as though this was the routine for a televised revue on "The Roarin' Fifties" instead of a motion picture. Who knows, maybe it was meant to be a dress rehearsal for a tv show. Otherwise, it's pretty much of a waste of production morale at one of Europe's most modern film studios. — *Holl.*

Paso Doble
(W. GERMAN-COLOR-16m)

Berlin, Sept. 21.
A Cikon Film production, Berlin. Features entire cast. Written and directed by Lothar Lambert, based on an idea by Albert Heins. Camera (color), Helmut Roettgen; editing, Lambert; assistant director, Dagmar Beiersdorf; music, Albert Kittler, "Brutto Netto" Group. Reviewed at Filmbuehne am Steinplatz, Berlin, Sept. 19, '83. Running time: 90 MINS.
Cast: Ulrike S. (Mother), Albert Heins (Father), Susanne Stahl (Daughter), Cristoph Wellemeyer (Son), Mustafa Iskandarani (Voiceless Spaniard), Morteza Ghazanfari (Persian masseur), Dorothea Moritz (Neighbor), Stefan Menche (Father's Office College), Jutta Kloeppel (Prostitute), Beate Kopp (Busybody Tourist), Monika Keller (Dance Teacher), Carina Conti (Transvestite), Erika Rabau (Singer), Paco Gil (Trans-

vestite Dancer), Semra Uysallar (Waiter), Lothar Lambert and Dagmar Beiersdorf (Vacationing Pair in Spain).

Lothar Lambert's "Paso Doble" is the Berlin Underground director's "graduation film" from the "no budget" category to the "low budget" bracket. The boost up the ladder came as a result of a new subsidy system in Berlin, whereby low-budget projects by beginners and promising talent can find needed backing with more or less the assurance of finding a public in the city's studio-theatres as well. It was Lambert's Underground prestige at these modest arthouses in fact, that made him an attraction in the first place.

"Paso Doble" still contains enough of Lambert's personal tics to satisfy his fans at home and abroad (note the retro in his honor at the Toronto fest last year), but the main difference is that he has discarded his rambling improvised methods for a definite narrative line — and thus proved himself to be a quite competent director of wacky, humorous family melodrama. Undoubtedly, a good deal of the credit goes to thesp Albert Heins, new to Lambert's corps and an inspirational idea man to boot. Heins, and other Berlin and international talent who mosey over to the Lambert Underground scene for the fun of it between other professional jobs, and add caliber to the commercial switch; as a result, they tend to make Lambert's Underground "star" Ulrike S. look better than ever as a rough-cut thesping talent in her own right.

This is the story of an average middleclass family — husband and wife, with teenage son and daughter — who spend their vacations in Spain at their summer home on the Mediterranean coast. This year, however, the father (Heins) wants the mother (Ulrike S.) to take dancing lessons in order to broaden their contacts and mix in better with the crowds.

One thing leads to another in the marriage bed and there's a family spat, so Ulrike attaches herself to a friendly Iranian masseur (to soothe her headaches) while Heins suddenly finds himself attracted to a young, voiceless waiter in Spain — it's enough to even discard his protective toupee. The kids, meanwhile, take it all in with a grain of salt, although neither feels the parents have nurtured into emotionally balanced adults. After the affairs have run their course, everything's back to "normal" again.

Pic has a number of humorous scenes, while Lambert's usual dips into promiscuity are held to a minimum. Hopefully, the director will iron out the rough edges in this trial run and go on to bigger and better things in the low-budget

feature realm, specializing in the laid-back melodrama with comic twists. —Holl.

A Time To Die
(COLOR)

Dull period action-revenger.

An Almi Films release of a Carnation International Pictures production. Produced by Charles Lee. Directed by Matt Cimber. Stars Rex Harrison, Rod Taylor, Edward Albert Jr. Screenplay, John Goff, Cimber, William Russell, from a story by Mario Puzo; camera (CFI color), Eddy van der Enden, Tom Denove; editor, Byron (Buzz) Brandt, Fred Chulack; music, Robert O. Ragland; additional music, Ennio Morricone; additional scenes and action direction, Joe Tornatore, assistant director, Peter Carpenter; sound, Lewis Rosen, Jeff Richard; art direction, Frank Rosen, John Thompson; set decoration, Michael Stewart; second unit camera, Nicholas von Sternberg; post-production supervisor, Russ Tinsley; stunt coordinator, Eddy Donno. Reviewed at RKO National 1 theatre, N.Y., Sept. 30, 1983. (MPAA Rating: R). Running time: 91 MINS.

Michael Rogan..........Edward Albert Jr.
Bailey.....................Rod Taylor
Von Osten..................Rex Harrison
Dora........................Linn Stokke
Genco Bari..................Raf Vallone
Vrost......................Cor Van Rijn
Mrs. Rogan.................Lucie Visser

Filmed in Europe in 1979 under the title "Seven Graves For Rogan," "A Time To Die" emerges as a would-be "film noir," harking back to the dark pictures of the late 1940s but lacking their style and punch. Market potential for the film, currently being given a hard-sell emphasizing the participation of "The Godfather" author Mario Puzo (as story writer), is dim.

Edward Albert Jr. (adding an associate producer credit here in addition to his rarely-used "Junior" to avoid viewer confusion with papa Eddie) stars as Michael Rogan, a World War II vet who sets out circa 1948 to avenge his wife's murder by the Nazis. Six villains (including a Hungarian and a Sicilian officer) are his targets, with the film's original title probably hinting at Rogan's destiny to fill plot No. 7.

Improbably, Rogan is aided in this grim mission by a CIA operative Bailey (Rod Taylor), who believes that by giving the lone wolf a hand in killing nonentities he can delay and protect Von Osten (Rex Harrison), being groomed by the U.S. as West German s next chancellor. Along the way, Rogan picks up a lovely teammate, Dora (Linn Stokke).

Though the film boasts direct-sound English-language dialog handled by even the European supporting cast (instead of the bad dubbing that is usual in actioners of this type), "Die" is a tedious, unappealing exercise.

With perfunctory and often extraneous action-stunt scenes credited to another, it is difficult to assess director Matt Cimber's con-

tribution to the project. Also known as Matteo Ottaviano, this B-picture helmer is better known as (husband and) director of Jayne Mansfield in "Single Room Furnished" and director of Pia Zadora in "Butterfly" & "Fake Out." —Lor.

Zwischen Den Bildern
(Between the Pictures)
(W. GERMAN-COLOR/B&W-DOCU-16m)

Berlin, Sept. 23.

A three-part documentary produced by the Stiftung Deutsche Kinematek Berlin, in co-production with Second German Television (ZDF), Mainz. TV producer, Hans Peter Kochenrath; production manager, Helmut Wietz. part I: "Editing in the Narrative Film," directed by Heide Breitel, Klaus Feddermann, Hans Helmut Prinzler; camera (color, b-&-w), Jody Saslow, Gregory von Berblinger; special effects, Gerd Vany; sound, Dena Schutzer, Steve Marlowe, Hans Martin; narrator, Monika Hansen, Peter Fitz; music accompaniment, Joachim Baerenz. Part II: "Editing in the Documentary Film," directed by Heide Breitel and Hans Helmut Prinzler, based on an outline by Helmut Herbst; camera (color, b-&-w), Carlos Bustamante, Jody Saslow, Wolfgang Knigge; sound, Sabine Eckhard, Dena Schutzer; narrator, Monika Hansen; collaborator, Wolfgang Mai. Part III: "On the Indolence of Perception," directed by Klaus Feddermann and Helmut Herbst; camera (color, b-&-w), Helmut Herbst; sound, Alf Olbrich; editing, Renate Merck. Reviewed at the DFFB Screening Room, Berlin, Sept. 17, '83. Running time: 174 MINS. (each part, 58 MINS.)

Upon viewing the three-part documentary "Between the Pictures," produced by the German Kinemathek for Second German Television (ZDF), one wonders why other film archives have never bothered to do the same for the sake of film schools, university film classes and film buffs. This is an exemplary job done on a very difficult subject: the editing of a film, or (as Europeans tend to say) the power of montage.

Four filmmakers and teachers at the German Film and Television Academy Berlin (DFFB) worked on the three "teaching documentaries:" Heide Breitel, Klaus Feddermann and Helmut Herbst on Prinzer on Part One, "Editing in the Narrative Film;" Breitel and Prinzler on Part Two, "Editing in the Documentary Film;" and Feddermann and Helmut Herbst on Part Three, "On the Indolence of Perception." On grounds of quality alone in argumentative exposition, plus key interviews, there's little doubt that the series will go into semi-commercial distribution for seminar showings at numerous German film institutions and special arthouses as well. In any case, this is what has happened in the past in regard to a prior archival series on camera techniques, also the docus by special-effects expert Helmut Herbst.

Part One, "Editing in the Narrative Film," is a salute to the American cinema. it begins with excerpts from Edwin S. Porter's

"Cripple Creek Barroom" (1898) and "The Great Train Robbery" (1903), then shifts into high gear with D.W. Griffith's "The Lonedale Operator" (1911) and "The Battle at Elderbrush Gulch" (1913), and singles out John Ford's "Stagecoach" (1939) for special consideration. Westerns by William S. Hart and Sam Peckinpah are also included, the idea being to show how showdowns between gunfighters were handled over the years in Hollywood.

The "learning" element in this part is enhanced by two interviews — with Dorothy Spencer, who edited John Ford's "Stagecoach" and was familiar with the legendary director's manner of making a film; and with Robert L. Wolfe, who worked on all of Sam Peckinpah's westerns. There's also an exposition on editing machines and tables from the turn-of-the-century up to the present.

Part Two, "Editing in the Documentary Film," leans a bit too heavily on films of favorite documentarists to make its conclusive points, but the excerpts in general treat the historically, often-neglected German contribution to the field: Guido Seeber's "Departure of the Saxon China-Fighters" (1900), Wilhelm Prager and Nicholas Kaufmann's "Ways to Strength and Beauty" (1925), Walter Ruttmann's "Berlin — Symphony of a Great City" (1927), Ella Bergmann-Michel's "Street Salesman" (1930) and Leni Riefenstahl's "Triumph of the Will" (1935). Bergmann-Michel, in fact, is a rediscovery, for her amateur docus lay buried for years.

These pre-WW2 docus are then contrasted with postwar West German examples, also relatively unknown as a whole: Peter Nestler's "A Worker's Club in Sheffield" (1965) and Klaus Wildenhahn's "In der Fremde" (Far from Home) (1967), made by two of the leading documentarists in the country (Nestler now working in Sweden). Interviews with Joris Ivens and his editor Helen van Dongen on the making of "Spanish Earth" (1937), together with clips from the classic docu on the Spanish Civil War, round out the film.

Part Three, "On the Indolence of Perception," is packed with one tickling and provocative interview after another, for the field here is the experimental film. Those expounding their theses on camera include Werner Nekes, the husband-wife team of Jean-Marie Straub and Daniele Huillet, Alexander Kluge and Klaus Wyborny. Nekes takes his art very seriously, Straub and Huillet ramble on about diverse topics for the sheer fun of it, Kluge is out to pull the viewer's leg with a half-baked exposition on editing and Wyborny raises some pretty tough questions on the legitimacy of edited reality in the narrative feature.

Excerpts from Part Three incude Jean-Luc Godard's "Le Gai Savoir" (1968), Neke's "Mirador" (1978), Straub's "Not Reconciled" (1965), Kluge's "The Patriot" (1979) and Wyborny's "The Scenic Sacrifice" (1980), among others. What's missing in this section, however, is a discussion of Sergei Eisenstein's principles of montage — or the Soviet experiments as whole in the 1920s. But the desire to stay close to home — that is, to German film history — is understandable. — *Holl.*

Boku No Oyaji To Boku
(My Stiffnecked Daddy & Me)
(JAPANESE-COLOR)

Vancouver, Oct. 11.

A Nikkatsu Children's Films Production. Produced by Yoshiteru Yuki. Directed by Shun Nakahara. Features entire cast. Screenplay, Kiku Kachima, Takahisa Katsume; camera (color), Massaru Mori; music, Takahiko Ishikawa. No further credits available. Reviewed at National Film Board Theatre, Vancouver, (2d Annual Vancouver Kidfest), Sept. 27, 1983. Running time: **89 MINS.**

With Isao Natsuki, Akemi Higashiyama, Miki Sanjo, Masayuki Hidaka.

Though well-meant this hamfisted kidpic about tensions within a working class family is marred continuously by sloppy camerawork and even more slapdash scripting. Director Shun Nakahara manages basically attractive material with ineptitude. he fails repeatedly in distinguishing the "real" scenes from the various daydreams indulged in by protagonist Tatsuo, an unhappy child who fights tooth and nail with his bad-tempered dad, Takeshi.

Takeshi, a moody gardener in his 40s has already alienated daughter Yoko. Due to a shortage of living space she has been farmed out to an aunt. Takeshi never keeps his promise of building a new home at the foot of Mt. Fuji. When Tatsuo unearths his granny's diary, which reveals the grossly antisocial conduct of his dad when a boy, family tensions are resolved. The building of a new home commences.

The many dreams of frustrated Tatsuo: himself a fearless Ninja warrior; his dad, a popular nitery crooner; his hunt for the treasure trove of Lord Takeda, are all poorly dotted through the narrative. So poorly that when dad falls victim to some daredevil motorcyclists on a craggy road, and he smashes up his truck, you fail to see the episode as anything but a fantasy.

All of the location camerawork is wobbly. The print under review was very muddy, with no depth of focus to speak of. All performances are hammy and awkward. The Westernized score flits from ersatz country & western thru even more ersatz Mantovani-style strings. A well-below-average kidpic that has no real export potential. —*Gran.*

Il Principe Di Homburg
(The Prince of Homburg)
(ITALIAN-COLOR)

Rome, Oct. 7

A D.L.F. release (for Istituto Luce and Italnoleggio), produced by Fabrizio Lori for RAI-TV Channel 3 and Arsenal Cinematografica. Stars Gabriele Lavia, Monica Guerritore. Written and directed by Gabriele Lavia, based on the play by Heinrich von Kleist. Camera (color), Tonino Nardi; editor, Roberto Perpignani; art director, Giovanni Agostinucci; music, Giorgio Carnini. Reviewed at Cinecitta, Rome, Oct. 7, 1983. Runr.ing time: **95 MINS.**
Homburg .... Gabriele Lavia
Natalie d'Orange .... Monica Guerritore
Prince Elector .... Massimo Foschi

Helmer-diva Gabriele Lavia, new star of the Italian stage, makes his big screen directing debut with a skillful film adaptation of his hit with "Prince" on stage. Heinrich von Kleist's 1811 "Prinz Friedrich von Homburg" is brought to life with brisk pacing and bold characterizations. Though a certain amount of horseback riding is thrown in to dissolve some of the staginess, Lavia's "modern" approach required respecting Kleist's poetic dialog, which keeps artifice firmly in the foreground. In the end, retaining this unnatural language pays off in some stirring, impassioned monologs. Mainly a tv item, "Homburg" could draw art house audiences of the sort who enjoyed Eric Rohmer's "Marquise Von O," based on work by the same author.

Pic very much aims at being a cultural experience. At the same time it recreates an age of high Romanticism that could appeal to a wider audience — magnificent villas with gardens, fountains, and salons; a pair of unfortunate aristocratic lovers; the pomp and splendor of fairy-tale armies and officers. The young prince of Homburg (Gabriele Lavia) is introduced as a romantic prone to losing himself in trance-like daydreams.

When awake, he is a brilliant cavalry officer. By having his men charge the enemy before the appointed time, he wins an important battle for his beloved commander, the Prince Elector (Massimo Foschi). Far from being grateful, the Elector follows the letter of the law and sentences Homburg to death for disobeying orders. He will rescind the sentence only if the young man declares the law is unjust. But being noble in more ways than one, Homburg refuses to do so, and prepares to die for the sake of principle.

Pic's basic conflict thus boils down to a very abstract question about the Law that isn't a burning issue for most viewers. Those who tune out can sit back and enjoy an intense Monica Guerritore as Natalie d'Orange, as she courageously tries to get Homburg off the hook with her uncle, the Elector. Surprisingly, what looks like a sure case of tragic love has an up ending — happily, because Natalie and Homburg are so passionately played they win our sympathy, almost in spite of the play.

Camerawork is spare and rigorous, Tonino Nardi's lighting properly moody and nocturnal, and Roberto Perpignani's cutting commendably fast.

Pic was screened in Venice's Italian Showcase this year.

— *Yung.*

Krzyk
(The Scream)
(POLISH-COLOR)

San Sebastian, Sept. 20.

A Polish Corporation for Film Production "Zespoly Filmowe," Unit KADR film presented by Film Polski. Written and directed by Barbara Sass; camera (color), Wieslaw Zdort; production manager, Ryszard Straszewski; music, Wojciech Trzcinski; sets, Jerzy Sajko; sound, Krzysztof Grabowski. Features Dorota Stalinska, Stanislaw Igar, Krzysztof Pieczynski, Iga Cembrzynska, Anna Romantowska. Reviewed at Cine Victoria Eugenia (San Sebastian), Sept. 19, '83. Running time: **92 MINS.**

"The Scream" fittingly begins and ends with the closeup of a woman screaming in utter desperation; after an hour and a half of overacting and sordid settings, audiences may also wind up screaming, albeit internally. Helmer Barbara Sass has hit on a fascinating if not novel subject (treated majestically in the Argentine film "La Raulito" about seven years ago), that of a grownup, half-demented waif who lives an underground existence in the streets and slums of Warsaw, a sort of potential bagwoman.

In this case the girl manages to get a job in an old-age home scrubbing floors and cleaning latrines. There she strikes up a sort of friendship with an invalid who is given special care and treatment due to his wealth and former position. The girl also latches on to a discontented orderly, and on the nights she doesn't sleep in a railroad station, or with her alcoholic mother in a hovel, she stays with the young man, her first sincere attachment.

When the orderly, after waiting five years to get a proper apartment (he lives in a self-made shack), is turned down by the housing authority because someone else has bribed the official in question, the distraught girl tries to get the money for him, ultimately pleading with the invalid for it. When he refuses, she smashes his head with a bottle and screams, for he is the symbol of the cause of her misery and oppression.

Though on occasion the waif's plight is touching, Dorota Stalinska exaggerates the girl's gumchewing grimaces and bouncy walk to such an extent that the character becomes ludicrous instead of pathetic. Message seems to be straight from the Party line: the oppressed girl wreaks vengeance upon the corrupt official and thus obtains social justice. However, after the girl kills the nasty old man, she learns the charges of corruption and bribery against him were unfounded.

—*Besa.*

Separate Ways
(COLOR)

Minor romantic opus.

A Crown International release of a Hickmar Prods. presentation of a 13 Valentine Associates production. Executive producer, Marlene Schmidt. Produced and directed by Howard Avedis. Stars Karen Black, Tony Lo Bianco. Screenplay, Leah Appet; camera (Deluxe color), Dean Cundey; editor, John Wright; music John Cavacas; songs, Bonnie Becker, Cavacas; sound, Art Names; assistant director, David R. Osterhout; art direction, Chuck Seaton; production manager, Reid Freeman; stunt coordinator, Gene Hartline; associate producer, Bill Kawata. Reviewed on Vestron Video vidcassette, N.Y., Sept. 18, 1983. (MPAA Rating: R). Running time: **92 MINS.**
Valentine Colby .... Karen Black
Ken Colby .... Tony Lo Bianco
Annie .... Arlene Golonka
Jerry ....David Naughton
Karen ....Sharon Farrell
Burney ....Jack Carter
Huey .... William Windom
Woody ....Robert Fuller
Jason Colby ....Noah Hathaway
Also with: Walter Brooke, Jordan Charney, Sybil Danning, Angus Duncan, Monte Markham, Bob Hastings, Katherine Justice.

Lensed in 1979 under the title "Valentine," "Separate Ways" is a small-scale romantic film released in 1981 and currently a pay-tv and homevideo title, reviewed here for the record.

Karen Black toplines as Valentine, an unfulfilled housewife married to former racing car driver (now running an inherited car dealership into the ground) Ken Colby (Tony Lo Bianco). Studying art at a local college, Valentine takes up romantically with a young student (David Naughton) after she sees her husband having an affair on family's boat, named after her (and film's original romantic title).

Ultimately she splits, getting a waitress job at a low-down nightclub run by Jack Carter. The Colbys finally reconcile, with a lightweight climax of hubby winning a racing trophy.

Husband-and-wife filmmakers Marlene Schmidt and Howard Avedis (latter an Iraqi emigre director formerly billed as Hikmet Avedis) have fashioned a romantic drama in the vein of Claude Lelouch's hit "A Man And A Woman" that is attractively lensed (by since-graduate to major pics Dean Cundey) but lacks bite. Acting by a big cast is okay and should help in attracting an audience in eventual tv broadcast slottings. Appearing in a small role as couple's young son is Noah Hathaway , currently toplining in the German fantasy epic "The Never-Ending Story" but not making much of an impression here.—*Lor.*

BMX Bandits
(AUSTRALIAN-COLOR)

Sydney, Sept. 25.

A Nilsen Premiere Pty. production. Produced by Tom Broadbridge, Paul Davies. Directed by Brian Trenchard-Smith. Features entire cast. Screenplay, Patrick Edgeworth, based on a screenplay by Russell Hagg; camera (color), John Seale; music, Colin Stead, Frank Strangio; production design, Ross Major; editor, Alan Lake; associate producer, Brian D. Burgess. Reviewed at Colorfilm theatrette, Camperdown, Sydney, Sept. 21, 1983. Running Time: 90 MINS.

Duane O'Connor . . . . David Argue
Povic . . . . John Ley
Judy . . . . Nicole Kidman
PJ . . . . Angelo d'Angelo
Goose . . . . James Lugton
The Boss . . . . Brian Marshall

Said to be the first feature film made to cash in on the worldwide craze among young teenagers for BMX bikes, "BMX Bandits" is a fast-moving comedy-chase-thriller geared for the under-16 audience. It certainly provides a different kind of entertainment for this age group, probably one much closer to their own reality. If the kids decide they want to experience the BMX phenomenon at the cinema, the film could hit the jackpot. It's scheduled for a Christmas release Down Under.

Director Brian Trenchard-Smith is an experienced hand at this kind of thing and, relieved of the necessity to inject the gratuitous violence of his last film, "Turkey Shoot" ("Escape 2000" is its U.S. title), he does a good job. Story, a kind of update on the 1946 British film "Hue and Cry," involves three young teenagers, Judy, PJ and Goose, BMX fanatics, who accidentally stumble on a hidden cache of two-way radios belonging to a local gang of bankrobbers. The kids decide "finders keepers," and start selling the radios tuned to the police band — to their friends, causing traffic-control chaos. Thwarted in his plans to rob a local payroll, the gang boss dispatches his two most incompetent hit men to find the kids and get back the radios. From then on, the film is an extended chase with the teenagers easily outwitting the hapless villains.

Photographed in Panavision by John Seale (winner of the 1983 Australian Film Award for Best Photography for "Careful He Might Hear You"), the film looks great; it was shot last summer in and around the beach suburb of Manly, north of Sydney.

There's plenty of Disney-style comedy from the hopeless thugs, amusingly played by David Argue and John Ley, and the three teenagers, too, emerge as real people (though they don't appear to have families), especially Nicole Kidman who's a real find and future star material as the self-confident Judy.

The stuntriding is excellent and there is the usual quota of comic car crashes and near misses. Younger children might be a bit scared by a scene where, threatened by the villains, who are wearing horror-comic rubber masks, Judy hides out in a cemetery at night, falls into an open grave, and is confronted by a rat; but otherwise the thrills take second place to the comedy.

Credits are tops down the line.
—*Strat.*

Die Matrosen Von Kronstadt
(The Sailors of Kronstadt)
(WEST GERMAN-COLOR)

Berlin, Sept. 19.

A Stern TV, Hamburg, coproduction with Second German Television (ZDF), Mainz. Features entire cast. Directed by Juergen Klauss. Screenplay, Theodor Schuebel; camera (color), Klaus Guenther; costumes, Ilse Dubois; tv producer, Franz Neubauer. Reviewed at ZDF Screening Room, Berlin, Sept. 19, '83. Running time: 120 MINS. -

Cast: Siemen Ruehaak (Perepelkin), Gottfried John (Petrichenko), Pinkas Braun (Trotsky), Gert Haucke (Koslovsky), Dietrich Mattausch (Sinoviev), Werner Kreindl (Kusmin), Josef Froehlich (Tuchachevsky), Petra Maria Gruen (Lisa), Dorothea Moritz (Mother).

Juergen Klauss has carved a reputation in quality tv feature film production. He's made the documentary "Bread And Films" (1980), "One Way Ticket" (1981), "The Border" (1981), "The Barricade" (1982) and now "The Sailors of Kronstadt" (1983). Judging from the success of these aired productions, the transfer to cinema presentations in selected arthouses and film archives/institutions is expected.

The city of Kronstadt was the scene of the first uprising against the newly-installed Communist Party in Russia. It occurred in March, 1921, and the insurgents were the same sailors at the Kronstadt naval base who were the bulwark of Bolshevik support during the October Revolution. Lenin put down the revolt ruthlessly.

First, Kronstadt itself. It's situated on Kotlin island in the Gulf of Finland, and was the official port for St. Petersburg until a canal was constructed direct to the heart of the capital (1875-85). The port is ice-bound five months of the year, making it possible to walk across the ice to Finland in the winter. Kronstadt witnessed four

naval mutinies at the dawn of this century — in 1905, 1906, 1917 and (depicted in Klauss' film) 1921.

And the reason for the mutiny? Lenin sought to feed his ravaged state by inaugurating a system of "war communism," whereby grain was taken from the peasants by forcible requisitioning for urgent distribution in urban and war-zone areas, the rest left over to be distributed among the peasants themselves and less needy of the population.

Instead of working as planned, however, shortages in every sector became so extreme that peasant uprisings occurred in the summer and autumn of 1918 — followed by the insurrection among the sailors at Kronstadt in 1921.

"The Sailors of Kronstadt" is a semi-documentary, semi-theatrical reconstruction of the events. The characters are fictional so far as the common people and the mutinous sailors are concerned, but the figures of Trotsky and Sinoviev are pretty close to real persons drawn from a vibrant page in history. Everything unspools in a studio with stage props and stylized acting performances. The audience is to experience the reconstruction of an event.

Well acted by several name thesps, "The Sailors of Kronstadt" will find a hip aud among Soviet history buffs, to be sure. Pic is also a fine example of how German tv productions amount on occasion to a full-fledged seminar on political questions.—*Holl.*

Giovanni
(DUTCH-COLOR)

Amsterdam, Sept. 16.

A Studio Nieuwe Gronden production. Produced by Rene Scholten. Stars Truus te Selle. Written and directed by Annette Apon. Camera (color), Theo Van de Sande; editor, Ton de Graaff; sound, Eric Langhout; art direction, Hadassah Kann. Reviewed at the Movies, Amsterdam, Sept. 16, 1983. Running time: 90 MINS.

"Giovanni," a film for festivals and art houses, is a lowbudgeter interesting for style and structure, which runs out of steam three-quarters of the way through.

De facto star of the 16m blowup, shot in 13 days, is a hotel room, eclipsing the importance of the central player, Truus te Selle, and aided by some skillful sound and image making.

Annette Apon, who wrote and directed, came up with a scenario that's not only open ended but has an open beginning and open middle. She experiments here, in a gamble which doesn't fully come off, by mixing naturalistic photography and te Selle's realistic acting with some deliberate attitudinizing in other performances.

A docu director with one credit ("The Waves"), she has organized

some good camera work and an excellent mix of natural sound, dialog and occasional music, all well edited.

Story sees Diane, a fashion photographer (te Selle) in Rome. She has an assignment, but also wants to look for Giovanni, a man she once knew. She takes a room in a hotel. Viewers see it before her arrival and when she enters. Pic then never leaves the room.

When Diane goes out, the camera stays behind, the mike goes on listening. They register who comes in, how the light and the street noises change with the hours. The maid and the valet (and some unexpected visitors) nosey around, into her bag, look at her photos.

The mike catches sounds in the street, in the buildings, the people in the next room. There is little dialog.

While Diane is in , she makes a few telephone calls, but never has a real conversation with anybody. She's tense. She can't sleep. She puts the tv on, only to switch it off.

While she is out an adulterous couple, on the run from the wronged husband, shelter a short while in her room.

Giovanni comes in and leaves a note. She'll never find it. A man, bleeding from a gun wound, climbs in the window, rests, climbs out again.

The room is a shambles when she comes back, and she is promptly suspected by the police — no one exactly knows of what. She leaves the hotel after less than 48 hours. The maid cleans the room for the next guest. End of film.

"Giovanni" is gripping during three quarters of its length, largely due to te Selle's fascinating portrayal. — *Wall.*

Aux Sources De La Coleur, De Son Et De L'Animation
(The Beginnings of Color, Sound & Film Animation)
(FRENCH-COMPILATION-B&W/COLOR)

A Service des Archives du Film, Centre National de la Cinematographie (Bois d'Arcy) compilation, organized by Franz Schmitt. Reviewed at Museum of Modern Art, N.Y., Oct. 2, 1983. Running time: 120 MINS.

"The Beginnings Of Color, Sound and Film Animation" is a diffuse compilation film which, unlike the excellent Bois d'Arcy archive presentations dealing with Melies and the Lumiere Brothers, tackles too many subjects. Pic does offer 24 complete early films plus a 1958-produced short survey of early sound experiments.

Highlight of the film is the final selection, Ladislas Starevitch's 1925 two-reeler "The Eyes Of The Dragon." Beautifully tinted, this stop-motion animation tale of a legendary Chinese fantasy world boasts beautiful, meticulously crafted miniatures and stop-motion effects that defy the usual constraints on the medium. For example, Starevitch's dancing insects include a mosquito of such thin proportions that conventional use of an armature for the repositioning process to animate the figure can be ruled out. This short film should be made available on its own, with a soundtrack added.

Another wonderful segment is a French travelog filmed on the U.S. West Coast, "En Suivant Le Soleil Sur L'Ouest" (Following the Sun Into the West), undated but apparently shot in the 1920s. Besides its recording of arresting period locales, short is a classic example of professional tinting, with many scenes combining subtle multicolors that fool the eye into believing that color film stock was used in lensing rather than monochrome, tinted later.

The remainder of the film lacks focus. Color is demonstrated by various tinted films made before 1910 by the Lumiere brothers, Pathé's "Le Moulin Maudit" (The Mill), a 1909 short which demonstrates subtle use of tinting. Some of the color effects are crude, particularly in Georges Melies' "Paris-Monte Carlo Race In Two Hours" (1905), in which the automobile has a red smear applied in quick-and-dirty fashion.

Early sound experiments are covered perfunctorily, with Roger Goupillieres' 1958 compilation short "Le Cinema Parlant en 1900" (The Sound Film In 1900) included. It incorporates excerpts of films synchronized with sound recorded on cylinders for playback in theatres. On view is Coquelin as "Cyrano de Bergerac," Mariette Sully singing in "La Poupee" and a comedy short, "Big Boots," featuring synchronized sound effects. Beyond this quickie survey, sound is represented in the form of a musical track for an 18-minute film "L'Assassination du Duc de Guise" (1908) by Andre Calmettes. This static film set in the era of King Henry III sports nice tinting but is too lengthy (it should be shown alone) and creates a dead patch in the middle of the film.

Animation emphasizes the work of Emile Cohl, Emile Reynand and others in dated material of mainly academic interest. The Starevitch beauty at the end serves as a welcome antidote to some rather dull material. —Lor.

Deal Of The Century
(COLOR)

Caveat emptor.

Hollywood, Oct. 18.

A Warner Bros. release, produced by Bud Yorkin. Exec producers, Jon Avnet, Steve Tisch, Paul Brickman. Directed by William Friedkin. Features entire cast. Screenplay, Paul Brickman; camera (Technicolor), Richard H. Kline; editor, Bud Smith; sound (Dolby Stereo), Willie Burton; production design, Bill Malley; associate producer, David Salven; assistant director, Terrence A. Donnelly; music, Arthur B. Rubinstein. Reviewed at the Academy of Motion Picture Arts & Sciences, Beverly Hills, Oct. 18, 1983. (MPAA rating: PG.) Running time: **98 MINS.**

Eddie Muntz	Chevy Chase
Mrs. DeVoto	Sigourney Weaver
Ray Kasternak	Gregory Hines
Stryker	Vince Edwards
Gen. Cordosa	William Marquez
Col. Salgado	Eduardo Ricard
Lyle	Richard Herd
Babers	Graham Jarvis
Harold	Wallace Shawn

"Deal Of The Century" transforms the military-industrial complex into a minimally intelligent simplex and, having redefined the target, misses it completely. Director William Friedkin doubtless had something important on his mind he wanted to satirize, but lost sight of it in trying to adapt to young comedy standards.

Friedkin starts with the rather sound notion that whoever manufactures weapons bears some responsibility for their use, an idea not a fresh thought to the current century nor the several preceding it. Next, he's attracted to the irony that most deadly machinery is sold for peace-keeping, admittedly amusing but also not original.

For a moment, he almost stumbles across the interesting possibility that most of today's expensive military machinery probably won't ever work the way it's supposed to, making all the fascination with it rather farcical. But Friedkin meanders past that one, except for a couple of obvious sight gags.

Whatever madness he did discover in the world of arms dealing might have been handled still with some sympathetic comedic characters and a light touch. But Friedkin doesn't come up with those, either.

Chevy Chase is at his worst as a self-centered, greedy, bargain-basement gun peddler in South America who lucks into a deal to palm off a lot of erratic drone fighters to a dictator, William Marquez.

To do so, he'll try to talk his conscience-stricken pal, Gregory Hines, out of converting to Christianity just long enough for a last minute killing (literally) and talk his girl friend, Sigourney Weaver, into bed with Marquez to assure the sale.

And those are the good guys.

Chief villain is Vince Edwards as the head of defense contractor whose survival depends on selling the planes, regardless of consequence. Looking like Godfather Gone Gadget, Edwards is certainly villainous enough, but Friedkin and writer Paul Brickman never make clear why he's worse than Chase.

Worse still, "Century" is one of those annoying films where the most bizarre things will happen in one scene — like a missile-firing plane gone amok over San Diego — and then never be mentioned again. Given everything else, however, that's probably a blessing.

"Century" also insists on mixing stark realism in otherwise supposedly funny scenes. How funny is it to watch Chase wrestle a machine-gunned bloody body for a suitcase of money?

The audience seemed to enjoy the film most when Chase or Hines are solving ordinary social vexations with the large armory they have in their car trunks. If so, Friedkin may have missed the whole point even more than it seems. —Har.

Apocalipsis Canibal
(Night Of The Zombies)
(SPANISH-ITALIAN-COLOR)

A Motion Picture Marketing release of a Dara Films/Beatrice Film production. Executive producer, Sergio Cortona. Directed by Vincent Dawn. Features entire cast. Screenplay, Claudio Fragasso, J.M. Cunilles; camera (Telecolor), John Cabrera; editor, Claudio Borroni; music, Goblin, under the direction of G Dell'Orso; production design, Antonio Velart; makeup, Giuseppe Ferranti; English-language version by A.B. Services. Reviewed at RKO Warner 1 Theatre, N.Y., Oct. 15, 1983. (No MPAA Rating; self-applied equivalent X rating). Running time: **100 MINS.**

With: Margit Evelyn Newton (Lea), Frank Garfield, Selan Karay, Robert O'Neil, Luis Fonoll, Gaby Renom, Ester Mesina, Victor Israel.

"Apocalipsis Canibal," also known as "Hell Of The Living Dead," is a haphazardly constructed European horror film lensed in 1980 in the wake of George A. Romero's international hit "Dawn Of The Dead." Its U.S. release title, "Night Of The Zombies," avoids confusion with Romero's fiercely protected "Dead" monicker, but unfortunately duplicates exactly the 1981 release title of Joel M. Reed's American film in the undead genre. Horror fans, used to endless title changes, will sort out the confusion in due course.

Picture is aimed squarely at the gore market, attempting to gross-out young viewers rather than offer edification. (It's being released with the increasingly common "No one under 17 admitted" ad come-on rather than an MPAA rating.)

Story is set mainly in Papua & New Guinea, where a so-called "Hope Centre" scientific installation has had a deadly leak, emitting green smoke which turns technicians and nearby natives into zombies with a hankering for human flesh. Terrorists occupy a U.S. consulate in an unidentified Spanish city, demanding that the Hope Centres worldwide be destroyed; but the local authorities destroy the terrorists instead.

Visiting Papua to investigate native disturbances are two of the dumbest aggregations imaginable: an Italian tv news crew led by pretty newshen Lea (Margit Evelyn Newton) and a squad of soldiers on a search & destroy mission. Eventually teaming up, these protagonists are endlessly beset by hungry zombies throughout the film, but much to the delight of an audience, they never seem to take matters seriously. Quickly discovering that the way to kill a zombie is to shoot it in the head ("Apocalipsis," as do most other imiative European pics, steals George Romero's premise without explanation), the heroes keep forgetting this in later scenes, wasting hundreds of bullets aimed at zombie torsos.

The zombies bear a varied set of cheap makeup jobs, tending towards sepulchral grey, and amusingly shamble about in imitation of singer Joe Cocker heading for his microphone. Also funny here is the dubbed dialog, which resurrects surefire B-movie cliches ranging from "I don't like the sound of those drumbeats" to the more appropriate "Something eatin' ya?" Three scenes vying for the silliest moment award: Lea's cameraman approaching the undead after numerous killings and asking them to "Hold still" for a photo; Lea suddenly (early on) declaring "I've got to meet them alone," stripping to the waist and marching off covered with body paint for an encounter with grainy stock-footage natives; and, memorably, a soldier yelling "Let go of her" rather than shooting from the hip when the ghouls grab Lea late in the proceedings.

Alas, the Continental filmmakers, including one pseudonym-sounding director "Vincent Dawn," have erected formidable barriers to anyone enjoying this film's camp value. First and foremost are the closeups of extras munching on red meat in cannibal-fashion, as well as other types of butcher-shop effects including a rat emerging from a woman's abdomen, the heroes' vomiting and natives feeding on maggots in corpses. Escalating sensationalism and an easing up on international censorship have made such scenes all too common.

Beyond its tiresome gross-outs, "Apocalipsis" is a mishmash of random footage, integrating endless stock footage filler of flora, fauna and natives into the unmatching new scenes. Color processing is relentlessly ugly and variable in terms of grain, timing, etc. Only pro credit is a rhythmic musical score by the Italian rock group Goblin, but it can't save this nihilistic mess. —Lor.

Parahyba Mulher Macho
(Parahyba Woman)
(BRAZILIAN-COLOR)

Rio de Janeiro, Oct. 12.

An Embrafilme distribution of a CPC-Centro de Producao e Comunicacao production. Features entire cast. Associate producers, Embrafilme, Helena Lundgren, Anita Harley, Sky Light Cinema, Luiz Pastore, Guide Vasconcelos. Directed by Tizuca Yamasaki. Screenplay, Yamasaki, Jose Joffily Filho, based on biographic novel "Anayde Beiriz — Passion and Death in the Revolution of '30," by Jose Joffily (Record Publishers); music, Paulo Moura; art direction, Yurika Yamasaki; editing, Lael Rodrigues; camera (Eastmancolor), Edgar Moura; direct sound, Juarez Dagoberto; sound editing, Walter Goulart; executive producer, Liane Muhlenberg; production director, Walter Schilke; assistant director, Vitor Lustosa. Produced by Carlos Alberto Diniz. Reviewed at Hotel Meridien screening room, Rio de Janeiro, Oct. 12, 1983. Running time: 88 MINS.

Anayde Beiriz ....Tania Alves
Joao Dantas ....Claudio Marzo
Joao Pessoa ....Walmor Chagas
Augusto Caldas ....Jose Dumont
Colonel Jose Pereira .....Oswaldo Loureiro

Also. Jose Mario Austregesilo, Chico Dias, Germano Hayut, Fernando Teixeira, Alvaro Freire, Braulio Tavares, Aldemar de Oliveira and Grande Otelo.

"Parahyba Mulher Macho" is the story of Anayde Beiriz, a woman who became responsible for a political murder in 1930 that highly influenced Brazilian history. Young and beautiful (although, according to historians, not as beautiful as portrayed by Tania Alves in the film), Anayde was audacious and the kind of woman who would later be labeled "liberated." In her time, political power in the state of Paraiba (at the Brazilian northeast) was disputed by two rival groups: the Liberal Alliance, leaded by Joao Pessoa, and the Republican Party, whose chief, Colonel Jose Pereira, waks a close friend of journalist Jaoa Dantas, son of a traditional and politically influential family of Paraiba, of whom Anayde Beiriz would become lover.

Not afraid of scandals, Beiriz took her passion for Dantas beyond the boundaries of the moral standards of that time. When Dantas' apartment was invaded by state police, a number of confidential letters and photographs were taken and publicly displayed. A few days later, Joao Pessoa, then chief politician of Paraiba, was murdered by Dantas in a restaurant in Pernambuco.

Main preoccupation of director Tizuca Yamasaki was to equally circulate among the general aspects of the Paraiba politics and the particular feelings of a couple not especially interested in the political events. Aim is partially achieved, though in both cases lacking the involvement of Yamasaki's "Gaijin," on the Japanese immigration to Brazil. Neverthe-

less, facts are narrated with no articulation problems and the production convincingly stages some street disturbances in locations mainly distributed through Pernambuco.

Acting is good, with Tania Alves in the role originally conceived for Sonia Braga. Tania is very attractive and a fine actress ("Cabaret Mineiro"), tending to overact due to the ambiguity of her character, for most historians wonder to what extent the feminism inherent to Beiriz' persona'ity was a cultural component. Historians, in fact, have come to a number of restrictions not so relevant to the film as a product of the artist-oriented minds.

In this sense, "Parahyba Mulher Macho" is doubtless a fine work. Well-photographed and edited (actually, twice edited and finally relesed in an 88-min. version), it has the standard expected from the author of "Gaijin." Perhaps it is not a product of the same sensibility, but it is equally important to tell a story about local history with literary imagination and cinematic skill. —Hoin.

Yuki
(Yuki-Snow Fairy)
(JAPANESE-ANIMATED-COLOR)

Vancouver, Oct. 9.

A Mushi Co. Production for Nikkatsu Children's Films. Produced by Ei Ito. Directed by Tadashi Imai. Animation director, Shinji Tuji; written by Akira Miyazaki, from a story by Ryusuke Saito; music, Chito Kawachi. No further credits available. Reviewed at Robson Square Cinema, Vancouver, (2d Annual Kidfest), Oct. 9, 1983. Running time: 88 MINS.

Vet helmer Tadashi Imai, whose distinguished left-wing career goes back 50 years, no doubt enjoyed the message of this stilted parable about peasant solidarity overthrowing land barons, samurai marauders, etc. Doubtless Imai also did little more than supervise the work of animator head Shinji Tuji. Unhappily, facial expression and bodily grace in this cartoon are both severely limited.

A 13-year-old Goddess, Yuki, is sent on a mission to earth by her grandparents. Her task is to purify the lower world with snow. She joins a band of beggars living next to a village owned by greedy landlord Goemon, whose white stallion, she tames. Her heroic example emboldens the villagers to drive out their various foes.

Only after 50 minutes does the cartoon come vividly to life in a brief montage during the farmers' night raid on the samurai camp. Though scenic backgrounds are often exemplary, their painterly virtues do not belong in a cartoon in such numbers. Animation has to be more than merely eye-catching if it is to succeed as drama, too.

A Westernized score is an asset, but the film is difficult to distinguish clearly from Saturday morning cartoons, apart from its socialist content. Could stir up some interest for paycable. — Gran.

Mercedes Sosa, Como Una Pajaro Libre
(Mercedes Sosa, Like A Free Bird)
(ARGENTINE-COLOR-DOCU)

Buenos Aires, Oct. 18.

A Dispro release of a Daniel Grinbank-Pino Farina production. Produced by Kiko Tenenbaum. Features entire cast. Directed by Ricardo Wüllicher. Camera (Eastmancolor), Miguel Rodriguez; second unit cameramen, Daniel Karp, Aldo Lobotrico, Jose Trela and Hugo Colace. Reviewed at the Sarmiento theatre, B.A., Oct. 6, 1983. Running time: 75 MINS.

Cast: Mercedes Sosa, Ariel Ramirez, Charly Garcia, Leon Gieco, Piero, Antonio Tarrago Ros. Musicians: Jose Luis Castiñeira de Dios, Domingo Cura, Oscar Alem, Nicolas Brizuela, Omar Espinosa.

Mercedes Sosa, who regularly tours all over the world, is one of the most-acclaimed and most-widely known Argentine female pop singer. At home she is admired not only for her talent, but also for her civic courage in opposing totalitarianism and defending human rights. She is one of the few performers still blacklisted in state o&o radio and tv stations on the eve of the transition to democracy.

Although middle-aged, left-winger Sosa has become a cult figure for Argentine youth, who see in her a combination of Indian features, untamable spirit and lyrical gifts, a symbol of the timeless vernacular stand against oppressors.

This documentary records her triumphal comeback to Argentina when the ban on her personal appearances was lifted. Crowds filled soccer stadiums in Buenos Aires, Tucuman (her native town), La Plata and other cities, wildly cheering her while engaging in chants challenging the military rulers.

Sosa has cleverly broadened her original folkloric repertory with songs by contemporary composers and lyricists. A few of the most famous unusually accompany her in concerts and recordings, as do Ariel Ramirez, Charly Garcia, Leon Gieco, Piero and Antonio Tarrago Ros in this film, adding attraction, marquee value and an updated look.

Shot in 16m and blown up to 35m, pic shows Sosa warbling 16 themes, relating her life to the camera, answering questions in press conferences and recording. Reportedly limited by a low budget, director Ricardo Wüllicher has lensed just that, not attempting either a deeper human approach to Sosa or an aesthetically creative enhancement of his work. But the sheer force of the singer's art and personality save the effort,

making it a valuable item for tv and homevideo after its theatrical run. Technical credits are acceptable despite some flaws. — Nubi.

For Love Or Money
(AUSTRALIAN-B&W/COLOR)
DOCU — 16m)

Sydney, Oct. 13.

A Filmmakers' Co-operative release of a Flashback Films production. Produced by Megan McMurchy, Margot Oliver, Jeni Thornley. Directed by McMurchy and Thornley. Script, research, McMurchy, Oliver, Thornley; music, Elizabeth Drake; editor, Margot Nash; still photography, Erika Addis; sound Pat Fiske; narrator, Noni Hazlehurst. Reviewed at Academy Twin Cinema, Paddington, Oct. 11, 1983. Running time: 108 MINS.

Voices: Jane Clifton, Diane Craig, Nick Enright, Vivienne Garrett, Richard Meikle, Margot Nash, Robyn Nevin, Emu Nugent, Justine Saunders, Kay Self, Carole Skinner, Maureen Watson.

An extremely ambitious, dedicated and comprehensive documentary feature about working women in Australia, "For Love Or Money" is bound to capture plenty of attention Down Under and generate debate as well.

Using copious amounts of footage culled from the National Film Archive — actuality footage as well as very many clips from feature films — the well-crafted docu covers a lot of ground, starting with the early convict days of the colony, in the 1780s, when thousands of women were transported from England for petty crimes and when women convicts frequently rioted against dreadful conditions and bad food.

Film is divided into four chapters: Part 1, Hard Labor, covers this convict period and continues until 1914, taking in the growth of cities, divisions of labor, and the suffragette movement (Australia was, in fact, one of the first countries in the world to give women the vote). Part 2, Daughters of Toil, continues until 1939, taking in the role of women during the Great War and the uneasy peace that followed. Part 3, Working for the Duration, takes us to 1969, and in its coverage of World War II looks at the way women were brought into the workforce to fill positions vacated by men; the film also explores the debate over equal pay for women in considerable depth. The arrival of thousands of migrant women in the postwar period is also seen as a factor. Finally, Work of Value, brings us to the present day and the growing feminist and peace movements.

As can be seen, "For Love or Money" endeavors to tell the most comprehensive story of Australian working women over a 200-year period, and also covers the plight of aboriginal women in some detail. It becomes rather too much for one film to bear, and as a result superficiality creeps in as vitally important subjects are rather sketchily treated. It also has all the hallmarks of a committee-made film, and lacks the exhilaration, anger and even the humor of such similarly themed US documentaries as "Union Maids" or "The Life and Times of Rosie the Riveter;" indeed, there's an overriding humorlessness which could be inherent in the subject but which may prevent the message being carried over to a wider audience. Length may also be a factor.

Filmmakers have obviously been given enormous help by the National Film Archive, yet they have treated the sometimes rare old footage in a cavalier fashion; excerpts are not identified, thus the viewer may have difficulty deciding which clips come from newsreels and which from fiction films (this is true of the early silent material). When very well known feminist themed films such as "My Brilliant Career" or "Caddie" are used to make a point the device works, but all too often scenes are wrested from a feature and presented completely out of context.

No doubt "For Love or Money" was made with total commitment, and very often it succeeds in relating present customs and conditions back into history. It will obviously be of the greatest interest to Women's Film Groups and Festivals all over the world, but its message is so important it shouldn't be limited to such audiences.

Narration tends to emphasize the rather doleful approach of the film rather than celebrate the achievements of women in Australia. Again, the enthusiasm and dedication of all concerned is notable. — *Strat.*

Yentl
(COLOR)

A star is borne. To a point.

Hollywood, Oct. 26.

An MGM/UA release of a United Artists presentation of a Barwood production. Produced by Barbra Streisand, Rusty Lemorande. Executive producer, Larry De Waay. Stars, and directed by Streisand. Screenplay, Jack Rosenthal, Streisand, based on "Yentl, The Yeshiva Boy" by Isaac Bashevis Singer; camera (Technicolor), David Watkin; editor, Terry Rawlings; music, Michel Legrand; lyrics, Alan Bergman, Marilyn Bergman; production design, Roy Walker; art direction, Leslie Tomkins; set decoration, Tessa Davies; costume design, Judy Moorcroft; sound (Dolby), David Hildyard; asst. director, Steve Lanning. Reviewed at the MGM Studios, Culver City, Oct. 26, 1983. (MPAA Rating: PG.) Running time: 134 MINS.

Yentl	Barbra Streisand
Avigdor	Mandy Patinkin
Hadass	Amy Irving
Papa	Nehemiah Persoff
Reb Alter Vishkower	Steven Hill
Shimmele	Allan Corduner
Esther Rachel	Ruth Goring
Rabbi Zalman	David De Keyser

Barbra Streisand becomes the latest to join the growing ranks of performer auteurs with "Yentl," a large-scaled but intimate musical she has been nurturing ever since she became a film star 15 years ago.

Carefully and lovingly done in every respect, pic starts out well, but ultimately bogs down due to repetitious musical numbers and overly methodical telling of a rather predictable story. Streisand's legion of fans, undoubtedly hungry after not having seen her in a full-blown leading role for more than four years, will surely flock to see this, and the sizable middle-aged public that occasionally emerges for the right film also reps a possible target audience.

Given her longtime superstar status and meticulous, demanding reputation, it is not surprising either that Streisand has made the move into the director's chair, or that the result is so thoroughly professional. (Contrary to some published claims, however, Streisand is not the first woman to become a writer-director-star on a major studio feature — Elaine May did it on "A New Leaf" — although Streisand is a quadruple hyphenate by virtue of producing as well.)

Based on a short story by Nobel Prize laureate Isaac Bashevis Singer, "Yentl" tells the tale of a young Eastern European woman, circa 1904, who disguises herself as a boy in order to pursue her passion for studying holy scripture, an endeavor restricted exclusively to men in orthodox Jewish culture.

Moving from her native village and passing as a pubescent boy, Yentl has no problem in the scholarly world, but tragi-comic results stem from the romantic situation her presence creates. Befriended by her brash, attractive fellow student Avigdor, wonderfully played by Mandy Patinkin, Yentl falls in love with him, but naturally can't do anything about it.

When Avigdor is prevented from marrying his lovely fiancee Hadass (a china doll Amy Irving) through a technicality of religious law, Avigdor pushes Yentl to marry Hadass in his stead. This she does, and although Yentl rationalizes the postponement of the marriage's consummation for a long time, she can't get away with her disguise forever, resulting in a unavoidably melancholy but hopeful conclusion.

Expository sequences between Yentl and her ailing father, perfectly essayed by Nehemiah Persoff, fully express the woman's frustration and bursting desire to fulfill her potential. Most moving aspect of the film, in fact, is its depiction of a character who is dedicated to excelling, to reaching beyond the limitations her society imposes upon her, and this is excitingly conveyed in the first song.

Yentl's situation and the detailed evocation of the distinctive Jewish society remain interesting throughout, but the trajectory of the story itself is self-evident despite the plot twists, and the payoffs seem a long time in coming.

Each scene is about just one thing, and there is no subtext — not to mention subplots — to fill out and enrich what increasingly appears as a one-note film.

Songs by Michel Legrand, with lyrics by Alan and Marilyn Bergman, have been carefully planned as interior monologs for Yentl (only Streisand sings here) and to advance the narrative. Nevertheless, tunes tend to slow the action down and eventually seem to meld together due to their musical similarity and identical manner of treatment; generally, numbers have Streisand peforming in lipsynch for part of the time, with montage of action and even some dialog mixed in.

Then there's the question of dramatic credibility where Yentl's masquerade is concerned. In terms of absolute verisimilitude, all the characters should have been played by younger performers, but given the already unrealistic aspect automatically supplied by pic's status as a musical, benefit of the doubt will surely be extended by viewers.

Disguised as a man via short hair, cap and wire-rimmed glasses, Streisand reminds by turns of David Brenner and Woody Allen, which doesn't hurt the comic scenes. But some of these, especially one which forces Streisand to sleep in the same bed with Patinkin, remind that we've recently been down the path of sex-role change and ambiguity before,

most notably with "Tootsie" and "Victor/Victoria." The result here is distinctly less entertaining and edifying for all its nobility of intent.

As both performer and director, Streisand is nothing if not energetic. She's constantly vibrant and inventive before the camera, and does a perfectly creditable job of staging the action. In league with ace cinematographer David Watkin, who has imbued the interiors, at least, with gorgeous, Vermeerlike lighting, Streisand has created a fine-looking period piece which cannot have been easy to mount.

Working on Czech locations and in English studios, production designer Roy Walker has impeccably fashioned an alien, vanished world, and Judy Moorcroft's costumes are equally impressive.

—*Cart.*

The House
(Husid)
(ICELANDIC — COLOR)

Sydney, Oct. 18.

A Saga Film production. Produced by Jon Thor Hannesson. Directed by Egill Edvardsson. Features entire cast. Screenplay, Snorri Thorisson, Bjorn Bjornsson, Edvardsson; camera (Fujicolor), Thorisson; editors, Thorisson, Evardsson; music, Thorir Bladursson; art director, Bjornsson. Reviewed at Academy Twin Cinema, Paddington, during Scandinavian Film Week, Oct. 13, 1983. Running time: 90 MINS.

Bjorg	Lilja Thorisdottir
Petur	Johann Sigurdarson
The Medium	Helgi Skulason
Foster-father	Baldvin Halldorsson
Foster-mother	Margaret Olafsdottir
Aunt	Thora Borg
Violinist	Helga Oskarsdottir
Little girl	Unnur Berglind

As filmmakers, the Icelanders are nothing if not economical. In his feature film debut, director Egill Edvardsson brought in this enjoyable litle thriller on a budget of $US270,000, neatly avoiding the rushed or penny pinching look of many cheapies.

Those Icelanders are also passionate cinemagoers. When this pic played on its home patch earlier this year it was seen by 70,000 in its 10-week season, around one-third the nation's population. And the locals pay twice the regular admission prices for the privilege of seeing native fare.

Icelandic lingo and dubbing costs are listed as the chief obstacles in the way of international distribution and, if they can be surmounted a film like "The House" could find a niche on television in nations where subtitling or dubbing is acceptable. Pic unspooled in Australia as part of a festival of 10 Scandinavian films.

Simple at the outset, but gaining in complexity and ambiguity as it rolls along, plot has a young couple moving into an old house. She teaches deaf children, he is a struggling composer, a vivid contrast in the worlds of silence and of music. House, or rather its other unfriendly inhabitants moving wraith-like among the gloom, gradually becomes more menacing to Bjorg (Lilja Thorisdottir) particularly after she is left alone when Petur (Johann Sigurdarson) leaves town for a few days. There are a medium, a coffin, nightmarish visions of screaming, contorted faces. Are they ghosts? Or is Bjorg reliving some long supressed childhood experiences? Either way, she undergoes a torrid time until she meets a violent death.

This is well acted, well written and well directed drama — and all for $US270,000. That's a steal.

— *Dogo.*

O Chico Fininho
(Skinny Chico)
(PORTUGUESE-B&W-16m)

Vancouver, Oct. 6.

A BeiFilm Production. Produced, directed by Serio Fernandes. Features entire cast. No writing credit. Camera (black and white), Joao Bourdain de Macedo; editor, Fernando Manuel; music, Rui Veloso. No further credits available. Reviewed at Robson Square Cinema, Vancouver, (2d Annual Vancouver kidfest), Oct. 6, 1983. Running time: 64 MINS.
Chico Fininho .... Vitor Norte
Cenoura .... Manuel Guilherme Almeida
Reporter .... Luis Pereira de Sousa
Lena .... Helena Melc
Ze .... Jose Luis Oliveira
Phonas.............. Sergo Malpique Lopes

Somebody in the sunstruck city of Oporto has finally caught up with Richard Lester's fettlesome frolic, "A Hard Day's Night" — 20 years too late! This numbskull revamping of dumb kids on the prowl features some of the worst use of Steadicam apparatus on record. Listlessly we track (in murky monochrome) the aimless itinerary of rock musician Skinny Chico as he and his hangers-on boozily bore one another while dusk settles.

Skinny and his buddies are Americanized teens (each looks well past 25 years) whose taste in music has to be heard to be believed. They're so cool, man, and like groovy, y'know? Right on, compadre! Any poor soul who submitted to the atrocius rock here unleashed would be as dazed as Skinny. Director Fernandes' visuals are a potpourri of avant-garde and counterculture nonsense that has been kept under covers for a decade.

Tech credits are even less than rock bottom. A total writeoff for export. —*Gran.*

Making Out
(W. GERMAN-COLOR)

Hollywood, Oct. 23.

An SRC Film Release. Produced by Wolf C. Hartwig. Director, Walter Boos. Features entire cast. Screenplay, Gunther Heeler; camera (color), Klaus Werner; editor, George Stiehle; set design, Laslo Varga. No other credits. Reviewed at AMC Hawthorne Theatre, Hawthorne, Calif. Oct. 23, 1963. (MPAA Rating: R). Running time: 94 MINS.

Cast: Jessie St. Clair, Nona Phillips, Sandra Gayle, Brigette Lee, Karja Benet.
(English-dubbed soundtrack)

A nasty little movie, reviewed here for the record, "Making Out" is a West German sexploitation pic, probably softened for American release and poorly dubbed into English. Pic is packaged as a teenage sex romp, featuring an ad with a scantily-clad vixen who doesn't even appear in the movie, but whose appeal is clearly to dirty old men. Boos has made a long series of these pics under an overall title of "Schulmadchen" (Schoolgirls).

Nothing about "Making Out" makes much sense. A series of "erotic" tales is strung together as stories told by students preparing for a production of "Romeo and Juliet." Shakespeare this stuff is not. Rather, the stories feature such unpleasant excuses to display some flesh as blackmail, alcoholism and shoplifting.

Attitude towards sex here is reminiscent of the wild and crazy guys (Steve Martin and Dan Aykroyd) who appeared several years ago on "Saturday Night Live," lusting after everything in sight — except when they did it, it was meant to be a parody. — *Jagr.*

The Devonsville Terror
(COLOR)

Interesting but highly derivative horror outing.

A Motion Picture Marketing release of a New West Films production. Executive producers, Jochen Breitenstein, David Du-Bay. Produced and directed by Ulli Lommel. Features entire cast. Screenplay, Lommel, George T. Lindsey, Suzanna Love; camera (Pacific color), Lommel; editor, Richard Brummer; music, Ray Colcord; additional music, Ed Hill; sound, Bruce Malm, John Huck; production manager, Ron Norman; assistant director, Bruce Starr; special photographic effects, David Hewitt; makeup, Erica Ueland; second unit director, Breitenstein; second unit camera, Joerg Walther; set design, Priscilla van Gorder; special effects, Matthew Mungle, George Rogers; historical consultant, Elizabeth Trevelyan; co-producer, Charles Aperia; associate producers, Tim Nielsen, Bill Rebane. Reviewed on Embassy Home Entertainment vidcassette, N.Y., Oct. 22, 1983. (No MPAA Rating). Running time: 83 MINS.
Jenny Scanlon .... Suzanna Love
Matthew Pendleton .... Robert Walker
Dr. Warley .... Donald Pleasence
Walter Gibbs .... Paul Willson

Filmed in 1982, "The Devonsville Terror" has prolific German director Ulli Lommel dabbling in the witchcraft genre with mixed results. Positive entertainment values of a burn 'em at the stake picture are unfortunately diluted by imitative special effects gimmickry in this item, currently available to homevideo fans.

Set in the New England town of Devonsville (actually filmed mainly in Wisconsin), picture opens with three accused witches tortured and executed in 1683 by townsfolk. On the 300th anni of the event, three young women move to town and quickly arouse the suspicions of the current residents of the insular community.

Jenny Scanlon (Suzanna Love) is the new elementary school teacher in from Princeton, N.J.; Monica (Deanna Haas) is a disk jockey and Chris (Mary Walden) is an environmentalist at the local lake testing the water for toxins. Since all three are highly independent outsiders, they are potential victims in a horror film.

Jenny is befriended by the young caretaker of lake cabins Matthew Pendleton (Robert Walker), but the rest of his family is out to get her, especially after she informs her school class of the heretical notion that in early religions God was supposed to be a woman.

Though the witch-hunting is based on prejudice, it turns out that Jenny is a supernatural agent, sent to wreak vengeance on Walter Gibbs (Paul Willson) who has just killed his wife. An unresolved subplot has the local doctor Warley (Donald Pleasence) suffering from a curse (his ancestor was the witches' executioner) in which his body is infested with worms (shown in icky closeups).

"Devonsville Terror" is okay as a suspense film until the finale, when Jenny is being burned at the stake but is saved by supernatural intervention. The staging exactly imitates the special makeup effects climax of "Raiders Of The Lost Ark" (even the soundtrack keyboards music imitates John Williams' climactic theme from that picture). It's a flattering nod by a B-filmmaker to the big guys, but originality would have been more appropriate.

Once again in the lead role in a Lommel pic (she's the director's wife), Love is appealing in or out of her clothes, styled here with a close-cropped red hairdo to resemble Jamie Lee Curtis. Name costars Walker and Pleasence have their moments but are underutilized in guest spots. Tech credits are fine, particularly the moody camerawork handled by Lommel himself. — *Lor.*

Star 80
(COLOR)

Murder of a centerfold.

Hollywood, Oct. 26.

A Ladd Company release through Warner Bros. Produced by Wolfgang Glattes, Kenneth Utt. Features entire cast. Directed, written by Bob Fosse, based in part on "Death Of A Playmate" by Teresa Carpenter. Camera (Technicolor), Sven Nykvist; editor, Alan Heim; music, Ralph Burns; art direction, Jack G. Taylor Jr., Michael Bolton; set decoration, Ann McCulley, Kimberley Richardson; visual consultant, Tony Walton; costume design, Albert Wolsky; sound, David Ronne; associate producer, Grace Blake; assistant director, Wolfgang Glattes. Reviewed at The Burbank Studios, Burbank, Oct. 26, 1963. (MPAA Rating: R.) Running time: 102 MINS.
Dorothy Stratten .... Mariel Hemingway
Paul Snider .... Eric Roberts
Hugh Hefner .... Cliff Robertson
Dorothy's Mother........... Carroll Baker
Aram Nicholas .... Roger Rees
Geb .... David Clennon
Private Detective .... Josh Mostel
Eileen .... Lisa Gordon
Nightclub Owner............. Sidney Miller
Photographer .... Keith Hefner
Bobo Weller .... Tina Willson
Betty .... Shelly Ingram
Exotic Dancer .... Sheila Anderson
Meg Davis .... Cis Rundle
Robin .... Kathryn Witt

Bob Fosse takes another look at the underside of the success trip in "Star 80," an engrossing, unsentimental and unavoidably depressing account of the short life and ghastly death of Playmate-actress Dorothy Stratten. As seemingly authentic and vivid a telling of this fairy tale with a tragic ending as anyone could want, pic will automatically assume a high profile in the marketplace due to Fosse's name and glamor attendant the Playboy mystique, and this should be enough to assure good openings in urban situations. But it's probably too dryly morbid for extended mass consumption.

Stratten was a sweet, voluptuous blonde who became a popular Playmate of the Year in Playboy, appeared in a few films, all of which are forgettable except for Peter Bogdanovich's "They All Laughed," and was brutally killed by her estranged husband in a murder-suicide in 1980.

Unfortunate story of this briefly bright shooting star caught the fancy of the media, having been the subject of Teresa Carpenter's investigative "Death Of A Playmate" article in The Village Voice, which helped the writer win a Pulitzer Prize and is credited as a basis for this film, and also having inspired the 1981 telepic "Death Of A Centerfold: The Dorothy Stratten Story" with Jamie Lee Curtis. Bogdanovich has long been working on his own memoir of their relationship, due out in book form.

Although not mentioned here, it is said that Hugh Hefner had high hopes for Stratten to become the first genuine star to emerge from the Playboy empire. In any event, the gal must have had something special to attract the prolonged attention of such eminent men as Hefner, Bogdanovich and Fosse, even if it was just that she possessed an innocent, unspoiled quality that nearly everyone found enchanting.

As played here by a newly proportioned Mariel Hemingway, Stratten is a virginal, extremely insecure teenager — almost a baby, really — in Vancouver who is swooped down upon by small-time hustler Paul Snider. Although doubtlessly in love with his discovery, Snider uses Stratten as his ticket to the big time in L.A., getting her in the door at Playboy and becoming her socalled manager once her career is underway.

Although Snider convinces Stratten to marry him, their relationship heads straight downhill, as he finds himself as unwelcome in Hollywood as she is embraced. Hardly insane, Snider nevertheless becomes unhinged through personal jealousy and general bitterness, and ultimately drags his wife down with him rather than just letting go.

Including a fair amount of interview format scenes to supply exposition, Fosse the screenwriter has taken an extremely schematic approach to the material, none-too-subtly foreshadowing such doomladen personality traits as Snider's violent streak and his wild jealousy. Climactic bloodbath is also introduced in little snippets from the very beginning, thus embuing entire pic with a sense of sadness and dread.

Director succeeds admirably in showing Stratten as a willingly malleable girl ready to be shaped by any strong man who comes along, but that it fails to be emotionally moving is due to the fact that Fosse's style is almost entirely geared to externals. The physical trappings and dramatic movement are all down pat, but one never gets inside the characters at all, rendering the experience detached and even a bit icy. As presented, it's more than a case history, but far less than great drama.

Given Stratten's passivity and pliability, histrionics fall to the Snider character, and Eric Roberts gives a startlingly fine performance as this pathetic loser, a man with no talents of his own who quickly blows the one lucky break he ever got. Slimy, obnoxious and hideously dressed, character is not the most appealing individual with whom to spend time, and fact that he's centerscreen throughout much of the film could represent a major turn-off to audiences.

Hemingway undergoes a wonderful transformation from small town girl to glamor queen, looks great and does a fine job throughout. Cliff Robertson is eminently plausible as Hefner, who enjoys a fatherly relationship with Stratten but is appalled by Snider.

Most of the characters are called by their real names, the one major exception being the Bogdanovich figure. Fosse seems to have gone out of his way to avoid any direct resemblance to the actual director, having cast English actor Roger Rees of "Nicholas Nickleby" and making the character shy and very soft-spoken. Good, if brief, support

is also offered by Carroll Baker as Stratten's mother, David Clennon as a friend of Snider's and Josh Mostel as a private investigator.

As can be expected of any Fosse film, craft and technical aspects are super slick and professional, notably Sven Nykvist's lensing and Alan Heim's editing. Tony Walton is credited as visual consultant; and photos of Hemingway prominently on display throughout unerringly evoke the w.k. Playboy look.

Fosse has dedicated the film to the late writer Paddy Chayefsky.
—*Cart.*

Mot Haerlige Tider
(Happy Days Are Here Again)
(SWEDISH – COLOR)

Stockholm, Oct. 20.

A Nordisk Tonefilm AB Svensk Filmindustri Swedish Film Institute production, AB Svensk Filmindustri release. Written and directed by Kjell Jerselius. Executive producer, Ingemar Ejve. Features entire cast. Camera (Fujicolor) Lasse Bjoerne; production design and costumes, Mona Theresia Forsen; editor, Lars Hagstroem; production management, Bjoern Henrickson, Susanne Ruben; music uncredited. Reviewed at the Roeda Kvarn theatre, Stockholm, Oct. 20, 1983. Running time, 92 MINS.
Jackie .... Pia Green
Carl-Adam .... Stig Engstroem
Yvonne .... Anki Liden
Vanja .... Helena Brodin
Arvid .... Jan Malmsjoe
Svempa .... Eddie Axberg
Katrin .... Lis Nilheim
Bosse .... Greger Lindquist
Peder .... Leif Ahrle
Marre .... Cecilia Walton
Lena .... Claire Wikholm

"Happy Days Are Here Again" is a first feature by Kjell Jerselius, a young film scholar with tv as his brief training ground for picture making. The training has been insufficient. His little triangular love-story comedy drags its dramatic feet at every turn and is embarrassingly stiff-jointed and overexplicit in its general story telling. Audience attendance after film's first week in Swedish theatres does not bode well even for domestic boxoffice although popular Swedish tastes have been catered to in plot and setting. The three main protagonists converge with friends for a midsummer holiday outing and erotic intrigue on a small island in the most idyllic of lake districts.

Jerselius has Jackie (Pia Green) look up her former lover Carl-Adam (Stig Engstroem) on his holiday island without giving him any warning. Ten years have gone by since she ran out on him also without warning. She is a woman who likes to act on impulse. Also on impulse, she has brought along a just-divorced, slightly older girlfriend (later to be matched with the island's local fisherman, played incongruously by Jan Malmsjoe, the fear-inspiring bishop of Ingmar Bergman's "Fanny and Alexander"). Jackie and Carl-Adam used

to be active in left-wing political work. He has since gone into a solid business career and furthered the latter by heading for marriage with the boss' daughter Yvonne (Anki Liden).

On the island, Jerselius fails in his hopes of having the triangle interplay twist and sparkle with anything remotely resembling old Howard Hawksian comedy. All characters and situations move leadenly in his hands. it makes things no better that Carl-Adam is robbed of sympathy by being depicted as too wishy-washy to be worthy of the attention of any woman but a mother. The surrounding characters are tired cliché renderings of common folks as the good guys and gals and rich folks as the utter fools. All are fairly nice and handsome to look at, and the camera is allowed to nearly fall asleep doing so. — *Kell.*

Going Berserk
(COLOR)

Candy gets sticky.

Hollywood, Oct. 28.

A Universal Pictures release. Produced by Claude Heroux; executive producer, Pierre David. Features entire cast. Directed by David Steinberg. Screenplay, Dana Olsen, Steinberg; camera (color), Bobby Byrne; editor, Donn Cambern; music, Tom Scott; production designer, Peter Lansdown Smith; set decorator, Marc Meyer; sound, Joe Kenworthy; associate producer, Denise Di Novi; assistant director, Dan Kolsrud. Reviewed at Hollywood Pacific Theatre, Oct. 28, 1983. (MPAA Rating: R.) Running time: 85 MINS.
John Bourgignon .... John Candy
Chick Leff .... Joe Flaherty
Sal De Pasquale .... Eugene Levy
Nancy Reese .... Alley Mills
Ed Reese .... Pat Hingle
Patti Reese .... Ann Bronston
Mrs. Reese .... Eve Brent Ashe
Grandmother Reese .... Elizabeth Kerr
Sun Yi .... Richard Libertini
Angela .... Dixie Carter
Dr. Ted .... Paul Dooley

John Bourgignon (John Candy) may be from Melonville, but he lacks the wit and inspired lunacy that we have come to expect from residents of that town made famous on Second City TV. "Going Berserk," which features Candy and SCTV vets Joe Flaherty and Eugene Levy, shoots a bit lower (and raunchier) than the now pay-cable Canadian series, but will probably be satisfying only to devout fans.

One of the big problems here is the writing. Though pic is directed and penned by David Steinberg (with Dana Olsen), usually no slouch in the comedy department, he has gone for a considerably less-sophisticated approach than Candy, Levy and Flaherty and company brought to SCTV as writers.

Also missing is a unifying concept (like a renegade tv network) to tie the bits together. The plot, involving the marriage of chauffeur

and part-time drummer Candy to the daughter of a Congressman while a quasi-religious sect tries to knock-off the politician, lacks credibility and continuity.

Steinberg has opted for a series of sight gags over the great character bits tackled by SCTV. The trio cuts such a comical appearance though, that Steinberg manages to hit a few bullseyes.

Playing the drums or in an aerobics class, the hee-haw faced Candy is irresistible. Brainwashed "Manchurian Candidate" style into killing his father-in-law to be, Candy is offishly funny in isolated moments.

Almost as amusing is Eugene Levy as Sal Di Pasquale, a sleazy but likable porno filmmaker who could be a second cousin of Samy Maudlin. Flaherty has his moments, too, one in a bit as the patriarch of Father Knows Best.

Still other gags fall flat, like Candy in a "Blue Lagoon" parody, because they rely too heavily on slapstick rather than humor that comes out of the situations.

Production values are fine, but the direction does nothing to help propel what is a clumsy plot to begin with. — *Jagr.*

Biddy
(BRITISH-COLOR)

London, Oct. 11.

A Sands Film Production. Produced by Richard Goodwin. Directed and written by Christine Edzard. Features entire cast. Camera (color), Alec Mills; music, Michael Sanvoisin. No other credits. Reviewed in London, Oct. 11, '83. Running time: 86 MINS.
Biddy .... Celia Bannerman
The Mother .... Patricia Napier
Tom .... Sam Ghazoros; Luke Duckett, Miles Parsey, David Napier
Mathilda ... Kate Elphick, Sabine Goodwin, Emily Hone
Susan .... Sally Ashby
Mr. Tove .... John Dalby
The Wife .... Amelda Brown

"Biddy," which recounts the transition to a lonely old age of a Victorian-period nanny, gradually forgotten by her former charges, is an atmospheric item made with loving care by director Christine Edzard. However, halting pace and ineptitude in the sound department will make for dim b.o. performance, even in arthouse locations.

Pic is at its most imaginative as it charts the rearing of the children in Biddy's care, whom their nanny regales with slabs of poetry and traditional wisdom. But the interest thins a little when Biddy is on her own.

A real downer, given the fact that Biddy never stops talking, is that all voices were post-synched. It's almost a relief, therefore, when the camera turns from faces to objects.

Celia Bannerman convincingly underplays her role as nanny and observer of passing life. Camera style and script keep the other characters at a distance.

The pic, shot entirely on sets constructed at producer Richard Goodwin's London dockland base, effectively captures the mood of life in a 19th-century household. With more ambition, director Edzard could realize a real talent for observing people and places.

— *Japa.*

To All A Goodnight
(COLOR)

Carbon copy terror picture.

An Intercontinental World Distribution Corp. production, in association with Four Feaures Partners Ltd., presented by Sandy Cobe. Executive producers, Alex Rebar, Rick Whitfield. Produced by Jay Rasumny. Directed by David Hess. Features entire cast. Screenplay, Rebar; camera (Fujicolor; prints by MGM), Bil Godsey; editor-2d unit director, William J. Waters; music arranged by Rich Tufo; sound, Itzhak Magal; productions manager, Evzen W. Kolar; production design, Joe Garrity; set decoration, Sharon West; stunt coordinator, John West Buchanan; special effects makeup, Mark Shostrum; second unit camera, Bryan England. Reviewed on Media Home Entertainment vidcassette, N.Y., Oct. 24, 1983. (No MPAA Rating). Running time: 84 **MINS.**
Nancy . . . . Jennifer Runyon
Alex . . . . Forrest Swanson
Melody . . . . Linda Gentile
T.J. . . . . William Lauer
Leia . . . . Judith Bridges
Mrs. Jensen . . . . Katherine Herrington
Ralph . . . . Buck West
Polansky . . . . Sam Shamshak
Trisha . . . . Angela Bath
Sam . . . . Denise Stearns
Tom . . . . Solomon Trager

Made in 1980, "To All A Goodnight" is a poor terror film closely resembling in format innumerable other psychotic slasher pics. Unreleased theatrically (the Christmas motif has not proved a popular one for the genre), it is currently on the market as a videocassette.

California-lensed film is set at Calvin Finishing School For Girls (to be taken literally), where two years ago a femme died during Christmas vacation by falling from a balcony during a sorority prank. In is present-day holiday season, a madman dressed in a Sant Claus outfit is bloodily killing girls and their boyfriends.

Corny revenge-themed opus is cheaper-looking than most, with the obligatory pre-credits tease a hurried affair. Main film is slowly-paced filler, with standard gore effects as each cast member is dispatched. Presentation is not satirical, but with chichès intact, including a retarded gardener Ralph (Buck West) and a nerdy kid, Alex (Forrest Swanson) to be sexually initiated by one of the pretty girls.

Without disclosing the payoff, there are two nuts in Santa costumes, whose identities are easy to guess. Acting is okay by the no-name cast, but director David Hess displays little style and the anti-climax ending is perfunctory. Tech credits are unimpressive.

— *Lor.*

Dracula Blows His Cool
(Graf Dracula (Beisst Jetzt)
In Oberbayern)
(W. GERMAN-COLOR)

A Martin Films release of a Lisa/Barthonia production. Executive producer, Martin Friedman. Directed by Carlo Ombra. Features entire cast. Screenplay, Grunbach & Rosenthal; additional dialog, Don Arthur; camera (color), Heinz Hölscher; music, Gerhard Heinz. Reviewed at Anco Theatre, N.Y., Oct. 21, 1983. (MPAA Rating: R). Running time: 90 **MINS.**
With: Gianni Garko (Stan/Count Stanislaus), Betty Vergès (Countess Olivia), Giacomo Rizzo (Mario), Linda Grondier (Linda), Bea Fiedler, Ralf Wolter, Alexander Grill, Herta Worell, Tobias Meister, Ellen Umlauf, Herbert Stiny, Laurence Kaesermann.

"Dracula Blows His Cool" is a 1979 West German sexploitation comedy modeled after George Hamilton's "Love At First Bite." In release domestically the past year and finally opening in Manhattan, minor opus is reviewed here for the record. Pic's original title translates as "Count Dracula Bites Again in Upper Bavaria," but its English-language title was meant to be "Dracula Sucks," also an early rejected monicker for Hamilton's film. Ultimately, Philip Marshak's 1979 release starring Jamie Gillis used the "Dracula Sucks" name.

Premise resembles Howard W. Koch's 1958 pic, "Frankenstein 1970," in poking fun at and updating horror material by placing a European men's magazine photographer Stan (Gianna Garko) in his ancestors' Bavarian castle snapping photos of unclad models against spooky backdrops. As with Hamilton's 1978 hit film, picture makes the most of the resemblance between vampire garb and decadent contemporary fashions, with lots of musical filler on the dance floor of the local disco.

Stan's great-grandfather, Count Dracula (Garko again in dual role) is housed in the basement with Countess Olivia (Betty Vergès), preying on locals but yearning to return to his native Transylvania. In film's lightweight format, the bites leave no telltale toothmarks on anyone's neck, no one is killed, and a silly happy ending has the castle converted into Hotel Dracula, with room service featuring a much-desired bite on the neck (or other part of the anatomy, this being a softcore sex film) for each tourist.

Burdened with execrable English-language dubbing of unfunny double-entendres, "Dracula" is attractively lensed on sunny Bavarian locations, with the mountains, forests and fields offering no horror atmosphere. Chief selling point is plentiful female nudity on display, including the beautiful Vergès, previously seen in the German film, "The Fruit Is Ripe," who makes a most striking Vampirella-style Countess Olivia.

Disappointment for the fans comes in Italian thesp Gianni Garko's unimpressive handling of the title role. For the record, over a dozen new Draculas or Dracula/-Nosferatu imitations were made in a production burst for films and tv beginning in 1978, starring actors Louis Jourdan, Klaus Kinski, Frank Langella, Hamilton, Gillis, Garko, Richard Lynch, Dick Shawn, Gerald Fielding, Enrique Alvarez Felix, Judd Hirsch, Michael Nouri, Peter Lowey, Johnny Harden, Christopher Berneau, Andres Garcia, Louise Fletcher (as "Mamma Dracula" and even Fabian Forte (in the 1978 Mexican pic "La Dinastia Dracula").

— *Lor.*

I Paladini - Storia D'Armi E D'Amori
(Hearts in Armor)
(ITALIAN-COLOR)

Rome, Oct. 18.
A.P.I.C. release, produced by Nicola Carraro for Vides International and released world-wide by Warner Bros. Features entire cast. Written and directed by Giacomo Battiato. Camera (Technicolor), Dante Spinotti; editor, Ruggero Mastroianni; art director, Luciano Ricceri; costumes, Anna Cecchi; music, Cooper and Hughes. Reviewed at International Recording, Rome, Oct. 17, 1983. Running time: 98 **MINS.**
Rolando . . . . Rick Edwards
Ruggero . . . . Ron Moss
Bradamante . . . . Barbara De Rossi
Isabella . . . . Tanya Roberts
Marfisa . . . . Zeudi Araya
Atlante . . . . Maurizio Nichetti
Rinaldo . . . . Leigh McCloskey
Gano . . . . Giovanni Visentin
Ferrau . . . . Tony Vogel

One of the season's big budget productions from Vides — "Hearts in Armor" is a landmark in several ways. Pic was written and directed by Giacomo Battiato, a newcomer who made a name for himself in commercials and tv ("Martin Eden"), as a pictorially striking and emotionally appealing fairytale, concocted out of Medieval legends and embellishments of love and war (read sex and violence). The film is a clever and probably successful attempt to use Italo talent behind the camera and American actors in front of it to create an exportable motion picture. It received a hefty material boost from a much-heralded pre-sale to Warner Bros., and production values show the money has been well spent. One can imagine it as the first of a long series of Round Tables all'Italiana.

In pic's completely imaginary world, a holy war is going on in which Christian knights and Saracen warriors are interlocked by affairs of the heart. Bradamante (Barbara De Rossi), perhaps the screen's first woman knight, is more interested in Ruggero, the Saracen leader (Ron Moss), than the Crusades; for love of him she gives up her prisoner, his sister Isabella (Tanya Roberts). Ruggero likewise forgets there's a war on when he's in Bradamante's arms, until the girl he left behind, the beautiful Marfisa (Zeudi Araya), comes to remind him of his duty.

Meanwhile the musclebound Christian champion Rolando (Rick Edwards) has fallen hard for Isabella and also finds his lust for bloodshed waning. After defeating the three dreaded Saracens (the film's only real heavies, who come on in the wildest costumes yet), Rolando and Isabella, Bradamante and Ruggero give up warfare and walk into the sunset together.

Pic has no pretensions of being more than simple entertainment — luckily, because it lacks the symbolic-psychological resonance of a genuine fable. What it does do is use the fairy tale setting, beefed up with characters, dress and sets, to create an engrossing and visually exciting tale, with a sophistication unusual for Italo fantasy product. "Hearts" owes much of its appeal to the team effort of a fine technical crew. The clashes between individual Christians and Saracens is accompanied by Cooper and Hughes' stirring music, and choreographed in personalized suits of armor designed by Anna Cecchi that are stars in themselves. Art director Luciano Ricceri puts Byzantine cathedrals in the midst of the wilderness, while Dante Spinotti's camera carves a wonderland out of forests and Mt. Etna gorges.

Heading the cast are two neophyte thesps, Rick Edwards and Ron Moss, chosen for their romantic comic book looks; ditto one of "Charlie's Angels," Tanya Roberts, whose fetching purple dress suffers progressive deterioration through a series of attempted rapes and dagger fights. Barbara De Rossi wins sympathy as the sentimental but courageous Badamante. — *Yung.*

Kono Ko Wo Nokoshite
(These Children Survive Me)
(JAPANESE-COLOR)

Tokyo, Oct. 18.
A Shochiku release of a Shochiku-Hori Planning co-production. Produced by Hideo Sasai, Akira Tojo and Hiroshi Kanezawa. Directed by Keisuke Kinoshita. Features entire cast. Screenplay, Kinoshita, Taiichi Yamada, based on book by Takashi Nagai; camera, (color), Kozo Okazaki; art direction, Masataka Yoshino; music, Tadashi Kinoshita; sound, Mitsura Shimado; lighting, Takehiko Sakuma; editing Yoshi Sugihara. Reviewed at Shochiku Central, Tokyo, Oct. 18, 1983. Running time: 128 **MINS.**
Takashi Nagai . . . . Go Kato
Midori Nagai . . . . Yukio Toake
Midori Nagai . . . . . . Masatomo Nakabayashi

Kayano Nagai	Mami Nishijima
Tsumo	Chikage Awashima
Makoto Nagai	
(as adult)	Takashi Yamaguchi
Masako Migishi	Shinobu Otake
Shizuko Migishi	Ai Kanazaki
Dr. Sagawa	Toyoshi Fukuda

Some observers consider it ironic that the "Christian" soldiers of the American republic, in their fight against the "godless hordes" of the Japanese Empire during World War II, dropped an atomic bomb almost directly on top of the largest Catholic churches in Asia.

Still, the wartime experiences of the members of Nagasaki's Christian community are the stuff of which an intriguing, challenging and morally complex film could have been made: patriotically devoted to a country with a long history of persecuting them, abjured from worshipping false gods yet virtually commanded to regard the Emperor as divine, incinerated by their brothers in Christ.

Leaving largely unexplored the many dramatic possibilities available to him, director Keisuke Kinoshita instead opted to make yet another how-Japan-suffered-in-wartime tearjerker, in the process distorting the reality of both Christianity in Japan and nuclear war.

"Kono Ko Wo Nokoshite" is based on the writings and experiences of Dr. Takashi Nagai, a Christian surgeon who, along with his son, daughter and mother-in-law, survived the bombing of Nagasaki and who, on his death bed in 1951, secured from his children the promise that they would always strive to oppose war.

War, it has been observed, is seldom a congenial time for civil liberties, and wartime Japan was certainly no casebook study in libertarian principles. Even as distorted a film as the WWII extravaganza "Dai Nippon Teikoku," made quite clear that Christians were often severely harassed by the authorities, especially by the kempeitai (security police). The cult of the Emperor was at its height and Christians were asked whom they loved more, the Son of God or the Son of Heaven, with no consolation prizes awarded those who gave the wrong answer.

Suffice it to say a film about WWII-era Japanese Christians in which not one of the characters suffers at the hands of the authorities is about as realistic as a film about WWII-era Japanese-Americans in which not one of the characters is sent to a relocation camp.

Kinoshita resorts to exaggeration, the technique often favored by artists not completely familiar with their subjects.

Accentuating the positive, eliminating the negative, Kinoshita enlarges and distorts what is already an extreme perception my many

Japanese of Christians as prototypical Westerners not completely in touch with their emotions: slightly ethereal heads-in-the-heavens, almost insufferbly understanding goody-two-shoes, seldom if ever given to discouraging words.

Although the Japanese are not, by any means, a religious people, they are capable of holier-than-thou attitudes when it comes to the subject of wartime suffering. More often than not, "Kono Ko Wo Nokoshite" is less a plea for pacifism than an attempt to reinforce the notion of Japan's unique insight into human suffering, having been the only country in the world to have undergone an atomic bombing.

Nagai's son, exhorted by his father to prevent any repetitions of Nagasaki, grows up to become a journalist and files stories from battlefields around the world. Having seen with his own eyes that nuclear weapons were not used in any of the conflicts he covered, he "breathed a sigh of relief."

This eyewitness reporter serves to reassure Japanese audiences that, since 1945, no one has suffered as grievously as they did. As if to underline this point, the film concludes with a dramatic recreation of the Nagasaki bombing, complete with smoldering ruins and charred human remains.

To suggest that there are worse fates than a nuclear attack is to deny the Japanese their pre-eminent position as victims, yet advances in conventional weapons technology have served to blur the line between the effects of full-scale conventional and limited nuclear exchanges.

"Kono Ko Wo Nokoshite," in addition to encomiums from Pope John Paul II, has received the official blessing of the Ministry of Education. This seal of approval means while the film has not been an enormous hit during its roadshow engagement, it will undoubtedly continue to generate income for Shochiku in the form of rentals to schools.—Bail.

Die Schwarze Spinne
(The Black Spider)
(SWISS-COLOR)

Zurich, Oct. 16.

Europa Film SA Locarno release of a Pica-Film AG (Eduard Steiner) production. Directed by Mark M. Rissi. Features entire cast. Screenplay, Walther Kauer, based on a story by Jeremias Gotthelf; dialect adaptation, Peter Holliger; camera (color), Edwin Horak; sound, Florian Eidenbenz, Peter Begert; lighting, Rolf Knutti; special effects, Giacomo Peier, Cornelius Defries, Bruno Reithaar; costumes, Edith Roth; art direction, Knutti; editor, Evelyne von Rabenau; music, Yello, Veronique Muller. Reviewed at the Cinema Frosch, Zurich, Oct. 12, '83. Running time: 95 MINS.

Cast: Beatrice Kessler, Walo Lueoend, Peter Ehrlich, Walter Hess, Henrik Rhyn, Peter Schneider, Christine Wipf, Michael Gempart, Sigfrit Steiner, Hanny Scheuring, Stephan Litchtensteiger, Peter Luechinger, Benjamin Kradolfer, Hansjoerg Bahl, Peter Holliger, Juergen Bruegger, Rene Bill, Peter Fischli, Sergio Catellani, Curt Truninger, Clem Dalton, Lorenz Wuethrich, Fridolin Zaugg, hans Gaugler, Hannes Daehler, Dominik Daehler, Hans Wittwer, Sigmund Oberli, Barbara Grimm, Corinne Hirt, Greti Jakob-Gugger, Hans Minder, Walter Krumm, Rosali Nydegger. Theatre 1230.

The 19th century Swiss author Jeremias Gotthelf's story, "The Black Spider," is valued as a classic example of an early horror tale set in the peasant milieu of a typical Swiss landscape, the Emmental, in the middle ages. Subjugated by a merciless knight ruling over the village, the peasants are forced to labor way beyond their strength. One farmer's wife, a beautiful, sensuous woman from outside the village, makes a pact with the devil to help the men fulfill their task. The prize is a newborn, unbaptized baby.

When the time comes, the woman cheats the devil of his reward by having the child baptized right after birth. As a revenge, the village is afflicted by a black spider spreading death, plague and pestilence until a courageous young woman succeeds in catching the spider and locking it up.

Curiously enough, this dramatic legend with its symbolic connotations (the spider as the incarnation of evil) yet popular language, has never before been filmed. Swiss composer Heinrich Sutermeister made it into an opera in 1936 as did Willy Burkhard in 1949. In his film version, Mark M. Rissi has tried to place the Gotthelf tale into a contemporary context via a frame story involving a group of young drug addicts. Cheated by a dealer and desperate for supply, they break into a chemical plant where they involuntarily trigger off an ecological disaster a la Seveso. They flee into a nearby farmhouse, where one of the girls dies from an overdose and another, on a drug trip, hallucinates the "Black Spider" story.

The topical framework, probably conceived with an eye on the youth audience less familiar with the Gotthelf original, seems contrived and unconvincing. It taxes the patience of those expecting the "Black Spider" tale; for others it seems too thin and superficial to stand on its own. The intended juxtapostion of two ages and use of a parallel situation (drug addiction, pollution, etc., as today's black spiders) do not quite jell.

Filmic values are on the conventional side. Lensing by Edwin Horak is above par, but Evelyne von Rabenau's editing is occasionally choppy. Performances are average, even by such seasoned performers as Sigfrit Steiner and Walo Lueoend. Standing out, part-

ly due to their flashier roles, are Beatrice Kessler as the woman pacting with Satan and Peter Ehrlich as the evil knight who also ends up a black spider victim.

—Mezo.

The Man From S.E.X.
(BRITISH-COLOR)

A Group 1 release of a Lindsay Shonteff Prods./Palm Beach Enterprises picture. Produced by Elizabeth Gray. Directed by Lindsay Shonteff. Features entire cast. Screenplay, Jeremy Lee Francis; camera (Technicolor), Bill Paterson; editor, Gerry Ivanov; music, Simon Bell; sound, Tony Jackson; production manager, Matthew Raymond; assistant director, John Wain, Peter Jacobs; special effects, Chris Verner. Reviewed on Catalina Home Video vidcassette, N.Y., Sept. 9, 1983. (MPAA Rating: R). Running time: 95 MINS.

Charles Bind	Gareth Hunt
Jensen	Nick Tate
Carlotta	Fiona Curzon
Lucifer Orchid	Gary Hope
Stockwell	Geoffrey Keen
Merlin	John Arnatt
Scarlet	Toby Robins
Vice president	Don Fellows

"The Man From S.E.X." is a failed British imitation of the James Bond films, lensed in 1978 and marginally released in the U.S. before its current vidcassette availability. Pic, a sequel to the 1976 "No. One Of The Secret Service," was originally titled "Licensed To Love And Kill," and circulated under the alternate moniker "Undercover Lover."

Indie filmmaker Lindsay Shonteff, best known Stateside for his 1964 "Devil Doll," is actually lampooning his own work here, particularly the 1965 Bond imitation "The Second Best Secret Agent In The Whole Wide World," which starred Tom Adams as agent Charles Vine. In "S.E.X.," Gareth Hunt portrays Charles Bind, a well-tailored British agent sent out by his boss Stockwell (Geoffrey Keen, who coincidentally has had similar roles in recent Bond pics) to fetch Lord Dangerfield (Noel Johnson) from the U.S., presumed missing.

The enemy is Senator (a naturalized U.S. citizen born in England) Lucifer Orchid (Gary Hope), bent on taking power in America by substituting doubles created by plastic surgery for the U.S. veep, agent Bind and others. Working from an Atlantic island base, he hires a mercenary Jensen Fury (Nick Tate) to carry out his dirty work.

Shonteff errs in stretching the Bond formula of tongue-in-cheek sex and violence beyond the breaking point, adopting a live-action comic strip style familiar from his more successful 1972 picture "Big Zapper." People blow up in a puff of smoke at will, fight scenes are likely to have fists crashing through solid walls and the requisite special effects gimmicks are similarly hokey. Shot in England, the half of the film set in America is unconvincing, as are several lame attempts at U.S. accents.

As Jensen nicknames him in the film, Gareth Hunt as Bind is indeed "Stiff," whether playing this role or the interchangeable double. Rest of the cast is routine, with various pretty girls (including Ingmar Bergman's actress daughter Anna) delivering occasional nude shots, but falling wide of the mark expected in an R-rated (and thereby more liberated) Bonder. Though there are some outlandish scenes, Shonteff doesn't deliver the sci-fi overtones of his similarly-plotted "Second Best..." 1965 picture. Tech credits reflect a low budget. — *Lor.*

Papy Fait de la Resistance
(Gramps Is In The Resistance)
(FRENCH-COLOR)

Paris, Nov. 1.

AMLF release of a Christian Fechner production. Directed by Jean-Marie Poire. Screenplay, Poire, Christian Clavier, Martin Lamotte, based on an original story idea by Clavier and Lamotte; camera (color) Robert Alazraki; art director, Willy Holt; costumes, Catherine Leterrier; editor, Catherine Kelber; sound, Daniel Brisseau; music, Jean Musy; makeup, Paul Lemarinel; production manager, Henri Brichetti. Reviewed at the Havas screening room, Neuilly, Oct. 25, 1983. Running time: 105 MINS.

With: Christian Clavier, Michel Galabru, Gerard Jugnot, Martin Lamotte, Dominique Lavanant, Jacqueline Maillan, Jacques Villeret, Josiane Balasko, Michel Blanc, Jean-Claude Brialy, Jean Carmet, Bernard Giraudeau, Thierry Lhermitte, Jean Yanne, Julien Guiomar, Jacques Francois, Roland Giraud, Pauline Lafont, Jeffrey Kime, Jean-Paul Muel, Roger Carel, Carole Jacquinot, Bruno Moynot, Patrick Petit-Jean, Alain Jerome, Sebastien Fechner.

There are a few good laughs in Jean-Marie Poire's "Papy Fait de la Resistance" but they derive mainly from performance, rarely from script or direction. "Papy" is a star-crammed lampoon on French Resistance heroics during World War II. A legit spinoff of the original story by Martin Lamotte and Christian Clavier was staged last season by the Splendide cafe-theatre company, whose troupers are among the no-less than 13 top-billed actors in the film.

Despite the big budget gloss (film's ad slogan boasts that it "cost more than the Allied invasion") script betrays the skit-minded theatrical origins of its writers and comes out a lumpy grabbag of gags surrounding a family of celebrated musicians who join the Resistance in spite of themselves when a German High Command outfit is billeted at their Paris mansion. Director Poire keeps this overblown romp moving at a breathless pace, but lacks the imagination to give the situations purely cinematic verve. Which leaves it to the actors to inject the missing punch.

Fortunately several of the stars manage to rise above the material. Stage veterans Jacqueline Maillan is happily on hand as the family's intransigent matriarch and provides some classy comic moments, as does comedienne Dominique Lavanant, who steals the show in story's funny epilog (several characters are reunited 30 years later on a tv talk show to discuss what really happened). Another highlight is provided by pudgy Jacques Villeret, who makes a late appearance as Hitler's crooner half-brother and provokes hilarity with a takeoff of Julio Iglesias.

Among other talent is Gerard Jugnot, as an hysterical French collaborator bent on vengeance; Jean Carmet as the family head who becomes a victim of his own grenade, Michel Galabru as "Papy," the doddering grandfather veteran of the Great War, and scripters Clavier and Lamotte, with the latter cast as "Super-Resistant," a cross between Zorro and Fantomas, who sends around the plate after saving a group of Frenchman from a German execution squad. Roland Giraud, a relative newcomer to film, does a smooth comic send-up of the Good German Officer, a stereotype especially familiar to French films about the war and the Occupation.

Also present in cameos are Jean Yanne, Thierry Lhermitte, Josiane Balasko, Michel Blanc and Bernard Giradeau, who makes a pointless appearance which lasts all of 15 seconds, but still has his name above the title.

Pic is a smash locally, and is holding its own against a competing new Jean-Paul Belmondo vehicle. Despite topbilled talent, it will need a hard sell in foreign markets, and first-rate subtitling.

—Len.

Acqua E Sapone
(Soap And Water)
(ITALY-COLOR)

Rome, Oct. 28.

A CEIAD/Columbia release, produced by Mario and Vittorio Cecchi Gori for Intercapital Film. Stars Carlo Verdone, Natasha Hovey. Directed by Carlo Verdone. Screenplay, Franco Ferrini, Enrico Oldoini, Verdone; camera (Technicolor), Danilo Desideri; editor, Antonio Siciliano; art director, Franco Valchi; music, Fabio Liberatori. Reviewed at America Cinema, Rome, Oct. 27, 1983. Running time: 105 MINS.
Rolando .... Carlo Verdone
Sandy Walsh .... Natasha Hovey
Wilma Walsh .... Florinda Bolkan
Grandma .... Elena Fabrizi

Versatile comedian Carlo Verdone is famous for his bizarre character creations and fresh humor. His latest picture, "Soap and Water," misses on both scores. As title suggests, pic is cleaned-up Italo mainstream comedy, and a strictly local item. Helmer's admirers may be disappointed, but pic has the simplicity and familiarity that could make it click onshore.

Chubby, boyish Rolando is one of Verdone's key characters, the poor Roman slob on the lookout for a job. Though he has a teaching degree, the closest he's gotten to students so far is as a janitor in an English high school run by priests and nuns. By intercepting a call for one of the teachers, Rolando lands a job tutoring 15-year-old American top model Sandy Walsh (Natasha Hovey). Her sophisticated mother (Florinda Bolkan) is gullible, indeed, to fall for his pose as a learned priest, especially when he keeps popping out with Roman dialect and it's obvious he can't speak a word of English.

Luckily, Rolando's embarrassing language problem is neatly solved when it turns out Sandy speaks Italian. It doesn't take her long to unmask Rolando, but she agrees to keep quiet in exchange for trips to pastry shops, pizzerias and amusement parks, all of which Mama has strictly forbidden.

Eventually the real priest turns up and Rolando is ignominiously cast out of the Walsh mansion. But one night Sandy appears on his doorstep and presses him to take her to bed. He hesitates; she insists. Every man's fantasy is chastely consummated off-screen. The next morning Sandy tiptoes out of the room and returns to her mother as a woman.

Funniest moments involve Rolando's Roman grandmother, limned by unrepressed character actress Elena Fabrizi in the great tradition. Otherwise "Soap" is wishy-washy, without many bubles. The hands of veteran scripters Franco Ferrini and Enrico Oldoini outweigh helmer's natural talent for on-target caricature; except for a wicked priest and nun, everyone gets soft-soaped. Even Sandy's ambitious mother is portrayed by Bolkan as loving and interested in her daughter's happiness. Newcomer Hovey as the poor little rich girl lacks the tough of malicious perversity that would have fleshed out the character of the child star.

Instead of bringing the character to life, pic is jazzed up with glamorous fashion shows and modeling sessions.

Technical credits are standard.

—Yung.

Le General de l'Armee Morte
(The General of the Dead Army)
(FRENCH-ITALIAN-COLOR)

Paris, Nov. 1.

UGC release of a Films 66/UGC-Top 1/Films A2/Antea Cinematografice/RAI coproduction. Produced by Michel Piccoli and Ludivine Clerc. Stars Piccoli, Anouk Aimee, Marcello Mastroianni, Gerard Klein. Directed by Luciano Tovoli. Screenplay, Jean-Claude Carriere, Tovoli, Piccoli, based on novel by Ismail Kadare; camera (color), Luciano Tovoli, Peppino Tinelli; editor, Noelle Boisson; costumes, Karl Lagerfeld; art director, Alessandro Bell'Orco; makeup, Peppino Banchelli; sound, Guillaume Sciama. Reviewed at the UGC Biarritz theatre, Paris, Oct. 26, 1983. Running time: 105 MINS.
General Ariosto ...... Marcello Mastroianni
Benetandi .... Michel Piccoli
Countess Betsy .... Anouk Aimee
General Krotz .... Gerard Klein
The specialist .... Sergio Castellito
The Minister .... Daniele Dublino

Actor Michel Piccoli and Italian cinematographer Luciano Tovoli fought for years to get the "General of the Dead Army," a novel by Albanian writer Ismail Kadare, onto the screen. To judge from the basic story line, their passion is understandable, and final credits have Piccoli as co-star, co-screenwriter and co-producer. But the final product is flaccid and dull, due mostly to poor direction by Tovoli, here making his directing debut in theatrical features.

Piccoli, Tovoli and Jean-Claude Carriere adapted this tale of an ambitious Italian general and an army chaplain who are sent by their government to exhume the remains of over 3,000 soldiers who fell on an Albanian battle field a decade earlier. Manipulated by an aristocratic war widow, who wants them to bring back the body of her husband, who disappeared at the front under mysterious conditions, the pair embark on their mission, where they are soon joined by a German officer assigned to a similar operation.

Intending a macabre comic parable, spiced with satire, Tovoli and company shoot wide of their mark. The promise of escalating absurdity — notably concerning the systematic roundup of skeletons and dogtags — is never kept, so that the deepening disarray of the protagonists has virtually no dramatic relief.

Tovoli fares weakly with his actors as well. Marcello Mastroianni seems utterly lost as the Italian general, and Piccoli is only slightly more in control as the chaplain. A chief casting error is Gerard Klein as the Dr. Strangelove-like German, again inadequate in a stylistically demanding part, especially in a climactic drinking showdown with Mastroianni. Anouk Aimee brings her beauty to the part of the seductive widow, but not much else.

Tech credits, notably the lensing (by Tovoli and Peppino Tinelli), are fine, but this is a sad waste of a promising idea and a couple of usually fine male leads.

Billing will certainly help sell the film, but it will need a lot of pushing. —*Len.*

City Of The Walking Dead
(SPANISH-ITALIAN-COLOR)

A 21st Century Distribution release of a Lotus International (Madrid)/Dialchi Film (Rome) production. Produced by Diego Alchimede. Directed by Umberto Lenzi. Stars Hugo Stiglitz, Laura Trotter. Screenplay, Piero Regnoli, Toni Corti; camera (Eastman color), Hans Burman; editor, Daniele Alabiso; music Stelvio Cipriani; assistant director, Riccardo Petrazzi; art direction, Mario Molli; makeup, Giuseppe Ferranti, Franco di Girolami. Reviewed at Embassy 2 Theatre, N.Y., Nov. 5, 1983. (MPAA Rating: R). Running time: **92 MINS.**
Miller ....Hugo Stiglitz
Sheila ....Laura Trotter
Major Holmes ....Francisco Rabal
Dr. Anna Miller ...Maria Rosaria Omaggio
General Murchison.............Mel Ferrer

"City Of The Walking Dead" is the awkward U.S. release title for Umberto Lenzi's 1980 science fiction/horror opus, "Nightmare City." Routine and highly derivative, picture carries a 1984 copyright date on print courtesy of distrib 21st Century, designed to confuse future lazy film historians.

Star of many a Mexican film, Hugo Stiglitz toplines as tv newsman Miller who witnessed monsters attacking at a local airport. (Film's setting is unidentified but, with English-language street signs, is supposed to be in the U.S. However, cars bearing European license plates are a giveaway of Spanish lensing site.) A nuclear spill at a power plant, a la "The China Syndrome," has created these monsters, noted for their cheap, black-tar-on-face makeup.

When Miller interrupts a tv disco dance show with this news, he is yanked off the air by orders of General Murchison (Mel Ferrer), afraid of panic. Monsters are ultra-strong, with an indestructible cellular structure caused by radioactivity. They can be stopped by destroying their control center or, as Ferrer puts it: "Aim for the brain." Premise and ensuing battles are identical with a dozen other imitations of George A. Romero's "Dawn Of The Dead," however these monsters are akin to vampires, feeding on human blood (needed to replenish their decaying red blood cells) rather than cannibalizing their victims. As usual, victims become infected and add to the monster population.

Since the prolific Lenzi is a seasoned pro, having directed three or four action films per year since 1960, "City" is better made than most films of this type, but lacks the humorous gaffes that make grade-Z junk watchable. Print viewed had murky color and poor definition, looking like a 35m dupe. Acting consists of walk-throughs, with several cast members, including a glum Ferrer, articulating in English. — *Lor.*

The Wars
(CANADIAN-COLOR)

Toronto, Nov. 2.
An International Spectrafilm Distributors Ltd. Release. Produced by the Canadian Film Development Corp. and Famous Players Limited; a coproduction of Nielsen-Ferns International Limited, the National Film Board of Canada, and Polyphon Film-und-Fernseh. Produced by Richard Nielsen. Directed by Robin Phillips. Features entire cast. Executive producer, Robert Verrall. Screenplay, Timothy Findley, based on his novel "The Wars," camera (color), John Coquillon; editor, Tony Lower; art director, Daphne Dare; costumes, Ann Curtis; special effects, Colin Chilvers; assistant director, Tony Lucibello; sound, Joseph Champagne; associate producer, Robert Linnell; music, Glenn Gould. Reviewed at the Fine Arts Theatre, Toronto, Nov. 1, 1983. Running time: **120 MINS.**
Robert Ross ....Brent Carver
Mrs. Ross ....Martha Henry
Mr. Ross ....William Hutt
Rowena Ross ......Ann-Marie MacDonald
Miss Davenport ....Jackie Burroughs
Captain Taffler...............Jean Leclerc
Lady Barbara d'Orsey ......Domini Blythe
Captain Leather ....Alan Scarfe
Lady Emmeline ....Margaret Tyzack
Nurse Turner ....Barbara Budd

"The Wars," marking the feature film helming debut of ex-Stratford Festival artistic director Robin Phillips, is a lushly photographed period piece, evoking the time before World War I and the dilemma of young men leaving their secure environs and heeding the call to war. But it's loaded with heavy-handed symbolism and is ineffective in its attempts to extend its theme that war goes beyond battlefields to the internal wars of the psyche.

Based on Timothy Findley's award-winning novel, story focuses on Robert Ross (Brent Carver), a young man born to a genteel Toronto family prior to WWI. The icy Wasp clan is headed by a tight-lipped matriarch (Martha Henry) and an ineffective, duty-bound father (William Hutt), who provide paltry roots for rebellious Robert.

Robert is especially attached to his invalid sister Rowena (Ann-Marie MacDonald), who dies in an accident. An incident follows the death — a need for Rowena's pet rabbits to be killed, despite Robert's furious protests. This precipitates a family quarrel, which sends Robert off to the Great War. His mother laments, "We're all cut off at birth with a knife and left at the mercy of strangers," and Robert departs against her wishes.

He participates in the requisite rites of passage, including the visit to a brothel and a steamy affair with a British lady. His final act of defiance emerges on the battlefield, when he overrides his commanding officer's orders and decides to liberate a barn full of horses, echoing the earlier rabbit scene and again challenging powerful parental figures at whatever cost.

There is authority in Phillips' direction, despite Findley's cumbersome script. The time and place are evoked with delicate art direction and with the mystical keyboard of Glenn Gould's score. Phillips extracts some well-crafted moments from many of his Stratford (and now Grand Theatre) thesps, including Carver, Henry, Hutt and a wise Jackie Burroughs as the aged, compassionate narrator Miss Davenport. It's refreshing to see a group of Canadian actors who lend a repertory ambience to the pic.

There are hints of themes that could have been fleshed out, such as the use of Canadians at the frontlines of the British Army, in the same vein as "Gallipoli." But overall aim to depict wars on all levels is unsuccessful, although the pic is stylish fare that's lovely to look at. — *Devo.*

The Country Girls
(BRITISH-COLOR)

Cork, Oct. 22.
A London Films Production. Executive producers, Mark Shelmerdine and David Conroy. Producer, Aida Young. Director, Desmond Davis. Stars Sam Neill, Maeve Germaine, Jill Doyle, John Kavanagh, Niall Toibin. Screenplay, Edna O'Brien from her own novel; camera (color), Denis Lewiston; editor, Timothy Gee; sound mixer, Pat Hayes; costume designer, Gwenda Evans; art director, Arden Gantly. Screened at Cork Festival of Film, Cork, Oct. 21, 1983. Running time: **100 MINS.**

Set in Ireland in the mid-'50s "The Country Girls" sketches the lives of two girls from rural Ireland through schooldays in a severe convent to adolescence, breaking from home for city life and emigration. The simple tale has translated well to the screen, and although lacking in strong drama there is tragedy and humor.

Desmond Davis, who has lensed two other Edna O'Brien stories, "The Girl with Green Eyes" and "I Was Happy Here," has drawn standout performances from his unknown leads, Maeve Germaine and Jill Doyle, contrasting their respective pseudo-sophistication male is not entirely convincing, but performances in smaller roles from Niall Toibin, John Kavanagh, Desmond Nealon, Anna Manahan and Agnes Bernelle are memorable.

Camerawork has caught the atmosphere of the piece, both on locations and in interiors. This is not a spectacular, but a pleasant entertainment which is visually satisfying. —*Max.*

Die Schaukel
(The Swing)
(WEST GERMAN-COLOR)

Munich, Oct. 27.
A Coproduction of Pelemele Film, Munich, Roxy Film Luggi Waldleitner, Munich, Project Film in Filmverlag der Autoren, Munich, and Bayerischer Rundfunk (BR), Munich; world rights, Filmverlag der Autoren, Munich. Produced by Eleanore Adlon. Features entire cast. Written and directed by Percy Adlon, based on a novel with same title by Annette Kolb. Camera (color), Juergen Martin; arts direction, Heidi Luedi; costumes, Regine Baetz; music, Peer Raben, employing motifs from Mozart, Chopin, Rossini, Boieldieu, Joh, Strauss, and folk music; sound, Rainer Wiehr; editing, Clara Fabry; tv-producer, Benigna von Keyserlingk. Reviewed at Odysee Kino, Munich, Oct. 26, '83. Running time: **130 MINS.**
Mathias Lautenschlag ......Anja Jaenicke
Otto Lautenschlag ......Joachim Bernhard
Gervaise Lautenschlag ....Lena Stolze
Hespera Lautenschlag .....Susanne Herlet
Herr Lautenschlag ....Rolf Illig
Mme Lautenschlag....Christine Kaufmann
Mme Lautenschlag's Mother..Jenny Thelen
Gartenmarie ....Elisabeth Bertram
Prof. Dr. Fritz Emanuel
von Zwinger ....Guenther Strack
Mrs. von Zwinger.........Dorothea Moritz
Lhombre ....Ulrich Tukur

Frau Erlendicht ....Irm Hermann
Baronin James ....Anja Buczkowski
Oberst von Ried-
Recours ....Gustl Weishappel
_____

"The Swing" is an adaptation of Annette Kolb's novel with same title (published in 1934, awarded the Munich Literature Prize in 1951). The inspiration for the feature undoubtedly came from Percy Adlon's earlier documentary on "Fraulein Annette Kolb," featuring interviews with the authoress (born 1870, died 1967).

Both the book and film are best described as autobiographical chronicles. Their theme is turn-of-the-century Munich, a single year in the period before 1914 and the outbreak of World War I. It was a time when both the aristocracy and the bourgeois, aristocratic families had their last day in the sun as members of the feudal-democratic nobility and society of art connoisseurs. Kolb's own family — the Lautenschlags — belonged to this circle via the latter contact: her father was the royal garden architect in Bavaria, a postion that didn't pay quite enough money for a family of six (plus a mother-in-law), but allowed enough comforts in a city that prided itself on a broadly cultivated range of art and leisure.

"The Swing" is not, strictly speaking, a narrative feature film. Its two hours plus are devoted almost entirely to fashioning an impressionistic picture book of people and places, art monuments and fashionable gatherings, the types and personalities who made Munich one of the major European art capitals just before the disaster of a world war. The film also shows, effectively, that the aristocracy itself had withered in the vine — to the point of joining with Austria in a metaphorical dance-of-death as the clouds of war gathered. Adlon offers this visionary forecast through the eyes of Mathias Lautenschlag, the girl of 15 with a boy's name and the mannerisms of an impertinent tomboy, pooh-poohing everything about her in a splurge of ordinary witticisms.

Adlon stays close to his source at all times. Undoubtedly, the film would have been better off as a three-part tv-serial production instead of a feature-film production pegged for arthouse release. Nevertheless, a festival push could put it over the top for the keyed "special screenings" promo in Germany and around Europe.

"The Swing" follows the activities of the Lautenschlag family, this remembrance cued in the beginning by the burning down of the Glass Palace in Munich in 1931 (the construction, in 1854, was a cultural monument situated just across the street from the Lautenschlag home). From there, the impressions drift to Christmas celebrations, the opening of a garden-architectural exhibition by Herr Lautenschlag, piano lessons by Mme. Lautenschlag (Annette Kolb's French-born mother), the arrival of the royal Bavarian family at the garden exhibition, a guest performance by Eleanora Duse at the National theatre, and a pair of musical recitals and balls. The novel's line of development compares the daily life of the Lautenschlag family with that of their neighbors, the Von Zwingers (he's a Prussian physician, she's from a wealthy British family, and their brood of five children about the same age as the Lautenschlag kids), but this segment of the film falls pretty much by the wayside due to the film's desire to present a panorama of the times.

Strikingly lensed, with eye-catching costumes and decor, "The Swing" is also ably acted by principals and bit-players. Christine Kaufmann as Mme. Lautenschlag is a standout thesp, whose role as the confused and distracted French wife and mother, ill at ease in Bavaria, could have easily carried the film, given a stronger narrative line. Indeed, the only missing ingredient to make this a cinema attraction is a proper dramatic scenario, but the same fate has greeted other historical film chronicles. Possibly, "The Swing" would have been better off as a faithful-to-the-source art film in the strict sense of that term: a three-hour-plus tv special with dramatic highs and lows in each aired part of the serial.

As it is now, a reading of Annette Kolb's "The Swing" in printed form would greatly enhance the film experience for insiders.—*Holl.*

Les Mots Pour le Dire
(Words To Say It)
(FRENCH-COLOR)
_____

Paris, Oct. 26.

UGC/Europe 1 release of a Stephan Films/Filmedis/Belstar/TF 1 Films/UGC-Top 1 coproduction. Produced by Vera Belmont. Stars Nicole Garcia, Marie-Christine Barrault. Directed by Jose Pinheiro. Screenplay, Suso Cecchi D'Amico, Marie-Francoise Leclere, Jose Pinheiro, and Marie Cardinal, based on the latter's book; camera (Eastmancolor), Gerry Fisher; sound, Pierre Befve; editor, Clair Pinheiro; music, Jean-Marie Senia; costumes, Olga Pelletier; makeup, Ron Berkeley; art director, Yvan Maussion; production manager, Linda Gutenberg. Reviewed at the UGC Champs-Elysees theatre, Paris, Oct. 20, 1983. Running time: 92 MINS.
Marie ....Nicole Garcia
Eliane ....Marie-Christine Barrault
Professor Talbiac ....Claude Rich
The analyst..............Daniel Mesguich
Francois..................Jean-Luc Boutte
Michele ....Michele Baumgartner
Bertheas...........Jean-Louis Foulquier
Marie's father ....Robin Renucci
Marie (child) ....Violaine Gonce
_____

Nicole Garcia and Marie-Christine Barrault give excellent portraits of troubled women in "Les Mots Pour le Dire," an adaptation of Marie Cardinal's acclaimed autobiographical novel about her struggle to overcome the neurotic consequences of a strained relationship with her mother.

Production went through a long gestation period, during which Andre Techine was to direct from a screenplay he had prepared. Reported difficulties ended in Techine's departure, however, and Jose Pinheiro was brought in to helm. Despite one's worst fears for the project, Pinheiro has delivered a finished product of considerable style, intelligence and feeling.

Director attracted attention here with his first feature, "Family Rock," a low-budget 1981 film about a very together young couple and their two kids who haul a merry-go-round around France in a battered bus and carry on a healthy bohemian existence. Apart from a strong cinematic sense and feeling for atmosphere, the picture demonstrated a genuine affection for and skill with actors. It's mostly the latter quality that gives "Les Mots Pour le Dire" its emotional impact.

Pinheiro has made his transition into mainstream commercial filmmaking with honors, but not without bumps. Inevitably there are compressions and simplifications of Cardinal's book — the script is by Suso Cecchi d'Amico, journalist Marie-Francoise Leclere and Pinheiro himself, with the author also credited. For example, the book spans a 10-year period, while the film packs everything into a neat three-year stretch. This creates a credibility strain, since the narrative spine of the tale is the protagonist's innumerable visits to a psychoanalyst, who silently hears out her tormented past. Despite the stylish shortcuts and visual "refrains" Pinheiro makes of these confession sections, her exorcism of mental wounds does come across somewhat too glossily.

Otherwise, this is solid adult commercial fare, sensitively directed and acted, and splendidly photographed by Gerry Fisher. It should have no trouble finding overseas pickups, and topbilled Garcia and Barrault could wind up competing for prize nominations at the next French Cesar Awards.

Garcia plays the Cardinal character, and Barrault is her mother in both flashbacks and contemporary scenes. Their pasts are attached to Algeria, where the family lived on a wealthy estate. Barrault has been traumatized by the death of her first child, and blames her husband, who never told her he was tubercular. Garcia is born to them when the mother's hatred is at a peak, and the daughter grows up in an atmosphere of emotional harshness and ambivalence.

With the independence of Algeria, the family is repatriated to France, where Garcia marries and has a famly, and Barrault, idle and impoverished, sinks into bitter intransigence, making her daughter's existence a living hell.

Film opens at Garcia's crisis point, when she suffers from anxiety and uterine hemorrhages and one day collapses in a subway car. Taken to a clinic where her uncle (Claude Rich) practices, she is advised to undergo surgery. But suspecting that her bleeding is psychosomatic, she dredges up the courage to undergo analysis.

In a more episodic part, Barrault is both terrifying and pathetic as the overbearing mother, who walls herself up in her loneliness, pride and deep hurt until it kills her.

Supporting cast is fine down the line, with stage wunderkind Daniel Mesguich, celebrated for his extravagance as both director and actor, surprisingly restrained as the Freudian psychoanalyst, whose laconic couchside manner at times drives Garcia to distraction. Cardinal, by the way, has a small, slyly symbolic part as a film editor at the tv station where Garcia finds work.
—*Len.*

Forraedderne
(The Traitors)
(DANISH-B&W)
_____

Copenhagen, Oct. 25.

A Nordisk Film A/S production (with the Danish Film Institute) and release. Features entire cast. Based on Eric Aalbaek Jensen's novel "The Chalk Line," Screenplay, Ole Roos with Erling Jepsen, Jorgen Kastrup, Bent Kielberg. Directed by Roos. Camera (B&W), Peter Roos; executive producer, Bo Christensen; production manager, Karsten Groenborg; editor, Joergen Kastrup; music, Ib Glindenmann; production design, Bent Kielberg; costumes, Annelise Hauberg. Reviewed at the Palads Theatre, Copenhagen, Oct. 25, 1983. Running time. 110 MINS.
Hardy ....Allan Olsen
Bertel ....Ole Meyer
Helga.................Sanne Salomonsen
Bennedsen ....Baard Owe
Gudrun.......................Lisbet Dahl
Physician..................Frits Helmuth
Hotel porter ....Hans Chr. Aaegidius
Sivertsen ....Stig Hoffmeyer
_____

"The Traitors" is filmed in black & white, director Ole Roos says, to emulate pictures of World War II as remembered via oft-repeated newsreel footage from the period. Whether this will add to the pleasures of present-day filmgoers is less than likely. It does not add much to the director's esthetic viewpoints either. He likes to have his cameraman do dramatic close-ups of details that may or may not, have a symbolic tie to the story itself, which is about a couple of youngsters who, on New Year's Eve 1945, go AWOL from a Danish army corps of volunteers, just back from fighting along with the Germans on the Russian front.

The boys are now being hunted by both their SS-like superiors and by members of the Danish resistance movement. While trying to reach their childhood homes in some remote part of the country, they kill a couple of their officers and find temporary refuge in a cottage where one of them has a bad wound nursed by a Jewish refugee girl. She later joins them, more or less voluntarily, on their further flight, and by-now solidly enamored couple is closely watched during a lot of explicit lovemaking.

While wanting to be taken serious as a meaningful statement about the comparative innocence, foolishness and general alienation of youngsters fighting either for and against the Nazis, film also tries to hold a steady course as an outright thriller. Film fails on both counts by too much ham-fisted setting-up of too-obvious psychological counterpoint along with equally over-explicit melodrama and pictorial symbolism. There is some good acting by the two main protagonists and some awful acting by otherwise more discreet older professionals and by several amateurs roped in from the pop music field.

"The Traitors" is based on a much more soft-spoken and truly dramatic novel in which author Erik Aalbaek Jensen has the Good Guys and the Bad Guys walking very close together along the invisible chalkline of wartime morals. Ole Roos' film version virtually carries its message on billboards and delivers its dramatic points like a salesman holding up his wares as if they were divine offerings. Apart from official Danish film weeks, "The Traitors" will hardly earn any ticket to foreign travel. —*Kell.*

The Champions
(HONG KONG-COLOR)

Hong Kong, Oct. 20.
A Raymond Chow Presentation for Golden Harvest. Directed by Yuen Chun Yeung. Stars Yuen Biao, Cheung Kok Keung, Dick Wei, Lee Choi Fung, Ko Hung. Executive producer, Yuen Wo Ping. Screenplay, Yuen Chun Yueng; action choreographers, Yuen Brothers; associate producers, Chan Pui Wah, Leung Kong Wah; camera (color), Ma Kwun Wah, Sung Kong Wah; editor, Cheung Yiu Chung. Reviewed at State Theatre, Hong Kong, Oct. 19, 1983. Running time: **100 MINS.** (*Cantonese soundtrack with English subtitles*)

The Yuens' freelance group of martial arts specialists has been consistent in turning out kung fu-comic fare that is visually entertaining, non-offensive and requires no intellectualizing. The gut street-level creativity is what they're really good and known for.

And this is evident in their latest outing — "The Champions," a modern comedy about football. Knowing that the formula kung fu

is passe, the Yuen family of stunt men wisely incorporated some untried ideas into their predictable movie fare and that is to give their kung fu-comic film a face lift, thus the main theme is football, athletes and acrobatic footwork cum kung fu tricks and spiced with all the basic ingredients of Yuen's non-stop action package.

The end result turns out to be a pleasant and enjoyable film with impeccably-choreographed action sequences.

The stunts of the leads are believable, brisk, good and professional-looking. Again, the storyline (the underdogs make good) and acting are secondary. Only the action scenes count and there are plenty to meet the eye. First a barefoot match, then a couple of football games and a hilarious tango dance sequence of two rivals that was ingenously executed.

The supposedly grand finale is the football match that pits the good team against the corrupt team and whoever loses will have to give a leg. The match, unfortunately, does not take place in a grand football field, but in some obscure sand lot that truly weakens the impact. It shows that low-budget look which could be the reason for the pics failure.

"The Champions" may remind some of Cantonese films made in the '60s, when production design looked unpretentiously cheap.

"The Champions" could have been better had the producers pursued their intentions with more quality as they have the right action concept and stars. Properly re-edited and spruced up, the film can still be marketed to action markets abroad. —*Mel.*

National Lampoon Goes To The Movies
(COLOR)

Batting .000 in laughs.

A United Artists picture (MGM-UA Entertainment); a Matty Simmons production. Produced by Simmons. Directed by Bob Giraldi (segments 1, 2), Henry Jaglom (segment 3). Features Robby Benson, Richard Widmark, Ann Dusenberry, Peter Riegert. Screenplay, Tod Carroll, Shary Flenniken, Pat Mephitis, Gerald Sussman, Ellis Weiner; camera (Movielab color; prints by Technicolor), Tak Fujimoto (#1, 2), Charles Correll (#3); editor, James Coblentz, Bud S. Isaacs; music, Andy Stein; sound, James La Rue, Charles Wilborn; assistant directors, Tony Brand, Jerry Ballew; production manager, Leonard Bray; second unit director-associate producer, Kenneth Charles Dennis; assoc. producer, Michael David Stotter; art direction, Alexander A. Mayer. Reviewed on Home Box Office, N.Y., Nov. 2, 1983. (MPAA Rating: R). Running time: **89 MINS.**

1. Growing Yourself
Jason Cooper	Peter Riegert
Liza	Diane Lane
Susan Cooper	Candy Clark
Diana	Teresa Ganzel

2. Success Wanters
Dominique Corsaire	Ann Dusenberry
Paul Everest	Robert Culp
Nixos Naxos	Titos Vandis
Nicky	Bobby DiCicco
Agent/emcee	Joe Spinell
First Lady	Margaret Whitton
President	Fred Willard
Helena Naxos	Olympia Dukakis
Jeff Steele	Gary Cookson
Secretary	Mary Woronov
Dr. Kleiner	Dick Miller

3. Municipalians
Brent Falcone	Robby Benson
Stan Nagurski	Richard Widmark
Samuel Starkman	Christopher Lloyd
Junkie	Barry Diamond
Mousy	Elisha Cook
Mrs. Falcone	Julie Kavner
Sergeant	Sam Gilman
Lawyer	Henny Youngman
Crazed husband	Bill Kirchenbauer
Crazed wife	Irene Forrest
Vice cop	Harry Reems

Filmed in January 1981, "National Lampoon Goes To The Movies" illustrates the peril of film comedy production: if it isn't funny, what do you do with it? Never released theatrically for obvious reasons, picture finally surfaced on cable tv with the crudely superimposed new title "National Lampoon's Movie Madness" and is reviewed here for the record.

Problem is in the writing, with one-joke routines and poor targets for satire. First two segments (helmed by Bob Giraldi) aim at unlikely film genres for lampooning: the self-actualization genre of "An Unmarried Woman" and the Harold Robbins-Sidney Sheldon glamor-success story (funnier when played straight). Henry Jaglom's "Municipalians" kids the Joseph Wambaugh school of police stories to ill effect. A fourth segment by Jaglom, spoofing disaster films, ended up on the cutting room floor in this edition, along with its performances by Allen Goorwitz, Marcia Strassman, Kenneth Mars and Jaglom regulars Patrice Townsend, Michael Emil and Zack Norman. (Project's original co-scripter P.J. O'Rourke is also missing from the final credits.)

Opener, "Growing Yourself," showcases Peter Riegert (comic actor who later starred in "Local Hero") as a husband who sends his wife (Candy Clark) away so that both can "find" themselves. Repititious spoof of self-analysis features one good scene, as busty Teresa Ganzel talks herself into an orgasm, as well as a dumb running in-joke which accidentally came true later, with Riegert trying to drag everyone to see an overlong Rainer Werner Fassbinder film (culminating in the posthumous release this year of his "Berlin Alexanderplatz," not the "In The Year Of 13 Moons" called a 6-hour epic here).

"Success Wanters" is an elaborately staged mockout of many films, dealing specifically with a young woman becoming a successful and revengeful business tycoon. Cute Ann Dusenberry is appealing as the girl who schemes to take

over a margarine empire and put butter magnates out of business after they "butter bang" her at a Dairy Companies convention. Key targets are such films as "The Greek Tycoon," "The Betsy," "Bloodline" and even "Emmanuele," but the switches on the genre's cliches aren't as amusing as the originals' kitsch.

"Municipalians" features a miscast Robby Benson as a goody-goody young L.A. cop teamed with ultra-cynical Richard Widmark, making fun of "The New Centurions" and similar films. The sight gags don't work and jokes are dated, as in Benson doing a singalong with looney Christopher Lloyd of "Feelings," left over from tv's "The Gong Show." Benson's predictable transition to a cynical tough guy is amateurishly acted while Widmark's dead-on performance is accurate but unfunny. As with the other two segments, the supporting cast is wasted.

Debuting director Giraldi (better known as maestro of music videos like Michael Jackson's "Beat It" and Miller Lite beer tv commercials) delivers static scenes and little visual interest while Jaglom fails to bring the improv humor of his own comedies to bear here. Technical credits are variable, with poor sound-synch and weak production values during Jaglom's segment. Dr. John warbles a boring "Going To The Movies" song to bookend the film, which has an unfinished quality to its lack of a host or transition material (just panning shots on cartoon illustrations between segments). —*Lor.*

Vive la Sociale!
(FRENCH-COLOR)

Paris, Oct. 26.
Fox-Hachette release of a Laura Productions/Hachette-Fox coproduction. Produced by Gerard Guerin. Associate producer, Rene Cleitman. Stars Francois Cluzet, Robin Renucci, Elisabeth Bourgine, Jean-Yves Dubois, Yves Robert, Judith Magre. Directed by Gerard Mordillat. Screenplay, Gerard Mordillat, Jacques Audiard, Louis-Charles Sirjacq; camera (Fujicolor), Francois Catonne; editor, Michel Catonne; art director, Theo Meurisse; music, Jean-Claude Petit; costumes, Caroline De Vivaise; sound, Michel Vionnet; production manager, Eric Lambert. Reviewed at the Marignan-Concorde theatre, Oct. 20, 1983. Running time: **95 MINS.**
With: Francois Cluzet, Robin Renucci, Elisabeth Bourgine, Jean-Yves Dubois, Yves Robert, Judith Magre, Jean-Pierre Cassel, Maurice Baquet, Emmanuelle Debever, Claude Duneton, Henri Genes, Camille Grandville, Bernadette Le Sache, Micheline Luccioni.

Growing up working class and left-wing is not a subject that's often been treated by French filmmakers (most of whom are of middle class backgrounds), but "Vive la Sociale" has the merit (among others) of dealing with just that.

'Director Gerard Mordillat, who grew up in Paris' popular 20th arrondissement, has nonetheless rejected the usual literal semiautobiographical mode of many newcomers, and has instead opted for a serio-comic manner that mixes satire, sentiment, theatrical convention and musical comedy to mostly winning effect.

Mordillat, 34, who previously made two films that used purely documentary footage to fictional ends (both were codirected by Nicolas Philibert) follows the funnysad growing pains of a young Parisian, born into a narrowminded communist/anarchist household in the early 1950s. Despite, or probably because of the heavy air of leftist sentiment he has breathed all through his young years, he finds himself drifting towards the reefs of bourgeois ideals. After an uninspired try at factory labor, he decides to create a catering service with some buddies, and travels around the country hosting banquets and weddings of all sizes and social classes, from makeshift popular affairs in high school gyms, to fancy galas on chateaux lawns.

"Vive la Sociale" (the title is multi-referential and untranslatable) is full of wistful charm, warmth and good-humoured ribbing. Mordillat gives full vent to his talents for colorful psychological and social anecdotes, many of which are apparently true. One of these (cited widely by local critics) shows the blinkered Communist dad, delightfully played by Yves Robert, who is shocked to find "Stalin" defined as a "dictator" in a crossword puzzle in L'Humanite, the French Communist newspaper.

Mordillat's direction is alert and frequently inventive, as in an amusing sequence in which the protagonist inadvertently gets mixed up in the May 1968 student revolts and discovers that the riot cop after his hide is a childhood buddy. Rather than cart him off to jail, latter offers him a lift home in the paddy wagon. In a marvelous, nostalgic coda to the scene, the police van disappears off screen to reveal the two friends as they were when kids, sitting on the hood of a car and gazing off wonderingly from the vehicle.

An appealing cast is led by Francois Cluzet as the forlorn prole who narrates his own story, sighs over his mediocrity and walks in and out of his own flashbacks, as if past and present had no barriers. Cluzet, spotted by Diane Kurys for her 1977 feature, "Cocktail Molotov" and who played Isabelle Adjani's bicycle-freak brother-inlaw in Jean Becker's "One Deadly Summer," is one of the most promising young screen faces

around locally and it's a wonder more producers aren't after him.

Rest of the casting offers a bright mix of reliable veterans (Robert, Judith Magre as the anarchist mom, Jean-Pierre Cassel, Maurice Baquet) with versatile newcomers like Robin Renucci and Jean-Yves Dubois, as Cluzet's catering colleagues, and Elisabeth Bourgine, who provides personable romantic interest as a Hungarian-born musician whom Cluzet falls in love with at first sight and marries. (She horrifies father-in-law Robert by telling him that her family emigrated to Paris, not Moscow, because there are concentration camps in the USSR.)

Tech credits stylishly match the vivacity of script, direction and performance, and it's worth noting that lenser Francois Catonne is one of the most versatile of France's new generation of cinematographers.

Some knowledge of France's social and political humors might help one better enjoy certain gags, but picture could easily charm non-French viewers with its knowing dosage of mirth and melancholy. —Len.

Los Dos Mundos De Angelita
(The Two Worlds of Angelita)
(COLOR-16m)

Stillborn story of average people.

A First Run Features release, presented by the Puerto Rican Foundation for the Humanities, of a Jane Morrison production. Produced and directed by Jane Morrison. Features entire cast. Screenplay, Jose Manuel Torres Santiago, Rose Rosenblatt, Morrison; additional story material, Tato Laviera; camera (DuArt color, 16m), Affonso Beato; additional photography, Jose Garcia; editor, Suzanne Fenn; music, Dom Salvador; production manager-associate producer, Lianne Halfon; assistant director, Michael Waxman; sound, Pam Yates; production design, Randy Barcelo. Reviewed at Carnegie Hall Cinema, N.Y., Oct. 29, 1983. (No MPAA Rating). Running time: 72 MINS.
Angelita . . . . Marien Perez Riera
Fela . . . . Rosalba Rolon
Chuito . . . . Angel Domenech Soto
Dona Angela . . . . Delia Esther Quinones
Also with: Pedro Juan Texidor, Idalia Perez Garay, Bimbo Rivas, Geisha Otero, Malik Mandes, Roberto Rivera Negron, Nena Rivera, Sandra Rodriguez, Carlos Perez Riera, Angie Gonzalez.

"The Two Worlds Of Angelita" is an earnest but uninvolving lowbudget film depicting the problems of an average Puerto Rican family moving to New York City and trying to cope with a new environment. By scrupulously avoiding the usual elements of popular Latino cinema (comedy, sex, glamor, violence), Gotham-based filmmaker Jane Morrison has come up with a dull picture of very limited commercial interest.

Marien Perez Riera toplines as the nine-year-old Angelita, a bright child who has trouble making friends when she and her mom Fela (Rosalba Rolon) move to New York to join her "papi" Chuito (Angel Domenech Soto). Big stumbling block for both daughter and dad proves to be inadequate knowledge of English, hurting Angelita at school and preventing Chuito from landing a good job.

Weak storyline broadcasts all the film's main themes on the surface, with little diversion or development. After mainly chatty scenes with neighbors and relatives, pic ends abruptly with Angelita's blank expression when her dad literally takes a hike to join a training program in Connecticut.

There are knowing verbal references to popular entertainment here, as Angelita play-acts tv soap operas with her favorite doll or makes a comparison to tv bomba Iris Chacon. Other than some invigorating soundtrack hits by Salsa star Willie Colon, "Angelita" lacks a popular link to its potential audience. Tech credits, including resonating direct-sound recording, are just adequate. —Lor.

Hospital Massacre
(COLOR)

Routine terror pic capitalizing on universal fear of being hospitalized.

A Cannon Films release of a Golan-Globus production. Executive producer, Geoffrey Rose. Produced by Menahem Golan, Yoram Globus. Directed by Boaz Davidson. Stars Barbi Benton. Screenplay, Marc Behm; camera (TVC color), Nicholas von Sternberg; editor, Jon Koslowsky; music, Arlon Ober; sound, Jonathon Stein; assistant director-assoc. producer, John Thompson; assoc. producer, Christopher Pearce; art direction-set decoration, J. Rae Fox; makeup master, Alan Apone; makeup, Kathy Shorkey. Reviewed on MGM-UA Home Video vidcassete, N.Y., Oct. 15, 1983. (MPAA Rating: R). Running time: 88 MINS.
Susan Jeremy . . . . Barbi Benton
Harry . . . . Chip Lucia
Jack . . . . Jon Van Ness
Dr. Saxon . . . . John Warner Williams
Dr. Beam . . . . Den Surles
Dr. Jacobs . . . . Gay Austin
Nurse Dora . . . . Gloria Morrison
Nurse Kitty . . . . Karyn Smith
Hal . . . . Lanny Duncan

"Hospital Massacre" is a slowly paced terror film which has had minor theatrical release (primarily in England) ahead of its current availability on videocassette as part of Cannon Films' distribution deal with MGM-UA. Other than an escalating mood of hospital-related paranoia and some alluring skin footage of diminutive actress Barbi Benton, pic has little to offer fright fans.

Picture had a very curious production history. It was filmed in December 1980 as "Be My Valentine, Or Else ..." but lost the race to debut off-season as "holiday" hor-

ror fare in February 1981 to an earlier Canadian pic "My Bloody Valentine."

The film then adopted, appropriately given its content, the title and ad campaign of a Cannon project for Jill St. John entitled "X-Ray," but though completed in time for the Cannes 1981 market, it was not released and missed out on the business 20th-Fox earned in early 1982 with a similar Canadian pickup ("The Fright") that was retitled "Visiting Hours."

Finally retitled "Hospital Massacre," pic concerns a psychotic killer named Harold, who 19 years ago (illustrated by another corny childhood opening) had his Valentine card laughed at by Susan (Barbi Benton when full-grown) and her brother. He kills the brother right away, but allows the resentment against Susan to fester for 19 years.

We meet Sue again the week before Valentine's Day, visiting an L.A. hospital to pick up test results stemming from a routine checkup relating to her job promotion. Mad Harold (clad in doctor's getup and surgical mask) kills Sue's femme doctor and switches her X-rays. When a substitute medico, Dr. Saxon (John Warner Williams), sees these phony X-rays, he concludes Sue is desperately ill and orders her to be kept in hospital for observation and possible surgery. Harold is on the loose, meanwhile, building up an impressive body count with gory murders of staff and patients.

Though this hospital is unnaturally and unconvincingly as underpopulated as the one holding Jamie Lee Curtis in "Halloween II," director Boaz Davidson preys upon the viewer's natural fear of helplessness in such an institution to create an increasing mood of paranoia. Star Benton, with her perpetual toothy grin, does not express the requisite fear, but oh what a body the former pinup displays. It is on view during a lengthy closeup examination scene which, probably unwittingly, comments on the current trend away from fantasy, towards the strictly clinical (and explicit) in both the horror and sex film genres. Otherwise, there are very dull stretches between murders. Tech credits are adequate. — Lor.

Make Them Die Slowly
(Cannibal Ferrox)
(ITALIAN-COLOR)

An Aquarius Film Releasing release. Executive producer, Antonio Crescenzi. Written and directed by Umberto Lenzi. Features entire cast. Camera (color), Giovanni Bergamini; editor, Enzo Meniconi; music, Budy/Maglione. Reviewed at Liberty theatre, N.Y., Nov. 6, 1983. (No MPAA Rating; self-applied equivalent rating). Running time: 91 MINS.
With: John Morghen, Lorainne de Selle, Brian Redford, Zora Kerowa, Walter Lloyd,

Robert Kerman, John Bartha, Meg Fleming, R. Bolla, Venantino Venantini, (El Indio) Rincon.

"Make Them Die Slowly," originally titled "Cannibal Ferrox" for its overseas release, is a perfunctory brutality exercise pitched at undiscriminating, violence-seeking audiences. Lensed in fall 1980 on South American and New York City locations, pic is belatedly getting U.S. release.

Two stories are crosscut: young Gloria Davis and her brother Rudy and friend Patricia are vacationing in Colombia in search of a small village where Indians have been exported as cannibals committing atrocities. Gloria is researching her NYU doctoral thesis in anthropology, proving cannibalism as an organized native practice is a myth created by Conquistadors and other white oppressors.

Back in Gotham, policemen Lt. Rizzo (porn actor R. Bolla) and Ross (Venantino Venantini) are searching for drug dealer Mike Logan who is involved in a murder. Mike is in Colombia prospecting for emeralds and teams up with Gloria and her companions.

Horror format used by filmmaker Umberto Lenzi is as old as Tod Browning's 1932 classic "Freaks;" the viewer is shown that the white heroes (specifically, sadistic, cocaine-crazed Mike) are the villains persecuting hapless Indians, with the Indians retaliating monstrously and brutally. One is bound to have ambivalent feelings, though the target minority audience is being stroked with a corny "get whitey" message.

Film's ultraviolence is unexciting, merely grotesque: blonde second-lead heroine strung up by the chest in emulation of Richard Harris in "A Man Called Horse;" Mike castrated on camera, and even a realistic cannibalism scene. Since the ASPCA does not monitor European filmmakers, there are numerous distasteful scenes of animals being killed on camera.

Though Lenzi's mixed bag of Continental and U.S. actors articulate in English, the post-synch dubbing is sloppy. His only personal touch in a routine assignment is having the two heroines sing "Red River Valley" to keep their spirits up while the Indians prepare to torture them. Cynical epilog has Gloria receiving her PhD. with all traces of cannibalism and savagery hushed up.

—Lor.

Thessaloniki Film Fest

Revenge
(GREEK-COLOR)

Thessaloniki, Oct. 8.

A Nicos Verguitsis coproduction with the Greek Film Centre. Written and directed by Nicos Verguitsis. Stars Antonis Kalatazopoulos, Yota Festa, Panos Eliopoulos, Thalia Aslanidou, George Moschides, Angela Brouskou, Demetris Poulicacos, Ira Papamichael. Camera (color), Andreas Bellis; music, Demetris Papademetriou, editing, Yannis Tsitsopouloosets, Nicos Verguitsis-Rallou Koundourou; costumes, Maria Harami. Reviewed at the Thessaloniki Film Fest, Oct. 8, 1983. Running Time: 110 MINS.

This is the second feature film by Nicos Verguitsis, a talented young filmmaker who turned a simple story into a fresh and sensitive picture which won five prizes at the Thessaloniki fest, including best director and a share best picture prize.

It is a skillful directorial effort, heartily applauded at the fest, which should have good prospects at the boxoffice with young audiences. It might well attract international attention with proper handling.

The central character of the story is a man, 30, who on the night of an earthquake, decides to enjoy life and everything hitherto forbidden him. He runs to see Eva, his best friend's girl, with whom he was once in love. Their relationship, however, dissolves because of his failure to respect her personal life. After a period of intense loneliness they try again, only this time the three of them will live together.

His cinematic fantasies remain his sole refuge since he still has not learned how to get what he wants. The only thing he knows for sure is that he must begin to live. In the end, he is revealed to be the one who denounced his friend to the authorities for his political beliefs.

Verguitsis has done a good job of telling this simple story with a flair for evoking the right atmosphere with sensitivity and freshness. He has intentionally left the identifications vague in order to describe the uncertainty prevailing with young people of today, but the political element added in the last part of the picture is a weak point in the film.

Thesping all around is excellent with prize-winning performances by three players, Demetris Poulicacos, Antonis Kafetzopoulos and Yota Festa. Photography by Andreas Bellis is superb. The musical score written by Demetris Papademetriou is a definite asset. All other technical credits are good.

—Rena.

Ypoguia Diadromi
(Underground Passage)
(GREEK-COLOR)

Thessaloniki, Oct. 8.

Apostolos C. Doxiades and Greek Film Centre coproduction. Written by Doxiades, Petros Tatsopoulos. Directed by Doxiades. stars Yannis Fertis, Betty Livanou, George Moschidis, Pavlos Kontoyannidis. Camera (color), Andreas Bellis, Aris Stavrou; music, Michalis Gregoriou; editing, Takis Yannopoulos. Reviewed at the Thessaloniki Film Festival, Oct. 8, 1983. Running Time: 128 MINS.

This is the first picture by new filmmaker Apostolos Doxiades who, though he has turned out a film with many flaws, makes a promising start. He won the prize for best picture by a new director at the Thessaloniki Festival.

His picture is a modern thriller with vague political references. Based on an uninspired script and with an uneven pace and structure, abounding in political and social suggestivity, its prospects will be slim both locally and abroad.

Centering the action around his central hero, Minister of Industrial Development Costas Kavadias, he presents him with two crises. The first concerns his wife, Irene, who tries to commit suicide despite his efforts to understand the cause of her frustrations. The second is serious trouble caused in his electoral district by a dangerous leakage of toxic elements from a local factory. The inhabitants of the area, headed by his old friend, Dr. Michalis Liaskos, demand the closing of the factory. Meanwhile, his assistant is informed that the minister's wife has been meeting secretly with a onetime fellow activist from the Junta era, a relationship that could be especially dangerous in leading to extremists' action in the matter of the factory.

Kavadias tries to settle the matter as quickly as possible, but is too late. His wife is already there with Ioannou, the old friends now playing opposite roles. Agents of the Secret Service arrive on the scene and lead the action to its final conflict.

Doxiades, though he shows a directorial knowhow, could not overcome the weakness of his script. The storyline is uneven, poorly developed and slow. The political plot and the characters involved are not well defined. Some influences of foreign filmmakers on similar subjects are seen on the surface but are not well assimilated.

Acting as a whole is good, particularly the key performance of Yannis Fertis and Pavlos Kontoyannidis. The film has technical polish due to effective photography by Andreas Bellis and Aris Stavrou and music by Michalis Gregoriou, plus otherwise good technical credits.

—Rena.

Glykia Symmoria
(Sweet Bunch)
(GREEK-COLOR)

Thessaloniki, Oct. 8.

A Nicos Nicolaidis production, written and directed by Nicolaidis. Stars Dora Masclavanou, Takis Spyridakis, Takis Moschos, Despina Tomazani, Lenia Polykrati, Alsis Panayotidis, Constantinos Tzoumas; Camera (color), Aris Stavrou; music, George Hatzinassios; editing, Andreas Andreadakis. Reviewed at the Thessaloniki Film Fest, Oct. 8, 1983. Running time: 140 MINS.

This is the third picture by Nicos Nicolaidis, a prize-winning director in previous festivals who scores again with this film, winning five prizes.

It is a skillful, offbeat sort of picture, brought off well and definitely aimed at a young audience, due to its theme. Despite excellent cinematography, unfortunate choice of subject matter makes it a waste of talent of all concerned. For this reason it will easily find its way to festivals and art houses here and abroad, but its exploitation prospects are moderate.

The plot involves a group of young people who lead an unconventional way of life. They are misfits, self-excluded from society, having reached a point of no return and are seeking for something in which to believe and die for. Along the way, they steal, cheat, and make love with the same indifference and apathy that marks their other deeds. Someone, however, spies on their deeds and police raid their house, killing them.

According to its filmmaker, the point of the story is that where violence may lead youth today, cynical youths with no ideals will be the victims of eventual global fascism.

However, his story is unbelievable, by Greek standards at least, and will certainly embarrass people. Still, Nicolaidis paints his characters well, making them convincing, even touching. He presents them as lonely, desperate people who deep inside are longing for real love, companionship and tenderness. He unfolds his film with speed and a modern rhythm that reflects its suspenseful mood. Stunning visual effects evoke an unusual atmosphere of violence and eroticism that makes the film worth watching.

Performances for the most part are excellent, especially that of Takis Spyridakis who won a special prize at Thessaloniki for his performance. The striking camera work by Aris Stavrou was awarded the prize for best photography as well as the costumes by Maria Leonardou Vartholomeou, the editing by Andreas Andreadakis and sound by Marinos Athanassopoulos. —Rena.

O Fonias
(The Killer)
(GREEK-COLOR)

Thessaloniki, Oct. 8.

A Christos Manguos production. Written and directed by Takis Christopoulos, based on play by Metsos Efthymiadis. Stars Vaguelis Kazan, Nicos Kalogueropoulos, Timos Perlengas, Emilia Ipsilanti. Camera (color), Sakis Maniatis; music, Michalis Christodoylidis; Editing, Antonis Tempos. Reviewed at the Thessaloniki Film Fest, Oct. 8, 1983. Running Time: 90 MINS.

This is a failed transfer to the screen by Takis Christopoulos of the Metsos Efthymiadis play, screened at the Information Section of the Thessaloniki Fest. The confined sets give it a static style not likely to appeal to foreign audiences and confines it to home consumption.

The title character is a man who killed his friend because the latter had insulted his mother. On his return from prison to the house of his married sister, he tries to find out who had denounced him to the police as there was no eye-witness when he committed his crime.

He worshipped his mother as a saint while in reality she was a whore, which he did not know. He learns it from his sister, who denounced him. When he leaves her house after this revelation, he is killed by one of his old pals because he was responsible for the death of a fellow he denounced in prison as a drug addict, in order to shorten his own sentence.

Most of the picture is static and uneventful. The director also failed with his actors with the exception of Vaguelis Kazan in the title role. All other technical credits are up to standard. —*Rena*.

Prosohi Kindynos
(Caution: Danger)
(GREEK-COLOR)

Thessaloniki, Oct. 8.

A Georges Stampoulopoulos co-production with the Greek Film Centre. Written and directed by George Stampoulopoulos. Stars Titos Vandis, Katerina Razelou, Costas Halkias, Dora Sitzani, Andreas Vaioos, Danis Katranidis. Camera (color), Demetris Papaconstantis; music, Christodoulos Halaris; editing, Aristidis Karydis Fucks. Reviewed at the Thessaloniki Film Festival, Oct. 8, 1983. Running Time: 120 MINS.

Georges Stampoulopoulos had already indicated by his previous films that he is a skillful filmmaker. This new picture confirms that promise, winning four prizes at the Thessaloniki Festival. It is a violence-packed thriller with many shock qualities, strong meat by all standards, which will find its way to the box office, though many people will find its subject disgusting.

Murder, violence and incest are the three elements involved in this story about a peculiar criminal family. The father — master of his two sons and a daughter — is a murderer, a thug and a thief imposing his authority on them by violence. Protected by the local police, he is the terror and fear of the whole surrounding region. Isolated in a forbidding quarry at the end of a solitary road, he lives with his children by setting deadly traps for passing cars and robbing their occupants.

About 20 people have been murdered this way in the "accident" set by this satanic murderer. His sexual relationship with his daughter and brutal maltreatment of his sons revolts the younger one who

tries to escape from this infernal life with the help of a woman who loves him.

The oldest son, however, seeks to take over and replace his father in both the robbery operations and in his sister's bed. He fails in both, kills his sister and sets fire to their shack.

Stampoulopoulos has built up a violent atmosphere loaded with sexual lust, and brutality, unfolding it with a quick pace until its final climax. Though the characters of the story are not well defined, Titos Vandis, as the father, turns in a memorable interpretation and rightly won the best actor prize at the fest. Andreas Vaioos, as one of the sons, shared the best supporting actor prize; Katerina Razelou as the daughter is equally good.

Another asset of the picture is the music by Christodoulos Halaris, which effectively underscores the film and won the best music prize. Editing of the film by Aristidis Karydis Fucks gave the film its quick pace and won the picture its fourth prize. All other technical credits are good.—*Rena*.

To Tragoudi Tis Epistrofis
(Homecoming Song)
(GREEK-COLOR)

Thessaloniki, Oct. 10.

A Yannie Smaragois co-production with the Greek Film Centre. Written by Yannis Smaragdis, Th. Valtinos, Yannis Kakoulidis. Directed by Yannis Smaragdis. Stars Stathis Yallelis, Katia Dandoulaki, Vaguelis Kazan, Vassilis Kolovos, Sperantza Vrana. Camera (color), George Arvanitis; music, Demetris Papademetriou, Thymios Papadopoulous; editing, George Triantafyllou. Reviewed at the Thessaloniki Film Festival Oct. 10, 1983. Running time: 90 MINS.

This is the second long feature film by young filmmaker Yannis Smaragdis who did not manage this time to turn out the picture expected. Unfortunately, this is a disappointing adaptation of a great theme, a weak rendering of a story he failed to present in its right dimensions. So local boxoffice chances are moderate as is the foreign market.

The plot introduces a young man who returns to his homeland after 11 years of living as a political exile in Sweden. The only member of a resistance group to evade capture, he returns full of longing and nostalgia with bittersweet memories.

Upon arrival in Greece he boards a ship for Crete where he left his girl and his friends. He finds the girl married and his friends quite different. It is difficult to adjust to the new life he encounters in his homeland. The people are living a new way of life different from what they had dreamed of and fought for. He refuses to sell his property to his

friends who have a real estate enterprise selling land to forcigners, prefering to live alone with his remembrances. Smaragdis' flat direction resulted in a disappointing picture. It is true he was not helped by actor Stathis Yallelis whose expressionless portrayal of the returnee adds nothing to the story. On the other hand, the beautiful presence and talent of Katia Dandoulaki is wasted in an underplayed love story.

The photography by George Arvanitis captures the fascinating Cretan landscape. Other technical credits are up to standard.

— *Rena*.

The Dresser
(BRITISH-COLOR)

Superb acting may put it on top.

Hollywood, Nov. 10.

A Columbia Pictures presentation of a Goldcrest Films-World Film Services Production of a Peter Yates-Ronald Harwood Film. Produced and directed by Peter Yates. Features entire cast. Screenplay, Ronald Harwood; camera (Rank Film Lab Color), Kevin Pike; editor, Ray Lovejoy; music, James Horner; production design, Stephen Grimes; art direction, Colin Grimes; set decoration, Josie Macavin; sound, David John; wardrobe supervisor, Rosemary Burrows; associate producer, Nigel Wooll; assistant director, Andy Armstrong; makeup, Alan Boyle. Reviewed at Warner-Hollywood Studios, Nov. 10, 1983. (No MPAA Rating at presstime). Running time: 118 MINS.

Sir	Albert Finney
Norman	Tom Courtenay
Oxenby	Edward Fox
Her Ladyship	Zena Walker
Madge	Eileen Atkins
Frank Carrington	Michael Gough
Irene	Cathryn Harrison
Violet Manning	Betty Marsden
Lydia Gibson	Shelia Reid
Geoffrey Thornton	Lockwood West

Two of the most indelible screen performances of the year — by Albert Finney and Tom Courtenay — lift producer-director Peter Yates' film adaptation of the play "The Dresser" to the realm of the commercially accessible, an important boxoffice point for a picture that recreates a little patch of theatre tradition in the provinces of World War II Great Britain.

Adapted by Ronald Harwood from his 1980 London comedy-drama (which later earned Tony nominations for Courtenay and for best Broadway play of 1981), this December release for Columbia is indisputably one of the best films ever made about theatre. It's funny, compassionate, compelling, and in its final moments pulls off an uncanny juxtaposition between the emotionally and physically crumbling Finney and the character he's playing on stage for the 227th time, King Lear.

Finney and Courtenay, who could both be nominated for best actor Oscars insofar as they share almost equal screen time, deliver performances that are startling in their cumulative impact. Finney portrays an aging, spoiled, grandiloquent actor-manager of a traditional English touring company whose dedication to his art creates chaos for those around him. The only character who can handle the old actor is his gofer-valet Norman, played with an amazing dexterity and energy by Courtenay. While air raid sirens whistle in the background and Finney is cracking under the pressure of moving a troupe of broken-down actors around a bombed-out countryside, Courtenay is a well of single-minded resourcefulness, scheming one minute, cajoling the next, indulgent, loving, devoted as much to his man-servant role as Finney is to his acting.

Courtenay's performance is so varied and intricately shaded that once when his character playfully steps out of its homosexual roots to effect a brief tough, sneer-like pose the result is jolting. Finney's breakdown on a public street, his thundering authority at stopping a departing train so his bundled-up troupe can clamber aboard, and his ability to suggest a wreck of a man who still has flashes of brilliance tinges his character with the brush of tragedy, all the more dramatic because of the comic environment.

For a picture hitched so tightly to the human tangle of Finney and Courtenay, Yates brings to the film, much of it shot at Pinewood, a strong visual sense of the British experience in wartime. And the whiff of greasepaint, particularly notable when aide Courtenay goads Finney into his makeup for Lear, lends the tawdry dressing room world of touring theatre its most physically felt detail.

Around Finney, who is addressed only as Sir, stir the motley company members, either crippled or old or generally frayed because everyone else is fighting the war. Edward Fox plays a limping actor resentful of Finney's autocracy. Cathryn Harrison (Rex Harrison's granddaughter) is sharply credible as a young stage assistant. Eileen Atkins is resonant in a deceptively important role as the stage manager, and Zena Walker is Finney's self-consumed wife and leading lady of the company. A wonderful turn is delivered by Lockwood West as an older and grateful aspirant playing the Fool to Finney's Lear.

Playwright and screenwriter Harwood was once a member of an English rep company run by the late, flamboyant British actor-manager Donald Wolfit (1902-'68) and Harwood is said to have based much of his story on his experiences with Wolfit and his troupe.
— *Loyn.*

Le Marginal
(The Outsider)
(FRENCH-COLOR)

Paris, Nov. 5.

Gaumont/Cerito Rene Chateau release of a Cerito/Films Ariane coproduction. Produced by Alain Belmondo, Alexandre Mnouchkine, Georges Dancigers. Stars Jean-Paul Belmondo. Directed by Jacques Deray. Screenplay, Deray, Jean Herman; camera (color), Xaver Schwarzenberger; music, Ennio Morricone; editor, Albert Jurgenson; makeup, Charly Koubesserian; costumes, Paulette Breil. Reviewed at the Paris Theatre, Paris, Nov. 4, 1983. Running time: 101 MINS.
With: Jean-Paul Belmondo, Henry Silva, Claude Brosset, Pierre Vernier, Roger Dumas, Carlos Sottomayor, Tcheky Karyo, Maurice Barrier, Michel Robin.

Jean-Paul Belmondo's new actioner, breaking all-time boxoffice records in France, is another anonymous star vehicle that will please only the initiated.

"Le Marginal" casts him as a lone-wolf cop with extralegal methods who rips into a powerful drug ring operating out of Marseilles and Paris, and finally disposes of its inaccessible chieftain by executing him and passing off the deed as an internecine gangland incident. Dirty Jean-Paul.

Jacques Deray, a veteran of French thrillers, cowrote the screenplay with noted crime novelist Jean Vautrin, who writes for the cinema under the pseudonym Jean Herman. Between the two of them, few cliches and stereotypes of the genre are ignored. What makes this potpourri of sordid incident even less enticing is the absence of humor, an element that made previous Belmondo pics more palatable.

Belmondo, who turned 50 last April, is still in extraordinary physical shape and as usual does his own stuntwork. Among the obligatory setpieces here is one in which the actor leaps from a helicopter onto an escaping speedboat. There is, of course, the inevitable urban car pursuit, and a foot chase across dangerous highways and railyards.

Henry Silva has been imported to play the chief villain, and Belmondo's real-life girlfriend, Carlos Sottomayor, a Brazilian-born singer, provides some dispensable romantic interest as the hero's hooker bedmate.

Tech credits are okay. —*Len.*

Les Princes
(The Princes)
(FRENCH-COLOR)

Paris, Nov. 8.

AAA release of an ACC-Babylone Films coproduction. Produced by Ken and Romaine Legargeant. Stars Gerard Darmon, Muse Dalbray. Written, directed and scored by Tony Gatlif. Camera (color), Jacques Loiseleux; sound, Bernard Ortion; editor, Caludine Bouche; art director, Denis Champenois; costumes, Miruna Boruzescoux and Rose-Marie Melka; production manager, Thierry Barbier. Reviewed at the Marignan-Concorde Pathe cinema, Paris, Nov. 5, 1983. Running time: 100 MINS.
Nara .... Gerard Darmon
The grandmother .... Muse Dalbray
Zorka .... Celine Militon
Miralda .... Concha Tavora
Petiton .... Dominique Maurin
Bijou .... Marie-Helene Rudel
Schoolteacher ...... Anne-Marie Philippe
Samson .... Farid Chopel
Chico .... Hagop Arslanian
Leo .... Tony Gatlif

Newest directing revelation in a local season full of heartening surprises is Tony Gatlif. His "Les Princes" is a film about gypsies, made by an insider. Gatlif, 35, is an Algerian-born gypsy whose family of 15 came to France in the early 1960s. After a delinquent youth in various reform institutions he found his way into a dramatic con-

servatory, and from there his passion for stage and film took root. He has previously directed a feature, "Le Terre au Ventre" (1978), which dealt with Algerian Independence, but seems to consider "Les Princes" his first real work.

Gatlif walks a fine line between the sordid and the poetic in this despairing drama about a gypsy family torn from a sedentary existence in a dreary lower-income housing block and condemned to a wretched nomadic state.

There is neither complacency nor apology in the portrait of Gatlif's sullen anti-hero, played with angry immediacy by Gerard Darmon. He is violent, intractable and macho, rejecting his young wife because she has allowed a social worker to talk her into using birth-control pills. Though he has a job on a construction site, he willingly takes part in various deals and thefts. There is little to render him sympathetic, but such is Gatlif's skill and Darmon's performance, that his destiny concerns the viewer.

Darmon's harsh rebellion is counterbalanced by the remarkable portrait of his grandmother, a colorfully clothed ancient who bears gypsy traditions but still has the youthful curiosity to learn how to write, aided by Darmon's daughter. Muse Dalbray, octogenarian actress and author, who's only made one film previous to this, provides some beautiful moments of humour and pathos. Screen stardom can sometimes begin at 80.

Good as Gatlif's direction often is, he loses control of his objectivity when it comes to portraying members of society, and gives way to unfortunate caricature, notably in the grotesque characterization of a German journalist who barely hides self-serving arrogance and condescension beneath a veil of false concern.

There are some other good characterizations like Darmon's three cheap hood brothers-in-law — played by Hagop Arslanian, Tony Librizzi and Gatlif himself — who awkwardly try to bring about a reconciliation between Darmon and their sister. Latter (Concha Tavora) is a demure but obstinate girl, who hangs around the family's residence in the hope of seeing her daughter, and regaining favor in her mate's blinkered eyes. When they are evicted from the home and must take to the road, she follows at a respectful distance.

Tech credits are excellent, and Gatlif also takes credit for the fine musical score. This is a film that will certainly travel the festival trail with panache and find interested response primarily in foreign art house precincts. —*Len.*

A Christmas Story
(COLOR)

Ghost of Christmas Past.

Hollywood, Nov. 12.

An MGM/UA release. Produced by Rene Dupont and Bob Clark. Directed by Bob Clark. Features entire cast. Screenplay, Jean Shepherd, Leigh Brown, Bob Clark, adapted from novel, "In God We Trust, All Others Pay Cash" by Jean Shepherd; camera (Medalion color), Reginald H. Morris; editor, Stan Cole; music, Carl Zittrer, Paul Zaza; production designer, Reuben Freed; art director, Gavin Mitchell; set decorator, Mark Freeborn; costume designer, Mary E. McLeod; sound mixer, Alan Bernard; associate producer, Gary Goch; assistant director, Ken Goch. Reviewed at MGM/UA studio, Los Angeles, Nov. 11, 1983. (MPAA rating: PG.) Running time: 94 MINS.
Mother .... Melinda Dillon
The Old Man .... Darren McGavin
Ralphie .... Peter Billingsley
Randy .... Ian Petrella
Flick .... Scott Schwartz
Schwartz .... R.D. Robb
Miss Shields .... Tedde Moore
Scot Farcus .... Zack Ward

For those who want to get their Christmas off to an early, idealized start before the real thing sets in, "A Christmas Story" should fit the bill nicely. Based on Jean Shepherd story, "A Christmas Story" is a version of Christmas as it exists only in the imagination. Though it is told through the eyes of a child, adults should find more to respond to in this nostalgic look at growing up in the '40s.

In his radio program, novels and PBS shows, Shepherd has always been best at evoking the texture of life as it used to be in his midwest childhood. It was a time of innocence and charm "when all was right with the world." "A Christmas Story" is true to that spirit without being cloyingly sentimental or phoney.

The films works almost as an illustrated monolog complete with narration by Shepherd. A bunch of vignettes about family life and small-town Americana in the mid-'40s are tied together around a rather flimsy plot device.

What Ralphie (Peter Billingsley) wants for Christmas more than anything in the whole world is a Red Ryder "range model air rifle." There seems to be a conspiracy against him getting one, however. While mother and teacher warn him that he'll only poke his eye out, visions of the Red Ryder dance in his head.

As Ralphie pines for something he has no power to do anything about, his life becomes vividly alive thanks to numerous well observed details. His younger brother Randy (Ian Petrella), for instance, hasn't eaten willingly in three years and his father (Darren McGavin) leaves a "stream of obscenities over Lake Michigan" as he waits to become a major winner in a crossword contest.

Director Bob Clark ("Porky's") and production designer Reuben Freed have lovingly recreated the look and feel of an era populated by Little Orphan Annie decoder rings, Ovaltine, and overloaded electrical outlets. Performances by McGavin, Melinda Dillon as the mother and especially the kids, bullies and classmates included, adds to a genuine feeling of family warmth.

With his hornrimmed glasses and voice-over narration by Shepherd, Ralphie seems more like a grown-up than a nine-year-old. "A Christmas Story" is an adult's view of childhood kids may find corny. — *Jagr.*

Young Warriors
(COLOR)

Cautionary tale re: teen vigilantes given a diffuse treatment. Okay exploitation chances.

A Cannon Films release of a Star Cinema production. Produced by Victoria Paige Meyerink. Exec producers, Mark Cohen, George Foldes; coproducers, Lawrence D. Foldes, Russell W. Colgin. Directed by Lawrence D. Foldes. Stars Ernest Borgnine, Richard Roundtree, Lynda Day George. Screenplay, Foldes, Colgin; camera (color), Mac Ahlberg; editor, Ted Nicolaou; music, Rob Walsh; assistant directors, Michael Sourapas, Carol Lewis; production manager, Gordon Wolf; production design, Karl Pogany; art direction, Richard S. Bylin; sound, Brian DeMellier, Rod Sutton; special makeup effects, Douglas J. White; animation sequences, Adam Slater; special effects, John Eggett. Reviewed at UACI Rivoli theater 1, N.Y., Nov. 13, 1983. (MPAA Rating: R). Running time: **103 MINS.**

Lt. Bob Carrigan	Ernest Borgnine
St. John Austin	Richard Roundtree
Beverly Carrigan	Lynda Day George
Kevin Carrigan	James Van Patten
Lucy	Anne Lockhart
Scott	Tom Reilly
Stan	Ed De Stefane
Fred	Mike Norris
Prof. Hoover	Dick Shawn
Ginger	Linnea Quigley
Jorge	John Alden
Heather	Britt Helfer
Animation instructor	Don Hepner
Tiffany Carrigan	April Dawn

"Young Warriors" is an overly-ambitious teen exploitation film that mixes the popular drive-in formulae of hijinks, violence and sex tease with an uncomfortable overlay of preachiness. Cannon pickup is likely to do fair off-season business.

Filmed last year in British Columbia and Southern California as "The Graduates Of Malibu High," a title it retains by way of introduction, picture limns the effects of crime and violence on teens three years after graduation, now attending Pacific Coast College. After an opening reel devoted to fraternity initiation revelry and sight gags, pic becomes melodramatic with the gang-rape and murder of Tiffany Carrigan (April Dawn) by thugs in a black van sporting a death's head insignia.

While her father (Ernest Borgnine) follows normal procedures as a police officer, Tiffany's brother Kevin (James Van Patten) feels frustrated and organizes his frat members to hit the streets and root out the killers. They quickly extend their efforts towards violently confronting any crime encountered, building up an impressive arsenal of automatic weaponry in the process.

The comic-strip fantasy elements here, culminating in a cantina shootout in which Kevin wields a machine gun in emulation of the slow motion blood pack finale of Sam Peckinpah's "The Wild Bunch," do not mix well with numerous debates by Kevin with his dad, girl friend and teachers regarding the violent crime problem in the U.S. Filmmaker Lawrence Foldes' specific juxtapositions are very heavy-handed, as in crosscutting between Kevin's girlfriend (Anne Lockhart) crying on his mom Lynda Day George's shoulder and footage of Kevin being serviced by a street hooker prior to the final shootout.

Acting is okay, with the star-billed trio in relatively brief roles and Van Patten stuck with an unplayable assignment of belligerent student by day/G.I. Joe by night. Other offspring talent Anne Lockhart and Mike Norris visually resemble their famous forebears June and Chuck, but have little to do. Comic actor Dick Shawn adds a welcome wry touch as Van Patten's equivocal philosophy prof. Tech credits, particularly the visuals and special effects, are good. —*Lor.*

Nate and Hayes
(COLOR)

Nifty swashbuckler is marketing challenge.

Hollywood, Nov. 9.

A Paramount release of a Phillips-Whitehouse production. Produced by Lloyd Phillips, Rob Whitehouse. Directed by Ferdinand Fairfax. Stars Tommy Lee Jones, Michael O'Keefe. Screenplay, John Hughes, David Odell; Screenstory, Odell, based on a story by Phillips; camera (Rank Film Lab color), Tony Imi; editor, John Shirley; music, Trevor Jones; production design Maurice Cain; art direction, Jo Ford (Fiji), Dan Hennah, Rick Kofoed; costume design, Norma Moriceau; sound (Dolby), Don Reynolds; second unit director, Michael Horton; second unit camera, Bob Hughes; special effects supervision, Peter Dawson; assistant director, Bert Batt. Reviewed at the Paramount Studios, L.A., Nov. 9, 1983. (MPAA Rating: PG.) Running time: **100 MINS.**

Captain Bully Hayes	Tommy Lee Jones
Nathaniel Williamson	Michael O'Keefe
Ben Pease	Max Phipps
Sophie	Jenny Seagrove
Count Von Rittenberg	Grant Tilly
Louis Beck	Peter Rowley
Reverend Williamson	Bill Johnson
Mrs. Williamson	Kate Harcourt
Moaka	Reg Ruka
Auctioneer	Roy Billing
Mr. Blake	Bruce Allpress
Ratbag	David Letch
King of Ponape	Prince Tui Teka
Fong	Pudji Waseso
Gunboat Captain	Peter Vere Jones
Count's Lieutenant	Tom Vanderlaan
Gun Operator	Mark Hadlow

"Nate and Hayes" is an agreeably surprising exception to the general rule that, "They don't make 'em like they used to." Filmed and acted with considerable panache and laced with boistrous humor, pic recalls such pirate sagas as "The Crimson Pirate" as well as the rollercoaster adventurism of "Raiders Of The Lost Ark," and should please young, mainstream audiences with its irreverent attitude. Getting them in to see it, however, represents a considerable marketing challenge, given the unlikely genre, non-descript title and off-season release date. Odds are stacked against it, but Par has a better film here than anyone had a right to expect.

Lensed under the title "Savage Islands," tale begins somewhat unpleasantly, as pirate Tommy Lee Jones blithely wipes out half of a native tribe in the wake of a guns sale gone bad. Prolog displays a highly jocular attitude toward violent death, complete with Jones making James Bond-style cracks when he dispatches enemies, all of which comes on a little strong as an aperitif.

Jones is captured for his crimes, and remainder of the narrative is told as a flashback from his prison cell. While hardly a noble, "good" pirate in the mold of Errol Flynn in "The Sea Hawk," Jones still has morals and standards, something that cannot be said for his former partner but now bitter enemy, Captain Ben Pease (Max Phipps), a odious a backguard as ever stalked a poop deck.

This comes clear when Phipps savagely invades the island paradise where Jones has deposited the engaged couple of Michael O'Keefe and Jenny Seagrove, who intend to follow the former's uncle missionary work there. Murdering most of the inhabitants and leaving the righteous O'Keefe for dead, Phipps kidnaps the lovely Seagrove, which leads eventually to O'Keefe and Jones banding together with the latter's men to search the seas for the woman they both love.

As imaginatively scripted by John Hughes and David Odell, yarn is chock full of solid laughs and bright developments, and the villainy is of a particularly high order. Phipps' Ben Pease is so rank you can smell him, and he always has another trick up his sleeve even when the forces of good seem to have him cornered at last. Thanks to Phipps' delicious performance, he is, as the saying goes, a man you love to hate.

Backing him up are Grant Tilly as a German naval officer who hopes to gain advantage for the empire by an alleigance with Phipps, and a certain Prince Tui Teka, who plays a monstrously fat native chieftan who one can well imagine lunching on babies and dining on virgin maidens.

But most central to the film's success is Tommy Lee Jones. His physical prowess has never been in doubt, but rarely, if ever, has he been allowed to exhibit his rambunctious sense of humor onscreen before, and he has a field day with this role. He conveys enough meanness to make him a dangerous character throughout, and his good ol' boy accent, while initially anachronistic, ultimately generates considerable amusement in context.

In comparison with all the other colorful characters, Michael O'Keefe's more earnest fellow seems a little bland, but thesp still carries off the part with some dash. Jenny Seagrove is simply wonderful as the damsel in distress.

Given the age-old adventure format, style counts for everything here, and British documentary and tv director Ferdinand Fairfax, in his feature debut, has supplied plenty of it, keeping both the camera and the story moving at a tremendous pace.

As lensed by Tony Imi on various South Pacific locales, as well as in New Zealand studios, pic has a richly colored look. Contributions by costume designer Norma Moriceau, production designer Maurice Cain and editor John Shirley are also notable.

Best of all, however, is Trevor Jones' score, which is rousing in the John Williams sense without seeming imitative, and which significantly multiplies the impact of all the action. — *Cart.*

The Being
(COLOR)

Short but not sweet horror pic.

Hollywood, Nov. 8.

A BFV release. Produced by William Osco. Directed by Jackie Kong. Features entire cast. Screenplay, Kong; camera (color) Robert Ebinger; editor, David Newhouse; music, Don Preston; art director, Alexia Corwin; sound, Rod Junkins; make up-special effects, Mark Bussen; associate producer, Kent Perkins. Reviewed at the Hollywood Pacific Theatre, Hollywood, Nov. 8, 1983 (MPAA rating: R). Running time: **79 MINS.**

Garson Jones	Martin Landau
Mayor	Jose Ferrer
Marge Smith	Dorothy Malone
Mayor's wife	Ruth Buzzi
Mortimer Lutz	Rexx Coltrane
Laurie	Marianne Gordon Rogers
Dudley Ford	Kent Perkins

At a relatively short 79 minutes, "The Being" ends not a moment too soon. Even for the genre of mutant creature horror pics there is remarkably little going on here, with most of the film a search-and-destroy mission. Appeal is strictly for diehards.

("Being" was lensed in 1980 under the title "Easter Sunday" —Ed.)

The inclusion of "name" performers does little to enhance the by now predictable course of events of the film. A small town in Idaho is experiencing the disappearance of people at an epidemic rate. Crusading cop Rexx Coltrane tries to solve the mystery but gets no cooperation from the mayor, Jose Ferrer, who doesn't want to endanger the potato traffic, or state scientist Martin Landau, who swears the nuclear dump outside of town is as safe as a kitchen.

Well, it's not, and some kind of creature is emerging from the primordial muck. The scientific explanation advanced by Landau is laughable and the best scenes in the pic are the ones that recognize the comic value of the material.

The hunt for the creative is a boring series of bloody pursuits, each revealing a bit more of the thing's appearance. He's not much to look at and the wait isn't worth it. The Being appears only briefly.

The acting is pedestrian at best with the characters, especially Dorothy Malone, wandering around in a world of their own. Lighting is consistently dark and other production values are primitive.—*Jagr.*

Allies
(AUSTRALIAN-COLOR-DOCU-16m)

Sydney, Oct. 9.
Cinema Enterprises presentation of a Grand Bay film. Produced by Sylvie Le Clezio. Coproduced by Allan Francovich. Executive producers, David Roe and Cinema Enterprises. Directed by Marian Wilkinson. Camera (color), Philip Bull; editor, Sara Bennett; music, John Stuart, Greg Maclain; research, Marian Wilkinson, William Pinwill, Denis Freney, George Munster. Reviewed at Australian Film Commission theatrette, North Sydney, Oct. 7, 1983. Running Time: 96 MINS.

"Allies" is an Australian followup to the American feature docu "On Company Business" (1980) which was an exhaustive examination of the activities of the CIA. The director of that film, Allan Francovich, came to Australia to present it at the Sydney Film Festival that year, and returned to promote its theatrical distribution via Le Clezio Films. Aussie audiences regularly quizzed Francovich on possible CIA involvement Down Under, and "Allies," which he coproduced with Sylvie Le Clezio, seems to be the answer to those questions.

Film opens by sketching in the beginnings of a close U.S.-Australian involvement in the dark days of World War II when General MacArthur was based on Melbourne and then, using old news-

reels and contemporary interviews in the by-now time-honored style of this kind of docu, explores the Communist scares of the late '40s and early '50s, the establishment of ASIO, the local CIA equivalent and CIA involvement in Indonesia and Vietnam.

Pic also covers the close relationship between President Lyndon Johnson and Prime Minister Harold Holt, and the tension that grew between the two countries when a labor government under Gough Whitlam was elected in 1972 and ministers in the government started to criticize President Nixon's Vietnam policies to the extent that liaison between Washington and Canberra was virtually severed. The film concludes by suggesting that the present Labor Prime Minister, Bob Hawke, is much more acceptable to the Reagan White House than his predecessor was to Nixon.

There is naturally controversial material here. Australian audiences will shudder to hear former U.S. Ambassador Marshall Green say: "President Johnson always thought that Australia was the next large rectangular state beyond El Paso and treated it accordingly," and writhe with embarrassment to see former U.S. Ambassador Ed Clark present Holt with a token payment for a year's rent on the strategic Pine Gap facility in Central Australia — one peppercorn!

There is plenty of conflicting evidence: William Colby and Marshall Green both strenuously deny any CIA involvement in the dismissal of the Whitlam government in 1975 (still a very emotional issue here), while convicted spy Christopher Boyce, serving 40 years for espionage, suggests one motive for his treason was the discovery that CIA was deliberately deceiving the Australian government (he was based on Pine Gap at the time), and Victor Marchetti seems certain there was CIA involvement.

"Allies" appears to have been carefully researched and is impeccably constructed by director Marian Wilkinson, a journalist making her first film. Film should generate, or even reactivate, passions Down Under and will be of considerable interest to students of CIA activities and Southeast Asian politics, as well as anyone interested in Australia.

The film has been attacked by ASIO, which has accused its makers of being funded by the KGB, an accusation that, given the people involved, seems so manifestly absurd one can only concur with former Prime Minister John Gorton who says he found ASIO operatives "stumblebums." — *Strat.*

My Breakfast With Blassie
(COLOR-16m)

Effective no-budget conversational comedy.

An Artist Endeavours Intl. presentation of a Lautrec/Legend Prods. production. Conceived, produced and directed by Johnny Legend, Linda Lautrec. Stars Andy Kaufman, Freddie Blassie. Camera (color, video), uncredited; editors, Legend, Lautrec, Lynne Margulies; music Linda Mitchell; billed as "a Bill Stern/Neal Wiener Amusement." Reviewed at Thalia theatre, N.Y., Nov. 10, 1983. (No MPAA Rating). Running time: 60 MINS.
With: Andy Kaufman, Freddie Blassie, Lynne Elaine, Laura Burdick, Linda Burdick, Linda Hirsch, Bob Zmuda.

"My Breakfast With Blassie" is an amusing takeoff on Louis Malle's hit "My Dinner With Andre." Aimed at the homevideo market, pic's low technical quality is a problem, but it merits playoff in college campus and other nontheatrical situations via 16m format (transferred from original videotape to film).

The art of the put-on requires an ability to play straight, and "Breakfast" features two masters of the form, here improvising comfortably at an L.A. fast food emporium, comic actor Andy Kaufman and pro wrestler-manager Freddie Blassie. Though the Wallace Shawn-Andre Gregory two-hander film is being lampooned, Blassie & Kaufman quickly assert their own personalities, and by interacting with various bystanders in the restaurant, they depart markedly from the original concept.

Central conceit is based on the two performers' massive egos: Kaufman proclaiming "I'm a famous tv star" to anyone foolish enough to come within earshot, while Blassie indulges in humorously sexist and misanthropic patter typified by his tirades against the "pencil-neck geeks" of the world. Blassie dominates most of the film with exaggerated anecdotes of his exploits as a wrestling champ noted for introducing biting to the sport, with Kaufman playing straight man. Kaufman wears a neck brace and self-servingly discusses his latter-day wrestling bouts with women, culminating in a serious injury when he got in the ring with a male pro.

Improvisation is far removed from the tightly-structured and rehearsed monologs of Malle's "Andre" picture, as Blassie & Kaufman spoof banalities with their pointless discussions of food between anecdotes. Running gag revolves around cleanliness, both adopting a paranoid fear of being infected by physical contact (e.g., handshakes) with their fans, cueing insult-laden confrontations with several girls sitting at a nearby table. Picture's attempt to shock is on a sophomoric level,

with a misguided climax when an obnoxious fan (Bob Zmuda) visits the duo and breaks up their meal (at dessert time) with novelty-shop simulated mucus and vomit.

Amateur filmmakers Johnny Legend and Linda Lautrec lensed this encounter in August 1982 via a three-camera setup, with what appears to be a real-time, one-day shoot. Visuals are murky and variable sound recording favors Blassie. — *Lor.*

Nogare No Machi
(Escape Route)
(JAPANESE-COLOR)

Tokyo, Nov. 7.
A Toho release of a Tanaka Promotion production. Produced by Jinichi Tanaka, Toshiuki Nakazawa and Toshio Sakamoto. Directed by Eichi Kudo. Features entire cast. Screenplay, Kudo, Motomu Furota, from book by Kenzo Kitagata; camera (color), Masahiro Kishimoto; art direction, Akira Takahashi; sound, Ichiro Tsujii; lighting, Toshio Takashima; editor, Osamu Tanaka; assistant director, Yusuke Narita. Reviewed at Toho Central, Tokyo, Oct. 31, 1983. Running Time: 120 MINS.
Koji Nagai .... Yutaka Mizutani
Hiroshi .... Hiroyuki Sakamoto
Makiko Endo .... Chiemi Kai
Detective Kuroki .... Isao Natsuki
Kinuyo .... Mitsuko Kusabue
Nakayama .... Kunie Tanaka
Yonekura .... Shinsuke Shimada
Hatta .... Umi Ato
Watanabe .... Ichiro Zaitsu

Japan's large middle class, it has been observed, is middle-class to an extreme not seen since the days of George Babbitt. And, to judge by the evidence of "Nogare No Machi," the members of the lower class in this country are really and truly low.

Rather than devoting their energies to pulling themselves up into the middle class, these lowborn lowlifes indulge in that habit social workers have been trying to break them of for generations: mindless violence. With fists, knives, swords and guns, they pummel, stab, slice and shoot friends, fellow workers, lovers and even, on occasion, people they don't particularly like. Oddly, they haven't yet figured out how to make it pay off, in improved socio-economic status.

While serving as an almost laughable confirmation of middle-class suspicions about extreme behavior by the lower class, "Nogare No Machi" undercuts the widely-held myth about the extreme control exercised by studio heads over the filmmaking process. It is doubtful anyone looking at this film will consider it the product of a company which worships the boxoffice and stymies the creative process. On the contrary, this is an indulgent work demonstrating the noncommercial extremes to which artistic "freedom" can be carried.

Delivery truck driver Yutaka Mizutani, falsely arrested on a murder charge, is released, but gets into an altercation with a fellow employee, quits his job, unintentionally kills Ichiro Zaitsu, the gangster lover of girl friend Chiemi Kai's mother, does battle with the dead man's compatriots, kills or wounds several, swipes a car, drives north with a boy who has run away from an orphanage, is followed on a motorcycle by best friend Shinsuke Shimada, who dies on the way of some consumptive disorder and whose body Mizutani burns on a funeral pyre, shortly after which he angrily stabs the orphan boy's uncle, then runs off with the lad into the mountains, where he is surrounded by both the local and Tokyo cops.

In the final analysis, the film is nothing more than color-coded melodrama, with the main characters taking care to make themselves easily identifiable. This is very poorly written melodrama, characterized by lapses that would irritate were it possible to work up any interest in the story.

The acting is of a piece with the rococo screenplay and visuals. Truly bizarre is the eyeball-rolling performance of Ichiro Zaitsu.

Story, acting and direction combine to prove extremism in the pursuit of art is no virtue. —Bail.

Silkwood
(COLOR)

Was it fact or fiction?

Hollywood, Nov. 15.

A 20th Century-Fox release of an ABC Motion Pictures presentation. Produced by Mike Nichols, Michael Hausman. Executive producers, Buzz Hirsch, Larry Cano. Directed by Nichols. Stars Meryl Streep, Kurt Russell, Cher. Screenplay, Nora Ephron, Alice Arlen; camera (Deluxe color), Miroslav Ondricek; editor, Sam O'Steen; music, Georges Delerue; production design, Patrizia Von Brandenstein; art direction, Richard James; costume design, Ann Roth; sound, Larry Jost; associate producers, Joel Tuber, Tom Stovall; assistant director, Hausman. Reviewed at the 20th Century-Fox Studios, West L.A., Nov. 15, 1983. (MPAA Rating: R.) Running time: **128 MINS.**

Karen Silkwood	Meryl Streep
Drew Stephens	Kurt Russell
Dolly Pelliker	Cher
Winston	Craig T. Nelson
Angela	Diana Scarwid
Morgan	Fred Ward
Paul Stone	Ron Silver
Earl Lapin	Charles Hallahan
Max Richter	Josef Sommer
Thelma Rice	Sudie Bond
Quincy Bissell	Henderson Forsythe
Gilda Schultz	E. Katherine Kerr
Mace Hurley	Bruce McGill
Wesley	David Strathairn
Curtis Schultz	J.C. Quinn
Carl	Kent Broadhurst
Georgie	Richard Hamilton
Jimmy	Les Lannom
Walt Yarborough	M. Emmet Walsh
Doctor at Union Meeting	Graham Jarvis
Los Alamos Doctor	James Rebhorn
Pete Dawson	Ray Baker

A very fine topical biographical drama, "Silkwood" represents an impressive return for director Mike Nichols after an eight-year layoff from dramatic filmmaking, and also marks another career triumph for star Meryl Streep. Exquisitely structured and written, this is another nuclear-themed story, albeit a true one, as it concerns Karen Silkwood, a nuclear materials factory worker who mysteriously died just before she was going to blow the whistle on her company's presumed slipshod methods and cover-ups. Pic's quality and illustrious talent insures strong b.o. in urban centers, with probable good results in store elsewhere.

At first glance, Karen Silkwood appears an unlikely candidate for liberal heroine. A lowdown, spunky and seemingly uneducated Southern gal whose three kids live elsewhere with their father, Silkwood works long hours at a tedious job in Oklahoma which presents the constant threat of radiation contamination.

Her home life is rather more unconventional, as she shares a rundown abode with two coworkers, b.f. Kurt Russell and a lesbian friend, Cher. Their lives are very much those of the young, rural working class, and filled pretty much with getting through the day and finding recreation with booze, dope and their lovers.

The complexion of their domestic life takes a turn when blonde cowgirl beautician Diana Scarwid moves in with Cher, and at work, Silkwood finds herself increasingly at odds with management after she becomes involved with a union committee fighting decertification of the union at the plant. While working with suspicious superior Craig T. Nelson, Silkwood casually discovers he is doctoring photo negatives to conceal deficiencies in their products, deficiencies which could cause catastrophies down the line at breeder reactors.

Silkwood mentions this on a union visit to Washington, D.C., and she is instructed to collect concrete evidence in preparation to giving the story to the N.Y. Times. The rest is history, as the 28-year-old woman's car was found wrecked at the side of the road she was driving en route to meeting the newspaperman at the airport.

Silkwood's death in 1974 was officially ruled an accident, but the story became a cause celebre in the media and among anti-nuke proponents. Upon the film's release, commentators will undoubtedly explore the fact vs. fiction aspects of the case history, and while writers Nora Ephron and Alice Arlen have not presumed to "solve" the mystery of her contamination at the plant and subsequent death, they have strongly suggested she was poisoned by an individual in management.

Scenarists have plotted the tale with estimable intelligence, laying little seeds and inferences throughout the early going which later pay off in the way of very satisfying dramatic and character revelations. Without belaboring it, they and Nichols create a general atmosphere of contamination via a proliferation of junk food, constant cigaret smoking, oil refinery exhaust and the obvious nuclear materials; the American Cancer Society couldn't make a more effective cautionary advertisement if they tried.

Pic is constructed to build slowly to a boil, and the solid craftsmanship approach has also been taken by Nichols, who turns in as plain and functional a piece of direction as he has ever offered. Enamored at earlier stages of his career of visual tricks and elaborate one-take, planar staging, Nichols here is entirely at the service of his material and players, and result is an almost entirely satisfying job.

Lensed in generally soft, bluish hues by Miroslav Ondricek on location and at the Studios at Los Colinas outside Dallas, film's visual coolness may have rendered it less emotionally devastating and moving than it might have been, and a slow-motion repeat of a climactic scene before fadeout comes across as the only significant miscalculation.

Large audiences, as well as the Oscar voters, were knocked out by her work in "Kramer Vs. Kramer" and "Sophie's Choice," but for the straggling unconverted, who have found her rather cold or inaccessible in the past, this could really be Meryl Streep's breakthrough picture. With darker hair than usual and a freewheeling southwestern accent, actress conveys a fantastic sense of earthiness, even baldiness, which has never been associated with her before, at least onscreen. Technically, her skills are as apparent as ever, but she also lets her personality loose here, and her performance is a thrill to behold.

Kurt Russell holds down the fort admirably as a man who loves her, but become so disturbed by the changes he observes that he momentarily leaves her. Cher also has some wonderful moments, none better than in an intense argument scene with Streep which turns into a lovely reconciliation. Diana Scarwid is low-keyed but still outrageous as Cher's lover, and the quartet's domestic trials provide some welcome comic relief to the otherwise heavy drama.

In supporting roles, Craig T. Nelson is very strong as Silkwood's chief nemesis, Fred Ward impresses yet again as a square-shooting unionite, and Sudie Bond stands out as another radiation victim at the plant.

Various production elements are first-rate all around, and Georges Delerue's score effectively combines country elements with romantic-tragic lyricism. —Cart.

A Night In Heaven
(COLOR)

But not for the audience.

Hollywood, Nov. 18.

A SLM Presentation of a Koch/Kirkwood Production for release by 20th Century-Fox. Produced by Gene Kirkwood, Howard W. Koch, Jr. Director, John G. Avildsen. Screenplay, Joan Tewkesbury; camera (color), David Quaid; editor, John Avildsen; production designer, William Cassidy; sound, Les Lazarowitz; costumes, Anna Hill Johnstone; set decoration, Nicholas Romanac; music, Jan Hammer; associate producer, Barry Rosenbush; assistant director, Alan Hopkins. Reviewed at The Egyptian Theater, Hollywood, Calif., Nov. 18, 1983. (MPAA Rating: R.) Running time: **80 MINS.**

Rick	Christopher Atkins
Faye	Lesley Ann Warren
Whitney	Robert Logan
Patsy	Deborah Rush
Mrs. Johnson	Carrie Snodgress
Slick	Sandra Beall
Shirley	Alix Elias
Eve	Amy Levine
Jack Hobbs	Fred Buch
Dancer	Deney Terrio

The disappointment of "A Night in Heaven" is particularly heightened by the notable talent associated with the film: producers Gene Kirkwood and Howard Koch, Jr., director John Avildsen, screenwriter Joan Tewkesbury, and star Lesley Ann Warren. The result, uncertainly centered on a married college instructor's sexual obsession with a male exotic dancer, is a disservice to all of them.

Twentieth Century-Fox, which released the film sans any advance press screenings, will lure spotty coin from the curiosity seekers, but prints are destined to a fast shelving.

The premise is promising enough: older woman (Warren) is drawn to younger boy (Christopher Atkins), in an alliance framed by the youth's daytime life as a student in the woman's class and his nighttime odyssey as a wildly popular male stripper. The fact that Warren flunks him in her speech class and is then speechless to find Atkins that same evening grinding his pelvis in her face in a nightclub called "Heaven" as the raunchy emcee grabs her hand and flattens it against his crotch underscores the yahoo appeal of the film. An hour later Warren and Atkins repeat the crotch scene without any urging from a third party. MPAA rating is an R; a few years back the torrid scene, with fast glimpse of male genitalia, would have earned an X.

Point, however, is that male dancer scenes and the single love scene are the only commercial draw of the film. Everything else — the reasons for a broken marriage, the political principles of a husband (Robert Logan) who quits a high-paying NASA job, the reasons that propel hordes of screaming women to stuff $20 bills into jock straps — is mere excelsior. Structurally and thematically, the film is damaged by an effort to say too much about too many different subjects.

Left to shore up the distended storyline is the interplay between Warren and Atkins. Warren's performance is sexually credible; no tigress, her character is basically gentle and passive. She may be in sexual limbo with her husband but the film lacks sufficient motivation to make her actions with Atkins believable. As for Atkins, he indeed makes a jump from "The Blue Lagoon" as the resourceful sex object who somehow remains likable.

Dancer Deney Terrio, who initially proposed the story idea to producer Kirkwood, Carrie Snodgress as Atkins' waitress-mom, Deborah Rush as Warren's equally frustrated sister, and sexpot Sandra Beall complete the support. Logan's aerospace husband is a sturdy portrayal, but it's a role too attractive to support Warren's betrayal of him.

Crowd scenes in the male nightclub are Avildsen's strength here. But film, shot in environs of Orlando, Fla., flatly skims the surface of events and the melodramatic conclusion between Logan and Atkins defies credibility. Production values are undistinguished. *—Loyn.*

Amityville 3-D
(COLOR)

Shallow and tired.

Hollywood, Nov. 18.

A Dino De Laurentiis production released through Orion Pictures. Produced by Stephen F. Kesten. Directed by Richard Fleischer. Script, William Wales; camera (Deluxe Color), Fred Schuler; editor, Frank J. Urioste; music, Howard Blake; art director, Giorgio Postiglione; set decorator, Justin Scoppa; sound, Manuel Topete; costumes, Clifford Capone; special effects, Michael Wood; assistant director, Joe Reidy; Reviewed at the Hollywood Pacific Theatre Nov. 18, 1983. (MPAA rating: PG.) Running time: 105 MINUTES.

John Baxter	Tony Roberts
Nancy Baxter	Tess Harper
Elliot West	Robert Joy
Melanie	Candy Clark
Harold Caswell	John Beal
Emma Caswell	Leona Dana
Clifford Sanders	John Harkins
Susan Baxter	Lori Loughlin
Lisa	Meg Ryan

"Amityville 3-D" proudly announces that it is not a sequel to "The Amityville Horror" or "Amityville II: The Possession." Even so there is hardly anything original about the picture. A new cast of characters and the addition of 3D does little to pump new life, supernatural or otherwise, into this tired genre. Okay special effects and good production values may generate moderate interest at the boxoffice.

This time around a doubting tom journalist (Tony Roberts) and his partner (Candy Clark) expose a occult hoax only to have their intervention literally backfire on them.

Roberts ignores the warnings of Clark and his estranged wife (Tess Harper) and thinks nothing of the sudden death of the realtor (John Harkins). His teenage daughter (Lori Loughlin) and her friend (Meg Ryan) can't resist the temptations of the house either, despite a series of strange occurrences.

Robert Joy as a psychic scientist seems too young for the role of a man supposedly wise in the ways of the spirit world, but his crazed eyes do suggest that he's seen some things normal people haven't.

The story itself involving the daughter being swallowed up by the forces which apparently live in a well in the basement of the house, moves along at a snail's pace enlivened from time to time by some nice special effects and 3-D images.

One suspects that the real reason for this film's existence is to hurl objects at the audience, which it does rather effectively. Images tossed about by the ArriVision 3-D process include a man being engulfed by flies, a pole impaling a car and a free floating Frisbee.

The film's finale featuring the explosion of the haunted house complete with flying bodies and furniture was designed by Michael Wood, Jeff Jarvis and the rest of the effects crew from "Poltergeist."

The flying objects are fun, but director Richard Fleischer and writer William Wales try to inject a level of seriousness the subject can't hold. The film would have worked better played for laughs. *— Jagr.*

Terms Of Endearment
(COLOR)

Excellent holding fare, on balance.

Hollywood, Nov. 16.

A Paramount Pictures release, produced, directed and written by James L. Brooks, based on a novel by Larry McMurtry. Co-producers, Penny Finkelman, Martin Jurow. Camera (Metrocolor), Andrzej Bartkowiak; editor, Richard Marks; sound, James Alexander; production design, Polly Platt; costumes, Kristi Zea; assistant director, Albert Shapiro; makeup, Ben Nye, Jr.; art direction, Harold Michelson, set design, Sandy Veneziano; music, Michael Gore. Reviewed at the Bruin Theater, L.A., Nov. 16, 1983. (MPAA rating: (G.) Running time: 130 MINS.

Emma	Debra Winger
Aurora	Shirley MacLaine
Garrett	Jack Nicholson
Flap	Jeff Daniels
Sam	John Lithgow
Teddy	Huckleberry Fox
Tommy	Troy Bishop
Vernon	Danny DeVito
Patsy	Lisa Hart Carroll
Rosie	Betty R. King
Edward	Norman Bennett
Janet	Kate Charleson

Teaming of Shirley MacLaine and Jack Nicholson at their best makes "Terms Of Endearment" an enormously enjoyable offering for Christmas, adding bite and sparkle when sentiment and seamlessness threatens to sink other parts of the picture.

It's a double pleasure to see Nicholson back in just the kind of role that catapulted him to stardom, playing a devilish, boozing astronaut who lives next door to MacLaine who has overlayed her libido with too many years of stifled feelings for everyone.

As writer and director, James L. Brooks has not made too clear what "Terms" is supposed to be about and, most of the time, it seems to be about too much, setting up situations and then skipping out of them as it tries to compress 30 years of a family relationship.

At the core is mother MacLaine and daughter Debra Winger, fondly at odds from the beginning over the younger's impending marriage to likeable, but limited, Jeff Daniels. Literally, it's just one cut to the next; then Winger is a mother and moving away from Texas to Iowa, where she becomes a mother a couple of more times; talks to MacLaine every day, carries on an affair with John Lithgow while Daniels dallies at college with Kate Charleson.

Plotwise, MacLaine and Nicholson are first introduced as she watches him come home next door drunk. Then it's several more years before the film finds them together again as he makes a stumbling pass at her over the fence. Then it's several more years before they're together again and she finally agrees to go out to lunch.

If that seems disjointed, it is. But the encounters between these two — always reminiscent of Hepburn and Bogart — are so much fun, it really doesn't make much difference. And when their romance starts to warm up, they are terrific and continue to be when it cools down and ripens into something else.

When they're missing from the action, Brooks has even more trouble concentrating on other single aspects of the picture, finally getting trapped into an overlong, lingering involvement with the sadness that finally befalls the characters. But tears will flow, no doubt.

Forgetting structure, though, Brooks' dialog is wonderful throughout and all the characters carry off their assignments beautifully, even down to Danny De Vito and Norman Bennett as MacLaine's other suffering suitors.

Production designer Polly Platt and makeup artist Ben Nye, Jr. make the 30-year time stretch completely acceptable, enhanced naturally by Andrzej Bartkowiak's camerawork. And ably at the controls of all of this, to be sure, is Brooks the director.

Early on, MacLaine tells Winger, "You aren't special enough to overcome a bad marriage." But "Terms Of Endearment" is certainly special enough to overcome its own problems. *—Har.*

Son Contento
(I'm Happy)
(ITALIAN-COLOR)

Rome, Nov. 19.

A Titanus release, produced by Gianfranco Piccioli for Hera International. Stars Francesco Nuti, Barbara De Rossi. Directed by Maurizio Ponzi. Screenplay, Franco Ferrini, Enrico Oldoini, Francesco Nuti, Maurizio Pinzi; camera (Eastmancolor), Carlo Cerchio; editor, Sergio Montanari; sets, Guido Josia. Reviewed at Ariston Cinema, Rome, Nov. 18, 1983. Running time: 95 MINS.

Francesco Giglio	Francesco Nuti
Paola	Barbara De Rossi
Falcone	Carlo Giuffré

In the wake of last season's surprise hit "Me, Chiara and Darkness," helmer Maurizio Ponzi and star Francesco Nuti have tried to rack up another winner with similar ingredients: a winsome, appealing leading man, comedy, music, a love story and honest emotions. "I'm Happy" undeniably has all this, yet lacks the previous film's sparkle and originality, conflict and building tension.

Predictions for its national reception in a difficult season are reserved, even if it will probably garner some fest kudos and industry awards.

Basically pic is the story of a young couple's breakup. It traces hero Francesco (Francesco Nuti) through the stages of initial pain, a long period of suffering and slow recovery; then a fleeting reunion and ultimately a philosophical acceptance that a beautiful romance has ended. He is a nightclub performer and his work takes a nosedive after Paola (Barbara De Rossi), his live-in mate of six months, packs her bags and leaves him for another man. Trying to drown his sorrows in drink, Francesco winds up an unfunny comedian with a string of cancelled contracts. He is so despondent he forgets to feed his canary, which dies from starvation.

This marks the turning point in his depression. He works his way back to the top, meets Paola by chance at a party, and they spend the night together. But a quick look at the relationship sends her off again. Francesco, he says, loves his work more than her — or at least he uses their real-life affair as material for his irreverent art.

There is precious little material to fill a feature film and pic's pace is slow. Though De Rossi demonstrates once again she is a sensitive and developing young actress, the camera does not glamorize her. Nuti dominates the film in every sense, and it is only thanks to his talent as a comic and Dudley Moore-style appeal that his seemingly incessant presence on the screen is not wearying.

High points are Nuti's arch interrogation of a mailman whom he believes to be Paola's new lover, and a musical parody of an English song (written by Nuti himself) whose lyrics are nonsense words.

Maurizo Ponzi's lensing is unobtrusively professional; ditto for Carlo Cerchio's photography. An elegant jazz track provides a commentary as tastefully subdued as the story, and like it is just a little too predictable this time around.
— *Yung.*

Una Mujer Sin Amor
(A Woman Without Love)
(MEXICAN-B&W)

Hollywood, Nov. 14.

A Televicine International release through Plexus Film Distributors (formerly Columbia in U.S.) of an Internacional Cinematografica S.A. production. Produced by Sergio Kogan, Oscar Dancigers. Directed by Luis Bunuel. Features entire cast. Screen-

play, Jaime Salvador, based on novel "Pierre et Jean" by Guy De Maupassant; camera (b&w), Raul Martinez Solares; editor, Jorge Bustos; music, Raul Lavista; art direction, Gunther Gerzso; sound, Rodolfo Benitez; assistant director, Mario Llorca. Reviewed at the Landmark Theaters Screening Room, West L.A., Nov. 14, 1983. (No MPAA Rating). Running time: 85 MINS.
Don Carlos Montero . . . . Julio Villareal
Rosario . . . . Rosario Granados
Julio Mistral . . . . Tito Junco
Miguel . . . . Javier Loya
Carlos . . . . Joaquin Cordero
Carlitos . . . . Jaime Colpe Jr.
Luisa . . . . Elda Peralta
With: Miguel Manzano, Eva Calvo.
(In Spanish; English subtitles)

Made in 1951 and reviewed now for the record, "Una Mujer Sin Amor" is one of four films by the late Luis Bunuel recently acquired and packaged for American theatrical premieres by Plexus Film Distributors in conjunction with Televicine International. Pics are currently being debuted one at a time in Los Angeles and New York.

Except for such international successes as "Los Olvidados," "El," "Nazarin" and "The Exterminating Angel," the 20-odd films made by Bunuel in Mexico, 1946-1965, have gone largely unseen in this country, and Bunuel's own relatively negative assessment of them has had to be taken at face value.

The two "premieres" recently unveiled in L.A., "El Bruto" from 1952 and "Susana" from 1950, have proved considerably superior than their reputations might have indicated, but "Una Mujer Sin Amor" is undeniably a melodramatic potboiler, and might easily have been ground out in the Hollywood of the era as a routine vehicle for Joan Crawford or Barbara Stanwyck.

Pic presents a beautiful young woman (Rosario Granados) stuck in a loveless bourgeois marriage with middle-aged antique dealer Julio Villareal. Their young son runs away from home and is returned to them by handsome stranger Tito Junco, who eventually tries to lure Rosario out of her marriage, but is finally rebuffed.

Cut to 25 years later, and the couple's younger son inherits over 1,-000,000 pesos (a hefty sum in those days, at least) from a mystery man in Brazil. It would be obvious to even the most dimwitted viewer that the deceased was old Tito, and that he was the father of the beneficiary, but the characters don't own up to the fact until the final reel. In the meantime, family relations are torn at the seams, particularly due to the bitterness and jealousy of the older son, the one who had been saved by the gentleman so many years before.

Bunuel's caustic touches are only evident in the frank cruelty of some of the emotional confrontations, so by any standard this has to be considered among his most blatantly "commercial" and impersonal efforts. It's of little intrin-

sic interest and, for repertory programmers, it will necessarily assume low priority in Bunuel festivals in future years. — *Cart.*

Au Nom de Tous les Miens
(For Those I Loved)
(FRENCH-CANADIAN - COLOR)

Paris, Nov. 15.

CIC release of a Producteurs Associes (Paris)/TF 1 Films Productions (Paris)/Les Productions Mutuelles Limitees (Canada) coproduction. Produced by Jacques Eric-Strauss, Claude Heroux. Exec producers, Andre Djaoui and Pierre David. Stars Michael York. Directed by Robert Enrico. Screenplay, Enrico and Tony Sheer, from the book by Martin Gray and Max Gallo; camera (color), Francois Catonne; art director, Jean-Louis Poveda; editor, Patricia Neny; costumes, Corinne Jorry; music, Maurice Jarre; sound, Claude Hazanavicius and Harrik Mary; documentation, Naciba Sator; production managers, Francois Peltier, Peter Ivanov (Hungary), Roger Heroux (Canada). Reviewed at the U.G.C. Normandie theatre, Paris, Nov. 12, 9183. Running time: 145 MINS.
Martin Gray (age 40)/
Martin's father . . . . Michael York
Martin Gray (age 20) . . . . . . Jacques Penot
Dina Gray . . . . Brigitte Fossey
Martin's mother . . . . Macha Meril
Martin's grandmother . . . . . . Helen Hughes
Dr. Celjmaster . . . . Jean Bouise
Mokotow . . . . Wolfgang Muller

With "For Those I Loved" mainstream commercial cinema and television again take a crack at turning the unspeakable horror of the Holocaust into a bankable big-budget spectacular, complete with palatably unpalatable verities of history and the indespensable heavy dose of moral uplift and affirmed faith in the tenacity of the human spirit. Sigh.

But if audiences are indeed eager for this sort of thing, then the Robert Enrico cinema/tv adaptation of the Martin Gray memoir, produced as a Franco-Canadian venture, and filmed in good part in Hungary — where the city of Budapest gives the film's best performance as the city of Warsaw — is as much deserving of commercial success as some other equivalent follies, like the American miniseries "Holocaust" and Claude Lelouch's "Les Uns et les Autres," to which it is somewhat superior, if only on a technical and mimetic level.

Martin Gray, a Polish immigrant who lived through the heroic tragedy of the Warsaw Ghetto and survived the fathomless horrors of the Treblinka death camp, came into the public spotlight in 1971 with his "as told to.." memoir, "For Those I Loved," in which, spurred on by a recent personal tragedy in which his wife and children perished in a forest fire in the south of France, he recounted his past, intending a celebration of the life force, and a solemn homage to those he loved and lost.

Gray's brutally peripatetic past is indeed the stuff of film bio-epic

dreams, but the good intentions and paralyzing respect of director Enrico (who co-scripted with Tony Sheers) for the subject and its protagonists often reduce the film to a familiar gallery of cliches and stereotypes about Jewish perserverance and courage and Nazi evil and oppression.

Then again, such criticism as can be lodged against characterization can only be provisional since this 150 minute theatrical film is the moviegoer's digest of the complete eight-hour miniseries, which will eventually air in France on the Tf 1 web, coproducer of this production. As usual, there is the inevitable feeling of cutting, and condensation, with the intimate elements getting a summary treatment.

Understandably, Enrico appears to have squeezed as much of the spectacular elements into his cinema version and the scenes of the Warsaw Ghetto and the eventual uprising occupy a major portion of screen time. Which is just as well, since these sequences are the best in the film, executed with a technical proficiency and epic sweep.

But another dramatic setpiece of more questionable effect is the recreation of the Treblinka death camp, where Gray lost his mother and brothers, but from which he managed to escape and make his way back to Warsaw in time for the Jewish insurrection.

Though it will probably have many an average filmgoer cringing, the scene in which a squad of prisoners must empty a gas chamber of its grisly contents and throw them in a communal grave only illustrates how ill-equipped conventional, literal-minded filmmaking is in treating something that escapes description and comprehension.

Meticulous documentation, art direction, and camerawork and a battery of compliant extras ready to strip and hold their breaths as asphyxiated corpses are just not enough. It's no surprise that some local scribes have expressed outrage and distaste at this undertaking.

British actor Michael York is sole topbiller as the mature Martin Gray in the framing scenes (set just after the 1970 forest blaze that killed his family), and as Gray's Resistance leader father in the Warsaw flashbacks scenes. Anonymous dubbing and insufficient screen time makes it difficult to say if his performance has anything more to it than mere surface presence.

Young screen newcomer Jacques Penot is the real dramatic star of the theatrical cut, and is adequate as the teenage Gray, growing up and through a series of harrowing, but ennobling tragedies. Macha Meril is the mother, Jean Bouise a doctor friend, and

Brigitte Fossey the young woman whom Gray meets, marries and loses in his new post-war existence in America and France. All these roles are probably padded out at length in the full miniseries.

Much care has been lavished on the look of the film to certify its attempted authenticity, so it's all the more grating that the sound of the film — French — should follow international convention with some of the actors faking Eastern European accents, while others speak in home-spun Gallic pronunciation.

— Len.

Eishockey-Fieber
(Hockey Fever)
(NORWEGIAN-COLOR)

Luebeck, Nov. 5.

A Film Group 1A/S and Norsk Film A/S Co roduction, Oslo. Features entire cast. Directed by Oddvar Bull Tuhus. Screenplay, Tuhus, Bjarne Roenning; camera (color), Halvor Naess; editing, Bjoern Breigutu; music, Geir Boehren, Bent Aserud. Reviewed at Luebeck Film Fest, Nov. 5, '83. Running time: **103 MINS.**

Cast: Rune Dybedahl, Liv Osa, Rolf Soeder, Sverre Anker Ousdahl, Jorn Donner.

Oddvar Bull Tuhus's "Hockey Fever" delivers just what the title promises: a fast-moving, Hollywood B-style sports film. The plot is as conventional as they come: after a poor season on the ice and at the gates, a new coach and a new manager are hired to set things right. Both of these newcomers, however, have different views of the game's moral principles, the coach on the side of self-pride and the manager pushing dirty tactics when necessary. In the middle of it all is a promising hockey player who has to make a choice between his girlfriend and his fellow players.

Well, with Jorn Donner (former director of the Swedish Film Institute) in charge as the coach, the team overcomes all adversities in the course of the season to come from the bottom of the standing right into the playoffs. —Holl.

Rebetico
(GREEK-COLOR)

Athens, Nov. 8.

A Rebetico EPE company coproduction with the Greek Film Centre. Produced by George Zervoulacos. Screenplay, Sotiria Leonardou, Costas Ferris. Directed by Costas Ferris. Stars Sotiria Leonardou, Michalis Maniatis, Nicos Kalogueropoulos, Themis Bazaca, Costas Tzoumas. Camera (color), George Zervoulacos; music and songs, Stavros Xarhacos; lyrics, D. Gatsos; editor, Yanna Spyropoulou; sets and costumes, Man. Maridakis. Reviewed at the Danaos Cinema of Athens, Nov. 8, 1983. Running time: **120 MINS.**

Since this ambitious picture was overlong at its screening at the Thessaloniki Film Festival and filmmaker Costas Ferris said he was going to trim it to two hours, it is being reviewed in its final release form.

"Rebetico" is a very good musical drama for all audiences, based on a true story, that of a popular singer of "rebetica" songs, and won five prizes at the Thessaloniki Film Festival, including a tie for best picture. Its prospects are very good locally because it has many ingredients of exploitation and could find its way into the foreign market due to its original music and background. It is already selected as the Greek entry at the 1984 Berlin Festival.

The plot covers a period of 40 years when the heroine, Marica, was born in 1917 in Smyrna, Turkey, till her death in Athens. She was seven years old when, in 1922, the Greek population of Smyrna was deported to Greece as refugees and Smyrna was burnt down by the Turks.

Three years later Marica's parents work as musician and singer in a has-den joint. Her mother falls in love with the owner, Thomas, and her father kills her in front of Marica's eyes. At the age of 17, Marica runs off with a wandering juggler but he deserts her a little later with a baby in her arms. She returns to Thomas' place where she played the tambourine and sang with her childhood friend, Georgakis, and bouzouki player Babis. Marica soon achieves the fame she has sought. Babis persuades her to work in a new better place and when Georgakis is exiled by the Metaxas' dictatorship Marica accepts his offer. There she shares the floor with Babis and his girl friend Rosa. The rivalry between the two women leads Rosa to suicide. In 1941, during the German occupation, the joints are closed but when they re-open Babis has a new girl. Marica, disappointed and frustrated, sends her daughter to a convent school and decides to go on tour to America. But on her return to Greece in 1956 she is killed accidentally.

Ferris succeeded in transferring onto the screen the story of this popular singer through the turmoil of one of the most eventful historic period of Greece. Generally the picture is effective though there are some flaws in the screenplay which is deficient in certain areas. Besides, with the new editing and trimming, some sequences end abruptly. Also a deeper insight into the character of the heroine was not given which should explain better the passion which prevailed in her life. But the director has recreated the period well and evokes an authentic atmosphere. This film is an unusual reflection of those times.

Acting as a whole is very good particularly the key performance of Sotiria Leonardou handling the many emotional levels of the heroine. She is really an impressive find, and rightly won the prize for best actress at the festival. Worthy of mention are, also, Themis Bazaca and Nicos Kalogneropoulos, who both got prizes for best supporting roles. The rest of the cast lends colorful support.

The excellently balanced lensing by George Zervoulacos makes the sets part of the plot without letting them overwhelm the story. Particularly outstanding are the music and original songs by Stavros Xarhacos who won also a special prize at the festival. All other technical credits are good. — Rena.

Mystere
(ITALIAN-COLOR)

Rome, Nov. 24.

A Titanus release, produced by Tris Film Productions. Stars Carole Bouquet. Directed by Carlo Vanzina. Screenplay, Carlo and Enrico Vanzina; camera (Technicolor), Beppe Maccari; editor, Raimondo Crociani; art director, Paola Comencini; music, Armando Trovaioli. Reviewed at Adriano Cinema, Rome, Nov. 23, 1983. Running time: **94 MINS.**

Mystere . . . . Carole Bouquet
Colt . . . . Philip Coccioletti
Ivanov . . . . John Steiner
Pamela . . . . Janet Agren

Carlo Vanzina's "Mystere" kicks off as all flash, fun and fantasy, but runs out of steam almost at once. This lame tale of secret agents and microfilm, crooked cops and "mysterious" prostitutes, neither takes itself seriously nor has the wit to play it tongue-in-cheek. Carole Bouquet is an eye-catching presence and the most attractive thing about the picture. But implausible plot limits commercial prospects.

Unrivaled queen of the beautiful girls working Via Veneto, Mystere (Bouquet) is an icy sophisticate who drives a Ferrari and packs a pistol in her evening bag. She and best girlfriend Pamela (Janet Agren) accept a tandem assignment in a hotel room, where Pamela steals a gold lighter containing microfilm. It shows an assassination attempt on the life of an American diplomat and reveals the face of the gunman to be a Russian agent, Ivanov (John Steiner).

Pamela slips the lighter into Mystere's bag but before she can retrieve it, is killed by a faceless assassin in white oxfords with a cane, who drives a black sports car. A handsome police detective, Colt (Philip Coccioletti) interrogates Mystere and beds her. Just as he is about to solve the murder, the head of his special section takes him off the case.

So it goes. Story is stretched far beyond its natural length, padded with every clichéd scene in the book and slowed down with excess dialog. Viewers will fret over the many implausibilities. Why doesn't Pamela's murderer ask her where the lighter is before he kills her? Why does the sinister character in the subway chase Mystere all over the place, if he only wants to say hello?

Though riveting in her transparent black dresses, Bouquet seems about as much a woman of the streets as Catherine Deneuve in a Chanel ad.

Marguerite Gauthier would look like a vulgar tramp in comparison. A far cry from the hard-boiled school of seamy low-life, "Mystere" paints the profession as all glamor, fun and easy money. Ditto the supposedly tough cop.

American thesp Coccioletti, a newcomer, projects some of the attractive nice-guy masculinity of Harrison Ford, whom he resembles. — *Yung.*

The Big Score

(COLOR)

Dirty Fred in action.

An Almi Films release of a Po' Boy Production. Executive producers, Harry Hurwitz, David Forbes. Produced by Michael S. Landes and Albert Schwartz. Directed by Fred Williamson. Stars Williamson. Screenplay, Gail Morgan Hickman; camera (TVC color), Joao Fernandes; editor, Dan Loewenthal; music, Jay Chattaway; sound, Ray Cynoszynski; assistant director, Marvin Towns Jr.; production manager, William Tasgal; stunt coordinator, John Sherrod. Reviewed at RKO Warner 2 theater, N.Y., Nov. 27, 1983. (MPAA Rating: R). Running time: **88 MINS.**

Frank Hooks	Fred Williamson
Davis	John Saxon
Gordon	Richard Roundtree
Angi Hooks	Nancy Wilson
Parks	Ed Lauter
Easy	D'Urville Martin
Goldy Jackson	Michael Dante
Koslo	Bruce Glover
Mayfield	Joe Spinell
J.C.	Frank Pesce
Jumbo	Tony King
Cheech	James Spinks
Huge	Karl Theodore
Kowalski	Ron Dean

As his eighth directorial assignment, Fred Williamson's "The Big Score" is an unexceptional action picture. Low-budget entry should do fair business at urban action houses.

Film is reportedly based on one of several Gail Morgan Hickman scripts originally written for the "Dirty Harry" film series and acquired in the mid-1970s from Clint Eastwood by Williamson when Eastwood put aside the hit character (temporarily, it proved, given the upcoming "Sudden Impact" feature).

Despite the Chicago locale, Williamson's narcotics cop role of Frank Hooks is firmly rooted in "Dirty Harry" terrain — bounced from the force after a bag of money disappears in a large-scale drug bust. Freed from red tape and the department's rules, Hooks ruthlessly dispatches the bad guys, leading to the inevitable villain in a Williamson film, Joe Spinell.

Before sputtering out in an uneventful anti-climax, pic is fun in the early reels, carried by the camaraderie between Williamson and his fellow cops played by action stars John Saxon and Richard Roundtree as well as no-nonsense thesping by his superior, essayed by Ed Lauter. Film lags with musical numbers by Ramsey Lewis and Nancy Wilson, latter merely okay in her film acting debut as Hooks' quasi-estranged wife.

Tech credits are adequate, with bright, functional lensing of Chicago neighborhoods by cinematographer Joao Fernandes (previously known under his pseudonym "Harry Flecks" on pioneer porn films

such as "Deep Throat" and "Devil In Miss Jones"). Jay Chattaway's invigorating musical score punches up Williamson's trademark footchases. —*Lor.*

El Maule

(The Maule River)
(CHILEAN-COLOR-DOCU-16m)

Santiago, Chile, Nov. 17.
Directed and edited by Patricio and Juan Carlos Bustamante. Reviewed at Espacio Cal, Santiago, Chile. Running time: **90 MINS.**

Shot during 1981 and edited last year, "El Maule" follows this river across Chile's narrow girth until it reaches the sea. Centuries ago it marked the southern frontier of the Inca empire and, for several centuries, it was a divisory line beyond line which the native Araucanians fiercely resisted the Spanish conquistadores.

Patricio Bustamante studied film at the San Francisco Art Institute, brother Juan Carlos is a painter. Their docu, with considerable empathy, encompasses men in his relationship with nature and shows the environmental conditions that determine an often timeless life style. Peasants and others live and work in conditions that have sometimes varied little in over 100 years.

Although carefully avoiding anything reminiscent of a tourist's eye view, there are beautiful views of the countryside and telling scenes and interviews with the inhabitants. Conversations with a local poet and historian tend to be too provincial and much weaker, and the filmmakers' view of the riverside cities is also less impressive.

"El Maule" obtained local art house exhibition. If re-edited to just under an hour, it could well obtain tv exposure in Chile and even abroad.—*Amig.*

Scarface

(COLOR)

Strong in language and violence, crime opera packs a b.o. wallop.

Hollywood, Nov. 28.
A Universal release of a Martin Bregman production. Produced by Bregman. Coproducer, Peter Saphier. Executive Producer, Louis A. Stroller. Directed by Brian DePalma. Stars Al Pacino. Screenplay, Oliver Stone; camera (Technicolor, Panavision), John A. Alonzo; editors, Jerry Greenberg, David Ray; music, Giorgio Moroder; art direction, Ed Richardson; visual consultant, Ferdinando Scarfiotti; set design, Blake Russell, Steve Schwartz, Geoff Hubbard; set decoration, Bruce Weintraub; costume design, Patricia Norris; sound, Charles Darin Knight; second unit director, David Dreyfuss; assistant directors, Jerry Ziesmer, Joe Napolitano. Reviewed at Universal Studios, Universal City, Nov. 28, 1983. (MPAA Rating: R). Running time: **100 MINS.**

Tony Montana	Al Pacino
Manny Ray	Steven Bauer
Elvira	Michelle Pfeiffer
Gina	Mary Elizabeth Mastrantonio
Frank Lopez	Robert Loggia
Mama Montana	Miriam Colon
Omar	F. Murray Abraham
Alejandro Sosa	Paul Shenar
Bernstein	Harris Yulin
Chi Chi	Angel Salazar
Ernie	Arnaldo Santana
Angel	Pepe Serna
Nick The Pig	Michael P. Moran
Hector The Toad	Al Israel
Banker	Dennis Holahan
Shadow	Mark Margolis
Sheffield	Michael Alldredge
Seidelbaum	Ted Beniades
M.C. At	
Babylon Club	Richard Belzer
Luis	Paul Espel

"Scarface" is a grandiose modern morality play. Excessive, broad and operatic at times, pic also possesses an engaging topicality and packs a punch which will undoubtedly be appreciated by general audiences round the world. Subject of beaucoup publicity already via a heavy paperback book campaign as well as the potential X rating brouhaha, pic is bloody but really no more brutal than many other films in recent years, although odds are that it contains more four-letter words than any picture to date. Strong b.o. seems in store.

Although dedicated to Howard Hawks and Ben Hecht, film nowhere acknowledges that its origins lie in the 1932 Howard Hughes production directed by Hawks and adapted by Hecht, with help from other hands, from the novel by Armitage Trail. Contours of the saga are very similar to those of the original, as the nearly three-hour effort charts the rise and fall of an ambitious young thug who for awhile becomes the biggest shot in gangsterdom, but ultimately is just too dumb to stay at the top.

To its credit, this is a remake which, for once, is plausibly justified by actual real-world circumstances. Docu prolog recounts how some 25,000 criminals entered the United States in 1980 during the boatlift from Mariel Harbor in Cuba. Among them, per this fiction, was one Tony Montana (Al Pacino), who quickly proves his stuff by coming out of a blown drug deal with both the money and the cocaine, a feat which impresses local Miami kingpin Robert Loggia.

Thanks to the fact that he has nerves of steel and ice in his veins, Pacino moves up fast in the underworld and establishes a crucial personal link with Bolivian cocaine manufacturer Paul Shenar. Seeing that Loggia is softer than he is, and not too secretly coveting his woman, blonde WASP goddess Michelle Pfeiffer, Pacino finally breaks with his boss and, about two-thirds of the way through the action, knocks him off, thereby becoming top dog himself.

All this is brought off by scripter Oliver Stone and director Brian DePalma in efficient, sometimes

stylish fashion. But the final hour devoted to Pacino's wallowing in ludicrous amounts of drugs and money and his ultimate demise, seems both overly extended and wildly obvious. The evil represented by cocaine is demonstrated quite clearly enough in the deterioration of Pfeiffer, an addict who marries Pacino after he bumps off Loggia, but after awhile people are seen snorting the stuff so often it seems like a running gag.

Hawks and Hecht came up with the idea of having the Scarface figure and his sister carry on a nearly incestuous, Borgia-like relationship, and DePalma and Stone have followed suit here. Having shown his Achilles heel by not killing an adversary due to the presence of latter's wife and kids, Pacino immediately thereafter kills his oldest friend because he suspects him of having dallied with his sister. Always amoral, Scarface becomes a total monster with success, and he pays the price.

World depicted is obviously a cesspool, and none of the characters is allowed any redeeming characteristics, except for the moment when Pacino spares the women and children. This will prevent any liberal moralizers from criticizing "Scarface" as they did "The Godfather," on the basis that the "family" was too likable, but it will also allow viewers to enjoy the carnage on a primal level, as the dozens of men mowed down undoubtedly deserve their desserts.

Filmmakers have carefully added a notation at the end to the effect that characters on view are in no way intended to represent the Cuban-American community at large. At the same time, both Bolivian and American officials are explicitly implicated in the success of international drug operations.

Performances are all extremely effective, with Pacino leading the way as a thug who talks straight, keeps his word and takes no bull from anyone. Steven Bauer is winning as his right-hand man, Pfeiffer does well with a basically one-dimensional role, Mary Elizabeth Mastrantonio is warm as the sister, and Loggia has numerous strong moments as the boorish boss. Paul Shenar is outstanding as the cool, well-bred Bolivian.

Lavish work by art director Ed Richardson and visual consultant Ferdinando Scarfiotti emphasizes the vulgarity preferred by these nouveau riche types, and John A. Alonzo's lensing is expressive of the same ends. Giorgio Moroder's synthesizer score evokes classical motifs at times, and also includes numerous disco-oriented tunes. —*Cart.*

Apinan Vuosi
(In the Year of the Ape)
(FINNISH-COLOR)

Luebeck, Nov. 5.

An Elokuvatu Ottajat Oy Film Production, Helsinki. Features entire cast. Directed by Janne Kuusi. Screenplay, Kuusi, Harri Sirola, based on Sirola's novel "Abiturientti;" camera (color), Tahvo Hirvonen;. editing, Anne Lakanen, music, Pekka Rechardt. Reviewed at Luebeck Northern Film Days Fest, Nov. 5, '83. Running time: 94 MINS.

Cast: Heikki Salomaa, Elina Hurme, Rea Mauranen, Kari Vaeaenaenen, Esko Salminen.

A debut pic from Finland receiving its preem at Luebeck's Scandinavian fest (the "Northern Film Days"), Janne Kuusi's "In the Year of the Ape" describes in experimental cutting fashion the fantasies of a young man of 20 just before his matriculation exams. The title makes use of a play on words in Finnish between "ape" and "abitur" (the matriculation exam that has to be passed in order to enter the university). Undoubtedly, pic's comic images hit home among the young aud at Luebeck on a late Saturday night, for at times the place went up for grabs.

Our young anti-hero acts and performs pretty much as a monkey in a tree: he's all arms and legs strapped onto a sturdy, uneasy body in the bloom of puberty. The difficulties of searching for a first love — the girl he likes doesn't return the compliment — is aggravated by an affair with a flighty, giggling maid in class and a brush with the unmarried, liberated sociology teacher. The lad's romping fantasies collide continually with reality, and that's the pic's message and amusement. In such a theme, it's pretty much of a one-man-show — but Heikki Salomaa is an interesting character to behold in grappling with the self, and helmer Kuusi doesn't resort to gratuitous sexploitation to entice a larger audience.

"In The Year Of The Ape," also gets in a few good whacks at middleclass, bourgeois standards of living in Finland. The boy spoofs his parents' marital habits at a home Christmas celebration, and another pair of fossilized parents in a home replete with a year-around swimming pool allow for more finger-pointing. What's missing, however, is a perspective on the young man himself. In the end, one is more or less sure that the ape will forever remain an ape. Either that, or the director himself is still wrestling in vain with his own libido.
— *Holl.*

Tsumikikuzushi
(Knocking Down Building Blocks)
(JAPANESE-COLOR)

Tokyo, Nov. 15.

A Toho release. Produced by Seiji Kuroda and Mari Isono. Directed by Mitsumasa Saito. Features entire cast. Screenplay, Kaneto Shindo, based on the book by Takanobu Hozumi; camera (color), Kaneshige Tabata; art, Masateru Mochizuki; sound, Hideo Okubo; lighting, Mitsuo Onishi; editor, Toyoji Nishimura; asst' director, Nobuaki Inosaki; music, Kentaro o Haneda. Reviewed at Toho screening room, Nov. 15, 1983. Running time: 111 MINS.

Kosuke Honami .... Makoto Fujita
Michie Honami .... Ayumi Ishida
Yuko Honami .... Noriko Watanabe
Kiyoshi Takeda .... Ryuzo Hayashi
Yoshiko .... Sayoko Ninomiya
Takako .... Akiko Kazami
Noriko .... Yuka Sudo
Akiko Sasahara .... Mizue Arimoto

This Toho release is, unfortunately, a perfectly faithful adaptation of a superficial work operating on the belief that raising a problem is as good as dealing with it. The problem is juvenile delinquency, though most Westerners may find the evidence offered to be less than frightening.

The juvenile delinquency of the film's heroine confirms that a true story, which "Tsumikikuzushi" is, does not necessarily make a good drama. The instances of anti-social behavior presented here hardly justify feature-length treatment.

For Yuko (Noriko Watanabe), daughter of actor Kosuke Honami (Makoto Fujita) and wife Michie (Ayumi Ishida), straying from the straight and narrow does not mean a life of hard drugs, casual sex and the commission of various felonies, but wearing a lot of garish makeup, dressing in bad taste, spraypainting her bedroom pink, sniffing paint thinner (infrequently), skipping school (occasionally) and slapping her mother around the room (once), all the while continuing to live at home.

Even granting that this young girl's case is indicative of widespread social dysfunction, the film is maddeningly vague about causes and cures, eschewing analysis for "feeling." Yuko goes off her rocker because of the cold war between her parents, brought on by papa's dalliances. Left unexplored is the intriguing possibility that a childhood disease which permanently changed the color of her hair from black to red left her feeling more than a little alienated from this ethnically homogeneous society.

Director Mitsumasa Saito and scenarist Kaneto Shindo, undoubtedly aware of the essentially tame nature of this story, attempt to juice matters up by turning a trendy section of Tokyo into a Boulevard of Broken Dreams, peopled by dispirited youths. To see this particularly overworked imagination.

Saito and Shindo borrow from, of all films concerned with inexplicably naughty little girls, "The Exorcist." For an outburst by a would-be Linda Blair, this comes across as pretty weak tea.

Performances are solid with, unfortunately, the exception of Noriko Watanabe's uneven Yuko. As this young screen newcomer is at the center of the action, this results, on occasion, in exceptionally gaping holes.

By unwittingly presenting the manageable dimensions of the juvenile delinquency problem, the film, in spite of itself, demonstrates the enviable strength of this society. That "Tsumikikuzushi" has attracted such widespread attention here only goes to prove that, in a country as placid as Japan, it doesn't take much to attract a crowd. — *Bail.*

Hero
(BRITISH-W. GERMAN — COLOR)

A Mirror Films Production, Cambridge, in collaboration with Second German Television (ZDF), Mainz. Executive producer, Benny Kay; associate producer, Christoph Holch (ZDF). Features entire cast. Written, directed, co-photographed, and co-edited by Alexandre Rockwell. Music: The Rolling Stones, David Bowie, John Hassle, Mader, David Hykes, Judy Garland. Reviewed at the Independent Feature Film Market (Cinema 3), New York, Oct. 12, '83. Running time: 106 MINS.

Cast: Paul Rockwell, Kim Flowers, Mika Yamada, Cody Maher, Willie Blue House Johnson, Sandy Bull.

If there ever was a hint of evidence that some Yank indie helmers have been influenced in visual manner by German filmmaking, then it's to be found in Alexandre Rockwell's "Hero," the film that impressed many foreign observers at this year's Independent Feature Film Market in Gotham. Rockwell's earlier indie feature, the $12,000-budgeted "Lenz" (1981), also benefited from a German literary connection: it was a loose adaptation of Georg Büchner's novella of the same title, which in turn chronicled a young writer (Jakob Michael Reinhold Lenz, 1751-1792) and his drift into insanity.

"Hero" recalls Werner Herzog's "Fata Morgana" (1970) in both pictorial beauty and thematic context. Both directors are preoccupied with crippled individuals (psychologically and spiritually as well as physically) who are isolated from society and modern civilization in a desert polluted with technological debris and human waste. Similarities are to be found, too, in the choice of pop-music on the respective sound tracks: David Bowie for Rockwell, Leonard Cohen for Herzog.

Rockwell is a master at juxtaposing images, much in the manner of Herzog, but other German directors as well. For "Hero" he employs a New York City Checker Cab with the words "Fast-Bender" blazoned on its side-door. Further,

some of the early financing for this film project came from Second German Television (ZDF), the station's producer, Christoph Holch, having seen the filmmaker's low-budgeted feature "Lenz" at a Forum of Young Cinema screening during the 1982 Berlin Film Festival. "Hero," in fact, will be aired this December on ZDF, per late reports.

"Hero" is a journey to nowhere. The cab sets out from an overcrowded urban community (probably Los Angeles), and winds its way across the deserts of the Southwest on its way to the town of Truth or Consequences in New Mexico. Along the way, the party gets marooned in a ghost-town, and they spend the rest of the time searching for their destination, as it were, in the shadow of John Ford's Monument Valley.

The group includes a 15-year-old handicapped lad, Paul, who is always taking pictures with his instant camera; a Mexican miss, Kim, who drives the cab aimlessly until it breaks down, a Japanese girl, Mika, who is mostly silent but can speak American English without a flaw if she so wishes; a cowboy-type hitchhiker, Cody, who runs off at the mouth most of the time and seems to be completely lost in his own environment (the humorous side of the story); and an American Indian guide, who appears on the scene rather abruptly and seems to represent an ephemeral spirit from the ancient past. Kim and Mika are Paul's "adopted sisters."

Undoubtedly, many of the metaphors and symbols can be interpreted with some clarity upon a second and closer viewing of the film and its style of expression. For now, let's just say that "Hero" has a lot to do with the American Dream in a manner reminiscent of Samuel Beckett and Edward Albee in their "theater of the absurd." Rockwell, in his own synopsis of the film, admits that the desert landscape is a metaphor for isolation, and that the journey draws upon the mythology of escapism in American culture. Cody, the caricature of a cowboy, lugs a suitcase around with him that contains "valuable information on America," and his last scene has him fighting Custer's Last Stand with an imaginary army to preserve his right to a mythology. Paul's adopted sisters are strong parallels to the American Indian, an outcast in his own land.

The film ends on a note of metamorphosis. The Indian guide, Willie Blue House Johnson, tells Paul as he dies about a mouse who aspired to become an eagle in order to achieve his vision, implying that by transference, society's victims can one day become whole human beings.

Some visual metaphors don't quite work within the reality of the setting.

But the images are often breathtaking, and "Hero" could go down as a major film-poem in the American independent film movement. It's a gem. — *Holl.*

Garçon!
(FRENCH-COLOR)

Paris, Nov. 16.

AMLF release of a Renn/Sara Films coproduction. Produced by Alain Sarde, Claude Berri. Stars Yves Montand. Directed by Claude Sautet. Screenplay, Sautet and Jean. Loup Dabadie; camera (color), Jean Boffety; art director, Dominique Andre; editor, Jacqueline Thiedot; sound, Pierre Lenoir; music, Philippe Sarde; makeup, Jackie Reynal; costumes, Olga Pelletier; production manager, Antoine Gannage. Reviewed at Gaumont Ambassade theater, Paris, Nov. 14, 1983. Running time: **102 MINS.**

Alex	Yves Montand
Claire	Nicole Garcia
Gilbert	Jacques Villeret
Francis	Bernard Fresson
Gloria	Rosy Varte
Marie-Pierre	Marie Dubois
Coline	Dominique Laffin
Simon	Yves Robert

Claude Sautet's newest scanning of the discreet anxiety of the bourgeoisie is called "Garçon!" and its hero is a chief waiter in a fashionable Paris restaurant. As portrayed with panache by Yves Montand, he is a blustering philanderer who nonetheless wears his tinsel heart on his sleeve, an aging egotist who has maintained the seductive elans of childhood. His profession reflects him perfectly: he serves others, without giving of himself.

Without really fully exploiting the possibilities of the protagonist's metier and decor, Sautet and co-scripter Jean-Loup Dabadie have written an engaging, sometimes touching, comedy-drama about a man who has little more emotional substance than a soufflé and who rides many a personal crisis because he remains aloof and self-centered. But Sautet and Dabadie know the recipes for audience empathy: how can you hate a man whose sole ambition — which he finally realizes — is to open an amusement part on a piece of coastal property left him by his father?

The restaurant scenes, fluidly acted, directed and designed — the Paris brasserie is a quintessential studio set by Dominique Andre — are among the film's highlights, but are, alas, little more than a colorful backdrop to the script's more conventional initimist concerns.

Dramatic prominence is given to Montand's personal agitations as he loses one (young) girlfriend, dodges the desperate advances of an (older) well-heeled mistress, and enters into a short-lived re-

lationship with a divorcee language-instructor (Nicole Garcia). He also has to put up with a problematic fellow waiter and roommate (Jacques Villeret), whose deep commitment to the wife and children he left contrasts sharply with Montand's flitting nature.

Sautet has served his film with smooth technical skill (as in the numerous tracking shots that describe the hero's unchecked impulses) and a sympathetic direction of actors: in addition to Montand's appealing swagger, there is Villeret's beautifully-drawn portrait, and Bernard Fresson as a tyrannical restaurant chef. Ladies, led by a gracious Garcia, all add emotive weight to the drama.

Sautet's indulgent studies of the French middle-class may not be everybody's dish, but "Garçon!" is as attractively executed as some of the helmer's earlier successes. It should have good chances in markets familiar with the director.

—*Len.*

Sleepaway Camp
(COLOR)

The horror formula is tired out.

A United Film Distribution Co. release of an American Eagle Films production. Executive producer, Robert Hiltzik. Produced by Michele Tatosian and Jerry Silva. Written and directed by Robert Hiltzik. Features entire cast. Camera (Technicolor), Benjamin Davis; editor, Ron Kalish, Sharyn L. Ross; music, Edward Bilous; songs, Frankie Vinci; sound, Rolf Pardula; assistant director, Richard Feury; production manager, Carl Clifford; production design, William Billowit; stunt coordinator, Cliff Cudney; special mechanical effects, Ed Fountain; special makeup illusions, Edward French. Reviewed at UA Rivoli 2 theater, N.Y., Nov. 27, 1983. (MPAA Rating: R). Running time: **84 MINS.**

Mel	Mike Kellin
Angela	Felissa Rose
Ricky	Jonathan Tierston
Judy	Karen Fields
Paul	Christopher Collet
Ron	Paul De Angelo
Ben	Robert Earl Jones

Filmed mid-1982 in upstate New York, "Sleepaway Camp" is a tired version of various teen-oriented horror film formulas. Amateurish production is too little and too late.

Story is set at Camp Arawak, a summer camp for young teens of both sexes, given to the usual hijinks. After an obligatory opening teaser sequence involving a boating accident, picture jumps forward eight years with pretty brunette Angela (Felissa Rose) and her cousin Ricky (Jonathan Tierston) sent off to camp.

Telegraphed immediately and underscored repeatedly in Robert Hiltzik's unsuspenseful direction and script, Angela is the shy girl turned mad killer whose true identity (the usual gender switch used in countless similar films since William Castle's classic "Homici-

dal") is revealed in the anticlimactic finale. With each killing, the camera unwisely lingers on Ed French's phony-looking fake torsos and makeup effects.

Acting is awful, with pros like the late Mike Kellin and Robert Earl Jones ill-served in this format and youngsters grating on the viewer. Many static shots use the archaic technique of actors rushing in and out of view at frame left and right, as in a theater piece. Chief difference of this film from dozens of others is the focus on younger kids rather than the adult counselors. —*Lor.*

Perdoa-Me Por Me Traires
(Forgive Me For Betraying Me)
(BRAZILIAN-COLOR)

Rio de Janeiro, Nov. 7.

An UCB release of a N.J. Filmes production. Features entire cast. Directed by Braz Chediak. Screenplay, Gilvan Pereira, Nelson Rodrigues Filho, Joffre Rodrigues, Braz Chediak, from play of same title by Nelson Rodrigues; camera (Eastmancolor), Helio Silva; music, Chico Buarque de Hollanda; song "Mil Perdoes" sung by Gal Costa; musical direction, Radames Gnatalli; editing, Rafael Valverde; sound, Roberto Leite; assistant director, Sindoval Aguiar and Nelson Rodrigues Filho; production director, Luiz Acerbi; executive producer, Joffre Rodrigues; associate producers, Joaquim Martins and J.B. Tanko Filmes. Reviewed at Cine Rian, Rio de Janeiro, Nov. 7, 1983. Running time: **95 MINS.**

Judith	Vera Fischer
Gilberto	Nuno Leal Maia
Raul	Rubens Correa
Glorinha	Lidia Brondi
Nair	Zaira Zambelli
Madame Luba	Henriette Morineau
Dr. Jubileu de Almeida	Sadi Cabral
Mother	Virginia Valli
Doctor	Jorge Doria
Nurse	Angela Leal
Aunt Odete	Monah Delaci
Pola Negri	Anselmo Vasconcelos

No Brazilian dramaturgist has ever shown the same capacity of Nelson Rodrigues to deeply explore the human weaknesses, desires and anxieties. His plays, written from 1947 to the late '70s, show, along with his few novels and daily chronicles on the press, a unique sense of truth, cruelty and humor, associated to a constant search for modernity and formal discipline that makes him comparable to playwrights of the level of O'Neill, Williams or Albee.

Rodrigues' plays have been adapted for the Brazilian cinema since the '50s, to generally poor results. After the "cinema novo" several directors were again inspired by his plays, but often rethinking them in order to substract a substantial part of their content (in life, Rodrigues was a target for frequent attacks from intellectuals due to hs conservative ideas). Other producers tried to concentrate on the sexual implications found in most of Rodrigues' work, reducing them to empty sex films, even "pornochanchadas."

"Perdoa-me Por Me Traires" is a fine exception to that rule, and doubtless one of the most consistent, honest and relevant adaptations of his plays. Written in 1957, it deals with jealousy, infidelity, psychoanalysis, and the relations of power within a family or a society — which would be developed in another play, "Viuva Porem Honesta" (Widow Yet Honest). It is the story of a husband madly jealous of his wife, who declares himself insane and asks to be interned in a clinic, while his wife actually betrays him and their teenage daughter is induced to work in a whorehouse.

Production was directly supervised by two sons of the author, Nelson Jr. and Joffre Rodrigues, who also collaborated on the screenplay. Director Braz Chediak was responsible for two other Rodrigues' adaptations: "Bonitinha mas Ordinaria" (1981) and "Album de Familia" (1982). Chediak strictly follows the original text, just introducing or taking off a few scenes, but cinematically interpreting with outstanding fidelity the impact and strength of the play.

Such achievement is due, in great part, to the casting. Rubens Correa and Jorge Doria are two superb Rodriguean actors. Lidia Brondi was in two other Rodrigues' films ("Bonitinha mas Ordinaria" and "Beijo no Asfalto") but here she seems a bit more free to portray a sensual character, who absorbs all the guilts and conflicts of her family. Nuno Leal Maia (in Rodrigues' "A Dama do Lotacao") is here carefully directed to avoid overacting. And veteran names, as Henriette Morineau and Sadi Cabral, harmonize with talented newcomers such as Anselmo Vasconcelos and Zaira Zambelli.

Chediak brings to his cast a seldom achieved atmosphere of anguish and discreet nonsense present in all Rodrigues' works, not to mention his refined sense of humor. Despite its small budget even for local standards (around $120,000), the film, as the play, transcends its immediate appearance turning out to be a fascinating trip inside the human soul. It is unquestionably one of the most respectful tribues to the memory of the Brazilian writer, who died two years ago. —*Hoin.*

Premiers Desirs
(First Desires)
(FRENCH-W. GERMAN-COLOR)

Paris, Nov. 23.

AMLF release of a T. Films/Sara Films/Rialto Film (Berlin) co-production. Produced by Alain Terzian. Features entire cast. Directed by David Hamilton. Technical advisor, Serge Leroy. Screenplay, Bertrand

Levergeois, Philippe Gautier, Michael Erdmann; camera (color), Alain Derobe: sound, Michel Kharat; music, Philippe Sarde; makeup, Florence Fouquier; art directors, Eric Simon, Jerome Clement, Jean-Philippe Reverdot; editor, Francois Ceppi; production manager, Philippe Lievre. Reviewed at the Marignan-Concorde Theater, Paris, Nov. 22, 1983. Running time: **90 MINS.**

Cast: Monica Broeke, Patrick Bauchau, Inger Maria Granzow, Emmanuelle Beart, Anja Shute, Bruno Guillain, Stephane Freiss, Charli Chemouni, Serge Marquand.

Photog David Hamilton offers up his usual canvas of soft lighting, nubile nymphettes and tepid eroticism in "First Desires," his fourth outing as film director. As with his previous ventures, this one is low on plot, characterization and feeling, and the story's climactic dramatic moment is callously treated as a pretext for the heroine's sexual initiation.

Hamilton's indifference here goes so far as to have someone else (filmmaker Serge Leroy) deal with the players — listed as a technical advisor in the pressbook. Leroy appears in the credits as "director of actors." For Hamilton, cinema is merely an animated extension of his photographic work.

Script, by Bertrand Levergeois, Philippe Gautier and Michael Erdmann, gives Hamilton the opportunity to focus his lens on three young vacationing girl-friends who are washed up on a coastal French island when their barque capsizes during a storm.

There they find, not a comfortless desert rock and some virile Robinson Crusoe, but a typical affluent island community and some cute young bucks to give them a conventional dose of summer romance.

But one of the girls (Monica Broeke) of virginal romantic stamp, becomes infatuated with the island's handsome millionaire owner (Patrick Bauchau), whom she mistakenly believes has saved her from drowning. Bauchau is, in fact, happily married to a lovely concert pianist, but Broeke, confident of his requited interest, bides her time until the wife takes off for a concert tour in South America.

Then, screenwriter's fate steps in. The tv reports that the pianist has been killed in a plane crash and Bauchau retires in despair to his bedroom. Broeke follows and offers night-long consolation. The morning after, she rises, fulfilled, and runs off ecstatically to join her friends. And that's all, folks.

If you're interested in finding out what happens to Bauchau, don't ask Hamilton or his scripters. Commercial chances are about the same as Hamilton's other pictures. —*Len.*

London Film Festival

An Englishman Abroad
(BRITISH-COLOR)

London, Nov. 22.
BBC Television production. Produced by Innes Lloyd. Directed by John Schlesinger. Stars Alan Bates, Coral Browne. Screenplay, Alan Bennett; camera (color), Nat Crosby; art director, Stuart Walker; music, George Fenton. Reviewed at London Film Festival, Nov. 21, 1983. Running Time: **63 MINS.**
Guy Burgess .... Alan Bates
Herself .... Coral Browne
Claudius .... Charles Gray
Rosencrantz .... Harold Innocent
Guildenstern .... Vernon Dobtsheff
Mrs. Burgess .... Molly Veness

In complete contrast to his last, rather calamitous, theatrical venture, "Honky Tonk Freeway," John Schlesinger has redeemed himself with this modestly-conceived but richly textured television movie. The story is based on a real incident which occurred in Moscow in 1958 when Australian actress Coral Browne was playing Gertrude in a production of "Hamlet" being staged as part of a British-Russian cultural exchange program.

On opening night at interval, a drunken Englishman bursts into her dressing-room and throws up in her wash-basin. He also steals her gin, cigarets, soap and makeup. She discovers he is Guy Burgess, a notorious traitor of the Cold War period, a member of the Foreign Office who had spied for the Soviets and defected. That night a note is pushed under her door — an invitation to lunch. After much difficulty (and with no help from the British Embassy) she finds the apartment where Burgess is living with his male lover, and though lunch is a spartan affair (tomatoes, grapefruit and garlic), the actress feels drawn to this charming man whom she at once despises for his treason and pities for his loneliness and isolation.

Alan Bates, who rose to screen stardom in Schlesinger's first feature, "A Kind of Loving," 21 years ago, is superb as Burgess: paunchy, down-at-heel, a disgraceful figure, he still retains his humor and charm. He misses, he says, the gossip from England, and finds it hard to converse with "the Comrades" ("Not strong on irony, the Comrades!") and longs to see "the old Mum." Browne, while not diminishing the man's treachery, warms to his humanity and undertakes to help him obtain new clothes from London on her return.

The screenplay by Alan Bennett is concise, witty and perceptive, and beautifully handled by Schlesinger. Art director Stuart Walker deserves a special nod for convincingly converting parts of Glasgow into Moscow. One is tempted to think that Schlesinger, who himself has been an Englishman abroad, warmed to the theme of cultural isolation and has consequently been inspired to make one of his best films, if certainly his most modest. Pic gets an almost immediate airing on BBC television. (Pic may have originated from Bennett's 1977 play, "The Old Country. — Ed.) — *Strat.*

The Store
(U.S.-DOCU-COLOR)

London, Nov. 20.
A Zipporah Films production. Produced & directed by Frederick Wiseman. Camera (color), John Davey; editor, Wiseman. Reviewed at London Film Festival, Nov. 18, 1983. Running Time: **118 MINS.**

Since 1967, Boston-based Frederick Wiseman has regularly produced one feature-length documentary a year (with the exception of an unfortunate attempt at a feature, "Seraphita's Diary," in 1982). A highly respected figure in the worldwide docu movement, Wiseman concentrates on studying American institutions (a mental home, high school, hospital, police station, the Army, etc.) and in his latest, and first in color, "The Store," the subject is one of the country's most famous retail establishments, the Nieman Marcus store and corporate headquarters in Dallas.

Result is mainly of academic interest, for there's little drama taking place in this refined environment; when Wiseman explored the daily dramas of people on welfare, or cops in the precinct house, or soldiers on maneuvers, his style was given substance by the material. Here we see sales staff doing their pitch with wealthy customers, behind-the-scenes staff pep talks, long-range promo planning by advertising execs, a black woman employee being interviewed for possible advancement. It's not exactly world-shattering material.

At the very end of an overlong film, Wiseman films the company's 75th anniversary dinner and we meet Stanley Marcus himself, an engaging character whom guest speaker Art Buchwald praises for the position he took during the McCarthy era. Marcus might well have been a very interesting subject for a docu, but as it stands "The Store" must count among Wiseman's lesser efforts. — *Strat.*

Ghost Dance
(BRITISH-W. GERMAN-COLOR)

London, Nov. 20.
A Looseyard Ltd. production, in association with Channel 4 and ZDF. Written, produced & directed by Ken McMullen. Features entire cast. Camera (color & b/w), Peter Harvey; editor, Robert Hargreaves; music, David Cunningham, Michael Giles, Jamie Muir. Reviewed at London Film Festival, Nov. 19, 1983. Running Time: **96 MINS.**
Leonie .... Leonie Mellinger
Pascale .... Pascale Ogier
George .... Robbie Coltrane
With Dominique Pinon, Stuart Brisley, Jacques Derrida.

Avant-garde item which seems to have been inspired by French director Jacques Rivette, "Ghost Dance" is a visually impressive exercise. Shot in London and Paris, it revolves around the inconsequential adventures of a French girl (Pascale Ogier) and an English girl (Leonie Mellinger), both of whom emerge as sprightly characters. Plotless pic covers a lot of ground, including psychoanalysis and ghosts, dreams and the cinema, Karl Marx and Franz Kafka, cargo cults and electrodes. Dialog is mostly English, but French track is subtitled.

Though hard to fathom at a single viewing, pic is continually engaging both because of helmer Ken McMullen's strong visual sense and also because of his very welcome sense of humor. Though film will have extremely limited possibilities in the market, it does suggest McMullen is worth watching and that, if he wanted, he could move into the mainstream (as have other avant-garde directors in recent times) with good results.

Film also boasts an excellent music score (featured in a 2½-minute blank screen overture) and impressive 16m photography.
—*Strat.*

Those Glory Glory Days
(BRITISH-COLOR)

London, Nov. 20.
An Enigma Production, for Goldcrest. Executive Producer, David Puttnam. Produced by Chris Griffin. Directed by Philip Saville. Features entire cast. Screenplay, Julie Welch; camera (color), Phil Meheux; editor, Max Lemon; art director, Maurice Cain; sound recording, David Crozier. Reviewed at London Film Festival, Nov. 17, 1983. Running time: **95 MINS.**
Julia .... Zoe Nathenson
Julia, journalist .... Julia Goodman
Mrs. Herrick .... Julia McKenzie
Mr. Herrick .... Peter Tilbury
Toni .... Sara Sugarman
Tub .... Cathy Murphy
Jailbird .... Liz Campion
Coalhole .... Elizabeth Spriggs
Himself .... Danny Blanchflower

Latest in the ambitious David Puttnam "First Love" series for tv, premiered on Channel Four the same night it screened at the London Film Festival, "Those Glory Glory Days" is a slight comedy which doesn't appear to have the same potential as others in the series, such as "Experience Preferred But Not Essential."

Scripter Julie Welch recalls her schooldays in 1961 when she and three girlfriends were enthusiastic soccer fans and champions of the local Tottenham Hotspur football team. Pic opens very well indeed with the adult Julia, a sports journalist, trying to cover a soccer game from an all-male press gallery and then being given a ride home by her childhood idol, soccer star Danny Blanchflower (who engagingly plays himself). But after this cheerful prolog, with a winning performance from Julia Goodman as the adult Julia, the flashback bulk of the pic, with its rather strained performances and humor, is a disappointment. The four schoolgirl soccer fans have moments of charm, but the young actresses tend to mug rather too much. And most of the adults — Julia's bickering parents, a pompous schoolmistress — are pure caricature.

Pacing is rather slow (this kind of light comedy needs a lot more zip to make it work) and basically the material is on the thin side.

— *Strat.*

Saigon — Year Of The Cat
(BRITISH-COLOR)

London, Nov. 20.

A Thames Television Production. Produced by Verity Lambert, Michael Dunlop. Directed by Stephen Frears. Features entire cast. Screenplay, David Hare; camera (color), Jim Howlett; editor, Oscar Webb; music, George Fenton; production design, David Marshall. Reviewed at London Film Festival, Nov. 17, 1983. Running Time: 103 MINS.
Barbara ....Judi Dench
Bob Chesneau ....Frederic Forrest
The Ambassador ...........E.G. Marshall
Jack Ockham ....Josef Sommer
Frank Judd ....Wallace Shawn
Mr. Haliwell............. ... Chic Murray
Quoc . ...Pichit Bulkul
Trinh ....Yim Hoontrakul
Donald Henderson .. ..Roger Rees
Nhieu ....Po Pau Pee
Debbie.................Deborah Eisenberg

Premiered the first day of the London Film Festival, "Saigon — Year Of The Cat" is an ambitious movie-for-television set in Vietnam in 1974-5. With U.S. forces withdrawn from the beleaguered country following the Paris peace talks, the only question remains whether the Vietcong will negotiate with President Thieu (which the U.S. Ambassador believes they will) or take over the whole country, including Saigon. First half focuses on a middle-aged British woman (Judi Dench) who works in a bank and who, out of frustration, initiates an affair with a younger man, a CIA agent (Frederic Forrest) working out of the U.S. Embassy.

Having established Dench's character rather effectively in opening scenes, scripter David Hare then shunts her aside to concentrate on Forrest, presented as being almost the only American who cares about what will happen to pro-American South Vietnamese if and when Saigon falls. Best performance comes from E.G. Marshall as the Ambassador who waits too long in anticipation of a nego-

tiated settlement and is forced to lead the panicky exit by helicopters from the embassy roof.

Interesting theme isn't given full justice by pic's rather tentative treatment and the fuzzy script. Stephen Frears, a director who has mainly worked in tv but who, in 1971, helmed the engaging theatrical private-eye comedy, "Gumshoe," does an okay job with the material.

Lensing took place on locations in Thailand, with Thai actors playing Vietnamese characters (and speaking Thai). Considering its budget, all concerned did a good job in conveying the panic and desperation of the hours leading up to the evacuation. However, pic's chances seem limited to tv and videocassette. —*Strat.*

Im Zeichen Des Kreuzes
(Due to an Act of God)
(WEST GERMAN-COLOR)

London, Nov. 25.

A Common Film Produktion, with Cikon Film, for WDR and SFB. Producer by Herman Wolf. Directed by Rainer Boldt. Features entire cast. Executive producer, Helmut Wietz. Screenplay, Hans-Rudiger Minow; camera (color), Karl Kases; editor, Elke Boische; art director, Winifried Hennig; music, Jens-Peter Ostendorf. Reviewed at London Film Festival, Nov. 23, 1983. Running time: 101 MINS.
Christine Bensch ....Renate Schroeter
Jorg Bensch ....Wigand Witting
Veronika Wichmann .....Johanna Rudolph
Michael Bensch ....Mathias Nitschke
Eva Wichmann................Antje Magen
Gerd Wichmann ....Karl-Heinz von Hassel
Suchow ....Werner Schwuchow
Gotsche ....Rainer Christian Mehring

Following the impact of nuclear disaster tv movies like "The Day After" and "Testament," here's a modestly styled but quietly-devastating German tv movie about another kind of nuclear disaster — the accidental spillage of lethal nuclear waste. Setting is timeless, peaceful countryside, and story centers around two families, a doctor who, with his wife and son, are visiting the area from the city, and a local family who live in a picturesque village and with whom they're acquainted.

Disaster happens when a petrol tanker, speeding along the narrow roads, collides with a convoy carrying the waste, incident not shown on screen, but well-prepared with earlier scenes of the vehicles heading towards each other from different directions. Explosive impact comes suddenly and unexpectedly.

During the impact, canisters containing the waste split open, and the whole area is polluted. Once the authorities realize what's happened, they take draconian measures to seal off the area and isolate the modern plague, with the frightened villagers herded into church are ordered to stay there. Film ends with the villagers break-

ing out of their confines and being gunned down by the military.

Towards the end, an official states that it is impossible for cans containing nuclear waste to break open in this kind of traffic accident: point made by director Rainer Boldt and writer Hans-Rudiger Minow is that the apparently impossible can sometimes happen.

Shot in 16m, pic makes the most of its low budget and the result is an extremely effective, if chilling, drama of ordinary people caught up in extraordinary events. Acting is natural, credits fine. —*Strat.*

The Aerodrome
(BRITISH-COLOR)

London, Nov. 20.

BBC Television production. Produced by Kenith Trodd. Directed by Giles Foster. Features entire cast. Screenplay, Robin Chapman, from the novel by Rex Warner; camera (color), Kenneth McMillan; editor, Clare Douglas; production designers, Geoff Powell, Tim Harvey; music, Carl Davis. Reviewed at London Film Festival, Nov. 20, 1983. Running Time: 91 MINS.
Roy..........................Peter Firth
Air Commander ....Richard Johnson
The Rector ....Richard Briers
Mark ....Dominic Jephcott
Bess ....'...............Natalie Ogle
Eustasia.......................Jill Bennett
Mary ....Mary Macleod
Florence.....................Mary Peach
Dr. Faulkner..............Geoffrey Chater

An ambitious telefilm, unveiled in the British section of the London Film Festival, "The Aerodrome" is an adaptation of a 1941 novel by Rex Warner in which, along the lines of "Things to Come," the author wrote of Britain in the future. Filmmakers have taken the risky step of keeping Warner's original concept and filling pic with the technology of the '50s and '60s, already old-fashioned by today's standards. It doesn't quite come off.

Setting is a peaceful English village where Roy, the 21-year-old hero, is living with his supposed parents, the Rector and his wife, and in love with the vivacious Bess. The Air Force has built a mysterious aerodrome close by, and Roy's friend, Mark, is a pilot there. At his birthday party, the Rector tells Roy he's not his real father after all. Soon after, at a village fete, the Rector is deliberately machine-gunned to death by Mark, who is appointed by the Air Commodore as the new Rector in his place. Gradually the Air Force takes over, making its own rules and absorbing the villagers; Roy becomes a pilot himself when he discovers Bess, whom he has married, may be his sister and that she's also secretly having an affair with Mark.

Plotting is extremely complicated, and the well-realized notion of the mysterious, obviously Fascist, Air Force which gradually takes over every aspect of civilian life,

eventually takes second place to some convoluted narrative involving Roy's search for his real parents. The peculiarly black English humor of the early scenes ("I feel a bit cut up," says Mark after gunning down the Rector) gives way to rather dated melodramatics. Acting is okay, with Richard Johnson a stand-out as the evil Air Commander, and Natalie Ogle charming as the sensual Bess. One problem for audiences is that the village and aerodrome are never placed in any context; the outside world never gets a look in. This was presumably a feature of the novel.

Technically, film is good, with an apt music score by Carl Davis.
—*Strat.*

The Gold Diggers
(BRITISH - B/W)

London, Nov. 25.

A British Film Institute Production. Produced by Nita Amy, Donna Grey. Directed by Sally Potter. Stars Julie Christie. Screenplay, Rose English, Lindsay Cooper, Sally Potter; camera (black and white), Babette Mangolte; editor, choreographer, Potter; music, Lindsay Cooper. Reviewed at B.F.I.-Theatrette, London, Nov. 23, 1983. Running time: 87 MINS.
Ruby ....Julie Christie
Celeste ....Colette Laffont
Ruby's mother ....Hilary Westlake
Expert.......................David Gale
Expert's assistant.............Tom Osborn
Tap Dancer ....Jacky Lansley

With a relatively long production history behind it, "The Gold Diggers," Sally Potter's first feature film, emerges as a strongly feminist, all-woman effort which is likely to have an extremely limited audience.

The radical filmmaker can either coat the pill in the trappings of commercial cinema and thus hope to get his/her message across to a large audience; or he/she can be resolutely uncompromising, as in this case, and thus risk preaching only to the converted.

Lacking a narrative, film concerns two women, one blonde (Julie Christie) who is trying to relive her childhood in spartan conditions in icy Yukon country where her father was a gold prospector (actually shot on locations in Iceland), the other black (Colette Laffont), who works in a bank and seeks to gain information from her patronizing male employers about the meaning of money and how it's controlled. Described as "a musical adventure," pic contains some songs and dancing, but little humor.

Christie's presence may spark some initial interest, but the actress has self-sacrificingly submerged herself into the concept of the film and becomes a symbol. It's not really a performance. Males are caricatured, natch. The gleaming black-and-white (35m) camerawork of Babette Mangolte is a major plus.

Basically, film will be limited to women's film festivals or festivals where feminist avant-garde will find audiences. Commercial and tv prospects seem to be extremely slim, as no concession whatsoever is made to the uninitiated viewer.

During production, pic was called "Gold", but a title change was necessitated to avoid confusion with the Michael Klinger production of the same name.

— *Strat.*

Meantime
(BRITISH-COLOR)

London, Nov. 23.

A Central Production, in association with Mostpoint Ltd. Produced by Graham Benson. Devised and directed by Mike Leigh. Features entire cast. Camera (color), Roger Pratt; editor, Lesley Walker; art director, Diana Charnley; music, Andrew Dickson; sound, Malcolm Hirst. Reviewed at London Film Festival, Nov. 22, 1983. Running time: 104 MINS.

Barbara	Marion Bailey
Mark	Phil Daniels
Colin	Tim Roth
Mavis	Pam Ferris
Frank	Jeff Robert
John	Alfred Molina
Coxy	Gary Oldman
Hayley	Tilly Vosburgh

Mike Leigh's first feature, "Bleak Moments" (1971), won him critical kudos but no commercial success, and he's divided his time between legit and television ever since. Now he returns with his second independent feature "Meantime," an outstanding example of his art, but also destined to be a very difficult picture to sell. Festivals and tv sales are indicated.

The subject is a working-class family living in a small apartment in London's sleazy East End. Frank, the father, is out of work and so are his two teenage sons, cynical Mark and simple-minded Colin. Mavis, Frank's wife, spends most of her time playing bingo. Her sister, Barbara, has succeeded in moving out of this depressing environment and is married to John, a businessman. But the marriage is unhappy, and they have no children. She takes pity on Colin, and tries to help the youth, arousing his brother's jealousy.

There's little plot as such: Leigh follows his characters as they drift their boring lives away, though the main emphasis is on Colin, who tries half-heartedly to form a relationship with Hayley, a local girl, or spends aimless hours with his skin-head friend, Coxy. Invited by his aunt to work as a decorator in her home on the other side of London, Colin at first loses his way there and then finds his brother made it there before him.

Leigh, credited with "devising," rather than scripting, the film, obviously cares for his characters and there's no patronizing here.

Film may sound dull, but it's rich in very British humor, with the wonderful actors perfectly capturing every tiny detail of their characters.

Stand-out is Tim Roth as the unfortunate Colin, but Phil Daniels (Mark) and Pam Ferris and Jeff Robert (their parents) are also beyond praise; indeed, every member of the cast is excellent. Despite the humor, downbeat tale of working-class problems, sans solution, will have trouble finding a large audience, more's the pity. Credits are tops, and there's an interesting, quirky music score by Andrew Dickson.— *Strat.*

Luotuo Xiangzi
(Rickshaw Boy)
(CHINESE-COLOR)

London, Nov. 20.

Beijing Film Studio production. Directed by Ling Zifeng. Features entire cast. Screenplay, Ling (based on the novel "Camel Xiangzi," by Lao She); camera (color), Wu Hansheng, Liang Ziyong; art director, Yu Yiru; music, Qu Xixian. Reviewed at London Film Festival, Nov. 20, 1983. Running time: 117 MINS.

Xiangzi	Zhang Fengyi
Huniu	Siqin Gaowa
Liu Si	Yan Bide
Fuzi	Yin Xin
Mr. Cao	Li Tang
Er Qiangzi	Li Xiang

In many ways the most accessible of new Chinese films for Western audiences, "Rickshaw Boy" is a downbeat love story set in Beijing in the 1920s and adapted from a novel by Lao She (1898-1966). The young hero, Xiangzi, arrives in the city from the west of China and sells his camels to raise money to rent a rickshaw from old Liu Si. The latter's daughter, Huniu, takes a shine to the young man and, in defiance of her father, tricks Xiangzi into marrige by pretending she's pregnant.

Her plans go awry when her father sells his business and disinherits her, but when she finds herself genuinely pregnant her marriage starts to improve. It ends tragically, however, when she dies in childbirth and her young husband is left destitute, forced to sell his rickshaw to pay for her funeral. Even a shy pauper girl he is attracted to suffers a tragic fate: sold into a brothel, she hangs herself. Xiangzi is left alone.

Lacking the overt political content of so many Chinese films, "Rickshaw Boy" succeeds as a simply told love story among the impoverished people of pre-war Beijing. Period setting is handsomely captured, thought the print caught had some shaky lab work. Veteran 66-year-old director Ling Zifeng tells the story in a straightforward way, getting very good performances from his actors, especially Mongolian actress Siqin Gaowa as the initially unappealing

but ultimately rather tragic Huniu. Fine music score by Qu Xixian is another plus.— *Strat.*

Good And Bad At Games
(BRITISH-COLOR)

London, Nov. 22.

Portman Quintet Films production. Produced by Victor Glynn. Executive producers, Iran Warren, Tom Donald. Directed by Jack Gold. Features entire cast. Screenplay, William Boyd; camera (color), Wolfgang Suschitzky; editor, Laurence Mery-Clark; production designer, Herbert Westbrook. Reviewed at London Film Festival, Nov. 21, 1983. Running time: 85 MINS.

Quentin (Wog) Niles	Martyn Stanbridge
Cox	Anton Lesser
Frances Mount	Laura Davenport
Alistair Mount	Dominic Jephcott
Joyce	Frederick Alexander
Harrop	Graham Seed
Colenso	Ewan Stewart

The exclusive British private school system (perversely known as public schools) comes under attack in this rather schematic pic which spans a 10-year period in the lives of its characters, all members of the Upper Crust.

In 1973, five senior boys, led by the appalling Mount, share a study together and a similarly elitist point of view of the world. Among them, Niles — popularly known as Wog because his family hails from Singapore — is something of an outsider and only tolerated because he's excellent at sports. Under Mount's leadership, all five mercilessly bully Cox, a junior boy they all call Animal.

Ten years later, Niles still plays cricket every weekend with his old friends, but is stuck in a thankless job and lives an otherwise lonely existence. He is approached by Cox, who claims to be a journalist, but who seems to be out for a belated revenge on his persecutors. Meanwhile, Niles is taken to bed by Frances, Mount's bored wife.

William Boyd's screenplay seems to suggest that the victim of repeated school bullying may wind up either as a Leftist (Cox has a poster of Che Guevara in his scruffy apartment, and also one for Solidarity), or as a terrorist; on the other hand, the chief bully, Mount, is apparently doing something unmentionably nasty in Northern Ireland. Pic emerges as over-written and a bit contrived, though the ensemble acting is good and Jack Gold's direction always competent. However, Lindsay Anderson's 15-year-old "If...." remains the definitive film to date on the phenomenon of the British upper-class education system. — *Strat.*

Tianyunshan Chuanqi
(Legend of Tianyun Mountain)
(CHINESE-COLOR)

London, Nov. 20.

A Shanghai Film Studio production. Directed by Xie Jin. Features entire cast.

Screenplay, Lu Yanzhou; camera (color), Xu Qi; editor Zhou Dingwen; art directors, Ding Chen, Chen Shaomian; music, Ge Yan. Reviewed at London Film Festival, Nov. 18, 1983. Running Time: 125 MINS.

Feng Qinglan	Shi Jianlan
Luo Qun	Shi Weijian
Song Wei	Wang Fuli
Wu Yao	Zhong Xinghuo
Zhou Yuzhen	Hong Xuemin
Xiao Lingyun	Huang Xuejiao
Ling Shu	Liu Han

Sixty-year-old Xie Jin, who attended the screening of "Legend of Tianyun Mountain" at the London Film Festival, is probably China's best-known director; his 1964 pic, "Two Stage Sisters," remains one of the finest Chinese films seen in the West, though because of it he found himself out of favor with the authorities and was unable to work for many years. His two most recent films, "Legend of Tianyun Mountain" (1980) and "The Herdsman" (1982) both deal with the purges of the past and rehabilitation in the post-Gang of Four period, a subject obviously still a burning issue in China.

Told in flashback, pic opens in 1978 with Song Wei running an office overseeing the rehabilitation of former so-called "rightists" while her husband, Wu Yao, in charge of the office, is away on sick leave. Her attention is brought to the case of Luo Qun, a former geologist, whose applications for rehabilitation have been refused by her husband. Pic flashes back to 1957 when Song Wei and Luo Qun were lovers, though she left him when he became politically suspect and eventually he married her former best friend, Feng Qinglan. Xie Jin contrasts the loveless marriage of Song and the autocratic Wu with the close relationship of the impoverished but courageous Feng and Luo. Song finally gets Luo rehabilitated, though at the cost of her marriage and not before Feng has expired.

By Western standards, film is best described as a political soap opera, complete with an occasional song. Abundant use of the zoom lens is as distracting here as it was in all those spaghetti westerns, but obviously the film is made with great feeling and passion, and this certainly comes through. Color is crisp and attractive and a special effects set-piece (the bursting of a dam) is well handled.

Hard to see even the best Chinese films making commerical inroads into the art-houses of the West just yet, but the time is coming. Meanwhile, this is a fascinating and important film, which apparently was a huge success at home although (for fairly obvious reasons) its export has been delayed until now.— *Strat.*

At The Cinema Palace - Liam O'Leary
(IRISH-COLOR & BW-DOCU)

London, Nov. 22.
A Poolberg production, for the Irish Film Board. Produced by Donald Taylor Black, James Hickey. Executive producer, Kieran Hickey. Written & directed by Donald Taylor Black. Camera (color), Sean Corcoran; editor, Patrick Duffner; music, Bill Whelan. Reviewed at London Film Festival, Nov. 21, 1983. Running time: 53 MINS.

An affectionate tribute to 73-year-old Liam O'Leary, the cheerful Irish film enthusiast, author and sometime filmmaker actor, who keeps Ireland's only film archive in his Dublin apartment. With a devotion to film similar to that of the late Henri Langlois, O'Leary speaks with passion about his love for the medium.

Donald Taylor Black, a former programmer of the Cork Film Festival, unfolds O'Leary's life story via interviews with the man himself and his many friends. In the late '20s, O'Leary had helped to form the Irish Film Society in order to get the banned Soviet classics like "Potemkin" seen in Ireland. For a while he was a producer at the Abbey Theater, and also directed a couple of documentary films, including "Portrait of Dublin" (1952). He also acted in a couple of forgotten B-pictures of the early '50s ("Stranger At My Door" and "Men Against The Sun") before leaving Ireland in frustration and joining the British Film Institute's National Film Archive, where he worked as Acquisitions Officer for several years.

O'Leary is also an acknowledged expert on the Irish-American director Rex Ingram, and one of his books is devoted to Ingram's career.

Among those who pay tribute to O'Leary in this well-made docu are British directors Lindsay Anderson and Michael Powell, and Irish actor Cyril Cusack. Black's film is an important tribute to one of the world's great 'behind-the-scenes' pic enthusiasts. — *Strat.*

Sudden Impact
(COLOR)

Dirty Harry in the suburbs.

Hollywood, Dec. 5.
A Warner Bros. release. Produced, directed by Clint Eastwood. Stars Eastwood. Executive producer, Fritz Manes. Screenplay, Joseph C. Stinson, story by Earl E. Smith, Charles B. Pierce, based on characters created by Harry Julian Fink, R.M. Fink, camera (Technicolor, Panavision), Bruce Surtees; editor, Joel Cox; music, Lalo Schifrin; production design, Edward Carfagno; set decoration, Ernie Bishop; sound, Don Johnson; associate producer, Steve Perry; assistant director, David Valdes. Reviewed at The Burbank Studios, Burbank, Dec. 5, 1983. (MPAA Rating: R.) Running time: 117 MINS.
Harry Callahan . . . . Clint Eastwood
Jennifer Spencer . . . . Sondra Locke
Chief Jannings . . . . Pat Hingle
Captain Briggs . . . . Bradford Dillman
Mick . . . . Paul Drake
Ray Parkins . . . . Audrie J. Neenan
Kruger . . . . Jack Thibeau
Lt. Donnelly . . . . Michael Currie
Horace King . . . . Albert Popwell
Officer Bennett . . . . Mark Keyloun
Hawkins . . . . Kevyn Major Howard
Leah . . . . Bette Ford
Mrs. Kruger . . . . Nancy Parsons

The fourth entry in the lucrative "Dirty Harry" series, "Sudden Impact" is a brutally hard-hitting policier which casts Clint Eastwood as audiences like to see him, as the toughest guy in town. Body count here is extraordinarily high, and everything is pitched for maximum action impact, so general audiences should feel they got their money's worth.

Since the series began in 1971, domestic rentals for the various entries have remained highly consistent. Original registered $18,000,000 in rentals, "Magnum Force" (1973) tallied $20,100,000, while "The Enforcer" (1976) chalked up $24,000,000. There's no reason current installment shouldn't fall in the same ball park.

As usual, homicide detective Harry Callahan is seen taking no end of bull from his department superiors due to his rough-house tactics. Described as "the one constant in an ever-changing universe" by an adversary and as "a dinosaur" by his boss, Harry represents the "eye-for-an-eye" school of justice and puts theory into practice whenever possible, endangering his continued existence on the force in the process.

"Sudden Impact" sends Harry out of his normal jurisdiction in San Francisco to research a case with connections to coastal San Paulo (most of the pic was lensed in scenic Santa Cruz). While there, he bumps into Sondra Locke, who is extracting her own brand of vengeance on a group of individuals who, some years back, savagely raped both her and her younger sister.

Locke's murderous character, as well as the setting, brings to mind Eastwood's first feature as a director, "Play Misty For Me," and also raises an interesting parallel to Harry's modus operandi which, unfortunately, is not explored as thoroughly as it might have been.

Local police chief Pat Hingle tries to bar Harry from behaving as usual in his community, but that doesn't prevent a slew of shootings that is surprising in its volume even in this context. Everyone in the picture carries a firearm, one bigger than the next, and it's safe to say no one feels shy about using them.

Any moral compunctions one may have about both Eastwood's and Locke's actions are shoved aside by the fact that all their victims are irredeemable scum, and the Dirty Harry pictures as a group feed in no small measure on the public's general attitude that the criminal justice system in the U.S. is far too lenient with certified criminals. If only there were more Dirty Harrys around.

This is the first entry in the series to have been directed by Eastwood himself, and action is put over with great force, if also with some obviousness and too much reliance on characters, particularly Harry, being in the right place at the right time.

As Harry, Eastwood has all his moves down pat and is effective as always. Locke looks astonishingly like Tippi Hedren did in Hitchcock's "Marnie" and, with the exception of a sympathetic black cop played by Albert Popwell, nearly everyone else in the cast represents a menace to Harry in one way or another.

Tech contributions are thoroughly pro, and an amusing end title discourages customers from attempting to imitate any of the stunts performed in the picture. —*Cart.*

Io Con Te Non Ci Sto Piu'
(I'm Not Living With You Anymore)
(ITALIAN-COLOR)

Rome, Nov. 30.
A P.I.C. release, produced by Bernardo Bertolucci for Fiction Film. Stars Monica Guerritore, Victor Cavallo. Directed by Gianni Amico. Screenplay, Amico, Francesco Tullio Altan, Enzo Ungari; camera (Technicolor), Antonio Nardi; art director, Giorgio Postiglione; editor, Roberto Perpignani; music, Fernando Falcao. Reviewed at Capranica Cinema, Rome, Nov. 30, 1983. Running time: 93 MINS.
Marco . . . . Victor Cavallo
Clara . . . . Monica Guerritore
Tina . . . . Coralla Maiuri

This is a classic love triangle between a young couple and the rich girl next door. Gianni Amico, noted tv helmer of quality product, attempts a foray into the more popular genre of Italo comedy, playing on its rules and boundaries in "I'm Not Living With You Anymore." Attesting to the serious nature of the enterprise is the sponsorship of Bernardo Bertolucci, who produced for Fiction Film. But the relatively novel approach doesn't produce enough entertainment value to capture the large audiences it's aimed at. Nor does pic ultimately succeed in saying anything new about male-female relations, or in making much of a statement about its target genre. Prospects offshore look limited.

A hard-working young woman, Clara (Monica Guerritore), and her unemployed boyfriend Marco (Victor Cavallo) have been evicted from their home and are about to break up when they miraculously stumble across an apartment for rent, rarer than icebergs in Italy. Unable to pass up the opportunity they move in, but a violent quarrel sends Clara running to neighbor Tina (Coralla Maiuri) for a place to sleep.

With Tina's support, Clara has the wall separating the two apartments moved so the girls will have more space. Later, when Marco and Tina begin sleeping together, the wall shifts again. Occupants switch apartments as they switch lovers, until finally the building can stand no more and collapses around them.

This essentially three-character film throws a lot of weight on the trio of thesps. Monica Guerritore is worthy and convincing as the hard-headed Clara, demonstrating her talent for comic as well as dramatic roles. Victor Cavallo and Coralla Maiuri are attractive performers in many ways, but are so tossed about by the needs of the script they never emerge as believably motivated characters.

Pic has a clever structure, but limited concrete development. Amico short-changes emotions and privileges strange antics. However, these bits of business have no significance to the story as a whole, and help neither its flow nor audience involvement.— *Yung.*

Christine
(COLOR)

Needs a trip to a garage.

Hollywood, Dec. 1.
A Columbia release of a Columbia-Delphi/Richard Kobritz production. Produced by Kobritz. Coproducer, assistant director, Larry Franco. Exec producers, Kirby McCauley, Mark Tarlov. Features entire cast. Directed by John Carpenter. Screenplay, Bill Phillips, based on the novel by Stephen King; Camera (Metrocolor, Panavision), Donald M. Morgan; editor, Marion Rothman; music, Carpenter, in association with Alan Howarth; production design, Daniel Lomino; set design, William Joseph Durrell Jr.; set decoration, Cloudia; special effects supervisor, Roy Arbogast; sound (Dolby), Thomas Causey; associate producer, Barry Bernardi. Reviewed at the Directors Guild of America Theatre, L.A., Dec. 1, 1983. MPAA Rating: R. Running time: 110 MINS.
Arnie Cunningham . . . . Keith Gordon
Dennis Guilder . . . . John Stockwell
Leigh Cabot . . . . Alexandra Paul
Will Darnell . . . . Robert Prosky
Rudolph Junkins . . . . . . Harry Dean Stanton
Regina Cunningham . . . . . Christine Belford

George LeBay .... Roberts Blossom
Buddy .... William Ostrander
Mr. Casey .... David Spielberg
Moochie .... Malcolm Danare
Rich .... Steven Tash
Vandenberg .... Stuart Charno
Roseanne .... Kelly Preston
Chuck .... Marc Poppel
Michael Cunningham ...... Robert Barnell

"Christine" seems like a re-tread. Novelist Stephen King's lucrative stock-in-trade seems to be dreaming up new entities which can be possessed and then wreak havoc on unsuspecting individuals, as with the hotel in "The Shining" and the dog in "Cujo."

This time it's a fire-engine red, 1958 Plymouth Fury that's possessed by the Devil, and this deja vu premise, combined with the crazed vehicle format already exploited in Steven Spielberg's "Duel" and the 1977 feature "The Car," makes "Christine" appear pretty shop-worn. Nevertheless, the combined King-John Carpenter names, along with a highly effective campaign by Columbia, angur well for potent initial grosses during the upcoming holiday season.

Title character's nasty personality is neatly established in an assembly line prolog, which leaves one man dead and another injured. Jump to 1978 and Christine is a broken-down junker. Nevertheless, she's the object of love at first sight for misfit high school student Keith Gordon, who purchases her despite objections from his parents and best friend, and restores her to her 1950s glory.

Just as Christine becomes rehabilitated, Gordon also undergoes a transformation, evolving from campus klutz to Mr. Cool and acquiring the foxiest girl in school, Alexandra Paul, in the process. But when the couple begins making out at a drive-in movie, Christine begins acting strangely, and nearly knocks off Paul in a fit of romantic jealously.

At the same time, Christine also has her assets. In the old days, Gordon was an easy mark for the school bullies, who delighted in pushing him around and stepping on his glasses. But with Christine on his side, Gordon need no longer take any of this from the local cretins, who are systematically eliminated by the vengeful vehicle.

The specific artistic merits of the various Stephen King screen adaptations to the side, "Carrie" probably remains the most effective of these simply because it offered a human inroad; the poor girl was so besieged by her friends and acquaintances that some satisfaction could be taken from the retribution she visited upon them.

Similarly, "Christine" works well for awhile in that it represents the revenge of the nerd. The baddies here, effectively represented by William Ostrander, Malcolm Danare and Stuart Charno, are undiluted creeps, and undoubtedly deserve their fates.

Unfortunately, Gordon's initially appealing character changes too quickly, so that for most of the running time he comes off as an arrogant, cold young fellow whose unconditional loyalty to his wheels seems inexplicable and ultimately offputting. One never understands why he stands by his car to the extent that he totally alienates a loving young lady, his best friend and his parents. Despite the outstanding craft with which it's all carried off, story ultimately seems pretty silly.

Director Carpenter's principal challenge was to create a real character of the car, and in this he has succeeded admirably. Flashy auto dominates everything, its jealousy is effectively, and sometimes humorously, conveyed, and some of the best sequences involve incidents in which the car miraculously restores itself to pristine condition after having been banged up and even torched. Technically, the film is outstanding, and Carpenter's choice of lenses and widescreen work is as astute as ever.

As dubious as the material is, pic has been mounted as well as could be imagined. Gordon manages both sides of his character's personality exceedingly well, but is restrained in the later sections by an imposed coldness and uncommunicativeness. John Stockwell is very appealing as his jock buddy, Alexandra Paul is fetching as his g.f., and Robert Prosky steals all his scenes as a cantankerous garage owner.

Good use has been made of 1950s rock tunes, which are the preference of Christine, and tech credits, particularly Donald M. Morgan's lensing, Marion Rothman's editing and Daniel Lomino's production design, are all excellent.

On balance, however, this is just another film where a great deal of talent has been applied to a less than worthy cause. — *Cart.*

Of Unknown Origin
(CANADIAN-COLOR)

Rodent deja vu.

A Warner Bros. release of a Pierre David and Lawrence Nesis presentation. Executive producer, David. Produced by Claude Heroux. Directed by George Pan Cosmatos. Features entire cast. Screenplay, Brian Taggert, from novel "The Visitor" by Chauncey G. Parker 3d; camera (Film House color), Rene Verzier; editor, Robert Silvi; music, Ken Wannberg; sound, Don Cohen; assistant director, John Fretz; production supervisor, Roger Heroux; production design, Anne Pritchard; art direction, Rosemarie McSherry; set decoration, Serge Bureau; post-production supervisor, Bill Wiggins; special effects makeup, Stephan Dupuis. Reviewed at UA Rivoli 1 theater, N.Y., Nov. 28, 1983. (MPAA Rating: R). Running time: 88 MINS.

Bart Hughes .... Peter Weller
Lorrie Wells .... Jennifer Dale
Eliot Riverton .... Lawrence Dane
James Hall .... Kenneth Welsh
Clete .... Louis Del Grande
Meg Hughes .... Shannon Tweed
Hardware salesman .... Keith Knight
Dan Errol .... Maury Chaykin
Peter Hughes .... Leif Anderson

"Of Unknown Origin" is the second Canadian-made horror film acquisition about rats released this year by Warner Bros., following "Deadly Eyes," and is of negligible commercial or artistic value. A similar segment in Universal's four-part film "Nightmares" barely maintained interest in the topic for 25 minutes, while "Origin" is padded out to a very tedious feature length.

Title is taken from the encyclopedia entry which lists no genealogy for rats, with a rather large, intelligent and nasty example of those rodents warring here with New York banking executive Bart Hughes (Peter Weller). Picture is set in Manhattan, but was filmed in November 1982, in Montreal.

With his wife (Shannon Tweed) and young son (Leif Anderson) off vacationing with grandpa, Hughes is left alone in his refurbished brownstone apartment to work on drafting an important consolidation plan for his trust company. Adding to the pressure on him is a noisy rodent, the dispatching of which rapidly becomes an obsession for Hughes.

Never horrifying, though creepy at times, film misguidedly attempts to be a definitive treatise on the danger of rats, with several characters launching into boring lectures on rat lore. Nadir occurs when Hughes ruins a business dinner by telling everyone, during the main course, about the pros and cons of rats, including their being eaten routinely in the Philippines as a form of "stringy chicken."

Toplined Weller alternates a drowsy walk-through with scenes of effective intensity in what amounts to a one-man show, underscored in hokey manner by a tv film clip of Spencer Tracy in "The Old Man And The Sea." Lovely Playboy mag pinup Tweed is wasted in a phoned-in role as his wife, with story structure avoiding any sense of jeopardy or viewer involvement by isolating Hughes alone with his rat. Greatest fear is that his house will be ruined before he can brain the beastie with his trusty baseball bat.

Tech credits are pro, though the many extreme closeups of a real rat do not generate the intended scares. "Willard" is still champ in this genre. — *Lor.*

La Tragedie de Carmen
(The Tragedy of Carmen)
(FRENCH-COLOR-16m)

Paris, Nov. 25.

MK2 release of an Alby Films/Antenne 2 coproduction. Produced by Micheline Rozan. Directed by Peter Brook. Adaptation, Marius Constant; camera, (color, 16m), Sven Nyk-Brook, based on the short story of Prosper Merimée and the opera of Georges Bizet, Meilhac and Levy. Musical direction, Marius Constant. Camera, (color, 16m), Sven Nykvist; production designer, Georges Wakhevitch; editor and executive producer, Pierre Jourdan; artistic collaborators, Philippe Nahon (music) and Maurice Benichou (director); sound, Georges Prat. Reviewed at the Publicis Matignon Theater, Paris, Nov. 20, 1983. Running time of each of three films: 80 MINS.
Carmen .... Helene Delavault,
                    Zehava Gal, Eva Saurova
Don Jose .... Howard Hensel,
                        Lawrence Dale
Micaela .... Agnes Host,
                    Veronique Dietschy
Escamillo .... Jake Gardner,
            John Rath, Carl-Johan Falkman
Zuniga .... Jean-Paul Denizon
Lillas Pastia .... Alain Maratrat
Gacia .... Tapa Sudana

It was probably inevitable that Peter Brook's phenomenally successful chamber version of Bizet's "Carmen" would wind up on film, and the director's intention to avoid the usual pedestrian transcription is praiseworthy. But Brook has betrayed his production. Abetted by Pierre Jourdan, who supervised the editing, he has sapped his stage hit of its intrinsic theatrical juice, and those who see it without having sat through the stage version may be wondering what all the fuss was about.

Rather than make one film, Brook has made three, using the three casts that alternated throughout the week during the show's extraordinary run at the Bouffe du Nord theater, the dilapidated playhouse in the north of Paris, where Brook has been based for years.

The three-cast policy was in good part dictated by the heavy physical demands of live opera performance. For film, such an approach is unnecessary technically, and has proven to be commercially disastrous as well.

Brook thought to recreate the theatergoer's experience and sense of ritual by offering spectators the choice they had to make for the legit night out. No doubt, he managed only to confuse and put off the audience.

Among the most appreciated aspects of Brook's original production were its unusual intimacy and the scrapping of conventional opera trappings. With the aid of writer Jean-Claude Carriere and composer Marius Constant, he remolded "Carmen" to a compact 80 minutes, transforming opera into musical drama. No less important, he gave the principal roles to young singers, reminding us that (like Romeo and Juliet), the heroes of Prosper Mérimée and Bizet are not pushing stolid middle age (as most star system productions of "Carmen" would have us believe). On stage, Brook's "Carmen" rediscovered its youth, vigor and dramatic purpose.

On film, it has lost most of its assets. Brook transformed the Bouffe du Nord into a film studio, hired the excellent Georges Wakhevitch to design a series of suggestive playing spaces that are neither theatrical nor cinematic, and brought in the no less-brilliant Sven Nykvist to photograph it (in 16m). These two glorious names do not prevent the film (or films, though all three have the same mise-en-scene and length) from lacking visual and dramatic excitement. Because, apart from the beautiful overhead shots that bookend the drama, most of the scenes are shot in bland closeups and edited arbitrarily, the essential theatricality is undermined in nearly every sequence.

The players are not to blame. This reviewer could only view the film with Helene Delavault and Howard Hensel, and their performances pretty much duplicate their fine stage portrayals. But, mediated by an unsubtle camera, they lose their dramatic credibility and force.

The films were co-produced by the Antenne 2 tv web. Ironically, home audiences will only get to see one of the casts, that starring Eva Saurova and Lawrence Dale.
— *Len.*

Un Jeans E
Una Maglietta
(Jeans and a T-Shirt)
(ITALIAN-COLOR)

Rome, Nov. 4.
A Titanus release, produced by Franco Calabrese for Gloria Cinematografica. Stars Nino D'Angelo. Directed by Mariano Laurenti. Screenplay, Franco Calabrese, Piero Regnoli and Laurenti; camera (Eastmancolor), Giuseppe Berardini; editor, Carlo Broglio; art director, Franco Calabrese; music, Franco Chiaravalle and Nino D'Angelo. Reviewed at Esperia Cinema, Rome, Nov. 2, 1983. Running time: **85 MINS.**
Nino .... Nino D'Angelo
Anna Maria .... Roberta Olivieri
Waiter .... Enzo Cannavale
Bombolo .... Bombolo

Mariano Laurenti's "Jeans and a T-Shirt" is a Grade C teen beach picture featuring pop singer Nino D'Angelo and a Capri setting. Pic's glaring technical and artistic demerits have not kept it from climbing into the top 10 on national charts, presumably thanks to star's personal following. He warbles six fully orchestrated numbers — many recent hits — in pic's brief span.

Plot, such as it is, has young Nino as a lowly ice cream vendor at a posh Capri club, frequented by rich snobs. He falls for a saucy girl named Anna Maria (Roberta Olivieri), but her industrialist father, who obviously lacks a sense of radical chic, slaps her around when he finds she is dating a "nobody." The father's hard line miraculously melts away after a man-to-man talk with Nino's protector (Enzo Cannavale), a waiter posing as a baron who hopes to marry a fat woman from Texas, whom he mistakenly believes to own oil wells. Pic closes with the young couple rolling on the beach in a lusty slow-motion embrace.

The romantic story is punctuated by broad humor, mostly slapstick and gestural, from Laurenti's stock players Cannavale and Bombolo. Principals are singularly inexpressive but look the part, like characters from the popular photographed comic books whom they resemble. Capri is unrecognizable.
— *Yung.*

Men From The Gutter
(HONG KONG-COLOR)

Hong Kong, Nov. 8.
A Shaw Brothers presentation by Run Run Shaw. Produced by Mona Fong. Directed by Simon Lan Nei Tsai. Stars Pai Piao, Wang Jung, Lo Mang, Miao Chiao Wei, Chen Pei Hsi, Li Hai Sheng. Screenplay, Li Pai Ling; camera (color, Lan Nei Tsai); art director, Huang Jui Min; music, Stephen Shing, So Chun Hou. Reviewed at Jade Cinema, Hong Kong, Nov. 5, 1983. Running Time: **100 MINS.**
(Cantonese Soundtrack with English subtitles).

"Men From The Gutter" is exactly what it is ... a failed attempt to create a believable and classy "film noir" gangster, commercial action film. Locally, this entry bombed critically and financially at the boxoffice.

Director Simon Lan Nei Tsai is an ex-cinematographer who showed some promise last year with "Brothers From The Walled City." But even mild success in Hong Kong can often transform young and inexperienced production men into pretentious, self-indulgent visual filmmakers. They are gifted with rich imagery but usually have a poor storyline, incapable of telling a story straight bout contemporary society, weak screenplay and underdeveloped characterizations.

The objective seems to be to just please the eyes and to hell with intellectual content and proper motivations of social ills and realistic issues in an urban city like Hong Kong. "Men From The Gutter," like many others, got trapped in calculated camera work showing graphic violence, car carnage and moody night shots.

Meant to be a hard-hitting social drama turned soft, it actually tells two stories. Huang Pai-won, Liu Nar-kwong and Lung Tien-shey are three ex-cons and cellmates who join forces and skills to rob a jewelery store and in the process kills a cop. Another story in parallel form is introduced which concerns a drug king syndicate, to be murdered by professional killer Pai Pao. Then, two competent police officers get to know their activities and whereabouts and an ambush is arranged to capture them. An exciting gun battle in the streets ensues and that's about all to wrap up the photoplay.

The lead stars are real uglies which must have been intentional but feminine lead Chen Pei-si who did so well in "Cream Soda and Milk" proves once again the extent of her dramatics even in a minor role of a convict's pregnant girlfriend. One sits through this eyeball exercise feeling tired and feeling nothing but gives the director a chance to practice his craft. He should do better in his next project.
— *Mel.*

Kanakerbraut
(WEST GERMAN-COLOR)

Berlin, Nov. 11.
A Deutsche Film-und Fernsehakademie Berlin (DFFB) Film Production. Features entire cast. Directed by Uwe Schrader. Screenplay, Schrader, Daniel Dubbe; camera (color), Klaus Mueller-Laue; sets, Folker Ansorge, Brigit Gruse; sound, Uwe Thalmann; production manager, Hans W. Mueller, Dieter Kirsten. Reviewed at Studio am Kurfuerstendamn, Berlin, Nov. 11, '83. Running time: **62 MINS.**
Cast: Peter Franke (Paul), Brigitte Janner (Lisa), Gerhard Olschewski (Businessman), Nikolaus Dutsch (Weigert), Alfred Raschke (Guenter), Steffi Lang (Ramona), Grete Jochmann (Secretary), Rainer Pigulla (Worker), Alex Zander (Security Driver), Volker Hanft (Man in Mirror), Margie Ellgaard (Woman in Car).

A diploma film at the Berline Film & TV Academy (DFFB). "Kanakerbraut" (colloquial for "friend of a foreign worker") introduces a promising new talent to the proliferating Berlin film scene: Uwe Schrader. When the hour-long feature was unspooled recently at the Hof Film Festival, it had to be repeated by popular demand and won broad critical praise. It is, indeed, a polished, professional piece of work made on a low-budget of around $15,000 over two weeks

There isn't a story to speak of. It's about Berlin bars and dives, but particularly about a 40-year-old loser named Paul. His wife has left him, he works parttime at odd jobs, and spends the rest of the time hanging around in a dingy room, visiting peep-shows, and swigging beer in a bar right out of Lionel Rogosin's "On the Bowery" (1954) — to which this film bears an affinity in theme and narrative style. One day, Paul meets Lisa, who has been nicknamed "Kanakerbraut" for hanging around with a Turkish foreign-worker (Berlin has a large Turkish population); they hit it off for a while, but Paul is inconsequent and loses Lisa to a self-styled "businessman" in the bar one evening. He tries to pull off a hold-up at one of the places he worked, but fails miserably. In the end, he's become a lonely, dissolute, incurable barfly at one of the lowest dives in Berlin.

An atmospheric film, requiring little dialog but nevertheless a fixed script, "Kanakerbraut" is made with a light hand and a perceptive eye for nuance and particularly the human condition. The three principals are all professional actors (working for little or no salary), while the cameraman (Klaus Mueller-Laue) has worked with several New German Cinema helmers. Pic was lensed on Super-16m and then blown up to 35m for release.

Undoubtedly, "Kanakerbraut" will draw fest attention in view of the critical success already experienced at Hof. Chances are equally good for a commercial run in German cinema and abroad in Europe. —*Holl.*

De Mannetjesmaker
(The Powerbroker)
(DUTCH-COLOR)

Amsterdam, Dec. 6.
A C.E.C. Production. Produced by Hans Klap. Features entire cast. Directed by Hans Hylkema. Screenplay, Hylkema, Ton Vorstenbosch; research, Rudie van Meurs; camera (color), Dirk Teenstra; sound, Lukas Boeke; editor, Ot Louw. Reviewed at City Theater, Amsterdam, Nov. 15, 1983. Running Time: **115 MINS.**
Ben Mertens .... Gerard Thoolen
Mieke Mertens .... Celia Nufaar
Hendrik Ouderkerk ... Carol van Herwijnen
Herbert van der Wall ...... Kenk van Ulsen
Joke van der Wall .... Marjon Brandsma
Olga Müller .... Kitty Courbois
Dr. Posthuma .... Siem Vroom

Hans Hylkema's first feature, following work in shorts and fictionalized docus, has given rise to extensive coverage by reviewers and political correspondents.

Film depicts a political scandal in the '60s. Ministers and other establishment figures (and their sometimes adulterous wives) are shown under fictitious names, but played by lookalike actors.

The screenplay follows closely a series of articles by an outstanding investigative journalist; but while the story, about morphine and shenanigans in the highest circles in The Hague, will probably draw many Dutch cinemagoers, it seems of little interest abroad.

Even younger natives, who had not reached the age of political awareness in the '60s, will have some difficulties in following the finer points of the plot. A Dutch p.r.-man (Mertens), inspired by the use of television during the Kennedy election of '63, sells his services to the then-ruling Catholic party in the Netherlands with great success.

He even advises on speeches, parliamentary tactics, and, finally, the composition of the government. He is admitted to the inner circle of the higher-ups. He always had a booze-problem and, when the stress of political and amorous machinations becomes too much for him, his physician treats him with severely controlled doses of morphine.

A society doctor on the make steps in and, without consulting the physician, gives the flack as much morphine as he wants, free of charge. He also provides him with a seaside flat where he can meet various femmes.

In return the medic seeks advancement and becomes the head of the highest medical government body, at which time he drops Mertens cold. No more free morphine, but the address of another doctor who sells it dearly.

Mertens, under the influence of drugs and alcohol, gives an interview to a weekly, wherein he boasts about his connections, his influence, and calls ministers by their nicknames. Result: questions in Parliament, an official hushup — everybody drops Mertens like the proverbial hot potato. He finds out that the fine gentlemen, whom he considered his personal friends, considered him not more than a useful instrument.

Mertens, without money, abandoned by all except his ex-wife and his secretary, finally dies in the hospital, due to an unexplained overdose of morphine.

He had had a mysterious visitor that day. There's the first question mark. The society doctor and the drugselling medico have been charged by a third doctor, but neither the legal nor the medical authorities saw reasons for any trials. Question mark number two. Both remain unanswered.

Pic is not overly lucid as to the political happenings. On the personal side, Mertens emerges as the fall guy who wallowed in the glory of his temporal power, but did not look for money or official position for himself. He is acted outstandingly by Gerard Thoolen.

All acting is of a very high standard. Marjon Brandsma, Kitty Courbois, Siem Vroom especially excel in smaller parts.

Hylkema's directing of actors is good, but overall he is hampered by his scenario. Credits are adequate. —*Wall.*

Nocturna
(COLOR)

Musicalized spoof of vampire films.

A Compass International Pictures release of a Nai Bonet Enterprises Ltd. production. Executive producer, Nai Bonet. Produced by Vernon P. Becker. Directed by "Harry Tampa" (Harry Hurwitz). Features entire cast. Screenplay, "Tampa" (Hurwitz), based on story by Bonet; camera (DeLuxe color), Mac Ahlberg; editor, Ian Maitland; music, Reid Whitelaw, Norman Bergen; songs performed by Gloria Gaynor, Vicki Sue Robinson, Moment of Truth, Heaven 'N' Hell Orchestra, Jay Siegel; sound, Joel Goldsmith; production manager, David Wolfson. Reviewed on Media Home Entertainment vidcassette, N.Y., Oct. 28, 1983. (MPAA Rating: R). Running time: 83 MINS.

Nocturna	Nai Bonet
Jugulla	Yvonne de Carlo
Count Dracula	John Carradine
Theodore	Brother Theodore (Gottlieb)
R.H. Factor	Sy Richardson
Jimmy	Tony Hamilton
Brenda	Monica Tidwell
B.S.A. prez	Adam Keefe
N.Y. vampire	John Blyth Barrymore

Made in 1978 and released the following year by Compass Pictures Int'l, "Nocturna" is an oddball vampire comedy currently in homevideo distribution. Designed as a vanity vehicle for dancer-actress-producer Nai Bonet, picture never hits its stride, though there are amusing moments.

As with several other horror comedies of its period, especially the hit "Love At First Bite," "Nocturna" capitalizes on the swing in fashions which made decadence and "evil" part of the disco-night life scene. Nai Bonet toplines as Nocturna, granddaughter of Count Dracula (John Carradine) who at age 126 is last in the family line. She falls in love with rock guitarist Jimmy (Tony Hamilton) and leaves Transylvania to be with him on tour in New York.

Film's romantic theme is that Nocturna can become a human by sharing a mortal's love. Main emphasis is on comedy and music, however, with many numbers allowing Bonet to display her body and brand of belly-dancing adapted to disco.

Director Harry Hurwitz (using the nom-de-film Harry Tampa he's also adopted on exploitation assignments) provides some laughs, with standup comic Adam Keefe reprising his Boris Karloff vocal impression and Brother Theodore committing to celluloid snippets of his funny "angry at the world" monologs. John Carradine's old-age version of the Count is a throwaway, as is Yvonne de Carlo's turn at a different vampire styling than she used in tv's "The Munsters."

Bonet is a sexy vamp, with plenty of skin footage for her fans, but her flat dialog readings are amateurish. Best scene for her, which indicates where a better film could have been built, has Nocturna strolling down the tough streets of Manhattan at night, bubbling "I love it" to what appear to be real-life extras (derelicts, etc.). The allure and inverted glamour of the sleazier aspects of the Big Apple is viable subject matter for filming, heretofore left to the domain of unwatchable punk-new wave features and cornball drug-prostitution exposés. — *Lor.*

Reuben, Reuben
(COLOR)

Really cuts the mustard.

Hollywood, Dec. 6.

A 20th Century-Fox International Classics release of a Taft Entertainment Co. presentation of a Walter Shenson production. Produced by Walter Shenson. Coproduced by Julius J. Epstein. Features entire cast. Directed by Robert Ellis Miller. Screenplay, Julius J. Epstein, based on a novel by Peter De Vries; camera (color) Peter Stein; editor, Skip Lusk; production designer, Peter Larkin; music, Billy Goldenberg; sound, Larry Hoff; costume design, John Boxer; associate producers, Philip B. Epstein, Dan Allingham. Reviewed at Taft Entertainment Co. offices, West L.A., Aug. 9, 1983. (No MPAA Rating available). Running time: 101 MINS.

Gowan McGland	Tom Conti
Geneva Spofford	Kelly McGillis
Frank Spofford	Roberts Blossom
Bobby Springer	Cynthia Harris
Lucille Haxby	E. Katherine Kerr
Dr. Haxby	Joel Fabiani
Edith McGland	Kara Wilson
Mare Spofford	Lois Smith
Dr. Ormsby	Ed Grady
Tad Springer	Damon Douglas

Offbeat Christmas surprise about a leching, alcoholic Scottish poet making the New England campus circuit could propel the career of British actor Tom Conti while serving well the reputations of director Robert Ellis Miller and veteran screenwriter ("Casablanca") Julius Epstein.

"Reuben, Reuben" is a delicious pickup for 20th Century-Fox Intl. Classics and a mid-December opening tied to a narrow two-house run in L.A. and New York could do ripe business. Pic's own merit shored up by imaginative extra-effort marketing pitch could spill over to broader boxoffice in January.

Made by The Taft Entertainment Co. and produced by Walter ("The Mouse That Roared") Shenson, his first U.S. film in a decade, "Reuben" is exceptionally literate, with lines that carom with wit from the superb adaptation by Epstein of a 1964 Peter De Vries novel. Epstein, with De Vries' blessing, merged three separate stories in the novel into the character of the rascal poet on the slide. The bizarre, ironic ending of the film is also Epstein's conception, as is the introduction of an old English sheepdog, the title character.

Helmsman Miller draws solid performances from debuting actress Kelly McGillis, whose chic blonde Vassar looks interestingly contrast, in this case, with her character's farmyard roots. She becomes the all-consuming obsession of Conti as he lurches from one bottle and bed to another. Two of his sexual conquests on the poet's college town circuit are nicely and avariciously played by Cynthia Harris and E. Katherine Kerr, and Roberts Blossom is particularly oaken-solid as young McGillis' grandfather. Deft performance is also turned in by Kara Wilson as the protagonist's estranged wife.

But the film is a tour-de-force act for Conti in this, his first U.S.-made film. Material is fodder for a versatile actor and poet Gowan McGland's character, per the filmmakers, is a blend of self-destructive poets by Dylan Thomas (who once lived a spell at DeVries' house) and Brendan Behan (whose maniacal fear about losing his teeth is integrated into McGland's own nightmare in a dentist's chair).

Playing a drunk, Conti is hard to beat. One scene with Conti in a commuter train trying to balance a jiggly glass of booze is uproarious.

Most importance, Conti captures the vulnerability of a man whose plunge into darkness suggests the emotional time most closely associated with 4 a.m.

In retrospect, the bite of the ending seems perfect. — *Loyn.*

Les Comperes
(The Co-Fathers)
(FRENCH-COLOR)

Paris, Dec. 1.

AAA release of a Fideline Films/DD Productions/EFVE Films. Written and directed by Francis Veber. Stars Pierre Richard and Gérard Depardieu. Camera (Eastmancolor), Claude Agostini; art director, Gerard Daoudal; editor, Marie-Sophie Dubus; costumes, Corinne Jorry; sound, Bernard Aubouy; music, Vladimir Cosma; production manager, Jean-Claude Bourlat. Reviewed at the Marignan-Concorde theater, Paris, Nov. 28, 1983. Running time: 92 MINS.

François Pignon	Pierre Richard
Jean Lucas	Gérard Depardieu
Christine	Anny Duperey
Paul	Michel Aumont
Tristan	Stephane Bierry
Jeannot	Roland Blanche
Milan	Philippe Khorsand
Ralph	Jean-Jacques Scheffer

"Les Compères" is brisk, amusing and warm-hearted, and far and away the best of Francis Verber's male-bonding farces, which have included the 1973 feature, "L'Emmerdeur" (A Pain in the Ass), both installments of "La Cage aux Folles," and the recent local commercial smash, "La Chevre," one of the top grossing domestic pics of 1981. "Les Compères" should be an attractive commodity for many foreign markets.

"Les Compères" is a follow-up to "La Chevre," throwing together once again the unlikely figures of Pierre Richard and Gérard Depardieu, and the opposition of neurotic tenacity and burly vulnerability again produces a comedy team of charm and high spirits rare in contemporary movie comedy. Richard and Depardieu play off one another with more humanity than did Lino Ventura and Jacques Brel, or even Michel Serrault and Ugo Tognazzi.

This may be due to presence of Veber behind the camera. The scripter showed clear eyed ability in his helming debut in "La Chevre," and his direction here is even better — the film has rhythm, color and feeling. Veber is probably the best executor of his own material and the success of these last two films should prod him on to future twin-hat activity. (Veber is also co-producer of "Comperes," along with Richard and Depardieu.)

The basic idea here is the same as in "La Chevre:" the search for a missing person conducted by an improvised Sherlock-Watson association. Veber has conceived an even more clever comic motor: Anny Duperey, as an anguished mother dissatisfied with the way police are handling the investigation into the disappearance of her son. Little confident in her hubby's own method, she appeals to old boyfriends for help.

The first is Depardieu, an aggressive investigative journalist; the other is Richard, a suicidal schlemiel who bursts into tears at the slightest contrariety. To insure their concern, Duperey has to tell each that he is in fact the father of the missing boy, but doesn't expect to have both finally on the trail.

Veber deftly spins out a bright series of variations on the curious picture of two males of disparate personalities claiming paternity of a boy they've never seen before, and locking horns with each other when it's not with the adversaries that Veber sprinkles along their path in the South of France. Although there are a few soft spots, the situations are blithely set up and dovetailed, and the whole skips to a perfect sentimental conclusion.

Duperey is near-perfect in her catalyzing role, as are Michel Aumont, as the real father, and Stephane Bierry, as the missing son, who's put out to discover two more dads (when one was already too much (the boy's screen name, by the way, is Tristan, presumably an affectionate nod to Veber's famous great-uncle, Tristan Bernard, the humourist-playwright). Other roles are stock, but freshly portrayed. Tech credits are good.

— *Len.*

El Norte
(The North)
(COLOR)

American indie epic bodes critical and some commercial warmth.

Cinecom International/Island Alive release of an Independent Productions film, Santa Monica. Produced by Anna Thomas. Directed by Gregory Nava. Feature entire cast. Screenplay, Gregory Nava, Anna Thomas; camera (color) James Glennon; sound, Robert Yerington; film editor, Betsy Blankett; music by Gustav Mahler, Samuel Barber, Giuseppe Verdi, The Folkloristas, Melecio Martinez, Emil Richards, Linda O'Brien. Reviewed at the Independent Feature Film Market, New York, Oct. 11, 1983.

(No MPAA rating.) Running time: 139 MINS.
Cast: Zaide Silvia Gutierrez, David Villalpando, Ernest Gomez Cruz, Alicia del Lago, Eraclio Zepeda, Stella Quan, Rodolfo Alejandre, Emilio del Haro, Rodrigo Puebla, Trinidad Silva, Abel Franco, Mike Gomez, Lupe Ontiveros, John Martin, Ron Joseph, Larry Cedar, Sheryl Bernstein, Gregory Enton, Tony Plana, Diane Civita, Jorge Moreno.

The reported hit of the recent Telluride festival, Gregory Nava's "El Norte" (produced by Anna Thomas) appears to be headed for commercial release in Yank art houses and for further exposure at international fests — where the reaction could scale the same heights of critical European appreciation as Robert Young's similarly thematic "Alambrista!" (1978).

At last word, the film is destined for one of the sections at the Cannes Film Fest next spring, after a launch in the States this winter.

An American Playhouse production for Public Television, "El Norte" significantly follows other recent AP hits into cinema distribution and thus effectively boosts the status of Yank indies on the arthouse circuit.

This is, indeed, the first epic in the history of the American Independents: a large-scale 35m on a modest budget production that has to be experienced emotionally as well as viewed for itself over a two-hours-plus running time. Each section in the three-part film lasts approximately 45 minutes, and will probably be presented in a tv series under three titles relating to "Guatelmala," "Mexico" and "Southern California."

The Guatemalan seg has a folkloric character about it. This republic peopled mostly by Indians was once a great center of the Mayan civilization before Columbus, and the population has retained its colorful costumes, traditions and mode of life since Mayan times. We are introduced to a closely knit family in a picturesque setting, but the paradise is deceiving: the central highlands is noted for its coffee and cotton export, the crops picked by the Indians for low wages under tyrannical overseers. The recent (1982) military coup by dissident army officers has led to a wave of political violence and terror, whereupon some 200,000 Guatemalans have sought refuge in Mexico or elsewhere "to the north" (thus the film's title).

The Mexican seg deals with a brother and sister, the two surviving members of this Guatemalan Indian family (their parents have been murdered during an insurrection), on their way north in search of a contact, who might help them to cross the border illegally into California. They have sold a silver necklace to finance the journey, but are now facing abject poverty with only prostitution and ghetto

slavery open as options. Worse: they have been preyed upon by a guide whose aim was to kill them during a night crossing for whatever money they have saved. Then a chance meeting with the searched-for contact leads to a precarious crossing over the border via a pipeline-system infested with rats. This is the strongest of the three parts.

The American seg finds the brother and sister living as Mexican illegals in Los Angeles, he as a waiter in a plush restaurant and she, first as a sweatshop assistant and then as a servant for a rich family. They go to night school to learn fundamental English, and appear to be on their way up the social and economic ladder — when tragedy strikes again. The girl has contracted a form of typhus transmitted by rats, but cannot be taken to a hospital in time due to her illegal "wetback" status. The boy, meanwhile, has to make a choice between going to Chicago to accept a promising job and leaving his sister behind to fend momentarily for herself. The ending ties all the threads of the preceding action together while offering a new dramatic twist of its own.

If all this sounds familiar, then accept the epic as a free-style updating of John Steinbeck's "The Grapes of Wrath." There are several parallels to be found here, particularly in the dramatic structure of both works. It's also a film that will immediately win the sympathy of the viewer with the plight of aliens in southern California and along the Rio Grande border. Perhaps it is too much of a tearjerker in the long run.

"El Norte" attracts on another level, however. It is beautifully lensed and comes across as a kind of giant Renaissance canvas. There were the problems helmer Nava and producer Thomas faced on location in Mexico and in finishing the project at all. "El Norte" is a milestone in American Independent filmmaking. —*Holl.*

A Flower In The Raining Night
(TAIWANESE-COLOR)

Taipei, Nov. 18.
A Montage Film Co. presentation and production. Produced by John Chang Mei Chun, Chang Yen Quan. Directed by Wang Toon. Stars Lu Hsiao Feng, Yu Chong Chua, Ying Ying, Su Ming Ming. Planning, Wade C. Yao; Screenplay, Hwang Chung Ming; associate producer, Wu Meng Lin; camera (color), Lin Hun Chung, art director, Wang Toon; editor, Shang Chan-Chen; music, Chang Hun I. Reviewed in Taipei, Taiwan, Golden Horse Awards, Nov. 17, 1983. Running time: 100 MINS.
(Mandarin soundtrack with English subtitles)

A most distinguished "new wave" Taiwanese film for 1983, brought about by more relaxed

censorship laws in the country, "A Flower In the Raining Night" won in the recent Golden Horse Awards for best actress category (Lu Hsiao Feng).

A Golden Torch Award at the 28th Asia-Pacific Film Festival from the Intl. Catholic Organization of Cinema and Audio-Visuals in Asia, for "outstanding artistic expression of positive human values" also helps.

It is one of Taiwan's current box-office bonanzas.

Films about prostitutes are now a dime-a-dozen and many have gotten awards before since dramtic content and opportunities are ample. But this one has more to offer as a touching film of artistic merit that is warm, inspiring and a penetrating cinematic representation of human nature.

"Flower" is a realistic story of a prostitute, Pai-Mei, who faces up to her past and undertakes the slow and difficult process of transformation to build a new future for herself as a respectable farm girl. Pai-Mei is played with earthy energy and power by Lu Hsiao-Feng), once known only for portraying sexpot roles and she herself underwent changes in her showbiz career to prove that she is more than just a "body."

Sold to a foster daughter when she was a baby and then sold again as a child into prostitution by her family, Pai-Mei is a woman who's been a classic victim of circumstance and prejudice. The pics animating social consciousness, sensitive presentation of a touching subject, plus high artistic presentation both visually and verbally, are some of the film's strong merits. Some sequences are overlong and could stand drastic editing.

Photographed and maturely directed by Wang Toon with restraint, the film captures the wide emotional range of actress Lu who ages from young girl to a pro (who later used a customer to have a child) to a hard working pregnant farm hand without worldly material things and a loving mother. It shows that with courage, determination and inborn wisdom, anyone can change one's fate. The beauty of rural life and community spirit to help people in need are also projected in an unpatronizing way. Added honor is Ying Ying's winning of best supporting actress laurels as the concerned mother.

The movie ends positively with hope as the audience sees a different woman. Here is a manifestation of the universal theme of courage and an expression of the original author's desire to possibly express the concept about the equality of life.

The success of "A Flower In The

Raining Night'' will assure its exhibition in international film festivals outside Taiwan. — *Mel.*

Kehraus
(Clean Sweep)
(WEST GERMAN-COLOR)

Berlin, Nov. 12.

A Solaris Film, in collaboration with Maran-Film, production, Munich. Hans Weth, producer. Features entire cast. Directed by Hans Christian Mueller. Screenplay, Mueller, Gerhard Polt, Carlo Fedier; camera (color), James Jacobs; sets, Winfried Hennig; editing, Thea Eymesz; costumes, Gudrun Schretzmeier; sound, Michael Lau; production manager, Guenter Prantl. Reviewed at Minilux, Berlin, Nov. 12, '83. Running time: **90 MINS.**

Cast: Gerhart Polt, Gisela Schneeberger, Dieter Hildebrandt, Nikolaus Paryla, Jochen Busse, Hans Guenther Martens, Karl Obermayr, Helena Rosenkranz, Hans Stadtmueller, Peter Welz.

The German cinema of late has turned to light comedies and satires featuring well-known tv personalities to boost attendance. It's a healthy sign. Indeed, it's a wonder that a very funny and quite pungent comedy like Hans Christian Mueller's ''Kehraus'' (the word has a variety of double meanings in the direction of ''sweep away'' or ''make a clean sweep,'' or simply ''clean sweep,'' as chosen for a fitting title here). The protagonists are Gerhard Polt (who assisted on the script and dialog), Dieter Hildebrandt, Gisela Schneeberger, and others. They belong to German TV's best cabaret team of satirists, along with helmer Mueller.

This is the story of a friendly and good-natured Bavarian truck-driver type who gets drawn into signing seven insurance policies by a slick operator — costing him (after he's figured it out) a round figure amounting to about half of his salary. Naturally, he figures he can right the error by simply going to the insurance company in Munich and paying a visit on the shady insurance salesman.

One door leads to another, however, and he's hardly making any headway at all — until he stumbles onto a brace of hidden cameras in the office building observing the coffee breaks and general moping around on the job. The monitoring screens are in the offices of the big bosses in the penthouse, who decide to make a ''clean sweep'' of the sixth floor personnel to save on overhead — just at the moment the Bavarian bullhead appears on the scene.

One good turn deserves another, so the inhospitable secretary who's been givieng him the runaround tells the hero he can find the dodging salesman at the company party that night during the carnival (Fasching) celebrations. It's here that helmer Mueller pulls out all the stops. All the characters, from top bosses all the way down to delivery boy, are shown to be oddballs with one hangup or another. The result is that a German-style Marx Brothers climax takes place as the whole place goes up for grabs in the course of accentuated merrymaking. In the end, all is righted due to the budding romance between the loser and the secretary.

''Kehraus'' is ready made for the home aud, and yet it could be easily appreciated by a foreign public at a German Film Week or possible fest spinoff — provided care is taken in preparing subtitles. —*Holl.*

A Nos Amours
(To Our Loves)
(FRENCH - COLOR)

Paris, Nov. 26.

Gaumont release of a Livradois/Gaumont/FR3 co-production. Executive producer, Micheline Pialat. Associate producer, Emmanuel Schlumberger. Directed by Maurice Pialat and Arlette Langmann. Camera (color), Jacques Loiseleux; art director, Jean-Paul Camail; editor, Yann Dedet; sound, Jean Umansky; costumes, Valerie Schlumberger; music, Henry Purcell's ''The Cold Song,'' performed by Klaus Nomy. Reviewed at Gaumont Champs-Elysees theater, Paris, Nov. 26, 1983. Running time: **102 MINS.**

Suzanne . . . . Sandrine Bonnaire
Her father . . . . Maurice Pialat
Her mother . . . . Evelyne Kerr
Robert, her brother . Dominique Besnehard
Anne . . . . Annie-Sophie Maillé
Luc . . . . Cyr Boitard
Michel . . . . Christophe Odent

Director Maurice Pialat has always been keenly interested in young people and has devoted some of his most perceptive productions to their disarray and problems, including his first feature, ''L'Enfance Nu'' in 1968, and the more recent ''Passe Ton Bac D'Abord'' (1979), to which this film is a sort of followup.

''A Nos Amours'' tells of a 15-year-old girl in sexual freefall, mildly disturbed by what she calls her ''dry heart.'' Despite her youth she feels incapable of making any genuine emotional attachments to her boyfriends, and feels no scruples about the unbridled promiscuity she has slipped passively into. Pursued by the boy she has broken up with, for no concrete reason, she responds to social and family pressures by marrying someone she doesn't love, and some time later takes off for the States with one of her other bedmates.

Like several of Pialat's previous works, this film went through some production difficulties and was interrupted for several months. Reportedly, the screenplay, written by Pialat and his usual collaborator, Arlette Langmann, underwent important modifications, including the introduction of some improvised dramatic scenes and the increased screen time for the girl's father, played with quiet, sometimes insidious authority by Pialat himself.

These factors may in part explain the unsatisfying patchwork feeling of the film, a lack of overall cohesiveness and occasional sloppiness of direction and editing. At his best, Pialat has an acute eye for detail, gesture and behavior, and the best scenes here are those in which he observes, with clarity and restraint, the listless social movements of the heroine (beautifully portrayed by newcomer Sandrine Bonnaire) and her guardedly confidential relationship with her father.

But at his worst, Pialat trades on undisciplined improvisations and shrill dramatic moments. Particularly irritating are the scenes of neurotic family squabbling, in which Bonnaire engages in screaming and slapping bouts with a repulsively hysterical mother (Evelyne Kerr) and goonish, tyrannical brother (played by Dominique Besnehard, a local casting director). And there is a long unrehearsed climactic sequence, in which Pialat makes an unexpected appearance during a family banquet and poisons its air of hypocritical detente, that's particularly exasperating in its self-indulgence, complacency and lack of dramatic rigor.

Nonetheless, ''A Nos Amours'' has been greeted with a rare unanimity of critical raves and strong public response. Despite all that, this film probably won't bring Pialat the international recognition that's unjustly and repeatedly escaped him until now. — *Len.*

London Film Festival

Wagner
(BRITISH-HUNGARIAN-
AUSTRIAN-COLOR)
London, Nov. 27.

A London Trust Cultural production of a Richard Wagner (Austria)/Ladbroke (UK)/Hungarofilm/MTV film. Produced by Alan Wright, executive producers, Derek Brierley, Florian Endre. Directed by Tony Palmer. Stars Richard Burton. Screenplay, Charles Wood; camera (Technicolor), Vittorio Storaro; editor, Graham Bunn; production design, Kenneth Carey; costume design, Shirley Russell; music, Richard Wagner, additional music, Ivan Fischer; conducted by Georg Solti. Reviewed at the London Film Festival, Nov. 26, 1983. Running time: **300 MINS.** **MINS.**

Richard Wagner . . . . Richard Burton
Cosima . . . . Vanessa Redgrave
Minna Wagner . . . . Gemma Craven
Ludwig Ii . . . . Laszlo Galffi
Pfistermeister . . . . John Gielgud
Pfordten . . . . Ralph Richardson
Pfeufer . . . . Laurence Olivier
Franz Liszt . . . . Ekkehardt Schall
Nietzsche . . . . Ronald Pickup
Hans von Bulow . . . . Miguel Herz-Kestranek
Mathilde Wesendonck . . . . Marthe Keller
Otto Wesendonck . . . . Richard Pasco
Richter . . . . Stephen Oliver
Mrs. Taylor . . . . Joan Plowright
Meser . . . . Arthur Lowe
Crespi . . . . Franco Nero

There's nothing particularly intimate or revelatory about the new five-hour (plus intermission) ''Wagner'' on the German 19th-century composer. So, the minimal delights of this lengthy biography come from the overblown and absurd elements of this film. However, director Tony Palmer certainly lacks the finesse of Ken Russell when it comes to mixing the outrageous and historical.

Although the composer has figured in a number of recent films (''Ludwig,'' ''Parsifal''), one has to go back 40 years to uncover an earlier biopic. The new film begins in Dresden in 1848 when Richard Wagner (Richard Burton) was beginning to gain notoriety for his compositions and grand, heroic operas. He was also actively involved in the movement for a unified Germany. The latter episode contributes several battle sequences for the film and is the cause of his flight to Switzerland and France.

So begins a 40-year trek across Europe for the most part as a stateless artist. Brunt of the first part deals with his self-imposed exile with part two beginning with his introduction to Ludwig II who becomes his patron. Along the way there are mounting bills, political scandals and Faustian pursuits.

The most curious aspect of the film is that one might have anticipated a warmer homage. As embodied in script and performance, Wagner is a loutish, insensitive, manipulating bigot. And while the film is handsomely mounted, very little is seen of the actual operas which might have at least justified some of the composer's mania for money.

Burton's performance as Wagner presents an almost entirely unsympathetic picture. He is ruthless about securing money at the cost of his marriage, ideals and friendships. So, when a performance in Paris is sabotaged as a result of Wagner's anti-Semitic remarks, one remains unmoved. Burton puts on such a fierce front, it's impossible to detect any humanity in Wagner's character.

Vanessa Redgrave and Gemma Craven as Wagner's wives have largely thankless roles. Craven particularly, as his long-suffering first wife, must endure her husband's thoughtlessness while Redgrave remains oblivious to, and in fact shares, his cold-blooded penchant for extracting favors.

For buffs, the film's biggest draw is watching England's acting knights — Olivier, Gielgud, Richardson — working together for the first time on screen. Gielgud, who also narrates much of the film, has the largest and most satisfying role. Conversely, Olivier mugs outrageously, winding up the loser of the three.

Remaining cast is of little note. Ronald Pickup's Nietzsche is perhaps the most interesting supporting character as he is at first attracted, then repelled by the composer. However, Laszlo Galffi as Ludwig II fails to convince as the foppish monarch inspired by Wagner's Lohengrin.

Chief attraction remains the visual components of the film which beautifully capture the era. Vittorio Storaro's camera, Shirley Russell's costumes and the production design of Kenneth Carey are dazzling to an extent that one wonders why such a small fraction of this talent emerges in script, direction and performance.

Plans are to four-wall "Wagner" in the U.S. to qualify for Oscars in December. However, even were it to secure some technical nominations, there's little likelihood the film will secure commercial distribution. Production simply fails to humanize or generalize its subject and pace is plodding. A nine-hour television production also exists but one suspects a case of more being less. — *Klad.*

Fords On Water
(BRITISH-COLOR)

London, Nov. 28.
British Film Institute production. Produced by Nita Amy, Jill Pack. Executive producer, Peter Sainsburg. Features entire cast. Directed by Barry Bliss. Screenplay, Bliss, Billy Colvill; camera (color), Russell Murray; editor, Neil Thomson; art directors, Ian Watson, Caroline Amies; music, Keith Donald. Reviewed at London Film Festival, Nov. 26, 1983. Running time: **81 MINS.**
Winston......................Elvis Payne
Eddie........................Mark Wingett
Beryl..................Kathryn Apanowicz
Mac...........................Jason Rose
Winston's father.............Allister Bain
Anne..................Michele Winstanley
Madeline......................Kate Rabett

This is a "buddy" movie in which an upwardly mobile black youth, Winston, meets a dejected working-class white youth, Eddie, when they're twice involved in violent incidents (Eddie saves Winston from a beating, Winston hits Eddie when driving his car). Since both are unemployed and Eddie is rejected by his stuffy girlfriend, they head north together on a voyage of optimistic discovery.

Newcomer Barry Bliss, helming his first feature, shows directorial promise: his handling is imaginative and inventive. He's hampered, however, by a muddled script, written by himself and Billy Colvill, which seems to strive for cynical comedy as well as a bleak view of a Britain filled with unemployed workers, growing militancy, and a smothering military presence; the narrative is aimless and the humor is thin on the ground.

Lead actors are excellent. Elvis Payne, as Winston, is a dead ringer for Eddie Murphy and has something of the American actor's menacing charm; Mark Wingett is

something like a very young Michael Caine.

"Fords On Water" (the title is meaningless and a put-off) is a very uneven film, but it does suggest a new British director and a couple of new British actors may be on their way. It's a case of the part overcoming the shortcomings of the whole. —*Strat.*

L'Ultima Diva: Francesca Bertini
(The Last Diva: Francesca Bertini)
(ITALIAN-COLOR/B&W-DOCU)

London, Nov. 28.
An Antea-RAI TV Production. Produced by Enzo Porcelli. Written & directed by Gianfranco Mingozzi. Camera (color), Luigi Verga; editor, Antonio Fusco; music, Egisto Macchi. Reviewed at B.F.I. Theatrette, London Film Festival, London, Nov. 25, 1983. Running time: **81 MINS.**

Francesca Bertini, born in 1892, was the first Italian film star and one of the world's great screen actresses of the early silent period. She made her first pic in 1907 and as recently as 1976 was still before the cameras, playing Burt Lancaster's sister in Bernardo Bertolucci's "1900." Director Gianfranco Mingozzi, himself a feature film director of some repute, has successfully reintroduced modern audiences to this fascinating woman. Bertini today is apparently as feisty, single-minded and capricious as she was in her heyday.

Actress claims many of her best early films were destroyed, but clips from some are shown, especially "The Serpent," one of her first. Bulk of this tribute, though, is devoted to a presentation of the 1915 "Assunta Spina," an adaptation of a famous novel by Salvatore di Giacomo, which (pre-dating neo-realism by some 30 years) was shot on the streets of Naples. Film is credited to Bertini's costar, Gustavo Serena, but she claims he only aided her and that she really was the director.

Certainly she gives a very modern performance as a working-class woman who goes astray while her husband is in prison, and the film looks to be quite impressive. Mingozzi intercuts between the film itself and closeups of Bertini watching herself and commentating unselfconsciously ("She's good looking, isn't she?" "What a profile she's got!"). Accompanying her during the screening is the grandson of the film's original producer.

To end his tribute, Mingozzi intercuts between two versions of "Odette" which starred Bertini in the same role, that of a mother who loses touch with her daughter: first version was made in 1915 and the remake was done as a talkie in 1934 by French director Marcel

L'Herbier. Effect of seeing actress play the same role 19 years apart is extraordinary.

"The Last Diva" is a must for all interested in the history of the cinema or in the star system. Only flaw is the opening, a clip from "Sunset Boulevard," dubbed into Italian, apparently meant to be a comment on Hollywood stardom. It doesn't work, and could be cut.—*Strat.*

Journal de Campagne
(Field Diary)
(FRENCH-ISRAELI-COLOR)

London, Nov. 25.
Les Films d'Ici production, produced by Richard Copans. Written & directed by Amos Gitai. Camera (color), Nurith Aviv; editor, Scheherazade Saadi. Reviewed at London Film Festival, Nov. 24, 1983. Running time: **85 MINS.**

A controversial documentary made by Israeli filmmaker Amos Gitai about the occupation of the West Bank and the Gaza Strip by his country's armed forces.

Gitai, who obviously feels for the displaced Palestinians, had trouble making his film: time and again, officials, soldiers, authorities try to stop the filming, covering the camera lens or threatening to smash it. But filming event won, as Gitai and his team photographed local farmers, occupying soldiers taking photos of themselves, life in the towns and markets, and an interview with the Arab mayor of Nablus, crippled after a bomb attack.

Israeli soldiers come across as naively enthusiastic about retaining the "occupied territories" since the land is so beautiful and historic, though one suggests it should be returned to the Palestinians for the sale of peace.

"Field Diary" is deliberately provocative, but a fascinating document of both Palestinian life and the lives of the Israelis coming to live in the new settlements in this troubled part of the world. Technically okay. —*Strat.*

Gorky Park
(COLOR)

'Park' turns into a maze.

Hollywood, Dec. 12.
An Orion Pictures release, produced by Gene Kirkwood and Howard W. Koch Jr. Directed by Michael Apted. Exec producer, Bob Larson. Screenplay, Dennis Potter, based on novel by Martin Cruz Smith; camera (Technicolor), Ralf D. Bode; editor, Dennis Virkler; sound, Simon Kaye; assistant director, Dan Kolsrud; associate producers, Efrem Harkham and Uri Harkham; production design, Paul Sylbert; music, James Horner. Reviewed at Beverly Hills Screening Room, L.A., Dec. 12, 1983. (MPAA rating: R.) Running time: **128 MINS.**
Arkady Renko................William Hurt
Jack Osborne.................Lee Marvin
William Kirwill...........Brian Dennehy
Iamskoy......................Ian Bannen
Irina......................Joanna Pacula
Pasha....................Michael Elphick
Anton...................Richard Griffiths
Pribluda.....................Rikki Fulton
General..................Alexander Knox
Golodkin......................Alexei Sayle
Prof. Andreev............Ian McDiarmid

There's enough menace and romance in "Gorky Park" to appeal to many, especially those helped by the memory of Martin Cruz Smith's successful novel. But it clearly suffers from an attempt to cram too much into two hours.

At the center, however, William Hurt is superb as a Moscow militia detective caught between his desires to be simply a good cop and the unfathonable motives of the secret Soviet government, all complicated by a unexpected love for Joanna Pacula.

Director Michael Apted sets Hurt up well with the discovery of three mutilated, faceless bodies in the city's Gorky-Park, leading Hurt to suspect this all the affair of the dangerous KGB and much to be avoided by plodding policemen such as himself.

Urged on by politically-connected Ian Bannen, Hurt stoically starts to collect clues which the audience must watch for carefully lest complete confusion set in quickly. (Again, the task must be simpler for those who had the leisure to read the book.)

Very quickly, Hurt's investigation brings him into contact with Lee Marvin, a wealthy American who enjoys high privilege in important Soviet circles, obviously not simply because he's a successful trader in sables.

Hurt also meets Pacula who, in honored tradition for a mystery, knows more than she's willing to tell about both Marvin and the victims. Gradually, their mutual need for survival turns into more carnal desires, followed by love.

In his pursuit for truth, Hurt receives a big boost from Brian Dennehy, whose character is unfortunately the most baffling and irritating of all. Though excellently played by Dennehy, this New York City detective is totally mystifying in his ability to move about Moscow in his own search for the killer of his brother, one of the three in the park. Thus the film's reliance on Dennehy to help Hurt out of trouble seems constantly too pat.

Marvin also counts among the many good performers, though his motives must be closely watched or lost in the rapidly developing rush to a conclusion.

Apted, cinematographer Ralf D. Bode and production designer Paul Sylbert have done an excellent job in making Helsinki stand in for Moscow, where they were denied access for filming. If "Gorky" accomplishes anything well beyond its immediate story, it conveys an acceptable portrait of what modern life may be like in the Soviet capital, complete with bureaucratic infighting.

Obviously, "Gorky" is also trying to tell something, too, about the commonality of mankind, regardless of the political backdrop. At this, it succeeds in part, but also fails because the unfamiliar setting finally makes it hard to understand completely what its people are up to. — *Har.*

Marvin And Tige
(COLOR)

Lachrymose but resistable.

Hollywood, Dec. 6.
A Major Films Release of a Marvin Film Partners production. Produced by Wanda Dell. Executive producer Frank Menke and Dell. Directed by Eric Weston. Features entire cast. Screenplay, Dell, Weston; based on novel by Frankcina Glass; camera (Deluxe Color), Brian West; editor, Fabien Dahlen Tordjmann; music, Patrick Williams; art directors, Paul Rhudy, Frank Blair; set decorators, Scott Stevens, Tanya Moontaro; costumes, Cheryl Kilborn, Christine Goluding; sound, Bud Alper; associate producer, Elayne Ceder; assistant director, Joan Feinstein. Reviewed at MGM/UA, Hollywood, Dec. 6, 1983. (MPAA Rating: PG). Running time: 104 MINS.
Marvin Stewart..........John Cassavetes
Richard Davis..........Billy Dee Williams
Vanessa Jackson......Denise Nicholas-Hill
Tige Jackson..............Gibran Brown
Brenda Davis.........,.....Fay Hauser
Carrie Carter...............Georgia Allen

Eric Weston's "Marvin and Tige" may give you a cry, but it's not a good cry or one that is earned by the characters and situations. Good intentioned as it may be, pic plays with feelings and makes the excessive emotions it generates suspect. Christmas appeal for family audience is limited.

Based on a novel by Frankcina Glass, screenwriters Wanda Dell and Eric Weston have included every cliché in the book to demonstrate the loneliness of two misfits. John Cassavetes is Marvin, apparently a gentleman at heart, who has fallen on hardtimes and supports himself by collecting deposit bottles. Marvin is a middle class bum if there ever was one.

Tige is an 11-year-old back street kid who may not live to see 12. Deserted by his father at an early age, he is left to his own devices after his mother dies. Marvin saves him from committing suicide one night and takes him under his wing.

The struggling youth, nicely played by Gibran Brown, goes through all the predictable steps. He resists Marvin's affections at first, becomes close and then becomes deathly ill. While the kid is in the hospital, Marvin digs up his father (Billy Dee Williams), who is married with three kids and reluctant to take on another.

Williams, like all the people here, turns out to be a good man at heart and ultimately does the right thing. No one seems to be any the worse for wear in this world and emotional scars are covered with a Band-aid.

Marvin is presented as a wise man, but his advice to Tige doesn't seem to be drawn from real life. Situations appear to be staged only to elicit a particular response and tug at the heart strings in a calculated fashion. This film may make you angry as your eyes inevitably cloud over.

Good performances by Cassavetes and Brown are undermined by poor development. There is no history or depth to provide a basis for their feelings.

Production values are adequate and glimpses of Atlanta in the background provide a relief from the hot-house drama. — *Jagr.*

To Be Or Not To Be
(COLOR)

Brooks remakes Lubitsch.

A 20th Century-Fox release of a Brooksfilms production, produced by Mel Brooks. Directed by Alan Johnson. Exec producer, Howard Jeffrey. Screenplay, Thomas Meehan, Ronny Graham, based on previous film directed by Ernst Lubitsch and written by Edwin Justus Mayer; camera, (Deluxe Color), Gerald Hirschfeld; editor, Alan Balsam; sound, Gene S. Cantamessa; associate producer, Irene Walzer; production design, Terence Marsh; costumes, Albert Wolsky; assistant director, Ross G. Brown; art direction, J. Dennis Washington; music, John Morris. Reviewed at Gotham Theater, N.Y., Nov. 30, '83. (MPAA rating: PG.) Running time: 108 MINS.
Frederick Bronski ....Mel Brooks
Anna Bronski ....Anne Bancroft
Lt. Sobinski ....Tim Matheson
Col. Erhardt ....Charles Durning
Prof. Siletski ....(.........Jose Ferrer
Sasha ....James Haake
Capt. Schultz............Christopher Lloyd
Ravitch ....George Gaynes
Ratowski ....George Wyner
Dobish ....Jack Riley.
Lupinski ....Lewis J. Stadlen
Sondheim ....Ronny Graham

With the solid farcical underpinning of Ernst Lubitsch's 1942 "To Be Or Not To Be" giving Mel Brooks his most disciplined comic structure since "The Twelve Chairs," his glossy remake of the

original Carole Lombard-Jack Benny starrer is very funny stuff indeed, though its boxoffice chances are hard to call.

Maintaining some of the dramatic core of the original, but played mostly for Brooks-style laughs, the convoluted tale of a Warsaw thea-

Original Film

Hollywood, Feb. 17.
United Artists release of Alexander Korda-Ernst Lubitsch production: directed by Lubitsch; screenplay by Edwin Justus Mayer, form story by Lubitsch and Melchior Lengyel. Stars Carole Lombard, Jack Benny; features Robert Stack, Felix Bressart, Lionel Atwill, Stanley Ridges, Sig Ruman. Camera, Rudolph Mate; editor, Dorothy Spencer; art, Vincent Korda; special effects, Lawrence Butler; asst.-directors, William Tummel and William McGarry. Previewed at Westwood Village, Feb. 17, '42. Running time: 90 MINS.
Maria Tura ....Carole Lombard
Joseph Tura ....Jack Benny
Lieut. Stanislav Sobinski .....Robert Stack
Greenberg ....Felix Bressart
Rawitch ....Lionel Atwill
Professor Siletsky ....Stanley Ridges
Col. Ehrhardt ....Sig Ruman
Bronski ....Tom Dugan
Producer Dobosh ....Charles Halton
Actor-Adjutant ....George Lynn
Capt. Schultz................Henry Victor
Anna ....Maude Eburne
Makeup Man ....Armand Wright
Stage Manager ....Erno Verebes
General Armstrong......Halliwell Hobbes
Major Cunningham ....Miles Mander
Captain ....Lelle Dennison
Polish Official ....Frank Reicher
William Kunze ....Peter Caldwell
Man in Bookstore.........Wolfgang Zilzer
Polonius in Warsaw......\.......Olaf Hytten
Reporter ....Charles Irwin
Second Reporter ....Leland Hodgson
Scottish Farmer ....Alec Craig
Second Farmer ....James Finlayson
Prompter.....................Edgar Licho
Gestapo Sergeant ....Robert O. Davis
Pilot ....'....Roland Varno
Co-Pilots ....:......Helmut Dantine
                            Otto Reichow
                        Maurice Murphy
Polish R.A.F. Flyers............Gene Rizzl
                            Paul Barrett
                            John Kellogg

trical troupe that winds up saving the Polish underground during the Nazi occupation does have some potential hurdles to clear. Primarily, appeal of the film will be concentrated among older audiences, and b.o. competition could be intense. Also to be considered: cute Nazis and roly-poly Gestapo officers hardly have universal lure.

Although Brooks is technically only in on "To Be" as producer and actor (film was directed by Alan Johnson and adapted from the original by Thomas Meehan and Ronny Graham), his personal contempo brand of parodic jokiness, ethnic humor and musical satire colors the entire project. Thankfully missing are the outhouse humor and gratuitous offensiveness that have plagued most of his recent self-generated comedies.

Here Brooks sustains, with varying success, a full-fledged role as Frederick Bronski, vainglorious head of a tawdry theatrical company whose shows run the spectrum

from cheap vaudeville turns to "Highlights From Hamlet." Mainstay of the film is a superbly sustained comic performance by Anne Bancroft, as Bronski's wife, in the real-life Brooks couple's first tandem costarring acting job.

Plot moves into motion when Bancroft embarks on a nightly backstage rendezvous with a handsome Polish airman (Tim Matheson) who, along with his colleagues in a London-based Polish flying unit, inadvertently feeds Bancroft's name and the identities of Warsaw resistance leaders to a presumed Polish patriot (Jose Ferrer).

When Matheson realizes Ferrer is actually a Nazi hireling, he parachutes back into Warsaw to prevent Ferrer from delivering the blacklist to local Gestapo chief Charles Durning.

Remaining progression of events is keyed to the theatrical troupe's various masquerades as Nazi officials, notably Brooks' impersonations of Ferrer (complicated when the latter's body turns up) and, in a wacky escape finale, as Hitler.

Durning is a standout as the buffoonish Gestapo topper and Bancroft's pseudo-seduction of him, and Ferrer, are among the pic's highpoints. Bancroft's sustained delights are not matched by Brooks, who seems to be trying too hard (especially at dramatic junctures) and draws on too many past bits (notably his "Springtime For Hitler" pieces in "The Producers") to be truly captivating.

Supporting cast is strong indeed, with Matheson a perfect romantic foil and James Haake, as Bancroft's swishy dresser, moving from broad gay posturing to genuine pathos as the Nazis begin their lavender roundup. Lavish production includes several musical set pieces (capped by the opening Brooks-Bancroft rendition of "Sweet Georgia Brown" in Polish), which lend the film a once-traditional Hollywood veneer. —*Step.*

Uncommon Valor
(COLOR)

Okay grind actioner.

Hollywood, Dec. 9.
A Paramount Pictures release, produced by John Milius & Buzz Feitshans. Directed by Ted Kotcheff. Stars Gene Hackman; features cast. Exec producer, Kotcheff. Screenplay, Joe Gayton; camera (Movielab Color), Stephen H. Burum; editor, Mark Melnick; sound, Joe Kenworthy; production design, James L. Schoppe; art direction, Jack G. Taylor, Jr.; associate producers, Burton Elias, Wings Hauser; assistant director, Craig Huston; music, James Horner. Reviewed at Paramount Pictures, Hollywood, Dec. 8, 1983. (MPAA Rating: R). Running time: 105 MINS.
Col. Rhodes ....Gene Hackman
MacGregor ....Roger Stack
Wilkes ....Fred Ward
Blaster ....Reb Brown

Sailor	Randall "Tex" Cobb
Scott	Patrick Swayze
Johnson	Harold Sylvester
Charts	Tim Thomerson
Lai Fun	Lau Nga Lai
Jiang	Kwan Hi Lim

All of the top talent involved — especially Gene Hackman — is hardly needed to make "Uncommon Valor" what it is, a very common action picture that should grind fine enough through the expected marketplaces.

Though produced by John Milius and Budd Feitshans, directed by Ted Kotcheff and written by Joe Gayton, "Valor" nonetheless has nothing to say that can be heard above the sound of gunfire. On the plus side, the picture does resort to less foolishness than usually required to enlist a ragtag band of soldiers on an impossible mission.

Hackman does as much as he can as a grieving father obsessed with the idea that his son remains a prisoner 10 years after he was reported missing-in-action in Vietnam. Financed by oil tycoon Robert Stack, whose son is also missing, Hackman puts together his small invasion force and two-thirds of "Valor" is consumed introducing the characters and putting them through various practice drills for the rescue which will predictably be tougher than they planned on.

Stateside, they manage to carry off their high-explosive rehearsals with a minimum of interest from their neighbors and the U.S. government, which is only around enough to complicate — but never thwart — their hopes of attacking a foreign nation.

True to a long tradition of war films, by the time the tough really get going it's only a question of who won't come back from the dangerous mission. But at least each of the main characters in "Valor" does his best to make you care whether it's him.

For the thoughtful, Hackman does quote a couple of lines of Julius Caesar before heading into battle, but not enough to get this one into the art houses. — *Har.*

Brontë
(U.S.- IRISH-COLOR-16m)

A Charlotte Ltd. Partnership production in association with Radio Telefis Eireann. Executive producers, Richard Seader, Maurice Levine. Produced by Sonny Fox. Directed by Delbert Mann. Stars Julie Harris (as Charlotte Brontë). Screenplay, William Luce; camera (color, 16m), Ken Murphy; editor, Martin Duffy; music, Arthur Harris; sound, Dermot Monyihan; production design, Alan Pleass; assistant director, Ronnie Patterson; wardrobe, Theresa Hughes; dialog coach, Christine Harger. Reviewed at Bruno Walter Auditorium, Lincoln Center, N.Y., Nov. 14, 1983. (No MPAA Rating). Running time: **88 MINS.**

"Brontë" is an engrossing and entertaining film of Julie Harris' one-woman show on the life of Charlotte Brontë. Handsomely filmed Sonny Fox production merits non-theatrical and tv exposure for discriminating audiences.

Adapted by playwright William Luce from his radio play "Currer Bell, Esq.," (Charlotte Brontë's pen name), "Brontë" differs from most filmed or taped transcriptions of one-man shows in its realistic lensing on location, with Irish exterior and house doubling convincingly for the Yorkshire setting. In this respect, the film has a precedent in Siobhan McKenna's 1971 "Here Are Ladies" (also filmed in Ireland). While McKenna's one-woman theater piece was augmented on film by supporting performances by Abbey Theatre players, Julie Harris appears solo here, suggesting the presence of Charlotte's father, servants or visitors on screen by handling both ends of conversations.

Picture takes place in 1849, when Charlotte has returned home to her father from her sister Anne's funeral. Recalling old grudges and a hard life which has taken all her siblings ("I've struck back with 'Jane Eyre,' " she notes regarding two sisters who died as children), Harris as Brontë uses props in the parsonage family home to jog her memory of earlier times. Marriage, "that obnoxious subject," is recalled as she wanders through an adjoining cemetery. Her father, Rev. Patrick Brontë, had opposed her getting married, and Charlotte reviews wistfully her unrequited near-affair with a married teacher in Brussels.

Artfully paced by Luce and director Delbert Mann, with moments of wit and light-hearted anecdotes balancing the serious mood, picture builds up a cumulative sense of loss as Brontë admonishes: "Don't knit human ties too closely; we must leave them someday." The colorful characters in her life: Aunt Branny, dissolute brother Branwell, sister Emily, fire & brimstone preacher William Grimshaw (her dad's predecessor in church) and others have passed on.

Using a slight but consistent accent, Harris gives an arresting performance, commanding attention with her voice rather than histrionics. She is ably abetted by Mann's subtle camera moves, natural-looking lighting through the house's windows and effective technical work by the Irish crew. Tinged with melancholy, this picture is a miniature treasure.—*Lor.*

The Body Is Willing
(HONG KONG-COLOR)

Hong Kong, Nov. 20.

A Golden Harvest presentation and release. Executive producer, Raymond Chow. Producer, Leonard Ho. Directed by David Lai. Stars Chen Wai-man, Emi (Amy) Shindo, Kaoru Oda, Michael Ling. Screenplay, George Ma; camera (color), Bob Thompson; editor, Cheung Yiu Chung; music, Michael Lai; theme song composed by Nobuyuki Sakuraba. Reviewed at State Theater, Hong Kong, Nov. 19, 1983. Running time: **98 MINS.** *(Cantonese soundtrack with English subtitles)*

The body may be willing but this limp piece of local erotica will not make it as a passable love story nor as soft core for overseas market. Started by local photographer-turned-director Ho Fan, another director (David Lai) was called in later to finish this oddity that combined a Japanese actress known for her screen purity (Amy Shindo) in her first daring role and charismatic, well-tattooed kungfu actor, Chen Wai-man. The idea is to create celluloid chemistry but this works better off than on screen. Nothing much can be said about this effort except its good hype and publicity stunt that helped at lot at the domestic b.o.

Shindo plays a middle-aged Japanese recording star on a promotional Hong Kong tour, accompanied by her spoiled sister (Kaoru Oda). Shindo meets her ex-lover, Chen, and the old flame burns again. For complications, a tycoon said to bed any celebrity he wishes for a price, is being given the cold treatment by the Japanese lady who's still carrying a torch for Chen, as proved by their unabashed semi-nude lovemaking in her hotel room.

Losing face, the tycoon resorts to dirty games to tarnish the image of the "lady." But all ends well as the Chen out fights them all in full fury during the final reel. Sadly, the love sequences look forced and the sensuous parts plain funny. Cast and director did try desperately to make a swinging pic, but succeeded only in making this sexploitation exercise look tediously ridiculous. — *Mel.*

Land Der Raeuber Und Gendarmen
(Land of Robbers and Gendarmes)
(WEST GERMAN-COLOR-16m)

Berlin, Dec. 3.

A Westallgaeuer Film Production. Features entire cast. Directed by Leo Hiemer and Klaus Gietinger. Screenplay, Gietinger; camera (color), Marian Czura; sound, Kurt Eggmann; music, Nightwork; editing, Wolfgang Raabe, Monika Theuner. Reviewed at Kant Kino, Berlin, Dec. 3, '83. Running time: **96 MINS.**

Cast: Anna Starke, Walter Nuber, Norbert Kerkhey, Anke Guenzel, Peter Krammer.

Leo Hiemer and Klaus Gietinger's "Land of Robbers and Gendarmes" appears at first glance to be a low budget offbeat "Heimatfilm" — that is, one of those mountain-greenery pics turned inside out by young German filmers to comment on German society as it is today. There's enough of that kind of social commentary in this personal spoof of one of the country's best known and best loved genres, but there's also much more: this is a satire on New German Cinema itself. It's a film about the making of an updated "Heimatfilm" in the lovely Allgäu region of southern Germany at the foot of the Alps.

Filmmaker happens to be known as Alexander Dummerle, a nom de plume, as it were, for Alexander Kluge, whose docus and essay-features are concerned primarily with sociopolitical problems in the contemporary Federal Republic of Germany. "Land of Robbers and Gendarmes" doesn't have a narrative line to speak of, but the figures are all too familiar in this provincial area and so too is the general film-theme of "Fascism and Growing War Danger." One has only to review the all-too-serious thematic content of NGC pics in the wake of Werner Herzog and Rainer Werner Fassbinder, Wim Wenders and Volker Schlöndorff, to note that the Left filmers in the movement have been steadily losing contact with the general public.

Film satires on NGC helmers appear to be becoming commonplace of late. Wolfgang Quest and Axel Voigt's "Warmest Congratulations" (1982) spoofed the popular worker, or proletariat, films of the last decade. Now Leo Hiemer and Klaus Gietinger have appeared on the scene with "Land of Robbers and Gendarmes," taking a potshot at the equally popular treatment of a genre that scores with the American Western as a perennial favorite. Perhaps a satire on femme filmers is in the offing, too.

"Robbers and Gendarmes," however, needs a great deal of savvy to unravel the in-jokes. Its weakness is the shucking of a story to sew all the loose ends together. Yet that, too, is pretty much in line with the nutcracker treatises on celluloid by Kluge & Co. — *Holl.*

Sei Zaertlich, Penguin
(Be Gentle, Penguin)
(WEST GERMAN-COLOR)

Berlin, Dec. 2.

A Regina Ziegler Film Production, Berlin. Features entire cast. Directed by Peter Hajek. Screenplay, Peter Weibel, Hajek, Fritz Mueller-Sherz; camera (color), Jacques Steyn; sets, Horst Furcht, Edwin Wengoborski; costumes, Katharina Schumacher; Reviewed at Berliner Werbung Screening Room, Berlin, Dec. 2, '83. Running time: **96 MIN.**

Cast: Marie Colbin (Nina), Heinz Hoenig (Mick), Petra Jokisch, Rainer Hunold, Helga Uhlig, Robert Schaefer, Andreas Mannkopff, Andre Heller.

Well-known in European film circles as a tv film reporter — whose Austrian-based series together with Helmut Dimko, "Apropos Film," has been aired over 100 times — Peter Hajek ventured for the first time into a feature film prod of his own with "Be Gentle, Penguin." Pic is a sex comedy with enough bare flesh to titillate, but it also has a satirical edge that spoofs such anomalies as matching "Lonely Hearts" by computerized tests and whatnot. The hero is also a macho type, a gym instructor, who can't satisfy his girlfriend from whatever angle or position he exercises on the mat.

The twist is in the title: when Mick catches on to the wiles and ways of being gentle in the love act, it turns out to be in a swimming pool — and he also drowns himself in the process. To make a long story short, the thorny path to mutual bliss is finally traversed with a goodly measure of wit and elan.

Credits are a cut above the average, particularly the lensing and thesping (Marie Colbin is a promising Austrian newcomer). What's lacking is a tighter script and that usual deficiency in German-funded pics, polished dialog. Yet Hajek as a debut helmer has scored higher than most Teutonic helmers this past season -- a name to watch. —Holl.

Teddy Baer
(SWISS-B&W)

Zurich, Nov. 27.

Rex Film AG Zollikon release of a Rolf Lyssy production. Written and directed by Lyssy. Stars Lyssy. Executive producer, Bernard Lang; coproducers, Eugen and Walter Schoch; camera (black and white), Hans Liechti; sound, Hans Kuenzi; art direction, Kathrin Brunner; editor, Helena Gerber; music, Bruno Spoerri; costumes, Yolanda Gambaro, Elisabeth Krog; lighting, Felix Meyer. Reviewed at the Movie 2, Zurich, Nov. 24, '83. Running time: 107 MINS.
Teddy Baer ....Rolf Lyssy
Loredana Reinhardt .....Renate Schroeter
Frank Klee ....Christoph Schwegler
Nelly Baer ....Erna Bruenell
Silvia Balsam ....Franziska Kohlund
Hugo Balsam ....Ueli Mueller
Otmar Fischli ....Walo Lueoend
Dr. Traber ....Inigo Gallo
Walter Otto Mueller............Edi Huber
Agnes Bosch................Yvonne Kupper
Mayor Steiger ....Hans Joachim Frick
Krummenacher......Hans Heinrich Ruegg
Barbara Wildhaupt ....Susanne Peter

Rolf Lyssy's 1978 comedy, "Die Schweizermacher" (The Swissmakers), became the alltime top Swiss boxoffice hit. Three years later, the Zurich director was not quite so lucky with another comedy, "Kassettenliebe" (Cassette Love), about a computerized marriage agency. Lyssy's latest entry, which he wrote, produced, directed and stars in, is "Teddy Baer" (not Bear), name of the leading character, a Swiss film director whose similarity to a helmer named Lyssy is certainly more than accidental.

The film opens with Baer winning a Best Foreign Film Oscar, Switzerland's first, for a (fictitious) film called "A Waltz For My Mother" (incidentally, the title of a script Lyssy worked on some years ago but which never materialized). In reality, Switzerland never won a Best Film Oscar, but was nominated three times: 1970 for Maximilian Schell's "First Love," 1973 for Claude Goretta's "The Invitation" and 1981 for Markus Imhoof's "The Boat Is Full."

After going through the expected hoopla as the new local celebrity, Baer tries to set up his next picture, "The Safe," about an actual, as yet unresolved robbery from the Zurich police headquarters, but finds that fame alone, even including an Oscar, fails to open the doors to financing. Although his name value is exploited in many ways, potential investors shy away from putting up the needed coin. Lyssy, of course, speaks from experience, his own as well as that of most other Swiss filmmakers, even with hit films to their names.

Finally, Baer cracks and is put away in a psychiatric clinic. After his recovery, he goes about a new project: the experiences of a Swiss film director who has just won an Oscar.

"Teddy Baer" was filmed in black and white, as a homage to Groucho Marx whom Lyssy personifies in one of the film's key sequences. Incidentally, poster art shows him in typical Groucho makeup, cigar and all, with an Oscar statuette in his hand.

Whether the general public will go for such a "filmmaker's film," filled with local inside gags and allusions to actual persons and institutions, seems questionable, at least outside Zurich where it was made. But Lyssy has the necessary light touch to bolster his story with visual gags and colorful characters. The opening sequence, for example, is a gem. Acting for the first time in front of the camera, Lyssy displays a surprisingly sure flair for comedy timing. The (too numerous) supporting roles range from average to below par. Hans Liechti's black and white lensing is pro, and Helena Gerber's tight editing is an asset. —Mezo.

D.C. Cab
(COLOR)

Strong holiday starter.

Hollywood, Dec. 9.

A Universal release of an RKO and Universal presentation in association with the Guber-Peters Co. Produced by Topper Carew. Coproducer, Cassius Vernon Weathersby. Executive producers, Peter Guber, Jon Peters. Features entire cast. Directed, screenplay by Joel Schumacher, story by Carew, Schumacher. Camera (Technicolor), Dean Cundey; editor, David Blewitt; music, Giorgio Moroder; production design, John J. Lloyd; art direction, Bernie Cutler; set decoration, Hal G. Gausman; costume design, Roberta Weiner; sound (Dolby), Will Yarbrough; assistant director, Newton D. Arnold; associate producer, Peter V. Herald; second unit directors, M. James Arnett, Alan Oliney; second unit camera, Rex Metz. Reviewed at Universal Studios, Universal City, Dec. 8, 1983. (MPAA Rating: R.) Running time: 90 MINS.
Albert ....Adam Baldwin
Tyrone ....Charlie Barnett
As Herself.....................Irene Cara
Myrna ....Anne De Salvo
Harold...........................Max Gail
Miss Floyd.................Gloria Gifford
Bongo Lennie ....DeWayne Jessie
Baba ....Bill Maher
Mr. Rhythm ....Whitman Mayo
Samson ....Mr. T
Mr. Bravo ....Jose Perez
Xavier....................Paul Rodriguez
Buzzy ....David Barbarian
Buddy ....Peter Barbarian
Ophelia ....Marsha Warfield
Dell ....Gary Busey
Cubby ....Bob Zmuda
Arnie ....Jim Moody
Denise....................Denise Gordy
Matty ....Alfredine P. Brown
Ambassador's Son ....Scott Nemes
Ambassador's Daughter ......Senta Moses
Claudette..................Jill Schoelen
Maudie ....Diana Bellamy

More funky than funny, "D.C. Cab" represents the only hip, youth-slanted comedy any of the studios are releasing this Christmas, and on that basis alone should provoke plenty of b.o. action over the next few weeks. Universal shrewdly moved up pic's opening date to capitalize on lack of similar competition, is prominently featuring the redoubtable Mr. T in its ads, and will undoubtedly also court black audiences, who will note that nearly half of the major roles are filled by blacks.

Premise is a comedy natural: a second-rate taxi company in the nation's capital forced to make do with dilapidated cars and a rag tag band of drivers finally rises to the occasion when threatened with possible extinction. To be sure, a diverse and colorful lot of characters has been assembled. Nominal head of the company is aging hippie Max Gail, who is married to aloof Jewish princess Anne De Salvo. Arriving on the scene is young enthusiastic innocent Adam Baldwin, who in the course of earning his hack's license makes the rounds with other drivers, who include jivey Charlie Barnett, Rastaman DeWayne Jessie, aspiring pimp Paul Rodriguez, musclemen David and Peter Barbarian, "token white" Gary Busey and Mr. T, who resents the fact that big-time pimps and pushers have more influence on the street than he does because of their glamorous cars.

Amiability of the characters and non-stop nature of the frenetic action is sufficient to make "D.C. Cab" a perfectly passable, even likable picture, but it's a pity that more effort wasn't expended in the direction of pumping up the laugh quotient. Dialog itself prompts very few laughs, and a quick rewrite by a gagman would have made a lot of difference.

Writer-director Joel Schumacher also seems to have bent over backward to avoid sociological or political humor. Seldom-used Washington, D.C. setting is of no intrinsic importance to the story and, except for a few glimpses of the White House, the Lincoln Memorial and Dulles Airport, pic could have been shot anywhere (and apparently was; some of the settings look like L.A., and much was lensed on the backlot).

Not that this film should have emphasized its politics-laden setting, but the unusual populace found in the city, with the country's movers and shakers (and international diplomatic community) on the one side and a mass of poor blacks on the other, clearly provides plenty of material for comic commentary which is unexploited here. A given monolog by Johnny Carson or Bob Hope includes more political barbs than are to be found here.

With a soundtrack so full of music, one also suspects a little room could have been found for some dancing, and perhaps for a little warbling by Irene Cara, who appears very briefly as herself in the back of a cab.

But these are all might-have-beens. Hijinx on view are harmless enough, and pic is carried by its energetic spirit. Performers carry on in uniformly broad style, a you-can-do-it attitude is espoused, and ending sends everyone out happy. It's a decent snack, if hardly a full meal. —Cart.

That Day, On The Beach
(TAIWAN-COLOR)

Taipei, Nov. 19.

A Central Motion Picture Corp. and Cinema City Co. production and release. Directed by Yang Teh-Chang. Stars Mao Hsuei-Wei, Sylvia Chang, Hsu Ming, Teresa Hu. Screenplay, Yang Teh-Chang, Wu Nieh-Chien; camera (color), Chang Huei Kung, Christopher Doyle; art director, Yang Teh Chang, Lee Pao Lin, Tu Da-Hsiung. Reviewed at the Asia-Pacific Film Festival, Taipei, Nov. 18, 1983. Running Time: 167 MINS.
(In Mandarin with English subtitles.)

Here's a mannered Taiwanese style of filmmaking that is an example of chic high fashion passivity in Asian movies.

"Beach" is a stylish, dreamily photographed, sensitively acted and intelligently presented mature Mandarin movie. Its inherent French-influenced ambiance could have worked against it in garnering more major awards besides best cinematography in the Asia Pacific International Film Festival as the jurors seem to have favored the more Taiwanese way of moviemaking.

"That Day, On The Beach" tells the story of two close friends (Sylvia Chang and Teresa Hu) who meet in Vienna after not seeing each other for years. Hu is now a

successful concert pianist and
Chang is a career woman with
business in Europe. During the reunion, they share and talk about
their childhood, reminisce and
mourn for their lost loves. Hu for
Chang's doctor brother, forced by
the strict family to marry somebody else, and Chang for her supposedly solid marriage that failed.

As if inspired by Nicolas Roeg's
fancy editing in "Bad Timing,"
Stanley Donen's marital disintegration in "Two For The Road"
and Alan Pakula's flashback style
in "Sophie's Choice," the film flits
smoothly from present to past, innocent childhood, insecure adolescence to worldly adulthood like a
smooth flow of loose summery
ideas

Long (almost three hours with a
ten-minute break) the lead actresses act out their roles with
ladylike elegance and suavity.
Slow paced like a romantic ballad,
there is nothing primitive here.
Chang's husband apparently disappeared one day on a deserted
beach (possible suicide), but his
death is never confirmed.

This artistic piece of artistic Taiwanese film should do well in festivals, college circuits and art
houses.—Mel.

The Man Who Loved
Women
(COLOR)

Major Burt Reynolds mis-
fire.

Hollywood, Dec. 9.

A Columbia Pictures release, produced by
Blake Edwards and Tony Adams. Directed
by Edwards. Exec producer, Jonathan D.
Krane. Stars Burt Reynolds, Julie Andrews.
Screenplay, Edwards, Milton Wexler, Geof-
frey Edwards; camera (Metrocolor), Haskell
Wexler; editor, Ralph E. Winters; sound,
Don Sharpless; production design, Roger
Maus; assistant director, Mickey McCardle;
associate producer, Gerald T. Nutting; art
direction, Jack Senter; music, Henry Manci-
ni. Reviewed at the Academy of Motion Pic-
ture Arts & Sciences, Beverly Hills, Dec. 9,
1983. (MPAA rating R.) Running time: 110
MINS.
David....................Burt Reynolds
Marianna................Julie Andrews
Louise....................Kim Basinger
Agnes....................Marilu Henner
Roy......................Barry Corbin
Courtney................Cynthia Sikes
Nancy..................Jennifer Edwards
Janet......................Sela Ward
Al........................Ben Powers
Svetlana..................Elle Bauer
Enid......................Denise Crosby

"The Man Who Loved Women"
may do for Burt Reynolds' girl-
chase films about what "Stroker
Ace" did for his car-chase films,
that is to say, not much. "Women"
is truly woeful, reeking of produc-
tion-line, big star filmmaking and
nothing else.

Once again, Reynolds appears
as the irresistible, yet sensitive,
modern man in search of something fulfilling in his life. Given his

good looks, charm and vivacity —
and in this case lots of money as a
successful sculptor — he is devilish-
ly attractive to women, but has a
problem with which one is for him,
a problem that has bothered him in
several other pictures.

This time, Reynolds' angst is ex-

Original Film
(L'Homme Qui Aimait Les
Femmes)
Paris, April 26.

UA release of Les Films Du Carrosse — UA
production, features entire cast. Directed by
Francois Truffaut. Screenplay, Truffaut,
Michel Fermaud, Suzanne Schiffman; cam-
era (Eastmancolor), Nestor Almendros,
editor, Martine Barraque-Curie; music,
Maurice Jaubert. Reviewed at Publicis,
Paris, April 18, '77. Running time: 119 MINS.
Bertrand....................Charles Denner
Genevieve..................Brigitte Fossey
Delphine..................Nelly Borgeaud
Helene..................Genevieve Fontanel
Martine....................Nathalie Baye
Bernadette................Sabine Glaser
Fabienne..................Valerie Bonnier
Vera......................Leslie Caron
Liliane....................Nella Barbier

amined in flashback from his
funeral in the words of his psychiatrist, Julie Andrews. And they
are terrible words, to be sure.
From the start, the psychobabble
she spouts is so stilted and stupid
that it raises false hopes that
"Women" must surely be a satire,
and perhaps a promising one. Then
the terrible realization sets in that
her dialog is supposed to be taken
seriously, right to the fadeout with
the audience finally groaning
laughs in desperation.

As Andrews rambles through
Reynolds' romantic past, there's
an unpleasant feeling for about an
hour that this film is never going
to get started, followed for another
50 minutes by the equally unpleasant feeling that it may never
end.

Had not director Blake Edwards
been fooling around with an
"American extension" of François
Truffaut's 1977 film of the same title, there probably was a better
picture contained here in Reynolds' one really amusing sojourn
into a bemused, adulterous affair
with Kim Basinger.

She's great as Houston millionaire Barry Corbin's kinky wife,
given to stopwatch dalliances in
dangerous places. But even this
joke is a bit overdone. The sequence does, however, introduce a
wonderful bit player — Ben Powers — as a garage attendant who
completely steals a scene from the
star. At any rate, the Basinger romance remains the one segment
that demonstrates those involved
might have come up with an
acceptable attitude otherwise
missing from the entire project.

"Women" also has one of those
annoying plot-turns that's used
just enough to get past the moment
and then largely ignored for the remainder. Together in her high-rise

office, Reynolds and Andrews are
suddenly rocked by an enormously powerful earthquake that makes
them realize their real romantic
interest in each other.

The quake sways the office, dis-
lodges furniture and undoes the
paintings. But once it's over, of
course, they resume their chat
with no thought that perhaps the
world outside has come to an end.
And sure enough, it hasn't since for
the rest of the picture, there's no
sign in L.A. or Beverly Hills that a
grain of sand has ever shifted.

Ultimately, Reynolds' libido
costs him his life, prompting Andrews to observe, "Well, there you
have it. It's finally over." Finally,
indeed. —Har.

Signes Exterieurs
de Richesse
(Outer Signs of Wealth)
(FRENCH-COLOR)

Paris, Dec. 6.

GEF/CCFC release of a Via Produc-
tions/GEF/TF 1 coproduction. Produced by
Christian Ferlet. Stars Claude Brasseur, Jo-
siane Balasko, Jean-Pierre Marielle. Direct-
ed by Jacques Monnet. Screenplay, Monnet,
Alain Godard; camera (Eastmancolor), Phil-
ippe Welt; art director, Serge Douy;
costumes, Annie Perier; sound, Alain
Lachassagne; editor, Pierre Gillette; music,
Johnny Hallyday, Pierre Billon, Eric Bouad.
Production manager, George Valon. Re-
viewed at the U.G.C. Biarritz Theatre, Paris,
Dec. 5, 1983. Running time: 90 MINS.
Gigi......................Claude Brasseur
Beatrice..................Josiane Balasko
Bouvier..................Jean-Pierre Marielle
Sylvie..................Charlotte de Turckheim
Gerard..................Roland Giraud

"Signes Exterieurs de Richesse"
is a routine romantic comedy that
fails to make the most of a good
comic situation. Claude Brasseur
is a well-to-do socialite veterinarian thrown into a tailspin by a
young neophyte tax inspector,
played by Josiane Balasko, the
plump, bespectacled cafe-theatre
writer-performer. To save his
bank account, Brasseur resorts to
seduction and, when that fails, attempts emotional blackmail by
performing a mock operation on
Balasko's cherished mutt. The
plan works in a way not intended
and Brasseur and Balasko wind up
in each other's arms.

Script by director Jacques Monnet and Alain Godard steers occasionally toward promising farce
complications, but the interest is
more in sentimental attractions of
two utterly dissimilar characters.
Only notes of welcome absurdity
are struck by the reliably amusing
Jean-Pierre Marielle, as Bras-
sour's quack accountant, and
Charlotte de Turckheim and
Roland Giraud, as a couple who divorce for tax benefits.

Pic doesn't size up as a strong-
enough Gallic comedy for Anglo-
Saxon markets. — Len.

Le Grand Carnaval
(The Big Carnival)
(FRENCH-COLOR)

Paris, Dec. 8.

Gaumont release of a Partner's Produc-
tion/Alexandre Films/Carthago Films/TF 1
Films/Soprofilms/SFPC coproduction. Produced by Ariel Zeitoun. Stars Philippe Noiret,
Roger Hanin. Directed by Alexandre Arcady.
Screenplay, Arcady, Alain Le Henry, Daniel
Saint-Hamon; camera (color), Pierre
Lhomme; production designer, Jacques Buf-
noir; music, Serge Franklin; editor, Joelle
Van Effenterre; sound, Guillaume Sciama;
costumes, Mic Cheminal and Ugo Pericoli;
second unit director, Luc Besson; executive
producer, Tarak Ben Ammar; production
manager, Michel Frichet. Reviewed at the
Gaumont Ambassade Theater, Paris, Dec. 7,
1983. Running time: 130 MINS.
Etienne Labrouche.........Philippe Noiret
Leon Castelli..............Roger Hanin
Sylvette Landry............Fiona Gelin
Norbert Castelli.........Jean-Pierre Bacri
Gaby Atlan................Gerard Darmon
Walter Giammanco.........Peter Riegert
Armande Labrouche.........Macha Meril
Simone Castelli.........Marthe Villalonga
Pierre-Marie Labrouche....Patrick Bruel
Remy Castelli.............Richard Berry
Hendricks................Edward Meeks
Benjamin Fitoussi.........Jean Benguigi

Alexandre Arcady checks in
with the third (and supposedly)
last instalment of his "Pied-Noir"
sagas, dealing with the mores and
manners of Algerians of French
extraction. Arcady struck boxoffice gold with his 1979 debut, "Le
Coup de Sirocco," which tapped a
huge audience of repatriates from
North Africa after Algerian independence in 1962. He was promptly offered a far larger budget for
his second film, "The Big Pardon," a kind of Jewish "Godfather" opus, in which Arcady's
modest talents as a minority
chronicler were lost in production
gloss and poor genre cribbing.

"Le Grand Carnaval" is even
bigger in concept and execution,
aspiring to fresco proportions in its
depiction of a small town in Algeria at the moment of the Allied invasion of North Africa in 1942. Arcady again falls back on his knowledge of Hollywood movies to compose the gallery of American soldier types who figure in the action.

The Yank silhouettes, however,
are basically present as dramatic
catalysts, as their liberation of a
sleepy Algerian town — film was
mostly shot in Bizerte, Tunisia —
throws its inhabitants into a semi-
anarchic state. With his usual co-
scripters, Alain Le Henry and
Daniel Saint-Hamon, Arcady has
attempted a serio-comic mosaic of
individual response and comportment.

The film is ambitious and, technically, it is sound. But Arcady is
not up to the task of sweeping
socio-historical impressionism.

He is more at home with vignettes of Algerian regulars. Roger
Hanin is once again on hand as the
director's quintessential "Pied-
Noir," big-hearted and big-
mouthed, a direct descendant of a
Raimu personage from a Marcel

Pagnol comedy. In fact, the spirit of Pagnol hovers over some of the film's best comic moments, truculent and chuckly, even if much of it may now seem familiar.

Hanin faces off costar Philippe Noiret. Hanin is a local barkeep who's tagged by a business-minded GI (Peter Riegert, in the most substantial and appealing of the Yank roles) as collaborator in a black market operation. Noiret is the town mayor and a prosperous colonialist.

While Hanin goes about setting up a thriving night spot in an abandoned hangar, Noiret is going through male menopause crisis. He begins an affair with his uninhibited young governess (played by lovely newcomer Fiona Gelin), but his wife (Macha Meril) gets wind of the liaison and throws Gelin out. Hanin takes her in as a waitress, which immediately creates tension between Hanin and Noiret, both friends from childhood (Hanin's mother had been a domestic at Noiret's family estate).

The resolution of the quarrel reflects the sentimentality of the script. Hanin's club is smashed up one night by a gang of hired thugs. Hanin immediately suspects Noiret behind the act, loads his shotgun and heads for the estate with murder on his mind. But when he gets there he learns of the death of Noiret's father, who has left a confession revealing he'd had an affair with Hanin's mother and that the barkeep and the mayor are half-brothers. The two forget their differences and social standing and become inseparable companions.

A constellation of minor characters rotates around these central situations, and depend much on the talents of the performers. Fortunately, Arcady has rounded up a solid supporting cast, including Gerard Darmon, Jean-Pierre Bacri, Richard Berry (in a late cameo as one of Hanin's sons, an Allied fighter pilot who returns home to fall in love and marry Gelin) and Martha Villalonga, again playing Hanin's boisterous mate (as she did in "Coup de Sirocco").

Credits list as second unit director Luc Besson, a young director who debuted last year with the promising low-budget, black-and-white sci-fi actioner, "The Last Combat," and one assumes he played a considerable part in the staging of the more spectacular sequences, like the opening landing of Allied forces on an isolated Algerian beach.

Arcady has also been skillfully aided by lenser Pierre Lhomme and production designer Jacques Bufnoir, who help make this Arcady's best-looking production. Pic is no doubt a good ad for exec producer Tarak Ben Ammar, who runs Tunisia's studio facilities operation, and who coproduced under his Carthago Films.

Despite its deep-running dramatic weaknesses, "Le Grand Carnaval" has enough polish, vivacity and exotic aspects to make it viable in the international marketplace. — Len.

Sag Nein!
(Say No!)
(W. GERMAN-COLOR-DOCU)

Berlin, Dec. 1.

A coproduction of the Freie Film Redaktion, Hamburg, and the Pro-jekt Filmproduktion im Filmverlag der Autoren, Munich. Produced with means of the Hamburg Film Fund. Executive producer Michael Bittins (Radiant Film). Directed by Stefan Aust. Camera (color), Eckhard Dorn, Reiner Schaeffer, Lucas Maria Boehmer, Josef Vilsmeier BVK, Peter Maiwald BVK, Nils Bolbrinker; editing, Barbara Hennings, Maria Jonderko. Reviewed at Kant-Kino, Berlin, Dec. 1, '83. Running time: 100 MINS.
With (in alphabetical order): Joan Baez, Christoph Bantzer, Harry Belafonte, Wolf Biermann, Jeanne Bitschewskaja, bots, Lubov Carsianovskaja, Franz Josef Degenhardt, Ida Ehre, Maria Farantouri, Fasia, Udo Lindenberg & his Panikorchester, Liederjan, Gisela May, Nuova Compagnia di Cato Popolare, Gianna Nannini, Peter Ruehmkorf, Irmgard Schleier, Hanna Schwarz, Hannes Wader, Konstantin Wecker, Floyd Westerman, the Hamburger Friedenschor, and others.

Subtitled "A Concert for Peace," Stefan Aust's docu on a Hamburg concert in September draws upon a well-known peace statement by Wolfgang Borchert for its highly emotional and exclamatory title: "Say No!" This poetic piece of antiwar literature was read at the concert by the respected Ida Ehre, actress and director, who produced the related Wolfgang Borchert play, "Draussen vor der Tuer" (The Man Outside), in 1947 at her Hamburg Kammerspiele theater.

Ehre was one of approximately 100 singers, performers and artistic and literary personalities from European (East as well as West) and North and South American countries, all of whom assembled in the German port city as part of the Peace Movement initiative throughout the so-called "hot autumn" (referring to mounting demonstrations to protest the installation of both Pershing missiles and SS-20s).

A Peace Concert in Hamburg deserves attention for any number of reasons, but not the least of which was the disastrous bombing attack by the Allies in late summer of 1943 — 55,000 died in the fire-storm that raged for 10 nights. Thus, the docu opens with an archival recollection of that event — almost 40 years to the day — and pairs these destructive scenes with peace protests occurring almost daily across Germany in Mutlangen, Bitburg, and elsewhere.

Further, the concert attracted some 50,000 for the 12-hour program on the Heiligengeistfeld meadow (also site of the beginnings of West German TV) before the old bunker surviving the war, where the stage was erected. Aust's team of cameramen worked as agilely as can be expected in this post-Woodstock age — in fact, he appears to have 10 times the amount of footage necessary to record the event, and easily could have assembled a sequel Part II (featuring footage regretfully dropped from Part I).

The stars of the show were such name performers as Harry Belafonte (the key figure in today's peace concerts), Joan Baez, and Floyd Westerman from the States, along with Udo Lindenberg (leading pop star in both West and East Germany), as well as Franz Josef Degenhardt, Konstantin Wecker and Wolf Biermann from West Germany. To these should be added East European performers: Gisela May (East Germany), Cieslav Niemen (Poland), Jeanne Bitschewskaja and Lubov Carsianovskaja (both from the Soviet Union). There were moments of "solidarity" with Chilean exiles and anti-atomic-weapon soldiers in the West German Army. With such personalities on display, "Say No!" is assured of a supportive run in German and European cinemas from the preem in mid-November until a possible wind-down via Sov-Yank negotiations.

Docu is exceptional for topnotch lensing of event and editing of footage. — Holl.

London Film Festival

Celso and Cora
(AUSTRALIAN-FILIPINO-DOCU-COLOR)

London, Nov. 26.

A Gary Kildea Films production in association with Australian Film Commission, Institute of Philippine Culture and N-AV Productions (Tokyo). Produced, directed, photographed (color), and edited by Gary Kildea. Reviewed at London Film Festival, Nov. 25, '83. Running time: 109 MINS.

Australian documentarian Gary Kildea observes the lives of a young Filipino couple in "Celso and Cora," his first feature-length endeavor. The film arrives at the London fest already acclaimed with top honors at the Nyon and Chicago festivals. Therefore, it's a bit of a shock to discover a rather straight-forward and overly long production which attempts to capture the nature of the extreme poverty of the principals.

The couple ekes out an existence at odd jobs including selling cigarettes in front of a fashionable Manila hotel. However, what they earn never attains the full intended impact. Certainly, their one-room hovel suggests a modest income but Kildea fails to establish either a comparison to western standards or a disperity of wealth within the city.

Instead, there is scene after scene examining their mundane daily routine. In the course of almost two hours, the couple separates, is reunited, discovers their son has pneumonia and is malnourished and Celso encounteres a city ban forcing him from his favored location. Apart from the Tagalog dialog, the situations might easily exist in any major metropolis.

Result is neither satisfying in its observation or social implications. It's just so much talk and not enough resolution. And lacking contrast, the film fails too as an ethnographic study.

Kildea's one-man filmmaking operation shows some strain in the technical departments of "Celso and Cora." Length, subtitles and a lack of tension contribute to a very limited theatrical future. Television sales prospects are only slightly better despite the prestige the film has thus far received on the festival circuit. —Klad.

Farmers Arms
(BRITISH-COLOR)

London, Dec. 2.

A BBC Television production. Produced by Ann Scott. Directed by Giles Foster. Features entire cast. Screenplay, Nick Darke; camera (color), Nat Crosby; editor, Clare Douglas; music, Ilona Sekacz. Reviewed at London Film Festival, Nov. 29, 1983. Running time: 60 MINS.
Geoff....................Philip Jackson
Wally.........................Colin Welland
Mrs. Casson.................Brenda Bruce
Sherman....................Ray Charleson
Carol.......................Rowena Roberts
Harry......................Mary MacLeod
Alvin.................Kenneth MacDonald
Mr. Brown.................Jonathan Cecil

Though its concerns are substantial, the television format of "Farmers Arms" lessens its impact. Set in a small seaside village in Cornwall, and with rather too many characters for its short running time to accommodate, it's about the impact of a U.S. Marine base on the neighborhood and the discovery that nuclear weapons are stored there. Geoff, a local farmer in love with Carol, who works in the gas station, is jealous of Sherman, a Yank who starts dating his girl. Sherman himself is perturbed by his own pacifist sentiments, at odds with his training. And a middle-aged woman, Mrs. Casson, disrupts a village meeting being addressed by Mr. Brown, who's from The Ministry, when he suggests that Britain could survive a nuclear war.

Best scene in film is the village meeting, with beautiful performances from Brenda Bruce as the anti-nuclear activist and Jonathan

Cecil (looking and acting very much like that past stalwart of English cinema, Richard Wattis) as the Man from the Ministry. Also very good is Colin Welland, better known as a screenwriter ("Chariots of Fire"), as a local landowner.

But none of these intriguing elements is given time to develop: here, surely was material for a feature-length contemporary comedy, with stubborn Cornish villagers standing fast against U.S. Marines —the sort of territory, in fact, that "Local Hero" mined so effectively. As it is, the film never really gets off the ground, and finally it just peters out into a non-ending. Pity, because all the elements were there, and the talent, for a fine movie. —*Strat.*

Kukurantumi - The Road To Accra
(GHANAIAN-COLOR)

London, Nov. 18.
IP Verlag and Filmproduktion in association with Afromovies Ltd and North German Television. Produced by Peter Wohlgemuth-Reinery. Directed by King Ampaw. Screenplay, Ampaw, Ralf Franz, Thilo Kline; camera, (color), Eckhard Dorn; editor, Anja Cox; music, Amartey Hedzoleh; production design, Harry F. Banks; sound, Winfried Bornschein; set design, Charles Ansong, Kobina Smith. Reviewed at the BFI Preview Theatre, London, Nov. 16, 1983. Running time, 83 MINS.
```
Addey ................Evans Oma Hunter
Abena ........................Amy Oppiah
Bob ........................David Dontoh
Mary ....................Dorothy Ankomah
Mensah......................George Wilson
Kofi ....................Ernest Youngman
Seewaa ........................Rose Flynn
Boafo ................Felix Asant Larbi
Alhaji ......................Kwesi France
Old Man ..................Emmi L. Lawson
```

"Kukurantumi," the feature debut of German film school trained Ghanaian helmer King Ampaw, is a low key item with plenty of dramatic interest. Pic is accessible for non-African audiences, but lacks sufficient thrills to promise b.o. performance.

Pic's theme is the contrast between the noise and corruption of Ghana's capital city of Accra and the steadier pace of life in rural Kukurantumi. The central character is a truck driver who carries passengers between the two places.

When the truck comes to grief, the driver Addey has to hawk the stolen watches of a jailed friend and offer his daughter in marriage to a wealthy merchant in order to secure the funds for a new machine. The girl flees with her boyfriend, Bob, to Accra, where she holes up with a mutual friend who has taken to whoring to survive.

The film, which runs at the pace of tv soap, ends with the girl reconciled to the ways of the city, and setting up home with the merchant from whom she formerly fled.

Professional actor Evans Oma Hunter gives a standout performance as the father divided between loyalty to family and friends, and the need to survive. Other performers, mostly amateurs, make an uneven showing.

Filmed by a largely German crew, the pic looks stylish.
—*Japa.*

Med Allt A Hreinu
(On Top)
(ICELANDIC-COLOR)

London, Dec. 5.
A Bjarmaland s.f. production, produced by Jakob Magnusson. Features entire cast. Directed by Agust Gudmundsson. Screenplay, Studemenn, Gudmundsson; camera (Eastmancolor), David Bridges; editor, William Diver; art director, Anna Th. Rognvaldsdottir; music, Studmenn, Grylurnar. Reviewed at London Film Festival, Dec. 4, 1983. Running time: 102 MINS.
With: Egill Olafsson, Ragnhildur Gisladottir, Eggert Thorleifsson, Jakob Magnusson, Anna Bjornsdottir, Valgeir Gudjonsson, Tomas Tomasson, Thordur Arnason, Asgeir Oskarsson.

A musical from Iceland has to be a novelty, and though "On Top" is a very slight affair it has the merits of good humor and bouncy music. Inspiration seems to be the pop films of nearly 20 years ago that launched The Beatles and The Dave Clark Five, though level of comedy and invention here is comparatively low.

Slight plotline has a mixed girl-boy group split up and go separate ways, with the girls trying to grab gigs away from the boys. Musical numbers aren't confined to the concerts themselves as the characters break into song at every opportunity, and so do the people they meet (there are even singing cops!)

Film has apparently been a big hit in Iceland, where its director, Agust Gudmundsson, is known as a pioneer, having helmed the very first Icelandic feature film, "Land And Sons" as recently as 1980; this is his third effort.

Despite pleasant musical numbers, appealing players, bright photography and unusual locales, film won't make much of an impact internationally. Storyline, which has been thin from the beginning, simply stops when the male group arrive in Copenhagen thinking they've got a date at the Tivoli (it was a hoax on the part of the girls). They arrive, and the film simply stops, making for a frustrating finale.—*Strat.*

Acceptable Levels
(BRITISH-COLOR)

London, Dec. 2.
Frontroom Productions, with Belfast Film Workshop. No producer credit. Directed by John Davies. Features entire cast. Screenplay, Gordon Hann, Ellin Hare, Alastair Herron, Kate McManus, Robert Smith, Davies;

camera (color), Smith; editor, Hare; art directors, Herron, McManus, Smith; additional music, Nick Garvey. Reviewed at British Film Institute Theatrette, London, Nov. 30, 1983. Running time: 103 MINS.
```
Sue ........................Kay Adshead
Simon ....................Andy Rashleigh
Tony McAteer.............Patrick Higgins
Roisin McAteer ............Tracey Lynch
Kathleen McAteer .......Sally McCaffery
Frank McAteer..............George Shane
Major Green ................Paul Jesson
Jill ......................Frances Barber
Andy......................Ina McElhinney
Ricky ....................Derek Halligan
Lawrence ....................Doyne Byrd
Father Docherty ........Michael Gormley
```

A scathing attack on the way the British media, specifically television, operates in Northern Ireland, "Acceptable Levels" is for the most part a strong, gutsy film about the making and un-making of a tv documentary.

A BBC team is making a series of programs on Britain's children: one episode is to be set in Belfast and to concentrate on the effect of the "troubles" on kids. Sue, a researcher, becomes friendly with the McAteer family whose young daughter, Roisin, she sees as typifying the attitudes of Catholic children. Simon, a celebrated producer, arrives, and a local camera/sound crew is hired.

During the filming of an interview in the McAteer home there's trouble outside in the street: one of the child's girlfriends is dead, apparently killed by a plastic bullet. The crew films the body, and later interviews other children who accuse the British soldiers of firing indiscriminately into the crowd and who also deny there was any kind of riot, which the British claim was the reason for the shooting. However, back in London, Simon gives way to various subtle pressures (mostly of his own making), and the dynamic footage ends up on the cutting room floor.

All of this is powerfully told, and much of it rings true. The setting-up of the interview, the presence of soldiers and subtly bullying police in the streets, the tv crew enjoying excellent food and wine in their hotel after a hard day in the slums — details like these are forcefully presented. It's unfortunate, then, that the film's impact is blunted by excessive length and discursiveness, problems also to be found in John Davies' previous film about Ireland, "Maeve." No less than six writers worked on "Acceptable Levels," and it shows: there are clear indications of a "committee" at work behind the scenes instead of one filmmaker's personal vision. Consequently, the film rambles along for the first 40 minutes or so, and includes scenes which work in themselves but which add nothing to the overall film and could easily be excised. Editor Ellin Hare wasn't nearly ruthless enough. An added problem is that in some of these early scenes the Belfast accents are virtually impenetrable:

English subtitles seem mandatory for screenings outside Ireland.

With some modifications, "Acceptable Levels" could attract quite a wide audience; certainly festivals are indicated. But this is one of those instances where a little less would be very much more. Acting is very good down the line, and the camerawork of Davies' long-time collaborator Robert Smith is tops.
—*Strat.*

Seventeen
(DOCU-COLOR)

London, Nov. 20.
A De Mott/Kreines Film Production. Produced, directed, photographed and edited by Joel De Mott and Jeff Kreines. Production assistant, Peter Esmonde. Reviewed at the London Film Festival Nov. 19, 1983. Running time: 112 MINS.

"Seventeen" is an intriguing documentary film that offers an insider's perspective on a group of working class kids as they pass through their final year of high school in the Indiana town of Muncie.

The project was commissioned as part of the "Middletown" series for PBS, but shelved because of the bad language and immoral behavior depicted in the film.

However, nothing in the pic, which was made by two filmmakers who lived with their subjects for a continuous 12-month period, rings untrue. And although the kids are rude to their teachers, smoke dope and get drunk, the portrait of the community is sympathetic.

Central character in the docu is a hyperactive girl whose relationship with a black schoolfriend causes many problems. Although she postures somewhat to the cameras, the result is candid and revealing.

Concentration throughout is on the white community and how it relates to fellow blacks in scenes that include uproarious cooking and government classes, basketball matches and a drunken "kegger" orgy.

Dramatic themes such as the pregnancy of a black schoolgirl and a fatal car accident are followed through within the pic which, nevertheless, remains episodic in structure. — *Japa.*

The Weather In The Streets
(BRITISH-COLOR)

London, Dec. 2.
Rediffusion Films production, with BBC Television and Britannia TV. Executive producer, David Nicholas Wilkinson. Produced by Alan Shallcross. Directed by Gavin Millar. Features entire cast. Screenplay, Julian Mitchell, from novel by Rosamond Lehmann; camera (color), John Hooper; editor, Angus Newton; music, Carl Davis; art director, Don Homfray; costume designer, Amy Roberts. Reviewed at London Film Festival, Nov. 30, 1983. Running time: 133 MINS.

Rollo	Michael York
Olivia	Lisa Eichhorn
Kate	Joanna Lumley
Etty	Rosalind Ayres
Lady Spencer	Faith Brook
Mrs. Curtis	Isabel Dean
Mr. Curtis	Sebastian Shaw

Whatever attributes the original novel possessed, this film version of "The Weather In The Streets" is very much ado about very little. It takes almost two and a quarter hours to tell a very old story indeed: in the period between the wars, a vivacious young woman, Olivia, has an affair with a married man, gets pregnant, has an abortion, and winds up alone, sadder but wiser.

Hardly world-shattering material these days, even with first-class production values and a stalwart cast of British actors. Former film critic Gavin Millar, who now works in television, brings little that's fresh to what are essentially hoary old clichés, and his pacing is exceptionally slow.

The film's one plus, and it's a major one, is the fabulous performance of Lisa Eichhorn as Olivia. The actress has never been better, and makes basically mundane material come alive in a way that's wonderful to watch. Radiant when she's in love, she is subsequently heart-rending when reduced to the pain and fear and indignity of a back-street abortion. Eichhorn is so very good that it's even more saddening that her work is to be found in such a predictable and lethargic context. —Strat.

Mandi
(Market Place)
(INDIAN-COLOR)

London, Dec. 2.

A Blaze Film Enterprises production. Produced by Freni M. Variava, Lalit M. Bijlani. Directed by Shyam Benegal. Features entire cast. Screenplay, Shama Zaidi, Pt. Satyadev Dubey, Benegal; camera (color), Ashok Mehta; editor, Bhanudas Divkar; music, Vandraj Bhatia. No other credits provided. Reviewed at London Film Festival, Dec. 1, 1983. Running time: 163 MINS.

Rukmani-bai	Shabana Azmi
Zeetnat	Smita Patil
Tungrus	Naseeruddin Shah
Agarwal	Saeed Jaffrey
Gupta	Kulbhushan Kharbanda
Basanthi	Veena Gupta
Nadira	Soni Razdan
Kamli	Ila Arun
Photographer	Om Puri
Mrs. Shantivedi	Gita Siddarth

Shyam Benegal is, internationally speaking, one of the top three Indian directors (with Satyajit Ray and Mrinal Sen); his latest film, "Market Place" is an interesting development for him, and not an entirely satisfactory one.

Pic could almost be re-titled "The Best Little Whorehouse In North India;" set in a small provincial town, it's about a brothel which has seen better days. However, this appears to be a uniquely Indian institution: prostitutes also entertain local dignitaries with erotic songs and dances, and the place also acts a kind of home for dispossessed girls, who are, nevertheless, expected to take part in the usual activities.

When the film begins, the Madam (Shabana Azmi) is under pressure from Mrs. Shantivedi (Agita Siddarth), leader of the Women's Reform Group (and the kind of moral crusader to be found the world over) to close the brothel down. Gupta (Kulbhushan Kharbanda), a slightly shady developer, is buying up the land, and the town is due for redevelopment: the municipal council, many of whose members have been customers over the years, now want the place closed too. Gupta offers the Madam some cheap land he bought outside the town limits, so she and the girls pack up and go off to start anew, but it proves to be the end of an era. Matters are complicated by the fact that the brothel's leading "star," Zeetnat (the splendid Smita Patil) has caught the eye of the callow young son of a local bigwig, not knowing she's actually his half-sister.

Script is based on a short story, obviously much expanded for this overlong film. There is some very broad comedy, involving a laughably inept cop, which doesn't play well by Western standards, and the mystical elements in the final reel are, for the uninitiated, rather obscure. For the most part, though, it's a fascinating film, filled with interesting characters and some of India's best actors. Plenty of songs, too, which add to rather than detract from the story, as they're well integrated. As mentioned, some comedy scenes don't work, and two long, drunken monologs from Naseeruddin Shah, playing the brother's simple-minded factotum, are a trial.

Shot in rich colors by Ashok Mehta, the film looks great, though the print caught had uncomfortably noisy patches on the soundtrack. Theatrical potential outside Indian audience territories looks to be iffy because of film's length and obscurities, though the Benegal reputation will help. Incidentally, for a film about prostitution, the film contains not even a single kiss.—Strat.

Leipzig Film Fest

Aufstehen Und Widerset-zen
(Stand Up and Resist)
(W. GERMAN-COLOR-DOCU-16m)

Leipzig, Nov. 24.

A documentary by Klaus Volkenborn and Johann Feindt, West Berlin. Camera (color), Feindt, Klaus Schrader, Lothar Woite, Norbert Bunge; editing, Volkenborn. Reviewed at Leipzig Film Fest, Nov. 24, '83. Running time: 85 MINS.

With "Concert for Peace" performances by Udo Lindenberg & the Panikorchester, Franz Josef Degenhardt, bots, and others.

Docu filmers from West Berlin, Klaus Volkenborn and Johann Feindt, are not new to the Leipzig Fest of political shorts and documentaries. They won a top honor in 1979 for "Irreconcilable Memoires," dealing with the Spanish Civil War and the Nazi Condor Legion; were on hand again in 1982 with "Henry Ford, or What Is a Man Worth?" and won another fest prize this year (a Golden Dove) for "Stand Up and Resist."

"Stand Up and Resist" records a "Concert for Peace" show in the spacious Waldbühne for the May 1982 Peace Concert, which forms the backbone of the film (title stemming from a song sung by the bots pop-group from the Netherlands). The rest of the film is polemical in using editing techniques to make fun of the Reagan visit in particular, but this team hardly matches such gifted docu satirists as Chris Marker and Alexander Kluge.

Save for a comment by one of the performers at the beginning of the docu — "we're against atomic weapons on both East and West" — one might gather that the filmmakers have greased the pan to point the blaming finger at only the Reagan Administration. It's also more than suspect to see political figures from the Berlin Senate used as additional bait-material, considering that this peace concert is being conducted in West Berlin with full permission of a democratic society and government. Going after Big Game is considered fair play by a free press, while aiming one's docu sights lower at the local gentry only serves to narrow the scope of the message down to personal prejudices.

Lastly, what the performers have to say in their songs and dramatic readings is more than enough for a film on "Artists for Peace." Why should the filmmakers hog the floor for their own sequestered statements? If the reader is interested in giving a peace concert the onceover, then the tip of the scales goes to Stefan Aust's "Say No!" —Holl.

No More Hibakusha
(CANADIAN-COLOR-DOCU-16m)

Leipzig, Nov. 22.

A National Film Board of Canada Production, Montreal. Written, directed and photographed (color), by Martin Duckworth. Editing, Huguette Laperrierre. Reviewed at Leipzig Film Fest, Leipzig, Nov. 22, '83. Running Time: 56 MINS.

Docus on Hiroshima and the dropping of the first atom bomb on a civilian population tend to be pretty grisly experiences, particularly since the American State Dept. has recently granted permission for archival use of film footage shot by Yank cameramen shortly after the bombing of the Japanese city. Martin Duckworth approaches the issue from a different angle in "No More Hibakusha," one that appeals to humanity through eyewitness accounts by survivors. This National Film Board prod received support from church groups and was far and away one of the most moving and sensitive pics shown at the Leipzig Fest of political docus.

The handful of Hiroshima survivors are shown, first, at their daily routines. Then the commentary makes clear that many have kept silent about their status, for the simple reason that the stigma of "hibakusha" makes them and their children and grandchildren outcasts in their own society. Since radiation afflictions can be passed on from generation to generation in some cases, the children of a victim (as shown in the film) are not considered appropriate marriage partners. Others are now bedridden and are dying a slow and painful death — nearly four decades later.

The occasion for the making of the docu was a Peace March in New York, to which Hiroshima survivors were invited in order to hear them tell their stories amid church and social groups engaged in the cause of peace and against the use of atomic weapons. It's rather remarkable to hear some American youngsters in these talk sessions express nearly total ignorance on what the Hiroshima bomb meant in physical and human destruction. But the courage it took for the survivors to talk about the tragedies to their families is even more remarkable, for (as stated) it is the Japanese sense of "shame" that has kept them silent all these years.

When one of the survivors talks of trying to save an older sister from the wreckage of their home, together with another sister who was shortly to die from her own wounds, the story and its retelling try the man's courage to the utmost. He was a primary schoolboy when the bomb fell, whose scars go far deeper into his person than just the physical wounds on his body. One listens humbly, —Holl.

Wien Retour
(Return To Vienna)
(AUSTRIAN-COLOR-DOCU-16m)

Leipzig, Nov. 22.

A documentary Film by Ruth Beckermann and Josef Aichholzer, featuring interview with writer Franz West (Weintraub) on the period 1924-1934. Only credits available. Reviewed at Leipzig Film Fest, Leipzig, Nov.

22, '83. Running time: 96 MINS.
With Franz West (Weintraub).

Docus dealing with historical personalities often suffer from a sheer lack of shooting time to allow the one being interviewed to unspool his biographical story at his own leisure and in his own manner. Ruth Beckermann and Josef Aichholzer's "Return to Vienna" is a welcome exception to the norm for the subject, Franz West (Weintraub), is not only highly literate (he's a professional journalist), but also a truly gifted storyteller with a balanced view of history as it unfolded a half-century ago in one section of Austria in the Viennese Jewish community of Leopoldstat.

Weintraub returned to this so-called "Matzohs Island" in 1924 at the age of 14, his family deciding to move back to Vienna after a long stay in the German city of Magdeburg (near Berlin). The period of the next 10 years was a heady one for a youth in his teens aiming to finish his education at the university, for during this time the Social Democrats in the fall of the Austrian-Hungarian monarchy hoped to turn the tide against the entrenched reactionaries and nationalists. Some 60,000 Jews had recently settled in this area, many coming from the eastern section of the defeated Hapsburg empire. "Red Vienna" was a byword at the time.

Weintraub, who changed his name to West upon emigrating to England in the 1930s, recalls street battles and daily humiliations at the hands of non-Jewish Austrian citizens, due to the fact that his "classical Jewish countenance" couldn't be mistaken in the crowd. He also frankly explains why he slowly drifted away from the Jewish tradition, about his involvement politically in the Labor Movement of the time, and his aborting of a university career in favor of journalism and politics. One can almost anticipate his thought processes as, before a still and observant camera, West explains why and how one event after another inched him towards making the key decision in his youth adult life: he became a member of the Communist Party.

At the end of the story, with West jumping from the past briefly to the present, he recounts his disappointment over the Warsaw Pact invasion of Czechoslovakia during the so-called "Prague Spring" of 1968. Immediately, he turned in his card and left the Communist Party. "Return of Vienna" was chosen by the Leipzig fest committee for showing in an ad hoc program at the Casino Theatre, not far away from the venue of competition screenings, the Capitol Theatre.

That the Soviet Invasion of Prague was openly mentioned in a selected film during the festival has to be some kind of first. Archival footage is kept to a modest minimum to allow for as much "oral history" as this all-embracing life-account requires. Helmers Beckermann and Aichholzer score as exemplary historical documentarists.—*Holl.*

Erinnerung An Eine Landschaft
(Remembrance of a Landscape)
(EAST GERMAN-COLOR-DOCU)

Leipzig, Nov. 20.
A DEFA Dokumentarfilm Studio production, German Democratic Republic. World rights, DEFA Aussenhandel, East Berlin. A documentary Film by Kurt Tetzlaff. Only credits available. Reviewed at the Leipzig Film Fest, Nov. 20, '83. Running time: 84 MINS.

Little doubt, one of the best contemporary "schools" for the documentary film is composed of a group of dedicated East Germans: Karl Gass, Wilfried Junge and Hans-Eberhard Leupold, Juergen Boettcher, Volker Koepp, Gitta Nikel, Karlheinz Mund and Kurt Tetzlaff. Each year at the Leipzig Fest for political docus, one of the side-bar events focuses on a new, or newly released, documentary by one of these filmers and, often enough, it's the fruit of a long period of precise observation of both theme and subjects.

Much like the National Film Board of Canada, the DEFA Dokumentarfilm Studios set out to chronicle the lives of local citizens by attempting to take the very pulse of society itself. In the milestone docu by Junge and Leupold, "Paths of Life" (1981), the period of observation covers some 18 years — from the first day of school for six-year-old kids in a provincial town to young adulthood today. Much the same is true of Kurt Tetzlaff's "Remembrance of a Landscape," unspooled in an Special Event screening at Leipzig.

The landscape referred to in the title is an area just south of Leipzig, where three villages (one celebrating its centennial) have to be abandoned and wiped off the map completely to allow for strip-mining of brown coal (or ignite), a necessary source of energy in the GDR for the next 20 years. Nevertheless, the uprooting of a community is a painful sociological process, particularly when traditions and graveyards are being tampered with.

Tetzlaff went to the area with his camera team, interviewed everyone of importance for the project (public officials, community leaders, ordinary people) in advance, recorded the abandonment and destruction of the homes, and then wrapped everything up by inter-viewing many of the same local citizens in their new homes and apartments a couple of years later. Apparently, the docu project covered some four to five years in all.

"Remembrance of a Landscape" is one of those docus that could easily backfire sometime in the future by posing the simple question: was it worth it to eliminate three rural communities for a massive hole in the earth and just 20 years more of handily available raw energy? Further, brown coal used in factories tends to belch out of smokestacks a hazardous amount of acid-rain sulfur. These questions, of course, are not treated directly in the docu treatise, but an observant viewer can easily draw the logical conclusions from the factual premises offered.

Since both East and West European lands face pretty much the same responsibilities so far as ecology versus technology is concerned, a documentary like Tetzlaff's "Remembrance of a Landscape" would make excellent discussion material for a conference or seminar on today's burning sociopolitical issues. Hopefully, more international docu fests will book this one (and other relevant GDR pics) for the upcoming circuit.
—*Holl.*

The Keep
(BRITISH-COLOR)

May keep until New Year's.

Hollywood, Dec. 14.
A Paramount Pictures release, produced by Gene Kirkwood and Howard W. Koch Jr. Written and directed by Michael Mann from a novel by F. Paul Wilson. Features entire cast. Exec producer, Colin M. Brewer. Camera (Metrocolor), Alex Thomson; editor, Dov Hoenig; sound, Robin Gregory; production design, John Box; assistant directors, Roger Simons, Ray Corbett; associate producers, Theresa Curtin, Richard Brams, Gavin MacFadyen; costumes, Anthony Mendleson; visual effects, Wally Veevers, Robin Browne; art direction, Herbert Westbrook; Alan Tomkins; makeup, Nick Maley; special effects, Nick Allder, music, Tangerine Dream. Reviewed at Paramount Studios, Hollywood, Dec. 14, 1983. (MPAA rating: R.) Running time: 96 MINS.

Glaeken Trismegestus	Scott Glenn
Eva	Alberta Watson
Woermann	Jurgen Prochnow
Father Fonescu	Robert Prosky
Raempffer	Gabriel Byrne
Dr. Cuza	Ian McKellen
Alexandru	Morgan Sheppard
Tomescu	Royston Tickner

"The Keep" is a Christmas giveaway and not worth that at half the price, as Paramount Pictures will probably discover soon enough. Buried deep within its mysterious exterior lies that chilling Hollywood question: How do these dogs get made?

From a trade standpoint, however, "The Keep" does display an unusual credit: "Assistant footsteps editor." Given the end result, it's not clear why a journeyman footsteps editor would have needed help at all. "The Keep" does not shy from excess anywhere along the way.

•After his promising debut with "The Thief," this is writer-director Michael Mann's second feature, testimony again to the one-step-forward, two-steps-back career theory. Fortunately for him, Scott Glenn has built up more credits to date to hide this one behind. As for the rest of the largely foreign cast, they should not expect to become American stars overnight.

Since the writing of F. Paul Wilson's novel preceded the release of "Raiders Of The Lost Ark," it cannot be said there is any connection. But "Keep" certainly seems inspired somehow with the idea that if one exploding Nazi was big box-office in "Raiders," then a bunch of them should be even better.

The Germans in question have arrived at a small Rumanian village, unaware and unafraid that the keep where they will be headquartered has an uneasy history. You can tell that by the silver crosses and the old man who takes care of it and talks in riddles.

Their commander, Jurgen Prochnow ("Das Boot"), is a nice guy despite his job with the Wehrmacht and it's obviously hardly his fault that his troops are gradually being eaten alive and blown apart by an unseen force that moves smokily through the keep.

But he has a tough time telling that to the miserable S.S. major, Gabriel Byrne, who shows up to take over and teach the rebellious villagers a lesson. Once in command, Byrne plays the whole part as if still angry at the barber who cut his hair two inches above his ears.

Professorial Ian McKellen is brought from a concentration camp to help solve the mystery, and brings his imminently assaultable daughter, Alberta Watson. While she's being raped, the monster emerges from his fog and blows those bad guys apart, making a friend of her father.

Somewhere across the dark waters, all this commotion wakes up Glenn, who sets out for the keep to make sure the monster doesn't use the professor to get out, even though it does keep the old man busy enough in the keep to give Glenn time to bed Watson in the local hotel.

Since Glenn's eyeballs sometime glow and flash light when he's annoyed, it's clear Watson will never get a straight answer when she asks, "Where are you from?" And by the time the bullet holes start glowing green when Glenn's shot, she's stopped asking.

Not surprisingly, before it all ends, the monster gets most of the Nazis and then turns his attention to Glenn. Having presumably been lifting weights for several centuries, both the creature and Glenn have developed terrific traps at the back of their necks, making the final look like Showdown at Muscle Beach. But Glenn has this fabulous flashlight and the monster is soon done for.

At the end, Watson keeps looking fearfully over her shoulder, as if more might be coming ... but it's only a freeze frame.

Maybe an assistant footsteps editor is hired to help people get out of the theater. — *Har.*

Flirt
(ITALIAN-COLOR)

Sorrento, Dec. 12.

A Gaumont release, produced by Paolo Infascelli for Komika Film. Stars Monica Vitti, Jean Luc Bideau. Directed by Roberto Russo. Screenplay, Roberto Russo, Vitti, Silvia Napolitano; camera (Eastmancolor), Luigi Kuveiler; editor, Alberto Galliti; art director, Giuseppe Mangano; music, Francesco De Gregori. Reviewed at Sorrento Encounters, Sorrento, Dec. 11, 1983. Running time: 103 MINS.
Laura .... Monica Vitti
Giovanni .... Jean Luc Bideau

An Italo comedy starring, and in part written by, Monica Vitti, "Flirt" has had decent onshore trade and is eligible for adjacent Mediterranean markets. The presence of Swiss thesp Jean Luc Bideau has not hurt the picture in Italy, adding rather an aura of quality to what is basically pretty standard fare.

Story traces the tribulations of Laura (Vitti), who after 22 years of marriage to Giovanni (Bideau) suddenly discovers her husband is mad.

Giovanni's particular form of schizo behavior consists in believing he is having an affair with a girl named Veronica, in reality only a figment of his imagination. First jealous of her husband's girlfriend, Laura finds it is much worse to lose the man she loves to a phantom.

"Flirt" has a serious side, but steers mostly through the safer waters of comic misunderstanding, jealousy and frustrated attempts to right a wrong situation. And things do get righted in the end: after a hospital stay, Laura decides to let Giovanni bring "Veronica" home and live à trois. She starts cooking for three. In the end nature takes it course and Giovanni, tired of merely imaginary satisfactions, dumps Veronica as suddenly as he created her.

Bideau plays the short-circuited husband with a believable alternation of warmth and psychotic distraction. A new face in Italian films, he is able to hold his own against the powerful presence of Vitti, who tends to k.o. most of her costars early in the picture. Looking better than ever in "Flirt," she is a trifle too glamorous and elegant in the role of the ordinary wife, prepared to make any sacrifice to hold on to her man.

Former still photographer Roberto Russo makes a dignified helming debut, having mastered the basic rules of the genre and a serviceable technique. — *Yung.*

Two Of A Kind
(COLOR)

Even Durning couldn't save this one.

Hollywood, Dec. 15.

A 20th Century-Fox release of a Joe Wizan-Roger M. Rothstein production. Produced by Rothstein, Wizan. Directed, screenplay by John Herzfeld. Stars John Travolta, Olivia Newton-John, Charles Durning. Camera (Deluxe color); Fred Koenekamp; editor, Jack Hofstra; music adaptation, Patrick Williams; production design, Albert Brenner; art direction, Spencer Deverell; set design, Kandy Stern, Diane Wager; set decoration, Marvin March; costume design, Thomas Bronson; sound (Dolby), Bud Alper; associate producers, Michele Panelli, Joan Edwards, Kate Edwards; second unit director, John Moio; assistant director, Fredric Blankfein. Reviewed at the 20th Century-Fox Studios, West L.A., Dec. 15, 1983. (MPAA Rating: PG). Running time: 87 MINS.
Zack Melon .... John Travolta
Debbie Wylder .... Olivia Newton-John
Charlie .... Charles Durning
Ruth .... Beatrice Straight
Earl .... Scatman Crothers
Gonzales .... Castulo Guerra
Beazley .... Oliver Reed
Stuart .... Richard Bright
Oscar .... Vincent Bufano
Terri .... Toni Kalem
Ron .... James Stevens
Mr. Choliner .... Jack Kehoe
Detective Staggs .... Ernie Hudson

"Two Of A Kind" is an embarrassment of the first order. Apparently, the notion of repairing the "Grease" team of John Travolta and Olivia Newton-John was sufficiently to lure 20th Century-Fox into this venture. Film will undoubtedly do better biz than Travolta's earlier "Moment To Moment," but it immediately assumes a similar standing in his career. Fox can count itself lucky for whatever b.o. the pic generates through New Year's, for there won't be much steam left in it past that point.

Aside from the presence of the two stars, confection has all the earmarks of a bargain-basement job. Sets are as constricted as those for live, three-camera sitcoms, and many of the so-called New York location scenes possess an obvious back-lot look. Supporting cast overacts down the line, and even the extras look wrong (since when do the majority of male diners at the Plaza Hotel in New York wear polyester with open shirts?).

Script's only vaguely amusing conceit presents itself at the beginning, when God returns from a vacation and, finding the world gone to seed in the interim, announces to four of his angels that he's going to wipe out the human race and start over again. For some reason, the angels disagree with His assessment of contemporary humanity and urge Him to reconsider His decision based on whether or not a random man can prove himself possible of genuine goodness.

So Travolta, a self-styled inventor of such inane items as edible sunglasses, is selected as the guinea pig, just in time to find him robbing a bank in order to pay off a debt to the mob. Bank teller Olivia Newton-John, fired for flirting with the stick-up man, actually makes off with the dough, spends lots of it on new clothes and furniture, gets to somewhere between second and third base with Travolta on her (new) couch, is witness to a food fight at the Plaza and gets saved by Travolta after being taken hostage by a gunman in a climax as breathlessly exciting as that of last week's rerun of "Chips."

Both stars have been better on virtually any other occasion, and the talented trio of Charles Durning, Beatrice Straight and Scatman Crothers is thoroughly wasted. Oliver Reed oozes through the proceedings as a Lucifer figure.

Pic is not a musical, but does feature three tunes chirped by Newton-John, as well as a duet with her and Travolta. An MTV version of one of them has been showing for a couple of weeks, but visual material on view there is not present in the picture. — *Cart.*

L'Art d'Aimer
(The Art of Love)
(FRENCH-ITALIAN-COLOR)

Paris, Dec. 14.

Parafrance release of a Naja Films/Distra/Mars International Film/Impexi/2T Produzione (Rome) coproduction. Produced by Marcel Albertini. Associate producer, Jacques Nahum. Features entire cast. Directed by Walerian Borowczyk. Screenplay, Borowczyk, Wilhelm Buchheim, Enzo Ungari, inspired by the "Ars Amatoria" of Ovid; camera (color), Noel Very; art directors, Gianlito Burcchiellaro, Mario Ambrosino; costumes, Luciana Marinucci; editor, Borowczyk; music, Luis Bacalov; production manager, Victor Beniard. Reviewed at the Monte-Carlo theater, Paris, Dec. 12, 1983. Running time: 101 MINS.
Cast: Michele Placido, Marina Pierro, Massimo Girotti, Laura Betti, Philippe Lemaire, Philippe Taccini, Pier Francesco Aiello, Antonio Orlando, Mireille Pame, Simonetta Stefanelli.

"L'Art d'Aimer" looks like a third-rate boulevard sex farce relocated in a Roman bath house. Walerian Borowczyk, who coscripted and directed, drew inspiration for his latest essay in eroticism from the "Ars Amatoria" of the Latin poet, Ovid, who, as portrayed by Massimo Girotti, is seen regularly expostulating on the art of seduction before a sparsely occupied amphitheatre of eager young Roman bucks.

But nothing much funny or titillating happens on the way to the forum in this embarrassing libertine romp, which purports to illustrate the master's teachings with an episode about a young Roman housewife (Marina Pierro) entertaining a lover while her soldier husband (Michele Placido) is away at the wars.

Laura Betti and Philippe Lemaire are also in on the hanky-panky, but none of the performances invites comment (and the French dubbing is dreadful). Production is tacky. Fellini can sleep tight. —*Len.*

Ziggy Stardust And The Spiders From Mars
(COLOR)

Hollywood, Dec. 15.

Twentieth Century-Fox International Classics presents a Miramax release of a Mainman production in association with Pennebaker Inc. and Bewlay Bros. S.A.R.I. Producer for Pennebaker Inc., Edyth Van Slyck. Directed by D.A. Pennebaker. Camera (color), James Desmond, Mike Davis, Nick Doob, Randy Franken, Pennebaker; assistants, Phillip Mesure, Steve Lysohir; editor, Lorry Whitehead; music mix, David Bowie and Tony Visconti with Bruce Tergesen; costumes, Freddie Buretti and Kansai; makeup, Pierre Laroche; music, Bowie, Jacques Brel, Mick Jagger, Keith Richards, Lou Reed. Reviewed at 20th Century-Fox Studios, Hollywood, Dec. 15, 1983. (MPAA rating: PG.) Running Time: 91 MINS.

David Bowie claims to have finally shaken off the self-destructive influence of Ziggy Stardust, the early, and still most memorable alter-ego of his multi-charactered career, and he seems eager to get audiences, long fascinated with the persona, to do the same. This technically deficient film, shot 10 years ago but only now getting a release, should make the divorce final.

But as flawed as this in-concert production is, Bowie's current high profile, via a record-breaking world tour, a platinum-plus LP and two previous film appearances this year, probably insures strong initial business before fan word-of-mouth kicks in. Given the fact that Bowie no longer performs most of the musical material preserved in this film, homevideo market potential seems guaranteed, however.

The "Ziggy Stardust" album was a watershed for both Bowie and rock music. Through Ziggy, Bowie brought a theatricality to rock which forever changed both the performance and production elements of the form, while elevating Bowie to international prominence.

Bowie-Ziggy's androgynous costuming, flame-red hair and full face makeup are still outrageous, and just as amusing, today, but the film often delivers the "wrong" kind of laughs, and little of the genuine significance of the show shines through.

D.A. Pennebaker, who'd previously applied his cinema verité approach to the still-fascinating Bob Dylan rockumentary, "Don't Look Back," and the "Monterey Pop" film, captured Bowie's "last" concert at London's Hammersmith Odeon in 1973. Pic has been in various stages of completion since, with Bowie finally remixing the soundtrack last year in anticipation of his first concert tour in five years.

Film embraces all the worst aspects of the verité style—wobbly camera work, dim lighting and, new mix or not, less than terrific audio. Shot in 16m, original negative from the film has several problems with it, according to 20th-Fox, and some new lab work is anticipated before a large print run is made.

Bowie's concert performance, moreover, is far from his best, perhaps partially owing to the fact that the Hammersmith Odeon show came at the end of a world tour which had begun in 1972. Same show played L.A. that year, and the performance here remains vividly etched in the memories of those in attendance.

Film does point up, however, how vastly improved Bowie's singing is these days, and how much better he is at bringing all the elements together smoothly, if not as excitingly. He also looks a lot better these days.

Included are 17 songs, spanning several albums in addition to "Ziggy Stardust," and featuring a rendition of Jacques Brel's "My Death" not found on any Bowie disk. Performances are raggedly intriguing at best, dismal and laugh-provoking at worst.

"Ziggy" includes some brief backstage sequences in addition to the concert, but in contrast to the richly beguiling offstage glimpses of Dylan which Pennebaker delivered in "Don't Look Back," the behind-the-scenes looks at Bowie, while enlivened by some by-play between him and ex-wife Angie, offer few revelations. —Kirk.

Echoes
(COLOR)

Disappointing supernatural suspense pic.

A Continental Distributing release of a Barry E. Rosenthal presentation. A Herberval Production in association with Seidelman/Nice Presents Inc. and Shiffman Group Inc. Produced by George R. Nice, Valerie Y. Belsky. Directed by Arthur Allan Seidelman. Stars Richard Alfieri, Nathalie Nell. Screenplay, Richard J. Anthony; camera (Movielab color), Hanania Baer; editor, Dan Perry; music, songs, Stephen Schwartz; additional music, Gerard Bernard Cohen; assistant director, Carol Polakoff; production manager, Fred Berner; sound, John Keene Wilkinson, Robert W. Glass Jr., Robert M. Thirlwell; art direction, Neal Deluca; set decoration, Frank Cocarro; special effects, Peter Kunz; stunt coordinator, Harry Madsen; choreography, Dennis Wayne; paintings by Frank Mason; abstract art by Renaldo De Juan. Reviewed on VidAmerica vidcassette, N.Y., Oct. 20, 1983. (MPAA Rating: R). Running time: **89 MINS.**

Michael Durant/
Alberto Serrano .... Richard Alfieri
Christine .... Nathalie Nell
Lilian Gerber .... Mercedes McCambridge
Michael's mother .... Ruth Roman
Mrs. Edmonds .... Gale Sondergaard
Sid Berman .... Mike Kellin
Stephen .... John Spencer
Ed .... Paul Joynt
Danny .... Leonard Crofoot

Filmed in Manhattan in 1980 and currently available on videocassette, "Echoes" is a romantic suspense picture with a supernatural plot device which doesn't pay off. Despite a good cast, film lacks the urgency and spectacular effects to attract attention in the thriller market (pic had a brief L.A. theatrical run earlier this year).

Richard Alfieri toplines (and pleasantly sings the out-theme) as Michael Durant, a Gotham art student who not surprisingly falls in love with Christine (played by the beautiful French actress Nathalie Nell), a successful ballet dancer. Durant, who has asthma causing wheezing attacks, is plagued by recurring nightmares in which he is caught in the arms of a woman by a mustachioed man who stabs and drowns him.

On the advice of his pal Stephen (John Spencer), Durant visits a psychic (Gale Sondergaard) who informs him he is the reincarnation of a Spanish artist who lived in the 19th century. Questioning his mother (Ruth Roman) Durant becomes convinced his unborn twin brother (the fetus miscarried during pregnancy) was the reincarnation of the killer from his memory-dream, and he hallucinates the man as an apparition pursuing him on the subway and at a party.

Though Alfieri is a handsome, engaging actor, the role has him becoming boorish and very unsympathetic as he becomes consumed with his dream. His art career, managed by gallery owner Lillian Gerber (Mercedes McCambridge) goes nowhere; he drives away Christine with his unreasonable possessiveness and is booted out of art class by his teacher (played by the late Mike Kellin). Anti-climax has a car accident resolving the dream paranoia, with a happy ending unconvincingly tacked on.

Main defect in Richard J. Anthony's screenplay is that Christine bears no relationship to the anti-hero's dream-life. In romantic supernatural tales, some mythic or emotional resonance is usually created by linking characters on more than one level of existence, but that doesn't occur here, leaving a void. As directed by Seidelman, the strong supernatural factor comes off as merely a gimmick.

Thesping is fine down the line, with Gale Sondergaard particularly persuasive among the vet talent as a psychic. Cinematographer Hanania Baer contributes a stunning opening crane shot in Manhattan's theatre district, not matched by the mundane dream sequences that follow. —Lor.

War Of The Wizards
(TAIWANESE-COLOR)

A 21st Century Distribution release of an Eastern Media Film Prods. Ltd. production, in association with JAD Films Inc. Produced by Frank Wong. Directed by Richard Caan, Sam Arikawa. Features entire cast. Screenplay, F. Kenneth Lin; camera (color), Mike Tomioka; music, Lawrence Borden; special visual effects, Arikawa. Reviewed at 42d St. Empire theater, N.Y., Dec. 10, 1983. (MPAA Rating: PG). Running time: **72 MINS.**

With: Richard Kiel, Charles Lang, Betty Noonan.

"War Of The Wizards" is the U.S. release version of a 1978 Taiwan film originally titled "The Phoenix." Picture is a colorful, but silly juvenile fantasy adventure, rendered very difficult to watch (and listen to) by idiotic U.S. dubbing and editing.

Period tale concerns a young fisherman named Thai, who finds a treasure chest underwater containing the legendary Magic Vessel of Plenty and Bamboo Book. The golden Vessel creates material wealth whenever he wishes, and attracts the attention of various villains (who comically kill each other in an escalating violence sequence, each trying to get at the hero) and wizards. Ultimately Thai falls in with two beautiful sisters, marrying one and setting up a ménage a trois.

The sisters are stooges for their evil aunt Flower Fox, who steals Thai's Vessel and demands the (still underwater) Bamboo Book from him. Thai escapes aboard that mythic bird The Phoenix to Fairy Mountain, where he acquires super powers from the Sun and Moon and battles with Fox and her huge henchman (played by U.S. guest star Richard Kiel).

Truncated film is of interest mainly for its gaudy costumes and sets, saturated with bright red and other primary colors. Special effects are cheap animated rays, poor miniatures and sloppy optical printing, with the Phoenix a stiff papier maché creation on the level of U.S. junk monsters such as the Giant Claw of the 1950s. The hero, credited as "Charles Lang," mugs incessantly while Kiel is embarrassing as a strong, silent retard. Fans of phony beards and hairpieces will probably get the most out of this junker. —Lor.

Tva killar och en tjej
(Two Guys And A Gal)
(SWEDISH-COLOR)

Copenhagen, Dec. 8.

A Svensk Filmindustri AB production and release. Features entire cast. Original story and script, Brasse Braennstroem, Lasse Hallstroem, Magnus Haerenstam. Directed and edited by Hallstroem. Camera (Eastmancolor) Roland Lundin, Thorbjoern Andersson; production design, Lasse Westfelt; costumes, Inger Pehrsson; music, Anders Berglund and opera excerpts; production management, Waldemar Bergendahl, Gisela Bergquist, Eva Larsson. Reviewed at International Film Teknik screening room, Copenhagen, Dec. 8, 1983. Running time, **110 MINS.**

Thomas .... Brasse Braenstroem
Klasse .... Magnus Haerenstam
Anna .... Pia Green
Lena .... Ann-Cathrine Froejdoe

In Sweden, actors Brasse Braenstroem and Magnus Haerenstam just have to have their names mentioned for audiences to smile happily. And when the two appear in a feature directed by Lasse Hallstroem, the boxoffice at home is assured. The threesome has cowritten Hallstroem's new effort, "Two Guys and a Gal," named to indicate a link with their previous comedy film, "A Guy and a Gal," but probably to be marketed abroad as "Happy We." Film, something as curious as a slow-motion romp of a comedy, deals with the reunion of Thomas (Braenstroem), Klasse (Magnus Haerenstam) and Anna (Pia Green) who 16 years ago made up a comedy trio on their university's amateur stage. Now, they are asked to do their trio act again at a friend's wedding. They decide instead to write entirely new material, but find it troublesome to do so. Times are different, nostalgia has turned sour, and, worst of all, since then Klasse and Anna have been married and divorced. It was a friendly divorce, but jealousy raises its ugly head when Anna starts an affair with Thomas, who has really been through a divorce war and is now alone with his little son. He always was sweet on Anna anyway.

Hallstroem has precious material for serious comedy here, but wastes the extraordinary talents of his three actors by having them run around in feet-dragging circles about the travail of their self-imposed writing chore. Klasse's jealousy is hardly touched upon until the last reel. Neither are the indicated difficulties of being a lone father developed very far as a theme. What is left is a mild-mannered surface probing into joys-of-adult-friendship.

Hallstroem and company offer some amusing insights along with displays of poetic wit beyond ordinary sitcom limits. Generally, however, it is left to the actors themselves to strike sparks from meager lines and setups — and sparks do fly from their line delivery as well as from their body language.

Since Anna works backstage at the Stockholm opera, some very amusing interplays between onstage performances, opera music in general and straight action pepper an otherwise rather dull narrative. Film has a nice production dress, it looks good and sounds good, but has very little apart from the acting and a few sharp lines to keep it afloat as an export item.
—Kell.

Los Viajes De Gulliver
(Gulliver's Travels)
(SPANISH-COLOR-ANIMATED)

Madrid, Dec. 17.
A Crus Delgado/Art Animacion production. Directed by Cruz Delgado. Script and adaptation of Jonathan Swift's book by Gustavo Alcalde; story board, Javier G. Inaraja; animators, Basilio Gonzalez, Maria Carmen Sanchez, Pedro D. Cavilla and Pedro Jorge Gil; animation supervisor, Gonzalez; set designs, Antonio Navarro; backgrounds, Angel S. Chicarro, Mauro Cáceres, José Maria Zumel; camera (Eastmancolor) José Maria Sanchez; editor, José Luis Berlanga; music, Antonio Areta. Reviewed at Cine Vergara, Madrid, Dec. 17, '83. Running time: 82 MINS.

Producer-director Cruz Delgado is best known for an animated feature he made about seven years ago, "The Magic Adventure," and more recently for the animatd tv series, "Don Quixote." This version of "Gulliver's Travels" is his most ambitious project so far. In 82 minutes of mostly full-animation he retells part of Jonathan Swift's yarn, singling out Gulliver's adventures in Brobdingnag, interspersing five musical numbers and creating some new characters to amuse moppets.

On the whole, item is well-done, professional and should prove commercial in virtually all world markets, especially for audience ranging in age from three to eight. Delgado's best creations here are a nasty, slinking cat which tries to gobble up Gulliver in the land of the giants, and a court jester who is jealous of Gulliver usurping the position as the prince's favorite.

Gulliver himself, his girlfriend Glundalich, Prince Flinap are more standardized, but should come across okay for the toddlers.

Delgado adds a miscellany of adventures that befall Gulliver: the attack of a giant crab, a gorilla let loose by the wicked buffoon who seizes Gulliver and threatens to crush him, an adventure in a fish bowl in which Gulliver must "ride" the beast, a duel with a hornet in which Gulliver brandishes a rapier against the insect's stinger, as well as the opening and closing adventures in a tempestuous sea.

Animation is, for the most part, well handled and geared to very young audiences; backgrounds and sets are well designed and quite intricate. Perhaps weakest are the musical numbers, ranging from a full-dress court dance to a little piece sung by the buffoon. Item is being released in Spain for the Yuletide season and should do good biz. Pic would have its best theatrical playoffs during school holildays and is a natural for tv and cable markets.

In Spain, pic was released preceded by a 15-minute short by Cruz Delgado titled "Molecula."
—Besa.

Growing Up
(TAIWANESE-COLOR)

Taipei, Nov. 19.
A Central Motion Picture Corp. production and release. Directed by Chen Kun-ho. Stars Cheng Chu-Fong, Neo Cheng-Tse. (No other credits provided.) Reviewed at the Golden Horse Awards, Taipei. Nov. 18, 1983. Running Time: 100 MINS.

(Mandarin soundtrack with English subtitles.)

"Growing Up" is a funny and heart-tugging dramatic account about the simple experiences of an illegitimate boy from his precocious youth and unsure adolescence to steady manhood. His mother marries an older man mainly for security and is willing to raise her young son properly with loving care, a good environment, proper education and solid-family background. All the main characters have done nothing blatantly wrong, but all have to pay the price for the security that all are searching for as grownups. It won the best film prize recently at the Golden Horse Awards.

For a change, we experience the pains and joys of normal childhood devoid of deranged activities so commonly portrayed in contemporary films.

This is truly an amiable and deeply moving film in grand Taiwanese style full of simplistic, true to life incidents as if carved from personal experiences of the writer and director. There's a lot of humanity here, balanced beautifully with humorous sequences with soulful performances from kids, pimply youths and accomplished adults. The growing up process is actually seen through the eyes of a young girl who silently idolizes the once misunderstood youth who grows up to be a responsible gentleman.

"Growing Up" is actually an upbeat film with uncommon brilliance to watch out for, to love and to remember though it seems to be a variant of Japanese films such as "Muddy River" and "Tokyo Twilight," which also dramatize the turmoil of the younger generation.

And unlike other films in this category, it does not suggest that the young family unit, educational system and society in general have defaulted on their moral obligation to provide an environment in which children can accept themselves. It shows there are a few headaches, but the shaping of the future depends on the individual's inner strength and resources.
—Mel.

Skoenheden og udyret
(The Beauty & The Beast)
(DANISH-COLOR)

Copenhagen, Nov. 4.
A Per Holst productin (with The Danish Film Institute), Kaerne Film release. Features entire cast. Original story, script and directed by Nils Malmros; camera (Eastman-color) Jan Weincke; production management, Ib Tardini, Janne Find; editor, Birger Moller Jensen; music, Gunnar Moeller Pedersen and excerpts from Henry Purcell's "Dido & Aeneas;" production design, Peter Hoejmark. Reviewed at the Dagmar, Copenhagen, Nov. 3, 1983. Running time, 88 MINS.
The Father .... Jesper Klein
Mette .... Line Arlien Soeborg
The Mother .... Merete Volstedlund
Joenne .... Carsten Joergensen
Drude .... Eva Scholdager
Lars .... Jan Johansen
Mini .... Brian Theibel
Joennes friend .... Michael Noergaard
Soesser .... Lone Elliot

Behind the bombast of its title, Nils Malmros' "The Beauty & The Beast," the writer-director's first feature since "The Tree of Knowledge" for which he won worldwide acclaim, while producer Per Holts enjoyed equally globe-spanning sales, lies a finely honed miniature treatment of an eternal theme: a father alone with his daughter in the days of her sexual awakening.

The father, a writer of sorts and generally an easygoing fellow (played with breath carefully held in check by comedy actor Jesper Klein) is alone over Christmas with his 16-year-old daughter Mette only because the mother is hospitalized with a precarious pregnancy. Between visits to the hospital, father and daughter were to have enjoyed holiday meals together and also to have given the nursery of their small house a paint job.

Mette, however, is off most of the time with her friends for afternoons of sleighriding and skating or evenings at the disco of their provincial town. She has a nice rapport with her father, and he has a similar rapport with her friends. He recognizes that his little girl is growing up and it does not bother him particularly until Joenne turns up.

Joenne is slightly older than Matte. He is a would-be-photographer who one evening gets Mette sufficiently intoxicated on eggnog for her to shed blouse and brassiere and pose for some semi-nude pictures. Joenne is not really a bad sort even if youthfully one-track-minded about getting Mette to bed down with him. He even has a sound esthetic viewpoint about portrait photography working better with the model partly undressed.

After having tried to join him (in on-the-rocks drinking of whiskey), rather than fight him, the father now threatens Joenne with charges of pornography. His little demon of jealousy (some may want to find incestuous feeling expressed here) also nudges the father into following Mette sneakingly around and this way making a bit (not too much, Malmros is firm believer in understatement) of a fool of himself by insisting on joining in her friends' wintersports and disco fun.

The father is a pretty tender beast and the daughter is a pretty robust beauty who kids daddy with the viciousness of innocence by referring to his sorry looks and increasing waistline and even his halitosis. When things finally come to a head between them, she hugs him with a true child's need and makes a confession that is as comically ironic as it is warmly beautiful.

Working again in total empathy with Malmros is cinematographer Jan Weincke, who has every frame lit and composed as to enhance its inner vitality rather than its more obvious dramatic potential.

Malmros uses music sparingly, but with particular poignancy for the cognoscenti. Words from the libretto of Henry Purcell's opera "Dido and Aeneas" are heard sung on the soundtrack when they serve as direct parallels to the feeling of the action. "The Beauty & The Beast," fortunately, also has qualities of general audience identification that should bring it out of its obvious festival circuit and into theaters of more select programming everywhere. —*Kell.*

The Forest
(COLOR)

Rotten horror film in the California woods.

A Fury Films Distribution Ltd. release of a Wide World of Entertainment presentation; a Commedia Pictures productions. Executive producer, Frank Evans. Produced and directed by Don Jones. Features entire cast. Screenplay, Evan Jones; camera (color), Stuart Asbjorsen; editor, uncredited; music, Richard Hieronymus, Alan Oldfield; sound, J.L. Clark; art direction, Sandra Saunders; makeup, Dana Wolski. Reviewed at Times Square 42d St. theater, N.Y., Dec. 10, 1983. (MPAA Rating: R). Running time: 85 MINS.
Steve ....Dean Russell
John ....Michael Brody
Sharon ....Elaine Warner
Charley ....John Batis
Teddi ....Ann Wilkinson
Mother ....Jeanette Kelly
John Jr. ....Corky Pigeon
Jennifer .. ..Becki Burke
  Also with: Tony Gee, Stafford Morgan, Marilyn Anderson, Don Jones (forest ranger).

Made in 1981, "The Forest" is a lame horror film adding supernatural elements to the overdone mad killer on the loose format. Local newspaper ads retitled pic "Terror In The Forest" in a futile attempt to spice up the contents.

Two married couples (appearing to be in their 30s) venture from smoggy L.A. to a woodsy hiking vacation, with an argument separating the men from the women at the outset. In the woods, a hermit John (Michael Brody) lives in a cave and stabs unwary visitors with his hunting knife, later cannibalizing them for food. The woods are also haunted by his dead wife (killed by John for her infidelity with each and every deliveryman and serviceman visiting their home) and their two kids, whose suicidal death drove John crazy.

As John picks off the cast members one by one, film presents an odd gimmick of the kids' ghosts appearing to one of the hiking wives Sharon (Elaine Warner), helping her to escape daddy's murderous attacks. Their and mom's ghostly appearances do not help the rest of the cast however.

Cheaply lensed with adequate direct-sound recording, "The Forest" is dull and silly rather than scary. Filmmaker Don Jones, who previously co-directed the tongue-in-cheek "The Love Butcher," provides some feeble moments of black humor in the dialog and cannibalism subplot, but generally delivers a routine cheapie. Killings feature plenty of blood but do not deliver the special makeup effects fans of this genre are accustomed to getting. Matching of day-for-night shots is extremely poor.

Acting is feeble, particularly by the kids, with Sharon's husband Steve portrayed by Dean Russell as a helpless, crying wimp, providing an easy target for the fans' derogatory comments back at the screen. The lowkey madman, Michael Brody, is an older dead ringer who could easily play Nick Nolte's dad or older brother.
—*Lor.*

On The Run
(AUSTRALIAN-COLOR)

Down under over and out.

A Cineworld release of a Pigelu production. Executive producer, Bill Anderson. Produced and directed by Mende Brown. Stars Paul Winfield, Rod Taylor. Screenplay, Michael Fisher; camera (Colorfilm color), Paul Onorato; editor, Richard Hindley; music, Laurie Lewis; sound, Ken Hammond; stunt direction; Grant Paige; assistant director, Martin Cohen; associate producer, Tony Walker. Reviewed at 42d St. Anco Theater, N.Y., Dec. 10, 1983. (No MPAA Rating). Running time: 101 MINS.
Harry ....Paul Winfield
Payette ....Rod Taylor
Paul ....Beau Cox
  Also with: Shirley Cameron, Ray Meagher, Danny Adcock.

"On The Run" is an old-fashioned, entertaining 1982 Aussie action picture for which there seems no discernible audience. B-movie fans will eventually catch up with the simple pleasures of this well-made but minor opus after its unheralded current theatrical release.

Surefire (but antiquated) formula rests upon the power of a cute young waif to soften a crusty, self-absorbed man. Protagonists this go-round are Paul Winfield as Harry, a U.S. escaped convict living in Australia who has to care for young Paul (Beau Cox), an orphaned boy from New Caledonia who only speaks French. The two are thrown together (in action-chase format) when Harry's employer, international hit man Payette (Rod Taylor), who is Paul's uncle, threatens to kill the boy when he witnesses a killing.

Travelling amidst scenic sites in the environs of Sydney, twosome is befriended by a dwarf car salesman en route to an exciting climax staged atop a mountainside pinnacle.

Acting by Winfield is firstrate, and should ensure U.S. tv interest in this vehicle. Cox is endearing as the youngster, but Taylor is not very convincing as the ultra-ruthless killer. Equal billing problem is neatly solved by placing Winfield and Taylor's names on screen in the form of a cross before the title card. Tech credits are adequate for a low-budgeter, Mende Brown's first feature film after producing the Anthony Quayle-hosted syndicated series, "The Evil Touch," a decade ago. — *Lor.*

Un Homme à Ma Taille
(A Man of My Measure)
(FRENCH-W. GERMAN/COLOR)

Paris, Nov. 30.
Prodis release of a GPFI/Gemme Production/Janus/Trinacra Films/FR 3 coproduction. Produced by Jean-Claude Fleury. Exec producer, Patrick Delauneux. Directed by Annette Carducci. Features entire cast. Screenplay, Carducci, Annick Rousset-Rouard; camera (color), Armand Marco; sound, Paul Lainé; editor, Bob Wade; art director, Noele Galland and Utal Reichardt; music, Pierre Bachelet; production manager, Stephan Heyne. Reviewed at the Marignan-Concorde theater, Paris, Nov. 29, 1983. Running time: 91 MINS.
Victoire ....Liselotte Christian
Babette ....Anemone
Andre ....Daniel Russo
Georges ....Thierry Lhermitte
Samuel ....Volker Brandt
Paul ....Francis André-Loux
Lisa ....Emmanuelle Riva

Annette Carducci, born in Germany, came to Paris as a student and stayed to work in the film business. She punctures some accepted notions about the French Lover in her filmmaking debut, "Un Homme à Ma Taille," a romantic comedy about a German girl in Paris, inspired by the director's personal experiences.

Heroine, who comes from a Francophile German family, has many romantic illusions and several inches above most of her boyfriends. Both factors create insurmountable obstacles, as Victoire (as she was brazenly dubbed by her mother at the height of World War II) makes her nearsighted way through the arms of several potential French gallants, including a pea-brained sports-crazy dentist (Daniel Russo), a liberated young sociologist (Thierry Lhermitte) who doesn't believe in monogamy, and a stuffy Jewish intellectual (Volker Brandt). But the emotionally myopic girl apparently falls across Monsieur Right

Carducci's direction is plain and the portraits of Gallic males tend too much towards caricature to be trenchant, but there is some anecdotal charm in this view of Franco-German mesentente.

Carducci found a unknown for the lead: Liselotte Christian, a tall, blond, blue-eyed German, whose lack of acting experience adds a gauche charm to the part. Anemone shares topbilling with Lhermitte as Christian's homely local confidante.

Pic was produced with aid from a new Franco-German state production fund. —*Len.*

G
(SWEDISH-COLOR)

Copenhagen, Oct. 29.
A Svensk Filmindustri AB/Filmslussen/-Swedish Television/SVT 1 production, AB Svensk Film release. Features entire cast. Original story and script Staffan Hildebrand, Goeran Gester, Joakim Schroeder. Directed by Staffan Hildebrand. Camera (Fujicolor) Goeran Gester, Lennart Peters, Lil Trulsson; production design, Jan Oequist; editor, Goeran Gester; music, the Barn and Reeperbahn rock groups; executive producer, Anders Birkeland. Reviewed at the Tivoli Bio, Copenhagen, Oct. 28, 1983. Running time: 100 MINS.
Robban ....Joakim Schroeder
Alexander ....Sebastian Hakansson
Kim ....Niclas Wahlgren
Mia ....Ulrica Oern
Robban's mother ....Ewa Froeling
Mia's father ....Lasse Stroemstedt
Sudden ....Dominik Henzel
Kristoffer.................Magnus Uggla

"G" is an overly ambitious attempt at combining the ordinary straight youth feature about teenagers getting involved with drugs, seeking a solution in the community of rock groups and losing their way, then finding it again in the fumblings of early sex.

Writer-director Staffan Hildebrand has reached large youth audiences on home territory with his film, but it is doubtful if "G" (named for a Stockholm disco) will stand up as an export item outside Scandinavia and/or limited tv programming elsewhere, since its solutions to all the plot's problems are both pat in a very bourgeois way and highly unlikely in any real-life youth context.

Kim has a homosexual flirt with the moustachioed manager of "G," but it is the latter who gallantly pushes him back in the direction of nubile young Mia. Robban has a cozy afternoon tea with his mother (Ewa Froeling of "Fanny & Alexander" after just 48 hours stealing and smoking and dealing hash and capture by the narcotics squad. And Alexander, lead singer with the rock group Barn, is lured away to the Nazi Rockers of Reeperbahn, but soon rejoins in his more innocent original herd. All of this with nary a hair misplaced on the heads of the nicely performing youngsters.

Some of the musical interludes work quite nicely like intelligent video spots, but the more narrative action is paler than bland. The Barn (which means "children" in Swedish) and Reeperbahn are real-life groups who perform with high professional gloss. —*Kell.*

Piranha II
(The Spawning)
(ITALIAN-U.S.-COLOR)

A Saturn International Pictures release of a Chako Film production. Executive producer, Ovidio G. Assonitis. Produced by Chako van Leuwen, Jeff Schectman. Directed by James Cameron. Features entire cast. Screenplay, H.A. Milton; camera (Technicolor), Roberto D'Ettore Piazzoli; editor, Roberto Silvi; music, Steve Powder; sound,

Piero Fondi; assistant director, Ruggero Salvadori; production manager, Umberto Sambuco; special makeup effects, Giannetto De Rossi; special effects, Antonio Corridori, De Rossi, Gilberto Carbonaro. Reviewed at UA Rivoli 1 theater, N.Y., Dec. 10, 1983. (MPAA Rating: R). Running time: **95 MINS.**

Anne Kimbrough	Tricia O'Neil
Tyler	Steve Marachuk
Steve Kimbrough	Lance Henriksen
Chris Kimbrough	Ricky G. Paul
Raoul	Ted Richert
Allison	Leslie Graves

Also with: Carole Davis, Connie Lynn Hadden, Arnie Ross, Tracy Berg, Albert Sanders, Anne Pollack.

Made in 1961, "Piranha II The Spawning" is a routine monster film, unrelated to Joe Dante's 1978 comedy "Piranha" or the 1972 William Smith adventure "Piranha, Piranha." Pic has played off in most territories before invading the Big Apple and is reviewed for the record.

Idiotic sci-fi premise has U.S. government genetic engineering experiments creating a deadly form of grunions (hinted at being used in the Vietnam war). A missing canister of fertile eggs of these mutant fish (called piranha for horror fans' sake) turns up in the wreck of a ship near the Caribbean resort of Club Elysium and the beasties start chewing up vacationers.

Film's title refers to the grunions' annual mating ritual of spawning on the beach, taking place during the first full moon after the spring equinox, at which time those nasty humans go out and catch the horny devils for a fish fry. Film's lame script pokes fun at the Club Med-type resort and match of human and fishy mating rites.

Nominal human interest plot has Club Elysium scuba diver Anne (Tricia O'Neil) teaming up romantically and investigatively with a visiting incognito biochemist Tyler (Steve Marachuk) to discover and blow up the fish, while her estranged husband Steve (Lance Henriksen) looks out for the welfare of the locals as the film's Roy Scheider-esque cop.

By employing a familiar cast of American actors and recording the picture in well-synched direct-sound English, exec producer Ovido Assonitis follows up his similar made-in-America horror pics "Beyond The Door," "Tentacles," and "The Visitor" with an Italian-crewed film which easily passes as All-American. Special effects experts come up with convincing gore for the victims, but the monsters are laughably phony, flying around on wires in the manner of bats or giant dragonflies from 1950s horror cheapies. Silliest moment is provided by yet another imitation of "Alien," when a flying fish bursts out of the chest of a corpse in the local morgue to attack a nurse. The concept of monsters attacking outside their normal habitat (e.g., Bruce coming out of the water onto Robert Shaw's boat in "Jaws") is an interesting one, well and truly muffed here. — *Lor.*

Sahara
(U.S.-COLOR)

Arid in every sense.

Sydney, Dec. 21.

A Fox-Columbia (Australia) release (MGM/UA) in U.S. and Canada of a Cannon Group presentation of a Golan-Globus production of an Andrew V. McLaglen film. Produced by Menahem Golan and Yoram Globus. Executive producer, Teri Shields. Directed by McLaglen. Stars Brooke Shields. Screenplay, James R. Silke; director of photography (color), David Gurfinkel; production designer, Luciano Spadoni; music, Ennio Morricone; assoc. producer, Rony Yacov; production manager, Omri Maron. Reviewed at Hoyts Entertainment Center, Sydney, Dec. 20, 1983 (Commonwealth film Censor rating: Not recommended for Children). Running time: **104 MINS.**

Dale	Brooke Shields
Jaffar	Lambert Wilson
Von Glessing	Horst Buchholz
Rasoul	John Rhys-Davies
Beg	Ronald Lacey
Cambridge	John Mills
R.J. Gordon	Steve Forrest
Andy	Perry Lang
String	Cliff Potts
Browne	Terence Hardiman

Coproducer Menahem Golan reportedly hatched the idea for "Sahara" when Mark Thatcher, son of the British Prime Minister, disappeared in the desert during an international car rally.

As it turns out, the Thatcher case would probably have made a far more intriguing, convincing, and dramatic yarn than the silly scenario offered here.

An old fashioned B-grade romantic adventure, directed in pedestrian fashion by Andrew V. McLaglen, "Sahara" is lamentably low on excitement, laughs and passion.

Whatever drawing power its leading lady Brooke Shields possesses, it's unlikely to overcome this film's deficiencies, and box-office outlook in the U.S. figures to be as arid as the denominative desert. Pic opened in Sydney to indifferent results.

James R. Silke's screenplay, set in 1927, has Shields as heiress to a car company who promises her dying daddy (Steve Forrest, who might be thankful he is merely called on to utter a few banalities before croaking) that she'll win the world's toughest endurance rally driving the car he designed.

Young women were not supposed to take part in rallies through the Sahara, let alone win, in the '20s, so wily Brooke disguises herself as a man, complete with wig and moustache.

Julie Andrews (a la "Victor/Victoria") she ain't, but she fools Horst Buchholz, her arch rival in the event, and everyone else.

Soon after the race starts, she discards her "disguise" and reverts to Brooke the beautiful, only to receive a beating and a mouthful of sand when she's captured by Arab thug John Rhys-Davies. Handsome sheikh Lambert Wilson saves her from his clutches and falls mildly in love with her. Brooke's heart and mind are still set on winning that race but she's distracted again when barbaric desert warrior Ronald Lacey captures her and throws her into a leopard's cage.

All that, and she still manages to win the race and wander off into the sunset with the sheikh.

The plot is predictable, the dialog is dopey, and the characters wafer-thin, the villains projecting about as much menace as the camels which plod across the shifting sands.

How sad to see that fine actor John Mills demeaning himself in the menial role of "Cambridge," a former professor who unaccountably winds up as the Sheikh's slave.

Director McLaglen and most everyone else treat it all tongue in cheek, as a sort of "Brooke of Arabia Meets The Great Race." All, that is, except Shields, who gives a brittle, superficial performance, alternately pouting and snarling and occasionally simulating ecstasy while looking vague and distant when registering any emotion in between.

Despite the appeal of the Israeli locations (including the Judean wilderness, the old port of Jaffa, and the Negev desert), the audience is likely to be asking itself the same question posed early in the piece by one of the race contestants when he wakes from a nap: "Are we there yet?" —*Dogo.*

Loose Connections
(BRITISH-COLOR)

London, Dec. 2.

An Umbrella-Greenpoint Films production, in association with National Film Finance Corp. and Virgin Films. Produced by Simon Perry. Directed by Richard Eyre. Features entire cast. Screenplay, Maggie Brooks; camera (Eastmancolor), Clive Tickner; editor, David Martin; music, Dominic Muldowney, Andy Roberts; associate producer, Paul Cowan. Reviewed at 20th Century-Fox theatrette, London, Nov. 29, 1983. Running time: **96 MINS.**

Harry	Stephen Rea
Sally	Lindsay Duncan
Axel	Jan Niklas
Kay	Carole Harrison
Kevin	Gary Olsen
Laurie	Frances Low

Richard Eyre's second theatrical feature (following "The Ploughman's Lunch"), handsomely produced by Simon Perry ("Another Time Another Place"), is an exceedingly amiable comic battle of the sexes. Sally (Lindsay Duncan), together with two girl-friends, has built a jeep in which to drive from London to a feminist conference in Munich, but at the last moment one friend fails her driving test and another's husband won't let her go, so Sally is left on her own. She takes a newspaper ad for a fellow driver, seeking a female non-smoking vegetarian, who speaks German and knows something about car engines. The only applicant is Harry (Stephen Rea), who claims to fill all the requirements except sex, and furthermore claims he's gay. Needless to say, Harry's a liar.

The trip to Munich is one comic disaster after another. On the first night, Harry, camping outside Sally's hotel, finds his tent demolished in a sudden rainstorm and is arrested for vagrancy. Later, he inadvertently sets fire to the jeep while fiddling with the wiring. Despite these disasters, and others, the odd couple are drawn to each other, and the inevitable happens. However, a traditional "happy ending" is sensibly avoided.

The screenplay by Maggie Brooks (a talented newcomer also responsible for the script in a London Film Festival short entry, "Too Drunk To Remember") provides two engaging and very modern characters in Harry and Sally, and both roles are played to perfection by Stephen Rea and Lindsay Duncan. It's not a film of hearty laughs, but of continual quiet chuckles, and most of all it's pleasant to spend time with these people. The script also keeps a few surprises up its sleeve.

Richard Eyre handles the film in a relaxed manner and, as in "The Ploughman's Lunch," stages his climax against a real background, in this case an international soccer match being played in Munich. Clive Tickner's location photography is exemplary. Pic should do very good business in Britain, and elsewhere, too, where quality British product has a following.

Film bears a 1984 copyright tag, but was selected to close the London Film Film Festival. A very happy choice. —*Strat.*

Ups & Downs
(CANADIAN-COLOR)

Vancouver, Dec. 27.

An Astral Films release of a Quest Films Production. Produced and directed by Paul Almond. Associate Producer, Michael Hadley. Features entire cast. Screenplay, Almond, Lewis Evans; camera (color), Peter Benison; editor, Yurij Luhovy; sound, David Evans; music, Bo Harwood; production designer, Glenn Bydwell. Reviewed at the Park Theater, Vancouver, Nov. 23, 1983. Running time: 97 MINS.

Arthur (Sherlock) Holmes ...Colin Skinner
Chip......................Andrew Sabiston
Drifty.....................Gavin Brannan
Penelope ....Leslie Hope
Sam ....Margo Nesbit
Mouse ....Alison Kemble
Emmie..................Sandy Gauthier

Established Canadian filmmaker Paul Almond, whose early films were notable for their moody atmospherics, has done a volteface with this preppie comedy that offers a cast of non-professionals. Unknowingly, Almond is following in the footsteps of British school-

master Colin Finbow, who has made a trio of feature-films with inexperienced school children over the past four years. Finbow's "Children's Film Unit" has cooperated with the Institute of Contemporary Arts on such films as "Captain Stirrick," a period action-pic.

Almond's script adheres to the tried and the true: relationships, amorous and antagonistic, among a handful of rebellious youths marking time in a gilded cage. Roommates Chip and Drifty vow to foil housemaster Holmes in their crusade to smash every rule in the school.

Drifty needs distraction badly as his mum is dying of cancer. Emmie and Santi have more severe problems. She suffers from epilepsy and is the butt of her fellow pupils' ill-feeling. He is an angry scion of a wealthy South American family. Mouse longs for romance. Her roommate Sam simply wants to lose weight. And so it goes.

Almond has succeeded in finding fresh faces, but has provided them with the stale characters to be found in any book of preppie cliches.

The principals do remarkably well. Sandy Gauthier has a tough, shut-off mien that suits the role. Alison Kemble is no less effective as the shy, bookwormish Mouse.

Peter Benison's camerawork is firstrate throughout, and editor Yurij Luhovy is no slouch, either. Essentially, this is a crisply produced and slickly handed venture, with the stress upon wholesome clean-living youth. It will gratify the teen audience that is fed up with leering sex and mindless violence. — *Gran.*

El Diablo Y La Dama
(The Devil and the Lady, or The Itinerary of Hate)
(MEXICAN-FRENCH-COLOR)

Mexico City, Nov. 27.

Produced by SINC, S.A. (Mexico) Les Films du Passage (France), in collaboration with Conacite 2, Estudios America, and the French Foreign Relations Ministry. Stars Catherine Jourdan. Directed by Ariel Zuniga. Screenplay, Zuniga, Carlos Castanon; camera (color), Toni Kuhn; music, Agustin Lara, Beto Mendez; editor, Beto Mendez; editor, Claire Painchault. Reviewed at Pecime screening room, 16th Muestra Internacional de Cine, Mexico City, Nov. 27, 1983. Running time: 98 MINS.

America................Catherine Jourdan
Jimmy................Carlos Castanon
Lover and old man .....Richard Bohringer
Singer...................America Cisneros
Women with scar ....Patricia Meyer
Killer..............Juan Manuel Gonzalez

Completed barely a month ago, the Mexican-French coproduction "El Diablo y la Dama" is a pretentious effort to bring life a collage of themes from Mexican cabaret pics of the 1940s.

This is Ariel Zuniga's fourth feature, which seems like a deliberate

attempt to alienate the serious film audience he has attracted with past efforts such as "Apuntes" (1974), "Anacrusa" (1978) and "Uno Entre Muchos" (1981).

The mock-surrealist film is distinguished by beautiful photography, incomprehensible and apparently-arbitrary editing and boasts no discernible storyline.

The film attempts to delve into Mexico City's night-time world of cabarets and gangsters, of the sleazy underworld dealings and murder, of love and hate. This is underscored by playing Mexican composer Agustin Lara's "Cabellera Negra" over and over. The sparse dialog — in Spanish and French — uses the lyrics as a code to penetrate into the film's themes, but Catherine Jourdan's heavy accent makes even this difficult.

The film revolves around its themes without reason or rhyme and follows no chronological order.

The characters are America (Jourdan), a French performer who has an erotic nightclub act, "El Diablo y la Dama," that uses a devil dummy in masturbatory fashion. There is her lover, Jimmy (Carlos Castanon), a thief and adventurer. And America is haunted by her former lover and father figure, played by Richard Bohringer. She runs away with Jimmy, traveling the nightclub circuit throughout the Mexican republic. The film here takes on surface aspects of a "road movie," as the two travel en route to hell carrying the devil with them.

"El Diablo" is interesting only for what it attempts to do: applying a new approach to a Mexican genre picture. But it wears thin very quickly and winds up merely pretentious. — *Lent.*

The Last Affair
(HONG KONG-COLOR)

Hong Kong, Dec. 7.

A Pearl City Studio Production, released by Golden Harvest. Directed by Tony Au. Stars Chow Yun Fat, Do Do Cheng, Han Man-Chik, Season Ma, Kim Toech; camera (color), Bill Wong; art director, William Chang. (No other credits provided). Reviewed at State Theater, Hong Kong, Dec. 7, 1983. Running time: 100 MINS.

(Cantonese with English subtitles)

Oh, to be young, beautiful and in love in Paris ... what a beautiful thought. But not when the affair is between Chow Yun Fat, Do Do Cheng, Han Man Chik and for added complications, a Frenchwoman, Shophie, in Tony Au's stylish but empty directorial debut, set in paris.

It's appropriately titled "The Last Affair," and let us hope it is indeed the last unless they do a horror thriller for a sequel.

Patrick Tam's "Nomad" was pretentiously bad and irritatingly chop-suey in style by trying to be

westernized, but then "The Last Affair" came along.

Do Do takes a vacation to attend her friend's wedding in Paris, also to be away from Hong Kong and her businessman husband. Her marriage is falling apart. She visits her best friend, Han Man, who now works in a Vietnamese restaurant. On one of her shopping sprees (a good device to insert a lot of travelog footage), she meets Chinese violinist Chow in the Metro. Naturally, they meet again and fall in love. She does not know of Chow's previous active sexual activities in Paris.

Along the way, viewers are treated to lifted adaptation of sequences from "Last Tango In Paris." Art director Au is just that, an art director, and only suitable for the visual parts in the same manner that Chow's limitations as an actor never leave the level of just looking handsome. A film cannot rely on fashionable cinematography and an actor cannot survive on smiles and clothes to portray a Chinese bohemian in Prais without an inborn flair and total graps of the role.

In this case, director and actor are sadly miscast. The Chinese ladies fare better though they sound extremely sentimental as they talk about food and ribbons. The pacing of the movie is one long drawl, tied up too neatly in the end.

The film is meant to be a serious, dramatic love story with a tragic ending. Chow Yun Fat looks unbelievable as a serious violinist who reads French comic books, speaks dubbed French and drinks expresso. Supporting roles are equally funny looking, from the Chinese "Picasso" painter to his girl friend, Season Ma, in a minor role. Chow keeps taking a bath as if telling the audience the Chinese are cleaner than the French who supposedly don't wash before or after lovemaking.

Chow evidently reminds a great many ladies of their dream lover. To an extent, some puritans might find the movie immoral, with adultery, free love and nudity, but it is quite harmless in its insistence on the verities of romantic pulp fiction for modern audiences. The film is overlong, self-indulgent and painfully contribed, but a nice try to shoot a film outside Hong Kong. It is patently absurd in the sense that it is how a Chinese who wants to project a French image would handle the entire affair. —*Mel.*

1984

January 4, 1984

Le Bal
(The Ball)
(FRENCH-ITALIAN-ALGERIAN-COLOR)

Paris, Dec. 14.

AMLF release of a Cinéproduction/Films A2/Massfilm (Rome)/O.N.C.I.C. (Algiers) coproduction. Produced by Giorgio Silvagni. Features entire cast. Directed by Ettore Scola. Screenplay, Scola, Ruggero Maccari, Jean-Claude Penchenat, Furio Scarpelli, based on the stage production of the Theater du Campagnol, from an original idea by Jean-Claude Penchenat; camera (Fujicolor), Ricardo Aronovich; musical direction and original music, Vladimir Cosma; musical advisor, Armando Trovaioli; choreography, D'Dee; occupation tango, Jacques Bense; production designer, Luciano Ricceri; costumes, Ezio Altieri, Françoise Tournafond; editor, Raimondo Crociani; makeup, Otello Sisi; exec producer, Franco Committeri; associate producer, Mohamed Lakhdar Hamina; production managers, Pierre Saint-Blancat and Giorgio Scotton. Reviewed at the Publicis screening room, Paris, Dec. 13, 1983. Running time: **112 MINS.**

Cast: Etienne Guichard, Régis Bouquet, Francesco de Rosa, Arnault Lecarpentier, Liliane Delval, Martine Chauvin, Danielle Rochard, Nani Noël, Aziz Arbia, Marc Berman, Geneviève Rey-Penchenat, Michel Van Speybroeck, Rossana Di Lorenzo, Michel Toty, Raymonde Heudeline, Anita Picchiarini, Olivier Loiseau, Monica Scattini, Christophe Allwright, François Pick, Chantal Capron, Jean-François Perrier, Jean-Claude Penchenat.

Ettore Scola's film of the smash French legit musical, "The Ball," lacks the stage original's tour de force exhilaration and its sheer delight in bodies in movement. "Le Bal" was born as a collective creation by the members of the Theater du Campagnol who, under the overall direction of Jean-Claude Penchenat (a former collaborator of director Ariane Mnouchkine), literally danced out a social history of France in the last four decades.

Through a three-hour marathon of waltzes, foxtrots, tangos, boogie woogies, jitterbugs, bebops, two-steps, twists, cha-chas, rhumbas, the Campagnol dancers wittily and gracefully retraced manners, mores and changing styles in a kaleidoscopic theatrical fresco. Audiences in France and abroad pulsated with every changing rhythm, and the critics raved.

This abstract whirl of choreography and social gesture becomes relatively lethargic and lead booted in Scola's hands. There is a formal fidelity to the stage production: a single set (a typical French ballroom), no dialog, and the tableaux structure — the popular ball in Popular Front society of 1936 (Scola's addition, in fact), the German Occupation of the early '40s, the Liberation, Saint-Germain-des-Pres, the '50s and the Algerian War, May 1968, the present day. And the Italian director has recruited many of the original Campagnol company. But he betrays the show essentially.

It's not entirely his fault. There was no apparent way Scola could recreate the theatrical "experience" of "The Ball," with the spectator as privileged wallflower. And naturally the very nature of cinema, as opposed to theater, almost completely nullifies the pleasure of watching a virtuoso ensemble performance in non-stop metamorphosis. Sitting in front of Scola's film, one can't help looking ahead anxiously to "A Chorus Line" on the screen.

Where Scola stumbles seriously is in his cinematic viewpoint. He has cut, added, compressed and reshaped the original tableaux, which can be justified. But he also selects for the viewer, giving precedence to the closeup rather than the long-shot. The stage picture was like a Jacques Tati comedy — you could select any one of numerous images in a teeming, deep-focus composition. Scola offers each detail, each gesture, one by one, and since what he shows us is often facile or caricatural, it loses its charm and freshness. And he thus de-emphasizes the show's physicality and choreographic verve.

Audiences unfamiliar with the show may respond to the unusual concept, and some of the humour and characterizations of the original still work in front of the camera. But Scola hasn't really gone far enough in his screen transcription, and "Le Bal" is not profoundly different from the "canned theater" of the old days, technically polished, but a pale shadow of the initial packaging. —*Len.*

Maruja en el Infierno
(Maruja in Hell)
(PERUVIAN-COLOR)

Huelva, Dec. 9.

A Producciones Inca Films S.A. production. Produced by José Perla Velaochaga, Andrés Nobl. Executive producer, Emilio Moscoso. Directed by Francisco José Lombardi. Features entire cast. Camera (color), Pili Flores Guerra; screenplay, José Watanabe, Edgardo Russo, based on Enrique Congrains' book "No una sino muchas muertes;" art direction, special effects, José Watanabe; music, Arturo Kike Pinto; editor, Augusto Tamayo. Viewed at Huelva Film Festival, Dec. 9, 1983, in competition. Running time: **90 MINS.**

Maruja	Elena Romero
Alejandro	Pablo Serra
Doña Carmen	Doña Carmen
Malagua	Oscar Vega
Manuel	Julio Vega
Taxi driver	Jorge Rodriguez Paz
The Gang	Manuel Rodriguez, Juan Carlos Alarcón (as Pepe), Juan Alberto Díaz, José Luis Herrada

Even weirder than Doña Carmen's cottage industry is the fact that, according to exec producer Emilio Moscoso, such places actually exist in Lima. She manufactures glasses out of discarded bottles and her work force consists of inoffensive lunatics she collects off the city streets and, of course, does not pay.

She becomes the target for a band of juvenile delinquents who are joined by Alejandro, an unemployed shantytown youngster. To stake out the place and discover where she keeps her money, the gang commissions Alejandro to deliver and sell an insane old man to her. While trying to do so, he meets Maruja, Doña Carmen's godchild, who is as much a prisoner of this strange factory as of its hellish environment and has not lost hope of a better life.

Maruja and Alejandro immediately feel attracted towards each other and, after considerable complications, and much violence, they eventually succeed in breaking away together. Francesco Jose Lombardi is one of Peru's best-known directors.

"Maruja in Hell" is not one of his major achievements from an artistic point of view. Elena Romero (Maruja) has an attractive personality and considerable possibilities as an actress; Pablo Serra (Alejandro) also does well, but Lombardi's handling of the actors, particularly the lunatics, is uneven and a major shortcoming. Although realistically made, it often lacks the ring of truth and the statement about society Lombardi at times seems to imply, does not come off; the required bedlam atmosphere of the factory only works very intermittently.

Lombardi's "Maruja" has played for over two months in Lima, becoming one of the most successful Peruvian films ever; the explanation lies in its combination of colloquial six-letter words, a long sex scene and the very considerable violence of the film's last segment. These ingredients might carry the film in other Latin countries but, although it will probably surface at other fests, it is not very likely to break out any further. —*Amig.*

La Trace
(The Trace)
(FRENCH-SWISS-COLOR)

Paris, Dec. 14.

Fox-Hachette release of a NEF/Hachette Premiere/FR 3/Little Bear/Nickelodeon/Cinéthèque/Radio-Télévision Suisse Romande coproduction. Produced by Claude Nedjar, Bertrand Tavernier. Directed by Bernard Favre. Features entire cast. Screenplay, Favre and Tavernier; camera (Fujicolor), Jean-François Gondre; art director, Patrice Mercier; sound, Roger Letellier; music, Nicola Piovani and Marc Perrone; editor, Emmanuelle Thibault; costumes, Marie Malterre; exec producer, Bernard P. Guiremand. Reviewed at Studio 407, Paris, Dec. 12, 1983. Running time: **103 MINS.**

Joseph	Richard Berry
His wife	Bérangère Bonvoisin
His sister	Sophie Chemineau
Accordeonist	Marc Perrone
Immigrant worker	Robin Renucci
Girl at carnival	Jean Manson

And: Roger Jendely, Marie-Christine Grudzinski, Pierre Forget, Attillio Bus, Dina Zanone, Sonia Gessner, Alain Lenglet, Louis Beyler, Philippe du Janerand, Emilio Danna.

The best historical films are like time machines — they whisk you back into the past, and for a couple of hours make you feel like you're reliving an epoch, and not just looking dispassionately at some meticulously arranged wax works. Bernard Favre's "La Trace" is a fine time-machine picture, but its appeal is not ostentatious or spectacular and doesn't deal directly with any momentous event. It attempts something more difficult: a description of a time and place, as dimly perceived by a protagonist who doesn't know, and doesn't particularly care, what's going on beyond his own sphere of immediate experience.

"La Trace" is set in the Alpine Kingdom of Savoy in 1859, at the moment that it became part of France. Its hero is a Savoyard peasant, who lives in a mountain village with his wife and two children. During the winter months he must leave his family and make his way across the mountains into Italy, hawking small wares to village womenfolk. Favre's film is the story of that one winter's itinerary, from which the protagonist returns to discover that he is now a Frenchman.

Obviously the historical interest is not decorative and there is little here that is highly dramatic. Favre has previously edited and himself made ethnological documentaries (this is his first fiction feature) and his relationship to his material is like that of a warmhearted ethnologist. He is of Savoyard origins and is deeply interested in tracing his roots. He's done so with clarity, respect and discreet feeling. There's no sense of slumming or hindsight condescension in his portrait of the peasant and the numerous personages he meets on his trail.

No doubt, the presence of director Bertrand Tavernier, as co-scripter and coproducer, has been essential. Tavernier, who directed two of the best French historical films of the last decade ("Que La Fete Commence" and "Le Juge et l'Assassin"), helped Favre shape his original screenplay and give each scene maximal resonance, since a major aim here is to obliquely illustrate the social changes that are going on around his uncomprehending hero. The sequences sometimes vary in effect and there are patches of dullness, but the overall impression is that of a genuine moment plucked out of time and skillfully scanned.

Richard Berry confirms his talent and ranges in the difficult central role, which involved months of harsh on-location photography in the snow-bound Alps and the learning of the historical Savoyard dialect and some Italian (some later scenes are set in Milan, in the process of industrialization). His peasant-peddler is simple, canny, thickheaded, impertinent and touching.

Other parts are episodic but deftly portrayed, including Robin Renucci as a former village boy who's gone down into the Italian cities to become a factory labourer, Jean Manson, as a girl Berry briefly meets at a carnival, Sophie Chemineau, as the peasant's religious sister, whom he visits after losing his donkey and goods in a mountain crevice, and Bérangere Bonvoisin as Berry's demure spouse. Composer Marc Perrone, who wrote some of the wistful music for the film, appears in the apt role of the northbound Italian accordionist whose instrument enthralls Berry. (Nicole Piovani, who has worked for the Taviani brothers and Marco Bellocchio, shares co-credit for the picture's fine score.)

Favre makes fine use of the splendid Alpine vistas and Jean-Francois Gondre registers as a fine new French cinematographer.

"La Trace" has already been well-received in several international fests and could peddle its cinematic charms in art house climes. In any case, a solid debut by a writer-director of certified talents. —*Len.*

Rocking Silver
(DANISH-COLOR)

Copenhagen, Nov. 30.
A Film-Cooperativet Danmark 1983 ApS/Europa Film/The Danish Film Studio production, Nordisk Film A/S release. Features entire cast. Original story and script and directed by Erik Clausen. Camera (Eastmancolor) Morten Bruus; production design, Viggo Bentzon; costumes, Gitte Kolvig; editor, Ghita Beckendorff; music, Leif Sylvester Petersen; rock music supervision, Ivan "Melvis" Haagensen. Reviewed at the Danish Film Institute Main theater, Copenhagen, Nov. 30, 1983. Running time: **93 MINS.**
Benny ....Leif Sylvester Petersen
Frank........................Erik Clausen
Buller ....Bjorn Uglebjerg
Michael ....Hans Frellesvig
Connie......................Eva Madsen
Johnny ....Jens Okking
Johnny's wife ....Pia Stangerup
Tina ....Sanne Gundlev
Martin.......................Don Martin

"Rocking Silver," writer-director Erik Clausen's third feature film, again made in musical cooperation with actor-singersongwriter Leif Sylvester Petersen, is more or less a "road picture" bumping along in the tracks of the team's highly successful "Circus Casablanca," but similar foreign sales can hardly be expected this time, since Clausen is relying mostly on carelessly slapped-together episodes of stagy satirical sketch character along with a muddled narrative about a '50s rock group that gets back together to pay musical tribute to a dead longshoreman comrade and to get out of the various ruts they have been mired in for the past 20 years.

The writing is either over-emphatic or much too loose for many of the film's episodes to work. When the re-united group is being exploited by a ruthless manager to perform as backing group for the rhetroic of a right-wing politician, its lead singer, well hidden, pulls a knife on the man's sex, and the satirical fun turns clumsily vicious.

Whole series of popular Leftish or generally humanistic causes and points are illustrated with similar crudeness. Elsewhere, a more friendly kind of fun and traditional social melodrama is on display, while the washing and drying-out of a bum (played by Erik Clausen himself) constitute true comic relief. —*Kell.*

Tchao Pantin
(So Long, Stooge)
(FRENCH-COLOR)

Paris, Dec. 18.
AMLF release of a Renn production. Stars Coluche. Produced and directed by Claude Berri. Screenplay, Berri and Alain Page, from latter's novel; camera (Eastmancolor) and artistic collaborator, Bruno Nuytten; music, Charlélie Couture; art direction, Alexandre Trauner; editor, Hervé de Luze; sound, Jean Labussière; makeup, Didier Lavergne; executive producer, Pierre Grunstein; associate producer, Christian Spillemaecker. reviewed at the AMLF screening room, Paris, Dec. 15, 1983. Running time: **100 MINS.**
Lambert ....Michel Colucci (Coluche)
Bensoussan ....Richard Anconina
Lola.......................Agnès Soral
Bauer ....Philippe Léotard
Rachid ....Mahmoud Zemmouri

Coluche, the abrasive stand-up comic who dropped his stage image to become France's favorite screen teddy bear, plays it straight in "Tchao Pantin," a sordid psychological thriller helmed by his mentor, producer-director Claude Berri.

The funnyman flirted disastrously with pathos in his last vehicle, "La Femme de Mon Pote," directed by Bertrand Blier, and it's hard to say how his fans will react this time, though the pre-release hype about the birth of a tragedian should draw on curiosity value. For other markets this is a mostly well-made but predictable vehicle that trades heavily on familiar themes of urban sleaze, solitude and world-weariness.

Coluche is cast as a man going quietly to seed as a night attendant in a Paris gas station. Though his former employment and tragedy are not immediately revealed, it turns out he once was a respected police inspector who dropped out of sight after his junkie son died of an overdose and his wife walked out.

But he is jolted out of his alcoholic stupor by a young Arab (Anconina) who nightly stops by the station on a stolen motorbike. Slowly a guarded friendship evolves between the two, unshaken even by

the boy's confession that he peddles hard drugs.

When the youth is killed one night in front of the station by a pair of mysterious assailants, Coluche sets out to avenge his death with the aid of a Punk girl, whom the boy had been seeing. The trail leads to the Arab drug dealer who employed Anconina, and duly not only exacts vigilante justice, but also gets to humiliate the underworld kingpin manipulating the heroin network. Coluche falls in love with the girl but the promise of a rebirth is cut short when he is shot down in a gangland reprisal.

Berri wrote the script with Alain Page, who adapted his prize-winning novel. The initial premise of a friendship between the ex-cop and the young dope pusher is the most interesting part, even if the rapport is not always psychologically plausible (why does Coluche not react to Anconina's confession of his activities?). The second half of the film degenerates into a fairly routine "Death Wish" revenge drama, with an obvious tragic end for its hero, on the doorstep of a new life.

Coluche gives a credible reading of the derelict cop numbed by drink and self-disgust, but about 30% of his composition is the makeup. Though his alcohol-soaked expressions are often inexpressive, Berri never fails to hit Coluche with huge closeups that nudge the viewer with "Look, folks, he's acting" insistence. Coluche has the makings of a good dramatic player, but this is mostly self-conscious apprentice work, not really deep and never genuinely moving.

Acting kudos go instead to Anconina who confirms his talent in the employ of basically sympathetic felons. Good thing for the star that Anconina gets bumped off halfway through the picture, or he'd completely steal the show. Agnès Soral is touching as the Punkster who wants out with Coluche, and Philippe Léotard does his best as a police inspector who looks the other way when Coluche goes on the warpath.

Berri, apparently no stranger to the social netherworld of Paris, directs well, apart from his indulgences with his star and a dreadfully staged final sequence (in which, believe it or not, a black cat crosses Coluche's path just seconds before he's gunned down).

Tech credits are excellent, with Bruno Nuytten at the camera and veteran production designer Alexandre Trauner insuring meticulous squalor. French pop artist Charlélie Couture has composed some tunes that will probably help the soundtrack LP onto local charts. —*Len.*

Bomben Auf Berlin
(Bombs Over Berlin)
(WEST GERMAN-B&W-DOCU)

Berlin, Dec. 12.
A compilation documentary film produced by Chronos Film, Berlin. Bengt von zur Muehlen, producer. Written, compiled, and directed by Irmgard von zur Muehlen. Editing, Petra Heymann; music consultant, Wolfgang de Gelmini; narrators, Liselotte Rau, Uta Hallant, Mona Seefried; texts selected by eyewitness accounts by Ursula von Kardoff, Inge Deutschkron and others. Reviewed at Pallette in Zoo Palast Cinema Center, Berlin, Dec. 12, '83. Running time: **90 MINS.**

Irmgard von zur Muehlen (wife of Chronos producer Bengt von zur Muehlen) has established a reputation since 1979 as one of the leading femme docu filmers on the German film scene, her specialty being the historical compilation film. Thus far, she has to her credit four medium-length docus on personalities and traditions, five shorts, and two feature-length historical docus: "Thalia in Ruins" (1982) and "Bombs over Berlin" (1983), both referring to Berlin before, during, and after World War II.

"Bombs over Berlin" impresses particularly in its conceptual approach to a wartime experience that has undoubtedly left its scars upon large numbers of the surviving German population — it's a women's view of the "Life Between Fear and Hope" (as the pic's subtitle states the viewpoint). The selected texts underscoring the docu footage is from letters and diaries kept by women-eyewitnesses, while the narration itself is delivered by legit thesps in a polished and sympathetic manner. Since the film is constructed along chronological lines, the dramatic element is heightened as the bombing increases and the city is buried under its own rubble.

It would be difficult to estimate how many cameramen contributed originally to the making of this compilation film, but a hats-off tribute can be detected throughout in the manner in which the clips and footage are selected and juxtaposed for effect. In order to place the docu in its proper focus as an historical record, the von zur Muehlen producer-director team preemed "Bombs over Berlin" Nov. 18, the 40th anniversary (if such can be said) of the first British bombing in the so-called "Fight for Berlin" that carried on thereafter almost unbroken until the bitter end in April 1945.

For the record, beginning in November 1943, a total of 310 air-attacks by the Allies culminated in 47,000 tons of bombs on Berlin. On Nov. 18, 1943, alone, a total of 402 British bombers flew their first dangerous mission with a load of 1,815 tons of bombs. Throughout 1944, the air raid alarms on 134 days totaled over 137 hours; in 1945, for just four months, they totaled 147 hours in 81 days. This means Berliners spent half of the last 18 months of the war under alarms of threatened and actual bombing.

What is more, the German cameramen dutifully took photos and lensed footage of the catastrophic bombings, all of which was reviewed in the Ministry of Propaganda and then mostly marked for secretive storage in archives on the grounds that the general public didn't need to see photographed misery but required instead images of diverting mirth or simply enthusiastic (sic) support for the Third Reich and the Fatherland.

Irmgard von zur Muehlen pairs these contrasting records to show both the truth and the veneer; and when the accounts in diaries and letters are read to accompany these contrasting images on the screen, the poignant moments of an all-embracing human drama are felt. It is this "universality" that gives the documentary its integrity, for fire-bombings are much in discussion today in the aftermath of the "The Day After" and "Testament."

So far as historians are concerned, there is much to be praised in "Bombs over Berlin." Unknown or neglected footage is presented. We see Unter den Linden and Berlin-Mitte as it was in the mid-1930s before the war entered the consciousness of Berliners: buildings that have since disappeared, and architectural treasures that are now lost forever. Then, as the war-machine begins to move, the city takes on a new profile: the bombastic Speer architectural plans, the spacious Hitler-commissioned Reichskanzlei (designed "to humble minor potentates"), and women taking over jobs for their men now on the fighting fronts. Finally, as the bombs begin to fall and the war effort mounts, we see Wilhelm Furtwängler conducting the Berlin Philharmonic in the Borsig factory, Göbbels and Göring visiting the bombed-out sites in the city, and performing personalities like Heinz Rühmann, Curt Jürgens, and the Hiller Girls doing their stuff to quiet the worried public.

Finally, there are the ruins that speak for themselves. On Feb. 3, 1945, the center of Berlin between Alexanderplatz and the Brandenburg Gate was laid level by 937 bombers in what scores as probably the height of the "total war" experience: 2,541 dead, 714 missing, 1,688 wounded and 119,057 homeless. It was a moment of reckoning for British bombers; for the bombings of London by Germans throughout 1940 had totaled 222 dead, 428 injured, and 9,000 homeless. Sometimes, statistics take on flesh-and-blood in a documentary — as in the case of "Bombs over Berlin." — *Holl.*

Dead Wrong
(CANADIAN-COLOR)

Vancouver, Dec. 27.

A Comworld International release of a Sounder Productions film. Produced and directed by Len Kowalewich. Executive producer, Tony Parsons. Features entire cast. Screenplay, Ron Graham; camera (color), Doug McKay; sound, Larry Sutton; editor, Jana Fritsch; music, Karl Kobylansky; art director, Ian Thomas; costumes, Trish Keating. Reviewed at Ridge Theatre, Vancouver, Dec. 20, 1983. Running time: **93 MINS.**

Sean Phelan	Winston Rekert
Priscilla Lancaster/'Penny'	Britt Ekland
Mike Brady	Dale Wilson
Insp. Fred Foster	Jackson Davies
The Stranger	Alex Daikun
Bahama Jones	Leon Bibb
Didi	Annie Kidder

Canadian Broadcasting cameraman Len Kowalewich has brought in a viable thriller for under $1,-000,000 that looks as though it cost thrice as much. Shot under the title, "The Colombian Connection," Kowalewich's pic was the first feature to benefit from 50% salary deferrals from the local branches of IATSE. "Dead Wrong" is Kowalewich's directorial debut.

Drug smugglers find that gullible fisherman Winston Rekert is the right sucker to sail a cargo of grass and coke from Colombia. Little do the bad guys know that the Canadian Mounties have been keeping tabs on the smugglers all the way. Undercover agent Britt Ekland falls for the young seadog, who mainly wants to get out from under the hassle that his old chum, Dale Wilson, has mismanaged. Both the Vancouver Mafia and the Canadian Armed Forces tangle with the innocent abroad.

The one quality that "Dead Wrong" has in its favor throughout is the crisp, imaginative lensing of Doug McKay. Though the tall tale, said to be based upon fact, is brazenly padded out to the requisite 93 minutes, every shot shows the eye of a craftsman. If only the same could be said for Ron Graham's script!

Fortunately, the cast imparts a degree of dignity to the low-keyed reprise of "Treasure Of The Sierra Madre," with obligatory double cross derring-do. Both Rekert and funnyman Jackson Davies are warm performers, as are Leon Bibb and Annie Kidder, sister of Margot. There's a tongue in cheek attitude on the part of this quartet that is perfectly judged.

Editor Jana Fritsch has cleverly cut around a very low shooting ratio with a style that at first seems eccentric, then becomes quaint.

"Dead Wrong" is short on thrills, but packs in the local color, and the sight of sails in the sunset. Nothing highly original goin' on here, but a cruise that beguiles for the duration. —*Gran.*

Isfugle
(Ice Birds)
(DANISH-COLOR)

Copenhagen, Dec. 13.

A Metronome with The Danish Film Institute production, Warner & Metronome release. Original story and script, Hans Hansen and Soeren Kragh Jacobsen. Directed by Kragh Jacobsen. Camera (Eastmancolor) Dan Lausten; editor, Jansu Billeskov Jansen; music, Kenneth Knudsen; production design, Henrik Moeller-Soerensen; production management, Michael Christensen, Henrik Moeller-Soerensen; costumes, Jette Termann. Reviewed at the Dagmar, Copenhagen, Dec. 12, 1983. Running time: **110 MINS.**

John	Peter Hesse Overgaard
Rene	Michael Ehlert Falch
Vivi	Mette Munk Plum
Rene's father	Dick Kaysoe
John's mother	Rita Angela
John as a boy	Alex Svanbjerg
Rene as a boy	Casper Bengtson

In Danish ornithology, an ice bird (alcedo atthis) is similar in looks and feeding habits to a kingfisher. The ice bird is not migratory, on the contrary it stays put during the cold Scandinavian winter. Writer-director Soeren Kragh Jacobsen is not inclined to carry the symbolism of his psychological thriller feature's title, "Ice Birds," too far. He seems satisfied with having suggested his main protagonists' ability to brave the freezing winds of their native habitat. But that, too, is an empty conceit, since one of his protagonists is clearly headed for a fall.

In a psychological thriller that is also a romantic melodrama turning on a case of male bonding, John, a peaceful, 30-year-old chief operator at the main console of a power plant, is drawn towards Rene, a brooding, harddrinking, at times boisterous loner and social dropout who has his old Thunderbird set on a collision course with his rich father, the latter supposedly guilty of Rene's mother's death.

Rene is turning into a regular terrorist. John wants no part in the terrorism but otherwise has new vistas opened to him by Rene's more innocently expansive gestures. And Rene is, of course, similarly charmed by John's quiet pleasures: listening to classical music and nursing sick birds of all sizes back to flying health.

While the built-in tensions of the male bonding is soon diluted by the appearance of the girl who will soon lead John to matrimony, the friendship itself is neither described nor explored in any depth. It is just taken for granted that John will indiscriminately follow Rene on his course of self-destruction. John reaches out, but cannot ultimately stop Rene from falling. Film has lot of juggling with various symbolic artifacts, especially concerning flame, fire and bird life. It also has nicely balanced acting in leads whose psychological potential however remains unexplored.

The cinematography by Dan Lausten has much in the way of sheer pictorial drama to commend it, but the general suspense of the action is handled rather clumsily and/or edited to death.

"Ice Birds" has more ambitions than Kragh Jacobsen can handle. He seems especially burdened by a script from which he has failed to weed out both the many instances of cloying symbolism and sequences that are just plain inexplicable in the dramatic context. The general production values are excellent and film is sure to attract some attention on the festival circuit. As an international sales item, it is hardly migratory. —*Kell.*

Los Refugiados de la Cueva del Muerto
(The Refugees from Dead Man's Cave)
(CUBAN-COLOR)

Huelva, Dec. 6.

An ICAIC production directed by Santiago Alvarez. Feature entire cast. Screenplay, Alvarez, Rebeca Chavez, Alfredo del Cueto, based on Mario Rojas' "Dead Man's Cave;" camera (color), Ivan Napoles; music, Leo Brouwer, Silvio Rodriguez; edited, Roberto Bravo, Lina Baniela; art director, Jose Manuel Villa. Reviewed at Huelva Film Fest, Dec. 6, 1983. Running time: **75 MINS.**

Cast: Rene de la Cruz Jr., Javier González, Reinaldo Lopez, Jos Pascual, Alberto Pujol, Jorge Trinchet, Orlando Casin, Dagoberto Gainza, Rogelio Meneses, Mora Heset, Ramiro Herrero, Joel Nuñez, and Raul Pomares.

Santiago Alvarez has earned a considerable and well-deserved international reputation as a maker of documentary films. Here he attempts a sort of historical reconstruction: the aftermath of the frustrated assault on the Moncada army barracks in 1953, with dictator Fulgencio Batista's troops fanning out over the countryside, capturing or killing the youngsters who took part in the attack.

Although brief, the film never makes up its mind in which genre it is trying to develop the story. At times it approaches its subject as if Alvarez' aim were a close documentary reconstruction; at others, the director seems to be trying for a fictional approach. And, towards the end, a further element is introduced through a short interview on the Moncada attack with Fidel Castro. One of the film's major aims is to show the peasants' solidarity with the fleeing students, but there is an unfortunate tendency to indulge in the sort of revolutionary rhetoric that was in vogue during the '60s and early '70s.

As a result the film is neither a powerful historical reconstruction nor a moving fictional interpreta-

tion of events. The Moncada subject could have become a telling experience either way but, as it stands, does not come to life.
—*Amig.*

Adiós Miami
(Bye Bye Miami)
(VENEZUELAN-COLOR)

Huelva, Dec. 6.

A producciones Doble Ele C.A. production. Directed by Antonio Llerandi. Features entire cast. Screenplay, Fausto Verdial; camera (color), Hector Ríos; music, Chuchito Sanoja; sound, Josué H. Savedra; edited by José Garrido. Reviewed at Huelva Film Fest, Dec. 6, 1983. Running time: **100 MINS.**

Cast: Gustavo Rodriguez, Tatiana Capote, Hernán Letjer, Isabel Hungría, Koke Corona, and Alicia Plaza.

Like the 1981 Argentine film "Easy Money" (Plata Dulce), Venezuela's "Bye Bye Miami" is set in Latin America's recent boom years and deals with those who took advantage of the situation to make a fast (and not necessarily honest) buck, until the bubble burst. They are then left out in the cold, while this largely artificial period of prosperity comes to an end.

Oswaldo Urbaneja (Gustavo Rodriguez), a 40ish, nouveau riche executive, picks up a race horse at an auction, discards a pregnant mistress, finds a new girl friend (Tatiana Capote) and, when he returns home, is informed by his daughter that she is pregnant and that his son has been suspended from school.

In spite of cracks in his real estate deals, Oswaldo decides to go to Miami with his new mistress, a tv actress with the contours of a Playboy centerfold. After a few days of living it up, devaluation and the breaking crisis back home put an end to the spree. Oswaldo's firm goes bankrupt and he is exposed as a swindler by the Caracas press. In Miami, Venezuelan credit cards are no longer honored, Oswaldo is bounced from his hotel and his girl leaves him to fly home.

With no money left, he tries to get a job, washes dishes and, ever more unshaven and unkempt, becomes a derelict who drifts around Dade County. Finally, in a witty ending, he starts a new life by pretending to be an exhausted Cuban refugee.

The social and economic background of the boom that became a bust is shared by many Latin countries and liable to surface again in South American films. Llerandi's version of this theme can expect to have a successful run on its home screens, but is unlikely to gain much international exposure. Thesping is uneven, but Koke Corona, in a minor role (Oswaldo's son), emerges as a young actor with considerable potential.

At times farcical and at others close to the telenovela genre, "Bye Bye Miami" is flawed in its screenplay and editing; other technical credits are all right but Llerandi's know-how as a director is still limited. —*Amig.*

Amada
(Amada)
(CUBAN-COLOR)

Huelva, Dec. 8.

An ICAIC production. Directed by Humberto Solas. Features entire cast. Screenplay, Nelson Rodriguez, Solas, based on Miguel Carrion's novel, "La Esfinge;" camera (color), Livio Delgado; music, Leo Brouwer; edited by Nelson Rodriguez. Reviewed at Huelva Film Fest, Dec. 8, 1983 in competition. Running time: **95 MINS.**

Cast: Eslinda Nuñez, César Evora, Silvia Planas, Andres Hernández, Oneida Hernández.

Humberto Solás' "Lucia" was the film that, together with Gutierrez Alea's "Memories of Underdevelopment" put Cuban films on the map in the late sixties, but Solás' recent work has not fulfilled the promise of his early features. "Cecilia," which competed at Cannes in 1982, did poorly, from both a critical and a commercial point of view and his latest, "Amada," is just as unlikely to enhance his reputation.

At best, it is a stylistic exercise that tries to infuse new life into old-time melodrama; but, in spite of beautiful photography and Eslinda Nuñez's acting, the attempt does not come to life and often provokes unintended laughter from the audience.

The story deals with Amada, an unhappily married woman of the upper classes and her love for a younger man to which she never dares commit herself, due to the mores of her period and caste. One of Solás' mistakes may well have been that he stuck too closely to a literary form of period dialog which was probably drawn from Carrión's novel but sounds as ridiculous today as its equivalent in a contemporary telenovela is likely to appear to people in the mid-21st century.

The film's apparent attempt to explore the melodrama genre does not come off and, besides not working as entertainment, it becomes a somewhat futile exercise in style. After the actual story reaches its tragic ending, Solás appends a scene of a hunger march that also took place in 1914. This seems a rather sudden and arbitrary endeavour to show another side of events of the period; as if, the director feels the need to prove that he has not lost his social conscience.

However, in spite of the film's shortcomings, Nuñez's acting is very impressive and she well deserves her Huelva acting award. Period style acting at this level is definitely unusual in Latin-American films. —*Amig.*

Ardiente Paciencia
(With Burning Patience)
(W. GERMAN-PORTUGUESE-COLOR-16m)

Huelva, Dec. 9.

A Von Vietinghoff Filmproduktion GmbH. production in collaboration with Prole Film (Portugal) and on behalf of ZDF, 2d German TV Network. Features entire cast. Directed by Antonio Skarmeta. Screenplay, Skarmeta; camera (color), Joao Abel Aboim; music, Roberto Lecaros; editor, Agape Dorstewitz. Reviewed at Huelva Film Festival, Dec. 9, 1983, in competition. Running time: **79 MINS.**
Pablo Neruda . . . . .Roberto Parada
Mario Jimenez . . . . .Oscar Castro
Beatriz . . . . .Marcela Osorio
Rosa vda. de Gonzalez . . .Naldy Hernandez

Shot in Portugal with local technicians, "Ardiente Paciencia" was financed by German television its director and cast are Chilean and the film is spoken in Spanish. Earlier this year it won the top award at the Biarritz fest and at Huelva it also obtained the main prize (ex aequo with the Argentine "Wait For Me A Long Time"). At both fests audiences voted it most popular film. Berlin-based director Antonio Skarmeta is a writer whose works have been translated into several languages and he has also authored screenplays for German directors Peter Lilienthal and Christian Ziewer.

"With Burning Patience" takes place in Isla Negra, a Chilean seaside village where Nobel Prize winner Pablo Neruda lived until his death in 1983. It does not show the poet's relation with his peers, but presents an intimate view of him, in everyday life and contacts with the local people. Given Neruda's worldwide reputation and friends in many countries, he is obviously the local postman's best customer and, from the very beginning, it is clear that there is a friendly relationship between the aging poet and young Mario Jimenez who delivers his mail.

Mario falls in love with the local innkeeper's daughter and asks the poet for help because, in Beatriz's presence, he is at a total loss for words. He ends up courting her with quotes from Neruda's love poems which he passes off as his own.

The story line is quite simple: first, the relationship between poet and postman, with its father-son and teacher-disciple undertones; then, the love of Mario and Beatriz, her mother's opposition to the match and the poet's involvement, as a slightly bemused and friendly advisor and mediator.

Shaded in, at first in the background and coming to the fore as the film develops, are the events of the period: the Nobel Prize award and an extract of Neruda's acceptance speech (from which the film's title is drawn), his brief span as presidential candidate and, later, as Chilean ambassador to Paris (under the Allende regime), followed by the poet's return, the 1973 military takeover and, a few days later, his death.

The film ends with Mario's arrest after the coup.

"With Burning Patience" is a low-key fable, enhanced by witty dialog and considerable humor; the general atmosphere is both tender and unpretentiously poetic and the very simplicity of the ingredients may well account for the film's effectiveness.

Roberto Parada's physical resemblance to the late poet is striking and his performance is well matched with Oscar Castro's postman. Technical credits are OK, but the handling of the extras in some crowd scenes is below the production's general level.

The film only cost $200,000 and, when the 35m blowup becomes available, it stands a good chance of finding international outlets, both on its own merits and due to the interest the Neruda name could provoke in art house audiences. Both the poet's and Skarmeta's literary reputations should also help to develop an afterlife for the film in the non-theatrical market.—*Amig.*

Garota Dourada
(Golden Girl)
(BRAZILIAN-COLOR)

Rio de Janeiro, Dec. 18.

An Embrafilme release of a L.C. Barreto Production. Directed by Antonio Calmon. Feature entire cast. Screenplay, Calmon, Flavio Tambellini Jr.; camera (Eastmancolor), Carlos Egberto; art direction, Pedro Nanni; sound, Jorge Saldanha; editing, Vera Freire; music, Guilherme Arantes; songs by Arantes, Lulu Santos, Nelson Motta; opening credits, Ricardo van Steen, Ucho de Carvalho; produced by Fabio Barretto; associate producer, Embrafilme. Reviewed at L.C. Barreto Screening room, Rio de Janeiro, Dec. 17, 1983. Running time: **105 MINS.**

Cast: Bianca Byington, André de Biase, Sérgio Mallandro, Roberto Betaglin, Andréa Beltrão, Geraldo D'El Rey, Carlos Wilson, Ricardo Graça Mello, Marina, Claudia Magno.

This is the second part of a trilogy, initiated with "Menino do Rio" (The Boy From Rio) two years ago and to be followed by "Menina Veneno" (Poison Girl) in 1985. It is the Brazilian version of the "beach movies" of the '50s, produced by Luiz Carlos Barreto (here associated with his son Fabio, who directed "India, the Daughter of Sun"), a producer traditionally concerned with the commercialization and final quality of his product.

Director Antonio Calmon is the same of "Menino do Rio" and the plot uses the same characters: a young surfer (Biase), now abandoned by his wife (Magno), decides to go away to the wild beaches of the Brazilian south coast, with his friend Zeca (Sergio Mallandro), a rock singer tired of the endless tours and attention of hundreds of female fans. While surfing, wind surfing and flying, both experience affairs with pretty young girls and are predictably threatened by rivals, in an atmosphere of music, freedom and mysticism.

Young sports, lovely landscapes and healthful people are the basic elements for a commercially positive result of this item oriented for teenagers. Using a pretty, young actress, Bianca Byington, and a popular tv comedian, Sergio Mallandro, was a good step by Barreto to improve domestic revenues over "Menino do Rio." Yet the problems and conflicts among the characters are no different from those in Hawaii or Australia — and a fine set of songs also helps the pic to be salable beyond local audiences.

Further accomplishments could not be expected from a beach movie. The surfing scenes could easily be improved, as could the latent sensuality of the plot. Nevertheless, aerial sequences are fine and "Golden Girl" offer attractive images and sounds for almost two hours through a professional technical standard. Maybe it is not too much, but it is sufficient to make the item noticeable by its target audience.—*Hoin.*

F.F.S.S. Cioé: "Che Mi Hai Portato a Fare Sopra A Posillipo Se Non Mi Vuoi Piu' Bene?"
(F.F.S.S.)
(ITALIAN-COLOR)

Rome, Dec. 27.

A Gaumont and Reteitalia release, produced by Mario Orfini and Emilio Bolles for Eidoscope productions. Stars Renzo Arbore, Roberto Benigni. Directed by Renso Arbore. Screenplay, Renzo Arbore, Luciano De Crescenzo; camera (Eastmancolor), Renato Tafuri, art director, Franco Vanorio; editor, Anna Napoli; music, Renzo Arbore and others. Reviewed at Barberini Cinema, Rome, Dec. 21, 1983. Running time: 111 MINS.
Film director/
talent scout .... Renzo Arbore
Lucia Canaria .... Pietra Montecorvina
The Beige Sheik .... Roberto Benigni

Tv showman Renzo Arbore has written and directed another way out comedy, after his controversial '82 hit, "Pap' Occhio" (In The Pope's Eye). Protesting the unauthorized use of his name and person this time is another illustrious Roman, Federico Fellini. Pic's massive publicity campaign, including the Arbore-Fellini feud, explains entry's strong start around the country.

Pic is a 100% Italo item that will have difficulty being understood beyond domestic screens and RAI-TV antenna range, due to its high saturation of local references. One of its major ploys is to spotlight guest appearances by well-known tv figures. While these personali-

ties may cause a gasp of delighted recognition onshore, their bits will seem unaccountably humorless to those not in the know.

Taking its cue from the attention span of channel-hopping tv audiences. "F.F.S.S." dispenses with storyline, logic and structure. Arbore plays a double role. One is a ringmaster-film director who is shooting a film called "Federico Fellini South Story," based on a script which has blown out the window of Fellini's study while the Maestro is in the bathroom and which providentially falls into Arbore's convertible.

Meanwhile, a curly-haired Neapolitan Arbore in loud shirts is a third-rate talent agent trying to promote a lowly singer named Lucia Canaria. They fail on local tv, but on the taunting advice of a goofy rock star called "The Beige Sheik" (Roberto Benigni) they try their luck in Milan, at RAI-TV, and finally at the San Remo song fest. It is here that chance offers Lucia a crack at the bigtime, and her powerful, raucous voice — in spots throughout the film — blasts out a protest song called "South" that brings the house down.

The North-South polemic is a running theme that gives pic a minimum of depth. It also accounts for some of the better jokes.

Arbore hosted a bizarre variety show called "The Other Sunday," the source of many "F.F.S.S." comics as well as pic's jabberwocky nonsense humor. Dialog is largely ad-libbed, which makes for tedious moments of stalling and repetition. Actors seem virtually undirected. Suffering from this particularly is newcomer Pietra Montecovina, the singer with a soulful, little girl face who plays Lucia in a number of different keys — sometimes silent and waiflike, at other times bold, glib and sophisticated.

She is at her best away from Arbore, as in the hilarious (but too long) scene in jail (she has been arrested for stealing an apple), when she stumbles across a "sanctuary" to Sophia Loren — "Her" cell — and the diva appears to her as a saint, advising the girl to "grab her chance." —*Yung.*

Over The Brooklyn Bridge
(COLOR)

Pleasant, old-fashioned Big Apple romance.

An MGM-UA Entertainment/Cannon Group release of a Golan-Globus production for City Films. Produced by Menahem Golan, Yoram Globus. Directed by Golan. Stars Elliott Gould, Margaux Hemingway, Sid Caesar, Burt Young, Shelley Winters, Carol Kane. Screenplay, Arnold Somkin; camera (Metrocolor), Adam Greenberg; editor, Mark Goldblatt; music, Pino Donaggio; sound, Nigel Noble; assistant director, David Womark; production manager, Carl Clifford; art director, John Lawless; post-production supervisor, Karen Koenig; associate producer, Christopher Pearce; fashion show sequence by Tracy Mills. Reviewed at Westside screening room, N.Y., Jan. 11, 1984. (MPAA Rating: R). Running time: 106 MINS.
Alby Sherman .... Elliott Gould
Elizabeth Anderson .. Margaux Hemingway
Uncle Benjamin .... Sid Caesar
Phil Romano .... Burt Young
Becky Sherman .... Shelley Winters
Cheryl Goodman .... Carol Kane
Eddie .... Robert Gosset
Marlena .... Karen Shallo
Also with: Jerry Lazarus, Francine Beers, Leo Postrel, Rose Arrick, Matt Fischel, Lynnie Greene, Amy S. Ryder, Sal Richards, Leib Lensky, Lou David, Tom McDermott, Zvee Scooler, Mort Freeman, Marh Gutzi.

"Over The Brooklyn Bridge" is producer-director (and Cannon Group chairman) Menahem Golan's love letter to New York City: a warm and pleasant romance similar to the type of films topliner Elliott Gould (and George Segal, as well) used to make 10 or 15 years ago. Boasting an outstanding (and promotable) supporting performance by Sid Caesar as Gould's bossy uncle, the picture (geared to the audience that attended "My Favorite Year") should do okay business when released later this year through MGM-UA, following its current debut in Tel Aviv.

Screenplay by the late Arnold Somkin (who died in 1982 before production began, and to whom "Bridge" is dedicated) is short on laughs but very effective in portraying a loving, romantic view of New York and its melting pot of ethnic groups. As directed by Golan, and cheerfully lit by cameraman Adam Greenberg, the Big Apple is a paradise where even 42d Street and the subways are sources of glamor rather than the clichéd eyesores they represent in most recent N.Y.-lensed films.

Gould stars as Alby Sherman, owner of a Brooklyn eatery who dreams of buying a posh restaurant on the East Side in midtown Manhattan. His love affair with an aristocratic Catholic girl from Philadelphia (Margaux Hemingway) raises the ire of his Jewish family, particularly the patriarch Uncle Benjamin (Sid Caesar), a women's underwear manufacturer who would rather have Alby marry his fourth cousin Cheryl (Carol Kane).

The basic conflict, as Alby must choose between his dream girl and career advancement (Uncle Benjamin offers a key loan with strings attached) is not developed beyond the plot gimmick stage, but "Bridge" works well as an actors' vehicle. Leads Gould and Hemingway are solid in the central roles, with standout support from a large cast. Given perhaps his best opportunity in an off-and-on film career to date (including his starring assignments for William Castle in the 1960s), Caesar is very funny as a man who tries to run everyone else's lives for them. He is extremely moving at the film's moment of catharsis, enduring Gould's ultimate rebellion in a strong last-reel scene set at an engagement party.

Kane is delightfully droll as the virginal intellectual whose demure exterior hides a rather kinky fantasy-sex life. There are also nice spots for an Italian pal played by the ubiquitous Burt Young and a variety of other ethnic types.

Release title is a bit weak, with the dialog plugging most of the discarded monikers for this project: "Alby's Special," "Alby's Delight" and "My Darling Shiksa." The marketing challenge is to find an audience for a nice little film which avoids contemporary hooks in favor of romantic-comedy formulas that worked well in the late 1960s.
— *Lor.*

Segni Particolari: Bellissimo
(Distinguishing Marks: Handsome)
(ITALIAN-COLOR)

Rome, Jan. 7.

A C.I.C. release, produced by Giovanni Di Clemente for Rual Cinema Corporation RCC. Stars Adriano Celentano, Federica Moro. Written and directed by Castellano and Pipolo. Camera (Eastmancolor), Danilo Desideri; art director, Bruno Amalfitano; editor, Antonio Siciliano; music, Gino Santercole. Reviewed at America Cinema, Rome, Jan. 6, 1984. Running time: 83 MINS.
Mattia .... Adriano Celentano
Michela .... Federica Moro

Popular entertainer Adriano Celentano stars in two or more vehicles a year with the same, apparently sure-fire formula; "Distinguishing Marks: Handsome" is no exception. A well-packaged comedy, written and helmed by veterans Castellano and Pipolo, pic has done very well at the holiday b.o. and will appeal to related markets.

Once more Celentano finds himself in the role of an irresistible bachelor who scorns matrimony until the last reel. The setting is a scenic town on Lake Como, where Mattia (Celentano), a super-successful novelist, lives alone and fights off the excessive attention of the ladies with the help of his next-door neighbor Michela (Federica Moro).

As soon as his latest conquest mentions the word Marriage, Mattia tells her she will have to pass muster with his "daughter" Michela. The teenage neighbor obligingly finds fault with the prospective bride and breaks off the affair.

However, Michela is in love with Mattia herself. Their 25-year age difference poses a problem for the writer, but he gets over his scruples by pic's end at the altar.

The whole story is framed by Mattia confessing his illicit love affairs to an understanding priest.

The appeal of Celentano's films lies in their brazen exaggeration, magic and camera tricks in which only the scripters' imagination is the limit. A motorcyclist shows off popping a wheelie and Mattia, not to be outdone, rears his sportscar up on its back wheels for a run down the road. Michela needs a hand in an exam; Mattia types an essay for her on a roll of toilet paper and sends it unwinding past the window of the exam room on helium balloons.

Another typical piece of Celentano humor is reversing stereotypes, for better or worse. Mattia falls for an African woman whose parents don't like whites; he spends a fortune on suntan lotion trying to darken his complexion. Mattia the sex-object walks down the street while women faint, drive their cars into telephone poles and try to pinch him.

However many times he does it, Celentano never seems tired or out of patience with the role of the boundless egoist. His youthful co-star Federica Moro is not only a pretty face, but a professional and talented comedienne full of saucy verve and self-assurance. —Yung.

Angel
(COLOR)

Dull tale of teen hooker.

Hollywood, Jan. 12.

A New World release of an Adams Apple/Sandy Howard production. Produced by Roy Watts, Donald P. Borchers. Executive producers, Mel Pearl, Don Levin. Features entire cast. Directed by Robert Vincent O'Neil. Screenplay, O'Neil, Joseph M. Cala. Camera (CFI color), Andy Davis; editors, Charles Bornstein, Wilt Henderson; music, Craig Saffin; art direction, Stephen Marsh; sound, Craig Felburg; assistant director, Betsy Pollack. Reviewed at the New World Screening Room, Los Angeles, Jan. 11, 1984. MPAA Rating: R. Running time: 92 MINS.

Lt. Andrews	Cliff Gorman
Mosler	Susan Tyrrell
Mae	Dick Shawn
Kit Carson	Rory Calhoun
Killer	John Diehl
Angel/Molly	Donna Wilkes
Crystal	Donna McDaniel
Lana	Graem McGavin
Patricia Allen	Elaine Giftos
Jenkins	Mel Carter
Yo Yo Charlie	Steven Porter
Ric Sawyer	David Underwood

"Angel" is the first in-house production of the "new" New World. On the evidence, one is obliged to say that the difference between the old New World and the new New World is the difference between good sleaze and dull sleaze. To put the bottom line upfront, Roger Corman would never have made a picture about a Hollywood Boulevard hooker who never takes her clothes off and never turns a trick, but that's exactly what "Angel" is. Premise is good, and ad campaign makes the most of the story's exploitable angles, so initial biz may provide sufficient payoff relative to investment. But pic itself has little to offer.

Eponymous character is an underaged (about 15) prostie who leads a Jekyll and Hyde existence, since by day she's a straight-A student at an exclusive high school who fends off potential suitors by claiming her mother insists she's too young to date.

Film devotes little time to her mundane classroom life, however, better to focus on her unusual extracurricular activities. Angel struts her stuff up and down the Boulevard in the company of other girls as well as transvestite Dick Shawn and gun-toting Rory Calhoun, a former Western cowboy under the illusion he is really Kit Carson.

Moving it all along is the seemingly inevitable psycho who's out there knocking off hookers right and left. The sicko's got a mommy complex, Angel's got a daddy problem, and the whole lot of them are so unappealing that parents everywhere could use this film as a pretext to keep their daughters as far away from Los Angeles as possible.

As stated, basic dramatic situation does hold some potential, but filmmakers appear both reluctant to take it to the limit as exploitation, and incapable of confronting its serious, real-life dimensions. Instead, film falls into a deadly middle ground of hackneyed characters and cliched sequences which fail to engage interest on any level.

Presumably, Angel is working the streets in order to pay for her education, but one has to wonder where the money comes from since she rejects — undoubtedly with good reason — every potential customer who comes her way. It's also difficult to figure out how she gets such good grades when she spends all her free time stomping the pavement.

One eyebrow raiser is that the psycho-killer here is introduced in precisely the same manner Eric Roberts' Paul Snider character is first glimpsed in "Star 80" — doing sit-ups, with his face rising right into the camera.

All cast members seem to have been just punching the time clock on this one. Susan Tyrrell puts in one of her specialty crazed acts as Angel's lesbian landlady, Cliff Gor-

man is uniformly grim as a policeman on the killer's case, Calhoun at least brings an amiability to the cowpoke, while Donna Wilkes is all surface effects in the lead. One would never guess Shawn is loaded with talent from his lackluster turn as the drag queen.

Tech credits are merely serviceable. —Cart.

Hot Dog ... The Movie
(COLOR)

Can't cut the mustard.

Hollywood, Jan. 9.

An MGM/UA rlease of a Hot Dog Partnership production, produced by Edward S. Feldman. Executive producer, Christopher W. Knight; coproducer Mike Marvin. Directed by Peter Markle. Features entire cast. Screenplay, Mike Marvin; camera (CFI Color), Paul G. Ryan; editor, Stephen Rivkin; music, Peter Bernstein; art director, Don DeFina; set decorator, Carl Arena; sound, Wolf Seeberg; costumes, Shari Feldman; stunt coordinator, Max Kleven; associate producer, Tim Tennant; assistant director, Paul Kimatian. Reviewed at MGM/UA Studio, Hollywood, Jan. 9, 1983. (MPAA rating: R.) Running Time: 96 MINS.

Dan	David Naughton
Harkin	Patrick Houser
Sunny	Tracy N. Smith
Rudi	John Patrick Reger
Squirrel	Frank Koppola
Sylvia Fonda	Shannon Tweed
Kendo	James Saito
Slasher	George Theobald

"Hot Dog ... The Movie" attempts to be a party pic on skis aimed directly at a teen audience. Instead it plays, as these pictures often do, as a dirty old man's fantasy of what teenagers want. Solid action sequences, appealing scenery and timing of its release when there's not much else around for young audiences, should give it modest success at the boxoffice.

The title of the picture refers to a type of free-form skiing known as hot dogging which combines dance-like choreography with dare devil jumping. Action takes place on the slopes of Squaw Valley Resort at Lake Tahoe, but accent is on indoor recreation and skiing comes off simply as a way to meet girls.

Fresh from the farm in Idaho, Harkin (Patrick Houser) is the new kid on the block. On the way to compete at the World Freestyle Championship he picks up a feisty hitchhiker (Tracy N. Smith) who becomes the film's romantic interest of sorts.

Romance hardly seems to be the point here. What counts instead is having a good time and finding someone to sleep with. One character, Squirrel (Frank Koppola), a spaced-out imitation of the Sean Penn character in "Fast Times At Ridgemont High," spends his time at a party propositioning every woman in sight as a running gag.

Harkin does as well on the social scene as he does on the slopes, falling in with the "fun-loving" rat

pack led by party-boy Dan O'Callahan (David Naughton). Naughton's New York street smarts, down to his New York Mets cap, is indeed an oddity on the slopes. Could he have learned to be a hot dogger dodging traffic in Manhattan?

Other than who sleeps with whom, the main dramatic tension of the film is supplied by the competition with a nasty Austrian world champ, Rudi Garmischt (John Patrick Reger) and his crew of Rudettes. The rivalry culminates in an every man for himself "Chinese downhill," which looks like a sequence from a James Bond film, complete with villainous costumes.

The resemblance to an 007 pic is probably not accidental since producer Mike Marvin is the man who designed the striking skiing and parachuting escape in "The Spy Who Loved Me."

"Hot Dog ... The Movie" looks best when it's on the slopes and the ski photography by Paul G. Ryan is firstrate. A crew of world-class free-stylers gets ample opportunity to show its stuff and much is shown in slow motion.

Shannon Tweed, Playboy Playmate of The Year in 1982, also gets a chance to show her stuff. She turns up from time to time in a different ski outfit which she is more than likely to take off. Her charms are ample but her performance is surpassed by newcomer Smith who conveys a convincing rough-around the-edges quality.

Voluptuous women are literally on display throughout the picture and anyone with a modicum of sensitivity will probably object to the blatant sexism. Women invariably have no last names when introduced and everything needed to know about any women is disclosed with the statement, "she's taken." —Jagr.

Il Tassinaro
(The Cabbie)
(ITALIAN – COLOR)

Rome, Jan. 5.

An Italian International Film release, produced by Fulvio Lucisano for Italian International Film. Starring and directed by Alberto Sordi. Screenplay, Age and Scarpelli, Sordi; camera (color), Sergio D'Offizi; art director, Massimo Razzi; editor, Tatiana Casini Morigi; music, Piero Piccioni. Reviewed at Metropolitan Cinema, Rome, Jan. 4, 1984. Running time: 125 MINS.

Pietro Marchetti	Alberto Sordi

With Giulio Andreotti, Federico Fellini and Silvana Pampanini as themselves.

"Taxi Driver" it isn't.

"The Cabbie" is a plotless, self-adulating Alberto Sordi vehicle, an old school comedy short on laughs and ideas. In spite of these defects, helmer-star's personal following and screen charisma have pulled it to the top of Italo Christmas charts. Foreign markets will be those where the comic is already a popular quantity.

The Age and Scarpelli/Sordi script shows a few days in the life of Pietro Marchetti (Sordi), an honest, hard-working Roman taxi driver whose life is all cab and family. Opening with an at-home New Year's Eve celebration, pic praises the simple joys of Pietro's existence: a comfy house in old Rome, a portly but faithful wife, son studying to be an architect, grandpa cooking in the kitchen.

Outside this haven lies the violent, heartless world of the big city, which Pietro is at pains to keep a secret from the innocents at home. A fare steals his Christmas bankroll; a woman snarls that her teenage kids have turned out all wrong and smoke pot; an elderly Englishman and his attractive young wife have Pietro drive them to a secluded park and try to seduce him.

"Cabbie" casts tasteless slurs at two other groups of foreigners: a prostitute's casual put-down of Japanese clients, and an extended scene of banqueting "sheiks" flinging mashed potatoes at their guests, while Pietro looks on in disgust.

Nothing seriously comic or dramatic occurs in the picture. Most of the footage shows Pietro behind the wheel of his cab, jabbering away to fares while the back projection changes the scenery most irregularly, and the cab turns without Pietro needing to move the steering wheel.

Highlights of the pic are supposed to be three illustrious personages who ride in Pietro's cab. Only Silvana Pampanini, who parodies herself as an aging movie star, is up to tv skit level. Federico Fellini and Giulio Andreotti, one of the country's leading politicians, are thrown away in awkwardly improvised scenes. Pietro/Sordi is so thrilled and honored to have them in his cab/film, anything they could say or do is redundant. Mainly they just sit there looking embarrassed and uncomfortable, no doubt wondering how they let themselves get talked into such an inanity.

Andreotti uses the occasion to air his disapproval of unrestricted university admissions. Fellini merely tries to get Pietro to shut up and drive him to Cinecittà in peace. — *Yung.*

Backstage At the Kirov
(U.S.-DOCU-COLOR)

Hollywood, Jan. 13.

Armand Hammer Production. Directed and written by Derek Hart. Executive producer. Kenneth Locker. Produced by Gregory Saunders and Locker. Camera (16m Kodak), Ivan Strasburg; editor, Kenneth Levis; music, orchestra of the Kirov Theater, conducted by Eugene Kolobov; sound, Mike McDuffie; assistant director, Jeff Michelson;

second unit photography, Steve Harrison. Reviewed at the Goldwyn Theater. Academy of Motion Arts & Sciences, Los Angeles, Jan. 12, 1984. (No MPAA rating). Running time: **80 MINS.**

Principal cast: Kirov dancers Galina Mezentxseva, Konstantin Zaklinsky, Altyani Assylmuratova.

First theatrical release from Armand Hammer Prods., and shot entirely in Leningrad with a Western film crew, "Backstage At The Kirov" deftly mixes the images of the ballet rehearsal hall with footage of performance (in this case, the second act of "Swan Lake").

Film opened last month in Seattle and San Francisco, hits New York and L.A. later this month and has already won some festival awards (Cine Gold Eagle, among them). Careful hand-picked distrib plan, initially tied in many cases to benefits for dance and ballet groups, should draw not only patrons of the art but even the less discriminating, drawn by word of mouth.

Knowledgeable dance film fans will make comparisons with "The Children Of Theatre Street," U.S.-Russian documentary filmed in 1977, also at the Kirov Ballet school in Leningrad. In fact, the beautiful oval-faced young dancer in "Backstage at the Kirov," Altyani Assylmuratova, was seen as a young student in director Robert Dornhelm's "Children Of Theatre Street."

Current film earns especially high marks for director Derek Hart and British cinematographer Ivan Strasburg's exquisite touch with the rich detail of ballet preparation and training. Closeups, from the reflection of an eyelash in a dressing room mirror to the bountiful but never tiresome use of images of ballerinas' twirling feet, strongly contribute to the artful look of the film.

A bouquet of roses is also due editor Kenneth Levis, for an exceptionally fluid rhythm, and to the producers' apt archival touches, from some footage of turn-of-the-century St. Petersburg, some of it courtesy of the Hoover Institute at Stanford U. Quality of the color, to the layman's eye, seems not at all diluted by fact the picture was shot in 16m Kodak and blown up to 35m.

Obviously abetted by Hammer's 50-year history of business and cultural associations with Russia (he first went to the USSR in 1921 as a young medical doctor), production was further supported by the global network of Hammer Prods.' parent company, Occidental Petroleum Corp.

Chief preoccupation in the film, which in turn serves as a kind of Western celebration of the 200th anniversary of the Kirov Ballet, is the behind-the-scenes interest in the corps de ballet. The faces of the young girls are sometimes captured with the suggestion of a painter's brush.

Some purists will no doubt object to the shots of "Swan Lake" in which the lens occasionally cuts off dancers' arms and feet, but the film, in its style and precision, goes a long way to framing the elusive quality that makes the Kirov great.—*Loyn.*

El-Nimr El-Asswad
(The Black Tiger)
(EGYPTIAN-COLOR)

Cairo, Dec. 19.

Produced by Atef Saleh and Co.; Stars Ahmed Zaki, Wafaa Salem. Directed by Atef Saleh. Screenplay, based on novel by Ahmed Abue Fath, Besher El-dik; camera (color), Samir Farag; editor, Rashida Abdel-Salam; music, Gamal Salama. Reviewed at Cinema City, Cairo, Dec. 19, 1983. Running time: **120 MINS.**

Atef Saleh is one of the grand directors of the Egyptian motion picture industry. For more than a quarter of a century, his films have been milestones of Egyptian cinema. "The Black Tiger" is a splendid surprise marking his return to cinema after a long absence.

Saleh has mustered all his long experience and skill in the first half of his film. Cinematographer Samir Farag, editor Rashida Abdel-Salam, composer Gamal Salama and actor Ahmed Zaki all contribute to Saleh's effort.

First half takes an illiterate Egyptian to W. Germany to find work. Alone on foreign soil, Ahmed develops in many directions — landing a job, learning Arabic and German and even becoming a boxing champ. Throughout the voyage to Germany the young man recollects his simple past and divorced parents in quick flashbacks.

Many weak points dot the second half of the script, adapted from a novel by journalist Ahmed Abue Fath. The young man shifts from poverty to wealth and back to poverty without clear dramatic justifications. His affair with a German girl (Wafaa Salem) and related discrimination remain vague.

The hero is a religious young man, probably from his training as a boxer with the Moslem Brotherhood, and becomes a model member of the faith. Loss of faith culminates with Egypt's defeat in 1967. The war and its significance are the weak points of the film by Saleh, who seems unwilling to tackle clearly the issues at stake. —*Fari.*

Canicule
(Dog Day)
(FRENCH-COLOR)

Paris, Jan. 10.

UGC release of a Swanie Productions/UGC-Top 1/TF 1 Films Production/Cinétélé co-production. Produced by Norbert Saada. Stars Lee Marvin, Miou-Miou, Jean Carmet, Victor Lanoux. Directed by Yves Boisset. Screenplay, Boisset, Michel Audiard, Dominique Roulet, Serge Korber and Jean

Herman, from novel by Jean Vautrin (Jean Herman); camera (Fujicolor), Jean Boffety; editor, Albert Jurgenson; art director, Jacques Dugied; music, Francis Lai, directed by Christian Gaubert; sound, Jean-Louis Ducarme; costumes, Rosine Lan; makeup Joël Lavau; production manager, Guy Azzi. Reviewed at the UGC Normandie theater, Paris, Jan. 4, 1984. Running time: **101 MINS.**

Jimmy Cobb ....Lee Marvin
Jessica ....Miou-Miou
Socrate ....Jean Carmet
Horace ....Victor Lanoux
Chim ....David Bennent
Ségolène ....Bernadette Lafont
Torontopoulos ....Jean-Pierre Kalfon
Lily ....Grace de Capitani
Marceau.....................Henri Guybet
Snake ....Pierre Clementi
Noémie Blue ....Tina Louise
Le Barrec ....Jean-Claude Dreyfus

Lee Marvin starts 1984 on an animal farm. Playing a killer on the run, the Yank actor hides out with the pigs in a barn in the midst of French cornfields. By the end of a harvest of gratuitous violence and brutish sex, the pink porkers show up as the most civilized inhabitants on the homestead.

Marvin, a dude gunman with a flamboyant legend and a moll (Tina Louise) from back home, leads a gang of French robbers into a police ambush while snatching dollars from a delivery truck at a bank in a provincial French city.

Making no concessions toward dramatic probability, "Canicule" then follows Marvin, who, a red carnation in his buttonhole intact, makes a miraculous escape from lethal police crossfire. While an army of gendarmes combs the surrounding farmlands with dogs and helicopters, the gangster arrives as an uninvited guest of a family of French hicks.

Each member of the clan rivals the others for bestiality and perversion. Victor Lanoux is the farmer, a voyeur and fetishist, who poses as a scarecrow to spy on nude girls camping nearby in the summer heat, and ends up clubbing them to death. Apart from the wine bottle, his delights include a collection of female underwear that he keeps locked away in a locker.

No less depraved, Bernadette Lafont is his crippled, nymphomaniac sister who preys on the farm's immigrant workmen and lusts after Marvin's rugged, white-haired virility. After the gangster is taken prisoner by Lanoux and his brother (Jean Carmet), who hope to snatch his loot, the filthy slattern becomes his murder victim while trying to seduce him.

The farmer's apparently submissive and victimized wife is played by Miou-Miou, who pacts with Marvin to help him escape, but in fact is interested only in using him for her own ends, which include the murder of her husband.

Her only son (David Bennent, the diabolical child in "The Tin Drum") is a crazed imp, doped out on gangster mythology, who wants to steal Marvin's thunder, and finally does so in a conclusion that breaks the implacably nihilistic logic of the script.

Director Yves Boisset, and his team of screenwriters, which include dialog writer Michel Audiard, and Jean Vautrin, also the author of the source print thriller, make no demands on their audience's imagination. Situations and characters are attacked head-on, without nuance.

· The city police are incompetent, the country gendarmes are dismally stupid, and the other gangsters who covet the booty are treacherous and oily puppets.

The killings are spelled out with graphic insistence, the sex depicted crudely and the humor conveyed laboriously. Nevertheless, the film was coproduced by French television and forbidden by the state review board only to children under 13.

The Yank star, called upon only to do a replay of his tough guy screen image, manages to escape being tainted by the grossness of story and treatment. Even in the pic's conclusion, after the action has cut its corny swath through a crop of horror and obscenity, Marvin manages to retain some dignity, despite a cop-out ending which has him commit suicide and the kid claim the gangster's scalp to an admiring national media.

— *Len.*

Scalps
(COLOR)

Cheapo horror lacks hair-raising qualities.

A 21st Century Distribution release of an American Panther Prods. production. Produced by The Eel (T.L. Lankford). Written and directed by Fred Olen Ray. Features entire cast. Camera (Quality Color), Brett Webster, Larry van Loon; editor, John Barr; music, Drew Neumann, Eric Rasmussen; sound, John Patrick Mitchell; assistant director, Jeff Vernon; special makeup effects, Chris Biggs, others; second unit director, Lankford; additional photography, Bryan England. Reviewed at Criterion 6 theater, N.Y., Dec. 30, 1983. (MPAA Rating: R.) Running time: **82 MINS.**
Dr. Howard Machen . . . . .Kirk Alyn
Dr. Reynolds . . . . .Carroll Borland
D.J. . . . . .Jo Ann Robinson
Randy . . . . .Richard Hench
Kershaw . . . . .Roger Maycock
Ellen . . . . .Barbara Magnusson
Ben .Frank McDonald
Louise . . . . .Carol Sue Flockhart
Billy Iron Wing . . . . .George Randall
Prof. Treatwood . . . . . .Forrest J. Ackerman

Lensed in Aqua Dulce, Calif. in 1982, "Scalps" is an amateurish horror effort which poses the question (all-too-frequently raised in recent shock films): "How much dull filler will the fans sit through while waiting for an explicit gore scene?" Commercial prospects are limited to product-hungry situations.

Hackneyed storyline involves an archeological expedition sponsored by Prof. Machen (Kirk Alyn), which has six college students disturbing the Black Trees Indian burial ground in the desert. The spirit of Indian renegade Black Claw (known for his black magic expertise) possesses the youngsters singly, cuing gory killings and scalpings.

Floridian filmmaker Fred Olen Ray, now based on the west coast, accomplishes very little with this low budget exercise. The 16m blowup is grainy and extensive night scenes feature some of the worst shot matching (level of darkness varies almost comically shot-to-shot) on record. Gore content, including blood pumped out liberally after a decapitation and cheapo masks, is the picture's only drawing card for horror audiences.

Film buffs had better arrive on time, since topliner Kirk Alyn (who played Superman in the 1948 Columbia serial) appears briefly at the outset sending his students on ahead, and comes back for just one scene at film's end. Also in cameo roles are Carroll Borland (she was featured in Tod Browning's 1935 "Mark Of The Vampire") as Alyn's university boss, and ubiquitous professional fan Forrest J. Ackerman flashing a monster magazine at the camera. Final credit warns the viewer to watch for "Scalps II, The Return Of D.J." next summer, but based on this offering that seems an idle threat. —*Lor.*

Deathstalker
(COLOR)

Low-budget blood-and-sorcery item for fast playoffs.

Hollywood, Jan. 5.

A New World release of a Falo Alto production. Produced by James Sbardellati Coproducers, Hector Olivera, Alex Sessa. Features entire cast. Directed by John Watson. Screenplay, Howard Cohen; camera (color), Leonardo Rodriguez Solis; editors, John Adams, Silvia Ripoll; art direction, Emilio Basaldua; music, Oscar Cardozo Ocampo; costume design, Maria Julia Bertolt; makeup special effects, John Buechler; sound, Norman Newcastle; associate producer, Frank Isaac; assistant director, Amerik Von Zaratt. Reviewed at the Aidikoff Screening Room, L.A., Jan. 4, 1984. (MPAA Rating: R.) Running time: **80 MINS.**
Deathstalker . . . . .Richard Hill
Codille . . . . .Barbi Benton
Oghris . . . . .Richard Brooker
Kaira . . . . .Lana Clarkson
Kang . . . . .Victor Bo
Munkar . . . . .Bernard Erhard
Salmaron . . . . .August Larreta
Toralva .Lillian Ker
Gargit . . . . .Marcos Woinsky
Nicor . . . . .Adrian De Piero
King Tulak . . . . .George Sorvic
Young Man . . . . .Boy Olmi

"Deathstalker," the first official release of the new year, is yet another low budget sword and sorcery item. It also apparently marks the first New World picture to have been lensed in Argentina, the country which seems to have replaced the Philippines on Roger Corman's favored nations list. With bountiful action and acres of naked flesh, both male and female, film pretty accurately captures the intended heavy metal look, but limp script and threadbare production values relegate this to quick-as-possible playoff status.

Tale has been stripped to the mythological bare bones. Brawny Mr. Deathstalker is like a wandering, masterless samurai, always ready to rape and pillage at a moment's notice. Fact that his king's sexy daughter, Barbi Benton, is being held prisoner by nasty, dome-headed wizard Munkar doesn't in the slightest inspire him to noble, heroic thoughts, but when he learns that seizing Munkar's magical amulet and chalice will give him a monopoly on mystical powers, he sets his sights on Munkar's castle.

During his travels, Deathstalker, whose emotional range is something less than that of Conan, runs across various creatures, both human and beastly. The most notable of these is lusty blonde Lana Clarkson, whose unique displays of topless swordswomanship decidedly rep pic's highlight.

To further divert the boys in the audience, plenty of footage is given over the carryings-on in Munkar's harem, which include some heavy metal-style and mud wrestling.

It all comes down to a climactic gladiatorial tournament, winner of which will presumably inherit the aging Munkar's position. Unfortunately, these proceedings are rushed through in an unceremonial way, and take place in an arena in which it looks like papier-maché hadn't yet dried before filming. It's also too bad they didn't let Clarkson stick around at least long enough to compete in the games.

Director John Watson seems to know what he's after, but numerous constraints, undoubtedly financial in nature, have conspired to keep film in the cheesy category. As Deathstalker, Richard Hill has the requisite biceps, but his blond wig makes him look like the brother of last year's late, unlamented Yor. His skull decorated with what looks like a partial spider's web, Bernard Erhard makes an effective villain.

Tech contributions are on the creaky side. —*Cart.*

Warriors Of
The Wasteland
(I Nuovi Barbari)
(ITALIAN-COLOR)

A New Line Cinema release of a Deaf International Films S.R.L. production. Produced by Fabrizio De Angelis. Directed by Enzo Girolami Castellari. Features entire cast. Screenplay, Tito Carpi, Castellari from Carpi's story; camera (Telecolor), Fausto Zuccoli; editor, Gianfranco Amicucci; music, Claudio Simonetti; sound, Massimo Loffredi; production design, Antonio Visone; stunt director, Riccardo Pitrazzi; special effects, Germano Natali. Reviewed at UA Rivoli 1 Theater, N.Y., January 15, 1984. (MPAA Rating: R). Running time: **87 MINS.**
Skorpion . . . . .Timothy Brent
Nadir . . . . .Fred Williamson
Alma .Anna Kanakis
Moses . . . . .Venantino Venantini
Also with: George Eastman, Enzo G. Castellari, Massimo Vanni, Andrea Coppola, Zora Kerova, Patsy May McLachlan.

"Warriors Of The Wasteland" is a chintzy Italian science fiction film lensed in late 1982, imported for U.S. action audiences. Other than the marquee name of the ubiquitous Fred Williamson, imitative picture has little to offer in urban bookings and looks to soft b.o.

The problem with "Warriors," originally titled "The New Barbarians," is endemic to the score of other recent Italian films of this ilk: going to the well once too often. Pic is akin to the 50th re-use of the same piece of carbon paper.

Visual model here is mainly George Miller's Aussie-made hit "The Road Warrior," with elements of Hal Needham's "Megaforce" and other pics. The story structure goes back even further, resembling Cornel Wilde's unsung sci-fier of 1970 "No Blade Of Grass," itself in turn influenced by Ray Milland's 1962 classic "Panic In Year Zero."

Set in 2019, nine years after a nuclear war, Castellari's "Warriors" has two lone heroes, Skorpion (Timothy Brent, a/k/a Italian actor Giancarlo Prete) and Nadir (Fred Williamson) aiding a group of religious wanderers led by Moses (Venantino Venantini) who are beset by a band of violent meanies, the Templars.

Castellari stretches the leather and bondage motif of the baddies in "The Road Warrior" to a satirical outer limit here, evidenced by Nadir referring to the Templars as "the big bad queers" after they rape Skorpion in a most outré manhandling of an action film hero. Perhaps this merger with gay films is the logical outgrowth of the recent blitz of muscleman pictures, but will probably be too far out for general audiences. Final gunfight is stolen from Sergio Leone's "A Fistful Of Dollars," with Skorpion even wearing a poncho.

Derivative package includes a cute little blonde kid as auto mechanic, reminiscent of the Feral Kid in "The Road Warrior," plus dialog from "Escape From New York," (already slavishly copied by Castellari in his "1990: The Bronx Warriors" and upcoming release "Escape From The Bronx"). The mistake is an overuse of slow motion, and in place of Miller's exciting high-speed action scenes, the car chases here (including Skorpion's souped-up late-1960s Pontiac Tempest) look to be occurring at 25 mph.

Acting is flat, with cast articulating in English, but post-synch dialog is very artificial. Williamson has some fun moments, especially when a beautiful black girl is presented to him by the good guys, but even he must suffer through many pompous lines of dialog. Castellari, who played Mussolini in the recent tv miniseries "The Winds Of War," appears in a supporting role as one of the Templars. — *Lor.*

Champions
(BRITISH-COLOR)

Hollywood, Jan. 10.

An Embassy release in association with Ladbroke Entertainments Ltd. of a United British Artists production. Produced by Peter Shaw. Features entire cast. Directed by John Irvin. Screenplay, Evan Jones, based on the book "Champion's Story" by Bob Champion and Jonathan Powell; camera (Rank color), Ronnie Taylor; editor, Peter Honess; music, Carl Davis; art direction, Roy Stannard; set decoration (U.S.), Ninkey Dalton; sound (Dolby), David Hildyard (U.K.), Michael Evje (U.S.); associate producer, Eva Monley; assistant director, Bert Batt (U.K.), Tommy Lofaro (U.S.); second unit director/camera, Arthur Wooster. Reviewed at the Embassy Screening Room, Los Angeles, Jan. 9, 1984. MPAA Rating: PG. Running time: 115 MINS.

Bob Champion .... John Hurt
Josh Gifford .... Edward Woodward
Burley Cocks .... Ben Johnson
Jo .... Jan Francis
Nick Embiricos .... Peter Barkworth
Valda Embiricos .... Ann Bell
Dr. Merrow .... Judy Parfitt
Mary Hussey .... Alison Steadman
Barbara .... Kirstie Alley

The true story of "Champions" is a genuinely stirring and heroic one, that of how successful English jockey Bob Champion, stricken with cancer in 1979, endured chemotherapy and came all the way back to win the grueling Grand National Steeplechase two years later. Very much in the "Chariots of Fire" vein of athletes triumphing by virtue of grit and conviction, film undeniably has its moments of swelling emotionalism, but falls noticeably short of its potential due to lumpy construction and insufficient streamlining.

Some trimming would seem in order to cut off some of the flab, which might enhance seemingly middling b.o. prospects. Pic opened in Nashville and Albuquerque test engagements Friday (13).

After a soaring horseback opening and a Kentucky vacation dalliance with sexy veterinarian Kirstie Alley, Champion discovers he has cancer, and fully the first half of the film is given over to his hospitalization and ensuing harrowing treatment, which entails endless needles, sickening hair loss, drastic emaciation and generally depressing conferences with doctors.

Given the confines of "popular" entertainment, screenwriter Evan Jones and director John Irvin have taken all the medical materials as far as they could. On the one hand, they can be congratulated for not flinching in the face of singularly unpleasant facts, for showing, as much as anyone would want to see, the actualities of gruesome cancer treatment.

On the other hand, they face the possibility of audiences turning off the film in the early going or, worst of all, not going near it to begin with.

Even after he is cured, Champion faces an extraordinary uphill battle just to get in shape to ride a horse again, not to mention actually winning the daunting four-and-a-half-mile, 30-fence Grand National. Not only is Champion in dreadful condition, but his favorite horse, Aldaniti, has become crippled in the interim and was almost "put down."

Slowly, Champion brings himself back to strength, with the steady support of his trainer. Unfortunately, this upward dramatic arc is accompanied by a simultaneous love story which is no more credible for the fact that it happens to have been true.

A pert young lady named Jo appears out of nowhere to begin visiting the jockey when he's at his lowest in the hospital, and there's never a clue to her motivation. He's in no position to offer her anything, and may not even live, so their relationships possesses all the believability of a fairy tale.

From that point on, Jo is given nothing to do but smile inanely in response to everything Champion says, and their scenes together, which become more frequent as the story progresses, all fall flat for lack of any meaningful interaction.

A truly dynamic portrayal of a love story which must have been fraught with certain difficulties in reality might have picked the pic up by its bootstraps, but as it stands it just bogs down the otherwise successful forward movement.

Climactic scene, that of the protagonist winning the Grand National, is a motion picture natural, one of the most famously employed, of course, by "National Velvet" 40 years ago.

Director Irvin, who demonstrates his considerable directorial skills throughout, strongly captures the immense physical difficulty of the race, the awesome jumps of which cause a great many riders not to complete it at all. Effective slow motion shots show the horses grazing the leafy, thorny hurdles and coming down hard at the end of their vaults.

Certainly, few could resist the scene of Champion's triumphant finish. But just as it was a tortuous road for the rider to get there, it is also a bumpy ride for the viewer, almost a reward held out like a carrot through the nearly two-hour running time.

Champion himself was a consultant on the picture, and few, if any, alterations of the truth were permitted in this telling. Under the circumstances, some artistic shorthand that wouldn't have betrayed essential truths might have been useful.

Crucially, John Hurt does a first-rate job in the leading role, and put himself through what, for him, are becoming the usual physical rigors in order to play it. With his head and even eyebrows shaved for much of the time, Hurt is painfully convincing as a cancer victim, and he also gets across the character's joy at the later heartening events in his life. — *Cart.*

Broadway Danny Rose
(BLACK & WHITE)

Woody Allen gets back to basics, and boxoffice looks respectable.

Hollywood, Jan. 10.

An Orion Pictures release produced by Robert Greenhut. Written and directed by Woody Allen. Stars Allen, Mia Farrow. Exec producer, Charles H. Joffe. Camera (B&W), Gordon Willis; editor, Susan E. Morse; sound James Sabat; production design, Mel Bourne; costumes, Jeffrey Kurland; associate producer, Michael Peyser; assistant director, Thomas Reilly; music, Dick Hyman. Reviewed at the Directors Guild of America, Jan. 9, 1984. MPAA rating: PG. Running time: 84 MINS.

Danny Rose .... Woody Allen
Tina Vitale .... Mia Farrow
Lou Canova .... Nick Apollo Forte
Himself .... Milton Berle
Himself .... Sandy Baron
Himself .... Corbett Monica
Himself .... Jackie Gayle
Himself .... Morty Gunty
Himself .... Will Jordan
Himself .... Howard Storm
Himself .... Jack Rollins
Ray Webb .... Craig Vandenburgh
Barney Dunn .... Herb Reynolds

"Broadway Danny Rose" is a delectable diversion which allows Woody Allen to present a reasonably humane, and amusing gentle character study without sacrificing himself to overly commercial concerns. Even so, it should fare much better than his last three boxoffice bothers.

Since it's been more than a decade since Allen has gone completely for comedy, it remains pointless to wish he would try once more, though many still do. It may be equally hopeless to await another "Annie Hall" or "Manhattan." But "Danny Rose" is certainly more complete than "Zelig," more satisfying than "A Midsummer Night's Sex Comedy" and certainly more everything than his disastrous "Stardust Memories."

With "Danny Rose," Allen assumes a character that totally suits him without having to play it for laughs or challenge the audience to accept the unacceptable.

He's perfect as a small-time, good-hearted Broadway talent agent, giving his all for a roster of hopeless clients who, should success ever fall upon them, prove ungrateful anyway. He is, indeed, the fellow just outside the frame or unrecognizable in the background of the celebrity photos on his wall.

Agent's career is fondly recalled here by a group of Catskill comics (all played by themselves) sitting around over coffee, focusing mainly on Allen's attempt to revive the career of an aging, overweight, boozing lounge singer, beautifully played by Nick Apollo Forte.

One of Forte's many problems that Allen must deal with is a floozy of a girlfriend. And it's truly one of the picture's early delights that this sunglassed bimbo is actually on screen for several minutes before most of the audience catches on that she's Mia Farrow.

For the actress, this is a wonderful career turn, just about the most outrageous character she's ever played, terrific all the way. When she talks about redecorating Allen's place in bamboo and pink, the sheer tackiness of the notion is only relieved by Gordon Willis' black and white photography, even though the decorating is never done.

Through Forte and Farrow, Allen becomes the target of a couple of hit men, generating a few dandy laughs reminiscent of early Allen pictures. But Allen the director still keeps the focus neatly on the personality of his main character, overwhelmed by events yet persevering in his nicety.

He will not succeed, of course; his kind never do. But for those like Danny Rose, failure brings its own rewards, even if it's less than he obviously deserves. — *Har.*

Crackers

(COLOR)

Small deal on a Frisco street.

Hollywood, Jan. 23.

A Universal release of an Edward Lewis production. Produced by Lewis, Robert Cortes. Directed by Louis Malle. Features entire cast. Screenplay, Jeffrey Fiskin, suggested by the film "Big Deal On Madonna Street" written by Suso Cecchi D'Amico, Mario Monicelli, Agenore Incrocci, Furio Scarpelli; camera (Technicolor), Laszlo Kovacs; editor, Susanne Baron; music, Paul Chihara; production design, John J. Lloyd; set decoration, Hal Gausman; costume design, Deborah Nadoolman; sound David Rome; assistant director, James Quinn. Reviewed at Universal Studios, Universal City, Jan. 23, 1984. (MPAA Rating: PG.) Running time: **92 MINS.**

Weslake ....Donald Sutherland
Garvey ....Jack Warden
Dillard ....Sean Penn
Turtle.......................Wallace Shawn
Boardwalk ....Larry Riley
Ramon ....Trinidad Silva
Maxine.................Christine Baranski
Jasmine ....Charlaine Woodard
Maria ....Tania Valenza
Lazzarelli ....Irwin Corey
Don Fernande ....Edouard DeSoto
Slam Dunk ....Anna Maria Horsford
Artiste ....Mitchell Lichtenstein
Mrs. O'Malley ....:....Marjorie Eaton

A mild little caper comedy with plenty of sociological overtones, "Crackers" comes as a letdown from director Louis Malle after the satisfying accomplishment of "Atlantic City." With a flimsy plot that is perhaps rightly treated in a throwaway manner, film basically consists of a wide assortment of character riffs which are offbeat enough to provide moderate moment-to-moment amusement but don't create a great deal of comic impact. Commercial prospects are limited. World preem took place at the U.S. Film and Video Festival in Park City, Utah Monday (23).

Pic was "suggested" by Mario Monicelli's 1956 Italian hit, "Big Deal On Madonna Street," and while it has been legitimately rethought for the new setting of the Mission District of San Francisco, one can still feel the Latin blood in its veins and sense that it would all sound funnier and more convincing in Italian.

As in dozens of tenement-set plays from "Street Scene" on, virtually all the action takes place within or very near the central setting, in this case a pawnshop owned by shameless profiteer Jack Warden. His buddy, Donald Sutherland, is out of work, and all but a few of the other characters make up a rainbow microcosm of today's unemployed.

There's Larry Riley, a flashy black pimp whose only lady walks out on him and leaves behind her baby; Sean Penn, a Southern, would-be musician who commits petty robberies with illegal alien Trinidad Silva and puts the make on the latter's sexy sister at great risk to his neck; Sutherland's sidekick Wallace Shawn (from Malle's

"My Dinner With Andre"), who is aptly named Turtle and bears a strong physical resemblance to Jean Renoir's Octave character in "Rules Of The Game;" man-eating metermaid Christine Baranski; maid and aspiring prostie Charlaine Woodard, and a nutty safecracking expert played by (Professor) Irwin Corey.

The alliances and love affairs that evolved so naturally in the courtyard-bound French and Italian films of the 1930s and 1940s seem a bit more farfetched in the big city environs here, and despite the economic imperatives that are clearly established, there is no desperation to be felt driving this motley crew to rob Warden.

Rather, Sutherland merely dreams up the idea of busting into his friend's safe, and the others, boasting no particular criminal skills, just willingly go along for the ride. Characters are basically likable, but prevailing attitude is casually amoral in the mode of numerous other Malle films, particularly "The Thief Of Paris."

Screenwriter Jeffrey Fiskin has had some fun playing off the conventional stereotypes of the assorted ethnic characters, and Malle has applied a light spirit to this ensemble acting piece. But none of the characters' actions has real consequences, rendering the film all too innocuous despite its intermittent charms.

Thesps all do fine jobs, and the production team has succeeded in making the Mission seem like the ultimate melting pot. —Cart.

Scandalous

(COLOR)

Disappointing try at sophisticated comedy.

Hollywood, Jan. 18.

An Orion release of a Sellers-Winitsky/De Haven/Raleigh Film production. Produced by Arlene Sellers, Alex Winitsky. Coproducer, Martin C. Schute. Executive producer, Carter De Haven. Directed by Rob Cohen. Stars Robert Hays, John Gielgud, Pamela Stephenson, Jim Dale. Screenplay, Cohen, John Byrum, story by Larry Cohen, Rob Cohen, Byrum. Camera (Technicolor), Jack Cardiff; editor, Michael Bradsell; music, Dave Grusin; production design, Peter Mullins; art direction, John Siddall, Brian Ackland-Snow; set decoration, Harry Cordwell; Stephenson's costume design, Krizia; assistant director, Derek Cracknell. Reviewed at the Orion Screening Room, L.A., Jan. 17, 1984. (MPAA Rating: PG.) Running time: **94 MINS.**

Frank Swedlin.................Robert Hays
Uncle Willie..................John Gielgud
Fiona Maxwell Sayle ..Pamela Stephenson
Inspector Anthony Crisp.........Jim Dale
Simon Reynolds ....M. Emmet Walsh
Lindsay Manning ....Nancy Wood
Francine Swedlin ....Conover Kennard
Bob Wow Wow ....Bow Wow Wow

"Scandalous" is just another bit of proof that sophistication ain't what it used to be. It takes a lot of skill to make a suspenseful romantic comedy soufflé, and this self-consciously cheeky attempt never

overcomes the painfully intense artificiality of its premise. Just as there was never any compelling reason to make this harmless concoction, nor will there be much reason for audiences to pay to see it.

Filmmakers have tried to graft as many modernistic trappings onto the proceedings as possible, to the point of dressing Sir John Gielgud in an S&M black leather outfit at one point and gratuitously dragging in a concert by English punk group Bow Wow Wow. But such stags at trendiness only underline how unanchored the film is to anything remotely relevant to current audiences, and how ephemeral a bauble it really is.

Robert Hays, looking dashing, plays a famous tv newscaster anxious to prove his stuff as a hard news reporter. When he thinks he's uncovered a spy conspiracy on a flight to London, he jumps at the bait represented by voluptuous Pamela Stephenson, who is partnered with Gielgud.

Shortly thereafter, Hays finds himself accused of the murder of his wife, obnoxious Scotland Yard inspector Jim Dale begins snooping around, and it all becomes a question of who is doing what to whom. The problem is, one could hardly care less.

Hays, Stephenson and Gielgud are all engaging performers capable of lending lilt to a line, and fact that they fail to make this anything but a frivolous time killer is no fault of theirs.

Tech credits are standard.

—Cart.

The Buddy System

(COLOR)

Whose love is it, anyway?

Hollywood, Jan. 13.

A 20th Century-Fox release. Produced by Alain Chammas. Directed by Glenn Jordan. Features entire cast. Screenplay, Mary Agnes Donoghue; camera (DeLuxe color), Matthew F. Leonetti; editor, Arthur Schmidt; music, Patrick Williams; production designer, Rodger Maus; costumes, Joe Aulisi; assistant director, Peter Bergquist. Reviewed at 20th Century-Fox Film Corp., Los Angeles, Jan. 13, 1984. (MPAA rating: PG.) Running time: **110 MINS.**

Joe ....Richard Dreyfuss
Emily ....Susan Sarandon
Carrie ....Nancy Allen
Mrs. Price..................Jean Stapleton
Tim ....Wil Wheaton
Jim Parks ....Edward Winter

Subject of love and friendship in relevant, contemporary setting receives treatment in this unpretentious but winning romantic comedy. Well-crafted script and sharp characterizations by debuting screenwriter Mary Agnes Donoghue give Richard Dreyfuss, Susan Sarandon and Nancy Allen dishy roles, and, under Glenn Jordan's intelligent direction, they all

deliver with rich, identifiable portraits.

Project was the last to be initiated under former 20th Century-Fox production president Sherry Lansing, in the twilight of her reign in late '82, and Fox wisely pushed up the release from fall, '83 to the comparative calm now current. Film opens in 14 markets and 200 houses and the pic's warmth and its billing (Dreyfuss' first picture since "Whose Life Is It, Anyway?" in late '81) could generate upbeat word-of-mouth and boxoffice sustenance.

The first American film of producer Alain Chammas, former Warner Bros.' production head in Europe, "The Buddy System," as entitled, is the signature for characters who decide to scrap the obligatory mating ritual after a disastrous roll in the sack and live as friends instead.

As sandwiched among complications galore — which number space cadet Allen as Dreyfuss' self-consumed girlfriend, 10-year-old newcomer Wil Wheaton as Sarandon's bright and desperate son, and Jean Stapleton as Sarandon's over-protective mother — the buddy system inextricably develops into love between Dreyfuss and Sarandon. You know the outcome from the first reel but telegraphy in this case is not ruinous because the execution is stylish, the dialog is telling and brisk, and the characters are etched with verve and flavor.

Dreyfuss, an incurable romantic, lives in an old wooden house by a canal in Venice, Calif., struggling to be a novelist while working as a security guard at an elementary school, where an encounter with Sarandon's son triggers the plot. Dreyfuss, touching on the qualities that have earmarked his best work, is vulnerable and likable, especially in his pursuit of his dream girl, Allen, who, in turn, hits every mark of a woman who can only love herself, but is even lovable in that single-minded absorption. At one point, she says she wants to have a baby "so I can grow." Dreyfuss dryly remarks that it's usually the baby who needs to grow.

Sarandon is a feast of anxious ineptitude. She crackles with authenticity, living as a dependent single mother under Stapleton's rather ugly manipulation (Stapleton's role, both as written and played, is the single disharmony in the picture), Sarandon catches a certain contemporary woman with singular exactitude. She runs a battery of steno tests (under the wonderfully baleful eye of steno tester Tom Lacy), crazily balances motherhood and daughterhood, and hurtles through a love affair with an attorney that is as masochistic as is Dreyfuss' fling with Allen. As the lover who discards her, Edward Winter is a sharp identifiable touch and his self-absorption counterpoints Allen's, giving the film an unstrained but pleasing coherence.

Writer Donoghue makes points with economy. Her son shouts at her, "What's wrong with you? Why can't you ever make anybody love you?" "It's not my job to force somebody to love me," Sarandon replies. "Love isn't a trick you play on someone else."

Her true love, Dreyfuss, later, and casually, casts another angle on the nature of loving and dreaming when he realizes he hasn't got what it takes to be a writer. A talented amateur inventor, Dreyfuss' attention is turned toward loving what he can do.

Generally, wit and charm propel events. Early scenes of the young son uncomfortably suggest a smart kid you can't stand, but actor Wheaton levels out to the landmines in the role as written. Music and production design serviceably contribute to the desired tone.
— *Loyn.*

Reckless
(COLOR)

Even bike films have their flat tires.

Hollywood, Jan. 20.
An MGM/UA release, produced by Edgar J. Scherick and Scott Rudin. Directed by James Foley. Features entire cast. Screenplay, Chris Columbus; camera (color), Michael Ballhaus; editor, Albert Magnoli; production design, Jeffrey Townsend; associate producer, Robert F. Colesberry; exec producer, Carol Baum; assistant director, Gary Daigler; art direction, Anamarie Michnevich; music, Thomas Newman. Reviewed at MGM Studios, Culver City, Jan. 20, 1984. (MPAA rating: R.) Running time: **90 MINS.**
Johnny Rourke . . . . Aidan Quinn
Tracey Prescott . . . . Daryl Hannah
John Rourke, Sr. . . . . Kenneth McMillan
Phil Barton . . . . Cliff De Young
Mrs. Prescott . . . . Lois Smith
Randy Daniels . . . . Adam Baldwin
Peter Daniels . . . . Dan Hedaya
David Prescott . . . . Billy Jacoby
Donna . . . . : Toni Kalem

Since reinventing the wheel for young filmgoers has proved successful recently, it's certainly impossible to say that "Reckless" has no commercial possibilities. But beyond that it can only be said it is brazenly trite.

If there is an audience out there not yet tired of an alienated, cycle-riding ruffian and his romantic attraction for a "nice" middle-class girl who's too good for him, then "Reckless" is just the film for them.

If there is an audience out there not yet tired of sexless sex scenes composed of a lot of rolling around in the altogether without showing much, then "Reckless" is just the film for them.

At least, the couple in question, Aidan Quinn and alluring Daryl Hannah, give their parts the best that could be expected and had

both been bringing the performances freshly to screen 30 years ago, they would have been considered major discoveries.

But Kenneth McMillan is wasted as the cliche drunken father who provides an unwholesome home life for Quinn, thus justifying the lad's taking Hannah on late-night lark, vandalizing the school and other good, unhappy teenage stuff like that.

All the other roles — from cleancut boyfriend to football coach — are equally cardboard.

The romance is played against the dreary backdrop of an eastern industrial center, asking whether any of these youngsters will ever escape the town. A better question would be what other town would want them. — *Har.*

Der Fall Bachmeier
(The Bachmeier Case)
(W. GERMAN-COLOR)

Berlin, Jan. 4.
A coproduction of the Hamburger Kino-Kompanie And Hark Bohm Film Productions, Hamburg, with financing from the Hamburg Film Fund and Maran Film. Producer, Natalia Bowakow. Distributed by Filmverlag der Autoren. Written and directed by Hark Bohm. Camera (color), Slawomir Idziak; sets, Uta Reichardt; sound, Hans-Joachim Bahr; editing, Moune Barius; production manager, Hans-Christian Hess. Reviewed at Zoo Palast Cine Center, Berlin, Jan. 4, '83. Running Time: **90 MINS.**
Marie Sellbach . . . . Marie Colbin
Martin Birkhoff . . . . Michael Gwisdek
Julia . . . . Christine Limbach
Tina Germer . . . . Angela Schmidt
Heimo Germer . . . . Werner Rehmm
Herbert Schulz . . . Eugeniusz Pirwieziencew

One of the founders and major figures in the organization of the Filmverlag der Autoren, Hark Bohm always made sure that his children-and-youth film productions drew at the boxoffice as well as meeting certain esthetic and critical standards. These included: "Chetan, the Indian Boy" (1972), "North Sea Is a Murderous Sea" (1975), "Moritz, Dear Moritz" (1977), and "Im Herzen Des Hurrican" (In the Heart of the Hurricane) (1979). Only the last-named revealed a doubt as to where his audiences lie, going through a change of titles between its preem at the 1980 Berlinale and pic's general release.

Now Bohm has latched onto a well-publicized murder tale to make "The Bachmeier Case," changing his working title at the last minute from "No Time for Tears" to make ample use of the built-in publicity the on-going court proceedings provided. At the same time, writer-actor-director Burkhard Driest also made a film about Marianne Bachmeier, "Anna's Mother," skedded to preem at exactly the same time as Bohm's film. Observers have noted that two films on the same theme could help each other, and this seems to

be just the case: top German news and film mags, Der Spiegel and Tip, have featured the tandem productions on front covers.

Further, Marianne Bachmeier has become a kind of household name in Germany. She's an attractive woman and mother in her late twenties, who recently killed with a pistol the sex-murderer of her seven-year-old daughter during the latter's court trial in Luebeck. The case of a mother taking revenge and justice into her own hands hit the headlines of the boulevard press, and was followed in detail by Stern mag (along the lines of Life magazine) in a series of reportage stories.

Bohm, as a practicing lawyer (alternating with his work as a filmmaker), took a personal interest in the case. As the Filmverlag press book for "The Bachmeier Case" indicates, he appeared regularly in court since May 1981, interviewed Bachmeier herself at length, and made the acquaintance too of her lawyers and counselors. Out of these year-long investigative sessions, he then attempted to make a feature film — first, however, with the idea of Bachmeier playing herself in a documentary portion, while Austrian thesp Marie Colbin interpreted a fictional alter ego given the name of Marie Sellbach. Later, Bohm abandoned the documentary segment altogether.

"The Bachmeier Case" is docu-fiction, or docu-drama. As such, the viewer has to be completely cued on the details of the real-life story, or drama, to catch the nuances in the film and overlook the expected weaknesses of patch-editing time sequences. More or less the same approach to documentary narrative was used in Volker Schlöndorff's "Circle of Deceit" (1980), based on Nicolas Born's novel (and related Stern mag stories) dealing with the Lebanon Crisis; and Margarethe von Trotta's "The German Sisters" (1981), based on the rather widely publicized true-story of Gudrun Ennslin (a member of the Baader-Meinhof group of German terrorists). Since all of these films deal directly or indirectly with such penetrating realities as death, murder, and suicide, the question of film ethics has to be raised at the outset — that is, do "boxoffice" or "career" play a role, too, in the director's "concern" for the thematic content?

"The Bachmeier Case" feeds on the sensational side of the story far too much to allow for even a warming to the central figure. Since the German viewer presumably knows the outcome in advance, Bohm has placed all his cards on a review of the case's morbid facts: the mother-to-become-murderer retraces the stages of her daughter's killing from her disappear-

ance to the strangling scene to the very grave on a dark night to swear revenge — and then killing the culprit in broad daylight by shooting him in the back in the courtroom.

The rest is Colbin's performance as Sellbach/Bachmeier. Given a stronger directorial hand to expand her role beyond a stilted scenario drawn from court records and factual observation, she might have carried the film on her fiery performance alone. As it is now, she shifts between voluptuous wildcat and hysterical avenger — nailed down, as she is, to a one-dimensional character prone to high-pressure emotional release. It's the opening scenes that convince the most: a mother trying to maintain a close relationship with a daughter while running a bar on the Hamburg waterfront and, at the same time, having time for affairs with both the father of her child and another casual acquaintance on the job. She also has to contend with a well-to-do family who want to adopt her daughter against her will.

Bohm has made two films, instead of one. And he might have been better off following his lawyer instincts and stayed with a predominantly documentary approach to the whole affair. "The Bachmeier Case" suffers by not having a script to speak of.

Tech credits otherwise are a cut above average. Pic should have a hefty spinoff in German-lingo territories familiar with court sensation, but without a supportive fest it has only limited offshore appeal on the arthouse circuit.
— *Holl.*

When The Mountains Tremble
(DOCU-B&W/COLOR)

A Skylight Pictures release and production, produced by Peter Kinoy. Directed by Pamela Yates and Thomas Sigel. Camera (16m color/B&W), Sigel; sound recordist, Yates; editor, Kinoy; music, Ruben Blades; orchestration, Carlos Franzetti; production manager, Ntathu Mbatha; camera assistants, Mike Barry and Javier Bajana; associate editor, Tom Crawford; sound editor, Margie Crimmins. Reviewed at Preview Theatre, N.Y., Jan. 12, 1984 (No MPAA rating). Running time: **83 MINS.**
Historic recreations cast: Chuck Portz, Shawn Elliot, Eddie Jones, Linda Segura, Shelly Desai, Ron Ryan.

Currently making nontheatrical rounds at benefit exhibitions and events at several U.S. cultural institutions, "When The Mountains Tremble" fares well as a documentary with its equal doses of information and drama. It's fair in quality but less so in its treatment of the issues, relentlessly criticizing U.S. policy in Central America.

There is limited theatrical potential in this film, but drumming up a patronage will be as difficult for this political docu as any other.

Pamela Yates, a photojournalist and documentary filmmaker who's worked frequently for European tv stations; Thomas Sigel, a New York cameraman of docus as well as music videos (Talking Heads' "Burning Down The House"), and Peter Kinoy, writer and editor of political docus, have collaborated once before, on "Resurgence," a docu about the Ku Klux Klan.

For this project, shot over six months in the Indian highlands of Guatemala, the trio assigned narration chores to a young Indian peasant woman who lost members of her family in the long, bloody struggle between the peasant guerrilla forces and the Army (fighting for the landed gentry-backed government).

The narrator, Rigoberta Menchú, has become understandably radicalized by her ordeals. At one point, she says in Spanish (pic uses English subtitles) that any kind of U.S. aid, economic or military, will guarantee a sustained bloodbath.

That the bloodbath continues is clearly documented in "When The Mountains Tremble." Juxtaposed against colorful and peaceful images of Guatemalan culture are the sinister scenes of youngsters preparing for and engaged in jungle warfare. Pic comes to a chilling climax with its close look at the aftermath of a massacre of civilians.

The filmmakers also scripted and photographed, in black and white, two scenes for the viewer's historical background, one set in a CIA outpost and the other at a dinner with a Guatemalan president and U.S. ambassador. The American officials are all portrayed as smarmy and singularly concerned with the interests of U.S. corporations in Central America.

Sigel and Yates coproduced and codirected the First Run Features release with Deborah Shaffer ("The Wobblies"). --*Binn.*

Surf II
(COLOR)

Satire of beach films ensures there won't be a "Surf III."

Hollywood, Jan. 13.
An International Film Marketing release, produced by George G. Braunstein and Ron Hamady. Written and directed by Randall Badat. Features entire cast. Exec producers, Frank D. Tolin, Lou George. Camera (De-Luxe Color), Alex Phillips Jr.; editor, Jackie Cambas; assistant director, D. Scott Easton; art direction, Jeff Staggs; costumes, Carin Berger. Reviewed at UA Cinema, North Hollywood, Jan. 12, 1984. MPAA rating: R. Running time: **91 MINS.**
Menlo ....Eddie Deezen
Sparkle ....Linda Kerridge
Daddy O ....Cleavon Little
Beaker ....Peter Isacksen
Chief Boyardie ....Lyle Waggoner
Chuck ....Eric Stoltz
Bob ....Jeffrey Rodgers
Cindy Lou ....Corinne Bohrer
Lindy Sue.................Lucinda Dooling
Chuck's Dad...............Morgan Paull
Chuck's mother ....Ruth Buzzi
Jocko ....Tom Villard
Jocko's mother ....Carol Wayne
Jocko's father ....Terry Kiser
Bob's mother ....Brandis Kemp
Bob's Father ....Biff Maynard

There is ever so slight a smile in the title of "Surf II" since there never was a "Surf I." But there is joy aplenty in the probability that there will never by a "Surf III" to follow the slight outlook for this one.

Given the state of the world generally, it's no surprise that a certain number of young people are given to the challenge of standing on top of a board at the edge of the ocean. And there have even been films over the past few decades that have tapped into this amazing pastime for amusement.

At its best, if there were such a thing, "Surf II" seems to want to satirize these previous efforts while adding the charming idea that what was really missing before was endless scenes of teenagers eating garbage. Not junk food, but genuine garbage.

The reason some of them do this is they have been drinking an awful soda pop concocted by nerdish Eddie Deezen, out for revenge on the surfers. He's unwillingly assisted by Linda Kerridge and willingly assisted by the usual money-hungry parents.

But the real question raised by a picture like "Surf II" is not why teenagers eat garbage but why otherwise respectable performers like Cleavon Little, Morgan Paull, Ruth Buzzi and Lyle Waggoner lend their names to it.

Oh yes, some of the girls remove their tops. — *Har.*

Fantozzi Subisce Ancora
(Fantozzi Takes It On the Chin Again)
(ITALIAN-COLOR)

Rome, Jan. 6.
A Titanus release. Produced by Bruno Altissimi and Claudio Saraceni for Maura International Films. Stars Paolo Villaggio. Directed by Neri Parenti. Screenplay, Leo Benvenuti, Piero De Bernardi, Neri Parenti, Villaggio; camera (Eastmancolor), Alberto Spagnoli; art director, Maria Grazia Pera; editor, Sergio Montanari; music, Gambrini. Reviewed at Reale Cinema, Rome, Jan. 6, 1984. Running time: **84 MINS.**
Ugo Fantozzi..............Paolo Villaggio
Pina Fantozzi ....Milena Vukotic
Silvania ....Anna Mazzamauro
Surgeon ....Alessandro Haber

Actor-helmer team Paolo Villaggio and Neri Parenti return to the screen with the fourth in their comedy series "Fantozzi." The further misadventures of the put down, exploited, hapless office clerk offer enough excellent skits and gags to keep audiences laughing from beginning to end. The problem is that repetition has set in and the routines look more than

a little dèja vu, which may be a factor in only fair domestic box-office.

Besides Mediterranean and Latin market pickups, the whole Fantozzi series merits circulation as a curiosity item at Italo cinema roundups, being perhaps the only type of local comedy capable of appealing to widely diverse audiences. Though deeply rooted in the Italian landscape and social scene, Fantozzi is a character based on the universal humor of the little guy who is pushed around and humiliated by all and sundry, and whose efforts to fight back only land him into deeper trouble.

When his daughter (who is so ugly even Fantozzi has difficulty telling her apart from a chimp in the pet shop) gets pregnant, Fantozzi (Villaggio) and his tiny wife Pina (Milena Vukotic) go to see the blustering "father" for a reckoning. They narrowly avoid getting raped before they beat a hasty retreat.

Next Fantozzi takes his savings and goes to the hospital to find a doctor willing to perform an abortion; when he finally locates a surgeon (Alessandro Haber), they put him on the operating table instead. Unable to find the patient's file and turning a deaf ear to his pleas, the surgeon performs a sex change operation. Through the intercession of the President of the Republic, Fantozzi is put back together again, but by the time he gets out of the hospital his daughter has given birth to a six-armed, trumpeting monster (never seen, but heard). The only thing Fantozzi can do is pass around baby pictures at the office, to the puzzlement and horror of his coworkers.

The office is Fantozzi's world; he is the victim of every kind of maliciousness, callousness and piece of ill luck that goes on. While the entire building empties at 9:05 as workers race off to their second jobs and favorite pastimes, Fantozzi is left alone to cover for them with the inspector, cranking a series of cardboard silhouettes around and stamping furiously on pieces of paper.

The gags are quick and surrealistic; the irony is effective and barbed. Villaggio is as appealing as ever in the central role, aided by fine character actors like Vukotic and Anna Mazzamauro, the office siren.—*Yung.*

Rue Barbare
(Barbarous Street)
(FRENCH-COLOR)

Paris, Jan. 10.
Parafrance release of a Films de la Tour/Farena Films/International Project coproduction. Produced by Adolphe Viezzi. Directed by Gilles Behat. Features entire cast. Screenplay, Behat and Jean Vautrin, based on David Goodis' "Street of the Lost;" camera (Eastmancolor), Jean-Francois Robin;

art director, Frédéric Astich-Barré; music, Bernard Lavilliers; sound, Paul Lainé; editor, Geneviève Vaury; production manager, Guy Perol. Reviewed at the Publicis Champs-Elysées theater, Paris, Jan. 8, 1984. Running time: **107 MINS.**
Daniel Chetman ....Bernard Giraudeau
Emma the Red ....Christine Boisson
Paul Chetman ....Jean-Pierre Kalfon
Georges Chetman ....Michel Aumont
Hagen ....Bernard-Pierre Donnadieu
Yougo ....Jean-Pierre Sentier
Temporini ....Pierre Frag
Carla Chetman ....Nathalie Courval

"Rue Barbare" is another misguided attempt to adapt American dime novelist David Goodis to the screen. After Jean-Jacques Beineix and his day-glo adaptation of Goodis' 1953 book, "The Moon in the Gutter," it's the turn of Gilles Behat, a former rock guitarist turned actor and filmmaker, to tackle the author's "Street of the Lost," published shortly before "Moon."

Behat is far from Beineix's glitzy aesthetic, but his treatment has its own arty pretentions and wallows in a finally numbing blood-and-thunder atmosphere. "Rue Barbare" is full of sound and fury signifying not much, although the stated intent was to make a parable about violence and the impossibility of neutrality in an anarchic society. (Behat, by the way, takes an opening series of shots that seem to spoof the prolog of "Moon.")

Bernard Giraudeau has the lead as a man who has retired from the violences of his quarter and professes an I-Don't-Want-To-Get-Involved philosophy. But predictably, he commits an action that gets him involved up to his neck, and he must have a showdown with the mug who terrorizes the district in order to assert his individuality.

The personage is a former street tough himself who has clung for 10 years to a job (railway workman), a fragile wife, and a family of derelicts.

Giraudeau fits the bill outlined in the script, displaying a virile torso and brooding animal vigor, though he's powerless against shallow characterization. Bernard-Pierre Donnadieu also supplies the physical requirements as his terrifying nemesis, a primping bull who struts menacingly, packs a mean punch, gets chauffeured around in an English taxi, but is really an insignificant cog in a larger wheel of tyranny and lawlessness.

Other actors do their best with shabbier parts, including Christine Boisson, sultry proprietress of a neighborhood hangout, Jean-Pierre Sentier, Donnadieu's vicious knife-throwing associate, and Michel Aumont and Jean-Pierre Kalfon, Giraudeau's flotsam father and jetsam brother.

Behat and Vautrin transpose the action from an American urban slum to a blighted European suburb, a limbo of social outcasts, forbidding lots and abandoned factories. But they betray the anonymity of Goodis' world by stereotyping the human fauna as a clichéd assortment of freaks, leather-jacketed delinquents and punk thugs. The look of "Rue Barbare" is closer to pictures of "The Road Warrior" ilk (with a nod to the western and samurai epics) and its fashionable dosage of blood, sleaze and sex will probably appeal to the teen crowd.—*Len.*

Blame It On Rio
(COLOR)

Quick before it melts.

Hollywood, Jan. 24.

A Sherwood Production and Sidney Kimmel Presentation of a 20th Century-Fox release. Produced and directed by Stanley Donen. Executive producer, Larry Gelbart. Stars Michael Caine, Joseph Bologna, Valerie Harper, Michelle Johnson. Screenplay, Charlie Peters, Gelbart; camera (Metrocolor), Reynaldo Villalobos; editor, George Hively, Richard Marden; music, Ken Wannberg, Oscar Castro Neves, art director, Marcos Flaksman; set decorator, Yeda De Mello Lewinsohn; sound, Jim Willis; associate producer, Robert Relyea; assistant directors, Scott Easton, Jose Joaquim Salles. Reviewed at 20th Century-Fox, L.A., Jan. 24, 1984. (MPAA Rating: R.) Running time: 110 MINS.

Matthew Hollis	Michael Caine
Victor Lyons	Joseph Bologna
Karen Hollis	Valerie Harper
Jennifer Lyons	Michelle Johnson
Nicole Marques	Jose Lewgoy
Signora Botega	Lupe Gigliotti

Elements that signal hope for a lush lark of a movie — amorous lunacy in Rio courtesy of exec producer and cowriter Larry Gelbart, producer-director Stanley Donen, and costars Michael Caine and Joseph Bologna — hit a flat note in this Sherwood Prods./Sidney Kimmel Presentation. Boxoffice for distributor 20th Century-Fox when film opens wide national run Feb. 17, must count on a fast takeoff.

Central premise of a secret romance between Caine and the love-smitten daughter of his best friend (Bologna) while the trio vacations together in torrid Rio may be adventurous comedy. Zany comedic conflict, however, is offputting, even at times nasty, in this essentially dead-ahead comedy that sacrifices charm and a light touch for too much realism.

Newcomer Michelle Johnson, in her maiden jump from modeling to acting, comes off as callow and disagreeably spoiled in key role of buxom daughter lusting after dad's best buddy (she's topless a lot, too, but that's life on those beaches at Rio).

Caine and Bologna play colleagues in a Sao Paulo coffee company whose marriages are toppling — Bologna is getting a divorce and Caine's wife (Valerie Harper) tells Caine while couple is packing for Rio that she's splitting for Bahia in a separate vacation.

Donen gets sharp, comic performances from Caine and Bologna. Caine's character is weak but never unlikable, even after tumbling hard and conceding emotional involvement with the girl. It's craftsmanship of a smooth order.

Bologna, bachelor-to-be making out wherever he can, is equally adept in role of uptight parent. Their inevitable confrontation scene, when Caine spills all, is well written by Gelbart and co-writer Charlie Peters. But the writers press their luck in final scenes

when wife Harper bombs in and it turns out she's been Bologna's secret paramour. Bologna to Caine: "At least your wife isn't somebody's daughter!" Exactly, but import of scene is to sort of balance the sexual ledger. It doesn't work.

Reprise of leading characters in pastiche of scenes before end credits is another flaw, surprisingly dated touch for a seemingly worldly comedy.

Harper hasn't much to do, and other principals aboard the vacation party, Demi Moore (Jackie Templeton on tv's "General Hospital"), who plays Caine's daughter, is darkly morose. Expectedly, she disapproves of her father sleeping with her friend Johnson, but role is left in limbo and exists in a vacuum.

Shot entirely on location, film disappoints in its conventional use of Rio. Noticeable by its absence is a desired mirthful, exotic physical texture — despite shots of parrots, red splashes of tomatoes and melons, and a nighttime macumba wedding on moonlit sands. Too often, filmmakers have a pair of principals stop cold at some street corner or cliffside to watch, like wooden tourists, the travelog before them. Brazilian art director Marcos Flaksman, however, swaths the vacationeers' tropical home in great gaudy designs.

Flaksman's touch captures the spirit of the outing better than any other element. Certainly, the music doesn't, an inconsistent blend of American pop and Brazilian rhythms. Brazilian composer Oscar Castro Neves' sounds, especially accompanying a beachfront drive, should have occupied the whole score.

Narrative device by Caine and Johnson that occasionally interrupts action is fine, and the film indeed enjoys funny moments, as when Bologna shouts at his daughter, "You made love with a man who is 43 — it's obscene!" But for Donen and others, the sum of the parts is a sore note. —*Loyn.*

Les Dalton en Cavale
(Escape from Grumble Gulch)
(FRENCH-U.S.-COLOR-ANIMATED)

Paris, Dec. 20.

Gaumont release of a Gaumont/FR 3/Hanna-Barbera coproduction with Dargaud publishing house. Executive producers, Philippe Landrot, Bob Maxfield. Alain de Lannoy; directed by William Hanna, Joseph Barbera and Morris Gascinny; animation directors, Juan R. Pina, Carlos-Alfonso Lopez; camera (color), Charles Flekal; editors, Larry Cowan, Pat Foley; sound, Alvy Dorman, Phil Flad; music, Claude Bolling, Shuki Levy, Haim Saban; production manager, Benedicte Aulois; mixing, Antoine Bonfanti. Reviewed at the Gaumont Colisée Theater, Paris, Dec. 20, 1983. Running time: 85 MINS.

Voices (French track): Jacques Balutin, Roger Carel, Marion Game, Bernard Haller, Gerard Hernandez, Jacques Thebault, Pierre Tornade, Pierre Trabaud.

Lucky Luke, the poor, lonesome cartoon cowboy made in France by Morris and René Grascinny, has bit the celluloid dust in his first transatlantic crossing to the Hanna-Barbera studios, coproduce of this third cinema version of the comic strip created in 1946. Gaumont, the FR 3 tv network, and Dargaud, publisher of the Lucky Luke albums, have also added their names to this Franco-American coproduction, which will certainly not advance the cause of the Gallic comic strip in the U.S.

Fans of the famous phlegmatic cowboy, his sententious horse, Jolly Jumper; his goofy mutt, Rantanplan, and Luke's enemies, the chronically imbecilic Dalton Brothers, are bemoaning the diluting modifications made in cartoon. Co-creator Morris Gascinny, who has codirecting credit with Hanna and Barbera, agreed to have Luke's ever present cigaret replaced by a blade of grass, and a whole gallery of ethnic secondary characters was banished from the drawing boards. The violence has also been toned down so that Luke, the man who "draws faster than his shadow," is virtually reduced to chatty inertia.

And inert this feature cartoon certainly is. Adapted from several albums by Morris and Gilberte Gascinny, widow of the strip's coauthor, the picture merely strings out a dull series of episodes pitting Luke against the Daltons. Despite all the prestigious talent involved, there's no verve, imagination or rhythm. The very young may like it, but its scrappy animation may look more at home on the television screen. —*Len.*

Le Bon Plaisir
(FRENCH-COLOR)

Paris, Jan. 25.

MK2 release of an MK2-S.F.P.C. Films A2 co-production. Produced by Marin Karmitz. Stars Catherine Deneuve, Michel Serrault, Jean-Louis Trintignant. Directed by Francis Girod. Screenplay, Girod and Françoise Giroud, based on her novel; camera (Eastmancolor), Jean Penzer; art director, François de Lamothe; sound, André Hervee; music, Georges Delerue; editor, Geneviève Winding; production manager, Gerard Crosnier. Reviewed at the Marignan-Concorde theater, Jan. 20, 1984. Running time: 108 MINS.

Claire	Catherine Deneuve
The President	Jean-Louis Trintignant
Minister of the Interior	Michel Serrault
Herbert	Michel Auclair
Pierre	Hippolyte Girardot
The First Lady	Claude Winter
Mike	Matthew Pillsbury
Julie	Alexandra Stewart

French president Jean-Louis Trintignant, stone-faced father to his nation, learns one day he's also daddy to a little bastard he'd sired 10 years earlier by former mistress Catherine Deneuve, who'd refused his demands that she abort, ended the relationship and raised the child alone.

Belated awareness of his paternity has him in a cold sweat. Deneuve never destroyed the compromising letter he'd written her at the time and had in fact been carrying it around all these years in her handbag — which she's just lost to a young purse-snatcher. Panicky that the letter could fall into the hands of the opposition and put the breaks on his glory march, the chief of state huddles with Minister of Interior Michel Serrault to plot some emergency measures.

Author-screenwriter Françoise Giroud, who adapted "Le Bon Plaisir" from her own recent novel, opts for an ironic comedy of political manners and uses her own experiences as minister in the cabinet of former French president Valery Giscard D'Estaing to paint some apparently composite portraits of people in high places (she denies that her fictional politicians are based on specific real-life figures).

Film has some mild psychological acuity and several good scenes, but overall effect is one of blandness, suggesting that politics and screen entertainment make for strange bedfellows when it's not a question of paranoid suspense or unbuttoned satire.

Despite adequate performances from Trintignant and Serrault, the scripter and director Francis Girod never fully resolve the dramatic problem of making stuffy, humorless politicians interesting as human beings.

Ironically, there is more tangible human interest in the parallel situation of the young purse-snatcher (Hippolyte Girardot) and his guarded relationship with a homosexual political journalist (Michel Auclair). Both become circumstantial victims in a turn of events that end with the return of the letter and the safeguard of the president's image.

Giroud is sharp in catching intransigent political figures in their moments of weakness or embarrassment. Claude Winter has one of the best bits as the long-suffering First Lady who suddenly vents her frustration and anger on her unsuspecting husband, informing him that once he's out of office, she's cut out of his life.

In the story's most effective setpiece, Trintignant "abducts" Deneuve and his son and has them brought out to his palatial Versailles retreat by helicopter, where the kid loses his pet cat and has the entire security force combing the vast grounds for the animal.

Trintignant has his most vulnerable moments here as he clumsily attempts to understand his own paternal feelings and make contact with his new-found son. When latter arrives on the stairs of the mansion, the president is disarmed when he says the house is his but,

then has to admit he doesn't know where the kitchen is.

Later, alone with Deneuve, he learns the boy was born and raised in America and exclaims triumphantly: "Then he could become President of the United States!"

Girod's direction respects the tone of Giroud's script, though to judge from his past works, restraint is not quite his thing. (Giroud has said that the ideal director would have been the late Jacques Becker, with whom she worked as writer for the marvelous 1946 comedy, "Antoine and Antoinette." In "Bon Plaisir," Deneuve lives in the fictional "Jacques Becker Square.")

Tech credits are fine down the line. Despite its dramatic inadequacies, glossy billing and curiosity value could put pic across as a good commodity in other markets.
— *Len.*

Slayground
(BRITISH-COLOR)

A Universal Pictures-Associated Film Distribution release of a Thorn EMI Films production, in association with Jennie & Co. Film Prods. Executive producer, Bob Mercer. Produced by John Dark, Gower Frost. Directed by Terry Bedford. Stars Peter Coyote, Mel Smith, Billie Whitelaw. Screenplay, Trevor Preston, from novel by Richard Stark; camera (Technicolor), Stephen Smith; editor, Nicolas Gaster; music, Colin Towns; sound, David John; production design, Keith Wilson; production supervisor, Ron Fry; assistant director, Steve Lanning, Henry Bronchtein (U.S.); special effects, John Richardson, John Morris, Al Griswald (U.S.); stunt arranger, Vic Armstrong, Victor Magnotta (U.S.); photography (U.S.), Herb Wagreich. Reviewed at Loews State 1 theater, N.Y., Jan. 29, 1984. (MPAA Rating: R). Running time: **89 MINS.**

Stone	Peter Coyote
Terry Abbat	Mel Smith
Madge	Billie Whitelaw
Costello	Philip Sayer
Joe Sheer	Bill Luhrs
Joni	Marie Masters

Also with: Cassie Stuart, Debby Bishop, Clarence Felder, Ned Eisenberg, David Hayward, Michael Ryan, Rosemary Martin, Malcolm Terris.

"Slayground" is an unengaging overly episodic British crime thriller suitable for undiscriminating action audiences.

Self-conscious direction by debuting helmer Terry Bedford, with experience as a cinematographer and tv commercials pilot, recalls in mood and look the flurry of stylish MGM British films noirs of 1970-71, such as "Get Carter" and "Villain." Peter Coyote toplines as Stone, a criminal at the end of his tether after an armored car robbery in upstate New York goes awry, leaving a little girl dead. Her dad vindictively hires a sadistic executioner (Philip Sayer) to kill Stone and his compatriots.

Degenerating into a series of barely-connected stalk-and-terror setpieces, "Slayground" segues mid-film to England, where Stone flees and takes up with an old pal Terry (Mel Smith), who has given

up crime and now lives with Madge (Billie Whitelaw), owner of a Blackpool amusement park. After another heist (this time stealing funds from a casino), Stone defeats the executioner in a dull but photogenic final reel set against the fun house backdrop of the empty amusement park.

Maintaining a grim mood of overcast skies, unsympathetic characters and general hopelessness, Bedford and screenwriter Trevor Preston fail to flesh out this tale beyond mere functional requirements. The overlay of backlighting, silhouette shots and gimmickry such as a blood-red color filter over the camera lens during the killings fail to enliven a perfunctory assignment.

Acting is adequate, with Mel Smith making a good impression as Coyote's pudgy pal. Tech credits, particularly the car stunts and special effects explosions, are good. — *Lor.*

The Lonely Guy
(COLOR)

For the desperately lonely only.

Hollywood, Jan. 27.

A Universal release. Produced and directed by Arthur Hiller. Executive producer, William E. McEuen. Coexecutive producer, C.O. Erickson. Stars Steve Martin. Screenplay, Ed. Weinberger, Stan Daniels, adaptation, Neil Simon, based on the book "The Lonely Guy's Book Of Life" by Bruce Jay Friedman; camera (Technicolor), Victor J. Kemper; editors, William Reynolds, Raja Gosnell; music, Jerry Goldsmith; production design, James D. Vance; set decoration, Linda DeScenna; costume design, Betsy Cox; sound, Larry Jost, Jimmy Sabat (N.Y.); special visual effects, Albert Whitlock; associate producer, Judy Gordon; assistant director, Jack Roe. Reviewed at Universal Studios, Universal City, Jan. 26, 1984. MPAA Rating: R. Running time: **90 MINS.**

Larry Hubbard	Steve Martin
Warren Evans	Charles Grodin
Iris	Judith Ivey
Jack Fenwick	Steven Lawrence
Danielle	Robyn Douglass
Merv Griffin	Merv Griffin
Dr. Joyce Brothers	Dr. Joyce Brothers
Schneider Twins	Candi Brough, Randi Brough
Rental Agent	Julie Payne

"The Lonely Guy" is Steve Martin's most naturalistic and least funny film comedy to date. Inevitably, some good laughs pop up here and there, but the dead air between them lasts much longer than ever before with Martin. This is certainly not the pic to regenerate b.o. interest in the comedian after the still mystifying failure of last year's "The Man With Two Brains."

Derived from a comic tome by Bruce Jay Friedman, premise has Martin bounced by sexpot girl friend Robyn Douglass and thereby banished to the world of Lonely Guys. He meets and commiserates with fellow L.G. Charles Grodin, who gets Martin to buy a

fern with him and throws a party attended only by Martin and a bunch of life-sized cardboard cutouts of celebs like Dolly Parton and Tom Selleck.

Finally, Martin meets cute blond Judith Ivey, who, having been previously married to six Lonely Guys, instantly falls for him. But Martin keeps losing her phone number and spends most of the pic trying to track her down. Finally, of course, they get together, while Grodin ends up with — of all people — Dr. Joyce Brothers.

Martin's trademark wacky humor is fitfully in evidence, but seems much more repressed than usual in order to fit into the relatively realistic world of single working people.

On the one hand, film could have been much funnier had it introduced Martin to more women in varied comic situations. On the other, true poignance could have been developed out of this material.

Unfortunately, the two strains keep fighting and beating each other down, thereby dampening the effect of both the comedy and the latent emotion.

Ultimately, Martin breaks out of the doldrums by writing a Lonely Guy Guide which becomes a bestseller. This momentarily wins him some girlfriends, as well as an appearance on "The Merv Griffin Show," where both Griffin and Brothers appear as themselves (Loni Anderson is also in for an amusing, uncredited bit).

Thesps all give it the college try, and Grodin is particularly engaging as a definitive sad sack. But the long stretches between genuine merriment drag the whole thing down irreversably.

Pic has a bright look and sound. While more sexually restrained than Martin's earlier films, it still features enough bawdy humor to earn its R rating. —*Cart.*

Undercover
(AUSTRALIAN-COLOR)

Sydney, Jan. 13.

A Roadshow Distributors release of a Palm Beach Pictures — Filmco Production. Produced by David Elfick. Executive Producer, Richard Toltz. Directed by David Stevens. Features entire cast. Screenplay, Miranda Downes; camera (Panavision, color), Dean Semler; editor, Tim Wellburn; music, Bill Motzing, with Bruce Smeaton, Dorothy Dodds; sound, Peter Barker; art director, Herbert Pinter; costume designer, Kristian Fredrikson. Reviewed at Roadshow Theatrette, Sydney, Jan. 10, 1984. Running time: **87 MINS.**

Libby McKenzie	Genevieve Picot
Fred Burley	John Walton
Max Wylde	Michael Pare
Nina	Sandy Gore
Theo	Peter Phelps
Arthur Burley	Andrew Sharp
May Burley	Caz Lederman
Alice	Susan Leith
Lionel	Wallas Eaton
Professor	Barry Otto

"Undercover" is another very good-looking Australian production set in the past, in this case the '20s. It seems that the public, both at home and overseas, prefer looking back on Australia as it was rather than exploring what it is today. This extremely handsome David Elfick production has as its background a true story and real characters, with focus of attention on Fred Burley, a businessman who pioneered new designs in women's underwear.

It's a theme with plenty of possibilities, most of them unfortunately missed in Miranda Downes' unfocussed screenplay. Film starts out as the story of Libby Mckenzie, an ambitious young career woman who leaves a deadend job in the little country town where she grew up to try her luck in the big city of Sydney. Eventually, she gets a job in the design department of Burley's company where she's inspired by the head designer, Nina, an independent woman who's as eccentric as she's talented.

At about this point, the screenplay shifts away from Libby to concentrate on Burley himself and his campaign to persuade his fellow countrymen and women to Buy Australian Products; while this theme may strike a local chord, it could well prove a bit chauvinistic for foreign audience. Climax is an extended fashion parade with musical numbers.

Elfick, whose previous productions have included "Newsfront" and "Starstruck," has ensured the film's budget is up there on the screen. Herbert Pinter's art direction is superb and has been beautifully photographed in Panavision by Dean Semler. Another major plus is the costume design by Kristian Fredrikson, who also designed the film's charming photo album credit-titles.

Despite all this quality on-screen, "Undercover" is a rather frustrating experience. David Stevens, who previously scored with the mini-series "A Town Like Alice" as well with his amusing first feature "The Clinic," seems unsure of the right mood for the film. Thus, some scenes are played for rather campy laughs, while others are old-fashioned melodrama.

Genevieve Picot, playing an early feminist, is a good actress but lacks warmth and humor; she has created a bad-tempered heroine who's hard to root for. John Walton is more effective as the enthusiastic Burley, but Michael Pare, the Yank actor who made an impact last year in "Eddie And The Cruisers," is wasted in a nothing part as a brash imported publicist.

Most enjoyable performance comes from Sandy Gore as Nina who visibly relishes the extravagancies of her character. The

suggestion of a lesbian attraction between Nina and Libby is raised, and then dropped like a hot potato; feminists in the audience are likely to greet the heroine's fadeout clinch with Pare derisively.

If it's trying to explore sexual roles in Australia in the '20s, "Undercover" doesn't really succeed; as a nostalgic look at the early days of the underwear industry, it is more successful. Roadshow will need to pull all the stops for the film to find a large audience domestically, while overseas results are iffy.—*Strat.*

The Power
(COLOR)

Ho-hum horror.

An Artists Releasing Corp. release through Film Ventures International. An Edward L. Montoro presentation of a Jeffrey Obrow Prods. production. Produced by Obrow. Directed by Obrow, Stephen Carpenter. Features entire cast. Screenplay, Carpenter, Obrow, from story by Obrow, Carpenter, John Penney, John Hopkins; camera (Getty color), Carpenter; editor, Obrow, Carpenter; music, Chris Young; sound, Earl Ghaffari; production design, Chris Hopkins; assistant director, John Hopkins; production manager, Samson Aslanian; post-production supervisor, John Penney; special makeup effects, Matthew Mungle. Reviewed at UA Rivoli 2 theater, N.Y., Jan. 27, 1984. (MPAA Rating: R). Running time: **84 MINS.**
Sandy .... Susan Stokey
Jerry .... Warren Lincoln
Julie .... Lisa Erickson
Tommy .... Chad Christian
Matt .... Ben Gilbert
Francis Lott .... J. Dinan Myrtetus
Ron Prince .... Chris Morrill
Lee McKennah .... Rod Mays

"The Power" represents a return to horror film basics: the requisite scares and flashy makeup jobs but little else to sustain viewer interest over the length of a feature. Also known during production as "Evil Passage," film is unrelated to the late George Pal's 1968 sci-fi thriller "The Power."

Supernatural tale concerns a tiny (two inches tall) Aztec idol, Destacatyl, which passes from hand to hand wreaking mucho havoc. Stolen by Francis Lott (J. Dinan Myrtetus) from a professor, it ends up in the possession of three Los Angeles high school students (Lisa Erickson, Chad Christian, Ben Gilbert) who use it during their amateur attempts to contact the spirit world.

The idol causes the death of a cemetery caretaker during one of the students' sessions, and the kids seek the aid of reporter Sandy McKennah (Susan Stokey) after she writes about the incident for her tabloid The Eyewitness. Sandy's boyfriend Jerry (Warren Lincoln) steals the idol, which possesses him, cueing familiar expanding-bladder makeup effects and general mayhem.

Filmmakers Jeffrey Obrow and Stephen Carpenter reprise low-budget versions of the levitating

and objects-flying-around-the-room special effects pioneered in "The Exorcist" at every opportunity, but fail to create interesting characters or situations. Makeup effects by Matthew Mungle vary in quality but deliver some effective grotesque faces as "evil" is mirrored on the visages of the least scrupulous players. Acting is unimpressive, as is a silly "three years later" epilog scene.

"The Power" departs from recent trends in the genre by being almost devoid of sexual content, except for a scary nightmare scene wherein Sandy imagines a dozen hands grabbing at her from beneath her bed.

Chris Young provides a suitably spooky musical score, which is overly derivative of Camille Saint-Saëns' "The Aquarium," previously used on the soundtrack of "Days Of Heaven." —*Lor.*

Aces Go Places III
(Our Man From Bond Street)
(HONG KONG-COLOR)

Hong Kong, Jan. 21.
A Cinema City Co. Ltd. production and presentation. Released by Golden Princess Distribution Co. Directed by Tsui Hark. Producers, Karl Maka, Dean Shek; coproducer and screenplay, Raymond Wong. Features entire cast. Production design, Nanshun Shi; art direction, Oliver Wong; camera (color), Bill Wong, Henry Chan; special effects, Rudolph Chiu, Joe Chan; editor, Tony Chow; music, Noel Quinlan; theme song written and sung by Sam Hui; special effects director, Don Yuen. Reviewed at President theater, Hong Kong, Jan. 20, 1984. Running time: **100 Mins.**
Cast: Sam Hui, Karl Maka, Sylvia Chang, Ricky Hsu Koon Ying, Naomi Otsubo, John Sham, Cho Tat-Wah, Peter Graves, Richard Kiel, Jean Mersant, Huguette Funfrock, Tsuneharu Sugiyama and Lerisa Momeyer. *(Cantonese soundtrack with English subtitles)*

Cinema City should be admired for its ability to consistently produce what local viewers want to see on the big screen, but be admonished for playing it too safe with its already patented slick commercial slapstick comedies. the only challenge is how to outdo, outbudget, outimitate and outexcess the stunts that have gone before. Now, there's "Aces Go Places-Number 3," obviously inspired by the 007 James Bond pics.

The first 30 minutes is very amusing, that's when King Kong (Sam Hui) is in Paris and meets a femme assassin Lerisa Momeyer. She lures the hero to the Eiffel Tower, where Kong meets once again Big G (giant Richard Kiel) and Thunder (Sugiyama). They engage in a frenetic fight on top of the Tower elevator. King naturally manages to escape and falls into the Seine via parachute.

Whilst underwater, a submarine shaped like a shark gobbles him and inside is a look-alike Mr. Bond (Jean Mersant), a supposedly special agent from the British Secret

Service. Assignment is to recover the jewels that belong to the Queen of England, (played to the hilt by look-alike Huguette Funfrock). Bond also assigns agent number 701 (Naomi Otsubo) to assist Kong in the mission. She is a beauty of course, a real charmer meant to capture the heart of Kong.

Then it's back to Hong Kong, and signs of the downtrend trail begin to show after a hilarious zipper comedy sketch with Karl Maka and a temporary maid. At that point, the screenwriter and director seem to have run out of ideas. There are fleeting gags, but the jokes are a series of superficial impossibilities, and the actors really have nowhere to go to develop believable characters in their assigned typecast roles as superheroes.

There are bits of creative gleam, like the assemblage of celebrity look-alikes. Hui's portrayal as Hong Kong's numero uno jewel thief is flogged to death. He remains handsome though, complete with his athletic slim grace which is still intact. The rest of the Cinema City gang do what they are expected to do — ham it up for laughs. The real scene stealer is a bald baby called "Junior" who has the best facial shots. Sylvia Chang does her usual cop kook turn with domestic problems, while Maka has his unsparing visual moments. The rest of the episodes are sadly either faded or formularized.

"Aces III" is a non-stop visual attack, an extravagant display of modern technology and special effects with antiseptic sexuality for the entire family trade to enjoy. It will also serve as an endurance test for those not familiar with the Cinema City style of a laugh-a-minute.

But CC churns out the surest film products hereabouts, and success of number III should ensure a number IV. To thinkers, this film can be a downright imbecilic effort, but its mass cretinism is what makes it sizzling hot and acceptable at the domestic box office. One really can't blame those involved in "Aces III" who wish to bask continuously in something that is a surefire Cantonese kitsch bonanza. — *Mel.*

Anna's Mutter
(Anna's Mother)
(WEST GERMAN-COLOR)

Berlin, Jan. 6.
A Planet-Film Production, Munich, in coproduction with CCC-Filmkunst, Berlin, and G & J (Gruner & Jahr) Film Production, Hamburg. Features entire cast. Distributed by Jugendfilm, Berlin, world sales, Cine-International, Munich. Produced by Marin Moszkowicz. Written and directed by Burkhard Driest, based on the Stern-book by Heiko Gebhardt. Camera (color), Lothar E. Stickelbrucke; sets, Dieter Baechle; costumes, Latona Vogel; makeup, Traute Koller; sound, Klaus-Peter Kaiser; editing,

Patricia Rommel; music, Kristian Schultze;
production manager, Eric Moss. Anja
Schmidt-Zaeringer. Reviewed at Filmbuehne
Wien, Berlin, Jan. 6, '84. Running time: **90
MINS.**

Marianne Grünwald	Gudrun Landgrebe
Ulrich, her friend	Rolf Zacher
Anna, her daughter	Verena Corinna
Gitte	Isolde Berth
Micha	Roger Fritz
Günter	Michael Simbruk
Reporter	Georg Marischka
Sonja	Sabrina Lorenz

"Anna's Mother" is Burkhard
Driest's first film as a director.
He's better known for his scripts
for Reinhard Hauff's films: "The
Brutalization of Franz Blum"
(1973), based on his own autobiographical data while serving a
prison term; "Fuses" (1974),
adapting a Franz Josef Degenhardt novel; "Paule Pauländer"
(1975), an authentic portrait of
poverty in sections of Germany;
and "Last Stop Freedom" (Slow
Attack) (1980), starring Driest in
another prison story with autobiographical touches.

From scripter to thesp to helmer
seem to be logical steps — in view
of his debut pic, "Anna's Mother,"
being another crime-and-prison
tale, the true story of one Marianne
Bachmeier.

"The Bachmeier Case" also happens to be the title-theme of Hark
Bohm's new pic (its previous
working title was "No Time for
Tears"), which means in effect
that both Driest and Bohm have
been racing each other in a good-
natured show of one-upmanship to
the boxoffice. Once it was known
that both directors were working
on the same film, the initial release
dates were set for the spring but,
like any feature exploiting the
daily headlines and magazine cover stories, the maxim of striking
while the iron is hot necessitated a
scurry for a convenient New Year
release. Undoubtedly, both films
thereby suffered under the pressure since the production credits
are sloppy.

Burkhard Driest and his producers have placed all their blue
chips on two promising p.r. angles:
(1) the well-known Stern mag publication titled "Anna's Mother,"
which chronicles the story of a
mother who took justice into her
own hands in an open courtroom
hearing by killing with a pistol the
man who had strangled her seven-
year-old daughter in a sex crime;
and (2) actress Gudrun Landgrebe, who had currently soared to
the top of the popularity ratings via
her performance in a German b.o.
winner, Robert van Ackeren's
"The Woman Flambee" (it
preemed at Cannes last year in the
Directors' Fortnight section).
Surely, these factors can indeed be
parlayed into a boxoffice win at
home.

The Bachmeier Case as a true
story, however, carries more drama in its reported media account

than this after-the-fact fiction narrative. Instead of hiring genuine
dialog writers (the bane of New
German Cinema), Driest as au-
thor-director simply spices the
sensational with questionable cultured references to Antonin Artaud
and sociocritical statements on
how the media tend to mangle the
human aspects of a courtroom
drama.

Landgrebe plays Marianne
Grünwald/Bachmeier like a sex-
bomb in the waning days of the
commercial movies in the 1950s.
Hardly a scene in which she appears is free of excessive stylization, some bordering on the maudlin and the downright corny. Worst
of all, the story itself — known by
heart by a vast majority of potential German moviegoers and other
devotees of the boulevard press —
loses its direction by molding an
apparent star image for Landgrebe. And at the cost of a real-life
tragedy.

Landgrebe, for German film
buffs, also played a hipped emancipated femme lawyer in Dorothea
Neukirchen's "Double Trouble"
(1982), a social comedy that
flopped and is better forgotten.

Opening scenes show the girl living with her mother and casual
friend in an idyllic country retreat,
the pot-of-gold for such a romantic
haven (dog and cat included) coming from the recent sale of a bar.
Soon Marianne and Ulrich weary
of clawing at each other whenever
their collective libido surfaces, and
he talks of shipping off to Goa
while she of opening another bar.
The new bar, in a nearby urban
area, is not only opened — it also
proves to be a commercial success, particularly with Marianne
on hand to attract the male customers. Throughout these sequences, Landgrebe struts around
in leather or peek-a-boo blouses.

Another couple appear regularly on the scene, a well-to-do doctor
and his wife. They want to adopt
the girl, and the deal is closed over
champagne one day — just as
Anna disappears. The rest is the
story of the child-murder and he
subsequent murder-case — the
emphasis here being not that of the
sex murderer, but Grünwald/Bach
meier's instead.

Only pluses are the polished lensing (Lothar E. Stickelbrucke) and
Rolf Zacher's performance as
Marianne's tough-but-tender playmate. "Anna's Mother" is for
sensation-seekers.—*Holl.*

Ronde de Nuit
(Night Patrol)
(FRENCH-COLOR)

Paris, Jan. 18.
AMLF release of a Sara Films/AMLF/-
Films A2 coproduction. Produced by Alain
Sarde. Stars Eddy Mitchell, Gerard Lanvin.
Directed by Jean-Claude Missiaen. Screen-
play, Missiaen, Claude Veillot, Marc Perrier,

from an original story idea by Missiaen;
camera (Fujicolor), Pierre-William Glenn;
editor, Armand Psenny; art director, Baptiste Poirot; sound, Michel Desrois; music,
Hubert Rostaing, Ivan Jullien; production
manager, Gérard Gaultier. Reviewed at the
Marignan-Condorde theater, Paris, Jan. 16,
1984. Running time: **95 MINS.**

Gu Arenas	Gérard Lanvin
Léo Gorce	Eddy Mitchell
Diane Castelain	Françoise Arnoul
Sissia Carpelli	Raymond Pellegrin
Mara	Lisette Malidor
Segalen	Gérard Desarthe
Christine	Amélie Prevost

Belatedly following the example
of former colleagues Bertrand
Tavernier and Pierre Rissient,
Paris press agent Jean-Claude
Missiaen last year took the plunge
into directing and came up with a
handsome, critical and commercial success with "Tir Groupé," a
modest urban thriller. Now he's
back with a second feature which
again reflects his buff tastes and
love of Hollywood action movies.
But it's a feeble effort that suggests Missiaen's talents lie elsewhere than in genre cribbing. (But
led the Paris b.o. in first week of
release with $391,000 in 25 city and
22 suburban houses. -Ed.)

"Ronde de Nuit" follows the adventures of a sort of Gallic
"Starsky and Hutch" police team,
with Gérard Lanvin and Eddy
Mitchell as super cool flics, idealistic and impetuous, barging their
way through a treacherous maze
of deceit, involving a crooked real
estate operation, barroom brawls,
high-caliber shootouts, and a kinky
black villainess. It all ends badly
as Mitchell is bumped off and Lanvin is transferred to a provincial
post.

Script offers us nothing we haven't seen before and better executed. Missiaen's personal addition is a penchant for multiple and
varied Paris-by-night settings and
a thick overlay of sentimentality
that clashes with the posturing
cops-and-robbers heroics. As
director, he has poorly assimilated
the teachings of his Hollywood
mentors Howard Hawks and Anthony Mann in his obsessive concern with gratuitous camera
movements.

Missiaen generously sows his
directorial path with numerous
buff citations and winks, helped by
the fact that he makes of Mitchell's
personage a film freak, who
adorns his apartment with huge
blowups of John Wayne and Burt
Lancaster (and boy, do Paris cops
have swell pads). The character's
very name is a buff nod, Léo
Gorce, in homage to the Dead End
kid Leo Gorcey. (Mitchell, a popular rock singer, is himself an inveterate film buff and presents
Hollywood favorites on French television.)

Helmer has announced a third
Paris thriller for this year, but he
probably needs subject matter further from the beaten track —*Len.*

Retenez Moi..Ou Je Fais Un Malheur
(To Catch a Cop)
(FRENCH-COLOR)

Paris, Jan. 18.
Gaumont release of a Imacité/Coline/TF1
Film Productions coproductions in association with Gaumont & Marcel Dassault
Productions. Produced by Pierre Kalfon,
Michel Gérard. Stars Jerry Lewis, Michel
Blanc. Directed by Gérard. Screenplay, Gérard, David Milhaud, Jean-François Navarre;
camera (Fujicolor), Jean Monsigny; art
directors, Gérard Viard and Philippe Ancel-
lin; editor, Gérard Le Du; music, Vladimir
Cosma. Reviewed at the Paris theater, Jan.
18, 1984. Running time: **90 MINS.**

Jerry Logan	Jerry Lewis
Laurent Martin	Michel Blanc
Marie-Christine	Charlotte de Turckeim
Carlotte Battucelli	Laura Betti
Farett	Maurice Risch

It is difficult to reconcile the high
reputation that Jerry Lewis enjoys
in France and the Yank comic's local screen debut (as actor only) in
this abysmal farce, which represents the kind of local commercial
comedy Lewis' buff following
wouldn't condescend to see. Is this
the best the comedian's Gallic
friends, admirers and backers (including Gaumont) could come up
with as a project? Depressing.

"Retenez Moi...Ou Je Fais un
Malheur" casts him as a Las Vegas cop on holiday at his ex-wife's
home in provincial France, where
he has a run-in with his former
mate's new hubby (Michel Blanc),
in fact a cop himself, working
undercover to expose an art smuggling ring, in which Lewis becomes
entangled as a hapless pawn.

Writer-director Michel Gerard
(also coproducer) shows little ap-
titude for story construction, gag
invention or helming basics in this
ragged alignment of sequences
designed to give its American star
free rein to his repertory of muggings, grimaces and idiot squeals
(except for a few unmistakable vocal effects, he is dubbed). Lewis
doesn't appear to have put his
heart into this one, and it's puzzling why he has committed himself to a film that will clearly not
advance his critical or commercial
fortunes.

English-language version, titled
"To Catch a Cop," is reportedly in
preparation, but pic's outlook
seems bleak. —*Len.*

Soldados De Plomo
(Lead Soldiers)
(SPANISH-COLOR)

Madrid, Jan. 13.
An Estela Films S.A., Brezal P.C., Anem
Films S.A., production. Directed by José
Sacristán. Features entire cast. Screenplay,
Sacristán and Eduardo Mendoza; camera
(Eastmancolor), J.A. Ruiz Anchía;
producers, Felix Tusell, José Luis Olaizola;
sets, Felix Murcia; editor, J.L. Matesanz;
music, Josep Mas. Reviewed at Minicine 1,
Madrid, Jan. 13, '84. Running time: **94 MINS.**

Andrés	José Sacristán
Don Dimas	Fernando Fernán Gómez
Blanquita	Silvia Munt
Elena	Assumpta Serna

Doña Mercedes.........Amparo Rivelles
Ramón.................Fernando Vivano

This is thesp José Sacristán's first pic as a director-writer, and as an opera prima is promising enough. Technically, item is up to snuff, with fine direction and excellent thesping all around. The script, however, misses the mark; it is jerky and never seems to make its point, with motivations of almost all the characters so blurred as to be incomprehensible.

Story revolves around a man returning from Mexico to his native Valladolid following a summons sent by a local lawyer. Andrés, the exile, learns he has inherited a huge, antiquated house that is virtually in ruins. Half-brother Ramón has his eyes on the property, apparently as a real estate investment, and offers Andrés a huge sum of money for it.

Though impecunious and a failure in life, Andrés balks at selling the old homestead until he has delved into his murky childhood, for at age six his father had apparantly committed suicide. Or did he? Andrés meanwhile seems to have a flirtation with the lawyer's daughter, and also with his half-brother's wife, but the reasons are never really spelled out. He is also being threatened by two of his brother's henchmen, who it later turns out are really taking their orders from a certain Pepe.

Unfortunately, most of the muddlement is never explained, and those explanations given only confuse matters more. At the end Andrés gets his hefty check and rides off on a train to Madrid with the lawyer's daughter in an adjoining compartment. The lead soldiers refer to some toys Andrés finds in the attic of the house, or are they an oblique reference to the defunct father? One needs more than a genealogical tree to figure out this family muddle. —Besa.

Rauschendes Leben
(Intoxicated Life)
(W. GERMAN-COLOR-DOCU-16m)

Berlin, Jan. 7.
A C&V Film production, Berlin. A documentary by Dieter Köster and Hannelore Conradsen. Camera (color), Köster, Jürgen Volkery; lighting, Volkery, Raoul Grass; sound, Theo Kondring, Grass; editing, Köster; mixing, Hannes Bojar (UNISONO); music, Roxy Music & Adaptionen; production manager, Volkery; shooting manager, Franziska Ruthe; assistant, Rainer Dellmuth. Reviewed at Arsenal-Kino, Berlin, Jan. 7, '84. Running time: 113 MINS.

When the husband-wife team of Dieter Köster and Hannelore Conradsen began making children's films for Sender Freies Berlin (SFB) — "Pretty Dull Vacation" (1980), "Drippel Droppel" (1981), "Berlin Wall Gang" (1981) — they scored the best critical ratings in the "Denkste" (Think So?) tv series. Then they won strong critical praise for a tv documentary in the "Under German Roofs" series for a portrait of a camping grounds on the North Sea, "A Bit of Heaven" (1982). This was followed by a self-made low-budget feature, "Berliners on Sunday" (Wild Bunch) (1983), winner of a Special Jury Prize at the Max Ophüls Competition in Saarbrücken last year.

The latest is a two-hour docu on the broad theme of West Berlin bars, titled "Intoxicated Life." Very much in the order of Lionel Rogosin's "On The Bowery" (1954), particularly in chronicling the dives of the city, pic offers a rather depressing view of wasted lives and end-of-the-street alcoholics. But make no mistake; Köster and Conradsen are more interested in the overall picture of drinking as a drug and an intoxicant. Some people — far too many for a healthy society not to be disturbed and even ashamed by the realities — are lushes from morn to eve and then worse through the night.

The fascinating aspect of "Intoxicated Life" is the structure of the film. The first few scenes are comically arranged: the human sponges before the camera play to an audience, undoubtedly because they feel a certain rapport with the filmmakers. This comic "optimism" gradually gives way to sketches of more despairing inebriates; we are also introduced to rather coarse and ill-mannered bourgeois types, people whose egos are reduced to zero without the opportunity in a bar to sprout peacock feathers before an admiring bunch of fellow-boozers. At the end, the lone impression is one of rather frightening "pessimism" — for this is what bars and saloons, cocktail parties and club operations are all about, then the civilized world seems to be drowning in its own cup.

One of Köster-Conradsen's best inspirations was to join a "moonlight cruise" on an excursion boat down the Spree River in West Berlin to Lake Havel. The outing on this particular night was booked by an association of barbers and beauticians. Once the singing and toasts have reached their drunken climax, the entourage disembarks in a stupor — the middle-class working citizen has now blown off enough steam to go back to a routine job early next week.

Then there's the blow-hard from Australia, a German native who travels six months of the year Down Under to buy and resell objects the richer class feels it cannot do without. The friendly merchant spends each available evening in a bar soothing his own ego, and how nice it is to run through the routine this evening before a camera! If Köster & Conradsen have found one of these types, they've stumbled at the same time over a score.

Occasionally, they film an event. A nightclub off the beaten path in Berlin features striptease by the customers. An Elvis Presley fan club mourns the anniversary of its idol's death with a solemn march down a boulevard, the teenagers moved to tears — until they hit their neighborhood bar for nostalgic rock 'n' roll and plenty of ale to drown their sorrows.

True, Berlin is a kind of Las Vegas. The bars, in comparison with other cities in West Germany, are open through the night. The saying goes (with a measure of truth) that if there are four street corners in Berlin, a "Kneipe" can be found on five of them. It is a tourist town as well, a wide-open "island" off the mainland catering to the needs of the all-expenses-paid businessmen and the merrymaking club member out on a spree to Germany's legendary city.

As for the docu's message, the filmmakers don't make any statements. The simple fact that literally gallons of beer are consumed daily by the German population is well known. Here, we note that there's little distinction made between young and old, rich and poor, reputable and degenerate, the conman and the helpless victim. Intoxication, in other words, is not only accepted in today's life, it's practically the sine qua non of society's social mores.

Perhaps too long as a documentary without commentary, "Intoxicated Life" is nonetheless only a portion of what could be actually presented in the film. Its saving grace lies in a certain respect Köster and Conradsen show to the people they film and the problem social drinking poses as a whole. — Holl.

Die Nacht Und Ihr Preis
(The Night And Its Price)
(W. GERMAN-COLOR-DOCU)

Berlin, Jan. 10.
A C&H Film Production, Berlin, in coproduction with Westdeutscher Rundfunk (WDR), Cologne, and Winkelmann Film Production, Dortmond. German distributor, Filmwelt. Directed by Richard Claus. Screenplay by Claus, Gerd Weiss, Adolf Winkelmann; camera (color), Reinhard Köcher, Claus; video, Franktek Brandt; editing, Adolf Winkelmann, Claudia Effner; music, Piet Klocke; tv producer, Alexander Wesemann. Reviewed at Lupe 1, Berlin, Jan. 9, '84. Running time: 107 MINS.

Richard Claus' "The Night And Its Price" scores as a documentary, although several scenes are improvised before the camera in a docu-fiction or docu-drama style. This is a peekaboo look at the underworld scene in the industrial area of the Ruhr, much in the manner of Robert van Ackeren's "Deutschland Privat" (Private Germany) (1982), a chronicle of homemade Super 8 filmmaking (including porno at its most naive).

Docu exploits its theme too much to be taken seriously as a socio-critical view of the seamy side of life. In fact, the bordello scene in which a lady of the night squeezes a few extra bucks out of a customer plays only for the voyeur — for the video camera is so sensitive to the faintest light that the whole sequence amounts to a kind of amateurish porno film.

Claus also spends a good deal of time visiting bedrooms of the working middle-class, as well as prison cells, discos, and wherever teenagers or on-the-town-money-spenders hang out to get their kicks.

There's no commentary to tie it all together, just patch-editing to give the impression that the camera-team is also out bumming around. —Holl.

P & B
(SWEDISH-COLOR)

Copenhagen, Dec. 19.
A Hans Alfredson/Svensk Filmindustri and Svenska Ord (Waldemar Bergendahl), AB Svensk Filmindustri release. Based on novel by Waldemar Hammenhoeg. Written and directed by Hans Alfredson. Camera (Fujicolor) Joergen Persson; production design, Stig Boquist; costumes, Inger Pehrsson; editor, Jan Persson; music, Gunnar Svensson, Sousa, ABBA. "It's Nice To Be Rich" sung by Agnetha Faeltskog; production management, Ann Collenberg, Eva Ivarsson. Reviewed at the Grand, Copenhagen, Dec. 18, 1983. Running time: 105 MINS.
Pettersson.............Stellan Skarsgaard
Bendel......................Allan Edwall
Mia..........................Lena Nyman
Agda.......................Lill Lindfors
Nilsson..................Bjoern Gustavson
Little Rodney.................Jim Hughes
Vreding...................Jan Blomberg
Angelica...................Eva Dahlman

"P & B," actor-writer-director Hans Alfredson's new feature comedy after last year's hit-beyond-home territory "The Simple-Minded Murderer," is a bit of a come-down to more run-of-the-mill social satire with unconvincing flashes of tragic insights. Still, film is full of mild smiles and droll situations, it also has superior acting in the leads, much mugging in supporting roles, plus handsomely-photographed Stockholm exteriors and a witty use of music, including Sousa's "The Thunderer."

The P & B banner, under which sails a couple of from-bumdom-to-riches Swedes named Pettersson and Bender, achieves a certain notoriety, even some respectability, for a short while until the bubble of easy money and rather innocent larceny (the ways and means, moods and manners of successful society in general are parodied) bursts, leaving the bums back where they started, definitely wiser and possibly better for their experience.

Since Bender (Allan Edwall) is an international drifter, Alfredson has some black-and-white flashbacks to prove him the tragic product of a Poland under the yoke of dictatorship. And when Pettersson (Stellan Skarsgaard) seems about to abandon the little waitress (Lena Nyman) who financed his first capitalistic venture, her suicide is interpolated as brutal fact amidst all the satirical fun & games. Tragedy may underscore the satirical fun & games. Tragedy may underscore the satirical points, but what is provoked is mostly embarrassment.

By taking his comedy too seriously, Alfredson has also kept it down to a mere chuckle-provoking level where a few loud guffaws in the old Alfredson tradition from his days of collaborating on feature films with Tage Danielsson would have served to break up a too polite atmosphere (the two men remain partners in various other stage and tv ventures under the aegis of their jointly-owned AB Svenska Ord company.

"P & B" wavers between straight dramatic narrative and a cut-up into a series of comedy sketches. The leading actors (including singing star Lill Lindfors) make the former believable, while the latter are nicely timed and executed without containing any true laugh relief. Of suspense film has practically none, its classic rags-to-riches-and-back theme being subjected strictly to set-piece developments. Some international sales were assured for "P & B" already during its production, and film preemed simultaneously in the capitals of Sweden, Norway and Denmark.—*Kell.*

Unfaithfully Yours
(COLOR)

The More the merrier.

Hollywood, Jan. 31.

A 20th Century-Fox release of a Joe Wizan-Marvin Worth production. Produced by Worth, Wizan. Exec producer, Daniel Melnick. Directed by Howard Zieff. Stars Dudley Moore, Nastassja Kinski, Armand Assante. Screenplay, Valerie Curtin, Barry Levinson, Robert Klane, based upon a screenplay by Preston Sturges; camera (Deluxe color), David M. Walsh; editor, Sheldon Kahn; music, Bill Conti; production design, Albert Brenner; set design, Dianne I. Wager, Lawrence J. Cuneo; set decoration, Rick Simpson; costume design, Kristi Zea; sound, Jery Jost; associate producer, Jack B. Bernstein; assistant director, Jerry Sobul. Reviewed at the 20th Century-Fox Studio, L.A., Jan. 31, 1984. MPAA Rating: PG. Running time: 96 MINS.

Claude Eastman	Dudley Moore
Daniella Eastman	Nastassja Kinski
Maxmillian Stein	Armand Assante
Norman Robbins	Albert Brooks
Carla Robbins	Cassie Yates
Giuseppe	Richard Libertini
Jess Keller	Richard B. Shull
Jerzy Czyrek	Jan Triska
Janet	Jane Hallaren
Bill Lawrence	Bernard Behrens

"Unfaithfully Yours" is a moderately amusing remake of Preston Sturges' wonderful comedy which, it might be remembered, was a commercial bust upon its release in 1948. Since becoming a star name, Dudley Moore has run either very hot or very cold at the b.o., never in between, but if the public is in the mood for a reasonably diverting sex comedy, this could pull some decent biz.

Lavishly mounted and astutely cast farce features Moore in the role of a big-time orchestra conductor who has just taken a much younger Italian screen star, Nastassja Kinski, as his bride. Moore suspects her of fooling around with dashing concert violinist Armand Assante, and core of the film consists of a fantasy in which Moore murders his wife, but makes it look as though Assante did it. He then tries to pull off such a scheme, with predictably incompetent results.

Sturges' film, which starred Rex Harrison as the conductor and Linda Darnell as his wife, offered three murder fantasies set to three different pieces of music. New effort limits Moore to just one imaginary plot, backdropped by Tchaikovsky's violin concerto.

In the early going, Moore snoops around after Kinski, sics private eye Richard B. Shull on her and voices his suspicions to his manager Albert Brooks, whose wife Cassie Yates is actually the one carrying on with Assante. Plot is just full enough of comic complications to keep things interesting, and director Howard Zieff and editor Sheldon Kahn have moved the proceedings along at an agreeably brisk pace.

Tale takes place in the upper reaches of New York cultural society, a world inhabited with ease by Moore, Kinski and Assante. Accomplished musician that he is, Moore is right at home on the podium or behind the piano, and his comic invention and frantic anxiety over his wife result in a generally delightful performance (Peter Sellers was originally announced for the role before he died).

Kinski exhibits hitherto unrevealed comic talents and a nice, frothy touch with this sort of light material. Assante looks just right and shows flair as a musical matinee idol, while Brooks virtually steals all his scenes and provides pic with some of its biggest yocks. Richard Libertini also provokes considerable mirth as Moore's towering Italian valet and cook.

Albert Brenner's rich production design aides greatly in creating the rarified atmosphere, and David M. Walsh's lensing is appropriately crips and bright for a comedy.

Film does run down a bit in the final reel or so, but it achieves much of what it attempts in the way of humor and emerges as a far from disgraceful re-do of a very strong original. —*Cart.*

Papa, Can You Hear Me Sing?
(HONG KONG-TAIWANESE-COLOR)

Hong Kong, Dec. 19.

A Cinema City Co. Ltd. production and release. Directed by Yu Kang-Ping. Stars Sun Yueh, Liu Juel Chi (Vicky Liu), Ng Siu Kong (Manfred Ng), Lee Li Qun, Jiang Shia. Produced by I.S. Wang, Karl Maka. Coproducers, Dean Shek, Raymond Wong. Production designer, Sylvia Chang, L.G. Jou; screenplay, Raymond Wong, Y.C. Yeh; camera (color), Y.C. Ho; art director, J.P. Pang; music, C.Y. Chen, S.C. Lee; editor, C.G. Hwang. Reviewed at President Theater, Hong Kong, Dec. 19, '83. Running time: 100 MINS.

(Mandarin soundtrack with Cantonese and English subtitles).

Hong Kong is good at making jet-paced slapstick comedy, the Philippines for its extremely melodramatic social dramas about poverty, but nobody in Asia can beat the Taiwanese when it comes to churning soap operas and tearjerkers. A perfect example is the multi-awarded Taiwanese soaper, "Papa, Can You Hear Me Sing?" which was originally known (when first released) as "Moonlight." After winning awards at the Golden Horse it was recently released in Hong Kong and was received with generally good response critically and commercially, considering that tear-stained photoplays are not currently in vogue in Hong Kong.

Produced by Cinema City (Taiwan), the production values are quite high, meaning, cinematography, script, storyline substance, music and especially the superb acting of Sun Yueh as "Uncle Dumb." What bogs down the film is the extremely unbelievable string of inter-related dramatic events that are meant to draw tears and emotional hooks. If Hong Kong prods effectively time each gag, Taiwanese films calculate each fatal situation one after the other so the final result is that of woeful extravaganza that is beyond the realms of reality.

"Papa" tells the story of "Uncle Dumb," a retired soldier who makes a living as a scrap collector. He rides a dilapitated bike early morning to conduct his lowly business. One morning in 1958, he finds an abandoned baby girl and raises her. She grows up into a beautiful young girl who can sing. As can be expected in this type of scenario, she gets discovered, finds big success, gets separated from her foster father and close friends as she zooms to the top of the pops.

During one of her concerts, "Uncle Dumb" dies, feeling rejected and dejected for his now very successful daughter has no time even to visit him. Naturally, the next sequence shows the singer taking out all her sorrow in a musical number that pays tribute to the poor bottle peddler.

Had the film been controlled from excessive wails and moans from a series of tragedies that the major characters received from life, this drama could have fared better. Meanwhile, new actress Liu Juel Chi (Vicky Liu) as the singing daughter and Manfred Ng as the sensitive composer who falls in love with the singer, brighten the screen with youthful vibrance. This film should have some legs in the Asian circuit and in Chinatown theaters abroad who may be homesick for some homegrown and fresh Taiwanese cinematic soaper.—*Mel.*

Hadley's Rebellion
(COLOR)

Will have to wrestle for biz.

Hollywood, Jan. 30.

An ADI Marketing release of the East India Trading Co. Production. Produced by Steve Feke. Executive producer R.J. Lewis. Features entire cast. Written and directed by Fred Walton. Camera (CFI color), David Golia; editor, Sam Vitale; music, Mike Post; production designer, Diane Campbell; art director, Martin Price; costumes, Erica Phillips; sound, Louis C. Williman; stunts, Don (Fox) Greene; associate producer, Marc Dodell and Susan Cooper; assistant director, Bob Bender. Reviewed at CFI screening room, Hollywood, Calif. Jan. 30, 1984. (MPAA Rating: PG) Running time: 96 MINS.

Hadley Hickman	Griffin O'Neal
Coach Ball	William Devane
Sam Crawford	Charles Durning
Bob McKenzie	Adam Baldwin
Linda Johnson	Lisa Lucas
Mr. Stevens	Eric Boles
Joe Forster	Dennis Hauge
Manual Hernandez	Israel Juarbe
Rick Stanton	Chas McQueen

"Hadley's Rebellion," a look at the problems of a teenager growing up set against the background of high school wrestling, could have been the dark side of "Breaking Away." Unfortunately it shies away from developing what is basically a sound premise. Consequently pic is unconvincing in either its attempt at portraying the harsh realities or small victories of teenhood. Either way commercial prospects are limited.

Hadley Hickman (Griffin O'-Neal), an import from the rural South attending a prep school in Southern California, sets the tone of the film early on when he announces in a voice-over that life for a teenager is basically rotten. The rest of the picture does nothing to dispel the notion and the mood is generally glum throughout.

Compared to recent teen pics like "Rumble Fish" and "The Outsiders," Hadley's problems are decidedly mundane and therefore more believable. Gang wars and petty crime are not the issues here, but the internal struggles to grow up, meet girls, have friends and find an identity. Hadley's one obsession is to be a great wrestler.

The conflicts set up by writer/director Fred Walton are recognizable and often painfully moving, but his characters can't carry the weight. They are not full-blooded people and only a strong performance can save them. William Devane, as Hadley's wrestling coach, makes the most of an underwritten role, but O'Neal does not yet have the presence to capture what's inside the head of his surly, remote character.

Much is made of Hadley's country origins which are supposed to form his character, but no scenes from his Georgia home are included and his problems in school could be those of any inexperienced youth away from home for the first time, regardless of where he's from.

And the people Hadley meets along the way are equally undeveloped. Charles Durning as Hadley's hero, an old-time wrestling champ turned alcoholic, is laughable, although the boy's need for the relationship is achingly real.

Similarly, his attempt at a love relationship is thinly drawn but full of youthful longing. Lisa Lucas is appealing as the townie girlfriend who mysteriously picks him up and then drops him just as abruptly.

Finally, at the end of the film after he has presumably grown up a bit, Hadley concludes that "a man has to do what he has to do." Too bad the film doesn't have the depth to explain why.

Production values are generally okay, but some scenes appear awkwardly staged and cinematography is ocassionally too pretty for the action. Numerous wrestling scenes are interesting at first, but tend to lose their visual punch. —*Jagr.*

P'tit Con
(Little Jerk)
(FRENCH-COLOR)

Paris, Feb. 1.

Gaumont release of a Gaumont International/Productions Marcel Dassault co-production. Produced by Alain Poiré. Features entire cast. Written and directed by Gérard Lauzier, based on his cartoon album, "Souvenirs d'un Jeune Homme." Camera (color), Jean-Paul Schwartz; production designer, Dominique André; editor, Georges Klotz; sound, Bernard Aubouy; music, Vladimir Cosma; production managers, Marc Goldstaub, Charlotte Fraisse. Reviewed at the Gaumont Colisée Theater, Paris, Feb. 1, 1984. Running time: 90 MINS.
Michel Choupon ....Bernard Brieux
Bob Choupon ....Guy Marchand
Annie Choupon ....Caroline Cellier
Alain Choupon ....Eric Carlos
Eric ....Philippe Khorsand
Maryse.................Claudine Delvaux
Rolande...................Josiane Balasko
Salima.....................Souad Amidou
Jeannot.....................Daniel Auteuil
Legionnaire ....Gérard Darrieu

Like his confrere Francis Veber, Gérard Lauzier is a screenwriter who may be best served by himself as director. A leading French comic-strip artist, Lauzier adapted two of his albums, "The Rat Race" and "Psy," to the screen in 1980 and 1981, but neither directors François Leterrier nor Philippe de Broca succeeded in reconciling the author's stark caricatures with sympathetic flesh-and-blood actors.

Now, with his second feature film as writer-director (his first was a sex comedy, "T'Empêche Tout le Monde de Dormir") Lauzier seems to have found a comfortable equilibrium between his often mean-spirited satiric penchant as cartoonist and the comprimises of mainstream commercial cinema. "P'tit Con" is above-average local comedy, skillfully written, smoothly directed and, most of all, finely acted.

Adapted from his own satiric cartoon, "Memoirs of a Young Man," film tells of the growing pains of a Parisian teenager, just turned 18 and chafing pseudo-poetically under the yolk of bourgeois servitude. Brandishing his received liberal notions, the youth (Bernard Brieux) declares war on his parents' narrow-minded materialism, moves from the family's cozy apartment into an upstairs maid's room and ventures out to taste life and love as a responsible citizen of the world.

Much of this is familiar stuff, but the optic is different: Lauzier's own social beliefs leans toward the conservative Right and his foolish (but likeable) protagonist's misadventures offer him the opportunity to settle some accounts with French Left-wing pretentions, hypocrisy and smugness.

Coming within closest artillery range of his poisoned spitballs is the super-cool Bohemian family, in whose bosom Brieux thinks he's finding solace and understanding. But the mother and her pseudo-

mystical artist mate merely invite the crestfallen boy to share their bed; the timid son heeds Brieux's naive advice about giving in to his sexual impulses and makes a pass at Brieux; and the bookish, chubby daughter, who gets orgasms dreaming about Joseph Stalin and Charles de Gaulle, turns out to be Brieux's first lover, after his long-suffering, ineffectual attempts to court an attractive young Arab girl, whom he shelters in her room along with her delinquent boyfriend.

Lauzier sides with the bourgeois parents, picturing them as basically decent, hard-working folk, perplexed with their son's rebellion and clumsily trying to make amends, though it brings them to the verge of divorce. Their son stirs in time from his dazed disillusion to prevent domestic catastrophe.

Lauzier has had obviously to water down the vitriol of his cartoon original (notably with the conventional happy ending), but what film loses in nastiness it gains in credible humanity. For this he is beholden to a solid, spirited cast, who soften the gratuitous barbs of his more facile characterizations.

Best of the players is Guy Marchand, delightfully touching as the befuddled dad, who fumes at his son's Marxist twaddle during a drive and then stalks down the street asking other motorists if he oppresses them. A deft comic performance. —*Len.*

Mi Manda Picone
(Picone Sent Me)
(ITALIAN-COLOR)

Rome, Jan. 25.

A Medusa release, produced by Gianni Minervini for A.M.A. Film and Medusa Distributione, in association with RAI-TV. SACIS world sales. Stars Giancarlo Giannini, Lina Sastri. Directed by Nanni Loy. Screenplay, Loy, Elvio Porta; camera (Eastmancolor), Claudio Cirillo; editor, Franco Fraticelli; art director, Elena Poccetto Ricci; music, Tullio De Pisoopo. Reviewed at Adriano Cinema, Rome, Jan. 24, 1984. Running time: 122 MINS.
Salvatore ....Giancarlo Giannini
Lucella Picone ....Lina Sastri
Coco ....Aldo Giuffré

A Neapolitan mystery (of sorts), Nanni Loy's "Picone Sent Me" manages to be intriguing in spite of the holes in its plot. Mixing comedy and thriller elements, "Picone" is really an absolutely serious film bent on revealing the mystery of how people live in Naples without jobs or an apparent source of income. Fest kudos will probably sound louder than the ring of the cash register at home, but pic has plenty of color and the draw of star Giancarlo Giannini to get it some merited play offshore.

Like helmer's popular "Cafe Express," "Picone" revolves around a humble hero who gets by on his wits alone. Salvatore (Giannini) set up an independent business in a big hospital; what this business consists of is giving information

about where to go to the confused public. Wearing a pair of unmatched shoes and carrying all his worldly possessions in a plastic bag, Salvatore is one of the many who survive in unorthodox ways, from black marketeers to basement bomb-makers, prostitutes, pimps, bookies, thugs. The point is that all of them (except Salvatore) are clients of the Mafia.

Salvatore's entry into this sinister world begins when he is asked by a young woman, Lucella Picone (Lina Sastri) to find out if her husband is in the hospital morgue. That morning he had set fire to himself in a crowded courtroom — a "protest" against working conditions in his factory — and was whisked away in a waiting ambulance.

You don't need to be Sherlock Holmes, or even Watson, to figure out whodunit and how. Tip-off is a joke early on in the film: "How do you tell a real ambulance from an unauthorized one? — The unauthorized one comes right away."

Salvatore smells a rat, too, and ingeniously gets hold of Picone's diary containing a list of business addresses — jewelry stores, butcher shops — and figures. Correctly deducing Picone is an "insurance" collector for the Mob, Salvatore decides he will make the rounds and pocket the take. He falls into a trap set by Picone — who never appears in the film — and gets out of it by the skin of his teeth. Pic has no definite conclusion, but simply ends with its central metaphor, the appearance of another wildcat ambulance.

Pic marks Giannini's happy return to Italian screens, older but as appealing as ever, more cunning but also more principled (or wiser) than in his Lina Wertmuller roles (he throws away a big Mafia bribe when it finally comes his way). Stage and screen thesp Lina Sastri is highly believable as his partner, more seductive with three kids hanging onto her old bathrobe than many a glamorous star.

Non-Italian viewers will find the picture of Naples a fresh one, ranging from patrician apartments to a long trip through the city sewage pipes. Script, co-penned by Loy and Elvio Porta, gives a comic touch to the most sordid surroundings, while making the city felt in its everyday reality. —*Yung.*

Louisiane
(Louisiana)
(FRENCH-CANADIAN-ITALIAN-COLOR)

Paris, Jan. 31.

Parafrance release of an I.C.C./Filmax/Antenne 2/Films A2/R.A.I. II co-production, in association with Superchanel/C.T.V. Television and the Société de Deeloppment de l'Industrie Cinematographique Canadienne. Produced by Denis Heroux, John Kemeny. Co-producers, Gabriel Boustani, Nader Atassi. Stars Margot Kidder, Ian

Charleson, Andréa Ferreol, Victor Lanoux. Directed by Philippe de Broca. Screenplay, Dominique Fabre, Etienne Perier, Chuck Israel, freely adapted from "Louisiane" and "Fausse-Rivière" by Maurice Denuzière; camera (color) Michel Brault; production designer, Jack Macadam; costumes, John Hay; editor, Hanri Lanoë; music, Claude Bolling; sound, Richard Lightstone, Jean-Charles Ruault; makeup, Joan Isaacson, Josiane Deschamps; production managers, Stéphane Reichel, Michel Nicolini. Reviewed at the Publicis Matignon Theater, Paris, Jan. 29, 1984. Running time: **187 MINS.**

Virginia Tregan	Margot Kidder
Clarence Dandridge	Ian Charleson
Charles de Vigors	Victor Lanoux
Mignette	Andréa Ferreol
Adrien de Damvilliers	Lloyd Bochner
Oswald	Len Cariou
Adrien junior	Larry Lewis
Morley	Raymond Pellegrin

"Louisiane," latest of the dual cinema/tv superproductions (three hours for cinemas, six hours in home-screen miniseries format) is a soggy family saga of Southern grit and inhospitality. Maurice Denuziere, author of the original bestselling source novels, and the makers of this French-Canadian-Italian opus, no doubt had an eye on that indestructible monument of historical romanticism, "GWTW," when they cast the mold for "Louisiane."

"Louisiane," too, has its antebellum plantation, Bagatelle, and its stalwart heroine, who clings ferociously to its soil through four decades of historical turmoil and domestic drama, tossing her braids and swishing her gowns with seductive wile and vengeful tenacity. She also wears out two husbands — the owner of Bagatelle, into whose heart she worms her way when she returns from studies in France to find her late parents' own land worthless, and a good-humoured Parisian aristocrat — before settling down to tranquil old age with her true love: the impotent plantation steward who has witnessed her romantic vicissitudes from the sidelines with passive devotion.

What film doesn't have enough of however, at least in this digest version, is sweeping spectacle and compelling dramatic interest. Despite the millions that were poured into it, "Louisiane," apparently conceived through a television optic, looks scrappy on the screen. In episodes like the Revolution of 1848 in Paris, and the devastations of the Civil War, accounting corners seem to have been cut for extras, sets and proper staging time.

Even in the scenes at the plantation, one doesn't have the impression of an imposing empire of slave labor and coffer-filling cotton crops.

Dramatically, principal handicap is Margot Kidder, too lightweight for the central role (and poorly dubbed in the French version, as are all the English-speaking players). Ian Charleson, a sturdier actor, looks ill-at-ease as her no-man man. Their rapport is supposed to provide the emotional spine of the story — but frankly, one couldn't give a damn.

Some more interesting supporting parts have been chopped down for the theatrical version, notably Victor Lanoux's appealingly casual Paris aristocrat, Andrea Ferreol's liberal-minded chambermaid, who marries a town blacksmith and loses him to a lynch mob incensed by his pro-Abolitionist stand, and Raymond Pellegrin's falsely civilized cotton merchant, who winds up rape-murdering Kidder's daughter.

Ironically, most important absentee here is historical Louisiana itself. Though most of the film was shot on location, the screenplay fails to dramatize the special sociocultural heterogeneity of the region, and its story could just as easily been set in another southern state of the period. International co-production requisites, with their casting and uniform language-track clauses, further water down the picture's period coloring.

Philippe de Broca is far from home both geographically and stylistically as last in line of French helmers to inherit the project (after Etienne Perier and Jacques Demy). Despite the uncongenital script, which takes its clichés seriously, de Broca doesn't come out of the affair too badly (and besides he married the leading lady). His direction is pedestrian but rarely embarrassing.

Apart from failure to suggest epic dimensions, production credits are otherwise sound, though Claude Bolling's score is a lazy potpourri of Dixie tunes and Negro spirituals. "Louisiane" will no doubt be more amply at home in its full-length on television screens.
— *Len.*

Comedy
(HONG KONG-COLOR)

Hong Kong, Jan. 20.
A Continental Century presentation and production, released by Golden princess Distribution. Presented by Albert Lee. Produced by Jeff Lau. Directed by Dennis Yu. Production controller, Wong Chung. Stars Cheng Jut Si, Dorothy Yu, Wong Ching, Tang Lan Hua, Wang Yue, Paul Ching, David Wu, Kuk Fung, Tin Ching. (No other credits provided by producers.) Reviewed at President Theater, Hong Kong, Jan. 18, 1984. Running Time: **98 MINS.**
(Cantonese soundtrack with English subtitles)

"Comedy" is the creation of the revamped Continental Century company, and marks the return of director Dennis Yu to the mainstream of commercial filmmaking. There were great expectations for this production, but they were hardly fulfilled as it is jam-packed with improbabilities and stereotyped characters borrowed from Cinema City's past hits in the genre.

"Comedy" is set in the late 1940s, when China was torn with conflicts among various underground, organized societies, in Mafia style. The center of the conflicts is in colorful and westernized Shanghai where the ringleaders reside. When the gang leaders from the 36 provinces gather in Shanghai to vie for the ringleader's throne, their possessions are stolen by three small-time hoodlums.

The three men are good friends and partners in petty thievery and have been making their living with con tricks at the nearby railway station. They are later mistaken as big shots from the powerful gangs at the Seven Heaven Hotel. Knowing the dangers, the three friends try to escape through a series of slapstick murders, along with their ladies in distress.

Very few good things can be said about this Cantonese comedy, except for the high level at production design, costumes and props from a lost era. There are also no marquee star names, only second billers.

Strangely enough, everyone has been unbelievably dressed to kill or charm. The acting and direction are very forced so the intended humor is lost in a muddle of unfunny sequences. There are lapses of high comedy, but the rest is plain lull, dull, ridiculous, idiotic, imitative, ludicrous and just plain tired jokes. —*Mel.*

El Caso Almeria
(The Almería Case)
(SPANISH-COLOR)

Madrid, Jan. 26.
A Multivideo S.A. production. Directed by Pedro Costa Muste. Producers, José María Cunillés, Isabel Mulá. Features entire cast. Screenplay, Manolo Marinero, Nereida B. Arnau, Muste; camera (Eastmancolor), José Luis Alcaine; editor, Pablo G. del Amo; music, Ricard Miralles. Reviewed at Cine Benlliure, Madrid, Jan. 26, 1984. Running time: **118 MINS.**

Mario Aguilar	Agustín Gonzalez
Col. Gonzalez Alarcón	Fernando Guillén
Enrique	Manuel Alexandre

Also: Margarita Calahorra, Pedro Diaz del Corral, Antonio Banderas, Iñaki Miramón, Juan Echanove, Muntsa Alcañiz. Echanove, Muntsa Alcañiz.

This is a taut, well-scripted and lively paced reconstruction of the events leading up to and the trial following a well-known Spanish case in 1981 in which three Civil Guards in Almería were accused and subsequently convicted of having tortured and then murdered three young men suspected of being Basque terrorists.

Despite rather static direction by neophyte Pedro Costa Muste, the script is brisk enough to maintain audience interest throughout the almost two hours of investigations and court trial. The centerpiece certainly is Agustin Gonzalez' superb performance as the prosecuting attorney.

Despite threats to himself and his wife, and the ominous power of the feared Guardia Civil hanging over him, the lawyer bucks the system, pushes on the investigation and overcomes lukewarm judges who try to stymie the proceedings at every step, and finally succeeds in trying and convicting the culprits, the leader of whom is presently serving a 25-year jail sentence.

Scripters have happily spared us overt violence or torture scenes; nonetheless they have imbued their film with a mood of ominous, threatening suppression almost psychologically inevitable upon seeing the uniformed Civil Guards on the screen. Many of the details of the case are still obscure, so the scripters have limited themselves to simply presenting the facts as they were uncovered during the investigation.

Due to its very "Spanishness," its gripping story and relevance to contemporary Spain, item could be of interest in nearly all markets.
—*Besa.*

Double Deal
(AUSTRALIAN-COLOR)

A Samuel Goldwyn Co. release. A Filmco Australia presentation for the TGP Group of a Rychemond Film Prods. Pty. Ltd. production. Produced by Brian Kavanagh, Lynn Barker. Written and directed by Kavanagh. Stars Louis Jourdan, Angela Punch-McGregor. Camera (Colorfilm color), Ross Berryman; editor, Tim Lewis; music, Bruce Smeaton; assistant director, Ross Hamilton; production supervisor, John Chase; sound, John Phillips; art direction, Jill Eden; associate producer, Carlie Deans. Reviewed on Cinemax, N.Y., Dec. 17, 1983. (No MPAA Rating.) Running time: **90 MINS.**

Peter Stirling	Louis Jourdan
Christina Stirling	Angela Punch-McGregor
June Stevens	Diana Craig
Young man	Warwick Comber
Det. Mills	Peter Cummins
Doug Mitchell	Bruce Spence
Mrs. Coolidge	June Jago
Sibyl Anderson	Kerry Walker

Filmed in 1981, "Double Deal' is an unappealing Aussie suspense film unreleased theatrically in this country, but appearing on pay-cable via the Samuel Goldwyn Co. Despite its use of Dolby stereo sound and widescreen Panavision lensing, dull picture is not a strong enough piece for theatrical use.

B-film story has fashion model and designer Christina (Angela Punch-McGregor) bored with her four-year marriage to cool businessman Peter Stirling (Louis Jourdan) and finding kicks with a young prowler (Warwick Comber). Young couple spontaneously wreck her house's interior and take off on the open road for a mini-crime spree, dressing in clown outfits to rob a remote store on the highway. Back home, the police investigate Christina's disappearance, which the prowler later turns into a kidnapping (half-consentual), demanding a stiff ransom.

Final reel features several predictable plot twists leading to a failed attempt at an ironical ending, revolving around Stirling's $1,000,000-plus Empress of Glengarry opal. Languorously paced film lacks the style of its B-film forebears, with filmmaker Brian Kavanagh substituting pointless crosscutting during the first reel that delays the narrative and opposes viewer involvement.

Topbilled Jourdan is suave and urbane in his walkthrough while the talented Aussie star Punch-McGregor is miscast as a beautiful, cigar-smoking mannequin. Playing his unnamed role exclusively in silver motorcycle garb, Comber is silly. Tech credits are okay, but contribute no atmosphere to this would-be "thriller." —*Lor.*

El Ultimo Grumete
(The Last Groomete)
(CHILEAN-COLOR)

Santiago, Jan. 6.

Produced and relesed by Chile Films. Executive producers, Paulina Morales, María Elena Wood. Directed by Jorge López Sotomayor. Features entire cast. Screenplay, López, Gerardo Cáceres, based on novel, "El último grumete de la Baquedano," by Francisco Coloane; camera (color), Domingo Garrido; sound, Alejandro Lyon; music, Carlos Fernández. Reviewed at Cine Imperio, Santiago, Jan. 5, 1984. Running time: **93 MINS.**

Cast: Gonzalo Meza, Domingo Tessier, Juan Cristobal Soto, Carlos Ramirez, Cora Diaz, Enrique Heine, Victor Mix, Teresita Rivas, Guillermo Altamirano, Alex López, Eugenio Claro.

"The Last Groomete," Chile Films' first feature in many years, deals with Alejandro, a 16-year-old schoolboy who runs away from home and embarks as a stowaway on the Navy's training ship, Esmeralda, in order to find his brother, lost somewhere in the neighborhood of Punta Arenas, at the bottom tip of Chile. Said brother, it turns out, lives on some Godforsaken southern island with the survivors of an almost-extinct Indian tribe. He has happily adopted their primitive way of life and no longer wants to return home to his mother and civilization.

Alejandro, instead of being put in the brig as a stowaway, is accepted on board as one more "groomete" (an obsolete Royal Navy term for apprentice sailors) and there he is grandfathered by an elderly sergeant who, many years before, had been a shipmate and friend of his father's.

Aimed at a family audience, the film is basically an old-fashioned youth-adventure story, frustrated by the inconsistencies of a screenplay that still required a great deal of work before being ready for shooting.

Filming in 16m and blown up to 35m by Movielab in N.Y., acting and technical credits are uneven. Much better use could also have been made of the Esmeralda, which was made available by the Chilean Navy; it is one of the "tall ships" that visited New York at the U.S. Bicentennial in 1976.

This first film by director Jorge López should do reasonably well on its home ground, thanks to intensive publicity on tv. — *Amig.*

Aussie Assault
(AUSTRALIAN-DOCU-COLOR)

Sydney, Jan. 31.

Hoyts Distribution release of a Sportsmaster Programs-Suatu Film Management Ltd. production. Producer, Garry Holt, Bill Scholer. Executive producer, Richard Tanner. Features entire cast. Written and directed by Harvey Spencer. Camera (color), Peter Hopwood, Alan Grice; editors, Peter Fletcher, Alan Lake, Lee Smith; sound, Bob Hayes, Steve Old, Randall Eve; music, Mario Millo; song, "Down Under," by Men At Work. Reviewed at Hoyts Warringah Mall Theater, Sydney, Jan. 26, 1984. Running time: **81 MINS.**

1983 was a vintage year for Australia's international image, with successes in such varied fields as pop music, movies and sport; for many the sporting highlight of the year came in September when, after 132 years in the possession of the New York Yacht Club, the America's Cup was won by the 12-meter yacht, Australia II. The suspenseful final race caught the imagination of the nation, and all over the country people stayed up most of the night to watch the live telecasts from Newport, Rhode Island.

Now, four months later, a feature documentary of the event has emerged which, unfortunately, fails in every way to recapture the excitement of the race itself. "Aussie Assault" is remarkable in many ways, but quality is not one of its accomplishments. It represents the most expensive documentary ever made in Australia, with an estimated budget of over $1,500,000, of which nearly half was apparently paid to the syndicates which mounted the Australian challenge for exclusive film coverage rights.

When one considers that the recent and very successful Paul Cox feature, "Man of Flowers," was made for a bit less than $250,000, the staggering costs of "Aussie Assault" is placed in some perspective. It is also the first feature film exhibited in Australia to be sponsored by a tobacco company, whose name is proudly displayed both before and after the feature.

But even with this vast budget, most of which, obviously, is not up there on the screen, the film is a mess. Awkwardly structured, confusing for the layman (the commentary makes continual use of yachting terms which will mean nothing to most people) and visually variable (to put it kindly), the film is a hard slog to the finish. The bottom line is that it's frankly boring, and the audience at the public session attended was visibly and noisily restless. Pic has opened quietly.

There are a couple of plusses, if minor ones. The final race is exciting (it couldn't not be) though even it is marred by the use of a fatuous race commentary. The music of Mario Millo is rousing, if conventional, and the use of the Men At Work standout, "Down Under," emerges as the liveliest thing in the picture. A sequence in which the camera tours the stately homes of Newport while actors on the soundtrack spout infantile gossip, is woefully inept; so is the occasional use of unnauthorized footage from an old black-and-white pirate movie (unidentified and unidentifiable, though it's better than any of the new footage) to press home the point that the executives of the New York Yacht Club kept firing broadsides (get it?) at the Aussie battlers. In addition, the film is presented, tv style, by Glenn Shorrock (of Little River Band), which merely adds more superfluous footage. Narration is by Ray Barrett.

In Australia, the film is too little and too late (and too poor) to achieve much; overseas, the childishly chauvinistic approach will be a turn-off. A pity, because the event would have made a marvellous documentary. The producers of "Aussie Assault," in going for bombast instead of subtlety, have made a failure about a great achievement. —*Strat.*

Magash Hakessef
(Fellow Travellers)
(ISRAELI-COLOR)

Tel Aviv, Jan. 21.

A Gad Lehsem Presentation. Produced by Yehuda Ne'eman and Ruchama Marton. Directed by Ne'eman. Features entire cast. Screenplay, Amnon Lord, Ne'eman, based on an original idea by Marton; dialog, Marton; camera (color), Hanania Bar; editor, Anath Lubransky; art director, Yoram Brazilai; music, Rafi Kadishsohn. Reviewed at the Paris Cinema, Tel Aviv, Jan. 21, 1984. Running time: **90 MINS.**

Cast: Giddi Gov, Yossi Polak, Shumuel Krauss, Yussuf Abu-Wards, Dahlia Shimko, Souhir Hani, Nurith Galron, Muhammad Bakri.

This kind of feature is bound to survive and find a niche in the international fest circuit, mostly because of the political arguments it generates regardless of its imperfect dramatic qualities.

The plot, while fictional, has been inspired by a number of real-life incidents, as it describes the ineffectual efforts of Israeli and Arab political moderates to build a bridge between the two warring factions in the Middle East. The main character is a pop singer, once a paratrooper in the Israeli Army, who has lived in West Germany and has been close there to the peace movement. On his way home he is entrusted with $250,000, designated to help toward the foundation of a new Arab university.

Once back home, the singer discovers most of his former friends have abandoned the idea of a peaceful struggle for Arab self determination in Israel and intend to use the money he has brought to buy the guns they need for their terrorist cells. As he is opposed to such a possibility, he refuses to hand over the money, and is supported in his attempt to send the money back by an Arab lecturer. Finally, hunted by both the Israeli Mossad and Arab extremists, he hits a blind alley from which there is no exit.

Billed as a political thriller, the story offers a valid point of view as far as the political situation in this part of the world is concerned, and manages to keep close to fairness in dealing with both parties.

The problem this picture will have to face is not on an ideological, but rather on a dramatic level. The story is pedestrian and manipulated throughout to fit in with the ideas it tries to present. Characters are cardboard deep and acting is indifferent, quite often because many of the parts have been cast against the grain.

To make matters even less comfortable, many of the problems which troubled director Yehuda (Judd) Ne'eman while shooting are reflected in the final results. The crew and the actors clashed all along, mostly because the film was shot in the summer of 1982, during the Lebanon operation, which heightened the polarization among political factions in Israel. This difference of opinon has infiltrated the work of the director, who never manages to pull his team together and wring out the plot's dramatic potential.

The loose editing, allowing sequences to go on long after they should have been terminated, leaves the impression that there was not insufficient material for a full-length feature, and camerawork lacks the style and rigor it had in the previous Ne'eman-Bar cooperation, "The Paratroopers."

Still, the subject is strong enough to attract a certain amount of curiosity, and it seems likely that it will do better abroad than at home.
—*Edna.*

Las Bicicletas Son Para El Verano
(Bicycles Are For The Summer)
(SPANISH-COLOR)

Madrid, Jan. 14.

An Incine-Jet Films production, presented by Alfredo Matas. Directed by Jaime Chavarri. Features entire cast. Screenplay, Salvador Maldonado' based on play of the same title by Fernando Fernán Gómez; exec producers, Alfredo and Helena Matas; assistant producer, Benjamin Benhamou; camera (Fujicolor), Miguel Angel Trujillo; editor, José Luis Matesanz; sets, Gil Parrondo; music, Francisco Guerrero, conducted by José Maria Franco Gil; costumes, Javier Artiñano. Reviewed at Cine Capitol, Madrid, Jan. 14, '84. Running time: **103 MINS.**

Dolores ....Amparo Soler Leal
Luis ....Agustín Gonzalez
Manolita ....Victoria Abril
Antonia ....Alicia Hermida
Maria ....Patricia Adriani
Also: Marisa Paredes, Carlos Tristancho, Gabino Diego, Aurora Redondo, Guillermo Marin, Emilio Gutierrez Caba, Laura del Sol, Miguel Rellan, Jorge de Juan, Marina Saura.

This is another film set in Civil War Spain, but concentrating mostly on the day-to-day life in Madrid during the three years (1936-39) it lay under siege by the Nationalist forces. Scripter Salvador Maldonado has adapted to the screen the very successful play of the same name which ran over a year in Madrid. As often happens in such cases, the result is very talky and lacks the dynamism of an original screenplay. Producer Alfredo Matas has tried to make the pic more cinematographic by hauling in a full-sized streetcar of the times, and shooting a few scenes in Old Madrid, using a couple of vintage cars. But the end result is still overwhelmingly more theater than cinema.

The charm of Fernando Fernán Gomez' play (Gomez has disassociated himself from the film altogether, as far as credits as concerned) was some snappy dialog and the fine thesping; some of this comes across in the film, but only intermittently.

Story tells of the life of a lower middle-class family during the war years; the father, brilliantly played by Agustin Gonzalez, runs a wine shop; the mother is rather bland and characterless; daughter, Manolita, has an affair with a soldier and bears an illegitimate child; her brother, Luisito, a gangly adolescent, makes out with the maid.

But for the most part the drama has somehow been lost in transposing from theater to film; though the bombs sometimes fall outside the family's home, and we are told they are hungry, one never feels as close to the war as in, says Jaime Camino's "The Long Vacations of 36," or even the post-war period piece, "The Bee-Hive," by Mario Camus.

Best performances are put in by the aforementioned Gonzalez as the father, and by Victoria Abril as the daughter. Gabino Diego as the son, is terribly miscast, a serious shortcoming since his is an important part. Pic is very local in scope. Even local audiences must by now be tiring of subjects dealing with the Civil War. — *Besa.*

Season Of Thunder
(DOCU-COLOR-16m)

Hollywood, Jan. 6.
A Southeast Asia Resource Center presentation. Produced by Charles Brucker, Jeffrey Chester. Camera (color), Scott Robinson; editor, sound, Ismael Saavedra; technical consultant, Joel Rocamora. Reviewed at the Landmark Screening Room, L.A. Jan. 6, 1984. (No MPAA Rating). Running time: 59 MINS.

This documentary on the increasingly rebellious minorities in the Philippines is part-anthropological and part-political, and works rather well on the first level and hardly at all on the second. Pic makes clear why some groups have good reason to be angry with the Marcos regime, but the more it

pushes into complex political territory, the more it fuzzes out into rhetoric and mindless generalities. Not touching at all on recent developments, including the killing of Benigno Aquino, this won't have much relevance to anyone not personally engaged in the struggle being depicted and thus has a playoff future limited strictly to politically and academically oriented arenas.

Opening shots show some exquisitely terraced rice farms in the mountain country of northern Luzon province, home of the tribal Igorota. These people have lived the same way for centuries, and proper indignation is generated when they are unceremoniously displaced by a massive government dam project and forced to live in ghastly resettlement communities. This relocation results in the death of a culture, something not to be visited upon any self-sufficient society.

Docu then jumps to southern Mindanao, an area allegedly dominated by the American Del Monte company. As it attempts to bring the burgeoning peasant revolt up to date, film displays more and more people bearing arms, and it is admitted that the New People's Army is Communist-backed, something that won't go down too well with the American liberals who presumably represent the film's primary audience.

Many factions make up those who oppose Marcos, and once this docu gets away from the specific injustice done the Igorots almost a decade ago, all sense of focus is lost. How the many groups from different parts of the country, including the particularly militant Moslems, who are not mentioned, can hope to pull together into a unified opposition front is not explored, and pic degenerates into the most simplistic kind of agit-prop in which footage of Marcos with President Reagan is to be booed and images of M-16-toting natives are to be cheered by knee-jerk radicals.

The Filipino predicament is a complicated one deserving of thoughtful treatment, since the situation can't help but heat up in coming years. But only the broadest brush strokes have been applied here.—*Curt.*

Esprit D'Amour
(HONG KONG-COLOR)

Hong Kong, Dec. 24.
A Cinema City Co. Ltd. presentation, released by Golden Princess. Directed by Ringo L.T. Lam. Stars Alan Tam, Cecilia Chan, Ni Shu Chun. Produced by Dean Shek, Raymond Wong; Karl Maka. Story, Raymond Wong, screenplay, Ko Chi Sum, Lo Kin. Raymond Fung; production designer, Nansun Shi, Raymond Fung; camera (color), Wong Chung Pui, Tong Po Seng; music, Violet Lam; art director, Ken Yee Chung Man; editor, Tony Chow. Reviewed at President Theater, Hong Kong, Dec. 24, 1983. Running Time: 98 MINS.
(Cantonese soundtrack with English subtitles)

Don't let the French title mislead you, this is a Cantonese movie. On the fourth anniversary engagement day for Alan Tam and Cecilia Chan, Alan nearly runs over a lovely girl who disappears before he can get over the shock. He makes it to his party and after dinner, the guests play with a board—to call on dead, wandering spirits.

Meanwhile, at the other part of the city, the girl (Ni Shu Chun), who was nearly run over, could not change her fate of being killed on the same day. She falls from the roof of her home accidentally after a fatal slip. The following day, Alan is given an assignment by his insurance company to investigate the case of accidental death. Strangely, the name and address of the insured coincide with the spirit contacted by the board.

One evening, Ni's spirit appears in Alan's apartment. Her mystical beauty intrigues him. A romance develops between man and the spirit and this love affair shocks Alan's family who later discovers this strange liaison with the underworld. The family tries its utmost to break them up, resorting to using a powerful exorcist to exorcise the roaming spirit. Will love survive? In a blithe romantic-horror film like this, you can bet that love will conquer all and esprit d'amour will survive all adversities.

Visually captivating, this well-designed and presented production is proving very popular with the locals during the holiday period (already grossed HK$12-million and still running). However, its appeal is generally limited to Asia and Chinatowns abroad.

The film is definitely commercial but in good taste, geared to Cantonese likes and has no serious cinematic significance for serious moviegoers. However, the entertainment values are high for the young market which Cinema City has managed to corner for the past couple of years and is the main reason for its still being the most successful indie company in Hong Kong. —*Mel.*

Saarbrücken Reviews

Pankow '95
(WEST GERMAN-COLOR)

Saarbrücken, Jan. 21.
A Pandora Film Production, Frankfurt. Features entire cast. Written and directed by Gabor Altorjay. Camera (color), Jörg Jeshel; music, Tom Dokoupil. Reviewed at Max Ophüls Competition, Saarbrücken, Jan. 21, '84. Running time: 82 MINS.
Cast: Udo Kier, Christine Kaufmann, Magdalena Montezuma, Dieter Thomas Heck, Anthony Ingrassia, Angelo Galizia, Tom Dokoupil, Karel Dudesek.

Following his sidebar prize at last year's Max Ophüls competition for "Tscherwonez" (1982), Hungarian-born Gabor Altorjay has attempted a kind of Orwellian

"1984"-oriented film fable on what it might be like to live under Big Brother in 1984 in Pankow of East Berlin. Everything in "Pankow '95" is scifi, yet any visitor to Socialist lands will recognize phenomena like lines before butchershops and other forms of highly regulated or institutional living.

Altorjay has cast several known figures from Werner Schroeter and Rainer Werner Fassbinder films: Magdalena Montezuma, Christine Kaufmann, Udo Kier. And there's a pop star named Dieter (Thomas) Heck who might increase the action at the wickets. But the story is rather lame as a whole: it takes place in a "nerve clinic" and features fantasy escapes to a tropical paradise, plus an occasional pop song to lighten the deadening atmosphere.

Despite the esthetic drift into an intellectual No Man's Land, Altorjay is a name to watch among German experimentalist and Underground filmers. —*Holl.*

Das Eismeer Ruft
(The Arctic Sea Calls)
(EAST GERMAN-COLOR)

Saarbrücken, Jan. 21.
A DEFA Film Production, East Berlin; world rights, DEFA-Aussenhandel, East Berlin. Features entire cast. Directed by Jörg Foth. Screenplay, Peter Wuss; camera (color), Wolfgang Braumann; music, Uwe Hilprecht. Reviewed at Max Ophüls Competion, Saarbrücken, Jan. 21, 84. Running time: 94 MINS.
Cast: Ute Lubosch, Heide Kipp, Carl-Heinz Choynski; Oliver Karsitz; Alexander Rohde, Viviane Schmidt, Thomas Gutzeit, Oliver Peuser, Ilja Kriwolutzky.

An entry in the Saarbrücken Fest's Max Ophüls Prize Competition, this children's film, Jörg Foth's "The Arctic Sea Calls," is Foth's first feature, and not a bad one so far as handling of kid thesps is concerned.

Tale is set in Prague of 1934, a city at this time speaking as much German as Czech — indeed, Franz Kafka has been deemed as one of the finest German stylists writing at the beginning of this century, and he scores too as a Czech writer living in Prague. All the kids in the film are German: Anton, Rudi, Rosi, Ferdi, ages 6-10. And in the Mark Twain tradition of "Tom Sawyer" and "Huckleberry Finn," they're out in search of adventure and exploration.

It happened that in the spring of 1934 a Soviet exploration vessel in the Arctic prompted a news event of some proportions: the Chelyuskin (about which a docu exists in Soviet film archives) was first stranded in a frozen sea, then sank after the crew abandoned ship. The fate of the crew was left in doubt for a spell as rescue efforts were made. Here, the kids in a Prague neighborhood hear about the tragedy and decide to join the rescue attempt on their own.

Their adventures into the outskirts of the city provide the humor, for each of these young troopers is assigned a special job, like carrying a homemade compass, cooking potato pancakes, and the like. One kid is funnier than the other, while the squirt in the expedition has the choicest inane lines and demeanor. Meanwhile, they're not making much progress by train, by cart, by foot — although they do manage to reach a relative's country cottage to spend a night. As the search continues to find the castaways, the parallel to the rescue of the ice-bound ship's crew takes on relevance. The kids hear on a radio that they're reported missing, but they don't give up until they find it's impossible to enter a dark tunnel because they are afraid of the dark, so they decide to return home.

Back in Prague they all get a good spanking, just as the rescue of the Chelyuskin crew is being announced on the radio. And all along the way, docu footage has been unspooled on the historical resuce mission. Why this historical background footage was used is not clear; instead of enhancing the tale, it tends to distract from it.. Without this tucked-away commentary, "The Arctic Sea Calls" might have accomplished its immediate purpose of being quite a delightful kidpic.

Credits are generally a plus, particularly the atmosphere of the times a half-century ago. —*Holl.*

Jagger & Spaghetti - Die Superbluffer

(Jagger & Spaghetti - The Supper Bluffers)
(WEST GERMAN-COLOR)

Saarbrücken, Jan. 19.
A Joachim Hammann Film Production, Munich, in collaboration with Second German Television (ZDF), Mainz; TV producer, Martin Büttner. Features entire cast. Directed by Karsten Wichniarz. Screenplay, Peter Buchholz, Stefan Schwartz; camera (color), Slawomir Idziak; music, Bodo Staiger. Reviewed at Max Ophüls Competition, Saarbrücken, Jan. 19, '84. Running time: **96 MINS.**
Cast: Sabine Kaack, Manfred Reddemann, Peter Buchholz, Stefan Schwartz.

After scoring with an impressive debut pic and combination diploma film at the Berlin Film & Television Academy, "No Land" (1981), helmer Karsten Wichniarz teamed with writer-actors Peter Buchholz and Stefan Schwartz to attempt a wacky comedy in the slapstick tradition of Laurel & Hardy, Abbott & Costello, Martin & Lewis, and so on. The gags, however, fall flat, while the pic itself appears to be simply an opportunity for thesps Buchholz and Schwartz — as "Jagger & Spaghetti — The Super Bluffers" — to strut their stuff before the camera.

Both Jagger (Schwartz) and Spaghetti (Buchholz) are losers. The former lives with his aunt and does little more than lay around thinking up deals; the latter runs a tv repair shop with the finesse of a bull in a china shop. Things go from bad to worse when Spaghetti takes on a hot deal to sell 200 stolen tv sets at the shop, just to save his business — at which time Jagger steps in to hopefully save the day by employing a oversized guru to fake their way out of the situation.

When all is said and done, the two are still in orbit with new schemes as a pair who have found each other to seek their fortune in life. Super bluffers Schwartz and Buchholz may style themselves, but not enough that they can script and topline film comedies. —*Holl.*

Parodontose Now

(Paradentosis Now)
(AUSTRIAN-B&W-16m)

Saarbrücken, Jan. 21.
A Hermann Dunzendorfer Film Production, Vienna. Features entire cast. Directed by Hermann Dunzendorfer. Screenplay, Dunzendorfer, Manfred M. Müller; camera (black and white), Paul Choung, Dunzendorfer; music, Karl Ellinger. Reviewed at Max Ophüls Competition, Saarbrücken, Jan. 21, '84. Running time: **80 MINS.**
Cast: Manfred M. Müller, Leopold List, Isidor Wimmer, Manfred Rott, Peter and Harry Sichrovsky, Fritz Walden, Elmar Prack, Peter Winkler.

As the title hints, Hermann Dunzendorfer's "Paradentosis Now" is a parody on Francis Coppola's "Apocalypse Now" — and as such, it's a treat for both the film buff and the Joseph ("Heart of Darkness") Conrad reader.

The twist here has to do with an Austrian dentist who has begun to handle his patients privately, instead of following the usual rules of state-controlled socialized medicine in the practice of dentistry. The case of Dr. Engelbert Lang follows the original story rather closely, but the jokes are in the images that make direct references to Coppola's film — that, and the dry Austrian narrative.

Recommended for insiders.
— *Holl.*

Der Sprinter

(The Sprinter)
(WEST GERMAN-COLOR)

Saarbrücken, Jan. 19.
A Reinery Verlag & Film Production, Remagen, Peter Wohlgemuth, producer. Features entire cast. Directed by Christoph Böll. Screenplay, Böll, Wieland Samolak; camera (color), Peter Fauhe; music, Paul Vincent. Reviewed at Max Ophüls Competition, Saarbrücken, Jan. 19, '84. Running time: **87 MINS.**
Cast: Wieland Samolak (Wieland Dietrich), Gerhard Olschewski (the Trainer), Renate Muhri (the Woman Shotputter), Miriam Spoerri (Wieland's Mother), Dieter Eppler, Wichard von Roell, Jürgen Mikol, Walter Goehrke.

One of the best pics by newcomers at Saarbrücken, Christoph

Böll's "The Sprinter" displays the same taste for social satire that won the director's uncle; writer Heinrich Böll, worldwide recognition. The butt of most of the jokes is sports — track meets, in particular — but the jabs also reach social attitudes on "being normal" (that is, "not gay" in this case).

Wieland Dietrich comes from a family with social standing, but he is an embarrassment to his father and a prayful hope to his mother. One day, he decides to show he can be as normal as anybody else, so first he goes to a dancing school and then to a sports store. One glance at a handsome young man in a track outfit, and he decides on the spot to become a sprinter. His new coach is only too delighted, for he just happens to be in need of another club member for track meets. After learning to run in the right direction, Wieland suddenly meets a femme shotputter on a day that he's racing — he falls in love then sprints joyfully to victory at the meet. A sprinter is born.

The mother is, of course, ecstatic that her son has proved himself overnight to be a man. The women's athletic coach is also overjoyed, for the shotputter is breaking records too by falling in love simultaneously with the gay sprinter. And since the two complement each other like David and Goliath's daughter, the laughs are aplenty — the biggest coming at a second meet at which the girl has to be strategically positioned on the field to inspire the lad to another victory. And vice-versa.

The only problem for the determined coach now dreaming of more track victories is how to keep the flame of romance burning. It appears, too, that an engagement will shortly lead to wedding bells, and then everything might just go down the drain. So an injection of hormones is in order. Result: our sprinter loses his hair. What happens after that is worth the price of a ticket to catch the twist at the ending.

Directed with a light hand and sharply acted by co-scripter Wieland Samolak, "The Sprinter" deserves more exposure on the fest circuit. This is another healthy sign that contemporary German cinema is finding its way out of the current b.o. crisis by fostering comedy-oriented directorial talent.
—*Holl.*

Giarres

(City Of Wolves)
(WEST GERMAN-B&W-16m)

Saarbrücken, Jan. 19.
A Reinhard von der Marwitz Film Production, Berlin. Features entire cast. Written and directed by Reinhard von der Marwitz. Camera (black and white), Wolfgang Pilgrimm; music, Peer Raben. Reviewed at Max Ophüls Competition, Saarbrücken, Jan. 19, '84. Running time: **90 MINS.**
Cast: Peter Schmittinger, Dieter Gärtig, Hieronymous Blösser, Beate Kopp, Margit-

ta Haberland, Bobby J. Moska, Christoph Eichhorn, Peter Gente, Gerhard Hoffmann, Dietrich Kuhlbrodt, Wolfgang Schlüns, Maximilan Weingärtner.

Reinhard von der Marwitz's "Giarres" is about two men who live with each other. Made on a mini budget, the director is also the manager of a gay bar in Berlin, Anderes Ufer. The title refers to a location in Sicily where, at the end of 1980, two male lovers apparently commissioned a third party to shoot them both in a double-suicide pact. The scene is reenacted in the film, the scene now having shifted to the port city of Hamburg.

The similarities with Rainer Werner Fassbinder's Genet-adaptation, "Querelle," are unmistakable. Atmospheric touches are the plus factors, but thesps perform in a stilted and showy manner while dialog amounts to little more than bits and pieces of narrative exchange. For insiders, who know the background details, there may be something here to chew upon. For even a hip fest audience, it's swimming upstream all the way.—*Holl.*

Kovacs

(WEST GERMAN-COLOR)

Saarbrücken, Jan. 22.
A Thomas Haaf Film Production, in coproduction with Phantaskop Film, Munich. Features entire cast. Written and directed by Thomas Haaf. Camera (color), Sabri Özaydin; music, Roman Schwaller. Reviewed at Max Ophüls Competition, Saarbrücken, Jan. 22, '84. Running time: **82 MINS.**
Cast: Manfred Zapatka (Kovacs), Georg Greiwe, Ernst Wilhelm Lenik, Franz Rampelmann, Luis Lamprecht, Helga Tölle, Gerlinde Eger, Werner Rom, Joseph Rothmann, Vivienne Newport.

Thomas Haaf, a grad of the Munich Film & TV Academy, bowed with "The Pale Man" (1978), and now has his second film in the Max Ophüls sweepstakes: "Kovacs." This is a modern German updating of the traditional robbery caper, like Jules Dassin's "Rififi" (1956), which brings together different types of individuals from social backgrounds to pull off a big job together. In this case, it's the robbery of an armored-car money-delivery service along the lines of an air-tight plan calculated to the minute.

The first half of the film presents the different types, most of them losers, as Kovacs, an engineer by trade, brings them all together to do the job. Then comes the robbery itself, and the twist in the end that finds everybody a loser again except Kovacs himself. — *Holl.*

Jäger Des Herzens

(Hunter Of The Heart)
(WEST GERMAN-COLOR)

Saarbrücken, Jan. 20.
A C&H Film Production, Berlin. Features entire cast. Written and directed by Peter Obrist. Camera (color), Bernd Heinl; music,

Andreas Darau. Reviewed at Max Ophüls Competition, Saarbrücken, Jan. 20, '84. Running time: **91 MINS.**

Cast: Eva Renzi (the Mother), Karl-Heinz von Kassel (the Father), Kai Buth (Manuel), Dietrich Mattausch, Elisabeth Volkmann, Erich Schumann, Beate Finckh.

———

A children's film by a debut helmer, Peter Obrist's "Hunter Of The Heart" is as pretentious as its title suggests. A boy in the pre-puberty stage becomes aware that his parent's relationship is falling apart. His own preference is for the mother, but she is the nervous type who ends up with a breakdown.

The boy is left alone with his computer game and increasing loneliness. He lapses into a dream world — nightmares at night and imaginary get-even daydreams in the classroom. He takes to spying on his father, who is having an affair with another woman. Then the lad begins to fight for his mother in his own way — until she's finally released from the clinic.

"Hunter Of The Heart" depicts the world of the well-to-do, but hardly any effort is made to analyze a family conflict nor try to tell a convincing story about adolescent fantasies. In fact, the film has no point of view at all. It's this kind of undigested kidpic fodder that makes it even an embarrassment to interpret a role, much less hold a young audience. Chances are that helmer Obrist wanted to make a children's film for grown-ups (as several noteworthy films, like Australia's "Storm Boy," have succeeded in doing) — but ended up missing the mark altogether.

— *Holl.*

Liebe Ist Kein Argument
(Love Is Not an Argument)
(WEST GERMAN-COLOR)

———

Saarbrücken, Jan. 20.

A Regina Ziegler Film Production, Berlin. Features entire cast. Directed by Marianne Lüdcke. Screenplay, Lüdcke, Leonnie Ossowski, based on a story by Ossowski; camera (color), Dietrich Lohmann; music, Günther Fischer. Reviewed at Max Ophüls Competition, Saarbrücken, Jan. 20, '84. Running time: **88 MINS.**

Cast: Erika Pluhar (Lea), Günther Lamprecht (Felix), Friedrich-Karl Praetorius (Max), Nine Hoger (Katharina), Heinz Schubert, Klaus Wendnemann, Karin Baal.

———

Marianne Lüdcke's "Love Is Not an Argument" marks her first solo venture into the realm of making films solely for the cinema. Her first films were made in collaboration with Ingo Kratisch (a fellow graduate at the Berlin Film and TV Academy): "Accord" (1971), "The Wollands" (1972), "Labor and Love" (1973), "Family Bliss" (1975), and "The Tanner Mill" (1976). Then she branched off on her own into tv productions: "Flutter" (1979) and "Fleeting Acquaintances" (1982). She presented "Love Is Not an Argument" at Saarbrücken for the Max Ophüls competition.

Pic is the story of a married couple in their forties with a teenaged daughter, the wife-mother falling for her daughter's boyfriend and then having an affair that spells the end to an idyllic middle-class family relationship. In the grand days of the Hollywood tearjerker and "confessional" romanticism, a film with a title like this one made Danish-born German emigrant director Douglas Sirk (Detleb Sierck) famous. Lüdcke has a lot to learn about movie psychology before attempting another feature of this sort. —*Holl.*

Chapiteau
(SWISS-COLOR)

———

Saarbrücken, Jan. 20.

A Cactus Film Production, Zurich, producers Edi Hubschmid, Theres Scherer. Features entire cast. Written and directed by Johannes/Flütsch. Camera (color), Pio Corradi; music, Rich Schwab. Reviewed at Max Ophüls Competition, Saarbrücken, Jan. 20, '84. Running time: **96 MINS.**

Cast: Thomas Ott, Otto Mächtlinger, Ingeborg Engelmann, Esther Christinat, Andreas Loeffel, Corinna Belz.

———

Johannes Flütsch, who previously collaborated with Manfred Stelzer (a fellow graduate of the Berlin Film & Television Academy) on a string of documentaries and docu-fiction features, has interested himself primarily in portrait sketches of outsiders in a well-to-do, socially and technologically advanced society. His "Flöz Dickebank" (1973), on a miners' colony; "We've Never Felt What Freedom Is" (1975), on carnival workers; "Long Way" (1977), on truckers; "Monarch" (1979), on a slot-machine gambler — each made in collaboration with other filmmakers — primed him for his first self-made docu: "Tenderness and Anger" (1981), about a gypsy family. That film, in turn, readied him for "Chapiteau," which deals with a traveling circus.

In general, this Swiss filmer documents people restlessly on the move, and he does it with a great deal of quiet sensitivity and communicative understanding. In the case of "Chapiteau," he has wed fiction with documentary to make a fine film on just what it may be like for a professional violinist to drop out of his rather routine existence to become a tractor-driver and tent-raiser for a circus caravan. There's little else to tell than that — yet the slow-moving style draws the viewer into the thread of a story, and provides for an experience that both teases and provokes.

Stories about dropouts are as old as intellectual moviemaking, one of the classics being Preston Sturges' "Sullivan's Travels" (1942). Flütsch's approach is simple: to show how a sensitive individual can refresh his spirit by observing life in a direct and rewarding manner. The violinist

leaves his orchestral job (applying for a temporary vacation, thus not really dropping-out at the beginning) and his girlfriend to follow a man who interests him as a dignified individual; he's an elephant-trainer whose advancing age is making it difficult to keep up with the rest.

But he also meets a girl in the caravan, and an affair begins. Then there's the struggling owners of the modest circus troupe, harried by an accident that hospitalizes one of the performers. So it comes about that our violinist himself might become a clown playing a violin in an act of his own at the end.

Pic's pluses are Flütsch's skilled directorial manner of blending fact with fiction, together with Pio Carradi's polished lensing "Chapiteau" might also score as a commercial item given more attention to a narrative line. As it stands, however, it deserves more exposure on the fest circuit.

—*Holl.*

K.u.K.
(AUSTRIAN-COLOR-16m)

———

Saarbrücken, Jan. 20.

A Bernhard Frankfurter Film Production, Austria. Features entire cast. Directed by Bernhard Frankfurter. Screenplay, Bernhard Frankfurter & Team; camera (color), Wolfgang Lehner; music, Gabi Kepplinger. Reviewed at Max Ophüls Competition, Saarbrücken, Jan. 20, '84. Running time: **80 MINS.**

Cast: Ludwig Grillich, Pilo Pichler, Gerhard Pöll, Ronald Meyer, Fritz Kohles, Elisabeth Eibl.

———

Bernhard Frankfurter's film "K.u.K." has a familiar clang for Austrians and Hungarians in the time of the Austrian-Hungarian Empire (the "k.u.k. in small letters being short for "kaiserl. und königl."), but the reference here could also be to the combination of "Kunst und Kommunikation" (Art and Communication) in view of the capital letters used.

In any case, this no-budget 16m film (blown up from Super-8 stock) is an exercise by students under Frankfurter's direction at an Institute for Journalism. Pic features Daisy, a nice-looking transvestite; Hurry Up, a communications freak; and Mickey, a Disney-inspired local reporter. And the setting is sometimes Hollywood as the center for mass-produced culture. A previous Frankfurter pic was the docu, "On the Road to Hollywood" (1982), dealing with Australian film emigration to Hollywood.

"K.u.K." was made for an insider audience, and appears to be a spoof of the Austrian film subsidy and TV/Media institutions. The grainy smeared-color style (common to blow-ups of Super-8 color stock onto 16m format) leaves very much to be desired on the visual plane. The lack of a suppor-

tive narrative line does help either, although Bernhard Frankfurter well deserved his platform at Saarbrücken to discuss film and cultural issues as they are at home. —*Holl.*

Deutschlandlied
(Song of Germany)
(WEST GERMAN-COLOR)

———

Saarbrücken, Jan. 20.

An Ernst Witzel Film Production, in collaboration with the Kuratorium Junger Deutscher Film. Features entire cast. Produced, written, and directed by Ernst Witzel. Camera (color), Jiri Stibr. Reviewed at Max Ophüls Competition, Saarbrücken, Jan. 20, '84. Running time: **90 MINS.**

Cast: Hans Hass Jr., Bernd Herzsprung, Hartmut Nolte, Isolde Barth, Hubert Suschka, Irene Schoenberger.

———

Ernst Witzel's "Song of Germany" is a debut feature made with support from the Kuratorum Junger Deutscher Film. Helmer Witzel had previously made a handful of shorts.

This is another of those nostalgia-packed glances over the shoulder to the heady student days of 1968. Last year in Saarbrücken, Dietrich Schubert's "Quite Far Away" treated the same theme with a setting off the beaten path in the neighborhood of Cologne. This time, in Witzel's version, the scene is the Palatinate.

A school reunion brings three old chums together again after each had gone his own way into one profession or another. After the class ceremonies and an evening of celebration, they're off with improvised camping gear into the woods on a drunken spree that will carry over the entire weekend. Between musing on the past they take to playing pranks to while the time away. The high point is reached when they visit an old veteran of WW II, an ex-stormtrooper type whose heart and soul was with the Nazis. And an anticlimax happens when a girl from the good old schooldays passes the night in one of the tents. More carousing, and the weekend of the long hangover reaches an end.

A low-budget pic with ideas too big to realize. —*Holl.*

Friedliche Tage
(Peaceful Days)
(W. GERMAN-COLOR-16m)

———

Saarbrücken, Jan. 18.

An Infrafilm Manfred Korytanski Production, in collaboration with Bayerischer Rundfunk (BR), Munich. Features entire cast. Written and directed by Richard Blank. Camera (color), Horst Schier; music, Loek Dikker. Reviewed at Max Ophüls Competition, Saarbrücken, Jan. 18, '84. Running time: **85 MINS.**

Cast: Katharina Thalbach (Hanna Rinkes), Branko Samarowski (Robert Kern), Hannelore Schroth (Silvia) Raphael Klachkin (Colonel Schönefeldt), Eva Mattes, Thomas Brasch, Laurens Straub.

———

Richard Blank's debut feature, after a string of tv productions, leaves little doubt that he has a penchant for Edgar Allan Poe and the Gothic novel, as well as Franz Kafka and the absurd theater of this century. His "Peaceful Days" describes a German city of the future, an Orwellian atmosphere of psychological oppression and urban alienation.

A woman has been picked up by the authorities to be committed to an asylum where public electrocutions take place in a kind of club restaurant. A guard assigned to the new arrival falls in love with her, and they escape together to wander from place to place, eventually booking into a pension-hotel. The woman is seeking her lost brother, finds him, and then witnesses his apparent suicide. The guard returns to the asylum and is promoted. What will happen to the woman is left open at the end.

A film of this peculiar nature is open to all sorts of intrepretation. But it's little more than intellectual fluff, and moves at such a snail's pace that the title fairly delivers what it promises: apathy and ennui. An eyecatching factor for film buffs is the mishmash aura of the postwar era in the outdated furnishings of the asylum. — *Holl.*

Gülibik
(WEST GERMAN-TURKISH-COLOR-16m)

Saarbrücken, Jan. 19.

A Provobis Film Production, Hamburg, in collaboration with the Kuratorium Junger Deutscher Film. Features entire cast. Directed by Jürgen Haase. Screenplay, Haase, Cornelius Bischoff, Cetin Öner; camera (color), Jürgen Grundmann, Fred Ebner; music, Zülfi Livaneli. Reviewed at Max Ophüls Competition, Saarbrücken, Jan. 19, '84. Running time: **103 MINS.**

Cast: Murat Güler, Nursim Demir, Ejder Akisik, Harun Yesilyurt, Gülseren Gürtunha, Orhan Aydin, Osman Diler, Gülibik the Rooster, the People of the Village of Sarihidir.

Jürgen Haase's "Gülibik' is a children's film set in Turkey, and is skedded for the upcoming kidpic fest of the Berlinale. Considering that West Berlin has a large population of Turks living in Kreuzberg and other sections of the city, the film is assured of a supportive audience.

The title refers to a rooster named Gülibik, raised by a young schoolboy in a Turkish village. Since the lad is now becoming acquainted with the ways of the world, he tries to experience everything that has to do with nature and village life. His older brother explains most of the facts of life to him, which in the process jumbles the truth even more but adds a comic touch to the events as a whole.

The family is poor. The father lives the life of a peasant who works the fields during the week and tries to sell his produce on the weekend. But prices are low and the future offers little hope of bettering their situation. So the father makes the

painful decision to enter his son's pet rooster in a cock-fight. The rest should be left to the viewer's own moviegoing expectations.

The docu-fiction approach offers several insights into rural life in Turkey, but the German dubbing is a mess and will not be a help in the Berlinale. —*Holl.*

Die Leichten Zeiten Sind Vorbei
(The Easy Times Are Over)
(WEST GERMAN-COLOR)

Saarbrücken, Jan. 21.

A PGF Film Production, Munich, Wolfgang G. Kreuse, producer, Features entire cast. Directed by Ulli Weiss. Screenplay, Weiss, Hartwig Nissen; camera (color), Wedigo von Schulzendorff; music, Hurricane. Reviewed at Max Ophuls Competition, Saarbrücken, Jan. 21, '84. Running time: **90 MINS.**

Cast: Heinz Hönig (Harry), Jan Fedder (Pit), Alexander Reichert, Margit Theiss, Kristina van Eyck, Karl Lieffen, Marie-Charlott Schüler.

Helmer Ulli Weiss came to directing from advertising films, as did his lenser Wedigo von Schulzendorff. This background is evident in nearly every camera setup in his debut pic, "The Easy Times Are Over." This style of filmmaking has become more popular since Jean-Jacques Beineix' "Diva" hit European screens — to say nothing of last year's Max Ophüls Prize winner, Niki List's "Cafe Malaria" (Austria). Weiss covers the Munich scene — cafes, galleries, clubs, hangouts, bookshops, and whatever — as thoroughly as any of the b.o. conscious New Generation of German directors of late.

"The Easy Times" is the story of two chums: one drives a taxi between romancing the ladies, the other is an artist who fumbles at everything. Both Harry and Pit wouldn't think of passing a day without spending a couple of hours together, although female companionship is always welcome. Harry chucked everything in the way of a career when his girlfriend of five years left him, but by driving his cab at night he doesn't have to worry much about easy company — until he meets, and later falls in love with, a mature lady running a bookshop.

As for Pit, he can't sell a single of his latest "glass sculpture" creations to a customer, so he destroys everything and looks for a new scheme on the side. He decides to rob a bank, but his best friend lets him down at the crucial moment when he is about to botch everything anyway. Further, his girlfriend, a thrush in the local rock 'n' roll scene, is having an affair. So, embittered, the would-be artist disappears from sight, which naturally worries his best friend.

One day, Harry gets a postcard from Pit on an island somewhere frequented by German dropouts. A reunion takes place in an idyllic

paradise, where the former bumbling artist is at least learning how instructive it can be to have blisters on the hand while repairing a villa. They part in the end, each going his own way with the realization that the easy times are over.

Weiss has told an amusing story with wit and charm. Thesps Heinz Hönig and Jan Fedder make a memorable pair. And the pic maintains a definite style from start to finish. The only weakness is in the shift of the scene out of Munich, where these "rock-cafes" and "long-drink joints" are peopled with costumed "in"-conscious clientele. As long as Weiss explores his own pop milieu with a critical eye — albeit that of an adman — the film works. Indeed, many of the camera setups are a stitch: shots under the armpits, mirror gimmicks, generous and glamorous lighting, clashing color patterns — it's all there.

Well worth a fest slot somewhere. —*Holl.*

Reise In Ein Verborgenes Leben
(Journey Into A Secret Life)
(WEST GERMAN-COLOR-16m)

Saarbrücken, Jan. 20.

A Regina Ziegler Film Production, Berlin, in coproduction with Sender Freies Berlin. Features entire cast. Written and directed by Hans Neuenfels. Camera (color), Hans-Günther Bücking; music, Heiner Goebbels. Reviewed at Max Ophüls Competition, Saarbrücken, Jan. 20, '84. Running time: **91 MINS.**

Cast: Stefan Wieland, Carlo Rola, Roland Schmid, Ram Murti, Josette Schäfer, Mark Gläser, Hajo Zörner, Frank Wittek, Mathais Niepelt, Susanne Peuscher.

Hans Neuenfels is a prominent legit director who has turned to cinema after making a name for himself in theatre and opera. His film debut, "Heinrich Penthesilea von Kleist" (1983), combined his stage production of Kleist's "Penthesilea" at the Schiller-Theater in Berlin with personal views on the Prussian dramatist's life. The stage production, by the way, utilized film projection from his latter film as extra intellectual fodder between acts.

Now Neuenfels has turned to Jean Genet's writing to make another personal statement on a famous author's vision. According to press information, the film was triggered after working on a production of Jean Genet's "The Balcony;" in any case, this is an encounter with Genet's own homosexual background and his autobiographical "Thief's Journal." The title of Neuenfels's film version is "Journey into a Secret Life," but a clear reference in image and text is made to Rainer Werner Fassbinder's "Querelle" as well. Arthur Rimbaud's writing are also included.

Anyone who has read Genet will know at the outset Neuenfels has but skimmed the surface. Pic is also much too theatrical to work any of the magic of the cinema. As for his personal view of Genet and Rimbaud, Neuenfels might find a gay fest somewhere interested in an odd collection of images dealing with toilets, prisons, and lighthouses on a barren seacoast. As for the rest of us, it's hardly worth giving the artist the benefit of the doubt on this outing. Better go see a Jean Cocteau film. Or better still: Genet's own directorial effort, the short feature "Un Chant d'Amour" (1952).—*Holl.*

Drinnen & Draussen
(Inside & Outside)
(AUSTRIAN-B&W-16m)

Saarbrücken, Jan. 20.

An Adi Mayer Film Production, Vienna. Features entire cast. Written and directed by Andreas Gruber. Camera (black and white), Hermann Dunzendorfer; music, Reinhold Keltzander, Johannes Prischl, and Grossgklockner. Reviewed at Max Ophüls Competition, Saarbrücken, Jan. 20. '84. Running time: **92 MINS.**

Cast: Heidi Baratta, Jan Kolar, Margarete Maurer, Alfons Stummer, Margarethe Mayer, Heinrich Heuer, Isidor Wimmer, Willi Seibetseder.

Andreas Gruber's "Inside & Outside" is the helmer's second feature after completing his courses at the Vienna Film and TV Academy with a diploma feature, "Everything Will Be Different Tomorrow" (1981).

This is a psychological study. A young student just entering upon her internship period is assigned to a psychiatric clinic for a year. There she meets an oddly intriguing patient, 30-years-of-age; he's been at the institution for four years, but firmly believes all the same that he will be released shortly. The problem, it develops, is a state of unrelieved psychological fear — something psychiatrists as a whole have a hard time to pin down and cure, it appears.

Gruber contrasts the patient's constant efforts to flee the institution with the rather dreary and hopeless atmosphere in the clinic itself. One begins to feel in the course of the tale that there's little difference between living "inside" or "outside" the institution so far as normality or acceptable mental health is concerned, particularly when the patient and the psychiatrist become too closely acquainted for the good of either. It's a praiseworthy effort at a knotty and complex theme.—*Holl.*

Hunderennen
(Dog Race)
(SWISS-COLOR)

Saarbrücken, Jan. 19.

A Bernard Safarik Film Production, Basel. Features entire cast. Directed by Bernard

Safarik. Screenplay, Jaroslav Vejvoda, Safarik; camera (color), Klaus Peter Weber. Reviewed at Max Ophüls Competition, Saarbrücken, Jan. 19, '84. Running time: **90 MINS.**

Cast: Josef Charvat, Pavel Landovsky, Sabine Rasser, Nina Svabova, Caroline Ramm, Peter Feyfar, Michael Schacht, Walo Lüond, Roger Thiriet.

Bernard Safarik's "Dog Race" is autobiographical docu-drama. It deals with the problems Czech emigrants had getting a visa to enter Switzerland following a stay in a refugee camp in Austria. Since this problem of East Europeans leaving Socialist countries to settle in the West has been a nagging sociopolitical one for most of the postwar period, the film has its relevance — although, in comparsion with Rolf Lyssy's "The Swiss Makers" (1979), it comes across as a variation on a popular theme.

"Dog Race" is based on Czech scribe Jaroslav Vejvoda's stories. Like Safarik in Base 1, Vejvoda in Zurich went through a decade of experiences as a refugee from Czechoslovakia in 1967. The chief protagonist is a painter who wants to leave Prague for the West for ideological and personal reasons. His way into the free world is anything but easy, not the least reason being that the two "states of mind" in East and West hardly allow for ready adoption. Pic chronicles in a dry, humorous manner how difficult any type of emigration in a European context is today, for hopes and dreams seldom correspond to the realities of seeking and finding asylum. —*Holl.*

Finder's Lohn
(Finders Keepers)
(WEST GERMAN-COLOR)

Saarbrücken, Jan. 19.
A M.M. Schwarz Film Production, Berlin. Features entire cast. Directed by M.M. Schwarz and Jan Fantl. Screenplay, Schwarz; camera (color), Axel Henschel; music, Horst Zinsmeister, Peter Lentz. Reviewed at Max Ophüls Competition, Saarbrücken, Jan. 19, '84. Running time: **84 MINS.**

Cast: Anni Luck, M.M. Schwarz, Birgit Anders, Rainer Hunold, Pumox.

Made with funding from the low-budget subsidy provided by the Berlin Film Fund, M.M. Schwarz and Jan Fantl's "Finders Keepers" scores as a neatly packaged idea for a short feature — over the long feature-length stretch, however, it becomes tedious and repetitive. More than likely, by editing pic down to a medium-length short, it could prove to be an audience winner on fantasy alone.

"Finders Keepers" leans heavily on the Hitchcock thriller genre for its narrative thread. A woman gets rid of her husband one dark night under a bridge, but there was a witness: a tramp sleeping under the bridge, who picks up an envelope she dropped that just happens to have her address upon it. When the eccentric tramp, who can manipulate natural happenings with extrasensory powers, returns the envelope to the distraught lady in her apartment, she grows all the more nervous and tries to buy him off with a finder's reward. Our tramp mimes his way into her heart after a while, then cuts off his beard — and in the end takes the place of the husband. It's evident at this point that he's one and same anyway.

Pic's main weakness is a dubbing gag: many of the "extras" in the story speak with the gravel voice of a Western hero in synchronized German tv airings.

— *Holl.*

Footloose
(COLOR)

'Flashdance Farmers' looks to bring home Bacon at the b.o.

Hollywood, Feb. 10.
A Paramount Pictures release, produced by Lewis J. Rachmil and Craig Zadan. Directed by Herbert Ross. Features entire cast. Exec producer, Daniel Melnick. Screenplay, Dean Pitchford; camera (Movielab color), Ric Waite; editor, Paul Hirsch; sound, Al Overton Jr.; production design, Ron Hobbs; choreography, Lynne Taylor-Corbett; assistant director, L. Andrew Stone; music, Miles Goodman, Becky Shargo. Reviewed at Paramount Studios, Hollywood, Feb. 3, 1984. MPAA rating: PG. Running time: **107 MINS.**
Ren . . . . Kevin Bacon
Ariel . . . . Lori Singer
Reverend Moore . . . . John Lithgow
Vi Moore . . . . Dianne Wiest
Willard . . . . Christopher Penn
Rusty . . . . Sarah Jessica Parker
Woody . . . . John Laughlin
Wendy Joe . . . . Elizabeth Gorcey
Ethel . . . . Frances Lee McCain
Chuck . . . . Jim Youngs
Burlington . . . . Douglas Dirkson

In addition to his usual directorial skill and considerable choreographic experience, Herb Ross brings to "Footloose" an adult sensibility often lacking in troubled-teen pics, resulting in a film that could play off across a broad marketplace.

To be sure, from its toe-tapping titles onward, "Footloose" is mainly a youth-oriented rock picture, complete with big-screen reminders of what's hot today in music video. And there's usually a stereo in sight to explain where the music's coming from, even on the side of tractors.

But by writing both the screenplay and contributing lyrics to nine of the film's songs, Dean Pitchford has come up with an integrated story line that works. The simple, singing yarn may not be profound or original, but it's at least as involving as many well-recalled Hollywood musicals of yore.

Essential to the result is young Kevin Bacon, superb in the lead part. At first glance, his punkish, big-city looks raises dread in the older heart that here comes another 107 minutes with an insufferable teenager carrying a grudge against the world.

But Bacon really just wants to get along in the small town he's been forced to move to from Chicago, bending more than halfway if allowed to. Sure to complicate his life, however, is pretty Lori Singer, a sexually and otherwise confused preacher's daugher, whose tease comes charged with a bully of a boyfriend, Jim Youngs. There will be trouble.

Singer's rebellion can be traced, rather, to John Lithgow, a hard-shell Baptist minister functioning as a one-man forum for the town's morals in addition to his daughter's, both fixated on the evils of "obscene rock and roll music" and any dancing thereto.

Striving to fit in, Bacon picks up a good friend in Christopher Penn, wonderfully portraying a hulking, thick-witted farmboy anxious for a little of life's excitement. And, naturally enough, Bacon will eventually discover more than friendship with Singer.

What's good about "Footloose" is that, young and old, the characters are essentially nice people living through a generation gap that's wide enough without becoming a hateful chasm. If both sides finally bridge the gap enough for a happy ending, even if predictably, so what?

Working on Lithgow's soft side, Dianne Wiest is terrific as his wife, as is Frances Lee McCain in a less-important part as Bacon's understanding mom. Lithgow turns in another solid performance.

But credit Ross with the consistently nice touches, which if detailed would spoil too much. Mention must be made, however, of Penn's ultimate preparations for the big dance.

Oh, yes, whether the kids will be allowed to stage a senior prom is the film's biggest question. And that may not seem like much compared to the usual teen-pic problem of whether gasoline or kerosene works best to torch the high school. But it's enough to tap toes to. — *Har.*

Weekend Pass
(COLOR)

Mass fare, worth docking for.

Chicago, Feb. 3.
A Crown International release produced by Marylin J. Tenser. Written and directed by Lawrence Bassoff. Coproducer, Michael D. Castle. Camera (Deluxe Color), Bryan England; Editor, Harry B. Miller III; sound, Mark Ulano; art direction, Ivo G. Cristante; assistant director, Dan Dugan; music, John Baer. Reviewed at Chicago Theatre, Chicago, Feb. 3, '84. (MPAA rating: R.) Running time: **92 MINS.**
Paul Fricker . . . . D.W. Brown
Lester Gidler . . . . Peter Ellenstein
Webster Adams . . . . Patrick Hauser
Bunker Hill . . . . Chip McAllister
Tina Wells . . . . Pamela G. Kay
Cindy Hazard . . . . Hilary Shapiro
Tawney Ryatt . . . . Graem McGavin
Heidi Henderson . . . . Daureen Collodel
Maxine . . . . Annette Sinclair
Bertram . . . . Grand L. Bush

If mass-directed popular films reflect broad social currents, Crown International's "Weekend Pass" is saying the public is yearning for gentle comedy with spice — but sans steamy sex and, finally, an undercurrent of old-fashioned patriotism.

Since Crown is canny at gearing its in-house productions to the cycles of broad audience taste, the company may be onto something. "Weekend Pass" looks in for respectable b.o. and — can it be true? — even a nod or two from condescending film reviewers.

Pic has four sailors fresh out of basic training in San Diego taking off for Los Angeles for fun and sex in any combination obtainable.

Quartet consists of familiar stereotypes — a clean-cut black kid (Chip McAllister), who used to be a ghetto gang member, a school cutup (D.W. Brown) who wants to be a standup comic, a bespectacled nerd (Peter Ellenstein) and an all-American sort (Patrick Houser) whose old girlfriend has gone to seed and sports, in the words of the swabby, "a dildo the size of the Hindenburg."

In its frenetic pursuit of fun and games, the group takes a number of wrong turns — a strip joint, a rumble in Watts and a tour of Venice beach — before making romantic connections.

The black sailor falls for a jazz exercise instructor. The comedy cutup meets a female counterpart. The nerd scores with the bespectacled daughter of a Naval officer. The all-American makes it with the last girl's cousin. Sex episodes are surprisingly discreet.

The journey, not necessarily the destination, of pics like these is important. "Weekend Pass" can be faulted for overdoing the "travelog" aspects of Los Angeles, apparently in an effort to flesh out its slender 92-minutes.

Balancing things is writer-director Lawrence Bassoff's handling of the material. He gets good performances from the young cast, making the principal characters sympathetic. Also made is the point that the sailors are pleasant chaps and diligent sailors, and not, as one girlfriend speculates, a group of goofballs who can't make it in civilian life. —Sege.

Kipperbang
(BRITISH-COLOR)

A United Artists Classics release of an Enigma TV Ltd. production in the "First Love" series for Goldcrest. Executive producer, David Puttnam. Produced by Chris Griffin. Directed by Michael Apted. Features entire cast. Screenplay, Jack Rosenthal; camera (Kay color), Tony Pierce-Roberts; editor, John Shirley; music, David Earl; sound, Derek Ball; art direction, Jeffrey Woodbridge; assistant director, Dominic Fulford; costume design, Sue Yelland; associate producer, David Bill. Reviewed at MGM/UA screening room, N.Y., Feb. 8, 1984. (MPAA Rating: PG). Running time: 80 MINS.
Alan .... John Albasiny
Miss Land .... Alison Steadman
Tommy .... Garry Cooper
Ann .... Abigail Cruttenden
Geoffrey .... Maurice Dee
Headmaster .... Robert Urquhart
Abbo .... Mark Brailsford
Shaz .... Chris Karallis

"Kipperbang" is a flat, understated attempt at romantic comedy, made for British television in 1982 as part of the "First Love" series, but virtually evaporating on the big screen. U.S. theatrical release via UA Classics comes sever-al months after the picture in videocassette form has been available in domestic video stores.

Writer Jack Rosenthal's consistently precious script matches the romantic problems of young adolescents (hero is 14) at a British school in 1948 with those of their elders, as the English teacher (Alison Steadman) must deal with an unplanned pregnancy, the father being the school groundskeeper (Garry Cooper).

Very thin material emphasizes running gags, most noxious of which is the kids reciting the nonsense phrase "P'Tang, Yang, Kipperbang" (pic's original title in Britain, pointlessly followed by a grunt, shortened for U.S. release) as an example of youngsters' codes and rituals. Young cast members throw away their dialog in mumbled, naturalistic readings, reducing potential chuckles to groaners.

Plot gimmicks, generally overemphasized, include the hero Alan (John Albasiny) dreaming of his first kiss with plain classmate Ann (Abigail Gruttenden), with attempted suspense generated as he is cast in a dull school play in which he is supposed to kiss co-star Ann in the final scene.

Device of a voiceover narrator turning most events into cricket match play-by-play (representing Alan's wish-fulfillment point-of-view) is overworked, as are the frequent references back to World War II (groundskeeper is fake war hero, leading to the predictable disillusionment of the hero).

Director Michael Apted appears uncertain how to approach this material, combining the general understatement with a coy approach to vulgar issues of adolescent sex (Alan and his two pals form the inevitable central trio of sex-obsessed young teens) and hyped-up crosscutting between the school play's climax and police arresting the groundskeeper.

Adult actors, especially Steadman, turn in good performances, but the kids are a drag. In his big finale scene, pouring his heart out to Ann, John Albasiny delivers his lines into the ground, inadvertently giving a worse performance than his intentionally incompentent nonacting during the school play. Tech credits are adequate. —Lor.

Against All Odds
(COLOR)

Sexy remake just misses.

Hollywood, Feb. 10.
Columbia Pictures release, produced by Taylor Hackford and William S. Gilmore. Directed by Taylor Hackford. Features entire cast. Exec producer, Jerry Bick. Screenplay, Eric Hughes based on 1947 film "Out Of The Past," written by Daniel Mainwaring; camera (Metrocolor), Donald Thorin; editors, Fredric Steinkamp, William Steinkamp; sound, Jeff Wexler; art direction, Richard James Lawrence; assistant director, Tom Mack; associate producer, William R. Borden; music, Michel Colombier, Larry Carlton. Reviewed at the Academy of Motion Picture Arts & Sciences, Hollywood, Feb. 10, 1984. (MPAA rating: R.) Running time: 128 MINS.
Jessie .... Rachel Ward
Terry .... Jeff Bridges
Jake .... James Woods
Hank .... Alex Karras
Mrs. Wyler .... Jane Greer
Caxton .... Richard Widmark
Tommy .... Dorian Harewood
Edie .... Swoosie Kurtz
Steve .... Saul Rubinek
Ed .... Pat Corley
Coach .... Bill McKinney

If not for a somewhat murky and misanthropic ending, "Against All Odds" would stand as a well-engineered second-try at 1947's "Out Of The Past," now considered a classic of its type. That and the names of director Taylor Hackford and Rachel Ward should be its main draws.

Obsessive love affairs are always interesting and this could be no different, especially with the alluring Ward as the one both Jeff Bridges and James Woods will go to any lengths for. On screen, there's simply something about Ward that makes that completely believable.

On the whole, "Odds" is definitely overplotted but still not that hard to follow. Bridges is a fading pro footballer with shady connections to Woods, a small-time L.A. bookie-hood who has been keeping house with Ward until she stabbed him and got away.

Jane Greer, who played Ward's role in the earlier version of the Daniel Mainwaring yarn, is now Ward's mean mother who owns the team Bridges is cut from and drove her daughter into associating with a low-life like Woods.

Greer is allied with suave, sinister Richard Widmark, lawyer in a rapacious real-estate deal who will turn out to be more than suspected at first. Alex Karras is Bridges' ally on the football team, but he, too, will turnout to be more than, etc.

These are the players and the action ranges all the way to remote Mexican areas whose scenic moods are captured nicely by cinematographer Donald Thorin, heating up the #2 love affair between Bridges and Ward.

Although all the performances are firstrate, the best scenes take place between Bridges and Woods, each projecting that special hatred men can have when in love — and having made love to — the same woman.

Hackford, unfortunately, does not seem as determined here to wrap matters up as neatly — and happily — as he did in "An Officer And A Gentleman" and the difference might mean millions at the boxoffice. "Odds" simply ends oddly.

There will be talk about a super-exciting auto race that takes place down — and often on the wrong side of — the stretch of Sunset Boulevard that winds treacherously for several miles west of Beverly Hills, a killer under normal conditions.

After having reached cliche dimensions in so many films, this chase seems freshly exciting, yet still vaguely irresponsible for filmmakers to indulge in, knowing some daredevils out there might be inspired to duplicate the thrill. But what can be said about that, except hopefully nobody connected with making the picture will ever meet the imitators on the wrong side of Sunset. —Har.

The Compleat Beatles
(DOCU-COLOR/B&W)

A TeleCulture Inc. release of a Delilah Films production. Executive producers, Stephanie Bennett, Jeannie Sakol. Produced by Stephanie Bennett, Patrick Montgomery. Directed by Montgomery. Written by David Silver; camera (new footage, color), Nick Hale, Peter Schnall, Djura Andjic, Joel King; editor, Pamela Page; sound, Nick Ware, Pat Heigham, Peter Miller, Dragan Andjic, Bill Fiege; London interviews by Tony Tyler; narrator, Malcolm McDowell; film research, Ron Furmanek, James Karnbach; newsreel announcers, Peter Kanze, Paul Killiam; additional narration, John Rousmaniere; still animation, Jeff Meyerowitz. Reviewed on Cinemax, N.Y., Feb. 7, 1984. (No MPAA Rating). Running time: 120 MINS.
Includes interviews with: Gerry Marsden, Allan Williams, Bill Harry, Tony Sheridan, Horst Fascher, Billy J. Kramer, Bob Wooler, George Martin, Nicholas Schaffner, Milton Okun, Bruce Johnston, Lenny Kaye, Wilfred Mellers, Marianne Faithfull, Billy Preston.

Hardly living up to its title, "The Compleat Beatles" is an educational, though lopsided documentary covering the history of the Beatles rock group. Made in 1982, film has been available primarily in homevideo form (as well as on cable tv via Universal Pay-TV distribution) and now looks to okay results from diehard fans in its theatrical release.

Film's strongest section is the opening 45 minutes tracing the group's origins from local Liverpool musicians during the 1956-61 period (taking the "Beatles" monicker in 1960 after earlier editions called "The Quarrymen," "Johnny & The Moondogs" and "The Silver Beetles") to British superstars in 1962-63. Interviews conducted by Tony Tyler are quite informative, particularly with Bill Harry, editor of Mersey Beat magazine (and ex-flatmate of John Lennon and group's original bassist Stuart Sutcliffe), tracing the struggling days of gigs in Liverpool's Cavern and other clubs as well as key training obtained in trips to Hamburg.

Fellow rockers Gerry Marsden (of Gerry & The Pacemakers), Tony Sheridan and Billy J. Kramer anecdotally paint a picture of the milieu, fleshed out by newsreel footage, numerous still photos and evocative vintage footage of the Beatles in performance. Formative influences and forerunners in America and the U.K., ranging from Little Richard to Lonnie Donegan (and his hillbilly style skiffle music) are effectively traced.

Documentary loses its force and thoroughness once the Beatles hit America in February 1964 as director Patrick Montgomery breezes through the next six years of the group's worldwide dominance in the music industry with numerous omissions and excessive telescoping of events. At the outset, the group's historic appearance on "The Ed Sullivan Show" is not included on screen, with a followup Washington, D.C. concert substituted.

None of the three surviving group members is interviewed, nor are many other key figures such as Yoko Ono, Allen Klein (the whole episode of Apple Records' financial problems is glossed over), Pete Best (original group drummer pre-Ringo Starr) and Richard Lester (director of Beatles films "Help" and "A Hard Day's Night") among others.

Lengthiest and best interview is with record producer George Martin, who, because the group's influential manager Brian Epstein died in 1967 and is thus present in the film only in old film clips, emerges as the most important creative force behind the Beatles (apart from the foursome themselves).

Taking personal credit (deservedly) for the electronics and instrumentation innovations of "Sgt. Pepper" and other records, Martin is exhaustively thorough in providing behind-the-scenes details of the Beatles' recording history. Docu frequently returns to him as its voice for the 1962-70 period.

Dramatically narrated by Malcolm McDowell, "Compleat Beatles" includes numerous performance excerpts. Director Montgomery presents a too-glib, perfunctory account of their peak days and decline, failing to update "common knowledge" material with new points-of-view.

For example, history of the "Magical Mystery Tour" phase is trite and misleading, with narration stating that the film was never released in America, when in fact it has latterly proved to be a solid draw in nontheatrical release here on college campuses.

Documentary rightfully emphasizes the less familiar aspects of the group's history, but takes a cavalier attitude towards key later events. Ending with Paul McCartney's quitting the group in April 1970 (which effectively broke up

the Beatles), picture utilizes oneliner captions to blithely describe what happened to Lennon, McCartney, Starr and George Harrison since then, a gimmick appropriate to fictional characters (a la "American Graffiti") but embarrassingly inadequate here.

This is not the complete story of the Fab Four, and future documentians will have to interview McCartney, Harrison and Starr (Lennon's death makes such a project incomplete by definition) as their starting point. —Lor.

The Smurfs And The Magic Flute
(La Flute a Six Schtroumpfs)
(BELGIAN-FRENCH-COLOR-ANIMATION)

An Atlantic Releasing Corp. release of a presentation by First Performance Pictures Corp. in association with Stuart R. Ross. A Studios Belvision (Bruxelles) Editions Dupuis (Paris) coproduction. Produced and directed by Jose Dutillieu. Screenplay, Peyo Culliford; adapted by Culliford, Yvan Delporte, from book by Culliford; camera (color), François Leonard, Jacques Delfosse, Marcel van Steenhuyse; editor, Nebiha Ben Milad, Michele Neny; music, Michel Legrand; songs, Delporte, Culliford; English-language version written and directed by John Rust; principal animators, Nic Broca, Marcel Colbrant, Louis-Michel Carpentier; animation supervision, Eddie Lateste; artistic supervision, Paulette Melloul; scribing-color supervision, Pros Cayman; timing, Jos Marissen. Reviewed at Embassy 49th St. theater, N.Y., Feb. 12, 1984. (MPAA Rating: G). Running time: 74 MINS.
(English-dubbed soundtrack)

"The Smurfs And The Magic Flute" is an uninteresting but innocuous animated feature film bringing the popular hit of books, tv and merchandising, the Smurfs (or "Schtroumpfs" as they were originally known in parts of Europe) to the big screen. Its success in U.S. distribution since just before the last Christmas season is more a testament to effective marketing and a vacuum of new, G-rated product than to the virtues of the film itself.

Weak, episodic storyline, set in the Middle Ages, has a bandit named Oilycreep stealing the magic flute (which has the power to cause people to dance uncontrollably when it is played) from Pee Wee at the king's castle. Pee Wee, whose dubbed voice vaguely resembles that of comic Pee Wee Herman, sets out on a dull trek with his pal Johan to retrieve the magical instrument.

Hypnotized by a friendly wizard, the twosome are transported to the land of the Smurfs, tiny blue creatures who all look alike and wear white hats and pants, except for their 542-year-old leader Papa Smurf, whose hat and pants are red. The Smurfs fabricate a second magic flute for Pee Wee, who ultimately bests Oilycreep in a final reel musical battle. Film has no

relationship to Mozart's opera "The Magic Flute."

Despite their billing and title come-on, the Smurfs do not appear (save for a tiny blue hand entering the frame at one point) until the second half of the film. A defensive song designed to demonstrate how individual Smurfs act like their names only proves that the character animation here lacks the differentiation of say, Disney's Seven Dwarfs.

The film utilizes rather limited animation techniques, with pretty but strictly static backgrounds against which the characters move. Absence of much fantasy material is disappointing and the labored gags aren't funny. The Smurfs themselves have irritatingly resonant voices and the premise of substituting the word "Smurf" for nouns and verbs in their language is run into the ground. Michel Legrand's soundtrack score (to which additional music has been added for the U.S. release version) is subpar.—Lor.

Le Joli Coeur
(The Charmer)
(FRENCH-COLOR)

Paris, Jan. 31.
AMLF release of a CAPAC-Films de la Colombe production. Produced by Paul Claudon. Stars Francis Perrin, Cyrielle Claire, Sylvain Rougerie. Directed by Perrin. Screenplay, Alex Varoux, Perrin, Claudon; camera (Eastmancolor), Didier Tarot; editor, Ghislaine sound, Michel Desrois; music, Yves Gilbert; production manager, Hubert Merial. Reviewed at the Gaumont Ambassade Theater, Paris, Jan. 29, 1984. Running time: 91 MINS.
With: Francis Perrin, Cyrielle Claire, Sylvain Rougerie, Patricia Carter, Michèle Bernier, Annie Jouzier, Barbara Willar, Jean-Claude Bouillaud, Régis Lespales, Jean-Paul Farré.

Local comedy favorite Francis Perrin hit paydirt with his helming debut in 1981, "Tete a Claque," which has encouraged him to direct another vehicle. "Le Joli Coeur" casts him as a whimsical tour guide who uses his talents as a benign seducer to sound out prospective mates for his timid, upright roommate and colleague.

When latter gets a crush on a pretty hospital psychiatrist, Perrin passes himself off as paranoid in order to gain her attention, but himself falls for her and resorts to various masquerades and phony crises to win her favors.

Perrin is a vivacious comedian who stepped from stage to screen without real difficulty and found screen popularity under the aegis of producer Paul Claudon, who has collaborated on the scripts of his films. But "Joli Coeur" is the feeblest of their films, a one-joke story Perrin fails to carry with his buoyant good humor.

At least he has a very pretty foil in Cyrielle Claire, a gracious new-

comer discovered by Alejandro Jodorowsky for his 1980 pic, "Tusk." — Len

---

In Our Hands
(COLOR-DOCU-16m)

Effective coverage of massive anti-nuke rally.

A Libra Cinema 5 Films release of a June 12 Film Group production. Produced by Robert Richter, Stanley Warnow. No director credited. Executive producer, Leon Falk; coordinating producer, Nina Streich; associate producer, Jacqueline Leopold; field producers, Brad Battersby, Eileen Braune, Roy Braune, Kevin Cloutier, Tom Cohen, Chana Gazit, Aviva Gellman, Linda Habib, Lora Hays, Katherine Herman, Joel Hinman, Mel Howard, Fran Kazui, Kaz Kazui, Barbara Kopple, Carole Michel, Cathy McClure, Sharon Sachs, Mary Salter, Judy Silverman, Rudd Simmons, Tom Simon, David Tapper, Chris Verges, Dean Wetherell, Barbara Zahm; camera (color), Robert Achs, Pedro Bonilla, Gary Corrigan, Gerald Cotts, Joseph Dell'olio, Steve Fierberg, Dick Fisher, Morris Flam, Anthony Forma, Robert Giraldini, Steve Harris, Douglas Hart, Terry Hopkins, Tom Hurwitz, Mike Jackson, Jeep Johnson, Allen Kinsberg, Ed Lachman, Hal Landen, Robert Leacock, Don Lenzer, Rick Liss, Vic Losick, William Markle, Neil Marshad, Stuart Math, Robert Nickson, Phil Parmet, Peter Pearce, Hart Perry, Sidney Reichman, Peter Schnall, Jim Scurit, Gene Searchinger, Nessya Shapiro, Thomas Sigel, Jonathan Smith, Buddy Squires, Burleigh Wartes, Alicia Weber, Jeff Weinstock, Brad Weiss, Oliver Wood; editors, Sharon Sachs, Anthony Forma, Donald Blank; supervising editor, Stanley Warnow; additional editing, Gloria Williams, Joan Morris; sound mixer, John Quinn; production manager, Robert Nickson; voice of atomic bomb survivors, Meryl Streep, Anne Twomy. Reviewed at Almi screening room, N.Y., Feb. 3, 1984. (No MPAA Rating). Running time: 90 MINS.
With: Helen Caldicott, Benjamin Spock, William Sloan Coffin, Randall Forsburg, Edward Markey, Maibritt Thorin, Roy Nichols, Jack Sheinkman, Cleveland Robinson, Coretta Scott King, Pete Seeger, James Taylor, Holly Near, Rita Marley, Peter, Paul & Mary, John Hall, House Of The Lord Choir, Are & Be Ensemble, Fred Moore, Judy Gorman Jacobs, Lucy Simon, Carly Simon, John Shea, Kathryn Walker, Jerry Stiller, Anne Meara, Roy Scheider, Bob Balaban, Orson Welles, Ellen Burstyn, Joan Baez, Judd Hirsch, Bianca Jagger, Susan Sarandon, Jill Clayburgh, Hiroshima and Nagasaki atomic bomb survivors.

"In Our Hands" is an admirable documentary covering the massive (reportedly 1,000,000-people strong) anti-nuclear weapons protest march held in New York City on June 12, 1982. Producers Stanley Warnow and Robert Richter have created a concise film from the voluminous material shot by dozens of volunteer filmmakers, which serves as a timely reminder of the scope of the event, and its implications of grass-roots sentiments.

Sharing several of the performers from the 1980 "No Nukes" film, "In Our Hands" is not a concert film but rather integrates the musical performances staged to entertain marchers at Central Park with speeches by nuclear freeze activists, interview material and wide-ranging views of the preparations and the march itself. Avowed goal of the picture to arouse ongoing disarmament fervor is undoubtedly optimistic, as it emerges as a record of an event that at most prescribes more rallies rather than a blueprint for action.

The march itself is very much a reminder of the peace and civil rights marches of the 1960s, though on a larger scale. Even the players, such as Pete Seeger and Dr. Spock, seem the same. Biggest difference is that the numerous policemen interviewed here all appear sympathetic to the demonstrators' cause, even when carrying off passive resistors on stretchers to jail in a June 14 followup rally of civil disobedience outside the major powers' U.N. missions.

Led by Helen Caldicott, of Physicians for Social Responsibility, film features many cogent speakers (including well-known celebrities) for the anti-nuclear cause, each interested in getting the message across to President Reagan. International scope of the movement is largely concentrated on a Japanese delegation of A-bomb survivors, whose pleas and testimony are movingly translated in voiceover by Meryl Streep and Anne Twomy.

Musical highlights include Pete Seeger's renditions of "If I Had A Hammer" and the very effective "Children's Cry" written by John & Joanne Hall and James Taylor, as well as Taylor's mellow reprise of his hit "You've Got A Friend."

Considering the diverse hands that contributed to it, film is technically smooth and probably could sustain a 35m blowup for wider distribution. —*Lor.*

Jacques Mesrine
(FRENCH-DOCU-COLOR)

Paris, Feb. 8.

Films Molière release of a Profil Productions/First U.V.P. Eurocitel coproduction. Directed by Hervé Palud. Conceived by Palud and Gilles Millet. Camera (color), Laurent Dailliand, Pascal Marti; editor, Roland Baubeau; music, Gil Slavin. Reviewed at the Olympic Balzac Theater, Paris, Feb. 6, 1984. Running time: **93 MINS.**

Five years after his death in a police ambush in Paris, French gangster Jacques Mesrine is the subject of two current theatrical films. First in release is this docu survey of his outlaw career, and former producer-turned-filmmaker André Genoves is shortly to release his own fictional treatment with Nicolas Silberg as Mesrine.

From his early days as a petty hood, involved in a series of holdups, kidnappings and murders on home ground and in exile in North America, to his more flamboyant peak as France's Public Enemy Number One and something of a media hero, particularly in his crusade against the inhumane High Security Quarters in local prisons, Mesrine remained an ambiguous figure whose life anti-hero allure is definitely the stuff of movies.

It's significant that screen star Jean-Paul Belmondo snatched film rights of Mesrine's 1976 autobiographical novel, "Death Instinct" (though he has so far hedged on going through with the picture).

Director Hervé Palud, in collaboration with journalist Gilles Millet, who did a scoop-interview with Mesrine, on the run after a spectacular prison break in 1978, and subsequently saw him again for a photo session, have essayed an objective recap of his life, without any overt pretentions to the analysis or editorializing.

Their film is an adroit assemblage of archive materials and interviews — with former cellmates, hostages, judges, lawyers and girlfriends supplying fascinating glimpses into an elusive often charming, hell-bent personality.

A highlight among the interviews is one (female) attorney's eye-witness description of Mesrine's incredible escape from the visitors' parlor of a prison, executed with the kind of panache and ingenuity that wouldn't be out of place in a classic Hollywood gangster melodrama.

Pic opens and closes with the evocation of Mesrine's death on the outskirts of Paris when clandestine police vehicles surrounded his car and a small army of police riddled him with bullets before he could retaliate. (His last girl friend, with him at the time, was seriously wounded but survived — she refused to endorse this film and demanded that two photos of her be cut.)

Despite the stance of objectivity, the filmmakers' outrage at what has often been considered a downright execution without trial is all to apparent; it is enforced by an interview with Mesrine's daughter, who tells how celebrating police chiefs invited her to share some champagne with her father's executioners. — *Len.*

Preppies
(COLOR)

Raunch comedy aimed at young audiences.

A Platinum Pictures release. A Playboy Channel presentation of a Chuck Vincent Prods. Ltd. film. Produced and directed by Vincent. Features entire cast. Screenplay, Rick Marx, Vincent, from story by Todd Kessler; camera (color), Larry Revene; editor, Clement Barclay; music, Ian Shaw; songs, Shaw, Vincent, Jonathan Hannah, Shannon MacLoughlin; sound, Dale Whitman; production manager, Per Sjostedt; associate producer, Bill Slobodian; assistant director, Josh Andrews; costumes, Robert Pusilo Studio; art direction, George C. Brown; stunt coordinator, Jerry Hewitt. Reviewed at Magno Preview 4 screening room, N.Y., Feb. 2, 1984. (MPAA Rating: R). Running time: **83 MINS.**

Robert (Chip) Thurston......Dennis Drake
Bayard....................Steven Holt
Marc.............Peter Brady Reardon
Roxanne................Nitchie Barrett
Jo.................Cindy Manion
Tip.............Katie Stelletello

Margot..................Katt Shea
Trini.............Lynda Wiesmeier
Suzy.............Jo Ann Marshall
Dick Foster.............Paul Sutton
Blackwel...............Leonard Haas
Louie.............Anthony Matteo
Dean Flossmore...........Leslie Barrett

"Preppies" is an okay exploitation comedy aimed at both the teenage drive-in movie audience and the somewhat older crowd for subsequent cable-tv exposure via co-backer The Playboy Channel. Promotable title and goodly share of sex-tease gags should generate decent returns in theatrical playoff.

The Rick Marx-Chuck Vincent screenplay pokes fun at the stereotype of Ivy League college students, in this case three freshmen at a college in New York State who are planning to be lawyers but are on the verge of flunking out.

Main plot device is the hiring of three local "townie" girls (Nitchie Barrett, Cindy Manion and Katie Stelletello) to seduce Chip Thurston(Dennis Drake) and his pals Bayard (Steven Holt) and Marc (Peter Brady Reardon) and prevent them from studying for a key economics exam over the weekend. Culprit is Thurston's cousin Blackwel (Leonard Haas), who stands to receive Thurston's multi-million dollar trust fund if latter flunks out of school.

The problem with this simple structure is that the protagonists are unsympathetic characters. Normally, in effective films ranging from Blake Edwards' 1957 "Mister Cory" to Peter Yates' "Breaking Away," the social stratum conflict is built around upwardly mobile lower-class figures for audience identifiction. "Preppies" ' heroes are the unpleasant, snooty guys from the other side of the tracks.

Perking things up are Katt Shea, delightful as Thurston's Bryn Mawr-accented unattainable "preppette" girl friend Margot, and Jo Ann Marshall as Suzy, an ebullient friend of the townie girls. The other female leads are mainly called upon to decorate the film in various degrees of undress, including busty Playmate Lynda Wiesmeier as Margot's naive pal.

Male leads are okay, though Peter Brady Reardon is called upon to overdo the grating Eastern accent. In for a nice bit as a handsome soap opera star that Suzy has a crush on is Paul Sutton, better known to the fans for his porno film appearances using the name Jerry Butler.

Director Vincent keeps things moving at a fast clip, but most of the verbal gags in a rather talkative script fall flat. Since the sight gags are often amusing, he would do well to shift the emphasis in future comedy efforts. Tech credits are fine down the line. —*Lor.*

Lassiter
(COLOR)

'Magnum' dresses up for a downer script.

Hollywood, Feb. 15.

A Warner Bros. release of a Golden Harvest production. Produced by Albert S. Ruddy. Executive producer Raymond Chow and Andre Morgan. Directed by Roger Young. Screenplay, David Taylor; camera, Gil Taylor (Technicolor); editor, Benjamin Weissman; music, Ken Thorne; production designer, Peter Mullins; art director, Alan Tompkins; set decorator, Jack Stephens; costumes, Barbara Lane; sound, George Stephenson; associate producer, Frederick Muller; assistant director, Patrick Clayton. Reviewed at Village Theater, Westwood, Calif. Feb. 15, 1984. MPAA rating: R. Running time: **100 MINS.**

Lassiter......................Tom Selleck
Sara.......................Jane Seymour
Kari.......................Lauren Hutton
Becker.....................Bob Hoskins
Breeze....................Joe Regalbuto
Smoke.......................Ed Lauter
Max Hofer.................Warren Clarke
Allyce......................Edward Peel
Askew......................Paul Antrim

"Lassiter" is a total formula picture designed to exploit the charm of Tom Selleck. Pic's success or failure should be a good barometer of Selleck's drawing power, since the film has little else to offer.

Selleck's big screen debut, "High Road To China," was a modest success, but inconclusive as to whether his television admirers would pay to see their hero. "Lassiter," in fact is not unlike a tv show with its attempt to pack as much into the time as possible — whether it fits or not.

Like a tv actioner, "Lassiter" features rapid plot turns, little character development, dozens of set pieces and lots of action.

Set in London 1934, "Lassiter" is part caper picture, part intrigue story. Nick Lassiter (Selleck) is an elegant jewel thief who is blackmailed by a coalition of the FBI and English police to liberate $10,000,000 in Nazi diamonds passing through London. Selleck resists, but really isn't given much choice since the alternative is a stay in a British prison.

The diamonds are to be transported out of London by none other than Lauren Hutton, playing German agent Countess Kari von Fursten. To help crack the fortress where the diamonds are kept, Lassiter elicits the help of his paramour Sara (Jane Seymour).

Lassiter's assignment leads him through a London underworld that has never looked more picturesque and quaint. Action jumps from a warehouse boxing match to a crowded marketplace to a sleazy nightspot as Selleck follows Hutton to the diamonds. The Countess, it seems, has some unusual tastes for pain and violence.

It is unlikely that a more skilled actress could have done more with the part as written, but as the countess, Hutton is totally unbelievable with her Germanic accent and evil habits. As the girlfriend, Seymour is wasted. Her role is basically to standy-by as Selleck races about trying to grab the diamonds and run.

Selleck's main adversary is not the Countess, but the cop who has put him up to it. Bob Hoskins as the dick is every bit as nasty here as he was in "The Long Good Friday," and is the only actor who brings any life to the film.

As Lassiter, Selleck has little range and relies basically on a smile and grimace to get by. The best thing about Selleck here is his clothes. Costumes by Barbara Lane are lush and Selleck, if anything, can wear clothes well.

What's missing in "Lassiter" is a sense of menace. In going for the glossy exterior, director Roger Young has created a cluttered lifeless film, full of exaggerated colors and textural inconsistencies. Script by David Taylor is loaded with phony dialog and a plot that is improbable without being surprising. — *Jagr.*

The Last Hunter
(ITALIAN-COLOR)

A World Northal release of a Flora Film-Gico Cinematografica production. Produced by Gianfranco Couyoumdjian. Directed by Anthony M. Dawson (Antonio Margheriti). Features entire cast. Screenplay, Dardano Sacchetti, from story by Couyoumdjian; camera (Technicolor), Riccardo Pallottini; editor, Alberto Moriani; music, Franco Micalizzi; sound, Alfonso Montesanti; assistant director, Edoardo Margheriti; production manager, Pasquale Vannini; production design-costumes, Bartolomeo Scavia; makeup, Massimo Giustini. Reviewed at 42d St. Apollo theater, N.Y., Feb. 11, 1984. (No MPAA Rating). Running time: 96 MINS.
Capt. Harry Morris ....David Warbeck
Jane Foster ....Tisa Farrow
Sgt. George Washington.........Tony King
Carlos ....Bobby Rhodes
Carol ....Margit Evelyn Newton
Major Cash ....John Steiner
Bartender.....................Alan Collins

"The Last Hunter" is an imitative Italian action film made in 1980. Its original title, "Hunter Of The Apocalypse," points more exactly at the picture's origins, lifting liberally for visual images and situations from both "The Deer Hunter" and "Apocalypse Now," but outfitted with a different (and rather dull) storyline to avoid accusations of plagiarism.

Set in Vietnam in 1973, tale has Capt. Henry Morris (David Warbeck) on a mission to destroy a Vietcong radio transmitter which is sending demoralizing messages to the Yankee troops. He's aided on the way by a ragtag group including war correspondent-cont-photographer Jane Foster (Tisa Farrow), minority GIs Sgt. George Washington (Tony King) and Carlos (Bobby Rhodes) as well as a bitter and nutty Major Cash (gueststar John Steiner), last-named filling the slot

Robert Duvall occupied in "Apocalypse Now."

Payoff has most of the players sent to the Happy Hunting Ground by the time Jane helps Morris escape from watery tiger cages (a la "The Deer Hunter") to conveniently find the transmitter nearby. Gimmicky resolution consists of Morris' best friend's girlfriend Carol (Margit Evelyn Newton) turning out to be the nasty voice of Ho Chi Minh trying to weaken our boys' fighting resolve.

Since his best friend committed suicide in a Saigon brothel at the beginning of the film by revolver (the Christopher Walken "Deer Hunter" role), finale is almost like bringing Meryl Streep in as the surprise villain. The same year, Newton played the uninhibited and undefeatable heroine in another European picture derived from these (and other) U.S. hits, "Apocalipsis Canibal."

"Last Hunter" is dull between its outbursts of action scenes. As in an earlier film directed by Antonio Margheriti, "Killer Fish," the model explosions are very good, mixed in with full-scale special effects work. Pic includes gratuitous, exaggerated gore effects as well.

Acting is fine, with British thesp David Warbeck serving well as Margheriti's gung-ho adventure hero (he represents the Italian helmer's cutrate version of Harrison Ford, having gone on to star in two imitations of "Raiders Of The Lost Ark," for Margheriti since "Hunter" was made).

Farrow is a game trouper, willing to get her hair mussed, but one wonders why Woody Allen doesn't give her a Stateside assignment alongside her sister, Mia, to save her from being typecast as an Italian B-movie denizen. —*Lor.*

The City Girl
(COLOR)

Intimate romance could click.

Hollywood, Feb. 1.
A Moon Pictures presentation. Produced, directed by Martha Coolidge. Executive producer, Peter Bogdanovich. Features entire cast. Screenplay, Judith Tompson, Leonard-John Gates, based on a story by John MacDonald, Coolidge; camera (Deluxe color), Daniel Hainey; music, Scott Wilk, Marc Levinthal; editors, Linda Leeds, Eva Gardos; art direction, Ninkey Dalton; set decoration, Elise Rowland; sound, Dan Latour; associate producer, Colleen Camp; assistant directors, Ray Elias, Robert Appelby. Reviewed at the Glen Glenn Sound Screening Room, L.A., Feb. 1, 1984. (No MPAA rating.) Running time: 85 MINS.
Anne ....Laura Harrington
Joey ....Joe Mastroianni
Gracie ....Carole McGill
Tim ....Peter Riegert
Steve ....Jim Carrington
The Stripper ....Lawrence Phillips
Monica ....Geraldine Baron
Rose ....Colleen Camp
Sugar....................Janice Greene
Ira.......................Rosanne Katon

Martha Coolidge's "The City Girl," which had its world premiere at the Berlin Film Festival Feb. 17, is actually a predecessor to the same director's 1983 indie hit, "Valley Girl." Begun in January, 1981 on Toronto locations, pic shut down the following month due to financial problems, only to have completed lensing a year later when Peter Bogdanovich came abroad as exec producer. Both pics are tales of mismatched romances, but are otherwise quite different in tone and intent, as the new film reps a hardnosed, if frequently funny, look at a young woman's attempt to forge a career and self-esteem. Without a U.S. distrib as yet, this is a small, intimate item which could develop a following a la John Sayles' pictures.

At heart, film is about the difficulty of finding a balance between career and personal relationships, with significant attention to the problem of establishing any genuinely satisfying romantic or sexual liaisons. Lead character of Anne is a young lady who, in an awfully serious way, is trying to get a foot up as a professional photographer. Joey, her sympathetic but very straight boyfriend, indulges her to a point but would rather have her fill the conventional woman's role, something it's obvious she won't do.

After a disastrous dinner for a business acquaintance of Joey's, to which Anne stupidly brings two floozies, the couple splits up, freeing Anne to pursue some of her fantasies. A backstage tryst with a male stripper doesn't live up to the heady buildup, an attempt at a wild night with two men ends in shambles, and Anne quickly finds herself in over her head when a local pimp she's been discreetly photographing trashes her apartment and is later killed by the girl she's been sheltering.

Most bracing aspect of Coolidge's treatment of the relatively plain material is her rigorously objective, unindulgent perspective. Much of Anne's behavior is rude and self-centered, and where her treatment of Joey is concerned, she's clearly in the wrong. One can easily imagine a different rendering of the material which would apologize for her misdeeds, but Coolidge's tough, clear-eyed view allows everything to appear for what it is.

In line with the director's approach, Laura Harrington, who plays Anne, and was previously seen as the teenage girl in "The Dark End Of The Street," does not sentimentalize her character, but engages the interest sufficiently to pull the viewer along with her many ups and downs. It's one of the more realistic and believable portraits of a modern woman to have been seen onscreen of late.

Supporting cast is full of colorful characters who supply the film with a good deal of exoticism and humor. Peter Riegert is outstandingly droll as a fellow who vies for Anne's favors at a party with self-styled cowboy Jim Carrington; their simultaneous seduction of her is a slow-burn comic gem. Carole McGill and Janice Green are lively and vulgar as the lowlifes, Lawrence Phillips is excellent as the striptease artist, while Colleen Camp, who is also billed as associate producer, knocks everyone else off the screen and eats them alive in her hilarious, all-too-brief appearance.

Pic does become a bit melodramatic toward the end with the pimp's violent death, and wrap-up is rather pat in a way not entirely consistent with the rough edges exposed up until then (final scene has characters going to a cinema which happens to be showing Bogdanovich's "They All Laughed").

Lensing is on the grainy side, while mostly Toronto locations are fresh and helpfully forbidding, in the sense that they represent another obstacle to be surmounted by the characters. Soundtrack is imaginatively strewn with early 1980s pop and new wave tunes. —*Cart.*

Nocaut
(Knockout)
(MEXICAN-COLOR)

Mexico City, Feb. 3.
Produced by Kinam Coop, S.C.I. Stars Gonzalo Vega, Blanca Guerra. Directed by José Luis García Agraz. Screenplay, José Luis García Agraz; camera (color), Angel Goded; music, Gerardo Suárez; editor, Carlos García Agraz. Reviewed at Pecime screening room, Mexico City, Dec. 3, 1983. Released for opening of Cineteca Nacional, Feb. 5, 1984. Running time: 100 MINS.
Rodrigo ....Gonzalo Vega
Lilia ....Blanca Guerra
López ....Guillermo Orea
Saúl Beltrán ....Wolf Ruvinskis
El Sultán ....Roberto Cobo

"Nocaut," the first feature film by "cine independiente" director José Luis García Agraz, comes close to what the phonetically-spelled title implies: a knockout.

The pic begins with a murder commited by the hero, Rodrigo (Gonzalo Vega). But what drives a man to crime? The film unfolds in an extended series of flashbacks as the young boxer slowly enters the world of professional boxing, and also the sordid world of crime that accompanies it.

Before he knows it, he is in over his head and can't get out, as he begins taking dives in the ring and becomes a hired thug to a Mafia boss. He strives for lost innocence, as he is on the run, wondering what has gone wrong with his life.

The story is not a new one by any means, but it is well told in a series of short scenes and abrupt cuts covering the main events in Rodrigo's life.

This is not another "Rocky," the underdog who achieves a personal victory. Rather it is the tale of a loser whose only crime lay in trying to make something out of his life, yet did not possess the foresight to note the danger signs as they appeared.

The acting is strong and the story moves briskly along.

With "Nocaut," García Agraz has established himself as a force in Mexican cinema showing that perhaps the independent cinema movement may point out new directions for Mexican commercial efforts. —*Lent.*

Gwendoline
(FRENCH-COLOR)

Paris, Feb. 16.

Parafrance release (S. Goldwyn in U.S.) of a Parafrance/Films del l'Alma/G.P.F.I. coproduction. Produced by Jean-Claude Fleury. Written and directed by Just Jaeckin, inspired by the comic strip by John Wilie. Camera, (color), André Domage; production designer and artistic director, Francoise Deleu; art director, André Guerin; makeup, Reiko Kruk, Dominique Colladant; costumes, Daniel Elis; editor, Michele Boehm; sound, Rene Levert, Michele Amsellem; music, Pierre Bachelet; production manager, Pierre Gauchet. Reviewed at the Marignan-Concorde theatre, Paris, Feb. 15, 1984. Running time: 102 MINS.

Gwendoline .... Tawny Kitaen
Willard .... Brent Huff
Beth .... Zabou
The Queen .... Bernadette Lafont
D'Arcy .... Jean Rougerie

Despite its vaunted source material and early promotional promise, "Gwendoline" is nothing to salivate about. Just Jaeckin's fantasy adventure about a lovely young innocent out in the cruel world has finally little to do with the once-scandalous 1930's erotic comic strip by John Wilie, in which the chaste but voluptuous young thing was continually being tied and chained and submitted to a variety of titilating punishments. If Jaeckin's heroine is trussed, it's only so she won't get away.

Nor is the screen Gwendoline the sort whose mere carnal presence is an affront to prudery and an incitation to dirty thoughts. California-born newcomer Tawny Kitaen (her real name!) is attractive enough and her natural gifts are amply displayed, but she's not the potential sex-bomb-without-a-fuse that the cartoon suggests. A cloistered virgin at first, Kitean develops conventionally, learning about love and budding to womanhood when the chips are down and her lover's life at stake.

The standardization of the original strip is also reflected in Jaeckin's introduction of a positive male figure: a macho adventurer who becomes the heroine's reluctant guide and protector and finally falls for her charms and affection. Kansas-born Brent Huff portrays the part as an Indiana Jones of fallible charm.

As for the original Gwendoline's guardian angel, U-69 (as much a sight for sore eyes as Gwen), she here become's the heroine's faithful sidekick, Beth, played with tomboyish perk and impertinence by local newcomer Zabou (not her real name!).

Finally Jaeckin's film is a falsely erotic live-action cartoon blending old and new recipes in camp romance, suggesting recasts of "Raiders of the Lost Ark," "Barbarella" and "Atlantis, the Lost Continent." In Jaeckin's screenplay, Kitaen leaves her Paris convent and journeys to the Far East in search of her entymologist father, who had disappeared while hunting a rare butterfly. In the company of Huff and Zabou, her adventures involve escape from leering Chinamen, cannibalistic savages, toxic sandstorms, and, as piece de resistance, a subterranean desert empire ruled by a diabolic Amazon (Bernadette Lafont).

Latter scenes are fitted out with extravagant studio sets and kinky costumes, though the more enjoyable scenes come early, when the charm works essentially through its three spirited young players and relatively relaxed direction.

A good majority of the film's $5,000,000 budget was reportedly supplied by early foreign sales. Young audiences may go for it, though "Gwendoline" will no doubt disappoint aficionados of the comic strip and sexual bondage freaks. France's state review board put no age restrictions on the opus.
— *Len.*

Wombling Free
(BRITISH-COLOR)

A Satori Entertainment release of an Ian Shand production for Rank Film Distributors. Produced by Ian Shand. Directed by Lionel Jeffries. Stars David Tomlinson, Frances De La Tour. Screenplay, Jeffries, based on book and BBC tv series by Elizabeth Beresford; camera (Rank color), Alan Hume; editor, Peter Tanner; music & songs, Mike Batt; sound, Cyril Collick; assistant director, Ray Frift; production supervisor, Geoffrey Haine; art direction, Jack Shampan; choreography, Eleanor Fazan; special effects, Bill Warrington, Brian Smithies; Womble heads' design, Smithies. Reviewed at Magno Preview 9 screening room, N.Y., Feb. 16, 1984. (No MPAA Rating). Running time: 96 MINS.

Roland Frogmorton ...... David Tomlinson
Julia Frogmorton ..... Frances De La Tour
Kim Frogmorton .... Bonnie Langford
Arnold Takahasi .... Bernard Spear
Doris Takahasi .... Yasuko Nagazumi
Surveyor .... John Junkin
Ernest .... Reg Lye

As the Wombles: Kenny Baker, Jack Purvis, Marcus Powell, Sadie Corre, Eileen Baker, John Lummiss, Brian Jones, Albert Wilkinson.

Voices of the Wombles by: Lionel Jeffries, David Jason, Janet Brown, Jon Pertwee, John Graham.

Made in Britain in 1977 as a feature spinoff of a popular BBC tv series, "Wombling Free" is an occasionally amusing but tiresome comedy for children. Featuring

The Wombles, furry creatures (portrayed by men in bulky costumes rather than puppetry or animation) responsible for literally cleaning up mankind's mess (litter) on Earth, picture is vaguely reminiscent of the Muppets' big-screen incarnations, but lacks the budget, wit and proper format to succeed.

Its belated domestic release (taking almost as long as The Smurfs' animated film to get here) augurs weak results this Easter, with film better suited to cable-tv broadcast.

Director Lionel Jeffries' own screenplay is overly episodic, shifting disconcertingly between the project's three types of footage: Wombles alone on screen (giving off a parallel-world aura somewhere between Gerry Anderson's strange "Thunderbirds" puppets and Jim Henson/Frank Oz's "The Dark Crystal" creations), Wombles plus people (The Muppets' format) and prosaic scenes of humans alone, overacting and pulling faces in kiddie film fashion.

Minor plotline has British Wombles, localed from Wimbledon to Scotland, suddenly becoming visible to humans, beginning with cute Kim (Bonnie Langford) who believe they exist. Later, Kim's parents (Frances De La Tour and David Tomlinson) also believe and can see the furry critters, who supposedly have been cleaning up after man, starting with the discarded apple core in the Garden Of Eden.

Non-adventures here include avoidance of having their Wimbledon burrow plowed under by a construction project, several amateurish, low-budget musical production numbers and a final "Keep Britain Tidy" rally for humans which culminates with children (a la "Pied Piper Of Hamelin") coming from everywhere to aid the Wombles in their chores.

Jeffries' attempts to shoehorn into the film messages about the oil shortage, anti-pollution sentiments and even a trite lament about the death of Britain's film theaters don't work. With Bernard Spear's dialect and jokes as the Frogmorton's Japanese neighbor (he makes Buddy Hackett and Jerry Lewis's oriental roles seem almost subtle by comparison), the film lapses into very poor taste.

The other lead actors are effective, Tomlinson even given a wise crack about "Mary Poppins" (one of his best screen roles) and tv comedienne De La Tour is a distinctive-looking talent. Among the Wombles (drolly voiced by Jeffries and others), Kenny Baker (R2-D2 in "Star Wars") as the littlest one, Bungo, is expressive and perky, skipping around in his bulky suit. Tech credits are fine. —*Lor.*

Les Tricheurs
(The Cheaters)
(FRENCH-W. GERMAN-COLOR)

Paris, Feb. 14.

Films Galatée release of a Films du Losange/FR3/Bioskop Films (Munich) coproduction. Produced by Margaret Menegoz. Stars Jacques Dutronc, Bulle Ogier. Directed by Barbet Schroeder. Screenplay, Schroeder, Pascal Bonitzer, Steve Baes; camera (color), Robby Muller; music, Peer Raben; art director, Maria Jose Branco; sound, Jean-Paul Mugel; editor, Denise de Casabianca; costumes, Catherine Meurice, Isabel Branco; executive producer Paolo Branco. Reviewed at the Gaumont Colisee Theater, Paris, Feb. 13, 1984. Running time: 94 MINS.

Elric .... Jacques Dutronc
Suzie .... Bulle Ogier
Jorg .... Kurt Raab
Toni .... Virgilio Teixeira
Casino manager .... Steve Baes
Aldo .... Claus-Dieter Reents
Boudha .... Karl Wallenstein
Engineer .... Robby Muller

Barbet Schroeder's "Les Tricheurs" is a slick but empty drama about gambling neurotics and a clever electronic swindle they engineer at the roulette wheel. Steve Baes, a professional habitue of international casinos, was the inspiration for many of the film's incidents and details and also worked on the screenplay, as did local critic-scripter Pascal Bonitzer.

Jacques Dutronc is a roulette addict who haunts the casino in Madeira and crosses the path of Bulle Ogier, who catches his eye because she happens to have the number "7" embossed on her shirt, and because the time of this encounter is 7:07. He asks her to accompany him to the game table for a week as a good luck charm and talks himself into believing she can wean him from his obsession.

Naturally, the inverse happens: Ogier herself gets the bug and cannot tear herself away from the casino. Their alliance meets an obstacle in the person of an even crazier gambler, Kurt Raab, a professional cheat. He wheedles Dutronc into joining his cause, which brings about a split between Dutronc and Ogier. The two men leave on an international round of casinos, cashing in everywhere with their illicit gimmicks.

But Dutronc and Ogier meet again months later in another casino and this time become inseparable. Hoping to win big enough to buy a chateau in Switzerland and retire there with Ogier, Dutronc hits on a scheme to cheat at the roulette wheel with a remote-controlled ball. The operation succeeds and the couple take off to Annecy to get their chateau. But in the meantime a new casino has opened in the vicinity.

The facile suspense of the casino sequences give the story a forward movement and tension, but Schroeder is unable to give any depth to his main characters, precisely because they are hollow puppets from the start and remain so in Dutronc and Ogier's glazed performances. Only Raab suggests the dizzy pinball soullessness of the inveterate gambler. Through him, the script makes some of its more observant dramatic points about its oft-treated subject matter.

Film is technically firstrate, and lenser Robby Muller does a cameo as the electronic wiz who manufactures the rigged roulette ball. It will need careful handling for specialized markets. — *Len.*

Victoria
(Victory)
(SPANISH-COLOR)

Madrid, Jan. 30.

A Tabaré, S.A. production. Directed by Antoni Ribas. Features entire cast. Screenplay, Ribas, Miquel Sanz; camera (Eastmancolor) Andreu Berenguer; editor Ramón Quadreny; assistant editors Teresa Alcocer, Margarida Bernet, Emilio Ortiz; sets, Jordi Berenguer; costumes, Consol Tura; exec producer, Jaume Behar; associate producer, Ferrán Repiso; historical coordinator, Miquel Sanz; music composition and arrangements, Manuel Valls Gorina; music conducted by Antoni Ros Marbá; assistant director, Jaume Santacana. Reviewed at Cine Proyecciones, Madrid, Jan. 30, '84. Running time: 142 MINS.

Lieutenant Rodriguez Haro . Helmut Berger
Jaume Canals............Xabier Elorriaga
Maria Aliaga ....Norma Duval
Lieutenant Colonel Bruguete.....Craig Hill
Commissaire Bravo Portillo Pau Garsaball
Palmira ....Carme Elias
Also: Artur Costa, Eva Cobo, Alfred Luchetti, Marta Sadurni, Josep Maria Angelat, Clotilde Duclos, Patrick Honoré, Joan Monleón, Jesús Guzmán, Stefano Palatchi, Agusti Ros, Santiago Maldonado, Xavier Palmada, Alfons Guirao, with cameo performances by Teresa Gimpera, Francisco Rabal, Antoni Ros Marba, Antoni Ribas.

Catalan helmer Antoni Ribas, after completing his former "La Ciutat Cremada" (The Burned City) in 1974, has been working on the present epic for the past three years. After months of lensing, the outcome is film running more than seven hours, set during three days in June 1917. This item, subtitled "The Great Adventure Of A People," is the first third. The first and second thirds of the historical epic are unspooling in two different theaters in Barcelona.

Ribas has aimed at recreating the political, social, military and intellectual atmosphere of that key year in Spanish history and he does this admirably. The production values are superb, Andreu Berenguer's splendid camerawork is crisp and gripping, the music has a majestic sweep suitable to the grandeur of the story, sets and costumes are a delight to see, and Ribas' imaginative direction takes full advantage of every situation. Occasional touches of humor lighten a well-paced script.

The political situation of Spain, especially in Cataluña province, around Barcelona, was particularly confusing in 1917, with the Alfon-

sine monarchy already tottering; strong labor union movements urging that the Russian revolution be seconded in Spain to topple capitalism and the bourgeois world; the military threatened by a schism; anarchists taking violent actions against the Establishment, and pro-Allied and pro-Axis sympathizers at each others' throats constantly.

Ribas captures this volatile world as he lurches back and forth between the salons of high society, the Montjuich barracks, and the prostitution-infested alleys of the Barrio Chino. As a vehicle, he uses two chief protagonists, a militant labor agitator, well played by the sympathetic Xabier Elorriaga, and a stiff, but wavering lieutenant, finely thesped by Helmut Berger.

At times the potpourri of interests, strategems and plottings becomes so thick that it is difficult to follow; but even those who may miss an occasional point are immediately caught up again by some scene of Barcelona low life, or an opera in the Liceo interrupted by the shouts of the factions, or naughty period musical numbers, or an occasional sex scene, often handled in a style reminiscent of pre-war Berlin expressionism. Admittedly the audience never gets very deeply into any of the characters, but the spectacle sweeps them along. With a few talky exceptions, near the close of the film, audience interest is maintained.

In its Madrid preem, dubbed into Castilian, item was received somewhat coolly. Pic might rack up some theatrical sales outside Spain, but its main appeal will probably be as a tv series. Some of the most savory scenes might run into censorship problems in more conservative countries. — *Besa.*

Motel
(MEXICAN-COLOR)

Mexico City, Feb. 2.

Produced by Abraham Cherem, Cherem & Mandoki, S.A. de C.V. Stars Blanca Guerra, José Alsonso. Directed by Luis Mandoki. Screenplay: Abraham Cherem, Jordi Arenas; camera (color), Miguel Garzón; music, Eduardo Diazmuñoz G.; editor, Francisco Chiu; Reviewed at Pecime screening room, Mexico City, Nov. 16, 1983. Released for the opening of the Cineteca Nacional, Feb. 4, 1984. Running time: 110 MINS.

Marta.......................Blanca Guena
Andrés Camargo ....José Alonso
Julian Vargas ....Salvador Sánchez
Carolina Lopez ....Carmelita González
Córdova ....Ignacio Retes
Andrés Pérez ....Salvador Garcini

From the opening minutes of "Motel," the audience realizes it is a murder mystery, but director Luis Mandoki is not interested in suspense.

It is rather the mediocre story of motel managers Marta (Blanca Guerra) and Andrés (José Alonso)

and how the dissatisfaction with their live-together relationship draws them into crime.

One knows in advance — through unchronological editing — who is killed and why. The heroes are even seen committing the act.

The film is filled with misogynistic attitudes and promotes an anachronistic view of women. The female murder victim deserves to die merely because she is a prattling old lady who doesn't know when to keep her mouth shut. Though the tension is carefully maintained, the plot contains several holes.

Although Mandoki's first feature is not completely satisfactory, its theme will attract a certain audience, especially with its overlong and dramatic sex scene which shows that there's nothing like a bloody murder to put some spark into your sex life. — *Lent.*

I Timi Tis Agapis
(The Price of Love)
(GREEK-COLOR)

Athens, Feb. 21.

An Andromeda Film co-production with the Greek Film Centre and the Greek Radio Television Channel I. Written and directed by Tonia Marketaki. Stars Anny Loulou, Toula Stathopoulou, Stratis Tsopanellis, Spyros Antiochos, George Ayovlasitis, Spyros Pantelios. Camera (color), Stavros Hassapis; music, Heleni Karaendrou; sets and costumes, George Patsas; editor, George Korras; singer of title song, Demetra Galani. Reviewed at the Opera Cinema, Athens, Feb. 19, 1984. Running time: 115 MINS.

This is the second picture written and directed by Tonia Marketaki who had indicated in her first picture, "John The Violent" (a prize winner at the 1973 Thessaloniki Film Fest), that she was a skillful and talented filmmaker kept from local production only by lack of funds.

This film is one of the best pictures of recent years and establishes her as one of Greece's top helmers. She does a professional job in telling a simple love story with realism and cinematic excellence through attention to detail, and good lensing and acting. The picture has very good prospects locally and potential sales abroad. It should also be heard from at festivals.

Based on the novel, "The Honour And The Money," by Constantine Theotokis, the story is set on Corfu island early in this century with two women as its central characters. Mother Epistimi and daughter Rene — Epistimi with three more children besides the elder daughter, and a drunkard husband — work in a factory to support the family. Andreas, a young man from a good but impoverished family falls in love with Rene and wants to marry her. Epistimi offers him half the amount he asks

as a dowry. Andreas wanted it to pay off the mortgage of his paternal house. As Epistimi refuses to give him what he asks, he persuades Rene to follow him, promising to marry her later.

Things, however, take a bad turn for the young lovers. Andreas losses the support of his political friends and cannot earn money as a smuggler. He asks a greater amount from Epistimi to save his house and marry Rene. Epistimi refuses again, but when she learns that her daughter is with child abandoned by her lover, she hits Andreas, throwing her keys at the same time to him to get all her possessions. However, Rene is the one who refuses now to marry him. Disgusted by his behaviour she prefers to go to Athens, where nobody knows her, to work and support her child.

Though the pace limps in the first part, the film comes across beautifully, shot on authentic backgrounds which are visually captivating. Marketaki respected the novel's period setting and its dramatic structure, paying greater attention to detail not only in prevailing at the time. While she had no obvious intentions of raising social or political issues, several emerged from the right rendering of this love drama.

Anny Loulou gives a sensitive performance as Rene and Toula Stathopoućou as Epistimi is particularly remarkable. Color camera work by Stavros Hassapis is frequently striking, making the Corfu scenery part of the plot. The pic is effectively scored by Heleni Karaendrou. All other technical credits are good. — *Rena.*

Love Streams
(U.S.-COLOR)

Winner from John Cassavetes

Berlin, Feb. 26.

An MGM/UA Entertainment and Cannon Group release of a Cannon Film Production. Produced by Menahem Golan and Yoram Globus, executive producer, Al Ruban. Directed by John Cassavetes. Features entire cast. Screenplay, Cassavetes, Ted Allan, based on the play by Allan; camera (Metrocolor), Ruban; editor, Georg Villasenor; music, Bo Harwood. Reviewed at the Berlin Film Festival (competing), Feb. 26, 1984. Running time: **136 MINS.**

Sarah Lawson	Gena Rowlands
Robert Harmon	John Cassavetes
Susan	Diahnne Abbott
Jack Lawson	Seymour Cassel
Margarita	Margaret Abbott
Albie Swanson	Jakob Shaw
Debbie Lawson	Risa Blewitt
Ken	John Roselius
Agnes Swanson	Michelle Conaway
Eddy Swanson	Eddy Donno

Closing film at the Berlin Film Festival, John Cassavetes' "Love Streams" (note: picture won the Golden Bear) shapes up as one of the filmmaker's best, both artistically and commercially, in some time. Emotionally potent, technically assured and often brilliantly insightful, the picture is guaranteed to generate controversy and critical wranglings. It's a work of great ambition and, as with his earlier films, likely to divide reviewers into two distinct camps, with no one sitting on the fence.

Reflecting the title, the plot begins with two separate flows. Robert Harmon (Cassavetes) is a successful writer from the Gay Talese school currently researching the subject of love for sale on a first-hand basis. Inter-cut is Sarah Lawson's (Gena Rowlands) story — an emotionally erratic woman proceeding through a divorce and custody case.

Despite the seeming incompatibility of their two worlds, one waits and wonders how the two principals will eventually meet. When Sarah and her mountain of luggage arrive at Robert's door, the assumption initially is to take her as a former wife. Only later do we learn that they are brother and sister. Still, before these two currents converge, there's considerable emotional terrain to be explored. Robert is revealed as a pushy, unpleasant sort who nonetheless has his better points.

Presumably, for his novel, he's turned his home into a girls' dorm which he surprisingly dismantles when a former wife arrives unannounced with their 8-year-old son. This circumstance opens up a vivid exploration of his efforts to be a real father countered by his strong instincts to maintain a certain lifestyle.

Sarah's situation is markedly different. Despite good intentions, she trips herself up during the custody hearing. Thus, her husband, Jack Lawson (Seymour Cassel) winds up victorious in court. The casting her suggests a continuation of Cassavetes' 1971 "Minnie And Moskowitz," although no direct antecedents are implied to that story.

So, while Robert takes his son to Las Vegas to effect a reconciliation of sorts, Sarah is in Europe attempting to sort out and carve out a new life for herself. Both efforts prove less than wholly successful with Robert concluding life is a "series of suicides, divorces and broken kids."

"Love Streams" is never as dour as Robert would like to picture it, thankfully. When the two characters are, in their opinion, at the end of their tether, they have each other. And in Cassavetes and Ted Allan's story, this allows them to perform some crazy, out-of-character actions which are indeed life-affirming.

One can nit-pick about the picture's length and use of repetition but these are minor points in the overall strength of the production. The dramatic rollercoaster ride of frightening and funny moments leave little room for indifference. Cassavetes' films will never attract enormous numbers but there's no reason this film cannot surpass the excellent returns of "A Woman Under The Influence" with proper marketing of critical reviews and the exploitation of powerful word-of-mouth response.

Fears that Cassavetes would be swallowed up and spit up unrecognizable by the Cannon Group simply are untrue. The film bears his unique signature of visceral drama with extra ordinary, natural performances and unfussy, vivid images. "Love Streams" is a considerable artistic achievement from the Cassavetes' canon. —*Klad.*

The Black Cat
(ITALIAN-COLOR)

A World Northal release of a Selenia Cinematografica production. Produced by Giulio Sbarigia. Directed by Lucio Fulci. Features entire cast. Screenplay, Biagio Proietti, Fulci, from story by Proietti, based on story by Edgar Alian Poe; camera (Technovision, Eastmancolor), Sergio Salvati; editor, Vincenzo Tomassi; music, Pino Donaggio; sound, Ugo Celani; assistant director, Victor Tourjansky; second unit director, Roberto Giandalia; stunt coordinator, Nazzareno Cardinali; makeup, Franco di Girolamo; special effects, Paolo Ricci; dubbing editor, Nick Alexander. Reviewed at 42d St. Apollo Theater, N.Y., Feb. 11, 1984. (MPAA Rating: R). Running time: **91 MINS.**

Mr. Miles	Patrick Magee
Jill Travers	Mimsy Farmer
Inspector Gorley	David Warbeck
Policeman	Al Cliver
Mrs. Grayson	Dagmar Lassander
Inspector Flynn	Geoffrey Copleston
Maureen	Daniela Dorio

Filmed in 1980 on British locations and Rome studio interiors, "The Black Cat" is a perfunctory supernatural horror film, representing a respite from prolific Italian director Lucio Fulci's recent zombie epics. Belated domestic release augurs weak b.o. performance in a depressed horror film market.

Not related to several earlier films of this title, including the well-remembered Bela Lugosi-Boris Karloff opus of 1934, "Black Cat" toplines the late Patrick Magee as Mr. Miles, an experimenter in the paranormal who tries to tape record messages (from crypts and gravesides) from the dead.

As a series of mysterious deaths occur in his small British village, the police, led by Scotland Yard inspector Gorley (David Warbeck) sent in to help the locals, are stymied, while a visiting American photographer Jill Travers (Mimsy Farmer) obtains evidence which points towards Miles' cat as the culprit.

Script uses a supernatural crutch to explain how a cat could plan and execute crimes seemingly requiring human intelligence, with Miles and his cat fighting for control in a mutually mesmerizing power struggle.

Director Fulci overuses the technique of tight closeups of the characters' (and cat's) eyes, while otherwise capturing some effective foggy night atmosphere shots and wideangle cat's point-of-view photography. The film draws on motifs from several Edgar Allan Poe stories, including a trite ironical climax that is virtually identical to the payoff scene in Fulci's 1976 picture "Seven Black Notes" (released in the U.S. in 1979 as "The Psychic"). Acting here, including one of Magee's last roles, is subpar, not helped by the approximate post-synched dialog. — *Lor.*

Splash
(COLOR)

Romantic mermaid bodes a comedy hit.

Hollywood, Feb. 17.

A Touchstone Films presentation of a Buena Vista release. Produced by Brian Grazer. Executive producer, John Lenox. Directed by Ron Howard. Features entire cast. Screenplay, Lowell Ganz, Babaloo Mandel, Bruce Jay Friedman, from a screen story by Friedman based on a story by Grazer. Camera (Technicolor), Don Peterman; editors, Daniel P. Hanley, Michael Hill; music, Lee Holdridge; production design, Jack T. Collis; art director, John B. Mansbridge; set decoration, Philip Smith, Norman Rockett; costume design, May Routh; sound, Richard S. Church; swimming choreographer, Mike Nomad; special visual effects supervisor, Mitch Suskin; mermaid design, Robert Short; underwater camera, Jordan Klein; assistant director, Jan. R. Lloyd. Reviewed at Goldwyn Theater, Hollywood, Feb. 17, 1984. (MPAA Rating: PG). Running time: **111 MINS.**

Allen Bauer	Tom Hanks
Madison	Daryl Hannah
Freddie Bauer	John Candy
Walter Kornbluth	Eugene Levy
Mrs. Stimler	Dody Goodman
Mr. Buyrite	Shecky Greene
Dr. Ross	Richard B. Shull

Touchstone Films, Walt Disney Prods.' springboard to broader audience appeal, takes the plunge with surprisingly charming mermaid yarn notable for winning suspension of disbelief and fetching by-play between Daryl Hannah and Tom Hanks. Opening wide (700 houses), the $11,000,000, PG-rated pic contains the nice, light kick of naughty family entertainment to give "Splash" allure to both traditional Disney patrons and the young adult spectrum that Touchstone was designed to attract.

Although film is a bit uneven, production benefits from a tasty look, an airy tone, and a delectable, unblemished performance from Hannah who couldn't be better cast if she were Neptune's daughter incarnate. Hanks, as a Gotham bachelor in search of love, makes a fine leap from sitcom land, and John Candy as an older playboy brother who has a penchant for looking up girls' dresses, is a marvelous foil.

Producer Brian Grazer and director Ron Howard, abetted by Don Peterman's New York and Bahamas lensing, achieve a sense of the same crispness associated with their last outing, "Night Shift." "Splash," which took four years to get off the ground through two studio turnarounds (one at UA, another at the Ladd Co.), is essentially a clever variation on Disney's old "Herbie" and "Flubber" series. But for Disney, whose only affiliation with the credits is by way of the Buena Vista distrib tag, the veneer this time is definitely new for the company.

The mermaid's fin materializes into human legs when she leaves the water and, a la Lady Godiva, blonde tresses covering her breasts, Hannah greets the city of New York via a looming POV of her naked derriere as she approaches a group of goggle-eyed tourists at the Statue of Liberfty. In short order, unseen but made repeatedly clear, she and Hanks hit the sack. Candy supplies a lot of the film's bawdy touchstone, in language and deeds.

Such does Disney signal its stretch into post-family fare. No big deal except that it is for Disney, and the moments are humorously executed.

Screenplay by Lowell Ganz, Babaloo Mandel and Bruce Jay Friedman is marred by some glaring loopholes in its inner structure but story is a sweet takeoff on the innocence mythology and sensuality associated with mermaids. In fact, the concept of a tail becoming a pair of shapely legs goes all the way back to Annette Kellerman's mermaid figure in Universal's 1914, seven-reel fairy tale, "Neptune's Daughter." Interestingly, in that picture the mermaid is eventually trapped on land as a human woman — but not so in "Splash," where filmmakers take the ultimate dive and have Hannah and Hanks descend together into an acquatic womb.

(For mermaid movie buffs, MGM used the title "Neptune's Daughter" in 1949, with Esther Williams owning a swimming suit factory, and MGM followed up three years later with Williams playing the true-life story of Kellerman in "The Million Dollar Mermaid."

"Splash" goes a little crazy at the end, with a frantic military swooping down on the winsome Hannah. And Eugene Levy's obsessed scientist is too noisy a performance for the film's romantic tone. Had helmer Howard kept Levy in check, anticipating Levy's softer characterization at the end, film's evenness of tone would have been greatly enhanced. Candy's comic performance, on the other hand, is a terrific, less stressful anchor to the proceedings.

Film's unqualified funny scene belongs to Hannah, voraciously gnawing through big lobster shell in a posh Gotham restaurant. Hannah's transformation on land when subjected to salt water works up bright surprises. Hanks' desperate vulnerability is on the mark, and the film's opening minutes, in a gauzy black and white, flashback cruise ship sequence, give the story a classy launching. —*Loyn.*

Le Garde du Corps
(The Bodyguard)
(FRENCH-COLOR)

Paris, Feb. 21.

UGC release of a Uranium Films/UGC-Top No. 1/Yvon Guezel coproduction. Produced by Dany Cohen, Georges Glass and Yvon Guezel. Stars Jane Birkin, Gérard Jugnot, Sami Frey. Directed by François Leterrier. Screenplay, Letterier and Didier Kaminka, from an original idea by Yves Kermorvan. Camera (color), Eduardo Serra; art director, Loula Morin; editor, Claudine Bouché; production manager, Alain Darbon. Reviewed at the U.G.C. Normandie theater, Paris, Feb. 20, 1984. Running time: 100 MINS.
Barbara ....Jane Birkin
Paul.........................Gérard Jugnot
Julien ....Sami Frey
André....................Didier Kaminka
Claudine ....Nicole Jamet
Yvette..................Jacqueline Doyen
Jocelyne ....Evelyne Didi

"Le Garde du Corps" is a comic variation on a suspense situation used by Alfred Hitchcock in "Suspicion." Has a young woman in fact married a man who intends to do away with her?

In François Leterrier's comedy the question isn't asked by the bride (Jane Birkin), deliciously oblivious to anything but the charm of her soft-voiced husband (Sami Frey), but by Birkin's jilted suitor (Gerard Jugnot), who learns that Frey's two previous wives died in curious accidents and that the

disconsolate husband collected on handsome insurance policies.

So Jugnot decides to trail the couple on their honeymoon and protect his true love from the possible machinations of her irresistible spouse.

Scripters Leterrier and Didier Kaminka spoil much of the fun by tipping the viewer off early to the fact that Frey is indeed a villain, and the latter part of the story is played mostly for suspense as he plots to do away with both Jugnot and Birkin in a rigged car accident.

Birkin, Frey and Jugnot (a comic from the cafe-theater scene) form a charmingly disparate trio and much of the story is set in touristy Morocco, but this is mostly routine commercial fodder for local tastes. —*Len.*

This Is Spinal Tap
(COLOR)

Amusing spoof of heavy metal bands, but b.o. outlook spotty.

Hollywood, Feb. 28.

An Embassy release of a Spinal Tap production. Produced by Karen Murphy. Directed by Rob Reiner. Screenplay, music lyrics, Christopher Guest, Michael McKean, Harry Shearer, Reiner. Camera (CFI color), Peter Smokler; supervising film editor, Robert Leighton; editors, Kent Beyda, Kim Secrist; production design, Dryan Jones; costume stylist, Renee Johnston; sound (Dolby), Bob Eber; assistant director, Donald Newman. Reviewed at Deluxe Laboratories, L.A., Feb. 27, 1984. (MPAA Rating: R.) Running time: 82 MINS.
Marty DiBergi ....Rob Reiner
David St. Hubbins ....Michael McKean
Nigel Tufnel ....Christopher Guest
Derek Smalls ....Harry Shearer
Mick Shrimpton...............R.J. Parnell
Viv Savage....................David Kaff
Ian Faith ....Tony Hendra
Tommy Pischedda ....Bruno Kirby
Jeanine Pettibone ....June Chadwick
Bobbi Flekman ....Fran Drescher
Belinda ....Joyce Hyser
Cindy ....Vicki Blue
Guest appearances by: Paul Benedict, Patrick Macnee, Billy Crystal, Fred Willard, Ed Begley Jr., Zane Busby, Howard Hesseman, Paul Shaffer.

For music biz insiders, "This Is Spinal Tap" is a vastly amusing satire of heavy metal bands. For others, it might prove an amusing diversion, but that won't be enough to help at the b.o., where rock 'n' roll pics have dropped like flies in recent seasons.

Thanks to its tremendously knowing send-up of the posturing, attitudinizing and, in its view, overwhelming stupidity of heavy metal scene, "Spinal Tap" joins such previous pics as "American Hot Wax" and "Get Crazy" as films that were weak commercial entries but continue to be cherished by the cognescenti for their astute observations of music world realities and foibles.

Director Rob Reiner has cast himself as Marty DiBergi, a filmmaker intent upon covering the

long-awaited American return of the eponymous, 17-year-old British rock band. Pic then takes the form of a cinema-verité documentary, as Reiner includes inteviews with the fictional musicians, records their increasingly disastrous tour and captures the internal strife which leads to the separation of the group's two founders.

First shock to greet the band upon arrival in the U.S. is that its new album, "Smell The Glove," isn't in the stores, reason being that the album cover art has been judged sexist. Sporting enormous herpes sores, band leaders proceed with the tour despite ever-dwindling houses, reaching bottom when they find themselves booked at a Washington State Air Force base.

Group comes apart at the seams when the obnoxious girlfriend of one of the founders imposes herself as a manager, then books it as a supporting act to a puppet show at a Themeland amusement park.

Reiner and cowriters Christopher Guest, Michael McKean and Harry Shearer, who also appear as main band members, have had loads of fun with the material, creating mock 1960s tv videotapes of early gigs and filling the fringes with hilariously authentic music biz types, most notably Fran Drescher's label rep and Paul Shaffer's cameo as a Chicago promo man.

Lead players are right on target delivering pompous nonsense to Reiner's interviewer, and rough, from-the-hip shooting style perfectly fits the subject, even if, on a formal level, the real life docu approach is occasionally violated by cross cutting and other, more conventional, techniques.—*Cart.*

Harry & Son
(COLOR)

Newman bats 0 for 4.

Hollywood, Feb. 21.

An Orion release. Produced, screenplay by Paul Newman, Ronald L. Buck, suggested by the novel "A Lost King" by Raymond DeCapite. Directed by Newman. Stars Paul Newman, Robby Benson. Camera (Deluxe color), Donald McAlpine; editor, Dede Allen; music, Henry Mancini; production design, Henry Bumstead, set decoration, Don Ivey; sound, Howard Warren; associate producer, Malcolm R. Harding; assistant director, David McGiffert; second unit director, Stan Barrett; second unit camera, James Pergola. Reviewed at the Directors Guild Theatre, L.A., Feb. 21, 1984. (MPAA Rating: PG). Running time: 117 MINS.
Harry.......................Paul Newman
Howard.....................Robby Benson
Katie........................Ellen Barkin
Tom ....Wilford Brimley
Sally........................Judith Ivey
Raymond......................Ossie Davis
Siemanowski ...,.........Morgan Freeman
Nina...............Katherine Borowitz

Lawrence.................Maury Chaykin
Lilly ....Joanne Woodward

Fuzzily conceived and indecisively executed, "Harry & Son" represents a deeply disappointing return to the director's chair for Paul Newman. Cowritten and coproduced by the star as well, pic never makes up its mind who or what it wants to be about and, to compound the problem, never finds a proper style in which to convey the tragicomic events that transpire. Newman's name may help initially, but b.o. prospects appear fair at best.

Newman the director scored heavily on his first time out with "Rachel, Rachel" in 1968, and emerged honorably with both "Sometimes A Great Notion" and, on television, "The Shadow Box." This time, however, he has been unable to find any sort of dramatic focus, and film lurches uncomfortably between Newman and screen son Robby Benson on the one hand, and between life crisis analysis and offbeat behavioral antics on the other. Result is an underdeveloped hodgepodge which just doesn't play.

Opening scenes are perhaps the strongest, as Newman gets fired from his job as a Florida construction worker due to an ailment which momentarily blinds him. One might imagine that his union could help him find a desk or supervisory post somewhere, but in any event he comes up empty-handed, which gives him the excuse to goad his son into expanding his horizons beyond polishing cars and pretending to be a young Hemingway.

Emphasis then swings startlingly away from Newman over to Benson, whose motivations are impossible to decipher as he moves on to supposedly amusing but pointless stints as a box assembly line worker and an auto thief, just as he tries to patch things up with former g.f. Ellen Barkin, who's now pregnant by someone else.

Newman and brother Wilford Brimley halfheartedly try to convince Benson to enter Brimley's retail business, and the rumblings of a relationship between widower Newman and eccentric neighbor Joanne Woodward are hinted at, but basically it's a question of many situations introduced but none carried through to any meaningful resolution.

As presented, Newman's character is in a position either to give up on life or make a fresh start, and perhaps film's overriding frustration is that he goes nowhere. One is made to care for this man at the outset, but then he just mopes around and indulges in occasional irrational flareups while Benson pursues his inane interests. Structurally, it's a mess.

After such fine performances in

Newman's earlier directorial efforts, it's a surprise to see this much thespian talent go to waste here, but none of the cast members can do much with these underdrawn characters.

Nor has editor Dede Allen been able to impose much sense of order on the proceedings. Since pic never finds its bearings, it feels laborious and exhaustingly overlong at 117 minutes.

Without belaboring the point, this is an unfortunate misfire in which some potentially good ideas never took off. —*Cart.*

Emmanuelle 4
(FRENCH-COLOR)

Paris, Feb. 20.

AAA/Sedpa release of a Sara Films/ASP Productions coproduction. Produced by Alain Siritzky. Written and directed by Francis Leroy and Iris Letans, from a story by Emmanuelle Arsan. Camera, (color) Jean-François Gondre; music, Michel Magne; art director, Jean-Baptiste Poirot; editor, Hélène Plemiannikov; makeup, Josée de Luca; costumes, Laurence Heller; production manager, Christine Gozlan. Reviewed at the Marignan-Concorde theater, Paris, Feb. 19, 1984. Running time: 90 MINS.
Sylvia .... Sylvia Kristel
Emmanuelle .... Mia Nygren
Marc .... Patrick Bauchau
Donna .... Deborah Power
Maria .... Sophie Berger
Suzanna .... Sonia Martin
Nadine .... Dominique Troyes
Rodrigo .... Gerard Dimiglio
Santano .... Christian Marquand

Emmanuelle, that arch-hedonist of page and screen, is back in new erotic adventures and — a new body. The makers of this fourth installment of the softcore series have conceived a clever exit visa for Sylvia Kristel, who has become completely identified with the role since the first smash episode directed by Just Jaeckin in 1975.

Film opens with Kristel running into an ex-lover (Patrick Bauchau) at a Beverly Hills party and fleeing in panic, fearful of renewed contact with a man who has made her suffer. Kristel decides the only way to guarantee her freedom is to change her body. So she flies off to Brazil to see an esthetic surgeon and submits to a complete face- and body-lift.

And presto-chango! Enter 23-year-old Swedish model Mia Nygrén in the title role. In her new body, Emmanuelle is so green she has to get deflowered all over again, and she heads for a nearby bar to pick up a suitable hunk of man for the chore.

What follows is the familiar roundelay of couplings (AC/DC), masturbation, sex talk and the like, served up against lush travelog backdrops. In the end, Nygren, having sufficiently broken in her new body, decides her heart still belongs to Bauchau and heads for Paris for a reunion, without revealing her secret, of course.

The lovely Nygren should have no trouble weaning fans of the series away from the Kristel image, and the producers have rounded up other attractive cinematic forms for the viewer's delight. Those who found satisfaction in previous Emmanuelle adventures should have no complaint with this one.

"Emmanuelle 4" was shot for 3-D and regular projection. Only latter version is being run in Paris, while provicials have the privilege of ogling the screen through their special glasses. This review is based on the flat version (so to speak).

Francis Giacobetti (who helmed "Emmanuelle 2") was credited director on pic. But his name disappeared somewhere during production, though the producers say it will be reinstated in overseas prints. Locally, scripters Francis Leroy and Iris Letans are being cited as codirectors. —*Len.*

Racing With The Moon
(COLOR)

Likable item with teen appeal. Could generate acceptable business.

Hollywood, Feb. 18.

A Paramount release of a Jaffe-Lansing production. Produced by Alain Bernheim, John Kohn. Directed by Richard Benjamin. Stars Sean Penn, Elizabeth McGovern. Screenplay, Steven Kloves. Camera (Movielab), John Bailey; editor, Jacqueline Cambas; music, Dave Grusin; production design, David L. Snyder; set design, Jeannine Oppewall; set decoration, Jerry Wunderlich; costume design, Patricia Norris; sound, Jerry Jost; associate producer, Art Levinson; assistant director, William S. Beasley. Reviewed at the Paramount Studios, L.A., Feb. 17, 1984. (MPAA Rating: PG.) Running time: 108 MINS.
Henry (Hopper) Nash .... Sean Penn
Caddie Winger .... Elizabeth McGovern
Nicky .... Nicolas Cage
Mr. Nash .... John Karlen
Mrs. Nash .... Rutanya Alda
Mrs. Winger .... Kate Williamson
Sally Kaiser .... Suzanne Adkinson
Grethen.................... Shawn Schepps
Alice Donnelly .... Julie Philips
Bill........................ Michael Talbott

"Racing With The Moon" is a sweet, likable film that doesn't contain the usual commercial "elements" normally expected these days in youth pics but might catch on anyway, particularly with teenage girls. Working in a more straightforward, serious mode, Richard Benjamin confirms the directorial promise he displayed in "My Favorite Year," and Sean Penn and Elizabeth McGovern are good as the romantic leads. With shrewd marketing in the late winter season, Paramount should be able to generate some quite acceptable biz for this first effort from the Jaffe-Lansing production unit at the studio.

By asserting quite traditional and conventional qualities, film manages to seem distinctly different from most contempo youth stories which stress casual, even cynical attitudes about relationships and sex. What distinguishes it, in fact, are that the teenagers here are basically good, decent people who want to do the right thing and are motivated by positive, not cheap, values.

Period and setting are highly reminiscent of that hit from 13 years ago, "Summer Of '42." In fact, time frame is Christmas of '42, and Penn and his rowdy buddy Nicolas Cage have just a few weeks left until they join the Marines.

Penn becomes dazzled by a new face in the California coastal town, McGovern, whom he takes to be a rich girl since she lives up in the "Gatsby" mansion. Shyly but relentlessly, he makes rather cute plays for her attention and, to his amazement, she finally responds and they fall in love.

A wrong-side-of-the-tracks type, Cage gets his g.f. pregnant, and after a disastrous, but wonderfully staged, attempt to hustle some sailors at pool, Penn forces himself to enlist McGovern's help in raising $150 for an abortion for his friend's gal. This leads to melodramatic complications and an ultimate revelation of McGovern's socal status, as well as to a resolution of their relationship.

Clearly, story is hardly earthshaking and, if anything, edges dangerously toward the bland for considerable stretches. This is such a white bread world that Cage's turbulent, urban-type character seems at times like an unnatural element; why does only he talk like a character out of "Mean Streets?"

But first-time scenarist Steven Kloves has created two nice leading characters, nicely essayed by Penn and McGovern. Hitherto identified with social misfit roles, Penn is an offbeat but plausible romantic figure capable of giving an edge to this sort of conventional fellow. In a roller skating sequence, he also exhibits great flair for physical comedy which he will hopefully exploit to fuller advantage on a future occasion.

McGovern is absolutely lovely and brings her character fully to life, seeming remote at first but flowering with the advent of romance. Other performers merely fill in the background.

"My Favorite Year" was one of the most genial of recent comedies, and now, after two films, director Benjamin shows a consistently generous attitude toward his characters and an inclination to emphasize their most exemplary traits. "Racing With The Moon" is not precisely Capraesque, but Benjamin reminds of Capra at times in his desire to get at the fundamental humanity beneath both the comedy and the melodrama.

Mendocino locations offer an eyeful, period details are charming without overwhelming the slight story, and lenser John Bailey has captured it all with a subdued but lush palette. —*Cart.*

Med Lill-Klas I Kappsaecken
(Little Klas In The Trunk)
(SWEDISH-DANISH-COLOR)

Copenhagen, Feb. 6.

An AB Sandrew Film (Stockholm), Swedish Television (Malmoe) and A/S Nordisk Film (Copenhagen) production, AB Sandrews release. Based on novel by Gunnel Linde. Script by Linde and Ulf Andree. Directed by Ulf Andree. Features entire cast. Camera (Eastmancolor) Bo Blomberg; production management, Bjoern Fredlund, Erik Overbye, Caroline Reichhardt; editor, Jerry Graensman; music, Monica Dominique; production design, Gert Wibe, Karin Hjort Suby; costumes, Pia Myrdal. Reviewed in Danish-dubbed version (director Finn Heriksen) at the Palads, Copenhagen Feb. 3, 1984. Running time, 92 MINS.
Annelie .... Maja Ekman
Nicklas .... Marten Ekman
Aunt Tinne .... Birgitta Andersson
The Mother .... Viveka Dahlen
The Father .... Stefan Ekman
Hotel Maid.................. Helle Hertz
Hotel Porter.................. Ole Thestrup
Zoo Emcee................. Poul Bundgaard
Girl in sport car .... Ingrid Janbell

"Little Klas In The Trunk" has all the ingredients of classical farce — a horse hidden in a hotel room and later in a sleeping-car and the attempts of its child owners to distract various grown-ups from noticing horse-manure in their beds and whinnying from cupboards, etc. Director Ulf Andree misses them all blatantly. Not even a fat hotel porter's maneuvering of an old-fashioned trunk (containing, of course, the horse) though a narrow door succeeds in raising as much as a chuckle.

Film was seen along with its tartget audience, kiddies up to the age of eight, and laughter was only to be registered occasionally and then rarely on any intended cue.

Story is based on a book by Gunnell Linde, known for her baroque kiddie entertainments, but the script she has fashioned along with director Ulf Andree is painfully ignorant of the basic mechanics of visual farce and of dramatic and narrative logic as well. The two small children who smuggle a tiny pony from Copenhagen, where they have won it in a zoo lottery, are played by siblings of the famous Ekman acting dynasty, but they are left floundering like fish.

Television stations, finding it hard to fill their afternoon kiddie spots, might wish to divide "Little Klas" up in parts and show it locally dubbed versions, but they will need audiences of the kind that still find it exhilarating that people on a screen move at all.—*Kell.*

Misunderstood
(COLOR)

Somber father-son drama. A toughie to market.

Hollywood, Feb. 24.
An MGM/UA release of a United Artists and Producers Sales Organization presentation of an Accent Films/Keith Barish production in association with Vides Internazionale. Produced by Tarak Ben Ammar. Executive producers, Keith Barish, Craig Baumgarten. Directed by Jerry Schatzberg. Stars Gene Hackman, Henry Thomas. Screenplay, Barra Grant, based on the novel by Florence Montgomery. Camera (Technicolor), Pasqualino De Santis; editor, Marc Laub; music, Michael Hoppe; production design, Joel Schiller; set decoration, Franco Fumagalli; costumes, Jo Ynocencio; sound, Arthur Rochester; associate producer, Mark Lombardo; assistant director, Bernard Farrel. Reviewed at the MGM Studios, Culver City, Feb. 23, 1984. (MPAA Rating: PG.) Running time: **91 MINS.**

Ned	Gene Hackman
Andrew	Henry Thomas
Will	Rip Torn
Miles	Huckleberry Fox
Kate	Maureen Kerwin
Lilly	Susan Anspach
Mrs. Paley	June Brown
Lucy	Helen Ryan
Ahmed	Nadim Sawalha

Quite a few tears flowed around the world due to Henry Thomas' last film, "E.T.," and he keeps his record intact with "Misunderstood," a somber and largely unsentimental study of a rift and ultimate reconciliation between father and son. Lensed in 1982 in Tunisia, pic has already opened in Japan and was recently picked up for domestic distribution by MGM/UA. Marketing challenge is formidable, and it would be easy for this one to get lost in the shuffle, but audiences looking for an emotional 90 minute will get what they're looking for.

Barra Grant's screenplay is based on Florence Montgomery's turn-of-the-century novel, and an end credits line adds that this is a "remake and adaptation" of Luigi Comencini's 1967 Italian pic "Incompreso," written by Leo Benvenuti, Piero De Bernardi, Lucia Drudi Demby and Giuseppe Mangione and starred Anthony Quayle as a British Consul stationed in Rome.

New version places former postwar black marketeer and now shipping magnate Gene Hackman in a palatial home in Tunisia. His wife, seen in mostly silent flashbacks in the person of Susan Anspach, has just died, and Hackman has a tough time breaking the news to his seven-or-eight-year-old son, Thomas. In his opinion, his other son, Huckleberry Fox, is simply too young to comprehend what's happened.

Deeply grieved, Hackman nevertheless continues to be absorbed by his work and unthinkingly neglects and rebuffs the real needs of his boys. It's not that Hackman is cruel, but he's a rather old father for such young kids, has no knack for playing with them or winning their confidence, and just doesn't know how to relate to them.

When his relative Rip Torn suggests Hackman is too stern with the boys, that he expects too much of them, the latter protests he's trying to treat Thomas like a grownup. Thomas tries the best he can, but the fact remains he's not a grownup and needs something more than school and a governess.

Without playmates other than his kid brother, Thomas takes off on his own in the desert country from time to time, briefly entering the Arab world (pic could have used even more local color and adventurous sidestrips).

But basically, he's a model of comportment and Thomas and little Huckleberry Fox are as lovable as two boys can be, kidding around and trying to keep stiff upper lips under truly trying circumstances. Their behavior is a continuing highlight of the film, maintaining interest even when not much is happening.

Ultimately, Thomas is seriously injured in a fall, and he and Hackman finally break through to each other in a climax of undiluted emotionalism. The delirious monolog Thomas is asked to deliver would probably be beyond any child actor, but the essentials get through to strong effect.

In the original film, the boy dies in the end. Director Jerry Schatzberg, who handles his chores in solid, straightforward fashion throughout, is reportedly unhappy with recutting executed by the producers, and pic ends with a freeze frame which fudges the outcome. But it still plays effectively enough.

Hackman's character forces him into something of a straightjacket, and the suspicion persists that the father really doesn't feel nearly as deeply for his sons as he evidently did for his wife. A few glimpses of genuine care or warmth might have helped.

Technically, film is highly polished, although Michael Hoppe's musical score cues the obvious emotional moments rather blatantly. —Cart.

Innocent Prey
(AUSTRALIAN-COLOR)

Sydney, Feb. 20.
Crystal Film Corporation production, executive produced by David G.B. Williams. Produced & directed by Colin Eggleston. Features entire cast. Based on a screenplay by Ron McLean; camera (color), Vincent Monton; music, Brian May; editor, Pippa Anderson; art director, Larry Eastwood. Reviewed at Crystal Film Corp. theaterette, Sydney, Feb. 17, 1984. Running time: **100 MINS.**

Kathy Wills	P.J. Soles
Joe	Kit Taylor
Rick	Grigor Taylor
Sheriff Virgil Baker	Martin Balsam
Phillip Nicholas	John Warnock
Gwen	Susan Stenmark
Ted	Richard Morgan
Hooker	Debi Sue Voorhous

Filmed in Dallas and Sydney with a U.S.-Australian cast of no great reknown, "Innocent Prey" is a mildly suspenseful thriller which tries to emulate numerous Hollywood pics about distressed damsels besieged by crazy, knife-wielding killers.

While pic is short on originality and imaginative flair, it probably contains enough blood-curdling moments to keep devotees of the genre sitting still, if not drawn to the edge of the seats.

Absence of big names in the cast, cliched dialog and slow pacing, particularly in the second half, will likely restrict the film's potential to tv in most territories, although fast theatrical playoff might pay off in some urban centers.

Director Colin Eggleston could have wrought more thrills and chills from the script if he had not allowed the narrative to telegraph so many of its punches in advance, and Brian May's thunderous music exacerbates the pic's heavy-handed feel.

Story opens in Dallas where Kathy (P.J. Soles) introduces her Aussie friend Gwen (Susan Stenmark) to her apparently successful husband, Joe (Kit Taylor).

It soon emerges that beneath that smooth exterior, Joe is a fraud and worse, a raving loony with homicidal tendencies. We know he's the violent type when he slashes a hooker in the shower. Kathy witnesses the crime, and the cops arrest Joe, who escapes from the asylum and returns to the house to terrorize her. Kindly sheriff Baker (Martin Balsam) arrives in the nick of time.

Kathy flees to Australia where she thinks she is safe at last, sharing a harborside mansion with Gwen. Alas, their landlord Phillip (John Warnock) is a mother-fixated sicko who spies on his tenants via video cameras in every room (mysteriously, no one ever notices the electronic eyes).

All too predictably, Joe turns up in Sydney, much blood is splashed around the walls and swimming pool, and May's score becomes even more frenzied, leading the audience to expect that Jaws I, II and III are about to leap out of the water.

Vincent Monton's lensing is OK. As for acting, Kit Taylor is merely called on to look wild-eyed and demonic, P.J. Soles looks wide-eyed and scared, Martin Balsam looks avuncular, and John Warnock looks sick. —Dogo.

Snow, The Movie
(AUSTRALIAN-COLOR)

Sydney, Feb. 15.
A Snowfilm Production. Produced by Eve Ash. Directed by Robert Gibson. Features entire cast. Screenplay, Lance Curtis, Geoff Kelso, Peter Moon, David Argue, Robert Gibson; camera (color), Martin McGrath, Tim Smart; editor, Gibson; sound, Steve Edwards; original music, George Worontschak; additional music by Split Enz, Dire Straits, The Sports. (No Commonwealth Film Censor rating). Reviewed on Syme Home Video videocassette, Sydney, Feb. 14, '84. Running time: **73 MINS.**

Darren	David Argue
Wayne	Lance Curtis
Bruno	Peter Moon
Bruce	Tom Cottage
Uncle Jack	Geoff Kelso
Pam	Jeanine O'Donnell
Pepi	Peppie Angliss
Hamish	Eddie Zandberg

In 1981-82 feature film production in Australia exploded at an alarming rate, fuelled by the government's 150% tax concessions, which were subsequently pulled back to 133%, and which clamped the brakes on an industry which appeared to be careening downhill on the way to a terrible accident.

Government's move was too late to avert a few minor disasters, like "Snow, The Movie" a so-called comedy which is almost entirely mirthless, plotless, characterless, shapeless and witless.

In common with a number of those 1981-82 celluloid mishaps, this pic has never been released theatrically here, but managed to find outlets on videocassette and on an Adelaide (South Australia) tv station.

According to the producers, some international deals have been firmed and others are pending, mostly for tv play-off. The hope is that it won't be billed as an Australian production, because it's the kind of film which will give Oz cinema a bad name.

It's such an incoherent mess, it's no surprise to find five writers, including the director, credited. Between them, they have concocted a silly story about two youths who win a car in a radio station contest, and set off for a snow resort for what is evidently intended to be a fun-filled weekend.

There is no joy for the Two Stooges or the audience on the slopes, and, indoors at the chalet, it's grimmer still, with a resident sex thereapist who doubles as floor-show compere, a tacky wet t-shirt contest, and a talent quest which is as bereft of talent as everything else in this production. —Dogo.

L'Etincelle
(Tug of Love)
(FRENCH-COLOR)

Paris, Feb. 6.
UGC release of a Madeleine Films/TF 1 Films Production/UGC — Top 1/Stand'Art coproduction. Produced by Gilbert de Goldschmidt. Executive producer, Michel Zemer. Stars Roger Hanin and Clio Goldsmith. Written and directed by Michel Lang, based on Robert Rousson's "Gene and Dale." Camera (color), Bernard Zitzermann; music, Vladimir Cosma; editor, Georges Klotz; art director, Jean-Claude Gallouin; sound, Philippe Lemenuel; reviewed at the UGC screening room, Neuilly, Feb. 6, 1984. Running time: **99 MINS.**

Maurice	Roger Hanin
Dale	Clio Goldsmith

Mike	Simon Ward
Bob	John Moulder-Brown
Patricia	Lysette Anthony
Kathryn	Polly Adams
George	Frank Crompton
Grany	Myrtle Devenish
Lindsay	Alec Sabin
Shelley	Angela Cheyne
Dr. Willenstein	Jacques Maury

Writer-director Michel Lang, who first hit commercial paydirt in 1975 with a comedy of youthful Gallic sex shenanigans on British soil, "A Nous Les Petites Anglaises," is back across the Channel for more mature romantic comedy in his seventh feature, "L'Etincelle." It's an engaging effort, with Lang at his relaxed best as scripter and helmer and a couple of buoyant performances by its stars, Roger Hanin and Clio Goldsmith.

Hanin is a French restaurateur in London whose heart misses a beat when he meets vivacious young Goldsmith, a radio announcer for a local station who makes a film buff gaffe during a broadcast and gets a friendly phone call from Hanin pointing out her error. When he reveals he's French and learns of Goldsmith's half-Gallic parentage, they agree to a casual rendezvous.

Much separates the two — not only age and social background, but also Goldsmith's English archeologist husband (Simon Ward), and the baby she's carrying. Drawn by their mutual joie de vivre, they become friends. Hanin, a divorcee with a grown-up son (John Moulder-Brown) and local antiquarian girlfriend he doesn't really love, gently presses for something other than a platonic friendship, but she resists a change of status and refuses to admit openly that her marriage doesn't suit her.

Hanin's dissatisfaction turns to jealousy when his son, who's just as uncommitted to his girl as dad is to his, meets and takes a similar interest in Goldsmith. They too become buddies, with Moulder-Brown unable to get any closer to her than Hanin.

A strain sets in between the restaurateur and the disk jockey, but Hanin suddenly finds himself indispensable when Goldsmith goes prematurely into labor, with her husband away on an overseas excavation and her regular doctor on vacation. Hanin takes charge of the situation, so much so that he's mistaken for the real father by hospital staff.

Hubby Ward flies in to see her, but immediately announces he must return to the archeological site. Shocked by his callously unfamilial attitude — the baby's health is jeopardized by the early birth — Hanin punches him down the stairs.

Inevitably the marriage breaks up, but Goldsmith insists on her independence before renewed pressures from Hanin and Moulder-Brown. Yet she succumbs to Hanin's charms in the end and they decide to link up, while his son goes back to his neglected friend (Lystte Anthony).

Lang's talents as scripter and helmer seem to have found compatible material in Robert Roussen's source story, and the filmmaker has imbued his main characters with warm sensibility and some pertinently humorous observations. With the exception of Moulder-Brown, appealing as the son, the Britons tend toward stereotype and caricature, though Ward's stuffy archeologist is an adroit two-dimensional representation.

But it's Goldsmith and Hanin who make the film. She gives a radiant performance, subtly suggesting she may be in love with Hanin, knowing she could well end up with him, but fiercely independent in her decision to get there to her own speed. Hanin, who in recent films has seemed on the verge of wearing out viewers with his semi-paternal Mediterranean types, here shows what a good actor he is when the role and director, keep his tics in check. He offers some wonderful comic moments, as in one scene where he goes into a stammering panic in the middle of a deserted London park when Goldsmith thinks she may deliver her baby right there on the grass.

Attractively packaged, film suffers from some seemingly unjustified dubbing of English characters (why should Britons be speaking French among themselves?) but this annoyance probably doesn't extend to the English-language version, titled "Tug of Love."
— Len.

Eszkimo Asszony Fazik
(Eskimo Woman Feels Cold)
(HUNGARIAN-COLOR)

Budapest, Feb. 17.
A Dialog Studio, Mafilm, production. Directed and written by Janos Xantus. Camera (Eastmancolor), Andras Matkocsik; music, Gabor Lukin, Mihaly Vigh. Reviewed at Hungarofilm theatrette, Budapest, 11 Feb., 1984. Running time: **110 MINS.**
Mari	Marietta Mehes
Laci	Boguslaw Linda
Janos	Andor Lukats

Janos Xantus is a new name who shows some promise, though his first feature, "Eskimo Woman Feels Cold," is a distinctly uneven affair. The tale of a bizarre menage a trois, with a strong musical motif, it begins with the central character, Laci, stabbed to death outside his house one morning.

Flashbacks explain that Laci, a gifted but charmless concert pianist who flits back and forth from Budapest to London, fell in love with Mari, the blonde wife of the deaf-and-dumb Janos, who works in a zoo. Mari wants to become a rock singer, and the infatuated Laci gives up his own classical music career to help her.

Meanwhile, the tragically inarticulate and jealous Janos finds himself playing drums for the group. When Mari finally ankles for the U.S., Janos kills Laci (though why he didn't do it far earlier remains a mystery).

The whole film is based on style rather than substance: it really doesn't make much sense, but Xantus has plenty of visual ideas that make the overlong pic watchable. Boguslaw Linda makes an irritating hero; Marietta Mehes, though, has moments as the rather wan heroine. Best performance comes from Andor Lukats, outstanding as the deaf-mute husband whose frustrations drive him to murder; it's a compelling piece of acting.

Maybe next time out, Xantus will apply his undoubted talent to a more coherent narrative; in this first feature, he's flexing his artistic muscles and the results show more promise for the future than actual achievement; but he bears watching. — Strat.

American Taboo
(16m-COLOR)

Student prizewinner for special outlets only.

Hollywood, Feb. 22.
A Steve Lustgarten production. Produced by Lustgarten, Sali Borchman, Ron Schmidt. Directed, screenplay by Lustgarten. Additional dialog, Jay Horenstein, Nicole Harrison. Camera (color), Lee Nesbit, Lustgarten, Eric Edwards, Mark Whitney; editors, Lustgarten, Schmidt; music, Dana Libonati, Dan Brandt; sound, Schmidt. Reviewed at the Vista Theatre, L.A., Feb. 21, 1984. (No MPAA rating.) Running time: **87 MINS.**
Paul Wunderlich	Jay Horenstein
Lisa	Nicole Harrison
Michael	Mark Rabiner
Maggie	Katherine King
First Model	Ki Skinner
Second Model	Suzette Taylor
Lisa's Mother	Dorothy Anton

Winner of last year's best student film Academy Award, "American Taboo" is a mix of heavy doses of amateurism with a bolder approach to sexuality than most Yank pics dare take. Shown commercially in a one-nighter at the Vista in Hollywood and being marketed on a date-by-date basis by the writer-director, pic bears too many earmarks of student filmmaking to be acceptable outside of specialized and campus venues, but is too essentially serious and somber to become a midnight item.

Tale of obsessive lust has at its center a curiously, even infuriatingly, passive figure, a 30ish fellow who fancies himself a photographer, but earns his keep as a pro lenser's studio assistant. He keeps his distance from the seemingly available models who pass through his life, but becomes fascinated by a nubile, teenage neighbor girl, snapping photos of her from a distance.

After one or two uneventful encounters with her, he allows himself to be shanghaied by her to the seashore, where she teases and flirts with him. Despite plenty of chances, he never makes a move on her, until finally, back at her mother's house, she seduces him.

This lights his fuse and there follow a couple of highly convincing, virtually real-time lovemaking sequences of considerable explicitness, bordering on the hardcore but more powerful in the mostly negative emotions they express.

Because of the fuzzy motivations of the characters, it's a bit difficult to define exactly what these emotions are, but these are far from the typical, idealized sex scenes one usually sees — they're brutal, uncomfortable and startling, partly because they seem real and partly because the "taboo" involved concerns the question of whether or not the girl is the young man's daughter.

Film could have been much more engaging if the fellow seemed to have anything going for him but, as played by Jay Horenstein, he's relentlessly dour, humorless and expressionless, with such a low opinion of himself that he never dares assert himself. He's such a dullard that it's impossible to believe the women in the film — not only the lively teenager, but his boss' wife — could throw themselves at him in the forthright manner shown.

While showing some talent for composition and quiet observations, writer-director Steve Lustgarten indulges his material too much, allowing scenes to run on too long and not getting to the point quickly enough.

But he has been quite successful in coaching a strong performance out of Nicole Harrison as the bracingly confident Lolita, and in attacking the subject of illicit sex so directly, but without exploitation.
— Cart.

Family Light Affair
(HONG KONG-COLOR)

Hong Kong, Feb. 10.

A Shaw Brothers production and presentation. Produced by Mona Fong. Directed by Alfred Cheung. Stars Anthony Chan (Chan Friend), Hui Ying Hung, Chao Wen Yin, Wu Yung Chi, Ku Feng, Lo Lieh, Tung Piao, Aldred Cheung, Liang Chung Ming. Screenplay, Chan Friend, Alfred Cheung; camera (color), Yang Ping Tang; editors, Shao Feng, Ma Chung Yao; art direction, John Hau; theme song by Chung Shao Feng, Chan Friend; music, Stephen Shing, So Chun Hou. Reviewed at Pearl Theater, Hong Kong, Feb. 9, 1984. Running Time: **100 MINS.**
(Cantonese soundtrack with English sub-titles).

Alfred Cheung is a brilliant 28-year old director now under contract with the Shaw Brothers. He was literally unknown to the local industry until the release of the modestly funded (HK$1,000,000) comedy, "Let's Make Laugh" last year which grossed HK$17,000,000 at the domestic boxoffice.

"Family Light Affair" is Cheung's second feature at the Clearwater Bay Studio and is sadly not being accepted by Cantonese viewers who expect any successful director to merely follow the predictable formula of repeating oneself. Cheung did not, as "Family" is a brilliant but erratic black comedy-melodrama. But there is no doubt that he is no flash in the pan in the creative department and given more time and opportunities, will emerge into a major Hong Kong filmmaker.

His new pic is a series of funny, touching, charming vignettes of manners and madness in modern Hong Kong. It is a form of inspired Cantonese comedy. The film has cinematic lunacy, enchanting performances from the lead and supporting charactgers and Cheung's kind of endearing touches of sensitivity, compassion and understanding of human nature.

The story is simple. Tony Chan is a farmer who brings his wife Hui Ying Hung and two daughters, Chao Wen-yin and Wu Yung-chi, from Mainland China to Hong Kong to join his father Ku Feng. All crave for a better life and believe that Papa made it big in the big city but realize soon enough that he is a poor coolie who can't even pay rent for his cubicle bed space and was really better-off as a farmer in China. What happens is a series of events that vividly show how the provincial family copes with the maddening city life amidst winter weather, lack of money, hunger, strange people, cops, ruffians, rough residents, and some newly found friends. There are numerous incidents that portray the tough urban existence as experienced by newcomers to the insensitive, cold cement jungle of a fast-moving city.

Hong Kong is lovingly presented like a Christmas tree aglow with countless neon lights at night as if to soften the harshness of daytime.

But despite the zany sequences that touch both the heart and mind, the film as a whole is an eclectic work.

The film definitely has many merits as the first half is stylishly funny while the second half suddenly bursts into high melodrama, with an "unbalanced" artificiality in an attempt to possibly incorporate serious dramatic sentiments. Proper editing of the last hour and insertion of new scenes more in the style of the first half would surely improve the picture into a more solid and unified production.

"Family Light Affair," despite its flaws, is a little film that deserves bigger attention. Cheung is a versatile director who refuses to be typecast. There are very few moments that do not display a vigorious and very fresh creative Hong Kong talent. —*Mel.*

Chords Of Fame
(DOCU-COLOR-16m)

A Pretty Smart Co. film. No distrib set. Executive producer, David Sternburg. Produced by Sternburg, Mady Schutzman, Michael Korolenko. Directed by Korolenko. Written by Schutzman; camera (Deluxe color, 16m), John Newby; editor-associate producer/co-director/post-production supervisor, John Bloomgarden; assistant director, Randy Sabasala; sound, Richard Murphy; musical direction/arrangements, Schutzman, Bill Burnett; interviews by Korolenko; funding assistance from American Film Institute, National Endowment for the Arts and Channel 4 (G.B.). Reviewed at Film Forum 1, N.Y., Feb. 19, 1984. (No MPAA Rating). Running time: **88 MINS.**

With: Bill Burnett (portraying Phil Ochs). Interviews with: Abbie Hoffman, Jerry Rubin, Pete Seeger, Oscar Brand, Odetta, Dave Van Ronk, Tom Paxton, Eric Andersen, Jack Newfield, Meegan Ochs, Michael Ochs, Sonny Ochs, Jim Glover, Mike Porco, Peter Yarrow, Bob Gibson, William Worthy, Harold Leventhal, Deni Frand, Sammy Walker, Ramsey Clark.

"Chords Of Fame" is an unsuccessful documentary portrait of Phil Ochs, folksinger of the 1960s. Composed of talking-head interviews, song performances by his friends and misguided "dramatic recreations" of incidents in his life, pic fails to justify itself or Ochs' importance worthy of feature-length treatment.

As several of the arm's length-interviewees state, Ochs, coming out of Ohio State U. to enter the protest movement of the 1960s as a self-styled writer and singer of "topical music," had limited musical and writing talent, but made a strong contact with audiences and had several fine songs which hold up well today. That he was a comparatively minor figure alongside such people as Pete Seeger, Bob Dylan, Joan Baez, etc. becomes increasingly clear as the docu unfolds. His final deterioration, lapsing into a silly (though pointed) imitation of Elvis Presley routine and finally near schizophrenia before committing suicide in 1976 is tastefully docu-

mented, except for an unwise juxtaposition montage of four photos linking Ochs with Hendrix, Morrison and Joplin in a variation on the cornball "matyrs roll-call" of the 1960s.

Fundamental error by filmmakers Michael Korolenko, Mady Schutzman and David Sternburg regrettably duplicates that made three years ago in the "Beatlemania" fiasco: using an imitation actor instead of sticking with footage of the subject (Ochs) as well as lapsing into padded, diffuse montages of 1960s events and trends. "Chords Of Fame," titled after an Ochs' song dealing with the perils of selling out for the big bucks, a topic frequently alluded to here by the interviewees, constantly strays from its subject to inadequately recall the times (and not the man) in an unintentionally near-parody fashion. As for that imposter, Bill Burnett delivers okay vocal carbons of Ochs' singing style but his acting is weak and the gimmick results in only a couple examples of Ochs' own voice being on the soundtrack, a very disappointing tribute to the performer.

Highlights along the way (which, if the dramatized Burnett footage and nostalgia montages were excised could yield a short piece for educational tv) include funny recollections by fellow Yippies Abbie Hoffman and Jerry Rubin, with latter conveying the energy and honesty of Ochs as a fellow Ohioan who maintained a "gee whiz" attitude to life. Solid performances of Ochs tunes by various folk stars also include emotional renderings by his Ohio State roommate Jim Glover. Pic ends with everyone joining in an a cappella version of Ochs' "Crucifixion" and Ochs himself performing "I Ain't A-Marching Anymore" filmed at a club date in 1967.—*Lor.*

Running Hot
(COLOR)

Not so hot.

A New Line Cinema release of a Highroad Prods. production, in association with Wescom Prods. Executive producer, Dimitri T. Skouras. Produced by David Calloway. Written and directed by Mark Griffiths. Features entire cast. Camera (color), Tom Richmond; editor, Andy Blumenthal; music, Al Capps; sound, Gerald B. Wolfe; assistant director, Steve Buck; production manager, Dennis Hoffman; production design, Katherine Vallin; art direction, Anthony Cowley; set decoration, Kathy Orrison; special effects, Roger George, Frank De Marko, Dick-Albains; co-producer, Zachary Feuer. Reviewed at UA Rivoli 1 Theater, N.Y., Feb. 24, 1984. (MPAA Rating: R). Running time: **95 MINS.**

Charlene Andrews	Monica Carrico
Danny Hicks	Eric Stoltz
Officer Trent	Stuart Margolin
Ross (pimp)	Virgil Frye
Tom Bond	Richard Bradford
Shane	Louise Baker
Officer Berman	Joe George
Angie	Laurel Patrick
Ex-con in desert	Sorrells Pickard
Danny's father	Ben Hammer
Jenny	Juliette Cummins

"Running Hot" is an extremely silly action picture, provoking the type of unintentional laughs and comments yelled back at the screen which bode poor word-of-mouth (except for seekers of camp entertainment). Opus was shot under the title "Lucky 13," frequently referred to by the characters and a far more appropriate monicker.

Story has 17-year-old Danny Hicks (Eric Stoltz) given a death sentence for killing his father, but escaping from the policeman, Trent (Stuart Margolin), transporting him to prison. On the run, he seeks refuge with a 30-year-old prostitute, Charlene (Monica Carrico), who has been a sort of groupie for Hicks at the trial, writing him love letters as well.

They steal a vintage Cadillac convertible from Charlene's former pimp (Virgil Frye) and hit the road, headed for Arizona to hide out with Hicks' younger sister. Duo's nonadventures are intercut with Trent's dogged detective efforts tracking them down. Film pays off with a revelation that Hicks is innocent of the murder charge and then a nihilistic climax that neatly kills off all the principal characters.

With many rock songs on the soundtrack attempting to distract the viewer from the dull footage, "Hot" proceeds fitfully (with many fadeouts between sequences) from one gun-toting confrontation to another, each so awkwardly staged by writer-director Mark Griffiths that laughter is generated instead of thrills. The currently trendy young boy-older woman romantic matchup doesn't work, nor does the overused plot gimmick of incest.

Newcomer Monica Carrico is promising here, boasting a dancer-femme weightlifter's body, but too closely styled in look and personality to Candy Clark to make a distinctive impression. Redhead Eric Stoltz is alternately too bland or merely unsympathetic, as filmmaker Griffiths seems to be avoiding any audience identification with him, in view of the upcoming "let's waste the cast" finish. Virgil Frye as the pimp and Sorrells Pickard as a tough rustic type who hankers after the Cadillac have arresting though brief turns.

Pic looks cheap and (in its interiors at least) sleazy, with underlit photography. As with the recent exploitation hit "Angel," one comes away feeling cheated.
— *Lor.*

La Discoteca
(The Discotheque)
(ITALIAN-COLOR)

Rome, Feb. 9.

A Titanus release, produced by Franco Calabrese for Gloria Cinematografica. Stars Nino D'Angelo. Directed by Mariano Laurenti. Screenplay by Franco Calabrese, Piero

Regnoli and Mariano Laurenti. Camera (Color), Giuseppe Berardini; art director, Francesco Calabrese; editor, Carlo Broglio; music, Nino D'Angelo and Franco Chiaravalle. Reviewed at the America Cinema, Rome, Feb. 8, 1984. Running time: **86 MINS.**

Nino	Nino D'Angelo
Maria	Roberta Olivieri
Romy	Cinzia Bonfantini
Bombolo	Bombolo
Hotel directors	Enzo Cannevale

Not taking any foolish chances on the follow-up to their surprise hit "Jeans and a T-Shirt," producer Franco Calabrese and helmer Mariano Laurenti have simply duplicated cast, crew and story line in "The Discotheque." The homely little warbler from sub-Naples, Nino D'Angelo, is back with four new tunes, bleached blond hair still in his eyes and teen partner Roberta Olivieri still in his heart. Pic has started strong and could ditto the success of "Jeans" on home territory. Pic's theme and star are the key to its boxoffice, and foreign markets will have to take this into consideration.

Setting is split between a Southern beach (Positano) and Northern ski resort (Merano). Nino is a humble pizza maker in love with a sharp-tongued little vixen named Maria (Olivieri), whose higher social standing prevents him from telephoning her at home ("Father wouldn't like it"). When he has to follow the tourist trade into the Italian Alps, his best friend, who is supposed to be a go-between on the phone, betrays his trust and splits the couple up, temporarily.

Meanwhile, in the mountains, Nino is very much out of his element. Tall, blond German youths pick on him constantly and his boss Enzo Cannevale, in lederhosen and a Hitler moustache, makes life tough. Romy, the hotel owner's beautiful daughter, falls hard for Nino, but he remains true to the girl he left behind. Again, her higher social class, money and foreignness are emphasized as divisive obstacles.

Pic's appeal seems to reach beyound D'Angelo's teen followers to family audiences attracted by strong, homey values and comic strip romantic plot.

Unphotogenic by any standards, D'Angelo turns his defects to advantage in the role of the poor boy fighting for his dignity. His handicaps — poverty, slight stature, barely average looks, no connections and an inability to speak anything but Italian dialect — are made up for by inner qualities: friendliness, loyalty, unpretentiousness and a sensual voice. The strength of the character overrides glaring thesping and technical inadequacies.

The discotheque of the title provides a marginal sequence or two where D'Angelo flops as John Travolta. The comic duo of Cannevale and Bombolo offer intervals of slapstick so broad it would

look overdone in an animated cartoon. — *Yung.*

Occhio Malocchio Prezzemolo E Finocchio

(Evil Eye)
(ITALIAN-COLOR)

Rome, Jan. 28.

A Medusa release, produced by Franco Poccioni, Giorgio Venturini and Luciano Martino for Filmes International, Nuova Dania and Medusa Distribuzione. Stars Johnny Dorelli and Lino Banfi. Directed by Sergio Martino. Screenplay, Bruno Corbucci, Mario Amendola, Franco Verucci, Franco Bucceri, Roberto Léone, Romolo Guerrieri, Sergio Martino; camera (color), Giancarlo Ferrano; art director, Antonello Gelling; editor, Eugenio Alabiso. Reviewed at America Cinema, Rome, Jan. 27, 1984. Running time: **100 MINS.**

Altomare	Lino Banfi
Giovanna	Milena Vukotic
Elena	Janet Agren
Corinto	Mario Scaccia
Gaspare	Johnny Dorelli
Agent	Renzo Montognami

A two-episode comedy of standard stamp, Sergio Martino's "Evil Eye" spoofs superstition and popular magicians. Packaged without excess imagination, pic hasn't done more than middling with the local audiences it was made for, who may finally be on the lookout for something new. Foreign markets will be those where stars Johnny Dorelli and Lino Banfi are drawing cards.

All told, the Banfi episode is probably the funnier of the two. The squat, bald comedian plays Altomare, a thriving appliance store owner whose Neapolitan quaking at portents of bad luck ruins him totally. While mate Giovanna (Milena Vukotic) tearfully emotes in front of the tv soaps and teenage daughter runs around with a biker-turned-Hari Krishna freak. Altomare invokes all the charms and spells he knows to defeat the malignant influence of his next-door neighbor Corinto (Mario Scaccia). Between fighting with the black maid who keeps voodoo dolls in her closet and consulting with experts on how to get rid of the "evil eye" that beleaguers him, Altomare has his hands too full to look after business, which naturally goes to the dogs.

Climax comes the night the shopkeeper decides to pluck out the "hair of misfortune" growing somewhere on Corinto's body that is supposed to be the cause of his ill luck. There is also time for a subplot with aerobic gymnast Janet Agren, bent on persuading Altomare to finance a new apartment in exchange for her athletic body. Vukotic and Scàccia, both pros worth far more than the silly plot, are better used as Altomare's dippy wife and leering nemesis.

Dorelli's segment is less colorful. Nice-guy Gaspare (Dorelli), a hack magician who plays country towns, one day meets a dying old

witch who passes real magic powers on to him, much to his surprise. The only stipulation is that he bring her a pistachio ice cream cone the day she asks for it, otherwise he loses his supernatural gifts.

Given the limitless range of feasts Gaspare can now perform, pic unleashes its powerful imagination and illustrates his powers by showing him make it rain; having him *fail* to solve the problem of a young woman who gives men a high-voltage electric shock when they try to touch her; and filling up a tacky office with "clients."

The only magic in the episode is provided by a rival wizard who challenges Gaspare to a televised duel. But by then Gaspare has lost his powers (the old pistachio ice cream problem) and can only try to fake it with the connivance of his agent, Renzo Montagnani.

Since neither is any more entertaining in total defeat than they were at the pinnacle of success, viewers are left watching the other wiz levitate a girl and then hypnotize the stars into waltzing out of the room — which is what a sensible film-goer would have done some time ago. — *Yung.*

El Avvocato

(The Lawyer)
(EGYPTIAN-COLOR)

Cairo, Feb. 14.

Written, produced and directed by Raafat El-Mihi. Stars Adel Iman, Yousra, Isaad Younis. Camera (color), Maher Radi; art director, Nehad Bahgat; editor, Said El-Sheikh; music, Haney Shenouda. Reviewed at Cinema City, Ciaro, Jan. 29, 1984. Running time: **125 MINS.**

Hassan	Adel Imam
Wife	Yousra
Sister	Isaad Younis

Comedy is the dramatic art most inimical to injustice and prejudice, and has been absent for long years in Egyptian cinema.

Now, Raafat El-Mihi's "The Lawyer" finally provides a high standard film comedy starring Adel Imam, top comedian in the Arab world, as Hassan Abdel-Rahim, a lawyer (also known as Hassan Spinach) with rare finesse.

Imam provides the character's essence when he casually remarks that any attempt to interpret factual underdevelopment in scientific terms is in itself non-scientific, and that underdevelopment creates its own code. This is also the key to the film itself, as the lawyer utilizes the distance between law and reality to reverse the facts, prove the innocent guilty and the guilty innocent.

Finally trapped, he goes to jail but manages to escape. The kind guard, serving the jail masters and spending his vacations in their homes, remains inside, smoking a discarded cigar. Explaining his attitude to the lawyer, the guard says

"You the gentry fight each other, but I believe in earning a living..."

El-Mihi highlights contemporary Cairo from the taxicab crisis, the queues to buy Egyptian cigarettes as well as the serious contradictions between justice and law — between what is said and what is done. He does it with coherent dramatic development through the four characters — lawyer, judge, policeman and teacher — with a realism rarely found in national cinema.

Achievement of El-Mihi in his second film (he debuted with "Eyes That Never Sleep"), lies in his ability to reveal the dramatic context of comedy with a realistic style tinged with surrealism, involving various prisoners.

Nehad Bahgat's decor is outstanding. So are Maher Radi's cinematography and Said El-Sheikh's editing.

El-Mihi selected his cast with care, drawing insight from each performer in the main as well as the lesser roles.

Adel Imam is a virtual genius in a role filled with bitter irony. Yousra in her first comedy confirms that a gifted performer is one who can excel in all roles. —*Fari.*

Constance

(NEW ZEALAND-COLOR)

Auckland, Feb. 9.

A Mirage Films release of a Mirage production. Produced by Larry Parr. Directed by Bruce Morrison. Features entire cast. Screenplay, Jonathan Hardy; camera (color), Kevin Hayward; costumes, Judith Crozier; music, John Charles; art direction, Ric Kifoed; makeup, Anne Pospischil; Abby, Francia Smeets; production design, Richard Jeziorny; editing, Phillip Howe; production supervision, Dorthe Scheffman. Reviewed at St James Thearette, Auckland, Feb. 8, 1984. Running time: **102 MINS.**

Constance Elsworthy	Donogh Rees
Simon Malyon	Shane Briant
Sylvia Elsworthy	Judie Douglass
Alexander Elsworthy	Martin Vaughan
John Munroe	Donald MacDonald
Richard Lewis	Marc Wignall
Errol Barr	Graham Harvey
Noeline	Hester Joyce

"Constance" is a highly stylized film about a beautiful young woman living in Auckland in 1946 who dreams she is a Hollywood superstar. If plot developments and characterizations are not always credible or are reduced to stereotypes, that may be part of the fantasy, a non-reality which reflects Constance's dream. The picture should be judged on its own terms, where artificiality seems to be equated with glamor, rendering literal-minded criticism beside the point.

As played by Donogh Rees in her first film role, Constance is given to such contrived charades as dressing as Marlene Dietrich at parties and singing along to a recording of Dietrich's hit, "Falling In Love Again." Her vocal timing is so out of synch that it must be deliberate, perhaps to show that her talent is not the match of her ambition. But if she is not going to make it in show business she certainly models a succession of smart '40s clothes with great dash (a new outfit for every scene) and with a fine disregard for the less than affluent status of the character.

The style of these garments and the cleverly lit Auckland locations, survivors of the period, are perhaps the film's major appeal.

Ree's stiffness of manner may be director Bruce Morrison's idea of the artificiality of the concept as a whole. Constance's male admirers, and most of the supporting players, are cast, dressed and made up to this pattern. Imported actor Shane Briant has the right air of handsome, predatory decadence as a visiting Hollywood still photographer. There is an outburst of sexual violence during a photo session which is given the blurred-lens, freeze-frame, jump-cut treatment, and it makes an effective contrast to the film's otherwise sharply focused sedate pace.

Black and white footage from the 1946 features, "Gilda" and "Brief Encounter" underlines the style of the time, but realism is destroyed by a live interlude on the cinema stage, preceding the screening of "Gilda," which features a riveting nude female dancer, Entertainment in Auckland, 1946, was never like that. —*Dub.*

Moord In Extase
(Murder In Ecstasy)
(DUTCH-COLOR)

Amsterdam, Feb. 17.

A Tuschinski Film Distribution release of a Maggan Films production. Produced by Henk Bros. Directed by Hans Scheepmaker. Features entire cast. Screenplay, Felix Thijssen, based upon the novel by A.C. Baantjer; camera (Fuji color), Rob van der Drift; editor, Victorine Habets; stunt coordinator, Dicky Beer; music, Arthur Cune; sound, Victor Dekker. Reviewed at Tuschinski Theater, Amsterdam, Feb. 14, 1984. Running time: **99 MINS.**
De Cock .... Joop Doderer
Vledder .... Ron Brandsteder
Monique .... Manouk van der Meulen

Banking on the popularity of bestselling author A.C. Baantjer's detective novels and their hero, police officer De Cock, producer Henk Bos went for the matter-of-fact approach that made the unassuming books successful in Holland and Belgium. De Cock is the alter ego of the author, who, recently retired after 28 years as a detective in Amsterdam's busiest precinct the red light and drugs district, penned 28 tomes (so far), all fact-based.

Main asset of "Murder in Ecstasy" (much murder, little ecstasy) is undoubtedly Joop Doderer, popular tv-comedian and legit actor, in the central part.

Doderer (who may be remembered as the South African securi-

ty official in Otto Preminger's "The Human Factor") imbued De Cock with the reticent kindliness, intelligent decency and sly humor the cop's fans would expect; he stands out as the only actor of stature in a motley cast of at best serviceable, at worst amateurish, thesps. Pic could develop legs in the Low Countries. Prospects abroad seem iffy.

Story, complex and not always gripping, concerns a string of murders following the hold-up of a cash transport; the driver is but the first victim. As one stiff follows another, so do the suspects in De Cock's fertile mind. Ultimate payoff is very violent, which does not please De Cock: the old sleuth is tender-hearted.

The screenplay tightens the meandering novel to better effect, while keeping three main characters in focus: De Cock; his not too-bright, impetuous young assistant Vledder, and, the sex-interest, model Monique.

Tyro helmer Hans Scheepmaker opts for quick action throughout, and on the whole succeeds. Some stunts, however, come much too pat for audience-involvement due to too taut editing. Location shooting is a plus, in the cool, rain-washed or hazy light in this part of the world.

What this workaday whodunit does best, apart from Doderer's contribution, is to evoke the look and feel of notorious Old Amsterdam, a bad old city with a neighborly heart. That heart has all but vanished, so that, on its home ground, pic may have a nostalgic appeal. — *Ewa.*

Les Cavaliers de l'Orage
(The Horsemen of the Storm)
(FRENCH-YUGOSLAV-COLOR)

Paris, Feb. 20.

Gaumont release of a Carthago Films/Jadran Films (Zagreb)/TF 1 Films Production/SFPC coproduction. Produced by Tarak Ben Ammar. Stars Marlene Jobert, Gerard Klein, Vittorio Mezzogiorno. Directed by Gérard Vergez. Screenplay, Vergez and Daniel Boulanger, freely inspired by Jean Giono's "Deux Cavaliers de l'Orage;" camera, (color) André Diot; art director, Jean-Jacques Caziot; editors, Nicole Dedieu, Jean-Pierre Roques; music, Michel Portal; costumes, Danielle Colin Linard; sound, Michel Bouleu; production manager, Bonis Gregoric; executive producers, Carlo Lastricati, Guy Delooz. Reviewed at the Gaumont Ambassade theater, Paris, Feb. 19, 1984. Running time: **105 MINS.**
Marie .... Marlene Jobert
Jason .... Gerard Klein
Gorian .... Vittorio Mezzogiorno
Ange .... Wadeck Stanczak
Colonel Debars .... Pinkas Braun
Emilie .... Agnes Garreau
Castaing .... Hanns Zischler
General .... Jean Rougerie
Sokoloff .... Emil Ruben

This Franco-Yugoslav coproduction, freely inspired by a novel by the Provençal writer Jean Giono, tells of two brothers, peasant horsebreeders from the south of

France, who become bitter rivals for the affections of an immigrant doctor (Marlene Jobert) during World War I.

Filmed in good part in the Balkans, action begins in France in the years before the Great War and later moves to the Dardanelles, where the elder brother (Gerard Klein) is mobilized. When her military husband dies, Jobert is assigned as medic to the same region, accompanied by the younger brother (Wadek Stanczak), who is her ambulance driver.

Their eventual reunion sparks tension, especially when Klein and Jobert finally become lovers. The war itself provides additional complications with the arrival of the Russian soldiers in Salonica and the companionship of a Franco-Serbian officer with progressive notions (Vittorio Mezzogiorno) who lands in military prison with Klein for having joined the Russians in singing the Internationale. Jobert and Stanczak engineer their escape and the three men make their way towards Serbia. But the brothers' feud anew and fatally wrestle each other off a cliff face. Jobert, who is court-martialed and imprisoned, meets Mezzogiorno years later in Paris and learns how the brothers died.

Gerard Vergez's film reprises the swaggering cloppity-clop and romantic schmaltz of old-fashioned male adventure yarns, but the director is unable to make one believe totally in the enterprise. The acting is too dull to rejuvenate the hackneyed theme of sibling rivalry and the action scenes are staged without enough genuine feeling for sweeping epic contours. (Despite an apparently high budget and co-production benefits, the battles seem deleteriously undermanned.)

With the exception of Michel Portal's discreetly effective score, other production credits reflect pic's pallid approach to its pseudo-Homeric intentions. It may appeal to undemanding audiences, but will need a hard sell abroad.
— *Len.*

The House Where Death Lives

Dull, old-fashioned gothic horror.

A New American Films release of a Trauma Associates Ltd. picture, a John Cofrin production. Executive producer, Cofrin. Produced by Alan Beattie, Peter Shanaberg. Directed by Beattie. Features entire cast. Screenplay, Jack Viertel from a story by Beattie, Viertel; camera (Metrocolor), Stephen Posey; editor, Robert Leighton; music, Don Peake; sound, Mark Harris; art direction, Steven Legler; assistant director, David Blocker; associate producers, David Charles Thomas, Thomas Viertel. Reviewed at 42d St. Times Square theater, N.Y., Feb. 7, 1984. (MPAA Rating: R). Running time: **82 MINS.**
Meredith Stone .... Patricia Pearcy
Jeffrey Fraser .... David Hayward
Gabriel .... John Dukakis
Ivar Langrock .... Joseph Cotten

Phillip .... Leon Charles
Duffy .... Alice Nunn
Wilfred .... Patrick Pankhurst
Pamela .... Simone Griffeth

"The House Where Death Lives" is a painfully slow-paced and old-fashioned gothic horror film, made in 1980 and originally titled "Delusion." Once planned for release by the since-defunct The International Picture Show Co., picture has had territorial release over the past two years via Gotham-based New American Films as well as pay-tv exposure, ahead of its current Manhattan debut.

Trite tale unfolds in flashback (bookended by the heroine writing this story to her dad), concerning a young man, introverted nurse Meredith (Patricia Pearcy) arriving at a mansion to take care of crippled Ivar Langrock (Joseph Cotten). Another newcomer to the Fairlawn estate is Gabriel (John Dukakis), Langrock's suspicious-looking 16-year-old grandson who has been living in a commune.

Overly expository opening reels introduce (with a straight face) many clichés of the gothic format: a face seen at an upstairs window of a room that is always kept locked, a heroine prone to wandering inquisitively about the house and grounds, etc. One by one, cast members are dispatched by a sudden bonk on the head from a blunt instrument (it turns out to be a leg from a table) until the final reel reveals who the crazy is. Wedged into the package for the umpteenth time is a case of incest as a long-ago incident and plot motivator.

Director Alan Beattie fails to generate suspense or atmosphere in a picture that remains low-key even during violent scenes. Acting is more than competent, with red-headed, fair-complexioned Patricia Pearcy making a distinctive impression in the rather limited central role and Cotten (in his most recent screen appearance) thoroughly professional in support. Despite its release title linking the film with the overworked "blame it on the house" horror genre, pic's locale is neutrally plain and there are no supernatural overtones.
—*Lor.*

Kids From Shaolin
(CHINA-COLOR)

Hong Kong, Feb. 9.

A Chung Yuen Film Production. Released by Sun-Luen Film Co. Directed by Chang Hsin Yen. Produced by Liu Yet Yuen; Executive producer, Fu Chi, Lam Ping Kwan. Leung Kwong Kin. Stars Jet Lee, Wong Chiu-Yin. Screenplay, Leung Chi Keung, Ho Shu Hua; Camera (color), Chau Pak Ling. Reviewed at Nanyang Theater, Hong Kong, Feb. 8, 1984. Running time: **100 MINS.**
(Mandarin soundtrack with Cantonese and English subtitles)

Jet Lee is a name to remember. His reflexes are fast, he moves gracefully with macho elegance, knows his martial arts without being menacing and has the sympathetic, teenage innocence and wholesome aura that Jackie Chan used to possess. He comes on like a Disney hero and does not resort to Chan's "toilet humour." His name is easy to remember and conjures images of a jet-propelled star from Hong Kong ... but he is from Mainland China.

Lastly, he has the boy-next-door image and is not built like a truck driver. Jet first gained public attention in 1982 when the film "The Shaolin Temple," directed by Chang Hsin Yen, was released.

It was a major film, a breakthrough in martial arts films as it was not only shot on location in China, but also used the country's top martial arts champions and actors from the renowned Henan opera in cooperation with Hong Kong production team. But one performance and personality stood out from the rest and upstaged the never before filmed sights of China. That was Jet Lee. The public response was tremendous and it was inevitable to star him in "Kids From Shaolin" to prominently compete with Hong Kong-made product for the Lunar New Year.

The film starts with a gang of thieves looting a village headed by the Lung family. Tin Lung, a Shaolin graduate, escapes with his brother and seven other boys. They hide in the Phoenix village which is situated on one of the river banks of Likiang. Lung trains the boys in kung fu so that they can seek revenge later. The plot has been done before, but the difference is the eye-filling locale and the incorporation of a sub-plot in the form of romance laced with comedy.

Across the river is a family with eight daughters. The father is Pao Seng-feng, known for his swordsmanship of Wudong and wants to have a son to be his succesor. After several attempts, Pao's wife finally delivers a baby and all the misunderstandings between the Lung and Pao families were resolved after a bit of fighting to ward off the villains.

"Shaolin Kids" is a visual martial arts pic, old fashioned in style and execution but fast moving, laden with human sentiments and forgotten values about respect for elders, discipline, kinship, dignity and courtship before marriage. The film is engaging and entertaining.

One cannot help but notice the improved cinematography, technical qualities of the production, the right balançe of talking and fighting sequences, and the Hong Kong-type pacing. It is definitely an improvement from the '82 "Shaolin Temple." "The Kids From Shaolin" should have long and strong legs for the action markets outside Hong Kong. It has the added appeal of being entirely filmed in fascinating locales not yet polluted by neon signs and discos. —*Mel.*

Epilogo
(Epilog)
(SPANISH – COLOR)

Madrid, Feb. 10.

A Ditirambo Films S.A. production; associate producer, La Salamandra. Features entire cast. Written and directed by Gonzalo Suárez; camera (color), Carlos Suárez; sets, Wolfgang Burman; editor, Eduardo Biurrun; production director, Jose Jacoste; music, Juan Jose Garcia Caffi; made with participation of Spanish Television. Reviewed at Cine Amaya, Madrid, Feb. 3, 1984. Running time: 89 MINS.
Ditirambo .... Jose Sacristan
Rocabruno .... Francisco Rabal
Laina .... Charo Lopez
Ana .... Sandra Toral
With Manuel Zarzo, Cyra Toledo, Jose Arranz, Manuel Calvo, Sonia Martinez, Martin Adjemian, Chus Lampreave, David Velez

In 1967 helmer Gonzalo Suárez made a whimsical, way-out experimental film called "Ditirambo" in which he let his imagination stray over alternately real and imagined adventures of a sort of antihero and writer. As an offbeat film, with no apparent rhyme or reason, it mustered an underground following of local film aficionados, but went busy at the boxoffice.

Now, 17 years older, Suarez casts a nostalgic eye back upon his creations, which first came to light in one of his novels written in the early 1960s. Hence title of pic, "Epilog." Though by now Suarez' technique is more polished, the zaniness of the original film is maintained in this droll exercise in indulgence which is given a lift by presence of two topnotch Spanish thesps, José Sacristán and Francisco Rabal.

Sacristán and Rabal are Ditirambo and Rocabruno, two writers in search of new plots and stories. But the latter's pen has run dry, causing Ditirambo to crash his former partner's pastoral hideaway and try to verbally bludgeon him into pounding the old Underwood again. Rocabruno ultimately is convinced to do so, if his former buddy will bring around his wife and they can recreate their love triangle of olden days.

Yarn is told with many digressions, asides, flashbacks; though we are told at the beginning that Rocabruno has finally committed suicide and Ditirambo has been awarded the Nobel Prize, none of it seemingly is to be taken literally by the audience, as Suarez continues his filmic games, eschewing any attempt at "reality."

As in the original "Ditirambo," there are touches of humor, a few gags, snippets of philosophical dialog and some plain cussedness as the chums go at each other and think up skits, which are then served up to us as mini-films.

The clowning is Suarez's way of indulging himself. Seventeen years after "Ditirambo," there isn't much difference in this update. — *Besa.*

Teppanyaki
(HONG KONG-COLOR)

Hong Kong, Jan. 27.

A Golden Harvest presentation and release. Executive producer, Raymond Chow. Directed by Michael Hui. Stars Michael Hui, Sally Yeh, Frances Yip, Lo Hoi Pang, Tsou Mei I, Michael Lai, David Cheung, Paul Ng, Hui Ying Sau. Production supervisor, Louis Sit; associate producer, Olivia Mok Bassett. Production designer, David T. W. Chan; camera (color), Larry Shiu; editor, Cheung Yiu Chung; music, Chris Babida. Reviewed at Queen's Theater, Hong Kong, Jan. 26, 1984. Running Time: 100 MINS.
(Cantonese soundtrack with English subtitles)

Michael Hui is one of the biggest stars of the Cantonese film industry with his comedies that have been copied frequently by fellow domestic filmmakers. He returns to the screen after an absence of about three years and to the high profile of showbiz as a solo act without equally known brother Sam Hui.

"Teppanyaki" is Hui's hilarious smorgasbord of Cantonese-flavored comedy sketches loosely linked in a one-line storyline. The title is a Japanese style of cooking.

Hui portrays a poor refugee from China who marries a rich, fat lady whose father owns a restaurant that features Teppanyaki-type cuisine. Hui works there and is completely overpowered by his father-in-law and henpecked by an extremely suspicious, spoiled wife.

Two lovely co-stars were unfortunately misused here merely as decorative pieces. Singer Frances Yip looks ridiculous in a fright wig playing second fiddle to everyone including a dog, and Sally Yeh serves as "Bo Derek" to Hui's dull kitchen life.

In Cinema City's "Aces Go Places," the scene stealer was a baby, but in this Golden Harvest production, the attention-getter is an old man who plays Hui's grandfather.

"Teppanyaki" tries to combine the slapstick antics of Jerry Lewis and Blake Edwards' satire in a scenario built around the restaurant business, Oriental food, domestic traumas, bizarre characters, an exotic tropical location outside Hong Kong and the business of cooking and eating. It is altogether an engaging comedy, if one is not too critical with the disjointed and often hollow efforts of the director-producer. The theme of the "underdog" is elaborated upon often to create sympathy and elaborates on man's idiocies in his struggle to have fun in life.

The film definitely has vitality and features a cross section of middle-class Hong Kong lunacy. The problem here is that with all the present advantages of popular stars, co-stars, Philippine scenery and colorful characters, they have no specific destination.

But "Teppanyaki's" moving spirit is inoffensively amiable and the strong determination of Hui's

harmless inventiveness to entertain is intact. They are welded on to the kind of adult pop cartoon strip that is unremarkable, but entertaining.

His viewers will enjoy his humor and high escapism.—*Mel.*

Xafnikos Erotas
(Sudden Love)
(GREEK-COLOR)

Athens, Feb. 10.

A George Tsemperopoulos coproduction with the Greek Film Center written and directed by George Tsemperopoulos, based on the novel "Talgo" by Vassilis Alexakis. Stars Betty Livanou, Antonis Theodoracopoulos, Nikitas Tsakiroglou, Thanassis Papagerguiou, Sophia Seirli, T. Papadakis, Nicos Pilayos, George Tountis. Camera (color), George Panoussopoulos; music, Stamatis Spanoudakis; art director Nicos Perrakis. Reviewed at the Atheneon Cinema, Athens, Feb. 10, 1984. Running time: 100 MINS.

This is the first fiction picture directed by George Tsemperopoulos who has only one documentary picture to his credit "Megara," a prize winner at the Thessaloniki Film Festival some years ago. This film marks a turning point to his career and establishes him as one of the promising new film directors in this country. By using a love story from a Greek novel he adapted it into a film with a quality of reality through excellent lensing and good acting. It is a noteworthy picture which, although dealing with a typical unconventional love affair, is not confined by Greek boundaries, giving it a cosmopolitan aspect. The picture being released currently in Athens first run theaters is doing extremely well. Foreign prospects against stronger competition will be fair.

Based on the novel "Talgo" by Vassilis Alexakis, the script describes the love affair of a young woman, Heleni, married to a second husband and mother of a teenage son from her first marriage. An ex-ballet dancer, Heleni is bored to death by her dull conventinal life with her second husband, when she meets Gregori, an executive with the Greek Section of the European Common Market, who came from Paris to visit his mother. He is married to a French woman and father of two children.

He falls in love with Heleni and when he returns to Paris they communicate by phone until he asks her to join him in Lisbon where he had to attend a convention. Heleni on the pretext of feeling very tired leaves her husband to go to Paris. Instead she goes to Lisbon to meet Gregori.

They spend a week there full of love, Heleni is ready to sacrifice everything to live with her lover. But she realizes that Gregori does not want to ruin his marriage. Bitterly disappointed she leaves him early in the morning of the day of their departure while he is still asleep, to give an end to an affair which would not lead anywhere.

George Tsemperopoulos, wishing perhaps to avoid the pitfall of filming a melodrama, has turned out a picture which lacks the pathos, deeper emotional insight and dramatic tension which would distinguish this love story from any other similar one. The use of flashbacks and certain lapses in the script lead to an unevenness in the film's structure. But these weak spots of the script and direction are overcome by the visually striking outdoor sequences on the film and the beautiful background.

Betty Livanou gives a sensitive performance handling the emotional levels of the story. She had won a State Prize for her performance as Heleni. Antonis Theodoracopoulos, a legit actor makes his screen debut as Gregori, and he is equally good. However, both of them as lovers do not create the romantic sparks that would be expected.

Nikitas Tsakiroglou as Heleni's husband is good as well as the rest of the cast. Credits are tops especially lenser George Panoussopoulos, a film director himself, whose camera work is outstanding. Some of the most effective shots in the film are long to be remembered: When Heleni is standing at the end of a rock looking at the waves of Atlantic Ocean dreaming to go far away, or/and when she strolls in the night at the pier where fishermen get ready to sail, and some other.

The music by Stamatis Spanoudakis is a definite asset as well as the title song. The overall art direction for the picture by Nicos Perrakis has certainly contributed a lot to the beauty of this picture.

— *Rena.*

Schatjes!
(Darlings!)
(DUTCH-COLOR)

Amsterdam, Feb. 8.
A Meteor Film/The Movies release of Chris Brouwer & Haig Balian. Directed by Ruud van Hemert. Features entire cast. Screenplay, Van Hemert; camera (color), Theo van de Sande; editor, Ton de Graaff; music, Van Hamert; sound, Georges Bossaers; Reviewed at The Movies, Amsterdam, Feb. 3, 1984. Running time: **98 MINS.**

Madelon Gisberts	Akkemay
John Gisberts	Peter Faber
Danny Gisberts	Geert de Jong
Thijs Gisberts	Frank Schaafsma
Jan-Julius Gisberts	Pepijn Somer
Valentijn Gisberts	Olivier Somer
Pete Stewart	Rijk de Gooijer
Dennis	Erik Koningsberger

Credit Movies Film Productions and Ruud van Hemert with hitting on a novel approach in Dutch film entertainment. They've come up with a zany version of the war between parents and children. It may well delight Dutch teen and preteen audiences and amuse postteens who enjoy farcical aggressiveness and irreverence towards generally accepted codes — including those of Dutch kidpic filmmaking. "Darlings!" could reap sizable b.o. success at home, and might attract audiences offshore.

In his theatrical debut, helmerscripter-composer Ruud van Hemert, after 14 years of television work for Holland's progressive, self-willed web VPRO, aimed at egghead aficionados of popular VPRO-shows he helped put together: spoofs of the burghers and celebrations of bad taste. However, per van Hemert, the most potent influence was Hollywood picture making, discernible in "Darlings!" in an unflagging accent on direct action, shooting for impact, cutting for speed.

Pic, at the outset, plunges into farce, heavily spoofing the military on an air base; then lunges into the mutual terrorizing of bickering parents Peter Faber and Geert de Jong and their rebellious brood. And it never lets up.

It's one rib-tickling or scandalous situation after another, as teenage son Frank Schaafsma blows up his parents' bedroom, teenage daughter Akkemay (well-remembered as the quietly seductive nymphet in Lili Rademakers' "Menuet") attacks her mother for going after tennis-coach Erik Koningsberger, whom they both want and Akkemay gets).

The two small boys, Pepijn and Olivier Somer, are funny as the rear guard resistance in the all-out war in the family home. Faber, who is a helicopter pilot at the nearby air base, and his knowledgeable sidekick Rijk de Gooijer, watching the goings-on below, see Faber's house barricaded by barbed wire. A siege by the military (lifted from umpteen gangster pics) fails to dislodge Faber's offspring. The appropriately cynical ending has the pursuing parents buried forever under a sandslide as the kids drive off merrily — into a future not all that different from what they despised in their parents' life.

Buffs will notice sundry quotes from American genre pics. But one needn't be a buff to spot Faber's pastiche of Jack Nicholson in "The Shining," mad grin, axe and all. The single "romantic" turn of Akkemay and Koningsberger in love has pink lighting, slow motion, and, for once, soft music. The adult actors, limning caricatures, ably adapt their proven talent to Van Hemert's purposeful direction. But the teens and tots, playing it straight, elicit most interest.

Van Hemert succeeded in creating the effect of determined anarchy he went for within most of his action-filled situations. But, as one situation follows another, pic as a whole tends to lose some of its steam, because there is no storyline to speak of, and no build-up of characters to support a modicum of audience identification. "Darlings!" is a circus. — *Ewa.*

Berlin Film Fest

Les Voleurs De La Nuit
(Thieves After Dark)
(FRENCH-COLOR)

Berlin, Feb. 27.
A Parafrance production and release. Produced by Michel Gue. Directed by Sam Fuller. Features entire cast. Screenplay, Fuller and Olivier Beer, based on Beer's novel, "Le Chant des enfants morts." Camera (color), Philippe Rousselot; art direction, Dominique Andre; editor, Catherine Kelber; music, Ennio Morricone. Reviewed at the Berlin Film Festival (competition), Feb. 27, 1984. Running time: **92 MINS.**

Isabelle	Veronique Jannot
François	Bobby Di Cicco
Inspector	Victor Lanoux
Isabelle's Mother	Stephan Audran
Louis Crepin	Claude Chabrol
Corinne Desterne	Camille de Casabianca
Jose	Andreas Voutsinas
Morell	Micheline Presle
Zoltan	Sam Fuller

French critics have long admired the work of American director Sam Fuller. However, in his maiden effort on their turf, the veteran filmmaker comes up short of his best U.S. pictures.

"Thieves After Dark" is a contemporary yarn of two young, unemployed people who concoct a series of petty crimes for money and revenge. Though awkward in execution, their offenses go well until an irony of fate implicates them in murder. It's a case of deceiving appearances which ultimately leads to tragic consequences.

Shown in its English version, the story centers on François (Bobby Di Cicco), an American-reared, French-born cellist unable to land a job who encounters the similarly situated Isabelle (Veronique Jannot) — an art historian — in an employment office. An ineffectual supervisor prompts a chair throwing incident with Isabelle and François whisks her out of the office.

The two become lovers and, after failed attempts to mount an act as street musicians, Isabelle suggests they seek revenge on three of the more offensive employment interviewers. They decide to break into their apartments and steal some valuable trinkets.

The premise of the film is both intriguing and conforming to Fuller's penchant for off-center characters. In this case, one is reminded of "They Live By Night's" criminal couple transferred to the big city and faced with modern problems.

The director's twist occurs when one of the victims, unaware of the young couple's presence, falls from his window to his death while engaging in secret voyeuristic pursuits. Initially, Isabelle believes she is responsible for the fall — a misconception shared by police investigators.

The prime failing of the film is its unhurried pace up until this moment. Its second half — a pursuit and desperate flight — finds Fuller on surer ground both for action and irony. There's a real sense of frenzy and danger as the couple manages to elude the police and stay one step in front of their hunters.

Also contributing to the picture's awkwardness is some stilted dialog coupled with the disappointing dubbing of English voices for the French performers. This is particularly acute when Ennio Morricone's excellent score is absent.

Teaming of Di Cicco and Jannot provides potent chemistry but Lanoux, as their pursuer, is never fully established to provide the type of menace which would elevate the tension. Technical elements, apart from sound, are strong, suggesting better results from foreign playdates than possible U.S. distribution.

While far from vintage Fuller, "Thieves After Dark" has the director's unique flavor. Commercial prospects are uneven, but reports of the picture being a catastrophe are certainly overblown. It is a light entertainment with exploitable and playable components. — *Klad.*

Morgen In Alabama
(A German Lawyer)
(WEST GERMAN-COLOR)

Berlin, Feb. 23.
An FFAT Production, Munich, in coproduction with Pro-jekt Filmproduktion im Filmverlag der Autoren and Rübezahl-Film; world rights, Futura Film, Munich. Stars Maximilian Schell. Directed by Norbert Kückelmann. Screenplay, Kückelmann, Thomas Petz, Dagmar Kekulé; camera (color), Jürgen Jürges, Renato Fortunato; music, Markus Urchs; sets, Winfried Hennig, Franz Bauer, Michael Aldmüller; sound, Hay von Zündt; ass't directors, Renate Leiffer, Peter Carpentier; production managers, Jo Schäfer, Florian Richter; production, Inge Richter. Reviewed at Berlin Film Fest (competition), Feb. 23, '84. Running time: **126 MINS.**

Cast: Maximilian Schell, Lena Stolze, Robert Aldini, Wolfgang Kieling, Katrin Ackerman, Dr. Manfred Rendl, Reinhard Hauff, Jörg Hube.

Norbert Kückelmann specializes in films dealing with court records and trials: "The Experts" (1972), "Shooting Practice" (1974), "Fear Is A Second Shadow" (1975), and "The Last Years of Childhood" (1979). Now comes the fifth: "A German Lawyer," investigating the current sociopolitical phenomenon of neo-Nazi groups in Germany. The German title refers in a loose context to Bertolt Brecht's writings (particularly a song in "Mahagony"), and thus the teasing title "Tomorrow in Alabama." The historical frame-of-reference, however, has to do with a recent bombing in Munich during Oktoberfest celebrations, the blame placed entirely on right-wing extremist groups. Since the film ends exactly on the same note as the Oktoberfest incident, "A German

Lawyer" scores as a docu-drama portrait.

Another Austrian film, Walter Bannert's "The Heirs" (1982), has also hit the headlines of late. It, too, deals with young kids joining neo-Nazi youth clubs, then gradually becoming so prone to violence that cold-blooded murder is the outcome. When Bannert's film played West Germany, threats were made on theater owners and a fire-bombing war attempted in Mannheim.

Kückelmann views the danger through the eyes of an investigation lawyer (Maximilian Schell). During a political rally a shot is fired out of the crowd in the direction of a state minister (an actor dubbed with the familiar voice of Hans Dietrich Genscher, head of the German Foreign Office). The lad is apprehended by the police and the papers immediately link him to leftist terrorists. The lawyer, however, suspects otherwise after looking into the boy's background and noting his membership in a reactionary youth club.

The twist comes at the moment when it's evident via tv-and-photo news coverage that the supposed assassination attempt amounted to little more than a shot in the air — a warning, so to speak. Eventually, the boy goes free for lack of convincing evidence. The focus of the film shifts to the neo-Nazi organization itself. It isn't long before a different youth kills a number of innocent political exiles, then commits suicide on the spot. So when the boy in question also disappears from sight, the worst is feared — and happens. During a Munich gathering, the boy again walks into a crowd and blows himself up, killing many as it happened at the aforementioned Oktoberfest.

Kückelmann has made a kind of stretched-out "Z" along the lines of the German experience and with a subplot that oddly parallels such Yank detective thrillers as "Anatomy of a Murder" and the Schell-toplined "Judgment at Nuremburg" (for which he won an Oscar). But in order to win auds for this political-thriller at home and abroad, he has to trim at least a half-hour out of the meandering plot. Lensing by Jürgen Jürges is a major plus. — *Holl.*

Nankyoku Monogatari
(Antarctica)
(JAPANESE-COLOR)

Berlin, Feb. 26.
A Nankyoku Monogatari Seisaku-Iinkai production, with Gakken Co. Ltd. and Kurahara Productions. Produced by Masaru Kakutani and Koretsugu Kurahara. Directed by Koreyoshi Kurahara. Features entire cast. Script, Tasuo Nogami, Kan Saji, Toshiro Ishido, Koreyoshi Kurahara; camera (Fujicolor), Akira Shiizuka; editors, Akira Suzuki, Koreyoshi Kurahara; sound, Kenichi Benitani; music, Vangelis; sets, Hiroshi Tokuda; dog trainers, Tadaomi Miya.

Reviewed at Zoo-Palast, Berlin (Berlin Film Festival Competition), Feb 21, 1984. Running time: 137 MINS.
Cast: Ken Takakura, Tsunehiko Watase, Eiji Okada, Masako Natsume, Takeshi Kusaka, Shigeru Koyama, Shin Kishida, Takashi Obayashi, Keiko Oginome.

Three years in the making, on freezing Antarctic locations, "Antarctica" is, first of all, a very handsomely made epic of endurance and fortitude, not by men but by a pack of husky dogs. Unusual premise, and totally realistic handling, give the film plenty of punch, but vastly excessive running time and rather awkward structure mitigate against it, finally. Pruning is indicated, and a fine film is still in there somewhere.

Set in 1957, pic takes almost an hour before it gets to the main theme. A Japanese Antarctic expedition, relying heavily on a team of 15 husky dogs, is forced through circumstances to leave the mutts behind, chained, at the base-camp. Up to this point, the film — though confirming the bond between dogs and men when the dogs help their masters when snow-blindness affects them — has really taken far too much time to set up the situation, especially as none of the expedition members are established as interesting characters in their own right. But with the abandonment of the dogs comes the drama, as some manage to free themselves from their chains and fend for themselves during the punishing winter months, catching fish trapped in the ice, or killing seals or even sea-birds. One by one, the critters perish, one falling from a high cliff, two drowning in icy water. But, finally, the expedition returns and the two dog handlers (who've been wracked with guilt for a year) see the two surviving dogs on the horizon: to a pounding Vangelis score, and an inevitable slow motion, the woofers run towards the men — but instead of going for the jugular, as one might have expected after being abandoned for a year, there's a joyful ending.

It's certainly a super-production, with extremely handsome photography of magnificent icy vistas. The dogs are the stars, of course, and though the film is presumably aimed at animal-lovers, there may well be distress at the apparent cruelty to the dogs during shooting: there are some very nasty moments indeed involving the unfortunate animals. The actors hardly get a look in, and scenes back in Japan during the ordeal of the hounds are all superfluous, only adding to an already inflated running time. The Vangelis score is an obvious plus.

With drastic editing and restructing, "Anarctica" could do biz around the world. Artistically, its considerable merits are compromised by its sheer size and length. Fox Classics has it for the U.S.
—*Strat.*

Klassenverhältnisse
(Class Relations)
(W. GERMAN-FRENCH-B&W)

Berlin, Feb. 22.
A Coproduction of Janus Film & TV and Hessischer Rundfunk (HR), Frankfurt, in collaboration with NEF-Diffusion, Paris. Features entire cast. Written and directed by Jean-Marie Straub and Danièle Huillet, based on Franz Kafka's fragment-novel "America" and the rediscovered novel "The Lost One." Camera, William Lubtchansky; staging, Georg Brommer; lighting, Jim Howe; sound, Louis Hochet; editing, Straub/-Huillet. Reviewed at Berlin Film Fest (Competition), Feb. 21, '84. Runnning time: 126 MINS.
Cast: Christian Heinisch (Karl Rossmann), Reinald Schnell (Stoker), Anna Schnell (Line), Klaus Traube (Captain), Hermann Hartmann (Head Purser), Jean-Fançois Quinque (Stewart), Mario Adorf (Uncle Jakob), Gérard Semaan (Schubal), Friedrich Wilhelm Vobel (Pollunder), Willi Dewelk (Chauffeur), Anne Bold (Klara), Tilman Heinisch (Green), Aloys Pompetzki (Servant), Burchkhardt Stoelck (Mack), Harun Farocki (Delamarche), Manfred Blank (Robinson), Katrin Bold (Chief Cook), Alf Bold (Waiter), Libgart Schwarz (Therea), Nazzareno Bianconi (Giacomo), Alfred Edel (Head Wiater), Andi Engel (Head Porter), Franz Hillers (Taxi Driver), Klaus Feddermann (1st Policeman), Henning Feddermann (2nd Policeman), Laura Betti (Brunelda), Georg Brintrup (Student), Thom Andersen (Guile).

Of Franz Kafka's three posthumously published fragmentary novels — "The Castle" (1925), "The Trial" (1926), and "America" (1927) — it's "America" that's the least known and quite unjustly so. More than likely, this is due to the failure of Max Brod, Kafka's biographer and close friend, to interest theater associates in doing a stage version of the material. Even in the seventh art, "America" has proven to be unfortunate: Orson Welles filmed "The Trial" (1962) and Rudolf Noelte "The Castle" (1968) (with Maximilian Schell), but nobody dared the third part of the trilogy until Jean-Marie Straub and Danièle Huillet attempted the same under the title "Class Relations."

Undoubtedly, the rechristening of the Kafka original — known to admirers of the literary genius under two versions, Brod's titled "America" and Kafka's own "The Lost One" (rediscovered recently) as cited among his private papers — is to give Straub and Huillet (a husband-wife team) the chance to cloak their project in their usual political-impact ideology. "Class Relations" (why not "Class Enemies"?) says something about America from the directorial as well as the literary perspective, make no mistake, just as it's sure that the "K" in Karl Rossmann (Kafka's protagonist in "America") has a lot to do with Josef K in "The Trial" and with the author's own obsessive preoccupations.

This is a faithful adaptation of the original. The text is spoken with a cadence peculiar to German theater, and the film unfolds like chapters in the book. The Charles Dickens-inspired "The Stoker" has the 16-year-old youth Karl Rossmann from Prague landing in New York in the pre-WW1 days when jobs were scarce for immigrants just off the boat, the main impression being that of a friendly contact with the ship's stoker. Thereafter comes the meeting with rich Uncle Jakob, a self-made man with a large transport firm under his charge. This brush with the industrial world leads to the predictable break, and the lad is then an elevator boy in the Hotel Occidental — only to lose this job due to his acute sense of justice in an environment of pettiness and hypocrisy, represented by the criminal figures of Delamarche and Robinson. Not even a guardian-angel figure in the person of the Head Cook can rescue him now. His last job is as a servant before departing from new employment at "The Great Natural Theatre of Oklahoma" — the note on which both the book and novel end.

Piecing this difficult film together in the midst of a film festival is like scaling Mount Everest from the inside (to steal a routine from Peter Sellers and his Goon Shows) — the terrain of both Kafka and Straub have to be coordinated in the consciousness to catch the refined nuances. In any case, the first reading of "Class Relations" is positive — save for the theatricality of the whole affair. Max Brod finally has his wish fulfilled, but the filmic aspects are hardly vintage Straub. But even this is to underscore the importance of "Class Relations" to both the German film scene and the Berlinale program at the midway point.

Static camera positions and subtle lighting are the aesthetic pluses, plus many thesp performances. Libgart Schwarz as Therese in a long monologue framed in the light of a window makes for a particularly fascinating figure, for she speaks Straub/Huillet's rhythmically directed texts in a perfected cadence. By contrast, Mario Adorf as Uncle Jakob remains a character actor of plumb coarseness fairly exuding Kapitalistic Amerika. Reinald Schnell (a respected artist-filmmaker in his own right) gives another meaningful "performance" as the ship's stoker. The one puzzler is Christian Heinisch as Karl/Kafka Rossmann: an innocent knee-deep in the muddy waters of injustice needs a shade of supple humanity to make him vulnerable.

Catch "Class Relations" if you're a Straub fan. But don't swallow it whole if you're a Straub/Huillet admirer. —*Holl.*

Das Arche Noah Prinzip
(The Noah's Ark Principle)
(WEST GERMAN-COLOR)

Berlin, Feb. 22.
A Coproduction of the Munich Film & Television School and Solaris Film, Munich, in collaboration with Maran Film, Munich. Features entire cast. Written and directed by

Roland Emmerich. Camera (color), Egon -Werdin, Thomas Merker; sets, Annette Deiters, Roger Katholing; music, Hubert Bartnoloma; editing, Tomy Wigand. Reviewed at Berlin Film Fest (Competition), Feb. 22, '84. Running time: **100 MINS.**

Cast: Richy Müller (Billy Hayes), Franz Buchrieser (Max Marek), Avival Joel (Eva Tompson), Mathias Fuchs (Felix Kronenberg).

Roland Emmerich's debut film, "The Noah's Ark Principle," also happens to be his diploma project at the Munich Film and Television School, as well as an "author's film" supported by the Kuratorium Junger Deutscher Film. And, as has happened in the past in the cases of Werner Herzog and Johannes Schaaf and Jean-Marie Straub, the Berlinale reached out its hand by selecting the pic as an official entry in the competition.

Film is a scifier along the lines of George Lucas (not "Star Wars," but his student-days short "THX-1138" in 1965 at the UCLA Cinema School) and the typical tv spacelab serials. It's the story of a pair of skilled astronauts experimenting in the year 1997 with a weather station far out in the stars, the idea of the experiments on "Florida Arklab" (an American-European joint enterprise) being to determine the effect of experiments on weather and climate. However, evil powers are at work in the background: the research lab is ordered to fiddle with the weather over Saudi Arabia in view of a Western invasion of that country — by setting up a smoke screen to insure surprise.

This ploy, unfortunately, means a catastrophe could take place in the Indian Ocean: a flood just like in the days of Noah and his ark. The commander refuses to pull off the experiment as his technician gradually comes to realize what's going on. Houston ground command dispatches two other astronauts to carry the experiment through to its proper military conclusion which, in turn, leads to a shoot-out in the lab, the good guys winning in the end. A man and a woman astronaut return to Earth and recount their story, then are whisked away to disappear conveniently and close the records for good on the blatant military venture.

The story is too threadbare to convince, and there isn't much excitement to knit all the loose ends together. Emmerich is content to show that he's technically adept at playing with Cinemascope and stereo, even though the end result is a

hollow shell without dialog or a strong narrative line to make the events jell. That isn't enough to score at a competitive international film festival, but he could do well as a quaint item on the upcoming fest circuit. Lensing by Egon Werdin is a plus, ditto the Bavaria Studios special effects. — *Holl.*

Xue, Yong Shi Re De
(Blood Is Always Hot)
(PEOPLE'S REPUBLIC OF CHINA-COLOR)

Berlin, Feb. 24.

China Film Export Corp. presentation of a Beijing Film Studio production. Produced by Yang Kebing. Directed by Wen Yan. Screenplay by Zong Fuxian and He Guofo, based on the stage play. Camera (color), Ru Shuiren; art direction, Shao Ruigang; editor, Zhan Quiang; music, Zhang Piji. Reviewed at the Berlin Film Festival (Competition), Feb. 23, 1984. Running time: **107 MINS.**

Luo Xingang	Yang Zaibao
Jiang Dingan	Fang Haiging
An Min	Mai Wenyan
An Kai	Mei Xi
Li Ziliang	Cheng Guodian
Xia Bingshi	Lu Fei
Sun Jianfang	Xie Fang
Shen Hua	Liu Kinyi
Song	Guan Shuzhen
Zhang	Wang Yunia
Song Qisozhen	Yin Kin
Fang Ying	Jin Kangning

Mainland China's "Blood Is Always Hot," competing at the Berlin festival, provides some pleasant surprises for viewers familiar with Chinese productions. The film is among the most dramatically complex and visually interesting from the fledgling film nation. Yet, finally it emerges as still rather bland by Western standards and far from the breakthrough picture observers keep hoping to view.

Story centers around a silk printing and dyeing factory. The plant's new director is an honest, aggressive sort with visions of moving into international marketing. However, his progressive steps are repeatedly stymied by petty bureaucrats and official red tape.

Woven into the main plot are a series of intertwining tales involving a number of plant workers. These vignettes allow both a breadth of romance and comedy to offset the underlying political concerns of the filmmakers.

The mix of popular front comedy with "Norma Rae" sociology sounds better than it plays. The real eye-opener of the film is the portrait of black marketeering, graft and petty officialdom running through the story. This element is only muted in the film's conclusion when we are told that this was the practice of the recent past which, according to the filmmakers no longer exists.

Performances and sentiment are rooted in the Capra tradition with goodness prevailing in the clinch. Too often characters make political statements rather than genuinely hitting an emotional chord. Still, the picture is decidedly more watchable and compelling than recent Chinese festival selections.

Also noticeably more dynamic is the visual style and pacing which only seizes up toward the conclusion. Commercial prospects remain extremely limited but "Blood

Is Always Hot" certainly provides encouraging signs from behind the Great Wall. —*Klad.*

Woenno-Polewoj Roman
(A Front Romance)
(USSR-COLOR)

Berlin, Feb. 20.

A Sovexport release of a Filmstudio Odessa production. Directed and written by Petr Todorovskij. Features entire cast. Camera (color), Valeri Blinov; art direction, Valentin Konovalov; music, Igor Kantjukov and Petr Todorovskij. Reviewed at the Berlin Film Festival (competition), Feb. 19, 1984. Running time: **88 MINS.**

Sascha Netushilin	Nikolai Burljavev
Ljuba Autipowna	Natalia Andrejtschenko
Vera	Inna Tshurikova
Kowikow	Victor Proskurin
Dubrowski	Z. Gerdt

Soviet entry in the Berlin festival, "A Front Romance," is a hoary tale of unfulfilled passion with minimal prospects outside the Eastern Bloc. Pedestrian effort lacks strength in either the areas of action or characterization to grab western audiences and should promptly find its place nestled in Soviet film weeks.

Story opens in the spring of 1944 in the camps along the front lines of the European arena. Sascha, a lowly soldier, develops an impossible desire for a woman fighter involved with one of the officers. She is aware of his yearning but does nothing to make his lot easier.

After peace is declared, the characters resume their lives but several years later, Sascha recognizes the woman — Ljuba — selling muffins in the streets of Moscow. The old attraction once again flares up, especially since her lover has died and Ljuba is faced with raising a young daughter.

However, the man has since married and his growing relationship threatens to topple his marriage to the proper Vera. Nonetheless, Sascha persists and one senses the woman is merely playing him for the fool until she can establish a permanent, secure position with a party functionary.

As is usual with Soviet films, the tale is extremely chaste and one has to fantasize the more sensual elements with difficulty. Natalia Andrejtschenko conveys the allure of Ljuba with facility but Nikolai Burljavev is much too awkward to suggest the danger of the situation. In very much a secondary role, Inna Tshurikova's Vera manages a few poignant moments.

Technical credits are unspectacular in that has to be an easily forgettable endeavor. "A Front Romance" recalls earlier, superior Soviet pictures and one is hard pressed to explain its presence as a festival contender. —*Klad.*

Mona Ja Palavan Rakkauden Aika
(Mona and the Time of Burning Love)
(FINNISH-COLOR)

Berlin, Feb. 28.

A National Filmi Óy production. Directed by Mikko Niskanen. Features entire cast. Screenplay Pekka Parviainen, Anna-Leena Harkonen, Arja Tiainen, Timo Humaloja, Taavi Kassila; camera (color), Pertti Mutanen; sound, Seppo Anttila; editor, Marjatta Niiranen; music, Matti Bergstrom, Pelle Milijoona. Reviewed at Berlin Film Festival Market, Feb. 27, 1984. Running time: **106 MINS.**

Mona	Anna-Leena Harkonen
Henkka	Markku Halme

With Liisa-Maija Laaksonen, Veli Keskivali, Sari Mallinen, Erkki Pajala.

It took five writers to concoct this youth pic, directed by one of Finland's most respected helmers, Mikko Niskanen. Title is extremely misleading, since Mona's "burning love" is not physical but spiritual. She's an apparently ordinary 16-year-old Helsinki girl, who goes about with a group of teenagers who spend their time boozing and having sex. Mona stays virginal, though, to the irritation of her new boyfriend, Henkka. Even when they go off on a weekend with the group, he gets no further than a naked cuddle.

About halfway through the film, Mona gets converted to Jesus by an earnest religious group, and her young life is transformed. Fadeout suggests (somewhat implausibly) that other members of her group will get that old-time religion too.

Pic would be great for Moral Majority unspoolings were it not for the rough language and nudity in the first (and livelier) half. Anna-Leena Harkonen, who collaborated on the script, is a youthful looker with acting ability. Tech credits are pro, though English subtitles are often misspelled.

—*Strat.*

De Stille Oceaan
(The Silent Ocean)
(DUTCH-BELGIAN-COLOR)

Berlin, Feb. 20.

A De Eerste Amsterdamse Filmassociatie van 1980 production, with Man's Film SPRL. Produced by Hans Klap. Directed by Digna Sinke. Script, Annemarie van de Putte; camera (Fujicolor), Albert Vanderwildt; editor, Jan Wouter van Reijen; sound, Lukas Boeke; music, Peter Vermeersch; executive producers, Conny Brak, Marion Hansel. Reviewed at Zoo-Palast, Berlin, at Berlin Film Festival (In Competition), Feb. 18, '84. Running time: **106 MINS.**

Marian Winters	Josee Ruiter
Emil Winters	Josse du Pauw
Rita Winters	Monique Kramer
Emilia Winters	Andrea Domburg
Frits Rosmeyer	Julien Schoenaerts
Enrique	Rafi Nahual
Miguel	Luis Granados

An earnest drama about a Dutch woman journalist just back after a lengthy stay in an unnamed Latin American country. Marian is one of those people who does everything wrong. She arrives home too late to see her father, who just died. She has tried to help a Latin American activist, Enrique, by going through the formality of marriage with him; but because she doesn't live with him, the authorities catch on and he's threatened with deportation from Holland. And she resents the way her mother and sister have treated her brother, Emil, who's mentally retarded; they've placed him in an institution from which she "rescues" him, but she makes everything worse than it was before.

With its infuriating heroine and downbeat, pessimistic mood, "The Silent Ocean" is rather heavy going. First feature by femme helmer Digna Sinke is seriously intentioned, but humorless and lethargic. Halfway through the film it's revealed why Marian looks so unhappy all the time: back in Latin America, she'd been in love with a man who was arrested and subsequently murdered. She'd found his body, with others, on a lonely beach, an image that still haunts her. Ending has Marian decide to kill Emil and herself, but only succeeds in killing her brother.

It's hard to feel much for Marian, who is manifestly making a mess of her own life and everybody else's. Josee Ruiter gives an adequate, if monotone, performance. On the other hand, Josse du Pauw is excellent as the unfortunate Emil. 16m blow-up is a bit grainy. Film was shot in Holland, Belgium and Spain (for the Latin American flashbacks) and means well even if it is, in the end, a plodding attempt to deal with the theme of how the people of the First World can help those not so well off, whether they be political refugees or mental patients. — *Strat.*

Mann Ohne Gedächtnis
(Man Without Memory)
(SWISS-COLOR)

Berlin, Feb. 28.
A Kurt Gloor Films Production, with the Bundesamt für Kultur Bern, ZDF Mainz, SRG Bern. Executive Producer, Rudolf Santschi. Written and directed by Gloor. Features entire cast. Camera (color), Franz Rath; editor, Helena Gerber; sets, Bernhard Sauter; costumes, Sylvia de Stoutz; sound, Hans Künzi; music, Jonas C. Haefeli. Reviewed at the Gloria Palace, Berlin, Feb. 27, 1984. Running time: 90 MINS.
The man....................Michael König
Lisa Brunner..............Lisi Mangold
Dr. Essner ....Hanelore Essner
Dr. Schellbert............Rudolf Bissegger
Dr. Hubert................Siegfried Kernen
Sister Mehret............Esther Christinat
Jonas ....Laszlo I. Kish
Hauri...................Ueli Eichenberger
Mrs. Schroeder.................Tina Engel

Three years ago, Kurt Gloor brought to the Berlin Festival one of the most interesting items in competition, "The Inventor." He is back and once more offers one of the strongest entries, surprisingly bypassed by the official jury.

The subject is by no means new and several other filmmakers such as Francois Truffaut ("L'Enfant Sauvage"), Werner Herzog ("Kaspar Hauser") or Reinhard Hauff ("A Knife in the Head") have treated similar themes. But Gloor chooses to give his plot a different slant and sticks faithfully to his guns, never erring in his approach.

The protagonist is a man found one grey morning by the side of the road, and picked up by the Swiss police under suspicion of vagrancy. What appears at first to be no more than a routine case soon becomes a baffling mystery, for the man has no identification papers and seems to have lost both memory and the power of speech. The normal police treatment, intimidation and a touch of violence, has no effect. Despairing of solving the riddle by themselves, the investigators move the man to a psychiatric ward, hoping science might help.

Gloor uses this basic situation to assess the reaction of modern society to someone who is alien, willingly or not, and refuses to conform. As the case is reviewed, all the traumas that have been inseparable from the subconscious of our period, emerge one after the other. It starts with the suspicion that the man is possibly a dangerous terrorist, if not at least an unwanted foreigner exploiting Swiss welcome, not to mention various other possibilities. Maybe he is a journalist out to get the medical institutions in trouble. Maybe he is a left wing psychiatrist infiltrating the establishment.

With no help from the patient, who persists in not speaking, in spite of the fact that he evidently understands what he is being told — his intellectual faculties are not harmed — as he easily defeats one of the doctors treating him, at chess, new solutions are reviewed, but none is accepted. Now the therapists care who he is and start worrying why he has to do what he does, enclose himself in a sort of voluntary autism which rejects the rest of the world.

For them, there is only one goal, to make the man talk or at least to find an adequate diagnosis to explain his silence. He is entitled to this diagnosis, but even more so is the society around him.

Under Gloor's expert guidance, it become evident the doctors are as much in need of help as he is. They cannot cope with anything outside what they consider the realms of accepted social behavior and are willing to go to the limits in order to have all men behave according to the same standards. The man's silence arouses aggression and by the end of the film it is clearly suggested that instead of helping they are quite capable of harming him, just to make him conform.

The questions the film raises such as the right of a man to be silent if he so wishes and the rights of the society around him to infringe on his privacy, or the duty of the medical profession that according to some has the obligation to treat anyone defined as sick by them, whether he likes it or not, are suggested intelligently, without taking one step beyond the straightforward presentation of the plot.

The dialog uses a lot of computer expressions, the man described alternatively as someone who has erased his memory banks, or has pulled out the plug. No attempt is made to show the doctors as the villains of the play and there is no idealization of the silent person. The style is dry, efficient, matter-of-fact, with glimpses of humor relieving the seriousness.

Thus, a therapist covers the cage of his parrot to shut him up, before he sets out to make his patient talk; another defines pessimism as long-term optimism; still another protests that patients aren't in the hospital to enjoy themselves, which would justify his rough treatment of them.

Even better, Gloor builds a solid Swiss background, implying all criticisms concerning over-pedantic conduct, mistrust of aliens in general, and many of the other points that have been often highlighted by the new Swiss cinema.

If there is a weak point, it is the sort of justification it finally supplies for this character, hinted at and gradually elaborated upon, through his nightmares. It may be the one preachy feature in an otherwise irreproachable, if sometimes rather too restrained and intellectual film.

Technical standards are high and the film, which has had its share of awards from some of the secondary juries, should find a solid audience in festivals and art circuits. —*Edna.*

Das Autogram
(The Autograph)
(WEST-GERMAN-FRENCH-COLOR)

Berlin, Feb. 25.
A Provobis Film, Berlin, in coproduction with Von Vietinghoff Film Production, Berlin, and Euro-America-Films, Paris, in collarboration with Second German Television (ZDF), Mainz. Features entire cast. Written and directed by Peter Lilienthal, based on the novel "Cuarteles de Invirno" by Osvaldo Soriano. Camera (color), Michael Ballhaus; editor, Siegrun Jäger; sound, Hartmut Eichgrün; sets, Lilienthal; music, Juan José Mosalini, Claus Bantzer; art direction, Georgio Carrozzoni; tv producer, Christoph Holch. Reviewed at Berlin Film Fest (Competition), Feb. 25, '84. Running time: 92 MINS.
Cast: Juan José Mosalini, Angel del Villar, Anna Larreta, Hanns Zischler, Nicolas Dutsch, Georges Geret, Pierre Bernard Douby, Vito Mata, Luis Lucas, Dominique Nato, Agostinho Faleiro, Asdrubal Pereira, Roman Pallares.

Peter Lilienthal's "The Autograph" can be viewed as the last film in an unofficial trilogy of docu-fiction features on Latin America, the two earlier films being "The Country Is Calm" (1975) and "The Uprising" (1980). There was also an important docu on free elections in Chile, "La Victoria" (1973). All leave little doubt that Lilienthal, raised in South America (Uruguay, Argentina) after the family emigrated from Germany in 1939, is a filmmaker as much attracted by political events in Latin America as he is with the contemporary West German experience.

"The Autograph" at this year's Berlinale also had its parallel in the official Argentine entry, Héctor Olivera's "Funny Dirty Little Wars," one of the real finds at the fest. Both are based on novels by Osvaldo Soriano, a respected Argentine writer whose themes treat his country's record of dictatorships in the post-World War II period. This one is set in a provincial village and the story comes across as a moral parable rather than a self-contained or probing narrative.

Two likable individuals, a musician and a boxer, are commissioned by the authorities to come to the town to participate and perform in a folk festival. As soon as they arrive at the station, however, they are met by brutal military police and searched for evidence of conspiracy or insurrection. This brings the two together, particularly when the chances are good that the population will support them as spokesmen for freedom of conscience. The songwriter, Galvan, is already suspect to the secret police for the lyrics in the songs he composes and sings, while the boxer, Rocha, has been brought here as a setup loser to the army's champion.

A kind of showdown occurs when an autograph is requested by gangster-type enforcers of the public peace — the fighter gives it, the singer refuses. The rest is then constant harrasment and orders to leave the city at once — that is, after the folk festival is over and the boxer has lost his rigged fight. Each decides to resist in his own way, however, even though the cause is lost at the outset. In the end, the friends are back on the train again, lucky to be alive after a series of dangerous adventures.

Tale (filmed on locations in Portugal) is too simplistic to be effective. Dialog and performances by nonprofessionals are commendable, as usual in Lilienthal's films. But the festival version was the dubbed-into-German one for some inexplicable reason, a faux pas that aggravates. —*Holl.*

Kidco
(U.S.-COLOR)

Berlin, Feb. 22.
A 20th-Century-Fox Film Corp. production. Produced by Frank Yablans, David Niven Jr. Features entire cast. Directed by Ronald F. Maxwell. Screenplay, Bennett Trainer; pro-

duction manager, Marty Katz. No other credits. Reviewed at Kinderfilmfest, Berlin International Film Festival, Feb. 22, 1984. Running time: **104 MINS.**

Dickie Cessna	Scott Schwartz
Nene Cessna	Cinnamon Idles
Belle Cessna	Tristine Skyler
June Cessna	Elizabeth Gorcey

This delightful film — a special acquisition at the Kinderfilmfest where American participation is usually non-existent — re-works a standard formula for kiddie films; children protest adult domination, retaliate, and eventually win on their own terms, including a new respect from the adults. Child audiences will be sure to identify with the young rebels and love the film.

The patriotic free enterprise theme of "Kidco" is established early, in the red white and blue titles. Locale is that kiddie-film paradise of soft rolling hills and blue skies, the ranch country of Southern California. Eleven-year-old Dickie, played with likable boyish charm by Scott Schwartz, uses his business flair in pursuit of "big bucks."

Before sleeping at night, Dickie prays for commercial success. On the wall above his bunk are pennants proclaiming "General Motors" and "Ford." Enlisting his sisters and other kids in a manure-peddling scheme that pays off handsomely, Dickie calculates his riches on his computer.

Adult competitors find their own businesses suffering from their moppet rivals. The battle is on, the community takes sides, a media blitz ensues, and the kids are hauled into court. They argue their own case, turning the legal proceedings to their advantage. Their persuasive defense, their solidarity and the evident justice of their cause engage our sympathies.

Everything is solved in the final moments, as the children emerge from the courthouse to discover a huge demonstration of children massed to hail them. There are plenty of clenched fists aloft, chants, and banners proclaiming "Equal Rights for Kids" and "Sufferage for Kids." But there's no cause for parents to worry, as the "Kidco" revolution is benign and simply good fun.

Aimed at a kid audience, "Kidco" casually uses "hell," "screw," etc. And a nubile teenage girl has a job preventing her teenage Romeo from getting his hand under her blouse. Kiddie films are today more grownup with words than the Andy Hardy epics were, but "Kidco" still partakes of an obsolete segregation — the film is devoid of black, Hispanic or Asian children.

"Kidco" is the first American film to participate in the Kinderfest. Limited to 35m, the Kinderfilmfest receives inquiries from U.S. producers about 16m offerings, shorts and features, but cannot program them in the main event, only in a 16m sidebar. Thus U.S. participation in the Kinder-

filmfest is small, as U.S. producers rarely make 35m films for children. — *Hitch.*

Akelarre
(Witches' Sabbath)
(SPANISH-COLOR)

Berlin, Feb. 27.

An Amboto Films production, produced by Eusko Jaurlaritza. Directed by Pedro Olea. Features entire cast. Script. Olea, Gonzalo Goikoetxea; camera (Eastmancolor), Jose Luis Alcaine; editor, Jose Salcedo; sound, Eduardo Fernandez; music, Carmelo Bernaoloa; art director, Felix Murcia. Reviewed at Zoo Palast, Berlin Film Festival (In Competition), Feb. 26, 1984. Running time: **105 MINS.**

Garazi	Silvia Munt
Amunia	Mari Carrillo
Acevedo	Jose Luis Lopez Vazquez
Fermin	Walter Vidarte
Unai	Patxi Bisquert
Inigo	Inaki Miramon

A familiar tale of a witch-hunt in which the Christian establishment is once more presented as torturing innocent people until they confess to supposed crimes of witchcraft they never committed. Setting is a Basque village, still run along feudal lines. The local landowner, Fermin, is troubled by growing unrest among the peasants, while his indolent son, Inigo, is outraged because his former girl, Garazi, has a new lover, the peasant Unai. Before long, an inquisitor, Avecedo, has arrived in the village and, since Garazi's grandmother had been burned as a witch, she's a natural suspect. Under vicious torture, she confesses, also implicating her elderly friend, Amunia, who suffers a similar fate.

Pedro Olea's film has nothing much new to say about the subject, but it is handsomely made and finely acted, especially by Silvia Munt as the tormented Garazi and Mari Carrillo as the old woman who is eventually burned to death. Top acting honors, however, go to veteran Jose Luis Lopez Vazquez as the merciless inquisitor. Pic suggests that, in this case at any rate, the conflict is not only between Christianity and Paganism, but also between the feudal ruling class and the peasants.

Pacing is slow in the first half, but things pick up toward the end as Unai and his friends attack Inigo's men, who are taking the condemned "witches" to the city for sentencing; the unpleasant Inigo, who had raped Garazi while she lay helpless in a prison cell after undergoing torture, gets his just desserts.

Torture scenes are not too rugged, though the implications of horror are there. Overall, pic is a worthy rep for Spain, though its impact inevitably pales in comparison with the masterpiece on this subject, Carl Dreyer's "Day of Wrath," "Witches' Sabbath" should not be confused with the recent Hungarian film by Janos Roz-

sa which has the same English title. — *Strat.*

Marlene
(WEST GERMAN-COLOR-B&W- DOCU)

Berlin, Feb. 25.

An Oko Film Karel Dirka Production, Munich. World sales, Futura Film, Munich. A Documentary with fictional elements directed by Maximilian Schell. Script, Meir Dohnal, Schell; camera (color), Ivan Slapeta; editing, Heidi Genée, Dagmar Hirtz, Nobert Lill; sets, Heinz Eickmeier; production manager, Peter Genée. Reviewed at Berlin Film Fest (out-of competition), Feb. 24, 1984. Running time: **96 MINS.**

Let's start by saying that "Marlene" was, far and away, the most impressive film presented in the official program at this year's Berlinale. Unspooled out of competition, the run on tickets was as madly frustrating for the festival organization as it was at last year's Venice fest for David Gill and Kevin Brownlow's "Unknown Chaplin." Little doubt, film buffs and movie star-gazers will see this fiction-documentary more than once, although the general public without film savvy may have a bit of trouble figuring out the perspective angle and may also be disappointed by not seeing Marlene Dietrich in person in a film obviously for and about her.

Maximilian Schell visited Marlene Dietrich in her Paris apartment for a full week of taped interviews, many excerpts of which have already been printed in a German newspaper. Each day, he was there for 4 to 5 hours, and ending up with some 15 hours of material. Dietrich refused to be on camera — on the understandable grounds that she has already been "photographed to death." That being the case, and considering that she was born in Berlin in 1901, what comes through? Quite fortunately: the running thoughts of a highly intelligent and self-protective entertainer on the craft it takes to be one of the great stars of the silver screen.

This is a patchwork documentary. At times when Dietrich speaks about a certain film or performance, the appropriate clip is provided to extend the conversation into a visual statement. In between, photographs and stage appearances, newsreels and prior filmed interviews are provided to fill in gaps where her own presence on camera might have knitted everything better into a compact whole. Then there are the improvised scenes, particularly with the editors of the film as scenes are discussed and the proper bridges in the tape-to-image text are seemingly made on the spot, that bring a certain fictional spontaneity to the experience. At certain points, the personality of Schell himself muscles to the forefront — in general, quite legitimately, for

without him there would have been no film document of this nature at all.

In regard to personal impressions, "Marlene" disturbs in more ways than one. An interview with an aging screen star not only highlights a lot of truth-vs.-gossip episodes in the actress's life (incidents with Josef von Sternberg and Hollywood's higher echelon of studio personalities), but also places the lady herself under the lamp of time — indeed, it's once made quite clear that a piece of family-background information is better off forgotten than dragged out from under the rug for the umpteenth time. Miss Dietrich also states that she never saw her films on the screen, nor does she ever desire to do so — and she regularly contradicts herself in an overall estimate of her own career from personal or emotional perspective.

This said, the rest is up to the viewer to accept or reject what he likes about Dietrich and, more important, what Schell himself wants to say about her. And on this latter aspect, Schell does not seem all that sensitive to a great German and American actress now nearing her 82d birthday, although respect and admiration are evident from beginning to end. It's the portrait itself on the editing-table that fascinates him — and the audience.

Of all the footage that's presented, the clips on her early silent film career (she supposedly was a movie extra as early as 1918) intrigue this reviewer the most. That, and Dietrich's expressive voice that prickles in the beginning and wins out over everything in the end. There's particularly one line that haunts: as a day's chores of interviewing draws to an end, she asks Maximilian and his crew when she can serve the pastries she had made herself that morning for the occasion. —*Holl.*

Hector
(SPANISH-COLOR)

Berlin, Feb. 20.

A Jose de Orbe production. Produced by De Orbe, Pepe Fernandiz. Directed and written by Carlos Perez Ferre. Features entire cast. Camera (color), Jordi Morraja, Federico Ribes; editors, Pablo G. del Amo, Juan San Mateo; sound, Alfonso Pino; music, Toti Soler, Ovidi Montllor; art director, Alejandro Soler. Reviewed at Atelier am Zoo, Berlin (Berlin Film Festival, Mediterranean Panorama section), Feb. 18, 1984. Running time: **85 MINS.**

Hector	Ovidi Montllor
Antonio	Julio Mira
Father	Aldo Sanbrell
Nuria	Lali Espinet
Grandmother	Rosario Guillem
Don Eliseo	R. Sansilvestre
Young Hector	Paris Soler

A brilliant central performance from Ovidi Montllor (remembered for his role in "Poachers" a few years ago) is the mainstay of this rather grim film about impoverished farmers in a remote part of Valencia. People are moving away from the district, but Hector stays on to tend his goats, together with his old grandmother and sadistic father, who regularly beats his son. It's a lonely, pathetic existence, and in the end Hector turns on his father and stabs him to death before hanging himself.

Extremely downbeat saga is relieved by luminous thesping and a rich visual style, plus some superbly menacing music. Film was shot in two languages: Castilian Spanish plus the language of the region, Alcoyano. Hard to see a commercial career for the film outside Spanish territories, but it's worth catching all the same. In addition to Montller, there's a bewitching cameo from Lali Espinet as the lovely girl who tries, not very successfully, to seduce Hector. This scene, plus one where Hector is amorously involved with one of his goats, could prove a problem for tv transmission.

—*Strat.*

Doomed Love
(U.S.-COLOR)

Berlin, Feb. 20.

An Independent Feature Project presentation. Produced, written and directed by Andrew Horn. Dialog, Jim Neu; camera (color), Carl Teitelbaum; editors, Steve Brown, Charlie Beasley; sets painted by Amy Sillman, Pamela Wilson; sound, Ulrich Kilian; original music; Evan Lurie; "Beach Song" and "Kitchen Song" by Lenny Pickett and Neu. Reviewed at the Minilux, Kino 5, Berlin, Feb. 20, 1984. Running time: **75 MINS.**

Andre .... Bill Rice
Lois .... Rosemary Moore
Bob .... Allen Frame
Psychiatrist .... Jim Neu
TV pair .Charles Ludlam, Blackeyed Susan

The most serious drawback of this practical joke is its length. At 75 minutes it overstates its case, its punches are pulled and lose much of their effect.

The original intention was obviously to send up soap operas by focusing on their banalities. This is clear from the first moment, when an off-screen voice introduces the narrative in a text made almost entirely of evergreen song titles. The first scene shows a suicide hanging himself, just to create the atmosphere. Later on the viewer is immersed in classical melodrama about a professor of European literature who can't forget an early love which probably had a tragic ending. When he finds someone to console him, it turns out she is married to a very nice, sympathetic young man who is prepared to go to considerable lengths to help the professor out of his depression.

For the rest of the film, Andrew Horn does his best to keep it on a two-dimensional level. For instance, there is no three-dimensional scenery, everything is played against painted backdrops. That means the image has no depth by itself. The dialog is carefully matched, every line being selected on the ground that it was used at least 1,000 times before.

Platitudes and cheap philosophies are repeated twice and more.

While the clever intellectual approach is to be appreciated, it is obvious that the straight faces of the actors and the corniness of a script couldn't really be appreciated by anyone outside the trade.

—*Edna.*

Arztinnen
(Lady Doctors)
(E. GERMAN-SWEDISH-SWISS-COLOR)

Berlin, Feb. 27.

A DEFA Studios Potsdam-Babelsberg Production with Manfred Durnick Productions, Swedish Television and Monopol Films, Zurich. Executive Producer, Dorothea Hildebrandt. Directed by Horst Seeman. Features entire cast. Written by Seeman, based on the play by Rolf Hochhuth; camera (color), Otto Hanisch; editor, Bärbel Bauersfeld; sets, Georg Wratsch; costumes, Inge Kistner; music, Seeman. Reviewed at the Zoo Palast, Berlin, Feb. 27, 1984. Running time: **106 MINS.**

Dr. Katia Michelsberg ....Judy Winter
Dr. Lydia Kowalenko ....Inge Keller
Dr. Riemenschild ....Walter Reyer
Dr. Böblinger ....Rolf Hoppe
Dr. Werner Michelsberg..Michael Gwisdek
Tom ....Daniel Jacob

This was probably the most embarrassing entry in the official competition in Berlin. Whatever made the East Germans offer this American tv-style soap opera whose entire plot takes place in West Germany and whose obvious goal is to blast the corruption and the decadence of the Federal Republic is not altogether clear, but it certainly is not an example of good taste or high cinematic level.

Adapting the Rolf Hochhuth play to the screen was done with very little imagination, the result a gabby torrent of dialogs, shot at best in a conventional way. The point it tries to make, that the medical profession in the West is all graft, promiscuity and selfish pretense, is crammed down the audience's throat and no punches are pulled to leave something for the imagination. Defective drugs are sold that the manufacturers do not want to assume the danger of killing their own reputation; better kill people, they argue.

A girl dies on the operating table and all the woman surgeon can say in her defense is that things like that happen and it is all for the progress of science. The investigation into the accident is killed through political string-pulling, doctors are invited to review favorably new drugs for under-the-table benefits transferred directly to Swiss bank accounts and, to make all this nice and dozy, a single family is involved in all the proceedings.

Needless to say, all these characters live a dissolute life, families are broken because of sheer personal amibition and finally the kids pay for their parents' sins.

All is delivered in stentorian tones, the dramatic devices and the acting leaving much to be desired. Seeing how determinedly

everyone involved plunges ahead, without the shadow of a smile, one can't help hoping "General Hospital" will take over, so at least it might be sort of entertaining for a while, which this film isn't.

Beyond this, having the East Germans produce this kind of preachy film about their Western counterparts reeks of old-time propaganda.

When last year someone suggested, jokingly or not, to open the Festival with a Disney yarn about a family from the East crossing the border to the promised land of the Occident the East Germans were furious and rightly so, because it was a direct slap at their regime. Why this wouldn't principle work in the opposite direction, when the East denigrates the West, is not at all evident. —*Edna.*

Bless Their Little Hearts
(U.S.-B&W)

Berlin, Feb. 21.

An Independent Feature Project presentation of a film produced, directed and edited by Billy Woodberry. Features entire cast. Script, Charles Burnett; camera (black and white), Burnett, Patrick Melly; titles, Bill Harris; music, "Nobody Knows You When You're Down And Out," arranged by Archie Shepp, "Lost In A Dream," Little Esther Phillips. Reviewed at the Delphi Theatre, Berlin, Feb. 21, 1984. Running time: **80 MINS.**

Charlie Banks .... Nate Herd
Andais Banks ....Kaycee Moore
Banks children ....Angela, Ronald and
                       Kimberley Burnett
Gene......................Eugene Cherry
John......................Lawrence Pierott
Duck......................Ernest Knight
Pasquale......................Ellis Griffin

It took all of $25,000, put together by several funds in the States, to help this film materialize. Without a glance at the credits, one registers immediately, from the film's first shots, a kinship with such earlier efforts of black filmmakers, on an independent basis, to reflect the plight of their community, notably a film such as "Killer Of Sheep," presented by the Forum a couple of years ago with considerable success. It has the same quality of black-and-white cinematography, most of the editing being done in the camera, the script which sounds improvised even when it isn't, non-professional actors with a remarkable on-screen presence.

What the film tries to capture is that depressing feeling of impotence which descends upon an adult when he suddenly finds himself unemployed, his whole life turned upside down. He faces empty spaces of time, his schedule is overturned, his position in his family is endangered and he has no idea what he can do to redress the situation.

Woodberry does a very good job of showing the man's utter confusion and lack of preparation to handle such a situation, long sequences stressing the loneliness

imprisoning the characters, as well as the creeping feeling of inadequacy and preparation to face life on its own terms.

Woodberry and Burnett refrain from idealizing their hero. Charlie Banks, no hero at all, is having an affair which he finds as difficult to sustain as his married life. This only adds to the authenticity of the venture, which gives the impression of a documentary in its rough, uncouth style, one which rises to some hairy climaxes. Woodberry often lets himself be dragged by one sequence for too long, no argument about the necessity to transit to the audience the heavy feeling of the man on the screen, justifying this sort of needless immobility. In other words, while there is no doubt this is true to life, one would wish the picture to be more concise.

Attentive camera work, lavishing much attention on close ups, very good interpretation by the three Burnett kids, but also by the adult non-actors, is a big help. It's a respectable effort which could find an audience either in festivals, which have been interested lately in this sort of modest independent American enterprise, or in those neighborhoods which might recognize the fatality and desperate acceptance of conditions as part of their own experience. But they might not like to be reminded.

— *Edna.*

Orengen, Der Forsvandt
(The Boy Who Disappeared)
(DANISH-COLOR)

Copenhagen, Feb. 17.

A Per Holst Film production, Kaerne Film release. Original story and script and directed by Ebbe Nyvold. Features entire cast. Camera (Eastmancolor) Jan Weincke; production management, Ib Tardini; production design, Palle Arestrup; editor, Niels Pagh Andersen, Sys Jondahl, Janus Billeskov Jansen; music, Kenneth Knudsen. Reviewed at the Palads, Copenhagen, Feb. 16, 1984. Running time; **85 MINS.**

Jonas ....Mads M. Nielsen
Lena......................Mille Reingaard
Jonas' mother ....Kirsten Olesen
Jonas' father ....Kjeld Noergaard
Tom, the ex-pilot ....Ole Ernst

"The Boy Who Disappeared," Danish entry in the Berlin Fest's Children's Section, may find it hard to find an audience beyond the captive one of tv kiddie slot programming on state monopoly networks. Although pretty to look at and featuring a couple of charming faces and excellent performances by the two juvenile leads, writer-director Ebbe Byvold's first feature is lamentably short on reasonable psychology and hence of genuine suspense.

The boy of the title role is Jonas (Mads M. Nielsen), 13, and his reason for bolting the home arena (along with an average of 2,000 other Danish kids annually) is the performances of his parents, a weepy mom and a dad given to excessive party drinking and marital sidestepping. Still, the household seems pretty well ordered and Jonas displays a very responsible attitude to both his older sister and his kid brother.

Jonas also looks in prime physical health and not suffering any obvious neuroses. His preoccupations are sane and normal, and when he finally ups and runs out, he soon establishes his own well-ordered household in some neck of the woods where he befriends a girl of his own age and the uplikely character of an expilot of clear voice, bright eyes and steady hands in spite of his daily downing of a quart of Glenfiddich.

It is, however, fresh-faced Jonas who remains the most unlikely character in a story which vaporizes in the thin air above all the nicely composed and lensed frames. Never for a second does the director attempt any probing of the boy's postulated inner conflicts, nor does he depict the boy's home anywhere nearly nightmarish enough to scare any robust kid convincingly. Film's production dress is handsome, an expert job along with Kenneth Knudsen's music which, unfortunately, gets to serve mostly as an underscoring of the film's missing drama.—*Kell.*

The Curse Of Fred Astaire
(U.S.-COLOR)

Berlin, Feb. 25.

A Monstermaker production in association with 24 FPS. Produced, directed and written by Mark Berger. Features entire cast. Camera (color), Berger, Peter Aaron, Jack Yaeger; editor, Steve Brown; choreography, Clinton Smith, Peter Anastos; art direction, Robert Edmonds; music, Ed Hee, John Czerkowicz, lyrics, Mark Berger. Reviewed at the Berlin Film Festival (market), Feb. 25, 1984. Running Time: 83 MINS.
Clio Grant....................Clio Young
Helen Grant................Mary Jennings
Memphis ....ᵧ................Alan Brooks
Joan Grant ....Jill Larson
Jane Grant ....Kelly Piper
Luce ....Clark Piper
Guardian Angel/Drunk .....Byron Thomas
The Virgin.................Margaret Tien

"The Curse of Fred Astaire" is one of those bad pennies which continues to pop up at film festival markets. Completed two years ago, this musical variation of Faust has gone through a series of versions but remains amateurish and sophomoric in each incarnation.

Clio Grant (Clio Young) is an unattractive, overweight homosexual who dreams of stardom as a tap dancer. The fact that he has two left feet is only a minor irritation to him as he persists through dance classes and odd jobs.

However, fate, in the form of a supposed talent agent, ensures fame and fortune in exchange for his immortal soul. Clio assumes it's a gag but the day of reckoning

soon arrives for the ill-equipped hoofer.

It's curious Berger would be drawn to this subject, considering its recent variant in Brian De Palma's "Phantom of the Paradise." De Palma's film clearly is superior in every way and Berger's modest resources can in no way touch the verve, budget or originality of the earlier picture.

Young lacks the charisma or talent someone such as Craig Russell could have provided the central role. And Berger's attempts at social satire and comedy are simply ham-fisted and embarrassing, though some of the gags in the later sections of the film are effective.

Commercial prospects for "The Curse of Fred Astaire" remain dim in any form and one suspects the filmmakers had better change cleats before they go tapping on further buyers' doors.—*Klad.*

Naughty Boys
(DUTCH - B&W)
Berlin, Feb. 24.

A Tiger Films production. Produced by Kees Kasander. Directed and written by Eric de Kyper, based on themes from Noel Coward and Marcel Proust. Camera, (B&W) Michael Houssiau; editor, France Duez; art direction, Ben van Os; music, Mark Naes. Review at the Berlin Film Festival (non-competing), Feb. 23, 1984. Running Time: 107 MIN. .
Daisy ....Linda Polan
Jeremy ....Rik Roesems
Jack ....Jack Post
Paul.......................Paul Ruven
Willie ....Paul Vestraten
Emile ....Emile Poppe
Gerard....................Gerard Lemaitre
Steve ....Steven van Galen
Walter ....Michel Israel

Dutch filmmaker Eric de Kuyper is back on the festival circuit with his second feature "Naughty Boys." While the new offering is a decided improvement over his "Casta Diva," the film is assuredly for the art house set, catering to a highly specialized crowd.

The setting is an English manor house where a group of young men are consumed with mini-dramas during the small hours of the night. De Kuyper dispenses with anything resembling a plot thrust, isolating moments through stunning visuals and the odd flash of literal or pictorial cleverness.

However, his best moments are isolated and brief require a real devotion to his style to sustain the film's full running length. By conventional practices, one could easily trim the picture into a brief, dazzling short subject and lose the carefully conceived sense of ennui. In the process the irony of the title would be lost even if the subject became more accessible.

Definitely a problem picture in terms of marketing, "Naughty Boys" is likely to be a habitue of specialized and festival screenings. De Kuyper's is a minimalist with a savage sense of humor

which is easily lost amid the striking images, long takes and great passages of silence characterizing his work. Yet, patience pays off in his off-beat tempos and he packs in a feeling of wonder and surprise in the proceedings. —*Klad.*

El Tango Es Una Historia
(Tango Is History)
(MEXICAN-COLOR)

Berlin, Feb. 22.

Produced by the Filmoteca de la UNAM, . Cooperativa Cambalache, Frente Argentino de Cineastas. Directed by Humberto Rios. Camera (color), Miguel Ehrenberg, Guillermo Navarro, Gónzalo Infante, Mario Luna, Gastón Ocampo, Humberto Rios; music, Astor Piazzola, Osvaldo Pugliese, Susana Rinaldi; narration, Gastón Martinez Matiella. Reviewed at the Delphi Theatre, Berlin, Feb. 22, 1984. Running time: 62 MINS.

There have been many attempts in the past to link music with history and to see in the development of a national kind of music a reflection of the political and historical struggles it has gone through.

This is what Mexican filmmaker Humberto Rios trying to do here for the tango and Argentina, using as his stepping stone a tango fest which took place in Mexico during the summer of 1980, which featured some of the best-known Argentine exiles at the time, such as Astor Piazzola, Osvaldo Pugliese and singer Susana Rinaldi.

Using the traditional form of the tv documentary, Rios sees in the three stars whom he interviews, representatives of different generations, therefore different approaches to music and life in general. Pugliese stands in for the older times, his music recalling calmer periods in Argentine history, if there ever was such a thing. Piazzola, who has brought a whole new set of ideas and musical phrases to the tango, is revealed as an innovator, whose contribution brought a new lease on life to the tango, while Rinaldi is shown as the almighty protesting voice of this kind of music. Stock shots from outstanding moments in recent Argentine history are featured to give added weight to this argument.

The argument is fashionable, but not altogether convincing in this context, while the immediate impact the film might have had in July 1983, when it was first shown and the Argentine government was still under sharp international criticism which this film joined, has been dulled by recent political developments after the last elections.

Still, the best part of it is by far the music it offers and the correct emphasis it puts on its characteristics. Rios has done an effective job covering the fest, and as far as the Berlin Forum of the Young Cinema was concerned, this was an auspicious opening for a series of tango films played at midnight at

the Delphi in front of capacity houses who have never known the glories of Carlos Gardel and his like. — *Edna.*

Kusameikyu
(JAPANESE/FRENCH-COLOR)

Berlin, Feb. 20.

A Toei presentation of a Films du Jeudi, Pierre Braunberger production. Directed by Shuji Terayama. Features entire cast. Written by Terayama, Risei Kishida, from short novel by Kyoka Izui; camera (color), Tatso Uzuki; editor, Tomoyo Oshima; sound, Katsuhide Kimura; executive producers, Hiroko Govaers, Eiko Kujo; music, J.A. Seazer. Reviewed at the Minilux Kino 5 Berlin, Feb. 20, 1984. Running time: 40 MINS.

Cast: Hiroshi Mikami, Takeshi Wakamatu, Keiko Nitaka, Juzo Itami, Miko Fukuya. English narration: Alexandra Stewart.

Filmmaker Shuji Terayama has a sound reputation as an avant-garde creator who has the knack to appeal to audiences outside the limited realm of the profession. His films, in the past, have appeared both on commercialized and specialized circuits and one, "Pastoral Hide 'n' Seek," carried the Japanese flag at Cannes.

Indeed, some of the ideas prevalent in that film seem to reappear in this 1979 featurette in the description of a young man's search for a tune and lyrics of a song he heard in his childhood.

His search leads him through different levels of reality, he delves into his subconscious, stress the inner conflicts of an adolescent who believes the key to his future is in one souvenir of the past, and elaborates on Freudian hangups, the son searching for the image of his disappeared father and doubting the identity of his mother, with whom he lives.

The visual style, as usual with Terayama is flamboyant, the English text is appealingly read by Paris-based Canadian actress Alexandra Stewart and, at 40 minutes, this should easily become a favorite in the cineclub and art club circuits.—*Edna.*

Berenice
(FRENCH-B/W)

Berlin, Feb. 22.

A Festival d'Avignon & Les Films Du Dimanche Production. Executive producer, Françoise Mazerat. Directed by Raul Ruiz. Features entire cast. Screenplay, Jean Racine play (1670); camera (black and white), Françoise Ede, Francis Lapeyre, Gregoire Venteo; editor, Martine Bouquin; sound, Jean Claude Brisson, J.P. Fenié, Ph. Lemeneul; music, Maurice Ravel, Reynaldo Hahn, Alber Roussel. Reviewed at the Minilux Kino 5, Berlin, Feb. 22, 1984. Running time: 105 MINS.
Bérénice.................Anne Alvaro
Titus ....Jean Bernard Gullard
Antiochus ....Jean Badin
Paulin......................Frank Oger
Arsace ....Claude Dereppe
Phénice...................Clarisse Daull

This unusual item stands very little chance of becoming a blockbuster, but in its own special way, it should find a niche for itself in a specialized market. Partly financed by the theater festival in Avignon, which covered the print and shooting expenses, this may well rate as one of the finest and most original tributes paid by cinema to French classic playwright Jean Racine. It is in no way a screen adaptation of a play in the conventional meaning of the word, nor a transition, but rather a new way of breathing life into material usually considered apt for the upper shelves of pretentious libraries.

Racine's play about Berenice, the queen from the East, the daughter of Herod, and her love for Roman emperor Titus, which was to be sacrificed to reasons of state, is a typical example of the clash between logic and emotion, with undercurrents of racist hints, the Romans refusing to accept any empress who is not pure Latin, and feminism, indicated by the willingness of one man to sacrifice his beloved to another without really inquiring about her feelings.

But as it is usually presented on stage or available in writing, its embellished rhymes are so long-winded, and its niceties of style so intricate, that for the larger part of the audience it is at best a museum piece.

Now comes Raul Ruiz, a Chilean filmmaker whose reputation as a noted avant-gardist has been soundly established in the last 10 years since he has moved, for political reasons, to Paris. He takes the original text and turns it into a shadow play. Berenice appears as the only real person in all this, the rest of the characters being represented most of the time by shadows, which she sometimes tries to touch, to grab or to reject, but who are never seen clearly enough to be identified. In very long shots, Ruiz lets the text speak for itself, uncluttered by the normally heavy machinery of a classical stage production.

This strange combination results in something Ruiz himself terms as "expressionist cinema put at the use of a Mexican melodrama," a pretty accurate description of the form and content of this film. Actors are asked to use mainly their voices, which they do beautifully, except for Anne Alvaro who, in the last scenes has to display all the pain and frustration of a woman sacrificed in spite of herself.

The result is highly intelligent cinema, not of the entertaining sort, to be sure, but a perfect hymn to the glories of the French language and the art of Racine. It shouldn't be selected for neighborhood cinemas, but any self-respecting university with a French department should be proud to use it in its courses.—*Edna.*

Him
(U.S.-COLOR-16m)

Berlin, Feb. 20.
Executive producers, Albert Milgrom and Alice M. Larson, for Ananda Productions, St. Paul, Minn. Produced by Oleg Danilov. Features entire cast. Directed by Wictor Grodecki; assistant director, Beth Johnson; screenplay, Grodecki, based loosely on Oscar Wilde's "Salome;" camera (color), Andrzej Kamrowski; sound, Paul Auguston. No other credits. Reviewed at Messe (Market), Berlin International Film Festival, Feb. 20, 1984, within special showcase of Independent Feature Project. Running time: 73 MINS.

In effect, "Him" is a Polish fiction feature produced in English in the U.S. Writer-director Wictor Grodecki, cameraman Andrzej Kamrowski and the film's chief actor, Piotr Probosc, are all Polish professionals. Producer Oleg Danilov is Russian-born. They connected with Minnesota producers Alice Larson and Albert Milgrom to create a brooding three-character drama of incest and disintegrating family relationships. An early version was seen at the Montreal festival last year.

"Him" (formerly "Our House") takes place in a rented mansion by the sea. The house is felt as a symbol of an oppressive enclosure of prison, within which the characters struggle both against one another and within themselves. The film was shot on Lake Superior with American actresses Phyllis Wright and Shirley Diercks.

Well-known in East Europe as a singer-poet-actor, the attractive young Probosc has appeared in Polish, Spanish and West German features. He was recently awarded one of Poland's highest theater honors for his lead role in the Warsaw hit musical, "Junkies," written and directed by Grodecki. The two had teamed also for Jean Genet's "The Maids" on the Warsaw stage.

As director of "Him," Grodecki faced the special problems of working in an alien tongue and in a foreign clime. At 25, Grodecki left Poland for the U.S. last April to present his "Polanski and Poland" at Filmex in Los Angeles. A graduate of Lodz, he worked with cameraman Kamrowski, a classmate, on eight shorts. "Him" is their first feature.

"Him" producer Danilov, in the U.S. for five years, had been production manager of George Cukor's U.S./USSR coproduction, "The Bluebird," in 1975 and also had worked on numerous Soviet productions. —*Hitch.*

Wanderkrebs
(Itinerant Cancer)
(WEST GERMAN-COLOR)

Berlin, Feb. 27.
A Herbert Achternbusch production, written, produced and directed by Achternbusch. Features entire cast. Camera (color), Jorg Schmidt-Reitwein; editor, Micki Joanni; sound, Heike Pillemann, Brian Greenman;

music, Gustav Mahler, Janet Baker, Michael Ranta, Hartmut Geerken, Hans Jurgen Buchner, Du Depp; art director, Peter Grenz; executive producer, Dietmar Schneider. Reviewed at Zoo Palast (Berlin Film Festival, Official Section, Out of Competition), Feb. 26, 1984. Running time: 92 MINS.
Waldler.............Herbert Achternbusch
Prime Minister ....Franz Baumgartner
Waldler's wife......Annamari Bierbichler
P.M.'s Secretary ....Sepp Bierbichler
Japanese Woman ......Judit Achternbusch
Bride....................Waltraut Galler
Bridegroom ....Dietmar Schneider

Herbert Achternbusch is a prolific, Munich-based one-man-band who had two films in the Berlin Fest, "Rita Ritter" in the Forum and "Itinerant Cancer" in the official section, out of competition. He has a following, especially as he has problems with government funding from time to time because of the anti-establishment nature of his films. But his sense of humor is very much an acquired taste and doesn't travel much outside Bavaria.

His latest film has him playing the lead as an Everyman, with black painted mustache, who leaves the peculiar factory where he works in company of a Japanese woman tourguide (played by a German actress, a typical example of Achternbusch humor). He winds up in the office of the Prime Minister, who has a false black beard and is trying to call the U.S. President on the line; the P.M. drinks Heinz tomato sauce (ketchup?) direct from the bottle, and is worried because his daughter is marrying the Leader of the Opposition.

The Achternbusch character takes with him everywhere a dog, dead 20 years and stuffed with gold. He also comes up with meaningful statements such as "Those who govern us always keep us afraid."

For the viewer not on the director's very specific wavelength, "Itinerant Cancer" is something of an ordeal; acting is mechanical, camerawork flat and uninteresting, pacing leaden. One gimmick is that some scenes are shot with circular masking, and it was allegedly technical problems involving this format that caused the film's appearance at the festival to be postponed for several days. But there's no obvious reason why the optical device should make any difference whatsoever to the projection, so the postponement seems like just another Achternbusch joke. — *Strat.*

El-Sabti-Fat
(What Will We Do On Sunday?)
(TUNISIAN-FRENCH-COLOR-16m)

Berlin, Feb. 22.
A SATPEC-Vendredi Films production Directed by Lotfi Essid. Features entire cast. Script, Essid, Chaibi Raouf; camera (Eastmancolor), Acacio de Almeida; editors, Philippe Gosselet, Moufida Tlatli; sound, Dominique Vieillard, Mongi Bellamine;

music, Mohammed Abdel Waheb; sets, Odile la Gentil. Reviewed at Atelier am Zoo (Berlin Film Festival, Mediterranean Section), Feb. 21, 1984. Running time: 87 MINS.
Nouri ....Mahmoud ban Jacoub
Kamoun ....Noureddine Kasbaoui
Nouri's Father ...Hamda Mohamed Hamza
Prostitute.................Brigitte Ariel
Housewife......................Noel Leiris
Nathalie................Dominique Goron
Transvestite............Philippe Planquois

A slight, quietly appealing film set in Paris on a warm summer Sunday. Two North Africans, Nouri from Algeria and Kamoun from Tunisia, join forces to spend the day together though they're not very sure what to do. Leaving the slums of the Arab quarter, they pass familiar Paris landmarks, flirting with women and engaging in rather desultory relationships. They wind up in the apartment of a friendly young man, who turns out to be a transvestite.

An unquestionably minor, but rather charming, film about two undemanding people whose day is filled with hopes and disappointments. Technically only so-so, but the music and songs (by Hadj Mohammed El-Anka) are excellent.
—*Strat.*

Gore Vidal: The Man Who Said No
(U.S.-COLOR-DOCU-16m)

Berlin, Feb. 24.
Produced, directed, photographed (color), and edited by Gary Conklin, for Alcon Films (Pasadena, Calif.); sound, Alan Linnell. Reviewed in Information, Berlin International Film Festival, Feb. 24, 1984. Running time: 90 MINS.

Novelist, playwright, essayist, political observer, talk-show raconteur Gore Vidal, scion of a political dynasty, is subject of a new biographical documentary produced by Gary Conklin, who earlier had produced documentaries about Raymond Chandler, Paul Bowles, Rufino Tamayo and artists of the Weimar Republic.

"The Man Who Said No" depicts Vidal, the private man, as well as the literary personality. Most of the film is devoted to Vidal's participation in California politics, in a state where showbusiness celebrities have often figured prominently in public office.

Vidal, the platform orator, running for elected office, is a new facet of his persona, and acquits himself well. Vidal's wit and intellect, which we take for granted, are here supplemented with facts and solid information on California problems.

Film was shot at a six-to-one ratio in 1982 during the primary campaign for the Democratic nomination as U.S. Senator. Vidal emerged second in a field of 11 candidates, losing to California ex-Governor Jerry Brown. One scene depicts the two adversaries on the dais together, about to clash in debate, and being introduced by the chairman.

One scene shows Vidal confronting managers of ARCO (California's third largest concern) with charges of tax evasion. Another depicts Vidal on foreign policy, defending self-government for Central Americans, free from military intervention by the U.S. And another scene has Vidal coolly deflecting a query about how his homosexuality complicates his politics. Throughout these meetings with voters, Vidal remains poised and charming, as expected, but he delivers straight talk on specific issues, sometimes becoming ironic and acerbic, even boldly iconoclastic.

Boxoffice predictions for a feature-length docu on California politics of two years ago seem grim, but the film may do well in special situations because of Vidal's reputation, especially in an election year.

"The Man Who Said No" has been seen in art-houses in Los Angeles and San Francisco and seems a likely candidate for public television. —*Hitch*

O Bom Burgues

(The Good Bourgeois)
(BRAZILIAN-COLOR)

Berlin, Feb. 22.

An Encontro Producoes Cinematograficas Ltda. production, with Embrafilme. Produced by Paulo Thiago. Directed by Oswaldo Caldeira. Features entire cast. Script, Doc Comparato, Caldeira; camera (color), Antonio Penido; editor, Gilberto Santeiro; sound, Jose Luiz Sasso; music, Paulo Moura; art director, Paulo Chada; executive producer, Angelo Gastal. Reviewed at Atelier am Zoo, Berlin (Berlin Film Festival, Special Screenings section), Feb. 22, 1984. Running time: 105 MINS.
Lucas ....Jose Wilker
Neuza ....Betty Faria
Thomas ....Jardel Filho
Joana (Patricia) ....Christiane Torloni
Lauro ....Anselmo Vasconcellos
Billy ....Nelson Dantas
Raul ....Nelson Xavier
Antonia ....Nicole Puzzi
Velho ....Jofre Soares

Set in the early '70s, a time of political turmoil in Brazil, "The Good Bourgeois" is about a rather ambivalent banker who secretly works for the Communist Party of Brazil. His wife is totally unaware of his double life, as he embezzles money from the bank to pass on to political extremists. He also supports financially a Far Left terrorist group, even though the party strongly disapproves his action. He discovers that his sister, Patricia (known to the revolutionaries as Joana), is a member of this group, but makes only a half-hearted attempt to persuade her to quit. Meanwhile, Lucas is flirting with the Far Right, sharing Antonia, a mistress of a prominent Rightist.

When the terrorist group kidnaps the Swiss ambassador and makes demands on the government, tragedy results and Patricia is in the position of betraying her

brother, who supplied the group with funds.

For the non-Brazilian, the plot is rather confusing with the motives of Lucas never made very clear. But the film is crisply and confidently made, with competent acting and the usual quota of sex and violence familiar from many other Brazilian pics. Maybe one has to be better versed in Brazilian politics of the time to appreciate all the allusions helmer Oswaldo Caldeira is obviously making. As is, the film registers as a well-made political thriller. —*Strat.*

Chile, No Invoco Tu Nombre In Vano

(Chile, I Do Not Call
Your Name In Vain)
(CHILEAN-FRENCH-
DOCU-COLOR)

Berlin, Feb. 23.

Produced by Amigos de la Cinemateca Chilena, Paris. Directed and edited by the Cine-Oio Collective. Music: Isabel Parra. Reviewed at the Berlin Film Fest, Berlin, Feb. 23, 1984. Running time: 85 MINS.

This first full-length, comprehensive documentary about the growing resistance to the Pinochet regime in Chile offers a wealth of material that will probably be a must for any respectable news archive. Shot at home, naturally without permission, by a Chilean who smuggled the footage later to Paris piece meal, and arranged for entire post-production process there, the film understandably does not carry any personal credits, which could put contributors in considerable danger.

For indeed, this recapitulation of events leading to and resulting in the five "Days of National Protest," couldn't please Santiago authorities. Starting with scenes of street arrests and women demonstratively gagging themselves in public as a means of pressure to discover something about their missing husbands and sons, the film gradually follows the smoldering intensity of the discontent among the working classes, including those same teamsters who once upon a time were instrumental in toppling the Allende government.

There are many impressive sequences in which Chileans display unusual courage, attacking the rulers and publicly demanding their demise. Some of the footage was obviously shot under dire conditions, evident mostly in the night sequences, but in any case their documentary value is certain.

As a matter of fact, this is the first audio-visual testimony of such scope, indicating the exasperation which has led many people to voice their protests out loud.

As the film advances, the clashes between the law and the protestors reach increasingly higher notes, violence explodes, women are arrested in the street, and one

leader of the teachers' union is even prepared, when released from jail, to elaborate on the new methods of torture introduced by the jailers. At another moment, blank-faced police officers, about to order their men to open fire, are asked by those in front of them whether they do not fear the day when someone else will take the reins. Which doesn't stop the ensuing violence and the increasing number of victims from one "Day of National Protest" to another.

It is almost incredible that people dared to hold a camera in such instances and that they found so many persons to voice their complaints in spite of the growing number of protestors (according to the film, about 2,500) and the violent threats to their lives.

If there are any defects they are on a cinematic level. It seems that for political reasons all the different factors and speakers for different unions had to be kept in the film to allow for a political balance in the representation of the insurgents. On the other hand, this leads to many repetitive sequences. What's more, if the chronological presentation of the facts does seem logical, there is no real attempt to organize the material into a more cohesive unity, which would not nly show what is going on in Chile but would also explain it.

The reverence towards material which was so difficult to obtain is understandable, and certainly the footage should be preserved as it is for archival purposes. For public display however, some serious tightening would be in order.

—*Edna.*

Signals Through The Flames

(U.S.-DOCU-COLOR)

Berlin, Feb. 20.

A Mystic Fire Productions picture, coproduced by Rachel McPherson. Produced and directed by Sheldon Rochlin, Maxine Harris. Camera (color), Rochlin; editors, Rochlin, Harris; sound, Harris; music, Carlo Altomare. Reviewed at Atelier am Zoo, Berlin (Berlin Film Festival, Special Screenings Section), Feb. 19, 1984. Running time: 97 MINS.

Interesting documentary about The Living Theater and its prime movers, Julian Beck and Judith Malina. Pic is made in a deliberately jagged style, complementing the abrasive, radical theories of the pioneering theater company. This won't endear it to the uninitiated, nor will it be admired by most tv programmers (photography is, frankly, awful). Yet the subject is interesting enough, as are the people, to make it worth seeing.

Beck and Malina formed Living Theater in 1947 in New York and key productions included "The Connection" and "The Brig," both seen in black-and-white excerpts from the eventual film versions.

After "The Brig," the theater was forced to close due to money problems, and Beck and Malina now live in Rome, where much of the docu was shot. Also included are scenes from Living Theater productions in France, Italy and Germany. The group was actively involved in the mini-French Revolution of 1968 (graphically seen via newsreel footage) and the Becks were jailed in Brazil for their activities.

Audience response to Beck and Malina, and the film, will be a matter of taste. But helmers Sheldon Rochlin and Maxine Harris have made a useful and informative pic about The Living Theater's contribution to legit over the last 35 years, even though had they made a somewhat more professional pic they might have found an even wider audience. As it is, bookings and audiences will be limited.

—*Strat.*

Rikos Ja Rangaistus

(Crime and Punishment)
(FINNISH-COLOR)

Berlin, Feb. 26.

A Villealfa Filmproductions Oy production, produced by Mika Kaurismaki. Directed by Aki Kaurismaki. Features entire cast. Script, Aki Kaurismaki, Pauli Pentti, based on novel by F.M. Dostoevsky; camera (color), Timo Salinen; sound, Mikael Sievers; editor, Veikko Aaltonen; sets, Matti Jaaranen; music, Shostakovich, Schubert. Reviewed at Berlin Film Festival Market, Feb. 21, 1984. Running time: 91 MINS.
Rahikainen (Raskolnikov) .Markku Toikka
Eeva (Eva) ....Aino Seppo
Inspector ....Esko Nikkari

There have been many screen versions of Dostoevsky's novel, but this contemporary Finnish version emerges as one of the most successful. Pared-down structure has Rahikainen (Raskolnikov), a worker in a slaughterhoue though a former law student, go to the house of the man who had three years ago killed his fiancee in a drunken hit-and-run accident, and shoot him. "Why?" asks the victim. "You'll never know," says the murderer. Before he can leave, Rahikainen is confronted by Eeva, who works for a catering company; he tells her he's the killer, and tells her his name. But she doesn't reveal his name to the police inspector in charge of the case. Indeed, she starts seeing the young murderer, making her lecherous boss jealous.

"Crime and Punishment" is gripping screen entertainment, with intensely strong acting from all the principals and some particularly fine photography, in pristine color, on various locations around Helsinki; indeed, the city itself becomes a character in the film. More problematical is the use of English rock songs on the soundtrack, which seems at times inappropriate, yet gets marks for originality (and the numbers are good, with the group unidentified in press handouts).

One of the best Finnish films of recent years, "Crime and Punishment" could gain international art house distribution and find a reputation for itself. It deserves to.

—*Strat.*

Die Frau Ohne Körper und Der Projektionist
(The Woman Without a Body and the Projectionist)
(WEST GERMAN-COLOR)

Berlin, Feb. 24.

A Visual Film Production, Munich, in coproduction with RTL Luxembourg and Second German Television (ZDF), Mainz. Features entire cast. Written, directed, photographed and edited by Niklaus Schilling. Technology and sound, Stefan Meisel; technical assistant, Thomas Meyer; video script, Silke Jaenicke; organization, Andrea Jonischkies, Klaus Gengnagel, Jutta Dickel-Meyer; administration, Elfriede Mayer; editing computer, Gusty Feinen; sound mixing, Marc Spielmann; studio, RTL-productions; adviser, René Steichen; tv producer, Janique Hastert, Herbert Knopp; sets, Gretel Zeppel; music, Michael Rüggeberg. Reviewed at Berlin Film Fest (Special Screening), Feb. 24, '84. Running time: **106 MINS.**

Cast: Liane Hielsche·, Gabriel Barylli, Gunther Malzacher, Elke Haltaufderheide, Alexander Osteroth, Mathias Eysen, Klaus Münster, Christop Lindert, Gerhard Acktun, Hildegard Buss, Jürgen Göbel, Günther Handwerker, Uwe von Schumann, Charls Brauer, Melanie Tressler, Nino Korda, Katja Borsche, Isolde Barth.

Niklaus Schilling's "The Woman Without a Body and the Projectionist" is an experimental film. It's an attempt to make a transfer from videotape to celluloid via a laboratory process, presently considered expensive and questionable but surely a commercial and artistic possibility for the future. As an experiment, this is a curiosity piece well worth a festival slot for appreciation and discussion. As a reconverted film to be presented in cinemas, it simply won't work as presented at the Berlinale for the simple reason that it still appears to be more video than film.

This is the tale of a successful woman tv reporter whose "Tele-Zeit" broadcasts have won her a coveted magazine award ("TV's Woman of the Year") for the second time. She is also an adventuress, seeking her erotic pleasures in dark corners of cinemas on occasion just for kicks, and it's here she is discovered in an act of love by a shy young projectionist in a rundown movie house. The projectionist, Michael Blank, is infatuated by the tv personality, Mara Weyland, and he follows up on his chances by using her lost key (he stole it from her purse in the cinema) to enter her apartment. This eventually leads to his first affair with a mature woman, which rocks him to the foundation of his psyche and makes a possessive idiot out of him. He begins to spy on her and one day disrupts the airing of one of her broadcasts. Result: a public institution also has been shaken.

So much for the story that intrigues more than the process used to deliver its pictorial images. "The Woman Without a Body and the Projectionist" (title refers to the head shots used regularly in tv reportage) was filmed entirely on one-inch videotape and later copied on 35m film by use of a special technique. All the tricks of video pans and zooms are superimposed on the film narrative, even to the point of annoyance and distraction. Further, the method has not been perfected enough to "erase" the video graininess, with the result that genuine clarity of an esthetic nature is only possible in closeups.

One has the feeling, sometimes, of watching a B-movie produced by the Monogram or Republic Studios in Hollywood's heyday. This seems to be intended by helmer Schilling and producer Elke Haltaufderheide. On that score this video-film works. —*Holl.*

Flight To Berlin
(W. GERMAN-BRITISH-COLOR)

Berlin, Feb. 21.

A Road Movies Filmproduktion, in association with The British Film Institute, for Channel 4 (London). Produced by Chris Sievernich. Directed by Christopher Petit. Features entire cast. Script, Petit, Hugo Williams, from novel by Jennifer Potter; camera (color), Martin Schafer; music, Irmin Schmidt; editor, Peter Przygodda; art director, Rainer Schaper; sound, Jon Ralph, Lothar Mankewitz; associate producers, Walter Donahue, Peter Sainsbury, Lynda Myles. Reviewed at Studio Kino, Berlin, Feb. 20, 1984. Running time: **91 MINS.**
Susannah .... Tusse Silberg
Nicholas .... Paul Freeman
Julie .... Lisa Kreuzer
Edouard .... Jean-Francois Stevenin
Jack .... Ewan Stewart
Eddie Constantine ...... Eddie Constantine
(English soundtrack)

Christopher Petit's third feature is a dazzlingly made modern thriller, though lovers of neatly structured plots with satisfactory ending in which everything is explained may not appreciate its qualities. Petit, an ex-film critic, isn't interested in the perfect plot, as he showed in his critically acclaimed first feature, "Radio On;" it's not the story so much as the characters and the background details that are exciting here.

And "Flight to Berlin" is exciting. It opens, brilliantly, as Susannah is taken from a Berlin apartment in the middle of the night by plainclothes police and driven speedily through the city streets. In the police station she's interrogated but, as the sparse narration tells, "They asked me the wrong questions." The questions they ask concern why Susanah was in the apartment of a known criminal but, as is discovered, when the inevitable flashbacks begin, she has other problems. She has flown into Berlin after her involvement with the death of a woman in mysterious circumstances. She checks into a seedy hotel and calls her elder sister, Julie (seems the sisters hardly know each other, and have been brought up in separate cities, Susannah in London, Julie in Berlin).

Gradually she becomes enmeshed with a group of mysterious characters who hover around Julie, including a French businessman, a self-confident young Englishman, with whom Susannah has an instant affair, and actor Eddie Constantine, who floats around the edges of the film lending his formidable presence to conjure up allusions to other films.

There are plenty of refcrences for film buffs to spot, some of the most obvious being to "Blow-Up" as well as to Petit's earlier films (and his very underrated detective movie, "An Unsuitable Job For A Woman," from the P.D. James novel). But it's not just a buff film, for the elliptical script, excellent acting and, above all, the extraordinary location camerawork of Martin Schafer, combine to make compulsive viewing, even if, in the end, the answers remain elusive.

There's also plenty of humor in the film, with small details such as a Japanese tourist struggling with a huge city street map in the background of a scene, or the very amusing dialog of Constantine (his comments on President Reagan's film career are memorable).

Performances are all very good, with newcomer Tusse Silberg a find as Susannah. Irmin Schmidt's jazzy score is apt and the film is expertly edited by Peter Przygodda.

By its nature, "Flight to Berlin" won't be a huge grosser, but it should get critical support and will probably be featured at a major festival this summer, so very healthy runs in specialized cinemas are indicated. It opens in two London cinemas early in March.
— *Strat.*

Death And The Singing Telegram
(U.S.-DOCU-COLOR/B&W-16m)

Berlin, Feb. 21.

Production, direction, camera (color/black & white), editing by Mark Rance. Reviewed at the International Forum of Young Cinema, Berlin International Film Festival, Feb. 19, 1984. Running time: **110 MINS.**

This family saga chronicles five years of discord and death, but with some happy moments, as the young producer-director Mark Rance documents his own relatives in leisurely unstructured action. He's more than a cameraman, he's a participant, sometimes speaking from behind the camera.

At times seeming to be unaware that they are being photographed as part of a film, but at other times protesting that implacable camera, these relatives engage spontaneously in the typical pursuits of middle-American families, including shopping for caskets and quarreling about inheritances — thus the death motif of the title.

Like our own lives, these lives on the screen combine little decencies and little atrocities in small-scale action. There are no big incidents in this film, no major revelations about our society. There are no sudden penetrating insights into the human condition. Nor is this a didactic documentary that investigates, explicates issues, or marshals imposing facts. Instead, we merely watch the dear old folks sicken and waste away, watch them buried; then we see their progeny, now middle-aged, develop their own symptoms and began for the first time to confront their own impending deaths. Meanwhile, the camera records it all.

Shooting over a five-year-period during visits home between work assignments as a cinema pro, Rance was able to observe changed conditions periodically as his family's fortunes and misfortunes shifted and sorted out.

Although slow and overlong, the film gives us occasional glimpses of authentic people beset by their humanity and struggling to keep control and maintain dignity. But occasional glimpses are enough when one goes to the movies. The film is cluttered with family memorabilia that doesn't communicate well to strangers in the audience. It's too privatized. Rance doesn't persuade one to care.

Rance had been a film student of Richard Leacock at the Massachusetts Institute of Technology. Leacock warns his students that it's not enough that a subject be true, it must also be interesting, to justify the shooting. Rance seems at time to have forgotten this precept: as cameraman, having shot some scenes that are true, but not interesting, he should have allowed Rance, the editor, to delete them.

Nevertheless, Berlin Festival audiences appreciated "Death and The Singing Telegram." And last October, the film won two prizes at the Nyon International Film Festival in Switzerland, an all-documentary event. —*Hitch.*

Derman
(Remedy)
(TURKISH-COLOR)

Berlin, Feb. 22.

A Gulsah Film Production. Directed by Serif Goren. Features entire cast. Script, Ahmet Soner, from novel by Osman Sahin; camera (color), Erdogan Engin; editor, Serif Goren; sound, Erkan Esenboga; music, Yeni Turku Gurubu. Reviewed at Atelier am Zoo, Berlin (Berlin Film Festival, Mediterranean Section), Feb. 22, 1984. Running time: **88 MINS.**
Muruvvet .... Hulya Kocyigit
Sehmuz .... Tarik Akan
Tahsin .... Talat Bulut
Bahar .... Nur Surer

Serif Goren, who did such a splendid job of directing "Yol" following the instructions of then-imprisoned Yilmaz Guney, proves he's a helmer to watch in his own right with "Remedy" (the Turkish title can also mean "solace"). Set in mountain country near the Iranian border, tale tells of young midwife, sent from Ankara to work at a medical center in the Anatolian village of Aladay. She never makes it there; a sudden, violent snowstorm cuts off all roads and she's given accommodation in the home of Tahsin and Bahar. Conditions are very uncomfortable; it's cold, and the city woman is forced to sleep in the same room as the rest of the family (an amusing touch has the husband, Tahsin, aroused by her perfume, making love with his wife).

After one aborted attempt to continue her journey, she decides to stay the winter, partly because she's become attracted to Sehmuz, a huntsman who, it's discovered, is wanted by the police for killing the men who'd slain his wife and children. Climax comes when the midwife and the fugitive help get a sick and pregnant woman to safety in the nearest hospital.

First half of the film is excellent, but novelettish aspects creep in towards the end, and the resolution is disappointing. But "Remedy" definitely indicates Goren is a helmer to watch and suggests the impressive visual and lyrical qualities of "Yol" came from him (just as the first post-prison solo Guney film, "The Wall," despite its tough theme, was artistically disappointing). What Goren needs is a stronger script, and he could emerge as Turkey's leading director. Opening part of "Remedy" is marvelous, with the tiny bus crawling through the snowbound countryside, a mysterious first encounter with Sehmuz by the roadside, and the arrival in the tiny village, whose inhabitants are minutely observed with insight and humor.

Hulya Kocyigit gives a warm performance as the city woman stranded in this icy wilderness, who is called "The Remedy" by the locals. Print shown in Berlin was, unfortunately, appalling and so heavily scratched it was sometimes difficult to tell if it was supposed to be snowing or not. If a decent copy can be found, no reason why "Remedy" can't play the festival circuit this year, and with honors. —*Strat.*

Repo Man
(U.S.-COLOR)

Berlin, Feb. 28.

A Universal film release of an Edge City production. Produced by Jonathan Wacks; executive producer, Michael Nesmith. Directed and screenplay by Alex Cox. Features entire cast. Camera (Technicolor), Robby Müller; art direction, J. Rae Fox, Linda Burbank; editor, Dennis Dolan; music, Steve Hufsteter, Tito Larrna, Los Plugz, Iggy Pop. Reviewed at the Berlin Film Festival

(non-competing), Feb. 26, 1984. Running Time: 94 MINS.

Bud	Harry Dean Stanton
Otto Maddox	Emilio Estevez
Leila	Olivia Barash
Miller	Tracey Walter
Lite	Sy Richardson
Debbi	Jennifer Balgobin
Plettschner	Richard Foronjy
Lagarto Rodriguez	Del Zamora
J. Frank Parnell	Fox Harris
Marlene	Vonetta McGee

A surprise hit of the Berlin festival's Info Show, "Repo Man" shapes up as a potential sleeper on the order of "Flashdance" or "Risky Business" at the boxoffice. While the title, referring to the people who repossess cars from those behind on their payments, might suggest a low-budget, gritty, realistic venture, the truth exists somewhat on the other end of the spectrum. However, the assured narrative and visual skill of filmmaker Alex Cox assures the film of more than a cult following. With the proper marketing, the picture has the potential to be an enormously popular success.

Plot descriptions for "Repo Man" are difficult and misleading. The more conventional aspects of the script deal with an aimless young man, wonderfully underplayed by Emilio Estevez, who falls in with a crowd of repo men and takes to the "intense" lifestyle with ease. His friends, meanwhile, are either on the dole or ekeing out an existence through petty crime.

Cox establishes the offbeat nature of the film from the start. In the opening scene, a state trooper stops a speeder and on a routine check of his trunk is blasted by a flash of light leaving him merely a smoldering pair of boots. This aspect of the story, centering on a '64 Chevy Malibu, begins to have significance only later.

The initial plot thrust involves Otto Maddox (Estevez) and Bud (Harry Dean Stanton), the veteran repo man who teaches him the ropes. Bud's Repo Code affects Otto's dress (conservative), style (never carry a gun, never damage a car) and method (always take amphetamines). Overall it's a colorful, bizarre lifestyle.

However, these are certainly tame facets as a story of alien invaders evolves. Suddenly, government agents, citizens groups and mad scientists enter the scene in a fast and furious chase for ownership of the Malibu. The Repo men become involved when a $20,000 bounty is placed on the vehicle.

This wonderfully original stew is a kind of "Skip Tracer" meets "Not of This Earth" with shadings of "Liquid Sky" and the pandora's box aspect of "Kiss Me Deadly." Yet there's no clear sense of homage or imitation — Cox is a true innovator and a stylist who displays the skill of a real up and comer.

The ever reliable Stanton turns in yet another indelible portrait of a seamy lowlife while Estevez

registers for the first time as a charismatic and talented actor. Also of note are both the driving score and Robby Müller's striking, evocative camera, particularly in the night sequences.

"Repo Man" has the type of unerring energy that leaves audiences breathless and entertained. —*Klad.*

Hungarian Week

Muzsika
(Music)
(HUNGARIAN-DOCU-COLOR)

Budapest, Feb. 17.

A Magyar Television production. Written and directed by Miklos Jancso. Camera (Eastmancolor), Janos Kende. No further credits available. Reviewed at Hungarian Film Laboratory, Budapest, Feb. 11, 1984. Running time: 55 MINS.

Miklos Jancso has contributed a loving, inventive, personal entry into a series of one hour films in which well known European directors have paid tribute to their respective cities. (First off the rank, Ermanno Olmi's "Milan 83," was the closing night film at last year's Venice Film Festival.)

As the title indicates, Jancso sees Budapest as a city of music, and he uses music of every imaginable kind: military music, folk songs, rock concert, popular standards, and of course the great classical works of Magyar composers. Accompanying the marvelous soundtrack are images of one of Europe's most beautiful old cities, seen through the sometimes amused eye of the director and his cameraman, Janos Kende.

The short but memorable pic is based on juxtapositions. Jancso moves from the brassy music of a military parade celebrating the country's National Day to a beautifully simple image of a mother with her baby — the military band is seen both through her apartment window and on television. Young girls march beside the Danube singing a traditional song, and the camera pulls back to reveal the pianist in one of the city's modern hotels playing a standard item by Hungarian Joseph Kosma, the melody of "Autumn Leaves," with the girls still seen through the hotel window. As the images change, so does the musical soundtrack. And so it goes.

Jancso himself wanders through a few scenes, and his film crew is seen reflected in windows or mirrors. A choir is seen singing in the rain, with the camera pulling back to reveal it's an artificial, cinema-effects, rainstorm.

In contrast to the mass choirs and rock groups, one Budapest citizen sings to himself on a city tram, while another plays "The Internationale" on the violin at a high spot overlooking the city. Jancso even manages to add a

scene involving naked women, who (for no particular reason) are seen besporting themselves in a city fountain.

All in all, a loving Valentine to the music and the capital city of his home country.—*Strat.*

Gyertek El A Nevnapomra
(The House-Warming)
(HUNGARIAN-COLOR)

Budapest, Feb. 17.

A Dialog Studios, Mafilm, production. Directed and written by Zoltan Fabri, based on a short story by Ferenc Karinthy. Camera (Eastmancolor), Gyorgy Illes; music, Gyorgy Ukan. Reviewed at Hungarofilm, Budapest, Feb. 13, 1984. Running time: 122 MINS.

Luca Peteri	Ildiko Piros
Dr. Egon Brenner	Istvan Bujtor
Laszlo Haudek	Ferenc Kallai
Laszlo Biro	Gabor Madi Szabo
Andrea Biro	Csilla Herczeg
Robi	Pal Macsay
Menyhert Hollan	Laszlo Inke

Basically, "The House-Warming" is a lot like all those Hollywood pics in which an intrepid investigative journalist uncovers a crime and cover-up in high places. Unfortunately, veteran director Zoltan Fabri has disdained the classical structure for such films, and has chosen to open his film with a 40-minute sequence detailing the events leading up to the crime, and the crime itself, before even introducing his reporter-heroine. This robs the tale of all suspense, presumably intentionally.

Opening sequence exposes the new Capitalist class in Hungary. A group of privileged middle-aged men gather to celebrate the house-warming of one of them: he's built a country place from his ill-gotten gains, and even managed to wangle a road with street lights be constructed leading up to it. He and his cronies eat and drink one of the most lavish meals in screen history, before their drunken revels are rudely interrupted by the daughter of one of them, who's eloping with her boyfriend against Dad's wishes; the drunken parent shoots the boy in the head, though not fatally. At a subsequent investigation, the host takes responsibility for the shooting, claiming he thought the youth was a prowling dog.

Enter the woman reporter, Luca, who hears about the case from her lover, a doctor who treated the wounded boy. Sniffing out a story, she starts making herself a nuisance among the big-wigs, and suffers various harassments (disconnected phone, stolen car, electricity cut off) before she even loses her job. But she keeps investigating.

Fabri, whose career dates back to the early '50s and who has made some fine films in the past, is obviously intent on exposing the privileged executive class who, the film suggests, are ripping off the rest of the country. But this is all established in the opening sequence (rather well) leaving the rest of the film, now lacking any mystery, redundant. Film looks good and thesping is fine, but, considering the fact that the source is a short story, the two hour-plus running time is manifestly excessive. Scenes go on and on, long after the point has been made.

Thus, a potentially important subject is trivialized and an opportunity for a tough dramatic expose is missed. — Strat.

Istvan, A Kiraly
(Istvan, The King)
(HUNGARIAN-COLOR)

Budapest, Feb. 17.

A Budapest Studio, Mafilm, production. Directed by Gabor Koltay. Based on a Rock Opera by Miklos Boldizsar; music, Levente Szorenyi; lyrics, Janos Brody; camera (Eastmancolor), Tamas Andor. Reviewed at Hungarofilm, Budapest, Feb. 13, 1984. Running time: 95 MINS.
King Istvan ....Laszlo Pelsoczy
Sarolt ....Kati Berek
Gisela ....Bernadette Sara
Abbot Astrik ....Victor Mate
Koppany ....Gyula Vikidal
Torda ....Gyula "Bill" Deak
Laboro ....Fero Nagy
Reka ....Ottilia Kovacs
Sur ....Sandor Szakacsi
Solt ....Sandor Soros
Bese ....Peter Balazs

A film of a live performance of a popular Rock Opera about Hungarian King Istvan I (970-1038), who brought Christianity to the country.

Director Gabor Koltay, whose other rock film, "The Concert," was a great success locally two years ago, has crafted a fine record of the event, obviously inspired by American concert films. With creative use of freeze-frame and slow motion, plus fine lensing and sound recording (with a Dolby Stereo mix), he couldn't have done better for the original musical.

Istvan's assumption of the throne marked the beginning of the end of old pagan ways in Hungary, and was marked with a Civil War, won by the King. The music score by Levente Szorenyi and Janos Brody is vigorous and lively, as befits the subject. Actors and singers are likewise fine.

The film should mop up locally, since the Rock Opera itself was very popular and the record album selling well. Overseas possibilities are very much in doubt, though.
—Strat.

A Csoda Vege
(The End Of The Miracle)
(HUNGARIAN-COLOR)

Budapest, Feb. 17.

A Hunnia Studio, Mafilm, production. Directed by Janos Veszi. Script, Veszi, Edit Koszegi; camera (Eastmancolor), Tibor Mate; music, Veszi. Reviewed at Hun-

garofilm, Budapest, Feb. 14, 1984. Running time: 84 MINS.
Irma ....Dana Medricka
Kamilla ....Vlasta Fabianova
Bozsi ....Klari Tolnay
Peter.......................Tamas Major
Gyorgy ....Vlastimil Brodsky
Jutka ....Mari Torocsik

A pleasant first feature about old people. Peter dies rather suddenly leaving behind two ex-wives, the sisters Irma and Kamilla, and Bozsi, his ex-mistress. They all live in an apartment house for geriatrics. Along comes Peter's oldest friend, Gyorgy, an expatriate who lives in Canada. He's happy to be back in Budapest after many years, and for a while it seems likely he might marry one of the three women; but it's not to be.

It's a modest but quite charming little film, with pleasant performances all round, but definitely not for young audiences, since it's single-minded concerned with old people and their foibles. Location photography around Budapest is an asset.—Strat.

Maria - Nap
(Maria's Day)
(HUNGARIAN-COLOR)

Budapest, Feb. 17.

An Objektiv Studio production, with Hungarian Television. Directed by Judit Elek. Script, Gyorgy Petho; camera (Eastmancolor), Emil Novak. No further credits available. Reviewed at Hungarofilm, Budapest, Feb. 4, 1984. Running time: 115 MINS.
Julia Horvath ....Edit Handel
Maria Gyulai.......................Eva Igo
Ignac Szendrey ....Sandor Szabo
Arpad Horvath ....Tamas Fodor
Pal Gyulai ....Imre Csiszar
Istvan Petofi.................Lajos Kovacs

Reminiscent of those Soviet films based on Chekhov works, "Maria's Day" is an intimate family story which takes place during a reunion of the Szendrey family at a country house in September 1866. Julia, the elder daughter of Ignac Szendrey, had been married to the famous Hungarian poet and patriot Sandor Petofi (who had died in 1849 fighting for Hungary's independence from Austria); her second husband, Arpad Horvath, is unpopular with other members of the family, who would like to see Julia leave him. Julia, who knows she has cancer, is also concerned about her son, Zoltan Petofi, who has become a loose-living alcoholic and is also seriously ill; the boy has been raised by his uncle, Istvan. Also in the house is Julia's beautiful younger sister, Maria, who is celebrating her name-day; she is happily married to Pal Gyulai.

Much of the film is taken up with family arguments, culminating in the unexpected death (from cholera) of the apparently healthy Maria. Though well acted by the ensemble cast, and eloquently photographed by Emil Novak, the film lacks the insights and flashes of humor which make the Soviet pics of

this type so memorable. Director Judit Elek tends to handle it all on one rather monotonous note, and the film lacks tension and a sense of accelerating drama as a result. Better suited for television than cinema release. —Strat.

Delibabok Orszaga
(The Land of Miracles)
(HUNGARIAN-B&W)

Budapest, Feb. 17.

A Budapest Studios, Mafilm, production. Directed by Marta Meszaros. Script, Balazs Vargha, based on "The Inspector General," by Nikolai Gogol; camera (b&w), Miklos Jancso Jr.; music, Zsolt Dome. Reviewed at Hungarofilm theatrette, Budapest, Feb. 11, 1984. Running time: 84 MINS.
The Mayor....................Jan Nowicki
Karikas ....Marek Kondradt
Mayor's wife ....Teri Tordai
Mayor's daughter ....Kati Rak
Karikas' servant.............Adam Szirtes

Gogol's "The Inspector General" has been filmed a few times in the past, most prominently the 1950 Henry Koster version which was a vehicle for Danny Kaye.

Now distaff Magyar helmer Marta Meszaros has a go at the familiar tale of the corrupt mayor and corporation of a small provincial town who hear that an inspector from the city is coming, incognito, to check up on them and who mistake a wayward traveller for the V.I.P. So, they dine him, wine him, bribe him — and even offer him the mayor's wife and/or daughter.

There are still some laughs in the subject, though comedy doesn't seem to be exactly where Meszaros is at. Too often she seems to be taking it all a bit too seriously. Thesping is fine, with Jan Nowicki, the Polish actor seen in many Meszaros films, giving one of his best performances as the corrupt mayor. The film is handsomely photographed in glittering black and white by Miklos Jancso Jr. Continual rain in exterior scenes seems a needless gimmick, but provides some attractive images. But overall, "The Land of Miracles" seems better suited to tv, as it lacks the punches needed for it to make much of a theatrical career.
—Strat.

A Hatarozat
(The Resolution)
(HUNGARIAN-B&W-DOCU)

Budapest, Feb. 17.

A Bela Balazs studio production. Directed by Gyula Gazdag, Judit Ember. Camera (black and white), Peter Jankura. No further credits available. Reviewed at Hungarofilm, Budapest, Feb. 15, 1984. Running time: 102 MINS.

Shot in February, 1972, and finally released (bearing a 1983 date), "The Resolution" emerges as quite the most remarkable documentary about the inner working of the system in a Communist country. There are no actors here: what is in the film is real.

The opening scene is of a small meeting of Communist Party officials from a regional district: they are discussing the alleged misconduct of the chairman of a local farm cooperative. It's suggested that the man has taken too large a salary, boosted his expense account, and employed (in some unstated capacity) a criminal who is now serving a six-year jail term for (believe it or not) running a brothel! They decide the chairman must go, but the decision is up to the co-op membership.

Next, a meeting of the board of this particular co-op. The Party officials state their case: the chairman must go. But, one by one, the chairman's colleagues rise to defend him, pointing out that the co-op was in dire financial straits before his leadership.

The climax comes at the annual general meeting of co-op members: again, the party officials make it perfectly clear they want the chairman fired for his alleged misconduct. A (rather peculiar) secret ballot is taken: the rank and file votes for the chairman to stay. The film ends as it began with a small meeting of the same party officials; they admit they handled the whole thing badly, and talk of strategy for the future. A closing title explains that nine months late the chairman of the co-op resigned.

Although by its very nature it is not a film likely to have a theatrical career, "The Resolution" could well be successful at festivals or on television; it's really a must for students of Eastern Europe.

Here the viewer can see, as never before, how Communism works at the grassroots level, and the sequence where the rank and file stubbornly rejects the advice of the party representatives is, in this context, quite devastating. No wonder the material has taken 12 years to reach the screen.

Black and white photography of Peter Jankura is faultless, always seemingly homing in on the right face at the right time. Editing makes the most of the impending drama.

Needless to say, when Judit Ember and Gyula Gazdag started shooting the film, they couldn't possibly have known how it would turn out. Result is one of the major documentaries of recent years.
—Strat.

Boszorkanyszombat
(Witches' Sabbath)
(HUNGARIAN-U.S.-COLOR)

Budapest, Feb. 17.

An Objektiv Studios, Mafilm, — Robert Halmi Inc. (New York) production. Directed by Janos Rozsa. Screenplay, Istvan Kardos; camera (Eastmancolor), Janos Kende; music, Zdenko Tamassy; sets and costumes, Gyula Pauer; special effects, Roy Field. Viewed at Voros Csillag theater, Budapest, Feb. 10, 1984. Running time: 88 MINS.
The wicked stepmother ..Dorottya Udvaros
Sleeping Beauty ....Eniko Eszenyi

The Brothers Grimm .... Robert Koltai
Zoltan Papp
Old man .... Antal Pager
Grandson .... Imre Kamondy

A lavish fantasy boasting top special effects, costumes and design, plus some rich ideas, though lacking the required light touch to stir it all together for the perfect brew.

Idea is that all the famous fairy-tale characters — Little Red Riding Hood, "Snow White and the Seven Dwarfs," "Cinderella," characters from "The Wizard of Oz," etc. — gather together for a great event: the awakening of Sleeping Beauty after her 100 years sleep.

Forgotten in the crush is the man who loved her before a spell was cast over her; he's now a doddering old man. Also on hand are the brothers Grimm, creators of so many fairy-tales. But Snow White's wicked stepmother is up to no good; she doesn't see why the villains in fairy-tales should always fare so poorly, so she gains the support of a gang of witches, wolves and other such villains, plus a giant, and turns the tables on the rest, imprisoning them and demanding that the Grimms re-write fairy-tale history. Needless' to say she doesn't get away with her dastardly scheme.

All the elements are here for a classic fantasy pic, but somehow — despite the endless care lavished on the visual side — it doesn't come off. Trouble is mainly that helmer Janos Rozsa (best known for a very different kind of children-themed film, "Sunday Daughters" (1979), which achieved theatrical release in the U.S.) is telling an allegory here about the dangers of rewriting history.

He lets the serious side of the story overwhelm what should have been a light-hearted souffle. Result is a declamatory pic with long speeches which will bore many youngsters; and the one note playing of it all makes it something of an endurance test.

No gain saying that the special effects, handled in London by a veteran team headed by Roy Field, are tops; the film has a superb opening of witches in flight which promises more than is ever delivered thereafter. Sets and costume design (Gyula Pauer) are also pro, as is lensing by Janos Kende. Would that Rozsa had had a bit more *fun* with the whole notion: all the wonderful images from childhood are here, but the Message takes over with too much of a vengeance. —*Strat.*

Konnyu Testi Sertes

(Light Physical Injuries)
(HUNGARIAN-B&W)

Budapest, Feb. 17.

A Hunnia Studio, Mafilm, production. Directed by Gyorgy Szomjas. Script, Ferenc Grunwalsky, Szomjas; camera (black and white), Grunwalsky; music, Tamas Somlo; sound, Andras Elek. Reviewed at Hungarofilm, Budapest, Feb. 12, 1984. Running time: 85 MINS.
Eva .... Mariann Erdos
Csaba .... Karoly Eperjes
Miklos .... Peter Andorai
With Edit Abraham, Vera Molnar, Erzsi Czerhalmi, Laszlo Szabo.

An abrasive contemporary comedy-drama, "Light Physical Injuries," which proved to be one of the best films shown in the 1984 Hungarian Film Week, is the work of an imaginative and gifted director, Gyorgy Szomjas, whose "Bald Dog Rock" (1981) had a similar impact. Pic is slated to represent Hungary in competition at the Berlin Film Festival.

The central character is Csaba, a rather anti-social, quick-tempered character who's been jailed for stabbing a man during a drunken brawl. On his release, he discovers that his wife, Eva, has brought another man, Miklos, into their apartment and is living with him. A divorce is quickly arranged, but with living accommodation in Budapest being in short supply, Csaba and Eva are forced to share their former marital home, which means sharing kitchen and bathroom too, hardly convenient when you still love your ex-wife and she's living with a man you can't stand, and the apartment walls are thin.

That's the basic plot: simple in the extreme, but used by Szomjas as a starting point for some bruising observations about working-class life in today's Budapest. While most of the drama — and comedy — centers around the menage-a-trois — plus Csaba's occasional girlfriends — a number of 'witnesses' are also introduced to propel the plot (such as it is) forward: Csaba's mother, a rather foolish woman always clutching official documents, who refuses to believe anything bad about her son; a nosey neighbor, forever spying on the threesome from across the way; and a former school-friend of Eva.

The three principal actors are unquestionably splendid. Mariann Erdos, a newcomer who looks a lot like French actress Fanny Ardant, is the sulky, infuriating, capricious Eva; Karoly Eperjes makes a wonderfully unsettling character out of the wiry, rather dangerous Csaba; and Peter Andorai, known for his roles in some Istvan Szabo films, is transformed as the repulsive Miklos, Eva's paunchy, sleazy, side-burned lover.

Film was made on a very low budget by Magyar standards, on the basis of a two-page outline. Hungarian release version (which has been a great success) included a few color sequences and tinted black and white; but Szomjas now says he prefers the 'international,' totally black and white, version which was shown officially here and which goes to Berlin. However, some critics who caught the part-color version found it an improvement.

Pic is an expert blend of dark comedy and gritty social drama, not to mention some uninhibited sexual situations. Dialog is apparently more authentic than in most Hungarian films, using plenty of gutter talk: there's an engaging sequence introducing Csaba's old grandmother, who warbles a very bawdy song. Attitude of the police in the film, who invade the privacy of the apartment on more than one occasion, is scary.

All in all, an engrossing, intelligent and often very funny film. —*Strat.*

Naplo

(Diary)
(HUNGARIAN-B&W)

Budapest, Feb. 17.

A Budapest Studio, Mafilm, production. Directed and written by Marta Meszaros. Camera (black and white), Miklos Jancso Jr.; music, Zsolt Dome. Reviewed at Hungarofilm, Budapest, Feb. 13, 1984. Running time: 106 MINS.
Juli .... Zsuzsa Czinkoczi
Magda .... Anna Polony
Janos .... Jan Nowicki
Juli's Father .... Jan Nowicki
Grandpa .... Pal Zolnay
Grandma .... Mari Szemes
Tomas .... Tamas Toth

Marta Meszaros has apparently wanted to make "Diary" for 15 years or more (her first feature, "The Girl," was made in 1968). Dedicated "for my children," it's an intensely personal autobiographical story, though the child in the film is named Juli, not Marta.

Meszaros was the daughter of Hungarian sculptor Laszlo Meszaros, a Communist who moved his family to the U.S.S.R. in 1936 when Marta was five years old.

"Diary" begins in 1947, when young Juli returns from Moscow to Budapest, accompanied by an elderly Hungarian couple. Her parents are dead, we discover in flashbacks; her beloved father was purged and forced into hard manual labor, while her mother, left alone, also died after a difficult childbirth resulting in a dead baby. Juli is delivered into the hands of Magda, the old man's younger sister, and takes an instant dislike to her new foster-mother, a rigid disciplinarian who soon leaves her job on a newspaper to become director of a prison. Juli misses her parents and hates school, frequently playing hookey to go to the movies.

But she takes a liking to Janos, a friend of Magda's, a man who reminds her of her father (both roles are played by Jan Nowicki) and who is chief engineer at a large factory. She develops a crush on Janos, which alienates her still further from the embittered Magda. And her world is turned upside down when, in the early fifties, the Stalinist purges come to Hungary too, and Janos is imprisoned, just as her father had been.

It's a strong tale of an unhappy childhood being endured at a grim time in Eastern European history, and the finely textured black and white photography of Miklos Jancso Jr. (the helmer's stepson) emphasizes the bleakness of Juli's world. Indeed, it's rather a cold, unemotional film, although a decisive return to form for Marta Meszaros whose recent work, often in French coproductions, had been getting more and more trivial. This is an important film, and obviously a controversial one: it bears a 1982 date, and has been held up for over a year, presumably becuase of its touchy theme.

It could make its mark abroad on its subject and intensity. Zsuzsa Czinkoczi is effective as young Juli. —*Strat.*

Atvaltozas

(Point of Departure)
(HUNGARIAN-COLOR)

Budapest, Feb. 17.

A Tarsulas Studio, Mafilm, production. Directed and written by Istvan Darday, Gyorgyi Szalai. Camera (Eastmancolor), Ferenc Pap, Laszlo Poros. No further credits available. Reviewed at Hungarofilm, Budapest, Feb. 14, 1984. Running time: 274 MINS.
Gabor Pasztor .... Gabor Csordas
Wanda Pasztor .... Amaryllis Tamas
Grandfather .... Miklos Jaky
Marta .... Marta Rimoczi
Intellectual .... Gabor Body

Undoubtedly one of the most interesting and talked about pics unveiled during the 1984 Hungarian Film Week, "Point of Departure" (or "Metamorphosis") is a frustrating mixture of the very good and the very bad.

Somewhere inside this excessively long, four-and-one-half hour marathon (already cut down from eight hours, apparently) is a major two-hour film struggling to emerge. It's to be hoped that further cutting is not out of the question. In any event, this version was shown in the Forum section of the Berlin Film Festival.

Pic's events take place entirely within a two-story suburban house (there are no exteriors until the very end). Living here is a very old man, deeply involved in writing his memoirs and going about his set routine. His granddaughter, Wanda, lives in the house too with Gabor, her husband, a poet and intellectual. Gabor and his friends spend endless hours in deep debate about the state of art in Hungary, among other themes, and wants to start a new cultural magazine. He neglects his wife, and is unenthusiastic about her desires to have a baby. Wanda's younger cousin, Marta, a ballet dancer, also lives in the house, and seems totally preoccupied with her own little world. Eventually Wanda leaves, and Gabor brings a new mistress to the house. The old man dies, leaving the house to Wanda and the furniture — and his collection of old photographs — to Marta, who promptly sells them.

Though it might seem hard to understand how such a long film could be made from such a small subject, helmers Istvan Darday and Gyorgyi Szalai have managed it, mainly by forcing the viewer to endure the agonizingly boring debates and arguments of Gabor and his friends.

All this intellectual masturbation might have some significance for local audiences (but at such length surely even on home ground audience potential will be severely diminished), but has almost none for foreigners, though no gainsaying scenes are well photographed, as is the entire film, by Ferenc Pap and Laszlo Poros. These debate scenes, dominated by men while the women mostly provide more drinks on cue, also feature more smoking than in a dozen other pics put together: obviously the fate of Hungary's tobacco industry is in no danger.

If the scenes with Gabor and his pals are dull, through sheer repetition, the scenes with the women and the old man are riveting. Seeing the grandfather pore over his old photos, or exercise his dog, or even watch television or make breakfast, is hypnotic. Uncommonly beautiful is a sequence where Marta dances nude and Wanda, quietly watching, kisses her lightly and then goes off to make love with her husband. The beauty and grace of so many of these scenes make the inclusion of so much uninteresting debate all the more regrettable. — *Strat.*

Te Rongyos Elet!...
(Oh, Bloody Life!...)
(HUNGARIAN-COLOR)

Budapest, Feb. 17.

A Dialog Studio, Mafilm, production. Written and directed by Peter Bacso. Camera (Eastmancolor), Tamas Andor; music, Gyorgy Vukan. Reviewed at Hungarofilm, Budapest, Feb. 12, 1984. Running time: **108 MINS.**

Lucy Sziraky	Dorottya Udvaros
Captain Matura	Zoltan Bezeredy
Baron Samoday	Odon Rubold
Kiptar	Laszlo Szacsvay
Theater Director	Andras Kern

Internationally speaking, Peter Bacso's most successful film has been "The Witness," a comedy set in the Stalinist '50s, made in 1968 but held up for many years and released only in the early '80s. With "Oh, Bloody Life!...," Bacso returns to the same period, but the results are meager.

The pic opens very well, promising more than is subsequently delivered. Lucy, a young actress, finds herself unexpectedly playing the lead in a stage musical about a woman tractor-driver when the

star is incapacitated. She's a success, even though her tractor knocks over some of the scenery. After the show, the lecherous director accompanies her back to her apartment with seduction in mind, contract in hand. Just at the wrong moment, the police burst in. It seems that Lucy was formerly <u>married</u> to an aristocrat, and though they've been divorced for years and he now lives in Paris, she's considered a part of the old bourgeoisie, a "class enemy."

As a result she's forced to leave her apartment, her career and Budapest itself and join other "class enemies" — former landowners, industrialists, aristocrats and military chiefs — doing manual labor in an isolated farming village.

So far, so good: but having set up an engaging premise, Bacso's invention apparently deserts him. Rest of the overlong pic is a slowly-paced slog involving Lucy's romantic entanglements with (1) a younger former Baron; (2) the local police chief; and (3) the local party leader, a schoolteacher. Despite a valiant performance from Dorottya Udvaros, and some effective supporting players, plus attractive camerawork, the bulk of the film works neither as comedy nor as drama. The very subject seems a bit dated by now.

For the record, there is one very amusing scene: the lustful police chief, stark naked, advances on the equally naked Lucy who suddenly produces a gun and forces the poor man to sing for his supper. It's a bright moment in an otherwise dull film. — *Strat.*

Kiralygyilkossag — Egy Merenylet Anatomiaja
(Regicide — Anatomy of an Assassination)
(HUNGARIAN-COLOR & B&W)

Budapest, Feb. 17.

An Objektiv Studio, Mafilm, — Hungarian Television production, in association with Rudas Filmproduktion KG. Written and directed by Peter Bokor. Camera (Eastmancolor, B&W), Sandor Sara, Sandor Kurucz. Reviewed at Hungarofilm, Budapest, Feb. 12, 1984. Running time: **92 MINS.**

King Alexander I	Karoly Mecs
Louis Barthou	Laszlo Inke
Ante Pavelic	Istvan Avar
Kerin	Gyula Szersen
Gustav Persec	Lajos Balazsovits
Jelka Pogolerec	Eniko Toth

And, as themselves: Pierre Mondanel, Paul Marabuto, Rene Massigli, Marguerite Ronserail.

On Nov. 10, 1934, Alexander I, King of Yugoslavia, arrived in Marseilles on an official visit and was welcomed by the French Foreign Minister, Louis Barthou. As the two men drove slowly in an open car away from the quay and up a city street, an assassin fired a number of shots which instantly killed the King and fatally wound-

ed Barthou; the gunman was clubbed to death by police.

This combination of interview and enacted drama, plus the dramatic newsreel of the assassination itself, makes for a fascinating investigation into who was responsible for the killings. Pierre Mondanel, then chief of the French Criminal Police and now a sprightly 94-year-old with apparent total recall, is interviewed as are others involved with the investigation. Acted sequences fill in the details.

The plotters were apparently members of Ustashi, a Croatian secret society seeking independence for Croatia from the rest of Yugoslavia, and working with the backing of Mussolini and Hitler. The murder of Yugoslavia's King was seen as a first step in a destabilization campaign directed against the country.

By its very nature, "Regicide — Anatomy of an Assassination" seems better suited for tv rather than cinema, though in countries where there are still groups of militant Croations, hostility towards the pic may well be expected. Director Peter Bokor has done an excellent investigative job, and the dramatic sequences are well handled. All credits are pro. — *Strat.*

Hanyatt-homlok
(Helter-skelter)
(HUNGARIAN-COLOR)

Budapest, Feb. 17.

A Budapest Studio, Mafilm, production. Directed by Gyorgy Revesz. Script, Miklos Vamos, from his short story; camera (Eastmancolor), Ferenc Szecsenyi; music, KFT Group. Reviewed at Hungarofilm, Budapest, Feb. 12, 1984. Running time: **76 MINS.**

Ferenc Deak	Andras Kern
Wife	Gyorgyi Tarjan
Mother	Zsuzsa Banki
Father	Laszlo Mensaros
Grandfather	Tamas Major
Professor	Lajos Oze
Woman	Judit Hernadi
Inquisitor	Peter Haumann

A light-hearted political fantasy filled with local references which will make it an unlikely prospect for exportation. Veteran director Gyorgy Revesz, whose 1962 film "Land of Angels," played at several festivals but who hasn't been heard from much lately, has contrived a briskly-paced tale of a successful writer who finds himself in a nightmare situation. He's just been awarded the Ovidon Prize for literature (Ovidon is a brand of birth-control pills!) and is celebrating with friends and relations, when the police come and unceremoniously haul him up before a tribunal: he's accused of a murder committed in 1949 although, as he reasonably points out, since he wasn't born until 1950 he can't be guilty. This it seems is no excuse: the crime was committed by his father, and somebody in the family has to pay for it.

In-jokes about contemporary Hungarian society abound, though

there are a few gags that any audience will appreciate (for instance, as the hero is led to the scaffold, a cloakroom attendant checks his coat). And the last few minutes are effective as the entire population of Hungary drives, lemming-like, into a giant concentration camp having been led to believe they're all going to West Germany.

Main plus the film has a pacing and brevity, and as such it's a model for more long-winded contemporary Magyar productions. Andras Kern is a rather bland hero. Production credits are fine.
— *Strat.*

Felhojatek
(Passing Fancy)
(HUNGARIAN-COLOR)

Budapest, Feb. 17.

A Hunnia Studio, Mafilm, production. Written and directed by Gyula Maar, from the short story "Budapest Cloudscape," by Tibor Dery. Camera, (Eastmancolor), Emil Novak; music, Gyorgy Selmeczi. Reviewed at Varus Csillag theater, Budapest, Feb. 11, 1984. Running time: **92 MINS.**

Dr. Gyorgy Racz	Jiri Menzel
Lajos Nemeth	Miklos Tolnay
Marta	Mari Kiss
Anny	Cecilia Esztergalyos
Kata Buchler	Hana Maciuhova
Professor Buchler	Jiri Adamira
Woman at Party	Mari Torocsik

"Passing Fancy" is an enjoyable, elegant, old-fashioned comedy set in the '20s. Dr. Gyorgy Racz, a rather befuddled character, returns by train to his native Budapest after 10 years absence and before long is spotted by his oldest friend, Lajos Nemeth, as he sits in a cafe. Immediately, Racz finds himself involved in a series of complicated love affairs and liaisons surrounding his friend, with a trio of beautiful women and a couple of jealous husbands around the corner.

The plot and settings are rather similar to those classic Lubitsch comedies of bygone years. Czech filmmaker Jiri Menzel gives a wonderfully droll performance as the bewildered hero, and is ably supported by a top cast of players, some of them fellow Czechs. Director Gyula Maar, who usually makes rather more serious films, shows he has the requisite light touch.

There's a lot of talk, but it's all quietly amusing and at the end there's a poignant note in a fade-out revelation. Production values are excellent. — *Strat.*

Szeretok
(An Afternoon Affair)
(HUNGARIAN-COLOR)

Budapest Feb. 17.

A Dialog Studios, Mafilm, production. Directed by Andras Kovacs. Script, Tibor Gyurkovits; camera (Eastmancolor), Miklos Biro; music, Gabor Presser. Reviewed at Hungarofilm, Budapest, Feb. 13, 1984. Running time: **84 MINS.**

Vera	Mari Kiss
Tamas	Gyorgy Cserhalmi

Mother	Nora Tabori
Tibor	Gabor Reviczky
Tamas' wife	Ottilia Borbath
Friend	Andras Balint
Man at Party	Peter Andorai

An unexceptional romantic drama in which Vera, a divorcee aged about 30, spends most of her time agonizing about the secret affair she's having with Tamas, a married man.

As the English title suggests, it's a case of love in the afternoon (the Hungarian title means, simply, "Lovers"). Vera lives with her mother, who thinks she should settle down, and arranges some disastrous blind dates. A night with an old friend also ends badly. Vera half believes that Tamas will leave his wife and marry her, until by chance when in hospital for a minor operation, she discovers that her lover is the proud father of a new baby.

Mari Kiss is excellent as the vulnerable, anguished Vera, but the film doesn't have much that's new to say about fidelity. —Strat.

Tank
(COLOR)

What a little Sherman can do.

Hollywood, March 9.

A Lorimar Presentation of a Universal Pictures release. Produced by Irwin Yablans. Directed by Marvin Chomsky. Features entire cast. Screenplay, Dan Gordon; camera (Metrocolor), Don Brinkrant; editor, Donald R. Rede; production designer, Bill Kenney; music, Lalo Schifrin; sound, Bill Tague; set designer, Richard McKenzie; costumes, James Tyson, Ann Lambert; associate producer, Richard McWherter; assistant director, Don Roberts. Reviewed at the Hollywood Pacific theater, Hollywood, March 9, 1984 (MPAA rating: PG.) Running time: 113 MINS.

Zack	James Garner
Sheriff Buelton	G.D. Spradlin
LaDonna	Shirley Jones
Billy	C. Thomas Howell
Deputy Euelid	James Cramwell
Sarah	Jenilee Harrison
Sergeant Tippet	Dorian Harewood
General Hubik	Sandy Ward
Elliott	Mark Herrier
Governor Sims	J. Don Ferguson

James Garner, as a career-soldier who fights small-town injustice with a Sherman tank, is sufficiently strong in his signature role of affable maverick to give this otherwise uneven and preposterous film some Sherman tracks at the boxoffice.

Press material describes budget "in the $6,000,000 range." If true, this Georgia-shot adventure-drama with doses of comedy should turn a green ledger for Lorimar and distrib Universal. The audience appeal of loners-against-corruption is here refashioned with the hero inside a marauding Sherman tank, taking on a maniacal southern sheriff in defense of integrity and family. Unlike similar vengeful characterizations played by Clint Eastwood, Charles Bronson, and Sylvester Stallone, Garner's persona gives the events a softer, more human, and at times bemused edge.

Film is latest theatrical outing for director Marvin Chomsky (Emmy-winner for "Inside the Third Reich," "Holocaust" as well as such features as "Evel Knievel") working from a script by Dan Gordon. Film also marks first of a multi-pic deal between producer Irwin Yablans and Lorimar. Filmmaker's design is aimed at broad, even "Smokey And The Bandit," yahoo elements. Result is a marketable film that sacrifices coherence and consistency of tone.

First 10 minutes, showing Garner's arrival on an Army base (in reality, Ft. Benning) are terribly slow; relationship is ploddingly established with wife Shirley Jones and teenage son C. Thomas Howell (Ponyboy in "The Outsiders"). It's amazing that contemporary filmmakers would rely on such dead-ahead, uninspired narrative to get a film going.

Pace finally picks up when Garner gets in trouble for bashing a deputy who had slapped around a prostitute in a bar. The action triggers outrage by the local sheriff, another signature role by G.D. Spradlin, who gets even with Garner by framing his son and sending the boy to a despicable work farm.

Well, what to do. Garner personally owns a Sherman tank, somehow the long-tinkered payoff of his years in the service. At this point, the film seems to be serious, the son languishing in jail thinking he's the pawn in his dad's playful moment with a hooker. Garner is full of emotional pain. Wife Shirley Jones (who essentially has little to do) stamps her feet. Garner can't get any sleep. Then he gets in his tank, revs it up, mows down the sheriff's jail, and makes the nasty deputy who started the whole mess strip to his socks on a public street and handcuffs him to a telephone pole. Next he assaults the prison work camp with his Sherman, rescues his son, and the pursuit to the Tennessee line is on.

At this point, after some nominally heavy father-son dramatics, film strips gears and shifts from neutral to farce. The crazed sheriff and his dim deputy, once serious objects of scorn, become characters in a comic strip panel. The familiar, tired, entertainment cliché that turns almost every southern town into a collection of William Faulkner's Snopses-turned-clowns is wearing awfully thin.

Effective work, though, is delivered by Spradlin and James Cramwell, with latter playing the lackey to a gawkish tilt.

As film grinds on, Garner, notwithstanding a tank injury, seems to lose vigor. Jenilee Harrison is a fetchingly innocent prostitute who tags along for the bumpy ride.

Ideally, the film should be mean and hard all the way. As it is, the bad guys get their PG desserts by falling ker-plunk in the mud.

—Loyn.

Killpoint
(COLOR)

Stoic police pic for action trade.

A Crown International Pictures release of a Killpoint Prods. production. Produced by Frank Harris, Diane Stevenett. Executive producers, Roger Jacobson, Dana J. Welch. Directed by Harris. Features entire cast. Screenplay, Harris; camera (Metrocolor), Harris; editor, Harris; music, Herman Jeffreys, Daryl Stevenett; sound, Gene Lehfeldt, Nelson Tharp; assistant director-production manager, Diane Stevenett; art direction, Larry Westover; set decoration, Jennifer Chung; special effects, Ron Adams; fight choreography, Leo Fong; stunt coordinators, Rick Avery, Gene Lehfeldt. Reviewed at UA Rivoli 1 theater, N.Y., March 11, 1984. (MPAA Rating: R). Running time: 89 MINS.

Lt. James Long	Leo Fong
Agent Bill Bryant	Richard Roundtree
Joe Marks	Cameron Mitchell
Nighthawk	Stack Pierce
Anita	Hope Holiday
Candy	Diana Leigh (Stevenett)

"Killpoint" is a perfunctory police picture made in a semi-documentary fashion that reduces audience involvement. Prospects on the action circuit are okay.

Filmmaker Frank Harris (who takes five credits on the pic) has sought to out-do Louis de Rochemont and Jack Webb in low-key realism, but the result is dull. Dozens of members of the Riverside Calif. police department plus the local coroner's office and people off the street fill most of the "acting" roles, and several lead players are so ice-cold in their performances that the film seems remote instead of exciting.

Leo Fong, a Chinese-American martial arts expert, toplines as Lt. James Long, a cop troubled by his wife's rape and murder, who is assigned to work with government agent Bill Bryant (Richard Roundtree) in catching the killers who have stolen automatic weapons from a National Guard armory and are creating mayhem by selling them to local criminals and gangs. Stack Pierce portrays Nighthawk, the key gunrunner, whose boss, played behind dark glasses by Cameron Mitchell, is a nut who gets his jollies torturing and killing women.

Fong, whose immobile but strong-featured visage suggests an Oriental counterpart to Woody Strode, is unimpressive, a totally unemotional nonactor. Pierce's one-note "Mr. Cool" is counterproductive, Mitchell is silly and guest star Roundtree tarnishes his "Shaft" superhero image by getting blown away in routine fashion. Technically merely adequate, "Killpoint" delivers none of the fun that once made B-features so enjoyable. —Lor.

Mike's Murder
(COLOR)

Debra's renown might help.

Hollywood, March 1.

A Ladd Co. release through Warner Bros. of a Skyeway production. Executive producer, Kim Kurumada. Directed, screenplay by James Bridges. Stars Debra Winger, Mark Keyloun, Darrell Larson. Camera (Technicolor), Reynaldo Villalobos; editors, Jeff Gourson, Dede Allen; production design, Peter Jamison; art direction, Hub Braden; set decoration, Chris Westlund; music, John Barry; additional music, Joe Jackson; sound, Willie Burton; associate producer, Jack Larson; assistant director, Albert Shapiro. Reviewed at The Burbank Studios, Burbank, Feb. 29, 1984. (MPAA Rating: R). Running time: 97 MINS.

Betty Parrish	Debra Winger
Mike	Mark Keyloun
Pete	Darrell Larson
Patty	Brooke Alderson
Phillip	Paul Winfield
Sam	Robert Crosson
Richard	Daniel Shor
Randy	William Ostrander

Finally entering release this week after a protracted postproduction period, "Mike's Murder" proves an intriguing, if not entirely successful, suspenser and paranoid mood piece. Resolutely a small, serious film, it may benefit from its delay due to star Debra Winger's greater-than-ever popularity, but queasy atmosphere and fundamentally depressing subject matter will probably prove insurmountable in terms of b.o.

Pic was made quickly and cheaply by James Bridges during the summer of 1982. Reported negative reactions at sneaks in northern California prompted drastic recutting. In addition, a score written by pop musician Joe Jackson, now all but discarded, was issued on an A&M soundtrack album several months ago.

It would be interesting to know if the original cut contained any turn-off bloody scenes, for perhaps the most compelling aspect of Mike's Murder" is a conceptual one, the fact that it is a film about contemporary violence without any overt violence in it. Modern filmmakers from Sam Peckinpah and Arthur Penn on have stated that it is necessary to display violence in order to condemn it, but Bridges has proved to the contrary in perhaps making the first non-exploitative, non-sensationalist film about American mayhem and urban dread.

Mark Keyloun's Mike is a casual, off-and-on-again lover of Winger. He's a tennis teacher who earns additional dough as a small time drug dealer. Unfortunately, with his sideline activities come some unsavory characters, notably the uncouth, impulsive Peter, convincingly played by Darrell Larson.

After he's attempted to go straight, Keyloun is lured into acting as a go-between in a major cocaine transaction, and they stupidly lift a small portion of the haul for themselves. In short order, Keyloun is killed for the offense and Larson is informed by a former associate that he's "a dead man."

A modestly successful bank employee, Winger's character, is deliberately played as a nice, average young woman to spur audience involvement, and to encourage a "this could happen to anyone" frame of reference.

When she learns of Mike's death, she spurns friends' advice and begins investigating the realties of Mike's world, meeting some of his lawless friends and ultimately being threatened by the desperate Larson.

With its consciously repetitive scenes of driving around Los Angeles streets, film attempts a contemplative approach to the material and mood of impending doom, and in this is reminiscent both of Alfred Hitchcock's "Vertigo" and Jacques Demy's neglected "Model Shop," the latter one of the most effective evocations of the L.A.

lifestyle. It's clear what Bridges is trying to get at, and while he doesn't entirely pull it off, the attempt is both interesting and admirable — up to a point.

As usual, Winger is wonderful to watch at all times, but her character is something of a cipher, and lack of any psychological angle holds down the film's ultimate achievement. Bridges may have wanted to convey a general sense of big city paranoia, but restricting the threat to the specifics of the drug trade prevents the film from being as overwhelmingly scary as it might have been.

Setting the action in many of the posher areas of L.A., rather than in obviously seedy sections, is an ironic stroke, and the film is full of very accurate slices of life and on-the-button behavioral details.

Lead performances are all strong, including Keyloun's as the doomed youth. Paul Winfield holds center screen during a long sequence in a low-key, fascinating performance as a well-heeled drug dealer, and William Ostrander is perfect as his kinky, well-muscled houseboy.

Replacing Jackson's score is a very evocative contribution by composer John Barry, and all other tech aspects are excellent.
— *Cart.*

Un Ragazzo E Una Ragazza
(A Boy And A Girl)
(ITALIAN-COLOR)

Rome, Feb. 14.
A Medusa release, produced by Claudio Bonivento for Numero Uno Cinematografica and Dean Film. Stars Jerry Calà and Marina Suma. Directed by Marco Risi. Screenplay, Furio Scarpelli, Marco Risi; camera (Eastmancolor), Beppe Maccari; editor, Alberto Gallitti; art director, Massimo Razzi; music, Manuel De Sica. Reviewed at C.D.S., Rome, Jan. 26, 1984. Running time: **96 MINS.**

Calogero ....Jerry Calà
Anna ....Marina Suma
Carmen ....Monica Scattini

Spats, break-ups and make-ups of a winsome pair of young lovers. Neohelmer Marco Risi (son of veteran Dino Risi) demonstrates precocious commercial savvy in putting together a sentimental comedy aimed at young audiences. Pic has hit its target locally and should interest related Mediterranean markets.

A winning choice was coupling pudgy Milanese comedian Jerry Calà and Southern beauty Marina Suma, two rising stars of Italo light comedy. Setting is the University of Milan, where Anna (Suma) and Calogero (Calà) are students. Poor but in love, they rent an apartment and move in together, living in Bohemian bliss till Anna accidentally gets pregnant. Calogero is too immature to be supportive in critical moments, and her decision to

have an abortion marks a turning point in their relations. She leaves, then returns. Another quarrel (she's a success academically and financially; he's not), another split. Anna is pregnant again and has the baby without telling Calogero until almost a year later. He tracks mother and child down in Naples, where Anna has found happiness with another man.

Calà and Suma make an appealing pair without having to exert their thesping talents much. Monica Scattini easily outshines both in a brief appearance as Calogero's deliciously malicious old girlfriend.— *Yung.*

The Hotel New Hampshire
(COLOR)

Tony Richardson tackles John Irving.

Hollywood, March 2.
An Orion release of a Woodfall film. Produced by Neil Hartley. Coproducer, Jim Beach. Executive producers, George Yaneff, Kent Walwin, Grahame Jennings. Written and directed by Tony Richardson, based on the novel by John Irving. Stars Jodie Foster, Beau Bridges, Rob Lowe, Nastassja Kinski. Camera (Deluxe color), David Watkin; editor, second unit director, Robert K. Lambert; music, Jacques Offenbach, arranged and conducted by Raymond Leppard; production, costume design Jocelyn Herbert; art direction, John Meighen; sound (Dolby), Patrick Rousseau; associate producers, Bill Scott, Norman Twain; assistant director, Bill Scott. Reviewed at the Directors Guild Theatre, L.A., March 2, 1984. (MPAA Rating: R). Running time: 110 MINS.

Franny ....Jodie Foster
Father........................Beau Bridges
John ....Rob Lowe
Susie The Bear ....Nastassja Kinski
Iowa Bob ....Wilford Brimley
Junior Jones................Dorsey Wright
Lilly........................Jennie Dundas
Chip Dove/Ernst ....Matthew Modine
Frank ....Paul McCrane
Ronda Ray ....Anita Morris
Miss Miscarriage ....Amanda Plummer
Mother.........................Lisa Banes
Egg.............................Seth Green
Freud.......................Wallace Shawn
Doris Walex/
  Screaming Annie ....Gayle Garfinkle
Sabrina ....Jonelle Allen

While it is decidedly not to all tastes, "The Hotel New Hampshire" is a fascinating, largely successful adaptation of John Irving's 1981 novel. In making his best picture in years, writer-director Tony Richardson has pulled off a remarkable stylistic tight-rope act, establishing a bizarre tone of morbid whimsicality at the outset and sustaining it throughout. It's difficult to imagine a b.o. breakout to a wide public for this, but college crowd and upscale audience could be drawn if properly handled.

Multitude of characters and sprawling nature of Irving's novel made for a heavy challenge in the adaptation, but Richardson has compressed the events with notable skill. Tale is even more difficult to describe than that of Irving's

"The World According To Garp," but it concerns an eccentric New England family that, spurred on by an ever-searching father, establishes a new hotel in locale after locale and mutates in the process.

Among the unusual family members is Jodie Foster, who must endure a punishing gang rape and a prolonged fascination with the young man who did it on her way to self-fulfillment; her brother, Rob Lowe, an impossibly good-looking fellow who takes on most of the women in the cast but has a special love for his sister; their "queer" brother Paul McCrane, and their little sister, Jennie Dundas, who, like the leading character of "The Tin Drum," remains small physically, but who becomes a famous author by writing an autobiographical book, "Trying To Grow."

Also virtually part of the family by association, if not by blood, are black jock Dorsey Wright, who proves enormously helpful in times of need; voluptuous hotel waitress Anita Morris, who develops an infatuation with Lowe, and Nastassja Kinski, a girl so insecure and uncertain of herself that she hides most of the time inside an enormous bear suit.

First section of the film presents wild comedy and tragedy simultaneously, and it is in the difficult task of setting this dual tone that Richardson succeeds so well. Foster's rape, and the death of grandpa Wilford Brimley, are hardly laughing matters, yet Richardson has been able to place them within the context of the many unexpected and downright weird things that happen to this family, and that make up the fabric of life as a whole.

Pic's major themes concern dreaming and pushing through whatever is necessary to realize oneself, but it is also about the heavy price that sometimes must be paid to live a life. Fact that the world view expressed is such a loony one does not diminish the importance of dire occurrences; to the contrary, it allows the tragedy to coexist palatably with the black comedy to almost surreal effect.

Story becomes darker in the second half, after what's left of the family moves to Vienna. Hotel they take over there is littered with whores and terrorists, and it's here that the libidos of the youngsters go on the rampage, as Foster has a tryst with Kinski and reunions with her rapist, who's now become a radical pornographer, and Lowe becomes the only lover of virgin anarchist Amanda Plummer.

Pursuing their taboo mutual obsession to the limit, Foster and Lowe finally get it on in a marathon encounter so as to free themselves once and for all, and ultimate couplings prove somewhat more conventional.

Artistically, picture marks a career high point for Richardson, who scored heavily with "Tom Jones" 20 years ago but has not had a solid international hit since that time. Despite the many story and character threads and shifts in locations, film moves with impressive confidence and fluidity, both from shot to shot and scene to scene. For this, top marks should go, not only to the director, but to cinematographer David Watkin and editor (and second unit director) Robert K. Lambert.

Skillfully using locations in Quebec province and the Montreal area, production designer Jocelyn Herbert has evoked numerous different settings, and overall look is extremely handsome. Music adapted from works by Jacques Offenbach also works very well.

For the most part, cast has put over these not-quite-real characters in marvelous fashion. Lowe is the fulcrum for much of the action, and he emerges as the brightest of the bunch, proving he's not just a pretty face.

In her most adult role to date, Foster does a fine job, and Wright, Dundas, McCrane, Morris, Plummer, Brimley, Kinski (despite being hidden by her costume) and Matthew Modine also shine. Only Beau Bridges and Lisa Banes as the father and mother fail to come to life, and it's hard to know whether this is the fault of the actors or the characters. —*Cart.*

Forced Entry
(COLOR)

Morbid case study of a rapist-psycho killer.

A Century International (CI) Films release of a Jim Sotos production for Productions Two. Produced by Sotos, Henry Scarpelli. Directed by Sotos. Features entire cast. Screenplay, Scarpelli; camera (Getty color), Aaron Kleinman; editor, Felix di Leone, Jim Markovic, Drake Silliman; music, Tommy Vig; sound, Gary Rich; assistant director, Katherine Connolly; associate producer, Sandy Charles. Reviewed at Criterion 5 theater, N.Y., March 10, 1984. (No MPAA Rating). Running time: **83 MINS.**
With: Tanya Roberts, Ron Max, Nancy Allen, Robin Leslie, Michelle Miles.

"Forced Entry" is a downbeat, technically subpar exploitation film about a rapist. Filmed in 1975 under the title "The Last Victim," with a new, re-edited version reportedly prepared in 1980, picture is reviewed here for the record.

"Entry's" main point of interest is its status as a skeleton in the closet for two currently prominent actresses, Tanya Roberts and Nancy Allen, since it was made before either one got her career into gear. Roberts has a leading role (and despite the genre, avoids any nude scenes) while Allen is in briefly as a hitchhiker.

Ron Max portrays Carl, a gas station worker who is, as cliché would have it, a normal boy-next-

door type that no one would suspect is an habitual rapist and murderer. Picture opens in a particularly negative film noir fashion with nighttime visuals of Carl driving around the city, voicing over an "I hate whores" rap loaded with violent verbal imagery. Ensuing rapes and murders are presented with hokey slow-motion photography that seems more like padding than style.

"Entry" winds up with a very lengthy sequence of Carl invading the home of a young housewife (Roberts) and abusing her in a well-acted, but hardly entertainment segment. The only suspense is when will Tanya strike back and get rid of this menace, once and for all.

Photography and editing are crude. The film's rating by the Motion Picture Assn. of America is in question; apparently the 1975 "Last Victim" received a PG, but the new version was never rated; pic's poster and advertising proclaim an unsubstantiated R rating. —*Lor.*

Szegeny Dzsoni Es Arnika
(A Duck and Drake Adventure) (HUNGARIAN-COLOR)

Budapest, Feb. 17.
A Budapest Studio, Mafilm, production. Directed by Andras Solyum. Script, Ervin Lazar; camera (color), Lorand Mertz; music, Istvan Martha. Reviewed at Voros Csillag theater, Buddapest, Feb. 10, 1984. Running time: **81 MINS.**
Johnny .Tamas Puskas
Arnika .Zsuzsa Nyertes
The Sorceress . . . . .Mari Torocsik
King Ostor . . . . .Istvan Bujtor

A fantasy for children in which a princess falls in love with a commoner and wants to marry him. The king doesn't object, but the young lovers fall under the spell of a wicked sorceress who turns the princess into a duck leaving her boyfriend, Johnny, in human form; alternatively, Johnny becomes a drake and the princess reappears. This is obviously a highly inconvenient state of affairs, so the couple sets out on a long journey to find a wizard who'll break the spell. Thus the scene is set for a classic fairy tale, with strange encounters along the way and the inevitable happy ending.

Director Andras Solyum, making his first feature after tv and experimental films, has some fun with the subject, but fails to give the pic the epic sweep required to make it really memorable. "The Wizard Of Oz" it's not, though there are similarities at times. The young leads are acceptable, and veteran actress Mari Torocsik has fun with her role as the wicked witch. Special effects and camera-

work are up to par. In all, agreeable, if minor, family entertainment. — *Strat.*

Police Academy
(COLOR)

This was the fuzz that never was.

Hollywood, March 6.
A Ladd Co. release through Warner Bros. of a Paul Maslansky prod. produced by Paul Maslansky. Directed by Hugh Wilson. Features entire cast. Screenplay, Neal Israel, Pat Proft, Hugh Wilson, from a story by Israel and Proft; camera (Technicolor), Michael D. Margulies; editor, Robert Brown, Zach Staenberg; music, Robert Folk; production design, Trevor Williams; set decorator, Steve Shewchuck; sound, David Lee; costume design, Christopher Ryan; assistant director, Michael Zenon. Reviewed at Warner Bros., March 6, 1984. (MPAA rating: R.) Running time: **95 MINS.**
Carey Mahoney . . . . .Steve Guttenberg
Lt. Harriss . . . . .G.W. Bailey
Commandant Lassard . . . . . .George Gaynes
Larvell Jones . . . . .Michael Winslow
Karen Thompson . . . . .Kim Cattrall
Moses Hightower . . . . .Bubba Smith
George Martin . . . . .Andrew Rubin
Leslie Barbara . . . . .Donovan Scott
Sgt. Callahan . . . . .Leslie Easterbrook
Tackleberry . . . . .David Graff
Laverne Hooks . . . . .Marion Ramsey
Chad Copeland . . . . .Scott Thomson
Kyle Blankes . . . . .Brant Van Hoffman
Hooker . . . . .Georgina Spelvin

Without its R-rated material, this action-comedy, centered on a clutch of loser-recruits in a police academy, would appear to find its natural market in the under-17 age group. That's how thin the material is.

A handful of riotous scenes notwithstanding, the intended young adult audience is likely to find the film derivative and predictable. Ladd Co. needs a quick break out of the gate.

Film has one ace for word-of-mouth among the raunchy male set. Not surprisingly, scene is triggered by porno actress Georgina Spelvin ("The Devil In Miss Jones") in a rare (for her) mainstream albeit very brief role.

Writers Neal Israel, Pat Proft and Hugh Wilson take a page from the famous Julie Christie-Warren Beatty restaurant scene in "Shampoo" and refocus it on a police commander standing before a podium addressing a hall full of VIPs. Result is uproarious, thanks to George Gaynes as the commander.

Unfortunately, filmmakers reprise the gag at the end, with star Steve Guttenberg the victim, and the repetition goes far to undermine whatever bouyancy the film has established.

Shot in Canada and, with exception of top-billed Guttenberg, utilizing actors with an even array of screen time in misfit roles, "Police Academy" at its core is a harmless, innocent poke at authority that does find a fresh background in a police academy. Women in the film, such as Kim Cattrall as an Ivy League-type and Leslie Easter-

brook as a busty sergeant, have almost nothing to do. Black actress Marion Ramsey as a timid-voiced trainee is fine in the film's most vivid female part.

Cowriter Wilson, who created "WKRP In Cincinnati," makes his feature film debut as director, and his scenes are short and fragmentary. He gets a fresh comic performance from Michael Winslow as a walking human sound effects system (the film's most appealing turn). Film is also the feature debut of G.W. Bailey (Sergeant Rizzo in "Mash") who capably handles the obligatory feverish drill sergeant role.

Bubba Smith, as a florist, takes a stretch from his Miller's Lite beer commercials, David Graf is solid as a manic gun-lover who helps an old lady get her cat from a tree by shooting it down, and George Martin and Donovan Scott round out primary support.

Through it all, Guttenberg is a likeable rogue in a role that's too unflappable to set off any sparks. Concluding mayhem in the streets, which brings the best out of the young recruits, is too pat for anybody but pre-teens.

Music credits, from diverse performers, are bright contribution. —*Loyn.*

Carmen
(FRENCH-ITALIAN-COLOR)

Paris, March 6.
Gaumont release of a Gaumont/Production Marcel Dassault/Opera Film Produzione (Rome) co-production. Produced by Patrice Ledoux. Stars Julia Migenes-Johnson, Placido Domingo, Ruggero Raimondi, Faith Esham. Directed by Francesco Rosi. Screenplay, Rosi and Tonino Guerra, based on the story by Prosper Merimee and the opera by Georges Bizet; musical direction, Lorin Maazel; choreography, Antonio Gades; camera (Eastmancolor), Pasqualino de Santis; art direction and costumes, Enrico Job; editors, Ruggero Mastroianni and Colette Semprun; sound, Herald Maury, Guy Level, Hugues Darmois; makeup, Francesco Freda, Adalgisa Favella, Marie-Helene Dugget; production manager, Alessandro Von Normann. Reviewed at Gaumont, Paris, March 2, 1984. Running time: **152 MINS.**
Carmen . . . . .Julia Migenes-Johnson
Don Jose . . . . .Placido Domingo
Escamillo . . . . .Ruggero Raimondi
Micaela .Faith Esham
Dancaire . . . . .Jean-Philippe Lafont
Remendado . . . . .Gerard Garino
Frasquita . . . . .Lilian Watson
Zuniga . . . . .John-Paul Bogart
Lillas Pastia . . . . .Julien Guiomar

As with Joseph Losey's "Don Giovanni," Gaumont general manager Daniel Toscan du Plantier has again called upon a renowned director with no previous professional contact with opera, Francesco Rosi, whose best films have been unadorned realistic dramas with socio-political topicality. But, unlike Losey, Rosi doesn't even have the advantage of theater experience. From his usual genre to that of the frilled folklore of Bizet's opera was a big step. But the filmmaker has not found the artistic legs to make it.

Except for some meek attempts at choral formations, he hasn't even tried to stylize the work on the screen. Instead we get neo-realistic opera: some historical accuracy in costume and setting and a reading of the drama that reflects more Rosi's preoccupations than the needs of Lyric ,Theatre/Cinema. He might have made a credible straight dramatic picture of Prosper Merimee's source novella, but his filmed opera is a lumbering cultural mammoth, overblown and graceless.

Music lovers will probably find their due here, as some of the most expensive voices in the business warble Bizet's melodies with Dolby stereo magnificence.

But dramatically the film is feeble. Julia Migenes-Johnson is high-spirited and alluring in the title role, but Rosi finally insists more on her humane qualities than her demoniac sense of fatalism, and the imposed concept reduces the actress-singer to a passivity in the last act that saps the work of its point and power.

But she is a plum next to Placido Domingo's Don José, which flirts with disaster. A beautiful voice, but a uniformed lump in front of the cameras. Had Rosi had a more believable actor-singer in the role, he might have come out of this with more honors. But Domingo is an unavoidable deadweight.

Ruggero Raimondi is a chilly,Escamillo, but he at least has credible bearing and photogenic line. Faith Esham's Micaela is limpid and touching.

Viewers who dread bullfighting are advised to come five minutes late. For openers Rosi offers, in a protracted slow-motion sequence, the grisly sight of a wounded bull being given the coup de grace by a matador (which a clumsy insert close-up reveals to be Raimondi).
— *Len.*

Children Of The Corn
(COLOR)

Stephen King name should insure profitability for this supernatural thriller.

Hollywood, Feb. 25.

Hal Roach Studios and New World Pictures presentation of a Gatlin Production in association with Angeles Group Inc. and Iverness Productions Inc. Released by New World Pictures in association with Cinema Group Venture. Produced by Donald P. Porchers and Terrence Kirby. Executive producer, Earl Glick and Charles J. Weber. Directed by Fritz Kiersch. Screenplay, George Goldsmith, based on a story by Stephen King; camera (CFI color), Raoul Lomas; editor, Harry Keramidas; music, Jonathan Elias; art director, Craig Stearns; set decorator, Crickett Rowland; sound, Jon "Earl" Stein; special effects, Max W. Anderson; associate producer, Mark Lipson; assistant director, Susan Gelb. Reviewed at New World screening room, Century City, Calif. Feb. 24, 1984. (MPAA rating: R.) Running time: **93 MINS.**
Dr. Burt Stanton ....Peter Horton

Vicky Baxter ....Linda Hamilton
Diehl ....................R.G. Armstrong
Isaac ....John Franklin
Malechai ....Courtney Gains
Job.........................Robby Kiger
Sarah ....AnneMarie McEvoy
Rachel ....Julie Maddalena
Joseph ....Jonas Marlowe
Amos......................:......John Philbin

Possibly the most supernatural thing about Stephen King's work is its omnipresence. His films and books appear with regularity and seemingly little lapse time between the two. Sensing the sure-fire appeal of a King work, New World has attempted to stretch a short story into a feature. "Children Of The Corn" is predicatably thin considering the source material, but New World may be right about appeal. Pic should be a profitably indie entry based on King's name above the title.

As in all King product, "Children Of The Corn" calls for a suspension of logic and appeals to the audience's hunger for the miraculous. Part Manson family religiosity and part "Shining" occultism, "Corn" is definitely planted on familiar ground.

"Children Of The Corn" presents a normal couple, played by Peter Horton and Linda Hamlton, thrust into supernatural occurrences while on a cross-country trip. Horton is a newly graduated doctor on his way to start his internship in Seattle. Somewhere in Nebraska the couple happen on the children of the corn, a band of vicious youngsters who have murdered the adults and established a religious community worshiping a mysterious deity of the corn fields.

Led by Isaac (John Franklin), an adolescent with an old man's demeanor, the band of outsiders displays a sinister attraction. Shrouded in pseudo-Christian mythology, the children are more appealing then the mundane reality of the adults.

Film is rather slow moving as it attempts to fill out the sparse material. The discovery and explanation of the town's secret creeps along through deserted buildings overgrown with corn. Hamilton is eventually abducted and literally must bear her cross of corn before she is rescued by Horton, assisted by two young holdouts, Job and Sarah (Robby Kiger and Anne-Marie McEvoy).

Director Fritz Kiersch and/or King seem to play both ends against the middle, neither accepting nor denying the supernatural occurrences. Though the children are more interesting, it is hard to root for them as the audience might sympathize with the villain in a Hitchcock film.

As the well-meaning doctor, Horton is simply a boring character. As he pleads that any religion without love and compassion is evil, he is earnest but unconvincing. Hamilton is livelier and attempts to inject a little life into their relationship, but the dramatic ploy of subjecting a troubled relationship to extreme danger still doesn't have the power to make the viewer care what happens.

As for its real reason for being, "Children Of The Corn" does have a few good scare scenes but special effects are surprisingly disappointing, especially the film's climax. The final confrontation with the ultimate evil that "lives between the rows" features some ordinary animation and foggy effects, but no terror.

Production looks first rate and art direction by Craig Stearns suggests a hidden evil around every corner. Unfortunately when confronted, it doesn't amount to much.
— *Jagr.*

Desiderio
(Desire)
(ITALIAN-COLOR)

Rome, March 13.

A Gaumont release, produced by Opera Film Produzione in collaboration with RAI-TV Channel 2. Stars Fanny Ardant. Directed by Anna Maria Tatò. Screenplay, Vincenzo Cerami, Anna Maria Tatò; camera (color), Giuseppe Rotunno; art director, Dante Ferretti; editor, Ruggero Mastroianni; music, Nicola Piovani. Reviewed at Fiamma Cinema, Rome, March 9, 1984. Running time: **96 MINS.**
Lucia ....Fanny Ardant
Vincenzo ....Leonardo Treviglio
Mariolina ....Francesca Rinaldi
Mother ....Francesca De Sapio
Father ....Carlo Giuffrè
Grandmother ....Isa Danieli

Fanny Ardant plays the role of a sensual Italian signora in this tale of passion and memory, stronger on atmosphere than story. Principally art house entertainment for Ardant aesthetes, "Desiderio" is too light-weight and unconvincing to raise much interest outside Italo-French Gaumont lands.

Lucia (Ardant) misses the boat to Greece to join her husband and so decides to make an unscheduled visit to her childhood home in the South. She is estranged from her parents (Francesca De Sapio and Carlo Giuffrè), an ill-matched pair of Southern gentry, but still enjoys seeing her doting grandmother (Isa Danieli), who casts out the Evil Eye and interprets dreams.

Almost at once a dark, brawny youth from the village (Leonardo Treviglio) develops a disturbing fixation on the beautiful out-of-towner, who can't keep herself from responding to his animal-like magnetism. Their mutual attraction culminates in a convenient hotel room. Apparently beleaguered with guilt at her own comportment, Lucia knocks the boy out with an ashtray and flees.

She is joined by a knowing little girl (excellent child thesp Francesca Rinaldi), who is running away from her First Communion party, and together they spend the rest of the day ducking Lucia's paramour, who has come to and is plenty mad.

Though pic tries to fill out these bare bones with Lucia's memories of childhood, her mother's madness, her father's incorrigible womanizing, "Desiderio" feels empty at the center. A major problem is that helmer Anna Maria Tatò never gets Lucia off the ground as a character, or succeeds in involving the audience in her sufferings and problems (if she really has any.) Flash-backs seem only tenuously related to the adult Lucia, and leave her motives, feelings and final choices murky and uncompelling.

Treviglio has a brooding, slightly sinister face that fits his part. Out-of-place detail continually distracts in the film, which — though weak in the dialog department — has some riveting visuals to tout: Ardant's mask-like face, the ancient city on the sea, Giuseppe Rotunno's white-hot outdoor photography, contrasting with the dark interiors inhabited by ghosts.

The plaintive musical score is by Nicola Piovani. — *Yung.*

Tukuma
(DANISH-COLOR)

Copenhagen, Feb. 20.

A Crone Film production, supported by the Danish Film Institute, Metronome Film release. Original story and script, Klaus Rifbjerg, Joself Tuusi Motzfelt, Palle Kjaerulff-Schmidt. Features entire cast. Directed by Kjaerulff-Schmidt. Camera (Eastmancolor) Dirk Bruel, Birger Bohm; production management, Nina Crone, Lise Lense-Moeller, Joergen Hinsch; editors, Kasper Schyberg, Camilla Schyberg; music, songs, Rasmus Lyberth, Fuzzy, Johannes Petersen, Joergen Fleischer. Reviewed at the Dagmar, Copenhagen, Feb. 20, 1984. Running time: **100 MINS.**
Erik ....Thomas Eje
Soerine ....Naja Rosing Olsen
Rasmus ....Rasmus Lyberth
His wife ....Agga Geisler
Elisabeth..............Benedikte Schmidt
Otto ....Rasmus Thygesen
The Ghost ....Erik Holmey

"Tukuma," Palle Kjaerulff-Schmidt's first feature film in 15 years, represents a change in his and writer Klaus Rifbjerg's usual theme (Danes mirrored in nostalgic-romantic realism). Both this time have gone to Greenland, the world's largest island and no longer a colony but an integrated, albeit mildly rebellious, part of the Kingdom of Denmark. Here they have fallen into the traditional double trap of being overawed by the grandiose natural scenery and of being correspondingly sentimental about the proverb-spouting wisdom of the natives. The result is too much cinematography of icebergs, hunting from dogsleds, and closeups of faces supposed to ooze natural sagacity.

The Greenland word of the title means "man in too much of a hurry," and young Thoms Eje in the lead role of suicidal, recently divorced Erik comes to Greenland to find out how and why his hang-gliding brother died in a crash. He moves in with young Soerine (Naja Rosing Olsen) who will not say whether her half-caste son Nikki was fathered by the brother. Erik proceeds through some sleepwalking (Thomas Eje's acting consists mainly of large eyes and an open mouth in a face of stoic innocence) and meetings with his brother's ghost.

Film has some asides of environmental observation. It also starts out to launch some classic drama (pregnant woman on dogsled across endless icy wastes, little boy being attacked and presumably eaten by vicious dogs, racial tension mounting), but no sooner started than the camera moves swiftly to find renewed rest in the magnificence of landscapes while tedium and stale dialog are allowed to take over from drama.

"Tukuma," on the strength of its superb cinematography and of the severity of its underlying theme, is assured representation of the Danish colors on the festival circuit. As feature film drama, its values are, like the greater part of an iceberg, hidden under a shiny surface of empty good looks. — *Kell.*

Boardinghouse
(COLOR)

Tape-to-film horror pic hits a new low.

A Coast Films release of a Bluestarr Films production. Presented by Howard Willette; produced by Peter Baahlu. Directed by Johnn Wintergate. Features entire cast. Screenplay, Jonema; camera (color, video), Jan Lucas, Obee Ray; editor, uncredited; music, Kalassu, 33⅓ & Jonema; assistant director, Lanny Williamson; technical advisor, Willette; creative consultant, Toni Covington. Reviewed at Criterion 5 theater, N.Y., March 3, 1984. (MPAA Rating: R). Running time: **89 MINS.**
With: Hawk Audley (Jim; also as the gardener), Kalassu (Victoria), Alexandra Day; Joel McGinnis Riordan, Brian Bruderlin, Tracy O'Brian, Belma Kura, Mary McKinley, Rosane Woods, Elizabeth Haill, A'Ryen Winter.

"Boardinghouse" is a nearly unwatchable assemblage of footage that fits in the horror genre, though fans of the form should be warned that it was videotaped in 1982, and inadequately transferred to film for current theatrical release. With "no refunds" policies proliferating (partly because of such awful junkers as this one), caveat emptor.

Technically inept opus expediently piles almost all its plot and story content into inserts of computer display listings, leaving the live-action footage for frequent displays of cheap, fake gore (which looks strange given the variable-color nature of this tape-to-film transfer) and semi-improvised, sub-porno quality dialog and nudie scenes.

Set in a nondescript Los Angeles house (no spooky mansion atmosphere) which, as usual, is blamed for a series of murders and accidental deaths taking place, story concerns the effects of a Professor Hoffman and wife, Nobel-prize winners for their research in the occult and telekinesis (evidently a new category for the Swedes), whose daughter killed them and is now on the rampage at their house, turned into a boardinghouse for pretty young women by its current owner Jim (Hawk Audley, who doubles as the film's inevitable key suspect, a sinister gardener wearing a truly phony goatee). Not wanting to be original, incest turns out to be the reason for the murders that set this creaky plot in motion.

As the girls are picked off one by one, the viewer is treated to such boring material as a bar of soap that levitates and a chromakey-style superimposed monster image that is thrown in from time to time. Scene construction is so poor that during an exposition scene with the police (who like the rest of the cast look like school chums who showed up for the videotaping with no preparation) there is a sudden fade to black right in the middle of a speech, as if one of the cameramen ran out of tape. No retakes, please.

Late in the picture, several scenes are thoroughly overexposed, but the spoiled footage is included in the final print. Pic's presenter, Howard Willete, uses as comeon a process dubbed "Horror Vision," supposedly the old gimmick of using visual and sound warnings to the audience when they should look away from the screen, but this is just another bad joke.

The frightening thing about "Boardinghouse" is not that it is terrible, but that it opens a Pandora's box for future no-budget, no-effort taped horror films. —*Lor.*

Baby
(WEST GERMAN-COLOR)

Berlin, Feb. 25.

A Basis-Film Verleih Production, Berlin, in coproduction with Westdeutscher Rundfunk (WDR), Cologne; production manager, Clara Burckner, tv producer, Wolf-Dietrich Brücker. Features entire cast. Written and directed by Uwe Friessner. Camera (color), Wolfgang Dickmann; music, SPLIFF; editor, Tanja Schmidtbauer. Reviewed at Berlin Film Fest (Forum), Feb. 25, '84. Running time: **114 MINS.**
Cast: Udo Seidler (Baby), Reinhard Seeger (Pjotr), Volkmar Richter (René), Frank Marwitz (Tilo), Harald Kempe (Mark), Jeanette Radlinski (Marina), Sylvia Woiczechowski (Bärbel).

Uwe Friessner, graduate of the Berlin Film Academy, scored with a rather impressive debut film, "The End Of The Rainbow" (1979), a docu-drama on a juvenile delinquent in Berlin played by a nonprofessional with a similar court-record as the one on the screen. Now he's back with another Berlin story, "Baby," featuring a young body-builder type who earns his pay as a bouncer at a disco and dreams of opening his own athletic club one day. Instead, he falls in with a couple of conmen and petty thieves.

Baby, the protagonist of this docu-fiction thriller, is played by an amateur actor using his own slang, dialect, and reverse euphemisms to the point of needing subtitles even for a German audiences. The same goes for everyone in the film — make no mistake, Friessner has attempted to capture the lingo of the streets and discos in all its pristine purity. On that score, he's made a quite significant contribution to the urban ethnographic genre.

The drawback is that he forgot to tell a story over the two-hours-long stretch of collected episodes in life and times of a young innocent enticed down the road to crime and murder. It starts with a rumpus at the disco, during which Baby gets the worst of it in a gang-up by a bunch of thugs — until he resorts to a baseball bat (!) and wreaks his vengeance on one of the assailants, nearly killing him in the process. The police pick him for questioning on an assault charge, but two friends at the disco hire a lawyer to argue his case, and eventually set him free. In the meantime, the conmen use his car and his apartment for their own purposes. These illegal activities get Baby deeper into a mess than before, for the petty crooks put the heat on our innocent to join them in a small-time robbery. It works, and they all divide the money.

Next comes a bigger heist at a supermarket. Baby loses his nerve at the last minute and kills a watchman, but the getaway appears to be successful. After the loot is divided, and Baby has afterwards invested in converting an abandoned factory loft into a sports club, he and one of the two cronies notice that they are suddenly under police surveillance. When the news comes that the third party in the hold-up has been picked up at the airport, they face a dead end — there's nowhere to go on this urban island called West Berlin (situated in East Germany far from the West German mainland), that is, without passing a control point.

Friessner's handling of nonprofessionals is commendable, and Wolfgang Dickmann (one of Germany's ace lensers) gives the pic a polish seldom seen in Berlin productions. This is an action pic for and about men in the broadest manner of speaking. It's also a film that accurately reflects the Berlin scene down to the last detail. The weakness, however, is in the script: "Baby" starts well, then begins to wander for long stretches into the realm of fiction-documentary. —*Holl.*

Moritz In Der Litfassäule
(Moritz Inside the Advertising Pillar)
(EAST GERMAN-COLOR)

Berlin, Feb. 27.

A DEFA Film Production, Johannisthal Film Unit, East Berlin; world rights, DEFA Aussenhandel, East Berlin. Features entire cast. Written and directed by Rolf Losansky, based on a children's book by Christa Kozik. Camera (color), Helmut Grewald; sets, Jochen Keller; music, Karl-Ernst Sasse. Reviewed at Berlin Film Fest (Film Mart), Feb. 27, '84. Running time: **85 MINS.**
Cast: Dirk Müller (Moritz), Dieter Mann (his father), Walfriede Schmitt (his Mother).

Rolf Losansky is a specialist in making children and youth films, many of which he penned the scripts for as well as directed. His ninth kidpic for DEFA in East Germany is the delightful "Moritz Inside the Advertising Pillar" (or "Litfassäule," as it's commonly known in Germany). Tourists and visitors to Europe can pick up nearly all the information necessary for a cultural night on the town by referring to this round, hollow ad-pillar on street corners. Often enough, the pillar's inner space is used to store street-cleaning equipment — in this case, it becomes the hiding-place of a runaway boy nine-years-old.

Moritz lives in a provincial town in the German Democratic Republic, is a dreamer during school hours, and is so pokey in everything he does that neither his parents nor the teachers know quite what to do with him, particularly since his three older sisters are prim and proper youngsters. His life is all the more difficult because his father, a bank employe, is orderly to the extreme and is regularly putting up a "Do Not Disturb" sign on the door to his study. The trouble starts when Moritz "forgets" to show his parents the bad marks he's been getting at school — and, one day, rather than face the medicine at home, he simply throws his school workbook away in a nearby creek.

The next step is to run away from home — that is, to the "litfassäule" on the town square in which to hide away with his duffel-bag and blanket. But the advertising pillar is already occupied — by a cat right out of an animated children's cartoon! As the story unwinds, it becomes clear that the cat is Moritz's alter ego partner, something concocted out of his fantasy. And the blending of fact and fiction goes even further: Moritz meets a young girl from a touring circus troupe, who later turns out to have been the cat in transposed form. Then there's the real-life friendly street-cleaner, who stores his brooms in the pillar and takes an interest in Moritz's problems without betraying him to the authorities or his parents. In fact, the street-cleaner makes up in his person for the seeming lack of trust on the part of Moritz's own father, who let him down at the moment it counted the most.

"Moritz Inside the Advertising Pillar" reveals a great deal about times and customs in East Germany, particularly the pace of life in a small provincial town. But this is also a human tale with twists along the way to provide wit. —Holl.

Mother's Meat and Freud's Flesh
(CANADIAN-COLOR)

Berlin Feb. 22.

An East of the Acropolis film. Produced by Louise Burns, executive producer, Simon Davies. Directed and written by Demetrios Estdelacropolis. Features entire cast. Camera (color), Jason Levy, Jean Lebeaux, Andre Guimond; editors, Louise Burns, Jean Leveaux; special makeup effects, Greggordon Hilderbrand, Greggordon Pastuszko; music, Trio. Reviewed at the Berlin Film Festival (non-competing), Feb. 22, 1984. Running Time: 97 MINS.
Esther......................Esther Vargas
Lucie/Demira ..Demetrios Estdelacropolis
Psycho-Dentist...................Rotwang
Speed.......................E.J. Sullivan
Porno Director...........George Agetees
Harry...................Harry Karagopian
Gore Twin Boy.............Rick Trembles
Gore Twin Girl............Michelle Tardif
Hollywood Producer .....Lawrence Joseph

"Mother's Meat and Freud's Flesh" is a low-budget, low-talent effort squarely aimed at the midnight movie crowd. If that faction doesn't rebel at the irritating, amateurish efforts of this Canadian production, it will be a major miracle. By comparison, the early works of John Waters are both tasteful and technically polished.

The vanity effort by Demetrios Estdelacropolis has the writer-director cast as a gay porno film star with malevolent intents against his ditzy mother. As he's decided to enter a new line of work, she arrives from New York for a visit. He promptly foists her on a lecherous, senile country singer and proceeds to make one last porno and take the money and run.

The simple plot line sounds more appealing and lucid than Estdelacropolis can effect. It is primarily a rant lacking humor or insight, crudely produced and offensive to virtually every minority and majority group in society.

Estdelacropolis attempts to shock through language and the depiction of sexual acts but clearly there is no purpose to his out-

rage. Esther Vargas as the mother is an unpleasant Barbi doll with 22 phrases randomly repeated by pulling an unseen string. One assumes this is a considerably larger vocabulary than at the filmmaker's personal disposal.

Picture's sole professional credit comes from the soundtrack of existing tunes from West German pop group Trio and the credits display an originality and candor which eludes the rest of the film. —Klad.

Wildrose
(U.S.-COLOR)

Berlin, Feb. 22.

New Front Films presents an Ely Lake Film Company production. Produced by Sandra Schulberg. Directed by John Hanson. Screenplay, Hanson and Eugene Corr, based on a story by Hanson and Schulberg; camera (Eastmancolor), Peter Stein; editor, Arthur Coburn; art direction, Shirley Morton, Cate Whittemore; music, Bernard Krause, Gary Remal. Reviewed at the Berlin Film Festival (non-competing), Feb. 22, 1984. Running time: 95 MINS.
June Lorich.................Lisa Eichhorn
Rick Ogaard..................Tom Bower
Pavich.........................Jim Cada
Karen......................Cinda Jackson
Ricotti....................Dan Nemanick
Katri Sippola................Lydia Olson
Timo Maki.................Bill Schoppert
Doobie.....................James Stowell
Billy......................Stephen Yoakam

"Wildrose" emerges as a successful follow-up for many of the filmmakers involved with the critically acclaimed "Northern Lights." An unconventional combination of romance, social issues and women's rights accounts for the film's unique quality. It's also a strikingly well-crafted picture bolstered by strong central performances.

Set in Minnesota's Mesabi Iron Range, the tale focuses on June Lorich (Lisa Eichhorn), a lode driver relegated to pit crew duty after a series of riffings. The job shift brings her face to face with male resentment of female workers as well as romance with a fellow worker, Rick Ogaard (Tom Bower).

One of the picture's greatest assets is the script's balance of social and human elements. Essentially it is a personal story and not political cant. And this is further reflected in the moving, natural performance by Eichhorn in a decidedly unglamorous role.

Without losing involvement for the viewer, the film manages to make its points about the area, its people and June's situation in an unhurried fashion. One feels a strong sense of the rather startling environment and a real bond with the two central characters, particularly Lorich.

Eichhorn presents a determined woman who is nonetheless fraught with doubt. She is anxious about her relationship and distraught about her former husband, now an unemployed alcoholic. This feeling

of instability is heightened when further firings affect her and she must grapple with the possibility of looking for new work.

Bower also registers well as her pit co-worker and lover and the supporting cast, including many non-professionals, seem authentically cut from the land. These aspects plus the extraordinary, vivid camerawork by Peter Stein represent a truly distinctive entertainment way from the mainstream.

Based on an idea by John Hanson (director) and Sandra Schulberg (producer), "Wildrose" should easily find a niche in the marketplace. Modestly produced for $1,-000,000, the film has the look and quality of a studio low-budget of a considerably higher cost. And while it lacks a "high-concept" appeal, the picture should have no problem capitalizing on its quality and reviews to build an audience for itself. —Klad.

Where's Eno?
(U.S.-COLOR-16m)

Berlin, Feb. 25.

A film by Eno One Productions, New York. Directed by D.E. Fischer; screenplay, Duvette Huma; separate Swedish and New York crews; performers, Rusty Fischer, Brigitta Engstrom, Mike Carolan. Reviewed at Messe (Market), Berlin International Film Festival, Feb. 25, 1984. Running time: 79 MINS.

Presumptuously describing itself in program notes as a "Woody Allen-like film," this low-budget amateur indulgence lacks any humor or evidence of talent. Produced by Swedes, with Swedish performers speaking awkwardly in English, this work has no clear nationality, identity, personality or purpose. Story is simply a series of disconnected set-pieces or one-joke comic turns for leading man Rusty Fischer playing Eno, impractical dreamer and con man. Humor is on the high-school level.

"Where's Eno?" opens and closes in a theater as Eno, a charming cad who lacks charm, joins his cast, crew and backers to see his new film, this film. They sleep. But Eno loves it, even when the screen goes black but the soundtrack continues, explaining that the production had run out of money. As the film within the film ends, the investors scream for their money back. They're entitled.

The Eno character is a youngish bearded gambler, lecher and swindler, who cheats even his own small son at cards. Episodic in structure, the film has Eno on an odyssey of various unfunny misunderstandings, a la the Abbott-Costello "Who's On First?" routine. Similarly, Eno breaks up serious business meetings of stuffed shirts with his madcap be-

haviour and outrageous puns.

Commercial prospects for this strange Swedish-American hybrid seem negligible. —Hitch.

Carry Greenham Home
(BRITISH-COLOR)

Berlin, Feb. 25.

A film produced, directed, photographed (color), and edited by Beeban Kidron, Amanda Richardson. Title song, Peggy Seeger, "We Are Singing For Our Lives" Cassia Kidron. Reviewed at the Minilux Kino 5, Berlin, Feb. 25, 1984. Running time: 66 MINS.

It is certainly impressive that two young girls, barely out of film school and still in their early 20s, managed to get their film accepted into the Forum selection. It has a lot of energy and features one of the most unusual public protest movements of late. The British women who have surrounded the Greenham Common military base since 1981, after they found out it was intended as one of the sites for American nuclear missiles, warrant a documentary, possibly a long and detailed one, for which the Kidron-Richardson effort could serve as an early sketch, but not much more.

Inflamed by their deep conviction that the Greenham syndrome is less important for its pacifist purposes and more for the effective way women proved they can organize, the two filmmakers are closer to a feminist tract than a balanced documentary on rearmament, which could have been suggested by the title. In the light of what it shows, this title could even be interpreted as an invitation for women to bring the spirit of female unity and purposefulness demonstrated at Greenham, into their own homes.

The truth is that what is presented on screen too often resembles a big happy reunion, with singalong ditties raising the spirits. The scuffles these women have with a woman reporter who doesn't really understand that feminism in this instance is more of an issue than pacifism, the pranks played on the soldiers on base, rhymes like "whose side are you on" indicating that on one side there are suicide, homicide and genocide, on the other, the protesting women, even the hardships they encounter (one woman gives birth to her baby, while camping outside Greenham) are all a happening, but not much more.

Which could be attributed to the enthusiasm of the two girls who were so infatuated with the material they shot on video (it was transferred to film only at the last stage) that they didn't care to go much deeper into it, such as really dwelling on the personal problems of these women who went through a drastic change in lifestyle, which certainly reflected on all those surrounding them.

Also, the premise that males as such are responsible for war-mongering and women alone realize the folly in this (at least this is the way characters are divided for the audience), is a rather simplistic one. In the final count, this seems to be most effective as a film that could trigger arguments and discussions in a public debate, more than a film which could stand on its own. — *Edna.*

State Of Wonder
(BRITISH-COLOR)

Berlin, Feb. 29.
An Ultraviolet Ltd. production, produced by Michel Mercy, Michael Donovan. Directed and written by Martin Donovan. Camera (color), Nick Gifford; editor, Timothy Gee; sound, Derek Williams; music, Alan Gill, Michael Parker; art director, Kaelon; costumes, Dorothea Smylie Tait; coproducer, John Furse. Reviewed at Atelier am Zoo, Berlin (Berlin Film Festival, Special Screenings Section), Feb. 28, 1984. Running time: 113 MINS.

Pichirica	Nigel Court
Capt. Benson	David Meyer
"Jesus"	Tony Meyer
Russell	James Telfer
Dana	Annie Chaplin
Father Daniel	Martin Donovan
Sgt. Bigwell	Barrie Smith
Jude	Tony Edridge
"Princess" Vicky	Anja Schute
Zoltan	Michael Halphie
P.C. Foster	David Capri

The synopsis of this new British pic describes it as being "an allegorical film of almost naive simplicity..." That's putting it mildly.

Setting is a tiny Irish village where a mop-topped blond youth, Pichirica, is the local child of nature, a simpleton with simple values. A squad of soldiers led by Captain Benson arrives on a mysterious mission, as does a city journalist, Russell, who strikes up a friendship with a local girl, Dana. It's the night of a celebration at the village hall, where the local priest, trendy young Father Daniel, sings a locally composed song he hopes will reach the finals of the Eurovision Song Contest. Meanwhile, we discover the soldiers are looking for members of a militant peace movement (though there doesn't appear to be any establishment nearby for the peaceniks to demonstrate at). Pichirica stumbles across the peace activists and mistakes their leader for Jesus.

Hard to see what audience the makers of this contrived piece of nonsense had in mind. Simplistic allegory (the traitor among the peaceniks is even called Jude) doesn't work on any level, and most members of the cast are enthusiastic rather than effective as actors. Nigel Court creates a singularly unconvincing character out of Pichirica, while the gimmick of casting twins to play the opposing forces — Captain Benson and the Peace Group leader — remains just a gimmick.

On the plus side, there's some attractive lensing on Irish locations from Nick Gifford, and the film can be noted for introducing another member of the Chaplin clan to the screen; Annie Chaplin is no conventional looker, but radiates warmth and, with better roles, could make an interesting performer.

Quite the most bizarre character in the film is Father Daniel, played by director Martin Donovan himself. First seen writing his sermon and listening to a Walkman, this trendy priest (who seems to be a distant relative to the character played by Bing Crosby in "Say One For Me") mutters "Let's get this show on the road" as he enters the church to hold Communion, and dons a red tux to sing a Barry Manilow-style number, "Peace of Mind is No Crime," at the local hop. One of his parishoners describes the good Father as "a bit on the pop side," which is no exaggeration.

Theatrical possibilities look to be tough indeed for this doubtless well-intentioned but frankly inept effort. One is left wondering how such a concept and screenplay got financial backing in the first place. —*Strat.*

Vater Und Sohn
(Father And Son)
(W. GERMAN-COLOR-
B&W-DOCU-16m)

Berlin, Feb. 26.
A Xenon Film, Hamburg, in coproduction with Second German Television (ZDF), Mainz. A documentary with fictional elements written and directed by Thomas Mitscherlich. Camera (color), Michael Busse; editor, Stefanie Möbius, Angela Meister; sound, Anke Apelt; music, Igor Stravinsky, Claude Debussy; TV producer, Christoph Holch. Reviewed at Berlin Film Fest (Perspectives section of Forum), Feb. 26, '84. Running time: 85 MINS.
Cast: Alexander Mitscherlich, Gert Heinz (the Father), Thomas Mitscherlich, Dan Hussmann (the Son), Wildried Grimpe (the Teacher), Gerd Kunath (the Mentor), Helke Sander (a Woman).

Thomas Mitscherlich's documentary, "Father And Son," uses fictional elements on occasion to explore a relationship he, the filmmaker, had over the years (but particularly in his childhood) with his famous father, psychoanalyst Alexander Mitscherlich of the "Frankfurt School" of the 1960s. Mitscherlich, for the record, died June 26, 1982, age 73 in the middle of his son Thomas's film project that began in 1982 and ended with preem of "Father And Son" at the Berlinale. He was the head of the Sigmund Freud Institute form 1960 to 1976, and among his many books was "The Inability To Sorrow" (pub. 1967), written together with his wife Margarete.

Thomas Mitscherlich underscored his documentary with the statement: "A film about myself, about my father Alexander, and a little bit about the Federal Republic of Germany." The turnout at the Academy of Fine Arts for the Forum presentation was an SRO event, the timeslot allowing for lengthy discussion afterwards. Little doubt, both the documentation in clips from film and on the father and the son's confessional approach to a close but controversial family relationship will attract an intellectual audience. Yet this is more of a reflective discourse than it is a film.

Two aspects of "Father And Son" recommend it to students of history, psychology, and the arthouse documentary. This is a film of humor and self-effacing, critical integrity: Thomas Mitscherlich admits that his spiritual father was Herbert Marcuse, and that he himself "wrestled" with his father without much hope of ever really coming out on top or winning a family or personal argument — yet striving to do so all the same even posthumously in this film.

It's also a film of insights: clips of the Marcuse-Mitscherlich debate at the height of the Student Reform movement, showing a vibrant personality, are contrasted with the last filmed moments of an aged and incapacitated patriarchal figure struggling to maintain a flow of coherent thought before the camera.

As a filmmaker with a conceptual point-of-view, son Thomas has the distinct advantage over father Alexander in "Father And Son." Yet he balances everything out by framing the docu within a fictional train-ride: along the way the filmmaker is confronted by a woman passenger in the same compartment (femme filmer Helke Sander), the latter in turn questioning Thomas Mitscherlich on just what he's up to in stealing the thunder from a parental god. It's this subjective twist that delights — that, and several other witty lines in the script and autobiographical commentary on growing up in a household of intellectual give-and-take. Also, the fictional sketches of a childhood in the 1950s capture the spirit of the times . —*Holl.*

Greystoke: The Legend Of Tarzan, Lord Of The Apes
(U.S.-BRITISH-COLOR)

Jungle action is the apeman's strongest suit.

Hollywood, March 6.
A Warner Bros. release. Produced by Hugh Hudson, Stanley S. Canter. Directed by Hudson. Features entire cast. Screenplay, P.H. Vazak, Michael Austin, based on the story "Tarzan Of The Apes" by Edgar Rice Burroughs; camera (Technicolor, Super Technoscope), John Alcott; editor, Anne V. Coates; music, John Scott; production design, Stuart Craig; supervising art director, Simon Holland; art director, Norman Dorme; set decorator, Ann Mollo; special makeup effects, primate costume design and creation, Rick Baker; special visual effects, Albert J. Whitlock; costume design, John Mollo; MacDowell's costume design, Shirley Russell; sound (Dolby), Ivan Sharrock; associate producer, Garth Thomas; assistant directors, Ray Corbett, Simon Channing-Williams; second unit camera, Egil Woxholt. Reviewed at The Burbank Studios, Burbank, March 5, 1984. (MPAA Rating: PG.) Running time: 129 MINS.

The Sixth Earl of Greystoke	Ralph Richardson
Capitaine Phillippe D'Arnot	Ian Holm
Lord Esker	James Fox
John Clayton, Tarzan Lord of the Apes	Christopher Lambert
Miss Jane Porter	Andie MacDowell
Lady Alice Clayton	Cheryl Campbell
Jeffson Brown	Ian Charleson
Major Jack Downing	Nigel Davenport
Sir Hugh Belcher	Nicholas Farrell
Lord Jack Clayton	Paul Geoffrey
Captain Billings	Richard Griffiths
Willy	Hilton McRae
Buller/Prince Max Von Hesse	David Suchet
Sir Evelyn Blount	John Wells

Eight years after it was first announced, Warner Bros.' grandly scaled "Greystoke: The Legend Of Tarzan, Lord Of The Apes" has hit the screen. Result is a generally absorbing but dramatically uneven epic adventure, much better in its jungle-set first half than after Tarzan is brought back to Edwardian England. Curiosity value, more realistic approach to the legend and beautiful production should be able to pull considerable b.o. across the general audience age spectrum, although the capricious fancy of teenagers will have to be caught in order for pic to push into profit.

Shot in Cameroon, West Africa, as well as the U.K., production cost $33,000,000, including $6,000,000 in overhead and interest, with Warners reportedly in for $21,000,000.

One of the main selling points of "Greystoke" is that it adheres much more closely to the original Edgar Rice Burroughs story than have the countless previous screen tellings of Tarzan stories. While a little obligatory vine swinging is on view, this is principally the tale of the education of the seventh Earl of Greystoke, first by the family of apes which raises a stranded white child and eventually accepts him as its protector and leader, then by a Belgian explorer who teaches him language, and finally by the aristocracy of Britain, which attempts to make him one of their own.

Shipwrecked in Africa, Lord and Lady Clayton fashion a makeshift jungle home, have a son and soon die. Adopted by apes, the infant naturally learns to communicate and behave like those around him. Little Tarzan is portrayed at ages six months, five and 12, and character's transformation from helpless toddler to experienced, intelligent hunter reps one of the film's chief fascinations.

Tarzan sees his first white men when a group of colonialists arrives on what seems like an expedition to eliminate the entire wildlife population of the area. These pompous ruffians are wiped out by some pygmies, but Belgian captain Ian Holm is saved by Tarzan and, after teaching him some English with a French accent, takes him back to the fabulous English estate of his grandfather, played by Ralph Richardson in his final role.

This is where both Tarzan, and the film, get into trouble. Up to this point, director Hugh Hudson, in his first outing since the Oscar-winning "Chariots Of Fire," imposes a stately, but reasonable, pace. Original screenplay by Robert Towne (who substituted the pseudonym P.H. Vazak after the project was taken away from him) reportedly concentrated almost exclusively on jungle material, and a rather abrupt shift of tone is perceptible after the shift to England.

With the exception of the warm, slightly batty Richardson, nearly all the Englishmen on view are impossible, offensive snobs, and main thrust of the second half consists of the umpteenth revisionist putdown of the titled upper class, in order to provide justification for Tarzan's ultimate rejection of his blood heritage. Despite a blossoming romance between Tarzan and the American Jane, pic struggles to sustain viewer interest through the second half, and does so largely due to Richardson's performance, which ends with a dignified, moving death scene.

Structure is clearly designed to present the wild, instinctive side of man on the one hand, and the cultured, "civilized" side on the other, but the deadening, demoralizing process of Tarzan's introduction into society is demonstrated in a heavyhanded fashion that drains the interest and excitement that has been built up painstakingly.

Frenchman Christopher Lambert is a different sort of Tarzan. Tall, lean, firm but no muscleman, and facially resembling Jean-Paul Belmondo, he moves with great agility and mimics the apes to fine effect. One also feels for him when society straps him in a monkey suit, and while one suspects the tradition of eccentricity among English nobility might even have accommodated this fellow, one can hardly wait for him to chuck it all and head back to the jungle.

Ian Holm is helpfully energetic as the enterprising Belgian, James Fox, in his return to major films after a 14-year absence, is the personification of stiff propriety, and Andie MacDowell smiles her way through as the eternally sympathetic Jane.

On a production level, film is a marvel, as fabulous African locations have been seamlessly blended with studio recreations of jungle settings. In some instances, the apes have been endowed with overly human emotions, but Rick Baker's primate suit creations — and performances of those within them — are generally outstanding, as they needed to be for audience acceptance of the realistic approach.

Also superior are John Alcott's lush cinematography and work of a large team under production designer Stuart Craig and supervising art director Simon Holland. John Scott's music also contributes strongly. —*Cart.*

Un Amour de Swann
(Swann in Love)
(FRENCH-WEST GERMAN-COLOR)

Paris, Feb. 16.

Gaumont release (Orion Classics in U.S.) of a Films du Losange/Gaumont/FR 3/SFPC/Bioskop Film (Munich) coproduction, with the participation of the French Ministry of Culture. Produced by Margaret Menegoz. Stars Jeremy Irons, Ornella Muti. Directed by Volker Schlöndorff. Screenplay, Peter Brook, Jean-Claude Carrière, Marie-Helene Estienne, Schlöndorff, based on Marcel Proust's "Un Amour de Swann;" camera (color), Sven Nykvist; music, Hans-Werner Henze; production designer, Jacques Saulnier; costumes, Yvonne Sassinot de Nesle; editor, Françoise Bonnot; production managers, Marc Maurette, Philippe Allaire; associate producer, Nicole Stephane. Reviewed at Gaumont, Neuilly, Feb. 15, 1984. Running time: 110 MINS.

Charles Swann . . . . Jeremy Irons
Odette de Crecy . . . . Ornella Muti
Baron de Charlus . . . . Alain Delon
Duchesse de Guermantes . . . . Fanny Ardant
Mme. Verdurin . . . Marie-Christine Barrault
Chloé . . . . Anne Bennent
Madame Cottard . . . . Nathalie Juvet
Young man . . . . Nicolas Baby

Gaumont's production of "Un Amour de Swann" was earmarked for critical tar-and-feathering even before it went before the cameras last year, with Proustians of all persuasions declaring it couldn't be done. Some dwelled on the irony of a French literary masterpiece being brought to the screen by a German, with a Briton and an Italian in the leads. Others shuddered at the announcement that Alain Delon, following the defections of Michel Piccoli and Michael Lonsdale, was to play the Baron de Charlus, one of Marcel Proust's supreme comic characterizations.

Volker Schlöndorff's film is not sacrilege — merely a disappointment. One did not really expect a miracle, but the makers of the adaptation seemed to have their sights held at a reasonable level — only "Swann in Love," the second part of the first volume of Proust's monumental book, was to be filmed, with material borrowed from later sections to provide an epilog to the story, complete in itself, and dramatically pliable for the purposes of an average-length motion picture.

Given that, one did have a right to hope for a film of some exceptional dramatic and cinematic merit, with perhaps some rubbed off brilliance from one of the great works of world literature. Schlöndorff fails, not so much because he hasn't found an equivalent for Proust's extraordinary style, but because he has no substantial style of his own, no controlling design to impose on the material. His fastidious application makes for a film of attractive-surfaces and little depth or feeling.

In other words, it's fairly dull. Certainly there's enough opulence here for oglers of period films, with the best collaborative talent money can buy (on an over $3,000,000 budget): Yvonne Sassinot de Nesle's exquisite costumes, Jacques Saulnier's art direction (pic was shot on actual locations, notably the elegant Chateau of Champs-Sur-Marne) and Sven Nykvist's lovely photography (though more than just beauty is expected from him).

But all else is shaky, beginning with the screenplay by Jean-Claude Carrière and Peter Brook (who was supposed to direct the film, but backed out when his legit "Carmen" turned into a runaway smash).

In "Swann in Love," Proust created a sort of blueprint for the rest of his "Remembrances of Things Past" with the story of a Parisian dandy, Charles Swann, who falls in love with and pursues a social-climbing demi-mondaine, Odette de Crecy. His passion becomes so obsessive and his jealousy so overpowering that he gradually cuts himself off from the brilliant high society circles — the time is the mid-1880s — that he has succeeded in penetrating, despite his Jewish origins. Finally he seals his social doom by marrying Odette, though he no longer loves her.

Rather than reshape the material in new cinematic terms (as Harold Pinter did in his screenplay), Brook and Carrière merely do a cut and paste job on the text, lifting, transposing and dovetailing episodes and dialog from all over the novel and concentrating them into a single 24-hour period: Day in the Life of Swann, begin with his late morning rising, and following him on his daily rounds, which mostly revolve around pestering Odette. Set at the end of the story, the script thus traces his neurotic behavior as it peaks and breaks like a fever.

The intention is to crystalize the novel's central themes and dramatic movements, but the conventionally linear method is inadequate. Too much about what has gone before is taken for granted, and viewers unfamiliar with Proust (which, outside of France, is most of the world) will simply not grasp what all the fuss is about. The writers desperately throw in some flashbacks, especially for the famous "cattleyas" scene (in which Swann and Odette have their first sexual contact in a carriage) but they are banally realized by Schlöndorff.

The performances might have salvaged the film, but Jeremy Irons — who will certainly provide a promotional locomotive for British and American playoffs — is not up to the difficult central role. He provides the exterior credentials smoothly, but the turbulence and complexity of Swann's jealous passion lack jagged conviction. One tires of his foppish single-mindedness and tends to side with poor Odette, lusciously but vaguely incarnated by Ornella Muti. (Both are dubbed).

Other performances range from good to indifferent, with the exception of — surprise! — Delon, who is both marvelously comic and touching as Charlus, the middle-aged homosexual aristocrat, whose own vain amorous pursuit of a young man is a parallel to Swann's actions. Script's best idea was to flesh out the Baron's presence here as Swann's friend and confidante, since his role is mostly developed in the later volume, "Sodom and Gomorrah" (one local newsweekly sarcastically tagged its cover story on the film: Sodom and Gaumont). Delon's announced return to serious acting after a chain of anonymous thriller vehicles was good news which his performance here confirms. —*Len.*

Mesrine
(FRENCH-COLOR)

Paris, March 8.

Parafrance release of a G.R. Production. Produced by Claude Bourillot. Features entire cast. Written and directed by André Genoves. Camera (Eastmancolor), Jean-Claude Couty; editor, Martine Rousseau; sound, Pierre Befve; music, Jean-Pierre Rusconi. Reviewed at the Marignan-Concorde theater, Paris, March 5, 1984. Running time: 110 MINS.

Jacques Mesrine . . . . Nicolas Silberg
Sylvia . . . . Caroline Aguilar
Besse . . . . Gerard Sergue
Broussard . . . . Michel Poujade
Lelievre . . . . Louis Arbessier
Charlie Bauer . . . . Claude Faraldo
Tillier . . . . Jean-Pierre Pauty

André Genoves, who traded in his producer's cap for that of writer-director and made his debut with an unambitious erotic comedy, "Les Folies d'Elodie," aims somewhat higher for his second film. "Mesrine" is a fictional biopic about the late French gangster, about whom a feature docu already appeared on local screens a few weeks ago. (Yet another docu, treating the legal aspects of Mesrine's death in a police ambush in 1979, has been announced for French television.)

One half-expected Genoves' version to be conventionally romanticized, glorifying an anti-hero who was by some starry-eyed accounts unusually intelligent, often flamboyantly charming and possessed with a gentleman-adventurer sense of humor. After all, Genoves cast the part with Nicolas Silberg, a romantic lead at the Comedie-Française (who co-starred in Paul Vecchiali's "Drugstore Romance") and, as his girlfriend, Caroline Aguilar, the Mexican-born model who is Madame Genoves in real-life.

Just the contrary: in Silberg's credible, unglamorous performance — and his physical resemblance to the real Mesrine gives the pic's best moments an uncanny sense of authenticity — Genoves takes the gangster's myth off its pedestal, picturing Mesrine as a slightly paunchy, humorless and quick-tempered hood with a big chip on his shoulder.

Accordingly, if Mesrine's exploits are inevitably spectacular, his image as a crusader against a dehumanizing society — he led a vigorous campaign against the cruel high security blocks in French prisons — is played down as little more than the incidental gripe of an clever, unusually lucky outlaw who was his own best publicity man. On the other hand, his capacity for brutality is dwelled upon in sequence in which he sequestered and inflicted painful wounds on a journalist who had questioned Mesrine's honor.

Unfortunately, Genoves' thesis is hindered by a screenplay that lacks pertinent analysis of a social phenomenon and direction that is at worst trite and at best routine. But there is ample gunplay, prison breaks, robberies, kidnappings and general mayhem to make this a watchable thriller, spiked by the knowledge of a real-life incident at the basis of most episodes. —*Len.*

Stanley
(AUSTRALIAN-COLOR)

Sydney, Feb. 23.

An Andrew Gaty presentation of a Seven Keys production. Produced by Gaty. Directed by Esben Storm. Features entire cast. Story by Storm and Gaty; exec producer, Brian Rosen; script consultant, Stanley Mann; assoc. producer, Warwick Ross; production manager, Antonia Barnard; camera (color) Russell Boyd; production designer, Owen Williams; editor, William Anderson; music, Wil-

liam Motzing. Reviewed at Seven Keys theatrette, Sydney, Feb. 20, 1984 (Commonwealth Film Censor rating: M). Running time: 103 MINS.

Norm Norris	Graham Kennedy
Amy Benton	Nell Campbell
Stanley Dunstan	Peter Bensley
Sir Stanley Dunstan	Michael Craig
Berger	Max Cullen
Morris Norris	David Argue
Dorris Norris	Susan Walker
Sheryl Benton	Lorna Lesley
Lady Dunstan	Betty Lucas
Patty Norris	Joy Smithers
Reg	Jon Ewing

The eponymous character is a young oddball who lives alone on a yacht, rollerskates to work and causes upheaval in his father's boardroom by proposing that the company market pet food which humans can eat along with Fido and Felix.

Straitlaced dad, one of the world's richest men, desperately wants his son to be normal and is prepared to go to any lengths, up to and including ordering junior to have a brain operation, so Stanley runs away and boards with what he assumes to be a normal Australian family living a typical suburban existence.

Stanley is soon wondering what "normal" means when he discovers the head of the family is a closet homosexual whose lover is tring to blackmail him into leaving his wife, who it turns out, is having an affair with the president of the local bowling club; the son is dealing in heavy drugs; and the daughter is pregnant by her black boyfriend.

It's a fresh, witty premise for a sharp-edged comedy which unfortunately fails to deliver as much as it promises.

Script lacks punch and consistency, missing more often than it hits, and director-screenwriter Esben Storm allows the narrative to lapse into pure farce in the last reel or so, as Stanley is pursued by his father's butler-cum-private detective and three klutz henchmen.

Pic's chief weakness is the casting of Peter Bensley, as Stanley. Formerly a regular in one of Australian TV's lesser soap operas, Bensley was recruited for the title role after the producers were turned down by Mel Gibson, and were blocked by Actor's Equity from importing Tom Conti or Anthony Andrews. His deadpan delivery and expressionless face weigh heavily, reducing Stanley to an insipid character, when more projection and style were required.

Another drawback is the lackluster performance by Graham Kennedy as the suppressed gay lurking behind the macho family-man front. Kennedy, a "Tonight" show compere turned actor, proved his worth in films like "Don's Party" and "The Odd Angry Shot" but here he is awkward and unconvincing. Similarly, Max Cullen, another gifted thesp, is nei-

ther funny nor credible as the butler, not helped by his strongly-strangled accent.

Nell Campbell fares better as the hard-to-woo object of Stanley's affections, and Jon Ewing has a delightful cameo as a shoeshop proprietor with a foot fetish.

Boxoffice prospects in Australia are fair at best, and while the pic's value theatrically overseas is questionable, it would be passable entertainment on the small screen. —*Dogo.*

The Ice Pirates
(COLOR)

Quick, before it melts.

Hollywood, March 12.

A JF Production released through MGM/UA. Produced by John Foreman. Directed by Stewart Raffill. Features entire cast. Screenplay, Raffill and Stanford Sherman; camera (Metrocolor), Matthew F. Leonetti; editor, Tom Walls; music, Bruce Broughton; art director, David M. Haber, Ronald Kent Foreman; set decorator, John M. Dwyer; set designer, Mark Poll, Bill Skinner; sound, Morris Harris, Dean Hodges; special effects, Max W. Anderson; motion control photography, Praxis Filmworks; costumes, Daniel Paredes; associate producer, Dennis Lasker; assistant director, Bill Carroll. Reviewed at MGM/UA screening room, Hollywood, March 12, 1984. (MPAA rating: PG). Running time: 96 MINS.

Jason	Robert Urich
Princess Karina	Mary Crosby
Roscoe	Michael D. Roberts
Maida	Anjelica Huston
Killjoy	John Matuszak
Zeno	Ron Perlman
Supreme Commander	John Carradine

"The Ice Pirates" is a dim-witted slow-moving space spoof aimed at a pre-adolescent audience. It may have aimed too low.

Film has been in the can since June and MGM/UA has decided to let it out at a slack time when picture might do some business. Thanks to an amusingly self-mocking ad campaign, pic might open fairly well, but in short order even kids should stay away from this one.

Production is dismal in every department. Special effects are hardly that and better visuals are probably available at the local video arcade. Photography by Matthew F. Leonetti is consistently grainy and dark.

On a plot level, picture's attempt at campiness totally misfires. A hearty band of pirates led by Robert Urich joins forces with Princess Karina (Mary Crosby) to help find her explorer father and a newly discovered water supply in the next galaxy.

Water, or lack of it, is the root of all evil in this mock universe and the pirates travel about stealing from the rich and giving to the poor, of course. Curious inconsistency — after a day flying about, pirates settle down at their favorite bar for, yes, a drink.

As for the bar itself, scene, like many here, is ripped off verbatim from the well-known interplanetary space bar in "Star Wars." "The Ice Pirates" has not an ounce of originality of its own.

Acting is not so much bad as absent; there are no characters developed in the film. Urich struts around in a curly wig romancing the Princess until they finally retreat to an "environmental chamber" featuring Muzak and greeting card visuals.

Urich and sidekick Michael D. Roberts get into constant scrapes and escape not by their own ingenuity but through editing that often jumps ahead to the next scene.

Visually, picture is about on a par with the old Flash Gordon serial, using the likes of dressed-up cars for vehicles of the future and a warehouse basement for a futuristic environment. Costumes are a cross between swashbucklers and knights of the round table.

Picture is ultimately disturbing in its contempt for the audience's intelligence, even children. At 96 minutes, it ends not a moment too soon. —*Jagr.*

Musical Passage
(DOCU-COLOR)

A Ginger Group Production, New York, 1984, released by Films Incorporated. Producers, Jim Brown, David Karpoff, Ginger Turek. Directed by Brown. Second unit director, George C. Stoney; camera (color), Brown; editor, Paul Barnes; sound, Turek, Chat Gunter, Jerry Bruck, Frank Halzer, Fran Daniels. Reviewed at Times Square Screening Room, New York, March 14, 1984. Running time: 73 MINS.

The title, "Musical Passage," puns the notion of travel or transition, as these Soviet Jewish musicians pass from the oppressive restricted atmosphere of committeeized culture in the USSR, to the exhilaration of playing their music in artistic freedom in the U.S.

Now safely here and pursuing successful careers as individuals, and collectively as the Soviet Emigre, these musicians remember the difficulties of that rite of passage. Gathered in small groups for shirt-sleeved rehearsals, they dispute among themselves in English — was their escape luck?

No, they finally decide. They marvel that they endured, and prevailed, after months and often years of Soviet harassment and surveillance that followed their application for travel visas. They lost jobs, were blacklisted, forced to sell precious things, to live on savings. Families were forced to emigrate in stages, get the young ones out first.

"Musical Passage" seems assured of exposure on public television, and 16m distribution can connect it with schools and churches. But theatrical audiences are the first target, per the 35m blowup and bookings being arranged by Films Inc., following the film's March 21 debut in Manhattan.

This is the third of a musical-documentary trilogy produced by Jim Brown and wife Ginger Turek.
— *Hitch.*

Ein Mann Wie EVA
(A Man Like EVA)
(WEST GERMAN-COLOR)

Berlin, March 2.

A Horst Schier and Laurens Straub Film Production, Munich, in collaboration with Atlas Trio Film, Impuls Film, and Maran Film. Stars Eva Mattes. Directed by Radu Gabrea. Screenplay, Gabrea, Straub, after an idea by Schier and Straub; camera (color), Schier; sets, Jörg Neumann; editor, Dragos-Emanuel Wittkowski. Reviewed at Royal Palast, Berlin, March 2, '84. Running time: **86 MINS.**

Cast: Eva Mattes (EVA), Lisa Kreuzer, Werner Stocker, Charles Regnier, Charly Mohamed Huber, Carola Regnier, Albert Kitzl, Towje Kleiner, Sybille Rauch.

The E.V.A. in Radu Gabrea's "A Man Like EVA" might just as well be R.W.F., for this is a thinly veiled exploitation feature on Germany's best known and most discussed New German Cinema filmmaker, the late Rainer Werner Fassbinder. Since his tragic death in June 1982, two documentaries and a handful of books have been written about the prolific filmmaker, most of them uncomplimentary and seemingly produced for a fast mark. There's no reason why "A Man Like EVA" should be reviewed as anything different.

Fassbinder fans will note immediately the multiple references to stages of RWF's career, particularly the early 1970s. There are also a slew of confidantes and "family" figures right out of real life, and here their actions are a giveaway that the frame of historical reference is a good decade later (when he was completely in charge and the film team avidly protected his and their interests). Eva Mattes (thus the title) plays RWF with a commendable flair for mimicry, and there's one scene of a voyeuristic nature in which she makes an attempt to charge her performance with emotional depth.

As for the narrative line EVA/RWF is shooting a fictitious Dumas adaptation, "Lady of the Camelias," in a hideaway villa. Verdi's "La Traviata" floods the track. —*Holl.*

The Story of Chaim Rumkowski And The Jews of Lodz
(SWEDISH-DOCU-B&W-16m)

Produced by P O J Filmproduction AB and Swedish Television STV1, 1983. Presented in the U.S. by the Cinema Guild, New York. Director: Peter Cohen; writer Bo Kuritzen; historical consultant, Lucjan Dobroszycki. Narrated in English. Reviewed at Global Village, N.Y., March 16, 1984. running time: **60 MINS.**

Winner this year as Best Film in the 10th annual Film and Video Documentary Festival, of Global Village, New York, this extraordinary work is one of the best documentaries on the Nazi Holocaust.

A Swedish film, now in U.S. release, "The Jews of Lodz" is especially noteworthy for its meticulous documentation and calm and austere narration (in English), which traces chronologically the gathering horror as 300,000 Jews in the Polish city of Lodz were corraled, then decimated (of 3,000,000 Jews who died throughout Poland).

With painful irony, this film details how a Jewish Council was formed in Lodz by the Nazis to facilitate the orderly extermination of the Jews. Chairman of the council was Chaim Rumkowski, a charismatic political organizer who was cleverly able to delay but not halt the implacable Nazi process.

Personalizing the moral dilemma of Jewish elders elsewhere in Nazi-occupied Europe who were forced to collaborate with the Nazis in order to save some of the beleaguered Jews, the film concentrates on Rumkowski, a popular public figure in the Lodz ghetto, chosen by the Nazis as chairman of their council because of Jewish faith in his leadership. Rumkowski established a vast bureaucracy that he closely administered to social services within the ghetto — schools, health care, sanitation, fire and police, food rationing, etc. Also, Rumkowski attempted to convert the ghetto into an industrial center of value to the Nazi war machine, making the Jews indispensable and thus insuring their survival until the Allied victory.

But Rumkowski's strategy was doomed to failure, as the ghetto was progressively depopulated by Nazi roundups of Jews over several years. Finally, the ghetto by now almost empty, Rumkowski himself was shipped to Auschwitz, where he was torn to pieces by Jews there who felt he had betrayed and misled them.

Thus, "The Jews of Lodz" is a heroic tragedy of misguided genius — forcing us to ask ourselves what we would have done, what other alternatives were at hand? "The Jews of Lodz" is a horror tale and a history, little known except to scholars of the Holocaust. Finally, it is heartbreaking, sparing its viewers nothing.

Skillfully using rare archival photographs taken by Jewish Council photographers and other ghetto inhabitants, the film traces not only Rumkowski's frenzied efforts to impeded the Nazi deportations of Jews, but also his curious megalomania. Rumkowski suppressed dissent and promoted himself as a kind of messianic paterfamilias, his face omnipresnt in ghetto newspapers, posters, postage stamps and paper currency. Indeed, many photographs in "The Jews of Lodz" come from the large numbers of albums published to honor Rumkowski.

Given the recent popular interest in Holocaust topics, "The Jews of Lodz" will find its home naturally on public television and in 16m distribution to the religious and educational communities. But in addition, if carefully marketed, especially with a well-chosen congenial companion film, "The Jews of Lodz" should find audiences in selected theatrical situations in major American cities. — *Hitch.*

Berlin Film Fest

Haunted
(U.S.-COLOR)

Berlin, Feb. 20.

Post Mills Productions, with WBGH Boston. Produced by Stanley Plotnick. Co-produced by Cynthia Mitchell. Written and directed by Michael Roemer. Stars Brooke Adams, Jon de Vries, Ari Meyers, Trish van Devere. Camera (Eastmancolor), Franz Rath; editor, Terry Lewis; sound, Flora Moon; executive producer, Peter Cook. Reviewed at Atelier am Zoo, Berlin (Berlin Film Festival, US Non-Majors section), Feb. 17, '1984. Running time: **119 MINS.**

Jo ....Brooke Adams
tom ....Jon de Vries
Jackie ....Ari Meyers
Donna ....Trish van Devere
Fran.......................Audrey Matson
Steve ....Mark Arnott

Superb acting and some subtle scripting are the hallmarks of this rather gloomy tale of personal relationships. The title is misleading, in that this isn't a horror film, at least not in the traditional film sense.

The story begins as Jo (Brooke Adams) returns home after an absence and a failed marriage to see her mother, who is seriously ill, and her sister, a proud new mother. Both daughters were adopted into a very strict Catholic family, from which Jo rebelled, got pregnant at 16 (the baby was adopted, too), and rejects religion. Her husband follows her and there's a violent scene between them. Gradually, as if she didn't have enough problems of her own, Jo gets drawn into the world of her mother's neighbors. Another marriage, between writer Tom (Jon de Vries) and his hysterical wife Donna (Trish van Devere) is breaking up, and their bright 12-year-old daughter Jackie (Ari Meyers) is caught in the middle. Jo befriends the child, then finds herself so disapproving of Donna's violent outbursts that she interferes quite blatantly — nearly fatally — in a situation that's none of her buisness.

Adams is outstanding as the ambiguous Jo, who does everything wrong and can be seen a dangerous manipulator of other people's lives, having made something of a mess of her own. It's a subtle, complex character. Trish van Devere, as the hysterical and possibly mentally deranged Donna has a flashier role and really gets her teeth into it; the confrontations between these two are beautifully handled. Meyers is totally assured and touching as young Jackie.

German-born Michael Roemer isn't a prolific filmmaker (only one film between "Haunted" and his first feature, "Nothing But A Man," in 1965), and he has done an intelligent job here. However, the downbeat subject and basically unresolved ending will make it an exceedingly difficult sell. TV sales are indicated. Lensing of Franz Rath, which looks like a 16m blowup, is rather flat. —*Strat.*

The Terence Davies Trilogy
(BRITISH-B&W)

Berlin, Feb. 24.

A British Film Institute production and release. Written and directed by Terence Davies. Camera (black and white), William Diver; editors, Mick Audsley, William Diver. No other credits. Reviewed at the Berlin Film Festival (non-competing), Feb. 24, 1984. Running time: **84 MINS.**

Robert Tucker
(middle-age) ....Terry O'Sullivan
Robert Tucker
(old age) ....Wilfred Brambell
Robert's mother ....Sheila Raynor

Shot between 1976 and 1983, three short subjects by filmmaker Terence Davies are now being distributed by the BFI as a feature outing. The three installments — "Children," "Madonna and Child," and "Death and Transfiguration" — tell the story of Robert Tucker from youth to his dying gasp. Although far from an encouraging tale, the trio of stories comprise one of the best endeavors from the BFI in artistic quality and in raw emotional power.

Story begins with young Tucker's days in an austere boys' school. It is a cold, bloodless environment of discipline and ridicule. His home life is equally bleak with his parents' relationship viewed as violent and loveless. Yet, there is a tremendous sense of loss in the boy when his father dies in this section's conclusion.

In "Madonna and Child," Tucker is an adult working in a grim office. Still living with his mother, he is a closet homosexual, fraught with guilty feelings. The final section sees his mother's death and Tucker emotionally adrift. Events move backward and forward in time to his old age, informed in a hospital and the dire memories of his earlier years.

Overall tone is downbeat which limits the film's commercial prospects. Nonetheless, the persistent vision is riveting and the emotional struggle aims straight for the heart. The obvious comparison here is to the Bill Douglas trilogy with which Davies' work compares very favorably.

Seen together there are obvious time and character inconsistencies. However, these aspects in no way diminish the thrust of the story or the power of the message. What is, at times, disconcerting are the complicated structures of flashforwards and flashbacks within individual sections. And this complexity coupled with the unrelenting dreariness make viewing the films somewhat painful even if in the final analysis one is moved by the whole.

Davies' control of all artistic and technical components of the film is assured. Yet, one suspects he could have benefited from greater outside input to enable a wider accessibility through levity or contrast.

Picture has already scored well in festival situations but conventional distribution will be quite difficult. Specialty screenings and art house life should easily enhance the reputation of Davies and his films.
— *Klad.*

Hrafninn Flygur
(Flight Of The Raven)
(ICELAND-SWEDISH-COLOR)

Berlin, Feb. 26.

A coproduction of F.I.L.M. (Reykjavik), Viking Film (Stockholm) and the Swedish Film Institute. Produced by Bo Jonsson. Directed and written by Hrafn Gunnlaugsson. Camera (Fujicolor), Tony Forsberg; editor, Gunnlaugsson; art direction, Karl Juliusson, Gunnar Baldursson; music, Hans-Erik Phillip. Reviewed at the Berlin Film Festival (non-competing), Feb. 26, 1984. Running time: **108 MINS.**
Gest . . . . Jacob Thor Einarsson
His sister . . . . Edda Bjorgvinsdottir
Thor . . . . Helgi Skulason
Thor's brother . . . . Egill Olafsson
Erik . . . . Flosi Olafsson
Wachter . . . . Sveinn Eidsson

If Sergio Leone had directed a Viking saga, it might very well look and sound something like Iceland's "Flight of the Raven." This energetic, visually striking yarn of revenge has a breathtaking energy which translates well internationally and bodes well for the picture's prospects outside Scandinavia.

The story has vague allusions to Leone's "Once Upon a Time in the West" insofar as it concerns a young man's search for the men who killed his father when he was a boy. Now fully grown, Gest, the Irish boy, seeks out the murderous Vikings, who also ran off with his young sister. The Nordic brothers — Thor and Erik — have fled Norway for political reasons and have set up in barren Iceland.

Gest initially kills a couple of brothers' henchmen in such a way that the highly superstitious siblings believe it must be retribution from the gods. Subsequently, brother turns against brother and, after Thor has Erik killed, the human reality of the Irish gunslinger comes to light.

Combining the mythic quality of the era with brisk pacing, Gunnlaugsson moves his story along with dash and style. Both the stunning camerawork and Ennio Morricone-style music elevate the basic simplicity of the narrative into extraordinary filmmaking.

Despite the obvious inexperience and technical limitations of the young Icelandic film industry, film shows no strains of amateurism. Gunnlaugsson, at times, masks his limited resources through clever editing. However, there appears to be some tension in his balance between stark simplicity and stunning polish. The frills, particularly the overpowering score, might be toned down to greater entertainment returns.

Casting is quite strong, performing to type, and there's a nice irony in the split loyalties of Gest's sister who has had a child by Thor. Latter aspect allows for a nice full circle aspect at the story's conclusion.

Marketing in North America may prove somewhat tricky as the picture has both exploitable art house and mainstream elements. Nonetheless, there's obvious appeal in boxoffice for this one-off endeavor. Possibility exists to open selected markets and build to wide release stressing action elements for this visceral flight of fantasy.
— *Klad.*

Husty
(JAPANESE-COLOR)

Berlin, Feb. 24.

A Cine Centers Kobushi Production; world rights, Daiei International Films, Tokyo. Features entire cast. Directed by Toshio Gotoh. Screenplay, Hideka Nagasasa, Gotoh; camera (color), Shun Yamamoto; editor, Jun Nabeshima; music, Kentaro Haneda; sets, Muneo Naganuma. Reviewed at Berlin Film Fest (Children's Films), Feb. 24 '84. Running time: **88 MINS.**
Cast: Akemi Makamura (Saeko), Yuichi Saito (Jiro), Hisashi Igawa, Momoko Kohci, Kei Yamamoto.

Helmer Toshio Gotoh was at the Berlin Fest a few years back with "The Old Bear Hunter," unspooled also in the Children's Film Festival of the Berlinale. Now he's back with another tale of a young boy and his dog: "Husty."

In a small village near the sea live a boy and his young pup, Husty. He makes the acquaintance of a young girl, and the three become inseparable on occasion. She is well on her way to becoming a pianist, but a car accident injures an optic nerve and soon she may be blind.

The boy receives a second blow when his full-grown pup is taken away from him for special training. But Husty is to be trained as a seeing-eye dog for the young friend next door. Thus, boy and dog and blind girl remain friends and closely attached to each other.

"Husty" is a bit too programmed to work as a narrative story, but credits are a plus down the line. Highly recommended for youth and children film fests.
— *Holl.*

A Mort l'Arbitre
(Kill the Referee)
(FRENCH-COLOR)

Paris, March 7.

Planfilm release of a Lira Elephant/TF 1 Films Productions/RTZ coproduction. Produced by Raymond Danon. Directed by Jean-Pierre Mocky. Screenplay, Mocky, Jacques Dreux, based on the novel, "The Death Penalty," by Alfred Draper; camera (Eastmancolor), Edmond Richard; art directors, René Loubet, Marielle Robinson, Gérard Moiteaux; editors, Catherine Renault, Mocky; music, Alain Chamfort; sound, Luc Perini, Lucien Yvonnet; production manager, Pierre Darcay; executive producers, Daniel Deschamps, Maurice Illouz. Reviewed at the Marignan-Concorde theater, Paris, March 3, 1984. Running time: **82 MINS.**
Rico . . . . Michel Serrault
Maurice . . . . Eddy Mitchell
Martine . . . . Carole Laure
Teddy . . . . Laurent Malet
Granowski . . . . Jean-Pierre Mocky
Albert . . . . Claude Brosset

"A Mort l'Arbitre" is the second French manhunt suspenser in a year, and, like Yves Boisset's "Prize of Peril," is from an Anglo-Saxon print source. Director Jean-Pierre Mocky and coscripter Jacques Dreux drew their film from "The Death Penalty," by Alfred Draper, a British university professor who witnessed a real-life example of mob violence when a group of frenzied soccer fans maimed a hapless referee after a university game.

Mocky tries to dramatize a similar situation, transposed to France, by keeping screen time and real time as close as possible (though there are inevitable temporal ellipses, since the action begins before a soccer game, and reaches its climax sometime after it's over).

Eddy Mitchell is the cool, self-confident referee whose auxiliary ambitions include trying to call the shots in Carole Laure's bed. But their nascent idyll is interrupted by the gang of motley fans who are after his goat for ruling against their team in a game judgment.

There follows a hot nocturnal pursuit as the mob, led by a particularly rabid Michel Serrault, trails the unfortunate lovebirds through a tv station, a shopping center, a suburban apartment complex, and, finally, an underground quarry. In the course of the chase some accidental deaths occur, which,

rather than braking their rage, only whips it up further.

Mocky, who has a critical following here for a handful of personal, anarchistic thrillers like "Solo," scores his most effective points in the first part of the film, skillfully recreating the morbidly mindless excitement often attendant on sports events.

Once the pursuit begins, "A Mort l'Arbitre" takes the shape of a conventional thriller with occasional flashes of unusual incident. As fastpaced and watchable as it is, Mocky's picture would have been more barbed with an even short running time.

Mocky, who himself plays the role of a blasé cop in no hurry to get to the scene of a possible crime, uses his found decors vividly notably the modern residential complex designed by Ricardo Bofill for the suburb of Noisy-Le-Grand, which cinematographer Edmond Richard milks for all its sinister value. —*Len.*

Dorian Gray Im Spiegel Der Boulevardpresse
(The Image of Dorian Gray in the Yellow Press)
(WEST GERMAN-COLOR)

Berlin, Feb. 20.

An Ulrike Ottinger Film Production, Berlin; producer, Renée Gundelach. Features entire cast. Written, directed, photographed (color), and sets designed by Ulrike Ottinger. Music, Peer Raben; editing, Eva Schlensag. Reviewed at Berlin Film Fest (Forum), Feb. 20, '84. Running time: **150 MINS.**
Cast: Veruschka von Lehndorff (Dorian Gray), Delphine Seyrig (Frau Dr. Mabuse), Tabea Blumenschein (Andamana), Toyo Tanaka (Hollywood), Irm Hermann (Passat), Magdalena Montezuma (Golem), Barbara Valentin (Susy), Hanno Jochimsen (Herr von Welt), Jonatan Briel (Dr. Spiegelwelt), Horst Berzrath (Mr. Standard Telegraph), Gary Indiana, Joy Peters.

The queen of the Berlin Underground filmmakers, Ulrike Ottinger began her career a decade ago with a portrait of a local conceptual artist, "Berlin Fever — Wolf Vostell" (1973), and went on to make a string of produced-directed-scripted-photographed-designed offbeat features on the surrealist world of art and cinema: "Laokoon & Sons" (1974), "The Bewitchment of the Drunken Sailors" (1975), "Madame X — An Absolute Ruler" (1977), "Portrait of a Woman Drinker," (Ticket of No Return) (1979), "Freak Orlando" (1981), and now "The Image of Dorian Gray in the Yellow Press" (1983). Nearly all of these were made in collaboration with, or starring, Tabea Blumenshein, while other regulars in her cast have included Magdalena Montezuma and Delphine Seyrig.

There's a lot going for Ottinger when her Underground features unspool in Berlin, for here the actors blend into the set design like pieces of gorgeous furniture. Further, the Berlin Underground scene is so lively that the local audience delights in each and every nuance of Ulrike's extravagance. Yet it's a presumption to think that even an opening niter, at the Forum of Young Cinema at the Berlinale will give "Dorian Gray" the legs needed to ankle abroad on the arthouse circuit, although playoffs are possible at fest catering to the offbeat and the exotic.

"The Image of Dorian Gray in the Yellow Press" has relatively little to do with Oscar Wilde's classic "The Picture of Dorian Gray" (pub. 1891) as a narrative tale, but it has everything to do with its inspirational source: Georges Charles Huysmanns's "A Rebours" (Against Nature) (pub. 1884). Both Huysmanns and Wilde offered prototypes of decadence and figures of the occult world, for whom hedonistic tastes and hypersensitive sensations take preference over the common things in life — yet both are redeemed by their commitment to idealism and aestheticism. Ottinger simply transposes these dandy-personalities of Paris and London to her own Berlin demi-monde.

Veruschka, a well-known cover-girl mannikin, plays a unisex Dorian Gray wandering from set to set. Delphine Seyrig is Frau Dr. Mabuse. Magdalena Montezuma is Golem. On occasion, these figures are given other names. That's about the extent of Ottinger's thematic concept. Insofar as German film history is concerned, the key is the chain of Humunculus-Golem-Mabuse fantasy headliners from the silent period to almost the present. Mabuse, head of an international press cartel, decides to create an artificial Dorian Gray of her own — one who is young, rich, and beautiful — and then send her/him out into the world under cover of a yellow press thirsting for just such a phenomenon. After two-and-a-half-hours of static pictures and operatic poses, one assumes he has seen a collection of rushes — and waits for the film to be cut for commercial release. But no Ottinger apparently cannot part with images of her own creation, and thus as a filmmaker overtaxes the patience of her audience.—*Holl.*

Tiznao
(VENEZUELAN-COLOR)

Berlin, Feb. 24.
A Tiznao Films Production. Produced by Fernando Arias and Gualdino Ferreira. Written and directed by Dominique Cassuto de Bonet, Salvador Bonet. Features entire cast. Camera (color), Salvador Bonet; edited by Dominique Cassuto de Bonet; sound, Alfredo Oronoz; music, Miguel Angel Fuster. Reviewed at the Delphi Cinema, Berlin, Feb. 24, 1984. Running time: **90 MINS.**
With Flor Maria Belisario, Domingo Antonio Lovera, Francisca Hernández, Pablo Alejo, Candida Tovar de Macero, Juan José Yañez, Abilio Antonio Molina, Natividad Belisario, Natividad Graterol, David Lares Gualdino Ferreira da Silva, people of the village San Francisco de Tiznados.

This painstaking document, put together by a husband and wife team who invested over three years in its preparation, is right up the alley of the spirit prevalent in this year's edition of Young Cinema Forum. It is effective both as an ethnographic document of a dying society and as an additional image of Latin America and its specific problems.

The Bonets lived three years in a small village, San Francisco de Tiznado, a place twice doomed and now nonexistent. Already on their arrival, most of the population was on its way out, looking for better places to make a living and create a future. The second and final condemnation is the government's decision to build a dam, which may well profit the economy of the entire country, but will leave San Francisco de Tiznado deep under water.

The film proclaims its theme from the first shot, as it records the exodus of the last villagers who had stuck there to the end, under a heavy, pitiless sun, towards their new place, a slum for which they will have to pay out of their own meagre resources.

Then it goes back to record the creeping despair of a simple and surprisingly cheerful congregation, slowly shrinking as day after day more people are defeated by the economic conditions in the village, and prefer to join family or relatives in more prosperous surroundings. Nostalgia for the past combines with present day frustration as the rural community disintegrates. Already only old people and a child, through whose eyes the story is told are still living there, churches fall into disrepair, the houses are crumbling. Still, there is a certain charm in this place and its people which the film transmits nicely, whether by carefully listening to old stories, following the village drunk, or via the backward representative of the law.

As it goes on, the expropriation system, whereby the evacuees are offered pennies for their present dwellings and obliged to move to another place, whether they like it or not, is shown in subdued, but very critical tones. The prefect who assures everybody they had been offered fair prices for their homes, but doesn't like it when he is given a similar amount for his, the paradoxical situation that old people — they are the only ones left — have to start their life anew when they lack the energy to do so, all in clearly stated, and indeed one of the evicted old ladies prefers to die in her own bed, even if nothing is stated that plainly.

Using the villagers to play their own story, the Bonets opted for a technique that would take into account the presence of the filming crew, for it is evident that the participants are aware of the camera and tend quite often to play to it. But by explaining there is a film being made about the village, it justifies their attitude. At one point, the eight-year old girl who is the main protagonist approaches the jeep of the crew to ask them whether, as filmmakers, they couldn't do anything to stop the downward process.

Camera work is daring at times, some scenes played in almost complete darkness, letting the voices of the persons take over, numerous closeups affectionately record the deep-wrinkled, weather-beaten faces, and allow some characters a margin of comic relief, welcome in this sort of subject. Traditions are carefully preserved in the way these people address each other and music intrudes only when absolutely necessary.

Certainly limited by its subject matter, its slow, deliberate tempo and the particular technique chosen, to a specialized audience, this item nevertheless stands a good chance at playing at many other festivals later this year, and some already intend to book it. — *Edna.*

Romancing The Stone
(COLOR)

Romantic adventure with a light touch looms an instant winner.

Hollywood, March 21.
A 20th Century-Fox release of an El Corazon Producciones S.A. production. Produced by Michael Douglas; coproducers, Jack Brodsky, Joel Douglas. Directed by Robert Zemeckis. Stars Michael Douglas, Kathleen Turner. Screenplay, Diane Thomas; camera (Panavision, Deluxe color), Dean Cundey; editors, Donn Cambern, Frank Morriss; music, Alan Silvestri; title song, Eddy Grant; sound, Bill Kaplan; production design, Lawrence G. Paull; art direction, Augustin Ituarte; set decoration, Enrique Estevez; assistant director, Joel Douglas; production manager, John Schofield; second unit director-stunt coordinator, Terry Leonard; costume design, Marilyn Vance; costume supervisor, Gilda Texter; second unit camera, Richard Hart; choreographer, Jeffrey D. Hornaday; optical effects, Peter Bloch, Kerry Colonna; mechanical alligator effect, Chris Walas Inc. Reviewed at Avco Theater, L.A., March 21, 1984. (MPAA Rating: PG). Running time: **106 MINS.**

Jack Colton	Michael Douglas
Joan Wilder	Kathleen Turner
Ralph	Danny DeVito
Ira	Zack Norman
Juan	Alfonso Arau
Zolo	Manuel Ojeda
Gloria	Holland Taylor
Elaine	Mary Ellen Trainor

As an early spring entry, "Romancing The Stone" looks like a verdant possibility, the green growing thick at the boxoffice for another fundamental, time tested fun formula.

Ahead of release, "Stone" has been likened many times to another "Raiders Of The Lost Ark" but the similarity is really limited to the fact that both borrow freely from escapist traditions. Of the two, "Stone" is lighter by far and most successful when it is.

Living alone with her cat, Kathleen Turner writes romantic novels and cries over the outcome, blowing her nose on "buy tissue" reminders and assuring friend Holland Taylor that one day the writer's life will pick up for real.

It's certainly less exciting than that of Turner's sister, currently missing a husband somewhere in Colombia. When Taylor inquires, "Have they found the body yet?" it's typical of the delights in Diane Thomas' script that Turner deadpans "Only the one piece."

Naturally, Turner receives a package mailed from South America just ahead of sister's phone call that she's been kidnapped and will die if Turner doesn't deliver the contents of the package south of the border as soon as possible.

Heading for the jungles in her high heels, Turner is like a lot of unwitting screen heroines ahead of her, guaranteed that her drab existence is about to be transformed — probably by a man, preferably handsome and adventurous.

Sure enough, Michael Douglas pops out of the jungle, saving her life once but then becoming an unwilling helper, then an avid swain and finally an even more ambitious accomplice in turning the contents of the package to their advantage.

The expected complications are supplied by the kidnappers, Danny DeVito and Zack Norman, in rivalry with a local murderous official, Manuel Ojeda — all in pursuit of the same treasure. Though amusing, DeVito and Norman are a bit more bumbling than necessary but Ojeda stays closer to the mark as a menace whose silliness is self-contained.

Best of all the supporting players is Alfonso Arau, who first appears as a certified danger to the couple but becomes an ally because of a fortunate pastime.

Director Robert Zemeckis keeps all of this going beautifully, punctuated by thousands of gunshots that rarely do anybody any harm, even with machine guns fired at close range.

Given the outlook, "Stone" probably won't need any excuses later as to why it didn't do business. But this is one time the filmmakers can't blame the marketers. Since serving as the film's coproducer, Jack Brodsky has since gone on to become ad-pub-promo chief at 20th, which is distributing the pic. —*Har.*

Anou Banou Or Daughters Of Utopia
(WEST GERMAN-DOCU-COLOR)

Berlin, Feb. 27.

An Archange Film Productions with the ZDF (Second German TV Channel). Written and directed by Edna Politi. Camera (color), Nurith Aviv; editor, Elisabeth Waelchli, Politi; sound, Dani Natowich. Reviewed at the Akademie die Kunste, Berlin, Feb. 27, 1984. Running time: **85 MINS.**

This documentary about six Israeli pioneer women fits nicely into this year's Berlin Forum program, which focused on ethnography, paid a tribute to the production efforts of the Second German Channel in the frame of "Das Kleine Fernsehspiel" (The Little TV play), and included many subjects of political and social relevance.

Indeed, filmmaker Edna Politi, a Lebanese-born Israeli based now in Paris, fills the bill nicely on all the levels. The film was commissioned by German TV, and Politi, well known for her leftist political stands and her pro-Palestinian opinions (her first film was "For the Palestinians, an Israeli Testifies") has worked her way carefully to light up the Middle East conflict, being faithful to her position but also never tampering with the material.

The bulk of the film consists of six long interviews with women who went to Israel, then Palestine, in the '20s, and are now looking back at the dreams they had once and the reality they have bred. The narrative titles between the interviews suggests some of Politi's own opinions, and the Israeli-Arab conflict is featured more by the reluctance of subjects to go further than a certain point into this matter, rather than the opinions voiced.

Still, the outcome is evident: there is a certain common denominator in the reticence to deal with this matter, and an interview with a Communist activist of the same generation offers the alternative, if very radical view, of someone who has already reached conclusions the other women are not as yet prepared to accept.

Since the film was shot before the summer of 1982, the Lebanon War is not referred to, but the human background could be helpful in understanding some of its aspects. Also, Politi comes back time and again to the status of women in the Israeli society, less flattering than it is usually considered to be.

One topic on which interviewees are very explicit is their relative disenchantment with Israeli society as it is today in comparison with what they hoped, at the time, it would grow into. These criticisms, as painful as they may be, are made without bitterness, somewhere behind them lurking the hope that present situation may still be only temporary and will improve somewhere in future.

Politi deals in a straightforward way with all this material and even when she does not agree with the people she talks to, she allows them to express themselves freely, a bond of sympathy somehow being suggested between them. While it is doubtful if this would be right for normal commercial theatrical release, it might easily fit in with specialized programs and tv programming. —*Edna.*

Slapstick Of Another Kind
(COLOR)

Limited chances for a one-joke fantasy comedy.

Hollywood, March 23.

An International Film Marketing and Entertainment Releasing Co. release of an S. Paul Co. production, produced in association with Serendipity Prods. Executive producers, Hank Paul, Larry Sugar, Dan Murphy. Produced by Steven Paul; line producer, Patrick Wright. Directed by Steven Paul. Stars Jerry Lewis, Madeline Kahn, Marty Feldman. Screenplay, Steven Paul, based on Kurt Vonnegut's novel "Slapstick;" camera (MGM color), Anthony Richmond; editor, Doug Jackson; supervising editor, Ross Albert; music, Morton Stevens; sound, Bill Teague, Chip Garamella; assistant director, Benjamin Legrand; production design, Joel Schiller; set decoration, Albert Heintzelman; special effects makeup, Robert Zraick, Steve Laporte, Ve Neill; technical director, Ariel Levy; special effects; William D. Nipper, Tim O'Connell; special visual effects, Private Stock Effects Inc.; additional visual effects, MGM Labs; associate producer, Murray Schwartz; casting, Dorothy Koster-Paul. Reviewed at Paramount Theater, Hollywood, March 23, '84. (MPAA Rating: PG). Running time: **87 MINS.**

Wilbur Swain/Caleb Swain	Jerry Lewis
Eliza Swain/Letitia Swain	Madeline Kahn
Sylvester	Marty Feldman
Dr. Frankenstein	John Abbott
U.S. president	Jim Backus
Col. Sharp	Samuel Fuller
Anchorman	Merv Griffin
Ambassador Ah Fong	Pat Morita
Alien father (voice)	Orson Welles

Also with: Virginia Graham, Ben Frank, Cherie Harris, Robert Hackman, Eugene Choy, Ken Johnson, Peter Kwong, Richard Lee-Sung, Steve Aaron, Becca Edwards, Steven Paul, Patrick Wright.

Special Visual Effects Unit Credits
Private Stock Effects: producer-supervisor, C.N. Comisky; technical director, Ken Jones; exec producer, Larry Benson, production design-second unit director, John Muto; camera, Dennis Skotak, George Dodge; stop-motion animation, Ernest D. Farino; special visual consultant, Robert Skotak; technical consultant, Austin McKinney; production manager, Steve Fagerquist.

Formerly released in Germany in a substantially different version, a re-edited "Slapstick Of Another Kind" is now opening in America two years after it was filmed. Picture is a kind-hearted quirky comedy based on Kurt Vonnegut novel "Slapstick," but is essentially a one joke affair stretched out over 87 minutes. Star cast including Jerry Lewis, Madeline Kahn and the late Marty Feldman, plus literary interest in Vonnegut should provoke some initial, but shortlived, boxoffice interest. Longer life is possible as a cult item.

Film is built around the birth of twins so ugly that they are sequestered by their rich and famous parents, Jerry Lewis and Madeline Kahn. In reality kids are messengers from another planet sent to straighten out problems on earth. Lewis and Kahn play dual roles as the parents and kids with the help of cosmetic facial flaws.

Secret of the twins is their hidden super intelligence which is only present when they are together. They conceal their intelligence thinking that adults want them to be dumb like they are. What there is of a plot involves attempts by midget Chinese, the planet's most advanced species, to capture the twins and use their mental powers for their own profit.

Picture manages a few good gags but tone is generally inconsistent vacillating between slapstick, fairy tale and social satire. Laughs are more subtle than the belly variety and Lewis is mostly subdued here. Spectacle of the twins putting their misshapen heads together is funny only once, but repeated frequently.

Vonnegut's whimsical atmosphere doesn't come through enough, possibly because of the obvious moralistic tone of the picture. Simplistic observations about how people should "begin to listen with their hearts" and treat each other like family are well-meaning but reek of a kind of '60s philosophy which belies the superior intelligence supposedly at work here.

There are, however, some definite fringe benefits in the film. Voice-over of the alien father who masterminds the twins' visit to earth is supplied by Orson Welles. Sam Fuller, acting rather than directing, is thoroughly amusing as Col. Sharp, headmaster of a sadistic military school. Fuller plays his part without once removing his cigar from his mouth.

Marty Feldman is delightful as Sylvester, faithful servant to the twins. Equipped with busy eyebrows and his signature bulging eyes, Feldman is all mischief here, one of his last roles.

Special effects such as the Chinese mini-missile and the twins' thought waves are cheerfully primitive. The low-budget feel of the production actually adds to the charm of the film. Paul's direction seems haphazard at times as if he couldn't always decide in what direction to lead this shaggy dog story. — *Jagr.*

The Stone Boy
(COLOR)

Terrific rural drama.

Hollywood, March 15.

A TLC Films release. Produced by Joe Roth, Ivan Bloch. Executive producer, James G. Robinson. Directed by Chris Cain. Stars Robert Duvall, Glenn Close. Screenplay, Gina Berriault; camera (DeLuxe color), Juan Ruiz-Anchia; editor, Paul Rubell; music, James Horner; production design, Joseph G. Pacelli; art director, Stephanie Wooley; costume design, Gail Viola; sound, Milton "Robby" Robinson, Josh Bleibtreu; associate producers, Daniel M. Farrell, David G. Hermelin; assistant director, Steven J. Tramz. Reviewed at the UA Coronet, Westwood, March 15, 1984. (MPAA rating: PG). Running time: **93 MINS.**

Joe Hillerman	Robert Duvall
Arnold Hillerman	Jason Presson
Andy Jansen	Frederic Forrest
Ruth Hillerman	Glenn Close
George Jansen	Wilford Brimley
Lu Jansen	Gail Youngs
Amalie	Cindy Fisher
Gary	Mayf Nutter
Nora Hillerman	Susan Blackstone
Eugene Hillerman	Dean Cain

Compelling drama of a midwestern farm family's shattering adjustment to a tragic death in the family represents a strong acquisition for 20th Century-Fox' new speciality film label, TLC Films. Director Chris Cain, in only his second feature, draws a remarkably restrained and moving performance from debuting child actor Jason Presson, who plays central role of a 12-year old brother who accidentally and tragically slays his older, beloved brother with a shotgun in the opening moments of the film. Toplining Robert Duvall and Glenn Close as the parents, with exceptional support from Wilford Brimley, Frederic Forrest and Gail Youngs (Duvall's real-life wife), the production's quiet power and momentum signals solid returns in TLC's speciality house venue.

Film should light up the career of hitherto little-known director Cain (his only other film was a skid row derelict drama, "Sixth and Main," released seven years ago). Pic also marks a smash screenplay debut by Gina Berriault, a novelist and Humanities prof at San Francisco State who adapted the script from one of her short stories in her book "The Infinite Passion of Expectation."

Shot last summer under producers Joe Roth and Ivan Bloch in Great Falls, Montana, production's sorrowful subject matter as family is rendered dazed and grief-stricken by the death of the older son, while young responsible brother retreats behind a wall of guilt, never lapses into sentimentality or melodrama. While a catch comparison might be a rural "Ordinary People," "The Stone Boy," in its inarticulate characters whose feelings tear them apart, is a singular and highly accessible film. The theme is about healing, not loss, and result strongly benefits from structural economy and rich, appealing lensing by Juan Ruiz-Anchia whose sparing masters and long shots always heighten the drama.

Duvall unthinkingly compounds the dazed misery of his younger son by stoically fostering a family attitude that denies the boy communication and love at a time when he desperately needs it. On the periphery are neighboring relatives (Forrest and Youngs) whose marriage is marred by philandering on the husband's part, by miscarriages on the wife's. Frowzy and downtrodden, Youngs (sister of actor John Savage and united on the screen for the first time with husband Duvall) plays a crucial role in the young boy's reawakening, while the youth's low-key grandfather, wonderfully played by Brimley, is the family's sole member to fully comprehend and effectively react to the turbulence the boy endures.

Film is continually marked by taut, dramatic scenes. The pastoral opening moments, jolting when a shotgun gets caught in a barb wire fence and blasts the teenage brother (played by Dean Cain, the director's son), are excruciating as the young boy sits numbly by his brother's body while the dawn turns to daylight. His return to the family kitchen to tell his parents and sister (Susan Blackstone) what has happened propels the narrative line from turmoil to misunderstandings to its ultimate compassion.

During the boy's runaway odyssey to Reno, film builds its momentum and Presson's final explosion of long-suppressed feeling comes unexpectedly in a bus when the boy spots a young, carefree mother sitting alone with her baby. In the film's most emotional moment, the

boy moves into the empty seat beside the mother and spills his anguish to the stranger. The brief role of the girl is splendidly played by Linda Hamilton.

Others in sharp supporting roles are Cindy Fisher as Forrest's short-lived fling and Mayf Nutter as a happy singer on the road.
—*Loyn*.

Almonds And Raisins
(BRITISH-B&W-DOCU)

Berlin, Feb. 26.
A Brook Productions and Willowgold Production, London. (TeleCulture release in U.S.) Produced by David Elstein and Russ Karel. A Documentary Film directed by Russ Karel. Screenplay, Wolf Mankowitz; camera (black and white), Jacee Laskus; editor, Christopher Barnes; sound, Andy Rovins; music, John Altman; sets, Ralph Steadman; production manager, Mary Oppé. Reviewed at Berlin Film Fest (Information Show), Feb. 26, '84. Running time: 90 MINS.
With a commentary by Orson Welles and featuring, in interviews, Herschel Bernardi, Joseph Green, Zvee Scooler, Seymour Rechtzeit, Leo Fuchs, Miriam Kressyn, David Opatashu.

For those who follow film history, Russ Karel's documentary, "Almonds and Raisins," is a real treat. This is an historical chronicle with clips from features, still-photos, posters, and other memorabilia on the Yiddish cinema in several countries at the beginning of the sound period. Docu's counterpart in West Germany last year was Hans Peter Kochenrath's "Das Jiddische Kino" (The Yiddish Cinema), aired on Second German Television (ZDF) in April 1983 to accompany a Filmforum series of broadcasted Yiddish feature films. For the record, Yiddish films have been restored by Sharon Pucker Rivo and Miriam Saul Krant at the National Center for Jewish Film of Brandeis University in the U.S. — in fact, much of the material in both Kochenrath's and Karel's documentaries has been supplied by this archival source.

"Almonds and Raisins" traces the forgotten phenomenon of some 300 films made in the Yiddish language, nearly all of them during the early sound period (wherein the language could be heard) up to the time of the Second World War. Accompanying this docu on the program of the Info Show was Edgar G. Ulmer's "Fishke der Krumer" (1938), produced for audiences in the Jewish quarter of lower New York City; pic was long believed lost, but was then found and completely restored by the Brandeis center (it's now in release under the title "The Light Ahead").

In "Almonds and Raisins" Karel revives the New York period from 1900 to 1920, the years in which more than a million and a half Jews migrated from Eastern Europe to the Lower East Side. Many of these emigrants went on later to found Hollywood, practically

speaking, while the first talkie only missed by a commercial hair of being filmed in the language it thematically embraced: Alan Crosland's "The Jazz Singer" (1927). That film alone spurred the making of a string of Yiddish talkies, which in turn played Yiddish cinemas until the culture was gradually assimilated into the American experience.

Orson Welles narrates, and among those interviewed are Herschel Bernardi and the Polish/Yiddish/American filmmaker Joseph Green, who made some of the last expressions of Yiddish cinematic art — "Yidi mit'l Fidl" (1936) and "A Brivele der Mamen" (1938) — in Poland before the curtain rang down tragically. Besides Green, the American features by Maurice Schwartz ("Tevye," 1939) and the aforementioned Ulmer are singled out as an additional masterpieces in the movement. Particularly of interest is the manner in which the commentary traces historical change-of-perspective through the films as they were produced. Missing is the crucial early silent period, particularly a word for the record on the Soviet/Russian/Yiddish film productions (four produced between 1925 and 1933); yet that might have meant a second docu altogether.

This docu scores as a must-see on the grounds alone that some 12,000,000 once spoke Yiddish, and the language today is kept alive by noted writers, like the Nobel Prize winner Isaac Bashevis Singer, and the publication of Yiddish journals: e.g., "Di Goldene Kejt" in Israel and "Sowetisch Hejmland" in the USSR. One day, a modern Yiddish film along the lines of Joan Micklin Silver's "Hester Street" might be produced again for an appreciative public.—*Holl.*

Moscow On The Hudson
(COLOR)

Well-acted picture for a very limited audience.

Hollywood, March 19.
A Columbia Pictures release, produced and directed by Paul Mazursky. Stars Robin Williams. Screenplay, Mazursky and Leon Capetanos; camera (Metrocolor), Donald McAlpine; editor, Richard Halsey; sound, Dennis Maitland; production design-coproducer, Pato Guzman; costumes. Albert Wolsky; assistant director, Alex Hapsas; music, David McHugh. Reviewed at the Academy of Motion Picture Arts & Sciences, Beverly Hills, March 19, 1984. (MPAA rating: R). Running' time: 115 MINS.
Vladimir Ivanoff . . . . Robin Williams
Lucia Lombardo . . . . Maria Conchita Alonso
Lionel Witherspoon . . . . . . Cleavant Derricks
Orlando Ramirez . . . . Alejandro Rey
Boris . . . . Savely Kramarov
Anatoly . . . . Elya Baskin
Yuri . . . . Oleg Rudnik
V's grandfather . . . . Alexander Beniaminov
V's mother . . . . Ludmila Kramerevsky
V's father . . . . Ivo Vrzal
Sasha . . . . Natalie Iwanow
Lionel's grandfather . . . . Tiger Haynes

L's mother . . . . Edye Byrde
L's stepfather . . . . Robert MacBeth

"Moscow On The Hudson" is a sweet, beautifully performed picture that unfortunately wanders around several patriotic themes that are worth remembering without necessarily being worth paying for the reminder.

Directed by Paul Mazursky with his usual unusual touches, "Moscow" would be in a lot of trouble without a superbly sensitive portrayal by Robin Williams of a gentle Russian circus musician who makes a sudden decision to defect while visiting the U.S.

As Mazursky sees it, Williams thus becomes one more in a flood of immigrants who still are coming to this country and discovering virtues that those already here many times forget. Of course, they also encounter the faults, as well.

But "Moscow" gets this across more with mood than message, building satisfying scenes and images without really latching onto an involving story beyond the question — never much in doubt — of whether Williams will fit in.

That aside, the entire film is full of performers working way beyond the material. Cleavant Derricks is especially good as a department store security guard who saves Williams from the KGB and takes him home to live in Harlem. Maria Conchita Alonso is also spirited as Williams' Italian girlfriend with her own hopes for America, which don't necessarily fit his. Their romance is useful, even if finally unbelievable.

With the kind of awkward title that usually goes on audio-visual materials for high schools, "Moscow On The Hudson" would serve well enough there for the civics class. But it would play even better over in the drama department. Unfortunately, major-studio releases need a broader audience than either or both. —*Har.*

Rita Ritter
(WEST GERMAN-COLOR)

Berlin, Feb. 25.
A Herbert Achternbusch Production. Features entire cast. Written and directed by Achternbusch. Camera (color), Jörg Schmidt-Reitwein; sound, Sylvia Tewes; editor, Ulrike Joanni; makeup and costumes, Ann Poppel. Reviewed at Berlin Film Fest (Forum), Feb. 25, '84. Running time: 93 MINS.
Cast: Annamirl Bierbichler, Christiane Cohendy, Armin Müller-Stahl, Barbara Valentin, Eva Mattes, Sepp Bierbichler.

Literary director Herbert Achternbusch turns out talky features of an autobiographical nature as fast as he can pen a satirical essay. In many ways, he is quite gifted at a turn of a phrase or setting up, with the equally talented lenser Jörg Schmidt-Reitwein, a camera shot to allow the thesps (usually himself) as much space as Charlie Chaplin did in asserting his other self as the supreme object of contemplation.

In "Rita Ritter" (one of three Achternbusch pics programmed at the Berlin fest) Achternbusch only appears as an "extra," the main roles left to stock performers and professional thesps: Annamirl Bierbichler, Sepp Bierbichler, Christiane Cohendy, Eva Mattes, Barbara Valentin and Armin Müller-Stahl. The script is one of the wittiest and most entertaining since "Bye Bye Bavaria" (1977).

A writer without much success in love and letters decides to change his sex and becomes a woman named Rita, honoring a former lover. As Rita, the woman playwright, she discovers that one of her dreams is being staged by a director in Paris, who invites her to attend performance. She goes, and who should Rita the writer find in one of the performing roles but Rita the former lover. Love erupts again like a volcano — and it doesn't seem to make such differences as to the mistaken identities. The walk through Paris to the Eiffel Tower is a stitch!—*Holl.*

El Señor Galindez
(Senor Galindez)
(SPANISH-COLOR)

Berlin, Feb. 28.
An Ibercine production, produced by Severino Pascuel. Features entire cast. Directed and screenplay by Rodolfo Kuhn, from the stage play by Eduardo Pavlovsky. Camera (Eastmancolor), Angel Luis Fernandez; editor, Roberto Fandino; sound, J.R. Ibiricu; art director, Aldo Guglielmone. Reviewed at Zoo Palast, Berlin (Berlin Film Festival, Official Section, Out of Competition), Feb. 27, 1984. Running Time: 87 MINS.
Beto .... Hector Alterio
Pepe .... Joaquin Hinojosa
Eduardo .... Antonio Banderas
Maria .... Maria Casanova
Coca .... Cecilia Roth
Sara .... Luisa Rodrigo
Maria Luisa .... Laura Culat
Rosi .... Lourdes Amor
Noemi .... Roberta Kuhn
Stripper .... Ella

A gripping pic about the dreadful banality of fascist torturers, "Senor Galindez" was originally seen as a stage production in Argentina in the early '70s. In the light of the tragedies that befell that country later in the decade, the piece takes on an even greater impact. Now filmed by Argentine expatriate Rodolfo Kuhn, and with Argentine actor Hector Alterio in the lead role, the material makes for a haunting production.

The play was obviously inspired both by Samuel Beckett and Harold Pinter; Beto is a happily married man who loves his wife and daughter, while his partner Pepe is a loner who gets off on watching a stripper in a nightclub. They work for the never-seen eponymous Galindez, who gives them tele-

phoned instructions. Their headquarters is an isolated building, set up for the purposes of torture, and on this particular day they've been told to train a new recruit, Eduardo, who has to learn all the tricks of the trade. And, while awaiting their latest victims, the obliging Galindez sends them a couple of prosties to "play with."

Quietly horrifying tale shows its theatrical origins, but has a fascination and grimly humorous appeal. Thesping is first rate, with Alterio a standout as the sinister family man and Joaquin Hinojosa also impressive as the more obviously sadistic character.

Technically tops, film is a timely reminder that evil lurks behind the most bland façades. It's to be hoped that, with a new democratic government in Argentina, the film will be shown there in the near future.—*Strat.*

Cenerentola '80
(Cinderella '80)
(ITALIAN-FRENCH-COLOR)

Rome, March 22.
A C.D.E. (Compania Distribuzione Europea) release, produced by Roberto Malenotti for RAI-TV Channel 2, TVC-Television Center, and Stand'Art. Directed by Roberto Malenotti. Stars Bonnie Bianco and Pierre Cosso. Screenplay, Ugo Liberatore, Ottavio Alessi and Roberto Malenotti; camera (Technicolor), Dante Spinotti; editor, Angelo Curi; art director, Paolo Biagetti; music, Guido and Maurizio De Angelis, sung by Bonnie Bianco and Pierre Cosso. Reviewed at Barberini Cinema, Rome, March 21, 1984. Running time: 115 MINS.
Cindy .... Bonnie Bianco
Mizio .... Pierre Cosso
Marianne .... Sandra Milo
Prince Gherardeschi .... Adolfo Celi
His wife .... Sylva Koscina
Harry .... Vittorio Caprioli

Roberto Malenotti's "Cinderella '80" takes off from the clever idea of updating an old fairy tale into a modern-day, tongue-in-cheek teen musical. Though the material often feels forced to fit the mold, pic has some strong moments thanks to the appeal of debuting American singer-actress Bonnie Bianco in the title role. Principally packaged for Italo and French markets (costar is young French thesp Pierre Cosso), pic has high production values and could be picked up elsewhere.

Cindy is a natural child who has been raised by her father (Vittorio Caprioli), owner of a Brooklyn pizza parlor. Her stepmother is a vain, foolish virago who hates Cindy but dotes on her two legitimate sisters, whom she is taking to Rome to study classical music.

But the real talent of the family is Cindy; she attends a performing arts academy right out of "Fame" and does the vocals to her own rock songs. Tagging along to Rome at her father's insistence, she joins the band of an incognito Roman prince, Mizio (Cosso), in rebellion

against his stuffy parents (Adolfo Celi and Sylva Koscina).

Pic climaxes at a grand ball in Mizio's house where fairy godmother-astrologer Sandra Milo gets Cindy out of dungarees and into a decent evening dress. In this version, Cinderella loses her shoe by throwing it at the Prince when she discovers his real identity and that he's been slumming to court her.

Sumptuous interiors, Dante Spirotti's lush camerawork and a fine cast of supporting actors, notably Vittorio Caprioli as the Brooklyn pizza maker and Adolfo Celi as Mizio's snobbish père, add a quality touch to the just for fun rags to riches tale. Guido and Maurizio De Angelis's music is up and down, bleeding into watered-down disco at times, but Bianco belts out a few solid numbers. In spite of scripting difficulties with all the American characters, she manages to stay natural throughout the film. Cosso, with a moony, teen idol face, stretches credibility as Prince Charming. Both have been badly dubbed into flat, nuance-less Italian. — *Yung.*

Bianca
(ITALIAN-COLOR)

Rome, March 23.
A C.I.D.I.F. release, produced by Achille Manzotti for Faso Film. Directed by Nanni Moretti. Stars Moretti and Laura Morante. Screenplay by Moretti and Sandra Petraglia. Camera (color), Luciano Tovoli; editor, Mirco Garrone; music, Franco Piersanti. Reviewed at Eden Cinema, Rome, March 23, 1984. Running time: 96 MINS.
Michele .... Nanni Moretti
Bianca .... Laura Morante
Neighbor .... Remo Remotti
Italian teacher .... Giovanni Buttafava

Nonconformist helmer Nanni Moretti has been the *enfant terrible* of the Italian cinema since his surprise hit "Ecce Bombo" opened the door to youthful comedian-directors in 1978. In spite of fanfare, "Bianca" has gotten off to a slow start. Part of the reason may be pic's glum finale, outstripping the querulous humor that is the director's trademark. Another factor could be that pic's introverted, personal theme doesn't strike young adult audiences with the same force of recognition as in previous films.

Pic is producer Achille Manzotti's break-away venture from routine comedies into the land of serious, festival-directed cinema. "Bianca" may go to Cannes and certainly deserves fest exposure.

Tale centers on Michele (Moretti), a young mathematics teacher dismayed in an ultra-liberal, alternative high school. The "Marilyn Monroe School" is the source of a number of good gags, ranging from the insufferably hip faculty to jukeboxes in every classroom.

A school psychiatrist is on hand to analyze not the students but the

staff; Michele a hopeless neurotic and foot fetishist, is sane enough to steer clear of him. Happy family life is his obsession and he meddles in his friend's affairs in a doomed attempt to keep their relationships intact and "normal." A few who have deviated from Michele's fixed schemes of happiness are found murdered, and the police suspect him.

Desperately longing for companionship but terrified of involvement, Michele falls in love in spite of himself with the French teacher, Bianca (Laura Morante, a newcomer more interesting than her respective roles, which in this case is to look beautiful, mysterious and demure). The victim of Michele's hyperbolic jealousy, Bianca too is fated to disappear. Michele's long, meandering confession to the police chief is anti-climactic.

A talented comic, on the screen Moretti is less an actor than a flawed human being with twitches, quirks and a cracked voice, able to create a powerful bond with the audience. As a murderer he is as preposterous and sympathetic as Chaplin's Monsieur Verdoux. In his obstinate refusal to accept the sad realities of life, he remains trapped between the mindless idiocy of the Marilyn Monroe School and a hopeless yearning to be part of the ideal family he spies on across the courtyard. — *Yung.*

The World Of Tomorrow
(COLOR/B&W-DOCU-16m)

A film from An American Portrait Production Unit, of Media Study, Buffalo and New York. Project director, Gerald O'Grady. Producers and directors, Lance Bird and Tom Johnson. Screenplay, John Crowley; narrator, Jason Robards; historical consultant, Warren Susman; editor, Kate Hirson. No other credits. Reviewed at Film Forum, New York, March 8, 1984. Running time: 78 MINS.

This documentary about the New York World's Fair of 1939-40 — attended by 40,000,000 in its short life of 15 months, cut short by World War II — is "The World of Tomorrow," a term derived from the futuristic theme of the Fair. The film reaches back 45 years, using stock footage and old ballads, to what may now seem to have been a happier, simpler time.

It is an appealing film, more urgent than nostalgic, because it contains parallels and reverberations that make it timely today; a kind of warning.

The narration, written with poetic grace by John Crowley and spoken with rough sentimentality by Jason Robards, asks us to pretend Robards is now an older man, remembering how it was long ago, when he visited the Fair at age 10. It's a useful conceit to evoke an elegiac remembrance of things past (although in actuality Robards never visited the Fair, only its San Francisco counterpart, a comparatively minor twin).

Having set a tone and established a format, Robards tours the fairgrounds, re-visiting the General Motors Futurama super-exhibit, the Billy Rose Aquacade, the many foreign pavilions, the amusements and scientific wonders and architectural marvels. President Franklin D. Roosevelt's opening-day speech, in the first television broadcast, set the tone of faith in a democratic and technologically modern America. He and others still live on film in "The World of Tomorrow," affirming America's faith in its future, including such figures as New York Mayor Fiorello H. La Guardia, Fair czar Grover Whalen, Henry Ford, J. Edgar Hoover, and such popular personalities as Bill (Bojangles) Robinson, Ethel Merman, Mickey Rooney and Judy Garland. "Happy days are here again," said the nation, now that the Great Depression had ended, a naive optimism symbolized by the Fair itself.

"The World of Tomorrow," in genre a compilation documentary recycling fragments of old promotional films, newsreels, home movies, cartoons and junk memorabilia, is entirely successful as entertainment, culture or social history. The New York Council for the Humanities, and the National Endowment for The Arts through the Independent Documentary Fund of WNET/13, New York, abetted by the Corporation for Public Broadcasting, the Ford Foundation and the Pew Memorial Trust all deserve applause. —*Hitch.*

Among The Cinders

(NEW ZEALAND-
W. GERMAN-COLOR)

Berlin, Feb. 20.
A Pacific Films production, in association with NDR and New Zealand Film Commission. Produced by John O'Shea. Directed by Rolf Haedrich. Features entire cast. Script, O'Shea and Haedrich, from novel by Maurice Shadbolt; camera (color), Rory O'Shea; editors, Inge Behrens, John Kiley; music, Jan Preston; art director, Gerry Luhman. Reviewed at Atelier am Zoo, Berlin (Berlin Film Festival, Special Screenings Section), Feb. 18, 1984. Running time: **99 MINS.**
Nick Flinders ....Paul O'Shea
Hubert Flinders ....Derek Hardwick
Beth Flinders ....Yvonne Lawley
Sally.......................Rebecca Gibney
Glenys ....Amanda Jones
Helga Flinders ....Bridget Armstrong
Frank Flinders ....Maurice Shadbolt
Derek Flinders ....Marcus Broughton
Kate ....Ngaire Woods
Michael ....Christopher Hansard
Sam Waikai ....Ricky Duff
Mrs. Waikai...............Harata Solomon

World preemed in the Special Screenings section at the Berlin fest, "Among the Cinders" is a "coming-of-age" pic adapted from the novel by Maurice Shadbolt. Helmer Rolf Haedrich, who's made films in Germany since 1958, came to New Zealand to direct and also wrote the screenplay together with vet producer John O'Shea. Adaptation uses a considerable amount of first-person narration to help tell the tale of a 16-year-old boy, Nick, going through adolescent traumas. He lives with his devoutly religious parents in a rural part of the country, and when his best friend, a Maori, dies in an accident when they're out climbing together he feels responsible. He goes to live with his grandparents, but when his grandmother expires, grandfather — without telling the boy the old lady is dead — abruptly decides to set out with the lad on a hiking tour. It might make sense in the novel, but it doesn't in the film.

Overall, and despite handsome photography by Rory O'Shea of the glorious New Zealand countryside, the film is a distinct disappointment. Screenplay is awkward and filled with risible dialog (such as, "It's hard to find a real man these days," spoken by a voluptuous blonde, first discovered bathing naked in a lake). Even more of a problem is the acting. Apart from a modestly professional performance by Derek Hardwick as the grandfather, the cast appears amateurish; dialog is delivered flatly, players move awkwardly and without conviction. Though he tries hard, young Paul O'Shea is really not up to his demanding role.

Television sales are indicated on pic's handsome locations and visual dress, but theatrically this will be a hard slog outside home territory.
—*Strat.*

The Big Lever
(U.S.-COLOR-DOCU-16m)

Berlin, Feb. 20.
A production of Appalshop, Whitesburg, Kentucky. A film by Frances Morton. Running time: **60 MINS.**
Reviewed at Messe (Market), Berlin International Film Festival, Feb. 20, 1984.

This delightful documentary was produced by Appalshop, an Appalachian film/video collective in Kentucky, with funding from the National Endowment for the Humanities and other sources. Technically, thoroughly professional, even if it lacks the slickness and super-star narrators of network documentaries like "CBS Reports."

In addition, film has a special intimacy and affection for these mountain folks that the producers would probably overlook in their zeal to confirm the L'il Abner stereotypes. Film is authentic down-home Americana and thoroughly entertaining, even if documentaries almost by definition are supposed to be tedious and didactic.

In "The Big Lever" the time is 1978 and Richard Nixon is cautiously emerging from his self-imposed exile after resignation in 1974. For his debut Nixon accepts an invitation to visit Leslie County, Kentucky, rock-ribbed Republican redoubt in the heart of largely Democratic Dixie. Grassroots local politicos greet Nixon at the airport and local mountain folk cheer him in a big welcoming rally at the sweltering high-school gymnasium. Nixon is genuinely grateful for this confirmation of acceptance.

Thus "The Big Lever" explores perverse party loyalty through the Nixon visit and also through the up-and-down career of the incumbent county Judge-Executive, host of Nixon who loves to embrace him for photographers. This man subsequently seeks re-election despite a Federal conviction for vote fraud conspiracy, and wins.

These mountain voters hear and applaud the full gamut of political oratory, from such profound Nixonisms as "America is worth living for" to the campaign promises of the fat lady running as cook for the local jail — "I've been cooking for 26 years. Vote for me — I'll feed you good if you get in jail."

"The Big Lever" demonstrates, states one bemused Southern professor, "how deeply corruption is engrained in the political life of America — as American as Mom and apple pie. And terrifying."

Some scenes come close to the social satire films of Preston Sturges in kidding small-town American life. But this is authentic documentary, no Hollywood, and a microcosm of national politics, of special interest in an election year. Where else would we learn that a Kentucky candidate must spin good yarns and must memorize not only the names of all his constituent voters but the names also of their kids and dogs? "I hope you live two thousand years and never die!" is a favorite farewell of Kentucky candidates. Appalshop gets it all with its merciless yet humorous eye.

"The Big Lever" has participated in many U.S. and foreign festivals. Other Appalshop films deal with Appalachian history and culture, aging, energy and the environment, women and social issues. Appalshop is involved in Kentucky television, conducts photography workshops, produces Roadside Theater, and produces and distributes recordings of mountain music. —*Hitch.*

Committed
(U.S.-B&W-16m)

Berlin, Feb. 25.
A Production of Story Films, New York; co-produced, co-written and co-edited by Sheila McLaughlin and Lynne Tillman. Camera (black and white), Heinz Emigholz; original music, Phillip Johnston. Reviewed at Interna-tional Forum of Young Cinema, Berlin International Film Festival, Feb. 25, 1984. Represented at Berlin by Independent Feature Project, New York. Running time: **77 MINS.**
Frances Farmer ....Sheila McLaughlin
Lillian Farmer ....Victoria Boothby
Clifford Odets ....Lee Breuer
Dr. Taylor ....John Erdman
Dr. Kraus..................Heinz Emigholz

"Committed" is a fiction narrative film derived from facts about the trouble life of Hollywood star and political activist Frances Farmer. Close to docu-drama in form, "Committed" suffers from that curse of struggling New York independents, low budget, which prevents filmmakers Lynne Tillman and Sheila McLaughlin from fully developing the fascinating and complex raw material of Farmer's life, especially its cultural and political context.

An alumna of the famed Group Theater in New York, where she appeared on stage in Clifford Odets' "Golden Boy" (in the role taken by Barbara Stanwyck in the film adaptation), Farmer was politically left liberal-radical and journeyed to the U.S.S.R. before age 21. Arriving in Hollywood during the scandal of her Soviet trip, Farmer embarked on a lightning career that exploited her stunning blond beauty, much as Marilyn Monroe was to do several decades later. But within 10 years, Farmer had earned a dubious and disturbing reputation as a troublemaker. An alcoholic, she was arrested for drunk driving, publicly quarreled with her shrewish mother about her politics, and was shut away in a mental hospital for five years, subjected to electroshock and drug therapy, ultimately lobotomized, then released into the custody of her parents, her life shattered. Farmer is sensed as a victim of "the system" — Hollywood and the McCarthyites and vindictive doctors. She is committed (to the asylum) because she was committed (to progressive causes).

Drawing upon the facts of the extraordinary Farmer saga, the filmmakers compress time and events into a few key scenes that are played as intense but static dramatic confrontations — Farmer against her mother, Farmer against the psychiatrists, Farmer against the legal authorities determined to punish her for allegedly promoting Communism. Farmer is shown also in long dramatic monologs, rather more rambling than introspective, as nurses and mental patients move about in the background. Farmer is seen in bed in another scene, the dupe and plaything of playwright Odets, opportunist who abandoned the idealism of Broadway for a lucrative screenwriting career

These and other episodes the Farmer story are not linked in a continuous narrative thrust, and thus are merely interesting when they should have been electrifying.

In addition to defects of script and direction, filmmaker McLaughlin is inadequate physically and temperamentally for the demanding role of Farmer.

Because a mini-cult about Farmer has grown from recent revival of several of her Hollywood films of the 1930's and 1940's, further abetted by the 1982 "Frances" of Jessica Lange (an Oscar nominee as Best Actress), the chances of "Committed" to find audiences in special art-house situations are encouraging. For promotional purposes, the film can be exploited in terms of its connections to popular concerns with militant feminism, oppressive machismo, bureaucratized psychiatry, and right-wing political intolerance. Public television — which happily will accommodate minority tastes, controversy and imperfect but worthwhile endeavors — also seems a likely bet for "Committed."

—*Hitch.*

Keine Zufällige Geschichte
(Not By Coincidence)
(WEST GERMAN-COLOR)

Berlin, Feb. 22.
A Charlotte Kerr production in association with Sokol Film. Written and directed by Charlotte Kerr. Camera (color), Peter Braumuller; sound, Heiko Hinderks; editor, Rosemarie Stenzel-Quast. Reviewed at the Berlin Film Festival (non-competing), Feb. 22, 1984. Running Time: **89 MINS.**
With Jules Dassin, Melina Mercouri.

As films on filmmakers and film performers go, "Not By Coincidence" fares rather well. Focusing on the lives of director Jules Dassin and his wife, actress (and Greek culture minister) Melina Mercouri, the picture is a vignettish, often intriguing study on what appears to be, on the surface, an odd artistic union.

The main asset of the film is writer-director Charlotte Kerr's ability to comprehend the Dassin-Mercouri relationship. There's a real sense of what attracted the two to each other and what has kept the relationship strong and balanced. However, this is only a small element in the documentary which also addresses their artistic careers and personal lives.

The use of film clips to chart the two careers is hardly exhaustive and some choices of sequences are indeed odd, as are omissions. The rambling nature of the study suggests a lack of initial focus and the probability of mountains of footage left on the cutting-room floor.

Still, there are some priceless moments in the course of the 90 minutes. Majority of this material centers on Dassin's blacklisted years, his battles at MGM and a brief vignette in Hollywood recently with other former blacklistees. Dassin's yarns are humorous and insightful, but Kerr finds no easy way to incorporate them into the film without tipping the focus and even-handedness of the venture.

Venture should find some television interest although the subjects don't have quite the profile, topicality or notoriety of recent documentary profiles on Marlene Dietrich and Jerry Lewis. There's also potential classroom use more for insights into working than in the actual films involved in Dassin and Mercouri's lives. —*Klad.*

The Hunters Of The Golden Cobra
(ITALIAN-COLOR)

A World Northal release of a Gico Cinematografica-Regal Film production. Produced by Gianfranco Couyoumdjian. Directed by Anthony M. Dawson (Antonio Margheriti). Features entire cast. Screenplay, Tito Carpi, from story by Couyoumdjian; camera (Eastman color), Sandro Mancori; editor, Alberto Moriani; music, Carlo Savina; special effects, Apollonio Abadesa; dubbing editor, Nick Alexander. Reviewed at 42d St. Times Square theater, N.Y., March 10, 1984. (No MPAA Rating). Running time: **94 MINS.**
Bob Jackson .... David Warbeck
June/April .... Almanta Suska
Capt. David Bracken .... John Steiner
Uncle .... Alan Collins
Yamato .... Protacio Dee

"The Hunters Of The Golden Cobra" is an unspectacular Italian adventure film, lensed in 1982 in the Philippines under the title "Raiders Of The Golden Cobra" and, not surprisingly, heavily derived from the worldwide hit "Raiders Of The Lost Ark." Trender is okay filler for action audiences.

British actor David Warbeck (whose post-synched dialog varies from a Yank accent in opening reels to his own Blighty voice in later reels) toplines as soldier-of-fortune Bob Jackson, working on missions in the Philippines during World War II with a British officer Bracken (John Steiner). He's tabbed by the Allies to return to an island jungle (site of film's one-year-earlier teaser opening) to retrieve a stolen idol, the Golden Cobra, worshiped by the native religious cult of doped-up Awoks, and believed to possess incredible powers.

Besides Bracken, Jackson is aided on his mission by June (Almanta Suska) and her uncle (Alan Collins), searching for June's twin sister April, who was lost in the jungle many years ago, and whom Jackson encountered in his first visit there, finding her to be a white queen lording it over the natives. After several double crosses, Jackson and April escape with the golden idol in a nicely-staged volcanic eruption climax.

Filmed on a low-budget and generally small scale (but including director Antonio Margheriti's usual quota of topnotch miniatures and special effects explosions), "Cobra" is of interest due to its careful transfer of the basic gimmicks of George Lucas/Steven Spielberg's "Raiders" to a new story and setting. Instead of Nazis, the supernatural totem of absolute power is being contested by the Japanese here, and numerous scenes recall the look & action of the original: opening and closing escape to a seaplane with blowdart natives in pursuit; hero thrown into a dungeon that fills with snakes; heroine kidnapped in an open-air market; even Warbeck exclaiming "I'm making this up as I go along" when caught in a tight spot, a la Indiana Jones.

Oddest touch is the film's unintentional predictive aspects: the baddies are named Awoks, a year or more before Lucas's race of Ewoks were made public in "Return Of The Jedi;" and dual-role-playing femme lead Almanta Suska is virtually a European double for Kate Capshaw, later to get the "Indiana Jones And The Temple Of Doom" plum part. Serendipity at work, no doubt.

Acting by a troupe of Margheriti regulars is okay, and for fans of this genre Warbeck and Margheriti have recently teamed up for another unauthorized "Raiders" pic, "The Ark Of The Sun God," filmed in Turkey.—*Lor.*

Smartgransen
(Beyond Sorrow, Beyond Pain)
(SWEDISH-DOCU-COLOR)

Berlin, Feb. 28.
A coproduction of SAFTRA and JOA Film and the Swedish Film Institute. Produced, written and directed by Agneta Elers-Jarleman. Coproducer, Lisabeth Gabrielsson. Camera (Eastmancolor), Peter Ostlund, Sten Holmberg, Jonas Hallqvist; editors, Dubravka Carnerud, Jarleman; music, Gunnar Edander; sound, Peter Ekvall, Mats Klyvare. Reviewed at the Berlin Film Festival (non-competing), Feb. 28, 1984. Running time: **74 MINS.**
With Jean Montgrenier, Agneta Elers-Jarleman.

A documentary of resounding power and depth, "Beyond Sorrow, Beyond Pain" cannot but help affect those who view it. The highly emotional first-hand nature of the material escapes pretention and self-consciousness to emerge a deeply felt, compelling and heartbreaking experience.

Filmmaker Agneta Elers-Jarleman focuses on former classmate and lover Jean Montgrenier, who was involved in a life-shattering auto accident in 1977. The accident resulted in extensive surgery on Montgrenier's face which left him blind, partially paralyzed and seemingly unable to bear or communicate.

Continuing his story five years later, Jarleman relates his progress as he begins to walk and, through songlike noises, attempts to communicate. Although an extraordinary development, Montgrenier has long since been labeled a hopeless case by hospital authorities and Jarleman's attempts to have him reclassified are generally fruitless.

Another important aspect of the documentary is Jarleman's incorporation of interviews with Montgrenier's friends who have over the years stopped visiting him. They serve as a tragic Greek chorus but in no way are intended as a finger-pointing exercise.

The most poignant element of the film is the manner in which Jarleman manages to address the probable frustration of her subject. The camera captures his often futile attempts to make himself understood. Clearly, he is not a hopeless case but because of ineffectual authorities one assumes further progress will be unlikely.

Length and the inability to market non-fiction features obviously makes "Beyond Sorrow, Beyond Pain" a highly doubtful theatrical release in most markets. However, both the craft and power of the message suggest strong television sales and festival screenings. Also, with strong exposure and reviewers, picture could make strong inroads in non-theatrical and specialized situations. — *Klad.*

Freiwild
(Fair Game)
(WEST GERMAN-POLISH-COLOR)

Berlin, Feb. 20.
A CCC-Filmkunst Production, Berlin, in coproduction with Film Polski, Warsaw, Film Group Zodiak; Artúr Brauner, producer. Stars Sharon Brauner. Directed by Jerzy Hoffman. Screenplay, Hoffman, Jan Purzycki, based on a story by Art Bernd and a manuscript by Paul Hengge and Bogdan Wojdowski; camera (color), Jerzy Goscik; sets, Maciek Putowski; costumes, Marta Kobierska; music, Andrzej Korzynski; editor, Zenon Piorecki; sound, Leonard Ksiezak; mixing, Dieter Schwarz; production manager (Zodiak), Wilhelm Hollender; production manager (CCC-Filmkunst), Wolf Brauner. Reviewed at Studio am Havelchaussee, Berlin, Feb. 20, '84. Running time: **90 MINS.**
Cast: Sharon Brauner (Ruth), Anna Dymna (Rachel), Günter Lamprecht (Kleinschmidt), Matthieu Carrière (Knoch).

Jerzy Hoffman's "Fair Game" — a coproduction between Film Polski and Artur Brauner's CCC-Filmkunst Studios in West Berlin — was lensed on location in Poland and in the CCC-Studios. That makes it a kind of first in the developing new line of coproductions between East and West lands. But even more: this also happens to be one of the most sensitively human feature films made on the Warsaw Ghetto and the Holocaust theme that has yet appeared.

"Fair Game" never loses sight of being a human drama, one that affects all the individuals in the film (whether good or bad, evil or indifferent, courageous or self-effacing). There are few, if any, stereotypes — and no "messages" of underscored statements at the cost of shelving the narrative line. Also, the perspective is through the eyes of a young girl of 12 or 13, who manages (accidentally or miraculously) to survive that chain of horrible historical events in Poland from 1939 to 1944. At the end, she is lost from our field of vision, but the spiritual force ofher presence is still felt — to the extent that one tends to view the film as a moral parable.

The story begins when Poland falls under the heel of the Third Reich. Ruth is rounded up with her mother and other women for transport to a secret place of execution in a woods — she escapes due to her mother's instinctive ingenuity in pushing her from the truck at an opportune moment. Next she is picked up by a friendly Polish farmer and hidden away in a shed; his wife, however, happens upon the secret and betrays both the girl and her husband at the same time, much to her ultimate regret. While in prison, Ruth is helped again at the last second due to her lithe frame: she is able to squeeze through a convenient hole in the make-shift jail; but the others, who have generously helped her, perish.

The girl is forever on the run — sometimes eating the food thrown to swine to calm her stomach pains, often helped by a sympathetic individual who simply takes pity on her without asking questions. In the final sequence, it's a Polish lad of her own age, working as a photographer's assistant allied with the Nazis. The boy hides Ruth from his boss, but danger rears its ugly head again with the arrival of a menacing SS-man (Matthieu Carrière) sent to overrule a compliant German commandant (Günter Lamprecht) and clean up the nest of Polish resistance in the area. The girl is discovered. Meanwhile, another execution is to take place in a quarry — and a secret resistance leader, a German woman attaché (Anna Dymna) to the commandant, prepares a trap for the Nazi officer. The plan goes awry in the end, but another surprise twist leads to a deadly shootout and then has the Jewish girl floating down a river stream on a raft in the fateful year of 1944. She is never heard from again.

Tightly directed and lensed from a camera-eye perspective by Jerzy Hoffman, "Fair Game" should find a positive echo an international fests and is assured of an arthouse run with proper handling. Sharon Brauner has to carry the entire film as the main figure always on camera, and her performance convinces on the energy expended alone. "Fair Game" is headed for a preem at an international fest, at last reports. — *Holl.*

Triumphs Of A Man Called Horse
(MEXICAN-U.S.-COLOR)

Ho-hum sendoff of a Western hero.

A Jensen Farley Pictures release of a film produced by Redwing Prods. S.A. in association with Transpacific Media Prods. and Hesperia Films S.A. Produced by Derek Gibson. Executive producer, Sandy Howard. Directed by John Hough. Stars Richard Harris. Screenplay, Ken Blackwell, Carlos Aured, based on story by Jack DeWitt and a character by Dorothy M. Johnson; camera (CFI color), John Alcott, John Cabrera; editor, Roy Watts, music, George Garvarentz; sound, Manuel Rincon; assistant director, Kuki Lopez; production design, Alan Roderick-Jones; art direction, Marilyn Taylor; production executive, Keith Rubinstein; associate producer, Donald R. Borchers; creative consultant, Sandra Bailey. Reviewed on HBO, N.Y., March 9, 1984. (MPAA Rating: PG). Running time: **84 MINS.**

Man Called Horse	Richard Harris
Koda	Michael Beck
Redwing	Ana De Sade
Capt. Cummings	Vaughn Armstrong
Elk Woman	Anne Seymour
Sgt. Bridges	Buck Taylor
Gance	Simon Andreu
Perkins	Lautaro Murua
Durand	Roger Cudney
Winslow	Gerry Gatlin
Mason	John Davis Chandler
Big Bear	Miguel Angel Fuentes

"Triumphs Of A Man Called Horse" reduces the large-scale Westerns "A Man ..." and "The Return Of A Man Called Horse" into a lowgrade B-picture format. Filmed in Mexico, Montana and Arizona in 1982, this picture was marginally released by Jensen Farley Pictures and is reviewed here for the record.

Producer Sandy Howard, following the current trend of aiming at series of films rather than mere sequels, set out here to create a new spinoff of his previous hits by casting Michael Beck as Koda, halfbreed son of Shunka Wakan (Richard Harris). As a transitional film, "Triumphs" falls flat, with original series star Harris killed off after half an hour.

Paternalistic theme is that Harris, the English nobleman who has spent 30 years with the Sioux indians, and his son are the only ones who can protect their adopted tribe from the Gold Rush white settlers who are greedily overrunning their land. A kindly army officer (Vaughn Armstrong) supports them in their efforts to keep the peace and uphold the treaty, but whites are staging killings on both sides to foment a war.

"Triumphs" pays mere lip service to those "elements" that worked in its predecessors: there is a suggestion of ESP and mysticism in Beck's nightmares and prescience concerning his father's death and other events; vet Anne Seymour follows Judith Anderson and Gale Sondergaard in the now gimmick role of tribal elder Elk Woman; highlights such as the chest-hoist ritual scene are featured in old flashback footage.

Beck's stilted, "proud" dialog readings are a boring cliché from old-fashioned noble savage films; Harris gueststars in his own picture and the supporting cast is weak. Sole highlight is the beautiful Mexican actress Ana De Sade, who had a small role in "The Return Of A Man ..." and here plays a Crow indian with whom Beck teams up after she's been attacked by whites.

Silly finale, wrapped up in the whirlwind fashion of a tv series episode, has De Sade (armed with bow & arrow) and Beck in a convenient shootout with the baddies. The settlers promptly leave, the soldiers go back to Ft. Laramie and the Indians are left happily to their Black Hills land.

End credits crawl reminds that the U.S. ended up breaking the treaty and stealing the Sioux' land, but that a 1980 Supreme Court ruling gave it back to them (plus $105,000,000 in damages) and 40,000 Sioux live there now. That's the sort of material that could yield a passable motion picture. — *Lor.*

Der Lachende Stern
(The Laughing Star)
(W. GERMAN-COLOR-DOCU)

Berlin, Feb. 21.

A Luxor Film Peter Kern Production, in coproduction with Second German Television (ZDF), Mainz. A documentary written, directed, and photographed (color) by Werner Schroeter. Artistic collaboration, Peter Kern, Christel Orthmann, Franz Christoph Gierke, Bibiena Houwer; editors, Christel Orthmann, Schroeter; executive producers, Franz Christoph Gierke, Paul Simon; TV producer, Christoph Holch. Reviewed at Berlin Film Fest (German Series), Feb. 21, 1984. Running time: **110 MINS.**

One can think evil thoughts about Werner Schroeter's depiction of the Manila Film Festival at the beginning of his documentary, "The Laughing Star." And one can wonder why make this political pamphlet on the Philippines in view of the chain of recent events in that troubled corner of the globe.

"The Laughing Star" mixes aesthetic, baroque images with sociological commentary for the most part, even though the emphasis is clearly anti-Reagan in an "open letter" to Imelda Marcos at the outset. One sees what religion means to a superstitious population during a Way of the Cross procession at which the natives fairly mutilate themselves in a self-emulation ceremony. Interviewed authorities on life in the Philippines (mostly in English) explain the historical whys and wherefores of political and economic realities.

One can feel in excerpts from ethnographic docus included in this all-embracing portrait of a land and its people that this is a country of the Third World in the midst of revolutionary change by the very fact that it is dragging itself into the current century. Then there's those liberation clips from the World War II Yank propaganda films (Reagan appearing again in a patriotic American war feature) that contrast with the tv newsreels on dictatorship today. Surely, one can tie these and other loose ends together in one's own imagination without asking Schroeter to make the necessary bridges. Yet it would have been admirable if he had bothered to take a stand somewhere along the way all the same.—*Holl.*

Rape/Crisis
(U.S.-COLOR-16m)

Berlin, Feb. 27.

A Cinema Guild (New York) release of a production by the Criminal Justice Center, Sam Houston State University, Huntsville, Texas. Producers, Victor Strechter, Larry Hoover, Jerry Dowling. Written and directed by Gary T. McDonald. Camera (color) Bert Guthrie; sound, Wayne Bell; editor, McDonald; content consultants, Sylvia Callaway. Sherri Goode, Jef Schroeder. Reviewed at Messe (Market), Berlin International Film Festival, Feb. 27, 1984, within special showcase of Independent Feature Project. Running time: **87 MINS.**

Becky	Carla Phillips
Bob	David Kroll
Laurie	Suzanne Chesshire
Joan	Jennifer Johanos
David	Julius Sharp
Sharon	Sheila Tesar

Dedicated to the Austin Rape Crisis Center, this earnest but overlong docu-drama reconstructs real-life rape encounters and the devastating psychological consequences experienced by the victims. Some officials and volunteer trainees of the ARCC perform in the film, which appears impeccably accurate but slow and portentous.

Patrolmen of the Austin Police Department also act, or re-enact, the roles they actually perform a real-life when summoned to investigate a rape. Similarly, other nonprofessionals interpret roles that elucidate other aspects of rape — prosecuting and defense attorneys, lab technicians, jailers, a nurse.

"Rape/Crisis" focuses on the experience of the rape victim and the trauma she undergoes during the aftermath, rather than on the violence and melodramatic cliches of the rape itself. Thus, as the film begins, the rape has already taken place. The victim is interrogated by the police, friends comfort her, later a suspect is apprehended and grilled. Because this sketchy storyline is inter-cut with documentary footage of a classroom training session for volunteer ARCC counselors, characterizations are necessarily one-dimensional and dramatic tension is minimal. Nevertheless, these dramatic scenes, in combination with the documentary interpolations, are informative and provide insight into the suffering of the victim and the compulsive sexual violence of our society.

A first fiction work by a young Texan, "Rape/Crisis" won the Grand Prix at the Mostra du Film d'Epernay in France and the Golden Athena as Best Feature Length Documentary at the Athens International Film Festival. It was telecast in New York on the Independent Focus series at WNET Channel 13.

McDonald's previous films, all documentaries, have dealt with prisoners serving life sentences, the philosophical and social issues involved in the concept of punishment, the mentally handicapped offender, and related topics.

— *Hitch.*

Tod Dem Zuschauer

(Death To The Spectator)
(WEST GERMAN-COLOR)

Berlin, Feb. 27.

An experimental film produced, directed, photographed (color), and edited by Vlado Kristl, in collaboration with the Hamburg Film Bureau. Costumes, Silke Voszberg; commentator, Christina Elvers. Reviewed at Berlin Film Fest (Forum), Feb. 27, '84. Running time: 102 MINS.
Cast: Hans-Jürgen Masch, Kiev Stingl, Milan Horacek, Brigitta Grabenkamp, Angelika Oehms, Jürgen Schnitzler, Silke Pause, Gisela Frank, Uli Dörrie, Dietrich Kuhlbrodt, Harald Brütt, David Roberts, Michael Kellner.

As the title hints, and as the reputation of Vlado Kristl warrants, "Death To The Spectator" is a fun film for a well attended international film festival like the Berlinale. When it was unspooled here, the public at the Forum greeted the scheduled screenings with warm appreciation for here was finally the needed rib-tickling break after hours of committed viewing. It's indeed the kind of film experience that fairly cries for a response from the audience, simply because filmmaker's primary concern is to provoke the viewer with whatever means are at his disposal.

In this case, it's a static and observant camera set up on a street in Hamburg. The object of its observation is a man leaning against a car or building waiting and waiting and waiting for something to happen. His dog waits, too, for his master to make a move in one meaningful direction or another. And the viewer waits for the dog at regular moments to break the monotony of the whole affair. Then, after a splash of caricatures on the screen, the audience takes collective notice of having sat there in the theater for nearly two hours of distracting amusement — and begins to dribble out into the foyer for other refreshments. One returned on this occasion to seek a friend who had stayed behind: "Helmut?" — "Dead!" responded a wag in the audience.

Thank the god of bleary-eyed film buffs that experimental filmers in Germany like Vlado Kristl and Hellmuth Costard are still around and kicking at the annual Berlinale. And the same goes for the Berlin Underground and the far-out cine-feminists. Their calculated insanity brings a welcomed and often hilarious note of sanity into the proceedings. Like the Marx Brothers, if Kristl wasn't making films, he would surely have to be invented to warm the cockles of the festivalier. — *Holl.*

Taubenjule

(Pigeon-Jill)
(EAST GERMAN-COLOR)

Berlin, Feb. 27.

A DEFA-Studio Production, Berlin Film Group, East Berlin; world rights, DEFA Aussenhandel, East Berlin. Features entire cast. Directed by Hans Kratzert. Screenplay, Margot Bleicher, based on Edith Berger's children's book, "The Girl with the red Pullover;" camera (color), Helmut Grewald; editor, Erika Lehmphul; sound, Rolf Prochazka; music, Christian Steyer; production manager, Uwe Klimek. Reviewed at Berlin Film Fest (Children's Films), Feb. 27, '84. Running time: 69 MINS.
Cast: Ruth Reinecke (Mother), Eckhard Becker (Father), Hans-Peter Reinecke (Klaus Kürbs), Jördis Hollnagel (Jella), Christa Löser (Betty Kojanke), Johannes Wieke (Father Jennert), Jürgen Rothert (Kalle Maschke), Jürgen Trott (Cuno Zack), Uwe Geyer (Teacher), Sina Fiedler (Secretary).

Hans Kratzert's "Pigeon-Jill" is highly recommended for those interested in the day-to-day life of young people in the German Democratic Republic. It's the story of a girl from the country who leaves behind a childhood paradise to accompany her parents to the big city. The conflict spills over into the parents' world as well: the father is a construction foreman and has to move on to this new position, while the mother prefers to follow her natural vocation of gardener back in a rural setting.

The twist comes when the girl, 11, is given a brace of pigeons as a going-away present. But after realizing city-life is not for pigeons used to open spaces, she takes them back to the land and sets them free. The pigeons, however, decide to stay with their owner and fly back to roost with Jella as is natural to homing-pigeons. Meanwhile, the girl has acclimated, too.

Nice human tale, and quite representative of East German craftsmanship in the genre.— *Holl.*

Flussfahrt Mit Huhn

(River Trip With Hen)
(WEST GERMAN-COLOR)

Berlin, Feb. 25.

A Frankfurter Filmwerkstatt Production in coproduction with Hessischer Rundfunk (HR), Frankfurt. Features entire cast. Producer, Michael Smeaton. Written and directed by Arend Aghte. Camera (color), Jürgen Jürges; sets, Thomas Bergfelder; music, Matthias Raue, Martin Cyrus; editor, Yvonne Kölsch; sound, Jochen Hergersberg; costumes, Stephanie Polo; production manager, Gudrun Ruzickova. Reviewed at Berlin Film Fest (Children's Films), Feb. 25, '84. Running time: 100 MINS.
Cast: Julia Martinek (Johanna), David Hoppe (Robert), Fedor Hoppe (Alex), Uwe Müller (Harald), Hans Beerhenke (Frandpa), Erika Skrotzki (Else), Barbara Stanek (Eva), Andreas Mannkopf (Heinz), Jockel List (Ulf), Julian Moscherosch (Peter).

The best kidpic to appear on the German film scene this season, Arend Aghte's "River Trip with Hen" has all the adventure of a Mark Twain Mississippi tale, along with distinctive local touches that amuse throughout and often tickle to the bone. There's little doubt that Aghte — already well known as a diversified talent in art and letters — will be a name to watch

"River Trip with Hen" comes across like Howard Hawks's Missouri River epic, "The Big Sky" (1953), via a narrative thread supplied by a diary — and it could very well be that the dramatic storytelling drive is taken from Hawks' cinema as a whole. And the chief protagonist of the film, Robert, a youth of 12, draws his inspirational fantasy for the river trip from the books of Twain, Stevenson, and Melville.

Tale begins with a girl's parents deciding to spend a vacation together with a cousin, thereby leaving the kids from both families together with an accommodating grandfather. It turns out that this is just what Robert has been waiting for: he now has the chance to explore the Weser River in his backyard to its mouth at the North Sea — the stretch from the heart of Germany northward being unknown territory to him. For the trip he plans to take along two neighboring lads, both younger and compliant to his schemes, but the girl Johanna (the visitor to the family) is unexpected and agreed upon only with reluctance. It is Johanna, however, who keeps the daily chronicle of the adventure in a school notebook. A hen, called Gonzo, joins the crew at the last minute.

Once the kids have stolen away at night to their awaiting motorboat, it's open water and a fast current. They haven't contended with grandpa, however, who sets out after them in the same spirit of adventure while, at the same time, concealing the news of the runaways to the respective mothers. He nearly catches up with them on several occasions, but the kids keep slipping through his grasp

Along the way the explorers float through military maneuvers under a camouflage and find themselves trapped in a dungeon of an abandoned factory, but with a bit of ingenuity they fare well despite mishaps. So, too, does grandpa — he bluffs his way along with questioning parents on the phone until, by chance, everybody comes together for a brief surprise visit at the parents' vacationing resort. After that semi-climax, the kids make peace with grandpa and continue on together to the mouth of the Weser and the open sea.

Tightly directed, charmingly acted (with the kids regularly stealing the show), and sharply lensed (Jürgen Jürges), "River Trip with Hen" deserves further fest exposure and should bring home the bacon at international kidpic fests. —*Holl.*

Mississippi Triangle

(U.S.-COLOR/B&W-DOCU-16m)

Berlin, Feb. 26.

A production of Third World Newsreel and the Film News Now Foundation. Producer and project director, Christine Choy. Directors, Choy, Worth Long, Allen Siegel; camera, (color/black & white), Choy, Kyle Kibbe, Ludwig Goon (with three crews); sound, J.T. Takagi, Sylvie Thouard; music, Lee Ray, Eugene Powell, Kee Wing, Leon Penson, Fred McDowell, Eddie Cussick; editor, Siegel. Reviewed at International Forum of Young Cinema, Berlin Festival, Feb. 26, 1984 (one of four screenings at Forum). Running time: 110 MINS.

The triangle is the Mississippi River Delta, but it's also the complex three-cornered relations among the whites, blacks and the 5,000 Chinese of northwest Mississippi. Long the most backward and least prosperous of the states, with a debilitating cotton-based economy and pockets of immense wealth amid the general poverty, Mississippi has a nasty history of tri-racial tension and strife that includes a century of discrimination and segregation of Chinese.

The little-known story of Chinese communities in Mississippi is the topic of this film, but by extension the facts and lessons of the film apply as a pattern to Asian-Americans throughout the country. It's a sad story of a small ethnic minority, visibly identifiable, culturally exotic, quite different often in appearance and language, cut off from the majority.

In the mid-1800s, Chinese males had been cargoed into the U.S. like human freight for manual labor on railroads. They were kept isolated, rarely could intermarry, imported Chinese brides where possible, struggled to survive. In time, the Chinese established small businesses, especially groceries, and came to achieve over the years a measure of economic self-sufficiency, even respect. Although still largely isolated socially, their retail firms brought them especially into contact with black sharecroppers shopping on credit.

Through old footage, still photos, family vignettes and interviews with ancient survivors, "Mississippi Triangle" documents this corner of Americana, which is not a pretty picture. Because of festering racism, three separate crews were needed, all-white, all-black and all-Chinese. The film is an investigation, trying to piece together what happened to those early Chinese, but also with some guesses about what will happen in the future, now that the bright young Chinese-Americans are well-educated, assertive and determined to break out of the ancestral rut.

The Delta music — blues, gospel, country-western and spirituals — conveys a strong feeling for the culture of the region, supplementing and reinforcing the visuals. Chinese traditions are expressed through scenes of weddings, funerals, mah-jong games, church services, business deals, cooking, dining and dancing.

Major funding was provided by the National Endowment for The Humanities ($220,000), with additional funding from the John Simon Guggenheim Memorial Foundation ($20,000), the National Endowment for The Arts ($11,000), and the Film Fund.

Now in its second decade, Third World Newsreel is a film-video collective that produces, acquires and distributes works on minority issues, women's rights, prisons, housing, labor relations, community organizing. Target-audiences see these works in union halls, churches, schools, governmental and private social agencies, and community centers.—*Hitch.*

Alley Cat
(COLOR)

Entertaining but silly action picture.

A Film Ventures International release of an Ordoñez-Waters production. An Edward L. Montoro presentation of a Dragonfly Prods. picture. Produced by Robert E. Waters, Victor Ordoñez. Directed by Eduardo Palmos, Victor Ordoñez, Al Valletta. Features entire cast. Screenplay, Waters; camera (United color), Howard Anderson 3d; editor, Robert Ernst; editorial consultant, Emmett R. Alston; music, Quito Colayco; music supervision, Igo Kantor, Doug Lackey; sound, Jon Huck; assistant director, Mary Ellen Woods; production design, Robert Lee; set decoration, Mannie Lee; stunt coordinator, Lita Vasquez; special makeup effects, Melanie Kay; associate producer, Robert A. Gronsky. Reviewed at UA Rivoli 1 theater, N.Y., March 24, '84. (MPAA Rating: R). Running time: 82 MINS.

Billie Clark	Karin Mani
Johnny	Robert Torti
Hooker	Britt Helfer
Scarface	Michael Wayne
Thomas	Timothy J. Cutt
Boyle	Jon Greene
Charles	Jay Fisher
Rose	Claudia Decea
Kate Clark	Rose Dreifus

Its production dating back a couple years, Film Ventures' new release "Alley Cat" is an entertaining oddity on the action circuit, of more interest to B-movie connoisseurs than general audiences.

Though the advertising promises something in the female revenge-vigilante vein, a la "Ms. 45" or "Lovely But Deadly," the picture delivers a softer approach and a silly storyline. Young Billie Clark (Karin Mani) is a martial arts expert who insists on jogging at night in her L.A. neighborhood despite the obvious susceptibility to criminals. A contrived vendetta develops between her and several thugs who first attempt to steal her car tires one night, later mug her grandparents (grandma dies) and subsequently are interrupted, while raping a woman, by Billie who makes a citizen's arrest.

Filmmakers mock the judicial system (leading the film into campy territory) with a young district attorney who can't present a case properly and an asinine judge who lets the thugs go and ends up throwing Billie in the slammer for alleged abuses. She resists lesbian advances in the county jail and upon release is aided by her cop boyfriend in doing away with the thugs.

Utilizing a gritty, realistic visual style (one case where a low budget helps avoid glamor or gloss), "Alley Cat" transcends its rather limited premise by the apt casting of lead player Karin Mani. Looking like a Latino version of 1960s actress Yvonne Craig, Mani has a terrific body, impressive high-kicking action skills in fight sequences and a peppy manner that overcomes obvious acting inexperience. Her strong presence, combined with a library music action score, conjures up the fun Russ Meyer action pictures of the 1960s, toplining Haji or Tura Satana.

The rest of the cast is unexciting, with writer-co-producer Robert E. Waters repeating the device of his 1977 film "Death Force" (a/k/a "Fighting Mad") in awarding associate producer credits to half a dozen of the leading thesps. Three directors collaborated on this opus, but lacking the clout of the "Airplane"-"Top Secret" team of Zucker, Abrahams and Zucker, they signed the film collectively using the *nom de film* of "Edward Victor."

Film's plentiful quota of nude scenes will probably prove a boon in ancillary cable and homevideo action.—*Lor.*

Razorback
(AUSTRALIAN-COLOR)

Sydney, March 27.

A UAA Films Ltd. presentation of a McElroy & McElroy production. (WB release outside Australia.). Produced by Hal McElroy. Directed by Russell Mulcahy. Stars Gregory Harrison, Arkie Whiteley. Screenplay, Everett De Roche, from novel by Peter Brennan; camera (color, Panavision), Dean Semler; music, Iva Davies; editor, Bill Anderson, assisted by Jeanine Chialvo; sound, Tim Lloyd; 1st assistant director, Stuart Freeman; 2nd unit director, Arch Nicholson; associate producer, Tim Sanders; production design, Bryce Walmsley; art director, Neil Angwin; special effects, Mark Canny; "Razorback" design and construction, Bob McCarron. Reviewed at Greater Union Theatrette, Sydney, March 26, 1984. (Commonwealth Film censor rating: M) Running time: 94 MINS.

Carl Winters	Gregory Harrison
Sarah Cameron	Arkie Whiteley
Jake Cullen	Bill Kerr
Benny Baker	Chris Haywood
Dicko Baker	David Argue
Beth Winters	Judy Morris
Danny	John Howard
Turner	John Ewart
Wallace	Don Smith
Andy	Mervyn Drake
Magistrate	Redmond Phillips
Counsel	Alan Beecher
Lawyer	Peter Schwartz
Louise Cullen	Beth Child
Wagstaff	Peter Boswell
Male Newscaster	Brian Adams
Female Newscaster	Jinx Lootens
Himself	Don Lane

A razorback is a particularly nasty species of feral pig, vicious and brainless, which is found in Australia's outback. "Razorback," a late but nonetheless welcome entry into the "Jaws" cycle, involves a giant of the species which runs amok with spectacular abandon.

The handsome Hal McElroy production, which introduces an inventive new action director in Russell Mulcahy, should bring home the bacon for local distrib Greater Union. (Warners has it for the rest of the world).

Screenplay by Everett De Roche, an experienced writer of thrillers, from a book by Peter Brennan, starts with a bang with a sequence sure to grab Aussie audiences: Jake Cullen (Bill Kerr) is minding his grandchild in his isolated homestead when the place is attacked by the unseen porker who wounds the old man and disappears with the infant: parallels with a notorious and recent case involving a dingo (wild dog) and a missing baby will be instantly evident Down Under. The distraught granddad is brought to trial for killing the kid, but acquitted, and he becomes obsessed with getting the giant beast to clear his name and avenge his bereavement. Kerr gives another solid performance in the role.

Enter Judy Morris who, though sixth in the billing, is probably the best known Australian thesp in the film. She plays — somewhat surprisingly — an American tv journalist who arrives in this remote spot to do a story on the slaughter of the kangaroos. She comes up against a couple of manic brothers (Chris Haywood, David Argue) who run a kangaroo meat factory, and barely escapes rape. She is left behind, however, to become the next victim of the razorback, thus fulfilling the kind of impactful but truncated role Janet Leigh did in "Psycho." Morris is good, and to non-American ears, at least, her Yank accent is passable.

Next to arrive in this God-forsaken place (the boondocks of Australia haven't looked so depressing since Ted Kotcheff's "Outback") is her husband, Carl (Gregory Harrison), who doesn't believe she fell down a mine shaft, the story put out by the locals.

Rest of the film is built around the increasing attacks of the maddened monster, with cast members dropping like ninepins before the beast is most satisfactorily, and spectacularly, destroyed.

The plot may be a bit familiar, but "Razorback" is no quickie: it's an extremely handsome production, beautifully shot by Dean Semler (who also made a major visual contribution to "The Road Warrior"), sharply edited by Bill Anderson, and given a top visual sheen by production designer Bryce Walmsley and art director Neil Angwin.

Above all, it introduces a new director of considerable talent in Russell Mulcahy. Mulcahy first came to local attention when he won the experimental (General) section of the 1976 Greater Union Awards at the Sydney Film Festival and has since carved out a distinguished career making dynamic video clips for the likes of Elton John, Rod Stewart, Paul McCartney, Billy Joel, Kim Carnes, Little River Band and others. He takes to features like a duck to water, handling the actors and the narrative with confidence.

Above all, Mulcahy directs with a physicality found only in Australia in the films of George Miller, and though "Razorback" lacks the mythic qualities that made "The Road Warrior" so outstanding, Mulcahy could eventually find himself in the same league. He also knows his Sam Peckinpah movies, and his comic villains, wonderfully enacted by Chris Haywood and David Argue, are closely related to the outrageously funny-but-dangerous types L.Q. Jones and the Strother Martin used to do so well.

As for the razorback itself, it works just about all the time. A specially constructed mechanical monster, which would frighten the life out of Miss Piggy, it's artfully photographed (and cut) to give it maximumum impact (the Dolby track is a plus, too). In short, it's at least as convincing as the shark in "Jaws."

Pic keeps the gore down to a minimum, and is further helped by a lively music score by Iva Davies. Mention should also be made of Arkie Whiteley, who had a small role in "The Road Warrior," but who looks like being a major female star for future Australian movies — she has looks and appeal.

"Razorback" opens locally at Easter, and prospects look very bright. Overseas biz could be similarly healthy, especially in countries like Japan where top quality action pays off. — *Strat.*

Wonderful Copenhagen
(DANISH-COLOR)

Copenhagen, March 15.

A Hanne Hoyberg, Wonderful Copenhagen production with The Danish Film Workshop, The Danish Film Institute, A/S Nordisk Film release. Directed by Jenoe Farkas. Original story and script by Farkas, Al Hansen; camera (Eastmancolor) Lars Johansson, Jenoe Farkas; editors, Farkas, Jens Bidstrup; music, Funtime, ADS, Teddy Nelson. Reviewed at the Delta Bio, Copenhagen, March 14, 1984. Running time: **90 MINS.**

Danish-Hungarian Jenoe Farkas shot most of his "Wonderful Copenhagen" over several years in workshop-fashion as a more or less private affair, intending it to emerge as a tribute to the fun and funny insights life among metropolitan bohemians and their more bourgeois friends of the fringe had given him. He was encouraged by several film professionals to blow up his modest footage to a theatrical release and in this he was clearly ill advised.

Farkas has built a collage of very old-fashioned experimental shots. Film has no cinematic energy and only scattered bits of humor or compassion. Its interest in its characters seems limited to the candid camera view. —*Kell.*

Strikebound
(AUSTRALIAN-COLOR)

Sydney, March 27.

A TRM Production, in association with Film Victoria. Produced by Miranda Bain, Timothy White. Written, directed by Richard Lowenstein, from unpublished book, "Dead Men Don't Dig Coal" by Wendy Lowenstein. Camera (color), Andrew De Groot; editor, Jill Bilcock; music, Declan Affley; production design, Tracy Watt; costumes, Jennie Tate. Reviewed at Australian Film Commission theatrette, Sydney, Jan. 6, 1984. Running time: **101 MINS.**

Wattie Doig	Chris Haywood
Agnes Doig	Carol Burns
Idris Williams	Hugh Keays-Byrne

With Rob Steele, David Kendall, Declan Affley, John Flaus, John Howard, Tony Hawkins, Marion Edward, Nik Forster.

Four years ago, 19-year-old film school student, Richard Lowenstein, made a short film called "Evictions" which dramatized events during the Great Depression in Melbourne. Now, Lowenstein has made an accomplished low-budget feature about a coal strike in Victoria's Gippsland district in 1927, which brought to prominence one of Australia's first Communist unions.

This is nostalgia without the gloss: as befits the subject, "Strikebound" is a grim, gritty film about workers engaged in a life and death struggle against the mine owners. Many of them are Welsh, and so naturally there are haunting ballads to be sung in times of respite, but there's no hint of romanticism here: it smacks of the truth. The militant miners and their families not only struggle against management and police, but against scab labor brought in to take their jobs.

Pic was filmed where it happened, with an old coal-mine reopened for location filming. The very young crew, and especially cinematographer Andrew DeGroot, deserve praise for their efforts. Shooting was on Super 16m and the blow-up to 35m is excellent.

Leads are played with complete conviction by Chris Haywood and Carol Burns as a husband and wife who were leaders of the miners. Lowenstein has book-ended his film with brief footage of the real life Wattie and Agnes Doig, elderly now but who have obviously lost none of their fighting spirit over the years. Presence of the real characters obviously adds another dimension to the roles portrayed so well by Haywood and Burns in the bulk of the film.

Because of its militant approach to the subject, film will need careful handling to find an appreciative audience at home and overseas. Lowenstein has based his screenplay on the research carried out over the years by his mother, Wendy Lowenstein, for her unpublished book "Dead Men Don't Dig Coal."
—*Strat.*

The House Of God
(COLOR)

Unfunny and unreleasable.

Hollywood, March 24.

A United Artists presentation. Produced by Charles H. Joffe, Harold Schneider. Directed, screenplay by Donald Wrye, based on the novel by Samuel Shem, M.D. Camera (Technicolor), Gerald Hirschfeld; supervising editor, Bob Wyman; editor, Billy Weber; music, Basil Poledouris; production design, Bill Malley; set decoration, Bob Checchi; sound, Barry, Thomas; associate producer, John Lugar; assistant director, Jerry Bellew. Reviewed on Z Channel, L.A., March 24, 1984. (No MPAA rating). Running time: **108 MINS.**

Dr. Roy Basch	Tim Matheson
Fats	Charles Haid
Dr. Wayne Potts	Michael Sacks
Jo Miller	Lisa Pelikan
Dr. Worthington	Bess Armstrong
Dr. Leggo	George Coe
Officer Quick	James Cromwell
Dr. Sanders	Ossie Davis
Chuck	Howard Rollins Jr.

"The House Of God" is another one of those notorious, circa 1979 United Artists pics which was deemed unreleasable theatrically and, like "National Lampoon's Movie Madness" and "Safari 3000," is now surfacing on Los Angeles' Z Channel. Actually, this and "Movie Madness" make a perfect pair, in that both are tasteless comedies totally devoid of laughs.

Source novel by Samuel Shem, M.D., is a cult classic along the lines of "Catch-22" among medical school students, as it points up the insanities that accompany life and death in a big city hospital.

Donald Wrye's pic version becomes instantly offputting. A group of young interns is shown around the facility by obnoxious hipster Charles Haid, whose groundrules for hospital practice are supposed to be hilarious because they are the precise opposite of what one expects (have as little contact with patients as possible, never believe what they say, etc.).

Entire first reel is filled with Haid's grating harangues, and temptation to check out at an early stage is exceedingly strong. What one is rewarded with for hanging in there is the suicide of one of the interns and, in what is unquestionably the low point, an autopsy which Bess Armstrong feels compelled to perform topless.

Comparisons wth "Catch-22," or "Mash," for that matter, are apt, in that such potential black comedy needs a firm grounding in reality in order to work, and "The House Of God" is just nonsensical from the outset.

Story attempts to turn serious in the stretch, as earnest intern Tim Matheson quits in disgust at how unfair, corrupt and desensitizing the whole system is, but then climbs back aboard when a friend needs emergency care. Unfortunately, none of the characters exists beyond one dimension, and it's a relief when it's all over.

Wrye's direction is devoted exclusively to obvious effects, and much of the film alternates between indiscriminately cut high and low wide-angle compositions, with many repetitive tracking shots down those hospital corridors as actors rush to keep up with the camera.

Cast is a young, attractive one, but all are defeated by the misguided approach to the material. On view briefly as a supporting player is Sandra Bernhard, pre-"The King Of Comedy."

Pic was lensed in Philadelphia, with some locationing in Boston. Tech credits are okay. —*Cart.*

Maybe It's Love
(HONG KONG-COLOR)

Hong Kong, March 12.

A Shaw Brothers production and presentation. Directed by Angie Chen. Stars Cherry Chung (Chung Chong Hor), Tong Chun-Yip Ken, Kam Lin-Ling, Ku Feng. Camera (color), Bob Huke; music, Noel Quinlan. (No other credits provided by producer.) Reviewed at Jade Theater, Hong Kong, March 10, 1984. Running time: **91 MINS.**
(Cantonese soundtrack with English subtitles)

"Maybe It's Love?" No! It's definitely a hateful Hong Kong Cantonese cinema creation with a fried rice mentality. In other words, yet another cross-breeding of unrelated elements and ingredients in an effort to create a commercial film with the high-minded pretentiousness meant to be taken seriously. After all, the director studied abroad and that is a social status in a place like Hong Kong.

There's nothing new here, merely local adaptations of segments from various foreign pics. The cast and weird characters have been naturally localized with a gallery of Hong Kong misfits to amuse the innocent, the gullible and seekers of things kinky.

But the confused scenario can't decide what type or genre to follow and the director succeeds in making moviegoers bewildered. What ails "Maybe It's Love" is that it tries too hard to accomplish all, so that it becomes a carnival of feeble fabrications projected by the supposedly creative minds that possibly went haywire by the time the final sequence was shot. The end result is an irritating, erratic work that will leave many with a feeling of creeping misery for the producer of this very flawed effort.
— *Mel.*

New York Nights
(COLOR)

Life in the slow lane.

A Bedford Entertainment release of an International Talent Marketing Inc. production of a Roman Vanderbes film. Produced by Vanderbes. Directed by Simon Nuchtern. Features entire cast. Screenplay, Vanderbes; (loosely based without credit on Arthur Schnitzler's play "Reigen"); camera (Technicolor), Alan Doberman; editor, Victor Zimet; music, Linda Schreyer; songs, Schreyer, Rod Stewart, Peter Newland, Dave Immer & Tom Bernfeld, others; sound, Rick Waddell; art direction, Frank Boros, Patrick Mann; assistant director, Keven Dowd; production manager, William Milling; costumes, Donna Williams; associate producer; John Maddocks; Steadicam operator, John Corso. Reviewed at UA Rivoli 1 theater, N.Y., March 31, '84. (MPAA Rating: R). Running time: **102 MINS.**

Brooke, debutante	Corinne Alphen
Jesse, rock star	George Ayer
Lenore Woolf, author	Bobbi Burns
Werner Richards, photographer	Peter Matthey
Christina, model/wife	Missy O'Shea
Harris, husband	Nicholas Cortland
Nicki, prostitute	Marcia McBroom
Margo, porno star	Cynthia Lee
Owen, financier	William Dysart

- Also with: Tamara Jones (young model), Thomas Happer (gigolo), Michael Medeiros (Foster, porno director), Willem Dafoe (punk boyfriend), Gordon Press (chauffeur).

"New York Nights" is a poorly conceived, strictly surface-effects update of the oft-filmed "La Ronde" based on Arthur Schnitzler's play "Reigen," best-known via Max Ophüls' classic 1950 all-star French film. Theatrical chances are poor, with picture aimed clearly at the low-involvement voyeur end of the pay-cable market.

"Nights" was filmed in Gotham at the end of 1981 but has been tied up in litigation. Some of the conflict remains, as director Simon Nuchtern is listed as "production director" in the one-sheet poster and awarded the unusual placement in the opening credits *before* the music, editor and writer-producer credit cards.

Nine segments, using Schnitzler's format of a circular chain with one character common to each adjacent episode, emphasize Manhattan's decadent side with rich folks seeking kicks. With dull dialog and none of the humor of previous versions, it all plays similar to a porno film without the porn, since R-rated sex scenes are seriously abbreviated. The kicker ending most segments is usually a verbal putdown, with many of the vignettes emerging as pointless filler.

Acting consists mainly of posing plus daytime drama (i.e., soap opera) readings. The only multi-dimensional character is created by Marcia McBroom (star of "Beyond The Valley Of The Dolls" in 1970), who brings energy to her role of a high-class call girl who poses as a sassy low-down street hooker or mulatto from Martinique depending on the client's whims. Her segment also offers the only structural novelty, in using a lesbian liaison to continue the film's chain temporarily.

Disco music score, highlighted by Rod Stewart's "Passion," is dated, but pic's tech credits are good.

For the record, other recent versions of "La Ronde" have been Jacques Lemoine's 1973 "Le Lit" (The Bed) with Ana Gaël and Terry-Thomas; Otto Schenck's 1973 Austrian "Reigen" (aka "Dance Of Love") with Senta Berger, Helmut Berger and Maria Schneider; Pierre Balakoff's 1982 U.S. hardcore porn film "Ring Of Desire" with Georgina Spelvin and Ron Jeremy; and Harry Alan Towers' new production "La Ronde '84" directed by Gerard Kikoine. — *Lor.*

A Generation Apart
(COLOR-DOCU-16m)

A City Lights Production Inc., New York. Executive producer, Danny Fisher. Producers, Jack Fisher, Ed Fields, in association with Peter Arnow. Directed by Jack Fisher. Screenplay, Fields; editor, Danny Fisher; music, Arnow. No other credits. Reviewed at Times Square Screening Room, New York, March 7, 1984. Running time: **56 MINS.**

How to deal with the Holocaust — the extermination of 6,000,000 Jews in Nazi concentration camps — is the topic of this one-hour documentary, produced by brothers Danny and Jack Fisher, filmmakers whose parents had miraculously survived. The parents, Esther and Alan Fisher, had endured much suffering and barely escaped death. Now two of their three sons, as cinema professionals in Israel and the U.S., used their own parents in their film-biography in an attempt to understand for themselves what their parents had gone through.

Thus "A Generation Apart" deals with the pain of evoking horrible memories and also deals with division, with apartness, as the Holocaust survivors and their children, and their children, attempt to understand that enormous crime, a genocide too vast to be comprehended.

Survival required toughness, and left scars, and perhaps killed a capacity to love children fully and to give tender guidance. Thus the Fisher parents seem apart and distant from their own sons. Resentment and guilt hang in the air during the film's long candid family confrontation. The eldest son concludes that the Holocaust must be acknowledged, but not allowed to corrupt family harmony; a certain soothing forgetfulness is necessary. In contrast, his younger brother argues for a dynamic and ceaseless attitude of protest and outrage regarding the Holocaust, keeping its memory alive.

In effect a family profile and a debate that probe old wounds, the film is inter-cut with old Fisher photographs and other footage that provide some relief from its demanding all-talk format. In another sequence reinforcing its theme of generations apart, another survivor and her grown daughter are seen separately and together in emotional discourse on the Holocaust.

Particularly with recent emphasis on Holocaust films, "A Generation Apart" seems a natural for public television and for specialized distribution in 16m to schools, public service agencies and the religious community. —*Hitch.*

Mrkáček Čiko
(Blinker-Čiko)
(CZECH-COLOR)

Berlin, Feb. 28.

A Filmstudio Barrandov Production, Prague. World rights, Czechoslovak Film Export, Prague. Features entire cast. Written and directed by Věra Plívova-Šimková. Camera (color), Antonín Holub; music Petr Hapka; sets, Vladimír Labský. Reviewed at Berlin Film Fest (Children's Films), Feb. 28, '84. Running time: **76 MINS.**
Cast: Filip Menzel (Mrkáček, the "blinker"), Jakub Štěpán (Šmatla), Vít Olmer (Hlava, the Father), Marie Málková (Hlavová, the Mother), Pavel Nový (Puštík), Michal Nesvadba (EX), Marcela Přichystalová-Peňázová (Korelka), Elena Strusková (Pekárková), Jiří Prýmek (Portér), Václav Helšus (Kubák).

Femme helmer Věra Plívova-Šimková has established a reputation as one of Czechoslovakia's leading directors of films for children and youth, having made 11 kidpics since 1964. She wrote and directed "Blinker-Čiko," a charming story naturally played by the young thesps and highly recommended for genre screenings on the fest circuit.

Čiko is the 10-year-old son of a diplomat: since his parents were assigned to a Latin American country, that's where he grew up. He's seen pretty much of the wide, wide world, but now he doesn't feel very much at home in Czechoslovakia — for, in Mexico, his mother taught him at home, and now he has to go to school. The boy "blinks" whenever he gets overexcited, and so he has trouble fitting in with other kids at first. But he meets a quite normal Huckleberry Finn lad, and together they decide to "live in the stone age" with chums and a dog during a summer vacation. It's here that Čiko learns about life at the grassroots — and matures into a young man in the process.

A real "greenpeace" ecology-minded nature pic! — *Holl.*

Sa mori ranit din dragoste de viata
(Fatally Wounded For Love of Life)
(RUMANIAN-BLACK & WHITE)

Washington, March 27.

A Romaniafilm production. Produced by Ioan Iuga-Lozinesti; world rights, Romaniafilm, Bucharest. Features entire cast. Directed by Mircea Veroiu. Screenplay, Anghel Mora; camera (b&w), Doru Mitran; editor, Mircea Ciociatei; art direction, Nicolae Schiopu; sound, Silviu Camil; music, Adrian Enescu. Reviewed at the United States Information Agency Theater, Washington, D.C., March 27, 1984. Running time: **92 MINS.**
Horatio .... Claudio Bleont
Sarka .... Gheorghe Visu
Inspector General .... Marcel Iures
Lola .... Tora Vasilescu
Caraman .... Virgil Andriescu

After a propitious beginning with his first feature, "Stone Wedding," in 1977 at Cannes (directed in tandem with Dan Pita), Rumanian director Mircea Veroiu did not emerge onto the international film scene again until 10 pictures later. His eleventh, "Fatally Wounded For Love of Life" is looking for festival slots and looks promising after years of moribund cinema from Rumania.

Seeking the safety of a retro on the glorious resistance, Veroiu offers up a thinly veiled political challenge to his countrymen weighed down by the current regime's incompetence. Like most resistance pics, it focuses on the relationship between two men working with the underground, but places it in 1934 just as the Green Shirts were coming into fascist power.

Horatio, a young student played by Claudio Bleont, joins forces with a more experienced circus tight-rope walker Sarka to engineer explosions of factories and similar insurrectionists activities to prevent the fascist take-over. A dialog-heavy beginning establishes their characters and lays out the theme of the courage and physical pain necessary for resistance work. They escape from Bucharest, up the river to safety. An inspection of a train forces them to hide in a water tower, submerged for the seemingly long duration of boots marching atop the freight cars.

The pace picks up when they visit a circus looking for protecton from Sarka's old friends. A sexy trapezist Lola seduces Horatio, and the brief physical interlude offers him his initial physical pleasures to offset the endurance tests of the Resistance. Sarka, meanwhile, is seized, and Lola comes again to the rescue, using her connections to spring him from a provincial jail.

Scenes of an attempted strike at the docks and its subsequent failure are sure to conjure up associations with late Seventies Poland. The two buddies are subsequently separated, and Horatio must take on the real responsibility of a resistance fighter and die. The final sequence shows him being hunted down after a headlong chase scene through a power-plant. On opposite sides of a ravine, Sarkas must watch Horatio get backed up to a cliff and handcuffed. As the inspector claps on the handcuffs, firmly securing his captive to his own wrist, Horatio leaps and takes the fascist with him in a salto mortale worthy of the name.

Acting kudos go particularly to Marcel Iures, who plays the inspector with insolence and suavity. The black and white cinematography is smoothly shot and edited but reflects the state of an industry that can afford only three takes, according to Veroiu. Technical credits remain sold in the pic, and the music is particularly fine-tuned to carry along the action through the innovative direction that perks up such a low-budget movie. An underwater sequence stays tense, and location shooting lends a feel for the authenticity of the Rumanian setting in the hills around Sibiu. Close attention to the details of subversive actions is necessary to understand the subtlety of the plot.

Strong possibilities for the festivial circuits, but the b&w lensing is sure to discourage even the arthouse circuit abroad. Pic has the intimacy and whispered intensity of much good European tv fare.
— *Kaja.*

Taxid Stin Protevoussa
(Journey to the Capital)
(GREEK-COLOR)

Berlin, Feb. 20.

A Greek Film Center production. Produced and directed by Takis Papayannidis. Features entire cast. Script, Papayannidis, Mary Dimopouzlou, Pavlos Matessis; camera (color), Alexis Grivas; editor, Giorgos Triantafyllou; music, Thanos Mikroutsikos. Reviewed at Atelier am Zoo (Berlin Film Festival, Mediterranean Panorama section), Feb. 20, 1984. Running time: **93 MINS.**

Cast: Kostas Kazakos, Despina Bebetheli, Stavros Mermigis, Katerina Karoussou, Vassilis Langos.

For the non-Greek viewer, relying on rather inadequate (and frequently misspelt, subtitles), "Journey to the Capital" is rather confusing, but giving the benefit of the doubt to the film, maybe for local audiences the picture makes sense. At any rate, it's a quietly gripping contemporary story about a young man, Manolis, who leaves his village after doing military service and goes to live with his uncle and cousins, Andreas and Lefteris. His uncle is still obsessed by violent images from trouble times of the past and everyone hopes things will be better for today's younger generation. But it doesn't work out that way.

Manolis gets a job in a factory, but there's industrial unrest and he winds up unemloyed. Andreas takes up with a rich girl and dies as a result of drug addiction. Lefteris turns to crime and winds up in prison. Film ends with Manolis returning to his village, where a factory is being opened.

Pic is rather ragged, with scenes ending abruptly before they've made their point. But as a depiction of a generation trying to find a better life than their parents enjoyed, the film is interesting and modestly effective. Camerawork by Alexis Grivas is a plus. —*Strat.*

Hasta Cierto Punto
(Up to a Certain Point)
(CUBAN-COLOR)

Berlin, Feb. 27.

A production of the Instituto Cubano de Arte y Industria Cinematograficos, La Habana. Produced by Humberto Hernández. Directed by Tomás Gutiérrez Alea. Screenplay, Juan Carlos Tabió, Serafin Quiñones, Gutiérrez Alea; camera (color): Mario García Joya; editor, Miriam Talavera; costumes, José Manuel Villa. Sound Germinal Hernández; music, Leo Brouwer. Reviewed at the Delphi Theatre, Berlin, Feb. 27, 1984. Running time: **68 MINS.**

Oscar . . . . .Oscar Alvarez
Lina . . . . .Mirta Ibarra
Arturo . . . . .Omar Valdés
Marian . . . . .Coralia Veloz
Diego . . . . .Rogelio Blain
Flora . . . . .Ana Vina
Claudio . . . . .Claudio A. Tamayo
Quinones .Luis Celeiro

For a filmmaker of Tomas Gutiérrez Alea's stature — the top feature film director of the Cuban industry and, after 25 years, still its best known representative — this is barely more than a trifle. Not only because at 68 minutes it is rather short change for a feature length program, but also because the treatment and construction of the script are lightweight, or have been cut to size from a more considerable dimension.

Those who had a chance to see the film earlier in Cuba attest it was at least a quarter of an hour longer then but, whether it was cut before allowed to travel abroad or not, this looks like one episode in a much larger project.

The theme is stated from the opening titles. It is all about machismo in what is otherwise a progressive, egalitarian and revolutionary society. The tone is light banter but, between the lines, Alea introduces some sharp criticisms of the malfunctions of Cuban socialism, and these criticisms may have caused the evident tampering with the finished product.

Oscar is a successful playwright who is given his first chance in films, to prepare a picture about the profound male chauvinism, deeply rooted in a society which has otherwise made great steps forward.

In his extensive research before writing the script, Oscar does many interviews, recorded on video and inserted throughout the picture, which indicate no self-respecting Cuban likes earning less than his wife or would dream of allowing her the same margin of personal freedom he feels he is entitled to. But the interviews go further and hint clearly the revolution is bogged down in lots of bureaucracy and indifference, remarks that sound pretty painful even if delivered in the spirit of constructive auto-criticism.

The trouble starts for Oscar when he meets a truly liberated woman who works on the docu, and has an affair with her, but does not dare to face the reality sqarely and make a choice between her and his wife. Which indicates that deep down he is no less a male chauvinist than the subjects he researches and, since it may be construed in a way that Oscar represents filmmaker Alea himself, the idea could possibly be that no male is yet qualified to deal with this theme.

While cutting is effective and the frequent use of video interviews inside the frame of the story is adroit, there is very little development of character or dramatic situation, everything is stock-in-trade stuff, a sketch which does not justify a full feature. One late interview explaining how Cuba is progressing by learning from its own failures looks very much a handy excuse for much of the previous criticism and one wonders whether the juxtaposition of documentary footage and fiction shouldn't have been given more room to develop.

Students of the Cuban cinema, so promising only a few years ago, will want to see this, a turning point, not for the better, which indicates the basic talent is still there, but like the bird in the allegory used by the film, it isn't allowed to fly freely. —*Edna.*

Der Schlaf Der Vernunft
(Reason Asleep)
(WEST GERMAN-B&W)

Berlin, Feb. 22.

An Ula Stöckl Film Production in coproduction with Common Film, Berlin, and Second German Television (ZDF), Mainz. Features entire cast. Written and directed by Ula Stöckl. Camera (black and white), Axel Block; music, Helmut Timpelan; editor, Christel Orthmann; production manager, Ulrike Herdin. Reviewed at Berlin Film Fest (Forum), Feb. 22, '84. Running time: **82 MINS.**

Cast: Ida di Benedetto (Dr. Dea Jannsen), Pina Esposito (Elena), Marta Bifano (Georgia), Stefania Bifano (Laura), Christina Scholz, (Johanna Erdmann), Christoph Lindert (Dr. Reinhard Jannsen), Therese Hämer (Girl Friend).

To her credit, femme helmer Ula Stöckl is still carrying the torch from film to film for the German cine-feminists. Her best feminist films were "The Cat Has Nine Lives" (1968) and "Erika's Passions" (1976) among a dozen features. Now, after a five-year pause, she's back with "Reason Asleep" in the Berlinale's Forum of Young Cinema.

"Reason Asleep" is about a woman gynecologist's inability to come to grips with both her private life and her professional world, the title referring to eery nightmares that creep up on her while her intellectual powers are asleep and the pent-up emotions take over. What these nightmares mean is anybody's guess, but they have certainly something to do with a husband who prefers her own assistant over herself, an aging mother living at home with two irascible daughters of their own mind and opinion (in eternal conflict with the mother), and a losing fight against a medical concern over the ill side effects of using birth-control pills. All this, of course, hints of breakdown and radical resistance.

Since the ideology contained in "Reason Asleep" is surely better expounded in a pro-and-con documentary than an convoluted feature film embracing an argumentative thesis, that leaves only the narrative line left to win a potential audience to see the film. And here Stöckl lacks both the finesse of a storyteller and the skill to win a degree of sympathy and understanding for the protagonist.

Ida di Benedetto (the Italian actress appeared also in Werner Schroeter's "Palermo or Wolfsburg") offers some fascination as a woman and mother standing between the old ways and customs (figure of the grandmother) and the arbitrary morals of the younger generation (the two daughters). But neither the screenplay nor the dialog present much to chew on in the long run, and her performance lacks conviction and luster. Story continuity is also patchy and (to this observer) even contradictory at crucial psychological moments. A plus is the greyish lensing effects by Axel Block in the nightmare or dream sequences.

A natural for the local femme film fest. — *Holl.*

34y Skoreil
(Fire on East Train 34)
(RUSSIAN-COLOR)

Sydney, March 29.

A Mosfilm production. Directed by Andrei Malyukov. Features entire cast. Screenplay, Vsevolod Ivanov, Malyukov; camera (Sovcolor, Scope), Yuri Gantman; music, Marc Minkov; art director, Tanya Lapshina. Reviewed at Academy Twin, Sydney, March 28, 1984. Running time: **81 MINS.**

Cast: Lev Durov, Alghimantas Masulis, Marina Shimanskaya, Helena Mayorova, Alex Fatjushin, A. Rishenkov, V. Ridzakov, V. Ezepov.

A three-year-old disaster pic in which a motley collection of characters travelling by night express from Moscow to Elekmonar find themselves in danger when a careless cigaret butt starts a fire which sweeps through the passenger coaches.

First part of the film, following the tradition of this kind of picture, introduces a motley collection of train passengers, including a honeymoon couple looking for a compartment where they can be alone, a black marketeer with a case-full of illegal money, a woman train conductor, with an unhappy love affair behind her, who's attracted to a man from her home town and lets him aboard though he doesn't have a ticket, a circus clown who's losing his eyesight, a snobbish horse-owner who cares more about horses than people, a pretty Aeroflot hostess and a soldier who starts to flirt with her, etc.

Having established its characters, pic gets on with the disaster. What's interesting here is that the actors look as if they were in real danger: the camera stays close enough to the action to show that no stunt-people were used, but the seemingly uncontrolled blaze gets terribly close to the characters.

Climax, where the bridegroom hurls himself under the train with a huge wooden post in an attempt to stop it ramming into another engine, is a knockout.

Although the characters in the film aren't particularly involving, the filmmakers show themselves well equipped to deliver some very exciting action. —*Strat.*

Frevel
(Mischief)
(WEST GERMAN-COLOR)

Berlin, March 18.

A coproduction of Hallelujah Film, Munich, together with Rapid Film, Metro Film, and Süddeutscher Rundfunk (SDR), Stuttgart. Features entire cast. Written and directed by Peter Fleischmann. Camera (color), Klaus Müller-Laue; music, Brian Eno; editing, Fleischmann, Margarete Nielsen. Reviewed at Studio am Kurfürstendamm, Berlin, March 18, '84. Running time: **90 MINS.**

Cast: Angelika Stute (Annette), Peter Fleischmann (Lohmann), Isolde Barth (Gilla), Balduin Baas (Dürkheimer), Horst Kummeth (Vesselitz), Dieter Moser (Watrin), Heike Marx (Kathi), Theo Mack (Häussler), Roland Kenda (Schäfer), Axel Olsson (Opferstock).

Peter Fleischmann makes his features few and far between, but until now he has scored with some impressive entries at international fests: "Hunting Scenes in Bavaria" (1968), "Calamity" (1970), "Dorothea's Revenge" (1973), "The Third Degree" (1975) and "The Hamburg Sickness" (1979). "Mischief" is his latest, but it's hardly the Fleischmann of old and is perhaps better off forgotten.

A police commissioner (played by Fleischmann) has an exceptional record for cracking crime cases, but this is because motivation for a crime hounds him in his working and free time until a satisfactory answer is produced. However, when a mother kills her own child and continues to maintain a quiet, wordless composure under questioning, he decides to neglect his own wife and family altogether despite a well-earned a vacation, and gets deeper and deeper involved in the young murderess' plight. Then he breaks all the rules and illegally seeks to free her from a sanitorium — to run away with her across the border, no less.

That's about the gist of the story — save that the walls of the commissioner's own common sense come tumbling down. In the end, he is as berserk as the girl with whom he has become infatuated.

Tale might have taken on needed flesh if the motivation had been made clear somewhere along the way: the story seems, in fact, to have been improvised in part. Also, Fleischmann, the actor, could use more camera hints from Fleischmann, the director; sometimes, he's positively puzzled by what's going on about him. Otherwise, credits are on the plus side.
—*Holl.*

The Secret Agent
(DOCU-COLOR-16m)

A Green Mountain Post/Human Arts Assn. Production, distributed by First Run Features, New York. Producers, Daniel Keller, Jacki Ochs. Directed by Ochs. Narration written by Laurie S. Block, John Crowley; narrator, Max Gail; camera (color-16m), Ochs; editor, Keller; sound editor, Margie Crimmins; original score, Country Joe McDonald.

Reviewed at Film Forum, New York, March 21, 1984. Running time: **60 MINS.**

The secrecy in "The Secret Agent" is the long coverup concerning the dangers of dioxin. a chemical poison within herbicides that has left a long trail of death, disability and ecological disaster. Years after dioxin's lethal properties were secretly known in the labs, the secret has come out, as documented in this courageous film.

Class-action suits against five chemical giants on behalf of 20,000 Vietnam veterans exposed to Agent Orange defoliant are in the courts, as is additional litigation relating to illnesses and deformities among offspring of these vets.

Aside from Vietnam-related cases, other suits concern dioxin contamination in the U.S., e.g., in agriculture and in such dumps and sites as Times Beach, Mo., where an entire town was evacuated.

"The Secret Agent" deals responsibly with these and other controversial topics in a comprehensive journalistic manner, compelling praise for objective reporting from even Dow Chemical, although Dow clearly emerges as the chief heavy in this drama, along with a gullible Pentagon.

Oddly beautiful but ominous, like a circling buzzard, are shots of low-flying U.S. military aircraft lazily spraying 11,000,000 gallons of Agent Orange in picturesque patterns over river bottom-land and rice paddies. The film includes shots from Vietnam today, of deformed babies, born to Vietnamese parents possibly contaminated by Agent Orange.

Thus, in a sense, the Vietnam war is still on, as both the Vietnamese and the Americans continue to suffer, a deadly legacy that mocks peace.

A final prediction comes from the American mother of a deformed child, born with 22 defects, fathered by a G.I. who had worked with Agent Orange in Vietnam — "This has become the age of accountability."

"The Secret Agent" is grim stuff that leaves a viewer disquieted and fearful he's seeing only the tip of a very big iceberg. —*Hitch.*

Femmes de Personne
(Nobody's Women)
(FRENCH-COLOR)

Paris, March 7.

Parafrance release of a T. Films/FR 3 coproduction. Produced by Alain Terzian. Written and directed by Christopher Frank. Camera (Eastmancolor), Jean Tournier; music, Georges Delerue; art director, Dominique André; editor, Nathalie Lafaurie; sound, Michel Desrois; makeup, Jackie Raynal; costumes, Yvette Frank; production manager, Philippe Lievre. Reviewed at the Marignan-Concorde theater, Paris, March 5, 1984. Running time: **106 MINS.**

Cecile	Marthe Keller
Isabelle	Caroline Cellier
Adeline	Fanny Cottençon
Gilquin	Jean-Louis Trintignant
Antoine	Philippe Léotard
Marc	Patrick Chesnais
Julie	Elisabeth Etienne
Patrick	Pierre Arditi
Arnaud	Karol Zuber
Dubly	Marcel Bozonnet

Franco-British novelist Christopher Frank has been prominent as a local screenwriter for the past decade. A stage author and director as well, Frank turned to filmmaking in 1982. But "Josepha," a drama about an acting couple on the skids, suffered from some pretentious writing, miscast lead roles and generally drab direction.

All the more reason then to be surprised by his second film, "Femmes de Personne," a poignant group portrait of women working in a Paris radiological clinic trying to cope on the domestic front. The writing is mostly fresh, the direction fluid and assured and the acting excellent down the line.

Frank's script smoothly interweaves the personal stories of two clinic doctors, Caroline Cellier and Marthe Keller, both strong-willed and intelligent, and a younger nurse, Fanny Cottençon, more fragile and confused.

Keller is a divorcee, with a young son, who buffers her solitude with one-night stands. But she has an eye for Jean-Louis Trintignant, a successful businessman, whose daughter attends the same school as her kid. They get involved but she soon realizes the relationship is a fruitless one and puts an end to it.

Colder and more calculating, Cellier has all the comforts of middle-class domesticity, but bridles under the shallow placidity of it all. With a young daughter of dating age and another child on the way, she can no longer tolerate the bland passivity of her husband and resorts to a perverse remedy to wake him up: she pays the clinic's beautiful young receptionist to lure him into a brief fling.

Cottençon leads an after-hours life of breathless promiscuity, but the mask of bohemian smugness cracks when an old flame turns up. Her attempted suicide brings all three women momentarily together in a fine scene of feminine solidarity.

As director, Frank has this time betrayed neither script nor cast and the film's smooth but varied textures ow much to Jean Tournier's lensing, Dominique André's art direction and Nathalie Lafaurie's editing, especially for the early expository part.

Hopefully, pic will pave the way to more substantial roles for Keller, a vibrant, subtle actress whose international career has not given her the parts that she deserves. Good as all the women are, the menfolk are no less vivid. Patrick Chesnais is pathetically fine as Cellier's perplexed mate, and Philippe Léotard is reliably derelict as Keller's homosexual friend, who camps out in her apartment when he wants to escape his own private pains. —*Len.*

Ne Chochu Bytj Vzroslym
(I Don't Want To Be Grown-Up)
(SOVIET-COLOR)

Berlin, Feb. 22.

A Mosfilm Studio Production, Moscow; world rights, Goskino, Moscow. Features entire cast. Directed by Yuri Chulyukin. Screenplay, Georgi Kushnirenko, Valeri Vladimirov, Valentin Makarov; music, Gennadi Gladkov, Igor Kantyukov; sets, Pyotr Kisselyov. Reviewed at Berlin Film Fest (Children's Films), Feb. 22, '84. Running time: **77 MINS.**

Cast: Natalya Varley, Yevgeni Steblov, Yevgenia Melnikova, Yuri Nikulin, Yevgeni Yevstigneyev, Vladimir Saizev, Yelena Valyishkina.

Yuri Chulyukin's "I Don't Want To Be Grown-Up" tickles the funny bone via the story line. Here's a situation in which the parents are sure they have brought a genius into the world, so they decide to help the kid along as best they can in the way of training and education. The poor lad thus has a full slate of activities to cope with daily: judo with mother, poetry with father. And that's only the beginning for the six-year-old whiz-kids: he gets extra lessons in music, chemistry, painting, even astronomy. Even his health diet is controlled: nature foods in the raw.

One day, however, Pavlik get the chance to visit his grandmother. What happens — he can eat what he likes, and begins to enjoy life. Of course, this leads to a clash between granny and the parents. And when the boy decides to run away from home to find himself, this leads in turn to a new friendship with an older 17-year-old maid. The girl wants to help her young friend to return home, but by chance the lad first appears on a live tv broadcast — and amazes everyone by reciting Shakespeare! The parents, naturally enough, are both proud and taken aback by their self-centered tactics. Warm and human. —*Holl.*

Echt Tu Matsch
(Too Much, Man)
(WEST GERMAN-COLOR)

Berlin, Feb. 19.

A Denkmal Film Production, Munich, in coproduction with Sender Freies Berlin (SFB). Features entire cast. Directed by Claus Strigel, Bertram Verhaag. Screenplay, Strigel; camera (color), Michael Teutsch; sets, Thomas Deutschmann; music, Neumann; editor, Strigel. Reviewed at Berlin Film Fest (Children's Films), Feb. 19, '84. Running time: **88 MINS.**

Cast: Mine Gruber (Bastian), Ulrike Neumann (Uli), Michael Gahr (Head Master Zander), Astrid Boner (Frau Radke), Ottfried Fischer (House Master Unertl), Willy Lenik (Herr Schneider), Karl-Heinz Windhorst (Herr Paschke), Jockel Tschiersch (Herr Dinkel).

The twist in Claus Strigel and Bertram Verhaag's "Too Much, Man" is the remote possibility of a schoolmaster's liberality extending to such a point that the kids can temporarily take over seventh-grade classes in a school to turn the tables on teachers, so to speak. Naturally enough, the incentive to learn is off and running when the students themselves are running affairs, and the poor teachers are going to get it in the neck for doing such a miserable job of teaching in the past. Yet the theme has its surprises, too: there are both teachers and students who are aching to try a new experiment — even when the kids bring hammocks and easy chairs into the classroom.

It's when the kids investigate the hatching of eggs in the biology class that their natural curiosity is aroused to ask questions. This leads eventually to even asking grandparents about what it was like under National Socialism. The damper is put on the experiment when some spoil sports decide it's time to take advantage of the situation and overrule the headmaster on just about everything. — *Holl.*

Everlasting Love
(HONG KONG-COLOR)

Hong Kong, March 18.

A Johnny Mak Production Ltd. presentation. Directed by Michael Mak. Stars Lau Tak Wah, Irene Wan, Loletta Lee, Ng Man Tat Leung Chieu May. Executive producer, Johnny Mak. Produced by Terence Chang. Screenplay, Manfred Wong; production manager, David Wong; assistant director Jobie Wong; camera (color), Gary Ho; sound recording, Wong Kwok Hung. Reviewed at Hong Kong Lab. Preview Room, Hong Kong March 17, 1984. Running time: **98 MINS.**
(Cantonese soundtrack with English subtitles).

Andy Lau (Lau Tak Wah) is the reigning matinee idol king of Cantonese film, vintage '84. He takes the crown away from the aging Chow Yan Fat who got waylaid and was marred by bad publicity generated by his personal life. Critically acclaimed for his secondary but stunning supporting role in Ann Hui's "Boat People," Lau sizzles to boxoffice bonanza with the release of Johnny Mak's "Everlasting Love," directed by his younger brother Michael.

Latest femme draw is Shaw's contract player Cherry Chung, who can attract patrons to theaters, so Lau should generate the attention "Everlasting Love" rightfully deserves.

The film was first titled "Lonely 15-Chapter Two" as a followup to the highly successful "Lonely Fifteen" (directed by David Lai), later changed to "Love Story."

Michael Mak finally makes his individual mark as a maturing film director. The pic is not a grand epic, but it can be praised for its earnest desire to tell a dramatic story in a straightforward manner without the self-consciousness of a commercial director trying hard to be taken seriously. Story suffers from a commonplace scenario about the rich and the poor, the born losers and born winners.

It centers on a young, comely nightclub hostess, P.K. (Irene Wan). A teenage mother, she supports her year-old baby, a kid brother and semi-delinquent sister. P.K. makes enough money to feed her family and she works hard, but her popularity in the club arouses jealousy from less attractive colleagues and this leads to a series of fights and mishaps.

It is a sordid life that seems to be without hope and P.K. can be compared to a doomed woman trapped in a low environment she cannot escape. One day, a light of hope appears in the form of a handsome, young Eric (Andy Lou) who works in hospital. To P.K., he represents the type of clean-cut man she has been longing to meet. They fall in love and P.K. is introduced to his rich family. She is overwhelmed by her inadequacies and insecurities. There are cultural, social and educational gaps and she tries to reform. It is a long, hard climb and when things are getting better ... a series of discouraging situations arise to further complicate the road towards a better life.

Hong Kong's high and low societies are beautifully and realistically captured on camera and the romantic melodramatic sequences give ample opportunities for Lau and Wan to act out their sympathetic roles as impassioned, star-crossed lovers with conviction. Altogether an entertaining contemporary production with fine acting, tight editing and generally top technical credits despite its old-fashioned story development and updated soap opera sense. Mak's romanticism should appeal to the young market and viewers interested in things associated with today's bustling Hong Kong. — *Mel.*

The Dorm That Dripped Blood
(COLOR)

Generally routine stalking horror opus.

A New Image Releasing release of a Jeff Obrow Prods. production, in association with Wescom Prods. Produced by Jeffrey Obrow. Directed by Obrow, Stephen Carpenter. Features entire cast. Screenplay, Obrow, Carpenter, Stacey Giachino; camera (Getty color), Carpenter; editors, Obrow, Carpenter ; music, Chris Young; assistant director, Jon Hopkins; production manager, Samson Aslanian; sound, Patrick Moyroud, Chris Hopkins; makeup/special effects, Matthew Mungle; stunt coordinator, Stephen Sachs; art direction, Charlotte Grant; production consultant, Robert L. Newman. Reviewed on Media Home Entertainment vidcassette, N.Y., March 25, 1984. (MPAA Rting: R). Running time: **85 MINS.**
Joanne ....Laurie Lapinski
Craig ....Stephen Sachs
Brian ....David Snow
Patti ....Pamela Holland
Bobby Lee ....Dennis Ely
John Hemmit ....Woody Roll
Also with: Daphne Zuniga, Jake Jones, Robert Frederick, Chris Morrill, Chandre, Billy Criswell.

"The Dorm That Dripped Blood" is a low-budget, low-interest version of the familiar (especially since "Friday The 13th" 's success) horror formula of a mysterious killer sequentially picking off the lead players in an isolated location. Picture was made in 1981 under the title "Death Dorm" (which is retained in the end credits) and was renamed "Pranks" before its present moniker; it was released theatrically in 1983 with no N.Y. playdate and is reviewed here as it gains exposure in the homevideo and cable-tv media.

Minimal storyline has Joanne (Laurie Lapinski) and several helpers staying behind at college to clean out the equipment and furnishings of dorm Dayton Hall, due for renovation, while everyone goes on vacation. They're sitting targets for a mad killer who builds up an impressive body count before Joanne and her friends even begin to suspect something's wrong halfway through the picture.

As usual, a weird-looking simpleton John Hemmit (Woody Roll) is suspected but turns out to be a good guy. As with most pictures of this type, film suffers from the fact that *it is not about anything,* i.e., there is no interesting story material to distract or captivate the viewer apart from the necessary filler of murders and wandering around footage between murder scenes. "Dorm" also proves that the familiar wish to go against the grain and avoid the genre's obligatory "save the heroine; punish the monster" ending is not so appealing when put into effect. Nihilistic twist finale comes off as just as corny as obeying the format cliche would be.

Claustrophobic production features a forgettable cast and variable gore effects. Same production team later made another horror pic, "The Power," also an unambitious formula effort. — *Lor.*

First Contact
(DOCU-COLOR/B&W-16m)

Produced and directed by Bob Connolly and Robin Anderson, in association with the Institute of Papua New Guinea Studies. Distributed in U.S. by Filmmakers Library, New York. Associate producer, Dick Smith; narrator, Rich Oxerburgh; camera, Tony Wilson, Dennis O'Rourke; sound, Ian Wilson; editor, Stewart Young, Martyn Down; music, Ron Carpenter. Reviewed at Filmmakers Library screening room, New York, March 22, 1984. Running time: **58 MINS.**

An Oscar nominee this year as best feature documentary, "First Contact" has been seen in recent months in theatrical bookings at the Film Forum, N.Y. and with the Landmark chain in Southern California, as well as in museums, universities and other special screenings.

"First Contact" won prizes at festivals in Nyon (Switzerland), San Francisco, Sydney, American Film Festival (New York), and the Grand Prix, Cinema du Reel, Fifth International Festival of Ethnographic and Sociological Films, Paris, in addition to invitational participation at the non-competing London and Margaret Mead film festivals, latter in New York. Thus "First Contact" is another excellent example of continuing high-quality filmmaking from Australia.

"First Contact" uses a formula, by now well-established in many documentaries, of combining old B&W footage taken many years ago, inter-cut with new color materials shot in the present that interprets and reappraises the past by today's standards. It's a reliable structural device that lends itself to valid retrospective reassessments when done well. The secret is to choose the right topic and to find the right past and present footage, which can result in exciting and valuable cinema.

"First Contact" concerns the remote Highland aborigines of Papua New. Guinea today, as they see themselves today in old 1930s movie footage, see themselves as simple people living for millenia in isolated mountain valleys. This old footage was shot by three brothers from Australia, prospectors burning with gold fever.

"That's how we used to be," cry the old New Guinea natives, recognizing themselves in the Leahy footage on the screen. "We'll keep this picture for each generation to see, so they can say that's us." Does that sound like vicious primitive savages? They laugh at themselves and have no animosity toward the whites who had exploited them, good-naturedly watching the screen images and reliving old memories.

The white Leahys had traveled to New Guinea with the usual tale of bringing civilization to naked heathens. To demonstrate their benevolence and the power of their weapons, the Leahys executed a few pigs and shot a village chieftain and his elders who had defied their authorities. Gramophones, tin cans, axes and other modern trappings further awed the natives.

The brothers soon had the natives subdued in fear and fascination, working at slave wages digging for gold, aided by native superstitions about the divine origins of supermen with white skins. "First Contact" is more than a curious anthropological document about primitive culture — the Stone Age caught on celluloid for a time capsule — it's also about the things we do to one another in our lust for riches.

The natives had thought — what proof had they to the contrary? — they were the only people on earth, a quarter-million of them, alone in these high valleys. Now they realized they shared the planet and they laugh at their earlier simplicity, watching themselves on the screen as they were then.

Two of the brothers, still alive as old men and filmed in their Australian homes, also smile in remembrance, but their faces grow hard when they justify their frequent use of deadly force. "I didn't go up there to get a suntan," explains one, "I went up there for the love of James Leahy, and I didn't do too badly."

Such casual colonial racist confessions are inter-cut with old Australian newsreels showing giant dredges and hoses despoiling the mountain beauty. —Hitch.

One Night Stand
(AUSTRALIAN - COLOR)

Sydney, March 26.

Hoyts Distribution release of a Michael Edgley International presentation, in association with Astra Film Productions. Produced by Richard Mason. Directed and written by John Duigan. Executive producer, Simon Wincer; associate producer, Julia Overton; camera (color), Tom Cowan; editor, John Scott; music, William Motzing; production designer, Ross Major. Reviewed at Hoyts Theatrette, Sydney, March 2, 1984. Australian censor rating: M. Running time: 94 MINS.
Sam .... Tyler Coppin
Sharon .... Cassandra Delaney
Brendan .... Jay Hackett
Eva .... Saskia Post
Themselves .... Midnight Oil

The current crop of nuclear war-themed pictures has so far come up with a disaster movie ("The Day After"), a family weepie ("Testament") and a boy's adventure ("WarGames") and all have been effective in their different ways. No one has yet treated the whole subject as a colossal bad joke, which Stanley Kubrick did to devastating effect with "Dr. Strangelove" which capped and temporarily ended the previous cycle of such pics. While not to be compared with that particular classic, Australian John Duigan has attempted in "One Night Stand" the very difficult task of making a rather nervously amusing exploration of an almost unbelievable situation.

It's New Year's Eve on a hot summer night in Sydney. The previous week has seen peace activists demonstrating against visiting U.S. nuclear ships, while news and tv reports indicate a crisis situation in Europe. Sharon and Eva, however, are oblivious to what's going on outside their immediate

area of interest: two very average Aussie teenagers, they share an apartment in the old part of the city and are more interested in dating boys than hearing about threats of war.

Sharon works at the Sydney Opera House, where the very popular local group Midnight Oil is having an SRO New Year concert in the largest auditorium; the girls meet up after the show, intending to go to a party, but they never make it. Over a transistor radio comes the news nobody thought was possible: nuclear war has broken out in Europe and North America, and bombs have already dropped on U.S. facilities in Australia: everyone is warned to stay where they are.

Thus begins a long, long night. The two girls are joined by two young men: Brendan, who works as a cleaner in the Opera House, and Sam, an American sailor who's jumped ship. They while away the time exploring the vast building, engaging in nervously banal chatter, and even playing a game of strip poker. With the dawn, however, the enormity of the situation finally comes through, and at the same time the realization that there are more lethal bombs to come.

Pic builds inexorably to a truly shattering climax, yet doesn't rely on special effects or histrionics. Duigan seems to suggest that, in Australia at least, the world will end not with a bang nor exactly a whimper, but with a puzzled question-mark. His film deals with the most horrifying of subjects, but he plays it for a kind of flip humor as his four characters struggle to cope with a situation beyond their understanding, and don't really know how to tackle it, or how to get through what may be their last night on earth.

It's a daring approach, uniquely different for an Australian feature, and sometimes it treads a very thin line between working and appearing banal. But overall, and despite some rather strident acting early on, it does work, and the final impact is considerable.

Duigan even introduces footage from Fritz Lang's "Metropolis" (the film which played the Opera House cinema that fatal evening)

Technically, "One Night Stand" is one of the best Aussie pics, though its budget was comparatively modest. Tom Cowan's photography is outstanding, with early exteriors providing images of Sydney never seen before: the girls' apartment building, for instance, comes out looking totally artificial and very strange via Cowan's inventive lensing. Production design is tops, and there's a state-of-the-art sound mix.

Whether the public will respond is the big question. Hoyts have prepared a clever ad design for local

release (the four characters sheltering under colored umbrellas with the nuclear cloud behind them) which is eye-catching. Presence of Midnight Oil, one of the most popular groups in Australia right now, is an obvious plus. But will audiences go for Duigan's delicate blend of styles? Pic doesn't fit snugly into any particular category, and this may be unsettling enough to prevent wide audience acceptance.

Pic definitely has international possibilities on its off-beat treatment of the theme, though again it's clearly not everyone's idea of what a nuclear film should be like. Added to which the fairly accurate Australian dialog, which is often deliberately banal, may not travel.

All told, a film of originality, invention and daring which deserves to find audiences but could be too offbeat to connect with the kids it's aiming at. — Strat.

The Good Fight
(DOCU-COLOR/B&W-16m)

A production of the Abraham Lincoln Brigade Film Project, released by First Run Features, New York. Produced and directed by Noel Buckner, Mary Dore, Sam Sills. Narrated by Studs Terkel. Voice of La Pasionaria, Colleen Dewhurst; voices of Father Coughlin and of Ernest Hemingway, narrating his "The Spanish Earth;" project historian, David Paskin; camera, Stephen Lighthill, Peter Rosen, Joe Vitagliano, Renner Wunderlich; editor, Buckner; animation, Patty Curran; music, Wendy Blackstone and Bernardo Palombo. Previewed on March 22, 1984, at Film Forum, New York. Running time: 98 MINS.

The fight for the freedom and independence of Loyalist Spain during the 1936-39 civil war pitted a polyglot International Brigade of 40,000 civilian soldiers from 51 nations against the well-equipped rebel armies of Gen. Francisco Franco, leading fascist officers and troops from Spanish Morocco and aided by the Nazi Condor Legion of Junker bombers, with Italian fighter planes from Mussolini, trying out new weaponry as a dress rehearsal for World War II.

The fight in Spain was lost, but not before 3,200 Americans had fought with distinction in the Abraham Lincoln Brigade, within the International Brigade. Poorly equipped, about half the Americans died in Spain, another 700 were wounded. Having risked losing their U.S. passports and citizenship by going to Spain surreptitiously, to fight for a foreign flag, Lincoln veterans returned home after the Loyalist defeat to encounter suspicion as "premature anti-fascists." Branded Communist sympathizers, blacklisted for years, unable to get work, many paid dearly for their good fight.

This tough and ironical film does not nostalgize that period nor make heroes of the volunteers. Narrated by Studs Terkel, "The

Good Fight" fills a gap in our social history. It was barely produced in time, as few survivors remain. Of 130 located and audio-taped, most were in their 70s, some died during the filming, 11 appear in the film.

"The Good Fight" intercuts color interviews with the veterans with black & white archival footage, newsreels, still photographs, posters and other Depression-era memorabilia. Also included are clips from Walter Wanger's "Blockade," written by John Howard Lawson, leader of the imprisoned Hollywood 10, starring Henry Fonda as a Spanish peasant fighting Franco.

Two of the veterans dispute the lessons of the good fight in Spain, one says the Spanish defeat was merely one lost battle within World War II that ended in victory and that the Spanish civil war gave the democracies time to react and to arm.

But there are the doubts of another veteran who says the Spanish defeat is a metaphor for the human condition, a permanent series of lost causes, with greed and bungling triumphing as always over human aspiration and lofty intention.

Both share a common pride in their long-ago sacrifices. They had done their best then and like the others had continued to do so since, in civil rights marches and for other causes, up to the present.

"The Good Fight" premiered theatrically in February in Boston, hometown of the young filmmakers collective that made the film with $225,000 of funding from the National Endowment for The Humanities. It can probably build on early dates in selected theatrical situations in other big cities, before settling down with 16m distribution and public tv. —Hitch.

Fremtidens Boern
(Children of the Future)
(DANISH-SWEDISH-DOCU-COLOR)

Copenhagen, March 15.

A Per Holst Film with The Danish Film Institute, The State Film Central, Denmark's Radio/TV and Sweden's Channel 2 TV production, Kaerne Film release. Original conception, script and directed by Ove Nyholm. Camera (Eastmancolor) Alexander Gruszynskl, Bjoern Blixt; production management, Benni Korzen, Henrik Fleischer, Jensz Arnoldus, Jane Graun; production design, Soeren Skjaer, Josef Svoboda; special effects, Preben Seltoft, Jacob Bonfils; optical effects, Roy Field; editor, Lizzi Weischenfeldt; music, excerpts from Beethoven's Ninth Symphony; English narration, Colin Gosden. Reviewed at the Grand, Copenhagen, March 15, 1984. Running time: 60 MINS.

Ove Nyholm's "Children of the Future" has lots of cannily shot and crafted footage of life with and within the DNA molecule (the cell nucleus is seen floating like a planet in its own universe), but this is just window dressing for his docu's main interest, which lies in the provocative statements about genetic engineering offered in long interviews with genetic scientists and scholars.

"Children of the Future" had its world preem recently at the Palais de l'Europe in Strasbourg where a Danish member of the European Council is using it in his proposal towards an amendment to the U.N. and European Declarations of Human Rights: "Man must retain the right to be born different from others ... the right to be born unmanipulated." Although Nyholm's film is sober and seemingly neutral in its attitude towards genetic engineering, his sympathy lies clearly with those who warn against its application to human life. —*Kell.*

Iceman
(COLOR)

Frozen assets no help.

Vancouver, April 10.

Universal release of a Norman Jewison-Patrick Palmer production. Produced by Jewison and Palmer. Directed by Fred Schepisi. Features entire cast. Screenplay, Chip Proser, John Drimmer; camera (Technicolor), Ian Baker; editor, Billy Weber; music, Bruce Smeaton; art directors, Leon Ericksen and Josan Russo; costume designer, Rondi/Johnson; sound, Frank Warner; associate producer, Charles Milhaupt. Reviewed at Robson Square Cinema, Vancouver, March 31, 1984. (MPAA Rating: PG). Running time: **99 MINS.**

Dr. Stanley Shephard	Timothy Hutton
Dr. Diane Brady	Lindsay Crouse
Charlie (The Neanderthal)	John Lone
Whitman	Josef Sommer
Dr. Singe	David Strathairn
Dr. Vermeil	Philip Akin
Loomis	Danny Glover
Mabel	Amelia Hall
Hogan	Richard Monette
Maynard	James Tolkan

A latecomer in the newfangled genre that includes the 1980 Ken Russell extravaganza "Altered States," "Caveman," "Greystoke," "Quest For Fire" and even John Carpenter's 1982 Universal remake of "The Thing (From Another World)," Aussie helmer Fred Schepisi's second U.S. feature (after the 1982 "Barbarosa") inevitably suffers from the contents of its predecessors.

There are simply too many sequences here that, however well dramatized, remind the viewer of Miguel Godreau's antic apeman in the Russell pic. The locations used here are similar to those caught in the Carpenter frightshow.

Explorers at a remote Arctic outpost unearth an adult male Neanderthal hunter, encased in a block of ice for 40,000 years. Rivalry between dull-as-dishwater medicos and humane anthropologist Timothy Hutton centers upon the biochemical secret of the eons-spanning hibernation.

Idealist Hutton longs to communicate with the "find," dubbed Charlie. He engages in a painstaking encounter session in the deluxe vivarium that houses the iceman, who seems to be on a suicide mission as his primitive psychology is thawed out.

Newcomer John Lone, a Broadway dancer, steals the show, aided by clever makeup, as the sleeper rudely awakened. As a sexless doctor, her hair rudely shorn, Lindsay Crouse is Hutton's equal in the dourness stakes.

Chip Proser and John Drimmer's script courts the preposterous and slides kneedeep into absurdity. The lack of appealing characterizations for supporting players aids and abets this sad process of slippage into silliness.

It is to the credit of helmer Schepisi that "Iceman" is fairly intense whenever the central pair are thrown together. The director

has failed to extend the genre beyond its already established range, but his failure is an honorable one. He has overcome a maudlin musical score from Bruce Smeaton and has wrung out the tension from standard scenes. However, Schepisi has indulged his obsession with so-called "natural" man and with the nitty-gritty of ethnology.

The Norman Jewison-Patrick Palmer production is a handsome one, made with the best in intentions, but hamstrung by the uninspired scripting and the rent-a-thesp performances.

Aussie lenser Ian Baker has shot "Iceman" with panache, both for the claustrophobic interiors and the vast, icy wasteland that surrounds the principals. In the print viewed the Dolby Stereo track was a shade fuzzy, and some dialog may elude all but the most attentive listener.

"Iceman" was shot in Vancouver, at Panorama Studios, and at Steward, British Columbia, as well as near Churchill, Manitoba, Canada. — *Gran.*

Up The Creek
(COLOR)

And with a b.o. paddle.

Hollywood, April 3.

An Orion Pictures release, produced by Michael L. Meltzer. Directed by Robert Butler. Exec producers, Louis S. Arkoff and Samuel Z. Arkoff. Screenplay, Jim Kouf; camera (DeLuxe Color), James Glennon; editor, Bill Butler; coproducer, Fred Baum; production design, William E. Hiney; assistant director, Daniel McCauley; music, William Goldstein. Reviewed at the Directors Guild of America, Hollywood, April 2, 1984. (MPAA rating: R). Running time: **95 MINS.**

Bob	Tim Matheson
Heather	Jennifer Runyon
Gonzer	Stephen Furst
Max	Dan Monahan
Irwin	Sandy Helberg
Rex	Jeff East
Braverman	Blaine Novak
Tozer	James B. Sikking
Dean	John Hillerman
Rocky	Mark Andrews
Roger	Will Bledsoe
Reggie	Grant Wilson
Lisa	Julie Montgomery
Molly	Jeana Tomasina
Cork	Romy Windsor

Welcome back, Samuel Z. Arkoff (with son, Louis): "Up The Creek" is just exactly what a 1980s American International Picture would be if he were still running AIP, meaning it looks more expensive than it was, has moments of originality (but not too many to confuse the audience) and will take in every dollar it's entitled to. Pic is being distributed by AIP's successor company (following Filmways), Orion Pictures.

The key line of dialog arrives when the boy asks the girl, "Are you here for the raft race?" and she replies, "No. We're here to get laid." Nothing gets much more complicated than that and the high

school crowd who might fantasize that this is what college is really like won't care who wins the boat race, anyway.

On one raft are four likeable misfits, Tim Matheson, Stephen Furst, Dan Monahan and Sandy Helberg, who have been assured of graduation if they win. They are pitted against a quartet of rich ruthless preppies led by despicable Jeff East, who will go to any lengths to win.

Somewhere between both boats is pretty Jennifer Runyon, once romantically involved with East, but now bedding Matheson anytime the raft's ashore. Not surprisingly, the woods are also full of lots of other girls who do not believe in completely dressing for the great outdoors.

Elsewhere in the hills is a band of disqualified military school rafters, led by Blaine Novak, seemingly determined to sink everybody else with an excessive performance. But they are ultimately responsible for changing the course of the river with dynamite.

That creates an interesting aspect about "Creek," aside from the obvious. When the river starts running crazy, there are several sequences that either reflect director Robert Butler's elaborate staging or deft use of models. And it's to the credit of him and his crew that it's impossible to say which.

There's also a nifty scene in which the good guys play charades with a dog in order to find out where the bad guys have the hostage. In fact, it's the film's best scene, but smart dogs do not certify a hot sexploitation picture, so its best the audience doesn't find that out until later. — *Har.*

Hard To Hold
(COLOR)

Rock singer meets child psychologist.

Hollywood, April 10.

A Universal Pictures release of a D. Constantine Conte Production. Produced by Conte. Executive producer, Joe Gottfried. Directed by Larry Peerce. Features entire cast. Screenplay, Tom Hendley; based on story by Hendley, Richard Rothstein; camera (Technicolor), Richard H. Kline; editor, Bob Wyman; music, Tom Scott; additional music, Rick Springfield; production designer, Peter Wooley; set decorator, Philip Abramson, set designer, Joseph G. Pacelli; costumes, Rosanna Norton; sound, Willie D. Burton; associate producer, Kurt Neumann and Dana Miller; assistant director, Steve Barnett. Reviewed at Directors Guild, Hollywood, Calif., March 30, 1984. (MPAA Rating: PG.) Running Time: **93 MINS.**

James Roberts	Rick Springfield
Diana Lawson	Janet Eilber
Nicky Nides	Patti Hansen
Johnny Lawson	Albert Salmi
Owen	Gregory Itzen
Casserole	Peter Van Norden
James Roberts Band:	
Keyboard	Bill Mumy
Guitar	Tony Fox Sales
Drums	Mike Baird
2. Hard To Hold Credits	
Bass	Robert Popwell

In his feature film debut, Rick Springfield gets a chance to combine his two previous careers: as a soap opera heartthrob and a rock 'n' roll heartthrob. "Hard to Hold" is a skin-deep romance wrapped around a forgettable rock score. Even Springfield's primarily pre-teen audience may find "Hard To Hold's" high gloss hard to watch.

James Roberts (Springfield) is a rock star at the top of his game until he encounters Diane (Janet Eilber), an uptight child psychologist. He literally runs into her car and it's love at first sight. Though they have nothing in common, musically or otherwise, he chases her around San Francisco while going through the creative block of the suffering sensitive artist.

In one of the film's cute moments, he arrives outside her window to serenade her with her favorite music — a Tony Bennett imitator. That, of course, melts the ice and the scene leaps ahead to the bedroom. No matter that the couple has barely had a civil conversation to this point.

Director Larry Peerce's method through the ups and downs of the predictable romance is to jump from one beautiful location to another with frequent costume changes. Characters can't stay in one place long enough to resolve a crisis. And for further distraction, Springfield appears in a sailor outfit, jogging suit, rock garb and various states of undress.

All the moving about, pretty people and nice sets, however, don't pump any life into the characters. Cliched plot developments, such as the death of Diane's father (Albert Salmi), don't deepen the relationship, they trivialize it. The passion is make believe and the film remains on one level.

"Hard To Hold" was probably aiming for a fairytale glow, but the couple doesn't have the appeal to involve the audience in the romance. Eilber is cold and grumpy while Springfield is too good to be true.

More palatable is Patti Hansen as Springfield's songwriting partner. She supposedly represents the dark side that rocker Rick is moving away from. Though her posing at badness is exaggerated, former model Hansen is never boring to watch and puts some fire into her performance, despite the silliness of the part.

Springfield tries hard but is simply not a strong enough actor to overcome the hollow material. Eilber is attractive but her performance is too full of mannerisms to expose the character.

Production values are fine but almost work against the picture. "Hard To Hold" relies too much on its good looks to carry it. A nighttime view of S.F. from the top of the Fairmont Hotel looks good only if there is nothing going on in front of it. — *Jagr.*

Le Leopard
(The Leopard)
(FRENCH-COLOR)

Paris, April 2.

UGC release of a Fidebroc/Films A2/-UGC-Top 1 coproduction. Produced by Michelle de Broca. Stars Claude Brasseur and Dominique Lavanant. Directed by Jean-Claude Sussfeld. Written by Alain Riou, Sussfeld, Jean Amadou; camera (Fujicolor), François Catonné; editor, Jacqueline Thiedot; music, Claude Boling; art director, Eric Simon; production manager, Ginette Mejinski. Reviewed at the Clichy-Pathé cinema, Paris, April 1, 1984. Running time: 94 MINS.

Lartigue	Claude Brasseur
Pauline	Dominique Lavanant
Nick Denver	Marius Weyers
The Colonel	Max Megy
Latimer	Nini Crepon

This is the latest in local productions with exotic African settings and bears more than a casual resemblance to last year's Philippe de Broca romantic comedy-adventure "The African," in which sophisticated Catherine Deneuve and uncouth Philippe Noiret fought ivory poachers and each other in picturesque Kenya.

Replace Deneuve and Noiret with Dominique Lavanant and Claude Brasseur, emphasize the headlong adventures rather than the hotheaded romance, and you pretty much have "The Leopard," shot on location in no less picturesque Zimbabwe. As an extra added attraction, throw in South African actor Marius Weyers, who played the bumbling hero of "The Gods Must Be Crazy," the sleeper hit from Botswana that still has French moviegoers lining up at the pay windows.

Director Jean-Claude Sussfeld means to provide audiences with the good old-fashioned fun of the mindless cliffhanger. He and his screenwriters have not bothered much with plausibility or characterizations. They merely concoct a breathless chain of incident: pursuits, kidnappings, rescues, more pursuits, kidnappings, rescues and a big, literally explosive, climax à la James Bond to rid the world of evildoers (Weyers among them).

The action moves too quickly for one to be bored, but the zigzag plotting only rarely attains the level of giddy preposterousness that would make it genuinely entertaining. Still, there are some delightful scenes, as when Lavanant and Brasseur make a galloping getaway across the savannah — on ostriches!

Lavanant, a wryly amusing comedienne from the cafe-theater scene, plays a prudish novelist whose popular detective series, inspired by the personality of an old flame, is now considered outmoded. Brasseur is a rugged secret service man who resigns after a botched mission and decides to try his hand at espionage fiction.

They meet at the editor's office and take an immediate dislike to each other. But the Hitchcockian murder of a prominent physicist on the editor's doorstep incites Lavanant to live out her fantasies with a solo investigation and Brasseur to re-enlist in the service. Their separate paths collide in Africa where they become reluctant allies and together outwit their foe. — *Len.*

Where The Boys Are '84
(COLOR)

Tame update.

Hollywood, April 10.

A Tri-Star Pictures release of an ITC Production. Produced by Allan Carr. Executive producers, Terry Donnelly and Jeff Apple. Directed by Hy Averback. Screenplay Stu Krieger and Jeff Burkhart; suggested by Glendon Swarthout's novel; camera (Technicolor), James A. Contner; editor, Melvin Shapiro and Bobbie Shapiro; production designer, Michael Baugh; sound (Dolby), David Schneiderman; costumes, Marla Denise Schlom; choreography, Tony Stevens, music, Sylvester Levay; associate producer, Denis Pregnolato; assistant dirctor, Maximillian Bing. Reviewed at Orion screening room, Century City Calif., April 5, 1984. (MPAA rating: R). Running time: 95 MINS.

Jennie	Lisa Hartman
Scott	Russell Todd
Carole	Lorna Luft
Sandra	Wendy Schaal
Chip	Howard McGillin
Laurie	Lynn-Holly Johnson
Barbara	Louise Sorel
Maggie	Alana Stewart
Tony	Christopher McDonald
Camden	Daniel McDonald

"Where The Boys Are '84" is a film with modest expectations and even on those terms it's a bit disappointing. Despite the " '84" added to the title of the original 1960 film, pic seems surprisingly conservative and old fashioned at heart. R rating is more for language than nudity, which also may disappoint its target audience. Attraction of fun in the sun should still be good for lively action at the boxoffice.

"Where The Boys Are '84" is not a remake of the original, though both are indebted to Glendon Swarthout's novel. Supposed new twist is that the film is told from the girl's point of view, but these are hardly women of the '80s.

As the quartet of students readies for their Easter break in Ft. Lauderdale, Laurie (Lynn-Holly Johnson) speaks for them all when she announces that "all you need is a bikini and a diaphragm."

These are practical girls out for a good time, but when it comes down to it, what they really want is to fall in love. They start out with visions of "ten days in Sodom and Gomorrah," but what they get is really quite tame.

Plot is basically an excuse for hijinx at the beach with assorted problems of the heart getting ironed out in the end. Main wrinkle is the double-barreled attention aimed at Jennie (Lisa Hartman), the serious member of the group. Courted by wimpy musician Camden Roxbury 3d (Daniel McDonald) and hitchhiking acquaintance (Russell Todd), she must make a choice and the results are not surprising.

The rest of the group is filled out by Carole (Lorna Luft), whose boyfriend has tracked her to Florida, and aristocrat Sandra (Wendy Schaal), who regards Ft. Lauderdale as a slum until she gets arrested and falls for a cop.

The girls don't necessarily leave the beach older and wiser, but they do their best to have a good time. Director Hy Averback keeps up the frantic pace usually set in teen pics, lest the audience's attention wanders. Most scenes seem to have at least 100 bodies, all healthy and attractive, falling over each other.

Picture still doesn't totally deliver on its promise for a good time. Maybe a more authentic sounding rock soundtrack would have helped. The girls, too, seem a bit old for the college life. Or maybe nostalgia just isn't what it used to be. —*Jagr.*

Laisse-Beton
(FRENCH-ALGERIAN-COLOR)

Paris, March 26.

Luna Films release of a Marion's Film/-Films de l'Atelier/FR3/ONCIC, Algiers coproduction. Features entire cast. Produced by Jean-Marc Henchoz. Written and directed by Serge Le Peron. Technical advisor, Edgardo Cozarinsky; camera (color), Maurice Giraud; sound, Jean-Louis Garnier; editor, Jean-François Naudon; music, Jean-Pierre Mas; reviewed at the Gaumont Ambassade theater, Paris, March 25, 1984. Running time: 88 MINS.

Brian	Julien Gangnet
Nourredine	Khalid Ayadi
Jerry Lee Lewis	Youcef Rajai
Mini Meuf	Noelle Ciccodicola
Huguette Moreau	Manuela Gourary
Gilles More	Jean-Pierre Kalfon
Mick	Christian Bouillette
Rachid	Cherif Boudjelal

Serge Le Peron, a Cahiers du Cinema critic who has had some filmmaking experience in fictional and docu shorts, makes a promising feature debut with this drama about two youngsters in a drab working class suburb of Paris trying to escape to more romantic climes.

Their geographic ideal: San Francisco — the city as perceived in an old Scopitone and home movie made by the father of one of the boys, who toured there in the '60s as a flash in the pan rock star. Now dad is doing a prison term and mom makes ends meet with a job in a nightclub (which apparently involves some prostitution). The son, Brian, and his best friend, Nourredine, an Arab who shares his hopes, shoplift goods in a nearby supermarket and sell them to a local dealer to raise the fare to the west coast of their celluloid dreams.

But reality and betrayal disrupt their plans. During a filching session at the mart, Brian is nabbed by security men and taken to the police station. When the police threaten serious repercussions for his still-jailed dad, the youngster breaks down and squeals on his friend.

The former friends later meet in a duel of honor on a back lot, refereed by schoolmates and other locals, but the fight is cut short when Brian falls on a rock and is rushed to his apartment as police arrive.

In the film's final and most touching scene, the lad comes to in his own room and finds standing before his movie screen his father, who has just been released from jail. The boy switches on his projector, catching the idolized parent in its rectangle of light. Past and present, dream and reality, father and son, have been reconciled, the image seems to say.

Le Peron's own youth was spent among the cramped horizons documented in his film and his view of life among the lower income housing projects, dangerous backlots and constricting super highway belts of the northern outskirts of Paris is convincingly evoked.

There is little of the sordid or gratuitous naturalism that infects most other films of this sort, though as his own scripter, Le Peron doesn't always succeed in giving greater relief or freshness to some of the secondary or peripheral characters and incidents. A scene in which some youths insensitively have some fun with an elderly, docile local gendarme (who seems to have a screw loose) has the tacked-on quality of a souvenir that the director absolutely wanted in his film, but didn't quite know how to integrate.

Julien Gangnet and Khalid Ayadi, the youths, are credible in their first acting efforts. Noteworthy among the adults are Jean-Pierre Kalfon in an episodic part as Brian's absent but adored father, and Manuela Gourary, sweetly dimwitted as the boy's still sexy mother.

Tech credits are sound. Edgardo Cozarinsky, a Chilean-born filmmaker based in France since 1974, is technical advisor. — Len.

Angela
(CANADIAN-COLOR)

An Embassy Home Entertainment (vidcassette) release of a Zev Braun production for Classic Films and Canafox Films. Executive producer, Braun. Produced by Julian Melzack, Claude Heroux. Directed by Boris Sagal. Stars Sophia Loren. Screenplay, Charles Israel; camera (Bellevue Pathé color), Marc Champion; editor, Yves Langlois; music, Henry Mancini; sound, Patrick Rousseau; assistant director, Charles Braive; production managers, Claude Léger, Bob Gray; production design, Seamus Flannery; art direction, Keith Pepper; set decoration, Ronald Fauteux; stunt coordinator, Erik Cord; camera operator, Richard Ciupka; associate producers, Alfred Pariser, Leland Nolan. Reviewed on Embassy Home Ent. vidcassette, N.Y., April 4, 1984. (No MPAA Rating). Running time: 91 MINS.

Angela Kincaid .... Sophia Loren
Jean Labrecque .... Steve Railsback
Ben Kincaid .... John Vernon
Hogan .... John Huston
Coco .... Michelle Rossignol
Marie Labrecque .... Luce Guilbault

"Angela" is a competently made but uninvolving melodrama shot in Montreal at the end of 1976. Reviewed here for the record as it finally appears in the homevideo market, domestically unreleased film had foreign playdates only.

Production history was a troubled one, with directors Benjamin Manaster and Sidney J. Furie replaced and the late Boris Sagal taking over. As with other tax shelter-financed entries during the Canadian production boom, pic is copyrighted by a financial institution, the Montreal Trust Co.

Prolog is set during the Korean War, with Angela Kincaid (Sophia Loren) giving birth to a child while her husband Ben (John Vernon) is off fighting. Upon his return, Ben accuses her of promiscuity, does not believe the kid is his and then ends up in jail on a long stretch after Angela finks on him concerning a gun-running caper for local gangster Hogan (John Huston).

Shifting 20-plus years ahead to 1976 (with Loren and several other cast members not aging at all), Angela is a successful restaurant manager who falls in love with a young man Jean Labrecque (Steve Railsback) who is actually her son, whom she had given up for dead, kidnapped as an infant by Hogan and given to foster parents.

Melodrama pays off with a vengeful husband Ben released from prison gunning for Angela plus Angela's inevitable realization that she has unwittingly been engaged in incestuous relations.

Atmospherically filmed, picture is unfortunately flat and suffers from an emotionally unsatisfying ending. General format, including, a fine, melancholy Henry Mancini musical score, recalls the surprise 1976 hit "The Sailor Who Fell From Grace With The Sea:" a sexually repressed mature (and beautiful) woman letting go in a torrid affair. Unfortunately, though the handsome Sophia Loren is well-cast, film's erotic content is nil and would qualify for roughly a PG rating if submitted for same.

Performing is rather low-key, with Steve Railsback playing the son's part as so friendly and pleasant the character comes off as slightly retarded. Guest star John Huston is effective in a tailor-made role of the local gangster, playing checkers all day with his black henchman at a cafe, and carrying obvious mythological overtones as he carelessly determines the destinies of the other characters.

—Lor.

Rebelote
(FRENCH-B&W)

Paris, April 2.
Films de l'Atalante release of a Garance/Films Elementaires coproduction. Produced by Dominique Vignet and François Nocher. Features entire cast. Written and directed by Jacques Richard. Camera (b&w), Dominique Brenguier; art directors, Denis Mercier, Anne Grossouard-Slaveska; editor, Luc Barnier; makeup, Anne Deleris, Isabelle Blanchard; music, Pierre Jansen. Reviewed at the Marais theater, Paris, March 30, 1984. Running time: 80 MINS.

With Jean-Pierre Leaud, Christophe Bazini, Olga Georges-Picot, Jacques Robiolles, Tina Aumont, Mado Maurin, Maurice Garrel, Philippe Castelli, Gabrielle Lazure, Dominique Maurin, Vince Taylor.

"The first truly silent film since the advent of sound in 1927" boasts the press book for this oddity, produced in 1983 and first shown at the Cannes Film Festival that year.

Jacques Richard is a 30-year-old avant-garde filmmaker with a high regard for the pioneers of the cinema. For "Rebelote," his valentine to the silent era, he tried to play by the old rules as far as possible: black and white photography, inter-titles, stylized performances, and, a specially composed score to be played by live musicians as the film unspools. (Pic was accompanied by a small string orchestra during the early part of its Paris firstrun last month, though this review caught pic in a print with a recorded soundtrack.)

"Rebelote" is a sympathetic curiosity, but not much more than that. Richard may indeed have sat through endless hours of old Feuillades, Fairbanks and Griffiths at the Cinémathéque in his day, but to conceive and execute a film as was done 60 years ago is as vain and impossible an effort as trying to now compose a stage play with iambic pentameter, choral passages, and masked players.

Besides which, Dominique Brenguier's lensing fails to capture the photographic splendor of the old silent cinema. At times, "Rebelote" seems to pay a backhanded salute to the silent image as has come down to contemporary viewers in duped or faded prints. In mint copies, the well-photographed silent movie was as crisp and sharply defined as today's sophisticated productions.

The script itself is a lampoon of old film melodrama, reset in a contemporary context. Jean-Pierre Leaud is a hapless delinquent trying to survive the consequences of a turbulent, unhappy childhood and abortive attempts at professional and romantic equilibrium. But Richard's parody is short on invention and the cast ill-at-ease with imposed acting conventions from an era long gone (but not forgotten).

Pic's curiosity value could give "Rebelote" some festival invitations, but it will probably have trouble finding a voice for solid commercial playoffs. —Len.

Vive les Femmes!
(Long Live Women!)
(FRENCH-COLOR)

Paris, March 20.
UGC release of a Protecrea/UGC-Top1/TF1 Films coproduction. Produced by Dagmar Meyniel. Features entire cast. Directed by Claude Confortes. Screenplay, Claude Confortes and Jean-Marc Reiser, based on the latter's cartoon album; camera (Eastmancolor), Renato Berta; art director, Alexandre Trauner; editor, Martine Barrque; music, Nicolas Errera; costumes, Edith Vesperini; sound, Dominique Levert; production manager, Armand Barbault. Reviewed at the UGC Biarritz theater, Paris, March 19, 1984. Running time: 87 MINS.

Mammouth .... Maurice Risch
Bob .... Roland Giraud
Viviane .... Catherine Leprince
Ginette .... Michelle-Brousse
Pauline .... Pauline Lafont
Patrick .... Georges Beller
Mimi .... Michele Bernier
Albert .... Maurice Bacquet

"Vive les Femmes!" is another attempt to adapt comic strip material to the screen. Co-adaptor/director Claude Confortes, who staged a successful legit version of the Jean-Marc Reiser cartoon a few seasons back, has rounded up top technical collaborators for the film — including Alexandre Trauner, set designer, and lenser Renato Berta — but the glossy packaging is one of the things that works against the material, which cries out for black-and-white photography to approximate the stark, caricatural style of the cartoon.

Reiser, who died of cancer last year before shooting was completed (he wrote the dialog for the film), won great favor with critics and public for his strips about libidinous, slobbering, vulgar humanity. In "Vive les Femmes!" he depicted young Parisian types on the make, with men and women of equally lecherous tastes, though the latter get the upper hand through manipulative prowess.

Confortes does some good casting with Roland Giraud, as a macho swinger, and Maurice Risch, as an uncouth, unloved fatty. Both provide some very funny bits and come close to reproducing the gross Reiser male in flesh-and-blood. The ladies, Catherine Leprince and Michelle Brousse, fare less well.

The aggressive vulgarity of Reiser's strip doesn't sit well in Confortes' visualization, which despite the superficial continuity offered by the actors, is little more than a string of blackout sketches of uneven effect and little internal development. The players sometimes break the realism of the presentation by addressing asides to the camera, but the gimmuck is neither new nor adequate. Reiser's cartoons would be better suited to film animation, where the author's graphic humor could at least be preserved. —*Len.*

Aldo et Junior
(Aldo and Junior)
(FRENCH-COLOR)

Paris, April 4.

A.A.A. release of a S.E.D.P.A./TF1 Films coproduction. Produced by Jo Siritzky. Stars Aldo Maccione. Directed by Patrick Schulmann. Screenplay, Schulmann, Georges Wolinski, based on the latter's comic strip. Camera (Fujicolor), Robert Alazraki; art director, Raoul Albert; editor, Aline Asseo; music, Schulmann; songs, Wolinski and Pierre Papadiamandis; sound, Alix Comte; production manager, Pierre Saint-Blancat. Reviewed at the Ponthieu screening room, Paris, March 31, 1984. Running time: 105 MINS.
Senior .... Aldo Maccione
Fernande .... Andrea Ferreol
Junior .... Riton Liebman
Paul .... Luis Rego
Thorok .... Nico Il Grande
Max .... André Nader
Meredith .... Sylvie Nordheim

"Aldo and Junior," ex-Parafrance boss Jo Siritzky's first independent production under his new S.E.D.P.A. banner, is an overextended and unfunny live-action screen adaptation of a popular cartoon album by Georges Wolinski, who worked on the screenplay with Patrick Schulmann. Latter is the young director who made a big commercial splash in 1979 with his first feature comedy, "Et la Tendresse? Bordel," but has been treading water since. His helming here often borders on amateurism.

Entire film is tailored to its star, Aldo Maccione, the hulking Italian comic whose mock macho antics have earned him a certain popularity here, which explains the film's title: the original comic strip was called "Junior."

Maccione plays a former revolutionary of the May 1968 student uprising generation who has gone through a bad marriage and ended up raising his son, Junior, alone. The boy isn't quite a chip off the old hippy block, however, since he develops as a clean-faced, utterly straight A middle class-minded young man, worried about dad's future.

The odd father-son relationship is supposed to be the motor of the film, but the screenplay evolves as a series of poorly articulated episodes that only incidentally reflect the initial premise. Longest, and worst, of these concerns Maccione and Junior (played by Riton Liebman, the precocious youngster in Bertrand Blier's "Get Out Your Handkerchiefs") separately plotting to extract a young man from a high class male bordello where he is forcibly employed. The sequence is executed with all the grace and

energy of a third-rate sex farce performed by a geriatric cast.

Maccione is sometimes vulnerably sympathetic as the perplexed dad, but he's helpless against the indigent script and direction. Andrea Ferreol has a stupid secondary role as Maccione's amorous neighbor. Other casting is poor.
— *Len.*

Dance Music
(ITALIAN-COLOR)

Rome, March 13.

A D.M.V. release, produced by Galliano Juso for Metrofilm, Filmes International, Nuova Dania Cinematografica, National Cinematografica. Features entire cast. Directed by Vittorio de Sisti. Screenplay by Mario Amendola and Bruno Corbucci. Camera (Eastmancolor), Giorgio Di Battista; editor, Daniele Alabiso; art director, Claudio Cinini; choreography, Steve Mustafa; music, Paolo Casa. Reviewed at Del Vascello Cinema, Rome, March 12, 1984. Running time: 101 MINS.

There's more flash than dance in this blatant spinoff.

One of the first Italo "Flashdances" to hit the screens, "Dance Music" is a hodgepodge of recent American teen pics with no identity of its own. Despite bursts of modernistic shooting and editing techniques, story line is stale and unconvincing. Pic was strong in Germany but has done only moderate trade here with youthful patrons onshore and looks like a long-shot elsewhere.

Though pic's shortage of originality is deliberate, story line is straggling. Hoofing talent, left to the young cast who were presumably also picked for their screen presence, is unexceptional. Tale has a bunch of kids living together in an apartment-dance studio, where they work on their numbers in colorful leotards in front of a full-length mirror. When they're not dancing they're washing cars and waiting tables to keep body and soul together and save the fare to New York, where an "audition" is being held.

The youthful cast seems to execute all its own footwork without the benefit of doubles. None appears to be a professional actor and pic is hampered by unconvincing, inexperienced thesps called on to carry a thin script forward on the strength of ensemble acting.

Helmer Vittorio De Sisti is to be credited with good slow-and-stopmotion lensing and camera tricks that inject some life into the dance numbers, staged in some of Italy's most beautiful locales. —*Yung.*

Midt om natten
(In The Middle Of The Night)
(DANISH-COLOR)

Copenhagen, March 2.

A Nordisk Film with Medley records, Knud Thorbjoernsen and The Danish Film Institute

production, Nordisk Film release. Features entire cast. Directed by Erik Balling. Based on original story by Kim Larsen. Script, Henning Bahs, Balling; camera (Eastmancolor), Claus Loof; production management, Tom Hedegaard, Lene Nielsen; production design, Henning Bahs; music, Kim Larsen; musical arrangements, Henning Pold, Soeren Wolff; editors, Finn Henriksen, Leif Axel Kjeldsen; stunt coordinator, Eddie Stacey. Reviewed at the Imperial, Copenhagen, March 1, 1984. Running time: 128 MINS.
Benny .... Kim Larsen
Arnold .... Erik Clausen
Susanne .... Birgitte Raaberg
Elderly Bum .... Holger Boland
Charles .... Buster Larsen
Police Lietenant .... Frits Helmut
Susan's Father .... Ove Sprogoe
Charles' wife .... Judy Gringer
Spacy .... Allan Olsen
Bumand .... Poul Bundgaard
Also Holger Boland, Ellen Winther Lembourn, Anders Hove, Henning Sprogoe, Lea Risum Broegger, Morten Fusinger, Jesper Milsted, Toommy Frederiksen, Leif Sylvester Pedersen, Jimi Hoegh Daneilsen, Martin Vieth.

In his first feature after 13 years and as many entries in the perennially boxoffice-topping "Olsen Gang" feature comedy series, writer-director Erik Balling has turned to a big-scale adventure story, filled with topical political asides and by-the-ways, some music, some comedy and some bloodoozing drama.

"The Middle Of The Night," an original story by singer-songwriter, entertainer and now actor Kim Larsen, has been scripted by Balling and Henning Bahs into a plot involving friendship between two men in their 30s being put to the test by unemployment at a time of political unrest.

Pragmatic Arnold (Erik Clausen) and easy-going Benny (Kim Larsen) are plumbers out of work and into a lot of moonlighting. They are also the leading spirits in a collective of younger counterculture strays. In their abandoned factory home, they face the assaults of chain & leather gangs and populist politicians. In between, they also have to cope with sensationalist journalism and tv panelists, and until everything explodes in raw and not too deftly choreographed violence, they go their merry way about living right and poking fun at The Establishment.

Balling has too many current subjects up for satirical treatment at the same time. This makes for unwieldy drama and for a story line that too often goes slack. Too many minor characters are allowed to appear as strictly schtick performances, but Larsen and Clausen in the leads remain convincing throughout — along with newcomer Birgitte Raaberg as the young woman who sleeps with one of them because the other one, whom she loves, is too shy to ask. Film has production design of a high order. Larsen's songs are sung by himself in a way that blends naturally into the dramatic context. "In The Middle Of The Night" is short on art house finesse, but it has a robust air about

it and enough satirical punch on currently universal issues to carry it through the fest circuit —*Kell.*

The House By The Cemetery
(ITALIAN – COLOR)

An Almi Pictures release of a Fulvia Film S.R.L. production. Produced by Fabrizio De Angelis. Directed by Lucio Fulci. Stars Catriona MacColl. Screenplay, Fulci, Dardano Saccheti, Giorgio Mariuzzo, from story by Elisa Livia Briganti; camera (Luciano Vittori color), Sergio Salvati; editor, Vincenzo Tomassi; music, Walter Rizzati; makeup special effects, Giannetto De Rossi, Maurizio Trani; stunt coordinator, Nazarreno Cardinali; assistant director, Roberto Giandalia. Reviewed at RKO Warner 1 theater, N.Y., March 31, '84. (No MPAA Rating; selfimposed equivalent X Rating). Running time: 78 MINS.
Lucy Boyle .... Catriona MacColl
Norman Boyle .... Paolo Malco
Ann .... Ania Pieroni
Bob Boyle .... Giovanni Frezza
Mrs. Gittelson .... Dagmar Lassander
Dr. Freudstein .... Giovanni de Nari

"The House By The Cemetery" (Quella Villa Accanto Al Cimitero), made in 1981, is prolific Italian director Lucio Fulci's riposte to Stanley Kubrick's hit "The Shining," delivering effective scenes of tension and fright but severely limiting its appeal by reliance upon extraneous payoffs of extremely realistic bloodletting and gore. U.S. distributor Almi Pictures is releasing the picture with the familiar "No one under 17 will be admitted" ad line to tap the fringe audience for explicit violence.

Storyline has the nuclear Boyle family moving into Oak Mansion in the small town of New Whitby (near Boston), where dad Norman (Paolo Malco) is to spend six months on a research project while wife Lucy (Catriona MacColl) and son Bob (Giovanni Frezza) enjoy a "vacation" at the gloomy site. A killer in the basement is iteratively murdering everyone in sight, and turns out to be one Dr. Freudstein, a mad scientist banned from the medical profession in 1879 and still alive by experimenting on himself using cells from the corpses of his victims.

Picture suffers from poor continuity, as its abbreviated running time has had plot and transition scenes sacrificed in favor of leaving the gore intact. After one excruciatingly effective scene of a large bat attacking Norman, there is a drastic jumpcut to an unrelated scene wherein Norman is uninjured, but later in the film he reappears with a properly bandaged hand.

Location lensing in New England and Manhattan is a plus (interiors were shot in a studio in Rome) but Fulci overdoes the zooming and racking of focus, as well as near parodying the Italian practice of tight closeups of eyes filling the anamorphic wide-screen. English dubbing is only approximate and haphazardly synchronized.

A Fulci regular, British actress Catriona MacColl (currently in the U.S. miniseries "Last Days of Pompeii") is fine as the frightened mother while blonde moppet Giovanni Frezza (the kid in another recent Italian release "Warriors Of The Wasteland") is a surefire audience surrogate as her imperiled son. Frezza's seeming hallucinations of a little girl playmate from Oak Mansion are used to deliver an ending similar to Jack Nicholson's ultimate fate in "The Shining." — *Lor.*

Las Amantes Del Señor De La Noche

(The Lovers of the Lord of the Night)
(MEXICAN-COLOR)

Mexico City, March 15.

Produced by Isela Vega for Cinematografica Fenix, S.A. Stars Elena de Haro and Isela Vega. Directed by Vega. Screenplay, Vega; camera (color), Angel Bilbatua; music, Pedro Pacencia and Pancho Saenz; editor, Manuel Landeros. Reviewed at Churubusco Studios screening room 1, Mexico City, March 14, 1984. Running time: **97 MINS.**
Amparo ....Isela Vega
Venusita ....Elena de Haro
Don Venustiano
.............Emilio (El Indio) Fernández
Pedro ....Arturo Vázquez
Saurina.....................Irma Serrano
Maid ....Lilia Prado

Actress Isela Vega shows in her directorial debut with "Las Amantes del Señor de la Noche" she can produce a marketable and entertaining product. The pic features newcomer Elena de Haro as Venusita, daughter of Don Venustiano, played by Emilio (El Indio) Fernández. Venusita means "Little Venus," and De Haro takes the name seriously as she perks to the growing desires of adolescence brought on by Pedro (Arturo Vázquez), son of a local merchant. The merchant, afraid her son will marry this small-town girls, sends Pedro off to the U.S. to study.

The girl, driven crazy by her first taste of love, turns to her governess Amparo (Vega) for help and the two seek out the aid of the town witch Saurina (Irma Serrano), who uses black magic to kill the merchant and bring the boy back home.

The script, also by Vega, ably deals with Mexican superstitions and belief in black magic, while avoiding a kitsch humor that could have easily overwhelmed the film. The tone is carefully maintained and even Serrano's outlandishness works to carry the pic's theme to its logical conclusion: a blood sacrifice to atone for lost innocence and as payment to the powers of darkness.

The nature of Venus' family life also reflects popular Hispanic attitudes such as the power of the

patriarchal society where a man is fully justified for killing his wife and her lover; and a daughter is denied a son's inheritance.

"Las Amantes del Señor de la Noche" has proved Vega's power as a director to manipulate images and storyline into an entertaining low-budget whole. —*Lent.*

Kaddish
(DOCU-B&W)

A Ways and Means Production, New York. Producer, director, editor, Steve Brand; Associate producer, Robert Rosenberg. Camera (black & white), Robert Achs; original music, Andy Statman; maps, Mayin Lo; artwork, Barbara Soloway Statman; Major funding provided by the National Endowment for The Humanities. A presentation of New Directors/New Films series, from the Film Society of Lincoln Center and the Dept. of Film of the Museum of Modern Art, New York. Previewed in Lorimar screening room, New York, March 30, 1984. Running time: **92 MINS.**

The documentary "Kaddish" is a family saga of death and heartbreak. The suffering is redeemed in its final moments by belated realizations and by a guarded hope — not optimism, but a certain affirmation.

"Kaddish" concerns a Jewish family, the Kleins, caught in the Nazi Holocaust as it engulfed Hungary. As World War II began, it seemed inconceivable to the Hungarian Jews that mass genocide was the Nazi goal. Their Jewish elders counseled faith and patience, withholding the terrible truth from their people, fearful perhaps of causing panic.

Zoltan Klein's son, Yossi, although born an American, inherits the Holocaust trauma of his father. Yossi's spiritual odyssey is the center of the film. Yossi dedicates himself while at school and in early manhood to a militant Jewish activism, encouraged by his father.

But Yossi's activism is mixed with doubts, as he explains on camera and as voice-over for archival news footage and old home movies. Morally and intellectually, Yossi searched for his own identity and life-purpose, aware that the heavy shroud of the Holocaust burdened his life.

The kaddish is now complete. It is a process and a lesson that many children, Jews and non-Jews, go through in a search for selfhood. Dramatically, the kaddish as a catharsis and as a re-structuring is a staple in American theater.

Producer-director Brand, ex of the N.Y.U. film school, children's television, and A.B.C. News 20/20 — has made an important film of lasting value in his first independent documentary venture. The film has theatrical possibilities if properly marketed.
—*Hitch.*

El Dia Que Murió Pedro Infante
(The Day Pedro Infante Died)
(MEXICAN-COLOR)

Mexico City, March 12.

Produced independently by Películas Mambo. Stars Humberto Zurita. Directed by Claudio Isaac. Screenplay, Isaac; camera (color) Nicolas Echevarría; music, Nicolas Echevarría; editor, Rodolfo Montenegro; production manager, Alejandro Liceaga. Reviewed at Condominio Cinematográfico screening room, Mexico City, March 12, 1984. Running time: **90 MINS.**
Pablo Rueda ....Humberto Zurita
Laura ....Delia Casanova
Julia ....Chela Braniff
Elena....................Luz María Jerez
Adriana.......................Tina Baker
Gabriel ....Joisé Angel Garcia
Anselmo ....Alfonso Arau
Elsa ....Leticia Perdigón
Editor ....Pedro Armendariz
Neighbor ....Carmen Salinas
Rodolfo ....Miguel Angel Ferriz
Worker...............Juan Angel Martínez

Claudio Isaac's second pic, "The Day Pedro Infante Died," comes as a pleasant suprise. The independent film, produced by a group of eight persons as Películas Mambo, deals with the life of young artist-writer Pablo Rueda (Humberto Zurita).

The title, apparently misleading, is not. The artist-writer was born the day Infante died. He was delivered into a world on the death of the Mexican film and song hero. In the same year (1957), the Angel of the Independence monument fell from her perch during a large earthquake.

Rueda sees the symbolism inherent in these two symbols: the death of a myth and the fall of independence. He lives an existential life as he reacts to the world around him and sees the limited independence he really has.

Rueda is viewed in how he relates to those around him, his unsuccessful love affairs, his friends and his neighbors. He moves in a society that for him holds only a semblance of order and he defines his role by how he responds: through his drawings and writing.

The film, clearly autobiographical, is parallel to that of the young writer as he goes to publish his second book, much as Isaac must encounter the critics with his second film. He anticipates the confrontation.

In the film, an editor (Pedro Armendáriz) gives Rueda the benefit of the doubt, telling him that even though he has a unique vision of the world, it is elitist and won't sell.

The same can be said about the film. It is personal and unique, but also uncompromising and probably won't draw crowds at the box-office. But Isaac wants to make a film that says something about the world he lives in, and that is what he achieves.

He has grasped the fundamentals of film and tells his story through images and juxtaposition of scenes. The use of sound and

music corresponds perfectly with the images making tone an important aspect of the picture.

"The Day Pedro Infante Died" establishes Isaac as a voice to be reckoned with in Mexican cinema, but will find its strongest audiences in art film houses.—*Lent.*

Hookers On Davie Street
(CANADIAN-DOCU-COLOR-16m)

Toronto, March 21.

Pan-Canadian release of a Spectrum Films Production. Produced and directed by Janis Cole and Holly Dale. Camera (color, 16m), Nancy Blue, Paul Mitchnick; editors, Cole and Dale; sound, Aerlyn Weissman; music, The Crusaders. Reyiewed at National Film Board screening room, Toronto, March 21, 1984. Running time: **86 MINS.**

Docu team of Janis Cole and Holly Dale, who probed prison life in their Genie Award-winning "P4W: Prison for Women" have staked out new territory — prostitution — in their riveting "Hookers on Davie Street." It's a natural for festival circuits and specialized venues, notably women's groups. With careful handling of this hot topic it could attract a commercial run, especially here where the country is in the midst of a federal investigation into pornography and prostitution.

Davie Street in Vancouver is an unusual strip for prostitutes across Canada: it's pimp-free. hookers get to keep whatever they make and don't have to pay anyone for protection. There's a solidarity among those who work the area that propels them to each other's defense if they meet up with bad tricks. And there's a panoply of humanity here: male and female prostitutes, transvestites, juvenile hookers, transsexuals.

What makes the docu especially effective is Cole and Hall's compassion for the subject and establishment of trust with the prostitutes. The film combines actual footage of street solicitations with talking-head interviews. Real portraits are fleshed out.

While there's humor and warmth in the confessions, the overall tone is one of urgency.

Big plus is that there's no intrusive narration. The street action and interviews are self-sustaining and powerful. Tech credits, aside from some muffled street sounds, are fine. The camera was mounted in a van across from the main corner of Davie Street and caught the prostitutes soliciting their tricks. This docu offers a mainline injection of real life. —*Devo.*

Pessi Ja Illusia
(Pessi and Illusia)
(FINNISH-COLOR)

Berlin, Feb. 28.

A Finnkino Oy production. Directed by Heikki Partanen. Features entire cast.

Script, Erkki Makinen, Riitta Rautoma, Jorma Kairimo, Partanen, from the book by Yrjo Kokko; camera (Fujicolor), Henrik Paersch; editor, Rautoma; music, Kari Rydman. Reviewed at Berlin Film Festival (Children's Section), Feb. 26, 1984. Running time: **77 MINS.**

Spiderman ....Jorma Uotinen
Illusia ....Annu Marttila
Pessi ....Sami Kangas
Captain ....Raimo Gronberg
Soldier ....Esa Suvilehto
Mother Mouse..............Eija Ahvo
White Death ....Pauli Pollanen
Jay ....Rabbe Smedlund

This very beautiful and most original fantasy film for children was inspired by a book written during World War II by a Finnish officer, Yrjo Kokko. Set in splendid forests, among soldiers anxiously awaiting an attack in the front line, pic introduces Illusia, a petite fairy who descends to earth from the rainbow where she lives with her parents. She meets Pessi, a furry little gnome, and they spend the summer happily together, although the evil Spiderman clips Illusia's wings while she sleeps.

Comes the icy winter, Pessi helps to make shelter for his small friend, though he falls ill after an encounter with White Death. All ends happily, as in the best fairy stories, but not before the little couple runs into all sorts of danger.

Mixture of reality (the soldiers) and fantasy (Pessi and Illusia and the strange creatures they encounter) works by virtue of its imaginitive invention and beautiful acting. Closest comparison is with Stanley Donen's "The Little Prince" (though "Pessi and Illusia" mercifully lacks songs) and indeed Jorma Uotinen, who plays the sinister Spiderman with balletic grace, is not too different from Bob Fosse's Snake in the earlier film.

Obviously very tricky to market internationally, nonetheless pic deserves to be seen for its beauty and its disarmingly direct approach to the fantasy. Makeup and costumes are great, with the gay Jaybird (Rabbe Smedlund) a particularly beautiful creation. Spiderman and White Death (Pauli Pollanen) are suitably creepy, the latter meeting a sticky end at the hands of the resourceful Pessi.

Forest locations, in summer and winter, are spectacularly lensed by Henrik Paersch. Delightful pic copped the UNICEF prize at Berlin and was one of the most popular items in the Children's section of the Fest. — *Strat.*

Les Morfalous
(The Vultures)
(FRENCH-COLOR)

Paris, April 2.

A.A.A./Cerito Rene Chateau release of a Cerito Films/V. Films/Soprofilms/Carthago Films coproduction. Produced by Alain Belmondo. Stars Jean-Paul Belmondo. Directed by Henri Verneuil. Screenplay, Verneuil, Michel Audiard, Pierre Siniac, based on Siniac's novel. Camera (Fujicolor), Edmond Se-

chan; art director, Jacques Saulnier; editor, Pierre Gillette; sound, Alain Sempé; music, Georges Delerue; production-manager, Jacques Juranville. Reviewed at the Gaumont Ambassade theater, Paris, April 1, 1984. Running time: **105 MINS.**

With: Jean-Paul Belmondo, Jacques Villeret, Michel Constantin, Michel Creton, François Perrot, Marie Laforet, Robert Lombard, Caroline Sihol.

Jean-Paul Belmondo's breezy macho charm is all that matters in "Les Morfalous," latest in the French actor's chain of commercial blockbusters. Helmed by Henri Verneuil, the veteran commercial filmmaker who has directed Belmondo in seven previous hits, this desert adventure set in wartorn Tunisia in 1943 dilutes the traditional ingredients of action, suspense and romance so nothing will interfere with the spotlight fixed on its center-stage star.

Belmondo walks nonchalantly through the part of a French Foreign Legionnaire, embarked with a detachment of comrades to retrieve 6-billion francs of gold bullion from a French bank in a deserted Tunisian town. No sooner do the trucks pull up at their destination, than th legionnaires are decimated in a German ambush.

Only survivors are, of course, Belmondo, mates Michel Constantin, and Michel Creton, and Jacques Villeret, an overlooked artillery officer from an earlier massacre. They immediately lock horns on what to do with the gold, with Constantin advocating fulfillment of their original mission and Belmondo pushing to split the booty among themselves.

The action unfolds with the dreary predictability and directorial anonymity that one has come to expect of a Belmondo vehicle. The only surprise here is that the actor has no daredevil stunts with which to impress his vast following. Apart from wielding a machine gun, and beating up Constantin, Belmondo has rarely appeared less physical in an action picture.

The dialog by Michel Audiard, an habitual scripter for Belmondo, reaches new depths in crassness and vulgarity. Tech credits are routine, despite the top-ranking collaborative talent hired. — *Len.*

The Black Room
(COLOR)

Unappealing horror picture.

A CI Films release of a Butler-Cronin production. A Lancer Prods. picture. Executive producer, Douglas P. Cronin. Produced by Aaron C. Butler. Directed by Elly Kenner and Norman Thaddeus Vane. Features entire cast. Screenplay, Vane; camera (color), Robert Harmon; editor, David Kern; music, Art Podell, James Achley; sound, Robert Marts; Steadicam operator, Andrew Mart; art direction-set decoration, Yoram Barzilai; assistant director-associate producer, Ami Amir; post-production supervision, Butler; makeup artist, Silvia Florez. Reviewed at 42d St. Empire theater, N.Y., March 23, 1984.

(MPAA Rating: R). Running time: **87 MINS.**
Jason ....Stephen Knight
Bridget ....Cassandra Gaviola
Larry ....Jim Stathis
Robin.....................Clara Perryman
Sandy ....Geanne Frank
Lisa ....Charlie Young
Terry ....Christopher McDonald
Milly... ....Linnea Quigley

"The Black Room" is a pretentious, thoroughly unappealing horror picture whose poster and advertising promise a dark, sexy opus that does not materialize on screen. Filmed in January 1981, delayed release looks to grim box-office.

The script by Norman Thaddeus Vane (who also takes a codirector credit) awkwardly meshes two separate stories: (1) Jason (Stephen Knight) is a California artist living with his beautiful model sister Bridget (Cassandra Gaviola). He suffers from a blood disease that requires replacement of his blood at least twice a week, and duo are given to ensnaring unwary young visitors in their mansion's Black Room, photographing their sex acts through a one-way mirror, and then killing them for their blood. Corpses are neatly buried in coffins in the garden.

(2) Larry (Jim Stathis) is a young married man having sexual problems with his wife Robin (Clara Perryman). Larry answers Jason's ad for a low-cost home in the Hollywood Hills and starts acting out his sexual fantasies in the Black Room with various women he picks up. Unbeknownst to him, Jason and Bridget are killing his partners for their blood.

Absurd finale has both Jason and presumably normal sister Bridget turning into zombies after Larry, and Robin kill them, a supernatural tangent not justified by the preceding footage and guaranteed to anger a paying audience.

Film's sole highlight is a lengthy, showcasing role for the exotically beautiful model-turned-actress Cassandra Gaviola (aka Gava), who later had small parts in "Conan The Barbarian," "Night Shift" and "High Road To China." Casting of Stephen Knight, who looks like an entirely different nationality, as Gaviola's brother is an error.

Technically, the film is sloppy, with frequent shots from the window side (peering into the Black Room) producing mirror images of the watcher. Picture is also an object lesson for itinerant filmmakers in how not to use the Steadicam. — *Lor.*

Fariaho
(Vagrants)
(EAST GERMAN-COLOR)

Berlin, Feb. 24.

A DEFA Film Production, Babelsberg Film Unit, East Berlin; world rights, DEFA Aussenhandel, East Berlin. Features entire cast. Directed by Roland Gräf. Screenplay,

Martin Stephan, Gräf; camera (color), Jürgen Brauer; sets, Georg Wratsch; music, Günther Fischer; production manager, Dieter Anders. Reviewed at Berlin Film Fest (Info Show), Feb. 24, '84. Running time: **92 MINS.**

Cast: Franciszek Pieczka (Fussberg), André Hiller (Achim), Arianne Borbach (Marianne), Jaecki Schwarz, Marylu Poolman, Heide Kipp, Achim Schmidtchen, Werner Godemann.

After establishing himself as a top cameraman in the German Democratic Republic, Roland Gräf turned to directing features himself in the 1970s. His best known pics are "The Flight" (1977), "P.S." (1978), and "Exploring the Brandenburg Marshes" (1982). Now he's made a remarkable portrait on life in the GDR in the postwar Fifties, "Vagrants," unspooled at the Berlinale in the Info Show.

"Vagrants" is about a group of outsiders. Sebastian Fussberg travels from village to town with his puppet-show, these miniature theatres being popular throughout southern Germany and particularly rural Bohemia in Czechoslovakia going back to the Middle Ages — indeed, in the time of the Hapsburg Empire, they constituted an effective form of Czech resistance by advocating the use of local dialects and beloved folktales.

Fussberg is just this type of stubborn individualist. During WW II, he was imprisoned with his partner by the Nazis in a concentration camp; he came away with his skin, but his friend and partner was executed. So he tries to reconcile himself with the past by taking his friend's grandson on his trips, hoping one day to pass everything on to the youngster to keep the tradition of traveling puppet-theaters alive. Everything goes well at first, but then the duo becomes a trio when a runaway girl joins the troupe — it's only a matter of time before Achim and Marianne are attracted to each other. The old puppeteer, however, is also captured by the young girl's spirit.

Gradually, the pent-up remorse in the old puppeteer erupts into an open war with society as a whole. Considering that the times are what they are (a period of stark poverty in Germany, particularly in the East), the old man has to adjust in any case to find peace of soul. As for the young couple, here too a brief romance leads to departure. In the end, the life of vagrancy is discarded for assimilation in an urban community — which, in fact, doesn't hint that any of the personal problems pinpointed in the film are liable to be solved in the future.

One of the more thought-provoking pics to emerge from East Germany in recent months, "Fariaho" (pronounced in a lyrical fashion FAR-I-A-HO) bears a strong reference to Theodor Storm's "Pole Poppenspäler" (pub. 1874). This

popular tale in German literature also features a wandering puppet-theater troupe and deals with the question of happiness from a moral standpoint. Thus, "Vagrants" leans on the same Kasper figure to search for the meaning of life in the GDR during the immediate postwar period, offering a lot for the observant public to chew on.
—*Holl.*

Der Gemeindepräsident
(The Town Mayor)
(SWISS-B&W)

Zurich, March 11.

Cactus Film Zurich production and release. Written and directed by Bernhard Giger. Stars Mathias Gnädinger. Screenplay, Martin Hennig, Peter Bichsel; exec producer and production manager, Theres Scherer; camera (black and white), Pio Corradi; sound, Hans Kuenzi; lighting, Werner Santschi; costumes and art direction, Marianne Milani; editor, Fee Liechti; music, Ben Jeger. Reviewed at the Movie 1, Zurich, March 8, '84. Running time: 90 MINS.

Cast: Mathias Gnädinger, Peter Freiburghaus, Paul Born, Eva Schär, Janet Haufler, Christof Vorster, Max Begert, Franz Mummenthaler, Christine Kohler.

Bernhard Giger, Swiss film writer and critic, made his first feature, "Winterstadt" (Winter City), in 1981. Shown at the Locarno Film Festival that year, it grabbed some critical attention, but failed to make it commercially. Giger's second film, "Der Gemeindepräsident" (The Town Mayor), has a much better chance.

The mayor of an unidentified Swiss provincial town, a burly, quiet, politically liberal type, is confronted with two crises at the same time which deeply influence his political career and personal life. One is a protesting youth group's occupation of an empty house owned by a local architect who, supposedly, bought it to have it renovated. It now turns out, however, he merely acquired it as an object for speculation.

The mayor half-heartedly tries to straighten things out with the occupants, unaware at first of the owner's hypocrisy, but to no avail. The architect had helped him along in his political career and the mayor refuses to believe in his dishonesty until he is faced with undeniable proof.

The second crisis is a personal one. The widowed mayor's closest friend, a homosexual taxi driver, falls to his death after a fight with his young lover. Following the accident, rumors are flying that the mayor himself might be gay — almost a political death sentence for a small town leader. Unable to cope with these crises, he resigns and will probably leave the town for good.

Giger narrates the simple story in an unobtrusive, realistic style, a bit slow-moving at first, but always believable. Pio Corradi's ex-

cellent black-and-white lensing is a big help in creating the desired drab atmosphere of a former village grown into a small town in just 20 years, with all the disadvantages of not being a city yet and not a village anymore.

The picture's number one asset is the performance of Swiss actor Mathias Gnädinger, but secondary parts are also a bit underwritten. A special nod is due Ben Jeger's brilliant, mood-evoking music score.
—*Mezo.*

Friday The 13th — The Final Chapter
(COLOR)

Solid b.o. prospects for Blood Bath #4.

Hollywood, April 12.

A Paramount Pictures release, produced by Frank Mancuso, Jr. Directed by Joseph Zito. Features entire cast. Screenplay, Barney Cohen, based on story by Bruce Hidemi Sakow; coproducer-production manager-assistant director, Tony Bishop; camera (Movielab color), João Fernandes; editor, Joel Goodman; production designer, Shelton H. Bishop 3d; music, Harry Manfredini; sound, Gary Rich; art director, Joe Hoffman; exec producers, Lisa Barsamian, Robert Barsamian; special make up effects, Tom Savini; special effects coordinator, Martin Becker. Reviewed at Paramount Studios, April 12, 1984. (MPAA rating: R.) Running time: 91 MINS.

Jimmy	Crispin Glover
Trish	Kimberly Beck
Sara	Barbara Howard
Rob	E. Erich Anderson
Tommy	Corey Feldman
Paul	Alan Hayes
Samantha	Judie Aronson
Jason	Ted White
Ted	Lawrence Monoson
Mrs. Jarvis	Joan Freeman
Doug	Peter Barton
Tina	Camilla More
Terri	Carey More
Nurse Morgan	Lisa Freeman
Axel	Bruce Mahler

Only thing different this time out is Paramount's chance to open on Friday, the 13th. More to the point, is the rentals history of the "Friday" genre: the first one (in 1980) returned $17,000,000, "Part II" dipped to $9,500,000, and "Part III" (with 3-D) regained ground with $15,000,000. Horror has lost some blood at the boxoffice since the last Crystal Lake rampage in '82, but followers of this particular mix of teenage sex and disembowelment should make the returns of this third sequel respectable.

Subtitled "The Final Chapter" (but don't count on it), pic marks third "Friday" go-around for producer Frank Mancuso Jr., son of the Paramount exec. Four other productions hands are all aboard for at least a second time, including composer Harry Manfredini, whose signature has accompanied the whole quartet.

Opening line of film — "I don't want to scare anyone, but Jason is still out there" — is film's only laugh, aside from unintended chuckle in the credit roll for First Aid. Everyone in sight of the lake gets it this time, except for a little boy with a fetish for masks who slaughters the crazed Jason and the boy's older sister (Corey Feldman and Kimberly Beck).

That leaves a dozen others who don't make it. More accurately, most are butchered after making it — by bowie knife, by spear, by hacksaw, by axe, by harpoon, by kitchen knife and surgical knife.

Latter killing, of dishy Nurse Morgan (Lisa Freeman) is film's most outrageously graphic as surgical blade is plunged high into her sternum as she's gutted straight down through the length of her

body. Two seconds of this is like two hours. Pic is an R and film (not for the first time) underscores fact that X in the MPAA's mind is not in practical terms a judgment related to violence.

Last-named killing of dishy Nurse Morgan (Lisa Freeman) is film's most outrageously graphic as surgical blade is plunged high into her sternum as she's gutted straight down through the length of her body. Two seconds of this is like two hours. Pic is an R and film (not for the first time) underscores fact that X in the MPAA's mind is not in practical terms a judgment related to violence. (Especially for films released by the majors — *Ed*).

Of course, nobody is expected to take this stuff seriously. Given, however, the consistency pro production value, the evisceration on parade is not campy. Film doesn't deal in imagination, just bloody cutaways. Implausibilities abound as ever, and several "Friday the 13th" veteran players make brief appearances in an opening flashback compilation of old footage.
— *Loyn.*

Strawanzer
(The Bums)
(AUSTRIAN-WEST GERMAN-COLOR)

Vienna, April 1.

An Arabella (Vienna) with Almaro Film (Munich) and Satel Film (Vienna) production, Cineart/Hans Peter Hofman (Vienna) release. Directed by Peter Patzak. Stars Elliott Gould. Original story and script, Wolfgang Einberger; camera (Eastmancolor) Dietrich Lohmann; music, Peter Zwetkoff; production design, Peter Manhardt; costumes, Heidi Melinck; special effects, Willy Neuner; production management, Herbert Reutterer, Jochen Losse-Klug, Eduard Meisel, Adolf Lehner. Reviewed in Austrian Films section of the Viennale in Urania screening room on March 31, 1984. Running time: 102 MINS.

Willie	Elliott Gould
Josef	Heinz Moog
Willie's wife	Andrea Jonasson
Willie's son	Danny Hirsch
Erwin	Andreas Goenczoel
Rainer	Hanno Poeschl
Girl In Black Leather	Evi Meisel
Boy In Black Leather	Klaus Kelterborn

Peter Patzak, an all-round able filmmaker, did not have much luck in the theaters with this Elliott Gould-starring feature whose Austrian title "Strawanzer" is a friendly slang word for bum. The non-success must largely be attributed to obvious technical shortcomings of the film as released. If the editing seems choppy, to put it mildly, this is quite obviously not the editor's fault but due to lack of vital footage to edit at all; characters, for instance, drop out of frames where they clearly were intended to remain. Script may have similar holes in it, since too often the characters' behavior leaves one completely up in the air.

"Strawanzer" is a male-bonding, father-figure and son or maybe a bum-bonding story about an alienated old railroad employee now living in the loft of an abandoned theater where he takes in Willie (Elliott Gould), an architect who occasionally leaves his wife and son to go on drink and morphine binges that have him in an almost totally derelict state. He clings only to a Leica through the lens of which he claims to see life more clearly. What the camera does see and record is the murder of a youth in a gangfight among black leather toughs. The possession of the prints will later lead to Willie's being chased by a motorcycle gang without his really knowing why. He is busier with his own latest problem, he has kidnapped his more than willing to be kidnapped son. Most of the film, however, describes Willie's and the old man's wanderings or stumblings through various railroad station restaurants.

Heinz Moog plays the old man with a certain stubborn warmth and dignity, while Elliott Gould most of the time is asked to resort to his most stumble-bummish routines. He breaks out of the latter, however, in one glorious scene of tap-dancing. Otherwise, he mostly staggers and mumbles (he is dubbed into German by Austrian singer Ludwig Hirsch) and rolls his eyes. Since there is no logic of any kind in the bonding between the two men, and due to script and editing lapses, no suspense, physical or psychological is ever achieved. Even with Elliott Gould's name as a marquee value, "Strawanzer" would seem destined for shelving if rather radical re-editing cannot save it. — *Kell*.

Swing Shift
(COLOR)

Unlikeable characters sink this World War II-era pic.

Hollywood, April 11.

A Warner Bros. release of a Lantana production. Produced by Jerry Bick. Directed by Jonathan Demme. Stars Goldie Hawn, Kurt Russell. Exec producers, Alex Winitsky, Arlene Sellers. Screenplay, "Rob Morton;" camera (Technicolor), Tak Fujimoto; editor, Craig McKay; sound, Tommy Overton; production design, Peter Jamison; costumes, Joe I. Tompkins; associate producer, Charles Mulvehill; assistant director, C.A. Myers, art direction, Bo Welch; music, Patrick Williams. Reviewed at The Burbank Studios, April, 1984. (MPAA rating: PG). Running time: 100 MINS.

Kay	Goldie Hawn
Lucky	Kurt Russell
Hazel	Christine Lahti
Biscuits	Fred Ward
Jack	Ed Harris
Annie	Sudie Bond
Jeannie	Holly Hunter
Laverne	Patty Maloney
Violet	Lisa Pelikan
Edith	Susan Peretz

With all the heartwarming heroics to choose from on the homefront in World War II, "Swing Shift" tries instead to twist some consequence out of a tawdry adulterous tryst by a couple of self-centered sneaks. Picture's credible patriotic background does not override the fact that these were not people worth fighting a war for.

Great drama, to be sure, does not depend on likeable characters and a better script might have found something here to justify such extended attention to the pair's lust to create their united states while everybody else tries to save one. But the writing and acting are too flat for the challenge.

(Screenplay is credited to the pseudonymous "Rob Morton;" Ron Nyswaner, Bo Goldman and Nancy Dowd were listed as the writers while "Swing Shift" was in production last year.—*Ed*.)

Even worse, "Swing Shift" sports a pretension that it has something important to say about the feminist significance in women being forced out of their traditional home roles to build war materials the men needed overseas.

For women, that's a proud historic point, indeed, but "Swing Shift" betrays all that every time the whistle blows at the factory. What women are really interested in, the film says, is men.

"Shift" gets into difficulty right from the start because adultery rarely works well in fiction unless the audience comes to dislike the husband before the wife finds solace in the arms of another man. But on the eve of the war, Goldie Hawn and Ed Harris are your basic nice young couple living modestly in a Santa Monica cottage until Pearl Harbor demands he immediately volunteer.

Hawn fretfully sees him off to war and somewhat timidly goes to work at an aircraft factory where she draws the immediate romantic interest of Kurt Russell. Though there are later script references to Russell's heart problem and suggestions that he feels bad he isn't somewhere getting shot at, Russell otherwise acts from the beginning like 4-F is fairly fortunate.

He is not for a moment put off by Hawn's initial protests that she's married to a sailor overseas. But given the situation, her protests are pretty feeble and, after all, results prove what he's said all along: When women say "no," they really mean "yes." (Another point that should warm modern women to the film.)

Bearded by Hawn's neighbor/co-worker Christine Lahti, the lovers spend the war having loads of fun, dancing, smooching, bedding and riding with the top down. This apparently goes on for several years though time references in the picture are extremely jarring.

Eventually, hubby Harris shows up unexpectedly and is heartbroken over his wife's infidelity. But "Swing Shift" seems more concerned that Harris' arrival drives Russell into a one-nighter with Lahti, upsetting Hawn who upsets Lahti while poor Harris crawls back to the war, presumably hoping if the Japanese become better shots he won't ever see this wonderful group again.

But Harris eventually comes home for a happy ending that suggests everything that went before is justified because, after all, war is tough on everybody.

Though there are many offscreen rumors about who should really be blamed for this mess, there's no question that considerable technical praise should go to cinematographer Tak Fujimoto, production designer Peter Jamison and costumer Joe I. Tompkins. They have created an evocative period that brims with patriotism and feeling for a lifestyle and values worth defending.

It's a shame that everything going on behind and about the main characters in "Swing Shift" seems important and they do not.—*Har*.

Silu Huayu
(Along The Silk Road)
(CHINESE-COLOR)

Vienna, April 4.

A Xi'an Film Studio production, China Film Export and Import Corporation (People's Republic of China) release. Directed by Yan Xueshu. Story and script created collectively by the Gansu Song & Dance Ensemble. Camera (Fujicolor), Chen Wancai. Stars He Yanyun as Yingniang and the Gansu Ensemble. Reviewed in the Chinese Week section of the Viennale in the Middle Theater of the Urania Palace, Vienna, April 3, 1984. Running time: 100 MINS.

In a series of dance tableaux, director Yan Xueshu has the Gansu Song and Dance Ensemble tell the story of beautiful Yingniang's adventures "Along The Silk Road" where, during the Tang Dynasty (A.D. 618-907), she was recorded in famous murals to have been kidnapped by a dance and acrobatics troupe manager and later to have been freed through a ransom paid for her painter-father by a Persian merchant who in his turn had once been saved in a sandstorm by the painter.

The filmed dance drama is short on real narrative and dramatic strength and long on costume and decor opulence. The dancing would seem to be not too far removed from Western ballet dancing, but the director and the cameraman have more feeling for spectacle than for the rhythms and movements of dance: the dancers are allowed to crowd each other out of the wide-screen frame again and again, and the switches between masters and closeups rarely if ever serve to enhance anything but the twists of the plot, never the turns of the bodies.

There are some acrobatics and even an instance of fanciful aerial dancing full of strength and beauty, but most things come off bumpily rather than silken. In general, the Gansu Ensemble has been ill-served with this filmed mirror of their undoubtedly superior and exciting efforts. Outside of package presentation in chinese film weeks, "Along The Silk Road" will be no thoroughfare to Western acclamation in theaters, and due to its wide-screen format, it will not be squeezable into tv programming. Production date was not revealed, but it would seem to be of recent vintage.—*Kell*.

Unfinished Business
(CANADIAN-COLOR)

Hollywood, April 12.

A Zebra Films with the National Film Board of Canada in associaiton with the Canadian Broadcasting Corporation production. Produced by Annette Cohen and Don Owen, associate producer, Dorothy Courtois Lacour. Written and directed by Don Owen. Camera (color), Douglas Kiefer; art direction, Barbara Tranter, Ann Pepper; editors, Peter Dale, David Nicholson; original music, Patricia Cullen, songs, Parachute Club, Alta Moda. Reviewed at the Nosseck Screening Room, Los Angeles, April 10, 1984. Running Time: 90 MINS.

Izzy Marks	Isabelle Mejias
Jesse	Peter Spence
Matthew	Leslie Toth
Peter Marks	Peter Kastner
Julie Marks	Julie Biggs
Carl	Chuck Shamata
Jackie	Jane Foster
Larissa/Larry	Melleny Brown

Don Owen's "Unfinished Business" continues the story the filmmaker began 20 years ago in "Nobody Waved Goodbye." a groundbreaking Canadian feature. Sequel picks up with the original young couple, now divoced, experiencing the travails of parents with a rebellious 17-year-old daughter.

The new film is very much the daughter Izzy's (Isabelle Mejias) story — fresh and with few strings connected back to the inspirational picture which is little known outside Canada and the festival circuit. Like her estranged parents, Izzy is at a point in her life where she is confused and directionless. This allows for a certain degree of support from her parents who relate strongly to that situation but, by and large, they attempt to instill practical, traditional values in their daughter.

A high school senior, Izzy is days away from her finals yet balks at the prospect of completing her education. She finds diversions in dope, friends, a rock club and a group of anti-nuke activists. The clash between pressures from her parents and the seemingly more meaningful pursuits of the radicals sends her into the streets for a different kind of education.

Although a common enough story, "Unfinished Business" has a raw energy whch is touching and deeply felt. This is aided to a great extent by Mejias' natural screen charm and Owen's strong feel for the street atmosphere which figures strongly in the narrative.

As the story evolves, Izzy develops a strong emotional attachment to a young jack-of-all-trades at a new wave club. He, in turn, is connected to the anti-nukers through his father, an ex-lawyer who's dropped out for the cause. Also weaving through the film is her attachment to a fellow student on the verge of a breakdown and, of course, the rollercoaster relationship she attempts to cope with and between her parents — a radio commentator and a director of commercials.

While the middle section of the film is sometimes too busy with plot. Owen manages to maintain interest through his careful delineation of a situation of emotional disintegration. The sense of things falling apart in Izzy's life is keenly observed, leaving the audience breathless with concern for her plight.

Film concludes with Izzy planning to leave Toronto for Montreal with Jesse, the Mr. Fixit of the rock club, much in the same way her father initially ran away 20 years earlier. The new wrinkle is that she catches wind of the radical's plot to explode a bomb at a nuclear plant and wrestles with her need to inform the police of the situation.

Reprising their earlier roles, Peter Kastner and Julie Briggs provide the cognoscenti with an added emotional pull to the story. The remaining supporting roles range from good to excellent, but in general one feels these parts are underdeveloped. Exception is Mejias who proves an extraordinary anchor to the helter-skelter story elements. Her genuine rapport with the camera as mentioned is a major reason for the film's success.

Technical elements are strong in pic with particular praise going to the imaginative and evocative sound mix. Music by Parachute Club and Alta Moda hits the mark nicely and Doug Kiefer's camera captures the gritty nature of the story accurately.

Basically a small, intimate portrait, "Unfinished Business" seems an ideal pickup for a studio classics division or indie company. Theme and music tie-in should help pic's appeal to youth market through universal theme and attractiveness of cast for respectable commercial dividends. — Klad.

Warming Up
(AUSTRALIAN-COLOR)

Sydney, April 10.

A JNP Films production. Produced by James Davern. Directed by Bruce Best. Stars Barbara Stephens, Henri Szeps, Screenplay, Davern; camera (color), Joseph Pickering; music, Mike Perjanik; editor, Szolt Kollanyi; sound, Ross Linton; art director, Michael Ralph; associate producer, Terri Vincent. Reviewed at Atlab theaterette, Epping, Sydney, April 4, 1984. Running time: 84 MINS.
Juliet Cavanagh-Forbes . Barbara Stephens
Sgt. Peter Sullivan .... Henri Szeps
Mrs. Marsh .... Queenie Ashton
Randolph .... Adam Fernance
Ox .... Lloyd Morris
Snoopy .... Tim Grogan
Lennie .... Ron Blanchard

A quietly amiable, but very slender, romantic comedy, "Warming Up" has some pleasant ideas and agreeable characters, but not enough substance to sustain a theatrical feature these days. As a telemovie, it could fare better.

Pic, scripted by producer James Davern, intros a feisty divorcee, Juliet (Barbara Stephens), who tires of the jock she's living with (in a super Sydney apartment) and ankles together with her 10-year-old son, Randolph, who for obvious reasons prefers to be known as Andy. Seems Juliet, a ballet teacher, has acquired a ballet school in a small country town, but on arrival they discover the place has burned down.

The staunchy feminist Juliet also runs foul of local police sergeant Peter Sullivan (Henri Szeps) when she defends herself against what she assumes to be an attack from a violent biker gang, only to discover they're harmless lads who are members of the town football team — and the lawman is their coach. Rest of the film charts the romance between the independent woman and the equally independent cop, complicated by the fact that she starts to train his footballers in classical ballet while he secretly teaches her son the rudiments of football, a sport she despises.

Stephens and Szeps are pleasant actors and seasoned professionals and the film is never really dull when they're around. But they're not given much to do and, as a comedy, "Warming Up" is crucially lacking in laughs, though the climactic football game, with the leading players doing some neat ballet steps on the sports field and consequently tripping to victory, is a modestly amusing notion.

Queenie Ashton registers as an elderly local of eccentric habits who's fond of quoting Chairman Mao, while newcomer Adam Fernance is good as the boy who wishes his mother wasn't quite so fixated against sporting activities but loves her just the same.

Technically okay in every department, pic represents the first feature outing for the team that packages "A Country Practice," currently Australia's most popular television soaper, and its television antecedents are apparent in every frame, although it was lensed on 35m for cinema release. — Strat.

Naturens Haemnd
(Nature's Revenge)
(SWEDISH-DOCU-COLOR)

Vienna, March 27.

A Jarl & Lindkvist Film production, AB Svensk Film Industri (SF), Stockholm, release. Original script and directed by Stefan Jarl. Camera (Eastmancolor), Per Kaellberg, Ejnar Bjarnason; production management, Suzanne Branner; editor, Anette Lykke-Lundberg; music, Ulf Dageby. Distribution within Sweden, Folkets Bio. Reviewed at the Urania, Vienna as official Viennale entry on March 27, 1984. Running time: 76 MINS.

Having made a minor fortune on his semi-fictional feature "A Respectful Life" (about heroin abuse among Swedish youth), writer-director-documentarist Stefan Jarl undertook a working journey through a Swedish countryside which he found badly polluted, mostly by chemicals meant to increase crops and standards of living. And he found true the words of Friedrich Engels who in 1878 stated that "for each instance of Man's manipulating Nature, Nature takes its own revenge."

The revenge, according to Jarl, who interviewed Swedish farmers en route but who avoided most official statistics as well as industry and science spokesmen, takes the shape of cancer, inflicted upon humans in 80 cases by chemical fertilizers, industrially colored foods, etc. And if it is not cancer, it is heart trouble, muscle decline or neuroses. Jarl's film might have been inspired by Rachel Carson's "Silent Spring," but sometimes it looks more like parallels to Picasso's "Guernica," when the camera closes in on the death struggle of insects and birds hit by aerial discharge of chemical refuse. Unavoidably, the animals remind us of Man's Fate as well.

Even when the images are at their most gruesome, any suspicion about "Mondo Cane" trickery can be put to rest. Jarl never manipulates even if he does juxtapose his death scenes with gorgeous cinematography of nature and animal life in unimpaired freedom. He intersperses talks with farmer families inflicted with illnesses caused by chemicals and shots from a children's cancer ward in a Gothenburg Hospital with digressions in a spoken (English-dubbed and written by Jarl and Torsten Naeslund) about the Mau-Mau freedom struggle in Kenya and may be a bit too fanciful here, but he is soon back on home ground where he has audiences by the throat. Early sales via the Berlin fest and other venues have already proven interest for "Nature's Revenge" internationally. Film has been picked up for distribution in all German-speaking territories. Where theatrical release is not possible, tv programming all over the world would seem assured. — Kell.

Angst
(Fear)
(AUSTRIAN-COLOR)

Vienna, April 2.

A Gerald Kargl Filmproduktionsgesellschaft GmbH production and release. Directed by Gerald Kargl. Original story and script, Gerald Kargl, Zbigniew Rybczynski. Camera (Eastmancolor), Rybczynski; editor, uncredited; music, Klaus Schulze. Reviewed in Austrian Films section of the Viennale on April 2, 1984 in Urania Palace screening room. Running time: 82 MINS.
The murderer .... Erwin Leder
Elderly woman .... Edith Rosset
Her daughter .... Sylvia Rabenreither
Man in wheelchair .... Rudolf Goetz

Is it at all feasible that a young man is sprung from prison for good behavior after having served 10 years for matricide only to go on a 24-hour wanton murder spree, actually eating and drinking the blood of one of the victims along with, through interior monolog, recounting evil events in his childhood to justify his current misdeeds? It should be added to the question that the killer knows nothing at all about his three victims, an elderly mother, a wheelchair-bound and retarded crippled son and a pretty daughter. They just happen to return to the suburban estate the man has broken into to find find shelter.

The writer and the director of "Fear," a psychological blood and gore feature, has an anonymous psychiatrist state at the end that all the things we have seen are just expressions of hatreds that have lain fallow during the man's 10 years in prison, and that he must be deemed sane enough to be condemned to a lifelong prison stretch without possibility of pardon. Director Gerald Kargl claims he has based his film and writer-cameraman Zbigniew Rybczynski's film on a case history only slightly fictionalized.

Fiction or fact, "Fear" has been slickly filmed with a fireworks display, flashy camera angles and other fancy footwork. It is also so soaked in blood and violence that it unavoidably will make even a hardened shocker audience wonder what on earth is the matter with this guy — and not the protagonist, the filmmaker. The way the story is told, it has no redeeming human interest value, let alone any attempt to temper things with sympathy or the nervous wit that otherwise belongs to the horror genre. It is hard to see how "Fear" would gladden any theater audience's hearts or guts, and few tv stations would ever get away with programming this film even in the most pretentious of art slots. Film has caused controversy but achieved very little boxoffice on home grounds. — Kell.

De Leeuw Van Vlaanderen
(The Lion of Flanders)
(BELGIAN-COLOR)

Brussels, Feb. 7.

A Belga Films release of a Ministerie van de Vlaamse Gemeenschap/BRT/KRO/Kunst en Kino production. Produced by Jan van Raemdonck. Directed by Hugo Claus. Screenplay, Hugo Claus, based on Hendrik Conscience's "The Lion of Flanders;" camera (Eastmancolor), Walter van den Ende; music, Ruud Bos; editor, Ludo Troch and Guido Henderickx; production manager, Gérard Vercruysse; unit manager, Jef Van De Water; first assistent director, Stijn Coninx. Reviewed at the Albert I theater, Paleis voor Congressen, Brussels, Jan. 27, 1984. Running time: 106 MINS.
Robrecht de Bethune .. Frank Aendenboom
De Chatillon .... Theu Boermans
Jan Breydel .... Jan Decleir

Pieter de Coninck ......Julien Schoenaerts
Johanna van Navarre ..Josine Van Dalsum

Heralded as the most expensive Flemish feature to date (just over $1,000,000), "The Lion of Flanders" is a drastically cut theatrical version of a four-part television series. Narrative is very abrupt, charactors are left undeveloped, motivation doesn't make much sense and sub-plots got heavily mutilated in what looks like a hasty pruning down of the 200-minute tv material.

The Flemish novelist-playwright and part-time filmmaker, Hugo Claus, wrote and helmed this heavyhanded adaptation of the famous historical novel by Hendrik Conscience, a romantic and epic account of the revolt against France of the Flemish municipalities and their victory at the Battle of the Golden Spurs in 1302.

First hour depicts the events that lead to the battle. A lot of charactors are sketchily introduced. The French are all depicted as thoroughly corrupt and depraved: a bunch of decadent traitors and vile murderers. Johanna van Navarre tops everyone as the bloodthirsty wife of the weak King Philip the Fair, a demoniac witch who hates the Flemish. The oppressed Flemish victims are, on the contrary, monuments of virtue and bravery. Those broad contrasts fit the nationalistic bill of the original novel, but don't make the film very believable for a contemporary audience.

To make matters worse, the director doesn't seem to know if he should treat his naive material seriously or tongue in cheek. Sometimes he lingers endlessly on the fanatical issues, at other times a sword fight scene looks as silly as a gunfight in an Italian western. At the end, the audience doesn't know whether "The Lion of Flanders" is a choker or a costumer.

Acting, with domestic thesps as the Flemish, and Dutch actors in the French armour and garments, is very uneven. The stilted dialog that remains after the cuts isn't any help in making the characters credible or giving them any human resonance.

To be fair, Claus wasn't given the necessarily big money to give an epic dimension to the proceedings. But even within the limits of the budget, the film looks poor, static and shows inadequate feeling for the medieval times. It furthermore lacks the drastic sweep that one expects from this sort of dated material. Despite all the bloody terror, "The Lion of Flanders" is anaemic. —*Pat.*

Tien Shia de Yi
(The World's Best Men)
(TAIWAN-CHINESE-COLOR)

Vienna, March 29.

A Central Motion Pictures Corp. of Taiwan production, Sunny Overseas Corp. (Taiwan) release. Directed by King Hu. Original story and script, King, Hsiao Yeh, Wu Nien-chen. Executive producer, Hsu Kuo-liang. Production manager, Ming Chi; camera (Eastmancolor), Chou Yeh-hsing; editor, King. Stars Tien Fung, Tang Pao-yun, Chuei Tai-ching, Cheng Pei-Pei. Hua Hsuen-hsuen. Reviewed as official entry in the 1984 Viennale on March 28, '84 at the Urania, Vienna. Running time: 99 MINS.

Popular roaming Hong Kong filmmaker/director King Hu (aka Djintjuan Hu) returns to the largest of possible of screens and to comico-historical epic material with "The World's Best Men" (also marketed abroad as "All The King's Men"). It should easily be sold into Chinese-speaking areas everywhere as popular entertainment of a nice quality level, but it is hard to take it seriously as a festival entry (it gave the local Chinese population a lot of guffaws, however, at a late evening showing).

The time of the story is 960, last year in the reign of the Emperor Chou, who suffered from epilepsy. He did not want his enemies to know, used devious means to get a famous doctor from the south to apply acupuncture more or less on the sly. Getting the doctor to come also involved bribing a famous painter with the gift of a princess as a model. Some switched heirloom pieces of jade came to play a role, too. Plus, of course, much court intrigue.

Film features only a little in the way of action acrobatics, but a lot of low comedy in settings of serious-minded production design. There is less overacting than Western audiences have come to expect from Chinese films. Story unfolds as a series of episodes, but the narrative flow of this rather forgettable epic is maintained nicely throughout. —*Kell.*

Milano '83
(Milan '83)
(ITALIAN-DOCU-COLOR-16m)

Vienna, April 3.

A Trans-World Film/RAI-3 (Rome) production and release. Written, directed, camera (Eastmancolor, 16m) and edited by Ermanno Olmi. Music, Mike Oldfield; production management, Marcello Ciena, Tony Amendola; executive producer, Giacomo Pezzali. Reviewed in the Information Section of the Viennale at the Urania Palace on April 3, 1984. Running time: 67 MINS.

Ermanno Olmi's docu "Milano '83," later to take its place among other famous filmmakers' looks at The Culture Capitals of Europe in a RAI tv series, is getting its first showings in theaters where it is sure to disappoint audiences who have come to expect the more genuinely heart-tugging and certainly more artistically refined viewpoints from the maker of "The Tree Of Wooden Clogs." As a documentarist, Olmi has only too obviously done everything himself, doing Milan on the run between rushing crowds with his hand-held camera — and most of the time in darkness, too. His shots are rarely in focus, and as to their composition, it will take a very staunch Olmi supporter to find them any more than haphazard.

Olmi himself has declared that his purpose has just been to record the collective rituals of a big city going about its 'round-the-clock business, but any such recording seems to have been beyond his practical powers. Film has no narration, which would be fine if Mike Oldfield's high-strung sing-song-cum-electronics music had not been so monotonously persistent. Olmi's name plus outside-Italy tv stations' commitment to the series will bring "Milano '83" to millions of home screens, only to have viewers search frantically for other channels after the first five minutes. They will have missed only repetitions of a once-stated theme and style: film-flam-cum-noise. — *Kell.*

Karambolage
(Carom)
(AUSTRIAN-COLOR)

Vienna, March 29.

A Neue Studio-Film GmbH production. Jupiter Film (Vienna) release. Directed by Kitty Kino. Original story and script, Kino, Reinhard Meier. Camera (Eastmancolor), Tamas Ujlaki; production design, Christoph Kanter; music, Heinz Leonhardsberger. Reviewed in Austrian Films section of the 1984 Viennale in Urania Palace screening room on March 29, 1984. Running time, 100 MINS.

Judit ....Marie Colbin
Lilo ....Renee Felden
Ernst ....Gehard Reuhmkorf
Hans ....Florentin Groll
Max ....Helfried Edinger
King ....Wilfried Baasner

Kitty Gschoepf aka Kitty Kino in "Karambolage" (the U.S. expression for this collision in the games of billiards is "carom,"while the British call it "cannon"') has a story that at least on paper reads like great stuff. A young woman, bored with, and abused by, her bourgeois-artistic friends, forsakes them and her own art studies in favor of pursuing a career as a pool player. She becomes a national champion, but just as she thinks she has finally gained equality if not superiority among males, the latter either turn their backs on her or their exposed fronts — to rape and thus degrade her again.

Unfortunately, Kitty Kino has turned this material into a long-winded film featuring not very much of either the visual excitement of billiards or the young woman's forays into male territory. Instead, we get truckloads of bar and poolroom nostalgia (complete with buxom barmaid who helps everybody, but cannot help herself) and clichéd sneering at the bourgeois crowd, and practically all men, as drunks, impotents or just plain weaklings. In the lead, Marie Colbin has moments of animal gusto to dispel her general air of morose boredom. "Karambolage" may make it in situations specializing in Women's Film but hardly anywhere else apart from some tv programming (again riding on the coattails — if there are such — of feminism).—*Kell.*

Raffl
(AUSTRIAN-COLOR)

Vienna, April 1.

A TTV-Film (Christian Berger) with ORF production, Cineart (Hans Peter Hofmann) release. Directed by Christian Berger. Based on an idea by F. C. Schmidt. Story and script by Berger, Markus Heltschl. Camera (Fuji-color), Berger; editor, Tina Frese; music, Bert Breit; production design, Lois Weinberger; costumes, Otto Kollross; production management, Helga Berger, Christoph Rohrbacher. Reviewed as official entry in the 1984 Viennale at the Urania on March 31, 1984. Running time: 100 MINS.

Raffl ....Lois Weinberger
His wife ....Barbara Weber
His daughter ....Barbara Viertl
The vicar ....Dietmar Schoenherr
The city friend ....Art Brauss

Christian Berger, a veteran tv director tired of adhering to run of the mill narrative standards, did his own producing, writing, directing and camera work on "Raffl." The result may disappoint him, since tv programming in more serious slots will probably be his film's ultimate fate although a cult adoration may spring up around it securing it some art house showings and a festival circulation (it had already been accepted at Directors' Fortnight Cannes).

Filmed mostly in puritanically clean frames with only a few dashes of Eisenstein-like action movement (columns of soldiers moving crosswise over a snowclad mountain slope), "Raffl" aims to tell most of its story in Carl Th. Dreyeresque contemplation of facial details. This way, everything is meant to be expressed through psychology, while all obvious possibilities of straight dramatic treatment are avoided most carefully.

Based on facts, film has poor, indebted, morose mountain farmer Raffl in the Tyrolean Alps point the way for French occupation forces in 1810 to the hiding place of famous freedom fighter Andreas Hofer. He does it for a reward he never receives. He does it out of the underdog's twisted drive towards some kind of a redemption. He has sought the advice first of the vicar, but has been turned away. His life is all toil and as played by Lois Weinberger he does have a certain stubborn dignity to make him look like just a bit more than a beast of burden. In a single sequence of great humor, Raffl declines to give away his information to the French commander before he has been allowed to partake in the latter's sumptuous breakfast.

Hofer is never seen. And after the betrayal, Raffl is chased out of town and picks up a new and more lucrative way of life as a storage worker in a big city far away. But happy he is not. Rather he finds he has been robbed of more than his reward, he has lost his roots, his identity; in short, himself. When he one day cannot even find his old clothes, he does not want to live any longer. The question that remains for audiences at this point is whether this footnote character to history merits so much interest, and whether exploration of the truly one-dimensional life has not already run aground on the mountain rocks of the very first few frames. —*Kell.*

Lin-jia Puzi
(The Lin Family Shop)
(CHINESE-COLOR)

Vienna, April 2.

A Beijing Film Studio production, China Film Corp. release. Directed by Shui Hua. Based on short story by Mao Dun. Script by Xia Yen. Camera (Eastmancolor), uncredited. Stars Xie Tian. No further credits available. Reviewed as a Chinese Week entry in the Viennale on April 1, 1984 in the Urania Middle Theatre. Running time: **90 MINS.**

"The Lin Family Shop" was made in 1959, but stands up today as a thoroughly modern film drama with a shopkeeper family and its troubles during a period of war and economic crisis (1931) at its center. Film is based on a short story by Mao Dun, a writer in disgrace during the Cultural Revolution, as were director Shui Hua and his film.

Today, the artists and their work (lead actor Xie Tian had also been pushed aside for "too individualistic portrayals") are all bestowed with new honors, and "The Lin Family Shop" is finally on its way to world acclamation via festivals and other specialized venues. It could easily reach art houses eventually.

With the Japanese attacking Shanghai and with the Kuomintang authorities abusing their power, Lin and his family have their mixed goods shop constantly threatened with bankruptcy. If they don't have to pay bribes, they are forced to pay excessive rates on bank loans. Competing merchants also gang up on the Lins, and when one day a Kuomintang official wants the Lin's teenage daughter to be his concubine in exchange for safe-guarding the shop, Lin resorts to measures not quite worthy of him.

Story is told in a series of swift portraitures (the teenage daughter is as sweet and as wantonly cruel as any teenager anywhere) that merge naturally with plot developments. Tension keeps rising until an explosion of tempers is depicted through a grandiose riot scene. There is lots of local, historical color but never so much as to distract from the common human interest pull of the drama and its characters. Xie, almost a Jack Lemmon lookalike, offers a subdued per-formance of great strength. Nor do the other actors resort to the theatrical gesturing and yelling Western audiences have come to expect from the Chinese via Hong Kong's kung fu offerings. —*Kell.*

Alexyz
(COLOR-16m)

St. Paul, March 8.

A Huaca Ltd. release of an Elizabeth Converse/Daniel Richter production. Produced and directed by Converse, Richter. Screenplay, Converse; camera (color), Flip McCarthy; additional camera, Benjamin Goldstein; editors, Ben Annand, Stanley Vogel, Connie Sheets; music, John Aschenbrenner; sound, Maryte Kavaliauskas, Jeb, Peter Evans, Bruce Jehle; production manager, Jonathan Sinaico; assistant directors, Debbie Keller, Jan Worthington. Reviewed at Film in the Cities screening room, St. Paul, March 4, 1984. Running time: **78 MINS.**
With: Elizabeth Converse, Daniel Richter, Timothy Shelton, Gerda Shepard, Elena Hall, Helen Sinclair, Carl Tasha, April Kinsberg, Kim Rilleau, Ted DeColo, Eddie Euler, Bill Rabinovitch, B.H. Williams.

Shot in and around Provincetown, Mass., "Alexyz" is an earnest indie effort that, in its exploration of one woman's tussle with a predatory, male-dominated world, doesn't quite gather the power it could. The film, completed in 1982 on a $150,000 budget, is too often at odds with its own good intentions; alternating between an offhand verite style and clunky, stiffly acted scenes, "Alexyz" shouldn't be written off completely.

It's obviously one from the heart for filmmakers Elizabeth Converse and Daniel Richter (whose son appears in the movie), as they coproduced, directed and star. "Alexzy" tells the story of a photographer fed up with the sexual harassment — blatant or otherwise — hampering her life and career in Manhattan.

She takes up summer residence at a friend's cabin on the Cape, where two very different men enter her life. One, played by Richter, becomes her lover. The other (Timothy Shelton) is a thick-headed macho type who after spying on her and trying to win her over, ultimately rapes her on the beach.

Subtitled "The Rape of Love," "Alexyz" has in its favor some smart usage of dreamlike home-movie footage intercut with harsh scenes of violence. (On her first day at the beach, Alexyz witnesses a man slug his girlfriend.) The contrasts are often effectively ironic. Also, a good score by John Aschenbrenner adds a layer of class to the project

Despite some observant touches, the general technical and thematic result is rather slack. There's some clumsy phallic symbolism only a pre-teen would miss; the rapist is seen early on stroking his rifle between his legs, etc. Despite an inherently powerful subject, the film's elements never quite mesh.

To Converse and Richter's credit, the movie ends on a resonant note of hope for its victim. At the climax, a pistol-bearing Alexyz confronts her attacker but decides that life, even with its emotional scars, can go on. There's no Dirty Harry-style vengance to save the day here. It's just too bad that "Alexyz'" overall impact is muddied by some fuzzy, uneven acting and nothing new in the writing.
— *Phil.*

Warum Die UFOs Unseren Salat Klauen
(Why The UFOs Steal Our Lettuce)
(WEST GERMAN-COLOR)

Vienna, March 31.

A Cine-Contor (Martin Haussler) production, currently possessed by the Berliner-Bank (West Berlin). Directed by Hansjürgen Pohland. Original story and script, Heinz Freitag, Pohland. Camera (Eastmancolor), Atze Glanert; editor, Christi Pohland; production design, Norbert Scherer. Reviewed as an entry in the "Cinema Nobody Likes" section of the 23d Viennale in the Urania on March 30, 1984. Running time: **92 MINS.**
Peter ....Tomas Pieper
Monica ....Ursula Monn
UFO General ....Curd Jürgens
U.S. General ....Alexander Kerst
Film-Hitler ....Kurt Raab
Peter's Mother.............Hildegard Knef
UFO Stewardess ....Pavla Ustinov

By having the Viennale pay the Berliner-Bank 500 Deutsche Mark, German film historian and author of the recently published book about The World's Worst Movies, "Kino wie es keiner mag — Die Schlechtesten Filme der Welt," Rolf Giesen was given the loan of Hansjürgen Pohland's farce feature "Why the UFOs Steal Our Lettuce" for a special fest showing. Film was released in three theaters in 1979, ran for only two days, was seen by practically nobody and was then — when producer Martin Haussler had (as he remains) absconded — taken over by the Berlin Bank. Rolf Giesen, who thought only one print existed, has found a total of 14 prints were made. He will present "Why The UFOs ..." again shortly in special showings in Berlin along with other "worst movies."

It seems the Berlin Film Authority originally granted Häussler's project considerable production aid because it wanted to throw work to West Berlin film studios. Film, however, was then made entirely on location and obviously in a very haphazard way. Well-known acting talent cannot really have known in what context their efforts were put, but film's original working title may give a hint: "Berliner Ballade, II" indicated this was to be a followup on another farcical and star-studded entertainment that had turned into a sizable boxoffice hit. Director Pohland's name always had respect. He, too, must have been astonished at what was to follow even if he, to-day, insists he finds his film quite successful.

Story has Curd Jürgens in a jump-suit with some Martian trimmings sitting with his fellow space creatures (one of them Peter Ustinov's daughter Pavla) in a large UFO-bubble (actually a botanical garden hot house) receiving televised reports on the progression of the experiments of a young earthling biologist who is experimenting with cross-breeding various lettuce specimens to generate explosive energy. The biologist has several run-ins with comical policemen, an encounter with his long-lost mother (Hildegard Knef), and a romance with a baker's daughter with whom he sets up an experimental garden. The U.S. Army, Russian paratroopers, a film crew doing a Hitler film, and many other elements are introduced, none followed through with any instance of the logic that even insanity must have to work as comedy.

The very badness of this film will, of course, assure it some new status, and it really is enough of a mess to make it hold its own in any Worst Movies Ever context. Outside of special event slotting at festivals however, "Why The UFOs ..." cannot be expected to travel very far into theatrical space outside German-speaking territories.—*Kell.*

The Bounty
(COLOR)

Superior remake, with Anthony Hopkins smashing as a sympathetic Capt. Bligh.

Hollywood, April 17.
An Orion release of a Dino De Laurentiis presentation. Produced by Bernard Williams. Directed by Roger Donaldson. Stars Mel Gibson, Anthony Hopkins. Screenplay, Robert Bolt, based on the book "Captain Bligh And Mr. Christian," by Richard Hough. Camera (Technicolor, J-D-C anamorphic process), Arthur Ibbetson; editor, Tony Lawson; co-editor, Barrie Vince; music, Vangelis; production design, John Graysmark; art direction, Tony Reading; set decoration, Bob Cartwright, Louise Carrigan; costume design, John Bloomfield; sound (Dolby), John Mitchell; special effects supervisor, John Stears; assistant director, David Tringham; second unit camera, Doug Milsome. Reviewed at the Coronet, L.A., April 17, 1984. (MPAA Rating: PG). Running time: **130 MINS.**

Fletcher Christian .... Mel Gibson
Lt. William Bligh .... Anthony Hopkins
Admiral Hood .... Laurence Olivier
Captain Greetham .... Edward Fox
Fryer .... Daniel Day-Lewis
Cole .... Bernard Hill
Young .... Philip Davis
Churchill.................... Liam Neeson
King Tynah .... Wi Kuki Kaa
Mauatua .... Tevaite Vernètte
Adams .... Philip Martin Brown

"The Bounty" is an intelligent, firstrate, revisionist telling of the famous tale of Fletcher Christian's mutiny against Captain Bligh. Well-done in all departments, film is particularly distinguished by a sensational, and startlingly human, performance by Anthony Hopkins as Bligh, heretofore one of history's most one-dimensional villains. Sea faring high adventure tales used to be a staple of kids' imaginations, a proposition more dubious now, and making this familiar story more complex and shaded than it's traditionally been may render it a questionable big b.o. performer, which it must be for the Dino De Laurentiis presentation to recoup its $20,000,000-plus negative cost.

The two previous big-scale versions of the yarn were both made by MGM, first in 1935 starring Clark Gable and Charles Laughton directed by Frank Lloyd, then in 1962 toplining Marlon Brando and Trevor Howard under Lewis Milestone's direction. Earlier pic won a best picture Oscar and is generally regarded as a classic, although staging now looks awfully stodgy and Laughton's nastiness is strictly of the hissable variety. Despite its visual qualities, remake was overstuffed and went wildly over budget.

Present film was initiated by director David Lean, who brought Robert Bolt abroad to write two projected pix, "The Lawbreakers" and "The Long Arm," which were to have told, for the first time, the entire "Bounty" saga. Lean eventually moved on, and De Laurentiis, having paid for the construction of a replica ship, decided to condense Bolt's script to the proportions of a single feature.

Unlike many current re-dos of vintage pix, this is a remake with a reason, that being the exoneration and rehabilitation of the reputation of William Bligh. A British Naval court-martial, which serves to frame Bolt's dramatization, ultimately absolved Bligh of blame for the mutiny, and he went on to enjoy a distinguished career.

Until now, however, writers have tended to overlook this detail and portray Bligh as a little Hitler who was finally overthrown by Christian, a romantic hero. Thanks to the new slant and the work of Hopkins (who was originally signed by Lean), Bligh is not exactly likeable, but he emerges for the first time as an understandable, even sympathetic, man.

After Bligh sits down to defend himself to Admiral Hood, played with dispatch by Laurence Olivier, and chief prosecutor Edward Fox, pic cuts back to 1787, when good friends Bligh and Christian decide to team again for a voyage to Tahiti, purpose of which is to transport breadfruit, a possible cheap staple food for slaves, to Jamaica.

Bligh's only untoward act during the voyage is his month-long effort to battle storms around Cape Horn in order to make a shortcut to the South Pacific. Ultimately, the Bounty takes the long way around, and crew is rewarded for its time at sea by the gorgeous, sexually open women of Tahiti (among its other distinctions, this is the first candidly topless version of the story, although it still got a PG rating).

During the months in paradise, the men understandably become lazy and dissolute, Fletcher Christian impregnates the daughter of the local king, and Bligh alone seems to resist the pleasures of the flesh.

When it comes time to set sail again, the general resistance to the idea forces Bligh to impose strict measures in order to make the crew shape up, and three deserters are put under the lash. For his part, Christian is in a deep romantic funk, and Bligh's rash decision to once again attempt passage via Cape Horn is simply too much.

The mutiny itself, formerly shown as a more ceremonious affair, is here presented as a chaotic mess, with Christian nearly delirious. Bligh's subsequent 4,000-mile voyage to safety in an open boat is depicted as the amazing, arduous achievement that it was, and is intercut with the gradual deterioration of morale among the mutineers, who briefly return to Tahiti and then find their final destination on remote Pitcairn Island.

Greater emphasis could have been placed on the interaction of the men with the Tahitians, and the ultimate fate of some of the mutineers is not fully explained. Overall, however, Bolt has done a fine job of reinterpreting familiar material, and has come to grips with the admittedly conservative theme of how the breakdown of civilization and its rules results in selfish anarchy.

Most of all, he has written a great role in Bligh, and Hopkins, who even resembles Laughton at times, has masterfully conveyed the complexity of a man whose nature and official responsibilities conspired with circumstances to bring infamy upon himself. It's a great performance, and marks the first time Hopkins has really broken through like this onscreen.

Tailor-made physically to fit the mold of old-style heroes, Mel Gibson gets across Christian's melancholy and torn motivations in excellent fashion. Remainder of the men have suitably raffish looks and personalities, with Daniel Day-Lewis, as an oily officer, and Liam Neeson, as a particularly insubordinate crew member, standing out.

Physically, film is everything an epic and high-adventure fan could want. Roger Donaldson, a young director from New Zealand whose previous pictures were "Sleeping Dogs" and the excellent "Smash Palace," has mounted the drama with considerable impact.

Tahitian and New Zealand locales have been maximized by the lush lensing of Arthur Ibbetson, John Graymark's production design is tops, and Vangelis' score is of a low-keyed, brooding nature.

As the best rendition of this classic story, "The Bounty" is the exception to the rule that remakes are inferior to the originals.
— Cart.

The Voyage Of Bounty's Child
(AUSTRALIAN-DOCU-COLOR)

Sydney, April 16.
A Look Film Productions production. Produced by Will Davies. Directed by Michael Edols. Script, Cecil Holmes; narrator, Leo McKern; camera (color), Edols; editor, Richard Francis-Bruce; sound, Bronwyn Murphy; assistant cameraman, Wayne Taylor; production coordinator, Bee Reynolds; executive producer, Richard Tanner; associate producer, Martin Cohen. Reviewed at Roadshow theaterette, Sydney, April 9, 1984. Running time: **94 MINS.**

With renewed interest in the events known as the Mutiny on the Bounty which occurred in April 1789, via the upcoming Dino De-Laurentiis version of this much-filmed saga, this interesting documentary may spark some interest. Pic is a record of a voyage made last year in an open boat by a direct descendant of the much-maligned Captain Bligh, following the same course the deposal naval officer and his loyal men themselves took 195 years ago.

Bligh's descendant is Captain R.W. Bligh-Ware, who gathered eight volunteer crew members to join him (Bligh had 18) on the hazardous 4,000-mile voyage from Tonga via Fiji, Vanuatu, the Great Barrier Reef of eastern Australia, and finally to what is today Indonesian Timor. With the benefit of the notes made by his forebear in a meticulously kept diary, plus his own seagoing experience, Bligh-Ware and his sometimes disaffected crew weather the journey, and a violent storm, to safety.

All is captured on film, obviously under considerable difficulties, by documentary filmmaker and cinematographer Michael Edols, and the results make for interesting, if not exactly enthralling, viewing. At its present length, pic is too long, though for those with a particular interest in the subject it's probably not enough. Pruning will make it much more accessible to a general audience, and the material is all there to make it work.

A definite plus is the narration which purports to be the thoughts of the original Bligh and which is beautifully written by vet helmer Cecil Holmes and spoken with considerable relish by Leo McKern. Witty, amusing text does a lot to cover the dull spots. Bligh-Ware is seen briefly enacting the role of his ancestor, and the likeness to contemporary portraits of Capt. Bligh is remarkable. While every film of the Mutiny on the Bounty seen to date has cast Bligh as the villain, there's a major reversal here: Fletcher Christian is denounced as a scurvy mutineer and the courage and tenacity of Bligh and his loyal followers is given full credit.
—Strat.

Don Chisciotte
(Don Quixote)
(ITALIAN-COLOR)

San Francisco, April 12.
Sacis release of a production by Teatro Popolare di Roma in collaboration with RAI-2 — Istituto Luce. Directed by Maurizio Scaparro. Screenplay, Rafael Azcona, Tullio Kezich and Scaparro, from novel by Miguel de Cervantes, camera, (color), Luigi Verga; editor, Nino Baragli; music, Eugenio Bennato; set design, Giantito Burchiellaro and Roberto Francia; costumes, Lele Luzzati. Reviewed at the San Francisco Film Festival (Castro), April 12, '84. (No MPAA Rating.) Running time: **100 MINS.**
Don Quixote .... Pino Micol
Sancho Panza .... Peppe Barra
With: Els Comediants of Barcelona, Medini's Circus, Il Teatro dei Pupi Siciliani dei fratelli Pasqualino (Pasqualino Bros. marionettes).

The theatrical production on which this pic is based (although this is not a "filmed play") is subtitled "fragments of a theatrical discourse." Therein rests the problem: fragmentized, experimental Quixote is unfulfilling and is this production also claustrophobic.

The adaptation, set in a musty, abandoned warren of stages, tilts more at the wind of rhetoric than windmill dragons.

Quixote, goaded on by a bemused, oft-frustrated Panza, fights his usual battles. But this time they are too illusory, too contained, ultimately stifled by the spatial hem-in of the production design.

The two principals are fine, with the attendant ensembles all of pro thesping quality.

Considering that the collaborators on this project have essentially a legit background, the transfer to film is commendable. But as a pic, this Quixote will have minimal commercial possibilities in the U.S. —*Herb.*

Ultimas Tardes
Con Teresa
(Last Evenings With Theresa)
(SPANISH-COLOR)

Madrid, April 3.

A Samba Films and Impala S.A. coproduction, with collaboration of TVE (Spanish Television). Directed by Gonzalo Herralde. Screenplay, Herralde, Juan Marsé, Ramón de España, based on novel of same name by Marsé. Producer, Pepón Coromina. Camera (color), Fernando Arribas; production manager, Andrés Coromina; editor, Anastasi Rinos; sets, Felipe de Paco, Ramón Olives, Alicia Nuñez; music, J.M. Bardagi. Reviewed at Cine Avenida, Madrid, April 3, '84. Running time: 105 MINS.

Manolo ....Angel Alcázar
Teresa.....................Maribel Martin
Maruja ....Patricia Adriani
Cardenal......................José Bódalo
Hortensia ....Cristina Marsillach
Also: J.M. Cervino, Monica Randall, Marta Molins, Alberto Closas, Charo Lopez, Angel Jové, Alfredo Marchetti.

Talky, monotonous meller set in and around Barcelona in 1957. The book may have been better, but the film drags painfully from scene to scene, never building any insight into the characters or arousing any interest in their two-dimensional lives. The fact of the scene being Franco Spain seems purely fortuitous, since the occasional political references to inchoate Communist cell activity add nothing to the story line.

Triangle around which the weak plot is spun consists of a macho, small-time hood trying to be a Spanish John Travolta, an expressionless upper class blond who's twice caught reading a history of Socialism, and an earthy servant girl (by far the best performance in the picture).

The beefy type, who walks throught half the film baring his chest, posing with his profile, or riding a motorcycle in a black leather jacket, first makes out with the servant, and then moves up to the young daughter of the rich family, after the servant is carted off to a hospital. The doctors don't know what to make of her case, and she dies.

The small-time, swaggering sharpie ekes out his delinquent existence stealing motorcycles and trying to pass counterfeit bills. But after the servant's death, the society gal is whisked off by her parent and the hood is tracked down for speeding by the police.

Aside from the mostly indifferent acting, there is a terrible musical score which surges up melodramatically at the worst possible moments. Direction by Gonzalo Herralde is discreet; he does what he can with the no-win script.

The best performances are cameos by thesps such as José Bódalo, Charo López, Mónica Randall and Alberto Closas. Maybe the film would have been better if they had played the leads. — *Besa.*

From Somalia With Love
(Lettres d'Amour en Somalie)
(FRENCH-COLOR)

A production of Les Films du Losange and FR 3, Paris. Produced by Nicole Flipo. Written and directed by Frederic Mitterrand. Camera (color), John Cressey; sound, Pierre Camus; editor, Luc Barnier; music, Jean Wiener; narrator (in English), Mitterrand. A presentation of New Directors/New Films series, from the Film Society of Lincoln Center and the Dept. of Film of the Museum of Modern Art. Reviewed at 57th St. Playhouse, N.Y., April 12, 1984. Running time: 100 MINS.

"From Somalia with Love," produced by the nephew of France's president and narrated by the filmmaker in English, is an impressionistic documentary-essay that uses the troubled East African nation of Somalia as the environment for a highly personal privatized memoir.

The film's style, risky and demanding, places "Somalia" within a certain tradition of French documentary — significant but peripheral — that seeks to break away from the usual dry didactic expectations and confines of the typical documentary. Instead, such French documentaries, notably those of Chris Marker, are frankly, even intimately autobiographical and self-reflexive. These films are characterized by placement within an exotic geographical context; also, they use non-stop intellectual narration, often commenting ironically against the visuals.

But this formula, which can be challenging for audiences capable of responding to its demands, is a failure in the case of "Somalia." Seeking originality, Mitterrand gives us affectation. Lacking a deeply felt base, the film becomes mannered and pretentious, such that the "New Directors" series audience became audibly alienated. Yet this was an audience, we can assume, predisposed to partaking in a special cinema ex-

perience. But one notes the boos were counterpointed by some applause, indicating the search for an enlargement of documentary expressiveness deserves continuing support.

"Somalia" takes place within the head of Mitterrand, as his voice-over, as he remembers and laments and longs for an absent lover, someone never seen but sensed in the opening images of an empty rumpled bed. As Mitterrand drones on in blurred English, visuals of Somalia begin. We learn Mitterrand is apparently on assignment to shoot a documentary reportage that includes scenes of Somalia's terrible poverty and horrendous problems of starvation and disease, especially among refugees of desert warfare. Intercut are interviews with Somalian authorities of the military dictatorship, backgrounded by clips from old newsreels explaining former colonial rivalries between Britain and Mussolini's Italy. The war with Ethiopia, and its on/off alliance with the USSR, further complicate Somalia's present.

In the manner of a travel diary, "Somalia" is incomplete and fragmentary. And it is so insistently subjective, for Mitterand the man, that his film as a professional work of at least some objective validity is imperiled. In short, the film becomes the victim of its own style. Although beautifully photographed in a fascinating country with striking visual imagery, "Somalia" is damaged further by its relentless and obtrusively self-sentimentalizing narration.

Although the film's theatrical future in the U.S. seems doubtful, the New Directors/New Films series merits praise for having brought the film from France —*Hitch.*

Improper Conduct
(Mauvaise Conduite)
(FRENCH-DOCU-COLOR)

A Cinevista presentation of a coproduction of Les Films du Losange and Antenne-2. Produced by Margaret Menegoz, Barbet Schroeder, Michel Thoulouze. Written and directed by Nestor Almendros and Orlando Jimenez-Leal. Camera (color), Dominique Merlin; sound, Daniel Delmau and Phil Pearl; editor, Michel Pion; English-language narrator, Geoffrey Lawrence Carey. A presentation of the New Directors/New Films series, from the Film Society of Lincoln Center and the Dept. of Film of the Museum of Modern Art. Reviewed at 57th St. Playhouse, N.Y., April 12, 1984. Running time: 115 MINS.
(In English, French and Spanish, with English subtitles.)

Completed only a few weeks earlier, "Improper Conduct" won the Grand Prix at the XII International Human Rights Film Festival in Strasbourg, France. It has already played in Paris to good notices at two theaters for three weeks.

"Improper Conduct" is an important film of lasting value. Remarkably, it is codirected by a busy Oscar-winning cinematographer, Nestor Almendros, who shot "Sophie's Choice" and 40 other features, in collaboration with Orlando Jimenez-Leal, who directed the feature "El Super" several seasons back. The two men had worked together once before, in 1961, in Cuba during the early days of the Castro regime, on an ethnographic short.

The improper conduct of "Improper Conduct" is daring to express individualism in Cuba, which this year marks 25 years under Castro. During the period 1959-1984, 10% of the Cuban population fled, thousands of others were imprisoned and many still are.

Among the dissidents who left and/or were jailed and mistreated, then expelled, are the two dozen men and women who describe their ordeal in "Improper Conduct." Of this group, some are editors, poets, artists; indeed, some were Castro's former officials and friends.

Although a long film, heavily reliant on talking heads, time flies in "Improper Conduct," and supplementary visuals and stock footage provide variety.

A survey of Cuban political dissidence in general, "Improper Conduct" emphasizes homosexuality as a crime in Cuba — a crime, but one capable of reformation. In sweeps, police round up gays on the streets and in bars, then pack them off to remote labor camps for years of rehabilitation. Other gays are denounced by anonymous informers. Extravagant behavior, or effeminancy, or long hair, or any deviation from a narrowly defined norm, can lead to imprisonment.

But masculine-appearing gays can "pass" and survive in Cuba. Some become prominent in government, especially within the military and the police, where machismo is almost a cult. Indeed, Cuba seems consecrated to images of male virility, in its obsession with military preparedness. "Improper Conduct" postulates that Castro himself, like Hitler, is machismo personified, a manly celibate wedded to his political duty, married to his nation.

Speaking in excerpts from a 1979 interview on French tv, Castro concedes some harsh measures against dissidents have taken place, but defends his policy as justifiable expedience to preserve the revolution.

Castro's self-defense contrasts dramatically with testimony from ex-prisoners, e.g., poet Armando Valladares, who describes prison horrors, including the torture and rape of child-prisoners, witnessed during his 22 years behind bars for "ideological diversionism." Valladares was released by Castro after a personal appeal from French President François Mitterrand and is seen in news footage at Orly airport, Paris, in an emotional re-union with his wife.

Other Cuban dissidents — interviewed in Madrid, London, Paris, Rome, New York and Miami — similarly describe a repressive Cuba very different from that seen by foreign visitors on controlled tours.

"Improper Conduct" also ex-presses the disenchantment of former Castro supporters. Susan Sontag, speaking in French, says "one of the Left's weaknesses has always been a difficulty in dealing with questions bearing on the moral and political aspects of sex ... It's a heritage, in a way a puritan one, that is deeply imbedded in the morals of the Left. The discov-ery that homosexuals are being persecuted in Cuba shows how much the Left needs to evolve."

Homosexuality in "Improper Conduct" is a metaphor, of course, for the generalized suppression of civil liberties in Cuba — a persecu-tion that victimizes all religious, moral, and political transgres-sions.

These and other ideas are dis-cussed in "Improper Conduct" with great intelligence and dignity. Memories of hardship in prison, and other sad events, are told with austere restraint. But also there are occasional moments of hilari-ous Cuban self-mockery, as ex-pri-soners describe their battle of wits against their guards.

Despite a certain prejudice against documentaries in the theatrical environment, "Im-proper Conduct" clearly can find its place before sophisticated au-diences in congenial art theaters. In addition, its 16m future with universities, civil liberties groups, the artistic community, et al., and to public television, seems as-sured. —Hitch.

Nightsongs
(COLOR)

Modern immigrant drama. Limited b.o. potential.

San Francisco, April 14.
No distrib set. An FN Films production in association with American Playhouse. Produced by Thomas A. Fucci, Written and directed by Marva Nabili. Camera, (color), Ben Davis; editor, Fritz Liepe; music, R.I.P. Hayman. Reviewed at San Francisco Film Festival (Ghirardelli), April 14, '84. (No MPAA Rating.) Running time: 116 MINS.
Chinese/Viet Woman ....Mabel Kwong
Fung Tak Men ....David Lee
Fung Leung..................Victor Wong
Fung Lai Ping ....Ida F.O. Chung
Fung Mei Fun...................Rose Lee
Fung Tak Sing ....Roger Chang
Gang Recruiter... ....Geoff Lee

Pic, in a way a Chinese version of "Hester Street," was filmed by director-writer Marva Nabili, an Iranian expatriate who spent, she says, five years on the project, in-cluding a four-month job in a gar-ment factory in New York's China-town.

It's clearly put together with care and feeling and offers poig-nant insights into the adaptation problems of the modern American immigrants. Nabili's tour guide into this adjustment is lovely Chi-nese Viet refugee Mabel Kwong, separated from her family in the Far East and come to live with relatives she's meeting for the first time.

The project is out of FN Films of the U.S., but opts for English sub-titles, mandatory because even the Chinese who have been here for some years prefer to hang on to their culture and language.

Nabili's yarn is episodic, often slow-moving and repetitive, yet builds to a pre-ordained tragic cli-max, although the victim of the tragedy comes as a surprise. Voice-over poetry, from the book "Women Poets of China," is ascribed to the newcomer and serves as her only method of com-municating — with her host fami-ly and with the audience; as a plot device the lyrical language is ac-ceptable, but not always, or neces-sarily, as an attention-holder.

Ethnic audiences in urban areas will find "Nightsongs" fetching and, if the larger, "outside" au-dience can be attracted, they will find it informative and often com-pelling in its tale of labor, educa-tion and culture-generation gaps.

Technicals are efficient, and Nabili has much success in urging crisp performances out of an es-sentially non-pro cast. Strongest performance comes from Victor Wong, once a "Second City" troup-er, as the mah jong-smitten father. —Herb.

Stop Making Sense
(DOCU-COLOR)

Well-made rock perform-ance film; limited b.o. poten-tial.

Hollywood, April 23.
A Talking Heads Film production in associ-ation with the Arnold Amusement Group. Produced by Gary Goetzman. Executive pro-ducer, Gary Kurfirst. Directed by Jonathan Demme. Features the Talking Heads. Cam-era (Technicolor), Jordan Cronenweth; edi-tor, Lisa Day; conception, lighting for the stage, David Byrne; visual consultant, Sandy McLeod; sound (Dolby), Billy Youdelman; assistant director, Joseph A. Viola. Reviewed at the Warner Hollywood Studios, L.A., April 23, 1984. (No MPAA Rating). Running time: 88 MINS.
Features: Bernie Worrell (keyboards), Alex Weir (guitar), Steve Scales (percus-sion), Lynn Mabry, Edna Holt (backup vo-cals), Tina Weymouth (bass), Jerry Harrison (keyboards, guitar), Chris Franz (drums), David Byrne (lead vocals, guitar).

As befits the nature of the band it showcases, "Stop Making Sense" is a carefully made, technically su-perior rockumentary starring that highly individualistic art school dance band, the Talking Heads. World preemed Tuesday (24) night as the closing attraction at the San Francisco International Film Festival, pic is currently being shopped for domestic distribution and, as always for rock concert features, its potential in theatrical release is highly questionable; mu-sic pics toplining groups much more popular than the Heads have made little impact at the b.o. High-ly selective openings in carefully chosen theaters, tied in with con-current release of a live album, would seem the best way to go, and good response should be found down the line in cable and vidcas-sette markets.

On conceptual and technical lev-els, this is probably the best ex-ecuted film presentation of a con-cert since Martin Scorsese's "The Last Waltz," and perhaps it's no coincidence that this one, too, was directed by a musically hip feature helmer, Jonathan Demme. Unlike "The Last Waltz," however, which boasted a whammo star cast of performers, "Stop Making Sense" (which doesn't make much sense as a title) spotlights only one band, one whose fans are probably a bit older and more upscale than is the rock norm.

Film was lensed over three nights in December 1983 at the Pantages Theatre in Hollywood, but crowd is kept at a significant distance visually, and there are very few cutaways to audience reactions. Were it not for the audi-ble response at the ends of num-bers, one might forget this is a live show, such is the rigorous visual control Demme and Heads leader David Byrne impose upon the pro-ceedings.

Concept is both intriguing and in-structive: the first of 16 numbers offered, the band's early classic "Psycho Killer," features Byrne alone onstage singing to the ac-companiment of his guitar and a tape player in front of an exposed rear theater wall.

Bassist Tina Weymouth joins him for the second tune, and as drummer Chris Franz joins them for the third number, and guitarist Jerry Harrison enters for the fourth, the raw backstage back-drop begins to be filled in.

Backup singers, a bongo player and a keyboardist pitch in begin-ning with the fifth song, and by the time the rhythm section arrives for the recent hit, "Burning Down The House," the band is complete and totally revved up.

Slow buildup is effective, not only musically, but in illustrating how the skeleton of the band was built up around Byrne. He remains the esthete he was at the begin-ning, but the addition of black mu-sicians and African influences has made Talking Heads one of the most rhythmically exciting and danceable bands around.

Thereafter, colors, words and various slides are projected from time to time to arty effect on black screens behind the band on the huge stage. Even more self-conscious, and striking, are light-ing designs credited to Byrne and superbly captured by cinematog-rapher Jordan Cronenweth. At times, intricate lighting patterns, often involving light from the floor and handheld mini-spots, result in images more closely associated with studio photography than live, on-the-spot work.

Although all the performers get their share of close-ups, Byrne re-mains centerstage virtually throughout (Weymouth warbles one number, "Tom Tom Club"), and he is certainly one of the most unlikely of rock stars. Intense, se-vere in looks and vocally limited, he indulges in considerable spastic dancing, and his trademark move-ment, with head bobbing back and forth, resembles that of an ostrich. But he can also boogey with the best of them, and he emerges as a compelling, if remote, personality.

Even surpassing the visuals is the brilliantly clear sound work. Touted as the first film to use direct-to-film digital rerecording technology, it has a perfect bal-ance in Dolby stereo, and lyrics come across as clearly as imagina-ble.

Perhaps because of the au-dience's remove and the sense of complete control exercised over the show, film doesn't convey the all-stops-out abandon that some re-cent Talking Heads live gigs have possessed. But the band is seen and heard to good advantage here, and their fans should be generally pleased.—Cart.

Nacional III
(National III)
(SPANISH-COLOR)

Sydney, April 16.
An InCine-Kaktus-Jet S.A. production. Produced by Alfredo & Helena Matas. Direct-ed by Luis Garcia Berlanga. Features entire cast. Screenplay, Rafael Azcona, Berlanga; camera (Eastmancolor), Carlos Suarez; edi-tor, Jose Louis Matesanz; art director, Ro-man Arango. Reviewed on Network 0/28, Sydney, April 11, 1984. Running time: 105 MINS.
The Marquis ....Luis Escobar
Luis Jose ....Jose Luis Lopez Vazquez
Chus ....Amparo Soler Leal
Father Calvo............Agustin Gonzalez
Alvaro ....Jose Luis de Villalonga
Segundo ....:.....Luis Ciges
With Chus Lampreave, Angel Alvarez, Francisco Llinas.

The senile Marquis de Le-guineches and his crazy family first appeared to great effect in Luis Garcia Berlanga's domestic smash of 1978, "La Escopeta Na-cional" (The National Shotgun), which also had some international festival success. The characters returned with less success in the 1981 sequel, "Patrimonio Nacional" (National Patrimony), and now the same team has produced a third film, "Nacional III," which bears a 1983 date and has just been aired on Aussie television.

Third time around the joke is definitely wearing a bit thin. The Marquis has now sold his Madrid apartment and lives in a small flat with his foolish son, Luis Jose, his servant/mistress, Viti, and incongruously, the family priest, Father Calvo. The death of his father-in-law brings about a reunion with Luis Jose's estranged wife, Chus, who has liquidated her assets in preparation for ankling the country.

With the failure of the 1982 attempted coup, the strongly anti-Socialist Leguineches decide it's definitely time to go, but how to leave the country carrying all their accumulated wealth without having it confiscated? Jose Luis won't trust a professional "courier" (i.e., smuggler), so the family contrives to hide the loot under a huge plaster cast and have Jose Luis travel to Lourdes (across the border in France) to be "cured." But even in France, the advent of Mitterand's Socialist government has the family seeking new pastures, and last seen they're heading for Miami.

Berlanga, whose early career was noted for some excellent films, takes a few rather obvious swipes at the changes which came to Spain after the Socialist government was elected (porno films, etc.) There's lots of talk as the characters jabber away at each other furiously, but the actors are all good, especially Luis Escobar as the Marquis and Jose Luis Lopez Vazquez as his idiot son. The extended climax, with Lopez Vazquez swathed in plaster and trying to scratch himself, or relieve himself, provides most of the laughs.

Presumably this is the last of the series, and one can only hope the gifted Berlanga will return to less obvious and more relevant subjects for his satirical vision.

—*Strat.*

Dietrich Bonhoeffer: Memories And Perspectives
(DOCU-B&W-16m)

Berlin, Feb. 20.

A Cinema Guild (New York) release of a Trinity Films (Minneapolis) production. Producers, Bain Boehlke and Gerald Drake. Directed by Boelhke. Camera (b&w), Gregory M. Cummins; sound, Mathew Quast; editor Cummins/Editronics; narrator, Oliver Osterberg; voice of Bonhoeffer, George Sutton. Reviewed in Information section, Berlin International Film Festival, Feb. 20, 1984. Running time: **93 MINS.**

"Dietrich Bonhoeffer" is an extraordinary documentary of a man's spiritual journey to death.

Bonhoeffer, a prominent Christian theologian in Nazi Germany — upper class, cultured, well-educated — could have survived the war by conformity and silence. He chose instead to engage for years in clandestine anti-Naxi activities and ultimately to conspire with other Germans in an unsuccessful attempt to assassinate Hitler. Caught by the Gestapo and imprisoned for two years, Bonhoeffer at age 39 was hanged by piano wire in the last days of the war.

The Bonhoeffer epic of courage is well documented in Germany today but oddly this is the first film ever on the man. Ironically, it is produced not by Germans but by an American, Bain Boehlke, totally inexperienced in cinema.

The "memories and perspectives" of the title refer to recollections about Bonhoeffer, a Confessionalist pastor within the Lutheran Church, by his surviving family, friends and church colleagues. Speaking in English, or in German with English subtitles, they offer a testament or eulogy to a deeply religious man who was unafraid morally and physically.

Bonhoeffer's anti-Nazi work began well before the war when he realized, after painful internal debate, that his Christian duty was not a passive abstraction but required deliberate and even daring action to eradicate Naziism. Also using stills and stock shots, the film reconstructs Bonhoeffer's spiritual odyssey as he moves from doubt to a conviction that violence against evil is morally justifiable. Able to travel to the U.S. before the war, and to neutral Switzerland during the war, Bonhoeffer always returned to Nazi Germany to continue his risky underground work, certain of his moral duty.

Because of American cinema's current, if belated, awareness of the Holocaust, "Bonhoeffer" makes an invaluable contribution to documenting historically another aspect of that Nazi period. But in a sense, the film goes beyond that old Nazi monster, because it reverberates with speculations about how far we will go for what we believe.—*Hitch.*

Die Andere Seite Der Welt
(The Other Side Of The World)
(WEST GERMAN-COLOR)

Berlin, April 17.

A Hanno Brühl & Westdeutscher Rundfunk (WDR) production, Cologne. Directed by Hanno Brühl. Features entire cast. Screenplay, Brian Phelan; camera (color), Peter Kaiser; sets, Brigitte Kämper; costumes, Ulla Maiwald; editing, Ellen Turecek; tv-producer, Hartwig Schmidt. Reviewed at SFB Screening Room, Berlin, April 16, '84. Running time: **91 MINS.**
Cast: Hildegard Kuhlenberg (Susanne Krüger), Eric Bergkraut (Klaus Krüger), Hans Schulze (Father), Dorothea Moritz (Mother), Klaus Wennemann (Rolf, the Cameraman), Hans Kremer (Toni, the Cam-

era Assistant), Bernd Birkhahn (Erik, the Director), Wilfried Grimpe (Wolfgang, the Editor), Polo Espinoza (Jesus, the Gautemalan).

Hanno Brühl's "The Other Side of the World" follows in the director's line of fiction-documentaries begun a decade ago as a social-conscious filmmaker working with Westdeutscher Rundfunk (WDR) in Cologne. Brühl has also made a name for himself in the documentary and reportage fields, both of which surface in this feature film drawing on material supplied by British scriptwriter Brian Phelan.

The Phelan original deals with South Africa and the problem every tv reporter faces in witnessing and recording human tragedies. Brühl has simply shifted the focus to a Latin American country, by inference Guatemala (in view of one of the thesp extras in the film). The story is charged with contemporary relevance, too, for certain tv footage used in the story stems from clips made by four Dutch tv cameramen just before they were killed. Make no mistake: the Brühl/Phelan concern for the media's role in delivering daily shocking news on the tube over an evening meal is at the heart of the theme.

Susanne Krüger (Hildegard Kuhlenberg) works for a tv station in Cologne (WDR, by implication) and accompanies a tv crew to Latin America, and there they photograph a massacre after it has taken place. The girl's conscience has thereby been aroused on the matter of human rights, and she has carried this new-found sense of injustice back home with her to the family table. This, in fact, is where the story starts in the film: each night is spent wrestling with a nightmare of seeing women and children wantonly murdered by death-squads.

Susanne's parents have retired, and now live quietly in a country home. For the mother, what happens "on the other side of the world" is of little interest; and she can't understand why her daughter has given up going to church on Sunday. The father attempts to play a compromising role, but can offer only a measure of understanding. The husband, a bank employe, wonders if his wife's job at a tv station hasn't left her more confused than liberated.

It's when the girl meets her former camera-team, and then has to work on the editing of the footage with the director, that she begins to notice the discrepancy between fact and fiction, reality and news broadcasting, indifference and engagement. The story of her search to find an answer has its twists too: the husband slowly becomes engaged when Amnesty International once comes into discussion, and the heroine is able to re-

solve some of her second-thoughts by visiting an activist center in Cologne for a soul-cleansing talk. No ultimate answer is given in the end, but the questions raised in this tightly narrated tale are vital and thought-provoking. Credits are a plus.—*Holl.*

Annie's Coming Out
(AUSTRALIAN-COLOR)

Sydney, April 16.

A Film Australia production. Produced by Don Murray. Directed by Gil Brealey. Script, John Patterson, Chris Borthwick, from the book "Annie's Coming Out" by Rosemary Crossley; camera (color), Mick von Bornemann; editor, Lindsay Frazer; sound, Rodney Simmons; music, Simon Walker; art director, Mike Hudson; executive producer, Don Harley. Reviewed at Film Australia theaterette, Lindfield, Sydney, April 2, 1984. Running time: **93 MINS.**

Jessica Hathaway	Angela Punch McGregor
David Lewis	Drew Forsythe
Annie O'Farrell	Tina Arhondis
The Judge	Charles Tingwell
Vera Peters	Monica Maughan
Dr. John Monroe	Mark Butler
Sister Waterman	Philippa Baker
Sally Clements	Liddy Clark
Dr. Rowell	Wallas Eaton
Harding	John Frawley
Hopgood	Alistair Duncan
Metcalf	Simon Chilvers

Although some of the names have been changed, "Annie's Coming Out" is based on a true story which caused something of a stir in Australia a few years ago. Annie is a teenage girl who suffered brain damage at birth and became a spastic. Her parents, who came from rural Victoria, were told by doctors that she would never get better, and since treatment in their part of the state was almost impossible, Annie was placed in a home for spastic children in Melbourne. By the time she was in her mid-teens, the child looked no older than eight or nine and had become like all the other spastic kids in the home: another statistic.

Then a therapist, Rosemary Crossley, started work at the home and came to believe that Annie, while physically greatly incapacitated, was mentally alert and even advanced in her intelligence. Once the child passed the legal age of consent, 18, Crossley fought a battle on her behalf, and against the wishes of her parents, to have her released from the home.

In the film, Crossley has become Jessica Hathaway, a determined young woman whose bitter fight to "rescue" Annie finds her in conflict with the conservative doctors and staff who run the home, and who believe these spastics are little more than human vegetables. Matters come to a head in court, with a judge finally visiting Annie in the home to determine for himself if the girl can really communicate via signs and symbols as Jessica claims. Result is foreshadowed by the film's title (also the title of Crossley's book about the events), and should leave few dry eyes in the audience.

This is a custody case pic with a difference, and has emerged as a rare feature from Film Australia, an organization better known for its documentary output.

He tells the moving story straightforwardly and economically, getting good performances from most (not all). Angela Punch McGregor as Jessica and Drew Forsythe as her long-suffering boyfriend are good, while young Tina Arhondis, herself a spastic, is deeply moving as Annie (it was originally planned to have the real Annie play herself, but once she left the home, and was given a better diet, she grew so rapidly this became impossible). Also noteworthy in small roles are Charles Tingwell as the kindly judge and Simon Chilvers as Jessica's lawyer. Some of the actors playing members of the hospital staff appear too much like stock villains, however.

"Annie's Coming Out" is certain to move a lot of people, and also raises questions about the way the physically retarded are treated, as if they were also mentally retarded. On the commercial front, the big hurdle is to persuade audiences to come to see a film in which a spastic is a central character; once they do, they should surrender to the drama of it all, especially knowing it really happened.
— *Strat.*

Ciske The Rat
(DUTCH-COLOR)

Amsterdam, March 30.

A Concorde Film release of a Sigma Film production. Produced by Matthijs van Heijningen. Directed by Guido Pieters. Features entire cast. Screenplay, Karin Loomans, based on the novel by Piet Bakker; camera (color), Frans Bromet; editor, Ton Ruys; music, Erik van der Wurff; art direction, Dick Schillemans; sound, Victor Dekker. Reviewed at City Theater, Amsterdam, March 29, 1984. Running time: **104 MINS.**
Ciske ....Danny de Munk
Marie ....Willeke van Ammelrooy
Cor ....Peter Faber
Mr. Bruis ....Herman van Veen
Inspector Muyskens ....Rijk de Gooyer
Jans ....Linda van Dyck
Aunt Chris ....Carolien van den Berg
Uncle Henri ....Willem Nijholt

"Ciske The Rat," first made into a successful film by the late Wolfgang Staudte in 1955, is an evergreen popular novel of Dickensian proportions, penned 40 years ago: a sentimental tale, in which a toned-down Dutch "Dead End Kid" in the dire years of the Great Depression finds his feet in the cruel world. Staudte called his film "A Child Needs Love" and that could also be the motto of the new "Ciske."

But while local partiality to the book and the energetic promotion of 14-year-old Danny de Munk,

playing the 11-year-old eponymous hero, has given the film an impressive start at the local boxoffice, it remains a curiously unmoving entertainment. Chances offshore are questionable.

For their third feature in tandem, scripter Karin Loomans and helmer Guido Pieters opted for 1934: a lean and hungry year of recession in the mean streets where poverty and unemployment hold sway and mounted police pursue desperate rioters.

So far, so good — the riots are historical; the sets and Amsterdam locations suggest realistic impressions of Ciske's drab surroundings. So do the adults and kids who people them.

But pic's approach to story and main characters remains resolutely contempo, and this creates an uneasy clash of basic material and filmization.

The omnipresent Danny de Munk is a case in point: the boy is an enthusiastic actor and undoubtedly a gifted young entertainer; but the way his lusty singing voice, his sturdy charm and pert facial expression are used stems from the streetwise kids of today rather than from the shy, furtive, "ratty" little loner from a broken home of the '30s. This robs the central character of much of his potential pathos.

Willeke van Ammelrooy excels as Ciske's shrill and hardhitting mother (she meets her fate when Ciske inadvertently kills her with a breadknife). But even bit players and nonpro children shine as Frans Bromet's obsevant camera catches them.

Pic's main failures are its stylistic inconsistency and structural weakness. Each of the (too) many episodes comes to a halt before the next one starts up from scratch. There is no narrative flow to carry on emotion, and a surfeit of music cannot really bridge the gaps.

It may have something to do with pic's history: it was reportedly cut from 168 minutes. (Parts unseen may yet surface in a planned serial on Dutch television). — *Ewa.*

Signal 7
(COLOR)

Art house b.o. possible with careful handling for cabbies' saga.

San Francisco, April 13.

No distrib set. Produced by Don Taylor and Ben Myron. Directed, and story by, Rob Nilsson. Camera (color, video), Geoff Schaaf and Tomas Tucker; editor, Richard Harkness; sound, Philip Perkins and Mark Berger; art director, Hildy Burns and Steve Burns; music, Andy Narrell; associate producer, Roy Kissin. Reviewed at San Francisco Film Festival (Gateway Theater screening), April 13, '84. (No MPAA Rating.) Running time: **92 MINS.**
Speed ....Bill Ackridge
Marty ....Dan Leegant

Johnny ....John Tidwell
Steve ....Herb Mills
Roger ....Don Bajema
Phil........................Phil Polakoff
Setts ....Don Defina
Tommy ....Frank Triest
Hank ....Jack Tucker
Bert ....David Schickele
Paul ....Paul Prince
Director..................... Bob Elross

If for no other reason — and there are plenty of reasons — "Signal 7" is a must-see for anybody who ever has had anything to do with an audition of any kind because of a long, brilliant audition scene early in this picture.

The truth in this segment, in which two failed actors turned cab drivers seek a role, any role, in a revival of "Waiting for Lefty," is so acute that it couldn't have been written — and wasn't. Like everything in "Signal 7," the audition seg was improvised following basic suggestions from excellent director Rob Nilsson (who was co-director on "Northern Lights" and is in post-production on Bruce Dern starrer "On the Edge.")

If there were Oscars for obscurant roles in obscurant pics, one would be mandated for Bob Elross, who essays the director in this audition seg, which should be clipped, bronzed and mounted.

The entire pic is a standout in the improv genre. Nilsson never permits a scene to elongate into tedium or repetition, usually the glaring fault of this sort of picture, whether a docu or docudrama. "Signal 7" is, per Nilsson, a salute to improv maker John Cassavetes but to some will be far more entertaining than several of Cassavetes' films.

The film bespeaks economy in several ways: Its cost was well under $1,000,000; it was shot on three-quarter inch videotape (with an estimable job of transfer to film) over some 60 hours on four nights, much of the footage caught within taxi cabs; its storyline is taut, simple, and served handsomely by a jazz score from Andy Narrell.

The two major characters, hackies played by Bill Ackridge and Dan Leegant, both middle-aged, tired, failed but never defeated, are limned superbly — never camera-conscious and certainly encouraged by the fact they're "reading" their own material. Film spends a long night with them and fellow cabbies through a string of amiable dirty jokes, a hackie's murder, labor union problems, discourses on family anguish and frequent references to the leads' pro acting ambitions.

Nilsson never lets this tale of quiet desperation get out of hand or grow mawkish. His frequent footage of the rain-slicked streets of Frisco during cab rides is reminiscent of "Taxi Driver," but little else here is derivative. The yarn is rife with originality and humanity.

Whether it can be sold to an audience remains to be seen. But the pic will take careful, nurtured ad-promo handling and could score decently at the b.o. on the strength of reviews and word of mouth.
— *Herb.*

Sixteen Candles
(COLOR)

A bit of light, but not much heat.

Hollywood, April 26.

A Universal release of a John Hughes Film. Produced by Hilton A. Green. Directed and written by John Hughes. Features entire cast. Executive producer, Ned Tanen; camera (Technicolor), Bobby Byrne; editor, Edward Warschilka; production design, John W. Corso; sound, Jim Alexander; music, Ira Newborn; set decoration, Jennifer Polito; associate producer, Michelle Manning; assistant director, Newton D. Arnold. Reviewed at Avco Cinema Center, Westwood, Calif., April 26, 1984. (MPAA Rating: PG.) Running time: **93 MINS.**

Samantha	Molly Ringwald
Geek	Anthony Michael Hall
Jake	Michael Schoeffling
Jim Baker	Paul Dooley
Mike Baker	Justin Henry
Randy	Liane Curtis
Caroline	Haviland Morris
Long Duk Dong	Gedde Watanabe
Howard	Edward Andrews
Dorothy	Billie Bird
Helen	Carole Cook
Fred	Max Showalter

Cream puff of a teen comedy about the miseries of a girl turning 16 turns out to be an amiable, rather goldilocked film. Tone of the film, despite some raw language, brief nudity in the shower and carnage at a high school party, actually suggests the middle America of a Norman Rockwell Saturday Evening Post cover. As such, pic veers from the contempo youth genre film. PG rating is apt. Teen action and sex crowds may be hard sells, but Universal could reap rewards from budding adolescent groups who can identify with the turbulence about growing up in a nice family.

For the girls, there's Molly Ringwald as the film's angst-ridden centerpiece. Formerly seen as John Cassavetes' daughter in "Tempest," Ringwald is engaging and credible. For the boys, there's a bright, funny performance by Anthony Michael Hall, a hip freshman wimp called Ted the Geek. There's also a darkly handsome high school heartbreak kid (Michael Schoeffling), a merciful brisk pace, some quick humor (visual and verbal), and a solid music track (which MCA is pushing on both album and cassette).

Film is the initial foray under exec producer Ned Tanen's indie flag and the directorial debut of John Hughes, who scripted and who also wrote a couple of "Lampoon" movies, not to mention "Mr. Mom." Film was shot last summer in the Chicago area and the tree-lined midwest aura is flavorful backdrop.

Flaws in the film are an overload of stock characters (from eccentric grandparents to smart kid brother, latter played by the boy in "Kramer Vs. Kramer," Justin Henry), one tiresome running character gag (a weird Chinese kid), and a pretty spineless premise tied to the consequences on an insecure girl whose 16th birthday goes unremembered. Core of the film is mix of "Sweet Sixteen" fantasy and some on-target observations and fresh laughs. — Loyn.

Another State Of Mind
(COLOR)

Hollywood, April 24.

A Coastline Films release of a Stuart/Small Production. Written, produced and directed by Adam Small & Peter Stuart. No other credits available. Reviewed at the Beverly Center Cineplex, L.A., April 24. (No MPAA rating.) Running time: **78 MINS.**

An earnest attempt to dispel some of the general public's anxious perceptions of the hardcore punk-rock scene, "Another State Of Mind" is also an interesting sociological study of how youthful idealism can come a cropper of "reality." In its own way, that's a point which helps make punkers seem less like some strange new manifestation and more like an extension of previous teen generations' own search for self.

But the people most likely to learn something from the film will probably find the barely adequate technical side of the production off-putting, and given the relatively small hardcore constituency, basically limited to a few big cities on each coast, prospects for the pic would seem restricted to the specialized theatrical and ancillary markets.

Pic follows a U.S.-Canada tour by L.A. punk groups Social Distortion and Youth Brigade in the summer of 1982 aboard a decrepit bus bought from proceeds of a concert here. What began as a noble mission, to spread the punk gospel and open some minds about the lifestyle rather than rake in the big bucks, rapidly unravels as money, food, parts for the bus and the tensions of 11 people crammed into small quarters grow larger.

Along the tour route, filmmakers interview group members and local punk fans and come away with some intriguing character studies which demonstrate just how unmonolithic the scene and its followers truly are. General impression that the scene is a violent one is rejected by most participants — slam dancing just looks rough, the punks say — although an interview with a femme punker from Montreal who "beats up faggots" for spare change is rather chilling by virtue of her matter-of-factness.

That attitude, however, is balanced by the members of Minor Threat, a Washington, D.C., punk band, who are part of a no drugs-no-booze-no casual sex sub-movement of the scene, and the genuinely sweet-spirited idealism of many of those depicted. Principals are seen as the teenagers they are — the oldest band member is 21 — full of energy, altruism and the conviction that they can make the world a better place — or at least a different one.

Shot in both 16m and on videotape, print screened was a 16m version, and somewhat out-of-synch. A 35m release print is being readied for its theatrical bow in L.A. —Kirk.

Ayoub
(Patience)
(EGYPTIAN - COLOR)

Cairo, March 5.

Produced by Mamdouh El-Leithy for Egyptian TV. Stars Omar Sharif. Directed by Hani Lashin. Screenplay, Mohsen Zayed, based on a story by Nagib Mahfouz; camera (color), Abdel-Moneim Bahnasi; editor, Adel Mounir; art director, Abdel-Moneim Shokri; sound, Magdi Kamel; music, Moustapha Nagi. World sales: Egyptian TV. Reviewed at Cinema Cairo, March 5, 1984. Running time: **120 MINS.**

Ayoub	Omar Sharif

With Foad El-Mohandes, Madiha Yousri, Moustapha Fahmi, Athar El-Hakim and Mohmoud El-Milige.

"Ayoub" marks the return of the Egyptian cinema's biggest international star, Omar Sharif, to a national picture after 20 years of offshore assignments in Europe and the U.S. It is also notable as the first theatrically released picture made by Egyptian television.

Psychodrama about a millionaire (Sharif) who suddenly finds himself paralyzed in Cairo Airport, in spite of riches and success, is bound to be read in terms of star's own life, adding interest to a simple plot. Ayoub, the millionaire, is escorted to an office in the airport to rest, where he realizes his sudden paralysis is psychological in origin and can only be cured by facing up to the sordid steps in his climb to wealth. He tries to recall images of his happy past, days of innocence, friends of his youth. But the past cannot return, and nothing remains in the end except death.

The temptation is strong to connect the story with Sharif's depression following his return to his native land, after achieving success abroad and living more than half his life with the myth of the "star." Pic's finest moments are Sharif's expression of anxiety over having cut his ties to his sentimental past. A scene with a barber and another listening to Om Kalthoun are very effective dramatically.

Eventually, to clear his conscience, Ayoub writes down the truth about how he amassed his wealth and is murdered by a powerful interest group that doesn't wish to have its methods and secrets revealed. Viewers may have trouble identifying with the woes of millionaire Sharif, particularly as "Ayoub" means a symbol of patience and suffering, which the character is obviously intended to embody. This weakness, however, doesn't sink the film, which is a feather in the cap of Egyptian tv and producer Mamdouh El-Leithy, and heralds a new talent behind the camera, Hani Lashin. — Fari.

They're Playing With Fire
(COLOR)

Danning with faint praise.

Hollywood, April 27.

A New World release of a Hickmar production. Produced, screenplay by Howard Avedis, Marlene Schmidt. Directed by Avedis. Camera (Deluxe Color), Gary Graver; editor, Jack Tucker; music, John Cacavas; art direction, Rosemary Brandenburg; sound, Bill Fiege; associate producers, Ernest Kaye, Tim Siu; assistant director, Herman Grigsby. Reviewed at the Hollywood Pacific, L.A., Apr. 27, 1984. (MPAA Rating: R.) Running time: **96 MINS.**

Diane Stevens	Sybil Danning
Jay Richards	Eric Brown
Michael Stevens	Andrew Prine
Bird Johnson	Paul Clemens
Lillian Stevens	K.T. Stevens
George Johnson	Gene Bicknell

When Roger Corman owned New World Pictures, films as bad as "They're Playing With Fire" were never allowed to run as long as 96 minutes. But, as they did on "Angel," the company's new honchos have come up with an effective — if widely deceptive — ad campaign, and this first of the perhaps 10 or 12 Sybil Danning starrers for 1984 could rack up some profitable b.o. totals.

Ads feature the ubiquitous Danning as an English professor who's going to give an advanced education to "Private Lessons" star Eric Brown. That part all takes place in the opening minutes, with the next section of the seemingly endless plot devoted to a hairbrained scheme Danning and slimy husband Andrew Prine have concocted to milk inheritance millions from latter's dotty grandmother and nasty mother.

From there, pic segues into a lame horror-suspense meller, as several characters are dispatched by a masked lunatic who seems like a refugee from one of the "Friday The 13th" opuses and even rises from the dead after having seemingly been killed — so what else is new?

Such are the close, affectionate feelings the characters have for their friends and close relatives that they exhibit absolutely no reactions upon finding them murdered. Or maybe that's merely director Howard (formerly Hikmet) Avedis' idea of effective underplaying on the part of his thesps.

In any event, this is a failure on all levels, including the quality of the print caught, which makes the film look like it was processed in a bathtub and is full of brown splotches and variable colors.

For Sybil watchers, pic does offer up three nude scenes which effectively show off her total tan, but eroticism is nowhere present. If this makes money, the ad department will be due for a raise.

— *Cart.*

Caged Women
(ITALIAN-FRENCH-COLOR)

A Motion Picture Marketing (MPM) release of a Beatrice/Imp. Ex. Ci./Les Films Jacques Leitienne production. Directed by "Vincent Dawn" (Bruno Mattei). Features entire cast. Screenplay, P. Molteni, Oliver Lemat; camera (Telecolor; prints by Getty), Luigi Ciccarese; editor, Bruno Mattei; music, Luigi Ceccarelli; art direction, Maurizio Mammi; production manager, Sergio Cortona; assistant director, Claudio Fragasso; makeup, Marcello di Paolo. Reviewed at UA Rivoli 1 theater, N.Y., April 27, 1984. (MPAA Rating: R). Running time: 96 MINS.
Laura/Emanuelle ....Laura Gemser
Dr. Moran ....Gabriele Tinti
Warden ....Lorraine de Selle
Also with: Maria Romano, Ursula Flores, Raul Cabrera.

"Caged Women" is a shoddy women-in-prison picture, filmed in Rome in 1982 under the title "Emanuelle Reports From A Woman's Prison." It s theatrical life is limited to slumming film buffs and fans of old-fashioned shock gimmicks.

Perfunctory storyline has undercover reporter Emanuelle (Laura Gemser, who has essayed the globe-hopping character in more than a dozen films since "Black Emanuelle" in 1975) is thrown into Santa Catarina women's penitentiary, pretending to be one Laura Kendall, a prostitute, in order to gather information to expose prison corruption and brutality directed against the inmates. That she does, after dull pic runs through the usual array of genre cliches, with emphasis upon lesbianism and sadism. Dubbing is atrocious and color processing variable.

Highlight for fans of this material is a lengthy scene of the heroine attacked by rats, notable for Gemser letting some rather repellent critters sit on her shoulders. Elsewhere, director Bruno Mattei (using his nom de film of Vincent Dawn) essays such filler as Laura's crusty old cellmate Pilar, whose only friend is a pet cockroach, and tangential action at a neighboring men's prison where the focus of attention is on a comic-relief effeminate inmate.

Stars Gemser and her real-life husband Gabriele Tinti (here playing a sympathetic inmate/doctor) have made 20 films together since 1975, more than such prolific teams as Charles Bronson-Jill Ireland and Richard Burton-Elizabeth Taylor. Not surprisingly, they both look wornout and sullen during their turns here, even in the requisite softcore sex couplings.

Duo found time to crank out a companion film, also in 1982, titled "Emanuelle's Escape From Hell," and also featuring the pretty Italian actress Lorraine de Selle, who portrays the wicked warden in "Caged Women." On a higher plane, Gemser (using the name Moira Chen) and Tinti were also featured that year in the Hall Bartlett-Michael Landon telefilm "Love Is Forever." —*Lor.*

Atemnot
(Gasping)
(AUSTRIAN-COLOR)

Vienna, March 29.
A Neue Studio Film production, Cineart (Hans Peter Hoffman) release. Directed by Käthe Kratz. Original story and script by Peter Turrini. Camera (Eastmancolor) Christian Berger; editor, Susanne Schett; music, Konstantin Wecker, Dead Nittels; production design, Angela Hareiter; costumes, Susi Heger; production management, Monika Maruschko. Reviewed as official entry in the Viennale at the Urania on March 28, 1984. Running time: 95 MINS.
Tina ....Henrietta Cejpek
Gerhard ....Johannes Silberschneider
Tina's mother ....Maria Martina
Gerhard's father ......Hubert Kronlachner
Gerhard's mother ....Maria Singer
Sigi ....Sigi Maron
Karl ....Armin Felsberger
Wegrostek.............Paul Wolff-Plottegg
Sister Fidelitas ....Paola Loew

"Gasping" has been seen by some Austrian critics as a clumsy anti-establishment tirade, but writer Peter Turrini's and director Käthe Kratz' first joint feature is rather, to use a double metaphor, a tongue-in-cheeky film about alienated youth using all the clichés of such films in a subtly ironic, often self-satirizing way and employing the cinematic language in almost an extremity of perfection ("Gasping" has shots, lighting, color and production design to call Michelangelo Antonioni films to mind).

Story has two youngsters, rich girl Tina and blue collar worker Gerhard, as inmates in a mental institution after unsuccessful suicide attempts. They feel softly attracted to each other, have a rendezvous in a toilet booth and perform an amorous underwater ballet in the swimming-pool; but sex as such does not seem to mean much to them.

We get to know their well-meaning but comically helpless parents who were obviously not instrumental in driving the youngsters to their suicide attempts. Was society to blame? Yes and no. Turrini and Kratz use social indictment bombast mostly as an added tragicomic effect. Reasons for the general alienation must run deeper in history and society and the filmmakers are not meaning to analyze, just to tell their story in jolts of poetry and/or violence.

When the youngsters are released they find a kind of peace when they join a group of occupiers of condemned houses, but of course that idyll is soon broken up by police looking for, and finding, narcotics. Here as everywhere else, audiences are left to guess at what is what and when is a joke a joke and not a serious statement. Tina and Gerhard are returned to the mental institution only to run away again. Both have been rather vague of expression all through the film, which again leaves them as open question marks

"Gasping" is a delight to look at, and as soon as its oblique way of telling its story finds its narrative rhythm, it is also a delight to listen to.

Obviously, what was once called an art house item should not have trouble finding a theatrical audience sympathetic to it. —*Kell.*

Nunca Fomos Tão Felizes
(We Have Never Been So Happy)
(BRAZILIAN-COLOR)

Gramado, April 10.
An Embrafilme release of a Salles & Salles, Embrafilme, L.C. Barreto, Imacon Comunicação, Morena Filmes, Movi & Art and Cinefilmes production. Features entire cast. Produced and directed by Murilo Salles. Screenplay, Alcione Araujo, based on the novel, "Alguma Coisa Urgentemente," by João Gilbert Noll; adaptation, Jorge Durán, Murilo Salles; camera (Eastmancolor) Tadeu Ribeiro; editing, Vera Freire; costumes and set design, Carlos Prieto; sound editing, Valéria Mauro; dubbing and mixing, Robert Carvalho; music, Sergio G. Saraceni; executive producer, Mariza Leão. Reviewed at Embaixador Theatre, Gramado Film Festival, April 10, 1984. Running time: 90 MINS.
Cast: Claudio Marzo, Roberto Bataglin, Suzana Vieira, Antonio Pompeu, Meiry Vieira, Marcus Vinicius, Enio Santos, Fabio Junqueira, José Mayer, Angelo Rebello, Tonico Pereira.

This is the debut as a director of Murilo Salles, cinematographer for "Dona Flor," "Eu te Amo" and "Cabaret Mineiro."

His first film effort deals with an apparently simple, yet complex, plot. After eight years away from his teenaged son, studying in an interior religious school, the father decides to pick him up and bring him to an empty apartment in a big city (Copacabana Beach, Rio) for an undisclosed reason.

Later we realize the father's intent was to kidnap the Swiss ambassador to Brazil and escape to Europe with the boy. But his political activity is revealed step by step, through strange behavior. The son finds out about mysterious relations between his father and a cabaret dancer, a strange wealthy woman who owns the apartment, and a recently murdered terrorist.

Son is Roberto Bataglin, who appeared in "Golden Girl." Father is Claudio Marzo, a well-known tv star.

Salles tries to concentrate the action in the youngster's solitude, reinforced by the idea that something may happen at any moment. He is helped by cinematography of Tadeu Ribeiro (Salles' former assistant) and fine art direction by Carlos Prieto. He fails to escape, however, from reiterative dialog and inconsistensy of dramatic action.

Yet, "Nunca Fomos Tão Felizes" proves a fine professional work, a testimony about a political period of influence over most Brazilians now in their 30s.

Work is fit by any international standards and representative of the new Brazilian cinema. Salles' maturity as a film director will not take long, as it did not take long for him to become one of the finest Brazilian cinematographers.

—*Hoin.*

Feroz
(Ferocious)
(SPANISH-COLOR)

Madrid, April 11.
An Elias Querejeta production, directed by Manuel Gutiérrez Aragón. Screenplay, Querejeta and Aragón; camera (color), Teo Escamilla; editor, Pablo G. del Amo; sets, Gerardo Vera; production manager, Primitivo Alvaro; music by Coro Infantil Villa de Madrid. Features Fernando Fernán Gómez, Frederic de Pasquale, Elene Lizarralde, Javier Garcia and Julio César Sanz. Reviewed at Palacio de la Música (Madrid), Apr. 11, '84. Running time: 110 MINS.

Spanish helmer Manuel Gutiérrez Aragón has done a complete turnaround from such previous pics as "Demons in the Garden" and "Maravillas." Here he sets his sights on a whimsical fable about a bear trying to become a *mensch*. The result is an unpalatable hybrid of a film which scores neither as comedy nor drama. As a "fable," it is just embarrassingly silly.

Somewhere in mountainous northern Spain a young man, shackled to a cabin, escapes into the woods. After being pursued by a pack of hounds, who seem rather more friendly than menacing as they occasionally glance at the camera, he holes up in a cave and by the following spring has turned into the semblance of a bear. (In fact, he is very obviously a man in a large bear suit.)

He is then brought into the home of a writer (Fernando Fernán Gómez), who attempts to make a "real person" out of him. The bear talks with the clear voice of his former Spanish self, is taught to use a home-computer and enjoys a singalong of "La Cucaracha."

At the end, when invited to have tea in a private house, the bear is attacked by a dog, whom he kills; this forces him to flee back to the mountains where, after another winter, he turns back into a human being. Every now and then touches of wry humor come across, but on the whole they are lost as the man in the bear suit shuffles from scene to scene and is even taken to an office to work as a computer operator. Commercial prospects: zilch.

— *Besa.*

Caged Fury
(FILIPINO-COLOR)

A Saturn International Pictures and Shapiro Entertainment Corp. release of an LEA Prods. production. Produced by Emily Blas. Directed by Cirio H. Santiago. Features entire cast. Screenplay, Bobby Greenwood; camera (Imperious color), uncredited; editor, uncredited; music, Ernani Cuenco; sound, Rolly Rota; assistant director, Barbara Greenwood; production manager, Santiago Garcia; casting, Jim Wynorski. Reviewed at Cine 42 Screen 1 theater, N.Y. April 21, 1984. (MPAA Rating: R). Running time: 84 MINS.
Denise................Bernadette Williams
Linda......................Jennifer Laine
Also with: Taffy O'Connell, Catherine March, S.P. Victoria, Mari Karen Ryan, Ken Metcalf.

"Caged Fury" is a dull, low-on-action women's prison film made in the Philippines. It packs none of the B-movie fun of its forebears, which flourished on the drive-in circuit in 1970-74.

Plot device is reminiscent of "The Manchurian Candidate" and "Telefon." In contemporary Vietnam, American girls (as well as local girls who consorted with G.I.'s during the war) are rounded up and put in camps to be brainwashed (by elecric shock-aversion methods) into becoming zombie-like agents. Taking an unwise cue from Richard Brooks' "Wrong Is Right," film has them turned into "human bombs," exploding themselves (wearing vests containing explosives) back home in order to kill important people nearby.

While a U.S. officer (Ken Metcalf) tries to swap a renegade Vietnamese general, wanted by his people, for the girls, the heroines attempt to escape from the camp in a series of laughably executed "action" scenes. Finale involving a train, tanks and U.S. helicopters is thoroughly unconvincing hokum.

Chief surprise here is in the casting, done by Jim Wynorski, former New World Pictures publicity man who is latterly an indie writer-director. While the Filipinos made films in this genre of the 1970s inevitably gave employment to Pam Grier, Jeanne Bell, or others, no black actresses appear in "Caged Fury." The actresses on view here give tired walk-throughs, indistinguishable from the "zombies" in the cast. Tech credits are subpar, with dialog articulated in English but inadequately post-synched.
— Lor.

Cento Giorni A Palermo
(100 Days In Palermo)
(ITALIAN-COLOR)

Rome, April 10.
A Titanus release, produced by TV/Cine 2000 Coop and C.L.C.T. (Palermo). Stars Lino Ventura and Giuliana De Sio. Directed by Giuseppe Ferrara. Screenplay by Giorgio, Giuseppe Ferrara and others; camera (color), Silvio Fraschetti; editor, Mario Gargiulo; art director, Antonio Visone; music, Vittorio Gelmetti. Reviewed at Barberini Cinema, Rome, April 17, 1984. Running time: 108 MINS.

Gen. Carlo Dalla Chiesa......Lino Ventura
Emmanuela...............Giuiiana De Sio
Capt. Fontana........Stefano Satta Flores
Banker.............Adalberto Maria Merli

Financed by contributions from an impressive array of associations — the region of Sicily and other local government organizations, trade unions, anti-drug leagues, film industry groups (the list of sponsors that unrolls in the final credits is seeming endless) — "100 Days in Palermo" was conceived as a film against the Mafia. As such, it is a collective cry of outrage at the murder of the Italian state's anti-Mafia prefect Gen. Carlo Alberto Dalla Chiesa and his wife.

Made by two film co-ops, pic was released here by Titanus with great success, and may point to a rebirth of interest in films with social themes. Star Lino Ventura should assure wider trade. Subject and particularly veiled references to political figures and local facts could be a limitation for other markets.

Helmer Giuseppe Ferrara paints the figure of Dalla Chiesa, who made his reputation organizing a nationwide battle against the Red Brigades, with sympathetic admiration. Ventura injects the rigid general with enough burning idealism, integrity and selflessness to blow him up to truly heroic proportions on screen. With the emotional support of his understanding young wife Emmanuela (Giuliana De Sio), Dalla Chiesa goes to Sicily and launches a practically one-man campaign to root out Mafia leaders and unblemished political supporters.

Film's implication (made at the time by the newspapers) is that the super-prefect was sent to Sicily as a figurehead by political forces too interconnected with organized crime to give him the powers he needed to clean the place up. Even in the absence of an effective anti-Mafia law, the general proves too efficient at his job. When he starts checking the banks that have been laundering mob money, a certain banker makes a phone call to a certain minister; the minister calls Dalla Chiesa; the general doesn't heed the warning and is soon eliminated.

Pic does well to focus on the prefect's public struggles, building suspense not around the assassination, a foregone conclusion, but around the intricate workings of the mob machine and the unequal battle between the forces of good and evil.

Disappointingly, filmmakers (and the long list of Giorgio Arlorio's cowriters contribute to a collective feeling) keep to generalities. They don't, or can't, get specific about the public figures hinted at as linking Mafia, state and high finance (a connection most people would agree existed before they saw the film). Given the many unanswered questions the film raises, viewers may be left as doubtful as the locals, embodied in the Capt. Fontana character played by Stefano Satta Flores, about whether such a deep-rooted evil can ever be eradicated, if even the legendary warrior-general failed.— Yung.

O Baiano Fantasma
(The Ghost From Bahia)
(BRAZILIAN-COLOR)

Gramado, April 17.
An Embrafilme release of a Palmares Producôcs/Embrafilme production. Produced by Maracy Mello, Denoy de Oliveira. Features entire cast. Directed by de Oliveira. Screenplay, Denoy de Oliveira; camera (Eastmancolor), Aloisio Raulino; editing, Milton Bolinha, Renato Neiva Moreira; art direction, Leo Leoni; sound, David Penington; sound track, De Oliveira; music, Julinho Vicente, Luiz Carlos Gomes, De Oliveira; production director, Wagner Carvalho. Reviewed at Embaixador Theatre, Gramado Film Festival, April 17, 1984. Running time: 100 MINS.
Cast: José Dumont, Maracy Melb, Regina Dourado, Luiz Carlos Gomes, Raphael de Carvalho, Paulo Hesse, Benedito Corsi, Renato Consorte, Carlos Bucka, Julio Calasso, Sergio Mamberti.

The biggest surprise at the XII Gramado Film Festival, "O Baiano Fantasma" got the awards for best film, best director and best actor, and is one of the finest Brazilian films of the last years.

José Dumont is Lambusca, a northeastern Brazilian who goes to São Paulo in search of a job. He gets work as a money collector, not realizing he is actually getting involved with a kind of local Mafia. When a "client" dies of a heart attack, his life becomes complicated, and Lambusca is turned into a target for bandits, policemen, everybody.

Deeper, "O Baiano Fantasma" is a dramatic panel of life in a big city like São Paulo. Dialogs are rhythmic, in the tradition of the popular literature (cordel) of Brazilian northeast. Dumont's performance is more than outstanding, as are the music by Denoy and partners, the sets by Leo Leoni and the cinematography by Aloisio Raulino, who captures the magic and the mystery of nightlife in São Paulo.

Sequences are elaborated frame to frame, and so are the characters, who include workers, prostitutes and policemen. Authentically funny, yet dramatic, "O Baiano Fantasma" is faithful to the Brazilian culture and costumes. It almost brings to life the smell of Brazil and some of its sequences, like the one in which the drunken northeasterner meets a São Paulo Japanese late at night in a desert street, should be inscribed in an anthology of Brazilian cinema.

By far the best film by Denoy de Oliveira (who previously directed "A Amante Muito Louca" and "Sete Dias de Agonia"), "O Baiano Fantasma" is one of the most poetic and poignant local items in a long time, despite its apparent lack of ambition. Being essentially Brazilian, it must be seen as such, for it makes no concessions in terms of a "universal" language. Yet, "O Baiano Fantasma" is a perfectly articulated feature, with high technical standards.

It is not part of the "Brazilian Super Cinema" in terms of production (actually, it is a small-budget film by current local standards). Still, it is by no means intended only for selective audiences. It is the best testimony that, though concerned with the efforts to improve the technical standards of Brazilian cinema, quality is still a matter of talent, and not only a consequence of the size of the budget. —Hoin.

Tukana
(PAPUA NEW GUINEAN-COLOR)

A production of the North Solomons Provincial Government, Papua New Guinea, and the Institute of Papua New Guinea Studios. Executive producer, Graeme Kemelfield. Directed by Chris Owen; codirected by Albert Toro. Screenplay, Toro, Owen, from story by Toro; camera (color), Owen; sound, Les McLaren; editor, McLaren. A presentation of the New Directors/New Films series, from the Film Society of Lincoln Center and the Dept. of Film of the Museum of Modern Art. Reviewed at the 57th St. Playhouse, N.Y., April 8, 1984. Running time: 120 MINS.
(In Tok Pisin, with English subtitles.)

Audiences familiar with Third World cinema will be instantly at home with "Tukuna" as it deals with problems endemic to the so-called developing or emerging nations. Although rarely seen in the U.S. except for such specialized series as the New Directors/New Films, these films, even as fiction works with invented characters and plot, are in effect documents or documentaries that describe the devastating social upheavals that beset dozens of new nations that achieved statehood during the post-World War II dissolution of the great European empires.

A recurrent theme of these films concerns the village-boy-gone-wrong. The boy is always sensed as a tiny microcosm of big cultural changes. Having apprehensively left the stability and traditions of his isolated village, the youth goes away to a technical school, can't adjust to it, does badly, drops out, and drifts into rootlessness among bad companions, drop-outs like himself. The young man thus becomes progressively alienated from his parents, forsaking his original ideals, resenting the narrowness and taboos of village elders.

That's the formula. But this is not to say that "Tukuna" is another mechanical reworking of a cliché; it is not. "Tukuna" is lively and original and intelligent, although it is overlong and stiffly acted by non-professionals.

"Tukuna" fits the formula but that merely confirms the strength and validity and omnipresence worldwide of its story and theme. All these troubled tricontinental young men are brothers — there are millions of them — with the same hardworking and baffled parents back home in the village, and with the same homely and neglected fiancée patiently waiting.

But while his loved ones wait in the village, the boy in the newly created industrial town becomes fascinated by blue jeans, beer and motorbikes. In the case of "Tukuna," subtitled "What Went Wrong?" the young man becomes a tractor driver for Bougainville Copper, which pays him well to plunder the Papua New Guinea landscape. He becomes Westernized, but at what a cost — the film leaves the future open, an unstated menace.

"Tukuna" was screened last November at the third annual Hawaii International Film Festival in Honolulu, as Papua New Guinea's second or third feature. Coscenarist, codirector Albert Toro plays Tukuna; his codirector Chris Owen shot "Tukuna," having had extensive background in anthropological documentary. The film is spoken in Tok Pisin, a richly idiomatic English-based vernacular.

Commercial prospects for "Tukuna" seems dubious although special houses with a loyal clientele, perhaps in university towns, are a possibility. —*Hitch.*

A Proxima Vitima
(The Next Victim)
(BRAZILIAN-COLOR)

Gramado, April 9.

An Embrafilme release of a Raiz Produ ções Cinematogáficas, Embrafilme and Taba Filmes production. Features entire cast. Directed by João Batista de Andrade. Screenplay, Lauro Cesar Muniz; camera (Eastmancolor), Antonio Meliande; editor, Renato Neiva Moreira; costumes, art direction, Heraldo de Oliveira; music, Marcus Vinicius; production director, Wagner de Carvalho; assistant director and dubbing director, Mario Masetti; executive producer, Assumpção Hernandes de Andrade; associate producers, Alamo Filmes and Beca. Reviewed at Embaixador Theatre, Gramado Film Festival, April 9, 1984. Running time: **94 MINS.**

Cast: Antonio Fagundes, Louise Cardoso, Mayara Magri, Gianfrancesco Guarnieri, Othon Bastos, Aldo Bueno, Esther Goes, Goulart de Andrade, Denise del Vecchio.

Jose Batista de Andrade's previous feature, "O Homem que Virou Suco," got the Gold Prize at Moscow's 1981 Film Festival. Director is an artist committed to social issues and the discussion of factual aspects of Brazilian social life. "A Proxima Vitima" is set in São Paulo over the period of November 1982 elections for Congress and governors.

David (Antonio Fagundes) is a tv journalist covering a series of murders involving prostitutes. The action is slowly centered on David himself and in the broad reality involving him, his marital problems, his disenchantments with the tv orientation and with the political life. Getting closer to the prostitutes' life, he merges into the world of criminality and police corruption, at the same time he witnesses the claims and demands of his fellow workers in the streets of São Paulo.

Actual scenes of political manifestations are mixed with the fictional material. The technical improvement of Andrade's work is evident: his camera is lighter, moves easier and, as in "Suco," he manages to capture relevant aspects of the life (and the underground) of a city like São Paulo. Acting by Fagundes, Louise Cardoso and Mayara Magri are outstanding, but Andrade's insistence on obvious political statements makes them often repetitive and may well dilute their original power.

On the other hand, Andrade's narrative option seems sometimes confusing and one often may wonder about the direct relation between the crimes and the political perplexity of the character. For some reason, director is reluctant to keep his story in a clear track, thus jeopardizing the spectator's involvement, which is not as strong as in "Suco."

Nevertheless, "A Proxima Vitima" is a faithful portrait of the universe Andrade tries to discuss. Cinematography and editing are fine, and film doubtless achieves an international standard. As a crafty and very personal work, "A Proxima Vitima" reveals the existence of a serious and professional filmmaker, concerned with the final quality of his product and the improvement of a type of film both politically committed and competitive. —*Hoin.*

Gracias Por El Fuego
(Thanks For The Light)
(ARGENTINE-COLOR)

Buenos Aires, April 6.

NormaVigo release of an Horacio R. Casares Prods. production. Directed by Sergio Renán. Features entire cast. Screenplay, Juan Carlos Gené, Renán, based on Mario Benedetti's novel; camera (Eastmancolor), Alberto Basail; editor, Luis César D'Angiolillo; art direction, Tita Tamames, Rosa Zemborain. Reviewed at the Ambassador theater, B.A., April 5, 1984. Running time: 90 MINS.
Edmundo Budiño ....Lautaro Murúa
Ramón Budiño ....Víctor Laplace
Dolly.....................Bárbara Mujica
Susana.......................Dora Baret
Gloria ....Graciela Dufau
Hugo.....................Alberto Segado
Aunt ....Nelly Prono
Junior son ....Gabriel Lenn

Reteaming of director Sergio Renán and novelist Mario Benedetti raises hopes they will match their achievement with "La Tregua" (The Truce) (1974), the only Argentine pic so far nominated for an Oscar. But this lackluster opus is below expectations mainly due to the shortcomings of a script that resorts most of the time to dialog to tell the story of an autocratic pater familias instead of showing through action what would have been the nuances of his character and the dramatic charge of his behavior.

Benedetti's plot takes place within upper-class Uruguayan circles. In the film the place of action is not identified, which doesn't help the believability of tycoon Lautaro Murúa's confrontations with his workers and his sons, his calm encounters with mistress Graciela Dufau and the ambiguous relationship with elder son Víctor Laplace that will lead the troubled young man to suicide (not before having had an affair with sister-in-law Bárbara Mujica, clashes with wife Dora Baret and brother Alberto Segado, and understanding with his father's lover and, among other things, a fruitless effort to become master of his own life). Most of these developments are rather abruptly introduced into the story, lacking the narrative and psychological justifications to make them convincing.

Players lend their professional ability to the shallow parts alloted them. Camerawork has the players in profile or semi-profile a good deal of the time, thus blocking their in-depth communication with viewers. Other technical credits are generally okay.
—*Nubi.*

Verdes Anos
(Green Years)
(BRAZILIAN-COLOR)

Gramado, April 9.

A Diotriboidera Nacional release of a Z Produtora Cinematografica production. Features entire cast. Producer, Sergio Daniel Lerrer. Directed by Carlos Gerbase, Giba Assis Brasil. Screenplay, Alvaro Teixeira, from novel, "Os Verdes Anos," by Luiz Fernando Emediato; camera (Eastmancolor), Christian Lesage; editing, Alpheu Godinho; art direction, Marlise Storchi, José Arthur Camacho; sound, Roberto Carvalho; music, Nei Lisboa, Augusto Licks; Nelson Coelho de Castro; costumes, Marta Biavaschi; assistant direction, Roberto Henkin; production design, Giba Assis Brasil, Carlos Gerbase, Werner Schunemann Alex Sernambi, Roberto Henkin. Reviewed at Embaixador Theatre, Gramado Film Festival, April 9, 1984. Running time: 90 Mins.
Cast: Werener Schunemann, Marco Antonio Breda, Xala Felippi, Carlos Gruber, Márcia do Canto, Marco Antonio Sório, Sérgio Lulkin, Zé Tachenco, Angel Palomero, Luciene Adami, Monica Schimiedt, Marta Biavaschi, Haydée Porto.

Rio Grande do Sul, a state at Brazil's south end, is one of the country's richest areas and a traditional meat and wine producer. Film industry, however, is not one of its priorities. It is no secret that almost 100% of the 80 Brazilian features produced every year comes from Rio de Janeiro and São Paulo. Therefore, the efforts of Rio Grande do Sul producers in making a film must be acknowledged.

In fact, "Verdes Anos" is the first 35m feature produced by a young group (some teenagers, some in their early 20s) after some successful experiences with features produced in Super 8 and released at previous Gramado Festivals. Their theme is the same now: the life of the generation of the '70s (their own) living in Rio Grande do Sul under years of political repression in Brazil.

"Verdes Anos" concentrates on three days in the lives of a group of teenagers: school problems, first loves, dance parties, fights, juvenile frustrations, etc. It suffers from lack of experience in many aspects. However, it is also surprisingly well narrated and acted, and has the help of experienced technicians and artists such as cinematographer Christian Lesage.

One can feel the unity of the crew, from production itself (item reportedly cost as little as $50,000, unbelievably low even by Brazilian standards) to all steps of the filmmaking, including the acting.

Under these circumstances, directors Carlos Gerbase and Giba Assis Brasil have managed to create a number of funny and dramatic situations. Timing is mature, above the average of local production, even though the screenplay frequently fails to provide strong dramatic cornerstones.

"Verdes Anos" is a successful first professional experience of a homogeneous group coping with the problem of producing in Rio Grande do Sul, but already with a second feature ready and two others in post-production. Doubtless it is a major contribution (not subsidized by Embrafilme) to decentralize Brazilian production and create an operative filmmaking pole in the south, while expressing aesthetic and political viewpoints worth seeing —*Hoin.*

Fast Talking
(AUSTRALIAN-COLOR)

Sydney, April 16.

An Oldata Pty. production. Produced by Ross Matthews. Directed and scripted by Ken Cameron. Features entire cast. Camera (color), David Gribble; music, Sharon Calcraft; editor, David Huggett; production design, Neil Angwin. Viewed at Film Australia Theatrette, Lindfield, April 3, 1984. Running time: 93 MINS.
Steve Carson..................Rod Zuanic
Vicki Arnold ....Toni Allayis
Moose ....Chris Truswell
Redback.....................Steve Bisley
Sharon Hart ....Tracy Mann
Ralph Carlson ....Peter Hehir
Yates......................Denis Moore
Al Carson ....Gary Cook

Ex-schoolteacher Ken Cameron's second theatrical feature (after last year's very successful "Monkey Grip") is another youth-themed pic, this time dealing with younger kids. Indeed, the inspiration seems to have been Francois Truffaut's "The 400 Blows," and comparisons aren't odious at all.

Set in the western suburbs of Sydney, "Fast Talking" centers around young Steve Carson, about 14, a likeable, cheerful youngster whose future looks exceedingly bleak. He comes from a broken home, his mother has run off with a baker and his father, who half-heartedly trains racing grey-hounds for a living, is a hopeless drunk. Steve has an older brother heavily into drugs, and it's through him that Steve has started pushing marijuana to his fellow-students. However, when stronger drugs are proposed, Steve draws the line.

His best friends are Vicki, a girl his age but much more mature, and the amiable Moose; he also has a dog and a craving to own a motorbike. He befriends the part-owner of a junkyard, Redback (Steve Bisley), an ex-con who tries to help the boy build a bike. Red-back is one of the few sympathetic adults in the film; another is Miss Hart (Tracy Mann), a new teacher at the school (most of the other teachers are presented as grossly inadequate or totally uncaring).

Pic ambles along in a relaxed, good-natured fashion, and is filled with genuine humor as it deals un-patronizingly with Steve and his mates and their problems. Came-ron skilfully combines scenes of rich comedy without losing sight of the fact that the future for these disoriented young people, older than their years, is probably one of reform schools and prisons. It's an indictment of modern society, but not in the least bit heavy.

Performances are all tops, with Rod Zuanic, as Steve, a real find; he gives an unaffected, totally pro-ressional performance. Cameron and his cameraman, David Grib-ble, have chosen some unusual lo-cations, such as vast mountains of scrap paper which form a back-drop to some key scenes.

Technically, "Fast Talking," though obviously a low-budgeter, rates with the best Aussie pics. The ending is open, though suggesting not much of a future for Steve who has trashed the office of his hated deputy-principal, accidentally set fire to it, and stolen a car with which to escape. Like Jean-Pierre Leaud at the end of Truffaut's film, he achieves a dream of sorts — rid-ing off on his motor-bike — but for how long?

In a market saturated with youth pics, this one is the genuine article. It should do good biz Down Under, and deserves international expo-sure. —*Strat.*

Eine Firma Für De Ewigkeit
(A Firm Forever)
(WEST GERMAN-B&W)

Berlin, April 9.

A coproduction of Rolf Gmöhling Film, Berlin and Futura Film, Munich, in collabo-ration with November-Film; world rights, Futura Film, Munich. Features entire cast. Written and directed by Rolf Gmöhling. Cam-era (b&w), Claus Deubel; Uli Köhler; edit-ing, Gabriele Herms; sound, Gottlieb Renz; music, Claus Deubel, Paul Esslinger; sets, Paul Miller; costumes, Nils Jastram. Reviewed at Yorck-Kino, Berlin, April 7, '84. Running time: **86 MINS.**
Cast: Jim Kain (Arno Noppe), Rudolf Schwarz (Director Freddersen), Peter Schlesinger (Doctor), Karl-Heinz Grewe (Program Director), Siegfried Zimmer-schied (German Chancellor), Bernd Henkels (Colonel), Klaus-Dieter Fröhlich (TV Moder-ator), Hans-Joachim Kaiser (Herr Ritzer), Ilse Schmalzigaug (Frau Radl), Joachim Schnabl (Civil Servant at Employment Of-fice), Julius Ziehmer (Reporter), Hildegard Bauer (Erika), Gerhard Joachimsthal (Egg-man).

Rolf Gmöhling's "A Firm Forev-er" is another bit of tickling evi-dence that the Berlin Underground is still as alive and kicking as ever. This low-budget pic (made from an inheritance the director fortunate-ly received) was lensed in 16m and then printed in the laboratory in brownish sepia-like tones for pre-sentation a year ago in a Berlin Underground showcase in fact, one of the large old houses illegally oc-cupied by squatters called "Eis-zeit" (Ice Age).

This is an amusing commedy with a Kafkaesque or George Or-well bent. A bedridden patient for 10 years with shattered nerves, Arno Noppe is finally announced cured by his friendly practicing medicine man, so off he goes into the wide, wide world (like Peter Sellers' Mr. Chance in "Being There") to make himself useful. The outside world has changed in the meanwhile, however, and our adventurer finds himself in a world in which nobody in particular has a working job.

Not even the West German Chancellor can function, for the latest elections show he had not reached the required 5% vote clause. So no party at all is in gov-ernment, and the president of the Federal Republic is off somewhere on a round-the-globe trip and hasn't reported in for months.

Noppe goes to the unemploy-ment bureau in search of a job, but with everyone avoiding work as a policy it's hard to find anything save for a fireworks company, "a firm forever" according to its ads. Here, he finds the fireworks are used by the employees for their own use, right off the modest as-sembly line. Even when he himself is appointed to the position of fore-man, and decides to make deliver-ies for orders that have been ne-glected in the head office until now, enterprise becomes little more than outfoxing the others on the job

to disturb in the end the public peace.

A worker publicly on the job merits a tv broadcast. Noppe is brought into the tv studio by a re-porter, only to note that here an in-terview with a Nobel Prize winner for mathematics has been faked to air anything at all.

Thus, it makes little difference whether a real, live working man has been bagged for a tv special or not. At this point the twist could have been beefed up into an absurd comedy, but Gmöhling unfor-tunately lets his wacky story peter out just when it is getting inter-esting.

A debut helmer with talent, Gmöhling has made a quite re-spectable feature out of a situation resembling Jean-Luc Godard's "Alphaville" and futuristic sci-fiers common to Yank independent filmmaking. —*Holl.*

Laylat El-Kaped Alla Fatma
(The Night They Arrested Fatma)
(EGYPTIAN-COLOR)

Cairo, April 10.

A Traytel release produced by Tara Film. Stars Faten Hamama. Directed by Henri Barakat. Screenplay by Barakat and Abdel-Rahman Fahmi, based on a story by Sekiena Fouad. Camera (Color), Wahid Farid; art director, Onsi Abou-Seif; editor, Enayat El-Sayes; music, Omar Khairat; sound, Gamil Aziz. Reviewed at Mist Cinema, Cairo, March 26, 1984. Running time: **120 MINS.**
Fatma . . . . Faten Hamama
El-Sayed . . . . Shoukri Sarhan
Galal 1 . . . . Mohsen Nohi'El-din
Galal 2 . . . . Salah Kabil
Zakiya . . . . Layla Fahmi
Hapashi . . . . Aly El-Sherif

"The Night They Arrested Fat-ma" is a dramatic rendition of Egypt's July Revolution (1952) as seen through the eyes of a girl waiting to be married.

Fatma (actress Faten Hamama, whose input included supervision of all stages of production) refuses to go abroad with her lover, a poor fisherman seeking work, so she can bring up her two orphaned brothers. Like Penelope waiting for Ulysses to return, Fatma spends the time behind her sewing machine. When the lover finally comes back, Fatma's brother Galal has him arrested and sent-enced to 15 years in prison, then tries to have Fatma locked up in a mental institution.

Story is told in flashbacks, with Fatma sitting on the roof of her house, threatening to jump if Galal goes through with sending her to the asylum, while neighbors and townsfolk look on.

Parallels to Egyptian history are unmistakable — Galal is clearly meant to represent the self-pro-claimed "heroes" of the July Revolution who switched sides be-tween Egypt and England as self-

interest dictated and who traf-ficked in arms; Fatma is the ally of the popular resistance move-ment.

An artificial and unjustified hap-py ending is not very convincing after a freeze frame on Fatma be-ing taken away by police. Also weak is pic's opening, a popular wedding ceremony in Port Said with no relation to the story. Only the central part of the film finds its pace and style, following the struc-ture of folklore and heroic epic.

Veteran helmer Henri Rarakat shows an expert touch at interject-ing documentary footage of the war in Port Said and using Omar Khairat's theme music. He directs a fine cast of thesps, particularly Hamama, Mohsen Moh'Eldin, and Salah Kabil. —*Fari.*

Los Santos Inocentes
(The Holy Innocents)
(SPANISH-COLOR)

Madrid, April 9.

A Ganesh Producciones Cinematograficas S.A. production, in collaboration with Spanish Television (RTVE). Directed by Mario Ca-mus. Screenplay, Antonio Larreta, Manuel Matji and Camus, based on novel by Miguel Delibes; camera (Eastmancolor), Hans Bur-mann; editor, José Mariá Biurrun; producer, Julián Mateos; sets, Rafael Palmero; music, Antón Garcia Abril. Reviewed at UIP screen-ing room, Madrid, April 9, '84. Running time: **105 MINS.**
Paco . . . . Alfredo Landa
Azarias . . . . Francisco Rabal
Régula . . . . Terele Pávez
Don Pedro . . . . Agustin Gonzalez
Señorito Iván . . . . Juan Diego
Miriam . . . . Maribel Martin
Also: Belén Ballesteros, Juan Sáchez, Agata Lys, Mary Carrillo, José Guardiola, Manuel Zarzo.

"The Holy Innocents" is a slow-paced, somewhat overlong but nonetheless poignant rural drama zeroing in on the abysmal class differences still existing in some sectors of modern Spain, especial-ly in the holdings of the rural aris-tocracy. Delibes' novel, as well as this film, have deliberate political overtones, since they underline the misery and ignorance in which parts of Spain's population still lived — in the 1960s. In fact, for the first quarter hour of the film it is hard to tell whether the action is placed in modern times or in the pre-war era, the era of Luis Bú-ñuel's "Las Hurdes."

This is the sort of film that would have incensed the Franco govern-ment, since it portrays the black-est of Spains which is not really representative of modern Iberia as a whole.

Story concerns a wretched, im-poverished family working on the estate of an aristocratic family in the province of Extremadura in the 1960s. Each of the members of the poor family is spotlighted for a part of the film, but the stories are interlocking and at the end provide a coherent narrative. There is the paterfamilias, a pathetic laborer brilliantly played by Alfredo Landa, whose main purpose in life seems to be allaying the capricious ire of his almost feudal employers and helping one of them in birdhunting parties.

His wife is also long-suffering, and scrapes along with phrases to the aristocrats like "Order us, we are here to obey." Their daughter is a vegetable-like paralytic; the son is doing his military service, an eccentric uncle who washes his hands with his own urine goes mad when his pet bird is callously shot by the "señorito."

Camus includes some gripping scenes, such as the aristocrats showing off before a French ambassador that their help knows how to write their own names (which they laboriously accomplish); or that of poor Paco, after falling from a tree and breaking his leg, being made to go out to a bird shoot and helping the señorito, despite his pain and weakened state.

All elements of pic combine to present a devastating condemnation of the Spain of 20 years ago, and perhaps still that of today. Thesping is first-rate throughout, with Francisco Rabal giving a stellar performance as the doddering uncle who ultimately reaps revenge.

Camerawork is fine, screenplay excellent, and Garcia Abril's music perfect, but rather too short; editing tends to be a bit jerky at times.

All in all, item is memorable, and undoubtedly is one of the year's best from Spain and a strong contender as the probable Spanish official entry at the upcoming Cannes event. — *Besa.*

Vigil
(NEW ZEALAND-COLOR)

Auckland, N.Z., April 17.
A John Maynard production in association with the Film Investment Corp. of New Zealand and the New Zealand Film Commission. Directed by Vincent Ward. Produced by John Maynard. Camera (color) Alun Bollinger; production design, Kai Hawkins; editor, Simon Reece; music, Jack Body; screenplay, Vincent Ward and Graeme Tetley; sound, Graham Morris; costumes, Glenys Jackson; executive producer, Gary Hannam, associate producer, Piers Davies; production manager, Bridget Ikin; assistant director, Timothy White. Reviewed at Columbia-Warner preview theater, Auckland, April 14, '84. Running time: **90 MINS.**
Elizabeth . . . . Penelope Stewart
Ethan . . . . Frank Whitten
Birdie . . . . Bill Kerr
Toss . . . . Fiona Kay

"Vigil" is the strongest, most personally inspired film to come out of New Zealand to date. In form and content, and in its detailed and immaculate concern with visual imagery, it establishes in a single blow the place of its creator, 27-year-old Vincent Ward, as a unique film talent.

"Vigil" has been a time in the making. After completing two award-winning short features, "A State Of Siege" (Golden Hugo winner at Chicago) and "In Spring One Plants Alone" (Grand Prix co-winner at Cinéma du Réel in France) he began work on this, his first feature. It was four years in gestation before a 10-week shoot in a remote valley during a wet winter and early spring of 1983.

Ward's landscape is archetypal New Zealand but universal as well. His four main characters, locked as certainly within themselves as within the primeval valley they occupy and farm, constantly confront each other and withdraw as in the manner of an ancient dance.

Central figure is 11-year-old Toss (Fiona Kay), on the threshold of womanhood and caught in the tragedy of the death of her father and the coincidental arrival of a stranger, Ethan (Frank Whitten). It is primarily through her eyes, actions and interpretation of events, that the impact of Ethan's presence upon the household is registered.

While Toss is fascinated by Ethan's mysterious aura, her mother Elizabeth (Penelope Stewart) is reawakened from a joyless marrige, and her grandfather Birdie (Bill Kerr) finds a comrade for his eccentric pranks and grandiose mechanical inventions.

The remarkable quality of the film is the way it gives fresh resonance to universal themes. Ward's canvas contains the detail of old woodcuts found in brassbound bibles. Hawks swoop like angels of death down the ravines of rainforest mountains; the act of searing off lambs' tails assumes the significance of an age-old rite.

The director is supported strongly in realization of his vision by the superb photography of Alun Bollinger, cameraman on Ward's two short features, and Jack Body's music, which never overpowers but blends subtly with sound effects and images.

The acting of the principals is never found wanting. Kerr, in a role that gives full rein to his skilled comic gifts, is particularly fine, while Stewart, an Australian actress, finds both the remoteness and innate sexuality within Elizabeth. Whitten personifies expertly the ominous aloneness of Ethan.

But it is young Fiona Kay who is the essential touchstone of the piece and with her Ward has discovered a near-perfect alter ego. Her Toss is imbued with restless inner intensity that is always compelling. Her elfin quality resides in the truest sense of that description, mischievously supernatural, never cute.

"Vigil" is filmmaking at its finest and most satisfying. It will not be an overnight commercial blockbuster in cinemas throughout the world, but it seems destined to do strong business on the increasingly lucrative art film circuits.
— *Nic.*
(Film is first Kiwi feature to be in competition at 1984 Cannes Film Fest. —*Ed.*)

Conquest
(ITALIAN-SPANISH-MEXICAN-COLOR)

A United Film Distribution Co. (UFDC) release of a Clemi Cinematografica S.r.l. (Rome)-Golden Sun (Barcelona)-Producciones Esme S.A. (Mexico) coproduction. Produced by Giovanni Di Clemente. Directed by Lucio Fulci. Features entire cast. Screenplay, Gino Capone, Jose Antonio de la Loma Sr., Carlos Vasallo, from story by Di Clemente; camera (Telecolor), Alejandro Alonso Garcia; editor, Emilio Rodriguez Oses; editing supervision, Vincenzo Tomassi; music, Claudio Simonetti; art direction, Massimo Lentini; makeup/masks, Franco Rufini. Reviewed at UA Rivoli 1 theater, N.Y., April 21, 1984. (MPAA Rating: R). Running time: **89 MINS.**
Maxz . . . . Jorge Rivero
Ilias . . . . Andrea Occhipinti
Ocron . . . . Sabrina Siani
Also with: Conrado San Martin, Violeta Cela, Jose Gras Palau, Maria Scola.

"Conquest" is a stupefyingly bad fantasy import, vaguely resembling the popular "Quest For Fire" and "Conan The Barbarian" films in format. Playoff at U.S. action cinemas will result in weary customers suffering from eye strain.

Pic marks the fifth film by the prolific Italian director Lucio Fulci to be released Stateside within the last year, the others being horror films. His only trademark on display here in fantasyland is extraneous gore.

Non-story has two mythic warriors wandering around the countryside and battling with an assortment of furry man-beasts, sent out by a demonic demigod Ocron (Sabrina Siani, heroine of a dozen of these Italian fantasy films recently). Lacking any sense of continuity, purpose or script logic, their episodic trek becomes tedious in a hurry.

The cryptic absurdities here include monsters who like to launch themselves into action from (off-screen) trampolines; inappropriate use of blue-animated magic bows and arrows; Ocron feeding on the brains of her victims; and a pair of dolphins coming out of nowhere to save one of the heroes when he falls into the ocean while being crucified. Film's climax of Ocron turning into a wolf and running off into the sunset with a mate after a hero finally "kills" her is just another cause for jaws to drop in the audience.

Lamely attempting to create atmosphere, Fulci's visuals offer a nonstop array of smoke, sunlight and filtered distortion, creating a general sort of soft blur that is a projectionist and audience's nightmare. Even when he turns off the distorting effects, the viewer has to suffer through underlit night or cave scenes.

Cast is helpless under the circumstances, and Siani has to play her entire role naked, with gilt paint on her body and her face covered by a gold mask. Aggressive electronic rock music score, in Dolby stereo, is by Claudio Simonetti, formerly of the Italian group Goblin (who scored many memorable horror films such as "Deep Red," "Suspiria" and "Dawn Of The Dead"). —*Lor.*

Didi Der Doppelgänger
(Didi And His Double)
(WEST GERMAN-COLOR)

Berlin, April 15.
An UFA Film Production, Berlin, producer, Wolf Bauer; coproduction with ZDF, Mainz. Directed by Reinhard Schwabenitzky. Features Dieter Hallervorden. Screenplay, Christian Rateuke, Hartmann Schmige, based on a theme by Walter Kempley; camera (color), Charly Steinberger; sets, Jan Schluback; music, Harold Faltermeyer, Arthur Lauber; editing, Clarissa Ambach, production chief, Werner Mietzer; production manager, Klaus Michael Kühn. Reviewed at Royal Plast, Berlin, April 15, '84. Running time: **90 MINS.**
Cast: Dieter Hallervorden (Bruno Koob/Hans Immer), Tilo Prückner (Brazille), Hans-Joachim Grubel (Otto), Ruth Maria Kubitschek (Heidi), Barbara Nielsen (Molly), Götz Kaufmann (Heinrich), Gerhard Burkart (von Pösel), Elfi Eschke (Sylvia), Winfried Glatzeder (Pete), Arno Jürging (Eck), Karl Schulz (Reinhold), Manfred Lehmann (Charly).

Didi Hallervorden has become a household word in Germany — a comic personality on tv and the film screen with a gift for mugging and play-on-words gags in the tradition of German Kabarett. Hallervorden himself comes from the Berlin cabaret scene, but became known chiefly for his TV series, "Nonstop Nonsens'," beginning in 1975 and ending in 1980 when Didi moved over to making movies. His record of b.o. hits is impressive: "Ach Du Lieber Harry" (1980), "Alles im Eimer" (When It Rains, It Pours) (1981), "Der Schnüffler" (The Snooper) (1982), and now "Didi and His Double."

For the sake of comparison with Yank comics, Didi Hallervorden comes across like a Red Skelton at his mugging best. Even the gags are the same: mistaken identify ploys, ine face of an Indian rubberman that registers everything from childish disappointment to grim optimism in spite of everything, and a taste for good old-fashioned slapstick as in the heyday of the silent comedians.

"Didi and His Double" has Hallervorden playing both the head of a multi-cartel (Hans Immer) and a down-and-out bartender (Bruno Koob), look-alikes from the opposite of the tracks in West Berlin. The plot has the usual twists stemming from a switching of roles due to a suspected kidnapping caper (the switch would also allow the big boss to get away for a long weekend with a young girlfriend), and the laughs are mainly rooted in the hopeless cause of a bunch of fumbling gangsters as well as Koob doing his best to imitate Immer in his penthouse office. And one of the chase scenes with acrobatics and runaway vehicles through the streets of Berlin is very well handled, both on location and at the cutting table. Hats off to helmer Reinhard Schwabenitzky.

But it's Dieter Hallervorden himself who proves that he's more than just a comic adept at mimicry this time around. The plot allows him the opportunity to start with two completely opposite roles, and then gradually bring them in the course of the movie closer to one another — until Koob really does step into Immer's shoes, while the latter sinks into oblivion so deeply as to end up running a bar of his own.

What's lacking in "Didi and His Double" is the sharp edge. The plot is a mite too loose and easy-going, the gags a hit-or-miss affair, and the dialogue geared to stereotype humor instead of a sound narrative line. Too often thesps are wasted, and Didi Hallervorden is capable of much more than pic demanded. All the same, this is the best director yet to handle the comedian, and the b.o. returns hint that they will be together again on another venture. — *Holl.*

The Natural
(COLOR)

Redford slugs a triple, at least.

Hollywood, May 4.
A Tri-Star release. Produced by Mark Johnson. Exec producers, Roger Towne, Philip M. Breen. Directed by Barry Levinson. Stars Robert Redford. Screenplay, Towne, Phil Dusenberry, based on the novel by Bernard Malamud. Camera (Technicolor), Caleb Deschanel; editor, Stu Linder; music, Randy Newman; production design, Angelo Graham (L.A.), Mel Bourne (N.Y.); art direction, James J. Murikami (L.A.), Speed Hopkins (N.Y.); set decoration, Bruce Weintraub; costume design, Bernie Pollack; costume design for Close, Basinger & Hershey, Gloria Gresham; sound (Dolby), Jeff Wexler, Chris McLaughlin, James Stuebe; associate producer, Robert F. Colesberry; assistant director, Chris Soldo, Patrick Crowley. Reviewed at the VIP Screening Room, L.A., May 4, 1984. (MPAA Rating: PG). Running time: 134 MINS.
Roy Hobbs . . . . Robert Redford
Max Mercy . . . . Robert Duvall
Iris Gaines . . . . Glenn Close
Memo Paris . . . . Kim Basinger
Pop Fisher . . . . Wilford Brimley
Harriet Bird . . . . Barbara Hershey
The Judge . . . . Robert Prosky
Red Blow . . . . Richard Farnsworth
Gambler . . . . Darren McGavin
The Whammer . . . . Joe Don Baker
Sam Simpson . . . . John Finnegan
Ed Hobbs . . . . Alan Fudge
Young Roy . . . . Paul Sullivan Jr.
Young Iris . . . . Rachel Hall
Ted Hobbs . . . . Robert Rich 3d
Bump Bailey . . . . Michael Madsen

"The Natural" is an impeccably made, but quite strange, fable about success and failure in America. In his first screen role in four years, and his first credit of any kind since directing the Oscar-winning "Ordinary People," Robert Redford plays an aging rookie who takes the baseball world by storm in one season while dealing with demons from his past and present. With its deliberate style and remote characters, pic is not exactly fodder for the masses, but the commercial veneer, and Redford's name, should generate substantial b.o. action.

While remaining faithful to Bernard Malamud's 1952 novel in many regards, scenarists Roger Towne and Phil Dusenberry have drastically altered some major elements, most notably Malamud's despairing ending. Film thereby has become the story of the redemption of a born athlete whose life didn't unfold as anticipated.

Opening sequences present farmboy Roy Hobbs showing natural skill as a ballplayer and, upon the death of his father, carving his own magical bat, dubbed "Wonderboy," from the wood of a lightning-struck tree.

Some years later, Hobbs, now in the person of Redford, leaves farmgirl honey Glenn Close to head for the big time in Chicago, and raises the eyebrows of ace sportswriter and cartoonist Robert Duvall when he strikes out the majors' greatest hitter (Joe Don Baker, looking a lot like Babe Ruth) in an impromptu exhibition.

In Chitown, however, he is lured to the hotel room of mysterious temptress Barbara Hershey, who shockingly shoots him down.

Sixteen years later, in 1939, Redford arrives on the dugout steps of New York Knights manager Wilford Brimley, who has no desire to play a rookie of retirement age. But after the Knights' right fielder dies going after a home run ball, Brimley is forced to put Redford into the lineup, and due to his brilliant play, fans of the lowly Knights begin to catch pennnant fever.

Naturally, everyone wants to know where this sensation has been all his life, but Redford remains taciturn in the extreme, allowing neither the other characters nor the audience in on his secret.

When Redford starts bedding down with bad girl Kim Basinger, he goes into a horrendous slump, only cured when Close re-enters his life. Traditional melodrama here rears its head, as Redford is poisoned by Basinger, bribed by team owner Robert Prosky to blow the pennant playoff game with the Pirates and blackmailed by Duvall, all before stepping up to the plate in the bottom of the ninth with two men on and two out, and the Knights down 2-0.

Looking fit and trim and fulfilling the fantasies of any man who ever wanted to play in the majors, Redford is perfectly cast as the wary, guarded Hobbs. All the man wants is to be the best who ever played the game, and any attempts to get further under his skin are thwarted by the conception of the piece. Despite his heroic stature and all-American demeanor, he remains distant and secretive, and the sneaky curve ball thrown to him by fate represents the eternal monkey wrench in the American dream.

The female characters leave behind a bad taste, however, since they schematically and simplistically stand for the archaic angel-whore syndrome. Whenever he goes for harlots like Hershey or Basinger, Redford is in big trouble, from which he must be rescued by Close. Even as a convention from the era depicted, this doesn't go down too well.

Supporting roles have been wonderfully filled by topflight character actors Duvall, Brimley, Prosky and Richard Farnsworth. Excellently playing the substantial part of a big league gambler is Darren McGavin, who curiously goes unbilled and unmentioned in any press material.

Pic marks a big step up production-wise from "Diner" for director Barry Levinson, whose style looks to have been heavily influenced here by cinematographer Caleb Deschanel. Young lenser displays his customary brilliance, and the darkness of many of the scenes, which conveys the downside of Hobbs' dream, strongly evokes the work of his mentor, Gordon Willis.

Exteriors were shot in Buffalo, N.Y., where the War Memorial Stadium, built in the 1930s, was pressed into service for most of the baseball scenes. Period details, especially the old-time uniforms and mitts, are great, save for one anachronistic matter, that of the pennant playoff game being played at night. Night baseball was, in fact, introduced in Cincinnati in 1935, but big contests like this or the World Series were never played under lights until years later. A quibbling point, perhaps, but one that baseball purists will make note of.

All production hands have contributed to make this as lush and rich-looking a film as possible, and Randy Newman's score, which evokes Aaron Copland at times, is a major plus. —*Cart.*

Firestarter
(COLOR)

Special effects dominate okay Stephen King pic.

Hollywood, May 3.
A Universal release of a Dino De Laurentiis presentation. Produced by Frank Capra Jr. Directed by Mark L. Lester. Features entire cast. Screenplay, Stanley Mann, based on the book by Stephen King; camera (Technicolor), Guiseppe Ruzzolini; music, Tangerine Dream; editor, David Rawlins; sound, David Hildyard; associate producer, Martha Schumacher; art direction, Giorgio Postiglione; special effects, Mike Wood, Jeff Jarvis; assistant director, David Whorf. Reviewed at the Century City Plitt, May 3, 1984. (MPAA rating: R). Running time: 115 MINS.
Andrew McGee . . . . David Keith
Charlie McGee . . . . Drew Barrymore
John Rainbird . . . . George C. Scott
Captain Hollister . . . . Martin Sheen
Vicky McGee . . . . Heather Locklear
Irv Manders . . . . Art Carney
Norma Manders . . . . Louise Fletcher
Dr. Pynchot . . . . Moses Gunn
Dr. Wanless . . . . Freddie Jones

Fourth Stephen King novel to hit the screen within a year comes enflamed with largest gallery of name players of any King adaptation. But on the King scale ("The Shining" being best) "Firestarter" falls into the level of achievement repped by "Cujo" and "Christine." That's sufficient to signal moderate profit margin for this special fire effects bonanza, toplining Drew Barrymore, David Keith, Martin Sheen and a terrific salvage job by George C. Scott as a crazed, charming, deadly government operative.

Performances and characterizations are solid for the genre but pic's stars are special effects team Mike Wood and Jeff Jarvis, whose pyrotechnics — flying fireballs, fire trenches, human balls of fire — create the film's impact. Story of a nine-year-old girl who can en-flame objects and people by power of her will balances human concern of a pursued and loving father and daughter (Keith and Barrymore) against a clandestine government agency that wants to use the girl's power for nefarious ends. Agency is headed by Sheen, with Moses Gunn and Scott as a chilly support group.

Shot in North Carolina (where production offices in Wilmington area inspired permanent filmmaking facility for presenter Dino De Laurentiis), film marks the first major picture for director Mark L. Lester ("Class of '84," "Roller Boogie," "Truck Stop Women"). He gets a terrific performance from a bulky Scott, whose serpentine villainy lights up the film, and quite credible work from all other principals, who include, in tiny screen time, Art Carney and Louise Fletcher as a kindly farm couple, and early victim Heather Locklear (her film debut).

Script by Stanley Mann ("Eye Of The Needle") is quite faithful to the novel, but cinematically that loyalty is damaging. Picture's length, nearly two hours, can't sustain the material. Pacing is slack and pic sags in the middle when Keith and Barrymore are entrapped by intelligence agents in a plantation mansion. The result is a plodding tempo rather than the kind of romp the story demands.

Despite horrific fires, film's intention is suspense, not horror. Suspense factor is aided by fact that Keith as the father has powers of telepathetic suggestion, but pic's explosion arrives too late. All production values are pro. — *Loyn.*

---

10 Violent Women
(COLOR)

Erratic but enjoyable women's prison film.

A New American Films release through Aquarius Releasing of a Cinema Features Inc. production. Produced and directed by Ted V. Mikels. Features entire cast. Screenplay, James Gordon White, Mikels; camera (Movielab color), Yuval Shousterman; editor, Mikels; music, Nicholas Carras; sound, Vernon Lombard; production design, Mike McClusky. Reviewed at 42d St. Selwyn theater, N.Y., May 5, 1984. (MPAA Rating: R). Running time: 96 MINS.
Samantha .... Sherri Vernon
Maggie .... Dixie Lauren
Bri Terry .... Georgia Morgan
Madge .... Jane Farnsworth
Leo .... Ted V. Mikels
Vickie .... Anne Gaybis

"10 Violent Women" is a strange women's prison film which will be of interest to followers of that specialized genre. Made in 1978, pic was released regionally in 1982 and is reviewed on its belated first appearance in New York.

Convoluted storyline (punctuated by freeze-frames and announcement titles-over as gags) opens with eight women miners getting frustrated with their work and

turning to crime. They successfully pull off a jewelry store robbery, but are nabbed (roughly halfway through the film) by narcs when they try to sell them cocaine obtained from Leo the fence (Ted V. Mikels, the director, in a support role).

Action in stir is generally routine, except for a memorably overdone turn by Georgia Morgan as the extremely butch head guard, who likes to doff her mannish uniform at night, put on frilly nightgowns and force the prettier inmates to submit to everything from humiliation to whippings. After a much too easy escape from behind bars, heroines Samantha (Sherri Vernon) and Maggie (Dixie Lauren) mark time unconvincingly until a shah whose sacred scarab ring they stole (in the jewel robbery) invites them onto his yacht, drops criminal charges and whisks them off in an absurd happy ending.

"Women" is the sort of odd B-movie that proliferated over a decade ago for regional and drive-in circuit use (when budgets under $50,000 per film were possible), but since then tv action shows have obviated the production of such pictures. Filmmaker Mikels, for example, made an interesting actioner "The Doll Squad" in 1972 with Francine York starring as the leader (named Sabrina) of a trio of tough female undercover agents, which was the prototype of "Charlie's Angels."

Though too kinky in spots for general audiences (Mikels as Leo is killed gruesomely by a "heroine" stabbing him repeatedly with her spiked heel), "Women" is technically adequate low-budget action fare. Its title defies precise calculation, since only three or four heroines are in the spotlight at any one time. —*Lor.*

Dhrupad
(INDIAN-COLOR)

San Francisco, April 21.
No distributor. Directed by Mani Kaul. Camera (color), Virendra Saini; editor, Ashok Tyagi; musical performers, Ustaad Zia Mohiuddin Dagar, Ustaad Zia Fariduddin Khan Dagar. (No additional credits available.) Reviewed at San Francisco International Film Festival (Castro), April 21, '84. (No MPAA Rating.) Running time: 72 MINS.

This is a numbingly esoteric history of a Hindi musical genre, Dhrupad, dating at least as far back as 1670 and possibly as old as 300 B.C., per subtitled comments of artists. There are long, static sequences of solos, duets and trios, mostly instrumental, on the rudra, veena, sarod, tabla and sitar. Music is quite austere, often ethereal. Some of the lensing attempts to reflect the architectural history of the land.

Pic played the Friscofest on same program with Satyajit Ray's "Deliverance" and drew a large,

attentive crowd. But "Dhrupad" has little international commercial value save for music academicians.

Technicals are adequate, but a greater variety of shots and cuts would have been welcome.
— *Herb.*

Breakin'
(COLOR)

Spirited dance quickie should clean up.

Hollywood, May 3.
An MGM/UA Entertainment and Cannon Group release of a Golan-Globus production. Produced by Allen DeBevoise, David Zito. Executive producers, Menahem Golan, Yoram Globus. Directed by Joel Silberg. Features entire cast. Screenplay, Charles Parker, DeBevoise, Gerald Scaife; story by Parker, DeBevoise; camera (Metrocolor), Hannania Baer; supervising editor, Mark Helfrich; editors, Larry Bock, Gib Jaffe, Vincent Sklena; production design, Ivo G. Cristante; set decoration, Julie Kaye Towery; musical numbers staged, choreographed by Jaime Rogers; musical score, Gary Remal, Michael Boyd; music supervisor, Russ Regan; costume design, Dana Lyman; sound (Dolby), Steve Nelson; assistant director, Marita A. Karrell. Reviewed at the MGM Studios, Culver City, May 2, 1984. (MPAA Rating: PG) Running time: 87 MINS.
Kelly ...,.................... Lucinda Dickey
Ozone ...... Adolfo (Shabba-Doo) Quinones
Turbo .... Michael (Bongaloo Shrimp) Chambers
Franco .... Ben Lokey
James .... Christopher McDonald
Adam .... Phineas Newborn 3d
Electro Rock 1 .... Bruno (Pop N' Taco) Falcon
Electro Rock 2 .... Timothy (Poppin' Pete) Solomon
Electro Rock 3 .... Ana (Lollipop) Sanchez
Rap Talker .... Ice T

The spirit of the late Sam Katzman lives in Golan-Globus' "Breakin'," the first feature film entirely devoted to the breakdancing craze. In the late 1950s, Katzman specialized in identifying the latest teenage fad and getting it up on the screen practically overnight. In the same vein, "Breakin' " began shooting only in February, and hit the nation's theaters May 4, which surely represents a 1980s record. Light-spirited and innocuous, pic will delight anyone who enjoys breakdancing and will undoubtedly rack up a nice profit based on the minimal investment.

On a plot level, concoction is too derivative of "Flashdance" for its own good, as the premise once again is untrained, but highly skilled and imaginative, street dancers versus the stuffy, inflexible dance establishment.

Filmmakers have also played it safe in focusing the action on a nice, middle class white girl, whereas breakdancing is almost exclusively the domain of blacks and Latinos. Script also shys away from the possibility of interracial romance so latent in the story.

Aside from these fainthearted choices, however, film is quite satisfactory and breezily enter-

taining on its own terms. Serious dance student Lucinda Dickey (who, it should be pointed out, obviously does all her own dancing) is fed up with her life as a waitress, but becomes instantly turned on to street dancing when introduced to it by fellow student Phineas Newborn 3d, who nicely puts over his character's gayness without it being spoken.

Dickey becomes friendly with ace breakdancers Adolfo (Shabba-Doo) Quinones and the aptly named Michael (Boogaloo Shrimp) Chambers, two of L.A.'s most celebrated performers on the scene. This pair and numerous other youths put on some amazing displays on the street and in local clubs and ultimately, joined by convert Dickey, conquer academic prejudices at a professional dance audition, which leads to Broadway.

Climactic scene of a stage production number bears an unfortunate parallel to the finale of "Staying Alive," but is happily cut short. Essentially, filmmakers held in mind that the only *raison d'etre* for the pic was the dancing, and there's plenty of it. Quinones and Chambers shine in their specialty, and are perfectly respectable in the dialog sequences.

Filmed in energetic style on L.A. locations, pic is marred in two regards. Breakdancing is so spectacular that it is best viewed in uninterrupted takes, and director Joel Silberg (who took over from original helmer David Wheeler) has felt the need to cut too frequently and include too many closeups which impair overall perspective. Also, Ben Lokey, as Dickey's dance teacher, has been made unrealistically villainous, which introduces an unneeded taste of melodrama.

Given its quickie status, production looks and sounds fine. End credits announce a sequel, "Electric Boogaloo." — *Cart.*

Purple Hearts
(COLOR)

Okay prospects for small-budget actioner.

Hollywood, May 2.
A Ladd Co. release through Warner Bros., produced and directed by Sidney J. Furie. Screenplay, Rick Natkin and Furie; camera (Technicolor), Jan Kiesser; editor, George Grenville; sound, Ron Judkins; associate producer, Rick Natkin; assistant director, Juncq Amazan; art direction, Francisco Balangue; music, Robert Folk. Reviewed at The Burbank Studios, May 1, 1984. (MPAA rating: R.) Running time: 115 MINS.
Don Jardian .... Ken Wahl
Deborah Solomon .... Cheryl Ladd
Wizard .... Stephen Lee
Hanes .... David Harris
Zuma .... Cyril O'Reilly
Market .... Lane Smith
Gunny .... Lee Ermey
Hallaway .... Annie McEnroe
Brenner .... Paul McCrane
Larimore .... Drew Snyder
Bwana .... James Whitmore, Jr.

"Purple Hearts" is a systematically simple love story set against the Vietnam War, with the action largely overwhelming the romantic time-outs. Pic has already been playing select engagements without creating great excitement, but that's okay for what's obviously a restrained expenditure.

Producer-director Sidney J. Furie says the film came in for $2,800,000, a wonder these days that puts the results in favorable perspective, meaning it's not one to raise the familiar cry, "How could they spend so much money on *that?*"

Ken Wahl is a handsome young and dedicated doctor in Vietnam where he meets a beautiful young and dedicated nurse, Cheryl Ladd. They fall in love, but as in countless war romances before it, their passion is complicated by various forms of impending doom.

Between kisses, they assure each other that they hope one day to return Stateside and do medical good together forever. But then he's killed — but no he isn't — and then she's killed — but (fill in the blank) — and it looks like they may never live happily ever after.

Warwise, Furie gets a lot more going giving the action sequences and the hospital carnage considerable grit. By any measure, Vietnam was not a fun war.

Wahl is solid in the lead and Ladd hangs in there in a less demanding part. Supporting roles are generally good, with particular notice going to David Harris as a ghetto-bred corpsman forced by medical scarcity to function as a skilled surgeon under fire.

He's the most interesting character to pass through the story, which unfortunately has no larger place for him.—*Har.*

Chesty Anderson — U.S. Navy
(COLOR)

An impressive cast in a silly comedy.

A Coast Films release of a Cinefilm Group Industries (in association with Shelby Associates) production. Executive producer, Philip Hacker. Produced by Paul Pompian. Directed by Ed Forsyth. Features entire cast. Screenplay, H.F. Green, Pompian; camera (color), Henning Schellerup; editor, credit unknown; assistant director, Arello Blanton; production manager, John Burrows. Reviewed at 42d St. Selwyn theater, N.Y., May 5, 1984. (MPAA Rating: R.) Running time: **89 MINS.**

Chesty Anderson	Shari Eubank
Tina Marlowe	Dorrie Thomson
Coco Daniels	Rosanne Katon
Pucker	Marcie Barkin
Peter	Fred Willard
The baron	Frank Campanella
Vincent	Timothy Agoglia Carey
Senator Dexter	George Cooper
Don Cheech	John Davis Chandler

Also with: Scatman Crothers, Mel Carter, Constance Marie, Dyanne Thorne, Betty McGuire, Brenda Fogerty, Joyce Gibson, Uschi Digard, Pat Parker, Betty Thomas.

"Chesty Anderson — U.S. Navy" is a relatively obscure exploitation film shot in 1975, released the following year by the since-defunct Atlas Films and just arrived in New York as a second feature. Chief interest here is the cast, combining many voluptuous pinups of a decade ago with a number of familiar character players later to become famous troupers.

Shari Eubank, who had just starred in Russ Meyer's "Super Vixens," portrays the titular character, a Wave in the U.S. Navy whose younger sister is kidnapped and killed by local Mafiosi — the Baron (Frank Campanella) and Vincent (Timothy Agoglia Carey) for having photos that would incriminate a Mafia-controlled corrupt senator (George Cooper).

Anderson sets out with three of her fellow servicewomen to find the missing sister, but their adventures on land (for a service comedy, film contains absolutely no seafaring action) play second fiddle to silly gags. Ultimately, a government undercover agent (Fred Willard) unravels the case and collars the baddies.

Besides Willard, whose straight-ahead thesping resembles his more familiar persona as a (former) regular on the "Real People" tv series, there are glimpses of the ebullient Scatman Crothers as a pool hustler and even a cameo by Betty Thomas of "Hill St. Blues." For pulchritude, Eubank is upstaged by the superstructures of costars Rosanne Katon and Dorrie Thomson, plus numerous other starlets, including Dyanne (of the "Ilsa" sex and gore films) Thorne as a nurse in a lengthy burlesk-style "Doctor will see you now" segment, Joyce Gibson and Uschi Digard, also of "Super Vixens." Surprisingly, there is very little nudity here.

Acting honors go to Carey, who is way over the top "winging it" with stream-of-consciousness Italian expressions and an hilarious limping-jiggling gait. The young heavy of 1960s pics, John Davis Chandler, pops up as a gangster henchman who gets fed to a carnivorous plant, in explicit homage to "The Little Shop Of Horrors." For obvious reasons, good or bad depending upon one's point-of-view, no one makes films in this vein anymore. —*Lor.*

Hardbodies
(COLOR)

Strictly for middle-aged lechers.

Hollywood, May 4.

A Columbia Pictures release of a Chroma III Production. Produced by Jeff Begun and Ken Dalton. Directed by Mark Griffiths. Features entire cast. Screenplay by Steve Greene, Eric Alter and Griffiths from a story by Greene and Alter. Camera (Deluxe color), Tom Richmond; editor, Andy Blumenthal; production designer, Gregg Fonseca; set decorator, Anne Huntley; sound, David Brownlow; associate producer, Judy Mooradian; assistant director, Eric M. Brieman. Reviewed at The Burbank Studios, May 4, 1984. (MPAA Rating: R.) Running Time: **88 MINS.**

Scotty	Grant Kramer
Kristie	Teal Roberts
Hunter	Gary Wood
Rounder	Michael Rapport
Ashby	Sorrells Pickard
Lana	Roberta Collins
Kimberly	Cindy Silver
Rag	Courtney Gains

"Hardbodies" is the kind of vision of Southern California Woody Allen might have in a nightmare, so exaggerated is the pursuit of fun in the sun. In fact it's become a way of life with boys chasing and girls chasing a BBD — bigger, better deal. With more than its share of bouncing breasts, low-budget Columbia indie pickup should generate initial boxoffice interest, but probably more among an older leering crowd rather than a teenage audience.

Though pic satirizes the sexual appetites of the white middle-aged middleclass American male, it is really made for them — teens will probably find it too hokey.

Plot chronicles the arrival at the beach of three 40-ish swinging singles. Their techniques are hopelessly out of date, so they employ the help of waterfront Lothario, Scotty (Grant Kramer), to show them the ropes.

After a change of costume and a few tips from the pro, the luck of the three gents does actually change, but there's a fly in the suntan ointment. Hunter (Gary Wood) starts messing with Scotty's girlfriend (Teal Roberts) and must be taught a lesson.

But all seriousness aside, point of the pic is to party. Though it takes place at the beach, indoor sport is what the overgrown boys have in mind. The trio, aptly described as "dumpy, frumpy and lumpy," seem to be making up for a lifetime of repressed desires. Anyone in a bathing suit is fair game.

Women here have little purpose for existence other than as the fuel for male fantasies and, when one protests she is more than an "airhead, dingaling and bimbo," there is little evidence to support her claim.

Director Mark Griffiths has a good eye for the ingredients of the Southern California good life featuring a bed with a car dashboard control-panel which turns the room into a disco. Griffiths might have managed a decent satire of '80s narcissism if his heroes were not victims of the same sensibilities. Roberts' decision to go back to school and move in with Scotty at the end of the picture is comically wholesome after what's preceded it.

As for the cast, Kramer and Roberts are predictably pretty and bland, but Courtney Gaines as Scotty's beach bum sidekick brings some eccentric humor to a character reminiscent of the Sean Penn role in "Fast Times At Ridgemont High." (Every teen comedy seems to have one.)

Chubby but lovable Michael Rapport supplies ample opportunity for sight gags as one of the three musketeers and Gary Wood is suitably slippery and unlikeable as the most lecherous. Sorrells Pickard is also likeable as the fertilizer magnate who is finally too decent to stay with his buddies. The girls, needless to say, look great.

Production values are adequate despite oversights such as sunset passing for sunrise. "Hardbodies" tries hard to have a good time, but somewhere along the line the good clean dirty fun becomes tiresome and offensive.—*Jagr.*

Alphabet City
(COLOR)

All style, no substance in contempo Gotham *film noir*.

An Atlantic Releasing release of an Andrew Braunsberg production. Produced by Braunsberg. Executive producers, Thomas Coleman, Michael Rosenblatt. Directed by Amos Poe. Features entire cast. Screenplay, Gregory K. Heller, Poe, from story by Heller; additional dialog, Robert Seidman; camera (color), Oliver Wood; editor, Grahame Weinbren; music, Nile Rodgers; sound, Richard Brause; production design, Nord Haggerly; art direction, Steven Lineweaver, Terence McCorry; assistant director, Aaron Barsky; production manager, Ben Gruberg; special makeup effects, Ed French; associate producer, Robert Friedman; coach-special consultant to director, Loyd Williamson; stunt coordinator, Harry Madsen. Reviewed at UA Rivoli 1 theater, N.Y., May 4, 1984. (MPAA Rating: R). Running time: **85 MINS.**

Johnny	Vincent Spano
Angela	Kate Vernon
Lippy	Michael Winslow
Mama	Zohra Lampert
Sophia	Jamie Gertz
Gino	Raymond Serra
Juani	Daniel Jordano
Tony	Kenny Marino

"Alphabet City" is an unsuccessful attempt to portray the subculture of Manhattan's underbelly (title refers to the area of lower Eastside Manhattan between avenues A through D) in a commercial film. Director Amos Poe, graduating from a series of 16m features to the mainstream, demonstrates style and nascent talent but lacks the narrative skill to make the picture work. Released film shows evidence of last-minute tinkering, indicated by its abbreviated running time and the absence onscreen of actress Laura Carrington, sixth-billed in the press materials.

Non-story, long on atmosphere but terminally thin on plot, presents a night in the life of Johnny (Vincent Spano), an Italian teenager who is a kingpin in the neighborhood drug and extortion rackets. Ordered by his gangster boss Gino (Raymond Serra) to torch the building where his mother (Zohra Lampert) and younger sister (Jamie Gertz) live, Johnny decides to chuck his lucrative lifestyle and flee for parts unknown with artist wife Angela (Kate Vernon) and their infant child.

Along the episodic way, Johnny makes his nightly rounds in his white Porsche, visiting a drug den out of Dante's Inferno, collecting payments from local bar owners, frightening off heirs apparent such as "hey man"-stereotype Juani (Daniel Jordano) and lecturing his sister and right-hand man Lippy (Michael Winslow) on cleaning up their acts (as prostitute and drug addict, respectively).

Poe, one of the few contemporary directors, along with John Flynn, Wim Wenders and Paul Schrader, who consistently recalls the Hollywood 1940s tradition of *film noir,* adopts an intermittently effective visual style of distortion, over-using pastel lighting and diffused light sources. At several points, cinematographer Oliver Wood's artily smeared shots look like Douglas Trumbull's lens flares (simulating UFOs) in "Close Encounters Of The Third Kind." Net effect is to distract the viewer from the weak storyline. Poe and his producer Andrew Braunsberg would have done better to emphasize more action footage, since the several fight and chase scenes on view are well staged and invigorating.

Cast consistently transcends the material, with rising young star Vincent Spano winning audience sympathy in the sketchy central role and Michael Winslow, reprising his sure-fire machine-gun vocal sound effects routine from "Police Academy," valuable as the comic relief sidekick. Jamie Gertz scores as the precociously sexy sister, but debuting actress Kate Vernon is stuck with a wimpy role as Spano's wife.

Curiously, producer Braunsberg's former collaborator Paul Morrissey (on the 1973 productions "Blood For Dracula" and 3-D "Flesh For Frankenstein"), has just completed directing his own film "Alphabet City" (since retitled variously "New York, Avenue D" and "Down Town"), which hopefully will boast a stronger storyline. — *Lor.*

Flor Do Desejo
(Flower Of Desire)
(BRAZILIAN-COLOR)

Gramado, April 10.

An Embrafilme release of a Star Films production. Features entire cast. Directed by Guilherme de Almeida Prado. Screenplay, Almeida Prado. Camera (Eastmancolor), Antonio Meliande; editing, Jair Garcia Duarte; art direction, Luiz Carlos Rossi; sound editing, Danilo Tadeu; mixing, Eduardo dos Santos; sound track, Almeida Prado; executive producer, A.S. Cecilio Neto; costumes, Leni Caetano. Reviewed at Embaixador Theatre, Gramado Film Festival, April 10, 1984. Running time: **103 MINS.**
Cast: Imara Reis, Caique Ferreira, Tamara Taxman, Raymundo de Souza, Matilde Mastrangi, Mário Benvenuti, Cida Moreyra, Luiz Carlos Arutin and the group, Premeditando o Breque.

This is a mostly senseless, though funny comedy involving almost anything that could come to the minds of the filmmakers over the writing or the shooting of the film. Basically an erotic comedy involving a seaport worker and a prostitute, it actually turns out to be a parody of other erotic comedies, while being punctuated by unexpected references to anything from old musicals to recent Brazilian economic and political problems.

Director Guilherme de Almeida Prado seems to be clearly inspired by the films of Carlos Reichembach, also from São Paulo, whose unconventional erotic comedies have generated polarized debates among Brazilian critics. Dealing with a screenplay (by himself), often surprisingly amateuristic, Almeida Prado manages to keep an attractive rhythm by moving his camera incessantly and cutting each shot in the precise moment (credit must be given the work of editor Jair Garcia Duarte).

Cast is very good, especially Imara Reis, Caique Ferreira and Tamara Taxman, while cinematography by Antonio Meliande is some of the most professional seen at the Gramado Festival, successfully alternating different levels of reality and dramatizing sequences at a diverse number of locations, from seaports and bordellos to bright landscape and mansions.

Although not intended to be more than a successful commercial movie, "Flor do Desejo" is often a positive surprise thanks to its irreverence and general quality of realization. It can be seen as a thesis that a sex comedy by no means, has to be foolish. — *Hoin.*

Cannes Fest

Abel Gance Et Son Napoleon
(Abel Gance and His Napoleon)
(FRENCH-DOCU-COLOR/B&W)

Paris, May 1.

A Cythere Films production and release. Produced, written, directed and edited by Nelly Kaplan, Camera (color), Jean Monsigny; music, Betty Willemetz and Hubert Rostaing. Reviewed at the C.N.C., Paris, April 26, 1984. "Un Certain Regard" selection at Cannes Festival. Running time: **60 MINS.**

The core of Nelly Kaplan's hour-long documentary on the making of Abel Gance's silent masterpiece is three eye-popping reels of film shot in 1925-26 during the production of "Napoleon" at the Billancourt studios and on location in various regions of France and Corsica. Later assembled into a feature-length docu of about six reels, "Autour de Napoleon," it was part of the inaugural program of the famous Paris art cinema Studio 28 in 1928, which also included the projection of the triptychs from the film.

Kaplan, Gance's assistant on his last films bought from him a good part of his personal archive, including the extant reels of "Autour de Napoleon." (Fragments of the film have been conserved by the Cinemathèque Française, and some of it was used by Kevin Brownlow in his 1967 docu portrait of Gance, "The Charm Of Dynamite.") Rather than attempt to reconstruct the original docu, she has made her own presentation, filling it out with other unique documents, including Gance's hand-written production diary and innumerable rare photographs and documents.

Inevitably that 60-year-old footage of an unsurpassed cinematic achievement being created by an inspired director, top-ranking technicians and a dedicated cast make this a priceless documentary, which will certainly find its way overseas in tv and non-theatrical situations.

Among the production sequences covered are the shooting of the famous snowball fight at the military school of Brienne, in which the chief cameraman scurries among the battling schoolchildren with portable camera strapped to his chest; the vengeance of young Bonaparte (Wladimir Roudenko) in the Brienne dormitory, prelude to the pillow fight that certainly inspired Jean Vigo when he made "Zero For Conduct," the "Marseillaise" sequence at the Club des Cordeliers; and the location work in Corsica, where Gance's collaborators innovated with some audacious traveling shots. Anybody who has marveled at "Napoleon" in its recent full orchestral renaissance will find complementary wonders in these glimpses of collective genius.

Michel Drucker, a popular, local broadcasting personality, narrates the presentation from the actual sound stages of the Billancourt studios (those used by Gance have since burned down and been reconstructed). Though Kaplan might have enlisted a more appropriate commentator, the selection of Drucker was apparently a concession for local network sales.
— *Len.*

Khandar
(The Ruins)
(INDIAN-COLOR)

Paris, May 1.

A Jagadish and Pushpa Chowkhani production for SRI BLC (P) Ltd. Written and directed by Mrinal Sen, from the novel by Premendra Mitra; camera (color), K.K. Mahajan; music, Bhaskar Chandavarkar. Reviewed at the C.N.C., Paris, April 27, 1984. "Un Certain Regard" selection at Cannes Festival. Running time: **102 MINS.**
With: Shabana Azmi, Naseerruddin Shan, Gita Sen, Pankaj Kapoor, Annu Kappor, Sreela Majumdar, Rajen Tarafder.

Mrinal Sen has been a frequent contributor to Cannes Festivals. Last year he was awarded the festival's jury prize for his "The Case Is Closed."

In "Ruins" three young men take a few days off from the noisy bustle of city life to relax in the crumbled remains of a mansion on a once feudal estate. There live an ailing old woman and her daughter, partial heirs to the decaying property. The daughter awaits the return of a lover who has abandoned her; and the mother, blind and senile, imagines one of the holidaying visitors is her child's lost suitor.

The situation unfolds at a leisurely pace with echoes of the underlying conflicts: betrayal and fidelity, escape and involvement, ruthlessness and compassion, but none is developed to expected theatrical effect. A vague, sleepy implication of loss and defeat hovers over everything against the background of fallen grandeur and broken dreams. One of the vacationing trio is a professional photographer who snaps a photo of the deserted daughter. When he gets back to the city he tacks it up on the wall of his room and that is the end.

Sen's treatment is filled with subtle nuances and the photography lends strange fascination to the setting of a vanished civilization, but the expected facing of the issues of the story is bypassed. The result is an atmospheric vignette, done with skill, taste and sympathy and competently interpreted, but without sufficient theatrical substance to hold the screen for 102 minutes. A slow-moving mood piece, it may find audiences in the art-houses. —*Curt.*

Le Jour "S"
("S" Day)
(CANADIAN-COLOR)

An Yves Rivard production for Cinsk Productions. Directed by Jean-Pierre Lefebvre. Screenplay, Lefebvre, Barbara Easto, Pierre Curzi, Marie Tifo. Camera (color), Guy Dufaux; editor, Barbara Easto; music, Jean-Pierre Lefebvre and Barbara Easto; sound, Claude Hazanavicious. Reviewed at the C.N.C., April 25, 1984, Paris. An "Un Certain Regard" Cannes Festival selection. Running time: **88 MINS.**
With: Pierre Curzi, Marie Tifo, Simon Esterez, Marcel Sabourin.

"S" stands for sentimental in the title of this one in which a fortyish man dedicates a day to remembering his sexual passions, the sensations he no longer experiences and the social groups he no longer frequents.

Jean-Baptiste Beauregard wakes up, his head filled with images of his past loves. He lets himself float on day dreams, passing again through his childhood fantasies, the vicissitudes of his adolescence, his marriage and divorce. He is jerked back into the present when his girl friend of the moment shows up as "S" day is done.

A popular Parisian revue by Rip before the war touched on a device used here. All Jean-Baptiste's girls are the same girl in differing costumes and hairdos, this to suggest everyone is basically faithful to a certain type — and also a clever salary-saving idea.

The tone of the film — for all its light once-over with psychoanalytical hints — is a mild put-down of the average-man protagonist whose love-life is, despite his brooding over it, commonplace to the point of banality. At least the approach makes no effort to be serious. "S" is the first letter in "standardized" and of "silly," too.

Pierre Curzi, amiable comic rather than romantic figure, plays for laughs, untroubled by any vain regrets the character may harbor, and Marie Tifo with quick-changes of costumes and wigs is all the women of the sentimental journey, an overlong one, brightened too seldom by a few bright moments.
—*Curt.*

Indiana Jones And The Temple Of Doom
(COLOR)

Noisy, overkill prequel headed for smash b.o.

Hollywood, May 7.

A Paramount Pictures release of a Lucasfilm Ltd. production. Executive producers, George Lucas, Frank Marshall. Produced by Robert Watts. Directed by Steven Spielberg. Stars Harrison Ford. Screenplay, Willard Huyck, Gloria Katz, from a story by Lucas. Camera (Rank color; prints by Deluxe), Douglas Slocombe; editor, Michael Kahn; music, John Williams; sound design (Dolby), Ben Burtt; production design, Elliot Scott; chief art director, Alan Cassie, set decoration, Peter Howitt; special visual effects supervisor, Dennis Muren at Industrial Light & Magic; costume design, Anthony Powell; mechanical effects supervisor, George Gibbs; second unit director, Michael Moore; choreography, Danny Daniels; associate producer Kathleen Kennedy. Reviewed at MGM Studios, Culver City, Calif., May 7, 1984. (MPAA Rating: PG). Running time: 118 MINS.

Indiana Jones . . . . Harrison Ford
Willie Scott . . . . Kate Capshaw
Short Round . . . . Ke Huy Quan
Mola Ram . . . . Amrish Puri
Chattar Lal . . . . Roshan Seth
Capt. Blumburtt . . . . Philip Stone

Also with: Roy Chiao, David Yip, Ric Young, Chua Kah Joo, Rex Ngui, Philip Tann, Dan Aykroyd, Pat Roach.

Special Visual Effects Unit Credits

Industrial Light & Magic; visual effects supervisor, Dennis Muren; chief cameraman, Mike McAlister; optical photography supervisor, Bruce Nicholson, ILM general manager, Tom Smith; production supervisor, Warren Franklin, matte painting supervisor, Michael Pangrazio; modelshop supervisor, Lorne Peterson; stop-motion animation, Tom St. Amand; supervising stage technician, Patrick Fitzsimmons; animation supervisor, Charles Mullen; supervising editor, Howard Stein; production coordinator, Arthur Repola; creative consultant, Phil Tippett. Additional optical effects, Modern Film Effects.

Additional Technical Credits

U.K. crew: assistant director, David Tomblin; production supervisor, John Davis, production manager, Patricia Carr. U.S. crew: production manager, Robert Latham Brown; assistant director, Louis Race. First unit: stunt arrangers, Vic Armstrong (studio), Glenn Randall (location); additional photography, Paul Beeson; sound mixer, Simon Kaye, chief modeller, Derek Howarth; chief special effects technician, Richard Conway; floor effects supervisor, David Watkins; research, Deborah Fine; post-production services, Sprocket Systems.

London second unit: second unit director, Frank Marshall; assistant directors, David Bracknell, Michael Hook, cameraman, Wally Byatt; floor effects supervisor, David Harris.

California unit: second unit director, Glenn Randall; director of photography, Allen Daviau; art direction, Joe Johnston; stunt coordinator, Dean Raphael Ferrandini; special effects supervisor, Kevin Pike; sound mixer, David McMillan; production coordinator, Lata Ryan.

Asian unit: assistant director, Carlos Gil. Macau: production supervisor, Vincent Winter; production manager, Pay Ling Wang; assistant director, Patty Chan. Sri Lanka: production supervisor, Chandran Rutnam; production manager, Willie de Silva; assistant director, Ranjit H. Peiris; steadicam photography, Garrett Brown; art direction, Errol Kelly; sound mixer, Colin Charles.

Aerial unit: second unit director, Kevin Donnelly; director of photography, Jack Cooperman.

Just as "Return Of The Jedi" seemed disappointing after the first two "Star Wars" entries, so does "Indiana Jones And The Temple Of Doom" come as a letdown after "Raiders Of The Lost Ark." This is ironic, because director Steven Spielberg has packed even more thrills and chills into this followup than he did into the earlier pic, but to exhausting and numbing effect.

End result is like the proverbial Chinese meal, where heaps of food can still leave one hungry shortly thereafter. Will any of this make any difference at the boxoffice? Not a chance, as a sequel to "Raiders," which racked up $112,000,000 in domestic film rentals, has more built-in want-see than any imaginable film aside from "E.T. II."

Spielberg, scenarists Willard Huyck and Gloria Katz, and George Lucas, who penned the story as well as exec producing with Frank Marshall, have not tampered with the formula which made "Raiders" so popular. To the contrary, they have noticeably stepped up the pace, amount of incidents, noise level, budget, close calls, violence and everything else, to the point where more is decidedly less.

Prequel finds dapper Harrison Ford as Indiana Jones in a Shanghai nightclub in 1935, and title sequence, which features Kate Capshaw chirping Cole Porter's "Anything Goes," looks like something out of Spielberg's "1941."

Ford escapes from an enormous melee with the chanteuse in tow and, joined by Oriental moppet Ke Huy Quan, they head by plane to the mountains of Asia, where they are forced to jump out in an inflatable raft, skid down huge slopes, vault over a cliff and navigate some rapids before coming to rest in an impoverished Indian village.

Community's leader implores the ace archaeologist to retrieve a sacred, magical stone which has been stolen by malevolent neighbors, so the trio makes its way by elephant to the domain of a prepubescent Maharajah, who lords it over an empire reeking of evil.

Remainder of the yarn is set in this labyrinth of horrors, where untold dangers await the heroes. Much of the action unfolds in a stupendous cavern, where dozens of natives chant wildly as a sacrificial victim has his heart removed before being lowered into a pit of fire.

Ford is temporarily converted to the nefarious cause, Ke Huy Quan is sent to join child slaves in an underground quarry, and Capshaw is lowered time and again into the pit until the day is saved.

What with John Williams' incessant score and the library full of sound effects, there isn't a quiet moment in the entire picture, and the filmmakers have piled one giant setpiece on top of another to the point where one never knows where it will all end.

Film's one genuinely amazing action sequence, not unlike the airborne sleigh chase in "Jedi" (the best scene in that film), has the three leads in a chase on board an underground railway car on tracks resembling those of a roller-coaster.

Sequence represents a stunning display of design, lensing and editing, and will have viewers gaping. A "Raidersland" amusement park could be opened profitably on the basis of this ride alone.

Overall, however, pic comes on like a sledgehammer, and there's even a taste of vulgarity and senseless excess not apparent in "Raiders."

Kids 10-12 upwards will eat it all up, of course, but many of the images, particularly those involving a gruesome feast of live snakes, fried beetles, eyeball soup and monkey brains, and those in the sacrificial ceremony, might prove extraordinarily frightening to younger children who, indeed, are being catered to in this film by the presence of the adorable 12-year-old Ke Huy Quan.

Compared to the open-air breeziness of "Raiders," "Indiana Jones," after the first reel or so, possesses a heavily studio-bound look, with garish reds often illuminating the dark backgrounds.

As could be expected, however, huge production crew at Thorn EMI-Elstree Studios, as well as those on locations in Sri Lanka, Macao and California, and in visual effects phase at Industrial Light & Magic, have done a tremendous job in rendering this land of high adventure and fantasy.

Ford seems effortlessly to have picked up where he left off when Indiana Jones was last heard from, (though tale is set in an earlier period), although Capshaw, who looks fetching in native attire, has unfortunately been asked to react hysterically to everything that happens to her, resulting in a manic, frenzied performance which never locates a center of gravity. Villains are all larger-than-life nasties.

Critical opinion is undoubtedly irrelevant for such a surefire commercial attraction as "Indiana Jones," except that Spielberg is such a talented director it's a shame to see him lose all sense of subtlety and nuance.

In one quick step, the "Raiders" films have gone the way the James Bond opuses went at certain points, away from nifty stories in favor of one big effect after another. But that won't prevent Spielberg and Lucas from notching another mark high on the list of all-time b.o. winners. —*Cart.*

Making The Grade
(COLOR)

For teens, but adults, too, if they can corral 'em.

Hollywood, May 10.
An MGM/UA and Cannon Group release of a Golan-Globus Production. Produced by Gene Quintano. Executive producers Menahem Golan, Yoram Globus. Directed by Dorian Walker. Screenplay by Quintano from a story by Quintano and Charles Gale. Camera (TVC color), Jacques Haitkin; editor, Dan Wetherbee; music, Basil Poledouris; art director, Joseph T. Garrity; set decorator, Leslie Morales; sound, Russel Williams 2d; costumes, Emily Draper; assistant director, Matia Karrel. Reviewed at MGM/UA Main Theater, May 9, 1984. (MPAA rating: R.) Running time: **105 MINS.**

Eddie Keaton ....Judd Nelson
Tracey Hoover...................Jonna Lee
Mr. Harriman ....Gordon Jump
Coach Wordman ....Walter Olkewicz
Nicky ....Ronald Lacey
Palmer Woodrow ....Dana Olsen
Rand ....Carey Scott
Bif.........................Scott McGinnis
Dice ....Andrew Clay

Cannon Films' "Making The Grade" aims a bit higher than the flood of teen comedies released in the last year, but still doesn't manage to hit its mark. Despite winning performances by a cast mostly of newcomers, and some genuinely funny moments, film can't avoid sinking to the food and party gags so familiar by now. "Making The Grade" is still a better-than-average romp and even an audience older than the teen target could respond once in the theater. Getting them there should present a marketing challenge for MGM/UA.

Pic is a role reversal comedy setup rather obviously in the early going, cross-cutting between a spoiled rich kid (Dana Olsen) and a streetwise New Jersey kid (Judd Nelson). Palmer Woodrow 3d (Olsen) must complete his senior year at prep school in order to secure his trust fund and be able to coast for the rest of his life. Unfortunately, school bores him and, besides, he has other travel plans.

Enter Eddie Keaton (Nelson). Chased by his bookie (Andrew Clay) and henchmen, Eddie hops the fence of a country club and literally runs into Palmer, who proposes the switcheroo backed by a $10,000 bonus at graduation.

Most of the humor generated by "Making The Grade" comes from the clash of cultures. Eddie arrives at the ivy league Hoover Academy in a Yellow Cab, dressed in a bright red polyester suit. Under the tutelage of Palmer's only friend (Carey Scott), Eddie must learn the ways of the preppie world. Predictably, he becomes too good at his new identity, totally embracing the privileges and style he's missed.

But Eddie doesn't abandon all his street ways and soons becomes a BMOC because he does whatever he wants and gets away with it. Crap games, porno pics in the dorm and general tweaking of the rich become commonplace.

Varied assortment of characters, though not always original, carry the film when the plot runs out of steam. The bookie of course, soon turns up at the manicured New England campus demanding his pound of flesh and generally complicating Eddie's disguise. Also in the way is Palmer's prissy girlfriend Muffy (Patrice Watson).

More problems. Eddie falls for the daughter of the school's patron and tries to act the blue blood. Palmer returns from his travels and further crowds what is already a crowded room and picture.

By the second half, the story becomes secondary to a rapid-fire succession of set pieces splendidly played by the ensemble cast. Particularly good is Walter Olkewicz as the overweight coach who ultimately saves the day with his Godfather impersonation. Nelson, too, is likable as he mugs his way through. Even better is Olsen as the loathsome Palmer, a character of unmitigated gall who proudly announces, "I'm rich, I don't have to be nice."

First-time director Dorian Walker has done a nice job in getting all the elements to work well together. Unfortunately picture straddles the line between a clever class comedy à la "Philadelphia Story" and just another "Porky's." In the latter category, Daniel Schneider as the Blimp is hopelessly overdone. Constantly stuffing food into one's face wears thin fast and begins to take on a cruel edge.

"Making The Grade" compares favorably with other films of its ilk, but the problem is it compares too often and too easily. "Diner," "Risky Business" and perhaps half a dozen other youth comedies come to mind while watching.

(Pic was filmed as "The Last American Preppy," but lost its title to the earlier, similarly themed Platinum Pictures' "Preppies." —Ed.) —Jagr.

Condores No Entierran Todos Los Dias
(Condors Don't Die Everyday)
(COLOMBIAN-COLOR)

Paris, May 1.
A Procinor Imds. production. Directed by Francisco Norden. Screenplay, Norden, Duni Kuzmanich, Antonio Montana, Carlos Jose Reyes, from the novel by Gustavo Alvarez Gardearzabel; camera (color), Carlos Saurez; editor, Jose Alcalde; sound, Heriberto Garcia; reviewed at the C.N.C., Paris, April 25, 1984. "Un Certain Regard" selection at Cannes Festival. Running time: **90 MINS.**
With: Victor Morant, Frank Ramirez, Isabelle Corona, Santiago Gardia, Luis Chiappe, Rafael Bohorquez, Edguardo Roman, Vicki Hernandez.

Francisco Norden's film is one of violent action depicting the massacre that took place in Colombia in 1948. the result of the conflict between conservative and liberal forces.

Its script traces the rise of an asthmatic cheese-monger from petty assassinations to be an underworld "brain" of organized crime. The plot maneuvering is often incomprehensible with the accent on gangster battles before us for motives that remain obscure. Its directorial inspiration has obviously been the U.S. films of a "Scarface" complexion. Frank Ramirez as the gnomish, cold-blooded paid killer is appropriately repellent in the central role. —Curt.

Hambone And Hillie
(COLOR)

Lillian Gish, way down west, with a dog.

Dallas, April 24.
A New World Pictures release of an Adams Apple Film Co. presentation of a Sandy Howard production, in association with Cineamerica Pictures Corp., VTC and Grahame Jennings. Produced by Gary Gillinghám, Howard. Directed by Roy Watts. Features entire cast. Screenplay, Sandra K. Bailey, Michael Murphy, Joel Soisson, based on a story by Ken Barnett; coproducer, Roger La Page; camera (Astral Bellevue Pathe color), Jon Kranhouse; eidtor, Robert J. Kizer; music, George Garaventz; sound, Richard Van Dyke; art director, Helena Rubinstein; exec producers, Mel Pearl, Don Levin; costumes, Kathy Estocin; stunt coordinator, Dan Bradley; animal trainers, Christie Miele, Clint Rowe, Jackie Martin, Paul Calabria, Cheryl Harris. Reviewed at Village Theatre, Dallas, April 24, 1984. (MPAA rating: PG.) Running time: **89 MINS.**

Hillie Radcliffe ....Lillian Gish
Michael Radcliffe ....Timothy Bottoms
Nancy Rollins ....Candy Clark
Tucker......................O.J. Simpson
The Wanderer ....Robert Walker
Lester Burns ....Jack Carter
McVicker ....Alan Hale
Roberta Radcliffe ....Anne Lockhart
Bert Rollins ....William Jordan
Jere ....Paul Koslo
Ellen.......................Nancy Morgan

We're overdue for a bona fide movie-star dog, the last one being "Benji" more than 10 years ago, ad this three-year-old spaniel-pekingese mongrel, Hambone, may be it. Neither as beautiful as Lassie nor as cute as Benji, Hambone is the ultimate dog-next-door, a lonely mutt so devoted to his grandmother-owner that he treks 3,300 miles cross-country to be reunited with her. It helps when his costar is the indomitable Lillian Gish, making her 103d film appearance, even though her hand-wringing role amounts to scarcely 10 or 15 minutes in actual screen time.

Editor-turned-director Roy Watts is working with tried-and-true formulas in this sappy, shamelessly sentimental triumph. With the lush, expressive score of George Garavarentz contributing to the melodrama, he takes an episodic script and turns it into an uneven but sometimes genuinely affecting story of innocent animals triumphing over the evils of the human world.

The action begins before opening titles, when kindly old Hillie Radcliffe (Gish) boards a New York-to-L.A. flight, but, unbeknownst to her, loses her beloved Hambone when he jumps free of his pet-carrier case and leads airport guards on a high-speed chase to freedom. The dog then calmly trots across the George Washington Bridge, finds the New Jersey Turnpike, and waits by the roadside until he's picked up by a trucker (O.J. Simpson in a nicely done cameo). The outlandish premise — that the dog is going to find Hillie in her L.A. suburb even though he's never been there — requires the utmost suspension of disbelief, but once given, the film becomes a pleasing, fast-paced travelog and variation on Disney's "Incredible Journey."

Since almost everything revolves around the animal action, it helps that every actor feels a compulsion to pour out his life story to Hambone during the dog's adventurous trip through slums, ghettos, farmland, desert mountains and suburbs on his way to a Southern California nirvana. The dog gets drunk, teams up with a viscious hand named Scrapper, liberates a dozen dogs from a canine prison run by junk-dealing Jack Carter, falls in love (with the aptly named Camille, a fluffy little terrier who meets a tragic end), suffers through a period of near-despair, befriends a crippled girl, faces wild wolves, helps kill three desparate assassins, and survives a parched-desert crossing. Helped only by children and a few kindhearted pet lovers (like Robert Walker, in a superb minor role as a laid-back '60s-style hobo), Hambone is the Robinson Crusoe of animal actors.

It all gets to be a bit much when Hambone begins reading interstate highway signs and signalling to his temporary owners when it's time for him to hit the road again and move west, but the director did have the good judgment, in one crucial scene, to not allow the dog to deliver Candy Clark's baby. The ending is no less harrowing for being predictable and sends everyone out on an emotional high. With careful handling and good word-of-mouth, "Hambone And Hillie" could play through the summer, especially in suburban situations which have had a dearth of children's pictures this year.

Technical credits are excellent, especially the naturalistic photography of Jon Kranhouse, the economical editing of Robert J. Kizer, mixing of Garavarentz' manipulative orchestral score, and the handling of Hambone by Christie Miele of Animal Actors of Hollywood. New World is opening the

picture slowly, with plans to platform it territory-by-territory.
—*Loom.*

Toy Soldiers
(COLOR)

Dumb hostage rescue film.

Hollywood, May 5.

A New World Pictures release, produced by E. Darrell Hallenbeck. Directed by David Fisher. Features entire cast. Screenplay, Fisher, Walter Fox; camera (CFI Color), Francisco Bojorquez; editor, Geoffrey Rowland; associate producer, Kevin Finnegan; music, Leland Bond. Reviewed at the UA Del Amo Theatre, Torrance, Calif., May 4, 1984. (MPAA rating: R.) Running Time: 91 MINS.

Sarge	Jason Miller
Buck	Cleavon Little
Amy	Terri Garber
Col. Lopez	Rodolfo De Anda
Larry	Douglas Warhit
Ace	Willard Pugh
Tom	Jim Greenleaf
Buffy	Mary Beth Evans
Monique	Tracy Scoggins
Boe	Tim Robbins
Jeff	Jay Baker
Trevor	Larry Poindexter
Rafael	Alejandro Arroyo

"Toy Soldiers" is just one of those madcap college romps, with some bloodshed and rape, as a bunch of fun-loving Beverly Hills rich kids take on a band of Central American guerrillas.

Pretty little Terri Garber and her wealthy young friends are on a yachting holiday overseen by tough captain Jason Miller, sailing sexily off the Central American coast. The fun bunch manage to ditch Miller on a lark, but unfortunately then find themselves ashore and captured by these mean fellows who speak in subtitles.

Anyway, Miller rescues Garber, but several of the other kids are still captive. Back in Beverly Hills, Garber mopes around the house and tries to persuade her rich dad to raise a rescue army. When dad refuses, she enlists Miller, his sidekick Cleavon Little and some neighborhood kids for the mercy mission.

Although it's clear she doesn't have much money for the effort, they apparently find a bargain store on Rodeo Drive or somewhere where they can get several machine guns, grenades, a bazooka, etc., and set off on the journey.

With just a few hours to go before the hostages are to be executed, they leave Los Angeles in a small twin-engine propeller plans that apparently travels nearly at the speed of light and without the need for refueling. And most of these amateurs parachute safely into the night while others land the plane in complete darkness on an unfamiliar field.

Along the way, they've laughed a lot and the lark just gets better as they go about blowing up the guer-

rilla stronghold and rescuing Muffy and Monique and the others from their fates worse than death. Only in Beverly Hills would you begin to find people selfless enough to risk their bright young futures.

Because of all the excitement, the pretty girls do heave a lot. But they largely keep their clothes on, in keeping with current wisdom that young filmgoers don't like a lot of blatant sex. "Toy Soldiers" also seems to assume that they don't like a lot of blatant intelligence, either.—*Har.*

Noites do Sertão
(Hinterland Nights)
(BRAZILIAN-COLOR)

Gramado, April 18.

An Embrafilme release of a Grupo Novo de Cinema/Embrafilme production. Produced by Tarcisio Vidigal, Helvécio Ratton. Features entire cast. Directed by Carlos Alberto Prates Correa. Screenplay, Prates Correa, Idé Lacreta, based on the novel, "Buriti," by Guimarães Rosa; camera (Eastmancolor), Tadeu Ribeiro; editing, Idé Lacreta and Amauri Alves; art direction, Anisio Medeiros, sound, Romeu Quinto; sound track and original music, Tavinho Moura. Produced in association with Cinematografica Montesclarense. Reviewed at Embaixador Theatre, Gramado Film Festival, April 18, 1984. Running time: 100 MINS.
Cast: Christina Aché, Debora Bloch, Carlos Kroeber, Carlos Wilson, Tony Ramos, Sura Berditchevsky, Milton Nascimento, Maria Silvia, Álvaro Freire.

Films like "Perdida" and "Cabaret Mineiro" defined Carlos Alberto Prates Correa as one of the finest Brazilian film directors. "Noites do Sertão" is a great challenge for any filmmaker, for it is inspired by a novel by Guimarães Rosa, an author who literally "invented" a new Brazilian language and places all his action in very subtle, almost imperceptible, moves of his characters.

Prates Correa chooses the literary approach: the spectator is invited to read the film as he would turn the pages of a book. The result is excellent. He captures the essence of Rosa's feeling and manages to trap the audience in a set of beautiful landscape, fine music and acting, and chronically precise camera movements.

Story is set in Minas Geraes (as is any work by Prates Correa) in the '50s, and involves moral codes surrounded by a permanent state of sensuality. Everything happens with the limits of a farm. Almost every image is superlatively beautiful and dialogs are deeply emotive, though one must make some effort to understand their meaning (even in Portuguese).

"Noites do Sertão" got the Quality Award in Gramado, besides the awards for best actress (Debora Bloch, in her first cinema performance), best cinematography, editing, sound, sound track, music and art direction. It is a completely mature work of a filmmaker

primarily concerned with the culture of his state and committed with every single element of the cinematic language.   —*Hoin.*

Cannes Festival

Fort Saganne
(FRENCH-COLOR)

Paris, May 13.

A.A.A. release of an Albina Productions /Films A2/S.F.P.C. co-production. Produced by Albina du Boisrouvray. Stars Gérard Depardieu, Philippe Noiret. Directed by Alain Corneau. Screenplay, Corneau, Henri de Turenne, Louis Gardel, from Gardel's novel; camera (Eastmancolor), Bruno Nuytten; music, Philippe Sarde; art director, Jean-Pierre Kohut-Svelko; costumes, Rosine Delamare, Corinne Jorry; sound, Pierre Gamet; editor, Thierry Derocles; production managers, Georges Casati, Bernard Loran, Henri Jaquillard. Reviewed at the Gaumont Ambassade theater, Paris, May 13, 1984. A Cannes Festival official selection (non-competing). Running time: 180 MINS.

Charles Saganne	Gérard Depardieu
Dubreuilh	Philippe Noiret
Louise Tissot	Catherine Deneuve
Madeleine de Saint Ilette	Sophie Marceau
Baculard	Michel Duchaussoy
Hazan	Robin Renucci
Embarek	Salah Teskouk
Lucien Saganne	Florent Pagny
Vulpi	Roger Dumas
Amajar	Said Amadis
Courette	Hippolyte Girardot
Bertozza	Jean-Laurent Cochet
Flammarin	Jean-Louis Richard

"Fort Saganne," which has checked in as one of France's most expensive films at a cost upwards of $6,000,000, is something of a throwback to the 1920s and '30s colonial sagas that thrived on local screens. Most were trite melodramas about love and honor that reinforced prevalent beliefs about the nation's imperialistic mission in colonial North Africa. Some of the better ones, often starring screen favorites like Jean Gabin or Pierre Richard-Willm, were pessimistic sagas of men enrolling in the Foreign Legion in the vain hope of putting distance between themselves and a shameful past, have become film classics, like Julien Duvivier's "La Bandera" or Jacques Feyder's "Le Grand Jeu."

Alain Corneau's film of Louis Gardel's prize-winning 1980 novel about an empire builder in the Sahara in the early years of the century, based on the real-life exploits of the author's grandfather, is often fine in its large-scale reconstruction of a time and place and a mentality, but falters in its attempts to inscribe well-detailed characters in its wide-screen canvas.

Despite three hours of screen time, "Fort Saganne" doesn't tell all that much about its protagonist, Charles Saganne, an aspiring young military officer of peasant stock who achieves quasi-legendary glory during the French penetration of the Sahara between 1910 and 1914. Gérard Depardieu, who cuts a smashing figure in des-

ert military garb, perched on a camel, followed by a column of faithful, taciturn Arab warriors, brings all his talent and presence to the role, but the immediacy of the personage is only intermittently felt. In a secondary role, costar Philippe Noiret is full-bloodedly excellent as the ambitious colonel seeking general's stars with his advocacy of aggressive military action in the Sahara.

The script by Corneau, Gardel and Henri de Turenne (an historian, journalist and docu writer-director), follows Depardieu, a young peasant who got cheated out of a proper officer training school by his father, as he makes his way to North Africa where he is posted in a garrison town, before getting his first assignment by Noiret. He quickly distinguishes himself as a natural leader and officer, and gets sent on a mission to Paris to bend opinion to the necessity of a hardline colonial policy.

The mission fails, but Depardieu manages to have a fling with a reputed woman journalist. The idyll is destroyed when he learns his efforts to prevent the marriage of his kid brother, who is getting the officer training he never had, result in tragedy.

He returns to the Sahara, where he soon overcomes his feelings of guilt and failure with a brilliant exploit involving a small army of dissident Arab tribes. His courageous deed brings him fame, the Legion of Honor and the hand of the daughter of local French Bourgeois residents, who have previously kept the socially inferior officer at a distance.

Depardieu buys the house in his native village he has coveted since childhood and moves in with his mate. But it is 1914. War erupts. The colonial dream is abruptly neutralized and Depardieu is sent to the front at the head of an Algerian platoon where he becomes one more victim in the massive, anonymous slaughter.

Without being an anachronistic apology of France's imperialistic past, or a revisionist chronicle, pic does admirably revive some of the epic sweep and romanticism of the old French sagas. Corneau, who has made his reputation in the thriller genre, has made the move from cramped urban decors to endless desert vistas with smooth professionalism. The earlier sequences of Depardieu's apprenticeship to arduous Sahara life convey a feeling of grandeur and lyricism. Bruno Nuytten's firstrate lensing, Jean-Pierre Kohut-Svelko's art direction and the costumes by Rosine Delamare and Corinne Jorry help make pic a visual oasis amid the arid human particulars.

Film is weakest in describing Depardieu's romantic relationships. His brief but intense affair with special guest star Catherine Deneuve, as the journalist who maneuvers him into bed provocatively, lacks fire and poignancy. And young Sophie Marceau, straight from her success in Gaumont's hit youth comedies, "La Boum" and "La Boum 2," gets insufficient screen time to make any impression as the young bourgeois girl who pines for Depardieu and later becomes his wife, then widow.

Other male supporting roles are good, including Roger Dumas, as a loud mouthed fellow officer, Hippolyte Girardot, as a military medic who came to the Sahara with the dream of playing his cello on a camel (he does), Robin Renucci, as a rich Jewish officer who becomes Depardieu's romantic rival, Florent Pagny, as Saganne's fragile brother, and Michel Duchaussoy, as a fanatical captain who avenges a slight suffered at Depardieu's hands by massacring a group of Arab warriors. Said Amadis, as a noble tribal chieftain whose leg Depardieu must amputate in the middle of the desert using only the contents of a tool box, and Salah Teskouk, as the protagonist's orderly, create fine silhouettes that make one regret their minimal screen time.

"Fort Saganne" opened the Cannes Fest Friday (11), the day of its national release. Cool fest reception could mean pic may have to undergo some cutting for overseas playoffs. Depardieu's growing stature will undoubtedly be a major factor in pic's commercial career. —Len.

Wo Die Grunen Ameisen Traumen

(Where The Green Ants Dream)
(W. GERMAN-COLOR)

Cannes, May 14.
An Orion Classics release of a Werner Herzog Filmproduktion, with ZDF. Produced by Lucki Stipetic. Directed and written by Herzog. Stars Bruce Spence. Camera (color), Jörg Schmidt-Reitwein; editor, Beate Mainka-Jellinghaus; music, Gabriel Fauré, Ernst Bloch, Klaus-Jochen Wiese, Richard Wagner, Wandjuk Marika; art director, Ulrich Bergfelder; sound, Claus Langer; production coordinator, Tony Llewellyn-Jones; script consultant and additional dialog, Bob Ellis; Aboriginal consultant, Gary Foley. Reviewed at Cannes Film Festival (In competition), May 14, 1984. Running time: 101 MINS.
Lance Hackett . . . . Bruce Spence
Miliritbi . . . . Wandjuk Marika
Dayipu . . . . Roy Marika
Cole . . . . Ray Barrett
Baldwin Ferguson . . . . Norman Kaye
(English-language dialog)

Once again the peripatetic Werner Herzog has traveled around the world to make a characteristically stylized movie about a clash of civilizations, a clash of worlds. This time his setting is central Australia and his theme is the confrontation between tribal Aboriginals

and a giant uranium mining company.

Aboriginal people of the Riratjingu tribe stand in the way of the bulldozers and diggers of the Ayers Mining Company, claiming their tribal land is being violated. Specifically, they explain that this particular holy place is where the green ants gather to dream, a 40,-000-year-old legend which, they fear, if desecrated, will bring disaster.

Reps of the mining company try cajolery and bribery to little effect, even buying an aged air force plane as a gift for the people; but the matter winds up in the Supreme Court where the legends and beliefs of Australia's original inhabitants clash with English law.

It's certainly the stuff of drama, and land rights versus mining issues have been very much in the news in Australia in recent years. Herzog, however, doesn't make the most of the subject. Though the film contains moments of brilliance and magic, they're few and far between. Mostly, the pic rambles along in a wayward fashion, filling in the running time with anecdotes, minor incidents and a plethora of eccentric characters, some much more interesting than others.

For example, there's a moment typical of Herzog at his best when an aboriginal stands up to speak in court and it's discovered that even the other aboriginals present can't understand him; he's the last survivor of his tribe and speaks a language known only to himself.

For every incident like this, and there are a few more, there are altogether too many uninteresting characters thrown in for no very good reason, such as an old lady looking for her lost dog (in the middle of the desert?)

Aboriginal actors are dignified and graceful. Lead Bruce Spence (the tall actor who played the 'copter pilot in "The Road Warrior") is sympathetic as an employee of the mining company who comes to feel for the plight of the aboriginals. Norman Kaye is also in top form as the head of the mining company and has an amusing couple of scenes where he brings two aboriginal leaders to Melbourne to impress them with contemporary urban life, only to get stuck in an elevator, not once, but twice. Australian screenwriter Bob Ellis, who helped Herzog on the local dialog, does a funny bit as a racist supermarket manager.

In the end, though, pic must be counted as a disappointment. Herzog doesn't seem sure how to end it (there are about three possible endings) and sets up an interesting situation only to do little with it. In Australia, pic may well stir some controversy over the emotive is-

sues raised, with lively pros and cons to be expected.

Technically pic is tops, with the weird desert landscape used to great advantage. Though pic is in English with an entirely Aussie cast, it was made with an all-German crew and is a totally German production. Orion Classics has it for the U.S. — Strat.

Un Dimanche A La Campagne

(A Sunday In The Country)
(FRENCH-COLOR)

Paris, April 17.
AMLF release of a Sara Films/Films A2 coproduction. Produced by Alain Sardé. Features entire cast. Directed by Bertrand Tavernier. Screenplay, Bertrand and Colo Tavernier, based on the novella, "Monsieur Ladmiral Va Bientot Mourir," by Pierre Bost; camera (Eastmancolor), Bruno de Keyzer; production designer, Patrice Mercier; costumes, Yvonne Sassinot de Nesles; editor, Armand Psenny; sound, Guillaume Sciama; music, Gabriel Fauré; additional music, Louis Ducreux, Marc Perrone; make-up, Eric Muller; production manager, Gérard Gaultier. Reviewed at the Gaumont Colisée theater, Paris, May 2, 1984. Competing entry at Cannes Festival. Running time: 94 MINS.
Mr. Ladmiral . . . . Louis Ducreux
Irene . . . . , ... Sabine Azema
Gonzague (Edouard) . . . . Michel Aumont
Marie-Therese . . . . Genevieve Mnich
Mercedes . . . . Monique Chaumette
Madame Ladmiral . . . . Claude Winter

Like the exquisite Gabriel Fauré music that echoes through it, "A Sunday In The Country" is touched with melancholy grace and subtle emotion. Working in a minor key, the eclectic Bertrand Tavernier has made one of his most luminously humane and personal films to date. Its selection for Cannes is good news that will probably help it find specialized situations in overseas art film markets.

With his wife Colo (who collaborated on "A Week's Vacation"), the helmer has adapted a 1945 novella by Pierre Bost, the gifted novelist and film critic whose screenwriting collaboration with Jean Aurenche produced some of the peak moments in the French cinema of the 1940s and '50s. The iconoclastic New Wave edged the team into retirement, but Tavernier, thumbing his nose at prevalent auteur notions, asked the veteran scripters to write his first feature effort, "The Clockmaker," in 1973. Bost died shortly after, but Aurenche has continued writing for Tavernier and others with undiminished fervor.

Filming Bost's tale of an aging academic painter who receives a visit from his grownup children was risky. The book's cinematic possibilities weren't evident, and its essence was in the author's fine prose and ironic sense of portraiture.

But Tavernier has brought it off with style, humor and feeling, being at once beautifully faithful to

Bost and true to his own universe; the father-child rapport has been a recurring theme in his work, and the helmer has taken artful delight with period reconstitutions in previous films.

Story is set in a country house on a Sunday in the late summer of 1912 (the time was left vague in the novella). Here Mr. Ladmiral, a septuagenarian painter who had earned some repute during the heyday of the Impressionists, lives out the last years of his life in the company of a taciturn housekeeper and in expectation of a weekend visit from a middle-aged son and his family.

On this particular Sunday the dutiful filial visit begins typically, with the usual banalities, peeves and minor incidents. But the day takes a different turn, momentous for the old man, with the unannounced arrival of his daughter, who now rarely comes to see him, though she has always been his adored favorite. She adores him, too (even if she's never liked his painting), but her independent life style, which contrasts with the plodding placidity of her brother, has kept her selfishly preoccupied.

Father and daughter spend an intensely private moment together, going for a ride in her car, dancing at a riverside dance hall. But a phone call from her lover in Paris sends her rushing in panic back to the city, leaving the old man heartbroken and alone, despite the other family presence.

A superlative cast brings the characters memorably to life. Acting on an inspired hunch Tavernier has given the lead role to Louis Ducreux, a veteran stage dramatist and director who makes his screen debut here at age 73. He's wonderful.

Sabine Azema, who gave the only signs of life in Alain Resnais' last picture, is radiant as the exuberant but secretly anxious daughter, and Michel Aumont, as her brother, suggests the hurt and disappointment beneath the mediocre bourgeois façade. Genevieve Mnich is quietly excellent as Aumont's small-minded, piously humorless wife, and Monique Chaumette unemphatically eloquent as the housekeeper.

Tavernier's direction is lyrically assured, attentive to his cast and to his camera, which glides across the lovely interiors and exteriors like an artist's brush across canvas. The film's final sequence, when the old man sees everybody off at the station and returns to his atelier to perhaps begin a new painting, is one of the most beautiful segments Tavernier ever directed.

Another hunch that pays off here is the decision to work with a different cinematographer (Tavernier's habitual lenser is Pierre

William-Glenn) — Bruno de Keyzer is a new name in French feature production, and his debut assignment is nothing short of stunning. Yvonne Sassinot de Nesles has designed some splendid period costumes, and art director Patrice Mercier has also done excellent work. —*Len.*

Forbrydelsens Element
(The Element Of Crime)
(DANISH-COLOR)

Cannes, May 13.

A Per Holst Production, Kaerne Film (Copenhagen) release. Directed by Lars von Trier. Original story and script, Von Trier, Niels Voersel; dialog translated into English by Steven Wakelam, William Quarshie; assistant and second unit director, Ake Sandgren; camera (Eastmancolor), Tom Elling; production design, Peter Hoimark; costumes, Manon Rasmussen; music, Bo Holten, performed by Ars Nova and The Danish Radio Symphony Orchestra; song "Der Letzte Tourist In Europa" by Mogens, Dam, Henrik Blichman, performed by Sonja Kehler; production management, Per Arman, Susanne Arnt Torp. Reviewed as official competition entry in the Cannes Film Festival at the New Festival Palais on May 12, 1984. Running time: 100 MINS.

Fisher ....Michael Elphick
Osborne ....Esmond Knight
Kim ....Me Me Lei (Lay)
Kramer ....Gerald Wells
Therapist ....Ahmed el Shenawi
Housekeeper ....Astrid Henning Jensen
Coroner ....Janos Hersko
His assistant..................Stig Larsson
First Lotto Girl.......:...Camilla Overbye
Second Lotto Girl..........Maria Behrendt
Schmuck of Ages ....Lars von Trier
(Dialog in English)

Visually and with reference to all production credits, "The Element Of Crime," Lars von Trier's Danish but from the outset English-dialog official Cannes competition entry, will stun even the most blasé international audiences. With superior direction of excellent, primarily English, players, with evocative imagery and murky poetic-philosophical threads running through a futuristic crime thriller plot, film is a natural for the further festival circuit as well as for more demanding theatrical situations everywhere (U.S. distribution is already being negotiated).

Through mere consistence of style along with the absurd logic of its narrative flow, Von Trier's work stands as a personal statement as well as an accomplished piece of filmmaking, forever thrilling in its use of *film noir* takeoffs mixed with "Blade Runner" comeons. Also, film has a sustained visual excitement through Von Trier and cinematographer Tom Elling's use of low-pressure natrium lighting. This makes for a particularly golden sepia in all frames, only intermittently allowed a dash of bright natural color (the blue light on top of a police car, the red of a flower, etc.).

Plot, told in peeling-off of character lawyers, has policeman Fisher (Michael Elphick, recently of

"Gorky Park") subject himself to hyponosis so he can, in his mind, return to the scene of the so-called Lotto Murders, crimes committed in a series against little girls.

From retirement in Cairo, Fisher travels to a desolate, derelict, possibly atomic war-devastated Central Europe. Here, he seeks the help of Osborne (Esmond Knight), his old police academy teacher and the author of the book "The Element Of Crime," which advises emulation of a criminal's behavior pattern as the best way to track down the criminal.

Soon, Fisher is sunk in a quagmire of red herrings, much obfuscation of justice, the antagonism of the new police chief (Gerald Wells whose looks and bearing recall Erich von Stroheim), involvement with a pretty whore (Me Me Lei) who turns out to have been the lover of the most likely suspect, Harry Grey. Grey remains elusive up to the moment where his character merges first with Osborne's, then with Fisher's own. Fear has made criminals of them all, in their minds as well as actually.

While the it-takes-a-thief-to-catch-a-thief theme is hardly very original, it is not beaten to death either. It serves mostly to bring Fisher through the eerie landscapes that are also, obviously, his own states of mind. Occasional bursts of very rough humor do nothing to soften his journey, they serve rather to add to his mounting desperation.

Where the finely twisted thriller clichés are given a pause, surreal elements are introduced: heads of dead horses rising slowly from sewer waters constitute a recurrent theme. "The Element Of Crime" will not stand too much probing of its philosophical points of view, but the film medium does not lend itself naturally to philosophy anyway.

Von Trier is clearly a feminine filmmaking artist from the start (his Film School gradute work, the 60-minute "Liberation Pictures," is a Channel Four-U.K. distribution pickup). After shooting "The Element Of Crime" as a 100% Danish production, but making it sound like a completely English film, Von Trier refused to allow Danish dubbing. — *Kell.*

The Ultimate Solution Of Grace Quigley
(U.S.-COLOR)

Cannes, May 15.

An MGM/UA and Cannon Films release of a Golan-Globus production for Northbrook Films. Produced by Menahem Golan and Yoram Globus. Executive producers, A. Martin Zweiback and Adrienne Zweiback. Stars Katharine Hepburn and Nick Nolte. Directed by Anthony Harvey. Screenplay, A. Martin Zweiback; camera (MGM color), Larry Pizer; editor, Bob Raetano; music, John Addison; costumes, Ruth Morley; associate pro-

ducer, Christopher Pearce. Reviewed at Cannes Festival (Market), May 14, 1984. (No MPAA Rating.) Running time: 102 MINS.

Grace Quigley ....Katharine Hepburn
Seymour Flint ....Nick Nolte
Emily Watkins ....Elizabeth Wilson
Dr. Herman ....Chip Zien
Muriel ....Kit Le Fever
Mr. Jenkins ....William Duell
Homer Watkins ....Walter Abel
  With: Francis Pole, Truman Gaige, Paula Trueman, Christopher Murney, William Cain, Howard Sherman, Jill Eikenberry, Michael Charters, Christopher Charters and Harris Laskaway.

Katharine Hepburn and Nick Nolte on the surface would seem to be an incongruous screen match, but in this black comedy dealing with voluntary euthanasia by the Geritol set, casting Hepburn as the spry, entrepreneurial mother figure who arranges for her peers' demise and Nolte as the gruff, hard-bitten and sarcastic hitman she hires, the two actors exude endearing though smarmy persona that impart a light-hearted and whimsical tone to otherwise unpleasant subject matter. Some viewers might find the notion of elderly folk lining up to get bumped off, having tired of the loneliness and mundane existence of fixed income realities, distasteful. One must suspend a lot of disbelief to accept the premise. But for the most part, pic doesn't know how or when to take itself seriously. Circumventing the touchy topic in the marketing strategy will prove to be no small task, but the attraction of the two leads should provide it with some respectable b.o. .

Pic opens with Hepburn as a lonely and economically strapped pensioner who lost her immediate family in a pre-war auto accident, but who has a zestful embrace for life nonetheless. Sitting across from her apartment one day, she inadvertently witnesses Nolte put a bullet into her money-grubbing landlord, and subsequently enlists him in her scheme to provide a "service" for her aging compatriots who wish to meet the hereafter ahead of schedule. Nolte is at first intolerant and skeptical, but soon warms to the idea when he realizes that his potential customers are really quite anxious and willing to be dispatched by a pro.

Hepburn gradually builds up the clientele until it has become a lucrative enterprise, both for her and for Nolte. The tables turn when Nolte refuses to rub out a typically rude New York cabbie for Hepburn, and he learns through his too-hip shrink (wonderfully overplayed by Chip Zien) that she'll go to the police and turn him in if he doesn't come through. Nolte embarks to "hit" Hepburn while she's on her way to a funeral for four of their "clients," botches it up, and ends up patching the relationship with Hepburn before the unsatisfactory ending is revealed.

There are some marvelous supporting performances by Elizabeth Wilson as the spinster who can't get arrested trying to get Nolte to put her out of her misery, William Duell as the nerdy neighbor of Hepburn, and Kit Le Fever as Nolte's girlfriend hooker with a heart of gold, whose tabletop striptease at a tea party for prospective willing targets is the pic's highlight. Walter Abel, Francis Pole, Truman Gaige, Paula Trueman and Christopher Murney's portrayals of old friends who wish to check out of the picture en masse tug at the heart strings, and represent one of the palatable moments about euthanasia that really works within the film's framework.

Script is well-paced, the dialog cutesy, the acting solid, particularly by the two stars. But after a rousing first hour, a patchy resolving of the Hepburn-Nolte relationship subsequent to his refusal to kill the cabbie leaves the viewer feeling cheated.

Lighting of key scenes is exemplary, Ruth Morley's costumes look great on Hepburn, and direction of Anthony Harvey pulls some juicy bits from the thesps. But the hurry-up finish remains a stumbling point in the storyline, and a limiter on generating more positive word-of-mouth. —*Silv.*

Dreamscape
(U.S.-COLOR)

Cannes, May 14.

A 20th Century Fox release (U.S.) of a Zupnik-Curtis Enterprises presentation of a Bruce Cohn Curtis production. Produced by Bruce Cohn Curtis. Coproducer, Jerry Tokofsky. Features entire cast. Directed by Joe Ruben. Screenplay, David Loughery, Chuck Russell, Ruben; camera (color), Brian Tufano; editor, Richard Halsey; music, Maurice Jarre; optical and special effects, Craig Reardon, Peter Kuran, Richard Taylor. (No further credits available). Reviewed at Cannes Film Festival (Market), May 13, 1984. (MPAA rating: R). Running time: 95 MINS.

Alex Garner ....Dennis Quaid
Dr. Paul Novotny ....Max Von Sydow
Robert Blair ....Christopher Plummer
The President ....Eddie Albert
Dr. Jane de Vries ....Kate Capshaw
Tommy Ray Glatman .David Patrick Kelly

First of Zupnik-Curtis Enterprises' four-pic slate (this one picked up by 20th Century Fox domestically), "Dreamscape" is a run of the mill sci-fi thriller that wastes some good performances in an intriguing but tediously executed storyline. Unspectacular stop-motion special effects à la Ray Harryhausen don't provide enough of a drawing card in these days of optical wizardry to merit more than a passing glance for buffs, somewhat longer looks for the less discriminating. There is, however, enough contrived suspense to pull a marginal share of the forthcoming 1984 b.o. bonanza. Manner in which Fox sells the pic will be a tougher task than merely getting teens to part with a fiver.

Film centers on "dreamlinking," the psychic projection of one person's consciousness into a sleeping person's subconscious, or his dreams. If that sounds far-fetched, it is. Central character is played with gusto by Dennis Quaid as Alex Garland, a reluctant ex-psychic who prefers to use his powers picking winners at the horsetrack and bedding available Los Angeles tootsies. Via a plot device, he hooks up with Dr. Paul Novotny (Max von Sydow), who runs a dream re search project at the local college that has an elaborate laboratory setup to study the phenomena. There he meets Dr. Jane de Vries (Kate Capshaw), Von Sydow's chief assistant who secretly lusts after Quaid, but only until he "eavesdrops" on her erotic dream that involves Quaid, and then it's no longer a secret. That's about where the love interest begins and ends.

Enter Christopher Plummer as Bob Blair, a secretive and despica ble government type who finances and oversees Von Sydow's re search, but covertly plans to use its results for sinister ends.

Von Sydow's top dreamlinking prospect before Quaid comes on the scene, Tommy Ray Glatman (David Patrick Kelly) is a cold, sneering psychopath who feels threatened by Quaid's similar talents, in one of the more hissable screen roles in some time. Resolution of the plot comes when Plummer decides to enlist Kelly to enter the anti-nuke nightmares of the President, limned with credibility by Eddie Albert, and assassinate the Chief Exec, whose plan to engage in arms reduction talks with the Soviets raises Plummer's ultra-conservative hackles.

Natch, Quaid (the good) and Kelly (the bad and the ugly) slug it out in the sleeping Albert's post-apocalypse dreamscape to an unsurprising conclusion. Horrific makeup effects outpunch the special effects in the finale sequence, and there's a surprise twist ending to dispatch the Plummer antagonist role.

Quaid and Capshaw are well cast and a good-looking screen couple, he charming and believable, she sexy, smart and lovable. Both would do better with more solid material. Von Sydow and Plummer are also well cast, but are not required to do more here than the perfunctory. Kelly stands out as heinous all around, in temperament as well as looks — a great guy to hate.

Joe Ruben's direction is fine, but his scripting with David Loughery and Chuck Russell lacks a strong foundation to build upon. Effects men Craig Reardon, Peter Kuran and Richard Taylor leave only a cursory effect on screen. Art direc-

tion, production design and camerawork are way beyond the story's merits.

Despite its shortcomings, pic should be okay to fill screentime between the blockbuster bookings.—*Silv.*

Irreconcilable Differences

(U.S.-COLOR)

Cannes, May 15.

A Hemdale presentation of a Warner Brothers release. Produced by Alex Winitsky and Arlene Sellers; executive producer, Nancy Meyers. Directed by Charles Shyer. Screenplay, Nancy Meyers and Shyer. Camera (Technicolor), William Fraker; editor, John Burnett; art direction, Ida Random; music, Paul de Senneville. Reviewed at Cannes Festival (Market), May 14, 1984. Running time: 114 MINS.
Albert Brodsky .... Ryan O'Neal
Lucy Van Patten Brodsky .... Shelley Long
Casey Brodsky .... Drew Barrymore
David Kessler .... Sam Wanamaker
Phil Hanner .... Allen Garfield
Blake Chandler .... Sharon Stone
Bink .... David Graff
Dotty Chandler .... Beverley Reed

"Irreconcilable Differences" begins strongly as a human comedy about a nine-year-old who decides to take legal action to divorce her parents. Unfortunately, this premise is soon jettisoned for a rather familiar tale of a marriage turned sour as shown step-by-step. Set in the world of Hollywood writers and filmmakers, the story is also more fun for the cognoscenti than the average filmgoer.

The film shapes up as too long and erratic to rate as a winner. However, some good figures might be registered with clever marketing and appeal of the name cast. Also, some trimming and more humor would be a real boost to picture's eventual commercial appeal.

Drew Barrymore plays the youngster who hires lawyer Allen Garfield (formerly Goorwitz, once previously Garfield) to bring parents Ryan O'Neal and Shelley Long to court. The sudden kids' rights activist wants to free herself of either's custody and move in with their former housekeeper.

On the witness stand the seeds of her dissatisfaction emerge in the three principals' testimony. It is regrettably an uninspired and improbable device to tell the yarn. An anatomy of a marriage without a great deal of perception emerging.

The stages in Albert (O'Neal) and Lucy (Long) Brodsky's relationship begin when he's hitchhiking to California and she picks him up in her fiancé's car. Of course, he affects her growing doubts about union with her sailor boyfriend when he encourages her to pursue her interest in writing children's stories. He, by the way, is about take a teaching post at UCLA's film department.

Circumstance conspires to land Albert a job writing, then directing in Hollywood. As his fame grows, the relationship begins to show signs of strain. Albert succumbs to a fantasy lifestyle and the crunch occurs shortly after he turns Svengali for a carhop.

Lucy initially suffers the leper status of an ex-Hollywood wife. However, she rallies with the publication of her book "He Said It Was Going To Be Forever," while Albert falls victim to ego and a disastrous musical version of "Gone With The Wind."

The charting allows for some humorous and insightful observations of tinseltown morés. It will no doubt spawn a guessing game as to how much Meyers and Shyer have culled from their own lives and those of others in the community. However, the device does little to enhance the initial premise of the film.

Clearly, the first half of the film is light and vignettish before it hits any substantive drama relating to the events which touched off the court case. It's a case of too little, too late and too many injokes weakening the recipe.

O'Neal and Long spark off a nice romantic chemistry but really need a better vehicle to show off their craft. Barrymore is largely wasted as their child turned accuser while Wanamaker and Garfield turn in effective support work.

Technical work is smooth but Shyer's debut as a director demonstrates only modest command of the medium. He and Meyers had previously written "Private Benjamin" but curiously, the new film is much more sympathetic to its male character in the final balance.

While "Irreconcilable Differences" does not have irreconcilable problems, it is in need of some serious tightening. Picture doesn't quite carry off balancing the comic and poignant elements of the story as it stands. Nonetheless, there are bright moments throughout and initial response should be good if brief. —*Klad.*

De Weg Naar Bresson
(The Way To Bresson)
(DUTCH-COLOR-B&W-DOCU)

Cannes, May 13.

A Frans Rasker Film, Amsterdam. A Documentary Film written, directed, and edited by Jurriën Rood and Leo de Boer. Camera (color), Deen van der Zaken; sound, Joris van Ballegoyen. Reviewed at Cannes Film Fest (A Certain Regard section), May 13, 1984. Running time: 54 MINS.
With: Robert Bresson, Louis Malle, Dominique Sanda, Paul Schrader and Andrei Tarkovsky in interviews.

Documentary films on famous filmmakers are usually only as good as the people being inter-

viewed, and in this regard Jurriën Rood and Leo de Boer's "The Way To Bresson" is a beaut. Not only do they get Robert Bresson before the camera (one of the hardest directors to get even on the phone, as the docu shows), but they also interview helmers Andrei Tarkovsky, Louis Malle, and Paul Schrader, as well as Bresson thesp Dominique Sanda.

Bresson has made only 13 films in just over 40 years of filmmaking. His style has been the subject of several good film books, but few critics have ever dared to interpret it with any degree of success. One of the best writers on Bressonian aesthetics was the late André Bazin, but another is writer-filmmaker Paul Schrader in a book titled "Transcendental Cinema" (honoring not only Bresson, but Ozu and Dreyer).

Naturally enough, the documentarists have read all these sources on the director to whom they openly confess allegiance and something bordering on veneration.

The film is divided into segs titled "camera," "actors," "theory," etc. Each seg has an illustrative film clip to underline the spoken word or written test. All in all, this is a fine one-hour tv docu or introductory trailer to a Bresson retrospective.

Nevertheless, it only scratches the surface and is much too short to really do the cinema master due honor and credit. Further, the award ceremonies at last year's Cannes fest, at which Bresson and Tarkovsky were doubly awarded, only sours the occasion. —*Holl.*

Nadia
(U.S.-COLOR)

Cannes, May 13.

A Dave Bell/Tribune Entertainment (Chicago) in association with Jadran Film (Yugoslavia) production. Tribune Entertainment release for North America; Cori Films (London) elsewhere. Directed by Alan Cooke. Story and screenplay by James T. McGinn. Executive producer, Jim Thompson. Features Leslie Weiner, Johann Carlo, Joe Bennett, Carrie Snodgress, Jonathan Banks, Carl Strano, Karrie Ullman, Simone Blue. No credits given for camera (Eastmancolor), music and editor. Reviewed as a Cannes Film Festival Market presentation at the Olympia 5, May 13, 1984. Running time: 100 MINS.

Tribune Entertainment, normally engaged in production and distribution of tv programs, will give "Nadia" a try at the U.S. theatrical circuit first. Done entirely on Yugoslavian locations, thought to look like Bucharest and smaller Rumanian towns, feature is an only slightly fictionalized retelling of the growing up and into fame of Rumania's teenage triple gold medal winner in the 1976 Montreal Olympic Games, petite gymnast Nadia Comaneci.

It seems fame had its usual not-so-golden price to pay. Nadia's parents were divorced over the issue of whether a star upbringing was good for the child (Carrie Snodgress is grimly radiant as the typical movie, or rather sports heroine, mother). Nadia is taken away from the able and enthusiastic coach (played with a hustler's charm by Joe Bennett) by a chauvinistic Communist Party sports official. Nadia is not allowed to enjoy disco life with a boyfriend. Nadia's partner-in-sports breaks with her in a fit of career jealousy. And Nadia takes to consoling herself with overeating.

Everything, including Nadia's return to sports with a solid 9.95 point gymnastic win in Fort Worth, Texas, before "retiring" (she is 22 today) is told in a smooth, but dramatically rather unconvincing way by British tv graduate Alan Cooke. It would take a sports specialist to find any fault with Leslie Weiner and Johann (it IS a girl's name) Carlo's gymnastic performances emulating the feats of the younger and older Comaneci herself, and both have the moody charm, brown eyes and fragile shape of their model. Although the film fails to be explicit about the shape and form of its heroine's retirement, it provides what must be labeled good, clean entertainment for audiences who like their sports mixed with plenty of appeal to heart and tear ducts. — *Kell.*

The Jigsaw Man
(BRITISH-COLOR)

Cannes, May 14.

Produced by S. Benjamin Fisz, executive producer Muhred Sirpa. Directed by Terence Young. Screenplay by Jo Eisinger based on the novel by Dorothea Bennet. Camera (Eastmancolor), Freddie Francis; editor, Derek Trigg; music, John Cameron. Reviewed at Cinema Olympia, Cannes, (Market) May 13, 1984. Running time: **91 MINS.**
Philip Kimberley/
Kuzminsky .... Michael Caine
Admiral Scaith .... Laurence Olivier
Penelope Kimberley .... Susan George
Jaime Fraser .... Robert Powell
Sir James Chorley· .... Charles Gray
Milroy .... Michael Medwin
General Zorin............,.... Vladek Sheybal
Vicar..................... Anthony Dawson

Producer Ben Fisz has wanted to do a film on British-born, Soviet spy master Kim Philby in the worst way for more than a decade. And although "The Jigsaw Man" is based on a fictional Philby, it certainly succeeds in portraying and conveying and executing him in the worst way.

Complex, yet inane, the spy versus spy shenanigans of this trouble-plagued production don't add up to very much on either the artistic or commercial ledgers. Despite the presence of a prestige cast, this big-budget effort is a minor effort steeped in the romanticization of the world of double agents, moles and traitors. It is an unsophisticated and improbable yarn for quick international

playoff and, likely, a direct cable sale in the U.S.

Rather than tracing the historic roots of the British double agents, the story begins in the recent past in Moscow. Sir Philip Kimberly, a contemporary of Philby and Burgess, is informed he has become an embarrassment to his Soviet hosts. However, rather than arranging his death, they give him a new identity aided by some radical plastic surgery.

The 62-year-old emerges quite unconvincingly as Michael Caine and after a few laps is meant to look years younger. While the papers and news broadcasts herald his funeral, the KGB issues an ultimatum directing him to return to England and retrieve an old list of their payroll employees they believe he stashed away years earlier.

Now called Kuzminsky, Kimberley defects at passport control, then escapes his British protectors. His old British colleague, Admiral Scaith (Laurence Olivier) sets about to find the Soviet and assigns Fraser (Robert Powell), who conveniently lives with Kimberley's daughter (Susan George), to the task.

The underpinnings of the plot are certainly far more serious and provocative than as executed by scriptwriter Joe Eisinger and director Terence Young. Both the breezy pacing and indifference to tying things up neatly produce a larkish quality to the proceedings. Old-rivalries between Kimberley and Scaith and the identity of a high-ranked traitor (easily determined) are lightly brushed over and quickly forgotten.

The independently financed production had to close down during shooting when funds ran out and the finished film hardly suggests the eventual financial bailout was merited. Caine and Olivier's reteaming a decade after "Sleuth" is far from magical and the supporting players have thankless roles. Technical work is competent but far from inspired.

"The Jigsaw Man" can't quite decide whether it's supposed to be fun or taken as gospel. It certainly is no competition for either Fleming or LeCarré, ranking as the cinematic equivalent to espionage's "deep sleeper." —*Klad.*

Heart Of The Stag
(NEW ZEALAND-COLOR)

Cannes, May 14.

A New World Pictures release of a Southern Light Pictures Inc. production. Produced by Don Reynolds, Michael Firth. Directed by Firth. Stars Bruno Lawrence. Screenplay, Neil Illingworth, from a story by Firth; additional writing by Firth, Martyn Sanderson, Bruno Lawrence; camera (color), James Bartle; editor, Mike Horton; music, Leonard Rosenman; production design, Cary Hansen. Reviewed at Olympia, Cannes (Market), May 13, 1984. Running time: **91 MINS.**

Daley .... Bruno Lawrence
Cathy Jackson .... Mary Regan
Jackson .... Terence Cooper
Mrs. Jackson .... Anne Flannery
Farmhand .... Michael Wilson

The best New Zealand films ("Smash Palace," "Bad Blood") all seem to deal with violent family relationships in remote parts of the country. "Heart Of The Stag," a New World pickup, is no exception and, despite some weaknesses in Neil Illingworth's screenplay, emerges as a quality drama of considerable intensity.

Bruno Lawrence, remembered for his fine performance in "Smash Palace," is Daley, a drifter who arrives by night at a large sheep ranch seeking work. He's soon attracted to Cathy (Mary Regan), daughter of the truculent ranch-owner, Jackson (Terence Cooper). Though the girl avoids him, Daley patiently woos her, however, until she reveals to him her secret, that her father has been forcing her to commit incest with him for several years.

This revelation comes as no surprise to the audience, since Illingworth's script reveals it at the very beginning. The drama could have been developed in a more interesting way if the viewer had only the same information as Daley, though on the other hand the denouement wouldn't have been hard to guess and Daley is rather slow in finding out the truth. Once the secret is out, the couple decides to take off, but is pursued by the vengeful Jackson for the film's exciting finale.

The fact that "Heart Of the Stag" works as well as it does is almost entirely due to the performance of its two leads. Lawrence is very strong as the rough-at-the edges but basically tender loner who finds himself drawn to the vulnerable, manifestly unhappy Cathy, beautifully played by Regan. Magnificent North Island locations form a backdrop to this intense tale which, with a little more development and incident might have worked even better.

As is, it doesn't quite pull together the various elements to make for a totally satisfactory drama, and may be a hard sell, especially for audiences looking for a bit more action than the film delivers.

There could be a place for the pic at a festival somewhere, though, as a worthy rep for New Zealand. A further plus is the evocative score by Hollywood vet Leonard Rosenman. — *Strat.*

La Femme Publique
(The Public Woman)
(FRENCH-COLOR)

Paris, May 5.

A Hachette-Fox production and release. Produced by René Cleitman. Stars Francis Huster, Valerie Kaprisky, Lambert Wilson. Directed by Andrzej Zulawski. Screenplay,

Zulawski and Dominique Garnier, from latter's novel; camera (Eastmancolor), Sacha Vierny; art directors, Bohden Paczowski, Christian Siret; costumes, Olga Berlutti-Squeri, Jean Zay; makeup, Michel Deruelle; sound, Harald Maury, Elvire Lerner, Joel Belledent; music, Alain Wisniak; editor, Marie-Sophie Dubus; production manager, Paul Maigret. Reviewed at the Publicis screening room, Paris, April 30, 1984. Running time: **114 MINS.**

Lucas Kesling............... Francis Huster
Ethel .... Valerie Kaprisky
Milan Mliska .... Lambert Wilson
Elena .... Diane Delor
Photographer .... Roger Dumas
Ethel's mother .... Yveline Ailhaud
Ethel's father .... Patrick Bauchau
Gertrude .... Gisele Pascal
Pierre .... Jean-Paul Farré

Andrzej Zulawski's last film, "Possession," competed at the Cannes festival in 1981 and won Isabelle Adjani an acting prize. His new picture, "La Femme Publique," was rejected for current edition by the fest selection committee, and some have been trying to stir up controversy with claims that it shocked the selectors. That would be odd, since it's not quite as repellent as "Possession," though it's just as morbidly hysterical.

Zulawski is a mortal enemy of rational, measured filmmaking. Excess is the key to each scene. The actors all seem afflicted with St. Vitus' Dance. The camera, too. Characters don't converse as much as rant, they don't interact, but collide. Copulation, brutality and murder are everyday activities.

Zulawski's vision of the world is sick and sordid. Cinematically this is at first fascinating, but the director's monotonously high-pitched conception of dramaturgy, his puppeteer-like attitude towards actors, and his penchant for facile shock effects and bloated symbolism tend to numb the viewer into indifference. "La Femme Publique" is just a pulp metaphysical turn by an unusually clever technician, though lovers of the sensational may turn on to it as a potential cult item.

There's plenty of madness, but little method or meaning in this convoluted tale of an inexperienced actress who lands a role in a film based on Dostoyevsky's "The Possessed" gets bedded and then bounced out by its rabid pseudo-German director and winds up playing a real-life role subbing as the dead girlfriend of a Czech immigrant, who is manipulated by the filmmaker into committing a political assassination.

Valerie Kaprisky gives her all as the aspiring thesp without much personality, though it's never more than a fair sub-Adjani exercise in uninhibited psychodrama. Her big scenes here are a series of lewd, nude convulsive dances for a voyeuristic photographer, but they don't hold a candle to the Adjani exorcism scene in the subway tunnel in "Possession." What's a nice, talented girl like Kaprisky doing in a freak show like this?

Francis Huster is the rabid, pretentious filmmaker, and for once the actor's narcissism finds some effective employ. Lambert Wilson plays the coerced Czech, who has some sexual tangos with Kaprisky before being set as a decoy to cover the monstrous political plot that never is adequately explained.

Sacha Vierny's lensing is superbly sinister, rendering the Paris locations as uninviting as the Berlin sites in "Possession," and there is matchingly good art direction by Bohden Paczowski and Christian Siret.—*Len.*

Taxidi Sta Kithira
(Voyage To Cythera)
(GREEK-COLOR)

Cannes, May 15.

A Cinema Center of Greece with Channel 4, RAI, Greek Television, ZDF and Theo Angelopoulos production, Cinema Center of Greece (Athens) release. Original story and script, Theo Angelopoulos, Th. Valtinos, T. Guerra; Directed by Theo Angelopoulos. Camera (Eastmancolor), Giorgos Arvanitis; production design, Mikes Karapiperis; music, Helen Karaindrou; editor, Giorgos Triantafyllou; costumes, Giorgos Ziakas. Reviewed at Cannes Film Festival (competing), May 15, 1984. Running time: **149 MINS.**
Old Man .... Manos Katrakis
Voula .... Mary Chronopoulou
Antonis .... Dionyssis Papayannopoulus
Old Woman .... Dora Volanaki
Panayotis .... Giorgos Nezos
Police Captain .... Athinodoros
Harbor Master .... Michalis Yannatos
Spyros .... Akis Kareglis
Longshoremen Union
   Leader .... Vassilis Tsaglos
Alexandros .... Julio Brogi
His wife .... Despina Geroulanou

In his seventh feature, "Voyage To Cythera," Theo Angelopoulos, Greece's past master of the highly artistic political film, is less political than before and more artistic than ever. In fact, artistry mixed with plenty of murky symbolism tends to lead him sometimes to excess in this dream-story of an old Communist Civil War fighter who returns from many years of Russian exile, armed with a violin and a stubborn will *not* to come to terms with his past or his present.

Filmed on Athens, Piraeus and various mountainous locations in mostly grey, rain-soaked weather, "Voyage To Cythera" never actually has its protagonists reach the island of the title. Cythera is Greece's second largest island, just south of the mainland. Its population consists mostly of elderly people who have returned from abroad to live on their pensions. It is off the beaten tourist track. If the old man eventually reaches Cythera, he will still be out of any contemporary context. But even if we, at the end, see him left adrift on a raft, reunited with his long-abandoned wife, we know the Civ-

il War will never leave his soul, as it will not ever let anybody else in Greece free of its shadow.

The old man is received in Athens by his stage director son. He meets his wife of old again. With son, wife and a daughter he goes to a village to which he has property claims that annoy the authorities who want to turn the place into a ski resort. He bedevils everybody by his stubborn behavior; he sets fire to an old outhouse in which they at first think him hidden, and he is generally never where they expect him to be. The police try to get a foreign ship to take him aboard, but then have to settle for placing him on the raft. While the son takes time out to have sex in a theater aisle with an actress, the entire family seems most of the time to be passively in pursuit of the wandering old man.

While most of the film is told in stark frames that are peopled with austere faces, humor shines through here and there, especially toward the end where longshoremen brave the bad weather to stage a song and dance festival and more or less dedicate it to the old man and his wife. There are shades of the Felliniesque here, but most of the time audiences are left with impressively mounted scenes of inner and outer counterpoint and plenty to guess about. Film is long but never boring.

It is obviously bound for further festival exposure and for art house programming, but nobody will have a really easy time with "Voyage To Cythera" and many will have the feeling of having been left stranded on shores of quicksand symbolism. —*Kell.*

Pallet On The Floor
(NEW ZEALAND-COLOR)

Cannes, May 15.

A Mirage Films production. Produced by Larry Parr. Directed by Lynton Butler. Features entire cast. Screenplay, Martyn Sanderson, Butler, Robert Rising; camera (color), Kevin Hayward; production supervisor, Dorthe Scheffmann; editor, Patrick Monaghan; production designer, Lyn Bergquist; costume designer, Christine West; music, Bruno Lawrence, Jonathan Crayford. Review at Cannes Festival (Market) May 15, '84. Running Time: **90 MINS.**
Basil Beaumont-Foster ...... Bruce Spence
Sam Jamieson .... Peter McCauley
Sue Jamieson .... Jillian O'Brien
Miriam Breen .... Shirley Gruar
Stan Breen .... Alistair Douglas
Larkman .... Tony Barry
Jack Voot .... John Bach
Joe Voot .... Marshall Napier
Brendon O'Keefe .... Terence Cooper

Closing sequence in which a car containing two villainous characters is driven by one somewhat flawed hero into a ravine and certain death is the best thing about "Pallet On The Floor," first feature from Kiwi helmer Lynton Butler.

Unhappily, the climax is a long time coming, and prospects for

this miscued black comedy outside of its homeland must be counted as bleak.

Plot based upon the novel by Ronald Hugh Morrison is potentially not a bad yarn, but is muddled in the execution. It's difficult to warm to any of the characters, the acting is inconsistent, some of the dialog is indistinct (either from a bad mix or inarticulate phrasing) and in setting and style, Butler has given the pic a depressingly gloomy, somber tone.

We're in a small town in a desolate part of the New Zealand coast, circa 1966. The men spend their days working in a slaughterhouse and their nights getting drunk at the local hotel. Truck driver Jack Voot tries to rape Sam Jamieson's young, pregnant Maori wife Sue, a fight ensues and he dies, but this is passed off to the dim-witted police as an accident. Brother Joe Voot is intent on revenge, but he too is dispatched.

Miriam and Stanley Breen know the truth behind the deaths, and they make life difficult for Jamieson by blackmailing him, until faded English aristocrat Beaumont-Foster puts an end to them and himself by driving over the cliff.

It's mostly a downbeat experience, made more so by dimly lit interiors and night scenes, and a sultry jazz-blues score by Bruno Lawrence and Jonathan Grayford.

Bruce Spence is evidently meant to provide some comic relief as Beaumont Foster but the lanky Aussie (who was terrific in "The Road Warrior") is an unconvincing Englishman and the script gives him few opportunities to work up laughs.

Peter McCauley fares better as Jamieson, but Jillian O'Brien gives a shallow performance as his wife, and the villains are straight out of stock.

Title, incidentally, apparently refers to the Maori preference for sleeping on a mattress on the floor rather than a regular bed, and there is some byplay about the differences between Maori and white cultures, but it is not well developed.—*Dogo.*

Rouge Midi
(FRENCH-COLOR)

Paris, May 5.

An Abilene Films/Paris Occitanie Films production. Produced by Alain Dahan. Directed by Robert Guediguian. Screenplay, Guediguian and Frank Le Wita. Camera (color), Gilberto Azevedo; sound, Antoine Ouvrier; editor, Catherine Poitevin; art director, Michel Vanestein; makeup, Maité Alonso. Reviewed at the C.N.C., Paris May 3, 1984. In "Perspectives on French Cinema" series at Cannes Festival. Running time: 110 **MINS.**
With: Ariane Ascaride, Martine Drai, Raul Gimenez, Gérard Meylan.

"Rouge Midi" is an example of a film with ambitions but without the means to fulfill them. Writer-

director Robert Guediguian aims at a family epic tracing several generations of Italian immigrants who settled on the outskirts of Marseilles in the early years of the century.

Some of the scenes are good enough to suggest the helmer could have pulled off the project on a comfortable budget. But the film skimps badly when it should be filling in, then leaps ahead several years without warning, often leaving the viewer confused and without bearings. One follows a personage only to have him die offscreen without explanation. The historical background, like the growth of fascism in the region in the mid-1930s, is merely suggested, and the war years simply passed over.

Best limned characters are two friends who follow different paths in life, but remain warmly attached. One marries, works in a factory for a time, then takes a job as a chauffeur to a rich woman, whom he quits when she tries to make a pass at them. The other becomes a local pimp, participates in gunrunning to Spain during the Civil War, and gets involved in other illegal activities. Film later follows the children of the first man, whose wife inexplicably turns up in a wheelchair.

A rich subject, but a skeleton of a film. —*Len.*

Thé à la Menthe
(Mint Tea)
(FRENCH-COLOR)

Paris, May 4.

An Entreprises Françaises de Production/Films A2 coproduction. Produced by Gilles Ricci. Written and directed by Bahloul Bahloul. Dialog, Jean Curtelin; camera (color), Charlie van Damme, editor, Jacques Witta; art director, Chantal Giuliani; sound, Richard Castro; music, Lahlou Tighrent; production manager, Jean-Claude Patrice. Reviewed at the C.N.C., Paris, May 4, 1984. A "Perspectives on French Cinema" selection at Cannes. Running time: **95 MINS.**
With: Abdel Kechiche, Chaffia Boudraa, Dominique Pinon, Malik Bowens, Jean-Luc Boutte, Anne Canovas, Pauline Laffont, Jacques Rispal.

"Mint Tea" offers a ruefully comic glimpse into the life of a young Algerian who has come to Paris to seek his fortune but has only managed to sink into the teeming netherworld of petty criminality in the capital's immigrant quarter.

But he must put on an elaborate, finally botched charade when his mother, to whom he has spun out a fabulous lie of social success in his letters, arrives unannounced for a several month visit. Though apparently naive and utterly unfamiliar with French language and customs, she gradually takes stock of her boy's demeaning existence and drags him home to Algeria.

Bahloul Bahloul, 34, Algerian-born, but settled in Paris since 1971 where he has worked as a tv cameraman and directed a couple of shorts, makes a promising debut in features with this bittersweet tale, which skillfully juggles irony, satiric observation and emotion.

But the film's big plus is Chaffia Boudraa's enchanting performance as the tradition-minded, warm-hearted mother, who disembarks in France in native peasant garb and the disarming obliviousness of an innocent, yet displays more spunk and resilience than one at first grants her.

She illuminates a charming sequence in which she leaves her son's cramped maid's room in quest of matches, and after several fruitless encounters, gets guidance from a slightly embarrassed traffic cop. Grateful, she brings him a tray of mint tea and leaves in it the middle of the street so the cop can help himself.

And she is heartbreaking in the penultimate scene when the son returns from prison and finds his mother dancing in the street to earn money (she had earlier chided him for dancing in a neighborhood cafe). The moment of mutual recognition and the despairing embrace in full view of the crowd is memorably pathetic.

Abdel Kechiche is appealing as the young Arab bamboozled by the gaudy illusions of Paris, but not yet fully corrupted. Supporting cast is good and the production is modest but professional. Original language version is in French and Arabic. —*Len.*

Ahlam El Madina
(Dreams Of A Village)
(SYRIAN-COLOR)

Cannes, May 12.

A National Syrian Film Office Production, Damascus. Directed by Mohammed Malass. Screenplay, Malass, Samir Zikra; camera (color, Ordohan Engine; editor, Haitham Kovalty. Reviewed at Cannes Film Fest (Critics Week) May 12, '84. Running time: **120 MINS.**

Cast: Bassel Abiad (Dib), Hicham Chkhreifati (His Little Brother), Yasmine Khlat (The Mother), Ragiq Sbai (The Grandfather).

Syrian cinema has moved recently into the forefront of Arab film production of late with a string of socially oriented features. And one might add neo-realist "street films" are back in vogue throughout the Arab world, if entries at international fests are any indication. Mohammed Malass' "Dreams Of A Village" is a prime example of this trend.

Upon the death of his father in the village of Kuneitra, young Dib moves with his mother and younger brother to Damascus to seek a life of great security at the home of the grandfather. It is 1950 and the military dictatorship in Syria is about to collapse.

Against this background, as the Middle East explodes politically (nationalization of the Suez Canal, Egypt and Syria forming an Arab Union, war with Israel), the boy grows up witnessing brutality all about him: in his own family, among the neighbors, between people on the street.

The harshest lesson is his grandfather's own meanness to his daughter-in-law, the boy's mother — whom her father finally forces to marry again for convenience sake — and witnessing the death of his brother in a senseless quarrel.

Too drawn out and rambling for offshore chances, pic is nonetheless impressive as a debut feature. Malass is a creator to watch, so, too is Yasmine Khlat as the mother. —*Holl.*

Silver City
(AUSTRALIAN-COLOR)

Cannes, May 15.

A Limelight Production (Hoyts Distribution in Australia). Produced by Joan Long. Directed by Sophia Turkiewicz. Features entire cast. Script, Thomas Keneally, Turkiewicz; camera (Eastmancolor), John Seale; music, William Motzig; editor, Don Saunders; art director, Igor Nay; costumes, Jan Hurley; sound, Mark Lewis. Reviewed at Cannes Festival (Market), May 15, 1984. Running time: **101 MINS.**

Nina .... Gosia Dobrowolska
Julian .... Ivar Kants
Anna .... Anna Jemison
Viktor .... Steve Bisley
Helena .... Debra Lawrance
Mrs. Bronowska .... Ewa Brok
Young Daniel .... Joel Cohen
Mr. Roy .... Tim McKenzie
Max .... Dennis Miller

A passionate love story set against a background of post-war European immigration into Australia is the theme of "Silver city," an extremely handsome production which introduces a vibrant new actress Gosia Dobrowolska. She plays Nina, a young Polish girl who arrives, bereaved and alone, in Australia in 1948 and becomes one of thousands of citizens of so-called Silver City, a migrant camp outside Sydney. There she meets a fellow Pole, Julian, a former law student, and falls in love with him although he's married to one of her best friends. He leaves his wife and for a while they live together until he discovers that his wife is pregnant and decides to return to her.

The background to this affair is vividly etched in. Well-meaning but officious immigration staff show little sympathy for the displaced people in their care. Camp orders are given in German, a language most of these refugees would prefer to forget; men and women, even husbands and wives, are forced to sleep in separate dormitories; outside the camp there is racism and sexism at a time when Australians were insular and myopic about world events.

Nina rejects a local suitor (Tim McKenzie) who has corresponded with her, gets a job as a cleaning woman in a small town hospital, but finds herself unable to make friends and barely escapes rape via hostile local youths. Life in the city is better for a while, but still alien and forbidding.

This is a film for anyone who has ever left the country of their birth to start a new life in a strange land. Polish audiences around the world should be deeply moved by the beautifully handled tale, but migrants of any nationality should respond. Pic is technically of a high standard, with lush Panavision lensing by John Seale and fine production dress.

Director Sophia Turkiewicz, a graduate of the Australian Film and Television School, where she studied under Jerzy Toeplitz, came to Australia from Poland aged three with her mother; there are thus strong autobiographical elements here which have provided her with rich material for her first feature. She was aided on the screenplay by Thomas Keneally, prize-winning author of "Schindler's List."

There are flaws in the film. Some minor characters are overacted, and there are a few rather pedestrian moments. But overall "Silver City" is a top quality pic, though the title is a bit meaningless and even misleading.

Best of all, Polish actress (now resident in Australia) Gosia Dobrowolska looms as a major discovery and has some of the qualities of Hanna Schygulla. She's a radiant personality and handles the demanding role with great skill. Also notable are Ivar Kants as her lover, Anna Jemison (the wife in "Smash Place") as his deceived wife, and Steve Bisley as a cheerful Pole who makes a success of his new life. Story is told in flashback as the former lovers meet, many years later, on a train and recall their early days in Australia. It draws the film to a neat, affecting conclusion. —*Strat.*

Torchlight
(U.S.-COLOR)

Downbeat yarn of a marriage that founders on drugs.

Cannes, May 13.

Film Venture International release of a UCO Film presentation. Produced by Joel Douglas. Coproducer, Michael Schroeder. Exec producer, Manuel Rojas. Directed by Tom Wright. Story and screenplay by P.S. Martin and Eliza Moorman. Camera, Alex Phillips; music, Michael Cannon; art direction, Craig Stearns. Reviewed at Cannes Film Festival, May 13, 1984 (Market). (No MPAA Rating). Running time: **91 MINS.**

Lillian Gregory .... Pamela Sue Martin
Jake Gregory .... Steve Railsback
Sidney .... Ian McShane
Al .... Al Corley
Rita .... Rita Taggart
Richard .... Arnie Moore

"Torchlight" is largely a family affair. Pamela Sue Martin, who costars with Steve Railsback and Ian McShane, is cowriter of the screenplay, as well as taking associate producer credit, while her husband, Manuel Rojas, is exec producer. Between them they've fashioned a film which opens on a deceptively light-hearted note but develops in downbeat style. Careful marketing will be needed for pic to find its audience.

In its opening sequences, the plot depicts the love-at-first-sight romance and marriage of Martin and Railsback. She's a successful artist, he's a wealthy construction boss, but the first cracks appear when he decides on early retirement and she wants to resume her painting. Enter McShane, a sinister and larger than life pusher, and Railsback's downfall progresses until he becomes a physical and mental wreck, left without wife or home.

First meeting between Martin and Railsback, when she's hired to do some painting on a high-rise construction and is carried to the top in an outdoor cage, belies the drama that is to follow, but intermittently the screenplay introduces a number of irrelevant scenes which have little bearing on the plot — as when he deliberately wrecks his foreman's car and then gives him a new one; when he pierces her ears so she can wear the diamond earrings he has bought as an anniversary gift; and particularly when she's decorously covered in a bubble bath while an old friend tries to get her involved in cocaine.

The film gets into its dramatic stride after the meeting with McShane at an art exhibition. Ironically, she's the one who is prepared to sample mouth-to-mouth cocaine inhalation, while he resists. But not for long, and he quickly turns into a full-blown addict, racing downhill with grim determination. Though rather predictable, there is a message to be exploited and that could help its ultimate performance.

As an actress of some experience in films and television, Martin has written for herself a role which allows her to reach the highs and lows of elation and despair, and she is at her best when portraying the happier moments, even though her dramatic scenes are sincerely done.

Railsback has a demanding role and mainly fills it convincingly, but McShane as the sinister pusher is a grossly overdrawn character. Al Corley and Rita Taggart are okay in limited secondary roles.

Although somewhat patchy to start, Tom Wright's direction develops smoothly as the plot progresses. Craig Stearns has designed some sumptuous set-

tings, while Michael Cannon's music, including the theme song "All The Love In The World," nicely complements the on-screen action.
— *Myro.*

Real Life
(BRITISH-COLOR)

Cannes, May 14.

A Bedford Production. Produced by Mike Dinseen. Directed by Francis Megahy. Stars Rupert Everett. Screenplay, Megahy, Bernie Cooper; camera (color), Peter Jessop; editor, Peter Delfgou; music, David Mindel. Reviewed at the Olympia Cinema, Cannes, May 14, '84. Running time: **90 MINS.**

Tim	Rupert Everett
Laurel	Cristina Raines
Kate	Catherine Rabett
Robin	James Faulkner
Anna	Isla Blair
Leon	Norman Beaton
Gerry	Warren Clarke
Jackie	Lynsey Baxter
Carla	Annabel Leventon
Lipton	Michael Cochrane

First feature from seasoned British television director and writer Francis Megahy, "Real Life" is a charming little romantic comedy about a young Londoner whose Walter Mitty fantasies melt into reality.

Pic's leisurely pacing and low-key tone will likely restrict its theatrical potential, and tv would seem to be the best shot in most territories.

A big plus is the presence in the lead role of Rupert Everett, who toplines in the official British entry in this year's Cannes festival, "Another Country." Clearly emerging as a major-league talent, Everett shot to prominence in the U.K. in 1982 in the West End stage production of "Another Country." An artful and handsome thesp, his performance in "Real Life" gives the film a sustaining interest.

Casting of Catherine Rabett as one object of Everett's desires and fantasies could hold some curiosity value; a London model and dancer, Rabett enjoyed a brief burst of international fame when the press seized on her relationship with Britain's Prince Andrew.

In "Real Life" she is not required to do much more than give Everett the brushoff, and at the finale rekindle her interest in him, but she handles that well enough.

Pic progressses slowly until Everett starts feeding stories about the theft of a Rembrandt from a national art collection to Fleet Street journalists. That he finds two reporters gullible enough to swallow his concoctions about a gang of unemployed youths, masterminded by a Mr. Big, working to support South African guerrillas is difficult, although not impossible, to believe.

He invents these tall stories to relieve the tedium of his domestic life (he thinks his mom and pop are tragically living in the past-the '60s) and to impress his friends and especially Cristina Raines as a mysterious but highly sexy American lawyer who is on the run from her enraged husband.

Everett turns to her when Rabett spurns him, and his older woman fantasy becomes deliciously true. That can't last, of course, which is why Rabett comes back into the picture, but meantime there is the real Rembrandt thief, understandably upset about the publicity he's getting, to deal with. Luckily the ever-vigilant police are on the spot.

Script by Megahy and Bernie Cooper offers a decent quota of laughs, mostly on the gentle, wry side rather than side-splitters.

As noted, Everett remains the center of attraction throughout, and Raines works splendidly with him. Also a treat are James Faulkner and Isla Blair as his oh-so-trendy parents. Tech credits are pro. — *Dogo.*

The Silent One
(NEW ZEALAND - COLOR)

Cannes, May 14.

A Gibson Films Production. Produced by Dave Gibson. Directed by Yvonne Mackay. Stars George Henare, Telo Malese, Rongo Tupatea Kahu and Reg Ruka. Screenplay, Ian Mune from the novel by Joy Cowley; exec producer, David Compton; camera (color), Ian Paul; designer, Tony Rabbit; editor, Jamie Selkirk; underwater photography, Ron and Valerie Taylor; music, Jenny McLeod. Reviewed at Cannes Festival (market), May 13, '84. Running time: **95 MINS.**

Jonasi	Telo Malese
Paui Te Po	George Henare
Luisa	Pat Evison
Tasiri	Anzac Wallace
Taruga	Rongo Tupatea Kahu
Etika	Jo Pahu
Bulai	Reg Ruka
Aesake	Anthony Gilbert

Entering the recordbooks as the first New Zealand feature by a woman director, Yvonne Mackay's "The Silent One" is a handsomely shot, intriguing but uneven fable set on a mythical Polynesian island (actually the Cook Islands).

Title character is a native boy who mysteriously emerges from the sea as a baby and is adopted by Luisa, one of the villagers. The boy, Jonasi, is set apart from the others because he is different — he neither speaks nor hears, communicating by sign language, and seems to possess supernatural powers — and he is increasingly feared and resented.

Reviled by the village priest as an evil spirit and unwittingly caught up in a power struggle between the chief and an ambitious rival, Jonasi seeks solace swimming and playing with an albino turtle, having more affinity with the sea world than the humans who do not understand him.

After a fairly languorous first half, the pace picks up and excitement mounts when the atoll is devastated by a violent storm (excellent special effects are deployed here) and attempts are made to kill both boy and turtle. A shark attacks and kills the assailant (creatures of the sea evidently look after their own) and both escape. Closing sequence suggests that the boy transmutes himself into a turtle.

Subject matter will not be universally accessible, but pic should hold some appeal to the under-15 age group as a moderately engrossing boy and his amphibious friend saga in the style of Henri Safran's boy and his pelican click Aussie film "Storm Boy."

As could be expected, the acting from the mostly Polynesian cast is spotty, ranging from capable to different emotional states quite effectively. Conversely, Anzac Wallace (who plays the title role in "Utu," another Kiwi offering in Cannes) is way over the top as the challenger, and George Henare is one-dimensional as the priest. Pat Evison is okay as Luisa, make-up disguising the fact that she is white.

Mackay, graduating to features after cutting her teeth on documentaries and tv dramas, has fashioned a visually striking picture which makes excellent use of the location, a paradise on earth. Underwater photography by Aussie sub-acquatic experts Ron and Valerie Taylor is tops, Jenny McLeod's score nicely enhances the changing moods, and the crystal-clear Dolby mix is another plus. — *Dogo.*

Argie
(ARGENTINE-COLOR-16m)

Cannes, May 14.

Produced, written and directed by Jorge Blanco. Features Jorge Blanco, Christine Plisson, Christine Von Schreitter, Ella Blanco, Philip Hartley, David Jones, Bill Evans, et al. Camera (color), Michel Amathieu and Jeanne Lapoirie; editor, Jorge Blanco; sound, Raoul Juarez and Laurent Daussy; special effects, Roger Bollengier. Reviewed at Cine Miramar, Cannes (Critics Week), May 13, '84. Running time: **85 MINS.**

The exploits and misadventures of an "Argie" in London during the Falklands war in the summer of 1982, with director Jorge Blanco himself playing the eponymous part, is handled with a strong dose of humor and considerable impartiality in a film which might find legs in art and university circuits round the globe.

Despite the constant shaking of a hand-held camera and some rather pointless simulations of Brits fighting Argies, pic delves purposefully into the personality of a ne'er-do-well Argentine trying to scrape together a living in London. Though made by an Argentine helmer, item is self-mocking in respect to the lead character and is scripted well enough to keep audience interest throughout.

The "Argie" in question follows a British pub-dancer back to her home, seizes her, and is about to rape her (to get even with the English), but she unexpectedly starts to speak Spanish to him and suggests they'd be more comfortable on her bed. He agrees, but while she is changing he falls asleep. The next morning, after explaining he is carrying out his own "war" against the empire, he must sneak off with his clothes in his hand, but is seen by the house's owner.

The girl consequently loses her rented digs, but the Argie follows her. An ambivalent love-hate relationship springs up between them as they wander through the streets, take the train to Brighton, and finally wind up working in bit parts in a film about Latin American guerrillas who are shot by the military.

Blanco throws in a surprise ending. Both he and Christine Plisson put in good performances; dialog is lively throughout, with occasional stock footage of the Falklands War used as a backdrop. At the end, the matter of culpability and justification for the war take second place to the personality of the exile himself. —*Besa.*

R.S.V.P.
(U.S.-COLOR)

Cannes, May 13.

A Platinum Pictures release of a Playboy Channel presentation in association with Chuck Vincent Prods. Executive producer, Vincent. Produced and directed by John and Lem Amero. Features entire cast. Screenplay-production design, LaRue Watts; camera (color), Larry Revene; editor, Lem Amero; music, Ian Shaw; sound, Trevor Black; production manager, John Amero; assistant director, Bill Slobodian; set decoration-costumes, Fabian Stuart. Reviewed at Olympia 8, Cannes Market, May 13, 1984. (No MPAA Rating). Running time: **80 MINS.**

Mr. Edwards	Ray Colbert
Mrs. Edwards	Veronica Hart
Linda Edwards	Lynda Wiesmeier
Grant Garrison	Harry Reems
Toby	Adam Mills
Patty De Foie Gras	Allene Simmons
Polly	Lola Mason
Rhonda Rivers	Katt Shea

Everybody's fantasies of a wild Hollywood party ending in seismographic catastrophe are fulfilled by this quick-paced, sexy production featuring the classic stars of erotic cinema.

In the trendy chambers of a Hollywood judge, all the guests at a party to celebrate a blockbuster exposé book, "Picnic Lunch," are assembled to defend themselves, after the party has ended in what appears to be a murder. After the usual bedroom antics, catering disasters, and boy-meets-daughter-of-director-and-gets-part machinations, the body in the pool turns out to be the governor.

The politicians invited to join in the festivities do not survive the decadence, and a sniff of amyl-nitrate, a popular erotic stimulus, does in the gov in the middle of a seduction. Experienced actors make the difference, especially an aging Hollywood gossip columnist called Polly (played by Lola Mason), parodying the lusty scoop-seekers.

Hollywood's beautiful people are portrayed as beautiful bodies, willing and able to enjoy a good orgy. All the old jokes find their way into amusing vignettes, for funny fare that fulfills Playboy Channel's promised erotica. The technical credits are better than average, except for the shaky camera used to create the earthquake that breaks up the party. —*Kaja*.

The Cold Room
(BRITISH - COLOR)

Cannes, May 14.

A Manson International presentation of a Jethro Films Production for Mark Forstater Films. Produced by Forstater, Bob Weis. Directed and written by James Dearden. Stars George Segal. Camera (color), Tony Pierce-Roberts; editor, Mick Audley; production design, Tim Hutchinson; music, Michael Nyman; associate producer, Raymond Day. Reviewed at Ambassade, Cannes (Market), May 14, 1984. Running time: **92 MINS.**

Hugh ....George Segal
Carla/Christa ....Amanda Pays
Lily......................Renee Soutendijk
Bruckner..................Warren Clarke
Erich.....................Anthony Higgins
Headmistress ....Ursula Howells

"The Cold Room," a modestly intriguing psychological thriller, marks the feature debut (after a couple of interesting shorts) of director James Dearden, son of the late Basil Dearden, one of the major British helmers of the '40s and '50s. There's obviously talent in the family, for it's a very confident first feature, intelligently directed and always interesting to look at. Dearden's screenplay, though, leaves a bit to be desired.

Story centers around an attractive if sulky British teenager (played by Amanda Pays, a looker introduced herein) who joins her father (George Segal) for a yacation in (of all places) East Berlin. Though Dad makes every effort to win her affection, she hates him for unexplained reasons, and is peeved because he has a German mistress (Renee Soutendijk) in tow. Spending time in her tiny room in an old-fashioned hotel, she gradually comes under the spell of another girl who lived in the same house during the war and who fell in love with a Jew hiding in the cold room of her Nazi father's butcher shop.

Plot is hardly original, but given some fresh touches via Dearden's unfussy style and tight pacing. Segal is relaxed as the baffled father who can't get through to his daughter and fears she may be going insane. Pays is a find as the possessed girl, but Dutch actress Soutendijk has almost nothing to do as Segal's girlfriend. Tony Pierce-Roberts' location cinematography deserves a nod, and film

music buffs should go for the score by Michael Nyman, who previously toiled on "The Draughtsman's Contract."

Film, which has already been telecast in U.S. via Home Box Office, is being sold as an exploitationer, which it most decidedly is not. Indeed, sex and violence are virtually absent. Rather, it's an imaginatively handled drama which manages to surmount some rather obvious cliches in plotting surprisingly well. Dearden bears watching. — *Strat.*

Wonders Of Life
(HONG KONG-U.S.-DOCU-COLOR)

Hong Kong, May 1.

An Ed Kong-Robert Endelson Pictures release and Edko Enterprises (H.K.). Directed by Kong. Produced by Kong and Endelson. Narration, Edward Setrakian. Screenplay, Hank Whittermore, Ken Vose and Sybil Rosen; camera (color), Lloyd Freidus; editors, Endelson, Leslie Mulkey; sound editor, Dough Smith; sound mixer, Aaron Nathanson; research consultants, Dr. Glenn Barrenkolt, Dr. Henry Washburn, Dr. Roland Cammerer, Hillery Harris; music by Vangelis, Jean-Michel Jarre, Pachelbel. Reviewed at Edko Towers Preview Room, Hong Kong, April 30, 1984. Included in Market Section at Cannes Film Festival. Running time: **90 MINS.**
(Available in Cantonese soundtrack with English subtitles and English version)

"Wonders Of Life" is an enlightening, entertaining and educational documentary which was only produced and directed by Hong Kong-born (but raised in Canada) Ed Kong (son of film distributor Joey Kong), in collaboration with Robert Endelson, whose best known feature length American pic is the 1977 actioner "Fight For Your Life." This is their second venture, the first being "Rising Sun," a docu on the rise of Japanese militarism in Asia. It made Hong Kong boxoffice history in 1980, as it clicked with $HK10,000,-000 with a Cantonese soundtrack.

Kong's "Wonders" traces the origin of life and dabbles in new frontiers in science that is on the verge of "redesigning" future generations. The latest photographic techniques were utilized to take viewers inside the human body to witness life, living forms and body functions not prominently seen before on the big screen. Using fiber-optic camera, the visuals capture the actual moment of conception when a human egg is penetrated by the sperm, forming one single cell. This cell is shown as it divides and multiplies into a human being.

Meanwhile, the soundtrack informs about genes and hormones. The script could have been better and more fascinating if some wit and tongue-in-cheek humor had been incorporated to brighten the rather lackluster voice-over. There

is also a tame segment dealing with male and female sexuality. The scenario then jumps into the animal kingdom where creatures struggle for life in a dog-eat-dog or just be-eaten existence.

"Wonders Of Life" diverts into test-tube babies and how a new breed of animal such as the wingless chicken can be created in the laboratory. The last subject dealt with is the wondrous and complex human brain whose workings modern science is still trying to unravel. This is a well-made film that can be sold for theatrical release, but has the added advantage of being a perfect vehicle for tv either for commercial or informative school use.

Released in Hong Kong last year with an all-Cantonese soundtrack, it took an encouraging $HK5,000,-000 boxoffice gross. Per Kong, there are three versions available with different language tracks, tabbed soft, semi-soft and plain hard versions to suit censorship laws of the buyers, territories and distribs. On the technical side, the quality of the visuals varies understandable and expected as some material was garnered or selected from existing archive material and library newsreels, then incorporated with the new.

The presentation, though, is very tidy, orderly, clear and very easy to follow, all positive qualities that can also be seen in "Rising Sun." The same applies to the appropriate compilation "soundtrack" music. "Wonders Of Life" will be shown in Cannes in the fest's market section.

The successful selling of this film may inspire Kong and his collaborators in the completion of their most ambitious project to date, something about China and its history. The two Kong films with English tracks are scheduled to be shown in Hong Kong later this year as a double feature. — *Mel.*

Splitz
(U.S.-COLOR)

Cannes, May 14.

A Film Ventures Intl. release of an Edward L. Montoro presentation. Produced by Kelly Van Horn and Stephen Low. Directed by Domonic Paris. Stars Robin Johnson, Raymond Serra, Patti Lee, Chuck McQuary, Barbara M. Bingham and Shirley Stoler. Screenplay, Paris, Bianca Littlebaum, Harry Azorin, and Van Horn; art direction, Tom Allen; exec producer, Low; director of photography (color), Ronnie Taylor; choreography, Matthew Diamond; composer, George Small. Reviewed at Les Arcades Cinema, Cannes (Market), May 14, '84. Running time: **83 MINS.**
Gina.......................Robin Johnson
Joan...........................Patti Lee
Chuck....................Chuck McQuary
Susie ....Barbara M. Bingham
Dean Hunta ....Shirley Stoler
Vito ....Raymond Serra
Louie ....Martin Rosenblatt
Tony......................Sal Carollo

Another campus comedy looking to hitch a ride on the coattails of

"Animal House" and "Porky's," this undistinguished effort is lamentably light on wit — either cheerful vulgarity or the off-the-wall variety — energy and creative flair and seems destined to quickly flunk out at the boxoffice.

Helmer Domonic Paris assembled enough elements to cook up a feast: good-looking girls, gangsters, the tyrannical teacher everyone loves to hate, college sports and lotsa rock 'n' roll songs, but they're delivered as an unappetizing stew.

Pin most of the blame on the script, credited to four writers (Paris among them), which lurches from one mirthless situation to the next while offering very little to keep the viewer amused or interested.

Threadbare plot follows an all-girl band, The Splitz, who are trying to attract a wider and better behaved audience than the handful of freaks who inhabit the dives into which their klutz of a manager (Chuck McQuary) books them.

As if they don't have enough problems with their career, the femmes decide to help a sorority house which is threatened with extinction by the malevolent dean of Hooter College (Shirley Stoler) unless they can beat two other sororities at a series of sporting contests.

"Strip" basketball and wrestling in lingerie are excuses to display some shapely bodies, and there is the obligatory shower scene, but real t&a devotees will probably feel they are not getting their money's worth.

With the Mob on their side (father of one of the girls is a cardboard cutout Mafia type) The Splitz are soon, although not soon enough, on their way to rock 'n' roll stardom, and the Phi Beta house is triumphant.

Playing the three band members, Robin Johnson (who may be remembered from the otherwise forgettable "Times Square") Patti Lee and Barbara Bingham struggle with the below-average dialog, and the Stoler character seems to be a straight but inferior copy of the physically formidable gym coach in "Porky's."

The music is a strange hybrid of vintage rock (Del Shannon), '70s new wave (Blondie), '30s ragtime and original songs written and performed by various New York artists including the Clonetones and Diane Scanlon. None of the new material appears to have hit potential.

Tech credits are mostly okay, although a few of the interiors, judging by the screening caught, were murky, surprising considering the director of photography, Ronnie Taylor, won a shared Academy Award last year for "Gandhi."
— *Dogo.*

Prince Jack
(U.S. - COLOR)

Cannes, May 14.

An LMF Production (Culver City), marketed in Cannes thru Shapiro Entertainment Corp. Written and directed by Bert Lovitt. Camera (Metrocolor), Hiro Narita. Executive producer, Jim Milio. Production design, Michael Corenblith; editor, Janice Hampton; music, Elmer Bernstein. Reviewed at Cannes Film Festival (Market) on May 14,1984 at the Olympia 5. Running time, 100 MINS.
Jack Kennedy . . . . Robert Hogan
Bobby Kennedy . . . . James F. Kelly
Lyndon B. Johnson . . . . Kenneth Mars
Joseph Kennedy . . . . Lloyd Nolan
General Walker . . . . Cameron Mitchell
Martin Luther King . . . . . Robert Guillaume
Russian Ambassador . . . . Theodore Bikel
The Cardinal . . . . Dana Andrews
Dealy . . . . Jim Backus

———

"Prince Jack" is an ambiguous little indie mock documentary about key events and private encounters during the Kennedy years. The ambiguity lies in writer-director Bert Lovitt's wavering between depicting Jack Kennedy as a tough wheeler-dealer and a politician of the grandest vision. Towards the end, when the Cuban missile crisis has been solved with Martin Luther King as a go-between, Lovitt settles for the latter point of view, having Jack talk about his great designs for Mankind in the future during a walk in swim-trunks on Cape Cod.

Martin Luther King is made to be the only thoroughly likable and almost all-around popular guy in this feature, and he is played with cool and quiet charm by Robert Guillaume, whereas none of the Kennedys, Robert Hogan as Jack, James Kelly as Robert and Lloyd Nolan as Joseph, bear more than very token likeness to their real-life models and certain exude absolutely none of their so indispensable charm and charisma.

It would seem that the greater policy decisions are depicted fairly correctly (Ole Miss, The Bay of Pigs), while most of the Inner Sanctum private talks in the Oval Office of the White House are obviously based on hearsay and guesswork. Kenneth Mars in his take-off on Lyndon B. is allowed to add many words of common sense to his supply of comic relief scenes.

The women in Jack Kennedy's life are mentioned only in passing — Marilyn Monroe is called Norma Jean, though, and in a cheap, leering way. There are nice cameos by Dana Andrews as the sensible Cardinal and by Theodore Bikel as the Russian ambassador, but it is the few interpolated spots of straight documentary footage that are really impressive and that may leave audiences wishing that the whole film had been made as a docu. It is great fun to hear Frank Sinatra sing "High Hopes For Kennedy" on the soundtrack in the opening sequence. Film is a very minor affair that has neither the scandalous nor the refreshing new insights to make it something out of the orginary as informative entertainment. — Kell.

Atomstodin
(Atomic Station)
(ICELANDIC-COLOR)

Cannes, May 15.

An Odinn Film production. Produced by Ornolfur Arnason. Directed by Thorsteinn Jonsson. Screenplay, Thorhallur Sigurdsson, Aranson, Jonsson, from the novel by Halldor Laxness; camera (color), Karl Oskarsson; editor, Nancy Baker; music, Karl Sighvatsson; production design, Sigurjon Johansson; costumes, Una Collins; associate producer, Sigurdsson. Reviewed at Directors Fortnight, Cannes, May 14, 1984. Running time: 95 MINS.
Ugla . . . . Tinna Gunnlaughsdottir
Bui Arland . . . . . Gunnar Hafsten Eyjolfsson
Cunnar . . . . Arnar Jonsson
Mrs. Arland . . . . Jonina Scott

———

Audiences hoping for a penetrating look at the postwar political situation in tiny Iceland, when controversy raged over the establishment of a U.S. nuclear base, will be disappointed with "Atomic Station." This adaptation of a 1948 novel by Nobel prize-winner Halldor Laxness uses the political events (which culminated in a riot outside the Parliament building in Reykjavik) very much as the background to a rather desultory romance about a pretty, spirited girl from the country who comes to the city to study music and works as a maid to a politician. Latter's snobbish wife and offspring are contrasted with the down-to-earth types the heroine meets at the home of her music teacher, but she has a yen for the politician while in the meantime having a baby by a man she meets only briefly.

Tinna Gunnlaughsdottir is as lively as the script allows as the heroine (named Ugla in the subtitles and Edda in the film's documentation), while Gunnar Hafsten Eyjollesson is a Martin Sheen lookalike as the politico. Scenes involving machinating government officials seem hardly convincing unless political life in Iceland at the time was really as totally naive as presented here. But, as noted, it's the heroine's story that assumes center stage, and it's hardly an original tale of unrequited love and rejection.

On its home ground pic has clicked (a third of the island nation's population has seen it), but foreign sales look to be doubtful. Music score is overpowering at times, and images rather uninspiring, given the locations available. Otherwise technically good.
—Strat.

Video Vixens
(U.S.-COLOR)

Cannes, May 11.

A Troma release of a Fieldstone Production, produced by Graham Place. An Aquifilm Co. picture. Directed by Ronald Sullivan. Screenplay by Joel Gross; camera (color) Arthur D. Marks; editors, Place, Marks; music, Jacques Urbont. Reviewed at the Star 3, Cannes Market. May 11, 1984. (MPAA Rating: R). Running time: 82 MINS.
Inge . . . . Robyn Hilton
Gordon Gordon . . . . Harrison Philips
Also with Cheryl (Rainbeaux) Smith, Sandy Dempsey.

———

"Video Vixens" fulfills its intentions by being an exploitation feature that looks like but never could be shown on tv, except for the late night blue movie market it aims at.

The president of KLIT, America's number one network according to this formula, decides to fight a conspiracy to unman America, which is the source of his paranoia. He goes for top ratings by airing at primetime an impromptu Academy Award ceremony for stag movies with clips that promise more violent threats to America's women than men.

Inge, Queen of Stag films, and Gordon Gordon, a principled and prudish film critic, host the show, which promises to liven up the Academy Award tradition of "90 minutes of boredom." (Which was never that short, even in 1972, the pic's copyright date.) (Per the director, pic was previously released that year sans rating under the title "Black Socks" — Ed.)

Scattered among the prurient but inexplicit, staggeringly bad black-and-white award winners, the producer rattles on about hexachlorophine closing the gender gap. The spoof is only moderately paced, with only suggestive sex, for mostly slob appeal.

The commercials reflect sparks of the "Kentucky Fried Chicken" style that resembles this attempt and ape known conventions of ads. With take off titles like "The Shrink Who Loved Me," one is rewarded with mostly poppycock. Best Director time sends up the endless love of self by pretenders to auteurism, with mate-and-a-half self-consciousness.

Competent fare for the genre, but more talk than action. Only real sex symbol is the late starlet of "Doc Savage" and other films, Robyn Hilton as a curvaceous lowbrow blonde, who should draw an appreciative market.

Technical credits good enough to be convincing tv, but it does not writhe enough for theatrical exploitation market. — Kaja.

Ellie
(U.S. - COLOR)

Cannes, May 12.

A Film Ventures International release of a Roudine-Wittman Films (Dallas) production, produced by Francine Roudine. Directed by Peter Wittman. Features entire cast. Screenplay, Glenn Allen Smith; camera (Eastmancolor), George Tirl; editor, John Davis; sets, Michael O'Sullivan; music, Bob Pickering, performed by Altanta and Charlie Pride. Reviewed at Cine Olimpia (Cannes Market), May 12, '84. (No MPAA Rating). Running time: 88 MINS.
Ellie . . . . Sheila Kennedy
Cora . . . . Shelley Winters
Tom . . . . Edward Albert
Sheriff . . . . Pat Paulsen
Preacher . . . . George Gobel

———

Main reason for making this film is to show off the teasing charms of 1983 Penthouse Pet Sheila Kennedy, who throws leering, innocent and not-so-innocent glances at the cast throughout the pic, who lopes through a field of flowers clad only in bra and panties and who is also chased by a tough on a motorcycle, and who sways, sashays and winningly shows off her charms; she does so in a wholesomely teasing way; with never a soupçon of even softcore libido to it. She utters insinuating lines steeped in a naughty Southern drawl.

A farcical backdrop story is provided to hang Kennedy's clothes upon, most of it rather silly, but useful enough in keeping the interest alive while the audience waits for Ellie to come on again. Shelley Winters again aptly plays the Big Mama, with four country cousin sons, who has knocked off two or three husbands after they have willed their assets to her. The last victim is Ellie's old dad, who's given a shove in his wheelchair and rolls down the hill to his watery death in a lake.

Ellie, who has been kept pure and virginal since puberty, but often is threatened by Big Mama's hulking sons, vows vengeance upon her father's assassins. One by one she predisposes them to "accidents" after enticing them with her alluring smiles and shimmying body. It's all handled lightheartedly and no sexplay is ever broached. Ellie remains evasively pure to the very end, until she polishes off the last of the sons by giving him a heart attack after multiple off-screen orgasms.

Pic might rack up some biz in less sophisticated areas and even offshore territories where a teasing sex comedy will be amenable to local censors. — Besa.

The Ninja Mission
(BRITISH-COLOR)

Cannes, May 14.

A New Line Cinema release (U.S.), world rights, World Film Alliance, of a VIC production, produced by Roger Lundey. Features Christopher Kohlberg, Hanna Pola, Bo F. Munthe. Exec producers, Charles Aperia and Guy Collins. Directed by Mats Helge; camera (color), Peter Stevenson; editor, David Gilbert; music, Danny Young; combat coordinator, Bo F. Munthe. Screenplay, credit unknown. Reviewed at Cannes Festival (market), May 14, '84. Running time: 101 MINS.

———

The CIA, the KGB and four ninja commandos on a mission to rescue an atomic physics prof and his daughter from the grasp of the Russians provide the negligible background story for virtually nonstop mayhem as the good guys machine-gun, garrotte, hack and dart-gun what seems to be half the Red Army.

This reviewer tallied about 10 dead on the Russian side and three or four on the Western side as ninja shenanigans alternate with slow-motion guts being spilled and aerobic death flips by the enemy who never seems to have heard of taking cover. But it's all nice bloody fun for those craving action.

Dubbed dialog is particularly expressionless, but Berlitz-clear for those whose English may be wobbly, and with content simplistically flat. Thesping is terrible, but there are enough bullets and darts flying about so that no one will notice. Direction of the action scenes is well handled, as are the special effects. Overall good production values should make item a suitable sell for action-oriented markets worldwide. —*Besa.*

Sentimental Reasons
(CANADIAN-COLOR)

Cannes, May 14.

MAG Enterprises and Gregory Earls presentation of a Jorge Montesi and Cinetel production. Produced and directed by Jorge Montesi. Screenplay by Peter Haynes, story by Montesi; camera (color), Gary Armstrong; editor, Harold Tichonor; music, Paul Zaza. Reviewed at Cannes Festival (Market), May 13, 1984. Running time: **86 MINS.**
Alex ....Jorge Montesi
Maureen ....Elaine Lukeman
Peter Gray ....Peter Haynes
Helmut ....Arvi Liimatainen
Izzy ....Israel Manchild
Joe Daniels ....Eric Shirt

Independently produced and largely non-pro credited "Sentimental Reasons" is an oddball thriller aspiring to much greater things than it can offer. The Edmonton-based production by Chilean Jorge Montesi is a shoestring offering with too many corners cut to be effective entertainment or creditable commentary.

Montesi stars as a hit man and former soldier of fortune called in by a former mercenary to sanction an Indian activist. A brief prolog establishes a botched mission in Africa with the principals. However, the Alberta locations prove an inferior substitute for these supposed Central African locales.

Although action is supposed to transpire over 48 hours, the prospect of incidents occurring that quickly is beyond belief. In short order, Montesi falls for a hooker on the run from her pimp, effects the assassination, then threatens both his life and those of former friends in his attempts to rid the prostitute of her vengeful, brutal benefactor.

Some intriguing ideas are bandied about, but Montesi and scripter Peter Haynes barely gloss the surface. Bargain-basement technical support and generally poor performances only serve to accentuate the film's already modest aspects.

Overall result is often unintentionally humorous, rarely thrilling and decidedly uncompelling dramatically. Needless to say theatrical prospects are dim, and Montesi and associates will require more than "Sentimental Reasons" to spark interest in future ventures. —*Klad.*

Zombie Island Massacre
(U.S.-COLOR)

Cannes, May 12.

A Troma release, distributed by Lloyd Kaufman, Michael Herz and the Troma Team. A presentation by David Broadnax, Michael Malagiero, Umberto di Leo. Exec producers, Malagiero, Abraham Dabdoub. Produced by Broadnax. Directed by John N. Carter. Features entire cast. Screenplay, Logan O'Neill, William Stoddard, from a story by Broadnax, O'Neill; camera (color), Bob Baldwin; editor, Carter; music, Harry Manfredini; art direction, Srecko Gall; sound, Rolf Pardula; production manager, Robert Russel; assistant director, Dwight Williams; special makeup effects, Dennis Eger. Reviewed at Cine Star (Cannes), May 11, 1984 (Market section). (No MPAA Rating.) Running time: **95 MINS.**
With: David Broadnax, Rita Jenrette, Tom Cantrell, Ian MacMillan, Debbie Ewing, Tom Fitzsimmons.

The trailer for "Zombie Island Massacre" prior to its projection in the Cannes market was snappier than the feature itself, concerned as it is with the voodoo adventure of a group of tourists on a small Caribbean island. The trailer was done tongue in cheek. The feature, however, goes at its subject straight, which is a great loss. (Pic was shot in Jamaica last year under the working title "The [Last] Picnic," with veteran Emmett Murphy credited at that time with screenplay, but now omitted from screen credits. -Ed.)

But audiences may burst out laughing anyway as they are fed a continuous line of cliches, inept exclamations, "Oh my God's" and dreadful non-acting. It's as though a real group of tourists had been enlisted to trip through the jungles and be eliminated in the standard ways of the horror genre — decapitations, strangling, pierced by spears, immolations in death traps and other claptrap.

Story concerns a busload of tourists who watch a voodoo rite involving the sacrifice of a lamb. The gory show arouses only their disgust, and they trudge back to the bus, only to find it won't start. In despair, they decide to hike off to a seemingly nearby house they had seen before, and are gorily eliminated one by one in the jungle and later in the house, in a series of rather silly massacres vaguely explained at the end of the film as being the work of Colombian "hit men" out to recover a cache of heroin.

No zombies ever surface on the screen. They do their dastardly deeds from behind the camera. Main attraction of pic may be pre-

sence of former Abscam congressman's ex-wife and Playboy pictorial subject Rita Jenrette, who can be seen briefly, once taking a shower and twice maneuvering in bed before her tourist duties interrupt the fun. More Jenrette and less mediocre special effects might have made pic more palatable. —*Besa.*

The Warrior And The Sorceress
(U.S.-COLOR)

Cannes, May 12.

A New Horizons release of a Roger Corman presentation. Produced by Frank K. Isaac Jr., John Broderick. Directed, written by Broderick. Story by Broderick, William Stout. Coproducers, Hector Olivera, Alex Sessa. Stars David Carradine. Camera (color), Leonard Solis; editor, Silvia Roberts; music, Louis Saunders; art direction, Emmett Baldwin; special effects, Richard Lennon; sound, George Stevenson; assistant director, Andrew Sargent. Reviewed at the Olympia 8, Cannes Film Festival Market, May 12, 1984. (MPAA Rating: R.) Running time: **76 MINS.**
Kain ....David Carradine
Zeg ....Luke Askew
Naja ....Maria Socas
Also with: Anthony DeLongis, Harry Townes.

"The Warrior And The Sorceress," (lensed last year under the title "Kain Of Dark Planet"), is quite a bit cheesier than Roger Corman's previous Argentine production, "Deathstalker," and even looks to have been made on some of the same sets. Blatantly lifted from Akira Kurosawa's "Yojimbo," late-in-the-cycle sword and sorcery item is a lowercase effort in all departments and has minimal potential even in quick-playoff release.

Derivative plot has holy warrior David Carradine arriving in an impoverished village where two rival clans vie for control of a water well and also lord it over helpless peasants.

As did Toshiro Mifune in "Yojimbo" and Clint Eastwood in "A Fistful Of Dollars," Carradine plays each side against the other to his own monetary gain, and even repeats the famous Kurosawa gag of laughing from a safe position above the village square as the two local forces go at each other.

Although sex doesn't seem to interest him, Carradine nevertheless spends quite a bit of time with "sorceress" Maria Socas, who endures running time being shuttled back and forth between the clutches of both evil factions. Although Socas' function in the plot remains unclear, she does have the distinction of having performed every one of her scenes in the picture topless, and her fabulous physique represents a decided distraction from the otherwise desultory goings-on.

Most eye-popping scene, however, is an exotic dance performed

by a woman with four breasts. If the special effects team was responsible for this effect, they deserve kudos for realism.

Predictably, it all ends up in a big melee, with Carradine mixing some quick swordplay with a few kung fu moves. Once he's eliminated all the baddies and left the spoils to the peons, he packs up his sword and informs Socas, "I travel alone." Too bad for him.

Virtually everyone save Carradine seems dubbed, and badly at that, and the pic's technical level is on a par with Italian sword and sandal epics of 25 years ago. —*Cart.*

Memorias do Carcere
(Prison Memoirs)
(BRAZILIAN-COLOR)

Cannes, May 14.

An L.C. Barreto and Regina Filmes production. Associate Producer, Embrafilme. Executive Producer, Mario da Salete. Directed by Nelson Pereira dos Santos. Adapation and screenplay from the novel by Graciliano Ramos, Pereira dos Santos; camera (color), José Medeiros and Antonio Luiz Soares; art director, Irenio Maia; sets, Adilio Athos and Emily Pirmez; costumes, Ligia Medeiros; editor, Carlos Alberto Camyyrano; sound, Jorge Saldanha. Reviewed at Cannes Film Festival (Directors' Fortnight) May 13, '84. Running Time: **187 MINS.**
Features: Carlos Vereza, Glória Pires, Jofre Soares, José Dumont, Nildo Parente, Wilson Grey, Tonico Pereira, Jorge Cherques, Jackson de Souza, Waldyr Onotre.

Nelson Pereira dos Santos' "Vidas Secas" (Barren Lives, 1963) first became a cornerstone of Brazil's Cinema Novo and, 21 years later, the film occupies an undisputed position as a classic of Latin-American cinema. With "Prison Memoirs" this director once again deals with a work by Graciliano Ramos, one of his country's most respected contemporary writers, and the result is an impressive film that should do well on its home ground, although its international exposure may well be limited by its three-hour length and the fact that much that is self-evident to Brazilian viewers may not be nearly as clear to foreign audiences.

Ramos' autobiographical story deals with the aftermath of an uprising in the northeast of Brazil against the Getulio Vargas dictatorship, which took place in the mid-'30s. At the time, the government not only arrested communists and members of the military who had taken part in the rebellion, but also took advantage of the situation to imprison a great many liberals, including writer Ramos. As he is transferred from prison to prison, ending up in a penal settlement on an island off the Rio de Janeiro coast, conditions constantly deteriorate. On the other hand, the writer's awareness of life, society and people from social strata other than his own increases and, although his health deteriorates considerably, he is much enriched by the experience.

For director Pereira dos Santos this vision of the Brazilian gulag of the '30s is a means for showing a microcosm of Brazilian society and he appears to use the successive prison environments to comment obliquely on present-day society and situations in his country, and much of this would also be valid for other parts of Latin America. It is, however, quite likely that this aspect of the film will by no means be as clear to foreigners as it is to Brazilians. A minor example would be the film's opening and closing music, which few people outside Brazil are likely to recognize as the country's national anthem (in Gottschalk's symphonic transcription). It would therefore be reasonable to conclude that "Prison Memoirs" will acquire different dimensions and connotations on its home ground and abroad.

In either case, however, Pereira dos Santos emerges as a mature filmmaker, fully in command of is craft and with a penetrating view of his country's mores. Technical credits are good and Carlos Vereza as Graciliano Ramos provides an outstanding performance in the difficult task of showing the development of a character whose role is basically passive and who, throughout, has to show what goes on within him by reacting to others rather than acting himself.

—*Amig.*

The Karate Kid
(COLOR)

Delightful victory for the underdog. Shapes up as a summer sleeper.

Hollywood, May 18.

A Columbia Pictures release of a Jerry Weintraub production. Produced by Weintraub. Executive producer R.J. Louis. Directed by John G. Avildsen. Features entire cast. Screenplay, Robert Mark Kamen; camera (Metrocolor), James Crabe; editors, Bud Smith, Walt Mulconery, Avildsen; music, Bill Conti; production design, William J. Cassidy; set design, Bill Matthews; set decorator, John Anderson; sound, Dean Hodges; martial arts choreography, Pat Johnson; associate producer, Bud Smith; assistant director, Clifford C. Coleman. Reviewed at National theater, Westwood, Calif., May 18, 1984. (MPAA Rating: PG). Running time: 126 MINS.

Daniel	Ralph Macchio
Miyagi	Noriyuki (Pat) Morita
Ali	Elisabeth Shue
Breese	Martin Kove
Lucille	Randee Heller
Johnny	William Zabka
Bobby	Ron Thomas
Tommy	Rob Garrison

John G. Avildsen is back in the "Rocky" ring with "The Karate Kid." More precisely, it is a "Rocky" for kids. Whether the mostly unknown cast and semi-exotic subject matter will have the same boxoffice punch for a youth audience as "Rocky" is hard to call. Same rousing ending and upbeat approach could make this a summer sleeper.

"The Karate Kid" follows the tried-and-true outline of "Rocky" almost point by point, with few variations. Daniel (Ralph Macchio) and his mother (Randee Heller) move from their home in New Jersey to sunny Southern California, which she describes as "the Garden of Eden."

Daniel has other ideas about the move and as he encounters the attacks of his schoolmates and problems with a would-be girlfriend (Elisabeth Shue), he is well established as an underdog from whom the audience can root.

Daniel's budding relationship with Ali triggers attacks by the bad kids. How do we know they're bad? They arrive on motorcycles (Daniel rides an old bicycle).

The leader of the pack (William Zabka), it turns out, is Ali's ex and he and his troup start taunting and working over Daniel.

Enter Mr. Miyagi (Noriyuki ["Pat"] Morita), the mysterious maintenance man who takes Daniel under-wing. Slowly revealing himself to be an exceptional person with hidden talents, the kicker comes when Daniel's adversaries follow him home and Miyagi single-handedly k.o.'s the whole group. Daniel is awestruck.

He wants Miyagi to teach him how to defend himself, but the old man resists until Daniel learns that karate is a discipline of the heart and mind, of the spirit, not of vengeance and revenge. Like Rocky, Daniel must go through a period of training and learn humility. And like "Rocky" the climax is a big fight, in this case the Valley Karate Championship.

In case there is any doubt about drawing sides, training Daniel's opponents is a Nazi-like ex-Vietnam Marine (Martin Kove), who instructs his troops to fight dirty. The offenders are all blond, with Daniel, a dark-haired Italian, and the Okinawan Miyagi bound together.

Seriously injured in competition, Daniel must show grace under pressure before he can can defeat his version of Apollo Creed. As a Talia Shire standin, Shue stands by and cheers-on her man. If anything, the "Rocky" formula is manipulative, and irresistible.

Aimed at a younger audience than "Rocky," the basic difference here is that Daniel gains his maturity under Miyagi's tutelage, and their scenes together are by far the best in the film. Miyagi's influence over Daniel is the meeting with a remarkable man which will stay with the boy for the rest of his life.

Morita, as Miyagi is simply terrific, bringing the appropriate authority and wisdom to the part. His timing and understated humor are also impeccable. On paper, Miyagi was probably not a great character, but Morita's performance makes him a memorable character.

Also right on the money, in a smaller, less dominating role, is Heller as Daniel's mother, who has totally mastered east coast Italian diction. Macchio is fine and likable as the boy, if perhaps a bit too straight to be realistic.

Avildsen and scripter Robert Mark Kamen shoot for a wholesomeness which stands out from the recent teen fare that has been full of easy sex. The relationship they draw between Daniel and Ali, however, is ridiculously childish (Daniel's mother accompanies them on dates), especially as the boy struggles for his maturity.

Soundtrack consisting of a bunch of ersatz rock 'n' roll also doesn't ring true. Picture, however, is well shot and karate scenes are briskly edited. But the heart of this film is the boy's triumph over heavy odds, just like "Rocky." —*Jagr.*

Memed My Hawk
(BRITISH-YUGOSLAV-COLOR)

Can't fly.

London, May 16.

A Peter Ustinov production in association with Jadran Film. Produced by Fuad Kavur. Coproduced by Brian Smedley-Aston. Directed by Ustinov. Stars Ustinov, Herbert Lom, Denis Quilley, Michael Elphick. Screenplay, Ustinov, based on the book by Yashar Kemal; camera (color), Freddie Francis; editor, Peter Honess; music, Manos Hadjidakis. Reviewed at the Bijou Theatre, London, May 14, 1984. (BBFC certificate: 15.) Running time: 105 MINS.

Abdi Aga	Peter Ustinov
Ali Safa	Herbert Lom
Memed	Simon Dutton
Rejeb	Denis Quilley
Jabbar	Michael Elphick
Hatche	Leonie Mellinger
Lame Ali	Vladek Sheybal
Kermioglu	Michael Gough
Sergeant Asim	Walter Gotell

"Memed My Hawk" is a thin comedy set in exotic climes which is likely to crash-land at the b.o. That's despite bravura performances from Peter Ustinov, who's also credited as writer and director, and a bevy of British actors.

Ustinov dominates the show as the feudal overlord of five villages in the Turkish hills. However, where he could have been evil and cruel, which might have been interesting, he's charmingly incompetent, which isn't.

The tendentious story starts with the young Memed fleeing to the hills with his beloved Hatche, who has been affianced to the Aga's boorish nephew. Having supposedly killed the ruler, he is enrolled in a band of rebels. Memed stages a putsch against the brigand leader in the tent of an opium-smoking carpet dealer before making two more attempts on the Aga's life. The latter is successful despite fact that the Aga now has half-hearted backing from central government.

There's something to cherish in the cast's attempt to play the Aga's henchmen and guerrilla warriors. However, the general effect is farce without any element of suspense or motivating message (something the original book had aplenty).

The high-flown dialog puts a further strain on credibility. —*Japa.*

Gremlins
(COLOR)

Special creature effects hit from Spielberg and Joe Dante.

Hollywood, May 19.

A Warner Brothers release of an Amblin Entertainment presentation. Produced by Michael Finnell. Exec producers, Steven Spielberg, Frank Marshall, Kathleen Kennedy. Directed by Joe Dante. Features entire cast. Screenplay, Chris Columbus; camera (Technicolor), John Hora; editor, Tina Hirsch; music, Jerry Goldsmith; sound, Ken King; production design, James H. Spencer; set design, William Matthews; set decoration, Jackie Carr; Gremlins created by Chris Walas; creature consultant, Jon Berg; production manager, Phil Rawlins; assistant director, James Quinn; special effects supervisor, Bob MacDonald Sr.; stunt coordinator, Terry Leonard; matte paintings, Dream Quest Images; matte artist, Rocco Gioffre; stop-motion animation, Fantasy II Film Effects; animation, Visual Concept Engineering; process photography, Bill Hansard. Reviewed at the Village Theater, L.A., May 19, 1984. (MPAA Rating: PG). Running time: 111 MINS.

Billy	Zach Galligan
Rand Peltzer	Hoyt Axton

Lynn Peltzer	Frances Lee McCain
Kate	Phoebe Cates
Mrs. Deagle	Polly Holliday
Sheriff	Scott Brady
Hanson	Glynn Turman
Pete	Corey Feldman
Futterman	Dick Miller
Grandfather	Keye Luke
Gerald	Judge Reinhold
Deputy	Jonathan Banks
Corben	Edward Andrews

Make room for adorable "Gremlins" dolls on the shelves and start counting the take for another calculated audience pleaser from the Steven Spielberg-Frank Marshall-Kathleen Kennedy team. But that's all that's here in this showy display of technical talent, otherwise nearly heedless of dramatic concerns.

Director Joe Dante is in full control of his extraordinarily realistic mechanical creatures, both lovable and hideous. And the preview audience — some in line by noon — were wild about it all.

In what story there is, amiable Hoyt Axton comes across a mysterious creature in Chinatown and takes it home as a Christmas present for his likable teenage son, Zach Galligan. With the gift, he passes along a warning from the inscrutable Chinese that the creature must never get wet, be allowed into the sunshine or fed after midnight.

For awhile, all is extremely precious as the little furry thing goes through an array of facial expressions and heart-warming attitudes. And there's also mixed in some genuine, if shopworn, amusement that Axton is a hopelessly muddled inventor and Galligan and mother Frances Lee McCain must put up with life with his labor-saving devices that are always more trouble than they're worth.

Given the warning that came with it, however, the creature inevitably is going to create problems, which the picture's initial sweetness suggests will probably be high-spirited but innocent. This is not to be and — given the explicit horror that follows — will probably be the reason "Gremlins" won't begin to approach "E.T." business. The change in tone will turn away the family-fun seekers.

Without giving away too much, suffice to say the first creature spawns a townful of evil, snarling, drooling, maniacal killer-creatures who are bound to cause a lot of woe before their predictable downfall.

But even here, Dante and crowd can't be content with sheer menace. In between snarls and drools, the evil creatures are just as likely to put on funny hats, sing Christmas carols or spin into some snazzy break dancing as they are to kill someone. Whatever is a grabber at the moment.

The humans are little more than dress-extras for the mechanics and it's not surprising the cast is finally credited in order of appearance.

But since "Gremlins" is so much his triumph, it should be noted the creatures were "designed, created and operated" by Chris Walas' company.—*Har.*

Finders Keepers
(COLOR)

Limited outlook for frantic caper comedy.

Hollywood, May 15.

A Warner Brothers release of a CBS Theatrical Films presentation. Produced by Sandra Marsh, Terence Marsh. Executive producer, Richard Lester. Directed by Lester. Stars Michael O'Keefe, Beverly D'Angelo, Louis Gossett Jr. Screenplay, Ronny Graham, Terence Marsh, Charles Dennis, based on novel, "The Next To Last Train Ride," by Dennis; camera (Technicolor), Brian West; editor, John Victor Smith; music, Ken Thorne; sound, Peter Hardford; art direction, J. Dennis Washington; assistant director, Christopher Newman; associate producer, Dusty Symonds. Reviewed at Warner Bros., Burbank, May 15, 1984. (MPAA Rating: R). Running time: **96 MINS.**

Michael Rangeloff	Michael O'Keefe
Standish Logan	Beverly D'Angelo
Century	Louis Gossett Jr.
Josef Sirola	Ed Lauter
Stapleton	David Wayne
Mayor Frizzoli	Brian Dennehy
Police chief Norris	John Schuck
Estelle Norris	Timothy Blake
Georgiana Latimer	Pamela Stephenson
Lane Biddlecoff	Jim Carrey
Agent Ormond	Jack Riley

Director Richard Lester returns to his pell-mell trademark and the result is maddening. Interesting cast is wasted, with bright exception of Beverly D'Angelo. Caper comedy, much of the action promisingly set on a train, is so edgy and fragmented that boxoffice outlook for this first CBS Theatrical-Warner Bros. linkup since "Table For Five" is highly spotty.

Using small towns in Alberta province to serve as representations of contemporary American West (which doesn't quite work, by the way), producers Sandra and Terence Marsh hang their frenetic tale of stolen money, chases and deceptions on several characters racing up and down a train enroute from California to Nebraska.

There's $5,000,000 in a coffin in the baggage car, there's a sexy neurotic (D'Angelo, who steals the movie), a bumbling con man (toplined Michael O'Keefe), a razor sharp con man (Louis Gossett Jr., on screen only briefly), a sweaty heavy (Ed Lauter), and a gregarious old train conductor (David Wayne).

Add an angry female Roller Derby team, a concluding encounter with a house that's being towed, a hideaway Vietnam defector, a blond moll in a veil, and a deputy's nymphomaniacal wife (a mildly humorous bit featuring Timothy Blake) and the parts add up to pieces that artlessly lurch and hurtle around. There's no sense of ensemble or a background tapestry.

Cinematically, the tone of the film is uneven, with some bucolic rural scenes that appear to be from another film. The editing makes one squirm. The material as scripted by Ronny Graham, Terence Marsh and Charles Dennis (from Dennis' book, "The Next To Last Train Ride") demanded a light, stylish directorial touch. Lester's touch isn't necessarily heavy — it's merely frantic; subsequent orchestration is one unrelenting clash of cymbals. — *Loyn.*

Viva la Vie!
(Long Live Life!)
(FRENCH-COLOR)

Paris, May 15.

UGC release of a Films 13-UGC-Top 1 coproduction. Produced, written and directed by Claude Lelouch. Stars Michel Piccoli, Charlotte Rampling, Jean-Louis Trintignant, Evelyne Bouix, Charles Aznavour. Script collaborator, Jerome Tonnerre; Camera (color), Bernard Lutic; art director, Jacques Bufnoir; sound, Harald Maury; editor, Hughes Darmois and Pauline Leroi; music, Didier Barbelivien. Reviewed at the UGC Normanide theater, Paris, May 13, 1984. Running time: **110 MINS.**

With: Charlotte Rampling, Michel Piccoli, Jean-Louis Trintignant, Evelyne Bouix, Charles Aznavour, Anouk Aimée, Laurent Malet, Raymond Pellegrin, Charles Gerard, Tanya Lopert.

Claude Lelouch reaches new depths in vacuity in his new film, "Viva la Vie." Produced in utmost secrecy, it finally was presented to the press with the request that it's plot not be revealed, since the narrative is conceived as a sort of cinematic Chinese puzzle, complete with final surprise solution(s).

With his usual technical virtuosity, Lelouch zigzags dizzily through a labyrinth of plot twists and genre lampoons. But all the hocus-pocus, actors' routines and hand-held camera acrobatics hide a gaping void. The answer to the puzzle is a howling cliché, the kind used by directors who don't know how to undo an intricate story-telling knot.

Lelouch's central situation concerns the simultaneous disappearance of an industrialist (Michel Piccoli) and a young actress (Evelyne Bouix) in inexplicable circumstances. Just as suddenly, both reappear, unable to remember what happened. They vanish again, return, vanish, etc.

Soon it becomes apparent that both have been kidnapped by extraterrestrials who want to use them as a mouthpiece to warn the earth on its dangerous nuclear antics.

But that's not it at all ...

An all-star cast has been rounded up by Lelouch for this futile charade, including Jean-Louis Trintignant, who gets to spout some gaseous observations on the art of acting (he plays Bouix' acting teacher-husband) and Charles Az-

navour as the mysterious owner of a Russian restaurant.

Tech credits ar flashy. Pic is drawing business locally and could tease its way into foreign situations, top name cast aiding. —*Len.*

Bastille
(DUTCH-COLOR)

Amsterdam, May 6.

A Euro-Centrafilm release of a MGS Film production. Produced by Anne Lordon and George Sluizer. Directed by Rudolf van den Berg. Screenplay, Annemarie van de Putte, Van den Berg, Leon de Winter, based on De Winter's story "La Place de la Bastille." Stars Derek de Lint. Camera (color), Toni Kuhn; sound, Piotr van Dijk; editor, Mario Steenbergen; music, Boudewijn Tarenskeen. Reviewed at Cinema International, Amsterdam, May 4, 1984. Running time: **105 MINS.**

Paul de Wit	Derek de Lint
Mieke	Geert de Jong
Nadine	Evelyne Dress
Midwife	Loudi Nijhoff
Professor Polak	Ischa Meijer
Mrs. Friedlander	Dora Doll

Rudolf van den Berg's controversial docus won him prizes, critical acclaim and at times vehement attacks. In style they tend more and more towards fiction, so the decision to make a feature, "Bastille," was not surprising. Neither was the meticulous care lavished on technical credits. Pic looks and sounds as if the budget had been several times higher than the final $230,000.

What makes surprise is debutant Van den Berg's decisive directing of actors, from children to very senior players, resulting in very good performances by all thesps (much better than expected from some), culminating in a cameo appearance by veteran actress Loudi Nijhoff, a small treasure of a performance as a retired midwife asked to remember details of a night 40 years ago. She does her best, but her mind starts to wander. She is perfectly lucid, but getting old and worn. Nijhoff is superb.

Nearly every sequence is good in itself, demands and gets attention. Unfortunately they don't jell. It's not the fault of the storytelling (except for a too loose and liberal use of flashbacks) — it's the story itself.

Paul de Wit was born during the war in an Amsterdam garret where his Jewish parents were hiding. Paul was brought up by foster parents, after his parents were sent to Auschwitz.

Paul is now a high school history teacher, happily married to non-Jewish Mieke. Paul is writing a book about the flight of the royal family to Varennes during the French revolution.

Paul likes to fantasize "what, if?" He believes Chance acts as a wonderfully arbitrary referee. he would like to believe in magic that would bring his perhaps imaginary twin brother to life, bring back his parents, find him roots. He fancies himself as neither Jew nor gentile; he does not believe in God, nor much in anything else. He does not quite fit into his life, so he uses his imagination to change the world to fit him.

Van den Berg tries to integrate a thriller (the search for the brothers), a romance with a Jewish girl in Paris, the quest for a definition of what it is to be a Jew, anger and anguish which have the same root, a man who follows his instincts, but would rather die of shame than show any feeling — some of these strands become loose ends, probably also on the cutting room floor.

Nevertheless, the problems raised, film's evident integrity, technical polish and outstanding level of acting should bring it interesting gate prospects, also abroad, in art houses, at festivals, and in ethnically interested quarters.
—*Wall.*

The Last Horror Film
(COLOR)

Poorly done horror satire, set at the Cannes Film Fest.

A Twin Continental Films release of a Shere Prods. Ltd. production. Produced by Judd Hamilton, David Winters. Directed by Winters. Features entire cast. Screenplay, Hamilton, Tom Classen, Winters; camera (Technicolor), Tom DeNove; editor, Chris Barnes, Edward Salier; music, Jesse Frederick, Jeff Koz; sound, David Stephenson; art direction, Brian Savagar; production design, Jeff Sharpe; assistant director, Devin Goldenberg; second unit director, Marty Ollstein; additional photography, John McCallum, Victor Petrashevitch, Mike Delaney; associate producer, Sean Casey. Reviewed on Media Home Entertainment vidcassette, N.Y., May 12, 1984. (MPAA Rating: R). Running time: **87 MINS.**
Jana Bates ....Caroline Munro
Vinny Durand ....Joe Spinell
Alan Cunningham ....Judd Hamilton
Marty Bernstein ....Devin Goldenberg
Stanley Kline ....David Winters
Susan Archer......Stanley Susanne Benton
Vinny's mother...............Mary Spinell
Bret Bates.................Glenn Jacobson
Girl in Jacuzzi ....J'len Winters
Stripper....................Sharon Hughes
Jonathan ....Sean Casey
Cowboy ....Don Talley
Reporter ....June Chadwick

"The Last Horror Film" is a low-grade vanity production filmed in part at the 1981 Cannes Film Festival. Retitled "The Fanatic" (to capitalize on picture's resemblance to "The Fan"), but as yet unreleased theatrically by its domestic distrib, film is available to homevideo fans.

It emerges as a professionally crewed home movie, with filmmakers, their families and several crew members pressed into service as actors. In a followup to his 1980 "Maniac" horror vehicle, character actor Joe Spinell again toplines as a schizophrenic modeled after the Travis Bickle cabbie in Martin Scorsese's "Taxi Driver."

As Vinny Durand, Spinell is N.Y.

cabbie infatuated with horror film star Jana Bates (Caroline Munro, who also starred in "Maniac"). He dreams of directing and starring with Bates in his own horror opus, "The Loves Of Dracula," and goes to the Cannes fest to try to interest her in the project. While he's there, numerous associates of Bates are gorily murdered, with Vinny the prime suspect. A surprise twist at film's climax resolves the mystery, but its effectiveness is nullified by a stupid ending in which the entire film (including numerous film-within-film segments) is revealed to be a movie Vinny is showing to his mom (played by Spinell's real mom).

Director David Winters, better known for his tv efforts, makes okay use of freebies, pressing into service the throngs of Cannes fest shutterbugs and gala crowds as unpaid extras (Isabelle Adjani, Isabelle Huppert, Karen Black, Kris Kristofferson and Marcello Mastroianni make unintended glimpse-only appearances as well). Regarding horror, he fails to have it both ways, pouring on the gore effects, sexploitation and stock slasher motifs while attempting to criticize the genre.

Most distressing is the film's cavalier on-screen citing of "Taxi Driver," the Hinckley/Jodie Foster/Reagan incident and even the killing of John Lennon as parallels to the story being told. Besides ripping off "Driver," picture carefully imitates Michael Powell's "Peeping Tom."

Ironically, the far-fetched premise that Cannes would honor a horror film (Bates beats out Julie Christie, Meryl Streep, Faye Dunaway and Jane Fonda for the best actress award in the jury vote here) is not that goofy; in retrospect, Adjani *did* win best actress at Cannes honors in 1981 for Andrzej Zulawski's pretentious horror opus "Possession." Even so, the picture plays as if it were taking place at Avoriaz or some other fantasy film fest rather than Cannes.

A sweaty Spinell is unbearably hammy in the lead role, trying for mock-pathos but yielding a camp performance. Well-cast British beauty Munro is done in by the post-synched dialog, with a neutral American voice dubbed in for hers. Sloppy production has many names misspelled in credits and on-screen (both Spinell's real name and character name are variously displayed in error). —*Lor.*

Buldoci a Tresne
(Bulldogs and Cherries)
(CZECH-COLOR)

Sydney, April 29.

A Barrandov Studios production of Ceskoslovensky Film. Directed by Juraj Herz. Features entire cast. Screenplay, Ivan Garis, Herz; camera (color), Jiri Machane; editor, Jaromir Janasek; music, Petr Hapka. No

further credits available. Reviewed on 0/28 TV, Sydney, April 28, 1984. Running time: **104 MINS.**
Cast: Marian Labuda, Miroslav Streda, Jiri Hrzan, Rudolf Hrusinsky, Josef Dvorak, Karel Effa, Vaclav Kovarik, Jirina Bohdalova, Lenka Korinkova, Dasia Veskrnova, Juraj Herz, Frantisek Nemec, Jan Schmid, Jana Radova, Jiri Menzel.

Juraj Herz was responsible for some fine Czech films in the late '60s, including the black comedy "The Cremator" in 1969. His recent work has been disappointing, and this 1981 effort (reviewed for the record) is no exception. It's a bland parody of gangster movies which spends a lot of time zapping around exotic locations (Rome, Vienna, Amsterdam, Prague), but almost none providing interesting characters or valid humor.

Marian Labuda plays Carmello Mushillo, a Mafia chief who runs foul of the Big Boss (Rudolf Hrusinski) and flees Italy, winding up in Prague with his two cohorts. He becomes involved with various ingenious local criminals, including three scurvy villains an a larcenous blonde.

Film is technically fine and looks as if it could have been expensive by Czech standards. But the script, by Herz and Ivan Garis, is very thin and the jokes either so local as to prove resistant to travel, or nonexistent in the first place. Acting is unrestrained and generally unamusing.

It's sad to see a talent like Herz wasted with such trivial material. The helmer himself plays a criminal who spends his time disguised as a rich Arab, while another fine Czech director, Jiri Menzel, is briefly glimpsed as a befuddled waiter. —*Strat.*

Hell's Kitchen Chronicle
(DOCU-COLOR-16m)

Famous New York neighborhood undergoing change.

A production of Lightworks Productions Ltd., N.Y. Coproduced and codirected by Maren and Reed Erskine. Camera (color), editing, narrator, Maren Erskine; research and sound, Reed Erskine; post-production, Women's Interart Center. Reviewed at Harold Clurman Theater, N.Y., April 9, 1984. Running time: **60 MINS.**

Warner Brothers' "Hell's Kitchen," 1939, a vehicle for the Dead End Kids, featured up-and-coming actor Ronald Reagan in a supporting role as a reformed crook who turns straight lawyer. Hell's Kitchen is like that, it changes people, and the changes Hell's Kitchen is undergoing today are the subject of this interesting documentary. This is "West Side Story" country, a tough district in Manhattan.

Novels, plays and films have often used Hell's Kitchen as a dramatic street scene for gangland thrillers and working-class love stories. Because Hell's Kitchen is

adjacent to Tin Pan Alley and Broadway, the district's former speakeasies, theatrical boarding houses and small hotels have figured in some of those breaking-into-show-business yarns.

Now much of that is changed. During hot summers, teenage boys no longer dive off the Hell's Kitchen docks. The ships and barges are gone.

This "Chronicle" details the efforts of Hell's Kitchen folks to preserve their community, rousting out the junkies and prostitutes. A militant Catholic priest is among the activists trying to save Hell's Kitchen from the bulldozers. Hell's Kitchen is proud of its "Theater Row," a dozen small legit houses on 42d Street west of Ninth Avenue, already a phenomenon in American theater.

In Hell's Kitchen today, retired vaudevilleans still turn out for nostalgia evenings, croaking forgotten tunes and hastening to display tattered press clippings. Some ladies are corseted breathlessly, heavily rouged, teetering on high heels. Some men with dyed hair gamely defy their years in youthful jackets. Hell's Kitchen for these troupers is their last engagement.

Now the Hell's Kitchen ethnic delis are becoming smart shops for the new high-rise condo clientele. Bodegas are out, boutiques are in. These are "disposable communities," the film says. The land is worth more than the buildings, fit only to be razed and supplanted by more profitable structures.

Wife-husband film team Maren and Reed Erskine — she shoots, he records sound — live in Hell's Kitchen and produced this film about their neighborhood with grants from Creative Artists Public Service, New York State Council on The Arts, the American Film Institute and the National Endowment for The Arts.

Part of the Erskine project was to compile oral-history interviews with ancient Hell's Kitchen residents, also to shoot and mount exhibits of still photographs for local display.

Their "Chronicle" film evolved from those projects and shows thorough research, including the use of old b&w newsreels and stills. Most visible is their affection for Hell's Kitchen, and their alarm about its fate.

"Chronicle" has been screened on television in Norway and Holland, is set for the Margaret Mead Film Festival, N.Y., in September, and will air via PBS in the fall.
— *Hitch.*

Mission Hill
(U.S.-COLOR)

Sydney, April 25.

A Still River Films produciton. Produced & directed by Robert Jones. Features entire cast. Associate producers, David Newhouse, Anne Jones; script, Anne & Robert Jones; camera (DuArt color), John Hoover; editor, William Anderson; sound, Mike Ryan; art director, nanny Starr; music, Don Wilkins. Reviewed on VHS Videotape, Sydney, April 25, 1984. Running time: **87 MINS.**

Danny Doyle	Brian Burke
Laura Doyle	Alice Barrett
Mrs. Doyle	Barbara Orson
Steve	Robert Kerman
Kevin	Daniel Silver
Bonnie	Nan Mulleneaux
Michael Doyle	John Mahoney
Freddie	Jerry Gershman
Smokey	Frank McCarthy
Bill Casey	Dick McGoldrich
Lenny	Paul Dunn
Valerie	Trish Holland

Dated 1982, this independently made Boston-based feature has emerged on the Filmways video label in Australia and is reviewed for the record.

Pic deals with the disintegration of a lower-middle class Boston family living in the Mission Hill district. Mrs. Doyle (Barbara Orson) has been abandoned by her drunken husband and is losing control of her three children. Daughter Laura (Alice Barrett) has a good job as a private secretary, but throws it over in favor of trying her luck as a singer. She takes up with a smooth musician (Robert Kerman) who eventually dumps her when he gets a crack at the big time in L.A.

Elder son Danny (Brian Burke) is in high school, but can't hack it and spends most of his time stealing car tapedecks and gambling with his buddies. When he graduates to pinching a new car from a lot, and gets involved in a hit-and-run, his fate is sealed. Second son, Michael (John Mahoney), who's just a kid, is seen starting on the same road via stealing comics from local store.

Situations unveiled are not unfamiliar, but benefit from a freshness in the treatment of the non-Hollywood filmmakers. There's a feeling here that the familiar characters are being seen for the first time. Relaxed, natural acting from all concerned helps, with Brian Burke and Alice Barrett standouts who could go further.

Chalk this up as a low-budgeter which indicates plenty of promise, though maybe a bit too familiar and insubstantial to make its mark. Good location lensing by John Hoover helps, and there's a good music score by Don Wilkins with several original and tuneful songs.

End credits include a dedication to Levi Hart, 1966-1980, indicating the film may contain biographical material. —*Strat.*

Silent Madness
(COLOR-3-D)

Okay depth effects in cornball horror pic.

An Almi Pictures release, presented by MAG Enterprises and Gregory Earls. A Sel-

im Picture Associates Ltd. production. Exec producer, Earls. Produced by Simon Nuchtern, William P. Milling. Directed by Nuchtern. Features entire cast. Screenplay, Robert Zimmerman, Milling; additional dialog, Nelson de Mille: camera (Precision color, ArriVision 3-D), Gerald Feil; editor, Philip Stockton; music, Barry Salmon; art direction, Brian Martin; sound, Rolf Pardula; assistant director, Michele Thibeault; production manager, Zimmerman; special makeup effects, Makeup EFX Labs (Allan Apone, etc.); script supervisor, Marvin Kitrosser; post-production, August Films Inc. Reviewed at RKO Warner 1 theater, N.Y., May 4, 1984. (No MPAA Rating). Running time: **97 MINS.**

Dr. Joan Gilmore	Belinda Montgomery
Mrs. Collins	Viveca Lindfors
Howard Johns	Solly Marx
Mark McGowan	David Greenan
Sheriff Liggett	Sydney Lassick
Dr. Kruger	Roderick Cook
Dr. Anderson	Stanja Lowe
Dr. Van Dyce	Ed Van Nuys

"Silent Madness" (known during production last year under the titles "Omega Factor" and "Night Killer") is a highly derivative terror film boasting some effective 3-D effects. Lacking the brand name of a "Friday The 13th" and coming very late in the current depth pic cycle, film looks to modest b.o. action.

Plot, a pastiche of innumerable formula horror films, has Belinda Montgomery toplining as Dr. Gilmore, a dedicated shrink at Gotham's Cresthaven Mental Hospital who discovers that due to a computer error a homicidal paranoid patient Howard Johns (Solly Marx) has been released instead of the docile John Howard. Hospital administrators led by Dr. Anderson (Stanja Lowe) attempt a coverup and Gilmore heads for the small town of Barrington (where Marx committed gruesome murders at a girl's school sorority many years ago) searching for the nut.

Aided by the local newspaper editor (David Greenan), she poses as an ex-Delta Omega sorority sister to check out Johns' old stomping grounds, at the sorority house run by suspicious-looking Mrs. Collins (Viveca Lindfors). Gilmore has to fight off both Johns (who has been killing girls again on campus with no one noticing) and a pair of malevolent hospital attendants sent to get rid of both Johns and her.

Laughably asinine dialog and tons of verbal plot exposition and explanations hurt the film, which is best viewed as a demonstration of 3-D effects. Cinematographer Gerald Feil, who scored with the 3-D "Friday The 13th Part 3," provides effective deep focus, plus intriguing overhead shots and tracking shots during chase sequences. The problem, as usual, is the intervening footage when the depth process isn't necessary: director Simon Nuchtern's dialog scenes are dull and give one time to notice the variable light intensity and dark fringes around the 3-D action. He also permits some awful overacting, which reduces an occasionally ultra-violent opus (Johns relies on

various outlandish and gory modes of killing) to mere camp. — *Lor.*

The Final Terror
(COLOR)

Trite horror opus lacks interest, despite big-name cast.

An Aquarius release of an Arkoff International Pictures presentation of a Watershed production. Presented by Samuel Arkoff. Produced by Joe Roth; coproducer, J. Stein Kaplan; associate producers, Gary Shusett, Anthony J. Ridio. Directed by Andrew Davis. Features entire cast. Screenplay, Jon George, Neill Hicks, Ronald Shusett; camera (Deluxe color), Andreas Davidescu (Andrew Davis?); editor, Paul Rubell, Erica Flaum; music, Susan Justin; sound, John Mason; assistant director, Luca Kouimelis; production manager, Jim Dennett; special makeup effects, Ken Myers; stunt direction, Jeannie Epper; exec in charge of post-production, Allan Holzman. Reviewed at Manhattan 1 theater, N.Y., May 18, 1984. (MPAA Rating: R.) Running time: **82 MINS.**

Zorich	John Friedrich
Cerone	Adrian Zmed
Windy	Daryl Hannah
Margaret	Rachel Ward
Mike	Mark Metcalf

Also with: Ernest Harden Jr., Akosua Busia, Lewis Smith, Cindy Harrell, Joe Pantoliano.

"The Final Terror" is a very poorly made (in 1981) horror picture finally released after an aborted (planned but unrealized) national launch set for last fall by since-removed distrib Comworld. Only possible interest here is presence of several stars of the future in the cast, but their assignments are brief. Among the numerous title changes on this film are: "Three Blind Mice," "Carnivore," "The Forest PrimEvil" and "The Campsite Massacre."

Director Andrew Davis (who may have doubled as cinematographer, given the suspicious-looking credit for same) delivers a sluggish, poorly lensed effort in the unrewarding campers-in-jeopardy genre. As cornily introed by the device of a scary tale around a campfire, a lunatic woman is on the loose in the woods, with four young couples as potential victims, along with a goofy guide (who turns out to be the nutcase's son).

Very little happens apart from red herring scares and killings here, with the potential "Deliverance" and "Southern Comfort" survival format dissipated by the presence of women, a horror pic necessity. Derived perhaps from the shooting title "Three Blind Mice," pic repetitively emphasizes a neck fetish, with most killings and threat of same involving throat-cutting or strangulation.

Producer Joe Roth and cohorts scored something of a coup in casting two of the (subsequently) hottest young actresses in Hollywood: Daryl Hannah and Rachel Ward, in the usually no-name interchangeable potential victim roles, as well as tapping Adrian Zmed for a male lead prior to his "T.J. Hook-

er" tv stardom. Unfortunately, the actresses are given nothing to do, not even exploitable nude scenes, and Ward's acting here is dreadful.

Tech credits are subpar, with the usual gore closeups for hardup horror fans. — *Lor.*

Uindii
(Races)
(JAPANESE-WEST GERMAN-COLOR)

Tokyo, April 29.

A Toho-Towa release. Produced by Kenichi Nakamura and Manfred Durniok. Directed by Masato Harada. Screenplay by Harada, Akinori Kikuchi, Yuji Izumi, Dar Sorrell, F.L. Horn, from a story by Izumi; camera (color), Witold Sobocinski; music, Akira Inoue. Reviewed at Yamaha Hall Tokyo, April 28, 1984. Running time: **110 MINS.**

Kei	Hiroyuki Watanabe
Anna	Chris
Sam	Leslie Malton
Leo	Claus-Theo Gartner
Barbara	Barbara Stanek
Denise	Olivia Pascal
Monique	Deborah Sasson
Gains	Dean Reed
Mr. Duffner	Patrick Stewart

The accumulated portrayals of Westerners in domestic films over the past several years are not calculated to promote the cause of international understanding.

However, "Uindii," in its treatment of a relationship between a Japanese and an American, is such a departure from the norm as to be almost revolutionary. Revolutionary because the Japanese and American who meet and fall in love are not treated as a Japanese and an American, but simply as a man and a woman.

The man is Kei (Hiroyuki Watanabe), a professional motorcycle racer who has a young daughter, Anna (played by a monomonikered Tokyo-based model, Chris), from his first marriage to a popular (foreign) vocalist. The woman is Sam (Leslie Malton), a professional motorcycle mechanic currently unemployed. Man and woman run into each other on the racing circuit and a romance develops slowly, with the little girl lending her help and approval.

Superficially a fairly conventional love story, it is told in an endearing, engaging manner and contains delightful surprises in characterization that perhaps can be best appreciated by someone familiar with the East is East/West is West philosophy underpinning the majority of "Japanese meets Foreigner" releases from the major studios. Kei, for example, is a completely international individual who survives without Japanese female companionship (all his girl friends are Caucasian), without expressing his deepest feelings in his native tongue (he is fluent in English), even without an occasional spiritually uplifting visit to the motherland (he never sets foot in Japan, but maintains an apartment in Berlin during the racing season, and lives in Canada in the off season). The breakup of his first marriage had nothing to do with his nationality and everything to do with his wife's opposition to his dangerous profession.

While far too many Japanese films dealing with Westerners make use of nonprofessional foreign actors, this pic features excellent performances by Leslie Malton, an American-born graduate of Britain's Royal Academy of Dramatic Arts and one of Germany's leading stage actresses, and Patrick Stewart, a member of the Royal Shakespeare Company and a veteran of stage and screen.

It's difficult to imagine a better choice than Watanabe to play a dashing athlete capable of setting feminine hearts aflutter, a classically handsome former model, he has the looks women of any country could fall for. Further, his English-language delivery is believably natural.

This is only the second feature directed by Harada, whose debut film in '79 was the cleverly constructed, Howard Hawks-influenced "Sarabe, Eiga Tomo Yo." It is worth noting that the two domestic films of the past decade which have been the most evenhanded in their treatment of foreigners are the one under review and Toho's "Rongu Ran," both directed by Japanese who have lived and worked abroad. — *Bail.*

Prince Charming
(HONG KONG-COLOR)

Hong Kong, May 8.
A Shaw Brothers presentation and release. Presented by Sir Run Run Shaw. Produced by Mona Fong. Directed by Wong Jing. Stars Kenny Bee, Cherry Chung, Maggie Cheung, Rosemund Kwan, Chen Pai-Chiang, Charlie Tsao, Chen Hui-min. Screenplay, Wong Jing; camera (color), Lan Nei Tsai, Li Hsin Yeh; sound, Hsu Jin Chin, Chung Chen Tao; music, So Chun Hou, Stephen Shing. Reviewed at Jade theater, May 7, 1984, Hong Kong. Running time: 100 MINS.
(Cantonese soundtrack with English subtitles)

Prince Charming is Kenny Bee and it is indeed a charming and captivating Cantonese comedy from Shaw Bros. that follows the light hearted style and the pop idol appeal of the male lead star (who also sings the soundtrack songs) along with some come-on femme screen favorites.

Pleasant, fast moving, uncomplicated and adorned with modern, colloquial verbal-visual comedy, the picture relates closely to the contemporary tastes of the Hong Kong youth market. The feature is proving to be a long running summer hit as producer Mona Fong hits the target once again as in Bee's "Let's Make Laugh" bonanza. It is the type of wholesome movie that Troy Donahue and Sandra Dee would have made, if they

had been doing Cantonese comedies during their heyday.

Bee plays an introverted and girl shy but wealthy young man persistently hounded by his parents to get romantically involved. Giving assistance in the way of the heart and girls in bikinis is Hong Kong-bred lothario Lolantho (Chen Pai-Chiang). They did their first training course in Waikiki Beach (shot on location) with disastrous results. They eventually end up in Hong Kong when Bee is asked by daddy to investigate the suspected business embezzlement of the company manager (Charlie Tsao). Bee is exposed once more to the two naughty ladies he met accidentally in Honolulu, Cherry Chung and Maggie Cheung (both Miss Hong Kong beauty contests graduates).

In order to check out secretly the discrepancy in the finances of the Hong Kong operation, Bee poses as the lowly chauffeur of his good friend Lolantho. As protective measure, manager Tsao summons his seductive cousin Rosemund Kwan to lure the unwordly millionaire bachelor from the boardroom to her bedroom which has been planned to end up in a church wedding.

But in this type of plot, the right boy gets the right girl and despite the mixups and petty quarrels, they end up in the right arms. Bee has Cherry and Chen has Maggie, while Rosemund ends up with the wedding gown and the floral arrangement.

There are many fashionably funny sequences here with universal appeal and one need not know Cantonese to comprehend the simple humor. Bee is now a fine comic actor who tends to be typecast in the same role while the three main ladies make lovely decorative objects, even in the most slapstick of situations. "Prince Charming" may not win awards but surely it is a winner at the domestic boxoffice. — *Mel.*

Der Beginn Aller Schrecken Ist Liebe
(Love Is Where The Trouble Begins)
(WEST GERMAN-COLOR)

Berlin, April 23.
A coproduction of Provobis Film Jürgen Haase, Hamburg, Helke Sander Filmproduktion, Berlin, and Second German Television, Mainz, Christopher Holch, tv producer. Stars Sander, Lou Castel. Directed by Sander. Screenplay, Sander, Dörte Haak; camera (color), Martin Schäfer; sets, Jürgen Rieger; music, Heiner Goebbels; editing, Barbara von Weitershausen. Reviewed at Yorck-Kino, Berlin, April 23, '84. Running time: 114 MINS.
Cast: Helke Sander (Freya), Lou Castel (Traugott), Rebecca Pauly (Irmtraut), Katrin Seybold (Anna), Monica Bleibtreu (Gisela), Malte Jaeger (Father), Uwe Bohm (Andres), Hark Bohm (Torsten), Ulrike S. (Vera), Roswitha Soukup (Marion).

Still the best femme helmer on the scene in Germany, Helke Sand-

er takes her time between productions to pour as much personal philosophical reflection into her films as possible. Obviously she feels a certain obligation to the women's lib movement in Germany and Europe in view of being the editor-in-chief of film mag Frauen und Film, but she doesn't hammer the theme to death by making features of a tiring repetitive nature for the "in" crowd, particularly exhibitors with "For Women Only" signs up in the windows. Her first short as a student at the Berlin Film and TV Academy, "Subjectivity" (1966), still rates a gem in only four minutes on the femme theme, while her first feature, "The All-Around Reduced Personality" (1977), is a New German Cinema classic.

One notes Sander constructs one film on top of another, so it's always advisable to go into the screening sufficiently oriented. Thus, for her latest pic "Love Is Where The Trouble Begins," its theme and motifs recall her prior "The Subjective Factor" (1981) and "The All-Around Reduced Personality." As the writer-director-protagonist of all these features (only in "Subjective Factor" did she use an alter-ego thesp to stand in for herself), she is able to fall back on not only relevant personal experiences but also describe with sometimes painful accuracy the ups and downs, the dreams and the reality, of the current women's movement.

"Love Is Where The Trouble Begins" is about two friends, Freya (Sander) and Irmtraut (Rebecca Pauly), who suddenly realize the former's longtime boyfriend is now the latter's fulltime lover. What's more, the male in the middle, Traugott (Lou Castel), is a jellyfish who can't choose between the two women in his life. His position is simply: "I have to be loved!"

Freya takes the hint and departs for a time to let everything settle. But love is such an inordinate emotion that she can't forget Traugott — even after she's thrown him out of her apartment as well as her life. Yet she's not prepared to make compromises either. But the more she broods, the angrier she gets — to the point of once tearing apart the office of her former boyfriend, who runs a doctor's practice as an exercise in humanitarian ideals. And so the story goes, from one encounter to another, until Traugott packs up one day and is off to serve in a medical corps in South America with his other girlfriend. Freya, on the banks of the Elbe, watches his ship pull out of Hamburg's harbor.

A bit too long at nearly two hours running time, "Love Is Where The Trouble Begins" is nevertheless rewarding cinema for film buffs who like witty dialog, sharp lens-

ing (Martin Schäfer), and a tale with plenty of human twists.
— *Holl.*

The Pit
(CANADIAN-COLOR)

A New World Pictures release of an Amulet Pictures Ltd. production. Executive producer, John C. Bassett. Produced by Bennet Fode. Directed by Lew Lehman. Features entire cast. Screenplay, Ian A. Stuart; camera (Medallion color), Fred Guthe; editor, Rik Morden; music, Victor Davies; art direction, Peter E. Stone; sound, John Megill; production manager, Donna Smith; assistant director, Christopher Danton; stunt coordinator, Karen Pike; special effects costuming, Dahl Delu, Yvonne Bromovitz Delu, Tracy Reid. Reviewed on Embassy Home Entertaiment vidcassette, N.Y., May 13, 1984. (MPAA Rating: R.) Running time: 96 MINS.
Jamie Benjamin .... Sammy Snyders
Sandra .... Jeannie Elias
Marg Livingstone ..... Laura Hollingsworth
Mrs. Lynde: .... Sonja Smits
Mrs. Benjamin................ Laura Press
Abergail .... Andrea Swartz

Filmed in Wisconsin by a Canadian company in 1980, "The Pit" (aka "Teddy") is an unsuccessful horror film that fails to adequately develop a very interesting (and rarely explored) genre premise: precocious child sexuality. Film was marginally released theatrically last fall and is now available on videocassette by virtue of distrib New World's deal with Embassy Home Entertainment.

Where previous horror pics such as "The Exorcist" and "Carrie" have skirted the taboo issue of youngsters' sexuality, screenwriter Ian A. Stuart addresses the topic directly here. Twelve-year-old Jamie Benjamin (Sammy Snyders) is a problem child, shunned by classmates and neighbors, and given to reading adult girlie magazines and peeping tom activities.

When going away on a house-hunting expedition, his parents leave Jamie in the care of a young babysitter-housekeeper, Sandra (Jeannie Elias), a college coed, who becomes disturbed when Jamie spies on her taking showers and makes sexual advances towards her.

Horror content occurs (and unfortunately turns the pic into a conventional monster opus in the later reels) when Jamie reveals his discovery of a pit in a nearby forest, containing four "trogs" (prehistoric furry little beasts). Afraid his little "friends" will starve, Jamie lures people who are unfriendly to him to the pit and pushes them in for the critters' meals.

Adding uneasily to this basic scifi/horror plot is the supernatural element of Jamie appearing to be under the influence of his teddy bear named Teddy, who (speaking with Snyders' voice, lowered), suggests he feed people to the trogs.

Unfortunately, pic's sexual premise gets lost as action segues to a typical hunt-down-the-monsters format, punctuated by unsuccessful attempts at black humor. Besides the symbolism of the pit and other motifs, film is ripe for analysis when local authorities repress all knowledge of the incidents after dispatching the trogs. A silly epilog scene at Jamie's grandparents' house is tacked on for the requisite horror film twist sendoff.

Director Lew Lehman's bright, cheery visuals are not conducive to the desired horror atmosphere, nor to the study of pathological sexuality. Acting is good. Monster suits design is unusual, but unconvincing. —*Lor.*

Tajemstvi Hradu V Karpatech
(Mysterious Castle In The Carpathians)
(CZECH-COLOR)

Sydney, April 29.

A Barrandov Studios production of Ceskoslovwnsky Film. Directed by Oldrich Lipsky. Features entire cast. Screenplay, Jiri Brdecka, Lipski; camera (color), Viktor Ruzicka; music, Lubos Fiser; editor, Miroslav Hajek; production design, Jan Zazvorka, Rudolf Stahl. Reviewed on 0/28 television, Sydney, April 28, 1984. Running time: **97 MINS.**
Count Felix Teleke....Michal Doclomanski
Salsa Verde...........Evelyna Steimarova
Ignac ....Vlastimil Brodsky
Baron Gore.................Milos Kopecky
Professor Ofranik........Rudolf Hrusinsky
Zutro ....Augustin Kuban
Vilja ....Jan Hartl

Anyone with fond memories of Oldrich Lipsky's 1978 comedy, "Nick Carter In Prague" (also known as "Adele Hasn't Had Dinner Yet") will doubtless welcome this 1981 followup, made with mainly the same team, behind the camera as well as in front, and in much the same style. Earlier film parodied comic-strip detective fiction, and this later entry has a rather more obvious, and welltrod, subject as it parodies horror movies.

Michal Docolomanski plays the intrepid hero once again, this time an opera singer (whose voice shatters glass) and who loves Salsa Verde (Evelyna Steimarova), who's also caught the lustful eye of evil Baron Gorc (Milos Kopecky). Gorc lives in a sinister ruined castle near the little town of Werewolfville, and despite the fact that the year is only 1897, has sponsored a manic inventor (Rudolf Hruskinsky)to come up with various"modern" inventions, including tv, film camera and tape recorder.

Some of the fun comes from the fact that all these inventions are in art deco style, and are the characteristic brainchilds of co-scriptwriter Jiri Brdecka. Pic's best joke comes when the tv, shattered after the hero sings a high note, comes up with the message, "The fault will be rectified!"

Plotting is rather labored and predictable, with the characters over-familiar and a bit stale. But

the inventions give plenty of pleasure, and the film is an amiable, cheerful, old-fashioned joke which, while not quite in the same class as its predecessor, still passes the time amiably enough. —*Strat.*

Hatta La Yattir El-Kokkhan
(The Smoke Should Not Fly)
(EGYPTIAN-COLOR)

Giza, Egypt, May 15.

Produced by New-Art Films. World sales, Trytel. Directed by Ahmed Yehia. Features entire cast. Screenplay, Moustapha Moharam, based on a story by Ihsan Abdel-Kodous; camera (color), Isam Farid; art director, Mahir Abdel-Nour; editor, Inayat El-Sayes; music, Gamal Salama; sound, Magdi Kamel. Reviewed at Cinema City, Giza, Egypt, May 15, 1984. Running time: **120 MINS.**
Cast: Adel Emam, Souhir Ramzi, Sanaa Shafie, Nadiya Arselan.

The story of the material rise and moral fall of a poor peasant boy in Egypt, this is Ahmed Yehia's best film to date and one of the most important Egyptian films of the year.

Thanks to the new free education laws following the July Revolution, a poor, fatherless boy (Adel Emam) is able to attend a posh law school, previously limited to the sons of aristocrats. At first he puts his nose to the grindstone and makes high grades; then he succumbs to the mocking taunts of the rich kids and eases up. All-night parties and fun replace the hours he used to spend with his books.

The first price Emam pays is the inability to love. Neither his poor childhood sweetheart nor the daughter of an ex-Pasha interest him.

Everything changes when his mother falls ill and dies. Emam vows revenge on his well-to-do schoolmates who refused him help in paying for expensive treatment his mother needed. But just at this moment the Open Door policy begins; Emam refuses a job at court in favor of setting up an office of commercial law.

Film makes the point that Emam's moment of illumination at his mother's death is also the beginning of his fall, as he decides to destroy everything, including himself. Cleverly reflecting the social scene before and after Nasser's death, pic shows the negative effects of the Open Door policy in terms of cost to the individual. Through his money Emam buys his way into the People's Assembly; through his money he forces the people who humiliated his childhood sweetheart to bow to her after their marriage.

Yehia and Emam are at the peak of their creative powers in this film. In his last films, Emam has carved out a portrait of the

young man in contemporary Egypt who struggles to learn and live well, but whom society trips up and turns into a criminal. The character is so recognizably true-to-life that the drama is heightened considerably. — *Fari.*

Abwärts
(Out Of Order)
(WEST GERMAN - COLOR)

Berlin, April 27.

A Coproduction of Laura Film, Mutoscop Film, and Dieter Geissler Filmproduktion, Munich; producers, Thomas Schühly, Matthias Deyle; coproducer, Dieter Geissler. Features entire cast. Written and directed by Carl Schenkel. Dialog, Frank Göhre; camera (Color), Jacques Steyn; sets, Toni Lüdi, editing, Norbert Herzner; music, Jacques Zwart. Reviewed at Royal Palast, Berlin, April 26, '84. Running time: **88 MINS.**
Cast: Götz George (Jörg), Renée Soutendijk (Marion), Wolfgang Kieling (Gössman), Hannes Jaenicke (Pit), Claus Wennemann (Heinz), Ralph Richter (Otto), Kurt Raab (Elevator Repair Man), Jan Groth (Porter), Ekmekyemez Firdevs (Cleaning Woman).

Newcomer Carl Schenkel came to filmmaking from journalism, debuting with the feature "Cold As Ice" (1981), and now has made one of the best action thrillers in contemporary German cinema: "Out Of Order." There's little doubt this actioner will do well on the commercial market, and pic could signal a new trend on the local scene to win back fading boxoffice.

"Out Of Order" is exemplary for its overall polished credits. Helmer Schenkel worked for a year-and-a-half on project. One of the frst collaborators he enlisted was Frank Göhre, a Hamburg writer with a deft pen for dialog — indeed, the team of Schenkel-Göhre, would put the majority of today's so-called "Autoren" writer-directors to shame. Here we have a story that takes place mostly inside of a broken-down elevator in a Frankfurt skyscraper, the drama contained in the fact that the breakdown occurred on a Friday evening and here we have a group of four social types (a woman and three men) trapped in a defective lift that may soon be their coffin as well.

Schenkel's casting is also remarkable. Götz George is an ornery Gentleman Jim macho type, and practically carries the film on his broad shoulders. Also impressive are Renée Soutendijk (a Dutch discovery of late), Wolfgang Kieling (burnt-out bookkeeper type soon to be replaced by the inevitable office computer), and Hannes Jaenicke (raw physical presence as an aggressive social dropout).

Pic moves at a fast clip. The dialog is tight and peppery, a constant game of one-upmanship and give-and-take encounters. Jacques Steyn's lensing is another major plus, particularly in the handling of in-tight shots within the confines

of the elevator, and so too the art direction (Toni Lüdi) in rendering a slick surface polish.

It's when the steel coils begin to snap and the elevator with its terrified passengers thunders down the shaft in abrupt intervals that the masks are stripped away rom the individuals in comic-tragic maneuvers. It turns out that the pair from an executive suite advertising agency (George and Soutendijk) are hard-edged types whose relationship in the elevator shifts a hundred degrees when it's revealed that she's in line to take over his job after climbing up the ladder from party-girl secretary. Kieling has chosen this very evening to rob the company's safe, and is about to run away somewhere forever — when the elevator fails, and he's left clutching a quarter-million in his suitcase. Jaenicke works out his frustrations against society by showing off his acrobatic skills, which then develops into a game of death as the antagonism mounts between him and George in the "cage" like two lions mauling each other for mating rights.

The rest follows the usual formula for catastrophe spectacles, but there are twists aplenty to please even sharp-eyed genre critics. And it's the humorous lines that make "Out Of Order" a special treat. Even the title in German has a symbolic twist stripped from the given English translation — it means "Going Down." — *Holl.*

Future Schlock
(AUSTRALIAN-COLOR)

Sydney, April 30.

An Ultimate Show production. Produced, written & directed by Barry Peak & Chris Kiely. Features entire cast. Camera (color), Malcolm Richards; art director, Ian McWha; music, John McCubbery, Doug Sanders; editors, Robert Martin, Ray Pond; sound, Murray Tregonning, Lindsay Wray, Don Borden; production manager, Ray Pond. Reviewed at Valhalla theater, Richmond, Melbourne, April 29, 1984. Running time: **75 MINS.**
Sarah....................Maryanne Fahey
Bear...................Michael Bishop
Ronnnie ....Tracey Callander
Alvin ....Tiriel Mora
Sammy ....Simon Thorpe
Cap'n Fruitcake.................Peter Cox
Sgt. Tatts ....Keith Walker
Skunk.....................Evan Zachariah
Bob ....Gary Adams
Trish.......................Deborah Force
Dr. Allen................Mitchell Faircloth
Simon ....Jason van de Velde
Lois.......................Tracy Harvey
Mrs. Christie..................Effie James
Mr. Christie..................Ron Granger
Minister ....Peter Moon
Il Revolto ....Tom Elovaris
Schoolteacher............Michael Eckersall
Newsreader ....Paul Harris

A chaotic, anrachic punk comedy, made a micro-budget, but with enough going for it to reach its target audience, "Future Schlock" is a mess, but fun.

Its enthusiastic creators, Barry Peak and Chris Kiely, are independent distributors/exhibitors who run the Valhalla cinemas in Sydney and Melbourne and specialize in repertory screenings as well as pics by Andy Warhol, John Waters and others. They know their audience, and made this, their first feature, with that specific audience in mind. Pic opened at Easter in Melbourne, and is already notching up cult status.

Set in the Victorian capital in the 21st century, the posits a post-civil war society in which the middle-class suburbanites defeated the non-conformists and then walled them up in a huge ghetto. Action centers around a ghetto watering hole, Alvin's where the locals meet to do their own thing. Leading lights are Sarah (Maryanne Fahey) and Bear (Michael Bishop) who do a brezzy nightclub act, often directing hostility against suburbanites who drop by on a slumming trip. Unknown to most of their audience is the fact that Sarah and Bear are also the famous Cisco and Pancho, intrepid ghetto-ites who drive from their sleazy compound in a Corvette to harass the police and suburbanites on the outside.

Their heroic assaults on the middleclass include such soups as placing live lobsters in toilet bowels at police headquarters; having Bear take the place of a government minister to announce that the brick veneer houses in which most suburbanites live are now unsafe and must be evacuated; or, by a similar ruse, announcing new "guidelines" for the middleclass, which include painting children green, sleeping with a duck on cold nights, undressing at parties, and burying the family car.

Film is a haphazard affair, with variable performances, uneven writing, and rough sound (with lip synch way off in several scenes). Yet such is the drive and enthusiasm of all concerned that it hardly matters; technical perfection would have been out of place in this kind of abrasive, punk, anti-establishment comedy.

As noted, acting is as hit and miss as the rest, but Fahey and Bishop score as the film's intrepid heroes, and the film unveils at least one new performer of considerable talent, Tracey Callander, who plays Ronnie, a suburbanite who joins the other two in a ménage a trois and embraces the ghetto life with abandon. Callander is excellent and could make her mark in other pics.

Considering it was made for under $80,000, pic is a remarkable achievement for all concerned. It may not travel, as its references and indeed its cast are resolutely from the Melbourne fringe and won't even mean as much in other Aussie cities. Title is inspired as much by John Landis' first feature, "Schlock,' as it is by Alvin Toffler.—*Strat.*

Turumba
(FILIPINO-COLOR)

A presentation of Les Blank/Flower Films, (El Cerrito, Calif.). Written and directed by Kidlat Tahimik. No other credits available. Reviewed on April 24, 1984 Film Forum, N.Y. Running time: **96 MINS.**
With: Herman Abiad, Katrin Luise.
(In Tagalog, with English subtitles.)

Debuted last June at New York's sixth annual Asian American International Film Festival, sponsored by Asian Cine-vision, "Turumba" has resurfaced in Manhattan's Film Forum.

Financed as a 45-minute documentary by East German television, the Filipino-made "Turumba" grew after its broadcast into a delightful fiction feature of twice that length that gently satirizes Western capitalism.

But "Turumba" is no heavy ideological tract, nor a grim propaganda diatribe against vulgrar acquisitiveness. No mention is made in "Turumba" of Americans, of Marcos, or of social unrest in faraway Manila, although all that is sensed as a distant menace.

In this isolated mountain village of the Philippines, the "turumba" of the title means the annual religious festival. But "turumba" also means a simple family life of dignity and worth, of Church-centered continuity, neighborhood stability, a sense of community, although with only marginal comforts for big families having many hungry children.

Having thus documented in its first half-hour the contented lifestyle of this remote village, "Turumba" then introduces a family of characters and its theme, implicit in its documentary prolog, of satisfaction with a close loving family, respect for elders and the traditional virtues, a life with monetary ambitions held to a minimum.

Although hardly a languorous tropical paradise among the bougainvillea, the "Turumba" village is offered by the filmmaker as a symbol of fulfillment. In contrast, the mindless pursuit of money is personified in the film by a West German department-store buyer whose arrival in the village upsets the serenity of the central family. She is plainly a threat.

During the turumba festivities, she spies his ingenious papiermaché toys being sold by the family, who are proud artisans. Recognizing the commercial potential of these toys if mass produced and shipped to Munich for the 1972 Olympics, she buys up everything in sight, orders more toys from the family, including 25,000 toy dachshunds with "Oktoberfest" insignia,

and sets the family on its ears to supply her demand.

Before long, the village band finds itself blaring "Deutschland Uber Alles," as the new prosperity spreads. But it could as well be any alien anthem, as the target villain of "Turumba" is a generalized Western obsession with materialism that corrupts Asian tranquillity.

Because the plot of "Turumba" is minimal, the German buyer is never closely characterized, as she is there merely to serve the parable. The family is the film's center — first threatened, then re-united, a final victory for a wiser alternative to Western economic agressiveness, which is repudiated. The "turumba" has triumphed as the film ends, as once more the annual religious festivities come round in the village.

Kidlat Tahimik is plainly a director to watch. His 1979 feature, "The Perfumed Nightmare," still enjoys a special following. His sly wit and his East-West insights are the core of his style.

The gentle humor of "Turumba," its theme and charming performances, can appeal to theatrical audiences, although its untested Filipino identity, unknown performers and slow pace make it a difficult sell. —*Hitch.*

El-Lanaa
(The Imprecation)
(EGYPTIAN-COLOR)

Cairo, March 15.
Produced by Aly Badrakan and Houssam Aly for Alexandria Films. Directed by Houssein El-Wakil. Screenplay, El-Wakil, Salah Gahin, based on Samuel Fuller's film, "Shock Corridor;" camera (color), Moustrapha Imam; editor, Said El-Sheik; art director and costume designer, Ounsi Abou-Seif. Reviewed at Cinema City, Giza, March 15, 1984. Running time: 120 MINS.
Hamdi .... Nour El-Sharif
Madiha .... Madiha Kamel
Shaker ....Mohammed Kamel
Moustapha ....Abdel-Rahman About-Zahara
Dr. Helmi ....Gamil Rateb
Homos Akdar...........Mohammed Nouh

"The Imprecation" is a first feature by Houssein El-Wakil, trained at the High Film Institute, where he graduated in 1968. His choice of Samuel Fuller's "Shock Corridor" as basis for his debut picture shows the influence Hollywood films have had on young filmmakers in Egypt.

Rewriting Fuller's psychodrama, set in a mental institution, with Salah Gahin, the dialog writer, El-Wakil sets pic in contemporary Egypt with recognizable characters. A newspaper reporter, Nour El-Sharif, pretends to be insane to be committed to an asylum, where he investigates a murder that has been committed. In this version, inmates of the "corridor" are familiar Egyptian figures — a young engineer involved

in a corruption scandal, a singer ruined by his agent, an Arabic-language teacher deceived by his beautiful wife, a physician who kills his wife to spare her the pain of cancer. This social framework goes hand in hand with a metaphysical puzzle, the distance that separates sanity and insanity. In the end, the reporter actually goes mad, a victim of the disease afflicting his society.

Pic is weakest in introducing extraneous characters for purely "entertainment" purposes, like the reporter's wife, who is made to sing in a nightclub at the beginning of the film, despite the fact she's a college student.

Helmer El-Wakil is skillful at stretching a limited number of locales with the aid of art director Ounsi Abou-Seif. Nour El-Sharif's reporter has clearly been influenced by Jack Nicholson's performance in "One Flew Over The Cuckoo's Nest," but manages to make it another in his long list of convincing roles. —*Fari.*

De Witte Waan
(The White Delusion)
(DUTCH-COLOR)

Amsterdam, April 21.
A The Movies release of a Jan Vrijman Cineproductie production. Produced by Jan Vrijman. Written and directed by Adriaan Ditvoorst. Stars Thom Hoffman, Pim Lambeau. Camera (color), Albert Vanderwildt; editor, Edgar Burcksen; music, Clous van Mechelen; sound, Pjotr van Dijk; art directin, Harry Ammerlaan. Reviewed at The Movies, Amsterdam, April 19, 1984. Running time: 101 MINS.
Lazlo ....Thom Hoffman
Mother ....Pim Lambeau
Aunt ....Louise Ruys
Jasja ....Guusje van Tilborgh
Doorman.....................Hans Croiset
Father ....Jules Croiset
Doctor ....Pamela Rose
Lili ....Hilde van Mieghem
Fuji ....Joe Hennes

With more than usual interest, Dutch buffs and the art house audience awaited the comeback of helmer Adriaan Ditvoorst with his first feature in six years. Ditvoorst was internationally hailed as a talent of stature after his first fcature, "Paranoia," in 1967. In the '70s, he directed two b.o. flops which, however, confirmed his marked pictorial gifts. "De witte wann," from Ditvoorst's own script, was produced by Jan Vrijman, himself a creative filmmaker of solid repute.

Disappointingly, pic met with a mixed reception from press and public, due to its wilfully baffling aspects which even wellwishers found hard to stomach. More's the pity, because there's much to be admired in striking images, excellent acting, firstrate photography, music and sound, rare perfectionism of technical credits generally. But future at the art house gates seems limited, as filmmaker does much to alienate the audience.

In brief, "Delusion" concerns Lazlo, a strong, silent hero who takes heroin for added strength. He despises addicts in general, along with most of the human race. Samurai-like in appearance, he meditates in an oriental posture under a mighty sculptured eagle, high on the roof of a disused factory; he paints surrealistically intriguing murals in the gutted building.

Thom Hoffman limns this proud and arrogant young man with great ability. However, the strongest impression is left by Kim Lambeau, a magnificent Belgian actress previously unknown in the Netherlands. She plays Lazlo's mother.

After an absence of 10 years, he returns to the decaying mansion where she lives alone, in order to help her: she has had a crippling accident. Mother, a solitary person like Lazlo, is a retired actress who lives with lines from "Cherry Orchard" on her lips and love and longing for her son in her heart.

Cherry blossoms on a bare tree in her dishevelled garden are but one sample of a surfeit of symbols caught by Albert Vanderwildt's masterly camera. The ending, an operatically conceived and beautifully executed melodramatic finale, has Lazlo killing his mother with a kiss — hence death as the ultimate gift of love.

Ditvoorst, first and foremost a forceful image-maker, scores in his usage of space and decor, while his direction of thesps owes much to current theatrical styles and performance art.

Pic is esthetically intriguing most of the time. It gets offputting, however, once one realizes many of its visually striking symbols and enigmas don't have far to go. Also, there are several ill-advised teases and unfunny put-downs which should have been cut to make for a clearer outline. Editing as such is commendable, especially considering the problems wayward motifs must have posed.

All in all, maker's supercilious disregard of a potential audience may have lost pic a sizable part of same. —*Ewa.*

Erlöst Oder Betrogen?
(Redeemed or Cheated?)
(WEST GERMAN-COLOR-DOCU-16m)

Berlin, April 17.

A Mario Offenberg Film Production, in collaboration with Sender Freies Berlin (SFB), Eberhard Kruppa, tv producer. Written and directed by Mario Offenberg. Camera (color), Rainer Koch, Meir Gregor; editor, W. Lindner. Reviewed at SFB Screening Room, West Berlin, April 17, '84. Running time: **55 MINS.**

Mario Offenberg, an Israeli professor living and teaching in West Berlin, makes regular trips to his homeland as an engaged social-political documentary filmmaker.

His best docus include "The Legacy Of Georgia T." (1982), filmed in East Germany and "Protest" (1983).

Now he's back with "Redeemed or Cheated?" — whose subtitle, "Israel's Oriental Jews," pinpoints the question raised in the documentary. This is a portrait of the Arab Jew, or the "Sephardim," the Jews of the Iberian Peninsula and the Mediterranean countries on the Arab side who adopted the Sephardic rite.

Offenberg's thesis is that the Sephardim (Oriental Jews) are second-class citizens in Israel today, much in the nature of the Western World (Europe and U.S.), comparing their standard of living with that of Third World countries.

Offenberg offers evidence for his point of view. He reviews historical facts, the important one being that between 1948 and 1961, a period of high immigration to Israel, 46.9% came from Europe, America, and Oceania (only Europe being significant), while 53.1% came from Asia and Africa. It meant Israel had two identities from the start as a new nation.

Offenberg uses clips from Israeli government-produced films to show how funds were raised abroad for the new state during the 1950s, then uses interviews with Oriental Jews to show the discrepancies in these same films.

The rest of this stimulating documentary is a search for answers among today's young generation in Israel. It's shown that the election of Oriental Jews to public office has helped a great deal.

Offenberg's answer to the situation is more utopian. He believes, apparently, that the current majority of Oriental Jews living in Israel — about 60% of the population — offers a mute possibility of making peace with Arab neighbors. In other words, Israel in an Arab world will continue to remain isolated unless the Oriental Jew, who describes himself as an Arab, too, can serve as an effective mediator.

"Redeemed or Cheated?" is too short an hour to cover all the ground of a complex theme; it only scratches the surface. But this is the first documentary of note to be made on the Oriental Jew in Israel. Among those interviewed, Victor Alush stands out: his religion is Jewish, his culture and education Arabic, his citizenship Israeli. Also, with a brood of 16 children, he's a hybrid to be taken seriously in the future. "Redeemed or Cheated?" is highly recommended for both the political historian and the film buff. —*Holl.*

Cannes Reviews (Competitive)

Under The Volcano
(U.S.-COLOR)

Cannes, May 18.

A Universal (U.S.), 20th Century Fox (foreign) release of a Michael and Kathy Fitzgerald presentation of an Ithaca-Conacine production. Produced by Moritz Borman, Wieland Schulz-Keil. Executive producer, Michael Fitzgerald. Directed by John Huston. Stars Albert Finney, Jacqueline Bisset, Anthony Andrews. Screenplay, Guy Gallo, from the novel by Malcolm Lowry; camera (color), Gabriel Figueroa; editor, Roberto Silvi; production design, Gunther Gerzeo; production supervisor, Tom Shaw; music, Alex North. Reviewed at Cannes Film Fest (In Competition), May 18, 1984. Running time: **109 MINS.**

Geoffrey Firmin, The Consul	Albert Finney
Yvonne Firmin	Jacqueline Bisset
Hugh Firmin	Anthony Andrews
Dr. Vigil	Ignacio Lopez Tarso
Dona Gregoria	Katy Jurado
The Brit	James Villiers
Bustamante	Carlos Riquelme
Diosdado	Emilio (El Indio) Fernandez
Herr Krausberg	Gunter Meisner
Dwarf	Rene Ruiz

Although it's said John Huston has wanted to film British author Malcolm Lowry's autobiographical masterpiece "Under the Volcano" for some 30 years, it was always a project fraught with difficulties. How would this remarkably difficult, introspective, pessimistic book about the descent into hell and oblivion of a self-destructive, impotent alcoholic be re-shaped as a major picture? Doubtless, some will feel Huston has had to make too many compromises, but overall the pic is a triumphant artistic success.

Story unfolds over a 24-hour period in November 1938 in the Mexican village of Cuernavaca where the former British Consul, Geoffrey Firmin (Albert Finney), guilt-ridden over the past and abandoned by his wife, is drinking himself to death. It's a time of celebration, the Day of the Dead, a day when death is celebrated ("Only in Mexico is death an occasion for laughter," says a friendly doctor). After a drunken night at a Red Cross function and then in bars, Firmin returns home to discover that Yvonne (Jacqueline Bisset), the wife he so desperately yearned for, has unexpectedly returned. The occasion provides only a momentary interval from hard liquor, however. Soon the couple is joined by his brother Hugh (Anthony Andrews), whose brief liaison with Yvonne had led to the breakup, on a doomed trip to a country bullfight in the shadow of a volcano.

Although this voyage into self-destruction won't be to the taste of many, there will be few unmoved by Albert Finney's towering performance as the tragic Britisher, his values irretrievably broken down, drowning himself in alcohol and practically inviting his own death. Reminding one at times of Charles Laughton, Finney, on-screen almost the entire film, is simply extraordinary; it's an extremely difficult role, and could easily have been over-played, but the actor encompasses the character with great distinction and one weeps for a human being so out of control and so tragic. Bisset and Andrews provide solid support, but this is Finney's film, and he should be up for a best actor prize at Cannes as well as earning another Academy Award nomination.

As regards the character's incapacity to help himself, Huston provides a useful analogy via a brief glimpse of Karl Freund's "Mad Love" (1935), a pic playing at the local cinema, based on the "Hands of Orlac" story which concerns a musician who loses his hands and has them replaced with the hands of a murderer; the hands kill, while the man is unable to stop the destruction. So it is with the Consul, he desperately wants to stop drinking, but can't.

Pic builds to a shattering climax in a cantina filled with low-lifes and prostitutes as the Consul meets his inevitable fate. Result will leave audiences drained.

Print at Cannes was rather soft and fuzzy in spots, but otherwise it looks technically good with Mexican locations well lensed by Gabriel Figueroa. Production notes mysteriously did not list the composer of the score, Alex North.

As noted, this will provoke pros and cons from supporters of the book, and will have to be carefully nurtured if it's to break out of limited major city runs. Word of mouth for Finney, and the great job done by Huston, should certainly help. — *Strat.*

Paris, Texas
(W. GERMAN-FRENCH-COLOR)

Cannes, May 19.

A Road Movies-Argos Films production in association with Westdeutscher Rundfunk, Channel 4 and Pro-ject Film. Produced by Don Guest. Executive producer, Chris Sievernich. Directed by Wim Wenders. Stars Harry Dean Stanton, Nastassja Kinski, Dean Stockwell, Aurore Clement, Hunter Carson, Bernhard Wicki. Screenplay, Sam Shepard; story adaptation, L.M. Kit Carson; camera (color), Robby Müller; editor, Peter Przygodda; music, Ry Cooder; art direction, Kate Altman; costumes, Birgitta Bjerke; sound, Jean-Paul Mugel; delegated producer, Anatole Dauman; associate producer, Pascale Dauman; assistant director, Claire Denis. Reviewed at the Cannes Film Festival (in competition), May 18, 1984. (No MPAA Rating.) Running time: **150 MINS.**

Travis	Harry Dean Stanton
Jane	Nastassja Kinski
Walt	Dean Stockwell
Anne	Aurore Clement
Hunter	Hunter Carson
Doctor Ulmer	Bernhard Wicki
Woman On tv	Viva Auder
Carmelita	Socorro Valdez
Crying Man	Tom Farrell
Slater	John Lurie

Stretch ....Jeni Vici
Nurse Bibs ....Sally Norvell

The European (German-French) coproduction, "Paris, Texas," under the direction of Wim Wenders, is one of the most beautifully lensed films at Cannes — hats off to cinematographer Robby Müller — and the entry is an odds-on favorite to walk away with a top prize at this year's fest. Nevertheless, at 150 minutes running time, the film takes on epic proportions and will thereby have its difficulties on both the commercial and arthouse circuits, unless it's whittled down by a half hour (relatively easy during the second half) to maintain the given momentum of the narrative line.

Wenders practically delivered the print to the projectionist from the laboratory, and it's reliably reported that the original footage ranged in the area of some five hours. Cutting it this close was probably not all that necessary in view of the long weeks he has taken to edit the print, but such timing is of the essence at Cannes.

This is the best Wenders film since "In The Course Of Time" (a.k.a. "Kings Of The Road," 1976), with which it has definite affinities. And one should add that finally a European director (living since 1979 in the States) has successfully interpreted America in English for the American arthouse trade. Given half a chance, he could have done the same with "Hammett" (1982), which cost him four years of his creative energies and left little behind except bitter memories. It thus appears that Wenders and his German-American producer, Chris Sievernich, have now evened the score.

"Paris, Texas" is a "road movie" — an odyssey, if you will. It's a man's journey to self-recognition, following the ancient formula that has its fulfillment when the awaited deed is done (with or without moral implication). In this case, a young boy of eight is reunited with his mother. That part of the tale is the least interesting, however.

What really impresses is the vision of writer-playwright Sam Shepard, upon whose "Motel Chronicles" short stories the original script was inspired and partially based. If Wenders had stayed close to this inspirational origin, he might have created a masterpiece on the contemporary American experience. Instead, he has dipped into occasional maudlin sentimentality and clichéd kidpic routine, too much in this overdrawn version to produce both a critical and commercial winner. All the same, the Cannes cut will please European crowds with their own vicarious views of American life and times. (One will have to wait and see if a new cut hits Yank screens.)

Pic is the story of a man wandering aimlessly along the Texas-Mexican border. When he collapses from exhaustion, a clinical doctor finds a name and address in his pockets and calls the patient's brother — to determine that Travis has been missing for four years. Travis' brother in Los Angeles, Walt (conveniently married to a French woman), is a billboard artist who took in the hero's boy four years ago when the mother literally left him on their doorstep. Now that Travis is back in the picture — he makes the trip to L.A., reluctantly but surely — he decides to win back the love of his son. Once he has done so, the pair's then off to Houston to find the missing mother, who works in a lonely-hearts kind of strip-joint for lonely individuals with a preference for talking over gawking. Soon the son is reunited with his mother in a modern, Yankee-style skyscraper motel. Travis, however, is mysteriously off in his pickup truck at the close, apparently full aware that amnesia victims or social dropouts don't have such fortunate rolls of the dice even in films.

Still, this need not be a factual film — European parables on the States are as legitimate as American metaphors about the Continent. What Wenders is apparently trying to say is that alienation and existential angst are just about the same on both sides of the Atlantic. "Paris, Texas," as even the title hints, equals "Europe, U.S.A."

It's indeed a beautiful film, one that will surely convince doubters that Müller is one of the cinema's best cameramen. He gives the story a surface polish that hints of Edward Hopper and Georgia O'Keefe Americana paintings. Some images are positively breathtaking.

As for Wenders' casual control of the actors, Dean Stockwell as Walt is a standout, while Harry Dean Stanton as Travis only comes alive in the interim segments when he recovers his taste for humanity. Aurore Clement as Walt's wife, Anne, fairly steals the show with her modest heart-tugging supportive role, while Nastassja Kinski is hampered in a part that drags the film out interminably during a duolog with Stanton at the end that is supposed to fit all the pieces together (it doesn't).

"Paris, Texas" is refined arthouse cinema, yet too slow and calculated to score in the boxoffice bigtime — unless a final cut is made. — *Holl.*

Another Country
(BRITISH-COLOR)

Cannes, May 12.

A Goldcrest presentation (Orion Classics in U.S.) with the National Film Finance Corporation. Produced by Alan Marshall. Directed by Marek Kanievska. Stars Rupert Everett. Executive producers, Robert Fox, Julian Seymour; script, Julian Mitchell, based on his original play; camera (color), Peter Biziou; music, Michael Storey; editor, Gerry Hambling; production design, Brian Morris; art director, Clinton Cavera. Reviewed at Cannes Film Festival (in competition), May 12, 1984. Running time: 90 MINS.

Guy Bennett	Rupert Everett
Tommy Judd	Colin Firth
Barclay	Michael Jenn
Delahay	Robert Addie
Devenish	Rupert Wainwright
Fowler	Tristan Oliver
Harcourt	Cary Elwes
Menzies	Frederick Alexander
Wharton	Adrian Ross-Magenty
Imogen Bennett	Anna Massey
Julie Schofield	Betsy Brantley

Julian Mitchell's adaptation of his successful West End play "Another Country" is an absorbing tale about life in a British public (i.e., private) boarding school in the 1930s. Story is supposedly based on the early friendship of Guy Burgess and Donald Maclean who, in the 1950s, spied for the USSR while working for the British government but defected to Moscow before they could be arrested.

Mitchell's contention is that the homosexuality of Burgess, called Bennett here, made him as much an outsider in the claustrophobic atmosphere of the British upper-crust as did Maclean's (Judd's) Marxism. The eventual resolution, of Bennett embracing Marxism as a form of resigned protest, seems a bit glib, but otherwise the film is in the main an absorbing look at this very effete and stifling world, though not as imaginative or daring as Lindsay Anderson's 1968 "if...," — which trod similar ground.

Audiences may find the early scenes a bit confusing, as there are plenty of characters vying for attention and it's sometimes a bit tricky to sort out who's who in the rigid hierarchy of this scholastic establishment (where, by the way, no one ever seems to study: there are no classroom scenes at all). But after a while attention comes to focus on the unhappy Bennett, hopelessly in love with another boy in the school.

Film is marvelously acted down the line, with Rubert Everett a standout as the tormented Bennett. Production is handsome, with sharp lensing by Peter Biziou and tight editing by Gerry Hambling.

Central drama is framed by a modern-day sequence in which a Yank femme journalist interviews the elderly Bennett in his cramped Moscow apartment: fade-out line is a winner, registering the exile's loneliness and isolation (though not quite with the same devastating effect as John Schlesinger's "An Englishman Abroad" in which Alan Bates played Burgess).

Pic will need careful handling for best results, for its hermetic mood and strongly critical look-back and an aspect of British society that hasn't changed much even today won't be to everyone's taste.

But as an exploration into the genesis of two traitors, it's an engrossing, if not totally riveting, experience.— *Strat.*

Bayan Ko
(My Country)
(FILIPINO-FRENCH-COLOR)

Cannes, May 17.

A coproduction of Malaya Films, the Philippines, and Stephan Films, Paris. Produced by Toni Gonzalez and Vera Belmont. Executive producer, Jeric Soriano. Features Phillip Salvador and Gina Alajar. Directed by Lino Brocka. Screenplay, Jose F. Lacaba, based on true incidents; camera (color), Conrado Baltazar; sets, Joey Luna; editor, George Jarlego, Robert Yugeco, Hero Reyes. Reviewed at Cannes Film Festival (Competition), May 17, '84. Running time: 108 MINS.

Turing	Phillip Salvador
Luz	Gina Alajar
Dhalee	Claudia Zobel
Carla	Raoul Aragonn
Boy Echas	Rez Cortez
Ka Ador	Venchito Galvez
Willie	Aristo Reyes, Jr.
Mrs. Lim	Lorli Villenueva
Mr. Lim	Normer Son
Mother of Turing	Gloria Guinto
Sister of Turing	Lucita Soriano

Also with: Joe Taruc and the PETA Kalinangan Ensemble.

One of the most impressive films shown at Cannes and a feature that reportedly had to be smuggled out of the Philippines to be screened for the first time at the fest, Lino Brocka's "My Country" (the title "Bayan Ko" was a popular protest song of the 1930s against U.S. domination of the Philippines, now converted to an anthem against the Marcos regime) is a heavy favorite at this writing for one of the top kudos on the Riviera. Certainly, as in the prior case of Yilmaz Güney's "Yol" (Grand Prix, 1982), the adventure behind the making of "Bayan Ko" will ensure wide theatrical release.

The film narrative is based loosely on two true, separate incidents rather widely known to Filipino audiences: a general strike, and a hostage case resulting in a shootout between police and gangsters in Manila. To these were added the extras of sexy nightclub scenes and a social melodrama to get the project past the censors unnoticed until the final editing stage. Since Brocka is a prolific commercial director with several sexpo/action pics to his credit, the ruse worked without a hitch, and the copy could be aired to Paris to the French coproducer in time for the world preem at Cannes.

For the record, Brocka churned out five other features last year — titles like "Hot Property," "Adultery" and "Your Body Is Mine" — but his international reputation rests securely on earlier socially engaged docu-dramas, films titled succinctly "Jaguar," "Insiang" and "Manila." "Bayan Ko" ranks with the best productions made in the Phililppines, although it's not his strongest and has some noticeable weaknesses in the story line.

This is a thriller with social punch, much in the fashion of Warner Brothers fare of the 1930s. The protagonist, Turing, works in a printing shop and has a way of losing his temper when things don't go right — which is quite often, as he is in debt and his wife is pregnant and needs special medicine to prevent a third miscarriage. In order to meet his obligations, he makes a deal with his employer not to join a budding labor union at the shop. That decision, of course, leads to misunderstandings as a general strike is about to be called.

Then there are his connections to a band of smalltime gangsters, who usually hang around a nightclub with striptease dancers. In the end, his wife is in the hospital due to a premature birth — meaning more debts and a financial dead end — and he's in a pack of trouble for agreeing to rob the printing company at the instigation of the thugs.

There's the expected shootout, but not before the media exploit the occasion of hostage-taking with a live broadcast featuring the trapped Turing to the outside world on tv (à la Warner Brothers via radio and newspapers in the early sound period). It's here that the social message comes across the strongest.

References to the assassination of Benigno Aquino can be read into the context of the plot, although this is on the periphery of the story. So, too, a parody of an official government celebration (like the Manila Arts Festivals under Imelda Marcos), using the occasion of an anniversary party thrown by the owner of the Jefferson Printing Co.

Brocka's pace in telling the story is a major plus, as are a good performance by Phillip Salvador as Turing and an exceptional one by Gina Alajar as his long-suffering but supportive wife Luz. Crowd scenes also are handled masterfully. Look for "Bayan Ko" to make the rounds of the season's festivals. —*Holl.*

Success Is The Best Revenge
(BRITISH-COLOR)

Cannes, May 18.

A DeVere and Gaumont production, Gaumont release. Produced and directed by Jerzy Skolimowski. Original story and script, Michael Lyndon and Jerzy Skolimowski. camera (Eastmancolor) Mike Fash; editor, Barrie Vince; production design, Vaytek; drawings, Feliks Topolski; music, Stanley Myers, Hans Zimmer. Reviewed as an official competition entry in the Cannes Film Festival at the Palais des Festival, May 18, 1984. Running time: **90 MINS.**
Alex Rodak . . . . Michael York
His wife . . . . Joanna Szerzerbic
Adam, their son . . . . Michael Lyndon
David, younger son . . . George Skolimowski
French Official . . . . Michel Piccoli

Monique de Fontaine . . . . Anouk Aimee
Dino Montecurva . . . . John Hurt

After "Moonlighting," London-based, longtime Polish exile Jerzy Skolimowski stays with the exile theme in "Success is The Best Revenge," his second Official Competition entry at Cannes in recent years.

"Success" deals with two main themes: how exile can become a trap, a temptation to coast along quite professionally on the artist-exile's most obvious obsession, and how the children of such exiles will sooner or later revolt against their exile status and insist on exploring their roots through personal confrontation with the country of their parents.

Story is told in parallels between teenager Adam (Michael Lyndon), who secretly prepares for combined punkdom and flight to Warsaw, and his father, Alex Rodak (Michael York), a Polish stage director about to put on another spectacular exile show at a London West End theater. Actually, the parallel lines are too rarely caused to influence each other, and the Adam story at long stretches seems almost forgotten, being allowed to emerge again only towards the end.

The sad plight of the younger generation of refugees is a theme well worth exploring, but Skolimowski really has much more to say in a satirical way — about the older generation that has turned exile into business.

As Rodak, York exudes youngish charm, irresponsibility and guts in indebting himself and his family to raise money for the show. He finally — against the wishes of his long-suffering wife (Joanna Szerbic) — gets the money from a cynical millionaire (John Hurt) who has his own shady reasons for entering the game as backer.

What Rodak lacks in loot, he has plenty of in artistic status: we see him awarded France's Legion of Honor by a French official (light mugging here by Michel Piccoli). He also has by his side Monique de Fontaine (Anouk Aimee) as a theater manager with possible off-stage designs on him.

It is commendable that Skolimowski using York (the last time it was Jeremy Irons) has cast an actor who looks like anything but a Polish stereotype for his lead. Otherwise, his casting, his use of cameos (Jane Asher and Mike Sarne among them), and his intermixing of very flashy cinematography with oddball characterizations of people and situations (from soccer field and courtroom) as often seems as haphazard as deliberate. Although mostly a shot-on-location film, production designer Voytek manages to make even its street scenes look like they were done in a studio.

Film's title is a slight twist of the 1920s adage about living well being the best revenge. It really does not apply too well, even as irony, to the story as it develops here, but the appeal — with the father-versus-son theme rather lost except in a sequence that has Adam being contemptuous of Alex' exuberant efforts when they are both playing soccer in Hyde Park — is mostly of the coyly intellectual kind.

Cannes competition participation should help "Success" into selected programming internationally, but true critical praise as well as audience cheering may prove hard to come by. — *Kell.*

La Pirate
(FRENCH-COLOR)

Cannes, May 22.

An AMLF release of a F.L.F.-Tango-Lola film coproduction. Produced by Olivier Lorsac. Direction and screenplay by Jacques Doillon. Camera (color), Bruno Nuytten; editor, Noelle Boisson; music, Philippe Sarde; sound, Jean-Claude Laureux. Reviewed at the Cannes Film Festival (official competition), May 21, 1984. Running time: **87 MINS.**
Alma . . . . Jane Birkin
No. 5 . . . . Philippe Leotard
Carol . . . . Maruschka Detmers
Girl . . . . Laure Marsac
Andrew . . . . Andrew Birkin

In production values and name casting, it would appear that "La Pirate" was seen as the commercial breakthrough film for the highly respected but idosyncratic French director Jacques Doillon. However, pic emerges as one of his least accessible and most emotionally oblique efforts to date. And despite the presence of name actors and a provocative subject, the film has limited appeal on either the home front or in international sales.

Complicated tale focuses sporadically on the relationships between the five principal characters. At its core, pivotal pairing is the renewed relationship between Alma (Jane Birkin) and Carol (Maruschka Detmers). However, this is complicated by presence of others, particularly Alma's husband Andrew (Andrew Birkin).

As with past Doillon efforts much of the picture is wall-to-wall dialog punctuated with shouting matches and quirky action. It produces a disquieting response for audiences unrelieved by the fact that the story lacks characters to embrace. The overall effect seems needlessly arty and distant.

Doillon telegraphs the outcome early on in proceedings. There can be no mistaking this *folie d'amour* where principals wield knives and guns with abandon. The question merely becomes whose patience will run out first and who will be on the receiving end. When the bodies do begin to fall, one greets the moment with relief rather than sorrow.

Performances by the actors caught in the love triangle are mercurial in nature and emotionally repelling. Slightly better are Philippe Leotard and newcomer Laure Marsac playing characters with no names. Both performances have an unsettling edge but lack the underpinnings of a *film noir* script to justify their mysterious nature.

Production values stress clean, cold values allowing for some striking immages from Bruno Nuytten. However, Doillon seems at a loss when it comes to composing for the wide-screen format.

"La Pirate" may gain some attention in festival slottings but commercial prospects outside France are highly dubious. One had hoped for some swashbuckling spirit, which never arises in this curiously titled film. — *Klad.*

Den' Dlinneje Notchi
(The Day Longer Than The Night)
(SOVIET-COLOR)

Cannes, May 17.

A Gruziafilm Production, Tbilisi (Georgian Republic), Soviet Union; world rights, Goskino, Moscow. Directed by Lana Gogoberidze. Screenplay, Zaira Arsenichvili, Gogoberidze; camera (color), Nugzar Erkomaichvili; art direction, Georgi Mikeladze; music, Guia Kantcheli. Reviewed at Cannes Film Festival (Competition), May 17, '84. Running time: **105 MINS.**
Cast: Deredjan Kharchiadze (Eva), Tamara Skhirtiadze (Eva as old woman), Guram Pirtzkhalaia (Spiridon), Irakli Khizanichvili, Manana Menabde.

Lana Gogoberidze's "The Day Longer Than the Night" scores as a rather conventionally made film-ballad about life and customs in Georgia at the turn of the century, with a chronological progression and a twist at the end that puts everything that went before it into the spotlight of the present. And like most ballads of life and death, love and sacrifice, the outcome is tragic for all the main characters. In between the separate episodes, a traveling troupe of actors and musicians tie the threads of the narrative together while offering a bit of commentary on their own.

It's the turn-of-the-century in this republic of striking natural beauty: lush hills and valleys, mountain streams and picturesque villages, the changing of the seasons and folkloric costumes — it's all there to feed the eyes and please the Georgian film buff. A pair of young lovers bathe in a stream and swear eternal love. Eva and Archil marry and plan for the future, but before they can have a child, he dies under mysterious circumstances. It's later revealed (but hinted by the troupe of actors) that her second husband, the rough and ruthless Spiridon, killed Archil in a fit of jealousy.

The years pass. Eva, always a blithe spirit, doesn't laugh anymore and refuses marital rights to her new husband at every opportunity; she even eats alone while simply serving her husband in the household. A child is adopted, and the young girl in growing up takes to her resolute father as much as to her dispirited mother.

Then comes the October Revolution and sometime in the early 1920s the Communists are seeking support in the village for the new times. Spiridon remains a rough-cut individualist, but when he momentarily joins the revolutionary movement, he wins the love briefly of Eva. It's when he abruptly reveals the crime burdening his conscience, however, that he loses Eva forever. He rides out to a mountain stream and kills himself.

Now Eva at 80 years of age has to answer to the questions of her grown daughter. She prefers the silence in her stilled heart instead.

Femme helmer Gogoberidze made the ranks of internationally respected women directors with "Some Interviews On Personal Questions" (1978). This time, although the theme is still female emancipation under the surface of the tale, she's demonstrated that poetic cinema is not her metiér. Pretty heavy-handed all the way down the line, save for the folkloric scenes of songs, costumes, and traditional ceremonies. — *Holl.*

Cal
(IRISH-COLOR)

Cannes, May 15.

A Warner Bros. release of a Goldcrest presentation of an Enigma production. Produced by Stuart Craig, David Puttnam. Executive producer, Terence Clegg. Coproducer-production designer, Stuart Craig. Directed by Pat O'Connor. Screenplay, Bernard Mac Laverty, based on his novel; camera (Rank Color), Jerzy Zielinski; editor, Michael Bradsell; music, Mark Knopfler; art director, set dresser, Josie Macavin; sound, Pat Hayes; assistant director, Bill Craske. Reviewed at the Cannes Film Festival (in competition), May 15, 1984. (No MPAA Rating). Running time: 102 MINS.
Marcella........:..........Helen Mirren
Cal.........................John Lynch
Shamie....................Donal McCann
Skeffington.............John Kavanagh
Dunlop..................Ray McAnally
Crilly....................Stevan Rimkus

An official entry from the Republic of Ireland in the Cannes Film Festival, "Cal" is a modest, well-made·brief encounter romance set against the ongoing "troubles." Initiated by coproducer David Puttnam and financed with British coin, pic reps a discreet, personal look at a potentially explosive subject, and limited b.o. prospects in arthouse venues loom for U.S. playoff.

Set in Northern Ireland (but lensed, for practical reasons, in the Republic), drama begins shockingly with a policeman being shot to death in his home. Although he tries to beg off further involvement in IRA-type activities, it's clear

early on that Cal, a 19-year-old Catholic, had some role in the murder.

A fellow with few prospects, extremely limited horizons, but essentially decent instincts, Cal toils fitfully with his father in a slaughterhouse, and shyly begins checking out an attractive older woman, Marcella, who has just begun working the local library.

However, unassumingly, Cal manages to insinuate himself into the woman's life, taking a job on her small estate and eventually moving into a ramshackle cottage there when his father's home is burned down by neighboring Protestants.

Although Marcella admits that her relationship with her husband had not been terrific before he died, Cal's guilt over having driven the getaway car for his cohort, the actual murderer, comes to haunt him more and more, particularly after their gentle affair begins.

The inevitable dilemmas and dead-ends implicit in the Northern Irish situation are made part and parcel of the personal drama, and no optimistic shadings are applied.

Story is presented so gingerly, and with such a desire to avoid overt melodrama, that it has only middling impact. As played by John Lynch, Cal remains a relatively anonymous figure, and Helen Mirren is such a strong, self-confident actress that it's somewhat difficult to understand why Marcella would go, even briefly, for such an unformed, unassertive youth.

Pic's basic intelligence and earnestness will inspire respect in some quarters, and director Pat O'Connor has done a decent job of mounting novelist Bernard Mac-Laverty's screenplay. But it's difficult to imagine audiences, particularly outside the British Isles, becoming too excited by this mute tale. —*Cart.*

Quilombo
(BRAZILIAN-COLOR)

Cannes, May 22.

A CDK production, produced by Augusto Arraes. Executive producer, Marco Altberg. Written and directed by Carlos Diegues. Camera, (color) Lauro Escorel Filho, Pedro Farkas; editor, Mair Tavares; scenery and costumes, Luiz Carlos Ripper; musical direction, Gilberto Gil; special effects, André Trielli; research coordinator, Everardo Rocha; songs, Gilberto Gil with lyrics by Walid Salomáo. Reviewed at the Cannes Film Festival (official competition), May 21, 1984. Running time: 120 MINS.
Zumbi....................Antonio Pompéo
Dandara.....................Zezé Motta
Ganga Zumba................Toni Tornado
Ana de Ferro.................Vera Fischer
Acaiúba...................Antonio Pitanga
Domingos José Velho....Mauricio do Valle

During the 17th century, when Brazil was still a colony contested by the Portuguese and Dutch, and the settlers' economy depended on

slave labor imported from Africa, the name Quilombo was given to the settlements established in the mountains by runaway slaves.

Carlos Diegues' film, one of the most expensive to be made in Brazil, deals with the specific story of Quilombo de Palmares, founded around 1650 and its leader Ganga Zumba. This was also the subject of the director's very first film, made in 1964.

First comes the rebellion and the establishment of the Quilombo community in the mountains under Ganga Zumba's wise leadership. However, once the Portuguese defeat the Dutch, they start to concentrate on the former slaves in the mountains, although their first attempts to attack the community are categorically defeated.

Later there are policy disagreements between Ganga Zumba and his godson Zumbi: the former accepts a peace treaty with the Portuguese (which is just about as fair as similar agreements with Indian tribes in the U.S. last century), while Zumbi opposes negotiating with the Portuguese, because he feels that in the long run, peace between the landowners and former slaves is impossible.

The blacks are finally defeated, but it still took the Portuguese several more decades to eliminate the survivors of the community in the mountains.

"Quilombo" is an epic story, and also a tale of Utopia, of the former slaves, left to their own devices, building a humane and equitable society. In this manner, Diegues simultaneously deals with the past and, indirectly, also comments on Brazil's present and future.

The fact that there are also economically deprived whites and Indians in the community, gives it an additional dimension.

Ganga Zumba, Zumbi and the women, Dandara and Acotirene, are powerful characters and Gilberto Gil's music and songs certainly help to create atmosphere and, for non-Brazilian audiences, give the film an exotic flavor. But, in spite of the subject's very considerable interest and the powerful story, the film does not quite come off.

This is partly due to the screenplay: the utopic lifestyle at the Quilombo is suggested but not clearly enough perceived or shown in action, which seriously limits what could have been one of the pic's most significant angles. Another fault may well be that, from a visual point of view, the film is somewhat lacking in style, particularly during its first segments where there are practically no sets and only the countryside, filmed rather flatly, which somehow makes it look too contemporary.

On the plus side there is strong acting (among others, Zezé Motta,

Antonio Pompeo, Toni Tornado and Alaide Santos), the already mentioned music and some impressive battle sequences towards the finale. But although exciting in parts, "Quilombo" as a whole does not reach the epic level that should have been its due.

Prospects in the U.S. would appear to be limited to art houses.
— *Amig.*

Ghare Baire
(The Home And The World)
(INDIAN-COLOR)

Cannes, May 22.

A National Film Development Corporation of India production. Directed by Satyajit Ray. Features entire cast. Script (from the novel by Rabindranath Tagore) and music, Ray; camera (color), Soumendu Roy; art director, Ashoke Bose; editor, Dualal Dutt; make-up, Ananta Das. Reviewed at Cannes Film Fest (In Competition), May 22, 1984. Running time: 141 MINS.
Sandip.................Soumitra Chatterjee
Nikhilesh................Victor Bannerjee
Bimala.............Swatilekha Chatterjee
Sister-in-law.....................Gopa Aich
Miss Gilby......Jennifer (Kendal) Kapoor
Headmaster...................Manoj Mitra
Amulya...................Indrapramit Roy
Kulada...................Bimal Chatterjee

Satyajit Ray, whose masterly "Apu Trilogy" of the mid-'50s, helped bring attention to Indian (especially Bengali) cinema in the west, comes up with a new adaptation of a novel by one of India's great writers, Rabindranath Tagore. Set in 1905, and dealing with momentous political events within the microcosm of a tense family situation, the film is full of burnished, glowing images, has three fine central performances, and many of the top qualities expected from Ray. However, in the context of his work, it is a minor film, and must be counted as a disappointment.

Lord Curzon, the British Viceroy, is pursuing the colonial policy of divide and rule by deliberately creating tension between Hindus and Muslims within Bengal. Story deals with an enlightened local landowner, Nikhilesh (Victor Bannerjee), who opposes the British policies, but yet is more moderate than his fiery friend, Sandip (Soumitra Chatterjee), a leader of a strongly nationalist movement which would boycott all foreign goods. Problem is, as Nikhilesh points out, Indian goods are simply not available to replace the hated imports (which include, sugar, salt and other essentials) so that it will be the poor people who will suffer as a result of the nationalist campaign.

There is tension between the two old friends for another reason: Nikhilesh's placid wife, Bimala (Swatilekha Chatterjee), who has for years observed an orthodox domesticity, has begun to be interested in other things, has learnt

English and started to take an interest in politics. She falls for Sandip's rather seedy charm, and steals money to support him. At fadeout, Sandip has left, but the trouble he has stirred up will result in tragedy for his friend.

Film has many similarities with a Ray masterpiece of exactly 20 years ago, "Charulata," which also had a triangular situation involving a lonely wife at a time of change. But comparisons emphasize the weaknesses of the new film, which relies far more on dialog (it's very talky) rather than visual interpretation and which is really rather too long for its own good.

There is a subtle finale which is typical of Ray at his best, and pic is lovely to look at, with the action rarely straying outside the couple's ornate home with, as Ray subtly indicates, its totally foreign furnishings (the camera lingers on an English teacup, English piano, etc.). Jennifer Kapoor does a neat bit as a gushy English teacher, and acting is fine down the line. But the Ray of old would have given us rather more visual invention than "The Home And The World" supplies. — *Strat.*

Enrico IV
(Henry IV)
(ITALIAN-COLOR)

Cannes, May 21.

A Gaumont release (Orion Classics for U.S.), produced by Enzo Porcelli for RAI-TV Channel 2 and Odyssia Film. Directed by Marco Bellocchio. Stars Marcello Mastroianni and Claudia Cardinale. Screenplay, Marco Bellocchio with the collaboration of Tonino Guerra, freely adapted from the play by Luigi Pirandello; camera (Technicolor), Giuseppe Lanci; art director, Leonardo Scarpa and Giancarlo Basili; costumes, Lina Nerli Taviani, sound, Remo Ugolinelli; music, Astor Piazzolla. Reviewed at the Cannes Film Festival, (official competition), May 20, 1984. Running time: **95 MINS.**
Enrico IV............Marcello Mastroianni
Matilda ....Claudia Cardinale
Young Enrico..............Luciano Bartoli
Young Matilda/Frida......Latou Chardons
Psychiatrist ....-......Leopoldo Trieste
Belcredi...................Paolo Bonicelli

Leaving the inward-looking family dramas that have occupied him in recent years ("Leap Into The Void," "The Eyes, The Mouth"), Marco Bellocchio returns to the theme of madness, and madmen as being saner than other people, with greater objectivity and a solid story. Helmer, with the assistance of scripter Tonino Guerra, has pared the venerable and dense Pirandello classic down to the bone and reconstructed it filmically. Result is an accessible and entertaining film that succeeds in capturing the essence of Pirandello's work. Pic has been sold to many territories in Europe and America on the strength of its prestige packaging, but could have a chance to reach larger audiences outside the art house circuit.

Film's engine and light is Marcello Mastroianni's performance as the mad nobleman who thinks he is Emperor Henry IV. After a fall from his horse during a riding party in Medieval costume when he was 26, Enrico spends 20 years in the sumptuous isolation of the family castle. His relatives surround him with costumed servants to humor his delusions and control his violent outbursts. Ranting and raving, making fun of his "counsellors," riding a rocking horse furiously till he drops from exhaustion, Mastroianni gives a sense of dignity, fire, pain, humor and humanity to the character.

Meanwhile, psychiatrist Leopoldo Trieste has concocted an offbeat scheme to "counter shock" his patient back to sanity. He plans to confront Enrico with a girl in the fatal riding party, Matilda. Matilda (Claudia Cardinale) is now in her 40s, but she has a daughter, Frida (Latou Chardons), who is the spitting image of her 20 years ago.

What no one knows is that Enrico isn't mad at all; he's acted the role of a madman all those years to escape from, and in some measure revenge himself upon, a society he sees as hypocritical, conventional, and emotionally sterile. Enrico, the wise fool, is shown to be justified when he takes off his mask and finds himself greeted with the angry indignation of his concerned friends and relatives.

A strong supporting cast is led by Claudia Cardinale as Enrico's great love, now a rich Baroness with a boorish husband. Though picture was made without the luxury of a lavish budget, art directors Leonardo Scarpa and Giancarlo Basili have gotten a great deal of mileage out of the scenic castle and surroundings. — *Yung.*

Cannes Festival

Once Upon A Time In America
(COLOR)

Cannes, May 20.

A Ladd Company through Warner Bros. (U.S.), PSO International (foreign) release. Produced by Arnon Milchan. Executive producer, Claudio Mancini. Directed by Sergio Leone. Stars Robert De Niro. Screenplay, Leonardo Benvenuti, Piero De Bernardi, Enrico Medioli, Franco Arcalli, Franco Ferrini, Leone; additional dialog, Stuart Kaminsky; based on the novel, "The Hoods," by Harry Grey; camera (Technicolor), Tonino Delli Colli; editor, Nino Baragli; music, Ennio Morricone; art direction, Carlo Simi, James Singelis (N.Y.); set design, Giovanni Natalucci; set decoration, Gretchen Rau (N.Y.); costume design, Gabriella Pescucci; sound, Fausto Ancillai; assistant directors, Fabrizio Sergenti Castellani, Dennis Benatar (N.Y.); executive in charge of production, Fred Caruso; production supervisor, Mario Cotone. Reviewed at the Cannes Film Festival (out of competition), May 19, 1984. (MPAA Rating [U.S. version]: R.) Running time: **227 MINS.**

David (Noodles) Aaronson .Robert De Niro
Max......................James Woods
Deborah............Elizabeth McGovern
Jimmy O'Donnell ....Treat Williams
Carol ....Tuesday Weld
Joe.........................Burt Young
Frankie Monaldi.................Joe Pesci
Police Chief Aiello...........Danny Aiello
Cockeye ....William Forsythe
Patsy ....James Hayden
Eve ....Darlanne Fleugel
Fat Moe ....Larry Rapp
Peggy ....Amy Ryder
    Also with: Scott Tiler (young Noodles), Rusty Jacobs (young Max/David), Jennifer Connelly (young Deborah), Mike Monetti (young Fat Moe), Adrian Curran (young Cockeye), Brian Bloom (young Patsy), Julie Cohen (young Peggy), Noah Moazezi (Dominic), James Russo (Bugsy), Karen Shallo (Mrs. Aiello).

After Sergio Leone's 12-year absence from the screen and resulting expectations surrounding his epic dream project, "Once Upon A Time In America" arrives as a disappointment of considerable proportions. As presented out of competition at the Cannes Film Festival in its 227-minute version, the only cut Leone said he will recognize as his own, sprawling saga of Jewish gangsters over the decades is surprisingly deficient in clarity and purpose, as well as excitement and narrative involvement.

Basic material and many of Leone's ideas are potent enough to prompt the feeling that the makings of an excellent film are in there somewhere, but it's far from having been realized. Implication is that the long version will be released in many foreign markets, but general audiences in any country will undoubtedly find the film trying.

Where the director's name is most respected, perhaps in Italy and France, full-length cut could settle in for nice runs. In the U.S., the Ladd Company through Warner Bros. will release a 150-minute cut, which will be evaluated here upon its opening next month.

As the title, and Leone's earlier masterful Westerns, would suggest, film is an imaginative flight of fancy about criminal life, but with a vividly realistic backdrop. Unlike "The Godfather" and most other mob stories, however, it is not about the Mafia or major organized crime, but focuses throughout on a small gang of hoods and their own friendships, loyalties and betrayals.

The fact that the characters, including lead Robert De Niro, are so brutal and essentially unsympathetic will undoubtedly put mass audiences off, but this is not what makes the drama fundamentally unsatisfying.

Rather, when one is asked to spend so much of the running time meditating on the emotional resonances of the characters' relationships and actions, as happens during the long, brooding, non-dialog sequences, one needs a set of moral codes to set everything in context. Amazingly, none is supplied, so the situations which are set up so elaborately never pay off.

Pic opens with a series of extraordinary violent episodes. It's 1933 and some hoods knock off a girlfriend and some cohorts of "Noodles" (Robert De Niro), while trying to track down the man himself.

Then, to the corny accompaniment of The Beatles' "Yesterday," action shifts to 1968, when the aging De Niro (with a superior make-up job) returns to New York after a 35-year absence and reunites with a childhood pal, Fat Moe (the excellent Larry Rapp). De Niro is clearly on a mission relating to his past, and his later discovery of a briefcase filled with loot for a contract is obviously a portent of something big to come.

Virtually the next hour, however, is devoted to showing how Noodles and his buddies began adopting lives of crime as kids on the Lower East Side.

There are perhaps 15 minutes of good anecdotal material here, mainly devoted to the boys' sexual initiation rites and the start of Noodles' lifelong love for Fat Moe's sister Deborah (beautifully personified in the early section by Jennifer Connelly), but this stretch in particular seems exhaustively devoted to the magnification of trivialities.

It's clear that a film is in trouble when some 100 minutes have passed without its finding a groove, and it isn't until action returns to the Prohibition era, and the gang's ascendence, that things pick up a bit.

A treacherous diamond robbery vaults them into the big money category, they blackmail the police chief and battle rival camps over labor rackets before a big disagreement over the idea of robbing the Federal Reserve Bank pits Noodles and best friend Max (James Woods) forever against one another.

Except for a brief coda, it all ends with a bizarre and truly mystifying confrontation in 1968. Last 40 minutes or so degenerate badly enough as it is without a story conclusion which leaves one entirely baffled as to what takes place. Final shot, it might be noted, is virtually identical to that of Robert Altman's "McCabe And Mrs. Miller."

Leone's pattern of jumping between time periods isn't at all confusing and does create some effective poetic echoes, but also seems arbitrary at times and, because of the long childhood section, forestalls the beginning of involvement. Because of the heavy violence upfront, one is braced for further carnage which, in fact, only pops up a couple of more times.

Most disturbing aspect of the tale is treatment of women

throughout. Presence of a chubby young girl who delivers sexual favors in exchange for sweets is mild compared to the excruciating rapes which De Niro commits on Tuesday Weld and, especially, Elizabeth McGovern.

Latter instance, which comes just before the intermission at 160 minutes, pretty much erases any sympathy built up for De Niro simply through prolonged exposure. Curiously, all the men remain bachelors throughout.

Slow film is never exactly boring but, unlike such similarly paced masterpieces as Luchino Visconti's "The Leopard" or Stanley Kubrick's "Barry Lyndon," methodical, contemplative style here doesn't yield eventual payoff emotionally or intellectually.

Rumored to have cost upwards of $30-40,000,000, but said at Cannes to have come in at $32,000,000, this is a big production, with gobs of extras in period dress, and sets and locations having been spread out from New York, Florida and Montreal to Paris and Rome.

Physical reproduction of downtown Manhattan streets recalls not only the "Godfather" pics but "Ragtime" in their verisimilitude, and the number of lavish sets offered up by art directors Carlo Simi and James Singelis is awesome.

Tonino Delli Colli's lensing is excellent, and one would hate to imagine the film without Ennio Morricone's score which, while spare, develops some haunting minor key themes.

Quiet and subtle throughout, De Niro and his charisma rep the backbone of the picture but, despite frequent threats to become engaging, Noodles remains essentially unpalatable. As his more hotheaded friend, James Woods is very fine, but it's hard to take McGovern, okay up until then, posing as a middle-aged woman in the 1968 section when she looks about 19. Other players are acceptable.

Since the Leone cut will supposedly not be available to American viewers, the following is offered for the record as a breakdown of the film's structure in its original version: Including titles, first 22 minutes take place in 1933, followed by 14 minutes in 1968.

Childhood-teenage years occupy subsequent 54 minutes, and after seven minutes back in 1968, 25 minutes are set in the 1920s after De Niro emerges from prison. After another seven minutes in 1968, major section of 61 minutes (bridging the intermission) unfolds in the 1920s-1933. Climactic sequence in 1968 lasts 30 minutes, while 1933-set coda and end credits run another seven minutes.

Given the decision of the Ladd Company and Warners, for better or worse, to cut the film by some 77 minutes, an enlightened approach

to confronting the accompanying controversy might be to showcase the director's version in one small cinema in a few key cities while widely distributing the trimmed edition. It's highly doubtful they would do this, but why not?

Billed on the end credit crawl as a PSO International release, this Arnon Milchan production bears an Embassy International Pictures copyright. —*Cart.*

Growing Pains
(U.S.-COLOR)

Cannes, May 18.
A New World Pictures release of a Kim Jorgensen production. Produced by Jorgensen. Executive producer, David Weisman. Directed by Bobby Houston. Stars Martin Mull, Karen Black. Screenplay, Houston, Joseph Kwong; camera (Metrocolor), Jan De Bont; editor, Barry Zetlin; music, Sparks; art direction, Jim Dultz; set decoration, David Glazer; costume design, Linda Bass, Jack Buehler; supervising producer, Alan C. Blomquist; associate producers, Steve Lane, Bill Ward; assistant director, Eric Jewett. Reviewed at the Cannes Film Festival (Market), May 17, 1984. (MPAA Rating: R.) Running time: 82 MINS.
Warren Fitzpatrick...........Martin Mull
Gladys Fitzpatrick...........Karen Black
Sister Serena ....Anne De Salvo
Kurtz ....Murphy Dunne
Piper ....Georg Olden

Made independently, provisionally acquired then let go by Disney, and finally picked up by New World, "Growing Pains" is a bratty, anarchic comedy which pits delinquent kids in guerrilla warfare against hopelessly lunatic adults. Fitfully funny and sometimes mean-spirited, this dark updating of the "Our Gang" formula is on the raunchy side, but would probably give parents more pause than youngsters themselves. With a strong sell, modest effort could yield some profitable early returns in wide breaks.

Early going presents a contempo nightmare version of Charles Dickens' institutions for wastrels, as the Bleeding Heart Orphanage is a gothic house of horrors run on the order of a high-security prison.

Lording it over the motley group of rascals are demented "sister" Anne De Salvo, who can't wait to throw the little buggers into isolation wards, and twisted Murphy Dunne, who has an electrified cattle prod ever at the ready.

Unfortunately, the moppets, who seem generally to be within a couple of years either side of 10, are not much more appealing, since they're surly, contentious and street-wise way beyond their years. As bad as conditions are in the orphanage, the kids go to great lengths to prevent being adopted, but finally one of them, Mouse, is taken away by pretentious rich folks Martin Mull and Karen Black.

Mouse doesn't like his lavish new digs in Santa Barbara much and, sensing this, his buddies (a street

tough, an intellectually inclined black, a dopey surfer type and a tomboy) escape in order to rescue him, and create rather predictable mayhem upon their arrival.

Much of the intended humor derives from sending up and destroying conventional, middle-class values, and the strafing approach to comedy invariably provokes a fair share of yocks. But there's also an underlying hostility toward organized society of any kind which, in this context, seems vaguely unpleasant and not entirely innocuous.

Performances are all as broad as could be, and lowbrow approach will probably maximize appeal for this sort of fare.

Low-budget item is technically okay, although visual quality, at least in print caught, was on the murky side. — *Cart.*

The Brother From Another Planet
(U.S. - COLOR)

Cannes, May 17.
An A-Train Films production. Produced by Peggy Rajski, Maggie Renzi. Directed, written, edited by John Sayles. Camera (Movielab color), Ernest R. Dickerson; music, Mason Daring; production design, Nora Chavooshian; art direction, Steve Lineweaver; costume design, Karen Perry; sound, Eric Taylor; assistant director, Craig Laurence Rice. Reviewed at the Cannes Festival (Market), May 16, 1984. (No MPAA rating). Running time: 104 MINS.
The Brother...................Joe Morton
Fly ....Darryl Edwards
Odell ....Steve James
Smokey ....Leonard Jackson
Walter ....Bill Cobbs
Noreen ....Maggie Renzi
Sam ....Tom Wright
Bernice ....Ren Woods
Rickey...........Reggie Rock Bythewood
Also with: John Sayles, David Strathairn, Rosetta Le Noire, Fisher Stevens, Josh Mostel, Michael Mantel, Jaime Tirelli, Edward Baran, Caroline Aaron, Herbert Newsome, Dee Dee Bridgewater, Sidney Sheriff Jr.

John Sayles takes a turn toward offbeat fantasy in "The Brother From Another Planet," a vastly amusing but progressively erratic look at the Harlem adventures of an alien who will undoubtedly be called a black E.T. Sci-fi angle gives the film a chance to reach a notably wider audience than have Sayles' previous three directorial efforts. Teen and college viewers rep the key target market, but an enterprising Yank distributor should attempt to arouse interest in the black community as well.

Financed on a shoestring by Sayles himself and almost entirely without the special effects generally associated with "alien" cinematic exploits, "Brother" begins with a tall, mute, young black fellow seeming to be dumped unceremoniously in New York harbor. Within minutes, he makes his way to Harlem, where his unusual, but not truly bizarre, behavior raises some cackles but in most respects blends into the neighborhood.

Roughly the first third of the action takes place in a local bar, and Sayles' outstanding talent with dialog is given free rein in the frequently funny comments and exchanges of the regulars.

Since he doesn't speak, the Brother represents a mostly passive character except for his mysterious healing powers, which not only enable him to cure physical injuries but to earn a job in a video arcade, since he can fix cantankerous video games with a pass of the hand.

On the subway, the Brother is given a fabulously entertaining display of ace cardsmanship by young Broadway legit thesp Fisher Stevens, and is later introduced to the pleasures of the flesh by jazz singer Dee Dee Bridgewater.

Pic is essentially a series of behavioral vignettes, and many of them are genuinely delightful and inventive. Once the Brother discovers the Harlem drug scene, however, tale takes a rather unpleasant and, ultimately, confusing turn, and much of the considerable promise and good will developed over the first hour is dissipated.

Pursuing the missing Brother around the streets of Harlem are two alien bounty hunters, one of whom is played by Sayles himself. Pair ultimately confronts its prey, but while a happy ending ensues, handling of the climactic section is quite awkward, as it's hard to tell exactly what's going on.

Ultimately, feeling persists that the full potential of this wonderful idea was not quite achieved, but pic does deliver enough pleasure, of both sophisticated and broadcased types, that it will surely be accorded a fine Stateside reception.

Because final reel or two tend to run down, film seems overlong, but, despite infinitesimal budget, tech credits and overall look are quite acceptable. — *Cart.*

Trauma
(WEST GERMAN-COLOR)

Cannes, May 18.
A Tura-Film production, Michael Wiedemann, Munich; world sales, Futura Film, Munich. Written and directed by Gabi Kubach. Features entire cast. Camera (color), Helge Weindler; sound, Günther Hahn; sets, Toni and Heidi Lüdi; costumes, Simone Bergmann; editor, Peter Przygodda; music, Paul Vincent Gunia. Reviewed at Cannes Festival (Market); May 16, '84. Running time: 103 MINS.
Cast: Birgit Doll (Anna), Armin Müller-Stahl (Sam), Lou Castel, Hanne Wieder, Jana Marangosoff, Eva-Maria Hagen.

Gabi Kubach's "Trauma" (previously known as "A Case in Itself") begins in a Munich detective agency, where Anna assists a fumbling private eye who has desires of becoming a budding author on the side. She decides to take on a missing person case herself and goes off to the Brittany coast in France to live in an abandoned house by the ominous sea, a house formerly occupied by Maria, the missing person.

She begins to have traumas and feels herself drawn to suicide, believing, too, that someone is out to kill her. A good-neighbor schoolteacher comes to her aid on more than one occasion, and finally her private eye boss ("Sam Schwarz") appears on the scene to unravel the mystery. The traumas go back to her childhood, when she was to look after her younger sister while their mother dalleid with a lover. The sister tragically died during a seaside vacation. All the same, someone is trying to drive her to suicide and the ending is best left to the viewer.

Lensing is a plus, but the rest is too jumbled to score anywhere.
— *Holl.*

Sakharov
(BRITISH-COLOR)

Cannes, May 18.

A Home Box Office presentation of a Titus Production. Executive produced by Herbert Brodkin. Produced by Robert Berger. Directed by Jack Gold. Stars Jason Robards, Glenda Jackson. Screenplay, David W. Rintels; camera (color), Tony Imi; music, Carl Davis; production design, Herbert Westbrook; editor, Keith Palmer. Reviewed at Cannes Festival (Market). May 17, 1984. Running time: 117 MINS.

Andrei Sakharov	Jason Robards
Elena Bonner	Glenda Jackson
Malyarov	Nicol Williamson
Kravtsov	Frank Finlay
Ludmilla Kovalov	Marion Bailey
Syshchikov	Michael Bryant
Pavel Leontiev	Paul Freeman
Valery Chalidze	Anton Lesser
Klavdia	Anna Massey
Sergei Kovalov	Joe Melia

With the dissident Russian physicist Andrei Sakharov in the international news again via his current hunger strike, "Sakharov" is a timely biography of a courageous man and his equally courageous wife. However, the story of Sakharov doesn't lend itself to a theatrical film and, despite laudatory intentions, the pic is not very successful. This Home Box Office release should be more at home on television.

Story begins as Sakharov (Jason Robards), one of the world's most distinguished scientists and winner of several honors in the USSR, becomes interested in the Human Rights movement and begins signing petitions and taking part in demonstrations. Warned by his colleagues, he first loses his senior position, together with half his salary, and then his job. When he persists, he and his second wife, Elena (Glenda Jackson), and her family are harassed and intimidated, but still the couple continue their fruitless campaign until they're exiled to the industrial city of Gorky, where they now live.

This could make dramatic material for a documentary film, or a book, but it stubbornly refuses to work as a fiction film, despite stalwart performances from Robards and Jackson. Pic is ultimately too static, too talky and too repetitive to sustain its length. Production dress is a bit scrappy, with Austrian locations uneasily subbing for the Soviet Union.

Climax comes with Elena's trip to Oslo to receive the Nobel Peace Prize on behalf of her husband, while the indomitable Sakharov is simultaneously involved in yet another demonstration back home.

Pic is well-meaning but a bit simplistic, and details don't ring true. Apart from the strong performances from the leads, as noted, there's a fine bit from Nicol Williamson as a fanatical KGB man.
— *Strat.*

Cheech And Chong's The Corsican Brothers
(U.S.-COLOR)

Cannes, May 19.

An Orion Pictures release of a C & C Brown production. Produced by Peter MacGregor-Scott; associate producers, Shelby Fiddis and Rikki Marin. Directed by Thomas Chong. Stars Cheech Marin, Chong. Screenplay, Marin, Chong; camera (Deluxe color), Harvey Harrison; editor, Tom Avildsen; art direction, Daniel Badin; music, Geo. Reviewed at the Cannes Film Festival (Market), May 18, 1984. (MPAA Rating: PG.) Running time: 87 MINS.

Luis	Cheech Marin
Lucien	Thomas Chong
Fucaire	Roy Dotrice
Princess 1	Shelby Fiddis
Princess 2	Rikki Marin
The queen	Edie McClurg
Princess 3	Robbi Chong
Gypsy	Rae Dawn Chong
Narrator	Laurie Maine

"Cheech And Chong's The Corsican Brothers" marks the stoned comedy team's first screen vehicle without drug humor and only a modest amount of rock 'n' roll. However, fans of the duo aren't about to be confronted by a major departure. Pic is very much in their raucous style and should maintain their popularity while doing okay at the boxoffice.

The swashbuckling parody actually opens in modern Paris with Cheech & Chong working as itinerant musicians. Gag is they're so bad, the crowds pay them not to play. Counting their cash in a café, they attract the attention of a gypsy, (Rae Dawn Chong), who, for a price, tells them of their noble origins.

Remaining yarn unreels in flashback during the French Revolution. Cheech & Chong are the illegitimate twins of a noblewoman and a commoner with the odd distinction of feeling pain only when it is inflicted on the other. This gag is milked to the limit.

Separated at a young age, Cheech returns after two decades in Mexico to discover Chong is now a revolutionary. Almost immediately they cross swords with heavy

Fucaire (Roy Dotrice) and are sentenced to the guillotine. However, a last-minute reprieve occurs when Fucaire prefers to torture the pair slowly.

Humor is largely derived from sexual themes including Fucaire's sado-masochistic tendencies, gay humor, double entendres and the like. In addition to the ethnic humor from Cheech's Hispanic background, there are Gallic gags ranging from bombs de terres (exploding potatos) to stone-hard bread used as karate sticks.

Overall effort is slapdash and borders on questionable taste. Nonetheless, this has proved a successful formula for the comedy team and there's no reason to believe it won't continue. At least, production values are of a slightly higher degree than usual.

Performances are broad, as usual, and the whole family works in "The Corsican Brothers." Wives Shelby Fiddis and Rikki Marin play lascivious princesses and serve as associate producers, and the director's daughters Rae Dawn and Robbi Chong show up in minor roles.

Still, one suspects the new effort won't have the legs of team's early hits. Initial boxoffice should be strong, but it will be difficult to maintain interest over the long run. The same off-filmed tale served as the basis for the 1969 Bud Yorkin-Norman Lear feature comedy "Start The Revolution Without Me," which remains the better picture, but its commercial fate was decidedly downbeat. —*Klad.*

The Bostonians
(BRITISH-COLOR)

London, May 14.

A Merchant-Ivory production for Rank and Rediffusion Films. Produced by Ismail Merchant. Directed by James Ivory. Stars Christopher Reeve, Vanessa Redgrave, Madeleine Potter. Screenplay, Ruth Prawer Jhabvala, based on the book by Henry James; camera (color), Walter Lassally; editors, Katherine Wenning, Mark Potter; music, Richard Robbins; production design, Leo Austin; art direction, Tom Walden, Don Carpentier; set decoration, Richard Elton; costume design, Jenny Beavan, John Bright, sound, Ray Beckett; assistant director, David Appleton. Reviewed at the Curzon cinema, London, May 10, 1984. A Directors Fortnight selection at Cannes Film Festival. Running time: 120 MINS.

Basil Ransome	Christopher Reeve
Olive Chancellor	Vanessa Redgrave
Verena Tarrant	Madeleine Potter
Miss Birdseye	Jessica Tandy
Mrs. Burrage	Nancy Marchand
Dr. Tarrant	Wesley Addy
Mrs. Tarrant	Barbara Bryne
Dr. Prance	Linda Hunt
Mrs. Luna	Nancy New
Henry Burrage	John Van Ness Philip
Mr. Pardon	Wallace Shawn
Henrietta Stackpole	Maura Moynihan
Mrs. Farrinder	Martha Farrar

Like the Merchant-Ivory-Jhabvala team's 1979 "The Europeans," this is a classy adaptation of a Henry James novel. The filmmakers have kept faith with their

source's distaste for the feminist movement in a way guaranteed to enrage present-day campaigners, but that's not likely to dent their regular following.

From the film's opening sequence at a women's meeting in late 19th century Boston, the dice are loaded against the feminist cause. The young Verena Tarrant offers an impassioned exposition of woman's sufferings only after being "touched" by the hands of her faith-healer father.

The charge of charlatanism is fixed by further displays of Mr. Tarrant's inspirational antics. Added to the indictment is an unsympathetic portrayal of journalist Mr. Pardon's plans to exploit Verena's gifts on a nationwide tour.

The emotional weight of the pic is carried by the relationship that evolves between Verena and Olive Chancellor. Latter is a mature spinster who attempts to secure her charge to the cause with a promise that she will never marry.

Central obstacle to Olive's ambition is Basil Ransome, a lawyer from the south with a persuasive tongue when it comes to wooing. His politics (which outrage Olive) are only lightly painted but, as depicted by Christopher Reeve, Basil's physical presence and native charm carry all before them.

The film's central problem is that Olive puts up little contest. Vanessa Redgrave brings a traumatized intensity to the part which frequently becomes unpleasant. Her final crime is to isolate the love-torn Verena from Basil in such a way that the mere sight of him in a crowd causes hysterics.

The film is ultimately convincing because of the central performance by newcomer Madeleine Potter as Verena who conveys all the dilemmas of a naive but strong-minded girl caught between her attachment to the cause and her longing for love.

A bevy of subsidiary characters illumines the film's message that people are more complex than their ideologies. Standouts are Jessica Tandy's Miss Birdseye, an elderly believer in "progress;" recent Oscar-winner Linda Hunt as Dr. Prance, a medic whose superficial espousal of the woman's cause barely covers a deeper understanding of human motives; and Mrs. Luna, played by Nancy New, who pursues Basil with traditional feminine guile.

The emotional transformations are mirrored in a geographical move from the cramped meeting rooms and lounges of Boston to the dramatic seashore locales filmed around Martha's Vineyard. It is there that Walter Lassally's camerawork reaches its apogee in a surreal scene where Olive Chancellor stalks the coastline, fearful that her beloved Verena is finally lost.

Ivory has a strong eye for moments of human contact and confrontation but occasionally falters with wide-open exteriors. — *Japa.*

A Breed Apart
(U.S.-COLOR)

Cannes, May 15.

An Orion Pictures release of a Hemdale-Sagittarius presentation. Produced by John Daly and Derek Gibson; associate producer, Dan Allingham. Directed by Philippe Mora. Screenplay by Paul Wheeler. Camera (Metrocolor), Geoffrey Stephenson; editor, Chris Lebenzon; art director, Bill Barclay; music, Maurice Gibb. Reviewed at the Cannes Festival (Market section), May 14, '84. Running time: **101 MINS.**

Jim Malden . . . . Rutger Hauer
Michael Walker . . . . Powers Boothe
Stella Clayton . . . . Kathleen Turner
J.P. Whittier . . . . Donald Pleasence
Charlie Peyton . . . . . . John Dennis Johnston
Huey Miller . . . . Brion James
Adam Clayton . . . . Adam Fenwick
Amy Rollings . . . . Jayne Bentzen

The visual splendors of North Carolina deserve top billing in "A Breed Apart." The tale of romance and chicanery in the backwoods simply lacks reason, dramatic tension or emotional involvement. Theatrical prospects for the Orion release remain unquestionably limited.

The core of the story centers on an obsessive bird egg collector's passion to secure specimens of a newly discovered breed of bald eagle. As the bird is protected by law, he has to hire a noted climber to illegally pilfer the shells. However, apart from the physical danger of reaching their lofty peak, he must contend with their protector, a reclusive mystery man who inhabits a secluded island.

Posing as a nature photographer, the climber enters the small community. He befriends a local woman who runs a fishing supply store and uses her to connect with his prime obstacle. The climber, Michael Walker (Powers Boothe) wins the quasi-conservationist Jim Malden's (Rutger Hauer), confidence and saves his skin from some angry hunters out for revenge.

Also figuring into the story is the unstated emotional bond between Malden and the storekeeper, played by Kathleen Turner, and her son who worships his independent ways. The liaison is eventually effected in some steamy sequences late in the story, but the nature of his timidity is never adequately explained — nor is there ever any clarity given to Turner's situation.

However, the film's biggest problem remains Walker's sudden change of heart which is completely out of character. The three leads have a hopeless task of fleshing out thinly developed roles despite their charisma. The narrative moves in the form of a series of non sequiturs.

Conversely, the technical credits, particularly Geoffrey Steph-

enson's camerawork, are rich and stunning. They are, needless to say, not enough to sustain the picture.

Ironically, while "A Breed Apart" wears the problems of a dramatic yoke, the filmmakers never crack the shell of its characters. Audubon would be proud of the effort, but Hemdale, the producers, should be prepared for the worst. —*Klad.*

The Naked Face
(U.S.-COLOR)

Cannes, May 17.

An MGM/UA release of a Cannon Group presentation. Produced by Menahem Golan and Yoram Globus. Direction and screenplay by Bryan Forbes, based on the novel by Sidney Sheldon. Stars Roger Moore, Rod Steiger, Elliott Gould, Anne Archer. Associate producer, Rony Yacov; camera (Metrocolor), David Gurfinkel; production design, William Fosser; editor, Philip Shaw; music, Michael J. Lewis. Reviewed at Cannes Festival (Market), May 17, 1984. (No MPAA rating.) Running time: **103 MINS.**

Dr. Judd Stevens . . . . Roger Moore
Lt. McGreavy . . . . Rod Steiger
Angeli . . . . Elliott Gould
Morgens . . . . Art Carney
Ann Blake . . . . Anne Archer
Dr. Hadley . . . . David Hedison
Mrs. Hadley . . . . Deanna Dunagan
Cortini . . . . Ron Parady

Taking a breather from his role as the much-loved spy 007, Roger Moore leads the star-studded and elegant production that marks Bryan Forbes' 25th year as a director. Based on Sidney Sheldon's first (but not first published) novel, "The Naked Face" foregoes the sex and minimizes the violence in a deliberately paced thriller, with setting shifted to Chicago.

Wearing glasses, Moore figures as Dr. Stevens, a psychiatrist being stalked but suspected by the police of masterminding the murders of a patient, his secretary and the apparent threats on his own life. The audience is clued-in from the first sequence in a cemetery where the doc visits wife's grave, that he's innocent. Rod Steiger plays a curmudgeon of a cop, embittered by doc's expert testimony in a case that cost a colleague's life. The cop's motives seem to get in the way of his finding the shrink's motives, so he's removed from the case, leaving the nice cop (Gould) to deliver the shrink into the hands of a jealous Mafioso.

The "family" has provided the shrink with one of his only successful cases, a Mafia bride who can't even bring herself to confess, much less make the couch an interesting indulgence. Anne Archer supplies the mysterious frustration as Ann Blake and, in the final scene, again in the cemetery, pays her dues for going outside the family with her problems. Dying in the doc's arms, she gives him a chance to adopt the 007 image he's trying to shed. Although he's sup-

posed to rid the role of the Bondian mannerisms, it's hard.

Art Carney almost steals the show as Morgens, a gumshoe living among dozens of clocks, whom the doctor hires for added protection. His time comes when he fingers a certain Don Vinton, a sobriquet not very well explained in pic. Morgens' presence manages to smoke out Gould, the sympathetic cop who turns out to be a stooge.

The sleek lensing in Chicago lends a nice sense of place and darkens progressively with the plot. Halfway through pic, everybody begins to look sinister, but Ron Parady as the sleazy Capo is archetypal. In his sewage and garbage plant, he gets off a few philosophical comments comparing his and the doc's respective contributions to modern living.

There is nothing excessive in all this, even though at times, things such as the music or the dialog threaten to become overdone. Bits such as a cripple, jumping on a Harley-Davidson, are delivered by helmer Forbes with such sleight of hand that Steiger's incredulous cop routine seems justified. Some of the twists and kinks, as well as the analytic sessions, seem to derive from a psychiatric imagination continually setting us up.

As an author with extensive experience, Forbes could have increased the suspense instead of solving the mystery about a quarter of an hour too soon. The pic works against Moore's Bond formula and image at the expense of its own tension. Cast is sure to be a big draw, even if their fans miss the action. — *Kaja.*

Le Chien
(The Dog)
(FRENCH-COLOR-16m)

Paris, May 15.

An Alice Productions film. Produced by Claude Bibas. Directed by Jean-François Gallotte. Screenplay, Irene Sohm. Camera (color, 16m), Etienne Szabo; editor, Christine Keller-Monge; music, Scorpions; sound, Jacques Gauron; art director, Pierre Gallotte, Guy Monbillard, Pierre Martin. Reviewed at the C.N.C., Paris, May 4, 1984. A "Perspectives on French Cinema" selection at Cannes Festival. Running time: **90 MINS.**

With: Micheline Presle, Veronique Silver, Jean-Luc Bideau, François Frapier, Marc Fege.

"Le Chien" is a mangy, distasteful drama about two batty brothers who try to shack up a drifter with their mother and then rival him for the sexual favors of a sluttish neighbor. The drifter turns out to be none other than the young men's long-departed father, and the neighbor his former mistress. When the latter is accidentally killed by the brothers, they arrange it so dad takes the rap.

Irene Sohm's screenplay piled up grotesque situations and neurotic tics, which director Jean-Fran-

çois Gallotte feverishly and artlessly splatters onto the screen. Ugly in content, "Le Chien" is no less hideous in form.

One's aversion is compounded by the fact that excellent actors such as Jean-Luc Bideau, Veronique Silver and notably Micheline Presle, have lent their talents to such a dubious script. Presle is the most unfortunate of the three, since she plays the mistress who tries to sexually initiate one of the brothers. —*Len.*

Fanny Pelopaja
(Fanny Strawhair)
(SPANISH-FRENCH-COLOR)

Cannes, May 16.

A Lolafilms S.A., Morgana Films S.A., Limpa P.C., Carlton Films production. Exec producer, Charles Durán. Written and directed by Vicente Aranda, based on novel "Protesis" by Andreu Martin. Camera (Eastmancolor), Juan Amorós; sets, Ramón Pou; editor, Teresa Font; Reviewed at Cannes Festival (Market), May 16, '84. Running time: **100 MINS.**

Fanny . . . . Fanny Cottençon
Andrés . . . . Bruno Cremer
Julián . . . . Francisco Algora
Nena . . . . Berta Cabré
Manual . . . . Ian Sera
Also: Paca Gabaldón, Eduardo MacGregor, Joaquim Cardona, Roberto Asla, Jordi Serrat, Marta Padován, Carles Sales.

Fanny is a tough Barcelona delinquent who has served several jail terms and holds up people in cars with her switchblade when she needs quick cash. Story, needlessly told in one long flashback, picks up when Fanny is working at a gas station in the sticks. But when she is tipped off that "Andrés" is back in Barcelona, she drops everything and hurries to the big city.

Andrés, we learn by a flashback, was a nasty cop who humiliated Fanny, killed her boyfriend and knocked out all her teeth, so that she now has to wear false ones (hence title of original novel, "Protesis," meaning false teeth). Fanny is dying to get even. After roughing her up, the cop was given the boot from the force for his brutality and is working as an armored car guard. Fanny and some friends, plus three pros, pull off the heist, but Fanny, instead of killing the ex-cop, merely slams him across the teeth with the butt of her gun.

But Andrés gets even and in a nasty, brutal scene murders Fanny's friends after they tell him where to find the girl. Rather than sate the spectator's aroused yen to see Andrés finally get his just desserts, pic ends in disappointingly low-key fashion. The love-hate relationship between Fanny and Andrés is not further explained, nor need it be.

Pic can keep a spectator on the edge of his seat, though the technique of building up tension during key scenes such as the van robbery is left at mid-stream. As an actioner, pic doesn't come across with enough punch. Fanny Cottençon does an excellent job of thesping as the tough straw-haired girl, and Bruno Cremer is thoroughly convincing as the despicable cop.

Item should do okay biz in Spain and France, and might find some offshore buyers — *Besa.*

Roadhouse 66
(U.S.-COLOR)

Cannes, May 21.

An Atlantic Releasing release. Produced by Scott M. Rosenfelt, Mark Levinson. executive producers, Thomas Coleman, Michael Rosenblatt. Directed by John Mark Robinson. Screenplay, Galen Lee, George Simpson, story by Lee; camera (United Color), Tom Ackerman; editor, Jay Lash Cassidy; composer, Gary Scott; music coordinator, Art Fein; production design, Chester Kaczenski; sound, Sunny Meyer; assistant director, Mary Ellen Woods; second unit camera, Bryan Duggan. Reviewed at the Cannes Film Festival (Market), May 20, 1984. (MPAA Rating: R.) Running time: **90 MINS.**
Johnny Harte...............Willem Dafoe
Beckman Hallsgood Jr. ....Judge Reinhold
Jesse Duran...................Kaaren Lee
Melissa Duran...............Kate Vernon
Sam.......................Stephen Elliott
Hoot..........................Alan Autry
Dink.................Kevyn Major Howard
Moss....................Peter Van Norden
Thelma.......................Erica Yohn

"Roadhouse 66" is a negligible youth meller that's unexciting in all departments. Despite its R rating, pic is so mild it could have been made back in the 1950s, where its sensibility clearly rests, and Atlantic Releasing will have to push hard to get any early mileage out of this one.

Plot is so thin it could have been written on a bar napkin. Spoiled Ivy Leaguer Judge Reinhold and hitchhiking hipster Willem Dafoe have to spend Labor Day weekend in little Bowman, Ariz., waiting for a new car radiator, and during their sojourn they raise some hell, find true love and win a local drag race. It's stuff that might barely get a passing grade in film school script courses but somehow gets made in the real world.

Pic's two dramatic highlights, a pool game and the auto race, in which the bad guy actually tries to sabotage the good guy by putting a real live scorpion in his car, would be right at home in a 1950s hood meller starring Richard Bakalyan and Sal Mineo.

One bright spot is Judge Reinhold, who wings it in high style as the upper class boy forced to acquire some street smarts overnight. Kate Vernon is quite attractive opposite him.

Some 21 rock and country tunes on the soundtrack divert the attention when nothing else does, which is often. Production-wise, pic is serviceable. —*Cart.*

681 A.D. The Glory Of Khan
(BULGARIAN-COLOR)

Cannes, May 16.

A Buyana Film Studio production, produced by Sidney H. Levine and Thomas L. Marshall. World rights, Globe Export. Exec producer, William R. Bloom. Features Anthony Genov, Stoyko Peyev, Marie Sir, Vanya Tavetkova, Anya Pencheva. Directed by Ludmil Staikov. Screenplay, Jules Minton and Sam Locke, based on the original screenplay "Khan Asparouch" by Vera Moutafchieva; camera (Eastmancolor), Boris Yonakiev; editor, John Duffy; music, Simeon Pironkov, Douglas Lackey and Gene Kauer. Reviewed at Cannes Festival (Market), May 16, '84. Running time: **90 MINS.**

This is the shortened 90-minute version of Staikov's "Khan Asparouch," originally madē in 1981, which ran four and a half hours. Item has been picked up by Globe Export for distribution worldwide as an epic actioner.

As such it is often spectacular enough, but largely monotonous and slow-paced since insights are never provided into the personalities of the main characters. The action scenes are skimmed over with little explanation; they lack poignancy and tend to be flat. The centerpiece of the film is the final battle between the combined Bulgar and Slav armies against those of the Byzantine emperor Constantine.

But, despite the really impressive array of troops used and the well-shot battle sequences, the fact of the Bulgar-Slav army being outnumbered 10 to one is never really brought across in the fighting, as the Romans seem to be turned back with relative ease.

Perhaps some of the depth and profundity that may have been included in the original version has been lost in this quickie edition of the Bulgar epic. The presence of the Roman Velasarius as a sort of Marco Polo-like observer doesn't really add much to the story, and when the Khan's wives die, little emotion is conveyed on the screen. Velasarius himself is to die at the hands of the Romans for refusing to falsify the Roman defeat, but even that is handled rather flatly.

— *Besa.*

Scream For Help
(U.S.-COLOR)

Cannes, May 16.

A Lorimar presentation. Produced and directed by Michael Winner. Executive producer, Irwin Yablans. Screenplay, Tom Holland; camera (color), Robert Paynter; editor, Arnold Ross; music, John Paul Jones, art direction, Tony Reading. Reviewed at Cannes Festival (Market), May 15, '84. (MPAA Rating: R.) Running time: **88 MINS.**
Christie Cromwell..........Rachael Kelly
Karen Cromwell Fox.......Marie Masters
Paul Fox.......................David Brooks
Brenda Bohle.................Lolita Lorre
Lacey Bohle...................Rocco Sisto
Josh Dealey ....Corey Parker
Janey.......................Sandra Clark
Bob Dealey ....Tony Sibbald

Filmmaker Michael Winner has earned his stripes with a string of exploitation films, notably "Death Wish." "Scream For Help," his latest, would appear to be familiar ground for Winner but it is, in fact, largely a parody of his past successes. Unfortunately, like his last foray into mirth, "Won Ton Ton," the new film is a dog.

Neither levity nor subtlety are Winner's forté and both are crucial to making "Scream For Help" work. The story centers on a teenage girl's unshakable belief that her stepfather is out to murder her mother. Events conspire to make it appear she's the girl who cried wolf too often. However, the audience realizes early on her instincts are sound.

When she finally secures the concrete evidence, it sets off an unpleasant reign of terror. The stepfather along with his girlfriend and her brother (actually husband) take mother and daughter by force and plan to stage murders which will secure them vast riches.

Despite the arch performances by the principals, the unsuspecting might still take the yarn as straight thriller laced with graphic violence. To ice the cake, Winner employs an overly melodramatic musical score to tip his hand. Needless to say the device is overused and the preciousness of the entire concept coupled with its questionable taste proves tiring and repugnant.

The necessity of this approach remains dubious. The story, though familiar, is probably more effective rendered in a traditional manner. The cast of newcomers largely seems ill at ease with the tongue-in-cheek approach while the technical components are crisp and fluid.

The chief failing here is the insistence on often stomach-turning violence. It chafes badly with the lighter, bizarre aspects of "Scream For Help," creating an unsettling mixture. Commercial prospects are thus limited to fast, saturation engagements aimed at exploitation markets. However, both action and comedy fans will feel cheated by the end result.

—*Klad.*

Ganga Maya
(FRENCH-COLOR)

Paris, May 15.

A Ludovic Segarra production. Produced, written and directed by Ludovic Segarra. Camera, Jean-Claude Larrieu; sound, Jean-Philippe Le Roux; editor, Chantal Piquet; music, Dominique Bertrand; production manager, Sarah Mondale. Reviewed at the C.N.C., May 4, 1984. A "Perspectives on French Cinema" selection at Cannes Festival. Running time: **97 MINS.**
With: Gilles Gesweiller.

A young Frenchman's journey up to Ganges river in India in search of spiritual renewal is the subject of "Ganga Maya," a first feature coproduced by the Antenne 2 tv web. Producer-writer-director Ludovic Segarra has devoted numerous shorts to the Far East and palpably put great feeling into this project. Though it finally misses its mark, the inevitable clichés are often swept aside by the affecting visual beauty of various scenes, which set it apart from the mere picturesque travelog item.

Pic follows the travels of a young man who has apparently reached an impasse in his life back home (leaving behind a girlfriend who pines philosophically for him in an irritating voice-over text) and heads for India in search of something else. Landing in Calcutta, he quickly has his bag and effects filched, and accepts an invitation to join a small cargo vessel traveling up the Ganges. The journey ended, he goes up into the hills and spends some time with a family of peasants, and subsequently continues on into the mountains, where he finally experiences the sought-after epiphany.

There is nothing more to the protagonist than the sympathetically thoughtful presence brought by the actor Gilles Gesweiller, so it's really hard to care about his inner experience. But the outer experience is often captured splendidly in Jean-Claude Larrieu's lensing. Segarra often proves he has a genuine sense of cinema, notably in a moving sequence in which an old Indian, who has died on the boat trip, is burned on a pyre on the river bank, as the vessel is hauled past in the background. — *Len.*

Pavlova
(BRITISH-RUSSIAN-COLOR)

Cannes, May 16.

A Frixos Constantine presentation for Poseidon Films (London). Written and directed by Emil Lotianou. Western version supervised by Michael Powell. Camera (color), Eugeny Guslinsjy; art direction, Boris Blank; music, Eugene Dogas; editors, I. Kalatikova, E. Galinka, J. Connock; associate producers, Eric Weissbergr (USSR), Serafim Karalexis, (U.S.), sound, Stan Fiferman. Ballets staged by Professor P. Gusev. Reviewed at Cannes Film Festival (market section), May 15, 1984. Running time: **132 MINS.**
Pavlova...................Galina Beliaeva
Victor D'Andre.................James Fox
Michael Fokine.........Sergei Shakourov
Diaghilev ....V. Larionov
Young Pavlova...........Lina Boultakova
Enrico Cecchetti........Georgio Dimitriou
Victor Stair..................Ivan Shykyra
Marius Pepita..................P. Gousev
Gatti Cassaza.............Martin Scorsese
Alfred Butt ....Bruce Forsyth
The Gardener ....Roy Kinnear
Saint-Saens.................Jaques Debari
Nijinsky...................Michael Padunin
Albert D'Andre.............Alkis Kritikos
Anastasia ....Anastasia Stakis

Subtitled "A Woman For All Time," this Anglo-Soviet coproduction was first presented at the 1983 Moscow festival and is now a prominent item in the Cannes market, where it has been receiving some hefty promotion.

(Paramount Pictures made a pre-buy for world rights to the film, less USSR, eastern Europe, Finland and India, but reportedly sold its rights back to Poseidon Films — *Ed.)*

By its very nature, "Pavlova" is destined to find its true theatrical audience from ballet addicts, but it also has potential for both cable and video, from which sources it is likely to recoup a substantial slice of its budget. Clearly it was not an inexpensive film to make, having studio interiors at Mosfilm in Moscow, and location filming in the U.S., Britain, France, Germany, Mexico and Cuba.

Anna Pavlova's short life — she died in 1931 at the age of 49 — embraces some landmark events in Europe and, of course, her native Russia. But while in Petrograd (now Leningrad) during the abortive 1905 uprising, she was already traveling the world when the revolution began and never returned to her homeland, although she had always planned to do so.

There is little doubt that the screenwriters have taken some dramatic license with the Pavlova story, but that's of little import. What matters, and what the film is all about, is to describe the career of the legendary ballerina, considered one of the greatest dancers of the century.

That she was dedicated is made evident from the early scenes in which she is totally captivated by watching ballet students in training. Her rise from corps de ballet to prima ballerina is sketchily told, but it is the performances of "Giselle" and "Swan Lake," for which she was universally famous, that illuminate the action.

While the emphasis is understandably on the title character, the story introduces more of the legendary personalities of the international ballet scene, notably Diaghilev, who, more than anyone else, shapes her career, Nijinsky, the famous dancer who ends in an asylum, and Alfred Butt, the distinguished London impresario, who gives Pavlova a two-year salary advance so she can bail out her husband who faces prison because of his debts.

Undoubtedly, the highlights are the dance sequences, magnificently devised by Professor Gusev, and the theatrical presentations, whether staged in Leningrad, Europe or Latin America, are played against sumptuous backgrounds. It is, in the main, a handsomely mounted production, augmented by authentic locations.

Of course, the action focuses on the title character, and as played by Galina Beliaeva, she is a determined but strong-willed personal-

ity, used to having her own way, whatever the cost to others. But it's as a dancer that her performance must be judged, and in this respect she has class. Her stage performances are totally inspired, though her more conventional thesping is sometimes less than convincing.

V. Larionov is dominant as Diaghilev, an artist who gives her pupils no pity until they've reached their zenith. James Fox portrays the weak but devoted man who becomes her husband in a rather colorless performance, but there are fascinating cameos from Martin Scorsese, Bruce Forsyth and Roy Kinnear.

Emil Lotianou's direction is brisk, despite a somewhat lethargic script. Eugene Dogas' music performed by the State Orchestra of the Bolshoi Theatre is a distinct plus, and other technical credits are okay. —*Myro.*

Bay Boy
(CANADIAN-COLOR)

Cannes, May 21.

An Orion Pictures International release of an ICC International Cinema Corporation presentation. Produced by John Kemeny and Denis Heroux. Executive producer, Frank Jacobs. Coproducer, Rene Cleitman. Direction and screenplay by Daniel Petrie. Camera (color), Claude Agostini; editor, Susan Shanks; production design, Wolf Kroeger; music Claude Bolling. Reviewed at the Cannes Film Festival (Market), May 20, 1984. Running time: **104 MINS.**

Jennie Campbell............Liv Ullmann
Donald Campbell.......Kiefer Sutherland
Sgt. Tom Coldwell.............Alan Scarfe
Father Chaisson.........Mathieu Carriere
Will Campbell................:...Peter Donat
Mary McNeil..............Isabelle Mejias
Saxon Coldwell................Lesh Pinsent
Dianna Coldwell...........Anne McKinnon
Joe Campbell.................Peter Spence
Chief Charles McInnes......Chris Wiggins
Father O'Meara.........Thomas Peacocke
Sister Roberts...........Josephine Chaplin
Blanche..................Stéphane Audran
Walt Roach...................David Ferry

Canadian-born director Daniel Petrie ("Resurrection," "Fort Apache, The Bronx," "Sybil," "The Dollmaker") has long cherished making a film about his early days in Nova Scotia. "Bay Boy" is the realization of that dream, but it's far from the pot of gold at the end of his rainbow. The gentle tale lacks the dramatic grit necessary to connect at the boxoffice although the film should earn respectable reviews and distribution in specialty situations.

Setting is a coastal mining community circa 1937. Principals are a family of non-miners barely eking out an existence during the Depression. Kiefer Sutherland, son of actor Donald, has the pivotal part of Donald Campbell, a teenager whose family envision his future with the clergy. He's more dubious about this path.

The family travails — father's precarious fortunes, brother's de-

bilitating disease, mother's profound religious guilt, etc. — are cut with humorous vignettes and insights. However, the plot later veers off into darker areas after Donald witnesses the murder of an old Jewish couple by a local policeman.

The killer, Tom Coldwell (Alan Scarfe), also happens to be the father of two girls for whom Donald pines. That and his terror of Coldwell's mean streak lead him to tell the police he did not see the murderer.

This facet of the story, as well as the aspects centering on pressures to enter the priesthood, come up short dramatically. Petrie pulls his punches in order to tie up ends neatly at film's fade. Even so, one is unclear about the title character's future or his relationship with another young girl. Certainly such elements as homosexuality, young love, murder and ethics would suggest more emotional power than is evident in this film.

Sutherland simply lacks the experience or charm to carry the picture as required in his role. Although top-billed, Liv Ullmann as his mother virtually disappears from the second part of the film and her performance, while strong, is thankless. Best turns belong to Scarfe — looking like a young Robert Shaw — as story's heavy, Mathieu Carriere as the priest sexually attracted to Sutherland, and Isabelle Mejias as an overpowering charmer.

Pic is handsomely mounted in all respects though music score tends to be intrusive at times. Story is much too busy and confusing to ultimately connect with mass audiences and direction remains carefree when one expects some bite.

"Bay Boy" appears headed for special handling route and, ironically, though regional in theme, should score best in urban areas — *Klad.*

Dorado — One Way
(WEST GERMAN-COLOR)

Cannes, May 17.

A Coproduction of Reinhard Münster Filmproduktion and Futura Film, Munich. Written, directed and edited by Münster. Features entire cast. Camera (color), Martin Theo Krieger; sound, Peter Schmidt; music, Gernot Voltz, Kurve, Oldenburg-Zielonka, Fliegenpilz; production manager, Joachim Rote; lighting and camera assistant, Axel Berger. Reviewed at Cannes Festival (Market), May 16, '84. Running time: **83 MINS.**

Cast: Uwe Schwalbe, Dominik Bender, Adriana Altaras, Uwe Büschken, Elisabeth Zündel, Peter Schmidt, Bruve Barthol, Peter Schlesinger, Sophie Daubier.

A diploma film made at the Berlin Film Academy, Reinhard Münster's "Dorado — One Way" is a lively, delightful and highly recommended spoof on filmmaking. It also shows how comically entertaining the Berlin Underground as a whole is these days.

The tale begins with the filmmaker in an apartment commune shooting a pic about a love relationship. Occasionally he does it in a freewheeling Lothar Lambert style, then he shifts over to the alienation effects of Jean-Marie Straub. When the girl is visited by a former boyfriend on the set, the filmer simply builds everything spontaneously into the plot as he goes along.

Then the style shifts to that of a road movie. The leads cross the border into Switzerland, and pick up a femme hitch-hiker. This allows for more aimless drifting across backroads and through lush countryside, Wim Wenders style. Sure enough, the hero finds out by accident that he's transporting cocaine hidden inside the paintings. He informs his contact back in Berlin that he wants a share of the payoff. This ploy, in turn, leads to a hired gunman in pursuit of the pair (read Peter F. Bringmann's "Theo Against The Rest Of The World" into the script at this juncture).

Once they reach Cannes, the film festival is on. There's a shootout, but the hero comes away unscathed. The last scene finds him in Berlin taking care of his girlfriend's (and his adopted) child while commenting on what's happened to the rest of the crew, including the erstwhile filmmaker.

"Dorado — One Way" benefits from a fun script and a light hand at direction by Münster. Pic also shared a Golden-TIP award at last year's Hof fest (with Uwe Schrader's "Kanakerbraut"). — *Holl,*

Blind Date
(U.S.-COLOR)

Cannes, May 15.

A New Line Cinema release of an Omega Pictures production in association with Wescom Productions. Produced, and directed by Nico Mastorakis. Exec producer, Dimitri Skouras. Stars Joseph Bottoms. Screenplay, Mastorakis, Fred C. Perry. Camera (color), Andrew Bellis; editor, George Rosenberg; music, Stanley Myers; songs, John Kongos; sets, costumes, Anne Marie Papadelis. Reviewed at the Cannes Film Festival (Market section), May 15, 1984. (MPAA Rating: R.) Running time: **99 MINS.**

Jonathon Ratcliffe.........Joseph Bottoms
Claire Parker................Kirstie Alley
David.....................James Daughton
Rachel.....................Lana Clarkson
Dr. Steiger....................Keir Dullea

Like most, this "Blind Date" turns out not to be worth the time. A U.S. exploitation thriller filmed in Athens, it carries on two simultaneous plots — that of a surgical killer of women on the loose and that of a young ad exec blinded and outfitted with a computerized implant that allows him to see and tape record shapes just enough to get around on his own.

As telegraphed in a slow-moving script not aided by equally dull direction, the two stories merge.

The killer is nailed and the ad exec saves a former girlfriend whom he has witnessed being raped years before. That's given him severe mental blocks, but she never knows either about that or that he's the one who rescues her. Expatriate Americans don't always have fun abroad. But all the women wear bikini briefs and are seen topless.

Repeated sequences of the surgical killer slicing up various women may be a turn-on for some who dig violence to women, but the gore is quite unnecessary. While the idea of an implant for the blind poses an interesting plot turn, the pic itself has all the earmarks of a nonstarter with limited appeal even in homevid. The actors all should have better things to do. — *Adil.*

Don't Kill God
(BRITISH-COLOR)

Cannes, May 16.
A Beamleaf Ltd. (London) production, Armand Rubin-Europex (Paris) release. Produced by Mubarak F. Al Sabah. Written and directed by Jacqueline Manzano. Camera (color) Daniele Nannuzzi; editor, Peter Taylor; music, Ennio Morricone; hymn sung by Barbara Henricks. Reviewed at Cannes Festival (Market), May 16, '84. Running time: **83 MINS.**

Writer-director Jacqueline Manzano is adamant that her first feature-length effort after several documentary shorts is not to be labeled as a docu. "Don't Kill God" can, however, hardly be considered as straight entertainment, whether artistic or not. Film is a carefully crafted mix of old and new (most of the new ones of her own making) documentary clips and some action sequences of obvious fictional character. Most of the docu footage shows the Pope having his hand kissed by the throngs in St. Peter's Square or being greeted by population and local dignitaries on his visits to Nigeria, the Philippines, Rio and elsewhere. The camera has not caught the assassination attempt on His Holiness but makes do with hovering over a still of the event.

The Pope is also seen briefly bidding Manzano welcome to the Vatican Gardens with her crew. John Paul II is clearly the hero of a film that soon emerges as a richly illustrated tract, extolling the virtues of true faith and warning against all the evils that threaten mankind through consumerism, armament and indulging in various vices.

The uplifting things in Life are seen as classical statuary and heard as choral singing, while the horrors are epitomized in snippets of Hitler, Mussolini, Stalin, Mao and Nasser parades and oratory, flashily staged scenes of battlefield action, a sex & dope orgy sequence, and fighting between gun-toting hippies who turn out to be survivors of a "Mad Max" style End of the World.

Ennio Morricone has been allowed to go to high-strung extremes with his score, and while Manzano and her technical team are clearly good at fixing real events on film, their staged action tends strongly towards the ludicrous. All through the film an anonymous, sonorous male voice accompanies the flow of pictures with words of dire warning and other rhetoric along lines such as these: "As they (surviving mankind) struggling to keep their footing on the slippery slope of the new barbarism, is there anything but faith which can provide them with firm support?"

Film's final warning repeats the title and goes on to say that by killing God, Mankind kills only itself. "Don't Kill God" was financed and produced by Mubarak F. Al Sabah, a Kuwaiti prince, and Faith in the film seems to encompass all true devotion to one Superior God, whether Catholic, Protestant, Muslim or Buddhist. It is hard to imagine this film in any commercial context, but its showing may prove an event in gatherings of religious groups or other humanistic rallies.
—*Kell.*

Reunion
(AUSTRALIAN-COLOR)

Cannes, May 17.
A South Australian Film Corp. presentation. Produced by Harley Manners. Stars Carmen Duncan, Michael Aitkens, Shane Briant, Nicholas Eadie, Redmond Symons and Annie Jones. Directed by Chris Langman. Screenplay, Graham Hartley, based upon the novel "When We Ran" by Keith Leopold; exec producer, Jock Blair; assoc. prod., Ron Saunders; camera (Eastmancolor), Ernie Clark; art director, Herbert Pinter; editor, Andrew Prowse. Reviewed at the Cannes Festival (Market), May 17, '84. Running time: **90 MINS.**

Eve	Carmen Duncan
Riley	Michael Aitkens
Chrissie	Annie Jones
Toe	Nicholas Eadie
Terrier	Shane Briant
Pitt	Redmond Symons

An actioner targeted primarily at the youth market, "Reunion" moves briskly from London to Sydney and the Barossa Valley in South Australia without managing to cover much territory emotionally. Item was conceived originally as a made-for-tv feature until the production company, the South Australian Film Corp. decided to angle it for theatrical playoff. First intention seems more realistic, since pic lacks the punch and scope to make it a big-screen event.

Carmen Duncan is a former West German terrorist on the run with her 15-year-old daughter (Annie Jones). They're pursued by Michael Aitkens and an Irishman and onetime lover of Duncan, who left London and the ranks of the Irish Republican Army in a hurry after shooting an IRA colleague.

The IRA dispatches two operatives (Shane Briant and Redmond

Symons) to track him down, and they join up with a revolting biker (Nicholas Eadie) who's sore because Duncan torched his car.

Australia is a mighty big continent, but through a series of scarcely believable lucky breaks, the IRA duo and biker find Duncan and daughter in an outlying part of the winegrowing region of the Barossa Valley, shortly before Aitkens shows up. Shoot-out in the winery has a predictable result.

Helming his first feature, Chris Langman does a tradesmanlike job technically but cannot overcome the holes in the script, and patches of unintentionally risible dialog.

Performances are mostly ordinary. Duncan frequently forgets her German accent, Aitkens and Briant are wooden, Symons' buffoonish character is hardly the image the IRA cultivates, and Jones' lack of experience shows. — *Dogo.*

Fear City
(U.S. – COLOR)

Cannes, May 17.
A Zupnik-Curtis Enterprises production. Produced by Bruce Cohn Curtis. Coproducer, Jerry Tokofsky. Executive producers, Stanley R. Zupnik, Tim Curtis. Directed by Abel Ferrara. Stars Tom Berenger, Billy Dee Williams, Jack Scalia, Melanie Griffith, Rossano Brazzi. Screenplay, Nicholas St. John; camera (Deluxe color), James Lemmo; editors, Jack Holmes, Anthony Redman; music, Dick Halligan; set decoration, Cricket Rowland; costume design, Linda M. Bass; sound, Jim Tannenbaum; assistant director, Peter Manoogian. Reviewed at the Cannes Film Festival (Market), May 16, 1984. (No MPAA rating.) Running time: **96 MINS.**

Matt Rossi	Tom Berenger
Al Wheeler	Billy Dee Williams
Nicky Piacenza	Jack Scalia
Loretta	Melanie Griffith
Carmine	Rossano Brazzi
Liela	Rae Dawn Chong
Frank	Joe Santos
Mike	Michael V. Gazzo
Goldstein	Jan Murray
Honey	Ola Ray

"Fear City" lives up to its title as a tough, nasty, big-league meller by throwing every element from the exploitation cookbook — gory violence, straight and gay sex, multiple murders, martial arts, raw-dialog, mobsters, drugs and gobs of female nudity — into the pot and letting them stew. Since male sensation seekers will certainly get their money's worth, Zupnik-Curtis production has plenty of b.o. value, but women won't like it — seediness of all of the characters and their milieu ultimately represents a turnoff.

Pic is set in the fleshpot of midtown Manhattan and is populated by strippers and the sleazy men who run their lives. Hovering above them are organized crime types on the one side and the cops on the other, and soon a third menace is introduced, that of a roving sicko who launches a systematic genocidal assault on the girls who work at the nude clubs.

This madman, like the countless others that have been seen onscreen in recent years, has his reasons, of course. A solitary, spartan type who is occasionally glimpsed in his loft writing an autobiographical account of his deeds called "Fear City," his martial arts-oriented beliefs have given him such a taste for purity that he thinks he's doing the world a favor by wiping out all these "dirty" girls.

His attacks are usually carried out with extremely sharp instruments, and some of them are awful bloody messes. Things finally get so bad that the girls stop working, which puts a major dent in business at strip joints and creates problems for B-girl talent agents Tom Berenger and Jack Scalia.

Teeming plot has Berenger trying to get things started again with old flame Melanie Griffith who, on the rebound, has embarked on a lesbian affair with Rae Dawn Chong and later gets hooked again on drugs. Nightspot operator Michael V. Gazzo is always sweating due to the money he owes, cop Billy Dee Williams is on everyone's case, and Berenger finally has to turn to gangland kingpins Rossano Brazzi and Jan Murray for help.

Mixed in with all this are flashbacks to Berenger's early career as a boxer, which he quit when he killed a man in the ring. Memories of this haunt him when he finally confronts the rampaging maniac in a dark alley for a to-the-death showdown, a battle which pits boxing skills vs. martial art techniques.

Pic overall amounts to a massive dose of urban paranoia. As in his earlier pictures, "Driller Killer" and the cult item "Ms. 45," director Abel Ferrara gives people who walk the streets of New York City a lot to worry about, and he's got really down and dirty with his material here in muscular style.

Lensed in New York and Los Angeles, production is big and impressive for its genre across the boards, although Dick Halligan's score is on the conventional side.
—*Cart.*

The Hit
(BRITISH-COLOR)

Cannes, May 19.
A Glinwod Films Ltd. presentation of a Central Productions-Recorded Picture Company production. Produced by Jeremy Thomas. Directed by Stephen Frears. Stars John Hurt, Tim Roth, Laura del Sol, Terence Stamp. Screenplay, Peter Prince; camera (color), Mike Molloy; editor, Mick Audsley; production design, Andrew Sanders; sound, Paul Le Marc; music, Paco de Lucia; title music, Eric Clapton; associate producer, Joyce Herlihy. Reviewed at Cannes Festival (Directors Fortnight), May 18, 1984. Running time: **97 MINS.**

Braddock	John Hurt
Myron	Tim Roth
Maggie	Laura del Sol
Willie Parker	Terence Stamp
Harry	Bill Hunter
Policeman	Fernando Rey

This astringent, sardonically funny thriller is only the second theatrical feature for director Stephen Frears since "Gumshoe" (1971), an engaging parodic private eye film with Albert Finney. Making a triumphant return to the big screen after prolific tv work, Frears and writer Peter Prince have taken a potentially familiar tale of a gangland betrayal and revenge and made something richly inventive and most entertaining.

Pic opens in London in 1972 as Willie Parker (Terence Stamp) fingers his fellow criminals and is warned that retribution will catch up to him eventually. Ten years later, Parker is living an apparently carefree existence in the Spanish countryside when four toughs kidnap him and kill his bodyguard. They hand him over to an experienced hit man, Braddock (John Hurt) and his novice sidekick, Myron (Tim Roth), who immediately eliminate four of the three kidnappers with a car bomb and set out to deliver their prisoner to the boss in Paris. It's a journey with plenty of diversion, a journey on which things keep going wrong.

Most disconcerting for the hitmen is that Parker is so relaxed and philosophical about his fate. Seems he's been expecting it all these years and is resigned to it. But it disturbs and disorientates the gunmen, because a victim *shouldn't* behave that way. A stopoff at a secret apartment provides a further problem: the apartment should have been empty, but it's occupied by an Australian criminal, Harry (Bill Hunter) and his young Spanish mistress, Maggie (Laura del Sol). After some procrastination, mainly because he likes Harry, Braddock decides the risk of witnesses is too great, and the Australian is gunned down while watching his favorite Melbourne football team in action on tv; Maggie is taken along as a hostage.

As the quartet heads north, Parker smoothly sets each one against the other in a series of beautifully written, directed and acted scenes. Pic eventually explodes in violence, but not at all the way one might have expected; indeed, until near the very end it manages to be continually surprising and playfully manipulative with the audience.

Acting is marvelous. Hurt is the experienced professional, certainly a change of pace for him. Terence Stamp give his best performance in years as the relaxed kidnap victim. Laura del Sol (Carlos Saura's "Carmen" star) is properly frightened but resourceful as Maggie. Fernando Rey has little to do as a cop. Bill Hunter gives a rich cameo as an over-the-hill gunman caught in the wrong place at the wrong time. He reacts by talking

non-stop, pathetically trying to hide his fear, and it's a gem of a performance.

Best of all, though, is Tim Roth, last seen as the simple-minded youth in Mike Leigh's "Meantime;" as a cocky little hood, a bit puzzled as to what's going on and wanting to assert himself a little, he creates a wonderfully detailed and sympathetic character out of what could have been a very minor role.

Spanish locations are well lensed by Mike Molloy, and the pic is technically fine down the line. It could do solid biz with good promotion on its originality, humor, suspense and style. It rates another nod for producer Jeremy Thomas, currently one of Britain's most original and creative producers.

— *Strat.*

Trial Run
(NEW ZEALAND - COLOR)

Cannes, May 18.

A Cinema and Television Prods. production, with the assistance of the New Zealand Film Commission. Produced by Don Reynolds. Directed, written by Melanie Read. Features entire cast. Camera (color) Allen Guilford; editor, Finola Dwyer; music, Jan Preston; production designer, Judith Crozier; assoc. producer, Alane Hunter; art director, Kirsten Shouler. Reviewed at the Cannes Festival (Market) May 18, '84. Running time: 90 MINS.
Rosemary .... Annie Whittle
Frances .... Judith Gibson
James .... Christopher Brown
Anne .... Phillipa Mayne
Michael .... Stephen Tozer
Alan .... Martyn Sanderson
Mrs. Jones .... Lee Grant

A low budget thriller, "Trial Run" is elevated above the run-of-the-mill by a strong feminist streak, courtesy of writer/director Melanie Read, and an ingenious, unexpected twist which puts a sting in the tale.

Slow to build, subdued in tone and enlivened by only a few dramatic flashpoints, pic does not possess enough exploitable elements to justify wide, theatrical release, but should play well on television in most markets.

Making her feature film debut, Read displays a style an flair which should see her graduate to bigger budget mainstream projects.

Deceptively simple plot has Rosemary (Annie Whittle) leaving her husband and two teenaged children to spend six months photographing and writing about penguins in an isolated part of the New Zealand coast. Family is none too pleased, especially son James (Christopher Brown), who is using his computer to program a training schedule to prepare her for a cross country race, but they get the chance to visit her at weekends. Also for company she has regular visits from independently spirited friend Frances (Judith Gibson).

Her presence in an old shack near the beach is not welcomed by either of her nearest neighbors, Alan (Martyn Sanderson) and Mrs. Jones (Lee Grant), and when windows are smashed, flowers are strewn around and blood is smeared over family photographs, it's clear someone is up to no good.

That person's identity, and the underlying purpose, are revealed in a skillfully written and directed climax. A shame the picture takes so long to get there. Acting is uniformly good, and production values don't seem to have been crimped by budget restraints. — *Dogo.*

Ordeal By Innocence
(BRITISH-COLOR)

Cannes, May 21.

An MGM/UA release of a Cannon Group Inc. presentation. Produced by Jenny Craven. Executive producers, Menahem Golan, Yoram Globus. Directed by Desmond Davis. Screenplay, Alexander Stuart, based on the novel by Agatha Christie. Camera (Eastmancolor), Billy Williams editor, Timothy Gee; music, Pino Donaggio, sound, Derek Ball; production design, Ken Bridgeman; assistant director, David Tringham. Reviewed at the Cannes Film Festival (Market), May 20, 1984. (No MPAA Rating.) Running time: 87 MINS.
Dr. Arthur Calgary ..... Donald Sutherland
Rachel Argyle .... Faye Dunaway
Leo Argyle .... Christopher Plummer
Philip Durrant .... Ian McShane
Mary Durrant .... Sarah Miles
Gwenda Vaughan .... Diana Quick
Kirsten Lindstrom .... Annette Crosbie
Inspector Huish .... Michael Elphick
Tina Argyle .... Phoebe Nicholls
Micky Argyle .... Michael Maloney
Maureen Cleeg .... Cassie Stuart
Jack Argyle .... Billy McColl

Cannon's "Ordeal By Innocence" is an old-fashioned drawing room whodunit from the Agatha Christie canon. The generally static, set-bound yarn has none of the allure of more sumptuous recent Christie film mysteries and looks very much like a modest television offering. However, one can recall easily more tense and better realized small screen Christie fare, suggesting the film has limited appeal in all venues.

Story centers on a research scientist, Arthur Calgary (Donald Sutherland), who returns to England after an Antarctic exploration. He carries with him an address book belonging to a man to whom he'd given a lift two years earlier. However, he discovers the owner has since been convicted of murder and executed and that he was, in fact, the dead man's alibi on the night of his alleged crime.

Calgary is horrified by the circumstance and perplexed when the dead man's family is indifferent to reopening the case. It becomes quickly apparent that almost everyone in the household had cause to murder the victim — the boy's mother. Husband Leo Argyle (Christopher Plummer) was having an affair with his secretary (Diana Quick); others had reason

to believe they were cut out of her will and another knew of a blackmail plot.

Playing amateur sleuth, Calgary displays neither smooth deduction nor a mania for justice. He is, as perceived by a local constable, a meddlesome bother. And the revelation of the true murderer is hackneyed and contrived.

The period setting (1958) is rather uninspired and performances lack any real spark. Faye Dunaway plays the victim in what amounts to a cameo in needlessly arty black and white flashbacks.

"Ordeal By Innocence" amounts to a quick programmer with questionable viability. Should be good for a week or two booked between runs of films with perceived boxoffice potential. — *Klad.*

Not For Publication
(U.S.-COLOR)

Cannes, May 19.

A North Street Films production. (No U.S. distrib.) Foreign rights, Thorn EMI. Executive producer, Mark Forstater. Produced by Anne Kimmel. Directed by Paul Bartel. Screenplay by John Meyer, Bartel. Camera (color), George Tirl; editor, Alan Toomayan; assistant director, Ira Halberstadt; production manager; Monty Diamand; costumes, Rondi Hilstrom-Davis. Reviewed at Cannes Film Festival (Market), May 18, 1984. Running time: 88 MINS.
Lois .... Nancy Allen
Barry .... David Naughton
Mayor Franklyn ...... Laurence Luckinbill
Doris .... Alice Ghostley
Troppogrosso .... Richard Paul
Odo .... Cork Hubbert
Woparico .... Barry Dennen
Jim .... Richard Blackburn

This hilariously trashy pic continues Paul Bartel's obsession with tasteless jokes, sight gags and kinky characters. Nancy Allen's energy is well invested in the lady reporter leading a double life as tabloid reporter Lois Thorndike and political volunteer Louise Thorn. The sleazy scandal sheet gives her little opportunity to do the meaningful investigative reporting she thinks would turn the paper back into the New York Enforcer her dear but dead father once edited.

Production designer Bob Schulenberg, who did three of Bartel's previous four films, has fun creating a suitably sloppy office for current editor Troppogrosso, played with greed and gusto by Richard Paul. He sends Allen to cover raids in a milk wagon trailing behind a classic '50s car serving as a mobile darkroom for their exposure of city smut.

Election year has inspired Mayor Franklyn (Laurence Luckinbill) to make a clean sweep through the porn shops and magazines, but Lois bursts into his office to warn him that it will cost him the youth vote. Her beauty and brains get her promoted to his personal assistant, as the plot moves into a campy love triangle involving Allen; Luckinbill and the photographer (David Naughton) she has·hired to work for the mayor, intending to use his work for The Informer.

The plastic fantastic apartment of Woparico, a pimp (Barry Dennen), builds to the final vinyl orgy at the Bestiary, a sex club, where Allen and Naughton deliver a song-and-dance number that stops the show, and provides a breather from the harrowing pace of the pic. Their animal costumes are just part of a running gag of same, stuffed trophies, and varying degrees of tame and wildlife.

A night on Long Island with the mayor exposes the complicity between the politico, the city's robberies and The Informer. Luckinbill turns total villain and bails out of the plane in which he is flying Allen and Naughton back to the city. Latter's zany psychic mom guides them in on a wing and a prayer to a crash landing in the Hudson, getting them to the press conference in time to threaten to expose Luckinbill. Allen saves the day, the city and her paper, changing its name to The Enforcer.

An engaging tale and innovative lensing make for a promising cult pic. Bizarre camera angles and wacky dialog cover up the uneven acting. Better part of the budget (provided by Thorn EMI) looks like it went into classic clothing, cars and collector's items.

— *Kaja.*

Les Années de Rêves
(Years of Dreams and Revolt)
(CANADIAN-COLOR)

Cannes, May 17.
Les Films Rene Malo presents a Films Vision 4 production. Produced by Claude Bonin, associate producer, Francois Labonte. Directed by Jean-Claude Labrecque. Screenplay, Robert Gurik, based on a story by Labrecque; camera (color), Alain Dostie; editor, Francois Labonte; art direction, Vianney Gauthier; sound, Serge Beauchemin. Reviewed at the Cannes Festival (Directors Fortnight), May 17, 1984. Running time: 94 MINS.
Claudette Pelletier ....Anne-Marie Provencher
Louis Pelletier ....Gilbert Sicotte
Yvette.................Monique Mercure
Adele ....Amulette Garneau
Marie ....Carmen Tremblay
Armand ....Roger Lebel
John ....Andre Mathieu
John-John ....John Wildman
Mathieu Pelletier ....Guillaume Lemay-Thivierge

Filmmaker Jean-Claude Labrecque continues the social history of Quebec as seen through the lives of one family he began in "Les Vautours," with "Les Années de Rêves." The prosperous and turbulent years of 1964 through 1970 provide the focus of the new film which ranks with the best of recent French-Canadian product.

Nonetheless the new film will have a difficult sales position in the marketplace. The historic fortunes of Quebec pictures have been a disappointment verging ón what many may consider the status of a jinx. Even art house penetration for "Les Années de Rêves" in major markets will be an obstacle despite its obvious quality.

The story centers on Louis Pelletier who marries Claudette in the film's opening section. Coincidentally, their wedding day coincides with police test runs for the imminent visit of Queen Elizabeth II. Although a roadblock sets off some heated moments, the matter is primarily comic.

Several years pass and the Pelletiers are now comfortably situated in Montreal which is enjoying a period of prosperity and attention thanks to Expo 67. Again, the situation is upbeat with the arrival of unexpected and scheduled family contributing to the merriment.

However, things grow dark as Louis loses his job at a printers. Mirroring his fortunes is the growing political dissatisfaction in Quebec leading up to the incidents of 1980 which triggered off martial law in the country.

Labrecque's thesis isn't about to win him applause from the province's separatist groups as he boldly suggests the dream was a sham. And while the film is generally assured and compelling entertainment, one can see the strains on the plot as the filmmaker attempts to cram in his political and social points in a trim 94 minutes.

The opening sections prove the most artistically successful simply because the characters enhance the period of hope. They are participants rather than shapers, allowing them a distance and objectivity they slowly lose as the drama progresses. As Louis becomes increasingly radicalized, some of the story's power is lost.

The downbeat ending also appears somewhat contrived in light of the preceding events depicted. Still, both artistic and technical work are well honed and the picture's best moments are often inspired.

"Les Années de Rêves" should set off heated debate and brisk business in Quebec but much of its political potency will be lost outside its borders. Some specialty and festival exposure seems assured but the pictures can't be expected to break out as a commercial powerhouse internationally.
— *Klad.*

Maria's Lovers
(U.S.-COLOR)

Cannes, May 15.
An MGM/UA and Cannon Films release of a Golan-Globus production. Produced by Bosko Djordjevic, Lawrence Taylor-Mortorff. Executive producers, Menahem Golan, Yoram Globus. Directed by Andrei Konchalovsky. Stars Nastassja Kinski, John Savage, Robert Mitchum, Keith Carradine. Screenplay, Gerard Brach, Konchalovsky, Paul Zindel, Marjorie David; camera (MGM color), Juan Ruiz-Anchia; editor, Jeanine Oppewall; music, Gary S. Renal; art direction, David Brisbin; set decoration, Lisa Fischer; costume design, Durinda Wood; sound, Robbie Robinson; second unit camera, Hanania Baer; associate producer, Rony Yacov; assistant director, Joseph Winogradoff. Reviewed at Cannes Festival (Market), May 14, 1984. (No MPAA rating.) Running time: 100 MINS.
Maria Bosic ....Nastassja Kinski
Ivan Bibic ....John Savage
Ivan's Father............Robert Mitchum
Clarence Butts ....Keith Carradine
Mrs. Wynic....................Anita Morris
Harvey..........................Bud Cort
Rosie ....Karen Young
Joanie ....Tracy Nelson
Frank ....John Goodman
Joe ....Danton Stone
Al Griselli ....Vincent Spano

The first American feature film by Russian director Andrei Konchalovsky, "Maria's Lovers" is a turbulent, quite particularized period romance about the sometime lack of synchronization of love and sex. Well performed but rather modest in its ambitions, pic should prove a serviceable, if unspectacular, b.o. attraction.

Best known on the domestic art house circuit for his last Soviet effort, "Siberiade," Konchalovsky is perhaps the first Russian director to have made a main-line Yank film with name performers. Although serious and not blatantly commercial, film is not an arty item and could be appreciated by general audiences, not only the cognoscenti.

Opening sequence makes use of excerpts from John Huston's great postwar U.S. Army documentary "Let There Be Light" to introduce the phenomenon of returning soldiers with psychological disabilities. Climaxing this is a mock verité interview with vet John Savage, who survived a Japanese prison camp and is terribly glad to be home in smalltown Pennsylvania.

His grizzled father Robert Mitchum gives Savage an understated welcome, and latter then has the misfortune of dropping by the home of his great love, Nastassja Kinski, just as she turns up in the grasp of another soldier, Vincent Spano.

Spano finally backs off, leaving the childhood sweethearts free to marry in a Russian Orthodox service (both this and the steeltown setting are intensely reminiscent of "The Deer Hunter"). A major problem crops up, however, when the deeply-in-love Savage, who has been successfully consorting with floozy Anita Morris upon his return, can't perform sexually with his anxious bride.

Savage's sustained failure ultimately sours the marriage, driving him to hit the road and leaving Kinski alone with her ancient grandmother until sexual weasel Keith Carradine wanders into town. Kinski, who turns out to be a virgin, finally succumbs to his slimy charms, and becomes pregnant. Drama's wrapup focuses on whether or not Savage will return to her under the new circumstances.

Konchalovsky's storytelling proceeds at a smooth pace and contains certain interesting wrinkles, such as Mitchum's discouraging his son from persuing Kinski because he himself is secretly interested in her (as he'd been in her mother), that help enrich the dramatic fabric.

Because the two leads genuinely love each other, however, the only problem between them is Savage's sexual dysfunction, and there's only one solution to that particular difficulty. Character spends so much time indulging in (understandable) self-hatred and pity that one's patience with him wears thin at times, and his abominable treatment of his wife once she becomes pregnant is exceedingly unsympathetic.

Kinski's character here reminds of a slightly more mature version of her Tess, and actress does a capable job, as do other cast members. Carradine, looking strangely like U.S. director John Waters with his pencil-thin moustache, has a field day as the womanizing vagabond, and he and Konchalovsky have written a nice tune which Carradine sings twice.

Tech credits are all very good.
— *Cart.*

Maya Miriga
(The Mirage)
(INDIAN · COLOR)

Cannes, May 19.
A Lotus Productions film (Delhi). Written and directed by Nirad N. Mohapatra. Features entire cast. Camera (color), Raj Gopal Mishra; editor, Bibekanand Satpathy; music, Bhaska Chandavarkar. Reviewed at Cannes Film Fest (Critics Week), May 18, 1984. Running time: 120 MINS.
Cast: Bansidhar Satpathy (the Father), Manimala (the Mother), Binod Mishra (Tuku), Manaswini (Prabha, his wife), Sampad, Sujata, Bibek, Shirangan, Tikina.

A debut pic by a young and talented documentarist, Nirad N. Mohapatra's "The Mirage" made an impact in the Critics Week section. It is a quiet and slow-moving film about family life, somewhat in the vein of Yasujiro Ozu's Japanese chronicles of daily life within an intimate familial structure.

Nothing much really happens in "The Mirage." Set in Orissa on a family estate, the central figure is a·retired schoolteacher with five children, four sons and a daughter. The oldest is also a teacher, whose wife at the beginning of the story is expecting a child.

Next in importance is the youngest son, the apple of the father's eye, who is studying in Delhi to become a civil servant. He's also newly married, and his wife refuses to stay at the family manor alone — so she returns home for the duration of her husband's studies. This decision sparks the first discord, for the girl has broken with tradition.

A child is born, and the aged grandmother dies. Rituals of life and death are performed for both. Slowly, however, the family structure begins to fall apart. Once the youngest son receives his civil servant papers, he prepares to leave the mansion for a residence in Delhi — and, in accordance with his father's wishes, he decides to support the education of another brother who wants to study. The father, an undisputed patriarch but also a firm believer in higher schooling, realizes he is himself responsible for sending his children away — and eventually leaving the parents alone and deserted by their own kin.

At the close, the mother is cooking dinner for two, while the father holds his tiny granddaughter in his arms, and asks: "When are you going to leave us too?"

Although sometimes too slow-moving to assure even the most comitted arthouse audience, "The Mirage" does deserve nevertheless some exposure on the fest circuit and in Indian Film Weeks.
— *Holl.*

Eva Sur Paysage Ordinaire
(Eva Against Ordinary Landscape)
(FRENCH-COLOR/B&W-16m)

Paris, May 4.
A Square Productions film. Written and directed by Emmanuel Ciepka. Script collaborators, Eva Roelens, Marie-Christine Vasquez, Catherine Adda; camera (color/b&w), Yves Lellouche, Emmanuel Ciepka; editor, Denis Jovignot; sound, Alain Contrault; art director, Myriam Bloede; makeup, Claire Lebon. Reviewed at the C.N.C., Paris, May 3, 1984. A "Perspectives on French Cinema" selection at Cannes Festival. Running time: **83 MINS.**
With: Eva Roelens, Jean-Claude Bonnifait.

"Eva Sur Paysage Ordinaire" is a trite study in alienation that would have looked dated 10 years ago. A young woman moves inexpressively through her daily routine of home and office, accompanied by the images and sounds of tv and advertisements. One day she meets a young man in a supermarket. He is in transit in Paris, scheduled to leave the next morning for a job overseas. She invites him home, they make love. After he leaves, she returns to her empty quotidian rituals.

Writer-director Emmanuel Ciepka splatters his film with media fragments culled during the French presidential campaigns in 1981 to point up the sterility of his protagonist's existence. It's old hat, as is the alternating use of color and black and white (the lat-

ter notably for the woman's apartment) and setting the film among impersonally modern apartment complexes and commercial towers. Technically the film is competent and Eva Roelens is an attractive camera subject, but banality comes of banality. —*Len.*

Sista Leken
(The Last Summer)
(FINNISH-SWEDISH-COLOR)

Cannes, May 21.
A Jörn Donner Productions release of MovieMakers AB (Stockholm) for The Swedish Film Institute and the Finnish Film Foundation and Jörn Donner production. Executive producer, Bert Sundberg. Directed by Jon Lindström. Screenplay, Lindstrom (based upon Walentin Chorell's novels "Agneta och lumpsamlaren" and "Sista Leken"); camera (Fujicolor), Peter Mokrosinski, Lasse Karlsson; editor, Lasse Lundberg; music, Ragnar Grippe; production design, Stig Limer. Reviewed at the Cannes Film Festival (Directors' Fortnight), May 20, 1984. Running time: **100 MINS.**
Viktor ....Sven Wollter
Karolina ....Agneta
Agneta's mother ....Aino Seppo
Viktor's wife ....Bibi Andersson
Agneta's father..........Thomas Laustiola

Some of the action of "The Last Summer," a Jörn Donner production of Finnish director Jon Lindström takes place in closed, dark rooms, some out in the brightly sunlit open. All the action has a claustrophobic feel due to the story's grim determination to remain gloomy and desultory throughout. The literary anchor of Walentin Chorell's two novels, on which the film is based, keeps the film from ever floating freely. Dialog is stilted to the point where it also makes the human interchanges in general incredible.

Bearded and close-faced Viktor (Sven Wollter) goes off on his usual summer trip to an archipelago where he buys up junk, but possibly also treasures for the antique shop his wife (Bibi Andersson) runs in Stockholm. The marriage is breaking up. On Viktor's last night at home, he raped his wife. Now, he seems perpetually on the lookout for some kind of erotic excitement among the womenfolk of the islands, where everybody seems to be as close-faced and tight with outward emotion as himself.

He befriends a little girl whose mother is either insane or forced to live as a recluse (when seen, she is usually naked and writhing). Viktor looks into other rooms. In those that are empty, he imagines the life (again very erotic) that might have been there once before.

An oppressive air hangs about the islands, their houses and their inhabitants. Viktor seems momentarily relieved in the company of the child and caresses her carefully while she sleeps naked in the sun. Their relationship remains innocent, however, but violence

enters the scene when Viktor decides to free the woman from her locked room. He kills her husband and, even if he avoids being accused of murder, the woman remains in seclusion and by now Viktor feels himself to be an unwanted person. He takes the child with him and sails off to the outer islands.

"The Last Summer" is full of supposedly Finnish Weltschmerz versus inner turmoil. After its Directors' Fortnight presentation at Cannes, film may move on to further minor fest exposure, but it's unlikely to pull sales outside selected Nordic territories, except for tv pickups. — *Kell.*

Palava Enkeli
(Burning Angel)
(FINNISH-COLOR)

Cannes, May 16.
A Skandie Filmi Oy production. Produced by Kaj Holmberg. Features entire cast. Directed by Lauri Torhonen. Screenplay, Claes Andersson, Hannele Torronen, Lauri Torhonen; camera (color), Esa Vuorinen; sound, Johan Hake; music, Hector; editor, Olli Soinio. Reviewed at Cannes Festival (Market), May 15, 1984. Running time: **106 MINS.**
Tuulikki Merinen ....Riitta Viiperi
Juhana Kokkala ....Tom Wentzel
Karin ....Elina Hurme
Katarina ....Eeva Eloranta
Mikko ....Juuso Hirvikangas
Saimi ....Helena Notkonen

One of the biggest-grossing releases in Finland this spring, "Burning Angel" is based on a true story about a 20-year-old nurse whose first job was in a country mental institution and who wound up insane herself. Tuulikki (Riitta Viiperi), despite her outward confidence, can't forget that her policeman-father had committed suicide, nor can she cope with her domineering mother. She gets a job far from home and is unprepared for the traumas of her work, especially when she's assigned a deeply disturbed woman patient, Katarina, who has apparently been driven insane by fears of "the Big Bang," and who eventually incinerates herself, using Tuulikki's lighter. The horrified girl responds by having a briefly passionate love affair with a senior doctor at the institution, but when she realizes the liaison means nothing to him, she starts to retreat into insanity herself.

Though the tale is not exactly unfamiliar (there are definite allusions to Robert Rossen's "Lilith"), it's well handled by director Lauri Torhonen, making his second feature (after "The Poet And The Muse" in 1978); he also worked as assistant director on both "Reds" and "Gorky Park." But the film stands or falls on the central performance, and Viiperi is most convincing as the vulnerable, naive young graduate nurse, the passionate, sensual lover, and finally as a deeply disturbed, even dangerous,

patient of the very hospital where she's been nursing. Depressing theme and rather long-winded treatment will make commercial chances outside Scandinavia very iffy, though pic ends on a cautiously upbeat note. But its lead actress should be heard from again.
—*Strat.*

Blood Simple
(U.S.-COLOR)

Cannes, May 17.
A River Road Production. Produced by Ethan Coen. Executive producer, Daniel F. Bacaner. Directed by Joel Coen. Features entire cast. Screenplay, Joel Coen and Ethan Coen; camera (Duart color), Barry Sonnenfeld; editors, Roderick Jaynes, Don Wiegmann; music, Carter Burwell; associate producer, Mark Silverman; production design, Jane Musky; special effects, Loren Bivens; art direction, (no credit available); first assistant director, Deborah Reinisch. Reviewed at Cannes Film Festival (Market), May 16, 1984. (No MPAA rating.) Running time: **97 MINS.**
Ray ....John Getz
Abby ....Frances McDormand
Marty ....Dan Hedaya
Maurice...............Samm-Art Williams
Visser ....M. Emmet Walsh

An inordinately good low-budget *film noir* thriller, "Blood Simple" first surfaced at the recent USA Film Festival in Dallas where it received positive notices. Written, directed and produced by brothers Joel and Ethan Coen, associated with "Evil Dead" filmmaker Sam Raimi, it is a finely crafted and intriguingly written picture that belies its $1-1,500,000 budget. Indeed, every cent, and then some, is up there on the screen. Picture is a real sleeper and a sure bet to be picked up by one of the U.S. majors' classics divisions, which will need to muster a campaign as terrific as the picture to draw out its full boxoffice potential.

Aside from the subtle performances, usually lacking in a film of this size, the observant viewer will find a cornucopia of detail. Director's attention to it takes what could have been a flat and lifeless canvas and paints a colorful, moody piece with a texture that's very true-to-life. The involving plot takes a twisty course as it unravels, and one wants to steer the characters straight when they take a wrong turn. Crux of the storyline is that the viewer knows the motivations of all the characters, while they are privy to only their own, thus making for audience around-the-bend anticipation.

Dan Hedaya plays Marty, a brooding owner of a Texas bar whose overbearing and oppressive attitude has taken its toll on his young wife Abby (Frances McDormand). She leaves him for a bartender at the joint. Incensed, Hedaya hires a sleazy, onerous malcreant named Visser (played with appropriate malice by M. Emmet Walsh) to kill his wayward wife and her boyfriend Ray (John Getz).

Walsh takes a snapshot of the lovers asleep in bed, doctors the photo to make it appear he's fulfilled the contract, and meets Hedaya at the bar after hours to collect. Upon payment, Walsh pulls out the wife's gun and shoots Marty dead in the chest. But the victim has swapped the photo and put it in the office safe before his demise, making Walsh's perfect crime not so.

Getz appears on the scene and finds the body and his lover's gun before the police get a chance and, believing she has killed her husband, panics. He cleans up the blood (there's a lot of it) and takes the body in his car to dump it out in the sticks, but on the way, Hedaya proves to be not quite dead yet. Getz, via a device borrowed from Edgar Allan Poe, drags Hedaya into a field and buries him — alive.

He then returns to McDormand, babbling that they must "keep our heads." She hasn't a clue what Getz is talking about, and goes to the bar to find out. Walsh, meanwhile, is trying to hammer his way into the safe to retrieve the doctored photo that links him to the murder that wasn't quite murder. Walsh hides in a closet upon McDormand's arrival, whereupon she sees the battered safe and assumes Getz was breaking into it, got caught by Hedaya, and killed him. Now she suspects Getz, and Walsh suspects both lovers are on to him.

Final confrontation between Walsh and the lovers is paced with mounting suspense, with a chilling face-off between McDormand and Walsh that's outright horrific.

Performances are top-notch all around, Walsh in particular conveying the villainy and scummy aspects of his character with convincing glee. Newcomer McDormand has an aura of animal desire about her that makes Getz' headlong plunge into a doomed situation all the more believable. Hedaya's Marty is a carefully etched study of desperation and tenacity, and Samm-Art Williams as a skeptical barhand is credible.

Sound and lighting are a real plus, and add much to the Hitchcock-esque look, as does the eye for detail of the art direction and production design. Catch it if you can. —Silv.

Comfort And Joy
(BRITISH-COLOR)

Cannes, May 17.
A Universal Pictures release of a Kings Road production. Produced by Davina Belling and Clive Parsons. Directed and written by Bill Forsyth. Camera (color), Chris Menges; editor, Michael Ellis; music, Mark Knopfler; art director, Andy Harris; production designer, Adrienne Atkinson; sound, Louis Kramer; associate producer, Paddy Higson; assistant director, Ian Madden.

Reviewed at the Cannes Film Festival (Market), May 17, 1984. Running time: **90 MINS.**
Alan .... Bill Paterson
Maddy .... Eleanor David
Charlotte .... C.P. Grogan
Trevor .... Alex Norton
Colin .... Patrick Malahide
Hilary .... Rikki Fulton
Mr. McCool .... Roberto Bernardi
Bruno .... George Rossi
Paolo .... Peter Rossi
Renata .... Billy McElhaney

In "Comfort And Joy," director-scripter Bill Forsyth sets up a wacko scenario about zany, off-center characters as he did in "Gregory's Girl," "Local Hero" and a first feature, "That Sinking Feeling."

But evincing much laughter over an unexpectedly funny couple living together, Forsyth abruptly switches into a more conventional plot. And it dissatisfies as much as the earlier section plays off so promisingly.

The two parts of the story don't work as a whole because the setup is so clever and isn't followed through.

Pic opens with a well-dressed kleptomaniac (Eleanor David) lifting goods at a department store, followed by a man (Bill Paterson). It turns out he's her lover and aware of her stealing. They return home, make love off camera and after a meal she announces she's leaving, telling him she forgot to tell him earlier. She takes everything in their home, too.

Depressed, he adopts a stiff upperlip attitude and goes to his job as an MOR radio station early morning deejay. He then becomes, innocently at first, a go-between as two warring Mafia families fight for territorial control of selling ice cream by van.

Unfortunately, the delightful and comically talented Eleanor Davis is gone from the audience's life, too. She never returns, but he dreams up a scheme to bring the two mobster families together and cuts himself in for a share of the profits.

David and Paterson are terrific together and almost every line between them is a joy. From the point she departs with no explanation the pic flashes a sparky moment or two, but it doesn't reach the high spots again. The title refers to the Christmas season when the pic takes place in a Scottish city (not identified).

However, the other players, who all speak with a clearly understandable Scottish accent, do come off well. Forsyth's direction is fine and keeps up the pace. And production values are solid. Editing, though, is slow in some latter sections.

There may be enough comfort, but there's not enough joy to make this one special or capable of having sustained commercial possibilities. The disappointment is palpable. —Adil

Vamping
(U.S.-COLOR)

Cannes, May 20.
Atlantic Releasing Corp. release of a Vamping Co. production. Exec produced by Nathan Boxer, Patrick Duffy, Frederick King Keller. Produced by Howard Kling. Directed by Frederick King Keller. Stars Patrick Duffy. Screenplay, Michael Healy with additional material by Robert Seidman; camera (color), Skip Roessel; supervising editor, Darren Kloomok; music, Ken Kaufman; production design, Howard Kling, Karen Morse, Stratton Rawson; associate producer, Rawson. Reviewed at the Cannes Film Festival (Market), May 19, 1984. (MPAA Rating: R.) Running time: **107 MINS.**
Harry Baranski .... Patrick Duffy
Diane Anderson .... Catherine Hyland
Raymond O'Brien .... Rod Arrants
The Fat Man .... Fred A. Keller
Benjamin .... David Booze
Lennie .... Jed Cooper
Jimmy .... Steve Gilborn

"Vamping" is a moody melodrama which deliberately evokes the '40s and *film noir* via its melancholy, doomed hero, a beautiful femme fatale, and some atmospheric jazz on the soundtrack. Tale unfolds in Buffalo, where down-and-out sax player Harry Baranski (Patrick Duffy) is so broke he's had to pawn his horn to the Fat Man (Fred A. Keller in a Sydney Greenstreet vein). Fat Man encourages Harry to rob the home of a recently deceased record company exec during the funeral, and during the breakin Harry also latches onto a priceless antique ring and some love letters. Catching a glimpse of the returning widow, Diane (Catherine Hyland), he becomes infatuated with her, and starts to follow her around, not realizing she's playing her own mysterious game. Also involved is her lawyer (Rod Arrants) who might be her lover, or the lover of her late husband.

Grainy location photography suffered in the very poor and sometimes mutilated print caught, but it's easy to see the mood Keller was striving for. He registers as an interesting director who's assimilated the old films he obviously likes and has wrought a few changes. Commercial chances are shaky, though, owing to the languid pacing which makes for an over-extended running time. On the other hand, interest in lead thesp (from tv's "Dallas") might help things along. He's good as the basically honest man caught up in a web of crime and intrigue. Also registering strongly, in her first outing, is Hyland as the apparently vulnerable widow who is actually much more than she seems. Ken Kaufman's score is a plus. —Strat.

Bloodbath At The House Of Death
(BRITISH - COLOR)

Cannes, May 16.
No U.S. distrib. A Wildwood Prods. production. Executive producers, Laurence Myers,

Stuart D. Donaldson. Produced and directed by Ray Cameron. Stars Kenny Everett, Pamela Stephenson, Vincent Price. Screenplay, Cameron, Barry Cryer; camera (color), Brian West, Dusty Miller; editor, Brian Tagg; sound, Marcus Thompson; assistant director, Ken Baker; production manager, Monica Rogers; art direction, John Sunderland. Reviewed at the Cannes Festival (Market), May 16, 1984. Running time: **93 MINS.**
Dr. Lucas Mandeville .... Kenny Everett
Dr. Barbara Coyle ..... Pamela Stephenson
The sinister man .... Vincent Price
Also with: Sheila Steafel, John Fortune, Gareth Hunt, Don Warrington, John Stephen Hill, Cleo Rocos, Graham Stark.

Fourteen murders occur on camera before the opening credits but this is a spoof, tailored for U.K. tv comic Kenny Everett. Oddball scientists, engaged in secret government work, gather at a British mansion where a few years previous 18 people were killed one night (the other four off camera) as depicted in the opening flashback.

Even stranger townsfolk belong to a weird sect led by Vincent Price, who has his menacing act down pat. If there is one major horror-thriller pic not spoofed in "Bloodbath," it hasn't been made yet. One lady scientist, for example, flashes back to killing her mother by mentally willing a wall-hanging can opener to slice off Mom's head — shades of "Carrie."

Everett's obvious talents are given too free rein. The pic, like its title, is wretched excess. Anything that works once is repeated two or three times. Director Ray Cameron makes his feature debut heavy-handed. Slight theatrical possibilities, it seems, even where Everett is known. — Adil.

Hundra
(U.S.-SPANISH-COLOR)

Cannes, May 18.
An Eric Bruckner and John Ghaffari presentation. Produced by Ghaffari, executive producers, Jose Truchado and Bruckner. Directed by Matt Cimber. Stars Laurene Landon. Screenplay by John Goff and Cimber, based on a story by Cimber. Camera (color), John Cabrera; editor, Claudio Cutry; music, Ennio Morricone; stunt coordinator, Javier Ingles. Reviewed at Cannes Festival (Market), May 17, 1984. Running Time: **100 MINS.**
Hundra .... Laurene Landon
Napatkin .... John Ghaffari
Drachima .... Marisa Casel

Obviously designed as a female Conan, "Hundra" lacks the energy or artistry to make a significant dent in the rapidly fading market for sword and sorcery pics. A trite script and heavy emphasis on violence further contribute to the limited appeal of the Spanish-lensed actioner.

Story centers on a female colony in some mythical locale which serves as a breeding ground for a warrior nation. It's unclear, but in the opening moments their village is raided and all killed perhaps because they too are emerging as a fighter cult.

Hundra (Laurene Landon) is the sole tribal survivor, having been away on a hunting trip during the attack. Seeking out a hermit, she is told "you are the ember of our fire of freedom" and proceeds to kill warriors and establish a new colony.

The quest leads to a walled city where Hundra seeks out a suitable breeder. Her choice is a sensitive doctor, which would most likely make her mother very happy. However, before she can effect her mission, many will die and the audience will suffer through the film's corny feminist tract. It's unlikely to win approval from activists.

Landon, in a variety of designer warrior outfits, gets to execute lots of physical feats but little acting ability. Still, she is Hepburn when placed beside the remaining cast members.

Technical work is okay, but Ennio Morricone's score seems like a patchwork of old themes. Direction is plodding and the film could easily stand considerable trimming to quicken the pace. Generally, the results are mediocre making the prospects of further exploits most unlikely. — *Klad.*

Ninja III - The Domination
(U.S.-COLOR)

Cannes, May 16.

An MGM/UA and Cannon Group release of a Golan-Globus production. Exec producers, Menahem Golan, Yoram Globus; associate producer, David Womark. Directed by Sam Firstenberg. Features entire cast. Screenplay and original story, James R. Silke; camera (Metrocolor), Hanania Baer; editor, Michael Duthie; music, Udi Haroaz, others; production manager, Womark; assistant director, Ann Cavalier; stunt coordinator, Steve Lambert; action choreography, Sho Kosugi; production design, Elliot Ellentuck. Reviewed at Cannes Festival (Market), May 16, 1984. (No MPAA Rating). Running time: 95 MINS.

Christie Ryder	Lucinda Dickey
Billy Secord	Jordan Bennett
Yamada	Sho Kosugi
The Evil Ninja	David Chung
Police sergeant	T.J. Castronova

With their new feature "Ninja III - The Domination" producers Menahem Golan and Yoram Globus have reunited members of the team that made their second entry in the martial arts series about the more deadly cousins of the Samurai: James Silke scripted, Sam Firstenberg directed and karate school master and actor Sho Kosugi plays one of the Ninjas and has handled the fight choreography as well. Still, the new outing into the never-never land of the world's trickiest controlled violence is done with quite a twist: the supernatural, exorcism, deadly laser eyes and many other action fireworks are employed to an extreme

that may seem silly but that will hardly detract from the pleasures of established Ninja audiences.

The twist has several quite humorous aspects, the least of which being that most of the Ninja action (swordplay, sickleblade-cutting, throwing of multi-pointed, killing stars, the use of feet claws and Caltrops plus fire-breathing and much more) is performed by a woman (dancer Lucinda Dickey of "Breakin'" who can turn her pretty, brown-eyed visage into a mask of true Evil at the crack of an Oriental Wizard's silken whip).

It seems that she, by chance — and because she happens to be blessed with ESP and a morbid interest in Japanese culture — from time to time bewilders her police officer boyfriend by unconsciously taking over the spirit of an evil Ninja on a visit to Arizona to carry on his wholesale killing of the police force that stubbornly has riddled him with bullets to the point where they think they have him safely stored away in the morgue.

Sho Kosugi is the Good Ninja who finally helps the American girl out of her predicament so she can return to her regular pasttime of working out to the music and singing of Pat Benatar. If the spirit is willing, the fun and a few thrills are there to be had. All production credits are nicely handled. — *Kell.*

Secret Places
(BRITISH - COLOR)

London, May 14.

A Skreba-Virgin production for the National Film Trustee Co. in association with the NFFC, Rediffusion Films and Rank Films. Executive producers, Al Clark, Robert Devereux. Produced by Simon Relph and Ann Skinner. Directed by Zelda Barron. Features entire cast. Screenplay, Barron, based on the book by Janice Elliott; camera, (Eastmancolor), Peter MacDonald; editor, Laurence Mery-Clark; music, Michel Legrand; production design, Eileen Diss; costume design, Jane Robinson; sound, David Stephenson, Keith Grant; assistant director, Relph. Reviewed at the Classic Haymarket, London, May 12, 1984. Also screening in Cannes Film Festival (Market). (BBFC certificate: 15). Running time: 96 MINS.

Laura Meister	Marie-Therese Relin
Patience	Tara MacGowran
Sophie Meister	Claudine Auger
Miss Lowrie	Jenny Agutter
Nina	Cassie Stuart
Rose	Anne-Marie Gwatkin
Barbara	Pippa Hinchley
Dr. Meister	Klaus Barner
Miss Trott	Sylvia Coleridge
Mrs. Mackenzie	Rosemary Martin

"Secret Places" is a pleasing evocation of schoolgirl life in England during World War II. Pic offers few surprises but sufficient small pleasures to promise slow but steady b.o. in select locations.

Based on a novel by Janice Elliott, the film recounts the initially hostile response of a group of adolescents to the enrollment of Laura Meister, a German refugee, in their all-girl school. Gradually her exotically winning ways and intelligence secure her enrollment

in the select circle which gathers in "secret places." Things turn sour, however, when a girl's father is killed in battle.

The plot, which often strays down the byways of nostalgia for schoolgirl innocence, is too diffuse to allow for serious treatment of the English attitude to aliens. Instead, it relates the psychological pressures which lead to Laura's attempted suicide.

The explanations of that act come thick and fast. The girl's father is imprisoned as an enemy alien. Her drug-addicted mother cracks up under the strain and disowns Laura from her hospital bed. Laura's brother, already disowned by his father for joining the Nazis, is killed in action. Laura also falls in love with an English boy who joins the air fore. The final blow for Laura is separation from her friend Patience following a tentative sexual encounter.

There's little psychological depth in the scripting but some topnotch performances. Marie-Therese Relin captures the gestures and looks of a girl whose emotional resilience conceals suffering. Tara MacGowran is right on as a repressed English girl and Anne-Marie Gwatkin is a standout in a minor part as the scholarly Irish Catholic Rose.

There's some overacting too. Cassie Stuart, the sexually adventurous Nina who is fated to become a GI bride, is a little too modern and ebullient. Claudine Auger's histrionics as Laura's mother are barely excused by the dialog reference to her mixed continental background.

Zelda Barron, making her directorial debut after a career in the continuity department of such films as "Reds" and "Yentl," has a sure touch. Helped by cameraman Peter MacDonald she neatly handles both the moments of emotional inensity and lyrical wonder. — *Japa.*

Boy Meets Girl
(FRENCH - B&W)

Cannes, May 16.

An Abilene production. Produced by Patricia Moraz and Alain Dahan. Direction and screenplay by Leos Carax. Camera (b&w), Jean-Yves Escoffier, Pascal Rabaud; editors, Nelly Meunier, Francine Sandberg; art direction, Serge Marzolff, Jean Bauer; music, Jacquee Pinault. Reviewed at Cannes Festival (Critics Week), Cannes, May 16, 1984. Running time: 90 MINS.

Alex	Denis Lavant
Mireille	Mireille Perrier
Bernard	Elie Poicard
Helene	Carol Brooks
Thomas	Christian Cloarec

French offering for the Critics Week, "Boy Meets Girl," presents an offbeat tale and talented first-time director. The unconventional, moody tone piece may not endear itself to audiences but certainly

will attract strong critical response and is a certain bet on the festival circuit.

The plot is open to a variety of interpretations but centers on a young man cruising the dark side of Paris. There are romance and encounters with flamboyant types before winding down to a downbeat, ironic conclusion. Largely vignettish, the story nonetheless has a poignant element reflected in the title which may attract other than the avantgarde.

Writer-director Leos Carax demonstrates both an assured hand with the technical and artistic components of film. His actors register effectively and the eerie combination of images, music and location provides an indelible quality to "Boy Meets Girl." — *Klad.*

The Ambassador
(U.S.-COLOR)

Cannes, May 17.

A Cannon Films release of a Golan-Globus-Northbrook Film production. Executive producers, Menahem Golan, Yoram Globus. Associate producer, Isaac Kol. Stars Robert Mitchum, Ellen Burstyn, Rock Hudson. Directed by J. Lee Thompson. Screenplay, Max Jack, based on Elmore Leonard's novel, "52 Pick Up;" camera (TVC Color), Adam Greenberg; editor, Mark Goldblatt; music, Dov Seltzer; production design Yoram Barzilai. Reviewed at Cannes Festival (Market), May 17, '84. Running time: 90 MINS.

Ambassador

Peter Hacker	Robert Mitchum
His wife Alex	Ellen Burstyn
Frank Stevenson	Rock Hudson
Mustapha Hashimi	Fabio Testi
Defense Minister Eretz	Donald Pleasence
Rachel	Heli Goldenberg
Tova	Michal Bat-Adam
Abe	Ori Levy
Assad	Uri Gavriel

Veteran British director J. Lee Thompson is in tight, energetic shape with "The Ambassador," a political thriller with a message about the meetings of open minds being the only possible solution to the Palestinian-Israeli conflict.

Peter Hacker, a U.S. Ambassador (played with monumental calm by Robert Mitchum) goes to highly unlikely and quite privately arranged extremes in pursuit of such a reconciliation. Ignoring warnings from his security adviser (Rock Hudson, leaner and swifter on his feet than in the heyday of his stardom) and the Israeli defense minister (Donald Pleasence, keeping his mannerism of facial contortions well under control this time), Hacker has meetings set up between the PLO and himself in the desert and between hundreds of students from Palestinian and Israeli campuses, both times with vicious bloodshed as the immediate result.

It is often asked what the President at home would say to all this private diplomacy, but then the film is not really all that serious about rhyme and reason in a plot that includes blackmailing of the ambassador when the Israeli Mossad (secret service) has made a film of the American diplomat's wife having enthusiastic sex (the ambassador neglects his marital duties for his other preoccupations) with a leading PLO intellectual and activist. No, the Mossad is not doing the blackmailing itself, it has handed the film over to the Palestinians. Security adviser Hudson has to step in again and again, gun in hand, to sort matters out. The ambassador's wife nearly gets killed before the couple can receive a thankful, candle-bearing crowd of students from both sides on their front steps.

Ellen Burstyn plays the ambassador's wife with abandon whether unclad or formally dressed. Her drinking problem is soon forgotten, and the ironic banter between her and Mitchum after she has been found out is carried by adult wit and a certain realistic weariness. Italy's Fabio Testi plays the lover who turns out to be PLO as a balancing act between the ludicrous and the sympathetic. Film's lack of more youthful roles of importance may slow its boxoffice appeal, but as an above the run-of-the-mill thriller with a claim to political realism, it could still make its way in the international marketplace. — *Kell.*

Lars i porten
(On The Threshold)
(NORWEGIAN-COLOR)

Cannes, May 14.
A Moviemakers Norway with Norsk Film production, Norsk Film release. Original story and script and directed by Leif Erlsboe. Executive producer, Dag Nordahl. Camera (Eastmancolor) Svein Kroevel; editor, Anne Marie Noerholm; music, Freddy Lindquist; production design, Torunn Mueller; costumes, Kari Elfstedt; production management, Hans Lindgren, Odd G. Iversen. Reviewed at Cannes Festival Market May 13, '84. Running time: 96 MINS.

Lars .... Magnus E. Haslund
Tobby .... Joachim Calmeyer
Lil .... Anne Katherine Krigsvill
Peter .... Peder Hamdahl Naess
Lars' Mother .... Anne Marie Ottersen
Lars' Father .... Frode Rasmussen

"On The Threshold" is a slice of pre-puberty life as seen and experienced by Lars, a 12-year-old working-class boy in Oslo in the '50s and cut with a very dull knife by writer-director Leif Erlsboe, a former sound technician and editor. He has also written several scripts for shorts and has based his helmer debut script on his own recollections of a Copenhagen (he is originally a Dane) boyhood.

Young Lars, played by the director's own son (Magnus E. Haslund, all innocent blue eyes and shy movements), is seen both as a watcher of adult life around him and as a participant who tries to

make up for what others do wrong. When his parents have prolonged fights, he sneaks a red, cut-out paper heart into his father's lunchbox; when a storekeeper abuses the whore-with-a-heart-of-gold living upstairs, Lars sneaks into the store to smear red paint on the faces of store mannequins, as often as not with results running counter to his good intentions.

Erlsboe's feature is filmed in colors that due to bad lighting lack gloss. The actors move leadenly through their old kitchen-sink realism clichés of situations and dialog. If Erlsboe's observations had been fresher and his sense of film rhythm keener, it might have made up for the lack of plot dynamics. Norwegian audiences will find "On The Threshold" fine for promoting some innocent '50s nostalgia and probably forgive film's male actors for wearing blue jeans with rolled up cuffs 10 years before that particular attire and style of wearing it reached Norway.
— *Kell.*

The Oasis
(U.S.-COLOR)

Cannes, May 16.
A Titan Films presentation. Produced by Myron Meisel and Sparky Greene. Executive producer, John Jay Schumann. Directed by Greene. Screenplay by Tom Klassen, based on a story by Meisel and Greene. Camera (color), Alexander Gruszynski; editor, Mary Bauer; production design, Woodward Romine; music, Chris Young. Reviewed at Cannes Festival (Market), May 15, '84. Running time: 92 MINS.

Matt .... Chris Makepeace
Jake .... Scott Hylands
Paul .... Richard Cox
Jill .... Dori Brenner
Alex .... Rick Podell
Eric .... Mark Metcalf
Louis .... Ben Slack
Anna .... Anne Lockhart
Jennifer .... Suzanne Snyder

An oft-trod tale of survivors in a desperate situation provides the story of "The Oasis." As the area has been cultivated many times and the film offers little novelty, this exploitation offering is likely to find once-fertile markets somewhat arid and unresponsive.

The situation casts nine survivors of an airplane crash in the middle of the desert with limited supplies and no clear indication of a safe route out. The by-the-book plot culls freely from staples such as "10 Little Indians" and more recent fare like "Survive" for a *de rigeur* unfolding. Who (and how) they will live and die becomes the focus with little care taken in the development of character.

While the technical components are well above average for this modestly budgeted item, the performances are uninspired and the script is banal. The familiarity of the situation often leads to unintentionally funny situations and dialog

and the emotional allegiances are telegraphed well in advance.

Respectable returns may be forthcoming for "The Oasis," but the producers would be well advised to go for fast playoff. The picture has no hooks other than the premise so marketing strategy will be an important element in its potential grossing power. — *Klad.*

Entre Tinieblas
(Dark Hideout)
(SPANISH-COLOR)

Cannes, May 15.
A Tesauro S.A. release of a Luis Calvo production. Exec producer Calvo. Features Cristina S. Pascual, Julietta Serrano, Marisa Paredes, Carmen Maura, Mari Carrillo, Lina Canalejas, Manuel Zarzo, Chus Lampreave, Berta Riaza. Written and directed by Pedro Almodóvar. Camera (color), Angel L. Fernandez; editor José Salcedo; sets, Pin Morales and Román Arango; costumes, Teresa Nieto; production director, Tadeo Villalba. Reviewed at Cannes Festival (Market), May 14, '84. Running time: 105 MINS.

Director Pedro Almodóvar has developed something of a youth cult following in Spain for his pics dealing with drifters and drugs. This item zeroes in on the same way-out ambience, providing some whimsical touches of humor, a strong dose of parody and not a little disrespect towards the Catholic Church and its minions.

First half hour of film is inventive and catchy, but story then loses its drive; the irony wears thin, though there are occasional outcroppings of clever burlesque. Story is spun around a nitery singer living in the lower depths of Madrid's drug and crime world. When her boyfriend dies of a dose of heroin and strychnine, Yolanda Bell, the dancer, decides to hide out in a convent where she knows two of the nuns who had asked her for an autograph backstage after a performance.

The four nuns and a chaplain are a weird lot, calling themselves the "humble redeemers," but each is known by a degrading nickname; one takes drugs herself; another is into self-mortification; a third keeps a pet tiger in the convent's garden, and the fourth writes sensationalist pulp literature under a pseudonym, based on the experiences of those "redeemed."

Since the convent is running short of coin, one of the swinging nuns decides to try to blackmail an aristocrataic dowager who has withdrawn her funding. Story comes to a head as a new mother superior arrives to take over the convent and the nuns organize a party to receive her.

Pic, produced over a year ago, did okay biz with youth audiences in its Spanish release, but so far hasn't been picked up for other territories. — *Besa.*

Stranger Than Paradise
(U.S.-B&W)

Cannes, May 17.
A Cinesthesia-Grokenberger Film production. Produced by Sara Driver. Executive producer, Otto Grokenberger. Directed, written by Jim Jarmusch. Features entire cast. Camera (b&w), Tom DiCillo; editors, Jarmusch, Melody London; music, John Lurie; sound, Greg Curry, Drew Kunin. Reviewed at the Cannes Film Festival (Directors' Fortnight), May 16, 1984. (No MPAA rating.) Running time: 95 MINS.

Willie .... John Lurie
Eva .... Ester Balint
Eddie .... Richard Edson
Aunt Lotte .... Cecilia Stark
Also with: Danny Rosen, Rammellzee.

"Stranger Than Paradise" is a bracingly original avant-garde black comedy. Begun as a short which was presented under the same title at some earlier festivals, film has been expanded in outstanding fashion by young New York writer-director Jim Jarmusch, and received a rousing reception at the Directors' Fortnight. Pic's minimalism and usual nature make it a hard sell commercially, although specialized cinemas could give it a go in brief runs.

A disciple of Wim Wenders who made one previous feature, "Permanent Vacation," in 1979, Jarmusch here has attempted a rigorously formal exercise, and it the formalism itself which contributes to the mounting hilarity as the film progresses.

Fragmented story is structured into three distinct sections, first of which (the initially-shot short film) takes place in New York City. Individual sequences within each section are presented in one sustained take, and are separated by blackouts.

Simple narrative has self-styled downtown hipster Willie (John Lurie) being paid a surprise, and quite unwelcome, visit by Hungarian cousin Eva (Ester Balint). Willie does nothing to conceal his displeasure at having to share his tiny apartment with this stranger, but when she finally leaves after 10 days, there seems to be a strange sort of affection between them even though they've shared nothing together except space.

Second section sees Willie and buddy Eddie (Richard Edson) deciding to head for Cleveland to visit Eva, who lives there with Aunt Lotte (Cecilia Stark), an ever-complaining old lady who insists upon speaking Hungarian to the annoyed young people. Once again, the characters do little of import together, spending this "vacation" staring at tv, watching a kung fu film and taking in the sights, such as Lake Erie in the dead of winter.

Part three has the trio abandoning the frozen wastes for Florida, where they check into an empty seaside motel and where Willie and

Eddie lose most of their money at the dog races.

However, when Eva suddenly comes into a huge stash of loot in wildly eccentric fashion, story manages to come full circle, but with an ironic twist.

Since plot doesn't count for much here, the style takes over, and Jarmusch has made such matters as camera placement, composition (in stunning black-and-white) and structure count for a lot. Long takes and often rigid camera positions seem indebted to the late Japanese director Yasujiro Ozu, and traces of Warhol and Godard are also to be found.

Happily, Jarmusch has moved beyond the obvious inherent subject of alienation to fashion a mordant comedy about missed connections, communication and lack thereof.

Lead thesp Lurie spends much of the running time acting like a boorish lout, but performance ultimatley proves enormously winning. Balint makes virtually no attempt at a Hungarian accent and assumes a deadpan, even blank stance, but also emerges quite sympathetically. Edson and Stark provide diverting comedy relief.

Technical contributions are very sharp despite meager budget.
— *Cart.*

The Inside Man
(SWEDISH-BRITISH-COLOR)

Cannes, May 18.

A Glinwood Films Ltd. (London) release of a Producers' Enterprises (London), Nordisk Tonfilm and Terra Film International (Stockholm) production in association with Hill Samuel, United Media Ltd. and AB Svensk Filmindustri. (No U.S. distrib set.) Executive producer, Ingemar Ejve. Associate producers; Calvin Floyd, Bjoern Henricson. Stars Dennis Hopper, Gösta Ekman, David Wilson, Cory Molder. Directed by Tom Clegg. Screenplay by Alan Plater, based on Harry Kullman's novel "The Fighter" and story by Clegg and William Aldridge; camera (Fujicolor) Jörgen Persson; music, Stefan Nilsson; title theme by Anthony More and Matthew Irving, sung by P.P. (Pat) Arnold; production design, Stig Boquist; editors, William Aldridge, Carina Ehn. Reviewed at Cannes Festival (Market), May 18, 1984. Running time: **100 MINS.**

Miller	Dennis Hopper
Mandell	Hardy Kruger
Larsson	Gösta Ekman
Kallin	Cory Molder
Baxter	David Wilson
Theresa	Cecilia Gregory
Astrid	Lena Endre
Lazlo	Janos Hersko
Receptionist	Lill Lindfors
Defense Minister	Leif Ahrle

The day has come where Dennis Hopper goes around telling other people to get haircuts. He does that as the uptight, sarcastic American security advisor to Hardy Kruger's electronics industry in a Sweden that hopes to be blessed with Kruger's latest invention, a laser weapon able to detect deeply submerged submarines. Sweden has had its share (180 of them, all supposedly Russian) in recent years, and Tom Clegg's feature "The Inside Man" hopes to combine the political thriller with the predicaments of an ordinary man caught up in hard-slugging superpower intrigue in connection with the theft of the small, cylinder-shaped laser contraption.

Film is not entirely successful in living up to its higher ambitions, but it should have a fair chance in the general action entertainment market. Clegg, whose best feature so far was the gritty prison film 'McVicar,'' works well in having the members of his international cast melt into the general fabric of his story.

Cory Molder is in the title role as the innocent Swedish Marine and ex-boxer with the farmboy looks who is planted by Swedish military intelligence (a good variation of the worldweary but stubborn cop given by Gösta Ekman) as the industrialist-inventor's chauffeur and told to do a lot of spying and yet not given any details about the whys and wherefores of his job. The young man takes a lot of beatings and so does a story line that soon seems to have everybody as villains up to the point where it's hard to continue caring.

Film has its share of bloody fight scenes and bits of looking and leering at sex in action that does not at all connect naturally with the narrative flow. The editing tends towards confusing the plot issues unnecessarily.

Along with coping with a lack of logic in the proceedings in general, audiences will also have to accept a hero who is neither clever nor a good fighter. But he is fast at getting on his feet again and wiping the blood from his face and body. In the latter department, he is helped by pretty Cecilia Gregory who also seems ready around the clock to supply him with slow or fast cars for very unconvincing chases. —*Kell.*

The Slim Dusty Movie
(AUSTRALIAN - COLOR)

Cannes, May 17.

A Greater Union Film Distributors (Australia) release, produced by Kent Chadwick. Directed by Rob Stewart. Features entire cast. Screenplay, Chadwick; associate producer, Brian Douglas; camera (Eastmancolor) David Eggby, additional photography, Dan Burstall; editor, Ken Sallows; art director, Les Binns; costume designer, Jany Hyland; music production, Rod Coe. Reviewed at the Cannes Festival (Market), May 15, '84. (Australian Commonwealth Film Censor rating: G.) Running time: **108 MINS.**

With: Slim Dusty, Joy McKean, Anne Kirkpatrick, Gordon Parsons, Honest John Moloney, Stan Coster, Buck Taylor, Jon Blake (Slim in his mid-20s), Dean Stidworthy (Slim aged 14), Sandy Paul (Joy in her early 20s).

Slim Dusty is the undisputed king of country music in Australia, the nation's biggest selling solo artist, and with the Dusty caravan on the road nearly continuously, probably its best-traveled.

This picture, part documentary, part musical, part travelog, charts his life from the day in 1937 when an 11-year-old kid named David Gordon Kirkpatrick decided to change his name and set his sights on becoming a country music star. Due to open in Mount Isa in outback Queensland in August, film will play at provincial centers up and down the east coast before segueing to Sydney and the other capitals.

Given the man's near legendary status, disk sales and enduring popularity as a concert attraction, his name probably ensures strong business in the bush, and fair to good b.o. in the cities.

However pic lacks enough ingredients to snare audiences who are not country and western enthusiasts, or at least the Slim Dusty twanging guitars and banjo, fiddle and yodeling version of the genre.

Overseas appeal therefore looks to be limited except in markets (Nashville, for example) where c&w is predominant. Producers are counting on the film's uniquely Australian flavor, the embodiment of the Aussie spirit in its star, and the depiction of the way the nation has changed and developed over nearly 50 years, to cross the bridge into foreign lands.

That's a neat idea, but is not carried through into the narrative with much effect. Dusty's formative years, his meeting with the singer who was to become his wife and co-star, and his time on the carnival circuit in the 1950s are told well enough in flashbacks, but the few moments of real drama, especially concerning the struggle he had to establish himself, are glossed over.

Bulk of the time seems to be taken up by Dusty and band performing at various venues around the country, and while there are dashes of color at some places (the Mount Isa rodeo, for instance), it makes for a fairly static spectacle.

Shots of the outback and land marks like Ayers Rock and the Sydney Opera House at least open up the picture, but they are mostly standard see-Australia postcard views.

In short, item will be a treat for Dusty devotees, but of marginal interest elsewhere. — *Dogo.*

De Grens
(Frontier)
(DUTCH-COLOR)

Amsterdam, May 15.

An Eerste Amsterdamse Filmassociatie production. Produced by René Seegers. Written and directed by Leon de Winter. Features entire cast. Camera (color), Eddy van der Enden; editor, Henk van Eeghen, Ine Schenkkan; music, Boudewijn Tarenskeen; sound, Kees Linthorst. Reviewed at Cinetone Studios, Amsterdam, May 8, 1984. A selection in "Un Certain Regard" section at Cannes Film Festival. Running time: **100 MINS.**

Hans Deitz	Johan Leysen
Rosa Clement	Angela Winkler
Marleen Ruyter	Linda van Dyck
Marcel Boas	André Dussollier
Andras Menzo	Hector Altério

Leon de Winter, who achieved critical and commercial success as one of the most original and inventive young Dutch novelists, has also made his mark in films. Ten years ago he dropped out of the Film Academy, together with René Seegers and Jean van de Velde, because they did not approve of the curriculum. Trio then founded First Amsterdam Filmassociation which has made three outstanding long docus (for tv), and two interesting features. They have also collaborated on a legit play.

"Frontiers," de Winter's first feature as a director, highlights his strength and his weaknesses. Strengths: the interesting thrillerish plot is interlarded with political motives and psychological problems which successfully bid for viewer's attention. Crowd scenes in this debut pic are handled with the assurance of an old pro. De Winter makes excellent use of color in his storytelling; also relying on the subtle and sophisticated score of Boudewijn Tarenskeen.

The weaknesses: helming does not tax full potential of a notable international cast. Thesps play scenes, but don't build up characters. A decisive flaw is the way his script chops up the story into bits and pieces which are flashed back and flashed forward, even sideways, until the story becomes unintelligible. De Winter does this intentionally, just as in some of his books dates are mixed up, events reversed, and time is manipulated. However, one can't turn back pages in a cinema, to find out where one is. What can be intriguing in a book may become just annoying in a film. It does in this case, the reason why the pic (shown in the "Un Certain Regard" program in Cannes) seems to be restricted to festival and avant-garde circuits.

That's a pity, because the three main motifs of the script could have been intertwined to form a gripping, exciting and thought-provoking film: First, the story of the foreign journalist who, in an unnamed South European country, tries to interview a leader of a terrorist movement which has not stopped its activities, although the revolution which it backed had succeeded five years ago. Secondly, the seemingly unbridgeable chasm surrounding a stagnant and comatose regional culture. Third, the subversive integration of violence into the characters of individuals and the daily life of communities. — *Wall.*

Hollywood Hot Tubs
(U.S.-COLOR)

Cannes, May 16.

A Manson International presentation of a Seymour Borde and Associates Production Produced by Mark Borde. Directed by Chuck Vincent. Features entire cast. Screenplay, Mark Borde, Craig McDonnell; camera (color), Larry Revene; editor, Michael Hoggan; art direction, Loma Lee Brookbank; music, Joel Goldsmith. Reviewed at Cannes Festival (Market) May 16, '84. (MPAA Rating: R). Running time: **102 MINS.**

Leslie Maynard	Donna McDaniel
Jeff	Michael Andrew
Eddie	Paul Gunning
Dee Dee	Katt Shea
Desire	Edy Williams
Crystal	Jewal Shepard

Adolescent pranks lead to a splashy if not steamy pic featuring the erotic equivalent of kids changing the "Hollywood" sign in the hills to "Hollyweed." To save young Jeff from the slammer, his parents get him a job mixing plumbing with pleasure in the Hollywood hot tubs.

Everything that can be done to, with, for, in or around hot water finds its way into a plot that tries to go from the quick and dirty to the gothic. A Hollywood hostess is trying to create a clientele for her Hollywood Hot Tubs business, and young Jeff's uncle has a plumbing business. The two mix and mate until the romantic lead finally makes it with his co-worker, a good girl looking for something deeper than the shallow water they work in. She is satisfied in the final innocuous scene.

Each half hour delivers a coupling in this not-too-funny comedy full of booze, broads and bubbles. The final party offers lookalikes of Burt Reynolds, Lauren Bacall and Bozo. Only the last is convincing. The kids, at whom this pic is aimed, witness more sex than they enjoy. The most promising moments come with Jewal Shepard, who takes the valley girl far beyond its usual dips.

Pic gives the pay-cable market what it needs, but can't keep the humor up for theatrical release. A very good premise simply sinks in the Hollywood hot tub. —Kaja.

Truckin' Buddy McCoy
(U.S.-COLOR)

Cannes, May 16.

A Bedford Entertainment release of an Omega Intl. Pictures presentation of a DeMarco/Blumenthal Production. Produced by Richard DeMarco and Richard Blumenthal. Features entire cast. Directed by DeMarco. Screenplay, Blumenthal, Herbert Dufine; exec producer; Ron Shapiro; camera (color), Mishal Suslov; art director, Paul Sussman; production coordinator, Doug Warrick. Reviewed at the Cannes Festival (Market), May 16, '84. (MPAA rating: R.) Running time: **82 MINS.**

Buddy	Terence Knox
Ellen	Myra Chason
Steel	Charles Rome Smith
Pete	Miguel Ferrer
Sally	Judy Cushing
Tony	James O'Hagen
Al	John Fleck

If truckin' pictures ever grind and belch their way back to mainstream popularity, this film will contribute absolutely nothing to that resurgence. "Truckin' Buddy McCoy" is a dismal exercise in nearly every department, except on a technical level where at least it is proficient.

Dopey dialog sounds like the actors are making it up as they go, and when they (or the scriptwriters) run out of ideas, which is often, forgettable country and western songs fill the gaps.

Light on action, totally lacking humor and baring a minimum of flesh, pic has next to nothing to offer audiences who got their kicks watching "Smokey And The Bandit" and "Convoy."

Title character is a simpleton whose big goal in life is to own a Mack truck, which he wins in a contest. Next, he embarks on a journey of self discovery, which involves driving to Texas and back, leaving behind his girlfriend who loves him but is not crazy about living in a mobile home.

On the road Buddy pals up with a veteran trucker, checks into a whorehouse, picks up a girl who turns out to be an S&M devotee, and has to get rough with a guy who takes the Mack for a joyride.

Then it's back to Los Angeles and the girlfriend; they get hitched and presumably truck on happy ever after.

It would not be fair to single out any thesp, for none deserves honorable mention. —Dogo.

Liberté la Nuit
(Liberty at Night)
(FRENCH-B&W)

Paris, May 15.

An Institut National de l'Audiovisuel production. Written and directed by Philippe Garrel. Camera, (b&w), Pascal Laperrousaz; editor, Dominique Auvray; music, Faton Cahen; sound, Jean-Pierre Fenie. Reviewed at the C.N.C., Paris, May 4, 1984. In "Perspectives on French Cinema" section at Cannes Festival. Running time: **90 MINS.**

With: Emmanuelle Riva, Maurice Garrel, Christine Boisson, Laszlo Szabo, Brigitte Sy.

"Liberté la Nuit," produced by the enterprising Institut National de l'Audiovisuel, the archive and experimental production arm of French tv, is a glum, empty drama about a man who tinkers in love and politics and loses on both fronts.

Writer-director Philippe Garrel, an avant-garde figure with a small, hardcore critical following here, sets his story during the Algerian War and deals with a man (Maurice Garrel, the helmer's father) whose involvement with the Algerian freedom fighters earns him the enmity of French rightwing nationalists, who murder his estranged wife (Emmanuelle Riva). Later Garrel becomes involved with a young Algerian woman, but the extremist gunmen finally catch up with him and execute him.

Garrel pretentiously attempts an analysis of personal relationships against a backdrop of political commitment, but the opaque script, spare black and white direction and poor acting (notably the usually excellent Christine Boisson, who's shrilly awful as Garrel's young lover) only reflect the thematic, emotional and artistic sterility of Garrel's often pseudo-Bressonian manner. Boring. —Len.

Door To Door
(U.S. - COLOR)

Cannes, May 17.

A Shapiro Entertainment presentation. Produced by Ken Wales. Exec producer, Robert H. Goodman. Directed by Patrick Bailey. Screenplay, Peter Baloff and Dave Wollert; camera (color), Reed Smoot; editor, Michael Brown; sound, Dave Anderson; assistant director, Tom Foulkes; production manager, Stratton Leopold. Reviewed at Cannes Festival (market); May 17, 1984. (No MPAA Rating). Running time: **85 MINS.**

Larry Price	Ron Leibman
Leon Spencer	Arliss Howard
Katharine Holloway	Jane Kaczmarek
Jimmy Lupus	Alan Austin

The dominant feature of "Door To Door" is the performance of Ron Leibman, as the glib, persuasive, smooth-talking traveling salesman who prefers to be styled an itinerant merchant. He has charm, too, and that helps him in his sideline activity, namely that of skilled conman.

The storyline is somewhat convoluted, dealing with the varied adventures of Leibman, an ace door-to-door man, who takes on board a struggling unsuccessful salesman, Arliss Howard, and involves him in one questionable activity after another, of the kind that would only deceive an absolute simpleton.

As it transpires, Leibman is not employed by the company for whom he is selling vacuum cleaners, and is being blackmailed by the company's chief detective. He is constantly trying to keep one jump ahead, even to the point of sinking his Cadillac in a river. As a conman, he tries paying for a new car by check after the banks have closed, trying to sell it to another dealer at a loss an hour later and, after a weekend in jail, driving off with a new car as a gift.

Apart from Leibman, there is a lowkey performance from Howard as the would-be salesman who is coached in the art of getting one's foot in the door and keeping it there. He provides hte slight romantic interest with Jane Kaczmarek, a lively and interesting screen personality. Alan Austin is a typical heavy as the blackmailer who predictably gets his comeuppance in the final reel. Patrick Bailey's direction keeps the action rolling at a steady lick. — Myro.

Beat Street
(U.S.-COLOR)

Cannes, May 22.

An Orion release. Produced by David V. Picker and Harry Belafonte. Directed by Stan Lathan. Features entire cast. Screenplay, Andy Davis, David Gilbert, Paul Golding, story by Steven Hager. Camera (Deluxe color), Tom Priestly Jr.; editor, Dov Hoenig; music produced by Belafonte, Arthur Baker; production design, Patrizia Von Brandenstein; costume design, Kristi Zea; choreographer, Lester Wilson; associate producer, Mel Howard. Reviewed at the Cannes Film Festival (out of competition), May 22, 1984. (MPAA Rating: PG.) Running time: **105 MINS.**

Tracy	Rae Dawn Chong
Kenny	Guy Davis
Ramon	John Chardiet
Chollie	Leon Grant
Lee	Robert Taylor
Henri	Dean Elliott
Luis	Franc Reyes

Also with: New York City Breakers, Rock Steady, Magnificent Force, Grand Master Melle Mel & The Furious Five, Afrika Bambaataa & The Soul Sonic Force, The System, Brenda K, Us Girls, Tina B, Jazzy Jay.

World preemed as a post-midnight out of competition attraction at the Cannes Film Festival, "Beat Street" is an impressively produced, music-loaded panorama of ghetto-derived contempo culture. Success of the recent "Breakin'" bodes well for the b.o. potential of this much larger Harry Belafonte-David V. Picker production, and this should prove to be the litmus test of how much crossover business can be done by an essentially ethnically oriented pic whose music has not been of the chart-topping variety up until now.

Boisterous film trades in the same elements as did last year's indie effort, "Wild Style," those being break dancing, rap music and graffiti art. Kids in ravaged South Bronx have developed these artistic styles on the streets and in clubs, and development is implicitly seen as a highly positive one in that they rep healthy alternatives to gang activity and other no-win ghetto options.

While eschewing polemics and societal analysis, "Beat Street" is socially conscious in the admirable sense that it conveys a real feeling of solidarity and purpose within its diverse community. In its own way, this is another film on the new American melting pot, and a quite upbeat one at that.

What exists of the plot is just slotted in between musical numbers, and rarely does even a dialog scene pass without someone clicking on a tape. Brothers Guy Davis and Robert Taylor meet college music composer-conductor Rae Dawn Chong (looking better than ever), who tries to help both of them raise their sights as a rapper and breaker, respectively, and she enters into a mild romance with Davis.

Meanwhile, Puerto Rican graffiti artist John Chardiet needs to provide for his girlfriend and baby, but is preoccupied by an unknown culprit who's defacing his work all over town.

Most spectacular and prolonged display of breakdancing comes relatively early in a big bash at Manhattan's Roxy, where two crews of dancers strut their stuff in dazzling fashion. Also great here is Afrika Bambaataa & The Soul Sonic Force.

When the story per se seems to be going nowhere fast, one of the characters meets an untimely death in the cause of his art, and huge finale back at the Roxy on New Year's Eve emerges as a tribute to him as well as a celebration of the teeming stew of cultural and musical influence being expressed in modern music. Grand Master Melle Mel & The Furious Five deliver a dynamite number in this sequence.

Despite the realism of the bombed-out backdrops, pic is pretty splashy and production number-oriented. Director Stan Lathan (who took over early in the shooting from original director, co-writer Andy Davis) has done an excellent job eliciting believable performances from the mix of actors and non-pros, and camera set-ups and editing generally show the dancing and art to good advantage.

Tom Priestly Jr.'s lensing, however, seems noticeably underlit, and general darkness (abetted by overcast winter weather most of the time) puts something of a damper on the excitement and enthusiasm.

Built up romantically in a big slow dance number, love affair between handsome Guy Davis (son of Ossie Davis and Ruby Dee) and Chong never visibly comes to anything, which is an emerging trend in breakdance films thus far.

—*Cart.*

Histoire du Caporal
(The Story of the Corporal)
(FRENCH-COLOR)

Paris, May 9.

A Lyric International/F.R. 3 coproduction, with the participation of the Ministry of Culture. Produced by Jean-Pierre Mahot and Humbert Balsan. Written and directed by Jean Baronnet. Camera, (color), Pierre Dupouey; editor, Jean Gargonne; sound, Jean-Philippe Le Roux; art director, Jean-Pierre Bazerolle. Reviewed at the C.N.C., Paris, May 3, 1984. In "Perspectives on French Cinema" section at Cannes Festival. Running time: 86 MINS.
With: Philippe Nahoun, Maurice Tuesch, Christian Defleur, Catherine Reynet, Paul Gobert.

"Histoire de Caporal" is a pacifist tale of a taciturn French peasant who, after three years at the front during World War I, decides the fighting is over for him and heads for the hills where he intends to live out the rest of the conflict in a mountain grotto.

Writer-director Jean Baronnet has adopted a subdued, non-psychological style for his story, related calmly and without spectacular effect. Early part of the film deals with the hero's life at the front, which is shown rather elliptically since he obviously did not have the means to depict war in its full intense horror. In an apparently key scene the peasant and a colleague are seen salvaging the necessary effects from the bodies of fallen combatants, including a German.

Later when the hero decides to desert, he quietly takes leave of his wife and makes his way into the mountains, where his skills permit him to live frugally. Soon he is joined by another deserter, from the city, who cannot stand the pastoral life, and leaves. But local police, aware the peasant is hiding in the area, finally ambush and shoot him down.

Despite an approach to a hackneyed theme that's far from the usual bellowing anti-war statements, Baronnet cannot avoid the platitudes of pacifist pictures. There's one scene here in which the protagonist, home on leave, argues with some blindly belligerent cafe habitués — that seems a listless redo of a scene in "All Quiet On The Western Front."

The almost documentary filming of the deserter's hermit existence finally becomes monotonous — one feels neither sorrow nor outrage when he is killed. — *Len.*

Yellow Hair And The Pecos Kid
(U.S.-SPANISH-COLOR)

Cannes, May 19.

A Continental Movie Productions and Cinestar presentation. Produced by John Ghaffari and Diego Sempere. Directed by Matt Cimber. Stars Laurene Landon, Ken Roberson. Screenplay by John Kershaw, Cimber; camera (color), John Cabrera; editor, Claudio Cutry; art direction, Jose Maria Tapiador; music, Franco Piersanti. Reviewed at the Cannes Film Festival (Market), May 18, 1984. Running time: 102 MINS.
Yellow Hair.............Laurene Landon
The Pecos Kid.............Ken Roberson
Colonel Torres.............Luis Lorento
Shayowteewah.............John Ghaffari
Flores.............Aldo Sambrel
Grey Cloud.............Isabella Gravi

The current ill fortunes of the western are unlikely to improve with the release of "Yellow Hair And The Pecos Kid." The Spanish-made oater is framed as an homage to Saturday afternoon serials of bygone days, but don't expect any olés from die-hard fans.

Tale centers on the quest for Indian gold which the title characters vie for with a Mexican general and renegade commancheros. Our heroes have the edge because they were raised by an Apache woman, and Yellow Hair (Laurene Landon) even claims to be part Indian. One suspects her heritage derives from her head band.

After a series of close calls running the usual gamut of western clichés, the duo finds the gold so eagerly guarded by the Inca-like Tulipan tribe. Their leader takes a shine to Yellow Hair — it is not amorous as she believes, but rather as a human sacrifice to their god.

Landon gets more of an opportunity to display some of her comic talents than afforded her by the same production team in "Hundra." However, the remaining cast is uniformly lackluster, particularly Ken Roberson as the Pecos Kid who has an unfortunate lisp.

Technical credits are good, but director Matt Cimber lacks the light touch which could have made the material work. Cimber also dots the action with needlessly violent action sequences which will further limit the picture's commercial potential.

"Yellow Hair And The Pecos Kid" looks like a quick siesta at the boxoffice. Threats of a next chapter at its close, are, thankfully, quite doubtful. —*Klad.*

Courage
(U.S.-COLOR)

Cannes, May 16.

No U.S. distrib. A Sandy Howard/Adams Apple Film Company production of a Robert L. Rosen film in association with VTV. Produced by Ronny Cox, Rosen. Exec producers, Mel Pearl, Don Levin. Directed by Rosen. Screenplay, Ronny Cox, Mary Cox; Camera (color), F. Pershing Flynn; editor, Steven Polivka; art direction, Don Nunley. Reviewed at the Cannes Festival (Market), May 16, '84. Running time: 90 MINS.
Pete Canfield.............Ronny Cox
Ruth.............Lois Chiles
Roger Bower.............Art Hindle
Colonel Crouse.............M. Emmet Walsh
Craig Jensen.............Tim Maier
Sonny.............William Russ
Stephanie.............Lisa Sutton
Clay Matthews.............Noel Conlon
Herb Jensen.............Anthony Palmer

Enter "Courage" in the why-was-it-made column. Three male friends go for a 72-mile marathon run in the desert (New Mexico) and are taken temporary hostage by a squad of militaristic-dressed civilians who are training for war and call themselves a citizens brigade. The three runners attempt to intervene on punishment imposed by a wayward female member of the brigade and are set free. Then they're pursued through the desert and in the nearby mountains.

Death ensues on both sides, but two remaining runners defy all odds and hobble to the finish line while the remaining baddies sit on motorbikes and surrender to police.

Plot is witless. Even the blood looks painted on. But the desert looks nice. Is there a moral here — that marathon runners should beware of mean vigilantes behind every rock? Otherwise, it's pointless and played off unconvincingly. Commercial possibilities? A no distance call.—*Adil.*

The Princess And The Call Girl
(U.S.-COLOR)

Cannes, May 19.

A Manley Productions release of a Highbridge Film Productions production. Directed by Radley Metzger. Features entire cast. Screenplay, Metzger, based on an original story by Peter Serbie. (No other credits provided.) Reviewed at the Cannes Film Festival (Market), May 18, 1984. (No MPAA Rating.) Running time: 91 MINS.
Cast: Cerol Levy, Victor Bevine, Shannah Hall, Chris Beach and Christine Swing.

Director-scripter Radley Metzger has been straddling the worlds of hard and softcore for some time, achieving success more often of late as a porno helmer ("The Private Afternoons Of Pamela Menn") under the pseudonym Henry Paris. In this softcore outing, Metzger combines the dramatic oafishness of hardcore with the sexual tedium of softcore, making the result suitable for unfussy sexpo fans only.

Plot has a high-priced call girl and her virginal lookalike friend swapping places for a number of uninteresting reasons. The latter, who lives with her wealthy family on New York's Beekman Place, flies to Monte Carlo to service several of the former's clients. The call girl, meanwhile, winds up substituting for the by-now sexually experienced "princess" at a fancy engagement party.

Given Metzger's characteristically glossy approach to the material, the film might have yielded a modicum of interest as a hardcore item. As a softcore pic, it's a snooze-producer. — *Sege.*

Le Sang des Autres
(The Blood Of Others)
(CANADIAN-FRENCH-COLOR)

Paris, May 20.

A Parafrance release of Filmax/Antenne 2/Films A2/International Cinema Corp. coproduction. Produced by Denis Heroux, John Kemeny, Gabriel Boustani. Executive producer, Lamar Card. Associate producers, Paulo de Oliveira, Christian Davin, Bashar Nasri. Directed by Claude Chabrol. Screenplay, Brian Moore, based on the novel by Simone de Beauvoir; additional French dialog, Jacques Levy; camera (color), Richard Ciupka; art director, Franoics Comtet; costumes, Pierre Cadot; sound, Patrick Rousseau, Jean-Bernard Thomasson; editors, Yves Langlois, Monique Fardoulis; music, Francois Dompierre, Mathieu Chabrol. Reviewed at the Paramount Mercury theater, Paris, May 18, 1984. Running time: **130 MINS.**

Helene	Jodie Foster
Jean Blomart	Michael Ontkean
Bergman	Sam Neill
Paul Perrier	Lambert Wilson
Gigi Grandjouan	Stephane Audran
Madeleine	Alexandra Stewart
Arnaud	Jean-Francois Balmer
General Von Loenig	Howard Vernon
Madam Blomart	Kate Reid
Madam Kotz	Monique Mercure
Raoul	Michel Robin
Mr. Blomart	Jean-Pierre Aumont
Madam Monge	Micheline Presle

(French-dubbed dialog)

Simone de Beauvoir's 1946 novel about social commitment and moral responsibility has been reduced to anemic dime-novel melodrama in this film scripted by Robin Moore and directed by Claude Chabrol.

De Beauvoir, whose books have never been filmed until now, reportedly is displeased with the results, but what did she expect from an internationally coproduced commercial picture in which lead casting must obey imperatives that are not primarily artistic. Jodie Foster and Michael Ontkean play the principals, who are both Gallics; actors, and dubbers, do their best, but a gulf remains between performance and personage.

Besides which, de Beauvoir's novel, dated as it seems now, is profoundly French in content and form, and it's hard to understand what its producers could have seen in this tale of some young Parisians sucked into the moral swamp of the German Occupation and the Resistance.

Moore's screenplay scraps the writer's intellectual structure for a bare, linear storyline that finally reflects little of the novel's essence and fills it in with a lot of clichés and two-dimensional characterizations. Again, definitive comment will be possible when the full, six-hour miniseries version airs, via HBO in the U.S.

The two-hour-plus version for theaters keeps Foster in focus throughout as a self-centered young woman working in a Parisian fashion house before the war and involved romantically with a young left-wing activist (Lambert Wilson). But politics and love don't mix well in their relationship, so she drops him for Ontkean, a young man of bourgeois background who has broken with his family in joining the workers' cause.

The outbreak of the war separates them, and when the German Occupation begins, she must steer her way through the pitfalls of collaboration, notably in her self-serving rapport with a German functionary (Sam Neill), who later commits suicide rather than denounce her role in a daring Resistance assassination.

To stay next to Ontkean, Foster engages in other underground operations. During an attempt to free an imprisoned freedom fighter, she is mortally wounded. Ontkean carries on in the Resistance, committed to activities in which innocent people will be victims.

Claude Chabrol has directed dully, failing to quintessentially recreate the atmosphere of Paris before and during the war. The scenes of the panicky exodus from Paris in June 1940 are particularly poor in their skimpy reconstitution. And he gets no better than middling performances from his French players, who, as is the case with the leads, seem only vaguely interested in what's going on around them.

"Le Sang des Autres" is meant to create some pathos and raise some vital questions about political and personal actions. It accomplished neither. —*Len.*

Fleshburn
(COLOR)

Dull survival pic, due for short b.o. life.

A Crown International Pictures release of an Amritraj production; a Fear Prods. picture. Executive producers, Ashok Amritraj, Sidney Balkin. Produced by Beth Gage. Directed by George Gage. Features entire cast. Screenplay, Beth & George Gage, from novel "Fear In A Handful Of Dust" by Brian Garfield; camera (Deluxe color), Bill Pecchi; editor, Sonya Sones; music, Arthur Kempel; additional music, Don Felder; sound, Lee Strosnider; assistant director-production manager, Mike Moder; special effects, Jim Hoagland; associate producer, Vijay Amritraj. Reviewed at RKO Warner I theater, N.Y., May 26, 1984. (MPAA Rating: R.) Running time: **90 MINS.**

Sam	Steve Kanaly
Shirley	Karen Carlson
Earl	Macon McCalman
Jay	Robert Chimento
Calvin Duggai	Sonny Landham
Jim Brody	Robert Alan Browne
Smyley	Duke Stroud

"Fleshburn," lensed last year in the Tucson area under the title of Brian Garfield's novel, "Fear In A Handful Of Dust," is a tedious, uneventful low-budget survival drama. Wearying rather than entertaining, B-picture has no perceptible audience in mind.

Filmmakers Beth and George Gage have a modest B-picture storyline to work with: Navajo Indian Calvin Duggai (pronounced "Do-Gay," played by Sonny Landham) has escaped from a mental hospital to wreak vengeance upon the people whose court testimony sent him there as a nutcase, after leaving several men to die in the desert in 1975 as a result of a tribal argument. He speedily captures Shirley (Karne Carlson), her husband Jay (Robert Chimento), a psychiatrist turned forest ranger Sam (Steve Kanaly) and another shrink Earl (Macon McCalman) and strands the foursome in the desert while he hovers around to make sure they don't escape and to prove his "medicine" is stronger than whitey's.

That's all she wrote, over 90 gruelling minutes of running time. At first, Sam's ingenuity in using cacti, rabbits and other materials at hand to prolong their lifespan is intriguing, but the orange-filtered visuals and static, low-on-action dramaturgy heads nowhere. Sam's unbelievable outwitting of Duggai at a nearby springs and non-ending are very disappointing payoffs for the wait.

Cast is capable in very sketchy roles, and Landham, effective as a heavy in Walter Hill's "48 Hrs.," has the strong face and physique to qualify for a "Conan"-style assignment. Background musical score is spare but promising in a Jerry Goldsmith-vein, and other tech credits are modest. Director Gage's earlier feature assignment was the stillborn trend pic "Skateboard," barely released by Universal in 1978.

Oddest touch here, and not reflected in film's content, is that a story about a Native American indian was backed in part by tennis star from India, Vijay Amritraj, who recently turned to acting in "Octopussy." —*Lor.*

Star Trek III
The Search For Spock
(COLOR)

Winning space saga guaranteed to please Trek fans.

A Paramount Pictures release of a Harve Bennett production, in association with Cinema Group Venture. Executive producer, Gary Nardino. Produced by Bennett. Directed by Leonard Nimoy. Features entire cast. Screenplay, Bennett, based on "Star Trek" (tv series) created by Gene Roddenberry; camera (Movielab color, Panavision), Charles Correll; editor, Robert F. Shugrue; music, James Horner; "Star Trek" tv series theme music, Alexander Courage; sound, Gene S. Cantamessa; special visual effects supervisor, Kenneth Ralston at Industrial Light & Magic; art direction, John E. Chilberg 2d; set design, Cameron Birnie, Blake Russell; set decoration, Tom Pedigo; executive consultant, Roddenberry; production manager, Michael P. Schoenbrun; assistant director, John Hockridge; costume design, Robert Fletcher; special makeup appliances, The Burman Studio; special (physical) effects supervisor, Bob Dawson; special sound effects, Alan Howarth, Frank Serafine; stunt coordinators, Ron Stein, R.A. Rondell; additional optical effects, Movie Magic. Reviewed at Paramount 30th Floor screening room, N.Y., May 23, 1984. (MPAA Rating: PG). Running time: **105 MINS.**

Kirk	William Shatner
McCoy	DeForest Kelley
Scotty	James Doohan
Sulu	George Takei
Chekov	Walter Koenig
Uhura	Nichelle Nichols
Sarek	Mark Lenard
David	Merritt Butrick
High priestess	Dame Judith Anderson
Saavik	Robin Curtis
Kruge	Christopher Lloyd
Capt. Styles	James B. Sikking
Alien at bar	Allan Miller
Spock	Leonard Nimoy

Also with: Robert Hooks, Cathie Shirriff, Phil Morris, Scott McGinnis, Phillip Richard Allen, Stephen Liska, John Larroquette, Sharon Thomas, Miguel Ferrer.

Special Visual Effects Unit Credits

Industrial Light & Magic: visual effects supervisor, Ken Ralston; cameramen, Donald Dow, Scott Farrar, Selwyn Eddy 3d; optical photography supervisor, Kenneth F. Smith; ILM general manager, Tom Smith; production supervisor, Warren Franklin; art direction, Nilo Rodis, David Carson; supervising modelmaker, Steve Gawley; creature supervisor, David Sosalla; matte painting supervisor, Michael Pangrazio; matte artists, Chris Evans, Frank Ordaz; animation supervisor, Charles Mullen; miniature pyrotechnics and fire effects, Ted Moehnke; editors, Bill Kimberlin, Jay Ignaszewski; production coordinator, Laurie Vermont.

"Star Trek III — The Search For Spock" is an emotionally satisfying science fiction adventure. Dovetailing neatly with the previous entry in the popular series ("Star Trek II — The Wrath Of Khan"), the Harve Bennett production (he also scripted) is helmed with a sure hand by debuting feature director Leonard Nimoy, who also appears briefly but to good effect as the indestructible half human/half-Vulcan Spock.

Relying upon clues (as revealed in flashbacks) cleverly planted in "Star Trek II," film centers upon a quest to seemingly bring Spock, the noble science officer and commander who selflessly gave his life to save "the many," back to life. Pic opens in a melancholy mood as the U.S.S. Enterprise limps home in damaged state. It is to be scuttled, as announced by Commander Morrow (Robert Hooks), and only the ship's engineer Scotty (James Doohan) has been reassigned to a flashy new ship The Excelsior.

Spock's friend, Admiral Kirk (William Shatner) is visited by Spock's Vulcan father (Mark Lenard, reprising a guest-star role he played in the tv series), who informs him that Spock's living spirit may still be alive via a mindmeld with one of Kirk's crew and must be taken to the planet Vulcan to be preserved.

Kirk discovers who the "possessed" crew member is, and with his other shipmates, steals the Enterprise out of its dock and sets off for Vulcan. Crosscut with this mission is footage of Kirk's scientist son (Merritt Butrick) and Vulcan science officer Lt. Saavik exploring the unstable Genesis planet where they find a young but rapidly aging Vulcan boy who appears to be a life-form regenerated from Spock's corpse, which had been left on Genesis.

The enemy are the Klingons, represented by one Commander Kruge (Christopher Lloyd) who defies an impending space treaty between the Klingon Empire and the Federation and attacks Saavik's ship, the U.S.S. Grissom (named for the late astronaut). Kruge attempts to steal the secret of the Genesis effect (life from lifelessness) but is outwitted by Kirk, who successfully arrives on Vulcan with Spock's regenerated body. In a ritualistic ceremony presided over by a high priestess (Dame Judith Anderson), Spock is reintegrated, spirit and flesh, and regains his memories with the help of his human friends in a moving conclusion, that promises not only a soon-to-come "Star Trek IV," but the prospect of the Nimoy-as-Spock character back in a starring role.

Bennett's script carefully captures the spirit of the Gene Roddenberry-created tv series, even providing satisfying (though brief) scenes spotlighting each member of the crew, including communications officer Uhura (Nichelle Nichols), who gets to state (and demonstrate) that "this isn't reality — this is fantasy."

Countering ongoing trends in science fiction and youth-oriented films, Nimoy's direction is people-intensive, with less of the zap and effects diversions of competing films. However, George Lucas' Industrial Light & Magic, under Ken Ralston's supervision, has delivered arresting miniature work and animation which, especially in the sequences of the Enterprise docking and departing, impart a sense of realistically vast scale (not looking like tiny models). The point is that the visuals do not overwhelm the performances, well-delivered by an ensemble rather than star cast.

James Horner elaborates effectively on his score from "Star Trek II," and his orchestral work (even including theremin-like effects) combines with Dame Judith Anderson's mystical three-word-incantation (when bringing Spock back to life) to conjure up pleasant memories of Robert Wise's classic "The Day The Earth Stood Still" and thereby link "Star Trek III" to science fiction tradition. Wise directed the first "Trek" feature but is no longer involved in the series.

"Trek III" will definitely satisfy the fans of the Paramount tv series and along with "Rocky III" demonstrates the effectiveness in a feature film series (unlike the Bond pictures and "Indiana Jones") of preserving a continuity in characters and stories from one adventure to the next. —*Lor.*

Streets Of Fire
(COLOR)

Rock 'n' Roll fable is long on style but low in content. Rocky b.o. road ahead.

Hollywood, May 29.
A Universal Pictures and RKO Pictures presentation of a Hill-Gordon-Silver production. Produced by Lawrence Gordon, Joel Silver. Directed by Walter Hill. Features entire cast. Screenplay, Hill, Larry Gross; camera (Technicolor), Andrew Laszlo; editor, Freeman Davies, Michael Ripps; music, Ry Cooder; special musical material supervision, Jimmy Iovine; sound, Jim Webb, Crew Chamberlain; production manager-executive producer, Gene Levy; assistant director, David Sosna; production design, John Vallone; art direction, James Allen; set design, Bob Schlafle, Martha Johnston; set decoration, Richard C. Goddard; costume design, Marilyn Vance; choreography, Jeffrey Hornaday; stunt coordinator, Bennie Dobbins; special effects, Howard Jensen. Reviewed at Universal Studios, L.A., May 24, 1984. (MPAA Rating: PG.) Running time: **94 MINS.**

Tom Cody	Michael Paré
Ellen Aim	Diane Lane
Billy Fish	Rick Moranis
McCoy	Amy Madigan
Raven	Willem Dafoe
Reva	Deborah Van Valkenburgh
Ed Price	Richard Lawson
Officer Cooley	Rick Rossovich
Clyde	Bill Paxton
Greer	Lee Ving

Also with: Stoney Jackson, Grand Bush, Robert Townsend, Mykel T. Williamson (The Sorels vocal group); Elizabeth Daily, Lynne Thigpen, Marine Jahan, Ed Begley Jr.

If there's a market for a theatrical that performs like a full-length music video, "Streets Of Fire" might ignite a trend. Boxoffice projection for this rock 'n' roll fable is cautionary in the extreme, however, because youth crowds addicted to MTV will likely continue to favor movies that explore more than a mélange of style and sound.

Assembled by the team that created the hit "48 Hrs." (director Walter Hill, producers Lawrence Gordon and Joel Silver, and writers Larry Gross and Hill), pic is a pulsing, throbbing orchestration careening around the rescue of a kidnapped young singer. The decor is urban squalor. The film alternately, and sometimes simultaneously, suggests the rhythm and texture of "Blade Runner," "Escape From New York" and "The Warriors" (the latter also a Hill-Gordon production).

Soundtrack album is terrific. Movie has 10 original songs — by Stevie Nicks, Jim Steinman, Ry Cooder (who scored), and the L.A. group The Blasters, among others — and musically the movie is continually hot, with lyrics charting the concerns of the narrative line, simplistic as it is.

Film also has undeniable texture. Smoke, neon, rainy streets, platforms of elevated subway lines, alleys and warehouses create an urban inferno in an unspecified time and place. Andrew Laszlo's lighting and John Vallone's production design, and Marilyn Vance's imaginative costuming, spill colors across the screen vividly and artfully.

But all form and no content is boring. There is no characterization to speak of, except in the case of Rick Moranis as an edgy and subtly humorous foil to the dead-ahead performances of Diane Lane as the kidnapped singer, Michael Paré as her former boyfriend and tough, handsome rescuer, and Amy Madigan as an adventurer in tow.

Lane, whose singing voice is dubbed, looks great and is cast expertly. So, for that matter, are Willem Dafoe and Lee Ving as leaders of the dreaded outlaw gang the Bombers. But the story is so deliberately thin, so tiresome a parody of action-romance films, that the exercise in visual and auditory imagination turns cynical very quickly.

Briefly seen as a stripper-dancer in the Bombers' hangout (where the Blasters perform "One Bad Stud") is Marine Jahan, who was the uncredited dancer in "Flashdance." —*Loyn.*

Le Juge
(The Judge)
(FRENCH-COLOR)

Paris, May 15.
A GEF/CCFC release of a GEF-Revcom/-TF1 Films/Trinacara co-production. Produced by Yves Rousset-Rouard. Executive producer, Denis Mermet. Directed by Philippe Lefebvre. Stars Jacques Perrin, Richard Bohringer, Daniel Duval. Screenplay, Lefebvre and Bernad Stora; camera (Eastmancolor), Jean-Paul Schwartz; art director, Jean-Claude Gallouin; editor, Youcef Tobni; sound, Jean-Pierre Ruh; music, Luis Bacalov. Reviewed at the Marignan-Concorde theater, Paris, May 15, 1984. Running time: **92 MINS.**

Judge Muller	Jacques Perrin
Inocenti	Richard Bohringer
Rocca	Daniel Duval
Regine Sauvat	Andrea Férreol
The doctor	Michael Lonsdale
Donati	Jean Benguigui

"The Judge" tells of a French examining magistrate bent on destroying a Marseilles drug ring controlled by an underworld kingpin whom the judge has arrested for carrying an unlicensed weapon. Conducting his own investigation, with the intermittent aid of a local police inspector, the magistrate comes dangerously close to his goal but is gunned down by gangsters.

Philippe Lefebvre, a tv helmer making his theatrical film debut, has transposed the true story of the judge, Michel, who was shot down in 1979 during a similar inquiry. Despite being based on fact, his film is rather conventional and superficial, developing without surprise or insight. No doubt the real event is more complex and fascinating than its fictional extrapolation.

Otherwise "Le Juge" is competent technically and passably acted, with Jacques Perrin as the aggressive magistrate, Richard Bohringer solid in a change of pace as a good guy cop, Daniel Duval as the gangster chieftain whose Achilles heel Perrin fails to find, and Jean Benguigui as Duval's wily attorney. —*Len.*

Der Bär
(The Bear)
(WEST GERMAN-COLOR-16m)

Berlin, May 23.
A Margarita Woskanjan Film Production, Berlin. Features entire cast. Written and directed by Don Askarjan, based on Anton Chekhov's one-act farce with the same title. Camera (color), Wladimir Woitinski; sets and costumes, Askarjan; sound, A. Arft, U. Thalmann; editing, S. Beckers; music, Johann Sebastian Bach, Donizetti, Dandrieu, Don Askarjan; assistant directors, M. Majerski, T. Podlesezki; German-language assistance, Peter Urban. Reviewed at Arsenal-Kino, Berlin, May 23, '84. Running time: **58 MINS.**

With: Hans-Peter Hallwachs (Smirnov), Elisabeth Rath (Popova), Hans Mandin (Luka).

Anton Chekhov has been filmed countless times, his short stories as well as his plays. And one of the most popular of student theater productions has to be his one-act farce, "The Bear," so it seems only natural that Armenia-born Don Askarjan should make a low-budget 16m short feature out of the classic.

Askarjan studied art history in Moscow before turning to filmmaking, working as an assistant director at Mosfilm studios in Moscow and Armenfilm at Yerevan in the Armenian Republic of the Soviet Union. In 1979, he emigrated to West Germany.

"The Bear" is filmed theater of a special sort. Askarjan filmed in an old Berlin villa with well-known stage thesps, and he attempts to place as much emphasis on the visual image as the spoken word. Results are still filmed theater, although some scenes are eye-catching. One inspiration that plays off is a hen roaming over the premises as though the place belonged to it. The use of natural light on occasion pays off too, and it's remarkable that the whole hour-long film was shot in 10 days over a New Year's holiday.

The story lends itself to a film exposition. The setting is a run-down mansion, whose widowed owner is still grieving over her dearly departed husband. Her only companion is the faithful but eccentric butler and jack-of-all-trades, Luka, who is a physical personification of a splendid mansion crumbling into filth and ruin (Askarjan found just such a place in the Berlin-Schlachtensee villa area). Then along comes an ex-calvary officer to collect an overdue debt: Smirnov, the next-door neighbor and equally-in-need houseowner, tries every means at his command to cajole the widow Popova into paying him the money. They get on each other's nerves for a while, then decide to fight a senseless duel, and end up declaring their mutual love for each other to resolve their differences.

Well acted by stage professionals, "The Bear" is on the level of programming one finds delivered up regularly on European television. Chekhovian cinema has become rather popular of late, and pic might find a slot on a retrospective slate of productions dealing with the works of the Russian master.—*Holl.*

L'Addition
(The Bill)
(FRENCH-COLOR)

Paris, May 21.

A UGC release of a Swanie Productions/TF1 Films Production/UGC - Top 1 coproduction. Produced by Norbert Saada. Executive producers, Norbert Chalon and Pierre Chalon. Directed by Denis Amar. Stars Richard Berry, Richard Bohringer, Victoria Abril. Screenplay, Denis Amar, Jean-Pierre Bastid, Jean Curtelin; Camera (color), Robert Fraisse; sound, Bernard Bats; art director, Serge Douy; editor, Jacques Witta; music, Jean-Claude Petit. Reviewed at the UGC Biarritz theater, Paris, May 15, 1984. Running time: **85 MINS.**

Bruno	Richard Berry
Lorca	Richard Bohringer
Patty	Victoria Abril
José	Farid Chopel
Minet	Fabrice Eberhard
Constantini	Daniel Sarky
Prison director	Jacques Sereys

"L'Addition" is a transparently contrived prison drama about a minor offender mired in a world of hardened criminals and vicious guards. Snubbing nuance and verisimilitude, director Denis Amar and writer Jean Curtelin shamelessly play on the frayed strings of audience manipulation to create terror and suspense, though the stock characterizations and obvious confrontations rob the tale of a genuine nightmare feel. It lacks the well-oiled mesh of good melodrama.

Pic's big plus is Richard Berry, who gives a semblance of substance to the central role of a young actor who lands in jail after having tried to intervene in the arrest of a pretty young kleptomaniac in a supermarket (Victoria Abril).

Behind bars everything goes wrong for the hapless Berry, who is first taken hostage in a prison break in which he is thought to be an accomplice. Not only does he get his sentence prolonged, but he also earns the undying hatred of the guard who was maimed during the break and holds Berry responsible. When Berry is transferred to a new prison, the psychotic guard (Richard Bohringer) follows, swearing to exact vengeance and cleverly setting some of the more brutal inmates on him.

When the actor realizes his situation will never improve and that a legal exit seems a faint possibility, he falls back on his talent to get him out; when Bohringer pays an expected night call to his cell Berry beats and trusses him, dons his uniform, and mimicking the guard's voice and pronounced limp, makes a clear getaway.

Curtelin, who revamped the original script by Amar and Jean-Pierre Bastide, is a proponent of the sledgehammer school of screenwriting, in which technicalities like credibility are shoved aside in the rush to get to the next big, dramatic sequence. Curtelin's manner finds perfect company in Amar's blunderbuss direction. The helmer, who made his feature debut with the 1980 film "Asphalte," still can't make one forget he's made a lot of commercials.

Abril is wasted as the young klepto who becomes Berry's lover-ally on the outside, and Bohringer repeats his usual hoarse-voiced nasty act, which is beginning to get monotonous. Among supporting roles, gifted comic Farid Chopel does a good turn as a vicious convict after Berry.

Serge Douy, son of the great French art director Max Douy, designed the principal set of a modern, spotless neon-lit prison, and promises to be a chip off the old block in the future if the opportunities arise. Other tech credits are sound.

"L'Addition" copped the grand prize at the recent Cognac Thriller Film Festival and has been doing fine in local bow. —*Len.*

Mardi Gras Massacre
(COLOR)

Gorefest in New Orleans, for horror addicts only.

An Omni Capital release. Written, produced and directed by Jack Weis. Assistant producer, John Stimac Jr. Features entire cast. Camera (color), Jack McGowan, Don Piel, Weis; editor, uncredited; music, courtesy of Westbound Records; sound, Rick Wigginton. Reviewed at 42d St. Selwyn theater, N.Y., May 26, 1984. (No MPAA Rating.) Running time: **93 MINS.**

With: Curt Dawson, Gwen Arment, Bill Metzo, Laura Misch, Cathryn Lacey, Nancy Dancer, Butch Benit, Wayne Mack, Ronald Tanet.

"Mardi Gras Massacre" had the makings of an atmospheric B-movie set in New Orleans, but emerges as a mere Grand Guignol exercise reminiscent of the Herschel Gordon Lewis ("Blood Feast") pictures of the 1960s. Extremely obscure feature is not listed in any fantasy reference books or film production charts but appears to have been lensed circa 1978.

Story concerns an unnamed nutcase who seeks out "evil" prostitutes and ritualistically sacrifices them on Tuesdays to an Aztec goddess whose name translates as "The Lady Of The Serpent Skirt." This leads up to Fat Tuesday (i.e., Mardi Gras), when he plans a three-girl sacrifice.

Frank, the cop on the case, falls in love with a heart-of-gold blond prostie named Shelley while he incompetently tries to track down the killer. Not surprisingly, Shelley (who proves to be amazingly forgetful, having met the killer at film's opening) is one of the three potential Mardi Gras victims until Frank and cohorts come to the rescue.

Location lensing at bars and strip-joints plus some flavorful quirky performances (particularly an ofay pimp who has his rhyming slang down pat) are "Massacre"'s highpoints. Unfortunately, the pic's raison d'être consists of repetitive gore stagings in which the killer ties each nude prostitute to a table, ceremonially cuts her hand and foot and then (switch to closeup of a well-matched rubber model torso) cuts open her chest to remove the heart as a sacrifice. Target audience for this old-hat attempt at shock is very limited.

Filmmaker Jack Weis directed a black-oriented period picture "Quadroon" in 1971 and announced an ambitious (but apparently unrealized) project entitled "Storyville" in 1973, the milieu later covered in Louis Malle's "Pretty Baby." With "Massacre," he has taken the low road, which leads directly to obscurity. —*Lor.*

Me'Achorei Hasoragim
(Beyond The Walls)
(ISRAELI-COLOR)

Tel Aviv, May 5.

An April Films Production. Produced by Rudy Cohen. Associate Producer: Katriel Schehori. Directed by Uri Barbash. Arnon Zadok, Muhamad Bakri. Screenplay, Benny Barbash and Eran Price with Uri Barbash; camera (color), Amnon Salomon; editor, Tova Asher; music, Ilan Wirtzberg; title song, Nurith Hirsch, Shimrith Or; Art director, Eitan Levi. Reviewed at the Berkey, Pathe, Humphries screening room, Tel Aviv, May 5, 1984. Running time: **97 MINS.**

Cast: Arnon Zadock, Muhamad Bakri, Assi Dayan, Hilel Ne'eman, Rami Danon, Boaz Shar'abi, Adib Jahashan, Roberto Polak.

This powerful drama, recently picked up by Warner Bros. for international distribution, is one of the best films to come out of Israel in some time. Director Uri Barbash, who has an impressive record of tv dramas, had difficulties making the transition to the big screen in his first theatrical feature, "Stigma," but has overcome both narrative and visual problems in a most satisfactory fashion.

The script focuses on a maximum security ward of an Israeli jail, using it as a representative image of the entire country's situation.

This maximum security ward houses side by side Israelis, most sentenced to long terms for criminal offenses, and Arabs, who have to serve even longer sentences, most for acts of terrorism.

The conflicts are many and varied, starting with the mutual rejection of the two factions, encouraged by the jail authorities who believe this is the best way to keep them under control, and going on to the personal problems of the different inmates, including drug addiction.

The introduction of a Jewish political prisoner, a peacenik whose independent initiatives in contacting the enemy have been his downfall, creates additional tension, for the Jewish inmates consider him a traitor responsible for promoting acts of terror. The Arabs, on the other hand, eye him with suspicion, for peace initiatives from the other side have never been accepted wholeheartedly.

But as the plot progresses and the clashes become more violent, it is evident that as much as they hate each other, both parties are victims and, finally, if there is one way out of the impasse, it is first of all to put up a common front against the manipulation of the jailers.

Barbash manages to avoid two obvious pitfalls: he does not make just another jailhouse drama; and does not adopt the stentorian tones of a preachy political picture.

He concentrates instead on each of his characters, never allowing them to be simply black or white, and he elicits powerful performances from Arnon Zadock as the leader of the Jewish inmates and Muhamad Bakri as his Arab counterpart.

If there is a flaw in this picture, it is mostly in the scenes showing the prison directors planning and preparing their policies. Hilel Ne'eman is far too obvious and superficial as the Machiavelian security officer who tries to pull all sorts of emotional strings in order to avoid any problems, and so are all the other actors of these sequences.

Art direction is impressive, with the film shot in a customs house, revamped for the occasion, rather than a real jail.

Chances at home will depend very much on political reaction of the audience. For the first time, an Israeli film depicts an avowed terrorist as a positive character, someone who is not a crazed extremist enjoying the idea of blowing people up, but an honest nationalist who believes this to be the only way to bring the opposite side to discuss the Palestinian problem realistically. The film doesn't praise him for it, but refuses the accepted position that any such person can be nothing but a villain.

This means the Israeli release will have to be timed carefully in order to avoid adverse reactions stemming from front page news. Abroad, it is probable a more objective audience will view it in a relatively dispassionate manner and will allow its sheer quality to prevail.—*Edna.*

Cannes Festival

The Shooting Party
(BRITISH-COLOR)

Cannes, May 16.

A Geoff Reeve Production. Produced by Geoffrey Reeve. Directed by Alan Bridges. Screenplay by Julian Bond, based on the novel by Isabel Colegate; camera (color), Fred Tammes; editor, Peter Davies; costume design, Tom Rand; music, John Scott, production designer, Morley Smith. Reviewed at the Cannes Film Festival (Market), May 16, 1984. Running time: **106 MINS.**
Lord Gilbert Hartlip .... Edward Fox
Lady Aline Hartlip .... Cheryl Campbell
Sir Randolph Nettleby .... James Mason
Lady Minnie Nettleby .... Dorothy Tutin
Cornelius Cardew .... John Gielgud
Glass .... Frank Windsor
Tom Harker .... Gordon Jackson
Lady Olivia Lilburn .... Judi Bowker
Lord Bob Lilburn .... Robert Hardy
Lionel Stephens .... Rupert Frazer
Count Tibor Rakassyi .... Joris Stuyk
Ida Nettleby .... Sarah Badel
Cicely Nettleby .... Rebecca Saire
Sir Reuben Hergesheimer .... Aharon Ipalé

A handsome historical homage to the proprieties and values of pre-World War I landed aristocracy in England, "The Shooting Party" revolves around a holiday spent on an estate in 1913, as an era ends, like the pic, with a whimper not a bang. Stuffed with characters and clever repartee, the story is a leisurely paced commentary on what happens when power and position decline to the level of dressing for dinner as a social statement.

Julian Bond's adaptation of the novel incorporates enough to make a promising miniseries, were it given the scope of a saga, as it so richly deserves. Such literary fidelity in such a brief space defies common sense.

James Mason as Sir Randolph is as world-weary as he is tired of his genuinely tiresome guests, and has done a splendid job replacing Paul Scofield who was injured on the first day of principal photography. Thesp credits resemble a Who's Who of the British stage, with Sir John Gielgud eclipsing the gentry in a brief appearance as a pamphleteering defender of animal rights, opposed to slaughter as amusement.

When a wild duck appears in the dining room for supper and turns out to be the pet of the young boy earlier seen arranging his toy soldiers, the threat of death and war is felt all too clearly. The expected death of the duck, when it gets loose into the fields where the men are shooting, does not come, in an unexpected restraint from further symbolism.

The voice-over of Sir Randolph's memoirs frames the events and formulates the concern he alone feels when he asks, "If you take away the proper function of the aristocracy, what can it do but play games too seriously?" He concludes in the final sequence that the shooting party made him lose his interest in killing, which strands the story in a dilemma with the Great War pending. What is the aristocracy to do then, if they are to help "God save the British Empire," as the dying peasant exhorts them?

The pleasure of watching dignified performances is balanced by the sense that the script intends to debunk their mystique with a class consciousness and autumnal tones. The final tribute to those who fell in action in the war occurs in a closing list before the credits roll.

Director Alan Bridges is very good at handling a story that tries to distinguish between the nobility and what is truly noble, without luxuriating in the sensational temptations of indulgent aristocrats, but the internal ambivalence of the script about its subject requires him to be subtle without depth.

The world's insatiable interest in the decline of the British Empire may not beef up the boxoffice on pics like this, but should prompt respectable pay-cable sales. —*Kaja.*

Old Enough
(U.S.-COLOR)

Cannes, May 20.

An Orion Classics release of a Silverfilm production, produced by Dina Silver. Directed and written by Marisa Silver. Camera (color), Michael Ballhaus; editor, Mark Burns; production design, Jeffrey Townsend; music, Julian Marshall; sound, Ed Novick. Reviewed at the Cannes Film Festival (Directors Fortnight), May 20, 1984. Running time: **91 MINS.**
Lonnie Sloan .... Sarah Boyd
Karen Bruckner .... Rainbow Harvest
Johnny Bruckner .... Neill Barry
Mr. Bruckner .... Danny Aiello
Mrs. Bruckner .... Susan Kingsley
Carla .... Roxanne Hart
Mrs. Sloan .... Fran Brill
Mr. Sloan .... Gerry Bamman
Diane Sloan .... Alyssa Milano

Orion Classics has a winner in "Old Enough," screening in Cannes' noncompetitive Directors Fortnight. The tale of friendship between two young girls of widely different social backgrounds has just the right balance of humor and insight to connect with audiences. "Old Enough" has emerged as one of the brightest entries.

Produced and directed by sisters Dina and Marisa Silver, the project evolved from Utah's Sundance Institute for Independent Filmmakers. Nonetheless, the simple story and modest budgeted effort need make no excuses for finished product. It easily exceeds either "The Ballad Of Gregorio Cortez" or "El Norte" — earlier Sundance-originated pictures — in its commercial appeal.

Story centers on 12-year-old Lonnie Sloan (Sarah Boyd) from an upper-class New York City family and slightly older Karen Bruckner (Rainbow Harvest) from blue-collar background. Both are at important emotional turning points when they meet on the street of the widely divergent economic neighborhood. It is an easily understandable attraction of opposites.

The young filmmakers acutely capture the sense of shared adventure as the two girls enter new, previously unknown worlds. One can readily perceive the breadth of common experiences and tensions which arise from differences in their upbringing. And an added dimension arises from the attraction developing between Lonnie and Karen's brother Johnny (Neill Barry).

On the surface, "Old Enough" would appear to be both predictable and familiar territory. However, the rendering is so vibrant and fresh, one can't help but be won over by its vitality. And the filmmakers demonstrate real talent in this first feature outing.

The mix of fresh faces and a few seasoned pros in cast all register indelibly. Both Sarah Boyd and Rainbow Harvest have burden of carrying the film, which they accomplish with ease.

Technical work is considerably above standard for a low-budget effort. Filmmakers have a real asset with German lenser Michael Ballhaus behind camera and haunting, evocative score by Julian Marshall enhancing grittiness and authority of the tale.

Silvers (daughters of filmmakers Joan Micklin and Raphael) are definitely names to reckon with in future. Initial outing has broader appeal than simply art and specialty market and should sell and play well outside English-language territories. "Old Enough" demonstrates real maturity for neophyte talents. —*Klad.*

Sole Survivor
(U.S.-COLOR)

Cannes, May 17.

An Intl. Film Marketing release of a Robert D. and Caren L. Larkey production. Produced by Don Barkemeyer. Executive producer, Sal Romeo. Directed, written by Thom Eberhardt. Stars Anita Skinner, Kurt Johnson. Camera (CFI color), Ross Carpenter. No other credits available. Reviewed at the Cannes Film Festival (Market), May 17, 1984. (MPAA Rating: R.) Running time: **90 MINS.**
Features: Anita Skinner, Kurt Johnson, Caren Larkey.

Anyone looking for a bottom-of-the-barrel suspenser need look no further than "Sole Survivor." Embarrassingly awful in every department, this is one of those films where 90 minutes seem an eternity, and where the story is so confoundingly convoluted it surely cannot be traced back to any of the few basic classical plots from which most tales derive. Made in 1982, pic went into limited regional release in January, and limited will remain the operative word.

Title stems from fact that young blond Anita Skinner is the only person to emerge alive from a major plane crash. Two red, demon-type eyes which momentarily appear behind the air controller's radar scope suggest some kind of monster is on the loose, but no such luck.

Instead, Skinner goes home, grapples boringly with sole survivor syndrome, tries to get her doctor, Kurt Johnson, to ask her out and, rather late in the game, has friends and acquaintances begin to be killed and wake up as zombies.

Keeping clear on the action through the muddled storytelling is no easy matter, and not worth it in any event, but it seems that behind the evil goings-on is a bitter has-been actress who is also a psychic, and played by co-presenter Caren Larkey.

Pic is a snoozer rather than a sleeper, and technically is rudimentary at best. — *Cart.*

Le Tartuffe
(FRENCH-COLOR)

Cannes, May 22.

A Gaumont release of a Les Films du Losange-D.C.-Gaumont-T.F. 1 films coproduction. Produced by Margaret Menegoz. Directed and adapted by Gérard Depardieu, based on the stage production by Jacques Lassale at the National Theatre of Strasbourg from the play by Molière. Camera (Kodak color), Alga Samuelson; editor and codirection, Helene Viard; art direction, Yannis Kokkos; costumes, François Barbeau; music, Rameau, Delalande, François Couperin, Gilles. Reviewed at Cannes Film Festival (Un Certain Regard selection), May 22, 1984. Running time: **138 MINS.**
Orgon .... François Périer
Tartuffe .... Gérard Depardieu
Elmire .... Elisabeth Depardieu
Laurent .... Noureddine El Ati
Madame Pernelle .... Paule Annen
Cleante .... Bernard Freyd
Marianne .... Helene Lapiower
Valere .... Jean-Marc Roulot
Damis .... Andre Wilms

Molière's classic stage farce "Tartuffe" serves as an unconventional directorial debut for Gallic star Gérard Depardieu. Also casting himself in the title role, Depardieu serves up a conventional rendering of the play, apparently derived from a recent stage mounting in Strasbourg. However, it's essentially a filmed version of a play with limited theatrical potential.

Story deals with the sway the title character, a supposed man of the cloth, has on a wealthy businessman. In turn, the rest of the rich patron's family and coterie remain suspicions of Tartuffe's intentions. In the end, Tartuffe is exposed as a fraud.

Produced on simple sets, the look of the film is quite visually stunning. Nonetheless, the action never escapes the proscenium arch and the limited use of music further intensifies the uncinematic nature of the piece.

Performances vary considerably with several performers emoting as if playing before a large audience. However, Depardieu handles himself well and François Périer as the nobleman of property is a treat to watch.

Despite several positive aspects, the length and simplicity of the screen adaptation suggest extremely limited theatrical life. Television prospects may be slightly better. However, there's not enough evidence in "Le Tartuffe" to verify Depardieu's skill behind the camera, which was the biggest question posed by this film.

—*Klad.*

Jenstchina U Tchetvero Jejeu Moujtchine
(A Woman And Her Four Men)
(SOVIET-COLOR)

Cannes, May 22.

A Lithuanian Studios production, Vilna, Lithuanian Republic; world sales, Goskino, Moscow. Features entire cast. Written and directed by Algimantas Puipa. Camera (color), Jonas Tamaskevicius; sets, Algirdas Nicius; music, Yuozas Sirvinskas. Reviewed at Cannes Film Fest (Market), May 16, '84. Running time: **90 MINS.**

With: Jurate Onatite, Antanas Shurna, Vidas Pyatkyavichus, Saulis Balandis

Some of the best films made in the Soviet republics in the past have emerged from the Lithuanian Studios in Vilna. At this year's mart screenings, it was another Lithuanian pic that won deserved critical attention: Algimantas Puipa's "A Woman And Her Four Men."

Set at the end of the last century in a small Baltic fishing-village, "A Woman And Her Four Men" weaves its magic as a moral parable — somewhat along the lines of William Synge's Irish play "Riders To The Sea" of Abbey Theater history. Both deal with the hand of fate, rugged sea fishermen, and the harsh life that brings out the best in humanity in the face of overwhelming odds.

The woman in the title refers at the outset to a recent widow; the body of her husband has been washed up on the beach. The woman is then taken into the humble cottage of a neighboring fisherman with two grown sons, the oldest of whom she eventually marries and bears a son. Almost the entire film is set among the rolling dunes and thatched-roofed fishinghuts, a natural paradise still untouched by industrial grime, while the emphasis is on the very rhythm of life and archaic customs and traditions: a wedding ceremony, a christening, death and familial departure. A recurring motif is a drum-beat on hollowed wood at a traditional marriage or celebration ceremony.

As the story goes, the older son disappears one day while on his way with the family's savings to repay a bank-loan; later, it's revealed that he encountered a robber, and they fought to the death for the prize of gold-pieces. Due to the shifting sands, the bodies are not found until years later, so the mystery is not unraveled in time to save the grandfather from going to prison for an unpaid debt. In the meanwhile, the woman marries again, to the second son, and bears two more children. Then another twist of fate enters the picture: this son dies in a rescue attempt to save shipwrecks on the open sea — a deed of valor that wins back the freedom of the grandfather.

Now having suffered the loss of three husbands, the woman is left with the patriarchal grandfather and three sons at the fishing-hut. The old man rebaptizes two of the boys to the names of his lost sons, and the third (still an infant) is christened by dropping him headlong into the open sea for a moment (as apparently by ancient custom).

Strikingly lensed with atmospheric touches to spur the story along, "The Woman And Her Four Men" is also supported by strong performances. Pic well deserves more fest exposure. —*Holl.*

Venus
(FRENCH-COLOR-3-D)

Cannes, May 17.

A T.Y. Productions and Goldfarb presentation. Produced by Pierre Benichou, Samuel Hadida. Directed by Peter Hollison. Stars Odile Michel. Screenplay, Jean Jabely. Camera (3-D, Fujicolor), Gerard Loubeau; editor, Alix Regis; music, Jean Louis d'Oraro; sound, Lucien Yvonnot; assistant director, J.P. Feuillebois. Reviewed at the Cannes Film Festival (Market), May 16, 1084. (No MPAA rating). Running time: **83 MINS.**

Venus ....Odile Michel
Florence..................Florence Guerin
Also with: Sophie Favier, Naldje Clair, Françoise Blanchard, Philippe Klebert, Riton Liebman.

"Venus" is like a Playboy pictorial on "The Girls Of The Mediterranean" in 3-D, and as such is a near-perfect voyeur's delight. Utterly brainless, sun-drenched item is overflowing with great bods and great softcore sex, which would augur well for its b.o. potential in the appropriate market except for the fact that it's so obviously dubbed.

Extent of full nudity and sex action harks back to the skin items of some 10 years ago, albeit with the added attraction of 3-D. Process is used obviously and jokingly in the early-going, but ultimately proves as easy on the eyes as what's on display.

Non-plot has some agreeable ad agency types in Paris auditioning nubile young things in a quest for the perfect girl to personify the new "Venus" sun tan oil. Scene of a procession of ladies rubbing the stuff on their upper bodies in hopes of winning the job reps a good indication of things to come.

Finalists are invited onto a yacht around Greece, where they work on their suntans and engage in some nicely staged lesbian encounters while waiting for the agency guys to make up their minds.

But, lo and behold, who should emerge from the sea but Venus herself, who objects to having her name commercialized and offers untold pleasures if the admen drop the product or change its name.

Although slight 3-D fuzziness and preponderance of medium and long shots disguises it to some extent, the unsynched dubbing is still apparent enough to crimp pic's chances Stateside. However, given the choice of getting these ladies' real voices or their unadorned physiques, there's no question of what's more important.

Director Peter Hollison has directed smoothly with absolute eye for skin flick priorities, and Jean Louis d'Oraro has composed a great schlock romantic score.

—*Cart.*

Die Olympiasiegerin
(The Woman Olympic Winner)
(WEST GERMAN-COLOR)

Cannes, May 22.

A Herbert Achternbusch Filmproduktion, Munich; world sales, Edition Bischoff (Exportfilm Bischoff), Munich. Features entire cast. Written and directed by Herbert Achternbusch. Camera (color),Jörg Schmidt-Reitwein; editor, Miki Joanni. Reviewed at Cannes Film Fest (Market), May 20, '84. Running time: **107 MINS.**

With Herbert Achternbusch, Annamirl Bierbichler, Gabi Geist, Tobias Frank.

Outside of the exceptional camerawork contributed by Jörg Schmidt-Reitwein (Werner Herzog's lenser, whose talents are regularly utilized to a minimum by director Herbert Achternbusch), there's little of cinematic interest to find in Achternbusch's "Woman Olympic Winner," one of three pics completed this season by the Bavarian scribe-filmer.

Pic makes reference in its title to the Berlin Olympics of 1936, as well as to Achternbusch's own conception at the time. Achternbusch's mother was a sports teacher, and in "Woman Olympic Winner" Achternbusch interprets the role of his own father. There are also visual metaphors in a restaurant on POWs in Nazi concentration camps. Pic consists of static camera shots in which Achternbusch does monolog bits (in one instance, reading from a hidden manuscript) or engages in lengthy dialog with his superstar Annamirl Bierchler. He can be very witty at time, even though the humor is distinctively Bavarian and is peppered with pungent vulgar terms.

In the long run, it's not so much how Herbert Achternbusch makes a movie, as how helmer Achternbusch features thesp Herbert in Kabarett-style numbers.—*Holl.*

Where Is Parsifal?
(BRITISH-COLOR)

Cannes, May 23.

A Terence Young production. Produced by Daniel Carrillo. Executive producer, Young. Directed by Henri Helman. Stars Tony Curtis, Cassandra Domenica, Erik Estrada, Peter Lawford, Ron Moody, Donald Pleasence, Orson Welles. Screenplay, Berta Dominguez D; camera (Rank color), Norman Langley; editors, Russell Lloyd, Peter Hollywood; music, Hubert Rostaing, Ivan Jullien; production design, Malcolm Stone; sound, David Crozier; assistant director, Allen Jones. Reviewed at the Cannes Film Festival (Un Certain Regard section), May 22, 1984. (No MPAA rating). Running time: **84 MINS.**

Parsifal Katzenellenbogen ......Tony Curtis
Elba ....Cassandra Domenica
Henry Board II ....Erik Estrada
Montague Chippendale......Peter Lawford
Beersbohm ....Ron Moody
Mackintosh..............Donald Pleasence
Klingsor ....Orson Welles
Ivan ....Christopher Chaplin
Ruth ....Nancy Roberts

Ludicrous beyond belief, "Where Is Parsifal?" is one of those pictures that makes one wonder how it got made at all. Frenetic, pathetic comedy has spun out of control even before the main titles are over, and commercial potential is nil.

Structurally, film is a varition on "You Can't Take It With You," except screenwriter Berta Dominguez D (who also acts under the name of Cassandra Domenica) forgot to put in any funny lines. Tony Curtis plays a frantic hypochondriac who lives in a castle with a bunch of nuts and hopes to sell his invention, a laser skywriter, either to tycoon Erik Estrada or rich gypsy Orson Welles.

Entire running time is devoted to breathless fretting and confusion as the family, such as it is, prepares to throw a dinner party for Estrada, who looks like Al Pacino in "Scarface" here, while trying to prevent Donald Pleasence from making off with all their belongings before Curtis can make millions from selling his skywriter.

It's all irrelevant to anything resembling entertainment, and Henri Helman has directed as if in desperate imitation of the 1960s comedy styles of Clive Donner or Joseph McGrath.

Actually, Ron Moody does get off some self-contained moments as a Prussian aide-de-camp, the score by Hubert Rostaing and Ivan Jullien is attractive and the production looks decent. But it's a fiasco from start to finish. —*Cart.*

The Secret Diary Of Sigmund Freud
(U.S.-COLOR)

Cannes, May 21.

A TLC Films release of a Dalyn International Ltd. presentation in association with Film 41st Avala Film. Produced by Wendy Hyland and Peer Oppenheimer, executive producers, David Raphel and Milos Antic. Directed by Danford B. Greene. Screenplay by Roberto Mitrotti and Linda Howard; camera (Deluxe color), George Nikolic; art direction, Miodrag Miric; music, V. Boris. Reviewed at Cannes Film Festival (Market), May 21, 1984. (MPAA Rating: PG.) Time: 99 MINS.

Sigmund Freud	Bud Cort
Martha Bernays	Carol Kane
Dr. Max Bauer	Klaus Kinski
Emma Herrmann	Marisa Berenson
Mama Freud	Carroll Baker
Ultimate patient	Dick Shawn
Herr Herrmann	Ferdinand Mayne
Pap Freud	Nikola Simic
Dr. Schtupmann	Rade Markovic

"The Secret Diary of Sigmund Freud" is likely to retain its anonymity in the marketplace despite its acquisition by TLC Films, the specialty division of 20th Century Fox. The comedy, which marks the directorial debut of film editor Danford Greene, is droll to the point that audiences may fail to see the joke. While far from offensive, this gentle yarn is in desperate need of something outrageous to move the action along and hammer home some humor.

Film traces Freud's life from childhood through to his early discoveries while still a young man. Much of this development is told in glib voice-over by Freud portrayer Bud Cort. The remaining humor is funnier in conception than execution.

An odd mish-mash of styles, the narrative lurches along in a series of vignettes only vaguely connected in theme. One is never quite sure whether the intent is purely comic or means to lace the tale with some reflective content.

According to the screenwriters, Freud possessed phobias for blood and the human anatomy which led him away from surgery and into research. A misunderstanding of the term "Practice" of medicine leads him into consultation and the study of the mind which, through the knowledge of one patient, leads to his initial pronouncements. It's pretty slim stuff to elicit a laugh.

Also meant to be funny are the liaison between Klaus Kinski, another doctor, and Freud's mother, played by Carroll Baker, and the offbeat relationship between Freud and lisping nurse Carol Kane. While these backfire, there's some fun from Dick Shawn's numerous deluded incarnations of famous historical characters. However, audiences will find the picture's efforts to please quite trying overall.

Given the fragility of the project, the actors give their best to uplift the material. Cort's concept of the man as a striver with dubious talents is quite effective, while Kane continues to be charming in a quietly overpowering manner. Filmed in Yugoslavia, the production values are solid and the locations contribute to establishing the period quality necessary for the yarn.

"The Secret Diary Of Sigmund Freud" may require more than tender loving care and TLC will have to persevere to find the picture's niche. Expect no more than modest results theatrically with ancillary rights making the final difference in bringing home a break-even figure. —*Klad.*

Varljivo Leto '68
(The Illusive Summer Of '68)
(YUGOSLAV-COLOR)

Cannes, May 22.

A Centar Film Production, Belgrade; world rights, Yugoslav Film, Belgrade. Features entire cast. Directed by Goran Paskaljevic; Screenplay, Gordan Mihic, Paskaljevic; camera (color), Aleksandar Petkovic; sets, Miljen Vuljanovic; camera (color), Aleksandar Petkovic; sets, Miljen Vuljanovic; music, Zoran Hristic. Reviewed at Cannes Film Fest (Market), May 20, '84. Running time: 90 MINS.

With: Slavko Štimac (Petar), Danilo Stojkovic (the Father), Mira Banac (the Mother), Mija Aleksic (the Grandfather), Sanja Vejnovic (Ruzenka), Dragana Varagic (the Teacher).

Set in the year 1968, when Yugoslav tv broadcasts were filled with news about Alexander Dubcek's "Communism With A Human Face" movement in Czechoslovakia, this is the story of how those revolutionary times were perceived in a land combining the social, political, and economical practices of both East and West Europe. The father in a family household somewhere in the province of Voivodina (neighboring Serbia) along the Danube River is a civil servant whose heart and soul belong to Tito and whatever the head-of-state says on current politics. Thus, the comically tyrannical father was against the student movement in Belgrade and the turnover of events in Prague during the hot summer months — until he noted on the newscasts that Tito himself gradually, and surprisingly, approved of them.

The hero of the tale is young Peter (popular young thesp Slavko Štimac), now in the bloom of puberty and suffering from a crush on every pretty girl, or femme teacher, he encounters in and out of the classroom. His father, naturally, disapproves of any and every romantic alliance on the grounds that the boy should be scoring high grades while soaking in principles of Marxism on the side. It's when the lad messes up his academic future at school (trying to get even with his gorgeous teacher at school for bathing bare with a beau down by the riverside), and falls in love with a Czech miss in a visiting youth band (thus having his first sexual affair one day, also down by the riverside), that things move along at a rib-tickling pace.

The joker in the deal is the boy's grandfather, who fakes chronic illness to get admitted to an old-age clinic, where he can while away his hours playing, and winning at, cards with the hospital administration and patients. Grandpa also helps Petar in learning the facts of life from an acknowledged expert.

If all of this sounds familiar, then it is: director Goran Paskaljevic has synthesized the Czech comedies of Milos Forman, Ivan Passer, and Jiri Menzel into a Yugoslav version — the particular film he salutes is Forman's "Black Peter" (1963), but another tip of the directorial hat goes to Menzel's "Closely Watched Trains" (1966), both chronicling the adventures of youth in heat in a similar witty manner.

Scripter Gordan Mihic supplies most of the laughs in the context of the story. Mihic spends a great deal of time among the common people, drawing his humor from bars and cafes, bus-rides and public celebrations, and wherever else the clowns of this world's social life assemble.

"The Illusive Summer Of '68" is all the more recommended in view of Paskaljevic's own experiences in Czechoslovakia at that time while studying at the Prague Film School (FAMU) under František Daniel (currently cochairman with Milos Forman at the Columbia University Film Department). With proper handling, pic could do well on the arthouse circuit and at Yugo Film Weeks. —*Holl.*

Model Behavior
(U.S.-COLOR)

Cannes, May 19.

An Arnold Kopelson presentation of a J. Christian Ingvordsen/Steven W. Kaman Production. Executive producers, Glenn R. Dubin, Henry Swieca. Produced by J. Christian Ingvordsen, Steven W. Kaman. Directed by Bud Gardner. Screenplay by Gordon Reynolds, Martin Kitrosser; camera (color), Steven W. Kaman; music, Andy Goldmark, Phil Galdston. Reviewed at Cannes Film Festival (Market), May 19, 1984. (No MPAA Rating.) Running time: 88 MINS.

Dino	Bruce Lyons
Richie	Richard Bekins
Becky Fairchild	Anne Howard
Monsieur Henri	Antonio Fargas
Serina	Cindy Harrell

Vivacious visuals and beautiful bodies let this pic do exactly what it's supposed to do, by turning on the youth market with a simple story of love on Madison Avenue. Lensing is appropriately slick to recreate everybody's fantasy of the world of fashion.

Two young guys try to crash into the world of glamorous models by passing themselves off as film folk, without knowing as much as the girls about what they should do. Pic's romantic interest, pretty Becky, bites but learns the truth when Richie's barracuda boss-lady tries to seduce him and lands him in a tangled web.

Super star Serina is the sex object of Dino's unbridled lust, and she is shown as a career girl who wants more than men or what they have to offer. Dino makes do with nightlife nibbles. The endless party scene at the club are inventive, backed by good disco music and fat with fantasy.

Technical credits are above average for the genre, and young actors are ambitious enough to do very good work here. Discreet nudity and minimal sex make it promising for tv use. —*Kaja.*

Mississippi Blues
(FRENCH-DOCU-COLOR)

Cannes, May 22.

An Odessa films release of an Odessa-Little Bear-Films A2 production with the U. of Mississippi. Produced and directed by Bertrand Tavernier and Robert Parrish. Camera (Fujicolor), Pierre-William Glenn; editors, Ariane Boeglin, Agnes Vaurigaud; sound, Michel Desrois, Dominique Levert. Reviewed at Cannes Film Festival (French Perspectives), May 22, 1984. Running time: 101 MINS.

"Mississippi Blues" is an oddball concoction of ideas and observations which meanders very much in the manner of the great river of its title. Nonetheless, the film has considerable charm in its parts and one can readily perceive interest for both non-theatrical and television sales.

The title suggests an emphasis on music and while the majority of footage does focus on blues and gospel singers, there are significant side trips into other venues. The filmmakers find time to discuss Faulkner as their base was Oxford, his birthplace, favorite "Southern" movies, the relationship of the church to politics and assorted social issues. It's far from a strict thesis film even if sections attempt to connect aspects of society too rigorously.

Directed by France's Bertrand Tavernier and American Robert Parrish, the view is definitely that of an outsider. One can readily appreciate the fascination they find with the music and its inter-relationships with this particular society.

Picture has a real asset in the quality of its images and overall excellence in technical departments. There's also an underlying sense of humor conveyed by the filmmakers both in the warmth they feel for their subject and directed back at themselves as benevolent intruders.

"Mississippi Blues" suffers slightly from a constantly shifting focus but isn't really trying on one's patience. Theatrical prospects are limited, but film should have a healthy life in other forms of distribution and exhibition.
—*Klad.*

Kaltes Fieber
(Cold Fever)
(WEST GERMAN-COLOR)

Cannes, May 19.
An OKO-Film, Karel Dirka, production, Munich. Executive producer, Rudolf von Bitter. Features entire cast. Written and directed by Joseph Rusnak. Camera (color), Lutz Konermann; sets, Volker Wach, Annette Deiters; sound, Manfred Thust; production managers, Jan Hinter, Hugo Schafer. Reviewed at Cannes Film Fest (Market), May 19, '84. Running time: **92 MINS.**
With: Klaus Rohrmoser (Pierre), Katharina Böhm (Babsie), Hans-Michael Rehberg (Schumann), Lisa Kreuzer (Silvie), Axel Milberg (Axel), Ulrich Tukur (Michael), Peter Luhr (Blumenfeld), Jan Paul Biczycki (the Writer), Ellen Umlauf (Lisa).

Winner of a German Film Prize, Joseph Rusnak's "Cold Fever" tackles a hot theme of both social and political importance: mercy-killing. This film doesn't pretend to seek answers, nor is it a dramatic exposition of the issues, but as a docu-drama it has its validity.

A pediatrician (Schumann) has founded an organization for mercy-killing, whereby people who wish to die but simply don't have the courage to perform the act themselves are helped along the way upon request. A young man (Pierre) simply gets paid for doing his job quietly and efficiently: at the outset, he enters an intensive-care ward of a hospital, finds the patient who's expecting him, and simply disconnects the tubes binding the victim to a living death.

Now comes the twist. When another patient changes his mind at the last minute, and opts to live after all despite the overwhelming odds against eventual recovery, Pierre is willing to back off — but Schumann feels the deed should be done in any case. Naturally enough, in view of Germany's past history on the question of euthanasia, Schumann's actions are rather controversial and frightening, to say the least.

The conflict mounts when Pierre falls in love with Silvie, who turns out to be one of Schumann's "cases." Silvie, however, manages to commit suicide on her own, unbeknowst to Pierre — who immediately suspects Schumann of having performed another of his self-justified acts of murder, and is determined to even the score.

Pic is too shallow in handling moral issues that need to be fully convincing, but the issue itself should guarantee a critical response at home and abroad.
— *Holl.*

Mob War
(U.S.-COLOR)

Cannes, May 21.
Reel Movies International release of a Bobby Davis Pictures Inc. production. Produced, directed and written by Davis. Score, Davis. No other credits available. Reviewed at the Cannes Film Festival, May 20, 1984. (No MPAA Rating). Running time: **88 MINS.**
Cast: Larry Hauck, R.J. Cox, Charlotte Sigmand, Andre Laborde, Richard Seelbach, Conrad Stevens, Robert White.

Each Cannes fest market brings its quota of pics that are patently amateurish. "Mob War," the creation of one Bobby Davis, fits that label. Rough sales are ahead.

Pic, set in New Orleans in the 1920s, is about rival factions of the mob shooting it out with confusing abandon. The acting, direction, photography, sound recording and scoring are woefully inadequate.

The film's few sex scenes threaten to turn hardcore. Unfortunately, they don't. "Mob Wars," distributed by Reel Movies out of Dallas, should play nicely at film schools as an example of how not to make a pic.—*Sege.*

Ghostbusters
(COLOR)

Gags & special effects scare pic misses its mark. Star names point to good but not smash b.o.

A Columbia Pictures presentation of a Black Rhino/Bernie Brillstein production, from Columbia-Delphi Prods. Executive producer, Brillstein. Produced and directed by Ivan Reitman. Features entire cast. Screenplay, Dan Aykroyd, Harold Ramis; camera (Metrocolor, Panavision), Laszlo Kovacs; N.Y. camera, Herb Wagreitch; editors, Sheldon Kahn, David Blewitt; music, Elmer Bernstein; theme song, Ray Parker Jr.; sound, Gene Cantamessa; sound design, Richard Beggs, Tom McCarthy Jr.; production design, John de Cuir; art direction, John de Cuir Jr., John Moore (N.Y.); set design, George Eckert; set decoration, Marvin March, Robert Drumheller (N.Y.); costumes, Theoni V. Aldredge; special visual effects, Richard Edlund at EEG; production manager, John G. Wilson, Patrick McCormick (N.Y.); assistant director, Gary Daigler, Peter Giuliano (N.Y.); special (physical) effects supervisor, Chuck Gaspar; stunt coordinator, Bill Couch; Steadicam operator (N.Y.), Ted Churchill. Reviewed at Loews State 2 theater, N.Y., May 23, 1984. (MPAA Rating: PG.) Running time: **107 MINS.**
Dr. Peter Venkman............Bill Murray
Dr. Raymond Stantz ....Dan Aykroyd
Dana Barrett ....Sigourney Weaver
Dr. Egon Spengler ....Harold Ramis
Louis Tully ....Rick Moranis
Janine Melnitz..................Annie Potts
Walter Peck ....William Atherton
Winston Zeddmore...........Ernie Hudson
Also with: David Margulies, Steven Tash, Jennifer Runyon, Slavitza Jovan, Michael Ensign, Alice Drummond.

Special Visual Effects Unit Credits
Entertainment Effects Group (EEG): visual effects supervisor, Richard Edlund; chief cameraman, Bill Neil; art director, John Bruno; optical supervisor, Mark Vargo; production supervisor, Richard Kerrigan; matte dep't supervisor, Neil Krepela; mechanical effects supervisor, Thaine Morris; modelshop supervisor, Mark Stetson; stop-motion animation effects, Randall William Cook; animation supervisors, Garry Waller, Terry Windell; chief matte artist, Matthew Yuricich; production coordinator, Laura Buff; head of Ghost shop, Stuart Ziff; Ghost shop advisor, Jon Berg.

Columbia's "Ghostbusters" is a lavishly produced but only intermittently impressive all-star comedy lampoon of supernatural horror films. Closer in scale at an estimated $32,000,000 negative cost to "It's A Mad, Mad, Mad, Mad World" and "1941" than modest spoofs such as the Bob Hope-Paulette Goddard "The Ghost Breakers," pic looks to good but not fantastic results in the summer b.o. sweepstakes.

Originally conceived as a John Belushi-Dan Aykroyd vehicle called "Ghostsmashers" before Belushi's death in 1982, "Ghostbusters" under producer-director Ivan Reitman makes a fundamental error reminiscent of the atypical 1946 Abbott & Costello picture "The Little Giant:" featuring a set of top comics but having them often work alone rather than as a team throughout. This format, together with the usual pauses to gaze at spectacular special effects, creates a comedy that works in fits and starts.

The Harold Ramis-Dan Aykroyd screenplay (which, curiously, gives its writer-actors the least interesting of the lead roles), takes as its main premise the idea played straight in Michael Winner-Jeffrey Konvitz' 1977 feature "The Sentinel:" a Manhattan apartment building inhabited by beautiful Dana Barrett (Sigourney Weaver) and her nerd neighbor Louis Tully (Rick Moranis) becomes the gateway for demons from another dimension (led by the Sumerian demigod Gozer) to invade the Earth.

To battle Gozer and other motley phantasms come the Ghostbusters, a trio of scientists who have been kicked off campus and are now freelance ghost catchers for hire. Dan Aykroyd is the gung-ho scientific type, Bill Murray is faking competency (he's had no higher education in parapsychology) and using the job to meet women, while Harold Ramis is the trio's technical expert; later, Ernie Hudson joins the team as an out-of-work black hardup for a job.

Weaver is their first customer, after she has a poltergeist episode in her kitchen. Servicing various other clients en route to fame, the Ghostbusters stockpile a horde of trapped ghosts which are set free when an EPA Investigator (William Atherton) opposes their unsafe procedures. Soon after, Weaver is possessed by a demon known as The Gatekeeper and Moranis by one called The Key Master. Together, they open the way for Gozer's invasion and a very flashy special visual effects climax.

Within the top-heavy cast, it's Murray's picture, as the popular comedian deadpans, ad libs and does an endearing array of physical schtick. Aykroyd, trying too hard, gets virtually no laughs, Ramis is along for the ride and Moranis is underutilized but quite effective when given screen time. Weaver is deliciously sexy both before and after her possession, adding heavy eye makeup and vamp poses to effect the transition. Annie Potts is cute as the heroes' secretary.

Under multi-Oscar-winner Richard Edlund's supervision, the film's visual effects offer quite a show, comparable in quality (most unusual for a spoof) to the targeted horror films. Several effects, such as a monster in the library and floating wraiths, recall earlier Edlund assignments "Poltergeist" and "Raiders Of The Lost Ark." Elsewhere, both puppet and stop-motion animation monsters provide original contributions, combining with topnotch animation and design work to yield satisfying results. Problem is the effects are far better than the film vehicle containing them.—*Lor.*

The Executioner Part II
(COLOR)

Amateur action film.

A 21st Century Distribution release. Produced by Renee Harmon. Directed by James Bryant. Features entire cast. Camera (Pacific color), no other credits available. Reviewed at Embassy 2 theater, N.Y., June 2, 1984. (MPAA Rating: R). Running time: **85 MINS.**

With: Christopher Mitchum (Lt. Roger O'Malley), Aldo Ray (Police commissioner), Antoine John Mottet (Mike), Renee Harmon (Celia Amherst), Dan Bradley, Jim Draftfield.

"The Executioner Part II" is an incompetent, cheaply made action picture, produced circa 1981-82. Its title seems intentionally designed to cause confusion, since the film has no relationship to several earlier pics called "The Executioner" (including a 1970 Columbia British-made spy effort), but is imitative of the 1980 Robert Ginty vehicle "The Exterminator." Soon to add further confusion are two more Ginty vehicles yet to be released, "Exterminator II" and "The Executioner: The Mission."

Chris Mitchum toplines as L.A. Homicide Lt. Roger O'Malley, tracking down a vigilante killer who is blowing up street criminals with hand grenades (each explosion is an insert of grainy old stock footage). Sans suspense, the killer turns out to be Mike (Antoine John Mottet), O'Malley's old army buddy who saved O'Malley's life in Vietnam, as shown in prolog footage. Both men are at war with a local gangster kingpin Antonio Casals, known as the Tattoo Man, who kidnaps O'Malley's daughter Laura and tortures her until a last minute rescue. Asinine ending has O'Malley letting his guilty buddy go, leaving town to set up a (shudder!) sequel.

Filmed silently on L.A. locations with a wobbly, often out-of-focus handheld camera technique and seemingly 1:1 shooting ratio, "Part II" is way below current technical standards of watchability. Dubbing is awful, with a maddening failure to put back footfalls or other appropriate background sound. Acting is generally below the level of a hardcore porn film. Mitchum *fils* is miscast, and his daughter looks old enough to be his elder sister. Aldo Ray is on screen for under a minute as Mitchum's blowhard boss, and producer Renee Harmon has herself written into the script as a most unlikely, matronly L.A. tv newscaster boasting a thick French accent. Her close-ups are lensed through a horse-blanket.

Credits included above for the record are skimpy, because the projectionist helpfully cut off the film before the end credits. — *Lor.*

Spasms
(CANADIAN-COLOR)

A Producers Distribution Co. release of a Cinequity Corp. and Martin Erlichman presentation. Produced with participation of Canadian Film Development Corp. & Famous Players Ltd. Executive producers, John G. Pozhke, Maurice Smith, Erlichman. Produced by Pozhke, Smith. Directed by William Fruet. Stars Peter Fonda, Oliver Reed. Screenplay, Don Enright, from novel "Death Bite" by Michael Maryk, Brent Monahan; camera (Medallion color), Mark Irwin; editor-postproduction supervisor, Ralph Brunjes; music, Eric N. Robertson; Serpent's theme music, Tangerine Dream; sound, Stuart French; assistant director, David Shepherd; production manager-coproducer, Gordon Robinson; coproducer, John Newton; art direction, Gavin Mitchell; set decoration, Patricia Gruben; makeup illusions, Dick Smith, Carl Fullerton, Stephan Dupuis; Monster: designer/producer, Raymond A. Mendez, mechanical effects, Lewis Gluck, model maker, Neal Martz; special (physical) effects, Brian Warner; stunt coordinator, R.L. (Bobby) Hannah; additional photography, Maris Jansons. Reviewed on Thorn EMI Videocassette, N.Y., May 28, 1984. (MPAA Rating: R.) Running time: **87 MINS.**

Dr. Tom Brasilian	Peter Fonda
Jason Kincaid	Oliver Reed
Susanne Kincaid	Kerrie Keane
Crowley	Al Waxman
Mendes	Miguel Fernandes
Dr. Claire Rothman	Marilyn Lightstone
Duncan Tyrone	Angus MacInnes
Allison	Laurie Brown
Capt. Noveck	Gerard Parkes
Rev. Thomas	George Bloomfield

"Spasms" is a low-grade Canadian supernatural horror film made in 1981 under the title "Death Bite," which is unreleased theatrically in U.S. and is now a video store shelf item. Pic bears a 1982 copyright by National Trust Co., typical of tax-shelter output.

Weak story hook has a huge serpent, supposedly a demon guardian of the Gates of Hell, captured and brought to America from an island near New Guinea. Supposedly, the serpent earlier killed the brother of Jason Kincaid (Oliver Reed) and left Kincaid with a gamy leg, care of his niece Susanne (Kerrie Keane) and (believe it or not) a telepathic connection with the serpent in times of violence, similar to the gimmick in the Faye Dunaway vehicle "Eyes Of Laura Mars."

A campus shrink turned ESP researcher Dr. Brasilian (Peter Fonda) is called in by Kincaid to help out, perhaps to prove a far-fetched scientific theory that snakes carry a virus that could account for telepathic powers. An evil religious fanatic Rev. Thomas (well-played as a bald heavy by erstwhile SCTV comedy director George Bloomfield) sends his henchman Crowley (Al Waxman) to steal the serpent.

Unconvincing fantasy film is mainly a tease, with the serpent monster creation glimpsed in only a few fleeting frames until fighting with Reed at film's end. Instead, a wideangle, blue-tint monochrome effect is used to represent the serpent's point-of-view during gory attacks, resembling the camera technique used in an earlier Ophidian feature that also starred Reed, "Venom." Similarly, special makeup effects by masters in the field such as Dick Smith remain as only brief moments in final cut.

Acting is poor, with Reed twitching in an overdone tortured perf. Mark Irwin's visuals are mainly underlit, apparently in an effort to hide the unsuccessful gimmickry. Oh yes, digressing from the film's forward narrative, the serpent gets to take time out to attack (or threaten) several shapely and barely clad women. Not much, but at least something for the fans.

— *Lor.*

Trap Them And Kill Them
(ITALIAN-COLOR)

A Megastar Pictures (N.Y.) release of a Fulvia Cinematografica/Gico Cinematografica/Flora Film production. Directed by Joe D'Amato (Aristide Massaccesi). Stars Laura Gemser. Screenplay, Romano Scandariato, Massaccesi; camera (Telecolor), Massaccesi; editor, Aldo Moriani; music, Nico Fidenco; art direction, Carlo Ferri; assistant director, Donatella Donati; production manager, Fabrizio de Angelis; special makeup effects, Fabrizio Sforza. Reviewed at 42d St. Liberty theater, N.Y., June 2, 1984. (No MPAA Rating.) Running time: **92 MINS.**

Emanuelle	Laura Gemser
Prof. Mark Lester	Gabriele Tinti
Maggie	Susan Scott
Donald	Donald O'Brien

Also with: Percy Hogan, Monica Zanchi, Anne Marie Clementi, Geoffrey Coplestone.

"Trap Them And Kill Them" is the retitled, belated U.S. release of the umpteenth (at least a dozen are circulating in theatrical, home-video or pay-cable distribution) Laura Gemser as Black Emanuelle feature to be imported. Unrated film (which would qualify for an X) emphasizes softcore sex, but as the title implies, is being marketed on the basis of its explicit gore footage, quite graphic though brief in running time. Pic was filmed as "Emanuelle And The Last Cannibals" circa 1977-78.

After an unconvincing title reading "This is a true story as reported by Jennifer O'Sullivan," tall tale opens with an extraneous segment of Emanuelle (Gemser) working undercover in a Manhattan nuthouse, taking a nude photo (and giving unexplained lesbian attention) of a young woman who has savagely bitten a nurse's breast in cannibalistic fashion.

Emanuelle is, once again, a reporter for the "N.Y. Evening Post," and, inspired by the nuthouse incident, she organizes an expedition led by Prof. Mark Lester (played by Gemser's real-life husband Gabriele Tinti) to seek out a tribe of cannibal indians on the Amazon river.

Many reels later, most of the party is sacrificed by the cannibals until Emanuelle ingeniously paints her belly with an ancient symbol and successfully masquerades as the indians' Goddess of the Waters to effect an escape.

"Trap Them" is adequately dubbed, with various accents rather than the usual neutral approach. It emphasizes the "mixed combo" sex scenes prevalent during the mid-1970s after the interracial hit "Mandingo" was released and is highlighted by the genuine sex appeal of the mature Italian actress who uses the anglicized stage name of Susan Scott. Gemser is her usual over-worked, cool self.

Location photography in Manhattan and in a South American jungle is okay though occasionally underlit, while the gore effects are fortunately phony-looking. — *Lor.*

Umi Isubame Joe No Kiseki
(The Miracle Of Joe Petrel)
(JAPANESE-COLOR)

Tokyo, May 28.

A Shochiku-Fuji release of a Mifune Production. Produced by Kazuyoshi Okuyama, with planning by Toshiro Mifune. Production assistant, Hisao Nabeshima. Directed by Toshiya Fujita; screenplay by Fujita, Eiichi Uchida and Fumio Kaminami, from an original story by Kozo Sasaki. Music, Ryudo Uzaki; art direction, Masateru Mochizuki; sound, Senichi Beniya; editing, Osamu Inoue; assistant director, Takao Nagaishi. Reviewed at Tokyo Rex Theater, May 25, 1984. Running time: **133 MINS.**

Joe	Saburo Tokito
Yoko	Miwako Fujitani
Sawaii	Kentaro Shimizu
Michi	Midori Satsuki
Yanamine	Yoshio Harada
Fisherman	Toshiro Mifune

"Umi Tsubame Joe No Kiseki" is all form and no content and serves to recall, without the intended irony, Mark Twain's cautionary remarks about the futility of trying to find any moral in "Tom Sawyer."

Technically top-notch, the film has the engagingly steamy/sleazy, neon-lit look of a Forties *film noir:* suit lapels are wide, shirts are loud, roscoes blaze. Stunt work, special effects, art direction, cinematography, even editing, the Achilles' heel of the major studios here — none of these can be faulted.

But the plot! Small-time punk shoots gangster kingpin, takes it on the lam to the Philippines, is spotted by his pursuers, and escapes, but only momentarily. Accompanying this skeletal excuse is a list of horrors awaiting any Japanese foolish enough to travel abroad outside of a tour group: among the "representative" Filipinos encountered here are bribe-taking cops, women of extemely easy virtue, fleet-footed thieves and trigger-happy soldiers.

Further complicating matters is the egregious miscasting of the two principals. Saburo Tokito — with his unique, not totally Japanese features — is physically perfect as the half-Filipino gunsel on the run, but is less than perfect when he opens his mouth and attempts to act. As Tokito's sweetheart, the ever-gorgeous Miwako Fujitani displays none of the grit and gravel necessary to survive the grind of working in a two-bit night club, leaving the viewer to wonder what a nice girl like her, etc.

Fortunately, the supporting cast includes the gifted character actor, Yoshio Harada who maintains the above-it-all stance and split-second timing of a very, very hip stand-up comedian.

The title of the film to the contrary withstanding, the only "miraculous" thing about "Umi Tsubame Joe No Kiseki" is its release.
— *Bail.*

Evita (Quien Quiera Oir Que Oiga)
(Evita - Who Wants To Hear May Hear)
(ARGENTINE-DOCU-COLOR/B&W)

Buenos Aires, May 22.
A Yasi presentation of a Macrocolor production. Produced by Mario Alvarez and Tito Vitali. Directed by Eduardo Mignogna. Written by Carlos Santiago Oves and Mignogna; camera (Eastmancolor), Marcelo Camorino; editor, Luis César D'Angiolillo; music, Lito Nebbia; off-screen singer, Silvina Garré. Features Flavia Palmiero; interviews with Ernesto Sábato, Silvina Bullrich, Jack Anderson, Juan José Sebrelli, Arnaldo Rascovsky, Dalmiro Sáenz, Armando Cabo, Paco Jaumandreu, Pascual Pellicciotta, José Pablo Feinman, Félix Luna, Antonio Cafiero, José M. Castiñeira de Dios, Arturo Mathov and others. Reviewed at the Normandie theater, B.A., April 26, 1984. Running time: **90 MINS.**

No wonder Andrew Lloyd Webber-Tim Rice's "Evita" has yet to be staged in Argentina. Both politically and emotionally, Eva Perón and all that was implied in her deeds are still hot potatoes for many people here.

In recent times a growing number of (mostly young) people have been seeking a historical, non-partisan approach to the mysterious forces that launched her from the camerinos shared by second-rate actresses up through the structure of power to become Juan Perón's alter ego, an idol wildly-cheered by the masses, an early victim of cancer and, finally, a myth. Eduardo Mignona's "Evita" is the first film aimed at fulfilling that goal.

Seemingly conscious of the love-hate subject he was working with, Mignogna chose an investigative path leading the less known facts of Evita's pre-1944 life mixed with interviews of noted historians, psychologists, writers, politicians and people who knew her before and after her ascent to power. Old newsreels in b&w depicting some of her most significant public appearances are also included.

Only fictional segment shows Evita, still an adolescent, boarding a train in Junin and travelling on it to Buenos Aires. Mignogna converts that trip in a symbolical journey to fate, using it to link the past and the future of Evita. The flashbacks, interviews and newsreel clippings are not chronologically intertwined but Mignogna has managed to keep a sort of continuity — sometimes informative, sometimes subjective — within individual sequences. Litto Nebbia's songs, sung by Silvina Garré off-screen, add effective lyrical praises of Evita.

Showing professional prowess in his first film, Mignogna has achieved an entertaining docu mainly thanks to an extensive research that provided him with many pieces of unknown (or partially known) data on Evita. He also shows skill in getting a wide sympathetic response to his heroine without resorting to the pamphlet-like style of other political documentarists.

Statements from the people interviewed by Mignogna are contradictory in some cases, but most of them have interesting information or thought-provoking insights. "Her illegitimate origin justifies her social rancor," opines psychologist Rascovsky. "Intellectuals of that time were unable to tell the difference between intelligence and wisdom, between erudition and culture; we were idiots," says formerly anti-Peronist writer Dalmiro Sáenz. "Evita was a woman chosen by the gods: she got all that she wanted and she died young," summarizes novelist Silvina Bullrich. "She was resentful, full of hate," claims old foe Arturo Mathov, a former congressman. Jack Anderson thinks "If Evita hadn't died Perón probably wouldn't have been ousted in 1955." But writer José Pablo Feinman cautions: "No individual alters the course of history; not even Eva Perón."

Technical credits are generally okay.—*Nubi.*

Ningyo Densetsu
(Legend of the Mermaid)
(JAPANESE-COLOR)

Tokyo, May 18.
An Art Theater Guild-Director's Company co-production. Produced by Shiro Sasaki and Susumu Miyasaka. Planning by Yosuke Taga. Directed by Toshiharu Ikeda. Associate producer, Yoshitaro Negishi and Isamu Yamamoto. Screenplay, Takuya Nishioka, from an original story by Kazuhiko Miyatani; camera (color), Yonezo Maeda; lighting, Yukio Inoue; music, Toshiyuki Honda; art, Tomio Ogawa; sound, Osamu Onodera; editing, Akimasa Kawashima; assistant director, Hirokazu Shiraishi. Reviewed at Toho screening room, Tokyo, May 14, 1984. Running time: **110 MINS.**
Migiwa Saeki . . . . Mari Shirato
Keisuke Saeki . . . . Jun Eto
Yohei Miyamoto . . . . Kentaro Shimizu
Hanaoka . . . . Takashi Kanda

Nobu . . . . Hiroko Seki
Mayor . . . . Toshitaro Emi
Oda . . . . Kazuo Kato

An otherwise useless film, "Ningyo Densetsu" does serve the useful purpose of illustrating that hearty appetites for cinematic violence are probably universal.

The climax of this drama of the deep is awash with blood as heroine Mari Shirato, the "mermaid" of the title, picks up her trusty trident, files off two of its points and then fatally punctures between two and three dozen attendees at a semi-formal reception.

The putative purpose of this mass slaughter is to demonstrate, as the heroine asserts, that no matter how many villains you may dispose of, there will always be others to take their place. The baddies of the film, determined to set up a nasty nuclear power plant in a fishing village, kill Shirato's husband. Later — much, much later — in the action, henchmen of the baddies toss Shirato into the sea, and guess whose rapidly decaying body she runs, or rather swims, into? After burning what's left of her spouse on a funeral pyre, she commences her aforementioned act of one-pronged revenge.

For her role, Shirato is required only to display her body periodically and to look angst-ridden. Kentaro Shimizu engages Shirato in some surprising vigorous and realistic-looking softcore love scenes, which means that "Ningyo Densetsu" can be said to have given at least two people a few moments of pleasure ... — *Bail.*

Stacy's Knights
(COLOR)

Meek B-movie about blackjack gambling fever.

A Crown International Pictures release of an American Twist Prods. presentation, in association with Golden Gaters Prods. Executive producers, David L. Peterson, Jim Wilson. Produced by Joann Locktov, Freddy Sweet. Directed by Wilson. Features entire cast. Screenplay, Michael Blake; camera (Deluxe color), Raul Lomas; editor, Bonnie Koehler; music, Norton Buffalo; sound, James Thornton; art direction-set decoration, Florence Fellman; production manager-assistant director, Jacqueline Zambrano. Reviewed on Vestron Video cassette, N.Y., May 28, 1984. (MPAA Rating: PG.) Running time: **96 MINS.**
Stacy Lancaster . . . . Andra Millian
Will Bonner . . . . Kevin Costner
Jean Dennison . . . . Eve Lilith
Shecky Poole . . . . Mike Reynolds
Mr. C . . . . Garth Howard
The Kid . . . . Ed Semenza

"Stacy's Knights" is a stillborn feature attempt to dramatize average people's hopes for hitting the jackpot in the casino world of blackjack. Filmed in 1982 under the more appropriate (if uncommercial) title of "Double Down," pic was marginally released

theatrically last year but is more suitable as low-key tv fare.

Weak cast is led by Andra Millian as Stacy, a shy young girl (termed "a mouse" by the casino surveillance staff) who goes to Reno with her drama school teacher Jean (Eve Lilith) to make a killing at the "21" tables. There they meet Will (Kevin Costner), a local boy with a fancy hat, who recognizes Stacy's card sense and amazing memory and suggests the trio go into partnership to break the bank at a casino run by nasty Shecky Poole (Mike Reynolds).

Both before and after the requisite training sequence, Stacy is met by a "knockout" put on her by Shecky: ordering his best blackjack dealer to get rid of the player by cheating. Will, whose dad was a famous cardsharp, takes Stacy to a guru-like expert known as The Kid (Ed Semenza) to learn the almost mystical secrets of counting in blackjack.

After the baddies get rid of Will, Stacy organizes a team of players to execute a "The Sting"-style assault on Shecky's casino, successfully taking home $611,000 in winnings.

Film's major failing is the absence of excitement or suspense during the gambling scenes, mechanically directed by Jim Wilson. Low-budget opus includes dated romantic montages and an unfortunate use of voice-over exposition laid in during transition driving-around footage.

Cast is inadequate, with lead Millian failing to blossom, even when she cornily removes her specs and is supposed to be glamorous (she later does an okay male-drag routine with moustache added to fool casino authorities). Costar Kevin Costner is a comfortable, engaging young performer in an underwritten role, who has since landed leading roles in "St. Louis Square" and upcoming Warner Bros. releases "Fandango" and "American Flyer." Tech credits are satisfactory.—*Lor.*

Hollywood High Part II
(COLOR)

Abysmal drive-in fare.

A Lone Star Pictures International production and release. Executive producers, Caruth C. Byrd, Lee Thornburg. Produced by Cotton Whittington, Colleen Meeker. Directed by Thornburg, Byrd. Fetures entire cast. Screenplay, Thornburg, Byrd, Whittington, Meeker; camera (CFI color), Gary Graver; editor, Warren Chadwick; music & songs, Doug Goodwin; sound, Jean Clark; production manager, Meeker; stunt coordinator, Ron Amos. Reviewed at Criterion 5 theater, N.Y., May 26, 1984. (MPAA Rating: R.) Running time: **85 MINS.**
Bunny . . . . April May
Rocky . . . . Brad Cowgill
Kiki . . . . Donna Lynn
Jock . . . . Drew Davis
Skip . . . . Bruce Dobos

Ginger ....Camille Warner
Chessie ....Alisa Ann Hull
Also with: Angela Field, Anne Morris.

Filmed in spring of 1981, "Hollywood High Part II" is an embarrassingly bad teen exploitation film. Instead of including frequent dull stretches to allow the target drive-in audience to trek to the refreshment stand, pic is an 85-minute forced break during which patrons will hide out waiting for the next feature to begin.

Sole story detail has the six leads snapping incriminating photos of the cop on the beach having sex with the class prude Chessie (Alisa Ann Hull), with the cop later blackmailing them in turn when he catches the boys cheating on their girlfriends by servicing a pair of man-hungry femme teachers. Film's cynical moral is that one has to go to bed with one's teachers in order to graduate.

Consisting 100% of padding and filler, "Part II" 's best use would be as anti-American propaganda if exported to Japan or the Eastern Bloc nations, where its portrayal of U.S. education could be taken as documentary evidence. —Lor.

Covergirl
(CANADIAN-COLOR)

A New World Pictures release of a Filmplan International production, produced in association with Canadian Film Development Corp. & Famous Players Ltd. Executive producers, Pierre David, Victor Solnicki. Produced by Claude Héroux. Directed by Jean-Claude Lord. Features entire cast. Screenplay-creative consultant, Charles Dennis; camera (Film House color), René Verzier; editor, Christopher Holmes; music, Christopher Stone; sound, Henri Blondeau; art direction, Michel Proulx; costume design, Jean-Claude Poitras; assistant director, John Fretz; production manager, Roger Héroux; post-production coordinator, Bill Wiggins; associate producer, Lawrence Nesis. Reviewed on Thorn EMI Video cassette, N.Y., June 2, 1984. (MPAA Rating: R.) Running time: **93 MINS.**
T.C. Sloane ....Jeff Conaway
Kit Paget ....Irena Ferris
Tessa ....Cathie Shirriff
Dee........................Roberta Leighton
Avril..................Deborah Wakeham
Harrison ....Kenneth Welsh
Cockridge ....William Hutt
Blitzstein ....Charles Dennis
Eva Randall ....Paulle Clark
Zara...............................Tiiu Leek
Joel ....August Schellenberg
Topsy ....Samantha Logan

"Covergirl" is an uninspired, glossy Canadian tax-shelter picture, lensed in 1981 under the title "Dreamworld" and marginally released this past January by New World in Denver and other regional dates. Purporting to show a behind-the-scenes glimpse of the glamorous world of New York modelling, pic plays in similar fashion to a tv-movie with nudity and swearing added, but minus name talent, making it neither fish nor fowl for theatrical use.

Beautiful blond Irena Ferris is introed here as Kit Paget, an up-and-coming fashion model who meets whiz-kid promoter T.C. Sloane (Jeff Conaway) in a traffic accident. Incident proves fateful, as Sloane gets a massive crush on her, takes over her career and quickly builds her into a world-famous model, designated the "Dreamworld Girl." Amidst numerous soap opera subplots, Sloane's empire almost crumbles as his key associate Harrison (Kenneth Welsh) stages a corporate coup to topple Sloane from power.

Under Jean-Claude Lord's direction, which emphasizes visual glitz and kitschy details, acting here is a bit arch with lead Conaway unfortunately overdoing a (perhaps unconscious) vocal impression of George Segal throughout in his brash, dislikeable role.

Writer-actor Charles Dennis' script suffers from gauche dialog (Cathie Shirriff at one point exclaims: "He's got a light meter where his heart's supposed to be," played straight) and fails to present a fresh point-of-view to the usual success story material. Ferris and cohorts are attractive, but well-budgeted opus (reportedly in the $5,000,000 range) could have benefitted from some star names.

All told forgettable film is unlikely to register in film history alongside the Rita Hayworth musical classic "Cover Girl" or even a well-received west coast-made porno title by that name released three years ago. —Lor.

Zärtlichkeit Und Zorn
(Tenderness And Anger)
(SWISS-DOCU-COLOR)

A production of Cactus Film Export (Zurich), produced by Toni Stricker. Written and directed by Johannes Flütsch; camera (Fuji color), Carlo Varini and Flütsch; assistant director, Bea Götz; sound, Andre Simmen; editing, Flütsch and Hannelore Künzi. Reviewed at Film Forum, N.Y., May 22, 1984. Running time: **90 MINS.**
In German, with English and French subtitles.

Winner of Switzerland's "Best Quality Award" in 1981 and the "Special Mayor's Award" at the Mannheim festival, as well as prizes from FIPRESCI (film critics) and from OCIC (Catholic film jury), "Tenderness And Anger" is a commendable but overlong odyssey film that wanders with the small Cesa family of gypsies through the village of Switzerland.

Impelled by ancient tribal memory or instinct or tradition, gypsies keep moving on down the road — indeed, the word "gypsy" is a racist epithet for itinerant vagabond. But in this film police harassment and village suspicion are also goads to travel. The Cesa family seems barely able to manage financially. They steal vegetables from fields, also sharpen knives and scissors door-to-door, living from hand to mouth.

But there are remarkable unity, affection and stability within the family. They are proud to be a minority of outsiders, nomadic and homeless but not without roots.

Once oppressed, largely exterminated in the Nazi deathcamps, European gypsies today are reduced in number, and so the fear of their strangeness has moderated. When they camp in the woods, as in this film, they are kept under surveillance.

The "tenderness and anger" of the title derives from the closeness and love within the family, contrasted with their open anger against government, any government, seeking to impose regulation and limitation upon them. The word "freedom" is very often on the lips of these gypsies, self-consciously describing and demonstrating their lifestyle for the camera.

Shot in a modified cinema-verité style, with director Flütsch audible behind the camera with provocative questions at times, the film concentrates solely on this one family of two parents, with two children, two dogs, plus two horses that draw their heavy wooden caravan. There are no visits to large gypsy encampments, such as one might expect in a film about gypsies.

The strength of the film is its intense preoccupation with this solitary family, cutting down vertically as an in-depth portrait. But the film's weakness, perhaps, is its lack of broad horizontal context, putting gypsy life into wider and more general perspective.

Three years old, "Tenderness And Anger" premiered in the U.S. during May at the Film Forum showcase in New York. Its continuing theatrical presence in the U.S. elsewhere seems limited to such small counterpart cinemas, for specialist audiences in big cities. Public television also seems a probable destiny. — *Hitch.*

Top Secret
(COLOR)

Funny material, but without that 'Airplane' potential.

Hollywood, May 22.

A Paramount Pictures release. Produced by Jon Davison, Hunt Lowry. Executive producers-directed by Jim Abrahams, David Zucker, Jerry Zucker. Features entire cast. Screenplay, Abrahams, Zucker & Zucker, Martyn Burke; camera (Metrocolor), Christopher Challis; editor, Bernard Gribble; music, Maurice Jarre; sound, Derek Ball; art direction, John Fenner, Michael Lamont; costumes Emma Porteous; assistant director, Barry Langley; choreography, Gillian Gregory; special effects, Nick Allder; special makeup effects supervision, Stuart Freeborn; stunt arranger, Joe Powell; second unit director-camera, Jack Lowin; associate producer, Tom Jacobson. Reviewed at UCLA, May 21, 1984. (MPAA Rating: PG.) Running time: **90 MINS.**
Nick Rivers ....Val Kilmer
Hillary ....Lucy Gutteridge
Nigel ....Christopher Villiers
Cedric ....Omar Sharif
Bookstore Owner...........Peter Cushing
Gen. Streck ....Jeremy Kemp
Martin ....Billy J. Mitchell
Dr. Flammond ....Michael Gough
Du Quois ....Harry Ditson
Deja Vu ....Jim Carter

After the ascendant success of "Airplane," writer-directors Jim Abrahams, David Zucker and Jerry Zucker have returned with one more venture into inspired silliness with "Top Secret," another bumptious tribute to all that was odd in old movies. Trio's followers will probably be happy and satisfied with this effort, yet short of overjoyed.

The attempted target this time is a combination of the traditional spy film and Elvis Presley musical romps, which in and of itself is funny to start with. And Val Kilmer proves a perfect blend of staunch hero and hothouse heartthrob.

But in a deliberate effort to do something different, the directors have unfortunately discarded an important ingredient of "Airplane's" success: The cast of matinee idols so closely identified with the originals.

Given the nature of comedy, it's hard to explain why the very presense of those familiar faces worked so well for a send-up and it's equally hard to say why "Secret" doesn't work so well without them. But it is so. And the one reminiscent turn here by Omar Sharif just proves the point.

Other than that, "Secret" shares the same wonderfully wacky attitude that allows just about any kind of gag to come flowing in and out of the picture at the strangest times, given a full framework of Kilmer as an American pop idol drawn into a plot to reunite Germany under one rule.

And how all of this gets started on the beach with "skeet surfing" is a bit beyond easy description, along with the parachuting fireplace, a magniloquent minuet and the unexpected sexual delights in dressing up like a cow.

As one character says, "It all sound like some bad movie," which of course is just exactly what it's supposed to be. And all the better for it. —*Har.*

Buried Alive
(ITALIAN-COLOR)

An Aquarius Releasing release of a D.R. Mass Communications production. Directed by Joe D'Amato (Aristide Massaccesi). Features entire cast. Screenplay, Ottavio Fabbri; camera (Telecolor), Massaccesi; editor, Ornella Micheli; music, The Goblins; assistant director, Franco Gandeli; art direction, Donatella Donati; set design, Ennio Michittoni; makeup, Cesare Bisco; production manager, Oscar Santaniello. Reviewed at 42d St. Selwyn theater, N.Y., June 9, 1984. (No MPAA Rating.) Running time: 84 MINS.
With: Kieran Canter, Cinzia Monreale, Franca Stoppi, Sam Modesto, Ana Cardini, Mario Pizzin, Klaus Rainer.

"Buried Alive" is a tedious, incoherent gore-horror film which vaults director Aristide Massaccesi (who uses the *nom de film* of Joe D'Amato) to a position of leadership in the current sweepstakes among Italian directors of unrated (equivalent to an X) and unwatchable pictures. Origin of the film is unknown, but it appears to have been produced circa 1980-81.

Narrative is rather difficult to follow, since exposition and character relationships are glossed over by Massaccesi and his scripter Ottavio Fabbri. After a cryptic opening reel, one gradually learns that the 22-year-old antihero Frank's wife (or maybe just girlfriend) Anna has died in a hospital. Frank is a taxidermy specialist and he injects fluid surreptitiously in Anna's corpse when she is on view at the funeral home, subsequently digs up her buried body, removes the entrails and preserves her in his bedroom.

Frank lives in a mansion with a creepy older woman Iris, who seems to be his governess from childhood though she might be a distant relative. She has taken care of him (sexually as well, it is implied) since his parents died in a car accident nine years ago. In the midst of various murders by the twosome of female passers-by, Iris and Frank plan a marriage, but get sidetracked when Anna's lookalike sister Eleonora shows up at the mansion.

Vague storyline is merely a hook for Massaccesi to display butcher-shop goodies which still have shock value for the target audience. Cheaply lensed opus (Massaccesi doubles as cameraman, per usual) attempts to create gothic atmosphere but fails due to inept storytelling, though pic boasts a solid keyboards jazz-rock score credited to "The Goblins," presumably the Italian group known heretofore as Goblin.

Acting and dubbing are miserable, and the long stretches of filler when nothing much is happening will try the patience of even the most dedicated gorehound. — *Lor.*

The Evil That Men Do
(COLOR)

Suitably violent Charles Bronson vehicle.

London, June 12.
An ITC Film Distributors release (Tri-Star Pictures in U.S.-Canada) of a Pancho Kohner/Lance Hool production. An ITC Entertainment presentation of a J. Lee-Thompson film. Produced by Pancho Kohner. Directed by J. Lee-Thompson. Screenplay, David Lee Henry, John Crowther, based on the novel by R. Lance Hill. Executive producer, Lance Hool; associate producers, David Pringle, Jill Ireland. Camera (CFI color), Javier Ruvalcaba Cruz; editor, Peter Lee-Thompson; music, Ken Thorne; second unit director, Ernie Orsatti; production supervisor, Marco Aurelio Ortiz; assistant director, Gordon A. Webb. Reviewed at the Leicester Square theater, London, June 10, '84. (BBFC Rating: 18.) (MPAA Rating: R.) Running time: 89 MINS.
Holland .... Charles Bronson
Rhiana .... Theresa Saldana
Moloch .... Joseph Maher
Lomelin .... Jose Ferrer
Max .... Rene Enriquez
Briggs .... John Glover
Randolph .... Raymond St. Jacques

An assembly-line Charles Bronson pic, "The Evil That Men Do" is another vengeance-glorifying actioner, with the star playing a hired gun lured out of retirement for one last assignment. The ITC production is slickly made and tightly scripted to a formula that has worked before and should still appeal to Bronson fans.

Pic is a Tri-Star domestic negative pickup and has already opened in several European territories, with U.S. release slated for September or thereabouts.

Target of Bronson's vengeance this time is Moloch (Joseph Maher), a specialist in torture and an advisor to several Central American regimes, who lives in Guatemala (impersonated herein by Mexico), surrounded by a squad of heavies and protected by an agency of the American government.

A more inept bunch would be hard to find, for Bronson cuts down the lot of them with casual ease and a surfeit of mayhem. Uncle Sam's agents, most of them, perish after a ritualistic car chase through the Guatemalan countryside and at one point, oddly, through some Guatemalan rivers.

Femme interest Theresa Saldana is called on to alternate between looking upset and looking worried. As the wife of one of Moloch's most recent victims, gruesomely tortured to death at the beginning of the film, she is allowed to slow up the mayhem briefly by raising the wider moral implications of Bronson's actions.

This introspection isn't allowed to intrude for long. In an age of vio-

lence, "The Evil That Men Do" is as violent as they come, exploiting the actions of the torturer to create a palpable sense of nervous anticipation by the audience. Viewers these days seem to need the frisson of torture to stay awake.

Film is tightly edited, with locations that evoke the seedy air of a run-down Latin country. Pic works as a thriller, with plenty of the continuous slam-bang action presumably expected by Bronson buffs.

Only question that remains is how long Bronson can continue to milk this formula before the genre goes stale. — *Mung.*

American Nightmare
(CANADIAN-COLOR)

A Mano Films Ltd. presentation, in association with Manesco Films Ltd., of a Kramreiter Lynch production. Executive producers, Anthony Kramreither, Paul Lynch. Produced by Ray Sager. Directed by Don McBrearty. Stars Lawrence S. Day, Lora Staley, Neil Dainard. Screenplay, John Sheppard, from story by John Gault, Steven Blake; camera (Quinn color), Daniel Hainey; editor, Ian McBride; music, Paul Zaza; sound, Dan Latour; art direction, Andrew Deskin; assistant director, David Pamplin; production manager, Bob Wertheimer; fight coordinator, Dwayne McLean; associate producer, Derrett Lee. Reviewed on Media Home Entertainment vidcassette, N.Y., June 5, 1984. (No MPAA Rating.) Running time: 87 MINS.
Eric .... Lawrence S. Day
Louise .... Lora Staley
Tony .... Neil Dainard
Tina .... Lenore Zann
Det. Skylar .... Michael Ironside
Motel manager .... Paul Bradley
Andrea .... Claudia Udy
Dolly .... Larry Aubrey
Fixer .... Mike Copeman
Isabelle .... Alexandra Paul

"American Nightmare" is a routine, low-budget 1982 Canadian-made terror picture, unreleased theatrically but available in videocassette format. Title apparently was inspired by a 1979 horror film retro under that name held at the Toronto Film Festival.

Lawrence S. Day toplines as Eric, a pianist searching the world of Sin City's (i.e., Toronto) bars, strip joints and hot sheets motels for his missing 18-year-old sister Isabelle (Alexandra Paul), who has drifted into prostitution and drugs. A fellow dancer at the Club 2000, Louise (Lora Staley) helps Eric in his search and becomes involved romantically with him, while other dancers and bystanders are being killed by a mystery man. The police, led by Sgt. Skylar (Michael Ironside), are getting nowhere on the case.

Gimmicky effort relies on cornball devices of an incest subplot and murderer's identity being ultimately revealed via a convenient hidden-camera videotape setup at a motel. Plenty of blood is spilled by the killer with a straight razor, but picture skimps on fantastic gore or makeup effects.

Filmmakers, who include executive producer-titles designer Paul Lynch (a horror genre vet with "Prom Night" and "Humongous" among his helming credits), have opted for a gritty, realistic approach that is unengaging and (until final reels with romance injected) unsympathetic to the characters.

Lead players are unimpressive but two of the small role femme victims subsequently have made career breakthroughs. Alexandra Paul, who appears here in the opening scene as the sexually aggressive Isabelle, has since had leading roles in John Carpenter's "Christine," the tv-movie "Getting Physical" and upcoming Kristy McNichol starrer "I Won't Dance." Blond Claudia Udy, who meets her maker in a bathtub, starred in the title role of the 1983 softcore hit "Joy." —*Lor.*

Dominique
(BRITISH-COLOR)

A Sword & Sorcery production, presented by Melvin Simon. A Grand Prize Prods. picture. Exec producer, Simon. Produced by Milton Subotsky, Andrew Donally. Directed by Michael Anderson. Screenplay, Edward & Valerie Abraham, from story by Harold Lawlor; camera (color), Ted Moore; editor, Richard Best; music, David Whitaker; sound, David Bowen, Bob Jones; production design, David Minty; assistant director, Brian Cook; production manager, Rufus Andrews. Reviewed on Prism Entertainment vidcassette, N.Y., June 4, 1984. (MPAA Rating: PG.) Running time: 95 MINS.
David Ballard .... Cliff Robertson
Dominique Ballard .... Jean Simmons
Tony, chauffeur .... Simon Ward
Ann Ballard .... Jenny Agutter
Also with: Ron Moody, Judy Geeson, Michael Jayston, Flora Robson, David Tomlinson, Jack Warner, Leslie Dwyer.

Packaged in its newly released videocassette form as "Domique Is Dead," "Dominique" is an unsatisfying British mystery thriller filmed in 1977, prepared for release but shelved by the since-defunct American Cinema Releasing banner, and previously shown via pay-tv outlet Showtime in 1979. Reviewed here for the record, opus was among the first 10 projects backed by real estate magnate Melvin Simon, many of which went unreleased, before he hit paydirt with "When A Stranger Calls," "Love At First Bite" and, later, the "Porky's" films.

A miscast Cliff Robertson heads an otherwise British troupe as an American stockbroker in England who appears to be doing a Charles Boyer ("Gaslight") number on wife Jean Simmons, trying to make her think she's losing her mind. With lots of suspects to choose from, the working-backwards script includes numerous twists but is ultimately repetitive and dull, with a simple scene such as digging up a coffin to see if the person's *really* dead repeated a second time, illogically, but fitting the writers' reliance upon extra plot twists. Various gimmicks, including a silly remote-control piano device, fall flat.

Robertson walks through his role with virtually no change in expression, and the starry supporting cast is given little to do. Sadly, co-producer Milton Subotsky, who a decade before was a prolific supplier (with partner at that time Max J. Rosenberg) of horror films, has lost his connection with the youth market. There are no young people in the cast here, and, as with his only other theatrical feature in recent years "The Monster Club," Subotsky has missed out completely on the popular horror film boom and what makes such pictures work. — *Lor.*

A Rare Breed
(COLOR)

Uninspired 'true life' story of a girl and her racehorse.

A New World Pictures release of a Carnoba Co. film. Executive producer, Kade Matthews. Produced by Jack Cox. Directed by David Nelson. Features entire cast. Screenplay, Garner Simmons, from a story by Stanley Canter; camera (color), Darrell Cathcart; editor, John O'Connor; music, Bob Sommers; sound, Fred Dresch; assistant director, Worth Keeter 3d; production manager, Mike Allen, Domenico Maxxone (Italy); art direction, Sara Robbins; set design, James Martin; European· coordinator, Drummond Challis. Reviewed on U.S.A. Home Video cassette, N.Y., June 9, 1984. (MPAA Rating: PG.) Running time: **94 MINS.**

Nathan Hill	George Kennedy
Jess Cutler	Forrest Tucker
Anne Cutler	Tracy Vaccaro
Luigi Nelson	Tom Hallick
Frank Nelson	Don DeFore
Lt. Oppo	William Hicks
Romano	Jerry Colbert

"A Rare Breed" is a cornball, by-the-numbers story of a racehorse and the pretty teenage girl who loves it. Filmed in early 1981 under the title (and horse's name) "Carnauba" at the Earl Owensby Studios in Shelby, N.C. (plus some globehopping second-unit footage), this Jack Cox production has been sitting on the shelf ever since, both theatrically (via New World Pictures) and in homevideo stores.

Uneventful but apparently true-life story has teen Anne (Tracy Vaccaro) getting a crush on filly Carnauba, bought at an auction for her by her dad Jess' (Forrest Tucker) friend Nathan Hill (George Kennedy). She helps raise the horse, but when it is sent to Milan for training, Anne stows away and ultimately is allowed to stay with Carnauba as it wins races in Italy and England.

Carnauba is kidnapped and held for ransom, with the kidnappers later grabbing Anne and Carnauba's handsome trainer Luigi Nelson (Tom Hallick) as well. Not suprisingly, everyone is rescued in the final reel amidst desultory ac-

tion footage filmed in North Carolina as an unconvincing substitute for the Italian locale.

As family entertainment, pic is dull in the extreme. A certain carelessness is apparent in script and direction, as when the head kidnapper repeatedly demands 2,000,000 lira in ransom, supposedly $350,000, when 2-billion (or more) is what the filmmakers had in mind.

Cast generally walks through these paper-thin roles, with drama and romance singularly lacking. The pretty heroine introduced here is actress Vacarro (19 at time of filming) who subsequently shed this overly wholesome routine and became a Playboy Playmate of the month as well as Blake Edwards' dreamgirl "Legs" (that's all that appeared on screen) in last year's "The Man Who Loved Women."

Perfunctory direction is by David Nelson, who also helmed producer Cox' political thriller "Last Plane Out," and is better known as the actor son of Harriet Hilliard and Ozzie Nelson. -- *Lor.*

Camila
(Camille)
(ARGENTINE-SPANISH – COLOR)

Buenos Aires, May 18.

GEA Producciones release of own coproduction with Impala (Spain). Directed by María Luisa Bemberg. Stars Susú Pecoraro and Imanol Arias. Screenplay, Docampo Feijóo, Juan B. Stagnaro and Bemberg; historical adviser, Leonor Calvera; camera (Eastmancolor), Fernando Arribas; music, Luis María Serra; art director, Miguel Rodriguez; set decoration, Esmeralda Almoncid; executive producer, Lita Stantic; costumes, Graciela Galán; production managers, Marta Parga and Clara Zapettini. Reviewed at the Atlas theatre, B.A., May 17, 1984. Running time: **105 MINS.**

Camila O'Gorman	Susú Pecoraro
Father Ladislao Gutiérrez	Imanol Arias
Mr. O'Gorman	Héctor Alterio
Doña Joaquina	Elena Tasisto
La Perichona	Mona Maris
Eduardo	Claudio Gallardou

With: Carlos Muñoz, Cecilio Madanes, Jorge Hacker, Héctor Pellegrini, Boris Rubaja, Juan Manuel Tenuta, Lidia Catalano, Zelmar Gueñol.

One of the best Argentine pictures ever and an instant blockbuster locally, "Camila" has the potential for international b.o. success if properly handled, with its combination of quality, content and the gripping real-life story of young Catholic socialite Camila O'Gorman and Jesuit priest Ladislao Gutiérrez, who fell in love in 1847, ran away and ended their intense relationship before a firing squad.

Camila's tragedy was filmed in 1912 with Blanca Podestá in the title role, but all projects to remake it were blocked either by secret maneuvering or open censorship. Influential rightwingers have also

managed to keep the story out of history books.

Maria Luisa Bemberg, top director who excelled last year with "Señora de Nadie" (Nobody's Wife), lost no time in taking advantage of the new democratic freedoms to turn out this dream of many Argentine filmmakers. Her opus has been chosen to compete at the Karlovy Vary fest.

The bloody tyranny of Juan Manuel De Rosas was at its peak — five years before he was overthrown — when Camila and Father Gutiérrez met in still-colonial-like Buenos Aires. Both unsuccessfully tried to repress their feelings when realizing that not only the director, but also the strict Mr. O'Gorman, the Church and a society plagued by fear, bigotry and prejudice would not understand, much less forgive them.

Eventually they fled B.A. for a hideout some 500 miles up the Paraná river, near Goya, Corrientes. They were labelled sacrilegious and Rosas ordered their capture. They lived happily for a time in a hut and founded a school for the children of nearby settlers, but Camila got pregnant before they were discovered by a grudging priest. The local commander, grateful for their teaching work and friendly behavior, gave them a chance to escape, but Gutiérrez devoted an entire night to praying and both surrendered the next morning.

Then everybody asked for their heads. Rosas not only was pressed by Church, society and his own instincts, but also by his political enemies, the freedom fighters exiled in neighboring countries, who denounced the Camila-Gutiérrez affair as proof of the corruption of the dictator's regime. Rosas ordered the execution of the young lovers, who were shot before the amazed inmates of a prison and buried within the same casket.

Pic's main asset is how Bemberg achieves a delicate balance between the human, almost innocently sincere sentiments igniting the lovers' hope to find a place far from the taboos, and the director's brave statement on how a merciless regime gets a greenlight for murder from social complicity, a sort of sinister civic consent. Bemberg has done a warm, and moving love story without losing sight of her intellectual stand against the pitiless side of political, religious and social powers.

Susú Pecoraro and Imanol Arias make one feel the honesty, the conflict of conscience and the romantic intensity of the wretched lovers. Héctor Alterio as Camila's father, a steely cattle baron, and Mona Maris as her grandmother, a lovable old lady with a past, also shine. Elena Tasisto and young Claudio

Gallardou are other key members of a generally able cast.

Fernando Arribas' superb lensing gives "Camila" a pictorial level rarely seen in Argentine cinema. Period feeling has been attained with production values above average. All other technical credits are good, as is Luis María Serra's score. — *Nubi.*

Notre Histoire
(Our Story)
(FRENCH-COLOR)

Paris, June 6.

An AMLF release (Spectrafilm for U.S.-Canada) of a Sera Films/Adel Productions coproduction. Produced by Alain Sarde. Written and directed by Bertrand Blier. Stars Alain Delon and Nathalie Baye. Camera (color), Jean Penzer; art director, Bernard Evein; sound, Bernard Bats; costumes, Michéle Cerf; editor, Claudine Merlin; music, Beethoven, Shubert, Eric Kemray, Bohuslav Martinu, Laurent Rossi; production manager, Gérard Crosnier. Reviewed at the Marignan-Concorde theater, Paris, June 5, 1984. Running time: **111 MINS.**

Robert Avranche	Alain Delon
Donatienne	Nathalie Baye
Emile	Michel Galabru
Duval	Gerard Darmon
Carmen	Sabine Haudepin
Traveller	Jean-Pierre Darroussin
Madeleine	Geneviéve Fontanel
Chatelard	Jean-François Stevenin
Florist	Ginette Garcin
Stranger	Nathalie Nell

The non-selection of Bertrand Blier's new film "Notre Histoire" ("Separate Rooms" in U.S.-Canada) for the Cannes film festival was one of this year's inevitable local "scandals," along with the rejection of Andrzej Zulawski's "La Femme Publique." Latter nonetheless managed to turn its snub into effective publicity, but "Notre Histoire" has been a weak performer at the wickets, and co-star (and coproducer) Alain Delon has given vent to his disappointment in a bitter public outburst against the festival and culture minister Jack Lang, implying political manipulation in selection procedures (Delon's sympathies lean to the Right).

Another, more cogent reason for the pic's rejection for Cannes is that this new film falls short of its mark. "Notre Histoire" has a more stylistically ambitious script and good cast than Blier's last picture (a commercial flop), "My Best Friend's Girl," but it is often downed by its self-conscious verbosity and plodding direction. Notably since "Buffet Froid," Blier has been moving away from the anarchic fireworks of his earlier comedies to a more studied, theatrical manner, with which he seems increasingly uneasy.

Delon plays a world-weary, beer-guzzling man who gets propositioned in a train compartment by an attractive young stranger (Nathalie Baye), has a brief fling with her and then refuses to part with her. Rather than return to his Paris home and his wife, Delon decides to install himself in Baye's Alpine chalet and comfortably go to seed with his substitute mate and a fridge full of beer.

Unable to dislodge him, Baye, a divorcée who has lost custody of her children and now abandons herself completely to random quickie sexual encounters (she has slept with all the married men in her neighborhood), calls on Delon's Paris pals, who come running but sway his self-destructive plan.

The long night that follows - in which the action spills out onto neighboring chalets where Delon becomes a sort of reluctant male hero in a sexual marathon with the frustrated housewife — occupies a good chunk of screen time and is meant to slip progressively into dream-like ambience. But Blier's direction of this sequence is lacking in the necessary spontaneity and camera judgment and fails to give accent to the bizarre chorus of males (all township husbands who have received favors from Baye) that shuffles about as witness to Delon's exploits.

The disconnected unrealty of the film (which leads to a trite conclusion similar to the end of Claude Lelouch's "Viva la Vie!") is reflected in Blier's dialog technique, by which Delon and Baye describe their actions in the third person — something Delon himself has been doing in real life in recent interviews! — beginning with the formula refrain: "This is the story of ..." (hence the film's title). For Blier's personages, language is an alienation device to insure the separation of action and reaction.

Delon and Baye are okay as the desparate protagonists, on the run from themselves, though the pathos of their existence rarely is felt amid the artifices of plot and dialog. Supporting parts are fine down the line, and film is polished technically, though the hodgepodge of musical excerpts that invades the soundtrack is poorly judged and irritating. —Len.

The Jupiter Menace
(DOCU-COLOR)

A Celebrity Releasing release of a Peter S. Davis and William N. Panzer presentation. A Youngstar production, in association with E.C. Monell; a Jupiter Menace Ltd. picture. Exec producers, Davis Panzer. Produced by Lee Auerbach. Directed by Peter Matulavich, Auerbach. Stars George Kennedy. Written by Matulavich, Alan Henry Coats; camera (Deluxe color), Robert Harmon; editors, David Schwartz, Greg Schorer; music, Synergy; sound, David Brownlow; production manager, Beth Tate; assistant director, Catrine Cash. Special visual effects: Midocean Motion Pictures, director-designer, Scott Bartlett; producer, Peter Bloch, exec producer, John C.B. Green; production manager, Michelle Tuton. Computer generated imagery: Digital Prods., exec producer, John Whitney Jr.; technical director, Gary Demos. Special photographic effects: producer, David M. Garber, in association with David Stipes Prods.; camera, Stipes; matte art-

ists, Dan Curry, Sean Joyce. Planet photography: Private Stock Effects, technical directors, Ken Jones, Bob Skotak; camera, George Dodge; visual consultant, Dennis Skotak. Time-lapse photography, Lou Schwarzberg; post-production supervisor, David Schwartz; visual consultant, Tom Southwell; associate producer, E.C. Monell; second narrator, Lindsay Workman. Reviewed on Thorn EMI Video cassette, N.Y., June 6, 1984. (MPAA Rating: PG.) Running time: **79 MINS.**

Made in 1981, "The Jupiter Menace" is a gee-whiz, scare documentary elaborating on the basic premise that our world will come to an end in December 1982 when the planetary alignment fulfills various prophecies by psychics, prophets and scientists foretelling doom. Since things still are running smoothly, theatrically unreleased docu is vaguely reassuring to watch on vidcassette, though it promises another truly devastating cataclysm by the year 2000.

Boasting top-notch special efects, model work and computer animation by experts such as underground filmmaker Scott Bartlett (who previously contributed to "More American Graffiti" and "Altered States"), "Menace" basically resembles the numerous goofball docus cranked out a decade ago by Sunn Classics and others to intrigue credulous audiences lured by hardsell ads and booked on a four-wall basis. Actor George Kennedy walks the viewer through an assortment of theories that forecast cataclysmic upheavals on Earth in the near future. Filmmakers cheat by interchangeably mixing real scientists and psychics with actors pretending to be "real" in their equally unconvincing explanations of why (and how) the Earth's poles are suddenly going to shift, plunging us into an instant ice age, or some such other quack notion.

An interesting segment midway spotlights on various groups of "survivalists," those friendly folks (spoofed in the 1983 Robin Williams flop film "The Survivors") who seem to have memorized Ray Milland's 1962 film "Panic In Year Zero" and are busily arming themselves in the belief that protection against one's fellow man is the best way to handle an impending natural disaster. The Stelle Community near Chicago, repped onscreen by technical expert Tim Wilhelm, are the type of people who would heartily endorse Dr. Strangelove's plans enumerated in the 1963 Stanley Kubrick film of that name, rather than recognize them as satire or a cautionary message. Lest one conclude they are on the right track, please note these folks are planning to build 2-3,000 airships (for completion by the year 1999) in which to hover above the Earth until it is safe to land again, at which future time they will form a new post-Apocalypse community called "Philadelphia."

A bit more frightening are the people of the Zarephath Horeb community in the Ozarks, who believe they're on a mission from God and stress war games and violent self-defense training. They mirror the existence of thousands of "normal" people who attend weekend military exercises, probably having overdosed on too many World War III movies which inevitably feature that clichéd scene of looters and nasty neighbors who will invade your hard-earned bomb shelter if you aren't ready to shoot them down.

Since the film's exec producers, Peter Davis and William Panzer, made the theatrically unreleased feature "St. Helens" in 1980, there is footage of the volcano erupting and mucho boring predictions of super-earthquakes worldwide. A computer simulation of a 12-point (Richter scale) earthquake is thoroughly unconvincing, as is a cheapo look at a video display purportedly showing us a flattopped sunken pyramid 40 miles off the Florida Coast.

For those who desperately want to believe in this nonsense, the next superconjunction of planets is due to occur May 5, 2000. If you thought the world ended in 1982, wait till you see what happens to it 16 years from now. —Lor.

Terre Brulante
(Burning Land)
(ISRAELI-COLOR)

Jerusalem, June 4.
A Y.N.I.L. Films Production. Produced by Yeud Levanon and Doron Eran. Written and directed by Serge Ankri. Camera (color), Yaakov Eizenman; editors, Nelly Guilad, Benny Kimron; sound, Yaakov Goldstein; costumes and art direction, Michelle Belin; music: Gerard Pullicino. Reviewed at the Berkey-Pathe-Humphries Studios, Givatayim, May 31, 1984. Running time: **94 MINS.**

With: Jacques Ovadia, Gerard Benhamou, Myriam Nataf, Alexis Dupont, Meir Suissa, Dahlia Malka, Laurence Sendrowicz.

In spite of its French title and the fact that it is a French-speaking film, Serge Ankri's first feature film is a 100% Israeli production, conceived, shot and processed entirely in this country. The shoestring budget on which it was kept, did not hinder Tunisian born Ankri from turning out a promising debut, using a theme with which he personally is familiar and giving it a new slant, by connecting it with current events.

Ankri's script deals with a Jewish family living in a Tunisian village, the disintegration of its rural traditions, on the one side, and more particularly the animosity of the surrounding Arab population which finally drives the family off its land.

The central character is the grandfather, a patriarchal figure who has always entertained the best relations with his neighbors. He feels he belongs to the land on which he lives and does not see in the fact that he is of a different creed than the majority of the population around him, an impediment to his continuing to live on this land; he, his children and their offspring, forever.

But with mounting Arab nationalism in Tunis, which is about to sever itself from French rule, Jews are being considered an undesirable alien element to be eliminated. Also, the younger generation does not have any real feeling for the land itself and is moving away, into town or even to France. Also, a brief romance between his younger son and the Arab orphan girl who has been raised by the family helps bring into focus the basic fact that complete blending with the local background is impossible.

A short intro and an even briefer epilog, showing Israeli bulldozers tearing down olive trees on the West Bank to make way for a new Jewish settlement, put the whole plot into the context of the Middle-East tragedy, hinting that what has happened to the Jewish family in Tunis 13 years ago is not dissimilar to the situation faced by the Arab population now living in Israel.

Ankri's main strength throughout the picture, is the sympathetic revival of a way of life in a simple, unadorned style that is close to certain ethnographic films. There is also something of the rough, unpolished acting one often finds in this sort of film, but some of the characters are worked in depth with obvious affection; this is particularly true of the grandfather, played by Jacques Ovadio, a poet and sometimes film reviewer now retired, making his film debut here. His presence is considerable and he lends the film much of its credibility.

Shot in 16m and blown up to 35m, on locations that Ankri maintains are very similar to the original Tunisian sites, the film, probably the first to deal seriously with the recent past of the Sephardic Jews prior to their immigration to Israel, should do well on the festival circuit and in specialized positions. In spite of some unsecure editing, technical credits are satisfactory. —Edna.

Rhinestone
(COLOR)

Mismatched Sly and Dolly in an off-the-wall comedy.

Hollywood, June 8.

A 20th Century Fox release of a Marvin Worth presentation of a Howard Smith production. Produced by Smith, Worth. Co-producers, Bill Blake, Richard M. Spitalny. Executive producers, Sandy Gallin, Ray Katz. Directed by Bob Clark. Stars Sylvester Stallone, Dolly Parton. Screenplay, Phil Alden Robinson, Stallone. Screen story, Robinson, based on the song "Rhinestone Cowboy" by Larry Weiss. Camera (Deluxe color, Panavision), Timothy Galfas; editors, Stan Cole, John Wheeler; music, Parton; music adaptation, Mike Post; production design, Robert Boyle; art direction, Frank Richwood; set design, Dianne Wager; set decoration, Cloudia; costume design, Tom Bronson; Parton's costume design, Theadora Van Runkle; sound (Dolby), Michael Evje; associate producers, Linda Horner, James Brubaker; assistant director, Duncan Henderson. Reviewed at the U.A. Egyptian theater, L.A., June 8, 1984. (MPAA Rating: PG.) Running time: 111 MINS.

Nick Martinelli	Sylvester Stallone
Jake Ferris	Dolly Parton
Noah Ferris	Richard Farnsworth
Freddie Ugo	Ron Leibman
Barnett Cale	Tim Thomerson
Father	Steven Apostle Pec
Mother	Penny Santon
Elgart	Russell Buchanan
Luke	Ritch Brinkley
Walt	Jerry Potter
Billie Joe	Jesse Welles
Maurie	Phil Rubenstein

Effortlessly living up to its title, "Rhinestone" is as artificial and synthetic a concoction as has ever made its way to the screen. Fortunately, everyone connected with the film seems to have known this, which takes a lot of the edge off the silliness, and there may be sufficient general curiosity in seeing the overdeveloped but mismatched pair of Sylvester Stallone and Dolly Parton square off to put this over commercially.

Doubts linger, however, since pic is pitched in such a way that may not satisfy the hefty core followings for either star. It remains to be seen whether or not Stallone's action fans will turn out to watch him attempt something he can't do, that is, sing, and Parton partisans could be put off by the constant ribbing the country-western scene receives here.

Directed in low-down, good-spirited vulgar fashion by Bob ("Porky's") Clark, who took over from Don Zimmerman after two weeks of lensing, film is a genuine oddball. Stallone's character, that of a Gotham cabbie whom singer Parton bets she can turn into a convincing country crooner in two weeks' time, is like no one ever encountered on earth before.

Uncouth loudmouth, who comes to be called "Hopalong Meatball" by Parton's pa, Richard Farnsworth, has no discernible talents whatsoever, so it's an uphill battle when Parton takes him down home to Tennessee to try to pump some real country feeling into his bulging veins.

When Stallone first opens his mouth, sound coming out is so gawd-awful that Clark offers up a montage of farm animals running and squawking in panic, a device probably not seen onscreen since the Ma and Pa Kettle series.

Unfortunately, things never get much better, but Parton covers up for him nicely enough to let him sort of squeak through, even if it's sex jokes which manage to initially win over the tough New York audience against which he's finally tested publicly.

Neither Stallone nor Parton stray at all from their past personae, and major shows are actually put on by their costume designers, since two leads seem to change their clothes every three minutes (which, considering how tight they fit, is no small achievement). Their romance, such as it is, consists of considerable innuendo and little action.

Practically stealing the picture is Tim Thomerson as Parton's old Tennessee flame. A beer-guzzling bar scene between him and Stallone is genuinely funny, and the amusement generated by Thomerson mounts steadily as his jealousy and simmering rage increase.

Script by Phil Alden Robinson and Stallone is chock full of weird lines, some of which are laugh-provoking but many of which are in the form of crude repartee and poor insults. Pic, which could easily have been cut by 10-to-15 minutes, features more than enough music, although Parton's songs and delivery are, as always, a pleasure.

Tech contributions are all proficient, but the product tie-in department put in too much overtime where the Busch Brewery was concerned. —*Cart.*

Girls Nite Out
(COLOR)

Standard slasher film, with a surprise ending.

An Aries International Releasing release of a GK Prod. production. Presented by Anthony N. Gurvis, in association with Concepts Unlimited. Exec producers, Kevin Kurgis, Richard Barclay. Produced by Anthony N. Gurvis. Directed by Robert Deubel. Features entire cast. Screenplay, Gil Spencer Jr., Joe Bolster, Kurgis, Gurvis; camera (TVC color), Joe Rivers; editor, Arthur Ginsberg; sound, Dale Whitman; production design, Howard Cummings; production manager, Patrick McCormick; special effects makeup, Tom Brumberger. Reviewed at 42d St. Cine Rialto 1 theater, N.Y., June 16, 1984. (MPAA Rating: R.) Running time: 96 MINS.
With: Julie Montgomery, James Carroll, Suzanne Barnes, Rutanya Alda, Hal Holbrook, David Holbrook, Lauren-Marie Taylor, Al McGuire, Matthew Dunn, Paul Christie, Richard Bright.

Filmed in 1982, "Girls Nite Out" is a routine slasher picture, offering little entertainment to already jaded horror pic fans. Film was test-released last year by Independent-International Pictures under the title "The Scaremaker," but reverted to its producers and is now playing more widely under the "Girls" monicker.

Yawn of a storyline has a mad-killer on the loose on the campus of Dewitt University set in Westville, Ohio, during a sorority scavenger hunt held at night. Cliche gimmick has history repeating itself: many years ago Dickie Cavanagh was jilted by his girlfriend and killed her during a scavenger hunt, for which he was incarcerated in the local Weston Hill Sanitarium. The victim's father Mac (Hal Holbrook) is the campus security guard trying to catch the killer.

Film is divided drearily into about four opening reels emphasizing youthful hijinks (somewhat overage for their roles players are silly rather than funny here), followed by deadly dull police investigation footage, headed by a detective played by Richard Bright. Bright's real-life wife Rutanya Alda is cast as a friendly waitress.

Killer dresses up in a bearsuit stolen from the male mascot to Dewitt's basketball team, and murders cast members in bloody, repetitive fashion with several knives strapped together as a makeshift claw. Lacking the nudity or special effects diversions common to this genre, film's only point of interest is a surprise ending. After planting fair clues (re: age and facial resemblance) the revelation of who the killer is proves to be a satisfying switch.

Tech credits and acting are unimpressive, with Holbrook's son David making his film debut as an outsider figure and prime suspect. — *Lor.*

The Pope Of Greenwich Village
(COLOR)

Flavorful but unsatisfying slice of life in Little Italy.

An MGM/UA Entertainment release, presented by United Artists, of a Koch-Kirkwood production. Produced by Gene Kirkwood. Directed by Stuart Rosenberg. Features entire cast. Screenplay, Vincent Patrick, based on his novel; camera (Metrocolor), John Bailey; editor, Robert Brown; music, Dave Grusin; sound, James Sabat; production design, Paul Sylbert; set decoration, George DeTitta; assistant director, Joseph Napolitano; production manager, Joseph Caracciolo; costumes, Joseph G. Aulisi; associate producer, Benjy Rosenberg; second unit director, Lawrence Tetenbaum. Reviewed at MGM/UA screening room, N.Y., June 12, 1984. (MPAA Rating: R.) Running time: 120 MINS.

Paulie	Eric Roberts
Charlie	Mickey Rourke
Diane	Daryl Hannah
Mrs. Ritter	Geraldine Page
Barney	Kenneth McMillan
Pete	Tony Musante
Burns	M. Emmet Walsh
Bedbug Eddie	Burt Young
Bunky Ritter	Jack Kehoe
Paulie's dad	Philip Bosco
Nunzi	Val Avery
Jimmy	Joe Grifasi
Ronnie	Tony DiBenedetto
Nicky	Ronald Maccone
Nora	Betty Miller

"The Pope Of Greenwich Village," set in Manhattan's Italian community, is a near-miss in its transition from novel to film, setting forth an offbeat slice-of-life tale of small-time guys involved in big trouble. Well-produced but overacted opus constitutes unusual counterprogramming from MGM/-UA for the prime summer season, and its b.o. performance will require substantial audience defection from the generally PG-rated fantasy and comedy fare currently dominating the market.

Vincent Patrick's adaptation of his bestseller retains the book's basic strength, its funny, colloquial dialog, while altering character motivations, turning verbal anecdotes into enacted scenes and laundering some potentially objectional material (as in attitudes toward blacks, who are generally absent on-screen here). Key protagonists are two young buddies (distantly related), Charlie (Mickey Rourke), a supervisor in a restaurant where Paulie (Eric Roberts) works as a waiter. Both are heavily in debt and headed nowhere, with the usual pipe dreams of escape, Charlie to a restaurant he plans to buy in New England and run with his exercise instructress girl friend Diane (Daryl Hannah) and Paulie, out to become rich via one-third ownership in a racehorse.

Fired from their jobs at film's outset due to a misdeed by Paulie, the two of them seek a way out via a crime caper initiated by Paulie, involving an older man Barney (Kenneth McMillan) as safecracker. Though coming away with $150,000 in cash, trio ends up in hot water due to Paulie's failure to inform his partners that the money belonged to a local organized crime bigshot Bedbug Eddie (Burt Young), as well as an accidental mishap during the caper that involves them in the death of cop Bunky Ritter (Jack Kehoe).

The leads' adventures in trying to stay alive make for a number of flavorful scenes in a vein reminiscent of Martin Scorsese's "Mean Streets," but ultimately "Pope" lacks the dramatic payoff and character insight that would yield a truly satisfying picture.

In the more colorful role, Eric Roberts takes a bit of getting used to as the naive kid on the make, but he delivers much of the film's humor and becomes an affecting figure. Mickey Rourke's glamorous assignment as dressed-to-the-nines Charlie (who has been made a much nicer guy than he is in Patrick's novel), consists mainly of surface effects which pall upon repetition, such as his sudden shifts from coolness to hot-headed slapping around of Paulie, or his overly Brando-inflected gimmick of punching walls and smashing furniture when irritated.

Rising young star Daryl Hannah is saddled with the nothing role of Charlie's conscience. In the 1950s, Eva Marie Saint invested such missions with suitable intensity, but it is a sign of the times that up until her inevitable confrontation scene with Rourke, Hannah is simply called upon to show off her alluring physique in exercise togs or revealing underwear.

Within the over-the-top acting format encouraged by director Stuart Rosenberg, Geraldine Page delivers the best performance as Jack Kehoe's mom, combining humor and near-pathos in a showy pair of scenes.

Tech contributions for the Koch-Kirkwood production (only Gene Kirkwood of the since-dissolved partnership takes a producer's credit on-screen, though Howard Koch Jr. also receives the same credit on the cover of a recently reprinted paperback tie-in) are excellent, particularly Paul Sylbert's design work and John Bailey's richly-textured lighting. —Lor.

Pinot, Simple Flic
(Pinot, Just A Cop)
(FRENCH-COLOR)

Paris, June 18.
An AMLF release of a G.P.F.I./Arturo Productions coproduction. Produced by Jean-Claude Fleury. Starring and directed by Gérard Jugnot. Screenplay, Pierre Geller, Christian Biegalski, Jugnot, Robin Katz; camera (color), Edouardo Serra; editor, Catherine Kleber; sound; Alain Lachassagne; art director, Loula Morin; music, Louis Chedid; technical advisor, Robin Katz; production manager, Charlotte Fraisse. Reviewed at the Marignan-Concorde theater, Paris, June 17, 1984. Running time: 90 MINS.
Robert Pinot . . . . Gérard Jugnot
Marylou (Josiane) . . . . Fanny Bastien
Tony . . . . Patrick Fierry
Morcy . . . . Jean-Claude Brialy
Vaudreuil . . . . Jean Rougerie
Blanchard . . . . Gérard Loussine
Rochu . . . . Pierre Mondy
Tom . . . . Pascal Legitimus
Craquette . . . . Claire Magnin

Gérard Jugnot, one of the café-theater personalities who has become a familiar screen comedy presence, goes it alone as star and director in this comedy about the misadventures of an ordinary Paris cop with Good Samaritan impulses.

Jugnot lends his bald, mustachioed teddy bear presence to the title role of a blundering, but well-meaning young patrolman who tenaciously tries to save a pretty young drug addict from her no-good dealer boyfriend.

The Christian Bieglaski-Pierre Geller script, adapted by Jugnot, respects the conventional mode of the loser-comic hero, with the star adding his own personal brand of wistful credibility and deceptive spunk. Despite the farcical settings, Jugnot's cop is believably human and likeable.

Comedy sometimes lapses into tasteless situations (a running gag involving a fellow officer who keeps getting his nose broken, for instance) and the rooftop pursuit climax is mostly mechanical and overlong; but there are enough good sequences to compensate for the flab.

As helmer, Jugnot does nicely with both comic and serious moments; there is a good feeling between Jugnot and pretty newcomer Fanny Bastien as the young junkie, and the police station routine is amusingly sent up. — Len.

Brady's Escape
(U.S./HUNGARIAN-COLOR)

Effective W.W. II adventure.

A Satori Entertainment release of a Robert Halmi Inc. production in association with Brady's Run Associates. Produced by Halmi. Executive producer, Jozsef Marx. Directed by Pal Gabor. Stars John Savage and Kelly Reno. Screenplay, William W. Lewis; story, Gabor; camera (color), Elmer Ragalyi; editor, Norman Gay; music, Charles Gross; art director, Jozsef Romvari; associate producer, Robert Halmi Jr. Reviewed at Magno 4 Preview Theater, N.Y., June 13, 1984. (No MPAA Rating). Running time: 96 MINS.
Brady . . . . John Savage
Miki . . . . Kelly Reno
Klara . . . . Ildiko Bansagi
Dr. Dussek . . . . Laszlo Mensaros
Wortman . . . . Ferenc Bacs
Csorba . . . . Dsoko Rosic
Moro . . . . Laszlo Horvath
Sweede . . . . Matyas Usztics

"Brady's Escape" is a lean, curious World War II action film that could benefit from the current wave of nostalgia for that last great blowout in which the forces of good were aligned clearly against the agents of evil. Briskly paced hunted vs. hunters plot line and the exotic element of Hungarian cowboys make this pic ideal for feevee exploitation, and could produce limited theatrical success.

Pic's very title makes it clear that downed pilot Captain Brady (John Savage) of the U.S. Army Air Corps (anachronistically called the U.S. Air Force in this pic) does eventually escape from Nazi-occupied Hungary. Further deflating the suspense is an opening establishing scene set in the present in which Wyoming rancher Savage (looking improbably young to be a grandfather) is forced to kill his protesting grandson's sick old mare. The rifle's roar brings on a flashback which makes up the rest of the picture.

Bomber pilot Savage and his navigator, Sweede (Matyas Usztics) run into heavy flack near Budapest and, with the rest of their crew dead, are forced to bail out over the Hortobagy plain. They're immediately confronted by the stern, rugged csikos, Hungarian-style gauchos portrayed as a noble equestrian people, embittered by the ravages of war. They're disposed initially to eliminate the Yank fly boys ("They're bombing us," one says), but cool Capt. Brady persuades them instead to send for Dr. Dussek (Laszlo Mensaros) to attend Sweede, badly injured in the parachute jump.

The csikos hide the airmen in their straw hutment village and Dr. Dussek's comely daughter Klara (Ildiko Bansagi) is assigned to teach Brady Hungarian in preparation for his escape. Horning in on the lessons with Dondi-like cuteness is csiko orphan kid Miki (Kelly Reno), a crack horseman like all the male villagers. The two quickly develop a buddy/hero-worship relationship which gives the plot its emotional glue.

Tension is supplied by a cruel Nazi officer who is obsessed with tracking down the enemy parachutists and detaches a whole company of storm troopers for the purpose (seems the Nazi's mother and sister were incinerated in the firebombing of Dresden and he's "going to kill every American pilot I can get my hands on"). Also hunting Brady is a plainclothes SS honcho whose contrived rivalry with the Nazi army officer seems a purposeless convention here. Soon, Sweede dies of his wounds and Brady is alone, a stranger in a strange land.

Savage, playing Brady as a cross between a swaggering southern good ole boy and laconic range-riding Marlboro man, impresses the csikos by breaking the toughest bronco on the Hungarian cowboys' ranch. Garbed in native costume and riding the scrubby brown plains with abandon, Brady soon fits right in. A romance of sorts begins to develop between the flyer and the doctor's daughter, but the horrors of war interfere. These are not cultured Germans who host Sunday chamber music teas for their captives. The Nazis torture the csikos for information (slicing them up slowly with knives is a favorite tactic here) and after the SS man is murdered, proceed to butcher the defiant horsemen of the village.

But with the aid of his noble steed and his inseparable companion, Miki (who's determined to go off to "Vyoming" with Brady), Savage makes his final dangerous and desperate break for the Tisza river and the safety of Tito's partisans in Yugoslavia. Recovering from a nasty wound in a manner only slightly more miraculous than Miki's rapid grasp of English, Brady makes it, but not without paying a price.

Cinematographer Elemer Ragalyi's evocation of the Hungarian countryside quite good and the fluid grace of the equestrian scenes provides a tranquil counterbalance to the war motif. Some of the Hungarian to English dubbing synchronization is off, however, and at least one crucial line of dialog was lost in an over-quick jumpcut. —Rich.

Conan The Destroyer
(COLOR)

Muscular followup in fantasyland.

Hollywood, June 25.

A Universal release of a Dino De Laurentiis presentation of an Edward R. Pressman production. Produced by Raffaella De Laurentiis. Executive producer, Stephen F. Kesten. Directed by Richard Fleischer. Stars Arnold Schwarzenegger. Screenplay, Stanley Mann; story, Roy Thomas, Gerry Conway, based on the character created by Robert E. Howard; camera (Technicolor, J-D-C widescreen), Jack Cardiff; editor, Frank J. Urioste; music, Basil Poledouris; production design, Pier Luigi Basile; art direction, Kevin Phipps, Jose Maria Alarcon; costume design, John Bloomfield; sound, Manuel Topete; "Dagoth" created by, Carlo Rambaldi; stunt coordinator, Vic Armstrong; creative make-up, Giannetto De Rossi. Reviewed at the Hollywood Pacific, L.A., June 25, 1984. (MPAA Rating: PG.) Running time: **103 MINS.**

Conan	Arnold Schwarzenegger
Zula	Grace Jones
Bombaata	Wilt Chamberlain
Akiro "The Wizard"	Mako
Malak	Tracey Walter
Queen Taramis	Sarah Douglas
Princess Jehnna	Olivia D'Abo
Man Ape/Thoth-Amon	Pat Roach
Grand Vizier	Jeff Corey
Togra	Sven Ole Thorsen
Village Heckler	Bruce Fleischer
The Leader	Ferdinand Mayne

A hundred times better than its ponderous predecessor, "Conan The Destroyer" is the ideal sword and sorcery picture. Loaded with action and pitched just right for maximum tongue-in-cheek humor, boistrous film stands as a fine summer entry from Universal and reps a good alternative to seeing "Indiana Jones" for the second or third time. B.O. should be muscular.

Dino De Laurentiis was shrewd in calling upon his old associate Richard Fleischer to direct, and vet Stanley Mann to write, this second installment in the Conan saga. Fleischer has had plenty of experience over the years handling this kind of high adventure piece, and it pays off here in a pic that any kid, or anyone who ever enjoyed this sort of thing as a kid, will relish.

Plot is appropriately elemental. Conan is recruited by sexy queen Sarah Douglas to accompany teenage princess Olivia D'Abo to a distant castle, wherein lies a gem that will supposedly unleash many secret powers.

Unbeknownst to Conan, Douglas has instructed her henchman Wilt Chamberlain to kill the muscleman once the mission is accomplished, and to deliver D'Abo back home with her virginity intact so that she can be properly sacrificed.

Along the way, group, which includes Conan's fool, Tracey Walter, also picks up amusing magician Mako and fiery warrioress Grace Jones, and all come in handy at various points as the band is required to fend off no end of baddies standing in its way.

Managing to survive, Conan is nonetheless wary on the trip back due to the imposing Chamberlain's apparent attempts to do him in, and he must finally do titanic battle with the monster Dagoth, a deliciously repulsive creation by Carlo Rambaldi.

Since this territory has been traversed many times before, the key is clearly in the telling, and filmmakers have been breezily imaginative in breathing fresh life into such material.

As Conan, Arnold Schwarzenegger seems more animated and much funnier under Fleischer's direction than he did under John Milius' in the original — he even has an amusing drunk scene. In his screen debut, Wilt Chamberlain is not exactly required to act, but the iconography he contributes is highly appropriate in this context, as he's one of the few people on earth who could conceivably represent a genuine threat to Conan.

Mako and Douglas emerge, strongly in limited roles, and if Walter's comic relief is less than scintillating, Grace Jones just about runs off with the picture. Coming on like a full-fledged star from her very first scene, singer throws herself into her wild woman role with complete abandon, fighting with frenzied enthusiasm and delivering lines with nifty innuendo. Preview audience howled its approval of her every move.

Lensed in Mexico, film also offers up numerous visual pleasures, from stark landscapes studded with visual effects such as a giant elephant skeleton or a glass castle in the middle of a lake, to a Hall of Mirrors sequence. Pier Luigi Basile's art direction is outstanding, and John Bloomfield's costume design may be even better.

Lenser Jack Cardiff contributes a customary fine job, and Fleischer's sharp, but not frantic, pacing, combined with Frank J. Urioste's ace editing, moves the film along at a perfect pace.

Coming in the wake of the ratings brouhaha over "Indiana Jones" and "Gremlins," this "Conan" may be in for some criticism concerning violence. Original was rated R, and bloody action has been toned down somewhat here, a highly appropriate move given the nature of the project. Plenty of people are stabbed, decapitated, sliced up and the like, but none of it is very explicit, and high degree of unreality takes the edge off any disturbing impact. —*Cart.*

Escape From Womens Prison
(ITALIAN-COLOR)

A 21st Century Distribution release presented by Dick Randall. A Cinema 13 Cooperativia production. Produced by Aldo Baglietta, Bruno Fontana. Directed by Conrad Bruegel. Features entire cast. Screenplay, Giovanni Brusatori, Fontana; camera (Staco color), Nino Celeste; editor, Pier Luigi Leonardi; music, Pippo Caruso; production manager, Roberto Carlevari; assistant director, Donatelli Batti. Reviewed at Criterion Center 5 theater, N.Y., June 22, 1984. (No MPAA Rating.) Running time: **83 MINS.**

With: Lilli Carati (Monica), Ines Pellegrini (Terry), Zora Keer, Franco Ferrer, Patrizia Fonara, Ada Poletta, Angela Doria.

"Escape From Womens Prison" is an obnoxious Italian exploitation film, lensed in 1978 under the more grammatically acceptable title "Breakout From A Women's Prison." Despite these comeon titles, film is not a prison picture, as it opens with the women already escaped.

Poorly developed story is sort of a femme variation on "The Desperate Hours:" four women bust out of an Italian prison and take hostage a bus filled with a women's tennis team, hiding out in the mansion of a local judge, who is also taken prisoner. The women subject their prisoners to forced lesbian sex acts and even ludicrously force a captured man to have sex with one of them, until the police lay siege to the house, infighting occurs among the foursome and a handy nihilistic ending is delivered.

Ludicrous film is laughable in spots, especially when the role reversals are carried to extremes. Filmmakers include timeouts for dialectical politics in the form of harangues, but crude dubbing renders such diversions meaningless. Nadir of the film is probably when the judge beats up and rapes the leader of the escaped foursome, in a turnabout cynically inserted to make the viewer side with the underdogs against the symbols of order: she is a political terrorist while the other three women are hardened criminals.

Two prominent cast members are wasted: Lilli Carati, a beautiful and popular starlet cast as the tough terrorist, and Ines Pellegrini, an Ethiopian actress featured by Pier Paolo Pasolini in his "The Arabian Nights" and "Salo," here marking time as a wide-eyed victim.

Tech credits are poor, especially the brackish color and generally underlit visuals. —*Lor.*

Night Of The Ghouls
(B&W)

Mediocre horror opus escapes from the vaults.

A Wade Williams presentation of an Atomic Prods. production. Executive producer, Major J.C. Foxworthy. Produced and directed by Edward D. Wood Jr. Screenplay, Wood; camera (b&w), William C. Thompson; editing supervision, Donald A. Davis; music supervision, Gordon Zahler; assistant director, Ronnie Ashcroft; art direction, Kathleen O'Hara Everett; costumes, Mickey Meyers. Reviewed on The Nostalgia Merchant vidcassette, N.Y., June 15, 1984. (No MPAA Rating.) Running time: **60 MINS.**

Criswell	Himself
Dr. Acula	Kenne Duncan
Lt. Dan Bradford	"Duke" Moore
Lobo	Tor Johnson
Sheila, white ghost	Valda Hansen
Capt. Robbins	John Carpenter
Kelton	Paul Marco
Crandel	Don Nagel
Darmoor	Bus Osborne

Also with: Jeannie Stevens (black ghost), Harvey B. Lynn (Henry), Margaret Mason (Martha), Clay Stone (young man), Marcelle Hemphill (Mrs. Foster), Tony Cardoza (Tony).

"Night Of The Ghouls" is a below-average B-picture, of interest since it is the 1959-lensed, theatrically unreleased sequel to the cult favorite "Plan 9 From Outer Space." After 25 years in the vaults, it now is available to home-video fans and is reviewed here for the record.

Narrated by Criswell, the late psychic who used to appear annually on Johnny Carson's "Tonight Show" with his "I predict" routine, "Ghouls" has the L.A. County Sheriff's office investigating strange goings-on at the old house on Willows Lake. Years before (a vague reference to "Plan 9"), a mad doctor had made monsters there, but everything was destroyed by lightning.

Currently, the fake swami Dr. Acula (Kenne Duncan, wearing a turban) is swindling gullible folks by pretending to reanimate dead relatives. Unbeknownst to him, Acula's fake powers were strong enough to actually bring back the dead, who, in the lore of this film, have 12 hours of freedom to walk on Earth every 13 years when called forth by a spirit medium. Led by Criswell, the undead attack, and Acula's assistant Sheila (Valda Hansen) is lured by a black-veiled ghost (Jeannie Stevens) to join them in the grave, as a real ghost rather than a fake one. Despite its title, film is not about ghouls, since there is no grave-robbing per se, nor any of the currently fashionable (in horror films) feeding on corpses.

The late filmmaker Edward D. Wood Jr. displays his usual minimal approach, utilizing barely-dressed sets (typically a blank wall with a lonely looking picture hanging on it), poor acting tending towards swishiness in the supporting cast and an assortment of silly sound effects and cheapo insert shots which lamely try to inject humor into a dull script.

For those who place Wood's work on a pedestal, beyond the usual critical standards, it should be recalled that both earlier directors (e.g., Edgar Ulmer) and contempo ones (John Sayles, Wayne Wang) have crafted effective pictures on similarly minuscule budgets, with no apologies necessary. —*Lor.*

Tibet — A Buddhist Trilogy
(BRITISH-DOCU-COLOR-16m)

A production of Thread Cross Films, Bath (U.K.), presented in U.S. by Orient Films, Orient Foundation, Seattle, Wash. Produced by David Lascelles. Written and directed by Graham Coleman. Camera (color, 16m), Lascelles; lighting and still photography, Michael Warr; sound, Robin Broadbank; editor, Pip Heywood; special effects, Rank Post Production; translations, Glenn Mullin; narration in English subtitles to Tibetan voices. Reviewed at Van Dam Theater, N.Y., June 8, 1984. Running time: **231 MINS.**

An independent production costing $125,000, financed in part by the Arts Council of Great Britain, and circulated to European festivals via the National Panel for Film Festivals, this four-hour trilogy has participated in festivals and has played theatrically in Los Angeles, San Francisco and Seattle.

Part One is closest to a conventional documentary, exploring a commune in India in which refugee Buddhist families and monks from Tibet live in harmonious primitive socialism, oddly combining Maoist with Gandhian principles. We see monks in both their private moments and in vigorous theological dispute, also gardening and painting murals. A carpet-making cooperative provides support for the commune, which is run by democratic decision-making with universal education, unprecedented in Tibetan culture.

Forced to flee from Tibet in 1959, when invading Chinese expelled him and his followers, H.H. the XIV Dalai Lama continues his reign from exile in India, a benign and popular figure. "When we look at it from this point of view," says the Dalai Lama, "the invasion of Tibet has been something good for the Tibetans, providing we can follow the right path in the future." His attitude is tolerant and forgiving, when one remembers that thousands of Buddhist monasteries and libraries were destroyed by the Chinese.

Part Two is set in a breathtaking North India mountainscape and uses a-day-in-the-life format to show the eternal rhythmic tilling of the fields by poor farmers and the daily monastic work and rituals of the Buddhist monks in their monastery above. This part ends with the ceremonial cremation of a brother, shot in close detail, but oddly with no horror even as we see the flesh sizzle, as by now we recognize the Buddhist concepts of impermanence, non-attachment, and acceptance of death.

Shot in a remote Buddhist monastery in Nepal, Part Three is relentless, a long traditional Tantric ritual of protection for the female deity Tara, condensed from five to two hours. The camera merely records everything, watching, without judgment, emphasizing the hands and faces of the worshipping monks. The only sound is the droning of chants and tinkling of bells for two hours. English subtitles render the Tibetan, sparingly but with surprising sophistication. No narration intrudes on the film to explain these strange visuals, which cast a spell. By now we are converts, or we are mesmerized or stultified or (doubtlessly a few of us) asleep. Quite rightly, to preserve its authenticity, the producers have shot this Buddhist performance in long takes, and without Western voice-over interpretations.

Pic is devoid of explanatory narration except for brief and austere comments in early scenes.

Already visible in a smattering of U.S. art cinemas, "Tibet" can doubtlessly exhibit further, in other cities and in the universities. Public television seems a likely prospect as well. —*Hitch.*

Paul Cadmus — Enfant Terrible At Eighty
(DOCU-COLOR-16m)

A Fairfield U. presentation, Executive Producer, Stephen L. Weber. Directed and produced by David Sutherland. Camera (color), Joe Seamans; editor, Michael Colonna; art director, George Petrakes; research and associate director, Phillip Eliasoph. Major funding provided by the Sara Roby Foundation, Forbes Inc., and Maupintours. Reviewed at the American Film Festival, N.Y., May 31, '84. Running time: **64 MINS.**

This film is a biographical portrait of octogenarian Paul Cadmus, since 1979 Academician at the National Academy of Design, and among the few survivors of the American Scene school of painting of the 1930s Great Depression era.

Cadmus at 80 is portrayed in his studio in Connecticut. Perhaps self-portrait is a more accurate term to describe this film, as Cadmus was involved closely in the daily production mechanics of making it

The film was pre-planned, story-boarded and rehearsed, including a 12-hour study film in Super 8m as a rough draft, before shooting began in 16m.

Cadmus' comments on life, his art, painting techniques, fellow artists, etc., were first audio-recorded, transcribed, compressed, then fed back to him on big cue-cards as a succinct distillation of his philosophy. Cadmus, on camera, then spoke his own thoughts naturally, rephrasing them spontaneously but with exactitude.

Similarly, some action in "Cadmus" was staged, in order best to bring out the Cadmus lifestyle and work habits. The result is a controlled and tight film, packed with information, that preserves an aspect of American cultural history.

The artist emerges as a striking personality, mild in manner while strong in character, cool and poised, handsome with full white hair, erect and alert in manner,

Cadmus is renowned for his studies of male nudes. His work includes, but is not limited to, updatings of Bosch, Breughel and Signorelli, adapted to modern locales such as YMCA locker rooms, parks and beaches, as satirical observations of the working-class in joyless pursuit of pleasure. "People's noses should be rubbed in all sorts of things — both pleasant and unpleasant," states Cadmus.

Debut of the "Cadmus" film coincides with publication of "Paul Cadmus," hardcover by Lincoln Kerstein, founding director of the New York City Ballet and brother-in-law of Cadmus. — *Hitch.*

Bachelor Party
(COLOR)

Lame teen comedy.

Hollywood, June 25.

A 20th Century Fox release of a Raju and Sharad Patel Presentation of an Aspect Ratio/Twin Continental production. Produced by Ron Moler and Bob Israel. Executive producer, Joe Roth. Directed by Neal Israel. Features entire cast. Screenplay, Neal Israel, Pat Proft from a story by Bob Israel. Camera (color), Hal Trussell; editor, Tom Walls; music, Robert Folk; art direction, Kevin Colin and Martin Price; set design, Mark Billerman; sound, Susumu Tokunow; costumes, Jeanne Mascia, Buddy R. Cone; special effects, Reel Effects, Inc., Martin Becker, Frank Inez, Ken Sher; associate producer, Gautam Das; assistant director, Jerry Sobul. Reviewed at Egyptian Theatre, Westwood, Calif., June 25, 1984. (MPAA rating: R.) Running time: **106 MINS.**

Rick Gassko	Tom Hanks
Debbie Thompson	Tawny Kitaen
Jay O'Neill	Adrian Zmed
Mr. Thompson	George Grizzard
Mrs. Thompson	Barbara Stuart
Cole Whittier	Robert Prescott

"Bachelor Party" is another case of adults giving the kids what they think they want. Picture is too contrived to capture the craziness it strains for and ultimately becomes offensive rather than funny. There may be a niche in the summer boxoffice for this kind of film, but chances are it won't last very long.

Filled with cartoon caricatures instead of people, "Bachelor Party" is built around a pre-nuptial celebration that seems to bring the worst out in people. Against the objections of her parents, Rick (Tom Hanks) is marrying Debbie (Tawny Kitaen) and Rick's friends decide to throw a bash for their departing pal.

While the film offers predictable shenanigans, such as a donkey snorting cocaine and an attempted suicide with an electric razor, main reason to see the pic is for Hanks' performance. Recalling a younger Bill Murray, he's all over the place, practically spilling off the screen with an over-abundance of energy.

As a carefree school bus driver, Hanks almost makes the film worth watching and several of the early scenes are promising. Kibbutzing with the nun-in-charge (Florence Schauffler), Hanks picks up his load of Catholic school boys, drives away from the school and all hell breaks loose on the bus with Hanks the ringleader.

Hanks also knows his way around in the kitchen, using a blow torch to cook meatballs and making a mean potato salad which consists of lettuce and whole potatoes. Unfortunately writers Neal Israel and Pat Proft surround Hanks with a bunch of run-of-the mill friends who act if they have never seen a woman before. Sexual attitudes throughout have scarcely gotten out of grade school with an underlying meanness and hostility towards women.

Tawny Kitaen as the girlfriend is the one woman who gets slightly better treatment, but even then her role amounts to little more than looking good (which she does) and smiling. Her main concern in life is that boyfriend Hanks will be unfaithful at his bachelor party. Possibility prompts a series of set pieces including a girl's night out at Chippendales, and Kitaen dressing up as a prostitute to spy on her would-be hubby.

In a silly subplot, Debbie's bourgeois father (George Grizzard) hires former boyfriend (Robert Prescott) to win back his daughter to path of righteousness. A pat preppie meanie, Prescott is hardly an apt target for Hank's hostility. Hanks is constantly baiting Grizzard's middle class respectability, but that too doesn't prove to be a very original or amusing contest.

Film does manage to collect a weird assortment of people for the party scene but visual look overall is cluttered and photography is consistently dark and occasionally out of focus. Director Neal Israel seems to have little touch for this kind of scatterlogical comedy.

"Bachelor Party" is proof that tastelessness requires taste and an inspired lunacy and spontaneity which, with the exception of Hanks' performance, is sorely lacking here. —*Jagr.*

My Friends Need Killing
(COLOR)

Dismal Vietnam vet as psycho B-picture.

A Nick Felix release of a Cinema Producers Center presentation. An LMN Prods. production in association with Mulmac Inc. Produced by Jack Marshall. Written and directed by Paul Leder. Features entire cast. Camera (color), Parker Bartlett; editor, Leder; music, Mark Bucci; sound, Anthony Coogan, Reuben Leder; techincal director, Steve Marlowe; San Francisco production

manager, Jack Pierce. Reviewed at 42d St. Selwyn theater, N.Y., June 19, 1984. (MPAA Rating: R.) Running time: **72 MINS.**
Gene Kline ....Greg Mullavey
Laura Kline ....Meredith MacRae
Gil ....Clayton Wilcox
Susan ....Carolyn Ames
Audrey ....Elaine Partnow
Also with: Roger Cruz, Laurie Burton, Bill Michael, Savannah Bently, Eric Morris.

For the seekers after bad movies (in the currently inverted value system among cultists), "My Friends Need Killing" is worth the hunt. Filmed in 1976 and only marginally released, this truly crummy B-picture not only belongs to the dismal genre of Vietnam aftershock but also manages to bungle its premise.

Greg Mullavey is seriously miscast as Gene Kline, a Vietnam vet who wakes up from a nightmare one morning and decides to visit several members of his platoon to kill them for misdeeds (slaughtering Vietnamese villagers) in which we was an unwilling participant. Kline behaves in the manner of a schizophrenic, though his underlying rationality is in question due to Mullavey's inconsistent performance.

Cheaply-made programmer (its 72-minute running time recalls the old Bs, but is still tedious to experience) is padded out with crosscutting back home during Kline's deadly visits, as his wife Laura (Meredith MacRae) worries about him and gets assistance from a local shrink in trying to analyze hubbie's disappearance and to find him.

Writer-director Paul Leder was obviously in a bad mood when he concocted this project, and film proves quite distasteful as Mullavey assumes the "sadistic" personalities of his "friends," torturing them and bloodily killing them.

"My Friends' " only virtue is its wacky conclusion, one of the goofiest twists imaginable. After stabbing his last target victim, the mean former sergeant, Kline confronts the sergeant's mucho pregnant wife with a knife — jumpcut to Laura and shrink rushing to the rescue. When the dynamic duo arrives, there is blood all over the bed, but believe it or not, Kline (who has already killed another friend's innocent wife after raping her) has delivered the baby, which is nestled in its happy mother's arms. Kline has hung himself in the backyard — end of movie.

Tech credits are poor, with very rough editing by the director. Leder's other credits include such junkers as "I Dismember Mama" and the inept 3-D opus "A-P-E" (aka "Attack Of The Giant Horny Gorilla").—*Lor.*

Ghost In The Noonday Sun
(BRITISH-COLOR)

Winnipeg, June 13.
A Tyburn Entertainment presentation of a World Film Services Cavalcado Films production. Produced by Gareth Wigan, executive producers, Thomas Clyde, Ben Kadish. Directed by Peter Medak. Screenplay by Evan Jones, additional dialog, Spike Milligan. Camera (color), Michael Reed; production design, John Howell; editor, Roy Lovejoy; music, Dennis King. Reviewed on First Choice (pay tv), Winnipeg, June 13, 1984. Running time: **93 MINS.**
Dick Scratcher ....Peter Sellers
Pierre Rodriguez.......Anthony Franciosa
Bill Bombay ....Spike Milligan
Bay of Algiers ....Clive Revill
Ras Mohammed ....Peter Boyle
Jeremiah ....Richard Willis
Parsely-Frack ....James Villiers
Kate ....Rosemary Leach
Abdullah ....Thomas Baptise
Hamdon...................Murray Melvin
Giacomo ....Bill Kerr

"Ghost In The Noonday Sun" arrives as a genuine surprise release (albeit on pay tv) not because of its quality but rather because of its very existence. The 1973 production which stars Peter Sellers had been believed by many key artistic contributors to be incomplete and unfinishable. However, perhaps because of pay's hunger for product, it now surfaces as an unpretentious comedy of modest merits unlikely to stir cries of revival or mainstream playoff.

Tale centers on Sellers, a cook on a pirate ship who murders his Arabian captain, becoming the sole possessor of the actual location where hidden booty has been buried. With this knowledge he assumes an uneasy command of the ship. His second, played by Anthony Franciosa, is just itching to take over but the seemingly crude, bumbling chef proves quite adept at keeping the secret and maintaining command.

Story evolves into a family oriented vein when the crew take on young Richard Willis, eager to learn buccaneering ways. Sellers believes he has mystical contact with the dead captain, so the act is partly insurance and partly as a refresher for his dimming memory. Franciosa also befriends the lad along with his accomplice Thomas Baptiste.

The original script by Evan Jones appears to be quite thin on tension and one imagines both Sellers and Spike Milligan (credited with additional dialog), as a rival bumbling pirate chief, camping and padding the antics during filming. Their efforts produce lengthy and tedious slapstick tracts.

("Ghost" was made independently for Columbia Pictures release, but was shelved a decade ago by the studio, reportedly due to the "too parochial" nature of its comic content. Originally Ernest Tidyman was credited with co-scripting, though he is no longer listed on screen. According to a recent biography of Sellers, the late comedian fired director Peter Medak during the filming, with Milligan taking over direction, but this has not been confirmed. — *Ed.*)

Filmed in Cyprus, the location work is quite handsome and remaining technical credits outshine the artistic components of the picture. Acting is largely uninspired and frantic with the story finally running out of steam rather than reaching a satisfying conclusion. — *Klad.*

Sydney Film Fest

Hotel New York
(U.S.-COLOR/B&W-16m)

Sydney, June 17.
An International Showcase release of a Zanzibar production. Produced by Jackie Raynal, Sid Geffen. Directed and written by Raynal. Dialog, Gary Indiana; camera (color/b&w, 16m), Babette Mangolte; editor, Suzanne Fenn; music, Lee Erwin; sound, Helene Kaplan. Reviewed at Sydney Film Festival, June 15, 1984. Running time: **84 MINS.**
Loulou ....Jackie Raynal
Sid ....Sid Geffen
Gary ....Gary Indiana
Landlord ....John Erdman
Director........................Tom Bucle
With: Jonathan Rosenbaum, Erroll Morris.

A funny, low-budget 16m featurette about a French femme filmmaker and her misadventures in Manhattan. Loulou is invited to show one of her films at the Museum of Modern Art and, despite the ponderously silly questions she gets from the miniscule audience after the screening (questions on structualism and feminism and whether the urinating scene was real or faked), she decides she likes New York and will stay for a while.

She takes a bed in an apartment shared by two bizarre women, paying exorbitant rent to a grasping landlord, and gets a job cutting a gay porn movie whose pretentious director talks like Samuel Fuller. And she meets, and marries, a middleaged film buyer for CBS who hates her film but thinks she can help his kinky son.

Manhattan film scene insiders should get plenty of yocks from this economically made and quite winning item. Director Jackie Raynal (a former cutter from Rohmer, Chabrol and Godard) plays Loulou herself with a wide-eyed innocence that works perfectly. Her real-life husband, Sid Geffen, also has lotsa fun with his role, especially in a sequence where he goes off looking for a younger lover for his wife and winds up in the Carnegie Hall Cinema watching Buster Keaton in "Sherlock Junior." (Geffen owns that theater in real life.)

"Hotel New York" is an exceedingly modest affair, but could find an audience if billed with another quality item of similar length. It ends on one of the brightest sightgags since the Broadway night opening of Jack Buchanan's show literally laid an egg in Vincente Minnelli's "The Band Wagon.
—*Strat.*

I'll Be Home For Christmas
(AUSTRALIAN-DOCU-COLOR)

Sydney, June 17.
A Brian McKenzie production. Produced by John Cruthers. Directed by Brian McKenzie. Camera (color), McKenzie; sound, Cruthers. Reviewed at Sydney Film Festival, June 16, 1984. Running time: **132 MINS.**

A painstaking documentary, shot over a two-year period, about a group of homeless, alcoholic men who live out in the parks and streets of Melbourne. Filmmaker Brian McKenzie, who previously made the award-winning short documentary "Winter's Harvest," obviously achieved considerable rapport with his subjects, and concentrates on five of them. But his film is way overlong at over two hours, and by his apparent inability to be more ruthless with his material, he has reduced the impact of the subject.

The men, of all ages and some with obviously good education, spend their time sitting around either in the open or in special hostels, drinking cheap wine and talking and arguing among themselves. Since their speech is often slurred, and the park where they meet is close to a main road, it's often very hard to pick up what they're saying. McKenzie eschews any commentary or titles, which might have bridged some gaps and helped him to edit the film more tightly: but the structure seems odd anyway, since we have to wait until the very end to discover the moving story that a youthful Irishman came out to Australia to be best man at his brother's wedding and stayed on, after his mother died, in this tragic and wasteful environment.

McKenzie, who says his film was "exploratory" in the beginning, originally planned a 50-minuter, and would have achieved much more if he'd disciplined himself to retain that length. Almost thirty years ago, Lionel Rogosin's "On The Bowery," a similar film in many ways to this one, managed to tell its tragic story in a little over an hour.

Visually the film is good, though as noted sound recording is not always up to snuff. — *Strat.*

Kemira: Diary Of A Strike
(AUSTRALIAN-DOCU-COLOR)

Sydney, June 17.
A Kemira Production. Produced and directed by Tom Zubrycki. Camera (color), Fabio Cavadino; editor, Gil Scrine; music,

Elizabeth Drake. Reviewed at Sydney Film Festival, June 10, 1984. Running time: 61 MINS.

"Kemira: Diary Of A Strike" ranks as one of the best documentaries ever made in Australia. It's theme is familiar enough: coverage of a bitterly disputed coal-miners' strike of two years ago centered on the N.S.W. South Coast industrial city of Wollongong.

The giant BHP company, Australia's largest, controlled coal-mines in the area has announced that 400 miners will lose their jobs — this despite the company having earned a staggering overall $300,-000,000 profit the previous year. Some 31 miners stage a sit-in deep below the surface, and their union battles in court for a moratorium on the sackings.

The miners' stand caught the attention of the nation when two trainloads of angry miners journey to the capital, Canberra, to protest outside Parliament House. When the then Prime Minister, Malcolm Fraser, refused to see a delegation, the miners literally smashed their way through glass doors into the Parliament building, a momentous event captured on prime-time tv. Soon after an apparent settlement was reached and the miners ended their sit-in; but they had been deceived, and the sackings continued and even accelerated.

Zubrycki, a sociologist turned filmmaker with one other docu under his belt ("Waterloo," 1981) has handled the subject with both intelligence and expert craftsmanship. Not content to end his film with the strike's end, he waited until he could follow the fortunes of the key strikers months later. Result makes for an exceptionally moving human document, as he discovers marriages have broken up and families scattered as the men are mostly still jobless. This is particularly touching in the case of one couple, the Wiltshires: the plucky wife had been to the fore in support of her husband during the 16-day sit-in, and now we find her left alone to look after her kids.

Pic is unusually well photographed (Fabio Cavadino), and imaginatively edited (Gil Scrine). Zubrycki has edited it to the bone, making the story unfold with economy and drive, never dwelling on the unnecessary but always injecting a touch of humor and humanity. Another rarity for this kind of film: a musical score by Elizabeth Drake was specially commissioned, and is a major plus.

Feature documentaries have seen surprising commercial success Down Under, and this one should be no exception. Overseas festivals are definitely indicated, and even an Oscar nomination isn't out of the question on this film's quality. — Strat.

The Neverending Story
(WEST GERMAN-COLOR)

A Warner Bros. release, presented by WB and Producers Sales Organization (PSO). A Bernd Eichinger/Bernd Schaefers production of a Neue Constantin Film GmbH picture, in collaboration with Bavaria Studios and WDR. Executive producers, Mark Damon, John Hyde. Produced by Bernd Eichinger, Dieter Geissler. Directed by Wolfgang Petersen. Features entire cast. Screenplay, Petersen, Herman Weigel; from (uncredited) a novel by Michael Ende; camera, (Technovision, Eastman color; prints by Technicolor), Jost Vacano; editor, Jane Seitz; music, Klaus Doldinger, Giorgio Moroder; sound, Milan Bor, Trevor Pyke; supervising sound editor, Mike le Mare; production design-set decoration, Rolf Zehetbauer; conceptual artist, Ul de Rico; special & visual effects supervisor, Brian Johnson; special effects makeup & sculpture supervisor, Colin Arthur; assistant director, Don French; production manager, Harry Nap; art direction, Gotz Weidner, Herbert Strabel, Johann Iwan Kot; costumes, Diemut Remy; second unit camera, Franz Rath; stunt coordinator, Tony Smart; exec in charge of production, Robert Gordon Edwards; coproducer, Günther Rohrbach; associate producer, Klaus Kähler. Reviewed at Warner Bros. screening room, N.Y., June 29, 1984. (MPAA Rating: PG.) Running time: 94 MINS.

Atreyu	Noah Hathaway
Bastian	Barret Oliver
Childlike empress	Tami Stronach
Cairon	Moses Gunn
Urgl	Patricia Hayes
Engywook	Sydney Bromley
Bastian's dad	Gerald McRaney
Teeny Weeny	Deep Roy
Koreander	Thomas Hill
Night Hob	Tilo Prückner

Additional Technical Credits
Scenery, creature and costume designer, Ul de Rico; chief animatronics engineer for mechanical special effects creatures, Giuseppe Tortora; special effects engineering supervisor, Ron Hone; special effects supervisor, Philip Knowles (main unit), Barry Whitrod (2d unit); illustrator-storyboard artist, Juan Japl; scenery painter, Friedrich Thaler; senior model maker, Martin Gant; chief molder, Antonio Paramo; additional dialog-dialog coach, Robert Easton; production sound mixers, Ed Parente, Chris Price.
Cloud effects unit: supervisor, Mike White; camera, Jair Ganor. Motion control unit: supervisor, Dennis Lowe; computer consultant, Nick Pollock; optical consultant, Dennis C. Bartlett; animator, Steve Archer; model maker, Bob Ballan; optical camera, Keith Holland. Optical and matte painting unit: optical supervisor, Bruce Nicholson; matte painting supervisor, Michael Pangrazio; matte painters, Jim Danforth, Chris Evans, Caroleen Green, Frank Ordaz; supervising matte photographer, Craig Barron.

Wolfgang Petersen's "The Neverending Story" is a marvelously realized flight of pure fantasy. Already a hit in West Germany, where the underlying book by Michael Ende (who took his name off the picture) is a longstanding success, pic's domestic b.o. fate through Warner Bros. release (in a prime summer slot originally earmarked for "Supergirl" which WB ceded to Tri-Star for a yearend berth) will depend upon whether audiences are willing to sample the related fantasy genre in the record numbers with which they have attended sci-fi and horror pics over the last decade.

With the support of top German, British and U.S. technicians and artists plus a hefty $27,000,000 budget (highest for any film made outside U.S. or USSR), helmer Petersen has improved on pic's immediate forebear, Jim Henson/Frank Oz' 1982 "The Dark Crystal," by avoiding the audience turnoff of too much unrelieved strangeness. This fantasy world contains myriad unusual creatures, created by sophisticated animatronics, puppetry, makeup effects, stopmotion animation and opticals, but there are also identifiably human actors there as well as a framing story that, through deft crosscutting, keeps the whimsy rooted in everyday reality.

Film opens with a little boy, Bastian (Barret Oliver), in an unidentified U.S. town (actually lensed in Canada) lectured by his dad (tv actor Gerald McRaney) to stop daydreaming and adjust to the real world to improve his schoolwork. Bastian has been deeply affected by the death of his mother and is tormented by a trio of young bullies. Instead of going to class, he borrows a strange-looking book at a local bookstore and holes up in the school attic to read.

Book, titled "The Neverending Story," depicts a world known as Fantasia, threatened by an advancing force called The Nothing (represented by storms) which is gradually destroying all. Fantasia is a world created by the dreams and imagination of humankind on Earth, and as people lose hope and forget their dreams, turning to despair, Fantasia crumbles.

To save Fantasia, an ailing empress sends for a young warrior from among the plains people, Atreyu (Noah Hathaway) to go on a quest to find a cure for her illness (linked to Fantasia's destruction) and deliver it to her at her Ivory Tower. On his journey, Atreyu meets many fabulous creatures such as the vast Rock Biter, a flying luck dragon named Falkor (marvelously executed with both full-scale and animated techniques) that transports him in exhilarating footage reminiscent of the "Superman" features, and a vast turtle-like creature named Morla in a swamp, large as an island. He must pass through gates guarded by huge stone sphinxes, which have eyeslits that open and flash white death rays at fearful passers-by, much in the manner of the robot Gort in the sci-fi classic "The Day The Earth Stood Still."

Completing his quest, Atreyu meets the empress (Tami Stronach, a preternaturally beautiful young girl) in her tower and discovers that only a human boy can save her and Fantasia by giving her a new name. Bastian fills the bill, and pic's satisfying finale resembles classic fantasy such as E.R. Eddison's novel "Mistress Of Mistresses," as Fantasia remains only in the form of a single grain of sand in the empress' hand, and Bastian is empowered with unlimited wishes by which to recreate it from his own imagination.

Filming at and backed by Munich's Bavaria Studios, "Story" benefits from special effects technicians working overtime to create a new-look world. Mattes and bluescreen work are exemplary, suffering from none of the "blue spill" or other defects that have marred earlier classics such as the revered Alexander Korda "The Thief Of Baghdad." In terms of scale and plastic personality, the creatures are a hit, except one large wolf-like monster named Gmork that chases Atreyu and is an unscary letdown when finally viewed full-face.

Director Petersen, whose way with actors was well-demonstrated in early personal pics such as "The Consequence" (starring Jürgen Prochnow) and "Black And White Like Days And Nights" (for tv, but released here theatrically, starring Bruno Ganz), has evidenced here and in "Das Boot" an ability to rein massive-scale projects that should keep him busy in filmdom's major leagues. Shooting in direct-sound English language for the most part (creatures are of course post-synched), film has no specifically European flavor, except in the effective casting of idealized leads, such as the handsome young Hathaway and young Camilla Sparv-esque Stronach. For his part, audience surrogate Barret Oliver as Bastian conveys the wide-eyed sense of wonder that makes fantasy literature (and film) an enduring genre.

Tech credits, extending over a long list of functions, are tops.

—Lor.

Purple Rain
(COLOR)

Smashing feature debut for rock star Prince.

Hollywood, June 29.

A Warner Bros. release of a Cavallo, Ruffalo & Fargnoli production. Produced by Robert Cavallo, Joseph Ruffalo and Steven Fargnoli. Directed by Albert Magnoli. Stars Prince. Screenplay, Magnoli, William Blinn; camera (Metrocolor), Donald L. Thorin; editors, Magnoli, Ken Robinson; production manager, Mike Frankovich Jr.; costume design, Marie-France, Lewis & Vaughan; production design, Ward Preston; set decoration, Anne McCulley; makeup, Richard Arrington; sound (Dolby), Bruce Bisena; lighting technician, Leroy Bennet; music, Michel Colombier; songs by Prince, The Time, Apollonia 6, Dez Dickerson. Reviewed at Warner Hollywood Studios, L.A., June 29, 1984. (MPAA Rating: R.) Running time: 104 MINS.

The Kid	Prince
Apollonia	Apollonia Kotero
Morris	Morris Day
Mother	Olga Karlatos
Father	Clarence Williams 3d
Jerome	Jerome Benton
Billy Sparks	Billy Sparks

Playing a character rooted in his own background, and surrounded by the real-life members of his Minneapolis-based musical "family," rock star Prince makes an impressive feature film debut in "Purple Rain," a rousing contemporary addition to the classic backstage musical genre.

Pic captures the essence of the current music scene, and the colorful Prince persona, very well indeed. Fans of the performer, who went triple-platinum with his last LP and is already charted with his first single from the film's soundtrack album, will be mightily pleased. Well-shot musical sequences, doubtless intended for additional musicvid cable and tv exposure, should enhance the pic's drawing power.

Director Albert Magnoli, making his feature bow, gets a solid, appealing performance from Prince, whose sensual, somewhat androgynous features are as riveting on film as they are on a concert stage. Supporting cast, drawn from the ranks of Prince-linked musical ensembles The Time and Apollonia 6 (né Vanity 6), fill in the textures and cadences of the scene with convincing naturalness, and femme love interest Apollonia Kotero is a beautiful, winsome presence.

Custom-tailored vehicle for the rocker spins the familiar tale of a youngster who escapes the sordid confines of his family life through music, ultimately becoming the better man and musician through the love of a "good woman" and the inevitable, self-redeeming confrontation with "reality."

Musical and romantic rivalry with a competing musician, played by The Time's leader Morris Day, and "The Kid's" (Prince) struggles with his own psyche and family pressures flesh out the story with both wit and drama.

The walls The Kid has built around himself stem from his home life, where father (Clarence Williams 3d) is an alcoholic, mentally disturbed musical burn-out who beats up his wife, Greek actress Olga Karlatos, and son in blind rages. The Kid sees his father's madness infecting both his music and his own personal life, and he tries burying himself even deeper in his music, with negative results to both.

Father's attempted suicide finally triggers the emotional catharsis which frees both his music and his spirit, and pic wraps with a joyous mini-concert which should have young film-goers dancing in the aisles.

Known for his sexually graphic musical imagery, most of Prince's songs in the film are relatively tame by his standards — and while the film is R-rated, nudity and language are only briefly vivid. Violence, including the suicide scene, is totally blood-free, a bit un-realistically so in the case of the suicide.

Concert sequences, by Prince, The Time, Apollonia 6 and Dez Dickerson, are splendidly realized musicvid-type affairs, awash in purple-hued smoky lighting atmosphere and right-on camera work.

Sound mix, still to be fine-tuned this week, is very punchy.—*Kirk.*

The Guest
(SOUTH AFRICAN-COLOR)

Distributed by R M Productions, London; A Ross Devenish and Athol Fugard Production. Produced by Gerald Berman. Directed by Devenish. Screenplay, Fugard; camera (color), Rod Stewart; sound, Ian Ross; editor, Lionel Selwyn; set designer, Jeni Halliday. Reviewed at Film Forum, N.Y., June 15, 1984. (No MPAA Rating). Running time: **114 MINS.**
Eugene Marais .... Athol Fugard
Dr. A.G. Visser .... Marius Weyers
Oom Doors (the farmer) ... Gordon Vorster
Tant Corrie
  (farmer's wife) ..... Wilma Stockenstrom

"The Guest" is the second film of a trilogy written by Athol Fugard, the famed South African dramatist, and directed by Ross Devenish, also South African. The others are "Boesman And Lena" and "Marigolds In August."

In addition to his formidable credentials as a writer of his own works, Fugard has another reputation as an actor, including his role as General Jan Christian Smuts in the Attenborough "Gandhi." Fugard's non-stop virtuoso performance in "The Guest" furthers that reputation. It is a demanding role, both subtle and demonic.

Based on the career of the South African naturalist, scientist of animal behavior and poet, Eugene Marais — a morphine addict for forty-five years, until his suicide at age sixty-seven — "The Guest" was produced in 1977 from an original Fugard screenplay and won two prizes at the Locarno festival that year.

Fugard plays Marais, a tortured figure undergoing great physical and psychic pain in withdrawal from his addiction. The characterization closely parallels Fugard's own alcoholism, from which he has recovered recently. Thus "The Guest" for Fugard is intensely personal and difficult, both as its author and principal performer.

The action of "The Guest" takes place in 1926, in a single setting, an isolated farm in the Transvaal, with a small cast. It is a contest of wills — the half-mad morphine addict at war with his own addiction, at war against the good will of his doctor and against the well-meaning intentions of a pious Boer family whom he badgers and manipulates and intimidates, testing to the limit their Christian charity and forbearance.

Unlike most of Fugard's works dealing with apartheid and its hu-man wreckage, "The Guest" deals instead with pain and suffering as preconditions for human achievements and awareness. "It hurts, therefore I am " and "The man who increases knowledge, increases sorrow" are Marais aphorisms that are dramatized and enacted by Fugard in "The Guest." The Marais-Fugard composite character is a man in torment, only occasionally and partially relieved of his agony, which touches us all.

A film of enduring relevance, "The Guest" unfortunately seems limited in its U.S. commercial potential because of its bleak, uncompromising theme, little-known locale and cast, and the difficulty at times with the clarity of the South African accents. — *Hitch.*

Hot And Deadly
(COLOR)

Boring action picture, with the CIA as bogeyman.

An Arista Films release, distributed by Saturn International Pictures. An Elliot Hong Prods. production, presented by Lou George. Executive producer, George. Produced and directed by Hong. Features entire cast. Screenplay-coproducer, Larry Stamper; camera (United Color), Stephen Kim; editor, Rob "Smitty" Smith; music, Ted Ashford, Paul Fontana; assistant director, Bill Poplar; production manager, Brandock Oaha; fight coordinators, Master Bong Soo Han, Master Tiger Yang. Reviewed at 42d St. Cine Rialto 1 theater, N.Y., June 16, 1984. (MPAA Rating: R.) Running time: **90 MINS.**
Tom .... Max Thayer
Janice .... Shawn Hoskins
Trigger .... Randy Anderson
Danny .... Lenard Miller
Phillip .... Bud Cramer

Made in 1981 under the title "The Retrievers' but just recently released domestically, "Hot And Deadly" is a substandard action cheapie loaded with martial arts fighting scenes. Director Elliot Hong (credited with one t on-screen, two t's on the one-sheet poster) did a poor job here, but went on to make the pleasant Johnny Yune vehicle "They Call Me Bruce" (aka "A Fistful Of Chopsticks").

After an annoyingly fake and cryptic opening reel (the import of which is only made known much later in the film), pic develops around a nondescript hero Tom (Max Thayer), recruited by a buddy to find fortune by joining the Company (i.e., the Central Intelligence Agency). Tom is quickly disillusioned when on a mission to pickup Danny (Lenard Miller), who's written an unpublished exposé of the CIA based on his experiences as an operative, an innocent bystander is ruthlessly murdered by his partner Phillip (Bud Cramer).

Tom protects Danny's sister Janice (Shawn Hoskins) against Phillip, subverts their mission, and goes on the lam with Janice in tow.

While attempting to get the manuscript published, duo also finds time to fall in love (with a truly silly insertion of the 1960s-standard lyrical interlude montage plus balladover, right in the middle of a reel of chases) and to try and spring Danny from his captors.

Hong fails to find a tone for this nonsense, mixing some tongue-in-cheek action gags with the usual ruthless ultraviolence. Acting is flat and color quality is relentlessly ugly.—*Lor.*

The Alien Factor
(COLOR)

Okay monsters in primitive film.

A Cinemagic Visual Effects production. Written and directed by Donald M. Dohler. Features entire cast. Camera (Quality color), Britt McDonough; editors, Dohler, Dave Ellis; music-sound effects, Kenneth Walker; sound, Ellis; assistant director, Anthony Malanowski; makeup & special effects, McDonough, Larry Schlechter ("Inferbyce" insect), John Cosentino ("Zagatile" tall creature); title sequence-add'l photographic effects-stop motion animation, Ernest D. Farino. Reviewed on VCI-Media Home Entertainment vidcassette, N.Y., June 13, 1984. (No MPAA Rating.) Running time: **80 MINS.**
With: Don Leifert (Ben Zachary), Tom Griffith (Sheriff), Richard Dyszel (Mayor Wicker), Mary Martens (Edie), Richard Geiwitz (Pete), George Stover (Steven), Eleanor Herman (Mary Jane), Anne Frith (Dr. Ruth Sherman), Christopher Gummer (Clay), Don Dohler (Ernie), Dave Ellis (Rich), Johnny Walker (Rex), Tony Malnowski (Ed Miller).

"The Alien Factor" is a home-made monster picture, shot in Maryland in 1976 and syndicated to television three years later. Its theatrical potential is limited, as evidenced by it being pulled after only a one day's run this spring when it debuted at a 42d Street theater.

Extraterrestrials crashland near the city of Perry Hill and begin killing local residents (male only, as potential girl victims luckily escape in a switcheroo on the usual horror film format). Mayor Wicker (Richard Dyszel) is loath to call in outside assistance or inform the populace, as (a la "Jaws' "-much imitated plotline) he's afraid of scotching a pending amusement park complex to be built nearby.

An astronomer, Ben Zachary (Don Leifert), drops by and appoints himself monster-hunter, efficiently dispatching the critters with ingenious homemade weapons. It turns out, unsurprisingly, that Zachary is also an alien, sent from his home planet to deal with the situation.

Non-actors here, including many of the crew members doubling before the camera as per usual for a lowbudgeter, have trouble reciting the merely functional dialog, which links the picture to campy efforts of the 1950s. Visual effects vary in quality (one can literally see the tabletop onscreen when Ernest Farino's stop-motion "Leemoid" monster is superimposed over the live action) with the men-in-monster-suits providing the film's highlights. Most imaginative design is John Cosentino's seven-foot "Zagatile" creature in an outfit worn by Cosentino himself, combining disparate elements of earlier screen monsters into a distinctive new look. — *Lor.*

Mystery Mansion
(COLOR)

Mild family adventure.

A Pacific International Enterprises (PIE) release of an Independent Film Prods. production. Produced by Arthur R. Dubs. Directed-created by David E. Jackson. Features entire cast. Screenplay, Jack Duggan, Arn Wihtol, Jackson; camera (CFI color), Milas C. Hinshaw; editor, Stephen Johnson; music, William Loose, Jack K. Tillar, Marty Wereski; sound, Richard Pitstick; assistant director, Zachari Brown; production manager, William Humphrey; set design, William Holdeman. Reviewed on Media Home Entertainment vidcassette, N.Y., June 13, 1984. (MPAA Rating: PG.) Running time: **95 MINS.**

Sam	Dallas McKennon
Gene	Greg Wynne
Mary	Jane Ferguson
Susan	Randi Brown
Billy	Lindsay Bishop
Johnny	David Wagner
Fred	Barry Hostetler
Willy	Joseph D. Savery

"Mystery Mansion" is a 1983 family adventure film evidently made for the regional theatrical market, but popping up instead on vidcassettes. Mild pic, lensed in Oregon, is inoffensive and lacks excitement.

Story, with very slight supernatural overtones, concerns Susan (Randi Brown), a young girl sent on vacation with her little brother Johnny (David Wagner) to stay with their aunt and uncle (Jane Ferguson, Greg Wynne). She is haunted by recurring nightmares and memories concerning the disappearance in 1889 of her ancestor Rachel, whose family was terrorized by bank robbers. Rachel's parents were killed, but the girl's body was never found, with the events shown in intercut flashbacks.

Susan and Johnny, together with neighbor Billy (Lindsay Bishop) and a friendly old neighbor Sam (Dallas McKennon) alternate exploring for a missing treasure (linked to Rachel's ancient disappearance) with a boating trip on the river. A pair of escaped convicts terrorize everyone, but are ultimately frightened off by Sam and his fake spook effects in the title house where Rachel once lived. Happy ending ties matters up neatly, regarding the treasure, missing Rachel's whereabouts, etc.

Cast is unimpressive and film's pacing is slow, but attractive views of Oregon locations provide some diversion for an undemanding audience. —*Lor.*

Beach House
(COLOR)

Aimless teens and sand programmer, east coast style.

A New Line Cinema release. A Sidney Abusch and Galaxy Industries Prods. presentation of a Marino Amoruso production. Executive producer, Abusch. Produced by Amoruso. Directed by John Gallagher. Features entire cast. Screenplay, Gallagher, Amoruso; camera (TVC color), Peter Stein; editor, Victor Kanefsky, John Bloomgarden; music, C.P. Roth; songs, Adam Roth; sound, Ron Harris; assistant director-associate producer, Randy Ostrow. Reviewed on Thorn EMI Video cassette, N.Y., June 24, 1984. (MPAA Rating: PG.) Running time: **75 MINS.**

With: Ileana Seidel (Cecile), John Cosola (Anthony), Kathy McNeil (Cindy), Richard Duggan (Jimmy), Spence Waugh (Kathy), Paul Anderson (Baby), Adam Roth (Googie), Chris Phillips (Nudge), Jonathan Paley (Drake), Marino Amoruso (Michael), Dana Nathan (Angela), Richard Warren (Frankie), Eddie Brill (Snooky), Nancy Quinn (Janey), Regan Kennedy (Billy), Bobby Amoruso (Louie), Al Wheatley (Marty), John Amoruso (Police chief).

"Beach House" is an unsuccessful feature ill-advisedly attempting to adapt the format of west coast surf and sand frolics to the Jersey shore. Filmed in Ocean City and Avalon, N.J. several seasons back under the title "Down The Shore," tame entry was released marginally in 1982 and is currently a homevideo entry.

Slim premise derives from cultural clash as a folksy group of Italian kids from Brooklyn, headed by handsome Anthony (John Cosola) go to Ocean City for a week's vacation at the beach, staying at a house where kids from Philadelphia likewise are staying. Anthony falls for a cute blonde from Philly named Cindy (Kathy McNeil) and both groups spend their time drinking beer and dancing to rock music.

With unfunny, strictly functional dialog, and an absence of the wild gags and grossness that have made scores of teen comedies (culminating in "Porky's") work, "House" adds up to mere filler. Cast, which seems to be populated by friends and relatives of young producer Marino Amoruso, tries hard but makes little headway within the plotless format, which has no payoff, ending with a nothing dance number on the beach.

Reportedly, a plan was devised to convert the finished film into a trendy horror opus by adding footage of a mutated monster coming out of the ocean to threaten the protagonists, but even that hackneyed gimmick wouldn't have helped. No horror scenes are included in the film viewed here.
—*Lor.*

The Gods Must Be Crazy
(BOTSWANA-COLOR)

A TLC Films (subsid of 20th Century Fox) release of a C.A.T. Films presentation. Executive producer, Boet Troskie. Produced and directed by Jamie Uys. Features entire cast. Screenplay, Uys; camera (color), Uys, Buster Reynolds, Robert Lewis; editor, Uys; music, John Boshoff; sound, Chris Fellows; dialog replacement supervision, Avram D. Gold; assistant director, Kobus Kruger; sets, Wilhelm & Piet Esterhuizen; special effects, Paul Ballinger; narrator, Paddy O'Byrne. Reviewed at 68th St. Playhouse, N.Y., June 27, 1984. (MPAA Rating: PG.) Running time: **108 MINS.**

Andrew Steyn	Marius Weyers
Kate Thompson	Sandra Prinsloo
Xi	N!xau
Sam Boga	Louw Verwey
Mpudi	Michael Thys
Reverend	Jamie Uys
Jack Hind	Nic de Jager
President	Ken Gampu

Belatedly opening in America after becoming a runaway boxoffice success in many other countries such as Japan and France, "The Gods Must Be Crazy" is a tiresome comic fable by one-man-band South African filmmaker Jamie Uys, who shot the picture in Botswana (formerly Bechuanaland in the British Empire days) in 1979. Taken over by 20th Fox' TLC Films subsidiary after having test bookings last year by since-defunct Jensen Farley Pictures, "Gods" is an overlong, poorly dubbed string of sight gags which would play better to U.S. action audiences rather than the specialty sites currently earmarked by its distrib.

Uys' basic storyline, which shares thematic elements with cult pictures such as "Koyaanisqatsi" and other throwbacks to the 1960s, has Xi (N!xua), a bushman who lives deep in the Kalahari desert, setting off on a trek to destroy a Coca Cola bottle which fell from a passing airplane and by virtue of its strange usefulness as a utensil (thought to be thrown by the gods from heaven) has caused great dissension within his tribe.

Xi plans to throw the unwanted artifact of modern civilization off the edge of the world (actually a striking cliffside location revealed at film's Werner Herzog-esque climax), and in his trek encounters modern people who have trouble communicating with him. There is a clumsy, but personable, microbiologist Andrew Steyn (Marius Weyers), who is accompanying a lovely new schoolteacher from South Africa Kate Thompson (Sandra Prinsloo) to her posting in Botswana. Also interacting with them is the president (action pic vet Ken Gampu) of a Black African nation to the north, chasing communist terrorists across the countryside after they violently attempt to rub him out during a cabinet meeting. Ultimately, Xi proves to be instrumental in saving Kate's life when she and her schoolchildren are captured by the terrorists.

With the sort of crude dubbing not usually encountered outside of 42d St. grindhouses, "Gods" errs in way overdoing hackneyed comedy devices, such as a wearying use of speedup footage throughout to provoke a slapstick effect. Since stumbling hero Marius Weyers physically resembles the Aussie tv comedian Paul Hogan doing his patented Benny Hill routines, "Gods" unfortunately resembles a feature length version of such low humor tv sketches. Pic's success in France (where Jerry Lewis and the late Louis de Funès are so popular) is not surprising, nor is its conquering of unsophisticated markets, but the U.S. is another story.

Film's main virtues are its striking, widescreen visuals of unusual locations, and the sheer educational value of its narration concerning the bushmen and their folkways. In fact, the opening reel set deep in the Kalahari often resembles a low-budget, annotated version of "The Dawn Of Man" opening segment of Stanley Kubrick's "2001: A Space Odyssey," but with the attractive Botswana people playing themselves rather than having men in apesuits enacting the roles of primitives encountering new technology (here the Coke bottle).

Uys' sledgehammer direction is technically inadequate, with crude editing and other gimmickry destroying some very promising sight gags. His impulse to revivify the universally accessible silent comedy genre of Keaton, Chaplin, et al, is laudable, but his reach falls short.—*Lor.*

Bangkok Bahrain
(FRENCH-DOCU-COLOR)

Sydney, June 19.
A TF1-Amos Gitai production, in association with Channel 4 (U.K.). Written, produced, directed by Amos Gitai. Camera (color), Ronnie Katzenelson, Richard Copans; editor, Juliana Sanchez; sound, Olivier Schwab. Reviewed at Sydney Film Festival, June 18, 1984. Running time: **79 MINS.**

In introducing "Bangkok Bahrain" to the Sydney Film Fest audience, Israeli-born helmer Amos Gitai described it as part of a trilogy on "the anthropology of modernity" and the relationship between countries. In his earlier, controversial, "Field Diary," Gitai explored, with some force, the situation of Israeli occupation of Arab lands on the West Bank. New pic is far less successful.

As the title suggests, Gitai is exploring the movement of laborers from Thailand to the Persian Gulf. Men from Thai villages, seeking high wages, travel to countries such as Bahrain or Saudi Arabia to work on construction projects, while their wives often end up in Bangkok brothels. This dislocation of two societies could have been the material for an important docu, but Gitai is too indulgent and his structure too diffuse to make much impact.

Along the way we meet some strippers and bar-girls in Bangkok, plus a Thai film censor who talks about his work; and in Bahrain, a local prince shows us around his incredibly ornate and overfurnished home. But Gitai never really gets down to the nitty-gritty, and precious little is gleaned from his rather aimless filming.—*Strat.*

Cannonball Run II
(COLOR)

All-star action comedy is a shambles.

Hollywood, June 28.

A WB release of a Warner Bros./Golden Harvest presentation of an Albert Ruddy production. Produced by Ruddy. Executive producers, Raymond Chow and Andre Morgan. Directed by Hal Needham. Stars Burt Reynolds, Dom DeLuise. Screenplay, Harvey Miller, Hal Needham, Albert Ruddy, based on characters created by Brock Yates; camera (Technicolor), Nick McLean; editor, William Gordean, Carl Kress; art direction, Thomas E. Azzari; set decorator, Charles M. Graffo; music, Al Capps; sound, Darin Knight; assistant director, Tom Connors; costumes, Don Vegas, Kathy O'Rear; special effects, Philip Cory; animation, Ralph Bakshi. Reviewed at Warner Bros., June 27, 1984. (MPAA Rating: PG.) Running time: **108 MINS.**

J.J. McClure	Burt Reynolds
Victor/Chaos	Dom DeLuise
Veronica	Shirley MacLaine
Betty	Marilu Henner
Blake	Dean Martin
Fenderbaum	Sammy Davis Jr.
Jill	Susan Anton
Marcie	Catherine Bach
King	Ricardo Montalban
Homer	Jim Nabors
Don Don	Charles Nelson Reilly
Hymie	Telly Savalas
Sheik	Jamie Farr

Also with: Jack Elam, Richard Kiel, Don Knotts, Henry Silva, Frank Sinatra, Sid Caesar, Foster Brooks, Jackie Chan, Louis Nye, Tim Conway, Michael V. Gazzo, Alex Rocco, Joe Theisman, Doug McClure, Dub Taylor.

This film is so inept that the best actor in the pic is Jilly Rizzo. But he has a great advantage: he's only on screen five seconds and he doesn't have to talk. Sequel to the all-star, 1981 hit "The Cannonball Run" (that took in $35,378,000 in domestic rentals), which was in turn an embellishment of Roger Corman's "Cannonball" (1976), has, per Golden Harvest, already covered its $17,000,000 negative cost with foreign rentals and presales. Warners releases domestically but film actually opened in Japan last December. U.S. outlook, despite hot numbers of the last "Cannonball" and the huge all-star cast (at least 25 recognizable names), has to remain questionable.

A combination of cynicism and arrogance hover over the production. The film plays as if former "Cannonball" colleagues — producer Albert Ruddy, director Hal Needham and stars Burt Rey-

nolds, Dom DeLuise, Dean Martin and Sammy Davis Jr. — don't even have to make an effort anymore. It's the ole boy network kind of filmmaking, joined this time by Frank Sinatra (playing himself) and Shirley MacLaine, in terms not endearing.

Again, a bunch of crazies, in a disparate collection of cars, are engaged in racing across the country to collect a lot of money. Action on the road, as encounters with most of the supporting players resemble nothing more than day work for majority of the cast, is limited to dusty, desert highway scenes (filmed in Arizona). To depict the later momentum of the race, filmmakers engage Ralph Bakshi to show the race's progress in animation.

Execution is uninspired, laughs are hard to find, and the script by Ruddy, Needham and Harvey Miller is also difficult to locate. Reynolds' high-pitched laugh is wearing thin. Pic's frenzy, after very slow opening half hour, induces torpor. If ever there's need of a classic example to show how overcrowding a production with a ton of stars is self-destructive, this is it. —*Loyn.*

The Last Starfighter
(COLOR)

Terrific combo of human story and sci-fi effects.

Hollywood, July 6.

A Universal Pictures release. A Lorimar presentation of a Universal-Lorimar production. Produced by Gary Adelson, Edward O. Denault. Directed by Nick Castle. Features entire cast. Screenplay, Jonathan Betuel; camera (Panavision, Technicolor), King Baggot; editor, C. Timothy O'Meara; music, Craig Safan; songs, Safan & Mark Mueller; "Just One Star Beyond" song, Safan, Mueller, Melissa Manchester; sound (Dolby stereo), Jack Solomon; production design, Ron Cobb; art direction, James D. Bissell; set decoration, Linda Spheeris; set design, Beverli Egan, Jim Teegarden, Don High; costume design, Robert Fletcher; production manager, Kim C. Friese; assistant director, Brian E. Frankish; digital computer scene simulation, Digital Prods.; design makeup, Terry Smith; technical makeup, Werner Keppler, mechanical effects makeup, Lance Anderson; optical effects, Apogee Inc., Van der Veer Photo Effects, Pacific Title & Optical; visual effects coordinator, Jeffery A. Okun; stunt coordinator, Glen Wilder; Star Car built by Gene Winfield Special Projects; associate producer, John H. Whitney Jr. Reviewed at Universal Studios, L.A., July 6, 1984. (MPAA Rating: PG). Running time: **108 MINS.**

Alex Rogan	Lance Guest
Centauri	Robert Preston
Grig	Dan O'Herlihy
Maggie	Catherine Mary Stewart
Jane Rogan	Barbara Bosson
Xur	Norman Snow
Louis Rogan	Chris Hebert
Enduran	Kay E. Kuter
Lord Kril	Dan Mason

Additional Computer Animation Credits
Digital Prods.: technical executive, Gary Demos; production executive, Sherry McKenna; unit supervisor, Claudia Sumner; senior drafter-encoder, Kevin Rafferty; senior technical manager, Jim Rygiel; post production coordinator, Peggy Baker.

With "The Last Starfighter," director Nick Castle and writer Jonathan Betuel have done something so simple it's almost awe-inspiring: They've taken a very human story and accented it with sci-fi special effects, rather than the other way around. If the film attracts the crowds it should, maybe there's hope yet.

This is not to say the outer-space hardware and digital doo-dahs aren't all on a par with what's become commonplace; they are. But "Starfighter" employs them judiciously and, better still, has them anchored in a continuing earthly involvement.

Granting the fairy-tale elements, it's still impossible not to immediately like a teenager who stays home to patch up his mother's rundown, remote trailer park while the rest of the gang goes off to the lake on a lark. From then on, it's easy to share hero Lance Guest's hopes for a rewarding life.

If he gets a few breaks, like a college loan that doesn't come, Guest hopes to share his life with Catherine Mary Stewart, who is willing but afraid of the world beyond the last immobile mobile home at the corner.

Importantly, "Starfighter" has a clear fix on this mundane earthiness and art director James D. Bissell and production designer Ron Cobb have taken equal care with its detail as they do later with the dazzle of alien environments. And Castle and Betuel have inhabited the trailer park with a wonderful assortment of neighbors who remain significant throughout.

Among the few things Guest has going for him at the moment is a talent for a lone video game that was somehow dropped off at the camp when it should have been delivered to Las Vegas. And when he breaks the record for destroying alien invaders, Guest not only excites the whole trailer park, he attracts a visit from Robert Preston.

Sporting his familiar impish attitude, Preston is perfect as a somewhat ethically short-circuited headhunter from the Star League of Planets, in dire need of fighter pilots to defend the galaxy from evil invaders (with the fate of Earth also at stake).

This is not what Guest had in mind as a career but he's eventually lured by the challenge and excitement, encouraged further by lizard-like sidekick Dan O'Herlihy.

To cover the youngster's absence, Preston leaves behind a robot double, setting up a dual role for Guest which he handles beautifully. And Castle neatly keeps cutting between one Guest's adventures in outer-space and his double's difficulties in carrying out an earthly disguise, much of it very amusing.

There is never a moment that all of this doesn't seem quite possible, accompanied by plenty of building questions about what's going to happen next, though the set-up for a sequel is a bit overdone.

It's certainly no secret at the end that the producers hope to bring Guest back in more outer-space adventures, which may be well and good. But he'll only be leaving the trailer park this one time and it's the essential humanity of that which makes this edition of "The Last Starfighter" special. — *Har.*

Target Eagle
(SPANISH-MEXICAN-COLOR)

A Carlos Vasallo presentation of a Golden Sun S.A. (Spain) and Esme International (Mexico) production. Produced by Vasallo. Written and directed by Jose Antonio de la Loma. Stars Jorge Rivero, Maud Adams, George Peppard, Max von Sydow. Camera (Fotofilm color), Hans Burmann; editor, Emil Reed; music, Renato Serio, Daniele Patucchi; title song, Pino Donaggio; sound, Manuel Rincon; assistant director, Jose Ma Ochoa; car stunts, Remy Julienne; aerial and ski stunts, Kin Densalat; aerial camera, Ray Cottingham; second unit camera, Javier Garcia. Reviewed on VCL-Media Home Entertainment vidcassette, N.Y., June 30, 1984. (No MPAA Rating.) Running time: **99 MINS.**

David	Jorge Rivero
Carmen	Maud Adams
McFadden	George Peppard

Col. O'Donnell . . . . .Max von Sydow
Sam Fisher . . . . .Chuck Connors
Capt. Casado . . . . .Jose Maria Blanco
Laura . . . . .Susana Dosamantes

, "Target Eagle" is an okay international action picture, made at least a decade too late to have domestic theatrical use (in a market long since ceded to interchangeable martial arts fare). Pic played off at U.S. Spanish-language houses last year and has gone through several title changes since being lensed in Europe in 1982, such as "Playing With Death."

Jorge Rivero toplines as a most unlikely Jewish mercenary and globetrotter codenamed Eagle (because of a tattoo) hired by Spanish police chief O'Donnell (Max von Sydow, another ethnic casting stretch) to infiltrate a gang of heroin smugglers. A femme cop named Carmen (Maud Adams) is sent along to act as Eagle's contact. Punching up the storyline is a key subplot in which the same bad guys are involved in transporting uranium oxide to make plutonium bombs for sale to Libya or other aspiring nuclear powers.

With the usual stunts and modest-budget appeal to James Bond antics (with Bond veteran Maud Adams on tap), pic passes muster with lead players handling their own English-language dialog while minor players are dubbed. Credits are slightly anglicized, such as Jose Maria Blanco listed as one "Joseph White." Acting tends to be a bit wooden until an hour into the piece, when George Peppard enters as a ruthless baddie who was once in the Foreign Legion with Eagle. Using a cigaret holder prop, Peppard is very convincing as a ruthless, misogynistic villain, opening up new casting ideas for the usually heroic actor. —*Lor.*

The Muppets Take Manhattan
(COLOR)

Charming family pic from Henson and Oz.

A Tri-Star Pictures release presented by Jim Henson of a Frank Oz film, from Tri-Star/Delphi II Prods. Executive producer, Henson. Produced by David Lazer. Directed by Oz. Features entire cast. Screenplay, Oz, Tom Patchett & Jay Tarses, from story by Patchett & Tarses; camera (Technicolor; prints by Metrocolor), Robert Paynter; editor, Evan Lottman; music, Ralph Burns; songs, Jeff Moss; sound, Les Lazarowitz; production manager, Ezra Swerdlow; assistant director, Ron Bozman; production design, Stephen Hendrickson; art direction, W. Steven Graham, Paul Eads; set decoration, Bob Drumheller; Muppet special effects, Faz Fazakas; costumes, Karen Roston, Calista Hendrickson, Polly Smith; choreography, Chris Chadman; stunt coordinator, Victor Magnotta; second unit camera, Peter Norman. Reviewed at Columbia Pictures screening room, N.Y., June 20, 1984. (MPAA Rating: G.) Running time: **94 MINS.**
Kermit The Frog, Rowlf, Dr. Teeth,
   Swedish chef, Waldorf . . . . . . .Jim Henson

Miss Piggy,
   Fozzie Bear, Animal . . . . .Frank Oz
Gonzo, Chester Rat, Bill
   (frog), Zoot . . . . .Dave Goelz
Rizzo, the Rat, Gil (frog) . . .Steve Whitmire
Scooter, Statler, Janice . . . . . .Richard Hunt
Camilla, Lew Zealand,
   Floyd Pepper . . . . .Jerry Nelson
Jenny .Juliana Donald
Ronnie . . . . .Lonny Price
Pete . . . . .Louis Zorich
   Other Muppet performers: Kathryn Mullen (Jill the frog), Karen Prell (Yolanda Rat), Brian Muehl (Tatooey Rat), Bruce Edward Hall (Masterson Rat, Beth Bear), James J. Kroupa, David Rudman, Melissa Whitmire, Michael Earl Davis, Glenngo King, Tim de Haas, Cheryl Bartholow, Martin P. Robinson.
   Cameos: Dabney Coleman, John Landis, Joan Rivers, Gregory Hines, James Coco, Art Carney, Linda Lavin, Liza Minnelli, Vincent Sardi, Elliott Gould, Mayor Ed Koch, Brooke Shields, Frances Bergen.

Jim Henson and Frank Oz's "The Muppets Take Manhattan" is a genuinely fun confection of old-fashioned entertainment that will appeal to both children and their parents, weaned on Henson's syndicated tv series. Considerable challenge for fledgling distributor Tri-Star Pictures is to convince the populous teenage audience to sample this G-rated fare, virtually the only new title out this summer with that obsolete classification. Box-office performance for the third Muppets feature should fall somewhere between the $17,000,000 domestic rentals level of Universal-AFD's "The Great Muppet Caper" and the $32,000,000 earned by AFD's original "The Muppet Movie."

Just as "The Muppet Movie" limned a parallel world tale of how the Muppets came to Hollywood and achieved fame in their tv series, "Manhattan" poses a hypothetical story of Kermit the Frog penning a successful senior variety show, "Manhattan Melodies," at Danhurst College and deciding to take it to Broadway. A hit show will enable him to marry his sweetheart, Miss Piggy, but the Muppets realistically find it difficult to find backing and split up to various towns, working at odd jobs to support themselves.

Format allows director Frank Oz and script collaborators Tom Patchett and Jay Tarses to poke light fun at showbiz clichés while creating some comic tension as Kermit, working among rat (literally) waiters at a luncheonette, befriends the cute human daughter (Juliana Donald) of the immigrant owner (Louis Zorich), arousing Miss Piggy's uncontrollable jealousy. En route to the expected reuniting of the Muppet troupe and success on The Great White Way, a wonderful subplot has Kermit struck with amnesia and becoming a bigshot at an ad agency run by frogs with rhyming names, providing Henson and company with very funny ensemble frog humor.

Making atmospheric use of New York locations, film includes the sort of musical production num-

bers and honest sentimentality that differentiate Oz and Henson's approach from other contempo filmmakers. Mobility of the Muppet performances and several mass stagings involving a hundred or more puppets in simultaneous movement continue to effortlessly impress the viewer.

Among the small cast of featured actors (as opposed to Muppet players), newcomer Juliana Donald is a winning ingenue, utterly convincing in the difficult assignment of making one believe she is playing to a personage named Kermit, rather than the actuality of Jim Henson and several technicians hiding just out of frame manipulating the hardware that makes this screen magic work.

Pic boasts effective cameos (though not as potent as the first film), best of which are Joan Rivers comfortably ad libbing with Miss Piggy (played by Oz) and Dabney Coleman doing slapstick as an unscrupulous producer. John Landis, the film director for whom Oz has made several cameo appearances as an actor, returns the favor here in a cameo that is harder to identify than most. Tech credits are solid. — *Lor.*

Secret Honor
(COLOR)

Brilliant Nixon spinoff; dubious b.o. pull.

San Francisco, July 3.

A Sandcastle 5 Productions, Inc., in cooperation with the University of Michigan Department of Communications and Los Angeles Actors' Theatre release of a Robert Altman production. Executive producer, Scott Bushnell. Produced and directed by Altman. Stars Philip Baker Hall (one-person cast). Written by Donald Freed and Arnold M. Stone, from their one-act legit solo-drama; camera (Movielab color), Pierre Mignot; music, George Burt; art direction, Stephen Altman; editor, Juliet Weber; associate director, Robert Harders; sound, Bernard Hajdenberg. Reviewed at the Jack Wodell screening room, San Francisco, July 3, 1984. (No MPAA Rating.) Running time: **85 MINS.**
Richard M. Nixon . . . . .Philip Baker Hall

Admitting that "we don't know what we've got here," Robert Altman is quietly nudging "Secret Honor" into theatrical release. Filmed version of one-man play limning crack-up of a Nixon figure is Altman's third recent legit transference (following "Come Back To The 5 & Dime, Jimmy Dean, Jimmy Dean" and "Streamers"). Play opened in Los Angeles in the summer of 1983, then Altman backed its touring; lensing came during producer-director's stint as visiting professor at U. of Michigan, with students participating in the project.

Pic was first unspooled "secretly" at the Seattle film fest and now is being four-walled by Altman for one week at Frisco's Cannery art house 10 days before the start here

of the Democratic National Convention. Not even its director is certain of pic's fate after the booking here.

The monolog is described as "a fictional meditation" but emerges as a compendium of facts about the Nixon career tied to the thesis that he was the plaything of a sinister "committee" seeking global power. At heart, yarn is a putdown of the presidency and its attendant arrogance of power more than merely another knee-jerk swipe at the Nixonian litany.

Philip Baker Hall is so physically and verbally impressive in his ravings that, should pic get a commercial release in L.A., the Academy would be quite realistic in considering him for a best acting Oscar. Hall's range in stumbling through his study and wildly reminiscing into a tape recorder is text book thesping, and his resemblance to Nixon is often unsettling.

Altman ingeniously seized on the gimmick of four closed-circuit tv screens (not used in the legit version) to serve as cutaways and relief from constant one-shots of Hall. Even though Hall usually appears on the tv screens, this device serves, in a sense, to people the screen with another character. Pierre Mignot's lensing diminishes potential claustrophobia of the set and the story, and the original score by U.M. Prof. George Burt is swell embellishment.

There isn't likely a broad audience for "Secret Honor," yet pic is really too good to remain a secret for long. — *Herb.*

The Return Of Pom Pom
(HONG KONG-COLOR)

Hong Kong, June 22.

A Golden Harvest release of an A and B Film Production. Directed by Philip Chan. Stars Richard Ng, John Sham, Deanie Ip, Philip Chan, Wai Ying Hung, Tian Chun and Lam Ching Ying. (No other credits provided by producers). Reviewed at State Theatre, Hong Kong, June 21, 1984. Running time: **90 MINS.**
(Cantonese soundtrack with English subtitles)

"Pom Pom I," a low budget, domestic slapstick comedy made such a hit showing in the domestic market by grossing $HK20,000,000 this year that it is not surprising to have "The Return Of Pom Pom" rapidly on the screen to capitalize on its built-in success.

As can be expected from sequels, prequels and series pics, the followups are often disappointing as they are merely recaps and rehashes of the original idea. Such is the case of this particular Cantonese comedy.

The visual gags are predictable and the colloquial verbal jokes are already shopworn. However, it has the taste of the masses and mentality of a television addict which should guarantee its popularity with the patrons of "Pom Pom I." The scenario picks up where the original left off, with criminal investigator officer Richard Ng finally marrying longtime girlfriend. Deanie Ip, also a cop. His colleague John Sham who has the nickname Beethoven gets kicked out of his flat and decides to stay with the couple for a while.

Back in the police station, Ng and Sham are transferred to another department, headed by a hot-tempered Tian Chun who never did like the bumbling but well-intentioned detectives. Meanwhile, their former boss Philip Chan has been framed by a gangster and faces possible prosecution. The two friends decide to clear the name of their ex-boss by investigating and thus a series of complications that are better seen than described.

"The Return Of Pom Pom" has no potential abroad, except for the small Chinatown circuit as the film is strictly for the Cantonese-speaking crowd. It is an inoffensive, mechanical comedy-spoof, an unpretentious feature devoid of any intellectual content. It will likely hit the $HK20,000,000 mark locally.—*Mel.*

Style Wars
(DOCU-COLOR)

Sydney, June 20.
A Public Art Films production. Produced by Tony Silver, Henry Chalfant. Directed by Silver. Camera (color), Burleigh Wartes; editors, Sam Pollard, Mary Alfieri, Victor Kanefsky; narrator, Sam Schacht; sound, Richard Patterson, Larry Scharf. Reviewed at Sydney Film Festival, June 19, 1984. Running time: **67 MINS.**

A bright, spirited docu on what one hostile adult calls "a whole, miserable sub-culture." The subculture in question is really two: breakdancing and graffiti painting among teenagers in New York City.

Featuring such colorful characters as Seen, Kase, Crazy Legs, Frosty Freeze and Iz, pic takes the viewer into a multi-racial environment where kids relieve their boredom and frustration either via their spontaneous and extraordinary dancing, now taken up with great success in various Hollywood features, or risk arrest or injury to create often magnificent frescoes on the sides of subway trains or city walls.

Ebullience and energy (and talent) of the youngsters is contrasted with the stuffy attitudes of their elders, especially Mayor Ed Koch, who pontificates about jailing the kids and launches an expensive and seemingly rather absurd anti-graffiti campaign. Footage of railway yards heavily guarded by dogs and barbed-wire fences looks like extreme over-reaction to what, for the viewer, is a cheerful attempt to bring some life and color into a rather drab urban world.

Interestingly, Sydney Fest audience hooted with derision at a scene in which the graffiti artists present their work in a posh art gallery, and art types analyze the various creations.

"Style Wars" is made economically, well shot, tightly edited, and a lot of fun. It should certainly appeal to kids, and be an eye-opener for viewers unexposed to the whole graffiti, and breakdance phenomena.—*Strat.*

Knee Dancing
(COLOR/B&W)

Promising experimental feature.

A Doreen Ross film. Produced by Ross, Terry Logan, Paula Preston, Sara Pharo. Written and directed by Ross. Camera (color), Ted V. Mikels; editor, Ross; assistant editor-script supervisor, Preston. Reviewed on "Independent Focus," WNET-TV, N.Y., July 1, 1984. (No MPAA Rating.) Running time: **83 MINS.**
Laura Zuckerman ....Doreen Ross
Ivan, David,
Tony, Daddy................Terry Logan
Bargirl, operator, loudspeaker,
Lucky's mother ....Paula Preston
Janitor, psychiatrist,
pinballer, hippie...........Rob Thrasher
Old Laura...............Gertrude Clement
Teen Laura ....Tina Faulkner
Young girl Laura ....Chiah Tuck
Child Laura ....Roxanne Holland

"Knee Dancing" is a personal dramatic film about a young woman recalling her romantic affairs and childhood traumas. Indie filmmaker Doreen Ross shows promise has a helmer with ideas both visual and structural, but pic's 1960s-style experimental format is a barrier to audience acceptance. Made in 1982, pic has made the indie markets circuit with no domestic theatrical distribution deal, and preemed (unexpurgated and uncut) on WNET-TV's "Independent Focus" series.

Story unfolds in the form of color and black and white flashbacks detailing incidents in the life of Laura Zuckerman (Doreen Ross). Basic setting is a surrealistic white-on-white airport, with Laura hiding in the bathroom recalling her relationships. A key man in her life was Ivan (Terry Logan), a jazz pianist neighbor she met while in college and later married but could not get along with. She also has an affair with a brutish married man David Calloway (also played by Logan).

Earlier period flashbacks show her as a teen (played by Tina Faulkner) gang-raped by a gang of boys in the 1950s, and prior to that, forced to have incestuous sex by her ogre of a father (Logan again). After a long string of troubling scenes and imagery, pic ends on a hopeful note of Laura having relived all of her traumas and expressing the optimistic message of "I'll be fine."

Director Ross' experimental approach is overly gauche at times, incorporating shock effects (mainly sexual and virtually X-rated) which interfere with the gradually pieced together narrative. Her visual concepts, executed ably by cinematographer Ted V. Mikels, himself a busy indie film director, are arresting and frequently original within the stream-of-consciousness format popularized by Federico Fellini and other influential helmers in the 1960s.

Gimmick of casting lead actors in many multiple roles, definitively used by Lindsay Anderson in "O Lucky Man!" a decade ago, seems an affectation here, though lead player (and coproducer) Terry Logan delivers acceptably differentiated personae as the various men Laura has dealt with in her life. Filmmaker Ross is not well-served by casting herself in the central role, giving a perf that lacks dimension and seems overly influenced by the screen work of Ellen Burstyn. Tech credits reflect a very low budget. —*Lor.*

First Look
(DOCU-COLOR-16m)

A Riverfilms (N.Y.) production, distributed by Icarus Films (N.Y.). Produced and directed by Kavery Ditta; co-director, Veronica Selver. Camera (color, 16m), Don Lenzer, Burleigh Wartes; supervising editor, John Carter; sound editor, Alex Pfau; narrator, Harry Belafonte. Reviewed at Asian-American International Film Festival, N.Y. June 24, 1984. Running time: **60 MINS.**

"First Look" is really a double look — of Cubans at American art and of Americans at Cuban art. Separated since the Castro Revolution in 1969, Cuban and American artists have been cut off from one another, denied their usual cross-fertilization, as peripheral victims of the U.S. boycotts and embargoes against Cuba.

As spoken by Harry Belafonte, the narration is brief, factual, functional, non-inflammatory. The prolog establishes the political background, then gets onto its main topic, Cuban art.

The first half of "First Look" deals with the Cuban artists in Cuba, seen in their studios, homes and schools.

This survey demonstrates ethnic diversity, with both male and female Cuban artists of European, black and Asian origins, who show their work, extol their freedom and provide personal information. Although the aboriginal Indians of Cuba were exterminated by the colonizing Spaniards centuries ago, Indian art survives in the styles and motifs of certain artists.

The second half shows a two-months traveling Cuban art exhibit in San Francisco and New York, the first Cuban art to be seen in the U.S. since the Revolution. Widely reported in the U.S. media at the time, the fall of 1981, the exhibit is a treat and an education for the American public and for American artists who serve as hosts.

Already busy on the U.S. and foreign festival circuit, "First Look" is likely to do well in 16m distribution to colleges and art centers.
— *Hitch.*

Black Venus
(COLOR)

Okay softcore sexploitation, with a Continental flavor.

A Film Accounting Services Ltd. (Nassau, Bahamas) production, in association with Playboy Enterprises Inc. Executive producer, Harry Alan Towers. Produced by Andres Vicente Gomez, Juan Alexander, Robert Ausnit. Directed by Claude Mulot. Features entire cast. Screenplay, "Peter Welbeck" (Harry Alan Towers), from a story by Honoré de Balzac; camera (Fotofilm color), Julio Burgos, Jacques Assuerus; editor, Antonio Ramirez; musical arrangements, Gregorio G. Segura; art direction, Enrique Alarcon; production manager, Jose Mª Maldonado; production supervisor, Jesus Mª Lopez-Patiño. Reviewed on vidcassette, N.Y., June 24, 1984. (No MPAA Rating.) Running time: **95 MINS.**
Venus ....Josephine Jacqueline Jones
Armand ....Jose Antonio Ceinos
Jacques ....Emiliano Redondo
Madame Jean ....Helga Liné
Louise ....,.....Florence Guerin
Madame Lilli ....Mandy Rice-Davies
Marie.....................Karin Schubert

"Black Venus" is a classy-looking sex romance made last fall as an indie feature and already played off by its co-financer, The Playboy Channel paycabler. A throwback to the type of undressed period films that flourished before hardcore porn hurt softcore films at the boxoffice, pic has further potential in the homevideo market.

Screenplay by exec producer Harry Alan Towers (writing under his nom de film of Peter Welbeck) adapts a Balzac story about Venus (Josephine Jacqueline Jones), a beautiful model-cum-prostitute from Martinique who lives in Paris in the 19th century. She entrances a struggling young sculptor Armand (Jose Antonio Ceinos), who creates a striking full-figure art work of her called Black Venus.

As Venus moves up in local society, modeling for dress shop owner Madame Jean (Helga Liné) and shacking up as a companion to rich bisexual Madame Marie (Karin Schubert), Armand slips into a depression, unable to tolerate Venus' earning money to support them, either legitimately or by prostitution.

She later falls in love with a 17-year-old country girl in Paris, Louise (Florence Guerin) and duo seem to be living happily ever after at a Spanish villa of a fatherly art collector Jacques (Emiliano Redondo). Unfortunately, Jacques has stolen the Black Venus statue and Armand comes a-hunting, leading to a tragic conclusion.

Oldfashioned tale ironically is gussied up with handsome costumes, though its *raison d'etre* is obviously to have attractive women disrobe for the voyeur trade. Madrid-lensed settings are attractive, though a low-budget is evidenced by repetitive shots of an all-purpose single street locale.

The post-synched English language dialog is well-synched to actors articulating in English, but has that artificial, disembodied ring that is not up to domestic theatrical release standards. French helmer Claude Mulot, who made a stylish horror film starring Anny Duperey in 1969, "Blood Rose," does an okay job.

In the title role, statuesque (literally) and toothy Jones is a real looker in the Jayne Kennedy vein, though her acting ability is not demonstrated here. Vet Karin Schubert (who had a key role in the 1972 "Bluebeard" starring Richard Burton) has become a striking-looking mature actress, as has Spanish thesp Helga Liné, while Florence Guerin is a most alluring young French thesp. Actress Mandy Rice-Davies (of Profumo scandal notoriety two decades ago) is wasted in a minor role as a brothel keeper. —*Lor.*

All Of Me
(COLOR)

Wonderful supernatural comedy teaming Steve Martin and Lily Tomlin.

Hollywood, July 6.
A Universal Pictures release of a Kings Road Presentation. Produced by Stephen Friedman. Directed by Carl Reiner. Screenplay, Phil Alden Robinson, adapted by Henry Olek from novel by Ed Davis; camera (Technicolor), Richard Kline; editor, Bud Molin; music, Patrick Williams; production designer, Edward Carfagno; set decoration, Jerry Wunderlich; sound, Willie D. Burton; costumes, Ray Summers; assistant director, Albert M. Shapiro. Reviewed at Universal Screening Room, Universal City, Calif. July 6, 1984. (MPAA rating: PG-13.) Running time: **93 MINS.**
Roger Cobb ....Steve Martin
Edwina Cutwater..............Lily Tomlin
Terry Hoskins............Victoria Tennant
Peggy Schuyler ....Madolyn Smith
Prahka Lasa.............Richard Libertini
Burton Schuyler ....Dana Elcar
Tyrone Wattell ....Jason Bernard
Margo ....:....Selma Diamond

"All Of Me" is a true rarity in an era of high concept, prepackaged screen comedy — it's original. Picture should serve as a shot in the arm for the flagging screen careers of stars Steve Martin and Lily Tomlin and with the right handling should be a commercial hit though it was moved by Universal from a late summer slot to a September opening.

"All Of Me" plays more like an old fashioned screwball comedy than a contempo film, its premise of a woman dying and her soul in-

habiting half of another person's body being in the same vein as "Here Comes Mister Jordan" (remade by Warren Beatty as "Heaven Can Wait" in the 1970s). Emphasis is on human not high tech and the warmth of the characters makes the impossible plot plausible.

Also reminiscent of Preston Sturges comedy is the splendid assortment of the supporting cast. These are not pat characters, but people with faces and personalities who contribute to the action. Case in point is Selma Diamond as a secretary to Martin's overwrought attorney. Also excellent is Dana Elcar as the philandering head of the law firm to which Martin aspires to be partnered.

When he is not arranging divorce settlements for rich husbands, Roger Cobb (Martin) is a jazz guitarist and Jason Bernard, as his blind saxophonist friend Tyrone, is also a pleasure.

Martin's troubles really start on his 38th birthday when he inherits the soul of departing heiress and first-rank crank Edwina Cutwater (Tomlin). Circumstances under which this occurs, assisted by guru Prahka Lasa (Richard Libertini), are patently ridiculous, but acceptable because of the charm of the characters.

In his best comedy bits, Martin has always performed like a man possessed, someone consumed by conflicting impulses. As the receptor for Tomlin's soul, Martin is given a great opportunity to show off his superb body language. Screenwriter Phil Alden Robinson has created enough interesting situations for the Martin-Tomlin mismatch. Urinating, shaving and making love take on new proportions when a man and woman are trying to do it in the same body.

Unlike some of his other films which have relied too heavily on slapstick alone, Martin gets to play a person here with recognizable feelings. Both Martin and Tomlin change and grow because of their experience and find love at the end of the picture. It's crowd pleasing without being corny.

For all its clowning, "All Of Me" **makes some good points about taking chances and doing what you want** in life. Tomlin undergoes a transformation from a crabby sheltered poor little rich girl to a compassionate woman. It's a measure of her performance that even as a sourpuss she's irresistible.

One of the key ingredients to make this kind of comedy work is timing and much of the credit must go to director Carl Reiner who has never seemed more in control of his material. Robinson has supplied some snappy dialog and tech credits are firstrate throughout.

Music by Patrick Williams is appropriately understated and effec-

tive. Title tune, heard in snatches throughout and sung by Joe Williams in the last scene and over the final credits fits like a glove.
— *Jagr.*

Madhouse
(COLOR)

Right-to-work horror pic is a stinker.

A Chesham production. Produced by Peter Shepherd, Ovidio G. Assonitis. Directed by Assonitis. Features entire cast. Screenplay, Stephen Blakley, Robert Gandus, Shepherd, Assonitis; camera (Technovision, Technicolor), Roberto D'Ettore Piazzoli; editor, Angelo Curi; music, Riz Ortolani; sound, Piero Fondi; art direction, Stefano Paltrinieri; production manager, Roger Salvadori; assistant director, Stratton Leopold; exec in charge of production, Jacques Goyard. Reviewed on VCL-Media Home Entertainment vidcassette, N.Y., June 30, 1984. (No MPAA Rating.) Running time: **92 MINS.**
With: Trish Everly (Julia), Michael Macrae (Sam), Dennis Robertson (Father James), Morgan Hart (Helen), Allison Biggers (Mary), Edith Ivey (Samantha), Jerry Fujikawa (Mr. Kimura), Richard Baker (Sacha), Don Devendorf (Principal).

"Madhouse" is a below-average horror opus, representing a technical but not an artistic improvement for Italian filmmaker Ovidio G. Assonitis. Lensed in a right-to-work state (Savannah, Ga.) in 1980 in English with a U.S. cast, pic has less of a foreign flavor than the auteur's prior pics such as the 1974 "Beyond The Door" or "Tentacles." Its title continues to cause confusion, originally monickered "Scared To Death" (a name lost to William Malone's horror opus that year), later altered to "I Will Scare You To Death," "There was Once A Child" and finally "Madhouse," last named being identical to a British 1974 American International Pictures release starring Vincent Price.

Derivative story concerns the five days before Julia's (Trish Everly) birthday, as her twin sister Mary (Allison Biggers), suffering from skin eruptions and other disfigurements, escapes from a hospital ward, at which time gruesome murders begin. The real killer, whose identity is telegraphed stupidly early-on, is revealed after an hour, and the whole mess ends in a bloodbath.

With no nudity and unimaginative violence, pic has nothing to offer for genre fans and, not surprisingly, failed to get a domestic distribution pickup, appearing on vidcassette instead. Cast is weak and tech credits average. Failing to resolve the tensions or issues raised, Assonitis cops out pretentiously with an end title quote from George Bernard Shaw: "Life differs from the play only in this ... it has no plot, all is vague, desultory, unconnected until the curtain drops with the mystery unsolved ..." Unfortunately, too many filmmakers are content with mirroring life's banalities rather than creat-

ing an artifice or representation that used to be termed a photoplay. Assonitis didn't even understand what Shaw meant.—*Lor.*

Room 666
(DOCU-COLOR-16m)

Incisive experimental docu from Wim Wenders.

A Gray City release and production. Produced by Chris Sievernich. Directed by Wim Wenders. Camera (color, 16m), Agnes Godard; editor, Chantal De Vismer; music, Jurgen Knieper; sound, Jean Paul Mugel. Reviewed at screening, N.Y., July 3, 1984. (No MPAA Rating). Running time: **45 MINS.**
With Jean-Luc Godard, Steven Spielberg, Michelangelo Antonioni, Werner Herzog, Rainer Werner Fassbinder, Paul Morrissey, Susan Seidelman, Robert Kramer, Ana Carolina, Romain Goupil, Mike de Leon, Mahroun Bagdadi, Monte Hellman, Wim Wenders, Noel Simsolo, voice of Yilmaz Güney.

Filmed at the Cannes Film Festival in 1982, and shown in a shorter version on French tv that year, Wim Wenders' "Room 666" is an informative and often funny cinematic stunt. Pic is scheduled for release later this year in tandem with a longer docu by Wenders about Japanese director Yasujiro Ozu, tentatively titled "Tokyo."

Wenders' concept, simple yet novel, was to present a written list of questions on the future of cinema and its relationship to tv technology to a large number of film directors attending the Cannes Fest, admit them one by one to a hotel room, containing a tape recorder and a pre-set 16m camera holding one reel of film. With identical compositional framing, each participant is seated in a chair by a window, with a tv set playing next to him, its sound turned off, and permitted complete freedom (other than the time constraint imposed by the single film reel) to present a monolog on camera.

Wenders edited the results, comically choking off the dullards with a sudden blackout (minimalist filmmaking's equivalent to vaudeville tradition's "Get the hook!") and adding a brief, poetic framing story to put everything into context: a shot of an aged cedar standing by the highway, a tree old enough to have seen the entire history of photography, and cinema as well.

Stars of this format emerge as Jean-Luc Godard and Steven Spielberg, each one arguably the key director of, respectively, the '60s and the current decade. Godard addresses with both provocative insight and considerable background the issue of technological change, noting how tv esthetics are replacing cinematic standards. Stating that advertising-supported tv has adopted the representational and editing methods of Sergei Eisenstein's classic "Potemkin," he notes that one-minute "Potemkin''-style commercials work at that length because if they were longer they would face the problem of having to tell the truth about the product involved.

Addressing the tendency toward super-production films and tv miniseries, he notes that in the U.S. the trend is to make just one important film, in which the title is the key, not the content. The idea, per Godard, is to shoot less film but *release* more of it (e.g., the miniseries version) than in the past.

Spielberg begins his discourse with some self-serving analysis of how the inflation of film budgets has affected him since the ''Jaws'' days, but segues into several pointed and valuable observations concerning the trends for studio heads to approve only pictures made ''to please everybody,'' leaving no room for personal films. His seg is definitely an interesting one and takes ''Room 666'' out of the esoteric territory earmarked by most of the other helmers, each speaking for the most part in his or her native tongue (with English subtitles).

Werner Herzog is the only subject to direct himself actively, turning off the nearby tv set, taking off his shoes and socks, and even dramatically ending his spot by placing a couch pillow over the camera lens. He has no fear of tv, which he compares to a jukebox; ''tv never absorbs you like a movie; you can't turn off the cinema,'' is the subtitled translation. The late Rainer Werner Fassbinder, looking and sounding weary, defends personal and national-identity cinema against the current trend towards sensationalism in films.

Other speakers often resemble their film output, with Michelangelo Antonioni pacing around the room and asking numerous unanswerable questions, repeatedly stressing what he doesn't know; Monte Hellman proving to be as laconic as one of his pictures; and Paul Morrissey, acting glib yet sincere in his favoring of tv over filmmaking since the ''intrusion of the director does not exist on tv'' and because tv stresses people and characters.

Unfortunately, the third-world directors on view seem hung up with their own parochial issues and do not address Wenders' philosophical questions. The two women included, New York's Susan Seidelman and Brazil's Ana Carolina, seem a bit flustered and inarticulate, adding little to the discourse.

Minimalist in design, Wenders' experimental concept works and whets one's appetite for similar projects with other subjects. Failing to obtain the rights to use Bernard Herrmann's soundtrack music from ''North By Northwest'' in the background (reportedly, they

would have cost more than the filming did), he opted for outtracks by Jurgen Knieper, leftover from his scores of other Wenders features. They add a note of melancholy to link ''Room 666'' with the director's more familiar fictional odysseys. — *Lor.*

Laughterhouse
(BRITISH-COLOR)

London, July 2.
A Film Four International presentation of a Greenpoint Film. Produced by Ann Scott. Executive producer, Simon Relph. Directed by Richard Eyre. Stars Ian Holm, Penelope Wilton, Bill Owen. Screenplay, Brian Glover; camera (color), Clive Tickner; music, Dominic Muldowney; editor, David Martin; art direction, Jamie Leonard; sound, Dave Stephenson; production manager, Paul Sparrow. Reviewed at the Bijou Theatre, London, 2 July 1984. (BBFC certificate, PG.) Running time: 92 MINS.
Ben Singleton .... Ian Holm
Alice Singleton .... Penelope Wilton
Emma Singleton .... Emma Tague
Amos Lintott .... Bill Owen
Hubert .... Richard Hope
Tristram .... Aran Bell
Sylvia .... Rosemary Martin
Howard .... Stephen Moore
David Wolmer .... Patrick Drury

Despite its title, a pun on slaughter house, ''Laughterhouse'' is an amusing romp. The plot about an English eccentric and a flock of geese has curiosity value but insufficient dramatic thrust to secure wide appeal.

Pic plots the response of Ben Singleton, an academic-turned-goose farmer who's on the edge of financial and emotional collapse due to a strike of his workers following an accident on the farm. Balked in his attempts to terminate and package his 500 geese, Ben sets out on foot with his flock along the 100-mile road from Suffolk to London.

Judicious script editing could have focused the plot on the obstacles to Ben's anachronistic endeavor. Instead, the audience is led down the byways of such issues as media bias, trade unionism and family conflicts.

A dominant issue is the contrast between Ben's gentle farming methods and depersonalized factory farming. However, the question's never asked whether the dumb creatures prefer their protracted walk to the usual quick death.

Film also comments on the way in which the media circus turns the marchers from objects of ribald mockery to heroic telly stars by distorting Ben's message.

Serious efforts are made to develop dramatic tension as a counter to the prevailing nostalgia for simpler times. Director Richard Eyre gives a bleak slant to the constant bickering between husband, wife and daughter. He also attempts to conjure up the wild west through the characterization of farm hand Hubert and Dominic Muldowney's score, but ''Laugh-

terhouse,'' is the loser in any comparison to the western genre.

Most of the cast are allotted fairly one-dimensional roles. Ian Holm is persuasive as the neurotic Ben, ready to respond to any setback with a violent outburst or melodramatic whining. Penelope Wilton as his wife rarely lets drop her sourpuss look. By contrast, there's some comic pleasure on offer from the double act of Bill Owen and Richard Hope as farm workers.

Lenser Clive Tickner makes dramatic use of the East England landscapes swathed in the mist of early February. —*Japa.*

Filmex

Observations Under The Volcano
(DOCU-COLOR-16m)

Hollywood, July 3.
A Christian Blackwood Prods. release. Produced, directed, photographed by Blackwood. Editor, Ned Bastille; sound, Pam Katz; writings of Malcolm Lowry read by John Hurt. Features John Huston, Albert Finney, Jacqueline Bisset, Anthony Andrews, Michael Fitzgerald, Wieland SchulzKeil, Guy Gallo, Gabriel Figueroa, Tom Shaw, Emilio Fernandez, Rene Ruiz. Reviewed at Filmex, L.A., July 3, 1984. No MPAA rating. Running time: 82 MINS.

This is a well-observed behind-the-scenes look at the making of John Huston's serious, ambitious film version of Malcolm Lowry's ''Under The Volcano.'' Prolific documentarian Christian Blackwood, who distributes his own productions, was on Mexican locations with the film company around Cuernavaca during much of the lensing, and effectively demonstrates how numerous scenes were developed from the run-through and camera set-up stages through to completion.

A worthy effort on all counts, pic is a natural for fests and specialized venues, and down the line at revival houses would serve as an excellent companion piece to the Huston film.

More colorful than most on-location docus, due to the splendid native backgrounds and the impressive array of talent assembled around Huston, film quickly introduces the key participants, and a context is provided through John Hurt's readings of brief passages from Lowry prose and letters.

''Under The Volcano'' was shot, in August-October, 1983, in chronological order, and Blackwood's work presents selected sequences along the way, beginning with the Red Cross Ball, and proceeding to Jacqueline Bisset's return to her husband, played by Albert Finney, the bullfight, and the climactic scene in a cantina-whorehouse.

With seeming free reign on the set, Blackwood makes the viewer privy to Huston's conversations

with his actors, cameraman and writer. Director congratulates his collaborators profusely for jobs well done, is gentle in making suggestions or asking for something to be done over again, and at all times seems concerned with the task at hand.

Making use of excellent coverage, Blackwood sets up each scene, and on several occasions has been provided with actual finished sequences (where not, still photographs are employed), so that one can observe the fruits of all the effort of the cast and crew.

Interspersed throughout are brief interviews with creative personnel. Exec producer Michael Fitzgerald explains that Huston had absolute authority, and perhaps greater freedom than he ever enjoyed before, in the making of ''Under The Volcano;'' coproducer Wieland SchulzKeil sketches in some of the complicated production history. Finney likens his approach to his role to completing a jigsaw puzzle, and screenwriter Guy Gallo gives an idea of how he tackled his enormous task.

Docu offers particular pleasures to Huston buffs, as the 77-year-old director can be seen riding about in his personalized golf cart (a la ''Winter Kills''), playing poker with his pals (winning, of course) and being swarmed over by the frisky real-life prostitutes who were engaged to populate the fictional bordello. —*Cart.*

Anne Devlin
(IRISH-COLOR)

Hollywood, July 9.
An Aeon Films production with the assistance of Bord Scannan na hEireann/Irish Film Board and the Arts Council in association with RTE. Produced by Pat Murphy, Tom Hayes. Executive producer, Hayes. Directed, screenplay by Murphy. Stars Brid Brennan. Camera (color), Thaddeus O'Sullivan; editor, Arthur Keating; music, Robert Boyle; production design, John Lucas; costume design, Consolata Boyle; assistant director, Martin O'Mally. Reviewed at the Four Star (Filmex), L.A., July 8, 1984. (No MPAA rating.) Running time: 120 MINS.
Anne Devlin .... Brid Brennan
Robert Emmet .... Bosco Hogan
Also with: Des McAleer, Gillian Hackett.

Women's neglected role in history is the subject of ''Anne Devlin,'' highly sober, overlong, intelligent independent effort from Ireland. Historical drama was made and financed in the Republic, a rare feat, and represents the second feature by coproducer and writer-director Pat Murphy after her debut with ''Maeve'' a few seasons back. Slow pace makes this a specialized item for U.S. consumption, but film deserves exposure on the fest, art and college circuits.

Murphy based her script on the diaries of the title character, imprisoned for several years by the British for her part in the unsuccessful Dublin uprising led by Irish patriot hero Robert Emmet at the beginning of the 19th century.

The context of Devlin's story is loaded with intrigue and action, but Murphy's strategy — intended to demonstrate how women are kept on the periphery of history — keeps overly dramatic events at a minimum, at least until Devlin's arrest over halfway through.

Devlin was a young farmer's daughter in County Wicklow who agreed to help at the nearby house where Emmet and his fellow revolutionaries were living underground planning their assault on Dublin. Murphy presents Emmet earnestly and sympathetically, although some ideological discussions reveal him as perhaps too tied to the monied class to be sufficiently ruthless as a rebel leader.

Opening reels are decidedly on the slow side, and Murphy's plain, even-keeled, long-take style has both pros and cons, sacrificing in dynamism and excitement what it gains in clarity and thoroughness. Film picks up in purposefulness in the climactic section, with Devlin's absolute refusal to cooperate with her English captors or to confess even her own obvious involvement in the rebellion emerging as both the most personally absolute and politically radical act witnessed in the entire picture.

Although Devlin seems essentially reactive throughout, her attitude ultimately assumes heroic proportions due to the enormous strength apparent in her passivity. In the role, Brid Brennan is proud, unsentimental and triumphant, even though ending reveals she had to pay for her courageous stance in a sadly unexpected manner.

Other performances are solid, and tech credits, particularly Thaddeus O'Sullivan's fine lensing and Robert Boyle's classical-sounding score, are expert.

Points Murphy is making here all hold water, but often come clear well before she finishes treating them dramatically. Tighter telling would have sharpened this worthwhile effort even further.
—*Cart.*

duBEAT-e-o
(COLOR)

Self-styled cult musical for fringe audiences.

Hollywood, July 3.

An II-Z-II presentation of a duBEAT-e-o production. Produced, directed by Alan Sacks. Executive producers, Harold Halpern, Robert Zane. Screenplay, Mark Sheffler, based on an idea by Sacks. Narration written and performed by El Duce, Alan & friends. Camera (United color), Robert Primes; still photography, Ed Colver; editors, Linda Folk, Joe Zappala; music supervisors, Doug Moody, Phillip Raves; 'The Mentors' film by

Gary Pressman; art direction, George DiCaprio; set decoration, Ned Parsons, Virginia Parsons; costumer, Sunny Chayes; sound, John Nicholas; titles and graphics, Gary Panter; associate producer, Harry Landers; associate producer, post production, Eric Barrett; assistant director, Rick Nathanson. Reviewed at the Walt Disney Studios (Filmex), Burbank, July 3, 1984. (No MPAA rating.) Running time: 85 MINS.
duBEAT-e-o .... Ray Sharkey
Joan Jett .... Joan Jett
Benny .... Derf Scratch
Sharon .... Nora Gaye
Hendricks .... Len Lesser
Benny's nightmare .... Johanna Went
duBEAT-e-o's
  nightmare .... Linda (Texas) Jones

Seldom has a film seemed so intent on proclaiming itself a cult item as "duBEAT-e-o." Intentionally abrasive, self-consciously hip and off-puttingly "inside" in its humor and references, pic is as hermetic as its film director leading character and offers little to viewers who are not part of the hardcore punk scene depicted within. Technically superior despite an apparent low budget, film will undoubtedly emerge in some way in its self-appointed cult arena of midnight shows and fringe venues, but its market will remain limited to that.

Made by "Welcome Back Kotter" creator and telefilm producer Alan Sacks, "duBEAT-e-o" is a visual and aural hodgepodge of elements, including "current" dramatic scenes, concert footage, dream (or nightmare) sequences, black-and-white and color still photographs, tv monitor replays and laid-over comic narration by unseen spectators. It can't be denied that something is always going on to bombard the senses, but what it all adds up to is yet another allegory of the egotistical "genius" versus the venal moneymen.

Eponymous character, played with throttles-out relish by Ray Sharkey, is a real creep who's been working on a punk rockumentary featuring singer Joan Jett. Crippled financier Len Lesser decides to crack the whip and gives Sharkey 31 hours to finish the film, or else join him in the wheelchair brigade.

A crazed and tyrannical sweet-talker, Sharkey yanks his film editor Derf Scratch (of the punk group Fear) out of the gutter and ultimately chains him to the editing machine, then sort of supervises the final cut while lingering in the hay with luscious blonde bimbo Nora Gaye.

Much of the editing room banter and arguing rings true, but the thrust of the concoction is so repellent, and its justification so elusive, that the persistent temptation is just to tune out. Intercut still photographs by Ed Colver focus almost exclusively on violence, death and urban blight, and combination of these with some graphic sex-oriented shots would probably put pic into the X-rated category.

Aesthetically, with its heavy doses of callous violence and flashy technique, film recalls "A Clockwork Orange" from time to time. But its focus is too narrow for pic to lay claim to much seriousness, and humorous commentary scores only haphazardly. Like its unexplained title, "duBEAT-e-o" is a singular oddity. — *Cart.*

Sösken Pa Guds Jord
(Children Of The Earth)
(NORWEGIAN-COLOR)

Hollywood, June 14.

An A.S. Elan-Film production. Production team, Fred Sassebo, Kirsten Bryhni, Merete Lindstad, Arve Figenschow. Directed, written by Laila Mikkelsen, based on the novel by Arvid Hanssen. Dialog advisor, Hanssen. Camera (color), Rolv Haan; editor, Sassebo; music, Pete Knutsen; sets, Torunn Muller, Harald Egede-Nissen, Jan Bertheussen; costumes, Tone Skjelfjord; sound, Sassebo, Thomas Samuelsson, Jan Lindvik. Reviewed at the MGM Studios (Filmex), Culver City, June 13, 1984. (No MPAA rating). Running time: 80 MINS.
Margit .... Anneli Marian Drecker
Baela .... Torgils Moe
Krestian .... Odd Furoy
Simon .... Frode Rasmussen
Johanna .... Randi Koch
Arild .... Ernst Rune Huemer
Magdalena .... Eli Doseth
Vavva .... Merete Moen

A muted tale of petty feuds, looming violence and a girl's strange youth tinged with allegorical religious significance, "Children Of The Earth" alternates between the compelling and the obscure. Femme Norwegian writer-director Laila Mikkelson has managed to rivet attention on some very marginal characters in the forbidding wastes of northern Norway, but it remains difficult to see what she's driving at. A decent festival item, pic has little commercial potential.

Sporting strains of the Cain and Abel story and the Hatfield and McCoy battle in equal measure, drama is loaded with the unpleasant intrigues of small minds. Living on the barren coastline during the summer of 24-hour sunlight, drunkard Simon and his nearby brother Krestian have an ongoing feud. Local village idiot Baela, a dinosaur of a man, shuttles between them, and is in due time offered a sum of money by Simon to kill Krestian.

Witnessing all of this is pubescent orphan Margit, who lives with Krestian and his wife. She spends a great deal of time with Baela, is pursued by a consumptive teenager, is advised in religious matters by a saintly neighbor woman and is forced to care for a horrible wretch of a woman in her barn.

The threat of imminent violence hangs over everything, as the characters are forever lurching around carrying lethal tools such as axes, saws and scythes. Despite the fact that these seem to be highly religious people (erratic English subtitles seem to be trying

to equate the archaic language with Quakerese), they behave with increasing nastiness to each other, and the notion of "love thy neighbor" has obviously been banished.

Compounding the obscurity of the tale is Mikkelsen's intermittently awkward direction, which makes the action even harder to grasp. Film has been nicely shot by Rolv Haan and well scored by Pete Knutsen.

Much of the credit for making the pic absorbing has to go to Torgils Moe, who plays the giant simpleton Baela. Following any command obediently, almost making the earth quake with his every step and displaying awesome physical strength, character is developed into a fascinating creation by Moe, and considerable suspense is generated by the question of whether or not his nascent sense of morality will prevent him from carrying out Simon's order to kill Krestian.

Other performances are low-keyed. — *Cart.*

Notes From Under The Volcano
(DOCU-COLOR-16m)

Hollywood, June 30.

Produced, directed, photographed, narrated by Gary Conklin. Editor, Michael Toshiyuki Uno; sound, Daniel Camhi. Features John Huston, Guy Gallo, Albert Finney, Jacqueline Bisset, Anthony Andrews, James Villiers, Arturo Sarabia. Reviewed at The Burbank Studios (Filmex), Burbank, June 30, 1984. No MPAA rating. Running time: 54 MINS.

While continuously interesting, this documentary on the production of "Under The Volcano" represents a rather random sampling of on-the-set events. Filmmaker Gary Conklin has caught some valuable glimpses into John Huston's relaxed but firm working methods, but pic could have done with more varied material and more information, and comes in second to Christian Blackwood's more definitive docu on the same subject. Film looks to have been cut for hour-slot public and international tv length, and would work well there.

Curiously, both Conklin and Blackwood were present during some of the same stretches of shooting in Mexico, such as the opening and closing sequences, and the bullfight. Conklin also features material from a crucial patio drinking session among Albert Finney, Jacqueline Bisset and Anthony Andrews, and provides a decent look at how the thesps built up to their performances.

In good form in an interview, Huston amusingly expounds on his theory that, since World War II, God has not been "in strict attendance" and has been away, "probably on a bat." His legend is also furthered by hilarious scenes of hookers acting very physical with the director on the Farolito set, in shots similar but different from those in Blackwood's docu.

It's all amiable and engaging enough, but film suffers from its defiantly unanalytical approach. Conklin doesn't even suggest why "Under The Volcano" was such a difficult undertaking or how it was pulled together. Filmmaker had the chance to investigate many nuts and bolts matters in his narration, but simply doesn't seem inclined to go into depth or detail. Instead, he seems content just to show the filming of several sequences, which is of moderate, but limited, interest. —*Cart.*

Maria De Mi Corazon
(Mary My Dearest)
(MEXICAN-COLOR)

Hollywood, July 6.
An Azteca Films release. Produced by Manuel Barbachano Ponce, Universidad Veracruzana & Asociados. Executive producer, Hernan Littin. Directed by Jaime Humberto Hermosillo. Stars Hector Bonilla, Maria Rojo. Screenplay, Gabriel García Marquez, Hermosillo; camera (color), Angel Goded; editor, Gerardo Pardo; music, Joaquin Gutierrez Heras; art direction, Lucero Issac; sound, Fernando Camara; assistant directors, Miguel Angel Velazquez, Miguel Mora. Reviewed at the Azteca Screening Room (Filmex), L.A., July 5, 1984. (No MPAA rating). Running time: **100 MINS.**
Hector Roldan . . . . Hector Bonilla
Maria Torres Lopez . . . . Maria Rojo
Dr. Murguia . . . . Ana Ofelia Murguia
Blanquita . . . . Blanca Torres
Ward 3 Nurse . . . . Xochitl
Pepe . . . . Jose Alonso

Quite intriguing if not fully achieved, "Maria De Mi Corazon" is an independently produced Mexican feature which, like much of the Latin American literary new wave, effectively mixes fantasy elements with sociological observation. Influence in this case is understandable, given the presence of Gabriel Garcia Marquez as coscreenwriter, and result is one of the most serious and effective recent Mexican films to reach the U.S., presented at L.A. Filmex.

This 10th feature by young director Jaime Humberto Hermosillo was made in 1981-1982 under a cooperative arrangement with the U. of Vera Cruz film department and the Union of Independent Actors. Pic was lensed in 16m and blown up to 35m, numerous prominent thesps donated their services and Hermosillo and Marquez waived any production salaries, all in an attempt to help forge a new alternative to the normal commercial industry methods in Mexico.

Contempo tale is radically divided into two parts. A petty thief, Hector, returns from his nocturnal rounds to find a former flame, Maria, in his apartment clothed in a wedding dress. After sobbing out her story of having been left at the altar, she startlingly pulls off some magic tricks, such as drawing milk from the water tap, and the two shortly resume their affair, but more passionately than ever.

Convincing him to abandon his life of crime, Maria and Hector marry, and she trains him so he can join her in a professional magic act, dubbed "Lotario & Euridice." Just as their star begins to rise, however, Maria's van breaks down in the middle of nowhere, she hitches a ride on a bus and is dropped off with the rest of the weird-looking female passengers in a loony bin.

Naturally, the more she insists she's not crazy, the harder the authorities clamp down on her. Thinking she's just ditched him, Hector gives up on Maria, and second half of the drama details the tragic trajectory of the lovers tripped up by fate.

The fiery couple on the burn-out trail resemble many a doomed twosome in American *films noir,* and their physical attraction to one another is conveyed convincingly. Monkey-wrench Marquez and Hermosillo have thrown into the story midway is genuinely surprising, although the denouement is not, as the second half unfolds rather too predictably.

Although the time frame for the events of act two is impossible to gauge, it seems Hector abandons the idea of ever finding Maria all too easily, and neither does much to try to circumvent the trap they've fallen into.

Murky look of the film also puts a damper on things, as blowup from 16m robs images of their clarity and luster. Some visual correlatives to the dramatic flights of fancy would have helped substantially.

Nevertheless, this is a generally commendable effort, one that at least shows real promise for the burgeoning indie scene in Mexico. Performances by Hector Bonilla and Maria Rojo are strong. —*Cart.*

La Scarlatine
(Scarlet Fever)
(FRENCH-COLOR)

Hollywood, June 18.
A UGC (France) release. Produced by Paul Claudon. Directed, written by Gabriel Aghion. Camera (color), Robert Alazraki; editor, Christine Lack; music, Gabriel Yared; costumes, Elizabeth Tavernier; assistant director, Pierre Wallon. Reviewed at The Burbank Studios (Filmex), Burbank, June 17, 1984. (No MPAA rating.) Running time: **97 MINS.**
Features: Brigitte Fossey, Stéphane Audran, Christophe Malavoy, Hito Jaulmes.

Lightweight but amiable enough, "La Scarlatine" ("Scarlet Fever") is a French domestic comedy about a young boy raised in a nutty family dominated by three generations of single women. Rather frivolous goings-on are given some buoyancy by a group of energetic, talented performers, but pic is primarily a commercial diversion spiked with modest human insights. American preem was at Filmex, and film is not entirely without some domestic b.o. possibilities.

The Palazzi family, which somehow gets by financially in a rundown but spacious Paris apartment, consists of Grandma Genia, imprisoned in Egypt during World War II as a fascist and who notices everything that happens since she never seems to sleep; middle aged Minon (Stéphane Audran), a loud mouthed snoop who can't forget the good life they used to enjoy in the Middle East; attractive blonde Nicole (Brigitte Fossey); her curious son Roger, and a couple of ne'er-do-well brothers of the women.

Roger is full of mischief and ideas, is more interested in dating one of his school teachers than learning from her, and in fact takes her out on "dates." But everything falls to pieces when Nicole takes up with Jacques, a handsome fellow whose presence throws Minon into a frenzy.

As the romance escalates and the domestic turmoil mounts, pic takes a turn from comedy into fairly serious drama, an eventuality heightened by Roger's dismissal from school and old Genia's death.

It's all fluffy stuff, given a lining of substance through the feeling of possibly real events recalled by the writer-director and the efforts of the thesps. As usual, Fossey is a delight to watch, and the youngster playing Roger is very cute and always watchable.

Gabriel Yared's score in nice and simple, and contributions by all hands is creditably enthusiastic in a modest cause. —*Cart.*

Supergirl
(BRITISH-COLOR)

Okay gender variation in the superhero fantasy series.

Sydney, July 16.
A Tri-Star Pictures release (U.S.), Hoyts Distributors (Australia) release of an Artistry Ltd. production for Cantharus Productions. Executive producer, Ilya Salkind. Produced by Timothy Burrill. Directed by Jeannot Szwarc. Stars Faye Dunaway, Helen Slater, Peter O'Toole, Screenplay, David Odell (based on the comic-strip character); camera (Panavision, color), Alan Hume; editor, Malcolm Cooke; production design, Richard Macdonald; art director, Terry Ackland-Snow; music, Jerry Goldsmith; costumes, Emma Porteus; sound, Derek Ball, Robin Gregory; special visual effects, Derek Meddings; optical visual effects, Roy Field; travelling matte consultant, Dennis Bartlett; set decorator, Peter Young; special effects supervisor, John Evans; flying effects specialist, Bob Harman; models, Terry Reed, Roy Scott, Robert Scott, Tadeusz Krzanowski, Rodger Shaw; stunt coordinator, Alf Joint; process background camera, Ronald Goodman; visual effects camera, Paul Wilson; video coordinator, Chris Warren; matte artists, Doug Ferris, Charles Stoneham. Reviewed at Hoyts Entertainment Center, Sydney, July 15, 1984. (No MPAA Rating.) Running time: **114 MINS.**
Selena . . . . Faye Dunaway
Kara/Linda Lee . . . . Helen Slater
Zaltar . . . . Peter O'Toole
Nigel . . . . Peter Cook
Bianca . . . . Brenda Vaccaro
Alura . . . . Mia Farrow
Zor-El . . . . Simon Ward
Jimmy Olsen . . . . Marc McClure
Ethan . . . . Hart Bochner
Lucy Lane . . . . Maureen Teefy
Mr. Danvers . . . . David Healy
Pretty Young Lady . . . . . . Sandra Dickinson
Myra . . . . Robyn Mandell
Muffy . . . . Jenifer Landor
Mrs. Murray . . . . Diana Ricardo
Billy-Jo . . . . Nancy Lippold
Betsy . . . . Sonya Leite
Jodie . . . . Virginia Greig
Nancy . . . . Nancy Wood

Latest in the Salkinds' "Super..." series rings the sexual changes to tap new mileage out of the comic-strip fantasy genre. Result is an intermittently enjoyable spectacle, which might perform better than the last "Superman" outing if the kids identify with the winsome teenage heroine.

Supergirl is Kara, Superman's cousin, who journeys from her home on the planet of Argo to Earth to recover the missing Omegahedron Stone, life-force of her world, which has fallen into the clutches of the evil Selena (Faye Dunaway), a power-hungry sorceress. Landing near an exclusive boarding school for young ladies, Kara quickly adopts the name of Linda Lee and finds herself rooming with Lois Lane's kid sister, Lucy (Maureen Teefy). (Superman himself appears only as a poster on Lucy's bedroom wall: a throwaway line indicates the Man of Steel was off visiting another galaxy at the time, thus saving the producers the expense of ringing in Christopher Reeve, or indeed virtually any other player from the male side of the series, save for Marc McClure, who repeats as Jimmy Olsen). Rest of pic represents a struggle between the good of Supergirl and the evil of Selena with, as is usually the case, evil being a lot more fun.

Dunaway has a ball as Selena, giving a campy portrayal akin to her impersonation of Joan Crawford in "Mommie Dearest." "Never send a man to do a woman's job," she mutters angrily at one point, and her enjoyably over-the-top handling of the part could merit cult attention. She's ably backed by Brenda Vaccaro as her incredulous assistant, and Peter Cook as her sometime lover and math teacher at the girls' school.

Peter O'Toole makes a modest impression as Supergirl's friend and mentor, while Mia Farrow and Simon Ward, as her parents, have even smaller roles than Susannah York and Marlon Brando in the first "Superman." Back on Earth, Maureen Teefy is sweet as Lucy, and Hart Bochner registers as Ethan, a groundsman who catches Dunaway's lustful eye, but who falls in love with Supergirl instead. As for Helen Slater, she's a find: blond as Supergirl, dark-haired as Linda Lee, she's an appealing young heroine in either guise and should be heard from in the future.

David Odell's screenplay is filled with witty lines and enjoyable characters, but Jeannot Szwarc's direction is rather flat, partly compensated for by some of the performances.

There are some well-staged effects highlights, notably a violent storm that threatens the school and the climax in which Supergirl and Selena confront each other in the latter's mountain-top castle, though here the satanic monster conjured up by Selena to fight on her behalf would have been more suited to a horror film than to this kind of light-hearted comic-strip entertainment. Flying scenes are generally up to par, though at least once a wire is plainly to be seen.

Production is generally very handsome, with a big nod to production designer Richard Macdonald, whose sets are great.

Pic was caught at an advertised sneak where reaction seemed most favorable, with some sections of the audience responding particularly to Dunaway's bitchy villainess. Initial biz should be very brisk, when pic debuts Stateside via Tri-Star at Christmas. —*Strat.*

Splatter University
(COLOR)

Lowgrade terror pic.

A Troma Team release, presented by Michael Herz and Lloyd Kaufman. An Aquifilm Co. picture; a Richard W. Haines production. Produced by Haines, John Michaels. Directed by Haines. Features entire cast. Screenplay, Haines, Michaels, Michael Cunningham; camera (color), Fred Cohen, Jim Grib; editor, Haines; music, Chris Burke; songs, The Pedestrians; sound, Nick Delia; contributing writer-associate producer, Miljan Peter Ilich; special makeup effects, Amodio Giordano; add'l makeup effects, Ralph Cordero, Ron Darrier; creative consultants, Kaufman, Dan Lowenthal. Reviewed at Criterion Center 5 theater, N.Y., July 13, 1984. (MPAA Rating: R.) Running time: **77 MINS.**
Julie Parker . . . . Francine Forbes
Father Janson/
    Daniel Grayham . . . . Dick Biel
Cathy . . . . Cathy Lacommare
Mark . . . . Ric Randig
    Also with: Joanna Mihalakis, George Seminara, Dan Eaton, Sal Lumetta, Denise Texeira, John Michaels, Richard W. Haines.

"Splatter University" is a negligible stalk and slash terror picture, offering too little (and coming too late in the cycle) to impress hardened horror fans. Its proposed title "Splatter U." would have been more fun.

Amateur effort, boasting poorly timed color and the look of a grainy blowup from 16m, has a minimal plot concerning a new teacher at a N.Y. school, St. Trinians College (presumably a lame reference to the hit British comedy film series by Frank Launder and Sidney Gilliat).

Julie Parker (Francine Forbes) is the new sociology prof; her predecessor was killed last semester and not surprisingly, the body count among her students and colleagues is high during the pic's abbreviated 77-minute duration.

Characterizations are nonexistent, with the padding of subplots (between knife murders) revolving around Catholic issues, presented in poor taste. Identity of the killer is telegraphed very early.

Editor turned helmer Richard W. Haines evidences little prowess with actors or action sequences here. The gore is strictly of a bloodletting nature, extraneous enough to offend traditionalists and not creative enough to interest horror cultists. — *Lor.*

Revenge Of The Nerds
(COLOR)

Comedy on social rejects for simple minds. Shoulda been called 'Animal Mouse.'

Hollywood, July 16.
A 20th Century Fox release of an Interscope Communications production. Produced by Ted Field and Peter Samuelson. Coproducer, Peter MacGregor Scott. Exec producers David Obst and Peter Bart. Directed by Jeff Kanew. Features entire cast. Screenplay, Steve Zacharias, Jeff Buhai, from story by Tim Metcalfe, Miguel Tejada-Flores, Zacharias, Buhai; camera (Deluxe color), King Baggot; editor, Alan Balsam; music, Thomas Newman; production designer, James L. Schoppe; set decorator, Frank Lombardo; costume supervisor, Eddie Marks; sound, Al Overton Jr.; special effects, Joe Unsinn; choreographer, Dorain Grusman; assistant director, Terry Donnelly. Reviewed at UA Cinema 6, Marina Del Rey, July 15, 1984. (MPAA Rating: R.) Running time: **90 MINS.**
Lewis . . . . Robert Carradine
Gilbert . . . . Anthony Edwards
Stan . . . . Ted McGinley
U.N. Jefferson . . . . Bernie Casey
Betty . . . . Julia Montgomery
With: Tim Busfield, Andrew Cassese, Curtis Armstrong, Larry B. Scott, Brian Tochi, Donald Gibb, David Wohl, John Goodman.

Simple-minded romp about a group of freshmen outcasts doesn't qualify for the dean's list, but "Revenge Of The Nerds" shows more than enough smarts to deserve passing grades at the boxoffice.

From the outset, the nerds who have learned to feel more at home talking computers and grade point average, get a "real-world" education from the upperclass fraternity of jocks.

They are unceremoniously dumped from the Adams College frosh dorms by the football players, who have been rendered homeless after accidently setting fire to their own quarters.

Exiled to sleeping in cots on the men's gym the nerds are told they are welcome to stay there until basketball season begins. They suffer constant humiliations from the older students and ultimately decide to fight back.

Led by hometown buddies Lewis (Robert Carradine) and Gilbert (Anthony Edwards), the nerds rent a house that rightfully should be condemned, and in turn fix it up and form their own frat.

But breaking into the school's Greek fraternity group will not come easily because the council is chaired by Stan (Ted McGinley), a member of the jock frat, and his g.f. Betty (Julie Montgomery), enemies of the nerds and sticklers for the rules.

Ultimately, the nerds link up with the Tri-Lambda's, an all-black fraternity headed by U.N. Jefferson (Bernie Casey), and set about to turn the values of college world rightside up.

Though the picture features extensive cardboard stereotypes, belching and other bad taste humor, director Jeff Kanew moves the action swiftly to a convincing payoff.

Film contains a solid score, including Michael Jackson's "Thriller" tune and Kanew gets good perfs from his cast in typically good-guy, bad-guy roles. There's also ample t&a along the way.
—*Klyn.*

Children Of Pride
(DOCU-COLOR-16m)

Produced and distributed by Carole Langer Prods. (N.Y.). Written, directed and produced by Carole Langer. Camera (color, 16m), Robert Leacock; music, Tim Cappello; songs by Richie Havens; editor, Bob Brady. Reviewed at the American Film Festival, N.Y., May 31, 1984. Running time: **60 MINS.**

Winner of the 1984 Christopher Award as best television documentary and winner also of a blue ribbon at the recent American Film Festival, "Children Of Pride" tells the story of a Harlem man who le-

gally adopted and is caring for 18 handicapped orphans.

The story of "Children Of Pride" began 10 years ago when Kojo Odo — a black unmarried social worker, former civil-rights activist, then age 32 — came upon a one-armed eight-year-old black boy, unwanted and being shuttled about among foster homes. Odo adopted the boy, learned to calm his fears and violence, and in turn learned something about himself, his gift for reaching troubled "unadoptable" children and helping them to overcome their physical and emotional handicaps, leading to further adoptions.

Film is cinema verité in style, without narration, and without the cloying sentimentality that typifies fictional renderings of similar themes.

"Children Of Pride" was broadcast by PBS in March 1983, as part of the "Frontline" series, hosted by the late Jessica Savitch. The film is now being made available in 16m to schools, churches and social-service groups. —*Hitch.*

Deadline
(CANADIAN-COLOR)

Cannes, May 18.
A New Image Releasing release of a Mag Enterprises and Gregory Earls presentation. Executive producer, Gregory Earls. Produced by Henry Less. Directed by Mario Azzopardi. Screenplay, Mario Azzopardi and Dick Oleksiak; camera (Panavision, color), Fred Guthe; editor, Joseph Ruff and Harvey Zlateratz; music, Dwayne Ford, Carole Pope & Rough Trade. Reviewed at Olympia 7, Cannes Film Festival (Market), May 18, 1984. (No MPAA Rating.) Running time: **92 MINS.**
Steven Lessey . . . . Stephen Young
Elizabeth Lessey . . . . Sharon Masters
Sharon Lessey . . . . Cindy Hinds
Philip Lessey . . . . Phillip Leonard
David Lessey . . . . Todd Woodcroft
Burt Horowitz . . . . Marvin Goldhar
Darlene Winters . . . . Jeannie Elias

"Deadline" is a Canadian horror picture, filmed in 1979 under the title "Anatomy Of A Horror," and due for release this year by New Image Releasing.

This tortured and tortuous pic would have us believe that its hero is a famous screenwriter, master of suspense and violence. Pic itself is low on former, absurdly morbid on latter and reflects little that would make anybody famous. Lacking in imagination and immersed in moral speculation about the role of the writer in society and filmmaking, it wallows in self-consciousness worthy of a novice attempting to mask artistic pretensions in gore.

The serious professional writer protagonist is determined to write the horror pic to end all horror. Depicting writers writing is, of course, the least cinematic thing imaginable. So the narrative takes on the writer's imagination and tries to show how he loses the ability to distinguish reality from fiction. His wife has a nervous breakdown, his children despise him, he is hounded by critics and thought to be the perpetrator of gratuitous violence, all of which seems quite justified.

Stephen Young plays Steven, the writer, as if he had lost his glasses rather than his visionary literary talent.

When the writer finally lunges into orgiastic forgetfulness and wanton sex, the results get unintentionally hilarious. Although technical credits pass muster, the production is not burdened with talent. The premise of a deadline unleashing such violence smacks of the tortured artist, who has to be a known quantity or genius to raise the public's interest. Pic may be too arty even for the drive-in circuit. —*Kaja.*

Electric Dreams
(BRITISH-COLOR)

Lame computer romance.

Hollywood, July 13.

An MGM/UA Entertainment release, presented by MGM of a Virgin Pictures Ltd. production. Produced by Rusty Lemorande, Larry DeWaay. Executive producer, Richard Branson. Directed by Steve Barron. Features entire cast. Screenplay, Lemorande. Camera, (Rank color, prints by Metrocolor), Alex Thomson; editor, Peter Honess; music, Giorgio Moroder; production design, Richard Macdonald; art direction, Richard Dawking; set decoration, Peter Young; sound, Roy Charman; video supervisor, Ian Kelly; video graphics, Tim Boxell, Guy Dawson, Steve Lee; costumes, Ruth Myers; video dream created by Cucumber Studios; assistant director, Roger Simons, production manager, Craig Pinkard. Reviewed at MGM/UA screening room, L.A., July 12, 1984. (MPAA rating: PG.) Running time: **96 MINS.**
Miles . . . . Lenny Von Dohlen
Madeline . . . . Virginia Madsen
Bill . . . . Maxwell Caulfield
Voice of Edgar . . . . Bud Cort
Ryley . . . . Don Fellows
Frank . . . . Alan Polonsky

"Electric Dreams" attempts to be the first Disney film for the computer age. Billed as a computer fairytale, the picture wraps a conventional love story around a computer with a mind of its own. Result is a slight and silly story which probably won't please videogame fans or the audience searching for a good romance. Commercial prospects are modest at best.

Basic problem with the picture is its desire to humanize a computer and involve it in a love triangle. Complications of the heart do not program well. Whimsical fairytale mood too often comes out cutesy as when the principals bump shopping carts in the supermarket.

Bumbling young architect Miles (Lenny Von Dohlen) buys a computer to organize his life. Character is an updated version of the absent minded professor, not quite a nerd but socially backward.

When beautiful concert cellist Madeline (Virginia Madsen) moves into his San Francisco walkup, a most unusual courtship

starts. Miles' newly acquired computer starts rehearsing with Madeline through the walls of the house and, thinking that her neighbor is a closet musician, she starts to fall in love with him.

Miles in reality is wooing Madeline with his computer which not surprisingly starts to develop "human" feelings for the girl. Humanizing of the machine includes using Bud Cort's voice for the computer. Idea of a computer with a personality is certainly not new, having been done to great effect with HAL (voiced by Douglas Rain) in Stanley Kubrick's "2001."

Cort's personality as the computer Edgar is meddling and possessive, virtually taking over the running of Miles' life and love life. "Electric Dreams" tries to play it both ways by suggesting that computers are dangerous and can potentially control our lives and at the same time structuring the film around a dazzling collection of computer sights and sounds.

Unfortunately, computer graphics, including even an electric dream, and numerous synth-pop songs and spirited soundtrack by Giorgio Moroder, are not enough to mask the paucity and implausibility of the love story. Madeline somehow is kept out of her lover's apartment and doesn't discover his secret until late in the film.

In spite of Bud Cort's amusing turn as the voice of Edgar, computers cannot be convincingly anthropomorphized, and wide-eyed fairytale tone does not fit. Von Dohlen plays Miles as if the poor kid is in a daze, not a magical state. Only Madsen's performance begins to suggest a playfulness and infatuation that has nothing to do with computers. — *Jagr.*

'Frank' And I
(FRENCH-COLOR)

A Playboy presentation of a Gold Prods. picture, in association with Leeds Accounting Services. Executive producer, Harry Alan Towers. Produced by Wilfrid Dodd. Directed by Gérard Kikolne. Features entire cast. Screenplay, "Peter Welbeck" (Harry Alan Towers), from an anonymous Victorian erotic novel; camera (color), Gerard Loubeau; editor, uncredited; music, Marc Hillman; music conducted by J.L. Negro. No other credits available. Reviewed on vidcassette, N.Y., July 10, 1984. (No MPAA Rating.) Running time: **83 MINS.**
"Frank" . . . . Jennifer Inch
Charles Beaumont . . . . Christopher Pearson
Maude . . . . Sophie Favier
Mrs. Leslie . . . . April Hyde

" 'Frank' And I" is a rather flat (no pun intended) rendering of Victorian era romantic porno, funded by and recently broadcast by the Playboy channel and currently playing theatrically in France (via Eurogroup Films distribbery) under a title translating as "Liberated Lady."

Screenplay by exec producer Harry Alan Towers (using his *nom*

de film of Peter Welbeck) will be familiar to 1960s readers of "The Pearl" or other traditional erotica published by Grove Press, presenting a romantic tale of a young woman's adventures with inevitable "birchings" and other disciplining punctuating the usual softcore sex couplings.

A British writer, Charles Beaumont (Christopher Pearson), narrates the story as recollections, detailing his romance with a 16-year-old girl (Jennifer Inch), taken into his household as a wastrel he met on the road, disguised as a boy named Frank. "Frank" is in fact Frances, sent to London after her parents died in Canada, to stay with a Mrs. Leslie (April Hyde). Leslie turns out to be running a brothel, forcing young girls to work as her prostitutes, and Frances escaped, cutting her blond hair short and dressing as a boy.

In Beaumont's care, "Frank's" masquerade is quickly discarded and the young woman is initiated into more adult behavior by Beaumont's prior girl friend (planning to marry another man), Maude (Sophie Favier). Various minor adventures, including Beaumont beating Mrs. Leslie as punishment for her having mistreated "Frank," lead to duo finally getting married and living happily ever after.

Diminutive Jennifer Inch combines a childlike face with a very well-developed figure in the central role, but her acting is unimpressive, not helped by postsynched English dialog. Production values are low budget, with two European tours by Beaumont presented as still photos only.
—*Lor.*

C.H.U.D.
(COLOR)

Unappealing sci-fi/horror cheapie.

Hollywood, July 13.

A New World Pictures release of a Bonime Associates production. Produced by Andrew Bonime. Exec producer, Larry Abrams. Directed by Douglas Cheek. Screenplay, Parnell Hall; camera (TVC Color) Peter Stein; editor, Claire Simpson; music, Cooper Hughes; art director, Jorge Luis Toro; sound, Harry Lapham; special makeup effects, John Caglione Jr.; assistant director, Lewis Gould. Reviewed at New World Pictures screening room, L.A., July 12, 1984. (MPAA rating: R.) Running time: **110 MINS.**
George Cooper . . . . John Heard
Lauren Daniels . . . . Kim Greist
The Reverend . . . . Daniel Stern
Captain Bosch . . . . Christopher Curry
Wilson . . . . George Martin
Commissioner . . . . John Ramsey
Chief O'Brien . . . . Eddie Jones

Story of strange creatures lurking in New York City's underground passages never rises out of the gutter, making "C.H.U.D." a routine indie exploitation picture with little to offer beyond the curiosity of its initials.

Biggest problem here clearly sits above ground, where too much of Douglas Cheek's picture takes place following the opening sequence when a woman and her dog are snatched into the sewer by an unidentified ugly, presumably not of this planet.

The first half of the picture chokes on inane dialog and the establishment of the male and female leads (John Heard and Kim Greist) whose story doesn't connect with the main business at hand.

Their disappearance becomes apparent when they turn up absent for dinner at the Reverend's (Daniel Stern) soup kitchen.

Finally, the film comes to its own term — "Cannibalistic Humanoid Underground Dwelling" — the place where colonies of unfortunate souls have been living.

Plot takes an interesting turn upon the disclosure of a government coverup, when an official grudgingly admits "C.H.U.D." stands for something even more ominous.

Picture contains some unintentionally comic direction. In one scene, two officials simultaneously use the same expression to show their displeasure, making a dramatic situation laughable. For another, there's a perpetually dissatisfied distaffer in the police station who constantly rolls her eyes.

Audiences will surely roll their eyes when Greist turns from innocent fashion model to strike a pose right out of the "Conan" stories and proceeds to slice up one of the unwanted visitors late in the film.

Effects don't enhance pic's values either. The makeup on some of the supposedly grizzled characters in this low budget entry is laughable, and the creatures themselves are not terribly frightening.

Greist turns in the film's most appealing performance despite some of the silly things she is asked to do. John Heard puts in a good turn as her boyfriend while Daniel Stern performs admirably within the limited confines of the script.

New World sneak previewed the pic over the weekend. Undeniably long at 110 minutes, company said it will be making additional cuts in "C.H.U.D." before putting it into the marketplace. —*Klyn.*

The Camel Boy
(AUSTRALIAN-ANIMATED/
LIVE-COLOR)

Sydney, July 11.

An International Home Cinema release (U.S.) of a Yoram Gross Film studio presentation. Produced and directed by Gross. Features entire cast. Screenplay, Gross, John Palmer; director of animation, Ray Nowland; chief cameraman (color) and camera supervisor, Graham Sharpe; editor and post-production supervisor, Christopher Plowright; music, Bob Young. Reviewed at

Yoram Gross film studios, July 10, 1984. (Commonwealth Film Censor classification: G.) Running time: **72 MINS**.

Featuring the character voices of Barbara Frawley, Ron Haddrick, John Meillon, Robyn Moore and Michael Pate.

Latest offering by Australia's resident expert in matching animation with a live background, Yoram Gross, "The Camel Boy" is a well-spun adventure yarn pitched at the under-10 brigade.

While Gross' previous films have found a lucrative niche on cable and in the videocassette market in the U.S., with limited theatrical exposure, this one is planned for release in 25 cinemas in California next month.

Item should connect with the targeted teenies.

In part it's an affectionate look at the hardy explorers whose pioneering spirit literally put much of Australia on the map. Into the mix Gross adds a liberal dose of derringdo, a dash of gentle humor and some appealing characters — both human and animal — pitted against stock villains.

The hero, a young Arabic boy named Ali, sets off in the 1920s with his grandfather as camel drivers on an expedition across the Great Victoria desert in Western Australia. An excess of water — a violent storm — followed by a shortage of water, an attack by wild dogs, sandstorms and other mishaps force them to turn back, whereupon grandpop perishes and Ali returns to his homeland.

Story jumps 20 years ahead and focuses on Pewter, an Aussie lad who unwittingly finds himself on a ship exporting camels to the mythical Arab nation, Bhustan. On arrival, Peter is arrested on suspicion of being a spy, but luckily for him the arresting officer turns out to be Ali, and all ends well.

Some of Australia's best known actors provide the character voices, the high-standard animation is set against the impressive backdrop of some rugged Australian terrain, and Bob Young's lively score nicely enhances the moods. —*Dogo*.

East To West
(CHINESE-AMERICAN-DOCU-COLOR-16m)

Produced and distributed by Y Productions, Inc., New York. Produced by Yaping Wang and Janet Yang. Directed by Wang. Script and narration editor, Yang; camera (color, 16m), Eric Lau, Jean Tsien; sound, Ang Lee; editor, John Kwiatkowski; advisor, Shu Lea Cheang; narrator, Wang. Reviewed at Asian-American International Film Festival, N.Y., June 24, 1984. Running time: **00 MINS**.

In 1271, the Venetian merchant Marco Polo left the west for explorations in the east. Now that trek is reversed, hence the film's title "East To West." For a decade, U.S. news crews have worked over

China, but now the Chinese have come here to shoot us.

Yaping Wang, the youngest member of the prestigious Chinese Writers Assn. in Beijing, made an odyssey by Cadillac through 20 states in summer of 1982. Like Polo's "Travels," Wang has kept a diary, although his is on celluloid, a kind of Chinese "Innocents Abroad." Because several of his colleagues are American, the film is, in effect, a Chinese-American coproduction. Its original title was "Chinese Youths Discover America." Budget was $32,000.

Aside from the standard street-scenes of Manhattan, Washington, D.C., and Los Angeles, locations photographed in "East To West" included the World's Fair in Knoxville, "peasant" farms in Iowa, an Indian reservation, a Chicago slaughterhouse, a factory, a cattle ranch, a skid-row, supermarkets and an old-age home.

Throughout his journey of awe and discovery, Wang asks questions that are naive yet profound. Because Wang asks with respect, the Americans work hard for exact answers. Among them are Studs Terkel, I. M. Pei and Muhammad Ali.

The Disney Channel has an option on "East To West," and portions were shown on the CBS "Sunday Morning" of March 20, when Charles Kuralt interviewed Wang. Although theatrical possibilities of "East To West" are doubtful, the film seems a likely bet for public television, as it is charming and informative. — *Hitch*.

The Company Of Wolves
(BRITISH-COLOR)

Hollywood, July 11.

An ITC presentation of a Palace production. Produced by Chris Brown, Stephen Woolley. Executive producers, Woolley, Nik Powell. Directed by Neil Jordan. Screenplay, Angela Carter, Jordan, from the original story by Carter; camera (Rank color), Bryan Loftus; editor, Rodney Holland; music, George Fenton; production design, Anton Furst; art direction, Stuart Rose; makeup effects designer, Christopher Tucker; special effects supervisor, Alan Whibley; costume design, Elisabeth Waller; sound (Dolby), David John; effects unit director-lighting, Peter Macdonald; assistant director, Simon Hinkly. Reviewed at the Picwood (Filmex). L.A., July 10, 1984. (No MPAA rating.) Running time: **95 MINS**.
Granny .... Angela Lansbury
Father .... David Warner
Young Groom .... Stephen Rea
Mother .... Tusse Silberg
Rosaleen .... Sarah Patterson
Priest .... Graham Crowden
Bride .... Kathryn Pogson
Amorous Boy's Father .... Brian Glover
The Huntsman .... Micha Bergese
Amorous Boy .... Shane Johnstone
Alice .... Georgia Slowe
Also with: Terence Stamp (cameo).

Admirably attempting an adult approach to traditional fairy tale material, "The Company Of Wolves" nevertheless represents

an uneasy marriage between old-fashioned storytelling and contemporary screen explicitness. Initial feature production by Palace, the British distribution company, film treats the beast-within-the-man theme in the context of a teenage girl's nightmarish fantasies, but is seldom powerful enough to captivate completely. Good effects and production values will attract attention, but generally soft approach studded by occasional graphic sequences will make for a marketing challenge.

Virtually the entire film is the dream of the gravely beautiful adolescent Sarah Patterson. Within her dream are other dreams and stories told by other, all of which gives director Neil Jordan, who penned the screenplay with story originator Angela Carter, free imaginative rein, but which also gives the tale a less than propulsive narrative.

For unexplained reasons, wolves dominate the minds of Patterson and everyone else on view, and action starts with a beautifully filmed sequence wherein her older sister is chased and finally done in by a pack of the wild animals.

Patterson is taken in by her Granny, crisply played by Angela Lansbury, who relates the story of a young bride whose husband turned out to be a wolf. This sequence features the man in question bloodily tearing off his skin, transforming by gruesome stages into wolfly proportions, then being decapitated. Stuff is definitely not for little kids.

Another yarn revolves around aristocrats who become wolves at a wedding party, and climactic sequence unfolds something like a Bloody Red Riding Hood, as Patterson, despite ample warning, allows an obvious wolfman to meet her at Granny's place. Fortunately, one is spared the sight of Granny being gobbled up, but Mr. Wolf's change of appearance, as a wolf body seems to emerge from a human frame, is startling.

Literary critics often have commented upon the dark, grisly aspect of many classical fairy tales, and "The Company Of Wolves" is one of the few films to have explored this territory. Nevertheless, the seemingly obligatory mundane sequences involving Patterson's mother and father, and other subsidiary characters, are pretty bland, and no strong hook is provided to pull the viewer in.

On the upside, Anton Furst's elaborate forest settings, all created within studio confines, are lovely and reminiscent of some British pics of the 1940s. Jordan maneuvers well within them, even if Bryan Loftus' lush lensing is sometimes so dark that a claustrophobic feeling sets in. Makeup effects by Christopher Tucker and special effects supervised by Alan Whibley are outstanding along the lines pi-

oneered by Rick Baker, Dick Smith and Rob Bottin by such films as "The Howling," "Altered States," "An American Werewolf In London," "The Thing" and the music video "Thriller." — *Cart*.

Uforia
(COLOR)

Funny redneck comedy, but a tough sell.

Hollywood, July 11.

A Universal Pictures release. Produced by Gordon Wolf. Exec producers, Melvin Simon, Barry Krost. Written and directed by John Binder; camera (Deluxe Color), David Myers; editor, Dennis Hill; sound, Kirk Francis; coproducer, Susan Spinks; assistant director, Anthony Brand; production manager, Joseph Ellis; art direction, William Malley; set decoration, Carl Biddiscomb; associate producer, Jeannie Field; music, Richard Baskin. Reviewed at the Picwood Theatre (Filmex). L.A., July 10, 1984. (MPAA Rating: PG). Running time: **100 MINS**.
Arlene .... Cindy Williams
Brother Bud .... Harry Dean Stanton
Sheldon .... Fred Ward
Emile .... Robert Gray
Toby .... Darrell Larson

Critical favor at the film fests may be the last hope for "Uforia," an agreeable, amusing picture filmed in 1980 that has had its admirers within two major distributors without getting released. Based on its test marketings, "Uforia" has been unfortunately saddled with the opinion that it won't attract the audience most likely to enjoy it.

Launched in the fading days of Mel Simon Prods., pic was first part of his package at 20th Century Fox, then moved over to Universal where it now resides without immediate prospects for further effort there.

Though unquestionably a pleasure, "Uforia" nonetheless deals with that level of redneck Americana that has persistently defied boxoffice success, probably because the people it involves are themselves here, these films contain plenty of footage about drinking, sexing, watching tv and going to church, but never does a single scene take place at a movie theater.

Writer-director John Binder can boast a snappy, beautifully written piece of work featuring a sprightly cast of Cindy Williams, Harry Dean Stanton and Fred Ward, plus good support throughout, especially from Robert Gray and Darrell Larson.

A drifter whose only fortune in life is a cultivated resemblance to Waylon Jennings, Ward meets up with Williams in a small desert town where he's gone to link up with an old pal, Stanton, who's equally disreputable but has a good deal going as a tent preacher.

Ward's romance with Williams not only is complicated by his lack of character but her intense belief in UFOs, especially a vision that one is arriving any minute and the world must get ready. Though her sincerity is a bit hard to handle, both Stanton and Ward see a chance here to make a buck off the yahoos she has convinced. Naturally, they won't and the why-not is where the fun is. — *Har.*

L'Hirondelle et la Mesange (1920-1983)
(The Swallow And The Titmouse)
(FRENCH-SILENT-B&W)

Paris, July 13.

A Société Cinématographique des Auteurs et Gens de Lettres production (1920). Post-produced and presented by the Cinémathèque Française (1983). Directed by André Antoine. Screenplay, Gustave Grillet. Camera (black & white), René Guychard and (uncredited) Leonce-Henry Burel; edited by Henri Colpi; historical advisor, Philippe Esnault; music, Raymond Alessandrini (with additional themes by Maurice Jaubert). Reviewed at the Avignon Theater Festival, July 12, 1984. Running time (at 18 frames per second): 79 MINS.

Pierre Van Groot	Ravet
Michel	Pierre Alcover
Griet Van Groot	Maylianes
Marthe	Maguy Delyac

This film, produced and shot in 1920 and edited and prepared for public presentation 63 years later, had its world premiere last March at the Cinémathèque Française.

Its director, André Antoine, one of the pioneers of modern stage naturalism, who moved fluently to the film medium in 1915 (at age 57), perfected his esthetic ideas with "L'Hirondelle et la Mesange," shot entirely on location on the waterways of Flanders. An intransigent but inspired theoretician, Antoine was obsessed by verism in dramatic representation, and was naturally fascinated by photography and cinema. Several of his seven released features, notably "Le Coupable" (1916), and "La Terre" (1919), from the Emile Zola novel—brilliantly exposed the studio-bound artificiality of French production of the period.

"L'Hirondelle et la Mesange," his penultimate film, and his only picture made from an original screenplay, so disconcerted Charles Pathé that he refused to release it.

Set on twin canal barges (the "Hirondelle" and the "Mesange"), the film describes the increasingly tense and finally tragic relationship between the barge family and the taciturn young pilot hired to steer the vessels on their bi-annual transport of coal and building goods to regions of France devastated by The Great War.

The pilot easily wins the confidence of the captain, who sees in him a suitable husband for his young sister-in-law and a good hand on-board. But the young man remains sullen and elusive, hiding a sexual preference for his boss' spouse. The latter anxiously senses his furtive glances and, one day, alone with him on the barge, must fight off his advances.

When the captain finds out, his first impulse is to send him packing. But his wife informs him that the pilot knows they are smuggling diamonds into France. In fact, the young man had seen the captain bind the pouch of jewels to the

ship's rudder, to escape customs scrutiny.

The captain disguises his rage and leads his employee into thinking the proposed marriage with his sister-in-law is still on. During a bachelor's party in a border tavern, the captain feigns a drunken stupor, follows his treacherous pilot back to the barge, and catches him in the act of retrieving the diamonds. He knocks the young man into the water and drowns him with a barge pole. The barges continue their journey, "slowly moving through the waters that guard their secret" (as the final title reads).

This is the stuff of melodrama, but filmed with an insidious restraint and subtle realism that jarred with the conventions of the time. Antoine refused the cozy falseness of the studio, took his actors out on real barges, shooting even his interiors on location. The film's quiet naturalism, and the use of landscape and lighting, rather than dramatic overstatement, to help limn story and characters, gives this film much of its breathtaking modernity. It's not surprising that Pathé saw the film as an overextended travelog with minimal story interest.

Obviously much of the credit for the film's movement and rhythm must go to Henri Colpi, the brilliant editor who selected and shaped six hours of rushes into a sinuous 79-minute film. Though Colpi had the original screenplay and most of the intertitles to work with, the action at times departed from the original story, and the editor was often faced with odd shots that didn't seem to fit in anywhere. Colpi (who was born a year after the film was shot) seems to have cut the film that Antoine himself might have completed.

The Cinémathèque's restored print is beautiful, and the tinting, in sepia and blue tones, helps recreate the orignal splendor of the silent film. It was shot by one of the leading French cameramen of the period, René Guychard, who was apparently backed by Leonce-Henry Burel, then Abel Gance's cinematographer.

Future screenings will be unthinkable without Raymond Allessandrini's haunting score, performed by a small orchestra of eight. Allessandrini has aptly incorporated three musical themes by the great film composer Maurice Jaubert, notably the jaunty composition written for Jean Vigo's barge-set classic, "L'Atalante."

"L'Hirondelle et la Mesange" is a must for international festivals and retrospective sidebars, all the more so because its cost of presentation is not prohibitive. Modern audiences will discover a great

cinema pioneer whose work is not merely of academic interest.
—*Len.*

Overvallers in de dierentuin
(Robbers In The Zoo)
(DUTCH-COLOR)

Amsterdam, July 7.

A Concorde Film release of a Cine/Vista production. Produced by Gerrit Visser. Directed by Christ Stuur. Features entire cast. Screenplay, Felix Thijssen and Annie van den Oever, based on a book by Ciny Peppelenbosch. Camera (color), Rob van den Drift; sound, Vicor Dekker. Reviewed at Cinema International, Amsterdam, July 6, 1984. Running time: 92 MINS.

Ros	Lex de Regt
Plumming	Paul van Soest
Haas	Maurice Schmeink
Sonja	Miranda Sanders
Steef	Martin Versluys

The book on which pic is based is probably quite a nice tale for younger children: a villain with two helpers holds up a gas station; when their stolen car breaks down, they hide the loot in a zoo, but can't get it out again because of police surveillance and unforeseen complications. A girl of about 15 and a boy of about 12, both part-time helpers in the zoo, solve all the problems and everyone gets his or her just desserts.

Filmmakers obviously thought their pre-teen aud would be unable to follow the story unless every clue was spotlighted, every detail exaggerated, every character simplified. Even seasoned players in the cast act like puppets, and only the animals in the zoo behave naturally. — *Wall.*

Roommates
(U.S.-COLOR)

Munich, July 2.

A Rubicon Film Production, in coproduction with American Playhouse. Produced by Morton Neal Miller and Richard Mellman. Directed by Nell Cox. Screenplay, Miller, based on John Updike's "Christian Roommates;" camera (color), Jeff Jur; music, Alan Bacus; editing, Nicolas Smith, Marc Mille. Reviewed at Munich Film Fest, July 1, '84. (No MPAA Rating). Running time: 90 MINS.

Cast: Lance Guest (Ziegler), Berry Miller (Paula).

In "Roommates," a young man from a conservative Christian background and the plains of South Dakota arrives at Northwestern (circa 1960) to study premed. He has just left his girlfriend behind, with whom he is already destined to spend the great part of his adult life within the bounds of matrimony once he returns to become the town physician. His assigned roommate is a beatnik, doesn't study at all and feels that this hallowed educational institution is for the birds. Our straight-laced hero, Ziegler, wants out of the picture — but perhaps with patience and Christian persuasion the roommate can be converted to become a worthy member of the human race.

The opposite happens; Ziegler is gradually introduced to the joys of participating in a panty raid, gets a chance to drown his troubles and celebrate his scholastic achievements by joining his classmates in a chug-a-lug down at the students' beerhall across the city limits in Chicago, as Evanston is a dry town.

The final twist-of-fate is when one of the students in the dorm has a breakdown and is about to run headlong into a rainy night, and who should be the one to rescue the wayward spirit but the guru-roommate. That about settles it for Ziegler: he's ready to make amends and keep his roommate on until the end of the school term, simply by employing a pair of earplugs during the Indian-style meditation seances.

There are several pluses in "Roommates," but the pic's winning qualities are the thesp performances and the authentic period aura. Some scenes don't quite click on a professional directional level and low-budget seams can be detected throughout, but these are minor in relation to the whole. A sure fest choice. Originally made (à la "Testament") for the American Playhouse tv series, Nell Cox' pic has art house potential if the reported entanglement over film vs. tv acting fees is resolved.—*Holl.*

Hayal Halayla
(Night Soldier)
(ISRAELI-COLOR)

Tel Aviv, June 15.

Wagner-Hallig and a Cannon Films presentation of a Dan Wolman production. Written, produced and directed by Dan Wolman. Camera (color), Yossi Wein, editor, Shoshi Wolman; music, Alex Kagan. Reviewed at the Jerusalem Cinematheque, June 14, 1984. Running time: **87 MINS.**
With: Ze'ev Shimshoni, Iris Kaner, Hilell Neeman, Yiphtach Katzur, Yehuda Efroni, Sari Raz, Galina Swidansky.

One of the world premieres at the Jerusalem Film Festival, Dan Wolman's latest effort may well be his best, on a strictly technical level, but is his least satisfactory on a personal level.

Started as an exercise with his students at Tel Aviv U., Wolman found the necessary end-money to complete the project from a German distributor and from the Golan-Globus Cannon tandem and thus managed to finish a production which lingered on for over two years.

Thematicaly, his intentions are clear enough. He argues that the Israeli reality, building up the macho image of the warrior and construing military service as an ultimate proof of masculinity, creates distorted ideas in the nation's youth and leads them into a murderous path.

The plot, however, can't make up its mind which way to go. It starts as a thriller, with a murder in a wood, leading the audience to believe the story is about discovering the identity of a mysterious murderer, killing soldiers without any visible motive. But soon enough, the identity of the killer is revealed and some pretty clear hints about why he is doing it are supplied at an early stage. Then, there is another possible direction for the script to develop, for the murderer, who is also the protagonist, has an affair with an unsuspecting waitress. But again, there is very little tension or interest generated from this romance.

The real trouble is that the viewer is better informed than the characters on screen. One quite legitimately wonders how it is that not even the slightest police enquiry seems to bother the man in his actions. This may fit the thesis that he bears the seeds of his own destruction, but it doesn't make much sense on the screen. Also, the numerous references to the responsibility of the media in general, and television in particular, for creating these sorts of monsters, looks very much an afterthought that hasn't been quite worked into the pattern of the story.

Technically the film shows the most confident visual style visually ever displayed by Wolman. Yossi Wein's camera is efficient and effective, Shoshi Wolman (the director's wife) supplies brisk, professional editing.

Ze'ev Shimshoni and Iris Kaner, playing the leads, are certainly photogenic enough, but neither one of them seems to be able to make head or tails of his part. The audience may share their discomfort.
—*Edna.*

Best Defense
(COLOR)

A dud for Dudley Moore & Eddie Murphy.

Hollywood, July 18.

A Paramount Pictures release and production, in association with Cinema Group Venture. Produced by Gloria Katz. Directed by Willard Huyck. Stars Dudley Moore, Eddie Murphy. Screenplay, Katz, Huyck, based on Robert Grossbach novel "Easy And Hard Ways Out;" camera (Movielab color), Don Peterman; editor, Sidney Wolinsky; music, Patrick Williams; sound, Jerry Jost, Robin Gregory (Israeli unit); production design, Peter Jamison; art direction, Robert W. Welch 3d, Ariel Roshko (Israel); set decoration, R. Chris Westlund, Giora Porter (Israel); assistant directors, Jerry C. G. Grandey, Jerald B. Sobul, Nissim Levy (Israel); production managers, Austen Jewell, Robert Latham Brown, Haim Sharir (Israel); costume design, Kristi Zea; stunt coordinator, Everett Creach; miniature photography, Dream Quest Images. Reviewed at Directors Guild of America, L.A., July 18, 1984. (MPAA Rating: R.) Running time: **94 MINS.**
Wylie .... Dudley Moore
Landry .... Eddie Murphy
Laura .... Kate Capshaw
Claire .... Helen Shaver
Loparino .... George Dzundza
Jeff .... David Rasche
Brank .... Mark Arnott
Joyner .... Peter Michael Goetz
Holtzman .... Tom Noonan

The good news about "Best Defense" is that Dudley Moore and Eddie Murphy are both on screen a lot more than the advance gossip would have it. But that's also the bad news.

Since Paramount did not screen the picture very much prior to its opening, exhibitors have been complaining they were led to believe Murphy was a full costar and not a "strategic guest star" whose billing generated fears he was barely about.

But Murphy is allowed plenty of time here to do what he does — and seems to have padded that. And Moore is woefully way off for the rest. It is true that the pair never share a scene. But if they had, it presumably would have been written by (producer) Gloria Katz and (director) Willard Huyck, which is no promise of greatness.

Actually, Moore shot all his scenes around L.A. and it plays on screen as events of 1982. Then the production moved to Israel for Murphy's contributions, which take place in the film two years later but are intercut throughout. If this sounds a bit awkward, it is.

Moore is miscast as a washed-up engineer working for a failing defense contractor whose last hope is a gyro they are developing for a tank. The gyro, unfortunately, is working no better than Moore's marriage to Kate Capshaw, whose coolness has Moore lusting for his sexy supervisor, Helen Shaver.

By accident, Moore inherits the plans for a workable gyro sought by a wacko, murderous industrial spy played by David Rasche. When it promises to save his company, Moore gets the praise for its invention, a new respect from Capshaw and the amorous adulation of Shaver — plus unwanted attention from Rasche and the FBI.

Overseas two years later, tank comander Murphy is suffering through the results of all of this with a vehicle that refuses to function properly. While it crashes about, he curses and crazes and all those other Murphy things.

Finally, in one time frame, Moore rushes around trying to straighten out all the mistakes and save the gyro project while, in the other time frame, Murphy gets into a real shooting match that demands a reliable weapon.

Will any of this work to save Moore's project? To save Murphy's life? To save the audience from abject depression?

Well, as they say, two out of three ain't bad.—*Har.*

Paris Vu Par ...
Vingt Ans Apres
(Paris Seen By ... 20 Years After)
(FRENCH-COLOR/B&W)

A Gerick Films release of a JM Productions/Films A2 coproduction. Produced by Jean Santamaria and Marc Labrousse. Directed and written by Chantal Akerman, Bernard Dubois, Philippe Garrel, Frédéric Mitterrand, Vincent Nordon, Philippe Venault. Camera (B&W and color), Luc Benhamou, Anne-Claire Khripounoff, Pascal Laperrousaz, Romain Winding, Martin Schäfer; editors, Francine Sandberg, Bernard Dubois, Sophie Coussein, Kenout Peltier, Joëlle Barjolin; sound, François de Morant, Antoine Ouvrier, Jean-Luc Rault-Cheynet, Pierre Camus, Louis Gimel, Alix Comte; music, Michel Bernholc, Faton Cahen, Roger Pouly, Jean-Claude Deblais, Silvano Santorio, Jean-Marie Hausser, Jorge Arriagada. Production manager, Denys Fleutot. Reviewed at the Olympic Entrepot theater, Paris, July 17, 1984. Running time: **100 MINS.**
With: Maria De Medeiros, Pascal Salkin, Agathe Vannier, Julien Dubois, Daniel Mesguich, Christine Boisson, Jean-Pierre Léaud, Philippe Garrel, Tonie Marshall, Antoine Perset, Katerine Boorman, Sophie Melnick, Béatrice Romand, Pascal Rocard, Jacques Bonnafé.

"Paris Vu Par ... Vingt Ans Apres" is a mostly glum followup to the 1964 omnibus film made (for producer Barbet Schroeder) by six New Wave directors (Eric Rohmer, Claude Chabrol, Jean-Luc Godard, Jean Rouch, Jean-Daniel Pollet, Jean Douchet). Though the product of disparate sensibilities, that early sketch film tended to reflect a revolutionary movement that took the French cinema back into the streets after decades of studio-bound convention.

No similar trend dictated this new edition. The six directors — Chantal Akerman, Bernard Dubois, Philippe Garrel, Frederic Mitterrand, Vincent Nordon, Philippe Venault — are all young, but little binds them, other than perhaps the fact that their previous efforts have played Mitterrand's Olympic art house circuit. This film was produced by the Olympic's new production unit, Gerick Films.

Nor do the directors play by the basic ground rules. With one exception, none of the sketches takes its Paris setting at anything more than face value.

Ironically, the sketch that most ignores the basic premise is the best. Chantal Akerman's "J'Ai Faim, J'ai Froid" (I'm Hungry, I'm Cold") is a succint (12 minutes) and impudently funny short about two wierd Belgian girls who disembark in Paris one night, converse in a kind of absurdist patter, engage in some minor adventures, and then make their way off, Chaplinesque, into the distance. Akerman affirms an off-beat sense of humor here that promises to develop in future efforts. (She currently is working on a musical comedy).

Akerman opens the package promisingly, but the rest is mostly downhill. Bernard Dubois' "Place Clichy" (17 minutes) offers some shots of the major Paris square, but this tale of a mother and son who spat like lovers is disjointed and verbose.

Philippe Garrel's "Rue Fontaine," (17 minutes) offers old New Wave favorite Jean-Pierre Léaud the occasion to revive the neurotic tics of his career. His monolog of desperation in the first scenes has breathless pertinence, but the story has neither point nor substance.

Mitterrand's "Rue du Bac" at least pays attention to the street of the title in this evocation of dissipated romance. Mitterrand's camera moons along the Rue du Bac in the literary voice-over manner à la Marguerite Duras that characterized his first feature "From Somalia With Love," but the addition of actors here breaks the reflective mood the director has a certain knack in creating.

Vincent Nordon's "Paris-Plage" (13 minutes) describes minor goings-on around on indoor pool atop a Paris skyscraper, and Philippe Venault's "Canal Saint-Martin" (17 minutes) rather dimly recalls an old Marcel Carné classic such as "Hôtel du Nord" in a story about a depressed, suicidal young couple.

Collectively, this is a poor advertisement for the short or sketch film industry, though the Akerman nugget merits independent attention. — *Len.*

En Retirada
(Withdrawal)
(ARGENTINE-COLOR)

Buenos Aires, June 28.
An Artaediez presentation. Produced by Hugo Lamónica. Directed by Juan Carlos Desanzo. Stars Rodolfo Ranni. Screenplay, José Pablo Feinman, Santiago Oves and Desanzo; camera (Eastmancolor), Juan Carlos Lenardi; music, Baby López Fürst; art direction, Osvaldo Rey. Reviewed at the Monumental theater, B.A., June 28, 1984. Running time: 90 MINS.
Cast: Rodolfo Ranni, Julio De Grazia, Gerardo Sofovich, Edda Bustamante, Osvaldo Terranova, María Vaner, Lydia Lamaison, Villanueva Cosse, Vicky Olivares, Pablo Brichta, Norma Kaider, Jorge Sassi, Max Berliner.

As in his successful opera prima "El Desquite" (Revenge), former cinematographer Juan Carlos Desanzo turns out an effective thriller shrewdly spiced with sex and violence but also strengthened by a topical subject: it is the story of an ultrarightist goon who, after having "worked" for death squads, has been left unemployed by the advent of democracy.

As played by Rodolfo Ranni, he witnesses in disgust the rallies of political parties in Buenos Aires' streets. He loses contact with his former boss and, feeling abandoned, tries to sell what he knows to an unscrupulous publisher but ends killing a photographer who has taken pictures of him from a rooftop.

He also travels to his hometown, where he meets his former girl friend, goes to bed with her but fails when trying to make love to her. The following night, after seeing she has bedded a boyfriend, he kills the young man, then submits the girl to a savage torture seemingly similar to those he inflicted on female political prisoners and this way he overcomes his sexual impotency. Back in B.A., he attempts to blackmail a powerful industrialist who formerly employed his services to slaughter union activists but his former boss eventually intervenes to stop him.

Yarn unfolds smoothly, making room for some psychological insights that don't interfere with the action. The most gripping scene is the torture of the girl, enhanced by the superb acting of Edda Bustamante. Director Desanzo confirms his craftmanship in sustaining the story's interest with a brisk pace and competent handling of able players surrounding Rodolfo Ranni, who is on screen almost all the time, giving a restrained menace to his sinister character in a well-balanced performance.

Pic only loses steam in its last sequence which fails to combine situation and tension. With Ranni doing unconvincing acrobatics across rooftops for unclear reasons, then being attacked empty handed by a man he already has overpowered, it gives a weak end to an otherwise strong entertainment.

Good lensing, fast editing and unobtrusive music are pluses. —*Nubi.*

Savage Streets
(COLOR)

Powerhouse femme revenge pic.

A Motion Picture Marketing (MPM) release, presented by John L. Chambliss, Michael Franzese. A John Strong production; a Savage Street Prods. picture. Executive producers, Chambliss, Franzese. Produced by John C. Strong 3d. Directed by Danny Steinmann. Stars Linda Blair. Screenplay, Norman Yonemoto, Steinmann; camera (CFI color), Stephen Posey; editors, Bruce Stubblefield, John O'Conner; music, Michael Lloyd, John D'Andrea; sound, Arthur Names; assistant directors, Thomas Irvine, Nancy King; art direction, Ninkey Dalton; set decoration, Nancy Arnold; stunt coordinators, Al Jones, B.J. Davis; associate producer, Cleve Landsberg. Reviewed at Magno Preview 9 screening room, N.Y., July 18, 1984. (MPAA Rating: R). Running time: 93 MINS.
Brenda .... Linda Blair
Principal Underwood .... John Vernon
Jake .... Robert Dryer
Vince .... Johnny Venocur
Fargo .... Sal Landi
Red .... Scott Mayer
Rachel .... Debra Blee
Francine .... Lisa Freeman
Heather .... Linnea Quigley
Also with: Marcia Karr, Luisa Leschin, Ina Romeo, Jill Bunker, Mitch Carter, Richard DeHaven, Bob DeSimone, Susan Dean, Joy Hyler, Louis P. Zito, Brian Mann, Catherine McGoohan, Sean O'Grady, Rebecca Perle, Paul Shaw, Kristi Sommers, Troy Tompkins, Perle Walter, Judy Walton, Carol Ita White.

"Savage Streets" should prove to be a tonic for action film fans, delivering the kind of low-down, violent exploitation material that has been absent on screen of late, while avoiding the burned out clichés of recent martial arts and horror product.

Linda Blair toplines (in her most persuasive adult performance to date) as Brenda, an L.A. girl who turns vigilante when her mute younger sister Heather (Linnea Quigley) is brutally gang-raped by a local gang of toughs, the Scars, led by the particularly heinous Jake (Robert Dryer).

Pic unfolds as a tough update of the juvenile delinquency B-pictures of the 1950s, incorporating ineffectual adult authorities (John Vernon as the hardnosed but powerless high school principal, reunited with his "Chained Heat" costar Blair), warring groups of dislikeable good kids (the school cheerleaders led by blond Rebecca Perle, always itching for a catfight with Blair) and gangs of punks. The uncensored approach (film's violence earned it an X rating, later changed to an R upon appeal) pays off in deliciously vulgar dialog and well-directed confrontation scenes.

After not-so-hot performances in such pics as "Exorcist II," "Hell Night" and "Chained Heat," the grownup Blair emerges here as a tawdry, delightfully trashy sweater girl in a league with 1950s B-heroines such as Beverly Michaels, Juli Reding and Mamie Van Doren. Other acting standouts in a generally effective cast include Robert Dryer, totally malevolent as the tall, homicidal dude with a razor blade for an earring, who finally gets his just desserts from Blair in a manner recalling Steve McQueen's revenge on Karl Malden in "Nevada Smith," as well as Linnea Quigley in a convincing turn as the mute sister.

Indie pic had a troubled production history, with original director Tom DeSimone (who helmed Blair in "Hell Night") ankling shortly before cameras rolled in June of last year, then producer Billy Fine (who made "Chained Heat" with Blair) leaving after 11 days of shooting, and the production shutting down for lack of funds (with about one reel of material completed). Exec producers John Chambliss and Michael Franzese restarted in February of this year with John Strong 3d producing and finished the remaining four-plus reels. Final product, directed throughout the shoot by Danny Steinmann, is relatively seamless, though prominently credited Debra Blee (the Annette Funicello-esque star of "The Beach Girls") as one of Blair's best pals is curiously missing from many key scenes without explanation.

Hard rock musical score is a major asset. — *Lor.*

Nicaragua — No Pasaran
(AUSTRALIAN-DOCU-COLOR)

Sydney, July 19.
A Ronin Films (Australia) release of a Bradbury production. Produced and directed by David Bradbury. Camera (color), Geoffrey Simpson; editor, Stewart Young; sound, Toivo Lember; associate producer, Leah Cocks; narrator, Mark Aarons; script consultant, Bob Connolly. Reviewed at Academy Twin theater, Sydney, July 16, 1984. Running time: 73 MINS.

There have been several documentaries produced of late about Central America and especially about Nicaragua; this new effort by award-winning Aussie David Bradbury looms as one of the more interesting entries, especially when it gets in among the people and lets them have their own say.

No doubt where Bradbury's sympathies lie: with the beleaguered Sandinista government, in power since 1979, and the object of President Reagan's antipathy. In the main, film concentrates on one Sandinista leader, Tomas Borge, an engaging and charismatic character who talks freely about his background (his mother wanted him to be a priest, but he liked girls too much) and his original ambitions (to be a pilot or a movie producer).

He was tortured under the Somoza regime, and his ordeal is re-enacted (for a video camera) while he remarks that he felt only sorrow for his torturers. He also is filmed in his office, where a collection of crucifixes on the wall indicates a strong Christian connection, at a prison camp for Miskitu Indians (some of whom collaborated with the CIA-backed Contras, operating out of Honduras), and in Paris, on a current affairs television program (a telling moment comes when the program compère finishes his interview with Borge and switches to a story about Lebanon; from one trouble-spot to another, instant superficiality).

Bradbury also talks to a dissident Sandinista, Eden Pastora, who's now a Contra himself, and in one particularly good sequence films the ordinary citizens of Nicaragua in a marketplace talking about shortages with some criticizing the Sandinistas, others supporting them in obviously spontaneous debate. For the most part, people on camera support their government, and express bewilderment over Washington's attitude towards their country.

Bradbury, an Academy Award nominee for "Frontline" (about a news-photographer in Vietnam) is no historian; a brief sequence in which he tries to tell the history of Nicaragua in a nutshell comes over as glib and superficial. But his coverage of the country as it is today, and study of the people, is engrossing. Best sequence is during the visit of the pope, where the Pontiff becomes first impatient and then visibly angered when the huge crowd facing him starts (apparently spontaneously) to chant, "We want peace!"

Technically film is excellent, with crisp sound recording and sharp images, though one wonders at the necessity of having to identify President Reagan in writing on his first appearance; is there anyone who doesn't know who he is?
— *Strat.*

Wolf Lake
(COLOR)

Tedious, dated Vietnam hangover meller.

A Filmcorp Distribution release of a Melvin Simon Prods., Aztec Prods. and Lance Hool presentation. A Wolf Lake Prods. production. Executive producers, Melvin Simon, Paul Joseph. Produced by Lance Hool. Written and directed by Burt Kennedy. Stars Rod Steiger. Camera (CFI color), Alex Phillips Jr.; editor, Warner Leighton; music, Ken Thorne; sound, Armando Bolaños; assistant director, Jesus Marin; production manager, John Morrison; art direction, Agustin Ituarte; stunt coordinator, Jerry Gatlin. Reviewed on Prism Entertainment vidcassette, N.Y., July 11, 1984. (MPAA Rating: R.) Running time: **87 MINS.**
Charlie .... Rod Steiger
David .... David Huffman
Linda ...., ... Robin Mattson
Wilbur .... Jerry Hardin
George .... Richard Herd
Sweeney ....: Paul Mantee
Bush pilot .... Alan Conrad

Made in 1977-78 as an early entry from Melvin Simon Prods., "Wolf Lake" is a tortuous melodrama, not saved by a strong Rod Steiger performance. Picture received very limited theatrical release under the title "The Honor Guard" from Filmcorp and is reviewed here for the record upon its availability in homevid format, reverting to its original monicker.

Writer-director Burt Kennedy tips his hat here in the direction of his 1960s contemporary in the Western genre, Sam Peckinpah (at least one key scene recapitulates latter's "Straw Dogs") in this desultory tale of the sour feelings left on the home front after the Vietnam war. Pic is set in Canada in 1976 (though oddly filmed in Chihuahua, Mexico), where Vietnam deserter David (David Huffman) is living at Wolf Lake lodge with his girl friend Linda (Robin Mattson).

Four hunters trek to the lake for their annual outing, led by Charlie (Rod Steiger), whose son Danny was killed in Vietnam. When Charlie and his rifle toting pals find out David's a deserter, there's hell to pay.

Dreary format has the inevitable climactic violence delayed by pointless scenes of verbal parrying and some worthwhile (perhaps for excerpt purposes) bravura monologs by Steiger expressing the bitterness of flagwaving Americans who saw youngsters avoiding or deserting from the military service while their kids were toeing the line. Biggest mistake here is that all the violent payoffs, including killings and a gang rape, are telegraphed repeatedly by flashforwards and even a senseless prolog that turns out to be the pic's final scene inserted as the outset. This structuring turns everything into an anticlimax.

Outside of Steiger, pic has little to offer, with dull thesping by the rest of the cast and meager technical contributions. — *Lor.*

Filmex

Andrei Tarkovsky
(ITALIAN-DOCU-COLOR-16m)

Hollywood, July 15.
A Ciak Studio production. Executive producer, Franco Terilli. Produced, directed, written, edited by Donatella Baglivo. Camera (Cinecittá color, 16m), Cualtiero Manozzi. Reviewed at the Nuart (Filmex), L.A., July 14, 1984. No MPAA rating. Running time: **100 MINS.**
Features: Andrei Tarkovsky.
(In Russian and Italian: with English subtitles)

Although incomplete and unsatisfying on an informational level, this documentary on Russian director Andrei Tarkovsky is so in synch with the esthetics of its subject that one imagines it closely resembles the sort of self-portrait the director himself might have made had he been so disposed. Made for Italian tv, film had its world premiere at Filmex and is a good bet for repertory houses and college venues in non-theatrical distribution.

A highly serious, self-conscious film poet generally regarded as the leading contemporary Russian director, Tarkovsky has made only six films during his 22-year career, five in his native country and his most recent, "Nostalghia," in Italy.

Filmex screening of this documentary followed by just a few days Tarkovsky's difficult decision to seek ásylum in the West. Perhaps understandably, given the director's in-between status at the time this filmed interview was conducted, politics and his own relationship with the Soviet regime are not mentioned at all, although he admits that, "I can't imagine living away from it (his homeland) for too long."

Filmmaker Donatella Baglivo, who produced last year's excellent Filmex documentary entry, "Montgomery Clift," has set her conversation with the director at the ultra-Tarkovskian setting of a wooded stream, and there Tarkovsky holds forth on his difficult, wartorn childhood and the important role his mother played in his life, given the absence of his father. Section is laced with clips from his first feature, the 1962 "Ivan's Childhood," and Baglivo has also included nifty footage of Tarkovsky receiving the Golden Lion that year at the Venice Film Festival.

Admitting his strenuous seriousness, Tarkovsky waxes philosophic about his art, opining that, "I believe only poets will remain in the history of the cinema."

Baglivo includes clips from his russian films, "Andrei Rublev," "The Mirror" and "The Stalker" (although dubbed into Italian) and indicates total sympathy with his work, but asks no questions about their production, reception in the USSR (an apt inquiry, since not all of them were readily released there) and his standing in the industry.

Instead, she asks such faintly ridiculous questions as, "Do you like children?" and "Do you like animals?" As it happens, Tarkovsky is so eloquent and thoughtful that he can answer even this sort of query in an interesting manner, but surely there were more pertinent questions to be posed.

Docu is dedicated to the director's father, Arseny Tarkovsky, called by both his son and Baglivo the "greatest living Russian poet" (excerpts from his work are read on the soundtrack). Early in the film, Tarkovsky recalls how painful it was for him when his father left his family when Andrei was a boy, and, given Tarkovsky's current expatriot status, one is left to ponder the irony of the director now repeating his father's behavior in leaving behind a son.

Baglivo poses her questions in Italian, and Tarkovsky responds in Russian. English subtitles are abbreviated, attempting to sum up ideas rather than to fully translate the words. —*Cart.*

The Census Taker
(COLOR)

Okay black humor.

Hollywood, July 6.
A Seymour Borde & Associates release of an Argentum Prods. production. Produced by Robert Bealmer. Directed by Bruce Cook. Exec producer Gordon Smith. Written by Cook and Smith. Camera (uncredited color), Tom Jewett; music, Jay Seagrave; editor, Cook. Reviewed at Picwood Theater (Filmex), July 6, 1984. (No MPAA Rating.) Running time: **96 MINS.**
Harvey McGraw .... Garrett Morris
George ....:. Greg Mullavey
Martha .... Meredith MacRae
Eva .... Austen Taylor
Pete .... Timothy Bottoms

A black comedy in the vein of but on a quality level below "Eating Raoul," Bruce Cook's "The Census Taker" sustains a wacky air throughout, but piles its on-target humor at the beginning. This makes for a lopsided feature with limited potential in firstrun theatrical, although the well-cast players enhance chances for midnight and ancillary exposure.

"Saturday Night Live" alumnus Garrett Morris is very good as the title character, a door-to-door polltaker whose extreme inquisitiveness (sanctioned by federal law) raises the hackles of a bickering couple living in a middle-class southern California community. The put-upon pair (Greg Mullavey and Meredith MacRae) shoot Morris in forehead a half-hour into the epic, dispatching the comic to silent status as a corpse posing disposal problems for the rest of the film.

Interesting premise of a privacy-shattering census taker ("What are your bathroom habits?") should have been exploited for more running time. Director Cook and exec producer (and CBS exec) Gordon Smith's dialog was best in the interplay between Morris and his "hosts," as well as their two teenage kids.

The antics expand but the laughs dwindle upon arrival of Timothy Bottoms, a macho, kinky cop, and his sexy wife Austen Taylor. Mullavey and MacRae eventually let slip the existence of the dead fed wrapped in trash bags in the laundry room. In time, Bottom is shot, then Mullavey, leaving the conniving, less than distraught wives with an insurance windfall.

Cook doesn't muster up enough original frenzy to make the offbeat premise work. Pic lags in several points, taboo for the kind of comedy of weird manners he set out to film.

The performances, however, are all enjoyable, sometimes excellent, particularly Morris and MacRae. Taylor, in her feature debut, is fine as the blond bombshell, and Bottoms, looking more mature than previous screen work, also is satisfactory.

Script relies too much on sarcasm among the characters, and the players' line delivery is unrelievedly deadpan, except for Mullavey, okay in the pic's sole edgy, panic-stricken role.

World-preemed to mixed audience reaction at Filmex, version caught was reportedly the first answer print. Some color and sound had yet to be adjusted, but the lapses in continuity (illogical camera angles, and one character emerges inexplicably in a new shirt) presumably will not be corrected. —*Binn.*

'I'm Almost Not Crazy ... ' John Cassavetes: The Man And His Work
(DOCU-COLOR-16m)

Hollywood, July 19.

A Cannon Group presentation of a Golan-Globus production. Produced by Menahem Golan, Yoram Globus. Directed, written by Michael Ventura. Camera (Metrocolor), Gideon Porath; editor, Daniel Wetherbee; sound, Peter Tullo. Reviewed at the Four Star (Filmex), L.A., July 19, 1984. (No MPAA Rating.) Running time: **60 MINS.**

Features: John Cassavetes, Gena Rowlands, Seymour Cassell, Menahem Golan, Romy Dana, Ted Allan, Bo Harwood, Phedon Papmichael, Carole R. Smith.

Lensed a year ago during the shooting of "Love Streams," "I'm Almost Not Crazy ... ' " is an illuminating, responsive documentary about John Cassavetes and his directorial methods. Backed by Cannon Films, which also made "Love Streams," featurette by no means stands as a promotional piece, emerging rather as an evocative glimpse of one of filmdom's genuine mavericks. Apparently intended mainly for television, this deserves a place at fests and on Cassavetes programs at specialty houses.

Writer-director Michael Ventura, co-screenwriter of the 1980 feature "Roadie," championed Cassavetes while working as a critic for the L.A. Weekly and was commissioned by Menahem Golan to make this portrait. Looking more gaunt than before, almost resembling Humphrey Bogart in his 50s, Cassavetes is amusingly interviewed in his Cannon cutting room in front of a poster for the Lou Ferrigno "Hercules" picture, saying things like, "I hate entertainment," attacking money and the Hollywood way of making pictures, and generally showing himself as the unpredictable iconoclast he is.

It is made clear that virtually all of "Love Streams," which won the top prize at the last Berlin Film Festival, was carefully scripted, but one of the docu's highlights shows the lengthy preparation, and subsequent lensing, of an improvised sequence for the picture, wherein Gena Rowlands must try to make a serious little girl laugh. Cassavetes is seen in discussion with his wife (Rowlands), telling her not to worry about it but giving her no real direction, after which she delivers a bravura performance with is suspenseful since viewer knows she's totally on her own.

Brief clips from such earlier Cassavetes features as "Shadows," "Faces," "A Woman Under The Influence" and "Opening Night" are underscored by frequent commentary from the director, who insists all his films center on the problems of loving, and repeatedly voices his belief that

"Filmmakers should be aware they don't know anything."

Rowlands admits her husband has an affinity for characters who are crazy or, at least, eccentric, and other collaborators chime in with interesting, sometimes irreverent, remarks.

Ventura is entirely sympathetic to Cassavetes without being indulgent, and result is a vibrant, engrossing look at a worthy subject.

— Cart.

Reflections
(BRITISH-COLOR)

Hollywood, July 16.

A Court House Films Production for Film Four International. Produced by David Deutsch, Kevin Billington. Directed by Billington. Screenplay, John Banville. Camera (Kay color), Mike Molloy; editor, Chris Ridsdale; music, Rachel Portman; art direction, Martin Johnson; sound, Tony Jackson; costumes, Jane Boyd. Reviewed at Nuart Theater, L.A., July 15, 1984 (Filmex). (No MPAA Rating). Running time: **103 MINS.**

William Masters .... Gabriel Byrne
Edward Lawless .... Donal McCann
Ottilie Granger .... Harriet Walter
Charlotte Lawles .... Fionnula Flanagan
Michael Lawless .... Gerard Cummins

"Reflections" is a dark brooding domestic drama filmed in Southern Ireland for Britain's Channel Four. Heavily influenced by Ingmar Bergman, pic presents a psychological puzzle which is only partially satisfying when unravelled. Appeal is limited to arthouse or select television audiences.

Meticulously directed by Kevin Billington, film follows the arrival of a young academic, William Masters (Gabriel Byrne), as he takes up residence in the cottage house of a declining rural estate. Ostensibly he is there to complete his study of Sir Issac Newton which has become his life's work.

Film actually is structured around paradoxes in Newton's life. Masters envisions him as a "scientist hero," a man of action who was driven mad by his own discoveries. Newton's cold abstract approach to experience, copied by Masters, gradually unravels and his world comes apart.

In the countryside, Masters becomes part of a troubled family. He starts a hopeless affair with Ottilie (Harriet Walter) while secretly desiring her aunt (Fionnula Flanagan) who manages the family nursery while her boozing husband Edward (Donal McCann) does little more than drink.

Masters is a mere observer in this hothouse drama while constructing an elaborate scenario in his mind which misses the obvious facts of life. Seen through Masters' point of view, Billington and cinematographer Mike Molloy have created a cold scientific structure for the film.

Events occur as if under a microscope with characters always maintaining a stiff distance. Space

between people also is marked in the screenplay by John Banville as thoughts are never completed and just trail off into thin air. Lush Irish scenery is ancient and unchanging as well.

As reflected by Masters' state of mind, Billington has taken a very mannered approach to the material. While it is interesting to piece together the workings of Masters' mind, the effort ultimately reveals little.

Billington keeps his distance from the characters. Overall effect comes off as an analytical exercise, pretty to look at but not especially compelling or revealing. There is no sense that Masters has mastered anything or of going through an experience with him.

Performances are fine all around but since characters are more pitiful than likable, "Reflections" remains a film seen from the outside looking in.

— Jagr.

Lillian Gish
(FRENCH-DOCU-COLOR-16m)

Hollywood, July 16.

An Acapella Films production. Produced, directed by Jeanne Moreau. Camera (color, 16m), Thomas Hurwitz (U.S.), Pierre Goutard (France); editor, Noelle Boisson; music, Roland Romanelli; associate producer, Klaus Hellwig; assistant director, Susan Resnick. Reviewed at the American Film Institute (Filmex), L.A., July 16, 1984. (No MPAA Rating.) Running time: **54 MINS.**

Features: Lillian Gish, Jeanne Moreau.

'Tis the season of Lillian Gish. Honored earlier this year by the American Film Institute, the 90-year-old actress with a 72-year screen career thus far is the subject of this adoring documentary portrait by Jeanne Moreau. Designed as the first of several such studies by the French actress-director, of great American women of the cinema, nearly hour-long pic concentrates on Gish's upbringing and collaboration with D.W. Griffith. Most of the stories are familiar to buffs, but Gish is in top form here and film would be a solid offering are appropriate retrospective and non-theatrical circuits.

Gish-Moreau interview takes place in the former's lovely, old-fashioned New York apartment, and Gish herself is striking in a flowered red, black and gold silk Chinese gown.

Unfortunately, Moreau proves too intrusive a hostess, over-introducing her subject and cutting away too often to smiling reaction shots of herself. Also, someone should have told her she mispronounced some words, such as "guardian." But once Gish takes over, all is well, as she tells of her childhood theatrical days, vividly describes how she and her sister Dorothy met Griffith and began working for him, and concisely relates some of the familiar stories

concerning Griffith's philosophy of the cinema and the making of some of their great films.

Clips of good visual quality are on view from "The Birth Of A Nation," "Broken Blossoms," "Way Down East" and "Orphans Of The Storm," but musical accompaniment is distractingly below par and quite repetitive.

At a couple of points, Moreau gently pushes Gish into less familiar territory, such as how the latter's mother's health was ruined on World War I locations for "Hearts Of The World," but then she pulls back. Gish proves such a winning and responsive subject here that one wishes Moreau would have asked some more unexpected questions, but her personal life and career after Griffith are only lightly touched upon.

Docu, then, is far from definitive in any respect, but Gish continues to shine like the great star she has been virtually from the dawn of film history.—Cart.

Modern American Composers I
(BRITISH-DOCU-COLOR-16m)

Hollywood, July 14.

A Trans Atlantic Films production for Channel Four. Produced by Revel Guest. Directed by Peter Greenaway. Camera (color, 16m), Curtis Clark, Nic Knowland; editor, John Wilson; music advisor, Michael Nyman; music, John Cage, Meredith Monk; sound, Garth Marshall. Reviewed at the Four Star Theater (Filmex), L.A., July 14, 1984. (No MPAA Rating.) Running time: **104 MINS.**

Director Peter Greenaway, who made such an impression last year with "The Draughtsman's Contract," is represented this year with a pair of documentaries, each offering profiles of two avant garde American composer-performance artists. First film, combining two 50-minute-plus portraits of John Cage and Meredith Monk, employs a style, enhanced by John Wilson's editing, which meshes very well with the sensibilities of the artists, heightening the understanding and appreciation of Cage and Monk's work and underlying philosophies. Non-theatrical (educational), tv and cable markets would seem well suited to these efforts.

Both segments were shot in London as part of the New York/Almeida Festival. The Cage portion includes performances of a cross-section of the composer's work, in chronological order, filmed at a deconsecrated church in celebration of Cage's 70th birthday.

Cage's observations about the performance and his body of work in general are both illuminating and witty, and his comments on his attempts to allow for artistic "freedom" — i.e., spontaneity — within the confines of a structured, performance distill the creative dilemma concisely.

Within that context, Cage remarks in the film about his distaste for phonograph records, because they condition people to think that the recorded version is the "right" version, and any departures from that an "error."

In contrast to Cage, who uses everything from wood screws and portable radios to make his "music," Monk is downright traditional, using the voice, dance, film and music to make her creative points. Monk's approaches to these media, however, are just as individual as Cage's are in his way, and hers are perhaps more challenging to an audience's preconceptions of what "art" is.

Portions of Monk's "Ellis Island" film, demonstrating what she calls the "musicality of images," are seen here, as are performance pieces and solo vocal presentations of rather jarring intensity. Interview segs with Monk heighten comprehension of her underlying vision. — *Kirk.*

Gospel According To Al Green
(BRITISH/U.S.-DOCU-COLOR)

Hollywood, July 12.

A Film Four International presentation of a Mug Shot Prods./Channel 4 production. Produced, written and directed by Robert Mugge. Written by Mugge. Camera (color), Erich Roland; editor, Mugge; music, Al Green; sound, Terry Hillman, William Barth; music recording, Johnny Rosen, Paul Zaleski, Hillman. Reviewed at the Mark Goodson Theatre, AFI (Filmex), L.A., July 11, 1984. (No MPAA rating.) Running time: 105 MINS.

American soul music's deep roots in the black church have rarely been more dramatically demonstrated than in this documentary on Al Green, one of secular soul's most compelling performers who's now a Pentecostal minister and gospel-only singer. Film's finale, during which Green delivers a passionate, sweat-drenched sermon at his Memphis church, illustrates the close ties between black secular and gospel music styles with riveting intensity, and far better than the interviews and critical analyses which precede it. The power of those closing moments make the docu a must-see for Green fans of both musical persuasions, and specialized theatrical and ancillary markets should reap nice benefits.

Director-producer-writer-editor Robert Mugge, has previously taken looks at jazz musicians Sun Ra and Gil Scott-Heron.

Interviews with Green's pre-gospel producer Willie Mitchell, rock critic Ken Tucker and experts on black gospel and Pentecostal religion give background, both on the music scene and Green himself,

and Mitchell offers up a few intriguing anecdotes about the making of the performer's best-known pop hits, in addition to a tour of the Memphis studios where the records were made.

Green is also interviewed on his transformation, which occurred following a performance at Disneyland in 1973. As eloquent as Green is at the pulpit and on the stage of a military base's NCO club in this film, his spoken comments during the interview segs are often rambling, albeit fascinating, affairs which tend to circle the questions being asked. Some trimming, of his segs and those with the "experts," in favor of the musical performances might improve the overall punch.

As a pop music performer, Green's unforced sexuality and soaring, heat-filled falsetto whipped crowds into a frenzy. As this documentary demonstrates, Green's rapturous intensity in the cause of Jesus does no less. The church-music influences he brought to soul music have thus been returned to their original platform, and breathtakingly so.
— *Kirk.*

Polar
(FRENCH-COLOR)

Hollywood, July 8.

A Les Films Noirs presentation in coproduction with FR3. Executive producer, Patrick Delauneux. Directed, adaptation by Jacques Bral. Screenplay, dialog by Bral, Jean-Paul Leca, Julien Levi, based on the novel "Morgue Pleine" by Jean-Patrick Manchette; camera (color), Jacques Renoir, Jean-Paul Rosa Da Costa; editors, Bral, Anne Boissel, Noun Serra; music, Karl-Heinz Schafer; costumes, Olga Pelletier; sound, Gerard Barra; assistant director, Renald Calcagni. Reviewed at the Picwood (Filmex), July 7, 1984. (No MPAA rating.) Running time: 97 MINS.
Eugene Tarpon .....Jean-François Balmer
Charlotte Le Dantec .....Sandra Montaigu
Inspecteur Coccioli ....Pierre Santini
Jean-Baptiste Haymann..Roland Dubillard
Theodore Lyssenko ....Claude Chabrol

Made in 1982 by Jacques Bral, director of the well-regarded "Exterieur, Nuit," "Polar" is a tired, enervating *film noir* which illserves the reputation of the French as true connoisseurs of the *policier* tradition. A lesser entry in Filmex, pic is too derivative to stand any chance in U.S. distribution.

Jean-François Balmer plays a young detective world-weary before his time, a man for whom business has been so bad that he's on the verge of packing it in and returning to his native village.

Naturally, it's a beautiful dame who changes everything. Slinky Sandra Montaigu arrives at his door in the middle of the night, explaining that her roommate, a porno queen, has been murdered. Not anxious for a case but nevertheless somewhat intrigued, Balmer finds himself the center of attention for the cops, sleazy underworld types

and the dead girl's boyfriend, and eventually enters into a highly tentative relationship with Montaigu.

Balmer's fatigue with life is instantly contagious for the viewer, and pic proceeds at a deadly pace which is not quickened even by the standard genre conventions. Lead character's voice-over narration basically conveys how tired of it all he is, and what the world doesn't need right now is one more jaded private eye. Even the appearance of director Claude Chabrol as a pornography kingpin doesn't have any oomph.

Balmer somewhat resembles a younger Philippe Noiret, but without that actor's humor or inventiveness. Pic goes through all the familiar motions, but this ground has been tilled so many times in the past that it's pointless to undertake such an effort without having anything new to offer. — *Cart.*

Le Courage Des Autres
(The Courage Of Others)
(UPPER VOLTA-COLOR)

Hollywood, June 16.

An Inafri presentation. Produced by Jacob Sou. Directed, written by Christian Richard. Camera (color), Serge Dalmas; editor, Christian Allani; music, folk music of Upper Volta; costumes and decor, Magda Ouédraogo, Patricia Rol; sound, Jean-Pierre Honiel. Reviewed at The Burbank Studios (Filmex), Burbank, June 16, 1984. (No MPAA Rating.) Running time: 92 MINS.
With: Sotigui Kouyate, Samake Sali, Baha Kouyate.

Like many African films, "The Courage Of Others" demands to be judged by somewhat different standards than pictures from Westernized industries. Concerned neither with conventional narrative storytelling nor psychology, pic emerges more as a series of historical tableaux on the subject of slavery and the triumph over it, and holds the interest on that specialized basis. Worthwhile for fests, it has no commercial possibilities.

Christian Richard is a Frenchman living in Upper Volta who teaches film at the African Film Institute in Ouagadougou and made "The Courage Of Others" as his first feature following numerous shorts. Film's first half methodically shows how a group of villagers are rounded up by some marauding black slave traders and made to march long distances through bleak country on their way to presumed export.

At a certain point, a mysterious horseman begins surveying the situation and allows himself to be captured. Group's women are sold off to a tribal chieftain and soon the stranger is stung by a scorpion and left for dead.

Film thereupon comes close to becoming an action genre piece, as the mystical Man With No Name begins picking off the slave drivers with increasing frequency, culmi-

nating in a successful slave uprising. All of this is accomplished with scarcely any dialog, and what there is goes untranslated.

Initial section plays as a series of "Scenes From The Gathering Of The Slaves," with shot after shot depicting the chained victims slowly traversing the blistered landscape. Theoretically, this should be very boring, but it isn't. Experience is akin to taking a hike through unfamiliar terrain and having the opportunity to think, meditate, daydream or just look at the scenery.

Pace picks up a bit in the second half, although Richard has no idea how to stage or cut action for the camera. Tall, thin stranger is apparently helped in his combat by unexplained mystical or religious powers, but it is deeds, not words of philosophy, which count here, and his exploits have a moderately exhilarating effect after the long march of the first half.

Pic was very handsomely shot by Serge Dalmas, and overall is not a bad example of current indigenous African filmmaking.
— *Cart.*

Vidas
(Lives/Survivors)
(PORTUGUESE-COLOR)

Hollywood, July 17.

An Animatografo-Producao de Films, Lda. production. Chief of production, Carlos Mota. Directed by Antonio da Cunha Telles. Screenplay, Cunha Telles, Jose Sebag. Camera (Fujicolor), Acacio de Almeida; music, To Neto; assistant director, Hugo de Carvalho. Reviewed at the American Film Institute (Filmex), L.A., July 17, 1984. (No MPAA Rating.) Running time: 120 MINS.
Features: Pedro Lopes, Julia Correia, Maria Cabral, Carlos Cruz.

A hopelessly meandering, maddeningly unstructured piece of work, "Vidas" may or may not represent a surprising exposé of Lisbon's drug underworld to Portuguese audiences, but it's just a bad trip within the context of international cinema. Due to its moderate exoticism, pic holds the interest at times, but it lurches on and on to such an extent that it seems it will never end. Finally, mercifully, it just stops. An unfortunate entry in Filmex, film has zero commercial potential.

Even at its exorbitant two-hour length, ("Vidas," "Lives," or, as translated in the subtitles "Survivors") is unable to supply much basic information about its characters and their relationships to one another. What cowriter-director Antonio de Cunha Telles seems to have in mind is a portrait of two lost generations, one of the 1968 youth, now in their 30's, the other of kids half their age.

Older characters include two writers and a smooth intellectual who turns out to be a heavy drug dealer. With the bloom off their earlier activist political dreams, they are basically a weary, cynical lot, headed nowhere.

Taking the quicker road to hell are teenagers Lina and Pedro, who like to hang around a seamy disco operated by drug kingpin Carlos and spend a fair amount of screen time shooting up. Pedro's mother, one of the older writers, knows of her son's addiction but, astonishingly, does absolutely nothing about it, while Victor, the brainy dealer, tries to convince Lina to join him on a sea cruise aboard his yacht.

Story telling is wildly disjointed, as if many necessary scenes were either never filmed, or cut out. At one moment, Lina is getting high with Pedro, the next she's apparently Victor's date at an upscale dinner. Similarly, Victor is busted and jailed for his illegal dope activity, but shortly photographed, and thesps have a free and easy manner which makes the proceedings watchable. But it's a long haul to the end, and there's nothing there upon arrival. —Cart.

Eyes Of Fire
(COLOR)

Okay horror in novel setting.

Hollywood, July 13.

An Elysian Pictures presentation. Produced by Philip J. Spinelli. Directed, written by Avery Crounse. Camera (CFI color), Wade Hanks; editor, Michael Barnard; music, Brad Fiedel; art direction, Greg Fonseca; set decoration, John Stadelman; costumes, Bernadette O'Brien; sound, Susanna Tokunow; makeup, Annie Mansicalco; associate producers, Andrew Reichsman, Chris Baldwin; second unit camera, Don Devine; assistant director, Bruce Solow. Reviewed at the Four Star (Filmex), July 13, 1984. (No MPAA rating.) Running time: 106 MINS.
Will Smythe . . . . Dennis Lipscomb
Mr. Dalton . . . . Guy Boyd
Eloise Dalton . . . . Rebecca Stanley
Fay Dalton . . . . Sally Klein

"Eyes Of Fire" is an oddball all the way, a low-budget indie feature with big-league special effects, and an old-time pioneer tale with aspects of "Night Of The Living Dead" and "Poltergeist" grafted on. Inaccessibility of the characters and general mildness of the action severely limit involvement and commercial potential, but pic's unusual nature and weirdo appeal could find it a little niche in the horror-supernatural marketplace. It was lensed in late spring of 1983 under the title "Crying Blue Sky."

Drawing on folklore and legend concerning ghosts and witches in pre-Revolutionary America, writer-director Avery Crounse opens the action with zealous preacher Will Smythe nearly being lynched somewhere on the frontier in 1750. Saved by apparent magic, Smythe leads his small following out in search of the Promised Land and decides to settle in a valley feared

by the local Shawnee Indians for what turn out to be excellent reasons.

Once the group settles in, anything in the way of a plot largely disappears in favor of a barrage of shock and special effects sequences involving apparitions, ghouls and visions emerging from the ground and trees.

Ostensibly, it all has to do with the blood of history's haunted ones mingling together in the earth and materializing as a manifestation of the Devil, but it actually serves to show what nifty effects Crounse and his resourceful collaborators can come up with on a $1,000,000 budget. Film isn't really scary or gory enough for what's left of the hardcore horror audience, but on a technical level, effects and makeup are reasonably impressive, and Crounse can at least be acknowledged for having found a new setting for such goings-on.

Unfortunately, virtually all of the characters are so looney to begin with, and the situation is so fundamentally unreal, that it is impossible to take any of it seriously, thus encouraging a posture of detached amusement and mere curiosity as to what might happen next.

As an indie effort (shot on location in Missouri), it looks good, and, certainly, some of the craft and technical personnel will be heard from again. — Cart.

Scarred
(Street Love)
(COLOR)

Gritty tale of prostitution requires a hard sell.

Hollywood, July 17.

A Seymour Borde & Associates release of a Mark Borde/Rose-Marie Turko production. Produced by Turko, Borde. Coproducer, Dan Halperin. Executive producer, Seymour Borde. Directed, written, edited by Turko. Camera (Deluxe color), Michael Miner; supervising editor/post production, Miller Drake; art direction, Cecilia Rodarte; assistant director, Alex Cox. Reviewed at the Nuart (Filmex), L.A., July 17, 1984. (MPAA rating: R.) Running time: 85 MINS.
Ruby Star . . . . Jennifer Mayo
Carla . . . . Jackie Berryman
Easy . . . . David Dean
Jojo . . . . Rico L. Richardson
Sandy . . . . Debbie Dion
Rita Lili
First Trick . . . . Randolph Pitts
Last Trick . . . . Walter Klenhard
Barber Shop Pimp . . . . Haskell Anderson
Barber Shop Pimp . . . . Andre Waters
Barber . . . . Willie
Porno Producer . . . . Eddie Pansullo

"Scarred" is a serious slice-of-life study of teenage prostitution which did not start life as an exploitation film but is apparently growing up to become one. Covering the same turf as the recent New World hit "Angel," this very indie effort is much more realistic

and honest, but also cruder and less commercially pandering. Given the subject matter, a heavy exploitation push is the only way to go, with okay results looming.

Production on what was initially called "Red On Red" required almost four years of effort by producer-director-writer-editor Rose-Marie Turko, who began lensing on virtually no money at UCLA, was able to bring it to rough-cut form via American Film Institute and National Endowment for the Arts grants, and finished it once Mark and Seymour Borde picked it up. Distrib required that more nudity be inserted and will apparently release film under the title "Street Love."

Story is as standard as they come, with 16-year-old waif Jennifer Mayo forced to hit the streets when she can think of no other way to pay the rent and support her baby.

After working independently for a while, she finally relents and allows a relatively nice guy, David Dean, to become her pimp and, briefly, her lover. She gets accosted by the usual assortment of weirdos, tries porno films and finally, with another prostie friend, jumps off the downward-turning spiral.

Filming on Hollywood Boulevard, mostly at night, and on other natural locations, Turko almost by necessity has adopted a cinema-verité style which is quite raw but also results in moments of vivid realism and power. Lack of phoniness and sentimentality on the one hand, and relative absence of overt exploitation elements on the other, combine for an impressive believability overall, a quality underlined by the fact that it's impossible to differentiate between the actors and the real street people.

Also landing strongly in the plus column is the lead performance by Mayo. Obviously young (14½ when lensing began) but well developed physically and clearly no innocent, she seems incapable of reaching for easy audience sympathy and is free of mannerism or off-putting cuteness. More resilient than resourceful, she definitely lives up to film's title by fadeout.

Although presentable, pic does have its drawbacks commercially, notably a dark, grainy look resulting from the 16m to 35m blowup and a very erratic, hollow sound which resembles nothing more than cheap porno films of a decade ago. Male performances tend toward the exaggerated.

Ultimately, "Scarred" falls short of the seamless artistry and utter reality of Tony Garnett's "Prostitute," shown at Filmex a few seasons back, but beats stuff like "Angel" by a mile. —Cart.

Naitou
(The Orphan)
(GUINEAN-COLOR)

Hollywood, July 12.

A Syli Cinema presentation (Republic Of Guinea). Director general, Gillart Minot. Directed by Moussa Kemoko Diakite. Screenplay, Moussa Kemoko Diakite; camera (color), Laalioui Mohamed; editor, Ahmed Bouanani; music, The African Ballet Of Guinea; costumes, Jeanne Delavision. Reviewed at the Nueart Theater (Filmex), L.A., July 11, 1984. (No MPAA Rating.) Running time: 87 MINS.
Cast features The African Ballet Of Guinea; principal dancers: Fanta Kaba, Marie Camara, Italo Zambo, Nalo Camara, Jeanne Macaulay.

"Naitou" (The Orphan) is a highly specialized film primarily for dance aficionados or students of African culture. Part myth and part fairy tale, picture's commercial appeal is limited to festival and museum settings despite universal themes of the material.

Based on a Guinean legend, "The Orphan" is a primal dance drama concerning jealousy and retribution. In a two-wife household, number one becomes jealous of number two and poisons her. Each wife has a daughter on the verge of womanhood. Evil wife is resentful of her stepdaughter and tries to do away with her as well.

At this point, supernatural elements enter the picture to balance the scales of justice. In the film's finale, the evil wife is afflicted with leprosy, epilepsy and is transformed into a hunchback all conveyed in a frenzied dance.

Story is probably well known by a native audience but for those not familiar with the legend, picture is a bit confusing to follow.

Shot on a village location rather than in a dance studio, main attraction of the film is the glimpse of Guinean culture.

Film has no dialog and individual dance pieces are linked together by a narrative delivered in pantomime. In some ritualistic scenes all the village people appear in a variety of exotic locations including waterfalls, tropical jungle and village square. With peripheral action, film has a strong feel for the rhythms of local life.

Rhythms, in fact, are very much what the film is about as musicians playing an unusual assortment of percussion, vibe-like and stringed instruments are often in full view and accompany many of the dance scenes.

As for the dancing itself, style blends elements of modern dance with more traditional movement. Choreography is basically simple with elaborate costumes and props helping to create a mythical mood. Scenes such as the initiation of young girls into womanhood and the intervention of supernatural powers in human affairs are endowed with appropriate emotion and import.

Dances done at night by torch-light are visually and emotionally striking while some sections fall a bit flat to the unfamiliar eye. Costumes for an array of wildlife, particularly a lizard, are colorful and fun.

Production values do not detract from the action but are a little less polished than is customary. Lighting, especially in the broad daylight, tends to be too bright and cutting occasionally jumps abruptly from place to place in an attempt to bring elements together.

—*Jagr.*

Habanera
(CUBAN-COLOR)

Hollywood, July 19.

A Cuban Institute of Cinematographic Art & Industry (ICAIC) production. Produced by Jose Ramon Perez. Directed by Pastor Vega. Screenplay, Ambrosio Fornet; story, Vega, Fornet; camera (color), Livio Delgado; editor, Nelson Rodriguez; sound, Geronimo Labrada. Reviewed at the American Film Institute (Filmex), L.A., July 18, 1984. No MPAA rating. Running time: **108 MINS.**
Laura Durán .... Daisy Granados
Chilean Teacher .... Ely Menz
Leonor .... Marcia Barreto
Carlos Durán .... Adolfo Llauradó
Doctor .... Miguel Benavides
Other Doctor .... Cesar Evora
(In Spanish with English subtitles)

"Habanera" is a well-made but relatively banal women's picture from one of Cuba's top talents, Pastor Vega. Virtually without political or socially conscious content, this mid-age crisis drama about a psychiatrist losing her grip on both her professional and personal lives is almost shockingly similar to numerous European and American films of the same stripe, and will probably disappoint the many admirers of Vega's earlier effort, the 1979 "Portrait Of Teresa."

Most striking aspect of the pic to Yank eyes is that it portrays up close a strata of Cuban life seldom revealed, that of sophisticated, intellectual professionals who could as easily live and work in New York, Rio or Rome as in Havana.

In the early going, Laura Durán, played with lovely seriousness by Daisy Granados, Vega's wife, seems the picture of accomplished womanhood. As a medic, she's at the top of her class, able to counsel her patients wisely and advise her younger colleagues. As a wife and mother, she also appears to be a success, and claims her husband's fooling around won't bother her as long as she doesn't know about it.

Little by little, however, cracks open on the surface of her self-assurance, and she's ultimately devastated when she realizes one of her patients, an attractive young Brazilian girl unhappy over a romance with a married man, is having an affair with her husband.

This coincidence is pretty creaky

to begin with, and isn't helped by the fact that situation is discernable almost from the start. Laura's self-confident maturity seems to blind her to the common realities lying in front of her nose, and result is a melancholy tale of how a woman's solidarity with family, friends and coworkers breaks down due to elemental emotional occurences.

Characters are all very well delineated, but Vega seems tentative about the direction in which he wants to carry the film. Not interested in making a full-fledged soap, he indulges in several long, confessional-style monologs in the first section, suggesting he may be trekking into Ingmar Bergman territory. These are then dropped, and ultimate artisitc point becomes elusive.

References to the revolution, political struggle and the like are non-existent, and context of the film's production is evident at only a couple of moments, such as when Laura reminds a fellow doctor not to forget the "social" considerations regarding the functioning of the brain, and when she is glimpsed briefly firing a gun in what appears to be a military reservers training session.

Overall, film is a moderately interesting, but inadequately plotted, look at a fresh aspect of the new Cuba. —*Cart.*

The Californians
DOCU-COLOR-16m)

Hollywood, June 12.

Produced, directed, written, camera (color) by Alexander von Wetter. Additional camera, Don Biggs, Leisle Hebert; editor, Yeu Bun Yee; narrator, Jared Martin. Reviewed at the Warner Hollywood Studios, (Filmex), L.A., June 12, 1984. (No MPAA rating.) Running time: **90 MINS.**
Features: Paul Rodriguez, Kedric Robin Wolf, John Trudell.

"The Californians" is an ultra-conventional, classroom-style documentary on the history of the nation's most populous state. Dull pic contains a few pieces of interesting information, but nothing that couldn't fit on one sheet of paper, and sentimentalizes and indulges all ethnic and minority groups it mentions. Only audiences for this will be found among elementary school students and the most easily-pleased social and academic groups.

The history and current inhabitants of California clearly provide a wealth of material for any kind of documentary, straight or irreverent, so producer-director-writer-cameraman Alexander von Wetter's failure to come up with 90 minutes of lively footage here is all the more lamentable.

Von Wetter alternates between shots of contemporary California and its sometimes kooky citizens, and illustrated tellings of historical

events, such as the arrival of the Spanish, the Gold Rush, etc. Very mundane narration is abetted by commentary by some real-life figures of importance.

Given Von Wetter's particular interest in native Indians and their philosophy, and his penchant for pitting the purity of ethnic groups against high technology, it at first appears that the diretor has in mind a prosaic version of "Koyaanisqatsi." But film then continues to plod through history, using footage of the "Ramona" pageant and a community recreation of Fort Sutter to pass the time.

As usual, Chicano comedian Paul Rodriguez, presented both onstage and in a private interview, has some sharp and funny things to say, but crackpot performer Kedric Robin Wolf seems like a pointless holdover from the hippie era in context. —*Cart.*

Hey Babe!
(CANADIAN-COLOR)

Hollywood, July 15.

A Rafal production with the financial assistance of the Canadian Film Development Corp., l'Institut Quebecois du Cinema and Famous Players Ltd. Produced by Rafal Zielinski, Arthur Voronka. Executive producer, Morden Lazarus. Directed by Zielinski. Stars Buddy Hackett, Yasmine Bleeth. Screenplay, Edith Rey, from an original story by Rey, Zielinski; camera (color), Peter Czerski; supervising editor, Scott Conrad; editor, Afte Chiriaeff; music, Gino Soccio, Roger Pilon, Mature Adults; choreography, Lynn Taylor; sound, Richard Nicoli; associate producer, Gilbert Tinel. Reviewed at the Four Star (Filmex), L.A., July 14, 1984. (No MPAA Rating.) Running time: **105 MINS.**
Sammy Cohen .... Buddy Hackett
Theresa .... Yasmine Bleeth
Miss Wolf .... Marushka Stankova
Roy .... Vlasta Vrana
Miss Dolores .... Denise Proulx

Although entirely sweet and good-natured, "Hey Babe!" is a thin Canadian confection which, like its lead character, tries too hard to please. Lensed four years ago under the title "Babe" as the first feature of Rafal Zielinski and recut many times since, pic was seen in its world premiere at Filmex. Utterly commercial in intent, this is not a festival-type picture, although it was selected to open the Taormina Film Festival in Italy on July 19. Boxoffice prospects are slim.

After most of the lensing had been finished in Montreal and New York, production ran into financial trouble, which was only recently solved through the offices of Carolco. In the interim, director Zielinski went on to his second feature, "Screwballs," which New World released last year.

In essence, this is a January-December romance of sorts between an extraordinarily beautiful 12-year-old orphan girl with intense showbiz aspirations, and a washed-up vaudevillian who gradually takes her under his wing.

Yasmine Bleeth, a New York model who was 11 and 12 years old when film was made, highly resembles a young Brooke Shields. Without roots or a home, Bleeth courts detention in youth centers by conducting what amount to commando raids on tv stations and a dramatic arts academy in hopes of forcing her break in the performing world, lying left and right, stealing when need be and generally imposing herself on everyone she encounters.

Buddy Hackett easily etches the old-time entertainer who lives upstairs in an abandoned legit theater, drinks to forget his lost career and romance, and eventually teaches Bleeth some of the fundamentals she'll need to make it

Most of the script's dilemmas consist of the close calls Bleeth has with various authority figures in her selfish attempts to live life by her own street rules, and some of these are passably amusing. There's a modicum of pathos in her scenes with Hackett, and undemanding audiences could find the whole thing moderately entertaining, as some skill is evident in most departments.

But it's pretty fluffy, artificial stuff, and musical numbers aren't potent enough to pass muster with contempo rock and flash viewers.

Wearing an ever-changing, thrown-together hip wardrobe and gobs of loud makeup, Bleeth is the center of attention throughout, and she comes on so strong that her precocious, aggressive talents are almost scary. There is no doubt that she was some kind of discovery in 1980, although it remains to be seen how she can latterly fit within a more conventional context.

Despite production problems, technical aspects are all very slick.
—*Cart.*

The Philadelphia Experiment
(COLOR)

So-so sci-fier

Hollywood, July 29.

A New World Pictures release, produced by Douglas Curtis and Joel B. Michaels. Directed by Stewart Raffill. Features entire cast. Exec producer, John Carpenter. Screenplay, William Gray, Michael Janover; camera (CFI Color), Dick Bush; editor, Neil Travis; sound, Bob Gravenor; associate producer, Pegi Brotman; art direction, Chris Campbell; assistant director, Pat. Kehoe; costumes, Joanne Palace; visual effects, Max Anderson. Reviewed at the Academy of Motion Picture Arts & Sciences, Beverly Hills, July 9, 1984. (MPAA Rating: PG). Running time: 102 MINS.

David .... Michael Pare
Allison .... Nancy Allen
Longstreet .... Eric Christmas
Jim .... Bobby Di Cicco
Clark .... Kene Holliday

"The Philadelphia Experiment" had a lot of script problems in its development that haven't been solved yet, but final result is an adequate sci-fi yarn with a confined outlook.

Problems with the pic are common to all stories with a time-warp twist (the layers of future/past events tend to overlap until they flatten), but director Stewart Raffill and writers William Gray and Michael Janover have kept "Philadelphia" reasonably simple.

In 1943, Michael Pare and Bobby Di Cicco are sailors aboard a destroyer that's the center of a secret radar experiment which goes awry, throwing them into 1984, seemingly cross-circuited into another experiment taking place in that time.

Befriended in the future by Nancy Allen, the pair obviously are a bit bemused at their surroundings before Di Cicco fades again into the past, leaving Pare to develop a romance with Allen and try to find his own way back in time.

There are a lot of enjoyable moments in all this, but the story is confounded by unnecessary trouble Pare gets into defying authority instead of relying on it to solve his problems. But if Pare had simply gone to the navy of 1984 with his difficulty, there would be no need for the shooting and car chases that make up much of the action.

Difficulty in the development of the script over several years was always in the ending — and still is.
— *Har.*

Mr. Virgin
(HONG KONG-COLOR)

Hong Kong, July 18.

A Shaw Brothers production and release. Producer, Lawrence Fong; Executive Producer, Mona Fong. Directed by Chan Friend. Stars Alfred Cheung, Olivia Cheung and Hu Chun. Screenplay, Alfred Cheung. Reviewed at Jade Theater, Hong Kong, July 16, 1984. Running time: 96 MINS.
(Cantonese soundtrack with English subtitles.)

One needs good friends in show-biz to survive and a chance to experiment with the different aspects of filmmaking. Such is the case of Chan Friend who directs for the first time his ex-director and business partner Alfred Cheung who acts the male lead for the first time in this modern Shaws comedy that's been geared to recreate the tremendous success of "Let's Make Laugh."

In the case of "Mr. Virgin," it seems they formulated the title first, then tried to do a formula storyline around the general idea that must have been inspired by the likes of "Mr. Mom," "Arthur" and Woody Allen comedies.

The weakness and trivialities of the scenario are very prominent. Cheung is a young man who's been trying to eradicate his virginity without much success. It is also taboo for him to marry until he's 30 years old or, as his father explains, he will be jinxed for life.

But Cheung falls in love anyway with lovely Olivia Cheng (a beauty pageant title-holder who's no actress) who happens to be a funeral parlor makeup girl cum beautician in picturesque Macao. These two awkward characters and elements are combined to create contemporary Cantonese comedy. Some bits work, but most of the time they don't. The final outcome is an uneven, mawkish, self-conscious collection of little episodes that don't jell into a well-coordinated pic.

After a series of emotional and familial complications, Cheung finally loses his virginity to wife Cheng, a condition the hero to now has treated like a dreaded disease that is in need of antibiotics.

An interesting piece of novel casting is in having retired Taiwanese actress Hu Chun in a comeback role as the mother. "Mr. Virgin" is just doing average business and will not likely overshadow the director's first boxoffice blockbuster at Shaw's studio. — *Mel.*

Les Fauvres
(The Beasts)
(FRENCH-COLOR)

Paris, July 23.

A Gaumont release of a Transcontinentale/Accord Production/Super 7 coproduction. Produced by Lucien Duval. Directed by Jean-Louis Daniel. Screenplay, Jean-Louis Daniel. Philippe Setbon, Catherine Cohen; camera (Eastmancolor), Richard Andry; editor, Isabelle Rathery; art director, Olivier Paultre; sound, Jean-Marcel Milan; music, Philippe Servain; stunts, Gil Raconis; artistic advisor, Lucien Camezza; production manager, Serge Menard; associate producers, Alain Pancrezi, Jean-Pierre Voronowsky, Jacques Ristori, A. Grandgerard. Reviewed at the Gaumont Ambassade theater, Paris, July 1, 1984. Running time: 90 MINS.
Leandro .... Philippe Léotard
Berg .... Daniel Auteuil
Bela .... Gabrielle Lazure
Mimi .... Veronique Delbourg
Juliette .... Valérie Mairesse
Jeff .... Jean-Francois Balmer
Nino .... Florent Pagny
Keller .... Farid Chopel

"Les Fauvres" is another of those overblown dramas that mistakes sustained hysteria for dramatic force. The result is an unusually insipid pursuit thriller-cum-psychological study, in which the awfulness of script and direction is surpassed by some embarrassing acting from usually competent players.

Story deals with a young stunt car driver (Daniel Auteuil) who drops out of sight after his partner-spouse (Gabrielle Lazure) is killed during a meet. He later surfaces in a Paris private security patrol service where he hopes to forget his past. But Lazure's psychotic brother (Philippe Léotard), who's always had an incestuous attachment to sis, signs up as well with vengeance in mind and proceeds to set Auteil's colleagues against him.

The plot and characterizations are obvious, unlikely and loud. Auteuil somehow manages not to come out of the affair too badly as the tormented stunting ace, but Léotard's harmonica-tooting retard seems like a grotesque parody of the seedy roles the actor has tended too often to play; and Jean-Francois Balmer vies for worst acting laurels as a drooling sex maniac who works with Auteuil and has designs on his new girl friend. Most cast members overact in the worst fashion and the action sinks into shrill absurdity in no time.

Director Jean-Louis Daniel, 29, attracted serious critical attention with his first film "Le Trottoir des Allongés" (1977), which won some art fest prizes, and followed with a second feature in 1980. It is difficult to fathom here any qualities that he might have displayed in his previous efforts.—*Len.*

Sálvese Quien Pueda
(Save Themselves Those Who Can)
(ARGENTINE-COLOR)

Buenos Aires, July 24.

An Aries Cinematográfica Argentina production and presentation. Produced by Luis Osvaldo Repetto. Directed by Enrique Carreras. Stars Jorge Porcel, Alberto Olmedo and Mario Sapag. Screenplay, Salvador Valverde Calvo, Juan Carlos Mesa, Carlos Garaycochea and Carreras; camera (Eastmancolor), Antonio Merayo; art director, Alvaro Durañona y Vedia; assistant director, Ricardo Cuevas; production manager, Mario Faroni. Reviewed at the Ambassador theater, Buenos Aires, July 5, 1984. Running time: 85 MINS.
Cast: Jorge Porcel, Alberto Olmedo, Mario Sapag, Beatriz Bonnet, Carlos Garaycochea, Mónica Gonzaga, Marita Ballesteros, Nancy Herrera and María, Marisa and Victoria Carreras.

As it always happens at the beginning of the winter holidays, star comedians Jorge Porcel and Alberto Olmedo appear in a light-hearted pic aimed primarily at the moppet audience, who can't see them in the spicy revues they play

onstage and only partially understand the double entendre jokes on their tv shows. Another comic ace, Mario Sapag, presently at the top of the ratings scoreboard, adds drawing power to the cast.

Porcel & Olmedo are not this time the Abbott & Costello-like pair seen in their previous pics. In parallel stories, Porcel is a timid hotel detective wishing to play the bandoneon (the key instrument for tango) and Olmedo a chemist in love with a widow who has three daughters. Sapag, for his part, does impressions of famous people, as on his tv show.

Director Carreras seems to have kept in mind he was filming for the less discriminating audience.
— *Nubi.*

Meatballs Part II
(COLOR)

Tame sequel bodes lame b.o.

Hollywood, July 29.

A Tri-Star Pictures release of a Space Production. Produced by Tony Bishop, Stephen Poe. Executive producer, Lisa Barsamian. Directed by Ken Wiederhorn. Features entire cast. Screenplay, Bruce Singer, from a story by Martin Kitrosser and Carol Watson. Camera (Movielab color), Donald M. Morgan; editor, George Berndt; music, Ken Harrison; production designer, James William Newport; set decorator, Peg Cummings; set designer, Lou Mann; costumes, Sandi Love; sound, Bill Nelson; assistant director, Robert P. Cohen. Reviewed at Hollywood Pacific Theater, L.A., July 26. MPAA rating: PG. Running time: 96 MINS.
Jamie .... Archie Hahn
Flash .... John Mengatti
Nancy .... Tammy Taylor
Cheryl .... Kim Richards
Eddie.................... Ralph Seymour
Giddy .... Richard Mulligan
Hershey .... Hamilton Camp
Meathead................ John Larroquette
Albert .... Paul Reubens

As a PG entry in the summer crop of kiddie comedies, "Meatballs Part II" is probably too tame and inane even for the prepubescent audience it aims for. Trading on the name of the highly successful summer film from 1979, the sequel lacks the two ingredients that made "Meatballs" a hit — Bill Murray and a sense of humor. This is one summer camp kids won't want to go to.

Film does little to exploit its summer camp setting and instead throws together a bunch of elements that could take place anywhere. Jumbled together helter skelter are military bullies victimizing the good guys, girls looking for their first peek at male anatomy, gay jokes, and a bargain basement E.T. that looks like a Mr. Potatohead with eyes.

If that isn't enough, the Flash (John Mengatti) is a city kid on probation from something or other sentenced to spend his summer as a counselor-in-training at lovely Camp Sasquatch. He might have done better to stay in jail.

Mengatti who plays Flash like a streetwise version of Matt Dillon with a bit of Robert De Niro thrown in for good measure, goes about his business being cool until he is smitten by the innocent gaze of the lovely Cheryl (Kim Richards), a girl who gives new meaning to the word sheltered.

Essential element missing here, and one that made people respond to the original "Meatballs," is sympathetic characters. Hamilton Camp, as the commandant of the neighboring military camp that is trying to take over Sasquatch, is a cardboard fascist. Equally predictable is John Larroquette as his closet gay assistant. Richard Mulligan as the dotty camp owner is scarcely more convincing. Performances throughout do little to make an audience want to spend two hours with these people.

Paul Reubens, a.k.a. standup comic Pee-Wee Herman, is okay but under-used as Albert.

Climax in the boxing ring, with Flash showing more than his true colors, saving the day and winning the girl, tries to bring together all the elements with a supernatural whimsical ending but falls flat. By this point Bruce Singer's script has already let things get out of hand.

Direction by Ken Wiederhorn is competent but does nothing to make a whole out of the fragmented and not very funny material. Special effects involving the alien are definitely dime store variety and give the film an amateurish look. — *Jagr.*

Bete Balanco
(Swingin' Betty)
(BRAZILIAN-COLOR)

Rio de Janeiro, July 24.
An Embrafilme release of a CPC production. Executive producer, Tizuca Yamazaki. Produced by Carlos Alberto Diniz. Directed by Lael Rodrigues. Features entire cast. Screenplay, Rodrigues, Yoya Wurch; camera (Eastmancolor), Edgar Moura; art direction, Yurika Yamazaki; music, Cazuza, Roberto Frejat; musical direction, Liane Muhlemberg; editing, Leal Rodrigues; special effects, J.M. Efeitos Visuals; sound, Roberto Carvalho and Irapuan Jardim; production director, Walter Schilke. Reviewed at Embrafilme main screening room, Rio de Janeiro, July 23, 1984. Running time: **74 MINS.**
Bete Balanco ....Débora Bloch
Rodrigo ....Lauro Corona
Paulinho ....Diogo Vilela
Bia...........................Maria Zilda
Tony....................... Hugo Carvana
Deca..................Arthur Muhlemberg
Vitor ....Jessel Buss
Tininho ....Cazuza
With the groups Barão Vermelho, Lobão e os Ronaldos, Brylho, Celso Blues Boy and Metralhatxea.

The current reality of the cinema market in Brazil has determined a set of new strategies for producers. One is a tendency toward youth-oriented pics, as well as an increased concern with merchandising and with the technical standards of films. As it happens everywhere else, the market is determining the product, while auteuristic ideals tend to be left behind.

"Bete Balanco" is a film typically determined by the market. Cheap (around $50,000), clean, well-done, it tells the story of an inland Brazilian teenager whose dream is to become a famous rock singer in Rio de Janeiro. She manages to escape from her parents' tutelage and comes to Rio where, along with a photographer boyfriend, she will climb every step to make her dreams come true.

Director Lael Rodrigues (partner and editor of Tizuca Yamazaki's films, including "Gaijin," here debuting as director) keeps most of his film moving to the rhythm of a video music clip. In fact, a few videoclips were actually produced to be a part of the action, each showcasing a particular international standard.

Yet "Bete Balanco" is more than a succession of fine videoclips. Rodrigues is sensitive to the situations, the locations and the characters. Unlike other youth-oriented items, the characters here are closely related to real life. They are all teens, and they make music, consume drugs and enjoy sex. In short, they behave "normally," very much aided by fine dialog, an involving plot and a light director's presence.

Acting is uniformly fine by Debora Bloch (a young tv actress who debuted in features only a few months ago in "Noites do Sertão," by Carlos Alberto Prates, winning the Gramado Festival's award for best actress), Lauro Corona (also a tv actor, seen last year in Sergio Resende's "O Sonho Não Acabou") and Diogo Vilela (in the role of Paulinho, Bete's best friend and roommate in Rio). The presence of pop music is constant, of course, performed by popular rock groups such as Barão Vermelho and Lobão e os Ronaldos. In fact Bete's musical theme, composed by Barão's leader Cazuza, has been a hit on local FM stations months ahead of the pic's opening.

As a film exclusively committed to satisfying young audiences, "Bete Balanco" is an absolutely successful product. Production level, despite the low budget, is good, including bright cinematography and dynamic editing. The fine rock music, and touching characters could make "Bete Balanco" a saleable item — *Hoin.*

Go Tell It On The Mountain
(COLOR)

Powerful Black drama destined for PBS.

Hollywood, July 29.
A Learning In Focus production. Produced by Calvin Skaggs. Executive producer, Robert Geller. Directed by Stan Lathan. Features entire cast. Screenplay, Gus Edwards, Leslie Lee, based on the novel by James Baldwin. Camera (TVC color), Hiro Narita; editor, Jay Freund; music, Webster Lewis; production design, Charles Bennett; set decoration, Joe Rainey; costume design, Bernard Johnson; sound, Jim Hawkins; assistant director, Herb Gains. Reviewed at the Four Star (Filmex), L.A., July 15, 1984. (No MPAA Rating.) Running time: **94 MINS.**
Gabriel Grimes ....Paul Winfield
Aunt Florence ....Rosalind Cash
John Grimes ....James Bond 3d
Roy Grimes............Roderic Wimberly
Elizabeth Grimes ....Olivia Cole
Young Gabriel ....Ving Rhames
Esther......................Alfre Woodard
Deborah...................C.C.H. Pounder
Sister McCandless ....Linda Hopkins

"Go Tell It On The Mountain" is a superbly acted, admirably earnest adaptation of James Baldwin's first novel. Made by Learning In Focus via grants from the National Endowment for the Humanities, American Playhouse and the National Endowment for the Arts, pic premiered at Filmex but is apparently destined for television exposure on PBS rather than a theatrical release. Intense family drama has a particular appeal to black audiences, but integrity of the telling and Baldwin's name create crossover appeal as well.

Set in 1935 but featuring flashbacks spanning three decades, ambitious work documents two generations of extremely oppressed family life and how various youths attempt to make their break with it.

Central figure is Gabriel, who as a young man in the South runs away from home and becomes an up-and-coming Baptist preacher. Married but childless with meek fellow believer C.C.H. Pounder, Gabriel (played with vigor in the flashbacks by Ving Rhames) is seduced by Alfre Woodard and has an illegitimate son who grows up with his mother.

Remorseful about all this, Gabriel becomes irrevocably embittered when his ne'er-do-well son is killed at an early age, and the man, grown into the person of Paul Winfield, resettles and starts a new family in Harlem.

Reduced to subordinate status in his neighborhood church and a laborer by day, Winfield is a forbidding figure of pent-up rage, intolerance and casual cruelty to his second wife, sister and two sons. Insisting upon regular home Bible readings to the exclusion of any other pastime for his kids and mindless of any other interests or abilities they might exhibit, Winfield bears down on them mercilessly and even demands that his bright son John (the obvious Baldwin figure) return a city honor for writing achievement, so much does he hate and mistrust white folks.

Despite the restrictions at home, one son, Roy, clearly is headed for no good on the streets. On the other hand, John celebrates his 14th birthday by stealing off to Midtown to see his first motion picture, the Leslie Howard-Bette Davis "Of Human Bondage."

Unfortunately, because of the demands of squeezing a rich, incident-filled book down to 90 minutes of screen time, some of the situations and characters don't really pay off dramatically. John's first film experience, for instance, clearly makes a big impression on him, but he never discusses it with anyone and one doesn't know what the intellectual ramifications are for him.

Introverted, curious and smart, John is clearly "different" from those around him, and for this reason his conformist capitulation to his father at the end, in the form of an acceptance of Jesus at an emotional gospel meeting, doesn't quite ring true. With all that's come before, it's almost impossible to believe John will now just swallow his other interests and accept his father's world lock, stock and barrel.

Nevertheless, drama is consistently engrossing due to pointed scripting by Gus Edwards and Leslie Lee and expert performing by an outstanding cast. In an essentially unsympathetic part, Winfield is dynamite. As his sister and second wife, Rosalind Cash and Olivia Cole, respectively, hold their own in top fashion, and Alfre Woodard is supremely sultry as she finds young Gabriel's Achilles' heel. James Bond 3d most effectively conveys John's ambivalence, hopes and intellectual potential.

Director Stan Lathan has done a fine job with the actors and in staging the dramatic confrontations. Visual quality, at least in print on view, is on the murky and fuzzy side, which reduced the enjoyment. Period details are modest but effective. — *Cart.*

Joint Custody: A New Kind of Family
(COLOR-DOCU-16m)

A New Day Films release (Franklin Lakes, New Jersey). Executive producer, Kathy Kline. Produced and directed by Josephine Hayes Dean. Camera (color, 16m), Stuart Nash, John Hazard; sound, Lee Orloff, Samantha Heilweil, Peter Miller, Doug Vaughn; music, Peter Fish; editor, Marian Hunter. Reviewed at American Film Festival, N.Y., May 31, 1984. Running time: **85 MINS.**

Broken homes are a common setting for drama on television, but "Joint Custody" is different, as its theme is mended homes. These parents, four sets of them — all white, middle-class, employed and seemingly well educated — have worked out the calendars and logistics by which their children live equally and happily with both divorced parents. The parents have divorced one another but have not divorced their children.

Indeed, "Joint Custody" shows one case of an extended family network wherein divorced parents have re-married to new partners who also have children by previous marriages. One almost needs a genealogical chart to identify who's whose when six or eight head of children run screaming through the house.

This valuable new film on co-parenting — "custody" has such an institutional ring to it — demonstrates how these ex-spouses can share the joys and hardships of parenthood in a new kind of democratic collaboration that was perhaps missing in their defunct marriages. "Joint Custody" shows how a new kind of divorce settlement, now about five years old, is already working in thirty states. Dangers remain, however, as when irresponsible "ping pong" parents bounce their kids back and forth, causing them severe disorientation and personality disorders.

Given the high divorce rate in the U.S., with 85% of divorced women working, the increasing assertiveness of women demanding equal rights and careers, and the new recognition by the law and society that fathers must partake in child-rearing — given all that, "Joint Custody" connects importantly to American concerns.

— *Hitch.*

Hard Choices
(U.S.-COLOR)

Hollywood, July 15.
A Screenland/Breakout Prods. Two production. Produced by Robert Mickelson. Co-producers, Iris Sawyer, Anthony Kiser. Executive producers, William Kirksey, Toby Hubner, Wendi Friedman. Directed, written by Rick King. Story by Mickelson, King. Camera (DuArt color), Tom Hurwitz; editor, Dan Loewenthal; music, Jay Chattaway; production design, Ruth Ammon; costume design, Jeffrey Ullman; sound, Drew Kunin; associate producers, Ellen Sherman, Rob Nathan, Eric Freidheim, Loewenthal; assistant directors, Evan Dunsky, Dennis Benatar. Reviewed at the American Film Institute, L.A., July 13, 1984. (No MPAA rating.) Running time: **90 MIN.**
Laura Stephens .... Margaret Klenck
Bobby Lipscomb .... Gary McCleery
Sheriff Mavis Johnson .... John Seitz
Don .... John Sayles
Ben .... John Snyder
Josh .... Martin Donovan
Carl .... Larry Golden
Jimmy .... Judson Camp
Horton .... Wiley Reynolds III
Maureen .... Liane Curtis
Deputy Anderson .... J.T. Walsh
Terry Norfolk .... Spalding Gray
Preach .... John Connolly
Mrs. Lipscomb .... Ruth Miller
Blinky .... Thom McCleister

Spiked with curveball plot twists and in all ways a strange film, "Hard Choices" is a pleading social problems picture, a prison meller, an unlikely romance and a contempo thriller all rolled into one. A sense of social unjustice seems to be the motivating force behind the film, but the unexpected story turns lead to considerably

more interesting territory than the premise initially promises. This indie feature, which preemed at Filmex, has limited b.o. potential due to its unusual mixture of genres, but it does reveal some talent which will undoubtedly be heard from more decisively in future.

Writer-director Rick King, whose previous feature was the 1977 experimental cinema-verité effort "Off The Wall," starts this off with three poor white trash brothers trying to commit a petty robbery and killing a policeman instead.

Trio is quickly apprehended, and while the two older brothers are sent straight to prison, Bobby, who was waiting out in the getaway truck when the shooting occurred, is only 15 and endures incarceration not knowing whether he'll be tried as an adult or juvenile.

Enter Laura, a young woman who, with seemingly selfless devotion, runs a program to spring under-age kids from adult jails. At first, Laura seems like an insufferably earnest do-gooder, and one braces oneself for an hour of self-righteous harrangues about the evils of the criminal justice system and how prisoners ought to just be let go because they're just misunderstood victims of circumstance and society.

But then funding for Laura's program dries up, and she's so determined to help Bobby out that she visits an old college chum played by writer-director John Sayles, a big-time drug dealer who's only too glad to underwrite the hiring of a new lawyer because, as he puts it, kids need to be out there on the streets to become his future customers.

When Bobby has reached the end of his legal rope and appears headed for a life sentence from an adult court, Laura can't take it anymore, marches into the kindly sheriff's office with a gun and springs Bobby who, after a moment's hesitation, decides to accompany her.

Under the momentary protection of Sayles and his drug-running operation, the two flee to Florida and enter into a sexual affair. But, in true film noir fashion, the lovers-on-the-run are inevitably doomed, so it's only a matter of time.

Final point of the inherent social tract is the anticipated one, that the system leaves those trapped within its net no way out. However, King is to be commended for subverting conventional expectations at numerous points along the way, not only in the realm of plot but also in characterization.

Margaret Klenck's Laura intriguingly evolves from a noble, purposeful soul to a hopelessly confused and misguided one who will

even seduce a 15-year-old simply because he's been a victim. John Seitz is particularly impressive and sympathetic as the smalltown sheriff who recognizes that Bobby is not a bad egg but pays for his understanding ways. Gary McCleery is okay in the leading role, while Sayles seems to have had fun as the laid-back drug runner.

A mixed-bag of curiosities, pic is adequate on technical levels.

— *Cart.*

Noches Sin Lunas Ni Soles
(Nights Without Moons Or Suns)
(ARGENTINE-COLOR)

Buenos Aires, July 24.
A Vicente Vigo presentation of a Horacio Casares Producciones production. Produced by Daniel Portela. Directed by José Martínez Suárez. Stars Alberto De Mendoza and Luisina Brando. Screenplay, Martínez Suárez and Rubén Tizziani, based upon the latter's novel; camera (Eastmancolor), Alberto Basail; editor, Jorge Pappalardo; music, Roberto Lar; art director, Carlos T. Dowling. Reviewed at the Sarmiento theater, Buenos Aires, June 21, 1984. Running time: **90 MINS.**
Cairo .... Alberto De Mendoza
Ana .... Luisina Brando
Maidana .... Lautaro Murúa
Forger .... José Mará Gutiérrez
Páez .... Arturo Maly
Felix The Cat .... Cacho Espíndola
Muñeco .... Boy Olmi
Cairo's father .... Guillermo Battaglia
Cairo's mother .... Eva Franco
Informer .... Rudy Chernicoff

It is hard to imagine, much less explain, why the experienced people associated with this project didn't notice the flaws in the script, which lacks the clear motivations and unarguable details necessary to a convincing police story.

Here Alberto De Mendoza, as a convict soon to be freed, escapes from jail at the request of his best friend, who is dying in a neighboring country and who has asked him to deliver his part of a hidden booty. The friend doesn't appear on screen, so the viewer can only guess at the feeling linking him with the protagonist. There is just a verbal clue when De Mendoza reads aloud (despite being alone) the letter he has received.

While spending his first night in the refuge of the three gangsters who helped him to escape, De Mendoza exchanges some glances with Luisina Brando, a whore living with the gang's leader, and soon after they flee together, chased from then on by both police and villains. Although his picture is widely shown on tv, De Mendoza ventures into the streets without hiding his features, after having bedded Brando, of course, and fallen in love with her. Subsequent developments leave either loose ends or resort to incredible solutions, such as the sheriff suddenly figuring out — after three years of guessing — where the money is hidden.

The script shortcomings prevent the buildup of both suspense in the

main story and human warmth in the De Mendoza-Brando affair. Star names might help somewhat at the local wickets. Director Martínez Suárez — summoned at the last minute when originally inked helmer David José Kohon refused to lens the pic — apparently did best he could to attain decorous acting. —*Nubi.*

The Work I've Done
(U.S.-DOCU-COLOR-16m)

Hollywood, July 30.
A Blue Ridge Mountain Films production with the Television Laboratory of WNET/13. Produced, directed, written by Kenneth Fink. Camera (DuArt color), Don Lenzer, Gary Steele; editor, Sonya Polonsky; sound, Peter Miller, Roger Phenix; associate producer, Edward Gray. Reviewed at the Celluloid Services Screening Room, L.A., July 27, 1984. (No MPAA rating.) Running time: **54 MINS.**
Features: Thess Campell, Buddy Jones, John Kollock, Dot Ladyansky, Walter Unger.

"The Work I've Done" is an engrossing, sometimes touching documentary about the dilemma of retirement and how different people handle it. Recently unspooled at Filmex, hour-long study is the second effort by Gotham filmmaker Kenneth Fink, who two years ago surfaced with another fine look at working folk, "Between Rock And A Hard Place." Since it was produced in conjunction with WNET in New York, this will have its primary exposure on television, but might also prove a valuable addition to a non-theatrical library.

Fink found a good, representative focus for his film at the Budd Co. in Philadelphia, where his subjects worked as welders or janitors and where the union contract dictates "30 years and out" with full pensions for employees.

Docu is framed around the last day on the job for Thess Campell, a reserved, 54-year-old American Indian who looks considerably younger than his years and is clearly going to have a lot of time on his hands.

Fink then moves on to a union-sponsored trailer park in Florida, where he finds some good interview subjects, including one outgoing black man who sings Italian opera arias and another, sadder, one who is having psychological problems readjusting to his having nothing to do with his days after years of labor.

Although the workers here are all men, Fink rewardingly turns for a few moments to the challenge widows face after their husbands die. With great candor and generous humor, one Dot Ladyansky describes how she fully expected to live out her years alone, but at 68 decided to try to reverse her fate and soon landed a wonderful gentleman her own age. Ladyansky's description of how she seduced her new mate is pricelessly moving, the highlight of the picture.

One of the men is seen returning to the plant for the first time since his retirement, and the visit is filled both with hearty reunions and awkward moments. But Campbell's bow-out is a sadly perfunctory affair, with comrades stopping by for the obligatory so longs on an occasion of heavily mixed feelings.

Fink allows his subjects to fully voice the pros and cons of retirement, how on the one hand it represents what they've been looking forward to all along, but on the other leaves them with a sense of emptiness and lack of worth.

What the film does not take on, however, is the system itself, one which puts seemingly able people out to pasture well before their time. The majority of the men on view are decidedly of middle age, not real oldtimers, and on the face of it, it seems preposterous that a man of 54 should be forced to quit work if he doesn't want to. Pic leaves one wondering if this is a union or management-imposed requirement, and why it is so. When the retired worker revisits the factory, he urges his old pals to stay on the job, not to leave, but it's quite unclear what choice they have in the matter. —Cart.

Last Stand
(AUSTRALIAN-DOCU-COLOR)

Sydney, July 17.
A Captured Live production. Produced by John McLean. Directed and edited by Tony Stevens. Camera (color), John Whitteron; sound (Dolby stereo), Mark Opitz, Bronwyn Murphy; associate producer, Dirty Pool Artists Management. Reviewed at Village Cinema City, Sydney, July 17, 1984. Running time: 85 MINS.

"Last Stand" is a chronicle of the history and music of one of Australia's most commercially successful rock groups, Cold Chisel.

Band broke up at the end of 1983 after 10 years together, signaling its end with a mammoth farewell concert at Sydney's 12,000 seat Entertainment Center.

"Last Stand" lets the music say it all, conveying as best as film can the energy and excitement of their last concert. Concert footage is simple but comprehensive, throwing in a good balance of backstage, audience and frontstage shots; for a live performance, Dolby stereo sound is excellent.

Footage in between includes interviews with band members and colleagues and various events that mark different stages of the band's development or inspired their most well known songs, ranging from earliest footage ever taken of Cold Chisel in their days as a rough pub act, to their infamous appearance on the prestigous Countdown Awards in 1981, when the group

smashed its instruments as a protest against what it saw as the hypocrisy of the music industry.

The integrity Cold Chisel claimed to hold towards their music and fans, coupled with the band's reckless regard for bucking the system within the record industry, is constantly played up throughout the docu.

Docu is sure to consolidate its first release on the art cinema circuit in Australia and New Zealand, then homevid and tv. Band never broke into the U.S. or European markets in a big way, however, so it's unlikely pic will have appeal elsewhere. —Doch.

The Other Side Of A Gentleman
(HONG KONG-COLOR)

Hong Kong, July 17.
Always Good Film Co. Ltd. production and presentation. Released by Golden Princess. Directed by Lam Ling-Tung. Stars Alan Tam, Lin Ching-shia. Music and songs by Alan Tam. Reviewed at Isis Theater, July 17, 1984, Hong Kong. Running time: 98 MINS. (Cantonese soundtrack with English subtitles)

Uneducated, rough, irresponsible and outspoken Alan Tam is unknowingly chosen as a guinea pig by a group of university intellectuals as part of their psychology research. They want to find if love can mold him into a different person by changing him into a responsible and decent man.

Lin Ching-shia is the lady assigned to carry out the mission. What follows is a chain of events that is not only forced and predictable, but also beyond belief. Lin and Tam discover an attraction for each other and Tam naturally decides to improve himself to come up to the lady's educational and cultural background.

For complications, Lin is engaged to be married and she is perturbed with the fact that an innocent man has been victimized then dropped like a used tissue. She gets married anyway, but during the wedding ceremony something happens, just like in the movies.

What is wrong with the storyline is that it can't seem to decide whether to be serious or comic. The quality of the cinematography varies from sequence to sequence, while the acting is extremely calculated. As expected, there's a huge dosage of scruffy lingo and coarse Cantonese-style comedy. And while both the male and female players are still great-looking on screen, their matured 30s look cannot be disguised in their roles as teenage lovers. If one goes often to American films one won't be surprised to see variations of some scenes from "The Graduate" and "Two Of A Kind."

However, despite the failings of "The Other Side Of A Gentleman,"

the film is doing well at the box-office, which should prove once again that comedy, no matter how lackluster and unoriginal, still sells with the Hong Kong masses.

The film ends happily as the reunited lovers ride a motorcycle into a sea of Hong Kong traffic with the romantic message, true love does determine people's road to destiny. This gentleman sadly has no legs to move outside the domestic scene. — Mel.

Robbers Of The Sacred Mountain
(CANADIAN-COLOR)

A Paul Heller production, in association with Sanford Greenberg, Schulz Prods. and Sonesta Prods. An Intrepid Prods. picture. Executive producer, Heller. Produced by Keith Rotman. Directed by Bob Schulz. Stars John Marley, Simon MacCorkindale, Louise Vallance. Screenplay, Olaf Pooley, Walter Bell; camera (Film House color), Laszlo George; editor, Ralph Brunjes; music, Lalo Schifrin; sound, Owen Langevin; assistant director, Eduardo Rossoff; production design, Dave Davis; costume design, Aleida MacDonald; stunt director, Hubie Kerns; special effects, Lorencio Cordero, Jesus Duran. Reviewed on Prism Entertainment vidcassette, N.Y., July 12, 1984. (No MPAA Rating.) Running time: 97 MINS.
Dr. Falcon....................John Marley
Hank Richards.....Simon MacCorkindale
Tracey Falcon............Louise Vallance
B.G. Alvarez...............Blanca Guerra
Murdoch..................George Touliatos
Marques...................Jorge Reynoso

"Robbers Of The Sacred Mountain" is an okay pulp adventure film, inspired by the success of "Raiders Of The Lost Ark." Filmed in 1982 under the title "Falcon's Gold" as the first of the cable-backed feature films (by Showtime), pic is now available to homevideo fans.

The late John Marley toplines as Dr. Christopher Falcon, an archaeologist called away from an Arabian dig to Mexico where his expert opinion is needed on a recent find. Items, including a fertility goddess statuette much sought after by Falcon, turn out to be from a legendary treasure lost in a 1645 earthquake, containing materials from meteorites and thought to have supernatural powers.

A shady, fabulously wealthy industrialist Murdoch (George Touliatos) stakes Falcon to an expedition to find the rest of the Mexican treasure, with gungho reporter Archibald (Hank) Richards (Simon MacCorkindale) tagging along in hopes of writing about Falcon, and a beautiful Mexican woman B.G. Alvarez (Blanca Guerra) hired as guide. Falcon's feisty young daughter Tracey (Louise Vallance) stows away also.

Punctuated by frequent action sequences, treachery and twists, tale is an effective low-budget update of traditional serials and benefits from a more explicit sexiness (cable backing shows up in

frequent nude scenes by the striking Mexican actress Guerra, balanced by equal time skin displays by hero MacCorkindale) than its more famous big-screen competition. Cast is okay, though villainy is not hissable enough and despite supernatural and sci-fi teasing story elements, the plot payoff is conventional. — Lor.

Slavnosti Snezenek
(Snowdrop Celebrations)
(CZECH-COLOR)

Karlovy Vary, July 15.
A Czechoslovak Film Production, Barandov Film Studio, Prague; world rights, Ceskoslovensky Filmexport, Prague. Features entire cast. Directed by Jiri Menzel. Screenplay, Bohumil Hrabal, camera (color), Jiri Macak; music, Jiri Sust. Only credits available. Reviewed at Karlovy Vary Film Festival (Film Mart), July 15, 1984. Running time: 85 MINS.
Cast: Rudolf Hrusinsky, Jaromir Hanzlik, Jiri Schmitzer, Petr Cepek, Zdena Hadrbolcova, Josef Somr, Libuse Safrankova, Miloslav Stibich, Eugen Jegorov, Borik Prochazka.

This is the fourth time helmer Jiri Menzel and scribe Bohumil Hrabal have collaborated on a Czech film production — the others were Oscar-winner "Closely Watched Trains" (1964), the unreleased "Larks On A Wing" (1969) and "Cutting It Short" (1980). Now comes arguably the most original and personal of their team efforts, "Snowdrop Celebrations," based on a Hrabal book of short stories and portraying the writer's neighbors who live rather lusty and eccentric lives in the forest district of Kersko (near Prague in Bohemia). Pic may have been cut down from its original feature length to the present 85 minutes, but enough fare in is still there to gather and appreciate fully the filmmaker's intentions.

This is a warming human comedy on man's foibles, a universal tale that surely would have tickled the funnybone of Aristophanes or Chaucer, to say nothing of Jaroslav Hasek and Terry Southern. Nothing much happens in the film, save for an incident in the forest community. But this spurs a conflict between two rival hunting associations: a wild boar is shot in a schoolroom (on neutral territory) and that's enough to prompt a celebration in the local inn for both clubs in order to settle squatter's rights, so to speak. Naturally enough, the carousing leads to more conflicts and good-natured pranks, until at the end only a few take notice that a fatal accident to one of the revelers has taken place (exemplifying that tragedy is but the reverse side of comedy on the classical dramatic scale).

Czech film buffs thereby will notice a probable conscious similarity with other Czech comic classics, e.g., Milos Forman's "A Fireman's Ball," Ivan Passer's short

"A Sunday Afternoon," and Menzel's own "A Capricious Summer" and "Cutting It Short."

Pic begins with an overview of the community, most of the principal characters leading a lazy rustic existence in the lap of nature and being pampered by ritual visits to the village inn just down the road. One local chap (Rudolf Hrusinsky) has to steal away from his harridan of a wife to join his cronies, while a constable in the area does his best to keep the peace (that is, to keep the rival hunting clubs from going for each other's necks at every available opportunity). There's also a young couple who play pattycake in the kitchen between preparing dishes for the feast; an eccentric down the road who takes his goats grazing in an authentic Pontiac stashed away in his chicken-coop garage; a couple of signpainters who plaster motto-like messages all over the place (even in the wooden outhouses), and a crazy fellow on a wobbly bicycle who gets run off the road by a passing bus every time he's loaded with perishable edibles.

As for the wild boar, it's found hiding in a field during harvest time and is smoked out by a trio of intrepid hunters, only to run off wounded down the road to the village school before meeting its demise. That prepares the way for the celebration in the inn, where all the major fun takes place.

Credits are tops, the most amusing moments provided by deadpan thesp types and visual gags. This may be lightweight Menzel, but it's prime Hrabal from start to finish.
—Holl.

Seksmisja
(Sex Mission)
(POLISH-COLOR)

Munich, June 29.
A Film Polski Production, "Kadr" Film Unit, Warsaw; world rights, Film Polski, Warsaw. Features entire cast. Directed by Juliusz Machulski. Screenplay, Machulski, Jolanta Hartwig, Pavel Hajny; camera (color), Jerzy Lukaszewicz; sets, Janusz Sosnowski; music, Henryk Kuzniak; sound, Marek Wronko; editing, Miroslawa Garlicka; production manager, Andrzej Soltysik. Reviewed at Munich Film Fest, June 28, '84. Running time: 90 MINS.
Cast: Olgierd Lukaszewicz (Albert), Jerzy Stuhr (Max), Bozena Stryjkowna (Lamia), Buguslawa Pawelec (Emma), Hanna Stankowna (Tekla, Thecla), Beata Tyszkiewicz (Berna).

Juliusz Machulski's "Sex Mission" is the story of two scientists chosen as guinea pigs for a time experiment: they are to be placed in frozen hibernation machine, and then brought back to life after three years. In the meanwhile, however, the dreaded World War III has broken out, and life has been extinguished on Earth. What's more: the two survivors happen to be the only living specimens of the male sex in a new underground society composed entirely of women and test-tube babies. Further, not three years, but 50 years, have passed since that crazy scientist confined them to their icebox containers.

The jokes begin right away, as lovely, enticing young ladies happen on the scene to watch over them and monitor their every wish. One of the males, Max (Jerzy Stuhr), is a woman-chaser in any case, so the entire experiment of now being a surviving male in a female society is nothing short of being in heaven. As for his companion, Albert (Olgierd Lukaszewicz), love and sex are things he put out of his mind long ago as befitting a serious scientist — but he's quite willing to learn. So, too, is the curious Lamia (Bozena Stryjkowna), who discovers one day the mysteries of a kiss — that slight indiscretion, by the way, turns tyrannical Amazons into pliant kittens. Once this has been discovered, Max and Albert have their weapons to fight back.

The boys' object is to win as much leeway time as possible, for the Council of Women is now deciding on whether or not to "neutralize" the pair for their own good. The pair win a temporary reprieve as sociable guinea pigs, then discover that there's a way to get to the Earth's surface with special space-uniforms. Lamia gives into the kisses and decides to both help them and accompany them on their new mission, while another sturdy young miss wishes to stop the escape by whatever means possible — even if it means donning a space-uniform and following the culprits to the surface too.

Once there, it's evident that breathing fresh air hardly has a bad effect on anybody. And what's more: there's life on earth. Someone has been living after the holocaust in a real seashore paradise, while making periodic visits to the underworld in disguise. This last joke boosts the film after the basic routines have become repetitious.

Although not up to the standards of those quality Polish pics of the late 1970s, "Sex Mission" is nonetheless the best pic to emerge from the Warsaw studios over the past season.— Holl.

The Electric Valley
(U.S. DOCU-COLOR-16m)

Hollywood, July 17.
A James Agee Film Project production. Produced, directed, written by Ross Spears. Camera, Anthony Forma; editor, Melanie Mahohick; music, Kenton Coe; sound, John Jennings; narrator, Wilma Dykeman. Reviewed at the American Film Institute, L.A., July 16, 1984. (No MPAA rating.) Running time: 92 MINS.
Features: Barrett Shelton, Ed Falck, Henry Wiersma, David Lilienthal, Steve Humphries, Curt Stiner, Henry Clark, Sen. Albert Gore, George Palo, Louis Lowery, John Siegenthaler, Gen. Herbert Vogel, James Gilmore, John Prine, the Smith family, Harry Caudill, Aubrey Wagner, Beryl Moser, Jean Ritchey, Charles Hall, David Freeman.

"The Electric Valley" is a highly informative, worthwhile study of the embattled history of the Tennessee Valley Authority, from its beginnings in the Depression under FDR to its current controversial status as a major nuclear power center. Subject is on the dry side for theatrical situations, but opportunities for playoff exist in non-theatrical campus and television slots.

Using a wealth of newsreel footage and many contemporary, to-the-point interviews, producer-director-writer Ross Spears has created a satisfying portrait of what was behind the creation of the TVA, how it affected those benefited and displaced by it and how it recently became the dinosaur of the nuclear power industry.

Although the downside of some 3,000 families being pushed off their land is amply illustrated, pic resurrects the initial enthusiasm surrounding the TVA's early days. President Roosevelt's personal involvement in the project, designed to bring cheap electrical power to an impoverished area, is invoked via fascinating newsreel material, and pic succeeds in conveying an idea of the genius of original TVA director, Dr. Arthur Morgan.

Along the way, one glimpses how the overeducated Eastern boys heading up the project were regarded as virtual foreigners by the locals, how Wendell Wilkie and various business interests nearly toppled the venture early on and how a rift in TVA leadership, particularly between David Lilienthal and Morgan, resulted in the ouster of the latter.

Project's original purpose prevailed for about a decade, but the advent of the Manhattan Project changed all that, and the TVA appears to have survived the rollbacks of the Eisenhower administration largely because it had assumed such military importance.

Scandal and excess is shown as characterizing the TVA from the 1960s onward, as pollution and strip mining set in, accidents occured, the snail darter slowed things up, electrical costs soared and, with $2.2-billion already spent, construction on the mammoth Hartsville Nuclear Plant was stopped in May 1982. Current officials are left to admit that, with its confidence shaken, the TVA now needs to "redefine its role."

Material is sufficiently absorbing and complicated to easily fill out the 90 minutes given over to it, and Spears has done a fine job in rounding up interview subjects, both eminent and lowly, to offer diverse points or view. This is a solid documentary in all respects.
—Cart.

The Adventures Of Buckaroo Banzai: Across The 8th Dimension
(COLOR)

Quirky comic adventure demands patience.

Hollywood, Aug. 3.
A 20th Century Fox release of a Sherwood Productions presentation of a Sidney Beckerman production. Produced by Neil Canton and W.D. Richter. Executive producer Sidney Beckerman. Directed by Richter. Script by Earl Mac Rauch. Camera (Metrocolor-Panavision), Fred J. Koenekamp; editor, Richard Marks, George Bowers; music, Michael Boddicker; production designer, J. Michael Riva; art director, Richard Carter, Stephen Dane; set decorator, Linda DeScenna; set designer, Virginia Randolph; special effects supervisor, Michael Fink; costumes, Aggie Guerrad Rodgers; music supervision and sound design, Bones Howe; special makeup design, The Burman Studio, Inc.; sound (Dolby stereo), Michael Evje; associate producer, Dennis Jones; assistant director, Gary Daigler.
Motion control photography by Dream Quest Images. Animated visual effects by VCE, Inc.; 8th Dimension sequence by Greenlite Effects, Inc. Reviewed at 20th Century Fox screening room, August 1, 1984. (MPAA rating: PG.) Running time: 103 MINS.
Buckaoo Banzai . . . . Peter Weller
Dr. Emilio Lizardo/ Lord
  John Whorfin . . . . John Lithgow
Penny Priddy . . . . Ellen Barkin
New Jersey . . . . Jeff Goldblum
John Bigboote . . . . Christopher Lloyd
Perfect Tommy . . . . Lewis Smith
John Emdall . . . . Rosalind Cash
Professor Hikita . . . . Robert Ito
Reno Neveda . . . . Pepe Serna
President Widmark . . . . Ronald Lacey
Secretary of Defense . . . . Matt Clark
Rawhide . . . . Clancy Brown

"The Adventures Of Buckaroo Banzai" plays more like an experimental film than a Hollywood production aimed at a mass audience. It violates every rule of storytelling and narrative structure in creating a self-contained world of its own. There is no middle ground here — people will either love it or hate it. Quirky nature of the picture represents a real marketing challenge with prospects iffy.

First-time director W.D. Richter and writer Earl Mac Rauch have created a comic book world chock full of references, images, pseudo scientific ideas and plain mumbo jumbo. It's half serious, half parody and half make believe with the parts adding up to more than the whole.

So complete is the universe dreamed up for "Buckaroo Banzai" that the studio press kit contains "bios" of the characters in the film. The mythology of the "Banzai Institute" supplies a wealth of trivia for future Banzai scholars. It's the kind of picture that could generate Ph.D dissertations. It has already generated a mass of merchandising aimed at capturing the filmgoing audience's taste for the offbeat, including headbands, sweaters, t-shirts, pajamas, comic books, posters, toys and membership cards.

Buried within all this Banzai trivia is an indecipherable plot involving a modern band of Robin Hoods who go to battle with enemy aliens released accidentally from the eighth dimension as a result of Buckaroo's experiments with particle physics.

The search for the oscillation overthruster which allows Buckaroo and his jet car to pass through a solid mountain into the eighth dimension somehow endangers the future of the planet, both from the good aliens who want to contain the spread of the criminal element, and an all-out war between the U.S. and Russia. The latter in particular is a bit hard to follow.

"Buckaroo Banzai" has mixed more genres than a pulp novel. From "Raiders Of The Lost Ark" it borrows the idea of the scholar-hero. Buckaroo is a world-class neurosurgeon, physicist, race car driver and, with his band of merry pranksters, the Hong Kong Cavaliers (also a distinguished group of scientists in their own right) a rock 'n' roll star (in New Jersey, of course).

Richter and Mac Rauch have also fashioned elements of James Bond, "Star Wars," "Dr. Strangelove" and "Invasion Of The Body Snatchers" (Richter wrote the remake of last pic) into an original and off-the-wall synthesis of styles.

Unfortunately the blend of tone and mood falls flat as often as it succeeds. The "Dr. Strangelove" plot in particular is predictable, involving a crazed secretary of defense (Matt Clark), a president of the U.S. (Ronald Lacey) strapped up in traction, and an inept array of advisors.

More interesting is the "Invasion Of The Body Snatchers" undertone with the aliens assuming human form and passing for normal members of the community. It could mean something, but one is never sure if the film is being serious or tongue-in-cheek.

Major difficulty the film presents is in its shifting tone which makes it nearly impossible to get a handle on. What the filmmakers seem to be counting on is a leap of faith from the audience which will allow them to become a part of "Team Banzai."

In this regard they may have miscalculated the appeal of their characters; Buckaroo and crew are intermittently amusing, but are never really sympathetic or engaging. By relying too heavily on enigma the film actually distances the characters and objectifies the action. Plot is too convoluted for one to become caught up in and carried along by it.

As the great one (Buckaroo), Peter Weller presents a moving target that is tough to hit. Richter's gamble is that people will find him interesting enough to keep trying. Weller plays Buckaroo as an

implacable sort of character who may or may not be serious about what he's doing. He'd be more fun if he'd let the audience in on the joke.

Buckaroo's arch enemy, Lord John Whorfin in the body of mad scientist Dr. Emilio Lizardo, is played by a crazed John Lithgow who obviously relishes the chance to be stark raving mad. It is one of the most controlled out-of-control performances on the screen in recent years and is also very funny.

Also very funny is Jeff Goldblum, coming as if from another dimension as every mother's Jewish son hanging out with these cosmic renegades. Dressed as a cowboy from New Jersey, Goldblum's costume with full leg chaps is a howl.

The rest of Banzai's Hong Kong Cavaliers affect a vaguely punk look without much of a personality. Again performances are competent but distanced. Ellen Barkin does a turn as Buckaroo's mysterious girlfriend and looks great but is another emotionless character.

Visual style of the film is more high camp than high tech, though the execution by effects supervisor Michael Fink and large crew of assistants is distinct and in synch with the rest of the film. Production design has utilized more hardware than a junk yard, moving through an array of subterranean locations and seemingly endless rows of plumbing.

Photography by Fred Koenekamp effectively mixes the mundane with the fantastic all under a dark shadow. Richter appears to have accomplished exactly what he had in his mind's eye, but it is not clear exactly what he had on his mind. —*Jagr.*

Red Dawn
(COLOR)

Promising war pic sunk by moralism.

Hollywood, Aug. 6.

An MGM/UA release, produced by Buzz Feitshans and Barry Beckerman. Directed by John Milius. Screenplay, Kevin Reynolds, John Milius; camera (Metrocolor), Ric Waite; editor, Thom Noble; sound, Joe P. Kenworthy; exec producer, Sidney Beckerman; production design, Jackson De Govia; assistant director, Arne L. Schmidt; art direction, Vincent Crisciman; music, Basil Poledouris. Reviewed at the Academy of Motion Picture Arts & Sciences, Beverly Hills, Aug. 3, 1984. (MPAA rating: PG-13.) Running time: **114 MIN.**

Jed ....Patrick Swayze
Robert ....C. Thomas Howell
Bella ....Ron O'Neal
Streinikov ....William Smith
Andy ....Powers Boothe
Erica ....Lea Thompson
Matt ....Charlie Sheen
Daryl ....Darren Dalton
Toni ....Jennifer Grey
Danny ....Brad Savage
Aardvark ....Doug Toby
Mason ....Ben Johnson
Eckert ....Harry Dean Stanton
Bratchenko ....Vladek Sheybal

Teasdale ....Frank McRae
Morris ....Roy Janson

"Red Dawn" charges off to an exciting start as a war picture and then gets all confused in moralistic handwriting, finally sinking in the sunset. Director John Milius will probably lose the film's most obvious sympathizers by carrying the wrong message.

Even among an apparently unsympathetic trade audience at an advance screening, "Dawn" seemed to catch them for awhile with some patriotic fervor for the underdogs, but lost them to laughter with its subsequent cornball dialog.

Idea for the picture was both promising and probable: Sometime in the future, the United States stands alone and vulnerable to attack, abandoned by its allies. Rather than an all-out nuclear war Soviet and Cuban forces bomb selectively and then launch a conventional invasion across the southern and northwest borders, quickly conquering the central part of the country.

"Dawn" takes place entirely in a small town taken by surprise by paratroopers. Hardly have the opening titles gone by than the invaders are in the schoolyard, killing the students and quickly establishing that the villains in this piece will be villainous indeed.

Grabbing food and weapons on the run, a band of teens led by Patrick Swayze and C. Thomas Howell makes it to the nearby mountains as the massacre continues below. Eventually, their fear and confusion turns into rage at the rape and pillage and the teens become a tough troupe of guerillas.

When their first surprise attack on the invaders worked beautifully, it was clear that Milius had gotten the audience on the teenagers' side, equally fed up with what the Communists' had been getting away with. And the excitement built with each subsequent success.

At this point, the formula war picture would have the resistors grow in strength and move out — past, of course, some major final obstacle — to link up with the American armies still defending the country; losing a few favored players in the final moments. It wouldn't have been very original, but it would have been a good picture.

But at the height of their success, Milius has them suddenly betrayed off-camera by one of the teens and on-camera by a lot of self-doubt about the morality of what they're doing. Finally, the small band of originals is all that's left and they get shot up, too, leaving the winning of the war to a postscript. By then, the disappointed audience was hooting.

Swayze, Howell and the other youngsters are all good in their parts (forgiving them the dialog) and Ron O'Neal is splendid as the Cuban commander who doesn't know how to cope when he must defend against tactics that previously worked for him in the field.

Despite their billing, Ben Johnson and Harry Dean Stanton are hardly in the film. —*Har.*

Grandview, U.S.A.
(COLOR)

Cliched view of hinterlands.

Hollywood, July 20.

A Warner Bros. release of a CBS Theatrical Film. Produced by William Warren Blaylock, Peter W. Rea. Executive producer, Jonathan Taplin and Andrew Gellis. Directed by Randal Kleiser. Screenplay, Ken Hixon. Camera (Astro Color), Reynaldo Villalobos; editor, Robert Gordon; music, Thomas Newman; production designer, Jan Scott; set decorator, Bill Harp; sound (Dolby stereo), Kirk Francis; costumes, Wayne Finkelman; choreography, Lisa Niemi, Patrick Swayze; assistant director, Donald Heitzer. Reviewed at Burbank Studios, July 18, 1984. (MPAA rating: R). Running time: **97 MINS.**

Michelle "Mike"
Cody ....Jamie Lee Curtis
Tim Pearson ....C. Thomas Howell
Ernie "Slam"
Webster ....Patrick Swayze
Donny Vinton ....Troy Donahue
Candy Webster ....Jennifer Jason Leigh
Bob Cody ....William Windom
Betty Wells ....Carole Cook
Mr. Pearson ....Ramon Bieri
Cowboy ....John Philbin

"Grandview, U.S.A." attempts to be a slice of American pie, but unfortunately comes out mostly as processed food. The props are all there — the cars, the girls, the small-town life — but the feeling for the people isn't. Jamie Lee Curtis seems to be the only interesting person living there. Because of its location, film should generate some short-lived interest in middle America.

Set somewhere in the midwest, residents of Grandview are all recognizable — too much so. They're clichés. Ernie (Slam) Webster (Patrick Swayze) is a blue-collar man who enjoys smashing cars at the local raceway. "I'm good at it and it's the only thing that makes me different," he tells track owner Mike Cody (Jamie Lee Curtis).

But it doesn't make him different; in fact, it makes him the same as dozens of other small-town characters who were dreamed up in corporate studio offices to represent what the common folk are supposed to be like.

As high school classmates who eventually drift together, Swayze and Curtis are a mismatched couple generating little electricity. Swayze is good at playing a lovable loser but is basically a bore. As the independent woman who fights against the typically presented small-town corruption to keep her raceway, Curtis has much more going for her than Slam. One of the mysteries of the film is what she sees in him.

Another mystery is what Curtis' attraction is to 18-year-old Tim Pearson (C. Thomas Howell). Affair between an older woman and younger man is hardly a new element in film, and is another example of a commercially rather than artistically motivated choice.

Ramon Bieri is fine, keeping Howell's father basically sympathetic despite his patently greedy actions in trying to buy out Curtis' speedway for a golf course and housing development. Are all unscrupulous, small-town businessmen, or has that become a stereotype perpetuated in films like this one?

Script by Ken Hixon doesn't begin to tap the lifeblood of the American grain though mythical midwest location designed by Jan Scott looks authentic as does toned down photography by Reynaldo Villalobos. But the script shows little insight or originality in presenting life in rural America. Cars are everywhere but a five-minute Bruce Springsteen song says more about what they represent in people's lives than "Grandview, U.S.A." begins to suggest.

Ultimately pic is condescending in its view of small-town life in that characters are based on various preconceived notions. They come off the page and not out of their environment as did the people in the more successful American drama "Breaking Away." Only Jamie Lee Curtis has the screen presence here to make her character come alive.

Not only is the film condescending in its rendering of small-town folk, but by extension is condescending to its audience in thinking that this portrait will pass for the real thing.

The fault is not really with Randal Kleiser's direction which makes the most of the limited material and occasionally finds the right wistful tone. But indicative of the lack of imagination that infects the film are Howell's two dream sequences delivered MTV-style. His fantasy life comes more out of boxoffice considerations than his psyche.

There must be more interesting stories in Grandview than the ones in this film. —*Jagr.*

Cloak And Dagger
(COLOR)

Kid thriller should please adults too.

Hollywood, Aug. 2.

A Universal Pictures release of an Allan Carr production. Produced by Allan Carr. Executive producer C.O. Erickson. Directed by Richard Franklin. Script and screen story by Tom Holland. Story by Cornell Woolrich. Camera (Technicolor), Victor J. Kemper; editor, Andrew London; music, Brian May;

production designer, William Tuntke; art director, Todd Hallowell; set decorator, Hal Gausman; sound, Tom Causey; costumes, Ronald I. Caplan; assistant director, Katy Emde. Reviewed at Universal Studios, July 19, 1984. (MPAA rating: PG.) Running time: 101 MINS.
Davey Osborne . . . . Henry Thomas
Jack Flack/Hal Osborne . Dabney Coleman
Rice . . . . Michael Murphy
Kim Gardener . . . . Christina Nigra
George MacCready . . . . John McIntire
Eunice MacCready . . . . Jeanette Nolan
Alvarez . . . . Eloy Casados
Haverman . . . . Tim Rossovich
Morris . . . . Bill Forsythe

"Cloak And Dagger" is a taut, mostly engaging thriller that cleverly manages the trick of using a child as the hero of an espionage yarn without turning the film into a kid's story. While the film is basically a youth thriller and a vehicle for Henry Thomas, adults should not find the picture boring. Blend of Disney and Hitchcock should yield satisfactory results at the boxoffice.

Aussie director Richard Franklin is a longtime Hitchcock disciple as evidenced by his earlier filming of "Psycho II," but pic does not deteriorate into a slavish imitation of Hitchcock's style. Elements like a villain with missing fingers are incorporated into the story more in a spirit of fun.

Though pic is loosely based on the 1949 melodrama, "The Window," and credits a story by Cornell Woolrich who also wrote "Rear Window," Franklin's and screenwriter Tom Holland's intention is more a contemporary exploration of father-son relationships than an espionage plot which is a mere MacGuffin.

Davey Osborne (Thomas) is a normal 11 year old whose imagination sometimes blurs the boundary between fact and fiction. As an adult alter ego he has created the super hero Jack Flack to assist him in his flights of fancy usually carried out on a video game battlefield. Only this time he has stumbled onto a real-life spy adventure involving agents who are trying to sneak military secrets out of the country concealed in a videocassette of the cloak and dagger game.

Befitting any good Hitchcockian hero, no one believes Davey when he tells his tale of witnessing a murder by the enemy agents and the existence of the secret documents. The plot thickens and the only two allies Davey can find are his young girlfriend Kim (Christina Nigra) and the fearless Jack Flack (Dabney Coleman).

Less believing is Davey's father Hal Osborne, also played by Dabney Coleman. Hal fears his son is going overboard and kindly rebukes his fantasies. But in his guise as Jack Flack, costumed in grey leather military garb, Coleman becomes the boy's partner in crime.

The presence of Coleman as an extension of the adult part of the boy's personality is a canny device that not only reveals his relationship with his dad, but presents a way for the adults in the audience to relate to the child's drama. Thomas' performance also helps on this count as he reacts not as a precocious child grown up too soon, but as a likable and sympathetic person with fears and obvious limitations because of his age and experience.

Coleman also turns in a fine performance in the dual role of concerned father and fantasy figure who whispers instructions to the boy. Michael Murphy is convincing, as always, in the villain's role. As leader of the bumbling spy operation, Murphy is appropriately slimy and despicable. His confrontation at gunpoint with Thomas does, however, strain credibility.

In another Hitchcockian touch, John McIntire and Jeanette Nolan play an elderly couple who are not as benign and helpful as they seem at first.

Picture benefits from unfamiliar and interesting San Antonio locations nicely shot by Victor Kemper to suggest impending danger. Problem with any pic featuring kids is the lapse into cuteness and "Cloak And Dagger" is not immune, but it generally manages to overcome its shortcomings with a slick storyline. — *Jagr.*

Sesion Continua
(Double Feature)
(SPANISH-COLOR)

Madrid, July 21.

A Nickel Odeon production, produced and directed by José Luis Garci. Exec producer, José Esteban Alenda. Screenplay, Horacio Valcárcel and J.L. Garci; camera (Eastman-color), Manuel Rojas; sets, Julio Esteban; editor, Miguel Gonzalez Sinde; music, Jesus Gluck; production assistants, José Luis Merino and Valentin Panero; camera operator, Ricardo Navarrete; makeup, Romi Gonzalez; assistant director, Roberto Bodegas. Reviewed at Cinearte screening room, Madrid, July 20, 1984. Running time: 130 MINS.
José . . . . Adolfo Marsillach
Federico . . . . Jesus Puente
Mala . . . . Maria Casanova
Balboa . . . . José Bódalo
Pili . . . . Encarna Paso
Also with: Victor Valverde, Patricia Calot, Pablo Hoyos.

José Luis Garci's new pic "Double Feature" is a film made for other film lovers. From its opening "dedication" to a dozen of cinema's "greats" (mostly American, though Truffaut, Fellini and Bergman are included) to its closing frames, the film is Garci's often touching homage to and reflection upon cinema as a substitute for life, or as life itself.

The two main characters in the film, excellently played by Jesus Puente and Adolfo Marsillach, are Garci's alter egos: a couple writing a screenplay together, to be directed by José (Marsillach). Both men are so utterly absorbed in their world of cinema, which pervades every aspect of their lives, that rather than being a means to an end, it provides the meaning *per se* to their existences.

Whether ultimately this is desirable or not Garci leaves a moot point.

Using a supporting cast of José Bódalo and Encarna Paso, who appeared in Garci's "To Begin Again," along with Maria Casanova, a "steady" in earlier Garci films, helmer fashions a work that relies heavily on colloquial dialog and occasional flashes of humor. The lines, like the sets and everything else in the film, bubble with filmic allusions and the relations of cinema to the real world; for the most part they are delivered in a lighthanded manner.

As the two writers struggle to get their script written, the real world impinges upon them: José's teenaged daughters can no longer communicate with their father and finally drift away into their own world; Federico's (Puente) wife, too, is utterly alienated from her husband and takes herself off to a convent in Avila, without him particularly caring, so engrossed is he in the new script. Even the producer Balboa has ceased to communicate with the non-filmic world around him. It is only after his 19-year-old son dies that he is momentarily deeply moved. But after a touching monolog, his next utterance again refers to the film they are preparing.

It is always risky when filmmakers become introverted with their art and turn solipsist. Garci does not avoid all the pitfalls. The film runs far too long and could do with some cutting. The part with Maria Casanova, cast as a kind of magician-companion is nebulous. But even with some shortcomings, the film comes across as a profound and generally entertaining reflection upon filmic creation as a lifestyle. It once again attests to Garci's international status as an imaginative filmmaker. Pic is unlikely to have the broad appeal of "To Begin Again," but should garner attention in arthouse and "classics" release. —*Besa.*

Karlovy Vary

Lev Tolstoy
(SOVIET-COLOR)

Karlovy Vary, July 18.

A Mosfilm Production, Moscow; world rights, Goskino, Moscow. Stars Sergei Gerasimov and Tamara Makarova. Directed by Gerasimov. Screenplay, Gerasimov. Reviewed at Karlovy Vary Film Fest (Competition), July 16, '84. Running time: 180 MINS.
Cast: Sergei Gerasimov (Lev Tolstoy), Tamara Makarova (Tolstoy's Wife).

"Lev Tolstoy" (or "Leo Tolstoy" — take your pick) has been a film project Sergei Gerasimov reportedly has been wanting to make for some 12 years. And with this three-hour feature (the original version, unspooled at the Tashkent fest last May, was clocked at some four hours), Gerasimov won the Grand Prix at the Karlovy Vary Film Fest, the third time he has done so.

Those who enjoy literary figures in facsimile on a giant screen migh... be entranced by Gerasimov's "Tolstoy." As an actor, he does conjure up some resemblance to one of the great figures in world literature, but as a director he leaves much to be desired, for the film moves at a snail's pace. Pic recreates the last days of Tolstoy's life, a time when his thoughts were wrapped in peasant mysticism. It features the ongoing conflicts with his wife, dialog with his doctor-friend, and the final flight, at age 82, to the railroad station at Astapovo (where he died in the stationmaster's house). Tolstoy was a complex genius, one whose life and works sparked many controversies and are still open to many contemporary interpretations. Gerasimov's view is by no means doctrine.

"Lev Tolstoy" is best viewed as a treatise. If the same had been geared for a lengthy stage monolog it might have worked on the level of "interiorized theater." But as a film, this is little more than a brace of photographs sometimes put into motion. —*Holl.*

Putovani Jana Amose
(Jan Amos' Peregrination)
(CZECH-COLOR)

Karlovy Vary, July 20.

A Czechoslovak Film Production in two parts, Film Studio Barrandov, Prague. World rights, Ceskoslovensky Filmexport, Prague. Features entire cast. Directed by Otakar Vavra. Screenplay, Milos V. Kratochvil, Vavra, Camera, (color), Jaromir Sofr; sets, Karel Lier; music, Otmar Macha. Reviewed at Karlovy Vary Film Fest (out-of-competition), July 12, '84. Running time: 154 MINS.
Cast: Ladislav Chudik (Jan Amos Komensky), Jana Brezinova (Dorota Cyrilova), Marta Vancurova, Zuzana Ciganova, Jiri Adamira, Mikulas Huba, Oldrich Kaiser, Ota Sklencka, Leopold Haverl, Jirina Svorcova, Ctibor Filcik, Radovan Lukavsky, Pavol Mikulik.

Vet Czech helmer Otakar Vavra first teamed with scripter Milos V. Kratochvil some 30 years ago on an epic trilogy on Hussite history, "Jan Hus" (1954), "The Hussite Warrior" (1955), and "Against All" (1957). Now they're back with another lengthy, two-part historical portrait that might just as well be viewed as a continuation of the earlier venture: "Jan Amos' Peregrination," the story of Czech writer and teacher Comenius (Jan Amos Komensky, 1592-1670), a prominent member of the Church of the Bohemian Brethren whose long life and many travels extended the doctrine of Jan Hus (who died in 1415 at the stake in Constance) into the emerging literary world.

Comenius is renowned for spending 40 years of his life seeking to improve the educational systems of Europe; historians estimate that probably 80% of Western Europe in the 17th century was illiterate. "Jan Amos' Peregrination" is the story of his struggles as he combined his many talents (writer, philosopher, diplomat, educator) with his position as a priest in the Church of the Brethren (then still under Catholic persecution, due to the Hapsburgs' crushing the Bohemian Diet in 1621) to help the common people. In 1632, Comenius wrote in Latin "Didactica Magna," a landmark in the history of education that pleaded that education should be universal, regardless of sex, financial means or birth.

And he finished this work while on the run from church persecutors: first to Poland, then to England, Sweden, France and the Netherlands. In his old age, he saw many of his educational theories put into practice and lived to complete a 20-volume "Dictionary of the Czech Language" (unfortunately partially destroyed by enemies). One of his last friends and acquaintances was Rembrandt.

Pic is usual costume-and-sets epic, moving too slowly to entrance many viewers other than history buffs. Czech castles and locations in Bohemia and Moravia are eye-catchers, seemingly ready-made for Jaromir Sofr's sharp lensing talents. — *Holl.*

Nu-Daxne Sheng Su-She
(Girls' Dormitory)
(CHINESE-COLOR)

Karlovy Vary, July 20.

A People's Republic of China Film Production, Shanghai. Features entire cast. Directed by Chao Chun-chung. Screenplay, Yu Shan, Liang Yen-chung. Reviewed at Karlovy Vary Film Festival (Debut Competition), July 11, '84. Running time: 90 MINS.
Cast: Luo Yen, Hsu Ya, Chon Huang-mei, Li Hsia, Chiang I-ping.

Chinese femme helmer Chao Chun-chung graduated from the State Film School in 1964, but was unable to practice her chosen profession until 1975 due to a change in her country's political and creative climate during the late 1960s. She joined the Shanghai Film Studio as an assistant director and waited her turn to direct, which finally came with "Girls' Dormitory."

The film breaks new artistic ground, for Chinese films at least, by portraying student life at the university level. Several contrasting personalities are presented, while via flashbacks it's shown that one of the girls in the school dormitory has had a very difficult childhood. It seems that during the Cultural Revolution the girl's father, a writer, was arrested and then sentenced to work in the mines. The mother than left her family to marry a highly placed official, while the father died tragically in a mine accident. The young orphaned girl is raised by distant relatives. And when she now gets the chance to study at the university, she can only do so by disappearing mysteriously at night to earn her keep at a manual labor job.

The twist is that she meets her long-departed mother again, and soon discovers that a roommate in the dorm from a rich background is her half-sister. As expected in this sentimental, vail-of-tears treatment, identities are revealed in the end and the combined effort of her classmates leads to the girl's story being printed in the school paper. The heroine has won a coveted university scholarship, too.

Only for the committed Chinese film buff. —*Holl.*

The Inferno
(U.S.-DOCU-16M-
BLACK & WHITE)

Karlovy Vary, July 18.

A Robert M. Young Film Production. World rights, Robert M. Young. Directed by Young and Michael Roemer. Written, photographed and edited by Young. Reviewed at Munich Film Fest, June 28, '84. Running time: 58 MINS.

Robert M. Young's 1962 documentary, "The Inferno" (a.k.a. "Cortile Cascino, Sicily") was originally to be produced by NBC for its "White Paper" series, but the docu was then considered too controversial to be aired. The footage was to be discarded, but was rescued by Young, and later pieced together along the lines of his original concept for private and special showings. It was only when a copy was presented recently to the Museum of Modern Art that "The Inferno" got its first exposure. Shortly thereafter, the Munich Film Fest booked it as part of its retro tribute to Young. The film is reviewed here for the record.

Before making "The Inferno," Young and his then filmmaking partner, Michael Roemer, had made three other significant docus for the NBC White Paper series: "Sit-In" (1960), on the Civil Rights sit-ins in the South; "Angola: Journey To A War" (1961), on the growing rebellion in the Portuguese African colony; and "Anatomy Of A Hospital" (1962), a critical view of general hospitals. For "Sit-In" and "Angola" he won the Polk and Peabody awards for journalism and reporting, so it's easy to see why he left NBC after making this revealing and compassionate documentary on life in a Palermo ghetto.

This is a documentary with a narrative line, the story told mostly and metaphorically through the eyes of a woman and mother in the ghetto. It chronicles the despair of living under such hopeless and degrading conditions. Young follows the classic line for a social documentary, particularly those made for television to demonstrate a degree of social responsibility and to elicit an awareness of human suffering and travail.

Young and Roemer somehow won the confidence of the dwellers in the ghetto of Cortile Cascino, which allowed for filming without much gaping or inhibited movement before the camera. They show the limits of the ghetto first, indicating one of the boundaries is a railroad track on which children play rather dangerous games between the passages of freight cars. A shot of a crippled boy picking his way across puddles in the fouled area also indicates one is in an encampment with its own laws and social regulations. One has to struggle everyday to survive, and death is cheap and commonplace.

Young picks out a mother living in a delapidated hut, who describes the members of her family via voiceover. She mentions that her only hope for the future lies in one of her younger children, a girl who just might have the courage and good luck to leave the ghetto one day.

Then comes the chain-of-command that shows that probably nothing will ever change in "The Inferno": the young boys learn to steal early in life, for objects are bought and sold easily on both the legal and the black markets; rag-picking is a job that returns a fast coin or two, so preschool children are employed in the trade run by fathers or brothers; hygiene is practically nil, so babies die in infancy from lack of medicine and nourishment; the Mafia runs an illegal slaughterhouse, where boys learn the meaning of death early; prostitution is rampant, and young girls are recruited from the ghetto. The views of the Mafia in particular make this docu memorable as a statement on Sicilian ghetto life.

Pic deserves more fest exposure as one of the classic tv films made in the heyday of the on-the-spot, American-style, reportage docus.
— *Holl.*

Pensja Pani Latter
(Mrs. Latter's Pension)
(POLISH-COLOR)

Karlovy Vary, July 20.

A Film Polski Production, "Tor" Film Unit, Warsaw; world rights, Film Polski. Warsaw. Features entire cast. Directed by Stanislaw Rozewicz. Screenplay, Pavel Hajny, based on Boleslaw Prus' novel "The Emancipated;" camera (color), Jerzy Wojcik; sets, Tadeusz Wybult; music, Zdzislal Szostak; editing, Urszula Sliwinska; sound, Jan Czerwinski, Jerzy Blaszynski; production manager, Andrzej Soltysik. Reviewed at

Karlovy Vary Film Fest (Information Section), July 12, '84. Running time: 104 MINS.
Cast: Barbara Horawianka (Mrs. Latter), Halina Labonarska (Claire Howard), Hanna Mikuc (Maggie), Magda Wollejko (Joanna), Bronislaw Pawlik (Zgierski), Janusz Paluszkiewicz (Mielnicki), Jacek Borkowski (Casimir), Barbara Rachwalska (Martha).

Well known on the Polish film scene for his literary adaptations, Stanislaw Rozewicz' latest is based on Boleslaw Prus' "The Emancipated" (written in 1893), a realistic novel in the then new tradition of European writing. Another Prus novel, by the way, was adapted by Poland's Jerzy Kawalerowicz: "Pharaoh" (1966). As for the writer, his real name was Aleksander Glowacki (1845-1912); Boleslaw Prus was a pseudonym used in writing social and humorous commentary in a regular weekly newspaper column.

Set at the turn of the century when emancipated women in Poland were still the exception, four ladies at a girls' pension home are contrasted in lifestyles and views on how to get ahead in a man's world. Mrs. Latter runs the boardinghouse, a severe governess whose only weakness is her children and covering up their indiscretions. Her foil is Claire Howard, a militant emancipant of the British school with a distinct habit of nosing into everybody else's business. Then there are the younger women, a pair of tutors Maggie and Johanna, the central figure in the story being the long-suffering Maggie.

Maggie sticks up one day for her friend Johanna, who has been accused of living a generally immoral life — in fact, Mrs. Howard is sure she's now pregnant, and that the expectant father is Mrs. Latter's spoiled son, Casimir. This shakes up Mrs. Latter enough to seek a way to raise enough money to send her son abroad, for the girl's pension is not meeting all its own expenses. So Mrs. Latter sets off one day to see a rich landowner who once proposed to her, and on the way she meets a tragic end by falling into a river fully clothed and drowning.

Stylistically a recommended feature with polished credits, "Mrs. Latter's Pension" doesn't go anywhere as a story. The four femme thesps are particularly engaging as turn-of-the-century personalities groping for emancipation. Lensing by Jerzy Wojick is also a plus. — Holl.

Une Femme Pour Mon Fils

(A Wife For My Son)
(ALGERIAN-COLOR)

Karlovy Vary, July 18.
An Algerian Film Production. Features entire cast. Written and directed by Ali Ghalem, based on Ghalem's novel of the same title. Camera (color), Mahmud Lekhal. Reviewed at Karlovy Vary Film Fest (Competition), July 14, '84. Running time: 90 MINS.
Cast: Isma, Rahim Lalui, Farida, Shafia, Budra, Mustafa El Anka.

So-so Algerian feature about emancipation in a country where old traditions still clash with new ways. Based on a novel by the director, Ali Ghalem, "A Wife For My Son" is about a 16-year-old girl who is forced by her parents to give up her studies to marry a man she has never seen. What's more, the prospective husband has gone off to find work in France. Thus, he returns home only for the wedding and to get his young wife pregnant, then returns to France and a job that's better than anything he can find in his native land.

The twist comes when the girl rebels and walks out of her house, never to return. Instead, she goes to live with a commune of other young women to sort out her future for herself among women who understand her situation fully.

Idea has some value, but pic drags as a whole and doesn't impress in its emancipation theme.
—Holl.

Bota Jmenem Melichar

(A Shoe Called Melichar)
(CZECH-COLOR)

Karlovy Vary, July 20.
A Czechoslovak Film Production, Barrandov Film Studio, Prague. World rights, Ceskoslovensky Filmexport, Prague. Features entire cast. Directed by Zdenek Troska. Screenplay, Jana Knitlova; camera (color) Josef Hanus; music, Karel Wagner. Reviewed at Karlovy Vary Film Fest (Debut Competition), July 12, '84. Running time: 73 MINS.
Cast: Martin Sotola (Honzik), Magdalena Ledvinkova, David Rauch, Tomas Ruzicka, Regina Zahradnikova, Michaela Kreslova, Milada Stybrova, Eva Matejkova, Jana Vankova, Jirina Jelenska, Vaclav Mares.

A children's film, but an unusual one with three parallel stories on life's challenges in a school environment, "A Shoe Called Melichar" is the debut feature of FAMU (Prague Film School) grad Zdenek Troska, and the setting is a typical Prague elementary school. The school being newly constructed, the kids are required to change their shoes for slippers to attend certain classes. Further, the school unfortunately has been built next to a highway, which makes things a bit dangerous and disturbing for all concerned, particularly because of the noise and smog saturating the playground.

The youngest protagonist is a boy named Honzik, whose last stop was nursery school (he liked it better than first grade). On the ninth grade level, another lad has to get accustomed to growing up, and he takes an interest in Honzik's plight because he's sweet on the newcomer's older sister. Lastly, there's the new teacher, a young woman who now has to put aside her leisurely lifestyle, nourished at the university, for teaching respon-

sibilities. Everyone reaches "adulthood" in contrasting ways, while extra motivation is supplied by a schoolroom detective subplot: there's a thief loose in the cloakroom!

Okay for the kidpic circuit, as school scenes have a ring of authenticity. — Holl.

Ultimatum
(POLISH-COLOR)

Karlovy Vary, July 18.
A Film Polski Production, Warsaw. World Rights, Film Polski, Warsaw. Features entire cast. Directed by Janusz Kidawa. Screenplay, Jerzy Janicki; camera (color), Henryk Janas; music, Henryk Kuzniak; sets, Czeslaw Siekiera; editor, Jaroslaw Ostanowko; production manager, Henryk Parnowski. Reviewed at Karlovy Vary Film Fest (competition), July 13, '84. Running time: 90 MINS.
Cast: Stanislaw Michalski, Krzysztof Kiersznowski, Jan Jerusal, Marek Wysocki, Leon Niemczyk, Wienczyslaw Glinski, Wirgiliusz Gryn.

Vet Polish helmer Janusz Kidawa has made some rather good features over a long directing career that began back in 1961. One of his best was the satire "The Sinful Life Of Francisek Bula" (1980). And one of his minor efforts was the Polish competition selection at this year's Karlovy Vary festival "Ultimatum."

Based on a true incident but stretched as far as the imagination can reach, "Ultimatum" tells the story of four Polish terrorist refugees who strongarm a Polish embassy in a Western country (apparently West Germany, although the incident happened in 1982 in Switzerland). Their aim, per Kidawa, was to grab the headlines but all for different reasons: one revolutionary is a psycho killer, another a common criminal, the third an idealist, and the fourth a confused student.

During the hostage-taking at the Polish embassy, one of the office secretaries dies of unforeseen injuries and a lack of proper medicine. Then another embassy staff member is killed. When the police storm the place, the idealist notes the error of his ways and commits suicide. The rest is supposed to be a condemnation of a sensation-hungry media. A zero on every count.—Holl.

Faunovo Velmi Pozdni Odpoledne

(The Very Late Afternoon Of A Faun)
(CZECH-COLOR)

Karlovy Vary, July 16.
A Studio for Documentary Films, Kratky Film production, Prague; world rights. Ceskoslovensky Filmexport, Prague. Features entire cast. Directed by Vera Chytilova. Screenplay, Chytilova, Ester Krumbachova; camera (color), Jan Malir; music, Miroslav Korinek. Reviewed at Karlovy Vary Film Festival (Film Mart), July 15, 1984. Running time: 87 MINS.
Cast: Leos Sucharipa (the "Faun"), Lubise Pospisilova, Jiri Halek, Vlasta Spicnerova, Tereza Kucerova.

Czech film buffs with a recollection of an earlier collaborative effort between helmer Vera Chytilova and scripter Ester Krumbachova, "Daisies" (1965), will be amused by the passing presence of an identical type right out of that film in their latest feature — Chytilova's highly recommended "The Very Late Afternoon Of A Faun." Indeed, in many respects, this appears to be a very late sequel to "Daisies" and well deserves to be booked at international fests. (At last report, the pic was headed for competition at Montreal.)

A moral comedy molded around the well-known Don Juan theme and Debussy's piano piece, the film's protagonist is an aging lecher-type who spends most of his waking hours in pursuit of the fair sex. This is not to say that he succeeds in his aching endeavors, for the joy of such pursuit is often enough in the effort itself — at least that seems to be the director's point.

The hero awakes in the morning in his attic apartment and completes his morning libations under the assumption that the day is bound to have something in store for him if he only keeps his mind and heart on his work. So off he goes, gazing at each and every woman who passes by: some very old, some very young, but mostly lovely ladies in the bloom of youth. However, it just so happens that our pouchy playboy also has an office job to fill in the course of the day, one that's of course also peopled with appropriate damsels and particularly with a middle-aged siren of his own ilk who is on to just about all his devilish tricks. She, in turn, is continually in hot, angry pursuit of the "faun" as he prances off on his daily foolish forays.

The upshot of the comedy is that the faun gets foiled at nearly all his ploys to interest young ladies in his wiles, and he has to share this mutual disappointment with another old crony who stands on the sidelines rooting him on from adventure to adventure. Also, if the horn-rimmed glasses he wears do happen to resemble those of fellow-director Jiri Menzel, then there's another sure connection as well with Chytilova's earlier feature with Menzel in the lead: "The Apple Game" (1977), in which the same sort of protagonist (a hospital physician) constantly is chasing passing nurses.

Although "Faun" is pretty predictable plot-wise, there is nevertheless plenty of enjoyment watching the old boy refusing to give up after each and every charge onto the battlefield. One has only to keep paintings of the mythological satyr in mind throughout this experimental feature composed of bits and pieces of juxtaposed camera shots and excerpted footage to cull more from the movie experience. One has the feeling, too, that the film was put together by Chytilova completely on the editing table, where perhaps Krumbachova penned appropriate dialog as the two went along.

And naturally, the old guy gets his just deserts in the end when the real apple of his eye and perennial heartthrob, his elderly companion in the office, gets even with his meanderings by simply deciding to pack up and leave. Thereupon, the Don Juan finds himself shamelessly chasing his true love with a flagging and repentive passion.

The joy of this modest experimental feature is in the flair with which the whole is composed and delivered. The film buff will be amused from start to finish, while some moments are treasures — as when the flab on the playboy's belly is compared at one point with the bark of a tree trunk in a subtle visual blending effect. Vintage Chytilova, although chancy arthouse fare at best.—*Holl.*

Zanik Samoty Berhof
(The Doom Of The Berhof Lonely Farm)
(CZECH-POLISH-COLOR)

Karlovy Vary, July 15.
A Film Studio Barrandov, Second Production Group, Prague Production; world rights, Ceskoslovensky Filmexport, Prague. Features entire cast. Directed by Jiri Svoboda. Screenplay, Vladimir Körner, Svoboda, based on Körner's story with the same title; camera (color), Vladimir Smutny; music, Jozef Revallo. Reviewed at Karlovy Vary Film Festival (Competition), July 11, 1984. Running time: **91 MINS.**
Cast: Jana Brejchova, Ladislav Krivacek, Evelyna Steimarova, Milan Knazko, Marek Probosz, Zbigniew Suszynski, Leon Niemczyk, Petronela Vancikova, Lubomir Kostelka, Vit Pohanka, Stefan Misovic.

Helmer Jiri Svoboda began making features a decade ago upon graduating from FAMU, the Prague film school. The most successful of his earlier films was "Girl With A Shell" (1980), about a young girl's attempts to raise her younger brothers and sisters despite an alcoholic, divorced mother. Now he's in the competition at Karlovy Vary with a Czech-Polish coprod, "The Doom Of The Berhof Lonely Farm."

Pic is based on a novel by Vladimir Körner and deals with the troubles had in Czechoslovakia along the borders of Germany and Poland during the immediate months after World War II. At this time, bands of so-called "werewolves" were roaming the forests — that is, ex-German soldiers from the Sudeten area who felt they had to keep on fighting despite the certain loss of their properties and certain community rights now that a new government was about to be formed in Czechoslovakia. The

leader of this trio of werewolves is a nun, who has turned in her religious beliefs for a resistance code.

If that sounds a bit farfetched, the rest of the story is much more credible. On this lonely farm "occupied" by the German warmongers is an odd cross-section of the human race: a recently diseased mother (a Sudenten German), a drunken Czech father, a lonely and sensitive daughter in her early teens, a town prostitute hiding from the wrath of the villagers for consorting with the enemy, and various visitors who meet their death — until the newly appointed commissioner roots out the moral evil with a flank attack on the farm.

Well made, with fine thesping, but strictly home fare. — *Holl.*

City Dreams
(SYRIAN-COLOR)

Karlovy Vary, July 18.
A Syrian Arab Republic Film Production. Features entire cast. Directed by Mohamad Malas. Screenplay, Malas, Samir Zikra; camera (color), Ordean Engine. Reviewed at Karlovy Vary Film Fest (Competition), July 15, '84. Running time: **90 MINS.**
Cast: Basel Al-Abiad, Yasmen Al-Kalat, Rafek Al-Sobeay, Iman Zedan, Adeeb Shahada, Talhat Hamdy.

After a series of shorts, Syrian helmer Mohamad Malas has made his first feature, "City Dreams." It's about a 12-year-old who accompanies his mother and younger brother to Damascus to live with their grandfather. The boy has to pretty much support the family with a job as a tailor's assistant, while the grandfather is about as ornery as they come to the defenseless family. Since this is the 1950s, the boy witnesses the overthrow of the Syrian military regime (1954) and the first attempts at unity among the Arab nations. Some two years later in the film, the boy has become a wiser, maturing teenager. It's now 1956, the year of the Suez Canal crisis.

The better aspects of "City Dreams" have to do with the realistic portrayal of life on the streets of Damascus, but thesp performances are wanting in dramatic moments with credits as a whole subpar. — *Holl.*

Smriti Chitra
(Memory Episodes)
(INDIAN-BLACK & WHITE)

Karlovy Vary, July 18.
An Indian Film Production. Features entire cast. Directed by Vijaya Mehta. Screenplay, Laxmibai Tilak, based on her memoirs; camera, Mehta. Reviewed at Karlovy Vary Film Fest (Debut Competition), July 12, '84. Running time: **100 MINS.**
Cast: Suhas Jaoshi, Pallavi Patil, Ravindra Mankani, Suhas Joshi, Mangesh Kulkarni, Visvas Mehandale, Rekla Kamat.

Marathi-language cinema aver-

ages some 40 features annually. The main cities in this centrally located area are Bombay and Pune, and opportunities to make art films or unusual experimental pics are more plentiful than most anywhere else in India. One such film is debut feature by femme helmer Vijaya Mehta, "Memory Episodes."

This is the story of poetess Laxmibai Tilak, whose husband Naryan V. Tilak was a Sanskrit scholar. The 70-year-old writer reminsces about her past, providing a 20-year period for the film to cover as probably the most crucial years in her life.

Following Brahmin and Hindu custom, the 11-year-old Laxmibal is married off to her older husband Naryan, who shortly thereafter goes off on his own to find himself spiritually. It's before 1900 and gradually the husband decides to abandon his previous spiritual teachings and embrace Christianity instead. This poses a problem for the budding poetess, but gradually and independently she goes the same spiritual way herself.

"Memory Episodes" has a lot of technical drawbacks, but it does reveal a good deal about religion in India as it leaves old traditions behind to go new ways. — *Holl.*

Hoi Duiong Mau Da Cam
(Orange-Colored Bells)
(VIETNAMESE-COLOR)

Karlovy Vary, July 18.
A Vietnamese Film Production. Features entire cast. Directed by Nguyen Ngoc Trung. Screenplay, Nguyen Dinh Chinh; camera, (color), Dan Thu. Reviewed at Karlovy Vary Film Fest (Competition), July 10, '84. Running time: **90 MINS.**
Cast: The Anh, Hoang Cuc, Hong Puc, Le Cung Bac.

Vietnamese cinema is still struggling to make its mark on the international film festival scene. Up to now, the only features of note to emerge from the Hanoi Studios and its equivalent in Ho Chi Minh City (formerly Saigon) have been Hong Sen's "The Whirlwind Area," Phan Van Kho's "They Called Her Zao" and Huy Tank's "In The Region Of Sand And Wind."

Nguyen Ngoc Trung's "Orange-Colored Bells," in competition at Karlovy Vary this year, is about a former captain in the South Vietnamese Air Force, who has now retired to the life of a Buddhist monk. However, an old air chum and conspirator with the Americans finds him by chance, and uses the monk's past history to get him to plot against the new Socialist government. The monk initially refuses but eventually spills the beans about secret American bombing flights in the mid-1960s, during which napalm was wantonly used on agricultural fields, jungle foliage, and the like. It turns

out that this same spraying of poison from the heavens had indirectly caused the death of the former air force captain's wife, who committed suicide after giving birth to a deformed child. The monk's confession helps to clear his conscience and cleanse his soul.

Credits are subpar. Same theme was handled brilliantly, by and large, in Kon Ichikawa's "The Burmese Harp" (1956), albeit from a different perspective. — *Holl.*

Kono Ko Wo Nokoshite
(Children Of Nagasaki)
(JAPANESE-COLOR)

Karlovy Vary, July 18.
A Japanese Film Production. Features entire cast. Directed by Keisuke Kinoshita. Screenplay, Taichi Yamada, Kazuo Yoshida, Kinoshita, based on Takashi Nagai's book of same title; camera (color), Hirozo Okazaki. Reviewed at Karlovy Vary Film Fest, (Competition) July 12, '84.
Cast: Go Kato, Yukio Toake, Masamoto Nakabayashi, Mami Nishijima, Chikage Awashima.

Often compared with René Clair (whom the director once visited in France) and Frank Capra, Kiesuke Kinoshita made a string of highly popular social satires in the 1950s, perhaps the best to appear in the whole of Japanese cinema. Now, after many years of inactivity and neglected recognition of the body of his remarkable work, he's back in the competition at Karlovy Vary with "Children Of Nagasaki." It's a rather heavily sentimental feature on the dropping of the Atom Bomb there on Aug. 9, 1945. All the same, it has some saving features — not the least of which being thesp Chikage Awashima, one of Japan's most popular stars in the postwar period in the role of the grandmother.

Kinoshita built a career on poignant human tragedies, but will go down in the film history books as a master, too, of the social satire in which the characters were often more memorable than the films. His best features always demonstrated a professional polish: "The Port Of Blossoms" (1943), "A Morning With The Ozone Family" (1946), "Carmen Comes Home" (1951) and "Carmen's Pure Love" (1952) (two very popular films spotlighting a striptease dancer, the latter the first color feature in Japan), "A Japanese Tragedy" (1953), "Twenty-Four Eyes" (1954) (voted "Film of the Year"), "She Was Like A Wild Chrysanthemum" (1955), "Times Of Joy And Sorrow" (1957), "Candle In The Wind" (1957), "The Ballad Of Narayama" (1958) (its remake won the Golden Palm at Cannes last year), and "The River Fuefuka" (1960).

As for "Children Of Nagasaki," it's quite professionally made and acted. And it has a certain immediacy in view of its connection with

Kinoshita's earlier antimilitaristic "Morning With The Ozone Family" and "A Japanese Tragedy," both made in the immediate postwar period under the watchful eye of Occupation censors. Undoubtedly, "Children Of Nagasaki" could not have been made back then, so one has the feeling now of being introduced to Keisuke Kinoshita's own film testament — that is, a summary of the director's past personal convictions

Based on the originally banned writings of Takashi Nagai, a young doctor who witnessed the holocaust in the city of Nagasaki, the film is a flashback through the eyes of the writer-doctor's son as the latter returns home on a plane from a convention abroad. He recalls how his father fought valiantly with leukemia and the after-effects of being exposed to atomic fallout while treating the survivors. The doctor's own wife died, but his two little children survived and are cared for in the film by the grandmother (Chikage Awashima) while the bedridden father struggles against time to complete his memoirs and scientific research on the after-effects of the atomic bomb.

It's this tragic experience that forms the pic's core, better understood, however, via the eyewitness' spoken words than in the closing sequence which visually reconstructs that horrendous fire over Nagasaki. —*Holl.*

Eine Sonderbare Liebe
(Strange Love)
(EAST GERMAN-COLOR)

Karlovy Vary, July 13.
A DEFA Film Production, "Babelsberg" Group, East Berlin; world rights, DEFA Aussenhandel, East Berlin. Features entire cast. Directed by Lothar Warneke. Screenplay, Wolfram Witt; camera (color), Thomas Plenert; sets, Georg Wratsch; music, Jürgen Ecke; editing, Erika Lehmfuhl; production manager, Manfred Renger. Reviewed at Karlovy Vary Film Festival (Competition), July 13, 1984. Running time: **95 MINS.**
Cast: Christine Schorm (Sybille Seewald), Jörg Gudzuhn (Harald Reich), Mike Gregor (Holger Reich), Christa Lehmann (Sibylle's mother), Franz Viehmann (Hartloff), Peter Sodann (Krüger), Wilfried Puchar (Brigadier).

Lothar Warneke scores as one of the best directors presently on the scene in the German Democratic Republic. He's made a series of fine sketches of life in the GDR, the best being "Dr. Med. Sommer II" (1970), "Life With Uwe" (1974), "The Incorrigible Barbara" (1976), "Our Short Life" (1981) and "Apprehension" (1981). Now he's in the Karlovy Vary competition with the equally impressive "Strange Love."

Both "Apprehension" and "Strange Love" star Christine Schorm, in the former as a middle-aged career woman facing a threat of cancer of the breast, in the latter

as a career woman who puts her job before her heart and her life as a whole. She is one of the fine actresses working at DEFA at present.

Sybille runs a company kitchen, and has been doing her job well for 20 years, so her superiors give her an award at a company dance. There, bored stiff with it all, she meets another lonely soul at the bar, Harald, who knows what makes her a sourpuss, for he's going through the same middleaged crisis himself. After spending the evening together, the rest is making through the same middle-aged together although love seems to be hardly a question. Harald, in fact, needs a mother for his children. Sybille just wants to quit her job and dedicate her life to a home and family. For a while, it works.

The twist is that two strong personalities now have to conserve all their spare energies to win a couple of important matches in the battle of the sexes. And since Harald has recently survived the plight of his deceased wife's lingering illness, he's not about to make concessions just because Sybille wishes to reorganize the household and run things just like she did back at the company kitchen. So the expected showdown comes, and soon Sybille is back on the soup lines trying to figure out what went wrong in the first place. It doesn't take too long: what happened is that she fell in love somewhere along the line, but hasn't as yet melted enough into a flesh-and-blood woman to capture the heart of her mate. In the end, however, a busy signal on the phone back at the commonly shared household indicates there's still a chance to set things right, given one more opportunity.

Pluses in this social drama are the touches throughout that underscore certain pros and cons of living in a Socialist society, as well as the fine performances delivered by Schorm and her partner, Jörg Gudzuhn. The company party-and-dance is an unappetizing affair, one that cuts to the bone as rather cold and even petty bourgeois. Indeed, all the way through the film Warneke is offering constructive criticism of the system as it stands. Western-oriented pics have been handling themes like this for much of the postwar period, but seldom has an East European director reworked the same territory with the same sharp eye for credible detail.

"A Strange Love" also recalls a similar film and performance in a recent Soviet film: Yuli Raisman's "A Strange Woman," starring Irina Kupchenko as a career woman also trying to sort out an affair with a young lover. Lother Warneke deserves something at present like a retro at home or abroad

to put this thematic oeuvre in a proper critical light. Along with Hermann Zschoche, he is currently one of those directors whose few artistic failures are nevertheless of interest to the committed follower of national cinemas. — *Holl.*

Na Gospozhitsata I Neinata Muzhka Kompania
(For A Young Lady And Her Male Companions)
(BULGARIAN-COLOR)

Karlovy Vary, July 18.
A Bulgariafilm Production, Sofia. World rights, Bulgariafilm, Sofia. Features entire cast. Directed by Ivan Dobchev. Screenplay, Margarit Minkov, based on Mikhael Alekseyevich Kuzmin's short story "The Orchestra;" camera (color), Dimko Minov; sets, Georgi Goutsev; music, Kiril Donchev. Reviewed at Karlovy Vary Film Fest (Debut Competition); July 11, '84. Running time: **90 MINS.**
Cast: Plamena Getolva, Naum Shopov, Ivan Ivanov, Nikola Todev, Marin Mladinov, Stefan Iliev.

Bulgarian debut helmer Ivan Dobchev comes from theater directing and carved out a reputation in Plovdiv by tackling Shakespeare, Calderon, Chekhov and Mayakovsky. For his first feature film he has employed noted stage and screen actors.

The time is 1944 and the setting is Sofia. The war is drawing to a close, but the state police are still hunting for underground resistance fighters. It so happens that an orchestra with a torchsinger is performing in a nightclub known as the Titanic Bar. One of the honored guests also happens to be a hated state's attorney, and, with the blood of innocent people on his hands, he is assassinated by a resistance fighter. When the police arrive, suspects are rounded up for questioning, which throws the spotlight on the orchestra (indeed, the girl did innocently help the murderer to get away). The questioning leads to cruelty and death, the upshot being that the girl and her male companions harden into a resistance of their own.

Okay for debut pic, but nothing much beyond filmed theatrics to rave about. — *Holl.*

Einer Vom Rummel
(A Man From The Fun Fair)
(EAST GERMAN-COLOR)

Karlovy Vary, July 18.
A DEFA Film Production, East Berlin; world rights, DEFA Aussenhandel, East Berlin. Features entire cast. Written and directed by Lothar Grossmann, from a story by Harry Falkenhayn. Camera (color), Andrea Kofer. Reviewed at Karlovy Vary Film Fest (Debut Competition), July 13, '84. Running time: **90 MINS.**
Cast: Dirk Nawrocki, Renate Krossner, Jens Uwe Prose, Helmut Strassburger, Angela Brunner, Daniela Hoffmann.

Lothar Grossmann's debut film, from a novel by Harry Falken-

hayn, deals with an outsider, an 18-year-old youth who prefers hanging around carnivals and merry-go-rounds to holding a permanent job. There he can earn enough money to maintain his independence, while romancing the girls on the side.

A quarrel with his uncle who has been raising him leads to a decision to run away from home, which means he now has to earn his bread-and-butter on his own. Things are a bit tougher than expected, but he meets a mature woman who takes him in. She helps the lad to find himself, whereupon he gets a union job in a factory where he has to prove himself. In the end, he's become a bit more grownup than before.

A rather ordinary story with nothing special to recommend it.
— *Holl.*

Parexigisi
(Misunderstanding)
(GREEK-COLOR)

Karlovy Vary, July 18.
A Dimitris Stavrakas Film Production in collaboration with the Greek Film Center, Athens. Features entire cast. Written and directed by Dimitris Stavrakas. Camera (color), Stavros Chassapis; music, Michalis Grigoriou. Reviewed at Karlovy Vary Film Fest (Debut Competition), July 13,, '84. Running time: **90 MINS.**
Cast: Spyros Fokas, Alexis Damianos, Mimi Denisi, Giorgos Moschidis.

After turning from journalism to filmmaking and winning awards for his short "Betty," Dimitris Stavrakas has made his debut feature along the lines of the film noir tradition with "Misunderstanding." The thriller is about a petty criminal just released from prison who decides to try his luck on a "job" just one more time only to get caught in a web of vengeance and betrayal, and finding himself behind bars again. The protagonist is a goodhearted fellow all the same, and he dies in a road accident at the end trying to help the man who has aided him in a risky prison escape.

A film about society's losers, "Misunderstanding" starts well but loses ground as characters' motivations are simply jettisoned in favor of an ambiguous stream of rather pointless actions. Nevertheless, it's of some significance that Greek cinema today is being guided by filmmakers with a distinct liking for the crime thriller and related genre-oriented auteur films. This is still a fascinating film, despite its fragmented storytelling.
— *Holl.*

Ni-Jen Chang Chuan-Gi
(The Story Of Master Chang)
(CHINESE-COLOR)

Karlovy Vary, July 18.
A People's Republic of China Film Production, Peking. Features entire cast. Directed

by Li Wen-hua. Screenplay, Li Wen-hua, Tuy Yu, based on a play by Li Wen-hua; camera (color), Chen Yu-yuan. Reviewed at Karlovy Vary Film Fest (Competition), July 13, '84. Running time: **90 MINS.**

Cast: Shao Wan-lin, Hsin Ching, Hsian Hung, Chang Tie-chu, Huang Tsu-lei.

"The Story Of Master Chang" is in a theatrical manner with appropriate period sets and costumes dating from the turn of the century. Directed by the author, story begins during the fading days of the last Chinese Emperor of the Manchurian Dynasty (it ceased in 1912), and ends with the moral that art and social responsibility grow when ancient oppressive traditions are broken.

Master Chang is a native artist gifted in making clay figures, thus offering an opportunity to frequent the Emperor's court in Peking. He is exploited there by a wily merchant who manipulates his artistic talents under the guise of friendship. Years later, the artist's progeny down to the fourth generation find themselves in similar circumstances: a brother and sister continuing the artistic traditions of the Changs are beset upon by another greedy merchant. They eventually resist the second intrusion and break the family tradition at the same time by offering the secrets of their craft to the public at large.

Pretty predictable and rather stiffly performed filmed theater.
— *Holl.*

Taormina

Papierfuglen
(Paper Bird)
(NORWEGIAN-COLOR)

Taormina, July 23.
Produced by Bente Erichsen for Norsk Film A/S. Stars Elisabeth Mortensen. Directed by Anja Breien. Screenplay by Anja Breien and Knut Fladbakken. Camera (Color), Erling Thurmann-Andersen; editor, Lars Hagstrom; sound, Thomas Samuelson; music, Jan Garbarek. Reviewed at the Taormina Film Festival, July 23, 1984. Running time: **95 MINS.**
Helen Stousland . . . . . . Elisabeth Mortensen
Stefan Larre . . . . Per Sunderland
Paul Brenden . . . . Bjorn Floberg
Aasned . . . . Kjell Stormoen

Norwegian helmer Anja Breien, now on her sixth feature, continues to evolve as a director interested in psychological studies of difficult women. "Paper Bird" adopts a mystery yarn format to depict a woman's struggle to balance feelings, family, work and love. The detective story offers a modicum of suspense, but the real interest is the heroine. Pic will require special handling to pass to foreign markets, but could interest arthouse circuits.

Pic gets off to a strong start with the death of the heroine's father, who falls out of a window almost before her eyes. The police investigation strangely converges with

her defense of a smalltime drug pusher (she is a lawyer) which involves her personally more and more.

Helen Stousland (Elisabeth Mortensen) cannot keep her personal life out of this case. She works for a law firm that is involved with her father selling his property. Her client, the drug dealer, hints he was connected with her father. Sparks fly between Helen and her father's lover, even over details about the funeral. She feels attracted to the police inspector investigating her father's death, and seduces him. Meanwhile, her recently separated husband is a nuisance about the children.

All these elements somewhat sidetrack the viewer from the mystery, though they are interwoven with it. Breien's real interest is exploring Helen's interior world, which is made up, among other things, of a more-than-filial love for her father. The relationship is hinted at throughout the film, but only becomes explicit at the end when Helen "remembers" the events surrounding her father's death.

Elisabeth Mortensen steers a difficult course between being the cold, dispassionate lady lawyer and a troubled human being with hidden emotional problems. Breien wisely avoids sentimentalizing the figure, preferring to show a multisided woman instead of a standard screen heroine. — *Yung.*

Dvazhdy Rozhdennyj
(Born Again)
(SOVIET-COLOR)

Taormina, July 19.
Produced by Mosfilm. Stars Viatcheslav Baronov. Directed by Arkady Sirénko. Screenplay by Viktor Astaffiev and Evguény Fedorovsky. Camera (color), Elizbar Karavaév; art director, Alexandre Samulekin; music, Edisson Dénissov. Reviewed at the Taormina Film Festival, July 19, 1984. Running time: **85 MINS.**
Andrei Bouliguin . . . . . Viatcheslav Baronov
Mother . . . . Tatiana Doguileva

The Russian entry in competition at Taormina, "Born Again" is a stripped-down survivor-in-the-wilderness yarn that has a magnetic pull thanks to its very simplicity. Film recounts a true episode that occurred in 1942 when Nazi aviation sunk a Red Cross ship in the middle of the Arctic seas. The sole survivor, a young soldier, miraculously struggled back to civilization to tell what happened. Pic should have fest legs.

Helmer Arkady Sirénko shows a fine sense of timing in describing little Andrei Bouliguin's heroic trek through the icy wasteland. His obstinate determination not to give up, even though salvation seems impossible, is bolstered only by fleeting memories of his mother waiting for him back home and the bag of mail he has been entrusted

to deliver by his dead comrades.

His interminable trek is punctuated by the appearance every morning of a Nazi flying ace who returns over and over to finish him off, but for one incredible reason after another never succeeds. This comic book villain, shown sitting in the cockpit of his plane in unmatched studio closeups, acts as a kind of tragic nemesis who is defeated against all odds — obviously intended to echo the Germans' defeat during the war.

Andrei's mission, to tell the world about the Nazis' crime, is wisely left understated while the man-against-nature element is emphasized, with occasional bursts of humor. Viktor Astaffiev's simple, open face and his muttering to himself (virtually the only dialog) are all it takes to keep up sympathy with the character and interest in his plight. When, after surviving machine-gun strafing for three consecutive days, he downs the ace's plane with the single shot left in his rifle, his impossible victory comes across as the triumph of good over evil, David felling Goliath. — *Yung.*

Widziadlo
(The Phantom)
(POLISH-COLOR)

Taormina, July 27.
Produced by the Polish Film Production Company Zespoly Filmowe, Perspektywa Unit; foreign sales, Film Polski. Features entire cast. Written and directed by Marek Nowicki, based on a short story by Karol Irzykóvski, "Paluba." Camera (Color), Witold Sobocinski; editor, Krystyna Rutkowska; sound, Nikodem Wolk Laniewski; art director, Jerzy Sajko; music, Krzysztof Knittel. Reviewed at the Taormina Film Festival, July 27, 1984. Running time: **90 MINS.**
Cast: Roman Wilhelmi, Marzena Trybala, Hanna Mikuc, Mariusz Benoit, Mariusz Dmochovski, Anna Chodakowska, Olgierd Lukaszewicz, Dorota Kwiatkowska.

Seen in competition at the Taormina Film Festival, "Phantom" marks a late-career helming debut for Market Nowicki, a former cameraman who now teaches at the Lodz film school. Set in the early years of the century on an idyllic country estate, "Phantom" is a Polish costume picture with a certain degree of sophistication, a surprising amount of sensuality, and a special interest in dream sequences. As a Gothic ghost story it is not too exciting. Might have some fest outings.

Country gentleman Piotr Strumienski is haunted by the memory of his first wife, Angelika, whose passionate embraces he can't get out of his mind. Ola, his current wife, has had all she can take of his obsession and takes a lover, who becomes mysteriously paralyzed. While Piotr fantasizes about making love to Angelika in an abandoned house that is his private shrine to her, his young son Pavel gets his first taste of sensual experience

with a mute peasant girl. Piotr deliriously mistakes the girl for Angelika and shoots her. This unpleasant incident seems to being him to his senses for a while and, to the family's joy, he has Angelika's house razed. But just as things are taking a turn for the better the phantom reappears (Pavel's governess in disguise) and leads Piotr to a gruesome death.

Pic is full of beautiful women who strongly recall the fetching heroines of old Hollywood Bs (helmer is surely a fan) with their heavy makeup, tangled hair and perverse fascination. Nowicki updates the genre a bit with dream sequences, recurrent glimpses of female nudity (rare in a Polish film) and a sophisticated use of sound.

Witold Sobocinski's elegant photography exploits the beauty of the Polish countryside and its graceful, old-world charm.
— *Yung.*

Una Strana Passione/
Nicolo' Ou L'Enfant Trouve'
(A Strange Passion)
(ITALIAN-FRENCH-COLOR)

Taormina, July 21.
A Difilm release, produced by W.M.F. (Paris) and Difilm (Rome). Stars Fernando Rey, Brigitte Fossey, Saverio Marconi. Directed and written by Jean-Pierre Dougnac, based on Heinrich Von Kleist's novel "The Foundling." Camera (Color), Romano Albani; editor, Marie-Jo Audiard; music, Luis Bacalov. Reviewed at the Taormina Film Festival, July 21, 1984. Running time: **95 MINS.**
Piachi . . . . Fernando Rey
Elvira . . . . Brigitte Fossey
Nicolò . . . . Saverio Marconi
Saveria . . . . Agostina Belli

Jean-Pierre Dougnac, an actor and stage helmer, has chosen to adapt a literary work to make his debut behind the camera. And literary this "Strange Passion" is (title has already gone through changes and one only hopes French and Italo distribbers dream up something more attractive). Despite its top-flight cast headlining Fernando Rey and Brigitte Fossey and a stately, dignified tone, pic runs through its paces in predictable fashion without latching on to a strong point of view that could illuminate the tragic tale. For all its sensitivity, pic looks more like television than theatrical material.

The story itself has a perverse fascination. Von Kleist's tale has a wealthy man, Piachi (Rey), lose his little boy in a plague and adopt a ragged street urchin named Nicolò. Nicolò is indirectly responsible for the son's death, since it was because Piachi took him into his carriage that they were forced to stop in the lazaretto where the son falls ill. Nevertheless, Piachi is a kind and enlightened man and raises Nicolò to be his heir. In classic wild-child fashion, the boy' demonstrates a quick mind and talents of all kinds.

Nicolò (Saverio Marconi) grows up to be the pride of the family. He marries a suitable young lady to bear him an heir, then totally ignores her while offering his attentions to a bishop's beautiful mistress (Agostina Belli). Tragedy occurs when Nicolò conceives of a scheme to seduce his adoptive mother, Elvira (Brigitte Fossey), by masquerading as her long-lost love, whom he disocvers he resembles. The quasi-incest upsets Elvira's already fragile mental balance and plunges her into irreversible madness. When Piachi discovers what has happened, Nicolò exploits his legal rights and connections to throw his foster parents out of their own home. Piachi revenges himself on his demonic son (who still loves him) and refuses to repent of his crime, even on the gallows.

Rey and Fossey lend noble dignity to the figures of the two parents. Saverio Marconi gives Nicolò the psychological ambiguity of an "ideal" son who rebels against his parents' gift of love in an act of apparent madness, but he fails to make sense of that act. It is up to the viewer to guess why the tragedy occurs. Helmer seems to have concentrated on a faithful reproduction of the story at the expense of clarifying the characters' psychology. — *Yung.*

Na Strazy Swej Stac Bede

(I Shall Always Stand Guard) (POLISH-COLOR)

Taormina, July 27.
Produced by the Polish Film Productoin Company Zespoly Filmowe, KADR Unit; foreign sales, Film Polski. Features entire cast. Directed and written by Kazimierz Kutz. Camera (Color), Wisslaw Zdort; art director, Roleslaw Kamykowski; sound, Janusz Rosol; editor, Jozef Bartezak; music, Wojciech Kilar. Reviewed at the Taormina Film Festival, July 27, 1984. Running time: 116 MINS.
Cast: Krzysztof Kolberger, Iwona Swietochowska, Lidia Maksymoeicz, Marta Straszna, Andrej Golejewski.

Directed by award-winning veteran Kazimierz Kutz, "I Shall Always Stand Guard" is a muscleless exercise in dramatizing the work of the Polish resistance movement during the war. Seemingly made for audiences who have never seen a film before and don't know how to tell the good guys from the bad guys, it is too labored and naive to be of commercial interest, much less a festival entry as it was in Taormina (out of competition).

Story focuses on a young officer, Jan Klimza, who returns home in 1939 when Poland had ceased to exist as a country. Far from rebelling, Kutz shows, most Poles are out in the streets celebrating the arrival of the Nazis. While everyone is learning German, changing their names and kowtowing to the enemy, Jan sets about organizing a resistance network. Among his recruits is the sister of a wealthy pal, whose fervor for the cause is somewhat less than her interest in the man. Jan rejects her advances and she threatens to make him "pay for his stupidity."

When arrests start being made and the partisans rounded up, Jan hasn't a clue who could have betrayed them. The audience, alas, continues to receive "clues" and strong hints till the dramatic climax, when Jan makes the incredible discovery that it was his frivolous, would-be lover.

Dialog and acting of the principals is likewise handled with sledgehammer subtlety. Krzysztof Kolberger shores up the character of the resistance leader with such naive patriotism ("We must renew Poland!") that he is never entirely believable or likable. But then neither are any of the other characters, with the exception of an obese old lady who brilliantly diverts the Germans from arresting Jan by coming to the door nude.

Crowd scenes showing citizens lining the streets saluting the German occupiers are certainly a striking image, but Kutz plugs it in so often it starts to look like stock footage. The director's good or courageous intentions are small consolation for this film. — *Yung.*

Berget På Månens Baksida

(The Hill On The Other Side Of The Moon) (SWEDISH-COLOR)

Taormina, July 25.
A Sandrews release, produced by MovieMakers Sweden for The Swedish Film Institute, The Swedish Television/SVT 1, Sandrews and MovieMakers. Stars Gunilla Nyroos and Thommy Berggren. Directed by Lennart Hjulström. Screenplay by Agneta Pleijel. Camera (Eastmancolor), Sten Holmberg and Rolf Lindström; art director, Stig Boquist; editor, Lasse Lundberg. Reviewed at the Taormina Film Festival, July 25, 1984. Running time: 101 MINS.
Sonya ....Gunilla Nyroos
Maxim .'................Thommy Berggren
Foufa ....Lina Pleijel
Ann-Charlotte Leffler ......Bibi Andersson
Gustaf Edgren ....Ingvar Hirdwall

Though the doomed love affair of two 19th century Russian emigré intellectuals may seem like unlikely cinematographic material, helmer Lennart Hjulström, who directs the Folkteatern of Gothenburg, and scripter Agneta Pleijel inject it with the sensitivity and delicacy it needs to captivate. A festival film par excellence with good potential to find arthouse audiences.

Characters in the film are taken from real life, and truth is stranger than fiction, which accounts for the insignificant coincidence that the film's lovers have the same last name. Sonya Kovalevsky (Gunilla Nyroos) was the world's first woman professor of mathematics; born in Russia, she taught at Stockholm U. in the 1880s, when revolution was in the air and women's rights were under discussion. Exponent of the new current of thought is Maxim Kovalevsky (Thommy Berggren), a "friend of Marx, Engels, and Darwin," who hears Sonya lecturing and falls in love with her mind. With stubborn and misdirected honesty he refuses to tell Sonya he loves her — but he admires her emancipation enough to want to marry her.

Sonya, who is physically unattractive and insecure, feels idealized and limited within Max' picture of her. Madly in love herself, jealous and unhappy, she experiences all the ecstasy and torments love can bring. Her work wins her international acclaim, but it is not enough. Unable to bear not being able to bend Max to her will, or to live without him, she falls ill and dies.

The entire action is seen through the eyes of her young daughter from a previous marriage, an impassive and helpless observer of her mother's destruction.

Characters are cleverly drawn and brilliantly fleshed out by Gunilla Nyroos and Thommy Berggren, who split top acting kudos at the Taormina Festival. They make the vision of two people destroying their chances for happiness while being fully aware of what they're doing a heartrending sight.

Yet the film suffers from stasis, since all the "action" is in the depiction of more or less repetitive psychological states. By the time Sonya and Max have their final feud we're ready for the climax to arrive. Sticking too closely to historical record may have kept the filmmakers from dramatizing events more fully. Instead of just telling us what an exciting period the characters are living through, we could have been shown some of it.

Nevertheless, "Hill" is an unusually sensitive film, so wellcrafted it flows without the aid of music. A fine supporting cast is led by Bibi Andersson as a liberated woman novelist. — *Yung.*

Tightrope (COLOR)

Psycho-killer pic worthy follow-up for Eastwood.

Hollywood, Aug. 14.
A Warner Bros. release of a Malpaso production. Produced by Clint Eastwood, Fritz Manes. Directed, written by Richard Tuggle. Stars Clint Eastwood, Genevieve Bujold. Camera (Technicolor), Bruce Surtees; editor, Joel Cox; music, Lennie Niehaus; production design, Edward Carfagno; set decoration, Ernie Bishop; sound, William Kaplan; assistant director, David Valdes. Reviewed at The Burbank Studios, Burbank, Aug. 3, 1984. (MPAA Rating: R.) Running time: 117 MINS.
Wes Block ....Clint Eastwood
Beryl Thibodeaux.......Genevieve Bujold
Detective Molinari ....Dan Hedaya
Amanda Block ....Alison Eastwood
Penny Block ....Jennifer Beck
Leander Rolfe ....Marco St. John
Becky Jacklin ....Rebecca Perle
Sarita................Regina Richardson
Jamie Cory ....Randi Brooks
Melanie Silber...............Jamie Rose
Judy Harper ....Margaret Howell

Instead of choosing a complete change of pace from his popular tough guy persona, as he did in the past with "Bronco Billy" and "Honkytonk Man," Clint Eastwood has opted to follow his "Sudden Impact" smash with a halfway turnabout. "Tightrope" sees him comfortably in the role of a big city homicide cop, but also as a vulnerable, hunted man, a deserted husband, father of two daughters, a man whose taste for seamy sex nearly brings him down. A strong sell by Warner Bros. should net this interesting-effort some good late summer b.o. returns. Film will have its world preem as opening attraction at the Montreal World Film Festival Aug. 16.

Written and directed by Richard Tuggle, whose previous screen credit was the excellent "Escape From Alcatraz" script for Eastwood, pic trades extensively on the theme of guilt transference from killer to presumed hero which for so long was the special domain of Alfred Hitchcock.

Surface action is of a highly familiar sort, as an anonymous, ruthless killer, the only glimpse of whom one sees are of his distinctively, laced sneakers, stalks prostitutes and massage parlor girls in New Orleans' French Quarter. With few leads to work with, Eastwood has little success in coming up with any suspects, but he's working on familiar turf; since his wife left him for another man, he has been accustomed to taking his pleasure with the very sort of women upon whom the murderer is preying.

A fair amount of running time is given over to Eastwood's relationship with his growing daughters (older of whom is played by his real-life offspring, Alison). Opportunity to see the star in the relatively unfamiliar role of papa affords some very nice human moments which evoke both emotional warmth and tension. Genevieve Bujold smartly underplays her largely subordinate part of a rape counseling center director who at first challenges Eastwood to get more aggressive with the case and ends up in something resembling a romance with him. Potential for her character to remain a stock feminist is nicely transcended in both the writing and playing.

But the most intriguing aspect of the story is the personality parallel between the cop and killer. Albeit for different reasons, they're both interested in the same sort of woman, and the man in sneakers lets Eastwood know they're both cut from the same cloth in insidious fashion. Eastwood begins getting into hot water with his superiors when they learn their investigator has consorted with murdered prosties just prior to their deaths.

Becoming ever more daring, the killer goes so far as to set Eastwood up with a young man in a gay bar. Following every lead, Eastwood chats the blond fellow up, only to be overtly propositioned and asked how he knows he doesn't like boys if he hasn't tried them. "Maybe I have," Eastwood replies.

It all leads up to a rather predictable assault on the cop's home and daughters, and some sweating and soul-searching on his part. Director Tuggle resorts to some cheap shots at certain junctures, including a thrown-in shock nightmare and hokey lightning-and-thunder background effects.

Overall, however, action is well-handled, as Tuggle demonstrates ample storytelling talent and draws a multitude of nuances from his cast. Despite the kinky overtones, there is a small amount of sex and nudity, and ample opportunity for gore provided by the multiple murders has been deliberately ignored, as these scenes are consistently cut away from and left almost entirely to the imagination.

At 117 minutes, pic is too long, and could profitably have been cut by 10 minutes or so. Even with the considerable night shooting, lenser Bruce Surtees has taken his patented dark look to nearly perverse lengths; some of the action is downright difficult to see. One hates to imagine what this will look like on drive-in screens.

All other tech credits are solid.
— *Cart.*

Giuseppe Fava: Siciliano Come Me
(Giuseppe Fava: Sicilian Like Me)
(ITALIAN-COLOR)

Taormina, July 25.
Produced by RAI-TV Channel 3, Region of Sicily. Features entire cast. Directed by Vittorio Sindoni. Screenplay, Vittorio Sindoni, based on "The Sicilians" by Sindoni and Giuseppe Fava. Camera (Color), Alberto Manzi and Piero Schimmenti; editor, Romano Trina; music, Riz Ortolani. Reviewed at the Taormina Film Festival, July 25, 1984. Running time: 60 MINS.
Cast: Ida Di Benedetto, Leo Gullotta, Corrado Gaipa, Mariella Lo Giudice, Giuseppe Lo Presti, Mico Magistro, Anna Malvica, Ignazio Buttitta.

A compendium of excerpts from a tv series about Sicily today made by Giuseppe Fava and Vittorio Sindoni, "Giuseppe Fava: Sicilian Like Me" unfortunately now stands as a memorial to Fava, a journalist whose unflagging efforts to expose corruption and the inroads of the Mafia on his beloved island led to his murder earlier this year. Fava appears in the film as the interviewer who talks to representative Sicilians in cafés, clubs, and on the street. Director Sindoni re-edited highlights from the series into this hourlong video special.

Although documentary in intent, picture uses mainly actors to recreate the essence of Sicily. Some performances, like Ida Di Benedetto's as the mother whose son was killed by the Mafia and whom the judge fruitlessly attempts to silence at the hearing, are a bit above the lines; others, like the young man accused of being a hired assassin who explains how he got into working for the Mob, have a disturbing sense of tragedy.

Even more subtly revealing, perhaps, are improvised sections that show bands of children playing around ancient ruins, or a group of oldsters telling Fava why they never bring their wives to their card club. A unified picture of misery, unemployment and poverty emerges, showing the face of Sicily hidden from tourists and forgotten by legislators. — *Yung.*

Sheena
(COLOR)

Campy comic strip features mucho nudity for the kiddies.

Hollywood, Aug. 10.
A Columbia Pictures release from Columbia-Delphi Productions II. Produced by Paul Aratow. Executive producer, Yoram Ben-Ami. Directed by John Guillermin. Stars Tanya Roberts, Ted Wass. Screenplay, David Newman, Lorenzo Semple Jr. from story by Newman, Leslie Stevens, based on comic strip books "Sheena, Queen Of The Jungle" by S.M. Eiger, Will Eisner. Camera (Metrocolor, Panavision), Pasqualino De Santis; editor, Ray Lovejoy; music, Richard Hartley; production design, Peter Murton; art direction, Malcolm Middleton; set decoration, Ian Watson; wardrobe, costume design, Annalisa Nasalli-Rocca; sound (Dolby), Brian Simmons; special effects supervisor, Peter Hutchinson; special effects coordinator, Bob Nugent; animal coordinator and trainer, Hubert G. Wells; associate producers, Christian Ferry, Alan Rinzler; assistant directors, Pat Clayton, Tom Mwangi (Kenya), Michael Zimbrich (second unit); action unit camera, Moshe Levin; action unit sound, Daniel Brisseau; second unit director, Jack Couffer. Reviewed at the Samuel Goldwyn Theatre, Beverly Hills, Aug. 9, 1984. (MPAA Rating PG.) Running time: 117 MINS.
Sheena	Tanya Roberts
Vic Casey	Ted Wass
Fletcher	Donovan Scott
Shaman	Elizabeth of Toro
Countess Zanda	France Zobda
Prince Otwani	Trevor Thomas
King Jabalani	Clifton Jones
Jorgensen	John Forgeham
Bolu	Errol John
Juka	Sylvester Williams
Grizzard	Bob Sherman
Phillip Ames	Michael Shannon
Betsy Ames	Nancy Paul
Child Sheena	Kathryn Gant
Young Sheena	Kirsty Lindsay

There are plenty of laughs to be had in "Sheena," but it's quite impossible to tell how many of them were intentional. Attempt to install this 1930s jungle heroine in the pantheon of the contempo adventure icons fails to find a consistent tone, with dangerous result that audiences will be tempted to laugh at it rather than with it. Massive ad and promo push will assure some initial b.o., but Columbia's $26,-000,000 investment in this long-in-the-works project seems precarious.

Based on the comic strip books "Sheena, Queen Of The Jungle" by S.M. Eiger and Will Eisner, screenplay by David Newman and Lorenzo Semple Jr. aspires to the self-consciously humorous but nevertheless rousing spirit of the recent "Superman" epics. Male lead Ted Wass got the idea but, unfortunately, Tanya Roberts, as the eponymous character, and director John Guillermin take the monkeyshines far too gravely. Upshot is, the more serious the scene, the higher the camp.

Story cooked up by Newman and Leslie Stevens is acceptable: orphaned in deepest Africa, much like Tarzan, blonde-tressed Sheena is raised by a remote, noble tribe and appears to be the fulfillment of a prophecy concerning a mysterious lady who will protect it in dire times.

Yank tv producer Wass and his cameraman Donovan Scott arrive in the Kingdom of Tigorda to do a feature on Prince Otwani, an arrogant hotshot who has played football in the U.S. and speeds around the impoverished country in his Mercedes convertible. The prince knocks off his brother to assume power, Sheena's adoptive mother is set up to take the blame, Wass and Scott find themselves onto a breaking news story, the prince sets his band of mercenaries after them, and it's off to the races.

In the midst of all this, Roberts and Wass find the time to fall in love, even though she's initially disturbed by the "fur" on his chest. By contrast, he's not at all put off by her chest, which is exposed in all its glory to an extent surely unprecedented in a PG-rated film.

For the most part, pic is designed to please kids, even very young ones, and the brief National Geographic nudity of natives is traditionally acceptable in this content. Pleasing as Roberts' statuesque physique may be, however, it's eye-popping to see her indulge in an *au naturel* waterfall shower, or conduct an extended dialog scene with Wass totally in the buff, in a film like this. Result is a t & a kidpic.

As it happens, "Sheena" was rated PG the week before the PG-13 ratings category was implemented, but notwithstanding the MPAA's decision against retroactively judging pics which had already been rated, for the film to go out now as is makes a joke of the whole PG/PG-13 issue.

Sheena, her tribe and her animal friends ultimately rout all the baddies, and in this line a salute is in order to animal trainer Hubert G. Wells, who got a zoo-full of wild beasts to impressively perform on cue. Potential racial issues were blurred by casting native Africans in both good and evil roles, and by balancing Sheena's virtue with the low-down motives of the white mercenaries.

A pro when it comes to logistics and widescreen lensing, director Guillermin does a passable job with the action, but his essential seriousness collides head-on with prevailing cornball comedy. Same can be said of Roberts, whose eager, enthusiastic earnestness is at complete odds with the casually rollicking style of the other performers.

Fact that film was shot entirely on location in Kenya is an enjoyable plus. On the minus side, however, is Richard Hartley's music, which sounds so close to Vangelis' famous "Chariots Of Fire" score that, accompanied by endless prolog and epilog shots of Roberts riding her zebra in slow motion along a lake, it enters an uncomfortable zone between parody and absurd imitation.
— *Cart.*

Lunnaya Raduga
(Lunar Rainbow)
(SOVIET-COLOR)

Karlovy Vary, July 18.
A Mosfilm Production, Moscow; world rights, Goskino, Moscow. Features entire cast. Directed by Andrei Yermash. Screenplay, Valentin Yezhov, Yermash, based on a novel by Sergei Pavlov; camera (color), Naum Ardashnikov; sets, Vladimir Aronin; music, Aduard Artemyev. Reviewed at Karlovy Vary Film Fest (Debut Competition), July 13, '84. Running time: 112 MINS.
Cast: Vladimir Gostykhin, Igor Straygin, Vassily Livanov, Yuri Solomin, Georgi Tarotorkin, Natalia Saiko, Grazhina Baikshtite, Vladimir Kenigson.

This debut feature by Andrei Yermash (a relative of Filip Yermash, head of Soviet Cinematography) was lensed for both widescreen and 70m projection, the former unspooling at Karlovy Vary. Based on a novel by Sergei Pavlov, it's set in the 21st century at a time when the exploration of the planets is a thing of the past and further probings into the depth of the universe are on the agenda. Of course, this means danger, surprise, even tragedy for the intrepid astronaut.

An international space commission learns of four spacemen who have the capability to affect radio waves and magnetic fields, as well as transform themselves into different people. These powers, we are told, came into play after four astronauts made a research expedition to Oberon, Mercury's satellite, where a catastrophic accident occurred. The rest of the pic is about how the four spacemen get tracked down by the space security service.

Okay sci-fi, with some modest special effects. — *Holl.*

Joy Of Sex
(COLOR)

Lamentable teen sex comedy.

Hollywood, Aug. 3.

A Paramount Pictures release, produced by Frank Konigsberg. Directed by Martha Coolidge. Screenplay, Kathleen Rowell, J.J. Salter; camera (Movielab color), Charles Correll; editors, Allan Jacobs, William Elias, Ned Humphreys; sound, Pat Mitchell; art direction, Jim Murakami; assistant directors, Tony Brown, Don Heitzer; music, Bishop Holiday, Scott Lipsker, Harold Payne. Reviewed at Paramount Pictures, Hollywood, Aug. 2, 1984. (MPAA rating: R.) Running time: 93 MINS.

Alan Holt	Cameron Dye
Leslie Hindenberg	Michelle Meyrink
Max Holt	Charles Van Eman
Melanie	Lisa Langlois
Liz Sampson	Colleen Camp
Miss Post	Joanne Baron
Farouk	Danton Stone
Porter	Ernie Hudson
Carp	David H. MacDonald
Ed	Darren Dalton
Pittman	Robert Prescott
Ted	Paul Tulley
Coach	Christopher Lloyd
Candy	Heidi Holicker
Sharon	Cristen Kauffman
Jenny	Terry Wagner-Otis

The band is playing somewhere and somewhere hearts are light. And somewhere men are laughing and somewhere children shout. But there is no joy in "Joy Of Sex" — mighty Martha has struck out.

For more than five years, Paramount has wanted to paste some kind of a picture onto the title of the popular book, not caring much whether one had anything to do with the other. If nothing else, director Martha Coolidge has realized that limited dream and brought the picture to market, where it has been unceremoniously dumped.

This is Coolidge's first major-studio picture since the critical and financial success of "Valley Girl," which marked her as a special talent, bringing sensitivity to an insensitive subject while stretching low-budget dollars admirably.

But she shows none of that talent in "Joy," which is crude, decidedly

unfunny and a technical mess, far below usual studio standards. Carrying the hopes of a lot of other aspiring female directors into the major leagues with her, Coolidge has clearly not hit the homerun they sorely needed.

One of the other interesting footnotes about "Joy," too, is that it was once one of the vaunted National Lampoon projects when that group was running hot. But somewhere along the line their intense interest in getting their name in the title of films no longer applied to this one.

About the film itself, there's just not much more to note about another formula high school where libidinal urges are variously relieved by vandalism, drugs and the daunting of dippy adults.

It is interesting that as the high-school kids are introduced, one of the first is Colleen Camp, who played the mother in "Valley Girl," setting up a credibility problem right away despite her bobby sox and pigtails. Surely, the thought goes, if Camp doesn't turn out to be an undercover cop or something, this picture is in worse trouble than it seems to be already.

But it doesn't really make much difference when Camp's true identity is revealed since she just disappears from the picture shortly after causing some commotion. The main focus remains on whether the boys and girls will have sex or not, which is unfortunately probably inevitable.

On the continuity side, interesting little miracles occur, like when a couple are making love at the motel in room 319 and somebody chops down the door to 302 to get in. And high-school life is often marked by boom shadows creeping into the frame.

Coolidge assertedly made "Valley Girl" for $350,000 while "Joy" was reportedly budgeted around $5,000,000. Sometimes, it's amazing how those additional zeros add up to nothing. —*Har.*

The Woman In Red
(COLOR)

Lusty comedy should have late-summer success.

Hollywood, Aug. 9.

An Orion Pictures release, produced by Victor Drai. Written and directed by Gene Wilder, based on "Un Elephant Ça Trompe Enormement" by Jean-Loup Dabadie and Yves Robert. Exec producer, Jack Frost Sanders. Camera (Deluxe Color), Fred Schuler; editor, Christopher Greenburg; sound, Thomas G. Overton; production design, David L. Snyder; associate producers, Susan Ruskin, Xavier Gelin; assistant director, Michael F. Grillo; music, John Morris. Reviewed at the Academy of Motion Picture Arts & Sciences, Beverly Hills, Aug. 6, 1984. (MPAA rating: PG-13.) Running time: 87 MINS.

Theordore Pierce	Gene Wilder
Buddy	Charles Grodin
Joe	Joseph Bologna
Didi	Judith Ivey
Michael	Michael Huddleston
Charlotte	Kelly Le Brock
Ms. Milner	Gilda Radner
Richard	Kyle T. Heffner
Shelly	Michael Zorek

The perplexing sexing that goes on in "The Woman In Red" posits a healthy outlook for this late-summer comedy if word-of-mouth overcomes prevalent advance confusion that the title has something to do with John Dillinger, which it definitely doesn't.

The woman in red is simply a very sexy contemporary (Kelly Le Brock), hired as a model by a San Francisco city agency, bringing her into contact with a mundane bureaucrat, Gene Wilder, heretofore a contented family man.

But one look at Le Brock (though it's some look, with a tip of the skirt to Marilyn Monroe in "The Seven Year Itch"), and Wilder is ready to risk all for illicit romance. Un-

---

ORIGINAL FILM

Un Elephant Ça Trompe Enormement
(An Elephant Can Be Extremely Deceptive)
(FRENCH-COLOR)

Paris, Oct. 5.

Gaumont release of Gaumont International-Les Productions De La Gueville production. Stars Jean Rochefort, Claude Brasseur, Guy Bedos, Victor Lanoux, Daniele Delorme, Anny Duperey. Directed by Yves Robert. Screenplay, Jean-Loup Dabadie, Robert; camera (Eastmancolor), Rene Mathelin; editor, Gerard Pollicand; music, Vladimir Cosma. Reviewed at Club 13, Paris, Sept. 30, '76. Running time, 100 MINS.

Etienne	Jean Rochefort
Daniel	Claude Brasseur
Simon	Guy Bedos
Bouly	Victor Lanoux
Marthe	Daniele Delorme
Charlotte	Anny Duperey
Esperanza	Martine Sarcey
Mouchy	Marthe Villalonga

"Pardon Mon Affaire" (U.S. release title)

---

fortunately for him, he is not very adept at adultery.

The laughs roll along readily as Wilder tries one idea after another to sneak out on wife Judith Ivey and family to rendevous with Le Brock. Naturally, when it seems he's finally successful, the worst surprise awaits.

A wonderful diversion through all of this is Gilda Radner, a relatively plain fellow office worker who initially thinks she's the object of Wilder's wanderlust and is bitterly — and vigorously — disappointed when she finds out she isn't.

Joseph Bologna, Charles Grodin and Michael Huddleston also make a good cheering section for Wilder's efforts. But as writer-director-star, Wilder wins the credits. —*Har.*

Secrets
(BRITISH-COLOR)

A Samuel Goldwyn Co. release of an Enigma TV Ltd. production in the "First Love" series for Goldcrest. Executive producer, David Puttnam. Produced by Chris Griffin. Directed by Gavin Millar. Features entire cast. Screenplay, Noella Smith; camera (Kay color), Christopher Challis; editor, Eric Boyd-Perkins; music, Guy Woolfenden; sound, Chris Munro, Otto Snel; assistant director-production manager, Dominic Fulford; art director, Jeffrey Woodbridge; associate producer, David Bill. Reviewed at Lorimar screening room, N.Y. Aug. 13, 1984. (MPAA Rating: R.) Running time: 78 MINS.

Mother	Helen Lindsay
Dr. Jefferies	John Horsley
Louise	Anna Campbell-Jones
Sydney	Daisy Cockburn
Trottie	Rebecca Johnson
Jane	Lucy Goode
Paul	Richard Tolan

"Secrets" is a diverting, ultimately moving little comedy-drama made in 1982 as part of the British "First Love" series of telefilms made by David Puttnam. Well-directed by Gavin Millar, pic's theatrical future Stateside via Samuel Goldwyn Co. release is limited, though art house returns loom okay.

While maintaining the period romance format and young protagonists structure of the "First Love" series, "Secrets" departs in focusing on a mother-daughter relationship rather than a boy-meets-girl pairing. Set in 1963, Noella Smith's script concerns 13-year-old Louise (Anna Campbell-Jones), off to girls' boarding school after the death of her father. Mom (Helen Lindsay) is a middleaged woman, having given birth to Louise late in life.

Key plot diversion is the discovery by Louise of her father's secret books and materials of the Masonic Lodge, which she hides and takes to school with her. There, she initiates her girl friend Sydney (Daisy Cockburn) and later classmates Jane (Lucy Grode) and brainy but nerdy Trottie (Rebecca Johnson) in her interpretations of the rituals of Freemasons, made grotesque and comical by the girls' misunderstanding of the secret book's codes and abbreviations.

While Louise is learning the usual lessons in friendship and integrity at school, film's comic force derives from mom's jumping to the wrong conclusions when she finds a box of condoms in Louise's room at home. Not knowing that the contraceptive devices were innocently found (and misidentified as balloons) by Louise among daddy's kit of masonic materials, mom believes her daughter has been sexually involved with her 18-year-old cousin Paul and assumes the "trouble" she's having at school is a pregnancy. By the time the confusion is sorted out, "Secrets" turns briefly and movingly into a serious vein, as Louise realizes her close bond to her elderly mother and the importance of preserving for mom an untarnished memory of her presumably errant late husband.

As the mother, Helen Lindsay turns in a terrific performance, maximizing both the comic and sentimental nature of the material. Young players are okay, adhering to the lowkey thesping that typifies this series. Tech credits are suitable, though pic lacks period atmosphere, relying on verbal references, costuming and hairstyles to evoke the 1963 milieu. —*Lor.*

10 Tage In Calcutta
(10 Days In Calcutta)
(WEST GERMAN-DOCU-COLOR-16m)

Munich, June 30.

A Bioskop Film Produktion, Munich, in collaboration with Westdeutscher Rundfunk (WDR), Cologne. A documentary film by Reinhard Hauff on director Mrinal Sen. Written and directed by Hauff. Camera (color, 16m), Frank Brühman; sound, Sanjay Mukherjee, Willi Schwadorf; editor, Heidi Handorf; music, Vijay Raphava, Roa, Bhaskar Chandavarkar, Salil Chowdury. Reviewed at Munich Film Fest, June 30, '84. Running time: 82 MINS.

West German director Reinhard Hauff and Indian helmer Mrinal Sen have long been friends, and Hauff took the opportunity on one of his frequent trips to the subcontinent to interview Sen during one of latter's film projects.

Hauff has not only made a revealing portrait of Sen, but he's also filmed him in his own visual element: on the streets of Calcutta, amid crowds and among friends; at work and at leisure, and in conversation about his recent and pathbreaking films, from "Bhuvan Shome" (1969) to "Ruins" (1983).

The charm of this docu is the loose, spontaneous style of handling the interview questions and answers, together with Hauff's broad knowledge of both the subject and the films. Hauff knows the films quite well, and is able to relate the full body of the director's work to that peculiar Sen vision of his country and the people of Bengal.

The one aspect of the docu that offers food for thought is how Sen ever manages to bring a project to completion in the first place. He apparently starts out with little more than a general idea of a theme, then learns himself what it's all about while shooting on the set. This is testified to not only by Sen but by collaborators as well, for it's only on the editing table that the film really takes shape at all.

A fine documentary with credits all on the plus side. —*Holl.*

O Statecnem Kovari
(The Courageous Blacksmith)
(CZECH-COLOR)

Karlovy Vary, July 20.

A Czechoslovak Film Production, Gottwaldov Film Studio. World rights, Ceskoslovensky Filmexport, Prague. Features entire cast. Directed by Petr Sveda. Screenplay, Bohumil Steiner, Jaroslav Petrik, based on a fairy tale by Bozena Nemcova; camera (color), Jiri Kolin; music, Petr Ulrych; sets, Zdenek Roskopal. Reviewed at Karlovy Vary Film Fest (Debut Competition), July 12, '84. Running time: 83 MINS.

Cast: Pavel Kriz (Mikes, the Courageous Blacksmith), Jan Kroner (Matej), Jiri Knot (Ondra), Tana Cechovska, Jana Tomsu, Martina Gasparovicova (the three princesses), Vlado Müller (the village blacksmith), Petr Cepek (the Black King), Lubot Tokos (the King of Sadness).

Debut helmer Petr Sveda's "The Courageous Blacksmith" was made at the Gottwaldov Film Studio, which specializes in children's films and releases four features there annually. Story is taken from the now classic writings of Bozena Nemcova (1820-1862), the first Czech woman novelist, who made a reputation with romantic fairy tales drawn from the folk traditions and village life of the past century. Tale's original title was "The Courageous Mikes," referring to the young hero.

This is the tale of a young blacksmith and his two companions, a miller's helper and a farm lad, who journey through woods and meadows and across mountains in search of their fortune. Mikes takes with him his trusty blacksmith's hammer. One day, they happen upon a "sad kingdom," where three princesses have each strangely disappeared on their respective 18th birthdays. The Black King, it turns out, who hides out at the bottom of a deep well, is to blame. Mikes, despite the weaknesses of his companions, proves to have the courage and character to rescue the girls by overcoming supernatural forces, human failings, and mankind's evil.

Special effects and lensing are pluses, the rest only so-so. — *Holl.*

Los Zancos
(The Stilts)
(SPANISH-COLOR)

Madrid, July 23.

An Emiliano Piedra production, directed by Carlos Saura; screenplay, Carlos Saura and Fernando Fernán Gómez; camera (Eastmancolor), Teo Escamilla; music, Madrid Judeo-Spanish Musical Group; sets, Tony Cortes; editor, Pablo del Amo. Reviewed at Cinearte screening room, Madrid, July 23, '84. Running time: 95 MINS.
Angel . . . . Fernando Fernán Gómez
Teresa . . . . Laura del Sol
Alberto . . . . Antonio Banderas
Manuel . . . . Francisco Rabal
Also with: Amparo Soto, Enrique Pere, José Yepes, Adriana Ozores, Willy Montesinos Jesus Sastre and Grupo de Zancos de Madrid.

After the international success of "Carmen," Carlos Saura returns to his introspective world of former years in "The Stilts." The new yarn,

however, is shorn of all symbols and obsessive historical and personal flashbacks. Result is a humdrum story which breaks no new ground and is from start to finish unrelievedly downbeat. Pic is the official Spanish entry for the Venice Film Festival this year.

Story is set in a mountain resort outside Madrid. An elderly, recently widowed professor pays an autumnal visit to his summer cottage. After poking about for a few days and recalling his late wife and two daughters, he decides to turn on the propane gas reserves and blow himself to bits.

At the critical moment, an attractive neighbor (Laura del Sol) appears at the door of the shed and saves his life. She is married to a young fellow who with some friends, also disenchanted with life, have found some meaning to it all by doing skits on stilts for the locals.

The glum prof is introduced to them and is urged to write a little piece for the troupe. While doing so, he falls madly in love with the girl, 30 years his junior. She at first reluctantly reciprocates his advances, but then tires of his bothersome mooning and importuning. Undeterred, he continues to press his attentions. He even calls a friend to counsel him; latter wisely tells him to forget the girl. But the prof is unable to do so. He has filmed the stilt-players on video and now sits in his cold chalet endlessly pining over the images of the girl on the screen.

Realizing there can be no solution, he descends to the gas shed again but the second time there is to be no reprieve. He opens the gas and lights the match.

Fernán Gómez' thesping is fine, Laura del Sol looks pretty enough and the stilt players do their act nicely. However, there is a yawning void in this film; never are we given a hint that hope and redemption might ever be possible. We are left in the dark about the prof's family, his professional life or any intellectual interests he may have. Nor is it ever made clear why he commits suicide, since even his marriage, it is casually mentioned, wasn't all that happy.

Would a college prof in his 50s pull the plug when a 25-year-old girl with a husband and small child whom he has just met fails to requite his love? Scripters Saura and Fernán Gómez seem to think so.

The dreary theme, blighted love story and unhappy ending are apt to spell b.o. poison even for inveterate Saura fans. Better to bide one's time for the director's next dance project, "El Amor Brujo." —*Besa.*

My First Wife
(AUSTRALIAN-COLOR)

Sydney, July 30.

A Roadshow (Australia) release (Intl. Spectrafilm in U.S.) of a Dofine Production.

Produced by Jane Ballantyne, Paul Cox. Directed by Paul Cox. Stars John Hargreaves, Wendy Hughes. Screenplay, Cox, Bob Ellis; camera (color), Yuri Sokol; editor, Tim Lewis; sound, Ken Hammond; associate producer, Tony Llewellyn-Jones; art director, Asher Bilu. Reviewed at Roadshow Theatrette, Sydney, July 20, 1984. Running time: 95 MINS.
John . . . . John Hargreaves
Helen . . . . Wendy Hughes
Lucy . . . . Lucy Angwin
Hilary . . . . Anna Jemison
Tom . . . . David Cameron
Helen's father . . . . Charles Tingwell
Helen's mother . . . . Betty Lucas
John's father . . . . Robin Lovejoy
John's mother . . . . Lucy Uralov
Psychiatrist . . . . Ron Falk
Conductor . . . . Jon Finlayson
Kirstin . . . . Julia Blake
Barmaid . . . . Renee Geyer

A lacerating, emotionally exhausting drama about a marriage breakup, "My First Wife" manages to breathe new life into familiar material and reconfirms director Paul Cox ("Lonely Hearts," "Man Of Flowers") as one of Australia's leading talents. Pic also gives an opportunity for two of the country's best actors, John Hargreaves and Wendy Hughes, to shine in powerful, heart-rending performances as the couple involved.

Cox and coscripter Bob Ellis ring a few changes. This 10-year marriage is collapsing because the wife, not the husband, is having an affair, and it's the husband who desperately wants her back, willing to forgive and forget everything if only she'll return to him.

John works for a very up-market radio station where he plays classical records, accompanying them with erudite commentary. The son of Russian emigrant parents, he's emotional and distraught when his wife, Helen, tells him their marriage is over and that she's having an affair with another man, one of John's friends. John is reduced to tears, then to anger, and eventually to a suicide attempt, which fails. At the same time, Helen, who is obviously still very fond of him but no longer wants to live with him, can only stand by helplessly as he gradually loses his grip. Also at stake is their young daughter, Lucy, whom Helen unquestioningly believes should live with her.

Pic rings utterly true, with no false sentimentality, no firm ending (the problems remain unresolved at fadeout), and with both sides of the question fairly, if emotionally, presented. Cox has drawn on his own marital experiences, apparently, and the pain in the film is palpable. Hargreaves is immensely impressive as the beleaguered husband, while Wendy Hughes again confirms her glowing talent (Cox even includes, in a flashback sequence, a shot of the actress giving birth to her baby, taken from a documentary the director made a few years ago). Support players are solid, with a special nod to Anna Jemison as a warmhearted woman from the radio station who takes the distressed Hargreaves back to her home and bed.

Yuri Sokol's images are splendid, giving the film the same European look that distinguished "Man Of Flowers;" editing by Tim Lewis is very tight, and all other credits are pro.

Pic should nab solid reviews and score in the forthcoming Australian Film Awards, which will definitely help local biz. Overseas it also looks to make its mark in specialized houses and with careful handling. A major festival outing is also indicated. — *Strat.*

Mrtvi Ucia Zivych
(The Dead Teach The Living)
(CZECH-COLOR)

Karlovy Vary, July 18.

A Czechoslovak Film Production, Koliba Studios, Bratislava. World rights Ceskoslovensky Filmexport, Prague. Features entire cast. Directed by Martin Holly. Screenplay, Jiri Krizan; camera (color) Stanislav Szomolanyi; music Svetozar Stur. Reviewed at Karlovy Vary Film Fest (Information), July 10, '84. Running time: **87 MINS.**
Cast: Vladimir Kratina, Michal Docolomansky, Stefan Kvietik, Ctibor Filcik, Jana Krausova, Darina Simanska, Frantisek Kovar, Marian Slovak, Jan Kroner, Vlado Müller, Madia Hejna, Teodor Piovarci, Tatiana Kuliskova, Vladimir Barton.

The Slovak feature on display at Karlovy Vary, Martin Holly's "The Dead Teach The Living," is run-of-the-mill moral-message cinema, Socialist style. The main characters are a young surgeon on a hospital staff and an able young man in charge of an automobile repair shop. It so happens that one day the surgeon gives the auto mechanic a modest "bribe" to speed up the work on his car. All well and good, but then comes the kicker. The mechanic one day has to be operated on for stomach cancer, so he "bribes" the surgeon to do a decent job on the operating table.

Naturally, the surgeon obeys his conscience and refuses the money, whereupon the mechanic, in turn, is not sure whether or not the operation has been successful. It has, and integrity has won out again in the end.

Martin Holly has made some significant action pics and is a veteran Slovak director. Pic works on most levels but the script is laden with wooden lines and go-nowhere plot twists. With everything so cut-and-dry from the start, there's no room to present a few questions that don't have ready answers. — *Holl.*

Oxford Blues
(BRITISH-COLOR)

Teen-aimed romance of an American heel at Oxford.

Hollywood, Aug. 17.

An MGM/UA Entertainment release of an MGM presentation of a Winkast Film Prods. Ltd. production. A Baltic Industrial Finance Co. Ltd. film. Produced by Cassian Elwes, Elliott Kastner. Written and directed by Robert Boris. Features entire cast. Camera (Technicolor), John Stanier; editor, Patrick Moore; music, John DuPrez; production designer, Terry Pritchard; sound, Chris Munro; costumes, Pip Newberry; associate producer, Peter Kohn, David Wimbury; assistant director, Kohn; additional music, George Romanis. Reviewed at MGM/UA screening room, Aug. 17, 1984. (MPAA Rating: PG-13.) Running time: **93 MINS.**
Nick ....Rob Lowe
Rona ....Ally Sheedy
Lady Victoria ....Amanda Pays
Colin ....Julian Sands
Geordie ....Julian Firth
Simon.....................Alan Howard
Las Vegas Lady ....Gail Strickland

Dr. Ambrose ....Michael Gough
Dr. Boggs ....Aubrey Morris

At heart, "Oxford Blues" is really Rocky Goes To College. Though source material is MGM's 1938 Robert Taylor starrer, "A Yank At Oxford," treatment is decidedly modern and should appeal to the audience still waving the American flag from the Olympics. Presence of Rob Lowe in the leading role should also generate some excitement among young female fans.

In the original film, Lionel Barrymore borrows the cash to send athlete son Taylor over to Oxford. In "Oxford Blues," Lowe, a valet at the Dunes Hotel in Vegas, hustles the money at the crap table from a stake put up by an older woman (Gail Strickland) who picks him up.

Director and writer Robert Boris fails to establish a consistent tone to make his fairytale story believable Film opens to an airy outdoorsy scene with Lowe practicing his rowing skills. Tone changes almost at once when the real Nick Di Angelo (Lowe) hits the streets accompanied by a blaring rock soundtrack.

Nick's real reason for going to England is not to crew and certainly not for an education (students never seem to study in this film),

ORIGINAL FILM
A Yank At Oxford

Hollywood, Feb. 1.

A Metro-Goldwyn-Mayer release of Michael Balcon production. Stars Robert Taylor; features Lionel Barrymore, Maureen O'Sullivan, Edmond Gwenn, Vivien Leigh, Griffith Jones. Directed by Jack Conway. Screenplay by Malcolm Stuart Boylan, Walter Ferris and George Oppenheimer; original story by Leon Gordon, Sidney Gilliatt and Michael Hogan; based on an idea by John Monk Saunders; score by Hubert Bath and Edward Ward; camera, Harold Rosson; supervising editor, Margaret Booth; film editor, Charles Frend. Previewed at Village theatre, Westwood, Jan. 21, '38. Running time: **100 MINS.**
Lee Sheridan ....Robert Taylor
Dan Sheridan......Lionel Barrymore
Molly Beaumont .Maureen O'Sullivan
Elsa Craddock ....Vivien Leigh
Dean of Cardinal....Edmund Gwenn
Paul Beaumont ....Griffith Jones
Dean Snodgrass ........C.V. France
Scatters..............Edward Rigby
Cecil Davidson, Esq. ..Morton Selten
Ben Dalton ......Claude Gillingwater
Cephas ....Tully Marshall
Dean Williams .....Walter Kingsford
Wavertree ....Robert Coote
Ramsey ....Peter Croft
Tom Craddock ....Noel Howlett
Capt. Wavertree .....Edmund Breon

but to chase his dreamgirl, aristocrat covergirl Lady Victoria (Amanda Pays). Pays is indeed worthy of Lowe's attention, but it's hard to believe she's a dream that can come true.

Nick arrives at the stately halls of Oxford, again accompanied by a blaring rock soundtrack, with one thing on his mind — winning the

hand of his fair lady. Violating every tradition with his American "charm," Nick is like chalk grating on the blackboards of Oxford.

Film is at its best when it's building up the conflict between American brashness and British reserve. Problem is that initially Nick is so crass and unlikeable and concerned only with his own personal affairs, that it is hard to root for him against the Brits.

In a mock trial examining if the world would have been better off if Columbus hadn't discovered America, "Oxford Blues" appeals to the most jingoistic tendencies. It is only when Nick applies his anything goes attitude to something more than his own petty concerns that his Americanness becomes tolerable.

Climax is another example of a sporting contest which proves the hero has the right stuff to get the girl. Only the girl turns out to be another American. Must be a moral in there somewhere.

Lowe is suitably nasty as the streetwise Nick in a way that often passes for charm in films like this. Pays is indeed lovely but surprisingly accessible for the pedestal Nick has placed her on. As the American student lurking in the background, Ally Sheedy is equally appealing in her own tomboyish way.

Outstanding in a small bit as Nick's tutor is Michael Caine look-alike Alan Howard. Michael Gough does a John Houseman turn as the haughty headmaster.

Producer Elliott Kastner filmed without fanfare on location at Oxford and cinematographer John Stanier does a nice job with the tradition-laden halls as well as contributing some splendid rowing footage. But as far as films about Americans abroad, Laurel & Hardy's "A Chump At Oxford" is still more fun. —*Jagr.*

Sam's Son
(COLOR)

Michael Landon semi-autobiographical pic has new twist on sports appeal, javelin throwing.

Kansas City, Aug. 17.

An Invictus Entertainment release of a Worldvision Enterprises presentation. A Kevin O'Sullivan production. Written and directed by Michael Landon. Producer, Kent McCray, assistants, Marvin Coil, Gary L. Wohlleben; camera (color), Ted Voightlander; music, David Rose; art director, George Renne; editing, John Loeffler; set decoration, Dennis Peeples; casting, Susan Sukman. Reviewed at Show-A-Rama, Dallas, March, 1984. (MPAA Rating: PG.) Running time: **104 MINS.**
Sam Orowitz................Eli Wallach
Harriet Orowitz ....Anne Jackson
Gene Orowitz ...Timothy Patrick Murphy
Cathy Stanton ....Hallie Todd
Robert Woods ....Alan Hayes
Bonnie Barnes...............Jonna Lee
Gene Orman ....Michael Landon
Cy Martin................Howard Witt
Coach Sutter ....William Boyett

Ronnie Morgan . . . . John Walcutt
Lonnie Morgan . . . . . David Lloyd Nelson
Mr. Turner . . . . William H. Bassett
Jake Bellow . . . . Harvey Gold
Mr. Collins . . . . James Karen

"Sam's Son" represents a venture by Michael Landon, of tv fame, into feature filmmaking, and it sums as a picture of moderate entertainment values that should give its main appeal to the family trade. Drawing on his personal past, Landon has scripted a story with a variety of angles about a slightly built high school youth who has a knack for tossing the javelin, while getting himself crossways with school authorities over his unflinching belief that his strength derives from his long dark locks — in the '50s, yet.

The story actually hinges on a close relationship between young Gene Orowitz (Landon's real name), played by Timothy Murphy, and the father, Eli Wallach. He dreams of being a writer and pecks away at his typewriter in the wee small hours, but must support his shrewish wife, Anne Jackson, and family by managing the local movie theater. That the story hangs together as well as it does is largely due to Wallach's apt performance as an understanding father who solves the impasse between the son and the school principal by sending the boy into the javelin competition with his hair hidden under a bandage.

Story hits a melodramatic peak just this side of cornball, as Wallach suffers a heart attack while lugging a six-reel can of film to the theater booth atop the balcony. On his deathbed he hands over the completed manuscript that he pecked out in the wee hours, and of course, young Orowitz heaves the javelin almost out of the park as a tribute to his father. That's how it was in real life, with Landon winning a scholarship to USC. That led to bit parts in movies and television, and on to "Bonanza" and "Little House On The Prairie."

So Landon, himself, said, when introducing the picture to exhibitors at the annual Show-A-Rama held in Dallas last March. Invictus, is releasing the picture on a market-by-market game plan, the first being a three-theater showcase in K.C. that began Aug. 17.

Landon has little more than a bit part as Gene Orman, film star returning to his old home town for a world premiere of his latest picture, thus setting the flashback mood. Hallie Todd is suitably sweet as the schoolgirl who is loyal to Murphy, after he is tossed aside by swinger Jonna Lee, who switches her blond affection to football star and big bully, Alan Hayes. He has a high-point scene with Murphy, whom he has mercilessly chided, and is felled by a single blow to the

chops, the surprised onlookers being unaware that the slight javelin thrower had been into heavy weightlifting while training for the school meets.

Landon has embellished the picture with other effective vignettes, and Wallach's sincere interpretation of the liberal-minded father sets the picture above the usual tv fare.
—*Quin.*

The Act
(COLOR)

Cynicism laid on with a trowel.

An Artists Releasing Corp. release through Film Ventures International of a Sig Shore production. A Cine-U.S. Prods. picture. Executive producer, Ron Gorton. Produced by David Greene, Sig Shore. Directed by Shore. Features entire cast. Screenplay, Robert Lipsyte; camera (Technicolor), Benjamin Davis; editor, Ron Kalish; music, John Sebastian, Phil Goldston; songs, Sebastian, Goldston, Peter Thom; sound, William Daly, Richard Murphy; production design, Steve Wilson; assistant director, Mike Shore; production manager, Ron Gorton Jr. Reviewed on Vestron Video cassette, N.Y., Aug. 18, 1984. (MPAA Rating: R.) Running time: **94 MINS.**
Don Tucker . . . . Robert Ginty
Leslie . . . . Sarah Langenfeld
Julian . . . . Nick Surovy
Ron . . . . John Aprea
Dixie . . . . John Tripp
Harry-Kruger . . . . Eddie Albert
Mickey . . . . James Andronica
The President . . . . John Cullum
Deputy police chief . . . . Roger Davis
Frank Boda . . . . Pat Hingle
Corky . . . . David Huddleston
Elise . . . . Jill St. John
The hooker . . . . Arika Wells
The john . . . . Tom Hunter

"The Act" is an unappealing B-picture, reeking of cynicism concerning contemporary U.S. society's mores, filmed in 1982 under the title "Bless 'Em All." Pic was briefly released earlier this year and is now a curiosity for homevideo fans.

Film is currently the subject of a legal battle surrounding its distribution.

Presented in an awkward time-hopping structure (pic starts out mid-execution of a crime caper, violating the genre requirement of showing recruitment and planning first), "The Act" concerns a hotshot labor union lawyer turned presidential assistant Don Tucker (Robert Ginty) who engineers a deal to obtain a presidential pardon that will spring corrupt ex-labor boss Harry Kruger (Eddie Albert) from stir, to avoid a Gandhi-style hunger strike threatened by Kruger. In return for the pardon, the prez (John Cullum in a weird turn) demands and gets a $2,000,000 under-the-table re-election campaign "contribution" from current union boss Frank Boda (Pat Hingle).

Afraid of losing face when the word goes out that he was bamboozled, Boda orders his organizing chieftain Mickey (James Androni-

ca) to recover the cash, and Mickey hires an ex-con (Nick Surovy) who improbably brings along his instantly corruptible acting troupe to pull the heist. They take over N.Y.'s Savoy Hotel, robbing the payoff money while Tucker is upstairs dallying with a goodtime girl (Jill St. John).

Potentially interesting opus becomes silly due to the exaggerated venality of all the characters. Filmmaker Sig Shore, best-known for producing the hit "Superfly" (and its sequel), showed a sharper touch and far more credibility with a similarly cynical exposé of the recording industry, "That's The Way Of The World," starring Harvey Keitel, and written by "The Act's" scripter, Robert Lipsyte. Acting is earnest but unexceptional, and tech credits are on the cheap. — *Lor.*

Hoevdingen
(The Chieftain)
(NORWEGIAN-COLOR)

Haugesund, Aug. 19.
A Norena Film A/S (Oslo) release of As Film A/S production. Written, produced, directed by and starring Terje Talvik Kristiansen. Artistic producer, Vibeke Kleiydal Lökkeberg. Camera (Eastmancolor), Paul Rene Roestad; editor, Lillian Fjellvaer; production management, Hilde Berg, Petter Borgli; music, Geir Boehren, Bent Aserud; production design, Ingeborg Kvamme. Reviewed as a competition entry in the 12th Norwegian Film Festival at the Edda Theater, Haugesund, Aug. 19, 1984. Running time: **119 MINS.**
Arne . . . . Terje Kristiansen
Eva . . . . Vibeke Lökkeberg
Turid . . Tonje Kamilla Kleivdal Kristiansen
Torill . . . . Eva von Hanno
Tom . . . . Klaus Hagerup
Glass Works boss . . . . Arne Hesteness
Marti . . . . Mette Wesenlund
Tor . . . . Rolf Thrap-Meyer
Björn . . . . Espen Arneberg Boerset
Karl . . . . Geir Berdahl
Gunnar . . . . Björn Sundquist
Baby . . . . . Julie Marie Kleivdal Kristiansen

Terje Kristiansen, a hulking, friendly looking man in his Forties, wrote "Hoevdingen" (The Chieftain), produced the feature for his own and wife Vibeke Lökkeberg's As Productions, then directed himself in the lead along with other members of his family and circle of friends, including Lökkeberg in the female lead. Formerly, Kristiansen stuck to producing while his wife directed, for instance their highly acclaimed and border-crossing "Kamilla." Maybe Kristiansen has taken on too big a load this time, but there are many rewards of humorous and tragic insights to his effort in describing the Rise, Crawl, Fall and Final Redemption of The Male Chauvinist in the disguise of a free-spirited designer-artist closed in upon by the womenfolk and children of a past and a present marriage.

In spite of all his posturing and baboonish charm, this Chieftain is really at a perpetual loss when it comes to coping with any serious problem at home or at the glass

works where he is miserable even when promoted. At home, he busies himself with carpentry and is totally inept as a father. He always takes the easy way out and resorts to lies when his former wife from time to time pops up with renewed claims on his love and, particularly, what little money he has. He has temper tantrums and one day kills a kitten with his bare hands, causing his second wife (Lökkeberg) to up and leave him.

Some kind of a — very contrived — happy ending is accomplished when the film has wavered from home-movie technique to careful artifice like intricate flashbacks experienced via a television screen. Too many good intentions are left by the wayside, while others are clearly worked to death. The rather warm mood of the feature is maintained mostly through the acting of Vibeke Lökkeberg (her rather gaunt face has the classic beauty of a Martha Graham or an Isak Dinesen) and the mild-mannered non-acting of Kristiansen himself. Film is full of sly little references to local Norwegian phenomenae and sensitivities and it also has a lot of peeking through the curtains into the private life (frolicking in bathtubs, making love in fancy positions, etc.) of a famous film couple and so should do well on the theater circuit at home. Since especially Lökkeberg has avid aficionados among international festgoers, a limited international exposure may also be obtained by this very long-winded piece of tragi-comic self-indulgence. —*Kell.*

Stereo
(CANADIAN-B&W)

Hollywood, Aug. 11.
An Emergent Films Ltd. presentation. Produced, directed, written, photographed, edited by David Cronenberg. Reviewed at the Landmark Screening Room, L.A., Aug. 10, 1984. (No MPAA Rating.) Running time: **63 MINS.**
Features: Ron Mlodzik, Jack Messinger, Iain Ewing, Clara Mayer, Paul Mulholland, Arlene Mlodzik, Glenn McCauley.

Lensed in 1969 for a paltry $3,500, "Stereo" is now surfacing theatrically for the first time on the specialty circuit because it represents the initial feature film effort by David Cronenberg, Canadian director who has since gained reknown via such horror items as "They Came From Within," "Rabid," "Scanners" and "The Dead Zone." Billed with his follow-up feature "Crimes Of The Future" and his 1976 short "The Italian Machine," avant-garde item showed at the Vista in Hollywood on Aug. 15, and entire package is a highly esoteric one limited to similar venues in major cities and on campuses.

Shot in black-and-white without synch sound, "Stereo" carries built-in liabilities for audiences thanks to its technical limitations and aesthetic idiosyncracies. Basically a student effort (Cronenberg was 26 at a time), pic tests the viewer's patience and endurance even with its hour's running time due to its emphatically dry, scientific narration and deliberate emotional distancing.

Reminiscent by turns of Chris Marker's "La Jetée," George Lucas' short USC version of "THX 1138" and Jean-Luc Goddard's "Alphaville," as well the 1960s New York underground scene, film abstractly examines the situation at the Canadian Academy for Erotic Inquiry, where eight individuals have been subjected to telepathic surgery.

As the narrator drones on about the assorted desired and unanticipated effects of the operation, alternately strange and static scenes are presented which only occasionally bear any relation to the words being spoken. Long silences accompany the observation of anonymous characters performing largely indecipherable actions, and what little interest is generated, apart from the quality of the visuals, stems from notions of dominance and submission developed through telepathy and the creation of an "omnisexuality" out of the ashes of destroyed conventions.

Compositions and lighting show evidence of a strong artistic sensibility behind the camera, and to prove that one has talent with only $3,500 at one's disposal was accomplishment enough under these circumstances. Basically, it's dull stuff, but of interest to Cronenberg watchers as a revelation of his arty, experimental origins.—*Cart.*

Crimes Of The Future
(CANADIAN-COLOR)

Hollywood, Aug. 11.
An Emergent Films Ltd. presentation. Produced, directed, written, photographed, edited by David Cronenberg. Reviewed at the Landmark Screening Room, L.A., Aug. 10, 1984. (No MPAA Rating.) Running time: 63 MINS.
Features: Ronald Mlodzik (Adrian Tripod), Jon Lidolt, Tania Zolty, Paul Mulholland, Jack Messinger, Iain Ewing, William Haslam, Ray Woodley, Stefan Caernecki, Kafe Macpherson, William Poolman, Don Owen, Udo Kasemets.

Made in 1970 on a $20,000 budget, David Cronenberg's second feature film, "Crimes Of The Future," bears a strong similarity to his first outing, "Stereo," produced the year before. In now-beginning premiere revivals, pic will be of interest to hardcore Cronenberg cultists for the appearance of numerous of the director's themes and fetishes in embryonic form.

In his later commercial pics, Cronenberg has displayed a continuing obsession for such matters as bodily mutation and grotesque growths, aberrant medical experiments, massive plagues and futuristic architecutre. They're all present here, as the director concocts a bizarre, convoluted look at a future gone perverse.

As in "Stereo," periodic narration is used to cover lack of synch sound and dialog. The blank, effete Adrian Tripod wanders aimlessly from The House Of Skin, founded by his former mentor, Antoine Rouge, to the Institute of Neo-Veneral Disease, in an effort to elucidate the effects of Rouge's Malady, a vicious disease caused by one of Rouge's cosmetic creations.

The world's entire female population has evidently been wiped out, and the male population has turned to various, and disappointingly tame, alternative sexual fixations. Prime symptom of the illness is Rouge's Foam, a substance which leaks from bodily orifices and is sexually exciting in its initial stage, but deadly later on.

As he moves through the bleak but architecturally striking settings, Tripod begins to take on the dimensions of an Edgar Allan Poe hero, a doomed figure traversing a devastated landscape. Despite the intriguing premise and incidental kinkiness, however, there is no artistic or dramatic payoff, and one is left only with some nifty ideas in their baldest undeveloped states.

This effort shares with "Stereo" a confident visual style, with color in the bargain, and precious scientific narration which is sometimes amusing, but it's clearly the work of a talent just beginning to find its way. —*Cart.*

Nie Byla Slonca
(There Was No Sun)
(POLISH-COLOR)

Karlovy Vary, July 18.
A Film Polski Film Production, Warsaw; world sales, Film Polski, Warsaw. Features entire cast. Directed by Juliusz Janicki. Screenplay, Jerzy Ofierski, Janicki, based on Ofierski's novel of same title; camera (color), Jerzy Goscik; music, Janusz Hajdun; sets Andrzej Przedworski; production manager, Michael Szczerbic. Reviewed at Karlovy Vary Film fest (Debut Competition), July 15, '84. Running time: 90 MINS.
Cast: Ernestyna Winnicka (Chaja), Marian Kozlowski (Piotr), Krzysztyna Wachalko-Zaleska (Monika), Janina Nowicka (Mother), Juliusz Lubicz-Lisowski (Father).

Polish debut helmer Juliusz Janicki's "There Was No Sun" is set during the war years 1943-44. It's about a young Jewish woman on the run from transports to the death camps. She takes refuge one night at a farmhouse and being a doctor helps save one of the family members. A young man on the farm falls for her but nearly spills the beans on a trip to town by bragging too much over a beer or two. This brings collaborators into the game and there's a showdown between informers and the partisan fighters who happen upon the scene at a convenient moment. The girl takes off with the partisans, leaving behind a broken heart. In the end, the Nazis are in the picture too, rounding up hostages and wreaking revenge on the civilian population for losing the war.

"There Was No Sun" is not much of a picture. — *Holl.*

Street Hero
(AUSTRALIAN-COLOR)

Sydney, Aug. 6.
A Roadshow (Australia) release of a Paul Dainty Films Ltd. production. Produced by Julie Monton. Executive producer Paul Dainty. Directed by Michael Pattinson. Stars Vince Colosimo, Sigrid Thornton, Sandy Gore. Screenplay, Jan Sardi; camera (color), Vincent Monton; editor, David Pulbrook; production design, Brian Thomson; sound, Gary Wilkins; music, Bruce Smeaton; costumes, Norma Moriceau. Reviewed at Hoyts Center, Sydney, July 31, 1984. Running time: 100 MINS.
Vinnie . . . . Vince Colosimo
Gloria . . . . Sigrid Thornton
Bonnie Rogers . . . . Sandy Gore
Detective Fitzpatrick . . . . Bill Hunter
George . . . . Ray Marshall
Miss Reagan . . . . : Amanda Muggleton
Vinnie's mother . . . . Peta Toppano
Joey . . . . Peter Sardi
Ciccio . . . . Luciano Catenacci
'Frog' Freddo . . . . Tibor Gyapjas

Bursting with energy and high spirits, "Street Hero" is an intermittently successful and enjoyable youth pic in which the talents of director Michael Pattinson and his cast of excellent players frequently collide with an incoherent and top-heavy screenplay.

Set in the sleazier parts of Melbourne, pic revolves around 17-year-old Vinnie (Vince Colosimo), the son of a former hood who as a boy, witnessed his father's murder. Vinnie is making none-too-successful attempts at a boxing career, and is also a courier for chief mobster Ciccio, who thinks the lad will go far. But meanwhile he's also attending school, where he has an affectionate girlfriend, Gloria (Sigrid Thornton) and where he comes under the influence of a music teacher (Sandy Gore) who encourages him to become the drummer in the school band.

Jan Sardi's busy screenplay tries to pack in so much that it frequently collapses in total confusion. The 100-minute film consists of an amalgam of "Mean Streets," "Blackboard Jungle" and "Strike Up The Band," with dope dealing, corrupt cops (who, incredibly, turn out to be okay guys at fadeout) and Vinnie's brutal *de facto* father thrown in for additional good measure. It's too much of a good thing.

However, film gets by via helmer Pattinson's skills and the charismatic central performance of Colosimo. Director and actor first teamed two years ago in "Moving Out," a less ambitious but more controlled film, which was a modest success. Colosimo is definitely a comer, and his professional performance brings the mixed-up Vinnie very much to life. He's ably backed by Sigrid Thornton (the girl from "The Man From Snowy River") as his g.f., Bill Hunter as a cop whose motives the script makes obscure but whose presence is forceful, Peta Toppano as Vinnie's tragic mother, and— best of all — Sandy Gore as the music teacher. Gore, who always manages to bring humor and style to the sappiest part, is three-dimensional in a one-dimensional role.

The film has been given a self-styled "new wave" look and sound, via art direction by Brian Thomson ("Rocky Horror Picture Show") that's as busy as the script, costumes by Norma Moriceau ("The Road Warrior") and a soundtrack of almost non-stop rock numbers.

Specially composed for the film, these numbers, which should attract the desired youth audience, are performed by Leo Sayer, Dragon, Garth Porter (of Sherbert), Red Symons (from Skyhooks) and Sharon O'Neill. Soundtrack album should make the local charts, with a couple of singles indicated to, which will help boxoffice.

Interesting to compare "Street Hero" with recent North American youth-slanted movies, which tend to be almost plotless but filled with sex and bad jokes. This Aussie item, as indicated, is overburdened with plot, and eschews sex (just some chaste kissing) and gutter humor in favor of color and atmosphere. It's a bit of a muddle, but it's a good looking, energetic, amiable one.
—*Strat.*

Davitelj Protiv Davitelja
(Strangler Vs. Strangler)
(YUGOSLAV-COLOR)

Pula, July 22.
A Centar Film Production, Belgrade. Features entire cast. Directed by Slobodan Sijan. Screenplay, Sijan, Nebojsa Pakic; camera (color), Milorad Glusica; sets, Veljko Despotovic; music, Vuk Kelenovic. Reviewed at Pula Film Fest, July 21, '84. Running time: 93 MINS.
Cast: Tasko Nacic, Nikos Simic, Srdjan Saper, Sonja Savic, Rahela Ferari, Pavle Mincic, Marija Baksa, Branislav Zeremski.

Yugoslav helmer Slobodan Sijan is a filmmaker ready-made for the fantasies of the committed film buff. His record for making both entertaining and personal cinema is indisputable. Witness the naked fun and sharp wit in "Who's That Singing Over There?" (1980), "The Marathon Family" (1982), and "How I Was Systematicaly Destroyed By An Idiot" (1983). Now he's parodied the horror genre with the morbidly hilarious "Strangler Vs. Strangler."

Picture a homely looking red carnation flower-seller resembling an oversized Peter Lorre. He only gets ruffled when potential customers make fun of his carnations, whereupon he goes beserk for a moment and strangles the fair ladies out of sheer frustration. Back home in his dank abode sits his cranky old mother, a witch right out of Hitchcock's "Psycho." Then there's the hapless police inspector, another oddball along the lines of the "Pink Panther" series. Add to this a second strangler whose shy sexual hangups seem to propel him to deeds he doesn't quite understand himself.

The rest has to be seen to be fully appreciated. Suffice it to say that several classics of the horror film are touched upon via respectful references, such as Fritz Lang's "M" with Lorre, the original "Frankenstein" with Boris Karloff, and Christopher Lee's Dracula pics.

"Strangler Vs. Strangler" is a rare treat, all the more a howl in that this black comedy comes out of Belgrade. Pic deserves more exposure on the fest circuit, and could find a modest spinoff in arthouses leaning towards repertory cinema. —Holl.

Stigma
(GREEK-COLOR)

Karlovy Vary, July 18.
A United Filmmakers Production, Athens. Features entire cast. Written and directed by Pavlos Tassios. Camera (color), Theodoros Margas; music, Kyriakos Sfetsa. Reviewed at Karlovy Vary Film Fest (Competition), July 13, '84. Running time: 90 MINS.
Cast: Olia Lazaridou, Dina Konsta, Andonis Kafetzopoulos.

Greek helmer Pavlos Tassios has been on the scene since his debut feature in the late 1960s, "Wretched People" (1966). Others since then include "Lost Happiness" (1967), "Forbidden Desires" (1967), "Tormented Youth" (1968), "Rivals" (1969), "Yes, But..!" (1972), "Protectors" (1973), "The Big Boss" (1976) and "Special Wishes" (1980). All of these lean heavily on the melodramatic, sensationalist side.

His latest, "Stigma," treats a family tragedy. A young married couple has an incurably hydrocephalous infant. Since state laws protect the child's right to live, the couple gradually come to the decision that starvation may be a fitting form of the forbidden euthanasia. So the baby is to die a slow death. But the tables are turned; the couple begin to quarrel and eventually break off their relationship. Moral: the taking of an innocent life has its own price, one that leaves scars forever.

Credits are on the lean side, although theme is striking and thesp performances offer some convincing moments. —Holl.

Pasajeros de una Pesadilla
(Passengers Of A Nightmare)
(ARGENTINE-COLOR)

Buenos Aires, June 15.
An Aries Cinematográfica Argentina presentation and production. Produced by Luis Osvaldo Repetto. Directed by Fernando Ayala. Stars Federico Luppi and Alicia Bruzzo. Screenplay, Jorge Goldenberg, based upon the book "I, Pablo Schocklender," by Pablo Schocklender, as told to Emilio Petcoff; camera (Eastmancolor), Victor Hugo Caula; editor, Eduardo López; music, Oscar Cardozo Ocampo; art director, Emilio Basaldúa; assistant director, Alberto Lecchi; production manager, Mario Faroni. Reviewed at the Gran Rex theater, B.A., June 14, 1984. Running time: 95 MINS.
Fogelman . . . . Federico Luppi
Mrs. Fogelman . . . . Alicia Bruzzo
Junior son . . . . Gabriel Lenn
Elder son . . . . German Palacios
Daughter . . . . Gabriela Flores
Also with: Gilda Lousek, Nelly Prono, Dalma Milevos, Esteban Massari, Golde Flami, Jacques Arndt, Lydia Lamaison.

Some three years ago, blood dripping from the rear side of a car stationed one Sunday morning on the main street of a fashionable B.A. quarter led to the discovery, inside the trunk, of the bodies of a wealthy engineer and his wife. Their two sons, accused of the murder, ran away but were soon captured in what seemed the grotesque parody of a western; almost knocked down by cold and hunger, they were riding a horse near Mar del Plata. Afterwards they admitted their parricide and were jailed. The case not only made headlines but also horrified when gory details of the killings were leaked to the press.

But eventually some doubts arose. Schocklender Pére was the agent of a powerful British armaments company having dealings with the military. Suspicion shifted in that direction. Later on, the junior son, Pablo Schlocklender wrote — with the help of journalist Emilio Petcoff — a book revealing shocking secrets of his family which raised more doubts about who killed his parents. The verdict is still pending on this baffling affair.

As the mystery deepened and scandalous intimacies were revealed, producer-director Fernando Ayala and producer Luis Osvaldo Repetto bought the film rights of Pablo Schocklender's story, put it on the screen and attained an instant local success.

Story is told in flashbacks showing what Pablo (played by Gabriel Lenn) tells scripter-actor Jorge Goldenberg in jail. Shy, poor Jewish engineer Fogelman (fictional surname for Schocklender), played by Federico Lupp, marries an uninhibited Gentile girl, Alicia Bruzzo, without telling his domineering father. When their two sons and a daughter are in their late teens the couple, already enjoying a high status thanks to the fortune amassed by Luppi in secret business with a

general, face their major crisis: Bruzzo takes a lover, then some others, Luppi becomes homosexual with the eventual knowledge and approval of his wife, their relationships with their children deteriorate, neurotic and alcoholic Bruzzo indiscreetly steps into the dealings of Luppi with the military, then develops an incestuous infatuation with son Pablo. When their two sons want to leave for Israel to live in a kibbutz, she refuses to give her legal consent for their travel abroad.

All these and many other shocking angles of the real-life story have been handled expertly by Ayala. The enigma of who shot the couple is left to the viewer to unravel, although the strongest indication points to professional killers using the green Falcons of para-military units.

Bruzzo shines in her portrayal of Mrs. Fogelman; although being placed by the script mostly into limited situations she has managed to make one feel the sickness prompting her erratic, aggressive and vicious behavior. Luppi is also convincing despite the superficial treatment given his character. Technical credits are okay. —Nubi.

Balkaski Spijun
(The Balkan Spy)
(YUGOSLAV-COLOR)

Pula, July 30.
A Union Film Production, Belgrade. Features entire cast. Directed by Bozidar Nikolic and Dusan Kovacevic. Screenplay, Dusan Kovacevic; camera (color), Bozidar Nikolic; sets, Milenko Jeremic; music, Vojislav-Voki Kostic. Reviewed at Pula Film Fest, July 24, '84. Running time: 99 MINS.
Cast: Danilo Bata Stojkovic, Mira Banjac, Bora Todorovic, Zvonko Lepetic.

Based on a popular stage production presented two seasons ago at Belgrade's Atelier 212, "The Balkan Spy" was codirected by scripter Dusan Kovacevic and lenser Bozidar Nikolic. As drama, the layers of spoken text have a tense snowballing effect as a little guy's wild imagination drives him into a kind of self-destructive madness. Make no mistake: this is a sharply honed black comedy that is best understood by viewers familiar with Stalinist times and those dark postwar years stamped by a Personality Cult. The principal figure in this drama is thesp Danilo Bata Stojkovic, who scored a critical success in both Kovacevic's play and the film adaptation (voted at Pula a Golden Arena award as Best Actor).

Ilija, living peacefully with his wife and daughter in a quiet section of Belgrade, was once a mighty mite in the fear-laden 1950s. But those days are now over: he served his two-year prison term, and his more brutal brother sat out a longer four-year term. Outside of his complacent neighbors (one neighbor assembles a daily chorus ensemble for

the singing of romantic national hymns), life has treated him rather well even in passing him by in his advancing middle age.

Now comes a change in events. A stranger who has lived for a long time in Paris rents the quarters in back of Ilija and has apparently opened a tailor shop. One day, Ilija is called to the police station to ask about the whereabouts and goings-on in regard to the lodger. This triggers a nerve in our hero's consciousness: what if he is harboring a spy in contact with "imperialist forces" who could also be a danger to national security? Without any further ado and minus any extra police help (who think Ilija is a quack in any case), matters are taken into his own hands. He buys a camera and tape recorder, then takes a leave-of-absence at his job to follow the suspect spy around town as the latter makes his rounds. The lodger, it turns out, is innocently involved in fashions and trade shows. And the reason he has returned from Paris to Belgrade is to seek some advice and help from friends and colleagues in regard to how to help a drug-addicted son.

Gradually, Ilija gets more involved in his snooping activities. He calls in his brother, and together they dig up their Stalin pictures and related insignia out of the cellar. Then, as the two begin to close in on their prey, more Stalinist chums are called in to participate in the caper. The rest has to be seen: a kidnapping caper, brutality once again, and one of the ripest cases of paranoia ever seen on Yugoslav screens.

At the end, Ilija's wife has given into the same madness, while the daughter will have nothing more to do with her over-stressed father. Not even an apparent heart attack as Ilija's hysteria mounts can turn him from his stubborn, self-righteous ways.

Scripter Dusan Kovacevic also penned Slobodan Sijan's comic success, "The Marathon Family" (1982), while lenser Bozidar Nikolic ranks as one of the best cameramen presently working in Yugoslav cinema. Their "Balkan Spy" is a winner. It won the Golden Arena at Pula. —Holl.

Beyom Bahir Royim Et Damesek
(On A Clear Day You See Damascus)
(ISRAELI-COLOR)

Tel Aviv, June 9.
An Eran Riklis Production. Produced and directed by Eran Riklis. Screenplay, Eran Riklis, Gabriel Beristain; camera (color), Gariel Beristain; editor, Rina Benner; art direction, Dino Gershoni, Yoram Barzilai; sound, Kevin Greenwood, Itamar Ben Yaakov; additional photography, Avi Karpik, Rafi Rafaeli; music, May Music. Reviewed at Beth Lessin Cinema, Tel Aviv, June 8, 1984. Running time: 94 MINS.

With: Eli Dankner, Joseph Bee, Liron Nirgad, Daniel Wachsman, Muhamad Bakri, Asthar Shamir.

Eran Riklis started shooting this film, his first feature, some three years ago, as a graduation short for the National Film School in London. As shooting continued, the project grew in dimension, until he completed the full-length feature some months ago.

The film may attract some attention at home and abroad as it deals with a highly controversial topic, already broadly referred to in a couple of other Israeli features of late: the trial and conviction of a group of extremists from the left, who several years ago decided to start their own peace initiatives by contacting enemy agents. The most prominent figure, who has been repeatedly refused early release for good behavior, is a former army officer and kibbutz member Udi Adiv, and both the recently released "Fellow Travellers" and the not yet released "Beyond The Walls," are using this character as part of their format dealing with the political struggles in this area.

Riklis cast film director Daniel Wachsman in the role of Uri Sharon, a kibbutznik who is thrown in jail for his political activities. While Sharon himself is not the plot's center, he is certainly its inspiration, as the real conflict raised by the film is whether such initiatives are acceptable and how far can an Israeli afford to depart from legality in search of true merger of peoples and cultures in the region. All this is reflected in film's hero, a friend of Sharon and a composer who is trying to find a way of combining Oriental tunes with occidental sounds.

While the theme itself is valid, Riklis lacks the knowhow to build an acceptable plot around it, his film looking very much like a student's effort. The narrative style is botched, directing is heavy-handed, dramatic material insufficent to fill out a feature.

Acting is poor and chances on home market look dim. —*Edna*.

Montreal Fest

Windy City
(U.S.-COLOR)

Montreal, Aug. 17.

A Warner Bros. release of a CBS Theatrical Films presentation. Produced by Alan Greisman. Written and directed by Armyan Bernstein. Camera (Technicolor), Reynaldo Villalobos; editor, Clifford Jones; production design, Bill Kenney; costumes, Betsy Cox; music, Jack Nitzsche. Reviewed at the World Film Festival (competition), Montreal, Aug. 17, 1984. (MPAA Rating: R.) Running time: **102 MINS.**
Danny Morgan . . . . John Shea
Emily Reubens . . . . Kate Capshaw
Sol . . . . Josh Mostel
Mickey . . . . Jim Borrelli
Bobby . . . . Jeffrey DeMunn
Pete . . . . Eric Pierpoint
Marty . . . . Lewis J. Stadlen
Eddy . . . . James Sutorius

"Windy City" marks writer Armyan Bernstein's ("One From The Heart") maiden voyage as director of his own tales, and while the endeavor isn't always smooth sailing, the heart-felt nature of his subject is generally strong enough to weather the awkwardness of this story of romance, friendship and shattered dreams.

Chicago-set story echoes such recent U.S. male bonding films as "Diner" and "The Wanderers" with nods to "The Big Chill" and "The Return Of The Secaucus 7" in pointing out the differences between youthful aspiration and adult reality. Yet, there is no sense of slavish devotion to a format or formula as Bernstein boldly enters highly emotional territory much in the manner his protagonists brazenly saw themselves as pirates in their youth.

Focus is Danny Morgan (John Shea), the most obvious victim of failed ambition among a group of seven men. He's a writer forced to take odd jobs including delivering mail. In the latter capacity he meets Emily (Kate Capshaw), the woman who finally accelerates his maturation which ironically forces their estrangement.

Using an unconventional structure, pic unfolds in flashback concerning Emily and present to detail the last surge of the former boyhood allies. Also detailed is Danny's last desperate stab at averting Emily's marriage to a staid, secure businessman. The framework allows for a helter-skelter approach frought with vignettes and punctuated by emotion.

While the impending wedding sets a deadline for Danny and Emily's story, the imminent death of the gregarious Sol (Josh Mostel) from leukemia serves as the boundary for the film's other thread. Contrast is effective between Danny's constant blocking in his relationship with Emily and his agonized pleas to friends to fulfill Sol's ocean-going dream. The grand romantic gesturing proves to be a hit-and-miss device when it turns earnest but hits its mark in the most fanciful moments of the script.

Begun almost two years ago as "All The Sad Young Men," the film's delay should improve commercial prospects in light of success of "The Big Chill," and oddly "Romancing The Stone." Technical work is almost too polished but only real detriment is Jack Nitzsche's overtly romantic and unfluctuating music score which often telegraphs the intent of emotional scenes.

Cast is very strong although Shea is saddled with too much voice-over narration at top of picture. Capshaw finally gets a real opportunity to justify her charismatic qualities and Mostel shines in a full performance of comedy and poignancy.

"Windy City" curiously works, warts and all, and even when Bernstein forces the drama over the top. Warners could have a sleeper in the film with careful marketing to play a likely strong word-of-mouth growth. Prize prospects at Montreal look rosy for the debuting helmer. —*Klad*.

Choose Me
(U.S.-COLOR)

Montreal, Aug. 19.

An Island Alive production and release. Produced by Carolyn Pfeiffer and David Blocker. Written and directed by Alan Rudolph. Camera (Movielabcolor), Jan Kiesser; editor, Mia Goldman; production design, Steven Legler; costumes, Tracy Tynan; music (songs) performed by Teddy Pendergrass. Reviewed at the World Film Festival (noncompeting), Montreal, Aug. 18, 1984. (No MPAA Rating.) Running time: 106 MINS.
Nancy . . . . Genevieve Bujold
Mickey . . . . Keith Carradine
Eve . . . . Lesley Ann Warren
Zack Antoine . . . . Patrick Bauchau
Pearl Antoine . . . . Rae Dawn Chong
Billy Ace . . . . John Larroquette
Relph Chomsky . . . . Edward Ruscha
Mueller . . . . Gailard Sartain
Lou . . . . Robert Gould
Also: John Considine as the voice of Dr. Ernest Greene.

Offbeat, original and entertaining, "Choose Me" emerges as a truly novel film with strong appeal for hip audiences and beyond. The seemingly straightforward melodrama quickly changes its colors to reveal situations where nothing is as it seems and the apropos response is laughter not tears.

This is a precarious tightrope act emotionally but the high degree of artistry in front of and behind the camera effects an almost perfect balance.

Story centers on three unique people whose lives intertwine, mirror, diverge and reunite with ferocity. Dr. Nancy Love (Genevieve Bujold) is a mysterious open-line radio sex therapist unable to take hold of her personal problems. Mickey Deleon (Keith Carradine) appears to be a mythomaniac ne'er-do-well and Eve (Lesley Ann Warren) fluctuates between the role of a strong, capable bar owner and a hopelessly confused and vulnerable romantic.

Each of the principals seems to be projecting a false front. Eve uses a series of names in her daily calls to Dr. Love while the therapist, who answers Eve's ad for a roommate, introduces herself as Ann, the owner of an answering service. Mickey simply breezes into town spinning yarns of being a published poet, spy, mechanic and master of all skills.

Gradually the precarious relationships evolve between them and two others — Eve's sometime boyfriend Antoine (Patrick Bauchau), a gangster, and Antoine's wife Pearl (Rae Dawn Chong), a denizen of Eve's bar who hasn't revealed her true intentions to the woman.

The melodramatic underpinnings of the yarn are immediately apparent but writer-director Alan Rudolph plays against the drama as he forces the story into humorous extremes. Adopting elements of classic farce, the film offers a merry rollercoaster ride which is subtly illuminating and vigorously entertaining.

The surreal nature of the approach is handsomely captured in candy-box colored images from cameraman Jan Kiesser and the evocative sets of Steven Legler. The story unfolds largely at night which gives a *film noir* aspect to the proceedings and a further counterpoint emerges with the moody score and songs by Teddy Pendergrass.

Casting couldn't be better with Bujold, Carradine and Warren turning in their best work in some time. The principal trio have a keen appreciation for underplaying the most ludicrous elements of the plot to effect the greatest emotional and comical response.

While Rudolph has received considerable attention for such idiosyncratic films as "Welcome To L.A." and "Remember My Name," "Choose Me" goes even further in its diversions from mainstream filmmaking. Yet, this choice accounts largely for the film's artistic success and ultimate boxoffice cachet. He has made a film which is accessible to more than just a specialized audience while adopting shrewd economy financially (pic cost under $1,000,000).

Pic requires clever handling to snowball, it is offbeat in nature but has definite appeal to more than just the cogniscenti. —*Klad*.

Les Nuits De La Pleine Lune
(Full Moon In Paris)
(FRENCH-COLOR)

Hollywood, Aug. 24.

An Orion Classics (U.S.), A.A.A. (France) release of a Les Films du Losange-Les Films Ariane presentation. Produced by Margaret Menegoz. Directed, written by Eric Rohmer. Features entire cast. Camera (color), Renato Berta; editor, Cecile Decujis; music, Elli and Jacno; sound, Georges Prat. Reviewed at the Orion Screening Room, L.A., Aug. 24, 1984. (MPAA Rating: R.) Running time: 102 MINS.
Louise . . . . Pascale Ogier
Octave . . . . Fabrice Luchini
Remi . . . . Tcheky Karyo
Bastien . . . . Christian Vadim
Camille . . . . Virginia Thevenet
Marianne . . . . Anne-Severine Liotard

Currently premiering at film festivals in Montreal, Venice, Telluride and elsewhere and opening in New York in early September, "Full Moon In Paris" (as the title "Nights Of The Full Moon" has been rendered for domestic release) is another delightful and insightful look at French youth from Eric Rohmer. The fourth in the writer-director's "Comedies And Proverbs" series, film may not be as overtly titillating as his 1983 winner, "Pauline At The Beach," but will amply please his art house followers with its keen intelligence, good talk and excellent use of attractive new performers.

In all his films, but especially in his current series, Rohmer begins with elementary plots about the comings and goings of emotions between the sexes, frustrated desires, near-miss relationships and mismatched lusts. What actually happens in his stories is the stuff of the most banal little teenage love stories, but Rohmer almost invariably elevates his material to vastly amusing and sometimes profound levels with his precise and lucid structuring and writing, and his firm, but unemphatic, philosophical distance.

French proverb which introduces the action, and needn't be taken too seriously, runs, "He who has two women loses his soul. He who has two houses loses his mind." Slim, dark Pascale Ogier lives in the Paris suburbs with athletic Tcheky Karyo, but has reached the point where she wants to maintain a separate apartment in the city so she can pursue a more active social life than her b.f. wants.

Couple reaches an accord on this point, but it looks pretty clear that they're destined for a rupture sooner or later. Her best male friend, writer Fabrice Luchini, is happily married but can't stand the fact that Ogier doesn't want to sleep with him anyway.

Over the course of four winter months (diametrically opposed to the seasonal frame of "Pauline"), Ogier fulfills her wish of spending more time on her own in Paris, but watches as her friends, including her boyfriend, drift away from her into other romantic entanglements.

Diverting thrust of the film's first half is that it's all about partners who hardly spend any time with one another. Straying parties insist that they're happy with their mates, but still seek more happiness on the outside.

Another key to Rohmer's characterizations is that, no matter how intelligent, civilized and sophisticated they may be, they are still entirely vulnerable to emotional mistakes and prone to gaffes in matters of love and sex.

Young Pascale Ogier, daughter of prominent French actress Bulle Ogier, is an offbeat, large-eyed looker who remains centerstage virtually throughout, and admirably makes the swing from confident gal who calls all the shots to isolated woman who must learn to grow up. Another showbiz child, Christian Vadim, son of Roger Vadim and Catherine Deneuve, has a supporting role as a Keith Richards lookalike who picks up Ogier at a party. Tcheky Karyo is solid as Ogier's earnest lover.

Film is practically stolen, however, by Fabrice Luchini, young thesp who starred in "Perceval" for Rohmer several years ago and has now developed into a wonderfully witty, self-assured actor. All his scenes possess a special spark beyond that found in the rest of the film.

Renato Berta's lensing is lovely and simple, and contempo European schlock pop music is adroitly used in the backgrounds.—*Cart.*

Luther Ist Tot
(Luther Is Dead)
(WEST GERMAN-COLOR-16m)

Berlin, Aug. 9.

A PAN-Film production, commissioned by Haus der Kirche, Berlin. Features entire cast. Written and directed by Frank Burckner. Camera (color), Hartmut Jahn, Armin Faust, Tom Preiss; sets, Maya Dubois; music, Rainer Böhm, Reinhard Hoffmann, Dagmar Jaenicke, Bernhard Wageringel; editing, Goetz Meyer. Reviewed at Haus der Kirche Screening Room, Berlin, August 8, '84. Running time: **60 MINS.**
Cast: Ingeborg Drewitz (speaker), Hermann Treusch (Luther as Monk), Ulrich Kuhlmann (Luther as Rebel), Wolfgang Bathke (Luther as Junker Jörg), Gerhard Friedrich (Luther as Opponent of the Peasants), Eberhard Wechselberg (Luther as Prophet), Eric Vaessen, Manuel Vaessen, Rainer Johannes Kölble, Britta Toegel, Horstdieter Wildner, Rainer Pigulla, Ulrich Hass, Erich Schwarz, Andreas Bissmeyer, Krikor Melikyan, Wolfgang Unterzaucher, Jockel Baumann, Klaus Jepsen, Manfred Petersen, Walter Alich, Erika Fuhrmann, Peter Schlesinger, Helmut Kraus, Alexander Herzog, Frank Glaubrecht, Jons Dengler.

Frank Burckner's "Luther Is Dead" is filmed street theater. Last year, on the 500th anniversary of Luther's birth, the Evangelical Church and its Berlin research center at the Haus der Kirche decided to present a Berlin street performance with noted legit actors and literary and church personalities of the historical events associated with the name of the religious performer. The idea works well as theater, particularly if the audience is cued to the historical events beforehand, and it's not bad as a film either when a team of cameramen are cued on when to be where during a charged performance.

So far as "Luther Is Dead" is concerned, the performance crowned a series of cultural and religious events last year during the 500th anniversary across both East and West Germany.

Five different actors (the best known of whom is Hermann Treusch) interpret the positions of Martin Luther during key moments in his life: as monk, reformer, fugitive, political force in the Peasants' War, and prophet of times to come. Each actor offers a different perspective on the Protestant reformer, the whole being quite critical and reflective — particularly Luther's damning position on the peasants and their aborted revolt as they tried to follow in his footsteps as reforming revolutionaries.

Pic has some serious faults, for the camera teams could have used a dress rehearsal and elevated platforms for better shooting angles. Nevertheless, "Luther Is Dead" is impressive — particularly its thematic drive taken from a review of the facts upon Luther's death whereby costumed actors voice contrasting and contradictory opinions in open debate on the reformer and the upheaval he triggered by his words and deeds. Now that film (and videocassette) is completed, production is recommended for commercial as well as religioso mart. — *Holl.*

Los Sures
(U.S.-COLOR-DOCU-16m)

Five portraits of New York Hispanics.

A production of Terra Prods., N.Y., and the Television Laboratory at WNET/13, N.Y. Executive producer, David Loxton; coordinating producer, Kathy Kline. Produced and directed by Diego Echeverria; associate producer, Fernando Moreno; camera (color), Mark Benjamin, Alicia Weber; sound, Felipe Borrero; editor, Kathryn Taverna. Produced for "Non-Fiction Television" with funding primarily by the Independent Documentary Fund WNET/13 and by the New York Council for The Humanities. Reviewed at Mayflower Hotel, N.Y., Aug. 23, 1984. (No MPAA Rating.) Running time: **60 MINS.**

"Los Sures" was a Blue Ribbon winner at the American Film Festival in May and was also shown at the Latin American Film Festival in New York during July. The film will now connect with a larger public in late September, as one of several distinguished new U.S. documentaries that are scheduled for the New York Film Festival in Lincoln Center.

"Los Sures" is an impoverished neighborhood of Puerto Ricans in Brooklyn. The film documents the community — its struggles at self-help, its successes and failures — through the differing perspectives of five persons living there who embody, we presume, general "Los Sures" attitudes and values, despite their quite varied separate individualities.

It is therefore a kind of sociopsychological profile of a part of New York City, These are five episodes that blend into a single composite whole, to make a picture of inner-city life in the 1980s.

Some audiences will doubtlessly be shocked and depressed by "Los Sures," as life there is grim stuff. These decayed streets and crumbling tenements hardly seem congenial soil for cultivating dreams and ideals, yet somehow they grow there, at least for awhile, amid the crime and despair and apathy.

"Los Sures" is tentatively set for public tv broadcast this fall. Its 16m future to the non-theatrical market seems assured. —*Hitch.*

America and Lewis Hine
(DOCU-B&W/COLOR-16M)

A production of Daedalus Prods., N.Y., with the Television Laboratory at WNET/13, N.Y. Executive Producer, David Loxton; project coordinator, Kathy Kline; co-produced by Nina Rosenblum, Daniel V. Allentuck. Directed by Rosenblum. Written by Allentuck, John Crowley, L.S. Block; camera (color/b&w), John Walker, Robert Aachs, Kobi Kobiashi; editors, Lora Hays, Gerald Donlan; voice of Margaret Byington: Maureen Stapleton; voice of Lewis Hine: Jason Robards; narrator, Crowley; sound editor, Maurice Schell. Major funding by National Endowment for The Humanities, the Independent Documentary Fund (for "Non Fiction Television"), AGVA-Gevaert, and other foundations and individuals. Reviewed at invitational premiere at WNET/13, N.Y., June 26, 1984. (No MPAA Rating.) Running time: **60 MINS.**

Few films get off to such a fast start: "America and Lewis Hine" was completed in late June and is already scheduled for the New York Film Festival Sept. 29, as well as the Telluride, Nyon and Berlin festivals, and for a PBS nationwide telecast Oct. 18. The film is clearly one of the major American documentaries of recent years, a tribute to and rediscovery of a major artist, the pioneering American still-photographer, Lewis Hine, chronicler and portraitist of working class America.

"America and Lewis Hine" brings him back to life, and that period of our history. The film combines an extraordinary selection of Hine photographs — he had made 15,000 — with b&w stock footage from early U.S. social history, and with color interviews of several surviving Hine contemporaries, shot in the present. Skillful weaving of these visuals, also of voices and music, guided by intelligent and poetic narration, makes this film a unique character-study and social document of a man and his times. Perhaps more importantly, "America and Lewis Hine" is entertaining and dramatic as a theatrical experience.

Hine's first major body of work concerned Ellis Island immigrants at the turn of the century. In later years, he followed these newcomers as they built American cities and industries, shooting thousands of photographs in mines, mills, factories, sweatshops, slums, tenant farms, on the road, everywhere American.

For a period, Hine was photographer for the National Child Labor Committee, dedicated to social reform, often working clandestinely because some grownups liked the exploitation of children, profiting from it. Hine's pictures of childworkers tending dangerous machines, and working long hours in damp, dark mines, are heartbreaking. The children recognized him as an adult they could trust, someone who cared; who wanted them to have a childhood.

Later, in 1930, when work began on the Empire State Building, Hine was made official photographer. He documented the dangerous and exciting construction aloft, often swinging out precariously on mooring masts for a better angle, risky work at age 56. Alas, his photography for the FDR Administration of the mid-1930s seems to have suffered from bureaucratic infighting. Hine died penniless and near forgotten in 1940, at age 66.

After its initial impact in festivals and on television, "America and Lewis Hine" should become a standard in 16m distribution to schools, libraries and museums, a film of long-range value and popularity.
—*Hitch.*

Sta Je S Tobom, Nina
(What's Up, Nina?)
(YUGOSLAV-COLOR)

Pula, July 30.
A Union Film Production, Belgrade. Features entire cast. Written and directed by Gordana Boskov. Camera (color), Nevenka Redzic; sets, Divna Milosevic; music, Zoran Simjanovic. Reviewed at Pula Film Fest, July 22, '84. Running time: **98 MINS.**
Cast: Snezana Savic, Radko Polic, Miodrag Petrovic.

One of Yugolavia's few femme helmers, Gordana Boskov has here directed her first feature after making a number of documentaries and tv films, and result is a femme theme: a modern woman can't make up her mind between career as a champion with the fencing foils or

sacrificing everything for the love of her husband. The question is still left open at the end, even though it appears that the identity problem has been solved when the woman fights her way back into winning form after going through a series of imaginary traumas.

Pretty heavy on the symbolic side, pic also moves at a snail's pace. —*Holl.*

Angelan Sota/Angelas Krig
(Angela's War)
(FINNISH-COLOR)

Helsinki, Aug. 23.
A Jörn Donner production and release (Helsinki) in coproduction with Trebitsch International (Hamburg) and co-financed by the Finnish Film Foundation, Finnish TV-1, Swedish TV-2. Written and directed by Eija-Elina Bergholm. Based on novel by Jörn Donner. Camera (Eastmancolor), Kari Sohlberg; editor, Irma Taina; music, Esa Helasvuo; production design, Pekka Hilkamo; executive producer, Jörn Donner; production management, Jaakko Talaskivi. Reviewed at the Nordia Theater, Helsinki, Aug. 22, 1984. Running time: 97 MINS.
Angela Anders . . . . Ida-Lotta Backman
Thomas Schmidt . . . . Mathieu Carriere
Gabriel . . . . Jörn Donner
Jakob Anders . . . . Kim Gunell
Goldberg . . . . Erland Josephson
The Professor . . . . Matti Oravisti
Karin Berggren . . . . Birgitta Ulfsson

The hurt and conflicting emotions of the Finnish people at the end of World War II were far more complex than those of the other Scandinavian countries that had had German soldiers on their soil. For a while, Finland and Germany had actually been allies in fighting the Russians.

When the Russians won after all and the Finns tried to make a separate peace with them in 1943, Finland not only did not regain her lost Karelian territories but had to try to force the remaining German forces out of Lapland, an operation that was not accomplished until the Germans surrendered to the Allies in April-May 1945.

From having been seen by the world as shining paragons of patriotic vigor and virtue during their lone fighting of the invading Soviet forces in the winter war of 1939, the Finns now emerged with a reputation soiled by their collaboration, albeit forced, with the Germans.

With such a historical background, writer-filmmaker Jörn Donner had almost too much material to cope with in his novel "Angela's War," and in turning book into feature film, writer-director Eija-Elina Bergholm could easily have used both epic scope and an epic budget. Less has had to suffice, which leaves her film rather staccato and out-of-breath at times, but there is enough setting up of staging — areas for great emotion and held-back suspense — to make "Angela's War" a fest-worthy item (slotted for Venice competition ap-

pearance on Sept. 4), which should also see international sales in carefully nursed situations before it reaches its tv-programming destiny.

The larger wartime events are used to put Angela's love affair with a German army captain into a sensitive perspective that mirrors her own stubborn maintaining of her right to love the German and the wide range of reaction recorded by her wealthy bourgeois family, an elderly Jewish gentlemen and the friend-admirer of herself and of the Finn she originally had a love affair with but who is later reported dead as a war casualty.

Satire is used here as well as sharp social commentary, and there is also the mostly mute regarding of the whole scene and its *Dramatis Personae* by Angela's young brother, obviously an Alexander inspiration from Ingmar Bergman's "Fanny And Alexander."

There is good and strong playing in the Angela role by Ida-Lotta Backman, while Erland Josephson, Matti Oravisto, Birgitta Ulfsson and Jörn Donner himself get only the briefest opportunities to indicate the shadings they might have added to their secondary roles. German-speaking French actor Mathieu Carriere (Gudrun Landgrebe's prostie partner in "A Woman In Flames") hardly seems to be burning with any glow of passion to match Angela's when their nurse-patient relationship in the Lapland field hospital turns into at first heated bedding-down together and later into a lasting but doomed love affair. He has, however, a rather Leslie Howardian intellectual/sensitive look that makes it reasonable enough that Angela succumbs to his initial appeal to her love and pity.

Further developed, "Angela's War" would seem to have made excellent extended melodramatic fare, and film also seems to have the potential tv miniseries running in its veins. As it stands, however, audiences will have to contend themselves with intriguing hints at what might have been a truly great love-amidst-war story. All production credits are of the first order.
— *Kell.*

Drama In Blond
(WEST GERMAN-COLOR-16m)

Berlin, Aug. 8.
A Lothar Lambert Film Production, Berlin, in collaboration with Norddeutscher Rundfunk (NDR), Hamburg. Features entire cast. Produced, written, directed and edited by Lothar Lambert. With the cooperation of Dagmar Beiersdorf; camera (color), Helmut Röttgen; sound, Christian Moldt. Reviewed at Cine Service Screening Room, Berlin, Aug. 7, '84. Running time: 81 MINS.
Cast: Lothar Lambert (Gerhard), Dagmar Beiersdorf (Margot), Hans Marquardt (Hans), Stefan Menche (Reinhard), Ulrike S. (Hanna), Albert Heins (bank manager), Dor-

othea Moritz (bank employee), Erika Rabau (bar frau), Dieter Schidor (Lore), and the transvestite stars Joaquin La Habana, Kim, Paco Moreno, Jessica Lanée, Tara O'Hara and Claire de Montagne.

With his twelfth low-budget feature production, "Drama In Blond," prolific Lothar Lambert leaves little doubt that he is the undisputed king of the Berlin underground. This is among his finest, and it's to his credit that he's not been spoiled by working with a fatter-than-usual budget of some $20,000 (thanks to NDR-TV in Hamburg). Pic has already been booked blind by the Toronto fest, while Lambert's Paris public (after the astonishing success there of "Fräulein Berlin") is also said to be clamoring to see the film.

"Drama In Blond" is about down-and-out Gerhard (Lambert), a bank employee who suffers under both a nosy sister (Ulrike S.) and an equally busybody neighbor (Dagmar Beiersdorf), who has a mild crush on him. Both Gerhard and Dagmar are lonely souls. At the bank, Gerhard is attracted to Hans, a young employee who encourages him to go out come along one evening to see him in a new Berlin underground movie. Hans is playing a transvestite in the pic (made by Lambert too), and so the next step is for Gerhard to come along to the local transvestite club to see Hans' friends perform. This makes for some more delightful comedy, moreso when coupled with the funny bank scenes (where Gerhard's exploits at the club are mused over by his strait-laced colleagues).

The upshot is that Gerhard decides to don an assortment of glad rags himself and finally, after practicing a Lili Marleen number at home before the mirror, he goes up on the stage himself at the club. It's a howl — and so, too, a run-amok imitation of the show later at the bank. It's at the club that everyone gets into the act — including former Rainer Werner Fassbinder producer-actor Dieter Schidor as the transvestite "Lore" with a string of ad libs to bring the house down.

In the end, Gerhard is a flop as a transvestite stage star, but he has liberated himself to such an extent that he forms a liaison with both Hans and his neighbor Margot, and apparently everybody lives happily ever after.

Good fun from start to finish with hardly a lag in the narrative, "Drama In Blond" will unspool in due time in a tv slot and should put the intrepid do-everything helmer in the Big Time. Lothar and Dagmar are the lead figures, but the show is consistently stolen throughout by professional thesps Hans Marquardt, Albert Heins, and Dorothea Moritz. And Erika Rabau is worth seeing in a fine cameo as the "bar frau." — *Holl.*

Treffer
(Bull's-Eye)
(WEST GERMAN-COLOR)

Berlin, Aug. 8.

A Bavaria Atelier Film Production, Munich, in collaboration with Westdeutscher Rundfunk (WDR), Cologne. Producer, Michael Hild; TV producer, Alexander Wesemann. Released by Futura Film. Directed by Dominik Graf. Screenplay, Christoph Fromm; camera (color), Helge Weindler; costumes, Esther Walz; sets, Hubert Popp; sound Klaus Eckelt; production manager, Peter Sterr. Reviewed at Kant Kino, Berlin, Aug. 7, '84. Running time: 103 MINS.

Cast: Max Wigger (Albi), Dietmar Bär (Franz), Tayfun Bademosy (Tayfun), Barbara Rudnik (Conny), Beate Finckh (Mira), Guido Gagliardi (Leone), Hinrich Schafmeister (Chris), Rainer Grenkowitz (Alf).

Dominik Graf's "Treffer" (perhaps best translated into the colloquial "Bull's-Eye") is another example of the trend among new generation German directors to tell a story along commercial entertainment lines, rather than get caught in the self-centered labyrinth of the auteur cinema.

Graf was one of the five Munich-based filmmakers who collaborated on "Neon City" (1981) — his seg was titled "Running Blue" and won him a German Film Prize — after which he made "The Second Sight" (1982) on his own. "Treffer" is his second feature and his best, falling in the vein of his thriller short "Running Blue" and without the psychological hangups that marred "The Second Sight." Worth noting in all three Graf pics is the polished professionalism of lenser Helge Weindler.

"Treffer" is the story of three chums crazy about motorbikes who spend all their time and money on the sport. Not even girls get in the way of their friendship, although two make out with the ladies quite well while the third, a chubby imp, doesn't even bother. The three work as mechanics and assistant manager at a shoddy auto workshop — until the owner dies of a heart attack just when the future was looking a bit rosier for him. The trio get taken in a shady car deal and now have to pay off their debts or get beaten to a pulp by a local mobster in addition to losing all that they worked for.

Bulk of pic concerns how the trio try to pick up loose cash by staging car accidents to pressure victims into quick cash payoffs in order to forget the matter. This works for a while, until the biggest deal of them all requires a fatal head-on crash.

Scripter Christoph Fromm, a grad of the Munich Film School (HFF), penned the story and appears to have been inspired by Boaz Davidson's Israeli "Popsicle" youth series, also featuring three inseparable chums with one on the beefy side. He and Graf have caught the milieu and their story does move at a quick pace, but something is missing all the same — the trio are convincing without being comical or sympathetic. Some extra dialog would have tied key scenes together, too, for that matter.

On the plus side are the thesps and the action sequences, plus lensing. — Holl.

Zlatnata Reka
(Golden River)
(BULGARIAN-COLOR)

Karlovy Vary, July 18.

A Bulgariafilm production. Directed by Ivanka Grabcheva. Features entire cast. Screenplay, Georgi Bogdanov; camera (color), Emil Wagenstein; art director, Valentina Mladenova; music, Mitko Shterev. Reviewed at Karlovy Film Fest July 7, '84 (in competition). Running time: 112 MINS.

With: Mihail Mihailov, Peter Slabakov, Nicola Chiprianov, Stoine Pavlin, Pepa Nikolova, Nikola Todev, Ivan Janchev.

The Golden River may have been a peaceful back-country stream in the not-so-long-ago of Bulgaria's agricultural past but a cement plant now stands along its muddy banks. The site is typical of an industrialized future in which the villages are fast disappearing and new factories are attracting an influx of migrant labor, a situation common to many Eastern European provinces today, and specially relevant to Bulgaria, where within 25 years migration patterns have radically altered and virtually destroyed a once-colorful pastoral life.

Enter director Ivanka Grabcheva, who uses this situation to paint a portrait of a band of social "misfits" who find solidarity and affection in a provincial small town but within their own special circle, whose radius extends from the village tavern of card-players and hangers-on to the house of Old Vangel (Mihail Mihailov), who takes into his cramped cottage any outsider who can't find a place in "society."

Adapting his own sprawling, near-400-page novel (which contains no dialog), with many subplots, to this story of some half-dozen, unproletarian, "colorful characters," Bogdanov has collaborated with Grabcheva in what seems to be a frank and undidactic look at contemporary problems in a national production that has until last year focussed interest on historical themes in celebration of Bulgaria's 1,300th birthday.

There is "Smoothy" (Peter Slabakov), a guitar-strumming and balladeering ex-con, who holds center stage at the pub and attracts a gypsy girlfriend and others of easy virtue. There is the village railwayman who feels defeated by life and finally drowns himself; a young man in the group, who did a stretch for drunk driving, takes responsibility for the railwayman's wife and kids. The local constable is always checking up on why people are not working. The village philosopher curses the polluted stream where he finds no more fish. Old Vangel, who once was a ladies man himself in the city, willingly gives shelter without offering advice. Not a "positive hero" in the bunch.

Prying villagers are put in their place, while the film offers many folkish touches of provincial rituals (greeting newlyweds with short songs). Pulling all these threads together is story of the young man who must leave for the city after the accidental death of an uncle at a wedding party, in much the same way Old Vangel left for the city to make his own fortune years ago.

Director Grabcheva, a onetime film student of the late Konrad Wolf at Potsdam-Babelsberg Film Institute (GDR), and who is best known in Bulgaria as a director of children's films, emerges as a name worth watching in the West, although her reputation is well-established on home grounds.

Technical credits are a plus. Though film leaves one wishing to know more about some of the more forceful characters (Slabakov in particular is good and Grabcheva's sharp introductory sketch of Old Vangel in "retro style" makes you want her to dwell on him alone), film overall is a surprising composite and honest portrait of one aspect of contemporary Bulgarian life. Good for festival outings and special film weeks. — Milg.

O Pokojniku Sve Najlepse
(Nothing But Words Of Praise For The Deceased)
(YUGOSLAV-COLOR)

Pula, July 30.

A Centar Film Production, Belgrade. Features entire cast. Directed by Predrag Antonijevic. Screenplay, Antonijevic, Dusan Perkovic; camera (color), Tomislav Pinter; sets, Milenko Jeremic; music, Vojislav Kostic. Reviewed at Pula Film Fest, July 23, '84. Running time: 95 MINS.

Cast: Zvonko Lepetic, Radmila Zivkovic, Bora Todorovic, Bogdan Diklic, Petar Kralj, Pavle Vujisic, Dragolub Milosavljevic.

As a satire on the period of the Personality Cult and the Socialist Realist films made under Stalinist dictates, Predrag Antonijevic's "Nothing But Words Of Praise For The Deceased" comes across as a very impressive debut feature. Without doubt, Antonijevic has seen at the film school in Belgrade a broad selection of these "straitjacket" film productions of yore, and possibly the milestone Yugo fun pics on the same theme made a decade ago by Dusan Makavejev ("WR-- Mysteries Of The Organism"). Bata Cengic ("The Story Of My Family In The World Revolution") and Zelimir Zilnik ("Early Works").

Pic is set immediately after the war in a small Serbian village. The president of the people's council catches fish illegally by throwing grenades into a river, thereby stunning his prey and filling his baskets at will. One day he happens upon an unexploded bomb on the river bank — just what he needs, as gunpowder is now running low. Trying to defuse the bomb, however, he sends himself to his reward in the Happy Hunting Grounds of the Personality Cult. No matter: a school is named in his honor, and life goes on.

The new party chairman then shacks up with his predecessor's ready and willing widow. The newcomer, however, has designs to shake the village from its sleepy lethargy. In other words, a human-scale Animal Farm is organized to establish the proletariat of the peasants. In the end, as it comically turns out, another "hero of the people" has been benevolently consigned to the hereafter. And, of course, with nothing but words of praise for the deceased.

Although in parts a quite amusing satire, pic in general misses its mark by opting for excess over measured commentary. —Holl.

Cudo Nevidjeno
(Unseen Wonder)
(YUGOSLAV-COLOR)

Pula, July 30.

A Zeta Film, Budva, and Centar Film, Belgrade, Coproduction. Features entire cast. Directed by Zivko Nikolic. Screenplay, Sinisa Pavlic; camera (color), Stanislav Somolani; sets, Milenko Jeremic; music, Boro Tamindzic. Reviewed at Pula Film Festival, July 21, '84. Running time: 96 MINS.

Cast: Savina Gersak, Dragan Nikolic, Petar Bozovic, Boro Begovic, Tasko Nacic, Danilo Stojkovic, Velimir Zivojnovic, Boro Stjepanovic, Vesna Pecanac, Mirjana Kodzic, Slavko Stimac, Bogdan Diklic.

The opening night feature at the Pula arena, Zivko Nikolic's "Unseen Wonder" comes across as a stylized black comedy, quite amusing for the home crowd but mostly lost on the outsider. The setting is an oddball fishing village on the shore of a lake plentiful with fish and an idyllic scene to boot. For centuries the women here do most of the work — even the fishing — while the men-folk hang around the local inn, flirt with the waitresses, tell lusty jokes, and dream of one day seeking their fortune in America. The only person in the place who feels that the times are changing is a young man who hits upon the idea of creating a paradise here on earth: connect the lake to the neighboring sea by digging a tunnel through the obstructive mountain and then use the fertile land on the bottom of the lake for "three crops a year."

Naturally, such a novel idea needs an accomplice and this is supplied when an "unseen wonder" happens upon the scene. She's the new blond and sexy waitress, fresh from America, a native lass returning to her homeland to stay. She and the canal-builder appear to make an ideal pair, but her presence arouses the gentry and sparks a Hatfield-and-McCoy feud that leads to a bloody and tragic end.

Pic's drawback is that it doesn't really go anywhere.—*Holl.*

Ambassador
(The Ambassador)
(YUGOSLAV-COLOR)

Pula, July 30.

A Jadran Film (Zagreb), Kinema (Sarajevo), and Kinematografi (Zagreb) coproduction. Features entire cast. Written and directed by Fadil Hadzic. Camera (color), Zivko Zalar; sets, Zelimir Zagotta; music, Alfi Kabilja. Reviewed at Pula Film Festival, July 22, '84. Running time: 97 MINS.
Cast: Miodrag Radonovic, Elizabeta Kukic, Voja Brajevic, Zeljiko Königsknecht, Fabijan Sovagovic, Marija Kohn.

Fadil Hadzic, who won Golden Arenas in the past for "Official Position" (1964) and "Journalist" (1967), has now made his best feature in the genre of the political drama, "The Ambassador." It also scored as one of the best films presented in Pula, and though classical, rather oldfashioned cinema, it at least deserves a bit more exposure on the fest circuit.

This is a psychological as well as political drama. Within a time frame of 24 hours, a foreign Yugoslav foreign diplomat and ambassador to Western capitals faces a severe moral crisis within his own family. It appears that he has never paid much attention to his children, and after the mother's death (for which he also shares the blame) he witnesses how they turn against him. In the family villa, and on the anniversary of the mother's death, the daughter decides to commit suicide, for the young woman loved her mother above all and cannot stand the presence of her father's new girlfriend in the house (no matter how unobtrusive she may be). As for the teenaged son, he's as spoiled and ornery as teenagers come these days — outside of rock music, his only interest is girls and sex games up in his private quarters.

On this particular day, a working man arrives at the villa to repair the water boiler. He serves as a distant observer and moral commentator on the affairs that pass before his eyes. One of his conversations is with the ambassador on a speech he heard the latter deliver about the time when both were volunteers in the Spanish Civil War on the side of the people. Other observers are guests the ambassador has invited to dinner. They are all well-to-do professionals, a bit vague in their politics and hardly the moral leaders a Socialist country depends on

to go its own way between East and West. It's the discussions among these tired and complacent gentry that underscore the film's message.

Strongly directed with a tight script and sharp dialogue, "Ambassador" gains as well in lensing (by Zivko Zalar) and fine thesp performances. —*Holl.*

Mala Pljacka Vlaka
(The Little Train Robbery)
(YUGOSLAV-COLOR)

Pula, July 30.

A Jadran Film (Zagreb) and Kinema (Sarajevo) Coproduction. Features entire cast. Written and directed by Dejan Sorak. Camera (color), Karpo Godina; sets, Dusko Jericevic; music, Neven Franges. Reviewed at Pula Film Fest, July 27, '84. Running time: 97 MINS.
Cast: Bata Zivojinovic, Miodrag Krivokapic, Mustafa Nadarevic, Kruno Saric, Danko Ljustina, Fabijan Sovagovic, Tatjana Boskovic.

A debut film by the talented writer-director Dejan Sorak, "The Little Train Robbery" takes its cue (as the title hints) from Edwin S. Porter's "The Great Train Robbery" — the same film-within-a-film motif was also used recently in Phillip Borsos' Canadian feature "The Grey Fox."

It's the closing days of World War I, and in a rocky desert border area of Bosnia-Croatia (near where the war began), is a wind-blown part of the Balkans where robbers and gendarmes live peacefully side by side for the simple want of company. The head of the outlaw band is Todor the Terrible (Bata Zivojinovic), a lunkhead of gigantic proportions whose sidekicks are even slower on the pick-up than he is. One day, the brigands stop a traveling cinematograph on the road (run by a visionary named Tomaz Netahly), and they learn firsthand what a train robbery is all about. Everything they've been doing up to now on the dusty mountain pass seems like small peanuts compared to a train holdup, but where to fine one like those described in the newfangled movies?

While they're off looking, along comes a coach with a gentleman and a lovely miss abroad. The distraction of loot and beauty is just too much, and the lady (the sensuous Tatjana Boskovic) does indeed steal the show!

Next comes law and order to the region. Todor the Terrible is arrested. His best friend, the border gendarme, is tricked into handing him over to the authorities, who plan a hanging to rid the area forever of the bandits. Instead, after a comic twist at the gallows, the outlaw is required to switch places with the gendarme, and so the same show goes on as before with the single exception of switched identities.

Pic stalls out when the running gags begin to wear thin, but the wit-

ty dialog makes up for everything lacking in the way of action and belly laughs. Lensing by Karpo Godina is also a plus. —*Holl.*

Seraphim Polubes e drugie zhiteli zemli
(Seraphim Polubes and Other Humans)
(SOVIET-COLOR)

Karlovy Vary, Aug. 2.

A Mosfilm Studios Production. Directed by Viktor Prokhorov. Features entire cast. Screenplay, Alexander Alexandrov; camera (color), Pavel Lebeshev; music, Alexci Rybnikov; art director, Ludmila Kusakova. Reviewed at Karlovy Vary fest, July 9, 1984 (in debut film competition). Running time: 90 MINS.
With: Rodion Nakhepetov, Eduard Bocharov, Darya Mikhailkova, Vladimir Samilov, Nina Menshikova.

Seraphim Polubes lives in a small town in central Russia and, now retired as a stovefitter, likes to paint the walls of his simple peasant home with magical scenes from his fantasmagoric world, like "Russian Travellers in Africa Save Locals from Wolves at Night." A Russian "Grandma Moses," he is visited by jaded Moscow art expert Rodion Nakhepetov (best known for his role as cameraman in Nikita Mikhalkov's "A Slave of Love"), who is putting together a show of primitive art for a Paris exhibition.

Entranced by Polubes and his argumentative village buddies and the atmosphere of cordiality and kindness, bachelor Nakhepetov decides to hang around awhile instead of returning immediately to the Moscow rat-race and to sample the pleasures of a rural idyll. His stay among Serafim's circle of simple, though eccentric, "natural" types confirms what he considers his own artificial and shallow city life as a functionary who had long ago given up his own dreams of becoming a painter.

A young blonde on a motorcycle also catches his eye (Darya Mikhailkova), who figures in a nude-by-the-lake picture hanging on Seraphim's wall. Though half his age, the 18-year-old impresses him with her individuality and "inner truth and purity" (following a long line of Russian heroines from Pushkin's Tatiana to Turgenev girls and Tolstoy's Natasha in "War And Peace"). His discovery of a kindred soul belatedly coincides with the time for farewells and gathering pictures for the exhibition, striking portraits with large, staring eyes (suggesting the artist's own view of the world). Rather than face the possibility of never seeing his newfound inspiration again, Nakhepetov leaving the station impulsively jumps from the fast-moving train, pictures under arm, to quit his past and be regenerated by the young girl running to meet him. Though a little bruised he's now happy.

This first feature, which shared a prize here in the debut category, is by young director Viktor Prokhorov (early 30s), who did not come up via the usual Moscow Film School route (VGIK) but did a decade apprenticeship in documentaries and screenwriter Alexandrov ("One Hundred Days of Childhood"). Sure professionalism and a light touch give the village characters high screen energy while Nakhepetov appears the passive observer (as he does also in Gleb Panfilov's 1982 "Valentina," playing a similar character). The "return to the village" theme, with its implicit criticism of big-city sophistication, has an added interest here with emphasis on Soviet-style naive art, found also in the prototypical Soviet Georgian film biography "Pirosmani." Paintings in the film were all done by actual village primitives. Though story line is a bit schematic, film would do well in Soviet weeks and in ethnically-slanted programs, in addition to having interest for art buffs. — *Milg.*

Ardh Satya
(Half-Truth)
(INDIAN-COLOR)

Karlovy Vary, Aug. 2.

A Neo Films Production. Produced by Manmohan Shetty, Pradeep Uppoor, Vasanji Mamani, Shivanand Shetty. Stars Om Puri and Smita Patil. Directed and photographed by Govind Nihalani. Screenplay, Vijay Tendulkar, based on short story by S.D. Panwalkar; art direction, C.S. Bhali; music, Ajit Verman; editor, Renu Saluji. Reviewed at Karlvoy Vary (Czech.) Film Fest, July 8, 1984 (in competition). Running time: 118 MINS.
Anant Welankar .... Om Puri
Jyotsna .... Smita Patil
Anant's Father .... Amrish Puri
Inspector Lobo .... Naseeruddin Shah
Rama Shetty .... Sadashiv Amrapurkar
Inspector Patil .... Achyut Potdar
(In Hindi with English subtitles)

A fast-paced police story about an over-zealous cop who rides around the city on his motorcycle, whose sense of duty sometimes leads him to using violent means of persuasion during interrogations, who has connections with shady characters in high places, and who gets suspended from the force for his unorthodox methods of fighting crime is a staple of American television. In the Indian (Hindi) cinema, however, the subject is uncommon enough to become a boxoffice surprise and find audiences who welcome a "cinema of social conscience," in contrast to the tinsel world of commercial "Bombay movies" or the old-fashioned 3-hour family melodrama, with song and dance.

Govind Nihalani's new film, which earned lead Om Puri "best actor" prize here (shared) belongs to a handful of recent Indian films which have confounded the trends at the commercial wickets and the speculations of producers responsible for the huge output of a gargantuan film industry (768 features last year for a population of 700 million in 19 language states.) As a Bombay sub-inspector caught between a desire to do his job well and maintain his human dignity and a system whose injustices (police violence) have increasingly come under public attack, young Anant tries to measure up to the exacting duties of a professional conscience.

Nihalani successfully manages to transcend the genre and Om Puri the type to depict what ultimately becomes the tragedy of a young man who is out of place in a job urged on him by his father, a prototypical police officer, now retired. In the course of his duties around the precinct station he also gets first-hand knowledge of bribery connections with the politico Shetty, implicated in a murder case, but protected by some of Anant's very fellow-officers.

His moral righteousness carries him once too far when in his rage he beats a prisoner under interrogation so brutally that the prisoner dies. Suspended from the force, he must seek help from Shetty, who has now become a figure of importance. In the end, Anant refuses complicity and faces up to the responsibility for his deed.

Puri, whose craggy features and pock-marked face reflect stern duty in a role not geared to get immediate sympathy from Indian audiences, carries the film and even manages to finally reach a heroic plane in a definitely anti-heroic character. He is abetted by Smita Patil, who plays Anant's school teacher girl-friend, but who does not figure prominently in the story, despite Patil's strong boxoffice name at home and abroad.

Nihalani, who was second-unit cameraman on "Gandhi," has been quietly moving up to the the front rank of Indian filmmakers with three features in the last four years, after a decade as Shyam Benegal's cameraman. His 1980 story of man belonging to a marginal tribe, wrongfully accused of murder ("Aakrosh") convinced producers that hard-hitting social themes can make it commercially these days in the Hindi film world, where fantasy and illusion have been the norm. Nihalani spreads a broader canvas — power and corruption — in this new film, which is a must for Indian film weeks abroad or art houses specializing in Asian fare. —*Milg.*

U Raljama Zivota
(The Jaws Of Life)
(YUGOSLAV-COLOR)

Pula, July 30.

An Art Film (Belgrade), Croatia Film (Zagreb). Jadran Film (Zagreb), Union Film (Belgrade), and Kinematografi (Zagreb) coproduction. Features entire cast. Directed by Rajko Grlic. Screenplay, Grlic, Dubravka Ugresic; camera (color), Tomislav Pinter; sets, Stanislav Dobrina; music, Brana Zivkovic. Reviewed at Pula Film Fest, July 26, '84. Running time: **95 MINS.**

Cast: Gorica Popovic, Bogdan Diklic, Vitomira Loncar.

The most provocative film to appear at Pula, "The Jaws Of Life" is also the best feature Rajko Grlic has made in an already remarkable career of critical successes that include "Whichever Way the Ball Bounces" (1974), "Bravo Maestro" (1978) and "The Melody Haunts My Reverie" (1981). What makes his latest feature so satisfying is the loose comic flow of the narrative, the bittersweet perspective on the foibles of life, and the overall philosophical bent that springs from the very nature of the tale.

Here is a middleaged woman tv filmmaker, a bit on the chubby side, making a serial titled (rather tongue-in-cheek) "The Jaws Of Life." It's about a young office clerk, another lady on the chubby side, who is hungry for love and affection. Both women are at core lonely individuals, yet have an inner strength that spurs them both to risk all rather than let life pass them by completely. The irony is that although each woman is from a different walk of life (the filmmaker an intellectual, the office clerk simple and uncomplicated), the fate of one — quite naturally — affects the other. In other words, the creative process and the related search for self-knowledge and identity run parallel to each other throughout the tale. In fact, the two stories begin to converge toward the end after starting quite separately from one another.

The tv heroine — from the tv series "Stephie Cvek In The Jaws Of Life" — is a romantically inclined individual looking for the right man in her life, while at the same time open to whatever affairs or experiences may come her way. As it happens, she offers herself body and soul to various types of males: a macho Serb, a shy gay, a drunken poet. As for her filmmaking counterpart, she's turning down the suitors knocking on the door of her penthouse apartment, particularly a conceited Marxist critic and a beachboy hippy type. Dunja, our intellectual, somehow still prefers her ice cream dishes to a senseless roll in the hay.

In the end, the lonely clerk Stephie has run the gamut of social prototypes, only to discover that the man of her dreams may have been right there under her nose all the time. By contrast, Dunja faces for the first time the consequences of living a life apparently much too emancipated for her own good.

Credits are generally tops but hats off primarily to the two thesp performances and a sparkling script and story by the talented Dubravka Ugresic. —*Holl.*

Bakom Jalusin
(Behind the Shutters)
(SWEDISH-COLOR)

Karlovy Vary, July 17.

A Farago Film production (Swedish-Danish coproduction) for The Swedish Film Institute, Svensk Filmindustri and Nordisk Film. Producer, Katinka Farago. Direction and script by Stig Bjorkman. Features entire cast. Camera, Dirk Bruel; art direction, Kaj Larsen; editing, Sylvia Ingemarsson. Reviewed at Karlovy Vary Film Fest (in competition) July 17, '84. Running time: **98 MINS.**

With: Erland Josephson, Domiziana Giordano, Gunnel Lindblom, Lotte Tarp, Vlado Juras.

One of Sweden's top film critics as well as director of six features and seven documentaries, Stig Bjorkman ventures into Antonioni and Alain Robbe-Grillet territory in this would-be thriller about a Swedish writer (Erland Josephson) trying to cope with paranoidal jealousy over his actress wife (Gunnel Lindblom) and a disintegrating marriage by fleeing Sweden to exotic North Africa where he hopes to find salvation and to rediscover his own identity while working on a new novel heavily dependent on his own voyeurism.

In the bazaars and at the beaches of coastal Morocco he comes upon a young painter (Vlado Juras) and his Italian girlfriend (Domiziana Giordano, remembered from her major role in Andrei Tarkovsky's "Nostalghia") and assorted international types hanging about the drug scene. To the writer, they all become grist for his novelistic fantasies and, as the story develops, what is fantasy about disappearances of these characters and their erotic liaisons and what is real become intertwined. As fiction and reality continuously double on each other, the complicated story becomes enigmatic, surrounded by an evocative atmosphere of street sounds, interior monologs, and repetitive starings in mirrors and through venetion blinds.

Has the Italian woman on whom his imagination fastens been murdered by her boyfriend? Was she really found lifeless one morning outside his flat? And then the body, why did it disappear? While the viewer may follow with fascination (after all, it's a whodunit), he ultimately is hard put to fit clues together and make a case as to what the writer saw, knew or wrote.

Though primarily Josephson's film and well realized, "Behind The Shutters" would take more than one viewing to be able to separate the strands for a coherent story. Electronic score with guitar motifs suggesting strange, Arabic locale, and nice lensing of the expatriate North African scene are pluses, but the viewer is still unhappily at sea despite Hitchcockian twists and a now-we-see-it, now-we-don't exercise in murder. With this qualification, film could have some limited art house playoff. — *Milg.*

Love In A Fallen City
(HONG-KONG-COLOR)

Hong Kong, Aug. 5.

A Shaw Brothers production and release by Sir Run Run Shaw. Executive producer, Mona Fong. Produced by Lawrence Wong. Directed by Ann Hui. Based on the novel by Eileen Chang; camera (color), Anthony Hope; music, Lam Man-Yee, military advisor, Andy Neilson; art direction, Tony Au. Reviewed at Queens' Theater, Hong Kong, Aug. 4, 1984. Running time: **100 MINS.**

Cast: Cora Miao, Chow Yun Fat, Keung Chung Ping, Chiu Kao, Helen Ma, Winnie Chin, Chung king-pie, Kam Yin-Ling, Wong Man, Jovy Couldrey.

(Cantonese soundtrack with English subtitles).

If director Ann Hui made "Love In A Fallen City" first, followed by "Boat People," then most of the local critics and the general public could have been kinder to her "Fallen" pic.

"Success can kill success," remarked Ms. Hui during the Hong Kong Film Awards 1984. It is a well-known fact that it is more likely for a much touted or awarded artist to be knocked down by the media while the public demands fresher creative blood.

In the case of Hui's latest venture for Shaw Brothers, her love story feature proved to be difficult if not burdened as the masses expected her to come out with either "Boat People II" or something more powerfully potent, if not topical.

"Love In A Fallen City" was adapted from a best-selling woman's novel, written by well-respected Chinese author Eillen Chang, set in the colorful 40's of Hong Kong leading to its occupation by the Japanese. It tells the long drawnout affair of divorcee-widow Cora Miao who live aimlessly in Shanghai but moves to Hong Kong to be courted by rich, tall, dark, handsome, well-dressed and Cambridge-educated playboy Chow Yun Fat. It is a detailed encounter between the old fashioned lady who initially resists the charms and advances of the prospective lover, possibly husband.

Overly passive and repressed Miao wants respectability, not the non-status life of a concubine. She suffers so much from her nagging family due to the harshness of her failed marriage. Being the sixth daughter of once well-off family, Miao is more of a burden, until a high society matchmaker enters the picture.

There are many beautifuly staged romantic sequences, an elegant dinner party at Repulse Bay, napping on the beach, strollng to a Chinese opera and striding about touristy spots amidst a love song on the soundtrack. The director obviously wanted a movie of subtle emotions and action instead of blatant moods and fiery feelings. Hui succeeded in what she wanted and sure enough, the commercial aspiration will suffer from the literary ambiguities.

The pacing is slow with everybody fashionably dressed even during wartime, and the heavy recitatives may lull many to sleep. Hui seems to have forgotten the fact that many did not read the novel. Thus, it is a movie without punch, emphasized further by its stiff staging of events that needs an improvisational "air." There are also many flaws, like the re-creation of a battle wherein the English soldiers appear to be gunning down Japanese apparitions (enemies are not seen) and the abrupt ending to the trivial story of an ordinary woman who gets her prince charming in the final reel is anti-climactic.

Overlooking the oversized flaws, the production gloss is admirable, from the reconstruction of the historic Repulse Bay Hotel facade to the vaseline-smeared cinematography of the lost era of elegant British Colonialism in Asia to the occasional sparks of serious acting (too rehearsed in fact) of the lead characters. "Love In A Fallen City" is a big, good-looking photoplay that is far from perfect, but Shaw Brothers is showing definite signs of earnest sincerity in their deep desire to produce artistic movies with commercial values. Hopefully they will strike the perfect balance in their future projects. In the meantime, Ann Hui's international reputation alone could give this miscalculated production some prestigious exposure and mileage in countless minor film fests round the world. —*Mel.*

Neli Ti Rekov
(I Told You So)
(YUGOSLAV-COLOR)

Pula, July 30.

A Varda Film, Skopje, and TV Skopje Coproduction. Features entire cast. Directed by Stevo Crvenkovski. Screenplay, Rusomir Bogdanovski, Crvenkovski; camera (color), Ljubomir Vaglenarov; sets, Taki Pavlovski; music, Ljupco Konstantinov. Reviewed at Pula Film Fest, July 23, '84. Running time: 86 MINS.
Cast: Petar Arsovski, Risto Siskov, Blagoja Spirkoski.

Reportedly left on the shelf after its completion some six years ago, and only recently blown up to 35m from 16m stock, Stevo Crvenkovski's "I Told You So" bears an odd title for what is, in fact, a pretty decent historical film about Macedonia's struggle for freedom from Turkish oppressors back at the turn of the century. It's the time of the Ilinden Day Uprising in 1903 when, for some three months, a group of Macedonian revolutionaries fought a losing battle in the mountains

against frustrated Turkish troops. We follow the fate of several of these rebels as one by one they are betrayed by informers (in this case, Bulgarians) and tracked down by encircling troops.

Pic is made in the style of Italian spaghetti westerns and bears a resemblance, too, to Glauber Rocha's Brazilian epic "Antonio Das Mortes." —*Holl.*

Letu Odlocitve
(The Years Of Decision)
(YUGOSLAV-COLOR)

Pula, July 30.

A Viba Film Production, Ljubljana. Features entire cast. Directed by Bostjan Vrhovec. Screenplay, Branko Gradisnik; camera (color), Rodo Likon; sets, Janez Kovic; music, Jani Golob. Reviewed at Pula Film Fest, July 25, '84. Running time: 87 MINS.
Cast: Boris Ostan, Boris Cavazza, Slavko Jan, Damjana Cerne, Jozica Avbelj, Ales Valic.

Slovenian debut helmer Bostjan Vrhovec made "The Years Of Decision" after cutting his teeth on shorts and educational films. His approach to cinema is rather academic: he stuffs as much meaningful nonsense into a production as possible but fails to ensure that the story is going to work on its own merits in the first place. A son returns home from his tour of duty in the army to the manor of his father and grandfather, and here he begins to investigate the past and to learn details about his mother's mysterious death while working on his father's memoirs. Meanwhile, he has troubles in his own relationships with women, and it's through a similar family tragedy that he learns, the truth about his mother and father — and, theoretically, develops into a mature male.

Pretty predictable and strained story. —*Holl.*

Montreal Fest

Until September
(U.S.-COLOR)

Montreal, Aug. 23.

An MGM/UA Entertainment Co. release of a Michael Gruskoff production. Produced by Gruskoff; associate producer, Vincent Malle. Directed by Richard Marquand. Screenplay, Janice Lee Graham; camera (Metrocolor), Philippe Welt; editor, Sean Barton; production design, Hilton McConnico; music, John Barry. Reviewed at the World Film Festival (Hors Concurs), Montreal, Aug. 23, 1984. (MPAA Rating: R.) Running time: 95 MINS.
Mo Alexander . . . . .Karen Allen
Xavier de la Perouse . . . .Thierry Lhermitte
Philip . . . . .Christopher Cazenove
Isabelle . . . . .Marie Catherine Conti
Andrew . . . . .Hutton Cobb
Colonel Viola . . . . .Michael Mellinger
Sylvia . . . . .Nitza Saul
Carol . . . . .Rochelle Robertson
Jenny . . . . .Raphaelle Spencer
Marcia . . . . .Johanna Pavlis

Familiar tale of a star-crossed romance, "Until September" seems a pretty dubious candidate to draw large audiences. Despite handsome production values, a winning cast and a basic warmth, the underlying banality of situation will be a major stumbling block for wide popular success.

Set in Paris, plot centers on a young American woman stranded in the City of Lights when she becomes separated from a tour group headed for Eastern Bloc countries. Frustrated by airline and diplomatic red tape, she heads for the apartment of a woman she went to school with years earlier in the U.S. It turns out all for naught as friend has gone on vacation and the woman, Mo Alexander (Karen Allen), takes refuge in a modest hotel.

Temporary setback is put aright when a neighbor, suave banker Xavier de la Perouse (Thierry Lhermitte), checks on the woman's story for verification. It doesn't take much to guess that the two tenants are destined to hit it off romantically, even if there are some initial awkward moments.

Aside from Mo's travel complications, drama derives from the fact that Xavier is married with two children. Initially, appearances conform to the woman's terse description of a former French lover as "handsome, charming and a bit of a jerk." However, as story evolves, we learn it is a loveless union which exists primarily for social appearances.

However, filmmakers are not intent on making another "woman involved with a married man" or "doomed love affair" saga. Instead, a fanciful, unconvincing "love conquers all" scenario emerges. Either route in context would likely produce the same no-win situation on an entertainment level.

Allen makes the best of her feisty yet vulnerable heroine. It is a performance of great humor and subtle emotion. French heartthrob Lhermitte offers an oozing passion that suggests a wide international appeal once he lands the right vehicle.

Paris locations add a nice flavor to the effort but director Richard Marquand serves up no more than a competent, uninspired emotional stew. John Barry's musical score is appropriate and, thankfully, not overstated.

Upbeat ending doesn't betray the material and certainly won't affect boxoffice negatively. Yet, suspicion remains a lack of novelty in "Until September" will result in lackluster returns. One suspects both the relationship and the film won't last beyond October. —*Klad.*

Unerreichbare Naehe
(Final Call)
(WEST GERMAN-COLOR)

Montreal, Aug. 21.

An MFG Film GmbH, Munich production, in cooperation with WDR, Cologne, and Roxy-Film GmbH Co. KG, Munich. Produced and directed by Dagmar Hirtz. Screenplay, Hirtz and Margarethe von Trotta; camera (color), Dietrich Lohmann; editor, Hirtz; art direction and costumes, Heidrun Brandt; music, Nicolas Economou; sound, Hayo von Zuendt. Reviewed at the World Film Festival (competition), Montreal, Aug. 20, 1984. Running time: 93 MINS.
Ines . . . . .Kathrin Ackermann
Andreas . . . . .Klaus Gruenberg
Monika . . . . .Brigitte Karner
Sabine . . . . .Loni von Friedl
Beni . . . . .Benjamin Hembus
Neighbor . . . . .Berta Schwarz
Pic (the clown) .Pic

Highly respected for her abilities as an editor, Dagmar Hirtz proves to be an able and sensitive writer and director with her first feature, an intense story of the emotional sterility of young German singles with interesting observations on the love/hate relationship of Germans toward America.

Ines is a restrained professional woman making a tv documentary about a clown, played by the prominent mime Pic. Her best friend Monika attempts suicide, and together with Andreas, her friend and lover, she installs Monika in the apartment they share, where they have separate telephones and answering machines to relay their attempts to communicate. In stark contrast to Ines, Monika is a woman who has been repeatedly abandoned by men, who tire quickly of her traditional female traits and her dependency. Her need for love and demonstrative dedication to serving others is portrayed as a trap that prevents her from pursuing her career or achieving a balance and confidence to sustain her when she is alone.

The other characters are all alone, apparently by choice, but as the story develops, shown to be out of an inability to express their friendship. Most requirements of personal relationships are perceived by the characters as emotional blackmail, except for the long-suffering and sympathetic heroine, Ines. Kathrin Ackermann delivers an admirable performance in the type of role actresses covet.

Ines has a secret that she must allow to gestate before she reveals it to her extremely neurotic friends: a 16-year-old son in Richmond, Va., whom she has not seen since he was three, when she divorced the father and returned to Germany. The son is now writing letters seeking contact.

Ines is solicitous about her friends, although she seems to realize the limits of her concern, and she has effectively killed her maternal instincts. Her response to the distant child, who is never shown except in a snapshot, is confused at first, but becomes increasingly clear, as she lends a hand to Andreas, who writes books and acts like a jealous child when she explains what has been bothering her. The original German title captures the tentative psychological drama but is almost impossible to translate, the closest expression being "Impossible Intimacy." Hirtz herself chose the English title, apparently as a reference to the mechanized messages Ines and Andreas leave for each other.

The hand of Margarethe von Trotta is visible in the script in the schematic opposition of the two women trying to find a common ground, but there is an irresistible impulse to see a strong portion of autobiography drawn from the life of Hirtz, longtime companion of Maximilian Schell. Hirtz has integrated the elements very well, rendering a portrait of alienated adults clinging to the values of the 1960s. She demonstrates that, in order to live together, relationships should be less defined.

The predictable anxiety of the New German Cinema is present, but laced with ironic counterpoint, such as Andreas walking into a bookshop requesting his own book and noting that their bestseller seems to be the latest Marxist opus of the noted German sociologist Jurgen Habermaas. The intellectual and cultural snobbism also crops up in the heroine's horror of "the idea of becoming an American housewife."

Dialog is meaningful and ably delivered from characters who have something to say to a generation that may have found other group portraits of "The Big Chill" generation shallow or insufficient. Whether the German version of their problems in facing adult life will apply or be appreciated outside of Germany will depend upon very careful handling of a complex pic. It does lend insight into people trying to recover from emotional quarantine.

Particularly good festival fare, pic is blessed with a pace and rhythm that lightens up its philosophical load. Although the narrative stumbles in the first 20 minutes, as if scenes had been eliminated, the growth of the characters sustains interest. Notable is the very delicate addition of a subtle score toward the end, which is unobtrusive but builds a trust in the protagonist to make the right decision and go find her son. The cornerstone of such a successful personal film is integrity, and Hirtz exhibits this in both her technical competence and attempt at a message that cannot be distilled for Western Union. — *Kaja.*

Wenn Ich Mich Fürchte
(Fear of Falling)
(WEST GERMAN-COLOR)

Montreal, Aug. 24.

A Filmverlag der Autoren release of a Christian Rischert Produktion, with Multimedia. Produced and directed by Rischert. Executive producer, Christine Carben-Stotz. Stars Horst Buchholz. Screenplay, Rischert; camera (color), Xaver Schwarzenberger; editor, Margret Sager; art director, Winifried Henning; costumes, Anastasia Kurz; music, Eberhard Schöner; sound, Yves Zlotnicka. Reviewed at World Film Festival, Montreal (in competition), Aug. 23, 1984. Running time: 104 MINS.
Robert Feldmann . . . . Horst Buchholz
Johanna Feldman . . . . . Franziska Bronnen
Theo Schuster . . . . Tilo Prückner
Rita . . . . Constanze Engelbrecht
Robert's mother . . . . Herta Schwarz
Cleaning Lady . . . . Elma Karlowa

A familiar tale of male mid-life crisis "Fear Of Falling" is lifted from the usual rut by intelligent writing and direction and an extremely strong central performance from Horst Buchholz.

Latter plays a Munich film director disoriented after his actress-wife has left him. He decides to take a holiday in Italy, and lends his apartment to an old friend he hasn't seen since school days; but hardly has he started his trip when he's involved in a car accident and finds himself recuperating back home. So his personal problems are related to those of his friend (a chef in the restaurant atop Munich's high TV tower), his shop-lifting mother, his sex-obsessed cleaning lady, and the beautiful wife of a real-estate man with whom he has a brief affair.

At the same time he gets an idea for a new movie, based on events which took place historically around the tv tower (the Hitler-Chamberlain meeting of 1938, wartime devastation, the 1972 Olympics with the killing of Israeli athletes, etc.).

The film ends in a suicide, though the victim is not the character one might have expected. All in all, this is a quietly involving film, which plays well throughout, is filled with absorbing scenes and interesting characters, but which ultimately leave a feeling of frustration. The problems of the central character are familiar ones, basically, and the film comes up with no really new ideas. A fantasy sequence is miscalculated.

As noted, Buchholz puts over a sock performance as the troubled hero, and all the support actors are pro, with a special nod to Tilo Prückner as the unhappy friend. Lensing of Xaver Schwarzenberger also deserves favorable mention.
— *Strat.*

Stress
(FRENCH-COLOR)

Montreal, Aug. 23.

A presentation by Adolphe Viezzi and Jean Ardy of a co-production of Les Films de la Tour-F.R.3. Produced by Adolphe Viezzi. Directed by Jean-Louis Bertuccelli. Screenplay, Andre Grall, with dialog and adaptation by Alain Demouzon and Bertuccelli; camera (color), Ricardo Aronovich; set design, Frederic Astich-Barre; sound, Jean-Pierre Ruh; editor, François Ceppi; assistant director, Marc Cemin. Reviewed at World Film Festival, Montreal, (competition), Aug. 23, 1984. Running time: 89 MINS.
Nathalie . . . . Carole Laure
Alex . . . . Guy Marchand
Michel . . . . Andre Dussollier
Celine . . . . Anne Meson
Isabelle . . . . Isabelle Mergault
Madame D'Ambray . . . Germaine Montero
Gerard . . . . Patrice Kerbrat
France . . . . Nathalie Jouin
Concierge . . . . Claudine Berg
Delphine . . . . Sandrine Diaz
Beauty salon proprietor . . Veronique Silver
Client . . . . Hubert Noel

Although the English title of Jean-Louis Bertuccelli's latest pic would seem to be an overt bid to an audience beyond continental Europe, it says more about the experience of watching the pic than about its success as a thriller.

An extremely contrived plot begins at a chateau where a marriage is being engineered by a domineering mother. The groom either jumps or falls out of a window, and the story jumps forward to "Several years later" in Paris. Carole Laure plays Nathalie, a single mother being harrassed by a breather on the phone who ups the ante when he leaves a bloody beef heart on the seat of her car. The followup to that is a skewered heart labeled as that of her daughter in a package delivered to her at the beauty salon where she works as a manicurist.

The persecution of Laure never seems to develop into anything beyond a series of silly gestures, in part because she seldom registers any reaction beyond surprise, and in part because Bertuccelli does not build the requisite suspense.

Although the technical credits are slick, pic lacks credibility and is totally unsuitable as a flag-bearer in competition at Montreal. It almost caused a scandal by driving a few jurors out of the screening.

Guy Marchand does his best to turn the madman into a threatening but elusive presence, but in every scene the grinding wheels of the plot crush any potential interest in the characters. The name-value of the cast may attract some initial attention, but Bertuccelli's talent, demonstrated in his 1970 "Ramparts of Clay," is not visible in this failed attempt at a Hitchcock-inspired pic about obsesion. — *Kaja.*

L'homme a la Valise
(FRENCH-COLOR-16m)

Montreal, Aug. 23.

A production of the Institut National de la Communication Audiovisuelle. Produced by Sylvie Blum. Directed and written by Chantal Akerman. Camera (color), Maurice Perrimont, Marie-Cecile Thevenin; editor, Frederic Sandberg; sound, Jean-Claude Brisson; music (noise), Jerome Levy. Reviewed at World Film Festival, Montreal, (Cinema of Today and Tomorrow), Aug. 23, 1984. Running time: 60 MINS.
Woman returning . . . . . . Chantal Akerman
Henri . . . . Jeffrey Kime

Based on an autobiographical incident, pic reflects a period of frustration in avant-garde director Chantal Akerman's life, when she spent a month focusing an undue and unsatisfactory amount of attention on an unwelcome house guest. Akerman plays herself in this droll, one-hour pic, ideal for fest & some European TV markets, focusing on 14 days of being besieged by an uninvited guest in one's own home.

The commonplace that hell is other people finds a new twist in helmer Akerman's use of a soundtrack that enunciates and emphasizes every bothersome vibration emanating from another person. The woman who is back in her own apartment holes up in her room, only to be subjected to the clatter, flushing and footsteps she is unable to ignore or to live with.

Certain moments are very effective in this prolonged trauma, and all the more remarkable for their fleet, elusive appearance. The quick sight of a naked man in the bath unexpectedly in the morning, or his short chorus from the musical "Oklahoma!" lend the hilarity of the situation its impact. But for the most part, Akerman leaves the camera in a static position, observing the scene about her that records responses. Her reactions range from withdrawing her breakfast into her room to remaining there with her garbage for 28 days.

What is amusing about this pic is the slow build up of frustrating humor and sight-gags, although the half-hour it takes to get to them may go beyond frustration for many audiences. Akerman's name is guaranteed festival cache, and "L'homme" proves she has given feminism, her stock in trade, an ironic shading by playing the role of a fussy, fastidious woman detesting not just men but anybody who invades her space. Because Henri is only shown in three sequences, and then fleetingly, the problem of the film is the problem of a hermit, male or female, captivated by the imagined threat of another being beyond the door. His activities seem quite normal; it is hers that turns the existentialism of Roman Polanski's "Repulsion" into burlesque.
— *Kaja.*

The Last Oasis
(YUGOSLAV-DOCU-COLOR)

Montreal, Aug. 18.

A Centar film production. Produced by Milan Zmukic. Directed, written and photographed (color), by Petar Lalovic. Sound, Marko Rodic. Reviewed at Montreal Festival (Cinema of Today and Tomorrow section), Aug. 18, 1984. Running time: 91 MINS.

Very reminiscent of the Walt Disney feature-length "True Life Adventure" documentaries of some 30 years ago, "The Last Oasis" aims to entertain an unsophisticated audience with interesting photography and a chatty narration.

Photographed in a valley between the Danube and Brave rivers in Yugoslavia, the material concentrates on animals and birds mating and killing each other. Cheating is evident in the editing, as audience is led to believe an owl is watching a fox stalk a hedgehog when obviously the owl was nowhere near the other creatures. The commentary, in lightly acented American, is very facile, even containing lines like: "Night falls on the oasis."

Nonetheless, much of the material shot is quite beautiful, and even if theatrical chances are highly doubtful, at least tv might grab the pic and show it with or without a new narration.

Footage was apparently shot over a three-year period, but film never tells us exactly where this beautiful part of the world is located and why it has remained so unspoiled.
—Strat.

The Masculine Mystique
(CANADIAN-COLOR)

Montreal, Aug. 24.
Produced by the National Film Board of Canada. Executive producers, Robert Verrall, Andy Thomson. Produced and directed by John N. Smith and Giles Walker. Associate producer, Ken McCready. Written by Smith, Walker and Andrew Kitzanuk; camera (color), David Wilson; editor, David Wilson; music, Richard Gresko; sound, Jean-Guy Normandin. Reviewed at the World Film Festival, Montreal, Aug. 24, 1984. Running time: 87 MINS.
Blue .... Stefan Wodoslawsky
Alex .... Sam Grana
Mort .... Mort Ransen
Ashley .... Ashley Murray
Felice .... Felice Grana
Eleanor .... Eleanor MacKinnon
Char .... Char Davies

Great feminist appeal lurks in this docu-drama applying the principles of femme-lib films to the nascent men's lib movement, visible in several role-reversal pics. This NFB product has more wit and verve than most such socially-conscious attempts, because the characters are drawn from life and played by the originals. Scenes recreated and replayed by those who agonized through them increase the playfulness of seeing men behave as women did ten years ago as a decade of feminist films began.

Four men talk about their lives in interviews with the camera, with each other in a group-session of consciousness-raising, and play themselves along with their friends from real life in dramatizations of battles between the sexes. Filmed in Montreal in English, the narrative is really a comedy of characters, as the four men try to realize what impact women's lib has had, or not had, on

their relationships with their wives, lovers, or potential mates.

The strongest character is Blue, whose devotion to finding the perfect mate prompts generous gestures like foot massages and breakfast in bed for a woman who finds it stifling.

Also interesting is Alex, a married man conducting an affair on the side and rationalizing it as his own quest for freedom.

The structure of the film is sometimes frustrating, as the episodes quickly shift from character to character than back to their c-r sessions. But the material is fascinating, full of intrinsically complex human flaws and surprises.

The dramatic potential of seduction ruses and disappointments will hold an audience, and the dialog, obviously improvised on location, is full of clever insights and self-effacing wit.

There is a remarkable lack of exhibitionism in the four men exposing their love lives to the camera. The filmmakers deserve credit for arranging the ungainly material of psychology into a fine piece of entertainment funny enough to amuse television audiences throughout the world and possibly attract a specialized public into the art-house circuit. A very fine jazz score reinforces the fluctuating modern atmosphere. — Kaja.

Chiheisen
(The Horizon)
(JAPANESE-COLOR)

Montreal, Aug. 19.
A Shochiku production. Produced by Genshiro Kawamoto. Directed by Kaneto Shindo. Features entire cast. Screenplay, Shindo; camera (color), Teiji Mayajana; music, Hikaru Hiyayashi. No further credits available. Reviewed at World Film festival, Montreal (in competition), Aug. 19, 1984. Running time: 135 MINS.
With: Toshiyuki Nagashima, Kumiko Akiyoshi, Miwako Fujitani, Misako Tanaka, Maiko Kawakami, Hisashi Igawa.

Subject matter of veteran Kaneto Shindo's new pic is extremely interesting; his treatment, however, is somewhat disappointing.

Story concerns a young Japanese woman who, in 1920, comes to San Francisco as the purchased bride of a Japanese dirt farmer. It seems she agreed to be sold in order to repay a family debt. She's initially horrified to find herself in desolate and sparse surroundings, and with a husband who, though kindly, is to say the least primitive in his approach to love-making. But she endures, they raise four children, and make a go of their barren farm. Then comes Pearl Harbor, and Japanese, even if American citizens, are interned, enduring the rigors of a kind of concentration camp in Arizona, while the banks freeze their assets and their land is taken over by others. Post-war experiences re-

veal the death of the husband in a tree-felling accident (off-screen), the relocation of the family, with others, to Otay Valley, the return of the son from fighting in the Nisei unit in Europe, and the assimilation of the daughters into a U.S. lifestyle as they fall in love with and marry American men, against their mother's wishes.

Story is apparently based on the experience of Shindo's own sister, who left the family home in Hiroshima in the early 1920s and never returned to Japan; she died very recently.

Despite this personal input, and fascinating theme, pic remains surface and rather unsatisfactory. Handling is surprisingly stilted, especially when one considers Shindo made the remarkably cinematic "The Island" more than 20 years ago. Apart from the two impressive leads, supporting actors are a bit stiff, and dialog tends to be written and handled like theatrical speeches rather than given a more relaxed cinematic style.

Nonetheless, this saga of an uprooted family of Japanese is often gripping material. Lensing is fine, with the dusty, arid desert and evocative backdrop to the tale of this displaced woman who at first yearns for the rains and snows and flowers of her native home. Conflict between generations is neatly etched in, too.

With more subtle handling, "The Horizon" could have made more of an impact. As is, international theatrical possibilities seem unlikely, though tv in some markets is definitely indicated. — Strat.

Lekhayude Maranam - Oru Flashback
(Lekha's Death - A Flashback)
(INDIAN-COLOR)

Montreal, Aug. 19.
A Sathru International (Madras) production, with National Film Development Corp. Produced by David Kachappily Innocent. Directed by K.C. George. Features entire cast. Screenplay, George; camera (Technovision, Eastmancolor), Shagi; music, M.B. Srinivasan; editor, M.N. Appu. No further credits available. Reviewed at World Film festival, Montreal (Cinema of Today and Tomorrow section), Aug. 19, 1984. Running time: 168 MINS.
With: Natalin, Subha, Jayasree, Jayachitra, Sharada, Nedumudi Venu, Gopi, John Varghise.

This biopic of a popular film actress of southern India, who hanged herself in September 1980, after an unhappy love affair with one of her directors is, if overlong, a surprisingly rich exploration of some aspects of the Indian film scene.

Lekha's story is certainly not unfamiliar in its essentials. The teenage beauty's ambitious mother brought the girl from a Kerala village to the film capital Madras in July 1977. First section of the four-

part film deals with early frustrations and disappointments as mother and daughter live in poverty while going the rounds of producers and directors hoping for a break. Among others, they meet an opportunistic journalist who demands payment for a story he writes, and an assistant director who seduces the girl on the pretext of getting her a part. Before long, both mother and daughter are involved in high-class prostitution. In the second section, Lekha gets her first small role as a back-up dancer in a musical. By part 3 she's become a popular, highly paid star. In part 4, she wins best actress prize, and goes to live with a married director whose rejection leads to her suicide.

Main interest in the film is the revealing insights into Madras film production. Other Indian films, notably Shyam Benegal's "The Role," have explored the world of screen stars and filmmaking in the most prolific film producing country in the world. "Lekha's Death" goes further in covering all aspects of this curious sub-culture, the characters come vividly to life, and scenes of actual production, especially of the elaborate musical productions, are great fun. Lekha's lover is presented as being an "artistic" director, but juding from his description of his own film, he seems little more talented than the rest. Doubtless there has been fascination back home in identifying who's supposed to be who, though the film ends with the usual disclaimers.

Few credits were provided, so it's not possible to identify the various players, though the actress playing Lekha's pushy mother is especially good. Pic is definitely too long for non-Indian audiences, but is worth seeing for its insights into the Madras film industry and its humor. English subtitles, which refer to bit parts as "small rolls" could be improved. —Strat.

La Casa De Agua
(The House Of Water)
(VENEZUELAN-COLOR)

Montreal, Aug. 17.
A Prod. Cinematographicas Manicuare production. Produced and directed by Jacobo Penzo. Screenplay, Thomas Eloy Martinez, camera, Arthur Albert, editor, Giuliano Ferrioli, art director, Ramon Aguirre, sound, Hector Moreno, music, Juan Carlos Nunez, costumes, Laura Otero. Reviewed at Montreal Film Festival (Latin American Cinema), Aug. 17, 1984. (No MPAA Rating). Running time: 95 MINS.
Cast: Franklin Virguez, Elba Escobar, Doris Wells, Luis Rivas, Hilda Vera, Ricardo Blanco, Kiddio Espana.

A first feature by a young Venezuelan painter and film critic, "La Casa De Agua" incorporates the surrealistic style and political commitment of South American literature in imagery that vacillates between the sublime aspirations of a peasant boy with poetic potential and a gritty vision of the military oppression that plagues countries south of the border.

Loosely based on the career potential of noted poet and statesman Ruben Dario, the pic shows the road not taken when the young man rejects social advancement and prestige and returns to his dusty village on the shore to combat a certain General Gomez who reigns as a petty tyrant. Poet Cruz Elias Leon is the son of a fisherman whose suffering provides the narrative of a virtual martyrdom.

The first half-hour is a riddle in structure, with flash-forwards and flashbacks failing to create a tension between Leon's background in the barren fishing village and his grandiloquent posturing in the bohemian life of a student. At regular intervals throughout the pic, snatches of Leon's funeral procession suddenly remind the viewer of his tragic end, although the extent of the tragedy is not clear until director/writer Penzo introduces the curse of leprosy to ultimately confine the poet in an artistic and political quarantine following his capture and torture as an agitator.

While the first half of pic sketches the temptations of bourgeois life for the promising poet, complete with the sentiments of 1920s existentialism about what is real and what isn't, the second half lunges into punishments and tortures that are all too real, as Leon is cast into a house of water, immersed up to his elbows. The title is derived from Leon's flounderings in sequences that both begin and end the film. He has been horribly deformed by leprosy by the time he dies, and this physical apparition seems meant to symbolize the subjugated peasantry of Venezuela.

Although the film is designed with an artistic touch and photographed with great sensitivity, the narrative has too much ambition and it is scored like a soap opera. For the director to make his statements about class conflict and the apparently immutable politics of Venezuela, he reduces his characters to the beau geste. The actors are seldom able to rise above the melodrama of the situation.

Such films offer good festival fare because they are consistent with other artistic movements in South American art and literature, but commercial potential seems never to have been a consideration. The shreds of sequences from every phase of the poet's life that inaugurate the pic confuse rather than establish the much-needed frame of reference for foreign audiences.

This pic is furthermore problematic from the point-of-view of how peasants and banana republics are to be depicted in the cinema. If an American product depicted such a situation in this way, it would very likely come under attack for indulging in the clichés of half-understood conflicts. The perceptions of Penzo seem only to reinforce many a western estimate that South American political cruelties are rooted in the culture or national character and therefore irradicable. Pic provides good fodder for political cinema series. —*Kaja.*

Le Soldat Qui Dort
(The Sleeping Soldier)
(FRENCH-SWISS-COLOR)

Montreal, Aug. 25.

Jean-Marc Henchoz presents a co-production of Marion Films (Paris) and Xanadu Film SA (Zurich). Produced by Henchoz. Direction and screenplay by Jean-Louis Benoit. Camera (Fujicolor), Emmanuel Machuel; editor, Benoit; art direction, Christian Marti; costumes, Nadine Lefortier. Reviewed at the World Film Festival (competition), Montreal, Aug. 25, 1984. Running time: **108 MINS.**

Henri.....................Andre Wilms
The Boy.................Laurent Pahud
Mere Cazal..........Marie-Helene Daste
Suzanne.................Karen Rencurel
Boy's Mother..........Yvette Theraulaz
The Priest...............Guy Touraille

A brooding tale of the toll of war, "Le Soldat Qui Dort" is too introspective and aloof to suggest strong commercial prospects. Competing at the Montreal fest, pic is ideally suited to high-brow and specialty situations with some European television sales also likely.

Story is told from the vantage point of a 10-year-old French lad and begins eerily in a Gallic infirmary during the First World War. The boy's father is in a coma in the hospital where the youngster crawls along the floors as if he were crawling through battlefront fire.

Writer-director Jean-Louis Benoit continues with disquieting images as the boy is sent off to a serene village away from the fighting. On the train, he views rows of specter-like soldiers caked with mud and in the small hamlet is struck by the shell of a downed plane and the slightly eccentric villagers. Through it all he remains virtually mute and registers almost no emotion.

Under the care of an elderly woman, the boy is kept relatively safe from the ravages of war. However, when the woman's son is demobilized — a severe victim of front line fatigue — the film, at last threatens to turn emotional. It remains only a threat.

Henri, the soldier, is a mercurial character who flies up and down the emotional spectrum. Although one is never quite sure how the boy is reacting to his intense bouts of euphoria and depression, there seems little doubt he understands something is amiss.

The title suggests a broad ambiguity, so one can readily interpret different significances. The device is effective only to a point and one wishes the filmmaker had let up on his oblique approach to allow for a more dramatic finale.

Technical credits are competent, if at times self-consciously artistic and the performers are all quite capable in this Franco-Swiss production. A truly hard sell internationally which has only its undeniable pacifistic strain to lure the already committed. —*Klad.*

Mario
(CANADIAN-COLOR)

Montreal, Aug. 22.

A National Film Board of Canada production and release. Executive producer, Jacques Bobet; associate producers, Helene Verrier, Jean Beaudin. Directed by Jean Beaudin. Screenplay, Arlette Dion, Beaudin and Jacques Paris, inspired by the story "La Sabliere" by Claude Jasmin. Camera (color), Pierre Mignot; editor, Werner Nold; art direction, Denis Bocher; music, François Dompierre; sound, Bruce Nyuznik. Reviewed at the World Film Festival (competition), Montreal, Aug. 22, 1984. Running time: **97 MINS.**

Mario Leblanc..Xavier Norman Petermann
Simon Leblanc............Francis Reddy
Helene Boulanger.....Nathalie Chalifour
Father....................Jacques Godin
Mother....................Murielle Dutil
Social worker............Claire Pimpare
Receptionist............Christine Breton
Therapist...............Marcel Sabourin
Denis.,.............Jonathan Painchaud
Benoit.................Sylvain Cormier
Pierre.............Marc-Andre Vigneau

Jean Beaudin's "Mario" is a disturbing yarn centering on the relationship between two brothers, aged 18 and 10. The expected adulation of the younger title character is complicated by the fact he is mute, partially deaf and lives largely in a world of heroic imagination.

The dramatic possibilities inherent in the material — the older brother's devotion weighed against his first emotional contact with the opposite sex which threatens to destroy the special rapport — suggests a much stronger film than the one on view. Director Beaudin, who also cowrote the screenplay, quickly involves the audience in the somewhat offbeat tale but has significant problems in sustaining interest in both the characters and situations. Marketing will be forced to take the "art" circuit route where picture could attract some beneficial critical attention.

Filmed in the Magdalen Islands, story unfolds in visually stunning natural locations. Both the remoteness and uniqueness of the area prove assets to effecting a disquieting ambience.

Mario (Xavier Norman Petermann) is first viewed in makeshift mufti clutching a stuffed toy coyote. He inhabits a world of warriors and crusaders fueled by older brother Simon's (Francis Reddy) wild imagination. The relationship is simpatico and quite necessary in light of their parents' hard-working nature which consumes a short tourist season.

It is during one season that Simon meets Helene (Nathalie Chalifour) and an immediate spark is ignited between the two young people. Mario is not unmindful of what is occuring and it becomes increasingly more difficult to divert his brother's attention. Strain between the two is soon apparent but Helene's departure with her parents would appear to resolve the difficult period.

Instead, an accident prompts a local social worker to suggest Mario be removed to a special home on the mainland. It is an unhappy compromise, further aggravated when Simon takes him out for what will prove to be their last adventure.

"Mario" provides a lot of food for thought but brunt of nutrition comes from dazzling visuals from Pierre Mignot and François Dompierre's eerie score. The actual story remains unfocused, particularly its resolution which is bathed in ambiguity.

Also contributing to the positive aspects of the film are the performances by the three principal young performers. Petermann expresses volumes in his eyes while Reddy, as Simon, has the exuberance of youth so necessary to realize the drama of the piece.

A handsome production, "Mario" should realize some foreign sales in sophisticated markets and, despite a muted dramatic component, earn some thoughtful reviews. Combination doesn't suggest upbeat commercial prospects, a recurring problem for French-language production in Canada.—*Klad.*

Waterwalker
(CANADIAN-DOCU-COLOR)

Montreal, Aug. 26.

A National Film Board of Canada-Imago coproduction. Produced by Wilbur Sutherland, Dean Peterson. Written and directed by Bill Mason. Camera (color), Ken Buck; music, Bruce Cockburn, Hugh Marsh; editor, Mason; sound, Alan Geldart. Reviewed at World Film Festival, Montreal (Cinema of Today & Tomorrow section), Aug. 25, 1984. Running time: **83 MINS.**

Bill Mason is a dedicated, some would say fanatical, nature lover who is also an accomplished painter and filmmaker. His latest feature-length docu, made over a twelve-year period apparently, is in line with all his earlier work and features himself (sans family this time out) and his canoe in the beautiful setting of Lake Superior (which he calls "the biggest and most spectacular lake in the world.")

Trouble is that the main audience for the film, Mason's fellow nature lovers, would doubtless rather be out there in the wilderness hacking it than sitting in a theater or in front of a tv set watching a film about it.

For those not as single-mindedly committed as Mason to the joys of the wild, "Waterwalker" is rather too much of a good thing. Though Mason is a pleasant, if rather earnest, character and Ken Buck's photography is fine, and the scenery great, it's really a long 83 minutes. The relentless music score, including title song, doesn't help, and the rather folksy narration is grating at times.

So this is strictly for the converted. — *Strat.*

Que He Hecho Yo Para Merecer Esto

(What Have I Done To Deserve This?!!) (SPANISH-COLOR)

Montreal, Aug. 24.

A Tesauro S.A. and Kaktus S.A. Co-production. Executive producer Herve Hachuel. Directed and written by Pedro Almodovar. Stars Carmen Maura. Camera (Eastmancolor), Angel Luis Fernandez; editor, Jose Solcedo; music, Bernardo Bonezzi; art directors, Pin Morales, Roman Arango. Reviewed at World Film Festival, Montreal (in competition), Aug. 23, 1984. Running time: **100 MINS.**

Gloria	Carmen Maura
Antonio	Angel de Andres-Lopez
Cristal	Veronica Forque
Lucas	Gonzalo Suarez
Grandmother	Chus Lampreave
Toni	Juan Martinez
Miguel	Miguel Angel Herranz
Patricia	Amparo Soler Leal
Polo (chief Inspector)	Luis Hostalot

In introducing "What Have I Done To Deserve This?!!" to the festival audience at Montreal, helmer Pedro Almodovar said he didn't know whether he'd made a comedy or a tragedy. Most people would say the former, as this enjoyably bizarre tale of a Madrid housewife has plenty of laughs, though no denying an undercurrent of a more serious message.

Gloria, splendidly played by Carmen Maura, has a chauvinist husband, Antonio, who drives a taxi and gets involved in a strange plot to forge letters supposedly written by Adolf Hitler. Gloria's two sons are as mixed up as their father; one, aged 12, is a heroin dealer, while the younger seems to have gay tendencies and gets "adopted" by a lecherous dentist. Also living in the cramped apartment is Gloria's batty, myopic mother-in-law, who has a pet lizard she calls Dinero (Money). As if that weren't enough, one neighbor is a hooker while another is a bluenose whose daughter has mystical powers.

There are other strange characters, too, floating through this fast-paced tragi-farce which is sometimes bawdy, often tasteless, but never dull. This kind of comedy is very much a matter of taste. Helping it along is the photography of Angel Luis Fernandez — all bright primary colors — and the jaunty

music of Bernardo Bonezzi. Indeed, all credits are tops.

Almodovar has lots of serious points to make about sexism and the non-liberated Spanish housewife, as well as what's happening to families, especially kids, these days. He tends rather to overburden the plot with too many characters, but gets his quota of entertainment from his basically serious theme.

Among the highlights are a parody of a tv commercial for coffee which features leading Spanish actress Cecilia Roth, and a very funny scene in which helmer Jaime Chavarri gets to act the role of one of the hooker's more outrageous clients. —*Strat.*

Mouvement-Danse
(CANADIAN-DOCU-COLOR-16m)

Montreal, Aug. 18.

A Les Productions Image Inc./Les Productions La Gauchet Inc. production. Produced by Serge Ladouceur and Celine Thibodeau. Associate producer, Raymond Gravelle. Directed by Gilles Pare and Celine Thibodeau. Camera (color), Serge Ladouceur, editor, François Gervais, sound, Gilles Pare, Thierry Mooriaas, Dominique Chartrand. Reviewed at Montreal Film Festival (Cinema of Today and Tomorrow), Aug. 18, 1984. (No MPAA Rating.) Running time: **61 MINS.**

Director Gilles Pare has made his reputation in the Qubeçois cinema with documentaries about challenging if not impossible situations. He proved his mettle in making a potentially harrowing portrait of these paraplegics learning to choreograph their wheelchairs into an emotion-packed documentary.

The starting point is dance therapy for the physically handicapped who are perhaps too sensitive or simply not inclined to play handicapped basketball. Three young men, Alfred, Michel and Robert, take therapy beyond the confines of self-expression into the realm of performance. Their "dance" at the Saskatoon Dance Colloquim brings tears to both the audiences' eyes, within the doc and in the potential public for such a pic.

Their intentions to extend dance with the mechanical movement of wheel-chairs is, at first, potentially embarrassing, as they are contrasted with the strong, healthy dancers' bodies. But self-pity proves not to be a problem, as the boys demonstrate a witty attitude toward the attempts at perfection they see in ballet.

The musical theme from "Chariots Of Fire" builds as they perfect their own performance for their concert. Their courage to face normal dancers in a forum reserved for extremely artsy fare is more than a blow for freedom for the handicapped. It points up the validity of such a form, even juxtaposed to

ballet, in modern dance, which has become quite conceptual. Dancing in wheelchairs is no less bizarre than much of what has passed for the cutting edge of performance art. A piroutte in a chair is not an easy thing, but the boys perform them repeatedly quite well.

If the camera is confronted with special problems in photographing dance movements, it is sure to be taxed trying to capture the aesthetics of paraplegic choreography, which is focused as much in eye-movement as in coordination of wheelchair mobility. Where the camera can't keep up, the narration and music compensate, providing promising fare for public service broadcasting.—*Kaja.*

On A River Without Navigation Marks
(CHINESE-COLOR)

Montreal, Aug. 19.

China Film Export Corp. presents a Xian Film Studio production. Produced by Mi Baichao. Directed by Wu Tianming. Screenplay, Ye Weilin, camera (color), Liu Chang-xu; editor, Zhang Furong; art direction, Wang Shanan; music, Xu Youfu; sound, Chen Yudan. Reviewed at the World Film Festival (Hors Concurs), Montreal, Aug. 18, 1984. Running time: **89 MINS.**

Old Pan	Li Wei
Shi Gu	Hu Ronghua
Zhao Liang	Tang Quingming
Wu Aihua	Tao Yuling
Gaixia	Li Shulan

Currently enjoying a successful run in Mainland China, "On A River Without Navigation Marks" is a handsome melodrama which should enjoy some non-theatrical and specialty marketing outside its native soil. However, the old-fashioned sentiment and storytelling involved in the film, as with so many Chinese pictures, again bodes ill for prospects of mainstream release.

Story centers on three men who eke out a living on a river raft, fishing, transporting and trading. The period is the Cultural Revolution and the eldest, Pan, offers an insight into the old and new regimes. He is the voice of reason to Shi, a young man frustrated by his lot which includes a forced separation from the young woman he loves.

The complex plot includes a parallel story involving the young Pan — told in flashback — and a dramatic rescue of Shi's beloved. The screenplay also manages to thrust a faintly critical perspective of the previous regime which ousted a former territory director, portrayed here in the most glowing terms.

An underlying theme of self-sacrifice threads through the film, ending with Pan's unselfish gesture which saves the lovers at the cost of his life. The ennobling incident takes on mystic importance which

does not translate well to other cultures.

Also problematic is the seemingly unending series of hardships encountered by the principals which only Shi appears to confront with anger. At times one finds "On A River Without Navigation Marks" better titled "A Raft Of Problems" and possibly marketed to emphasize some unintentional humor.

Certainly the picture demonstrates a growing sophistication in films from the People's Republic both in its technique and story. However, this film isn't quite ready to bridge the span between Eastern and Western sensibilities. — *Klad.*

Vremia Jelanii
(Wishing Time) (SOVIET-COLOR)

Montreal, Aug. 20.

Sovexportfilm presents a Mosfilm production. Directed by Yuli Raizman. Screenplay, Anatoli Grebnev; camera (color), Nikolai Olonovski, art direction, Tatiana Lapshina; music, Alexander Belyaiev; sound, I. Urvantsev. Reviewed at the World Film Festival (competing), Montreal, Aug. 19, 1984. Running time: **100 MINS.**

Svetlana	Vera Alentova
Vladimir	Anatoli Papanov
Mila	Tatiana Egorova
Nilolai	Vladislav Strjeltchik
Dima	Edouard Izotov

Still active after more than 50 years of directing, octogenarian Soviet filmmaker Yuli Raizman presents "Wishing Time," a tale of emotional manipulation. And while less potent and accomplished than his recent Oscar-nominated "A Private Life" the picture has enough intriguing elements to merit exhibition beyond the festival circuit.

Central character is Svetlana, an unmarried beautician approaching 40. Although quite vivacious, the woman is convinced by a friend that she must settle down into a stable relationship. The friend suggests her boss, a musician, but it is a considerably older civil servant who finally perks Svetlana's interest.

After a quick courtship, the couple settle into a passionless arrangement. The woman's prime concern becomes furthering her husband's career and, at the same time, improving here social situation.

Although effected without a maniacal zeal, one appreciates the reverse Svengali aspect of the man's transformation. And when all elements appear in place, Raizman and writer Anatoli Grebnev provide the ultimate irony in having the man die from the pressure of adopting a style unsuited to his personality.

While technical work is quite good, it is really the central performances of Vera Alentova as Svetlana and Anatoli Papanov as her chosen mate which provide the greatest impact on the material. Nonetheless, Raizman's understated style loses dramatic points for the film's broader commercial prospects. "Wishing Time" should enjoy some specialty and festival life over the short haul. —*Klad.*

Pejzazi U Magli
(Foggy Landscapes)
(YUGOSLAV-COLOR)

Pula, July 30.

A Union Film Production, Belgrade. Features entire cast. Written and directed by Jovan Jovanovic. Camera (color), Radoslav Vladic; sets, Vladimir Jovanovic; music, Aleksandar Habic. Reviewed at Pula Film Fest, July 24, '84. Running time: 103 MINS.

Cast: Ana Marija Petricevic, Ljubomir Todorovic, Tihomir Arsic, Rade Serbedzija, Milena Zupancic.

Jovan Jovanovic was last seen with a feature at Pula back in 1971, when he competed with "Young And Healthy Like A Rose," the tale of an ex-con who goes off on a wild jaunt with a newly formed gang to set Belgrade afire with fear and trembling. Now, with "Foggy Landscapes," he's back to his old film tricks again. This time the focus is on the world of drug addicts and how they stay a step or two ahead of the authorities at all costs.

Some speeded-up, experimental-film-style clips at the outset hold the attention for a while, but in general this is a rehash of the oft-told drug scene and bored kids. —*Holl.*

Locarno

Öszi Almanach
(Autumn Almanac)
(HUNGARIAN-COLOR)

Locarno, Aug. 18.

A Hungarofilm Presentation of a Mafilm Production. Written and directed by Béla Tarr. Camera (color), Sandor Kardos, Ferenc Papp Buda Gulyas; editor Agnes Hranitzky; music, Mihaly Uigh; art direction, Agnes Hranitzky. Reviewed at the Morettina Film Center, Locarno, Aug. 17, 1984. Running time: 122 MINS.

Cast: Hedy Temessy, Miklos Szekely, B. Erika Bodnar, Pal Hetenyi, Janos Dezsi.

Bela Tarr, who was awarded a special mention in Locarno two years ago for his "Prefabricated People," returns now with an even more painful, scorching and unsettling image of Hungarian society. Unlike his previous effort, shot in black and white and creating a strong naturalistic impression of images taken in actual dwellings of the Hungarian proletariat, this one is located in a sort of hellish limbo. The entire movie is claustrophobically restricted into one apartment strewn with decadent remains of a bourgeois interior, lighted in a bizarre way, the frame usually divided between reddish tinges on the one side, and blue-grey ones on the other, all this briefly observed when the camera is not practically shoved

down the characters' throats, as it directs its pitiless eye at the very pores of the actors' skins, without allowing them a moment of respite.

Tarr has already shown in the past his predilection for this style, known as pseudo-documentary, but he takes it here one step further, into the realm of the abstract, in order to analyze the strange relations between two women and three men sharing the same quarters. An older woman owns the place and lives there with her son, who covets her money. Since she is ailing, a young nurse has moved into the premises, to administer to her daily shots, and she has brought with her a man who is her avowed lover. Joining the party is an older man, a teacher who obviously is seeking refuge from some money troubles he has.

It is hard to imagine a company of humans so dependent on each other, and yet capable of exuding more hatred and deviousness, people whose only escape from solitude is failure. For a young man (Tarr is 29) this image of human desolation brought to its climax is truly frightening.

Still, as talented as the director is at his craft, and as dedicated as his actors and his technical crew are, watching this fivesome taking each other apart relentlessly for over two hours, may well be too trying an experience for an average audience. Even those in the know will find it an anguishing moment that goes on nearly forever. — *Edna.*

Jenstchina U Tchetvero Ieieu Moujtchine
(A Woman And Her Four Men)
(LITHUANIAN– COLOR)

Locarno, Aug. 13.

A Sovexport Presentation of a Lithuanian Studios Production. Written and directed by Algimantas Puipa. Camera (color), Ionas Tamaskevicius; Art director, Algirdas Nicius; Music, Yuozas Birvinskas. Reviewed at the Morettina Film Center, Locarno, Aug. 12, 1984. Running time: 90 MINS.

Cast: Urate Onanite, Antanas Shurna, Vidas Petkevicius, Saulus Balandis.

Lithuaninan films are a rarity on the international film fest circuit, but Locarno appears to have a soft spot for them. In 1965, one such film got a special prize here, and now they are back in town trying to repeat that feat.

Inspired by a Danish novel of the last century, "Romance Of The Dunes" by Holger Drachmann, scripter-helmer Puipa moved the story into his own homeland, and advanced it a bit, so that it takes place at the turn of this century. But the film remains indebted in its spirit to the approach and style of the early Scandinavian directors, who often used this kid of poetical prose for their early films.

A strange woman, whose husband has drowned at sea, comes to

live with a family of fishermen, a father and his two sons. She is first the wife of the older borther, when he disappears, the younger one takes over, and at the end of the movie, she is left with the sons she has borne to both of them, and with the old father, the only one left alive.

This is a spare, bleak and moody movie, which uses the background, the sandy shores of the Baltic gradually invading these people's existence, the covered and gloomy skies and the threatening grey sea to full advantage, to stress the hardships of life, but also to accentuate, in contrast, the deep and complex humanity of its protagonists. There is a world of difference between their struggles against the forces of nature around them, which appears at least to be fair, and the devious ways of the town people nearby, where members of the family have to go from time to time were it only in order to lend some money that they are incapable of paying back because of crooked interests.

The film makes its points with the help of very little dialog, images are sufficient in their own right, climaxes are tuned down by editing which often skips points to go to the after-effects, and the screen presence of Onanite and Shurna is impressive. However the narrative line is not always very clear, whether because of subtitles shortcomings, or because, as Puipa said here, the film was recut by an editing committee at the Studio which considered its first version too long.

Considering that the entire production was made for a very low budget on the Soviet scale (about 400,000 rubles) and that director Puipa is only 33, it is certainly a nice realization. —*Edna.*

Il Bacio Di Tosca
(Tosca's Kiss)
(SWISS-DOCU-COLOR)

Locarno, Aug. 12.

A Rex Film Presentation of a T&C Film Production. Produced by Hans-Ulrich Jordi and Marcel Hoehn. Written and directed by Daniel Schmid. Camera (color), Renato Berta; sound, Luc Yersin; editor, Daniela Roderer; music, Giuseppe Verdi, Giacomo Puccini, Gaetano Danizetti. Reviewed on Piazza Grande, Locarno, Aug. 11, 1984. Running time: 87 MINS.

Cast: Sara Scuderi, Giovanni Puligheddu, Leonida Bellon, Salvatore Locapo, Giuseppe Manachini and artists living at the Casa Verdi, Mialno.

This intelligent and highly sensitive documentary is dedicated to an institution that had been established by Giuseppe Verdi and had been inaugurated shortly after his death in 1902, and now bears his name. This is a home for retired artists in Milan which Verdi, at the time, considered his most beautiful work. Visiting it today, through the eyes of veteran Swiss filmmaker Daniel Schmid one

can't help but agree with him.

What could have been a lachrymose review of luminaries of the lyrical stage, now relegated to their memories only, or alternatively, a grotesque image of has-beens living in a world of their own, becomes, through the sheer affection and admiration that transpires in every sequence, a tribute to artists who may have lost the physical requirements necessary to continue their careers on stage but are still as passionately enamoured in their profession, as perpicacious musically, and as keen to sing and perform as they ever were.

That the film is dedicated to the Casa Verdi, but bears the name of a Puccini opera, is explained by the fact that Tosca is the only heroine on the lyrical stage whose profession is that of an opera singer, in common with Schmid's protagonists. Furthermore, Tosca's kiss, in the opera, is the kiss of death and while never mentioned, the presence of an imminent end is felt throughout the film.

The main charm of the whole venture is the unusual personalities of the singers interviewed and followed by the camera. Included are Sara Scuderi, one of the great divas of the past, who lights up the screen with her presence and is both humorous, sensitive and passionate in her reactions; Giuseppe Manachini, who remembers how he decided to retire at the right time, but still keeps in a trunk all the costumes that made him famous on stage: Leonida Bellon, who still sports the true spirit of the heroic tenor; and composer-conductor Puligheddu, possibly the only characater in this film that is slightly grotesque, but also very amusing when he fixes dates with the camera. There is also an interview with Giulietta Simonato, one of the great mezzos of our time, who is now president of the friends of the Casa Verdi, who are responsible for keeping this venerable institution going, once the author rights left by the composer for this purpose had stopped, Verdi's works having gone into public domain some twenty years ago.

Schmid, who in most of his previous films has dealt with paroxysms of romanticism slipping into decadence and decay, stopped short of the last part, for once, to admire those who have lived their lives in that exalted climate that is the opera stage, and who continue to live in their own reality today, unblemished by the world that has changed around them.

Besides being a natural for film fests and art houses, this documentary should attract tv programmers everywhere. —*Edna.*

Campo Europa
(SWISS-COLOR)

Locarno, Aug. 13.
A Zoo Film Production. Produced by Patricia Plattner. Written and directed by Pierce Maillard. Camera (color), Patrice Cologne, Luc Weber; editing, Jean-Louis Gauthey; sets, Sabine Jeanson; costumes, Salika Wenger; sound, Pierre-Alain Besse; music, Jacques Robellaz. Reviewed at the Morettina Film Center, Aug. 13, 1984. Running time: **90 MINS.**
Cast: Lou Castel, Valerie Favre, Federico Queni, Camillo Milli, Nerses Boyadjian.

A young Swiss woman who hides from the possibility of facing real life in a deserted Italian summer colony, is informed that her brother, back in Geneva, has died. Her grief at this news, combined with the strange relationship she entertains with an Italian writer going through a creativity drought, her restlessness and difficulty to decide what her next step should be, these are the main ingredients of this disjointed and confused first feature, too often declamatory and self-indulgent.

Symbols are spread all over the place. Ther is an obvious refusal of life within the system, which appears to be the topic of the writer's concerns. There is clear indication that the world, according to director Pierre Maillard, is going through another cycle of decadence and destruction. The bankruptcy of protest and even terror are indicated as well, for the Castel character, says there is nothing now that can extinguish the terrible rage at the world around us. Drugs are discounted as well in this process, and the possibility of suicide is contemplated, but no real answer is supplied at the end. Which is the least of this film's troubles. For even its extensive use of intricate camera movements and its flair for visuals cannot disguise the repetitiousness of sequences and the exaggerated use of poses that appear too pretentious, as presented here. Even the actors do not appear to be very confident about their parts. While these shortcomings may be typical of ambitious first films, this will not make this picture's career any easier.—*Edna.*

L'Etat De Crise
(The State Of Crisis)
(FRENCH-WEST GERMAN-COLOR)

Locarno, Aug. 13.
A Films du Passage Production. Written and directed by Mamad Haghighat. Camera (color), Omar Eladi; editor Nicholas Barachin; sound, Harry Grigorian; music, Jean-Pierre Lefebvre. Reviewed at the Morettina Film Center, Locarno, Aug. 13, 1984. Running time: **80 MINS.**
Cast: Laurence Baudry, Laurent Chomel, Jacques Combe, Pascal Pistaccio, Pascal Sellier, Alain Thierry.

A former assistant to Iranian exiled director Sohrab Shahid Saless, 32-year-old Mamad Haghighat, who is Saless' countryman, shares with his tutor the predilection for very slow tempos, and the veneration for immobility on the screen, which should impart a sense of uneasiness to the audience, equal to that of the characters on screen. Also in Saless' spirit, there is very little dialog here, most points being made, repeatedly so, visually, and the absurdity of modern life in the West is as frustrating and tragic as it is for the older filmmaker.

After establishing despair and despondency through street scenes in Paris, (where the whole film is shot), by using a subjective camera, and after insisting often on the consumer society we live in, the film moves to its six protagonists, five boys and a girl. The boys face one of the worst plagues of the latest economic crisis in the West, unemployment and the girl is rejecting the absurd parental supervision combined with a refusal for financial support. Out of sheer despair and pointlessness, after failing in their attempt to rob, amateurishly, the Samaritaine department store, they decide that their only way to attract attention to their plight is to kidnap the children of the Labor Minister, and instead of ransom, demand that they be given regular work. Their plan backfires because society is too insensitive to their problem, the movie ending in tragedy and degradation.

If the film's message is, to quote the director-writer, that "terrorism will not solve the problems of unemployment," this sketchy plot will certainly not convince those who think differently. If it is intended as an expression of protest against the indifference of the majority to the miseries of certain minorities, against a society which consumes more than it needs and refuses to consider those who cannot afford the minimum they need, then Haghighat could have achieved the same thing in a much shorter and concise way. For with the typical reluctance of any filmmaker in his maiden effort, he cannot bear to part with may superfluous or repetitive shots.

Long sequences of hand-held camerawork hint that the pleasure of shooting in such instances was greater than the necessity of the sequence to the film itself. For a normal audience this will be an exhausting experience, possibly so intended in order to have it participate in the emotions of the protagonists, but hardly conducive to wide commercial distribution. Still, it will be interesting to see Haghighat's development, once he acquires more experience and self-control. —*Edna.*

L'Air Du Crime
(A Breath of Crime)
(SWISS-COLOR)

Locarno, Aug. 16.
A Citel Films Presentation of a Xanadu Films, Zurich, in coproduction with Marion Films, Paris. Executive Producer, Ruth Waldburger. Directed by Alain Klarer. Screenplay, Klarer, Jacques Baynac, Deva Pravasa, Claude Muret; camera (color), Hugues Ryffel; editor, Georg Janett; sets, Alex Ghassem, Pierre Gattoni; costumes, Marianne Monnier; sound, Luc Yersin; music Peer Raben. Reviewed at the Morettina Film Center, Locarno, Aug. 16, 1984. Running time: **95 MINS.**
Elena	Helene Surgere
Robert	Tcheky Karyo
Stutz	Jean Bouise
Alice	Laura Morante
Policeman	Hanns Zischler
Conductor	Peer Raben
Boatman	Walo Lüönd

In spite of the title and of the opening sequences, which suggest the possibility of a thriller, this is basically a self-destruction exercise, with clear symbolic undertones referring to present Swiss society.

A successful businessman, head of a trucking company, disappears one day, without leaving a trace. His wife takes over in the office, and his son, a musician, starts looking, not very energetically, for the missing parent. An Italian girl comes into the picture, possibly as the mother's confidante, possibly even lover, becoming the son's sidekick in his search.

But soon it is clear that the wife is systematically destroying the company she pretends to preserve in her husband's tradition while the son is perturbed to such an extent by the unexpected event that he loses his job with the Zurich Tonehalle Orchestra.

On an allegorical level, it would seem that the father who has dropped out of the picture, the mother who wishes to anihilate everything he left, and the son, whose impracticality leaves him quite incapable to deal with the problems he faces, are to be taken as symbols of a society falling apart. The faithful accountant who cannot stand the sight of all this desolation, ultimately commiting suicide, is part of the same picture, and so is the fact that the mysterious young girl is Italian, an alien factor which throws the careful Swiss out of their famous balance.

While all this may be true, the plot which has to carry this message is sadly neglected. Characters that are not sufficiently founded are brought in and taken out of the film by sheer caprice, and things happen off-screen which one would like to know about but are never explained.

Helene Surgere as the mother has good moments and Laura Morante manages again to suggest dark and mysterious proprieties hidden under a gorgeous figure. Tcheky Karyo as the son seems less confident of what is expected of him, but Jean Bouise as the accountant is once again reliable.

Given the infuriating slow tempo and the heavy-handed treatment of the story, it is probable that the handsome production values of this film will be restricted to a select audience before it reverts to the three tv partners, FR 3 in France, Swiss tv, and the Bavarian tv in West Germany, who helped finance the project. — *Edna.*

Le Roi De Chine
(The King Of China)
(FRENCH-COLOR)

Locarno, Aug. 18.
A Plaisance Productions Presentation co-produced with TF1, SSRT. Directed by Fabrice Cazeneuve. Screenplay, Marceau Ginesy, Jean-Marc Terasse, Fabrice Cazeneuve, based on story by Gregor Vartanian; camera (color), Bernard Dumont; editor, Michèle Gourot; sets, Jacques Rouxel; music, Michel Portal. Reviewed at the Moettina Film Center, Locarno, Aug. 17, 1984. Running time: **100 MINS.**
Cast: Marylin Even, Jean-François Balmer, Roger Jendly.

This strange little film, looking at the underbelly of Paris and the human refuse which populates it, takes some time to get used to, but once this is done, the three leading characters and their unseemly surroundings became strangely attractive.

The King of China is one Gregor Vartanian, a solitary man buying garbage from bums and winos, who bring everything they can lay their hands on to his warehouse. He pays them by the pound, treats them all fairly and keeps them all at a distance, except for Genie, a woman still young whose mind is only partly present, due to too much alcohol. The third personage in this drama is Emile, an older man, as much a bum and as drunk as all of Vartanian's other clients, yet imposing and unusual in his way.

The strange relationship which develops between this trio is nursed nicely along by a script that never gets too explicit, but hints gently in the right directions, allowing the viewer to reach his own conclusions. Director Fabrice Cazeneuve, in his first feature film, doesn't stay in control all the time and many details are left too hazy or unexplained, and his tempos, particularly in the first part of the film, tend to drag on, yet he manages to create a world apart for his characters to live in, a kind of latter day "Lower Depths," which after a while becomes entirely believable.

Also, what may appear at first as overacting on the part of Marylin Even and underacting by Jean-François Balmer as Gregor, turns out to be the right kind of performance in both instances. Swiss actor Roger

Jendly as the mysterious Emile whose identity is gradually revealed through the film, offers a nice balance between these two extremes.

Imaginative art direction and camerawork are immensely helpful here, as is the amazing collection of faces chosen to play the refuse suppliers to the Vartanian yard. Pic is quite an interesting item for those who have the patience to watch it blossom slowly.—*Edna*.

Donauwalzer
(Waltzes Of The Danube)
(AUSTRIAN-COLOR)

Locarno, Aug. 16.

A Team Films Presentation of a ORF/ZDF Production. Directed by Xaver Schwarzenberger. Written by Ulli Schwarzenberger, Susanne Philipp, Xaver Schwarzenberger. Camera (color), Xaver Schwarzenberger; editor, Ulli Schwarzenberger; sets, Frank Geuer, Peter Ecker, Laura Duda; costumes, Egon Strasser; sound: Rolf Schmidt-Gentner. Peter Hofmann; music: Bert Breit. Reviewed at the Morettina Film Center, Locarno, Aug. 16, 1984. Running time: **99 MINS.**

Judith . . . . Christiane Hörbiger
Taddek . . . . Hans Michael Rehberg
Georg . . . . Axel Corti
Father-in-law . . . . Hugo Gottschlich
Tetta . . . . Jane Tilden
Jakob . . . . Micha Prückner
Jakob's father . . . . Tilo Prückner

It is no wonder there is some stunning photography in this film. Director-cameraman Xaver Schwarzenberger has acquired a reputation for shooting Rainer Werner Fassbinder's last movies, and has without any doubt a keen eye for the visual aspects of cinema but he is doing less well where drama is concerned.

This is his second effort as independent helmer, and if the first time around, for "The Still Ocean," he got a prize in Berlin this time he is not likely to repeat. In the former film he was slow, deliberately, but the quality of the black and white photography and the earnestness of his tone, saved the day. Here, whether the script is based on fact, as suggested by the pressbook, or not, what promises, at least in the first part to be on par with expectations from Schwarzenberger, gradually slips into a ludicrous melodrama and climaxes in tragedy, which doesn't begin to move, for none of the characters is arresting enough to cause one to care about him.

It is about a Hungarian girl who is saved by an Austrian journalist in the midst of the 1956 uprising and brought to the West, while her boyfriend is arrested and condemned to 15 years in a forced labor camp. The girl marries her savior and when he dies, shortly after the marriage, she stays with her father-in-law in a small village called Tara, to become a much respected high-school teacher. Years later the man she had once loved and whom she

believed to be dead appears out of the blue and triggers a series of events that lead to catastrophe.

The production is carefully designed and shot, but obviously lacked the expert writing hand which would raise the characters out of their plodding banality and give the relationship between them a true tragic dimension. In some instances, stress on visual effects is almost grotesque, as in the entrance of a character into a funeral celebration in church, with such powerful backlight projected behind him, that some sort of mythical presence is expected, totally out of place in this instance.

Acting isn't very subtle, the only one whose presence is felt being Hugo Gottschlich, as the father-in-law, while Jane Tilden supplies a nice vignette as a devoted servant. Hörbiger and Rehberg, as the erstwhile lovers attempting to rekindle an old fire through a trip in Italy, are neither convincing nor particularly interesting to watch.

Coproduced by Austrian tv and the Second German Channel, the film will have trouble finding a market beyond the small screen.
—*Edna*.

Le Rapt
(The Kidnapping)
(FRANCO-SWISS-COLOR)

Locarno, Aug. 12.

A Television Suisse Romande, Telvetia & Antenne 2 Production. Executive Producer, Raymond Vouillamoz. Directed by Pierre Koralnik. Adapted by Pierre Koralnik and Jacques Probst from "La Separation des Races" by C.F. Ramuz; dialog by Jacques Probst; camera (color), Pavel Korinek; editor, Didier Periat; sets, Serge Etter; costumes, Erica Loup, Micheline Tercier, Suzanne Baud; sound: René Sutterlin; music by Serge Franklin. Reviewed at the Morettina Film Center, Locarno, Aug. 12, 1984. Running time: **100 MINS.**

Cast: Pierre Clementi, Daniela Silverio, Heinz Bennent, Elisabeth Kaza, Teco Cello, René Peier, Naara Salomon.

This rather elaborate adaptation of a novel by one of the leading Swiss writers of this century, Charles Ferdinand Ramuz, suffers from the typical difficulty of translating poetic ideas from the abstract imagery of a novel, into the concrete image of film. While theoretically the theme is very much uptodate, the movie lacks the subtlety that would suggest emotions and feelings without really exposing them, and contents itself with retelling plot in a straightforward fashion, quite insufficient in this case.

The starting point is very Swiss to begin with, as the audience is introduced to two villages, separated by a mountain. On the one side, there are blond people, on the other side dark people, and everything separates them, the mountain, their religious creeds, their languages and

their customs. It is clearly a microcosmic description of the relations between German Swiss on one side of the Alps, and the Italian Swiss, on the other side. The plot deals with one dark peasant, who, late in the season, kidnaps a blond girl and brings her to his house, knowing that once the snows settle in, she will have to stay there until next spring. By doing this he not only risks the vengeance of the girl's people, but also incurs the hate of his own village folk, who are suspicious of strangers and do not want to be accused of crime.

All sorts of parallels could have been drawn from such a story that are barely suggested but never developed here. If social aspects are too often lacking, the personal ones, which could have replaced them, aren't much better treated.

The relationship between the kidnapper and his victim is supposed to move from animosity to affection, but there is too little of either of these emotions coming through on the screen. Finally, the only character that does have some substance is that of the peddler, played by Heinz Bennent, the only existing link between the two villages all winter long. But his presence is one clear instance when poetic license works on paper but not on screen. For you can write that he is a sort of mythical character who knows no borders or limitations in his travels, but when you see him cross the mountains quite easily, in the picture, you wonder why it is impossible for others to do the same.

The best part of the film consists of technical contributions, for the sets, the costumes and the camerawork are more than adequate. Produced by French and Swiss TV channels, this is very much the kind of respectable project which will have a hard time finding a spot beyond small screens. —*Edna*.

Amadeus
(COLOR)

Physically well mounted, but disappointing translation of hit play to film. Modest b.o. chances.

Hollywood, Aug. 17.

An Orion release of a Saul Zaentz Co. presentation. Produced by Zaentz. Executive producers, Michael Hausman, Bertil Ohlsson. Directed by Milos Forman. Features entire cast. Screenplay, Peter Shaffer, based on his play. Camera (Technicolor, Panavision), Miroslav Ondricek; editors, Nena Danevic, Michael Chandler; music coordinator, John Strauss; music conductor and supervisor, Neville Marriner; production design, Patrizia Von Brandenstein; art direction, Karel Cerny, Francesco Chianese (Italy); opera set design, Josef Svoboda; choreography and opera staging, Twyla Tharp; costume design, Theodor Pistek; sound (Dolby), Chris Newman; make-up and wig design, Paul Leblanc; old Salieri make-up, Dick Smith; assistant director, Hausman; second unit director, Jan Schmidt. Reviewed at Gomillion Sound, L.A., Aug. 16, 1984. (MPAA Rating: PG.) Running time: **158 MINS.**

Antonio Salieri . . . . . . F. Murray Abraham
Wolfgang
   Amadeus Mozart . . . . Tom Hulce
Constanze Mozart . . . . . Elizabeth Berridge
Emanuel Schikaneder . . . . . . Simon Callow
Leopold Mozart . . . . Roy Dotrice
Katerina Cavalieri . . . . . Christine Ebersole
Emperor Joseph II . . . . Jeffrey Jones
Count Orsini-Rosenberg . . . . . Charles Kay
Parody Commendatore . . . . . . Kenny Baker
Papagena . . . . Lisabeth Bartlett
Frau Weber . . . . Barbara Byrne

On a production level and as an evocation of a time and place, "Amadeus" is loaded with pleasures, the greatest of which derive from the on-location filming in Prague, the most 18th century of all European cities.

With great material and themes to work with, and such top talent involved, film nevertheless arrives as a disappointment. Although Peter Shaffer adapted his own outstanding play for the screen, the stature and power the work possessed onstage have been noticeably diminished, and Milos Forman's handling is perhaps too naturalistic for what was conceived as a highly stylized piece. Essential drama remains sufficiently potent to absorb audience interest, and many who never saw it live may be greatly impressed. Strong biz looms in major city first-runs, but length and heavy dose of classical music mute chances for a widescale breakout.

"Amadeus" is Shaffer's fictionalized account, based on well-informed speculation, of the relationship between Viennese court composer Antonio Salieri and Wolfgang Amadeus Mozart, during the 10 final years of the latter's life. A caustic study of the collision between mediocrity and genius, of Salieri's consuming jealousy and his bitterness over God's unfair distribution of talent, play is based on the provocative premise that the manipulative Salieri may have intentionally caused Mozart's death in 1791.

Pic begins with Salieri's suicide

attempt more than 30 years later, and is framed by and narrated through a sort of confession the old man makes to a priest, in which he enunciates his rage at God and bemoans the fact that Mozart has already become deified, while Salieri's own reputation has become extinct.

Flashing back to 1781, film presents Salieri's first encounter with the 26-year-old prodigy; Mozart's coarse, childish way with his bride-to-be; his clownlike appearance before the royal court; Salieri's placement of a spy, in the form of a maid, in the Mozart household; his furious abandonment of God and his decision to try to destroy Mozart; Mozart's prodigious creativity in the writing of "The Marriage Of Figaro," "Don Giovanni" and "The Magic Flute," and, while literally on his deathbed, his feverish effort to finish his "Requiem Mass."

Shaffer has drawn Salieri as a character of Mephistophelian proportions, a man who needs to drag Mozart down in order to cope with his awareness of his own shortcomings. Part and parcel of this, however, is the marvelous irony that Salieri, with his erudition and superb musical scholarship, is one of the few who genuinely appreciates the exalted level of Mozart's accomplishments; Forman repeatedly shows Salieri discreetly savoring Mozart's operas from his box, even when he has already gone to great lengths to insure lackluster official receptions of the works.

Fueling the fire of Salieri's fury is Mozart's offensive personality. In opposition to the idealized, romanticized 19th-century view of the composer, Shaffer has written the character as an outlandish vulgarian to whom Salieri constantly refers as an "obscene child" and "the creature."

While this proved an interesting conceit in the theater, in the film the concentration on this one aspect of Mozart's character comes off as superficially one-dimensional, an effect emphasized by the fact that the weight of the drama has unfortunately been shifted away from Salieri to Mozart.

As the film progresses into its second half, one increasingly loses sight of Salieri in favor of Mozart's rantings and ravings. As played by Tom Hulce, Mozart emerges as the John McEnroe of classical music, an immature brat with loads of talent, but with little human dimension.

Elizabeth Berridge as Mozart's young wife, a lower-class girl clearly beneath her husband's station, acts on a similar one-note level, and the flat American accents and sloppy diction of both performers sometimes strike discordant notes amid the aristocratic splendor of the film

at large. Somehow, Forman's usual wizardry at casting has deserted him on both counts.

By contrast, F. Murray Abraham, an experienced Broadway stage actor, is quietly excellent as Salieri, even if he lacks the stature and authority of Paul Scofield and Ian McKellen, who excelled in the stage role in London and New York, respectively.

Other supporting parts are well filled, and the most striking performance in the entire picture is given by Jeffrey Jones, who makes a supremely elegant and entirely human Emperior Joseph 2d.

Opera buffs will delight in seeing bits of "Don Giovanni" staged in the extraordinary Tyl Theatre, the actual house where Mozart conducted the world premiere of the work some 200 years ago. Other locations, form theaters to castles, palaces, streets and apartments, are all sensational, although Miroslav Ondricek's cinematography, at least in the print caught, appears overly brown and murky.

Top-flight contributions have been made by production designer Patrizia Von Brandenstein, costume designer Theodor Pistek, choreographer and opera stager Twyla Tharp and music overseers John Strauss and Neville Marriner. Ample opera excerpts will delight some, but will probably seem excessive to non-aficionados. —*Cart.*

A Soldier's Story
(COLOR)

Gripping race relations drama. Should attract a wide audience.

Hollywood, Aug. 29.

A Columbia Pictures release of a Caldix Films Ltd. production. Produced by Norman Jewison, Ronald L. Schwary, Patrick Palmer. Exec producer, Charles Schultz. Directed by Jewison. Features entire cast. Screenplay, Charles Fuller, from his play; camera, (Metrocolor), Russell Boyd; editing, Mark Warner, Caroline Bigglestaff; music, Herbie Hancock; production designer, Walter Scott Herndon; set decorator, Tom Roysden; sound, Charles Wilborn; costumes, Tom Dawson. Reviewed at the Academy of Motion Picture Arts and Sciences, Beverly Hills, Calif., Aug. 28, 1984. (MPAA Rating: PG). Running time: **101 MINS.**

Capt. Davenport . . . Howard E. Rollins Jr.
Master Sgt. Waters . . . . Adolph Caesar
Capt. Taylor . . . . Dennis Lipscomb
Pfc. Wilkie . . . . Art Evans
Pfc. Peterson . . . . Denzel Washington
Pfc. "CJ" Memphis . . . . Larry Riley
Cpl. Cobb . . . . David Alan Grier
Lt. Bird . . . . "Wings" Hauser
"Big Mary" . . . . Patti LaBelle

"A Soldier's Story" is a taut, gripping film which features many of the old fashioned virtues of a good Hollywood production — brilliant ensemble acting, excellent production values, a crackling script (adapted from the Pulitzer Prize winning "A Soldier's Play" by its author, Charles Fuller), fine direct-

ion and a liberal political message. Story of a military murder at a black army base towards the end of World War II remains a tough sell and must rely on critical acclaim and favorable word-of-mouth.

Returning to the racial tensions he explored in his 1967 Academy Award winner, "In The Heat Of The Night," producer/director Norman Jewison is playing pretty much the same ballgame here. "A Soldier's Story" presents, as did "Heat," a situation in which a foregone conclusion proves erroneous, causing a reassessment of individuals' basic values.

In a role reminiscent of Sidney Poitier's Northern detective in "Heat Of The Night," Howard Rollins Jr. plays Captain Davenport, a prideful black army attorney called into Fort Neal, La., to investigate the murder of Sgt. Waters (Adolph Caesar). Rollins' arrival at this holding tank for black soldiers is cause for racial strife on both sides of the fence — the white officers are contemptuous and the black soldiers are proud.

Before a roadside murder, which opens the film, Waters served as the tough-as-nails manager of the base's black baseball squad. Talking out of the side of his mouth, Caesar is extraordinary in creating a character that is at once despicable and totally comprehensible.

Film is structured around a series of flashbacks as Rollins interviews the team members who represent a variety of black experience and attitudes, from the contemporary anger of Private Peterson (Denzel Washington) to the Uncle Tomish C.J. Memphis (Larry Riley).

Cutting a MacArthuresque pose in dark glasses, Rollins is a catalyst for the volatile and changing black-white relations. But the revelations in "A Soldier's Story" come not from the predictable humanist values and role reversal twists, but from the extraordinary depth of Fuller's script and the right-on-target performances.

Rollins is the calm in the eye of the storm against which the other actors can react. Art Evans as Waters' flunkie, Private Wilkie, reveals a life of humiliation and accommodation to the white man's world. As the arrogant modern black, Denzel Washington is totally convincing in communicating his impatience for Waters' kind of assimilation into the mainstream.

On the other side of the spectrum, C.J. Memphis (Larry Riley) is brilliant as the star ballplayer and country blues singer who represents the values of the old fashioned Negro Waters considers a blight on the race and wants to wipe out.

Fuller's script delves deep into the black psyche to reveal the wounds and compromises these men have

Original Play
A Soldier's Play

Negro Ensemble Co. (Douglas Turner Ward, artistic director; Leon B. Denmark, managing director) presentation of a play in two acts by Charles Fuller. Staged by Douglas Turner Ward; scenery, Felix E. Cochren; costumes, Judy Dearing; lighting, Allen Lee Hughes; sound, Regge Life; stage manager, Clinton Turner Davis; publicity, Howard Atlee. Opened Nov. 20, '81, at Theatre Four, N.Y.; $12 top weeknights, $14 weekend nights.

Cast: Charles Brown, Adolph Caesar, Peter Friedman, Samuel L. Jackson, Brent Jennings, Steven A. Jones, Eugene Lee, James Pickins Jr., Larry Riley, Cotter Smith, Denzel Washington, Stephen Zettler.

---

made in order to take their stand in the white man's army in which they ironically can't fight.

Jewison and his associates have succeeded in creating a cross-section of America in transition and production values are uniformly high. Crisp cutting keeps the film crackling with sparks on tension even in the second half when the sorting out of the murder mystery plot becomes a bit tedious and long-winded.

Cinematographer Russell Boyd strikes an appropriate summery tone and production design by Walter Scott Herndon adds the feel of the South in the '40s effortlessly.

Jazzman Herbie Hancock's score is also a plus supplemented by a hot blues number by Patti LaBelle and several tunes written and performed by Riley.

Jewison makes the most of the material all around and "A Soldier's Story" is totally compelling throughout, mostly on the strength of its performances. It is only after the curtain is down that the conventionality of the film starts to take hold. — *Jagr.*

Veselo Gostivanje
(The Merry Marriage)
(YUGOSLAV-COLOR)

Pula, July 30.

A Viba Film Production, Ljubljana. Features entire cast. Directed by France Stiglic. Screenplay, Branko Sömen, Stiglic, based on a novel by Miska Kranja; camera (color), Vilko Filac; sets, Mirko Lipuzic; music, Jani Golob. Reviewed at Pula Film Fest, July 22, '84. Running time: **97 MINS.**

Cast: Igor Samobor, Danilo Benedicic, Polde Bibic, Bert Sotlar, Darja Moskotevic, Milena Muhic.

France Stiglic's "The Merry Marriage," a literary adaptation, is the sixth part of a tv series produced for Slovenian audiences. Based on Miska Kranja's stories in a collection titled "His Uncles Told Him," the setting is Ljubljana in the 1920s. A young man is studying theology at a Catholic seminary, then decides to chuck everything and follow in his father's footsteps by becoming a musician. His mother, now a widow, is not much for the idea, for the lad has to join his older cousins in touring towns to play mostly at weddings. It's at one such "merry marriage" that he meets a lovely Hungarian lass and falls immediately in love. The girl is lame, however, and so the mother disapproves. Love wins out in the end, even though the two must part — apparently forever.

Okay literary adaptation for home auds. —*Holl.*

Bolero
(COLOR)

Inane romantic showcase for Bo Derek by husband John.

Hollywood, Aug. 31.

A Cannon Releasing release of a Cannon Group production for City Films. Produced by, starring Bo Derek. Executive producers, Menahem Golan, Yoram Globus. Written and directed by John Derek. Camera (Rank color), John Derek; editor (uncredited), John Derek; sound, William Randall; music, Peter Bernstein; music conducted by/love scenes scored by Elmer Bernstein; assistant director, Yousaf Bokhari; production design, Alan Roderick-Jones; associate producer, Rony Yacov; dialog coach, Mickey Knox. Reviewed at Pacific theater, Hollywood, Aug. 31, 1984. (No MPAA Rating; self-applied equivalent X rating.) Running time: **104 MINS.**

Ayre .... Bo Derek
Cotton .... George Kennedy
Angel .... Andrea Occhipinti
Catalina .... Ana Obregon
Paloma .... Olivia d'Abo
Sheik .... Greg Bensen
Robert .... Ian Cochrane
Evita .... Mirta Miller
Sleazy Guide .... Mickey Knox

There's a real good cartoon at the Hollywood Pacific this week in which a horse does funny things with Woody Woodpecker, followed by "Bolero" in which Bo Derek does funny things with a horse, her hair and a couple of men. Judging from the audience's reaction, the cartoon will be around longer.

But Bo gives Woody a run for it, especially when the lines written for her unique performing ability are penned by adoring husband John Derek and directed by that same adoring husband and photographed by a close relative whose entire career currently consists of Bo Derek.

When not lingering over his wife's private parts, photographer Derek has an obsession with extreme closeups of her face, presumably because as a writer he repeatedly pens lines about her being the "most beautiful girl in the world." Well, if this can be said delicately, Bo is not exactly a girl anymore and, pretty though she still is, those closeups are killing her here.

Such technical matters aside, "Bolero" is all about Bo's determination to lose her virginity after graduating from an English board-

ing school, which she flashes in farewell, setting the overall tone for the dramatic content to follow.

Accompanied by friend Ana Obregon and family retainer George Kennedy, Bo ventures first to Arabia where a sheik falls asleep in her arms, apparently having seen as much of the film as he wanted to.

Still unviolated, Bo moves on to Spain where she meets handsome bullfighter Andrea Occhipinti, setting up a special credit of "love scenes scored by Elmer Bernstein." Ready for womanhood, Bo utters the immortal lines:

"Do everything to me. Show me how I can do everything to you. Is there enough I can do for you so you can give ecstasy to me?"

Then the dog barks and the deed is done as Bo and Occhipinti rub against each other enough that the picture is being released without a rating. (This is doubtlessly for publicity value since physically there's nothing here more daring than an R and mentally nothing more challenging than a PG-4.)

But poor Bo no sooner has her initial introduction to amour than the new lover gets gored in a sensitive location, putting him out of commission. While he recuperates, she rides around the edge of the ocean on a pretty blond horse she just acquired.

Bo also arouses the wrath of Occhipinti's red-headed girlfriend. Apparently upset that she didn't get to go to the ocean, too, the woman attacks Bo with a knife, screaming "Beach, Beach!"

The picture ends with a wedding, a freeze frame and another extreme closeup. And as Woody Woodpecker said earlier on the bill, "I hope I don't see him anymore."

But it's her, Woody, it's her.
— *Har.*

Mirrors
(Marianne)
(COLOR)

Something awful this way comes.

A First American Films release of a Southern Cinema Ventures picture. A Cinema Systems Inc. production. Produced by John T. Parker, Stirling W. Smith. Directed by Noel Black. Stars Kitty Winn, Peter Donat. Screenplay, Sidney L. Stebel, from story by Stebel, Black; camera (CFI color), Michael D. Murphy; editor, Robert Estrin; music, Stephen Lawrence; sound, James Tanenbaum; assistant director, Michael Daves; production design, Ronald Weinberg; art direction, Ray Kutos; set decoration, Shirley Drevich; sound effects, Sam Fusco Shaw; creative consultant, Ray Bradbury; associate producer, Daniel Bossier; ass't producer, Jack Boasberg. Reviewed on Monterey Home Video cassette, N.Y., Aug. 24, 1984. (MPAA Rating: PG.) Running time: **88 MINS.**

Marianne .... Kitty Winn
Dr. Philip Godard .... Peter Donat
Charbonnet .... William Swetland
Helene .... Mary-Robin Redd
Gary .... William Burns
Chet .... Lou Wagner

Peter .... Don Keefer
Marie Laveau .... Vanessa Hutchinson

"Mirrors" is a mediocre supernatural horror pic, lensed in New Orleans in 1974 under the title "Marianne." Though rated (PG) in 1977, film had virtually no theatrical exposure, but is now available on vidcassette.

Poorly developed premise has Marianne Whitman (Kitty Winn) arriving with her young husband Gary (William Burns) at a N.O. hotel with a sinister-looking desk clerk Charbonnet (William Swetland) setting the stage for touristy views of the city.

After buying perfume from a sinister-looking black woman, Marianne begins hallucinating freely, seeing images in mirrors and wandering around in her white nightgown (as all good gothic heroines are wont to do). It turns out that an ages-old voodoo specialist Marie Laveau is attempting to take possession of Marianne, with mirrors serving as the instrument to snatch one's soul away.

Following her husband's death (from a presumed asthma attack), Wynn is hospitalized after a fainting spell, where kindly Dr. Godard (Peter Donat) befriends her. Considerable filler ensues until she finally is possessed by Marie Laveau.

Pic is technically deficient, with opening reel featuring poorly post-synched dialog that is an immediate turnoff. Wynn, fresh from a supporting role in "The Exorcist," is miscast, never expressing the sense of vulnerability and mounting paranoia needed in the role. Sole point of interest here is several scenes which presage Paul Schrader's 1981 "Cat People," also set in New Orleans, such as the heroine fleeing by train.

Renowned fantasy author Ray Bradbury is credited as creative consultant, and as an unfair comeon, his name figures prominently on the homevideo packaging. — *Lor.*

An Amorous Woman Of The Tang Dynasty
(HONG KONG-COLOR)

Hong Kong, Aug. 6.

A Shaw Brothers production and release. Produced by Overground Film Co. Ltd. Directed by Eddie Fong. Screenplay, Chun Tien Nan, Eddie Fong, Chui Kong Jian. Stars Alex Man, Patricia Xia, Zheng Guo Chu, Lin Hai Lin. No other credits provided. Reviewed at Shaw Brothers preview room, Clearwater Bay Studios, Kowloon, Hong Kong, Aug. 5, 1984. Running time: **100 MINS.** (Without cuts - Original version).

(Cantonese with English subtitles)

This costumed Shaw Brothers film was shown last May and had a more than reasonable boxoffice life (nearly $HK5,000,000) despite the fact that it was liberally butchered by the local censors. The artistical-

ly presented erotic heterosexual and lesbian (simulated) graphic acts were trimmed along with prolonged nudity.

Lovingly composed and presented, the supposedly well-researched steamy drama marked the auspicious debut of director Eddie Fong. Alex Man and Patricia Xia raised the level of local eroticism to Japanese standards with their daring love scenes. Here's a film that validates all the skin exposure projected on screen.

The amorous woman of the Tang Dynasty is Yu Yuen Kai (portrayed with conviction by Patricia Xia), scholarly, sensuous, young, beautiful and willing. The film begins with the poetess' efforts to absorb the Taoist path to immortality. But Yu develops a physical relationship with a wanderer called Chui (Alex Man) and when he leaves, she channels her sexual needs to her maid Luk (Lin Hai Lin). Yu and Luk are caught making love and banished to the outside world by the head of the monastery.

The lady was ahead of her time. She leads a bohemian life with intellectuals as she writes poems between parties. This gives the scenario plenty of space and opportunities to incorporate stunning visuals of orgies, rape, sword fights and an intimate look at the Chinese way of making love.

The screen recreation of the Tang Dynasty is sumptuous. It has been said that the Tang is the greatest of Chinese dynasties in terms of creative advancement among writers, poets, painters and sculptors. And among them is the female rebel Yu Yuen Kai, the lady who led and experienced what life had to offer and became the decadent trendsetter of her time. But all things must come to an end as tragedy strikes twice which eventually extinguished the life of this extraordinary woman of leisure-pleasure.

The period costumes, Chinese artifacts and traditions will please many foreign eyes. It is for this reason that foreign international film fest organizers should ask for this film with high artistic potential as an Asian entry. Sadly lacking though are samples of the poems written by u to validate her journey beyond the Valley of the Tank Dynasty.

Xia's interpretation as Yu is a bit too studied and a more carefree portrayal could have given her role more emotoinal dimension and dramatic shadings. But Alex Man as the very masculine wandering assassin is stunning to watch. Shaw Brothers must be congratulated for this meritorious work that went against their normal Cantonese fare. —*Mel.*

Flashpoint
(COLOR)

Thriller lacks believability.

Hollywood, Aug. 31.

A Tri-Star Pictures release of an HBO Pictures presentation, in association with Silver Screen Partners. Produced by Skip Short. Directed by William Tannen. Stars Kris Kristofferson, Treat Williams. Screenplay, Dennis Shryack, Michael Butler, based on book by George La Fountaine; camera (Metrocolor), Peter Moss; editor, David Garfield; sound, Courtney Goodin; production design, Paul Greimann; assistant directors, Arne L. Schmidt, Ken Gilbert; production manager, Carl Olsen; associate producers, Michael Appel, Francette Mace; music, Tangerine Dream; songs, Scott Richardson. Reviewed at the Directors Guild of America, Hollywood, Aug. 30, 1984. (MPAA rating: R.) Running time: **94 MINS.**

Logan . . . . Kris Kristofferson
Ernie . . . . Treat Williams
Sheriff . . . . Rip Torn
Brook . . . . Kevin Conway
Carson . . . . Kurtwood Smith
Roget . . . . Miguel Ferrer
Doris . . . . Jean Smart
Lambasino . . . . Guy Boyd
Hawthorne . . . . Mark Slade
Amarillo . . . . Roberts Blossom
Ellen . . . . Tess Harper

"Flashpoint" is a four-flusher that almost bluffs its way past disbelief, but audiences are likely to tire of its game very quickly.

As border patrolmen, Treat Williams and Kris Kristofferson make a fairly balanced team: Williams overacts while Kristofferson underacts and between the two of them there's the makings of one fairly mediocre performer. This is okay since "Flashpoint" doesn't require much more.

For various and not particularly interesting reasons, the pair is growing increasingly disenchanted with its border patrol work when Kristofferson discovers a wrecked jeep, a skeleton and $800,000 buried in the desert, apparently for some 20 years.

Kristofferson wants to get away with the money, but Williams isn't so sure and, while they debate, various dark-suited government agents start showing up among the cactus. If stuck in a theater with nowhere else to go, the question naturally arises, "What's going on here?" and director William Tannen takes advantage of that for a while to build some suspense about the origin of the money and what the bad guys are up to.

Unfortunately, amidst various bloodshed, the answer is revealed at the end and it's even sillier than this type of film usually falls back on. Suffice to say the whole picture turns out to be some sort of footnote to one of the most cataclysmic moments in American history, suggesting a conspiracy still continues but not caring much so long as Sheriff Rip Torn stays behind to cover Kristofferson's getaway.

The film opened with two girls featured prominently in the advertising along with the skeleton. The skeleton got a better part than either Jean Smart or Tess Harper. —*Har.*

Secerna Vodica
(Sugar Water)
(YUGOSLAV-COLOR)

Pula, July 30.

A FRZ Cronos Film (Belgrade) and Union Film (Belgrade) Coproduction. Features entire cast. Directed by Svetislav Prelic. Screenplay, Momcilo Kovacevic; camera (color), Branko Perak; sets, Marko Sanjevic; music, Goran Paljatic. Reviewed at Pula Film Fest, July 22, '84. Running time: **104 MINS.**

Cast: Sonja Savic, Svetislav Goncic, Velimir Bata Zivojinovic, Ljubisa Samardzic, Milena Dravic, Zoran Radmilovic.

About the only saving grace in Svetislav Prelic's "Sugar Water" is Sugar herself: thesp Sonja Savic, a natural talent who plays a young girl trying desperately to find an excuse to lose her virginity. The drawback, she believes, is an unappealing nose, so she decides to undergo surgery to correct the disfigurement. Furthermore, she's the tomboy type, so when the surgery takes place, she also discards her jeans for femme garb. When finally she has her first affair, it's with a boyfriend she's been tagging around with on bikes and such during her carefree teenage years.

A comedy for the home crowd.
—*Holl.*

Fatal Games
(COLOR)

Olympics-themed horror pic that should have been scratched.

An Impact Films presentation. Executive producer, William Kroes. Produced by Christopher Mankiewicz; co-produced by Rafael Buñuel. Directed by Michael Elliot. Features entire cast. Screenplay, Mankiewicz, Buñuel, Elliot; camera (United color), Alfred Taylor; editor-associate producer, Jonathon Braun; music, Shuki Levy; song, Levy, Deborah Shelton; sound, Rod Sutton; assistant director, Wendy Bernier; production manager, Patricia Stallone; art direction, Jay Burkhart; set decoration, Anne Kuljian; costume design, Shoko Saito; stunt coordinator, B.J. Davis. Reviewed on Media Home Entertainment vidcassette, N.Y., Aug. 25, 1984. (No MPAA Rating.) Running time: **88 MINS.**

Diane . . . . Sally Kirkland
Annie . . . . Lynn Banashek
Phil . . . . Sean Masterson
Frank . . . . Michael O'Leary
Lynn . . . . Teal Roberts
Nancy . . . . Melissa Prophet
Coach Drew . . . . . . Marcelyn Ann Williams
Sue . . . . Angela Bennett
Joe . . . . Nicholas Love
Shelley . . . . Lauretta Murphy

"Fatal Games" is a misguided, undernourished horror film, keyed in topically to the Olympics but failing to do much with its premise. Pic was lensed in 1982 under the title "The Killing Touch," but failed, as have so many fright films of late, to achieve theatrical distribution, going directly to homevideo instead.

Set at Falcon Academy of Athletics in Brookfall, Mass. (but filmed in California), pic follows the regimented modern horror format of seven youngsters, who have qualified for the national olympics trials, being killed one by one by a madman wielding a javelin.

Opening reels feature plentiful, mainly extraneous, nude scenes, replaced in last few reels by underlit, blue-filtered chase sequences that are pure eye-strain. In this pic's mythos, virtually all adult women are lesbians, or, in the complication that has been copied in scores of horror pics since William Castle's "Homicidal," perhaps of indeterminate gender. Latter gimmick fits, since film is concerned with dangerous and illegal training methods to compete with the East Europeans, such as administering hormones to retard the bust development of femme swimmers.

Suspense is nil, characterizations absent and musical score strictly repetitive and grating. Pic's major defect is that it never gets to the Olympics; it's just another campus "killer on the loose" exercise with no crowds and nobody noticing the missing persons' absence until it's too late.

Oddities here are several of the filmmakers popping up in acting roles; cowriter/coproducer Rafael Buñuel hardly doing credit to the memory of his illustrious dad Luis Buñuel; featured victim Melissa Prophet going on to become associate producer of "The Cotton Club;" cowriter of the theme song "Take It All The Way" Deborah Shelton earning a key acting role in Brian DePalma's "Body Double" and chief suspect Nicholas Love popping up here after toiling in various horror movies made by his brother-in-law Ulli Lommel. Quite a mishmash. —*Lor.*

Out Of Order
(DOCU-COLOR-16m)

A First Run Features, New York, release of a Documentary Research, Buffalo, N.Y. production. Produced, directed and edited by Diane Christian and Bruce Jackson. Camera (color), Jackson; sound, Christian, Michael Jackson, Barbara Copley. Funding from National Endowment for The Humanities, Levi Strauss and Co., Irving and Julia Jackson Literary Fund, and Roy (Bud) Johns. Reviewed at American Film Festival, N.Y., June 2, 1984. Running time: **89 MINS.**

Filmmakers Christian and Jackson have dealt once before with controlled institutionalized confinement, in their one-hour 1980 "Death Row," concerning 114 convicted men tediously awaiting execution at Ellis Prison, Huntsville, Texas.

The title of their new "Out Of Order" puns the idea that some nuns are leaving the controlled confinement of their holy orders, renouncing the Church's security and certitudes. Paradoxically, their lives are now in order, outside the Church, for the first time since their late girlhood, when they entered convent life.

In "Out Of Order," six dropout nuns, one co-filmmaker Diane Christian, describe why they entered and why they exited the religious life, left variously after six to 16 years.

Motivations to join the order include: mission, a sense of calling, deep conviction, social idealism, family example, pride, elitism, a fear or revulsion regarding sex and motherhood, even a teenage admiration for Deborah Kerr in John Huston's "Heaven Knows, Mr. Allison."

Motivations to drop out include: unwillingness to forfeit identity, a waning of original commitment, monotonous duties, disenchantment with ritual over righteousness, impatience with the Church's slow impact on community reform, lack of opportunity for advancement within a male-dominated structure, a growing futility and a certain panic that time is passing without personal realization, and a desire for normal companionship, dating, romance, sex and motherhood.

Cut from 26 hours, these six interviews are edited into a verbal montage by theme, creating fascinating character vignettes. Some are touching, some hilarious, and some are sad.

"Out Of Order" has participated in the recent American Film Festival among other fests, and is set for a fall telecast on PBS.

The film can have a long life in 16m release to churches and colleges, given its timely and timeless themes. It can manage as well in certain theatrical situations.
— *Hitch.*

Death Warmed Up
(NEW ZEALAND-COLOR)

Wellington, N.Z., Aug. 18.

The Tucker Production Co. in association with the New Zealand Film Commission. Directed by David Blyth. Produced by Murray Newey. Screenplay, Michael Heath, Blyth; camera (color), James Bartle; production design, Michael Glock; editor, David Hugget; music, Mark Nicholas; sound (Dolby), Michael Westgate. Reviewed at National Film Unit preview theater, Wellington, Aug. 13, '84. Running time: **85 MINS.**

Michael Tucker . . . . Michael Hurst
Sandy . . . . Margaret Umbers
Lucas . . . . William Upjohn
Jeannie . . . . Norelle Scott
Spider . . . . David Letch
Dr. Archer Howell . . . . Gary Day

"Death Warmed Up" is the second feature of N.Z. director David Blyth, whose "Angel Mine" raised the eyebrows of more conventional members of the film industry here a few years ago.

That first Blyth feature was

not entirely successful. "Death Warmed Up" is a horror film aimed at the young market in a style clearly labelled surreal-art deco-punk, with dollops of action and blood.

Michael Tucker (Michael Hurst) is programmed by genetic surgeon Dr. Archer Howell (Gary Day) into killing his parents. He is incarcerated in a psychiatric institution for the crime.

Some years later, Michael and friends travel to an isolated island where Howell now runs Trans Cranial Applications, experimenting on humans and turning them into mutant killing machines. Michael is seeking revenge and the saving of mankind.

The film has high production values. However, the acting fares less well in that it fails to achieve the high degree of archness which Blyth's filmmaking style demands, or that kind of simple sweetness that makes characters like Janet and Brad work in "The Rocky Horror Picture Show." The actors are not helped by a plot that runs out of ideas in the second half.

Nevertheless, there are strong performances from Hurst, bleached blond and looking not unalike a young Hollywood Alexander the Great, as the "hunter," and David Letch, as Spider, king of the mutants.

But the gem is a cameo by Jonathon Hardy, as Ranji Gandhi, the Indian owner of a fast food takeway shop on horrs island. His few moments of byplay with the sinister Dr. Howell ... "one piece of fish and make it snappy!" ... are a standout. —Nic.

Breaking The Silence:
The Generation After
The Holocaust
(DOCU-COLOR-16m)

A production of Documentaries For Learning, Mental Health Center, Harvard U., Boston. Coproducers, Eva Fogelman and Edward A. Mason; associate Producer, Henry Grunewald. Directed by Mason. Written by Fogelman; camera (color, 16m), Ben Achtenberg; sound, Tom Hill; music, Rosalie Gerut; editor, Achtenberg; narrator, Edie Wieder. Major funding provided by the Van Ameringen Foundation. Reviewed at Mayflower Hotel, N.Y., Aug. 25, 1984. Running time: 59 MINS.

Broadcast nationally via PBS during Holocaust Remembrance Week April 29-May 5, "Breaking The Silence" is set to open New York's Margaret Mead Film Festival Sept. 17. It is circulating further via 16m distribution to schools, cultural groups and religious communities.

A therapy film, yet more than that, "Breaking The Silence" was shot in three days in Boston, with four families of Holocaust survivors, and with their nine children,

now young adults, who break through the long silence of suppressed feelings (of guilt and rage and alienation) that separate the two generations.

Thus "Breaking The Silence" is primarily talk, with painfully honest self-revelations. The scenes derive from intensive awareness groups of survivor-children who explore the Holocaust experiences of their parents.

Intercut with these scenes are old b&w stock footage and stills (providing historical background to the Holocaust), a visit to an eighth grade class, and comments by psychotherapists, including Robert J. Lifton, author of works on Hiroshima survivors and on Vietnam veterans who also live with terrible memories. Lifton gives a final direction to the film by describing a new social movement among the children of survivors "toward being heard, toward making known what has happened to them, what they have been experiencing — an insistence on feeling, being true to their own history, confronting their own history."

Among groups collaborating with the film is the International Network of Children of Jewish Holocaust Survivors. The film was screened during May at the first international Conference of Holocaust Survivors, held in New York. Director Mason is a psychiatrist and professor at Harvard Medical School, with 25 years in the production of films and videotapes on mental health. —Hitch.

Trije Prispevki K
Slovenski Blaznosti
(Three Sorts Of Slovene Madness)
(YUGOSLAV-COLOR)

Pula, July 30.

A Viba Film Production, Ljubljana. Features entire cast. A feature film directed in three parts by Zare Luznik, Boris Jurjasevic, and Mitja Milavec. Screenplay, Zare Luznik (Part I), Boris Jurjasevic, Emil Filipcic (Part II), Diana Martinc, Mitja Milavec (Part III); camera (color), Rado Likon (Part I), Zoran Hochstatter (Part II), Vilko Filac (Part III); sets, Zdravko Papic; music, Zoran Simjanovic. Reviewed at Pula Film Fest, July 23, '84. Running time: 100 MINS.

Cast: Jozef Roposa, Desa Muck (Part I), Petar Bostjancic, Vladica Milosavljevic (Part II), Radko Polic, Majda Potokar, Milos Batellino, Simona Gruden (Part III).

"Three Sorts Of Slovene Madness" offers a chance for three new graduates of the Ljubljana Academy for Theater, Film, Radio and Television to show their stuff without Viba Film having to support separate debut features for all three. The general theme is madness, with the three stories intertwined in such a manner that one story seems to blend naturally into the next. Part I is titled "Chronicle Of Crime," Part II "Chronicle Of Madness," and Part III "Chronicle Of Resis-

tance." In other words, the despair at the beginning is resolved at the end in a sign of hope.

It's the "Chronicle Of Crime" segment that impresses from the acting side. A young boy witnesses at firsthand the cruelty of his father at home: the mother is beaten for trying to save money needed for the family, and this leads in turn to the moral ruination of the mother when she turns to alcohol for release. The boy grows up to become the goat of the school class, and then one day he kills a gang leader in a junkyard in self-defense. He is sent to reform school, and leaves that institution as a complete outsider indeed; his only friend is a girl bearing similar moral scars, who offers a sexual release as one antidote to oncoming madness.

Part II offers a journey through madness as such. The real world is blended into one of fantasy. An Orpheus seeks his Eurydice, following the general lines of the Orpheus legend. Part III has a mentally disturbed fellow on the brink of self-destruction, when he meets a young girl whose youthful and refreshing innocence offers a way out.

Credits are all on the plus side, and the whole comes across as a quite impressive diploma film and springboard to directing future features. Pic deserves exposure at fests primed for new directors and first features. —Holl.

Kral Drozdia Brada
(King Thrushbeard)
(CZECH-COLOR)

Karlovy Vary, July 18.

A Czechoslovak Film Production, Koliba Studios, Bratislava. World rights, Ceskoslovensky Filmexport, Prague. Features entire cast. Directed by Miloslav Luther. Screenplay, Tibor Vichta, Milos Ruppeldt. Luther, based on a story by the Brothers Grimm. Reviewed at Karlovy Vary Film Fest (Debut Competition), July 11, '84. Running time: 90 MINS.

Cast: Adriana Tarabkova, Lukas Vaculik, Marie Schellova, Gerhard Olschewsi, Zita Furkova, Marian Labuda, Bronislav Poloczek.

Czech and Slovak features based on fairy tales have a long tradition and appeal to old as well as young. The Brothers Grimm and Hans Christian Andersen often supply the stories and motifs, but so too the books of Czechoslovak writers Bozena Nemcova and Pavel Dobsinsky. In the case of Miloslav Luther's "King Thrushbeard," it's the Brothers Grimm supplying the source.

This is the story of a fickle princess named Anna, who repulses her suitors by laughing at them for even trying. So when Michal, a suitor from the neighbor from the neighboring kingdom, comes along, she makes fun of his beard by telling him it resembles a thrush. Thereupon, the princess' father grows angry, swearing to give his daughter's

hand to the first beggar to come along. This happens, and the princess soon regrets her spoiled ways. But she tries to make the best of things as a poor man's wife — only to discover she has married the kindly "King Thrushbeard" after all.

Miloslav Luther, the brother of ace cameraman Igor Luther (who has worked with Andrzej Wajda and Volker Schlöndorff), has made a number of tv pics in Czechoslovakia. This is his first feature, and one of promise for the future. Tech credits are on plus side. — Holl.

Nobena Sonce
(What A Sun!)
(YUGOSLAV-COLOR)

Pula, July 30.

A Viba Film Production, Ljubljana. Features entire cast. Directed by Jane Kavcic. Screenplay, Zelko Kozinc; camera (color), Valentin Perko; sets, Janez Kovic; music, Deco Zgur. Reviewed at Pula Film Fest, July 24, '84. Running time: 98 MINS.

Cast: Vesna Jernikar, Vida Juvanova, Branko Sturbej, Dare Valic, Marija Lojk-Trsar.

Jane Kavcic has made a number of widely acclaimed features for children and youth — indeed, he has become Yugoslavia's specialist in the field. His latest, "What A Sun!," features a teenager named Veronika who's not too pleased with the progress she's making at a vocational school, nor with her part-time job at a glass factory. All the same, she meets a young man at the factory whom she gradually falls for. Together, they manage to sort out their futures without relying too much any more on the misguidance of certain teachers or the rather helpless direction given by the girl's parents. It seems that the father's own hobbies and pipe dreams come before his concern for the good of his children, but a lesson is learned on both sides in the finale.

Authentic locations and the natural talents of the two young thesps make this a recommended youth pic for fests specializing in the genre. —Holl.

Rani Snijeg u Münchenu
(Early Snowfall In Munich)
(YUGOSLAV-COLOR)

Pula, July 30.

A Jadran Film (Zagreb), Centar Film (Belgrade), Makedonija Film (Skopje), Zvezda Film (Novi Sad), and FRZ Münchner coproduction. Features entire cast. Directed by Bogdan Zizic. Screenplay, Goran Massot; camera (color), Goran Trbuljak; sets, Zelimir Zagk ta; music, Ozren Depolo. Reviewed at Pula Film Fest, July 25, '84. Running time: 89 MINS.

Cast: Drago Grgecic-Gabor, Pavle Vujisic, Ute Fiedler.

Bogdan Zizic made a remarkable feature on Yugoslavs living in West

Germany as foreign workers, "Don't Lean Out The Window" (1977). And now he's made what scores as a equally representative sequel, "Early Snowfall In Munich."

This is the story of a young man who accompanied his Yugoslav parents to Munich some 16 years ago at the age of four. Now, at 20, he feels himself to be more a part of German culture and rearing than Yugoslav. He has attended German schools, speaks better German and Serbo-Croatian, and even has a longtime school chum whom he loves and wishes to marry. For the parents, who have only this son and have scrimped and saved for his future for years, the need to return immediately back home is now more urgent than ever. The father sends the mother on ahead of the family, and his hopes lay with the offer of opening a garage for his son, a gifted auto mechanic.

The upshot is that the son decides to play cat-and-mouse with his parents until the last minute, at which point he drops the bombshell that he has set the wedding date after all.

Cast with both Yugoslav and German actors, "Early Snowfall In Munich" doesn't aim any higher than to be a treatise on a rather widespread problem in a fiction feature. As such, it succeeds. Credits are also on the plus side, although script could have been tightened considerably. —*Holl.*

Montreal Fest

La Femme de L'Hotel
(CANADIAN-COLOR)

Montreal, Aug. 22.

A J.A. LaPointe (Canada) Film release by an ACPAV production. Produced by Bernadette Payeur. Directed by Léa Pool. Screenplay, Pool, Michael Langlois, collaboration by Robert Gurik; camera (color), Daniel Jobin, Georges Dufaux; editor, Michel Arcand; art direction, Vianney Gauthier; costumes, Gaudeline Sauriol; music, Yves Laferriere; sound, Serge Beauchemin. Reviewed at the World Film Festival (non-competing), Montreal, Aug. 21, 1984. Running time: 88 MINS.
Andrea . . . . Paule Baillargeon
Estelle . . . . Louise Marleau
The actress . . . . Marthe Turgeon
Simon . . . . Serge Dupire
First woman . . . . Gilles Renaud
Young woman . . . . Genevieve Paris
The manager . . . . :. . . . . Raymond Cloutier
The stranger . . . . Kim Yarosheyskaya

Swiss-born filmmaker Léa Pool creates an angst-ridden tale of loneliness and creative frustration in her Canadian debut, "La Femme de L'hotel." This introspective, arty yarn is surefire festival material with a decided feminist slant but highly questionable as a strict commercial outing.

Story centers on a filmmaker named Andrea (Paule Baillargeon) who returns to her native Montreal to do a musical drama with the emphasis on the latter element. Shortly after checking into the hotel of the title she has a brief brush with Estelle (Louise Marleau), an older woman with a strange, unsettling quality. A short time later, we see Estelle attempt suicide by taking pills and gin together.

One might suspect from the brief description that the film darts along at a frantic pace, but this couldn't be further from the truth. Each incident is prolonged and labored and imbued with a severe, self-conscious quality.

The story is rounded out by the presence of an actress playing the role of a singer in Andrea's movie and the filmmaker-within-the-film's brother.

As story evolves, Andrea and Estelle finally meet and exchange histories. It would appear that the script of the film being made has real life parallels to Estelle's life. The prospect of art imitating life and vice versa forms the core of the drama.

Pool offers nothing of novelty in her portrayal of the filmmaking process itself and the most strained, serious points on exchanged personalities. It comes off as highly pretentious and artistically insular stuff indeed.

Technical credits are generally smooth but the director fails to get much in the way of performance from her cast. Characters generally wind up adopting poses and attitudes but there's a genuine lacking of what goes into the creative spark. This is particularly unfortunate in the case of Louise Marleau's Estelle. Outside the fest circuit "La Femme de L'hotel" might stir up some interest in specialty situations and on television in Europe. —*Klad.*

Torn Allegiance
(U.S.-COLOR)

Montreal, Aug. 27.

An Overseas Filmgroup presentation of an SABC-Mandalay/Pro Gear production. Produced, directed and written by Alan Nathanson. Camera (color), Digby Young, andre Pienaar; editor, Peter Thornton; art direction, David Pulvermacher; music: Johnny Boshoff. Reviewed at the World Film Festival (non-competing), Montreal, Aug. 26, 1984. Running time: 97 MINS.
Sana . . . . Trevyn McDowell
Lt. Harry Wyckham . . . . . Jonathan Morris
Pvt. Stan Archer . . . . Ronald France
Henk . . . . Marius Weyers
Mother . . . . Shelagh Holliday
Maria . . . . Ilsa Schmidt
Charlie . . . . Paul Bosman

Oddball indie effort "Torn Allegiance," screened in a non-competition slot at Montreal fest, appears chiefly headed for the television sales route. Period drama set during the Boer War has more recent echoes in confrontations in such hot spots as Vietnam and Lebanon. Although handsomely mounted, pic's no-name cast and lack of drama suggest theatrical life will be limited to very selected action territories.

Title refers specifically to a British woman who has married a now dead South African Boer. However, the split loyalties subsequently apply to a British officer who is appalled by the carnage witnessed in the name of noble pursuits.

At outset, the British are checking Boer farms that may have hidden food and ammunition caches for the Dutch guerrilla fighters. A young officer searches one such place but it's not the one he'd been advised to inspect by his superiors. When he can secure neither a store nor information, he sacks and dynamites the spread.

Action leaves the British woman and her two daughters, one of whom is pregnant, homeless. They are then escorted to a camp but defiantly head home rather than face internment. Later they receive assistance from the Boer fighters.

Latter half of picture breaks down into bloody confrontation between the two sides. Brits are viewed with less sympathy, particularly one soldier with a mean streak that manifests itself in ruthless revenge including a sexual attack on the teenage daughter of the British-born Boer sympathizer. He gets his just desserts and the officer realizes the inhumanity of the situation, providing hope for more peaceful coexistence in future.

Message is sincere if treacly in "Torn Allegiance." This might have been more effective with a better cast and a music score that didn't try as hard to identify our emotional response. Location filming is good, but the pacing and direction are pedestrian under the guidance of tv helmer Alan Nathanson, who also wrote and produced. —*Klad.*

Carne de tu Carne
(Flesh Of Your Flesh)
(COLOMBIAN-COLOR)

Montreal, Aug. 25.

A presentation of Producciones Visuales. Produced by Berta del Carvajal and Fernando Baron. Directed by Carlos Mayolo. Screenplay, Elsa Vasquez, J. Nieto, Mayolo; camera (color), Luis Gabriel Beristain; editors, Luis Ospina, Karen Lamassone; art direction, Miguel Gonzalez; music, Mario Gomez Vignes; sound, Phil Pearle. Reviewed at the World Film Festival (Cinema of Latin America), Montreal, Aug. 24, 1984. Running time: 85 MINS.
Margareth . . . . Adriana Herran
Andres Alfonso . . . . David Guerrero
Enrique . . . . Josue Angel

Although "Carne de tu Carne" (Flesh Of Your Flesh) is dedicated to "Polanski And Corman," one can readily see the influence of Luis Buñuel and George Romero on this erratic, darkly comic, political mishmash from Colombia. Not quite direct enough to earn dates as an exploitation film, neither is the film truly suited to an art house thrust. It's caught somewhere in between, making commercial prospects very limited outside Spanish-language territories.

Story takes place in 1956 and vague references are made to the military dictatorship and the complicity of the rich which allows a reign of terror in the country. Focus is on a wealthy family and, initially, it appears we're in for a struggle over the will of its dead matriarch. This never fully evolves, nor is much made of political terrorism which crops up in the opening passages.

Instead, we are confronted with the incestuous relationship between members of the family. Nothing can quite prepare an audience for the odd twist (segueing into vampirism) in the plot. The ghoulishness is anything but organic and the overall effect is an unsatisfying, increasingly hysterical botch.

"Carne de tu Carne" shares some similarities with another recent Colombian effort, "Pura Sangre" by Luis Ospina (this film's co-editor). However, the earlier film, equally vampiric and unflattering to the bourgeoisie, had a tighter rein and a more cohesive plot. Here, director Carlos Mayolo takes a scattergun approach which erases intended irony in a curdling bloodbath.

Commercial prospects in U.S. and Europe theatrically are virtually nil. Still, with some trimming and dubbing, pic might be decent pay-tv fare with horror aspects accentuated. — *Klad.*

Bao And His Son
(CHINESE-COLOR)

Montreal, Aug. 22.

China Film Export presents a Beijing Film Studio production. Directed by Xie Tieli. Screenplay, Tieli, based on the novel by Zhang Tianyi; camera (color), Huang Xinyi; art direction, Tieli; music, Wang Ming. Reviewed at the Montreal World Film Festival (non-competing), Aug. 21, 1984. Running time: 94 MINS.
Bao Guowei Sr. . . . . Guan Zongxiang
Bao Guowei Jr. . . . . Liu Changwei
Hu Da . . . . Duan Lian
Guo Chun . . . . Bao Xun
An Shuzhen . . . . Gong Ying

Set in pre-1984 Mainland China, "Bao And His Son" is a handsomely produced tale of a devoted father and his ungrateful son. Basic situation hits a familiar chord but the extremes to which the drama is taken simply do not travel to outside cultures.

The widower Bao has only a modest income but has sacrificed virtually everything to ensure his son receives the best possible education. As the story opens, he has learned the young man has failed to pass his exams and will not go on to the next academic level. This provides him with an added financial burden his son in no way attempts to alleviate.

Added to the problem is the old man's total blindness to his son's self-centeredness and predilection for decadent pursuits. He is a peacock only interested in a good time, hanging out with the sons of rich men and looking his best. This general attitude can only lead to trouble and the eventual crumbling of the man's dream that his son will be an important and wealthy official.

Picture evolves as more a political allegory than a family drama and this fact limits its accessibility beyond the Great Wall. The junior Bao, by his association with the rich, lazy uppercrust, is a doomed species. There's no doubt that had he followed his father's selfless ways, he would be part of the future new order and successful in his endeavors.

Vet Chinese Helmer Xie Tieli gets the richest performances from his crew who've lovingly recreated the period. As for on-camera actors, the results may conform to party doctrine but they don't measure up to dramatic standards necessary to penetrate foreign markets. Pic's primary appeal is to special interest groups, so some fest slottings may be forthcoming. —*Klad.*

Nice A Propos de Jean Vigo
(FRENCH-DOCU-COLOR-16m)

Montreal, Aug. 21.
Produced by the Institut National de la Communication Audiovisuelle. Directed by Manoel de Oliveira. Camera (color), Jacques Boquin; editors, Janine Verneau, Françoise Besnier; sound, Jean-Paul Mugel. Reviewed at World Film Festival, Montreal, Aug. 20, 1984. Running time: **59 MINS.**

A promising concept proves to founder in this docu made for a French tv series, "Regard sur la France," in which foreign directors viewed French cities or provinces.

Manoel de Oliveira, known on the festival circuit for his able Portuguese pics such as "Francisca," chose to view Nice and the Cote d'Azur, where a community of Portuguese promised interviews in his native tongue.

Oliveira's other motivation lay in his admiration for Jean Vigo's "A Propos de Nice," extracts of which pop up frequently in this pic.

Oliveira presents three proposals at the opening of the film which he presumably intended to demonstrate. First, Nice is a city that lives off gambling. Second, Nice functions only for tourists. Third, fundamentally the locals are no more interesting than their guests. His prejudices are not sufficiently substantiated in this impressionistic, subjective work.

Sequences of a museum exhibit demonstrate the ancient foundations of the city, in stark contrast to the frolicsome feeling of the city

found in Vigo's work. Modern Nice and the Cote d'Azur are presented as elitist and elegant in comparison. Slow pans and long takes stretch out a concept about 30 minutes longer than is necessary.

The final sequence is an interview with the daughter of Vigo, which would have been more appropriate as an introduction, as she presents a portrait of her father as a young boy. Related oddities such as a Le Mans videogame and the Nietzsche path leading to the citadel where he conceived of Zarathustra, provide a kind of progress report on a city most viewers would prefer to like rather than dislike. A denunciation of the Riviera is not going to find much interest outside France, and on the festival circuit, it relies on Vigo's name to attract viewers for Oliveira to grind an ax that has nothing to do with Vigo. — *Kaja.*

Venido a Menos
(Gone To Seed)
(ARGENTINE-COLOR)

Montreal, Aug. 26.
A Filmstar production. Produced by Camilo Cappelleto. Directed by Alejandro Azzano. Screenplay, Azzano, Cappelleto; camera (Kodacolor), Diego Bonacina; editor, Miguel Perez; music, Pocho Lapouble. Reviewed at the World Film Festival (Cinema of Latin America), Aug. 26, 1984. Running time: **83 MINS.**

Alfredo Gomez Olaciregui . . Fernando Siro
Beba, his wife . . . . Fernando Mistral
Tia Meme . . . . Irma Cordoba
Dr. Montone . . . . Xavier Portales
Zenon . . . . Sebastian Larreta
Oscar Birolo . . . . Fernando Madanes

The Montreal festival program notes for "Gone To Seed" state that the film shot in 1981 and remains banned in Argentina. If true, the sensibilities involved are hard to fathom for outsiders, because the film appears to be a modest, rather cynical comedy about a phony who sponges off others and finally gets his comeuppance.

Dr. Alfredo Gómez Olaciregui (Fernando Siro) comes from a rich bourgeois background but has frittered away his money over the years. When the film begins, he moves with his alcoholic, frigid wife, his vacuous, pretty daughter and his reclusive, fascist son to live with and off his wealthy sister. Taking charge of his sister's finances, he manages to pay off some of his own bills, and resumes his gambling habit. He borrows and sponges from all, and when his daughter's boyfriend is invited to dinner, dad pours cheap local wine into an empty bottle with a fancy French label. He also enters into a shady deal with a Texas cattleman to bring a prize bull to Argentina for breeding purposes. When the animal dies of seasickness on the voyage, he has no scruples about providing the sperm of a donkey to his customers, though the results are catastrophic.

Siro plays this shallow charmer with relaxed skill, and there are plenty of quiet chuckles along the way. No doubt local allusions would give the film all the more impact were it to be seen at home. All other thesps are pro, and the pic is tightly paced at an uncluttered 83 minutes. Payoff has the shady hero jailed (it's his ungrateful son who calls the cops) but, after serving his sentence, emerging with new ideas for conning people.

Chalk down this satire about the dissolute Argentine aristocracy as a pic which probably won't spark too much international interest on its generally familiar theme, unless its domestic plight is well publicized as an aid to draw attention to it.
— *Strat.*

Reviewed At Venice

Les Favoris de la Lune
(Minions Of The Moon)
(FRENCH-COLOR)

Venice, Aug. 30.
A Philippe Dussart Production, in collaboration with the French Minister of Culture and RAI-TV1 (Rome). A Spectrafilm release (U.S.-Canada). World sales, Philippe Dussart, Paris. Directed by Otar Ioseliani. Features entire cast. Screenplay, Ioseliani, Gérard Brach; camera (color), Philippe Theaudiere; sound, Allx Comté. Claude Bertrand, Jacques Maumont; sound editing, Dominique Roy; music, Nicolas Zourabichvill; artistic collaboration, Catherine Foulon, Dimitri Eristavi, Leila Naskidachvill; editing, Dominique Bellfort; production manager, Michel Choquet; associate producer, Pierre André Boutang. Reviewed at Venice Film Fest (in competition), Aug. 29, '84. Running time: **101 MINS.**

Cast: Alix de Montaigu (Delphine Laplace), Pascal Aubier (Monsieur Laplace), Gaspard Flori (Christian Laplace), Emilie Aubry (Lucie Laplace), Hans Peter Cloos (Monsieur Duphour-Paquet), Maite Nahyr (Madeleine Duphour-Paquet), Julie Aubier (Sabine Duphour-Paquet), Baptiste Blanchet (Marc Duphour-Paquet), Jean-Pierre Beauviala (Colas), Mathieu Amalric (Julien), Christiane Bailly (Agnes), Rene Vo Van Mindh (Jean), Katja Rupé (Claire). Bernard Eisenschitz (Gustave), François Michel (Philippe), Fanny Dupin (Rivière), Vincent Blanchet (Pluton), Gabriella Scheer (Nicole), Marie-Claude Pouvesle (Christine), Marie Parra Aledo (Blanche).

Director Otar Ioseliani left the Georgian Republic of the Soviet Union some time ago after compiling an enviable international record with three features: "When the Leaves Fall" (1966) (Critics' Prize, Cannes 1968), "Once There Was a Song-Thrush" (1970) (Directors' Fortnight, Cannes 1974), and "Pastorale" (1976) (Critics' Prize, Berlin 1981). It took some five years for "Pastorale" to receive permission to leave the country, whereupon the director went with it to take up residence in Paris.

"Favoris de la Lune" (rough translation: "Minions Of The Moon") doesn't have a plot to speak of: it simply rambles along, like Ioseliani's other stories that rest

almost solely on a couple of key motifs to spur the action in one direction or another.

(U.S. distrib Spectrafilm is planning to release the pic next year with the title "Thieves" (Voleurs).)

Pic opens with a 19th-century salon painter doing a portrait of a nude to sell on the market, which later in our own time gets sold in Paris at an auction along with a magnificent set of porcelain. These bourgeois treasures, along with a handful of jewelry, then begin to trade hands among thieves and conmen, gunrunners and antique collectors, the guilty and the innocent. The fun is had in watching these objects change hands as familiar faces pass each other on streets or in cafés or even behind prison bars, until the painting has been cut down to the lady's head and the broken porcelain to a makeshift ashtray.

What Ioseliani is perhaps trying to say is that the human comedy can play wicked tricks on the pretentious and cruel jokes on the weak and unwary. None of the people is what society would term a "contributing" citizen, yet they all play their roles for better or for worse. Take the Jacques Tati-style policeman, for instance. He's as common in the social fabric as the aging prostitute with the cats on her bed, or the manner in which a casual affair is fabricated behind a café window in wordless dialog.

One feels compelled to compare Ioseliani to William Saroyan, for a Georgian director and an American-Armenian writer undoubtedly have much in common. But the French influence is also there, via scripter Gérard Brach, who undoubtably contributed much to the tale of twisting coincidences.

Film is the kind of sleeper that could develop into a winner on the arthouse circuit with proper handling. —*Holl.*

Il Futuro E' Donna
(The Future Is Woman)
(ITALIAN/FRENCH/
W. GERMAN-COLOR)

Venice, Aug. 31.
A C.I.D.I.F. release, produced by Achille Manzotti for Faso Film, U.G.C.SA. (Neuilly sur Seine) and Ascot Film GmbH. (Berlin). Directed by Marco Ferreri. Stars Hanna Schygulla, Ornella Muti. Screenplay, Ferreri, Dacia Maraini and Piera Degli Esposti; camera (color), Tonino Delli Colli; art director, Dante Ferretti; costumes, Nicoletta Ercole; editor, Ruggero Mastroianni; music, Carlo Savina. Reviewed at the Venice Film Festival (in competition), Aug. 31, 1984. Running time: **105 MINS.**

Malvina . . . . Ornella Muti
Anna . . . . Hanna Schygulla
Gordon . . . . Niels Arestrup

Marco Ferreri, masterful director of black humor Italian-style ("La Grande Bouffe," "Dillinger Is Dead"), strikes out at bat with "The Future Is Woman," sent to Venice in competition. Tale of a couple's *menage a trois* with a pregnant free spirit becomes absurd at the very start and never manages to find its way. Only ardent Ornella Muti fans will want to attend, in order to see her as a glowing pre-mama. Hanna Schygulla addicts will be disappointed.

At first glances Ferreri's approach to unwed motherhood — which he says inspired him to make the film — appears to be from a radical, pro-femme viewpoint. Lending their credentials are Dacia Maraini and Piera Degli Esposti, two well-known feminists who co-penned the script. It is not long, though, before the filmgoer begins to suspect someone is pulling his leg.

Anna (Schygulla) and Gordon (Niels Arestrup) have decided against bringing children into a world destined for nuclear annihilation. She is a marketing exec for a supermarket; he transplants trees. Their post-Sixties life-style includes frequent trips to the disco, and it is there they meet Malvina (Muti), a homeless young beauty expecting a child. She moves in and a succession of bonds develops between the characters.

Jealous of the intruder and swamped with neurotic anxiety, Anna attempts suicide. Then she and Gordon try to get rid of her, but Anna soon repents. Already she misses the baby, which she senses is destined to become hers.

Tragedy strikes. At a folk concert, a horde of kids break through the police lines to get in and cause a stampede. The one casualty: Gordon, trampled to death while trying to protect his women. Closer than ever, Anna and Malvina have the baby (off-screen) and Malvina hits the road, leaving Anna with the child she always longed for.

This improbable chain of events is shot in a riotous mesh of colorful images by ace cameraman Tonino Delli Colli, playing in and around Dante Ferreti's fantasy sets. No eccentricity is barred: friends come and go reciting Shakespeare, Anna screens old Garbo pics in her office over-the shopping aisles, and Anna and Malvina cavort in belly-hugging evening gowns through nightmarish discos.

All this sounds like more fun than it is. Pic takes itself seriously and flounders through portentious symbolism and dubious myths of motherhood. The only message that comes over clearly is helmer's fear of emasculating women (consistent with his last batch of films) and paranoia over the disappearance of the male sex, superfluous even for having babies.

Actors seem a little disoriented by it all. Muti closes herself off in splendid, Sphinxlike calm, Schygulla flutters around as a magnetic but undirected presence, and Arestrup, a passive tool, just waits quietly for his end. —*Yung.*

Paar
(The Crossing)
(INDIAN-COLOR)

Venice, Aug. 30.
An Orchid Films (Private) production, released by National Film Development Corp. of India. Produced by Swapan Sarkar. Directed by Goutam Ghose. Stars Naseeruddin Shah, Shabana Azmi. Screenplay, Partha Bannerjee, Goutam Ghose, from a short story by Samaresh Bose; camera (Eastmancolor) & music, Goutam Ghose; art director, Ashoke Bose; editor, Prasanta De; costumes, Neelanjana Ghose; Reviewed at Venice Film Festival (in competition), Aug. 29, 1984. Running time: 132 MINS.
Naurangia .... Naseeruddin Shah
Rama .... Shabana Azmi
With: Om Puri, Mohan Aghase, Utpal Dutta, Anil Chatterjee, Ruma Cuha Thakurta.

"Paar" is a grim, exhausting look at caste conflicts and poverty in contemporary India, which deserves festival exposure and kudos but which will be tough to sell, even to arthouse audiences.

Still, this impressive feature by youthful Goutam Ghose deserves to be seen on its no-holds-barred depiction of life for Untouchables both in the villages of troubled Bihar and on the streets of Calcutta.

Film opens in the tiny village of Korir, in the Monghyr district of Bihar; long-running antagonism between the Harijan (untouchable) villagers and the landowners has reached a climax when a Harijan scores a win in a local election. Riots ensue, and several are killed, with Harijan homes burned. Among the dead is a popular and progressive local schoolteacher. (These incidents are based on real events; as recently as January 1984, eight people, including children, were killed in a Bihar village.)

Fearing for his life, Naurangia (Naseeruddin Shah) and his pregnant wife Rama (Shabana Azmi) flee their village and arrive, destitute, in over-crowded Calcutta. They have an introduction to someone from their home district who may help Naurangia find a job; but he's nowhere to be found. So the couple join the thousands of homeless sleeping on the streets, until they agree to take a dangerous and bizarre job: to avoid paying transportation costs, an unscrupulous man wants them to swim across the wide, fast-flowing river with a small herd of pigs.

This climax, vividly presented, is a kind of calvary for the couple, as man and wife, and the frightened animals, brave the river and nearly drown, only to be paid a pittance at the end of it. It brings the drama to a gripping finale.

Ghose, who handled the excellent cinematography as well as composing the score, emerges as a top-rank Indian director with this film. Born in 1950, he has an important career ahead of him. His superb thesps, among the best and busiest actors in quality Indian films, are deserving of highest praise. Pacing is leisurely, of course, but for audiences willing to surrender themselves to the rhythm of this important and moving film, there will be ample rewards. —*Strat.*

La Neve Nel Bicchiere
(A Glassful Of Snow)
(ITALIAN-COLOR)

Venice, Aug. 27.
An Istituto Luce/Italnoleggio release, produced by Gianni Federici for Ve.Ga. Produzione and RAI-TV Channel 1. Directed by Florestano Vancini. Features entire cast. Screenplay, Massimo Felisatti, based on a novel by Nerino Rossi; camera (Color), Aldo Di Marcantonio; art director, Elio Balletti; editor, Enzo Meniconi; music, Carlo and Paolo Rustichelli. Reviewed at the Venice Film Festival, Aug. 27, 1984. Running time: 150 MINS.
Venanzio .... Massimo Ghini
Mariena .... Anna Teresa Rossini
Medea .... Antonia Piazza
Ligio .... Luigi Mezzanotte
Argia .... Anna Lelio
Widow .... Teresa Ricci
Nullo .... Marne Maitland
Don Angelo .... Peter Chatel

The saga of three generations of peasant sharecroppers in the Emilia Romagna region of northern Italy unwinds in two and a half hours, cut down from a much greater amount of material in its literary source, a novel by Nerino Rossi. Florestano Vancini's straightforward story-telling covers the distance with good craftsmanship, sensitivity and lively sympathy for the characters. Drama and emotion are present in a far lesser degree. Though its heart is in the right place, this Italnoleggio/Istituto Luce release, co-produced by RAI-TV, has a hard time getting off the ground. The result is dignified, but unexciting.

Tale begins with grandpa Nullo's decision to leave the back-breaking manual labor of canal-building in the Po Valley and start a new life as a sharecropper. Nullo (Marne Maitland) contracts with Don Angelo (Peter Chatel), a parish priest, to work his land. At the same time his elder son Venanzio (Massimo Ghini) becomes a carriage driver.

The peasants' will to change and better their situation is the theme running through the film. This is the light in which the early farm leagues appear, where Venanzio soon becomes a leader. As dreams of revolution fade, Venanzio turns to literacy as the poor people's best weapon in the social struggle.

Interwoven with these events are personal joys and sorrows: the death of the grandmother from Pellagra, Venanzio's marriage to Mariena (Anna Teresa Rossini), the birth of children. Vancini has a gift for portraying events with great naturalness and conviction.

Yet the very even-handedness of the picture works to its disadvantage in the end, keeping the story skimming the surface rather than diving in deeper at moments of greater dramatic interest. The first rumblings of Fascism are heard, Venanzio moves his family to a new house, and his sons leave home against his will. Only his youngest son is left to carry on his ideals.

Print screened in competition at Venice was noticeably faded in color, partly as a result of its 16m to 35m blowup. Thesping is excellent throughout, including work by many non-pros. — *Yung.*

Illusione
(Illusion)
(SWISS-COLOR)

Venice, Sept. 2.
A Frama Film International production, in association with Ananda Film-SSR/RTSI. Directed and written by Jerko V. Tognala. Camera (Eastmancolor). Giorgio Battilana; music, Mario Robbiani, Tognala; costumes, Lia Morandini. No further credits available. Reviewed at Venice Film Festival (non-competing). Sept. 2, 1984. Running time: 89 MINS.
Johnny Pista .... Dino Conti
Ramona Pista .... Adelheid Kock
Sissy Dollar ...... Franca Maria De Monti
Sarah Schupita .... Milva
Franz Kula/Rosa Foka .... Mary Laaf
The m.c. .... Alessandro Balducci
Johnny's mother .... Valerie Lush

"Illusions" is an enjoyably bizarre mystery comedy about a night-club magician whose wife and partner literally vanishes one night during their act. There seems to be no explanation and though Johnny searches (rather half-heartedly) for her, he soon has himself a new partner, who quickly becomes his mistress, too. Then, rather inconveniently, his wife reappears as mysteriously as she disappeared.

Alongside the main story of the magician-hero's odd predicament, there are a variety of interesting subsidiary characters, including the nightclub owner (Mary Laaf) who finds more success on stage in drag than he does in his male persona. Adelheld Kock is charming as the wife, while Franca Maria De Monti makes a lively contribution as the woman who replaces her. As the befuddled magician, Dino Conti is a bit too knowingly charming, but manages to suggest the bewilderment and at the same time the sense of new freedom the character experiences.

The denouement is satisfactorily offbeat and the whole film, tightly paced and professionally made, is modestly enjoyable throughout. It was made in the Italian part of Switzerland, with locations in Lugano and Bellinzona. —*Strat.*

Wundkanal
(Gun-Wound)
(W. GERMAN/FRENCH-COLOR)

Venice, Aug. 29.

A Quasar Film Production, Berlin, in association with Wieland Schulz-Keil (Paris). Produced by Heike Geschonneck, Wieland Schulz-Keil. Directed by Thomas Harlan. Screenplay, Yvette Biro, Harlan; camera (color), Henri Alékan; art direction, Max Berto; costumes and design, Carlo Cattaneo, Françoise Rabut; editor, Patricia Mazuy; production managers, Patrick Dumont, Ulrich Adomat, Norbet Lassek; video, Robert Kramer, Gérad Pierrard. Reviewed at Venice Film Fest (Special Program), Aug. 28, '84. Running time: 112 MINS.
With: Alfred "F" (Doktor "S"), Robert Kramer, Heike Geschonneck, Francoise Rabut, Rolf Niffuag, the voices of Libgart Schwarz, Peter Fitz, Margit Broich, Thomas Boothby.

___

Thomas Harlan's "Wundkanal" (also titled for a time "Doktor S." and "Execution For Four Voices") paired with Robert Kramer's "Our Nazi" to become the most talked about "special event" of the first week at Venice. The title refers to a term used to describe the trace of a bullet into the body (in this case the head or neck region) by which a person has been killed. In the course of the film, a man in advanced old age fiddles with a gun pointed at his own neck and at others while trying to put the final touches on a dialog between himself and a quartet of voices plaguing his conscience with questions.

The man is "Doktor S.," a Nazi war criminal guilty of killing over 11,000 people in White Russia and Lithuania 30 years ago during the Eastern Front campaign of World War II. Since the individual has now been set free (due to old age, after serving 18 years in prison), he feels a certain injustice has been done in that the whole truth has never been told. He wants to clear his conscience, so to speak, and director Harlan worked out a deal with him to tell his story together with a double (an East German actor named Erwin Geschonneck). This original ploy, however, fell through when Hungarofilm (an eventual coproduction partner) got cold feet at the last minute and canceled their part of the contract. So producer Wieland Schulz-Keil stepped in to rescue the project.

All the better, so far as the finished production is concerned, for a former Nazi war criminal tells his own story in his own way, thus one gets the opportunity to dig below the surface of unusual subject matter. As far as can be determined, this is the first time such a dialog has taken place on screen in which the criminal both affirms his Nazi atrocities and then denies everything in the very next breath when questioned further on the matter. The Nazi was bitterly disappointed at losing his post of being second-in-

command in the Nazi Secret Service when his long-lost brother returned home from America to visit the family at a very inopportune moment (just as the curtain on the war-theater was about to go up). The brother was rather outspoken in his criticism of Hitler and Nazism, which was to later cost him his life in Buchenwald. Meanwhile, "Doktor S." had to work his way back up in the party and SS by taking on the more gruesome task of liquidating civilians in Russia and Lithuania. When Harlan pushes his man against the wall with sharper questioning (via voices transmitted to Doktor S. by way of a tiny microphone taped to his subject's head) the viewer expects results. However, one goes away more puzzled than ever. —Holl.

Unser Nazi
(Our Nazi)
(W. GERMAN/FRENCH-DOCU-B&W)

Venice, Aug. 28.

A Quasar Film, Berlin, and Reass Film, Paris, coproduction, produced by Heike Geschonneck in association with Wieland Schulz-Keil and with the participation of the Bibliothéque Publique d'Information/Centre Pompidou, Paris. Directed and photographed (b&w), by Robert Kramer. Audio, Olivier Schwob; assistant director, Gérard Pierrard; editor, Sheherazade Saadi; sound editor, Yasha Aginsky; recording, Daniel Deshayes; video, Francis Garret; production managers, Patrick Dumont, Ulrich Adomat, Norbert Lassek. Reviewed at Venice Film Fest (Special Program), August 27, '84. Running time: 114 MINS.
With: Alfred Filbert (Doktor "S"), Thomas Harlan (the director), Hertz Natif (makeup man), Ursula Langmann (interpreter), Henri Alékan (director of photography), Jimmie Glasberg (camera opeator), Roland Allard (photographer), Heike Geschonneck (assistant director), George Liatard (double), Pierrot Devos (chief electrician).

___

Robert Kramer's "Our Nazi" was programmed in Venice as a special program presentation together with Thomas Harlan's "Wundkanal" (Gun-Wound), with good reason: Kramer's docu-fiction is about Harlan's film being made. One could argue that he has made a documentary about the process of filmmaking, but it's far more than that, for somewhere along the line he has become so involved in the thematic material that he has made an independent statement of his own.

Harlan is a German-born director (raised in various cultures and a multi-linguist), who also happens to be the son of a famous director who made films for Goebbels under the Third Reich: Veit Harlan. The son is trying to purge himself of his father's propaganda-laden past, and he does so by making a film featuring a Nazi criminal (forget his name: it's not that important even though he's identified in the film). "Our Nazi" (as Kramer tags him in

the title) had served 18 years in prison upon being convicted of killing 11,449 people on the Eastern Front during the war; he's now been released due to ill health, failing eyesight and just plain old age.

Apparently to "exonerate" himself, the former Nazi war criminal decides to address himself to the cameras in an on-going dialog with a film director harried by his family's past. This process of two quite opposite individuals involved in a film project spurred Yank filmer Robert Kramer to pick up his video-camera and start shooting.

Per reports, Kramer recorded on videotape some 80 hours of "rushes" on Harlan interrogating both the Nazi war criminal and himself on Germany's past shame. This video material was then transferred to 35m film stock with amazing visual results ("I simply filmed from the video screen") via a selective process to guarantee both objectivity and room for a subjective opinion on the matter. It's this personal viewpoint that makes the film. Kramer, in fact, raises questions only the viewer himself can answer: why are we fascinated by this criminal, and why do we rather willingly join Harlan's own quest for answers on the matter?

It's a film that haunts, and one that begs for a followup discussion on the issues it raises. At Venice, it was one of the major events of the first week. — Holl.

Jukkai No Mosukito
(The Mosquito On The Tenth Floor)
(JAPANESE-COLOR)

Venice, Aug. 31.

An N.C.P. production. Produced by Yoshihiro Yuki. Directed by Yoichi Tosaka Sai. Features entire cast. Screenplay, Yuya Uchida, Yoichi Tosaka Sai; camera (color), Masaru Mori; music, Katsuo Ohno. No further credits available. Reviewed at Venice Film Festival (Critics Section), Aug. 30, 1984. Running time: 110 MINS.
The policeman	Yuya Uchida
Girlfriend	Ann Lewis
Toschie	Kazuko Yoshiyuki
Rie	Kyoko Koizumi
Keiko	Reiko Nakamura
Bargirl	Junko Miyashita
Police chief	Kei Sato

___

A promising, if deeply pessimistic, first feature which reveals Yoichi Tosaka Sai a newcomer with visual flair and an uncompromising style, this tale of a city cop on the skids is unlikely to find its mark abroad, owing to a certain repetitiveness and gloomy theme.

Unnamed protagonist was once an efficient cop, but since his wife left him two years earlier, he's heading on a downward path. He drinks too much, he's deeply in debt, and he has a nasty habit of raping every woman he meets. Film charts his downfall mercilessly until he finally goes berserk and robs a bank.

Yuya Uchida, who co-authored the screenplay with the director, is memorable as the rogue cop, and indeed thesping is fine down the line.

But, despite the promise involved, Sai's debut feature is a depressing affair, which adds little to the theme of a man destroyed by women. The cop's teenage daughter treats him with disdain and sponges off him, while his wife (who left him for unexplained reasons) ignores him. His only comfort is a home computer, with which he plays obsessively.

The rape scenes are unlikely to endear the pic to women in western countries, and the central character is basically unsympathetic and frustratingly self-destructive. Though he puts the blame on the women in his life, he is obviously the problem.

The setting, which looks to be an unnamed provincial city, is used in exemplary fashion and the film gets by on its striking visuals and strong central performance. —Strat.

Noi Tre
(We Three)
(ITALIAN-COLOR)

Venice, Aug. 30.

An Istituto Luce/Italnoleggio release, produced by Antonio Avati for Istituto Luce/Italnoleggio, Due Film and RAI-TV Channel 1. Directed by Pupi Avati. Features entire cast. Screenplay, Pupi Avati, Antonio Avati; camera (color), Pasquale Rachini; art direction, Giancarlo Basili, Leonardo Scarpa; editor, Amedeo Salfa; costumes, Alberto Spiazzi; music, Riz Ortolani. Reviewed at the Venice Film Festival (in competition), Aug. 29, 1984. Running time: 90 MINS.
Amadè	Christopher Davidson
Leopoldo	Lino Capolicchio
Cousin	Gianni Cavino
Count Pallovicini	Carlo Delle Piane
Maria Caterino	Ida Di Benedetto
Giuseppe	Dario Parisini
Antonia-Leda	Barbara Rebeschini

___

Pupi Avati, the film board of Bologna who brought "A School Outing" to last year's Venice Film Festival, has turned up a whimsical bit of local lore, the brief sojourn of Wolfgang Amadeus Mozart in Bologna when he was 14, that is the starting point of "We Three." Story is lightweight and played for laughs, not biographical profundity. But helmer's affectionate sketches of provincial life have been slowly building an audience of fans over the years and pic's faithfulness to the form should bring it onshore trade. Offshore film could have life as a children's program.

"Amadè" (Christopher Davidson) and his father (Lino Capolicchio) arrive at the country estate of eccentric old Count Pallavicini (Carlo Delle Piane) and his wife (Ida Di Benedetto). The child genius is to take a prestigious music exam that will consecrate him officially as a composer. Scripters Pupi and Antonio Avati then imagine that Amadè lives a brief moment of happy, carefree childhood. At first he is snubbed by the count's son Giuseppe (Dario Parisini), but enmity soon turns into fast friendship. The two pals are joined by a pretty young neighbor, Antonia-Leda (Barbara Rebeschini) in various innocent frolics.

In the end Amadè deliberately tries to flunk his exam to remain with them, but to no avail. He can't escape his destiny.

Young thesps are high-spirited and attractive, but unconvincing as 18th century youths, English actor Davidson simply does not look the part; all three speak modern Bolognese slang and behave like the kids next door with permissive parents.

Deliberately putting aside musical questions (almost the entire score is a Mozart-like theme by Riz Ortolani), helmer concentrates on the human side of the composer and his presumed longing to be just another kid. The point remains suggested rather than developed. It is helmer's stock troupe that carries pic through its weak moments. Capolicchio lends dignity to the figure of Amadè's loving but ambitious father. —*Yung.*

El Balcón Abierto
(The Open Balcony)
(SPANISH-DOCU-COLOR)

Venice, Aug. 31.

A Tibidabo Films production for Television Española. Produced by José L. Garcia Arrojo. Directed by Jaime Camino. Features entire cast. Script, José Amoros; editor, Teresa Alcover; music, Emilio De Diego. Reviewed at Venice Film Festival (noncompeting), Aug. 31. 1984. Running time: 95 MINS.
With: José Luis Gómez (the voice of the poet), Amparo Muñoz, Antonio Flores, Berta Riaza, Alvaro De Luna.

Catalan director Jaime Camino has made a long-awaited, personal tribute to the great poet and dramatist Federico Garcia Lorca, who was senselessly murdered in August 1936, aged 38, in the early days of the Civil War. Lorca, whose best known work internationally is probably "Blood Wedding," was shot, together with two others, by supporters of Franco. His death was just one of countless atrocities during that tragic war, yet, as Camino shows, Spanish school children today have only a vague idea as to who Lorca was, and also hardly know what the Civil War was all about. Yet Lorca has influenced a whole generation of writers, poets and filmmakers, including Carlos Saura and Camino himself (whose excellent "The Long Vacation Of '36" dealt trenchantly with the war period).

Present film opens and closes with a re-enactment of the poet's death, seen at the beginning from the point of view of his murderers and at the end from the victim's.

Both scenes are shattering in impact. In between, Camino uses actor José Luis Gómez to read some of Lorca's poetry as a kind of narrative link for images from the writer's life; luminously shot scenes of Granada, the city where he was born, and also of Seville and New York, which he visited.

His homosexuality is touched on, but no motive is given for his murder. There are also richly handled dramatic sequences from his work, in which some of his favorite themes, notably involving a mother figure, come to life. All this is framed by school kids finding out about the dead man, examining photos of him (with Luis Buñuel and Salvador Dali pictured among others) and old newsreel footage.

Film is a bit indulgent at times, and the inclusion of a rather long breakdance routine in the New York sequence seems quite unnecessary. But overall, Camino's achievement is to bring the world of Lorca back for today's viewers in a most evocative way so we weep for the waste involved and for the wonderful works never written.
— *Strat.*

L'Inceneritore
(The Incinerator)
(ITALIAN-COLOR)

Venice, Aug. 27.

A Titanus release, produced by Bruno Sanguin for Tecnofilm Cinematografica (Padua). Stars Flavio Bucci, Ida Di Benedetto. Written and directed by Pier Francesco Boscaro Dagli Ambrosi. Camera (color), Roberto Girometti; art director, Lorenzo Forin; editor, Gianfranco Amicucci; costumes, Patrizia Zappaterra; music, Richard Benson. Reviewed at the Venice Film Festival (Vittorio De Sica section), Aug. 27, 1984. Running time: 90 MINS.
Hunchback .... Flavio Bucci
Mora .... Ida Di Benedetto
Fedora ...... Alexandra Delli Colli Groski
Grandpa .... Pietro Francescato

Screened in the Venice De Sica section for first and second features, "The Incinerator" is an absurdist comedy with moments of great vitality and ironic humor, made on the fringes of the industry under conditions that make its very existence remarkable. Youthful helmer Pier Francesco Boscaro Degli Ambrosi found funding for his project with the help of a group of Paduan industrialists and engaged two well-known actors to star, Flavio Bucci and Ida Di Benedetto. Money ran out and film sat on the shelf for three years before it was possible to resume shooting recalling actors and matching old material. Titanus, which is to release, has agreed to finance better sound and some crucial special effects missing from the end of the picture.

The audience for this film will be teens and young people attracted by its comic strip unreality, imaginative characters drawn from familiar

stereotypes and its general spirit of disillusionment with a violent and inhuman society. Pic has no real story, only a collection of situations that seem to be moving to an inevitable but at first mysterious conclusion.

Main characters are a hunchback (Bucci) who spends his time performing strange experiments on animals in his laboratory, the worldly young countess Fedora (Alexandra Delli Colli Groski) involved in strange games with her two Spanish bodyguards; and Mora (Ida Di Benedetto), a prostitute. Film opens with the bloody murder and dismemberment of a "student nurse" on her way home. As it proceeds the number of homicides multiplies dizzyingly.

Each victim is disposed of in a garbage bag and burned in the city incinerator. By the end almost the entire population of the town is lying around the street in black bags, waiting for the sanitation trucks to cart them away. The survivors all wear an amulet showing three monkeys: see/hear/speak no evil. Anyone trying to speak out against the slaughter is killed.

Degli Ambrosi works his way skillfully around budget limitations. Film is clearly patched together out of bits and pieces, but is cut so fast it doesn't matter. Most of it is very entertaining, with a tone as offhandedly provocative as "Rocky Horror Picture Show." Where it falters is in an over-long ending which needs to be considerably trimmed when the final "special effect" is added: the overloaded incinerator spewing forth an apocalyptic cloud. An interesting debut effort. — *Yung.*

Uno Scandalo Perbene
(A Proper Scandal)
(ITALIAN-COLOR)

Venice, Aug. 30.

A P.I.C. release, produced by Fulvio Lucisano for Italian International Films and Screen World in collaboration with RAI-TV Channel 2. Directed by Pasquale Festa Campanile. Stars Ben Gazzara, Giuliana De Sio. Screenplay, Suso Cecchi D'Amico; camera (color), Alfio Contini; art director, Enrico Fiorentini; editor, Antonio Siciliano; music, Riz Ortolani. Reviewed at the Venice Film Festival (in competition), Aug. 28, 1984. Running time: 119 MINS.
Amnesiac .... Ben Gazzara
Giulia Canella .... Giuliana De Sio
Camilla .... Valeria D'Obici

"A Proper Scandal" raised comment even before it was screened at Venice, because helmer Pasquale Festa Campanile's commercial savvy and skill at hitting the jackpot with formula comedies had never given rise to the suspicion he was a Golden Lion aspirant. Pic was direly misplaced in the competitive section. Locating it in Venice TV (P.I.C. release is the two-hour cut of a three-part television miniseries)

would have made more sense. Though Festa Campanile has shown the Midas touch with comedy, he is still untested at the boxoffice with historical mystery, and pic's commercial results may be less gratifying than usual.

Much would seem to depend on whether audiences can get involved in a great mystery story that filled the papers between the wars and kept the public interested for years. The Bruneri-Canella case begins in 1926, when an unidentified man (Ben Gazzara) in shabby clothes is caught stealing flowerpots from a cemetery in Turin. In the film scripted by Suso Cecchi D'Amico, he is brutally interrogated at a police station where he says he can't remember his name. Locked in a nightmarish mental asylum as a victim of amnesia, he is eventually identified from a newspaper photo as the wealthy Prof. Canella of Verona, missing in action during the war.

Gazzara plays the amnesiac as a gentleman who mildly submits to every mortification, until a beautiful young wife comes to reclaim him. Giulia (Giuliana De Sio) doesn't recognize the husband she lost many years before, nor he her. For reasons the film leaves unclarified, however, she decides to identify the stranger. Festa Campanile glosses over motivations and emotions with an embarrassingly obvious sex scene, and the couple is divinely united.

Their happiness is short-lived. The world intrudes in the form of a rival identification: another family, mistress and debtors claim Gazzara is a con man from Turin specializing in impersonations. In trial after trial, the true identity of Canella-Bruneri is debated. Gazzara spends most of the rest of the film in jail, with outings to search for "Bruneri." Film tries to keep audience guessing, but broadly hints at its own Bruneri hypothesis.

While Gazzara is likable and believable as the amnesiac/imposter, co-star De Sio opts for a modern interpretation of Mrs. Canella that is disturbingly out of period. Technically pic is filled with wobbly zooms and blatant small screen closeups. All seems aimed at a broad public, which may or may not respond to an old-fashioned puzzle done with a knowing, contemporary wink.
— *Yung.*

Rok Spokojnego Slonca
(The Year Of The Quiet Sun)
(POLISH-U.S.-W. GERMAN-COLOR)

Venice, Aug. 29.

A Film Polski, "Tor" Film Unit, Warsaw, coproduction with TeleCulture, N.Y.-Munich, and Regina Ziegler Filmproduktion, Berlin. Features Maja Komorowska and Scott Wilson. Written and directed by Krzysztof Marek Denys; music, Wojciech Kilar; costumes, Maria Biedrzycka; sound Wieslaw Dembin-

ski. Reviewed at Venice Film Fest (competition), Aug. 28, '84. Running time: 107 MINS.
Emilia . . . . Maja Komorowska
Norman . . . . Scott Wilson
The mother . . . . Hanna Skarzanka
Stella . . . . Ewa Dalkowska
David . . . . Daniel Webb
Hermann . . . . Vadim Glowna
Szary . . . . Zbigniew Zapasiewicz
The translator . . . . Tadeus Bradecki
The doctor . . . . Jerzy Nowak
Adzio . . . . Jerzy Stuhr

Present in Venice with two films (one in competition, the other in the tv section), Krzysztof Zanussi has accomplished just about the impossible in view of the hard times Film Polski and the Assn. of Polish Filmmakers have fallen upon since December 1981. His competing pic, "The Year Of The Quiet Sun," is the better of the two (the tv entry is a straightforward literary adaptation of Max Frisch's story, "Bluebeard"), although it will go down in the books as minor Zanussi in comparison with his strictly "Polish" productions.

It will, however, prove accessible to general audiences on the arthouse circuit and with proper handling prove once and for all that the gifted intellectual Polish director can handle an international production, given the right thematic material.

"The Year Of The Quiet Sun" takes place in Polish-occupied Germany immediately after World War II, a village near the newly drawn border that's now filled with a mixture of personalities and nationalities in view of a military inquest into the wartime atrocities at a POW camp. In short, this is a love story, between a Polish refugee from the east (probably an area that's presently a part of the Soviet Union) and an American soldier who is part of the inquest because he is one of the sole survivors of the camp.

Zanussi doesn't tell us why or how the American (Scott Wilson) should happen to fall in love with the shy and retiring widow Emilia (Maja Komorowska), but the tragedies of war are such that two lonely and silent individuals need only to communicate mutely with their hearts and awkwardly with strained gestures.

Emilia is living with her invalid mother in a dank, old apartment building amidst the rubble and ruins of a seemingly once-prosperous town. Her neighbors, all Poles, save for a single German (a former member of the Wehrmacht), are lost souls for the most part; the one exception is a next-door prostitute, a woman Emilia eventually takes pity on and helps to cross the border at the very moment when she is about to leave the place to join Norman in Berlin and become his bride.

For, meanwhile, her mother has made the ultimate sacrifice and refused medical treatment in order to die and leave her daughter a chance for happiness. Why this should be Emilia's only opportunity to join

Norman in the States at some time in the future is not explained. But Zanussi has made a metaphorical, symbol-laden feature, and not a story for its own sake.

Lead and supporting thesps are pic's saving grace, plus ace lensing in autumnal browns and yellows.
— *Holl.*

The Goodbye People
(U.S.-COLOR)

Toronto, Sept. 8.
An Embassy Pictures release of a Coney Island Prods. production. Produced by David V.Picker. Associate producer, Mel Howard. Direction and screenplay by Herb Gardner, based on his stage play. Camera (Deluxe color). John Lindley; editor, Rick Shaine; production and costume design, Tony Walton; set decoration, Chris Kelly; sound, Billy Daly; production manager, Mel Howard. Reviewed at the Festival of Festivals (Contemporary World Cinema), Toronto, Sept. 8, 1984. (MPAA Rating: PG.) Running time 104 MINS.
Arthur Korman . . . . Judd Hirsch
Max Silverman . . . . Martin Balsam
Nancie (Shirley) Scot . . . . Pamela Reed
Eddie Bergson . . . . Ron Silver
Michael Silverman . . . . Michael Tucker
Marcus Soloway . . . . Gene Saks

"The Goodbye People" marks stage author and director Herb Gardner's first foray into film direction. Based on his 15-year old stage flop of the same name, neither time nor the transferal of media has improved the story of three eccentric losers who band together in hopes of changing their luck.

Basically a one-set (albeit a beachfront location) human comedy, the film centers on Arthur Korman (Judd Hirsch), a man in his 40s trapped in a job he cannot stand. To relieve the tension stemming from his inability to chuck working at a toy firm, he makes a daily early morning excursion to Coney Island to watch the sunrise. It is there he meets Max Silverman (Martin Balsam), the former owner of a boardwalk hot dog stand.

Max still harbors dreams of reopening his eatery which have intensified since a recent heart attack. The susceptible Arthur soon finds himself caught up in the other man's grand scheme.

Matters are complicated by the arrival of Max' daughter Shirley (Pamela Reed). Long-absent from the scene, Shirley was unaware of her father's illness or subsequent plans to resurrect his emporium (Max' Hawaiian ecstasies). She too is a dreamer, having changed both her nose and name (Nancie Scot).

The uneasy alliance between these characters is treated in a glib fashion by Gardner. The dialog is superficial, laced with presumably comic barbs. However, underlying it all is an illsuited strain of sentimentality.

Nonetheless, his three actors defiantly attempt to overcome the shallowness of observation with their own humanity. Best of the lot is Reed who invests a genuine sense of vulnerability to Shirley-Nancie. Also strong are Michael Tucker as Max' lawyer son in a well-perceived generational clash with his father, and Ron Silver, Shirley's husband, who wants his old wife back but is willing to accept her new incarnation.

The side stories easily supercede the main thrust of the drama. A fur-

ther diminution of emotional power comes from the basically claustrophobic nature of the piece and Gardner's own pedestrian direction. Certainly, the former worked perfectly in the author's play and screen version of "A Thousand Clowns." But artistic lightning does not strike twice with "The Goodbye People."

Technical credits are good though uninspired but the score, largely composed of old chestnuts such as "Toot Toot Tootsie" and "California Here I Come," dates the piece in time and sentiment. The entire production seems ill-suited for the screen.

Commercial prospects are dim and Embassy, the film's distributor, will be fortunate to find dates outside major urban centers. Foreign theatrical also seem dubious although small screen and videocassette exhibition with older demographics should be slightly better.
— *Klad.*

The Prey
(COLOR)

Subpar stalker in the woods horror programmer.

A New World Pictures release of an Essex Distributing presentation. Produced by Summer Brown. Executive producer, Joe Steinman. Directed by Edwin Scott Brown. Features entire cast. Screenplay, the Browns; camera (Deluxe color), Teru Hayashi; editor, Michael Barnard; music, Don Peake, sound, Robbie Robinson; special makeup effects, John Carl Buechler; assistant directors, Jenny Townsend, Jesse Wayne; production manager, D.K. Miller; direction, Rober Holzberg; wildlife photography, Gary Gero; Steadicam operator, Randy Nolen; climbing stunts, Don Wilson. Reviewed on Thorn EMI Video cassette, N.Y., Sept. 3, 1984 (MPAA Rating: R). Running time: 80 MINS.
Nancy . . . . Debbie Thureson
Joel . . . . Steve Bond
Debbie . . . . Lori Lethin
Skip . . . . Robert Wald
Gail . . . . Gayle Gannes
Greg . . . . Philip Wenckus
Mark . . . . Jackson Bostwick
Lester Tile . . . . Jackie Coogan
Sgt. Parsons . . . . Gary Goodrow
Monster . . . . Carel Struycken

"The Prey" is an uneventful, assemblyline horror film, made in 1980 and booked regionally last November by New World Pictures. Pic was produced by Summer Brown, more famous as a femme porno filmmaker, for Essex Distributing, also mainly a hardcore porn outfit, but is a relatively tame R-rated opus.

Trite premise, nearly identical to numerous other films such as "The Final Terror," "Don't Go In The Woods" and "The Forest," has six young hikers in the Keen Wild woods picked off one by one by a stalking monster. It seems that a band of gypsies were burned to a crisp there in 1948, with one gypsy boy surviving and latterly getting mean.

Inane opus is padded out with irrelevant wildlife footage featuring insects, snakes, raccoons and owls and photographed with magnified closeups resembling "The Hellstrom Chronicle" (or some porno film's inserts). Weak script has no characterizations, with many scenes featuring inaudible murmuring instead of dialog. Corny epilog tries for an open ending (the next generation), as in every other horror film of this type.

The late Jackie Coogan, in one of his last film assignments, is rooted behind a desk as a friendly forest ranger. Gore makeup effects are okay, but kept to a minimum.—*Lor.*

A Family Affair
(HONG KONG-COLOR)

Hong Kong, Aug. 25.

A Cinema City Co. Ltd. presentation. Released by Golden Princess theater circuit. Produced by Karl Maka, Dean Shek, Raymond Wong. Directed by Shek. Stars Sam Hui, Olivia Chang, Shek, Jenny Yan, Melvin Wong, Helen Chan and Ben Ben. Screenplay, Lee Chun; camera (color), Henry Chan; production design, Wellington Fung; art director, Honny Lam; music, Mahmood Rumjahn; editor, Tony Chow. Reviewed at President theater, Hong Kong, Aug. 24, 1984. Running time: 98 MINS.

(Cantonese soundtrack with English subtitles)

In "A Family Affair," the supposedly made in heaven marriage of photographer Chan (Sam Hui) and interior designer Nancy (Olivia Chang) ends up in separation. They still love and care for each other, but can't live together anymore without barking at each other. Consequently, their cheerful and precocious children, Maisy (Helen Chan) and Tommy (Ben Ben) are living apart. Maisy is with mom while Tommy is with Dad and grandpa (Dean Shek, almost unrecognizable with a white wig).

Chan starts seeing Linda (singer Jenny Yan in a comedy role) while Nancy dates George (Melvin) Wong in yet another one of his stiff portrayals). The two kids and grandpa connive and plan how to get the estranged couple get back to each other's arms and to daddy's bedroom. But things don't always work out as planned, else how can the producers sustain 98 minutes of Cantonese high comedy.

Mushy but heartwarming, this mass-oriented domestic comedy, with the now patented fast-moving Cinema City formula, has found inspiration in such films as "Kramer vs. Kramer," "Table For Five" and "Mr. Mom." Meanwhile, child actor Ben Ben is endearing and captivating when not overacting. The dialog is often high pitched and deafening with the children's crying and shouting. Aside from that, Chang is lovely in fashionable dresses for every scene and Sam acts vulnerable enough to make one believe his heart-tugging marital problems.

"A Family Affair" should do well in the Chinatown circuits abroad.—*Mel.*

Frankenstein 90
(FRENCH-COLOR)

Paris, Sept. 5.

An AMLF release of a A.J. Films/TF 1 Films co-production. Executive producer, Louis Duchesne. Produced and directed by Alain Jessua. Stars Jean Rochefort, Eddy Mitchell, Fiona Gélin. Screenplay, Jessua, Paul Gégauff; camera (color), William Lubtchansky; art direction, Thierry Flamand, Christian Grosrichard; makeup, Reiko Kruk, Dominique Colladant; costumes, Cat Styvel; editor, Hélène Plemiannikov, music, Armando Trovajoli. Reviewed at the Gaumont Colisée theater, Paris, Sept. 4, 1984. Running time: 90 MINS.
Victor Frankenstein......Jean Rochefort
Frank....................Eddy Mitchell
Elizabeth.................Fiona Gélin
Adelaide..................Herma Vos
Inspector.................Ged Marlon
Commissioner.........Serge Marquand
Corona...................Anna Gaylor

Newest twist on the undying Frankenstein legend comes from france's Alain Jessua. His "Frankenstein 90" grafts a sentimental humoristic variation on the familiar plot, making of Victor Frankenstein a contemporary cybernetics genius (Jean Rochefort) who fits his monster with a microprocessor for a brain.

But the creature is as ugly and lovelorn as ancestor Karloff, always in search of a little cuddle. When his creator throws together a slinky, sexpot mate from the bodies of some murdered disco dancers, the creature is left cold. In fact he prefers the doctor's gentle girl friend (Fiona Gélin), who eventually warms up to the ungainly but sympathetic ogre, while the scientist himself pairs off with his female creation.

The script, by the director and the late screenwriter Paul Gégauff, manages some facile but amiable comic situations, but Jessua gropes unsuccessfully for the right macabre-satiric tone. Tale collapses irremediably in the final part concerning the monster's pilgrimage to Frankenstein castle (inexplicably relocated to the vicinity of Geneva!)

Eddy Mitchell, one of France's top rock singers, is amusing as the hulking eyesore with a good heart. An inveterate film buff, who presents his Hollywood favorites on French tv, Mitchell no doubt had fun with the part, affectionately sending up some monster pic lore. Rochefort and other players seem less at ease. — *Len.*

Wheels On Meals
(HONG KONG-COLOR)

Hong Kong, Aug. 25.

A Golden Harvest production and release. Executive Producer, Raymond Chow. Directed by Samo Hung. Story by Samo Hung. Stars Jackie Chan, Yuen Biao, Samo Hung, Richard Ng and John Sham. (No other credits provided.) Reviewed at State theater, Hong Kong, Aug. 24, 1984. Running time: 98 MINS.

(Cantonese soundtrack with English subtitles)

This jet-speed Cantonese comedy directed by funnyman martial arts expert Samo Hung is the type of attraction that motivates people from all walks of life to come out of their routine lives and jobs ... out in the open, then straight to the theaters. The mindless nonsense of "Wheels On Meals" has its own captive audience here and abroad.

Popular Jackie Chan, sidekick Yuen Biao and Samo with the cameo appearance of Richard Ng and John Sham (superb as asylum residents) are all united in sunny Barcelona, Spain. Jackie and Biao are fast food operators in a food mobile who get involved with a lovely senorita who is not only an expert pickpocket with a mother in a loony bin but is also a missing heiress. Here comes curly-haired Samo as a fumbling detective. The quartet then tries to avoid, outchase, out Kung-Fu, outsmart and outjump the baddies, with a happy ending in store.

Undemanding Golden Harvest regulars and devoted fans of Jackie Chan will smile at this concoction with initial boxoffice grosses proving that "Wheels On Meals" is another solid hit and run operation.

Though basically a Chan picture, Samo Hung is also to be admired for his comic abilities. —*Mel.*

Tir à Vue
(Fire On Sight)
(FRENCH-COLOR)

Paris, Sept. 6.

A Parafrance release of a Lira-Elephant Films production. Produced by Raymond Danon. Directed by Marc Angelo. Screenplay, Yves Mourot, from story idea by Lucas Belvaux; camera (Eastmancolor), Charles Vandamme; art director, Raoul Albert; editor, Nelly Meunier; sound, Michel Laurent; music, Gabriel Yared. Reviewed at Paramount Mercury theater, Paris, Sept. 4, 1984. Running time: 90 MINS.
Marilyn ....Sandrine Bonnaire
Richard..................Laurent Malet
Commissioner Casti.........Jean Carmet
Inspector Galo ....Michel Jonasz

"Tir à Vue," a first film by former assistant director Marc Angelo, is a harebrained Boy-Meets-Girl-Meets-Gun thriller about a young couple on a spree of robbery and murder pursued by a pair of cops who seem in no hurry to apprehend the culprits.

Laurent Malet is at his narcissistic worst as a young punk with a chip on his shoulder who burgles an arms shop and shacks up with a screwy girl who has a secret death wish. They have a roaring good time, committing holdups and shooting cops, but the fun is cut short by spoil-sport policemen Jean Carmet and Michel Jonasz, who conduct an investigation so pointlessly roundabout one begins to wonder if they're in the same picture.

Angelo's direction is perfectly attuned to the empty screenplay by Yves Mourot.

Malet's mate is played by 16-year-old Sandrine Bonnaire, who was so fine as the sexually uncentered girl in Maurice Pialat's acclaimed "A Nos Amours" last season. A few more inane roles like this and she may nip a promising career in the bud. — *Len.*

And Now, What's Your Name?
(HONG KONG-COLOR)

Hong Kong, July 29.

A Golden Harvest Production and release. Produced by Raymond Chow. Executive producer, Wallace Cheung. Directed by Albert Lai. Title song performed by Kenny Bee; story and screenplay, James Wong. Reviewed at State Theater, Hong Kong, July 28, 1984. Running time: 100 MINS.
Cast: Kenny Bee, Mei Suet, Tsang Hing Yue, Lai On Yee.
(Cantonese soundtrack with English subtitles).

"Everybody's got a price tag." Or "Everybody's selling something!" — that's the main theme of an atypical and underplayed contemporary Cantonese drama produced by Golden Harvest, starring current marquee come-on, Kenny Bee. The film fluently states the materialistic, unfeeling and noninvolvement attitude of city folks as seen through a young photographer called C.K. (Bee), as he encounters three kinds of women.

The first is a golddigging, glamorous film and tv star who is the mistress of many rich businessmen, the second is a comely night club hostess who can be hired by the hour but craves for a more lasting relationship and the third is a rich, spoiled rotten debutante who names all her lovers "Simon," then treats them like domesticated canines.

Idealistic and passive C.K. gets intimate with these "today" women and in the process experiences infatuation, a one-night stand mixed with disappointment and then career and social advancement.

The sensitively made movie actually shows how a young man can be eaten up by the establishment, its false values of social success and the preoccupation of keeping "face" in an environment that's generally motivated by the "you scratch my back, I'll scratch yours" way of life. Foreign movies that can be likened to this feature include "The Apprenticeship of Duddy Kravitz" and "Room At The Top."

Unfortunately, the presentation needed a considerable amount of punch and power to achieve its commercial aspirations, yet its simplicity and underplayed passions are some of the presentation's positive qualities since most Cantonese social dramas are often exaggerated to the point of high comedy.

Director Albert Lai (only 31 years old with two features to his credit) lets the major performers breathe sufficient realistic shadings into their roles and he has a wonderful eye for eccentric character details. Meanwhile, the cinematography provides an unflinching, honest look at contemporary Hong Kong's modern residents: the buyers and sellers, the users and the used, the winners and losers, the good, the cunning, the survivors and victims, and the ugly ones whose faces have been poetically stepped on by circumstances or fate. This is the civilized Hong Kong urban jungle where the go-getters get ahead unscathed and unhurt.

The freewheeling lifestyle is reflected in this picture made modestly for $HK1,600,000 which did not make a boxoffice dent ($HK4,600,000) but its universal theme may take it to some prestigious international film fests.

—*Mel.*

Walls
(CANADIAN-COLOR)

Toronto, Sept. 5.
A Jericho Films production. Producers, Christian Bruyere, Tom Shandel. Executive producer, Michael Chechik. Directed by Shandel. Screenplay, Bruyere; camera (color), Douglas McKay; editor, Barbara Evans; music, J. Douglas Dodd, Michael Oczko; art director, Graeme Murray. Reviewed at Toronto Film Festival, Sept. 5, 1984. Running time: 92 MINS.
Joan Tremblay . . . . Andree Pelletier
Danny Baker . . . . Winston Rekert
Ron Simmons . . . . Alan Scarfe
Curt Willis . . . . : . . . John Wright
Louis Martin . . . . John Lord

"Walls" is a prison reform drama that goes through some predictable paces and characterizations to make its point about humanizing abhorrent conditions in penal institutions.

Pic was inspired by a true hostage incident at a British Columbia penitentiary in 1975. Scripter Christian Bruyere transfers his stage play "Walls" to the screen with an inevitable loss of immediacy and tension.

Story concerns the efforts of a liberal prison classifications officer, Joan Tremblay (Andree Pelletier), to inject compassion and empathy into a prison system that sustains violence and dehumanizing practices. She aligns with a civil libertarian lawyer (Alan Scarfe), who's trying to make the case that solitary confinement is "cruel and unusual" punishment.

An incorrigible lifer, Danny Baker (Winston Rekert), is the focal point for info for Tremblay, all the while experiencing the indignity and accompanying madness of solitary. He's released from the "hole" for

a short time with his fellow inmates and works with Tremblay, only to be erroneously charged with drug possession and forced to go back to the concrete 8x10 cells. Faced with the prospect of solitary again, Baker and two cohorts take Tremblay and three other prison workers hostage. The result is a barrage of shots by the hardlined prison officials, killing Tremblay in the process.

Director Shandel time-hops from the outset of the hostage crisis to a flashback of the contributing cumulative factors. The pic becomes mired in predictable dialog from the two opposing camps. Graphic depictions of suicide attempts and drug mainlining add to the grim reality pic strives for.

Tech credits are fine, with some interesting camera angles from Douglas McKay. Rekert gives a tight performance as Baker in turmoil, spewing the embittered tirades that go along with the rage of being a lifer.

"Walls" was a Telefilm Canada Broadcast Fund project for indie UHFer CKVU in Vancouver. Pic doesn't have a distributor yet and downbeat subject matter won't assure commercial success, but a comfortable niche should be found on the fest circuit and on public TV stations. — *Devo.*

Mein Teema
(Main Theme)
(JAPANESE-COLOR)

Tokyo, Aug. 29.
A Toei release of a Haruki Kadokawa production, in cooperation with New Century Producers. Produced by Haruki Kadokawa. Associate producer, Yoshihisa Nakagawa. Written and directed by Yoshimitsu Morita. Camera (color), Yonezo Maeda; lighting, Kazuo Yabe; sound, Osamu Onodera; art, Tatsumi Nakazawa; editing, Akimasa Kawashima; assistant director, Shosuke Kaneko; magic, Hakufu Hiraiwa; fashion adviser, Kumiko Ogawa; music, Osamu Shiomura; theme song lyrics by Takashi Matsumoto. Reviewed at Shibuya Scalaza, Aug. 28, 1984. Running time: 101 MINS.
Shibuki Ogasawara . . Hiroko Yakushimaru
Ken Daitojima . . . . Hironobu Nomura
Wataru Omaezaki . . . . Kazuo Zaitsu
Shizuku Chitose . . . . Yumi Ota
Eri . . . . Jun Togawa
Kayoko Ise . . : . . . . Kaori Momoi
Cameraman . . . . Yuri Kurokawa

"Main Theme" starring Hiroko Yakushimaru is one half of a double-bill release (paired with the Tomoyo Harada starrer "Aijo Monogatari") from producer Haruki Kadokawa, following up on last year's hit pairing of two vehicles with the same stars.

"Theme" is the lesser picture of the duo, with its lead Yakushimaru annually losing her grip on that commodity demanded by audiences here of their "young idols," namely youth.

Yakushimaru (aged 20) plays a 20-year-old kindergarten teacher, but her character's mental and emotion-

al age are clearly much younger. She falls hopelessly in love with the divorced father of one of her pupils, but ends up finding happiness with an itinerant magician. Latter provides Yakushimaru with her first screen kiss, a passionless incident.

Writer-director Yoshimitsu Morita provides occasional instances of deadpan wit and some decent sight gags, but leads Yakushimaru and her costar Hironobu Nomura are ineffective.—*Bail.*

Äntligen
(At Long Last)
(SWEDISH-COLOR)

Stockholm, Aug. 29.
A Swedish Film Institute (SFI) release of Athena Film production for SFI. Original story and script, Christer Dahl and Ami Rolder. Directed by Dahl. Camera (Eastmancolor), Bengt Danneborn, Anders Cederholm. Editor, Göran Aslund, Dahl. Music (no credit given). Executive producer, Göran Guner. Production design, Tofte-Paer Lamberg. Reviewed at the Sandrews' Grand 1 on Aug. 29, 1984. Running time: 89 MINS.
Maria/Vita . . . . Ami Rolder
Ruth . . . . , ... Gudrun Brost
Gunnar . . . . Ulf Eklund
Peter . . . . Kenneth Risberg
Fjodor . . . . Torsten Flink

Having opened to absolutely strangling reviews three weeks ago, Christer Dahl's "Äntligen" (At Long Last) has seen a fast b.o. death. Feature is a semi-surrealistic mix of dream and cruel reality. Not even its message of the survival of the poetic mind comes through with conviction anywhere but in a mid-film sequence of the heroine and a forlorn folk singer finding a mutual sidewalk pitch for their film title tune.

Plot and dialog, concocted by director Dahl and his sister, cutesy Ami Rolder, has the latter running away from her ambition-burdened husband and his eternally rumbling machine for stamping out of plastic Halloween masks. Perhaps her initial exit is just a dream. She seems to have gifts as an angelic redeemer of lost souls' hopes wherever — in idyllic landscapes — she meets them. Then she is abruptly back with her husband and his machine, fighting him, making up (and love) with him, and finally, running off again (naked, of course).

Rolder is obviously a happy little exhibitionist of body and soul. The other players struggle valiantly to appear human, but most of the time they seem like the clumsily oversize adults in a kiddie comedy tv show, as if they had to try to act natural while having their bodies squeezed inside dolls' houses. Unless some Limboland with a fairy-tale tv station exists, "At Long Last" would seem to stand scant chance of having its back-home losses recouped via foreign sales. — *Kell.*

Venice Festival

L'Amour à Mort
(Love Unto Death)
(FRENCH-COLOR)

Venice, Sept. 2.
A Philippe Dussart and Les Films Ariane-Films A2 coproduction, Paris, in collaboration with the Centre National de la Cinématographie and French Ministry of Culture. Foreign sales, Roissy Film, Paris. Directed by Alain Resnais. Features entire cast. Screenplay, Jean Gruault; camera (color), Sacha Vierny; music, Hans Werner Henze; sets, Jacques Saulnier, Philippe Turlure; costumes, Catherine Leterrier; editors, Albert Jurgenson, Jan-Pierre Besnard. Reviewed at Venice Film Fest (competition), Sept. 1, 1984. Running time: 90 MINS.
Elisabeth Sutter . . . . Sabine Azema
Judith Martignac . . . . Fanny Ardant
Simon Roche . . . . Pierre Arditi
Jerome Martignac . . . . André Dussolier
Doctor Rozier . . . . Jean Daste
Anne Jourdet . . . . Genevieve Mnich
The specialist . . . . Jean-Claude Weibel
Michel Garenne . . . . Lou Castel
Juliette Dottax . . . . Françoise Rigal
Madame Vigne . . . . . . Françoise Morhange
————— •

The sole early entry in the Venice fest with solid chances to walk away with the Golden Lion, Alain Resnais' "L'Amour à Mort" (Love Unto Death) scores as one of the eminent French director's often groping concerns with the rigour and ascetics of love. This is sparse but rewarding cinema, although much depends on the viewer placing the film in its proper context as the third part of a trilogy that began with "Mon Oncle D'Amerique" (1980) and continued with "La Vie Est Un Roman" (1983), the latter unspooled here at the last Venice fest.

All three pics were made in collaboration with screenwriter Jean Gruault. Philosophical and theological concerns have occupied both Resnais and Gruault of late. In "Mon Oncle D'Amerique" it's material pleasures that dissatisfy; in "La Vie Est Un Roman" it's the search for happiness that makes life a trial, and now in "L'Amour à Mort" carries on with the use of the same four actors in both films: Sabine Azema, Pierre Arditi, Fanny Ardant, and André Dussolier.

Resnais leaves visual and textual hints all along the line to help the viewer sort out the message. There's first of all the names given to the four protagonists: Elisabeth (Azema), Simon (Arditi), and Judith (Ardant) are all biblical names chosen among the "fathers of the church" during the early centuries A.D. The colors used in decor and costumes are also key essentials: Martha is dressed in red, a symbol of love, while Simon is always seen clothed in the black of death.

The setting is an equally austere southern French town, Uzes (near Nimes), where an archaelogical dig on a site of Roman ruins is taking place under Simon's direction. It's at this isolated place that Simon meets Elisabeth, and for two months they experience an intense love that is then shattered by Simon's brief encounter with death. And here religion enters the picture, to try to explain why Simon is gradually forsaking Elisabeth's love to reach a final communion with death. The Catholic-Jewish pair turn to two friends, a husband-wife pair of protestant pastors: Judith (the humanist) and Jerome (the dogmatist). In the course of their discussions, Elisabeth decides to join Simon in death by committing suicide — the deed, however, presented as an act of hope as well as love, and with an open conclusion.

Pic is interspersed with musical interludes (composed by Hans Werner Henze) matched to a black screen or images of a "floating universe' (something like snow falling on a star-filled night). These interludes offer some keys to the film's complex esthetics. Perhaps not a masterpiece, "L'Amour à Mort" is nonetheless a major work of contemporary European cinema.

—*Holl.*

Bereg
(River Bank)
(SOVIET-COLOR)

Venice, Sept. 6.

A Mosfilm Productin. Moscow, in association with Westdeutscher Rundfunk (WDR), Cologne. Features entire cast. Directed by Alexander Alov and Vladimir Naumov. Screenplay, Yuri Bondarev, Alov, Naumov, based on Bondarev's novel with same title; camera (color), Valentin Zelenznyakov; sets, Yevgeni Cernyaev, Vladimir Kirs; editing, Yevgeni Suragiskaia; music, Tchaikovsky, Vivaldi, Handel. Reviewed at Venice Film Fest (competition), Sept. 5, 1984. Running time: 140 MINS.
Cast: Boris Serbakov (Nikitin), Natalya Belochvostikova (Emma), Bernhard Wicki (Werber), Kornelia Boia (Lola), Bruno Deitrich (Disman).

The Soviet entry at Venice, "Bereg" (River Bank), won the highest honors the Soviet film industry could give the film, and was unspooled once in its longer two-part version in the film mart at Cannes. For convenience sake it was apparently shortened for Venice, and thus the role of Bernhard Wicki doesn't really appear at all, although the actor is listed in the titles. Pic was made by the team of Alexander Alov (who died in the middle of the production) and Vladimir Naumov, with the script collaboration of Lenin Prize winner for literature, Yuri Bondarev, upon whose recent novel the film is based. This is an autobiographical story, and one can surmise the central role of the Soviet lieutenant, Nikitin, is an alter ego of Bondarev himself, for he not only participated in the "Great War," but also returned to Hamburg in the 1950s for a visit (per film narrative).

The war is just drawing to a close in 1945, and a Soviet battalion leaves Berlin to be reassigned to a town called Königsdorf near Hamburg. There a young Soviet army lieutenant Nikitin has an affair with a teenaged German girl named Emma. Years later, the soldier-writer returns to Hamburg on the invitation of his German publisher. Who should be his translator as well as an owner of an international bookstore but Emma. The two now have married others and have grown older, but their love is undiminished, and their few days together provide the occasion to review the past, before the next tearful departure.

Pic is directed quite straightforwardly with little in the way of poetic or nostalgic touches. Since Westdeutscher Rundfunk (WDR) had a hand in the production (on a socalled "services rendered" basis), Mosfilm could shoot exterior scenes in Hamburg. But so much doesn't really fit: the actress playing the German woman is a Soviet film personality, Natalya Belochvostikova, the hotel interiors are decidedly Russian (hardly a Hamburg establishment), and the sentimental and patriotic statements on the Great War are geared entirely to the Soviet home audience. What's left for the Western viewer is amusement over how the Soviets look upon Western free-wheeling ways. — *Holl.*

Kaos
(Chaos)
(ITALIAN-COLOR)

Venice, Sept. 3.

Produced by Giuliano De Negri for RAI-TV Channel 1 and Filmtre Productions. Features entire cast. Written and directed by Paolo and Vittorio Taviani, based on the novels of Luigi Pirandello. Camera (Eastmancolor), Giuseppe Lanci; art director, Francesco Bronzi; editor, Roberto Perignani; music, Nicola Piovani. Reviewed at the Venice Film Festival (out of competition), Sept. 3, 1984. Running time: 188 MINS.
"The Other Son"
The mother . . . . Margarita Lozano
"Moonstruck"
Batà . . . . Claudio Bigagli
Saro . . . . Massimo Bonetti
Sidoro . . . . Enrica Maria Modugno
"The Jar"
Zi Dimo . . . . Franco Franchi
Don Lollo . . . . Ciccio Ingrassia
"Requiem"
Salvatore . . . . Biagio Barone
The old patriarch . . . . Salvatore Rossi
Padre Sarso . . . . Franco Scaldati
Baron . . . . Pasquale Spadola
"A Talk With Mother"
Luigi Pirandello . . . . Omero Antonutti
The mother . . . . Regina Bianchi

Title of the latest effort by Paolo and Vittorio Taviani — five episodes taken from works by Luigi Pirandello which will be released simultaneously on big and small screens in Italy; sold by SACIS offshore in a flexible buy-by-the-episode format — refers to Pirandello's birthplace, a dialect form of the ancient Greek word "chaos." The picture itself is all clarity and light (albeit the moonlight of madmen and poets), a stunning display of imagination, free literary adaptation and technical control. Shown out of competition at Venice because its directors were on the jury, "Kaos" was not a prize candidate, a fact regretted by many. Besides being a thoughtful portrait of Sicilian life and history, pic is also highly entertaining. It should have excellent prospects for successful arthouse and small screen runs abroad.

The spirit of the film is in its opening, exultant aerial pans over the Sicilian countryside, revealing ancient temples and landscapes whose barren appearance, as Nicola Piovani's swelling score suggests, hides great richness and drama. The recurrent motif, a belled crow that rings music over the land as it flies, introduces the first episode, "The Other Son." An old woman follows a group of immigrants on their way to America. She has a letter for her two sons who left home 14 years ago, but the letter contains nothing but meaningless scribbles. At the same time she snubs a third son who loves her because of his striking resemblance to the bandit who raped her and killed her husband, bowling with his head.

"Moonstruck" is another grotesque tragedy, a mini-thriller with a werewolf for a hero. A young bride on an isolated farm discovers that every full moon her husband goes berserk and has to be locked outdoors to keep from harming her. The origin of the man's strange malady goes back to the time when, as an infant, his mother left him alone in a field all night exposed to the moon. The terrified girl turns to her mother for help, but only gets an offer of company during the next full moon, along with her lost love, Saro. She seizes the opportunity — possibly the only one in her life — to experience love, while her husband howls in agony outside the door.

Comedy takes over in "The Jar," helmers' most successful comic attempt to date. Much of the credit goes to superb casting of two veteran funnymen, Ciccio Ingrassia and Franco Franchi, who play adversaries involved in a bizarre dispute. Don Lollo (Ingrassia), a tryannical landowner, orders a huge clay jug to be delivered for the olive harvest. When it mysteriously splits open during the night, Zi Dimo (Franchi), a hunchback with an incredible glue capable of permanently joining anything together is called in. In the process of putting the pieces together, however, Zi Dimo remains trapped inside the jar, unable to get out because of his hump. He pits wits against Don Lollo until he tricks him into breaking the jar open himself.

"Requiem" is a somber essay about landless peasants who have to fight both boss and police to be allowed to bury their dead in a little mountain cemetery they have built. The landowner tells his daughter that allowing the peasants to bury their dead in a plot of ground is the best way to make them believe the land is theirs.

Death is also the starting point for "A Talk With Mother," in which Pirandello returns to his boyhood home and finds himself conversing with his mother's ghost about his sorrows. Omero Antonutti, one of the helmers' favorite actors, is remarkable in the role of the author. Soon, however, memory leads him to remember a joyful trip to "Pumice Island," where a band of children slide down a mountain of loose pumice into the sea.

Taviani followers will note all the directors' familiar trademark present in particularly refined form: the careful use of sound, ensemble acting just this side of naturalism, a preference for vast natural backdrops, and a social-historical analysis behind everything. The depiction of a literary-imaginary-magical-real world shows them at their best.— *Yung.*

Un Delitto
(A Crime)
(ITALIAN-COLOR)

Venice, Sept. 1.

A Solaris Produzioni (with RAI-1) production. Produced by Raffaello Monteverde. Directed by Salvatore Nocita. Stars Daniel Gélin. Script, Vittorio Bonicelli, from a novel by Georges Bernanos; camera (color), Bilasco Giurato; editor, Enzo Monachesi; music, Guido and Maurizio De Angelis. Reviewed at Venice Film Fest (non-competing, TV section), Sept. 1, 1984. Running time: 174 MINS.
Judge Freshville . . . . Daniel Gélin
Evangalina . . . . Margaret Mazzantini
Madame Louise . . . . Emmanuelle Riva
Grignoles . . . . Karl Heinz Heitman
Doctor . . . . Nino Castelnuovo
Celeste . . . . Denise Bosc
Evangalina Souricet . . . . Isabel Roussinova
Abbot . . . . Francisco Rabal

"A Crime," featured in the tv section at Venice, demonstrates all the perils of spotlighting what was originally designed as a tv miniseries in a feature film slot. At almost three hours, pic is hopelessly overextended if viewed as a *feature;* over three nights on the tube, it would play infinitely better. Print screened also suffered from below-par visual quality, seeming to be in soft focus throughout.

Story is basically an Ellery Queen-type mystery, with a rich old woman and a nameless stranger murdered on the same night in an Alpine village. The investigating judge (very well played by Daniel Gélin), notes that the night in question coincided with the arrival in the village of a new priest. Is there a connection?

Of course there is, though helmer Salvatore Nocita takes his time to reveal all the details. Apart from Gélin, Emmanuelle Riva scores as a morphine-addicted housekeeper with a sinister secret. — *Strat.*

Der Spiegel
(The Mirror)
(WEST GERMAN-COLOR)

Venice, Sept. 10. 1984.

A Von Vietinghoff Film Production (Berlin), in collaboration with "Das kleine Fernsehspiel" ZDF-TV (Mainz), Christoph Holch, tv-producer. Features entire cast. Written and directed by Erden Kiral, based on Osman Sahin's novel "The White Ox." Camera (color), Kenan Ormanlar; art direction, Nikos Perakis; costumes, Heidrun Brandt; music, Brynmor Jones; singer, Sümeyra Cakir; sound, Luc Yersin; ass't cameraman, Martin Gressmann; editing, Agape Dorstewitz. Reviewed at Venice Film Fest (competition), Sept. 3, 1984. Running time: 88 MINS.

Cast: Nur Sürer (Zelihan), Suavi Eren (Necmettin), Hikmet Colik (Kücük Aga), Vasilis Tsaglos (the diviner), Nikos Skiadas (Aga), Vera Deludi (the Mother).

"Ayna" is the Turkish title of the official German entry at Venice, meaning in translation "Der Spiegel" (The Mirror). And how this came about is a story in itself. Helmer Erden Kiral, a Turkish exile filmer, won a Silver Bear at the 1983 Berlin fest for "A Season In Hakkari," lensed in Turkey but not particularly liked by the authorities there. ZDF's Christoph Holch (of "Das kleine Fernsehspiel") and Berlin producer Joachim von Vietinghoff decided to back him for his next feature, and it promptly was invited to the Lido by Venice topper Gian Luigi Rondi upon screening it in Berlin on a last-minute selection jaunt.

And rightly so: next to the recently deceased Yilmaz Güney, Erden Kiral is Turkey's best director. He has a poetic touch, yet remains very close to real life in depicting human suffering.

"The Mirror," based on a story by a Turkish novelist, actually happened in a village dominated by a rich landowner. The son of the landowner has fallen for a peasant's wife, but being a rather decent man he first tries to win her favors by offering money, and then a mirror. The woman, ashamed, tells her husband about the money, but decides to hide the mirror under her pillow as a remembrance. The husband then holds to an ancient code-of-honor and lays a trap to kill his rival. He announces to the landowner that he is willing to spend the night in the village away from his wife and cottage, thus enticing the prospective lover to visit his wife in the night. The man comes, and is murdered by the husband.

But where to hide the corpse? A shallow grave is dug under the very spot in the cottage where the couple's white ox is kept in hopes that no one will ever look there. It works. Not even the local soothsayer can tip the landowner on where his missing son can be found, save to indicate it's "somewhere near." Searches, in which the husband participates, don't help either. It's the wife who can't stand the suspense anymore; nor can the husband — they both gradually lose their senses.

The rest is the story of the madness. One evening, the wife is found with her arms around the ox' neck, which enrages the husband to prompt a killing of the animal. It now appears that the woman in her delirium has made the step to accept the forbidden love offered by the sensitive lover, for whose death she now feels guilt and despair.

A remarkable film, simply told with sparse means. Pic was lensed on a Greek island, which scores as another overall oddity. Lensing and thesp performances are pluses, and with "The Mirror" Erden Kiral has joined the ranks of talented new European directors. —*Holl.*

Heimat
(Homeland)
(W. GERMAN-B&W/COLOR)

Venice, Sept. 3.

A Edgar Reitz Film Production (Munich) in association with Westdeutscher Rundfunk (WDR) (Cologne) and Sender Freies Berlin (SFB). Features entire cast. Directed by Edgar Reitz. Screenplay, Reitz, Peter Steinbach; camera (b&w, color) Gernot Roll; music, Nikos Mamangakis; casting/co-direction, Robert Busch; sets, Franz Bauer; costumes, Reinhild Paul, Ute Schwippert, Regina Bätz; sound, Gerhard Birkholz; editing, Heidi Handorf; executive producer, Inge Richter. Reviewed at Venice Film Fest (out of competition), Aug. 29-31. Sept. 1-2, 1984. Running time: 924 MINS.

Cast: Marita Breuer (Maria Simon), Dieter Schaad (Paul Simon, old man), Michael Lesch (Paul Simon, young man), Eva Maria Bayerwaltes (Pauline Kröber, born Simon), Rüdiger Weigang (Eduard Simon), Karin Rasenack (Lucie Simon), Gertrud Bredel (Katarina Simon), Willi Berger (Mathias Simon), Eva-Maria Schneider (Marie-Goot), Wolfram Wagner (Mathes-Pat), Kurt Wagner (Glasisch Karl), Karin Kienzler (Pauline Simon), Arno Lang (Robert Kröber), Mathias Kniesbeck (Anton Simon, older man), Markus Reiter (Anton Simon, young man), Rolf Roth (Anton Simon, teenager), Sabine Wagner (Martha Simon), Michael Kausch (Ernst Simon, older man), Roland Bongard (Ernst Simon, younger man), Ingo Hoffman (Ernst Simon, teenager), Peter Harting (Hermann Simon, older man), Jürg Richter (Hermann Simon, younger man), Johannes Lobewein (Alois Wiegand), Gertrud Sherer (Martha Wiegand), Hans Jürgen Schatz (Wilfried Wiegand), Gabriele Blum (Lotti Schirmer), Jörg Hube (Otto Wohlleben), Johannes Metzdorf (Fritz Pieritz), Alexander Schulz (Hänschen Betz), Marlies Assmann (Appolonia), Gudrun Landgrebe (Klärchesn Sisse), Helga Bender (Martina), Joachim Bernhard (Pollak), Hans-Günter Kylau (Hauptmann Zielke), Gerd Riegauer (Gschrey), others.

Edgar Reitz' "Heimat" (Homeland) is not only the fulfillment of all the hopes of New German Cinema over the past two decades, but should also go down as a milestone in contemporary film history.

Truly, as the vast majority of critics attending the Venice fest attest, there has never been anything like it before. By comparison, there's Erich von Stroheim's aborted nine-hour-long "Greed" and Rainer Werner Fassbinder's acclaimed 15½-hour "Berlin Alexanderplatz," but these were both literary adaptations and could be viewed as running chapters in a book. "Heimat" is something quite different.

This a family chronicle, set in a Hunsrück village (named Schabbach). It was the key film event at the Munich film fest last June, where it was viewed in its original 35m version, and it will be aired shortly in 11 parts as a tv serial in September-October, produced by WDR Cologne (Joachim von Mengershausen) and SFB Berlin (Hans Quiet). It took Edgar Reitz five years and four months to complete the roughly 16-hour (including "bridges" between the parts) version.

The team of helmer Edgar Reitz, screenwriter Peter Steinbach, and cameraman Gernot Roll collaborated previously on the making of the tv-film "Stunde Null" (1976), a similar portrait of postwar Germany set in a village near Leipzig as the American and Soviet troops converge on the same spot.

"Heimat" is a semi-autobiographical portrait of Reitz' own childhood in this hilly region between Frankfurt in Hessen and Saarbrücken in the Saarland (bordering Luxembourg), taken from newspaper accounts, word-of-mouth stories, and village chronicles of every sort.

Herewith the chronological breakdown of the story: (1) The Call Of Far Away Places, 1919-1928; (2) The Center Of The World, 1928-1933; (3) The Best Christmas Ever, 1935, (4) The Highway, 1938; (5) Up And Away And Back, 1938-39; (6) The Home Front, 1943; (7) Soldiers And Love, 1944; (8) The Americans, 1945-1947; (9) Little Hermann, 1955-1956; (10) The Proud Years, 1967-1969; and (11) The Feast Of The Living And The Dead, 1982 (which also serves as an epilog).

As the chronicle indicates, the early years are rather tightly strung together, while those in the postwar era are marked by giant leaps up to the present. Indeed, one has grown to know each member of the Simon family so well that the final quantum jumps are generally welcomed, for as in reading "The Forsyte Saga" or "Buddenbrooks" or "The Magnificent Ambersons," one fairly aches to see how everything will turn out in the end.

Maria is the central figure, played with disarming charm by Marita Breuer from a 19-year-old girl ready to embark on marriage to her death and burial at the end at the age of 82.

Maria, daughter of an established landowner in the area falls in love with the son of the village blacksmith, Paul (returning home dazed from the Great War), and marries him. They have two children, but Paul is restless and one day inexplicably leaves for America to try his fortune as an inventive radio technician. Maria can't explain his disappearance to herself but keeps faith all the same.

Next comes the period under the Third Reich, and the drama shifts momentarily to the fortunes of Paul's brother Eduard and sister Pauline, the former marrying a house madame from Berlin and rising to become village mayor, the latter marrying a well-to-do jewelry shopowner and settling down to a welcomed but brief prosperity. Reitz and Steinbach in the sections set in the 1930s offer a remarkably accurate sketch of the times. It's during this period that Maria meets a new love, Otto, who is building a new highway through the Hunsrück, and she becomes pregnant with a third son, Hermann, who then joins his older brothers, Anton and Ernst, as key figures in the later postwar episodes of the film.

Several important characters join in the story: Glasisch, the village original who is also the narrator; Lucie, Eduard's wife, who joins her husband as a comic interest in the early episodes; the grandmother of the Simon clan, Katharina, whose spiritual strength is absorbed by her daughter-in-law Maria, and then in turn passed on to Maria's own daughter-in-law Martha (who at the end of film stands as the third and final Earth Mother pillar of the Simon family tree).

The trio of performances by Gertrud Bredel as Katharina, Marita Breuer as Maria, and Sabine Wagner as Martha are outstanding, indeed, emotionally moving and credible down to the last detail in word and gesture, and should wipe out in a single stroke much of the usage of clichéd stereotypes customary in current German tv productions. For that matter, the thesp performances are the major plus all the way through "Heimat."

No one at Venice expected "Heimat" to take off in the critics' and public's estimation as rapidly and convincingly as it did: immediate sales to British and Italian television, bookings at festivals in London, New Delhi, Los Angeles, and elsewhere. One jury member frankly admitted he would have liked to see it judged in the competition.

This is the one superb example of how cinema and television can be wedded as complementary media. The shifts of black-and-white to color as just one prominent example: the tv version allows for "blending" the colors in such a way that, on one occasion, the passing of a bouquet of roses to Martha's hands at her wedding fairly illuminates in flowing contrasts a drab and dreary winter landscape.

Since Reitz had complete access to all the seasons over his many months of shooting, he could deal as he wished with both the film and video potentialities of the material. So he and ace lenser Gernot Roll have, when all's said and done, made two different, contrasting versions of the same project. Try to see both.

"Heimat" was unanimously voted the FIPRESCI critics' prize at Venice. — *Holl.*

Ninguém Duaz Vezes
(No One Twice)
(PORTUGUESE-COLOR)

Venice, Sept. 5.

A Grupo Zero/Paisá/Jorge Silva Melo Film Production (Lisbon) in collaboration with Janus Film and Fernsehen (Frankfurt) and Les Films du Passage (Paris). Produced, written and directed by Jorge Silva Melo. Camera (color), Acácio de Almeida; sets, Marcel Wengler; music, Hans Werner Henze; editing, Ana Luisa Guimarães. Reviewed at Venice Film Fest (competition), Sept. 4, 1984. Running time: **100 MINS.**
Cast: Michael König (Bernd Hoffmann), Luis Miguel Cintra (Carlos) Manuela De Freitas (Mariana), José Maria Branco (Mario), Zita Duarte (Maria Teresa), Luis Lucas (João), Glicinia Quartin (Amelia), Gina Santos (Mariana's Mother), Diogo Dória (Augusto), Rita Blanco (Sonia), Charlotte Schwab (Hanna Brauer).

Portuguese intellectual diretor Jorge Silva Melo studied at the London Film School, worked as an actor in Manoel de Oliveira's "'' e Soulier de Satin," founded his show theater group in Lisbon (Teatro da Cornucopia), and worked for a time as an assistnt to Peter Stein at the Schaubühne Ensemble in Berlin. His first film was an experimental 16m pic without commercial release: "Passagem ou a Meio Caminho" (1980).

At Venice, Silva made his debut, so to speak, with a head crammed full of intellectual ideas on identity crisis. The German painter Bernd Hoffmann (played by Michael König of the Schaubühne Ensemble) arrives in Lisbon to exhibit his paintings in an art show along with those of a Hanna Brauer, the latter deciding at the last minute not to make the trip to Berlin. All the same, Bernd is sure he has seen Hanna in a video clip on the exhibition, and desperately begins to search for her. Meanwhile, a Portuguese theater group is also going through a crisis with a production of Chekhov's "Uncle Vanya." Hanna later turns up dead; was it suicide or murder?

Silva has a way to go before he sorts out the bugs in his intellectual thinking, and pic is much too strongly influenced by theatrical notions.—*Holl.*

Angyali Udvözlet
(Annunciation)
(HUNGARIAN-COLOR)

Venice, Sept. 3.

A Hunnia Studio, Mafilm, Production. Directed and written by András Jeles, based on "The Tragedy Of Man," by Imre Madách. Camera (Eastmancolor), Sándor Kardos; music, István Mártha; editor, Margit Galamb; special effects, Zsuzsa Urhin; sound, Peter Laczkovich. Reviewed at Venice Film Festival (competition), Sept. 2, 1984. Running time: **101 MINS.**
Adam . . . . Péter Bocsor
Eve . . . . Júlia Mérö
Lucifer . . . . Eszter Gyalog

Hungary scored strongly at the other major fests this year via gritty black and white documentary-style features, for example, "Light Physical Injuries" in Berlin and "Intimate Diary" in Cannes. Venice competition entry is totally different, a semi-experimental, color fantasy built around a potted history of mankind and enacted entirely by children eight to 12. Result is very much an acquired taste.

Source is a mid-19th Century tome, "The Tragedy Of Man," by Imre Madách, in which Lucifer guides Adam and Eve through history so they can become aware of their future. During the story, Adam becomes in turn an Athenian general, a crusader in Byzantium, an astronomer in old Prague, Danton during the French Revolution and a witness of poverty in London brought about by (we're told) unrestrained capitalism.

Having each role played by a child results in the film looking like Alan Parker's "Bugsy Malone" meets Cecil B. De Mille, but project is woefully lacking in humor and will be an endurance test for the viewer not charmed by its central conceit. Indeed, it's hard to think of any kind of audience for this precious item which, despite rich color and attractive costumes, fails to find the needed mixture of charm and invention. The moppets do their best, but most of them obviously are acting by the numbers. It is probably a first that the Devil is enacted by a little girl.

This is the second feature of helmer András Jeles, who previously made the thoroughly charming (realistic) "Little Valentino" (1978). It at least indicates variety and contrast in Magyar cinema production, but seems destined to disappear without trace. —*Strat.*

Blaubart
(Bluebeard)
(W. GERMAN/SWISS-
COLOR-16m)

Venice, Aug. 31.

A Wesdeutscher Rundfunk (WDR) Cologne, and DRS, Zurich, coproduction. TV producers, Hartwig Schmidt, Martin Schassmann. Features entire cast. Written and directed by Krysztof Zanussi, based on Max Frisch's story with the same title. Camera (color), Slawomir Idziak; sets, Hans Eichin, Lothar Kirchem; costumes, Detlef Papendorf; editing, Liesgret Schmitt-Klink; music, Wojciech Kilar; sound, Gerhard Trampert. Reviewed at Venice Film Fest (Venice Tv), Aug. 30, 1984. Running time: **100 MINS.**
Cast: Vadim Glowna (Doktor Felix Schaad), Karen Baal (Lilian), Vera Tschechowa (Gisela), Ingrid Resch (Corinne), Elisabeth Trissenaar (Andrea), Maja Komorowska (Katharina), Margarethe von Trotta (Jutta), Barbara Lass (Rosalinde), Eberhard Feik (Public Prosecutor), Hans Paetsch (Judge), Guido Baumann (Defense Attorney), Leslie Malton (Maid).

There's not much cinematic to recommend in Krzysztof Zanussi's tv production, unspooled in the new "Venezia Tv" section. Instead of reaching a probably acceptable audience before a tube, accustomed to talking heads in a courtroom caper (reminiscent in this case of the heyday of Perry Mason on Stateside television), the 16m print shown in Venice left fest critics rather high-and-dry with mixed emotions as to just what to do with it (the same was true of other tv entries at fest).

Here we have a recent published story by Swiss writer Max Frisch, who has written a quite intellectually satisfying variation on the Bluebeard theme of a man with eight wives on his conscience. The twists in the story are the death of a call girl with the chief suspect being our "bluebeard," Felix Schaad of Zurich. Schaad pleads his innocence, and the women in his life are trotted into the courtroom before the camera to tell different parts of the story.

All well and good, but it makes for heavy concentration to follow the motifs as explicated: it seems Bluebeard Schaad is guilty after all via his own interior monolog, but by that time the audience has given up on the courtroom caper altogether. So — read the book.

Tv pic was lensed in 16m in both German and English versions, the latter shown here. —*Holl.*

Ybris
(Habris)
(ITALIAN-COLOR)
Venice, Sept. 4.

A RAI-TV Channel 3 production. Stars written and directed Gavino Ledda. Camera (color), Pietro Morbidelli; art director and costume designer, Morbidelli; editor, Tullio Cordanti; music, Pietro Sassu. Reviewed at the Venice Film Festival (competition), Sept. 4, 1984. Running time: **124 MINS.**
Gavino . . . . Gavino Ledda
Leonardo Do Vinci . . . . . . Giuseppe Lepori
Thiu Pulinari . . . . Giuseppe Becciu
Maria Concetta . . . . Pierfranco Olivieri

"Ybris" is an experimental first feature directed by Gavino Ledda, the shepherd-scholar whose autobiography was used by the Taviani brothers as the basis for their film "Padre Padrone." In this film Ledda's arduous self-education continues in a less structured, imagina-tive vein. This RAI-TV production is a serious work which makes no concessions to entertaining the audience.

Yet the picture has strong appeal all the same, thanks to forceful imagery and an original hero seen battling his demons. To make matters more complicated, Ledda, the writer and director, plays himself in the film. Story picks up where the Tavianis' picture left off.

After finishing his stint in the Army and getting a university degree, Ledda returns among the shepherds and peasants of his native Sardinian village. The people want nothing to do with him — they see him as having chosen a path (education) only the rich can follow. "He who doesn't work is a thief," is one of their proverbs. In addition, Ledda is suffering from an ulcer. He conquers his ailment with the help of Leonardo Da Vinci (Giuseppe Lepori), his symbolic mentor.

He retires to an old shepherd's dwelling to study truth and science. His struggle after knowledge unfolds in a totally imaginary world peopled with monsters and Greek goddesses, among others. After terrible torments, Ledda triumphs, conquering a host of local "devils" in insect garb and rediscovering his cultural roots in the earth itself.

Ybris or hubris is a Greek word meaning, among other things, the revolt of an individual against the gods and against his own origins. For the Greeks it was the gravest sin a man could commit, and Ledda, as a classicist, knows he must pay the price for his learning through suffering. In the end he assumes the goatskin clothes of ancient shepherds and "sows" Beethoven scores and little statues in the fields, after magically defecting a combine harvester and exploding the stone walls that are the boundaries of the fields.

All this symbolism makes the film at times fresh and startling; at other times practically impenetrable. If Ledda gets another shot behind the cameras, one can hope he makes a greater effort to keep the audience in mind.—*Yung.*

Detskij Sad
(A Childhood Garden)
(SOVIET-COLOR)

Venice, Sept. 7.

A Mosfilm Production, Moscow; world rights, Goskino, Moscow. Features entire cast. Written and directed by Yevgeny Yevtushenko. Camera (color), Vladimir Palyan; sets, Victor Yushin; music, Gleb May; sound, Vladimir Chiarun. Reviewed at Venice Film Fest (out of competition). Sept. 6, 1984. Running time: **143 MINS.**
Cast: Sergei Gusak (Zhenya), Svetlana Evstratova (the Woman Bandit), Galina Stachanova (the Nun), Sergei Bobovskij (Tolian), Nikolai Karachansev (Spiel), Klaus Maria Brandauer (the German Officer), Yevgeny Yevtushenko (the Chess Player).

Yevgeny Yevtushenko's "A Childhood Garden" was unspooled out-of-competition in view of the poet-filmer's presence on the international jury. This is an autobiographical sketch of his youth as the city of Moscow was being evacuated in 1941, although the characters are transposed to a poetic, experimental form of cinema. In general, it's too long and rather uninspired so far as style and cinematic finesse are concerned, but there are some rich moments here and there to warrant further exposure on fest circuits (provided one can get the poet himself to discuss just what he was trying to pack into certain images).

· Pic opens with Moscow in turmoil, as people are struggling at the train station to find a place on an already overcrowded transport. The train is headed for Siberia, where Yevtushenko himself was born, and a boy with a violin under his arm bids his tearful mother farewell. As German fighter planes are strafing train transports, the drama is heightened by everything going wrong from the start.

Along the way, the lad meets a woman bandit who fascinates him by her lust for life and booty. The lady in the end sees the errors of her ways and joins in the struggle to win the war as a way of cleansing herself of past sins. This is the central piece in the pic, and the one that makes the whole worth sitting through. "A Childhood Garden" resembles experimental films of the 1950s, particularly European symbolic tracts substituting metaphors for a narrative text. Watch for Yevtushenko playing the chess-player at the beginning: his acting performance is typical of the film's overall stylistic quality. Indeed, one has the feeling that an hour-long version would have been enough, minus the antiquated zoom shots. — *Holl.*

Claretta
(ITALIAN-COLOR)

Venice Sept. 7.

A Trans World Film, in collaboration with RAI-2, Rome. Executive producers, Toni Amendola; Giancarlo Marchetti; producer, Giacomo Pezzali. Features Claudia Cardinale. Directed by Pasquale Squitieri. Screenplay, Squitieri, Arigo Petacco; camera (Eastmancolor), Eugenio Bentivoglio; sets, Nicola Losito; costumes, Ezio Altieri; editor, Mauro Nonanni; music, Gerard Schurmann. Reviewed at Venice Film Fest (competition), Sept. 6, 1984. Running time: 127 MINS.

Cast: Claudia Cardinale (Claretta Petacci), Catherine Spaak (Roberta), Guiliano Gemma (Marcello Petacci), Caterina Boratto (Giuseppina Petacci), Miriam Petacci (played by herself), Nancy Brilli (Miriam Petacci as young woman), Lorenzo Piani (Gasperini), Angela Goodwin (Luisa), Maria Mercader (Princess of Montenevoco), Raffaela Curi (carabinieri officer), Mario Granato (prison director), Fernando Briamo (Mussolini).

Orson Welles' interview technique in "Citizen Kane" has been utilized in Pasquale Squitieri's

"Claretta," official Italian entry at Venice.

Pic proved to be controversial due to its subject-matter: this is the story of Claretta Petacci, the mistress for 10 years of Mussolini, killed with Il Duce in 1945. Since everyone is familiar with the photographs taken of the two hanging from a gas-station pole before a gaping crowd, and since the Italian government still keeps much of the Mussolini-Petacci records under lock-and-key, it's only natural that a film made on Claretta Petacci would be an eye-catcher.

The treatment derives from the cooperation with Claretta's still-living sister, Miriam Petacci, who makes a brief appearance at the outset when a television reporter named Roberta (Catherine Spaak) is assigned to make a tv film about Claretta and contacts this last remaining member of the family (an eye-witness to the events described). From this meeting in the film, at Claretta's tomb, it can be surmised that the only version one is going to get is that of the Petacci family. It's one-sided and sentimentalized to the point of excess.

The storyline covers from July 27, 1943 to the Petacci family's flight to Barcelona some six months later, together with material added on Mussolini and Claretta's death in 1945 as viewed primarily through cut and censored U.S. Army newsreels. Events are viewed entirely over the shoulder of Miriam (Claretta's younger sister) as the father and mother, together with the two daughters, leave Rome with a chauffeur to escape to the north.

Meanwhile, the story of the brother Marcella (a marine officer) is picked up along the way until he, too, joins the family at a later stage. The meeting between Claretta and Mussolini takes place in the Vittoriale estate of the poet d'Annunzio, the best moment in the film; in addition to Claudia Cardinale's respectable performance as she wrestles valiantly in a losing cause to add depth to the title role. — *Holl.*

Places In The Heart
(COLOR)

Beautifully made rural drama for a limited audience.

Hollywood, Sept. 7.

A Tri-Star Pictures release. Produced by Arlene Donovan. Executive producer, Michael Hausman. Written and directed by Robert Benton. Stars Sally Field. Camera (Technicolor), Nestor Almendros; editor, Carol Littleton; music, John Kander; production designer, Gene Callahan; art director, Sydney Z. Litwak; set decorator, Lee Poll, Derek Hill; sound, James Pilcher; costumes, Ann Roth; assistant director, Joel Tuber; special visual effects, Bran Ferren. Reviewed at Charles Aidikoff screening room, L.A., Sept. 6, 1984. (MPAA rating: PG.) Running time: 102 MINS.

Edna Spalding . . . . Sally Field
Margaret Lomax . . . . Lindsay Crouse
Wayne Lomax . . . . Ed Harris
Viola Kelsey . . . . Amy Madigan
Mr. Will . . . . John Malkovich
Moze . . . . Danny Glover
Frank . . . . Yankton Hatten
Possum . . . . Gennie James
Albert Denby . . . . Lane Smith

"Places In The Heart" is a loving, reflective homage to his hometown by writer/director Robert Benton. Picture is the first of a trio of rural dramas, which includes "Country" and "The River," to arrive. Flawlessly crafted, Benton crates a full tapestry of life in Waxahachie, Texas circa 1935, but filmgoers may find his understated naturalistic approach lacking in dramatic punch. Expansion beyond a core audience is possible, but unlikely.

Obviously drawing on his personal experiences and people he knew growing up, Benton remembers the rituals of everyday life: love, in all of its forms, birth and death. Death arrives early as Sheriff Spaulding (Ray Baker) is called away from his family dinner to corral an errant black youth who has got himself drunk and is firing off a pistol down by the railroad tracks.

When death comes, it comes casually but not by surprise, as Benton's people seem to be well prepared for any of the accidents of life. Spaulding's death leaves his wife Edna (Sally Field) and two children to pick up the pieces and reconstruct a life.

Edna is one of those no-nonsense gritty women who can roll up her sleeves and get down to work as she later proves in the cotton fields. Fields is solid in the lead role, but she is not the strong unifying character that can tie the strands of Benton's script together. Picture is comprised of individual struggles and crises and may have spread itself too thin in trying to do justice to all its characters.

Rather than building to a climax, pic peaks twice. First comes about two-thirds through when a tornado humbles everyone before the forces of nature. Central struggle of the film surrounds Edna's efforts to keep her land from foreclosure by

the bank, climaxing with a race to be the first to harvest the crop.

Aside from these two emotional highpoints, the film follows a leisurely pace and spends a good deal of time with an adulterous affair between Ed Harris and his best friend's wife (Amy Madigan), and later his attempts to win his own wife (Lindsay Crouse) back. Harris is the kind of man who doesn't miss his water till his well runs dry and succeeds in creating a moving portrait of a good-natured, but impractical lover.

"Places In The Heart" is deeply Christian in the feelings of love and brotherhood which seem to emanate from the tower of the courthouse and cover the whole town. It is the bond which links Edna with the two men who assist her in her struggle. Danny Glover makes a man of substance out of the transient black field worker who teaches her the ways of the cotton field and John Malkovich is totally believable as an embittered, blind World War I vet who also discovers his ties to the community.

Everyone has a place in the rituals of life in Waxahachie and Benton extends a loving understanding to their shortcomings and prejudices. Nestor Almendros' photography is not pretty, but high on feeling and atmosphere. It radiates a lived-in autumnal light.

John Kander's country flavored score also adds to the sense of place as does Gene Callahan's immaculate production design. But ultimately the credit must go to Benton for assemblying the ingredients — the cars, the food, even the weather — that put the heart into the production. —*Jagr.*

George Stevens: A Filmmaker's Journey
(DOCU-COLOR)

Deauville, Sept. 8.

A Creative Film Center production. Written, produced and directed by George Stevens Jr. Coproducer and supervising editor, Susan Winslow; associate producer, Toni Vellani; editor, Catherine Shields; music, Carl Davis; research, Caroline Stevens; sound editor, A.C. Warden; camera (color), Juan Ruiz-Anchia, Tom Hurwitz, Don Lenzer, Gerald Cotts, Harrison Engle, Robert Pierce; production manager, Gail Schumann. Reviewed at the Deauville Film Festival, Sept. 7, 1984. Running time: 110 MINS.

With: Jean Arthur, Fred Astaire, Montgomery Clift, Brandon de Wilde, James Dean, Douglas Fairbanks Jr., Cary Grant, Katharine Hepburn, Rock Hudson, Sam Jaffe, Alan Ladd, Joel McCrea, Fred MacMurray, Jack Palance, Millie Perkins, Ginger Rogers, Elizabeth Taylor, Spencer Tracy, Max von Sydow, Shelley Winters, Warren Beatty, Frank Capra, John Huston, Rouben Mamoulian, Joseph L. Mankiewicz, Alan J. Pakula, Fred Zinnemann, Pandro S. Berman, Hermes Pan, Ivan Moffat, Hal Roach, Jack Sher, Yvonne Stevens, Irwin Shaw, Toni Vellani.

George Stevens Jr.'s portrait of his famous director father does what any good docu on films and filmmakers should do: it gives the neophyte moviegoer the desire to discover the helmer's films in their entirety, and incites the buff to a new look at familiar classics. Completed only recently, "George Stevens: A Filmmaker's Journey" had its world premiere this month at the Deauville American Film Festival, where it was cited immediately as one of the highlights. Warm words from the French are particularly significant, since Stevens was never ranked as a Hollywood giant by the New Wave critics filmmakers (though one of their mentors, the late Henri Langlois, remained faithful in his admiration).

Using the traditional film clip-and-interview method, Stevens Jr. gives his portrait three distinct movement. The first deals with Steven's early days and motion picture apprenticeship as cameraman and gag writer at the Hal Roach studios, then his rise to director's status in the1930s with a series of evergreen social comedies, musicals and exotic adventure pictures. Silent movie buffs may be left a bit frustrated by the limited screen time accorded Stevens' formative years, but the selection of marvelous scenes from the sound features and the warm, admiring reminiscences of Katharine Hepburn, Frank Capra, Hermes Pan, Joel McCrea, Fred Astaire and Ginger Rogers, among others, make one quickly forget any imbalance.

Second section covers Stevens' service in the Army Signal Corps during World War II, where, as part of General Dwight D. Eisenhower's combat photography unit for the European invasion of 1944, he kept his own 16m color film diary of the Allied advance from Normandy into the Continent.

From the over four hours of footage shot by Stevens and his fellow cameramen, his son has culled about a quarter-hour of exciting scenes: D-Day, the Liberation of Paris, and the freeing of the Dachau death camp. The technical quality of this footage is quite good (it's clear that it's shot by professionals) and the fact of it being in color gives the subject matter a new sense of immediacy, exhilaration and pain (a final image of two Dachau inmates strolling arm-in-arm in the camp yard is especially haunting).

Stevens' post-war career is evoked in the last section. Profoundly impressed by what he had seen during the war, Stevens lost the desire to turn out any more entertainments, and turned to subject matter of mythic proportions with pictures like "Shane," "A Place In The Sun" and "Giant." The integrity of the director during the McCarthy period is also paid tribute by interviewees Joseph L. Mankiewicz and Fred Zinnemann, among others.

Stevens Jr. narrates with quiet modesty and feeling. He lets the interviewees do the essential portrait-painting of a humane, immensely gifted artist committed to his work, and resists the temptation to cite his dad's honors list, or make special pleas for more hotly contested pictures like "The Greatest Story Ever Told" (nonetheless, Max von Sydow was an inspired bit of casting as Jesus).

Clip selection and quality are first-rate, and intercutting of interviews and pic extracts deft. Stevens Jr. does some sharp editing by interweaving sections of "Gunga Din" with color footage from an unusual 16m production log Stevens made during the shot. Heady stuff, that.
— *Len.*

Crimes Of Passion
(COLOR)

Poorly scripted sexer.

San Francisco, Sept. 15.
A New World Pictures release of a Donald P. Borchers production. Produced by Barry Sandler and Borchers. Executive producer, Larry Thompson. Directed by Ken Russell. Stars Kathleen Turner, Anthony Perkins. Screenplay, Sandler. Camera (color), Dick Bush; editor, Brian Tagg; production design, Richard Macdonald; costumes, Ruth Myers; music, Rick Wakeman; sound, Christopher Ross-Leong; first asst. director, Pat Kehoe. Reviewed at the Regency III, S.F., Sept. 15, 1984. (No MPAA rating.) Running time: 101 MINS.
China Blue . . . . Kathleen Turner
Rev. Peter Shayne . . . . . . Anthony Perkins
Bobby Grady . . . . John Laughlin
Amy Grady . . . . Annie Potts

Coming off successful performances in "Body Heat" and "Romancing The Stone," the evocative Kathleen Turner thuds into a wall of inanity in this dismally written, Ken Russell-directed serio-comic examination of sexual morality among American savages.

Barry Sandler's painfully pretentious screenplay deflects the usual Russell outrageousness and traps the four principals (all other roles are momentary) into the most superficial of characterizations.

The sexuality of the picture is shabby, overt and gratuitously brutalizing, despite a string of failed one-liners. Turner, for example, suggests to "Reverend" Tony Perkins that he assume "the missionary position" and that she is about to "play the organ." One keeps waiting for Cheech & Chong to enter this clumsily contrived boudoir.

Whether "Crimes of Passion" can avoid an X remains to be seen. Not that Turner's nudity is so mitigating or that the incessant puns about vital organs so tasteless, but the mix of persistent sexual activity, including a lengthy S&M scene with Turner and a cop, may send the raters even deeper into the alphabet for a Z (zilch).

The picture, caught here at a sneak, is so redundant that it can be trimmed before the eventual, and likely ill-fated, theatrical distribution. It could have a career as a midnight movie for Russell cultists.

Turner leads two lives in "Crimes Of Passion." By day she is Joanna, a compulsively laboring sportswear designer. She is divorced — something about her husband sleeping with her best friend — and, according to her employer frigid when it comes to fellows. But by night she is, under a blond-banged wig, China Blue, the hottest $50 a trick hooker in the local combat zone.

She explains late in the film that prostitution is the safest place she can be, for no one knows her and she can be anything and anyone she wishes. That is just about all we are ever told about this potentially interesting, but vapidly scripted character.

Perkins' past also goes undetailed. So he has to lean on "psycho"-somatic credentials to portray a glib, sweaty, presumably ministerial, homicidal wacko who would like to be China Blue if only he had the right hormones.

There are moments while Perkins and Turner are playing Fric-and-Frac that one perceives the picture as a send-up of the American obsession with the orgasm. Yet Perkins' role is too menacing, and an ambivalence emerges about what is going on up there on the screen. Even near the climax, when the knife-holding reverend suddenly sits down at the piano to warble "Get Happy," the turn plays more silly than amusing.

Meshed into Perkins' panting pursuit of Turner is the failing marriage of electronics repairman John Laughlin and sexless spouse Annie Potts. After 12 years in the sack, he suddenly discovers she has no interest in his body — and never had. That it has taken him this long to analyze her frigidity suggests he has slept through the sexual and all other revolutions. Their scenes together are tedious and further marred by Laughlin's stiffness.

He is plopped into China Blue's bed via the plot device of being hired to follow her when she is suspected of bootlegging dress designs. The earth moves for the two of them, but the Richter scale reading — accompanied by a series of wall shadows during their lovemaking — doesn't rise above a decimal point.

Same with the picture. Whatever the intention, and despite the technical efficiency, "Crimes Of Passion" falls between the cracks. The fault line here is quite identifiable — it's in the screenplay. —*Herb.*

Exterminator 2
(COLOR)

A Cannon Releasing release of a Cannon Group presentation of a Golan-Globus production. Executive producers, Menahem Golan, Yoram Globus. Produced by Mark Buntzman, William Sachs. Directed by Buntzman. Additional scenes directed by Sachs. Stars Robert Ginty. Screenplay, Buntzman, Sachs; camera (TVC color), Bob Baldwin, Joseph Mangine; editors, Marcus Nanton, George Norris; music, David Spear; production manager, Jeffrey Silver; stunt coordinator, Ted Duncan; art direction, Mischa Petrow (N.Y.), Virginia Field (L.A.); makeup illusions, Ed French; post-production supervisor, Michael Sloan. Reviewed at RKO Warner 2 theater, N.Y., Sept. 15, 1984. (MPAA Rating: R.) Running time: 89 MINS.
Johnny Eastland . . . . Robert Ginty
X . . . . Mario Van Peebles
Caroline . . . . Deborah Geffner
Be Gee . . . . Frankie Faison
Eyes . . . . Scott Randolph
Spider . . . . Reggie Rock Bythewood
Red Rat . . . . Bruce Smolanoff
Head Mafioso . . . . David Buntzman

"Exterminator 2" is a silly and tiresome revenge actioner, unlikely to repeat the freak hit status of its 1980 predecessor.

Formula, patterned after a successful line of Charles Bronson films, is to create audience antipathy against young street punks of mixed racial backgrounds, allowing a stalwart avenger to be motivated to wipe them out at intervals, with plenty of action. Mark Buntzman, who produced the original "The Exterminator," here wears (and shares with William Sachs) too many hats, taking over James Glickenhaus' writing and directing assignments from #1 and ending up with a contradictory mishmash.

Reprising his title role as Vietnam vet Johnny Eastland, an uncomfortable Robert Ginty is supposedly spurred into renewed vigilante action when his flashdancing girl friend Caroline (Deborah Geffner) is at first savagely beaten and crippled and later murdered by the all-purpose punks, led by a messianic leader ("I am the streets") X (Mario Van Peebles). However, the crudely constructed film has Ginty, in his mythic steel helmet, army khakis and flamethrower uniform, randomly and unconvincingly incinerating punks right from the outset, including X's brother.

Crassly violating the "lone avenger" formula, Eastland is teamed with an old mate from Vietnam, Be Gee, your friendly neighborhood black garbageman who eagerly endorses Eastland's murderous cleanup policy. Sole interesting element on view is the weird sight of Be Gee's vast Mack garbage truck, armored and refitted as a sort of tank with remote-control machine-gun turrets by Eastland for the final confrontations with punks, who meanwhile are trying to take over New York City via armored car robbery and peddling Mafia-supplied drugs.

Ginty has one good scene wherein he manhandles a punk for information, but generally, the sadistic element of the first film (which had him ingeniously feeding bad guys to a meatgrinder, etc.) has been toned down. Geffner gets to show her nude body and dancing ability, while acting honors go to Van Peebles, creating a solid physical presence with his male version of Grace Jones.

Technically, film adheres to an ugly look in keeping with its theme, though why it took such a huge crew (over 300 people are credited with behind-the-camera contributions) to make a B-picture is mighty strange. Only real sense of humor in this "serious" comic strip approach comes in the song titles: "Exterminate Me (With Your Flame)," "Shake It To Bake It" and the ever-popular "Return To Cinder."

—*Lor.*

The River Rat
(COLOR)

Worthwhile rural drama looms as a tough sell.

Hollywood, Sept. 13.

A Paramount Pictures release of a Larson/Rickman production in association with the Sundance Institute. Produced by Bob Larson. Executive producer, Michael Apted. Written and directed by Tom Rickman. Stars Tommy Lee Jones. Camera (Technicolor), Jan Kiesser; editor, Dennis Virkler; music, Mike Post; production designer, John J. Lloyd; editor, Steve Mirkovich; set decorator, Joe Mitchell; sound, Jim Alexander; costumes, Peter Saldutti; assistant director, L. Andrew Stone. Reviewed at Paramount screening room, L.A., Calif., September 12, 1984. (MPAA Rating: PG). Running time: 93 MINS.

Billy . . . . Tommy Lee Jones
Jonsy . . . . Martha Plimpton
Doc . . . . Brian Dennehy
Wexel . . . . Shawn Smith
Vadie . . . . Nancy Lea Owen
Sheriff Cal . . . . Norman Bennett
Poley . . . . Tony Frank
Joyce . . . . Angie Bolling

"River Rat" is a worthwhile entry in the swelling field of rural dramas. First directorial effort by writer Tom Rickman, picture has a decidedly literary bent which tries to capture, not always successfully, the flavors of Southern, and especially Mississippi River, literature. Result is a bit overseasoned, but can still charm an audience willing to go with the flow. Finding a crowd, however, will be a difficult task.

One of the ingredients that gets the film off to a good start is Martha Plimpton as Jonsy, a local tomboy living with her grandmother (Nancy Lea Owen) at their riverside bait store. Jonsy is a practical girl more at home on water than land and Plimpton's performance is right on target, playing the girl with an impish vulnerability.

The first turn in the girl's fortunes comes when her father Billy (Tommy Lee Jones), whom she has never met, is paroled from prison and

returns home. Jailed for an accidental murder, Billy is sullen and guarded until Jonsy establishes a rapport, perhaps too easily.

"River Rats" starts out as a father-daughter relationship story and then explodes into a suspense genre tale when Billy's enigmatic parole officer, Doc (Brian Dennehy), comes looking for the payoff he was promised.

Rickman introduces elements of an old fashion treasure hunt down the river to Louisiana with undertones of gothic horror and regional superstitions. But he holds his cards too long and what are initially surprises become too drawn out.

At first Doc is hard to figure and Rickman cleverly keeps the audience guessing, but when he is ultimately revealed, he becomes almost comic in his evilness.

Similarly, the undercurrent of cajun mysticism never becomes a strong enough force to explain occurrences attributed to it. The arrivals of lightning bolts and runaway boats at precisely the right moment become contrivances rather than supernatural events.

The final revelation and vindication when the film is finished with its dark business also seems rather abrupt. Still the ride is fun and there are interesting people to meet along the way. Tommy Lee Jones makes Billy a likeable, sympathetic and moving character. Dennehy seems to be having the time of his life as the bad guy surpassed only by Tony Frank as an even worse bad guy.

Finally, "River Rats" is disarming in its simplicity, not unlike a Walt Disney adventure picture out on the river barge. — *Jagr.*

Toronto Festival

Sonatine
(CANADIAN-COLOR)

Toronto, Sept. 11.

Les Films Rene Malo presents a Cine II production. Produced by Pierre Gendron. Executive producer, Rene Malo. Directed and written by Micheline Lanctôt. Camera (Kodak color) Guy Defaux; editors Louis Surprenant, Lucette Bernier; music, François; sound, Marcel Fraser. Reviewed at the Festival of Festivals (Contemporary World Cinema) Toronto, Sept. 10, 1984. Running time: 91 MINS.

Chantal . . . . Pascale Bussieres
Louisette . . . . Marcia Pilote
Lambert . . . . Pierre Fauteux
Sailor . . . . Kliment Dentchev

Recent winner of the Venice fest's Silver Lion (for best first effort), actress-turned-filmmaker Micheline Lanctôt's "Sonatine" shapes up as a solid arthouse entry in all markets. In only her second effort behind the cameras, Lanctôt demonstrates considerable growth with both her narrative skill and in marshalling technical elements.

"Sonatine," meaning a brief, simple sonata, indicates with the ti-

tle that the film is meant to be about form and filmmaking rather than teenage suicide. Nevertheless, Lanctôt also delicately finds the depressive sense of isolation that makes kids more curious about death than life.

Constructed in three "movements," pic tells the story of a young girl infatuated with the bus driver on the route she takes. Only their behavior is shown, the emotion leaking out through tentative gestures and simple acts of human kindness. Chantal seems to grow up, at least physically, but lacks the courage to express her desires. One day, the bus stops, and a new driver is at the wheel.

The next movement quickly takes over, as Louisette, another teenager, stows away on a fishing boat, only to be discovered by a Bulgarian sailor whose language she cannot understand. Their evening on the boat is extremely tender, providing Louisette with refuge and understanding. Kliment Dentchev delivers a fabulous performance in an incomprehensible tongue.

In the third movement, the girls become frineds, united by a common desire to escape. The minimal use of dialog and clean camerawork are reinforced by a soundtrack that is confined to the point of view of teenagers die before they can be Walkman earphones.

The occasional glimpses into the environment shaping them reveals frequent discussions of union strikes, to which they are oblivious. Yet they become the victims of a successful strike one night, when they board the subway with handfuls of pills which they swallow on their way to the end of the line. They sit beneath a homemade sign challenging the world to stop them from dying. Public transportation workers abandon the trains and the teenagers died before they can be found.

By restricting her observations to the roads that lead nowhere, Lanctôt keeps the audience interested by promises of escape. Production values are tops, and the subtlety of the picture should give it a b.o. boost, particularly with the prestige of the prize won at Venice. — *Kaja.*

Mixed Blood
(U.S.-COLOR)

Toronto, Sept. 12.

Sara Films presents a Sef Saellite Films production. Produced by Antoine Gannage and Teven Fierberg. Executive producer, Alain Sarde. Direction and screenplay by Paul Morrissey. Camera (Eastman color), Stefan Zapasnik; editor, Scott Vickrey; art direction, Stephen McCabe; music, Andy Hernandez; additional dialog, Alan Browne. Reviewed at the Festival of Festivals (Contemporary World Cinema), Toronto, Sept. 11, 1984. (No MPAA Rating.) Running time: 97 MINS.

Rita la Punta . . . . Marilia Pera
Thiago . . . . Richard Ulacia
Carol . . . . Linda Kerridge

Toni . . . . Geraldine Smith
Juan the Bullet . . . . Angel David
The German . . . . Ulrich Berr
Hector . . . . Marcelino Rivera
Jose . . . . Rodney Harvey
Commanche . . . . Pedro Sanchez
Woman cop . . . . Carol Jean Lewis
Captain Kenzo . . . . Yukio Yamamoto

Filmmaker Paul Morrissey returns to the mean streets of New York City with the energetic and offbeat "Mixed Blood." Unlike Morrissey's earlier "Forty Deuce," his new outing stands a healthy chance of attracting a specialized audience with its odd, pleasing mixture of violence and perverse humor.

A tale of rival youth gangs tied into the city's drug scene, "Mixed Blood" paints a colorful story of kingdom building, corruption and revenge. Adopting an overblown style of performance, the picture maintains an edgy quality where one is often wondering whether to laugh or shudder at the proceedings. However, rather than resulting in an uncomfortable experience, the film emerges as a fun, enjoyable pastiche of genre moviemaking.

Brazilian actress Marilia Pera from "Pixote" arrives on the scene like some loud, conquering hero and with her son, Thiago (Richard Ulacia), and fashions a Hispanic ring of young teenagers to challenge an established Gang. After stealing a shipment intended for the reigning Puerto Rican Group, Rita la Punta (Pera) sets up her own operation.

When Puerto Rican gang boss Juan the Bullet (Angel David) calls for reprisals, one of Pera's gang members is thrown from a roof. But rather than curbing the fiery South American Ma Barker's operation, it only serves to make her more aggressive in dealing and fighting.

The success of the film will largely rest with how quickly audiences tap into its humorous vein. The urban jungle environment conveyed by Morrissey is filled with larger-than-life characters and performances that should tip his hand. Even such clichés as police complicity in the drug trade and gang warfare get a novel, skewed quality which is satisfying.

The offbeat nature of the piece is further reinforced by the mixture of pro and amateur talent and a variety of acting styles. Pera's matriarch is comically inspired and, despite a certain awkwardness, Ulacia manages to convey her son's combination of seemingly thick-headedness an street smarts. Also quite effective is Angel David as the blood thirsty rival drug czar.

A real asset to the production is its overall slick production values. Stefan Zapasnik's camerawork effects a cold, clean urban gloss to the picture while the Latin rhythms on the soundtrack contribute to its novel tempo.

Both "Mixed Blood's" decided violent strain and vivid dialog will limit possibilities in the theatrical mainstream, but in art and speciality areas it rates as Morrissey's most accessible venture to date. It should also ellicit strong sales in overseas markets and video exploitation with its combination of familiar genre elements and bizarre comic underpinning.—*Klad.*

Orson Welles à la Cinémathèque
(Orson Welles At The Cinematheque)
(FRENCH-COLOR)

Toronto, Sept. 14.
Produced by the Cinémathèque Française. Directed by Pierre-Andre Boutang. Editor, Françoise Collin. No other credits available. Reviewed at the Festival of Festivals (Stranger Than Fiction), Toronto, Sept. 14, 1984. Running time: **97 MINS.**
With Orson Welles, Henri Behar.

The first of a proposed series of interview/discussions with noted filmmakers, "Orson Welles à la Cinémathèque" is a filmed record of an in-person session at the august institution with the legendary cinéaste. Despite many reservations with the format and selection of material, the production has obvious merit for educational institutions, learned research, and with some trimming, specialized theatrical and conventional television play.

The actual event occurred some two years ago, so Welles' comments on upcoming projects provides an interesting historic footnote. He recently had been decorated with France's Legion of Honor and it's apparent from his mood and rapport with the audience that the filmmaker was filled with *joie de vivre* and prone to expansive statements.

Yet, due to length and the awkwardness of oral translation from English to French and vice versa, much of Welles' charm is lost on screen. Although clearly not the intention, one leaves with the sense that the tête à tête was organized by his severest detractors.

Aficiandos will be quite familiar with many of Welles' anecdotes, though several surprises do crop up in the course of his interplay. He categorizes Cecil B. De Mille and Alfred Hitchcock as the only two star directors in cinema history and confesses he detests the work of both.

Welles also insists the most important aspect of film is the actor, followed by everything else in front of the camera. The script rates third with him and he cites Federico Fellini ("you can make wonderful films without a script") as proof of his allegation.

What comes out primarily in the film are Welles' pronouncements on filmmaking. He insists the best acting moments are in black and white;

"working for posterity is vulgar;" the video revolution will occur within four months; "directors should be intelligent not intellectual;" and finally that "all you (the filmmaker) can do is imitate dreams, but you do a damn good job of it."

Much of his braggadacio must have enthralled the audience, but the flat technical style of the exercise wears on a cinema audience. Effort goes on much too long considering a general lack of content. Welles rightly chides the attending group for being too kind in their questioning and the proof results in a tame at-home session, minus any party libation. —*Klad.*

Listen To The City
(CANADIAN-COLOR)

Toronto, Sept. 15.
An International Spectrafilm release of a Sphinx film production. Produced by Ron Mann. Associate producer, Colin Brunton. Directed by Mann. Screenplay, Mann and Bill Schroeder, from an original story by Schroeder. Camera (Eastmancolor), Rene Ohashi; editor, Elaine Foreman; art direction, Barbara Dunphy; music, Gordon Deppe; sound, David Joliat. Reviewed at the Festival of Festivals (Perspective Canada) Toronto, Sept. 14, 1984. Running time: **87 MINS.**
Sophia ... P.J. Soles
Goodman ... Michael Glassbourg
Arete ... Sandy Horne
Hupar ... Jim Carroll
Arete's Father ... Barry Callaghan
Shadow ... Sky Gilbert
White ... Mary Hawkins
Green ... Real Andrews
Black ... Gary Augustynek
Peter ... Peter Wintonick
Preston Sturrock ... Bill Lord
Christie Hines ... Gigi Guthrie
Mayor ... Pete Griffin
Data Base ... Geets Romo

Award-winning documentarian Ron Mann ("Imagine the Sound," "Poetry in Motion") essays his first fictional theatrical with "Listen To The City." The ultra-sincere reflection on contemporary urban living will, however, have an extremely difficult time finding the ear of the public.

The prime obstacle of the film is Mann's inability to find a melodic tone to his piece. On one level it is a straightforward investigation of immoral, illegal business practices. Yet, this is only a small aspect of the overall film. Mann also injects a buffoonish city council as a comic sounding board to the story's more serious aspects, a touch of the poetic and almost enough musical numbers to place the film into a musical genre.

Final result is a sour cocktail with its elements out of balance. Essential story concerns a large corporation which is manipulating stock and worker sentiment through a proposed shutdown. The situation is being monitored closely by a television reporter (P.J. Soles) and ineffectually responded to by city officials.

The material sounds more promising than what one finally sees on

screen. The traditional elements of the tale, particularly the portrait of the media, are conveyed in the form of a primer while the more bizarre aspects of the story are played in broad strokes. The clash between styles is just too extreme for the film to embrace with grace.

Certainly part of the problem rests with Mann's insistence on casting a largely non-pro cast. With the exception of Soles (and a deleted scene filmed with Martin Sheen) his players have limited,or no prior screen experience, resulting in performances which are either flat or hysterical.

Technical work is fine, but one might have hoped for a more flamboyant style given the nature of the piece. Mann's heart appears to have been primarily centered in pic's musical aspects (which are strong) and in esoteric methods of conveying his social concerns. The latter element simply is strained out of all proportion.

"Listen To The City" won't make much noise in theatrical venues where playoff will be limited to arthouse circuit. Cable and cassette possibilities are perhaps marginally better, but the picture is hardly the breakthrough one anticipated after Mann's two striking feature-length documentaries.
— *Klad.*

Venice Festival

Ladies & Gentlemen
(ITALIAN-COLOR)

Venice, Sept. 3.
A C.D.E. release, produced by Nello Santi for Cinefin, Vides and Rete Italia. Stars Maurizio Micheli. Directed by Tonino Pulci. Screenplay, Pulci, Paola Pascolini and Claudia Poggiani; camera (color), Blasco Giurato; editor, Luigi Zita; art director, Antonio Visone; music, Mauro Pagani. Reviewed at the Venice Film Festival (De Sica section), Sept. 3, 1984. Running time: **90 MINS.**
Catello Coppola ... Maurizio Micheli
Carlotta ... Ania Pieroni
Isgrò ... Mario Maranzana
Paolino ... Adolf Belletti

"Ladies & Gentlemen," a remake Italian-style of René Clair's delightful "It Happened Tomorrow," was the most commercial entry on view in Venice's Italian Showcase. Regular production circumstances (i.e., an adequate budget) and experienced helming (Tonino Pulci is a stage director making his film bow) gave it a pro look that many of the Italian debuts lacked. Title refers to the "surreal" plot twist designed to increase pic's b.o. appeal, but the film had enough wit and style to keep it from looking grossly out of place at a festival.

Maurizio Micheli plays Catello, a luckless reporter specializing in celebrity gossip who is the office scapegoat. His one friend is old Paolino (Adolfo Belletti), the washroom at-

tendant of a big hotel. After Paolino dies, he sends Catello magic messages on the walls of public bathrooms announcing "the news of tomorrow." Paolino's signal from the Beyond is when Catello feels the sudden urge to rush into the nearest men's room. The system works, and overnight Catello becomes the prince of ace reporters, with one scoop after another.

Micheli, a stage comic, effortlessly carries the weight of the film on his own shoulders, making Catello into an utterly likeable fellow and toning down the inescapable bathroom humor of the story (*pace* René Clair). Aptly timed gags keep Catello moving from scoop to scoop with the help of girlfriend Ania Pieroni, a newcomer with screen presence. — *Yung.*

Nucleo Zero
(Nucleus Zero)
(ITALIAN-COLOR)

Venice, Sept. 6.
Produced by Michele Marsala for Diamant Film, a production for RAI-TV Channel 2 and TF1. Directed by Carlo Lizzani. Features entire cast. Screenplay, Ugo Pirro and Carlo Lizzani with Piero Travaglini, based on a novel by Luce D'Eramo. Camera (color), Ernesto Lanzi; editor, Franco Fraticelli; art director Pasquale Germano; music, Stelvio Cipriani. Reviewed at the Venice Film Festival (TV section), Sept. 6, 1984. Running time: **180 MINS.**
Dettore ... Patrick Bauchau
Lorenza ... Antonella Murgia
Marisa Martano ... Mirella Banti
Paolo ... Francesco Capitano
Prof. Brandi ... Paolo Graziosi
Commissioner ... Giacomo Piperno

Former Venice film fest topper Carlo Lizzani appeared on the Lido as a director in the "Venice TV" section with a special three-hour made-for-tv film on terrorism. Pic is a professional effort that veers into the cops and robbers genre. Its problem is that no clear viewpoint comes across regarding the host of characters it deals with, causing a loss of dramatic focus. Ho-hum entertainment will find its main audience on the small screen.

Multi-character story is obviously derived from a book (by Luce D'Eramo). Left-wing terrorists, driven underground by the sweeping police round-ups of recent years, decide to give up armed revolution for the time being. Instead they will be common criminals, thieves, and save their booty to use in the future when the time is ripe to resume armed terrorism.

Covered by solid civilian identities (doctor, maid, trucking boss, etc.), the group plans and executes three brilliant robberies in the same area within half an hour. This illustrates the superb organization of terrorist groups — and provides pic with its best moment, when personalities are forgotten and a simple thriller structure takes over. The audience inevitably roots for the crooks, who get away with all three hold-ups.

When the group is eventually caught, they face arrest calmly, knowing they will be judged by less severe laws as criminals than as terrorists. They also have a good lawyer — an honest man who is compromised because his son is a member of the band. Pic concludes with the rather obvious message that the passage of terrorsm through Italian society has left a permanent scar.

In the aftermath of the blackest years of shooting, the issue of terrorism seems to have lost some of its topicality, and needs special handling to bring it to life for audiences. This "Nucleus Zero" doesn't deliver. Helmer is obviously concerned to give an even-handed presentation of the characters, making them neither likeable nor monstrous, but believable human beings. Cast also follows the dangerous path of blank neutrality, maintaining a distant coolness towards their parts. Audience has no way to respond to this cautious portrait of terrorists in sheep's clothing.

—*Yung.*

Pianoforte
(Grand Piano)
(ITALIAN-COLOR)

Venice, Sept. 6.

A Gaumont release, produced by Renzo Rossellini and Manolo Bolognini for Opera Film Produzione. Stars Giulia Boschi and François Siener. Directed by Francesca Comencini. Screenplay, Comencini, Vincenzo Cerami; camera (Eastmancolor), Armando Nannuzzi; art director, Dante Ferretti; editor, Ruggero Mastroianni; music, Guido and Maurizio De Angelis. Reviewed at the Venice Film Festival (De Sica section), Aug. 31, 1984. Running time: 102 MINS.
Maria .Giulia Boschi
Paolo . . . . .François Siener
Alessandra . . . . .Giovannella Grifeo
Robertino . . . . .Karl Zinny
Maria's mother . .Marie-Christine Barrault

A bright film debut for Francesca Comencini, daughter of vet helmer Luigi and part of the Gaumont circle of talents (husband is company topper Daniel Toscan Du Plantier), "Pianoforte," a semi-autobiographical love story about a young couple struggling against heroin addiction, won a merited first prize in Venice's Italian Showcase. Story is sensitively told, thesps are well-directed, and for once budget was sufficient to make technical credits a plus and not a minus. It should have a moderate run on Franco-Italian screens and some fest replay.

Maria (Giulia Boschi) and Paolo (François Siener), a journalist, separate for a period to try to kick a drug habit. They apparently succeed and come back together, but after an idyllic vacation in Sri Lanka, they slide back into the stuff. Maria's resolve to get out at all

costs pulls her apart from Paolo, who kills himself.

This thin skeleton is filled in with perceptive glances at the heroine's inner emotions, her misfired attempts to become closer to her distant mother and her piano playing as a symbolic way out of the drug trap.

No stomach-churning details of needles plunging into veins are shown; helmer concentrates on the emotional effects, which are convincingly portrayed. If Comencini sometimes errs on the side of safe choices, she avoids most beginner's clichés and creates believable characters with real problems. Giulia Boschi, a newcomer with excellent prospects, is attractive, composed, exuberant and childlike as the part demands. François Siener gives the down-and-out reporter a kind of roguish appeal, but never connects with audience's sympathies — possibly the result of helmer's own identification with the girl and defensive attitude towards her.

Pic boasts a co-script by Vincenzo Cerami, quality camerawork (Armando Nannuzzi), sets (Dante Ferretti), editing (Ruggero Mastroianni) and a charming score from Keith Jarrett, Emmanuel Chabrier and Guido & Maurizio De Angelis. — *Yung.*

Una Notte Di Pioggia
(One Rainy Night)
(ITALIAN-COLOR)

Venice, Sept. 4.

Produced by Carlo Chemblant for Cooperativa Coala Spettacoli. Stars Paolo Cesar Pereio. Written and directed by Romeo Costantini. Camera (color), Alessandro Carlotto, Gaetano Valle; editor, Enzo Meniconi; art director, Vincenzo Medusa; music, Gianfranco Plenizio. Reviewed at the Venice Film Festival (De Sica section), Sept. 4, 1984. Running time: 90 MINS.
Giorgio Ferrari . . . . . . .Paolo Cesar Pereio
Mariana . . . . .Adriana Falco

Former art director Romeo Costantini goes behind the camera in a commendable helming début that was appreciated by audiences in the Venice Italian Showcase. Film is a kind of low budget "Silkwood," speaking out against the criminal abuses of a nuclear power center and misuses of scientific research. A difficult theme for onshore release, but with special handling pic might find a small audience.

Giorgio Ferrari (Paolo Cesar Pereio) is a nuclear physicist who invents an antidote to atomic fallout and radiation. Slowly, however, the honest scientist working in the service of humanity realizes his discovery is being appropriated by an unscrupulous multi-national which intends to test it out on human beings, deliberately murdering the helpless old people who live in a re-

mote mountain community. One murder follows another and the scientist is himself the last victim, but he leaves behind a videotape of his death addressed to a newspaper reporter.

Technical work is surprisingly good for this type of shoestring production, with convincing interiors of the nuclear plant and several spectacularly staged accident sequences.

Opening scene shows the mysterious gunning down of a transport crew and explosion of their truck, which was carrying equipment to the institute where Ferrari works. Another effective sequence is devoted to his exploration of the village of old folks on the mountaintop who, abandoned by children, church and state, have developed their own miniature society. The nuclear explosion that destroys them (the bomb is dropped by an invisible American pilot in the pay of the evil multi-national) is as shocking as the one that finishes off Lawrence, Kansas in "The Day After." Helmer stretches a minimum of special effects a long way.

Dour and unassuming, Paolo Cesar Pereio is not an immediately appealing hero, but his quiet determination to get at the truth surrounding his work wins audience sympathy. There are a few plot points that stretch credulity, but on the whole "Rainy Night" is effectively gripping. — *Yung.*

Il Mistero Del Morca
(The Mystery Of The Morca)
(ITALIAN-COLOR)

Venice, Aug. 28.

An Instituto Luce/Italnoleggio release, produced by Istituto Luce-Italnoleggio Cinematografica, RAI-TV Channel 2 and Arti Sceniche. Stars Mario Scaccia. Directed by Mario Mattalini. Screenplay, Alberto Ongaro and Mattalini. Camera (color), Antonio Nordi, art director, Carmelo Agate; editor, Ida Cruciani; music, Giovanna Marini. Reviewed at the Venice Film Festival (De Sica section), Aug. 28, 1984. Running time: 100 MINS.
Sergio . . . . .Gianenrico Bianchi
Franco . . . . .Filippo Bocalon
Romano . . . . .Stefano Cola
Marco . . . . .Stefano Gritti
Serena . . . . .Serena Decal
Prof. Dicobene . . . . .Mario Scaccia

Marco Mattolini was one of the more experienced helmers making their screen debuts in the Venice De Sica section, a showcase for first features. His years of stage directing show in this well-shot adventure film for children. Tale gets off to a lively start and holds interest while the mystery of the title is unraveled by four boys in the manner of Hardy Boys stories. Story's interest is Universal, and there should be no reason why this Istituto Luce-Italnoleggio release can't cross the border to other markets.

Pic is set in Venice in the late '30s, where the local kids play at being

grownups with "coins" they have invented called cimbanos, made out of flattened bottle caps. Sergio, Franco, Romano and little Marco have banded together and are frantically trying to save up to buy a shiny red canoe. Cost: 12,000 cimbanos. Just as they are about to reach their goal, their hoard is stolen from the clubhouse. At first they suspect a rival gang, but soon taunting messages signed "The Morca" send them all over Venice and the lagoon trying to discover the identity of the mystery robber. The discovery, when they make it, is a shock that brings a certain part of their innocent childhood to an end.

Characters are sharply drawn and all four young actors (Gianenrico Bianchi, Filippo Bacalon, Stefano Cola and Stefano Gritti) work wonderfully, thanks also to Mattolini's talent at directing them. Mario Scaccia is excellent as their wise old teacher, nicknamed "Dicobene" (meaning: am I right?). Serena Decal is the pretty but snooty girl Sergio wants to impress at all costs.

Pic's merit is its being entertaining without being condescending, silly or sentimental. Venice is a beautiful backdrop, almost devoid of adults, seemingly a children's kingdom made for adventure and imagination. The approaching darkness of the war, Fascism and anti-semitism is adumbrated without turning into a heavy message. — *Yung.*

Un Caso Di Incoscienza
(A Case Of Irresponsibility)
(ITALIAN-COLOR)

Venice, Aug. 29.

An Asa Film S.r.l. production for RAI-2. Directed by Emidio Greco. Stars Erland Josephson, Brigitte Fossey, Rüdiger Vogler. Script, Ruggero Guarini, Vittorio Marchetti, Greco; camera (color), Franco Lecca; art director, Franco Velchi; costumes, Maurizio Millenotti; editor, Alfredo Muschietti; music, Luis Bacalov. Reviewed at Venice Film Festival (non-competing TV section), Aug. 28, 1984. Running time: 135 MINS.
Erik Sander . . . . .Erland Josephson
Elisabeth . . . . .Brigitte Fossey
Anderson . . . . .Rüdiger Vogler
Milton . . . . .John Steiner
Crivelli . . . . .Claudio Cassinelli
Helga . . . . .Margareth Mazzantini
Meticulous Gentleman . .Graziano Giustini
George . . . . .Roberto Bisacco
Stover . . . . .William Berger
Colette . . . . .Giuliana Calandra

Shown in the television section of the Venice fest, "A Case Of Irresponsibility" is a prestige production from RAI which boasts three major European stars and looks sumptuous.

Tale is set in the early '30s and involves a journalist (Rüdiger Vogler) investigating the disappearance of a Swedish millionaire tycoon (Erland Josephson) a couple of years earlier. Focus of the investigator's attention falls on the missing man's mistress, elegantly played by Brigitte Fossey.

Film was designed to play on tv, presumably over more than one evening, and has been edited with this in mind; pacing is thus lethargic when compared to a feature film or movie of the week, but this should be no problem for home viewers. Resolution is not terribly hard to work out in advance, and script is a bit on the thin side, though Emidio Greco's direction makes the most of the material.

Film buffs will delight in a tantalizing clip from Dorothy Arzner's "Christopher Strong," with a luminous Katharine Hepburn featured.

— *Strat*.

Il Ragazzo Di Ebalus
(The Boy From Ebalus)
(ITALIAN-COLOR)

Venice, Aug. 30.

Produced by Alberto Pesce for Ebalus Coop. Stars Riccardo Cucciolla and Saverio Marconi. Written and directed by Giuseppe Schito. Camera (Color), Paolo D'Ottavi; editor, Otello Colangeli; art director-costumes, Elio Canestrari; music, Marcello Pasquali. Previewed at the Venice Film Festival (De Sica section), Aug. 30, 1984. Running time: **104 MINS.**

Old man of Corico	Riccardo Cucciolla
Marco	Saverio Marconi
Terrorist	Teresa Ann Savoy
Maria	Alida Sessa

Terrorism and Latin literature are the strange bedfellows of "The Boy From Ebalus," a helming debut seen in Venice's Italian Showcase. Director Giuseppe Schito normally works as literary consultant for a publishing house. Cooperative budget allowed pic to employ three name thesps in the cast, but script is too weak to hold audiences in thrall. Could have onshore tv use.

Pic's wholesome but credulity-stretching thesis is that an antidote to the violence and evil of terrorism which have led many good youth astray can be found in a return to nature. Spokesman and exemplar of the joys of bucolic life is an old peasant (Riccardo Cucciolla), who offers shelter to Marco (Saverio Marconi), a young terrorist on the run. Pursued by both police and members of his former band who want to keep him from talking, Marco runs away from his past with a gun and a thick wad of American dollars. In the rocky landscape of Puglia, he stumbles across the old peasant, who reads Virgil to him, and a pretty schoolteacher (Alida Sessa), also a Virgil fan, who drives him from one hiding place to another. But terrorist Teresa Ann Savoy is hot on his trail and Marco's fate is sealed.

There isn't much excitement to the chase and the ending is foreseeable long in advance. Probably the most dramatic thing in the picture is the ancient land dotted with trulli — stone huts — and sheep folds.

Thesp Riccardo Cucciolla is a big plus in the part of the old man who balances poetry with farming. The rest of the cast is adequate.

— *Yung*.

Country
(COLOR)

Gritty farm drama looms as a hit.

Hollywood, Sept. 15.

A Buena Vista release of a Touchstone Film. Produced by William D. Wittliff and Jessica Lange. Directed by Richard Pearce. Stars Jessica Lange, Sam Shepard. Screenplay, William D. Wittliff; camera (Technicolor), David M. Walsh; editor, Bill Yahraus; sound (Dolby stereo) Jim Webb, Scott Senechal; production design, Ron Hobbs; art direction, John B. Mansbridge; set decorator, John Franco Jr.; music, Charles Gross; assistant director, Al Nicholson. Reviewed at Gomillion Sound, Hollywood, Sept. 14, 1984. (MPAA Rating: PG). Running time: **109 MINS.**

Jewell Ivy	Jessica Lange
Gil Ivy	Sam Shepard
Otis	Wilford Brimley
Tom McMullen	Matt Clark
Marlene Ivy	Therese Graham
Carlisle Ivy	Levi L. Knebel
Arlon Brewer	Jim Haynie
Louise Brewer	Sandra Seacat
Fordyce	Alex Harvey
Cowboy	Jim Ostercamp

A gritty, gut-wrenching account of rural America which more than lives up to its advance rumblings, "Country" should reap a healthy b.o. harvest as Disney platforms the picture, hopefully with critical accolades as a boost.

Jessica Lange's pet project took a few well-documented detours on the road to getting produced, but it winds up firmly on the right track, with its basic theme of the classic struggle of the working man against the forces of government,

William D. Wittliff's screenplay recalls recent real-life events of how farmers have taken on loans with the government's blessing in order to expand and wind up faced with foreclosure when unable to keep up with the payments.

Lange, who coproduced with Wittliff, is the focal point, essaying the mother of the family faced with losing the farm which had been in her lineage for some 100 years, and fighting to keep together the land, as well as her husband and three children.

She and mate Sam Shepard are honest, hard-working people who pray at the dinner table, attend church and help their neighbors. It's just that his family, like 40% of the farmers in the area, is about to be victimized by get-tough government policies.

Lange sees the tragic effect on her neighbors, and witnesses first-hand her husband's violent, over-the-edge behavior in the wake of desparate circumstances.

But at "Country's" core is director Richard Pearce's deliberately paced establishment of the innerworkings of the family. It's buffered by David M. Walsh's cinematography, which captures the beauty and blemishes of the countryside.

Lange provides the heroic deeds, showing a rare strength in the most difficult of circumstances, but never losing touch with the sensitive side which finds her one night sobbing at the sight of her three children huddled together asleep, their instinctual way of uniting to shield themselves from the outside.

Almost overshadowed by Lange, is Sam Shepard, though he gives a quietly effective portrayal of the husband dealt a humiliating blow to his pride when the farm is fingered for liquidation.

Wilford Brimley gives a finely tuned characterization as Lange's father, who watches a farm that had been prosperous for the first and second generation begin to falter before his eyes.

Levi L. Knebel offers a nice turn as the teenage son, old enough to see what's happening to the family as he begins to mature, and Matt Clark plays a sensitive interpretation of the government rep reluctantly forced to start foreclosure proceedings.

"Country" provides a jarring testament to the sometimes forgotten heroes of American culture.

With a solid drama following "Splash," its highly successful spring comedy release, Disney's Touchstone banner is two-for-two with a couple of very different pictures. — *Klyn*.

The Times Of Harvey Milk
(U.S.-DOCU-COLOR-16m)

Toronto, Sept. 13.

A TeleCulture release of a Black Sands production. Produced by Richard Schmiechen and Robert Epstein. Associate producer, Greg Bex. Directed by Robert Epstein. Camera (color), Frances Reid; editor, Deborah Hoffmann; narrated by Harvey Fierstein; narration writers, Judith Coburn and Carter Wilson; music, Mark Isham; sound, Dan Gleich; sound editor, John Benson; photo research, Wendy Zheutlin; print media archivist, Robert Hawk. Reviewed at the Festival of Festivals, Toronto (Stranger Than Fiction), Sept. 12, 1984. Running time: **87 MINS.**

Harvey Milk was the toast of the San Francisco gay movement until his assassination, along with Mayor George Moscone, on Nov. 27, 1978. This straightforward docu tells the story of his rise as a politico in the 1970s, ultimately being elected to the city's Board of Supervisors.

An omniscient voice-over recounts Milk's early adulthood, noting he had known he was homosexual since the age of 14, but not until he decided to become a major political force in the Castro district of S.F. did it seem to matter.

Film becomes riveting halfway through when Milk is seen through tv footage of his political tenure. How he garnered the support of union leaders, turned to local issues with a sense of humor and ultimately put through the Gay Rights Bill is an interesting demonstration of minority rights vindicated through political activity.

Because the focus is Milk rather than the political situation that led to his death, his murderer gets rather short shrift. Dan White is portrayed as a WASP who found a constituency among sports fans and firemen. White's mere eight-year sentence for killing two public officials was such a mockery of justice that Milk became a martyr.

The pic could stop at this point, presenting a challenge to those concerned about the death of the defense of liberalism. Instead, it continues through the candlelight procession for Milk and a barrage of mournful witnesses following, which provides a catharsis, and for television, a more confined point of view without a radical edge. It remains just one strange life that had a short-lived galvanizing effect on the gay culture.

The docu pulls few punches and should make for informative and amusing entertainment on the arthouse circuit. It has a verve that festival-goers may remember from a bizarre little pic from the same director called "What Ever Happened To Susan Jane?" in 1982, about a suburbanite mingling in the San Francisco gay community.

The more astute watchers may find it a bit disingenuous that the pic credits the defeat of Proposition 6, which was actually due to more mainstream politicians like Jimmy Carter and Jerry Brown speaking out against it. And it is all too cavalier about the argument in defense of Dan White that attributed his murderous psychic condition to junk food. —Kaja.

Heartbreakers
(COLOR)

Top-notch study of modern mores.

Hollywood, Sept. 18.
An Orion Pictures release of a Jethro Films presentation of a Bob Weis production. Produced by Weis, Bobby Roth. Executive producers, Lee Muhl, Harry Cooper, Joseph Franck. Directed, written by Roth. Stars Peter Coyote, Nick Mancuso. Camera (Deluxe color), Michael Ballhaus; editor, John Carnochan; music, Tangerine Dream; set decoration, Florence Fellman; costume design, Betsy Jones; sound, Petur Hliddal; associate producer, Cass Coty; assistant director, Jack Baran. Reviewed at Gomillion Sound, L.A., Sept. 17, 1984. (MPAA rating: R.) Running time: **98 MINS.**
Arthur Blue ....Peter Coyote
Eli Kahn ....Nick Mancuso
Liliane ....Carole Laure
Charles King ....Max Gail
Terry Ray ....James Laurenson
Candy Keen ....Carol Wayne
Libby ....Jamie Rose
Cyd Mills ....Kathryn Harrold
Max ....George Morfogen
Warren Williams ....Jerry Hardin

Amusing and dramatic, sexy and insightful, "Heartbreakers" is one of the best American films in some time about contemporary relations between the sexes and men's emo-

tional lives. Study of two male best friends in their mid-30s' who experience convulsions in their careers, romances and their own relationship emerges as a potent portrait of modern mores and neuroses. Pic is also exemplary in its evocation of the current trendy L.A. scene.

Fourth feature effort by Bobby Roth, after the 1976 pic "Independence Day," "The Boss' Son" and "Circle Of Power," was filmed quietly early this year and is being released initially by Orion this week on the west coast only. Falling somewhere between a domestic art film and a commercially oriented meller, it's a tough sell, but a concentrated push à la "Choose Me," which it somewhat resembles, would be in order.

Film benefits from being a highly personal one, in that Roth's own concern for the characters and issues on display is deeply registered. At the outset, Kathryn Harrold breaks off a five-year relationship with bohemian loft artist Peter Coyote, who then decides to get in gear and prepare for an exhibition, having not had one in years.

His lifelong buddy, Nick Mancuso, is heir to a successful clothing concern and is committed to being uncommitted with women, preferring the singles' scene and a succession of one-night stands.

Remarkably, Coyote lands a show with L.A.'s hippest gallery and proceeds to turn out a series of erotic paintings of women in leather s&m and bondage garb, most of which are posed for by complaint tootsie Carol Wayne, whom Coyote and Mancuso share in the sack one evening.

At the same time, Harrold moves in with Coyote's more affluent rival painter Max Gail, while Mancuso gets worked up over beauteous, enigmatic art gallery assistant Carole Laure, Keen to the point of anouncing to his friend, even before he knows her, that he intends to marry her.

Bottled-up emotions and mismanaged moments lead to an explosion between the two men, which is plausibly motivated and equally believably patched up, even if it's unclear whether or not things will be able to continue as before.

Since it is theoretically about the two-way dynamics of a friendship, film is vulnerable to criticism on a structural level, as Roth is far more drawn to the more exotic art scene inhabited by Coyote than to the mundane business world in which Mancuso works; Mancuso invariably has to visit Coyote's turf, rather than the other way around, and this prevents Mancuso's character from possessing as much depth and three-dimensionality as his friend.

Nevertheless, what's up on the screen is always terrifically engag-

ing. If the men here are not as sensitive to women as they might be, the women can be equally rough and unpredictable. Harrold gives Coyote little solace after she leaves him and, just when it seems Laure will never drop her icy reserve with Mancuso, she lurches into sex with him, with the proviso that she will sleep alone. For her part, Wayne, initially just a buxom bimbo, develops into a real person as well, one who accepts how she's perceived by men but hasn't quite managed to transcend that limitation.

Coyote is superb in his best screen role to date, managing to maintain viewer sympathy even when his character is unreasonable and wrong, and producing genuine joy for him when his long artistic struggle finally pays off (kinky paintings by his character, named Arthur Blue, were done by artist Robert Blue).

Despite built-in limitations, Mancuso is appealing and holds his own, and admirably registers his confusion and desperation in his scenes with Laure, fine as the insecure but strong-minded knockout. Harrold, Gail and Wayne are all solid, and James Laurenson proves an adroit scene-stealer as the gallery owner.

Hip L.A. viewers will delight in the parade of current in-spots on display, including Fatburger, Spago, Duke's and the Sports Connectin. With great locations and fine lensing by longtime Rainer Werner Fassbinder collaborator Michael Ballhaus, film looks snazzy on a low budget, and Tangerine Dream score and a few well-chosen standards make for a good soundtrack.
—Cart.

Before Stonewall
(U.S.-DOCU-COLOR-16m)

Toronto, Sept. 16.
A production of Before Stonewall Inc. and The Center for the Study of Filmed History. Produced by Robert Rosenberg, John Scagliotti and Greta Schiller. Directed by Schiller. Camera (color), Sandi Sissel, Jan Kraepelin, Cathy Zheutlin; editing, Bill Daughton; music, Lori Seligman, Roy Ramsing; archival research, Andrea Weiss. Reviewed at the Festival of Festivals (Stranger than Fiction: World Documentaries), Toronto, Sept. 15, 1984. Running time: **87 MINS.**

The subtitle of pic, "The Making Of A Gay And Lesbian Community," indicates the historical perspective but not the range of the best of this year's flock of docus about homosexuality.

Archival footage from unidentified silent pics and even a Ronald Reagan cross-dressing musical, at the outset, reflects the pervasive existence of a gay sub-culture, before Rita Mae Brown begins the narration of how the underground demimonde grew into a flourishing, outspoken community.

In interviews with such celebrities as Allen Ginsberg and writer Ann Bannon, pic offers a wide range of testimony about vice-squad tactics, censorship, and witchhunts that included failed attempts to cleanse one of Gen. Dwight Eisenhower's battalions as well as the State Dept. of suspected homosexuals. The spectrum of gays includes blacks, Native American Indians, playwrights, bar owners, and even women who hate typing.

Historically, pic begins to show the closet door opening in Harlem in the '20s, through the increased emancipation of women during the war effort, and the culmination of a movement modeled on the Civil Rights movement provoked to full confrontation with authority in June 1969 at the Stonewall Inn in Greenwich Village. Two days of riots followed the bust of that gay bar, perceived by the filmmakers as the turning point for openly declared and demonstrated homosexuality. Hippies contributed a new, celebrity approach.

The new twist in an old theme is provided by director Greta Schiller's intertwining both lesbian and gay cultures, showing some of the internal conflicts between them. Interesting is the testimony from older gays about whether homosexuality should be considered a disease or a matter of choice.

Pic should find its way into the usual outlets for documentaries and enthusiastic reception on festival front. Good pacing and a sense of humor should draw larger audiences than the already-converted.
— Kaja.

Nothing Lasts Forever
(B&W/COLOR)

Weak fantasy comedy in a nostalgic vein.

Seattle, Sept. 10.
An MGM/UA Classics release of a Broadway Pictures production. Produced by Lorne Michaels. Written and directed by Tom Schiiler. Features entire cast. Camera (b&w, Technicolor), Fred Schuler; editors, Kathleen Dougherty, Margot Francis; musical arrangements, Cheryl Hardwick; art direction, Woods MacKintosh; optical effects, Computer Opticals; additional graphics, Ken Kneitel; coproducer, John Head. Reviewed at Crest Theater, Seattle, Sept. 9, 1984. (MPAA Rating: PG.) Running time: **82 MINS.**
Adam Beckett..............Zach Galligan
Mara Hofmeier ....Apollonia van
   Ravenstein
Ely ....Lauren Tom
Buck Heller ....Dan Aykroyd
Daisy Schackman ....Imogene Coca
Aunt Anita ....Anita Ellis
Eddie Fisher ....Himself
Father Knickerbocker..........Sam Jaffe
Hugo.......................Paul Rogers
Uncle Mort ....Mort Sahl
Swedish Architect ....Jan Triska
Helen Flagella ......Rosemary De Angelis
Lu ....Clarice Taylor
Lunar Cruise Director........Bill Murray

If "Nothing Lasts Forever" goes it will need special selling for special audiences. Overall, it's not unpleasant, but it's in a rush, making it difficult to savor, for instance, a clip from "Intolerance," while paradoxically, film's 82 minutes running time seems a bit long. Low-budget item was made over two years ago, and was caught during MGM/UA Classics' test run in Seattle.

A first feature film for producer Lorne Michaels and writer-director Tom Schiller, "Forever" is a filmed in black & white (with brief color sequences) mishmash of film styles of the 1940s, 1950s and 1960s, with old newsreel clips, some from old films, plenty of panoramas and aerials of New York City and surely one of the oddest love stories extant.

A comedy (perhaps) with few laughs; the love story (and problems) of Adam Beckett, well played by Zach Galligan, is the only unifying cord evident.

Beckett wants to be an artist in some future New York City that is ruled by the Port Authority, an institution that calls everyone to work, tells them when to stop, and regulates the influx of artists.

Beckett doesn't pass the test and is given a job regulating traffic in the Holland Tunnel. His boss is Buck Heller (Dan Aykroyd).

Along the way young Beckett has a brief love affair with artsy Mara Hofmeier (Apollonia van Ravenstein), is led underground to the *real* New York by Hugo (Paul Rogers), where Sam Jaffe as Father Knickerbocker rules.

Beckett inadvertently gets on a bus that turns out to be a Lunarcruiser, taking shoppers to the moon, and hears Eddie Fisher sing "Oh! My Papa" in the Galaxy Lounge, while under the scrutiny of steward-cruise director Bill Murray, who recognizes Beckett is not one of the regular moon-shoppers (cruises began in 1953).

In some manner Beckett is transported back to earth and to a successful concert as a pianist at Carnegie Hall. Earlier he had been run out of the hall when it was discovered his instrument was a player piano. He is then unmited with his true love, Ely (Lauren Tom), who also got back from the moon.

Apperances of Aykroyd, Mort Sahl (with no jokes), as a properly avuncular uncle, and Imogene Coca are cameos, as are those of Anita Ellis, who belts out a nice "It's Only A Paper Moon," and the late Sam Jaffe, high-lamaish as Father Knickerbocker. Bill Murray has a bit more to do as the laidback cruise director. —*Reed.*

Tu Solo
(You Alone)
(SPANISH-COLOR)

Madrid, Sept. 11.

A Serva Films production. Written and directed by Teo Escamilla. Camera (Eastmancolor), Antonio Escamilla; editor, Pedro del Rey; music, Antonio Solera and Vainica Doble; sound, Carlos Faruolo. Features students of the Madrid School of Tauromachy, among them Andrés Vázquez, Gregorio Sánchez, Luis Miguel Calvo, Joselito, Sevillita, Cesita. Reviewed at Cinespaña screening room, Sept. 10, 1984. Running time: 95 MINS.

Teo Escamilla, until now known as one of Spain's top cameramen, has turned to the subject of bullfighting for his first feature film, a kind of semi-documentary study of some of the kids attending Madrid's School of Tauromachy. With a hand-held shaky camera and a rather grainy print blown up to 35m Escamilla and his brother Antonio behind the camera limn a curious portrait of the kids' activities.

We see them trying out in a small bullring in Madrid's Casa de Campo Park with cape and *muleta* and an imitation wheelbarrow bull; they listen to explanations of their teacher. Escamilla also peeks into their humble family lives. Best parts of pic are the actual bullfight sequences, first with calves and very young bulls and eventually leading up to a bullfight in a large commercial ring.

This is clearly a film for lovers of the *corrida* who will be hooked by what other people, who decry the fiesta, will be put off by. One part of the film shows a village *capea,* where the bull is corralled and made sport of by the villagers; and, of course, all the bullfight sequences are real, as they happened, including one of a boy getting thrown on the horns and bruised in the eye.

Item may run into lotsa flack in countries with strong SPCA's. Pickup for tv, however, might be of interest to some webs. — *Besa.*

Teachers
(COLOR)

Topical comedy over-reaches for absurdity, but looms as a popular fall entry.

Hollywood, Sept. 21.

An MGM/UA Entertainment release of a United Artists presentation. Produced by Aaron Russo. Executive producer, Irwin Russo. Directed by Arthur Hiller. Stars Nick Nolte. Screenplay, W.R. McKinney; camera (Metrocolor), David M. Walsh; editor, Don Zimmerman; music supervisor, Sandy Gibson; production designer, Richard MacDonald; set decorator, John Dwyer; sound, Jerry Jost; costumes, Ruth Myers, assistant director, L. Andrew Stone; associate producer, Art Levinson. Reviewed at MGM/UA Studios, L.A., Sept. 20, 1984. (MPAA Rating: R). Running time: 106 MINS.

Alex	Nick Nolte
Lisa	JoBeth Williams
Roger	Judd Hirsch
Eddie	Ralph Macchio
Dr. Burke	Lee Grant
Herbert	Richard Mulligan
Rosenberg	Allen Garfield
Ditto	Royal Dano
Horn	William Schallert
Danny	Crispin Glover
Mrs. Pilikian	Zohra Lampert
Theresa	Katharine Balfour
Troy	Art Metrano
Diane	Laura Dern

Social drama and irreverent, often **broad comedy** underscore this story **of a zoo-like urban high school that's run like an asylum.** "Teachers" stars Nick Nolte as a **burned-out teacher** who's drawn back to his ideals. Pic makes stinging, **important** points about the **mess of secondary** public education, but **those points** are diluted gradually **by an overload** of comic absurdity. **Result is a film** that tries to have **it both ways** through doses of **truth and exaggeration.** The effect is unwieldy, **unsteady,** fragmented. **Outlook, nevertheless,** could be solid **because of an** abundance of commercial ingredients.

Catalyst to dark comedy is a lawsuit **brought against** the school district **for awarding** a diploma to a student **who can't** read or write. JoBeth Williams plays the attorney serving notice on the school and her confrontation with Nolte as the disillusioned teacher is aptly dramatized by one quick exchange of dialog: "There's nothing worse than a female lawyer with a cause," shouts Nolte. "Except a male teacher without one," fires back Williams.

Pic shreds an educational system dedicated to getting as many kids through the pipeline as it can. As the school district's lawyer puts it during a deposition hearing: "We're a business like everyone else."

Administration and faculty range from the intimidated to the incompetent to, in a truly hilarious performance by Richard Mulligan, the insane. It's a mark of the movie's comic exaggeration that the mentally defective Mulligan plays the most imaginative, brilliant teacher on the campus. (The hard-nosed blue collar campus site is nicely represented by Central High School in Columbus, Ohio; the abandoned school also served as production headquarters.)

Filmmakers engaged a large cast of well known performers: Lee Grant as calculating, ruthless school superintendent; Allen Garfield (who's forsaken his Goorwitz billing) as a teacher afraid of his student but who turns heroic; Royal Dano as a glum disciplinarian whose bizarre death, although funny, underscores the distractions of comic overreach in the story; Judd Hirsch as a vice principal protecting his school's reputation; William Schallert as the principal afraid of his shadow; and, in the central student role, Ralph Macchio as a street-smart but illiterate kid who triggers Nolte's reemergence as a teacher willing to lose his job for what is right. Macchio's performance is effective but a bit over-mannered.

Music sound track, composed entirely of original songs by the likes of Joe Cocker, ZZ Top, The Motels, and Freddie Mercury, among others, is a boxoffice asset but song placement in the narrative doesn't propel the plot as well as it might.

Nolte nicely captures the image of a rather shaggy 10-year veteran of the classroom, and Williams is okay as his zealous nemesis who harbors romantic yearnings from the days when Nolte was her teacher. Her near-strip in the high school corridor, in her desperation to spark Nolte to his old ideals, is yet another example of how pic's comedy defuses the effect of the strong theme.

Director Arthur Hiller can't quite avoid the sense of the material's manipulation although he does achieve sturdy results in Nolte's showdown with the school board in the vast emptiness of the school's gym. A subplot about a student who is made pregnant by a gym teacher has the earmarks of a scene from a tv movie. And when the incident is used by the board to crucify Nolte (who had taken the girl to a free clinic for an abortion) the plot connection defies credulity.

Script was written by 27-year-old debuting screenwriter W.R. McKinney from a story conceived by producer Aaron ("Trading Places") Russo and his brother and exec producer Irwin Russo. Latter capitalized on his 10 years experience as a teacher in New York. Movie is not as thematically effective as "Up The Down Staircase" (1967) or "Blackboard Jungle" (1955) because it lacks cohesion. However, between the cracks something significant is still being said about the plight of American education. — *Loyn.*

The Bear
(COLOR)

Busey is terrif as Bear Bryant, but film lacks drama. Strong potential in southern markets and for football fans.

Hollywood, Sept. 25.

An Embassy Pictures release. Produced by Larry Spangler. Executive producer, James Hearn. Directed by Richard C. Sarafian. Stars Gary Busey. Screenplay, Michael Kane; camera (Deluxe color), Laszlo George; editor, Robert Florio; production designer, George Costello; sound, (Dolby stereo), Anthony Santa Croce; music, Bill Conti, Charles Koppelman, Martin Bandier; set decorator, Maria Rebman Caso; costume designer, Ron Talsky; assistant director, Buck Edwards. Reviewed at the Directors Guild of America, Sept. 24, 1984. (MPAA rating: PG.) Running time: 112 MINS.

Paul (Bear) Bryant	Gary Busey
Mary Harmon Bryant	Cynthia Leake
Coach Thomas	Harry Dean Stanton
Pat Trammell	Jon-Erik Hexum
Mae Martin Bryant	Carmen Thomas
Grandson Marc	Cary Guffey
Joe Namath	Steve Greenstein

Billy .... D'Urville Martin
Tony Eason .... Eric Hipple

In "The Bear," Gary Busey does his best work since "The Buddy Holly Story," and Embassy Pictures has a very American biopic that should particularly generate quick dollars in the South, where the craggy Paul (Bear) Bryant forged a legend that transcended football. The Larry Spangler production should also draw quick box-office from football addicts of all regions. That's the good news.

On the downside, the pic suffers from the absence of any dramatic conflict. Another serious problem is the failure to get at the man behind the legend. If "Bear" had any flaws, if he ever argued with his wife, indulged any vices, committed any human transgressions, we don't see it here. (Film's treatment of the scandalous charge in a national magazine in 1963 that Bryant had fixed a game with Georgia shows him passing a lie detector test and confirms a later court ruling that Bryant had been libeled.)

Writer Michael Kane (who also scripted last fall's gridiron-themed "All The Right Moves") and director Richard C. Sarafian had the cooperation and direct help of Bryant, who died last year.

However, with all their research, the filmmakers don't sufficiently develop any secondary characters to play off Bryant and give the movie a dramatic momentum. It's all Busey, whipping teams into shape at Kentucky, Texas A&M, and Alabama, uncorking some wonderful locker room inspirations, turning boys into men out of an undeniably winning combination of tyranny and humanity.

Busey credibly ages 50 years in the film, from Bryant's playing days when Bama beat Stanford in the Rose Bowl to Bryant's emotional 1982 Liberty Bowl victory over Illinois, which ended his coaching career. Given Busey's comparatively young age, he is more credible in the stronger first half of the film but, throughout, the Bear's walk, body language, the cigaret dangling from his lips, the scratchy voice, and the spirit of the man are solidly rendered by Busey.

Jon-Erik Hexum is excellent playing the late Alabama quarterback Pat Trammel, but the dramatization of Bryant's best-known player, Joe Namath, (Steve Greenstein) is given short shrift. Bryant's pretty, proper Southern wife (Cynthia Leake) contributes little to the narrative, and family scenes are pallid. Harry Dean Stanton stands out in early scenes as Bryant's college coach.

Production values, except for a rather muddy dialog track at screening caught, are sharp. And football action, including juxtaposition of old clips (black and white and color) is great if you're a football junkie.

But "Bear" doesn't stand up to "Knute Rockne — All American" (Warner Bros., 1940) precisely because there are no characters like the Gipper to give the script punch. Embassy's toughest pull: getting females into the theaters. —*Loyn.*

Les Ripoux
(FRENCH-COLOR)

Paris, Sept. 19.

An AMLF release of a Film 7 production. Produced and directed by Claude Zidi. Stars Philippe Noiret. Screenplay, Zidi and Didier Kaminka, from an original story idea by Simon Mickael. Camera (Eastmancolor), Jean-Jacques Tarbes; editor, Nicole Saulnier; art director, Françoise De Leu; sound, Jean-Louis Ghetto; music, Francis Lai; production manager, Pierre Gauchet. Reviewed at the UGC Biarritz theater, Paris, Sept. 19, 1984. Running time: **107 MINS.**
René .... Philippe Noiret
Francois .... Thierry Lhermitte
Simone .... Régine
Natacha .... Grace de Capitani
Commissioner Bloret ..... Julien Guiomar
Pierrot .... Pierre Frag
Inspector Vidal .... Claude Brosset
Inspector Leblanc .... Albert Simono

Unlike the hit gag machines to which he has accustomed viewers, Claude Zidi's new film is a dramatic comedy about crooked Paris cops on the make ("Les Ripoux" is a back-slang term for a venal flic). The director, served by a tart, fluidly imaginative script by himself and Didier Kaminka, shows perfect ease on unfamiliar comic terrain.

Philippe Noiret is at his gruffly ironic best as a cynical veteran plainclothes policeman who plays the horses, lives with a former call girl, and pads his nest with bribes, petty rackets and occasional muggings of rich, undesirable pimps.

But his co-existence with the small-time felons, dealers and hucksters of his melting pot beat is threatened when he's teamed with a rookie inspector (Thierry Lhermitte), straight out of a provincial police academy and keen on making a career strictly by the book.

Unable to bring the cleancut Lhermitte around to his methods by reason, Noiret sets out to break his moral resolution by fixing him up with a young high-class prostitute, who has him wine-and-dine her in a super-expensive restaurant spending his entire salary in a matter of hours.

Utterly broke (and in headlong love with the prostitute) Lhermitte becomes dependent on the hypocritical paternalism of Noiret, who soon succeeds in weaning his partner from his unprofitably naive ideals. They form an efficient team, working their beat with impunity and outwitting the prying inquiries of their superiors.

But disciple outdoes master in proposing that they make off with the million-dollar booty at stake. Noiret and Lhermitte are faultless, together and separately, with former offering some memorable

moments of exasperated outrage and understaged irony, and latter credibly human in his total moral about-face.

Female roles take a back seat to the leads, but nightclub personality Régine is quietly genuine as Noiret's ex-hooker mistress, and Grace de Capitani charming as Lhermitte's expensive love interest.

Zidi and Kaminka got invaluable professional advice from a real cop, Simon Mickael (a pseudonym), credited with the original story idea. He's no doubt responsible for the wealth of realistic detail — notably in the depiction of Paris' notorious immigrant quarter, the Goutte d'Or, that puts to shame some of the non-comedy crime pictures France has been producing in abundance. —*Len.*

Body Rock
(COLOR)

Weak breakdancing pic arrives late in the trend.

Hollywood, Sept. 26.

A New World Pictures release in association with Angeles Entertainment Group and Inverness Prods. Produced by Jeffrey Schechtman. Co-executive producers, Phil Ramone, Charles J. Weber, John Feltheimer. Directed by Marcelo Epstein. Features entire cast. Screenplay, Desmond Nakano; camera (CFI color), Robby Müller; editor, Richard Halsey; sound (Dolby stereo) Lee Alexander; production design, Guy Comtois; art direction, Craig Stearns; costume design, Marlene Stewart; choreographer, Susan Scanlan; assistant director, Leon Dudevoir; associate producer, Chuck Russell; music, various artists. Reviewed at Aidikoff Screening Room, L.A., Sept. 25, 1984. (MPAA Rating: PG-13.) Running time: **93 MINS.**
Chilly D .... Lorenzo Lamas
Claire .... Vicki Frederick
E-Z .... Cameron Dye
Darlene .... Michelle Nicastro
Terrence .... Ray Sharkey
Donald .... Joseph Whipp
Magick .... La Ron A. Smith

New World's "Body Rock" would be in better shape if it lived up to its energetic soundtrack, but wobbly breakdance picture offers too little, and perhaps comes too late to capitalize on the craze, though it could do reasonable business with younger audiences.

Lorenzo Lamas stars as the supposedly street-wise Gotham youth, head of a group of city boys which specializes in trendy graffiti art and dancing.

Though diminutive La Ron A. Smith is the star attraction, Smith takes Lamas under his wing and teaches him the finer points of his craft. Lamas catapults ahead of his buddies when manager Ray Sharkey catches their act and persuades Lamas to leave his cronies and work for his club, though he never becomes more than an adequate performer.

Believing Lamas deserves the attention proves the picture's biggest obstacle. With its credibility in

doubt, "Body Rock" becomes a ho-hum affair.

Lamas shuns the apartment he shares with his mother, and leaves behind his pals and his girlfriend, Michelle Nicastro, for a spacious pad and a new mate in Vicki Frederick.

Director Marcelo Epstein moves things along, greatly aided by tunes from top-name artists assembled by music industry vet Phil Ramone (music supervisor of "Flashdance"), who also co-exproduced.

But while the music is lively, there's nothing substantial between the dance routines.

To its credit, the picture is pretty clean stuff, with only hints of sex. But New World, which has been having problems with the ratings board of late, obviously had to put in some extra work to tone the film down to PG-13.

Sometimes the tinkering is amusingly evident. In one scene, for example, Nicastro tells Lamas to go "screw" himself, which on screen she pronounces by putting her lower lip between her teeth. Since the word heard is not normally formed that way on the streets of New York, she perhaps was suggesting he go "find" himself.

What doesn't need translation are the dance sequences, excellently choreographed by Susan Scanlan, and Guy Comtois' production vision.

Nicastro emerges as a delightfully wide-eyed innocent who deserved more screen time. Smith provides the most cheerfully effective presence during his breakdance exhibitions, while Frederick and Sharkey fare adequately and supporting players are just okay. —*Klyn.*

Impulse
(COLOR)

Nasty and silly horror thriller self-destructs.

Hollywood, Sept. 28.

A 20th Century Fox release of an ABC Motion Pictures production. Produced by Tim Zinnemann. Directed by Graham Baker. Features entire cast. Screenplay, Bart Davis, Don Carlos Dunaway; camera (Deluxe color), Thomas Del Ruth; editor, David Holden; music Paul Chihara; production designer, Jack T. Collins; set designer, Spencer Deverill; set decorator, Jim Duffy; sound, Richard Bryce Goodman; costumes, John S. Perry; assistant director, Beau E.L. Marks. Reviewed at Egyptian Theater, Hollywood, Sept. 28, 1984. (MPAA Rating: R.) Running time: **88 MINS.**
Stuart .... Tim Matheson
Jennifer .... Meg Tilly
Dr. Carr .... Hume Cronyn
Bob Russell .... John Karlen
Eddie .... Bill Paxton
Margo .... Amy Stryker
Sheriff .... Claude Earl Jones

"Impulse" is an ugly little picture that would play better as comedy if it wasn't so mean-spirited. Filmmakers, however, insist on playing it straight, even to the point of tagging on a documentary-style epilog. Picture is neither gory nor fast enough to satisfy the action crowd; neither intelligent nor interesting enough for an adult audience — leaving almost no one to appreciate it.

Picture preys on the premise that when people are allowed to act according to their impulses, they will become violent, destructive and totally anti-social. Overall, "Impulse" presents a vicious and malevolent view of human nature. Fortunately is too ridiculous to be taken seriously.

Taking seemingly forever to get to the point, "Impulse" appropriates dose of Hitchcock here, a bit of "Invasion Of The Body Snatchers" there and ties it all together with a "Carrie"-like psycho-drama. Any suspense or curiosity the film generates in the first half is dissipated by inept story telling and awkward pacing.

Wholesome young couple Meg Tilly and Tim Matheson are literally called to Tilly's hometown when her mother (Lorinne Vozoff) blows her brains out while talking to her daughter on the phone. The fact that she's still alive is only the first of the implausible happenings in Sutcliffe.

Nothing is quite what it seems in this town and the dark undercurrents might have made for a better film if they were explored, not made into a cartoon. Upon their arrival Matheson and Tilly encounter a seething family feud between her father (John Karlen) and her brother (Bill Paxton).

For comic relief there is a scene in the bank in which people help themselves to money and another in a bar featuring an old flame of Tilly's showing her what real pain is about — he gruesomely breaks two of his own fingers.

The fun's not over yet. Kids set Tilly's car on fire while her old friend (Amy Stryker) tells her it's not easy having children.

All this nonsense goes nowhere as mysterious events are introduced and then dropped.

Editing by David Holden has no internal logic with the time sequence totally jumbled. The only way to tell that the day is done is that Tilly walks away into the sunset when it's over. The explanation for the town's destruction, when it finally comes, something about toxic waste in the milk, is hardly worth waiting for. A predictable government coverup operation is also included.

Performances are adequate given the material with Matheson more convincing as a doctor than a madman. Hume Cronyn as the old town doc who succumbs early to the mass mania is effective through he has little to do. Tilly too is underutilized, a role having no real flesh on its bones.

Thomas Del Ruth's photography keeps a nice lid on the color but Graham Baker's direction is generally as static as the story.—*Jagr.*

Night Shadows
(Mutant)
(COLOR)

Well-acted but silly horror thriller.

A Film Ventures International release of an Edward L. Montoro presentation of a Laurelwood production. Executive producers, Montoro, Henry Fownes. Produced by Igo Kantor. Directed by John (Bud) Cardos. Stars Wings Hauser, Bo Hopkins. Screenplay, Peter Z. Orton, Michael Jones, John C. Kruize from story by Jones, Kruize; camera (TVC color), Al Taylor; editor, Michael J. Duthie; music, Richard Band; sound, Jim Hawkins; production manager-associate producer, Nathaniel J. Dunn; assistant director, Mel Bishop; stunt coordinator, Lonnie R. Smith Jr.; special effects, Paul Stewart; special makeup effects, Eric Fiedler, Louis Lazzara; prosthetics, Dave Miller; sound effects, Gene Corso. Reviewed at RKO Warner theater, N.Y., Sept. 29, 1984. (MPAA Rating: R.) Running time: 99 MINS.
```
Josh .....................Wings Hauser
Sheriff Will Stewart .........Bo Hopkins
Mike.........Lee (Harcourt) Montgomery
Dr. Myra Tate ..........Jennifer Warren
Holly ....................Jody Medford
Albert ...................Marc Clement
Billy .....................Cary Guffey
Jack ......................Danny Nelson
Mrs. Mapes ........Mary Nell Santacroce
```

"Night Shadows," a.k.a. "Mutant," is a B-level horror picture which wastes some good acting in support of a trite, silly story. Outlook is okay in fast bookings.

Cornball science fiction premise (shared by no less than four other current films: "C.H.U.D.," "Impulse," "The Being" and "The Toxic Avenger") has toxic chemical waste creating instant (forget the science) monster mutations among the residents of the one-horse town of Goodland. Yankee visitors, the brothers Josh (Wings Hauser) and Mike (Lee Montgomery) become enmeshed in fighting both rednecks and monsters (sometimes redneck monsters) and, after Mike disappears mysteriously, the local sheriff (Bo Hopkins) and pretty school teacher (Jody Medford) join the survival crusade.

Director John (Bud) Cardos, who replaced original helmer Mark Rosman early in the shoot, handles routine action and fistfight scenes well and gets solid perfs from the principal performers, but the monsters (styled as white-faced Halloween zombies), don't show up en masse until an hour into the picture. Their slow gait, hands-reaching out threateningly mode is childishly executed, reducing film's horror potential to laughs as the good guys make familiar stands at a doctor's office or Kantor's (in-joke for producer Igo Kantor) Service Station.

Wings Hauser, currently scoring on-screen in a key supporting role in "A Soldier's Story," is well-cast as the brawling hero, his eyes appropriately bugging out at the sight of a ghoul. However, when the script calls on him to be able to punchout and escape from dozens of bloodthirsty monsters at once, he's stuck in a dumb joke. Bo Hopkins is again perfect as a southern lawman, a role quite similar (but with a boozing problem added) to his "Sweet 16" horror assignment. Former child stars Lee Montgomery (who has dropped his middle name Harcourt from his billing) and Cary Guffey have little to do here.

Special makeup effects are crummy, with that overused gimmick of air bladders under the skin (causing pulsating tumors on faces and hands) ready for the cinematic scrapheap. — *Lor.*

The Wild Life
(COLOR)

Pointless followup to "Fast Times At Ridgemont High;" attendance is strictly optional.

Hollywood, Sept. 25.

A Universal Pictures release. Executive producer, C.O. Erickson. Produced by Art Linson and Cameron Crowe. Directed by Art Linson. Features entire cast. Screenplay, Crowe; camera (Technicolor), James Glennon; editor, Michael Jablow; sound, Bud Alper; production design, William Sandell; assistant director, Albert Shapiro; coproducer, Don Phillips; music, Edward Van Halen, Donn Landee. Reviewed at Universal Studios, L.A., Sept. 24, 1984. (MPAA Rating: R.) Running time: 96 MINS.
```
Tom ..................Christopher Penn
Jim .................Ilan Mitchell-Smith
Bill .........................Eric Stoltz
Eileen ....................Jenny Wright
Anita ...................Lea Thompson
Tony ..................Brin Berliner
Harry ....................Rick Moranis
David ...................Hart Bochner
Donna ................Susan Blackstone
Julie .................Cari Anne Warder
Craig .................Robert Ridgely
Vince ..................Michael Bowen
Benny ..................Angel Salazar
Charlie ..................Randy Quaid
```

"The Wild Life" seems destined for success in some segments of the marketplace, a nice way of saying it is absolutely awful from the first frame but who's to judge what teenagers will like.

As the promotion proclaims, "Wild" is the work of the 'creators" of the profitable" "Fast Times At Ridgemont High," meaning producer (and now also director) Art Linson and writer (and now producer) Cameron Crowe. Unfortunately, Linson is no match for "Ridgemont" director Amy Heckerling and Christopher Penn does not do for "Wild" what brother Sean achieved earlier.

But Linson has incorporated all the trappings of nubility: vandalism, alienation, irresponsibility, substance abuse, promiscuity, voyeurism, allegorical adult authority, boderline adolescent insanity — and french fries.

It really makes no difference that none of this goes in search of a story. But, for the record, "Wild" has something to do with the last week of summer before high school starts again.

Penn is a wild and crazy prep wrestler who it would be tempting to say looks old enough to have been in high school for 10 years had this same observation not already been made about most of the people who ever appeared in these pictures. Having already shown a broader and better talent in "Footloose" and "Rumble Fish," Penn seems uncomfortably squeezed into the confines of class space cadet, even if Sean had not already previously defined the part completely.

Penn is friends with Eric Stoltz who has graduated already and is making his move into a swinging singles apartment. Though Stoltz is relatively responsible, finances force him to take Penn in as a roommate. But the picture really isn't about that, except that it allows for some wild and crazy action.

Stoltz is also the older brother of Ilan Mitchell-Smith, a mentally displaced 15-year-old with a fan's distant fixation on the Vietnam War and an adoration for one of its veterans, Randy Quaid. But the picture really isn't about that and Quaid's appearance is hardly more than a cameo.

Penn has a girl friend, Jenny Wright, who is and is not outgrowing him and Stoltz has a girl friend, Lea Thompson, who converts his rejection into a dalliance with married policeman Hart Bochner in the back of the donut shop. But the picture really isn't about that, except for flashes of bare breasts between threadbare dialog.

One bright spot, as usual when he's around, is Rick Moranis' presense as Wright's nerd boss at the department store, anxious to lure her into a quiet corner in home furnishings. But the picture really isn't about that, either, and more's the pity.

"Wild" really isn't about anything, except that it's about and out in release. And, given the wisdom of the Founding Fathers in 1776, nobody has to go unless they want to.
—*Har.*

Jaws Of Satan
(King Cobra)
(COLOR)

A United Artists release of a Bill Wilson production. Produced by Wilson. Directed by Bob Claver. Features entire cast. Screenplay, Gerry Holland, from story by James Callaway; camera (Technicolor), Dean Cundey; editor Len Miller; music, Roger Kellaway; sound, Carey Lindley; art direction, Robert Topol; set decoration, William Webb; assistant director for-second unit director, Dan Allingham; production manager-associate production manager-associate producer, Joel Douglas; post-production supervisor/-second unit producer, Peter W. Rea; second unit camera, Raymond Stella; makeup, Ron Figuly. Reviewed on Sl owtime, N.Y., Sept. 10, 1984. (MPAA Rati'ıg: R.) Running time: 92 MINS.

Father Farrow . . . . Fritz Weaver
Dr. Maggie Sheridan . . . . Gretchen Corbett
Paul Hendricks . . . . Jon Korkes
Monsignore . . . . .orman Lloyd
Evelyn . . . . Diana Douglas
Matt Perry . . . . Bob Hannah
Elizabeth Perry . . . . Nancy Priddy
Kim Perry . . . . Christina Applegate
Sheriff Tatum . . . . John McCurry
Mayor Thorpe . . . . Jack Gordan

"Jaws Of Satan" is an unsuccessful horror pic lensed in late 1979 under the title "King Cobra" as a pre-pickup for worldwide distribution by United Artists but shelved by the studio. It is reviewed here for the record, telecast as a pay-cable offering.

Made when a rash of snake films were getting produced, such as "Venom" and "Spasms," film relies on a hoary supernatural premise that Satan is materializing in the form of a large cobra, to do battle with southern priest Father Farrow (Fritz Weaver) whose family was cursed by a Druid priest long ago for persecuting his people. Inspired by the King Cobra's influence, an outbreak of fatal snake attacks is occurring in Weaver's town, but the mayor and leading local businessmen hush things up to avoid adverse publicity as a local greyhound dog racing track is due to open.

"Satan" relies too heavily on cliched scripting derived from the influential hit "Jaws," in both the central coverup premise (itself dating back at least to Henrik Ibsen's "An Enemy Of The People") and in having Weaver joined by two other cobra-hunters, a university herpetologist (Jon Korkes) and local doctor (Gretchen Corbett) to do battle with the beast.

Lacking the special effects demanded by modern audiences, "Satan" gets off to a terrible start by the obvious gaffe of a very noticeable protective glass partition suddenly materializing during the first reel snake attack aboard a train. Not only is the victim's reflection clearly visible on screen, but the poor snake goes "ping" when it haplessly strikes the glass with its head while we're supposed to believe it's making a deadly bite. Though Dean Cundey's atmospheric lensing and a moody score (with harpsichord motif) by Roger Kellaway help, pic never regains its credibility. Cast is mainly content to walk through. —Lor.

Far From Poland
(COLOR/B&W)

A film by Jill Godmilow in collaboration with Susan Delson, Mark Magill and Andrzej Tymowski. Directed by Godmilow. Camera (color), Jacek Laskus; sound, John Dildine; editing, Godmilow; research and translation, Tymowski; art director, Magill; assistant editor, Delson; production manager, Del-

son; piano, Michael Sahl. Reviewed at Magno Penthouse screening room, N.Y., Sept. 19, 1984. (No MPAA Rating.) Running time: 106 MINS.

Barbara Lopienska . . . . Honora Fergusson
Richard Fraser . . . . John Fitzgerald
Jill . . . . Jill Godmilow
Guard . . . . :Nels Johnson
Hanna Krall . . . . Elzbieta Komorowska
Mark . . . . Mark Magill
Anna Walentynowicz . . . . . Ruth Maleczech
Adam Zarewski . . . . Mark Margolis
Premier Jaruzelski . . . . John Perkins
"K-62" . . . . William Raymond
Jadwiga (voice) . . . . Elzbieta Czyzewska
Narrator . . . . John Dildine
Jan (voice) . . . . Olek Krupa

Thwarted by the Polish government authorities in her attempt to make a documentary about the Solidarity workers' movement, New York-based filmmaker Jill Godmilow undertook instead this talky and tortuous exercise in dialectical soul-searching which purports to challenge and dissect "the myth of documentary truth."

However, those few snippets of tv news clips and smuggled documentary footage in black & white used here indicate that a straightforward docu on the turbulent days of the Polish workers' national uprising in late 1981 might have been an electrifying work. But far removed (as indeed she was) from events in Poland, Godmilow chose to make a convoluted docudrama in which the filmmaker's own left-wing philosophical angst overshadows rather than illuminates the complex and far-reaching implications of the struggle spawned in the Gdansk shipyards.

Godmilow juxtaposes dramatic recreations of print interviews with representative Solidarity figures against a self-aggrandizing and somewhat self-pitying recreation of her own struggle to make this film. Hectored by her cynical, artsy videomaker boyfriend Mark about the inadvisability of the project ("You don't care about the Poles, you're using them"), she presses on, like the journalist who writes at length about how he couldn't get the story.

The bitterness of the workers' plight in a land where repression reigns, food is scarce and money is worthless paper, is communicated through dramatized conversations with sincere, but intellectually smug Polish emigrés and letters from the filmmaker's friends in Poland. Far more effective, however, are the recreated interviews with Anna Walentynowicz (the 55-year-old crane operator whose firing triggered the Gdansk shipyard strikes); Silesian coal miner Adam Zarewski and the former censor, "K-62."

Played with convincing indomitability by Ruth Maleczech, Anna embodies the limitless travail that's been the lot of Eastern Europeans of her war-torn, dislocated generation. The concreteness of her courage in the face of persecution by the workers' state she served for 30

years contrasts with the feeble ambiguity of the moralistic aphorisms ("are people basically good — or evil?") that the interviewer tries to extrapolate from the testimony of Anna's life.

The coal miner, given to black humor and grim realism concerning the possibility of social change is, quite simply, the salt of the earth — closer to the nub of the problems than either the union intellectuals or military bureaucrats will ever be. The censor has sold his soul for survival with Kafkaesque rationale ("censorship is good training for journalism") but he too is depicted as a victim.

Perhaps if she had concentrated on the real victims, Godmilow's film would have had more cohesion and impact. Instead much running time is given over to her dour, on-camera ruminations over the reconciliation of political conscience and artistic responsibility. When a fantasy epilog about General Jaruzelski under house arrest in 1988 and the filmmaker's closing litany of things she left out (the role of the Church, the CIA, international banks and Polish anti-Semitism) finally unfold, it's easy to speculate that the film's conclusion contains the seeds of a more interesting project.—Rich.

Le Futur Interieur
(The Future Interior)
(CANADIAN-COLOR)

Toronto, Sept. 13.

A Les Productions Monique Messier production. Produced by Messier. Written and directed by Yolaine Rouleau and Jean Chabot. Camera (color), Guy Dufaux; editor, Louise Suprenant; music, Alain Corneau, Ginette Bellavance. Reviewed at Toronto Festival of Festivals (Perspective Canada), Sept. 13, 1984. Running time: 63 MINS.
Cast: Veronique O'Leary.

A feminist study that tries too hard in tackling a wide range of political issues, "Le Futur Interieur" is a hybrid of poetic reflection and documentary. Its focus on the women's movement and the ultimate goal of world peace makes it a surefire femme fest entry, but commercial prospects are marginal.

A woman is riding on a train — destination unknown — reading the essays of Virginia Woolf and meditating on the need for women to use their influence to help men prevent war.

Film hops back and forth to this journey as a point of reference. Sprinkled throughout are a barrage of media snippets: early suffragette marches, antipornography demonstrations, antiwar rallies, women workers in World War II munitions plants, ERA newsclips and early '50s fashion shows.

High spots are found in interviews with the first woman graduate of Laval U. in Quebec and a meeting with an old suffragette remin-

iscing about her group's efforts to introduce a bill in Quebec giving women the right to vote on the same terms as men.

The most touching segment is a teary-eyed confession by a 40-year-old mother of five who is left by her husband during her last pregnancy, who feels society's contempt for women who bear too many children.

Directors Yolaine Rouleau and Jean Chabot are well-intentioned but the converted will cheer and the undecided will be overwhelmed by their approach. —Devo.

Seishun Zankoku Monogatari
(Cruel Story Of Youth)
(JAPANESE-COLOR)

Hollywood, Sept. 18.

A New Yorker Films release of a Shochiku production. Produced by Tomio Ikeda. Directed, written by Nagisa Oshima. Camera (color, widescreen), Ko Kawamata; editor, Keiichi Uraoka; music, Riichiro Manabe; art direction, Koji Uno. Reviewed at the Vista, L.A., Sept. 17, 1984. (No MPAA rating.) Running time: 97 MINS.

Kiyoshi Fujii . . . . Yusuke Kawazu
Makoto Shinjo . . . . Miyuki Kuwano
Yuki Shinjo . . . . Yoshiko Kuga
Akimoto . . . . Fumio Watanaba
Ito . . . . Shinji Tanaka
Terada . . . . Shinjiro Matsuzaki
Teruko Shimonishi . . . . Toshiko Kobayashi
Masahiro Shinjo . . . . Jun Hamamura
With: Shinko Ujiie, Aki Morishima, Yuki Tominaga, Kei Stato, Asao Sano, Kan Nihonyanagi.

(In Japanese: English subtitles)

Made in 1960, Nagisa Oshima's second feature film has only recently entered into U.S. release for the first time via New Yorker Films and is reviewed now for the record. Harsh, rigorously unsentimental and studded with numerous striking scenes, "Cruel Story Of Youth" will clearly be of interest only to ardent buff followers of Oshima and the Japanese cinema, but it's good to have on hand for the domestic repertory, as it offers bracing proof that the antisocial iconoclasm of the director of "In The Realm Of The Senses" and "Merry Christmas, Mr. Lawrence" stretches back to the very beginning of his career nearly 25 years ago.

Shot mostly on location on city streets and in some seaside areas, film features plot conventions which fall in line with the American juvenile delinquent pics of the 1950s, but stylistically and thematically it resembles nothing so much as Jean-Luc Godard's "Breathless," made in 1958.

Simple setup has Mako, a middle-class girl, falling in with a low-life student, Fujii, after he rescues her from an assault. Couple's initial sexual encounter, which takes place on some enormous floating logs, is directed with such remorseless precision as to take on a mesmerizing quality, and the Bernard Herrmann-esque scoring of the sequence adds to its haunting mood.

Girl scandalizes her family by moving in with the lout, and the two develop a money-making scam in which Mako hitches rides and induces the drivers to come on to her, at which point Fujii materializes to beat them up and rob them.

Trouble with some local small-time hoods, an abortion and ultimate arrest constitute the couple's downward spiral. Oshima acknowledges the time-honored convention for youth-on-the-run pictures that it's "society's fault" that kids have run amuck, but just as quickly slaps that liberal excuse down by positing that the young punks are just as greedy and money-loving as the bourgeois businessman they victimize. Youths may turn to crime out of anger at society, but that doesn't make them innocent.

Without question, film has more than its share of rough spots and slow stretches, notably towards the middle, but freshness and daring of Oshima's style obviously represented a major departure from the tradition-bound Japanese cinema at the time, and remains interesting as another example of the talent explosion that was happening around 1960 in many parts of the world.

Technically, film is excellent, and 35m print caught looked very good. A stupefying footnote to film history is provided in a climactic scene, in which a large, handprinted poster reading, "Paris, Tex.," looms prominently in the background. What the English-language sign was doing there in the first place is mystery enough, but fact that French producer Anatole Dauman, some 15 years later, brought Oshima to fame in the West with "In The Realm Of The Senses" and, this past year, backed Wim Wenders' "Paris, Texas," truly boggles the mind.—*Cart.*

Le Bon Roi Dagobert
(Good King Dagobert)
(FRENCH-ITALIAN-COLOR)

Venice, Sept. 6.

A Gaumont release, produced by Archimede International in association with Gaumont, Stand'Art, FR3, Filmedis and Operafilm. Directed by Dino Risi. Stars Coluche, Ugo Tognazzi and Michel Serrault. Screenplay, Gérard Brach, Age and Dino Risi; camera (color), Armando Nannuzzi; art director, Dante Ferretti; costumes, Gabriella Pesucci and Raffaella Leone; editor, Alberto Gallitti; music, Guido and Maurizio De Angelis. Reviewed at Venice Film Festival, Sept. 6, 1984. Running time: 112 MINS.
Dagobert . . . . Coluche
Pope Honorius & double . . . Ugo Tognazzi
Otarius . . . . Michel Serrault
Héméré . . . . Carole Bouquet
St. Eligius . . . . Michaël Lonsdale
Chrondielde . . . . Isabella Ferrari
Queen Nanthilde . . . . Karin Mai

Dino Risi has found congenial ground for his lusty tastes and crude sense of humor in the 10th century. Dagobert I was a historical figure, one of the legendary kings of France, of whom little survives except a song about him putting his trousers on inside out. Script by Risi, Gérard Brach and Age is free-wheeling fantasy that takes off from there. French thesp Coluche, the king of vulgarity, fills the title bill to a T. Audiences who go for royal chamberpot jokes may warm up to "Dagobert;" others will find it a lightweight and over-budget curiosity.

Story opens when the king's caravan, wending its way through a forest, is attacked by a horde of murderous barbarians. The sole survivors are Dagobert, his confessor, Otarius (Michel Serrault), and his prettiest wench (Isabella Ferrari). In thanksgiving for his salvation, Dagobert vows to make a pilgrimage to Rome to see the Pope.

Another trip, this time by boat, has further demonstrations of the king's insatiable carnality and bad digestion. When he finally arrives in Rome, he finds himself caught up in a complicated intrigue involving bogus popes (Ugo Tognazzi as original and imposter), scheming Byzantine princesses (Carole Bouquet) and a final betrayal by the power-hungry monk Otarius that has fateful consequences for the throne of France. The king, who never takes himself or his power seriously, is murdered by the vilest of his followers, his queen is deposed, and the serpent-like Bouquet ascends to the throne beside Otarius.

This cynical finale is hardly in keeping with the just-for-fun spirit of the picture, especially after the excellent Coluche wins the audience over to Dagobert's side despite all.

Standout technical credits (lensing by Armando Nannuzzi, Medieval décor by Dante Ferretti) lend richness to the thin story, ornamented with a bevy of buxom, blond, topless and anonymous concubines.
—*Yung.*

Tapetenwechsel
(Knock On The Wrong Door)
(WEST GERMAN-COLOR)

Berlin, Sept. 25.

A Georg Althammer and Monaco Film Coproduction. Features entire cast. Written and directed by Gabriele Zerau. Camera (color), Heinz Hölscher; sets, Michael Pilz; music, Jörg Evers; sound, Uli Winkler; editing, Annette Dorn; production manager, Jörg Schmitt. Reviewed at Zoo Palast Cine Center, Berlin, Sept. 24, 1984. Running time: 85 MINS.
Cast: Claudia Demarmels (Mona), August Zirner (Wolfgang), Rolf Zacher (Thomas), Erni Singerl (Frau Meier).

Femme helmer Gabriele Zerau did odd film industry jobs and worked as assistant director for Bernhard Sinkel and Thomas Koerfer before venturing out on her own with the debut feature "Knock On The Wrong Door" (direct translation of original title is "carpet change"). It's a light comedy with the talented Claudia Demarmels in the lead. She was the Swiss maid in Peter F. Bringmann's local b.o. comedy winner, "Theo Against The Rest Of The World."

"Knock On The Wrong Door" treats the age-old problem of apartment hunting. A young student of modest income may lose her apartment because the landlady wants to give the place to her son, so Mona goes out looking everywhere for another flat at a reasonable rent. Everywhere she turns leads to an adventure, for a young lady with Mona's charm and looks attracts suitors as in the sitcoms of the 1950s. In the end, and just when she is about to give up, along comes a white knight to her rescue whom she ran over with her bicycle at the start of the story.

Okay debut pic, but buried too deeply in clichés.—*Holl.*

My Farmors Hus
(My Granny's House)
(DANISH-COLOR)

Copenhagen, Sept. 5.

A Panorama release of Panorama Film (Just Betzer) with The Danish Film Institute production. Based on C.E. Soya's novel. Written and directed by Frode Pedersen. Camera (Eastmancolor) Dan Lausten; production design, Sören Kragh-Sörensen; music, Bent Fabricius-Bjerre; editor, Janus Billeskov Jansen; assistant director, Rumle Hammerich; costumes, Gitte Kolvig; executive producers, Just Betzer, Tivi Magnusson. Reviewed at Palads, Copenhagen, Sept. 5, 1984. Running time: 77 MINS.
Granny . . . . Bodil Udsen
Sörmand . . . . Mikkel Egelund
The Farther . . . . Sören Spanning
Johanne . . . . Kirsten Olesen
Vide . . . . Tammi Ost
Aunt Laura . . . . Birgitte Federspiel
Lillelund . . . . Olaf Ussing
Mrs. Agerlind . . . . Vera Gebuhr
Mrs. Tychsen . . . . Karen Marie Löwert

A sharply satirical, but also warmly satyric Danish writer, C.E. Soya, wrote "My Granny's House" in 1943 as a thinly disguised memoir of an early childhood spent in the heavily Victorian city apartment of his rich paternal grandmother, the latter of the Holy Monster variety bolstered by equal parts of egomania and hypocrisy. The boy of six proves to be her match, however. A devil lurks behind this Sörmand's angelic features. He does not give it a second thought when he has wantonly tripped his very favorite nurse, causing her to be hospitalized. He also gladly takes bribes to betray the trust of his widowed father and the latter's new lover. Granny wants any attempt at a new marriage thwarted and even administers poison to the lover so she can, she hopes, keep her grandchild with her forever.

Frode Pedersen, a graduate of Danish TV's kiddie entertainment department, has wanted to be very adult in his feature film debut, his "My Granny's House" has meticulous period decor and intricate frame-composing which succeed in slowing dramatic proceedings to episodic bursts, all too abrupt to sustain real suspense.

Granny is played with vigor and a fine measure of menace by Bodil Udsen, the fine actress who played Gertrude Stein on the Danish stage for more than a year. Mikkel Egelund is a fair match for her as Sörmand, equally believable when sweetly innocent as when innocently vicious. None of the other characters seems tempted by the director to rise above the role and clichés written for them. Where Soya's book contained rich bubbles of blackest humor, Pedersen's film never dares take itself lightly. Film will hardly suffer from confinement to the tv screen for which it is obviously destined if it is to enjoy any sales away from home.—*Kell.*

Almost You
(COLOR)

Almost a movie.

Mill Valley, Sept. 22.

A 20th Century Fox' TLC Films release of a Wescom production. Produced by Mark Lipson. Executive producers, Charles C. Thieriot, Sandy Climan, Stephen J. Levi. Directed by Adam Brooks. Screenplay, Mark Horowitz based on a story by Brooks; camera (color), Alexander Gruszynski; editor, Mark Burns; sound, Patricia Bennett, Lou Kleinman, Skip Lievsay; art director, Nora Chavoosian; sets, Leslie Pope; music, Jonathan Elias; first assistant director, Craig Laurence Rice. Reviewed at Mill Valley Film Festival, Sept. 22, 1984. (No MPAA Rating.) Running time: 96 MINS.
Erica Boyer . . . . Brooke Adams
Alex Boyer . . . . Griffin Dunne
Lisa Willoughby . . . . Karen Young
Kevin Danzig . . . . Marty Watt
Maggie . . . . Christine Estabrook
David . . . . Josh Mostel
Jeannie . . . . Laura Dean
Susan McCall . . . . Dana Delany
Ralph . . . . Miguel Pinero
Uncle Stu . . . . Joe Silver
Uncle Mel . . . . Joe Leon
Sal . . . . Daryl Edwards
Receptionist . . . . Suzzy Roche

20th Century Fox' specialized film arm TLC Films reportedly has "Almost You" set for February release, but there's no rush.

Main problem here is lifelessness of characters, compounded by weak direction. Not one of the four principals is interesting enough to care about.

Griffin Dunne, who coproduced "Baby It's You" and brought some of the crew with him to this one, is a young married fellow who feels trapped by his dull job, his dull wife (Brooke Adams) and the dull apartment in which he has lived since childhood. When his wife is injured in an auto accident, he takes up with her dull nurse (Karen Young) and then finds a friend in the dull actor b.f. (Marty Watt) of the nurse.

It's possible young marrieds might identify with Dunne's dilemma. It's also possible "Almost You" is almost a movie.

There is, though, momentary vitality provided by Josh Mostel as a family friend and Joe Silver and Joe Leon as Dunne's bosses-uncles in a garment factory. —*Herb.*

Cronica Dos Bons Malandros
(Story Of The Good Scoundrels)
(PORTUGUESE-COLOR)

San Sebastian, Sept. 20.

Produced, written and directed by Fernando Lopes. Camera, Manuel Costa e Silva; editors, Joao Carlos Gorjao and Manuele Gorja; sets, Teresa Lacerda; music, Rui Veloso. Features Joao Perry, Lia Gama, Maria do Céu Guerra, Nicolau Breyner, Paulo de Carvalho, Pedro Bandeira Freire, Duarte Nuno, Antonio Assuncao, Virgilio Castelo, Zita Duarte. Reviewed at Cine Victoria Eugenia (San Sebastian), Sept. 19, 1984. Running time: **80 MINS.**

"Story Of The Good Scoundrels" is a highly stylized, tongue-in-cheek film often bordering on the amateurishly silly, but providing an occasional laugh as Portuguese thesps ham up a story about robbing the Gulbenkian Museum in Lisbon.

Most of the pic whimsically delves into the backgrounds of the "good scoundrels," how some met in jail, or befriended prostitutes. One is a hopeful extra dreaming of being a star; another enjoys outrunning the cops.

The flashbacks are handled with exaggerated playacting, including an amusing takeoff on a Busby Berkley number with a gigantic revolving cake with three dancers circling about on it.

The robbery at the end of the film is shown schematically, on a computer screen. Some of the scenes are so bad they are amusing once you get into the mocking mood of the film. — *Besa.*

Christina
(SPANISH-COLOR)

A Playboy presentation of a Leeds Film Accounting Services Ltd. picture. Executive producer, Harry Alan Towers. Produced by Andres Vicente Gomez. Directed by Paco Lara. Features entire cast. Screenplay, "Peter Welbeck" (Harry Alan Towers), based on novels by Blakely St. James; camera (Fotofilm color), Alejandro Ulloa; editor, Antonio Ramirez; music, Ted Scotto; production manager, Jose Mª. Maldonado; art direction, Luis Arguello; production supervisor, Jesus Mª. Lopez-Patiñño. Reviewed on vidcassette, N.Y., Sept. 9, 1984. (No MPAA Rating.) Running time: **92 MINS.**

Christina . . . . .Jewel Shepard
Madame Rosa. . . . . .Karin Schubert
Antoinette . . . .Josephine Jacqueline Jones
Patrick . . . . .Ian Serra
Pablo . . . . .Enrique Johnson
Alain . . . . .Emilio Linder
Max . . . . .Tony Isbert
Brigitte . . . . .Pepita Full James
Jean . . . . .Emiliano Redondo

"Christina" is the third, and least interesting, of the European-made feature films from producer Harry Alan Towers, created for the Playboy Channel and various overseas theatrical and homevideo distributors. Softcore opus features plenty of nudity spotlighting attractive women, but not much more.

Bookended by threats of numerous sequels, pic limns the adventures of Christina (Jewel Shepard), a jetset playgirl and publishing empire heiress, who has a habit of being kidnapped for ransom. In fact, this episodic film consists solely of bad guys (and bad gals) nabbing her, having their way with her and then losing her to another antisocial group.

Along the way, Christina has a run-in with several femme veterans of Towers-Playboy's "Black Venus" film, but the ensuing martial arts fights by women are embarrassingly fake, as are director Paco Lara's cheaply staged action and chase sequences. Though pacing is much sprightlier than the average sex film, this exercise in voyeurism remains stillborn.

Having replaced first choice Monique Gabrielle (the memorable dream nude of "Bachelor Party") in the title role, Shepard displays a beautiful body and a toothy grin, but (partly due to weak material) creates no character meriting one's ongoing interest, whether or not the series of additional films materializes.

Pic's oddest touch is the recurring device (a la "Alice In Wonderland") of Christina falling asleep when in danger, cueing goofball dream sequences in which gloved hands roll Tinkertoy-size cars across her nude body. .

Domestically, pic might have had theatrical chances as a programmer but once again, Towers has opted for unacceptably haphazard dubbing, even though the actors articulate in English. — *Lor.*

Le Voyage
(FRENCH-COLOR)

Toronto, Sept. 12.

A K2 International Production/Egyptian Company for Cinema/TF1 Films Production. Produced by Herbert de Zaltza, Khalil Osman, Roger-Andre Larrieu. Written and directed by Michel Andrieu. Camera (color), Renan Polles; editor, Maureen Mazurek; sound, Michel Brethez; music, Michel Portal. Reviewed at Toronto Festival of Festivals (Contemporary World Cinema), Sept. 12, 1984. Running time: **100 MINS.**

Cast: Christophe Malavoy (Thomas), Victoria Abril (Veronique), Victoria Cavallo, Michael Jacob.

The topographic treats of Southern Europe overtake the action in "Le Voyage," a double-edged tale of potential powderkegs, but there's little emotional sustenance. It will be tricky to handle commercially.

Story revolves around Thomas (Christophe Malavoy) who, after being blackmailed, is forced to smuggle a car full of explosives to Egypt, where they will be sent to help terrorists in Cyprus.

Thomas runs the risk of being caught and imprisoned or even blown up by the sensitive detonators hidden in his Peugeot. He's joined by his girlfriend Veronique (Victoria Abril) on the volatile drive south from Switzerland. She's furious at him for getting involved in this dangerous mission, when it's clear that his politics are cloudy and confused. They're followed by enemies of the supplier as well as government agents.

But the journey centers on the evolution and confrontation of their relationship as well. Thomas accuses Veronique of betraying him with another lover; she calls him a jealous paranoid. They are alternately passionate and hostile, tender and mean-spirited. She abandons him and then returns during the course of their voyage, but when they finally solidify their commitment to each other it's simply too late.

It's clear from the beginning that both journeys are losing propositions. Despite the chemistry between Thomas and Veronique, it's curious to know why they're together in the first place. If it's simply physical pleasure, their ultimate emotional declaration is unconvincing.

Director Michel Andrieu uses clever camera devices — the light becomes progressively brighter until it is glaring white in Egypt, the place where the darkest possibilities lurk. The attractive thesps are in a no-win situation. The tension is sustained, but the resolution is unsatisfying. —*Devo.*

Antistrofi Metrissi
(Wrong Timing)
(GREEK-COLOR)

Athens, Sept. 20.

An A.V.I. Ltd.-Greek Film Center production. Directed by Panos Papakyriakopoulos. Features entire cast. Screenplay, Lila Habipl; camera (color), Nikos Kavoukidis; editor, Yannis Tsilsopoulos; sound, Antonis Bairaktaris; music, Giorgos Tsangaris; art director, Nikos Politis. Reviewed at Greek Film Center, Athens, Sept. 19, 1984. Running time: **96 MINS.**

Professor Markouzis . . . . . . .Yannis Voglis
Helen Markouzis . . . . .Kitty Arseni
Stefan Markouzis . . . . .Kostis Koukios
Stratos . . . . .Nikos Papakonstantinou
Anna . . . . .Agape Manoura
Despina . . . . .Loiska Avayannou
Maria . . . . .Lily Kokkodi

The problems of the political exile, who returns home after many years of absence, are explored in this honest but rather hermetic first feature by Panas Papakyriakopoulos.

Markouzis has lived for 30 years in Paris, where he's forged an academic career. Now, (the year is 1976), he decides to return home to Athens, bringing his reluctant wife and teenage son with him. Despite the fact that Greece is a democracy again. Markouzis finds things not as he expected. The students are more militant than ever, while his fellow faculty members at the university seem hidebound after years of conservatism. Further, many of his closest friends of former years are scattered to the winds; one spent years in Czechoslovakia and is a sick and tired man; another is a pompous opportunist; another went to Australia and apparently made a fortune; yet another has died.

The problems discussed in the film are specific ones, although they probably would relate to exiles from other countries where upheavals have occurred in recent years.

Lead actor Yannis Yoglis, himself active in politics (a member of the council of an Athens suburb), is quietly impressive . — *Strat.*

I Poli Pote Then Kimate
(The City Never Sleeps)
(GREEK-COLOR)

Athens, Sept. 20.

A Co-operative Filmmakers Ltd. Greek Film Center production. Executive producer, Vassilis Katsoufis. Written and directed by Andreas Tsilifonis. Features entire cast. Camera (Cinemascope, color) Christos Triandafillou; music, Yannis Kostidakis; art director, Yannis Tseklenis; sound, Lykourgos Vayiakis. Reviewed at Finos Filmstudio, Athens, Sept. 18, 1984. Running time: **96 MINS.**

Nicos . . . . .Christos Kalavrouzos
Polaloudas . . . . .Takis Moschos
Jeanie . . . . .Olia Stefanidou
Tsitas . . . . .Nikos Ziangos
Maharajah. . . . . .Sakis Boulas
Police Lieutenant . . . . .Dinos Makris

Plot of this debut feature by Andreas Tsilifonis is an overly familiar one about a middle-aged man, at sea for 20 years, who returns home to Athens to discover who was responsible for his younger brother's death.

The brother was a member of a biker gang and died in a "contra," an Athenian version of a chicken-run, in which rival bike riders hurtle towards oncoming traffic. Nicos, the film's hero, gets his old bike out of mothballs and, after seeking advice from a policeman friend, tries to join a gang. Needless to say, he's not taken very seriously until he proves his worth and courage, eventually winning a fatal race against the guy responsible for his brother's death, plus winning the love of a biker girl.

If the plot is a bit creaky, the script strives to be very up-to-date and is laced with racy street-slang, salty and apparently authentic. Supposedly the first Cinemascope film shot in Greece, it looks just great, with hard, shiny location photography by Christos Triandafillou, including some magnificently lit night scenes (which may, however, not show up well when the film is eventually shown on tv). Direction is quite inventive, apart from an unnecessarily arty (and unerotic) love scene, and acting is fine. The bike-race scenes are well staged.

Not a festival contender, but it could do well with the youth audience on its home turf, and certainly pinpoints a new director who shows promise for the future when he gets sharper and more original material to work with. —*Strat.*

Spiaccichicciacaticelo
(ITALIAN-COLOR)

Venice, Sept. 5.
Produced by Cinematografica Crisalide. Stars Carmine Faraco and Gianluca Favilla. Written and directed by Leone Creti. Camera (color), Fulvio Grubissich; editors, Creti, Giovanni Maniciotti; art director, Maurizio Petrangeli; music, Creti. Reviewed at Venice Film Festival (De Sica section), Sept. 5, 1984. Running time: **90 MINS.**
Claudio .... Carmine Faraco
Marco .... Gianluca Favilla
Claudio's father .... Nino Vingelli
Giulio .... Stefano Onofri
Bum .... Giangiacomo Colli

The untranslatable title is a password used by the two leads, aspiring young actors who can't get past the closed doors of Roman film companies. First helming effort by Leone Creti has all the hallmarks of the old-style Venice Italian Showcase: mostly amateurish shooting on an inadequate budget, and a few good ideas that got lost in the making. Chances for release are poor.

Nevertheless, there is something likeable about the characters and the realistic way their sad story is told. Marco (Gianluca Favilla) works parttime in a bar to make ends meet when he's not out beating the pavement in search of a film part. At night he sleeps in his car, parked outside the bar. Claudio (Carmine Faraco) lives at home, where he is tormented day and night by his father, who wants him to work in the family store and quit day-dreaming. Despite constant disappointments, the pair keep trying, reciting Shakespeare to themselves to "keep in practice." Once they seem about to get a part, only to have their hopes dashed at the last minute. In the end we find them taking a test to get jobs as public servants.

Technical problems betray pic's dire production circumstances: lensing is dark, dialog flat, script amateurish, dubbing awful. Only in a few moments of monolog does Creti manage to get some of film's bitter irony to come across, along with the rare one-liner, (e.g., "The avant-garde is like crime: it doesn't pay" is the translation). Thesps have enough talent to communicate that they are good actors within the context of the film, which makes

their failure to "make it" all the sadder. —*Yung.*

La Triche
(The Cheat)
(FRENCH-COLOR)

Paris, Sept. 17.
AAA release of a Productions du Daunou/Films de l'Equinoxe coproduction. Produced by Denise Petitdidier. Stars Victor Lanoux. Directed by Yannick Bellon; screenplay, Bellon and Rémi Waterhouse. Camera (Fujicolor), Houshang Baharlou; art director, Pierre Voisin; editor, Kenout Peltier; sound, Louis Gimel; music, uncredited. Reviewed at the Marignan-Concorde theater, Paris, Sept. 15, 1984. Running time: **100 MINS.**
Michel Verta .... Victor Lanoux
Nathalie Verta .... Anny Duperey
Bernard Mirande .... Xavier Deluc
The Morane brothers ..... Michel Galabru
Marilyn .... Valerie Mairesse
Manuel Garcia .... Roland Blanche
René Villedieu .... Guy Tréjean
Raymond .... Gérard Herold
Marianne .... \ .... Michele Simonnet
Jacky .... Jacky Laurent

Yannick Bellon, a former film editor, has been trying to reconcile commercial film and problem subject matter in the films she has directed, tackling thorny topics like divorce, rape and cancer. Now she turns to homosexuality in this tale of a bisexual police commissioner who risks his career and family when he takes a lover on his home turf.

Victor Lanoux is the Bordeaux cop who has managed to keep his homosexual affairs limited to brief out-of-town adventures. But a murder investigation in a local nightclub leads to an encounter with the establishment's young sax player, and subsequent meetings confirm a mutual passion.

They become lovers, though Lanoux' awkward search for meeting places brings the relationship to light in his immediate family, who react with expected horror. When the musician accidentally kills a blackmailing adversary, the resulting inquiry threatens to compromise Lanoux, who unsuccessfully tries to deflect the evidence. When police come to arrest him, the musician makes a consciously suicidal break to escape, and is shot dead by Lanoux' assistant, who has suspected the affair and wants to save his boss the inevitable scandal.

As scripter, Bellon often contents herself with the obvious (as in her exposure of smug bourgeois outrage) and plots clumsily, but she has done some of her best directing here, notably in dramatizing the central relationship. Lanoux and Xavier Leduc, a promising young newcomer, create an emotionally tangible center that is interesting in its development and crisis.

Of course, the depiction of homosexuality remains extremely timid — the sex is off-screen — and there is no great psychological depth, but Bellon has managed to

curb her penchant for demonstration and make a film of some dramatic viability. —*Len.*

In Punta Di Piedi
(All That Rhythm)
(ITALIAN-COLOR)

Venice, Sept. 2.
A D.A.C. release, produced by Gulliver 2000 Coop. Stars Marcello Modugno and Lara Nasszinski. Written and directed by Giampiero Mele. Camera (color), Ernesto Lanzi; art director, Piero Nastri; editor, Angelo Nicolini; music, Marcello Modugno, Ettore Fioravanti. Reviewed at the Venice Film Festival (De Sica section), Sept. 2, 1984. Running time: **93 MINS.**
Carlo .... Marcello Modugno
Elizabeth .... Lara Nasszinski
Silvana .... Debora Ergas

A first feature by youthful filmer Giampiero Mele, former assistant director and U.S.C. film school student. Though reportedly conceived before "Flashdance," "All That Rhythm" is banking on the continued popularity of the aspirant-hoofer genre to give it b.o. legs. Pic is technically accomplished, but just not very exciting. It has been pre-sold to many territories, but could come in under expectations, given flagging interest in reruns of "Fame" and such.

Made by a film co-op, pic works its way around budget limitations by hiring the relatives of famous people with bankable names. Leading the cast are Marcello Modugno (son of popular folksinger Domenico), Lara Nasszinski (cousin of Nastassja Kinski) and Debora Ergas (daughter of Sandra Milo and producer Morris Ergas). As thesps, though, none seems slated for greatness.

Carlo (Modugno), a college degree in hand, is pushed into working in his father's factory, even though what he really wants to do is be a folk-rock musician. He meets Elizabeth (Nasszinski), an American girl studying classical dance at the snooty temple of high art, the National Academy. She moonlights in discos performing slightly eroticized modern dance numbers.

The only new twist is that, instead of fulfilling her dreams to become a great ballerina, Elizabeth flunks her exams and decides it's time to go home. The happy ending is that Carlo decides to go with her.

Mele has a predilection for video musical numbers mixed with Italian-style break dance and free-form leaping around in groups on the Spanish Steps and the Via Appia Antica. All things considered, the touristy aspect of the film is probably more interesting than the choreography.

Modugno sings some tuneful numbers of his own composition.

— *Yung.*

Chi Mi Aiuta...?
(Who'll Help Me?)
(ITALIAN-COLOR)

Venice, Sept. 6.
Produced by Ugo Tucci for UTI Produzioni Associate. Stars Luca Barbareschi, Geppy Gleijeses and Marilù Prati. Written and directed by Valerio Zecca. Camera (color), Alfio Contini; art director, Beppe Mangano; editor, Mauro Bonanni; music, Carlo Siliotto. Reviewed at the Venice Film Festival, Sept. 6, 1984. Running time: **100 MINS.**
Carlo .... Luca Barbareschi
Paolo .... Geppy Gleijeses
Lili .... Marilù Prati
Sandro .... Victor Cavallo
Fritza .... Anna Melato

Valerio Zecca's first feature screened in Venice's Italian Showcase, "Who'll Help Me?" is a breezy, freewheeling account of young intellectuals and performing artists in Rome today. With a large number of musical interludes ranging from punk rock to classical, picture gives the schizophrenic impression of being aimed half at arthouse audiences and half at the youngsters who constitute the main film-going public in Italy. Still without a distributor at the time of its fest outing, pic can be expected to have an uphill struggle finding its way onto local circuits.

To its credit, pic has an underlying sincerity that breaks through many clichés; characters are convincing types. Carlo (Luca Barbareschi) and Paolo (Geppy Gleijeses) are roommates who end up falling for the same girl. Carlo is an incorrigible womanizer who carelessly splits his time between a rock band and a music academy. Paolo is a solitary, tormented intellectual who runs a bookshop. Lili, the girl in question (Marilù Prati), is a flighty, impulsive actress of avant-garde theater who can't make up her mind between the two. Story ends with Paolo's attempted suicide.

More interesting than the plot is the feeling Zecca gets across about these 30-year-olds without a purpose or future. Their artistic endeavors seem to be just for themselves and their friends. Anna Melato performs several electrifying rock numbers with her group, Lili rehearses a new play and Carlo practices on his violin. They rarely find an audience.

Everything is a bit too emblematic of a generation in crisis to set the screen on fire, but the film is sensitive and deserves a better fate than that of its characters.—*Yung.*

The Next One
(COLOR)

Farfetched fantasy.

An Allstar Prods. picture. Produced by Constantine Vlachakis. Written and directed by Nico Mastorakis. Stars Keir Dullea, Adrienne Barbeau. Camera (Technicolor), Ari Stavrou; editor, George Rosenberg; music, Stanley Myers; sound (Dolby), Nico Achladis; assistant director, James Lowe; production manager, George Iakovidis; production design, Paul Acciari; associate producers, Fred C. Perry, Steve Sustarsis. Reviewed on Showtime, N.Y., Sept. 12, 1984. (No MPAA Rating.) Running time: 105 MINS.

Glenn/The Next One ....Keir Dullea
Andrea Johnson ....Adrienne Barbeau
Timmy.................Jeremy Licht
Dr. Barnaby ....Peter Hobbs
Yanni ....Phaedon Georgitsis
Anna ....Betty Arvanitis

Nico Mastorakis' ''The Next One'' is a competently made but thoroughly unconvincing sci-fi romance. Filmed on Mykonos Island in Greece in the spring of 1981, pic was obviously aimed at theatrical release (replete with Dolby stereo) but failed to attract a U.S. distrib, debuting instead via pay-cable telecast.

The problem here is in the absurd premise and its illogical development. A well-cast Keir Dullea is washed ashore on a Greek Island, nursed back to health by Adrienne Barbeau, a widowed mother with young son Jeremy Licht. He seems to be suffering amnesia, but numerous insistent hints and visits to local churches payoff predictably in Dullea being a time traveller from the future, whose cloned brother went back 2,000 years further to be taken as Jesus Christ (forget the lack of logic in that these travelers are full-grown, not children).

Basic story unfolds in the manner of an episode of ''The Outer·Limits'' tv series of 20 years ago: balancing the fantasy gimmick and liberal thematic message with a romantic subplot, namely that of Barbeau's (unfortunately for voyeurs and her fans) G-rated level sexual encounter with the mysterious stranger Dullea. Lack of drama is a problem, until the arbitrary Greek locale comes into play when primitive islanders get angry at Dullea following his miraculous healing incident and then a fatal drowning accident killing off several children.

Storyline builds to Dullea's inevitable leavetaking, i.e., self-destruction, but not content with the ''There will be a next'' tagline, Mastorakis tacks on an absurd happy ending with another Dullea clone arriving on the same Greek beach in the same time period.

Touristy Mykonos Island visuals are okay, as is the English-language direct sound dialog. Presence of only token special visual effects is a real handicap for the film's acceptance by sci-fi fans. — Lor.

E Kathodos Ton Ennea
(The Descent Of The Nine)
(GREEK-COLOR)

Athens, Sept. 18.
A Greek Film Center Kronaka Film-ERT 1 coproduction. Directed by Christos Shiopahas. Features entire cast. Screenplay, Thanassis Valtinos, from his novella; camera (color),

Nikos Kavoukidis; music, Michalis Christodoulidis; editor, Giorgos Triantafyllou. Reviewed at Greek Film Center, Athens, Sept. 17, 1984. Running time: 127 MINS.

Nikitas ....Christos Kalavrouzos
Braditsas ....Antonis Antoniou
Koutsos ....Vassilis Tsanglos
Nassios ....Ilias Yannitsos
Georgouleas ....Christos Zorbas

An impressive adaptation of Thanassis Valtinos' 1963 novella of the same name, ''The Descent Of The Nine'' has finally been filmed, with the results almost completely satisfying.

Valtinos, who coscripted Theo Angelopoulos' ''Voyage To Cythera'' (prized at Cannes this year for its screenplay), seems interested in characters whose journeys basically end nowhere. Film is set in 1949, at the end of the Civil War, and deals with a party of nine ragged leftists who have been trapped in the mountains not far from Sparta, in the south, and who face a rugged trek through hostile terrain, down to the sea and, hopefully, safety.

But the countryside is alive with hostile troops, and these soldiers of the people seem also to have lost touch with their grass-roots support; twice local peasants aid them with food and water, then violently turn on them.

For these survivors of a lost cause, escape is only an illusion. The sea is tantalizingly near, to be glimpsed over the horizon, or even briefly waded into. But there's no escape. One by one, the members of the group are picked off, until finally the only survivor is the youngest, whose whole life is seemingly before him.

This is no action-packed drama of pursuit and escape, but rather a mellow, rather sad contemplation of the dying days of an era. The countryside through which these doomed men trudge so tortuously is idyllic, but they have no place in it. Aided by the exceptional cinematography of Nikos Kavoukidis, director Christos Shiopahas creates a mood not so much of suspense but of doom and resigned destiny.

Film was shot entirely on the rugged locations where the story unfolds. Pacing is admittedly slow, as befits the elegaic mood; some lighter editing, though, might improve international possibilities. Thesping is first-rate, and there's a discreet, lovely music score by Michalis Christodoulidis. —Strat.

Le Vol du Sphinx
(The Flight Of The Sphinx)
(FRENCH-COLOR)

Paris, Sept. 25.
A Distributeurs Associés of a compagnie Transatlantique de Films/Producteurs Associés Président Films/FR3 coproduction. Executive producers, André Djaoui and Jacques Eric-Strauss. Produced by Maurice Illouz and Daniel Deschamps,

Stars Miou-Miou, Alain Souchon. Directed by Laurent Ferrier. Screenplay, Alain Centonze, Ferrier. Camera (color), Jean- François Gondre; editor, Henri Lanoë; music, Michel Goguelat; art director, Jean-Pierre Kohut-Svelko. Reviewed at Club 13, Paris, Sept. 24, 1984. Running time: 106 MINS.

Tom ....Alain Souchon
Laura ....Miou-Miou
Mendel ....Jean Benguigui
Staubli ....François Perrot
Tournier ....Robin Renucci
Loussif ....Djelloul Beghoura

''Flight Of The Sphinx'' is a spiritless romantic adventure short on excitement and humor. Newcomer Laurent Ferrier has cowritten and directed with a solemnly nostalgic eye for genre clichés, but never succeeds in giving them new wings.

Film is latest in currently popular series of films about a guy and a gal and an exotic landscape (Africa) where they must triumph over natural and human enmities. With ''Romancing The Stone'' a smash on French screens, pic could benefit from the vogue locally, but will need a hard sell elsewhere.

Film's ill-assorted romantic couple is Miou-Miou, at her most self-consciously deadpan, and local pop singer Alain Souchon, whose lanky, puppy dog appeal has endeared him to many. But their personal rapport lacks movie magic. Miou-Miou looks especially silly in her Dietrich imitation, trekking across the Moroccan desert in high heels and gown.

''Sphinx'' is the name of a biplane piloted by Souchon, an embittered Frenchman who runs a local transport service in southern Morocco. When he crosses paths with Miou-Miou, she and her estranged lawyer husband (Robin Renucci) are plotting to prevent a Gallic arms merchant (François Perrot) from arriving at a scheduled appointment with a Middle East magnate.

Dramatic highlights in this predictable plot are few, with story unfolding at a snail's pace, and the action scenes staged without ingenuity or suspense. Attempts to fill in characterizations beyond the immediate needs of the story only add pointless screen time. —Len.

Next Of Kin
(CANADIAN-COLOR)

Toronto, Sept. 12.
An Ego Film Arts Production. Produced, written and directed by Atom Egoyan. Camera (color), Peter Mettler; editor, Egoyan; art direction, Ross Nichol; assistant director, Mark R. Battley; sound, Clark McCarron; music editor, Bruce McDonald; sound effects editor, Michele Moses. Reviewed at the Festival of Festivals (Perspective Canada), Toronto, Sept. 11, 1984. Running time: 72 MINS.

Peter Foster ....,....Patrick Tierney
George Deryan ....Berge Fazlian
Sonya Deryan ....Sirvart Fazlian
Azah Deryan ....Arsinee Khanjian
Mrs. Foster ....Margaret Loveys
Mr. Foster.............Thomas Tierney
Foster Counsellor ....Phil Rash
Deryan Counsellor ....Paul Babiak

A comical and promising premise is shattered by a shaky hand-held camera in this well-acted pic about a boy who decides to adopt a new family. In his first feature, Atom Egoyan shows a sure hand at directing actors but someone should have cautioned ''Put it on a tripod,'' when the camera was ready to roll.

Peter Foster is 23 years old and still living under the oppressive ambitions of his parents. Emotionally handicapped, he is taken to a family counselor who records sessions for families to play back for self-criticism. Peter also records his private thoughts on a tape recorder and is supposed to surrender his private world to their examination after a few weeks vacation in another city. Peter has, meanwhile, observed an Armenian family who came to the counseling center and, from their videotape, he knows they have a son they gave up for adoption at age two. He presents himself as the lost heir.

The scenes in the Armenian community have a full-bodied wit and ethnic flavor only possible by working with Lebanese Armenian originals. The problems of integrating into Canadian society in the subsequent generations are touched on, and Peter's total WASP-bred demeanor provides good foil.

The lunacy of Peter's new family has a human quality pointedly absent from the affluent household that has turned him toward catatonic despair. A cheerful denouement shows family should be a matter of choice, not birth, and Peter's speech to that effect at a family party is unnecessary.

This no-budget pic is unlikely to make it into theatrical distribution, and the camerawork may render it nearly unwatchable on a video screen. However, its director should be watched, and encouraged.
— Kaja.

Chewingum
(ITALIAN-COLOR)

Venice, Sept. 1.
A C.I.D.I.F. release, produced by Claudio Bonivento for Numero Uno Cinematografica. Stars Isabella Ferrari and Massimo Ciavarro. Directed by Biagio Proietti. Screenplay, Proietti, Osvaldo De Micheli; camera (color), Beppe Maccari; editor, Raimondo Crociani; music, Giancarlo Bigazzi. Reviewed at the Venice Film Festival, (De Sica section), Sept. 1, 1984. Running time: 100 MINS.

Mauro ....Mauro Di Francesco
Isabella ....Isabella Ferrari
Massimo ....Massimo Ciavarro
With Mara Venier, Fabrizio Temperini, Orsetta Gregoretti, Liliana Eritrei, Enrico Montuori, Carlo Mucari, Luca Ward, Marina Viro, Marina Occhiena, Anna Melato.

Noted tv helmer Biagio Proietti makes a long-awaited big screen debut with ''Chewingum,'' a sticky commercial package aimed at teen and pre-teen audiences. Pic somehow took a wrong turn and ended up in Venice's Italian Showcase, where it was mercilessly unappreciated by the sophisticated fest public. Yet with the market savvy of producer Claudio Bonivento behind it ("A Time For Loving," "Christmas Vacation") and current junior idols Massimo Ciavarro and Isabella Ferrari headlining, pic stands a chance of hitting its target, even though its rhythm misses a few of the beats that have made the films it is copying such moneymakers.

It's the last year of high school, noted for practical jokes and puppy love (sex is coyly hinted at, never shown). The characters are standard: Mauro (Mauro Di Francesco), the class clown who takes bets; Orsetta, the ugly duckling in love with handsome playboy Carlo (Carlo Mucari); Massimo (Massimo Ciavarro), a shy boy who hides the humiliating fact he works after school from his friends; and Isabella (Isabella Ferrari), a dazzling blond who transfers into the class

Young thesps are unruly actors and often seem out of control. Only the high-voltage extrovert Mauro Di Francesco is capable of bringing off comic lines, while romantic leads Ferrari and Ciavarro fail to convince as they embrace in front of a setting sun. But their local followers are numerous (both are ex-stars of the "fotoromanzi," photographed comic books) and score is a loud and long serenade of summer hits.

— *Yung.*

Liste Noire
(Black List)
(FRENCH-COLOR)

Paris, Sept. 11.

A Fox/Hachette release of an NEF/Hachette-Fox coproduction. Produced by Claude Nedjar and René Cleitman. Stars Annie Girardot. Directed by Alain Bonnot. Screenplay, Alain Bonnot, André G. Brunelin, Marie-Thérèse Cuny, based on "Nathalie ou la Punition" by Gérald Moreau; camera (color), Jean-François Robin; editor, Françoise Bonnot; art director, Patrice Mercier; sound, Paul Lainé; music, Alain Wisniak; production manager, Bernard P. Guiremand. Reviewed at the Marignan-Concorde theater, Sept. 5, 1984. Running time: **90 MINS.**
Jeanne Dufour . . . . Annie Girardot
Comm. Kalinsky . . . . . François Marthouret
David . . . . Bernard Brieux
Nathalie Dufour . . . . Sandrine Dumas
David . . . . Pascal Tedes
Pierre . . . . Paul Crauchet

"Liste Noire," Annie Girardot's first film in three years, is a strictly routine revenge thriller in which the actress dons a black raincoat and exacts stone-faced vengeance on a band of bankrobbers who have used her delinquent daughter as a decoy for a heist, having shot her and her boyfriend afterwards when they came to claim a part of the booty.

Script offers little for Girardot's talents and is mostly content to deploy a predictable quota of violence and pursuits as the heroine stalks her prey, shooting one hood, crushing another with a steam shovel and disposing of a third in a frantic car chase. Pic toys with serious themes like vigilante justice, but never gets beyond the glibly conventional in treatment.

Director Bonnot showed some ability in his first feature in 1980, "Une Sale Affaire," and confirms that basic storytelling skill here, but a first-rate story and script continue to elude him. — *Len.*

Revolutions, D'Ebats Amoureux, Epardus, Douloureux
(Revolutions)
(CANADIAN-B&W)

Toronto, Sept. 8.

A Canadian Filmmakers Distribution Centre release of an Osmosis Communications production. Produced, directed and written by Jean Marc Lariviere; camera (b&w), Kemp Archibald; editor, Lariviere; music, l'Ambulence se depeche poyr rien; sound, Marsh Birchard. Reviewed at the Festival of Festivals (Perspective Canada), Toronto, Sept. 8, 1984. Running time: 72 MINS.
A Woman . . . . Birgitte Haentjens
A Woman . . . . Sylvie Lacombe
A Young Woman . . . . Martha Wheaton
An Interviewer . . . . Louis Nolan

A brooding series of silences, "Revolutions" from Quebec is unlikely to escape out of the festival rut. This tale of three woman who share an apartment and the mundane activities of daily life does move at a revolutionary pace. Unfortunately its speed can be clocked at revolutions per hour.

Chock full of inane activites such as uncrating kitchen things, one cannot help but wonder how these women cope. If the message is: it's tough being a modern woman, then one can also say it's easy to have problems when your being is basically inert.

Multi-credited Jean Marc Lariviere certainly doesn't stint on the number of topics on which he touches, ranging from egoism to children. However, there's a decided lack of resolution or perception of his subject or even the basic skills of filmmaking beyond keeping images in focus. Commercially, this is nothing less than a quiet "Revolutions," and possibly a silent one. — *Klad.*

Pirata! (Cult Movie)
Pirate! (Cult Movie)
(ITALIAN-COLOR)

Venice, Aug. 29.

Produced by Paolo Ricagno, Valentino Schiavone and Sandro Signetto for Finzioni Coop. Directed by Paolo Ricagno. Features entire cast. Screenplay, Ricagno, Valentino Schiavone; camera (Eastmancolor), Claudio Meloni; editor, Ricagno; art director, Fausto Bonoveri; music, Jo Squillo & Eletrix, Art Fleury, Gaz Nevada, Great Cancer and Pirata. Reviewed at the Venice Film Festival, (De Sica section), Aug. 29, 1984. Running time: 95 MINS.
The Pirate . . . . Paolo Rocagno
Twins . . . . Gloria and Nadia Ferrero

Mother . . . . Luisella Ciaffi
Supreme Dreamer . . . . Ugo Gregoretti
Rock singer . . . . Jo Squillo

One of the few experimental works screened at Venice's Italian Showcase of young directors, "Pirate! (Cult Movie)" is an aggressive, wordless fantasy for younger audiences raised on tv, rock, comic strips and videogames. Though it may not reach cult status, neophyte filmer Paolo Ricagno's effort deserves a word of encouragement for using imagination to make up for shoestring budget. A second word might be to advise him to get some kind of a story next time.

A character called "Pirate" (played by Ricagno, on roller skates) is at war with "the Supreme Dreamer" (Ugo Gregoretti) who controls the minds of the populace through his "Hat Of Dreams" (television network).

This idea is merely the excuse for one long chase through a nightmarish, nighttime cityscape. The Pirate encounters, fights and flees its hostile denizens, alienated "videonegatives." A pair of black leather girls (Gloria and Nadia Ferrero) in a limo engage the hero in a violent sex scene at one point, but mostly pic flows on like an endless videoclip.

A commercial ace up the sleeve is the non-stop soundtrack featuring top Italian rock performers (Art Fleury, Jo Squillo, Gaz Nevada, Great Complotto). Music and lyrics, which were written expressly for the film, work together with machine-gun cutting in an endless wave of speed, energy and tension. Claudio Meloni's nighttime camerawork is appropriately sinister. — *Yung.*

Three Films By John Paizs
(CANADIAN-COLOR)

Toronto, Sept. 11.

A John Paizs Production. Produced by Paizs and Greg Klymkiw. Written and directed by Paizs. Camera (color) by John Coutts, Paizs, Tom Fijal; editor, Gerry Klymn, Paizs; sound, Klymn. Reviewed at Toronto Festival of Festivals (Perspective Canada), Sept. 11, 1984. Running time: 87 MINS.
Cast: "The Obsession Of Billy Botski:" Bridgette Graeff, John Paizs. "Springtime In Greenland:" Dean Dacko, Paizs. "The International Style:" John Harvie, Kathy Driscoll, George Toles.

Filmmaker John Paizs should be dubbed the king of kitsch in addition to his reputation as the Andy Warhol of Winnipeg. This trilogy of short films is wildly uneven, but displays an absurdist sensibility and a deadpan humor that could make it a late-night cult curiosity.

First entry, "The Obsession Of Billy Botski," is a ludicrous tale about a guy on the make who sashays into a party and spots Connie — a vision in a hot pink party dress and a platinum bouffant coiffure.

They rendezvous back in a motel room, she goes limp in his arms, and never wakes up. The whole scenario is a John Waters excursion, sprinkled with a hard-boiled narration and quick stiletto cuts.

"Springtime In Greenland" is the most effective journey into absurdity. In a mock Scandinavian accent, the narrator creates a sparkling travelog parody, as preparations are being made for the "First Sunday In Spring" parade in Greenland. This quickly changes into a pool party taken over by an obnoxious guest who challenges Paizs to a diving contest.

"The International Style" has a plot with more twists than a pretzel about an attempt to steal a secret formula, but it thuds quickly.

Paizs' efforts are amusing but erratic. The actors camp it up with the right amount of detachment. Tech credits are fine with some inventive camera angles. These three short films attest that local filmmaking is a lively pursuit in Canada. —*Devo.*

La Smala
(The Tribe)
(FRENCH-COLOR)

Paris, Sept. 19.

A UGC release of a T. Films/Films A2 coproduction. Produced by Alain Terzian. Stars Victor Lanoux, Josiane Balasko, Dominique Lavanant. Written and directed by Jean-Loup Hubert. Camera (color), Jean Charvein; art director, Jean-Baptiste Poirot; editor, Hélène Viard; sound, Jean-Philippe Le Roux; music, Michel Goguelat. Production manager, Philippe Lièvre. Reviewed at the UGC Normandie theater, Paris, Sept. 18, 1984. Running time: 90 MINS.
Robert . . . . Victor Lanoux
Simone . . . . Josiane Balasko
Rita . . . . Dominique Lavanant
Gégène . . . . Maurice Risch
Lucie . . . . Candida Romero
Priest . . . . Martin Lamotte
Intern . . . . Luis Rego
Cop . . . . Thierry Lhermitte

Jean-Loup Hubert, who debuted a few years ago with a slight but engaging romantic comedy with Isabelle Adjani and Thierry Lhermitte, "Next Year If All Goes Well," misses his comic mark with his second film about an eccentric family on the loose in Paris.

Victor Lanoux is head of the clan, unemployed and unrealistic, who cannot get over the fact that his frequently unfaithful wife now has hit the road for good. He's left in the lurch in a grim housing project, with five kids and a senile paralytic grandmother on his hands. The only thing that keeps the family from completely going to pieces is the presence of neighbor Josiane Balasko, a former rock and roll singer who's fallen on hard times and does housekeeping to stay afloat.

Balasko is keen on Lanoux, but he's only interested in finding his wife, and decides to head for Paris with the tribe in tow. Balasko winds up on the same train, on her way to see her family in the capital. Although fed up with Lanoux and his problems, she lodges everybody in the apartment of her brother who, in her absence, has undergone a sex change operation to become her sister (Dominique Lavanant).

Lanoux' quest finally proves fruitless, but the family gets its act together by recording a hit pop song and coming into its own with a winning lottery ticket. In the meantime, Lanoux and Balasko fall into the hay together and realize they're cut out for each other.

"La Smala," rambling and frenetic, as "Next Year If All Goes Well" was tidy and relaxed, utterly lacks what Hubert's debut effort was strong on — charm. Helmer is a former comic strip artist, and the coarse, anarchic tone of his film suggests a clumsily transposed cartoon, with everybody trying too hard to be aggressively funny and yet heart-warming. The attempted send-up of broken family values often sinks into callous bad taste, as in the business concerning the senile granny, whom the kids treat no better than a house plant; when she suddenly dies they leave her in a hospital corridor, since there's no cash to pay for a funeral. — *Len.*

Low Visibility
(CANADIAN-COLOR)

Toronto, Sept. 10.
A Noema Productions presentation. Produced by Tom Braidwood. Written and directed by Patricia Gruben. Camera (color), Paul Mitchnick, Kirk Tougas; art director, Renny Bartlett; sound, Nettie Wild, Larry Sutton; editor, Gruben; music and effects, Martin Gotfrit. Reviewed at the Festival of Festivals (Perspective Canada), Toronto, Sept. 9, 1984. Running time: **99 MINS.**
Mr. Bones . . . . Larry Lillo
Sgt. Nemitz . . . . David Petersen
Nurse Colville . . . . Penelope Stella
Gary Telfer . . . . Bob Metcalfe
Dr. Korona . . . . Jerry Wasserman
Nurse Knecht . . . . Brenda Robins

Out of one of the more interesting corners of the avant-garde comes this investigation into a man who wanders in out of the wilderness with a weird combination of amnesia, aphasia, and guilt. Initial focus fixes on his stay in the hospital and the amusing caricatures of hospital personnel trying to fit the subject's psychotic condition into pet theories.

Halfway through what appears to be a spoof of psychiatric investigations, pic turns a sharp corner into the dreadful dilemma of survival by cannibalism. For a brief moment, the point-of-view of the survivor reveals what he has done, permitting the audience a privileged vantage point, so that the imminent criminal charges challenge the sympathy that has been created for "Mr. Bones," as the hospital staff has dubbed him. Delightfully flaky

nurses offer foil for Mr. Bones.

Few fringe filmmakers are as good at directing actors as Gruben, and Larry Lillo develops a convincing portrait of traumatized insanity. Never hysterical or obvious, he unfolds the character as the point of unity in the film.

Pic will surely make the rounds of this year's fest circuit, although any controversy expected over the cannibalism theme is unlikely. Good taste forced Gruben to back away from that problem to make it more accessible for specialized programming. —*Kaja.*

Orinoko — Nuevo Mundo
(VENEZUELAN-COLOR)

Toronto, Sept. 14.
A Blanco Baldo Producciones Guakamaya presentation. Directed by Diego Risquez. Screenplay, Luis Angel Duque, Risquez. Camera (color), Marieta Perez, Andres Augusti; editor, Leonardo Henriquez; music, Alejandro Bianco Uribe. Reviewed at Toronto Festival of Festivals (Contemporary World Cinema), Sept. 14, 1984. Running time: **100 MINS.**
Cast: Shaman Yanomami, Kosinegue, Rolando Pena, Hugo Marquez, Diego Risquez.

Director Diego Risquez is carving a niche for himself with films that are without dialog but replete with diverse, symphonic soundtracks and visual splendor. First in "Bolivar" (1982), a history of Venezuela, and now in "Orinoko — Nuevo Mundo," the discovery of the New World, the genre is off and running. New pic is welcome fest fare, but a longshot commercially.

Filmed on location in Venezuela, "Orinoko" sets up its historical sweep by slowly panning the crystalline Orinoco River and focusing in on tribesmen in their daily rituals. This is the time prior to the conquest of America.

Enter a Spanish explorer, Christopher Columbus, who commands an expedition equipped with huge flags to stake out the land for the mother country. A missionary attempts to convert the natives, but they burn him on a cross. Walter Raleigh arrives in full regalia, complete with parrot perched on shoulder, and offers tribesmen gold coins. Other explorers already have laid claim to the same land and have built fortifications.

With nary a word spoken throughout, pic's effectiveness is dependent on fluid camerawork and sound. There is a medley of jungle noises, tribal grunts, warbling birds, and an assortment of percussion and violin solos. Images are frozen as paintings and combine the surreal with the tangible.

If the viewer tries to identify specific historical figures it can be tough going. But if that tendency is suspended, the film can be appreciated on a more mythological level, as the camera always returns to the river, which is the entry point

for discovery and the lifeline of the natives.

"Orinoko" is aesthetically inventive but seems overlong and tedious in parts because the "actors" are left with little to do than represent symbols of the old and new worlds. — *Devo.*

Berlin Zur Kaiserzeit
(Berlin In The Time Of The Kaiser)
(W. GERMAN-DOCU-B&W)

Berlin, Sept. 16.
A Chronos Film Production, Berlin. A documentary written and directed by Irmgard von zur Mühlen. Produced by Bengt von zur Mühlen. Editor, Petra Heymann; music, Wolfgang de Gelmini; advisers, Prof. Werner Knopp, Dr. Hans J. Reichardt; assistant, Wladimir Schilzow; optical effects, Studio Bartoschek; speakers: Martin Held, Carl Raddatz, Jürgen Thormann, Eva Katharina Schultz, Charlotte Joeres. Reviewed at Zoo Palast, Belrin, Sept. 15, 1984. Running time: **90 MINS.**

Chronos Film in Berlin under Bengt and Irmgard von zur Mühlen has released a series of important documentaries on the life-and-times of Germany in this century. An archive of rare historical materials was first painstakingly collected by Bengt von zur Mühlen, thus enabling him to produce a number of key historically oriented docus, like "Battle For Berlin," "Top Secret," "The Yellow Star" and the three made by his wife Irmgard: "Theater In Ruins" (1982), "Bombs On Berlin" (1983), and now "Berlin In The Time Of The Kaiser."

"Berlin In The Time Of The Kaiser" was made to accompany that extraordinary "Berlin Around 1900" art exhibit during the Berliner Festwochen (Berlin Autumn Arts Festival) in September. Pic runs 90 minutes and tries to cover the turn-of-the-century up to World War I from different perspectives: social, political, commercial, and cultural.

It's Kaiser Wilhelm who takes stage center, if for no other reason than he made very good newsreel footage. But then come the portraits of Berlin: streets in particular, but events of every kind (new inventions and official parades, for instance), and, of course, the stage and "Kintopp" stars of the day. One can almost feel the city growing.

Texts from diaries and letters are matched with appropriate photo and film material. The shops are described for nostalgia buffs, while the poverty in the working districts is similarly treated from eye-witness accounts but with weighted criticism. It appears that Berlin was sowing the seeds of its own downfall during the early balmy "Kaiserzeit" before two world wars would spell the end to the city's burgeoning hopes.

"Berlin In The Time Of The Kaiser" is the kind of docu historians and teachers are constantly in search of, to say nothing of film and histo-

ry buffs who will like those clips on old vaudeville routines. Docu's subtitle says everything: "Splendor And Shadow Of An Epoch." —*Holl.*

Karkalou
(GREEK-COLOR)

Athens, Sept. 20.
A Greek Film Center-Stavros Tornes production. Directed by Tornes. Script, Charlotte Van Gelder, Tornes, from an idea by Tornes; camera (color), Stamatis Yannoulis, Sakis Maniatis; editor, Despina Danae Maroulatou; sound, Christos Akalostos; music, Charlotte Van Gelder; art director, Stolios Anastasiadis. Reviewed at Greek Film Center, Athens, Sept. 18, 1984. Running time: **85 MINS.**
Stelios . . . . Stelios Anastasiadis
Taxi Driver . . . . Marios Karamanis
Five Faces of Woman . . . Ismene Kariotaki

"Karkalou," the third film of Stavros Tornes (who lived for many years in Rome), is about memory, levels of reality, creativity, dreams, games, etc. It is really only for the initiated, who will respond to its lovely images and almost entirely visual content.

Central character is a middleaged man (played with strength by a nonactor, Stelios Anastasiadis, a painter) who travels out into the rocky countryside past Corinth and meets a young taxi-driver who shares with him some mysterious and lyrical experiences. Other charters in the film include a variety of implacable women (played by the same actress), two chattering leftists, an old widow constantly pushing a pram, and an ice-cream salesman who gives the film its (meaningless) title.

Climax has the youth becoming a saint and the older man dying, as life goes in. It will enchant the few and doubtless infuriate the majority in its willful obscurities; but "Karkalou" is obviously the work of a dedicated artist, and deserves to be seen, especially at festivals where the personal and the offbeat are encouraged.—*Strat.*

Ostria
(South Wind)
(GREEK-COLOR)

Athens, Sept. 19.
A G. Karayannis Company-Greek Film Center production. Directed by Andreas Thomopoulos. Features entire cast. Screenplay, Thomopoulos, Katerina Gogou; camera (color), Takis Zervoulakos; music, Thanassis Bikos, OK Charlie; editor, Giannis Tsitopoulos; costumes, Andreas Sarantopoulos. Reviewed at Greek Film Center, Athens, Sept. 18, 1984. Running time: **88 MINS.**
Danae . . . . Betty Arvaniti
Aris . . . . Kostas Arzoglou
Nike . . . . Katerina Gogou
Minas' wife . . . . Themis Hazaka
Joseph . . . . Giorgos Sabanis
The Girl . . . . Rebecca Pauly

"Ostria" is a film which starts out as a rather intriguing look at members of the once-idealistic generation of the '60s, but which loses its way a bit and becomes too elliptical.

Three middle-aged couples, once pillars of the anti-establishment, now comfortably bourgeois, arrive on a remote beach for their first camping holiday. There's immediate tension in the air. One man, a doctor, is having a secret affair with the wife of another, an unpleasant businessman. The doctor's wife, a writer, is neurotic and timid. As for the other couple, the husband's an alcoholic looking for business favors, while the wife has decidedly kinky ideas.

As if these six characters weren't enough, on their first night they're disturbed by the arrival of a lovely, blond girl who pitches her flimsy tent not far from theirs and immediately and quite unself-consciously, goes for a nude swim. Next day's the same: this young tourist, engagingly played by the lovely U.S. actress Rebecca Pauly, hardly ever wears any clothes. Soon the three men are panting with lust, and the women are trying to be cool about it all.

With the stage set for an intriguing and possibly hedonistic romp, the film suddenly starts to muddy the waters with flash scenes in which characters *imagine* what they'd like to do. From then on, it's never very cle'r what *is* happening. Do the six invite the stranger for a dinner that turns into a drunken orgy? Does the businessman really kill the girl with his spear-gun (if so, why?), and do they then bury the body and leave?

Presumably the film is intended to be seen symbolically, with the young girl representing a free spirit (significantly, she turns out to be Greek, though they all initially assume she's a foreigner) that these middle-aged types would like to crush, but can't.

These apparent obscurities make it all a bit frustrating, but the film boasts superb photography by Takis Zervoulakos (filmed on location in Crete) and robust acting from the small cast. Cowriter Katerina Gogou is especially effective as the finnicky wife of the doctor who's aware her husband is being unfaithful.—*Strat.*

Loufa Ke Parallaghi
(Loafing And Camouflage)
(GREEK-COLOR)

-Athens, Sept. 20.
A Greek Film Center-Filmmakers Cooperation Ltd. Spentzos Film Ltd. production. Produced, directed and written by Nicos Perakis. Features entire cast. Camera (color), Yiorgos Panousopoulos; music, Nicos Mamangakis; editor, Yiorgos Triantafyllou; costumes, H. Perakis-Brandt; sets, Yiorgos Koliopandos. Reviewed at Greek Film Center, Athens, Sept. 17, 1984. Running time: 101 MINS.
Papadopoulos......Nicos Kalogeropoulos
Lambrou...............Yiorgos Kimoulis
Balourdos..............Takis Spyridak.s
Karamazov.......Fotis Polychronopoulos
Savidis............Yiannis Chadjiyiannis
Marlafekas ....∿......Paris Tselios.
The Colonel............Stavros Xenidis

The Lieutenant Colonel .Andreas Filippidis
The Major..........Christos Valavanidis
Cindy....................Rocky Taylor

"Loafing And Camouflage" is a breezy comedy about discontented conscripts of the Greek Army which is given added impetus by being set in 1967, the year of the Greek military coup which brought the junta of the colonels to power.

In fact, the sad sack hero of this engaging film, very well played by Nicos Kalogeropoulos, has the same name as the leader of the colonels — Papadopoulos — a fact that won't be lost on Greek audiences.

Prior to his conscription, the hero was a leading film cameraman at Finos Films, the country's largest producer of commercial movies, so naturally he's soon recalled from the icily inhospitable Bulgarian frontier post to which he is originally assigned and sent to work for the Armed Forces' television station, at that time the country's second tv channel (since de-militarized).

Here he becomes involved with a group making entertainment (of a sort) for the channel; this consists of editing patriotic news programs, filming the occasional pop-star, and translating Australian documentaries on sheep-shearing (probably obtained free, someone says derisively, from the Australian embassy). One member of his unit, nicknamed Karamazov, was the son of leftists and was born in the USSR, he did his training at the Tashkent Film School and naturally gets all the really dirty jobs.

With pompous officers trying to keep order, as well as a suspicious security man, the incompetent privates try to get away with whatever they can, including making an English-language porno film ("Maid In Greece") with army equipment and on army time. But of course things take a more sinister turn when the coup actually occurs, and the country that gave birth to democracy loses its freedom.

Director Nicos Perakis lived a long time in West Germany, where he worked as an art director ("The Tin Drum" among others) and directed a few films, including the successful "Bomber And Paganini" (1976); his previous Greek film, "Arpa Colla" (1982), was a big hit locally, and this new offering looks to be equally popular. It has overseas chances, too, on its bright and disrespectful mockery of the military regime in Greece and its amusing asides on army life. Acting is tops down the line, and the film is technically first rate. —*Strat.*

De Schorpioen
(The Scorpion)
(DUTCH-COLOR)

Amsterdam, Sept. 13.
A Euro Centrafilm release of a Movies Film Production. Produced by Chris Brouwer

and Haig Balian. Directed by Ben Verbong. Screenplay, Verbong, Pieter de Vos; camera (color), Theo van de Sande; editor, Ton de Graaff; music, Nicola Piovani; art direction: Dorus vanderLinden. Reviewed at Tuschinski theater, Amsterdam, Sept. 13, 1984. Running time: 98 MINS.
Loe Wolff...............Peter Tuinman
Anna...............Monique van de Ven
Karl Wissing...............Adrian Brine
William Kemp...........Henk van Ulsen
Mammy...................Rima Melati
Officer...................Huub Stapel
Snijder.................Senne Rouffaer

Ben Verbong's "Scorpion" preems here exactly three years after his "The Girl With Red Hair" (distributed in the U.S. by UA Classics). In an unusual deal for the Netherlands, Thorn EMI acquired all rights (outside Holland) before pic was relesed. It should find a sizable audience on screen and tube, mainly because of its intriguing looks.

Verbong makes use of an old, unresolved scandal about corruption in the Dutch army and the disappearance of some people in Indonesia in the '40s, of the Russian invasion of Hungary in '56, of the presence of Canadian and American soldiers in Holland, to imply that things are not necessarily safe or straightforward. Neither are people.

Loe Wolff (Peter Tuinman) is a truckdriver, divorced, with one kid and ex-wife in the States. His life is dull and drab. He gambles and loses his boss' money and tries to sell a truck to raise the fare to New York. But he's caught by the boss, who is surprisingly understanding: he'll provide visa and ticket to the U.S., even some traveling money, on condition that Wolff's passport will bear another name. The boss needs Wolff's passport, he says, to smuggle a Hungarian out of his occupied country.

Wolff agrees, but his departure is accidentally delayed and he discovers his truck is a total loss after a bad accident. The driver, supposedly Wolff, was burned to death.

Stubborn and obstinate he starts investigating. He's beaten up, shot at, framed, arrested. But "they" have power and connections, money. He can't win but becomes his own man, thereby keeping his dignity.

Wolff gets mixed up with Anna (Monique van de Ven). Her life is as lukewarm as his. They fall in love. At the happy ending she's become her own woman.

Peter Tuinman is impressive in his first lead. Monique van de Ven at her considerable best as the girl. Other thesping also is good, as are technical credits. But pic is mainly about events, not about people one gets to know or care about.

A film worth seeing because of the atmosphere created by Verbong and the lensing of Theo Van de Sande. —*Wall.*

Aijo Monogatari
(Curtain Call)
(JAPANESE-COLOR)

Tokyo, Sept. 10.
A Toei release of a Haruki Kadokawa Production. Produced and directed by Kadokawa. Screenplay by Sen Kenmochi, from the novel by Jiro Akagawa. Assistant producers, Hiroshi Sugawara and Koseuke Kuri. Camera (Color), Seizo Senmoto; art director; Tsutomu Imamura; editing, Noboru Suzuki; assistant director, Yoshisato Matsunaga; music director, Masato Kai; choreography, Miguel Godreau and Michael Shawn. Reviewed at Scalaza, Tokyo, Sept. 8, 1984. Running time: 110 MINS.
Miho Nakamichi........Tomoyo Harada
Haruko Nakamichi.......Mitsuko Baisho
Takuji Shinozaki......Tsunehiko Watase
Yoshiko Omori............Mariko Kaga
Hanaya No Onnashujin Atsuko Kawaguchi

"Aijo Monogatari" (literally, "A Story Of Affection," although "Curtain Call" is the designated English-language title) is a quintessential Haruki Kadokawa production. The theme song is sung by its thin-voiced, toplined star Tomoyo Harada, yet musical contributions by other artists — foreign and Japanese — add up to a very strong soundtrack LP, already in the Top 40 here. But about the best that can be said of the screenplay is that it fails to surpass the muddle-headedness of such past Kadokawa epics as "Yasei No Shomei" and "Sengoku Jieitai."

Being securely plugged into the zeitgeist, Akagawa has made his heroine an aspiring teenaged dancer whose stepmother (played by Mitsuko Baisho) manages a boutique. The central mystery of this young girl's life concerns the true identity of her father.

Harada's quest for her pappy: once it ends, so does the interest. Any remaining believability is swept away when she returns to Tokyo, passes a round of auditions and then — lickety-split — assumes the lead in a musical.

Accompanying Harada on her search is Tsunehiko Watase, a Kyushu potter whom the young girl initially (and mistakenly) assumes is the mysterious gentleman who, over the years, has sent her flowers on her birthday.

Though possessing a very supple and not physically unattractive body, Harada is a Jennifer Beals in need of a Marine Jahan. The many dancers who appear with her in the film's climactic production number seem to restrain themselves to make her look good.

The film is worth seeing for no other reason than it represents a startling attitudinal change for Kadokawa productions vis-a-vis Westerners. Notorious for his early films' harsh treatment of foreigners, particularly Americans (most pungent in "Ningen No Shomei"), he here shows a racially mixed couple simply out for a good time. Given that Kadokawa mirrors, rather than molds, public attitudes, this very well-acted film is a definite "up." — *Bail.*

Homecoming
(HONG KONG/CHINESE-COLOR)

Hong Kong, Sept. 2.

A Bluebird Movie Enterprises Ltd. and Target Film Co. Ltd. production and release. Executive producers, Xia Meng and Yim Ho. Directed by Yim Ho. Screenplay, Kong Liang; camera (color), Poon Hang Sang; music, Kitaro; editor, Kin Kin. Stars Si Quin Gao Wa, Josephine Koo, Xie Wei Xiang, Zhou Yun, Zhang Ju Gao, Ye Wai Zheng, Ceng Yu. Reviewed at Supreme Preview Room, Hong Kong, Sept. 1, 1984. Running time: **96 MINS.**
(Mandarin soundtrack with English subtitles; also available in Cantonese with English subtitles).

In "Homecoming," a young and attractive businesswoman in her 30s is harassed by the dehumanizing and materialist pressures of city life and decides to visit the small village of her birth and early youth. She meets her childhood acquaintances, especially her bosom friend, now a headmistress who is happily married with a daughter. Her presence causes some frictions and emotional tension among the locals due to her citified ways. The urbanized woman soon realizes the bonds of the past and affection are not sufficient to lessen the cultural gaps created through the years.

However, due to a continuing relationship with the desire to understand each other's environment and ideas, the two friends slowly establish an even stronger bond of friendship. They part in the end, but it seems to be just the beginning.

This is a sensitive story about the search for roots, identity, and the purpose of life, and also about deep kinship and life in a rural community. "Homecoming" is the much publicized return of 33-year old Cantonese director Yim Ho ("The Extras," "The Happenings") into the mainstream of Hong Kong filmmaking after an absence of a couple of years and the heralded rebirth of the local movie industry with the Hong Kong-Mainland China creative collaboration.

The nicest thing about the film is that the seemingly trivialities of life prove to be the keystones of the plot's simple structure. Ho's perceptive eyes, ears and heart for the nuances of behavior of the contrasting cultures are lovingly projected on the screen without taking sides.

Worthy to be shown at major international film festivals, pic should do well in the college-university circuit and art hosues.

Marvelous acting is provided by Si Qin Gao Wa as the conservative teacher-housewife Ah Zhen and elegant newcomer Josephine Koo as the modern Shan Shan (a.k.a.

Coral). Also to be commended are the fascinating country scenes of China, music of Kitaro and Kong Liang's screenplay which handled the delicate subject of contrasting life styles and doctrines.

There are two versions available, one with Mandarian soundtrack and the Cantonese version, which is said to contain a hit song. — *Mel.*

Tausend Augen
(Thousand Eyes)
(WEST GERMAN-COLOR)

Berlin, Sept. 17.

A Pro-ject Film Production im Filmverlag der Autoren, Munich, in collaboration with Radiant Film and Thorn EMI Video/ZDF. Producer, Martin Bittins. Features entire cast. Written and directed by Hans-Christoph Blumenberg. Camera (color), Martin Schäfer; sets, Christian Bussmann; editor, Helga Borsche; music, Hubert Bartholomae; sound, Reinhard Levin; costumes, Regina Troester; tv-producer, Willi Segler. Reviewed at Kant Kino, Berlin, Sept. 16, 1984. Running time: **92 MINS.**
Cast: Barbara Rudnik (Gabriele), Armin Müller-Stahl (Arnold), Karen Ball (Vera), Peter Kraus (Schirmer), Hannelore Hoger (Brigitte), Isolde Barth (Jutta), Ingeburg Thomsen (Marlene), Bettina Grühn (Minka), Susanne Aernecke (Susanne), Ann Flum (Pauline), Peter Behrens (Kargus), Mehmet Yandirer (Mehmet), Voker Eckstein (Engmann), Vera Tschechowa (Victoria), Gudrun Landgrebe (Lohmann).

"Thousand Eyes" is the first feature made by one of Germany's leading critics, Hans-Christoph Blumenberg. As the title suggests, it has a lot to do with peep shows, but it's rather difficult to say just why the motif plays such a central role. Like most everything else in the film, the metaphors are there for the viewer to dicker with as the story unfolds day by day over a week's time. In the end, one may simply give up unraveling both the title and the film's content.

Pic is set in Hamburg's inner city in winter. Gabriele is longing for sunny Australia and a recent lover who sends her taped messages from time to time to go along with a super-8m film: it was taken on the beach when they were a cooing couple. Now she's back home living in her parents' penthouse apartment (with swimming pool), attending courses in marine biology during the day, and working in a peep show at night to earn a couple extra bucks for a ticket back to Australia. Gabriele, it's made quite clear, has her dreams to keep her going.

Dreams are what makes the movie pull and tug in different directions. There's a friendly taxi driver, Schirmer (Peter Kraus, playing with flair), who takes her nightly to the peep show — because they both apparently share a yen for Down Under. There's the peep show manager, Arnold, who hankers for Gabriele, but is watched closely in turn by the cashier Vera, who reports his escapades to the femme boss, Lohmann. There's the sadder-but-wiser

coterie of peep-girls who trade words of tired truth in the dressing-room. There are a couple of love-sick types hanging around the peep show, one a young Turk who sketches his "dreamgirl" (Gabriele) from afar. And there's the saleslady in the video shop who vaguely recalls a similar Dorothy Malone small role (the saleslady in the bookstore) in Howard Hawks' 1946 "The Big Sleep," an observation only significant in view of Blumenberg's own book and docu on Hawks.

Put all this together and the formula comes out psycho-thriller. Outside of a couple of inside jokes for film buffs — walk-ons by Wim Wenders and Jean-Marie Straub, plus Aussie filmers in the super-8m seg — chalk this one up to a debut helmer's struggling to learn the secrets of his craft. Thesp performances are shallow and mannered, unfortunate since critic Blumenberg was noted for the might of his words. Is this "auteur" in need of a dialog coach? Major plus is the night lensing by Martin Schäfer. —*Holl.*

The Little Drummer Girl
(COLOR)

Uninspired adaptation of the espionage tome.

Hollywood, Oct. 5.

A Warner Bros.' release of a Pan Arts production. Produced by Robert L. Crawford. Executive producer, Patrick Kelly. Directed by George Roy Hill. Stars Diane Keaton. Screenplay, Loring Mandel, based on the novel by John Le Carré; camera (Technicolor), Wolfgang Treu; editor, William Reynolds; music, Dave Grusin; production design, Henry Bumstead; art direction, Helmut Gassner, Mikes Karapiperis (Greece), Ariel Roshko (Israel), Geoffrey Tozer (England); Diane Keaton's costumes, Kristi Zea; sound, Gunther Stadelmann; assistant director, Don French; second unit director, Michael Moore; second unit camera, Peter Rohe. Reviewed at The Burbank Studios, Burbank, Oct. 4, 1984. (MPAA Rating: R.) Running time: **130 MINS.**

Charlie	Diane Keaton
Joseph	Yorgo Voyagis
Kurtz	Klaus Kinski
Khalil	Sami Frey
Tayeh	Michael Cristofer
Mesterbein	David Suchet
Litvak	Eli Danker
Mr. Quilley	Thorley Walters
Helga	Kerstin De Ahna
Chairlady	Anna Massey
Katrin	Dana Wheeler-Nicholson
Rossino	Robert Pereno
Michel	Moti Shirin

George Roy Hill has made a disappointingly flat film adaptation of one of John Le Carré's top novels, "The Little Drummer Girl." Overlong and, for the most part, indifferently staged on a multitude of foreign locales, pic can't help but intrigue due to the intense subject matter, that of complex Israeli and Palestinian espionage and terrorism, and the combined names of Diane Keaton, Hill and Le Carré up top will mean some initial biz. However, the human story here never flowers, and the telling fails to deliver the punch it should.

Readers of the Le Carré tome will have some readjusting to do in order to accept the all-American Keaton in the role of Charlie, in the book a virulently pro-Palestinian British actress generally agreed to have been inspired by Vanessa Redgrave. Even without reference to the novel, one wonders for awhile at the incongruity of a Yank seemingly playing St. Joan and Shakespearean parts in an English repertory company.

No matter, though, for events quickly take Keaton out of the U.K. A team of Israeli operatives, led by the supremely self-confident Klaus Kinski, recruits her in Greece, breaks down her Arab sympathies and eventually puts her in place as an ideal agent.

Naturally, the true political positions of the numerous shady characters who surface in the early going are impossible to pin down, but Hill fails to subtly delineate the nuances of ambiguity essential to such an exercise, nuances so outstandingly drawn, for instance, in John Irvin's tv adaptation of Le Carré's "Tinker, Tailor, Soldier, Spy."

.Even more critically, a romance between Keaton and Joseph, her main Israeli contact, played by Yorgo Voyagis, never even threatens to ignite, much less catch fire. Chemistry between the two is simply nonexistent, and the emotional dynamic between them, which would have helped intensify the suspenseful period of their separation, is sorely missed.

Things pick up a bit in the middle-going, particularly during an admirably mounted sequence in which Kinski & Co. stake out a town square and railroad station waiting for terrorists to show up, and interest is increased further once Keaton successfully infiltrates a Palestinian camp near Beirut, undergoes rigorous military training and returns to Germany a well-prepared double agent.

Keaton's prey is a notorious Palestinian terrorist played by Sami Frey, and the French actor's great charm and warmth help make something valid of the film's climactic section. Ultimate resolution, however, proves rather pallid.

Keaton's loud, pushy, erratic showbiz character isn't all that easy to warm up to and, for an actress who set a fashion trend seven years ago, she sports an unbecoming new hairdo and strange, outsized clothes here. Performance isn't one of her better efforts. Best known for his looney roles, Kinski is cast against type and delivers a strong supporting turn.

Dialog is hardly inspired, but Loring Mandel's script ably manages to keep the complex plot relatively comprehensible. Director Hill, however, has his hands full just coping with the logistics of the story, many characters and countless locations, and imparts little of his customary slick stylishness to the proceedings; the number of camera setups in this film must rank among the all-time highs, each shot seems to last only about five seconds, and no overall shape or style is forged as a result.

· Locales, which include London, Mykonos, the Acropolis, ravaged Beirut and German cities, provided plenty of colorful backgrounds.
—*Cart.*

Gebroken Spiegels
(Broken Mirrors)
(DUTCH-COLOR)

Utrecht, Sept. 22.
A Tuschinski film distribution release of a Matthijs Van Heijningen production. Produced by Van Heijningen. Written and directed by Marleen Gorris. Features entire cast: Camera (color), Frans Bromet; editor, Hans Van Dongen; music, Lodewijk de Boer; art direction, Harry Ammerlaan; sound, Georges Bossaers. Reviewed at Rembrandt theater, Utrecht, Sept. 21, 1984. Running time: 105 MINS.
Diane . . . . .Lineke Rijxman
Dora .Henriette Tol
Bea . . . . .Edda Barends
Ellen . . . . .Coby Stunnenberg
Jean/Pierre . . . . .Eddy Brugman

Femme helmer Marleen Gorris' first pic, "The Silence Around Christine M.," was a success in half a dozen countries after festival screenings. Her second venture, "Broken Mirrors," similar in feminist outlook, but different in stylistic approach and emotional impact, may well again attract interest at festivals, in art houses and specialized situations.

Although pic leaves audiences in a sadder, less baffled mood than "Christine M.," it is the better film of the two, with a more balanced storyline and again, a clever script.

The basic story about prostitutes, their subsistence in an Amsterdam brothel and the liberating revolt of Diane and Dora, the two leading characters, ultimately ties in with the tragedy of Bea, a housewife and mother. She is clubbed and abducted by a pervert, fettered to a bed in a cold cellar, and slowly starved to death. Her murderer meanwhile photographs the stages of her agony, adding the prints to his collection of similar victims' snapshots.

This may sound corny, but isn't thanks to Edda Barends' impressive acting, Gorris' quiet and strong direction and Frans Bromet's observant camera. Not unlike the two most valiant prostitutes, Bea overcomes by opting out.

Pic never dwells on sex or violence — the effects are seen, not the deeds. It does not dwell on the men either, but on the women, adequately acted by all. — *Ewa.*

Garbo Talks
(COLOR)

Uneven New York comedy, too cute for its own good.

Hollywood, Oct. 4.
An MGM/UA Entertainment release of a United Artists presentation of an Elliott Kastner production. Produced by Burtt Harris, Kastner. Directed by Sidney Lumet. Stars Anne Bancroft, Ron Silver, Carrie Fisher, Catherine Hicks. Screenplay, Larry Grusin. Camera (Technicolor, prints in Metrocolor), Andrzej Bartkowiak; editor, Andrew Mondshein; music, Cy Coleman; production designer, Philip Rosenberg; set decorators, Philip Smith, John Godfrey; set dresser, John Oates, Jr.; sound, James Sabat; costumes, Anna Hill Johnstone; production manager-associate producer, Jennifer M. Ogden; assistant director, Alan Hopkins. Reviewed at MGM/UA screening room, October 3, 1984, Culver City, Calif. (MPAA Rating: PG-13.) Running time: 103 MINS.
Estelle Rolfe . . . . .Anne Bancroft
Gilbert Rolfe . . . . .Ron Silver
Lisa Rolfe . . . . .Carrie Fisher
Jane Mortimer . . . . .Catherine Hicks
Walter Rolfe . . . . .Steven Hill
Angelo Dokakis . . . . .Howard Da Silva
Sonya Apollinar . . . . .Dorothy Loudon
Bernie Whitlock . . . . .Harvey Fierstein
Elizabeth Rennick . . . . .Hermione Gingold
Also with: Richard B. Shull, Michael Lombard, Ed Crowley, Alice Spivak, Maurice Sterman, Antonia Rey, Court Miller, Denny Dillon, Karen Shallo, Adolph Green, Betty Comden (Garbo), Arthur Schlesinger Jr.

"Garbo Talks" is a sweet and sour film clearly not for all tastes. Packed with New York in-jokes,

not everyone will appreciate its aggressive charm. But beneath its cocky exterior, picture has a beat on some very human and universal truths. Low-key marketing approach by MGM/UA, at least on the Coast, offers the film little chance of finding more than a Woody Allen-type audience.

Premise of the film, one woman's lifelong obsession with Greta Garbo, is really a delightful idea. While she is seen in fleeting glimpses wearing capes and fleeing mysterious locations, the film is not really about Garbo, but what people make of their heroes.

Estelle Rolfe (Anne Bancroft) is a certifiable eccentric who has worshipped Garbo from afar since childhood, until the star has become woven into the fabric of her imagination. Her identification with Garbo has become a way for her to glamorize her day to day life.

Estelle is no ordinary housewife. Divorced from her husband (Steven Hill) because he doesn't want any more surprises, she is continually arrested for defending any and all causes and fighting the everyday indignities of life in N.Y. If not for Bancroft's spirited performance, Estelle would deteriorate into a caricature.

One of the weaknesses of the film is that screenwriter Larry Grusin's characters are often too stagey and theatrical. Consequently, "Garbo Talks" suffers slightly from the Neil Simon excess of being too delighted with its own wit.

At heart the film is sound, but unfortunately Estelle's health isn't and her last wish is to meet Garbo. Dutiful son Gilbert (Ron Silver) sets out on his personal quest for the holy grail and if his mother's obsession is meeting Garbo, his is finding her.

Though the reason for the quest wears thin, most of the stops along the way are fun. Silver takes a trip to Fire Island stalking the elusive Garbo. He doesn't find her but meets the perfectly likable Bernie Whitlock (Harvey Fierstein), who loans him a pair of pants.

The film is full of splendid little moments such as Silver camped out in front of Garbo's apartment building with burnt-out paparazzi Howard Da Silva drinking coffee from paper cups.

In a departure from her usual role as a cosmic princess, Carrie Fisher plays a Jewish American princess par excellence. As Silver's wife, she speaks two languages-"English and Gucci." When Fisher heads home to California, aspiring actress Catherine Hicks becomes his new love interest.

Not surprisingly, director Sidney Lumet has accurately and affectionately rendered the N.Y. milieu of delis and Central Park. Cast of Broadway stage regulars has perfectly mastered New York diction. Photography by Andrzej Bartko-

wiak bathes the film in a fairytale glow totally appropriate when searching for legends. —*Jagr.*

Atrapadas
(Trapped Women)
(ARGENTINE-COLOR)

Buenos Aires, Aug. 17.
An Argentina Sono Film presentation of an Carlos Luis Mentasti-Luis Alberto Scalella production. Directed by Anibal Di Salvo. Screenplay, Di Salvo, based upon a story by José Dominianni; camera (Eastmancolor), Carlos Torlaschi; music, Luis Maria Serra; editor, Darío Tedesco; art director, Santiago Elder; production manager, Miguel Torrado; assistant director, Miguel Angel Fernández Alonso. Reviewed at the Sarmiento theater, B.A., Aug. 16, 1984. Running time: 90 MINS.
Silvia . . . . .Leonor Benedetto
Pregnant woman . . . . .Betiana Blum
Susana . . . . .Camila Perissé
Graciela . . . . .Mirtha Busnelli
Warden Galindez . . . . .Cristina Murta
Maricarmen . . . . .Rita Terranova
Olga . . . . .Elvia Andreoli
Warden Castellanos . . . . . . .Adriana Parets
Daniel . . . . .Juan Leyrado
Fabián . . . . .Edgardo Suárez
Nacho . . . . .Gerardo Romano
Sara Stein . . . . .Inés Murray

"Atrapadas" is a successful Argentine counterpart to the U.S. "The Concrete Jungle," "Chained Heat" and other pics on women in prison, loaded with sex and violence, which have enjoyed a b.o. bonanza since censorship was lifted here. Anibal Di Salvo's opera prima includes the most daring softcore sex scenes seen so far in native films, helping it to sell nearly 1,000,000 tickets in its first few weeks of general release.

The central characters are Leonor Benedetto, caught during a hold-up, and Camila Perissé, leader of a sinister gang of inmates linked with some corrupt wardens and, through them, with the boss of a ring engaged in drug trafficking and prostitution. Lesbian Perissé administers the drugs among prisoners both to get lovers and to prepare them for the ruffian's ends when they are freed.

Benedetto refuses to surrender to Perissé's demands, is mercilessly beaten and eventually learns that the mobsters have killed her younger sister. With the help of accomplices and a good warden, she leaves prison one night for a few hours, kills the gangster and Perissé (who had been just freed) and returns to her cell, not leaving any clues.

Di Salvo, cinematographer of several films directed by the late Leopoldo Torre-Nilsson, proves he is a competent professional, attaining an effective — if superficial — entertainment.

Benedetto, Perissé, Mirta Busnelli and Rita Terranova give convincing performances, but Betiana Blum steals the picture with her irresistibly funny impersonation of an illiterate provincial girl candidly telling of her experiences with men.

Carlos Torlaschi's camerawork, Luis Maria Serra's score and Dario Tedesco's editing are pluses. Other credits are good. — *Nubi*.

1984
(BRITISH-COLOR)

London, Oct. 8.

A Virgin Films presentation of an Umbrella-Rosenblum production. Produced by Simon Perry. Executive producer, Marvin J. Rosenblum. Coproducers, Al Clark, Robert Devereux. Written and directed by Michael Radford. Stars John Hurt, Richard Burton, Suzanna Hamilton. Camera (color), Roger Deakins; editor, Tom Priestley; music, Dominic Muldowney; production designer, Allan Cameron; art directors, Martin Hebert, Grant Hicks; costume designer, Emma Porteous; sound, Bruce White; assistant director, Chris Rose. Reviewed at the Leicester Square theater, London, Oct. 7, 1984. (BBFC Rating: 15.) Running time: 120 MINS.

Winston Smith . . . . John Hurt
O'Brien . . . . Richard Burton
Julia . . . . Suzanna Hamilton
Charrington . . . . Cyril Cusack
Parsons . . . . Gregor Fisher
Syme . . . . James Walker
Tillotson . . . . Andrew Wilde

In this unremitting downer, writer-director Michael Radford introduces no touches of comedy or facile sensationalism to soften a harsh depiction of life under a totalitarian system as imagined by George Orwell in 1948. The pic's poetic intensity will, however, guarantee stronger b.o. performance than a 1955 screen version with Michael Redgrave, Edmond O'Brien and Jan Sterling which Michael Anderson directed. With careful handling that emphasizes the book's classic status and a standout performance by Richard Burton in his theatrical swansong, the Virgin Films release should prove profitable.

Burton, to whom pic carries a dedication "with love and admiration" as part of the end credits, is splendid as inner-party official O'Brien. Ironically, his performance as the deceptively gentle spur to Winston Smith's "thoughtcrimes," and then as the all-knowing interrogator who takes on the attributes of a father-figure to the helpless man whom he is intent on destroying, is something new in Burton's repertoire. It lacks any of the histrionics which were his hallmark.

Also strong is newcomer Suzanna Hamilton in the part of lusty seductress Julia who is the other agent of Smith's downfall. With the passionate impulsiveness of youth she lures him to carnal bliss in direct violation of Big Brother's campaign against interpersonal relations. The development of their incautious relationship is tellingly narrated.

However, it is John Hurt as Winston Smith who holds center stage throughout. Radford's images emphasize the character's tragic isolation as he submits to the propagandizing of mass rallies and an ever-babbling telescreen. He seeks forlornly for some hope within a society whose precepts he does not understand and which he finds increasingly difficult to tolerate. From the small rebellion of his free-thinking diary, an antidote to his daily activity as a rewriter of history, he is inexorably led to his braver stand. Hurt's craggy features help to eloquently project the agony to which his actions lead.

The film's message lies less in its political analysis, which retains the Orwellian disillusion with Soviet communism, than in its portrayal of the human need to dream a better life. Radford has peppered the film with fantasy sequences that capture those inner longings.

Smith's actions are counterpointed to the endless flow of propaganda from the ubiquitous never-silent telescreens. They channel the message of a society dependent upon keeping its members in a state of fever-pitch hysteria against the enemies within and without.

His treachery leads to Smith's protracted torture by O'Brien. The process is commonplace but Radford's images are extremely harrowing. As with the full-frontal nudity of the loving couple, the filmmaker reworks classic imagery for significance rather than exploitation. That seems to be the British censor's justification for a "15" certificate. The MPAA's rating board should please note.

Wisely, pic avoids the danger of anachronism by being set firmly in the late '40s period when the book was written. This adds to narrative interest. The bleak architecture of the period and urban landscape resonant of a London devastated by WWII bombing raids are used to telling effect, with topnotch set-design and location-dressing by Allan Cameron.

The film benefits not only from excellent photography by Roger Deakins, who did Radford's only previous feature "Another Time, Another Place," but also from a film-treatment process developed by Kay Laboratories which is the best solution yet devised for getting b&w tonal resonances on color film. Print caught for review had a sombre but occasionally stirring score by Dominic Muldowney. Additional music from the Eurythmics group was still in preparation.

"1984" stands out in today's market as an unusually serious and moving treatment of a story that could easily have been trivialized. Rather than attempting to adjust the horrors of its theme for easy watching, it journeys straight to the heart of the nightmare created by so many of the twentieth century's regimes. In showing the attempted rebellion of one individual against unbeatable odds it does provide a twinkle of hope in the gloom.
— *Japa*.

Night Of The Comet
(COLOR)

Derivative but enjoyable sci-fi comedy is headed for paydirt.

An Atlantic Releasing release of a Thomas Coleman and Michael Rosenblatt presentation, in association with Film Development Fund. Executive producers, Coleman, Rosenblatt. Produced by Andrew Lane and Wayne Crawford. Written and directed by Thom Eberhardt. Features entire cast. Camera (color), Arthur Albert; editor, Fred Stafford; music supervision, Tom Perry; sound, Steve Nelson; assistant director, H. Gordon Boos; production manager-associate producer, Nancy Israel; production design-special visual effects design, John Muto; set decoration, David Wasco; special effects, Court Wizard; makeup effects design, David B. Miller; second unit directors, Boos, Muto. Reviewed at Magno Penthouse screening room, N.Y., Oct. 4, 1984. (MPAA Rating: PG-13.) Running time: 95 MINS.

Regina . . . . Catherine Mary Stewart
Samantha . . . . Kelli Maroney
Hector . . . . Robert Beltran
Carter . . . . Geoffrey Lewis
Audrey . . . . Mary Woronov
Oscar . . . . John Achorn
Doris . . . . Sharon Farrell
Larry . . . . Michael Bowen
Willy . . . . Ivan Roth

"Night Of The Comet" is a successful pastiche of numerous science fiction films, executed with an entertaining, tongue-in-cheek flair that compensates for its absence of originality. Opening nationally Nov. 16, this low-budgeter stands to attract a sizeable audience as alternative to the major SF fare ("2010" and "Dune") debuting several weeks later.

"Comet" closely resembles in structure the prototype for end of the world cinema, Arch Oboler's 1951 Columbia feature "Five." When nearly everyone is out watching the arrival of a comet (last having visited Earth 65,000,000 years ago, when the dinosaurs disappeared), a few lucky people are indoors protected by steel walls from the comet's deadly rays. (Premise of course recalls "The Day Of The Triffids.") Survivors regroup and fight amongst themselves, attracted by an automated L.A. radio station signal, while the city's empty streets are littered with clothing and orange dust, all that remains of the bulk of humanity.

Baddies are scientists led by Geoffrey Lewis and Mary Woronov, partially protected in their underground installation but exposed to the comet's effects through an open ventilation system. They're rounding up unaffected survivors, draining them of their blood to perform tests to come up with a serum before they gradually turn into disfigured monsters, a number of which are prowling the city's streets (à la "The Omega Man"). Other key plot elements are liberally lifted from "Dawn Of The Dead" (and its shopping mall locale), "The Andromeda Strain" and even a gender switch on Roger Corman-Robert Towne's "Last Woman On Earth."

While SF fans are busy sorting out the influences, filmmaker Thom Eberhardt (whose previous feature was the minor "Sole Survivor") creates a visually arresting B-picture in the neon-primary colors style of the cult hit "Liquid Sky," aided by impressive technical contributions from cinematographer Arthur Albert and designer John Muto. Much of the film is played straight, including several effective special makeup effects scares, but what makes the picture work is a light-hearted approach, typified by the reaction of one of the heroines during a suspenseful, dangerous last reel scene: suddenly reunited with her sister, she exclaims: "What a great outfit," a non sequitur that is perfectly in character.

As the resourceful sisters who ultimately will be repopulating the planet, Catherine Mary Stewart (of "The Last Starfighter") and Kelli Maroney are delightful, providing, respectively, a believably feisty battler who can beat up monsters and a new, improved Valley Girl (pic was produced by Atlantic's "Valley Girl" creators and features frequent plugola on-screen for that film). Supporting cast has a solid turn by Robert Beltran, though his reunion with his "Eating Raoul" costar Mary Woronov is brief and unexciting. A virtually nonstop rock songs musical score supervised by Tom Perry adequately covers lulls in the action. —*Lor*.

The Blade Master
(Ator The Invincible)
(COLOR)

Surf's up in prehistoric fantasyland.

A New Line Cinema release of a Royal Film Traders presentation. Produced by John Newman. Executive producer, Alex Sussmann. Directed by David Hills. Stars Miles O'Keeffe. Screenplay, Hills (uncredited); camera (color), Federico Slonisco; editor, David Framer; music, Carlo Rustichelli; associate producer, Chris Trainor. Reviewed on Media Home Entertainment vidcassette, N.Y., Sept. 27, 1984. (MPAA Rating: PG.) Running time: 92 MINS.

Ator . . . . Miles O'Keeffe
Mila . . . . Lisa Foster (Raines)
Akronas . . . . Charles Borromel
Zor . . . . David Cain Haughton
Thong . . . . Chen Wong

"The Blade Master," filmed in Europe in 1982 under the alternate titles "Ator The Invincible" and "The Return," is a dull, incredibly silly fantasy adventure that will be remembered as the first (and hopefully last) prehistoric film in which the beefcake hero goes hang-gliding. New Line released the pic theatrically in February but there's no U.S. audience for this junk.

A quickie sequel to "Ator The Fighting Eagle," from which a five-minute recap montage is excerpted, "Blade" returns muscular Miles O'Keeffe as the good samaritan hero who has conquered the forces of nature, battling the power hungry Zor (played by David Cain Haughton, earlier the title star of "Caligula The Untold Story" from same director David Hills) and his wizard Sandur. Zor is after the knowledge possessed by scientist Akronas (Charles Borromel) and his invention, the "geometric nucleus," sort of a primitive atomic bomb.

With his oriental sage pal Thong (Chen Wong) and Akronas' pretty daughter Mila (Lisa Foster), Ator treks boringly to Akronas' castle. Film contains mucho filler and pointless plot tangents, prompting Mila to properly ask Ator at one point: "Wouldn't it have been easier if we had just gone on to the aid of my father?"

After Ator wrestles with a huge rubber snake (whose thick hoisting wires are clearly visible on screen), even faker than O'Keeffe's adversary in John Derek's "Tarzan" movie, pic reaches its risible nadir upon arrival at the castle. Ator sends his two pals on to sneak in the back way, while he suddenly floats out from a hill in a hang-glider, whose existence is both an anachronism and impossibility unless he built one from scratch in five minutes.

O'Keeffe has cranked out many made-in-Europe films since "Tarzan," but with the poor dubbing and nonscript he's a joke here. Lisa Foster (a Canadian actress a.k.a. Lisa Raines in the 1982 title role of "Fanny Hill") is a looker resembling Jennifer O'Neill. Director David Hills creates no atmosphere, with picture's exteriors never achieving any period feel. —Lor.

American Dreamer
(COLOR)

Fanciful but unspectacular romantic comedy. Could capture a sympathetic following but unlikely as mass market entry.

A Warner Bros. release of a CBS Theatrical Films presentation of a Krost/Chapin production. Executive producer, Barry Krost. Produced by Doug Chapin. Directed by Rick Rosenthal. Features entire cast. Screenplay, Jim Kouf, David Greenwalt, from story by Ann Biderman; camera (Prints by Technicolor) Giuseppe Rotunno; additional photography, Jan De Bont; editor, Anne Goursand; music, Lewis Furey; second unit director, William Watkins; production design, Brian Eatwell; art direction, Marc Frederix, Jeff Goldstein (U.S.); stunt coordinator, Chuck Waters; costume design, Michael Kaplan; miniature photography, Brick Price. Reviewed at Magno Preview 9 screening room, N.Y., Sept. 19, 1984. (MPAA Rating: PG.) Running time: **105 MINS.**

Cathy Palmer/Rebecca
Ryan . . . . JoBeth Williams
Alan McMann . . . . Tom Conti
Victor Marchand . . . . . . Giancarlo Giannini
Margaret McMann . . . . Coral Browne
Kevin Palmer . . . . James Staley
Karl Palmer . . . . Huckleberry Fox
Kevin Palmer Jr. . . . . C.B. Barnes
Ivan Stranauvlitch . . . . Leon Zitrone
Don Carlos . . . . Jean Rougerie
Inspector . . . . Pierre Santini
Malcolm . . . . Brian Eatwell

Inevitably to be compared (at some disadvantage) to this year's surprise hit "Romancing The Stone," which utilizes the same basic plot device of a femme romantic novelist living out her fantasy adventures for real, "American Dreamer" emerges as a pleasant throwback to earlier forms of Hollywood farce. Less than perfect casting and merely okay scripting spell yet another b.o. failure (fifth in a row dating back to "Back Roads") from CBS Theatrical Films arm, releasing through WB. Prospects for discovery and appreciation on the rebound, via either cable or network tv loom far better.

Problem here is that this type of vehicle, which appears tailormade to the talents of say, Doris Day or the late Natalie Wood two decades ago, has long since been co-opted by tv, making "Dreamer," despite its rich production gloss and unusual casting, appear to be a glorified telefilm. That's a shame given the generally entertaining results, but a roadblock that should have been addressed before production got the go-ahead.

JoBeth Williams toplines in the very showy dual role, beginning as a frustrated Ohio housewife, Cathy Palmer, literally sat on by her incredibly boring and paternalistic husband Kevin (James Staley). Hubbie would rather work on tomorrow's accounting in bed than make love to her. Winning a trip to Paris for writing a novel in the style of the hit Rebeca Ryan thrillers, Cathy jumps at the chance, even though Kevin nearly forbids it and ultimately refuses to go along.

Second reel of briskly paced pic takes us to Paris, with Cathy knocked unconscious by a speeding car driven by the Spanish Ambassador, Don Carlos (Jean Rougerie), but upon awakening in the hospital, she thinks she is actually the Rebecca Ryan character she has read about so avidly. Proceeding to live the part, she quickly amasses a vast, smashing wardrobe of Paris originals, using the felicitous gimmick of signing all bills "Rebecca Ryan, Hotel de Crillon," with the real hotel (mentioned prominently in the fictional Ryan books) vouching that indeed, that's where Ryan "lives."

Imposing herself upon an Englishman whom she presumes is her secretary (Tom Conti), but is actually the ghostwriter of the Ryan novels officially penned by his mother (Coral Browne), she keeps imagining everyone as villains and sure enough, they have something to hide. Principal baddie is the leader of the French opposition party (Giancarlo Giannini), whose pratfalls and escalating physical injuries parallel Herbert Lom's comedy antagonist function in the "Pink Panther" comedies.

Script and cast don't take things very seriously, typified by Conti interrupting a catchup exposition scene with mother Browne by rightfully asking "Why am I asking you?" since the whole scene is obviously just a filmic device in which he is mere spear-carrier. Director Rick Rosenthal wisely emphasizes the script's slapstick elements, yielding some uproarious physical comedy amid scenes of more conventional mock-intrigue and adventure.

Williams likewise maximizes the comedic potential of her roles, but though her career has been blooming of late with parts in hits such as "The Big Chill," and "Poltergeist," she lacks the marquee lure to carry an entire picture on her lovely back. Conti, continuing to follow threateningly in Dudley Moore's footsteps as an offbeat U.K. romantic hero, delivers some marvelous takes and is a solid foil to his leading lady. Ditto for Giannini, once again using his eyes to great advantage. Huckleberry Fox (of "Terms Of Endearment" and "Misunderstood") and C.B. Barnes make lovable kids, but James Staley as their Tim Conway-esque daddy is totally unbelievable in his straw man hissable role.

Given brief moments of true emotion and even horror (as when, late in the film, Williams becomes aware of her true identity and the arid existence awaiting her back home), pic might have worked better played straight rather than as farce. In any event, it fits with the current trend ("Cloak & Dagger," "Scandalous" and, yes, "Romancing The Stone") to adopt a tongue-in-cheek pose and is ably buttressed by lush lensing by Giuseppe Rotunno (Jan De Bont handling the L.A.-for-Ohio shoot) and solid technical contributions down the line. —Lor.

Dicht Hinter Der Tür
(Close Behind The Door)
(AUSTRIAN-COLOR)

San Sebastian, Sept. 22.
Written and directed by Mansur Madavi. Camera (color), Madavi; editor, Serge Sidi; sound, Ing. Reitmayer; music, Heinz Leonhardsberger. No other credits available. Features Erhard Pauer, Irene Kugler, Alfredo Solm, Nicola Filippelli, Karl Schmidt Werter, Answin Weissenbern. Reviewed at Cine Victoria Eugenia (San Sebastian), Sept. 21, 1984. Running time: **92 MINS.**

"Close Behind The Door" is an experimental, surrealistic film with Kafkaesque overtones in which a man who is holed up in his Vienna apartment is beset by manifestations of his fears.

Scripter-helmer Mansur Madavi drags out his pet hangups about the society surrounding him, though his indictments are never clearly spelled out. The oniric sequences include him opening up his living room door and being in a field, with Death telling him the moment and circumstance of his end; on another occasion he opens the door to a sea from which appears an obsessive offical who wants to question him.

Other vignettes see the man doing sketches on a paper which then come alive through animation

Item is well helmed and thesped, and production values are good, but the point, whatever it may have been, could have been made in a 20-minute short subject. —Besa.

A Flash Of Green
(COLOR)

Produced by Richard Jordan. Executive producer, Sam Gowan. Coproducer, American Playhouse. Directed by Victor Nuñez; editor, Nuñez; lighting director, Gus Holzer; sound, Stewart Lippe; music, Charles Engstrom; art director, Carlos Asse; costumes, Marilyn Wall-Asse, Dana Moser; production manager, Greg Hausch. Reviewed at New York Film Festival, Alice Tully Hall, Oct. 3, 1984. (No MPAA Rating). Running time: **131 MINS.**

Jimmy Wing . . . . Ed Harris
Kate Hubble . . . . Blair Brown
Elmo Bliss . . . . Richard Jordan
Brian Haas . . . . George Coe
Mitchie . . . . Joan Goodfellow
Jackie Halley . . . . Jean De Baer
Aunt Middie . . . . Helen Stenborg
Leroy Shannard . . . . William Mooney
Doris Rohl . . . . Isa Thomas
Ross Halley . . . . John Glover
Dial Sinnat . . . . Bob Murch
Nan Haas . . . . Joan MacIntosh
Borklund . . . . Bob Harris

This beautifully photographed, meticulously acted film is rigorously faithful to John D. MacDonald's 1962 novel about a small town Florida journalist who first serves and then turns against powerful local pols and businessmen determined at all costs to dredge and fill for profit a scenic, ecologically fertile bay. "A Flash Of Green" is one of a handful of pics to go into the New York Film Festival without a distributor, but its deeply textured storyline, balanced between individual moral dilemmas and the larger issue of environmentalism vs. institutional greed, certainly makes this indie effort worthy of theatrical showcasing.

Professionally hardboiled, personally easygoing Palm City reporter Jimmy Wing (Ed Harris) is grappling with a major life crisis as his brain-damaged wife lies dying in a hospital while his inarticulated love for his best friend's widow, Kat Hubble (Blair Brown) grows inexorably. Played with laconic understatement by Harris, Wing is a Palm County insider, with ancestral roots in the marshy, tropical land and an extensive network of friends, contacts and news sources.

One night, Wing is approached by egomaniacal county commissioner Elmo Bliss (Richard Jordan) to help the pol and his cronies gain title to land beneath publicly owned Grassy Bay for construction of a housing development worth millions to those with their thumbs in the pie. Wing is asked to gather blackmail dirt on members of the "S.O.B.'s" (Save Our Bay opposition group). Two years previously, Kat and other conservationists, backed by Wing's paper, fought off a bay development plan by out-of-towners. Now Wing's editors are playing ball with the rapine locals.

Although he wavers, Wing agrees to moonlight for Bliss, impelled perhaps by a need to distract himself from his painful personal problems. He rationalizes that refusing will only open the door for more vicious elements to attack Kat and others opposed to the development. Bliss (given stolid, brooding focus by Jordan) is a smooth redneck kingpin with designs on the governorship. He also has a rationale: dredging the bay means progress for Palm City and big money for the insiders. "The world needs folks like me — people with a raw need for power," Bliss tells Wing.

Wing soon dredges up muck on the daughter of a S.O.B. bankroller (she's having a motel affair with a younger lad) and a local amateur marine biologist (here doctorate was revoked for plagiarism many years past). Paradoxically, Wing's sympathies draw him to the environmentalists. Kat, in Blair Brown's effectively controlled portrayal, willfully uses Wing as an ally in the cause, but she remains emotionally aloof. So Wing's unrequited ardour smolders while his compromised position with Bliss leads him into a moral cul-de-sac.

Meanwhile, Bliss has broken his implicit promise not to play rough, and the environmentalists face increasingly nasty harassment from a local, pro-Bliss right-wing fundamentalist group, The Army Of God. Wing's breaking point comes when S.O.B. firebrand Jackie Halley (Jean De Baer) is abducted and flogged by sexually twisted, Klan-like thugs.

With the help of ex-alcoholic newspaper buddy Brian Haas (George Coe), Wing sets about to salvage his self-respect, win the love of Kat, and halt the development of Grassy Bay. He's only partially successful and pays a bitter price for his half victory, but out of Wing's fragmented life comes the potential for self-redemption.

Nuñez' evocation of the sleepy '60s Florida coast county is lovingly rendered and the director deserves credit for not undermining MacDonald's book, the concerns of which remain pertinent in America, 1984. —Rich.

L'Amour Par Terre
(Love On The Ground)
(FRENCH-COLOR)

A Spectrafilm release of an Arthur Cohn presentation of a La Cécilia production, in association with Ministère de la Culture. Produced by Martine Marignac. Directed by Jacques Rivette. Stars Jane Birkin, Geraldine Chaplin. Screenplay, Rivette, Pascal Bonitzer, Marilù Parolini, Suzanne Schiffman; dialog, Bonitzer, Parolini; camera (Kodak color), William Lubtchansky; editor, Nicole Lubtchansky; music, none; sound, Pierre Gamet; assistant director, Schiffman; set decorations, Roberto Plate; costumes, Renée Renard. Reviewed at Alice Tully Hall,

N.Y., Film Festival, Oct. 6, 1984. (No MPAA Rating,) Running time: 129 MINS.
Emily .... Jane Birkin
Charlotte .... Geraldine Chaplin
Paul .... André Dussolier
Clément .... Jean-Pierre Kalfon
Silvano .... Facundo Bo
Virgile .... Laszlo Szabo
Eléonore .... Sandra Montaigu
Adriana .... Eva Roellens
Béatrice .... Isabelle Linnartz

Jacques Rivette's "Love On The Ground" (a meaningless title) is a gamesplaying effort that unfortunately misses its opportunities for flights of fancy, remaining an Earthbound exercise. Rivette's loyal local following and the potent b.o. lure of stars Jane Birkin and Geraldine Chaplin augur good results in film's French release, but U.S. distribution by Spectrafilm faces an uphill battle.

A promising opening introduces three actors (Birkin, Chaplin and Facundo Bo) performing a Sunday night play in the rooms and corridors of their apartment. Among the casual spectators, who lurk just beyond the action (immediately setting up Rivette's usual duality between what is theater and what is "real" in his film) is a playwright Clément (Jean-Pierre Kalfon) whose work is being mangled by the trio. Instead of suing them, he hires them to enact a new play at his mansion the following Saturday, one performance only, with the fourth act to be delivered at the last moment. The two women also are invited to move into the mansion for rehearsals, and they accept.

What unfolds is a weak satire of gothic melodramas, loaded with portentous dialog and saddled with numerous rehearsal scenes of a boring play. Rivette's gimmick is to have the play be autobiographical, concerning Clément's triangular love affair with Béatrice (since disappeared) and Paul (André Dussolier), latter a nightclub magician who, à la Tyrone Power in "Nightmare Alley," has gone beyond tricks into truly supernatural actions. He is also at the mansion, exerting his powers over the two actresses, who briefly hallucinate future events involving themselves.

Rivette is working in familiar territory, not only from his previous films such as "L'Amour Fou" and "Celine And Julie Go Boating" but related other works by former collaborators such as Eduardo de Gregorio's "Sérail." The main problem is that his characters remain mere puppets in an elaborate, contrived game holding little intrinsic interest. Having the characters manipulate each other doesn't work since the plot changes are largely arbitrary, exemplified by an unconvincing, strictly functional, violent fight between Birkin and Chaplin midway through the film.

In place of fantasy, the film relies on well-disguised cuts to create the illusion of Chaplin and Birkin seeing themselves in their hallucina-

tions; a mysterious room upstairs which emits sound effects of the sea, birds and orchestra tuning up (about as exciting as someone playing a sound effects record) and arresting pastel painted sets at the mansion.

Within a tongue-in-cheek format poking light fun at all the roles-players, Chaplin and Birkin acquit themselves well though they're a bit too old for their parts. Kalfon is suitably sinister and Laszlo Szabo contributes several funny scenes as the unctuous "pussycat" of a butler/handyman working for Kalfon. Sandra Montaigu (star of "Lucie Sur Seine") has some sharp verbal exchanges as the current, disgruntled woman of the house.

Pat ending, in which many details are tied up neatly and characters indulge in a series of one-upsmanship games regarding the play's finale, is self-destructive, leading the viewer to wonder: is that all this was about? Obviously, Rivette is continuing his examination of theatrical devices but that was done far better in the serious context of his best film, "L'Amour Fou." — Lor.

Coracoes A Mil
(Heart-Pounding Beat)
(BRAZILIAN-COLOR)

Mill Valley, Sept. 27.

An A&B Productions presentation. Directed and written by Jom Tob Azulay. Camera (color), Miguel Rio-Branco; editor, Joao Carlos Mota. Stars Gilberto Gil. No other credits available. Reviewed at Mill Valley Film Festival, Sept. 27, '84. Running time: 80 MINS.

This is essentially a performance pic encumbered with a sometimes-embarrassing plot line and a sidebar travelog. A University teacher from Rio is ordered to follow Gilberto Gil's band around 30 cities and then do a thesis on the nature of musical mass communications. The teacher, Joel Barcellos, ends up in a romance with Gil groupie Regina Case.

Ultimately, their scenes together become fetching; there's a sweet charm to this silliness.

Pic appears to be a blow-up from 16m, and sound could be better. Minimal b.o. prospects loom. (Although Mill Valley fest translated title to "Heart-Pounding Beat," subtitle in opening credits is "One Thousand Hearts.") Best musical number is Gil's tribute to the late Bob Marley. —Herb.

Le Jumeau
(The Twin)
(FRENCH-COLOR)

Paris, Oct. 3.

An AAA release of a La Gueville/Fideline Films coproduction. Executive producer, Xavier Gélin. Produced by Danièle Delorme and Yves Robert. Directed by Yves Robert. Stars Pierre Richard. Screenplay, Yves Robert, Elizabeth Rappeneau, Boris Bergman, based on Donald Westlake's novel, "Two Much;" camera (color), Robert Fraisse; art

director, Jacques Saulnier; editor, Pierre Gillette; music, Vladimir Cosma, sound, Pierre Lenoir; production manager, Jean-Claude Bourlat. Reviewed at Club 13, Paris, Oct. 2, 1984. Running time: 100 MINS.
Matthias Duval .... Pierre Richard
Liz Kerner .... Carey More
Betty Kerner .... Camilla More
Volpinex .... Jean-Pierre Kalfon
Evie .... Andréa Ferreol
Ralph .... Jacques Frantz
Charlie .... Jean-Pierre Castaldi

"Le Jumeau" doesn't make the most of a brilliant black comedy premise and wobbles as an uncongenial vehicle for local comedian Pierre Richard. His rubbery agitations as harried innocent are insufficiently modified for a role that demands more ambiguity and fewer low comedy mannerisms.

Adapted from a Donald Westlake novel, "Two Much," film casts Richard as a penniless greeting card dealer who passes himself off as his own fictitious lookalike twin brother in order to court a pair of lovely American heiresses, identical twins.

His hoax only manages to land him in increasingly complicated situations as he winds up first engaged to then married to each. Bigamist in spite of himself, standing to inherit not one but two immense fortunes, Richard is literally run off his feet shuttling back and forth between twins. The pyrotechnic double play is especially problematic because he cannot tell the girls apart.

The twins' unscrupulous attorney, himself scheming after their inheritance, discovers the imposture and confronts Richard with the evidence. In an ensuing struggle, the lawyer is accidentally killed and, when Richard tries to burn the incriminating file, he also manages to burn the house down as well.

The blaze turns out to his advantage, since the charred remains of the lawyer are mistaken as one of the Richard "twins," and police suspect the murderer to be the attorney, presumably on the lam.

The sisters are already tipped off about Richard being the one and only. They don't mind though, and after leading him by the nose in a game of romantic musical chairs, let him know he can now double his pleasure guilelessly.

This sounds like darkly hilarious stuff, though the film, produced and directed by Yves Robert (who coscripted with Elizabeth Rappeneau and Boris Bergman) is rarely as funny as it could have been if writers and helmer had not chosen to water down the macabre cynicism of Westlake's story (which in fact ends by the protagonist murdering both twins and inheriting their fortunes).

Instead, film pictures Richard's character as an amoral but basically good-hearted skirt-chaser, spurred on by romantic appetite and a passive victim of it. Though he is hard-up for money, fortune-hunting is not his driving motivation.

Robert directs broadly, playing the mechanical set-up for what it's worth, though his handling of the major farce setpiece — a studio-shot sequence in which the camera cranes after a frantic Richard bouncing between the connecting apartments of is twin spouses — lacks the Swiss watch precision of good bedroom farce.

Camilla and Carey More (daughters of Yank playwright Julian More) are vivaciously photogenic as the real twins. Both are after Richard as hubby in order to qualify to inherit, though they later fall for him romantically. Jean-Pierre Kalfon is reliably sinister as the karate-chopping crooked lawyer, but Andréa Ferreol is underemployed as Richard's faithful secretary.

Pic should do well locally where Richard is still a comedy favorite. Overseas chances will depend on how well the catchy plot is played up in marketing. —*Len.*

Swordkill
(U.S.-COLOR)

Sydney, Oct. 4.
A Hoyts Distribution release (Empire Pictures in U.S.) of an Albert Band International Productions-Swordkill Productions-Empire Pictures-Harkham production. Produced by Charles Band. Directed by J. Larry Carroll. Features entire cast. Executive producers, Albert Band, Arthur H. Maslansky, Efrem Harkham, Uri Harkham; associate producer, Gordon W. Gregory; screenplay, Tim Curnen; camera (CFI color), Mac Ahlberg; editor, Brad Arensman; music, Richard Band; production design, Pamela B. Warner, Robert Howland. Reviewed at Hoyts Entertainment Center, Sydney, Oct. 3, 1984. (No MPAA Rating.) Running time: **80 MINS.**
Yoshimitsa . . . . Hiroshi Fujioka
Dr. Alan Richards . . . . John Calvin
Chris Welles . . . . Janet Julian
Willie Walsh . . . . Charles Lampkin
Detective Berger . . . . Frank Schuller
Dr. Carl Anderson . . . . Bill Morey
Dr. Pete Denza . . . . Andy Wood
Prof. Tagachi . . . . Robert Kino
Ellie West . . . . Joan Foley
Johnny Tooth . . . . Peter Liapis
Chidori . . . . Mieko Kobayashi

"Swordkill" is "Iceman" revisited. Protagonist in this Charles Band production is a 400-year-old Japanese samurai who, in the pre-credits sequence set in 1552, is wounded and then deep-frozen after a fall into an icy crevass when he fails to rescue his wife who's been kidnaped by members of a rival clan. Skiers in the present day find the body, which is shipped to an L.A. research institute, where an ambitious scientist sets about bringing him back to life.

Whereas Fred Schepisi's film was a thoughtful, intelligent look into what could follow from such an unlikely proposition, "Swordkill" takes a much more superficial approach. The ancient warrior recovers quickly, with seemingly no ill effects, though he is naturally puzzled to find himself in a world containing strangers who don't speak his language, plus television, fast cars, rock 'n' roll and muggers. He escapes from the institute after dis-

patching an intern who attempted to steal his sword and, pursued by police, scientists and a girl who wants to help him, heads off into the alien world of the 20th century.

What follows is perfectly predictable, but occasionally quite entertaining, thanks to a wry sense of humor and the authoritative presence of Hiroshi Fujioka as the samurai warrior in a time warp. Action scenes are conventionally staged, but undemanding audiences probably will derive some amusement from the incongruous confrontations. Supporting players are rather weak, with femme lead Janet Julian, supposedly an expert in oriental history, but looking as though she just stepped out of high school and more concerned about where her next pair of designer jeans is coming from, and John Calvin as yet another ludicrously villainous WASP scientist.

Mac Ahlberg contributes some crisp photography, and the pic is tightly edited by Brad Arensman; indeed, all technical credits are tops.

"Swordkill" just ended a very brief Australian release via Hoyts and is scheduled for U.S. distribution through Empire Pictures sometime during 1985. —*Strat.*

California Girls
(COLOR)

Minor musical travelog.

A VCL Communications presentation of a Westwind production. Executive producer, Alan Judd. produced by William Webb, Monica Webb. Written and directed by W. Webb. Features entire cast. Additional material, Al Music, Michael Sherman; camera (color), Eric Anderson; editor, Michael J. Duthie; second unit camera, W. Webb, Robert Barber; production manager, M. Webb. Reviewed on Media Home Entertainment vidcassette, N.Y., Sept. 29, 1984. (No MPAA Rating.) Running time: **83 MINS.**
Mad Man Jack . . . . Al Music
Mike . . . . Lantz Douglas
Jackie . . . . Mary McKinley
Joyce . . . . Alicia Allen
Chrissie . . . . Barbara Parks
Don . . . . Jim Benny

"California Girls" is an oddball feature, lensed in 1981 and released only on videocassette. Filmmaker William Webb has packed in as many full-length pop songs (hits by acts such as The Police, Blondie, Queen and Kool & The Gang) as possible, but this docu-style travelog is of only minor interest.

The problem is an absence of workable storyline and narrative footage. Structured around deejay Mad Man Jack (Al Music doing a variable and tiresome imitation of Wolfman Jack) running a contest to find the most exciting California girl, pic is over 80% shots of pretty girls in action, silent docu-style, while songs play on the soundtrack. We watch innumerable types of local leisure activities, including windsurfing, cheerleading, motorcycling, aerobic dancing, weight-

lifting, hang gliding, foxy boxing and mud wrestling, but the level of viewer involvement is too low to qualify even for drive-in movie slotting. As a cassette offering, it's tolerable background material.

Interjected is a lame subplot of three aspiring actresses trying to win the contest and a $10,000 prize by doing odd stunts in the nude outside Mad Man Jack's window. Oddest element here is that despite its plethora of hit music, film *does not* feature the Beach Boys' title song.
—*Lor.*

Una Donna Allo Specchio
(A Woman In The Mirror)
(ITALIAN-COLOR)

Rome, Oct. 4.
A Gaumont release. Produced by Enzo Gallo and Lello Scarano for Film International Co. for (Grandangolo Coop). Stars Stefania Sandrelli, Marzio C. Honorato. Directed by Paolo Quaregna. Screenplay, Quaregna and Fabio Carlini; dialog, Barbara Alberti; camera (color), Claudio Cirillo; art director, Elio Micheli; editor, Antonio Sioiliano; music, Gino Paoli. Reviewed at Brancaccio Cinema, Rome, Oct. 4, 1984. Running time: **88 MINS.**
Manuela . . . . Stefania Sandrelli
Fabio . . . . Marzio C. Honorato

First Italian hit of the season, "A Woman In The Mirror" has benefitted from a marketing campaign that strongly links it to last year's erotic top-grosser by Giovanni Tinto Brass, "The Key." Apart from a surface resemblance, however, pics have little in common. Stefania Sandrelli is once more the drawing card, irresistably appealing as a late-blooming softcore sex star (much softer in "Mirror" than the preceding "Key").

Erotica, though, is clearly secondary for helmer Paolo Quaregna, making his feature film bow. Audiences attracted by the sexy advertising lure may find pic more enjoyable as a modern love story (à la "Last Tango in Paris") but more neurotic than erotic.

During a colorful local carnival in Ivrea, a small town in northern Italy, nursery school teacher Manuela (Sandrelli) and Neapolitan Fabio (Marzio C. Honorato) meet during Mardi Gras. For three days and nights they engage in a series of lovers' trysts, experimenting with all the attitudes, feelings and games couples play, and reversing a number of stereotypes about sex, love, marriage, etc. At carnival's end, they separate. The woman refuses to exchange addresses and it is clear they'll never meet again.

Entire picture revolves around two images, repeated with variations: the two interlocked bodies in the bedroom, and the rowdy, orgiastic Mardi Gras going on outside.

There are plentiful scenes of Sandrelli and Honorato rendezvousing, but they are brief and modestly choreographed to avoid male frontal nudity. Actors run through the basic Kama Sutra positions with

neither embarrassment nor exuberance, kept in decorous shadow by Claudio Cirillo's lighting and accompanied by a romantic Gino Paoli score or, more interestingly, counterpointed with hand-clapping and other sounds. In both cases, the passion is neither glamorized, kinky, nor vulgar. Instead the ordinary, human side of the characters is coaxed out.

Script has gaps. Sandrelli is given little motivation for abruptly leaving what seems to be the ideal lover, and it is unsatisfying to see her decision — a crucial one for the film — passed off as female neurosis. Bad dubbing robs the picture of much of its color. Secondary characters — a poet, a madman, a bunch of friends participating in revelry — sorely need the sound of their real voices to come off on the screen.

Principals work well together. Sandrelli has an intrinsic sensuality that seems impervious to age. Honorato, a relative newcomer, is an appealing actor able to hold his own on the screen with great naturalness.
— *Yung.*

Prisoners Of The Lost Universe
(BRITISH-COLOR)

A Marcel/Robertson Prods. Ltd. production in association with United Media Finance Ltd. Executive producer, John Hardy. Produced by Harry Robertson. Directed by Terry Marcel. Features entire cast. Screenplay, Marcel, Robertson; camera (color), Derek Browne; editor, Alan Jones; music, Robertson; sound, Alan Gerhardt; stunt coordinator, Doug Robinson; special effects; Ray Hanson; optical effects, Ray Caple; prosthetics makeup, Aaron & Maralyn Sherman. Reviewed on VCL-Media Home Entertainment vidcassette, N.Y., Oct. 2, 1984. (No MPAA Rating.) Running time: **94 MINS.**
Dan Roebuck . . . . Richard Hatch
Carrie Madison . . . . Kay Lenz
Kleel . . . . John Saxon
Malachi . . . . Peter O'Farrell
Greenman . . . . Ray Charleson
Shareen . . . . Dawn Abraham
Dr. Hartmann . . . . Kenneth Hendel
Kahar . . . . Philip Van Der Byl

"Prisoners Of The Lost Universe" is a low-budget fantasy film shot in South Africa last year and cablecast by backer Showtime, now available on vidcassette as well as having theatrical bookings abroad. Pic is disappointingly unimaginative, even as program filler.

Imported American lead actors are trapped in a lame story, starting off with scientist Dr. Hartmann (Kenneth Hendel) and his cheap, flashing lights matter transmitter (lacking the sci-fi qualities of its predecessor in the classic "The Fly"). Convenient California earthquakes cause the doc and two innocent bystanders Carrie (Kay Lenz) and Dan (Richard Hatch) to be transported accidentally to another dimension and a planet Vonya.

Filmmakers Terry Marcel and Harry Robertson, latter a familiar horror film composer, have failed to concoct any interesting adventures for the heroes, who are simply captured and escape in a series of pointless skirmishes with local warlord Kleel (John Saxon, his voice lowered to indicate he's a meanie). Violence is comic-strip style with comical sound effects and even though this is a made-for-cable effort, no nudity is featured.

Motley supporting cast is styled with no consistency: one guy wears a Davy Crockett outfit, several others appear in Arab shieks' garb. The only mission is to get back home to Earth, which is accomplished too easily in the film's abrupt, who cares? nonending. Tech credits are undernourished, with the alien world and its (unexplained) English-speaking inhabitants looking like some ordinary African veldt. — *Lor.*

Massive Retaliation
(COLOR)

Clumsy survivalist thriller.

Mill Valley, Sept. 25.

A One Pass-Hammermark production: Produced and directed by Thomas A. Cohen. Executive producer, Steve Michelson. Stars Peter Donat. Screenplay, Larry Wittnebert, Richard Beban. Camera, Richard Lerner; editor, B.J. Sears; music, Harn Soper, Paul Potyen; sound, Philip Perkins; production manager-assistant director, Geoffrey de Valois. Reviewed at Mill Valley Film Festival Sept. 25, 1984 (No MPAA Rating.) Running time: **90 MINS.**
Kirk Fredericks . . . . Tom Bower
Marianne Briscoe . . . . Karlene Crockett
Lee Briscoe . . . . Peter Donat
Lois Fredericks . . . . Marilyn Hassett
Jackie Tolliver . . . . Susan O'Connell
Harry Tolliver . . . . Michael Pritchard
Eric Briscoe . . . . Jason Gedrick
Susie Barker . . . . Mimi Farina

"Massive Retaliation" is the initial theatrical feature for the Hammermark-One Pass production of Thomas A. Cohen and Steve Michelson, who previously paired for the theatrical docu "The Hungry I Reunion." Because Cohen lives in Mill Valley, filmfest world-preeming there of "Massive Retaliation," in first answer print form, made commercial sense.

The picture, focusing on survivalists settling in for an anticipated nuke attack, never finds its way out of a clumsy screenplay. Yarn starts as a fast-moving thriller; three couples evacuate to their countryside safehouse amidst radio and tv bulletins announcing nukes in the Gulf of Oman. The couples' children, meanwhile, are stranded in their van because of motor trouble and there is mounting fear about the youngsters' ability to reach survival central.

All of this early movement and pacing is helped by the musical score and appears to be developing as a satisfactory telefilm-level nuke suspense story.

Then the characterizations of the couples are either badly or barely etched and survivalist leader Peter

Donat becomes so blatant a baddie that the tale turns ludicrous. The message of "the real enemy" never takes hold because of the sketchiness of the principals.

Cohen should have tempered Donat's characterization. Marilyn Hasset and Tom Bowers do decent work within the framework of their one-dimensional roles. Popular Frisco stand-up comic Michael Pritchard just doesn't make it as the boozy husband of Susan O'Connell. —*Herb.*

Asalto En Tijuana
(Assault On Tijuana)
(MEXICAN-U.S.-COLOR)

A Filmadora S.A. coproduction with Metropolitan Million Dollar Prods. Produced by Abe Glazer. Directed by Alfredo Gurrola. Stars Mario Almada, Rozenda Bernal. Executive producer, Miguel Kahan; screenplay, Jorge Patino, Glazer; camera (color), Luis Medina. Reviewed at Cine 1, N.Y., Oct. 2, 1984. Running time: **85 MINS.**
Felipe . . . . Mario Almada
Sonia . . . . Rozenda Bernal
Osaka . . . . Noe Murayama
Pablito . . . . Paquito Cuevas
Joe . . . . Jorge Patiño
Santino . . . . Victor Junco
Raul . . . . Humberto Luna
Pepe Lemok . . . . Luis Accineli
Bruno . . . . Toño Infante
Killer . . . . : Ruben Recio

A fast-paced, intermittently gory Spanish-language actioner, "Asalto En Tijuana" was released in May at Hispanic cinemas in coproducer Metropolitan Theaters' Southern California exhibition chain. Brisk initial boxoffice results in the Cal-Mex market prompted talk of dubbing "Asalto" into English, but those plans since have been wisely shelved. Nevertheless, this caper pic about the theft of a world class racehorse from Tijuana's Caliente racetrack has excellent theatrical playoff potential for Latin American territories and prospects for a reasonable afterlife on U.S. Hispanic tv.

Plot centers around a scheme by a cabal of slithery, San Diego-based gangsters to steal "Excalibur," a $10,000,000 European racehorse which is due to make its Tijuana debut. From their lavish Stateside hacienda headquarters (complete with a swimming pool stocked with bilingual bimbo starlets) silver-haired villains Bruno (Toño Infante) and Killer (Ruben Recio) decide there's only one man for the job — Ensenada rancher and horse trainer, Felipe (Mario Almanda), who's also a commando veteran of the Korean war. Because Felipe is happily married to buxom cantina singer Sonia (Rozenda Bernal) and generally enjoying life on the rancho with his wife and son, Pablito, the hoods dispatch their chief hitman, Osaka (veteran Mexican film villain Noe Murayama) to exercise a little unfriendly persuasion.

Osaka and a bunch of thugs proceed to kidnap Pablito (beating Felipe's right-hand man, Raul, to a

crimson pulp in the process before blowing off his leg for good measure) and thus blackmail Felipe into participating. To demonstrate that there's honor among thieves, the gangsters offer the stoic hero $500,000 to organize the job.

Felipe heads for a Tijuana scrapyard where his old army buddy Joe is working and drinking the day away. Played with comic gusto by Jorge Patino, Joe leaps at the chance to make $50,000, agrees to stop boozing and reluctantly locates a third Korean vet, helicopter pilot Pepe Lemok (Luis Accineli) who's kicking heroin cold turkey in a Tijuana slum shanty. The team assembles and begins rehearsing its audacious plan to snatch the horse off the track with a helicopter *in midrace.*

Osaka ensures the jockey's cooperation by (what else) kidnaping his wife, and all goes well until Pepe gets rehooked on junk. No problema — Felipe knows a little bit about flying copters himself and the daring, if cockeyed and credibility-straining, horse heist is made.

Street-smart Felipe is not about to hand over the priceless nag until he gets his son back. However, a slight breach of contract leads to a bloodgusher denouement which is positively Jacobean in drilling home the message that crime, in any language, does not pay.

For a low-budget (around $300,-000) production, the camerawork does justice to the Mexico and California locations. Alfredo Gurrola's direction, like the performances, is sturdy and workmanlike. One hokey touch is a musical finale, loosely ripped-off from the "Chariots Of Fire" theme.—*Rich.*

Yaldei Hamdregoth
(Children Of The Steps)
(ISRAELI-COLOR)

Tel Aviv, Sept. 17.

A Zawta Production. Produced by Nissim Zion. Directed by Igal Pe'eri. Screenplay, Pe'eri, Shoshi Wolman; camera (color), Gad Danzig; editor, Shoshi Wolman; music, Alex Kagan. Reviewed at the Zawta Club, Tel Aviv, Sept. 16, 1984. Running time: **90 MINS.**
Cast: Ossi, Hillel, Eddie Goren, Hagith Beracha, Makhluf Albaz, Offer Gabai, Talma Plotkin.

Zawta is a cultural institution operated by Hashomer Hatzair, which has promoted progressive stage acts, plays and supported performers with an advanced political point of view.

Now it has decided to plunge into film production, tackling serious social and political subjects.

"Children Of The Steps" is its second feature and a vast improvement on the first, titled "83."

The film's title refers to the youth living in one of Tel Aviv's suburbs, partly a slum, who spend most of their time on the streets or on the steps of the Youth Club which sup-

plies the core of this plot. The relations between these kids, mostly of Oriental origin and from poor families, and the club's instructors, volunteers from a Hashomer Hatzair kibbutz, is the topic which really interested both producer Nissim Zion, who is Zawta's director, and first-time scripter-helmer Igal Pe'eri.

These relations have been bothering the Socialist movement in Israel lately, since the kibbutz, once considered the true representative of the working class, is now eyed suspiciously by the new proletarian class, which envies its relative economical ease and refuses its principles of communal life. In practice, this creates a gap between labor leaders and those they are supposed to represent, a gap featured in one of this film's first lines, when one of the slum kids says that in his neighborhood everyone votes for the Right, but they nevertheless frequent the Hashomer Hatzair Youth Club, for fun.

The entire film consists of such minute flashes adding up to an enlightening picture of the crisis as such, which it never attempts to solve one way or another. Its main appeal is the authentic and natural performances of the entire cast, all of them non-professionals who are indeed members of the Youth Club referred to in the film, aged 17-18.

The trouble with the entire project is that it lacks a real script to pull it together. The love triangle involving two of the deprived teenagers and a girl from an intellectual background isn't that original, and in order to give it some appeal, it has been cut from a linear development into a series of flashbacks, quite often confusing, adding a more intriguing dimension to the script. This is the reason editor Shoshi Wolman (wife of filmmaker Dan Wolman) receives a credit for the script as well.

Gad Danzig manages to get the best of the inexperienced protagonists with his 16m camera, the film having the gritty, unsteady feeling of a documentary.

For the time being the film is being shown only in Zawta's own 70-seat cinema, but may be headed for wider distribution. —*Edna.*

Souvenirs, Souvenirs
(Memories, Memories)
(FRENCH-COLOR)

Paris, Sept. 26.

A Gaumont/A.J.O. release of a Partner's Production/Gaumont/Canal Plus/TF 1 Films coproduction. Produced and directed by Ariel Zeitoun. Screenplay, Zeitoun, Daniel Saint-Hamont; camera (color), Bruno de Keyzer; art director, Jacques Bufnoir; editor, Geneviève Winding; sound, (Dolby stereo), Guillaume Sciama; music, Cyril Assous, Jean-Paul Dréau; lyrics, Pierre Grosz, Ariel Zeitoun; costumes, Mic Cheminal; production manager, Michel Frichet. Reviewed at the Gaumont Ambassade theater, Sept. 26, 1984. Running time: **124 MINS.**

Rego . . . . Christophe Malavoy
Antoine . . . . Jean-Loup Ragot
Hélène . . . . Gabrielle Lazure
Firmani . . . . Claude Brasseur
Nadia . . . . Marlène Jobert
Emma . . . . Annie Girardot
The principal . . . . Philippe Noiret
Samuel . . . . Jean Benguigui
Christian . . . . Michel Creton
Jean-Michel . . . . Jean-Claude Dauphin
Fressynet . . . . Philippe Laudenbach

"Souvenirs, Souvenirs" is producer Ariel Zeitoun's energetically promising debut as writer-director. Setting his story in Paris in the early '60s, when Algeria won its independence from France and the popularity of rock music was at its peak, Zeitoun follows the aspirations of two brothers and their divergent ambitions and fortunes. Though it derives from the overworked commercial trend that began with "American Graffiti," picture is saved from the banality of theme and situation by its vivid recreation of time and place, coherently fine performances and smart direction.

Like many debutant helmers, Zeitoun seems to have wanted to cram too much into his first film, and the script suffers from a welter of characters and incidents that are not always developed. But his skill as director outweighs the inadequacies of the scenario (developed with screenwriter Daniel Saint-Hamont) and his handling of the cast, which adroitly intermingles new young talent with veteran players in secondary roles (Philippe Noiret, Annie Girardot, Marlène Jobert and Claude Brasseur, notably).

The sibling protagonists (Christophe Malavoy and Jean-Loup Rajot) live in different worlds and see little of each other, but have implicit bonds of affection and understanding. Malavoy is just back from military service in Algeria, where he had sought refuge from the anxieties of showbiz ambition. His former impresario (Brasseur) has not forgiven his flight and is not eager to facilitate his comeback to a pop music scene he now controls. A determined, self-confident artistic director (Jobert) takes the stubborn young man in hand and guides him to a final triumph in a decisive public appearance.

His kid brother Rajot is still in high school and has no special talents, other than delinquent activities with his classroom chums. The first sight of his attractive new music teacher (Gabrielle Lazure) prompts him to a reckless courtship that eventually wins over the conventional objections of the demure prof. However, Lazure decides to return to her home town, but not before perjuring herself to save Rajot from a serious felony charge.

These stories are essentially trite, but Zeitoun's treatment has vivacity and poignancy. He knows how to suggest rather than overdramatize. Even the soundtrack, overburdened with inevitable period songs, is

well manipulated to increase the effect of scenes, both sprawling and intimate.

Malavoy is winning as the stubbornly aspiring pop artist (and performs his own lyrics). Rajot, a new face locally, is a revelation as the wild, passionate teen, prone to violence and suicidal rage, and Lazure is radiant as his older romantic conquest.

Among the veteran actors Brasseur, Jobert, and Giradot, as the brothers' understanding mom, give their best, and Philippe Noiret is marvelous as the convention-bound principal of Rajot's lycée.

Pic is technically first-rate, with evocative wide-screen lensing by Bruno de Keyzer (who shot Bertrand Tavernier's "A Sunday In The Country"), unfussy art direction by Jacques Bufnoir (who worked on Diane Kurys' "Entre Nous," produced by Zeitoun) sharp editing by Geneviève Winding, and masterly sound recording by Guillaume Sciama. — Len.

La Noche Más Hermosa
(The Most Beautiful Night)
(SPANISH-COLOR)

San Sebastian, Sept. 21.

A Luis Megino P.C. production with the collaboration of Television Española. Directed by Manuel Gutiérrez Aragón. Screenplay, Gutiérrez Aragón and Megino; camera (Eastmancolor), Carlos Suarez; editor, José Salcedo; production director, José G. Jacosta; sets, Gerardo Vera; special effects, Juan Marine; assistant director Antonio Isasi; sound, Carlos Faruolo. Reviewed at Cine Victoria Eugenía (San Sebastian), Sept. 20, 1984. Running time: 81 MINS.
Federico . . . . José Sacristán
Elena . . . . Victoria Abril
Bibi . . . . Bibi Andersen
Luis . . . . Fernando Fernán Gómez
Oscar . . . . Oscar Ladoire
Also: Pep Mune, Juanjo Puigcorbe, Maite Blasco, León Klimovsky, José Maria Pou, Eduardo McGregor.

Spanish scripter-helmer Manuel Gutiérrez Aragón scored at this festival two years ago with "Demons In The Garden" and followed up last spring with the disappointing "Feroz," latter one of the worst b.o. disasters in recent Spanish film history. Veering away now from fables, historical realism and symbolism, director has opted for the most difficult genre of all, comedy. The result left most funny bones in San Sebastian untouched. It turned out to be, for audiences, one of the most embarrassing nights as the familiar (in Spain) thesps labored for 81 minutes to be funny.

It's hard to say where the film went wrong, but much of the blame must be put on the screenplay by Megino and Gutiérrez Aragón who for some mistaken reason decided to include in the cast a well-known trans-sexual, Bibi Andersen (no relation to the great Swedish actress Bibi Andersson). Some of the other thesps, such as José Sacristán and Oscar Ladoire, have appeared in Spanish comedies but in this pic

simply cannot get into the swing of it. Victoria Abril and Fernando Fernán Gomez, both excellent actors, here come across deadpan, unable to cope with a script that is at best silly, at worst tiresomely dull.

Story concerns a tv exec who suspects his wife is cheating. He convinces the director of a film being shot for Spanish Television to make overtures to his wife to see if she remains faithful. When that doesn't work, he manages to get his boss (Fernán Gomez) to give it a try. Instead, the top TVE exec makes a play for Andersen who, unlikely as it may seem, is the husband's secret lover.

Miscellaneous, decidedly unfunny subplots include a love scene before the cameras with the wife playing Doña Inés in a "Don Juan," and two of her suspected lovers in the title role, each one trying to live "the most beautiful night" in his or her life.

The story is then left hanging in the air, suddenly cut off to a sudden ending as the wife acts out the part before tv cameras.

It is comprehensible that directors should yearn for a change of pace. However, after "Feroz" and this fiasco, it is to be hoped that Gutiérrez Aragón will return to his true métier. —Besa.

Een Dagje Naar Het Strand
(A Day At The Beach)
(DUTCH-COLOR)

Amsterdam, Sept. 17.

A Rust & Vreugd production. Produced by Gied Jaspers. Written and directed by Theo van Gogh, based on Heere Heeresma's novel. Camera (color), Willem Verboom; sound, Willem Hoogenboom; editor, Hoogenboom, Van Gogh; music, Willem van Eekeren and Rheiner Henzel. Reviewed at Cinetone Studio, Amsterdam, Sept. 17, 1984. Running time: 85 MINS.
Bernd . . . . Cas Enklaar
Walyne . . . . Tara Fallaux
Medusa . . . . Helen Hedi
Carl . . . . Emile Fallaux
Nicholaas . . . . Michiel Hanraath
Tonie . . . . Marie Kooyman
Barmaid . . . . Pamela Koevoets

A number of Heere Heeresma's books have been filmed. "A Day at the Beach," published in 1962, was a b.o. flop coproduced in England '69 by Paramount and Gene Gutowski, with a script by Roman Polanski ("the best I've ever written") and a gay cameo part played by Peter Sellers under the alias A. Queen.

Now Theo van Gogh (yes, Vincent was his great-great-great-uncle) has a second try. The result is a collection of superbly-acted sequences that never jell, although the storyline is simple.

Bernd, an alcoholic, fetches his little daughter Walyne from the home of her mother, who is married to Carl, an easy-going and successful advertising executive. He wants to give Walyne a good time; but his main aim, on this day as on all

others, is to get at as many beers and as much liquor as possible, without paying.

Walyne is not allowed in bars, so he loses her from time to time, but mainly due to the child, always finds her again, until the last time.

In the book the outing is a long destructive glide into oblivion. In the film it is rather a stroll, stopping at random to visit with people. The end does not appear inevitable and tragedy becomes a bad luck story.

Van Gogh must have felt this, because he brought Heeresma in during the editing stage to act as narrator, in an endeavor to link the separate scenes into an organic whole. It did not work.

Each sequence is perfectly executed with masterly photography. The acting is exemplary, not only by Cas Enklaar in his first film (mainly amateur) who appear on screen. It is not the fault of the editing (which is good), that pic emerges as just a series of episodes which happen to have the same protagonist. An overall structure and conception is lacking.

"A Day At The Beach" is fare for fests, art houses, and other special situations. It is a film well worth seeing, to savor its many good points, and deplore its one big failing. —Wall.

Fantasy Man
(AUSTRALIAN-COLOR)

Sydney, Oct. 1.

A Centaur Enterprises production. Produced by Basil Appleby, Darrell Lass. Written and directed by John Meagher. Stars Harold Hopkins, Jeanie Drynan. Camera (color), Lesnie; production design, Darrell Lass; music, Adrian Payne; editor, Rod Hibberd; sound, Ross Linton. Reviewed at Film Australia theater, Lindfield, Sydney, July 29, 1984. Running time: 79 MINS.
Nick Bailey . . . . Harold Hopkins
Liz Bailey . . . . Jeanie Drynan
Donna . . . . Kerry Mack
Neighbor . . . . Kate Fitzpatrick
Howard . . . . John Howitt
Art Teacher . . . . Colin Croft

"Fantasy Man" is a feeble low-budgeter about a boring officeworker in midlife crisis. Writer-director John Meagher brings no new insights to a hackneyed theme and the experienced, professional players are forced to struggle with some singularly banal dialog and predictable situations.

Nick Bailey (Harold Hopkins) works in a Sydney office (apparently the Dept. of Education), which he hates; he's also tired of his wife, Liz (Jeanie Drynan), and their admittedly hideous apartment. He spends a good deal of time locked in the shower, moping. He contemplates dalliance with a young woman (Kerry Mack) who operates an outdoor hamburger joint, while his wife considers an affair with a former flame, now a divorced decorator. Nobody actually does anything, and Nick's fantasies mostly involved images of cavorting in a sunlit field with the object of his dreams, images that were out of date 20 years ago.

The mood of the film is uncertain, but it seems as though Meagher took it all fairly seriously; most audiences won't. The hero's resolution is to take a new job in Brisbane, a fadcout which would seem to invite derision from cinemagoers (if the film ever sees the inside of a cinema) in Australia's other cities.

A number of songs on the soundtrack add nothing to this amateurish item.—*Strat.*

Asesinato en el Senado de la Nación
(Murder At The Nation's Senate) (ARGENTINE-COLOR)

Buenos Aires, Sept. 14.

A Norma-Vigo presentation of a Horacio Casares production. Directed by Juan José Jusid. Screenplay, Jusid and Carlos Somigliana; historical research, Mirtha Lobato; camera (Eastmancolor), José Maria Hermos; music, Baby López Fürst. Reviewed at the Opera theater, B.A., Sept. 13, 1984. Running time: 95 MINS.

De la Torre .... Pepe Soriano
Valdez Cora .... Miguel Angel Solá
Madame Rosa .... Martha Bianchi
Bordabehere .... Arturo Bonin
Pinedo .... Oscar Martinez
Duhau .... Alberto Segado
Don Alberto .... Villanueva Cosse
Yasky .... Salo Pasik
Unionist ....: ...... Manuel Callau

This is an account, more fictional than true, of events leading to the historic session (of July 23, 1935) at the Argentine Senate, when a former police chief, Valdez Cora, killed Senator Enzo Bordabehere. However his shots were aimed at another lawmaker, the famous democratic leader Lisandro De la Torre, who was accusing the government of having virtually sold the nation's meat trade to a monopoly of British packers.

Juan José Jusid and Carlos Somigliana's script has gone too far in changing and ignoring some key historical facts, presumably to avoid troubles with the descendants of the prominent people accused by De la Torre, who were acquitted by a majority of senators of the ruling Conservative Party who had won their seats through electoral fraud.

Story focuses much more upon the past of killer Valdez Cora than on the dramatic parliamentary charge against the political corruption of the time. After having been fired from the police by his own Conservatives due to his abuses, Valdez Cora becomes a bodyguard of fictional senator and cattle baron Don Alberto (in fact he was the bodyguard of Agriculture minister Duhau).

Pic shows him protecting Madame Rosa, owner of a luxurious whorehouse, and bedding a teenage prostitute, then being clubbed by Don Alberto for having used his

name in that maneuvering. His wife and daughter, fed up with his narrow-minded authoritarianism, abandon their one-room home. All this provides the pic with sex and other melodrama such as a torture session aimed at the boxoffice.

Brilliant performances by Pepe Soriano (De la Torre) and Miguel Angel Solá (Valdez Cora), supported by an able cast, are pluses, as well as José Maria Hermos' camerawork. Director Juan José Jusid confirms his technical prowess but his narrative still lacks heart when dealing with human conflicts. Other technical credits are okay. — *Nubi.*

Mountain Music Of Peru
(COLOR-DOCU-16m)

A production of Hazardous Films (Putnam Corners, N.Y.). Written, produced, directed, narrated and photographed (color) by John Cohen; sound, Richard Rogers, Rufus Cohen; editors, John Cohen, Jerry Michaels. Consultants, Patricia Oliarte, Jose Llorenz, Paul Doughty, Jorge Flores, Raul Romero. Reviewed at Margaret Mead Film Festival, N.Y., Sept. 18, 1984. (No MPAA Rating.) Running time: 60 MINS.

Produced with a grant of $20,000 from the John Simon Guggenheim Memorial Fundation, and with other funding, "Mountain Music Of Peru" is an anthropological document on film of the musical culture of the 7,000,000 Indians in the high Andes of Peru.

Like a musical travelog, but more than that, the film travels among towns and remote villages, tracing the musical heritage of the Indians, This is a strong heritage that still resists Western influences in the more than four centuries since the Spanish Conquest.

Rich headdresses, costumes, masks and make-up, derived from Inca times, enrich the film and give it a splendid color and vitality. Incongruously, expressing the unlikely blend of two antagonistic cultures, some dancers wear wristwatches and sunglasses.

In "The Dance Of The Old Men," Indian males satirize Western authority while attired in tuxedos, with canes and top hats, and in white-faced masks, with hunchbacks that denote their deformed morality. Elsewhere, blind musicians lay and beg in the streets, led about by small children.

Some dances celebrate the fertility of the alpaca flocks on which the itinerant Indians depend. The alpacas are pelted with flowers related to their seasonal melting, while the gods are praised in music for providing healthy animals.

Among Lima's 5,000,000 people, most of them living in terrible poverty, social and tribal networks survive through the use of music. Their popular "Huaynos" music provides identity and continuity.

"Mountain Music Of Peru" is the eleventh film of musicologist-filmmaker John Cohen, who

teaches at SUNY/Purchase. Picture represents the culmination of Cohen's many visits to Peru during the last quarter century. Its long-range viability in 16m to schools and on public tv seems assured. —*Hitch.*

Suzanne og Leonard
(Suzanne And Leonard) (DANISH-COLOR)

Copenhagen, Sept. 27.

An A/S Panorama Film release of Panorama (Just Betzer) production with the Danish Film Institute. Directed by John Hilbard. Screenplay, Anette Olsen, Bjarne Reuther, based on Reuther's novel; camera (Eastmancolor) Peter Roos; production management, Jens Arnoldus, Michael Obel; production design, Sören Skjär; editor, Grete Möldrup; music, Elisabeth G. Nielsen, Finn Verwohlt; stunts, Johan Thoren, Svenska Stuntgruppan. Reviewed at the Palads, Copenhagen, Sept. 27, 1984. Running time: 94 MINS.

Suzanne .... Pernille Falck
Leonard .... Ole Meyer
Suzanne's father .... Preben Neergaard
Suzanne's mother .... Fritze Hedemann
Vagn .... Troels Munk
The Swan .... Baard Owe
Nannah .... Tammy Ost

With "Suzanne And Leonard," writers Anette Olsen and Bjarne Reuther and director John Hilbard have fashioned a swift little feature item for youth audiences who will see shades of Bonnie & Clyde in the story's two young protagonists on the run through a wintry Denmark from a large police force, that suspects them of having committed several murders, and from gangsters. During the chase, Leonard feels sufficiently trapped to really commit a murder of his own, and though his flight with Suzanne goes on, we know his fate is sealed.

Writer Anette Olsen actually directed firm's early sequences but then fell ill, with John Hilbard, a journeyman director who has perfected his craft considerably since helming the "Bedside" porno spoofs for the now defunct Palladium Studios, took over at the helm.

Suzanne has well-to-do parents and is bored with the prospect of having to spend a weekend in the country with them. She is ready for adventure, but she also has a lot of common sense and thus turns out to be the perfect partner for Leonard when the latter, just escaped from prison, forces first a meal, then the family's car keys out of her at the point of a gun he does not even know to be unloaded.

From that point on, film is one long chase, interrupted by the traditional moments of repose and sexual idyll in some hideaway well-stocked with candles, wine, shampoo and mood music on LPs.

As Leonard, Ole Meyer gives one of his fine shy-but-resourceful performances. Newcomer Pernille Falck as Suzanné seems well in control of her acting, too. She is very pretty in a well-groomed upper middle class way and her smiles seem to rub off physically on Meyer's more common visage.

"Suzanne And Leonard's" story, its sustained, low-key suspense and the charm, hurt and innocence of its two lead players should help the film to cross borders and gain theatrical sales as well as its more obvious pickups by tv stations. — *Kell.*

Thief Of Hearts
(COLOR)

Slick but empty sex-romance.

Hollywood, Oct. 11.

A Paramount Pictures release of a Don Simpson-Jerry Bruckheimer production. Produced by Simpson, Bruckheimer. Directed, written by Douglas Day Stewart. Features entire cast. Camera (Metrocolor), Andrew Laszlo; editor, Tom Rolf; music, Harold Faltermeyer; visual consultant, Ferdinando Scarfiotti; art direction, Edward Richardson; set design, Blake Russell; set decoration, R. Chris Westlund; costume design, Michael Kaplan; sound (Dolby), Keith A. Wester; associate producer, Tom Jacobson; assistant director, Michael Grillo. Reviewed at Paramount Studios, L.A., Oct. 10, 1984. (MPAA Rating: R.) Running time: **100 MINS.**
Scott Muller . . . . Steven Bauer
Mickey Davis . . . . Barbara Williams
Ray Davis . . . . John Getz
Buddy Calamara . . . . David Caruso
Janie Pointer . . . . Christine Ebersole
Marty Morrison . . . . George Wendt

"Thief Of Hearts" is loaded with the patented Paramount elements — hunky, streetwise guy; unsatisfied, searching gal whose heart flutters at the sight of him and who needs to break out of her routine world; slick, but gritty, location lensing, and a throbbing synthesizer score, complete with one Giorgio Moroder tune. Unfortunately, these trendy trappings often work against the grain of what might have been a penetrating psychological study of two hopelessly mismatched but magnetically attracted people. Moderately successful, "American Gigolo"-sized b.o. results loom, at best.

Even though Steven Bauer is an outright criminal, a burglar who has spent at least part of his life in the pen, one is asked to sympathize with him since he aspires to a better lifestyle — he appreciates the art he steals, wears designer clothes, is learning to cook nouvelle cuisine, condescends to his lowlife, coketooting partner, and is not interested in women unless he really cares for them.

Among the items he loots one night from an opulent San Francisco home are the private diaries of the frustrated lady of the house. While mooning under her portrait, he gets off on learning her innermost secrets.

Since she's an up-and-coming interior designer, he comes on to her under the guise of hiring her to decorate his pad and, since he knows that she really wants, he gives it to her.

Her hubby, squirreled away writing his successful children's books, remains oblivious to the affair blossoming behind his back for a while, but finally exposes, not only the romance, but Bauer's true vocation. It all culminates in a violent act lifted directly from John Ford's great western, "The Man Who Shot Liberty Valance."

At the heart of the tale is a potentially viable study of a woman profoundly unsettled both by this overtly sexual man's impact upon her, and by a stranger's uncanny knowledge of her most intimate desires. Some of the quieter man-woman stuff is well managed by writer and first-time director Douglas Day Stewart, and Bauer and newcomer Barbara Williams have a handle on the main components of their characters.

Unfortunately, any notion of sustained subtlety or insight is pounded into oblivion by the relentless high-tech approach of which Paramount is the industry's leading practitioner. No opportunity is overlooked to trot out new threads, a hot song, sleek Bay Area locations and stylish sets, not to mention the lingering views of Bauer spreading suntan lotion all over his well-muscled bod. Many of the shots would be right at home in the pages of GQ.

Gun enthusiasts may also find here their favorite Hollywood picture since "Red Dawn," as Bauer finally seduces Williams as she tries out his pistol at his home practice range. —*Cart.*

Der Havarist
(Voyager)
(WEST GERMAN-COLOR)

Berlin, Sept. 26.

A Red Harvest Film Production, Wolf-Eckart Bühler, Munich, in coproduction with Norddeutscher Rundfunk (NDR), Hamburg, Westdeutscher Rundfunk (WDR), Cologne, and the German Federal Film Fund (FFA), Berlin. Features entire cast. Written and directd by Bühler, based on Sterling Hayden's book "Wanderer." Camera (color), Peter Fauhe; sets, Nikolai Müllerschön; sound, Martin Müller; editor, Giesela Castronari; music, Konstantin Wecker. Reviewed at Lupe 2, Berlin, Sept. 25, '84. Running time: **95 MINS.**
Cast: Burkhard Driest, Rüdiger Vogler, Hannes Wader (all three as Sterling Hayden), Hans-Michael Rehberg, Edgar Selge, and as guests Kristina Van Eyck, Klaus Emmerich, Michael Krüeger, Dieter Schidor, Hans Noever, Enno Patalas, Laurens Straub, Hans Gunther Pflaum, Roger Fritz.

German critic-filmmaker Wolf-Eckart Bühler first made an impressive docu about actor writer Sterling Hayden, "Pharos Of Chaos" (1982), which presented Hayden's viewpoint on a number of topics, but particularly the McCarthy years and his own role in the House Un-American Activities hearings (he comes down pretty hard on himself for his turncoat position back then). Now he's back with a first feature, loosely based on Hayden's book "Wanderer."

The myth of Hayden fascinates many today. As the story goes, he was a seaman, a partisan-fighter in World War II, then a Hollywood star and a Communist Party member, and finally a pitiful collaborator with the FBI and the McCarthy Committee in tattling on his Hollywood colleagues. All this ground is covered in his self-effacing biography, "Wanderer," and in the Bühler film.

"Voyager" comes across as filmed Readers Theater exercises. Three different actors — Burkhard Driest, Rüdiger Vogler, Hannes Wader — speak lines from the book in emotionless terms. The texts were selected to elucidate the seductibility of being in the national spotlight, the process of betrayal, and the pressure by the powers-that-be. The betrayal leads in turn to recantation and an escape into a wrestling with the self. The actors sit around — much as in the films of Jean-Marie Straub and Danièle Huillet — and "talk politics" in setting chosen as theatrical backdrops.

Since Hayden's own book offers three converging narrative points-of-view, there's much to defend in Bühler's approach to the subject. However, one would have hoped for a more accessible literary adaptation in movie houses than a political tract appropriate to a graduate course in political science. Recommended for the committed few, "Voyager" is otherwise pretty tough sledding. —*Holl.*

The Razor's Edge
(COLOR)

Bill Murray achieves an acting stretch in subpar remake.

Hollywood, Oct. 12.

A Columbia Pictures release of a Marcucci-Cohen-Benn/Columbia-Delphi production. Produced by Robert P. Marcucci, Harry Benn. Executive producer, Rob Cohen. Directed by John Byrum. Stars Bill Murray. Screenplay, Byrum, Murray, based on the novel by W. Somerset Maugham; camera (color, widescreen), Peter Hannan; editor, Peter Boyle; music, Jack Nitzsche; production design, Philip Harrison; art direction, Malcolm Middleton; set decoration, Ian Whittaker, Stuart Rose; set decoration (India), Saba Zaidi; costume design, Shirley Russell; sound (Dolby), Rene Borisewitz; associate producer, Jason Laskay; assistant directors, Ray Corbett, Laurent Bregeat (France), Kanwal Swaroop (India). Reviewed at the Samuel Goldwyn Theatre, Beverly Hills, Oct. 11, 1984. (MPAA Rating: PG-13.) Running time: **128 MINS.**
Larry Darrell . . . . Bill Murray
Sophie . . . . Theresa Russell
Isabel . . . . Catherine Hicks
Elliot Templeton . . . . Denholm Elliott
Gray Maturin . . . . James Keach
Mackenzie . . . . Peter Vaughan
Piedmont . . . . Brian Doyle-Murray
Malcolm . . . . Stephen Davies
Raaz . . . . Saeed Jaffrey
Louisa Bradley . . . . Faith Brook
Joseph . . . . Andre Maranne

Conceived as a major career departure for comic star Bill Murray, "The Razor's Edge" emerges as a minimally acceptable adaptation of W. Somerset Maugham's superb novel. Tonally inconsistent and structurally awkward, film does develop some dramatic interest in the second half, but inherent power of the material is never realized. Presence in the starring role of Murray will draw viewers out of curiosity, but pic's relative artistic failure will limit ultimate b.o.

This is the film that Murray insisted Columbia let him make if he appeared in "Ghostbusters," so even if "The Razor's Edge" doesn't earn a dime, Columbia will come out of the bargain very profitably indeed.

Due to the circumstances, then, pic has to be perceived as a very personal project for both Murray and his cowriter and director John By-

Original Film

20th-Fox release of Darryl F. Zanuck production. Stars Tyrone Power, Gene Tierney, John Payne, Anne Baxter, Clifton Webb, Herbert Marshall. Directed by Edmund Goulding. Screenplay, Lamar Trotti from novel by W. Somerset Maugham. Camera, Arthur Miller; music, Alfred Newman; editor, J. Watson Webb; dances, Harry Pilcer; special effects, Fred Sersen. Tradeshown N.Y. Nov. 18, '46. Running time: **146 MINS.**
Larry Darrell . . . . Tyrone Power
Isabel . . . . Gene Tierney
Gray Maturin . . . . John Payne
Sophie . . . . Anne Baxter
Elliot Templeton . . . . Clifton Webb
Maugham . . . . Herbert Marshall
Louisa Bradley . . . . . Lucile Watson
Bob MacDonald . . . Frank Latimore
Miss Keith . . . . Elsa Lanchester
Kosti . . . . Fritz Kortner
Joseph . . . . John Wengraf
Holy Man . . . . Cecil Humphreys
Specialty Dancer . . . . . Harry Pilcer
Princess Novemali Cebina Wright Sr.
Albert . . . . Albert Petit

rum. Maugham's 1944 novel, which was produced as a film by Darryl F. Zanuck at Fox two years later with with Tyrone Power in the lead, contrasted the spiritual quest of young American World War I veteran Larry Darrell with the pursuit of worldly eminence by snobbish socialite Elliot Templeton.

As children of the 1960s might be inclined to do, Murray and Byrum latched on to the Larry Darrell side of the story, which involves self-discovery through manual labor and learning at the feet of a guru in India, and have virtually jettisoned the Templeton angle, although the latter character pops up around the edges in the person of Denholm Elliott.

Further comparisons to the side, film opens with a happy-go-lucky and (in this story) surprisingly humorous Murray preparing to set sail for the European conflict. The horrors of war sober him up a bit, to the point that, when it's over, he is no longer certain he wants to marry his intended, pretty chatterbox Catherine Hicks.

Murray takes a job in a coal mine, reads a great deal and, while his old friends are being destroyed by the stock market crash, he's finally finding inner peace in the Himalayas.

Due partly to the scattershot presentation of scenes and the long time lapses, film is extremely jumpy and unsatisfactory up to that point. Indian mountain sequences, thanks to the impassive serenity of the landscapes, Murray's increased seriousness and a nice supporting turn by the delightful Saeed Jaffrey, give the picture some moorings, and the subsequent full-fledged arrival of Theresa Russell into the story livens things up considerably.

A former friend from the States, Russell has descended to a routine of drugs, drink and hooking in Paris' underworld, from which Murray resolves to rescue her. Hicks, by now long married to insolvent businessman James Keach even though she's still in love with Murray, conspires to wreck their planned marriage, and ends by doing much worse than that.

Most of the time, it seems that Byrum and Murray have all they can handle just getting the basic plot developments up on the screen. Regretfully absent is any sense of time passing, of spiritual and emotional feeling being deepened, of lives criss-crossing in meaningful ways.

At the same time, production itself, except for Shirley Russell's elaborate and extensive costumes, seems a bit threadbare. Chicago-area scenes were shot in Europe, and Paris locationing has yielded little in the way of local color or atmosphere. The trip to India was worth it, though.

As always, Murray is appealing, both when he's applying himself to his true needs in a serious manner on the top of the world. At the very least, film indicates that the actor has a potentially interesting future career outside the realm of the goofy. His essentially irreverent, iconoclastic attitude does bring unexpected and pleasant wrinkles to his characterization.

Although there's very little outright sex, Russell, sporting a striking Louise Brooks hairdo, gives the film a much-needed jolt of carnality, and her strong dramatic work significantly bolsters the second half. Hicks is good as the spoilsport gal who can't understand Murray's search, and remainder of the cast is okay.

Peter Hannan's grainy, atomized visual style with the camera doesn't give full play to the film's intended scope, and reminds of some of the late Geoffrey Unsworth's later credits. Jack Nitzsche's score threatens to overwhelm at times. — Cart.

For All People, For All Time
(DOCU-COLOR-16m)

A production of Valley Filmworks N.Y. Produced, directed and edited by Mark and Dan Jury. Camera (color, 16m), Dan Jury; sound, Mark Jury; original music, Shelton Leigh, Palmer and Company. Reviewed at the Margaret Mead Film Festival, Sept. 18, 1984. Running time: 75 MINS.

Bureaucratic bungling, governmental insensitivity, and good intentions gone awry — these are the themes of this new film by the Jury Brothers, about the creation of a new urban national park in Ohio.

The Jurys produced the notable feature-documentary "Chillysmith Farm" of several seasons ago, a work that was more personal than this film, as it was an intimate portrayal of birth and death within the Jury clan, set in Pennsylvania farm country.

This film concerns the four-year struggle of a residential community near Cleveland to retain its tranquil isolation, in one of the few undeveloped forests left in that part of the state. The National Park Service, within the Dept. of The Interior — first under Carter, then Reagan — implacably moves in with cash and bulldozers, buying out and forcing out 425 families, dispossessing them to create a national park without people.

After four years of resistance and litigation, 75 families remain today, but they seem doomed to expulsion. The Park Service even burns some of the vacated houses, as practice exercises for the fire department.

This is a film about the death of a community, defeated by big government acting in the name of the people.

Given the continuing attention of media to saving neighborhoods, and the see-saw of big versus little in our society, this film can have some lively distribution in 16m to specialized action-groups, urban planners conferences, and the like. Public television, of course, is its natural home. —Hitch.

Jack Kerouac's America
(COLOR)

Mill Valley, Sept. 21.
A John Antonelli production. Produced and directed by Antonelli. Coproducer, Will Parrinello. Executive producer, Marilyn Smith. Stars Jack Coulter. Screenplay, John Tytell, Frank Cervarich, Antonelli; camera (color), Jerry Jones; editor, Parrinello; sound, Gene Dougherty. Reviewed at Mill Valley Film Festival, Sept. 21, 1984. (No MPAA Rating.) Running time: 72 MINS.
Jack Kerouac .... Jack Coulter

This well-intentioned docudrama is a valentine to the late, great Beat writer (who died in 1969) that's delivered with so much sentimentality and romanticism that it may do a disservice to an interesting figure. Pic likely is headed for PBS, but it should be noted that Mill Valley fest audiences were so enamored three showings had to be skedded. Point also should be made that producer-director-coauthor Antonelli lives in Mill Valley.

Even though there are drop-in commentaries by Kerouac's Beatnik contemporaries and a running attempt to flesh him out via actor Jack Coulter, Jack Kerouac comes

to life only when he's shown in vidclips in appearances with Steve Allen and William Buckley.

There's a busyness to the pic with a mesh of a jazz score, narration, readings from the best of Kerouac, filtered views of his old homes and haunts.

According to poet Allen Ginsberg here, Kerouac "made a mythology of his whole life. He changed everybody." But that force is never apparent here. What is, is that Antonelli, in his dedication and devotion, has changed Kerouac. —Herb.

Body Double
(COLOR)

DePalma raids Hitchcock again, with commercial results.

Hollywood, Oct. 13.
A Columbia Pictures release of a Columbia-Delphi Prods. II production. Produced, directed by Brian DePalma. Features entire cast. Executive producer, Howard Gottfried. Screenplay, Robert J. Avrech, DePalma, story by DePalma; camera (Metrocolor), Stephen H. Burum; editors, Jerry Greenberg, Bill Pankow; music, Pino Donaggio; production design, Ida Random; set design, Bill Elliott, Charles Butcher; set decoration, Cloudia; costume design, Gloria Gresham; sound (Dolby), James Tannenbaum; assistant director, Joe Napolitano. Reviewed at the Samuel Goldwyn Theatre, Beverly Hills, Oct. 12, 1984. (MPAA Rating: R). Running time: 109 MINS.
Jack Scully .... Craig Wasson
Sam Bouchard .... Gregg Henry
Holly .... Melanie Griffith
Gloria Revelle .... Deborah Shelton
Jim McLean .... Guy Boyd
Rubin .... Dennis Franz
Drama Teacher .... David Haskell

Brian DePalma lets all his obsessions hang out in "Body Double." A voyeur's delight and a feminist's nightmare, sexpenser features an outrageously far-fetched and flimsy plot which merely serves as an excuse for extended sequences of visual virtuosity and some slumming in the netherworlds of perverse crime, low-budget filmmaking and pornography. It's an exploitable item for middle-range returns in quick playoff.

To his credit, DePalma moves his camera as beautifully as any director in the business today and on a purely physical level "Body Double" often proves quite seductive as the camera tracks, swirls, cranes and zooms towards and around the objects of DePalma's usually sinister contemplation.

Unfortunately, most of the film consists of visual riffs on Alfred Hitchcock, particularly "Vertigo" and "Rear Window." DePalma has said he's tired of critics claiming he lifts his inspiration from the late master, and recently even likened himself to Eisenstein instead. However, if he's tired of the comparisons, why does he keep running over the same ground time and again?

The first half of "Body Double" offers up virtually no storyline. Down-on-his-luck Hollywood actor Craig Wasson is fired from his job on a quickie vampire picture and, after catching his girlfriend in the sack with another guy, is befriended by fellow actor Gregg Henry, who invites him to housesit for him at a rich man's luxurious hilltop pad.

Before departing, Henry points out to Wasson that the home not only affords a great view of L.A., but of a bedroom in a house across the way, wherein a beautiful woman enacts an elaborate striptease dance at the same hour every evening.

Wasson digs the lady's act so much that he follows her the next day, when she is also pursued by a hideous-looking Indian. Long, virtually wordless sequence, which begins by car in the hills, continues at length in Beverly Hills' Rodeo Collection and winds up at the beach, is hypnotic and intriguing, and would be unqualifiedly wonderful had not DePalma done just about the same thing in the art museum in "Dressed To Kill" and, above all, had Hitchcock not done it all before in "Vertigo." It will be interesting to see if general audiences pick up on the precedents now that the Hitchcocks have enjoyed their recent successful reissues.

Pivotal murder scene occurs at about the midpoint, and it's an offensive lulu, being performed with an enormous power drill. Sequence occasioned multiple walkouts and catcalls at the preview screening caught.

Remainder of the film sees Wasson getting involved in the porno film world as a way of solving the murder in which he played an equivocal role. Cast in a sex pic, he wanders onto a set where a big-budget version of "Cafe Flesh" seems to be in production and, with some tail-end nudity excised, this sequence, accompanied by the likely hit song by Frankie Goes To Hollywood, "Relax," could stand independently as a music video.

Plot becomes increasingly outrageous/ludicrous (choose one) as it hurtles toward its climax, and DePalma tops it all off with a lighthearted demonstration of the film title's meaning.

Thesping by Wasson, Henry and former Miss U.S.A. Deborah Shelton, as the lady across the hill, is serviceable, while Melanie Griffith, with punky dyed hair and teensy voice, is just right as the porno queen. Guy Boyd proves an enormously effective scene-stealer as a skeptical police detective.

Technically, film is as slick as could be. Stephen H. Burum's ever-moving camerawork is aces, as are Jerry Greenberg and Bill Pankow's

editing, Pino Donaggio's score and Ida Random's production design.
—Cart.

Pale Passion
(HONG KONG-COLOR)

Hong Kong, Sept. 20.

A Shaw Brothers production and relese. Presented by Sir Run Run Shaw. Produced by Mona Fong. Directed by Chin Ping Hsing. Stars Ai Ti (Eddie Chan), Chiang Li Ping, Chin Yen Ling, Li Yen Shan, Hsia Ping and Chan Shen. Camera (color), Pan Heng Sheng; editors, Shao Feng, Ma Chung Yao; music, Lin Min Yi, Stephen Shing. Reviewed at Jade Theater, Hong Kong, Sept. 19, 1984. Running time: **98 MINS.**
(Cantonese soundtrack with English subtitles)

In "Pale Passion," factory worker then taxi driver Eddie Chan and Chiang Li-ping are lovers. She gets pregnant and though unwilling to marry Chan, she consents when he cuts off one of his fingers to prove his passionate love. The marriage doesn't work due to the erratic behavior and the roller coaster emotional makeup of Chan who is willing to love passionately, but quite incapable of showing it the normal way.

The husband and wife separate after her abortion, but his lusty passion for her continues. After a few years, he bumps into her at a restaurant and the haunting, taunting and begging to get her back at all costs begin. She is emotionally weak, mistress of a rich doctor, and a dramatic showdown develops. "Pale Passion" portrays the deranged type of love that blinds and motivates some people to tragedy.

Eddie Chan is a fine local actor who specializes in portraying neurotic men with inner rage and emotional outbursts. Too bad, this little low-budget film did not get the usual build up, so it did very badly at the boxoffice. Nevertheless, it is a fine local drama.

The acting of Chan and Chiang Li Ping as lovers shows conviction and understanding of their emotionally complex screen roles. —*Mel.*

Songwriter
(COLOR)

Likable musical vehicle for Willie and Kris.

Hollywood, Oct. 9.

A Tri-Star Pictures release. Produced by Sydney Pollack. Executive producer, Mike Moder. Directed by Alan Rudolph. Stars Willie Nelson, Kris Kristofferson. Screenplay, Bud Shrake. Camera (Metrocolor), Matthew Leonetti; editor, Stuart Pappe; music, Larry Cansler; original songs, Nelson, Kristofferson; production designer, Joel Schiller; set decorator, Barbara Krieger; sound (Dolby stereo), Arthur Rochester; costumes, Ernest Misko, Kathleen Gore-Misko; assistant director, David McGiffert. Reviewed at Charles Aidikoff screening room, L.A., Calif., Oct. 8, 1984. (MPAA Rating: R.) Running time: **94 MINS.**

Doc Jenkins . . . . Willie Nelson
Blackie Buck . . . . Kris Kristofferson
Honey Carder . . . . Melinda Dillon
Dino McLeish . . . . Rip Torn
Gilda . . . . Lesley Ann Warren
Arly . . . . Mickey Raphael
Corkie . . . . Rhonda Dotson
Rodeo Rocky . . . . Richard C. Sarafian

"Songwriter" is a good natured film that rolls along on the strength of attitudes and poses long ago established outside the picture by its stars, Willie Nelson and Kris Kristofferson, basically playing themselves disguised as fictional characters. Response to the film will depend on audience affection for Nelson and Kristofferson. Anticipating a stronger response in some areas, Tri-Star wisely has decided to go with a regional break before broadening its base.

"Songwriter" relies on the tried and true and is reminiscent of Jerry Schatzberg's "Honeysuckle Rose" from 1980 in which Nelson played a traveling musician with domestic problems. Probably the most surprising development in "Songwriter" is the film's image-breaking opening shot of Nelson without his trademark scruffy beard.

Brief opening collage establishes the younger days of Doc Jenkins (Nelson) and Blackie Buck (Kristofferson) as a performing duo before they go their semi-separate ways and revert to character.

Venturing into mogulling, as he calls it, Doc Jenkins is the saint of country music, loved and respected by everyone. Luckily Nelson has enough of a screen presence to support at least partially his deification.

As Blackie Buck, Kristofferson is still the outlaw with a heart of gold. He's a hard-loving, high-living, irresponsible sort who always comes through in the pinch, but who will probably never grow up and settle down, the film's final shot notwithstanding.

Cultivating this image for years, Kristofferson hasn't grown much as an actor and his best moments are on stage performing; fortunately they are in ample supply. His pose as the romantic troubador has, however, become a bit threadbare.

As a vehicle to carry the characters, Bud Shrake's script starts slow but eventually gets into gear to overcome its contrivances. Nelson is partnered with conniving music industry exec Rodeo Rocky (Richard C. Sarafian, the film director most recently having helmed "The Bear"), who hails from Chicago and is trying to reap the rewards of Nelson's talent without paying him for it.

Extricating himself from his tangle of failed business deals somehow ties in with Nelson reestablishing ties with his estranged wife (Melinda Dillon). One of the film's nicest scenes is Nelson's guitar duet with his young daughter.

Director Alan Rudolph, who took over for Steve Rash two weeks into the filming, is best at working with actors, and Lesley Ann Warren, in particular, is radiant as an up-and-coming, but reluctant, country/western singer. Until her character is subjected to an abrupt bout with drugs and drink, she is by far the most lively and original person in the pic.

Rip Torn does another superior job in a supporting role. As music promoteer Dino McLeish he maintains a scoundrel's edge while also being a likable character. Dillon, as Nelson's long-suffering wife, is also appealing in a role with rather limited range.

For fans there is plenty of music, though none of it is memorable. Each of the stars contributes several tunes including the title number from Nelson summarizing the struggles of the pure artist against the big bad businessman. There is one splendid moment in the recording studio as Nelson coaches his new discovery, Warren.

Sound and production values are fine and pic looks good all around.
—*Jagr.*

Cote Coeur, Cote Jardin
(Heart Side, Garden Side)
(FRENCH-COLOR)

San Sebastian, Sept. 22.

Produced and directed by Bertrand Van Effenterre; screenplay, B. Van Effenterre and Pierre A. Maubert; camera (color), Pierre-Laurent Chenieux; sound, Pierre Gamet; editor, Joele Van Effenterre; music, Serge Franklin. Features Betangere Bonvolsin, Julie Jezequel, Jean-François Stévenin, Jean-Jacques Biraud, Robin Renucci, Annie Kerani. Reviewed at Cine Victoria Eugenia (San Sebastian), Sept. 21, '84. Running time: **95 MINS.**

"Cote Coeur, Cote Jardin" is a talky, pretentious rural non-drama interspersed with highfalutin' poetic narration and utterance of "deep" philosophical lines on the state of the world, all presented in such a muddled way that it is not till halfway through the film that one can even start to piece together the relations between the characters.

Even at the end, it is still not entirely clear what all the fuss and endless yakking has been about. Most of the story concerns two half-sisters living in a house in the country near a canal.

There's also a literary clown who recites Rimbaud in front of school-children and whose body is found one night floating in the canal. A roving barge owner is accused, arrested by the police but then released. Finally the sisters take the train to Paris, leaving an audience guessing as to what it's all been about and what the title has to do with the film. —*Besa.*

Abenteuer Meiner Seele
(My Soul's Adventure)
(W. GERMAN-DOCU-COLOR)

Berlin, Sept. 25.

A Tantra Film Production, Hamburg. Written and directed by Moritz Boerner. Camera (color), Andreas Schulz; music, Ariel Kalma; sound, Wolfgang Liburg; editor, Boerner; production manager, Thomas Zastko. Reviewed at Filmbühne am Steinplatz, Berlin, Sept. 24, '84. Running time: **87 MINS.**
With: Antje Kraschinski, Ariel Kalma, Petra Grabenhorst, Jürgen Schmidt, Rudi Wormser, Karin Ruschke, Gunda Franchini, Albert Maria Bach, Margo Naslednikov.

As the title hints, Moritz Boerner's "My Soul's Adventure" is one of those docu-dramas constructed around the experiences of a sensitivity group over a six-day stretch. All the participants are young people with sexual or psychological hangups, although it's not at all clear whether some are there just for the fun of it because a camera happens to be peep-showing the whole affair.

This is a tickling but suspect pic in which the thin line between exhibitionism and voyeurism has been wiped out from the very beginning; the viewer is simply asked to relax as bodies and souls become entwined in tender, expectant confrontation.

Since Boerner's last feature, "Catch Your Dreams," was a similar male-female encounter with no holds barred (triple-X-rated fodder for the public under the guise of "sensual therapy"), one might say this is pretty much the same thing for the teenager too young to be permitted in to see the other stuff. "My Soul's Adventure" (invited to compete at the Mannheim festival) is sharply lensed in 35m, features a therapy class of likeable guys-and-gals and shows enough flesh to warm the blood in more fossiled veins. Also as a discussion-getter on sensual sensitivity, pic deserves a onceover. —*Holl.*

In Memory Of Malawan
(AUSTRALIAN-DOCU-B/W & COLOR-16m)

A production of Film Australia, Sydney; presented in U.S. by Australian Film Commission, L.A. Produced and directed by Ian Dunlop. Camera (color), Dean Semler; sound, Bob Hayes; editor and research, Phillippa Kirk; consultants, Dr. Nancy Williams, Ronald Berndt. Reviewed at Margaret Mead Film Festival, N.Y., Sept. 20, 1984. Running time: **92 MINS.**

Produced last year, "In Memory Of Malawan" uses footage and still photographs from the early 1970s, shot in Arnhem Land on the north coast of Australia. The entire film is devoted to a single, two-week-long event — a funeral and eulogy, with dance and ritual, as an Aborigine clan chief honors the memory of Malawan, his deceased father.

Doubtless a film of intense interest to anthropologists and to historians of funerary ceremonies, "Malawan" seems also to have more general interest.

As we catch glimpses in the background of the white man's encroaching industrialization, the foreground shows the wooden and tin shacks of the aborigines, spaced along a broad sandy beach, the sea in the distance. Children observe the adults, chanting and dancing — thus the laws of the clan are passed down. The narrator (unidentified) informs us that the white man has attempted to woo the aborigines with flour and sugar to accept his law, but they resist.

As documentation for ethnographers pledged to authenticity, and as a record of an ancient tradition that may soon vanish, "Malawan" has enduring value. Its utility for 16m distribution and for public television is doubtful, however.

—*Hitch.*

Firstborn
(COLOR)

Okay kids' rights drama.

Hollywood, Oct. 19.

A Paramount Pictures release of a Jaffe-Lansing production in association with Witt/Thomas Prods. Produced by Paul Junger Witt and Tony Thomas. Directed by Michael Apted. Exec producers, Stanley R. Jaffe and Sherry Lansing. Features entire cast. Screenplay, Ron Koslow; camera (Technicolor), Ralf D. Bode; editor, Arthur Schmidt; sound, John H. Bolz; production design, Paul Sylbert; costumes, Colleen C. Atwood; assistant director, Robert V. Girolami; coproducer, Ron Koslow; associate producer, Alice Shure; music, Michael Small. Reviewed at Regent Theatre, L.A., Oct. 19, 1984. (MPAA Rating: PG-13.) Running time: **103 MINS.**

Wendy	Teri Garr
Sam	Peter Weller
Jake	Christopher Collet
Brian	Corey Haim
Lisa	Sarah Jessica Parker
Dad	Richard Brandon
Mr. Rader	James Harper
Coach Gant	Richard E. Szlasa

Direction and smarts are passed up, not down the family tree in "Firstborn," an uneven but jarring drama which champions the rights of children to stand up and be counted and could yield Paramount some initial b.o. with the presence of Teri Garr and surehanded efforts from the male leads.

The picture takes a while to hit its stride, with Garr playing the confused divorced mother of two boys ages 15 and 10, who don't get much guidance since mom is going through her own trauma on the news that her ex of two years is about to remarry.

On the rebound and in a hurry to get on with her life, Garr takes up with rugged Peter Weller, a destructive drifter who moves into the house and, in short order, tears the family apart.

Christopher Collet, the oldest son, and brother of Corey Haim are suspicious of the directionless Weller from the outset and are only momentarily fooled when he tries to buy their trust.

Garr ignores the children's feelings, who harbor their resentments at school. The youngest gets into fights and the oldest, who becomes the focal point, challenges unsympathetic authority figures.

It is almost as if Garr forgets she has responsibilities as a mother, with Collet instead assuming the parental role.

In one instance, the couple leaves for a weekend retreat leaving behind only a note and some money telling the youngsters to fend for themselves. In another, Collet goes to the principal's office in his mother's place to bail his brother out of a jam.

Garr doesn't see things around her crumbling, her vision perhaps blurred by the cocaine and other foreign substances Weller has introduced. Things reach an all-time low when the kids come downstairs one morning to find the adults asleep on the couch, where they crashed after an evening of excesses.

Weller's pipe dream is becoming a restaurateur. He needs $10,000 for a down payment on a place, and will sell cocaine to raise the money. When Collet finds the stash in the couple's bedroom and hides it elsewhere all hell breaks loose in the house.

Though Weller's tough guy character provides a distrubing amount of emotional and physical bullying and later violence towards the children which goes largely unchecked, things build to a chilling and satisfying conclusion under the direction of Michael Apted ("Coal Miner's Daughter").

"Firstborn" goes too long without a clear direction, however, and shifts gears from drama to suspenser very abruptly.

Apted gets a strong performance from Weller, who essays a character ultimately so villainous it is easy to shudder when he appears on screen. Haim does an effective job as the resilient 10-year-old, a fine counterpart to Collet, who brings charismatic appeal to the role of a teenager with wherewithal beyond his years.

Garr does a competent job with her part, billed as her first leading dramatic role though the character though could have shown a little more savvy in the early stages of the pic, which Paramount also could easily have titled "Trading Places."

—*Klyn.*

Second Time Lucky
(NEW ZEALAND/-
AUSTRALIAN-COLOR)

Sydney, Oct. 18.

A United International Pictures (Australia) release of an Eadenrock Ltd.-Galatia Pte. production. Produced by Antony I. Ginnane. Directed by Michael Anderson. Stars Diane Franklin, Roger Wilson, Robert Helpmann. Screenplay, Ross Dimsey, David Sigmund, Howard Grigsby, form a story by Dimsey and Sigmund; camera (Panavision, Eastmancolor), John McLean; editor, Terry Paterson; production design, David Copping; music, Garry McDonald, Laurie Stone; costumes, Bruce Finlavson; coproducer, Brian W. Cook. Reviewed at Hoyts Entertainment Center, Sydney, Oct. 18, 1984. Running time: **98 MINS.**

Eve	Diane Franklin
Adam	Roger Wilson
The Devil	Robert Helpmann
Gabriel	Jon Gadsby
Devil's assistant	John-Michael Howson
Chuck	Bill Ewens
God	Robert Morley

"Second Time Lucky" is a tired, cliché-ridden fantasy-comedy in which the Devil makes a bet with God that if the world began all over again, Adam would make exactly the same mistakes. Amateurish script and storyline provide the basis for a lackluster example of antipodean "international" filmmaking, a mid-Pacific film which will doubtless sink fast when word of mouth gets around.

Adam, a bookish type, meets the equally serious Eve at a riotous party (you know they're both intellectuals because they both wear glasses). From there they're mysteriously transported, tactfully naked, to the Garden of Eden where Adam, coaxed by the Archangel Gabriel, manages to resist Eve's temptations. Next they're in ancient Rome, where Eve is about to marry Caesar and Adam is thrown to the lions. A quick rush forward in time to World War I, where Eve is a spy for the Germans and Adam an upright soldier. During prohibition, Eve is a gangster's moll and Adam a crusading cop, while in the present day Adam is a rock star and Eve is sent by evil impresario Sir Lew Seffer to persuade him to sing pro-instead of anti-nuclear songs.

It's all as witless as it sounds, and the fact that The Devil, overplayed by Robert Helpmann, is seen in every section (as the serpent, Caesar, a German officer, the chief gangster and Sir Lew) doesn't help matters much.

Whole concept is juvenile in approach and inane in execution, though the production designer deserves a nod for his passable sets. For helmer Michael Anderson, who 30 years ago was making such fine films as "The Dam Busters" and "Around The World In 80 Days," this marks a career low.

In the leads, U.S. talent Diane Franklin and Roger Wilson are pretty but cardboard, while Aussie tv personality John-Michael Howson flounces embarrassingly through his campy role as the Devil's assistant. Fastest possible playoff is the only hope for this clinker. — *Strat.*

Horror Vacui
(W. GERMAN-COLOR-16m)

Berlin, Oct. 3.

A Rosa von Praunheim Film, Berlin, in coproduction with Westdeutscher Rundfunk (WDR), Cologne; tv-producer, Joachim von Mengershausen. Directed by Rosa von Praunheim. Features entire cast. Screenplay, Praunheim, Marianne Enzensberger, Cecil Brown; camera (color), Elfi Mikesch; editing, Praunheim, Mike Shephard; sound, Shephard, Ian Wright; music, Maran Gosov; sets, Inge Stiborsky, Jürgen zum Brunnen, Volker März, Alexander Roob. Reviewed at Studio, Berlin, Oct. 2, '84. Running time: **85 MINS.**

With: Lotti Huber (Madame C.), Friedrich Steinhauer, Folkert Milster, Thomas Vogt, Ingrid van Bergen, Günther Thews, Joaquin La Habana.

Rosa von Praunheim's 32d film production, "Horror Vacui" — subtitled "Fear Of Emptiness" — takes its cues from historical German masterpieces, Robert Wiene's "Cabinet Of Dr. Caligari" (1919) and Fritz Lang's "Dr. Mabuse" (1922) and "The Testament Of Dr. Mabuse" (1932). However, the action refers entirely to the present: the new horror cabinet today is the Baghwan sect, based in Oregon but with footholds in both Switzerland (principally Zurich) and West Germany (discos in Berlin, but also hotels and restaurants and travel bureaus across the country).

Not only the Baghwans, but also the Moonies and the Jones suicide cult, are drawn upon for thematic material in sketching a loose story about a femme guru of the Optimal Optimism cult. Everything is, of course, fictional, and on the whole this is a satire on cultists of every ilk and gender. Here's a gay pair living in Berlin, both students attending the university (one an art major, the other in medical school). One day, they visit a cabaret where a modern Dr. Caligari type (Lotti Huber in a double role), puts one of the students under a trance — and thereby hooks him on joining her OO Cult. Much to his gay friend's dismay, he joins.

The rest is a journey through the labyrinth of a cult experience amid specially painted (in an abandoned factory) neo-expressionistic backdrops. Lotti Huber as the guru topper has some juicy lines and plays her role of Madame C. to the hilt. So, too, the so-called "Nightingale From Ramersdorf," Friedrich Steinhauer as her sidekick. This is another echo of "Dr. Caligari," for Steinhauer's undergone a brain operation and obeys his master's every wish. —*Holl.*

Shocking Cannibals
(Naked Magic)
(ITALIAN-DOCU-COLOR)

A Fury Films release of a PEA (Alberto Grimaldi) — Zarai production. Executive producers, Alfredo Castiglioni, Angelo Castiglioni. Directed and camera (Eastman color) by A. & A. Castiglioni. Music, A. Francesco Lavignino; original text, Alberto Moravia; narrator, Marc Mauro Smith. Reviewed at 42d St. Liberty theater, Oct. 13, 1984. (No MPAA Rating.) Running time: **98 MINS.**

"Shocking Cannibals" is an Italian shockumentary made in 1974 under the more accurate title "Naked Magic," currently imported as a gross-out exploitation film. Despite the prestigious names of producer Alberto Grimaldi (whose PEA banner coproduced) and highminded narration written by novelist Alberto Moravia, film is a relentlessly sensationalist look at primitive peoples that is very difficult to endure, even for hardened 42d Street grindhouse devotees.

The only cannibals here, and that's really stretching it, are an Indian tribe living on the Amazon river who pulverize the bones of their dead tribesmen and mix the dust with a banana mash for an annual ritualistic drink, meant to allow the dead folks' souls to go free into the next world.

Cheap thrills-seekers have plenty of non-cannibalistic activities to observe, ranging from primitive survival activities of African tribesmen living around the White Nile river, Ethiopian medical and metaphysical (exorcism) rituals, and that old standby, the Filipino healers who perform magical operations on camera, removing cysts, tumors and leftover props from "The Exorcist" out of people's bellies without leaving any sign of an incision.

Moravia's text intones against the evils of civilized man despoiling the primitives' world, but what we watch is an extremely narrow view of their existence, namely the rituals and both food-seeking and sacrificial slaughtering of animals. This is sheer exploitation, and the inclusion of nearly hardcore sex scenes on camera further ensures the picture an X rating, though the dozen or so fictional and docu-style brutality films (mostly Italian-made) currently floating around Stateside are not usually submitted to the MPAA's rating board. —*Lor.*

Tasio
(SPANISH-COLOR)

· San Sebastian, Sept. 20.

An Elias Querejeta production in collaboration with TVE. Written and directed by Montxo Armendariz. Camera (Eastmancolor), José Luis Alcaine; editor, Pablo G. del Amo; sets, Julio Esteban; costumes, Maiki Marin; music, Angel Illarramendi; sound, Bernardo Menz. Reviewed at Cine Victoria Eugenia (San Sebastian), Sept. 19, 1984. Running time: **95 MINS.**
Tasio (grownup) . . . . .Patxi Bisquert
Tasio (adolescent) . . . . .Isidro José Solano
Tasio (child). . . . : . . .Garikoitz Mendigutxia
Paulina .Amaia Lasa
Tasio's brother . . . . .Nacho Martinez
  Also: José Maria Asin, Paco Sagarzazu, Enrique Goicoechea, Elena Uriz.

"Tasio" is a touching, slow-paced and occasionally confusing first effort by Navarra filmmaker Montxo Armendariz tracing the childhood, adolescent and adult years of a humble Basque worker who toils in the mountains hunting and making coke (the kind distilled from coal).

Sensitive and profoundly respectful, the film, in part subsidized by the Basque government, resembles a ballad singing the praises of local Basque mores and culture. There are occasional digs at the priesthood, at the well-to-do exploiting the poor and at the Civil Guards, as the noble worker, Tasio, makes his honest way through life tending his coke pile, doing a bit of poaching, marrying a village lass and bringing up a daughter.

Though well directed and professionally lensed and edited by Querejeta's usual team of experts, item often drags, since there's not much of a story. The few potentially dramatic scenes, such as when Tasio confronts a man trying to cheat him, or the death of the wife, or an accident in which a boy falls into the coke oven, are purposely played down.

· Never made clear is what year the action is occurring; many will also be puzzled by the coke oven, basically a pile of dirt with smoke coming out of apertures. Also confusing are the time switches from childhood to adolescence, to manhood; finally, several of the actors bear considerable resemblance to each other so it is hard to distinguish Tasio from his friend, brother or father, since all wear similar dress and are of similar build.

Pic was well received in San Sebastian by audiences and critics. Armendariz shows considerable talent in this, his first effort. However, the story is rather too local and slow-paced to generate interest outside the fest circuits.—*Besa.*

The First Turn-On!!
(COLOR)

Implausible sex comedy lacks laughs.

Cranford, N.J., Oct. 17.

A Troma Inc. production and release. Produced by Lloyd Kaufman and Michael Herz. Executive producers, William E. Kirksey, Spencer A. Tandy. Directed by Michael Herz and "Samuel Weil." Features entire cast. Screenplay, Stuart Strutin; camera (color), Lloyd Kaufman; editors, Adam Fredericks, Richard King; art direction, Ellen Christiansen; costume design, Danielle Brunon; sound, Wendy Caplin; associate producer, Stuart Strutin; assistant director, Ilan Cohen. Reviewed at the RKO Cranford Theatre, Cranford, N.J., Oct. 16, 1984 (MPAA Rating: R). Running time: **82 MINS.**
Michelle Farmer/
  PA Announcer . . . . .Georgia Harrell
Mitch . . . . ,. . . .Michael Sanville
Henry. .Googy Gress
Annie Goldberg . . . . .Heidi Miller
Danny Anderson . . . . .John Flood
Mrs. Anderson . . . . .Betty Pia
Madame Gumbo . . . . .Gilda Gumbo
Lucy the hooker . . . . .Lara Grills
Barbara Billingham .Kristina Marie Wetzel
Ted . . . . : . . . . . .Ted Henning
Dreamgirl . . . . : . . . . . .Sheila Kennedy
Dwayne . . . . .Mark Torgl

"The First Turn-On!!" is the latest release (though pic was shot about a year ago) from indie producer-distributor Troma and has played in the U.K. prior to its current N.Y. unveiling. Pic is, at best, par for the previously charted Troma course and should do some quick business in swift theatrical playoff showing up as pay-tv filler.

Directed by the company's cotoppers Michael Herz and Lloyd Kaufman, who uses the *nom de film* Samuel Weil, comedy is strictly of the "can you outgross this?" sort and filmmakers apparently care not a whit about plot or plausibility. Set in a summer camp, director of which is more concerned with keeping costs down than saving a drowning camper, story is centered around four overaged campers who get trapped in a cave while exploring. Accompanied by their nature studies counselor, the kids, to while away the time, relate their first sexual experiences, thus enabling the film to shift back to flashback sequences.

Each, it turns out, is a big boaster and none of the tall tales is true. Most outrageous "remembrance" belongs to the counselor herself (Georgia Harrell) who tells of her great love for a nitwit (Mark Torgl) who reaches new screen heights in terms of physical repulsion, replete with a painful case of acne and bad table manners. Penthouse model Sheila Kennedy is an eye-pleasing relief in comparison.

Pic holds its big sexy payoff for the final moments when the protagonists, fearing death and unrelieved virginity, get naked in a pile, though sequence is comprised of very little that will offend watchdogs of morality (or please those that support this type of venture).

Performers down the line are too old for their roles and play them with exaggerated gusto, which gets tedious quickly. Tech credits are passable but nothing to write home about. —*Gerz.*

The Killing Fields
(BRITISH-COLOR)

Hollywood, Oct. 19.

A Warner Bros. release of a Goldcrest and International Film Investors presentation of an Enigma production. Produced by David Puttnam. Directed by Roland Joffé. Features entire cast. Screenplay, Bruce Robinson, based on the article "The Death And Life Of Dith Pran" by Sydney Schanberg. Camera (Kay labs color), Chris Menges; editor, Jim Clark; music, Mike Oldfield; production design, Roy Walker; art direction, Roger Murray Leach, Steve Spence; costume design, Judy Moorcroft; sound (Dolby), Clive Winter; special effects supervisor, Fred Cramer; stunt arranger, Terry Forrestal; associate producer, Iain Smith; assistant director, Bill Westley. Reviewed at The Burbank Studios, Burbank, Oct. 18, 1984. (MPAA Rating: R.) Running time: 141 MINS.
Sydney Schanberg . . . . Sam Waterston
Dith Pran . . . . Haing S. Ngor
Al Rockoff . . . . John Malkovich
Jon Swain . . . . Julian Sands
Military Attache . . . . Craig T. Nelson

A story of perseverence and survivial in hell on earth, "The Killing Fields" represents an admirable, if not entirely successful, attempt to bring alive to the world film audience the horror story that is the recent history of Cambodia. Intelligent, sober and perhaps even too austere, picture is terrifically successful in physically evoking its time and place, and is also the sort of tremendously ambitious project that can only be undertaken when an adventurous producer such as David Puttnam has carte blanche to make it his way. Warner Bros. release is a natural for prestige-oriented late year release, and strong reviews are a must to put it across to the intended upscale, educated target viewership.

Based on Pulitzer Prize-winning N.Y. Times reporter Sydney Schanberg's 1980 article "The Death And Life Of Dith Pran," film is designed as a story of friendship, and it is on this level that it works least well. The intent and outward trappings are all impressively in place, but at its heart there's something missing.

Action begins in 1973, with Schanberg, in the person of Sam Waterston, arriving in Cambodia and being assisted in his reporting by Dith Pran (Haing S. Ngor), an educated, exceedingly loyal native. Thanks to Dith Pran's ingenuity and resourcefulness, the two are able, against U.S. government wishes and ahead of all other journalists, to sneak downriver to a city accidently bombed by B-52s.

These vivid scenes set the stage for the fall of Phnom Penh, two years later, to the Khmer Rouge. The hectic evacuation of the U.S. Embassy is sharply depicted, as is the subsequent queasy mood at the French Embassy, where all the Westerners who chose to remain behind were detained.

As interesting as all these events are, film's main problems lie in these expository stretches. While lensing style is not documentary-like, approach to the characters and their place in the action verges on it, with the result that the principals' friendship and bonds of feeling have difficulty becoming palpable. Difficulty is compounded by the fact that much of the dialog is unintelligible or close to it.

In his article, Schanberg admitted that his professional behavior was often "relentless" to the point of seeming bossy and unfeeling to some. Unfortunately, his hard-driving aspect, the one typical of the reporter whose only thought is to get his story, is about the only side one sees. He's always in action, running from one hot spot to another, so the intimate, personal, human bond between him and his ever-faithful assistant is never sufficiently fleshed out in Bruce Robinson's screenplay.

Through a stupendous effort, and at great risk to his own existence, Dith Pran manages to save the lives of Schanberg and some colleagues after their capture by the victorious Khmer Rouge. Overwhelmed by this selfless act, Schanberg manages to protect Dith Pran for awhile at the French Embassy, but must ultimately face the fact that he can't reciprocate, and watches helplessly as his friend is forced to leave the compound for an unknown, doubtlessly dire, fate at the hands of the communists.

Dith Pran is transferred to a re-education camp in the Cambodian Year Zero, when "only the silent survive." Dith Pran would be a dead duck if he tipped his hand that he spoke English or French, and it is during the long camp and escape sequences, which are largely silent, punctuated only by occasional narration and untranslated Khmer dialog, that the film reaches its most gripping heights.

People are beaten or killed without apparent reason, children are taught the evils of family life and the old days, and countless corpses are dumped in "the killing fields" of the title. These countryside scenes are bracing, as well as being eerily beautiful. Given that over 3,000,000 of Cambodia's 7,000,000 citizens died during this period, they could have been a lot rougher, but quite enough is seen as it is.

Schanberg spent four years trying to track Dith Pran down, knowing all along that the chances of his friend's survival were slim. Given the odds, ultimate outcome was something of a miracle.

Film is something like an epic version of a previous Puttnam film about survival under impossible circumstances, "Midnight Express," but without the souped-up melodramatics. With material that's extreme enough already, first-time director Roland Joffé stages many scenes in a somewhat distant, off-hand manner, which is defensible but does reduce the personal element.

Because of the overall aesthetic, which does not go in for nuances of character, performances are basically functional, with Waterston registering little but determination and, later, angst. John Malkovich and Julian Sands are good, but quite subdued, as a photographer and the British correspondent, respectively. Fortunately, nonpro Haing S. Ngor is a naturally sympathetic and camera-receptive man, and he effectively carries the weight of the film's most important sequences.

Technically, film is aces, with Thai locations providing the closest possible replicas of the real thing. Chris Menges' cinematography and Roy Walker's production design are firstrate, while Mike Oldfield's score is uneven, strangely effective in spots and obtrusive in others.
—Cart.

La Guerre Des Tuques
(The Dog Who Stopped The War)
(CANADIAN-COLOR)

Montreal, Oct. 10.

A La Fête production. Produced by Rock Demers and Nicole Robert. Stars Cédric Jourdé, Julien Elie, Maripierre Arseneau-D'Amour. Directed by André Melancon. Screenplay, Danyèle Patenaude, Roger Cantin. Reviewed at the Cineplex, Montreal, Oct. 8, 1984. Running time: 89 MINS.

The first in a series of nine family-oriented films, "The Dog Who Stopped The War" is the sort of crisply-made allegory that should satisfy the kids and please the parents as well, although the subject matter is definitely not geared for the latter group.

Quasi-comedy, quasi-drama, film is set in rural Quebec, but locale plays no significant role in terms of confusing an international audience. By and large, plot focuses on two warring groups of kids who spend their Christmas holidays pelting one another with snowballs and trying to conquer a castle built of snow and ice.

By holiday's end, it becomes apparent that neither side can or should win this titanic struggle, that, in effect, war is futile. Although top-heavy with palatable morals, this doesn't detract from some genuinely comic moments and surprisingly taut performances from a cast of largely unknown neophytes, particularly from Maripierre Arseneau-D'Amour as the young lass torn between the two leaders of the rival gangs.

Script is both quirky and mildly provocative, and mercifully avoids the maudlin. Production values are impressive, all the more so considering film's $C1,000,000 budget.

Only real downer is the sloppy English dubbing of the original French-track version. It should be mentioned, however, that producer Rock Demers plans to re-dub 30% of English version.

Although film won't prove to be as memorable a fable as "The Neverending Story," it should keep kids from all corners of the globe mostly amused over their Yuletide break.
— Bro.

Give My Regards To Broad Street
(BRITISH-COLOR)

Hollywood, Oct. 23.

A 20th Century Fox release. Produced by Andros Epaminondas. Directed by Peter Webb. Features entire cast. Screenplay, Paul McCartney; camera (Rank color), Ian McMillan; editor, Peter Beston; music, McCartney; production design, Anthony Pratt; art direction, Adrian Smith; costume design, Milena Canonero; sound (Dolby), Bruce White; choreography, David Toguri; music produced and directed by George Martin; assiciate producer, Peter Manley; assistant director, Selwyn Roberts. Reviewed at the 20th Century Fox Studios, L.A., Oct. 22, 1984. (MPAA Rating: PG.) Running time: 108 MINS.
Paul . . . . Paul McCartney
Steve . . . . Bryan Brown
Ringo . . . . Ringo Starr
Journalist . . . . Barbara Bach
Linda . . . . Linda McCartney
Sandra . . . . Tracey Ullman
Jim . . . . Ralph Richardson
Harry . . . . Ian Hastings

Big star vanity productions are one thing, but "Give My Regards To Broad Street" is something else again. Characterless, bloodless and pointless, Paul McCartney's first film venture since "Let It Be" 14 years ago seems to exist in a vacuum, with nothing on its mind. It's even a waste musically, as only three of the 12 tunes offered up are new. Theatrical release will be of the here today, gone tomorrow variety.

Picture was no quickie, having begun lensing two years ago and having cost $9,000,000. Plenty of sets, locations and performers are on view, and production values are all slick.

It's hard to imagine that the former Beatle couldn't have invented a more imaginative artistic setting in which to place himself than this feeble concoction, the structure of which inherently frees it to pursue all manner of flights of fancy.

Set-up has McCartney dreaming that the master tapes for his new album, entrusted to an aide with a criminal record, have disappeared. Evil business types will take over his music company unless the tapes are produced by midnight, and McCartney spends the day imagining what might have become of them and recording some numbers in various spots.

It's all embarrassingly innocuous. McCartney moves through it all as if he didn't have a care in the world, and he's joined, to little effect, by his wife Linda, Ringo Starr and his wife, Barbara Bach. Only note of interest historically is that the film apparently marks the last screen appearance by the late Ralph Richardson, although he suffers the indignity of having his only scene stolen by a pet monkey.

Aside from the three, undistinguished-sounding new numbers, song score consists of five old John Lennon-McCartney tunes which have been rerecorded and other McCartney compositions which have been written since The Beatles broke up. — Cart.

Lovelines
(COLOR)

Worthless teen comedy.

Hollywood, Oct. 29.

A Tri-Star Pictures release of a Taines-Lloyd/Tri-Star-Delphi II production. Produced by Hal Taines, Michael Lloyd. Executive in charge of production. Gilles A. De Turenne. Directed by Rod Amateau. Features entire cast. Screenplay, Chip Hand, William Hillman, from story by Hand, Lloyd, Hillman; camera (Metrocolor), Duke Callaghan; editors, David Bretherton, Fred A. Chulack; music supervision, Lloyd; art direction, Robert K. Kinoshita; set decoration, A.C. Montenaro; sound (Dolby), Mark F. Ulano; associate producer, Hand; assistant director, Laura Andrus. Reviewed at the VIP Screening Room, L.A., Oct. 29, 1984. (MPAA Rating: R.) Runnng time: 93 MINS.

Rick Johnson ....Greg Bradford
Piper ....Mary Beth Evans
J.D. ....Michael Winslow
Jeff ....Don Michael Paul
Priscilla ....Tammy Taylor
Cynthia ....Stacey Toten
Beagle ....Robert Delapp
Godzilla ....Frank Zagarino
Hammer ....Todd Bryant
Lisa ....Jonna Lee
Theresa ....Robin Watkins
Brigit ....Claudia Cowan

"Lovelines" ought to be advertised with the warning that anyone who arrives after the beginning of the picture will miss the best part: the Tri-Star logo. Everything that comes after the beautiful white, flying horse would have been substandard even for a low-budget teen exploitation pic a decade ago, and b.o. results will be fitting with that.

Film's concerns are rooted even further back than that, in the mid-1950s, with rival all-white, squeaky clean high school students from Malibu High and Coldwater Canyon High in L.A., playing pranks on each other and occasionally occupying common turf for a battle of the bands.

Only acknowledgements that a few things have changed in 30 years come in the way of homages to the "Porky's" tradition (weenie gags, a formula which makes swimsuits come off in the water, a few four-letter words), and via some gratuitous breakdancing, which is woefully photographed. Even when it's trying to sound alternately punk and heavy metalish, music could not be more middle-of-the-road if it tried.

Segregated off in his own little corner of the film is black comedian Michael Winslow (of "Police Academy"), doing what amount to lame monologs into a battery of telephones, hence the title.

This one deserves a place along with "Where The Boys Are '84" on the most inaccessible shelf in Tri-Star's library. —Cart.

Terror In The Aisles
(COMPILATION-COLOR/B&W)

Poor recycling of footage for fast Halloween business.

A Universal Pictures release of a T.E.M. Programs International presentation of a Kaleidoscope Films Ltd. production. Produced by Andrew Kuehn, Stephen Netburn. Directed by Kuehn. Stars Donald Pleasence, Nancy Allen. Written by Margery Doppelt; camera (CFI color; prints by Technicolor), John A. Alonzo; editor-associate producer, Gregory McClatchy; original music, John Beal; additional music, Doug Timm, Richard Johnston; additional editing, Richard Goldstein; production executive, Martin Wesson; research-original treatment, John JB Wilson; sound, Gene Cantamesa; postproduction supervisor, Bea Dennis; assistant director-production manager, Vincent Arcaro. Reviewed at Universal screening room, N.Y., Oct. 23, 1984. (MPAA Rating: R.) Running time: 82 MINS.

"Terror In The Aisles" is a poorly conceived and executed compilation of sequences from (primarily) horror films, designed to do quick theatrical business during the Halloween season and later earn its keep as a homevideo item.

Picture's fatal problem stems from it having been made by coming attractions' trailer producers. Applying the rapid editing and juxtaposition techniques to a feature-length project results in simply ruining many classic film sequences rather than preserving them.

As its title suggests, the film is about terror rather than horror, and instead of fantasy it excerpts mainly shock scenes. Made for a joint venture by Universal Pictures' parent company MCA and Thorn EMI, it includes a surplus of clips from Universal films, reaching a nadir in the ridiculous overemphasis on a film such as U's forgettable "Nighthawks."

Tastelessness and lack of discrimination are evident in both the choice and arrangement of clips. Alfred Hitchcock's "To Catch A Thief" is excerpted to illogically introduce a segment (narrated by Nancy Allen) about sex and terror, cutting immediately to Brian De-Palma's "Dressed To Kill." The narration in general, by Donald Pleasence and Allen, is a mass of clichés about audience psychology and filmmakers' methods of manipulation. The only useful content is a Hitchcock interview (taken from the docu "Alfred Hitchcock: The Men Who Made The Movies") in which he explains his theory of suspense.

With only fleeting moments from pioneering films such as U's "Frankenstein," "Dracula" and "The Wolfman," "Aisles" emphasizes recent pictures and ignores foreign films (no H-G Clouzot, no German classics, just a brief glimpse of Dario Argento's "Suspiria") and domestic masters such as Val Lewton (we see Lynn Lowry in the "Cat People" remake but nothing from the original). Director Andrew Kuehn opens promisingly with Carol Kane in "When A Stranger Calls," the Columbia release that together with "Halloween" started the most recent horror film boom, but very quickly demonstrates an absence of any historical perspective.

Kuehn crosscuts embarrassingly between Laurence Olivier in "Marathon Man," Rutger Hauer in "Nighthawks" and Wings Hauser in "Vice Squad" for a lengthy segment on heinous villains that is an arbitrary selection upon which any viewer could improve. Elsewhere, his crosscutting mixes "Rosemary's Baby," "The Exorcist" and "The Omen," diminishing the power of each one, or moves to and fro between "Klute," "Ms. 45" and "The Seduction." The results are frustrating in the extreme.

Jack Nicholson in "The Shining" provides comic relief out of context, while hammy gags of Pleasence mingling with a fake movie audience to deliver his commentary fall flat. The black & white clips from Robert Aldrich's "What Ever Happened To Baby Jane?" and Hitchcock's "Strangers On A Train" and "Psycho" more than hold their own amidst more recent color footage. Though they receive no credit here, special makeup artists Dick Smith, Rick Baker and Rob Bottin, among others, are the true stars of the show with some of their best illusions displayed.

"Aisles" originally received an X rating, and has evidently been toned down with less gore footage in the R-rated release version (which has its roughest moments in scenes from "Scanners" and "The Thing" remake). Next time someone tackles a project of this nature, they'd be wise to rely on horror film scholars to aid in the selection process and then present individual scene excerpts intact so as to retain the qualities that made them work in the first place. —Lor.

Tail Of The Tiger
(AUSTRALIAN-COLOR)

Sydney, Oct. 2.

A Roadshow Distributors (Australia) release of a Producer's Circle production. Produced by James M. Vernon. Executive producer, Graham Jennings. Written and directed by Rolf de Heer. Features entire cast. Camera (color), Richard Michalak; production design, Judi Russell; music, Steve Arnold, Graham Tardif; editor, Suresh Ayyar; sound, Penn Robinson. Reviewed at Film Australia theaterette, Lindfield, Sydney, Oct. 2, 1984. Running time: 82 MINS.

Orville Ryan ....Grant Navin
Harry.....................Gordon Poole
Lydia Ryan ....Caz Lederman
Beryl ....Gayle Kennedy
Spike ....Peter Feeley
Rabbit.....................Dylan Lyle
Stan ....Walter Sullivan
Jack.......................Basil Clarke

"Tail Of The Tiger" is a quietly amiable children's film about an intelligent Sydney 10-year-old, Orville, who (as his name suggests) is obsessed with vintage airplanes. The local kids won't let him join their gang and fly model airplanes, but he stumbles upon an old man, Harry, who has a wrecked Tiger Moth in a shed near the docks. Orville spends his summer vacation helping Harry (who's at first suspicious of the boy) to repair and eventually fly the vintage aircraft.

Slight narrative works thanks to the relaxed performances director-scripter Rolf de Heer gets from the children. Toothy Grant Navin is sold as the young hero, while the film is practically stolen by the even younger Dylan Lyle, playing Orville's annoying little brother, Rabbit; young Lyle is funny and knowingly bright. Indeed the family scenes (as in "E.T.," there is no father around) are the best in the film, with Caz Lederman notable as the boys' long-suffering mother.

Pic's one major flaw is the injection of some awkward and unnecessary fantasy via three ghostly old pilots who pop up from time to time to encourage Harry and Orville, and even help them fight off an attack from a gang of kids.

Final sequences of the restored plane flying over the city of Sydney are joyful, though one wonders what the Dept. of Aviation would have to say about it all. The target audience of preteens won't worry too much about that, though, and will doubtless have a good time with "Tail Of The Tiger," while their parents won't be suffering either. —Strat.

Forever Young
(BRITISH-COLOR)

London, Oct. 19.

A 20th Century Fox release (U.K.) of a Goldcrest Films and Television production. Produced by Chris Griffin. Directed by David Drury. Executive producer, David Puttnam. Features entire cast. Screenplay, Ray Connolly; camera (color), Norman Langley; editor, Max Lemon; art direction, Jeffrey Woodbridge; costumes, Tudor George; sound, David Crozier. Reviewed at the Classic Chelsea, London, Oct. 4, 1984. (BBFC Rating: 15.) Running time: 84 MINS.

James ....James Aubrey
Father Michael ....Nicholas Gecks
Father Vincent ....Alec McCowen
Mary ....Karen Archer
John ....Joseph Wright
Paul ....Liam Holt
Cathy ....Jane Forster
Young Michael ....Jason Carter
Maureen ....Oona Kirsch
Alison ....Eileen Fletcher

Brenda ....Carol MacReady
Young James ....Julian Firth

"Forever Young" is the first item in David Puttnam's "First Love" series of lowbudget movies to debut theatrically in the U.K. It's a lacklustre account of a harrowing story whick is likely to be limited to small-screen playoff in most offshore territories.

Plot centers on the reunion of two men, a priest and a teacher, 20 years after the termination of their promising musical partnership. Initial joy at rediscovering each other is shattered by the revival of old resentments. The final showdown comes after the teacher, James, is seen on the floor with the mother of a boy whom priest Michael has befriended.

Ray Connolly's script wastes its potential by wandering down many byways. The forlorn young boy's interest in Roman coins and ambition to follow his hero into the priesthood does little to illumine the central conflict. Also irrelevant is the character of Father Vincent, a traditionally oriented antithesis to the rock-crazy cleric Michael.

Although director David Drury on his first theatrical outing, shows a sure touch in b&w flashbacks to traumatic moments in the late '50s, he fails to extract equivalent impact from his lead actors in their confrontational scenes. He also largely wastes two major sequences in a church hall disco. Tight scheduling and limited budget could be the explanation. —*Japa.*

Brothers
(AUSTRALIAN-COLOR)

Sydney, Oct. 19.
An Areflex Picture, produced by Terry Bourke. Executive producers, Frank Wilkie, Brock Halliday. Features entire cast. Directed and written by Rourke, from the book "Reflex" by Roger Ward; camera (Eastmancolor), Ray Henman; editor, Ron Williams; music, Bob Young; art director, Paul Tolley; sound, Bob Clayton. Reviewed on Syme Home Videocassette, Sydney, Oct. 17, 1984. Running time: **99 MINS.**
Adam Wild ....Chard Hayward
Kevin Wild ....Ivar Kants
Lani Aveson ....Margaret Laurence
Allison Levis ....Jennifer Cluff
Jenine Williams ....Alyson Best
Mrs. Williams ....Joan Bruce
Jim Williams................Les Foxcroft
Bill Mason ....Ricky May
Bureau Chief................Ken Wayne
Journalist ....Desmond Tester
Cameraman ....Roger Ward

An unappealing drama about an Australian journalist who survived a massacre of press people in Timor in 1975, "Brothers" is a total misfire. Made in 1982, but never shown in cinemas, it's reviewed for the record on its homevideo release.

There actually *was* a massacre of five Aussie pressmen in Timor nine years ago, and initially writer-producer-director Terry Bourke sets up quite a tense situation as he recreates that incident, but with seven journalists, two of whom manage to escape. These are the brothers of the film's title, and five years later the younger, Kevin (Ivar Kants) is living in a small New Zealand town and about to marry a local girl. Re-enter big brother Adam (Chard Hayward), who only wants to "rescue" Kevin from encroaching domesticity. Adam, a churlish, brutish character, dallies with the local prostie (Margaret Laurence) who attempts suicide when he throws her over, and also with a city girl (Jennifer Cluff) he meets on a train. He also gets beaten up at regular intervals, deservedly.

Adam is such an unpleasant protagonist that the audience has no one to root for, allowing inertia to set in early on. As a director, Bourke (who specializes in low-budget efforts of limited ambition) stages some set-pieces quite well, including the opening massacre and the climax in which Cluff is killed when the bus on which she's traveling is involved in an accident with a truck. As a writer, however, Bourke provides his characters with some depressingly banal dialog, and most of the dramatic scenes fall very flat.

Thesping is as good as can be expected under the circumstances, and technically film is okay, but it's such a downer that even on video it won't have many takers. — *Strat.*

Rush
(ITALIAN-COLOR)

A Cinema Shares International Distribution release of a Biro Cinematografica (Rome) production. Produced by Marcello Romeo. Directed by "Anthony Richmond" (Tonino Ricci). Stars Conrad Nichols. Screenplay & story, Tito Carpi; camera (Luciano Vittori color), Giovanni Bergmanini; editor, Vincenzo Tomassi; music, Francesco De Masi; production manager, Romualdo Buzzanca. Reviewed at 42d St. Selwyn theater, N.Y., Oct. 20, 1984. (No MPAA Rating.) Running time: **77 MINS.**
With: Conrad Nichols (Rush), Gordon Mitchell (the ruler), Laura Trotter, Rita Furlan, Bridgit Pelz, Richard Pizzuti, Osiride Pevarello, Paolo Celli, Luigi Filippo Lodoli, Daniel Stroppa.

"Rush" is a minor, highly derivative Italian action picture in the science fiction genre, which marks the return to theatrical distribution of the 1970s indie Cinema Shares Int'l: The director, Tonino Ricci signs his work Anthony Richmond, but that typically anglicized name will cause confusion with Jaclyn Smith's husband, the British cinematographer-director Anthony Richmond.

The film skimps on story and incident, preferring instead to rely on an Italian hero, whose stage name is the anglicized Conrad Nichols, decked out to closely resemble Sylvester Stallone in "First Blood." He's Rush, a muscular road warrior who, 10 years after a nuclear war has devastated the world, attempts to free the slave labor ruled by a despot (Gordon Mitchell). Pic is set at an oil refinery plus greenhouse. The basic conflict of people afraid to go back "outside" while Rush is there to inform them that radiation has dissipated and the Earth is becoming fertile again, is never borne out by the visuals (which have the people outside already).

After uneventful opening reels of minor fights and Rush in captivity, our smiling hero escapes, cueing a last half of him being chased through a forest which directly mimics "First Blood." For a futuristic film, "Rush" relies upon uniforms, vehicles and weaponry which seem left over from a World War II opus. Cheap production has poor special effects (puffs of smoke when grenades explode) and very fake fight scenes, likely to invite derision by action film audiences. Silliest touch is having the laborers in ordinary clothes, with pieces of transparent plastic (like raincoats) worn on top for "style."

A sequel has already been made, though the only suspense at the end of "Rush" is whether the perpetually sweaty and oiled-body (he seems ready to pose in a Mr. Universe contest) Nichols will get to take a bath. — *Lor.*

Busters Verden
(Buster's World)
(DANISH-COLOR)

Copenhagen, Sept. 28.
A Metronome release of Crone Film Production A/S (Nina Crone) with the Danish Film Institute and Danish Radio/TV production. Directed by Bille August. Screenplay, Bjarne Reuther, based on his novel. Camera (Eastmancolor), Fritz Schröder, Sören Berthelin, Birger Bohm; executive producer, Nina Crone; editors, Thomas Gislason, Jakob Gislason; production design, Sören Kragh Sörensen, Tove Robert Rasmussen, Thomas Heinesen; costumes, Françoise Nicolet; title song, Nana; music, Bo Holten; Film Institute consultant, Ida Zeruneith. Reviewed at the Dagmar Bio, Copenhagen, Sept. 28, 1984. Running time: **77 MINS.**
Buster ....Mads Bugge Andersen
His sister .....,......Katerina Stenbeck
Their father ....Peter Schröder
Their mother ....Katja Mieherenard
Joanna ....Signe Dahl Madsen
Joanna's mother ....Kirsten Rolffes
Stig Ole ....Martin Krakauer
Lars ....John Riedl
Mrs. Larsen ....Berthe Quistgaard
Shopkeeper ....Buster Larsen
Athletic coach ....Ole Thestrup
Teacher ....Jannie Fauerschou

In eight-year-old Mads Bugge Andersen, Bille August has found Freckle-Face Of The Year to play the lead in "Buster's World," a six-episode tv series that has been patched together to look — ever so slightly — like a feature film in the kiddie and family entertainment category.

Patchwork or not, "Buster's World" defies its tv origins by having a very special kind of magic. Magic is the key word, since young Buster has inherited the tools of the trade of his late magician uncle and now uses them, along with his vivid imagination, to overcome such handicaps as suffered by being a Very Small Kid in a world and a school of Very Big Bullies. Buster finds ways to cope with the rejection he experiences when he first — as a grocer's messenger boy — approaches the rich girl of his dreams (and particularly her mother).

All grownups in "Buster's World" are out-and-out caricatures. However, some of the kids seem real. Buster has a kid sister with a lame leg, annoyed with him when he tries to comfort her with made-up stories of other lame girls who succeed as dancers. She is thrilled, however, when Buster gives one of her tormentors at school a bloody comeuppance. A little bit of real life peeps through here and there, but not enough to distract from the film's real point, which is that a little bit of imagination serves to make the world a better place to live. Without Andersen's face, the film would be phony and coy. Instead, it comes through as a suburban fairy tale with tough little shades of Tom Sawyer. — *Kell.*

Jean-Louis Barrault — A Man Of The Theatre
(DOCU-COLOR-16m)

Washington, Sept. 22.
Produced by Helen Gary Bishop. Directed by Muriel Balash. Associate producer, Leone Jaffie; camera (color, 16m), Victor Johannes, Lawrence Yampolsky, Harold Seldon, François About, Dominique Dubose, Roger Labeyrie, Jean-Louis Dyer; editing, Catherine Brasier; music, Pierre Boulez, Jean-Pierre Stora. Reviewed at Cine screening room, Washington, D.C., Sept. 21, 1984. (No MPAA Rating.) Running time: **59 MINS.**

This documentary offers a lively and informative history of France's great actor Jean-Louis Barrault, whose career between "Children Of Paradise" and "La Nuit de Varennes" is not well-known outside France. The indefatigible actor an his companion, Madeleine Renaud, are easily documented in archival footage from their surrealist beginnings to Barrault's recent one-man show, in which he has been found to be a "traditionalist" mime.

Barrault tries to be explicit about the many phases of his career, offering insights into his feud with Andre Malraux, who provided Barrault's theater its first subsidy. Shown is Barrault's return to the Odeon theater for the first time since his expulsion in 1968, and why he considered the '68 riots an important form of theater. Testimony of Barrault's genius in both films and theater comes from Jeanne Moreau, Peter Brook, Pierre Boulez, whose music provides a noteworthy soundtrack, and many of his and Madeleine Renaud's admirers. Footage of their street theater in New York has a spritely air and clever use of color.

Barrault's own sense of humor is what carries the pic. His daring comparison of himself as a young man to Jean-Paul Belmondo and his confession that the early days of the Surrealist Atelier were devoted to "naked theater" because they could not afford clothes strike a welcome matter-of-fact balance to the worshipful tone of the filmmakers. At another point, he re-enacts his role as the dying mother in William Faulkner's "As I Lay Dying," noting the lugubrious side of his performance and laughing at himself.

Beyond the usual channels for films on the arts, the impact of Barrault on the careers of other actors should find a place for the pic in retrospectives and particularly on the festival circuit. —Kaja.

Samson og Sally
(Samson And Sally)
(DANISH-ANIMATED-COLOR)

Copenhagen, Oct. 1.

A Nordisk Film Distribution A/S release of Dansk Tegnefilmkompagni/Nordisk Film/-Swedish Television-Malmö with the Danish Film Institute production. Directed by (and story by) Jannik Hastrup, based on novel "Song Of The Whales" by Bent Haller. Executive producer, Ebbe Preisler. Narration consultant, Lena Gunlögsson; dialog, Li Vilstrup; design and animation, Jannik Hastrup, Kjeld Simonsen, others; background designs, Birthe Dalland; music, Jens Wilhelm (Fuzzy) Pedersen; camera (color), Jacob Koch; computer animation, Per Lygum, Sören Brink; Danish Film Institute consultants, Ulrich Breuning, Jörgen Melgard, Ida Zeruneith. Reviewed at the Palads, Copenhagen, Oct. 1, 1984. Running time: 60 MINS.
Voices:
Samson . . . . Jesper Klein
Sally . . . . Helle Hertz
The Seagull . . . . Per Pallesen
Moby Dick . . . . Preben Neergard
Captain Arhoff . . . . Olde Ernst
The Turtle . . . . Berthe Quistgard
The Dolphin . . . . Kirsten Peüliche

A veteran of Danish animated film, Jannik Hastrup has, for the first time, gone the Disney way with full animation, using 90,000 color drawings to tell the story of "Samson And Sally" as a mini-length (hour-long) cartoon feature. Hastrup has his animal characters speak and sing and even dance and perform music.

Story has two young whales, black and wise Sally and white and foolhardy Samson, learn about life in the high seas the hard way. They had been warned about the lurking dangers by their parents and other senior ocean citizens who particularly like to retell again and again the tale of their great forefather, Moby Dick, now believed to be living in some sunken Atlantis and waiting to come to the rescue of what is left of his species.

Having learned of their habitat's natural dangers and run afoul of its unnatural ones from oil-spills and modern Ahabs to nuclear waste, Samson goes off alone in search of

Moby Dick and finally finds him in his Atlantis (that turns out to be New York).

Film falls somewhere between the educational and the strictly entertaining. It takes its time getting through a rather jerky narrative and would seem to be of primary appeal to educational situations and particularly to tv kiddie programming. Since the dialog is sparse, dubbing into other languages than the original's Danish, should be a fairly easy job. —Kell.

Kassach
(ISRAELI-COLOR)

Tel Aviv, Aug. 4.

A Shapira films Presentation. Produced by Yossi Meshulam. Directed by Haim Gil. Screenplay, Aharon Bachar; camera (color), Yossi Wein; editor, Nissim Mossek; songs by Zohar Argov, Haim Moshe, Jacky Makeiten, Moshe Ghiyat, Hofni Cohen, Diklon, Avihu Medina, Shimi Tavori. Reviewed at Berkey-Pathe-Humphries Studios, Tel Aviv, Aug. 3, 1984. Running time: 90 MINS.
Cast: Hofni Cohen, Arieh Elias, Ilan Dar, Yona Elian, Makhram Khouri, Aharon Bachar, Pnina Rosenblum, Eyal Gefen.

This cheap exploitation movie with unpleasant racist undertones is the work of several highly regarded professionals, who were evidently chasing the fast buck. Director Haim Gil is a respected tv reporter and helmer, scripter Aharon Bachar is highly quoted as a columnist in Israel's biggest paper and producer Yossi Meshulam is a tv veteran respected for his knowhow.

All of them decided that a movie about Oriental pop-singers, better known here as "cassette singers" because they peddle their music on cassettes after being rejected by the record companies, couldn't possibly fail. These singers, with an enormous following among the younger set of Oriental origins, symbolize for many the culture gap existing in the country between Jews of different origins. Their partial boycott by diskeries and radio for a certain period of time was interpreted as a rejection by the European-oriented establishment, and was used as such many times in arguments about the nature of Israel's cultural life.

The film may be dedicated to these underground singing stars, but here they are depicted as either morons, drug addicts or jerks, while the d.j. who refuses to play them, and points out their ignorance in an insulting fashion, is nothing better than a decadent and disgusting snob.

There is very little plot in a feature designed to showcase as many song performances as possible, with a belly dance or two thrown in for good measure.

Early expectations that the film's lineup of singers would become overnight successes proved too optimistic. After strong initial re-

sponse, attendance dropped sharply, for once the audience being in complete agreement with the critics. —Edna.

Makedones Zografi
(Macedonian Painters)
(GREEK-DOCU-COLOR)

Thessaloniki, Oct. 2.

A Stavros Ioannou production. Directed by Stavros Ioannou. Screenplay, Yannis Guicas, Ioannou; narrated by George Geoglaris; camera (color), George Kolozis, Nicos Charalambides, editing by Vaguelis Christoulakis, George Zarvas. Reviewed at the Thessaloniki Film Festival, Oct. 2, 1984. Running time: 70 MINS.

This is a well-made documentary screened at the Information Section of the Thessaloniki Film Festival, which should do well as a tv item here and abroad.

It features two picturesque villages in Macedonia which were booming for almost a century (1830-1930) whenever the male population earned a lot of money working abroad. Returning home quite rich they built beautiful houses using popular painters to decorate them. Most of these houses are un-occupied now because the population has gone to live in the cities, but inside the painted masterpieces are preserved. Their subjects were taken mostly from Greek mythology: the gods on Mount Olympus, The Parthenon, Aesops' fables, Alexander the Great, etc.

Stavros Ioannou and Yannis Guicas worked for two years on this film in the picturesque villages of Klissoura and Nympheon. It is well photographed by George Kolozis and Nicos Charalambides with a narration describing the life of a lost era in these places unknown even to most of the Greeks. —Rena.

Gat In De Grens
(Gap In The Border)
(DUTCH-COLOR-16m)

Amsterdam, Sept. 15.

A NFI release of an Added Films Holland production. Produced by Dirk Schreiner. Directed by Froukje Bos and Ruud Schuitemaker. Features entire cast. Screenplay, Bos, Schuitemaker and Karel Eykman, based on novel by Guus Kuijer; Camera (color, 16m), Dirk Teenstra; editor, Ot Louw. Reviewed at Film Museum, Amsterdam, Sept. 11, 1984. Running time: 90 MINS.
Cast: Daan Dillo, Marcel Kunst, Nicky Schuitemaker, Arnold Gelderman, Tamar Baruch.

"Gap In The Border," planned as an adventure story for 12 to 16 year olds by Ruud Schuitemaker and Froujke Bos, had an adventurous history. When financing could not be found for a 35m feature, Dutch tv station Ikon suggested joint financing with Berlin Station SFB. Ikon wanted a mini-series of five half hours and SFB two segments running 45 minutes each (in German). During the editing, pro-

ducer Schreiner decided also to make a theatrical version. "Gap" should have possibilities internationally for tv and theater showings aimed at the younger teenage public.

Boy number one is 15 years old, bright, mischievous, from a progressive family. The second boy stammers and has rather old-fashioned parents. The Girl, a half-caste, was abandoned as a baby by her mother. Brought up in institutions, she craves an unfettered life.

The three run away, run into each other, gang up and become friends. They are chased by the authorities.

Undaunted by watching policemen, they make an appointment to meet next year skillfully misleading their captors as to the date.

Helmers, after several successful youth pics, have made a strikingly sympathetic film devoid of sex or violence that's captivating and funny. The three protagonists, all amateurs, behave naturally and creditably. The grown-ups, mainly antagonists, are very slightly overdone, but never caricatured. —Wall.

The Terminator
(COLOR)

Powerhouse sci-fi actioner could hit paydirt.

Hollywood, Oct. 24.

An Orion Pictures release of a Hemdale production of a Pacific Western picture. Produced by Gale Anne Hurd. Executive producers, John Daly and Derek Gibson. Directed by James Cameron. Stars Arnold Schwarzenegger. Written by Cameron, Hurd; camera (CFI color; prints by Deluxe), Adam Greenberg; editor, Mark Goldblatt; sound, Richard Lightstone; art director, George Costello; set decorator, Maria Rebman Caso; music, Brad Fiedel; costume designer, Hilary Wright; stunt coordinator, Ken Fritz; special Terminator effects, Stan Winston; special visual effects, Fantasy II Film Effects; stopmotion animation, Doug Beswick; assistant director, Betsy Magruder. Reviewed at the Directors Guild of America theater, Oct. 24, 1984. (MPAA Rating: R.) Running time: 108 MINS.
Terminator . . . . Arnold Schwarzenegger
Kyle Reese . . . . Michael Biehn
Sarah Connor . . . . Linda Hamilton
Traxler . . . . Paul Winfield
Vukovich . . . . Lance Henriksen
Matt . . . . Rick Rossovich
Ginger . . . . Bess Motta
Gun salesman . . . . Dick Miller

The earmarks of a hit light up this autumn surprise.

Advance-screened only at the last second, the production is a blazing, cinematic comic book, full of virtuoso moviemaking, terrific momentum, solid performances from the three leads, and a compelling story that weds a post-nuclear future to present-day Los Angeles. Orion can't lose, particularly in light of the Hemdale production's modest budget.

From the smart decision to cast against type and make Arnold Schwarzenegger a villainous cyborg (part man, part machine) to the filmmakers' tight focus and visual flair, "The Terminator" races like the wind. A cross between "Road Warrior" and "Blade Runner," the production is sure to bolster the career of little-known director James Cameron, a former art director and makeup effects specialist who has helmed only one other film ("Piranha II — The Spawning.")

The pic should also spark the heretofore modest careers of Linda Hamilton and Michael Biehn, who play heroic characters locked in a relentless pursuit from Schwarzenegger.

The clever script, cowritten by Cameron and producer Gale Anne Hurd (who met while Roger Corman proteges at New World), opens in a post-holocaust nightmare, 2029 A.D., where brainy machines have crushed most of the human populace. From that point, Schwarzenegger as the Terminator is sent back to the present to assassinate a young woman named Sarah Connor (Linda Hamilton) who is, in the context of a soon-to-be-born son and the nuclear war to come, the mother of mankind's salvation. A human survivor in that black future (Michael Biehn), through a "time displacement center," also drops into 1984 to stop the Terminator and save the woman and the future.

Shot on L.A. locations, the film catches contemporary pop culture with quick glimpses and mixes future and present images with verve and style. Without disturbing the elements of fantasy and suspense, Cameron skillfully complements the action with understated humor. A light running gag — until the character is blown away — is actress Bess Motta as a springy, dingy romantic who is never without her rock 'n' roll headset, even when making love.

The film's only stereotype is the police, dim-minded down the line, unaccountably absent in the heat of the worst urban mayhem, and only partially redeemed by the sensible, albeit very brief, presence of Paul Winfield.

The film's music track, with three of five songs performed by Tryanglz, is never intrusive but dramatically propels events, while Adam Greenberg's lensing and Mark Goldblatt's editing make solid contributions.

A major below-the-line talent is Stan Winston, whose special Terminator effects — especially when Schwarzenegger removes an eyeball to expose the machinery and red eyeball inside his brain — are scary without being hokey.

The shotgun-wielding Schwarzenegger, who at one point is doubled by a life-sized dummy, is perfectly cast in a machine-like portrayal that requires only a few lines of dialog. "I'll be back," he tells the

police sergeant before racing his car into the station and riddling everyone in it with bullets.

As the very physical hero, Biehn, in the role originally intended for Schwarzenegger, makes a strong impression, and Hamilton effectively bridges her path from innocence to fear to heroine. — *Loyn.*

Mannen fran Mallorca
(The Man From Mallorca)
(SWEDISH-COLOR)

Malmö, Oct. 8.

An SF/Europa Film release of Drakfilm with Svensk Filmindustri, The Swedish Film Institute, Sweden's TV-2, Filmhuset and Crone Film Sales (Copenhagen) production. Written and directed by Bo Widerberg, based on Leif G.W. Persson's novel "Grisfesten" (Pork Galore). Exec producer, Göran Lindström. Camera (Eastmancolor), Thomas Wahlberg; production design, Jan Oquist; editor, Widerberg; music, Björn Lindh; costumes, Karin Sundwall; production management, Brita Werkmäster. Reviewed at the Camera, Malmö, Oct. 8, 1984. Running time: 106 MINS.

Sgt. Jarnebring . . . . Sven Wollter
Sgt. Johansson . . . . . Tomas von Brömssen
Lt. Andersson . . . . Hakon Serner
Capt. Dahlgren . . . . Ernst Günther
Berg . . . . Thomas Hellberg
Fors . . . . Ingvar Hirdvall
Lt. Rundberg . . . . Tommy Johnson
Olsson . . . . Sten Lonnert

Director Bo Widerberg, has turned Leif Persson's book entirely into his own feature film, bearing the Widerberg stamps of wry humor, jump-cut editing, flashy cinematography in general and misanthropy in matters relating to Establishment values in particular. Along with technical gloss, his "The Man From Mallorca" has a sustained level of regular suspense, and as pure thriller entertainment it should follow Widerberg's 1976 "The Man On The Roof" easily into international sales on the bigger scale.

Action is laid in a grim, greyish Yuletide Stockholm, where two lower-rank plainclothesmen pursue their own leads towards the solution of first a post office robbery, then a couple of murders that at first would seem to have no interrelation at all. But they do tie up with the nightly escapades of a Justice Minister and with latter's total corruption.

What interests Widerberg is the way the investigation is stalled by interference from high places, and how the two lowly detectives really dig into the case with all kinds of primitive surveillance & pursuit techniques.

Excellent actors follow Widerberg's direction with spirited performances, and the Dolby Stereo sound, Thomas Wahlberg's camera (as steady on target as it is lively in its asides), plus Björn Lindh's muted music all contribute to the cinematic pleasure of this film. — *Kell.*

Pedro y El Capitan
(Pedro And The Captain)
(MEXICAN-COLOR)

Mexico City, Sept. 7.

Produced by Pedro Torres Castilla and Juan E. Garcia for Cine Imagen. Directed by Juan E.Garcia; assistant director, Maripi Saenz de la Cansada; screenplay by Maripi Saenz de la Cansada adapted from the play of the same name by Mario Benedetti; camera (color), Cuco Villarias; sound, Cato and Penélope Estrada; music, Gerardo Batiz; editing, Gerda Gatterer. Performed by the Teatro El Galpón from Uruguay, in exile in Mexico. Reviewed at the Abco screening room, Mexico City, Sept. 5, 1984. Running time: 137 MINS.

Pedro . . . . Humbolt Riviero
The Captain . . . . Rubén Yañez

Remaining non-speaking roles played by members of the Teatro El Galpón de Uruguay in exile in Mexico.

During their more than 10-year exile in Mexico, the Teatro El Galpón from Uruguay had a long successful run of the two-character play "Pedro And The Captain," by fellow countryman Mario Benedetti.

Unfortunately, the movie, by Juan E. Garcia, gives us only a filmed version of the play rather than a motion picture that finds cinematographic solutions to a static situation.

The film is a valiant effort to make a well-produced and intelligent film dealing with current Latin American problems, yet it is hindered in a variety of ways. Despite the excellent acting, the film's main problem is its lack of movement, something the director tries to alleviate from time to time with visual flashbacks, superimposed images and use of the traveling camera. However, the majority of the film is spent in dialog between Pedro (Rubén Yañez), a political prisoner, and the Captain (Humbolt Riviero), who interrogates him.

In fact, the entire first reel is a monolog by the Captain, as he sets the stage and offers us exposition; Pedro, alias Romolo, is married and has one child, a son. He and four others — bearing the aliases Gabriel, Rosario, Magdalena and Fermin — are involved in a Marxist anti-government group. Pedro was arrested for his political ideals and is at present being interrogated to betray the real names of his co-conspirators. The stage is set and it is Pedro's turn to talk. He speaks and the Captain speaks and the entire drama is reduced to a polemic, which does not a good movie make.

Yet with all this discussion, we never discover the nature of Pedro's political beliefs. Rather, we have a dialog between a torturer and the tortured, the eventual physical disintegration of Pedro counterpointed by the moral disintegration of the Captain. Benedetti has stacked the deck and we do not receive a fair argument. The Captain rationalizes his role; he is civilized and

only doing his job; he is defending his country from disorder. Pedro is free because he has already accepted his fate: he is a dead man who will never be reunited with his friends and loved ones. He is pure because of his lack of compromise.

The Captain represents brute power, someone who is not only following orders but also enjoys degrading and debasing his fellow man. Many prototypes can be found in the cliché of the Latin American dictator, of Somoza and Pinochet, within former political situations in Argentina, Uruguay and Brazil.

The movie does have its values and valid themes, and should prove popular in the arena of current political films, especially with today's interest in Latin America. — *Lent.*

No Small Affair
(COLOR)

Merely okay romantic youth comedy.

Hollywood, Oct. 3.

A Columbia Pictures release of a William Sackheim/Columbia-Delphi II production. Produced by Sackheim. Executive producer, George Justin. Directed by Jerry Schatzberg. Features entire cast. Screenplay, Charles Bolt, Terence Mulcahy; story by. Bolt; camera (MGM color), Vilmos Zsigmond; editors, Priscilla Nedd, Eve Newman, Melvin Shapiro; music, Rupert Holmes; production design, Robert Boyle; art direction, Frank Richwood; set design, Craig Edgar, Mark Poll, Rogert J. Schlafle, Donald High; set decoration, Arthur Jeph Parker; costume design, Jo Ynocencio; sound (Dolby), Arthur N. Rochester; assistant director, Chuck Myers. Reviewed at the Directors Guild Theatre, L.A., Oct. 29, 1984. (MPAA Rating: R.) Running time: 102 MINS.
Charles Cummings . . . . Jon Cryer
Laura Victor . . . . Demi Moore
Jake . . . . George Wendt
Leonard . . . . Peter Frechette
Susan . . . . Elizabeth Daily
Joan Cummings . . . . Ann Wedgeworth
Ken . . . . : . . . . . . Jeffrey Tambor
Stephanie . . . . Judy Baldwin
Mona . . . . Jennifer Tilly

"No Small Affair" is an okay coming-of-age romance in which the believability of the leading characters far outweighs that of many of the situations in which the script places them. Pic and players are amiable enough, but this probably isn't sufficient to overcome lack of any overt selling points to put it across in a strong way with the public.

Film has a long production history, as the former Rastar project began lensing in March 1981, with Sally Field and Matthew Broderick in the leads and Martin Ritt directing a script by Craig Bolotin. Production shuttered in New York after about 10 days due to Ritt's exhaustion, and producer William Sackheim had to wait almost three years to get it geared back up at Columbia with Jerry Schatzberg at the helm. Sackheim is the only constant factor on the project over the years.

Present film is set in San Francisco and has Jon Cryer as a 16-year-old who's precocious in still photography, but not much else, being difficult socially and unresponsive to girls his own age.

By chance, he snaps a shot of a sharp looking gal by the waterfront and, by chance again, he finds her singing in a seedy North Beach nightspot. Pretty gone on her by this time, he convinces her to pose for some pictures and, in a selfless effort to give her sluggish career a boost, he spends his entire life savings and gets her photo placed on top of 175 S.F. taxicabs (a tip of the hat to George Cukor's "It Should Happen To You" here).

Since most of those who respond to the photo are interested in something other than her singing talents, she is initially furious with Cryer.

Ultimately, however, she is invited to L.A. by a record company and, before she leaves, the inevitable occurs.

Basic material is highly conventional, and stock situations, such as his mother's disapproval, the girl's giving in to the lad's constant badgering and her ultimate capitulation, are as predictable as turkey at Thanksgiving.

But Schatzberg and leads Cryer and Demi Moore have managed to create two very credible and sympathetic (as opposed to sitcom) characters, and that carries the film a long way. Perhaps a bit too strange at first, Cryer settles into his role very nicely and finally manages to hold his own with Moore's character, who already seems to have had more than her share of hard knocks by her early twenties. For her part, Moore is both beautiful and delightful. Both show good promise for the future.

Most of the rest of the cast is in for comic relief. Ann Wedgeworth and Jeffrey Tambor are effective as Cryer's mother and her ex-hippie b.f., while Peter Frechette and Elizabeth Daily supply strong energy as the boy's brother and latter's fiancee. George Wendt is good as the club manager with a hot-and-cold relationship with Moore.

Vilmos Zsigmond has used S.F. locations evocatively, and Rupert Holmes' score, bolstered by some 14 tunes, is mostly enjoyable. Other tech credits are fine.—*Cart.*

Daddy's Deadly Darling
(The Pigs)
(COLOR)

Vanity horror film escapes from the vaults.

An Aquarius Releasing release of a D&R presentation of a Safia S.A. production. Executive producer, Donald L. Reynolds. Produced and directed by Marc Lawrence. Features entire cast. Screenplay, "F.A. Foss" (Lawrence); camera (CFI color), Glenn Roland Jr.; editor, Irvin Goodnoff; music, Charles Bernstein; sound, Lee Alexander; set design, Boris Michael; production manager, Bill Bushnell. Reviewed at 42d St. Liberty theater, N.Y., Nov. 3, 1984. (MPAA Rating: R.) Running time: 83 MINS.
Lynn Webster . . . . Toni Lawrence
Zambrini . . . . Marc Lawrence
Sheriff Dan Cole . . . . Jesse Vint
Doctor . . . . Walter Barnes
Miss Macy . . . . Katherine Ross
. Also with: Jim Antonio, Erik Holland, Paul Hickey, Iris Korn, William Michael.

"Daddy's Deadly Darling" is an unimpressive horror film, shot in 1972 under the title "The Pigs" and previously known as "Daddy's Girl." Something of a vanity production made by character actor Marc Lawrence, pic is reviewed in its (assertedly) Gotham debut.

Tale of two psychotics teaming up has Lawrence portraying Zambrini, an ex-circus aerialist now running a remote roadside cafe. He

keeps a dozen pigs out back and kills people, feeding the corpses to his pigs, who accidentally acquired a taste for human flesh after eating a drunk one day who had fallen asleep in a nearby field.

Enter Lynn Webster (Toni Lawrence), a pretty brunet who has escaped from Camarillo state mental hospital where she was interned for having killed her father after he raped her. Zambrini hires her as a waitress and helps dispose of the bodies (fodder for his pigs) when she starts killing local guys who make romantic advances.

Goofy melodrama emphasizes horror in its amplifed soundtrack of squealing pigs and wide-angle camerawork during the murder scenes. A phony supernatural element is introduced when a frightened neighbor Miss Macy (Katherine Ross, a middle-aged thesp who is definitely not young star Katharine Ross) complains to Sheriff Cole (Jesse Vint) that Zambrini's pigs are reincarnations of dead people. The good ol' boy sheriff replies sarcastically that there's not much he can do about it, since "dead people have no civil rights at all."

Lawrence, who previously directed in 1965 the John Derek-Ursula Andress melodrama "Nightmare In The Sun," marks time here with a threadbare budget. He has Vint ask the heroine several times whether she's related to Zambrini, and indeed, a strong facial resemblance implies that star Toni Lawrence is his daughter in this vanity effort. Another dumb in-joke has the same actor play her screen father in the first reel and then reappear as a hitchhiker at film's end so she can say "you remind me of my daddy."
—*Lor.*

Just The Way You Are
(COLOR)

Romantic comedy with a social message is an unsatisfying concoction.

An MGM/UA Entertainment release of an MGM presentation of a Leo L. Fuchs production. Produced by Fuchs. Executive producer, Jerry Zeitman. Directed by Edouard Molinaro. Stars Kristy McNichol, Michael Ontkean. Screenplay, Allan Burns; camera (Eastman color; prints by Metrocolor), Claude Lecomte; editors, Claudio Ventura, Georges Klotz; music, Vladimir Cosma; sound, Daniel Brisseau; art direction, François de Lamotte; assistant directors, Robin Katz, Marc Riviere; costume design, Jean Zay; production manager, Gerard Croce. Reviewed at Loews 83d St. 1 theater, N.Y., Nov. 3, 1984. (MPAA Rating: PG.) Running time: 94 MINS.
Susan Berlanger . . . . Kristy McNichol
Peter Nichols . . . . Michael Ontkean
Lisa . . . . Kaki Hunter
Sam . . . . Robert Carradine
Jack . . . . Lance Guest
Bobbie . . . . Alexandra Paul
François . . . . Andre Dussolier
Frank . . . . Timothy Daly
Steve . . . . Patrick Cassidy
Nicole . . . . Catherine Salviat
Earl . . . . Billy Kearns

"Just The Way You Are" is a glossy MGM romantic comedy featuring a fine cast, witty dialog and gags by scripter Allan Burns but precious little in the way of a payoff to attract the paying customer. It's a shame, since pic is diverting in parts and sports a social conscience to boot.

Troubled production history (recalling an earlier MGM flop, "Brainstorm") had the film, titled "I Won't Dance," shut down midway through production (commencing Nov. 1, '82) due to a "chemical imbalance" experienced by lead player Kristy McNichol. Pic finally restarted in December 1983.

McNichol toplines as Susan Berlanger, a flautist with a ballet company orchestra in an unidentified U.S. city (actually Toronto-lensed) who is crippled, wearing a leg brace and highly self-conscious about her condition. She has a romantic fling with Sam (Robert Carradine, quite affecting in a brief, key role) who at first makes a play for her ballerina pal Lisa (Kaki Hunter, making the best with a part that calls for too many "flat chest" lines). Her gamy leg creates a problem (love vs. pity) and Susan is glad to go on a European concert tour (30 minutes into the film), fleeing both Sam and her fiance, a gayboy stock broker (Timothy Daly), in a proposed marriage of convenience.

In France, she hits upon the clever notion of putting a cast on her leg to pose as a skiing casualty, rightly figuring that for once she will be accepted as normal, at a ski resort. There she falls in love with a handsome photographer Peter (Michael Ontkean) but is reminded constantly of her deception by the presence of a one-legged (car accident) ski magnate François (Andre Dussolier) who is romancing her French roomate Nicole (Catherine Salviat). Contrived happy ending is an unconvincing letdown.

Film is wildly uneven, best in its early North American segment which includes several hilarious scenes making fun of the way society treats the handicapped (especially a pertinent one when McNichol and Hunter try waiting in line at a movie theater). Last hour in France is strong in travelog elements but weak on comedy or pathos.

Picture does serve to adequately move young star McNichol into screen adulthood, often resembling the 1969 Patty Duke classic "Me, Natalie" in both theme and format. Supporting cast is excellent, though male lead Ontkean emerges colorless after an array of tantalizing partners for McNichol's affections precede him to the batter's box. Director Edouard Molinaro (best known Stateside for helming "La Cage Aux Folles" and its sequel) maximizes the comic potential but has trouble pulling it all together. Tech credits are solid. — *Lor.*

Double Decker
(HONG KONG-COLOR)

Hong Kong, Oct. 22.

A Peter Yung Production Ltd. presentation. Directed by Peter Yung. Stars Kitty Wai, Tom Poon, Fofo Mar, Eugene Chiang, Winnie Chin, Mark Cheng. Screenplay, Fong Ling-Ching, Peter Yung; camera (color), Sander Lee; editor, Fan Kung Wing; music, Chris Babida; art direction, John Hou; associate producer, Terence Chang. Reviewed at Hong Kong Lab. preview room, Hong Kong, Oct. 20, 1984. Running time: 98 MINS.
(Cantonese soundtrack with English subtitles)

"Double Decker" is the fourth feature film of Peter Yung, a U.S. trained photographer-cinematographer and ex-student of the late James Wong Howe.

The movie centers on three young people in modern-day Hong Kong, who want to be winners but are actually born losers. Tom Poon is Jim, a handsome man with dreams of being a top fashion designer but in the meantime a careless, disco-oriented youth incapable of achieving his ambition. His wayward girlfriend of the night called Cat (Kitty Wai) is pregnant and desperate for abortion money. Completing the trio is Fatty (Fofo Mar), son of a bakery proprietor who works as a waiter in a pizza parlor and idolizes his best friend Jim. Jim, Cat and Fatty all want a better life and believe emigrating to America is the cure-all. After a disastrous attempt at the American Embassy, all their dreams dissipate and they resort to kidnaping with tragic results.

Kitty Wai sheds her ingenue image established at Shaw Brothers for a stunning one as a coarse, sensuous, easy girl in the stray cat level. The biggest disappointment though is lead star Tom Poon, a lanky model with an excellent physical stance but sadly devoid of emotive ability.
—*Mel.*

Rive Droite, Rive Gauche
(Right Bank, Left Bank)
(FRENCH-COLOR)

Paris, Nov. 2.

A Fox/Hachette release of a T. Films/Films A2 co-production. Produced by Alain Terzian. Stars Gérard Depardieu, Nathalie Baye. Directed by Philippe Labro. Screenplay, Philippe and Françoise Labro. Camera (color), Pascal Marti; music, Michel Berger; art director, Geoffroy Larcher; editor, Martine Barraque; sound, Michel Desrois; production manager, Armand Barbault. Reviewed at the Club 13, Paris, Oct.29, 1984. Running time: 105 MINS.
Paul Senanques . . . . Gérard Depardieu
Sacha Vernakis . . . . Nathalie Baye
Babée Senanques . . . . Carole Bouquet
Pervillard . . . . Bernard Fresson
Catherine . . . . Charlotte de Turkheim
Guarrigue . . . . Jacques Weber

Top-billed pairing of Gérard Depardieu and Nathalie Baye (in

their first film together since "The Return Of Martin Guerre") should guarantee solid local returns for this dull, badly-written melodrama about an ethically sobered attorney who decides to defy the crooked high finance magnate he's been defending.

A sometimes unintelligible script trots out a mass of clichés, with powerful nasty Bernard Fresson (good as the shady financier ostensibly molded on a controversial French millionaire businessman) sending a small army of goons after Depardieu, who, with partner Jacques Weber, has established one of Paris' premier law offices through moral compromise. Armed with evidence proving Fresson's criminal dealings, Depardieu taunts him before millions of viewers on a television talk forum.

Baye steps into his life as a morally upright young divorcee who loses her public relations job because she's refused to sleep with a government functionary to aid her agency in securing a big contract. She rejects Depardieu's advances because he seems to her a part of corrupt society, but she tunes in to the tv show in which Depardieu bites the hand that's been feeding him, and immediatley rushes to a *rendezvous d'amour* with the transformed lawyer. Her committtment earns her harrassment not only from Fressons' toughs but also from her lover's bitchy wife, Carole Bouquet.

Writer-director Philippe Labro, a respected veteran French newsman who's been moonlighting as a commercial filmmaker since 1969, shows a weak hand at constructing a coherent, credible story and giving a fresh aspect to stock characterizations. Dip as he may into his own personal experiences as journalist, Labro provides a glimpse into the precincts of power and money that's closer to trite movieland convention than to real life.

Depardieu and Baye apply themselves dutifully to their parts, but without inspiration or surprises. Tech credits are glossy, as befits a film that is self-consciously doused with gorgeous shots of posh Parisian sites in which the action unfolds. —*Len.*

Silent Night, Deadly Night
(COLOR)

Santa the slasher, for those who hate Christmas.

Hollywood, Oct. 31.

A Tri-Star Pictures release. Produced by Ira Richard Barmak. Executive producers, Scott J. Schneid, Dennis Whitehead. Directed by Charles E. Sellier. Features entire cast. Screenplay, Michael Hickey based on a story by Paul Caimi; camera (Metrocolor), Henning Schellerup; editor, Michael Spence; music, Perry Botkin; production designer, Dian Perryman; set decorator, Linda Kiffe, set

dresser, Jim Stoddard; sound, Rod Sutton; costumes, Verkina Flower; assistant director, Denis Stewart. Reviewed at the VIP screening room. L.A., Calif., Oct. 30, 1984. (MPAA rating: R.) Running time: 79 MINS.
Mother Superior . . . . Lilyan Chauvan
Sister Margaret . . . . Gilmer McCormick
Pamela . . . . Toni Nero
Billy at 18 . . . . Robert Brian Wilson
Mr. Sims . . . . Britt Leach
Mrs. Randall . . . . Nancy Borgenicht
Captain Richards . . . . H.E.D. Redford
Billy at 8 . . . . Danny Wagner

"Silent Night, Deadly Night" is a nasty bit of business turning the arrival of Santa Claus into a red Christmas. Pic commits the blasphemy of turning America's best loved institution into a slasher. Results are quite (unintentionally) hilarious and for those few who hate Christmas, this could be their favorite film of the season.

Young Billy's worst holiday fears are realized when his parents are murdered by a highwayman Santa Claus. As Billy grows up so does his fear of Christmas and Santa Claus.

The orphanage where he is sent becomes a hothouse for his phobia, stoked by the unloving hardness of the Mother Superior (Lilyan Chauvan). In keeping with the mood of the film, young Billy is tied to his bed for being "naughty." By the time he emerges as a young man, he is a walking textbook of guilt and rage.

All those nice feelings find a way out when Billy (Robert Brian Wilson) conveniently goes to work at a toy store and at Christmas is forced to dress as Santa Claus. At first he just scares the dickens out of the kids, but than he really catches the Christmas spirit.

What follows is a rampage of gruesomeness and gore featuring an array of decapitations including death by impaling on antelope horns.

Director Charles E. Sellier's previous credits interestingly enough include such family fare as "Grizzly Adams" and his handling of the material, such as it is, is competent. Photography by Henning Schellerup is effective in suggesting a world where Santa Claus is capable of the most heinous acts.

Production design and other technical credits are a cut above the usual cut-and-kill fare, but overall look of the film, particularly locations, is bargain basement.

(Ironically, film's distributor has a hefty investment at the opposite pole in "Santa Claus — The Movie," due for release at Christmas 1985. — *Ed.*) — *Jagr.*

Marche à l'Ombre
(Walk In The Shadow)
(FRENCH-COLOR)

Paris, Nov. 2.

A Christian Fechner/Gaumont release of a Christian Fechner/Films A2 co-production. Produced by Christian Fechner. Stars Gérard

Lanvin and Michel Blanc. Directed by Michel Blanc. Screenplay, Blanc, Patrick Dewolf; technical advisor, Dewolf; camera (color); Eduardo Serra; art director, Carlos Conti; editor, Joëlle Hache; sound, Alain Lachassagne; music, Renaud, Téléphone, La Velle, Xalam; production manager, Bernard Marescot; additional music, Jacques Delaporte. Reviewed at the Gaumont Ambassade theater, Paris, Nov. 1, 1984. Running time: 90 MINS.
Francois . . . . Gérard Lanvin
Denis . . . . Michel Blanc
Mathilde . . . . Sophie Duez

Michel Blanc, the cafe-theater comedian who has been involved in some of the most successful local film comedies as actor and writer in recent years, makes his writing-directing debut with "Marche à l'Ombre," in which he co-stars with Gérard Lanvin. Film has opened here to powerhouse attendance scores, and has even bested the new Jean-Paul Belmondo film.

Blanc's flimsy script concerns a penniless musician (Lanvin) and his tag-along buddy (Blanc) who return to Paris after knocking about Mediterranean climes. The promise of work that had lured them back turns out hollow, and the two buddies end up down-and-out in a part of town inhabited by poor African immigrants. To make ends meet they transport stolen goods, but their fence is arrested and their abode raided by police. Finally, they decide to head out for New York, where Lanvin wants to find the pretty young dancer with whom he's fallen in love.

Despite its sketch-like structure and rather sudden conclusion (possibly contrived to leave audiences hungry for a sequel), "Marche à l'Ombre" is sympathetic fluff and Blanc shows some flair in the director's chair. Central theme of friendship remains only superficially treated: Lanvin is little more than a handsome foil to Blanc's hapless schlemiel, a Gallic Woody Allen-ish runt (who nonetheless has more luck in bedding the girls).

Tech credits are good. —*Len.*

A Nightmare On Elm Street
(COLOR)

Original fright feature should score in intended market.

A New Line Cinema release, presented by New Line Cinema, Media Home Entertainment and Smart Egg Pictures. A Robert Shaye production of an Elm St. Venture picture. Produced by Shaye. Executive producers, Stanley Dudelson, Joseph Wolf; coproducer, Sara Risher. Written and directed by Wes Craven. Features entire cast. Camera (Deluxe color), Jacques Haitkin; editor, Rick Shaine; music, Charles Bernstein; sound, James La Rue; assistant director, Nick Batchelor; production manager-associate producer, John Burrows; production design, Greg Fonseca; set decoration, Anne Huntley; mechanical special effects design, Jim Doyle of Theatrical Engines; special makeup effects, David Miller; second unit camera, Henning Schellerup. Reviewed at RKO National 2 theater, N.Y., Nov. 2, 1984. (MPAA Rating: R.) Running time: 91 MINS.

Lt. Thompson	John Saxon
Marge Thompson	Ronee Blakley
Nancy Thompson	Heather Langenkamp
Tina Grey	Amanda Wyss
Rod Lane	Nick Corri
Glen Lantz	Johnny Depp
Fred Krueger	Robert Englund
Dr. King	Charles Fleischer
Sgt. Parker	Joseph Whipp
Teacher	Lin Shaye

"A Nightmare On Elm Street" is a highly imaginative horror film that provides the requisite shocks to keep fans of the genre happy. Absence of a powerful dramatic payoff will limit its breakout potential, however.

Unlike the summer release "Dreamscape," which posed a nightmare vision within a far-fetched science fiction framework, "Elm Street" relies upon supernatural horror. Young teenagers in a Los Angeles neighborhood are sharing common nightmares about being chased and killed by a disfigured bum in a slouch hat who has knives for fingernails. It turns out that years ago, the neighborhood's parents took deadly vigilante action against a child murderer, who apparently is vengefully haunting their kids.

With original special effects, the nightmares are merging into reality, as teens are killed under inexplicable circumstances, starting with Tina Grey (Amanda Wyss), found dead in her room covered with blood. An interesting story structure has her start out as the film's heroine, with friend Nancy (Heather Langenkamp) taking over after Grey is killed early on.

Writer-director Wes Craven tantalizingly merges dreams with the ensuing wakeup reality but fails to tie up his thematic threads satisfyingly at the conclusion. Atmosphere is spooky with sustained suspense and amirable special effects work on a low budget. The young cast headed by Langenkamp is uniformly effective, for once believably aproximating the look and behavior of young teens. Adult cast is strictly functional, with Robert Englund properly frightening under tons of monster makeup and Langenkamp's screen mom, Ronee Blakley, scoring in one riveting scene when she reveals the neighborhood's dark secret. —*Lor.*

Joyeuses Paques
(Happy Easter)
(FRENCH-COLOR)

Paris, Nov. 2.

An AMLF/Cerito René Chateau release of a Cerito Films/Sara Films co-production. Produced by Alain Sarde and Alain Belmondo, Directed by Georges Lautner. Stars Jean-Paul Belmondo. Screenplay, Jean Poiret, based on his play; camera (color), Edmond Sechan; music, Philippe Sarde, stunt coordinator, Rémy Julienne; editor, Michelle David; art director, Dominique André; sound, André Hervée. Reviewed at the Gaumont Ambassade theater, Paris, Nov. 2, 1984. Running time: **96 MINS.**

Stéphane Margelle	Jean-Paul Belmondo
Julie Margelle	Marie Laforêt
Sophie	Sophie Marceau
Sophie's mother	Rosy Varte
Rousseau	Michel Beaune

Jean-Paul Belmondo takes a holiday from his usual run of action pictures with this adaptation of Jean Poiret's comedy, "Happy Easter," which enjoyed a long run on the Paris stage a few years ago. Belmondo hired Poiret to write the screenplay, but unwilling to leave well enough alone, also hired stunt specialist Rémy Julienne to coordinate the quota of dangerous stunting that Belmondo's public has come to expect.

The hybrid results are grotesque, with the original stage material sabotaged by Georges Lautner's broad direction and the star's clownish performance as a philandering husband who brings home a potential teen conquest (Sophie Marceau) and desperately passes her off as his daughter of an earlier marriage when his spouse (Marie Laforêt) walks in the door.

When the talk threatens to dominate, Lautner and Belmondo air out the action with some frenzied car and speed boat shenanigans around Nice, which have absolutely nothing to do with the central situation. A long pre-credits sequence highlights Belmondo's sexual athleticism as he zips from one mistress to the next.

The waste here is all the more regrettable because, between Belmondo and Poiret, "Joyeuses Paques" could have been a diverting screen comedy, but the film star is too preoccupied with his image to adapt himself accordingly. Ironically, the pic, which had a record launch (400 prints), has fallen far short of initial industry b.o. predictions. — *Len.*

Sapar Nashim
(The Hairdresser)
(ISRAELI-COLOR)

Tel Aviv, Aug. 2.

A Shapira Films presentation of an April Films Production. Produced by Rudi Cohen and Ya'akov Lifshin. Directed by Ze'ev Revach. Stars Revach. Screenplay, Hillel Mittelpunkt, Revach; camera (color), Amnon Salomon; editor, Alain Yakobovitz; music, Ilan Mokhiakh. Reviewed at the Zafon Cinema, Tel Aviv, Aug. 1, 1984. Running time: **90 MINS.**

Cast: Ze'ev Revach, Irith Sheleg, Tikwa Aziz, Ariel Furman, Moshe Ish Kassit, Ze'ev Berlinsky, Yossi Keynan, Rita Shukrun.

"The Hairdresser" is one more product from the assembly line of Ze'ev Revach, an immensely popular comic directing his own films, whose faithful audience on the local market makes each of his films surefire. By now, he has established a basic line: he plays two or more characters in each movie, exploits facial distortions to a surfeit and

uses schematic plots that are nothing more than a pretext for him to perform his antics.

This time he plays Victor, a poor assistant janitor in a big office building, and his long-lost twin brother, Michel, who has become a highly successful, gay hair stylist. The two are reunited when Victor, while cleaning an office, stumbles upon a pile of U.S. currency and helps himself to some of it. Terrified by his own courage, he calls his twin and asks for help. The twin agrees to replace him for a short while and return the money. The comedy of errors which follows is strictly predictable.

Nobody seems to have spent too much time either writing or preparing this production and all actors do far too much, inspired probably by Revach's excesses. For local consumption none of this is considered a drawback. Abroad, chances for a similarly appreciative audience are dim. — *Edna.*

Oh, God! You Devil
(COLOR)

Okay Part III for devilish George Burns.

Hollywood, Oct. 31.

A Warner Bros. release. Produced by Robert M. Sherman. Exec producer, Irving Fein. Directed by Paul Bogart. Stars George Burns. Screenplay, Andrew Bergman; camera (Technicolor), King Baggot; supervising editor, Randy Roberts; editor, Andy Zall; sound, Richard I. Birnbaum; production design, Peter Wooley; assistant director, Peter Bogart; music, David Shire. Reviewed at the Academy of Motion Picture Arts & Sciences, Beverly Hills, Oct. 30, 1984. (MPAA rating: PG.) Running time: **96 MINS.**

Harry O. Tophet/God	George Burns
Bobby Shelton	Ted Wass
Gary Frantz	Ron Silver
Wendy Shelton	Roxanne Hart
Charlie Gray	Eugene Roche
Billy Wayne	Robert Desiderio

After two turns as an amusing Supreme Being, George Burns proves to be an equally diverting demon in "Oh, God! You Devil," which should best the business of "Oh, God! Book II" but offer no new challenge to the success of the original.

The second attempt managed only a pale reminder of the first, mainly for lack of as satisfying a story and a costar to equal John Denver. This third has some of the same faults, but fortunately not all.

Director Paul Bogart and writer Andrew Bergman certainly have improved the chances by letting Burns loose as Lucifer and relegating Burns as God to little more than a cameo. This, to be sure, is not a theological assessment, only a note that the different direction works well for Burns' personality. As a comic, he's always been a bit devilish.

Not surprisingly, Burns' demon-in-chief is hardly very evil. Though he often refers to his love of pestilence and plague, Burns seems little more than a pixie who enjoys a bit of mischief. Even at the finale. God treats him as hardly worse than a Black Sheep twin brother.

Bergman's plot is unashamedly Faustian: Struggling musian Ted Wass is desperate for the break that will bring happiness and afford parenthood for him and wife Roxanne Hart. Repeated disappointment finally provokes him to cry: yes, you guessed it, "I would sell my soul to the devil."

Speeding along between pranks in his sports car (license plate: HOT), bad Burns picks up Wass' wail and a deal is soon struck, but not without considerable misgivings by Wass. Unfortunately, at this point Bergman and Bogart begin to get too complex with their tale.

Instead of moving Wass straight ahead toward fame and fortune with all the expected problems. Burns switches him with an already reigning rock star (Robert Desiderio) whose own pact with the devil has run out. This results in Wass' becoming Desiderio but still knowing he's really Wass while Desiderio becomes Wass and inherits pregnant Hart without knowing he's really Wass.

Unhappily, the story didn't need to get this involved and it winds up constantly trying to pull the picture apart, working against the comedy. By the time Burns as God heeds Wass' plea for salvation, it's almost too much for even Him to iron out satisfactorilly.

Burns is helped here by a fine cast. In addition to Wass and Hart, there's Ron Silver with an excellent rendition of a hotshot record company executive and, at the opposite extreme of Wass' life, Eugene Roche is delightful as the hopeless agent who's originally in charge of Wass' failing career.

Special effects are kept to a minimum. —*Har.*

Ave Maria
(FRENCH-COLOR)

Paris, Oct. 29.

An AAA release of a Films Galaxie production. Produced by Irène Silberman. Features entire cast. Directed by Jacques Richard. Screenplay, Jacques Richard, Paul Gégauff. Camera (Cinemascope/Panavision, color), Dominique Brenguier; editor, Luc Barnier; art directors, Dominique Barouh, Gilles Lacombe; sound, Jean-Paul Mugel; music, Jorge Arriagada; production managers, Roland Thenot, Bernard Lorain. Reviewed at the Publicis screening room, Paris, Oct. 25, 1984. Running time: **104 MINS.**

Adolphe Eloi	Feodor Atkine
Berthe Granjeux	Anna Karina
Ursula	Isabelle Pasco
Angélique	Pascale Ogier
Constance	Dora Doll
Mathieu	Bernard Freyd

"Ave Maria" caused some pre-release scandal last month with its poster, depicting a bare-breasted girl on a cross. Church organizations got the courts to ban the photo, but they probably won't find much to get excited about in the film itself, which offers an unconvincing attack on cult fanaticism.

Script by director Jacques Richard (who previously did "Rebelote," shot like a silent film of the '20s) and veteran scripter Paul Gégauff (this was his last film before his untimely death last year) follows the progress of a defrocked priest and his rabid mistress (Feodor Atkine and Anna Karina) as they prey on the religious convictions of a gullible farmland community.

Atkine and Karina, who pompously call themselves Holy Father and Holy Mother, hoodwink the hicks into accepting them as messengers of god. They induce their following to sell their land and sink all their money into the purchase of a small chateau, where the entire cult settles.

Only obstacle to their project is the recalcitrant daughter of a farmer who has obediently taken the rap for a swindle committed previously. She taunts the community with suggestions of rapports with the devil, and her outraged religious mentors viciously beat her to death in a night-long orgy of exorcism. To cover the crime, they induce her dad to denounce himself to the police as her accidental killer.

Richard fails to recreate the hothouse morbidity and religious terror the script obviously seeks, and the crucial performances by Atkine and Karina lack brimstone and fire conviction. Bernard Freyd is no less credible as the hapless farmer who is twice beguiled by the sadistic Tartuffes.

Also in the cast is Pascale Ogier, in her last screen role before her untimely death last month at age 24. She embodies the script's purely satiric aspect as an oddball young nun who receives divine messages during her periodic trances, and officiates a "Last Supper"-like congregation in a scene ill-inspired by Luis Buñuel. It's best to remember her luminous prize-winning performance in Eric Rohmer's "Full Moon In Paris." — Len.

Athalia
(ISRAELI-COLOR)

Tel Aviv, Oct. 14.

A Noah Films presentation of a Captial Studios production. Produced by Shmuel Shilo and Omri Maron. Associate producers, Nathan Hakeini and Danny Shik. Stars Michal Bat-Adam. Directed by Akiva Teveth. Adapted by Teveth and Zwi Kertzner from a Itzhak Ben-Ner novel; Screenplay, Kertzner; camera (color), Nurith Aviv; supervising editor; Danny Shik; editor, Reuven Kornfeld; music, Nahum Heiman. Reviewed at the Haifa Film Festival, Oct. 13, 1984. Running time: 80 MINS.

Cast: Michal Bat-Adam, Yiphtach Katzur, Dan Toren, Rafael Klatchkin, Gali Ben-Ner Yossi Polak, Yair Rubin, Ruth Geller.

Akiva Teveth and Zwika Kertzner, two young filmmakers who collaborated previously on short subjects, here attempt their first feature-length film, using a novel by one of Israel's foremost authors, Itzhak Ben-Ner.

"Athalia" is the story of a 40ish widow, mother of a 17-year-old girl, and her love affair with a frustrated 18-year-old, who, because of physical limitations, has been rejected from a crack military unit. Athalia is the kind of nonconformist who wants to live her life her own way, dresses differently talks differently and behaves differently than the rest of the kibbutz, thus attracting criticism which needs only the slightest incentive in order to turn into full rejection. The love affair, interpreted as highly immoral conduct, is more than sufficient to make her a pariah who has to be thrown out of the community.

The picture's main failing is in presenting society in a kibbutz as oppressive, conservative and out of touch with reality, with no redeeming features whatsoever, defusing the main conflict of its chief interest. Also, possibly out of inexperience, Teveth has difficulty in directing his actors to react to each other and quite often, it seems, they are more conscious of the camera than they are of their partners.

Still, some of the ingredients in this film are undeniably relevant. The slow degeneration of the highly idealistic kibbutz principles are glimpsed here and there (Athalia's senile father tries to dismiss Arab field hands, since using hired help is against kibbutz credos), the clash between the emotionally liberated mother smothered by her surroundings and her conformist daughter (soulfully played by the author's daughter, Gali), the narrow-minded ideals of masculinity and the tragedy of the 1973 war.

Michal Bat-Adam looks a bit youthful for the lead, but she is most convincing as a misplaced person who defies society, and Dan Toren offers a smooth portrayal of what ideal youth is like. Yiphtach Katzur, the protagonist of the "Lemon Popsicle" series, is too weak and confused as Athalia's lover to leave any lasting impression.

Nurith Aviv's camera and Danny shik's editing are highly efficient, and the film stands out as an above-average effort. —Edna.

Ti Ehoun Na Doun Ta Matia Mou
(What My Eyes Are Going To See)
(GREEK-COLOR)

Thessaloniki, Oct. 3.

A Theodore Maranguos production. Written and directed by Maranguos. Features Vaguelis Kazan, Petros Zarkadis, Costas Tsakonas, Yannis Evdemon, Katia Alexandrou.

Camera (color), Nicos Grammaticopoulos; music, Nicos Tatsis, sets-costumes, Stamatis Tsarouhas, Angelique Marangos; editor Andreas Andreadakis, sound by Nicos Doutsias. Reviewed at the Thessaloniki Film Fest, Oct. 3, 1984. Running time: 115 MINS.

Theodore Maranguos, aiming to present the situations that are troubling the Greek people today, wrote an overloaded script resulting in a comedy which may have appeal only to local audiences.

The story is centered on four friends who had spent their early life together. After some years one returns home to settle down. His brother takes him to meet their other two friends. One had come back from Germany where he had worked for years and the other had become a lawyer.

Through the efforts of his main characters to start a business, all the troubles of modern Greek life are described: air pollution, traffic, unemployment, false promises of politicians, destruction of surplus fruit production while there are still people starving in Africa, etc. As a result the film is neither an original social reconstruction nor a moving fictional interpretation, but rather an inventory. A tighter script and a bit more trimming would have yielded a better picture. Thesping all around is very good as are all technical credits. —Rena.

Edut Me' Oness
(Forced Witness)
(ISRAELI-COLOR)

Tel Aviv, Oct. 20.

A Cannon Group presentation of a Menahem Golan-Yoram Globus production. Stars Anath Atzmon and Uri Gavrieli. Associate Producers, Isaac Kol. Directed by Raphael Rebibo. Screenplay, Rebibo and Eli Tabor based on story by Rebibo; camera (color); Maurice Fellous; editor, Alain Jacobowicz; music, Dov Seltzer. Reviewed at the Shahaf Cinema, Tel Aviv, Oct. 16, 1984. Running time: 88 MINS.

Ronit .Anath Atzmon
Gabby. . . . . .Uri Gavriel
Police Inspector . . . . .Tzadok Tzarum
Belkin . . . . .Moscu Alkalay
Betty .Irith Frank

Raphael Rebibo, an Israeli filmmaker based in Switzerland, whose first feature effort, "La Bulle," was produced there, attempts with his first effort here to draw another Kafaesque image of modern society, trapped by its own devices. If "La Bulle" described the unsuspecting private citizen as victim of state-organized law, "Forced Witness" attempts to confront him (in this case her) with the rising violence prevalent around us, which in certain circumstances may affect every aspect of our life.

This is, at least, the intention behind this plot, about a divorced ballet teacher who witnesses a rape. She intends to testify in court against the culprit but the man's brother, a ruthless hood, intervenes, hoping to dissuade her, first through bribes and, when this doesn't work,

through threats and violence. The law is quite helpless, for by its nature it is applicable only when crimes have been committed accompanied by tangible proof. The man is careful to avoid any clear violation of the rules, nevertheless exercising a reign of terror on the teacher, reflected upon her current boyfriend who would like her to give up her righteous ideas of aiding justice, on her little boy and on her ex-husband.

The trouble is that Rebibo, uses characters as so many tools, manipulating them at will, never paying much attention to them as human beings. The division between good and evil is sometimes embarrassingly clearcut, and the acting is accordingly stilted and one-dimensional.

The Hebrew title, suggesting rape, attracted a mayhem-oriented audience which did not find the expected requisites and boxoffice results were poor. Abroad, with help from Cannon distribution, it may have more of a chance to be accepted, the way Rebibo intended it, as a cry of protest against modern society. —Edna.

Blame It On The Night
(COLOR)

Great music but lousy picture.

Hollywood, Oct. 31.

A Tri-Star Pictures release. Produced and directed by Gene Taft. Exec producer, Tony Wade. Features entire cast. Screenplay, Len Jenkin; camera (Technicolor), Alex Phillips; editor, Tony Lombardo; sound, David MacMillan; production design, Ted Haworth; assistant director, Jerry Ballew; associate producer, Rhonda Rosen-Lipnicki; music, Ted Whitfield, vocals, Ted Neeley. Reviewed at Orion Screening Room, L.A., Oct. 31, 1984. (MPAA Rating: PG-13.) Running time: 85 MINS.

Chris Dalton . . . . .Nick Mancuso
Job Dalton . . . . .Byron Thames
Shelly . . . . .Leslie Ackerman
Manzini . . . . .Dick Bakalyan
Melanie . . . . .Leeyan Granger
Animal . . . . .Rex Ludwick
Charlotte . . . . .Melissa Prophet
Colonel . . . . .Sandy Kenyon
Merry Clayton . . . . .Herself
Billy Preston . . . . .Himself
Ollie E. Brown . . . . .Himself

The relationship between a rock star and the 13-year-old son he's just met is painfully awkward in "Blame It On The Night," which features terrific music but such a limited rapport between the two leads that boxoffice for Tri-Star should fall short of tuneful.

Producer/director Gene Taft and the Rolling Stones' Mick Jagger developed the story, in which the son is forced to join father Nick Mancuso on tour following the death of the boy's mother, with whom the singer had obviously enjoyed a one-night stand way back but never saw again.

Byron Thames plays Job, straight-laced kid who addresses male grownups as "sir," which is only natural because he's been residing at a military school, and his repulsion is predictable when he is thrust into the world of the rock business.

With nothing in common, there is little reason for this pair to come together and watching these diametric opposites go through their machinations in Len Jenkin's screenplay is hardly eye-opening.

"Blame It On The Night's" brightest moments are supplied by Ted Neeley ("Jesus Christ Superstar"), who sings all of Mancuso's vocals and is responsible for much of the music.

Rock fans should also enjoy seeing Merry Clayton, Billy Preston and Ollie E. Brown appearing as themselves.

The uninitiated will have to settle for the sterotypical characters on the tour, who are at least more entertaining than watching the two leads. —Klyn.

La Tête Dans Le Sac
(Led By The Nose)
(FRENCH-COLOR)

Paris, Nov. 3.

A Parafrance release of a Trinacra/P.P.I./Films A2 coproduction. Produced by Yves Rousset-Rouard. Executive producer, Denis Mermet. Directed by Gérard Lauzier. Stars Guy Marchand. Screenplay, Gérard Lauzier, Edouard Molinaro; camera (color), Gérard De Battista; art direction, Serge Douy, Régis des Plas; editor, Georges Klotz; sound, Bernard Aubouy; music, Vladimir Cosma; production manager, Philippe Schwartz; associate producers, Roland Gritti, Serge Lebeau. Reviewed at the Marignan-Concorde theater, Paris, Nov. 2, 1984. Running time: 90 MINS.

Romain	Guy Marchand
Véra	Marisa Berenson
Eva	Fanny Bastien
Dany	Patrick Bruel
Patrick	Riton Liebman
Dr. Choulet	Jacques François
Said	Said Amadis
Sonia	Agnès Garreau
Malika	Christiane Jean

Gérard Lauzier, the cartoon satirist who began screenwriting in 1980 and recently turned to directing, provides a caustic portrait of white collar self-satisfaction in "La Tête Dans le Sac," his third film as writer-helmer. Lauzier is one of the few local comic strip talents who has been relatively successful in transposing his storyboard universe to the screen.

As in his previous film, "P'tit Con" (a commercial failure), the trump element of this new comedy is actor Guy Marchand. Thesp brings superb comic ability to the characterization of a smug, self-made businessman, undone by the sexual and professional vampirism of the younger generation. He has just turned 50 as the film opens and is "feeling fine." He has survived three marriages, has a beautiful mistress (Marisa Berenson) whom he keeps at a distance, runs a highly successful advertising agency and lives in posh bachelor comfort.

His preening self-confidence both on the job and in bed, hits a snag when long-toothed youth comes knocking at the door. Sexually assured, Marchand picks up and romances a pretty teen (Fanny Bastienne), who drags the snob into a social whirl of gay discothèques and drug parties, only to learn he's been had by a no-less contemptuous youth crowd. The young parvenu son of a friend whom he's taken on at the office not only walks off with his best collaborators to start his own agency, but also beds his mistress.

Lauzier's unrelenting misanthropy is still marred by some facile caricature (notably in his treatment of homosexual characters), but the overweening central role, faultlessly fleshed out by Marchand, brings out the best of the satirist's cynical penchant. Lauzier shows assurance in the director's seat and gets what he wants from the supporting cast, and the tech credits are polished. —Len.

Behind The Yellow Line
(HONG KONG-COLOR)

Hong Kong, Oct. 10.

A Shaw Brothers Presentation and Release. Produced by Sir Run Run Shaw. Directed by Hung Tai-Lai. Executive producer, Mona Fong. Stars Leslie Chung and Maggie Cheung. Title music track performed by Leslie Chung. (No other credits provided by producers.) Reviewed at Jade Theater, Hong Kong, Oct. 9, 1984. Running time: 98 MINS.

Fumbling and accident-prone Leslie Chung is on his way to work and bumps into lovely Maggie Cheung on the subway. From this trivial beginning, a series of unstructured, undisciplined and mostly unrelated sequences are strung together loosely to form a senseless romantic comedy with music. Chung later is pursued by a persistent rich, but extremely coarse heiress who fancies him while Cheung is being re-courted by her ex-lover with new proposals and flowers.

In "Behind The Yellow Line," the characters portrayed are definitely from Yuppieland as they roam aimlessly in fancy restaurants, swimming pools, tourist sights, well-appointed villas and other local middle class status symbols.

The cast behaves like poseurs rather than actors. Chung is a handsome-looking "teenager" at 29 who's also a recording star while Cheung's only current claim to fame is being a beauty pageant finalist.

The soundtrack is full of Cantonese pop songs and the visuals look very much like a music video. The possibilities of incorporating modern morality with love in a modern underground railway system simply went to waste. Neverthe-

less, the mixed-up ingredients are covered up by the glossy packaging and could mean another boxoffice hit for Shaw Brothers, with the patronage of the youth market. —Mel.

Nekatomeni Aeries
(Agitated Winds)
(CYPRIOT-COLOR)

Thessaloniki, Oct. 6.

A film of Council of Motion Pictures Productions. Written and directed by Yannis Ioannou. Features Kleoniki Zografou, Fatma Mehmet, Costas Heralambides Pieris Pieretis, Michalis Poulos, Liza Tsagaridou. Camera (color), Andras Gerö, Jan Borbely; music, George Spanos, Pieris Pieretis, Costas Haralambides; editing by Judit Köllany, George Katsouris; sound, Dinos Kitou, Bella Ivanfy. Reviewed at the Thessaloniki Film Festival, Oct. 6, 1984. Running time: 110 MINS.

This is a moving, well-made film based on true facts about the drama of Cyprus. Though it will do well at home it is doubtful if it will have any theatrical chance a abroad except for tv programs.

Two women are the main characters of the story, a Greek, Kleoniki Zografou and a Turk, Fatma Mehmet, who play themselves. They meet at Fatma's house and start talking, each one narrating incidents of her life.

In between their narration about their troubles, two musicians are shown riding on a cart to reach the village to attend a wedding. The bride is ready as are the groom and their families, but the wedding never takes place. The village is deserted and the houses destroyed.

It is a village where Greeks and Turks were living peacefully before and now only the two women stay there refusing to leave. Each narrates with simple words and in her own dialect the dramatic events, the misery and the troubles they had gone through with the rest of the population.

Production by Yannis Ioannou is a chronicle of the recent history of Cyprus. His aim is, perhaps, to convey the message that Greeks and Turks were living peacefully together, but alien factors had created their misery and provoked the catastrophe of their once-peaceful life.

The picture has excellent photography by Hungarians Andras Gerö and Jan Borbely. The musical background of original folklore songs and music is provided by George Spanos, Pieris Pieretis and Costas Haralambides.

All other technical credits are above standard. —Rena.

Shanghai Blues
(HONG KONG-COLOR)

Hong Kong, Oct. 9.

A Film Workshop Co. Ltd. Production, released by Golden Princess. Directed by Tsui Hark. Stars Kenny Bee, Sylvia Zhang, Sally Yeh. Story by Tsui Hark. (No other credits provided by producers.) Reviewed at President Theater, Hong Kong, Oct. 9, 1984. Running time: 98 MINS.
(Cantonese soundtrack with English subtitles)

The year is 1937: Kenny Bee and Sylvia Zhang meet under the Soochow Bridge during the bombing of Shanghai by Japanese planes. In the dark, the couple experience immediate mutual attraction and vow to meet again when the war is over, under the same bridge.

It is now 1947: Bee is a clown, musician and songwriter while Zhang has a hard as nails exterior but with a heart of gold. She works as a showbiz performer in a popular night club. Sally Yeh enters the picture, an innocent young girl looking for relatives in the city. The lives of the three get intermixed. There are misunderstandings, minor emotional complications, recriminations but true love wins in the end.

In "Shanghai Blues," Tsui Hark has created a good mixture of Cantonese pop comedy, sentimental romance and slapstick humor, laced with music, satire, and good taste.

All the lead performers are pleasant and act with verve, briskness and enthusiasm. Kenny Bee is vulnerably charming and Sylvia Zhang wonderfully inventive, while Sally Yeh does her Goldie Hawn imitation rather well.

Discriminating locals and foreign viewers seeking quality Hong Kong fun entertainment won't be disappointed. "Shanghai Blues" title refers to a song composed by Do-Re-Mi, Bee's name in the film.
—Mel.

The River
(COLOR)

Limited prospects for remote rural drama.

Hollywood, Nov. 7.

A Universal Pictures release of an Edward Lewis production. Produced by Lewis, Robert Cortes. Directed by Mark Rydell. Stars Mel Gibson, Sissy Spacek. Screenplay, Robert Dillon, Julian Barry, based on a story by Dillon; camera (Technicolor), Vilmos Zsigmond; editor, Sidney Levin; music, John Williams; production design, Charles Rosen; art director, Norman Newberry; set decorator, Jane Bogart; sound, David Ronne; costumes, Joe I. Tompkins; special effects, Ken Pepiot, Stan Parks; assistant director, Jerry Ziesmer. Reviewed at the Alfred Hitchcock Theatre, Universal City, Calif., Nov. 7, 1984. (MPAA Rating: PG-13). Running time: **122 MINS.**

Tom Garvey	Mel Gibson
Mae Garvey	Sissy Spacek
Lewis Garvey	Shane Bailey
Beth Garvey	Becky Jo Lynch
Joe Wade	Scott Glenn
Senator Neiswinder	Don Hood
Harve Stanley	Billy Green Bush
Howard Simpson	James Tolkan
Hal Richardson	Bob W. Douglas

The last of a trio of recent films to examine the hardships of rural life, "The River" puts fundamental American values to the test in a society that has come unglued. Stripped down to the bare essentials few people actually ever come into contact with, pic remains a rather private ordeal observed from the outside looking in.

There is a victory at the end, but not a sense of lasting triumph. While "The River" offers many fine moments and several strong performances, pic's failure to strike a universal chord or uncover new ground will limit its appeal at the boxoffice.

"The River" gets off to a good start with a series of immaculately constructed, self-contained scenes, each carrying its own dramatic punch. The characters are introduced — the hard-headed head of the household, Tom Garvey (Mel Gibson), his wife Mae (Sissy Spacek) and their two children (Shane Bailey and Becky Jo Lynch) — and their environment defined.

Setting the tone is the Garvey family battling the flood waters of the river to save their farm. Other problems include declining profits and overextended credit that force the farmers to sell off their land with hungry wolf businessman Joe Wade (Scott Glenn) waiting to pick up the pieces.

Screenwriters Robert Dillon and Julian Barry introduce all the traditional elements into the picture and attempt to come up with a coherent portrait of the life and times of working class rural America. Difficulty comes in trying to integrate the private lives of the Garvey family with the shared destinies of the community.

At the center of the action is the painfully proud and private Gibson who is basically too unemotional to hold the film together. He is a character without passion and the film suffers because of it. Director Mark Rydell has an obvious admiration and affection for his characters, but these people seem too much the construction of a liberal's imagination looking on in awe.

Picture takes an unexpected turn when financial pressures force Gibson to unceremoniously seek employment as a scab at a factory in a distant town. Cross-cutting and sound editing between factory and farm are meant to heighten Gibson's growing sense of community and the disharmony plaguing society.

Production designer Charles Rosen achieves a gritty realism, especially in the factory scenes, which accurately represents an America where neighbors are pitted against neighbors and society is unresponsive to their needs.

Glenn, as the silver-spoon kid and Spacek's former lover, is the film's most complex creation. Though he is the malignancy behind much of the farmers' troubles, Rydell allows him to maintain a level of humanity. Glenn succeeds at getting inside the skin of the character in a beautiful and sensitive performance.

At the heart of the film, of course, is the Garvey family and there are several lovely scenes, particularly with the children. As the son following in his father's footsteps, Shane Bailey captures the man inside the boy. However, many of the family scenes, looking for the big payoff, fall flat and are without the emotion implied. Love seems to be somehow linked with the weather and clinches are invariably framed by a flaming sunset.

"The River" offers a kind of constructed realism, something created to make a point, without capturing the natural dynamics of real life. Contributing to this effect is the hopelessly overstated score by John Williams which attempts to wring as much emotion as possible from every scene and bludgeons every emotional nuance.

On the plus side is Spacek who seems most at home with her role and is one of the few performers who can look graceful in heavy raingear up to her waist in mud.

As always, Vilmos Zsigmond's photography is a joy to watch with the incidental details, the faces, and the sets in the background sometimes overshadowing the action going on in the foreground.—*Jagr.*

Die Rückkehr Der Zeitmaschine
(The Return Of The Time Machine)
(WEST GERMAN-COLOR)

Berlin, Oct. 22.

A Telefilm Saar Film Production for Saarländischer Rundfunk, Saarbrücken. Producer, Ulrich Nagel. Directed by Jürgen Klauss. Features entire cast. Screenplay, Günter Kunert; camera (color), Michael Faust; sets, Friedhelm Beohem; sound, Werner Maier, Kurt Schubert; editor, Monika Solzbacher; production manager, Hans-Jürgen Niebuhr. Reviewed at ARD Screening Room, Berlin, Oct. 22, 1984. Running time: **116 MINS.**

With: Klaus Schwarzkopf (Dr. Beilowski), Peter Pasetti (Dr. Risolani), Siegfried Wischnewski (Prof. Danzke), Frank Hoffmann (Engineer Pfeil), Jan Nygren (Morges), Nicolas Lansky (Wernesberger), Brigitte Dryander (Amanda).

Jürgen Klauss' "Return Of The Time Machine" is based on original material penned by former East German (now settled in West Germany) poet and writer Günter Kunert. As the title hints, there's a touch of H.G. Wells in the story.

An H.G. Wells buff, Dr. Erasmus Beilowski who is an internal medicine physician, happens on a strange-looking machine in the backroom of an antique-handler, which he immediately recognizes as identical to the one described in the novel "The Time Machine." The period is 1925, long before space travel, so there's a lot of elbow room here for spoofing.

The fantasy-crazed doc calls all his cronies over one evening to talk about setting the time machine in motion. The group hits upon the plan to send a pecunious factory assistant off into the future.

The victim, a shy individual named Wernesberger, doesn't know at first what he's getting into. Then he realizes that a miscalculation in the device might leave him stranded in the future, and decides to chicken out at the last minute.

"The Return of The Time Machine" is too claustrophic in text and images. Just about everyone in the cast is a prominent tv thesp locked into stereotyped performances. —*Holl.*

Highpoint
(CANADIAN-COLOR)

Winnipeg, Oct. 27.

A New World Pictures release; Highpoint Film production. Produced by Daniel Fine. Executive producers, William Immerman and Jerry Pam. Directed by Peter Carter. Screenplay by Richard Guttman and Ian Sutherland. Camera (Eastman color), Albert Dunk; editor, Eric Wraite; art direction, Seamus Flannery; music, John Addison; stunt coordinator, Carey Loftin. Reviewed on videocassette, Winnipeg, Oct. 27. Running time: **88 MINS.**

Louis Kinney	Richard Harris
James Hatcher	Christopher Plummer
Lise Hatcher	Beverly D'Angelo
Rachel Hatcher	Kate Reid
Don Maranzella	Peter Donat
Banner	Robin Gammell
Centino	Saul Rubinek
Falco	Maury Chaykin
Alex	George Buza
Rich Customer	Ken James

Filmed in the fall of 1979, the tongue-in-cheek Canadian thriller "Highpoint" is unlikely to cause much stir with its recent regional release in the U.S. Certainly no one associated with the production can point to the title with conviction. It actually refers to the film's climactic clash atop Toronto's CN Tower.

The story begins with a frenzy as some bit of chicanery puts both the mafia and CIA on the tail of James Hatcher (Christopher Plummer), an industrialist. He's double-crossed both parties and proceeds to fake his demise and lay low with the loot.

For no apparent reason Louis Kinney (Richard Harris), an out-of-work accountant (possibly from bad movie deals), appears on the scene and through a quirk of fate becomes the bodyguard of Hatcher's sister Lise (Beverly D'Angelo) and invalid mother (Kate Reid).

The tone is intended to be droll with Harris cheerfully providing glib commentary on the soundtrack. As the story evolves, Hatcher's ploy becomes known by both the hoods and cops. He has apparently ferreted away $10,000,000 by pitting the two groups against each other. He also manages to make it appear that Kinney is a murderer, forcing the Brit to seek him out and clear his name.

With the constant go-round of pursuits and narrow escapes, the film is ideal for screenings on merry-go-rounds. Otherwise, it's largely a waste of some normally talented support people including Saul Rubinek and Maury Chaykin as hit men who are supposed to be funny and Peter Donat and Robin Gammell as the goony ganglord and CIA chief.

Picture is somewhat reminiscent of an earlier Harris effort, "99 & 44/100% Dead," and shows every sign of exceeding the earlier film's limited appeal. Reviewed for the record, don't stay home when this production turns up on paycable.—*Klad.*

White Elephant
(BRITISH-COLOR)

Wels, Austria, Oct. 19.

A Worlddc Production, London. Produced, conceived, and directed by Werner Grusch. Screenplay, Grusch, Ashley Pharoah; camera (color), Tom D. Hurwitz; music. Handel, African Brothers, Franco, Tabu Ley; editor, Thomas Schwalm; sound, Diana Ruston. Reviewed at Austrian Film Fest, Wels, Oct. 18, 1984. Running time: **99 MINS.**

With: Peter Firth (Peter Davidson), Abi Adatsi, Kwabena Holm, Owusu Akyeaw, Surfo Opoku, Toni Darko, Nana Abiri, Otchere Darko, Charles Annan, Klevor Abo, Samuel Amoah, Peter Sarpong (Bishop of Kumasi), Nana Seowg (High Priestess), Ejissu Jasantua (Fetish Priest), High Priest of Lake Bosomtwe, Frederick Lawluwi (Reverend in Anloga), A.N.K. Mensah (Herbalist in Anloga), People's Defence Committee (Anloga), Asugebe and Jasantua (Patron Ghosts of Ejissu Fetish-Priest School).

"White Elephant" was unspooled at the Austrian Film Fest in Wels because its director, Werner Grusch, is an Austrian and elected to present his low-budget feature there due to some support he received on the project from Austrian television. Pic was lensed entirely in English and was shot on location in Ghana.

"White Elephant" has a familiar theme: a young, fast-talking business technocrat arrives on the scene in a white Mercedes to bring change and riches (for the few) to black Africa — but it's he who is eventually seduced by the virgin paradise and finds himself in the end so disoriented that he is even willing to rethink his values.

A British engineering firm sends a successful young arm-twister (Peter Firth) to Ghana to convince the politicos there of the benefits of modernizing Ghana via the wonders of the microchip. Firth wants the Ghanians to discard their medieval living-and-working habits by establishing a fully automated plastic furniture factory, and since the initial bribes with the black leaders seem to be accepted, it's only a question now of "selling" the project to the local population. But here's the rub: the locals don't want the factory, for it upsets a whole way of life. The carpentry union works on a cooperative basis, so stuffing the pockets of the elite backfires in the end. That's not all: the fetish priests place a curse on Firth for even trying to contaminate a holy lake with factory waste.

All this leads up to a Robinson Crusoe ending. The juju-men have won for the time being — but it surely won't be long before another cock-and-bull technocrat happens upon the scene, and this time he just might be a black man in a black Mercedes. — *Holl.*

Kärntner Heimatfilm
(A "Heimatfilm" In Kärnten)
(AUSTRIAN-DOCU-COLOR-16m)

Wels, Austria, Oct. 22.
An Extrafilm Production, Vienna, in collaboration with the Federal Ministry for Education and Art, Vienna, and Radiotelevizije Ljubljana (Yugoslavia). A Documentary written and directed by Rudi Palla. Camera (color), Franz Schoys, Gerd Broser; editor, Henriette Fischer. With Janko Messner. Reviewed at Austrian Film Fest, Wels, Oct. 21, 1984. Running time: **80 MINS.**

A German or Austrian or Swiss-German "Heimatfilm" generally refers to a mountain-greenery romantic love story with comic and folk elements, a genre that was very popular among moviegoers shortly after World War II. In this case, however, the term is used ironically, for the documentary features a noted Austrian-Slovenian writer living in the southern Kärnten section of Austria (bordering the Yugoslav republic of Slovenia) who is proficient in both languages and cultures. This writer and resistance-fighter, Janko Messner, recounts the history of the Slovenian minority in Austria dating back to the aftermath of

the First World War, and he does so with wit and sarcasm, anger and belligerence.

Helmer Rudi Palla is a veteran cameraman and documentarist. For "Kärntner Heimatfilm" his subject is the Slovenes living across the border from Yugoslavia .

Janko Messner recounts the ups and downs of the Slovenes in Kärnten, laying important emphasis on the rights of minorities to resist assimilation, particularly when the overall loss is an identity and a culture with a rich tradition and literary heritage.

More than an ethnographic treatise, "Kärntner Heimatfilm" scores as a relevant social and political document as well — due largely to Messner's own place in Austrian and Slovenin history, arts and letters.
—*Holl.*

Lust In The Dust
(COLOR)

Bright prospects for funny oater.

Hollywood, Nov. 10.
A Fox Run production. Produced by Allan Glaser, Tab Hunter. Executive producers, James C. Katz, Robert Raymond. Directed by Paul Bartel. Stars Hunter, Divine. Screenplay, Philip Taylor; camera (CFI color), Paul Lohmann; editor, Alan Toomayan; music, Peter Matz; songs, Karen Hart; art direction, Walter Pickette; set decoration, Margot Kilbey, Al Eisenman; costume design, Dona Granata; sound, Frank Meadows; assistant director, Michael Schroeder; second unit camera, Leo Napolitano. Reviewed at the Granada Theatre, Santa Barbara, Nov. 10, 1984. (MPAA Rating: R.) Running time: **87 MINS.**
Abel Wood . . . . Tab Hunter
Rosie Velez . . . . Divine
Marguerita Ventura . . . . Lainie Kazan
Hard Case Williams . . . . . . Geoffrey Lewis
Bernardo . . . . Henry Silva
Father Garcia . . . . Cesar Romero
Nifa . . . . Gina Gallego
Big Ed . . . . Nedra Volz
Red Dick Barker . . . . Courtney Gains
Black Man . . . . Woody Strode
Mexican . . . . Pedro Gonzalez-Gonzalez
Clarence . . . . Daniel Firshman
Chang . . . . Ernie Shinagawa

As its title would indicate, "Lust In The Dust" is a saucy, irreverent, quite funny send-up of the Western, that recently moribund genre the industry is just now beginning to remember. Despite the dominant presence of cult star Divine and his/her repairing with Tab Hunter after their excursion in "Polyester," film's broad humor and accessible, basically uncampy tone create the possibility of a more general audience for this one. Caught at an advertised preview in Santa Barbara, pic should probably be opened in well-chosen, limited multiples in major cities, then be taken wider in relatively short order.

Shot independently in New Mexico last spring, film takes some of the old-time Western conventions

— the silent stranger, the saloon singer with a past, the motley crew of crazed gunslingers, the missing stash of gold — and stands them on their head with outrageous comedy and imaginative casting.

Prevailing attitude is established immediately via some florid narration and the sight of the outsized Divine making his way across the desert in full drag on a donkey. Upon meeting Hunter, the epitome of the straight-arrow hero of few words, Divine's character, Rosie, explains to him, in flashback, she's just been gang-raped by Geoffrey Lewis' bunch of Third World outlaws (and outlasted them all).

Duo arrives in the squalid little town of Chili Verde, where the entire populace seems to hang out at the cantina of Lainie Kazan, a boisterous, vulgar woman of the world who bears a suspicious resemblance to Divine.

It doesn't take too long to figure out that none of these people would be lingering in this God-forsaken outpost if it weren't for the gold said to be buried somewhere nearby. Middle stretch of the picture largely consists of some hilarious bedroom farce, main motivation for which is the fact that the map disclosing whereabouts of the treasure is tattooed on the derrières of Divine and Kazan, half on one cheek of each one. Whoever gets them together and matches up the two halves first will have a head start for the gold.

Outrageous tale penned by Philip Taylor is handled with fine high humor by director Paul Bartel, who smartly has pitched the comedy away from the limiting traps of campy inside jokes and towards the realm of the traditional (but very knowing) sex face.

In this, he has been aided by an expert cast led by Divine. Picture is Divine's for the taking, and take it he does with a vibrant, inventive comic performance. Divine's naughty, sugestive reactions are often riotous, and his eyes prove constantly alive and expressive on camera. Coproducer Hunter need do little but imitate Clint Eastwood's muffled, Man With No Name line readings and he does this efficiently, while Kazan matches Divine wisecrack for wisecrack and, in the inevitable barroom catfight, punch for punch, in a deliciously salacious turn.

Geoffrey Lewis scores strongly as the bad guy who quotes, and misquotes, the Bible and classical literature, Henry Silva and Cesar Romero have their moments as a gunfighter and priest, respectively, Nedra Volz is sweet as an over-the-hill bargirl, and Gina Gallego is wildly sexy as Kazan's main prostie.

Pic could perhaps have used more visual humor in the way of in-

ventive compositions and pictorial jokes, given the setting, but plenty of unexpected humor derives from Karen Hart's clever songs, belted by both Divine and Kazan. Dona Granata's costumes, are noticeably on the money, and editor Alan Toomayan astutely brought pic in at under 90 minutes.—*Cart.*

Gemini Affair — A Diary
(COLOR)

Cliched Hollywood non-success story.

A Matt Cimber production; a Gemini Affair-Moonstone picture. Produced and directed by Cimber. Screenplay, Harry Houydydu; camera (Movielab color), Colin Campbell; editor, Mark Michaels; music, Herschel Burke Gilbert; sound, Dick Pittstick; assistant director, Jeff Richard; production supervisor, Bethel Buckalew; art direction, Talie Cochrane. Reviewed on Unicorn Video cassette, N.Y., Oct. 17, 1984. (No MPAA Rating.) Running time: **93 MINS.**
Julie . . . . Marta Kristen
Jessica . . . . Kathy Kersh
Agnes Wilson . . . . Anne Seymour
Woody . . . . Rudy Durand
Bob . . . . John Hart

"Gemini Affair — A Diary" is emblematic of a recent phenomenon, unreleased feature films finally surfacing for the homevideo market. Shot in 1973, pic is a mildly interesting but woefully underproduced drama about young women "making it" in Hollywood and is reviewed here for the record.

Marta Kristen and Kathy Kersh, both good-looking blonds stuck in a near-sex film format which would probably get a soft X rating if submitted, topline as two girls from Indiana now in Los Angeles. Jessica (Kersh) has become a high-priced callgirl, while newly arrived Julie (Kristen) is an aspiring actress in town for her first screen test. Both have a warring relationship with the housekeeper (played by vet character actress Anne Seymour), taking care of a lavish mansion where Jessica lives as a "kept woman."

Producer-director Matt Cimber, more famous for his star vehicles for late wife Jayne Mansfield, Pia Zadora and latterly Laurene Landon, errs in rooting almost the entire film at the mansion, giving a claustrophobic (read: cheap) effect. The heroines talk about casting sessions and going out for tricks, but nothing is staged. After Julie unsuccessfully tries out prostitution, there is a rather tamely handled lesbian subplot between the two women, leading to an open ending implying each person has to find and be herself.

Gauche and smutty dialog (credited to a writer with the phony-sounding name of "Harry Houydydu") has Kersh swearing enough to qualify for Brian DePalma's recent "Scarface" remake. Acting and technical credits are okay, with "Gemini" containing one outstanding sequence in its latter half when Marta Kristen recalls an erotic incident of years ago, shot outside at night in one continuous take. This scene works in the same way as Bibi Andersson's erotic monolog in Ingmar Bergman's classic "Persona," and is almost strong enough to justify one's perusal of this minor failure.—*Lor.*

Magic Moments
(ITALIAN-COLOR)

Rome, Nov. 4.

A C.I.D.I.F. release. Produced by Gianfranco Piccioli and Gianni Stucchi for Hera International and RAI-TV Channel 3. Directed by Luciano Odorisio. Stars Stefania Sandrelli. Screenplay, Odorisio and Gaetano Stucchi; camera (color), Carlo Cerchio; editor, Sergio Montanari; art director, Elena Ricci Poccetto; music, Matia Bazar. Reviewed at Quirinale Cinema, Rome, Nov. 2, 1984. Running time: **110 MINS.**

Francesca	Stefania Sandrelli
Bo	Sergio Castellitto
Ben	Fabio Traversa

An offbeat, bittersweet comedy-cum-love story, "Magic Moments" has regrettably few of the things advertised in the title. As a gentle spoof on the movie nostalgia craze, it doesn't quite work, either. Helmer Luciano Odorisio's career got off to a flying start with prize-winning dramas "Authorized Educator" and "Chopin" (latter titled "Dear Maestro" in its U.S. release), and he would have done better to avoid this swim in the elusive Italo comedy market, young film author division, which works on other principles entirely.

For a start, lack of a strong male lead is keenly felt. While Stefania Sandrelli may draw initial fan interest, she can't carry the whole weight of the film on her chicly jacketed shoulders. Star quality makes her pic's center of interest, though her character, a tough tv director, isn't treated very sympathetically.

Sergio Castellitto plays Bo, the hapless hero, an aspiring script-writer emasculated by chronic unemployment and a writer's block. A misfired romance starts when Bo and Francesca (Sandrelli) cross paths. He gets starry-eyed at once; she, the cool professional, has a fling and forgets him.

Years later the pair meets again — and recouple fleetingly amid Bo's melancholy memories of "the way we were."

The hero is a pathetically nice guy, but it's obvious from the start he isn't right for restless, high-powered Francesca. Pic tapers off into grotesque sentimentality at the end when he looks up his old buddies and finds they're all disgraceful sell-outs. Practically turned out of the house by the woman he loves and torn from the child he thinks is his,

Bo can at least console himself with moral superiority.

Odorisio is good at capturing a feeling of superficial lives and loves, aided by Carlo Cerchio's moody, eye-catching camerawork and Elena Ricci Poccetto's sets. Fabio Traversa is a plus as a would-be producer who ends up running a cinemabilia boutique. — *Yung.*

Ich Oder Du
(I Or You)
(AUSTRIAN-COLOR)

Wels, Austria, Oct. 16.

A Dieter Berner and Hermann Wolf Production for Satel Film, Vienna, in collaboration with Austrian Television (ORF). Directed by Berner. Screenplay, Peter Mazzuchelli, Berner; camera (color), Wlater Kindler; editor, Ingrid Koller; music, Thomas Rabitsch, Hansi Lang. Reviewed at Austrian Film Fest, Wels, Oct. 16, 1984. Running time: **93 MINS.**
With: Hansi Lang, Beate Finckh, Karl Kröpfl, Hilde Berger, Wolfgang Ambros, Bobby Prem.

Dieter Berner's "I Or You," which received it preem at the Austrian Film Fest in Wels, is a tale of a gal and two guys, the girl played by the talented Beate Finckh and in much the same role as she had in Vadim Glowna's German pic "Desperado City" (1981).

Finckh is stuck on the rock singer, Hansi Lang (who also composed a share of the film's music, including the title song), but he's an irresponsible and spaced-out type. Then she meets a lad from the country, and becomes stuck on him — which upsets the rock singer. The conflict mounts to a showdown, and there is an idyllic moment when the true lovers try to make a go of it alone out in a country shack in a snowed-in landscape.

The twist comes when a pistol takes the place of fists and becomes the instrument of crime, despite the girl's efforts to keep both of her beaux on the straight and narrow. The ending (and much of the story) seems to be improvised patchwork, but pic drew a strong following at Wels among the younger crowd. — *Holl.*

Ake og hans värld
(Ake And His World)
(SWEDISH-COLOR)

Malmö, Nov. 7.

A Sandrews Film & Teater AB release of Sandrews Film & Teater AB with the Swedish Film Institute and Scentext AB production. Written and directed by Allan Edwall, based on novel by Bertil Malmberg. Camera (Eastmancolor), Jörgen Persson; production design, Anna Asp; costumes, Gertie Lindgren; music, Thomas Lindahl; editor, Lars Hagström, production management, Brita Werkmäster. Reviewed at Sandrews 1-2-3, Malmö, Nov. 7, 1984. Running time: **103 MINS.**

Ake	Martin Lindström
His father	Loa Falkman
His mother	Gunnel Fred
His sister	Katja Blomquist
His Grandmother	Ulla Sjöblom
Anne-Marie	Suzanne Ernrup
Bergström	Björn Gustafson
Ebenholtz/ murderer's son	Stellan Skarsgard
Kalle Nubb	Alexander Skargard
School principal	Allan Edwall
Sleeping girl	Anna Bergman

Ake (pronounced "O-keh") of actor-writer-director Allan Edwall's big-scale feature "Ake And His World" lives in a small Swedish 1930 community. He is the six year old son of loving parents, protected on all sides except for the phantoms of his childhood imagination. A pair of shoes protruding from under a cupboard has him run crying to his mother to tell excitedly about "a real-life monster."

Some of the adults in Ake's village are really grotesques that would scare anybody. There is a pretty young woman who in fits of madness in the midst of winter climbs trees and strips and accuses Ake of being The Devil. There is also Ebenholtz, a recluse, who occasionally comes out of his shadows to talk about his murderer-father while he himself does his level best to look like Boris Karloff on an off-day.

Ake is as shy as he is imaginative. He is also an honest little soul, and if he ever does anybody a bad turn or indulges in cowardice, he soon overcomes, if not his fears, at least his shortcomings in displays of subdued bravery.

Martin Lindström is well-chosen for this difficult role: never brash, never shrill, always pensive and muted, but beautifully alive in every shade of expression.

Allan Edwall, who played the dying theater manager in Ingmar Bergman's "Fanny & Alexander," takes a cameo role in his own film. The careful designing, crafting and directing of this childhood memoir, based on a 1924 novel by Bertil Malmberg, has otherwise kept him busy enough. Against the odds of having only snippets of dramatic narrative to work from, he has succeeded in evoking not only the small frights and pains, but also the sweet wonders of childhood in a way to dim eyes without falling into the traps of the maudlin or cloying.

Working with cinematographer Jörgen Persson (of "Elvira Madigan" fame) and a cast of otherwise not too type-cast Swedish actors, Edwall was given a free hand by Sandrews Film's managing director Göran Lindgren to go all out on all production credits, and these are firstrate. Film seems destined for major festival exposure and foreign sales into select situations. —*Kell.*

Malambo
(AUSTRIAN-B&W)

Wels, Austria, Oct. 19.

A Milan Dor Film Production, Vienna, in collaboration with the Austrian Ministry for Education and Art and the Vienna Film Fund. Written and directed by Milan Dor. Camera (b&w), Toni Peschke; sound Michael Etz; editing, Eliska Stibr; music, Flora St. Loup; sets, Christoph Kanter. Reviewed at Austrian Film Days, Wels, Oct. 19, 1984. Running time: **92 MINS.**
With: Klaus Rohrmoser (Chris), Miodrag Andrić (Mischa), Nirit Sommerfeld (Nada), Dietrick Siegel (Hans), Oliver Stern (Anatol), Dagmar Schearz (Rita), Georg Trenkwitz (Martin).

The Grand Prix winner at the recent Mannheim fest and a standout too at the Austrian Film Days at Wels, "Malambo" deserves more fest exposure. This is a delightful comedy, written and directed with a tongue-in-cheek nonchalance by debuting helmer Milan Dor (son of Yugoslav writer Milo Dor, who settled in Austria after the war).

"Malambo" takes its inspiration from the circus and fairground milieu that attracts sideshow performers of every ilk and trade. The pic's genial antihero is a young trouper from the provinces whose ambition is to follow in the footsteps of the Great Houdini: he tries to duplicate the escape artist's feats at every opportunity before small gatherings at country crossroads and small towns along the Danube, albeit with embarrassment and failure at practically every outing. To put it bluntly, Chris is a born loser although a likeable chap.

His counterpart on his adventures is a Yugoslav con-artist, Mischa, who lives off the goodwill of his sister in a modest flat, while Nada in turn has her heart set on marrying an Austrian straightlaced boyfriend in order to break out of her foreign-worker existence.

"Malambo" is a kind of Austrian version of Federico Fellini's "La Strada" — a humorous, melancholy glance at little people trying to accomplish one big feat in their otherwise modest lives. It's the visual gags that delight, along with deadpan rendering of one-liners by Mischa. Credits are all on the plus side, with black-and-white lensing by Toni Peschke standing out in particular. — *Holl.*

Morgen Grauen
(Morning Mist)
(AUSTRIAN-COLOR)

Wels, Austria, Oct. 16.

An Arion Film Production, Vienna, George Reinhart, producer, in collaboration Austrian Television (ORF), Vienna. Features entire cast. Directed by Peter Sämann. Screenplay, Hans Bachmann; camera (color), Hanus Polak; editor, Ingrid Koller; music, Georg Herrnstadt, Willi Resetarits. Reviewed at Austrian Film Fest, Wels, Oct. 16, 1984. Running time: **87 MINS.**
With: Albert Fortell, Hannelore Elsner, Barbara Rudnik, Hans Georg Panczak, Erwin Steinhauer, Erni Mangold.

TV helmer Peter Sämann hit it big with this actioner titled "Morgen Grauen," the word combination meaning both "Morning Mist" and "Tomorrow's Cruelty." It was presented in the "New Austrian Cinema" series at the Berlinale last February and did well in Austrian hardtops.

It's sometime in the future in a technocrat city. Everyone at the age of 16 receives an "energy chip" (computerized replacement for money) for all related "purchasing" purposes, but he can be liquidated by a roaming execution force if he misuses the chip for personal power or gain. The executors, Len and Jacob, are two different types — one efficient, the other brutally efficient — and when a girl, Sarah, enters the picture, the two part company. Sarah is on their hit list, and Len has had a soft spot for her in the past.

The rest is Len and Sarah on the lam, with Jacob in hot pursuit. In the end there's a shootout with a twist to resolve the thriller atop a modern building in the morning mist. Pic is well paced in its direction and tightly edited.—*Holl.*

Delitto Al Blue Gay
(Crime At The Blue Gay)
(ITALIAN-COLOR)

Rome, Nov. 2.

A Medusa release, produced by Globe Films. Directed by Bruno Corbucci. Stars Tomas Milian. Screenplay, Mario Amendola and Bruno Corbucci; camera (color), Marcello Masciocchi; art director, editor, Daniele Alabiso; music, Fabio Frizzi. Reviewed at Supercinema, Rome, Nov. 1, 1984. Running time: 96 MINS.
Nico Giraldi ....Tomas Milian
Venticello.....................Bombolo

Latest of the Inspector Giraldi police spoofs fathered by Bruno Corbucci is "Crime At The Blue Gay." Broad humor, slapstick and a pinch of action are the main ingredients of this strictly local series, which continues to be popular with Tomas Milian fans and B-comedy buffs.

Nico Giraldi (Milian) plays a shaggy, long-haired cop put on a transvestite murder case. Victim, a performer at the Blue Gay nightclub, was found dead in his dressing room. To uncover the evil-doers, Giraldi moves in with a blubbering petty thief named Venticello (Bombolo). Together they masquerade as a gay couple (Bombolo cross-dressing as a hideous hag) to become part of the underground scene.

When Giraldi's wife, who has just had a baby, stumbles upon her husband in questionable company, she makes a fuss that takes him till story's end to undo.

Locations shift to Berlin for the last part of pic, where a German film director is unmasked as a KGB agent responsible for the cabaret murder. He was after the victim's father, an atomic scientist.

If the plot's a mess, pic's rhythm is good, and Corbucci is a veteran at mixing fist-fights and muggings with an impromptu chariot-vs.-oar race. Pic is tongue-in-cheek in depicting the gay world, one enormous cliché of false eyelashes, boas and tearful scenes in the dressing room (when star performer "Colomba Lamar" discovers Nico is happily married.) The German spy ring is equally pasteboard. Milian and Bombolo deliver their standard Two Stooges performances. —*Yung.*

Falling In Love
(COLOR)

Modest outlook for minor De Niro-Streep romance.

Hollywood, Nov. 15.

A Paramount Pictures release of a Marvin Worth production. Produced by Worth. Directed by Ulu Grosbard. Stars Robert De Niro, Meryl Streep. Screenplay, Michael Cristofer. Camera (Technicolor), Peter Suschitzky; editor, Michael Kahn; music, Dave Grusin; production design, Santo Loquasto; art direction, Speed Hopkins; set decoration, Steve Jordan; costume design, Richard Bruno; sound, Les Lazarowitz; associate producer-production manager, Robert F. Colesberry; assistant director, Thomas J. Mack; additional photography, Ernie Miscelli; second unit camera, Peter Norman, casting, Juliet Taylor, Pat McCorkle. Reviewed at the Bruin Theatre, L.A., Nov. 14, 1984. (MPAA Rating: PG-13.) Running time: 107 MINS.

Frank Raftis.............Robert De Niro
Molly Gilmore ....Meryl Streep
Ed Lasky ....Harvey Keitel
Ann Raftis............. Jane Kaczmarek
John Trainer ....George Martin
Brian Gilmore............David Clennon
Isabelle ....Dianne Wiest

"Falling In Love" is a polite little romance, the ambition and appeal of which are modestly slight. Dynamic starring duo of Robert De Niro and Meryl Streep keeps the film afloat most of the time, but effects of this supertalented pair acting in such a lightweight vehicle is akin to having Horowitz and Rubinstein improvise a duet on the theme of chopsticks. Boxoffice prospects are moderate.

Those who have seen David Lean's post-war British favorite "Brief Encounter" will undoubtedly be reminded of that film, as new effort covers similar ground, that of a man and woman married to others who attempt to have a relationship and whose meetings depend to a great degree upon railway schedules.

In a day of wham-bam sex and action, very little actually happens in "Falling In Love." Screenplay by playwright Michael Cristofer attempts to create an interesting mosaic out of the principals' relationship, as snippets of conversations and selected moments of assorted rendezvous are presented in favor of sustained dramatic scenes.

Both De Niro, a construction engineer, and Streep, a graphic designer, have marriages which, while not unhappy, have settled into the routine. Meeting in Manhattan and on the commuter train to and from Westchester County, they are compelled to continue seeing one another, but are unsure where it's all headed. More quickly than Streep, De Niro decides he wants to have an affair, but she can't make up her mind, and major question becomes, "Will she or won't she?"

Problem is that the characters are rather superficially drawn, and their feelings don't seem deep enough. Because of their reticence and uncertainties, and because of the vaguely moralistic attitudes being suggested, one never feels a strong rooting interest in their relationship.

Streep, in particular, plays this in a lighter vein than is her usual wont.

She is, unfortunately, not well supported by the script; Streep laughs at much of what De Niro does and says, but has been given no witty lines of her own. She's a delight almost in spite of the character as written, and looks wonderful.

Scenes between De Niro and best friend Harvey Keitel remind one that it's been quite awhile now since their teaming in "Mean Streets," and the dramatic potency of what they're up to here is considerably weaker, to say the least. De Niro is charming and, like Streep, plenty of fun to watch, but he is very contained here compared to his usual work.

General approach by director Ulu Grosbard is conventional, although he and lenser Peter Suschitsky have admirably captured a strong dose of upscale New York atmosphere, with the particular assistance of the Rizzoli Bookstore on Fifth Avenue. Jane Kaczmarek delivers the one notable supporting turn as De Niro's wife; others are competent but strictly in for brief scenes. Dave Grusin's score is on the agreeably jazzy side. —*Cart.*

Missing In Action
(COLOR)

Gung-ho Chuck Norris actioner delivers.

Hollywood, Nov. 16.

A Cannon Films release of a Golan-Globus production. Produced by Menahem Golan and Yoram Globus. Executive producer, Lance Hool. Directed by Joseph Zito. Stars Chuck Norris. Screenplay by James Bruner, based on a story by John Crowther and Lance Hool; camera (Metrocolor), Joao Fernandes; editor, Joel Goodman; music, Jay Chattaway; sound, Jacob Goldstein; art director, Ladi Wilheim; costumes, Nancy Cone; assistant director, Gidi Amir; associate producer, Avi Kleinberger; stunt coordinator, Aaron Norris; casting, Fern Champion, Pamela Basker. Reviewed at the Hollywood Pacific, Nov. 16, 1984: (MPAA Rating: R.) Running time: 101 MINS.

Braddock ....Chuck Norris
Tuck ....M. Emmet Walsh
Ann....................Lenore Kasdorf
General Tran ....James Hong
Jacques..............Pierrino Mascarino
Vinh ....Ernie Ortega
Senator Porter ....David Tress

Cannon blew this Vietnam action meller onto 1,200 screens over the weekend, and given Chuck Norris' defined following and the redneck nature of this film, boxoffice figures should jump.

With the Philippines filling in for Vietnam jungles, with Norris kicking and firing away, with a likable sidekick in the black marketeering figure of M. Emmet Walsh, and with a touch of nudity in sordid Bangkok bars, writer James Bruner and director Joseph Zito have marshalled a formula pic with a particularly jingoistic slant: even though the war is long over, the Commies in Vietnam still deserve the smack of a bullet.

Norris plays a former North Vietnamese prisoner, an American colonel missing in action for seven years, who escapes to the U.S. and then returns to Vietnam determined to find M.I.A.'s and convince the world that Yanks are still imprisoned in Vietnam. Accompanying a Senate investigation committee to Ho Chi Minh City, Norris quickly forsakes politics and diplomacy for his special brand of search and destroy.

Norris' characterization, a kind of leashed fury, propels the comic book events, including one sly sequence in which Norris watches Spider Man on tv and then proceeds to emulate the cartoon hero by slithering up and down a tall building in old Saigon (the filmmakers manage a pretty good French colonial look with selective shots).

Physical scope of pic is ambitious, including one terrific action sequence with a boat, a munitions truck and a sedan on a pier in Bangkok, where Norris has unearthed his old Army buddy (Walsh) to help him prepare their amphibious assault on Vietnam.

The pair seemingly take on the entire Viet military. Asians in this pic are depicted with the identical villainy that Japanese soldiers had in World War II-era Hollywood pics. Next to theme and content of this pic, "Green Berets" is mellow stuff. — *Loyn.*

The Music Of The Spheres
(CANADIAN-COLOR)

Toronto, Nov. 14.
A Pan-Canadian release of a Lightscape Motion Picture production. Produced and directed by G. Philip Jackson. Coproducer, Nadine Humenick. Features entire cast. Screenplay, Jackson, Gabrielle de Montmollin; camera (color), Nadine Humenick; editor, Fred P. Gauthier; art director, James Stuart Allan; sound, Ross Redfern. Reviewed at the Bloor Cinema, Toronto, Nov. 13, 1984. Running time: **82 MINS.**
Melody . . . . Anne Dansereau
Andrew . . . . Peter Brikmanis
Paul . . . . Jacques Couture
The Bureaucrat . . . . Ken Lemaire
Einstein . . . . Kenneth Gordon
Security Officer . . . . Grant Roll
Dr. Moriarte . . . . Sandy Kaiser

A future global society controlled by supercomputers is the milieu for Canadian filmmaker Philip Jackson's first feature, "The Music Of The Spheres," which picked up the international jury award for "most promising first feature" at the 1984 Atlantic Film Festival in Halifax. Pic is strictly for sci-fi devotees who can forgive the low-budget quirks in favor of the convoluted plotline and ambitious message.

It's the 21st century and the world, no longer made up of individual nations, is run by a web of computers, headed by computer central — "The Beast." Melody (Anne Dansereau) is a highly skilled technician who can communicate telepathically with the Beast.

The current program, Project Ceres, is undertaken as a way to tap the earth's solar energy and prevent energy starvation. Melody receives messages from aliens outside the system that its execution is upsetting the ancient order of the universe, or the "music of the spheres."

She also has to contend with the Bureaucrat (Ken Lemaire), who cannot tolerate dissension because the logic of the system is perfect; her friend Andrew (Peter Brikmanis), who is part of the new order and helps to hook up Melody and the Beast; and her lover Paul (Jacques Couture), the brains behind the technology. The arguments of logic and order versus mystical and timeless universal balances are the pivotal points of dialog here, both in English and French.

Pic was shot on a budget of $C110,000 in bits and pieces as money became available, over a two and one-half year period, which shows in much of the continuity. The special effects that attempt to recreate Melody's psychic experiences and the dream sequences which use re-enactments of events are confusing, heavy-handed, and too-oft repeated. Non sequiturs abound.

Dansereau is convincing in her role as the psychically anguished Melody, and Brikmanis is cool and playful as the Doubting Thomas. —*Devo.*

Wodzeck
(WEST GERMAN-COLOR)

Hof, W. Germany, Oct. 25.
An Oliver Herbrich Film Production, in collaboration with the Nordrhein-Westfalen Filmbüro and Beyerischer Rundfunk (BR), Munich. Features entire cast. Written and directd by Herbrich, loosely based on Georg Büchner's novel "Woyzeck." Camera (color), sets, Tobias Siemsen, Josef Saubtjohansen; sound, Ana Mazur; editor, Romy Schumann; music, Andres Hofner. Reviewed at Hof Film Fest, Oct. 25, 1984. Running time: **82 MINS.**
. With: Detlef Kügow (Wodzeck), Ariane Erdelt (Maleen), Johannes Habla (Andres), Franz A. Huber (Foreman), Hans Beerhenke (Tramp), Charles Brauer (Doctor), Leo Bardischewsky (Professor), Georg Greiwe (Construction Worker), Regula Siegfried (Maleen's Shop Friend).

Oliver Herbrich's "Wodzeck" draws upon Georg Büchner's classic "Woyzeck" for its inspirational source (making use of a title twist in much the same fashion as Alban Berg did with "Wozzeck," the operatic version of same). For the record, Teutonic helmer Werner Herzog also adapted Büchner's "Woyzeck" (1978), with Klaus Kinski in the title role.

The hero this time is a shy and embittered factory worker, whose job is operating a gigantic press machine in a rather typical factory in the industrial Ruhr area of west Germany. One look at this assembly line, and it's pretty clear a human being is about to be dehumanized into a robot with little chance for a release of his pent-up emotions. His girl-friend, Maleen, begins to react against his possessive nature and inability to relax and have a bit of fun. Although she generally likes the good-natured Wodzeck, another man has entered her life.

Wodzeck begins to hear voices and let his imagination run wild — until the moment comes when he breaks down, buys a knife, and kills Maleen on the street. By this time he's not functioning as much more than a walking zombie.

"Wodzeck" has its eye-catching moments at the start of the story, then coasts along at a snail's pace thereafter over a familiar terrain of loneliness and madness until the murder is committed.—*Holl.*

Lieber Karl
(Dear Karl)
(W. GERMAN-AUSTRIAN-COLOR)

Hof, W. Germany, Oct. 28.
A Voissfilm Production, Munich, in collaboration with Bayerischer Rundfunk (BR), Munich, and Austrian Television, Vienna; Peter Voiss, producer. Features entire cast. Directed by Maria Knilli. Screenplay, Knilli, Wolfgang Paulus; camera (color), Klaus Eichhammer; sets, Mario Sedlmeier; editing, Knilli; music, Marran Gosov; costumes and make-up, Karin Gutberlet; sound, Fritz Baumann, tv-producers, Reinhard Stegen, Axel von Hahn. Reviewed at Hof Film Fest, Oct. 27, 1984. Running time: **90 MINS.**
With: Ulrich Reinthaller (Karl), Hans Brenner (Father), Krista Stadler (Mother), Elisabeth Prohaska (Hilde), Rudolf Wessely (Kubelka), Walter Prettenhofer (Bastian), Karl Friedrich (Residence Director), Vitus Zeplichal (Psychiatrist), Gertie Pall (Frau Reisenberger), Herbert Rhom (Doctor), Nico Seul (Hansi), Oliver Stern (Drunk), Johannes Kirchlechner (Student), Wolfram Paulus (Assistant), Karl Schippl (Chess Player), Daniel Olbrychski (Teacher).

"Dear Karl" is the debut feature of Austrian helmer Maria Knilli, who comes from Graz, but studied at the Munich TV and Film School, and was written together with Wolfram Paulus, another Austrian helmer trained at the Munich school.

This is a story of a young man from modest family means in a small Austrian town in the Styrian (or Steiermark) section of the country. The father runs a stationery store and wants his son to attend the university and perhaps one day bring honor to the family name by becoming a doctor. The boy, however, is sickly and shy, in addition to having a tough time of making the grade at school. There is some doubt whether he will be able to pass the matriculation exams, so a tutor (a family friend) has been secured.

The first half of the film is the slow buildup to passing the examination. The second half finds Karl at the university in Granz.

Primarily a mood piece, "Dear Karl" relies heavily on the motif of letters written home to tell its story. This might have been the key to the film's eventual success if the letters played a more revelatory role. As it is now, we don't know much more about Karl at the end than we knew at the beginning. —*Holl.*

Vidas Errantes
(Errant Lives)
(MEXICAN-COLOR)

Mexico City, Nov. 1.
A Películas Mexicanas-Películas Nacionales release of a Conacine, J.A. de la Riva & Assoc. and Churubusco Studios production. Directed by Juan Antonio de la Riva. Screenplay, J.A. de la Riva and Tomás Pérez Turrent; story, J.A. de la Riva; camera (color), Leoncio (Cuco) Villarias; editing, Luis Kelly; sound, Oscar Mateos; art direction, Josefina González de la Riva; sets, Guillermo de la Riva; music, Antonio Avitia and the group Me Cai; post-production, Jenny Kuri. Reviewed at the Condominio Cinematográfico, Mexico City, Oct. 31, 1984. Running time: **90 MINS.**
Francisco . . . . José Carlos Ruiz
Guillermo . . . . Ignacio Guadalupe
The Girl . . . . Josefina González
El Cristero . . . . Eduardo Sigler
El Gavi . . . . Juan Manuel Luevanos
Melo, the Carpenter . . José Manuel García
Maestra Laurencia . Gabriela Olivo de Alba
Prof. Lorenzo Francisco . . . . Javier Gómez
Don Copo . . . . Don Caspar Laviada
Doña Luisa . . . . Eugenia D'Silva
The Engineer . . . . Pedro Armendáriz

In his directorial debut, Juan Antonio de la Riva has made a small, quiet film with "Vidas Errantes" (Errant Lives), which comes as a change of pace in Mexican cinema.

The plot recounts the life of itinerant projectionist Francisco (José Carlos Ruiz), who travels the mountainous regions of the state of Durango in a truck, showing classic Mexican films to rural communities of lumberjacks and their families.

En route, he links up with a young man named Guillermo (Ignacio Guadalupe), who aids him in the trips, setting up the equipment, running the projectors, etc. They sleep in the truck, in cheap hotels or atop piles of old movie posters.

Francisco's dream is to stop this errant life and build a permanent cinema nestled in the forests outside the town where he was born. Over the years he has saved his money and has drawn up plans and blueprints on the back of vintage movie handbills. He and the boy, now accompanied by his young common-law bride (Josefina González) begin construction of the building, to be called Cine Analco, the old Indian name for Durango.

While workers continue the building, the three itinerates travel around showing their stock of films. One day, during the dry season the three stop to put out a potential forest fire. When they return to the village, they discover a fire has broken out at the construction site, and the dried timber frame of the new cinema goes up in smoke along with Francisco's dreams. At the end of the film, the three continue as before, visiting small remote mountain villages, bringing the inhabitants visions of classic melodramas.

"Errant Lives" is a type of road picture, with two friends involved in a series of episodes. These segments are broken by scenes from the films they show: "Los Hermanos del Hierro," the Tin Tan comedy "Calabacitas Tiernadas," the Indio Fernández classic "Pueblerina" and "El Gallo de Oro." These clips offer a type of homage to national cinema, of films that influenced the director's youth.

The relationship between the veteran exhibitor and Guillermo becomes that of father-son, teacher-student, as they travel together, learning to acccept life and what it has to offer. When Guillermo chooses a mate, Francisco accepts the fact that the boy is growing up.

"Errant Lives" is a quiet and absorbing film with a sense of honesty and simplicity that sets it apart from the bulk of Mexico's current film production. —Lent.

The Coolangatta Gold
(AUSTRALIAN-COLOR)

Sydney, Nov. 9.
A Hoyts Distribution (Australia) release of a Michael Edgley Intl.-Hoyts Theatres in association with Peter Schreck, Igor Auzins and John Weiley presentation. Produced by Weiley. Directed by Auzins. Features entire cast. Screenplay, Schreck; exec producers, Terry Jackman, Edgley; camera (Eastmancolor), Keith Wagstaff; editor, Tim Wellburn; sound supervisor, Phil Judd; production designer, Bob Hill; art director, Owen Paterson; associate producer, Brian Burgess; music, Bill Conti. Reviewed at Hoyts Center, Sydney Nov. 7, 1984 (Commonwealth Film Censor rating: NRC). Running time: 116 MINS.
Steve Lucas . . . . Joss McWilliam
Joe Lucas . . . . Nick Tait
Kerri Dean . . . . Josephine Smulders
Robyn Lucas . . . . , ... Robyn Nevin
Adam Lucas . . . . Colin Friels
Grant Kenny . . . . Himself
Gilda . . . . Melanie Day
Ballet teacher . . . . Melissa Jaffer
Karate teacher . . . . Paul Starling

Latest offering from the Hoyts Theaters-Michael Edgley stable "The Coolangatta Gold" is from director Igor Auzins and writer Peter Schreck (who combined on the slow-moving but visually stylish period outback drama "We Of The Never Never") and producer John Weiley.

A handsomely mounted contempo drama, pic represents a marked departure from the formulas which elevated "The Man From Snowy River" and "Phar Lap" to con-

siderable success here and, in the former's case, in the U.S.

This item lacks an emotional pull, but it offers enough ingredients to rack up good business with the youth market here.

Overseas prospects are hard to call, although the quintessential Australian setting and the themes it explores, laced with several lively pop songs and Bill Conti's score, are probably quite exportable.

Title denotes a gruelling contest (inaugurated for this film) on the Gold Coast resort in Queensland, in which superhuman young men swim, run and surf-ski over a 26-mile course.

In 1960, Nick Tait had finished second in the event. Haunted by that memory, he is determined to take his revenge by pushing and goading his elder son Colin Friels to take the title by beating Grant Kenny (Australia's real-life "Iron Man" champ) whose father had humbled Tait. Younger son Joss McWilliam resents the blatant favoritism Tait shows Friels and half-heartedly helps in training when he isn't pursuing beautiful ballet dancer Josephine Smulders and managing a struggling rock band.

Story livens up when Tait blames McWilliam for a motorcycle accident in which Friels luckily escapes injury. Fired up by this incident McWilliam dedicates himself to winning the Coolangatta Gold and casts Smulders aside while he undergoes an exhausting preparation.

Race itself, which occupies the last 15 or 20 mintues, is only moderately exciting. Outcome is not as the viewer might expect, but there is the predictable and corny reunion between McWilliam and Smulders at the fadeout.

Budgeted at around $A5,600,000 "The Coolangatta Gold" is an expensive pic by Aussie standards, and it looks it. Tech credits, particularly Keith Wagstaff's wide-angled photogrpahy, are tops, and Auzins keeps the narrative zipping along.

In his first pro role, McWilliam lacks resonance and conveys feelings in a fairly basic way, but he has an agreeable personality and his handsome looks are likely to win many femme admirers. Smulders, plucked out of ballet school for this picture, gets by with a fetching innocence and she too is a real looker. Their wordless seduction scene to the frantic beat of the Conti composition "Heartbeat" is a sizzler, one of the pic's few passionate interludes.

Tait, as the hard-driven father obsessed with winning, is effective if at times a touch too strident, and Robyn Nevin a his wife strikes a nice balance, torn between loyalty to her husband and love for her sons. Friels, not given much to work with, puts in an understated performance.

In an all-too-brief part, Paul Starling is impressive as a karate teacher whose serenity and supreme control help to curb McWilliam's hot-headed impetuousness.
—Dogo.

Schwarzer Bube
(Jack Of Spades)
(W. GERMAN-COLOR-16m)

Hof, W. Germany, Oct. 27.
A Toro Film Production in collaboration with Westdeutscher Rundfunk (WDR), Cologne. Directed by Vivian Naefe. Features entire cast. Screenplay, Klaus Bädekerl; camera (color), Gerard Vandenberg; sound, Ed Parente; editor, Tom Watts; music, Hubert Bartholomä. Reviewed at Hof Film Fest, Oct. 26, 1984. Running time: 60 MINS.
With: Hanno Pöschl (Werner), Sigfrit Steiner (Father), Heinrich Sauer (Hartwig), Katharina Raacke (Ellen), Inge Blau (Sabine).

Vivian Naefe's delightful short feature "Jack Of Spades" is about the game of poker as practiced in hotel suites and back rooms of inns across West Germany.

A cardsharp is cleaning up at a private poker party, and we see how he is able to use his wits to bluff and even (when necessary) cheat in order to win.

Once a year he visits his retired father, a former actor, on the old gentleman's birthday. The father has a surprise in store for after exchanging the usual amenities, a casual poker game with friends is staged. The three amateurs in the game suddenly go on a winning streak and, with a bit of finesse, the old man wins the sharp's Porsche! Even after the ruse is explained (the pic's most delightful twist), the con man's confidence has been shaken sufficiently to ruin his next outing.

Thesp performances are strong, particularly Hanno Pöschl as the cardsharp and Sigfrit Steiner as the father. A real plus is helmer Naefe's knack for telling a story with sometimes little more than gestures and telling closeups. —Holl.

Zu Hören Auf Hören
(Listening To Styrian Musicians)
(AUSTRIAN-DOCU-COLOR-16m)

Wels, Austria, Oct. 17.
A Cinedoc Production, Graz, in collaboration with Austrian Television (ORF), Vienna, Westdeutscher Rundfunk (WDR), Cologne, and the Austrian Ministry for Education and Art, Vienna. A Documentary written and directed by Heinz Trenczak and Ruth Deutschmann. Camera (color), Jiri Volbracht; music, Styrian folk artists; editor, Hanne Huxoll. Reviewed at Austrian Film Fest, Wels, Oct. 17, 1984. Running time: 86 MINS.

Hein Trenczak and Ruth Deutschmahn's "Listening To Styrian Musicians" deals with unique folk instruments and musicians in the Steiermark (or Styria) section of Austria, the capital city of which is Graz.

It starts out well with yodelers and zither-like instruments, and one wants to hear more. Then everything

is suddenly thrown to the winds for related but unnecessary material on how farmers, laborers and other ordinary folk live in this mountainous area.

Apparently, the filmers themselves forgot momentarily about listening to folk artists perfoim — and that's a pity.—Holl.

On The Road To Hollywood
(AUSTRIAN-DOCU-COLOR--16m)

Wels, Austria, Oct. 17.
A UFF-United Film Federation Production, Vienna. A documentary made in collaboration with the Austrian Federal Ministry for Education and Art, Vienna, by Bernhard Frankfurter. Script, Frankfurter; camera (color), Kurt Jetmar, G.P. Winter, Adriano Tuis, Hermann Dunzendorfer, Franz Riess; editor, Agnes Lenz. Reviewed at Austrian Film Fest, Wels, Oct. 17, 1984. Running time: 101 MINS.

Bernhard Frankfurter's docu on German and Austrian emigrants to Hollywood (and elsewhere in Europe), titled "On The Road To Hollywood" is better off forgotten.

The filmmaker received generous government support to make a docu on such personalities as the late Walter Reisch, Martha Feuchtwangler, Paul Henreid, Paul Falkenberg and many other personalities of the stage and screen, songwriting and arts and letters. He traveled to Prague, London, New York, Hollywood and many points in between, to interview key and aged figures on the past and the general topic of emigration. What he came back with is pretty much a disgrace — for Frankfurter has made himself the center of attention.

Frankfurter persists throughout in asking dumb questions. Even when the interviewee is off and running on an important subject, Frankfurter continually interrupts with oddball comments of his own.
—Holl.

Cosi' Parlo' Bellavista
(Thus Spake Bellavista)
(ITALIAN-COLOR)

Rome, Nov. 16.
A UIP release, produced by Mario Orfini and Emilio Bolles for Eidoscope Productions and Rete-4 TV. Directed by Luciano De Crescenzo. Features entire cast. Screenplay by De Crescenzo and Riccardo Pazzaglia, from a book by De Crescenzo; camera (Color), Dante Spinotti; editor, Anna Napoli; art director, Franco Vanorio; music, Claudio Mattone. Reviewed at Eden Cinema, Rome, Nov. 15, 1984. Running time: 92 MINS.
Prof. Bellavista . . . . Luciano De Crescenzo
Mrs. Bellavista . . . . Isa Danieli
Patrizia . . . . Lorella Morlotti
Giorgio . . . . Geppy Gleijeses
Cazzaniga . . . . Renato Scarpa
Concierge . . . . Benedetto Casillo

Bestselling writer-historian Luciano De Crescenzo goes behind and in front of the camera as helmer-actor for "Thus Spake Bellavista," based on his own book about today's Naples. Humorous sketches of the city, its joys, troubles and philosophy make a charming and fresh picture that is doing very good business in national release. This entertaining revisitation of the old stereotypes, corrected with a mild dose of realism, is the kind of picture that could move offshore with the right kind of handling.

Retired philosophy prof Gennaro Bellavista (De Crescenzo), hoary-headed but bright-eyed, holds daily "classes" for neighbors and concierges of his lordly apartment building, who raptly follow his teachings. Among other things, his unconventional wisdom divides the world into "Nordic" types ruled by "freedom". and "Southerners" ruled by love.

Bellavista's antagonist is Milanese exec Cazzaniga (Renato Scarpa, who moves into the building and introduces strange Nordic habits like reordering the mailboxes and making the concierges wear uniforms (most of them refuse). By pic's finish Cazzaniga is showing unmistakable signs of Neapolitanness himself, demonstrating that you are where you live.

Structured as chaotically as its colorful subject, "Bellavista" is a collection of anecdotes about the people of the city and their eccentricities. In the midst of all this looms the Camorra and unemployment.

Top-flight cast is rounded out by Isa Danieli as the uncontested head of the Bellavista household and young thesp Benedetto Casillo as a concierge. — *Yung.*

The Return
(ISRAELI-BRITISH-DOCU-16m)

Berlin, Oct. 22.
A B&S Film Production, Berlin. A Documentary by Michael Blum and Arthur Schrödinger. Camera (color), Werner Leckebusch, Arthur Ahrweiler, Denis Cullum; sound, Marion Dain, Norbert Weyer; editing, Ursula Höf, Sybille Windt. Reviewed at Berlin Film Mart Screening Rooms, Berlin, Oct. 22, 1984. Running time: **60 MINS.**

"The Return" is about Jewish people who have both immigrated to and emigrated from Israel for various reasons. It's made by a German-Jewish team — Michael Blum (the principal figure) and Arthur Schrödinger — and has no particular bones to pick, yet the theme is rather controversial so this docu should spark a sharp pro and con discussion wherever it's shown.

The idea is quite simple. Two Israeli families, one from Iran, one from London, are contrasted with each other via an interview technique that grows in depth and scope by matching the life experiences of both couples. Along the way, other individuals are introduced to broaden the theme and offer additional in-

formation and new perspectives on the issues. In the final analysis, one has a better understanding of why people decide to leave their homes in the Western world to immigrate to Israel, only to return after a few years; and why the dipping population factor continues to plague Israel in the face of inflation and a runaway economy, even though the yong nation is blessed with a backbone of committed settlers from various countries and an equally determined youth with strong beliefs in the future. —*Holl.*

Küchengespräche Mit Rebellinnen
(Kitchen Table Talk With Women Rebels)
(AUSTRIAN-DOCU-COLOR-16m)

Wels, Austria, Oct. 21.
A Documentary by the Project Group Women in Anti-Fascist Resistance under a collective direction. Written and edited by Karin Berger, Elisabeth Holzinger, Charlotte Podgornik, and Lisbeth N. Trallori. Camera (color, 16m), Gerda Lampalzer; music, Carla Bley. With Agnes Primoschitz, Johanna Sadolschek-Zala, Rosl Grossmann-Breuer, and Anni Haider. Reviewed at Austrian Film Fest, Wels, Oct. 21, 1984. Running time: **80 MINS.**

"Kitchen Table Talk With Women Rebels" was made by a film collective of women and features a handful of women rebels who risked their lives in the name of humanity during the anti-fascist struggle in Austria before and during World War II. Since each of these women — Agnes Primoschitz, Johanna Sadolschek-Zala, Rosl Grossman-Breuer and Anni Haider — has something to say and is willing to share her experiences with an open-eared camera team, the docu has historical value.

The women in focus resemble those found in Ernest Hemingway's "For Whom The Bell Tolls." They are tough yet tender champions of human rights and political freedom. They also suffered for their beliefs and in some cases underwent internment and mental and physical torture. The docu is a salute to bravery and determination, and it doesn't get lost in the labyrinth of contemporary feminist polemics. —*Holl.*

Der Prozess
(The Trial)
(WEST GERMAN-DOCU-COLOR-B&W-16m)

Mainz, Oct. 24.
A Norddeutscher Rundfunk (NDR) production, Hamburg; TV producers, Dieter Meichsner, Hans Brecht. A Documentary written and directed by Eberhard Fechner. Professional advice, Aladbert Rückerl; camera (color, 16m), Frank Arnold, Nils-Peter Mahlau, Bernd Schofeld; sound, Hans Diestel, Dieter Schulz; editor and artistic cooperation, Brigitte Kirsche; assistant director, Jannet Gefken; editing assistant, Sabrina Ziemer; special-effects camera, Heidi Möller; production manager, Herbert E.

Philipps, Günter Handke. Reviewed at the Mainz Conference of TV Critics, Mainz, Oct. 23, 1984. Running time: **270 MINS.**

Eberhard Fechner's 4½-hour documentary on the Holocaust, "The Trial," is an outstanding tv-sponsored production. It took five years to make, just as long as the Majdanek trial itself which took place in Düsseldorf and has been reckoned to be the last of the Nazi trials (due primarily to the age factor of testifying witnesses).

The Düsseldorf proceedings dealt with five prison guards accused of being implicated in the mass murder of some 250,000 people interned in the Lublin-Majdanek extermination camp (situated in eastern Poland and liberated by the Soviets). When the convictions were handed down in 1981, many impartial observers felt that the accused had been treated far too lightly in view of the evidence gathered. It was only after the appeals had been made to the high courts that Fechner's film could be released to the public — it will have its tv preem in three parts in late November on Germany's Third Channel.

Fechner exposed a total of 250 hours of docu footage; interviewed 70 key individuals from 20 cities in Germany, Poland, Austria, and Israel; and researched in archives in Warsaw, Lublin, Ludwigsburg, and Jerusalem for material on the liberation of the camp. The trial centered on the five accused, all former prison guards, but the real attention was upon the 26-eyewitnesses as a whole — for it's through their recollections that one learns a great deal about both the death camp and the people who ran it with such cold efficiency.

Then there are the judges, the state attorneys, and the defense lawyers. And lastly, there are people who might be termed "friends of the court" — in some cases journalists and chroniclers, in other cases historians and factual experts. Naturally enough, there are moments of high drama during the trial: the first confrontation in the courtroom between the former guards and prisoners, an underhanded tactic by one defense lawyer to discredit a witness on the basis of having worked as a prisoner in the poisonous-gas storage depot, and the moment in which the judge reads the sentences with a trembling hand.

"The Trial" doesn't really stop with these court proceedings. Fechner and NRD plan to turn over all 250 hours of footage to the Federal Film Archive in Koblenz, and the same to the Israeli archive. It means that any interested party can apply to view the material for study and research purposes. More than likely, too, "The Trial" will be given a rerun on German tv.

Fechner succeeds where others have failed: he reveals something about us that is painful and instructive — what would we have done if placed in the same situation as some of the more humanitarian guards, and what are our own feelings on the matter 40 years after the fact?
— *Holl.*

The Flamingo Kid
(COLOR)

Easy sell to ex-New Yorkers; may be tougher for rest.

Hollywood, Nov. 26.

A 20th Century Fox release of an ABC Motion Pictures presentation of a Mercury Entertainment production. Produced by Michael Phillips. Directed by Garry Marshall. Screenplay, Neal Marshall, Garry Marshall. Story by Neal Marshall. Camera (Deluxe color), James A. Contner; editor, Priscilla Nedd; production design, Lawrence Miller; art direction, Duke Durfee; set decoration, Fred Weiler; costume design, Ellen Mirojnick; sound, Peter Ilardi; associate producer-second unit director, Nick Abdo; assistant director, Stephen J. Lim; casting, Margery Simkin. Reviewed at 20th Century Fox Studios, L.A., Nov. 26, 1984. MPAA Rating: PG-13. Running time: **100 MINS.**

Jeffrey Willis	Matt Dillon
Phil Brody	Richard Crenna
Arthur Willis	Hector Elizondo
Phyllis Brody	Jessica Walter
Hawk Ganz	Fisher Stevens
Steve Dawkins	Brian McNamara
Joyce Brody	Carole R. Davis
Nikki Willis	Martha Gehman
Ruth Willis	Molly McCarthy
Fortune Smith	Leon Robinson
Carla Samson	Janet Jones
Alfred Schultz	Bronson Pinchot

Since "Porky's," it's been difficult for teenage coming-of-age films to wear a straight face, but "The Flamingo Kid" is a refreshingly realistic and likeable one. Set in 1963, which now seems like a never-never land of innocence and unquestionable values, pic has a modesty and charm along the lines of "Diner" and "Breaking Away," although its observations are not as densely packed or acutely made as those found in the latter films. Seriously intended comedy will especially appeal to current young adults who grew up around New York City. Positioning this as a Christmas attraction is a questionable tactic, however, since it has little built-in want-see and will need good reviews and word-of-mouth to flourish.

Previously known both as "Sweet Ginger Brown" and "Mr. Hot Shot," film sports the amusing trappings connected with 18-year-old Matt Dillon working for a summer at the El Flamingo Beach Club in Far Rockaway, N.Y. At its heart, though, story has to do with the critical choices facing a youth of that age and how they will help determine the rest of one's life.

Taken out of his rundown Brooklyn neighborhood one day to play cards with friends at the club, Dillon ends up getting a job there parking cars. With his good looks and winning ways, he is soon promoted to the vaunted position of cabana boy, and also attracts the attention of blonde UCLA student Janet Jones, with whom he has a skin-deep summer fling, and her uncle Richard Crenna, a sharp-talking sports car dealer who may be the richest man at the club and plays a mean game of gin.

A good kid but no brain, Dillon has been toying with the idea of going to college, which would fulfill the dream of his plumber father, but it doesn't take much convincing by Crenna for him to forget books in favor of a job selling Ferraris. Given his rebellion against the limited horizons represented by his family and Brooklyn, Dillon quickly comes to idolize the materialistic Crenna and parrots his crass philosophy in front of his appalled father.

When it comes to crunch, however, Crenna proves himself to be a lot less of a man than Dillon imagined, and Dillon saves himself from selling out his potential at an early age. His teenage impressionability is very well conveyed, as is his background of essential decency which ultimately brings about his correct moral decision.

In the meantime, there are plenty of colorful diversions at the club, which is festooned with an abundance of mild vulgarisms fitting with the nouveau riche status of the members. Place looks like Miami Beach North in 1963, what with the women's drastically teased hair and heavy makeup, self-satisfied old men, cha cha lessons, outrageous buffets and loose money.

Unlike most youth pics, this one concentrates on just one young man, not on a group, which somewhat limits the diversity of experience on view. It's also a rare one in that having sex is not the top priority of the male characters; in fact, when it finally happens to Dillon, it seems almost incidental to both him and the picture.

Dillon does a good job in his fullest, least narcissistic characterization to date. Playing down his looks by slicking his hair and wearing a porkpie hat, thesp relates to others more successfully here than before and effectively carries the picture.

Crenna seems a rather curious choice to play Mr. Slick, but hits the right notes as the big fish in the small pond who temporarily seduces Dillon to his way of thinking (the Crenna of over 20 years ago is also very briefly seen in a tv clip from "The Real McCoys"). Dillon's family is well represented by Hector Elizondo, Molly McCarthy and Martha Gehman, and Leon Robinson has some good moments as the only black employee at the club, a basketball player headed for Notre Dame.

Soundtrack is loaded with tunes of the period, and tech credits are good. Original screenplay by Neal Marshall was penned more than a decade ago, and director Garry Marshall (no relation) receives coscript credit (Bo Goldman, who was listed as a writer during production, is nowhere mentioned now). —*Cart.*

Deutschland Bilder
(Images Of Germany)
(W. GERMAN-COMPILATION-B&W)

London, Nov. 19.

A Big Sky Filmproduktion, in association with WDR and ARD. Produced by Werner Dütsch. Written, directed and edited by Hartmut Bitomsky, Heiner Mühlenbrock. Commentary, Jons Dengler. Reviewed at London Film Festival, Nov. 16, 1984. Running time: **61 MINS.**

From 1933 to 1945, feature films in German cinemas were accompanied by "inspirational" short subjects, prepared on behalf of the Nazi government. This documentary looks at excerpts from many of them, and notes the recurrent themes and ideas behind the image they created.

There's an emphasis on handsome men and women going about their work, whether in factories or on the land, with cheerful optimism; and there's also the repeated theme of parades and uniformity in sport and leisure as well. Later films, for instance "The Will To Live" (1944), show the German people overcoming adversity, via striking scenes of amputees still enjoying sporting activities.

The excerpts begin with the optimistic "We Have No Problems" (1933) about youngsters looking to the future, and continue with such self-descriptive titles as "The Beauty Of Work" (1934), "Holiday Fun" (1936) and "Women's Culture" (1942). All this old footage, confiscated by the Allies after the war, is beautifully shot and edited to get the Nazi message across.

"Images Of Germany" adds to the viewer's sum of knowledge about Germany during the Nazi period, and is a natural for fest exposure . —*Strat.*

Beverly Hills Cop
(COLOR)

Three in a row for Eddie Murphy, but no laugh riot.

Hollywood, Nov. 26.

A Paramount Pictures release of a Don Simpson/Jerry Bruckheimer production. Produced by Simpson, Bruckheimer. Directed by Martin Brest. Executive producer, Mike Moder. Screenplay, Daniel Petrie Jr., based on a story by Danilo Bach and Petrie Jr. Camera (Technicolor), Bruce Surtees; editor, Billy Weber, Arthur Coburn; music, Harold Faltermeyer; production design, Angelo Graham; art director, James J. Murakami; set decorators, Jeff Haley, John M. Dwyer; sound, Charles M. Milborn; costumes, Tom Bronson; assistant director, Peter Bogart. Reviewed at Paramount Pictures, Hollywood, Calif., Nov. 26, 1984. MPAA Rating: R. Running time: **105 MINS.**

Alex Foley	Eddie Murphy
Det. Billy Rosewood	Judge Reinhold
Jenny Summers	Lisa Eilbacher
Sgt. Taggart	John Ashton
Lt. Bogomil	Ronny Cox
Victor Maitland	Steven Berkoff
Mickey Tandino	James Russo
Zack	Jonathan Banks
Chief Hubbard	Stephen Elliott
Inspector Todd	Gilbert R. Hill
Det. Foster	Art Kimbro
Det. K. McCabe	Joel Bailey
Serge	Bronson Pinchot
Jeffrey	Paul Reiser

Eddie Murphy fans won't be disappointed as they streak to this certified Christmas profit center for Paramount Pictures. Working his brash persona to the hilt, under the brisk direction of Martin Brest and from a twisting but clean-lined screenplay by debuting screenwriter Daniel Petrie Jr., Murphy, it's no risk to predict, has now scored three hits in a row (following "48 HRS." and "Trading Places").

But filmgoers anticipating the laugh register of "Trading Places" will be a bit dismayed to find "Beverly Hills Cop" is more cop show than comedy riot. Also, expectations that Murphy's street brand of rebelliousness would devastate staid and glittery Beverly Hills are not entirely met in a film that grows increasingly dramatic as Murphy's recalcitrant cop from Detroit runs down the killers of his best friend.

Strong assists come from a deceptively likable performance from Judge Reinhold as a naive Beverly Hills detective, from by-the-book chief Ronny Cox, and from the serpentine villainy of Steven Berkoff, who plays an art dealer involved in nefarious endeavors.

Don Simpson and Jerry Bruckheimer, the "Flashdance" producers who now have bounced back from the lackluster "Thief Of Hearts," deftly hit the soundtrack button again with a terrific score from Harold Faltermeyer and solid contributing numbers from such off-screen artists as The Pointer Sisters and Patti LaBelle, among others.

Best moments arrive early when Murphy, bouncy, determined and vengeful, arrives in Beverly Hills in what old Detroit friend turned Beverly Hills art dealer Lisa Eilbacher correctly calls his "crappy blue Chevy Nova." The counterpoint between the scraggly dressed and incredulous Murphy and the palms, mansions and golden Rodeo Drive shops of glistening Beverly Hills is instantly provocative and funny. Film's single most satiric and hilarious scene is a sly encounter between Murphy and a gay, foreign assistant in Eilbacher's art gallery. Bronson Pinchot as the smarmy assistant denting the English language in a posh store is a great touch of local color. Audiences might not get it in Des Moines, but the scene typifies the high parody lamentably found wanting most elsewhere.

(Film was originally tagged for Sylvester Stallone and the finished product still carries the melodramatic residue of a hard, violent property, pre-Murphy.)

Shootout at the end, in the insidious Berkoff's Gatsby-like palace, is pic's weak point, as the carnage begins to suggest a mild takeoff of the concluding slaughter in "Scarface." As Murphy and his cohorts remarkably dodge hundreds of machine gun bullets richocheting off marble statuary, film momentarily ceases to be either dramatic or humorous.

Bruce Surtees' smooth cinematography suggests his lensing on "Risky Business," and production designer Angelo Graham's handiwork, particularly the bright mobiles and figure paintings in the art gallery, enrich the duchy-like environment. — *Loyn.*

Jungle Warriors
(GERMAN-MEXICAN-COLOR)

An Aquarius Films release of an Arnold Kopelson and Manson International presentation. A TAT film GmbH/Jungle Warriors GbR production, coproduced by International Screen Prods./Araiz-Condoy Producciones S.A./Popular Film GmbH. Executive producers, Monika Teuber, Francisco Araiz-Condoy. Produced and directed by Ernst R. von Theumer. Features entire cast. Screenplay, Robert Collector, von Theumer; camera (CFI color), Nicholas von Sternberg; editors, Juan Jose Marino, Warren Chadwick; music, Roland Baumgartner; sound, Klaus Peter Kaiser; art direction, Richard McGuire; assistant director, Barbara Schubert; stunt coordinator, Roberto Messina. Reviewed at RKO Warner 2 theater, N.Y., Nov. 23, 1984. (No MPAA Rating.) Running time: 93 MINS.
With: Nina Van Pallandt (Joanna), Paul L. Smith (Cesar), John Vernon (Vito), Alex Cord (Nicky), Sybil Danning (Angel), Woody Strode (Luther), Kai Wulff (Ben), Dana Elcar (Michael), Suzi Horne (Pam), Mindy Iden (Marci), Kari Lloyd (Brie), Ava Cadell (Didi), Myra Chason (Cindy), Angela Robinson (Monique), Louisa Moritz (Laura), Marjoe Gortner (Larry).

"Jungle Warriors" is a routine actioner filmed in Mexico last year, notable chiefly for its interesting B-film cast. Poor pacing loads all the action into the final reel, a ploy not likely to please the target audience.

Lame structure shoehorns two stories awkwardly into one package: A big drug deal is going down in a Latin or South American country between Cesar (Paul L. Smith) and Don Vito (John Vernon) while Pan American Drug Enforcement Agency leader Michael D'Antoni is out to bust them. He has a secret agent on the job, one of five U.S. models on location with their producer (Marjoe Gortner) and photographer (Nina Van Pallandt) for a shooting session in the jungle.

Cesar becomes suspicious and shoots down the models' plane, taking them captive, to be tortured by his incestuous half-sister Angel (Sybil Danning) and serve as playthings for his men. The girls escape in time for a final-reel shootout between Cesar's and Vito's forces, just as the government agents also arrive.

This mixture of women-in-prison (in Cesar's dungeons) and the usual drug action pic is unconvincing, with not enough nudity to satisfy the exploitation film trade. Substituted is flip dialog delivered by a host of slumming actors, of which Vernon is the hammiest and Smith extremely low-key as the oversize villain who goes crazy at the end. Van Pallandt is out of place as a macha femme and Danning, though well cast as an "Ilsa Of The SS"-type nasty person, has relatively little to do. Picture's main in-joke is that prominent actors in the cast are killed off suddenly and unpredictably.

Tech credits are adequate, including a direct sound English-language track. —*Lor.*

2010
(COLOR)

Overly ambitious space saga is a holiday disappointment.

Hollywood, Nov. 19.
An MGM/UA Entertainment of an MGM presentation. Produced and directed by Peter Hyams. Stars Roy Scheider. Screenplay, Hyams, based on the novel by Arthur C. Clarke; camera (Panavision, Metrocolor), Hyams; editor, James Michell; music, David Shire; sound design, Dale Strumpell; sound mixer, Gene Cantamessa; supervising sound editor, Richard L. Anderson; production design, Albert Brenner; set decorator, Rick Simpson; special visual effects supervisor, Richard Edlund; visual futurist, Syd Mead; assistant director, William S. Beasley; production manager-associate producer, Neil A. Machlis; associate producer, Jonathan A. Zimbert; makeup supervisor, Michael Westmore; special effects supervisor, Henry Millar; flying supervisor, Robert Harman; costume design, Patricia Norris; stunt coordinator, M. James Arnett; visual displays & graphics, Video-Image; video effects supervisor, Greg McMurry; additional optical effects, Cinema Research; casting, Penny Perry. Reviewed at Village theater, L.A., Nov. 16, 1984. (MPAA Rating: PG.) Running time: 114 MINS.
Heywood Floyd . . . . Roy Scheider
Walter Curnow . . . . John Lithgow
Tanya Kirbuk . . . . Helen Mirren
R. Chandra . . . . Bob Balaban
Dave Bowman . . . . Keir Dullea
HAL 9000 (Voice) . . . . Douglas Rain
Caroline Floyd . . . . Madolyn Smith
Dimitri Moisevitch . . . . Dana Elcar
Also with: Taliesin Jaffe, James McEachin, Mary Jo Deschanel, Elya Baskin, Savely Kramarov, Oleg Rudnik, Natasha Shneider, Vladimir Skomarovsky, Victor Steinbach, Jan Triska, Herta Ware, Arthur C. Clarke.

Additional Visual Effects Credits
Entertainment Effects Group (L.A.): visual effects supervisor, Richard Edlund; art director, George Jenson; camera (Super Panavision 65, color), Dave Stewart; editor, Conrad Buff; matte department supervisor, Neil Krepela; mechanical effects supervisor, Thaine Morris; model shop supervisor, Mark Stetson; optical supervisor, Mark Vargo; animation supervisors, Terry Windell, Garry Waller; chief matte artist, Matthew Yuricich; stop-motion animation, Randall William Cook; miniature mechanical effects, Bob Johnston; digital Jupiter simulation, Digital Prods.

Hype and heritage will unquestionably call out the queues for "2010," but MGM/UA can't count on seeing the same faces in line too many times. Sixteen years after the original, one sampling of the sequel will be sufficiently exciting for the older audience and, more importantly, probably too tame for the younger crowd who think science-fiction started with "Star Wars."

Working backwards from its determination to have "2010" as this year's Christmas picture to a tight Feb. 6 start date, MGM/UA may have made a very practical decision in resting producing, directing, writing (not to mention lensing) with one man, Peter Hyams. And it is to Hyams' credit that he got the ambitious job done under pressure.

Unfortunatley, Hyams does not possess the vision of Stanley Kubrick (whose own track record at the time helped him against some initial misgivings against "2001). But leave it to the buffs to debate the difference further; too much time and taste has changed to make comparisons between the two producer-directors very meaningful.

As the title proclaims, "2010" begins nine years after something went wrong with the Jupiter voyage of Discovery. On earth, politicians have brought the U.S. and Russia to the brink of war, but their scientists have united in a venture to return to Jupiter to seek an answer to Discovery's fate and the significance of the huge black monolith that orbits near it.

American crew is headed by Roy Scheider, haunted by his role in the original failure, John Lithgow and Bob Balaban. The Soviets want them along mainly for their understanding of HAL 9000, whose mutiny remains unexplained. If revived in the salvage effort, can HAL still be trusted?

In Hyams' hands, the HAL mystery is the most satisfying substance of the film and handled the best. Unfortunately, it lies again a hodge-podge of bits and pieces about the monolith, world peace, the mystical presence of astronaut David Bowman (Keir Dullea), all surrounded by technically respectable but otherwise uninspired celestial acrobatics.

And Hyams can usually be relied on for one plot turn that's totally unacceptable, but by the time it arrives in this one, it doesn't make much difference, other than to add suspense.

It's hard to accept that with war between their countries imminent on earth and all diplomatic relations ruptured, the Soviet side of the crew would suddenly follow Scheider blindly, led by his ghosts. But the big problem is the audience can't really follow at all, rushed along by too many Big Thoughts that aren't coming together in the monumentally important way Hyams hopes for. —*Har.*

Bog
(COLOR)

Sinks back into the mire.

A Marshall Films presentation of a Bog production in association with Nelsen Communications. Executive producer, Clark Paylow. Produced by Michelle Marshall. Directed by Don Keeslar. Stars Gloria De Haven, Aldo Ray, Marshall Thompson, Leo Gordon. Screenplay, Carl N. Kitt; camera (Cinema Processors color), "Wings" (Jack Willoughby); editor, John Montonaro; musical director, Bill Walker; assistant director, Stuart Gross; sound, Tim Turner; special effects, Richard Albain, Gerald Winchell; makeup, Erica Veland. Reviewed on Prism Entertainment vidcassette, N.Y., Nov. 17, 1984. (No MPAA Rating.) Running Time: 85 MINS.
Ginny Glenn/Adrianna . . Gloria De Haven
Sheriff Neal Rydholm . . . . Aldo Ray
Dr. Brad Wednesday . Marshall Thompson
Dr. John Warren . . . . Leo Gordon
Alan Tanner . . : . . . . Glen Voros
Chuck Pierce . . . . Rojay North
Dep. Jensen . . . . Ed Clark
Wallace Fry . . . . Robert Fry
Bog monster . . . . Jeff Schwaab

"Bog" is a homemade monster picture produced in 1978 and currently surfacing on homevideo. Various vet character actors fail to buoy up this made-in-Wisconsin cheapie.

A fisherman using a "Dupont lure" (dynamite instead of a rod and reel) unwittingly awakens a prehistoric monster living in the slime at the bottom of Bog Lake. Beastie, which appears onscreen in later reels as an ultra-fake looking rubber monster suit sporting big painted-on yellow eyes, kills the fisherman and various campers until local Sheriff Rydholm (Aldo Ray) whips into action. Aided by Dr. Wednesday (Marshall Thompson, who had fun in 1950s monster pics such as "Fiend Without A Face") and pathologist Ginny Glenn (topbilled Gloria De Haven), the sheriff captures the monster using a blood scent fish lure. Critter escapes and is anticlimatically killed by crashing a car into it.

Key subplot has the monster, which sucks all the blood out of its victims, reproducing by mating with human women, beginning with an old hag Adrianna (De Haven in a dual role). This story element is discussed but tastefully kept offscreen.

Dull film is poorly made, with terrible editing that includes frequent unintentional freezeframes between shots meant to cut smoothly together. — *Lor.*

Whoever Says The Truth Shall Die
(DUTCH-DOCU-COLOR/B&W)

Distribution by Minnesota Film Center, Minneapolis; produced by VARA-TV, Hilversum, The Netherlands. Produced by Frank Diamand. Directed by Philo Bregstein. Camera (color), Michel Pensato, Alan Jones, Vincent Blanchet, Ali Movahed, Richard Laurent; sound, Neil Kingsbury, Andre Vanin, Gianni Sardo; editor, Mario Steenberg. Pasolini poems read by Laura Betti. In English, French and Italian, with English subtitles. Reviewed at Paramount Screening

Room, New York, Nov. 14, 1984, as part of Gay Film Festival. Running time: **60 MINS.**

When murdered in 1975 at age 53, Pier Paolo Pasolini was at his peak, both as a film director and as a poet and novelist. Was his killer Pino The Frog, a 17-year-old male prostitute, who in claiming self-defense received a sentence of only nine years and was released in the fall of 1983? Alternatively, was there a conspiracy among right-wing fascist toughs to assassinate Pasolini — outrageous non-conformist, atheist and Marxist (although expelled from the Communist Party for homosexual scandals).

This interesting Dutch documentary reexamines Pasolini's entire career, using interviews of him and of his colleagues, still photographs, news footage, and clips from his "Accatone," "Hawks And Sparrows," "Teorema," "Oedipus Rex" and "The Gospel According To St. Matthew." Also excerpted is "Salo," Pasolini's final film, still banned in Italy by the Italian Film Censorship Commission for its "aberrational and repugnant scenes of sexual perversions."

Some attention is given to Pasolini's childhood with a fascist military father and anti-fascist mother, the murder of his young brother, apparently by fellow-partisans, his early schooling and literary endeavors. However, the film gives special emphasis to the pros and cons of Pasolini's death on a deserted beach near Rome.

Pasolini's screenwriter collaborator, Alberto Moravia, speculates that Pasolini's death was "an accident," a homosexual tryst between strangers where violent thrills got out of hand. Director Bernardo Bertolucci contradicts Moravia and instead surmises that neo-fascists committed the murder. Grisly photographs of Pasolini's battered body, including closeups, underscore the horror of his death.

Seconding Bertolucci's conspiracy theory is Laura Betti, Pasolini's close friend and actress in his films. She describes his militant anti-fascism and his 22 trials (always acquitted), charged variously with blasphemy against the church, obscenity and homosexual corruption of minors.

Betti's thesis is expressed in the film's title, that Pasolini spoke the truth and thus was doomed, "There was a license to get rid of him." By 1977, she had authored a book, "Pasolini: Legend Judgments, Persecution, Death," which she presented in public events and forums throughout Italy, hoping to cause the reinvestigation of the case.

This excellent cinematic biography of a film artist, and a murder mystery, conceivably could run in tandem with a congenial Pasolini feature as a strong double-bill in certain select bookings. One hopes as well to see it on public television, perhaps bookended by panel discussions. Long-term (but modest) 16m distribution, principally to colleges, is also indicated. —*Hitch.*

London Festival

Number One
(BRITISH-COLOR)

London, Nov. 16.
A Mark Forstater Production for Videoform Pictures/Stageforum. Produced by Forstater, Raymond Day. Executive producer, Warren Goldberg. Directed by Les Blair. Features entire cast. Screenplay, G.F. Newman; camera (color), Bahram Manocheri; editor, John Gregory; music, David Mackay; production design, Martin Johnson; sound, Peter Glossop; associate producer, Selwyn Roberts. Reviewed at London Film Festival, Nov. 15, 1984. Running time: **105 MINS.**
Harry (Flash) Gordon .... Bob Geldof
Billy Evans .... Mel Smith
Doreen .... Alison Steadman
Mike the Throat .... P.H. Moriarty
Terry the Boxer .... Phil Daniels
D-C Rogers .... Alfred Molina
D-C Fleming .... James Marcus
Brad Bookie .... David Howey
Teddy Bryant .... Ian Dury
The Wasp .... Ron Cook

British tv director Les Blair makes an engaging big-screen debut with "Number One," a colorful tale of London lowlife. International chances may, however, suffer from the insularity of the subject and the sometimes indecipherable London and Irish accents.

Harry (Flash) Gordon (Bob Geldof) is a smalltime gambler who hustles the snooker (similar to pool) halls, winning small amounts of loot here and there, but just as often getting into all kinds of trouble. A promoter (Mel Smith) pushes Harry into competing for Britain's professional snooker championship, though the bets are against him. Climax of the pic is the final match of the series.

Fine acting from the ensemble cast gives the film a naturalistic air that places it in the tradition of the "kitchen sink" dramas being made in Britain 25 years ago. Leader of rock group Boomtown Rats Bob Geldof is fine as the hustling hero, and a special nod also goes to Alison Steadman as his prostie girlfriend who watches her lover playing snooker on tv while absent-mindedly servicing a client.

Director Blair and writer G.F. Newman, who previously collaborated on some high class television movies, bring humor and a light touch to this slight, somewhat derivative tale. —*Strat.*

Slow Moves
(U.S.-COLOR)

London, Nov. 19.
A Jon Jost Production. Produced, directed, scripted, photographed, edited & scored by Jost. Sound, Rick Schmidt. Reviewed at London Film Festival, Nov. 17, 1984. Running time: 93 MINS.
With: Roxanne Rogers, Marshall Gaddis, Debbie Krant, Barbara Hammes, Geoffrey Rotwein, Bebe Bright, Roger Ruffin.

For 10 years, Jon Jost has been making experimental features on miniscule budgets. "Slow Moves," his latest, was brought in for $8,000 on a 4½-day shooting schedule using a two-man crew.

Pic is basically a two-hander about a couple who meet on the Golden Gate Bridge, start a love affair (off-screen), run into money trouble, and then drive across country on a spree that ends when he's gunned down robbing a store. For the leading roles, Jost chose two non-actors, Roxanne Rogers and Marshall Gaddis, and kept them apart so their first meeting was recorded on film in the opening scene. One of the film's flaws is that the hoped-for chemistry between these two strangers thrown into a close relationship doesn't really happen and they create uninvolving characters as a result.

It's an intriguing film, even though poor sound recording renders key dialog unintelligible and many crucial scenes take place off-screen. A digression to the Camera Obscura at San Francisco provides some lovely imagery. —*Strat.*

The Young Visiters"
(BRITISH-16m-COLOR)
London, Nov. 19.
A James Hill production for Channel Four. Produced, written and directed by James Hill. Based on a story by Daisy Ashford. Camera, Wolfgang Suschitzky; art director, Hazel Peiser; costumes, Susan Yelland; editor, Robert Hargreaves; sound, Ken Weston; music, John Cameron; associate producer, Geoffrey Helman. Reviewed at London Film Festival, Nov. 18, 1984. Running time: 93 MINS.
J.M. Barrie .... Alec McCowen
Daisy Ashford .... Carina Radford
Alfred Salteena .... Kenny Ireland
Ethel Monticue .... Tracey Ullman
Bernard Clark .... John Harding
The Earl Of Clincham .... John Bett
Edward Procurio .... Anthony Milner
Prince Of Wales .... John Standing
Minnit the Butler .... Brian Pringle

Although presented within a new kidfilm section of the London fest, this charming nine-year-old girl's view of life in late 19th century England should be a draw for grown-ups too.

Pic gets off to a slow start with an intro by "Peter Pan" writer J.M. Barrie and shots of the young authoress Daisy Ashford. Point is to establish "The Young Visiters" as the film of the book, thus enabling misspellings. After that, film moves with verve, accompanied by a scintillating score.

Story follows the fortunes of boorish fat man, Alfred Salteena, and his attractive young friend Ethel Monticue. When the sophisticated and wealthy Bernard Clark invites them both to stay, he quickly wins the affections of Ethel. Alfred is dispatched to London to learn the arts of a gentleman under the impecunious Earl of Clincham and Ethel is also introduced to London high life. After rejecting the advances of a forlorn Alfred, who secures a job with the Prince of Wales, she marries Bernard.

Narrative illogicality gives the film a dreamlike quality. Director James Hill emphasizes surreal elements such as a train that is actually a stable, inappropriately repeated landscapes and caverns entered through a glasshouse that lead into the lavish chambers of the aristocracy.

Singer Tracey Ullman and Kenny Ireland are standouts in their comic roles as Ethel and Alfred, and there's a fine supporting cast. Technical credits are fine. —*Japa.*

Majdhar
(BRITISH-COLOR)

London, Nov. 23.
A Retake Film & Video Collective production. Produced by Mahmood Jamal. Written and directed by Ahmed A. Jamal. Features entire cast. Camera (color), Philip Chavannes; art director, Fay Rodrigues; editor, John Dinwoodie; sound, Albert Bailey; music, Ustad Imrat Khan. Reviewed at London Film Festival, Nov. 21, 1984. Running time: 78 MINS.
Fauzia Khan .... Rita Wolf
Afzal Khan .... Tony Wredden
Rehana .. .. Feroza Syal
Arun .... Andrew Johnson
Gulshan .... Sudha Bhuchar
David .... Daniel Foley
Sandra .... Julianne Mason

An upbeat tale of the liberation of a young Pakistani woman in London, "Majdhar" (title is not translated) overcomes a rather tentative and occasionally clichéd script to provide a warm portrait of an interesting character.

Fauzia has recently arrived in London from Karachi to marry Afzal, who's been living in Britain for several years. However, he soon leaves her for another (white) woman, confidently expecting she'll simply go home. Supported by some loyal friends, she stays on, adopts western clothing and manners, aborts her husband's baby, gets a job in a travel agency, and has an affair with a rather dull English academic.

Made by a collective of Asian filmmakers whose aim is to challenge stereotyped images of minorities in the media, the film has a few stereotypes of its own. Though Rita Wolf is beautiful and confident in the leading role, she seems far too sophisticated to be the recent arrival she's supposed to be, while the case for old-fashioned Muslim values ("Once Pakistani girls get freedom they go completely mad") is stated rather obviously.

Nonetheless, this is an often charming and sometimes poignant film, with tv broadcasts indicated more than theatrical outings.
— *Strat.*

Roro Mendut
(INDONESIAN-COLOR)

London, Nov. 26.

An Elang Perkasa-Gramedia-Sanggar Film. Produced by Bambang Widitomo, J. Adisubrata, Hatoek Soebroto. Directed, scripted by Ami Priyono. Based on the novel by J.B. Mangunwijaya. Camera (Scope, color), Adrian Susanto; editor, S.K. Syamsuri; production design, A. Abidin; music, Franki Raden; sound, Okubo. Reviewed at London Film Festival, Nov. 25, 1984. Running time: **107 MINS.**

Tumenggung Wiroguno . . . . W.D. Mochtar
Roro Mendut . . . . Meriam Bellina
Pronocitro . . . . Marthias Muchus
Nyi Ageng . . . . Sunarti Soewandi

This is a lavishly mounted period piece set in the 17th century, a time of civil wars. Pic opens with galloping horses, a big battle and the beheading of the vanquished by the leader of the sultan's forces, Wiroguno. One of the spoils of war is the beautiful Roro Mendut, but before Wiroguno makes up his mind to take her as his mistress she has fallen for one of his young officers and escaped. Wiroguno pursues the lovers, and the pic climaxes with a duel on a beach with pounding surf in the background.

Though burdened with appalling English subtitles ("The houses have escaped!" cries an aide, meaning horses), the film's visual qualities are adequate compensation. On the basis of the two Indonesian films unspooled at the London fest, that country's filmmakers are using the Scope screen with considerable confidence and imagination. Acting is restrained, with W.D. Mochtar giving Wiroguno more depth than might have been expected. Meriam Bellina, as Roro, is a charmer. All technical credits are excellent.

—Strat.

Aderyn Papur
(...And Pigs Might Fly)
(BRITISH-COLOR)

London, Nov. 23.

A Red Rooster Film, in association with Sianel Pedwar Cymru. Produced by Linda James. Directed by Stephen Bayly. Features entire cast. Screenplay, Ruth Carter; camera (color), Richard Greatrex; art director, Hildegard Bechtler; editor, Scott Thomas; sound, Simon Fraser; music, Trevor Jones. Reviewed at London Film Festival Nov. 19, 1984. Running time: **75 MINS.**

Alun Owen . . . . Richard Love
Aunty Catrin . . . . Iola Gregory
Gwyn Owen . . . . John Ogwen
Idris Owen . . . . Robert E. Roberts
Gareth . . . . Llewelyn Jones
Granddad . . . . Stewart Jones
Kazuo . . . . Tasaki Noguchi
Naoyuki . . . . Yoshio Kawahara
(Dialog in Welsh)

A modest, perceptive study of contemporary life in a depressed village in North Wales, this Welsh-language pic succeeds because of its optimism and its positive approach to what could have been a dreary subject.

The village economy was based on a slate quarry which has closed down; every other house has a For Sale sign in front of it; most of the men are out of work, including Gwyn Owen (John Ogwen) whose wife has left him and is living in Liverpool.

The film's protagonist is Owen's younger son, Alun, confidently played by young Richard Love. Alun's older brother, Idris, is bored and anti-social and planning to join the Army which holds out promises of new horizons and adventure. Alun just wants to see the family together again.

A glimmer of hope comes with the arrival of two Japanese men, who rent a house in the village. Everyone jumps to the conclusion that they're businessmen who are going to reopen the quarry and provide work. The villagers rally round to impress the strangers, with whom they can't communicate at all — and by the time they realize the Japanese were only tourists after all, they have still regained enough confidence in themselves to face the future more positively.

Overcoming a lack of confidence is the theme of this well scripted (by Ruth Carter) and sympathetically directed (by Stephen Bayly) pic which, despite some flaws has a charm and integrity which transcend the meager budget. *—Strat.*

Jean Cocteau-Autoportrait d'un Inconnu
(Jean Cocteau — Self-Portrait Of An Unknown Man)
(FRENCH-DOCU-COLOR/B&W)

London, Nov. 16.

A JC Production, with Antenne-2 & French Ministry of Culture. Produced by Claude Chauvat. Directed by Edgardo Cozarinsky. Screenplay, Cozarinsky, Carole Weisweiller; camera (color, b&w), Jean-Louis Léon, Dominique Antoine; editors, Georges Klotz, Catherine Despratz. Reviewed at London Film Festival, Nov. 15, 1984. Running time: **66 MINS.**

Made to coincide with the 20th anniversary of the death of Jean Cocteau, this documentary presents a charming portrait of a contradictory, gifted, witty man.

Rather than produce the usual kind of tribute (containing interviews with people who knew the subject), expatriate Argentine helmer Edgardo Cozarinsky was lucky enough to obtain audio tapes and video and film footage of interviews Cocteau gave before his death. The late artist, author, poet and filmmaker had plenty of amusing anecdotes to tell about the golden age of the arts in France. His idols were Igor Stravinsky, Pablo Picasso ("king of junk dealers"), Erik Satie and Claude Debussy, among others. He recalls that Sarah Bernhardt called the Ballet Russes "jumping fleas," and pays a moving tribute to Raymond Radiguet, the youthful writer ("Devil In The Flesh") who died of typhoid aged 20.

Archive footage shows Cocteau in company with famous personalities of his time, including Charles Chaplin. There are plenty of excerpts from his films, including "Orpheus" and "Testament Of Orpheus," and from Jean-Pierre Melville's "Les Enfants Terribles."

Beautifully crafted docu contains rich and rare material about one of the century's most interesting artists, and is a natural for television screenings, festival participation and the college circuit. Theatrical possibilities are indicated, too, wherever this type of film portrait might find appreciative audiences.

—Strat.

Yr Alcoholig Lion
(The Happy Alcoholic)
(BRITISH-COLOR)

London, Nov. 23.

A Cine Cymru Ltd. production. Produced by Hayden Pearce. Written and directed by Karl Francis. Features entire cast. Camera (color), Roger Evans; art director, Hayden Pearce; editor, Aled Evans; sound, Patrick Graham; music, Ifor Ab Gwilym. Reviewed at London Film Festival, Nov. 19, 1984. Running time: **109 MINS.**

Alun . . . . Dafydd Hywel
Mam . . . . Gwenlliam Davies
Gwen . . . . Eluned Jones
El . . . . Eleri Evans
Auntie . . . . Glesni Williams
Maestro . . . . David Lyn
Die . . . . Reginald Mathias
(Dialog In Welsh)

Familiar tale of a hopeless alcoholic and his eventual redemption, this Welsh-language pic has a strong central performance from Dafydd Hwyel as the unfortunate man. However, writer-director, Karl Francis (who previously made "Giro City," aka "And Nothing But The Truth," with Glenda Jackson) tends to hammer his theme home repetitively and relentlessly, resulting in an overlong and, for the audience, charmless experience.

No doubting that Francis wanted to make an anti-alcoholism tract, and a plug for Alcoholics Anonymous, but subject has been handled better in several other films on the subject. Alun (Hywell), whose twin hobbies are singing in the local choir and boozing with his mates, loses his wife, his daughter, his job and almost his life before he gets a grip on himself, helped by a sympathetic musician friend and A.A. thesping is all fine, especially Hywel and Gwenlliam Davies as his sick old mother, but audiences are unlikely to respond to this downbeat tale.

The title is misleading, as there's precious little happiness in the film until the final reel. Technical credits are all fine given pic's modest budget. *—Strat.*

Pigs
(IRISH-COLOR)

London, Nov. 19.

A Samson Films production, with assistance from the Irish Film Board. Produced by David Collins. Directed by Cathal Black. Features entire cast. Screenplay, Jimmy Brennan; camera (color), Thaddeus O'Sullivan; art director, Frank Conway; editor, Se Merry; sound, Trevor O'Connor; music, Roger Doyle; executive producer, Kevin Moriarty. Reviewed at London Film Festival, Nov. 17, 1984. Running time: **78 MINS.**

Jimmy . . . . Jimmy Brennan
George . . . . George Shane
Tom . . . . Maurice O'Donoghue
Ronnie . . . . Liam Halligan
Orwell . . . . Kwesi Kay
Mary . . . . Joan Harpur

A promising feature debut about a group of misfits living in an abandoned house in Dublin, "Pigs" may not spark much boxoffice interest but could play well on television.

Director Cathal Black, who previously made the controversial documentary, "Our Boys," about the Christian Brothers, shows he's good with actors and displays a confident, fluid visual style, while working in the mostly confined conditions of the old house itself.

Scripter Jimmy Brennan, a novelist and playwright, acts the leading role, a man with a past who first arrives to "squat" in the house and is later joined by an assortment of others rejected by society. These include a small-time con-man, a mental patient, a youthful drug-pusher, and a black pimp and his wife.

As the film proceeds, we learn more about these characters, and especially Jimmy, who has served a spell in prison and is homosexual. Brennan's screenplay is more a series of character studies than a dramatic narrative.*—Strat.*

Sueño de Noche de Verano
(A Midsummer Night's Dream)
(SPANISH-BRITISH-COLOR)

London, Nov. 19.

A Cabochon Film Productions-Television Espanola SA production. Produced by Miguel Angel Perez Campos. Written and directed by Celestino Coronado. Stars The Lindsay Kemp Co. Based on the stage production by Kemp, David Haughton, from the play by William Shakespeare. Camera (color), Peter Middleton; production design costumes, Kemp, Haughton; art director, Carlos Dorremochea; music, Carlos Miranda. Reviewed at London Film Fest, Nov. 16, 1984. Running time: **80 MINS.**

Puck . . . . Lindsay Kemp
Hippolyta . . . . Manuela Vargas
Titania . . . . The Incredible Orlando
(Jack Birkett)
Oberon . . . . Michael Matou
Changeling . . . . François Testory
Lysander . . . . David Meyer
Theseus/The Beast . . . . Neil Caplan
Demetrius . . . . David Haughton
Hermia . . . . Annie Huckle
Helena . . . . Cheryl Heazelwood
Romeo/Bottom . . . . Atilio Lopez
Juliet/Flute . . . . Christian Michaelson
Starveling/Moon . . . . Javier Sanz

Shot in studios in Madrid last winter in a tight 12 days, this low-budget film version of the Lindsay Kemp Co.'s stage production of Shakespeare's "A Midsummer Night's Dream" is a unique and cheerful experience.

London-based Spanish director Celestino Coronado previously tackled the Bard with a bizarre version of "Hamlet" in 1976; his new effort is more sophisticated. The text has been almost completely eliminated in favor of mime, song and dance, the players invest their roles with doubtful sexuality (e.g., Titania is played by a man dubbed with the voice of a woman), and there's plenty of uninhibited nudity as the various lovers frolic through this artificial midsummer night.

With outrageous costumes and makeup, the fairy king and queen are splendidly campy characters. Kemp himself plays a fleet-of-foot Puck.

Pic could catch on as a cult item with late-night shows especially indicated. The play lends itself to this kind of way-out treatment. Given the miniscule budget, the film looks good and the rich music score is an added attraction. —*Strat.*

Ponirah Terpidana
(Ponirah)
(INDONESIAN-COLOR)

London, Nov. 26.
A Sukma Putra Film. Produced by Manoo Sukmajaya. Executive produced by Alex Dial. Directed, scripted by Slamet Rahardjo. Camera (Scope, color), Tantra Suryadi; editor, George Kamarullah; production design, Benny Benhardi; music, Eros Djarot; sound, Suparman Sidik. Reviewed at London Film Festival, Nov. 25, 1984. Running time: 105 MINS.
Ponirah . . . . Nani Vidya
Trindil . . . . Christine Hakim
Jarkasi . . . . Ray Sahetapy
Guritno . . . . Slamet Rahardjo
Djabarudi . . . . Bambang Hermanto
Wiwiek . . . . Lina Budiarti
Franky Darling . . . . Teguh Karya

A gutsy melodrama about a young woman who hates men, "Ponirah" is a confidently made saga which would not have been out of place in Hollywood 30 years ago.

Tale opens in 1964 as a man returns home from a business trip to find his beloved wife dying as she gives birth to a baby girl. A few years later, the little girl is with her older brother when he's killed in an accident. Blaming the child for the deaths of the two people he loved most, the father rejects her, and she's taken away by her nurse and cared for. But the nurse is forced to turn to prostitution to make ends meet, so young Ponirah grows up in a provincial whorehouse, hating all men.

Nani Vidya gives a vivacious performance as the eponymous heroine, but the film is stolen in the acting department by Christine Hakim as the devoted nurse. The director,

Slamet Rahardjo, plays a key role as Ponirah's teacher (revealed at fade-out to be more than that). Ending, with Ponirah in Djakarta to be sold to a leading pimp (named Franky Darling) goes over the top a bit, but until then Rahardjo's handling is exemplary, with good use of Scope and tight editing to drive the story along. The English subtitles, for once, are perfectly acceptable.
—*Strat.*

Dark Enemy
(BRITISH-COLOR)

London, Nov. 19.
A Children's Film Unit Production. Directed by Colin Finbow. Features entire cast. Script, Finbow and the Children's Film Unit; camera (color), Amos Richardson; sound, Robert Farr; music, David Hewson; make-up and costumes, Griselda Wallace. Reviewed at London Film Fest, Nov. 17, 1984. Running time: 82 MINS.
Aron . . . . Rory Macfarquhar
Barnaby . . . . Martin Laing
Garth . . . . Chris Chescoe
Ash . . . . David Haig
Ezra . . . . Douglas Storm
Ruth . . . . Jennifer Harrison
Rosemary . . . . Helen Mason
Beth . . . . Cerian Van Doorninck

The Children's Film Foundation is a registered charity (for tax purposes) in Britain which encourages children to participate in all aspects of filmmaking, both acting and scripting as well as technical assistance. The finished product — in this instance — is as amateurish as a high-school play and, for adults, about as much fun.

Gloomy tale is set in a pastoral British after a nuclear holocaust. Adults are dying out, and a group of children are living in a peaceful valley as farmers, though terrified of the Unknown that lies across the horizon. Bulk of the pic consists of a quest by young Aron to prove his manhood.

During his adventures outside the village, he discovers the truth about what happened to past civilization (as a result of greed, it's said) and meets his sister, a deformed "moon-child." Pic ends on a relentlessly depressing note.

Whole project seems to have been made with the attitude that children should be made to know the worst about their possible future and their materialistic present.

The miniscule budget is obvious from the poor technical qualities of the pic, and none of the acting rises above the amateur dramatic level.
— *Strat.*

Skazka Stranstvii
(A Fairy Tale Of Wanderings)
(RUSSIAN-CZECH-RUMANIAN-COLOR)

London, Nov. 19.
A Mosfilm-Barrandov Film Studio-Rumania Film coproduction. Directed by Alexander Mitta. Features entire cast. Screenplay, Yuli Dunski, Mitta; camera (Sovcolor),

Valeri Shuvalov; editor, Nadyezhda Veselovska; production design, Teodor Tezhik; music, Alfred Shnitke; sound, Yuri Rabinovich; choreography, A. Droznin. Reviewed at London Film Festval, Nov. 18, 1984. Running time: 103 MINS.
Orlando . . . . Andrei Mironov
Marta . . . . Tatiana Aksyuta
Gorgon . . . . Lev Durov
Mai as a child . . . . Ksjusa Pirjatinska
Mai as a young man . . . . . Valeri Storozhik
Brutus . . . . Baltabai Seytmamutov
The Plague . . . . Carmen Gali Pitaova
Aunt . . . . Marie Rosulkova

An inventive, timeless fantasy about the 10-year search of a young girl for her younger brother, kidnaped at Christmas by a villain disguised as Santa Claus.

The moppet was snatched because he possesses the secret of divining the whereabouts of gold. Setting out to find him, young Marta is befriended by Orlando, a self-styled physician-poet-philosopher. They have to trek over the top of a gigantic dragon, as big as a mountain, where they find a community of lazy people basking — dangerously it transpires — in the warmth of the beast. They escape from a tower prison by manufacturing a primitive flying machine, and survive a voyage over a stormy sea in a tiny sailboat.

In a downbeat scene two-thirds into the pic, the heroic Orlando succumbs after a deadly encounter with The Plague (in the shape of a voracious woman!) and Marta is left alone. After many years she finally finds her brother, now rich and greedy and ruling an evil empire.

Sets, costumes and effects are all tops, and glowingly photographed on picturesque locations. Tatiana Aksyuta plays Marta throughout the story, though she ages from about 10 years to 20, and the young actress brings it off. Other playing is in keeping with the extravagant mood sought by helmer Alexander Mitta, a vet at this sort of film.

Only drawback is the ragged editing, making it seem as though this version has been drastically reduced from a much longer original. The ending is surprisingly abrupt.
—*Strat.*

Fengkuel-lai-te-Jen
(The Boys From Fengkuei
(TAIWANESE-COLOR)

London, Nov. 23.
An Evergreen Production. Produced by Jung-Feng Lin, Hua-k'un Chang. Executive producer Kun-hou Ch'en. Directed by Hsiaohsien Hou. Features entire cast. Screenplay, T'ien-wen Chu; camera (color), K'un-hou Ch'en; editor, Ch'ing-sung Liao; sound, Chian-sheng Hsin; associate producers, Sheng-chung Liu, Shu-chen Hsu. Reviewed at London Film Festival, Nov. 22, 1984. Running time: 98 MINS.
Ah-ch'ing . . . . Ch'eng-tse Niu
Hsiao-hsing . . . . Hsiu-ling Lin
Ah-ho . . . . Tsung-hua T'o
Ah-jung . . . . Shih Chang
Kuo-tzu . . . . P'eng-chu Chao

A far cry from the action or broad comedy pics so prevalent in

Hong Kong and Taiwanese cinema, "The Boys Of Fengkuei" (also known as "All The Youthful Days") is a naturalistic tale of three bored youths who leave the village of Fengkuei, on a small island off Taiwan, to look for work and adventure in the city of Kaohsiung in the south of the main island.

First part of the film establishes life in the sticks, with the youths bored and restless as they lark about and try fitfully to occupy their time. One of the trio has a father unable to work after being disabled in a sporting accident. These provincial scenes use the Hokkien language authentic to the location.

Once on the main island (where the language is Mandarin), the youths meet up with the older sister of one of them, who helps find them factory work and somewhere to live. Their neighbors are an unmarried couple living together, and when the man is forced to flee from the police, the girl begins to develop a relationship with one of the young men.

Short on plot but long on atmosphere and an authentic feel for these characters and their lives, the film is low-profiled but engaging. Quality of direction and acting is good, indicating a genuine attempt to tell a truthful contemporary story.

Only drawback is an unfortunate soundtrack of classical music (Vivaldi and Bach) which is very jarring and which was apparently added to the export version of the film in place of the original track of local music and songs. —*Strat.*

Dune
(COLOR)

Enormous production rings hollow, but holiday biz should be strong.

Hollywood, Nov. 30.

A Universal release of a Dino De Laurentiis presentation. Produced by Raffaella De Laurentiis. Directed and written by David Lynch, based on the novel by Frank Herbert. Camera (Technicolor, Todd-AO), Freddie Francis; editor, Antony Gibbs; music, Toto; adaptation and additional music, Marty Paich; "Prophecy" theme by Brian Eno, composed by Brian Eno, Daniel Lanois, Roger Eno; production design, Anthony Masters; supervising art director, Pierluigi Basile; art director, Benjamin Fernandez; set decorator, Giorgio Desideri; mechanical special effects, Kit West; creatures created by, Carlo Rambaldi; special photographic effects, Barry Nolan; additional special visual effects, Albert J. Whitlock; costume design, Bob Ringwood; sound design, Alan Splet; sound (Dolby), Nelson Stoll; creative makeup, Giannetto DeRossi; additional units supervisors and cinematographers, James Devis, Frederick Elmes; model unit supervisor, Brian Smithies; associate producer-assistant director, Jose Lopez Rodero; casting, Jane Jenkins; U.K. casting, Maggie Cartier. Reviewed at Universal Studios, Universal City, Nov. 30, 1984. (MPAA Rating: PG-13.) Running time: **140 MINS.**

Lady Jessica	Francesca Annis
The Baron's Doctor	Leonardo Cimino
Piter De Vries	Brad Dourif
Padishah Emperor	
Shaddam IV	Jose Ferrer
Shadout Mapes	Linda Hunt
Thufir Hawat	Freddie Jones
Duncan Idaho	Richard Jordan
Paul Atreides	Kyle MacLachlan
Princess Irulan	Virginia Madsen
Rev. Mother Ramallo	Silvana Mangano
Stilgar	Everett McGill
Baron Vladimir	
Harkonnen	Kenneth McMillan
Nefud	Jack Nance
Reverend Mother	
Gaius Helen Mohiam	Sian Phillips
Duke Leto Atreides	Jürgen Prochnow
The Beast Rabban	Paul Smith
Gurney Halleck	Patrick Stewart
Feyd Rautha	Sting
Doctor Wellington Yueh	Dean Stockwell
Doctor Kynes	Max Von Sydow
Alia	Alicia Roanne Witt
Chani	Sean Young

"Dune" is a huge, hollow, imaginative and cold sci-fi epic. Visually unique and teeming with incident, David Lynch's film holds the interest due to its abundant surface attractions but won't, of its own accord, create the sort of fanaticism which has made Frank Herbert's 1965 novel one of the all-time favorites in its genre. What with the advance interest and big production values, biz should be solid through the holiday season, but it falls short of blockbuster status.

Set in the year 10,991, "Dune" is the story of the coming to power of a warrior savior and how he leads the lowly inhabitants of the Dune planet to victory over an evil emperor and his minions. This classical story with religious and political overtones was so fully detailed by Herbert that the book required numerous appendices and explanatory lists.

Lynch's adaptation covers the entire span of the novel, but simply setting up the various worlds, characters, intrigues and forces at work requires more than a half-hour of expository screen time, during which the viewer strains to keep track and is offered only the promise of a strong narrative in which to become involved. If anything, Lynch has been too faithful to his source material; in striving to retain as much of it as possible, he has overloaded the film with so many elements that many of them ultimately get lost in the shuffle.

The anointed one, Paul Atreides, travels with his regal mother and father to the desert planet, where an all-powerful "spice" is mined from beneath the sands despite the menace provided by enormous worms which gobble up harvesters in a single gulp.

The horrid Harkonnens conquer the city on Dune, but Paul and his mother escape to the desert. There Paul trains native warriors, achieves his full mystic powers, tames the worms and engages in final battle with the Harkonnens and the emperor.

Many filmmakers have expressed a desire to make "Dune" over the years, and handing the project to such an iconoclastic, offbeat talent as Lynch was a bold stroke on the part of Dino and Raffaella De Laurentiis. However, it must be said that, except for the weird touches here and there, little of Lynch's personality, as so strongly evidenced in "Eraserhead" and "The Elephant Man," surfaces here; the enormity of the production pretty well crushes his artistic distinctiveness.

At the same time, a great deal of imagination has been poured into physicalizing Herbert's universe, and Lynch can take credit for much of this. The vision of the future here is highly reminiscent of 19th century imaginings of it. The class structure is monarchistic, even feudal, in nature, and Anthony Masters' extraordinary production design emphasises heavy, carved woods and ornate gold leaf sculptural effects.

All down the line, the contributions of the production team are quite special, from Bob Ringwood's highly varied costumes and Carlo Rambaldi's nifty giant worms to Alan Splet's sound design, which provides an underlying hum of menace, and the assorted special effects, which include space travel, fiery projectiles, outrageous makeup (by Giannetto DeRossi) and much more. There's just about always something going on for the senses to appreciate.

Cast is also firstrate, even if players rarely get to sink their teeth into anything sustained. Francesca Annis and Jürgen Prochnow make an outstandingly attractive royal couple, Sian Phillips has some mesmerizing moments as a powerful witch, Brad Dourif is effectively loony, and best of all is Kenneth McMillan, whose face is covered with grotesque growths and who floats around like the Blue Meanie come to life. Kyle MacLachlan is solid and righteous as the good-looking hero. Unfortunately, rock star Sting is largely wasted as a second banana baddie.

Despite all the pluses, pic seems weighed down by all its diverse elements and plays rather heavily; the climactic spectacle is empty, the ultimate victory inevitable rather than hard-earned and exultant. Humor and the occasional light touch (something the most successful sci-fi pics have always had) are absent, as is a real relish and delight in the fanciful creation of other worlds.

—*Cart.*

Micki & Maude
(COLOR)

Hilarious pic is one of Blake Edwards' best.

Hollywood, Nov. 30.

A Columbia release of a Columbia-Delphi III/B.E.E. production. Produced by Tony Adams. Executive producers, Jonathan D. Krane, Lou Antonio. Directed by Blake Edwards. Stars Dudley Moore, Amy Irving, Ann Reinking. Screenplay, Jonathan Reynolds. Camera (Metrocolor, Panavision), Harry Stradling; editor, Ralph E. Winters; music, Lee Holdridge; song music, Michel Legrand; lyrics, Alan Bergman, Marilyn Bergman; production design, Rodger Maus; art direction, Jack Senter; set decoration, Stuart A. Reiss; costume design, Patricia Norris; sound, Jerry Jost; associate producer, Trish Caroselli; assistant director, Mickey McCardle; casting, Nancy Klopper. Reviewed at the Century Plaza, L.A., Nov. 17, 1984. (MPAA Rating: PG-13.) Running time: **118 MINS.**

Rob Salinger	Dudley Moore
Maude Salinger	Amy Irving
Micki Salinger	Ann Reinking
Leo Brody	Richard Mulligan
Dr. Eugene Glztszki	George Gaynes
Dr. Elliot Fibel	Wallace Shawn
Hap Ludlow	John Pleshette
Barkhas Guillory	H.B. Haggerty
Nurse Verbeck	Lu Leonard
Diana Hutchison	Priscilla Pointer
Ezra Hutchison	Robert Symonds
Governor Lanford	George Coe

"Micki & Maude" is a hilarious farce and takes its place with "A Shot In The Dark" and "10" as one of Blake Edwards' funniest films. For his part, Dudley Moore is back in top antic form, and Amy Irving has never been better. Pic may not rank first on the public's Christmas viewing list, but winning comedy should prove a durable b.o. commodity well into the new year after some of the season's other attractions have come and gone.

Debuting screenwriter Jonathan Reynolds, author of the hit Off-Broadway filmmaking satire "Geniuses," has constructed a farce of simple, classical proportions about a man who accidentally gets his wife and new girlfriend pregnant at virtually the same time. Although one can easily predict most of the resulting complications, they mostly come off as uproarious anyway thanks to the clever scripting and deft playing.

The host of a silly tv show which does features on things like the food at an election night celebration, Moore rarely gets to see his attorney wife (Ann Reinking) due to her hectic schedule, finding time only for a quickie in the back of a limousine.

On the job for his show, Moore meets comely Amy Irving, who easily seduces him on their next encounter. Premise is set up shortly thereafter, when both women announce that they are pregnant, and the career-minded Reinking startles Moore by deciding to turn down a major judicial appointment in order to have the baby.

Major unexpected wrinkle develops when Moore agrees to actually marry Irving, something in which he is encouraged by the fact that Irving's father is an imposing professional wrestler who will brook no nonsense when it comes to his daughter.

Despite Moore's status as a bigamist, premise proves acceptable within the comic framework because he clearly loves both women and cannot rationalize letting either of them down. He contorts and extends himself to the limit in order to treat each of his wives properly, even if he's ultimately doing them an enormous injustice, and only pauses to occasionally pour out his mountain of problems to his best friend, an effectively lowkeyed Richard Mulligan.

After the women are barely kept apart at the gynecologist's office, matters reach a peak of insanity when, natch, both go into labor at the same time and are delivering babies in adjacent rooms at the same hospital, with Moore racing between them.

Finally, of course, the truth will out, and both Irving and Reinking react with appropriate outrage at the coverup Moore has perpetrated. But there's more, and it must be said that, even if he has managed to conclude the film on an acceptably pleasant note, Edwards has fudged a bit by not being more specific in how the characters resolve their seemingly insoluable dilemma.

Only other notable flaw is that, as always, Edwards has let his film run too long; some tightening in the first half-hour or so would have helped. But, once again, the director has proved that he is a master farceur, probably the foremost practitioner on the scene today of the sort of romantic comedy at which Hollywood used to excel.

Dudley Moore's basic likeability is essential to making the film work, and his inventiveness throughout his performance here is prodigious and constant. Looking ravishing, Irving exudes a warmth unprecedented in her films to date and reveals a kookiness in her interplay with Moore which is also new for her. Selfassured and commanding, Reinking, known mostly for her dancing, does a fine job keeping up with prevailing top standards.

George Gaynes and Wallace Shawn have some good moments as the doctors of the ladies, and Lu Leonard provokes belly laughs as a heavyweight nurse who won't buy Moore's convoluted explanations of why he has two pregnant wives visiting the office. Former pro footballer and wrestler H.B. Haggerty is wonderful as Irving's pa.

Production itself is very modest, being mostly played out in studio sets of bedrooms and offices.

— *Cart.*

Mama Lustig ...?
(Mama Happy ...?)
(AUSTRIAN-DOCU-B&W-16m)

Wels, Austria, Oct. 20.

A Niki List Film Production, Vienna. A documentary by Niki List. Script, Christa Polster; camera, (b&w), Christian Schmidt, List; editor, List; music, Roli Krauss. Reviewed at Austrian Film Fest (Wels), Oct. 20, 1984. Running time: **80 MINS.**

Niki List won the Max Ophüls Prize at the Saarbrücken fest in 1983 for a comedy on the pop bar scene, "Cafe Malaria." His next was this docu on Downes Syndrome children, "Mama Lustig ...?" (here translated "Mama Happy ...?").

Christian is a 15 year old and has been living during weekdays in a home for Downes Syndrome victims that has a school attached for children like him. Weekends, however, he returns home to be with his mother and older brother. A full day during a family visit is the subject matter for the film.

Christian is seen with his mother and brother, as well as with the filmmaker, with whom he appears to have a special rapport. He is filmed doing ordinary things, like eating and performing small tasks around the house to keep him busy and active. The relationship with the family is the key to the boy's existence.

List demonstrates he has the talent to handle a demanding theme, for he treats the everyday more than the individual himself — and thus allows for a gradual unveiling of the circumstances in which a Downes child lives. It's a warm and quite sensitive documentary. —*Holl.*

Flügel und Fesseln/-L'Avenir d'Emilie
(The Future Of Emily)
(W. GER.-FRENCH-COLOR)

London, Dec. 3.

A Helma Sanders Filmproduktion, in coproduction with Les Films du Losange-Literarisches Colloquium. World sales by Munic Films, Munich. Produced by Ursula Ludwig, Nicole Flipo. Directed by Helma Sanders-Brahms. Stars Brigitte Fossey, Hildegarde Knef. Screenplay, Birgit Kleber; camera (Eastmancolor), Sacha Vierny; editor, Ursula West; art directors, Jean-Michel Rugon, Rainer Schaper; costumes, Rose Becker, Ulrike Schütte; music, Jürgen Knieper; sound, Gunther Kortwich. Reviewed at London Film Festival, Dec. 2, 1984. Running time: **106 MINS.**

Isabelle	Brigitte Fossey
Paula	Hildegarde Knef
Charles	Ivan Desny
Frederick	Hermann Treusch
Emilie	Camille Raymond

Also: The voice of Matthieu Carriere.
(French soundtrack)

World preemed at the London film fest, "The Future Of Emily" is a major film which should bring laurels for everyone concerned in its production. In her new film, Helma Sanders-Brahms explores mother-daughter relationships over three generations, in the confined space of a house by the sea and in the restricted time-span of about 24 hours.

Isabelle (Brigitte Fossey) is a successful film actress whose five-year-old daughter, Emily (Camille Raymond), is cared for by Paula and Charles (Hildegarde Knef and Ivan Desny), Isabelle's parents, while her mother is away making a film. Isabelle has completed a film in Berlin and flies to the small town in Normandy where her parents live; her costar, Frederick (Hermann Treusch) follows her, and checks into a small hotel.

That's the setting for a series of extraordinary effective scenes in which the lives of Isabelle and her parents are dissected. Paula, German-born, was herself an aspiring actress when she met and married Charles in the ruins of Berlin; she has always looked upon her daughter's career with a mixture of pride and envy. For Charles, Isabelle's lifestyle, and the fact that she never married Emily's father, is a constant source of shame.

The presence of Frederick prompts a crisis between Isabelle and her parents through a long night and morning of recriminations and a mixture of mutual love and hate.

Both Sanders-Brahms and Brigitte Fossey are mothers of young daughters, and there is obviously a strong autobiographical element in the pic. Little Camille Raymond gives one of the most naturalistic performances of a child since Fossey herself in "Forbidden Games" over 30 years ago. Indeed, at one point, when Emily buries a dead Seagull she found on the beach, her mother tells her that when she was her age she acted in a film about burying dead things — "and," she says, "it was my best film." Until now, because Fossey is quite remarkable as Isabelle. So too is Hildegarde Knef, absent from the screen for 10 years; her divided emotions towards her daughter are displayed with absolute conviction.

Ivan Desny gives fine support as her husband. Only weak link in the acting stakes is Hermann Treusch, giving a rather narcissistic performance as Isabelle's lover.

Superb lensing by Sacha Vierny is an added plus for this technically fine film. Version shown in London was French, but a German version also exists. It's a natural for arthouse distribution worldwide, and confirms Helma Sanders-Brahms as one of the top rank of German directors. — *Strat.*

A Certain Romance
(HONG KONG—COLOR)

Hong Kong, Nov. 10.

A Yon Fan Film production and release. Directed and produced by Man Shih Yon Fan. Screenplay, Man Shih. Stars Ng Mei Chi and Tang Hoi Kong. Music, title song performed by Samantha Lam. Reviewed at Golden Harvest theater, Hong Kong, Nov. 9, 1984. Running time: **86 MINS.**
(Cantonese soundtrack with English subtitles)

The story can be told in one sentence and "A Certain Romance" should not be confused with "A Little Romance," though both are bound to the same graceful idea of being cutesy and charming in the never-never-land of the mobile middle class that people will find either gently moving or sickeningly unreal.

A pleasant looking innocent schoolgirl glances briefly at a handsome young man and he glances back. He is a swimming coach, ballet instructor, an intellectual with a good physique and other things. This particular glance becomes a long-drawn excuse for 85 minutes of searching, thinking, swimming, swooning and longing. Every shot seems designed to delight the director, the performers and the cinematographer.

Yon Fan, however is earnest in his desire to create a mood feature film, a feminine feeling of young romance, a tale that conveys the fairy storybook message that fate should be left alone to resolve its romantic inclinations. Somehow, Prince Charming will meet his Princess lovely and vice versa. Meanwhile, the young lady (newcomer Ng Mei Chi, said to have been discovered at a department store) talks to friends, walks, writes in her diary, fantasizes about the mysterious young man in question, Gar Ming (portrayed by newcomer Tang Hoi Kong, rumored to have been discovered at a swimming pool). Luckily, both have close friends to talk about their trivial, growing-up murmurs of the heart.

It is sadly romanticized and packaged escapism without fun, subtle eroticism without titillation, life and love in a phony way without a speck of dirt and decay. However, the predictable happy ending demonstrates the richness of make-believe fantasies that movies can still offer.
— *Mel.*

City Heat
(COLOR)

Tongue-in-cheek actioner should please Clint/Burt fans.

Hollywood, Nov. 30.

A Warner Bros. release of a Malpaso/Deliverance production. Produced by Fritz Manes. Directed by Richard Benjamin. Stars Clint Eastwood, Burt Reynolds. Screenplay, "Sam O. Brown" (Blake Edwards), Joseph C. Stinson. Story by Brown. Camera (Technicolor), Nick McLean; editor, Jacqueline Cambas; music, Lennie Niehaus; production design, Edward Carfagno; set decoration, George Gaines; costume design, Norman Salling; sound, C. Darin Knight; assistant director, David Valdes. Reviewed at The Burbank Studios, Burbank, Nov. 27, 1984. (MPAA Rating: PG.) Running time: **97 MINS.**

Lt. Speer	Clint Eastwood
Mike Murphy	Burt Reynolds
Addy	Jane Alexander
Caroline Howley	Madeline Kahn
Primo Pitt	Rip Torn
Ginny Lee	Irene Cara
Dehl Swift	Richard Roundtree
Leon Coll	Tony Lo Bianco
Lonnie Ash	William Sanderson
Troy Roker	Nicholas Worth
Nino	Robert Davi
Dub Slack	Jude Farese
Fat Freddie	John Hancock

Clint squints, Burt clowns, both throw plenty of punches and behave just as their respective fans like them to in "City Heat," an amiable but decidedly lukewarm confection geared entirely around the two star turns. Although it evaporates from the mind instantly upon its conclusion, film probably delivers enough of the expected goods to make it pass muster as an initially potent holiday b.o. draw. Eastwood has been on a roll lately, and Reynolds has put a great deal of energy into recapturing his most familiar persona of charming rogue, so viewers will be able to settle in with them as if with old buddies.

The two actors have for years proclaimed their desire to work together, and it's a sign of how much the new Hollywood differs from the old that it has taken this long for them to find something that was mutually agreeable — Gable and Tracy or Grant and Stewart had no such problem. This will hardly go down as one of the highlights in either of their careers, but there remains a certain pleasure just in seeing them square off together in a good-natured arm wrestling match of charisma and star voltage.

Nevertheless, one might have hoped for material more exciting than this hokum. Blake Edwards rewrote the original script many times and was set to direct, but finally dropped out and has used the pseudonym "Sam O. Brown" ("S.O.B.") for his story and script credit, sharing the latter with Joseph C. Stinson.

Richard Benjamin replaced him in the director's chair and here displays competent professionalism, but less of the promising flair on view in his previous outings, "My Favorite Year" and "Racing With The Moon."

Set in an unnamed city around the end of Prohibition, plot is too convoluted to convey in detail and is treated so lightly in the telling that one hardly feels compelled to follow it conscientiously. Eastwood and Reynolds were old pals in their early days as cops, but the former has taken a dim view of the latter's jump over to the private detective business, resulting in a certain tension between them.

Reynolds' partner, Richard Roundtree, gets bumped off in the early going, and Reynolds spends the remainder of the picture attempting to play two mobster kingpins off one another, while Eastwood tries to decide whether Reynolds is trying to solve the case or is actually in cahoots with the baddies, who are up to no good with Roundtree's singer girlfriend Irene Cara and Reynold's sometime sweetie Madeline Kahn.

Structure provides the opportunity for intermittent fisticuffs, shootouts and assorted other interludes of mild violence, and some of these are carried to such ridiculous extremes that they represent send-ups of the sort of action with which both stars have come to be associated.

Some of the repartee is relatively amusing, and the two stars with tongues firmly in cheek, easily set the prevailing tone of lowkeyed facetiousness. Reynolds, working with great relish and rambunctiousness, seems subjectively to be on view considerably more than Eastwood, who nevertheless throws off so much star power and gets so much out of so little that he dominates whenever he's onscreen. Eastwood earned whatever he was paid just by the way he stalks down a street brandishing a shotgun and showing a nasty look in his eye.

Jane Alexander is saddled with the Lee Patrick role as Reynolds' office secretary and hopeful recipient of Eastwood's attentions. Madeline Kahn has a few screwball moments, while remainder of the cast fills out their roles in adequate fashion. As originally cast by Edwards, Marsha Mason had Alexander's part and Clio Goldsmith was going to play the Kahn role.

Production-wise, film is entirely a studio backlot job. Production designer Edward Carfagno has made full use of the Burbank Studios' New York streets in creating the period ambience, and Nick Mc-Lean has stylishly drenched the pic, perhaps a bit too much, in a brown glow. Norman Salling's costumes are sharp. —*Cart.*

Breakout
(BRITISH-COLOR)

London, Nov. 29.

An Eyeline Film, for the Children's Film and Television Foundation produced and directed by Frank Godwin. Features entire cast. Script, Ranald Graham, from the book "A Place To Hide" by Bill Gillham; camera (color), Ray Orton; editor, Gordon Grimward; music, Harry Robertson; sound, Stanley Phillips; art directors, Michael Rickwood, Richard Hornsby. Reviewed at London Film Festival, Nov. 27, 1984. Running time: **61 MINS.**

Donny the Bull	David Jackson
Keith	Ian Bartholomew
David	Simon Nash
Stephen	John Hasler
Phil	John Bowler

"Breakout" is a well-made kidpic which tells a suspenseful tale of two young birdwatchers kidnaped by a couple of runaway convicts.

Film avoids the smugly paternalistic tone of so many pics made for children and doesn't shirk from the genuine tensions of the story. One of the cons, Donny the Bull (David Jackson) is a rum-swilling giant who seems to have strayed out of "Great Expectations" and whose one aim — after buried loot is recovered — is to go (by boat) to Australia. The fact that the kids come to like this larger-than-life character, and in the end to try to keep him from being arrested, seems exactly right.

Simon Nash and John Hasler are standouts as the two boys, and the handsome location photography of Ray Orton provides some glorious scenery of the English countryside in summer. Very tight running time is another plus.

This seems an ideal children's film, which doesn't talk down to its young audience but will give them a genuinely exciting hour in the cinema. —*Strat.*

Starman
(COLOR)

Derivative but entertaining.

Hollywood, Nov. 29.

A Columbia Pictures release of a Michael Douglas-Larry J. Franco production, from Columbia-Delphi Prods. II. Executive producer, Michael Douglas. Produced by Larry J. Franco, coproducer, Barry Bernardi. Directed by John Carpenter. Stars Jeff Bridges, Karen Allen. Screenplay, Bruce A. Evans, Raynold Gideon; camera (MGM color), Donald M. Morgan; editor, Marion Rothman; music, Jack Nitzsche; production designer, Daniel Lomino; set decorator, Robert Benton, set designer, William Joseph Durrell, Jr; art director, Michael Gleason; Starman transformation, Dick Smith, Stan Winston, Rick Baker; visual consultant — second unit director, Joe Alves; special visual effects supervisor, Bruce Nicholson; sound (Dolby stereo), Tommy Causey; assistant director, Larry Franco; production manager, Tom Joyner; stunt coordinator, Terry Leonard; casting, Jennifer Shull. Reviewed at the Directors Guild Of America, Hollywood, Calif., Nov. 28, 1984. (MPAA rating: PG.) Running time: **115 MINS.**

Starman	Jeff Bridges
Jenny Hayden	Karen Allen
Mark Shermin	Charles Martin Smith
George Fox	Richard Jaeckel
Major Bell	Robert Phalen
Sergeant Lemon	Tony Edwards

Additional Visual Effects Credits
Industrial Light & Magic: supervisor of special visual effects, Bruce Nicholson; camera (VistaVision, color), Michael McAlister; supervising modelmaker, Ease Owyeung; matte painting supervisor, Michael Pangrazio; animation supervisor, Charlie Mullen; chief editor, Michael Gleason; ILM general manager, Warren Franklin; head effects animator, Bruce Walters.

There is little that is original in "Starman," but at least it has chosen good models. An amalgam of elements introduced in "Close Encounters Of The Third Kind," "E.T." and even "The Man Who Fell To Earth," "Starman" shoots for the miraculous and only partially hits its target. But despite serious shortcomings, pic ultimately manages to capture some of the glow that made its predecessors so successful. What it does have, however, may not be enough in the congested sci-fi Christmas market and "Starman" could prove to be a shooting star at the boxoffice.

The Starman (Jeff Bridges) arrives much like "E.T." — an alien in a hostile environment — but in an elaborate transformation scene he assumes human form. The body he chooses for his sojourn on Earth happens to belong to the dead husband of Jenny Hayden (Karen Allen) who lives alone in a remote section of Wisconsin.

As written by Bruce A. Evans and Raynold Gideon, story has frequent holes and lapses of plausibility which they try to patch over with exposition after the fact. Pic is like a jigsaw puzzle with missing pieces that director John Carpenter is never totally successful in weaving together in a full-blooded and human film, as "E.T." was able to.

Unlike its role-models, "Starman" takes a more intimate approach to the material, concentrating on the developing love story between a mortal and a spaceman. Bridges and Allen set off on a trip across the country to Arizona where the Starman must make his connection to return home. Why he came in the first place or exactly where that home may be are points that Carpenter obviously doesn't consider germane to his story.

As Bridges and Allen develop a connection and, eventually, affection for each other, heavies from the State Dept. are in constant pursuit, ready to make a lab experiment out of the alien. Richard Jaeckel as the head heavy is so one-dimensional and simplistic as to deny the immediacy and urgency of the hunt.

Also in pursuit is staff scientist Charles Martin Smith who is presented as a good guy whose kind heart and sound scientific principles have been corrupted by the evil government. As a character, he, too, is diluted and rendered un-believable by the superficiality of the story.

With little else credible going for it, "Starman" must rely on the love story to make it work and this doesn't kick into gear until the second half of the film, which may be too long to wait for some viewers. Allen and Bridges do establish a strange chemistry and the purity of their love and affection becomes quite touching in a strange way.

As the housewife who has not quite got over the death of her husband, Allen is fine at suggesting her vulnerability as well her longing. She also looks great. Bridges' performance, while totally different than anything he has ever done, relying mostly on monosyllables and stiff jerks of the neck, still projects his usual low-key good natured appeal. He may be motion pictures' first ordinary alien.

Film's finale is a virtual repeat of the climax of "Close Encounters" with a group of soldiers looking on in awe as the mother ship arrives for its passenger. Even their hostility is rendered impotent next to the Starman's cosmic love.

To the filmmakers' credit, special effects do not overwhelm the human elements in the picture, but on the other hand they are not especially striking or exciting either.

— *Jagr.*

Gimme An 'F'
(COLOR)

Dancing cheerleaders flunk out.

Boca Raton, Nov. 29.

A 20th Century Fox release of a Martin Poll production. Executive producers, Poll, Arnold Kopelson. Directed by Paul Justman. Features entire cast. Screenplay, Jim Hart; camera (CFI color; prints by Deluxe), Mario Di Leo; editor, Tom Walls; music, Jan Hammer; songs, Bob Gaudio; sound, Richard van Dyke; production design, Kim Colefax; art direction, Tom Randol; production manager, Patricia Carr; assistant director, Fred Baron; stunt coordinator, Cindy "Toad" Wills; choreographer, Steve Merritt; casting, Hank McCann. Reviewed at UA Movies at Town Center 6, Boca Raton, Fla., Nov. 28, 1984. (MPAA Rating: R.) Running time: **100 MINS.**

Tom Hamilton	Stephen Shellen
Roscoe	Mark Keyloun
Pam	Jennifer C. Cooke
Mary Ann	Beth Miller
Phoebe	Daphne Ashbrook
Lead Demon	Karen Kelly
Eileen	Sarah M. Miles
Bucky	John Karlen

"Gimme An 'F' " unsuccessfully converts the once-popular cheerleaders exploitation film format ("The Cheerleaders" and "The Pom Pom Girls" a decade or so ago) into an intended dance-oriented romp. Pic is unlikely to warrant a national release following its current regional bookings by distrib 20th Century Fox, and should play better on paycable.

Debuting feature director Paul Justman, who displays solid technical skills, has a meager premise to work with in Jim Hart's script. Story revolves around an annual clinic and competition for school cheerleading teams, held at Camp Beaver View, run by Bucky Berkshire, a.k.a. "Dr. Spirit" (John Karlen, hamming it up in the principal older generation role). Berkshire, who is working on obtaining Japanese financial backing for a chain of boutiques, bets his top instructor Tom Hamilton (Stephen Shellen) $10,000 that he can't get the Moline Ducks squad to win over the powerhouse Fudge High Falcons. If he loses, Hamilton must work another five years for Berkshire.

Teen antics and sexcapades at the camp are extremely mild, with film erring in offering almost no nudity for its target youthful/drive-in audience. In keeping with the recent hit "Footloose," there is an interesting role reversal, in which lead Shellen dances sexily in his underwear in a shower while femme cast secretly watch voyeuristically.

Dance numbers are overproduced, with the Ducks' predictable blossoming from awkward, mousey types to sexpots on stage coming off as unbelievable. Also, the use of dance doubles for several of the lead players is obvious. Thesping is adequate in context and musical score serviceable. —*Lor.*

Hot Moves
(COLOR)

Okay teen sex comedy.

A Cardinal Pictures release of a Cardinal Entertainment and Spectrum Cinema Prods. presentation. Executive producers, Ralph Kent Cooke, J. Don Harris, Martin Perfit. Coproducers, Paul A. Joseph, Luigi Cingolani. Produced and directed by Jim Sotos. Features entire cast. Screenplay, Larry Anderson, Peter Foldy; assistant director, Donald Newman; camera (CFI color), Eugene Shugliet; editor, Drake P. Silliman; art direction, George Costello; set decoration, Maria Caso; set dresser, Cindy Rebman; sound, Michal Mekjian; music, Louis Forestieri; stunt coordinator, B.J. Davis; costume design, Phillip Herzog Richards; choreography, Andrea Muller; casting, Al Onorado, Jerry Franks. Reviewed at RKO Warner 1 theater, N.Y., Nov. 23, 1984. (MPAA Rating: R.) Running time: **86 MINS.**

With: Michael Zorek, Adam Silbar, Jeff Fishman, Johnny Timko, Jill Schoelen, Debi Richter, Virgil Frye, Tami Holbrook, Monique Gabrielle, David Christopher.

"Hot Moves" is a slightly above average teen sex comedy, shot largely on the beach at Venice, Calif., thereby enabling the camera to ogle a wide array of uncovered flesh, both male and female. Reasonably conceived but predictable plot line makes it acceptable fare to young viewers, especially those in northern climes who can catch some vicarious rays during the current frost. Quick theatrical playoff should lead to vidcassette release by the thaw.

Hackneyed premise is that four teenaged boys each try in their own inimitable way to lure pretty girls into their clutches, horniest among them being pudgy Barry, energetically played by Michael Zorek in a virtual reprise of his role in last year's "Private School." Highlight for Barry (and male viewers) is the swiping of his father's telescope in order to get a closer look at the occupants of a nearby nude beach — populated only by young women, of course. Girls jog in slow motion through the surf, accompanied by vaguely familiar music, identified on the end credits as "Chariots For Hire."

"Serious" side of pic involves Mike's (Adam Silbar) frustrated attempts to bed his longtime but reluctant sweetheart Julie Ann (Jill Schoelen). They play cat and mouse, each toying with other game before coming to the conclusion that, well, sex isn't all that important if they really love each other.

With the exceptions of Zorek, Silbar and Schoelen, other performances tend toward caricature, due mostly to the underdeveloped screenplay. Monique Gabrielle, who appeared in "Bachelor Party," and Debi Richter are memorably attractive additions to the landscape.

Tech credits generally are fine, though short film is padded too much with pointless footage of various beach activities such as weightlifters working out on the sand while fascinated kids stand by. Director Jim Sotos, who also produced, takes a respite from his usual horror efforts and gets on the break-dance bandwagon with cinema verité-style scenes of head-spinning bodies, often repeated as a sort of cockeyed motif. —*Gerz.*

Desiree
(DUTCH-COLOR)

Amsterdam, Nov. 20.

The Movies distribution release of a Cosmic Illusion production. Produced by Norman de Palm. Written by De Palm. Directed by Felix de Rooy. Starring Marian Rolle. Dan Strayhorn. Camera (color), Ernest Dickenson; editors, Edgar Burcksen, Jacques Marcus; music, Ronald Snijders; sound, Gil Kraus, Anne Rodgers. Reviewed at Alhambra theater, Amsterdam, Nov. 19, 1984. Running time: **96 MINS.**

Desiree	Marian Rolle
Freddy	Dan Strayhorn
Mother	Cynthia Belgrave
Mrs. Resnick	Joanne Jacobson
Father Siego	Maxwell Glanville
Desiree as a child	Askina Touree

"Desiree" is a film with a complicated international history. Writer and director come from Dutch islands in the Caribbean. Norman de Palm is a writer, an actor and a Ph.D. in clinical psychology. Felix de Rooy is a legit and film director, actor, painter and art teacher.

De Palm saw a news story that on New Year's Eve 1980, in New York, a black woman burned her child in her oven in order to exorcise an "evil force" in the baby.

De Palm's film is based on his own play about this incident.

A Dutch film, set and shot in New York, with American actors, in English, "Desiree" should be of interest mainly for black audiences. During performance in an Amsterdam theater the blacks in the audience reacted passionately to the happenings on the screen.

Desiree (Marion Rolle) carries a carton around with her in which she imagines is her baby. She talks to it, feeds it, dresses and undresses it. Flashbacks tell her history. Father disappeared, the domineering mother gets the money to bring up her daughter from an ever-changing chain of "uncles." After mother's death, Desiree comes under the influence of the sect of the True Confessors of Father Siego. The sect has strange rules, for instance, no drinking of milk, and sex only with other True Confessors.

Desiree falls in love with the doorman of a chic apartment house where she cleans for a rich white woman. The woman sees to it that Freddy, the doorman, loses his job when Desiree becomes pregnant. Desiree loses her job, her man, her status as a True Confessor, and finally her mind.

Marian Rolle is extraordinary, managing a virtuoso performance full of deepfelt emotion. The only flaw is a certain theatricality, more due, probably, to writing and direction than to the actress.

"Desiree" never quite becomes cinema, but remains somewhat stagy, one or two cinematic sequences notwithstanding. The other performances are good, but not in the Marian Rolle class. Good tunes include vocals and arrangements by Rolle. Edgar Burcksen's editing is outstanding, other technical credits okay. —*Wall.*

The Surrogate
(CANADIAN-COLOR)

Winnipeg, Nov. 30.

A Cinepix release of a Cinepix Inc.-Telemetropole Intl. production. Produced by John Dunning and Don Carmody; executive producers, Andre Link, Andre Fleury. Directed by Don Carmody. Features entire cast. Screenplay by Carmody and Robert Geoffrian. Camera (Eastman), François Protat; editor, Rit Wallace; art direction, Charles Dunlop; music, Daniel Lanois. Reviewed at the Colony Cinema, Winnipeg, Nov. 25, 1984. Running time: **99 MINS.**

Frank Waite	Art Hindle
Anouk Van Derlin	Carole Laure
Lee Waite	Shannon Tweed
George Kyber	Michael Ironside
Dr. Harriet Forman	Marilyn Lightstone
Eric	Jim Bailey
Fantasy Woman	Jackie Burroughs
Maggie Simpson	Barbara Law
John Manion	Gary Reineke
Brenner	Jonathan Welsh

"The Surrogate" casts sultry leather-clad Carole Laure as both the savior and potential demise of a young couple's sexually troubled marriage. Despite the sexy come-on, the picture is essentially a violence-laced thriller that runs a familiar course. The material never comes near to touching its truly provocative nature suggesting a commercial strategy of quick, mass playoffs to attract the inquisitive and dispel disappointing word-of-mouth.

The story zigs and zags between pop psychology and the mounting body count inflicted by a maniacal killer. It's only by happenstance that the two elements of the film converge at any point. The whole affair is quite frantic and eventually quite predictable in a most disappointing way.

Story focuses on Frank and Lee Waite (Art Hindle and Shannon Tweed). He's a sports car salesman introduced as extremely hot-tempered. It turns out he used to be a nice guy but has been acting ornery since his wife turned increasingly frigid. His anger also manifests itself in blackouts that leave him wondering whether he's committed some unspeakable act.

So, his shrink (Marilyn Lightstone) suggests the couple try radical treatment in the form of a sex therapist specializing in unleashing repressed sexual fantasies. The woman (Laure) quickly opens the tap but the after-effect proves distasteful for Lee. Frank, too, is horrified at her power to egg him on sexually but he also notices he's getting fewer headaches.

Meanwhile, in the city (Montreal subbing for New York), a series of violent stabbings are going on which are not, surprise, overtly sexually related. Initially, they appear to have little to do with the couple other than in the link between a neighbor, a transvestite (Jim Bailey), who is seen lurking in the background at the scene of the crimes.

However, as victims turn up who are friends of the couple, they begin to fear a link may exist between the killings and the sex therapist. This, of course, would never do, even in as hackneyed an effort as "The Surrogate." So, the film boils down to a guessing game with liberal clues strewn about. Almost any scenario could evolve but the filmmakers opt for pointing a finger at the most sexually repressed character in the story.

Virtually every component of the film is lacklustre. Hindle is a truly colorless quasihero while Tweed (a former Playboy Playmate of the Year) demonstrates few assets beyond the physical. Only Laure begins to suggest, in flashes, the powerful dynamic possible here. Her mania for psychodramatic games can be quite chilling.

Don Carmody, best-known as the producer of the "Porky's"

films, makes a thoroughly forgettable debut as director and is credited with cowriting the script and coproducing. He effects quite a shoddy looking production with a murky soundtrack and curiously unflatteringly lit images from the normally professional and slick François Protat.

Produced under the initial title, "Blind Rage," "The Surrogate" is neither substitute nor improvement to such recent sexually themed fare as "Crimes Of Passion" and "Body Double." Commercial prospects for the new entry are considerably less than the two earlier pictures' as the film is disappointing in providing genuine shocks or in giving audiences a true sense of something risque. — *Klad.*

L'Année des Meduses
(Year Of The Medusa)
(FRENCH-COLOR)

Paris, Nov. 29.

Parafrançe release of a T. Films/FR3 coproduction. Produced by Alain Terzian. Stars Bernard Giraudeau and Valérie Kaprisky. Written and directed by Christopher Frank. Camera, Renato Berta; art director, Jean-Jacques Caziot; original music, Alain Wisniak; songs performed by Nina Hagen; sound, Bernard Bats; production manager, Philippe Lièvre. Reviewed at the Marignan-Concorde theater, Nov. 28, 1984. Running time: **110 MINS.**

Chris	Valérie Kaprisky
Romain	Bernard Giraudeau
Claude	Caroline Cellier
Vic	Jacques Perrin
Marianne	Béatrice Agenin
Lamotte	Philippe Lemaire
Pierre	Pierre Vaneck
Barbara	Barbara Nielsen

After a dull debut as writer-director, novelist-screenwriter Christopher Frank seemed to have found his manner in his second film, "Femmes de Personnes" a well-observed naturalistic study of several women struggling to assert their independence and equilibrium. However, with his third picture as helmer, the strain has returned in this overemphatic tale of a perverse teenage girl on the prowl along the beaches of St. Tropez.

Valérie Kaprisky, fresh from her undraped frenzy in Andrzej Zulawski's "The Public Woman," dons or undoes her bikini in the lead role, and Frank even goes so far as to have her repeat, in a lower key, her demonic nude dance of "Public Woman" for the story's somewhat Grand Guignolesque climax.

Still, Kaprisky is a definite plus in this awkwardly overwrought melodrama of desire, sexual manipulation and murder, creating a personage of disquieting ambiguity with less of the maniacal physicality of Zulawski's opus. As her mom, Caroline Cellier often steals the show as a still attractive woman, moving towards 40 and eyeing a summer romance with Bernard Giraudeau.

Giraudeau is the pivot of the drama, a beachside Casanova and sometime pimp who avoids Kaprisky like the plague while he angles for a sexual fling with Cellier. Mom finally lets herself go into Giraudeau's arms, while Kaprisky gives vent to her frustration by wreaking havoc among other vacationers.

Frank, who so skillfully interwove several narrative lines in "Femmes de Personne," plots clumsily here, injecting labored flashbacks (Kaprisky's early affair with her first victim, Jacques Perrin), some ludicrous voice-over commentaries to provide shortcuts when just the opposite is needed (a luncheon on the beach where Kaprisky exerts her divide-and-conquer fascination), and heavy-handed symbolic effects: Kaprisky is too obviously likened to a jellyfish, whose fatal role in the story is telegraphed with irritating insistence.

In an apparently semi-parodic mood, Frank even evokes "Jaws" in opening credits shots, and in some of Alain Wisniak's score, which is effectively dosed with some gutsy Nina Hagen tunes.

Frank's "one deadly summer" could benefit from trimming and reediting. As it is, an intriguing three-character sexual drama gets lost amidst a lot of soggy psychodramatics. — *Len.*

O Erotas Tou Odyssea
(Ulysses' Love)
(GREEK-COLOR)

Thessaloniki, Oct. 6.

A Sigma Film Kinimatografiki EPE coproduction with the Greek Film Centre, written and directed by Vassilis Vafeas. Featuring Costas Voutsas, Athenodoros Prousalis and Caterina Rodiou. Camera (color) and editor, Dinos Katsourides, sets and costumes, Damianos Zarifis, sound by Elias Ionesco. Reviewed at the Thessaloniki Film Fest, Oct. 6, 1984. Running time: **107 MINS.**

Ulysses	Costas Voutsas
His colleague	Athenodoros Prousalis
The girl (his love)	Caterina Rodiou
A woman singer	Hara Agueloussi
Yacht's owner	Yannis Goumas
His neighbor	Kariofilia Karabeti
Her roommate	Eva Moustaka
A young student	Menas Hatzisavas

This is a bittersweet comedy which should do very well locally and find profitable overseas sales, attracting attention on the festival circuit as well. It is the third film written and directed by Vassilis Vafeas who won the best director prize at the festival.

The central character is Ulysses, a middle-aged Greek, married and father of two children, who works in the accounting department of a company. While his family is away on vacation he is informed by the general manager of the company that he is fired.

Leaving his office, he wanders through the streets of Athens, a city still unknown to him though he has lived there all his life. He meets a girl who reminds him of the great love of his youth and starts following her. This pursuit leads him to encounters and funny situations he had never imagined. It is an escape from the misery of his everyday routine. Vafeas has created his own style by presenting in a humorous and satirical way situations of everyday life. He mingles realism and fantasy to describe the experiences of his hero, leaving the girl's identification vague.

Costas Voutsas' interpretation is touching as the simple and naive hero. He seldoms speaks, but with his expressions shows surprise and astonishment. He won a special prize at the festival for his role as well as for his career contribution in motion pictures.

The excellent photography by Dinos Katsourides is an added asset. —*Rena.*

Sword Of The Valiant
(BRITISH-COLOR)

W. Palm Beach, Dec. 1.

A Cannon Releasing release of a Cannon Group presentation of a Golan-Globus production, in association with Stephen Weeks Co. A London-Cannon Films Ltd. picture. Produced by Menahem Golan, Yoram Globus. Executive producers, Michael Kagan, Philip M. Breen. Directed by Weeks. Stars Miles O'Keeffe, Cyrielle Claire, Leigh Lawson. Screenplay, Weeks, Breen, Howard C. Pen; camera (Fujicolor, J-D-C Widescreen), Freddie A. Young, Peter Hurst; editors, Richard Marden, Barry Peters; music, Ron Geesin; sound, George Stephenson, Malcolm Davies; production design, Maurice Fowler, Derek Nice; set dresser, Val Wolstenholme; costumes, Shuna Harwood; action sequences director, Anthony Squire; second unit director, Sture Rydman; special effects supervisor, Nobby Clarke; special effects prosthetics, Daniel Parker; Green Knight head effects, Aaron Sherman; casting, Maude Spector. Reviewed at UA Village Green Movies 3, W. Palm Beach, Fla., Nov. 30, 1984. (MPAA Rating: PG.) Running time: **101 MINS.**

Gawain	Miles O'Keeffe
Linet	Cyrielle Claire
Humphrey	Leigh Lawson
Green Knight	Sean Connery
King Arthur	Trevor Howard
Seneschal	Peter Cushing
Oswald	Ronald Lacey
Lady of Lyonesse	Lila Kedrova
Baron Fortinbras	John Rhys-Davies
Black Knight	Douglas Wilmer
Friar Vosper	Brian Coburn
Morgan La Fay	Emma Sutton
Sir Bertilak	Bruce Liddington
Porter	Wilfrid Brambell

"Sword Of The Valiant" is a fanciful but uneven retelling of the Arthurian legend of Sir Gawain and The Green Knight, previously immortalized in verse and subject of a domestically unreleased 1972 film (starring Murray Head and Ciaran Madden) made by the same director as here, Stephen Weeks. Cannon production and release boasts an impressive cast but is unlikely to turn on contemporary audiences.

Weeks' glaring failure is to establish a consistent tone, opting instead for a mixture of romance, fantasy and mild sendup. It's a losing battle, especially since "Monty Python And The Holy Grail" definitively spoofed such material a decade ago.

Sean Connery, moonlighting here during the filming of "Never Say Never Again," perks matters up as the Green Knight, a magician who challenges King Arthur's court boastfully at film's opening with an ax contest. Finding no takers, the King (Trevor Howard in a guest role) offers to fight the Green Knight himself, at which point a young squire, Gawain (Miles O'Keeffe), volunteers to champion his king, is instantly knighted and beheads the magician. Unfortunately, the Green Knight's body magically finds its head, screws it back on and the tricky villain sentences Gawain to a year's grace in which to solve a riddle, after which his life will be forfeit.

Gawain, with his trusty squire Humphrey (Leigh Lawson), embarks on an episodic series of rather arbitrary adventures, all the while manipulated by the Green Knight and Morgan La Fay (Emma Sutton). Chief aspect of his riddle-solving quest involves Gawain rescuing (and frequently re-rescuing) the Princess Linet (beautiful French actress Cyrielle Claire) of the lost land of Lyonesse.

Burdened with silly-looking blond Prince Valiant tresses, O'Keeffe acquits himself well in the romantic lead role, aided by a bevy of top character actors. Connery, in particular, delivers a robust performance. Castle locations in Wales, Scotland and France are attractive, but production is deficient in its rather dull action sequences and fake-looking armor. Special effects are cutesy and not up to current standards. — *Lor.*

London Festival

Unfair Exchanges
(BRITISH-COLOR)

London, Nov. 29.

A BBC production. Produced by Kenith Trodd. Directed by Gavin Millar. Stars Julie Walters. Script, Ken Campbell, from an idea by Ion Will; camera (color), John McGlashan; production design, Derek Dodd; editor, Angus Newton; sound, Stephen Gatland; music, Bruce Cole. Reviewed at London Film Festival, Nov. 27, 1984. Running time: **70 MINS.**

Mavis	Julie Walters
Arthur	David Rappaport
Ronnie	Robert Kingswell
Danny	George Lapham
Sarah	Rosalind March
Mr. Wills	Bert Parnaby
Tim Rickett	Ken Campbell
Mavis' Dad	Joe Black

This intriguing conspiracy-theory pic treads a fine line between farce and thriller, and doesn't quite make it. The idea itself is a good one, though not new. Mavis (Julie

Walters) has left her gay husband and lives alone in London flat with her small son. One night the husband phones to say he's coming over; he doesn't, and next denies he called. Strange things seem to be happening with Mavis' telephone; there's hysterical laughter on the line, and other seemingly inexplicable occurrences.

Trying to discover what's happening, she meets a handful of highly eccentric people, including a lustful dwarf and a conspiracy-theory expert (played by scripter Ken Campbell, best known for his work as a fringe theater director). Solution is that the telephone company is taking over everybody with its universal spy network (a theory first promulgated in "The President's Analyst" [1967] by Theodore J. Flicker).

Gavin Millar gets good performances out of his cast, and includes some nice visual jokes (a telephone or a telephone company van is to be seen in every other shot); yet his overly tricky soundtrack, filled with overlapping conversations and noises, is needlessly confusing and seems likely to frustrate the viewer. Eventually the story has too many holes and too many questions remain unanswered. The difficult farce-thriller tone is only intermittently captured.

It may or may not be intentional, but in one scene Julie Walters wears pink pajamas in an apparent nod to her forthcoming feature film, "She'll Be Wearing Pink Pyjamas." —Strat.

Four Days In July
(BRITISH-COLOR)

London, Nov. 29.
A BBC Production. Produced by Kenith Trodd. Directed and devised by Mike Leigh. Features entire cast. Camera (color), Remi Adefarasin; production design, Jim Clay; editor, Robin Sales; sound, John Pritchard; music, Rachel Portman. Reviewed at London Film Festival, Nov. 27, 1984. Running time: 99 MINS.
Collette . . . . Brid Brennan
Eugene . . . . Des McAleer
Billy . . . . Charles Lawson
Lorraine . . . . Paula Hamilton
Brendan . . . . Shane Connaughton
Carmel . . . . Eileen Pollock
Dixie . . . . Stephen Rea

Still working in the naturalistic style of last year's magnificent "Meantime," Mike Leigh has come up with a pointed drama about two couples, one Catholic and one Protestant, living in Belfast. Although near neighbors, they have nothing in common but one thing: the wives are expecting their first babies, which will be born in the same hospital on the same day.

From this simple premise Leigh and his wonderful actors have fashioned a painfully accurate portrait of the divisions of Northern Ireland. Eugene (Des McAleer), the

Catholic man, is badly crippled after a shooting incident; Collette (Brid Brennan) has to devote as much time to him as to herself. They face a bleak future, though the prospect of parenthood excites them both. In one of the film's most moving scenes, Collette tries to help her husband's insominia by singing "The Patriot Game" to him. The Protestant, Billy (Charles Lawson), is a died-in-the-wool Ulsterman and a member of the Ulster Defense League. A beer-swilling, insensitive chauvinist, he still has his human side (when he's not drunk).

Pic is structured loosely with apparently improvised (actually rehearsed in workshops) conversations between the two couples and their friends. The climax comes when the two husbands face each other in the hospital waiting room and the two wives, with their new babies, are in adjacent beds while a midwife prattles away about nothing. Result may not be as quite as dramatically satisfying as "Meantime," but still shows that the loose approach pays off via acute insights into these people and the way they live. Acting, as in every Leigh film, is beyond praise, and the on-location camerawork in the troubled, wartorn city brings the tragedy of Northern Ireland vividly alive.

Unfortunately, the thick, authentic Ulster accents used by the entire cast are sometimes hard to penetrate and will diminish potential audiences for this fine film. —Strat.

Winter Flight
(BRITISH-COLOR)

London, Nov. 26.
An Enigma production for Goldcrest Films. Produced by Susan Richards and Robin Douet. Executive producer, David Puttnam. Directed by Roy Battersby. Features entire cast. Screenplay by Alan Janes; camera (color), Chris Menges; art, Adrienne Atkinson; costume, Sue Yelland; editor, Lesley Walker; music, Richard Harvey. Reviewed at the London Film Festival, Nov. 23, 1984. Running time: 103 MINS.
Mal Stanton . . . . Reece Dinsdale
Angie . . . . Nicola Cowper
Dave . . . . Gary Olsen
Hooker . . . . Sean Benn
Lara . . . . Beverly Hewitt
Kel . . . . Shelagh Stephenson
Doctor . . . . Michael Percival
Sergeant Bowyer . . . . Anthony Trent
Jack . . . . Tim Bentinck

"Winter Flight" is a bittersweet romance with deep resonances, some of which may be missed by non-British audiences. It's an impressive theatrical debut for Roy Battersby, with better b.o. prospects than other recent lowbudget items from David Puttnam's Enigma stable.

With a tight and witty script from Alan Janes, pic narrates the sometimes rocky development of a relationship between Mal, an innocent in charge of keeping birds off the runway at an airforce base, and the

somewhat more worldly Angie. The problems of getting to know each other are heightened when Angie reveals that her non-terminable pregnancy predates their acquaintance.

Pic plays the sophistication of military hardware and the brutality of training against the problems confronted by the young couple. In a lighthanded way, the contrast throws up questions about the relevance of the military apparatus in a world where just living is hard enough.

Although scenes of planes landing and soldiers exercising are often loosely connected to the central action, there's a link implicit in the institutionalized violence represented in the character of Hooker. Excellent camerawork by lenser Chris Menges and operator Mike Roberts reaches its apogee in action scenes involving Hooker as he beats up Mal and later uses a mechanical digger to destroy the car of his erstwhile girlfriend's new lover.

Love blossoms between the young couple thanks to Mal's impulsive gestures, which often surprise, and despite the secret that Angie can only hide before the baby is born. Reece Dinsdale gives energy and charm to the role of Mal. Nicola Cowper has problems giving life to the part of Angie once her belly begins to swell.

Film's chief downers are an uninteresting initial sequence and a conclusion which doesn't quite deliver given the long buildup. Excellent technical credits are rounded off by a riveting score. — Japa.

Sleeps Six
(BRITISH-COLOR)

London, Nov. 29.
A BBC Production. Produced and directed by James Cellan Jones. Stars Ben Kingsley, Diane Keen, Jeremy Child. Screenplay, Frederic Raphael; camera (color), John Hooper; production design, Don Homfray; editor, John Stothart; music, Richard Holmes; sound, John Murphy. Reviewed at London Film Festival, Nov. 26, 1984. Running time: 80 MINS.
Geoff Craven . . . . Ben Kingsley
Sherry Craven . . . . Diane Keen
Philip (Lord) Witham . . . . Jeremy Child
Bernie Pinto . . . . Alfred Marks
Goldie Pinto . . . . Nancy Roberts
Lady Jane . . . . Jackie Wood Smith
Chrissie . . . . Alisa Bosschaert

A year ago, the London Film Festival highlighted the BBC production "An Englishman Abroad," directed by John Schlesinger, which subsequently did the rounds at several international film festivals and played on PBS and cable in the U.S. This new BBC film is scripted by Frederic Raphael, who also wrote Schlesinger's "Darling" (1965) among many other excellent film and tv productions. In "Sleeps Six" he seems to be covering very old ground.

The basic notion of the film is that the British aristocracy is corrupt and can't be trusted — hardly a new theme. Jeremy Child is Lord Witham, a dissolute member of the upper crust, who, in the mid-1960s, befriends Geoff Craven (Ben Kingsley), a workingclass would-be film producer, and becomes his agent. The years go by and both men are fabulously rich and successful but there's one big difference: Craven is happily married and still very much in love with his wife, Sherry (Diane Keen), while the immature Witham still plays the field.

Bulk of the film takes place in a villa on the Riviera which has been rented by the friends (hence the film's unhelpful title) and where tensions are caused not only by the often rainy weather and the fact that builders are noisily constructing something next to the expensive swimming pool, but also by the fact that Witham's partner, Lady Jane, has sensibly dropped him and he's gone on a drunken binge as a result. He also picks up a well-endowed teenager who swims naked in the pool.

The basic problem with all this is that Witham, neatly characterized by Jeremy Child, is so obviously a snobbish ingrate from the start that his 18-year friendship with the sensible and affectionate Craven is hard to believe. Even harder to believe is the fact that his last-minute duplicity and betrayal should come as unexpectedly as it does.

Nonetheless, there's plenty of smart, bitchy dialog here, and a number of marvelous actors. Ben Kingsley displays his glowing talent yet again as the faithful, dogged Craven; Diane Keen is charming as his forthright wife, and Jeremy Child makes the awful Lord Witham a genuinely despicable character. There's also a neat cameo from Alfred Marks as a nouveau-riche member of the nobility.

Direction by James Cellan Jones tends to overemphasize what was already obvious in the script. Raphael's contempt for the upper crust of British society was revealed far more successfully in Clive Donner's "Nothing But The Best" back in 1964. — Strat.

Utsav
(Festival)
(INDIAN-COLOR)

London, Nov. 19.
A Film Valas Production. Produced by Shashi Kapoor, Dharampriya Das. Directed by Girish Karnad. Stars Kapoor. Screenplay, Karnad, from a play by Sudraka; dialog. Sharad Joshi; camera (color), Ashok Mehta; music, Laxmikant Pyarelal; lyrics, Vasant Dev; choreography, Suresh Bhat; sound, Hitendra Ghosh; editor, Bhanudas; art directors, Jayoo Pathwardhan, Nachiket; costumes, Lovleen Bains. Reviewed at London Film Festival. Nov. 17, 1984. Running time: 116 MINS.
Samsthanaka . . . . Shashi Kapoor

Vasantsena ....Rekha
Aditi ....Anooradha
Sajjal ....Shanker Nag
Charudatta.............Shenkhar Suman
Vatsyayana ....Amjad Khan

A lavishly produced comedy based on a 4th century Sanskrit play, "Festival" is the kind of Indian film rarely shown at Western festivals. Though the version shown in London has been "adapted" for western audiences (most of the songs have been eliminated, and the dialog well-dubbed into rather posh English), it still emerges as a delightful romp, full of larger than life characters and with a surprising amount of eroticism.

Basic plot concerns a married man who is seduced by a beautiful courtesan who, in turn, is trying to escape the lascivious attentions of a lustful nobleman. The Brahmin's passionate experiences with the courtesan make him a much better lover, and it's his wife who ultimately gets the best of the bargain.

There are plenty of subsidiary characters and subplots which occasionally confuse given the breakneck pace of Girish Karnad's direction. Viewers used to slowly paced Indian films are in for a surprise here, as the pic fairly belts along. Another surprise is the sexual content. Restrictions on screen kissing are obviously a thing of the past, and the sensuality of the love scenes is remarkable. There's even above-the-waist female nudity in one scene. —*Strat.*

Karnal
(Of The Flesh)
(FILIPINO-COLOR)

London, Nov. 26.
A Cine Suerte production. Produced by Benjamin Yalung. Directed by Marilou Diaz-Abaya. Features entire cast. Script, Ricardo Lee; camera (color), Manolo R. Abaya; editor, Marc Tarnate; production design, Fiel Zabat; music, Ryan Cayabyab; sound, Rudy Baldovino. Reviewed at London Film Festival, Nov. 23, 1984. Running time: 110 MINS.
Puring ....Cecille Castillo
Narcing ....Phillip Salvador
Mang Gusting...............Vic Salayan
Coryo ....Joel Torre
Doray................Grace Amilbangsa
Menardo ....Crispin Medina
Storyteller ....Charito·Solis

This Filipino pic is a fetid, grossly overstated melodrama set in a remote part of the Philippines in the '30s. Pic's hero, Narcing, brings his 18-year-old bride, Puring, home from Manila to meet the family. It proves to be a mistake, because she's a dead ringer for his mother, who killed herself some years earlier. This gets everyone very hot under the collar, especially Narcing's dad who, after much puffing and panting, almost rapes his daughter-in-law and is beheaded by his son for his pains.

Though apparently based on a true story (as published, the end

credits inform us, in Mr. & Mrs. Magazine), "Karnal" is wildly improbable as floridly handled by Marilou Diaz-Abaya, who earlier made the more interesting "Moral" (1982), which had a contemporary setting. Maybe its a question of a Third-World approach to drama that's so alien to Westerners as to be almost unwatchable; whatever the reason, it's far less interesting than the gritty urban political dramas of Lino Brocka or Mike de Leon coming from the Philippines.

Quality of acting is hard to judge: like the direction, it seems way over the top, with endless crying, screaming, breast-beating and carrying on. Some of the scenes of violence, though patently phony, are still so graphically handled as to make queasy members of the audience unwell.

Pic ends with the husband cutting his own throat in his prison cell while the wife, aided by a deaf mute who has lusted after her, painfully gives birth to a baby which she then kills. Story is related as a flashback by a narrator, a descendant of the family, who understandably seems quite upset about it all, even after so many years. —*Strat.*

Yoinchanhoksa: Mulleya
Mulleya
(The Wheel)
(SOUTH KOREAN-COLOR)

London, Nov. 25.
A Han Lim Cinema Corp. production. Produced by Chong Ung-ki. Executive produced by Kim Kap-ui. Directed by Lee Doo-yong (I Tu-yong). Features entire cast. Script, Im Ch'ung; camera (VistaVision, Eastmancolor), I Song-ch'un; editor, I Kyong-cha; music, Chong Yun-chu; sound, I Chae-ung; production design, I T'ae-u; Pae Yong-ch'un. Reviewed at London Film Festival, Nov. 25, 1984. Running time: 103 MINS.
Kil-rye ....Won Mi-kyong
Yun-po ....Shin Il-yong
Kim Chin-sa ....Ch'oe Song-kwan
His wife ....Mun Chong-suk
Ch'oe Chin-sa ....Pak Min-ho
Yun Pu-sa ....Ch'oe Song-ho

Korean films surface only sporadically at international fests, and rarely in competition at the major events. Yet the indications are that South Korea's film industry, producing 100 features a year, has plenty of talent and "The Wheel" is further evidence of this.

Set in the early days of the Choson dynasty (15th century), it's the story of a beautiful and vivacious woman crushed by the patriarchal society of her time. Kil-rye, performed luminously by Won Mikyong, is betrothed to a man who dies before the wedding. But, according to custom, she is effectively married and has to leave her home and live with her strict in-laws, where she does hard manual work and is not allowed to communicate with any men and most women.

One night a man breaks into her room and rapes her, the first time she has experienced sex. The act is repeated nightly until the man is caught and summarily killed, and she banished.

At a shrine she meets a kindly man who marries her and they find work as servants at what seems to be a monastery; but the chief priest also has rape on his mind, and is killed by the husband. The couple flee and arrive at the husband's family home where it seems he's a nobleman. Kil-rye's troubles aren't over, though; the family needs a male heir, and she can't get pregnant. Concubines are brought to her husband to no avail until it's accepted he's sterile. Then Kil-rye is forced to submit to a servant, who gets her pregnant and is killed for his pains.

The story is told in a series of rather complicated flashbacks, but builds to a powerful message on the plight of women in Korean society at this time. At the end, the pic has achieved the dimension of genuine tragedy. Visually it's outstanding, with rich images reminiscent of the finest of Japanese cinema, and director Lee Doo-yong (spelled that way on the print, but listed as I Tu-yong in the festival program notes), with 50 features behind him, is a talent worth exploring.

Biggest drawback, common to so many Third World films shown at foreign fests, is the poor English subtitling, with "chastity" constantly referred to as "chestity" and the use of such incongruous expressions as "You are goofing!" The original title, literally translated, means "A History Of Brutality To Women: O Spinning Wheel O Spinning Wheel." — *Strat.*

The Cotton Club
(COLOR)

Uneven but still commercial Coppola spectacular.

An Orion Pictures release of a Zoetrope Studios production. Produced by Robert Evans. Executive producer, Dyson Lovell; coproducers, Silvio Tabet, Fred Roos; line producers, Barrie Osborne, Joseph Cusumano. Directed by Francis Coppola. Features entire cast. Screenplay, William Kennedy and Coppola, story by Kennedy, Coppola and Mario Puzo, suggested by a pictorial history by James Haskins. Camera (Technicolor), Stephen Goldblatt; editors, Barry Malkin, Robert Lovett; production designer, Richard Sylbert; costume design, Milena Canonero; principal choreographer, Michael Smuin; tap choreography, Henry LeTang; music, John Barry; musical recreations, Bob Wilber; sound mix (Dolby), Jack Jacobson. Reviewed at the Magno screening room, N.Y., Nov. 9, 1984. (MPAA Rating: R.) Running time: 127 MINS.
Dixie Dwyer ....Richard Gere
Sandman Williams ....Gregory Hines
Vera Cicero ....Diane Lane
Lila Rose Oliver ....Lonette McKee
Owney Madden ....Bob Hoskins
Dutch Schultz ....James Remar
Vincent Dwyer ....Nicolas Cage
Abbadabba Berman ....Allen Garfield
Frenchy Demange ....Fred Gwynne
Tish Dwyer ....Gwen Verdon
Frances Flegenheimer ....Lisa Jane Persky
Clay Williams ....Maurice Hines
Sol Weinstein ....Julian Beck
Madame St. Clair ....Novella Nelson
Bumpy Rhodes ....Larry Fishburne
Joe Flynn ....John Ryan
Irving Stark ....Tom Waits
Winnie Williams.........Wynonna Smith
Sugar Coates ....Charles (Honi) Coles
Cab Calloway ....Larry Marshall
Lucky Luciano ....Joe Dallesandro
Holmes ....Woody Strode

The arrival of a new film by Francis Coppola brings with it the anticipation of greatness. His latest, "The Cotton Club," certainly isn't in the same league as his best pictures, but neither is it on the grim order of such recent efforts as "One From The Heart" and "Rumble Fish." For aficionados of the filmmaker, the latest effort may be a bit of a letdown, but it is by no means a disaster, nor is it a film lacking commercial appeal.

However, coming in at a reported $47,000,000, the '30s-era gangster saga set in the world of jazz music and dance will have a tough go at recouping its cost. Initial business should be quite brisk but the film's strongest point — its period music — is a doubtful long-term selling item for the prime movie-going audience.

Comparisons are inevitable between the new film and Coppola's highly successful "Godfather" efforts. Initial hoopla played up the reteaming of the filmmaker with "Godfather" cronies, producer Robert Evans and scripter Mario Puzo (given a story credit here). However, it subsequently became apparent, through on-set and court tangles, that harmony did not reign supreme during production.

The new film certainly doesn't stint on ambition. Four stories thread through and intertwine in the picture. While the earlier Coppola gangster efforts had a firm hand on the balance between plot elements and characters, "The Cotton Club" emerges as uneven and sometimes unfocused and its tone giddily goes from the coldly realistic to frenzied fantasy.

Focus is on Dixie Dwyer (Richard Gere), a cornet player in a small Gotham club. As the film opens in 1928, Dixie interrupts a solo to push a patron out of the way of a gunman's bullet. The thankful target turns out to be racketeer, beer baron and nightclub owner Dutch Schultz (James Remar).

Schultz is soon throwing work Dixie's way and hires his brother, Vincent (Nicolas Cage), as a bodyguard. He also asks the musician to act as beard and escort his mistress, Vera Cicero (Diane Lane), to various social functions. One such watering hole is the title Cotton Club owned by gangland peacemaker Owney Madden (Bob Hoskins) and operated by his righthand man, Frenchie Demange (Fred Gwynne).

Final thread involves club tap star Sandman Williams (Gregory Hines) who partners with his brother Clay (Maurice Hines) and has his eyes and heart set on chorus girl Lila Rose Oliver (Lonette McKee). Also in the background are both the Dwyer and Williams' family matriarchs, Schultz' wife, business manager and enforcer, the Harlem-based club's real and fictional performers, guests and colorful underworld characters. It's a roster which virtually demands a detailed program.

Dramatically, Coppola and co-screenwriter William Kennedy, juggle a lot of balls in the air. The relationships between the two sets of brothers is a more obvious link between the various strands of the plot. However, in neither case does one come away feeling the potential emotional impact has been realized.

The Williams brothers become estranged as Sandman breaks away from the act to seek his own fortune. Later, having acquired notoriety, he returns to the club and half-heartedly joins Clay on stage when patrons demand a reunion. However, the emotion of the moment has the two unable to complete the tap routine and ending with a warm embrace.

The Dwyers go their separate ways as Dixie assumes a film career (Pioneer Pictures' "Mob Boss") and Vincent turns into a trigger-happy gunman. Acting as go-between, Dixie effects the exchange of ransom money, when his brother kidnaps Frenchie. Despite the awkwardness of the situation, Dixie tries to spirit his brother away but Vincent meets a violent end.

The parallel stories of Dixie and Sandman's professional rise prove more potent, thanks largely to a mixture of romance, music and gangland involvement. Hines and McKee generate real sparks in their relationship and latter adds an interesting dimension as a light-skinned snger trying to hide her racial origins.

More complex, and less satisfying, is the hot-cold relationship between Dixie and Vera. Dixie's fear of Schultz and Vera's belief that the crime czar is her best ticket (he buys her a club) stall the prospects of a lasting union. However, as things heat up, Lane appears incapable of throwing off her cold exterior.

Highlights turly center with the gangsters' story and the many production numbers in the club. However, Coppola repeatedly frustrates one's appreciation of the musical elements by his continued cross-cutting to other action or truncating numbers. Not a single Cotton Club production is seen in its entirety.

Gere comes off well as both cypher and catalyst for the story. Any doubts about his ability to carry a picture can be dispelled with this film. And as an added bonus, he even does his own horn work. Also strong are Hines and McKee in the film's secondary story, but Lane is a genuine disappointment as Gere's love interest and as the ambitious singer (her voice dubbed once again) and club hostess tagging onto Dutch Schultz' coat tails.

Acting kudos go to Remar for a truly frightening portrait of the ruthless, erratic Schultz and to Hoskins and Gwynne who are a sheer delight whenever on screen. Gwynne's watch scene stands out as the film's best remembered nonmusical moment and seems likely to earn Gwynne critical honors. Also of note are the Living Theatre's co-founder, Julian Beck, as a silent, sinister enforcer; the effervescent Gwen Verdon as Ma Dwyer and singer Tom Waits as the club's maitre'd.

Coppola and Kennedy have taken great pains to research the era and come up with an interesting mix of real and created characters of great authority. The effort somewhat resembles "Ragtime" but, aside from the historical basis of the material, one clearly sees the nods to both gangster and musical films of the 1930s, particularly those with the Warner Bros. brand attached.

Kennedy effects a real stamp on the film and one only regrets a feeling that the collaborators hurried into production without a script fixed in stone. Although great liberties are taken, there's a touch of George Raft in Dixie, Vera seems a variation on Texas Guinan, Lila could be the young Lena Horne and the Williams brothers might have had their inspiration in the Nicholas brothers.

Technical work is generally first-rate with both sets and images providing an evocative rendering of the era. Original music by John Barry blends in nicely with Bob Wilber's reorchestrations of familiar period standards. Despite the fragments seen on screen, one can highly commend choreographic efforts of Hines, Michael Smuin and Henry LeTang.

"The Cotton Club" serves up more entertainment highs than lows. Coppola's heart appears to be more in tune with the realistic elements of the story, so the fantasy finale comes as a bit of a shock. still, so much good will have been served up in the picture that it's bound to please rather than irk audiences. The film should improve Coppola's personal stock and generate strong boxoffice returns even if it comes up short of being among the hallowed few topping the domestic theatrical gross figure of $100,000,-000. —Klad.

Mass Appeal
(COLOR)

Sleeper legit adaptation is a winner.

Hollywood, Nov. 2.

A Universal Pictures release of a Turman-Foster production, presented by Operation Cork Prods. Produced by Lawrence Turman and David Foster. Executive producer, Joan B. Kroc. Directed by Glenn Jordan. Stars Jack Lemmon. Screenplay, Bill C. Davis, based on his stage play; camera (Technicolor), Don Peterman; editor, John Wright; music, Bill Conti; production design, Philip Jeffries; set designer, Don Woodruff; sound, Barry Thomas; assistant director, James S. Simons; technical advisor, Father Joseph Battaglia. Reviewed at Universal Studios, Nov. 1, 1984. (MPAA Rating: PG.) Running time: **100 MINS.**

Father Farley ....Jack Lemmon
Mark Dolson ....Zeljko Ivanek
Monsignor Burke........Charles Durning
Margaret ....Louise Latham

Title may be a boxoffice misnomer, but Glenn Jordan-helmed adaptation of Bill C. Davis' Tony-nominated play is a sterling alternative to year-end film fare. Confrontation and growing rapprochement between a crafty, fat cat priest and a fiery, idealistic seminary student, performed to a winning hilt by Jack Lemmon and Zeljko Ivanek, spells a sleeper for Universal. Performances of toplined duo are sufficiently special to tap Oscar attention if the pic doesn't get lost in the theatrical rush.

A pickup of a Turman-Foster production, shot for $7,000,000 and change, and financed by San Diego millionairess Joan Kroc under her Operation Cork banner, pic is that comparatively rare instance of a film that improves upon its popular legit origins.

Davis the playwright confined his action to two characters, but Davis the screenwriter introduces two flavorful characters — a stern Monsignor played by Charles Durning and a self-styled housekeeper played by Louise Latham — who were only off-stage figures in the play. Dialog is crisp and frequently barbed. The feverish young seminarian calls Lemmon's spiritual executive a "Father Bojangles" who practices "song and dance theology."

"Going My Way" the film is not. Nor, on the other extreme, does it flirt with that scalding legit satire, "Sister Mary Ignatius ..." The Catholic-schooled writer Davis, while painting the Church hierarchy in the image of a corporate board, is really concerned with the human crucible of loyalty and commitment.

Ivanek's clear-eyed, passionate rebel represents the burnished ideal of moral faith, and he richly humanizes his character. When the boy's honesty, at the cost of his dream, compels Lemmon to shed his Nielsen rating mind-set, his need to be loved, and to become his own man for the first time in his clerical life the story of combatants turned allies builds to a gripping close.

Smoothly lensed by Don Peterman ("Flashdance") in the southern California locales of Riverside, Pasadena, and affluent Hancock Park in L.A., the production rewards with a multi-dimensional performance from Lemmon, whose humor, pathos, and survival instincts make his thrombosis of change particularly affecting.

Director Jordan has found a gratifying filmic context for what is essentially a three-character drama. And it's a film in which you lean into the dialog. Scenes such as the young zealot's first moment in the pulpit before what he considers a complacent, blue-haired congregation — he's prompted to shout that "the pursuit of the church is to become obsolete" — propel the movie's bright spirit with a spiritual viewpoint, which is no mean trick.

Durning is perfectly cast in his cunning, righteous role, although the film slips on a point of credibility by showing the monsignor wearing an emerald ring when, in the Catholic church, only a bishop would wear such a ring.

Latham's devoted but individual-minded housekeeper lifts a stereotyped role to a light, deft touch. Another strong contribution is Bill Conti's score, possibly his best to date. —Loyn.

Birdy
(COLOR)

Heavy, laborious drama offset by strong-performances.

Hollywood, Dec. 8.

A Tri-Star Pictures release, produced by Alan Marshall. Directed by Alan Parker. Executive producer, David Manson. Screenplay, Sandy Kroopf and Jack Behr, based on novel "Birdy" by William Wharton; camera (Metrocolor), Michael Seresin; editor, Gerry Hambling; sound, David MacMillan; production design, Geoffrey Kirkland; assistant director, Chris Soldo; associate producer, Ned Kopp; art directors, Armin Ganz, Stu Campbell; music, Peter Gabriel; casting, Juliet Taylor. Reviewed at MGM Studios, L.A., Nov. 30, 1984. (MPAA Rating: R.) Running time: 120 MINS.

Birdy	Matthew Modine
Al Columbato	Nicolas Cage
Doctor Weiss	John Harkins
Mr. Columbato	Sandy Baron
Hannah Rourke	Karen Young
Birdy's Father	George Buck
Birdy's Mother	Dolores Sage
Mrs. Columbato	Crystal Field
Renaldi	Bruno Kirby

Belying the lightheartedness of its title, "Birdy" is a heavy adult drama about best friends and the after-effects of war, but it takes too long to live up to its ambitious premise.

Matthew Modine stars in the adaptation of William Wharton's novel as the title character who had been missing in action and now, psychologically ill and institutionalized, spends much of his time naked, curled up in bird-like positions and speaking to no one.

These posturings stem from a childhood affinity to birds which he shared to a significant degree with Nicolas Cage, who himself is banged up from the fighting, but is brought in to try to communicate with his boyhood pal.

Though the camaraderie between the two is underscored via flashbacks from their more carefree days, under Alan Parker's direction the too-frequent images ultimately serve to disjoint "Birdy."

It is further stifled by a lack of dramatic advancement, making much of the two-hour pic laborious until the final payoff.

But despite these negatives, there are many strong elements, particularly the performance of Modine, who skillfully essays the offbeat troubled character, as well as Cage, sensitive and strong and fiercely loyal to his friend.

Supporting parts are excellently cast, particularly Sandy Baron as Cage's working-class father. In fact, Modine's heated confrontation with him over the sale of an automobile supplies "Birdy's" best moments. —Klyn.

Runaway
(COLOR)

Unintentionally funny, hi-tech Tom Selleck vehicle.

Hollywood, Dec. 8.
A Tri-Star Pictures release from Tri-Star/Delphi III Prods. Produced by Michael Rachmil. Written and directed by Michael Crichton. Stars Tom Selleck. Executive producer, Kurt Villadsen; camera (Panavision, Alpha color, Printed by Metrocolor), John A. Alonzo; editor, Glenn Farr; production design, Douglas Higgins; music, Jerry Gold-

smith; costume design, Betsy Cox; casting, Mike Fenton, Jane Feinberg, Judy Taylor; associate producer, Lisa Faversham; robot designs, David Durand; special robotic effects. Special Effects Unlimited, Broggie Elliott Animation; robotic spiders, Robotic Systems Intl., sound (Dolby), Rob Young; assistant director, Arne L. Schmidt. Reviewed at the Samuel Goldwyn Theatre, Dec. 7, 1984. (MPAA rating: PG-13.) Running time: 100 MINS.

Ramsey	Tom Selleck
Thompson	Cynthia Rhodes
Luther	Gene Simmons
Jackie	Kirstie Alley
Marvin	Stan Shaw
Bobby	Joey Cramer
Chief	G.W. Bailey
Johnson	Chris Mulkey

Tom Selleck, with a cop's short haircut and playing a workaday stiff who's afraid of heights, cuts a less dashing but more accessible figure in "Runaway" than in prior pictures. However, this Michael Crichton robotic nightmare won't be an easy pull for Tri-Star, despite the combination of Selleck and crazed robots who can wash dishes and fix dinner as well as go haywire and kill you.

Pic is so trite, once the robot mischief wears off, that the story seems lifted from Marvel Comics, with heat-seeking bullets and a villain so bad he would be fun if the film wasn't telling us to take this near-futuristic adventure with a straight face. Interestingly for rock fans, the devilish figure, an electronics wizard, is played by Gene Simmons, leader of the rock group Kiss, in his feature film debut. Simmons has a roaring time of it in what amounts to a non-musical parody of his rock persona.

In fact, Selleck's stardom notwithstanding, Simmons steals the movie, although Selleck fans will miss that point. Unfortunately, Crichton ("Westworld," "Coma") doesn't let campiness fly in the face of simplicity. The high-tech mayhem, which includes deadly spider robots with catchy sound effects that are programmed to kill, is played for melodrama.

Selleck's fem police partner Cynthia Rhodes, is an over-achiever and formula romantic foil to Selleck, who's a single parent raising a son. Departure may be fresh for Selleck but the comparative lack of his trademarked sardonic humor does cost the pic. His last, "Lassiter," for instance, is more winning and more stylish. "Runaway" is devoid of style.

To be sure, pic has its compensations: concept of helpmate robots that turn cranky and then dangerous is clever variation on programmed tin cans in other movies. And Kirstie Alley (the female lead in "Star Trek II" and a strong Maggie in last year's "Cat On A Hot Tin Roof" at the Mark Taper Forum) is splendid decoration as the villain's smitten fool.

The comparatively low-key, high-tech effects work to advantage, particularly during the last 15 minutes when vertigo victim Selleck is trapped in a hurtling outdoor freight elevator with those clackety spiders moving in on him. That scene, on a construction site at night, is terrific movie craftsmanship, as if Crichton had suddenly got it all together after it was too late. —Loyn.

A Passage To India
(BRITISH-COLOR)

Hollywood, Dec. 8.
A Columbia release of a John Brabourne and Richard Goodwin production in association with John Heyman and Edward Sands and Home Box Office. Produced by Brabourne, Goodwin. Directed, written and edited by David Lean, based on the novel by E.M. Forster and the play by Santha Rama Rau. Camera (Technicolor processing, Metrocolor prints), Ernest Day; music, Maurice Jarre; production design, John Box; art direction, Leslie Tomkins, Clifford Robinson, Rak Yedekar, Herbert Westbrook; set decoration, Hugh Scaife; costume design, Judy Moorcroft; sound (Dolby), John Mitchell; assistant directors, Patrick Cadell, Christopher Figg, Nick Laws, Arundhati Rao, Ajit Kumar; second unit camera and effects, Robin Browne; casting, Priscilla John. Reviewed at the Samuel Goldwyn Theatre, Beverly Hills, Dec. 6, 1984. MPAA Rating: PG. Running time: 163 MINS.

Adela Quested	Judy Davis
Doctor Aziz	Victor Banerjee
Mrs. Moore	Peggy Ashcroft
Richard Fielding	James Fox
Godbole	Alec Guinness
Ronny Heaslop	Nigel Havers
Turton	Richard Wilson
Mrs. Turton	Antonia Pemberton
McBryde	Michael Culver
Mahmoud Ali	Art Malik
Hamidullah	Saeed Jaffrey
Major Callendar	Clive Swift
Mrs. Callendar	Anne Firbank
Amritrao	Roshan Seth
Stella	Sandra Hotz

Fourteen years after his last film, David Lean has returned to the screen with "A Passage To India," an impeccably faithful, beautifully played and occasionally languorous adaptation of E.M. Forster's classic novel about the clash of East and West in colonial India. Magnificently crafted in the expected Lean manner and full of old-fashioned virtues of a sort that have largely disappeared from the modern cinema, the picture is not really a massive spectacle along the lines of the director's last four efforts, but rather marks something of a return to the more intimate character pieces of his mid-career. Potential b.o. depends first and foremost upon some strong reviews, as remoteness of the film's concerns and relative placidity of the drama don't earmark it as the stuff of mass entertainment of a highly commercial order.

Selling of the film inevitably will revolve around Lean, which is as it should be given his master status among directors. Unfortunately, an entire generation of filmgoers has grown up since the release of his most recent work, "Ryan's Daughter," and Columbia will have to make a very special effort to place the film intelligently in the marketplace.

Per the press materials, tale is set in 1928, a curious fact in that Forster's enduring novel was penned four years earlier. A young woman, Judy Davis, is taken from England to India by Peggy Ashcroft with the likely purpose of marrying the older woman's son Nigel Havers, the city magistrate of fictitious Chandrapore.

Intelligent and well brought up, Davis is not exactly a rebel, but chafes at the limitations and acute snobbery of the ruling British community. With her like-minded companion, Mrs. Moore (Ashcroft), she takes tea with pro-Indian British academic James Fox and a local medic, Aziz (Victor Banerjee), a native whose desire to both ape and please the English has become a way of life.

Breaking the general rule against racial intermingling, Banerjee invites the ladies on an expedition to the nearby Marabar caves, an excursion which ends in tragedy when a bloodied Davis returns to accuse the bewildered, devastated Banerjee of having attempted to rape her in one of the caves.

The British, of course, use the incident as an excuse to validate all their prejudices against all Indians. A trial follows and does not end predictably, but all the principal characters are changed drastically in its aftermath, in line with Mrs. Moore's opinion that, "India forces one to come face to face with oneself."

In his work as screenwriter, Lean has been extremely faithful to the source material, condensing the action cleanly and making coherent and comprehensible what, on the page, is sometimes ambiguous and difficult to entirely figure out.

Even if he has ignored the more mystical and political aspects of the book in favor of a more conventional emphasis on how the forces of nature and repressed sexuality serve to undo the heroine and those around her, Lean has succeeded to a great degree in the tricky task of capturing Forster's finely edged tone of rational bemusement and irony. While the long expository section might seem relatively slow and uneventful to mainstream contemporary audiences, it is nevertheless a masterful example of sustained mood setting and character orchestration.

Oddly, it is in the more overtly dramatic second half that the action bogs down at times. As in the novel, one never knows for sure what happened in the caves, but Lean fails to show the British pressuring Davis in developing her charges against Banerjee and thereby misses a critical connection between this one event and the larger picture of the East-West power balance.

Additionally, the one major change Lean has made lies in the ending. Forster concluded his novel with Banerjee's Aziz character delivering a revolutionary harangue. The film, it may be said, culminates in much more benign fashion.

The outstanding set of performances here is led by Peggy Ashcroft, a constant source of delight as the wonderfully independent and frank Mrs. Moore, and Judy Davis, an Australian actress who has the rare gift of being able to look very plain (as the role calls for) at one moment and uncommonly beautiful at another.

Banerjee, a leading Indian thesp, is excellent in his pivotal role, first appearing almost buffoonish as he tries to live up to the English model in all things, then conveying the deep bitterness he feels after his perceived betrayal by his imagined friends. James Fox and Nigel Havers are fine as representatives of opposite English attitudes, and Michael Culver lends an unexpected and highly attractive Scottish accent to his role as the prosecuting attorney in the trial.

Given the context, there might be some quarrel with the casting of Alec Guinness as a lightly comic Indian sage, but his long working relationship with Lean should, by rights, obviate any serious objections.

It's a given that any David Lean film will look great, and this is certainly no exception; the only esthetic surprise is that it has not been shot in the widescreen format.

Ernest Day, the first cinematographer other than Freddie Young to work with the director since Jack Hildyard shot "The Bridge On The River Kwai," has done an immaculate, genuinely impressive job, as have production designer John Box, costume designer Judy Moorcroft and all the other crafters.

Maurice Jarre's score, reminiscent at times of his music for "Ryan's Daughter," is relatively subdued and effective. At 163 minutes, film is Lean's shortest since "River Kwai," but a bit more tightening in the second half would have helped.—Cart.

Paroles et Musiques
(Words And Music)
(FRENCH-CANADIAN-COLOR)

Paris, Dec. 4.

An A.A.A. release of a 7 Films Cinéma/FR3/C.I.S. (Canada) coproduction. (Spectrafilm release in U.S./Canada.) Produced by Marie-Christine Chouraqui and Murray Shostak. Executive producer for Canada, Robert Baylis. Written and directed by Elie Chouraqui. Stars Catherine Deneuve, Richard Anconina, Christophe Lambert, Jacques Perrin. Camera (color), Robert Alazraki; art director, Gérard Daoudal; sound, Patrick Rousseau; music, Michel Legrand; songs, Legrand and Gene McDaniels (sung by Guy Thomas and Terry Lauber); editor, Noëlle Boisson; production managers, Henri Jacquillard, Daniel Szuster. Reviewed at Club 13, Paris, Nov. 30, 1984. Running time: **107 MINS.**
Margaux ....Catherine Deneuve
Jeremy ....Christophe Lambert
Michel ....Richard Anconina
Yves ....Jacques Perrin
Corinne ....Dayle Haddon
Peter ....Nick Mancuso
Charlotte ....Charlotte Gainsbourg
Florence ....Dominique Lavanant

Romantic French schmaltz from a former assistant and disciple of Claude Lelouch, "Words And Music" offers the familiar sight of Catherine Deneuve as the liberated contemporary woman, trying to juggle her professional and private responsibilities.

Here she is artistic director of a Paris record house who succumbs to the insistent charms of a young pop singer she is promoting (Christophe "Greystoke" Lambert, much less impressive and magnetic in the jungle of the city). Her romance is complicated by her two children (from whom she tries to hide the affair by putting Lambert out the door at 5 a.m.), and her estranged husband, a Yank novelist (Nick Mancuso), who has returned to New York to finish a book.

Lambert, too, has obligations that make his adventure with Deneuve difficult, notably towards his singing partner (Richard Anconina). Both have sworn to succeed together, but Lambert's increasing absences and apparent negligence leave Anconina solo for an important audition, for which he performs winningly.

He reluctantly decides to go it alone, but is only too glad to link up with the saddened Lambert when Deneuve and Mancuso are reconciliated. Together again, they go on to fame and fortune.

Writer-director Elie Chouraqui has dropped some of the sub-Lelouch showiness and old New Wave conceits that ran amok in his last picture, "What Makes David Run?", which only leave even barer a script of droning banality.

In a rush to get to what he considers the heart of the story, Chouraqui skimps on important exposition and characters, offering little idea of what Deneuve is like at her job, and introducing subsidiary characters played by Jacques Perrin and Dominique Lavanant, only to completely ditch them minutes later.

Technically the film is sloppy, presumably obeying Franco-Canadian coproduction clauses calling for some location shooting in Canada. Although most of the story takes place in Paris, with a final sequence supposedly set in New York City, Chouraqui has not taken any great pains to cover up the very unFrench guillotine windows that can be glimpsed on occasion, or the non-Gotham-style phone booth that figures in the Stateside denouement.

Nor is it explained why Lambert and Anconina, both French lads, write and sing their lyrics in accent-less English. A compromise for soundtrack recording marketing purposes apparently, though the Michel Legrand-Gene McDaniels songs do not stay in mind.

(Spectrafilm picked up film for North American theatrical distribution while it was still in production)
— Len.

Night Patrol
(COLOR)

Funny cheapo comedy.

Chicago, Nov. 30.

A New World Pictures release of a New World/Bill Osco presentation. Produced by Osco. Directed, coproduced, edited by Jackie Kong. Screenplay, Murray Langston, Bill Levey, Osco, Kong. Camera (color), Jürg Walthers, Hanania Baer; art direction, Jay Burkhardt, Bob Danyla; set decoration, Barbara Benz, Debbie Madalina; costume design, Terry Roop; sound design, Bob Biggart; associate producer, Jay Koiwai; assistant directors, Koiwai, Paul Leclair, Tom Jon. Reviewed at the United Artists Theater, Chicago, Nov. 30, 1984. (MPAA Rating R.) Running time: **82 MINS.**
Sue ....Linda Blair
Kent.....................Pat Paulsen
Kate ....Jaye P. Morgan
Dr. Ziegler...................Jack Riley
Capt. Lewis ....Billy Barty
Melvin ....Murray Langston
The Rape Victim ....Pat Morita

Surprise of surprises, New World's "Night Patrol" is more consistently amusing than Warner's "Police Academy," the much-slicker film that apparently spawned it. Given the low quality of the latter, that's not saying much. B.O. should be modest for a short period of time, but given "Patrol's" obviously minuscule budget, something is better than nothing.

This is an anything-for-a-laugh grossout comedy doting on wildly chaotic situations and gags of more than marginal bad taste. "Patrol" is candid about its intentions and lack of sophistication. Pic's technical credits are, for example, the worst (with the possible exception of hard-core porno) in recent memory.

More positively, the pic starts at a snail's pace but gradually picks up steam as one piece of outrageousness is heaped on the other. It's about a timid-soul of a Los Angeles policeman (Murray Langston, aka The Unknown Comic) who runs afoul of his midget captain (Billy Barty) and is transferred to a night-time beat where conditions are really rough.

The incompetent gendarme also aspires to be a standup comedian, performing with a paper bag over his face to conceal his moonlighting. He acquires a manager (Jaye P. Morgan) and meets with some success. When that occurs, a crook pops out of the woodwork committing robberies with a similar bag over the head.

"Night Patrol" doesn't take itself or its plot seriously for a moment. The pic's four writers (including producer William Osco and director Jackie Kong) employed a shotgun approach — spraying the subject with anything and everything hoping some of the bits stick.

There are grossout gags (a beefy diner waiter "cleans" a fork by rubbing it under a sweaty armpit), homosexual and lesbian sendups, sex bits of all descriptions and racial humor (an eatery run by a black proprietor will, says a visitor, accept "massa charge").

Pat Paulsen comes off amiably and funny as the naive cop's sardonic sidekick. Busty Linda Blair is largely wasted as the cop's love interest. Billy Barty overacts with gusto as the diminuitive police captain.

Overall, the good stuff just manages to outwit the bad. If only "Night Patrol" didn't look and sound so rotten. For reasons not explained but more confusing than funny, pic's opening credits unspooled in French. — Sege.

1919
(BRITISH-COLOR)

London, Dec. 3.

A British Film Institute production, in association with Channel 4. Produced by Nita Amy. Executive producer, Peter Sainsbury. Directed by Hugh Brody. Stars Paul Scofield, Maria Schell, Michael Ignatieff, Brody; camera (color), Ivan Strasburg; editor, David Gladwell; music, Brian Gascoigne; art director, Caroline Amies; costumes, Jane Robinson; sound, Mike McDuffy. Reviewed at Crown screening room, London, Nov. 30, 1984. Running time: **99 MINS.**
Alexander Scherbatov ......Paul Scofield
Sophie Rubin ....Maria Schell
The voice of
Sigmund Freud...........Frank Finlay
Anna ....Diana Quick
Young Sophie ....Clare Higgins
Young Alexander ....Colin Firth
Nina ....Sandra Berkin
Sophie's Father.............Alan Tilvern

The latest British Film Institute in-house production marks the feature debut of Hugh Brody, an anthropologist who previously made a docu, "People of the Islands," about Eskimos. It is hard to think of a greater contrast, since "1919" is a hermetic two-hander in which the leading role is taken by one of the English-speaking world's preeminent stage actors, Paul Scofield.

Pic attempts a revisionist look at the psychoanalytic theories of Sigmund Freud via the experiences of two elderly people who meet for the first time in 1984 knowing that back in 1919 they'd both been teenage patients of Vienna's most famous shrink. Sophie (Maria Schell) has been living for many years in America, and sees on tv an interview with Alexander (Scofield) which makes her determined to meet him. She goes back to the city of her childhood, and in Alexander's stuffy, memento-filled apartment the pair relive their hours on the most famous couch of all, deciding in the end that they didn't get as much help as they needed.

Alexander (played in the flashbacks by Colin Firth), seems to have been overly introverted and withdrawn, while young Sophie (Clare Higgins) was struggling with her feelings for a dominant father and her strong emotional attraction to an older woman (Diana Quick). Scene where Higgins and Quick go to bed together achieves added impact from the hitherto unrevealed fact that Quick is six months pregnant.

Freud himself is never seen, though his presence is naturally the dominating factor. He is effectively voiced by Frank Finlay.

Claustrophobic scenes between the old couple in the present and their younger selves on the analyst's couch are intercut with archive newsreel material depicting the revolutionary events going on outside the walls of Freud's consulting room. These scenes help to let some air into an otherwise rather stifling atmosphere.

Pic is sharply scripted by the director and Michael Ignatieff, and its relatively modest budget is up on the screen: it's first-rate in all technical departments. Paul Scofield takes every word and gently squeezes every possible nuance from it. He is perfectly teamed with Maria Schell whose recollections are more dramatic and moving and whose ultimate decision to return home indicates her acceptance of herself for what she is.

This is obviously a film which will need very careful handling if it's to find its audience, but the rewards will be there for viewers looking for fine acting and a fresh approach to the subject of Freud.
— *Strat.*

Protocol
(COLOR)

Pvt. Benjamin enters diplomatic service.

Hollywood, Dec. 15.

A Warner Bros. release, produced by Anthea Sylbert. Directed by Herbert Ross. Exec producer, Goldie Hawn. Stars Hawn. Screenplay, Buck Henry; camera (Technicolor), William A. Fraker; editor, Paul Hirsch; sound, Al Overton Jr.; production design, Bill Malley; assistant director, John Kretchmer; associate producer, Lewis J. Rachmil; art direction, Tracy Bousman; music, Basil Poledouris. Reviewed at The Burbank Studios, Dec. 14, 1984. (MPAA rating: PG.) Running time: **96 MINS.**

Sunny	Goldie Hawn
Michael	Chris Sarandon
Emir	Richard Romanus
Nawaf Al Kabeer	Andre Gregory
Mrs. St. John	Gail Strickland
Hilley	Cliff De Young
Crowe	Keith Szarabajka
Hassler	Ed Begley Jr.
V.P. Merck	James Staley
Lou	Kenneth Mars
Ella	Jean Smart
Donna	Maria O'Brien
Ben	Joel Brooks
Jerry	Grainger Hines
Mr. Davis	Richard Hamilton
Mrs. Davis	Mary Carver
Sen. Norris	Kenneth McMillan

Goldie Hawn's insistence on Saying Something Important takes a lot of the zip out of "Protocol," but the light comedy still has its moments for the forgiving. Against a headstart by other Christmas comedies, however, Hawn will have to hustle to get attention.

Moving far away from the disaster of "Swing Shift" and back toward the smash success of "Private Benjamin," Hawn is once again properly bubbly (and brainy), but one big problem here is an oh-so-obvious effort to reinvent the formula that boosted "Benjamin" to the heights.

In the former, she was a pampered Jewish princess thrust into the unfamiliar world of the Army; here, she's a sweet, unsophisticated cocktail waitress hurdled into the unfamiliar world of Washington diplomacy and Mideast travail.

In "Benjamin," Hawn's main adversary was a woman captain (Eileen Brennan) and ill-intentioned men; here, it's Gail Strickland as a devious, plotting protocol officer and more ill-intentioned men. In both Hawn's initially daffy adjustments are seasoned gradually by newfound inner strength and awakening to broader issues involved, culminating in triumph.

Formula doesn't work as well in "Protocol," partly because Strickland and gang aren't as much fun to foil as Brennan's bunch was and mainly because Hawn's character simply isn't as sharply delineated and the circumstances encountered are much more contrived.

Another main problem is that writer Buck Henry consumes too much initial running time trying to satirize the media stampede that

takes place when Hawn the unknown thwarts the assassination of a visiting Emir (Richard Romanus), making her an instant notable. Though there are some nice Henry touches along the way, as when a hometown newscaster intones that Hawn "graduated in the top 75% of her class and was a member of the hair-dressing club," the essential silliness of celebrity journalism is hardly a field for fresh comedy anymore.

Inspired by Hawn's popularity plus Romanus' lingering lust, Strickland and her youthful, cynical White House cronies plot to swap the unsuspecting patriot to Romanus for his harem in return for a needed military base in his country.

Consequently, a girl who can't even spell "protocol" when a job is offered to her in the protocol department is suddenly moving among the high mucky-mucks, making all sorts of mistakes that Hawn can make amusing with that particularly delightful daffiness she exudes. Unfortunately, this same uneducated, unsophisticated girl can also cite obscure provisions of federal law when necessary to thwart Strickland and maintain a proper feminist tone for the film, which is often jarring.

Eventually, Hawn gets wise to how she's being manipulated and the picture takes a turn toward "Miz Smith Goes To Washington," especially in her monolog about how bureaucrats have forgotten that they serve the people, not themselves. It's to Hawn's credit that she's established enough sweet sincerity by this point to make the dialog a bit touching and certainly important, but hardly hilarious.

This was obviously a difficult logistical picture for director Herbert Ross, with lots of scenes and many, many extras and sideshow action. He handles it very well with an experienced hand at "big" pictures.

Costar Chris Sarandon doesn't get to shine much as the one nice guy Hawn encounters in government, eventually becoming a romantic interest leading to — once again oh-so-obviously — a setup for a seqeul, complete with freeze-frame.—*Har.*

Invisible Strangler
(COLOR)

Underwhelming supernatural chokefest.

Delray Beach, Nov. 26.

A Seymour Borde & Associates release of a Jordan Lyon Prods. production, in association with New Century Prods. Produced by Earle Lyon. Executive producer, Fred Jordan. Directed by John Florea. Features entire cast. Screenplay, Arthur C. Pierce, from story by Lyon, Pierce; camera (color), Alan Stensvold; editor, Bud S. Isaacs; music, Richard Hieronymous, Alan Oldfield; second unit sequences directed by Gene Fowler Jr.; second unit camera, Nicholas von Sternberg; sound, William Edmondson; assistant director, Joseph Wonder; special effects, Roger George; associate producer, Robert Fitzger-

ald; casting, Edward Morse. Review at Delray Drive-In 2, Delray Beach, Fla., Nov. 25, 1984. (MPAA Rating: PG.) Running time: **85 MINS.**

Lt. Charles Barrett	Robert Foxworth
Candy Barrett	Stefanie Powers
Chris	Elke Sommer
Miss De Long	Sue Lyon
Coleen Hudson	Leslie Parrish
Bambi	Mariana Hill

Also with: Mark Slade, Frank Ashmore, Alex Dreier, Percy Rodrigues, Jo Anne Meredith, Cesare Danova, John Hart.

"Invisible Strangler" is an oddball police manhunt thriller, principally lensed in 1976 under the title "The Astral Factor" and completed several years later for ultimate 1984 release. Interesting cast, filled with actresses who first made their mark in the 1960s, fails to uplift a pedestrian premise.

Robert Foxworth toplines as Lt. Charles Barrett, an L.A. cop working on a string of strangulation murders of attractive women. Implausible and painfully underutilized gimmick has Roger Sands, jailed for matricide, escaping by using his study of psychic powers to become invisible. Sans suspense, it's revealed he's killing women who testified against him.

Picture becomes silly early on when it turns out that the invisibility adds nothing to sequences which could have been played naturalistically by a wily con staying one step ahead of the police. Guest victims have tiny roles, including highly billed Sue Lyon (who has no dialog). Exception is Elke Sommer, well-cast as a former beauty pageant winner.

Stefanie Powers has fun with role of Foxworth's practical joke-prone wife, perhaps warming up for her "Hart To Hart" tv series. Invisibility effects are minimal.—*Lor.*

Dream One
(Nemo)
(FRENCH-BRITISH-COLOR)

Paris, Dec. 12.

An NEF release of a NEF Diffusion (Paris)/Christel Films (London) coproduction, with the participation of Films A2 (Paris) and Channe Four (London). A Columbia Pictures release (U.S.). Produced by Claude Nedjar and John Boorman. Directed by Arnaud Selignac. Features entire cast. Screenplay, Selignac, Jean-Pierre Esquenazi, Telshe Boorman; camera (color), Philippe Rousselot; sets and special effects, Gilles Lacombe, Nikos Meletopoulos (Productions de l'Ordinaire); costumes, Michéle Hamel (Productions de l'Ordinaire); music, Gabriel Yared; editor, Tom Priestley; production manager, Michel Propper. Reviewed at George V cinema, Paris, Dec. 10, 1984. Running time: **97 MINS.**

Nemo (child)	Seth Kibel
Nemo (teen)	Jason Connery
Alice	Mathilda May
Mr. Rip/Benjamin	Nipsey Russell
Mr. Legend	Harvey Keitel
Rals-Akrai	Carole Bouquet
Boris/Nemo's father	Michel Blanc
Duchka/Nemo's mother	Katrine Boorman
Monkey	Dominique Pinon
Cunegond	Charley Boorman
Pushkin	Gaetan Bloom

"Dream One" is newcomer Arnaud Selignac's fond homage to the literary fantasies of his youth, but it lacks the invention and authority to fire the imagination of the viewer into a shared remembrance of early pleasures.

(Columbia Pictures acquired U.S. rights to the picture in a prebuy deal, but has not yet set a domestic opening for it within its 1985 release schedule. — *Ed.)*

Core of this tale is Jules Verne's sci-fi fantasy, "20,000 Leagues Under The Sea." Selignac's young protagonist is named Nemo, after Verne's famous nautical anti-hero, and the central setting is the submarine Nautilus, which lies rusting and abandoned on a beach.

Nemo is the son of a well-heeled Manhattan couple, who put him to bed before going out on the town. The vision of his parents perishing in a car accident sends the terrified child into the elevator which, instead of stopping on the ground floor, burrows through the earth and falls into space.

He finally lands on another planet, a twilight world of beaches, oases and mysterious grottos. Here he comes across the Nautilus and its sole survivor, Captain Nemo's monkey, who immediately warms to the boy as spiritual successor of his long-dead master.

Soon new characters, based on other childhood myths and legends, enter the picture. There is Alice, a delicate princess from Yonderland, sole survivor of a sea disaster that claimed her parents' lives; and Mr. Legend, a masked avenger who looks strikingly like Zorro, though he is not quite as romantically pure, and fails to hide his designs on poor Alice.

There are a couple of aristocratic Russian explorers, (who resemble Nemo's parents), a red-haired scamp, a beautiful creature from another planet and a black magician named Mr. Rip, who helps guide Nemo to young adulthood and fulfillment of his fantasies.

Selignac sets up a series of unexpected imaginary encounters that are not without charm, but the screenplay and direction fail to find an effectively exhilirating balance between parodic intent and the helmer's obvious delight in evoking the iconography of his childhood.

Pic, however, is first-rate in its production design, the work of a French collective of artists, Les Productions de l'Ordinaire, who conceived unusual studio facilities with a pair of bubble constructions erected near Paris, and visualized Selignac's dreamworld with imaginative economy and talent.

Their set for the Nautilus is superbly evocative of Verne's literary universe, and full credit is due them for the enchanting final image of the submarine, again operational with Nemo and the monkey at the helm, plowing through the twilight seas in search of the lost Alice.

Indecisiveness of Selignac's direction extends to the actors, who rarely find the tone called for. Though Mathilda May has somnambulistic grace as Alice, and Carole Bouquet is a perfect E.T. with sex appeal, the others range from passable to awful. Latter term applies to Harvey Keitel's inexpressive Mr. Legend, while French comedy favorite Michel Blanc is disconcerting as the (dubbed-in-English) Russian explorer. Nipsey Russell is Mr. Rip with his usual bonhomie.

Director John Boorman, for whom Selignac worked as assistant and still photographer on "Excalibur," coproduced "Dream One" and the final product is something of a family affair; Katrine and Charley Boorman, his kids, have roles; and their sister Telshe, is credited as co-scripter. One also notes Jason Connery, son of Sean, as the grown-up Nemo.

Another French player in this Franco-British coproduction is Dominique Pinon, as Nemo's man-sized monkey.

Pic is admirably photographed by Philippe Rousselot, who deserved much credit for the smart look of Jean-Jacques Beineix' "Diva."
— *Len.*

Heaven Earth Man
(BRITISH-DOCU-COLOR)

London, Dec. 3.

A YoYo Film, Video & Theater Production. Produced by Laurens C. Postma, Phillip Bartlett. Directed by Postma. Screenplay, Jonathan Frost; camera (color), David Scott, Billy Wo; editor, Hussein Younis; sound, Miranda Watts, Stanley Ko; music, David Hewson; narrator, Saul Reichling. Reviewed at London Film Festival, Dec. 1, 1984. Running time: **79 MINS.**

"Heaven Earth Man" is a documentary about the Triads, the ancient secret society that has evolved as a kind of Chinese mafia and which, according to this film, controls most activities in the British crown colony of Hong Kong, which will revert to mainland China in a few years time.

Pic contains some marvelous footage of Hong Kong itself, contrasting the very rich, chic neighborhoods with the squalor of the slums. This is where the Triads rule, per the film, recruiting young men and even schoolkids who have to go through a blood-drinking and oath-taking ritual before they can take part in extortion and other rackets such as pornography, prostitution and drugs.

Men are interviewed who have been or are still Triad members, with their identify often concealed for safety purposes. There's also a feisty old English social worker, Elsie Elliott, who talks about the endemic corruption in police and government circles which maintains the Triad system.

An interesting, well-made docu, it's a natural for tv slottings or fests specializing in this kind of product.
— *Strat.*

Don't Open Till Christmas
(BRITISH-COLOR)

A 21st Century Distribution release of a Spectacular (Trading) Intl. Films production. Produced by Dick Randall, Steve Minasian. Directed by Edmund Purdom. Stars Purdom. Screenplay, Derek Ford; additional scenes written and directed by Al McGoohan; camera (color), Alan Pudney; editor, Ray Selfe; music, Des Dolan; makeup, Pino Ferranti; special effects, Coast To Coast Ltd. Reviewed at Criterion Center 1 theater, N.Y., Dec. 8, 1984. (No MPAA Rating.) Running time: **86 MINS.**

Insp. Harris	Edmund Purdom
Giles	Alan Lake
Kate	Belinda Mayne
Cliff	Gerry Sundquist
Sgt. Powell	Mark Jones
Caroline Munro	Herself
Gerry	Kevin Lloyd
"Experience" girl	Kelly Baker
Sharon	Pat Astley
Det. constable	Des Dolan

"Don't Open Till Christmas" is a poorly made horror picture about a nut killing various Father Christmases (the British version of Santa Claus). Filmed a year ago in London by Rome-based producer Dick Randall and Massachusetts exhibitor Steve Minasian (latter one of the backers of Paramount's hit "Friday The 13th" film series), pic serves as a tawdry star vehicle for vet British character actor Edmund Purdom, who also directed.

Sad postscript here is that the maniacal killer is played by Alan Lake, who committed suicide several months ago, reportedly despondent following the death of his wife, Diana Dors. His sinister thesping in the final reels is the only thing that perks up this dull cheapie.

Purdom portrays Chief Inspector Harris, a harried Scotland Yard detective assigned to track down the nut who is killing Santas all over London. He ultimately is taken off the case for lack of results, replaced by his assistant Sgt. Powell (Mark Jones), who likes to wear a raffish hat and otherwise seems to be auditioning for the lead role in the tv show "Dr. Who."

Chief suspects, besides Purdom himself, include Giles (Lake), who pops in and out as an odd-looking newspaper reporter, and Cliff (Gerry Sundquist), present at several of the Santa attacks including one that murders the father of his girlfriend Kate (Belinda Mayne). Episodic presentation has a few okay twists until revelation that the maniac was traumatized as a boy at Christmastime.

Poorly scripted by British action and porno filmmaker Derek Ford, "Don't" is in slightly better taste than the recently notorious U.S. pic "Silent Night, Deadly Night." Its chief offenses include portraying numerous London Father Christmases as drunks plus a scene of one of them getting emasculated while relieving himself in a public restroom. To helmer Purdom's credit, a genre switcheroo has the iterated bloodletting directed at men, with vulnerable women only in danger as witnesses to the psycho's crimes.

Tech credits are ultra-cheap, with lots of shooting via available light and real-life extras ogling the camera on location. The beauteous British horror and fantasy film star Caroline Munro puts in a cameo appearance performing a rock song and dance number. — *Lor.*

Breakin' 2 Electric Boogaloo
(COLOR)

Sequel is okay as live-action comic strip.

Hollywood, Dec. 14.

A Tri-Star Pictures release of a Cannon Group film. Produced by Menahem Golan, Yoram Globus. Directed by Sam Firstenberg. Features entire cast. Screenplay, Jan Ventura, Julie Reichert, based on characters created by Charles Parker, Allen DeBevoise; camera (TVC color), Hanania Baer; editor, Marcus Manton; music, Mike Linn; song supervisor, Ollie E. Brown; music supervisor, Russ Regan; Production designer, Joseph T. Garrity; art director, Patrick E. Tagliaferro; set decorator, Jerie Kelter; sound, Mark F. Ulano; choreography, Bill Goodson; costumes, Dorothy Baca, David Baca; assistant director, David Womark. Reviewed at the VIP screening room, L.A., Calif., Dec. 13, 1984. (MPAA rating: PG). Running time: **94 MINS.**

Kelly	Lucinda Dickey
Ozone	Adolfo (Shabba-Doo) Quinones
Turbo	Michael (Boogaloo Shrimp) Chambers
Rhonda	Susie Bono
Byron	Harry Caesar
Mrs. Bennett	Jo de Winter
Mr. Bennett	John Christy
Lucia	Sabina Garcia

"Breakin' 2 Electric Boogaloo" is a comic book of a film, and, as in a cartoon, kids can get away with anything to have a good time. Characters are larger than life stick-figures who inhabit a kind of make-believe fantasy land. Pic is entertaining as long as it maintains a sense of freshness and spontaneity. Unfortunately, breakdancing may be a summer sport and Cannon's sequel (released this time through Tri-Star, not MGM/UA) compared to its summer hit is unlikely to cause as much of a stir at the boxoffice.

As a phenomenon, the hip-hop, breakdancing, sidewalk graffiti and rap music culture lends itself well to a comic book approach and to his credit director Sam Firstenberg doesn't try to interject too much reality into the picture. In some ways "Breakin' 2" is a throwback to the old film musicals where the good guys always overcome tremendous odds to prevail over some ruthless businessman. It's a childlike view of life, but that's what makes it fun.

This time around Ozone (Adolfo [Shabba-Doo] Quinones) and Turbo (Michael [Boogaloo Shrimp] Chambers) have turned their street dancing talents to teaching other disadvantaged youths at a rundown community club they've dubbed Miracles. Also returning from the original "Breakin'" is Kelly (Lucinda Dickey) who has become a little more successful and is uncertain if she wants to return to the neighborhood or get on with her career.

No time for subtlety here. when a stereotypical developer (Peter MacLean) and a corrupt politician (Ken Olfson) try to put up a shopping center where the community center stands, the kids decide to put on a show to raise the necessary $200,000. Writers Jan Ventura and Julie Reichert have sprinkled enough subplots throughout, such as Turbo's budding love affair and Kelly's parents hostility, to generate dance numbers at the slightest pretext.

"Breakin' 2" offers what may be the first breakdancing production numbers staged at various locations around East Los Angeles. Emphasis is on ensemble work rather than the individual theatrics often associated with breakdancing. All the spinning, popping and locking are still there, but with a new element of group choreography (by Bill Goodson). Still this is at least the fourth time around in film for the hip-hop culture and the whole business is starting to look a bit dated.

Luckily the lead cast brings a good-natured charm to their characters and some of the best scenes are the few quiet moments between dances. Quinones, in the older big-brother role, has a genuine screen presence and works well with the cherubic Chambers,

Jo de Winter and John Christy as Dickey's parents are adequate in rather ungratifying pat roles. Dickey herself has the appropriate measure of enthusiasm to overcome the unlikely nature of her character.

Costumes by Dorothy and David Baca are strictly street chic and keep up the visual interest. Street locations are also well chosen and probably served the dual function of being functional and cheap. Editing of dance sequences by Marcus Manton is crisp and lively as is the whole production when it isn't taking itself too seriously. —*Jagr.*

Tiger Town
(COLOR)

Touching baseball picture.

Sydney, Dec. 17.

A Buena Vista release of a Walt Disney production. Produced by Susan B. Landau. Directed, screenplay by Alan Shapiro. Stars Roy Scheider, Justin Henry. Camera (color) Robert Elswit; music, Eddy L. Manson; editors, Richard A. Harris, John F. Link; production design, Neil J. Spisak; costumes, Gary Jones. Reviewed on Syme Homevideo-

cassette, Sydney, Dec. 16, 1984. (No MPAA Rating.) Running time: **96 MINS.**
Billy Young ....Roy Scheider
Alex ....Justin Henry
Alex' father ....Noah Moazezi
Alex' mother ....Bethany Carpenter

Released theatrically only briefly in Detroit, this 1983 Walt Disney production made-for-cable has cropped up on videocassette Down Under and is reviewed for the record. Shelving of the pic is unrelated to its quality, as it's an excellent, genuinely touching, tale of a boy who manages to overcome the grief brought on by the unexpected death of his beloved father by putting into practice his father's last piece of advice: If you want something badly enough, you can make it come true.

Young Alex is a baseball fan and his hero is Billy Young, fading star of the local team, a once-great player with too many strikes against him. Roy Scheider plays Young with his customary insight and grim sincerity, and makes the character all-too-human in his frustrations with middle-aged failure. Alex is Justin Henry, as good herein as he was in "Kramer vs. Kramer."

Almost stealing the film, however, in a marvelous cameo role, is Naoh Moazezi as Alex' father. An overweight, chain-smoking, out-of-work assembly-line operator, Moazezi comes across, in his few scenes, as a loving, kindly man filled with wisdom except when it comes to his own health. His totally unexpected demise is almost as much a loss for the viewer as for his bereaved son.

However, Alex decides he must put his father's theory into practice, and what he wants most of all is for Billy Young to regain his old form. At this point, Alan Shapiro's excellent screenplay nudges over into "The Natural" territory: Young makes an unexpected comeback, but only when Alex is in the stadium, urging him on. Film's climax comes when Alex, on his way to the grand finale, is restrained by the school bully, his sworn enemy; without his unseen supporter, Young's game deteriorates. Will Alex get to the match in time to save the day?

There are no prizes for guessing the answer, and the fadeout is completely satisfactory. This is unquestionably an old-fashioned film, but it's handled by Shapiro with such sublime conviction, and it's so very well acted, that it's a pleasure to watch. —*Strat.*

The Initiation
(COLOR)

Same old horror premise.

A New World Pictures release of a Tom Vance-Leo Angelos, Georgian Bay Prods. Ltd., Joe Monzio presentation of a Bruce Lansbury Prods. Ltd. and Jock Gaynor Prods. production. An Initiation Associates

Ltd. picture. Executive producers, Lansbury, Gaynor. Produced by Scott Winant. Directed by Larry Stewart. Features entire cast. Screenplay, Charles Pratt Jr.; camera (Movielab color), George Tirl; editor, Ronald LaVine; music, Gabriel Black, Lance Ong; sound, John Pritchett; production manager-assistant director, John Colwell; set decoration, Ellen Freund; special effects, Jack Bennett; casting, Anita Dann, Lee Clark. Reviewed on Thorn EMI Video cassette, N.Y., Dec. 10, 1984. (MPAA Rating: R.) Running time: **97 MINS.**
Frances Fairchild ....Vera Miles
Dwight Fairchild ....Clu Gulager
Kelly/Terry ....Daphne Zuniga
Peter......................James Read
Marcia ....Marilyn Kagan
Jason Randall ....Robert Dowdell
Megan ....Frances Peterson
   Also with: Peter Malof (Andy), Deborah Morehart (Alison), Trey Stroud (Ralph), Patti Heider (Nurse), Paula Knowles (Beth), Joy Jones (Heidi).

"The Initiation" is a formula horror pic offering too little, too late. Filmed in Dallas-Fort Worth in 1983, this New World pickup was released regionally in May and is now available on videocassette.

Shopworn premise promises (but delivers only in the final reel) the spectacle of pretty young women terrorized by a maniac on Hell Night (see, for example, the 1981 Linda Blair vehicle) while pledging college sorority Delta Rho Chi. Plot contrivances, several of which are left dangling, revolve around Kelly Fairchild (Daphne Zuniga), a handsome brunet, who has had amnesia since age nine and is plagued by recurring nightmares involving her rich parents (Vera Miles and and Clu Gulager) and a mysterious stranger.

Her teaching assistant at college (James Read) is doing a doctorate on dreams and he performs experiments with Kelly, including hypnosis. Disappointing resolution solves the mystery but interjects new characters, thus cheating the audience. Gulager's key role is suddenly written out and, improbably, the other characters don't even notice he's missing halfway through the picture.

Pic is technically okay, with an impressive-looking (but not very atmospheric for horror) vast department store-mall location. Star Zuniga, credited as being "introduced" here, is an expressive youngster prominently featured in Rob Reiner's upcoming release "The Sure Thing." —*Lor.*

Every Picture Tells A Story
(BRITISH-COLOR)

London, Dec. 3.

A Flamingo Pictures-Every Picture Ltd. Production, in association with TSI Films and Channel 4. Produced by Christine Oestreicher. Directed by James Scott. Stars Phyllis Logan, Alex Norton. Screenplay, Shane Connaughton; camera (Technicolor), Adam Barker-Mill; production design, Louise Stjernsward; editor, Chris Kelly; music, Michael Storey; associate producers, Paddy Higson, Adam Kempton. Reviewed at London Film Festival, Dec. 1. 1984. Running time: **82 MINS.**

Agnes Scott ....Phyllis Logan
William Scott Sr. ....Alex Norton
William age 15-18......Leonard O'Malley
William age 11-14.........John Docherty
William age 5-8 ....Mark Airlie
Tocher ....Paul Wilson
Grandfather ....Willie Joss
Miss Bridle ....Natasha Richardson
Mr. Trimble..............Jack McQuoid

James Scott made the Oscar-winning short subject, "A Shocking Accident" a couple of years ago, a film in which a schoolboy was told about the unexpected death of his father. The climax of "Every Picture Tells A Story," a biography of the director's father, the artist William Scott (born 1913), is the death of William's father in an equally shocking accident: the man is killed while helping fight a shop fire.

William Sr. (Alex Norton) was from Northern Ireland, but his wife, Agnes (Phyllis Logan, last seen in "Another Time, Another Place") was Scottish, and young William's earliest memories take place at the close of World War I in Greenock, Scotland, when his dad unexpectedly returns home from the war. Husband and wife quickly quarrel about where they should live, and one day William Sr. simply ups and leaves, forcing his unwilling family to follow him to Ulster. There he gets a job as a sign-painter and encourages the artistic tendencies of his eldest son. After the accident, William Jr. is helped by grateful townspeople to attend art school in Belfast, and the film ends as he arrives in London to study at the Royal Academy.

This is thus a personal film in which the filmmaker pays tribute to his father and grandfather in glowing terms. Though discreetly, sometimes charmingly, handled, the fact remains that this is a rather small, ordinary story, and after the accident it really has nowhere to go but downhill. There's also some surprisingly clumsy structuring early on.

Despite these shortcomings, there are plenty of small pleasures to be derived from the pic, the period atmosphere is neatly captured, and the thesping is excellent throughout. Budget was obviously modest, but the quality is on-screen. — *Strat.*

On The Line
(Rio Abajo)
(SPANISH-COLOR)

Madrid, Dec. 2.

An El Iman S.A. and Amber Films Inc. production. Written and directed by José Luis Borau, based on original treatment by Borau and Barbara Probst Solomon. Exec producers, Borau and Steven Kovacs. Camera (Eastmancolor), Teo Escamilla; additional camera, Steven Posey, Mikhail Suslov; Joan Gelpi and Nicholas von Sternberg; sets, Philip Thomas; costumes, Sawnie Ruth Baldridge; editor, Curtiss Clayton; additional editor, Cary Caughlin; music, George Michalski, Armando Manzanero, Manuel Muñoz and Pam Savage; associate producer, Antonio Isasi-Isasmendi; production manager, José Jacoste; technical advisor, Paul Sanders;

south, Walter Martin. Reviewed at Cine Tivoli (Madrid), Dec. 1, 1984. Running time: **95 MINS.**

Bryant .... David Carradine
Mitch .... Scott Wilson
Engracia .... Victoria Abril
Chuck .... Jeff Delgar
Gabacho .... Sam Jaffe
Also with: Paul Richardson, Jesse Vint, Mitch Pileggi, Christopher Saylors, David Estuardo, Anne Galvin.
(Original soundtrack in English. Also dubbed Spanish version available.)

After his four-year odyssey, Spanish director José Luis Borau has finally succeeded in completing his first "American" film, shot entirely along the U.S.-Mexican border. The effort was worth the wait. "On The Line" is a well-directed, taut, fast-paced and poignant tale involving a relationship between two U.S. border guards and a Mexican prostitute.

The subject of border guards and illegal immigrants is one amply chronicled in cinema, but Borau adds a few new twists. Carrying the film on her shoulders is a superb performance by Victoria Abril as the virtually illiterate hooker who works in a dive in the "tolerated" prostitution strip on the Mexican side and who falls in love with a young border guard. Scott Wilson does a convincing job as the "heavy," also involved with the hooker but with no sympathies for the Mexicans. David Carradine is well-cast as a "coyote," a guide smuggling Mexicans across the border, while Jeff Delgar is the tyro guard bucking the system.

Pic never really takes a stand on the question of illegal entries, except for a line spoken by the late Sam Jaffe saying he sees nothing wrong with Mexicans heading north to seek work. Another view is expressed by Mitch, the tough guard, after an incident in which a wetback is killed and an official bi-national investigation is held north of the border. He spews out his indignation that he must sit down with Mexican officials in his own country and apologize for the accidental death of a Mexican.

Politics, however, are very much secondary to the story of the young guard's infatuation with the hooker, whom he ultimately marries in Mexico and smuggles up to the States only to be given away shortly by his hard-boiled rival. The girl later wreaks revenge upon the latter and pic ends touchingly with her writing her first letter in English to her husband who is under arrest in Texas.

Though directed by a Spaniard, pic comes across as though it were a solid Yank product and with a careful release could do well in the U.S. and other markets around the world in all media. For those non-Spanish audiences not yet familiar with the talents of Victoria Abril (she has been in a dozen topnotch Spanish films starting with Vicente Aranda's 1977 "Change Of Sex"), this film will be a revelation. Borau has steeped himself in the lore of the border and extracted a story that is both dramatic and convincing.
— *Besa.*

Bedroom Eyes
(CANADIAN-COLOR)

Edmonton, Dec. 11.
An RSL Films/Pan-Canadian release. Produced by Robert Lantos, Stephen Roth. Directed by William Fruet. Screenplay, Michael Alan Eddy; camera (color), Miklos Lente; production manager, Gerald Arbeid; costumes, Julie Ganton; music, John Tucker, Paul Hoffert; art director, Lindsey Goddard; editor, Tony Lower. Reviewed at Odeon 2, Edmonton, Alberta, Dec. 5, 1984. Running time: **95 MINS.**
Harry Ross .... Kennth Gilman
Alixe Barnes .... Dayle Haddon
Jobeth .... Barbara Law
Caroline .... Christine Cattell
Mary Kittrick .... Jane Catling

The odd good characterization, some passable acting and an initially interesting psychological angle fail to rouse "Bedroom Eyes" from being much more than a drowsy murder mystery with softcore sex scenes.

Story, filmed in Toronto, involves a successful stockbroker who, while jogging one night, inadvertently glimpses mysterious sexual goings-on in a townhouse. Attracted to a seductive red-haired woman inside, he returns to the house several times in the next few weeks to watch happenings involving two, sometimes three persons.

Concerned about his voyeurism, he undergoes therapy with a beautiful psychiatrist. She advises him to discontinue his activity. He sneaks back, however, just in time to catch the tail-end of a stabbing murder. Soon the panicked broker is both the prime suspect in a homicide and target of an unknown assailant.

In the meantime, the broker enlists the aid of the psychiatrist who tries, through hypnosis, to cut through a tangle of blocked memories and mistaken identities.

Direction and choreography are serviceable. Film is generally poorly paced, lacking, until its final minutes, the tautness and tension of a good thriller. Former Vogue model Dayle Haddon is a sympathetic shrink, while sultry Barbara Law is an effective femme fatale. — *Mojo.*

Johnny Dangerously
(COLOR)

Low-brow comedy escapes.

Hollywood, Dec. 18.
A 20th Century Fox/Edgewood Film Distributors release, produced by Michael Hertzberg. Directed by Amy Heckerling. Stars Michael Keaton. Exec producers, Bud Austin, Harry Colomby. Screenplay, Norman Steinberg, Bernie Kukoff, Colomby, Jeff Harris; camera (Deluxe Color), David M. Walsh; editor, Pem Herring; sound, Jerry Jost; production design, Joseph R. Jennings; assistant director, Bill Beasley; associate producer, Neil A. Machlis; costumes, Patricia Norris; music, John Morris; casting, Mike Fenton, Jane Feinberg, Marci Liroff. Reviewed at the UA Egyptian Theater, L.A., Dec. 17, 1984. (MPAA rating: PG-13.) Running time: **90 MINS.**
Johnny Dangerously .... Michael Keaton
Vermin .... Joe Piscopo
Lil .... Marilu Henner
Mom .... Maureen Stapleton
Dundee .... Peter Boyle
Tommy .... Griffin Dunne
Maroni .... Richard Dimitri
Sally .... Glynnis O'Connor
Young Johnny .... Byron Thames
Burr .... Danny DeVito
The Pope .... Dom DeLuise
Vendor .... Ray Walston
Cleaning Lady .... Sudie Bond

As a Christmas comedy, "Johnny Dangerously" ably brings up the rear. As often as possible, it also brings up women's breasts, male genitalia, various physical handicaps and whatever else will qualify it as this season's low-brow selection.

It does have a historic distinction: It took years under the old ratings system before "Cruising" raised the question, "If this is an R, what is an X?" After only a few months of the new system, "Johnny" poses, "If this is a PG-13, then what is an R?"

For the first 15 minutes, though, it does seem "Johnny" might turn out better than its long pre-release shelf life and advance talk suggested. Opening with a zip, young Byron Thames (worth checking for future projects) gets the 1930s gangster sendup off solidly as the good-hearted, honest lad forced to take up crime to pay for the operations on his multi-ailing mom, Maureen Stapleton.

Stapleton is also well-cast in her clichéd role, as are Peter Boyle as the good mobster and Joe Piscopo as the bad. At first, Richard Dimitri is fun as he mangles the English language, even the four-letter kind for a few times. However, too much is too much.

Deliberately overworking the Cagney mannerisms, Michael Keaton is initially good, too, in the title role, as is Griffin Dunne as Johnny's D.A. brother. Unfortunately, the material given all of them just gets worse and worse.

As a streetcorner pope extorting Keaton for cash, Dom DeLuise appears for only a few lines, none of them funny. It's Ray Walston's brief contribution that exemplifies the overall content of the film: as a blind news vendor, he gets hit in the head with a bundle of papers, restoring his sight. Then he gets hit again, turning him deaf. Hit a third time, he regains his hearing but loses his memory. Funny stuff.

With Amy Heckerling at the helm, this unfortunately was another of those films that was supposed to help establish the credibility of women directors in the industry. Too much shouldn't be made of that now.

After all, it took four men to write it. —*Har.*

Ronja Rövardotter
(Ronya - The Robber's Daughter)
(SWEDISH-COLOR)

Copenhagen, Dec. 11.
An AB Svensk Filmindustri/AB release of Svensk Silmindustri/AB Svenska Ord/Norsk Film A/S production. Executive producer, Waldemar Bergendahl. Directed by Tage Danielsson. Screenplay, Astrid Lindgren based on her own novel; camera (Eastmancolor), Rune Ericson, Mischa Gavrjusjov; production design, Ulf Axén; costumes, Lenamari Wallström, Bente Winther-Larsen; special effects and animation, Per Ahlin, P-O Ohlsson, Bengt Schöldström; music, Björn Isfält; choreography, Ivo Cramér. Reviewed at the Grand Copenhagen, Dec. 11, 1984. Running time: **125 MINS.**
Ronja .... Hanna Zcetterberg
Birk .... Dan Hafström
Mattis .... Börje Ahlstedt
Lovis .... Lena Nyman
Borka .... Per Oscarsson
Baldy .... Allan Edwall

A $2,100,000 budget is a big one for a Swedish feature, but "Ronya - The Robber's Daughter" looks like 10 times that much and like money well spent. Working from popular author Astrid Lindgren's novel and her own script, director Tage Danielsson has fashioned a combination of a Brothers Grimm fairy tale, a Robin Hood-ish adventure story and Romeo and Juliet romance-cum-melodrama.

During some undefined period of the Middle Ages, 10-year-old Ronya lives a protected life in an old mountain-top castle with her robber chieftain father, her mother and all the common robbers. She is hardly aware of her father's profession, until one day, venturing into the forbidding, but beautiful forest on the slopes below, she encounters Birk, a boy her own age and the son of another robber chieftain, her father's most bitter enemy.

Ronya and Birk explore the dangers and natural delights of the forest. They face and brave encounters with creatures such as the Gremlin-like Rump-Gnomes, the Greydwarfs and the terrible flying Witchbirds, too. Their real trouble, however, comes from their own familes, who will not permit them to see each other. The children are confused and bewildered by the attitude of the adults, but theirs is the ultimate victory, of course, when they succeed in reuniting the two robber families in a wittily choreographed song & dance fest.

Lindgren's screenplay and Tage Danielsson's direction tend to downplay the suspense and, especially, the horrors lurking in the woods. This may clear their adventure feature with censors, but it does make proceedings seem rather tame and episodic at times.

"Ronya - The Robber's Daughter" is cast with fine Swedish professionals, who all perform with vigor and a fine sense of the fun inherent in the story. Especially Allan Edwall has created a memorable and highly original figure, emulating a giant turtle, as the trusty robber Baldy. There is a good, wild gypsy glimpse in the eyes of little Hanna Zetterberg in the title role. —*Kell.*

What You Take For Granted
(COLOR-16m)

Docu-drama explores feminist sensibilities.

An Iris Feminist Collective Inc., Berkeley, release. Produced, directed, written and edited by Michelle Citron; camera (color, 16m), Frances Reid; production manager, Eileen Fitzpatrick; sound, Phoebe Bendiger; music, Karen Pritikin. Funded in part with grants from the National Endowment for the Arts and the Alumni Fund, School of Speech, Northwestern U. Reviewed at Paramount screening room, N.Y., Nov. 12, 1984, as part of Gay Film Festival. (No MPAA Rating.) Running time: 75 MINS.
Doctor (Dianna) . . . . Belinda Cloud
Truck driver (Anna) . Donna Blue Lachman
Cable splicer . . . . Mosetta Harris
Philosophy prof. . . . . Fran Hart
Sculptor . . . . Helen Larimore

At the end of this film appears a puzzling caveat or confession: "This film combines fictitious characters with documentary footage of women at work" "What You Take For Granted" is a fictional film using a cast of six women performers who speak lines and who act out fictionalized characterizations based upon the producer's interviews with 40 real-life women workers in non-traditional professions.

Four appear in solo monologs to the camera, each describing her difficulties in jobs that usually are for males only, and macho males at that. Although these four speak with the hesitations and cadences of everyday speech, they have in fact memorized or closely paraphrased their written lines, which succinctly summarize their job-place ordeals with male malice, sexual harassment and salary jealousies.

These monologs are intercut with lifeless dramatic scenes depicting a friendship between the two remaining characters, a relationship that ripens into a lesbian embrace as the film ends. These two fictional characters also speak their own monologs.

The film's form is a clumsy alternation of pseudo-documentary interview-monologs intercut with dramatized fictional scenes that are stiff and unpersuasive, shot in long static takes. One wishes the director had dealt directly with the original interview material instead of reworking it into soap opera.

The lesbian angle is a non sequitur and seems forced into the film. Although "What You Take For Granted" is part of the Gay

Film Festval, its gay angle is less than a subtheme. —*Hitch.*

Par Ou t'Es Rentré?
On T'A Pas Vue Sortir
(How'd You Get In?
We Didn't See You Leave)
(FRENCH-TUNISIAN-COLOR)

Paris, Dec. 18.
A Gaumont release of a Carthago Films production. Produced by Tarak Ben Ammar. Directed by Philippe Clair. Stars Jerry Lewis, Philippe Clair. Screenplay, Clair, Daniel Saint-Hamon, Bruno Tardon; camera (color), André Domage; art director, Jean-Michel Hugon; editor, Françoise Javet Frederix; reviewed at the Gaumont Ambassade theater, Paris, Dec. 17, 1984. Running time: 91 MINS.
With: Jerry Lewis, Philippe Clair, Marthe Villalonga, Jakie Sardou, Philippe Castelli.

Comedian Jerry Lewis seemed to touch bottom in his local film debut last year, but he has now appeared in another French-language farce (again as actor only) that reaches new depths in witlessness.

In this film, Lewis is under orders to Philippe Clair, a veteran director of Grade Z comedies, who also costars. Clair is not willing to be a foil, and ends up competing with Lewis in uninspired clowning, leaving the Yank little room to develop his own antics.

Lewis is cast as a private detective who is hired by a rich industrialist's wife to catch Clair, her mate, in *flagrant delicto* and provide evidence for divorce. But the two men instead become friends and find themselves on the lam together when Clair is pursued for larceny.

They escape to Tunisia (inevitably, because the film is produced by Tarak Ben Ammar, who has turned his homeland into a economical location-shooting and facilities mecca) where they are entangled in an international fast food war among Italian, Arab and Americanized Tunisian factions.

Lewis, post-synchronized with a fashionably comic Algerian accent, does what he is told without conviction. There's little one can do under a director who's idea of humor is a gym class full of fat, middle-aged matrons, whose every movement sends earthquake tremors through the building. — *Len.*

Tro, hab og kärlighed
(Twist & Shout)
(DANISH-COLOR)

Copenhagen, Dec. 7.
A Kaerne Film release of a Per Holst Film-produktion ad Palle Fogtdal production. Directed by Bille August. Story and screenplay by August and Bjarne Reuther, loosely based on latter's novels. Camera (Eastman-color), Jan Weincke; executive producer, Ib Tardini; production manager, Janne Find; production design, Sören Kragh Sörensen; editor, Janus Billeskov Jansen; music, Bo Holten; costumes, Françoise Nicolet, Manon Rasmussen. Reviewed at the Dagmar, Copen-

hagen, Dec. 7, 1984. Running time: 105 MINS.
Björn . . . . Adam Tönsberg
Erik . . . . : Lars Simonsen
Anna . . . . Camilla Söeberg
Kirsten . . . . Ulrikke Bondo
Also with: Thomas Nielsen, Lone Lindorff, Arne Hansen, Aase Hansen, Bent Mejding, Malene Schwarz, Kurt Ravn, Grethe Mogensen, Troels Munk, Elga Olga.

To be marketed abroad as "Twist & Shout," "Faith, Hope And Charity" (the translated title) is director Bille August's large-scale followup to his '60s meller "Zappa" (a Spectrafilm release in the U.S.) and looms as an even more impressive entry on the major film fest circuit along with solid foreign sales (Scandinavian territories are covered already).

This time around, cowriter Bjarne Reuther and wirter-director August have their teenage protagonists move up a notch in years. The boys still wear their hair short, but in dress they emulate the Beatles and either dance to or are members of Beatles-like bands. The girls wear blue blazers and flannel skirts. All are of lower middleclass suburban families and still very much tied to latter's manners and morals.

Björn is the winner type, Erik the loser. Björn has his first, radiantly happy love affair with Camilla, a waitress' daughter, but their love does not survive the illegal abortion she has to go through although they stay loyal and true till the end. Erik is the victim of a tyrannical father who keeps the mother bed-ridden and in a neurotic condition nearly to the point of killing her. Erik's timid attempts at revolt threaten to lead to his own at-home imprisonment.

In the Björn-Camilla story, everything develops along predictable lines without stepping into the pitfalls of cliché. The Erik story is full of mute suspense. Both stories merge beautifully although film does sag a bit around the end of its first two thirds.

Cinematography and all production credits are of the highest professional gloss. Bille August has the warmth, style, technical and dramatic skill to be ranked as a major European director. —*Kell.*

Chinese Boxes
(W. GERMAN-BRITISH-COLOR)

London, Dec. 3.
A Chris Sievernich Filmproduktion, presented by Palace Pictures. Produced by Chris Sievernich. Executive producers Stephen Woolley, Nik Powell. Directed by Christopher Petit. Feature entire cast. Screenplay, L.M. Kit Carson, Petit; camera (color), Peter Harvey; editor, Fred Srp; art directors, Edgar Hinz, Klaus Beiser; music, Gunther Fischer; costumes, Ulrike Schutte. Reviewed at Cannon Classic screening room, London, Nov. 29, 1984. Running time: 87 MINS.
Lang Marsh . . . . Will Patton
Zwemmer . . . . Gottfried John
Sarah . . . . : Adelheid Arndt
Harwood . . . . : Robbie Coltrane
Donna Johnson . . . . Beate Jensen

Eva . . . . Susanne Meierhofer
Alan . . . . Jonathan Kinsler
Crewcut . . . . : L.M. Kit Carson
Snake . . . . Chris Sievernich
Gunsel . . . . Christopher Petit

Almost a companion piece to his earlier film, "Flight To Berlin" (shown this year in the Cannes Directors Fortnight). "Chinese Boxes" sees British director Christopher Petit once more gleefully exploring the seedy side of West Berlin. It's a convoluted and densely-plotted thriller about an American innocent caught up in murder and mayhem when all he wants to do is catch the next plane out.

After a surprisingly clumsy opening sequence, in which the principal characters are awkwardly established, pic settles down with a murder on an underpass (Petit himself plays the unshaven gunman). The victim is an associate of Lang Marsh (Will Patton), whose girlfriend recently left for Amsterdam, expecting him to follow. That night, Marsh receives a visit from a young girl (Beate Jensen) with sex on her mind; when her body is found in his bathroom next day, having apparently died from a heroin overdose, Marsh discovers that (a) she was only 15 and (b) she was the daughter of an American diplomat. That's trouble.

Rest of the pic has Marsh fending off a variety of strange and sinister characters, including a drug kingpin (Gottfried John) and a portly U.S. customs official who, as beautifully played by Robbie Coltrane, is a dead-ringer for the late Jack Carson. Throughout, Petit's visual flair creates a superb atmosphere for this modern thriller.

Plot is, frankly, hard to unravel. Background seems to concern the reunification of Germany ("If you want to get a nation together, get the gangsters together"), and poor Lang is hopelessly caught up in the crossfire.

Dialog, by Petit in collaboration with L.M. Kit Carson (whose last credit was "Paris, Texas") is pithy and sharp, and despite a very low budget, entire film has a highly professional look. Camerawork of Peter Harvey is very fine, and there's a haunting music score by Gunther Fischer. All the actors appear to be postsynched, which slows down their performances a bit, especially in the first couple of scenes, but Fred Srp's editing is as brisk as his name.

Commercially, pic falls in the middle-ground between a genre thriller, which it is, and a high quality pic by a most innovative director, which it also is. Trouble is, art house audiences often reject this kind of film while embracing more obviously 'artistic' (i.e., classical) pics. However, "Chinese Boxes" should do well in most European countries, especially Germany and

France, and video life is obviously indicated. A major fest outing might help. — *Strat.*

Mrs. Soffel
(COLOR)

Dull drama in hurry-up bid for Oscars.

An MGM/UA release of an MGM presentation of an Edgar J. Scherick-Scott Rudin production. Produced by Scherick, Rudin, David A. Nicksay. Directed by Gillian Armstrong. Stars Diane Keaton, Mel Gibson. Screenplay, Ron Nyswaner; camera (Metrocolor), Russell Boyd; editor, Nicholas Beauman; music, Mark Isham; production design, Luciana Arrighi; art direction, Jacques Bradette; set decoration, Hilton Rosemarin, Dan Conley; sound (Dolby), David Lee; associate producer, Dennis Jones; assistant directors, Mark Egerton, Scott Maitland, Ron Bozman (Pittsburgh); second unit directors, Glenn H. Randall Jr., Bozman; casting, Margery Simkin. Reviewed at the MGM Studios, Culver City, Dec. 11, 1984. (MPAA Rating: PG-13.) Running time: 110 MINS.
Kate Soffel ....Diane Keaton
Ed Biddle ....Mel Gibson
Jack Biddle ....Matthew Modine
Peter Soffel ....Edward Herrmann
Irene Soffel ....Trini Alvarado
Margaret Soffel...........Jennie Dundas
Eddie Soffel ....Danny Corkill
Clarence Soffel ....Harley Cross
Buck McGovern ....Terry O'Quinn
Maggie ....Pippa Pearthree

The potential for a moving, tragic love story is clearly there, but "Mrs. Soffel" proves distressingly dull for most of its running time until it delivers a bracing breath of cold winter air towards the end. Being hurried into release in L.A. and N.Y. Dec. 26 to beat the Academy Awards deadline, pic has the prestige trappings of topliners Diane Keaton and Mel Gibson and Aussie director Gillian Armstrong in her Yank debut, but combo doesn't provide enough emotion or excitement to put it across as a mainstream b.o. attraction.

True story is set in Pittsburgh in 1901, and has Keaton, as the wife of Allegheny County Prison warden, Edward Herrmann, recovering from a long illness and resuming her rounds of quoting scripture to prisoners. She quickly takes a special interest in two cons on Death Row, brothers Mel Gibson and Matthew Modine, who are waiting to be hung for a murder they were convicted of committing during a burglary.

Presumably because of their good looks, the women of the community have taken the young men's cause to their hearts, and soon Keaton, who lives an uneventful, confined life with her family in quarters within prison walls, becomes stirred by Gibson.

Defying all reason, Keaton helps the brothers escape and thereby undergoes an instant transformation from respectable woman to fugitive outlaw. Given the chance to split up, the pair, with Modine, decides to stay together, and lead the authorities on a desperate chase across snowy country until inevitably being cornered.

The long first section of the film, probably unavoidably, is afflicted with the limitations imposed by its setting. The hulking prison is an oppressive enough place from the outside, and on the inside it is close to unendurable, especially as seen through the unaccountably dark lensing style adopted here by Russell Boyd.

For virtually all of the time up to the escape, Armstrong has little choice but to shoot the Keaton-Gibson encounters in a deadeningly routine succession of reverse shots, as the two look at each other from opposite sides of prison bars. When Keaton returns to her own quarters, things become even worse, as her husband is predictably written as a limited, by-the-books type who could never imagine his wife has desires which might exceed raising a family in the most conventional sense.

Structurally, pic has been designed so that once the escape is managed and the ill-fated lovers are together at last, a tremendous sense of exhilaration should be felt as they make their way across the wilderness. This does work to an extent, as aspects of "Bonnie And Clyde" and "Elvira Madigan" come into play, but is also undercut by the looming feeling that Keaton's character has genuinely ruined her life by pulling this stunt. There's no question of going back, and the actual amount of time she has with Gibson is pathetically short in view of the sacrifice made.

Final act does carry something of a charge, but it's not enough to make up for the long ride spent getting there. The two stars turn in good, pro jobs, but don't strike that special spark that might have pushed the film over the rough spots.

Armstrong and production designer Luciana Arrighi (who doubled, uncredited, as costume designer) have done an interesting job in conjuring up an unusual time and place, and Les Rubie and Paula Trueman are quite wonderful as an elderly couple who provide sanctuary for the runaways near the end. —*Cart.*

Safari 3000
(COLOR)

Weak car comedy.

An MGM/UA Entertainment release of a United Artists presentation of a Jules V. Levy-Arthur Gardner production. Produced by Levy, Gardner. Directed by Harry Hurwitz. Stars David Carradine, Stockard Channing, Christopher Lee. Screenplay, Michael Harreschou, from story by Levy, Gardner, Harreschou; camera (Panavision, Technicolor), Adam Greenberg; editor, Samuel E. Beetley; music, Ernest Gold; sound, David Hildyard; assistant director, Cedric Sundstrom; production supervisor, Jon Stodel; art director, Peter Williams; set decoration, Pat Bergh, Pat Furno; stunt coordinator, Eddie Stacey; second unit camera, Vincent Cox; associate producer, Robert Levy. Reviewed on MGM/UA Home Video cassette, N.Y., Dec. 8, 1984. (MPAA Rating: PG.) Running time: 91 MINS.
Eddie Miles ....David Carradine
J.J. Dalton ....Stockard Channing
Lorenzo Borgia..........Christopher Lee
Feodor ....Hamilton Camp
Freddie ....Ian Yule
Hawthorne ....Hugh Rouse
Victoria ....Mary Ann Berold

Once upon a time, stuntman Chuck Bail directed "The Gumball Rally" for Warner Bros., Paul Bartel directed David Carradine in "Cannonball" for New World and later on, Hal Needham piloted Burt Reynolds and friends in the "Cannonball Run" pictures. "Safari 3000" comes midway during this car-racing trend, with the novelty of location lensing in South Africa and Zimbabwe. Minor pic, inoffensive but not very stimulating, was originally titled "Rally" and "Two In The Bush," filmed in 1980, testbooked by MGM/UA in 1982, surfaced later on pay-cable and is now a homevideo entry.

Carradine toplines as a former Hollywood stuntdriver ("I'm a real Burt Reynolds," he cracks) competing in the African International Rally against Count Lorenzo Borgia (Christopher Lee), a descendant of the murderous family, and other teams from around the world. A gung-ho Playboy Magazine reporter, J.J. Dalton (Stockard Channing), tags along as Carradine's navigator.

Up until its who-cares, end-of-race ending, pic offers mild humor, effective camaraderie between the pleasant leads Carradine and Channing, and attractive visuals of the African landscape and fauna. Unlike the Reynolds' pics, the cast is thin, with other teams barely in evidence. —*Lor.*

Domani Mi Sposo
(Tomorrow I'm Getting Married)
(ITALIAN-COLOR)

Rome, Dec. 16.

A Titanus release, produced by Adriano De Micheli and Pio Angeletti for Intl. Dean Film. Stars Jerry Calà, Isabella Ferrari. Directed by Francesco Massaro. Screenplay, Massaro, Enrico Vanzina; camera (color), Giorgio Di Battista; editor, Alberto Gallitti; music, Detto Mariano. Reviewed at Reale Cinema, Rome, Dec. 15, 1984. Running time: 89 MINS.
Arturo ....Jerry Calà
Susie ....Isabella Ferrari
Simona ....Milly Carlucci
Rita......................Karina Huff

"Tomorrow I'm Getting Married" is a typical product of the Dean Film factory, cotton candy entertainment made with young audiences in mind. Pic has neither the sophistication of American product nor the earthiness of an older generation to Italo comedies. Milanese comic Jerry Calà, now an established star of the genre, is the principal drawing card. Pretty to look at but uninspired, it has grossed best in the boondocks.

Arturo (Calà), a young boutique owner from a small northern city, is engaged to be married the next day to Susie (Isabella Ferrari). Their hyper-traditional church wedding is all arranged; parents, guests and gifts are ready. All is threatened by a last-minute lovers' quarrel when Arturo is seduced by old flame Simona (Milly Carlucci). At a bachelor party, Arturo's buddies offer him a stunning stripper named Rita (Karina Huff) as a "present." He is too much in love with the bride to take advantage of the situation, and falls asleep on the girl's couch almost missing his wedding.

Sugar-coated fantasy for family audiences and girls dreaming of white wedding gowns hinges on the appeal of Calà, a solid professional who has developed his screen persona over a series of films and now has it down to perfection: an average-guy face, winning smile and constant stream of wisecracks. He more or less carries the show on his own, aided by the three girls, all blonds and very pretty. Enrico Vanzina's script is talky and peppered with Arturo's flashbacks to his skirt-chasing days as a bachelor and meeting his future wife. Helmer Francesco Massaro has it all under control.—*Yung.*

Fotografando Patrizia
(Photographing Patricia)
(ITALIAN-COLOR)

Rome, Dec. 7.

A DMV release, produced by Pietro Innocenzi for Globe Films, Dania Films, Filmes International and National Cinematografica. Directed by Salvatore Samperi. Stars Monica Guerritore. Screenplay by Riccardo Ghione, Edith Bruck and Samperi; camera (color), Dante Spinotti; editor, Sergio Montannari; art director, Maria Chiara Gamba; music, Fred Bongusto. Reviewed at Quirinale Cinema, Rome, Dec. 6, 1984. Running time: **102 MINS.**

Patricia . . . . Monica Guerritore
Emilio . . . . Lorenzo Lena
Arrigo . . . . Saverio Vallone

Softcore erotica entry featuring stage thesp Monica Guerritore is hampered by an awkward tale of brother-sister love scantier than the heroine's costumes. Salvatore Samperi, helmer of erotic hit "Malizia" a few years back, misjudges the dose of artiness required by the genre and pic gets quite a few unintentional laughs where thrills were obviously intended.

The extremely morbid atmosphere, Venice locales and plentiful nudity of the female star echo last season's Tinto Brass hit "The Key." Pic delivers plenty to ogle and has had a fair run with the men's magazine brigade, after which it should find a vidcassette audience.

Patricia (Guerritore), a successful fashion designer, leaves Milan and goes to live with her 16-year-old brother in Venice when the boy's guardian dies. Emilio (Lorenzo Lena), intelligent and moody, was a handicapped child and has been left

afraid to face the world. Big sister tries to get him out of the sepulchral family house and awaken his interest in life. Soon, however, her own unhealthy sexuality involves him in a punishing game of jealousy which culminates at last, to the exasperated audience's relief, in a final incest scene.

Pic bogs down in psychological overload early on when Patricia and Emilio's neuroses meet. She rushes around opening windows and chattering in her designer underwear; he buries himself in front of the tv (only hardcore glimpsed in the picture) surrounded by girlie magazines. Young thesp Lena, with his Marine crew cut and blue eyes, wins audience sympathy at once for his down-to-earth pessimism. Guerritore is a talented actress, but wastes histrionics on the ambiguous role of the sister-lover and comes out the weaker of the two characters. Camera can't seem to make up its mind between her lovely emoting face and body. Pic's most audacious scene centers not on the classy star but an extra, a bubble-headed model who seems to have wandered in from a neighboring hardcore set.

Title, which may be an appendage from an earlier version of the script, refers to the running theme of Emilio's voyeurism. More than taking pictures, he enjoys listening to his sister making love to b.f. Saverio Vallone through a bug he has planted in her room. Dante Spinotti's camerawork outdoes itself in creating a morbid atmosphere of light and shadow.—*Yung.*

Samuel Beckett —
Silence To Silence
(IRISH-DOCU-COLOR/B&W)

London, Dec. 3.

An RTE Production. Produced and directed by Sean O'Mordha. Written by Richard Ellman, Declan Kiberd; camera (color, b&w), Peter Dorney; editor, Martin Duffy; sound, Tony Doyle; narrator, Tony Doyle. Reviewed at London Film Festival, Nov. 29, 1984. Running time: **81 MINS.**

Made with the full cooperation of its subject, this excellent documentary on the Irish poet-novelist-playwright Samuel Beckett will be of considerable interest to anyone interested in 20th century literature.

Beckett, best known for his play, "Waiting For Godot," is an exponent of what the commentary calls "sumptuous minimalism," and he emerges from this portrait as a somewhat obsessive, introverted character, with a keen sense of humor. His childhood in Ireland is covered via family photographs, and his original manuscripts are shown ("Waiting For Godot," like most of his later work, was written in French).

Some distinguished actors, including Jack MacGowran, Patrick Magee and Billie Whitelaw, are seen

in excerpts from the plays. Music by Beckett's favorite composer, Schubert, proves an apt accompaniment.

Director Sean O'Mordha previously made a docu on James Joyce, to which this is a fine companion piece. Fest outings and tv exposure are musts for this informative and well-made pic.—*Strat.*

Tutti Dentro
(Put 'Em All In Jail)
(ITALIAN-COLOR)

Rome, Dec. 18.

A C.D.E. release, produced by Augusto Caminito for Scena Film. Stars Alberto Sordi. Directed by Sordi. Screenplay by Rodolfo Sonego and Sordi, with Caminito; camera (Eastmancolor), Sergio D'Offizi; editor, Tatiana Casini Morigi; art director, Massimo Rassi; Piero Piccioni. Reviewed at C.D.E., Rome, Dec. 17, 1984. Running time: **107 MINS.**

Annibalo Salvemini . . . . Alberto Sordi
Corrado Emilio Parisi . . . . Joe Pesci
Iris Del Monte . . . . Dalila Di Lazzaro
Mrs. Salvemini . . . . Giorgia Moll

For the last 20 years Alberto Sordi, one of Italy's most beloved veteran comics, has been directing half his pictures, most recently for the Scena Film company and producing-writing team Augusto Caminito and Rodolfo Sonego. After last Christmas' astutely written hit "The Cabbie," the group is back with a more balanced, ambiguous work, "Put 'Em All In Jail." Like its predecessor, pic's strength is in voicing the sentiments of the average guy about what's happening around him. Drawing on current headlines and recent scandals in the world of politics and high finance, pic succeeds in forging a strong bond of sympathy between the viewer and investigating magistrate Annibale Salvemini (Sordi), the honest but doomed judge who enters into a one-man battle against corruption that is stronger than he is. Pic's prospects for Christmas trade look excellent and could garner director-star new honors.

However, in spite of the Frank Capra-style theme of the lone honest man fighting on the side of right, pic remains closely tied to issues that have most resonance onshore. Not only does the script read like a collection of newspaper articles detailing the sweeping arrests of hundreds of political, financial and even religious figures on charges of corruption, tax evasion, and other illegal wheeling and dealing (a cathartic sequence bound to generate applause), but a number of characters bear a striking resemblance to well-known ministers and deputies, a joke that should be worth a good amount of laughter, if not lawsuits.

Perhaps in anticipation of trouble, pic pronounces all lookalikes innocent in the end, after mercilessly poking fun at them. Even when the physical resemblance isn't crucial, characters hit home because of

their easy identification with figures in the Italian news, like Joe Pesci's suave "mediator" Corrado Parisi, grand corrupter and puppetmaster who stays in the shadows while he moves the pawns. By the time Salvemini has been arrested, Parisi has woven a web of incriminating circumstantial evidence around the upholder of the law that leads straight to pic's somber ending. Salvemini himself is arrested and concludes that all you can hope for out of Italian justice is that one day it may become "unequal for all."

If Pesci makes a perfect international criminal, supremely sure of his own power, Sordi creates one of his most original and amusing characters, which keeps story in a light key. His magistrate is full of personality and human foibles, like his obstinate preference for wearing long hair and infatuation with decorative nightclub crooner Dalila Di Lazzaro, a weak link who accounts for most of pic's static moments. Pic's uncertain dubbing is particularly bad when she is made to mouth "By and By," not once but twice.

—*Yung.*

Sacred Hearts
(BRITISH-COLOR)

London, Dec. 3.

A Reality Production, for Film Four International. Produced by Dee Dee Glass. Written and directed by Barbara Rennie. Features entire cast. Camera (color), Diane Tammes; art director, Hildegard Echtler; costumes, Monica Howe; editor, Martin Walsh; sound, Moya Burns, Mandy Rose; music, Dirk Higgins. Reviewed at London Film Festival, Dec. 2, 1984. Running time: **89 MINS.**

Sister Thomas . . . . Anna Massey
Doris . . . . Katrin Cartlidge
Maggie . . . . Oona Kirsh
Sister Felicity . . . . Fiona Shaw
Sister Perpetua . . . . Anne Dyson
Sister Mercy . . . . Annette Badland
Mary . . . . Sadie Wearing
Lizzie . . . . Ann-Marie Gwatkin
Tillie . . . . Kathy Burke
Father Larkin . . . . Gerard Murphy
Father Power . . . . Murray Melvin
Dr. Taylor . . . . John Bett

The setting of "Sacred Hearts" is a convent-school in England in the early days of World War II, and it's apparently based in part on the experiences of director Barbara Rennie's mother, an orphan raised by the nuns. The indoctrination of impressionable young people has been treated often enough before in films.

All too often the jokes are a bit glib and cheap, and the nuns, especially Anna Massey as the hidebound Sister Thomas, are frequently caricatured rather than presented with any genuine depth.

Moral implications aside, the film is on safer ground when dealing with the girls themselves, all of them interesting characters. Doris (Katrin Cartlidge) is a newcomer who confides in her friend Maggie (Oona Kirsh) that she's not really a Catholic at all. When Doris starts asking Maggie about Catholic doctrine, she quickly comes to the conclusion that the rule that Catholics must not think for themselves but must believe and obey is uncommonly close to the fascist slogan of "Believe, Obey And Fight." Fadeout reveals that Doris is really a German Jew, terrified of a possible German invasion of Britain.

Though uneven in tone, pic is technically fine and, if it can be carefully distributed, has some chances on its anti-Catholic jokes and jibes. — *Strat.*

Le Vengeance du Serpent à Plumes
(The Vengeance Of The Winged Serpent)
(FRENCH-COLOR)

Paris, Dec. 4.

An AMLF release of a Renn Productions/AMLF coproduction, with the participation of the Mexican Film Institute Conacine. Executive producer, Pierre Grunstein. Directed by Gérard Oury. Stars Coluche. Screenplay, Oury and Danièle Thompson; camera (color), Henri Decaë; art director, Théo Meurisse; second unit director, Marc Monnet; second unit camera, Vladimir Ivanov; music, Michel Polnareff; sound, Alain Sempé; editor, Albert Jurgenson; production manager, Alain Dépardieu. Reviewed at the Gaumont Ambassade theater, Paris, Dec. 4, 1984. Running time: 105 MINS.
With: Coluche, Maruschka Detmers, Luis Rego, Philippe Khorsand, Farid Chopel, Josiane Balasko, Dominique Frot, Rodolpho de Souza.

"Le Vengeance du Serpent à Plumes," another hugely expensive comedy vehicle (after Claude Zidi's "Banzai" and Dino Risi's "Dagobert") designed for comedy star Coluche, is as low on invention as it is high on budget (over $6,000,000). Not even the technical savoir-faire of director Gérard Oury can save the frantically unfunny script he has patched together with Danièle Thompson, his daughter and frequent collaborator.

Remaining true to his vulgar low comedy mannerisms, Coluche plays a harmless boob who inherits his late grandmother's Paris apartment and finds the premises infested by some youths who are in fact a band of international terrorists. They are trying to spring their jailed leader before heading out to Mexico, where they plan to blow up the world's chiefs of state at the Cancún summit conference.

To keep Coluche from throwing them out, the group's sexiest member, Maruschka Detmers, seduces him, and on orders from the imprisoned chief, attempts, with increasing reluctance, to do away with him.

He finally wakes up to what's been happening, but too late: the anarchists have freed their colleague and have left for Mexico. Hurt and angry, Coluche follows and manages to foil the monstrous plot be-

ing hatched in the ruins of a Mayan temple, where the conference is to take place, and wins Detmers' heart, leading her finally into placid middle-class wedlock.

Oury and Thompson (latter separately authored the hit Gaumont "La Boum" youth pics) have seen more inspired days as gagwriters. Second half of the film, set in Mexico, falls back on the sort of frenetic spectacle at which Oury is an old pro, but the series of manic pursuits are arbitrary and singularly unzany.

Detmers is an attractive foil to Coluche's squeals, double-takes and tart rejoinders, but her characterization is neither credible nor consistent, and the other anarchists (Dominique Frot, Philippe Khorsand and Farid Chopel) are hardly more believable. — *Len.*

Rainfox
(DANISH-COLOR)

Copenhagen, Dec. 9.

A Nordisk Film Kompagni release of a Nordisk Film Studios production (with the Danish Film Institute/Christian Clausen). Directed by Esben Höjlund Carlsen. Screenplay and story, Lars Lundholm; camera (Fujicolor), Göran Nilsson; executive producer, Bo Christensen; editor, Rie Wanting; music, Ole Koch-Hansen; production design, Viggo Bentzon; costumes, Annelise Hauberg; inner monologs written by Peter Poulsen and spoken by Erik Wedersöe; production manager, Lene Nielsen. Reviewed at Palads Teatret, Copenhagen, Dec. 9, 1984. Running time: 96 MINS.
John Ericsson .... Keve Hjelm
Anette Swan .... Solbjörg Höjfeldt
Claude .... Leif Sylvester Petersen
Police lieutenant .... Ole Ernst
The Meat millionaire .... Axel Ströbye
Judge Swan .... Ole Brandstrup
Eggers .... Niels Alsing
Topper .... Jess Ingerslev
Scott .... John McEwan

"Rainfox" is a would-be Raymond Chandleresque crime thriller with a plot based on erotic tensions and evil doings among rich race horse owners more interested in making money on bets than in the nobility of their animals. Walking, with a wobble, down those shady tracks and side-stepping numerous corpses is John Ericsson, horse trainer and world vagabond in his 50s, now jobless and under suspicion of having doped the champion racer of film's title.

While plot gets murkier and murkier, the characters in Lars Lundberg's script talk much more than they move.

Höjlund Carlsen, who had a modest international hit with "Steppin Out," an adult divorce comedy of errors, has a good way with actors, too. What he cannot help, however, is their characters' contrived motivations.

Final denouement comes as a flat statement trivializing the film's whodunnit element. Although handsomely produced and containing several witty insights into track and horse lore, "Rainfox" lacks the

sheer animal excitement otherwise inherent in its theme and subject matter. The bets are on film's taking few international ribbons. —*Kell.*

Jungle Girl
(B&W-16m)

Experimental homage to the Republic serial.

Kent, Ohio, Dec. 1.

An experimental feature film in tribute to and loosely based on the 1941 Republic serial with the same title. Produced, written, directed and photographed by Richard Myers. Distributed by Myers. Kent State U., Ohio. Reviewed at Kent State, Kent, Ohio, Nov. 30, 1984. Running time: 100 MINS.
With: Mary Leed (Nyoka) and Jake Leed (Stanton).

For those film buffs with memories of the 1941 Republic serial "Jungle Girl," starring Frances Gifford as Nyoka and Tom Neal as Stanton, Richard Myers' tongue-in-cheek tribute and remake employing the same title will be a treat.

Even for those who weren't in the throes of early puberty some four decades ago, there's still enough here to send them off to a friendly collector or serial-purchasing library to catch a glimpse of the magic that went into the original.

"Jungle Girl" was inspired by a chance look-see again at the Republic serial, which Myers had seen as a nine-year-old at his neighborhood theater in hometown Masillon. The fact that the old hardtop was about to be demolished by wreckers undoubtedly meant to him the loss of a childhood dream-place. It spurred, too, a personal inquiry into the fate of Nyoka, played in the original by the winsome Frances Gifford. Shortly after this popular serial, she inked a contract with MGM, but then found her career cut short by a tragic auto accident in 1948 — resulting in a plastic surgery operation on her face. Gifford never adjusted psychologically to the misfortune, left the screen in 1953 and was later committed to a mental ward. Now pretty much forgotten, although recovered enough to live a quiet, retiring life in California, the former star agreed to meet with an ardent admirer, Myers, and this film was made.

Gifford does not appear in the film: her role and that of Stanton (Tom Neal in the original), are interpreted in a modern-day context by two veterans of Myers' filmmaking ouvre, Mary and Jake Leed. Myers' own mother adds an extra touch by speaking of past moviegoing as the Weslin Theater is being torn down. It's this combination of spoken reminiscences and recreated scenes matching originals in the serial itself that make this low-budgeter a warming homage to Republic and the glory days of the weekend serial. That, and the visuals employing

the full catalog of experimental camerawork. — *Holl.*

Vacanze In America
(Vacation In America)
(ITALIAN-COLOR)

Rome, Dec. 15.

A Columbia release, produced by Mario and Vittorio Cecchi Gori for C.G. Silver Films. Stars Jerry Calà and Christian De Sica. Directed by Carlo Vanzina. Screenplay by Enrico and Carlo Vanzina; camera (color), Claudio Cirillo; editor, Raimondo Crociani; music, Manuel De Sica. Reviewed at C.D.S. Rome, Dec. 14, 1984. Running time: 98 MINS.,
Peo .... Jerry Calà
Don Burro .... Christian De Sica
Alessio .... Claudio Amendola
Antonella .... Antonella Interlenghi
Mrs. De Romanis .... Edwige Fenech

Leader of the most recent wave of commercial teen comedies, helmer Carlo Vanzina is out to duplicate the success of his hit from last year, "Christmas Vacation," by reprising cast, style and a good part of the story from the earlier picture. Unfortunately, "Vacation In America" has none of the sparkle, not to mention originality, of its predecessor. Though the package has a built-in opening audience, pic is in a very minor key and probably won't climb to the top of the holiday flood of new releases. Unsophisticated storyline and careful skirting of vulgarity seem aimed more at provincial family audiences than city teens.

A fancy parochial boys' academy is taking a trip across the U.S. for vacation. Major faces in the group are Peo (Jerry Calà), an overaged wiseacre, eternal student and irrepressible skirtchaser, and Alessio (Claudio Amendola), the simple, nice son of a restaurateur who is himself chased from Central Park to Death Valley by rich girl Antonella (Antonella Interlenghi) when her own b.f. proves a dud.

Supervising the tour is a fussbudget young cleric, Don Burro (Christian De Sica, an eerie ringer for father Vittorio) and the knockout mom of one of the boys, played by Italy's favorite pin-up Edwige Fenech. A misunderstanding almost lands the unlikely couple in bed, but this tantalizing and long-threatened scene never materializes. If the chastity of the clergy is saved, Peo's nonstop efforts to deepen his knowledge of the American female are frustrated one after the other, and Antonella's seduction of Alessio is permanently deferred.

"Vacation" is an example of the new chasteness of young Italo comedy, and its changing market. Even though sex is the film's underlying thread, it is cleaned up and converted into innocent fun for family and very young audiences, whose curiosity is merely whetted by scenes of blue movies and gay parties in New York, sexy surfers on the California beach and Las Vegas callgirls. All is carefully handled to avoid nudity.

Scripting frères Carlo and Enrico Vanzina are adroit at mixing their standard assortment of characters and pacing their scenes. However, pic's mythic view of America through the bus window is distant and unreal; most character interaction takes place in nondescript hotel rooms, bars and diners. Scripters have spared no cliché about America, but fail to make them funny. In the end, national differences just boil down to hamburgers vs. spaghetti. —*Yung.*

Melvin, Son Of Alvin
(AUSTRALIAN-COLOR)

Sydney, Dec. 24.

A Roadshow release of a McElroy and McElroy production. Produced by James McElroy. Directed by John Eastway. Features entire cast. Screenplay, Morris Gleitzman; camera (color), Ross Berryman; production design, Jon Dowding; editor, John Hollands; music, Colin Stead; associate producers, Tim Sanders, Wilma Schinella. Reviewed at Balgowlah Cinema, Sydney, Dec. 21, 1984. Running time: **85 MINS.**

Melvin Simpson	Gerry Sont
Gloria Giannis	Lenita Psillakis
Alvin Purple	Graeme Blundell
Burnbaum	Jon Finlayson
Dee Tanner	Tina Bursill
Mr. Simpson	Colin McEwan
Mrs. Simpson	Abigail
Cameraman	David Argue
Mrs. Giannis	Ariathe Galani
Ferret	Greg Stroud
Streaky	David Beresh
Estelle	Katy Manning
Miss Fosdyke	Marian Callopy

Tim Burstall's "Alvin Purple" (1973) was an early commercial success for the reemerging Australian film industry; though hardly original, pic about a homely guy who's irresistible to women artfully took advantage of recently liberated censorship and mopped up locally. A sequel, "Alvin Rides Again" (1974) was less successful.

Now, 10 years on, a new production team has come up with a third film in the series, and the joke is thinner than ever.

It seems that Alvin (Graeme Blundell, reprising his original role) fathered a son, Melvin, in 1966, and the lad, now 18, has inherited his father's sexual chemistry though he himself is terrified of women. Gerry Sont plays Melvin with an air of bewilderment throughout, as well he might, for Morris Gleitzman's screenplay is almost totally devoid of humor and the uninhibited sexual encounters of the original film have been severely toned down to obtain a local M censorship rating.

Slight plot has a tv station (whose motto is "Truth, Justice, Ratings") assign a woman journalist (Tina Bursill) and an inept, accident-prone cameraman, to do a story on Melvin's reunion with his long-lost father. Meanwhile, Melvin has been befriended by a pretty Greek cinema usherette (Lenita Psillakis) who

wants to help him get over his anti-female phobias.

What laughs there are in this heavy-handed opus come from David Argue as the tv cameraman who, as the film goes on and his disasters multiply, is covered with more and more bandages; and Ariathe Galani as the heroine's black-garbed, over-protective mother whose first reaction, on seeing Melvin with her daughter, is to leap on him from a first-floor balcony like some avenging harpy.

Technically, the film is sometimes sloppy (a mike boom is reflected in glass), and a couple of comedy highlights — the collapse of a house during a party and the last-reel helicopter finals — go for little as a result of tacky staging.

First-time director John Eastway's direction is uninspired, as is the material he's given. Forced to compete with some big yearend releases Down Under, it's extremely doubtful that "Melvin" will set the cash registers ringing in the style of his dear old dad. —*Strat.*

Train d'Enfer
(Hell Train)
(FRENCH-COLOR)

Paris, Dec. 12.

A Fox/Hachette release of a Progefi/TF 1 Films/Canal Plus/Hachette Première/Les Productions Fox Europa coproduction. Produced by Christine Gouze-Renal. Directed by Roger Hanin. Features entire cast. Screenplay, Hanin, Jean Curtelin; Camera (color), Jean Penzer; music, Michel Legrand; art director, Jean-Claude Gallouin; editor, Youcef Tobni; sound, Bernard Ortion; second unit camera, Alain Levent; production manager, Philippe Verro. Reviewed at the Publicis screening room, Paris, Dec. 11, 1984. Running time: **90 MINS.**

Couturier	Roger Hanin
Salviat	Gérard Klein
Isabelle	Christine Pascal
Muller	Robin Renucci
Lacombe	Fabrice Eberhard
Le Goff	Xavier Maly
Jouffroy	Benoit Regent
Dalbret	Didier Sandre

The murder in 1983 of a young Arab, thrown to his death from a speeding train by some French soldiers on leave, inspired actor Roger Hanin to direct and appear in this film, intended as a virulent denunciation of racial hatred and violence. But "Train d'Enfer," produced by Hanin's wife, Christine Gouze-Renal, says little about racism, and says it ineptly.

For the script, Hanin called on Jean Curtelin, the shock trooper of French screenwriters. On the basis of this and his previous assignment (Denis Amar's "L'Addition"), Curtelin's fundamental concern seems to be bullying filmgoers into a programmed response. To achieve this end, he resorts to the most dated melodramatic methods.

There is not an ounce of courage in this film, which identifies racists as unmistakable goons, hysterics

and neo-Nazis (with blond hair, of course). The Arabs are mostly well-behaved and hard-working, with the exception of one subsidiary immigrant, a petty thief and pickpocket, though he's not hateful or violent.

The murder on the train remains the catalyzing incident of the story, sufficiently altered so as to avoid any legal hassles (the alleged real-life killers have not yet been brought to trial) or military protests (pic's culprits are not soldiers, but citizens of a small town near Paris — tarnishing the uniform is still a major screen taboo in France.)

Hanin casts himself in the part of the town's upright police commissioner trying to get the killers in the clink while staving off a potential race riot being stoked up by the extremist right-wingers.

Hanin directs limply, but there's nothing much he can do with a script that piles up incredible sequences and absurd dialog. Second part of the film turns into a ludicrous ripoff of Fritz Lang's "Fury" as the outraged white townspeople march on the city jail to claim the hides of some Arabs framed by the racists as rioters.

Law and order finally prevail, with only competent filmmaking biting the dust. Some usually fine actors have been assembled but "Train d'Enfer" does neither them nor the cause of racial tolerance any good. — *Len.*

L'Arbalète
(The Syringe)
(FRENCH-COLOR)

Paris, Dec. 5.

A CCFC release of a Candice Productions picture. Produced and directed by Sergio Gobbi. Screenplay, Gobbi, Daniel Ubaud; camera (Eastmancolor), Richard Andrey; editor, Robert Rongier; music, Jacques Revaux; art director, Frédéric Duru; fight coordinator, Guy de Rigo; sound, Jean-Pierre Delorme. Reviewed at Marignan-Concorde theater, Paris, Dec. 5, 1984. Running time: **90 MINS.**

With: Daniel Auteuil, Marisa Berenson, Marcel Bozzuffi, Daniel Ubaud, Michel Beaune, Didier Sauvegrain, Guy de Rigo.

"L'Arbalète" is a routine addition to the current vogue of mindless blood-and-thunder urban melodramas which the French are exploiting as much as the Yanks.

For his directorial comeback, Sergio Gobbi (who has recently been involved in some theatrical and homevid distribution ventures) leaves no ethnic stone unturned in this predictable tale of gangland drug warfare instigated by a fascist police inspector (Marcel Bozzuffi) who is hoping the various gangs will exterminate each other in their scrambling for a diverted drug shipment.

Hero of the affair is urban cowboy Daniel Auteuil, a former-hood-turned-cop who goes under cover to

prevent a massacre, but fails to save his friends, notably Daniel Ubaud (film's co-scripter), chief of a Vietnamese gang, and Marisa Berenson, a junkie streetwalker who becomes a pawn in Bozzuffi's deadly game.

All the local minorities check in during the story, with black, Arab and Vietnamese gangs facing each other off for a rumble or two. They all come out smelling sweet when a band of doped-out neo-Nazis show up, and with weapons supplied by Bozzuffi, mow down the blacks and Viets.

The macho heroics and backlot clashes leave little room for credible story development and characterization (though Bozzuffi is an always welcome baddie). Technically adequate, though market is glutted with this sort of product. — *Len.*

Behind The Veil
(CANADIAN-DOCU-COLOR-16m)

Toronto, Dec. 2.

A National Film Board Studio D production. Produced by Signe Johansson. Directed by Margaret Wescott. Written and narrated by Gloria Demes; camera (color, 16m), Susan Trow; editor, Rosemarie Shapley; research, Holly Dressel. Reviewed at Harbourfront Studio theater, Toronto, Dec. 1, 1984. Runing time: **126 MINS.**

This informative and controversial interpretation of the history and role of nuns in Europe and modern North American society ought to travel well. It is eminently suitable for television, divided as it is into two parts and covering a subject the anti-clerical inclinations of most filmmakers have left untouched.

The first part is dominated by interviews with three nuns working in the secular world and addressing such human instincts as falling in love, the sex drive, and the sublimation thereof into social work. Although it could be argued that more interviews would provide a wider perspective, the three women seem honest, speak frankly and provide a glimpse into the lives of thoroughly modern nuns.

Having established the social and intellectual work of contemporary sisters in the U.S., Ireland and Canada, second part of the picture turns to a history of the orders that developed out of pre-Christian Celtic cults in Ireland. Feminist revisionist history has put forth a theory of matriarchy and mother goddesses in former civilizations that is capsuled cavalierly in order to condemn the Catholic church's authority over women and their bodies. Historical aberrations such as Pope Joan and the vote in 900 A.D. on whether women had souls (by one vote, they got them) spice up the narration.

By projecting feminist authority into a more peaceable era, pic offers a vision of ordained sisters compensating for the disorder and probable destruction of a society governed by men. Pursuing the consequences of a belief in such feminist moral authority, pic shows recent political activism that has led nuns to throw blood on the walls of the Pentagon.

A soothing, superior voice masks the stridency of its narration. Technical credits and location shooting are quite competent. Director's long years as an editor guarantee an interesting rhythm, but the length will have to be reduced for the highly probable tv outlets in the Western world. —Kaja.

My Kind Of Town
(CANADIAN-16m-COLOR)

Vancouver, Dec. 18.
A Petra Films presentation of a Milltown Pictures Inc. production, in association with Teleflim Canada. Directed by Charles Wilkinson. Features entire cast. Screenplay, Charles Wilkinson; camera (color, 16m) David Geddes; editor, Frank Irvine; sound, Sandra Mayo, Paul Sharpe; music; Charles Wilkinson. Reviewed at the Ridge Theater, Vancouver, Dec. 17, 1984. Running time: 76 MINS.
Peter Hall . . . . Peter Smith
Sam The Mayor . . . . John Cooper
Astrid Heim . . . . Martina Schleisser
Michael Hall . . . . Michael Paul
Brad . . . : . . . . Michael Marks
Uncle Roy . . . . Roy Evarts
Frank Hall . . . . Frank Irvine
Margaret Hall . . . . Haida Paul

A lowbudget expansion of the awardwinning docu short "The Little Town That Did," Charles Wilkinson's debut feature "My Kind Of Town" takes a lighthearted look at jobless youth, the plight of British Columbia rural townships that have gone under during the recession that has fiercely gripped this province for two years, and the tenacity displayed by the singular Vancouver Island hamlet of Chemainus.

The townsfolk of Chemainus transformed their would-be ghost town into a successful tourist attraction by commissioning a set of huge murals depicting the colorful past of the locale, before the cowboys and loggers went thataway. Once the home of the "largest sawmill in the Commonwealth," Chemainus lost its staple industry and grabbed the brass ring before the exodus of the unemployed became complete.

Within a semidocumentary format, Wilkinson has spun out a tale of young love triumphing over the defeatism that overtakes talented Peter Hall (Peter Smith) when daily confronted by the lost hopes and dreams of his unemployed father, Frank. Peter starts a slow-burn affair with a photojournalist, Astrid, a West German newcomer to the island, while he awaits the results of an application to join the electronics workforce in Vancouver. Meantime he also endures the routine of compulsory community work after being convicted of vandalism.

Despite dialog that consists largely of small talk, and a ramshackle script, Wilkinson has lent a sprightly air to the humorous depiction of smalltown life. David Geddes' camerawork is clean and versatile; Frank Irvine's editing crisp and classical. The performances are variable, with Peter Smith a natural lead player but Martina Schleisser initially stolid and uneasy in front of the camera. Pic should find a ready home as an indigenous cable item, with appeal for all ages. —Gran.

Stico
(SPANISH-COLOR)

Madrid, Dec. 1.
A Serva Films production. Directed by Jaime de Armiñán. Screenplay, Armiñán and Fernando Fernán Gómez; camera (Eastmancolor), Teo Escamilla; editor, José Luis Matesanz; sets, Tony Cortés. Reviewed at Tecnison Studios, Madrid, Nov. 30, '84. Running time: 105 MINS.
Leopoldo Contreras
(Stico) . . . . Fernando Fernán Gómez
Gonzalo . . . . Agustin Gonzalez
Maria . . . . Carmen Elias
Also with: Amparó Boró, Bárbara and Vanessa Escamilla, Mercedes Lezcano, Manuel Zarzo, Manuel Torremocha.

Jaime "El Nido" de Armiñán's new pic falls somewhere between a comedy and a drama, never quite making up its mind which way to go. Fernando Fernán Gomez is good in his role as a washed-up college professor (the same part he recently played in Carlos Saura's "Los Zancos") and there are some droll moments in the film, but pic is ultimately too thin and feeble to interest audiences.

Yarn concerns an aging, down-and-out prof who happens to run into a former student, now a prosperous lawyer. He proposes to the lawyer and his wife that he become their "slave" for the remainder of his days, "slave" in the classical Roman sense; he would help about the house with chores in return for food, lodging and clothes.

After due hesitations, the couple agrees to take him on. The professor, who specialized in the classics, takes on the name of "Stico," commonly used for slaves at the time of the Caesars, and calls the lawyer "master." After at first creating a disrupting influence in the posh household, Stico gradually ingratiates himself to his "masters," their two daughters and even the other household help.

The story seems to take on a new tack when the prof learns that he has $200,000 due him from American royalties of books he has published, a discovery that coincides with the lawyer's finding himself in financial straits. Another twist comes when the lawyers' association is scandalized at any of its members having a "slave," and a radio reporter is on the verge of blowing the scandal sky-high. Unfortunately, neither lead is followed up, and pic ends tamely with prof being freed of his "servitude" during a First Communion ceremony of one of the children.

Film is Spain's official entry in next February's Berlin Film Festival.—Besa.

Za'am Utehila
(Rage And Glory)
(ISRAELI-COLOR)

Tel Aviv, Dec. 2.
A Zygmund B. presentation of an Avi Nesher & Itzhak Tzhayck production. Written and directed by Nesher. Camera (color): David Gurfinkel; editor, Tzhayek; costumes: Rina Doron; makeup: Zivit Yakir; sound: Nicholas Wensworth; special effects: Pini Kalvier; music, Rami Kleinstein. Reviewed at the Rav Chen Cinema, Tel Aviv, Dec. 1, 1984. Running time: 100 INS.
Eddie . . . . : . . . . Giuliano Mer
Noah . . . . Roni Pincovich
Dafna . . . . Hana Azulay
Angela . . . . Rona Frid
Pinocchio . . . . Tuvia Gelber
Colonel Caine . . . . Barry Langford
Martin . . . . Joseph Bee

Avi Nesher, a young director who already has three features to his credit, and a fourth one, ("She,") completed but unreleased, has put together here several episodes connected with the Jewish resistance against the British in Palestine during World War II, to fashion a thriller purported to be the most expensive film ever produced by an Israeli at home.

Taking place in Jerusalem in early 1942, it follows the secret operations of a Lehi cell (known abroad as the Stern Gang), and their efforts to take revenge upon a sadistic British colonel and his cohorts, who had captured and condemned to death one of the cell's members.

Visually, the film is quite satisfying, the reconstruction of the period, the quality of David Gurfinkel's camerawork, the many explosions and special effects, are all carefully tended to.

However, Nesher seems to have been carried away by details, ignoring both script and characters. Not only is the plot sloppily constructed, but it is historically objectionable, for it leaves on the scene only the Stern Gang and the British, turning a blind eye to the mainstream resistance organizations, as if they didn't exist at all, and failing to consider the enormous impact of the Holocaust on the Jewish population in Palestine.

All characters are two-dimensional and no information is supplied to infuse more interest in their actions. A point of interest raised early in the film, involving the possible existence of a traitor in the cell, is forgotten, and a love story develops on a secondary level, but doesn't lead anywhere.

Therefore, actors who could make quite an impact, if given the material to do so, are never more than puppets here, which is a pity, particularly in the case of Giuliano Mer, who seems endowed with a strong screen personality.

There is plenty of action, but it is not always clear why it takes place. All technical credits are above average, including soundtrack which incorporates music in the style of the '40s.

Initial reaction in the home market has been slow, possibly because audience is too familiar with the recent past to accept this almost abstract approach to it. —Edna.

The Killers
(U.S.-COLOR-16m)

Lowkey Bukowski adaptation.

Berlin, Dec. 13.
A Patrick Roth Film Production. Written and directed by Roth, based on Charles Bukowski's "Short Story." Camera (color, 16m), Patrick Prince; editor, Daniel Gross; music, Doug Lynner, Bill Boydstun; sound Jim Thornton; production manager, Jude Elliott; production, Claus Kenzenmeier, Bettina Morlock. Reviewed at Berlin Fair Screening Room, Berlin, Dec. 13, '84. Running time: 60 MINS.
With: Jack Kehoe (Harry), Raymond Mayo (Bill), Allan Magicovsky (Husband), Susanne Reed (Wife), Anne Ramsey (First Ragpicker), Susan Tyrrell (Susu, Second Ragpicker), Charles Bukowski (the Author).

Patrick Roth's "The Killers" was made in collaboration with popular L.A. cult scribe Charles Bukowski, whose stories about those living on the edge of society pretty much parallel his own existence as a wino, tramp and odd-job worker. Pic was completed three years ago, but bowed recently at the Hof fest in Germany after project got hung up in a financial pinch that prevented German-born, L.A.-based helmer Roth from completing it as desired.

Be that as it may, "The Killers," as the title indicates, is the murky tale of a senseless killing in a Beverly Hills mansion. Harry, an ex-insurance man and social dropout, meets Bill in an all-night cafe. Both are down on their luck, but Bill knows of a place in Beverly Hills that's a snap to burglarize. They agree to do the job together on a handshake, even though all of this is new to Harry. It's when they arrive on the scene that Harry begins to get cold feet, particularly when it becomes gradually clear that Bill is a maniacal killer.

During the robbery, the young couple in the villa wake up at the noise being made in the kitchen as silverware is being stashed away. Bill then takes charge completely, overpowers the husband and later kills him after playing with the man's destiny like a cat with a mouse. Meanwhile, Harry is spellbound by the figure of the lovely wife in bed, and gives way to his lower instincts to rape her. It's after this that Bill decides an extra witness need not be, so he kills the wife too as cold-bloodedly as he did before by simply cutting a throat.

At the finale, the two have walked away from the scene of their crime without even bothering to collect the valuables they originally came for. Harry wonders, however, why he's not feeling different as a human being now that he's become a clear accomplice to a brutal murder.

Pic comes across pretty much as an experimental theatrical piece set before a camera, and this also scores as the overall weakness. On the plus side are the performances and the slow, rather meditative pace in telling a low-key story without embellishment. The appearance of Bukowski at the outset as a kind of author's prolog is an extra treat. In fact, his laconic manner in commenting on the underbelly of social existence practically steals the show.
— *Holl.*

A Tu Per Tu
(On A First-Name Basis)
(ITALIAN-COLOR)

Rome, Dec. 11.

A D.A.C. release, produced by Carlo Valeri and Luciano De Feo for Adige Film 76. Directed by Sergio Corbucci. Stars Johnny Dorelli, Paolo Villaggio. Screenplay, Luciano Vincenzoni, Sergio Donati; camera (color), Danilo Desideri; editor, Ruggero Mastroianni; music, The La Bionda Brothers. Reviewed at Brancaccio Cinema, Rome, Dec. 10, 1984. Running time: **108 MINS.**

Emanuele Sansoni . . . . Johnny Dorelli
Gino Soisccaluga . . . . Paolo Villaggio

It's no secret that the golden age of Italian social comedy is long past. Films like "On A First-Name Basis" illustrate the way ripe ideas taken from newspaper headlines, which once might have been spun into a "Divorce Italian Style," are now run through the sanitizing mill, puffed up with a few standard gags and come out as empty entertainment. Aimed at the adult comedy market, pic has done fair business locally.

The pivotal character in "First-Name" is a high-powered financier whose wheeling and dealing has at last run him afoul of the law. In his flight from justice and search for hard cash, Emanuele Sansoni (Johnny Dorelli) barely has time to pack a suitcase full of incriminating documents on political figures and flee to Switzerland. A doltish taxi driver from the lower depths of Genoa, Gino Soiaccaluga (Paolo Villaggio), obediently chauffeurs him from country to country and gets entangled in his schemes. "Surprise" ending, foreseeable a long way off, reverses their rich man-poor man roles.

Veteran helmer Sergio Corbucci, an old hand at routine comedy, pads the story with a spurious love affair between the dumb cabbie and Sansoni, who dons feminine attire and a wig to disguise himself. At every gas station and hotel, dapper little Emanuele disappears and his bloated "sister" turns up, or vice versa. How Gino, who fails to notice the connection, could outsmart Sansoni and take his fortune away on a legal technicality, truly boggles the imagination.

Good pacing keeps the pic flowing smoothly. A gang of Mafia hitmen hot on Sansoni's trail are thrown in for action sequences here and there. The requisite touch of vulgarity is added with Gino's sluttish wife, who keeps answering the telephone while entertaining a muscular carabiniere. The considerable thesping talents of Dorelli and, especially, Villaggio (famous for his creation of pathetic losers) are largely wasted on pic's broad, conventional humor. Ditto a top-notch crew.

Naturally, the crooked politicians wriggle off the hook before Sansoni's documents can expose them about the only salient point pic makes. —*Yung.*

Mohan Joshi Haazir Ho
(Summons For Mohan Joshi)
(INDIAN-COLOR)

Rio de Janeiro, Nov. 28.

Produced by Saeed Akhtar Mirza Prods. Directed by Saeed Akhtar Mirza. Screenplay, Yusuf Mehta, Mirza; music, Vanraj Bhatia; camera (color), Virendra Saini; editor, Renu Saluja. Reviewed at Rio de Janeiro Film Festival, Nov. 26, 1984. Running time: **123 MINS.**

With: Bhisham Sahni, Dina Pathak, Naseeruddin Shah, Deepti Naval, Rohini Hattangady, Mohan Gokhale, Satish Shah, Amjad Khan.

The film opens with a ballad to Bombay, warts and all, full of love for the city, but at the same time with strong ironical undertones. The images on the screen complement the song, showing a city that is both lovely and full of squalor, but always teeming with life. The almost Brechtian distancing suggested by this introduction is sustained throughout the film.

Mohan Joshi is a dignified old gent who lives in a tenement building that is almost falling to pieces. He tries to persuade the landlord to make essential repairs but fails, for all the latter wants is that the people get fed up and leave, so that he can put this choice piece of real estate to more lucrative use.

Standing up for his rights, Joshi takes a lawyer (Naseeruddin Shah, winner of this year's best actor award at Venice), but finds that the endless lawsuit drains all his meager resources. At the beginning of the proceedings the rest of the slum dwellers are afraid to join Moshi but when, ages later, the trial comes to a climax and the judge decides to make a personal inspection of the tenement, they at last identify with his cause.

However, the judge's inconclusiveness puts an end to Joshi's hopes. This, plus the clubby atmosphere between his and the landlord's lawyers and the exhausting slowness of court proceedings, are part of a strong indictment of India's legal system which is depicted as something which, by its very nature, favors the rich and is of little use or comfort to the poor.

This theme is not developed in a preachy manner but through humor and satire and it is Joshi's steadfast, almost childlike, faith in law and lawyers which makes the outcome of his quest so poignant.

Made for $180,000, the film was shot in 16m. The blowup to 35m has its imperfections, but technical credits are otherwise satisfactory. The actual tenement building used as a location is very impressive and, although the leading roles are played by professionals, the rest of the cast is made up of actual slum dwellers and non-actors. —*Amig.*

Joe Louis — For All Time
(U.S.-DOCU-B&W/COLOR)

London, Dec. 3.

A Big Fights Inc. production, in association with ABC Enterprises. Produced by Jack Healy, Jim Jacobs, Bill Cayton, Peter Tatum. Budd Schulberg. Directed by Tatum. Written by Schulberg; camera (color/b&w), Isidore Manikofsky; editor, Anthony Zaccaro; music, Bill Zampino; narrator, Brock Peters. Reviewed at London Film Festival, Nov. 29, 1984. Running time: **87 MINS.**

A tribute to Joe Louis (1914-1981), the great heavyweight boxer and "Brown Bomber," this well-composed compilation docu not only celebrates a great boxing career but also pointedly attacks the Internal Revenue Service whose hounding of Louis, Budd Schulberg's script suggests, affected his career.

Through photographs and newsreel film, director Peter Tatum covers Louis' early career, including the famous Max Schmelling fights (Schmelling, at the time repping Nazi Germany, beat Louis the first time, was beaten the second). Other famous fighters seen in the footage here include the Baer brothers, Max and Buddy, Primo Carnera and Rocky Marciano.

Schulberg, whose feature screenplays often have involved boxing subjects, points out that, at the beginning of World War II, the patriotic Louis donated his entire fees from two championship fights to Navy and Army relief funds; despite this, he was taxed on the money he'd supposedly earned, and after his stint as a morale-booster in the Army, he found himself in the post-war period with accelerating debts, eventually owing the IRS a staggering $1,000,000. His debts forced him to take fights he would not otherwise have considered, and, after his final defeat, reduced him to swallow his pride and become, briefly, a wrestler.

For a while he was hooked on cocaine, and finally wound up as a host at Caesars Palace in Las Vegas, where this film ends with Frank Sinatra and others paying tribute to him shortly before his death.

Pic reveals that one of America's greatest heroes and role models was shabbily treated by the U.S. government. At the same time, everyone who knew Louis speaks of the man's decency and humanity. "Joe Louis — For All Time" is a very well made film of its type, and should succeed in informing new generations about one of the greatest boxers who ever lived.

"Joe Louis" opens with a few sequences on the career of the first black heavyweight champ, Jack Johnson, footage culled from the excellent 1970 docu named after the fighter. The earlier film was also produced by Big Fights Inc., though for the record it was directed by Jim Jacobs, not William Cayton (the producer) as listed by *Variety* in its original review. — *Strat.*

Isaac Littlefeathers
(CANADIAN-COLOR)

Edmonton, Dec. 7.

A Lauron Intl. release, in association with King Motion Picture Corp., Alberta Motion Picture Development Corp., Allarcom Ltd., Telefilm Canada, Canadian Broadcasting Corp. and Cinema Concepts. Produced by Barry Pearson and Bill Johnston; executive producers, Ron Lillie and Gerald Solway. Directed by Les Rose; screenplay, Rose and Pearson; camera (color), Ed Higginson; costumes, Mairin Wilkinson; music, Paul Zaza; production manager, Arvi Liimatainen; art direction, Richard Hudolin. Reviewed at Odeon 1, Edmonton, Alberta, Dec. 6, 1984. Running time: **94 MINS.**

Abe Kapp . . . . Lou Jacobi
Isaac Littlefeathers . . . . William Korbut
Jesse Armstrong . . . . Scott Hylands
Golda Hersh . . . . Lorraine Behnan
Moses Ankewat . . . . George Clutesi
Mike Varco . . . . Thomas Heaton

Shot in Edmonton, Alberta, "Isaac Littlefeathers" is a well-meaning, well-photographed tale of racial and religious prejudice that simultaneously tries to do too much and too little.

Pic revolves around teenaged Isaac Littlefeathers, illegitimate Metis ("half-breed") son of a shiftless hockey player and a young Indian woman. Littlefeathers has been adopted by Abe, a good-natured Jewish storekeeper who wishes to have him barmitzvahed.

Caught among Indian, Jewish and non-Jewish cultures, torn by feelings of hate, fear and love, Littlefeathers develops a reputation as a rebel and troublemaker. Some of his main adversaries are members of the fighting Varco family.

Eventually, a boxing match is arranged between Isaac and a member of the Varco clan, a bout which Littlefeathers wins. However, the Varcos retaliate by torching Abe's general store. Littlefeathers, in turn, gets a rifle and holds Mike Varco hostage. This serves as a pretext for a reunion between the youth and his real father.

While professionally shot and edited, pic never gets beyond its interesting premise. With the exception of Clutesi, who plays a Chief Dan George-style native, all characters are basically predictable types with predictable dialog. Movie is infected by both a blandness and a cuteness that prevents the viewer from feeling much of anything. "Isaac Littlefeathers" is also hobbled by poor continuity as elements from the 1940s, '50s and '60s are scrambled together. — *Mojo.*

Historias Violentas
(Violent Stories)
(MEXICAN-COLOR)

Mexico City, Nov. 24.
A Películas Nacionales-Películas Mexicanas release of a Conacite Dos, S.A. de C.V. production. Five separate episodes directed by Víctor Saca, Carlos García Agraz, Daniel González Dueños, Diego López and Gerardo Pardo. Screenplay, Pedro F. Miret; camera (color), Miguel Garzón; editors, Angel Camacho and Rodolfo Montenegro; music, Joaquín Gutiérrez Heras. Reviewed at screening room four of Cineteca Nacional, Mexico City, Nov. 22, 1984. Running time: **100 MINS.**
Alejandro . . . . Pedro Armendáriz
Girl. . . . . Alma Muriel
Also with: Enrique Rocha, Ernesto Gómez Cruz, Claudio Obregón, Alejandro Parodi, Diana Bracho and Rafael Villaseñor Kuri.

"Historias Violentas" (Violent Stories) is a collection of five tales by young Mexican filmmakers, recent graduates of either the CUEC (Centro Universitario de Estudios Cinematográficos) or the CCC (Centro de Capacitación Cinematográfica). All were written by Pedro F. Miret, based on his short stories.

The first and longest episode "Service â la Carte" (Servicio a la Carta), was directed by Víctor Saca. It involves a meek, mild-mannered character who is attacked in the hallway every morning by his neighbor.

The man's revenge is amusing and deserved, but strictly non-violent. Saca narrates the story well, and uses his cinematographic eye to relate the story both visually and with humor. The surprise ending draws all the more impact from this balance.

"New Fire" (Fuego Nuevo), directed by Carlos García Agraz, is perhaps the strongest of the stories and its humor and surrealist sense draws from a vision that links modern Mexico with its indigenous past.

A man arrives at what he believes will be a costume party. Instead, there is an elegant dinner party with everyone clad in tux and formal dress. The theme of the party had been changed at the last minute and our hero didn't receive the message. Thus, he comes dressed as an Aztec warrior, complete with club and shield. We see the reaction of the others to his bizarre dress before we are allowed to see for ourselves.

This savage nature of modern man is also the theme of the last episode, "Silent Night" (Noche de Paz), directed by Gerardo Pardo, which is also the weakest.

While the neighborhood sleeps, a car's horn suddenly blurts out an annoying blast which continues unabated. The neighbors gather round and try to find a manner to silence the car. As their frustrations build, they begin smashing it. When the car's owner emerges to protest, they turn on him and kill him.

They place the body inside the car and push it, with the horn still blaring, into a ravine. It's as simple as that. The sophisticated group of neighbors can now return to their bourgeois homes and get some shut-eye.

The seg's failure stems from misdirection, of leading the viewer to expect something more than will be given.

Sandwiched in between are two rather mediocre stories: "Reflections" (Reflejos), directed by Daniel González; and the "Last Showing" (Ultima Función), Diego López.

"Reflections" tells of a man (Pedro Armendáriz), whose plan to seduce his new date is thwarted by the appearance of a flying saucer and visiting Martians.

"Last Showing," which has more interesting possibilities, relates how a group of late-night filmgoers are trapped within a deadly practical joke. —*Lent.*

Un Eté d'Enfer
(A Summer In Hell)
(FRENCH-SPANISH-COLOR)

Paris, Dec. 19.
A CCFC release of an ATC 3000/TF 1 Films/Lotus Films coproduction. Produced by Benjamin Simon. Directed by Mickael Schock. Screenplay, Schock, Claude de Givray, based on a story by Jean-Pierre Tomasini; camera (Eastmancolor), Teo Escamilla; art director, Olivier Paultre; editor, Joëlle Van Effenterre; sound, Henri Roux; music, François Valéry. Reviewed at the Marignan-Concorde theater, Paris, Dec. 19, 1984. Running time: **105 MINS.**
With: Thierry Lhermitte, Véronique Jannot, Daniel Duval, Michel Devilliers.

The wave of anonymous domestic thrillers flows on with this commonplace actioner topbilling Thierry Lhermitte and tv actress Véronique Jannot. Set on the Riviera, but partially shot in Spain for coproduction purposes, tale has Lhermitte as a washed-up motorcycle champ who turns amateur detective and takes on a missing persons case.

Jannot, proprietress of a temporarily closed hotel, is the client, looking for her kid sister, whom Lhermitte discovers has been forced into a dope and prostitution ring, covered by a corrupt cop (Daniel Duval).

Everything one expects to happen happens. Lhermitte and Jannot become lovers after he is messed up by some junk dealers. Spurred on by this new commitment, Lhermitte, armed with a pistol, electronic equipment and some unexpected allies, goes after the villains, retrieves the sister, and has a final showdown with Duval, who is killed by a booby-trapped pinball machine rigged by the hero.

Newcomer Mickael Schock cowrote the not very credible script and directs without distinction. Lhermitte struggles in vain to give his stock characterization some texture, and Jannot looks at a loss for what to do with vacuous role.

Tech credits are adequate.
— *Len.*

Como Aman los Chilenos
(How Chileans Love)
(CHILEAN-COLOR)

Santiago, Nov. 16.
A CCN release of an Ansa Films production. Produced by Sandro Angelini and Alejo Alvarez. Executive producer, Jorge Sasia; camera (color), Ramón Orellana; music, José Luis Correa; editor, Alfredo Lewinsky. Reviewed at Cine Central, Santiago, Chile, Nov. 12, 1984. Running time: **95 MINS.**
With: Sandra Solimano, Exequiel Lavandero, Soledad Pérez, Violeta Vidaurre, Silvia Ebner, Rodolfo Torrealba, Patricio Torres, Tennyson Ferrada, Andrés Rojas Murphy, Yoya Martinez, Armando Fenoglio, Pina Brandt, Rubén Dario Guevera, Maggie Lay, Pedro Linares, Alfredo Herrera, Carlos Valenzuela, Sergio Silva, Patricia Larraguibel, Emilio Garcia, Clara Brevis, Yolanda Campos.

An American journalist arrives in Chile to study the love life of the locals and this serves as a pretext for a series of brief episodes which purport to illustrate same. The obvious intent is to provide picaresque entertainment, but the film lacks three ingredients that might have helped accomplish its objective: humor, wit and adequate craftsmanship.

Alejo Alvarez made his last film in 1967 and "How Chileans Love" is reminiscent of the pictures shot in this country during the 1950s and early 1960s. Acting is poor and technical credits are, at best, unimpressive. The gross manner in which a series of products are plugged in the film is another minus.

Made at a cost of approximately $100,000 the pic was launched with a strong publicity campaign on tv which should help initial boxoffice, but it lacks staying power. —*Amig.*

INDEX

A

A Contratiempo 4-28-82
A Mort l'Arbitre 3-21-84
A Nos Amours 12-7-83
A Rutana Pera 1-27-82
A Toute Allure 9-1-82
A Tu Per Tu 12-26-84
A Veces Miro Mi Vida 4-7-82
Aadharshila 2-10-82
Aaj-Kal-Parshur Galpa 2-24-82
Aakaler Sandhane 2-4-81
Aakrosh 2-4-81
Aar, El- 2-9-83
Abel Gance and His Napoleon (See: Abel Gance et Son Napoleon)
Abel Gance et Son Napoleon 5-9-84
Abenteuer Meiner Seele 10-17-84
Abierto Dia y Noche 12-15-82
About Judges and Other Sympathisers (See: Von Richtern und Anderen Sympathisanten)
About "The Wall" (See: Autour du Mur)
Absence of Malice 11-18-81
Absolution 12-2-81
Abuse 3-23-82
Abwarts 5-23-84
Acceptable Levels 12-14-83
Ace (See: Asso)
Ace of Aces (See: As des As, L')
Aces Go Places 2-17-82
Aces Go Places II 2-23-83
Aces Go Places III 2-1-84
Acqua e Sapone 11-9-83
Act, The 8-22-84
Acting: Lee Strasberg and the Actors Studio 10-7-81
Addition, L' 5-30-84
Addressee Unknown (See: Empfaenger Unbekannt)
Ademloos 11-24-82
Aderyn Papur 11-28-84
Adios Miami 1-4-84
Adj Kiraly Katonat! 3-2-83
Adon Leon 8-11-82
Adventures of Buckaroo Banzai: Across the 8th Dimension, The 8-8-84
Adventures of Enrique and Ana, The (See: Aventuras de Enrique y Ana, Las)
Adventures of Monica's Friends, The (See: Aventuras da Turma de Monica, As)
Aerodrome, The 11-30-83
Affaire d'Hommes, Une 12-9-81
Africain, L' 3-23-83
African, The (See: Africain, L')
After Love (See: Na De Liefde)
After Midnight (See: Nach Mitternacht)
Afternoon Affair, An (See: Szeretok)
Afurika Monogatari 6-10-81
Against All Odds 2-15-84
Agency 1-21-81
Agit 2-25-81
Agitated Winds (See: Nekatomeni Aeries)
Agonia 8-5-81
Agony (See: Agonia)
Agujero en la Pared, El 7-21-82
Ah Q Zhen Zhuan 5-26-82
Ah Ying 7-27-83
Ahava Ilemeth 10-27-82
Ahava Rishona 10-27-82
Ahlam el Madina 5-16-84
Aijo Monogatari 10-3-84
Ailes de la Colombe, Les 6-17-81
Air du Crime, L' 8-29-84
Airplane II: The Sequel 12-8-82
Airship, The (See: Luftschiff, Das)
Aiutami a Sognare 4-1-81
Ake and His World (See: Ake og Hans Varld)
Ake og Hans Varld 11-14-84
Akelarre 3-7-84
Akmar, Al 11-4-81
Akriet 12-30-81
Albert Pinto Ko Gussa Kyon Asta Hai 2-18-81
Album de Familia 11-4-81
Alcoholig Lion, Yr 11-28-84
Aldo and Junior (See: Aldo et Junior)
Aldo et Junior 4-11-84
Alexander der Kleine 1-19-83

Alexander the Little (See: Alexander der Kleine)
Alexandre 8-24-83
Alexyz 4-18-84
Ali au Pays des Mirages 7-29-81
Ali in Wonderland (See: Ali au Pays des Mirages)
Alien Contamination 9-14-83
Alien Factor, The 7-4-84
All by Myself 3-24-82
All Fired Up (See: Tout Feu, Tout Flamme)
All My Friends 2 (See: Amici, Miei, Atto 2)
All Night Long 3-11-81
All of Me 7-11-84
All Right, My Friend (See: Daijoobu, Mai Furendo)
All That Rhythm (See: In Punta di Piedi)
"...All the Marbles" 10-7-81
All the Right Moves 10-5-83
All the Wrong Clues (For the Right Solution) 8-12-81
All the Wrong Spies 4-27-83
Allegement, L' 8-24-83
Aller Simple, Un 8-26-81
Alles im Elmer 9-16-81
Alley Cat 3-28-84
Allies 11-16-83
Alligator Shoes 6-3-81
Allons Z'Enfants 4-22-81
Almeria Case, The (See: Caso Almeria, El)
Almonds and Raisins 3-28-84
Almost You 10-3-84
Alone in the Dark 7-28-82
Along the Silk Road (See: Silu Huayu)
Alphabet City 5-9-84
Alptraumfrau, Die 1-21-81
Als Diesel Geboren (See: Born for Diesel)
Als Je Begrijpt Wat Ik Bedol 3-16-83
Alsino and the Condor (See: Alsino y el Condor)
Alsino y el Condor 2-9-83
Altra Donna, L' 10-7-81
Amada 1-4-84
Amadeus 9-5-84
Amagi Goe 9-14-83
Amagi Pass (See: Amagi Goe)
Amantes del Senor de la Noche, Las 4-11-84
Amateur, The 2-17-82
Ambassador 8-29-84
Ambassador, The 5-23-84
America and Lewis Hine 8-29-84
America: From Hitler to M-X 1-5-83
American Dreamer 10-10-84
American Nightmare 6-13-84
American Pictures (See: Amerikanske Billeder)
American Pop 2-11-81
American Taboo 2-29-84
American Werewolf in London, An 8-19-81
Americana 5-27-81
Amerikanske Billeder 6-3-81
Ami de Vincent, L' 9-28-83
Amici, Miei, Atto 2 1-26-83
Amityville 3-D 11-23-83
Amityville II: The Possession 9-29-82
Amok 7-27-83
Among the Cinders 3-28-84
Amore Tossico 9-28-83
Amorous Woman of the Tang Dynasty, An 9-5-84
Amour a Mort, L' 9-12-84
Amour de Swann, Un 3-21-84
Amour des Femmes, L' 12-30-81
Amour Fugitif, L' 6-29-83
Amour Nu, L' 10-7-81
Amour par Terre, L' 10-10-84
Amy 3-25-81
An Bloem 9-21-83
Ana 3-23-83
Anametrissi 11-17-82
...And If We Don't Want To (See: Und Wenn Wir Nicht Wollen)
And Next Year at Balaton (See: Und Naechstes Jahr am Balaton)
And Nothing but the Truth (See: Giro City)
And Now, What's Your Name? 9-12-84
...And Pigs Might Fly (See: Aderyn Papur)
And the Ship Sails On (See: E la Nave Va)
And You'll Live in Terror! The Beyond (See: E Tu Vivrai nel Terrore! L'Aldila')
Andere Seite der Welt, Die 4-25-84
Andra Dansen 9-21-83
Andrei Tarkovsky 7-25-84
Android 10-13-82
Ange, L' 5-26-82
Angel 5-26-82
Angel 1-18-84
Angel (See: Anguelos)

B

C

D

E

Endangered Species 9-8-82
Endeavor (See: Nastojanje)
Endless Love 7-22-81
Endstation Freiheit 3-11-81
Enemies, The (See: Emenigos, Los)
Enemigos, Los 10-12-83 and 9-14-83
Energetic 21 11-3-82
Enfant Secret, L' 3-23-83
Engaldige Mordaren, Den 2-24-82
Engel aus Eisen 5-20-81
Englishman Abroad, An 11-30-83
Enigma 1-5-83
Enormous Changes at the Last Minute 9-21-83
Enrai 12-30-81
Enrico IV 5-23-84
Ente oder Trente 2-9-83
Enter the Ninja 4-7-82
Entity, The 11-3-82
Entre Tinieblas 5-23-84
Epilog (See: Epilogo)
Epilogo 3-7-84
Epitaph for Barbara Radziwill, An 9-21-83
Equateur 5-18-83
Equator (See: Equateur)
Erben, Die 11-17-82
Erendira 5-25-83
Ergostasio, To 8-25-82
Eric Clapton and His Rolling Hotel 4-22-81
Erinnerung an Eine Landschaft 12-14-83
Erlost oder Betrogen? 5-23-84
Erogena Zona 8-12-81
Erogenous Zone (See: Erogena Zona)
Erotas tou Odyssea, O 12-5-84
Erotica 9-9-81
Errand-Girl, The (See: Loeperjenten)
Errant Lives (See: Vidas Errantes)
Es Ist Kalt in Brandenburg – Hitler Toeten 5-27-81
Escape Artist, The 5-12-82
Escape from Grumble Gulch (See: Dalton en Cavale, Les)
Escape from New York 6-17-81
Escape from Womens Prison 6-27-84
Escape Route (See: Nogare No Machi)
Escape 2000 (See: Turkey Shoot)
Escapes Home (See: Uteky Domu)
Escarabajo, El 8-10-83
Eskimo Woman Feels Cold (See: Eszkimo Asszony Fazik)
Esperame Mucho 9-14-83
Espion Leve-Toi 2-24-82
Esprit d'Amour 2-8-84
Est-Ce Bien Raisonnable? 6-3-81
Estoy en Crisis! 9-15-82
Eszkimo Asszony Fazik 2-29-84
Etat de Crise, L' 8-29-84
Ete d'Enfer, Un 12-26-84
Ete Muertrier, L' 5-18-83
Etincelle, L' 2-29-84
Etoile du Nord, L' 4-14-82
Etrange Affaire, Une 3-24-82
Etrange Voyage, Un 5-20-81
Etwas Wird Sichtbar 3-10-82
Eu Te Amo 4-1-81
Eureka 6-8-83
Eva 8-17-83
Eva Against Ordinary Landscape (See: Eva sur Paysage Ordinaire)
Eva sur Paysage Ordinaire 5-23-84
Eva's Dreams 9-22-82
Evening Performance (See: Funcion de Noche)
Everlasting Love 4-4-84
Every Picture Tells a Story 12-19-84
Everybody Is Good (See: Todo er Mundo E Gueno)
Evil Dead, The 2-9-83
Evil Eye (See: Occhio Malocchio Prezzemolo E Finocchio)
Evil That Men Do, The 6-13-84
Evil Times (See: Zeit Is Bose, Die)
Evil Under the Sun 1-27-82
Evilspeak 1-27-82
Evita (Quien Quiera Oir Que Oiga) 6-6-84
Evita – Who Wants to Hear May Hear (See: Evita (Qien Quiera Oir Que Oiga))
Excalibur 4-8-81
Executioner Part II, The 6-6-84
Expensive Tastes 10-27-82
Experience Preferred but Not Essential 11-24-82
Explosion (See: Infigar, Al-)
Exposed 3-16-83
Exterminator 2 9-19-84
Eye for an Eye, An 8-19-81
Eye of the Needle 7-22-81
Eyes of a Stranger 4-1-81

Eyes of Fire 7-25-84
Eyes of the Birds (See: Yeux des Oiseaux, Les)
Eyes, The Mouth, The (See: Occhi, La Bocca, Gli)
Eyewitness 2-18-81
Ezhavathu Manithan 8-3-83

F

F.F.S.S. (See: F.F.S.S. Cioe: "Che mi Hai Portato a Fare Sopra a Posillipo se Non Mi Vuoi Piu' Bene?")
F.F.S.S. Cioe: "Che mi Hai Portato a Fare Sopra a Posillipo se Non Mi Vuoi Piu' Bene?" 1-4-84
Factory, The (See: Ergostasio, To)
Facts (See: Faktas)
Facture d'Orgue, La 9-16-81
Faelschung, Die 11-11-81
Fair Game (See: Freiwild)
Fairy Tale of Honzik and Marenka, The (See: Prohadka O Honzikovi A Marence)
Fairy Tale of Wanderings, A (See: Skazka Stranstvil)
Faits Divers 5-25-83
Fake-Out 5-26-82
Faktas 5-27-81
Falansterul 4-1-81
Falasha: Exile of the Black Jews 9-28-83
Falcon, The (See: Banovic Strahinja)
Falcon, The (See: Faucon, Le)
Faleze De Nisip 2-9-83
Fall Bachmeier, Der 1-25-84
Fall of Italy (See: Pad Italije)
Fall of the Rebellious Angels, The (See: Caduta degli Angeli Ribelli, La)
Falling in Love 11-21-84
Falling Stars (See: Zvezdopad)
False Eyelashes (See: Pestanas Postizas)
Familia Orozco, La 10-6-82
Family Affair, A 9-12-84
Family Album (See: Album de Familia)
Family Game, The (See: Kazoku Geemu)
Family Light Affair 3-7-84
Family Relations (See: Rodnia)
Family Rock 7-21-82
Famine, The (See: Bara)
Fan, The 5-20-81
Fanny and Alexander (See: Fanny och Alexander)
Fanny Hill 5-11-83
Fanny och Alexander 12-22-82
Fanny Pelopaja 5-23-84
Fanny Strawhair (See: Fanny Pelopaja)
Fantasies 11-11-81
Fantasma d'Amore 5-13-81
Fantasy Man 10-10-84
Fantomes du Chapelier, Les 5-19-82
Fantozzi Subisce Ancora 1-25-84
Fantozzi Takes It on the Chin Again (See: Fantozzi Subisce Ancora)
Far East 8-11-81
Far from Poland 10-3-84
Far from Where (See: Lontano da Dove)
Farewell (See: Proshchanie)
Farewell to My Native (or Beloved) Land (See: Saraba Itoshiki Daiachi (or Daichi))
Fariaho 4-11-84
Farmers Arms 12-14-83
Fast Talking 5-2-84
Fast Times at Ridgemont High 8-11-82
Fast-Walking 5-5-82
Fat Tilla (See: Dicke Tilla, Die)
Fatal Games 9-5-84
Fatally Wounded for Love of Life (See: Sa mori ranit din dragoste de viata)
Father and Child (See: Chichi To Ko)
Father and Son 5-6-81
Father and Son (See: Vater und Sohn)
Father by Accident (See: Padre por Accidente)
Father Will Beat Me Anyway (See: Otec Ma Zderie Tak Ci Tak)
Faucon, Le 9-28-83
Faunovo Velmi Pozdni Odpoledne 8-8-84
Fauvres, Les 8-1-84
Favoris de la Lune, Les 9-5-84
Favorite (Rock and Torah), The (See: Prefere (Rock and Torah), Le)
Favorites and Winners (See: Favoriti e Vincenti)
Favoriti e Vincenti 9-28-83
Fear (See: Angst)

Four Seasons of Natsuko, The (See: Shiki-Natsuko)
Fourberies de Scapin, Les 3-4-81
Four-Legged Man, The (See: Covek Sa Cetiri Noge)
Fourth Man, The (See: Vierde Man, De)
Fox and the Hound, The 7-1-81
Fox-Hunting (See: Vinatoarea de Vulpi)
Fracchia, La Belva Umana 1-27-82
Fracchia, The Human Beast (See: Fracchia, La Belva Umana)
Frances 12-1-82
Francisca 5-27-81
Francois Reichenbach's Japan (See: Japon de Francois Reichenbach, Le)
'Frank' and I 7-18-84
Frankenstein 90 9-12-84
Frau ohne Korper und Der Projektionist, Die 3-7-84
Fraulein Berlin 10-19-83
Freak Orlando 12-23-81
Freedom 3-31-81
Freiwild 3-28-84
Fremtidens Boern 4-4-84
French Lieutenant's Woman, The 9-9-81
Frevel 4-4-84
Friday (See: Vrijdag)
Friday Is Not the Weekend (See: Patek Neni Svatek)
Friday the 13th Part 2 5-6-81
Friday the 13th - Part 3 8-11-82
Friday the 13th - The Final Chapter 4-18-84
Fridays of Eternity, The (See: Viernes de la Eternidad, Los)
Friedliche Tage 2-8-84
Friend of Vincent, A (See: Ami de Vincent, L')
Friend or Foe 3-10-82
Friends, The (See: Yahalu Yeheli)
Frightmare 9-14-83
From a Far Country - Pope John Paul II 9-16-81
From Mao to Mozart: Isaac Stern in China 3-4-81
From Mysterious Buenos Aires (See: De la Misteriosa Buenos Aires)
From Somalia with Love 4-25-84
Front Line 3-18-81
Front Romance, A (See: Woenno-Polewoj Roman)
Frontier (See: Grens, De)
Fruehlingssinfonie 5-11-83
Fruits de la Passion, Les 5-27-81
Fruits of Passion, The (See: Fruits de la Passion, Les)
Fuenf Flaschen fuer Angelika 1-21-81
Fuerchete Dich Nicht, Jacob! 1-21-81
Fuga de Segovia, La 10-14-81
Full Moon in Paris (See: Nuit de la Pleine Lune, Les)
Fun (See: Hapnimia)
Funcion de Noche 10-14-81
Funeral Racket, The (See: Tomuraishitachi)
Funhouse, The 3-18-81
Funny Farm, The 3-16-83
Funny Money 6-29-83
Fuori dal Giorno 6-8-83
Furusato 8-10-83
Futur Interieur, Le 10-3-84
Future Interior, The (See: Futur Interieur, Le)
Future Is Woman, The (See: Futuro E' Donna, Il)
Future of Emily, The (See: Flugel und Fesseln/L'Avenir d'Emilie)
Future Schlock 5-23-84
Futuro E' Donna, Il 9-5-84

G

G 12-21-83
Gabriela 5-11-83
Gaki Teikoku 11-11-81
Gala 7-28-82
Galaxy Express 999 8-18-82
Galaxy of Terror 10-14-81
Gallipoli 8-5-81
Games of the Countess Dolingen of Gratz (Styrie), The (See: Jeux de la Comtesse Dolingen de Gratz (Styrie), Les)
Gandhi 11-24-82
Ganga Maya 5-23-84
Ganito Kami Noon, Paano Rayo Ngayon 12-23-81
Ganze Leben, Das 2-23-83
Gap in the Border (See: Gat In De Grens)
Gapi 9-1-82
Garbo Talks 10-10-84
Garcon! 11-30-83
Garde a Vue 10-7-81
Garde du Corps, Le 2-29-84

Gardener, The (See: Jardinier, Le)
Garota Dourada 1-4-84
Gary Cooper, Que Estas en los Cielos 2-4-81
Gary Cooper, Who Art in Heaven (See: Gary Cooper, Que Estas en los Cielos)
Gas 7-29-81
Gasping (See: Atemnot)
Gat in de Grens 10-31-84
Gates of Hell, The 5-25-83
'Gator Bait 9-14-83
Gazija 8-12-81
Gebroken Spiegels 10-10-84
Gedaechtnis 1-5-83
Geek Maggot Bingo 5-25-83
Geheimnis Meines Vaters, Das 1-6-82
Gehversuche 11-17-82
Gemeindeprasident, Der 4-11-84
Gemini Affair - A Diary 11-14-84
General de l'Armee Morte, Le 11-9-83
General of the Dead Army, The (See: General de l'Armee Morte, Le)
Generalprobe, Die 10-14-81
Generation Apart, A 4-4-84
Genocide 2-24-82
George Kuchar: The Comedy of the Underground 9-21-83
George Stevens: A Filmmaker's Journey 9-19-84
German Lawyer, A (See: Morgen in Alabama)
German Revolution, A (See: Deutsche Revolution, Eine)
German Sisters, The (See: Bleierne Zeit, Die)
Germany: Private (See: Deutschland: Privat)
Gespenst, Das 6-13-82
Get Crazy 8-10-83
Getting Even 4-22-81
Getting It On 8-31-83
Getting Over 5-20-81
Ghare Baire 5-23-84
Ghost Dance 11-30-83
Ghost from Bahia, The (See: Baiano Fantasma, O)
Ghost in the Noonday Sun 6-27-84
Ghost of Love (See: Fantasma d'Amore)
Ghost Story 12-16-81
Ghostbusters 6-6-84
Ghosts Galore 3-2-83
Ghosts of Cape Horn 1-7-81
Ghost, The (See: Gespenst, Das)
Giarres 2-8-84
Gib Gas - Ich Will Spass 5-18-83
Gift, The (See: Cadeau, Le)
Gimme an "F" 12-5-84
Ginga Tetsudo 999 (See: Galaxy Express 999)
Ginger Meggs 12-29-82
Giovanni 10-19-83
Girl from India 1-27-82
Girl from Thousand Lire Street, The (See: Ragazza di Via Millelire, La)
Girl with a Sea Shell (See: Divka s Musli)
Girl with the Horse, The (See: Pferdemadchen, Das)
Girl with the Red Hair, The (See: Meisje met het Rode Haar, Het)
Girls' Dormitory (See: Nu-Daxne Sheng Su-She)
Girls Nite Out 6-20-84
Girl's Tear, A (See: Lacrima de Fata, O)
Giro 2-16-83
Giro City 10-27-82
Giselle 10-6-82
Gita Scolastica, Una 9-14-83
Giuseppe Fava: Sicilian Like Me (See: Giuseppe Fava: Siciliano Come Me)
Giuseppe Fava: Siciliano Come Me 8-15-84
Give My Regrets to Broad Street 10-31-84
Glassful of Snow, A (See: Neve nel Bicchiere, La)
Glen or Glenda (1953) 5-27-81
Glosy 4-22-81
Glove, The 1-21-81
Glowing Autumn (See: Moeru Aki)
Glueck beim Haendewaschen, Das 2-2-83
Glut 9-21-83
Glutmensch 4-21-82
Glykia Symmoria 11-9-83
Go Tell It on the Mountain 8-1-84
Go West, Young Man 9-16-81
Goat, The (See: Chevre, La)
God's Gift (See: Wend Kuuni)
Gods Must Be Crazy, The 7-4-84
Goeta Kanal 6-2-82
Goin' All the Way 5-19-82
Going Ape! 4-15-81
Going Berserk 11-2-83
Going Down 10-13-82
Gold Diggers, The 11-30-83
Gold Er Liebe, Das 6-1-83

H

Heartbeeps 12-23-81
Heartbreakers, The 2-2-83
Heartbreaker 5-11-83
Heartbreakers 9-26-84
Heart-Pounding Beat (See: Coracoes a Mil)
Hearts in Armor (See: Paladini - Storia d'Armi e d'Armi, I)
Heartworn Highways 5-6-81
Heat and Dust 1-19-83
Heatwave 1-6-82
Heaven and Earth (See: Himmel und Erde)
Heaven Earth Man 12-19-84
Heavenly Hosts (See: Mennyei Seregek)
Heavy Metal 8-5-81
Hecate 11-10-82
Hector 3-7-84
Heidi's Song 11-17-82
Heimat 9-12-84
"Heimatfilm" in Karnten, A (See: Karntner Heimatfilm)
Heinrich Penthesilea von Kleist 3-16-83
Held for Questioning (See: Aufenthalt, Der)
Hell Night 9-2-81
Hell Train (See: Train d'Enfer)
Heller Wahn 3-2-83
Hello, Cane Stick (See: Sawasdee Mai Riew)
Hello, Taxi (See: Halo Taksi)
Hells Angels Forever 7-20-83
Hell's Kitchen (See: Kiez)
Hell's Kitchen Chronicle 5-23-84
Help Me Dream (See: Aiutami A Sognare)
Helter-skelter (See: Hanyatt-homlok)
Henry IV (See: Enrico IV)
Henry's Back Room (See: Henry's Bakvaerelsen)
Henry's Bakvaerelsen 9-1-82
Herbstkatzen 1-6-82
Hercules 8-31-83
Herdsman, The 6-15-83
Here Are Ladies 4-6-83
Hero 9-15-82
Hero 11-30-83
Herzlichen Glueckwunsch 2-9-83
Hey Babe! 7-25-84
Hey, Good Lookin' 8-25-82
Hi No Tori-2772 (See: Space Firebird 2772)
Hidden Dances (See: Verborgenen Taenze, Die)
High Country, The 9-16-81
High Risk 6-3-81
High Road to China 3-9-83
High Voltage (See: Visoki Napon)
Highpoint 11-14-84
Hill on the Dark Side of the Moon, A (See: Berg pa Manen's
    Baksida, Ett)
Hill on the Other Side of the Moon, The (See: Berget pa Manens
    Bakdisa)
Him 3-7-84
Him and Me 4-21-82
Himala 1-26-83
Himeyuri No To 8-4-82
Himmel und Erde 11-17-82
Hinterland Nights (See: Noites do Sertao)
Hipokuratesu-Tachi 11-18-81
Hirnbrennen 12-15-82
Hirondelle et la Mesange (1920-1983), L' 7-25-84
Histoire du Caporal 5-23-84
Histoire d'une Rencontre 9-21-83
Historias Violentas 12-26-84
History of the World - Part I 6-10-81
Hit, The 5-23-84
Hit and Run 9-1-82
Hiver '60 8-24-83
Ho Fatto Splash 1-7-81
Hockey Fever (See: Eishockey-Fieber)
Hocu Zivjeti 8-18-82
Hodiny 4-8-81
Hoero Tuekken 8-2-82
Hoevdingen 8-22-84
Hoi Duiong Mau Da Cam 8-8-84
Hole in the Wall, The (See: Agujero en la Pared, El)
Hole in the Windshield, A (See: Foro nel Parabrezza, Un)
Hollywood High Part II 6-6-84
Hollywood Hot Tubs 5-23-84
Hollywood Out-Takes & Rare Footage 3-23-83
Holy Innocents, The (See: Santos Inocentes, Los)
Hombre de Arena, El 10-19-83
Hombre del Subsuelo, El 10-7-81
Home and the World, The (See: Ghare Baire)
Home at Hong Kong 9-14-83
Home for Gentle Souls, A 11-4-81
Home Free All 9-7-83
Home Murders (See: Muertres a Domicile)

Home Village (See: Furusato)
Homecoming 10-3-84
Homecoming Song (See: Tragoudi tis Epistrofis, To)
Homeland (See: Heimat)
Homem que Virou Suco, O 8-12-81
Homesick (See: Xiang Qing)
Homework 9-1-82
Homme a la Valise, L' 8-29-84
Homme a Ma Taille, Un 12-21-83
Homme au Chapeau de Soie, L' 6-15-83
Homme Blesse, L' 6-8-83
Homme Fragile, L' 6-10-81
Hommes Preferent les Grosses, Les 9-2-81
Hon vong phu 9-21-83
Honeymoon (See: Medeni Mjesec)
Hong Kong, Hong Kong 8-24-83
Hong Kong Playboys 7-6-83
Honky Tonk Freeway 8-19-81
Honkytonk Man 12-15-82
Honneur d'un Capitaine, L' 10-20-82
Honoo No Daigo Gakusho 9-2-81
Hoodwink 5-27-81
Hookers on Davie Street 4-11-84
Hooray Brazil (See: Pra Frente Brasil)
Hopper's Silence 10-14-81
Horatio I.P.I. 5-18-83
Horizon, The (See: Chiheisen)
Horror Planet 12-1-82
Horror Vacui 10-24-84
Horse, The (See: At)
Horsemen of the Storm, The (See: Cavaliers de l'Orage, Les)
Hospital Massacre 11-9-83
Hostage - The Christine Maresch Story 5-11-83
Hot and Deadly 7-4-84
Hot Dog ... The Movie 1-18-84
Hot Moves 12-5-84
Hot Summer in Kabul, A 8-24-83
Hot Touch 1-5-83
Hotel Central (See: Hotel Tsentral)
Hotel des Ameriques 2-17-82
Hotel New Hampshire, The 3-14-84
Hotel New York 6-27-84
Hotel of the Americas (See: Hotel des Ameriques)
Hotel of the Stars 6-3-81
Hotel Polan and Its Guests (See: Hotel Polan und Seine Gaeste)
Hotel Polan und Seine Gaeste 5-26-82
Hotel Tsentral 9-14-83
Hound of the Baskervilles, The 6-15-83
Housata 3-11-81
House, The 11-2-83
House Arrest (See: En Residence Surveillee)
House Boat No. 70 (See: Awama Rakam Sabeen, Al)
House by the Cemetery, The 4-11-84
House in the Park, The (See: Haus im Park, Das)
House of Death (See: Pee-Mak)
House of Glass (See: Skleneny Dum)
House of God, The 4-4-84
House of the Long Shadows 6-29-83
House of the Yellow Carpet (See: Casa del Tappetto Giallo, La)
House of Water, The (See: Casa de Agua, La)
House on Sorority Row, The 2-9-83
House Where Death Lives, The 3-7-84
House Where Evil Dwells, The 5-19-82
House-Warming, The (See: Gyertek El A Nevnapomra)
Houston, Texas 4-22-81
How Chileans Love (See: Como Aman los Chilenos)
How I Was Systematically Destroyed by an Idiot (See: Kako Sam
    Sistematski Unisten Od Idiota)
How to Make It in the Movies (See: Wo Geht's Denn Hier zum Film?)
How Would You Say ... (See: Come Dire)
How'd You Get In? We Didn't See You Leave (See: Par Ou T'Es
    Rentre? On T'A Pas Vue Sortir)
Howling, The 1-28-81
Howling Fist (See: Hoero Tekken)
Hrafninn Flygur 3-21-84
Human Highway 8-18-82
Human Lanterns 10-20-82
Humongous 6-9-82
Hunderennen 2-8-84
Hundra 5-23-84
Hunger, The 4-27-83
Hunter of the Heart (See: Jager des Herzens)
Hunters of the Golden Cobra, The 3-28-84
Hunting Ground (See: Jaegerschlacht)
Hure und der Hurensohn, Die 3-24-82
Hurry, Hurry (See: Deprisa, Deprisa)
Husid (See: House, The)
Husty 3-21-84
Hysterical 5-25-83

I

I Am a Cat 9-15-82
I Am the Cheese 10-5-83
I Confess 8-12-81
I Dismember Mama 3-23-83
I Do 6-1-83
I Don't Want to Be Grown-Up (See: No Chochu Bytj Vzroslym)
I Hate Blondes 7-29-81
I Know That You Know That I Know (See: Io So Che Tu Sai Che Io So)
I Love You (See: Eu Te Amo)
I Love You (See: Je Vous Aime)
I Made a Splash (See: Ho Fatto Splash)
I Married a Dead Man (See: J'Ai Epouse une Ombre)
I or You (See: Ich oder Du)
I Ought to Be in Pictures 3-24-82
I Shall Always Stand Guard (See: Na Strazy Swej Stac Bede)
I, the Jury 6-2-82
I Told You So (See: Neli Ti Rekov)
I Want to Live (See: Hocu Zivjeti)
Iarba Verde de Acasa 3-25-81
Ice Birds (See: Isfugle)
Ice Pirates, The 3-21-84
Iceman 4-11-84
Ich oder Du 11-14-84
Ideiglenes Paradicsom 7-29-81
Idemo Dalje 8-18-82
Identification of a Woman (See: Identificazione d'una Donna)
Identificazione d'una Donna 6-2-82
Idolatrada, A 4-27-83
If I Were for Real 11-18-81
If I Were for Real (See: Chia-Ju Wo Shih Chen-Te)
If It Ain't Stiff It Ain't Worth a ... 4-29-81
If You Could See What I Hear 4-28-82
If You Know What I Mean (See: Als Je Begrijpt Wat Ik Bedoel)
Igman March, The (See: Igmanski Mars)
Igmanski Mars 8-17-83
Il Faut Tuer Birgitt Haas 9-2-81
Il Pap'Occhio 2-11-81
Ilektricos Anguelos 11-4-81
Ilha Dos Amores, A 5-26-82
I'll Be Home for Christmas 6-27-84
Illusion (See: Illusione)
Illusione 9-5-84
Illusionist, De 10-12-83
Illusionist, The (See: Illusionist, De)
Illusive Summer of '68, The (See: Varjivo Leto '68)
Ils Appelent Ca un Accident 9-29-82
'I'm Almost Not Crazy ...' John Cassavetes: The Man and His Work 7-25-84
I'm Blushing (See: Jag Rodnar)
I'm Dancing as Fast as I Can 3-3-82
I'm Getting a Yacht (See: Mi Faccio la Barca)
I'm Going to Be Famous 2-9-83
I'm Happy (See: Son Contento)
I'm in a Crisis (See: Estoy en Crisis!)
Im Land Meiner Eltern 6-30-82
I'm Not Living with You Anymore (See: Io con Te Non Ci Sto Piu')
Im Zeichen des Kreuzes 11-30-83
Image Before My Eyes 3-18-81
Image of Dorian Gray in the Yellow Press, The (See: Dorian Gray im Spiegel der Boulevardpresse)
Images of Germany (See: Deutschland Bilder)
Imagi Ningthem 2-10-82
Imagine the Sound 9-23-81
Imp, The 12-16-81
Imperativ 9-15-82
Imperative (See: Imperativ)
Imperial Japanese Empire, The (See: Dai Nippon Teikoku)
Imprecation, The (See: Lanaa, El-)
Improper Channels 4-22-81
Improper Conduct 4-25-84
Imprudent Lover, The (See: Ubetaenksomme Elsker, Den)
Impulse 10-3-84
In Broad Daylight (See: W Bialy Dzien)
In Just the Wink of an Eye (See: Kisap Mata)
In Memory of Malawan 10-17-84
In Our Hands 2-15-84
In Punta di Piedi 10-3-84
In Search of Famine (See: Aakaler Sandhane)
In September (See: En Septiembre)

In the King of Prussia 11-17-82
In the Land of My Parents (See: Im Land Meiner Eltern)
In the Middle of the Night (See: Midt om Natten)
In the Pope's Eye (See: Il Pap'Occhio)
In the White City (See: Dans la Ville Blanche)
In the Year of the Ape (See: Apinan Vuosi)
In Viaggio con Papa 1-5-83
Inceneritore, L' 9-5-84
Inchon 5-6-81
Incident of the Half-Meter, The (See: Hadisat an Nusf Meter)
Incinerator, The (See: Inceneritore, L')
Incomplete Eclipse (See: Neupline Zatmeni)
Incredible Shrinking Woman, The 1-28-81
Incubus, The 9-8-82
Indeks 4-22-81
Independence Day 1-19-83
Index (See: Indeks)
India, A Filha do Sol 6-2-82
Indian, Daughter of the Sun (See: India, A Filha do Sol)
Indian Story, An 2-10-82
Indiana Jones and the Temple of Doom 5-16-84
Indic, L' 5-25-83
Indiscretion, The (See: Indiscretion, L')
Indiscretion, L' 8-25-82
Inferno, The 8-8-84
Infigar, Al- 8-24-83
Information About a Kidnapping (See: Yukai Hodo)
Informer, The (See: Indic, L')
Ingenioer Andrees Luftfaerd 9-1-82
Inheritors, The (See: Erben, Die)
Initiation, The 12-19-84
In-Laws, The (See: Xi Ying Men)
Innamorato Pazzo 1-20-82
Innocent Prey 2-29-84
Ins and the Outs, The (See: Uns et les Autres, Les)
Insel im See 4-6-83
Inside & Outside (See: Drinnen & Draussen)
Inside Man, The 5-23-84
Inside Out 10-6-82
Instructor, The 7-20-83
Insult, The (See: Sertes, A)
Interdit aux Moins de 13 Ans (Lucie sur Seine)
Interrail 6-3-81
Interrupted Traces, The (See: Unterbrochene Spur, Die)
Inti Anti, Camino al Sol 10-27-82
Inti Anti, The Road to the Sun (See: Inti Anti, Camino al Sol)
Intimate Friends: An Historic Legend 3-31-82
Intimate Moments (See: Madame Claude 2)
Intoarcerea Din Iad 8-24-83
Intoarcerea Lui Voda Lapusneanu 4-1-81
Intoxicated Life (See: Rauschendes Leben)
Intre Oglinzi Paralele 4-1-81
Invisible Strangler 12-19-84
Invitacion, La 10-20-82
Invitation, The (See: Invitacion, La)
Invitation au Voyage 5-26-82
Invitation to a Trip (See: Invitation au Voyage)
Io, Chiara e lo Scuro 4-13-83
Io con Te Non Ci Sto Piu' 12-7-83
Io e Caterina 2-4-81
Io So Che Tu Sai Che Io So 9-29-82
Ion, Blestemul Parninthlui 2-11-81
Ion, The Curse of Land (See: Ion, Blestemul Parninthlui)
Irezumi - Spirit Of Tattoo (See: Sekka Tomurai Zashi)
Irreconcilable Differences 5-16-84
Is There a Frenchman in the House? (See: Y'at-Il un Francais dans la Salle?)
Is This Really Reasonable? (See: Est-Ce Bien Raisonnable?)
Isaac Littlefeathers 12-26-84
Isfugle 1-4-84
Island of Loves (See: Ilha dos Amores, A)
Island on the Lake, The (See: Insel im See)
Iso Valee 7-6-83
Issa's Valley (See: Dolina Issy)
Istvan, a Kiraly 3-7-84
Istvan, the King (See: Istvan, a Kiraly)
It Came from Hollywood 11-3-82
It Can't Be Winter, We Haven't Had Summer Yet (See: Ca Peut Pas Etre l'Hiver On N'A Meme Pas Eu d'Ete)
It Happened in Huayanay 7-29-81
It Is Cold in Brandenburg - Kill Hitler (See: Es Ist Kalt in Brandenburg - Hitler Toeten)
It Takes Two 9-1-82
It Was a Dream (See: Kung Mangarap Ka'T Migising)
Itineraire Bis 4-27-83
Itinerant Cancer (See: Wanderkrebs)
It's Handy When People Don't Die 10-14-81
It's Nice to Meet You 3-31-82

L

M

Maya 5-26-82
Maya Miriga 5-23-84
Maybe It's Love 4-4-84
Maybe This Time 4-22-81
Me, Light and Darkness (See: Io, Chiara e lo Scuro)
Me'Achorei Hasoragim 5-30-84
Meantime 11-30-83
Measure for Measure (See: Mera Spored Mera)
Meatballs Part II 8-1-84
Med Allt A Hreinu 12-14-83
Med Lill-Klas i Kappsaecken 2-29-84
Medeni Mjesec 8-17-83
Mediterranean, The 2-9-83
Megaforce 6-30-82
Megall Az Ido 3-10-82
Megilah '83 4-6-83
Mein Teema 9-12-84
Meisje met het Rode Haar, Het 10-7-81
Melanie 2-17-82
Melies (See: Melies et Ses Contemporaires)
Melies et Ses Contemporaires 10-12-83
Melody Haunts My Reverie, The (See: Samo Jednon Se Ljubi)
Melvin, Son of Alvin 12-26-84
Melzer 2-16-83
Memed My Hawk 5-23-84
Memoire Fertile, La 5-27-81
Memoirs of a Survivor 5-27-81
Memorial in Gdansk, The 1-27-82
Memorias do Carcere 5-16-84
Memorias do Medo 6-3-81
Memories, Memories (See: Souvenirs, Souvenirs)
Memories of Fear (See: Memorias do Medo)
Memory Episodes (See: Smriti Chitra)
Men from the Gutter 12-7-83
Men Prefer Fat Girls (See: Hommes Preferent les Grosses, Les)
Menino do Rio 2-10-82
Mennyei Seregek 9-14-83
Menuet 4-21-82
Mephisto 3-18-81
Mera Spored Mera 11-18-81
Mercedes Sosa, Como una Pajaro Libre 10-26-83
Mercedes Sosa, Life a Free Bird (See: Mercedes Sosa, Como una
    Pajaro Libre)
Mere, Une Fille, Une (See: Anna)
Merkozes 3-18-81
Merry Christmas, Mr. Lawrence 5-25-83
Merry Marriage, The (See: Veselo Gostivanje)
Mesrine 3-21-84
Message for Posterity, A (See: Nachwelt eine Botschaft, Der)
Meta 10-7-81
Metalstorm: The Destruction of Jared-Syn 8-24-83
Metin 10-13-82
Metropoli 9-21-83
Metropolis (See: Metropoli)
Meu-Peun 9-14-83
Mexico in Flames 9-1-82
Mezczyzna Niepotrzenbny 10-7-81
MGM Three Stooges Festival, The 5-11-83
Mi Faccio la Barca 1-21-81
Mi Manda Picone 2-8-84
Mi Socio 8-10-83
Mi Tia Nora 9-21-83
Miao Miao 10-27-82
Michiko 9-2-81
Micki & Maude 12-5-84
Microphone Test (See: Proba de Microfon)
Microwave Massacre 8-31-83
Midnight 1-5-83
Midnight Rehearsal (See: Hatasvadaszok)
Midnite Spares 2-9-83
Midsummer Night's Dream, A (See: Sogno di una Notte d'Estate)
Midsummer Night's Dream, A (See: Sueno de Noche de Verano)
Midsummer Night's Sex Comedy 7-14-82
Midt om natten 4-11-84
Mientras el Cuerpo Aguante 10-6-82
Mijlocas La Deschidere 4-1-81
Mikan No Taikyoku 10-13-82
Mike's Murder 3-14-84
Milan '83 (See: Milano '83)
Milano '83 4-18-84
Miles of Smiles, Years of Struggle 9-1-82
Milka 2-4-81
Milka, a Film About Taboos (See: Milka)
Mille Milliards de Dollars 3-24-82
Millennial Bee, The (See: Tisicrocna vcela)
Milo Barus — Der Staerkste Mann der Welt 2-9-83
Milo Barus — The Strongest Man in the World (See: Milo Barus — Der
    Staerkste Mann der Welt)
Milosz Ci Wszystko Wybaczy 10-7-81

Minami Jujisei 10-13-82
Minestrone (See: Minestrone, Il)
Minestrone, Il 3-4-81
Minions of the Moon (See: Favoris de la Lune, Les)
Minister's Wife, The (See: Mujer del Ministro, La)
Mint Tea (See: The a la Menthe)
Minuet (See: Menuet)
Miracle (See: Himala)
Miracle Fighters, The 8-25-82
Miracle of Joe Petrel, The (See: Umi Isubame Joe No Kiseki)
Mirage, The (See: Maya Miriga)
Mireasa Din Tren 4-1-81
Miris Dunja 8-18-82
Mirror, The (See: Spiegel, Der)
Mirrors 9-5-84
Mis 4-22-81
Mischief (See: Frevel)
Miserables, Les 11-3-82
Miss Lonelyhearts 5-25-83
Missing 1-27-82
Missing in Action 11-21-84
Mission, The (See: Ferestedah)
Mission Hill 5-23-84
Mission Thunderbolt 5-25-83
Missionary, The 11-3-82
Missioner, The (See: Auftrage)
Mississippi Blues 5-30-84
Mississippi Triangle 3-28-84
Mr. Leon (See: Adon Leon)
Mr. Mom 7-20-83
Mr. Virgin 8-1-84
Mrs. Latter's Pension (See: Pensja Pani Latter)
Mrs. Soffel 12-26-84
Ms. 45 5-6-81
Misterio 4-20-83
Mistero del Morca, Il 91-9-84
Misunderstanding (See: Parexigisi)
Misunderstood 2-29-84
Mitakhat La'Af 9-15-82
Mitten ins Herz 9-14-83
Mixed Blood 9-19-84
Mizu No Nai Puuru 7-21-82
Mniejsze Niebo 4-22-81
Mo Sheng De Peng You 3-9-83
Mob War 5-30-84
Model Behavior 5-30-84
Modern American Composers I 7-25-84
Modern Day Houdini 4-27-83
Modern Problems 12-30-81
Modern Romance 3-11-81
Moeru Aki 4-22-81
Moeru Yuja 8-18-82
Mohan Joshi Haazir Ho 12-26-84
Mohana 8-24-83
Moj Tata Na Odredjone Vreme 8-24-83
Molly 9-28-83
Moment de Bonheur, Un 6-3-81
Moment of Adventure, The (See: Momento dell'Avventura, Il)
Moment of Happiness, A (See: Moment de Bonheur, Un)
Momento dell'Avventura, Il 9-21-83
Momentos 6-10-81
Moments (See: Momentos)
Mommie Dearest 9-9-81
Mona and the Time of Burning Love (See: Mona Ja Palavan Rakkauden
    Aika)
Mona Ja Palavan Rakkauden Aika 3-7-84
Mond Ist Nur a Nackerte Kugel, Der 3-18-81
Money (See: Argent, L')
Monkey Grip 5-5-82
Monsignor 10-27-82
Monster Club, The 5-27-81
Monster Island 4-22-81
Montenegro 6-3-81
Montgomery Clift 5-4-83
Monty Python Live at the Hollywood Bowl 5-26-82
Monty Python's The Meaning of Life 3-23-83
Moon in the Gutter, The (See: Lune dans le Caniveau, La)
Moonlighting 5-26-82
Moonshine Bowling (See: Au Claire de la Lune)
Moon's Only a Naked Ball, The (See: Mond Ist Nur a Nackerte Kugel,
    Der)
Moord in Extase 3-7-84
Moral 2-2-83
Morfalous, Les 4-11-84
Morgen Grauen 11-14-84
Morgen in Alabama 3-7-84
Moritz Inside the Advertising Pillar (See: Moritz in der
    Litfassaule)
Morning Mist (See: Morgen Grauen)

Mort de Mario Ricci, La 5-18-83
Morte in Vaticano 9-15-82
Mortelle Randonee 4-13-83
Mortiz in der Litfassaule 3-14-84
Mortuary 9-28-83
Moscow on the Hudson 3-28-84
Mosque, The (See: Akmar, Al)
Mosquito on the Tenth Floor (See: Jukai No Mosukiito)
Mosquito on the Tenth Floor, The (See: Jakkai No Mosukito)
Moss-Covered Asphalt (See: Mahovina Na Asfaltu)
Most Beautiful Night, The (See: Noche Mas Hermosa, La)
Mot Haerlige Tider 11-2-83
Motel 2-22-84
Mother Lode 9-8-82
Mother Maria (See: Mat Maria [or Mat'r Marija])
Mother's Meat and Freud's Flesh 3-14-84
Mots pour le Dire, Les 11-9-83
Mountain, The (See: Berg, De)
Mountain Music of Peru 10-10-84
Mourir a Trente Ans 8-11-82
Mouvement-Danse 8-29-84
Move Along, There's Nothing to See (See: Circulez Y'A Rien a Voir)
Moving (See: Przeprowadzka)
Moving Out 10-13-82
Moyna Tadanta 4-1-81
Mrkacek Ciko 4-4-84
Mrtvi Ucia Zivych 8-22-84
Muddy River (See: Doro No Kawa)
Muerte de un Magnate 8-26-81
Muertres A Domicile 1-26-83
Muho Matsu No Issho 4-1-81
Mujer del Ministro, La 9-9-81
Mujer sin Amor, Una 11-23-83
Multo Prazer (See: It's Nice to Meet You)
Munasawagi No Hokago 5-26-82
Muppets Take Manhattan, The 7-11-84
Mur, Le 5-25-83
Murder at the Nation's Senate (See: Asesinato en el Senado de la
    Nacion)
Murder by Phone 1-26-83
Murder in Ecstasy (See: Moord in Exstase)
Murder in the Central Committee (See: Asesinato en el Comite
    Central)
Murs, Murs 5-27-81
Music (See: Muzsika)
Music of the Spheres, The 11-21-84
Musical Passage 3-21-84
Mutant (See: Forbidden World)
Mutant (See: Night Shadows)
Mute Love (See: Ahava Ilemeth)
Muzhyki 3-10-82
Muzsika 3-7-84
My Aunt Nora (See: Mi Tia Nora)
My Beloved 12-29-82
My Bloody Valentine 2-18-81
My Breakfast with Blassie 11-16-83
My Brother's Wedding 9-21-83
My Buddy's Girl (See: Femme de Mon Pote, La)
My Champion (See: Ritoru Chanpion)
My Country (See: Bayan Ko)
My Country, My Hat 6-29-83
My Dinner with Andre 9-16-81
My Farmors Hus 10-3-84
My Father's Secret (See: Geheimnis Meines Vaters, Das)
My Favorite Year 9-29-82
My First Wife 8-15-84
My Friend (See: Mi Socio)
My Friends Need Killing 6-27-84
My Granny's House (See: My Farmors Hus)
My Iz Djaza 9-7-83
My Kind of Town 12-26-84
My Love Letters 5-4-83
My Memories of Old Beijing 2-9-83
My Mother, My Daughter 9-9-81
My Road (See: Mai Roodo)
My Son, My Precious (See: Imagi Ningthem)
My Soul's Adventure (See: Abenteuer Meiner Seele)
My Stiffnecked Daddy & Me (See: Boku No Oyaji To Boku)
My Temporary Father (See: Moj Tata Na Odredjone Vreme)
My Trip with Dad (See: In Viaggio con Papa)
My Tutor 3-9-83
My Young Auntie 2-25-81
Mystere 11-30-83
Mysterious Castle in the Carpathians (See: Tajemstvi Hradu v
    Karpatech)
Mystery (See: Misterio)
Mystery Mansion 7-4-84
Mystery of the Morca, The (See: Mistero del Morca, Il)
Mystique 11-18-81

N

Na De Liefde 2-23-83
Na Gospozhitsata I Neinata Muzhka Kompania 8-8-84
Na Strazy Swej Stac Bede 8-8-84
Nach Mitternacht 6-16-82
Nach Wien 2-9-83
Nacht der Woelfe 6-23-82
Nacht des Schicksals, Die 7-21-82
Nacht und Ihr Preis, Die 2-1-84
Nachwelt eine Botschaft, Der 8-25-82
Nacional III 4-25-84
Nadia 5-16-84
Nagua 9-14-83
Naitou 7-25-84
Naked Face, The 5-23-84
Naked Love (See: Amour Nu, L')
Naked Magic (See: Shocking Cannibals)
Nameless Band, A (See: Orkestur Bez Ime)
Nana 3-23-83
Nankyoku Monogatari 3-7-84
Nantonaku, Kurisutaru 10-13-82
Naplo 3-7-84
Narayama-Bushi Ko 5-25-83
Narcissus and Psyche (See: Narcisz es Psyche)
Narcisz es Psyche 3-18-81
Nark, The (See: Balance, La)
Narrohut 11-17-82
Nasdednitsa Po Priamoi 10-6-82
Nastojanje 8-18-82
Nate and Hayes 11-16-83
National Lampoon Goes to the Movies 11-9-83
National Lampoon's Class Reunion 11-3-82
National Lampoon's Vacation 8-3-83
National Patrimony (See: Patrimonio Nacional)
National III (See: Nacional III)
Natural, The 5-9-84
Naturens Haemnd 4-18-84
Nature's Revenge (See: Naturens Haemnd)
Naughty Boys 3-7-84
Ne Chochu Bytj Vzroslym 4-4-84
Nedeljni Rucak 8-18-82
Needle, The (See: Pico, El)
Neger Erwin, Der 3-11-81
Neige 5-27-81
Neighborhood Barber, The (See: Coiffeur du Quartier des Pauvres,
    Le)
Neighbors 12-16-81
Neighbors (See: Lingju)
Neighbors (See: Vecinos)
Nekatomeni Aeries 11-7-84
Nelesita 8-10-83
Neli Ti Rekov 8-29-84
Nelly's Version 6-15-83
Nemo (See: Dream One)
Neptanitok 3-10-82
Nesting, The 4-22-81
Nesto Izmedju 6-1-83
Nestor Burma, Detective de Choc 4-14-82
Nestor Burma, Shock Detective (See: Nestor Burma, Detective de
    Choc)
Neupline Zatmeni 3-2-83
Neve nel Bicchiere, La 9-5-84
Never Cry Wolf 9-7-83
Never Say Never Again 10-5-83
Neverending Story, The 7-4-84
New Year's Evil 1-21-81
New York Nights 4-4-84
New York Ripper (See: Squartatore di New York, Lo)
News Items (See: Faits Divers)
Next of Kin 6-2-82
Next of Kin 10-3-84
Next One, The 10-3-84
Next Victim, The (See: Proxima Vitima)
Next Year If All Goes Well (See: Annee Prochaine Si Tout Va Bien,
    L')
Nicaragua - No Pasaran 7-25-84
Nice a Propos de Jean Vigo 9-5-84
Nice Dreams (See: Cheech & Chong's Nice Dreams)
Nie Byla Slonca 8-22-84
Night After Death (See: Noc Poslije Smrti)

Night and Its Price, The (See: Nacht und Ihr Preis, Die)
Night Crossing 12-30-81
Night Dreams 7-21-82
Night in Heaven, A 11-23-83
Night of Destiny (See: Nacht des Schicksals, Die)
Night of the Comet 10-10-84
Night of the Falling Stars (See: Notte di San Lorenzo, La)
Night of the Ghouls 6-27-84
Night of the Wolves (See: Nacht der Woelfe)
Night of the Zombies 7-20-83
Night of the Zombies (See: Apocalipsis Canibal)
Night of Varennes, The (See: Nuit de Varennes, La)
Night Patrol 12-12-84
Night Patrol (See: Ronde de Nuit)
Night River (See: Yoru No Kawa)
Night School 10-14-81
Night Shadows 10-3-84
Night Shift 7-14-82
Night Soldier (See: Hayal Halayla)
Night the Lights Went Out in Georgia, The 6-10-81
Night They Arrested Fatma, The (See: Laylat El-Kaped Alla Fatma)
Night Warning 9-14-83
Nightfall (See: Kopfschuss)
Nighthawks 4-8-81
Nightmare 10-14-81
Nightmare Lady, The (See: Alptraumfrau, Die)
Nightmare on Elm Street, A 11-7-84
Nightmares 9-7-83
Nights at O'Rear's 4-22-81
Nights Without Moons or Suns (See: Noches Sin Lunas ni Soles)
Nightsongs 4-25-84
Ni-Jen Chang Chuan-Gi 8-8-84
Niji o Kakeru Komodo Tachi 10-27-82
Nikolai Ghiaurov 4-1-81
Nimr el-Asswad, El- 1-18-84
Nimm die Nacht Weg 5-26-82
Nine Ways to Approach Helsinki (See: Yhdeksan Tapaa Lahestya Helsinkia)
1919 9-7-83
1919 12-12-84
1922 12-16-81
1984 10-10-84
1990: The Bronx Warriors 4-27-83
Ninguem Duaz Vezes 9-12-84
Ningyo Densetsu 6-6-84
Ningyo Girai 10-27-82
Ninja in the Dragon's Den 5-26-82
Ninja Mission, The 5-16-84
Ninja III - The Domination 5-23-84
Nishijin no shimai 4-8-81
No Charges Filed (See: Wa Koyedat Ded Maghoul)
No Clues (See: Nyom Nelkul)
No Cordiality for the Woman (See: Ualla Azae Lel Sayedat)
No Eran Nadine 6-2-82
No Grazie, Il Caffe Mi Rende .. Nervoso 12-22-82
No Habra Mas Penas ni Olvido 10-12-83
No Land (See: Kein Land)
No Mercy, No Future (See: Beruehrte, Die)
No More Hibakusha 12-14-83
No One Twice (See: Ninguem Duaz Vezes)
No Small Affair 11-7-84
No Terrace-House for Robin Hood (See: Kein Reihenhaus fuer Robin Hood)
No Thanks, Coffee Makes Me Nervous (See: No Grazie, Il Caffee Mi Rende .. Nervoso)
No West Runway - An Area Defends Itself (See: Keine Startbahn West-Eine Region Wehrt Sich)
No Yonamono 4-7-82
Noa At 17 2-24-82
Noah's Ark Principle, The (See: Arche Noah Prinzip, Das)
Nobena Sonce 9-5-84
Nobody's Perfekt 7-29-81
Nobody's Wife (See: Senora de Nadie)
Nobody's Women (See: Femmes de Personne)
Noc Poslije Smrti 8-24-83
Nocaut 2-22-84
Noche Mas Hermosa, La 10-10-84
Noches Sin Lunas ni Soles 8-1-84
Nocturna 12-7-83
Nogare No Machi 11-16-83
Noi Tre 9-5-84
Noites do Sertao 5-16-84
Nomad, The 12-15-82
Norman Loves Rose 4-28-82
Norte, El 12-7-83
North, The (See: Norte, El)
North Bridge (See: Pont du Nord, Le)
North Star, The (See: Etoile du Nord, L')
Nostalghia 5-18-83

Nostalgia (See: Nostalghia)
Not a Love Story: A Film About Pornography 9-16-81
Not by Coincidence (See: Keine Zufallige Geschichte)
Not for Publication 5-23-84
Notes for an African Orestes (See: Appunti per un Orestiade Africana)
Notes from Under the Volcano 7-11-84
Nothing but Words of Praise for the Deceased (See: O Pokojniku Sve Najlepse)
Nothing Lasts Forever 9-26-84
Nothing Left to Lose (See: Dies Rigorose Leben)
Notre Histoire 6-13-84
Notte di Pioggia, Una 9-19-84
Notte di San Lorenzo, La 6-2-82
"Now ... After All These Years" 6-16-82
Now and Everything (See: Jetzt und Alles)
Now and Forever 3-16-83
Nuclearvision 2-9-83
Nucleo Zero 9-19-84
Nucleus Zero (See: Nucleo Zero)
Nu-Daxne Sheng Su-She 8-8-84
Nudo di Donna 11-25-81
Nuit de Varennes, La 5-26-82
Nuits de la Pleine Lune, Les 8-29-84
Number One 11-28-84
Nunca Fomos Tao Felizes 5-2-84
Nuove Frontiere 4-22-81
Nuovi Barbari, I (See: Warriors of the Wasteland)
Nut in Action, A (See: Loco en Accion, Un)
Nutcracker 11-24-82
Nyom Nelkul 3-2-83

O

O Is for Oblomov (See: O Wie Oblomov)
O Pokojniku Sve Najlepse 8-29-84
O Sport, Ti Mir 7-29-81
O Wie Oblomov 6-16-82
Oasis, The 5-23-84
Ob Ich die Musik Nicht Hoere? - Sie Kommt Doch aus Mir 10-27-82
Obscene (See: Obszoen)
Observations Under The volcano 7-11-84
Obszoen 12-2-81
Occasioni di Rosa, Le 9-9-81
Occhei, Occhei 8-17-83
Occhi, La Bocca, Gli 9-8-82
Occhio Malocchio Prezzemolo e Finocchio 3-7-84
Occupation, The (See: Dakhal)
Occupied Palestine 11-4-81
Octavia 6-2-82
Octopussy 6-8-83
Odds and Evens (See: Pares y Nones)
Odio le Blonde (See: I Hate Blondes)
Odveta 4-8-81
Odyssey of the Pacific (See: Traversee de la Pacific)
Of the Flesh (See: Karnal)
Of Unknown Origin 12-7-83
Of Worms and Roses (See: Uod at Rosas)
Off the Air (See: Lo Leshidur)
Off the Wall 8-10-83
Officer and a Gentleman, An 7-21-82
Ohne Rueckfahrkarte 2-4-81
Oh, Bloody Life! ... (See: Te Rongyos Elet! ...)
Oh, God! You Devil 11-7-84
Oh, Sport, You Are Peace (See: O Sport, Ti Mir)
O'Hara's Wife 12-15-82
O.K. ... Laliberte 9-16-81
Okaasan No Tsushinbo 10-13-82
Okay, Okay (See: Occhei, Occhei)
Okinawa No Shonen 9-14-83
Okinawan Boys (See: Okinawa No Shonen)
Old Bear Hunter, The (See: Matagi)
Old Enough 5-30-84
Older Master Cute 8-12-81
Older Son, The (See: Starsi Syn)
Olelkezo Tekintetek 6-2-82
Olsen Banden over Alle Bjerge 12-23-81
Olsen Bandens Flugt over Plankevaerket 10-14-81
Olsen Gang Jumps the Fence, The (See: Olsen Bandens Flugt over Plankevaerket)
Olsen Gang over the Hill, The (See: Olsen Banden over Alle Bjerge)
Oltre la Porta 9-15-82
Olympiasiegerin, Die 5-30-84

Ombre Rouge, L' 1-6-82
On a Clear Day You See Damascus (See: Beyom Bahir Royim Et Damesek)
On a First-Name Basis (See: A Tu Per Tu)
On a River Without Navigation Marks 8-29-84
On Any Sunday II 7-22-81
On Golden Pond 11-18-81
On Love (See: Peri Erotos)
On Probation (See: Buergschaft fuer ein Jahr)
On the Far Side of Adventure (See: Mas Alla de la Aventura)
On the Fringe of Society (See: Prachachon Nork)
On the Line 12-19-84
On the Right Track 3-11-81
On the Road (See: On za Roodo)
On the Road to Hollywood 11-17-82 and 11-21-84
On the Run 12-21-83
On the Threshold (See: Lars i porten)
On the Time of Hellenes (See: Ton Kero Ton Hellinon)
On the Track (See: Etrange Voyage, Un)
On the Wrong Track 5-18-83
On Top (See: Med Allt A Hreinu)
On Your Feet, Crabs, the Tide's Up (See: Debout les Crabes, la Mer
    Monte!)
On za Roodo 5-26-82
Once Upon a Mirage 9-15-82
Once Upon a Rainbow 6-2-82
Once Upon a Time in America 5-23-84
One Among Many (See: Uno Entre Muchos)
One Could Laugh in Former Days (See: Vroeger Kon Je Lachen)
One Dark Night 2-2-83
One Deadly Summer (See: Ete Meurtrier, L')
One Down Two to Go 11-24-82
One from the Heart 1-20-82
100 Days (See: Sto Dni)
100 Days in Palermo (See: Cento Giorni a Palermo)
One Man's War (See: Guerre d'un Seul Homme, La)
One Night Stand 4-4-84
One Rainy Night (See: Una Notte di Pioggia)
One Way Ticket (See: Ohne Rueckfahrkarte)
One Way Ticket (See: Aller Simple, Un)
One-Armed Executioner, The 4-6-83
Onimasa 2-2-83
Only When I Laugh 9-16-81
Opcao, As Rosas de Estrada 8-26-81
Open Balcony, The (See: Balcon Abierto, El)
Open Day and Night (See: Abierto Dia y Noche)
Open Ends (See: Grenzenlos)
Open Eyes (See: Oyun La Tanum)
Opera in the Vineyard 8-17-83
Opera ve Vinci (See: Opera in the Vineyard)
Orange-Colored Bells (See: Hoi Duiong Mau Da Cam)
Ordeal by Innocence 5-23-84
Order of Death 3-30-83
Orderly, The (See: Paramedico, Il)
Orechi No Vedingu 5-4-83
Orengen, Der Forzvandt 3-7-84
Oridathu Oru Phayalvaan 3-30-83
Orientation Course (See: Concurs)
Orinoko - Nuevo Mundo 10-3-84
Orkestur Bez Ime 12-16-81
Orozco Family, The (See: Familia Orozco, La)
Oro, Plata, Mata 2-2-83
Orphan, The (See: Naitou)
Orson Welles a la Cinematheque 9-19-84
Orson Welles at the Cinematheque (See: Orson Welles a la
    Cinematheque)
Ostanovilsya Poyesd 4-6-83
Osterman Weekend, The 10-5-83
Ostria 10-3-84
Oszi Almanach 8-29-84
Otec Ma Zderie Tak Ci Tak 3-18-81
Oth Kayin 11-24-82
Othello 12-22-82
Other Side of a Gentleman, The 8-1-84
Other Side of the World, The (See: Andere Seite der Welt, Die)
Otoko Wa Tsurai Yo 7-29-81
Otto Er et naesehorn 4-20-83
Otto Is a Rhino (See: Otto Er et naesehorn)
Our Aunt Tao (See: Quan Shui Ding Dong)
Our Bodies Are Still Alive (See: Unsere Leichen Leben Noch)
Our Man from Bond Street (See: Aces Go Places III)
Our Nazi (See: Unser Nazi)
Our Parents Have the Foreigners' Work Permit C (See: Unsere Eltern
    Haben den Ausweis C)
Our Short Life (See: Unser Kurzes Leben)
Our Story (See: Notre Histoire)
Our Wedding (See: Orechi No Vedingu)
Out of Order 9-5-84
Out of Order (See: Abwarts)
Outcasts, The 8-3-83

Outer Signs of Wealth (See: Signes Exterieurs de Richesse)
Outland 5-20-81
Outlaw: The Saga of Gisli (See: Utlaginn (Gisla Saga Surssonar))
Outside the Day (See: Fuori dal Giorno)
Outsider, The (See: Marginal, Le)
Outsider in Amsterdam (See: Grijpstra & De Gier)
Outsiders, The 3-23-83
Over the Brooklyn Bridge 1-18-84
Overvallers in de Dierentuin 7-25-84
Oxford Blues 8-22-84
Oyun La Tanum 12-23-81

P

P & B 2-1-84
P4W: Prison for Women 9-9-81
Paar 9-5-84
Pablo Picasso 4-21-82
Pacific Banana 6-3-81
Pad, The (See: Meta)
Pad Italije 8-12-81
Padre por Accidente 7-21-82
Paesaggio con Figure 8-24-83
Painter, The (See: Maalaren)
Pajaros de Ciudad 10-14-81
Paladini - Storia d'Armi e d'Amori, I 11-2-83
Palava Enkeli 5-23-84
Pale Light of Sorrow, The (See: Lumina Palida A Durerii)
Pale Passion 10-17-84
Pallet on the Floor 5-16-84
Palombiere, La 6-15-83
Panelkapcsolat 8-25-82
Pankow '95 2-8-84
Papa, Can You Hear Me Sing? 2-8-84
Paper Bird (See: Papierfugien)
Paper Heart (See: Corazon De Papel)
Papierfugien 8-8-84
Papy Fait de la Resistance 11-9-83
Par Ou T'Es Rentre? On T'A Pas Vue Sortir 12-19-84
Paradis Pour Tous 9-15-82
Paradise 5-12-82
Paradise for All (See: Paradis Pour Tous)
Paradontosis Now (See: Parodontose Now)
Parahyba Mulher Macho 10-26-83
Parahyba Woman (See: Parahyba Mulher Macho)
Parallel Corpse, The (See: Parallelle Lig, Det)
Parallel Divergences (See: Divergenze Parallele)
Parallelle Lig, Det 3-24-82
Paramedico, Il 2-24-82
Parasite 3-24-82
Pares y Nones 10-6-82
Parexigisi 8-8-84
Paris Seen by ... 20 Years After (See: Paris Vu par ... Vingt Ans
    Apres)
Paris, Texas 5-23-84
Paris Vu par ... Vingt Ans Apres 7-25-84
Parodontose Now 2-8-84
Paroles du Quebec 9-2-81
Paroles et Musiques 12-12-84
Parsifal 5-26-82
Partfogol, A 3-10-82
Parti Sans Laisser d'Adresse 5-26-82
Partners 5-5-82
Party, The (Boum, La)
Party, Party 2-2-83
Party-2, The (See: Boum 2, La)
Pasajeros de una Pesadilla 8-22-84
Pasajeros del Jardin, Los 6-9-82
Pasla Kone Na Betone 8-10-83
Paso Doble 10-19-83
Passage to India, A 12-12-84
Passante du Sans-Souci, La 6-2-82
Passengers of a Nightmare (See: Pasajeros de una Pesadilla)
Passengers of the Garden, The (See: Pasajeros del Jardin, Los)
Passer-By of the 'Sans Souci' Cafe, The (See: Passante du
    Sans-Souci, La)
Passing Fancy (See: Felhojatek)
Passing Killer, A (See: Assassin Qui Passe, Un)
Passing, Roses of the Road (See: Opcao, As Rosas da Estrada)
Passion 6-2-82
Passionate People (See: Leidenschaftlichen, Die)
Passione d'Amore 5-20-81
Passions of Love (See: Passione d'Amore)

Q

R

S

Sezona Mira u Parizu 7-29-81
Shadow Dance (See: Java des Ombres, La)
Shadow of the Earth (See: Dhil Al-Ardh)
Shahzadeh Va Aloo 10-27-82
Shall the Cuckoo Sing at Night? (See: Pocukido Bame Un-Nka)
Shame, The (See: El-aar)
Shanghai Blues 11-7-84
Shaolin Drunkard 8-24-83
Shaolin Temple, The 2-24-82
Sharing the Secret 11-4-81
Sharky's Machine 12-16-81
Shcerzo del Destino in Agguato Dietro l'Angolo Come un Brigante di
    Strada 10-12-83
She Dances Alone 5-27-81
Sheena 8-15-84
Shi Zi Jie Tou 3-24-82
Shifshuf Naim 3-11-81
Shiki-Natsuko 7-1-81
Shilly-Shally (See: Wahadelko)
Shimmering Beast (See: Bete Lumineuse, La)
Shin Heike Monogatari: Shizuka To Yoshitsune 4-1-81
Shitoyakana Keda Mono 11-4-81
Shock, The (See: Choc, Le)
Shock Cops (See: Flics de Choc)
Shock Treatment 8-26-81
Shocking Asia 3-24-82
Shocking Cannibals 10-24-84
Shodh 4-1-81
Shoe Called Melichar, A (See: Bota Jmenem Melichar)
Shogun 12-23-81
Shoot the Moon 1-20-82
Shooting Party, The 5-20-84
Short Circuits (See: Court Circuits)
Short Cut (See: Postriziny)
Shot Pattern (See: Tir Groupe)
Showdown (See: Anametrissi)
Shrews Have Fun, The (See: Fierecillos Se Divierten, Los)
Shujakumon 4-22-81
Shut Up When You Speak! (See: Tais-Toi Quand Tu Parles!)
Sideroads (See: Itineraire Bis)
Siege 2-9-83
Sign of Four, The 5-18-83
Signal 7 42-5-84
Signals Through the Flames 3-7-84
Signes Exterieurs de Richesse 12-14-83
Signs and Wonders (See: Zeichen und Wunder)
Silence Around Christine M., The (See: Stilte Rond Christina M.,
    De)
Silence of the North 10-7-81
Silent Madness 5-16-84
Silent Night, Deadly Night 11-7-84
Silent Ocean, The (See: Stille Oceaan, De)
Silent Ocean, The (See: Stille Ozean, Der)
Silent One, The 5-16-84
Silent Rage 4-2-82
Silhouettes 4-28-82
Silkwood 11-23-83
Silu Huayu 4-18-84
Silver City 5-16-84
Silvestre 9-16-81
Simhasan 4-1-81
Simple-Minded Murderer, The (See: Engaldige Mordaren, Den)
Singles (See: Ma Femme S'Appelle Reviens)
Sing, Cowboy, Sing 6-16-82
Siroko Je Lisce 8-12-81
Sista Leken 5-23-84
Sisters of Nishijin (See: Nishijin no shimai)
681 A.D. The Glory of Khan 5-23-84
Six Pack 7-7-82
Six Weeks 12-15-82
Sixteen Candles 5-2-84
Sixth Gear (See: Sesta Brzina)
Sjecas Li Se Dolly Bell 8-5-81
Skazka Stranstvil 11-28-84
Skin, The (See: Pelle, La)
Skin of the Fool (See: Narrohut)
Skinny Chico (See: Chico Fininho, O)
Skleneny Dum 10-13-82
Skoenheden og udyret 12-21-83
Sky on Location, The 9-21-83
Skyline (See: Linea del Cielo, La)
Slap in the Face, A (See: Poshjetchina)
Slapstick of Another Kind 3-28-84
Slaughter in San Francisco 10-7-81
Slavnosti Snezenek 8-1-84
Slayer, The 10-27-82
Slayground 2-1-84
Sleepaway Camp 11-30-83
Sleeping Soldier, The (See: Soldat Qui Dort, Le)

Sleeps Six 12-5-84
Sleight of Hand (See: Jogo de Mao)
Slim Dusty Movie, The 5-23-84
Slingrevalsen 9-16-81
Sliozny Kapali 5-18-83
SL-1 6-29-83
Slow Boogie with Me (See: Suroo Na Bugi Ni Shite Kure)
Slow Moves 11-28-84
Slumber Party Massacre, The 3-31-82
Smaak van Water, De 9-15-82
Smala, La 10-3-84
Smaller Sky (See: Mniejsze Niebo)
Smartgransen 3-28-84
Smash Hit, A (See: Trhak)
Smash Palace 9-2-81
Smithereens 6-2-82
Smoke Should Not Fly, The (See: Hatta La Yattir El-Kokkhan)
Smokey and the Bandit - Part 3 8-17-83
Smokey Bites the Dust 11-4-81
Smorgasbord 6-8-83
Smriti Chitra 8-8-84
Smrt Sita Na Mieru 3-18-81
Smurfs and the Magic Flute, The 2-15-84
Snadji Se Druze 8-5-81
Snapshot Around the Family Table (See: Stop Cadru La Masa)
Snow (See: Neige)
Snow, The Movie 2-29-84
Snowdrop Celebrations (See: Slavnosti Snezenek)
So Fine 9-23-81
So Long, Stooge (See: Tchao Pantin)
So What (See: Eijanaika)
Soap and Water (See: Acqua e Sapone)
Sobrenatural 9-9-81
Society Limited (See: Feine Gesellschaft, Beschraenkte Haftung)
Soesken (or Sosken) pa Gud's (or Guds) Jord 9-7-83 and 7-11-84
Sofo Shel Milton Levi 5-27-81
Sogni d'oro 9-9-81
Sogno di una Notte d'Estate 9-21-83
Sok Od Sljiva 8-5-81
Soldados de Plomo 2-1-84
Soldat Qui Dort, Le 8-29-84
Soldier, The 5-26-82
Soldier Girls 4-22-81
Soldier's Story, The 6-3-81
Soldier's Story, A 9-5-84
Sole Survivor 5-30-84
Some Kind of Hero 3-31-82
Somehow, Crystal (See: Nantonaku, Kurisutaru)
Something Becomes Evident (See: Etwas Wird Sichtbar)
Something in Between (See: Nesto Izmedju)
Something Like That (See: No Yonamono)
Something Wicked This Way Comes 5-4-83
Sometimes I Look at My Life (See: A Veces Miro Mi Vida)
Son Contento 11-23-83
Sonata for a Redhead (See: Sonata pro Zrzku)
Sonata pro Zrzku 10-12-83
Sonatine 9-19-84
Sonderbare Liebe, Eine 8-8-84
Sonezaki Shinju 4-7-82
Song of Germany (See: Deutschlandlied)
Songwriter 10-17-84
Sonho Nao Acabau, O 6-9-82
Sons Die Before Their Fathers, The (See: Vor den Vaetern Sterben
    die Soehne)
Sophie's Choice 12-8-82
SOPOR 4-8-81
Sorcerer's Apprentice, The (See: Krabat)
Sorceress 2-16-83
Sorry I'm Late (See: Scusate il Ritardo)
Sorry to Have Imposed (See: Undskyid vi er her)
Sorte Fuger 9-21-83
Sound of the City: London 1964-73 7-29-81
Soup for One 4-28-82
South, The (See: Sur, El)
South Wind (See: Ostria)
Southern Comfort 9-23-81
Southern Cross, The (See: Minami Jujisei)
Southern Crossing 3-18-81
Southern Trail, The (See: Juzna Pateka)
Souvenirs, Souvenirs 10-10-84
Souvliste Tous! 11-4-81
Space Firebird 2772 7-21-82
Space Raiders 8-10-83
Spaced Out 12-16-81
Spacehunter: Adventures in the Forbidden Zone 5-18-83
Spaetlese 4-14-82
Spaghetti House 12-1-82
Sparsh 2-4-81
Spasms 6-6-84

Swamp Thing 3-24-82
Swann in Love (See: Amour de Swann, Un)
Sweet Bunch (See: Glykia Symmoria)
Sweet Dreams (See: Sogni d'Oro)
Sweet Hours (See: Dulces Horas)
Sweet Inquest on Violence (See: Douce Enquete sur la Violence)
Sweet Lies and Loving Oaths (See: Doux Aveux)
Sweet Pea (See: Piso Pisello)
Sweet Sixteen 9-28-83
Swing, The (See: Schaukel, Die)
Swing Shift 4-18-84
Swingin' Betty (See: Bete Balanco)
Sword and the Sorcerer, The 5-12-82
Sword of the Barbarians, The 10-5-83
Sword of the Valiant 12-5-84
Swordkill 10-10-84
Symphony of Love (See: Fruehlingssinfonie)
Syncopated Time (See: A Contratiempo)
Syndicate Sadists 3-30-83
Syringe, The (See: Arbalete, L')
System Ohne Schatten 8-24-83
System Without Shadow (See: System Ohne Schatten)
Szarza 10-7-81
Szegeny Dzsoni Es Arnika 3-14-84
Szerencses Daniel 3-2-83
Szeretok 3-7-84
Szivzur 3-3-82

T

Table for Five 2-9-83
Taer Ala El Tariq 11-4-81
TAG 4-28-82
Tag der Idioten 4-14-82
Tail of the Tiger 10-31-84
Tais-Toi Quand Tu Parles! 9-23-81
Tajemstvi Hradu v Karpatech 5-23-84
Take Away the Night (See: Nimm die Nacht Weg)
Take It or Leave It 5-4-83
Take 10,000 Francs and Settle Down (See: Prends 10,000 Balles et
    Casse-Toi)
Take This Job and Shove It 5-6-81
Talcum Powder (See: Borotalco)
Tale of Africa, A (See: Afurika Monogatari)
Tale of Love and Friendship (See: Storia d'Amore e d'Amicizia)
Tales of 1001 Nights (See: Pohadky Tisice A Jedne Noci)
Tales of Ordinary Madness 9-9-81
Talk to Me 9-15-82
Talmage Farlow 3-31-82
Talpra, Gyozo! 3-2-83
Taming of the Scoundrel (See: Bisbetico Domato, Il)
Tango della Gelosia, Il 11-25-81
Tango Es una Historia, El 3-7-84
Tango Is History (See: Tango Es una Historia, El)
Tank 3-14-84
Tanu, A 5-27-81
Tanya's Island 5-13-81
Taous, El- 11-3-82
Tapdancin' 4-22-81
Tapetenwechsel 10-3-84
Taps 12-9-81
Target Eagle 7-11-84
Tartuffe, Le 5-30-84
Tarzan, The Ape Man 7-29-81
Tasio 10-24-84
Tassinaro, Il 1-18-84
Taste of Sea, A (See: Sapore di Mare)
Taste of Sin, A 3-23-83
Taste of Water, The (See: Smaak van Water, De)
Tattoo 10-14-81
Tattoo (See: Tattoo [Irezumi] Ari)
Tattoo (Irezumi) Ari 7-21-82
Taubenjule 3-28-84
Tausend Augen 10-3-84
Taxi to the Loo (See: Taxi zum Klo)
Taxi zum Klo 6-10-81
Taxid Stin Protevoussa 4-4-84
Taxidi Sta Kithira 5-16-84
Tchao Pantin 1-4-84
Te Engle og Fem Loever 2-9-83
Te Rongyos Elet! ... 3-7-84
Teacher, The (See: Sensei)
Teachers 10-3-84

Teachers, The (See: Neptanitok)
Tears Are Flowing (See: Sliozny Kapali)
Teddy Baer 12-14-83
Teddy Bear (See: Mis)
Teenage Dreamers 5-26-82
Teenaged Girl (See: Sao Daet Deeo)
Tegnapelott 3-3-82
Teheran '43 7-29-81
Tema 7-29-81
Tempest 8-11-82
Temporary Paradise (See: Ideiglenes Paradicsom)
Temptation (See: Versuchung)
10 Days in Calcutta (See: 10 Tage in Calcutta)
10 Tage in Calcutta 8-15-84
10 to Midnight 3-16-83
10 Violent Women 5-9-84
Tender Mercies 12-29-82
Tender Spots (See: Czule Miejsca)
Tenderness and Anger (See: Zartlichkeit und Zorn)
Tenkosei 5-26-82
Tenth Brother, The (See: Deseti Brat)
Teppanyaki 3-7-84
Terceiro Milenio 11-25-81
Terence Davies Trilogy, The 3-21-84
Terminator, The 10-31-84
Terms of Endearment 11-23-83
Terra Roubada 2-10-82
Terre Brulante 6-13-84
Territory, The 3-16-83
Terror in the Aisles 10-31-84
Terror on Tour 9-7-83
Terrorists' in Retirement (See: Des 'Terroristes' a la Retraite)
Terry Fox Story, The 5-4-83
Terugtocht, De 3-18-81
Tesna Koza 8-17-83
Test of Strength (See: Kraftprobe)
Testa o Croce 2-9-83
Testament 10-19-83
Tete a Claques 4-14-82
Tete dans le Sac, La 11-7-84
Tex 7-28-82
Thalia Unter Truemmern 11-17-82
Thaneer Thaneer 2-3-82
Thanks for the Light (See: Gracias por el Fuego)
That Championship Season 12-8-82
That Day, On the Beach 12-14-83
That Was Jazz (See: Byl Jazz)
That's Why (See: Tim Padem)
The a la Menthe 5-16-84
Theatre in Ruins (See: Thalia Unter Truemmern)
Theatre of Shimmering Heat (See: Kagerouza)
Theme, The (See: Tema)
There Lived a Wrestler (See: Oridathu Oru Phayalvaan)
There Was a War When I Was a Child (See: Kodomo No Goro [or Koro]
    Senso [or Sensee] Ga Atta)
There Was No Sun (See: Nie Byla Slonca)
There Will Be No More Sorrows Nor Oblivion (See: No Habra Mas
    Penas Ni Olvido)
These Children Survive Me (See: Kono Ko Wo Nokoshite)
They All Laughed 8-19-81
They Call Him Hurricane (See: Jao Payu)
They Call That an Accident (See: Ils Appelent Ca un Accident)
They Don't Wear Black Ties (See: Eles Nao Usam Black-Tie)
They Were Nobody (See: No Eran Nadie)
They're Playing with Fire 5-2-84
Thief 3-25-81
Thief of Hearts 10-17-84
Thieves After Dark (See: Voleurs de la Nuit, Les)
Thing, The 6-23-82
Things Are Tough All Over 8-11-82
Third Key, The (See: Treci Kljuc)
Third Millennium (See: Tercerio Milenio)
34y Skoreil 4-4-84
36 Chowringhee Lane 2-3-82
This Is Elvis 4-8-81
This Is Spinal Tap 2-29-84
This Is the Way We Live (See: Ganito Kami Noon, Paano Rayo Ngayon)
Thorn in the Flesh (See: Stachel im Fleisch)
Thorvald and Linda (See: Thorvald og Linda)
Thorvald og Linda 2-24-82
Those Glory Glory Days 11-30-83
Thousand Billion Dollars, A (See: Mille Milliards de Dollars)
Thousand Eyes (See: Tausend Augen)
Thousand Little Kisses, A (See: Elef Neshikoth Ketanoth)
Thread, Background, Phosphorus (See: Fil, Fond, Fosfor)
Three Angels and Five Lions (See: Te Engle og Fem Loever)
Three Brothers (See: Tre Fratelli)
Three Crowns of the Sailor, The (See: Trois Couronnes du Matelot,
    Les)

Twinkle, Twinkle, Little Star 3-2-83
Twins, The (See: Jon Oddur og Jon Bjarni)
Twist & Shout (See: Tro, Hab og Karlighed)
Two Guys and a Gal (See: Tva Killar och en Tjej)
Two of a Kind 12-21-83
Two Stage Sisters 4-22-81
2010 11-28-84
Two Worlds of Angelita, The (See: Dos Mundos de Angelita, Los)
Tyrant's Heart or Boccaccio in Hungary, The (See: Zsarnok Sziva
   Avagy Boccaccio Magyarorszagon, A)
Tzlila Khozereth 2-17-82

U

U Raljama Zivota 8-29-84
Ualla Azae Lel Sayedat 11-18-81
Ubetaenksomme Elsker, Den 10-27-82
Ucna Leta Izumitelja Polza 8-18-82
Udenrigskorrespondenten 9-14-83
Uforia 7-18-84
Uiikendo Shaffuru 11-24-82
Uiin Monogatari - Jemin Y to S 4-6-83
Uindii 5-23-84
Uit Elkaar 4-22-81
Uliisees 6-1-83
Ultima Diva: Francesca Bertini, L' 12-7-83
Ultimas Tardes con Teresa 4-25-84
Ultimate Solution of Grace Quigley, The 5-16-84
Ultimatum 8-8-84
Ultimo Grumete, El 2-8-84
Ultimos Dias de la Victima, Los 5-5-82
Ulvetid 10-7-81
Ulysses' Love (See: Erotas Tou Odyssea, O)
Umi Isubame Joe No Kiseki 6-6-84
Unapproachable, The (See: Unerreichbare, Die)
Unattended Party, The (See: Festa Perduta, La)
Uncensored Cartoons 5-5-82
Uncle Scam 5-20-81
Uncommon Valour 12-14-83
Und Naechstes Jahr am Balaton 6-2-82
Und Wenn Wir Nicht Wollen 2-25-81
Undated Wedding 5-25-83
Under Fire 9-7-83
Under the Mosquito Net (See: Dibalik Kelambu)
Under the Rainbow 8-5-81
Under the Volcano 5-23-84
Undercover 2-1-84
Underground Man, The (See: Hombre del Subsuelo, El)
Underground Passage (See: Ypoguia Diadromi)
Undernose (See: Mitkhat La'Af)
Undisciplined Sailors, The (See: Ken Galasi)
Undskyid vi er her 1-7-81
Uneasiness After School (See: Munasawagi No Hokago)
Unerreichbare, Die 8-18-82
Unerreichbare Naehe 8-29-84
Unfair Exchanges 12-5-84
Unfaithfully Yours 2-8-83
Unfinished Business 4-18-84
Unfinished Game of Go, The (See: Mikan No Taikyoku)
Unhappy Hat, The (See: Boldogtalan Kalap)
Unimaginable (See: Akriet)
Unknown Chaplin 9-21-83
Uno Entre Muchos 8-25-82
Uns et les Autres, Les 6-3-81
Unseen, The 10-7-81
Unseen Wonder (See: Cudo Nevidjeno)
Unser Kurzes Leben 9-2-81
Unser Nazi 9-5-84
Unsere Eltern Haben den Ausweis C 2-16-83
Unsere Leichen Leben Noch 12-23-81
Unsuitable Job for a Woman, An 3-3-82
Untamable Shrews, The (See: Fierecillos Indomables, Los)
Unterbrochene Spur, Die 11-15-82
Until September 8-29-84
Uod at Rosas 4-21-82
Up the Creek 4-11-84
Up to a Certain Point (See: Hasta Cierto Punto)
Upir z Feratu 8-24-83
Uppercrust, The (See: Tuechtigen Gehort die Welt, Den)
Ups & Downs 12-28-83
Urgh! A Music War 4-7-82
Uteky Domu 3-4-81
Utilities 5-25-83

Utlaginn (Gisla Saga Surssonar) 3-31-82
Utopia 3-2-83
Utsav 12-5-84
Utu 2-9-83

V

Va Banque (See: Vabank)
Vabank 10-7-81
Vacanze in America 12-26-84
Vacation in America (See: Vacanze in America)
Vagrants (See: Fariaho)
Valentina 12-22-82
Valentina, Valentina 6-17-81
Valley Girl 4-13-83
Vammenes hazassag/Tullivapaa Avioliitto 2-25-81
Vamping 5-23-84
Van de Koele Meren des Doods 10-20-82
Van Morrison in Ireland 4-15-81
Variety 9-21-83
Variola Vera 8-18-82
Varjivo Leto '68 5-30-84
Vasili i Vasilisa 11-24-82
Vasily and Vasilisa (See: Vasili i Vasilisa)
Vassa 8-3-83
Vater und Sohn 3-14-84
Ve Noi Gio Cat 8-10-83
Vecinos 8-19-81
Vela Incantata, La 5-19-82
Veld van Eer, Het 4-6-83
Vengeance du Serpent a Plumes, Le 12-26-84
Vengeance of the Winged Serpent, The (See: Vengeance du Serpent a
   Plumes, Le)
Venido a Menos 9-5-84
Venom 1-27-82
Vent de Sable 5-26-82
Venus 5-30-84
Vera Storia della Signora delle Camelie, La 3-18-81
Verborgenen Taenze, Die 2-16-83
Verdammte Stadt 12-30-81
Verdes Anos 5-2-84
Verdict, The 11-24-82
Veritaaa', La 9-29-82
Vernon, Florida 10-14-81
Veronika Voss (See: Sehnsucht der Veronika Voss, Die)
Versuchung 2-10-82
Verszerzodes 3-2-83
Vertigo en Manhattan 4-22-81
Very Late Afternoon of a Faun, The (See: Faunovo Velmi Pozdni
   Odpoledne)
Veselo Gostivanje 9-5-84
Vestida en Azul 10-12-83
Via degli Specchi 3-2-83
Viadukt 3-2-83
Viajes de Gulliver, Los 12-21-83
Vicar of Olot, The (See: Vicario de Olot, El)
Vicario de Olot, El 6-17-81
Vice Squad 1-27-82
Vicious Circle (See: Chakra)
Victor Sjostrom - A Film Portrait 12-16-81
Victoria 2-22-84
Victor/Victoria 3-17-82
Victory 7-22-81
Victory (See: Victoria)
Vida e Sangue de Polaco 4-20-83
Vidas 7-25-84
Vidas Errantes 11-21-84
Video Vixens 5-16-84
Videodrome 2-2-83
Vie Continue, La 10-14-81
Vie d'Ange 4-22-81
Vie Est un Roman, La 4-20-83
Vienna Story - Gemini Y and S (See: Uiin Monogatati - Jemin Y to S)
Viens Chez Moi, J'Habite Chez une Copine 3-4-81
Vierde Man, De 4-27-83
Viernes de la Eternidad, Los 6-17-81
Vigil 5-2-84
Vigilante 1-26-83
Village Girl (See: Flickan i byn)
Village in the Jungle (See: Baddegama)
Vinatoarea de Vulpi 4-1-81
Violent Stories (See: Historias Violentas)
Virgin People 4-6-83

Visiting Hours 5-5-82
Visitors from the Galaxy (See: Gosti iz Galaksije)
Visoki Napon 8-5-81
Visszaesok 3-2-83
Vita E Bella, La 9-1-82
Viva la Vie! 5-23-84
Vive la Sociale! 11-9-83
Vive les Femmes! 4-11-84
Vivement Dimanche 8-17-83
Vlaschaard, De 4-13-83
Vlublen Po Sobstvennomu Zelanij 3-16-83
Vlucht regenwulpen, Een 3-10-82
Voce, La 9-22-82
Voice (See: Golos)
Voice, The (See: Voce, La)
Voices (See: Glosy)
Voie Lumiere, La 4-20-83
Vokzal dla dvoish 5-18-83
Vol du Sphinx, Le 10-3-84
Voleurs de la Nuit, Les 3-7-84
Volver 10-13-82
Volver a Empezar 4-14-82
Von Richtern und Anderen Sympathisanten 3-10-82
Vor den Vaetern Sterben die Soehne 3-10-82
Vormund und Sein Dichter, Der 8-26-81
Voros Fold 3-2-83
Vortex 10-6-82
Voyage, Le 10-3-84
Voyage au Pays de Rimbaud 9-21-83
Voyage d'Hiver, Le 10-12-83
Voyage of Bounty's Child, The 4-25-84
Voyage to Cythera (See: Taxidi Sta Kithira)
Voyage to Rimbaud Country (See: Voyage au Pays de Rimbaud)
Voyager (See: Havarist, Der)
Vreme, Vodi 8-5-81
Vremia Jelanii 8-29-84
Vrijdag 3-18-81
Vroeger Kon Je Lachen 5-11-83
Vulture, The (See: Dogkeselyu)
Vulture, The (See: Ha'ayit)
Vultures, The (See: Morfalous, Les)

W

W Bialy Dzien 4-22-81
Wa Koyedat Ded Maghoul 2-10-82
Wacko 2-9-83
Waga Hai Wa Neko De Aru (See: I Am a Cat)
Wagner 12-7-83
Wahadelko 10-7-81
Wait for Me a Long Time (See: Esperame Mucho)
Waitress 9-22-82
Wajda's Danton 5-11-83
Walk in the Shadow (See: Marche a l'Ombre)
Wall, The (See: Mur, Le)
Walls 9-12-84
Walls, Walls (See: Murs, Murs)
Waltz Across Texas 6-29-83
Waltzes of the Danube (See: Donauwalzer)
Wan Jia Deng Hou 3-24-82
Wandering Stars (See: Stelle Emigranti)
Wanderkrebs 3-7-84
Wanted: Good Looking Receptionist and Messenger with His Own
    Motorcycle (See: Se Solicita Muchacha de Buena Presencia y
    Motorizado con Motopropia)
War and Peace (See: Kreig und Frieden)
War of the Wizards 12-21-83
War of the Worlds - Next Century, The (See: Wojna Swiatow -
    Nastepne Stulecie)
War Story, A 7-21-82
War Years 8-17-83
WarGames 5-11-83
Warm Congratulations (See: Herzlichen Glueckwunsch)
Warming Up 4-18-84
Warning, One Woman May Be Hiding Another (See: Attention, Une Femme
    Peut en Cacher une Autre)
Warrior and the Sorceress, The 5-16-84
Warriors from the Magic Mountain (See: Zu)
Warriors of the Wastelands 1-18-84
Wars, The 11-9-83
Warum die UFOs Unseren Salat Klauen 4-18-84
Was Kostet der Sieg? 10-12-83
Was Tun Pina Bausch Ihre Taenzer in Wuppertal? 3-16-83

Wasted Lives (See: Kettevalt Mennyezet)
Wasteland (See: Pustota)
Water Water (See: Thaneer Thaneer)
Waterwalker 8-29-84
Wavelength 8-17-83
Waves (See: Golven)
Way Back Home (See: Terugtocht, De)
Way to Bresson, The (See: Weg naar Bresson, De)
We Are the Guinea Pigs 4-15-81
We Children from Bahnhof Zoo (See: Wir Kinder von Bahnhof Zoo)
We Have Never Been So Happy (See: Nunca Fomos Tao Felizes)
We of the Never Never 6-2-82
We Three (See: Noi Tre)
We Were German Jews 10-21-81
We Will Rock You 5-18-83
We Won't Commit Hara-kiri (See: ...E Noi Non Faremo Hara-kiri)
Weak Man, The (See: Homme Fragile, L')
Weather in the Streets, The 12-14-83
Weavers: Wasn't That a Time, The 12-9-81
Wedding, The (See: Boda, La)
Weekend Pass 2-15-84
Weekend Shuffle (See: Uiikendo Shaffuru)
Weg naar Bresson, De 5-16-84
Weggehen um Anzukommen 4-21-82
Weisse Rose, Die 11-17-82
Wend Kuuni 8-25-82 and 11-17-82
Wenig Sterben, Ein 12-2-81
Wenn Ich Mich Furchte 8-29-84
We're Getting Along (See: Koszonom, Megvagyunk)
Westen Leuchtet!, Der 9-1-82
What a Sun! (See: Nobena Sonce)
What Are Pina Bausch and Her Dancers Doing in Wuppertal? (See: Was
    Tun Pina Bausch Ihre Taenzer in Wuppertal?)
What Have I Done to Deserve This?!! (See: Que He Hecho Yo Para
    Merecer Esto)
What Makes David Run? (See: Qu'Est-Ce Qui Fait Courir David?)
What My Eyes Are Going to See (See: Ti Ehoun Na Doun ta Matia Mou)
What Now, Little Man? (See: Kleiner Mann Was Nun?)
What Price Victory? (See: Was Kotet der Sieg?)
What Will We Do on Sunday? (See: Sabti-Fat, El-)
What You Take for Granted 12-19-84
What're We Waiting for to Be Happy! (See: Qu'Est-Ce Qu'On Attend
    pour Etre Heureux!)
What's Up, Nina? (See: Sta Je S Tobom, Nina)
Wheel, The (See: Yoinchanhoksa: Mulleya Mulleya)
Wheels on Meals 9-12-84
When It Rains, It Pours (See: Alles im Elmer)
When the Mountains Tremble 1-25-84
Where Is Parsifal? 5-30-84
Where the Boys Are '84 4-11-84
Where the Green Ants Dream (See: Wo die Grunen Ameisen Traumen)
Where's Eno? 3-14-84
While the Body Resists (See: Mientras el Cuerpo Aguante)
White Delusion, The (See: Witte Waan, De)
White Dog 6-23-82
White Elephant 11-14-84
White Lions, The 7-20-83
White Magic (See: Byala Magia)
White Raven, The 8-26-81
White Red and Verdone Green (See: Bianco Rosso e Verdone)
White Rose, The (See: Wiesse Rose, Die)
White Umbrella, The (See: Witte Paraplu, De)
Who? 10-20-82
Who Dares Wins 7-14-82
Who Pulled the Plug? (See: Goeta Kanal)
Who Shall Live and Who Shall Die? 12-2-81
Whoever Says the Truth Shall Die 11-28-84
Whole of Life, The (See: Ganze Leben, Das)
Who's Knocking on My Door? (See: Kto Stuchitsya V Dverj Ko Mne?)
Who'll Help Me? (See: Chi Mi Aiuta ...?)
Whose Life Is It Anyway? 11-25-81
Why Albert Pinto Is Angry (See: Albert Pinto Ko Gussa Asta Hai)
Why the Charleston Nowadays? (See: Chikagoro Nazeka Chaarusuton)
Why the UFOs Steal Our Lettuce (See: Warum die UFOs Unseren Salat
    Klauen)
Wicked Lady, The 4-27-83
Widziadlo 8-8-84
Wie ein Fremder 1-6-82
Wielka Majowska 11-25-81
Wien Retour 12-14-83
Wife for My Son, A (See: Femme pour Mon Fils, Une)
Wife for My Son, A (See: Maraa Le Ibni)
Wild Bunch (See: Wilde Clique)
Wild Duck, The 9-7-83
Wild Field 8-5-81
Wild Flowers (See: Fleurs Sauvages, Les)
Wild Horse (See: Caballo Salvaje)
Wild Horses 2-9-83
Wild Life, The 10-3-84

X

Y

Z